ENCYCLOPEDIA

AMERICANA

INTERNATIONAL EDITION

COMPLETE IN THIRTY VOLUMES

FIRST PUBLISHED IN 1829

Scholastic Library Publishing, Inc.
Danbury, Connecticut

Library of Congress Cataloging-in-Publication Data

Main entry under title:
Encyclopedia Americana.—International ed.
   p.   cm.
"First published in 1829."
Includes bibliographical references and index.
ISBN 0-7172-0139-2
1. Encyclopedias and dictionaries.
AE5.E333   2006.
031-dc22
2005018141

Printed and Manufactured in the U.S.A.

PREFACE

The *Encyclopedia Americana* is intended to serve as a general reference resource for schools, colleges, and public libraries. In an era of increasingly specialized reference works, and of even more highly specialized journals and academic publications, it is occasionally forgotten that often the best introduction to a subject is the well-conceived, well-written overview provided by the general encyclopedia. Such an encyclopedia also has the ability to provide needed context, owing to the scope and depth of its coverage. The publication of the 2006 edition of the *Encyclopedia Americana* marks the set's 177th year in print and its 71st consecutive annual revision. While such figures do not absolutely ensure the integrity of an encyclopedia, the longevity of the *Americana* is surely a good indicator of the respect it has earned in the libraries of the United States, Canada, and elsewhere. The present edition continues traditions of service and accountability to the educational community established nearly two centuries ago.

The tens of thousands of articles in the *Americana* serve as a bridge between the worlds of the specialist and the general reader. Distinguished advisers have assisted the editors in organizing the information in their fields into convenient forms of presentation. In some instances articles of almost book length have resulted from the conferences between advisers and editors—for example, the articles on the United States and on the two world wars. In other instances the decision was to present facts briefly and specifically—for example, a definition of a technical term or the identification of a character in fiction. Thousands of such short entries are provided to meet the reader's needs for specific information.

The advisers have also assisted the editors in choosing leading authorities in each field to write the articles. After the contributor is selected—whether the area is physics or the theater, European history or sports—he or she is reminded of the need to write for the nonspecialist reader. The author is asked not to "write down" but to present facts and interpretations in an orderly way and in a direct style, as well as to explain technical terms when they are used. All articles in the *Americana* are carefully checked by the editors with these considerations in mind.

Because of this policy the *Americana*'s articles communicate to a wide range of readers. Young students are able to find the information they are seeking, and to understand what they read. Teachers, librarians, and adults in general satisfy their reference needs without losing time trying to comprehend technicalities for which they have no specialized preparation.

For this edition, in accordance with the *Americana*'s policy of continuous revision, many new articles have been prepared by either contributing authors or the editors, including those on subjects not covered in previous editions under their own headings. In addition, hundreds of articles have been revised by their original authors or by the editors. In a few instances articles formerly prepared by contributors have been amended by the editors, and in each such instance an asterisk (*) follows the name of the author.

In covering all areas the editors have sought to present information in an objective manner. As the *Americana*'s first editor, Francis Lieber (1798–1872), said in 1829, "My wish has been not to obtrude opinions but to furnish facts." At the same time, those facts need to be set in meaningful perspective, and this is what the contributors and editors have sought to do.

This edition of the *Encyclopedia Americana* is published in the belief that it provides an accurate and comprehensive picture of past and present times. Its editorial staff, advisory editors, and more than six thousand contributors have cooperated in producing an encyclopedia that is reliable, readable, and relevant to today's needs.

ARRANGEMENT OF CONTENTS

Volume 1, after this preface, contains the list of the *Americana* editorial staff members (page vii), the list of advisory editors (pages viii–ix), and the list of contributors (beginning on page x). These are followed by a key to pronunciation and a list of abbreviations used in the encyclopedia. Volume 30 contains the index. Preceding the index in that volume is a guide to the use of the index and a special list of abbreviations used in the index.

In the main text of the encyclopedia, articles are arranged alphabetically *word by word* rather than letter by letter: *North Dakota* precedes *Northcliffe*, *Wood Engraving* precedes *Woodbury*, and so on. In a series of articles with the same heading, the order of *persons, places,* and *things* is followed: *Bell, Alexander Graham* precedes *Bell* (city), which precedes *Bell* (thing). Further details on the alphabetizing system are given in the Guide to the Use of the Index (volume 30).

Names of persons and places are generally spelled in the encyclopedia as they are spelled in the country of origin. But standard anglicized forms are used for names of rulers, countries, and some major cities and geographical features—for example, *Henry*, not *Henri*, for kings of France; *Florence*, not *Firenze*, for the city in Italy. Names and other terms from languages that do not employ the Roman alphabet are transcribed according to established systems of transliteration.

The year-to-year revisions of the *Americana* sometimes require adding pages and, in some instances, dropping pages. As a result parts of the volumes have to be renumbered. Thus, when a new article fills more pages than the article or articles it has replaced, the new pages may be numbered with a figure plus a letter—for example, *237a, 237b,* and so on. Sometimes old material is dropped and new material added, or an article is transferred to a new heading, as when required by a change in a country's name. When the new or remaining material occupies fewer pages than the old, a page may be given a "telescoped" number such as *380–390.*

RESEARCH AIDS

The *Index* (volume 30) should always be consulted first in looking for information in the *Americana*. This index, with more than 350,000 entries, provides a complete guide to the contents of the encyclopedia. For every article in the set, there is an index entry, which also lists the other places in the encyclopedia where information on the subject can be found. In addition, the index has tens of thousands of entries on subjects that are covered in the encyclopedia but do not have separate articles of their own. Many subjects, especially major ones, are organized in the index in the form of extensive outlines.

Cross-References in the text of the encyclopedia—within articles, at the end of articles, or as separate entries—also lead the reader to related articles or provide the heading under which a subject is treated. Cross-references generally give the full title of the articles referred to, printed in capitals—for example, "See also UNITED STATES." Sometimes the abbreviations *q.v.* or *qq.v* (for the Latin words meaning "which see") are used.

Tables of Contents at the beginning of long articles help readers find coverage of specific topics they are investigating. Most of these tables contain page references to specific sections of the articles.

Bibliographies at the end of articles refer the reader to books or other materials for further research. Wherever possible books suitable for the general reader are included along with more advanced or specialized works. In addition every effort is made to ensure that divergent points of view on the subject discussed are represented in the bibliography.

SPECIAL FEATURES

The *Encyclopedia Americana* provides several features that organize information in a special way to benefit its readers. For example, separate articles appear on each of the centuries of the common era under their own headings, such as FIRST CENTURY and TWENTIETH CENTURY. These surveys cut across national boundaries to set political, social, and cultural events within an international perspective.

Separate articles on classic works of literature, philosophy, and economics and on major operas discuss these works more fully than can be done in the author's or composer's biography. There also are separate articles on the books of the Bible (for which references usually are based on the Revised Standard Version) and on significant historical documents, such as the Declaration of Independence and the Constitution of the United States, with some including the complete text of the document. Each letter of the alphabet is discussed in a separate article devoted to the letter's orthographic and linguistic history.

Articles on specialized areas of education, such as those on LEGAL EDUCATION, MEDICAL EDUCATION, and THEOLOGICAL EDUCATION, offer useful discussions of these fields for those contemplating advanced study in them or for those researching the various educational issues associated with each. These articles serve to complement the nearly booklength EDUCATION article itself as well as the various related education articles, such as LIBRARY and PRESCHOOL EDUCATION.

In entries for each of the states of the United States, there are sidebars identifying both prominent people associated with the state and key events in the state's history. Likewise shown are the names of all of those who have served as governor of the state, from the colonial era to the present.

ILLUSTRATIONS AND MAPS

Illustrations, in color or black-and-white, are used functionally in the encyclopedia to clarify and supplement the text. Drawings, diagrams, graphs, maps, and charts convey information that words cannot express as well. Photographs reveal the atmosphere of places and the personalities of people, show what objects look like, and make the reader a witness to important events in history.

Color maps appear with articles on continents, major countries, all U.S. states and Canadian provinces, and some major cities; black-and-white maps accompany many articles on smaller countries, islands, and other major cities. Most color maps are prepared by Hammond World Atlas Corporation. A convenient feature of many maps is an inset map that shows the location of the mapped area in relation to a larger unit—country, continent, hemisphere, or world. Most color maps are accompanied by map indexes listing the major geographical features shown and the inhabited places and their populations, with coordinates for locating them on the map. The map coordinates lead to the place-name, not to the dot or other locator symbol.

POPULATION FIGURES

Every effort is made to provide the latest available census figures or the most recent reliable estimates. For example, population data for the United States, the individual states, and cities and towns are based on the 2000 census. Populations for places in Canada are derived from that country's 2001 census.

PRONUNCIATIONS

Entries for names and terms whose pronunciation may be in doubt among users of the encyclopedia are supplied with pronunciations following the headword or, in the case of some surnames, as part of the headword. For foreign names the *Americana* generally gives the pronunciation used by native speakers of the language in question rather than the anglicized version. In some cases, however, both are shown. The symbols used and the sounds they represent are shown on page xcviii.

THE EDITORS

STAFF ACKNOWLEDGMENTS

Scholastic Library Publishing

President	Greg Worrell
Vice President and General Manager	Evan St. Lifer
Administrative and Financial Manager	Kevin Molina
Assistant to the General Manager	Margarita Heckler

Encyclopedia Americana

Editor-in-Chief	Michael Shally-Jensen
Managing Editor	Doris E. Lechner
Director of Art and Design	Nancy Hamlen

EDITORS

Patricia Bayer   Brian Feinberg
Karen Fairchild   Scott C. Monje
Veronica F. Towers

ASSOCIATE EDITORS

Rachel Barton   Laurie Hunt
Vadim Prokhorov   Joseph Richards
Lisa Torchiano   Craig B. Waff

COPY DEPARTMENT

Janine Stanley-Dunham (chief)   Judy Schweitzer
Judith Herrick Beard   Devon Towey
Robin Charney   Jessica Trichilo
Sharon L. Wirt

PRODUCTION

Production Editor	Patricia Raether
Publishing Application Design Specialist	Stephanie Grant
Indexer	Nutmeg Indexing

ONLINE EDITION

Editor, *Americana* Journal	Barbara Letta Cole
Internet Links Manager	Irina Balakina
Asset Manager	Lyndee Lou Stalter

PUBLISHING TECHNOLOGIES

Cyndie Cooper (director)   Linda K. Dillon
William Byler   Meghan O'Reilly Fiero
Raymond Casey   Emilia Urra Smith

PICTURE RESEARCH

Director, Photo Research	Cindy Joyce
Manager, Picture Library	Jane H. Carruth
Staff Assistant	Gwen Ruiz

LIBRARY

Emma Smith

ADVISORY EDITORS

PARTIAL LIST OF CONTRIBUTORS

AARON, RICHARD I., *Professor of Philosophy, University College of Wales, Aberystwyth; Author of* Our Knowledge of Universals

ABBOTT, HERSCHEL G., *Professor of Forestry and Wildlife, University of Massachusetts*

ABBOTT, R. TUCKER, *Delaware Museum of Natural History; Author of* Sea Shells of the World *and* American Seashells

ABBOTT, WALTER, SJ, *Editor of* The Documents of Vatican II

ABEL, DARREL, *Professor of English, Purdue University; Author of* American Literature

ABEL, WALTER, *Actor and President, American National Theatre and Academy*

ABELL, GEORGE, *U.S. Department of State*

ABETTI, GIORGIO, *Professor of Astrophysics, University of Florence, Italy; Director of Astrophysical Observatory of Arcetri-Firenze; Author of* The Sun *and* Stars and Planets

ABRAHAM, E. P., *Sir William Dunn School of Pathology, Oxford University*

ABRAHAM, GERALD E. H., *President, Royal Musical Association, Great Britain (1970–1974); Author of* Chopin's Musical Style, A Hundred Years of Music, Studies in Russian Music, *and* Tchaikovsky: A Short Biography

ABRAHAM, HENRY J., *Doherty Professor of Government and Foreign Affairs, University of Virginia; Author of* The Judicial Process *and* Freedom and the Court

ABRAMS, IRWIN, *Professor Emeritus, Antioch University*

ABRAMSON, JESSE P., *President, New York Football Writers' Association; President, Track Writers' Association of New York; Director, U.S. Olympic Invitational Track Meet*

ACKERKNECHT, ERWIN H., *Institute of Medical History, University of Zurich*

ACKLIN, R. I., *Marketing Analyst, Armstrong Cork Company*

ACOCELLA, JOAN, *Dance critic; Author of* Mark Morris; *Editor of* André Levinson on Dance: Writings from Paris in the Twenties

ADAMS, CHARLES J., *Director, Institute of Islamic Studies, McGill University, Canada*

ADAMS, DENVEL D., *National Adjutant, Disabled American Veterans*

ADAMSON, EDITH, *Library Consultant, Indian Affairs Branch, Department of Indian Affairs and Northern Development, Ottawa; Author of* Museums and Art Galleries, 1964 *and* Public Library Finance in Canada

ADLER, HELMUT E., *American Museum of Natural History*

ADLER, JACOB, *Professor of Accounting and Finance, University of Hawaii*

ADLER, LEONORE LOEB, *Author of* This is the Dachshund; *Editor of* Miniature Dachshund Digest

ADLER, SAMUEL, *Professor of Composition, Eastman School of Music of the University of Rochester; Author of* The Study of Orchestration

ADLER, SELIG, *Distinguished Service Professor of American History, State University of New York at Buffalo; Author of* The Isolationist Impulse *and* The Uncertain Giant

ADLOFF, RICHARD, *Research Associate, Hoover Institution, Stanford University; Coauthor of* Djibouti and the Horn of Africa

ADRIAN, CHARLES R., *Professor of Political Science, University of California at Riverside; Author of* State and Local Governments

ADROSKO, RITA, *Curator, Division of Textiles, Smithsonian Institution; Author of* Natural Dyes in the United States

AFRICA, THOMAS W., *Professor of History, State University of New York at Binghamton; Author of* Rome of the Caesars, Science and the State in Antiquity, *and* The Ancient World

AGARD, FREDERICK B., *Professor of Linguistics, Cornell University; Coauthor of* Spoken Romanian

AGNEW, L. R. C., MD, *Associate Professor of Medical History, University of California at Los Angeles*

AHLGREN, HENRY L., *Assistant Chancellor of University Extension and Associate Director of Cooperative Extension at the University of Wisconsin; Coauthor of* Crop Production; *Author of* Forage Crops

AKERS, CHARLES W., *Professor of History, Oakland University*

ALAUX, MICHEL J., *U.S. Olympic Coach, 1964, 1968; Head Coach, New York Fencers Club*

ALBERTSON, LEONA, *Librarian, Lake County Public Library, Leadville, Colo.*

ALBION, ROBERT G., *Gardiner Professor of Oceanic History and Affairs, Harvard University; Author of* Dictionary of Famous Ships

ALBRECHT, W. P., *Professor of English, University of Kansas; Author of* Hazlitt and the Creative Imagination

ALBRIGHT, ESTA LEE, *Librarian, Fairfax County Public Library, Carter Glass Branch, Reston, Va.*

ALBRIGHT, ETHEL W., *Andrew Carnegie Public Library, Anderson, Ind.*

ALBRIGHT, SPENCER D., *Professor of History and Political Science, University of Richmond; Author of* The American Ballot

ALBRIGHT, W. F., *Archaeologist; Author of* From the Stone Age to Christianity

ALBUS, JAMES S., *Project Manager for Sensor and Computer Control Technology, Mechanical Processes Division, National Bureau of Standards; Author of* Peoples' Capitalism: The Economics of the Robot Revolution

ALDEN, RAYMOND M., *Author of* Shakespeare; *Editor of* Poems of the English Race

ALDERSON, WILLIAM T., *Director, American Association for State and Local History; Author of* Historic Sites in Tennessee

ALDINGTON, RICHARD, *Author of* The Duke *and other books about Wellington*

ALDRIDGE, A. OWEN, *Professor of Comparative Literature, University of Illinois; Author of* Man of Reason: The Life of Thomas Paine

ALEXANDER, FRED, *Professor of Modern History, University of Western Australia*

ALEXANDER, LEWIS M., *Chairman, Department of Geography and Marine Affairs, University of Rhode Island; Author of* World Political Patterns, Offshore Geography of Northwestern Europe, *and* Regional Arrangements in Ocean Affairs

ALEXANDER, MARIE, *Painter; Member, Curatorial Staff, Museum of Modern Art, New York City*

ALEXANDER, MARY JEAN, *Author of* Handbook of Decorative Design and Ornament

ALEXANDER, PAUL B., *Assistant Professor of Geography, University of Montana*

ALEXANDER, PAUL J., *Professor of History and Comparative Literature, University of California at Berkeley; Author of* The Ancient World to 300 A.D.

ALEXANDER, R. S., *Professor of Physiology, Albany Medical College, Union University, Albany, N.Y.*

ALEXANDER, ROBERT J., *Professor of Economics and Political Science, Rutgers University*

ALEXANDER, SIDNEY, *Author of* Michelangelo the Florentine

ALEXANDER, WILLIAM M., *Professor of Education, University of Florida; Coauthor of* Curriculum Planning for Modern Schools *and* Independent Study in Secondary Schools

ALFORD, B. W. E., *Professor of Economic History, University of Bristol, England; Author of* Depression and Recovery? British Economic Growth, 1918–1939

ÁLISKY, MARVIN, *Director of Center for Latin American Studies and Professor of Political Science, Arizona State University*

In general, contributors are identified by the affiliations they had at the time they wrote for the *Encyclopedia Americana*.

ALLEN, CHARLES, *Coauthor of* The Little Magazine: A History and Bibliography

ALLEN, CODY H., *Head of Reference Department, Leon County Public Library, Tallahassee, Fla.*

ALLEN, EDWARD D., *Professor of Foreign Language Education, Ohio State University; Author of* The Changing Curriculum—Modern Foreign Languages

ALLEN, ELEANOR, *Associate Engineering Editor, SAE Journal*

ALLEN, FREDERICK G., *Professor and Chairman, Department of Electrical Engineering, School of Engineering and Applied Sciences, University of California at Los Angeles*

ALLEN, GAY WILSON, *Professor of English, New York University; Author of* The Solitary Singer: A Critical Biography of Walt Whitman; William James, A Biography; *and* Melville and his World

ALLEN, HORACE T., *Director of the Office of Worship and Music, United Presbyterian Church of the United States of America and the Presbyterian Church in the United States*

ALLEN, HUBERT L., *Assistant Professor of the Classics, University of Illinois; Director, Illinois-Princeton University Archaeological Expedition to Morgantina, Sicily*

ALLEN, JOSEPHINE D., *Historian, National Park Service, U.S. Department of the Interior*

ALLEN, LEE, *Author of* Kings of the Diamond

ALLEN, R. C., *Director, Kingwood Center, Mansfield, Ohio*

ALLEN, RICHARD SANDERS, *Author of* Covered Bridges

ALLEN, WALTER, *Professor of English Studies, The New University of Ulster; Author of* George Eliot

ALLEN, WILLIAM E. D., *OBE, FSA, Coauthor of* Caucasian Battlefields

ALLER, LAWRENCE H., *Professor of Astronomy, University of California at Los Angeles; Author of* Astrophysics and Gaseous Nebulae

ALLISON, JUNIUS L., *Professor of Law, Vanderbilt University; Former Executive Director, National Legal Aid and Defender Association*

ALLPORT, FLOYD H., *Author of* Theories of Perception and the Concept of Structures

ALLSOPP, BRUCE, *Reader in History of Architecture, University of Newcastle upon Tyne, England; Author of* A General History of Architecture

ALTICK, RICHARD D., *Professor of English, Ohio State University; Author of* Scholar Adventures *and* English Common Reader

ALTSTADT, AUDREY L., *Professor of History, University of Massachusetts at Amherst*

ALVEY, EDWARD, JR., *Professor of Education, Mary Washington College, Fredericksburg, Va.*

AMADON, DEAN, *Lamont Curator of Birds and Chairman, Department of Ornithology, American Museum of Natural History; Coauthor of* Curassows and Related Birds

AMAN, MOHAMMED M., *Dean, School of Library and Information Science, University of Wisconsin at Milwaukee*

AMANN, PETER, *Chairman, Section of Social Sciences, University of Michigan at Dearborn; Author of* The Modern World, 1650–1850

AMBROSE, STEPHEN E., *Eisenhower Professor of History, Kansas State University; Author of* The Supreme Commander: The War Years of Dwight Eisenhower

AMDUR, NEIL L., *Editor in Chief, World Tennis*

AMERINE, MAYNARD A., *Professor of Enology, University of California at Davis*

AMES, BARRY, *Associate Professor of Political Science, Washington University, St. Louis; Author of* Rhetoric and Reality in a Militarized Regime: Brazil After 1964

AMICK, CHARLES L., *Director of Engineering Services, Day-Brite Lighting Division, Emerson Electric Co., St. Louis, Mo.*

AMICK, HAROLD C., *Professor of Geography, University of Tennessee*

AMMON, HARRY, *Professor of History, Southern Illinois University; Author of* James Monroe: The Quest for National Identity *and* The Genet Mission

AMUNDSEN, DARREL, *Western Washington University*

ANAND, VIVODH, *New York University*

ANDERS, CURT, *Author of* Fighting Generals *and* Fighting Airmen

ANDERSEN, ARLOW W., *Professor of History, University of Wisconsin at Oshkosh*

ANDERSON, BARBARA GALLATIN, *Professor Emerita of Anthropology, Southern Methodist University*

ANDERSON, BRENT, *PE, Brent Anderson Associates, Inc.*

ANDERSON, CHARLES R., *Caroline Donovan Professor of American Literature, Johns Hopkins University; Author of* The Magic Circle of Walden

ANDERSON, EDGAR, *Curator of Useful Plants, Missouri Botanical Garden, St. Louis*

ANDERSON, GEORGE L., *Professor of English, University of Hawaii; Editor of* Masterpieces of the Orient

ANDERSON, HAROLD H., *Research Professor of Psychology, Michigan State University; Coauthor of* Studies of Teachers' Classroom Personalities

ANDERSON, HARRY H., *Executive Director, Milwaukee County Historical Society, Milwaukee, Wis.*

ANDERSON, HERBERT R., JR., *Manager, Material Process Technology, IBM Systems Development Division*

ANDERSON, JOHN B., *Professor, Department of History, College of the Holy Cross*

ANDERSON, JOHN D., JR., *Professor of Aerospace Engineering, University of Maryland*

ANDERSON, NORMAN G., *Department of Basic and Clinical Immunology, Medical University of South Carolina; Former Chief, Molecular Anatomy Section, Biology Division, Oak Ridge National Laboratory*

ANDERSON, ROBERT MAPES, *Professor of History, Wagner College; Author of* Vision of the Disinherited: The Making of American Pentecostalism

ANDERSON, ROBERT T., *MD, Professor of Anthropology, Mills College; Author of* Traditional Europe: A Study in Anthropology and History *and* Modern Europe: An Anthropological Perspective

ANDERSON, STANLEY V., *Associate Professor of Political Science, University of California at Santa Barbara*

ANDERSON, SYDNEY, *Curator, Department of Mammalogy, American Museum of Natural History*

ANDERSSON, THEODORE M., *Professor of German and Scandinavian, Harvard University; Author of* The Icelandic Family Saga

ANDRESEN, JACK, *Author of* Skiing on Water

ANDRESS, JOEL M., *Assistant Professor of Geography, Central Washington State College*

ANDREWS, F. EMERSON, *President, Foundation Center, New York City; Author of* Philanthropic Foundations

ANDREWS, THELMA, *Librarian, Abilene Public Library*

ANDREWS, WILLIAM L., *Distinguished Professor of English, University of North Carolina at Chapel Hill*

ANGLE, PAUL M., *Director, Chicago Historical Society; Author of* The Complete Lincoln-Douglas Debates *and* The Lincoln Reader

ANGLO, SYDNEY, *Senior Lecturer in the History of Ideas, University College of Swansea, University of Wales; Author of* The Great Tournament Roll of Westminster

ANGRIST, STANLEY W., *Professor of Mechanical Engineering, Carnegie-Mellon University*

ANGUS, W. S., *University of Aberdeen*

ANSCOMBE, ISABELLE, *Design Historian*

ANSELL, W. F. H., *Biologist, Department of Wildlife, Fisheries and National Parks, Zambia; Author of* Mammals of Northern Rhodesia

ANSLEY, DELIGHT, *Author of* The Good Ways

ANTAL, EVELYN, *Editor of* Frederick Antal's Hogarth and His Place in European Art

APPEL, MARTIN, *Director, Public Relations, WPIX, Inc.; Coauthor of* Baseball's Best: The Hall of Fame Gallery

APPLE, JAMES M., *Professor of Industrial Engineering, Georgia Institute of Technology*

APPLEBY, PAUL H., *Dean, Maxwell Graduate School of Citizenship and Public Affairs, Syracuse University*

APPLEBY, R. SCOTT, *Associate Director, The Fundamentalism Project, American Academy of Arts and Sciences; Professor of History and Director of the Cushwa Center for the Study of American Catholicism, University of Notre Dame*

ARBUCKLE, WENDELL S., *Professor of Dairy Science, University of Maryland; Author of* Ice Cream *and* Ice Cream Manufacture—Dairy Handbook and Dictionary

ARCHDEACON, THOMAS J., *Professor of History and Chair, Department of History, University of Wisconsin at Madison*

ARCHER, JOHN H., *Director of Libraries, McGill University; President, Canadian Library Association, 1966–1967*

ARCHER, STEPHEN M., *Captain, United States Navy (Retired); Secretary, Amateur Athletic Union*

ARCHIBALD, KENNETH C., MD, *Director of Physical Medicine and Rehabilitation, Jerd Sullivan Rehabilitation Center, Garden Hospital and Presbyterian Hospital of Pacific Medical Center, San Francisco, Calif.*

ARDAGH, JOHN, *Author of* The New French Revolution, France in the 1980s, *and* Rural France

ARENSON, JOSEPH T., *Counsel to the Public Administrator of New York County; Professor, Wills and Decedents' Estates, New York Law School*

ARESTY, ESTHER B., *Author of* The Delectable Past *and* The Best Behavior

ARIETI, SILVANO, MD, *Clinical Professor of Psychiatry, New York Medical College; Editor of* American Handbook of Psychiatry

ARMILLAS, PEDRO, *Professor of Anthropology, State University of New York at Stony Brook; Author of* Program of the History of American Indians

ARMITAGE, CLEMENT J., SJ, *Superior, Jesuit Missions, New York City*

ARMSTRONG, A. H., *Professor of Greek, School of Classics, University of Liverpool, England*

ARMSTRONG, BRIAN, *Associate Professor of Early Modern European History, Georgia State University*

ARMSTRONG, DONALD, MD, *Director of Microbiology Laboratory and Chief of Infectious Disease Services at Memorial Hospital, New York City*

ARMSTRONG, JOHN C., *American Museum of Natural History*

ARNALL, ELLIS GIBBS, *Governor of Georgia*

ARNASON, H. H., *Trustee, Solomon R. Guggenheim Foundation; Author of* History of Modern Art *and* Sculpture by Houdon

ARNETT, R. H., JR., *Florida State Collection of Arthropods, Gainesville*

ARNOLD, B. H., *Professor of Mathematics, Oregon State University; Author of* Logic and Boolean Algebra

ARNOLD, CHESTER A., *Professor of Botany and Geology and Curator of Fossil Plants, University of Michigan; Author of* Introduction to Paleobotany

ARNOLD, CHRISTIAN K., *Associate Director, National Association of State Universities and Land-Grant Colleges*

ARNOLD, EDMUND C., *Virginia Commonwealth University*

ARNOLD, HARRY L., JR., *Department of Dermatology, Straub Clinic, Clinical Professor of Dermatology, University of Hawaii School of Medicine*

ARNOLD, MARGARET J., *Librarian, Wellesley Free Library*

ARNOLD, MITCHELL, *Associate Professor of Music, Mundelein College*

ARNOLD, ZACH M., *Professor, Department of Paleontology, University of California at Berkeley*

ARNON, DANIEL I., *Professor and Chairman, Department of Cell Physiology, University of California at Berkeley*

ARONSON, JOSEPH, *Author of* The New Encyclopedia of Furniture

ARPER, ELIZABETH P., *Senior Librarian, Lubbock City-County Libraries, Lubbock, Texas*

ARRINGTON, LEONARD J., *Department of Economics, Utah State University*

ARTIBISE, ALAN F. J., *Director, School of Community and Regional Planning, University of British Columbia; Author of* Canadian Regional Development

ARTOLA, GEORGE T., *Associate Professor of Asian and Pacific Languages, Asian Studies Program, University of Hawaii*

ASCHER, ABRAHAM, *Professor of History, Brooklyn College; Author of* Pavel Axelrod and the Development of Menshevism

ASHBROOK, JOSEPH, *Editor of* Sky and Telescope *magazine*

ASHBROOK, WILLIAM, *Trustees Distinguished Professor of Humanities, Indiana State University; Author of* Donizetti *and* The Operas of Puccini

ASHDOWN, PAUL G., *Professor of Journalism, School of Journalism, University of Tennessee; Editor of* James Agee: Selected Journalism

ASHLEY, MAURICE, *Research Fellow, University of Loughborough, England; Author of* Life in Stuart England *and* The Glorious Revolution of 1688

ASHMOLE, N. PHILIP, *Assistant Professor of Biology and Assistant Curator of Ornithology, Peabody Museum of Natural History, Yale University*

ASHWORTH, JOHN, *Lecturer, Columbia University*

ASIMOV, ISAAC, *Associate Professor of Biochemistry, Medical School, Boston University; Author of* The Intelligent Man's Guide to Science

ASPATURIAN, VERNON V., *Evan Pugh Professor of Political Science, Pennsylvania State University*

ASPELL, P. J., OMI, *Professor of Philosophy, Oblate College, Washington, D.C.*

ASPINWALL, MARGUERITE, *Author of* Lost Treasure Trail

ASSAD, THOMAS J., *Professor of English, Tulane University; Author of* Three Victorian Travellers

ATHAY, R. GRANT, *Senior Research Staff, High Altitude Observatory, National Center for Atmospheric Research, Boulder, Colo.*

ATHERTON, JAMES S., *Author of* The Books at the Wake: A Study of Literary Allusions in Finnegans Wake

ATKIN, MURIEL, *Professor of History, George Washington University*

ATKINS, STUART, *Professor of German, University of California at Santa Barbara; Author of* Goethe's Faust *and* The Age of Goethe

ATLAS, JAMES, *Assistant Editor, New York Times Magazine; Author of* Delmore Schwartz: The Life of an American Poet, The Great Pretender, *and* Battle of the Books

ATTIG, CLARENCE J., *Professor of History, Westmar College*

AUBURN, NORMAN P., *President, University of Akron*

AUDET, LOUIS-PHILIPPE, *Professor, Faculty of Education, Université de Montréal, Canada*

AUGELLI, JOHN P., *Professor of Geography and Latin American Studies, University of Kansas; Coauthor of* Middle America: Its Lands and Peoples

AUSTERLITZ, ROBERT, *Professor of Linguistics and Uralic Studies, Columbia University*

AUSTIN, C. R., *Charles Darwin Professor of Animal Embryology, Cambridge University*

AUSTIN, GABRIEL, *Librarian, The Grolier Club, New York City; Author of* The Library of Jean Grolier

AVAKIAN, GEORGE, *Producer, Columbia Records*

AVALLONE, EUGENE A., *Associate Professor of Mechanical Engineering, City College of New York*

AVERY, EMMETT L., *Professor of English, Washington State University; Author of* The London Stage, 1700–1729

AVILA-PIRES, FERNANDO DIAS DE, *Director, Museu de Historia Natural, Universidade Federal de Minas Gerais, Cicade Universitaria, Pampulha Belo Horizonte, Minas Gerais, Brazil*

AVRICH, PAUL H., *Professor of History, Queens College*

AXELSON, ERIC, *Professor and Head, Department of History, University of Cape Town, South Africa*

AYALA, REYNALDO, *Associate Professor of Geography, San Diego State University at Calexico*

AYEARST, MORLEY, *Professor of Government, Washington Square College of Arts and Science, New York University; Author of* British West Indies

AYER, JOHN D., *Assistant Professor of Law, University of California at Davis*

AYERS, JAMES R., *Technical Adviser, U.S. Bureau of Yards and Docks*

AYLING, RONALD F., *Research Fellow, Drama Department, University of Bristol, England; Editor of* Sean O'Casey

BAATZ, M. A., *Academic Registrar, University of London*

BABEL, RAYONIA A., *Head of Reference, Aurora University Library*

BACHMANN, GLORIA A., MD, *Professor of Obstetrics and Gynecology and Chief, Division of General Obstetrics and Gynecology, Robert Wood Johnson Medical School, New Brunswick, N.J.*

BACHNIK, JANE M., *Department of Anthropology, University of North Carolina at Chapel Hill; Author of* The Japanese Household: An Organization of Self and Society *and* An Introduction to the Japanese Family

BACHRACH, BERNARD, *Professor, Department of History, University of Minnesota*

BACKMAN, JULES, *Research Professor of Economics, New York University; Author of* Pricing: Policies and Practices; *Coauthor of* Price Inflation and the Price Indexes

BACON, ELIZABETH E., *Professor of Anthropology and Asian Studies (Retired), Michigan State University; Author of* Central Asians Under Russian Rule, a Study in Culture Change

BACON, WALTER M., JR., *Professor of Political Science, University of Nebraska at Omaha; Author of* Behind Closed Doors: Secret Papers on the Failure of Romanian-Soviet Negotiations, 1931–1932

BADASH, LAWRENCE, *Associate Professor of History of Science, University of California at Santa Barbara; Editor of* Rutherford and Boltwood, Letters on Radioactivity

BADAWY, ALEXANDER M., *Professor of Art, University of California at Los Angeles; Author of* A History of Egyptian Architecture

BADGLEY, PETER C., *Director, Arctic and Earth Sciences Division, Office of Naval Research, U.S. Navy; Author of* Structural and Tectonic Principles

BADIA MARGARIT, ANTONIO M., *Faculty of Philology, University of Barcelona, Spain; Author of* Gramática catalana

BAGBY, WESLEY M., *Professor of History, West Virginia University*

BAILEY, DAVID B., *Manager for Technology Programs, Office of Science and Technology, Naval Air Warfare Center; Past Chairman, Technical Committee for Lighter-Than-Air Systems, American Institute for Aeronautics and Astronautics*

BAILEY, HELEN MILLER, *Chairman, Social Sciences, East Los Angeles College; Coauthor of* Latin America, the Development of Its Civilization *and* Our Latin American Neighbors

BAILEY, J. O., *Professor of English, University of North Carolina; Author of* Thomas Hardy and the Cosmic Mind *and* The Poetry of Thomas Hardy: A Handbook and Commentary

BAILEY, LLOYD R., *Associate Professor, Divinity School, Duke University*

BAINTON, ROLAND, *Titus Street Professor of Ecclesiastical History, Yale University; Author of* Here I Stand: A Life of Martin Luther *and* The Horizon History of Christianity

BAIRD, ROBERT N., *Assistant Professor, Department of Economics, School of Management, Case Western Reserve University*

BAKER, BURTON L., *Professor of Anatomy, University of Michigan*

BAKER, CARLOS, *Woodrow Wilson Professor of Literature, Princeton University; Author of* Ernest Hemingway: A Life Story

BAKER, DAVID J., *Music Reviewer,* New Haven Register; *Contributor,* Opera News

BAKER, FRANK, *Professor Emeritus of English Church History, Duke University; Textual Editor of the Oxford-Bicentennial Edition of the Works of John Wesley*

BAKER, KENDALL L., *Assistant Professor, Department of Political Science, University of Wyoming*

BAKER, MARVIN W., JR., *Associate Professor of Geography, University of Oklahoma*

BAKER, RICHARD B., *Director of Community Relations, University of Cincinnati*

BAKER, ROBERT S., *Professor of English, University of Wisconsin at Madison*

BAKHASH, SHAUL, *Professor of Government, George Mason University; Author of* The Reign of the Ayatollahs: Iran and the Islamic Revolution

BAKKEN, HENRY H., *Professor of Agricultural Economics, University of Wisconsin; Coauthor of* The Economics of Cooperative Marketing

BALABANIAN, NORMAN, *Professor of Electrical Engineering, Syracuse University; Author of* Electrical Network Theory *and* Fundamentals of Circuit Theory

BALAMUTH, WILLIAM, *Professor of Zoology, University of California at Berkeley*

BALCOMB, JOHN, *Public Information Officer, UNICEF, United Nations*

BALCOMB, KENNETH C., III, *Orca Survey, Whale Museum, Friday Harbor, Washington; Coauthor of* Marine Birds and Mammals of Puget Sound

BALD, F. CLEVER, *Professor of History, University of Michigan; Author of* Michigan in Four Centuries

BALDICK, ROBERT, *Fellow of Pembroke College, Oxford University; Author of* The Duel

BALDINI, MARIO, MD, *Brown University Institute for Health Science*

BALDINI, UMBERTO, *Director, Laboratories of Restoration, Florence, Italy*

BALDWIN, ROGER N., *Director, American Civil Liberties Union*

BALDWIN, WILLIAM L., *Professor of Economics, Dartmouth College; Author of* Antitrust and the Changing Corporation

BALL, HOWARD, *Professor, Department of Political Science, University of Vermont*

BALL, ROBERT HAMILTON, *Chairman, Department of English, Queens College*

BALLANCE, PAUL S., *Director of Libraries, Public Library of Winston-Salem and Forsyth County*

BALLANTINE, JOHN, *Lawn Tennis and Golf Correspondent, Times of London Newspapers; Author of* Thirty Years of Championship Golf *and* Cannonball Tennis

BALLESTEROS GAIBROIS, MANUEL, *Author of* Isabel de Castilla, Reina Catolica de España

BAMBERGER, CARL, *Editor of* The Conductor's Art

BAMBERGER, CURT, *Chemistry Consultant; Former Research and Development Chemist, Patent Chemicals, Inc., Paterson, N.J.*

BANCROFT, T. A., *Professor of Statistics and Director of Statistical Laboratory, Iowa State University*

BANES, SALLY, *Professor of Dance and Theater History, University of Wisconsin at Madison; Author of* Writing Dancing in the Postmodern Period

BANFIELD, A. W. F., *Department of Biological Sciences, Brock University, Canada; Author of* A Revision of the Reindeer and Caribou Genus Rangifer

BANGERT, WILLIAM V., SJ, *Adjunct Professor of Church History, Fordham University; Author of* A History of the Society of Jesus

BANISTER, JOHN R., *Director of Libraries, Bradley Memorial Library*

BANNER, JAMES M., JR., *Associate Professor of History, Princeton University; Author of* To the Hartford Convention

BANNON, JOHN FRANCIS, SJ, *Professor of History, St. Louis University; Author of* The Spanish Conquistadores—Men or Devils? *and* History of the Americas

BARAGWANATH, ALBERT K., *Senior Curator, Museum of the City of New York*

BARBASH, JACK, *Professor of Economics, University of Wisconsin; Author of* American Unions: Structure, Government and Politics

BARBER, BERNARD, *Professor of Sociology, Barnard College, Columbia University; Author of* Social Stratification

BARBER, JAMES ALDEN, JR., *National Defense University, Washington, D.C.; Author of* Social Mobility and Voting Behavior; *Coauthor of* The Military and American Society

BARCLAY, C. N., *Brigadier, British Army (Retired); Author of* The New Warfare

BARCLAY, ROBERT W., *Staff Writer, Aurora Beacon-News*

BARCLAY, WILLIAM, *Professor of Divinity and Biblical Criticism, University of Glasgow; Author of* The Mind of Paul

BARDACH, JOHN E., *Director of Hawaii Institute of Marine Biology, University of Hawaii; Author of* Harvest of the Sea

BARDEEN, JOHN, *Nobel Prize Winner in Physics, 1956 and 1972; University of Illinois*

BARGAR, B. D., *Professor of History and Acting Director of African Studies, University of South Carolina; Author of* Lord Dartmouth and the American Revolution

BARGER, EDGAR LEE, *Director, Agricultural Relations, Massey-Ferguson Inc.; Author of* Tractors and Their Power Units

BARGHOORN, ELSO S., *Fisher Professor of Natural History, Department of Biology, Harvard University*

BARK, WILLIAM C., *Professor of History, Stanford University; Author of* Origins of the Medieval World

BARKER, ALLEN V., *Professor, Department of Plant and Soil Sciences, University of Massachusetts at Amherst*

BARKER, EILEEN, *Professor of Sociology, London School of Economics and Political Science, University of London*

BARKER, ROBERT L., *President, Giant Schnauzer Club; Author of* Grooming the Giant Schnauzer

BARKER, STEPHEN F., *Professor of Philosophy, Johns Hopkins University; Author of* Induction and Hypothesis, Philosophy of Mathematics, *and* The Elements of Logic

BARKIN, SOLOMON, *Professor of Economics, University of Massachusetts; Author of* International Labor

BARKO, CAROL, *The New School for Social Research*

BARKSDALE, RICHARD K., *Dean, Graduate School, North Carolina College at Durham*

BARLOW, DAVID H., *State University of New York at Albany; Editor of* Behavior Therapy; *Coauthor of* Phobia: Psychological and Pharmacological Treatment

BARLOW, FRANK, *Professor of History, University of Exeter, England; Author of* William I and the Norman Conquest *and* Conquest to Magna Carta

BARNARD, HARRY, *Author of* Rutherford B. Hayes and His America

BARNES, DANIEL R., *Associate Professor of English, Ohio State University*

BARNES, FRANK, *Regional Chief of Interpretation, Northeast Regional Office, National Park Service, Philadelphia*

BARNES, H. J., *Master Lock Company*

BARNES, JOAN SEIDL, *Historian and Museum Consultant*

BARNES, JOSEPH W., *Rochester (N.Y.) City Historian*

BARNES, ROBERT D., *Professor of Biology, Gettysburg College; Author of* Invertebrate Zoology

BARNES, TREVOR J., *Department of Geography, University of British Columbia*

BARNETT, THOMAS A. M., *Professor of Old Testament, Anglican Theological College, Canada*

BARNHART, RICHARD, *Associate Professor of the History of Art, Yale University*

BARNICOAT, JOHN, *Principal, Falmouth School of Art, Cornwall, England; Author of* A Concise History of Posters

BARNUM, ROBERT H., *Rear Admiral, United States Naval Reserve—Ready Reserve*

BARON, MICHAEL S., *Director, Chicopee Public Library, Chicopee, Mass.*

BAROTT, HERBERT G., *Biophysicist, Bureau of Animal Industry, U.S. Department of Agriculture*

BARQUIST, DAVID L., *Associate Curator of American Decorative Arts, Yale University Art Gallery; Author of* American Tables and Looking Glasses in the Mabel Brady Garvan and Other Collections at Yale University

BARR, E. SCOTT, *Professor, Department of Physics, University of Alabama*

BARR, O. SYDNEY, *Professor of New Testament, General Theological Seminary, New York City*

BARR, ROBERT R., SJ, *John XXIII Center for Eastern Christian Studies, New York City*

BARRETT, EDWARD J., *Professor of Chemistry, Hunter College*

BARRETT, EDWIN B., *Professor of English, Hamilton College*

BARRETT, L. K., *Research Assistant, Harvard University*

BARRETT, MARY, *Librarian, King's College, Wilkes-Barre, Pa.*

BARRICELLI, GIAN PIERO, *Professor of Romance Languages and Comparative Literature, University of California at Riverside; Author of* Alessandro Manzoni

BARRINGTON, LOMA, *Librarian, West Bend Public Library*

BARRON, FRANK, *Professor of Psychology, University of California at Santa Cruz; Author of* Creative Person and Creative Process

BARRON, MILTON L., *Professor of Sociology, California State University at Fresno; Editor of* Minorities in a Changing World

BARRON, NEIL, *Editor of* Anatomy of Wonder

BARRY, JEANNE, *Director of Public Relations, De Paul University*

BARRY, KATHLEEN, *Associate Professor of Human Development, Pennsylvania State University; Author of* Susan B. Anthony: Biography of a Singular Feminist

BARSLEY, MICHAEL, *Author, Artist, and Television Writer; Author of* The Left-Handed Book

BARTHOLOMEW, PAUL C., *Professor of Government and International Studies, University of Notre Dame*

BARTLETT, C. J., *Reader in International History, University of Dundee, Scotland*

BARTLETT, IRVING H., *Professor of American Civilization, University of Massachusetts at Boston; Author of* Wendell Phillips, Brahmin Radical, Daniel Webster, *and* The American Mind in the Mid-19th Century

BARTON, H. ARNOLD, *Professor of History, Southern Illinois University; Author of* Hans Axel von Fersen

BARZANTI, SERGIO, *Associate Professor of Social Sciences, Fairleigh Dickinson University*

BARZUN, JACQUES, *Dean of Faculties and Provost, Columbia University; Author of* Berlioz and His Century

BASCOM, WILLIAM, *Professor of Anthropology, University of California at Berkeley*

BASHAM, A. L., *University of London; Author of* The Wonder that Was India

BASINGER, JEANINE, *Corwin-Fuller Professor of Film Studies, Wesleyan University*

BASKERVILLE, PETER A., *Professor of History, University of Victoria, Victoria, British Columbia*

BASSETT, REV. WILLIAM W., *Assistant Professor, School of Canon Law, Catholic University of America*

BASSHAM, JAMES A., *Research Chemist, Lawrence Radiation Laboratory, University of California at Berkeley*

BASTNAGEL, CLEMENT, *Associate Professor of Canon Law, School of Canon Law, Catholic University of America*

BASTOCK, MARGARET, *Fellow of St. Anne's College, Oxford University; Author of* Courtship: an Ethological Study

BATCHELDER, MURIEL G., *Librarian, Hyannis Public Library, Hyannis, Mass.*

BATEMAN, GARY C., *Assistant Professor of Biology, Northern Arizona University*

BATES, CAROLINE, *Senior Editor, Gourmet Magazine*

BATES, J. LEONARD, *Professor of History, University of Illinois; Author of* The Origins of Teapot Dome

BATES, JOSEPH D., JR., *Author of* Streamer Fly Tying and Fishing

BATES, MARGARET L., *Professor of Political Science, New College of the University of South Florida; Author of* A Study Guide for Tanzania

BATESON, FREDERICK W., *Fellow, Corpus Christi College, Oxford University; Author of* Wordsworth: A Reinterpretation

BATTELL, JACK STRALEY, *Coauthor of* The Best in Chess

BATTELLE, KENNETH, *President, Kenneth Beauty Salons and Products, Inc.*

BATTENHOUSE, ROY W., *Professor of English, Indiana University; Author of* Marlowe's Tamburlaine: A Study in Renaissance Moral Philosophy *and* Shakespearean Tragedy: Its Art and Its Christian Premises

BATTESTIN, MARTIN C., *Professor of English, University of Virginia; Author of* The Moral Basis of Fielding's Art

BAUGH, ALBERT C., *Professor of English Language and Literature, The College, University of Pennsylvania; Coauthor of* History of the English Language; *Editor of* A Literary History of England

BAUGH, RUTH E., *Professor of Geography, University of California at Los Angeles*

BAUMGAERTNER, IMRE VON, *Columbia University Lamont-Doherty Geological Observatory*

BAUSOR, SIDNEY C., *Professor and Head, Department of Biological Sciences, California State College, Pa.; Coauthor of the* Complete Guide to the Trees of North America

BAYER, PATRICIA, *Coauthor of* The Art of René Lalique; *Author of* Art Deco Interiors *and* Art Deco Architecture

BAYERSCHMIDT, CARL F., *Professor of Germanic Philology, Columbia University; Coeditor of* Scandinavian Studies

BAYLES, MICHAEL D., *Professor of Philosophy, University of Florida*

BAYLEY, NED, *Director, Animal Husbandry Research Branch, Agricultural Research Service, U.S. Department of Agriculture*

BAYLIS, THOMAS A., *Professor of Political Science, University of Texas at San Antonio; Author of* The Technical Intelligentsia and the East German Elite

BEACH, CECIL P., *Director of Libraries, Tampa and Hillsborough County, Tampa, Fla.*

BEACH, STEWART, *Author of* Samuel Adams: The Fateful Years, 1764–1776

BEACHAM, L. M., *Acting Director, Division of Food Chemistry and Technology, Food and Drug Administration*

BEADLE, NOEL, *Professor of Botany, University of New England, New South Wales, Australia; Coauthor of* Flora of the Sydney Region

BEAL, DENTON, *Director of Public Relations, Carnegie-Mellon University*

BEAMISH, F. E., *Professor of Chemistry, University of Toronto, Canada*

BEARD, JAMES FRANKLIN, *Professor of English, Clark University; Author of* The Letters and Journals of James Fenimore Cooper

BEARDSLEY, MONROE C., *Professor of Philosophy, Temple University; Author of* Aesthetics from Classical Greece to the Present

BEARDSLEY, RICHARD K., *Coauthor of* Twelve Doors to Japan *and* Village Japan

BEATSON, JAMES A., *Professor and Chairman, Department of History, New Mexico Highlands University*

BEATTIE, A. J., *Lecturer in Political Science, London School of Economics, University of London*

BEATTY, SAMUEL A., *Assistant Attorney General of Alabama; Former Dean, School of Law, Mercer University*

BEAVER, DONALD deB., *Associate Professor, Department of the History of Science, Williams College*

BECK, CURT F., *Professor of Political Science, University of Connecticut*

BECK, G. E., *Professor, Department of Horticulture, University of Wisconsin*

BECK, JAMES, *Professor of Art History, Columbia University*

BECK, LEWIS W., *Professor of Philosophy, University of Rochester; Author of* Studies in the Philosophy of Kant

BECK, RICHARD, *Editor of* Icelandic Poems and Stories

BECK, WILLIAM S., MD, *Professor of Medicine, Harvard Medical School; Tutor in Biochemical Sciences, Harvard College; Director of Hematology Research Laboratory, Massachusetts General Hospital; Author of* Human Design, Modern Science and the Nature of Life, *and* Hematology

BECKER, E. LOVELL, MD, *Professor of Medicine, Mount Sinai School of Medicine; Director of Medicine, Beth Israel Medical Center, New York City*

BECKER, JOHN, *Librarian, Otterbein College Library*

BECKER, ROBERT A., *Consulting Physicist and Former Director, Space Physics Laboratory, Aerospace Corporation, El Segundo, Calif.*

BECKERMAN, BERNARD, *Author of* Shakespeare at the Globe

BECKETT, R. B., *Editor of* Constable's Correspondence

BECKHART, BENJAMIN HAGGOTT, *Professor of Banking, Columbia University; Editor of* Banking Systems

BECKINSALE, ROBERT P., *Senior Lecturer in Geography, University of Oxford; Coauthor of* The Iberian Peninsula

BECKSON, KARL, *Associate Professor of English, Brooklyn College; Editor of* Great Theories in Literary Criticism

BÉDÉ, JEAN-ALBERT, *Professor of French, Columbia University*

BEDINI, SILVIO A., *Deputy Director, National Museum of History and Technology, Smithsonian Institution; Author of* The Life of Benjamin Banneker

BEDNAROWSKI, MARY FARRELL, *Professor of Religious Studies, United Theological Seminary of the Twin Cities; Author of* American Religion *and* New Religions and the Theological Imagination in America

BEEBE, LUCIUS, *Author of* The Big Spenders

BEEBE, MAURICE, *Professor of English, Temple University; Author of* Ivory Towers and Sacred Founts

BEELER, M. S., *Professor of Linguistics, University of California at Berkeley*

BEER, HARRY M., *Secretary-Treasurer, Canadian Headmasters' Association*

BEESLEY, MICHAEL E., *Professor of Economics, London Graduate School of Economics*

BEESON, PAUL BRUCE, MD, *Professor of Medicine, Department of Internal Medicine, Yale University School of Medicine*

BEGGS, JAMES M., *Office of the Secretary, U.S. Department of Transportation*

BEGLEY, VIMALA, *Department of Sociology and Anthropology, University of Iowa*

BEIER, ERNEST G., *Professor of Psychology, University of Utah; Author of* The Silent Language of Psychotherapy *and* People Reading

BEINERT, FREDERICA L., *Author of* The Art of Making Sauces and Gravies, The Art of Making Soufflés, *and* Now You're Cooking

BEISSWENGER, BLANCHE, *Secretary, German Shepherd Dog Club of America*

BELFORD, LEE A., *Professor, Department of Religious Education, New York University*

BELISARIUS, CONSTANTINE P., SJ, *Center for Eastern Christian Studies, Fordham University*

BELK, EVELYN SIMPSON, *Head Librarian, Garland-Montgomery Regional Library*

BELL, JOSEPH, *Associate Curator of Birds, New York Zoological Society*

BELL, WILLIAM GARDNER, *United States Cavalry; Editor of* The Armored Cavalry Journal

BELLER, ELMER A., *Professor of History, Princeton University*

BELLUSH, BERNARD, *Professor and Subchairman, Department of History, Bernard M. Baruch School of Business and Public Administration, City College of New York*

BELL-VILLADA, GENE H., *Professor of Spanish, Williams College; Author of* Borges and His Fiction: A Guide to His Mind and Art

BeMILLER, J. N., *Professor of Chemistry, Southern Illinois University*

BEMIS, SAMUEL FLAGG, *Author of* John Quincy Adams and the Union *and* A Diplomatic History of the United States

BENAGH, JIM, *Coauthor of* The Official Encyclopedia of Sports; *Author of* Incredible Athletic Feats

BENDER, ERNEST, *Professor of IndoAryan Languages and Literatures, Oriental and South Asia Regional Studies Departments, University of Pennsylvania*

BENDER, PAUL, *Professor of Law, University of Pennsylvania; Former General Counsel, Commission on Obscenity and Pornography*

BENDER, WILLIAM, *Professor Emeritus of Physics, Western Washington State University*

BENEDICT, MICHAEL LES, *Associate Professor of History, Ohio State University; Author of* The Impeachment and Trial of Andrew Johnson *and* A Compromise of Principle

BENÉT, LAURA, *Author of* Famous American Poets

BENET, SULA, *Professor of Anthropology, Hunter College*

BENJAMIN, HERBERT S., MD, *Cedars of Lebanon Hospital, Los Angeles; Author of* A Little Sickness Is Good for You

BENJAMIN, MARY A., *Director, Walter A. Benjamin Autographs, New York City*

BENNETT, BOYCE M., JR., *Professor of Old Testament, General Theological Seminary, New York City*

BENNETT, CHARLES E., *Member of U.S. Congress; Author of* Laudonnière and Fort Caroline

BENNETT, FLEMING, *Librarian, University of Arizona Library*

BENNETT, H. STANLEY, MD, *Professor of Biological Sciences, University of North Carolina at Chapel Hill*

BENNETT, JOHN F., *Lecturer in Embryology, Human Ecology, and Graduate Biology, San Jose State University*

BENNETT, JOHN W., *Chairman, Department of Anthropology, Washington University, St. Louis, Mo.*

BENNETT, ROBERT A., JR., *Assistant Professor of Old Testament, Episcopal Theological School, Cambridge, Mass.*

BENSMAN, JOSEPH, *Professor of Sociology, City College of New York; Coauthor of* Small Town in Mass Society

BENSON, OTIS O., JR., *Major General, U.S. Air Force (Retired); Consultant in Aerospace Medicine*

BENSTON, GEORGE J., *John H. Harland Professor of Finance, Accounting, and Economics, Emory University*

BENSUSAN, GUY, *Department of Humanities, Northern Arizona University*

BENTLEY, ERIC, *Author of* The Life of the Drama *and* The Playright as Thinker

BENTLEY, GERALD E., JR., *Professor, Department of English, University College, University of Toronto, Canada; Coauthor of* A Blake Bibliography

BENTLEY, J. M., *President, Canadian Federation of Agriculture*

BENZINGER, T. H., MD, *Director, Bioenergetics Laboratory, Naval Medical Research Institute, Bethesda, Md.*

BERAT, LYNN, *Yale University; Author of* Walvis Bay: Decolonization and International Law

BERENTSEN, WILLIAM H., *Professor of Geography, University of Connecticut; Coeditor of* Regional Development Processes and Policies *and* Beitraege zur raeumlichen Prozessforschung in den USA

BERG, DANIEL, *Manager, Insulation and Chemical Technology Research and Development, Westinghouse Research Laboratories*

BERG, ELLIOT J., *Department of Economics, Georgetown University*

BERG, KATHY L., *Reference Librarian, Tompkins County Public Library*

BERG, LINDA R., *Environmental Sciences Writer; Coauthor of* Environment

BERGEN, EDGAR, *Professional Ventriloquist and Entertainer*

BERGENDOFF, CONRAD, *President, Augustana College*

BERGER, M. MARVIN, *Associate Publisher, New York Law Journal; Member of the New York Bar*

BERGER, MORROE, *Director, Program in Near Eastern Studies, Princeton University*

BERGERON, DAVID M., *Professor of English, University of Kansas; Author of* Twentieth Century Criticism of English Masques, Pageants and Entertainments, 1558–1642

BERGH, NELLIE, *Artist-Craftsperson Embroiderer and Lecturer*

BERGHAHN, VOLKER R., *Professor of History, Brown University; Author of* Germany and the Approval of War in 1914, Modern Germany, *and* The Americanization of West German Industry

BERGIN, THOMAS G., *Sterling Professor of Romance Languages, Yale University; Author of* Dante

BERGSTEIN, STANLEY F., *Executive Vice President, Harness Tracks of America*

BERINGAUSE, ARTHUR, *Chairman, Department of English, Bronx Community College*

BERKEBILE, DON H., *Division of Transportation, Smithsonian Institution*

BERMAN, MILTON, *Professor of History, University of Rochester; Author of* John Fiske, the Evolution of a Popularizer

BERMAN, SIMEON M., *Professor of Mathematics, New York University; Principal Investigator, National Science Foundation Grant to New York University for Research in Probability Theory; Author of* The Elements of Probability, Mathematical Statistics, *and* Calculus for the Nonphysical Sciences

BERNATH, STUART L., *Author of* Squall Across the Atlantic: American Civil War Prize Cases and Diplomacy

BERNHARDT, ARTHUR D., *Assistant Professor, Department of Architecture, Massachusetts Institute of Technology; Author of* The Mobile Home Industry

BERNSTEIN, BRUCE H., *Assistant Professor, Department of Psychology, City University of New York*

BERNSTEIN, HARRY, *Chairman, Dance Department, Adelphi University*

BERNSTEIN, HARRY, *Professor of History, Brooklyn College; Author of* Modern and Contemporary Latin America

BERNSTEIN, IRWIN S., *Yerkes Regional Primate Research Center, Emory University*

BERNSTEIN, JEREMY, *Professor of Physics, Stevens Institute of Technology*

BERNSTEIN, NORBERT, *Librarian, Seymour Library, Auburn, N.Y.*

BERRILL, NORMAN J., *Strathcona Professor of Zoology, McGill University; Author of* The Living Tide *and* Growth, Development, and Pattern

BERRY, ERNEST B., *Associate Professor, School of Textiles, North Carolina State University; Author of* Textile Designing—Pure and Applied

BERRY, FREDERICK H., *Research Systematic Zoologist (Fishes), U.S. Bureau of Commercial Fisheries, Tropical Atlantic Biological Laboratory*

BERRY, GEORGE RICKER, *Author of* The Old Testament Among the Semitic Religions

BERTHOFF, ROWLAND T., *Professor of History, Washington University, St. Louis, Mo.*

BEST, CHARLES H., MD, *Director, Best Institute, University of Toronto, Canada*

BETTS, VICTORIA BEDFORD, *Art Consultant; Author of* Exploring Finger Paint

BEUKEMA, HERMAN, *Brigadier General, United States Army*

BEUTLER, ERNEST, MD, *Chairman, Division of Medicine, City of Hope Medical Center; Clinical Professor of Medicine, University of Southern California*

BEVIER, JANE, *Senior Librarian, Hollywood Regional Branch Library*

BEWLEY, LOIS M., *Professor Emeritus, School of Library, Archival, and Information Studies, University of British Columbia*

BEYER, CLARA M., *Acting Director, Bureau of Labor Standards, U.S. Department of Labor*

BIBBY, GEOFFREY, *Head of Oriental Department, Prehistoric Museum, Aarhus, Denmark; Author of* Testimony of the Spade

BICKELHAUPT, DAVID L., *Professor of Insurance and Finance, Ohio State University; Author of* General Insurance

BIDNEY, DAVID, *Professor of Anthropology, Indiana University*

BIELER, LUDWIG, *Professor of Late Latin and Early Medieval Latin, University College, Dublin, Ireland*

BIEN, DAVID D., *Professor of History, University of Michigan*

BIENVENU, RICHARD T., *Associate Professor of History, University of Missouri; Editor of* The Ninth of Thermidor: The Fall of Robespierre

BIERMAN, HOWARD, *Editor in Chief, Electronic Design*

BIERMAN, MARVIN, *R.C.A. Institutes*

BIGELOW, ARTHUR L., *Bellmaster of Princeton University*

BIGGAR, ROBERT J., MD, *National Institutes of Health*

BIGGS, ANSELM G., OSB, *Professor of History, Belmont Abbey College*

BILKEY, WARREN J., *Professor of Business, University of Wisconsin*

BILLIAS, GEORGE A., *Professor of American History, Clark University*

BILLINGS, MARLAND P., *Professor of Geology, Harvard University*

BILLINGSLEY, HOBIE, *Author of* Diving Illustrated

BILLINGSLEY, JOHN D., *Brigadier General, U.S. Army (Retired); Professor and Head of the Department of Ordnance, U.S. Military Academy*

BILLINGTON, MONROE, *Head, Department of History, New Mexico State University; Author of* Thomas P. Gore: The Blind Senator from Oklahoma

BILLINGTON, RAY ALLEN, *Author of* Frontier and American Culture, The Genesis of the Frontier Thesis, *and* Frederick Jackson Turner: Historian, Scholar, Teacher

BILOCERKOWYCZ, JAROSLAW, *Professor of Political Science, University of Dayton*

BINNEY, STEPHEN E., *Associate Professor of Nuclear Engineering, Oregon State University*

BIRD, HARRISON K., *Military Historian; Author of* Battle for a Continent, March to Saratoga, *and* Navies in the Mountains

BIRD, J. BRIAN, *Professor of Geography, McGill University, Canada*

BIRD, JUNIUS, *Curator of Archaeology, American Museum of Natural History*

BIRDSALL, RICHARD D., *Professor of History, Connecticut College; Author of* Berkshire County: A Cultural History

BIRDSEY, MONROE, *Professor of Botany, Miami-Dade Community College*

BIRENBAUM, ARNOLD, *Associate Professor of Pediatrics, Albert Einstein College of Medicine, Yeshiva University, New York City*

BIRNBAUM, NORMAN, *Professor of Sociology, Amherst College*

BIRNS, LAURENCE R., *Lecturer, Latin American Studies, The New School for Social Research; Author of* Chile: A Chronology and Fact Book

BISHOP, MORRIS, *Author of* A Survey of French Literature

BISHOP, THOMAS W., *Chairman, Department of French and Italian, New York University; Author of* Pirandello and the French Theater

BIZARDEL, YVON, *Honorary Director of the City of Paris*

BJORNESS, R. A., *Freeport (N.Y.) Sulphur Company*

BLACK, CHARLES WILFRED, *Librarian, Mitchell Library, Glasgow, Scotland*

BLACK, HAROLD S., *Author of* Modulation Theory

BLACK, JOHN D., *Professor of Zoology, Northeast Missouri State University*

BLACK, KENNETH, JR., *Dean, School of Business Administration, Georgia State University; Coauthor of* Life Insurance *and* Cases in Life Insurance

BLACK, MAX, *Professor of Philosophy, Cornell University*

BLACKALL, ERIC A., *Jacob Gould Schurman Professor of German Literature, Cornell University; Author of* The Emergence of German as a Literary Language

BLACKMAN, D. J., *Lecturer in Classics, Bristol University, England*

BLACKORBY, EDWARD C., *Professor of History, Wisconsin State University at Eau Claire; Author of* Prairie Rebel: The Public Life of William Lemke

BLACKSTOCK, PAUL W., *Professor of International Studies, University of South Carolina; Author of* The Strategy of Subversion *and* The Secret Road to World War II

BLACKWOOD, GEORGE D., *Professor of Political Economy, Boston University*

BLAHER, DAMIAN J., OFM, *Professor of Moral Theology and Canon Law, Holy Name College, Washington, D.C.; Author of* Thirty-two Answers to Questions in Moral Theology and Canon Law

BLAIN, JEAN, *Professor of History, University of Montreal, Canada*

BLAIR, KAREN J., *Professor of History, Central Washington University; Author of* The Torchbearers: Women and Their Amateur Arts Societies, 1890–1930

BLAKE, E. O., *Senior Lecturer in History, University of Southampton, England*

BLAKEMORE, HAROLD, *Secretary, Institute of Latin American Studies, University of London; Author of* Latin America

BLANCHARD, J. RICHARD, *University Librarian, University of California at Davis*

BLANCHARD, WENDIE, *Editor of* Creative Crafts *Magazine*

BLAND, DAVID, *Author of* A History of Book Illustration

BLANKSTEN, GEORGE I., *Professor of Political Science, Northwestern University*

BLANNING, T. C. W., *Lecturer in History, University of Cambridge; Author of* Joseph II and Enlightened Despotism *and* Reform and Revolution in Mainz

BLANSHARD, BRAND, *Author of* The Nature of Thought *and* Reason and Analysis

BLASER, H. WESTON, *Associate Professor of Botany, University of Washington*

BLAUSTEIN, ALBERT P., *Professor of Law, School of Law, Rutgers University; Author of* Law and the Military Establishment *and* The Military and American Society

BLEED, PETER, *Professor of Anthropology, University of Nebraska at Lincoln*

BLEICH, ALAN R., MD, *Assistant Clinical Professor of Radiology, New York Medical College*

BLESS, R. C., *Astronomy Department, University of Wisconsin*

BLEZNICK, DONALD W., *Head of the Department of Romance Languages and Literatures, University of Cincinnati; Coeditor of* Representative Spanish Authors

BLIER, SUZANNE PRESTON, *Department of Art, Vassar College*

BLIGHT, DAVID W., *Associate Professor of History and Black Studies, Amherst College; Author of* Narrative of the Life of Frederick Douglass, An American Slave *and* Frederick Douglass' Civil War: Keeping Faith in Jubilee

BLISTEIN, ELMER M., *Professor of English, Brown University; Author of* Comedy in Action

BLOCH, HOWARD R., *Associate Professor of Economics, George Mason University*

BLOCK, FARRIS, *Director of Information, University of Houston*

BLOCK, MARGARET E., *Reference Librarian, Eugene Public Library, Eugene, Oreg.*

BLODGETT, PHILIP R., *Director, Everett Public Library, Everett, Wash.*

BLOOM, ARTHUR L., *Associate Professor, Geological Sciences, Cornell University; Author of* Surface of the Earth

BLOOM, EDWARD A., *Professor of English, Brown University; Author of* Samuel Johnson in Grub Street

BLOOM, MURRAY TEIGH, *Author of* Money of Their Own: The Great Counterfeiters *and* The Man Who Stole Portugal

BLOOMFIELD, LINCOLN P., *Professor of Political Science and Director, Arms Control Project, Massachusetts Institute of Technology*

BLUME, WILLIAM W., *Author of* American Civil Procedure

BLUMENSON, MARTIN, *Author of* Kasserine Pass *and* The Duel for France

BLUMENTHAL, BOB, *Music Critic*

BLUNDEN, EDMUND, *Head of the Department of English, University of Hong Kong; Author of* Shelley: A Life Story

BOAK, ARTHUR E. R., *Author of* A History of Rome to 565 A.D.

BOARDMAN, JOHN, *Reader in Classical Archaeology, Oxford University; Author of* Greek Art

BOASE, THOMAS S. R., *President, Magdalen College, Oxford University; Editor, Oxford History of English Art series; Author of* English Art, 1100–1216 *and* English Art, 1800–1870 *in* Oxford History of English Art *series*

BOB, MURRAY L., *Director, Chautauqua-Cattaraugus Library System*

BOCK, HAL, *Hockey Writer, Associated Press; Coeditor of* The Complete Encyclopedia of Ice Hockey

BOCK, WALTER J., *Professor of Evolutionary Biology, Department of Biological Sciences, Columbia University*

BOCKHOP, CLARENCE W., *Professor and Head, Department of Agricultural Engineering, Iowa State University*

BODEMER, CHARLES W., *Professor and Chairman, Department of Biomedical History, School of Medicine, University of Washington*

BOERSMA, MICHAEL J., *Department of the History of Science, University of Wisconsin at Madison*

BOES, WARREN N., *Director of Libraries, University of Georgia*

BOGDAN, JOHN F., *Professor of Textiles, North Carolina State University School of Textiles; Author of* Carding and Combing, *in* The American Cotton Handbook, *vol. 1*

BOGERT, CHARLES M., *Curator, Department of Amphibians and Reptiles, American Museum of Natural History*

BOGUE, DONALD J., *Professor of Sociology, Director, Community and Family Study Center, University of Chicago; Author of* Principles of Demography

BOHLIN, J. DAVID, *Chief, Solar and Heliospheric Physics, NASA Headquarters*

BOK, BART J., *Professor of Astronomy, University of Arizona; Former Director of Steward Observatory*

BOLD, HAROLD C., *Professor of Botany, Plant Research Institute, University of Texas; Editor of* American Journal of Botany

BOLLAND, O. NIGEL, *Professor of Sociology, Colgate University; Author of* The Formation of a Colonial Society: Belize, from Conquest to Crown Colony; Belize: A New Nation in Central America *and* Colonialism and Resistance in Belize

BOLLENS, JOHN C., *Professor of Political Science, University of California at Los Angeles*

BOLTON, J. L., *Research Bureau, Canada Department of Agriculture*

BONANSEA, BERNARDINO M., OFM, *Professor of Philosophy, Catholic University of America; Coeditor of* John Duns Scotus, 1265–1965

BOND, DONALD S., *RCA Laboratories, Radio Corporation of America*

BOND, HORACE M., *Director, Bureau of Educational and Social Research, Atlanta, Ga.; Author of* The Education of the Negro in the American Social Order

BONDURANT, JOAN V., *Professor of Politics, University of the Pacific; Author of* The Gandhian Philosophy of Conflict

BONE, ROBERT C., *Professor of Government Emeritus, Florida State University*

BONEY, FRANCIS NASH, *Professor of History, University of Georgia*

BONICA, JOHN J., *Professor and Chairman, Department of Anesthesiology, University of Washington School of Medicine, Seattle, Wash.; Chairman of the National Institutes of Health Ad Hoc Committee on Acupuncture; Author of* The Management of Pain

BONNER, J. F., *Professor of Biology, California Institute of Technology*

BONNICK, B. J., *Cable and Wireless Limited, London*

BONNIWELL, WILLIAM R., OP, *Author of* The Liturgical Spirit of Lent, A History of the Dominican Liturgy, *and* The Martyrology of the Friars Preachers

BOOR, ELIZABETH E., *Administrative Librarian, Hannibal Free Public Library*

BOOTH, BRADFORD A., *Professor of English Literature, University of California at Los Angeles; Editor of* Nineteenth-Century Fiction

BOOTY, JOHN E., *Dean, School of Theology, University of the South*

BORDEN, SUSAN, *Librarian, Wayne County Public Library*

BOREN, HENRY C., *Professor of History, University of North Carolina; Author of* The Ancient World, The Gracchi, The Roman Republic, *and* Roman Society

BORGSTROM, GEORG, *Professor, Department of Food Science and Geography, Michigan State University; Author of* The Hungry Planet *and* Too Many

BOROMÉ, JOSEPH A., *Professor of History, City College of New York*

BOROW, RENA B., *Member of the Joseph Papp Yiddish Theater*

BORROFF, EDITH, *Professor of Music, State University of New York at Binghamton; Author of* The Music of the Baroque *and* Music in Europe and the United States

BORST, CHARLOTTE G., *Department of the History of Medicine, University of Wisconsin at Madison*

BOSART, LANCE F., *Professor, Department of Atmospheric Science, State University of New York at Albany; Editor (1981–84) of* Monthly Weather Review

BOSCH, RAFAEL, *Associate Professor of Spanish, New York University*

BOSKIN, JOSEPH, *Professor of History, Boston University*

BOSLEY, HAROLD A., *Minister, First Methodist Church, Evanston, Ill.*

BOSWORTH, C. E., *Professor of Arabic Studies, Department of Near Eastern Studies, University of Manchester, England*

BOUCHARD, JOYCE, *Librarian, Butte Free Public Library, Butte, Mont.*

BOULAY, HARVEY, *Assistant Professor of Political Science, Assistant Dean, The Graduate School, Boston University*

BOUQUET, A. C., *Cambridge University; Author of* Man and Deity

BOURGUIGNON, ERIKA, *Professor, Department of Anthropology, Ohio State University; Editor and Coauthor of* Religion, Altered States of Consciousness and Social Change; *Coauthor of* Diversity and Homogeneity in World Societies; *Author of* Possession

BOVÉ, PAUL A., *Professor of English, University of Pittsburgh*

BOWDEN, EDWIN T., *Professor of English, University of Texas at Austin; Editor of* The Satiric Poems of John Trumbull

BOWEN, JEAN, *Music Division, New York Public Library*

BOWEN, JOHN R., *Professor of Anthropology, Washington University*

BOWER, GORDON H., *Professor of Psychology, Stanford University; Coauthor of* Theories of Learning, Human Associative Memory, Asserting Yourself, Attention in Learning, *and* Introduction to Mathematical Learning Theory

BOWERS, DAVID A., *Professor of Banking and Finance, Case Western Reserve University*

BOWERS, PAUL C., JR., *Assistant Professor of History, Ohio State University*

BOWERS, Q. DAVID, *Author of* Coins and Collectors; *Columnist for* Coin World

BOWHILL, SIDNEY A., *Professor of Electrical Engineering, University of Illinois*

BOWIE, W. RUSSELL, *Special Lecturer, Virginia Theological Seminary*

BOWLES, GORDON T., *Professor of Anthropology, Syracuse University*

BOWLES, VIRGINIA K., *Director, Dover Public Library*

BOWMAN, FRANK PAUL, *Professor of Romance Languages, University of Pennsylvania; Author of* Montaigne, Essays

BOWMAN, JAMES E., JR., MD, *Associate Professor of Medicine and Pathology and Medical Director of the Blood Bank, University of Chicago; Consultant in Pathology, Division of Hospital and Medical Facilities, U.S. Department of Health, Education, and Welfare*

BOWMAN, RAYMOND A., *Professor of Oriental Languages and Literatures, University of Chicago*

BOWMAN, RAYMOND T., *Assistant Director for Statistical Standards, Bureau of the Budget, Washington, D.C.*

BOWMAN, THOMAS E., *Curator, Division of Crustacea, Smithsonian Institution*

BOWSFIELD, HARTWELL, *Provincial Archivist of Manitoba, Canada*

BOWSKY, WILLIAM M., *Professor, Department of History, University of California at Davis; Author of* Henry VII in Italy

BOXER, BARUCH, *Professor of Geography, Livingston College, Rutgers University*

BOYD, BARBARA GRAY, *Acting County Librarian, County of Alameda, Hayward, Calif.*

BOYD, JOHN D., SJ, *Professor of English, Fordham University*

BOYD, WILLIAM J. D., *Senior Associate, National Municipal League; Author of* Changing Patterns of Apportionment

BOYD, WILLIAM LOWE, *Distinguished Professor of Education, Pennsylvania State University*

BOYDELL, BRIAN, *Composer and Professor of Music, University of Dublin, Ireland*

BOYDEN, ALAN, *Professor of Zoology, Rutgers University*

BOYER, CARL B., *Author of* History of Mathematics

BOYER, KENNETH J., *College Editor, Bowdoin College*

BOYER, LEE E., *Harrisburg Area Community College, Pa.*

BOYER, PAUL S., *Associate Professor, Department of History, University of Massachusetts*

BOYLAN, JAMES R., *Editor,* Columbia Journalism Review, *Columbia University*

BOYLE, JOHN ANDREW, *Professor of Persian Studies, Victoria University of Manchester, England*

BRACE, C. LORING, *Professor of Anthropology, University of Michigan; Curator of Biological Anthropology, Museum of Anthropology, University of Michigan; Author of* The Stages of Human Evolution, *4th edition*

BRACE, RICHARD M., *Chairman and Professor, History Department, Oakland University, Rochester, Mich.; Author of* Making of the Modern World

BRACK, O. M., JR., *Professor of English, Arizona State University; Coeditor of* Bibliography and Textual Criticism: English and American Literature, 1700 to the Present

BRACY, WILLIAM, *Professor of English, Beaver College*

BRADBROOK, FRANK W., *Author of* Jane Austen and Her Predecessors

BRADDOCK, BILL, *Sports Department,* New York Times

BRADDY, HALDEEN, *Professor of English, University of Texas at El Paso; Author of* Cock of the Walk

BRADEEN, DONALD W., *Professor of Classics and Ancient History, University of Cincinnati; Coeditor of* Studies in Fifth Century Epigraphy

BRADEN, WALDO W., *Chairman and Boyd Professor, Department of Speech, Louisiana State University; Author of* Public Speaking: The Essentials *and* The Oral Tradition in the South; *Coauthor of* Speech Criticism

BRADLEY, ERWIN S., *Professor of History, Union College, Barbourville, Ky.; Author of* Simon Cameron, Lincoln's Secretary of War

BRADLEY, R. S., *Reader in Inorganic and Structural Chemistry, University of Leeds, England; Author of* High Pressure Chemistry

BRADLEY, ROBERT L., *Associate Professor of Food Science, University of Wisconsin at Madison*

BRADSHAW, DAVID, *Technical Consultant*

BRADSHAW, R., *Lecturer in Geology, Bristol University, England*

BRADY, NYLE C., *Director, International Rice Research Institute, Philippines*

BRAEMAN, JOHN, *Professor of History, University of Nebraska; Author of* Change and Continuity in Twentieth-Century America

BRAGG, SIR WILLIAM LAWRENCE, *Nobel Prize Winner in Physics, 1915; Author of* Atomic Structure of Minerals *and* Crystal Structure of Minerals

BRAKER, WILLIAM P., *Director, John G. Shedd Aquarium, Chicago, Ill.*

BRAMLETTE, M. N., *Professor of Geology, Scripps Institution of Oceanography*

BRAMMER, DANA B., *Director, Bureau of Governmental Research, University of Mississippi; Author of* A Manual of Mississippi Government

BRANCACCIO, RONALD R., MD, *Clinical Professor of Dermatology, New York University Medical Center*

BRANCH, DAVID R., *Assistant Director of the Medical Center for Public Relations, School of Medicine and Dentistry, University of Rochester*

BRANCH, M. A., *Director, School of Slavonic and East European Studies, University of London; Coauthor of* Finnish Folk Poetry: Epic

BRAND, REV. CHARLES D., *Episcopal Church*

BRAND, DONALD D., *Professor of Geography, University of Texas; Author of* Mexico, Land of Sunshine and Shadow

BRANDT, ELIZABETH T., *Librarian, Zion Public Library*

BRANDT, RICHARD B., *Professor of Philosophy, University of Michigan; Author of* Ethical Theory

BRANSCOMB, LEWIS M., *Albert Pratt Public Service Professor and Director, Science, Technology, and Public Policy Program, John F. Kennedy School of Government, Harvard University*

BRANT, IRVING, *Author of* James Madison *and* Storm Over the Constitution

BRATT, JAMES D., *Professor of History, Calvin College; Author of* Dutch Calvinism in Modern America: A History of a Conservative Subculture

BRATTAIN, WALTER H., *Nobel Prize Winner in Physics, 1956; Physicist, Bell Telephone Laboratories, Inc.*

BRAUDEL, FERNAND, *Author of* The Mediterranean and the Mediterranean World in the Age of Philip II

BRAUER, KINLEY, *Professor of History, University of Minnesota*

BRAUN, SIDNEY D., *Author of* Dictionary of French Literature

BRAUNTHAL, GERARD, *Professor Emeritus, Department of Political Science, University of Massachusetts at Amherst; Author of* West German Social Democrats, 1969–1982: Profile of a Party in Power

BRAYNARD, FRANK O., *Program Director, South Street Seaport Museum, New York City; Author of* Famous American Ships *and* S.S. Savannah, The Elegant Steam Ship

BRAZENOR, C. W., *Director, National Museum of Victoria, Melbourne, Australia*

BREDSDORFF, ELIAS L., *Head of the Department of Scandinavian Studies, Cambridge University; Author of* Hans Christian Andersen; *Editor of* Scandinavica: An International Journal of Scandinavian Studies

BRÉE, GERMAINE, *Kenan Professor in the Humanities, Wake Forest University; Author of* Marcel Proust and Deliverance from Time, Camus, *and* Gide

BREIT, PETER K., *Professor of Politics and Government, University of Hartford*

BRENNAN, J. WILLIAM, *Assistant Professor of History, University of Regina (Sask.); Editor,* Regina Before Yesterday: A Visual History, 1882 to 1945

BRENT, ROBERT A., *Professor of History, University of Southern Mississippi*

BRESLIN, THOMAS, SJ, *Fordham University*

BRESNAHAN, JOHN E., OSA, *Professor of Spirituality, Patristics, and Apologetics, Augustinian College, Washington, D.C.*

BRETT, BERNARD, *Author of* A History of Watercolor

BRETT-JAMES, ANTONY, *Head of Department of War Studies, Royal Military Academy Sandhurst, England; Author of* Wellington at War, 1794–1815

BREVAK, ALEXANDER, *Director, Division of Public Relations, Carnegie Institute*

BREWSTER, WILLIAM T., *Coauthor of* Introduction to the English Classics

BRICE, CAROL A., *Director, Hawaii Public Library*

BRICKMAN, WILLIAM W., *Professor of Educational History and Comparative Education, Graduate School of Education, University of Pennsylvania; Editor of* School and Society

BRIDGES, E. M., *University College of Swansea, University of Wales; Author of* The Soils and Land Use of the Area North of Derby *and* World Soils

BRIDGES, WILLIAM, *Curator of Publications, New York Zoological Park; Author of* Gathering of Animals: An Unconventional History of the New York Zoological Society

BRIEGER, GERT H., *Professor of the History of Health Science, University of California at San Francisco*

BRIGGS, ASA, *Provost of Worcester College, Oxford University; Former Professor of History, University of Sussex; Author of* The Age of Improvement *and* Victorian Cities; *Editor of* Chartist Studies

BRIGGS, KATHARINE M., *Author of* Fairies in English Tradition and Literature

BRIGGS, ROBERT T., *News Service, Caterpillar Tractor Company*

BRILLIANT, RICHARD, *Professor of Art History and Archaeology, Columbia University; Author of* Gesture and Rank in Roman Art, Arts of Ancient Greeks, *and* Roman Art

BRINNIN, JOHN MALCOLM, *Professor of English, Boston University; Author of* The Third Rose: Gertrude Stein and Her World

BRINTON, CRANE, *Author of* History of Western Morals, English Political Thought in the Nineteenth Century, *and* Lives of Talleyrand; *Coauthor of* A History of Civilization

BRINTON, HOWARD H., *Director and Lecturer, Pendle Hill Graduate School of Religion and Social Study*

BRISBIN, CHARLES E., *Chief Librarian, Hamilton Public Library, Ontario, Canada*

BRITT, STEUART HENDERSON, *Professor of Marketing and Advertising, Northwestern University; Former Editor of* Journal of Marketing

BRITTON, VIRGINIA, *Research Family Economist, U.S. Department of Agriculture*

BROCKETT, OSCAR G., *Professor of Theatre and Director of Graduate Studies in Theatre, Indiana University; Author of* History of the Theatre

BROCKWAY, WALLACE, *Coauthor of* Men of Music *and* The World of Opera

BRODERICK, JOHN F., SJ, *Professor of Ecclesiastical History, Weston College*

BRODIE, H. KEITH H., MD, *Professor and Chairman, Department of Psychiatry, Duke University Medical Center*

BRODIN, PIERRE, *Director of Studies, Lycée Français de New-York*

BRODY, BORUCH A., *Assistant Professor of Philosophy, Massachusetts Institute of Technology*

BROECKER, WILLIAM L., *School of Visual Arts, New York City; Author of* The Photographs of William Henry Jackson; *Editor of* Current 35mm Practice

BROGAN, OLWEN P. F., *Fellow of the Society of Antiquaries, London; Author of* Roman Gaul

BRONNER, EDWIN B., *Professor of History and Curator of the Quaker Collections, Haverford College*

BROOKS, CHARLES B., *Author of* The Siege of New Orleans

BROOKS, EDWARD M., *Professor of Geology and Geophysics, Boston College*

BROOKS, HUGH C., *Director, African Program, St. John's University*

BROWER, DANIEL R., JR., *Professor of History, University of California at Davis; Author of* The Russian City between Tradition and Modernity, 1850–1990

BROWN, BERTRAM S., *Director, National Institutes of Mental Health*

BROWN, DAVID H., *Professor of Biological Chemistry, Washington University School of Medicine*

BROWN, DONALD F., *Professor of Anthropology, Boston University*

BROWN, DOROTHY M., *Associate Professor of History, Georgetown University*

BROWN, ELIZABETH B., *Historical Librarian, American Institute of Aeronautics and Astronautics*

BROWN, FRANK A., JR., *Morrison Professor of Zoology, Northwestern University*

BROWN, GORDON S., *Dean of College of Engineering, Massachusetts Institute of Technology; Coauthor of* Principles of Servomechanisms

BROWN, HAROLD W., MD; *Clinical Professor of Pathology, Vanderbilt University; Author of* Basic Clinical Parasitology

BROWN, HARRY J., *Professor of History, Michigan State University; Coeditor of* The Diary of James A. Garfield

BROWN, IAN, *School of Oriental and African Studies, University of London*

BROWN, JOHN, *Lecturer in History, University of Edinburgh*

BROWN, LEWIS, *Chairman of the Board, Johns-Manville Corporation*

BROWN, MARVIN L., JR., *Professor of History and Political Science, North Carolina State University at Raleigh*

BROWN, MARYELLEN, *Secretary, Leavenworth City Library Board of Directors, Leavenworth, Kans.*

BROWN, NELSON C., *Professor, College of Forestry, Syracuse University*

BROWN, NORMAN O., *Professor of Humanities, University of California at Santa Cruz*

BROWN, PETER DOUGLAS, *Author of* William Pitt, Earl of Chatham *and* The Chathamites

BROWN, R. M., *American Bristle Corporation*

BROWN, RAYMOND E., *Auburn Professor of Biblical Studies, Union Theological Seminary, New York City; Author of the* Anchor Bible Epistles of John *and* Gospel According to John

BROWN, RICHARD L., *Librarian, Reading Public Library*

BROWN, ROBERT E., *Associate Professor of Music, Wesleyan University*

BROWN, RONALD, *Author of* Telecommunications

BROWN, ROYAL A., *National Paint and Coatings Association, Washington, D.C.*

BROWN, STUART GERRY, *Professor of American Studies, University of Hawaii*

BROWN, THEODORE M., *Assistant Professor of History, City College of New York*

BROWN, VERNON L., *Curator, Chase Manhattan Bank Museum of Moneys of the World, New York City*

BROWN, W. NORMAN, *Professor of Sanskrit, University of Pennsylvania; Author of* The United States and India and Pakistan, The Vasanta Vilasa, *and other books*

BROWN, WALLACE, *Professor of History, University of New Brunswick; Author of* The King's Friends *and* The Good Americans

BROWN, WILLIAM F., *Editor of* The American Field

BROWN, WILLIAM J., MD, *Chief, Venereal Disease Branch, State and Community Services Division, National Communicable Disease Center, Atlanta, Ga.*

BROWNE, MILLARD C., *Editor, Editorial Page, Buffalo* Evening News

BROWNE, WILLIAM P., *Professor of Political Science, Central Michigan University; Author of* Private Interests, Public Policy, and American Agriculture

BROWNELL, ROBERT L., JR., *U.S. Fish and Wildlife Service*

BROWNSTEIN, OSCAR, *Associate Professor of Speech and Dramatic Art, University of Iowa*

BRUCH, HILDE, MD, *Professor of Psychiatry, Baylor College of Medicine; Author of* Don't Be Afraid of Your Child; Studies in Schizophrenia; Eating Disorders: Obesity, Anorexia Nervosa and the Person Within; Learning Psychotherapy; *and* The Golden Cage

BRUCHEY, ELEANOR S., *Professor of History, Columbia University; Author of* The Business Elite in Baltimore, 1880–1914

BRUCKER, GENE A., *Professor of History, University of California at Berkeley*

BRUEGGEMANN, WALTER, *Professor of Old Testament and Dean of Academic Affairs, Eden Theological Seminary; Author of* The Vitality of Old Testament Tradition

BRUHNS, KAREN O., *Assistant Professor of Anthropology, San Francisco State University*

BRUMBAUGH, ROBERT S., *Professor of Philosophy, Yale University*

BRUNDAGE, AVERY, *President, International Olympic Committee*

BRUNELL, PHILIP, MD, *Professor of Pediatrics, University of Texas Health Science Center at San Antonio*

BRUNET, MICHEL, *Director, Department of History, University of Montreal, Canada*

BRUNS, FRANKLIN R., JR., *Associate Curator, National Postage Stamp Collection, Smithsonian Institution's National Museum of History and Technology, Washington, D.C.*

BRUNSTEIN, KARL A., *Department of Physics, University of Denver*

BRUNSWICK, NATASCHA, *Courant Institute of Mathematical Sciences, New York University*

BRUSH, JOHN E., *Professor of Geography, Rutgers University*

BRUSH, STANLEY E., *Associate Professor of History, University of Bridgeport*

BRUSH, STEPHEN G., *Professor, History of Science, University of Maryland; Coauthor of* Introduction to Concepts and Theories in Physical Science

BRUSHER, JOSEPH S., SJ, *Professor of History, University of Santa Clara*

BRUUN, GEOFFREY, *Author of* The World in the Twentieth Century

BRYAN, EDWIN H., JR., *Manager, Pacific Scientific Information Center, Honolulu, Hawaii*

BRYAN, HARRISON, *Librarian, University of Sydney, Australia*

BRYANT, SIR ARTHUR, *Author of* Samuel Pepys, The Man in the Making

BRYANT, DAVID J., *World Singles Bowls Champion (1966); Author of* Bryant on Bowls

BRYANT, MARGARET M., *Author of* Modern English and Its Heritage

BRYANT, WILLIAM CULLEN, II, *Coeditor of* The Letters of William Cullen Bryant (1794–1878)

BRYER, ANTHONY A. M., *Director of the Centre for Byzantine Studies and Professor of Byzantine Studies, University of Birmingham, England*

BUCHMAN, HERMAN, *Professor of Theatre Arts, State University of New York College at Purchase; Author of* Stage Makeup *and* Film and Television Makeup

BUCHSBAUM, RALPH, *Professor of Biology, University of Pittsburgh; Author of* Animals Without Backbones

BUCHTA, J. W., *Executive Secretary, American Association of Physics Teachers*

BUCK, FREDERICK S., *Author of* Horse Race Betting

BUCKINGHAM, F., *Creative Supervisor Merchandising, Massey-Ferguson Inc.*

BUCKINGHAM, WALTER, *Author of* Automation: Its Impact on Business and People

BUCKLEY, JEROME H., *Professor of English, Harvard University; Author of* The Victorian Temper

BUDDRUSS, GEORG, *Professor of Indology, University of Mainz, Germany*

BUDZYNSKI, THOMAS H., *Clinical Director, Biofeedback Institute of Denver; Assistant Clinical Professor, University of Colorado Medical Center*

BUENKER, JOHN D., *Professor of History, University of Wisconsin at Parkside*

BUERMEYER, EMILY L., *Librarian, Wyomissing Public Library*

BUGELSKI, B. R., *Professor of Psychology, State University of New York at Buffalo*

BULLOUGH, BONNIE, *Dean and Professor, School of Nursing, State University of New York at Buffalo; Coauthor of* The Emergence of Modern Nursing *and* New Directions for Nurses

BULLOUGH, DONALD A., *Professor of Medieval History, University of Nottingham, England; Author of* Age of Charlemagne

BULLOUGH, VERN L., *Dean, Natural and Social Sciences, State University of New York at Buffalo; Coauthor of* The Emergence of Modern Nursing; *Author of* History of Prostitution

BULMAN, LEARNED T., *Assistant Director, East Orange Public Library*

BULMAN, WARREN E., *President, Ohio Semitronics Inc.*

BUNZEL, RUTH L., *Professor of Anthropology, Columbia University; Coeditor of* The Golden Age of American Anthropology

BURBANCK, W. D., *Professor of Biology, Emory University*

BURCH, DEREK, *Director, Missouri Botanical Gardens*

BURCH, G. E., *The William Henderson Professor of Medicine and Chairman, Department of Medicine, Tulane University School of Medicine*

BURCHFIELD, J. D., *Department of History, Northern Illinois University; Author of* Lord Kelvin and the Age of the Earth

BURDETTE, FRANKLIN L., *Author of* Filibustering in the Senate *and* Lobbyists in Action

BURGESS, ROBERT H., *Curator of Exhibits, Mariners Museum, Newport News, Va.*

BURGESS, ROBERT L., *Professor, Department of Environmental and Forest Biology, SUNY College of Environmental Science and Forestry, Syracuse, N.Y.*

BURIAN, RICHARD M., *Department of Philosophy, Virginia Polytechnic Institute and State University*

BURKE, ARIANE M., *Research Associate, Archaeological Surveys of Canada, Canadian Museum of Civilization*

BURKE, ELLEN COOLIDGE, *Library Director, Alexandria (Va.) Library*

BURKE, FIDELIAN, FSC, *Academic Vice President and Professor of English, La Salle College*

BURKE, JAMES D., *Manager, Terrestrial Body Orbiter Development Program, Jet Propulsion Laboratory, California Institute of Technology*

BURKE, JOHN G., *Professor of History, University of California at Los Angeles*

BURKE, JOSEPH C., *Associate Professor of History, Duquesne University*

BURKE, MARY P., *Author of* Reaching for Justice: The Women's Movement

BURKE, REDMOND A., CSV, *University of Wisconsin at Oshkosh*

BURKETT, BARBARA N., *Professor of Biology, Gardner-Webb College*

BURKHEAD, JESSE, *Maxwell Professor of Economics, Emeritus, Syracuse University; Author of* Government Budgeting *and* State and Local Taxes for Public Education

BURKS, ARDATH W., *Professor of East Asian Studies, Rutgers University; Author of* Japan: Profile of an Industrial Power

BURKS, DAVID D., *Professor of History, Hunter College; Coauthor of* Evolution of Chaos: Dynamics of Latin American Government and Politics

BURLESON, DONALD R., *Professor of Mathematics, Rivier College, Nashua, N.H.*

BURLINGAME, MERRILL G., *Professor, Department of History and Government, Montana State University; Author of* Montana Frontier *and* History of Montana

BURN, ANDREW ROBERT, *Author of* Persia and the Greeks *and* The Lyric Age of Greece

BURNHAM, JACK W., *Chairman, Art Department, Northwestern University; Author of* Beyond Modern Sculpture *and* The Structure of Art

BURNHAM, JOHN C., *Professor, Department of History, Ohio State University*

BURNS, E. BRADFORD, *Professor of History, University of California at Los Angeles; Author of* A Documentary History of Brazil

BURNS, GEORGE W., *Acting President, Ohio Wesleyan University*

BURNS, ROBERT P., SJ, *Fordham University*

BURRILL, MEREDITH F., *Executive Secretary, Board on Geographic Names, U.S. Department of the Interior*

BURRIS, JOHN O., MD, *Associate Clinical Professor of Medicine, Columbia University College of Physicians and Surgeons; Danbury Hospital*

BURROW, MARTIN, *Professor, Courant Institute of Mathematical Sciences, New York University; Author of* Representation Theory of Finite Groups

BURROWS, WILLIAM, *Professor of Microbiology, University of Chicago*

BURSON, PHYLLIS S., *Library Director, Corpus Christi Public Libraries*

BURSTYN, HAROLD L., *Professor of Physics and Earth Science, William Paterson College; Author of* At the Sign of the Quadrant

BURTCHAELL, JAMES T., CSC, *Chairman, Department of Theology, University of Notre Dame*

BURTON, DONALD J., *Professor of Chemistry, University of Iowa*

BURTON, IAN, *Professor of Geography, University of Toronto, Canada*

BURTON, RICHARD I., *Director of Public Relations, Cleveland Museum of Art*

BURTT, EVERETT J., JR., *Professor of Economics, Boston University*

BUSH, DOUGLAS, *Author of* English Poetry

BUSH, G. W. A., *Lecturer in Political Studies, University of Auckland, New Zealand*

BUSH, ROBERT T., *Associate Professor of Physics, California State Polytechnic University at Pomona*

BUSHMAN, RICHARD L., *Professor of History, Boston University; Author of* From Puritan to Yankee: Character and the Social Order in Connecticut, 1690–1765

BUSTIN, ÉDOUARD, *Professor and Chairman, Department of Political Science, Boston University*

BUTCHER, DEVEREUX, *Author of* Our National Parks in Color

BUTLER, ALEXANDER R., *Professor, Department of Humanities, Michigan State University*

BUTLER, ANNIE L., *Professor of Early Childhood Education, Indiana University; Coauthor of* Early Childhood Programs: Developmental Objectives and Their Uses

BUTLER, JONATHAN M., *Coauthor of* The Disappointed: Millerism and Millenarianism in the Nineteenth Century

BUTLER, JOSEPH T., *Curator and Director of Collections, Sleepy Hollow Restorations, Tarrytown, N.Y.; Author of* American Antiques, 1800–1900

BUTLER, MARSHALL A., *Registrar, Montclair State College*

BUTLER, ROBERT N., MD, *Brookdale Professor of Geriatrics and Adult Development, Mount Sinai School of Medicine; Coauthor of* Human Aging

BUTT, RONALD, *Assistant Editor and Political Commentator, The Sunday Times (London); Political and Public Affairs Commentator of the Times; Author of* The Power of Parliament

BUTTERFIELD, SIR HERBERT, *Regius Professor of Modern History, Cambridge University*

BUTTINGER, JOSEPH, *Author of* The Smaller Dragon, A Political History of Vietnam, *and* Vietnam: A Dragon Embattled

BUTTON, KENNETH J., *Francis Bitter National Magnet Laboratory, Massachusetts Institute of Technology; Coauthor of* Microwave Ferrites and Ferrimagnetics

BUTWELL, RICHARD, *Chairman, Department of Political Science, State University of New York at Brockport*

BUZAN, LEROY R., *Technical Information Department, Research Laboratories, General Motors Corporation*

BYCK, ROBERT, MD, *Professor of Pharmacology, School of Medicine, Yale University*

BYRNE, FRANK L., *Professor of History, Kent State University; Author of* Prophet of Prohibition: Neal Dow and His Crusade

BYRNE, JOHN, *Sports Editor, Irish Echo*

CABANISS, ALLEN, *Professor of History, University of Mississippi*

CACHIA, PIERRE, *Muir Institute, University of Edinburgh*

CADE, TOM J., *Professor of Zoology and Research Director, Laboratory of Ornithology, Cornell University*

CADY, JOHN F., *Professor of History, Ohio University; Author of* Southeast Asia: Its Historical Development

CADZOW, HUNTER, *Assistant Professor, Department of English, University of Oklahoma*

CALBERT, HAROLD E., *Professor and Chairman, Department of Food Science and Industries, University of Wisconsin*

CALDWELL, HOWARD W., *Professor of American History, University of Nebraska; Author of* History of the United States, 1815–61

CALDWELL, JACQUES R., MD, *Chief, Section of Allergy and Rheumatology, Department of Medicine, University of Florida College of Medicine at Gainesville*

CALDWELL, ROBERT G., *Professor of Criminology, University of Iowa*

CALEF, WESLEY C., *Professor of Geography, Illinois State University*

CALLAN, EDWARD, *Professor of English, Western Michigan University; Author of* Albert John Luthuli

CALLEN, HERBERT, *Professor of Physics, University of Pennsylvania*

CALLENDAR, L. H., *Fellow, Royal Institute of Chemistry*

CALLENDER, JOHN BRYAN, *Associate Professor of Egyptology, University of California at Los Angeles*

CAMDEN, CARROLL, *Professor of English, Rice University; Editor of* Restoration and Eighteenth Century Literature

CAMERON, GEORGE G., *Author of* History of Early Iran

CAMPBELL, ALISTAIR, *Rawlinson and Bosworth Professor of Anglo-Saxon, Oxford University; Author of* Old English Grammar

CAMPBELL, ANGUS, *Director, Survey Research Center, University of Michigan*

CAMPBELL, DONALD F., *Professor of Astronomy, Cornell University; Associate Director, National Astronomy and Ionosphere Center*

CAMPBELL, JAMES, *Fellow of Worcester College, Oxford University*

CAMPBELL, ROSEMAE WELLS, *Special Collections Librarian, Tutt Library, Colorado College; Author of* Tops and Gyroscopes

CANBY, EDWARD TATNALL, *Associate Editor of* Audio *magazine; Author of* High Fidelity and the Music Lover *and* Home Music Systems

CANDELARIA, MICHAEL, *Assistant Professor, California State University at Bakersfield; Author of* Popular Religion and Liberation

CANFIELD, ARTHUR G., *Author of* Poems of Victor Hugo

CANN, D. B., *Soil Correlator, Research Branch, Canada Department of Agriculture*

CANNON, CLARENCE, *Representative in Congress from the 9th Missouri District; Author of* Procedure in the House of Representatives

CANNON, LEE, *Managing Editor,* Interior Design

CANRIGHT, JAMES E., *Professor and Chairman of Department of Botany, Arizona State University*

CANU, JEAN, *Professor of French Literature, American College in Paris*

CAPERS, GERALD M., *Professor of History, Newcomb College, Tulane University*

CAPRON, WALTER C., *Captain, U.S. Coast Guard (Retired); Author of* The U.S. Coast Guard

CAPSHAW, ANNE L., *Librarian, Texarkana Public Library, Texarkana, Texas*

CARDONA, GEORGE, *Professor of Linguistics, University of Pennsylvania; Author of* A Gujarati Reference Grammar

CARELESS, J. M. S., *Professor and Chairman, Department of History, University of Toronto, Canada; Author of* Canada: Story of Challenge; The Union of the Canadas; Brown of the Globe

CAREY, DAVID, *Director, Public Affairs, Moral Re-Armament*

CAREY, GEORGE W., *Professor of Government, Georgetown University; Author of* The Federalist Design for a Constitutional Republic *and* Basic Symbols of the American Political Tradition

CARLSON, BRUCE M., *Professor of Anatomy, University of Michigan at Ann Arbor; Author of* Foundations of Embryology *and* The Regeneration of Minced Muscles

CARLSON, LOREN D., *Chairman of the Division of Sciences Basic to Medicine, School of Medicine, University of California at Davis*

CARLSON, PHYLLIS D., *Library Assistant, Z.J. Loussac Library*

CARMER, CARL, *Author and Editor of* Rivers of America *Series*

CARMICHAEL, ANN G., *Professor of History, Indiana University; Author of* Plague and the Poor in Renaissance Florence

CARMICHAEL, RONALD L., *Professor of Engineering Management, School of Engineering, University of Missouri at Rolla*

CARMONY, DONALD F., *Professor of History, Indiana University; Editor,* Indiana Magazine of History

CARNEY, JAMES, *Author of* Studies in Irish Literature and History

CAROZZI, ALBERT V., *Professor of Geology, University of Illinois; Author of* Microscopic Sedimentary Petrography

CARPENTER, JAMES A., *Professor of Theology, General Theological Seminary, New York City*

CARPENTER, JOHN W., III, *Lieutenant General, U.S. Air Force (Retired); Commander, Air University*

CARPENTER, KENNETH, *Chief Preparator, Denver Museum of Natural History*

CARR, MICHAEL H., *U.S. Geological Survey, Menlo Park, California; Member, Mariner 9 and Viking Imaging Teams*

CARR, RACHEL E., *Author of* Japanese Floral Art

CARR, WILLIAM H. A., *Author of* The Basic Book of the Cat

CARRÉ, MEYRICK H., *Author of* Realists and Nominalists

CARROLL, JOSEPH, *Associate Editor,* Sports Illustrated

CARSE, JAMES E., *Professor of Religion, New York University*

CARSON, GERALD, *Author of* One for a Man, Two for a Horse

CARSTEN, FRANCIS L., *Masaryk Professor of Central European History, University of London; Author of* The Origins of Prussia *and* The Rise of Fascism

CARSTENS, PETER, *Professor of Anthropology, University of Toronto, Canada*

CARTER, EVERETT C., *Professor of Civil Engineering and Director of Transportation Studies Center, University of Maryland*

CARTER, GWENDOLEN M., *Professor of Political Science, Indiana University; Author of* The Politics of Inequality: South Africa Since 1948

CARTER, H. ADAMS, *Editor,* American Alpine Journal

CARTWRIGHT, JANET B., *Director, Hyde Park Free Library*

CARUSO, JOHN ANTHONY, *Professor of History, West Virginia University; Author of* The Mississippi Valley Frontier

CARVER, T. N., *Professor of Political Economy, Harvard University; Author of* Economic Functions of Government

CARY, VERONICA F., *Director, Free Public Library, Trenton, N.J.*

CASPER, GRETCHEN G., *University Fellow, University of Michigan*

CASPER, LEONARD, *Professor of English, Boston College; Author of* New Writing from the Philippines *and* Robert Penn Warren: The Dark and Bloody Ground

CASSAI, MARY ANN, *Public Relations Representative, New York Public Library*

CASSEDY, RUTH H., *Librarian, Frothingham Free Library, Fonda, N.Y.*

CASSIDY, GERALDINE R., *Director of Public Information for the City of Hawthorne*

CASSON, LIONEL, *Professor of Classics, New York University; Author of* The Mariners

CASSOU, JEAN, *Conservateur-en-Chef, Musée National d'Art Moderne, Paris; Author of* Situation de l'Art Moderne

CASTELLANI, JOHN A., *Librarian, Mount Vernon Ladies' Association*

CASTERAS, SUSAN P., *Affiliate Professor, University of Washington*

CATON-THOMPSON, GERTRUDE, *Governor, School of Oriental and African Studies, University of London; Author of* The Zimbabwe Culture

CAUGHEY, JOHN W., *Professor of History, University of California at Los Angeles; Author of* Bernardo de Gálvez in Louisiana

CAUGHLAN, GEORGEANNE R., *Associate Professor of Physics, Montana State University*

CAULFIELD, TOM, *Irish Echo*

CAVAN, RUTH SHONLE, *Professor of Sociology, Rockford College; Author of* Suicide

CAVANAGH, DENIS, MD, *Professor of Obstetrics and Gynecology and Director of Gynecologic Oncology, University of South Florida School of Medicine; Author of* Obstetrical Emergencies; Coauthor of Prematurity and the Obstetrician

CAVERT, SAMUEL McCREA, *General Secretary, National Council of the Churches of Christ in the U.S.A.*

CAZEL, FRED A., JR., *Professor of History, University of Connecticut*

CELARIER, JAMES L., *Associate Professor of Philosophy, University of Maryland*

CERWIN, HERBERT, *Author of* Bernal Díaz: Historian of the Conquest

CERZA, ALPHONSE, *Grand Historian of the Grand Lodge of Illinois (Freemasons); Author of* Anti-Masonry, Scottish Rite History of Illinois, *and* A Masonic Thought

CHACKAN, NICHOLAS, *Design Engineer, Westinghouse Electric Corp.*

CHADWICK, JOHN, *Reader in Classics, University of Cambridge; Author of* The Decipherment of Linear B *and* The Mycenaean World

CHADWICK, OWEN, *Regius Professor of Ecclesiastical History, Cambridge University*

CHAFFIN, ROBERT J., *Associate Professor of History, University of Wisconsin at Oshkosh*

CHALL, JEANNE S., *Professor of Education, Graduate School of Education, Harvard University; Author of* Learning to Read: The Great Debate

CHALMERS, DAVID M., *Professor of History, University of Florida; Author of* The Muckrake Years

CHAMBERLAIN, JOSEPH W., *Professor of Space Physics and Astronomy, Rice University; Author of* Physics of the Aurora and Airglow

CHAMBERLIN, WALDO, *Professor of History, Dartmouth College; Coauthor of* A Chronology and Fact Book of the UN, 1941–1964

CHAMBERS, RUTH, *Librarian, Cleveland Public Library*

CHAMPAGNE, ROGER J., *Professor of History, Illinois State University*

CHAN, WING-TSIT, *Anna Gillespie Professor of Philosophy, Chatham College*

CHANDLER, BRUCE, *Professor of Mathematics, New York University*

CHANDLER, DAVID G., *Head, Department of War Studies and International Affairs, the Royal Military Academy Sandhurst, England; Author of* The Campaigns of Napoleon *and* Dictionary of the Napoleonic Wars

CHANDLER, FRANK W., *Author of* The Literature of Roguery

CHANDLER, JAMES, MD, *Professor and Chairman, Department of Otolaryngology, University of Miami School of Medicine*

CHANEY, WILLIAM A., *George McKendree Steele Professor of History, Lawrence University; Author of* The Cult of Kingship in Anglo-Saxon England

CHANG, KUEI-SHENG, *Associate Professor of Geography, University of Washington*

CHANG, SEN-DOU, *Professor of Geography, University of Hawaii*

CHAO, Y. R., *Agassiz Professor of Oriental Languages, University of California at Berkeley; Author of* Grammar of Spoken Chinese *and* Language and Symbolic Systems

CHAPANIS, ALPHONSE, *Professor, Department of Psychology, Johns Hopkins University*

CHAPIN, KIM, *Sports Illustrated Magazine*

CHAPIN, SEYMOUR L., *Professor of History, California State University at Los Angeles*

CHAPLIN, JOHN B., *Assistant Chief Engineer, Bell Aerosystems Company, Buffalo, N.Y.*

CHAPMAN, C. RICHARD, *Research Assistant Professor, Departments of Anesthesiology and Psychology, University of Washington School of Medicine, Seattle, Wash.*

CHAPMAN, JOHN S., MD, *Professor of Medicine, University of Texas Health Science Center at Dallas*

CHAPMAN, ROBERT L., *Professor of English, Drew University; Editor of* Roget's Thesaurus

CHARANIS, PETER, *Voorhees Professor of History, Rutgers University*

CHARNEY, EVAN, MD, *Assistant Professor of Pediatrics, University of Rochester School of Medicine and Dentistry*

CHARNLEY, C. JOHN, *Senior Lecturer, Machine Tools and Automation, College of Aeronautics, Cranfield, England*

CHARTERS, ANN, *Professor of English, University of Connecticut at Storrs*

CHARTERS, SAMUEL, *Author of* Some Poems, Poets: Studies in American Underground Poetry since 1945

CHARYK, JOSEPH V., *President, Communications Satellite Corporation*

CHASE, GILBERT, *Author of* America's Music, A Guide to Latin American Music, *and* Music of Spain

CHATFIELD, CHARLES, *Professor of History, Wittenberg University; Author of* For Peace and Justice: Pacifism in America, 1914–1941, Peace Movements in America, *and* International War Resistance Through 1945; *Coeditor of* The Garland Library of War and Peace

CHATTOPADHYAYA, BRAJADULAL, *Assistant Professor in Ancient Indian History, Jawaharlal Nehru University*

CHEEVER, FRANCIS S., MD, *Director of Admissions, Harvard Medical School; Former Dean, School of Medicine, and Vice Chancellor, Health Professions, University of Pittsburgh*

CH'EN, DAVID Y., *Associate Professor of Chinese Literature, Ohio State University*

CHEN, SHIH-HSIANG, *Coauthor of* Modern Chinese Poetry

CHEN, THEODORE HSI-EN, *Chairman of the Department of Asian Studies and Director of the East Asian Studies Center, University of Southern California; Author of* The Maoist Educational Revolution

CHENEY, MARGARET, *Author of* A Brief History of the University of California

CHENG, C. K., *Professor of Sociology, University of Hawaii*

CHENG, TAO, *Associate Professor of Political Science, Trenton State College of New Jersey*

CHERNELA, JANET, *Department of Anthropology, American Museum of Natural History*

CHERNOFF, AMOZ I., MD, *Director and Research Professor, University of Tennessee Memorial Research Center at Knoxville*

CHESTNUT, HAROLD, *Manager, Systems Engineering and Analysis Branch, Information Sciences Laboratory, General Electric Company*

CHEYETTE, FREDRIC L., *Associate Professor of History, Amherst College*

CHILD, RICHARD B., *Professor of Law, New England School of Law*

CHILDERS, NORMAN F., *Professor of Horticulture, Rutgers University*

CHIPMAN, ERIC G., MD, *Office of Solar and Heliospheric Physics, NASA*

CHIPMAN, ROBERT A., *Professor of Electrical Engineering, University of Toledo*

CHIPP, HERSCHEL B., *Professor of the History of Art, University of California at Berkeley; Author of* The Theories of Modern Art

CHIRAS, DANIEL D., *Adjunct Professor, Environmental Policy and Management Program, University of Denver; Author of* Lessons from Nature: Learning to Live Sustainably on the Earth *and* Environmental Science: Action for a Sustainable Future, *4th edition*

CHOMCHAI, PRACHOOM, *Professor and Head, Department of Public Finance and Economy, Chulalongkorn University, Bangkok, Thailand; Author of* Chulalongkorn the Great

CHOPPIN, GREGORY R., *Professor of Chemistry, Florida State University*

CHOTKOWSKI, LUDMIL A., MD, *Former Chief of Medicine, Rocky Hill Veterans Home and Hospital, Rocky Hill, Conn.*

CHOU WEN-CHUNG, *Professor of Music, Columbia University*

CHRISTENSEN, JOHN W., *Vice President and Associate Director of Research, CBS Laboratories*

CHRISTENSON, C. L., *Professor of Economics, Indiana University; Author of* Economic Redevelopment in Bituminous Coal

CHRISTIANSEN, ANDREW J., SJ, *Fordham University*

CHRISTIANSEN, DONALD, *President and Principal, Informatica, Huntington, N.Y.; Editor Emeritus,* IEEE Spectrum *Magazine*

CHRISTOPHER, EVERETT P., *Professor, Plant and Soil Science, Department of Horticulture, College of Agriculture, Agricultural Experiment Station, University of Rhode Island*

CHRISTY, NICHOLAS P., MD, *Chairman, Department of Medicine, Roosevelt Hospital, New York City; Clinical Professor of Medicine, Columbia University College of Physicians and Surgeons; Editor in Chief,* Journal of Clinical Endocrinology and Metabolism

CHU, CHARLES J., *Professor of Chinese, Connecticut College; Author of* Chi Pai-shih, His Life and Works

CHU, CHARLES K., *Associate Professor of History, State University of New York at Fredonia*

CHURCH, WILLIAM FARR, *Professor of History, Brown University*

CIKOVSKY, NICOLAI, JR., *Associate Professor of Art, Vassar College*

CITTADINO, EUGENE, *Department of the History of Science, University of Wisconsin at Madison*

CLAPP, JOSEPH C., *Director, Public Relations and Alumni Affairs, William Jewell College*

CLAPP, VERNER W., *President, Council on Library Resources, Inc.*

CLARK, ANDREW HILL, *Vernor Professor of Geography, University of Wisconsin; Author of* Canada: A Geophysical Interpretation

CLARK, CHARLES E., *Chairman, Department of History, University of New Hampshire; Author of* Maine: A Bicentennial History *and* The Eastern Frontier: The Settlement of Northern New England

CLARK, DONALD B., *Professor of English, University of Missouri; Author of* Alexander Pope

CLARK, DONALD N., *Professor of History and Director of International Studies, Trinity University; Editor of* Korea Briefing, 1993

CLARK, GEORGE A., JR., *Professor of Biology and Curator of Ornithology, University of Connecticut at Storrs; Coeditor of* Perspectives in Ornithology

CLARK, GEORGE B., *Professor of Mining Engineering and Director of Rock Mechanics Research Center, University of Missouri at Rolla; Coauthor of* Elements of Mining

CLARK, HENRY AUSTIN, JR., *Owner and Director, Long Island Automotive Museum, Southampton, N.Y.*

CLARK, JAMES I., *Author of* Chronicles of Wisconsin

CLARK, JOHN W., *Professor of English, University of Minnesota; Author of* Early English: An Introduction to Old and Middle English

CLARK, MARK W., *General, U.S. Army (Retired); President, The Citadel*

CLARK, MOTHER MARY T., RSCJ, *Manhattanville College*

CLARK, ROBERT S., *Associate Editor, Stereo Review Magazine*

CLARK, THOMAS D., *Professor of American History, Indiana University; Author of* Frontier America *and* History of Kentucky

CLARK-KENNEDY, A. E., MD, *Author of* Edith Cavell: Pioneer and Patriot

CLARY, MARCUS, *Daimler-Benz of North America, Inc.*

CLAWSON, MARION, *Director, Bureau of Land Management; Author of* Uncle Sam's Acres

CLAYBOURNE, JOHN P., *Chief, Future Studies Office, Kennedy Space Center, Florida*

CLAYPOOL, L. C., *Manager, Escalator Department, Otis Elevator Company*

CLAYTON, PAUL B., *General Theological Seminary, New York City*

CLEGERN, WAYNE M., *Professor of History, Colorado State University*

CLELAND, HUGH GREGG, *Associate Professor of History, State University of New York at Stony Brook*

CLEMEN, RUDOLF A., JR., *Information Research Specialist, American National Red Cross*

CLEMENT, ANTHONY C., *Professor of Biology, Emory University*

CLEMENTS, ROBERT J., *Director, Comparative Literature Program, Graduate School of Arts and Sciences, New York University*

CLENCH, WILLIAM J., *Honorary Curator of Malacology, Museum of Comparative Zoology, Harvard College*

CLIFTON, JOE ANN, *Formerly President, Special Libraries Association; Author of* Computers in Information Data Centers

CLIFTON, ROBERT A., *Physical Scientist, Division of Nonmetallic Minerals, Bureau of Mines, U.S. Department of the Interior*

CLOSE, DAVID, *Associate Professor, Department of Political Science, Memorial University of Newfoundland; Author of* Nicaragua: Politics, Economics, and Society

CLOUDSLEY-THOMPSON, J. L., *Professor of Zoology, University of Khartoum, Sudan, and Keeper, Sudan Natural History Museum*

CLOUGH, SHEPARD B., *Professor of History, Columbia University; Author of* France: A History of National Economics

CLOUT, HUGH, *Reader in Geography, University College, London; Author of* The Geography of Post-War France

CLUNAS, CRAIG, *Research Assistant, Far Eastern Department, Victoria and Albert Museum*

CLUNIES-ROSS, SIR IAN, *Chairman, Commonwealth Scientific and Industrial Research Organization; Coauthor of* Australia and Nuclear Weapons

CLUTTON-BROCK, JULIET, *Institute of Archaeology, London; Coeditor of* A Review of the Canidae

COALE, BURTON V., *National Park Service*

COALSON, WINNIE F., *Associate Librarian, Virginia Intermont College*

COATES, CHRISTOPHER W., *Director, The Aquarium, New York Zoological Society; Author of* Tropical Fishes as Pets

COBB, SANFORD, *President, Association of American Publishers*

COCHRAN, WILLIAM G., *Professor of Statistics, Harvard University*

COCKCROFT, JAMES D., *Associate Professor of Sociology, Livingston College, Rutgers University; Author of* The Political Economy of Underdevelopment in Latin America

COCKERHAM, WILLIAM C., *Professor of Sociology and Medicine, University of Alabama at Birmingham; Author of* Medical Sociology, 5th edition *and* Sociology of Mental Disorder, 3d edition

COCKRUM, E. LENDELL, *Professor of Biological Sciences and Curator of Mammals, University of Arizona*

COENEN, FREDERIC E., *Author of* Franz Grillparzer's Portraiture of Men

COFFEY, ROBERT J., MD, *Professor and Chairman, Department of Surgery, Georgetown University Hospital*

COFFEY, THOMAS M., *Author of* The Long Thirst—Prohibition in America: 1920–1930

COFFIN, TRISTRAM P., *Professor of English and Folklore, University of Pennsylvania*

COFIELD, EUGENE P., JR., *Research Chemist, Scripto Incorporated*

COGAN, ROBERT, *Composer; Chairman of Theoretical Studies, New England Conservatory*

COHALAN, MSGR. FLORENCE D., *Professor of History, Cathedral College, New York, N.Y.*

COHAN, ALVIN S., *Director of Public Relations, Scientific Design Company, Inc., New York City*

COHEN, BERNARD, MD, *Associate Clinical Professor of Internal Medicine and Gastroenterology, Mt. Sinai School of Medicine*

COHEN, BERNARD L., *Professor of Physics, Department of Physics and Astronomy, University of Pittsburgh*

COHEN, DANIEL, *Science Writer, Author of* A Modern Look at Monsters

COHEN, DANIEL M., *Director of Ichthyology Laboratory of the Bureau of Commercial Fisheries, U.S. National Museum*

COHEN, GERSON D., *Jewish Theological Seminary of America*

COHEN, J. M., *Translator of* Don Quixote *and other Penguin Classics; Author of* History of Western Literature

COHEN, LAWRENCE S., MD, *The Ebenezer K. Hunt Professor of Medicine, Yale University School of Medicine*

COHEN, S. ALAN, *Associate Professor and Director of Reading and Language Arts Center, Ferkauf Graduate School of Humanities and Social Sciences, Yeshiva University; Author of* Teach Them All to Read

COHEN, SELMA JEANNE, *Editor of* Dance Perspectives *Magazine; Author of* The Modern Dance: Seven Statements of Belief

COHEN, SIDNEY, MD, *Director, Division of Narcotic Addiction and Drug Abuse, National Institute of Mental Health; Author of* The Drug Dilemma

COHEN, SOL, *Professor, Graduate School of Education, University of California at Los Angeles; Author of* Progressives and Urban Social Reform *and* Education in the United States: A Documentary History

COHEN, WILBUR J., *Dean, School of Education, University of Michigan; Former U.S. Secretary of Health, Education, and Welfare*

COHEN, WILLIAM, *Professor of Law, Stanford Law School; Coauthor of* The Bill of Rights: A Source Book

COIT, MARGARET LOUISE, *Professor of History, Fairleigh Dickinson University; Author of* Baruch; *Winner of the Pulitzer Prize for Biography, 1951*

COLAPIETRO, VINCENT M., *Professor of Philosophy, Fordham University; Author of* A Glossary of Semiotics

COLBERT, EDWIN H., *Curator, American Museum of Natural History; Author of* Evolution of the Vertebrates

COLBOURN, TREVOR, *Vice President for Academic Affairs, San Diego State University; Author of* The Lamp of Experience *and* The Colonial Experience

COLDWELL, DAVID F. C., *Professor of English, Southern Methodist University; Author of* Gavin Douglas

COLE, DAVID B., *Professor of Geography, University of Northern Colorado*

COLE, FAY-COOPER, *Author of* The Long Road from Savagery to Civilization

COLEMAN, ALICE LEE, *Reference Librarian, Little Rock Public Library, Little Rock, Ark.*

COLEMAN, F. X. J., *Associate Professor of Philosophy, Boston University; Author of* Contemporary Studies in Aesthetics

COLEMAN, HERBERT J., *Aviation Week and Space Technology*

COLEMAN, PETER J., *Professor of History, University of Illinois at Chicago Circle; Author of* The Transformation of Rhode Island, 1790–1860

COLEMAN, WILLIAM, *Professor, History of Science and History of Medicine, University of Wisconsin at Madison*

COLEMAN-NORTON, P. R., *Associate Professor, Department of Classics, Princeton University*

COLES, HARRY L., *Professor of History, Ohio State University; Coauthor of* Total War and Cold War

COLES, ROBERT, MD, *Research Psychiatrist, Harvard University Health Services; Author of* Erik H. Erikson: The Growth of His Work

COLETTA, PAOLO E., *Professor of History, U.S. Naval Academy*

COLLIER, CHRISTOPHER, *Association for the Study of Connecticut History*

COLLINGWOOD, FRANCIS J., *Professor of Philosophy, Marquette University*

COLLINS, BUD, *Columnist, Boston Globe; Coauthor (with Rod Laver) of* The Education of a Tennis Player; *Author of* My Life with the Pros

COLLINS, DANIEL A., DDS, *Author of* Your Teeth: A Handbook of Dental Care for the Whole Family

COLLINS, ELIZABETH BULLITT, *Librarian, Watsonville Public Library*

COLLINS, G. ROWLAND, *Dean, Graduate School of Business Administration, New York University*

COLLINS, HARVEY SHIELDS, MD, *Memorial Hospital, New York City*

COLLINS, HENRY B., *Bureau of American Ethnology, Smithsonian Institution, Washington, D.C.*

COLLINS, ROBERT O., *Professor of History, University of California at Santa Barbara; Author of* The Southern Sudan, 1883–1898; *Coauthor of* Egypt and the Sudan

COLLINS, WILLIAM R., *Major General, Assistant Chief of Staff for Operations and Training, U.S. Marine Corps*

COLSON, ELIZABETH, *Professor of Anthropology, Brandeis University; Author of* Tradition and Contract: The Problem of Order

COLTON, JOEL, *Professor of History and Chairman of Department of History, Duke University*

COMMAGER, HENRY STEELE, *Professor of History and American Studies, Amherst College; Author of* The American Mind; *Coauthor of* The Growth of the American Republic

COMMANDAY, ROBERT, *Music and Dance Critic, San Francisco Chronicle*

COMMON, R., *Reader in Geography, Queen's University of Belfast, Northern Ireland; Editor of* Northern Ireland from the Air; *Author of* The Relevance of the Hydrological Decade to Ulster

COMPTON, DALE L., *Director, Ames Research Center, National Aeronautics and Space Administration*

CONACHER, D. J., *Professor and Head, Department of Classics, Trinity College, University of Toronto, Canada; Author of* Euripidean Drama: Myth, Theme, and Structure

CONDRON, BOB, *Editor of* The Olympian *(magazine)*

CONE, CLARENCE D., JR., *Director, Cellular and Molecular Biology Laboratory, Veterans Administration; Author of* The Soaring Flight of Birds

CONFORTI, MICHAEL, *Director, Sterling and Francine Clark Art Institute*

CONKLIN, GLADYS, *Author of* The Bug Club Book: A Handbook for Young Bug Collectors

CONLEY, JOHN, *Professor of English, University of Illinois at Chicago Circle*

CONLEY, PATRICK T., *Professor of History, Providence College; Author of* Democracy in Decline: Rhode Island Constitutional Development, 1775–1841 *and* Catholicism in Rhode Island: The Formative Era

CONMY, PETER THOMAS, *Librarian, Oakland Public Library*

CONNELLY, OWEN S., JR., *Professor of Modern European History, University of South Carolina; Author of* Napoleon's Satellite Kingdoms *and* The Epoch of Napoleon

CONNIFF, MICHAEL L., *Professor, History Department, University of New Mexico; Author of* Black Labor on a White Canal: Panama 1904–1981 *and* Urban Politics in Brazil

CONNOR, CHARLES K., JR., *Charleston* Daily Mail

CONNOR, W. ROBERT, *Professor of Classics, Princeton University*

CONRAD, BARNABY, *Author of* La Fiesta Brava *and* The Encyclopedia of Bullfighting

CONRAD, HENRY S., *Professor of Botany, Grinnell College; Author of* How to Know the Mosses and Liverworts

CONRAD, SIMON, OFM CAP, *Public Relations Director, The Capuchins*

CONWAY, CATHERINE E., *Head Library Assistant, Lowell City Library, Lowell, Mass.*

COOK, GERHARD A., *Assistant Manager, Research Laboratory, Linde Division of Union Carbide Corporation*

COOK, MICHAEL J., *Professor of Intertestamental and Early Christian Literatures, Hebrew Union College—Jewish Institute of Religion*

COOKE, GEORGE W., *Head of Chemistry Department and Deputy Director of Rothamsted Experimental Station, England; Author of* Fertilizers and Profitable Farming *and* The Control of Soil Fertility

COOKE, HELEN J., *Professor of Economics, Newark College of Arts and Sciences, Rutgers University; Author of* The Role of Debt in the Economy

COOKE, JACOB E., *Author of* The Papers of Alexander Hamilton

COOLEY, HOLLIS R., *Author of* First Course in Calculus

COOLEY, MASON, *Associate Professor of English, Richmond College, New York City*

COOLING, B. FRANKLIN, *History Department, Pennsylvania Military College*

COONS, GEORGE H., *U.S. Department of Agriculture*

COOPER, DOUGLAS, *Author of* The Work of Graham Sutherland

COOPER, G. ARTHUR, *Paleobiologist, Smithsonian Institution*

COOPER, H. H. A., *Deputy Director, Criminal Law Education and Research Center, New York University*

COOPER, HELEN MARGARET, *Librarian, Wilson College*

COOPER, JOHN I., *Professor of History, McGill University; Author of* Montreal: A Brief History

COOPER, JOHN M., *Professor of Philosophy, University of Pittsburgh*

COOPER, JOHN W., *Assistant Professor of Philosophy, Calvin College*

COOPER, MARTIN, *Music Editor, London Daily Telegraph; Author of* French Music from the Death of Berlioz to the Death of Fauré

COOPER, RICHARD N., *Professor of Economics, Yale University; Author of* The Economics of Interdependence

COOPER, WILLIAM J., JR., *Associate Professor of History, Louisiana State University; Author of* The Conservative Regime: South Carolina, 1877–1890

COPE, MAURICE E., *Professor of Art History, University of Delaware*

COPE, ORVILLE G., *Associate Professor of Political Science, College of Idaho*

COPPAGE, NOEL, *Contributing Editor, Stereo Review*

COPPOLA, CARLO, *Instructor, Department of Modern Languages, Linguistics, and Area Studies, Oakland University*

CORBETT, JAMES A., *Professor of Medieval History, University of Notre Dame*

CORBETT, JOHN PATRICK, *Professor of Philosophy, University of Bradford, England*

CORCORAN, SARAH, *Librarian, Walla Walla Public Library*

CORDON, WILLIAM A., *Professor of Civil Engineering, Utah State University*

CORE, EARL L., *Professor of Biology, West Virginia University*

COREN, STANLEY, *Graduate Faculty of the New School for Social Research*

COREY, ALBERT B., *Author of* The Crisis of 1830–1842 in Canadian-American Relations

CORKRAN, DAVID H., *Author of* The Cherokee Frontier *and* The Creek Frontier

CORMACK, MALCOLM, *Curator of Paintings, Yale Center for British Art*

CORNELL, DAVID, *Professor of Chemical Engineering, Mississippi State University*

CORNELL, KENNETH, *Professor of French, Yale University; Author of* The Symbolist Movement

CORNER, GEORGE W., *Historian, Rockefeller Institute for Medical Research*

CORNEY, RICHARD W., *Professor of Old Testament, General Theological Seminary, New York City*

CORNMAN, JAMES W., *Professor of Philosophy and Chairman, Department of Philosophy, University of Pennsylvania; Author of* Metaphysics, Reference, and Language

CORPORA, THOMAS, *Member, Editorial Staff, United Press International*

CORSON, JAMES C., *Author of* Bibliography of Sir Walter Scott, 1797–1940

CORSON, JOHN J., *Coauthor of* Public Administration in Modern Society

COSENS, KENNETH W., *Sanitary Engineer, Alden E. Stilson Associates, Ltd.*

COSTELLO, CATHERINE L., *Director, Gloversville Free Library*

COSTELLO, DONALD P., *Kenan Professor of Zoology, University of North Carolina*

COSTIGAN, GIOVANNI, *Professor of History, University of Washington*

COSTIGAN, PETER, *Chief Political Correspondent, Melbourne* Herald

COTE, ALFRED J., JR., *Electronics Engineer, U.S. Naval Ordnance Laboratory*

COUDERC, PAUL, *Chief Astronomer, Paris Observatory; Author of* The Calendar

COULTER, ELLIS MERTON, *Regents Professor of History, University of Georgia; Editor of Georgia Historical Quarterly; Author of* The South During Reconstruction, 1865–1877

COULTER, JAMES A., *Professor of Greek and Latin, Columbia University*

COUNSILMAN, JAMES E., *Professor of Physical Education and Swimming Coach, Indiana University; Author of* The Science of Swimming

COUSINS, NORMAN, *Editor,* Saturday Review; *Author of* Dr. Schweitzer of Lambaréné

COVEY, ALAN D., *University Librarian, Arizona State University*

COVICI, PASCAL, JR., *Professor of English, Southern Methodist University; Author of* Mark Twain's Humor: The Image of a World

COWAN, L. GRAY, *Author of* The Dilemmas of African Independence

COWAN, RICHARD S., *Senior Botanist, Museum of Natural History, Smithsonian Institution*

COWAN, RUTH SCHWARTZ, *Assistant Professor of History, State University of New York at Stony Brook*

COX, JAMES M., *Professor of English, Dartmouth College; Author of* Mark Twain: The Fate of Humor

COXE, LOUIS, *Pierce Professor of English, Bowdoin College; Author of* Edwin Arlington Robinson

COXHEAD, ELIZABETH, *Author of* Lady Gregory

COYNE, WALTER A., *Director, Division of Program Support, Office of Information, U.S. Office of Education*

CRABTREE, THELMA R., *American Manchester Terrier Club*

CRAFTS, ALDEN S., *Professor of Botany, College of Agriculture, University of California at Berkeley*

CRAGG, GERALD R., *Author of* Reason and Authority in the 18th Century

CRAIG, GERALD M., *Professor of History, University of Toronto, Canada*

CRAIGMILES, JULIAN P., *Resident Director, Texas A&M University Agricultural Research and Extension Center, Beaumont*

CRAMER, D. L., *Research Assistant Professor, Department of Cell Biology, New York University School of Medicine*

CRANE, ROBERT I., *Director, South Asia Program and Ford-Maxwell Professor of South Asian History, Syracuse University*

CRANEFIELD, PAUL F., MD, *Professor of Physiology, Rockefeller University; Coauthor of* The Electrophysiology of the Heart

CRANTON, ELMER M., MD, *President, American Holistic Medical Association; Charter Fellow, American Academy of Family Physicians; Editor of* Journal of Holistic Medicine

CRANZ, F. EDWARD, *Rosemary Park Professor of History, Connecticut College*

CRAVEN, JOHN P., *Chief Scientist, Strategic Systems Project Office and Deep Submergence Project Office, U.S. Navy*

CRAWFORD, GEORGE, MD, *Assistant Chief of Infective Disease, Wilford Hall Medical Center at San Antonio*

CRAWFORD, MIRIAM I., *Curator, Conwellana-Templana, Samuel Paley Library, Temple University*

CRAWSHAW, NANCY, *Author of* The Cyprus Revolt

CREAN, HUGH R., *Chair, Restoration Department, Fashion Institute of Technology, State University of New York*

CRECELIUS, DANIEL N., *Professor of History, California State University at Los Angeles*

CRENSHAW, MARTHA, *Professor of Government, Wesleyan University; Author of* Revolutionary Terrorism *and* Terrorism and International Cooperation

CRESSEY, DONALD R., *Professor of Sociology, University of California at Santa Barbara; Author of* Principles of Criminology, The Structure and Functions of Organized Crime, *and* Theft of the Nation

CRILEY, RICHARD A., *Associate Professor of Horticulture, College of Tropical Agriculture, University of Hawaii*

CRIMMINS, TIMOTHY J., *Professor of History, Georgia State University*

CRIPPS, EDWARD J., SJ, *College of Philosophy and Letters, Fordham University*

CRIST, RAYMOND E., *Research Professor of Geography, University of Florida; Author of* Geography of Latin America

CRITCHFIELD, CHARLES L., *Associate Division Leader, Theoretical Division, Los Alamos Scientific Laboratory*

CRITCHFIELD, HOWARD J., *Professor of Geography, Western Washington University; Author of* General Climatology

CRITTENDEN, LUCY W., *Head Librarian, William A. Percy Memorial Library, Greenville, Miss.*

CROCKETT, JAMES UNDERWOOD, *Author of* Greenhouse Gardening as a Hobby

CRONON, E. DAVID, *Dean, College of Letters and Science, University of Wisconsin; Author of* Black Moses: The Story of Marcus Garvey and the Universal Negro Improvement Association

CRONQUIST, ARTHUR, *Senior Scientist, New York Botanical Garden; Author of* Basic Botany *and* Evolution and Classification of Flowering Plants

CROOKS, JAMES B., *Professor of History, University of North Florida*

CROPSEY, JOSEPH, *Professor of Political Science, University of Chicago*

CROSBY, ALFRED W., *Associate Professor of History, Washington State University; Author of* The Columbian Exchange: Biological and Cultural Consequences of 1492

CROSBY, MARSHALL R., *Chairman, Department of Botany, Missouri Botanical Garden; Coauthor of* A Dictionary of Mosses

CROSS, SIR A. RUPERT N., *Vinerian Professor of English Law, All Souls College, Oxford University*

CROSS, CLARK I., *Associate Professor of Physical Science, University of Florida*

CROSS, WILBUR L., *Professor of English, Yale University; Author of* The Development of the English Novel

CROSSER, WYTHE, *Reference Librarian, Mesa Public Library, Los Alamos, N.Mex.*

CROSSETT, LINDA, *Reference Librarian, Lockport Public Library, Lockport, N.Y.*

CROSSMAN, EDWIN J., *Curator, Department of Ichthyology and Herpetology, Royal Ontario Museum*

CROUCH, TOM D., *Chairman, Department of Aeronautics, National Air and Space Museum, Smithsonian Institution*

CROUSER, HERMAN H., *Engineer, U.S. Weather Bureau, Washington, D.C.*

CROWE, MICHAEL J., *Professor and Chairman, Program in the History and Philosophy of Science, University of Notre Dame*

CROWELL, CALEB, *Vice President, Educational Design, Inc.*

CROWELL, NORTON B., *Professor of English, Illinois State University*

CROWLEY, JAMES B., *Professor of History, Yale University*

CROXFORD, ROBERTA A., *Reference Librarian, Lewiston Public Library, Lewiston, Maine*

CROZIER, EMMET, *Author of* Yankee Reporters

CRUTZEN, PAUL J., *National Center for Atmospheric Research*

CULICAN, WILLIAM, *Reader in Ancient History, University of Melbourne; Author of* The Medes and Persians *and* The First Merchant Venturers

CULLEN, DOROTHY, *Librarian, Prince Edward Island Libraries*

CULLER, JONATHAN, *Class of 1916 Professor of English and Comparative Literature and Director, Society for the Humanities, Cornell University*

CULLY, KENDIG BRUBAKER, *Dean and Professor of Christian Education, New York Theological Seminary; Author of* The Teaching Church

CUMMINGS, MILTON C., JR., *Professor of Political Science, Johns Hopkins University; Author of* Congressmen and the Electorate; *Coauthor of* Democracy Under Pressure

CUMMINGS, PARKE, *Author of* The Dictionary of Sports

CUMMINGS, WILLIAM K., *Harvard University, Graduate School of Education; Author of* Education and Equality in Japan

CUNDICK, MAJOR RONALD P., *Chief of the Foreign Law Team, International Affairs Division of the Department of the Army, Office of the Judge Advocate General*

CUNNINGHAM, GLADYS, *Author of* Singer Sewing Book

CUNNINGHAM, JOHN T., *President, New Jersey Historical Society; Author of* New Jersey; America's Main Road, Newark, *and* This is New Jersey

CUNNINGHAM, K. S., *Fellow, Australian National Research Council; Former Director, Australian Council for Educational Research*

CUNNINGHAM, LUCILLE R., *Director, Hoboken Free Public Library*

CUNNINGHAM, NOBLE E., JR., *Professor of History, University of Missouri*

CUNNINGHAM, THELMA, *Library Director, Linden Free Public Library, Linden, N.J.*

CURRAN, CHARLES HOWARD, *Curator, Department of Insects and Spiders, American Museum of Natural History*

CURRAN, FRANCIS X., SJ, *Professor of History, Fordham University; Author of* The Churches and the Schools

CURRAN, JAMES B., SDB, *Public Relations Director, Salesian Fathers of St. John Bosco*

CURRAN, LINDA M., *Associate Section Manager, Battelle Memorial Institute*

CURRELL, DAVID, *Author of* The Complete Book of Puppetry

CURRENT, RICHARD N., *Distinguished Professor of American History, University of North Carolina at Greensboro; Author of* Old Thad Stevens

CURRIER, HELEN M., *Librarian, F.E. Parlin Memorial Library, Everett, Mass.*

CURRY, JANE, *Professor of Political Science, Santa Clara University*

CURTIS, GEORGE B., SJ, *Fordham University*

CURTIS, L. PERRY, JR., *Professor of History, Brown University; Author of* Coercion and Conciliation in Ireland, 1880–1892

CURTIS, MICHAEL R., *Professor of Political Science, Rutgers University; Author of* Great Political Theories

CURTISS, HOWARD C., JR., *Professor of Mechanical and Aerospace Engineering, Princeton University; Coauthor of* A Modern Course in Aeroelasticity

CURTISS, JOHN S., *James B. Duke Professor of History, Duke University; Author of* The Russian Army under Nicholas I, 1825–1855

CUSHMAN, JOY NELL, *Chairman, U.S. Olympic Synchronized Swimming Committee, 1960–1968; Author of* AAU Official Synchronized Swimming Handbook, 1956–1968

CUTBERTH, MILDRED L., *Head Librarian, Brookfield Public Library*

CUTLIP, SCOTT M., *Professor of Journalism, University of Georgia; Coauthor of* Effective Public Relations

CUTRIGHT, PHILLIPS, *Professor of Sociology, Indiana University*

CUTSHALL, ALDEN, *Professor of Geography, University of Illinois at Chicago Circle*

CZAP, PETER, JR., *Professor of History, Amherst College*

DA CAL, ERNESTO G., *Professor of Romance Languages, Queens College; Author of* Lengua y Estilo de Eça de Queiroz

DAHL, CURTIS, *Samuel Valentine Cole Professor of English Literature, Wheaton College (Mass.)*

DAHL, PHYLLIS, *Professional Liaison Department, La Leche League International*

DAIL, C. P., *Director, First Aid, American National Red Cross*

DALLEN, JAMES, *Assistant Professor of Religious Studies, Gonzaga University*

DALRYMPLE, CHARLES E., *Director, Lincoln City Libraries, Lincoln, Nebr.*

DALZIEL, CHARLES, *Professor of Electrical Engineering, College of Engineering, University of California at Berkeley*

DAMESHEK, WILLIAM, MD, *Coauthor of* Hemorrhagic Disorders

DAMJANOV, IVAN, MD, *Professor of Pathology, Jefferson Medical College, Thomas Jefferson University*

DAMKE, PAULA, *Associate Editor, Roller Skating Rink Operators Association Publications*

DANBOM, DAVID B., *Professor of History, North Dakota State University; Author of* 'Our Purpose Is to Serve': The First Century of the North Dakota Agricultural Experiment Station

DANBY, J. M. A., *Professor of Mathematics and Physics, North Carolina State University at Raleigh; Author of* Fundamentals of Celestial Mechanics

DANES, GIBSON A., *Dean, Division of Visual Arts, State University of New York at Purchase; Coauthor of* Looking at Modern Painting

DANGERFIELD, GEORGE, *Lecturer in History, University of California at Santa Barbara; Author of* The Era of Good Feelings *and* Chancellor Robert R. Livingston of New York, 1746–1815

DANGERFIELD, ROYDEN, *Executive Director, Midwest Universities Consortium for International Activities; Professor of Political Science, University of Illinois; Coauthor of* The Hidden Weapon: The History of Economic Warfare

DANIEL, DAN, *Editor of* The Ring Magazine

DANIEL, GLYN E., *Professor of Archaeology, Cambridge University; Author of* The Megalith Builders of Western Europe

DANIEL, HAWTHORNE, *Coauthor of* Happy Warrior

DANIEL, LOUISE J., *Professor of Biochemistry, Cornell University*

DANIEL, ROBERT L., *Professor of American History, Ohio University; Author of* American Philanthropy in the Near East

DANIELL, JERE, *Chairman, Department of History, Dartmouth College; Author of* Experiment in Republicanism: New Hampshire Politics and the American Revolution *and* Colonial New Hampshire: A History

DANIELS, GEORGE H., *Professor of History, Department of History, University of Alabama*

DANIELS, ROBERT V., *Professor of History, University of Vermont; Author of* The Nature of Communism *and* Studying History: How and Why

DANIELS, ROGER, *Author of* The Politics of Prejudice *and* Concentration Camps, U.S.A.

DANNEHY, LORRAINE K., *Librarian, Isaac C. Griswold Library, Whitehall, N.Y.*

DANOWSKI, T. S., MD, *Professor of Medicine, University of Pittsburgh; Author of* Clinical Endocrinology

DANSEREAU, PIERRE, *Professor of Ecology, University of Quebec*

DANTO, ARTHUR C., *Johnsonian Professor of Philosophy, Columbia University; Author of* Analytical Philosophy of Knowledge *and* Analytical Philosophy of Action

DANZIG, ALLISON, *Author of* The Racquet Game; *Coauthor of* Elements of Lawn Tennis

DANZIGER, JAMES N., *Professor of Political Science, School of Social Science, University of California at Irvine*

DARBY, WILLIAM J., MD, *Director, Division of Nutrition, Vanderbilt University School of Medicine*

DARROW, GEORGE M., *Consultant, U.S. Department of Agriculture; Author of* The Strawberry: History, Breeding and Physiology

DASHIELL, JOHN FREDERICK, *Author of* Fundamentals of Objective Psychology

DATSKO, JOSEPH, *Professor of Mechanical Engineering, University of Michigan*

DAUB, EDWARD E., *Assistant Professor, Department of History, University of Kansas*

DAUNT, JOHN G., *Professor of Physics, Stevens Institute of Technology*

DAUSTER, FRANK, *Professor of Romance Languages, Rutgers University; Author of* Breve historia del teatro hispanoamericano

DAUTERMAN, CARL CHRISTIAN, *Curator Emeritus, Metropolitan Museum of Art*

DAUTRICH, ELISABETH C., *Director, Hazleton Area Public Library*

DAVALL, GRACE, *Assistant Curator, Mammals and Birds, New York Zoological Park*

DAVALOS HURTADO, EUSEBIO, *Director General, Instituto Nacional de Antropologia, Mexico City*

DAVENPORT, HAROLD, *Rouse Ball Professor of Mathematics, Cambridge University; Author of* The Higher Arithmetic

DAVENPORT, MILLIA, *Author of* The Book of Costume

DAVENPORT, T. R. H., *Professor of History, Rhodes University, South Africa; Author of* South Africa: A Modern History

DAVIDS, JULES, *Professor of American Diplomatic History, Georgetown University*

DAVIDSON, BASIL, *Author of* A History of West Africa to the 19th Century, A History of East and Central Africa to the Late 19th Century, *and* The African Genius: An Introduction to Social and Cultural History

DAVIDSON, PHILIP G., *Program Adviser in Higher Education, The Ford Foundation, Bangkok, Thailand; Former President, University of Louisville; Author of* Propaganda and the American Revolution

DAVIDSON, RALPH H., *Professor of Ecology, University of Quebec; Author of* Insect Pests of Farm, Garden, and Orchard

DAVIDSON, W. A., *Grain Division, Agricultural Marketing Service, U.S. Department of Agriculture*

DAVIDSON, WILLIAM R., *Professor of Marketing, Ohio State University; Coauthor of* Retailing Management

DAVIE, GEORGE E., *Reader in Philosophy, University of Edinburgh*

DAVIES, ROBERTSON, *Professor of English, University of Toronto*

DAVIES, WILLIAM E., *Geologist, United States Geological Survey*

DAVIS, ALLEN F., *Professor of History, Temple University; Author of* Spearheads for Reform

DAVIS, AUDREY, *Chief, Extramural Program, National Center for Toxicology Research, U.S. Department of Health, Education, and Welfare*

DAVIS, CHARLES M., *Professor of Geography, University of Michigan*

DAVIS, DONALD R., *Curator, Division of Lepidoptera, Department of Entomology, Smithsonian Institution*

DAVIS, FREDERICK, *Professor of Law, University of Missouri*

DAVIS, GENE B., *Traffic Safety Editor, American Automobile Association, Washington, D.C.*

DAVIS, HAROLD E., *University Professor of Latin American Studies, American University; Author of* Latin American Leaders

DAVIS, HOWARD, *Professor of Art History, Columbia University*

DAVIS, JED H., JR., *Professor of Speech and Drama, University of Kansas; Coauthor of* Children's Theatre: Play Production for the Child Audience

DAVIS, JOSEPH A., JR., *Assistant to the Director, New York Zoological Society; Author of* Finding Out About Mammals

DAVIS, KAREN P., *Professor of Economics, Johns Hopkins University; Coauthor of* Medicare Policy: New Directions for Health and Long-Term Care

DAVIS, KENNETH P., *Professor of Forest Land Use, School of Forestry, Yale University; Author of* Forest Fire, Control and Use

DAVIS, R. H. C., *Professor of Medieval History, University of Birmingham, England; Author of* A History of Medieval Europe

DAVIS, ROBERT C., *Associate Professor of Sociology, Case Western Reserve University*

DAVIS, ROBERT CON, *Professor of English, University of Oklahoma; Author of* The Paternal Romance; *Coauthor of* Criticism and Culture

DAVIS, RONALD L., *Professor of History, Southern Methodist University*

DAVIS, STANLEY N., *Professor of Hydrology and Water Resources, University of Arizona; Author of* Hidrogeología; *Coauthor of* Hydrogeology

DAVIS, WAYNE H., *Professor of Zoology, University of Kentucky; Coauthor of* Bats of America

DAVIS, WILLIAM N., JR., *Chief of Archives, California State Archives, Sacramento, Calif.*

DAVISON, RODERIC H., *Professor of History, George Washington University*

DAWLEY, POWEL MILLS, *Professor of Ecclesiastical History, General Theological Seminary, New York City; Author of* Highlights of Church History: The Reformation

DAWSON, CHRISTOPHER HENRY, *Author of* Medieval Essays

DAWSON, JOHN W., JR., *Professor of Mathematics, Pennsylvania State University*

DAX, EDWARD R., *Director, Lane Public Library*

DEAK, ISTVAN, *Professor of History and Director, Institute on East Central Europe, Columbia University*

DEAN, ROBERT B., *Author of* Modern Colloids

DEAN, WINTON, *Author of* Georges Bizet, His Life and Work *and* Handel's Dramatic Oratorios and Masques

DE BEER, SIR GAVIN, *Director of British Museum (Natural History); Author of* Charles Darwin

DE CAPRILES, MIGUEL, *Professor of Law, University of California at San Francisco*

DECKER, A. MORRIS, *Professor of Agronomy, University of Maryland*

DECKER, ROBERT W., *Professor of Geophysics, Dartmouth College*

DeCONDE, ALEXANDER, *Professor of History, University of California at Santa Barbara*

DECSY, JÁNOS, *Department of History, Rutgers University and Douglass College*

DEEB, MARY-JANE, *Department of Government, American University; Author of* Libya since the Revolution: Aspects of Social and Political Development *and* Libya's Foreign Policy in North Africa

DeFRANCISCIS, ALFONSO, *Superintendent of Antiquities, Naples, Italy*

DeGARMO, LLOYD R., *Head Librarian, Compton College Library*

DEIBEL, TERRY L., *Professor of National Strategy, National War College, Washington, D.C.*

DEIMEL, RICHARD F., *Author of* Mechanics of the Gyroscope

DE JESUS, NELSON, *Chairman, Department of Romance Languages, Oberlin College*

DE KLERK, W. A., *Author of novels, plays, and essays in Afrikaans, including* Die Uur van Verlange *and* Die Jaar van die Vuuros

DeLANCEY, MARK W., *Professor, Department of Government and International Studies, University of South Carolina; Author of* Cameroon

DELEVORYAS, T., *Professor of Botany, University of Texas at Austin; Author of* Morphology and Evolution of Fossil Plants

DELL, HARRY J., *Professor of History, University of Virginia*

DELLINGER, ROBERT E., *Director and Distinguished Member, National Wrestling Hall of Fame and Museum, Stillwater, Okla.*

DELMAN, JUDITH, *Assistant to the National Director, American Montessori Society*

DELPH, GRACE S., *Director of Libraries, Flagstaff Public Library*

DELZELL, CHARLES F., *Professor of History, Vanderbilt University*

DEMONSABERT, WINSTON R., *Head, Extramural Program, Bureau of Drugs, Food and Drug Administration*

DE MONTEBELLO, PHILIPPE, *Director, Metropolitan Museum of Art*

DEMPSEY, FRANK J., *Director, Berkeley Public Library*

DEMPSTER, PRUE, *Author of* Japan Advances

DE NEVERS, NOEL, *Professor of Chemical Engineering, University of Utah; Author of* Technology and Society

DENNEY, REUEL N., *Professor of American Studies, University of Hawaii*

DENNIS, JESSIE McNAB, *Assistant Curator, Department of Sculpture and Decorative Arts, Metropolitan Museum of Art*

DENT, ALAN, *Drama Critic; Author of* Mrs. Patrick Campbell *and* Vivien Leigh

DENTAN, ROBERT C., *Professor of Old Testament Literature and Interpretation, General Theological Seminary, New York City; Author of* Holy Scriptures: A Survey *and* Preface to Old Testament Theology

DERBY, WILLIAM E., *Professor of History, State University of New York College at Geneseo*

DERRETT, J. DUNCAN M., *Professor of Oriental Laws, University of London; Lecturer in Hindu Law at the Inns of Court School of Law, London; Author of* Religion, Law and the State in India

DERRY, JOHN W., *Senior Lecturer in History, University of Newcastle upon Tyne; Author of* William Pitt *and* English Politics and the American Revolution

DERRY, THOMAS KINGSTON, *Coauthor of* A Short History of Technology

DE SANTIS, VINCENT P., *Professor and Chairman, Department of History, University of Notre Dame; Coauthor of* America's Ten Greatest Presidents

DESCH, JULIE ANNE, *Editor,* Chess Life

DESMOND, ROBERT W., *Author of* The Press and World Affairs

DESPRES, LEO A., *Professor of Sociology and Anthropology, University of Notre Dame*

DESROSIER, NORMAN W., *Director of Research, National Biscuit Company; Author of* Attack on Starvation *and* Technology of Food Preservation

DESSAINT, WILLIAM Y., *New University of Ulster*

DESSAUER, JOHN H., *Executive Vice President in charge of Research and Advanced Engineering, Xerox Corporation*

DE TERRA, HELMUT, *Adjunct Professor of History of Science, Columbia University; Coauthor of* Tepexpan Man

DEUTSCH, KARL W., *Stanfield Professor of International Peace, Harvard University; Author of* Politics and Government

DEUTSCH, SID, *Professor of Electrical Engineering, Polytechnic Institute of Brooklyn*

DE VAUCOULEURS, GERARD H., *Professor of Astronomy, University of Texas at Austin*

DeVILBISS, OTHO, *Director of Public Relations, Benevolent and Protective Order of Elks of the U.S.A.*

DE VILLAFRANCA, GEORGE W., *Professor and Chairman, Department of the Biological Sciences, Smith College*

DEVITA, VINCENT T., JR., MD, *Director of National Cancer Institute, National Institutes of Health*

DEW, GEORGE F. R., *Librarian, Lethbridge Public Library, Lethbridge, Alberta, Canada*

DEWINDT, EDWINA, *Bacon Memorial Public Library, Wyandotte, Mich.*

DEWS, PETER B., *Stanley Cobb Professor of Psychiatry, Harvard Medical School*

DIAMOND, MALCOLM L., *Professor, Department of Religion, Princeton University*

DiBENEDETTO, A. T., *Professor of Chemical Engineering, Director of Material Research Laboratory, Washington University, St. Louis, Mo.; Author of* The Structure and Properties of Materials

DIBNER, BERN, *Chairman of the Board, Burndy Corporation, Norwalk, Conn.*

DI CESARE, MARIO A., *Professor of English and Comparative Literature, Harpur College, State University of New York at Binghamton; Author of* Vida's Christiad and Vergilian Epic

DICHTER, ERNEST, *Department of Marketing, Mercy College, Dobbs Ferry, N.Y.; Author of* Packaging: The Sixth Sense, Motivating Human Behavior, *and* Strategy of Desire

DICKEN, SAMUEL N., *Professor of Geography, University of Oregon; Author of* The Pacific Northwest

DICKERMAN, EDMUND H., *Associate Professor of History, University of Connecticut*

DICKERSON, F. REED, *Professor of Law, Indiana University*

DICKIE, GEORGE T., *Professor of Philosophy, University of Illinois at Chicago Circle*

DICKINSON, JOSHUA C., III, *Research Associate in Ecology, University of Georgia*

DICKINSON, LEON T., *Professor of English, University of Missouri; Author of* A Guide to Literary Study

DICKINSON, RUTH ELY, *Librarian, Chester C. Corbin Public Library, Webster, Mass.*

DICKISON, ROLAND, *Professor of English, California State University at Sacramento*

DICKSON, FRANCES C., *4-H Information Specialist, Federal Extension Service, U.S. Department of Agriculture*

DICKSTEIN, MORRIS, *Professor of English, Queens College and the Graduate Center, City University of New York; Author of* Gates of Eden: American Culture in the Sixties

DIETZ, MARJORIE J., *Editor,* Home Garden Magazine; *Author of* Concise Encyclopedia of Favorite Flowering Shrubs *and* Concise Encyclopedia of Favorite Wild Flowers

DIETZE, ALFRED G., *Professor of Psychology, Michigan State University*

DIFFLEY, EDWARD J., *Librarian, Concord Free Public Library*

DIGGES, DUDLEY P., *Editorial Writer,* Baltimore Evening Sun

DIJKMAN, MARINUS J., *Professor of Tropical Botany, University of Miami; Author of* Hevea: Thirty Years of Research in the Far East

DILLON, JOHN M., *Regius Professor of Greek, Trinity College (Dublin); Author of* The Middle Platonists; *Editor of* Plotinus, Enneads

DILLON, MARY EARHART, *Professor of Political Science, Queens College; Author of* Frances Willard

DILLON, MERTON L., *Professor of American History, Ohio State University; Author of* Elijah P. Lovejoy, Abolitionist Editor *and* Benjamin Lundy and the Struggle for Negro Freedom

DILLON, RICHARD H., *Author of* We Have Met the Enemy *and* Meriwether Lewis

DIMOCK, EDWARD C., *Professor of Bengali and Bengali Studies, University of Chicago; Translator of* The Thief of Love, Bengali Tales from Court and Village

DIMOCK, MARSHALL E., *Author of* Public Administration

DIRINGER, DAVID, *Alphabet Museum and Seminar, Cambridge University; Author of* The Alphabet *and* The Illuminated Book

DI SANTOAGNESE, PAUL A., MD, *Chief, Pediatric Metabolism Branch, National Institutes of Health; Clinical Professor of Pediatrics, Georgetown University*

DISHMAN, ROBERT B., *Professor of Political Science, University of New Hampshire*

DITTERT, ALFRED E., JR., *Curator-in-Charge, Division of Research, Museum of New Mexico*

DIVER, WILLIAM, *Professor of Linguistics, Columbia University*

DIXON, THELMA B., *Librarian, Washington Parish Library, Franklinton, La.*

DOBBINS, CHARLES GORDON, *Assistant Director, Management Division, Academy for Educational Development*

DOBIE, J. FRANK, *Author of* The Flavor of Texas *and* Tales of Old-Time Texas

DOBLER, CLIFFORD I., *Professor of Business Law, University of Idaho*

DOBZHANSKY, THEODOSIUS, *Professor of Genetics, Rockefeller University; Author of* Genetics and Origin of Species *and* Evolution, Genetics, and Man

DOCKRILL, M. L., *Lecturer in War Studies, King's College, University of London; Coauthor of* Peace Without Promise: Britain and the Peace Conference, 1919–1923

DOCKSTADER, FREDERICK J., *Author of* Indian Art in America *and* Great North American Indians

DOCTOR, POWRIE V., *Chairman and Professor, Department of History, Gallaudet College; Editor,* American Annals of the Deaf

DODDS, GORDON B., *Professor of History, Portland State University; Author of* Oregon: A Bicentennial History

DODGE, PHILIP R., *Professor of Pediatrics and Neurology, and Head, Mallinckrodt Department of Pediatrics, Washington University School of Medicine*

DODSON, PETER, *Professor of Geology and Professor of Veterinary Gross Anatomy, University of Pennsylvania*

DOEBELE, WILLIAM A., JR., *Professor of City and Regional Planning, Harvard University*

DOELL, CHARLES E., *Author of* Elements of Park and Recreation Administration

DOHERTY, PAUL C., *Professor of English, Boston College*

DOLAN, JOHN P., *Professor of History, University of South Carolina*

DOMANSKI, BOLESLAW, *Professor of Geography, Jagiellonian University*

DONALD, DAVID, *Harry C. Black Professor of History and Director of the Institute of Southern History, Johns Hopkins University; Author of* Inside Lincoln's Cabinet, Lincoln Reconsidered, Charles Sumner and the Coming of the Civil War, *and* Charles Sumner and the Rights of Man

DONALDSON, GORDON, *Sir William Fraser Professor of Scottish History and Palaeography, University of Edinburgh, Scotland; Author of* Scottish Kings

DONNALLY, REAUMUR S., MD, *Staff, Washington Hospital Center, Washington, D.C.*

DONNELLY, JOHN PATRICK, SJ, *Associate Professor of History, Marquette University*

DONNO, ELIZABETH, *Professor of English, Columbia University*

DONOHOE, VICTORIA, *Art Critic*, Philadelphia Inquirer

DOOLING, DAVE, *Manager, NASA Microgravity Outreach, Infinity Technology, Inc., Huntsville, Ala.*

DORFMAN, J. G., *Professor, Institute for the History of Science and Technology, Moscow; Author of* Magnetic Properties of the Atomic Nucleus

DORN, WALTER L., *Author of* Competition for Empire, 1740–1763

DORR, FRANK, *Associate Editor of* Popular Science Monthly

DOUCET, MICHAEL J., *Professor of Geography, School of Applied Geography, Ryerson Polytechnic University; Coauthor of* Housing the North American City: Shelter and Society in Hamilton, Canada, 1830s–1980s

DOUGLAS, KENNETH, *Author of* A Critical Bibliography of Existentialism

DOUGLASS, WILLIAM A., *Coordinator, Basque Studies Program, University of Nevada at Reno*

DOUST, DOROTHY M., *Librarian, Tombstone Regional Branch Library*

DOVER, KENNETH J., *Professor of Greek, University of St. Andrews, Scotland; Author of* Lysias and the Corpus Lysiacum

DOWLIN, KENNETH E., *City Librarian, Arvada Public Library*

DOWLING, HERNDON, *Professor of Biology, New York University*

DOWNES, KERRY, *Honorary Lecturer in Fine Arts, University of Birmingham, England*

DOWNEY, GLANVILLE, *Distinguished Professor of History and of Classical Studies, Indiana University*

DOWNING, HOMER W., *President, Flat-Coated Retriever Society of America*

DOYLE, EUGENIE F., MD, *Professor of Pediatrics, New York University School of Medicine; Director of Pediatric Cardiology, New York University Medical Center*

DOZIER, EDWARD P., *Professor of Anthropology, University of Arizona; Author of* Pueblo Indians of North America

DRAGO, HARRY SINCLAIR, *Author of* Wild, Woolly and Wicked

DRAKE, FRANK D., *Director, National Astronomy and Ionosphere Center, Cornell University; Author of* Intelligent Life in Space; *Coauthor of* Murmurs of Earth

DRAKE, MICHAEL, *Professor in the Social Sciences, Open University, Milton Keynes, England; Author of* Population in Industrialization *and* Population and Society in Norway, 1735–1865

DRAKE, STILLMAN, *Professor, University of Toronto, Canada; Author of* Galileo Studies

DREHER, JOHN P., *Associate Professor of Philosophy, Lawrence University*

DRESSER, RICHARD C., *Director of Publications, Asphalt Institute*

DRESSLER, HERMIGILD, OFM, *Professor of Greek and Latin, Quincy College*

DREWES, HARM, *Bruinsma Hybrid Seed Company, Naaldwijk, Netherlands*

DREWS, ROBERT, *Professor of Classics, Vanderbilt University; Author of* In Search of the Shroud of Turin

DREYFUSS, HENRY, *Author of* Designing for People

DRISKEL, MICHAEL, *Assistant Professor of Art, Brown University*

DRIVER, HAROLD E., *Professor, Department of Anthropology, Indiana University; Author of* Indians of North America; *Editor of* The Americas on the Eve of Discovery

DRIVER, WILHELMINE, *Coauthor of* Ethnology and Acculturation of the Chichimeca-Jonaz of Northeast Mexico

DRUM, BOB, *President, Golf Writers Association of America*

DUBBEY, JOHN M., *Author of* The Development of Modern Mathematics

DUBINS, BARBARA, *Department of History, California State University at San Jose*

DUBOFSKY, MELVYN, *Professor of History, State University of New York at Binghamton; Author of* We Shall Be All: A History of the Industrial Workers of the World

DUBOIS, EDMUND L., MD, *Director, Collagen Disease Clinic, Los Angeles County General Hospital; Associate Clinical Professor of Medicine, University of Southern California School of Medicine; Author of* Lupus Erythematosus

DU BOIS, VICTOR D., *American Universities Field Staff*

DUBOIS, WARREN C., *President, Huguenot Society of America*

DUBOS, RENÉ J., *The Rockefeller University; Author of* Louis Pasteur: Free Lance of Science

DUCASSE, ANDRÉ, *Coauthor of* Vie et Mort des Français, 1914–1918

DUCHESNE-GUILLEMIN, J., *Author of* Hymns of Zarathustra

DUCKETT, MARGARET, *Associate Professor of English, University of Washington; Author of* Mark Twain and Bret Harte

DUCKWORTH, GEORGE E., *Giger Professor of Latin, Department of Classics, Princeton University; Author of* The Complete Roman Drama

DUDLEY, H. PHILIP, *Editor,* Shore Line Times, *Guilford, Conn.*

DUFEK, GEORGE, *Rear Admiral (Retired), U.S. Navy; Director, Mariners Museum, Newport News, Va.; Author of* Operation Deepfreeze

DUFFEY, DAVID MICHAEL, *Dog Editor,* Outdoor Life; *Author of* Hunting Dog Know How

DUFFIE, JOHN A., *Solar Energy Laboratory, University of Wisconsin at Madison; Coeditor and Contributing Author of* Solar Energy Research

DUIKER, WILLIAM J., *Professor of East Asian History, Pennsylvania State University; Author of* The Rise of Nationalism in Vietnam, 1900–1941 *and* The Communist Road to Power in Vietnam

DULCK, JEAN A., *Professor of English, University of Bordeaux, France*

DUMAS, ROBERT H., *City Librarian, Decatur Public Library*

DUMKE, GLENN S., *Chancellor, California State University and Colleges*

DUMMER, G. W. A., *Author of* Radio and Electronic Components *and* Modern Electronic Components

DUMOND, DWIGHT, *Professor of History, University of Michigan; Author of* Antislavery: The Crusade for Freedom in America

DU MOND, JESSE W. M., *Professor of Physics, California Institute of Technology*

DUNBAR, GEORGIA, *Professor of English, Hofstra University*

DUNCAN, ALASTAIR, *Consultant in 19th- and 20th-century decorative arts; Author of* Masterworks of Louis Comfort Tiffany *and* American Art Deco

DUNCAN, ALISTAIR M., *Reader in the History and Philosophy of Science and Technology, Loughborough University of Technology, England*

DUNHAM, K. C., *Director, Institute of Geological Sciences, London*

DUNLAP, FLORENCE B., *Reference Librarian, Gainesville Public Library*

DUNLOP, KATHLEEN E., *Professor of History, East Carolina University*

DUNN, JOSEPH, *Professor of Celtic Languages and Literature, Catholic University of America; Author of* A Grammar of the Modern Portuguese Language

DUNN, LESLIE C., *Author of* A Short History of Genetics; *Coauthor of* Principles of Genetics

DUNN, PAUL R., *Andover Newton Theological School*

DUNN, WALDO H., *Author of* English Biography

DUNNELL, ROBERT C., *Professor of Anthropology, University of Washington*

DUPREE, A. HUNTER, *George L. Littlefield Professor of American History, Brown University*

DUPREE, LOUIS, *American Universities Field Staff; Author of* Afghanistan: Land of Insolence

DUPREE, NANCY HATCH, *Afghan Tourist Organization, Kabul, Afghanistan*

DUPUY, R. ERNEST, *Author of* Compact History of the United States Army

DURAN, MANUEL, *Professor of Spanish and Portuguese, Yale University; Author of* Cervantes *and* Earth Tones: The Poetry of Pablo Neruda

DURAND, LOYAL, JR., *Professor of Geography, University of Tennessee; Author of* Economic Geography

DURANT, FREDERICK C., III, *Assistant Director, Astronautics, National Air and Space Museum, Smithsonian Institution*

DURHAM, J. WYATT, *Professor of Paleontology, Emeritus, University of California at Berkeley*

DURKIN, THOMAS A., *Board of Governors, Federal Reserve System*

DURNBAUGH, DONALD F., *Professor of Church History, Bethany Theological Seminary; Author of* European Origins of the Brethren *and* The Brethren in Colonial America

DUROST, WALTER N., *Adjunct Professor, University of New Hampshire; Coauthor of* Essentials of Measurement for Teachers; *Consultant to the Text Department, Harcourt Brace Jovanovich*

DVORNIK, FRANCIS, *Professor of Byzantine History, Dumbarton Oaks Research Library and Collection of Harvard University; Author of* Photian Schism

DWYER, JOHANNA T., *Director, Frances Stern Nutrition Center, New England Medical Center Hospital; Professor of Medicine and Community Health, Tufts University Schools of Medicine and Nutrition*

DYE, JOSEPH M., III, *Curator, Asiatic Art, Virginia Museum of Fine Arts; Adjunct Assistant Professor of Fine Arts, College of William and Mary*

DYE, LEE, *Staff Writer, Los Angeles* Times

DYER, EDWARD R., JR., *Executive Secretary, U.S. Committee for the International Years of the Quiet Sun*

DYER, HARRY, *Technical Editor of* Paper Trade Journal

DYER, HUBERT J., *Professor of Biology, Brown University*

DYKSTRA, MARY, *Director, School of Library and Information Studies, Dalhousie University*

DYNES, WAYNE, *Associate Professor of Art History, Hunter College; Author of* The First Christian Palace-Church Type *and* European Palaces from Late Antiquity to the Baroque

DYRNESS, ENOCK C., *Registrar, Wheaton College (Ill.)*

EADIE, JOHN W., *Professor of History, University of Michigan*

EAGLETON, CLYDE, *Author of* International Government

EAKER, IRA C., *Lieutenant General, U.S. Air Force (Retired); Author of* Winged Warfare

EALY, LAWRENCE O., *Professor of History, Rider College; Author of* Yanqui Politics and the Isthmian Canal

EAMES, ARTHUR J., *Professor of Botany, Cornell University; Author of* Morphology of Vascular Plants: Lower Group

EARLE, WILLIAM JAMES, *Associate Professor of Philosophy, Long Island University (The Brooklyn Center)*

EAST, L. R., *Chairman, State Rivers and Water Supply Commission, Victoria, Australia*

EASTON, H. H., *Chief Librarian, The Public Library, Winnipeg, Manitoba, Canada*

EASTON, STEWART C., *Author of* Roger Bacon and His Search for a Universal Science

EATON, JOHN W., *Assistant Professor, Department of Anthropology, Washington University, St. Louis, Mo.*

EATON, PAUL B., *Associate Professor of Metals Processing, Purdue University*

EATON, VINCENT L., *Chief Editor, Information and Publications Office, Library of Congress*

EBELING, VIRGINIA, *Librarian, Ohio County Public Library, Wheeling, W.Va.*

EBENSTEIN, WILLIAM, *Author of* New Political Thought *and* Today's Isms: Communism, Fascism, Capitalism and Socialism

EBERSOLE, ALVA V., *Professor of Spanish, University of North Carolina; Editor of* Calderón de la Barca: La desdicha de la voz

ECCLES, JOHN C., *Winner of the Nobel Prize for Physiology or Medicine, 1963; Author of* The Physiology of Nerve Cells

ECCLES, W. J., *Professor of History, University of Toronto; Author of* Frontenac the Courtier Governor, Canada under Louis XIV, *and* France in America

ECKLER, A. ROSS, *Director, U.S. Bureau of the Census*

ECKMANN, LEO, MD, *Chief, Department of Surgery, City Hospital, University of Bern, Switzerland; Author of* Tetanus

ECKSTEIN, HARRY H., *Distinguished Professor of Political Science, University of California at Irvine; Author of* Regarding Politics

EDDINS, BERKLEY B., *Associate Professor of Philosophy, State University of New York at Buffalo*

EDER, DORIS, *Author of* Three Writers in Exile: Pound, Eliot, and Joyce

EDGERTON, STEPHENIE, *Professor of Educational Philosophy, New York University*

EDGERTON, WILLIAM F., *Professor of Egyptology and Chairman, Department of Oriental Languages and Literature, University of Chicago; Author of* The Thutmosid Succession

EDIDIN, STEPHEN R., *Research Associate, Pennsylvania Academy of the Fine Arts*

EDINGER, LEWIS J., *Professor of Government, Columbia University; Author of* Politics in Germany

EDMUNDS, R. DAVID, *Professor of History, Indiana University*

EDWARDS, A. B., *Chief, Mineragraphic Investigations, Commonwealth Scientific and Industrial Research Organization, East Melbourne, Victoria, Australia*

EDWARDS, JUNIUS D., *Aluminum Company of America*

EDWARDSON, JOHN R., *Agronomist, University of Florida*

EFRAN, ELSA R., *Assistant Director, Office of Public Relations, University of Rochester*

EGAN, DESMOND, *Poet and Critic; Artistic Director, Gerard Manley Hopkins International Summer School, Monasterevin, Ireland*

EGAN, KEITH J., OC, *Assistant Professor, Historical Theology, Marquette University*

EGAN, ROBERT L., MD, *Professor of Radiology and Chief, Mammography Section, Department of Radiology, Emory University Clinic; Author of* Mammography

EGERTON, JOHN, *Author of* The Americanization of Dixie

EGGAN, FRED R., *Professor of Anthropology, University of Chicago*

EGGERTSEN, CLAUDE A., *Director of Program of Comparative Education, University of Michigan*

EGGUM, JANET M., *Librarian, Whitefish Bay Public Library*

EHRENBERG, WERNER, *Professor of Experimental Physics, Birkbeck College, University of London*

EHRMANN, HENRY W., *Joel Parker Professor of Law and Political Science, McGill University, Canada; Author of* Politics in France

EICHEL, ELLEN B., *Instructor, New School for Social Research, New York; Foodways Coordinator, National Foundation for Jewish Culture*

EICKWORT, GEORGE C., *Associate Professor of Entomology, New York State College of Agriculture, Cornell University*

EINARSSON, STEFÁN, *Professor of Scandinavian Philology, Johns Hopkins University; Author of* History of Icelandic Prose Writers (1900–1940) *and* A History of Icelandic Literature

EINHORN, ERIC S., *Professor of Political Science, University of Massachusetts at Amherst*

EISNER, JERRY D., MD, *Department of Social Medicine, Montefiore Hospital and Medical Center, Albert Einstein College of Medicine*

EITEMAN, DAVID K., *Professor of Finance, Graduate School of Management, University of California at Los Angeles; Coauthor of* The Stock Market

EKLOF, BEN, *Professor of History, Indiana University; Author of* Russian Peasant Schools, The World of the Russian Peasant, *and* Soviet Briefing: Gorbachev and the Reform Period

EKMAN, ERNST, *Professor of History, University of California at Riverside*

ELAM, CHARLES H., *Wayne State University Press; Editor of* The Peale Family: Three Generations of American Artists

ELIASON, NORMAN E., *Professor of English, University of North Carolina*

ELIOT, GEORGE FIELDING, *Major, U.S. Army (Retired); Author of* Bombs Bursting in Air, Victory Without War, *and* The Ramparts We Watch

ELKIN, A. P., *Author of* Australian Aborigines: How to Understand Them, Citizenship for the Aborigines, *and* Aboriginal Men of High Degree

ELKIND, DAVID, *Chairman, Eliot Pearson Department of Child Study, Tufts University; Editor of* Six Psychological Studies by Jean Piaget; *Coeditor of* Studies in Cognitive Development

ELKINS, HERVEY B., *Director of Massachusetts Division of Occupational Hygiene; Author of* Chemistry of Industrial Toxicology

ELKINS, T. H., *Honorary Professor of Geography, University of Sussex, England*

ELLARSON, ROBERT S., *Professor of Wildlife Ecology, University of Wisconsin*

ELLENBOGEN, LEON, *Associate Director, Professional Pharmaceutical Services; Chief, Nutritional Science, Lederle Laboratories*

ELLINWOOD, LEONARD, *Author of* The History of American Church Music

ELLIOT, JAMES L., *Professor of Astronomy and Physics, Massachusetts Institute of Technology; Coauthor of* Rings: Discoveries from Galileo to Voyager

ELLIOTT, GORDON R., *Department of English, Simon Fraser University, Canada; Author of* Quesnel, Commercial Centre of the Cariboo Gold Rush

ELLIS, DAVID M., *P. V. Rogers Professor of History Emeritus, Hamilton College*

ELLIS, JOHN TRACY, *Professor of Church History, University of San Francisco; Author of* The Life of James Cardinal Gibbons

ELLIS, RICHARD S., *Assistant Professor of New Eastern Archaeology, Yale University*

ELLIS, ROBERT A., JR., *Senior Research Physicist, Plasma Physics Laboratory, Princeton University*

ELLMANN, RICHARD, *Goldsmiths' Professor of English Literature, University of Oxford; Author of* The Identity of Yeats *and* James Joyce

ELSE, CAROLYN J., *Director, Pierce County Library, Tacoma, Wash.*

ELSEN, ALBERT, *Professor of Art History, Stanford University; Author of* Rodin; *Editor of* Auguste Rodin: Readings on His Life and Art

ELSHTAIN, JEAN BETHKE, *Centennial Professor of Political Science, Vanderbilt University; Author of* Public Man, Private Woman: Women in Social and Political Thought

ELTING, E. C., *Agricultural Research Service, U.S. Dept. of Agriculture*

ELTING, JOHN R., *Colonel, U.S. Army (Retired); Coauthor of* A Military History and Atlas of the Napoleonic Wars; *Associate Editor of* West Point Atlas of American Wars

ELTON, EDWIN J., *Professor of Finance, New York University*

ELTON, G. R., *Professor of English Constitutional History, Cambridge University; Author of* England Under the Tudors

EMELEUS, H. J., *University Chemical Laboratory, Cambridge University*

EMENEAU, MURRAY B., *Professor of Sanskrit and Linguistics, University of California at Berkeley*

EMERSON, THOMAS I., *Lines Professor of Law, Yale Law School; Author of* Toward a General Theory of the First Amendment; *Coauthor of* Political and Civil Rights in the United States

EMERY, IRENE, *Curator of Technical Studies, Textile Museum, Washington, D.C.; Author of* The Primary Structure of Fabrics

EMERY, SUE, *Editor, American Contract Bridge League Bulletin*

EMERY, WALTER B., *Professor, Communications, Ohio State University; Author of* National and International Systems of Broadcasting

ENGDAHL, RICHARD, *Principal Research Scientist and Fellow, Department of Mechanical Engineering, Battelle Memorial Institute, Columbus, Ohio*

ENGELBERGER, JOSEPH F., *Chairman, Transitions Research Corp.; Author of* Robotics in Practice *and* Robotics in Service

ENGLAND, NICHOLAS M., *Professor of Music, Columbia University*

ENGLAND, ROBERT, *Economist; Author of* Contemporary Canada

ENGLE, NATHANAEL H., *University of Washington*

ENGLE, T. L., *Professor of Psychology, Indiana University; Author of* Psychology: Its Principles and Applications

ENGLISH, DOROTHY, *Head, Pennsylvania Division, Carnegie Library of Pittsburgh*

ENGLISH, VAN H., *Professor of Geography, Dartmouth College*

ENGLISH, W. FRANCIS, *Dean, College of Arts and Science, University of Missouri; Author of* Pioneer Lawyer and Jurist in Missouri

ENGSTROM, ALFRED GARVIN, *Alumni Distinguished Professor of French, University of North Carolina at Chapel Hill*

ENTEEN, GEORGE M., *Associate Professor of History, Pennsylvania State University*

ENZLER, CLARENCE J., *Office of Information, U.S. Department of Agriculture*

EPPLE, WILLIAM S., *Director, Public Relations Department, National Dairy Council*

EPPS, ARCHIE C., III, *Dean of Students in Harvard College; Author of* The Speeches of Malcolm X at Harvard

EPSTEIN, PERLE, *Author of* The Private Labyrinth of Malcolm Lowry

ERBE, LAWRENCE, *Associate Professor, Department of Biology, University of Southwestern Louisiana*

ERICKSON, JOHN, *Professor of Politics, University of Edinburgh, Scotland; Author of* The Soviet High Command; *Coeditor of* The Military-Technical Revolution

ERICSON, RAYMOND S., *Music Editor, New York Times*

ERSKINE, JOHN, *Author of* The Elizabethan Lyric; *Joint Editor of* Cambridge History of American Literature

ESAU, KATHERINE, *Professor Emeritus of Botany, University of California at Santa Barbara; Author of* Plant Anatomy *and* The Phloem

ESCOLAS, EDMOND L., *Professor of Business Administration, College of Commerce and Industry, University of Wyoming*

ESPLIN, DON W., *Professor of Pharmacology, Department of Pharmacology and Therapeutics, McGill University*

ESPOSITO, VINCENT J., *Brigadier General, U.S. Army; Head, Department of Military Art and Engineering, U.S. Military Academy; Editor of* A Concise History of World War II

ESSIG, EDWARD O., *Professor of Entomology, College of Agriculture, University of California at Berkeley; Author of* History of Entomology

ESTABROOK, RONALD W., *Professor of Biochemistry, School of Medicine, University of Texas Health Center at Dallas*

ESTALL, R. C., *Reader in Geography, London School of Economics and Political Science, University of London*

ESTES, RICHARD D., *Museum of Comparative Zoology, Harvard University*

ETCHESON, WARREN W., *Professor of Marketing, University of Washington*

EVANS, BROCK, *Northwest Representative, Sierra Club*

EVANS, CHESTER E., *Chief, North Plains Branch, Soil and Water Conservation Research Division, U.S. Department of Agriculture, Agricultural Research Service*

EVANS, CINDY A., *University of Illinois*

EVANS, DAVID M., *Director, Potential Gas Agency, Colorado School of Mines*

EVANS, H. ROY, *President, International Table Tennis Federation*

EVANS, HOWARD E., *Professor of Entomology, Colorado State University; Author of* Wasp Farm; *Coauthor of* The Wasps

EVANS, PAUL, *Department of Political Science, York University, Ontario*

EVANS, RAYMOND A., *Research Leader, Pasture and Range Management, U.S. Department of Agriculture*

EVANS, W. H., *Staff Director, Special Projects, National Office Management Association*

EVANS-PRITCHARD, E. E., *Professor of Social Anthropology, Oxford University; Author of* The Azande

EVANSON, RANDALL, *Assistant Professor of Management, University of Wisconsin at Oshkosh*

EVENSEN, MARY K., *City University of New York*

EVES, HOWARD W., *Professor of Mathematics, University of Maine*

EWBANK, INGA-STINA, *Hildred Carlile Professor of English, University of London; Author of* Their Proper Sphere: A Study of the Brontë Sisters as Early-Victorian Novelists

EWEN, DAVID, *Author of* The World of Great Composers, Great Composers: 1300–1900, *and* Composers Since 1900, *and* Panorama of American Popular Music

EWERS, JOHN C., *Senior Ethnologist, Department of Anthropology, Smithsonian Institution*

EWERS, WILLIAM, *Author of* Sincere's Sewing Machine Service Book

EWING, A. C., *Editor of* The Idealist Tradition

EWING, DAVID PAUL, *Editor in Chief, Prentice Hall Computer Publishing*

EYRE, JOHN D., *Professor of Geography, University of North Carolina*

EYRING, HENRY, *Distinguished Professor of Chemistry, University of Utah*

EZELL, JOHN S., *Professor of History, University of Oklahoma; Author of* Fortune's Merry Wheel: The Lottery in America

FAGE, J. D., *Professor of African History and Director of Centre of West African Studies, University of Birmingham, England; Editor of* The Journal of African History; *Author of* Ghana: A Historical Interpretation *and* A History of Africa

FAHNESTOCK, ROBERT K., *Professor of Geology, State University of New York College at Fredonia*

FAIN, BUNA TURNER, *Director, Okefenokee Regional Library, Waycross, Ga.*

FAIR, MARVIN L., *Professor of Transportation, American University, Washington, D.C.*

FAIRBROTHERS, DAVID E., *Professor of Botany, Rutgers University*

FAIRCHILD, JANET D., *Library Director, Free Public Library of Verona, N.J.*

FALARDEAU, JEAN-CHARLES, *Professor, Department of Sociology and Anthropology, Laval University, Canada; Author of* Roots and Values in Canadian Lives *and* The Rise of Social Sciences in French Canada

FALCK, WILLIAM D., *Colonel, U.S. Army; Associate Professor of Military Art and Engineering, U.S. Military Academy*

FALK, MINNA R., *Professor of History, New York University; Author of* History of Germany

FALLS, CYRIL BENTHAM, *Chichele Professor of the History of War, Oxford University; Editor of* Great Military Battles

FALVO, CATHEY, MD, *Department of Community Medicine, New York Medical College*

FAMBROUGH, DOUGLAS M., JR., *Carnegie Institute of Washington, D.C.*

FAMILY, FEREYDOON, *Samuel Candler Dobbs Professor of Condensed Matter Physics, Emory University*

FANNING, LEONARD M., *Author of* Fathers of Industry

FANNING, RALPH, *Professor of History of the Fine Arts, Ohio State University; Coauthor of* The Italian Renaissance

FARBER, BERNARD, *Professor of Sociology, Arizona State University; Author of* Family: Organization and Interaction

FARBER, EDUARD, *Author of* The Evolution of Chemistry

FARKAS, ADALBERT, *Assistant Director of Research, Houdry Process and Chemical Co.*

FARNER, DONALD S., *Professor of Zoology, University of Washington; Coeditor of* Avian Biology

FARON, LOUIS C., *Professor of Anthropology, State University of New York at Stony Brook; Coauthor of* Native Peoples of South America

FARR, D. M. L., *Professor of History, Carleton University, Canada; Coauthor of* The Canadian Experience

FARRAR, KATHLEEN R., *Department of History of Science and Technology, University of Manchester Institute of Science and Technology*

FARRAR, MARGARET, *Crossword Puzzle Editor,* New York Times

FARWELL, BEATRICE, *Senior Lecturer, Department of Education, Metropolitan Museum of Art*

FASHENA, GLADYS J., *Professor of Pediatrics, Southwestern Medical College, University of Texas*

FATT, IRVING, *Professor of Engineering, University of California at Berkeley*

FAUCHER, DANIEL, *Honorary Dean, Faculty of Letters, University of Toulouse, France*

FAULK, HARVEY E., *General Anthony Wayne Chapter, Sons of the American Revolution*

FAURE, GUNTER, *Professor of Geology, Ohio State University; Author of* Principles of Isotope Geology *and* Strontium Isotope Geology

FAVRETTI, RUDY J., *Professor of Landscape Architecture, University of Connecticut at Storrs; Coauthor of* Landscapes and Gardens for Historic Buildings *and* For Every House a Garden

FAWCETT, N. G., *President, Ohio State University*

FAY, GERARD, *Author of* The Abbey Theatre: Cradle of Genius

FEATHER, NORMAN, FRS, *Professor of Natural Philosophy, University of Edinburgh, Scotland; Author of* An Introduction to Nuclear Physics

FEDER, HERBERT, *Department of Transmission Facilities, Bell Telephone Laboratories*

FEDER, KENNETH L., *Professor of Anthropology, Central Connecticut State College; Director of the Farmington River Archaeological Project; Author of* Frauds, Myths, and Mysteries: Science and Pseudoscience in Archaeology

FEDER, LILLIAN, *Professor of English, Queens College; Author of* Crowell's Handbook of Classical Literature

FEEN, HANS JØRGEN, Norwegian Whaling Gazette, *Sandefjord, Norway*

FEERICK, JOHN D., *Member of the New York Bar; Author of* From Failing Hands *and* The Twenty-Fifth Amendment

FEHREN, HENRY, *Author of* Christ Now *and* God Spoke One Word

FEHRENBACHER, DON E., *William Robertson Coe Professor of History, Stanford University; Author of* The Leadership of Abraham Lincoln; *Winner of the 1979 Pulitzer Prize in History for* The Dred Scott Case

FEIGIN, RALPH D., MD, *Professor of Pediatrics, Washington University School of Medicine, St. Louis, Mo.*

FEIGL, HERBERT, *Regents Professor of Philosophy, University of Minnesota; Coauthor of* Readings in Philosophical Analysis

FEINBERG, GERALD, *Professor of Physics, Columbia University; Author of* The Prometheus Project: Mankind's Search for Long Range Goals

FEINBERG, RICHARD A., *Professor, Department of Consumer Sciences and Retailing, Purdue University*

FEINBLATT, EBRIA, *Curator, Prints and Drawings, Los Angeles County Museum of Art*

FELIX, MICHAEL O., *Vice President and General Manager, Ampex Corporation*

FELL, H. B., *Professor of Invertebrate Zoology, Museum of Comparative Zoology, Harvard University*

FELLMAN, DAVID, *Vilas Professor of Political Science, University of Wisconsin; Author of* The Constitutional Right of Association

FELSENFELD, OSCAR, *Professor of Tropical Medicine and Hygiene, Tulane University School of Public Health; Adjunct Professor of Microbiology, School of Medicine; Chief, Division of Communicable Diseases, Tulane University Research Center*

FERACA, STEPHEN E., *Tribal Counselor, Bureau of Indian Affairs, U.S. Department of the Interior; Author of* Wakinyan: Contemporary Teton Dakota Religion

FERGUSON, DeLANCEY, *Professor of English, Brooklyn College; Author of* Pride and Passion: Robert Burns, 1759–1796; *Coeditor of* RLS: Letters to Charles Baxter

FERGUSON, E. JAMES, *Professor of History, Queens College; Author of* The Power of the Purse: A History of American Public Finance, 1776–1790

FERGUSON, FRANK, JR., MD, *Professor and Chairman of Department of Pharmacology, Albany Medical College of Union University*

FERGUSON, JOHN, *Assistant Professor of History, University of Texas*

FERGUSON, WALLACE K., *Professor of History, University of Western Ontario, Canada; Author of* Europe in Transition, 1300–1520

FERGUSON, WILFRED J., *Physicist; Head of Armor Materials Section, U.S. Naval Research Laboratory*

FERGUSSON, C. BRUCE, *Archivist of Nova Scotia; Associate Professor of History, Dalhousie University, Canada*

FERGUSSON, SIR JAMES, *Keeper of the Records of Scotland; Author of* The Curragh Incident

FERMI, LAURA, *Author of* Atoms in the Family *and* Atoms for the World

FERRATER MORA, JOSÉ, *Professor of Philosophy, Bryn Mawr College; Author of* Ortega y Gasset: An Outline of His Philosophy

FERRELL, ROBERT H., *Professor of History, Indiana University; Author of* America in a Divided World: 1945–72; *Editor of* Off the Record: The Private Papers of Harry S. Truman

FERRETTI, FRED, New York Times; *Author of* The Great American Marble Book

FERRILL, ARTHER, *Associate Professor of History, University of Washington*

FEUERWERKER, ALBERT, *Professor of History, University of Michigan; Author of* China's Early Industrialization; *Coauthor of* Chinese Communist Studies of Modern Chinese History

FEZANDIÉ, EUGENE H., *Professor of Mechanical Engineering, Stevens Institute of Technology*

FIELD, WILLIAM D., *Associate Curator, Division of Insects, Smithsonian Institution*

FIELDHOUSE, D. K., *Breit Lecturer in Commonwealth History and Fellow of Nuffield College, Oxford University; Author of* The Colonial Empires

FIERMAN, WILLIAM, *Professor of Uralic and Altaic Studies, Indiana University*

FIEVE, RONALD R., *Chief of Psychiatric Research, Lithium Clinic and Metabolic Unit, New York State Psychiatric Institute; Professor of Clinical Psychiatry, Columbia College of Physicians and Surgeons*

FIGLIO, KARL, *Wellcome Unit for the History of Medicine, Cambridge University*

FILLER, LOUIS, *Professor of American Civilization, Antioch College; Author of* Crusade Against Slavery

FILLIOZAT, JEAN, *Membre de l'Institut, Professeur au Collège de France, Paris; Author of* La Doctrine Classique de la Médecine Indienne

FILSON, FLOYD V., *Professor of New Testament Literature and History; Dean, McCormick Theological Seminary, Chicago*

FINAN, JOHN J., *Professor of Latin American Studies, School of International Service, American University, Washington, D.C.*

FINCH, ELEANOR H., *Secretary of the Board of Editors, American Journal of International Law*

FINCH, HERBERT, *Curator and University Archivist, Cornell University*

FINDLEY, JAMES S., *Museum of Southwestern Biology, University of New Mexico*

FINE, EVE, *University of Wisconsin at Madison*

FINE, JOHN V. A., *Ewing Professor of Greek Languages and Literature, Princeton University; Author of* Horoi: Studies in Mortgage, Real Security, and Land Tenure in Ancient Athens

FINN, ROBERT, *Music Critic, Cleveland Plain Dealer*

FINNEY, KENNETH V., *Department of History, North Carolina Wesleyan College; Author of* In Quest of El Dorado: Precious Metal Mining and the Modernization of Honduras (1880–1900)

FISCHER, ALBERT G., *Westinghouse Research and Development Center*

FISCHER, DONALD E., *Associate Professor of Finance, University of Connecticut*

FISCHER, G. L., *Public Library of South Australia*

FISCHER-GALATI, STEPHEN, *Professor of History, Wayne State University; Author of* Rumania: a Bibliographical Guide

FISHBEIN, DANIEL B., MD, *Centers for Disease Control, Atlanta*

FISHBEIN, SAM *Special Adviser, Flight Management Systems, National Air and Space Museum, Smithsonian Institution*

FISHER, JOHN, *Hunter College*

FISHER, LESTER E., DVM, *Director, Lincoln Park Zoological Gardens, Chicago*

FISHER, PAUL, *Director, Freedom of Information Center, University of Missouri*

FISHER, RUTH, *Public Relations Assistant, Department of Ophthalmology, University of Iowa*

FISHER, W. B., *Head of Department of Geography and Principal of the Graduate Society, University of Durham, England*

FISK, GEORGE, *Professor of Marketing, School of Management, and Director, Management Research Center, Syracuse University; Author of* Future Directions for Marketing

FITCH, ROBERT M., *Professor, Social Studies Education, University of Iowa; Coauthor of* Futures Unlimited *and* Modern Methods in Secondary Education

FITZGERALD, J. V., *Director, Tile Council of America Research Center*

FITZGERALD, THOMAS, *Assistant Chief Inspector, Department of Education, Dublin, Ireland*

FITZPATRICK, GARLAND M., *Consultant in Guidance, Connecticut State Department of Education*

FITZSIMONS, NEAL, *Consulting Engineer, Engineering Counsel; Author of* Civil Engineering History, Systems Engineering, *and* John B. Jarvis

FLAHERTY, TERESE, *Director, Grand Traverse Area Library Federation*

FLANAGAN, LOIS L., *Librarian, Dodge City Public Library*

FLANAGAN, THOMAS J., *Professor of English, University of California at Berkeley; Author of* The Irish Novelists, 1800–1850

FLANDERS, FRANCES, *Head Librarian, Ouachita Parish Public Library, Monroe, La.*

FLAXMAN, SEYMOUR L., *Executive Officer, Germanic Languages and Literatures, Graduate Center, City University of New York; Author of* Herman Heijermans and His Dramas

FLEAGLE, ROBERT G., *Professor of Atmospheric Sciences, University of Washington*

FLEMING, RICHARD H., *Professor of Oceanography, University of Washington*

FLEMING, SHIRLEY, *Editor of* High Fidelity/Musical America

FLESCH, PETER, *Department of Dermatology, University Hospital, University of Pennsylvania*

FLETCHER, ANGUS, *Professor of English, State University of New York at Buffalo; Author of* Allegory: The Theory of a Symbolic Mode

FLEXNER, JAMES THOMAS, *Author of* The Traitor and the Spy

FLINN, RICHARD A., *Professor of Metallurgical Engineering, University of Michigan; Author of* Fundamentals of Metal Casting

FLINK, STEVE, *Senior Correspondent, Tennis Week*

FLINTERMAN, PETER C., *Reference Librarian and Associate Professor, Miami University, Oxford, Ohio*

FLÖGE-BÖM, WOLF, *German Wirehaired Pointer Club of America*

FLORES, IVAN, *Consultant in Computer Design*

FLORIN, LAMBERT, *Author of the Western Ghost Town series*

FLORIPE, RODOLFO O., *Professor of Romance Languages, University of Minnesota*

FLOROVSKY, VERY REV. GEORGES, *Professor of Eastern Church History, Harvard Divinity School; Author of* Ways of Russian Theology

FOGLE, HAROLD W., *Stone Fruit Investigations Leader, Plant Industry Station, U.S. Department of Agriculture*

FOGLE, RICHARD HARTER, *Author of* Idea of Coleridge's Criticism

FOLMSBEE, STANLEY J., *Professor of History, University of Tennessee; Coauthor of* Tennessee: A Short History, History of Tennessee, *and* The Story of Tennessee

FOLSOM, JAMES K., *Professor of English, University of Colorado*

FOLTMAN, FELICIAN F., *Professor, New York State School of Industrial and Labor Relations, Cornell University*

FORAN, MAX, *Author of* Calgary: An Illustrated History *and* Calgary: Canada's Frontier Metropolis

FORBES, CLARENCE A., *Professor of Classics, Ohio State University*

FORBES, JOHN, *New York Times*

FORBES, R. J., *Professor of the History of Pure and Applied Sciences in Antiquity, University of Amsterdam, Netherlands; Author of* Man the Maker: A History of Technology and Engineering

FORD, ALICE, *Author of* John James Audubon

FORD, BARBARA J., *Professor, University Library Services, Virginia Commonwealth University; Formerly President, Association of College and Research Libraries*

FORD, JEREMIAH, DM, *Author of* Spanish Grammar *and* Exercises in Spanish Composition

FORD, JOHN T., CSC, *Associate Professor of Theology, Catholic University of America*

FORD, NEIL M., *Professor of Business, School of Business, University of Wisconsin*

FORMAN, CHARLES W., *Professor of Missions, Divinity School, Yale University; Author of* Christianity in the Non-Western World

FORMAN, SIDNEY, *Librarian, U.S. Military Academy*

FORSTER, MERLIN H., *Professor of Spanish and Portuguese, University of Illinois*

FORTE, ALLEN, *Professor of the Theory of Music, Yale University; Author of* Contemporary Tone-Structures

FOSTER, C. P., *Executive Director, Cordage Institute, Hingham, Mass.; Editor of* Synthetic Rope Manual

FOSTER, CHARLES H., *Professor of English, University of Minnesota; Author of* The Rungless Ladder: Harriet Beecher Stowe and New England Puritanism

FOSTER, J. B., *Assistant Director, British Columbia Provincial Museum, Victoria, British Columbia, Canada*

FOSTER, JOHN S., JR., *Vice President of Science and Technology, TRW, Inc.*

FOSTER, JOSEPH K., *Author of* Posters and Personality

FOSTER, L. H., *President of Tuskegee Institute*

FOTITCH, CONSTANTIN, *Author of* War We Lost

FOULET, ALFRED, *Professor of Romance Languages, Princeton University*

FOULKES, PETER, *Professor of German, University of Wales; Author of* The Reluctant Pessimist: A Study of Franz Kafka

FOWKES, ROBERT A., *Professor of German, New York University*

FOWLER, GARY L., *Assistant Professor of Geography, University of Illinois*

FOWLER, JOHN, *Architect*

FOWLER, KENNETH, *Lecturer in History, University of Edinburgh, Scotland; Author of* The Age of Plantagenet and Valois

FOWLER, SHIRLEY C., *Librarian, Village Library of Cooperstown*

FOWLES, GRANT R., *Professor of Physics, University of Utah*

FOWLIE, WALLACE, *James B. Duke Professor of French, Duke University*

FOX, ALLEN S., *Professor of Genetics, University of Wisconsin*

FOX, HAROLD W., *Professor of Marketing, DePaul University; Author of* The Economics of Trading Stamps

FOX, PAUL J., *Graduate Research Assistant, Lamont-Doherty Geological Observatory, Columbia University*

FRAENKEL, OSMOND K., *A General Counsel to the American Civil Liberties Union; Author of* The Sacco-Vanzetti Case

FRAME, J. SUTHERLAND, *Professor of Mathematics, Michigan State University*

FRANCIS, SIR FRANK, *Director and Principal Librarian, British Museum, London; Author of* Treasures of the British Museum

FRANCIS-WILLIAMS OF ABINGER, LORD , *Author of* The Rise of the Labour Party

FRANK, JOSETTE, *Author of* Your Child's Reading Today

FRANK, ROBERT G., JR., *Department of the History of Science, Harvard University*

FRANK, ROBERT N., *Wilmer Ophthalmological Institute, Johns Hopkins University School of Medicine*

FRANKFURT, HARRY, *Professor of Philosophy, Rockefeller University*

FRANKLIN, H. BRUCE, *Author of* Future Perfect: American Science Fiction of the 19th Century

FRANKLIN, S. HARVEY, *Professor of Geography, Victoria University of Wellington; Author of* Trade, Growth and Anxiety: New Zealand Beyond the Welfare State

FRANKLYN, JULIAN, *Author of* Shield and Crest

FRANTZ, JOE B., *Professor of History, University of Texas: Coauthor of* American Cowboy: The Myth and the Reality

FRANTZ, JOHN B., *Associate Professor of American History, Pennsylvania State University*

FRANZ, FRED W., *President, Watchtower Bible and Tract Society*

FRANZEN, GÖSTA, *Professor of Scandinavian, The University of Chicago; Author of* Prose and Poetry of Modern Sweden

FRASCONA, JOSEPH L., *Professor of Business Law, Graduate School of Business Administration and School of Business, University of Colorado; Author of* Agency

FRASER, ALLAN M., *Archivist, Province of Newfoundland, Canada*

FRASER, DOUGLAS, *Professor of Art History, Columbia University; Author of* Primitive Art

FRASER, MARY L., *Deputy Chief Librarian, Cape Breton Regional Library, Sydney, Nova Scotia, Canada*

FRASER, STEWART E., *Director, International Center, George Peabody College for Teachers; Author of* American Education in Foreign Perspectives

FRAZER, JOHN, JR., *Professional Genealogist to the National Society of Colonial Dames in the State of New York*

FRAZIER, WILLIAM H., MD, *Indian River Memorial Hospital, Vero Beach, Fla.*

FREDERICKSON, DONALD S., MD, *Director, National Institutes of Health*

FREDETTE, RAYMOND H., *Lieutenant Colonel, U.S. Air Force; Author of* The Sky on Fire

FREDRICK, LAURENCE W., *Chairman, Department of Astronomy, and Director, Leander McCormick Observatory, University of Virginia*

FREDRIKSON, E. BRUCE, *Professor of Finance, Syracuse University*

FREEBAIRN, DONALD K., *Director, Latin American Studies Program and Professor of Agricultural Economics, Cornell University; Coauthor of* Food, Population, and Employment

FREEBERNE, MICHAEL, *Lecturer in Geography, School of Oriental and African Studies, University of London*

FREEDLEY, GEORGE, *Coauthor of* A History of the Theatre

FREELANDER, DOUGLAS, *Assistant City Editor, Houston Post*

FREEMAN, ALBERT E., *Professor of Animal Science, Iowa State University*

FREEMAN, THOMAS W., *Reader in Geography, University of Manchester, England; Author of* Ireland *and* The Writing of Geography

FREIDEL, FRANK B., JR., *Professor of American History, Harvard University; Author of* Francis Lieber: Nineteenth Century Liberal

FREIER, GEORGE D., *Professor of Physics, University of Minnesota*

FREIREICH, EMIL J., MD, *Professor of Medicine, M. D. Anderson Hospital and Tumor Institute, University of Texas*

FRELICK, BILL, *Senior Policy Analyst, U.S. Committee for Refugees; Associate Editor,* World Refugee Survey

FREMANTLE, ANNE, *Author of* This Little Band of Prophets

FRENCH, HANNAH, *Psychiatrist*

FRENCH, OLIVER H., *Anesthesiologist, South Nassau Communities Hospital, Oceanside, N.Y.*

FRENCH, PETER A., *Professor of Philosophy, University of Minnesota; Author of* Individual and Collective Responsibility: The Massacre at My Lai

FRENCH, WARREN, *Professor of English, Indiana University-Purdue University at Indianapolis; Author of* John Steinbeck *and* J.D. Salinger

FRERE, S. S., *Professor of the Archaeology of the Roman Empire, Oxford University; Author of* Britannia, A History of Roman Britain

FREUND, GERALD, *Author of* Unholy Alliance

FREUNDLICH, IRWIN, *Coauthor of* Music for the Piano

FREY, J. WILLIAM, *Professor of German and Russian, Franklin and Marshall College; Author of* A Simple Grammar of Pennsylvania Dutch

FREY, KENNETH J., *Professor of Plant Breeding, Agronomy Department, Iowa State University*

FREY, RICHARD L., *President, International Bridge Press Association; Editor in Chief,* Official Encyclopedia of Bridge

FRIDLEY, RUSSELL W., *Director, Minnesota Historical Society; Author of* Minnesota: A Students' Guide to Localized History

FRIED, ADRIENNE, *Music Department, Hunter College*

FRIED, FREDERICK, *Author of* A Pictorial History of the Carousel

FRIED, JOHN H. E., *Professor of Political Science, City University of New York; Member of the United Nations Secretariat and UN Expert on International Law; Author of* The Relevance of International Law

FRIEDBERG, CHARLES K., MD, *Chief Cardiologist, Mount Sinai Hospital, New York City; Associate Clinical Professor of Medicine, College of Physicians and Surgeons, Columbia University*

FRIEDLAND, WILLIAM H., *Professor of Community Studies and Sociology, University of California, Santa Cruz; Coauthor of* Migrant: Agricultural Workers in America's Northeast

FRIEDLANDER, GORDON D., *Assistant Director, Burndy Library, Norwalk*

FRIEDLANDER, PAUL, *Director, Music Industry Program, Chico State University; Author of* Rock and Roll: A Social History

FRIEDLEIN, J. T., *Director, F. Friedlein and Co., Ltd., London*

FRIEDMAN, ARNOLD P., *Neurological Associates of Tucson, Tucson, Ariz.; Author of* Modern Headache Therapy; *Coauthor of* Headache: Diagnosis and Treatment *and* The Headache Book; *Editor of* Research and Clinical Studies in Headache

FRIEDMAN, DONALD W., *Director, Public Information and Publications, University of Connecticut*

FRIEDMAN, DORIS E., *Reference Head, Eau Claire Public Library*

FRIEDMAN, HARVEY L., *Assistant Professor of Government and Acting Director, Labor Relations and Research Center, University of Massachusetts*

FRIEDMAN, NORMAN, *Defense Analyst; Author of* Seapower and Space: From the Dawn of the Missile Age to Net-Centric Warfare

FRIEDMANN, ROBERT, *Professor of History, Western Michigan University; Author of* Mennonite Piety Through the Centuries

FRIEDMANN, WOLFGANG, *Professor of Law and Director of International Legal Research, Columbia University; Author of* The Changing Structure of International Law

FRIEDRICH, CARL J., *Eaton Professor of the Science of Government, Harvard University; Author of* The Age of the Baroque

FRIEDRICH, EDUARD G., JR., *W. C. Thomas Professor of Medicine, Department of Obstetrics and Gynecology, University of Florida College of Medicine; Coauthor of* Benign Diseases of the Vulva and Vagina

FRIERMOOD, HAROLD T., *Senior Director of Health, Physical Education, and Sports, National Board of YMCAs; Editor of* Handball Official Unified Playing Rules

FRIGUGLIETTI, JAMES, *Assistant Professor of History, Case Western Reserve University*

FRINGS, MANFRED S., *Director, Max Scheler Archives and Institute; Author of* Philosophy of Prediction *and* Max Scheler

FROEHLICH, KARLFRIED, *Associate Professor of the History and Theology of the Medieval Church, Princeton Theological Seminary*

FROHLICHER, S. V., *Teacher, Adult Education, Great Falls Public Schools*

FROMMER, HARVEY, *Coauthor of* Red on Red: The Autobiography of Red Holzman

FROST, PETER K., *Williams College*

FRUTON, JOSEPH S., *Eugene Higgins Professor of Biochemistry, Yale University; Coauthor of* General Biochemistry

FRYDE, EDMUND B., *Reader in History, University College of Wales, Aberystwyth*

FRYE, NORTHROP, *Professor of English, Victoria College, University of Toronto, Canada; Author of* The Well-Tempered Critic

FRYE, RICHARD N., *Aga Khan Professor of Iranian, Harvard University, and Director of the Asia Institute, Pahlavi University, Shiraz, Iran; Author of* The Heritage of Persia

FRYER, D. H., *Commander, Royal Navy (Retired)*

FRYER, DONALD W., *Professor of Geography, University of Hawaii at Manoa; Author of* Emerging Southeast Asia

FRYER, JOHN L., *Director of Research, Canadian Labour Congress*

FUCILLA, JOSEPH C., *Professor of Romance Languages, Northwestern University; Author of* Bibliographical Guide to the Romance Languages and Literature

FUESS, CLAUDE M., *Author of* Daniel Webster

FUGLISTER, FREDERICK C., *Oceanographic Institution, Woods Hole, Mass.*

FUKUDA, N., *Professor of Physics, Tokyo University of Education; Author of* Quantum Field Theory

FUKUI, HARUHIRO, *Professor of Political Science, University of California at Santa Barbara; Author of* The Party in Power: The Japanese Liberal-Democrats and Policy Making

FULFORD, ROGER, *Author of* Queen Victoria *and* The Prince Consort

FULLER, PETA J., *Coauthor of* The Wonderful Food of Provence

FULLER, R. BUCKMINSTER, *Comprehensive Anticipatory Design Scientist; Professor, Southern Illinois University*

FULLER, REGINALD H., *Professor of New Testament, Virginia Theological Seminary*

FULLER, ROBERT C., *Professor of Religious Studies, Bradley University; Author of* Religion and the Life Cycle

FULLER, SOPHIE, *Lecturer in Music, University of Reading; Author of* The Pandora Guide to Women Composers: Britain and the United States, 1629–Present

FULLER, WAYNE E., *Professor of American History, University of Texas at El Paso; Author of* The American Mail *and* R.F.D.: The Changing Face of Rural America

FURBER, HOLDEN, *Professor of History, University of Pennsylvania; Author of* Bombay Presidency in the Mid-Eighteenth Century

FURTH, HAROLD P., *Plasma Physics Laboratory, Princeton University*

FUTRELL, ROBERT FRANK, *Professor of Military History, Aerospace Studies Institute, Air University*

GABBEY, ALAN, *Lecturer in History and Philosophy of Science, Queen's University of Belfast, Northern Ireland*

GABEL, LEONA C., *Professor of History, Smith College; Editor of* The Commentaries of Pius II

GABRIEL, RALPH HENRY, *Professor of American Civilization, School of International Service, American University, Washington, D.C.; Author of* American Values *and* The Course of American Democratic Thought

GAERTNER, JOHANNES A., *Professor and Head, Department of Art and Music, Lafayette College*

GAGE, HARRY L., *Graphic Arts Consultant*

GAGLIANO, FELIX V., *Author of* Communal Violence in Malaysia: The Political Aftermath

GAIBROIS DE BALLESTEROS, MERCEDES, *Author of* Historia del reinado de Sancho IV de Castilla

GAILEY, HARRY A., *Professor of History, San Jose State University; Author of* A History of Gambia *and* A History of Africa in Maps

GALLAGHER, J. ROSWELL, *Chief, Adolescent Unit, Children's Hospital Medical Center, Boston, Mass.; Author of* Emotional Problems of Adolescents *and* Medical Care of the Adolescent

GALLETTI, PIERRE M., MD, *Professor of Medical Science, Division of Biological and Medical Sciences, Brown University*

GALLIGAN, JAMES M., *Brookhaven National Laboratory*

GALLIN, BERNARD, *Professor of Anthropology, Michigan State University; Author of* Hsin Hsing, Taiwan: A Chinese Village in Change

GALLMAN, ROBERT E., *Kenan Professor of Economics and History, University of North Carolina at Chapel Hill*

GALLOWAY, DAVID D., *Professor of American Studies, Ruhr University; Author of* Henry James: The Portrait of a Lady *and* The Absurd Hero

GANNON, MICHAEL, *Distinguished Service Professor of History, University of Florida; Author of* Cross in the Sand: The Early Catholic Church in Florida, 1513–1870

GANS, CARL, *Professor of Biology, University of Michigan*

GARAVENTA, LOUIS T., SJ, *Fordham University*

GARB, SOLOMON, *Science Director, American Medical Center, Denver, Colo.*

GARCIA DE SOUSA, LUIS, *Professor of History, Colegio Loyola, Belo Horizonte, Brazil*

GARD, ROBERT E., *Professor of Theatre Art, University of Wisconsin; Coauthor of* Community Theatre

GARD, WAYNE, *Author of* Frontier Justice *and* The Great Buffalo Hunt

GARDINER, C. HARVEY, *Research Professor of History, Southern Illinois University; Author of* William Hickling Prescott: A Biography

GARDINER, DOROTHY, *Author; Executive Secretary of the Mystery Writers of America*

GARDNER, ELDON J., *Dean, College of Science, Utah State University, Author of* History of Biology

GARDNER, HARRISON M., *Professor, College of Veterinary Medicine, Ohio State University*

GARDNER, MARY ADELAIDE, *School of Journalism, Michigan State University; Author of* The Inter American Press Association and Its Fight for Freedom of the Press, 1926–60

GARFIELD, DONALD, *Senior Editor, Museum News*

GARFIELD, ROBERT, *Associate Professor of History, Co-Director, Afro-American Studies Program, DePaul University; Editor of* Readings in World Civilization

GARFINKEL, BARRY D., MD, *Director, Division of Child and Adolescent Psychiatry, University of Minnesota Medical School; Coauthor of* The Adolescent and Mood Disturbance

GARGA, B. D., *Documentary Filmmaker and Film Historian; Member, Advisory Committee, National Film Archive of India*

GARLAND, GEORGE D., *Professor of Geophysics, University of Toronto, Canada*

GARLAND, PHYL, *Contributing Editor*, Stereo Review; *Author of* The Sound of Soul: The Story of Black Music

GARNER, JAMES W., *Author of* International Law and the World War *and* Law of Treaties

GARNER, RICHARD T., *Professor of Philosophy, Ohio State University*

GARRETT, WENDELL D., *Associate Editor*, Antiques *Magazine; Associate Editor of* Adams Family Correspondence

GARTLAND, JOHN J., MD, *James Edwards Professor of Orthopedic Surgery and Chairman of the Department of Orthopedic Surgery, Jefferson Medical College, Thomas Jefferson University*

GASTER, THEODOR H., *Professor of Religion, Barnard College, Columbia University; Author of* The Dead Sea Scriptures

GATELL, FRANK OTTO, *Professor of History, University of California at Los Angeles*

GATES, DAVID M., *Professor of Botany, University of Michigan; Author of* Energy Exchange in the Biosphere

GATES, PAUL W., *Professor of American History, Cornell University; Author of* Landlords and Tenants on the Prairie Frontier

GATZKE, HANS W., *Professor of History, Yale University; Author of* Germany's Drive to the West; *Editor and Translator of Clausewitz's* Principles of War

GAURI, K. LAL, *Professor and Chairman, Department of Geology, University of Louisville at Belknap*

GAY, PETER, *Professor of History, Yale University; Author of* The Enlightenment

GAYTON, A. H., *Professor of Decorative Art, University of California at Berkeley*

GAZLEY, JOHN G., *Professor of History, Dartmouth College; Author of* The Life of Arthur Young, 1741–1820

GEDDES, WILLIAM F., *Head, Department of Agricultural Biochemistry, University of Minnesota*

GEER, ELIZABETH D., *Librarian, Chapel Hill Public Library*

GEIGER, MAGGY, *Author of* The Window Box Primer

GEIRINGER, KARL, *Professor of Music, University of California at Santa Barbara; Author of* Brahms, His Life and Work *and* Haydn: A Creative Life in Music

GEIS, GILBERT, *Professor, Program in Social Ecology, University of California at Irvine; Coauthor of* Man, Crime, and Society

GEISMAR, MAXWELL, *Author of* Writers in Crisis *and* American Moderns

GEISON, GERALD L., *Assistant Professor of History, Princeton University*

GELB, IGNACE J., *Frank P. Hixon Distinguished Service Professor, Oriental Institute, University of Chicago; Author of* A Study of Writing

GELERNTER, DAVID, *Associate Professor of Computer Science, Yale University; Author of* Mirror Worlds; *Coauthor of* How to Write Parallel Programs: A First Course *and* Programming Linguistics

GELFAND, TOBY, *Fellow, Johns Hopkins Institute of the History of Medicine*

GELLMAN, LOLA B., *Department of Art, Queensborough Community College*

GENTRY, A. W., *Department of Zoology, British Museum (Natural History), London*

GENTZLER, J. MASON, *Department of Asian Studies, Sarah Lawrence College*

GEORGE, ALBERT J., *Author of* Lamartine and Romantic Unanimism

GERBER, DONALD A., MD, *Associate Professor of Medicine, State University of New York Downstate Medical Center*

GERBNER, GEORGE, *Dean, Annenberg School of Communications, University of Pennsylvania*

GERDTS, WILLIAM H., *Professor of Art History, Graduate School and University Center, City University of New York; Author of* Revealed Masters: 19th Century American Art *and* American Impressionism

GEROW, EDWIN, *Professor of Sanskrit and Asian Languages and Civilizations, University of Chicago; Author of* A Glossary of Indian Figures of Speech

GERSHENBERG, IRVING, *Assistant Professor of Economics, Rutgers University*

GERSHEVITCH, ILYA, *University Lecturer in Iranian Studies, Fellow of Jesus College, Cambridge University*

GERSHON-COHEN, J., MD, *Coauthor of* Comparative Anatomy, Pathology, and Roentgenology of the Breast

GERSON, NOEL B., *Author (under pseudonym Samuel Edwards) of* Barbary General: The Life of William H. Eaton

GERSON, THOMAS, *Coauthor of* Uncle Sam

GERTEINY, ALFRED G., *Professor of History, University of Bridgeport*

GERTSCH, WILLIS J., *Curator of Entomology, American Museum of Natural History; Author of* American Spiders

GERZINA, GRETCHEN HOLBROOK, *Associate Professor of English, Vassar College; Author of* Carrington: A Life *and* Racial Fictions: Black Characters in the Popular 18th-Century British Novel

GESSOW, ALFRED, *Chief, Aeronautics and Fluid Mechanics, Aerodynamics and Vehicle Systems Division, Office of Advanced Research and Technology, National Aeronautics and Space Administration*

GESTERFIELD, KATHRYN, J., *Librarian, Champaign Public Library*

GEYELIN, PETER, *Secretary, Franklin Institute*

GIBBONS, ALBERT E., SJ, *University of Detroit*

GIBBS, ALONZO, *Author of* Bethpage Bygones

GIBBS, FREDERIC A., MD, *Professor of Neurology, University of Illinois College of Medicine at Chicago; Author of* Atlas of Electroencephalography *and* Epilepsy Handbook

GIBBS, NORMAN H., *Chichele Professor of the History of War; Fellow, All Souls College, Oxford University*

GIBBS, RAFE, *Professor, University of Idaho*

GIBBS-SMITH, C. H., *Keeper of the Department of Public Relations and Education, Victoria and Albert Museum, London, England; Author of* Aviation: An Historical Survey

GIBSON, ARRELL M., *Professor of History, University of Oklahoma; Author of* Oklahoma: A History of Five Centuries

GIBSON, J. SULLIVAN, *Coauthor of* Soils: Their Nature, Classes, Distribution, Uses and Care

GIBSON, WALTER BROWN, *Author of* The Master Magicians; *Coauthor of* Houdini's Fabulous Magic

GIBSON, WILLIAM M., *Professor of English, New York University; Author of* A Bibliography of W. D. Howells; *Editor of* Mark Twain—Howells Letters

GIER, D. W., *Director of Science, Lea College*

GIESEL, JAMES T., *Associate Professor, Department of Zoology, University of Florida at Gainesville; Author of* The Biology and Adaptability of Natural Populations

GIFFORD, LEONA A., *Supervisor, Coolidge Corner Branch Library*

GIFFORD, PHILIP C., JR., *American Museum of Natural History*

GIGOUX, ZOE, *Librarian, Carnegie Public Library, Lawton, Okla.*

GILBERT, FELIX, *Professor of History, Institute for Advanced Study, Princeton, N.J.; Author of* Machiavelli and Guicciardini

GILBERT, MARY FRANCES, *Librarian, Wasco County Library, Oreg.*

GILBERT, RODNEY, *Author of* Unequal Treaties: China and the Foreigner

GILL, CLARK C., *Professor of Curriculum and Instruction, The University of Texas*

GILLESPIE, KAREN, *Professor of Business Education, New York University School of Education; Author of* Home-furnishings

GILLILAND, ERNESTINE, *Director, Hutchinson Public Library*

GILLIN, DONALD G., *Professor of History, Chairman of East Asian Studies, Vassar College*

GILLMAN, RICHARD, *Director, Public Affairs, Brandeis University*

GILMORE, MYRON P., *Gurney Professor of History and Political Science, Harvard University; Author of* The World of Humanism

GILMORE, RAYMOND, *Research Associate, Marine Mammals, Natural History Museum, San Diego, Calif.; Author of* Story of Gray Whale

GILMOUR, S. MacLEAN, *Norris Professor of New Testament, Andover Newton Theological School*

GIMBEL, JOHN, *Professor of History, Humboldt State University; Author of* A German Community under American Occupation: Marburg 1945–1952

GINGER, RAY, *Author of* Eugene V. Debs: A Biography *and* Age of Excess: The United States from 1877 to 1914

GINGERICH, OWEN, *Astrophysicist, Smithsonian Astrophysical Observatory; Lecturer, Harvard University*

GINSBURG, NORMAN S., *Director of Information Services, CBS Radio, New York City*

GINSBURG, NORTON S., *Director, Environment and Policy Institute, East-West Center, Honolulu; Editor of* The Pattern of Asia

GIORDANETTI, ELMO, *Professor of Romance Languages, Amherst College*

GIRARD, LOUIS, MD, *Professor and Chairman, Department of Ophthalmology, Baylor University College of Medicine; Editor of* Corneal Contact Lenses

GIRARD, RENÉ, *Andrew B. Hammond Professor of French Language and Literature, Stanford University*

GIRAUD, RAYMOND, *Professor and Chairman, Department of French and Italian, Stanford University*

GITTLEMAN, SOL, *Senior Vice President, Provost, McCollester Professor of Religion, Tufts University*

GITTINGS, ROBERT, *Author of* John Keats

GLASER, ARTHUR B., *Bell Laboratories; Author of* Integrated Circuit Engineering

GLASFORD, GLENN M., *Professor of Electrical Engineering, Syracuse University*

GLASHOW, SHELDON L., *Nobel Prize Winner in Physics, 1979; Professor of Physics, Harvard University*

GLASSER, GARY A., MD, *Professor of Gynecology and Obstetrics, Emory University School of Medicine*

GLASSIE, HENRY, *Associate Professor, Folklore Institute, Indiana University; Author of* Pattern in the Material Folk Culture of the Eastern United States; *Coauthor of* A Guide for Collectors of Oral Traditions and Folk Cultural Material

GLASSROCK, JEAN, *Director of Publicity and Coordinator of Special Events, Wellesley College*

GLAU, HELEN, *Alexander Mitchell Library*

GLAZEBROOK, G. DE T., *Author of* A Short History of Canada *and* A History of Canadian Political Thought

GLAZER, MICHAEL, *Member of the California Bar*

GLEAZER, EDMUND J., JR., *Visiting Professor, George Washington University; President Emeritus, American Association of Community and Junior Colleges*

GLEESON, AUSTIN M., *Associate Professor of Physics, University of Texas at Austin*

GLEESON, EMMET T., *Catholic University of America*

GLENDINNING, ROBERT M., *Professor of Geography, University of California, Los Angeles; Author of* Introduction to Geography

GLENN, CONSTANCE W., *Professor of Art and Director of the University Art Museum, California State University at Long Beach; Author of* James Rosenquist: Time Dust, Complete Graphics, 1962–1992

GLICK, THOMAS F., *Professor of History and Geography, Boston University*

GLOCK, ALBERT E., *Professor of Archaeology, Birzeit University*

GLOVER, RICHARD G., *Director, Human History Branch, National Museum of Canada*

GLUCKMAN, MAX, *Professor of Social Anthropology, University of Manchester, England; Author of* Custom and Conflict in Africa

GNAROWSKI, MICHAEL, *Assistant Professor and Co-ordinator of Canadian Studies, Sir George Williams University, Canada; Coeditor of* The Making of Modern Poetry in Canada

GODARD, BARBARA THOMPSON, *Professor, York University; Author of* Gynocritics/Gynocritiques: Feminist Approaches to Canadian and Quebec Women's Writing

GODBOLD, ALBEA, *American Secretary of the International Methodist Historical Society*

GODE, ALEXANDER, *Editor of* Interlingua-English Dictionary

GODFREY, BRIAN J., *Associate Professor of Geography, Department of Geography and Geology, Vassar College*

GODFREY, RICHARD T., *Director, News and Publications Service, Illinois State University*

GOEDICKE, HANS, *Professor of Near Eastern Studies, Johns Hopkins University; Author of* Re-Used Blocks from the Pyramid of Amenemhet One at Lisht

GOERING, JOHN M., *Professor of Sociology, Washington University, St. Louis, Mo.*

GOETHALS, PETER R., *Associate Professor, Department of Anthropology, University of North Carolina; Author of* Aspects of Local Government in a Sumbawan Village

GOFF, FREDERICK R., *Chief, Rare Book Division, Library of Congress; Editor of* Incunabula in American Libraries

GOFF, JOHN S., *Phoenix College; Author of* Robert Todd Lincoln

GOFFIO, FRANK L., *Executive Director, Care*

GOGGINS, LOTHARDUS, *Professor of Geography, University of Akron*

GÖHRING, MARTIN, *Director, Institute for European History, Mainz, Federal Republic of Germany*

GOHSTAND, ROBERT, *Associate Professor of Geography, California State University at Northridge*

GOKHALE, B. G., *Professor of History and Director, Asian Studies Program, Wake Forest University; Author of* Ancient India: History and Culture

GOLAS, PETER J., *Teaching Fellow, East Asian Research Center, Harvard University*

GOLD, CAROL, *University of Minnesota*

GOLD, JAY A., MD, JD, *Professor of Preventive Medicine and Bioethics, Medical College of Wisconsin*

GOLDBERG, BARRY S., MD, *Clinical Instructor, Department of Dermatology, Yale University*

GOLDBERG, J. B., *Fellow, British Textile Institute; Author of* Fabric Defects

GOLDBERG, SEYMOUR, *Director, Components Research and Development, EG&G Inc.*

GOLDBLITH, S. A., *Professor of Food Science and Executive Officer, Department of Nutrition and Food Science, Massachusetts Institute of Technology*

GOLDHIRSCH, LAWRENCE, ESQ., *Author of* The Warsaw Convention: Annotated

GOLDIN, AMY, *Contributing Editor*, Art News

GOLDMAN, RALPH M., *President, Center for Party Development, Catholic University of America; Author of* From Warfare to Party Politics

GOLDMAN, ROBERT B., *Chief Scientist, Philadelphia Group, Analysis, Inc.*

GOLDSMITH, TIMOTHY, *Professor of Biology, Yale University*

GOLDSTEIN, JONATHAN A., *Professor of History and Classics, University of Iowa*

GOLOS, ELLERY B., *Associate Professor of Mathematics, Ohio University; Author of* Foundations of Euclidean and Non-Euclidean Geometry

GOMEZ, ROSENDO A., *Professor of Government, University of Arizona; Author of* Government and Politics in Latin America

GONZALEZ, CATHERINE TROXELL, *Author of* Lafitte: Terror of the Gulf

GOOCH, BRISON D., *Professor of History, Texas A&M University; Author of* The Reign of Napoleon III *and* Europe to the Nineteenth Century: A History

GOOD, THOMAS L., *Professor of Educational Psychology, University of Arizona*

GOODALL, DAPHNE MACHIN, *Author of* Horses of the World

GOODELL, GEORGE S., *Professor of Economics, Kent State University*

GOODENOUGH, URSULA W., *Associate Professor of Biology, Biological Laboratories, Harvard University*

GOODFRIEND, JAMES, *Music Editor, Stereo Review*

GOODMAN, BENNY, *Clarinetist*

GOODMAN, EDWARD J., *Professor of History, Xavier University, Cincinnati, Ohio; Author of* The Explorers of South America

GOODMAN, SUSAN TUMARKIN, *Chief Curator, The Jewish Museum*

GOODMAN, WALTER, *Author of* The Committee: the Extraordinary Career of the House Committee on Un-American Activities

GOODNIGHT, CLARENCE J., *Professor of Zoology, Western Michigan University*

GOODRICH, JOSEPHINE BERRY, *Librarian, Cocoa Public Library*

GOODRICH, L. CARRINGTON, *Author of* A Short History of the Chinese People

GOODRICH, LLOYD, *Advisory Director, Whitney Museum of American Art; Author of* Thomas Eakins: His Life and Work *and* Winslow Homer

GOODSELL, LEONARD J., *Executive Director, Great Lakes Commission*

GOODSPEED, D. J., *Lt. Col., Canadian Armed Forces; Senior Historian, Directorate of History, Canadian Forces Headquarters; Author of* DRB: A History of the Defence Research Board of Canada; *Editor of* The Armed Forces of Canada, 1867–1967

GOODWIN, GEORGE G., *Curator, Department of Mammalogy, American Museum of Natural History*

GOODY, RICHARD M., *Director, Blue Hill Observatory, Harvard University*

GORAN, MORRIS, *Professor of Physical Science, Roosevelt University*

GORDON, ARCHER S., MD, *Director of Medical Research, Statham Instruments, Inc.*

GORDON, GLADYS, *Librarian, Watseka Public Library*

GORDON, IAN A., *Dean of Faculty of Languages and Literature, University of Wellington, New Zealand*

GORDON, LEONARD A., *Associate Professor of History, Brooklyn College*

GORDON, MATTHEW S., *Lecturer, Department of Theology, Boston College*

GORDON, MYRON, *American Museum of Natural History*

GORDON, RANDY, *Chairman, New York State Athletic Commission*

GORIS, JAN-ALBERT, *Director, Belgian Government Information Center, New York City*

GOSNELL, HAROLD F., *Author of* Machine Politics

GOSSNER, SIMONE DARO, *Natural History Magazine*

GOTESKY, RUBIN, *Professor of Philosophy, Northern Illinois University; Author of* Personality: The Need for Liberty and Rights

GOTH, ANDRES, MD, *Professor of Pharmacology and Chairman, Department of Pharmacology, University of Texas Health Sciences Center at Dallas; Author of* Medical Pharmacology

GOTTFRIED, KURT, *Professor of Physics, Cornell University*

GOTTLIEB, ROGER S., *Professor of Philosophy, Tufts University*

GOTTLIEB, SAMUEL, *Member of the New York Bar*

GOTTSCHALK, STEPHEN, *Author of* The Emergence of Christian Science in American Religious Life

GOULD, RICHARD A., *Professor of Anthropology, University of Hawaii*

GOVAN, JAMES F., *Head Librarian, Swarthmore College*

GOVE, SAMUEL K., *Director, Institute of Government and Public Affairs, University of Illinois*

GOYA, CAROLA, *Concert Dancer; Teacher of Ethnic Dance, School of Performing Arts, New York*

GRABAR, OLEG, *Professor of Fine Arts, Harvard University; Coauthor of* Islamic Architecture and Its Decoration

GRABB, WILLIAM C., MD, *Head, Section of Plastic Surgery, University of Michigan School of Medicine*

GRABINER, JUDITH, *Flora Sanborn Pitzer Professor of Mathematics, Pitzer College, Claremont, Calif.*

GRAD, FRANK P., *Professor of Law, Columbia University; Director, Legislature Drafting Research Fund, Columbia University*

GRAFF, SAMUEL, *Department of Biochemistry, College of Physicians and Surgeons, Columbia University*

GRAFLY, DOROTHY, *Editor and Publisher of* Art in Focus; *Author of* Parade of American Art

GRAHAM, C. D., JR., *Professor of Metallurgy and Materials Science, University of Pennsylvania*

GRAHAM, PAULINE A., *Head Librarian, Bethel Park Public Library*

GRALAPP, MARCELEE, *Library Director, Boulder Public Library*

GRAMPP, WILLIAM D., *Author of* Economic Liberalism *and* The Manchester School of Economics

GRANDE, FRANK D., *Lecturer in History, City College of New York*

GRANDJOUAN, CLAIREVE, *Associate Professor of Classics, Hunter College*

GRANT, EDWARD, *Indiana University*

GRANT, ELLSWORTH S., *Director, Connecticut River Watershed Council; Vice-Chairman, Governor's Clean Water Task Force*

GRANT, FREDERICK C., *Union Theological Seminary; Author of* The Economic Background of the Gospels *and* Ancient Judaism and the New Testament

GRANT, JAMES A., *Information Officer, Republic of South Africa Information Service, New York City*

GRANT, JAMES P., *President, Overseas Development Council, Washington, D.C.*

GRANT, RICHARD B., *Professor of French, University of Texas at Austin; Author of* The Perilous Quest: Image, Myth, and Prophecy in the Narratives of Victor Hugo

GRANT, ROBERT M., *Professor of New Testament, Divinity School, University of Chicago*

GRANT, VERNE E., *Professor of Botany, University of Texas at Austin*

GRANTHAM, DEWEY W., *Professor of History, Vanderbilt University; Author of* The Democratic South

GRATTAN-GUINNESS, IVOR, *Senior Lecturer, Enfield College of Technology, Middlesex, England; Author of* The Growth of Classical Analysis

GRAVER, LAWRENCE, *Professor of English, Williams College; Author of* Conrad's Short Fiction

GRAVES, ARTHUR H., *Brooklyn Botanical Garden*

GRAVES, F. CHARLES, *Director, New York Office, Public Communications, Church of Jesus Christ of Latter-day Saints*

GRAVES, FRED H., *Head Librarian, Cooper Union*

GRAVES, W. BROOKE, *Legislative Reference Service, Library of Congress; Author of* American State Government

GRAY, HAROLD E., *Sales Manager, Lord & Burnham, Division of Burnham Corporation*

GRAY, NANCY, *Head Librarian, Wilson County Public Library, Wilson, N.C.*

GRAYSON, GEORGE W., *John Marshall Professor of Government, College of William and Mary*

GREEN, ANNETTE, *Executive Director, Fragrance Foundation, New York City*

GREEN, CONSTANCE McLAUGHLIN, *Washington History Project, American University, Washington, D.C.*

GREEN, ELIZABETH B., *Librarian, Oconee County Library, Walhalla, S.C.*

GREEN, RICHARD A., *Director, American Bar Association Project on Standards for Criminal Justice*

GREEN, ROGER LANCELYN, *Author of* Lewis Carroll

GREEN, STANLEY, *Author of* Encyclopaedia of Musical Theatre *and* The World of Musical Comedy

GREEN, SUSAN, *Assistant Professor of English, University of Oklahoma; Author of* Women Critics, 1620–1820: An Anthology of Writings

GREEN, V. H. H., *Rector of Lincoln College, Oxford University; Author of* A History of Oxford University

GREENAWALT, KENT, *Professor of Law, Columbia University*

GREENAWAY, FRANK, *Keeper, Department of Chemistry, Science Museum, London, England*

GREENBERG, JOSEPH H., *Ray Lyman Wilbur Professor of Anthropology in the Social Sciences, Stanford University; Author of* The Languages of Africa

GREENBERG, LEON A., MD, *Professor of Physiology and Director of Laboratory Research, Rutgers University Center of Alcohol Studies*

GREENE, DAVID H., *Professor of English, New York University; Editor of* An Anthology of Irish Literature; *Coauthor of* J.M. Synge, 1871–1909

GREENE, FRANCIS A., SJ, *Loyola Blakefield School, Towson, Md.*

GREENE, SIR HUGH, *Director-General, British Broadcasting Corporation; Author of* The Future of Broadcasting in Britain

GREENE, JACK P., *Professor of History, Johns Hopkins University; Author of* Colonies to Nation *and* The Reinterpretation of the American Revolution

GREENE, MURRAY J., *Associate Professor of Philosophy, New School for Social Research; Author of* Hegel on the Soul

GREENFIELD, MICHAEL, MD, *Danbury Hospital, Danbury, Conn.; Author of* The Complete Vasectomy Reference Book; *Editor of* Williams Trends in Urology

GREENFIELD, THEO. J., *Department of the History of Science, University of Wisconsin at Madison*

GREENHILL, J. P., MD, *Author of* Obstetrics and Surgical Gynecology

GREENIDGE, K. N. H., *Forest Biologist, Department of Biology, St. Francis Xavier University, Canada*

GREENLEAF, WILLIAM, *Professor of History, University of New Hampshire; Coauthor of* U.S.A.: History of a Nation; *Author of* Monopoly on Wheels

GREENWOOD, PETER H., *Senior Principal Scientific Officer, Department of Zoology, British Museum (Natural History), London; Author of* The Fishes of Uganda; *Reviser of J.R. Norman's* History of Fishes

GREER, ROWAN A., *Professor of Anglican Studies, Yale Divinity School; Author of* Captain of Our Salvation

GREGG, ROBERT E., *Professor of Biology, University of Colorado*

GREGOR, A. JAMES, *Professor of Political Science, University of California at Berkeley; Author of* Young Mussolini and the Intellectual Origins of Fascism

GREGORY, HORACE V., *Author of* D.H. Lawrence: Pilgrim of the Apocalypse *and Coauthor of* History of American Poetry, 1900–1940

GREGORY, RUTH W., *Head Librarian, Waukegan Public Library*

GRELE, RONALD S., *Director, Oral History Research Office, Columbia University*

GRELLNER, LORETTA, *Author of* Art Form; *Extension Lecturer, Chicago Public School Art Society, Art Institute of Chicago*

GRENDON, FELIX, *Author of* Anglo-Saxon Charms

GRENIER, FERNAND, *President, Téléuniversité, University of Quebec; Author of* Quebec: Studies in Canadian Geography

GRIBBLE, LEONARD, *Author of* Triumphs of Scotland Yard, They Challenged the Yard, *and* Great Manhunters of the Yard

GRIER, HARRY D. M., *Director, Frick Collection, New York City*

GRIERSON, PHILIP, *Professor of Medieval Numismatics, Cambridge University*

GRIESS, THOMAS E., *Lieutenant Colonel, U.S. Army*

GRIFFENHAGEN, GEORGE BERNARD, *Director, Division of Communications, American Pharmaceutical Association; Editor of the* Journal of the American Pharmaceutical Association

GRIFFIN, BRENDA S., *Illinois State University; Coauthor of* Juvenile Delinquency in Perspective

GRIFFIN, CHARLES T., *Illinois State University; Coauthor of* Juvenile Delinquency in Perspective

GRIFFIN, JOHN A., *Director-Librarian, Lawrence Public Library, Lawrence, Mass.*

GRIFFITH, SANFORD, *New York University*

GRIFFITHS, DAVID E., *Reader in Molecular Sciences, University of Warwick, England*

GRIFFITHS, PAUL D., MD, *Fogarty International Scholar, The University of Alabama in Birmingham*

GRIFFITHS, RICHARD M., *Fellow, Brasenose College, Oxford University; Author of* The Reactionary Revolution: The Catholic Revival in French Literature (1870–1949)

GRIGG, AUSTIN E., *Dean of the Graduate School, University of Richmond*

GRINDSTAFF, CARL F., *Professor and Chair, Department of Sociology, University of Western Ontario; Author of* Population and Society: A Sociological Perspective

GRINSTEIN, LOUISE S., *Assistant Professor of Mathematics, Kingsborough Community College; Coeditor of* Calculus: Readings From the Mathematics Teacher

GRISWOLD, ALBERT H., *Assistant Dean, School of Engineering and Science, New York University*

GRISWOLD, ERWIN N., *Solicitor General of the United States; Former Dean of Harvard Law School; Author of* Fifth Amendment Today *and* Law and Lawyers in the United States

GROBSTEIN, CLIFFORD, *Professor of Biological Science and Public Policy, University of California at San Diego; Author of* Strategy of Life *and* Double Image of a Double Helix

GROENENDYKE, J. P., JR., *Corps of Engineers, U.S. Army*

GROENFELDT, JOHN S., *President, Executive Board, Moravian Church, Northern Province; Chairman, Executive Board, International Moravian Church; Author of* Becoming a Member of the Moravian Church

GRONDIN, JEAN, *Professor of Philosophy, Université de Montréal; Author of* Introduction to Philosophical Hermeneutics

GRONEMAN, CHRIS H., *Department of Industrial Arts, California State University at Fresno; Author of* General Woodworking

GRONINGA, CURT, *Administrative Assistant, City of Culver City, Calif.*

GROPP, ARTHUR E., *Librarian, Columbus Memorial Library, Pan American Union, Washington, D.C.*

GROSE, D. MICHAEL, SJ, *Fordham University*

GROSS, DEAN C., *Director, Harrisburg Public Library*

GROSS, FELIX, *Author of* Rhodes of Africa

GROSS, LEO, *Professor of International Law and Organization, Tufts University; Editor of* International Law in the Twentieth Century

GROSS, RICHARD E., *Professor of Education, Stanford University*

GROSSMAN, HAROLD J., *Author of* Grossman's Guide to Wines, Spirits, and Beers

GROSVENOR, MELVILLE BELL, *Chairman of the Board of Trustees and Editor in Chief, National Geographic Society*

GROUT, STUART, *Director of Academic Planning, Boston University*

GROVE, ALVIN R., JR., *Associate Dean for Commonwealth Campuses and Continuing Education, Pennsylvania State University*

GROVES, HAROLD M., *Author of* Financing Government *and* Federal Tax Treatment of the Family

GRUBE, ERNST J., *Associate Curator in Charge, Department of Islamic Art, Metropolitan Museum of Art; Author of* World of Islam

GRUBER, IRA D., *Professor of History, Rice University; Author of* The Howe Brothers and the American Revolution

GRUBERG, MARTIN, *Professor of Political Science, University of Wisconsin at Oshkosh*

GRUEN, ERICH S., *Professor of History, University of California at Berkeley; Author of* Roman Politics and the Criminal Courts, The Last Generation of the Roman Republic, *and* The Hellenistic World and the Coming of Rome

GRUNDFEST, JERRY, *Executive Director, Hall of Fame for Great Americans*

GRUNKEMEYER, MARILYN TRENT, *Department of Anthropology, University of North Carolina at Chapel Hill*

GRUNSCHLAG, DOV M., *Assistant Professor of Law, University of California at Davis*

GUBNER, RICHARD, *Clinical Professor of Medicine, State University of New York Downstate Medical Center; Secretary-Treasurer, American Society of Medicine Hydrology; Editor,* Medical Tribune *and* Hospital Tribune

GUENTHER, BRUCE, *Faculty of Religious Studies, McGill University*

GUENTHER, JOAN M., *Public Relations Manager, Buhl Planetarium and Institute of Popular Science, Pittsburgh, Pa.*

GUERLAC, HENRY, *Goldwin Smith Professor of the History of Science, Cornell University*

GUMMO, BLANCHARD, *Samuel H. Kress Professor of Art History, Bucknell University*

GUNDERSON, ROBERT G., *Professor of Speech and Theater, Indiana University; Author of* The Log-Cabin Campaign

GUNDERSON, SHERMAN E., *Professor of Economics, University of Wisconsin at Oshkosh*

GUNN, JOHN M., *Professor, Department of Rhetoric and Communication, State University of New York at Albany*

GUNNELL, JOHN G., *Professor of Political Science, State University of New York at Albany; Author of* Between Philosophy and Politics: The Alienation of Political Theory

GUNNING, GERALD E., *Professor of Biology, Tulane University*

GUPPY, NICHOLAS, *Writer and Ecologist*

GUPTA, BRIJEN K., *Director of Research and Development, Council on International and Public Affairs; Author of* Sirajuddaullah and the East India Company, 1756–1757.

GUSSIN, ARNOLD E. S., *Coordinator of Continuing Education, New York Botanical Garden*

GUSTAVSON, SANDRA G., *Professor of Insurance, Legal Studies, and Real Estate, University of Georgia; Coauthor of* Life Insurance: Theory and Practice

GUTHRIE, SIR TYRONE, *Author of* A Life in the Theatre *and* A New Theatre

GUTMAN, ALEXANDER B., MD, *Director of the Department of Medicine, Mount Sinai Hospital, New York; Professor of Medicine, Mount Sinai School of Medicine*

GUTMAN, ROBERT W., *Dean of Graduate Studies, Fashion Institute of Technology, State University of New York*

HAACK, SUSAN, *Lecturer, University of Warwick; Author of* Deviant Logic

HABER, TOM BURNS, *Professor of Comparative Literature and English, Ohio State University; Author of* A. E. Housman

HABIG, MARION, OFM, *Historian, St. Louis–Chicago Province of the Franciscans; Author of* The Franciscans

HABLANIAN, M. H., *Manager, Mechanical Components, Varian/Lexington Vacuum Division*

HACKENBROCH, YVONNE, *Senior Research Fellow, Western European Arts, Metropolitan Museum of Art*

HACKER, GRACE, *Acting Librarian, Superior Public Library*

HACKER, LOUIS M., *Professor of Economics, Columbia University; Author of* The Course of American Economic Growth and Development

HADLEY, ELBERT H., *Professor of Chemistry, College of Science, Southern Illinois University*

HAFEN, LEROY R., *Author of* Mountain Men and the Fur Trade of the Far West

HAGEN, KENNETH J., *Associate Professor of History, United States Naval Academy; Author of* American Gunboat Diplomacy and the Old Navy, 1877–1889; *Coauthor of* American Foreign Policy: A History; *Editor of* In Peace and War: Interpretations of American Naval History

HAGER, LOUISA WILSON, *Director, Bureau of Communications, National Board, Young Women's Christian Association*

HAGERTY, MARTHA M., *Town Librarian, Groton, Conn.*

HAGGERTY, ARTHUR J., *Director, Capt. Haggerty's School for Dogs, New York City*

HAGGERTY, CHARLES E., *Director, Danville Public Library*

HAGGERTY, JAMES J., SJ, *Fordham University*

HAGLAND, MARK M., *Managing Editor, Hospitals and Health Networks Magazine*

HAGOPIAN, JOHN V., *Professor of English, State University of New York at Binghamton*

HAGUE, JOHN A., *Professor and Director of American Studies, Stetson University*

HAHN, EMILY, *Author of* Romanic Rebels

HAHN, PIERRE, *Research Manager, Brain Research Institute, University of California*

HAHN, ROGER, *Associate Professor of History, University of California at Berkeley; Author of* The Anatomy of a Scientific Institution: The Paris Academy of Sciences (1666–1803)

HAI, AMBREEN, *Assistant Professor of English, Smith College*

HAILMAN, JACK P., *Professor of Zoology, University of Wisconsin at Madison; Author of* The Ontogeny of an Instinct: The Pecking Response in Chicks of the Laughing Gull (Larus atricilla larus) and Related Species; *Coauthor of* An Introduction to Animal Behavior: Ethology's First Century

HAIN, RAYMOND, *Catholic University of America*

HAITANI, KANJI, *Memphis State University; Author of* The Japanese Economic System: An Institutional Overview

HAJDA, LUBOMYR A., *Associate Director, Ukrainian Research Institute, Harvard University*

HALASI-KUN, TIBOR, *Professor of Turkic Studies, Columbia University*

HALCROW, HAROLD G., *Professor of Agricultural Economics and Head of Department of Agricultural Economics, University of Illinois*

HALDON, J. F., *Lecturer, Centre for Byzantine Studies, University of Birmingham, England*

HALE, HERBERT D., *Staff Member, Art News Magazine*

HALE, MASON E., *Curator, Smithsonian Institution; Author of* The Biology of Lichens

HALEVY, B. J., *Law Librarian, Osgoode Hall Law School of York University, Canada*

HALEY, GEORGE, *Professor of Romance Languages and Literatures, University of Chicago; Author of* Vicente Espinel and Marcos de Obregón

HALKIN, ABRAHAM S., *Professor of Hebrew, City College of New York; Professor of Jewish Literature and Institutions, Jewish Theological Seminary*

HALL, A. RUPERT, *Professor and Head of Department of History of Science and Technology, Imperial College of Science and Technology, University of London*

HALL, CALVIN S., *Director, Institute of Dream Research; Professor of Psychology, University of California at Santa Cruz; Author of* Theories of Personality, The Meaning of Dreams, The Content Analysis of Dreams, *and* A Primer of Freudian Psychology

HALL, CECIL E., *Professor of Biophysics, Massachusetts Institute of Technology; Author of* Introduction to Electron Microscopy

HALL, CLIFTON L., *Coauthor of* Readings in Educational History *and* Readings in American Education

HALL, COURTNEY ROBERT, *Professor of History, Queens College; Author of* History of American Industrial Science

HALL, D. G. E., *Professor, School of Oriental and African Studies, University of London; Author of* Burma

HALL, DAVID, *Professor of History, Boston University; Author of* The Faithful Shepherd: A History of the New England Ministry in the Seventeenth Century

HALL, E. RAYMOND, *Director, Museum of Natural History, University of Kansas*

HALL, EDWARD B., *Director, Washington County (Md.) Free Library*

HALL, ERIC J., *Professor of Radiology, Columbia University College of Physicians and Surgeons; Author of* Radiobiology for the Radiologist *and* Radiation and Life

HALL, G. D. G., *Fellow, Exeter College, Oxford University*

HALL, JOHN S., *Director, Lowell Observatory*

HALL, JOHN W., *Griswold Professor of History, Emeritus, Yale University; Author of* Japan: From Prehistory to Modern Times

HALL, JOHN W., *Professor of Insurance, Georgia State University; Coauthor of* Casualty Insurance

HALL, LEE, *President Emerita, Rhode Island School of Design*

HALL, MARIE BOAS, *Reader in History of Science and Technology, Imperial College, University of London*

HALL, ROLAND, *Reader in Philosophy, University of York, England*

HALL, T. MICHAEL, OSB, *Instructor in History, Catholic University of America*

HALLETT, CHARLES A., *Professor, Department of English, Fordham University*

HALLETT, H. F., *Professor of Philosophy, University of London; Author of* Benedict de Spinoza: The Elements of His Philosophy

HALLEWELL, L., *Ibero-American Bibliographer, Wilson Library, University of Minnesota; Author of* Books in Brazil: A History of the Publishing Trade

HALLGARTEN, PETER A., *Author of* Liqueurs *and* Côtes du-Rhône

HALLIDAY, IAN, *Astronomer, Herzberg Institute of Astrophysics, National Research Council, Canada; President, Royal Astronomical Society of Canada 1980–1982; Author of* Solid Particles in the Solar System

HALLMUNDSSON, HALLBERG, *Editor of* An Anthology of Scandinavian Literature

HALPERN, JOEL M., *Professor of Anthropology, University of Massachusetts at Amherst*

HALSTEAD, JOHN P., *Associate Professor of History, State University of New York at Buffalo; Author of* Rebirth of a Nation: The Origins and Rise of Moroccan Nationalism, 1912–1944

HALVERSON, KATHERINE, *Chief, Historical Division, Wyoming State Archives and Historical Department; Associate Editor of* Annals of Wyoming

HAMALAINEN, PEKKA KALEVI, *Professor of History, University of Wisconsin at Madison*

HAMBY, D. S., *Head, Department of Textile Technology, School of Textiles, North Carolina State University at Raleigh; Editor of* The American Cotton Handbook

HAMER, WALTER J., *Chief, Electrochemistry Section, National Bureau of Standards*

HAMIL, FRED C., *Professor of History, Wayne State University*

HAMILTON, CARL W., *City Librarian, Alameda Free Library*

HAMILTON, EDWARD P., *Director, Fort Ticonderoga; Author of* The French and Indian Wars

HAMILTON, GEORGE HEARD, *Professor of the History of Art, Williams College; Director, Sterling and Francine Clark Art Institute*

HAMILTON, HOLMAN, *Professor of History, University of Kentucky; Author of* Zachary Taylor

HAMILTON, R. W., JR., *President, Tarrytown Labs, Ltd.*

HAMILTON, W. E., *Director of Research, American Farm Bureau Federation*

HAMLEY, BRIAN L., *Chief Economist, National Australia Bank, Limited*

HAMLIN, CHRISTOPHER, *Professor, Lyman Briggs School, Michigan State University*

HAMMER, ELLEN J., *Author of* The Struggle for Indochina *and* Vietnam: Yesterday and Today

HAMMOND, N. G. L., *Professor of Greek, University of Bristol, England; Author of* History of Greece

HAMMOND, PHILIP C., *Professor of Anthropology, University of Utah; Author of* The Excavation of the Theater at Petra, 1961–1962: Final Report *and* A History of the Nabataeans, Studies in Mediterranean Archaeology

HAMNER, PHYLLIS, *Reference Librarian, Briggs-Lawrence County Public Library, Ohio*

HAMPSHIRE, STUART N., *Professor of Philosophy, Princeton University; Author of* Philosophy of Mind

HAN HONGKOO, *University of Washington*

HANCHETT, WILLIAM, *Professor of History, San Diego State University*

HAND, WAYLAND D., *Director, Center for the Study of Comparative Folklore and Mythology, University of California at Los Angeles; Editor of* American Folk Legend: A Symposium

HANDLER, A. BENJAMIN, *Professor of Planning, University of Michigan*

HANDLIN, OSCAR, *Carl M. Loeb University Professor, Harvard University*

HANDY, JIM, *Department of History, University of Saskatchewan; Author of* Gift of the Devil: A History of Guatemala

HANDY, ROBERT T., *Henry Sloane Coffin Professor Emeritus of Church History, Union Theological Seminary (New York City); Author of* Undermined Establishment: Church-State Relations in America, 1880–1920

HANFMANN, GEORGE, *Curator of Classical Art, Fogg Museum, Harvard University*

HANFORD, JAMES H., *Author of* John Milton, Englishman

HANNA, A. J., *Weddell Professor of American History, Rollins College*

HANNAH, PETER R., *Assistant Professor of Forestry, University of Vermont*

HANNEGAN, BARRY, *Soprintendenza delle Belle Arti, Venice*

HANNING, ROBERT W., *Professor of English and Comparative Literature, Columbia University; Author of* The Vision of History in Early Britain

HANNUM, HUNTER G., *Associate Professor of German, Mills College; Coeditor of* Modern German Drama

HANSELL, DOROTHY EBEL, *Editor of* Garden Journal

HANSEN, PETER S., *Head, Music Department, Tulane University; Author of* An Introduction to 20th Century Music

HANSON, CLARA A., *Librarian, Abilene Public Library*

HANSON, EARL PARKER, *Consultant, Departmento de Estado, Estado Libre Asociado de Puerto Rico; Author of* Transformation, The Story of Modern Puerto Rico

HANSON, ERIC J., *Professor and Head, Department of Political Economy, University of Alberta, Canada*

HANSON, SIMON G., *Editor of* Inter-American Economic Affairs

HARAKAS, STANLEY SAMUEL, *Archbishop Iakovos Professor of Orthodox Theology, Holy Cross Greek Orthodox School of Theology*

HARBAUGH, WILLIAM H., *Professor of History, University of Virginia; Author of* Power and Responsibility: The Life and Times of Theodore Roosevelt

HARBRON, JOHN D., *Associate Editor of the* Telegram, *Toronto; Canadian Editor of* Business Week

HARDIN, THOMAS L., *University of Illinois*

HARDING, WALTER, *University Professor of English, State University of New York at Geneseo*

HARDY, EDWARD R., *University Lecturer in Early Church History, Cambridge University; Author of* Christian Egypt: Church and People

HARGIS, BETTY, *Librarian, Bradley County Library, Warren, Ark.*

HARGREAVES, JOHN D., *Professor of History, University of Aberdeen, Scotland; Author of* Prelude to the Partition of West Africa *and* West Africa: The Former French States

HARING, DOUGLAS, G., *Professor of Anthropology, Syracuse University*

HARKINS, WILLIAM E., *Professor of Slavic Languages, Columbia University; Author of* Dictionary of Russian Literature

HARLAND, W. B., *Reader in Tectonic Geology, Cambridge University*

HARLEMAN, DONALD R. F., *Professor of Civil Engineering, Massachusetts Institute of Technology*

HARLEY, C. P., *U.S. Plant Industries Station*

HARLOW, ETHELYN, *University Archivist, University of Toronto, Canada*

HARMAN, GILBERT, *Professor of Philosophy, Princeton University; Author of* The Nature of Morality *and* Thought; *Editor of* On Noam Chomsky *and* Semantics of Natural Language

HARMAN, R. ALEC, *Coauthor of* Man and His Music

HARMSTONE, TERESA, *Executive Director, League of Women Voters of the United States (1970–1972)*

HARPER, DONALD V., *Professor of Transportation, Graduate School of Business Administration, University of Minnesota; Author of* Economic Regulation of the Motor Trucking Industry by the States

HARPER, ROBERT A., *Director of Engineering Relations, Columbia University*

HARRAR, ELLWOOD SCOTT, *James B. Duke Professor of Wood Science, Duke University; Author of* Hough's Encyclopaedia of American Woods

HARRIMAN, PHILIP L., *Editor of* Encyclopedia of Psychology; *Author of* Handbook of Psychological Terms *and* Modern Psychology

HARRINGTON, FRED HARVEY, *Professor of History, University of Wisconsin; Coauthor of* American History *and* History of American Civilization

HARRINGTON, JEAN, *Library Director, Public Library of Enid and Garfield County, Enid, Okla.*

HARRIS, H. S., *Chairman, Philosophy Department, Glendon College, York University*

HARRIS, L. DALE, *Associate Dean, College of Engineering, University of Utah*

HARRIS, LEON, *Author of* Only to God: A Life of Godfrey Lowell Cabot

HARRIS, MARKHAM, *Professor of English, University of Washington*

HARRIS, MEGAERA, *Historian, United States Postal Service*

HARRIS, MICHAEL H., *Professor of Library Science, College of Library and Information Science, University of Kentucky*

HARRIS, MICHAEL W., *Professor of History and African-American World Studies, University of Iowa; Author of* The Rise of Gospel Blues: The Music of Thomas Andrew Dorsey in the Urban Church

HARRIS, STEVEN, *University of Wisconsin at Madison*

HARRISON, C. WILLIAM, *Author of* The First Book of Hiking

HARRISON, EDWARD R., *Distinguished University Professor, Department of Physics and Astronomy, University of Massachusetts at Amherst*

HARRISON, JAMES P., *Associate Professor of History, Hunter College*

HARRJE, DAVID T., *Senior Research Engineer and Lecturer, Department of Mechanical and Aerospace Engineering, Princeton University; Editor of* Liquid Propellant Rocket Combustion Instability

HARRY, HAROLD W., *Consulting Biologist*

HARSLEM, ERIC, *Director of Technical Planning and Operations, Graphic and Color Systems Group, Inmont Corporation*

HART, DONN V., *Professor of Anthropology, Northern Illinois University; Author of* Riddles in Filipino Folklore: An Anthropological Analysis

HART, FRANCIS RUSSELL, *Author of* Scott's Novels: The Plotting of Historic Survival

HART, JEFFREY, *Editor of* Political Writers of Eighteenth-Century England

HART, RICHARD H., *Range Scientist, Agricultural Research Service, U.S. Department of Agriculture*

HARTIGAN, LYNDA ROSCOE, *Curator of Painting and Sculpture, National Museum of American Art, Smithsonian Institution*

HARTIN, J. S., *Director of Libraries, University of Mississippi*

HARTLEY, LODWICK, *Professor and Head, Department of English, North Carolina State College; Author of* Laurence Sterne in the 20th Century

HARTMAN, OLGA, *Research Associate, Allan Hancock Foundation, University of Southern California; Author of* Literature and Catalogue of the Polychaetous Annelids of the World

HARTMANN, ERNEST, MD, *Professor of Psychiatry, Tufts University School of Medicine; Senior Psychiatrist and Director of the Sleep Research Laboratory, West-Ros-Park Mental Health Center, Boston; Author of* The Functions of Sleep *and* The Sleeping Pill

HARTMANN, H. T., *Professor of Pomology, University of California at Davis*

HARTMANN, JACOB WITTMER, *Professor of Germanic Languages, Long Island University; Author of* Güngu-Hrolfssaga: A Study in Old Norse Philology

HARTMANN, ROBERT, *Adjunct Faculty, Graduate Musical Theatre Writing Program, Tisch School of the Arts, New York University*

HARTOG, JOHN, *Librarian, Public Library, Oranjestad, Aruba, Netherlands Antilles; Author of* Geschiedenis van de Nederlandse Antillen

HARTZOG, GEORGE B., JR., *Director, National Park Service*

HARVEY, M. J., *Associate Professor of Biology, Dalhousie University, Canada*

HARWARD, VERNON J., JR., *Professor of English, Smith College*

HASEGAWA, H. S., *Seismology Division, Earth Physics Branch, Canada Department of Energy, Mines and Resources*

HASELTINE, WILLIAM A., *Chief of Human Retrovirology, Dana-Farber Cancer Institute, Boston; Professor of Pathology, Harvard Medical School*

HASKINS, G. L., *Professor of Law, University of Pennsylvania*

HASLAM, MALCOLM, *Author of* In the Nouveau Style *and* Arts and Crafts Carpets

HASSRICK, ROYAL B., *Commissioner, U.S. Indian Arts and Crafts Board*

HATCH, CHARLES E., JR., *Historian, Office of Archaeology and Historic Preservation, National Park Service; Author of* The First Seventeen Years: Virginia, 1607–1624

HATCH, ROBERT A., *Assistant Professor, Program in History of Science, Technology, and Medicine, Department of History, University of Florida*

HATCHER, HARLAN, *President, University of Pennsylvania; Author of* Creating the Modern American Novel

HATFIELD, GARY C., *Assistant Professor of Philosophy, Johns Hopkins University; Author of* Mind and Space from Kant to Helmholtz

HATFIELD, GLENN W., *Associate Professor of English, University of Washington; Author of* Henry Fielding and the Language of Irony

HATHORN, RICHMOND Y., *Professor and Chairman, Department of Classics, State University of New York at Stony Brook; Author of* Tragedy, Myth, and Mystery, Handbook of Classical Drama, *and* Greek Mythology

HAUGEN, ARNOLD O., *Coauthor of* Field Archery and Bowhunting

HAUGEN, EINAR, *Victor S. Thomas Professor of Scandinavian and Linguistics, Harvard University*

HAUGHEY, JOHN C., SJ, *Corresponding Editor,* America Magazine

HAUS, MARY, *Director of Communications, Whitney Museum of American Art*

HAUSER, WALTER, *Associate Professor of Modern Indian History, University of Virginia, Coauthor of* Area Handbook on Jammu and Kashmir State

HAUSNER, MELVIN, *Professor of Mathematics, New York University*

HAVENS, MURRAY C., *Associate Professor of Government, University of Texas; Author of* The Challenges to Democracy

HAVIGHURST, ROBERT J., *Professor of Education and Human Development, University of Chicago; Author of* Society and Education in Brazil

HAWGOOD, JOHN A., *Author of* The Evolution of Germany

HAWKES, H. BOWMAN, *Professor of Geography, University of Utah*

HAWKINS, R. DAVID, *Chief Librarian, Dartmouth, Nova Scotia, Public Library*

HAWKLAND, WILLIAM D., *Professor of Law, University of Illinois; Author of* A Transactional Guide to the Uniform Commercial Code

HAWLEY, ELLIS W., *Professor of History, University of Iowa*

HAWORTH, W. BLAIR, JR., *U.S. Army Center of Military History, Washington, D.C.*

HAY, DAVID M., *Assistant Professor of New Testament, Princeton Theological Seminary*

HAY, DENYS, *Professor of History, University of Edinburgh, Scotland*

HAY, IAN D., MD, *Professor of Medicine, Mayo Medical School; Consultant in Endocrinology, Mayo Clinic*

HAY, LINDA R., *Assistant Professor, Graduate School of Applied and Professional Psychology, Rutgers University*

HAY, WILLIAM H., *Professor of Philosophy, University of Wisconsin*

HAY, WILLIAM M., *Assistant Professor, Graduate School of Applied and Professional Psychology, Rutgers University; Research Director of the Alcohol Behavior Research Laboratory, Rutgers University*

HAYES, BERNICE, *Librarian, Washington County Public Library, Belpre Branch*

HAYES, JOHN D., *Rear Admiral, U.S. Navy (Retired); Coauthor of* Concise History of World War I *and* Concise History of World War II

HAYES, KIRBY M., *Professor of Food Science and Technology, University of Massachusetts*

HAYES, RICHARD J., *Director of Technical Programs, National Aeronautics and Space Administration, Electronics Research Center, Cambridge, Mass.*

HAYES, ROBERT M., *Professor Emeritus, University of California at Los Angeles*

HAYES, WILLIAM F., *Director, Boise Public Library*

HAYES-McCOY, G. A., *Professor of History, University College, Galway, Ireland; Author of* Irish Battles

HAYNES, MARY, *Assistant to Curator of Mammals, Zoological Society of London*

HAYWARD, EDWARD BEARDSLEY, *Chief Librarian, Hammond Public Library*

HAYWARD, JANE, *Associate Curator, The Cloisters, Metropolitan Museum of Art*

HAYWARD, JOHN TUCKER, *Vice Admiral, U.S. Navy (Retired); President, Naval War College, Newport, R.I.*

HAYWOOD, DOROTHY C., *Chief Librarian, Lynn Public Library, Lynn, Mass.*

HAZEL, MICHAEL V., *Dallas County Heritage Society*

HAZELTON, NIKA, *Author of* The Best of Italian Cooking *and* The Cooking of Germany

HAZEN, ROBERT M., *Staff Scientist, Carnegie Institution of Washington; Clarence Robinson Professor of Science, George Mason University*

HAZLEHURST, G. CAMERON L., *Fellow of Queen's College, Oxford University; Author of* Politicians at War

HAZLETON, WILLIAM A., *Assistant Professor, Department of Political Science, Miami University, Oxford, Ohio*

HEALEY, JOHN W., SJ, *Associate Professor of Religious Studies, Iona College*

HEALEY, WILLIAM C., *American Speech and Hearing Association*

HEBBLETHWAITE, NORMAN, *Chief Librarian, Galt Public Library*

HECK, FRANK H., *Professor of History, Centre College of Kentucky; Author of* The Civil War Veteran in Minnesota Life and Politics

HECKEL, RICHARD W., *Professor of Metallurgical and Materials Science, Carnegie-Mellon University*

HECKERMAN, DAVID L., *Senior Editor,* Thoroughbred Record

HECKMAN, RICHARD A., *Associate Professor of History, Berea College; Author of* Lincoln vs. Douglas: The Great Debates Campaign

HEDGES, WILLIAM L., *Professor of English, Goucher College; Author of* Washington Irving: An American Study, 1802–32

HEDGPETH, JOEL, *Professor of Oceanography, Marine Science Laboratory, Oregon State University*

HEEZEN, BRUCE C., *Coauthor of* Face of the Deep

HEFFERNAN, JOHN B., *Rear Admiral, U.S. Navy (Retired); Former Director of Navy History, Department of the Navy*

HEFFNER, HUBERT C., *Distinguished Service Professor of Dramatic Literature, Indiana University; Author of* The Nature of Drama

HEIMAN, MICHAEL K., *Professor of Environmental Studies and Geography, Dickinson College*

HEIMERT, ALAN, *Powell M. Cabot Professor of American Literature, Harvard University; Author of* Religion and the American Mind

HEIMSCH, CHARLES, *Professor and Chairman of Department of Botany, Miami University, Ohio*

HEINE, RALPH W., *Professor of Psychology, University of Michigan; Coeditor of* Concepts of Personality

HEINE-GELDERN, ROBERT, *Manager, New Processes Research, Xerox Corporation*

HEINEMANN, EDWARD H., *Vice President, General Dynamics Corporation*

HEINRICHS, WALDO H., *Professor of History, University of Illinois*

HEINTZELMAN, ARTHUR W., *Keeper of Prints, Boston Public Library*

HEINZ, W. C., *Author of* The Professional *and* The Fireside Book of Boxing

HEISER, CHARLES B., MD, *Professor of Botany, Indiana University*

HEITNER, ROBERT R., *Professor of German, University of Illinois at Chicago Circle*

HELBURN, NICHOLAS, *Professor of Geography, University of Colorado*

HELLARD, ELLEN, *Capitol Regional Librarian, Frankfort, Ky.*

HELLIE, RICHARD, *Professor of History, University of Chicago*

HELMREICH, ERNST C., *Thomas Brackett Reed Professor of History and Political Science, Bowdoin College*

HELMREICH, JONATHAN E., *Professor of History and Dean of Instruction, Allegheny College*

HELMREICH, PAUL C., *Professor of History, Wheaton College (Mass.)*

HELPERN, MILTON, MD, *Chief Medical Examiner, City of New York; Professor and Chairman of the Department of Forensic Medicine, New York University School of Medicine; Visiting Professor of Pathology, Cornell Medical College; Coauthor of* Legal Medicine

HEMINGER, R. L., *Editor of* Republican-Courier, *Findlay, Ohio*

HEMMENDINGER, ARTHUR, *Physicist, Los Alamos Scientific Laboratory*

HEMMINGS, F. W. J., *Author of* Stendhal: A Study of His Novels

HEMMINGS, W. A., *Department of Zoology, University College of North Wales*

HENDEL, RONALD S., *Professor of Religious Studies, Southern Methodist University; Author of* The Epic of the Patriarch

HENDERSON, ALFRED J., *Professor of History, MacMurray College; Author of* London and the National Government, 1721–1742

HENDERSON, CHARLES N., *Former Director of Music, St. George's Church, New York City; Former Editor of* The American Organist

HENDERSON, GREGORY, *Fairbank Center for East Asian Research, Harvard University; Author of* Korea: The Politics of the Vortex

HENDERSON, JOE K., *Consulting Editor of* Runner's World; *Author of* Jog, Run, Race, *The Long-Run Solution, and* The Complete Marathoner

HENDERSON, KENNETH D. D., *Author of* Sudan Republic

HENDRICKSON, KENNETH E., JR., *Professor of History, Midwestern University*

HENINGTON, DAVID M., *Director, Waco Public Library*

HENKE, WARREN A., *Chairman, Division of Social Science, Bismarck Junior College*

HENLE, PAUL, *Professor of Philosophy, University of Michigan; Editor of* Language, Thought and Culture

HENNEMAN, JOHN B., JR., *Professor of History, University of Iowa*

HENNESEY, JAMES J., SJ, *Jesuit School of Theology, Chicago*

HENNESSEY, ROBERT, J., OP, *Associate Professor of Religious Studies, Albertus Magnus College*

HENRIKSEN, THOMAS H., *Senior Fellow, Hoover Institution, Stanford University; Author of* Revolution and Counterrevolution: Mozambique's War of Independence, 1964–1974; Mozambique: A History *and* The Struggle for Zimbabwe: Battle in the Bush

HENRIPIN, JACQUES, *Professor of Demography, Université de Montréal*

HENRY, SYLVIA, *Librarian, Long Island Collection, East Hampton Free Library, East Hampton, N.Y.*

HENSEL, J. W., *Professor and Chairman, Department of Vocational, Technical, and Adult Education, University of Florida*

HENSELMAN, FRANCES, *City Librarian, City of Long Beach Public Library, Long Beach, Calif.*

HENTOFF, NAT, *Coeditor of* The Jazz Makers

HENTY, MARGARET, *Conspectus Officer, National Library of Australia*

HERBERT, WALTER, B., *Director, Canada Foundation, Ottawa*

HERBIG, GEORGE H., *Professor of Astronomy, Lick Observatory, University of California at Santa Cruz*

HERING, DORIS, *Critic at Large,* Dance Magazine; *Director, National Association for Regional Ballet*

HERITY, MICHAEL, *College Lecturer, Department of Celtic Archaeology, University College, Dublin, Ireland; Author of* Irish Passage Graves: Neolithic Tomb-Builders in Ireland and Britain

HERIVEL, J. W., *Reader in the History and Philosophy of Science, Queens University, Belfast, Northern Ireland*

HERLIHY, DAVID, *Henry Charles Lea Professor of Medieval History, Harvard University*

HERMAN, ROBERT D., *Department of Sociology, Pomona College; Author of* Gambling

HEROLD, J. CHRISTOPHER, *Author of* Mistress to an Age: A Life of Madame de Staël

HERRICK, KENNETH W., *Professor of Insurance, Texas Christian University; Author of* Total Disability Provisions in Life Insurance Contracts

HERRIOTT, ROGER M., *Chairman, Department of Biochemistry, Johns Hopkins University*

HERSHBERG, THEODORE, *Acting Dean, School of Public and Urban Policy, Center for Philadelphia Studies, University of Pennsylvania; Author of* Philadelphia: Work, Space, Family and Group Experience in the Nineteenth Century *and* A Philadelphia Prospectus

HERSHKOVITZ, PHILIP, *Curator, Division of Mammals, Field Museum of Natural History*

HERSHKOWITZ, LEO, *Professor of History, Queens College; Coeditor of* New York Colonial Correspondence

HESKETH-WILLIAMS, D. M., *Hon. Secretary, Lhasa Apso Club (England)*

HESLIN, JAMES J., *Director, New York Historical Society*

HESS, ECKHARD, *Professor of Psychology, University of Chicago*

HESS, J. WILLIAM, *Archivist, Rockefeller Foundation*

HESS, ROBERT L., *Professor of History and Vice Chancellor of Academic Affairs, University of Illinois at Chicago Circle; Author of* Ethiopia: the Modernization of Autocracy

HESSE, MARY, *Professor of the History and Philosophy of Science, Cambridge University; Author of* Forces and Fields

HESTON, EDWARD, CSC, *Press Secretary, Second Vatican Council; Author of* The Press and Vatican II

HETHERINGTON, NORRISS S., *Director, Institute for the History of Astronomy, and Visiting Scholar, University of California at Berkeley*

HEWES, GORDON W., *Professor of Anthropology, University of Colorado, Boulder*

HEWES, JAMES E., JR., *Office, Chief of Military History, Department of the Army*

HEWETT, ROGER S., *Associate Professor of Economics, Drake University*

HEWITT, ESTELLA F., *Librarian, Oliver Wolcott Library, Litchfield, Conn.*

HEWITT, KENNETH, *Teaching Fellow, Department of Geography, University of Toronto, Canada*

HEWITT, MARGARET, M., *Director, Camden Free Public Library*

HEXTER, WILLIAM M., *Professor of Biology, Amherst College*

HEYDEBRAND, RUTH, *Social Sciences Institute, Washington University, St. Louis, Mo.*

HEYERDAHL, THOR, *Head, Norwegian Archaeological Expedition to Easter Island; Author of* Kon-Tiki

HEYMAN, ALBERT, MD, *Associate Professor of Neurology, Duke University Medical Center*

HIBBERT, CHRISTOPHER, *Author of* Agincourt

HICKMAN, GEORGE W., *U.S. Army (Retired)*

HICKS, ERNEST L., CPA, *Partner, Arthur Young & Company*

HICKS, JOHN D., *Author of* The Populist Revolt *and* Republican Ascendancy

HIEATT, A. KENT, *Professor of English, University of Western Ontario*

HIEBERT, RAY ELDON, *Author of* Courtier to the Crowd

HIESEY, WILLIAM M., *Department of Plant Biology, Carnegie Institution of Washington*

HIGGINBOTHAM, DON, *Professor of History, University of North Carolina*

HIGGS, DAVID, *Associate Professor of History, University of Toronto, Canada*

HIGHAM, ROBIN, *Professor of Technology and War, Kansas State University; Author of* Armed Forces in Peacetime: Britain 1918–1939 *and* The Military Intellectuals in Britain: 1918–1939; *Editor of* Aerospace Historian

HILBERG, RAUL, *John G. McCullough Professor of Political Science, University of Vermont*

HILDEBRAND, MILTON, *Professor of Zoology, University of California at Davis*

HILFER, ANTHONY C., *Assistant Professor of English, University of Texas*

HILL, FOREST G., *Professor of Economics, University of Texas at Austin; Author of* Roads, Rails and Waterways: The Army Engineers and Early Transportation

HILL, J. E. CHRISTOPHER, *Master of Balliol College, Oxford University; Author of* The English Revolution

HILL, JANE H., *Professor of Anthropology and Linguistics, University of Arizona; Coauthor of* Mulu'wetam, The First People, Speaking Mexicano, *and* Responsibility and Evidence in Oral Discourse

HILL, KENNETH, *Professor of Population Dynamics, School of Hygiene and Public Health, Johns Hopkins University*

HILL, MIRIAM G., *Associate Professor of Journalism, University of Alabama; Staff Writer, Birmingham News*

HILL, RALPH NADING, *Editor of* The College on the Hill, A Dartmouth Chronicle

HILL, RICHARD W., *Assistant Professor of Zoology, Department of Zoology, and Curator of Living Vertebrates, Museum, Michigan State University; Author of* The Comparative Physiology of Animals

HILL, ROBERT G., JR., *Professor of Horticulture, Ohio Agricultural Experiment Station and Ohio State University*

HILL, RONALD J., *Professor of Comparative Government, Trinity College; Coauthor of* The Soviet Communist Party

HILLARD, MARY HEDDA, *Economist, Business Conditions Section, Federal Reserve Board*

HILLERBRAND, HANS J., *Professor of History and Provost, Graduate School, City University of New York; Author of* World of the Reformation, Christendom Divided, *and* Luther's Sermons; *Past President, American Society for Reformation Research; American Editor, Archive for Reformation History*

HILLIER, MARY, *Author of* Pageant of Toys and Dolls *and* Dollmakers

HILLS, EDWIN S., *Professor of Geology and Mineralogy, University of Melbourne, Australia; Author of* Elements of Structural Geology

HILLWAY, TYRUS, *Author of* Herman Melville

HILTON, ORDWAY, *Examiner of Questioned Documents, New York City; Police Science Editor, Journal of Criminal Law, Criminology and Police Science*

HILTON, ROBERT C., *Director, Cary Memorial Library, Lexington, Mass.*

HILTS, VICTOR L., *Assistant Professor, Department of History of Science, University of Wisconsin at Madison*

HILU, VIRGINIA, *Editor of* Beloved Prophet (Letters of Kahlil Gibran and Mary Haskell)

HINDS, LILLIAN A., *Librarian, Tuscarawas Regional Campus Branch Library, Kent State University*

HINKLE, SAMUEL F., *President of the Board, Executive Department, Hershey Chocolate Corporation*

HINNEBUSCH, WILLIAM A., OP, *Professor of Church History, Dominican House of Studies, Washington, D.C.*

HINOJOSA, GILBERTO M., *Department of History, University of Texas at San Antonio; Consultant, Juarez Lincoln University, Austin, Texas*

HIRSCH, DAVID H., *Professor of English, Brown University; Author of* Reality and Idea in the Early American Novel

HIRSCH, JULIAN, *Hirsch-Houck Laboratories*

HIRSH, JOHN C., *Assistant Professor of English, Georgetown University*

HIRSH, RICHARD F., *Instructor, Department of Humanities, Virginia Polytechnic Institute*

HIRSHBERG, HERBERT S., *Dean, School of Library Science, Case Western Reserve University; Author of* Subject Guide to Reference Books

HIRSHBERG, JAN, *Graduate School of Education, Harvard University*

HIRSHBERG, RICHARD L., *Attorney at Law*

HIRT, HOWARD F., *Professor of Geography, Framingham State College*

HITCHCOCK, H. WILEY, *Professor of Music and Director of the Institute for Studies in American Music, Brooklyn College; Author of* Music in the United States *and* Ives

HITCHCOCK, JOHN T., *Professor of Anthropology, University of Wisconsin*

HITREC, JOSEPH, *Translator of Ivo Andric's* Bosnian Chronicle *and* The Woman from Sarajevo

HITTI, PHILIP K., *Author of* History of the Arabs *and* Lebanon in History

HOAR, L. J., JR., *Associate Professor of Spanish, Fordham University*

HOBAN, CHARLES F., *Research Professor of Education, University of Pennsylvania; Coauthor of* Instructional Film Research, 1918–1950

HOBBS, EDWARD H., *Dean, School of Arts and Science, Auburn University*

HOBBS, HERMAN H., *Professor and Chairman, Department of Physics, George Washington University*

HOCHHEISER, SHELDON, *Department of the History of Science, University of Wisconsin at Madison*

HOCHSTADT, HARRY, *Professor and Head of Department of Mathematics, Polytechnic Institute of New York; Editor of* SIAM Journal on Applied Mathematics; *Author of* The Functions of Mathematical Physics

HODGETTS, J. E., *Principal of Victoria College and Professor of Political Economy, University of Toronto*

HODGKIN, ALAN LLOYD, *Physiological Laboratory, Cambridge, England; Nobel Prize Winner in Physiology or Medicine, 1963*

HODGSON, EDWARD S., *Professor and Chairman, Department of Biology, Tufts University; Author of* Neurobiology and Animal Behavior

HODSON, H. V., *Provost, Ditchley Foundation, England*

HOENIGSWALD, HENRY M., *Professor of Linguistics, University of Pennsylvania*

HOEPRICH, PAUL, *Professor of Medicine and Pathology, Section of Infectious and Immunologic Diseases, Department of Internal Medicine, School of Medicine, University of California at Davis; Coauthor of* Fluids of Parenteral Body Cavities

HOEY, REID A., *Director, Onondaga Library System, Syracuse, N.Y.*

HOFFMAN, ERIC, *Formerly, American Philosophical Association*

HOFFMAN, GEORGE W., *Professor of Geography, University of Texas*

HOFFMAN, MARTIN, L., *Professor of Psychology, University of Michigan*

HOFFMAN, MIRIAM, *Member of the Joseph Papp Yiddish Theater*

HOFFMAN, SIDNEY, MD, *Attending Dermatologist, St. John's Espiscopal Hospital and St. Mary's Hospital, Brooklyn, N.Y.*

HOFFMAN, TONY, *Contributing Writer,* Equities *Magazine*

HOUNSHELL, DAVID A., *Assistant Professor of History, University of Delaware; Curator of Technology, Hagley Museum*

HOURANI, GEORGE F., *Professor of History, University of Michigan; Author of* Islamic Rationalism: The Ethics of Oabd Al-Jabbar

HOUSE, HUGH B., *Curator of Mammals, New York Zoological Society*

HOUSE, JOHN W., MD, *President, House Ear Institute, Los Angeles*

HOUSEHOLDER, FRED W., JR., *Professor of Classical Languages and Linguistics, Indiana University*

HOUSER, DAVID J., *Attorney at Law, Lecturer on Patent Law, University of Wisconsin Law School*

HOUSTON, JAMES, *Member, Canadian Eskimo Arts Council; Author of* Canadian Eskimo Art *and* The White Dawn

HOUSTON, JAMES M., *Fellow, Hertford College, Oxford University*

HOUTCHENS, LAWRENCE H., *Professor of English, Miami University, Ohio; Coauthor of* Leigh Hunt's Political and Occasional Essays

HOUTS, MARSHALL, *Author of* From Evidence to Proof, The Rules of Evidence, From Gun to Gavel, *and* Where Death Delights: Adventures in Courtroom Medicine

HOWARD, DEBORAH V., *Research Associate, Massachusetts Audubon Society*

HOWARD, EDWARD A., *Director, Evansville Public Library & Vanderburgh County Public Library, Evansville, Ind.*

HOWARD, EDWARD N., *Director, Vigo County Public Library, Terre Haute, Ind.*

HOWARD, FRANKLIN P., *Assistant Professor of Economics, University of Connecticut*

HOWARD, JOHN TASKER, *Author of* America's Music, The World's Great Operas, *and* This Modern Music

HOWARD, MICHAEL, *King's College, University of London, England; Author of* The Theory and Practice of War

HOWARD, PATRICIA, *Author of* Gluck and the Birth of Modern Opera

HOWARD, WILLIAM G., *Professor of German, Harvard University*

HOWARTH, T. E. B., *High Master, St. Paul's School, London; Author of* Citizen-King: The Life of Louis Philippe

HOWE, CHARLES W., *Professor of Natural Resource Economics, University of Colorado; Coauthor of* Interbasin Transfers of Water; *Author of* Benefit-Cost Analysis for Water System Planning

HOWE, JOHN, *Author of* Choosing the Right Dog

HOWE, W. ASQUITH, *Professor of Accounting, Temple University; Coauthor of* Cost Accounting

HOWELL, F. CLARK, *Professor of Anthropology, University of California at Berkeley; Author of* Early Man

HOWELL, KATHERINE, *Librarian, Wilmington Public Library*

HOWES, ALAN B., *Author of* Yorick and the Critics

HOWES, JOHN F., *Associate Professor, Department of Asian Studies and History, University of British Columbia, Canada*

HOWLETT, FREEMAN S., *Chairman, Department of Horticulture and Forestry, Ohio State University*

HOWTON, F. WILLIAM, *Assistant Professor of Sociology, City College of New York; Coauthor of* Mass Society in Crisis

HOWTON, LOUISE G., *Department of Sociology and Anthropology, City College of New York*

HU, C. T., *Gerald H. Read Professor of Education, Kent State University*

HUANG, SU-SHU, *Professor of Astrophysics, Northwestern University*

HUBBARD, PAUL, *Chairman, Department of History, Arizona State University*

HUBBARD, SUSAN M., RN, *Chief, Scientific Information Branch, National Cancer Institute*

HUBIN, ALLEN, JR., *Editor of* Best Detective Stories of the Year

HUCKER, CHARLES O., *Professor of History, University of Michigan; Author of* China: A Critical Bibliography

HUCKSHORN, ROBERT J., *Professor of Political Science, Florida Atlantic University; Author of* State Party Leadership; *Coauthor of* The Politics of Defeat

HUDSON, ALFRED BACON, *Associate Professor of Anthropology, University of Massachusetts*

HUDSON, JACK W., *Professor of Ecology and Systematics, Cornell University*

HUDSON, JAMES I., MD, *Assistant Psychiatrist, Mailman Research Center, McLean Hospital, Belmont, Mass.; Instructor in Psychiatry, Harvard Medical School; Coauthor of* New Hope for Binge Eaters: Advances in the Understanding and Treatment of Bulimia

HUDSON, JOHN A., *Librarian, University of Texas at Arlington*

HUDSON, WINTHROP S., *James B. Colgate Professor of the History of Christianity, Colgate Rochester Divinity School, Rochester, N.Y.*

HUGHES, ERIC, *Gymnastics Coach, University of Washington; Author of* Gymnastics for Men *and* Gymnastics for Girls

HUGHES, GERVASE, *Author of* Dvorak, His Life and Music

HUGHES, NATHANIEL C., JR., *Headmaster, St. Mary's Episcopal School, Memphis, Tenn.; Author of* General William J. Hardee

HUGHES, RICHARD E., *Professor of English, Boston College; Author of* Literature: Form and Function *and* The Progress of the Soul: The Interior Career of John Donne

HULBARY, ROBERT L., *Professor of Botany, University of Iowa*

HULL, GEORGE F., *Garden Editor and Chief of the Photographic Department, The Chattanooga Times and Post; Author of* Bonsai for Americans

HUMBY, MARJORIE, *Librarian, Waverly Public Library*

HUMPHREYS, R. A. LAUD, *Department of Sociology, Pitzer College*

HUNG, FREDERICK, *Professor of Geography, University of Guelph, Canada; Author of* La Géographie du thé

HUNKER, HENRY L., *Professor of Geography and Public Policy and Management, Ohio State University; Author of* The Study and Teaching of Geography

HUNNICUTT, ROBERT W., *Assistant Director of Public Affairs, National Rifle Association; Author of* Guide to the Shooting Sports

HUNSBERGER, CHARLES W., *Librarian, Monroe County (Ind.) Public Library*

HUNT, EVA, *Professor of Anthropology, Boston University; Author of* The Transformation of the Hummingbird

HUNT, ROBERTA McLEAN, *Consultant on Planning for Child Welfare, Community Council of Greater New York*

HUNT, WILLIAM DUDLEY, JR., *Architect; Author of* American Architecture *and* Encyclopedia of American Architecture

HUNT, WILLIAM R., *Professor of History (retired), University of Alaska; Author of* To Stand at the Pole, North of 53°, *and* Alaska: A Bicentennial History

HUNTER-STIEBEL, PENELOPE, *Principal, Rosenberg & Stiebel, New York City; Formerly Associate Curator, Metropolitan Museum of Art*

HURD, CHARLES, *Author of* The Compact History of the American Red Cross

HURD, DALLAS T., *Manager, Research—Lamp, Electronic and Refractory Materials, Lamp Metals and Components Department, General Electric Company*

HUREWITZ, J. C., *Professor of Government, Middle East Institute, Columbia University*

HURLBUT, CORNELIUS S., JR., *Professor of Mineralogy, Harvard University*

HURLEY, PATRICK M., *Professor of Geology and Geophysics, Massachusetts Institute of Technology; Author of* How Old Is the Earth; *Editor of* Advances in Earth Science

HURST, HAROLD EDWIN, *Hydrological Consultant to the Ministry of Irrigation, United Arab Republic*

HURST, J. WILLIS, MD, *Chief of Medical Service, School of Medicine, Emory University*

HUTCHINS, ROSS E., *Entomologist and Director, State Plant Board of Mississippi*

HUTH, HANS, *Curator of Decorative Arts, Art Institute of Chicago*

HUTH, JOHN F., JR., *Reporter, Plain Dealer, Cleveland*

HUTHMACHER, J. JOSEPH, *Richards Professor of American History, University of Delaware; Author of* Senator Robert F. Wagner and the Rise of Urban Liberalism

HUTNER, SEYMOUR H., *Haskins Laboratories, Pace University*

HUTTENHAUER, HELEN G., *Assistant in Publications, Board of Education of Baltimore County, Md.*

HUZAR, ELEANOR G., *Professor of History, Michigan State University*

HYATT, J. PHILIP, *Professor of Old Testament and Head of Department of Religion, Graduate School, Vanderbilt University*

HYATT, RUTH, *Head Librarian, Farmington Village Libraries*

HYDE, EARL K., *Senior Chemist, Lawrence Berkeley Laboratory, University of California at Berkeley*

HYER, PAUL V., *Professor of Asian Studies and History, Brigham Young University*

HYMAN, LIBBIE H., *Research Associate, Department of Living Invertebrates, American Museum of Natural History; Author of* The Invertebrates

HYNES, GEORGE P., *Librarian, Fort Dodge Public Library*

IANNINI, PAUL B., MD, *Chief, Infectious Diseases, Danbury Hospital, Danbury, Conn.; Assistant Professor of Medicine, Yale University; Author of* Psittacosis *in* Current Therapy

IBER, FRANK L., MD, *Professor of Medicine, University of Maryland, Baltimore; Author of* Diseases of the Liver, Gallbladder, and Bile Ducts *in* Principles of Internal Medicine

ICKIS, MARGUERITE, *Author of* Book of Christmas

IDZERDA, STANLEY J., *Editor, Papers of the Marquis de Lafayette, College of St. Benedict; Editor of* Lafayette in the Age of the American Revolution

IGGERS, GEORG G., *Professor of History, State University of New York at Buffalo*

IHDE, AARON J., *Professor of Chemistry and History of Science, Emeritus, University of Wisconsin at Madison; Author of* The Development of Modern Chemistry

ILARDI, VINCENT, *Professor of History, University of Massachusetts*

ILCHMAN, FREDERICK, *Museum of Fine Arts, Boston*

ILLIG, ALVIN, CSP, *General Manager, Paulist Press*

ILLINGWORTH, RONALD S., MD, *Professor of Child Health, University of Sheffield, England; Author of* The Normal Child, Babies and Young Children, Common Symptoms of Disease in Children, *and* The Development of the Infant and Young Child: Normal and Abnormal

IMARA, MWALIMU, *Director, Boston Center for Religion and Psychotherapy, Inc.; Staff Member, Psychological Counseling Center, Brandeis University; Author of* Dying as the Last Stage of Growth *in* Death: The Final Stage of Growth

IMPERATO, PASCAL JAMES, MD, *Professor and Chairman, Department of Preventive Medicine and Community Health, State University of New York Health Science Center at Brooklyn; Author of* African Folk Medicine *and* The Administration of a Public Health Agency

INBAU, FRED E., *Professor of Criminal Law, Northwestern University; Coauthor of* Truth and Deception: The Polygraph (Lie Detector) Technique

INGLES, LLOYD G., *Professor of Zoology, Fresno State College; Author of* Mammals of the Pacific States

INGLIS, STUART J., *Instructor, Astronomy, Chabot College, Valley Campus; Author of* Planets, Stars, and Galaxies

INGOLD, PETER R., *Assistant Professor, Department of Geography, University of Vermont*

INGRAHAM, CATHERINE A., MD, *Coauthor of* Introduction to Microbiology

INGRAHAM, JOHN L., *Professor Emeritus of Microbiology, University of California at Davis; Coauthor of* Introduction to Microbiology

INGSTAD, HELGE, *Author of* Westward to Vinland

IRVING, JOHN A., *Author of* The Culture of Canada

IRWIN, HOWARD S., *President, New York Botanical Garden, New York City; Coauthor (with Mary M. Wells) of* Roadside Flowers of Texas

IRWIN, RAY W., *Professor of History, New York University; Author of* Daniel D. Tompkins, Governor of New York and Vice President of the United States

ISAAC, RAËL JEAN, *Author of* Adopting a Child Today

ISACKS, BRYAN L., *William and Katherine Snee Professor of Geological Sciences, Institute for the Study of the Continents, Cornell University*

ISRAEL, CLINTON F., *Treasurer, Clarksburg Public Library*

ISTVANFFY, DANIEL I., *Author of* Alberta's Industry and Resources

ITZKOWITZ, NORMAN, *Professor of Near Eastern Studies, Princeton University; Author of* Ottoman Empire and Islamic Tradition

IVERS, LINDA M., *Librarian, Dorchester Branch Library, Boston Public Library*

IVERSEN, EDWIN S., *Chairman, Division of Graduate Studies in Marine Science, University of Miami Institute of Marine Science*

IVERSON, PETER, *Assistant Professor of History, University of Wyoming; Author of* The Navajos: A Critical Bibliography

IVES, COLTA FELLER, *Curatorial Assistant, Department of Prints, Metropolitan Museum of Art*

IVES, RONALD L., *Assistant Professor of Geography, Northern Arizona University*

IVRY, DAVID A., *Professor of Insurance, University of Connecticut*

JABLONSKI, DAVID, *Professor, Department of the Physical Sciences, University of Chicago*

JACKSON, B. DARRELL, *Department of Philosophy, College of Wooster*

JACKSON, BLYDEN, *Professor of English, University of North Carolina*

JACKSON, CLARENCE E., *Professor of Welding Engineering, Ohio State University*

JACKSON, DONALD, *Professor of History and Editor of George Washington Papers, University of Virginia*

JACKSON, GABRIELE B., *Professor of English, Temple University; Author of* Vision and Judgment in Ben Jonson's Drama

JACKSON, KENNETH T., *Mellon Professor of History and Social Sciences, Columbia University; Editor of* The Encyclopedia of New York City

JACKSON, MYRNA KANNER, *Department of English Language and Literature, University of Pennsylvania*

JACKSON, W. A. DOUGLAS, *Professor of Geography, University of Washington*

JACKSON, W. T. H., *Villard Professor of German and Comparative Literature, Columbia University; Author of* Medieval Literature: A History and a Guide *and* The Hero and the King

JACOBS, JOHN A., *Killam Memorial Professor of Science, University of Alberta, Canada; Author of* The Earth's Core and Geomagnetism; *Coauthor of* Physics and Geology

JACOBS, WALTER DARNELL, *Professor of Government and Politics, University of Maryland; Coauthor of* Modern Governments

JACOBSEN, HENRIETTA, *Administrative Coordinator, Office of the Chancellor, University of Texas System*

JACOBSON, FREDERICK L., *Author of* The Meek Mountaineer: A Climber's Armchair Companion

JACOBUS, WILLIAM W., JR., *Associate Editor, Engineering News-Record*

JAENEN, CORNELIUS J., *Professor of History, University of Ottawa, Canada*

JAFFE, JEROME H., MD, *Clinical Professor, Department of Psychiatry, University of Maryland School of Medicine*

JAHIEL, EDWIN, *Professor of French, University of Illinois*

JAKOBSON, KURT, *Chief, Agricultural and Marine Pollution Section, Office of Research and Monitoring, Environmental Protection Agency*

JAKOBSON, ROMAN, S. H. Cross Professor of Slavic Languages and Literatures, Harvard University*

JAMES, BEATRICE M., *Secretary, Council of National Library Associations*

JAMES, CLIFFORD L., *Professor of Economics, Ohio State University; Author of* Principles of Economics

JAMES, HAROLD, *Associate Professor of History, Princeton University; Author of* The Reichsbank and Public Finance in Germany 1924–1933: A Study of the Politics of Economics during the Great Depression; The German Slump: Politics and Economics, 1924–1936; *and* A German Identity, 1770–1990

JAMES, MARTIN, *Associate Professor of Art, Brooklyn College; Coeditor of* The Complete Essays of Piet Mondrian

JAMES, PAUL, *Hunter College*

JAMES, RALPH A., *Lawrence Livermore Laboratory*

JAMES, ROBERT V. R., *Principal Officer, Executive Office of the Secretary of the United Nations; Author of* Lord Randolph Churchill

JAMES, WALTER, *Author of* Wine, A Brief Encyclopedia

JAMIESON, PAUL F., *Editor of* The Adirondack Reader

JAMMER, MAX, *Professor of Physics, Bar-Ilan University, Israel; Author of* Concepts of Mass in Classical and Modern Physics *and* Conceptual Development of Quantum Mechanics

JANEWAY, R. C., *Texas Tech University*

JANICK, JULES, *Professor of Horticulture, Purdue University; Author of* Horticultural Science; *Coauthor of* Plant Science: An Introduction to World Crops

JANSEN, GUENTER A., *Director, Suffolk Cooperative Library System*

JANSON, ANTHONY F., *Art Historian*

JARETT, LAWRENCE, *Captain, USMS; Head and Professor of Law, Department of Maritime Law, United States Merchant Marine Academy; Author of* The Law of the High Seas in Peace

JAROCH, ROGER M., *Lieutenant Colonel, U.S. Marine Corps; Senior Fellow, Strategic Concepts Development Center, National Defense University*

JARRELL, HAMPTON M., *Professor of English, Winthrop College; Author of* Wade Hamilton and the Negro: The Road Not Taken

JARVIK, MURRAY E., *Professor Emeritus of Psychiatry and Biobehavioral Sciences, University of California at Los Angeles*

JASHEMSKI, WILHELMINA F., *Professor of Ancient History, University of Maryland; Author of* Letters from Pompeii *and* The Gardens of Pompeii, Herculaneum and the Villas Destroyed by Vesuvius

JAWETZ, ERNEST, MD, *Professor of Medicine, Professor and Chairman, Department of Microbiology, University of California School of Medicine at San Francisco*

JAY, EDWARD J., *Professor of Anthropology and Chairman, Interdivisional Committee on Asian Studies, California State University at Hayward*

JEFFARES, A. NORMAN, *Professor of English Studies, Stirling University*

JEFFERY, ARTHUR, *Professor of Semitic Languages, Columbia University; Author of* Qur'an as Scripture

JEFFREY, RICHARD C., *Author of* The Logic of Decision

JEFFREY, WENDELL E., *Professor of Psychology, University of California at Los Angeles*

JEHL, JOSEPH R., *Curator of Birds and Mammals, Natural History Museum, Balboa Park, San Diego, Calif.*

JELAVICH, BARBARA, *Professor of History, Indiana University; Coauthor of* The Establishment of the Balkan National States, 1804–1920

JELAVICH, CHARLES, *Professor of History, Indiana University; Coauthor of* The Establishment of the Balkan National States, 1804–1920

JELLINEK, GEORGE, *Music Director, Radio Station WQXR, New York City; Author of* Callas, Portrait of a Prima Donna

JELLISON, CHARLES A., JR., *Professor of History, University of New Hampshire; Author of* Fessenden of Maine

JENKINS, PETER, *Associate Editor, The Independent; Author of* Mrs. Thatcher's Revolution

JENKINS, ROMILLY J. H., *Professor of Byzantine History, Harvard University; Author of* Byzantium: The Imperial Centuries: A.D. 610–1071

JENKINS, VALERIE, *School Library Coordinator, Amherst Public Schools*

JENNER, R. W., *President, Cliffs Dow Chemical Company*

JENNINGS, BURGESS H., *Professor of Mechanical Engineering and Associate Dean, Technological Institute, Northwestern University; Author of* Environmental Engineering: Analysis and Practice

JENNINGS, FRANCIS, *Chairman, Department of History, Cedar Crest College*

JENNINGS, GORDON, *Technical Editor,* Cycle *Magazine*

JENSEN, JULIE M., *Professor of Education, College of Education, University of Texas at Austin; Editor of* Language Arts *Magazine*

JERUS, GEORGE R., *Vice President, Meyer Strong and Jones*

JESPERSEN, JAMES, *Staff Physicist, Time and Frequency Division, National Bureau of Standards, Boulder, Colo.*

JESSE, WILLIAM H., *Director of Libraries, University of Tennessee*

JEWELL, MALCOLM E., *Professor of Political Science, University of Kentucky; Coauthor of* The Legislative Process in the United States

JOHANNSEN, ROBERT W., *Professor of History, University of Illinois; Author of* The Union Crisis, 1850–1877 *and* Democracy on Trial

JOHNSGARD, PAUL A., *Professor of Zoology, University of Nebraska; Author of* Handbook of Waterfowl Behavior

JOHNSON, ARTHUR M., *Author of* Government-Business Relations

JOHNSON, B. EDGAR, *General Secretary, Church of the Nazarene*

JOHNSON, DONALD BRUCE, *Professor of Political Science, University of Iowa; Author of* National Party Platforms *and* The Dynamics of the American Presidency

JOHNSON, DOUGLAS W. J., *Professor of French History, University of London; Author of* France and the Dreyfus Affair

JOHNSON, E. GUSTAV, *Professor of Swedish, North Park College*

JOHNSON, E. N., *Professor of History, University of Massachusetts*

JOHNSON, EUGENE I., *Executive Director, Adult Education Association of the U.S.A.*

JOHNSON, GUY B., *Kenan Professor of Sociology and Anthropology, University of North Carolina*

JOHNSON, HARRY M., *Professor of Finance, University of Connecticut*

JOHNSON, HERBERT W., *Professor of Agriculture, University of Minnesota*

JOHNSON, HOWARD C. E., *Editor in Chief,* Chemical Week

JOHNSON, J. STEWART, *Curator of Decorative Arts, Brooklyn Museum*

JOHNSON, JAMES WILLIAM, *Professor of English, University of Rochester; Author of* Concepts of Literature *and* The Formation of English Neo-Classical Thought

JOHNSON, JANICE K., *Assistant to the Curators, Art Gallery of Ontario, Toronto, Canada*

JOHNSON, JOTHAM, *Professor of Classics, New York University; Author of* Monuments of the Republican Forum

JOHNSON, LUKE T., *Associate Professor of Religious Studies, Indiana University*

JOHNSON, OLIVE A., *Associate Librarian, University of Auckland Library, New Zealand*

JOHNSON, ROBERT W., *Professor of Industrial Administration, Purdue University; Author of* Capitol Budgeting *and* Financial Management

JOHNSON, RUDOLPH, *Librarian, University of Minnesota, Duluth Campus Library*

JOHNSON, S. F., *Professor of English, Columbia University*

JOHNSON, SUSAN R., MD, *Associate Professor of Obstetrics and Gynecology, University of Iowa College of Medicine*

JOHNSON, THOMAS A., *Metropolitan Desk Reporter, New York Times*

JOHNSON, THOMAS H., *Chairman, Department of English, Lawrenceville School; Editor of* The Poetical Works of Edward Taylor; *Coeditor of* Literary History of the United States

JOHNSON, VICTOR, MD, *Director, Mayo Graduate School of Medicine*

JOHNSTON, DONALD E., *Professor of Entomology and Environmental Biology, Acarology Laboratory, Ohio State University*

JOHNSTONE, J. K., *Professor of English, University of Saskatchewan, Canada; Author of* The Bloomsbury Group

JOLL, JAMES, *Stevenson Professor of International History, London School of Economics and Political Science; Author of* The Second International

JOLLIE, MALCOLM, *Professor of Biology, Northern Illinois University*

JOLLIFFE, HAROLD R., *Professor of Journalism, Michigan State University*

JOLLY, CLIFFORD J., *Associate Professor of Anthropology, New York University*

JONAS, ROBERT, *Library Director, West Orange Public Library*

JONES, AGNES M., *Breeder and Exhibitor of Cocker and Field Spaniels*

JONES, BURTON W., *Professor of Mathematics, University of Colorado*

JONES, CHARLES I., *Assistant Professor of Economics, Stanford University*

JONES, CINDY L. A., *Formerly, University of Colorado Health Sciences Center*

JONES, CLIFFORD R., *Assistant Professor of the History of South Asian Art, University of Pennsylvania*

JONES, ERNEST, *Author of* Sigmund Freud, Life and Works

JONES, GEORGE FENWICK, *Professor of German, University of Maryland*

JONES, GEORGE W., *Professor of Government, London School of Economics and Political Science*

JONES, H. G., *Curator, North Carolina Collection, University of North Carolina Library at Chapel Hill; Author of* North Carolina Illustrated, 1524–1984

JONES, HAROLD WELLINGTON, MD, *Editor,* Blakiston's New Gould Medical Dictionary

JONES, HARRY WILLMER, *Cardozo Professor of Jurisprudence, Columbia University*

JONES, HOWARD M., *Author of* The Theory of American Literature

JONES, JACK COLVARD, *Professor of Entomology, Department of Entomology, University of Maryland; Author of* The Circulatory System of Insects

JONES, JOHN BUSH, *Professor of English, University of Kansas; Editor of* W. S. Gilbert: A Century of Scholarship and Commentary

JONES, JOHN HALES, *Assistant Director for Records, Office of Admissions and Records, University of Delaware*

JONES, MABEL W., *Librarian, Waupun Public Library*

JONES, R. E., *Assistant Director of Studies, Royal Military College of Canada*

JONES, R. V., *Professor of Natural Philosophy, Aberdeen University, Scotland*

JONES, STEPHEN F., *Professor of Russian Studies, Mount Holyoke College*

JONES, STUART E., *National Geographic Magazine*

JONES, THOMAS C., *Assistant Professor of Medicine and Public Health, Cornell University Medical College*

JONES, TOM B., *Professor of Ancient History, University of Minnesota*

JONES, VIRGINIA C., *Director of Library Service, Carnegie Public Library, Paducah, Ky.*

JONES, WILLIAM J., *Author of* How to Raise and Train a Harrier

JONES, WILLIAM K., *Professor of Law, Columbia University*

JONTE, JOHN H., *Professor of Chemistry, South Dakota School of Mines and Technology*

JORDAN, AMOS A., JR., *Colonel, U.S. Army (Retired); Professor of Social Sciences, U.S. Military Academy*

JORGENSEN, PAUL A., *Professor of English, University of California at Los Angeles; Author of* Our Naked Frailities: Sensational Art and Meaning in Macbeth

JORGENSEN, RICHARD N., *Consultant, U.S. Department of Agriculture*

JOSEPH, JOHN, *Audenreid Professor of History and Archaeology, Franklin and Marshall College; Author of* The Nestorians and Their Muslim Neighbors

JOSEPH, NATHAN, *Formerly, Professor of Sociology, Herbert H. Lehman College, City University of New York*

JOSEPH, RICHARD, *Travel Editor of Esquire Magazine*

JOSPE, ALFRED, *National Director of Program and Resources, B'nai B'rith Hillel Foundations*

JOWSEY, JENIFER, *Adjunct Professor of Orthopedics, University of California at Davis; Author of* Metabolic Diseases of Bone *and* The Bone Biopsy

JOYCE, THOMAS, CMF, *Lecturer in Ecclesiastical History, Catholic University of America*

JOYNSON, R. E., *General Electric Research and Development Center*

JUDD, DEANE B., *National Bureau of Standards; Coauthor of* Color in Business

JUDGE, DONALD R., *Librarian, Mystic Seaport, Inc.*

JUDSON, THEODORE W., *Associate Professor, Process Engineering, General Motors Institute, Flint, Mich.*

JULY, ROBERT W., *Professor of History and Dean, Graduate Division, Hunter College; Author of* Origins of Modern African Thought *and* A History of the African People

JUST, THEODOR, *Field Museum of Natural History*

KABA, LANSINÉ, *Professor of History and Black Studies and Director of Black Studies, University of Illinois at Chicago; Author of* The Wahhabiyya

KACHLINE, CLIFFORD, *Historian, National Baseball Hall of Fame; Editor of* Official Baseball Guide, 1947–1967

KAFKER, FRANK A., *Professor of History, University of Cincinnati*

KAHN, DAVID, *Author of* Code-breakers

KAHN, ROBERT A., *Professor of History, Rutgers University*

KAISER, DAVE, *Feature Editor, Hoffman Publications Inc.*

KAKIUCHI, GEORGE H., *Associate Professor, Department of Geography, University of Washington*

KALMBACHER, GEORGE, *Taxonomist, Brooklyn Botanic Gardens*

KAMENETZ, HERMAN L., MD, *Chief, Rehabilitation Medicine Service, U.S. Veterans Administration Hospital, Washington, D.C.; Clinical Professor of Medicine, George Washington University; and Professorial Lecturer in Physical Medicine and Rehabilitation, Georgetown University School of Medicine*

KAMISAR, YALE, *Professor of Law, University of Michigan; Author of* Criminal Justice in Our Time

KAMMERER, JOHN C., *Hydrologist, Water Resources Division, U.S. Geological Survey*

KAMPION, DREW, *Editor of* Surfer Magazine

KANE, FRANCIS J., JR., MD, *Professor of Psychiatry, Baylor College of Medicine*

KANTOR, DAVID, *Director of Libraries, Volusia County, Fla.*

KANTOR, HARRY, *Professor of Political Science, Marquette University; Author of* Patterns of Politics and Political Systems in Latin America

KANTOR, THOMAS, MD, *Professor of Clinical Medicine, New York University School of Medicine*

KAPANY, NARINDER S., *Chairman of the Board and President, Kaptron, Inc.; Author of* Fiber Optics: Principles and Applications

KAPLAN, FLORA S., *City University of New York*

KAPLAN, HAROLD I., MD, *Professor of Psychiatry, New York Medical College; Co-editor of* Comprehensive Textbook of Psychiatry/II

KAPLAN, KAREN M., *Professor of Pediatrics, Biostatistics, and Epidemiology, Pennsylvania State University College of Medicine*

KAPLAN, LAWRENCE S., *Professor of History, Kent State University; Author of* Jefferson and France, NATO and the Policy of Containment, *and* Recent American Foreign Policy: Conflicting Interpretations

KARGON, ROBERT, *Professor of the History of Science, Johns Hopkins University*

KARLEN, DELMAR, *Professor of Law, New York University; Director, Institute of Judicial Administration; Author of* Anglo-American Criminal Justice

KARLSON, PETER, *Professor of Physiological Chemistry, Philipps-Universität, Marburg, West Germany*

KARP, THEODORE C., *Professor of Music, School of Music, Northwestern University*

KASER, DAVID, *Professor of Library Science, Indiana University*

KASFIR, NELSON, *Professor of Government, Dartmouth College; Author of* The Shrinking Political Arena; *Editor of* State and Class in Africa

KASH, DON E., *Professor of Political Science, University of Oklahoma; Coauthor of* Our Energy Future

KASPER, HIRSCHEL, *Professor of Economics, Oberlin College*

KATZ, IRVING, *Space and Information Systems Division, North American Aviation, Inc.*

KATZ, WILBER G., *Professor of Law, University of Wisconsin Law School; Author of* Religion and American Constitutions

KAUFFMAN, GEORGE B., *Professor of Chemistry, Fresno State College*

KAUFFMAN, ROBERT G., *Professor of Meat Science, University of Wisconsin at Madison; Author of chapter in* Science of Meat and Meat Products; *1970 Distinguished Teacher, American Meat Science Association*

KAUFMAN, GEORGE, *John F. Smith, Jr. Professor of Finance and Economics, Loyola University; Author of* U.S. Financial System

KAUFMAN, JAY, *Rabbi; Executive Vice-President, B'nai B'rith*

KAUFMAN, SAM, *Director, Public Relations, CARE, Incorporated*

KAUFMANN, WALTER, *Professor of Philosophy, Princeton University; Author of* Nietzsche: Philosopher, Psychologist, Antichrist; Hegel: Reinterpretation, Texts, and Commentary; *and* Religion from Tolstoy to Camus

KAVANAUGH, MARTIN, *Author of* The Assiniboine Basin

KAWATAKE, TOSHIO, *Professor of Literature, Waseda University, Japan*

KAY, ALAN S., *Department of the History of Science and Medicine, Yale University*

KAY, DAVID C., *Associate Professor of Mathematics, University of Oklahoma; Author of* College Geometry

KAY, MARSHALL, *Professor of Geology, Columbia University; Coauthor of* Stratigraphy and Life History

KAYE, DONALD, MD, *Professor of Medicine, Medical College of Pennsylvania*

KAYS, JOHN M., *Associate Professor of Animal Husbandry, University of Connecticut*

KAZEMI, HOMAYOUN, *Associate Professor of Medicine, Harvard Medical School*

KEARNS, FLORENCE M., *Librarian, James Memorial Library, Williston, N.Dak.*

KEATING, BERN, *Author of* Northwest Passage

KEEGAN, JOHN, *Senior Lecturer in War Studies, Royal Military Academy, Sandhurst, England*

KEELER, LOIS H., *Reference Librarian, Darien Library*

KEELEY, EDMUND, *Coeditor and Translator of* George Seferis: Collected Poems

KEENAN, EDWARD, *Professor of History, Harvard University*

KEENEY, ELIZABETH BARNABY, *Department of the History of Science, University of Wisconsin at Madison*

KEHR, ERNEST A., *Stamp News Bureau; Author of* The Romance of Stamp Collecting

KEITH, RUTH KING, *President, Historic Annapolis, Inc.*

KEITHAHN, EDWARD L., *Librarian and Curator (Retired), Alaska Historical Library and Museum, Juneau*

KELLAR, JAMES H., *Professor of Anthropology, Indiana University*

KELLER, CHARLES M., *Associate Professor of Anthropology, University of Illinois*

KELLER, DOUGLAS V., JR., *Otisca Industries, Ltd.*

KELLER, FRED, *Chief, Metallography Division, Alcoa Aluminum Research Laboratories, Aluminum Company of America*

KELLEY, DONALD R., *Professor of History, University of Rochester*

KELLEY, ROBIN D. G., *Professor of History, University of Michigan; Author of* Hammer and Hoe: Alabama Communists during the Great Depression

KELLOGG, CHARLES E., *Assistant Administrator, Soil Conservation Service, U.S. Department of Agriculture; Author of* Soil Survey Manual

KELLOGG, RUTH E., *Director, Elkhart Public Library, Elkhart, Ind.*

KELLY, JAMES R., *Commander, U.S. Coast Guard*

KELLY, LUCIE S., *Professor Emeritus, Columbia University School of Public Health and School of Nursing; Author of* The Nursing Experience: Trends, Challenges, and Transitions

KELLY, NORA, *Coauthor of* The Royal Canadian Mounted Police: A Century of History

KELLY, THOMAS, *Professor of History, University of Minnesota; Author of* A History of Argos to 500 B.C.

KELLY, WILLIAM C., *Professor of Vegetable Crops, New York State College of Agriculture, Cornell University*

KELSEY, HARRY E., JR., *Director, Michigan Historical Commission; Author of* Frontier Capitalist: A Life of John Evans

KELTING, HERMAN, *Assistant Professor of Real Estate, University of Florida*

KEMBLE, JOHN HASKELL, *Professor of History, Pomona College; Author of* The Panama Route, 1848–1869

KEMP, P. K., OBE, *Lieutenant Commander, Royal Navy (Retired); Author of* History of the Royal Navy

KEMPE, C. HENRY, MD, *Professor of Pediatrics, University of Colorado Medical Center*

KENDALL, HENRY M., *Coauthor of* Introduction to Geography

KENDALL, LANE C., *Colonel, U.S. Marine Corps (Retired); Former Adviser to U.S. Navy Sealift Command; Former Professor of Marine Transportation, U.S. Merchant Marine Academy; Author of* The Business of Shipping

KENNARD, C. H. L., *Department of Chemistry, University of Queensland, Australia*

KENNEALLY, JAMES J., *Associate Professor of History, Stonehill College*

KENNEDY, MICHAEL, *Author of* Portrait of Elgar

KENNEDY, STETSON, *Secretary, Ibizan Hound Club of America and World Federation of Ibizan Fanciers*

KENNER, HUGH, *Andrew W. Mellon Professor in Humanities, Johns Hopkins University; Author of* Samuel Beckett: A Critical Study *and* Wyndham Lewis

KENT, C. D., *Director, London Public Library & Art Museum, London, Ontario, Canada*

KENT, DONALD F., MD, *Overlook Hospital, Summit, N.J.*

KENT, GEORGE C., *Department of Plant Pathology, New York State College of Agriculture, Cornell University*

KENT, RAYMOND K., *Professor of History, University of California at Berkeley; Author of* Early Kingdoms in Madagascar: 1500–1700 *and* From Madagascar to the Malagasy Republic

KENT, ROBERT B., *Professor of Geography and Planning, University of Akron*

KENT, SARAH A., *Professor of History, University of Wisconsin at Stevens Point*

KENTER, BARRY, *Rabbi, Jewish Theological Seminary of America*

KERKER, MILTON, *Dean, School of Science, Clarkson College of Technology; Editor in Chief,* Journal of Colloid Science

KERMAN, JOSEPH, *Professor of Music, University of California at Berkeley*

KERN, ALEXANDER C., *Professor of English and Chairman, American Civilization Program, University of Iowa; Coauthor of* The Rise of Transcendentalism

KERN, ROBERT W., *Assistant Professor of History, University of New Mexico*

KERNAN, JULIE, *Translator of* Mare Escolier's Port-Royal, the Drama of the Jansenists

KERR, D. G. G., *Senior Professor, Department of History, University of Western Ontario, Canada; Author of* Canada: A Visual History

KERR, MALCOLM H., *Professor of Political Science, University of California, Los Angeles*

KERR, PAUL F., *Newberry Professor of Geology, Columbia University; Author of* Optical Mineralogy

KERSTEN, EARL W., JR., *Professor of Geography, Mackay School of Mines, University of Nevada at Reno*

KESTERTON, W. H., *Professor of Journalism, Carleton University, Ontario, Canada; Author of* A History of Journalism in Canada

KETAY, KENNETH R., DMD

KETCHAM, RALPH, *Professor of American Studies, Syracuse University; Author of* Benjamin Franklin *and* James Madison: A Biography

KETCHUM, CAROL Q., *Merchandising Assistant, Fuller Brush Company*

KETELLAPPER, H. J., *Professor of Botany, University of California at Davis*

KETTL, DONALD F., *Professor of Political Science, La Follette Institute of Public Affairs and Department of Political Science, University of Wisconsin at Madison*

KEYSER, CARL A., *Professor of Engineering, University of Massachusetts*

KGWARE, W. M., *Vice Chancellor and Rector, University of the North, South Africa; Author of* Education for Africans

KIDDER, MARY C., *Iowa State University*

KIDNEY, WALTER, *Author of* The Architecture of Choice: Eclecticism in America, 1880–1930

KIELY, EDMOND R., *Professor of Mathematics, Iona College*

KIKER, JOHN E., JR., *Professor of Environmental Engineering, University of Florida; Coauthor of* Sewerage Planning; *Consultant (1954–1968), United States Public Health Service*

KILBORN, KENYON, *Director, Editorial Services, Radio Corporation of America*

KILBOURNE, EDWIN D., MD, *Professor of Microbiology and Chairman of Department of Microbiology, Mount Sinai School of Medicine, New York City*

KILBY, CLYDE S., *Professor of English, Wheaton College (Ill.); Author of* The Christian World of C. S. Lewis

KILGOUR, RUTH EDWARDS, *Author of* A Pageant of Hats, Ancient and Modern

KILHAM, WALTER H., JR., *Fellow, American Institute of Architects*

KILLEN, GEOFFREY P., *Head of Faculty, Technology Department, Stratton College, Biggleswade, Bedfordshire, England; Author of* Egyptian Woodworking and Furniture *and* Ancient Egyptian Furniture, *vols. 1 and 2*

KILLIAN, JAMES R., *Chairman of the Corporation, Massachusetts Institute of Technology; Author of* Scientists Serving Eisenhower

KILMISTER, CLIVE W., *Professor of Mathematics, University of London*

KIM, ROY U. T., *Professor of Political Science, Drexler University*

KIMBALL, IRENE, *Acting Librarian, Welsh Public Library*

KIMBALL, STANLEY B., *Professor of History, Social Science Division, Southern Illinois University*

KIMBALL, WARREN F., *Associate Professor of History, Rutgers University; Author of* The Most Unsordid Act: Lend Lease, 1939–1941

KIMBLE, GREGORY A., *Professor and Chairman, Department of Psychology, University of Colorado; Author of* Foundations of Conditioning

KIMBROUGH, W. D., *Professor of Horticulture, Louisiana State University*

KIMMICH, CHRISTOPH M., *Associate Professor of History, Brooklyn College*

KING, ALLEN L., *Professor of Physics, Dartmouth College; Author of* Thermophysics

KING, DONALD, *Keeper of Textiles, Victoria and Albert Museum, London*

KING, JERE CLEMENS, *Professor of History, University of California at Los Angeles; Author of* Generals and Politicians *and* Foch Versus Clemenceau

KING, JOHN A., *Professor of Zoology, Michigan State University*

KING, MONIQUE, *Musées Nationaux, Paris*

KING, RONOLD W. P., *Professor of Applied Physics, Harvard University*

KING, RUSSELL, *Lecturer in Geography, Leicester University; Author of* Land Reform: The Italian Experience *and* Sicily

KING, THELMA R., *Director, Steele Memorial Library of Chemung County, Elmira, N.Y.*

KING, W. JAMES, *Senior Curator, Power and Communications Collections, Henry Ford Museum*

KING, WILLARD L., *Author of* Melville Weston Fuller: Chief Justice of the United States (1888–1910)

KINGDON, ROBERT N., *Professor of History, University of Wisconsin*

KING-HAMMOND, LESLIE A., *Dean of Graduate Studies and Project Director for the Philip Morris Fellowships for Artists of Color, Maryland Institute College of Art; Author of* We Wear the Mask: The Ethos of Spirituality in African-American Art, 1750–Present

KINGSBURY, ROBERT C., *Associate Professor of Geography, Indiana University; Author of* South Asia in Maps

KINGSLAKE, RUDOLF, *Director, Optical Design Department, Apparatus and Optical Division, Eastman Kodak Company*

KINGSLEY, DARWIN P., III, *Vice President, United States Squash Racquets Association*

KINNARD, WILLIAM N., JR., *Associate Dean, School of Business Administration, University of Connecticut; Author of* Industrial Real Estate

KIP, ARTHUR F., *Professor of Physics, University of California at Berkeley*

KIRBY, S. WOODBURN, *Major-General, British Army; Coauthor of* The War Against Japan

KIRK, NEVILLE T., *U.S. Naval Academy; Coauthor of* Sea Power: A Naval History

KIRK, PAUL L., *Author of* Crime Investigation: Physical Evidence and the Police Laboratory

KIRK, VIRGINIA C., *Library Director, Asbury Park Public Library*

KIRKENDALL, RICHARD S., *Professor of History, Indiana University; Executive Secretary, Organization of American Historians; Author of* The Global Power *and* The Truman Period as a Research Field

KIRKLAND, JAMES I., *Paleontologist, Utah Geological Society*

KIRSCH, BERNARD, *Assistant Editor,* New York Times Sports Almanac *1967, 1968, 1969*

KIRSCHNER, EDWIN J., *Author of* The Zeppelin in the Atomic Age

KIRWAN, SIR LAURENCE P., *Director and Secretary, Royal Geographical Society, London; Author of* The White Road

KISH, GEORGE, *Professor of Geography, University of Michigan*

KISSAM, PHILIP, *Professor of Civil Engineering, Princeton University; Author of* Surveying Practice

KISSNER, ARTHUR J., *Chief Librarian, Fitchburg Public Library, Fitchburg, Mass.*

KITCH, EDMUND W., *Professor of Law, University of Chicago*

KITTO, H. D. F., *Author of* Greek Tragedy: A Literary Study

KLAMAN, SAUL B., *Vice Chairman, BEI GOLEMBE, Inc.; Author of* The Postwar Residential Mortgage Market

KLAPP, ORRIN E., *Professor of Sociology, San Diego State University; Author of* Models of Social Order

KLAUBER, LAURENCE M., *Consulting Curator of Reptiles, San Diego Zoological Society; Author of* Rattlesnakes

KLAUS, KENNETH B., *Alumni Professor of Music, Lousiana State University; Author of* The Romantic Period in Music

KLAWITER, RANDOLPH J., *Professor of Modern Languages, University of Notre Dame; Author of* Stefan Zweig's Novellem

KLEBANOW, DIANA, *Assistant Professor, Department of History, University of Connecticut*

KLEIN, DONALD W., *Associate Professor of Political Science, Tufts University; Coauthor of* Biographic Dictionary of Chinese Communism, 1921–1965 *and* Rebels and Bureaucrats: China's December 9ers

KLEIN, FANNIE J., *Associate Professor of Law, New York University School of Law; Associate Director, Institute of Judicial Administration*

KLEIN, J. DOUGLAS, *Assistant Professor, Department of Economics, Syracuse University*

KLEIN, MARTIN J., *Professor of the History of Physics, Yale University*

KLEIN, PHILIP S., *Professor of American History, Pennsylvania State University; Author of* President James Buchanan, A Biography

KLENE, JOANNE, *Librarian, Bellwood Public Library*

KLINE, HARVEY F., *University of Alabama; Author of* Colombia: Portrait of Unity and Diversity; *Coeditor of* Latin American Politics and Development

KLINE, HIBBERD V. B., JR., *Chairman, Department of Geography, University of Pittsburgh*

KLINE, KATHERINE G., *Researcher, Albright-Knox Art Gallery, Buffalo, N.Y.*

KLINE, MORRIS, *Professor of Mathematics, New York University*

KLINE, RONALD R., *Department of General Engineering, University of Wisconsin at Madison*

KLING, MERLE, *Professor of Political Science, Washington University, St. Louis, Mo.*

KLING, SAMUEL G., *Attorney at Law; Author of* The Complete Guide to Everyday Law

KLINGER, GEORGE, *Editorial Director, Drug Topics*

KLOTS, ALEXANDER B., *Department of Entomology, American Museum of Natural History; Coauthor of* Living Insects of the World

KLOTS, ELSIE B., *Author of* The New Field Book of Freshwater Life; *Coauthor of* Living Insects of the World

KNACHEL, PHILIP A., *Associate Director, Folger Shakespeare Library*

KNAPP, BETTINA L., *Professor of Romance Languages, Hunter College and Graduate Center, City University of New York; Author of* Gerard de Nerval: The Mystic's Dilemma

KNAPP, GREGORY, *Associate Professor, Department of Geography, University of Texas at Austin*

KNAUERHASE, RAMON, *Associate Professor of Economics, University of Connecticut*

KNEITEL, THOMAS, *Editorial Director, CB Radio/S9 Magazine; Author of* CB'ers SSB Handbook, 103 Simple Transistor Projects, *and* Registry of U.S. Government Radio Systems

KNICKERBOCKER, KENNETH L., *Professor of English, University of Tennessee; Author of* Writing About Poetry

KNIGHT, DAVID M., *Lecturer in History of Science, University of Durham, England*

KNIGHT, FRANKLIN W., *Associate Professor of History, Johns Hopkins University; Author of* Slave Society in Cuba During the Nineteenth Century

KNIGHT, FRANKLIN W., *Leonard and Helen R. Stulman Professor of History, Johns Hopkins University*

KNIGHT, OLIVER, *Professor of History, University of Texas at El Paso; Author of* Following the Indian Wars

KNIGHT, RUSSELL W., *Editor of* Elbridge Gerry's Letterbook

KNIGHT, VERNON, MD, *Professor and Chairman, Department of Microbiology, Baylor College of Medicine, Houston, Texas*

KNIGHT, VIRGINIA CURTIN, *Consulting Editor,* Current History

KNIGHTON, C. S., *Magdalene College, Cambridge University*

KNOLL, ANDREW H., *Department of Geological Sciences, Harvard University*

KNOLL, SAMSON B., *Dean of the Faculty, Monterey Institute; Coauthor of* The Development of Historiography

KNOWLES, MALCOLM S., *Associate Professor of Education and General Consultant in Adult Education, Boston University; Executive Director, Adult Education Association of the U.S.A.; Author of* The Adult Education Movement in the United States

KNOX, JOHN, *Author of* Marcion and the New Testament: An Essay in the Early History of the Canon

KNOX, MARGARET R., *Librarian, Arlington Public Library, R.I.*

KNOX, R. S., *Professor, Department of Physics and Astronomy, University of Rochester*

KOBISKE, RONALD A., *Professor of Physics, Milwaukee School of Engineering*

KOCHMAN, RICHARD, MD, *St. Luke's Hospital, New York City*

KODJAK, ANDREJ, *Head of the All-University Department of Slavic Languages and Literatures, New York University*

KOENIG, RT. REV. MSGR. HARRY C., *Archdiocese of Chicago*

KOENIG, LOUIS W., *Professor of Government, New York University; Author of* The Chief Executive *and* The Invisible Presidency

KOETJE, TODD A., *Assistant Professor of Anthropology and Associate Director of Archaeological Services, Indiana University of Pennsylvania*

KOFRANEK, ANTON M., *Professor of Environmental Horticulture, University of California at Davis*

KOGAN, NORMAN, *Director, Center for Italian Studies, University of Connecticut*

KOHLSTEDT, DONALD W., *Library Director, Grand Rapids Public Library*

KOHN, MISCH, *Professor of Art, California State University, Hayward*

KOINZAN, ANNIE, *Reference and Interlibrarian, North Central Regional Library, Wenatchee, Wash.*

KOJIRO, YUICHIRO, *Professor of Architecture, Meiji University, Tokyo; Author of* Architectural Beauty in Japan *and* Forms in Japan

KOLLAR, F., *Seismology Division, Earth Physics Branch, Department of Energy, Mines and Resources, Ottawa, Canada*

KOLLER, LEWIS R., *National Research Corp., Cambridge, Mass.*

KOLM, HENRY H., *Francis Bitter National Magnet Laboratory, Massachusetts Institute of Technology*

KOLSKY, HARWOOD G., *Professor Emeritus of Computer Engineering, University of California at Santa Cruz*

KOMAR, ARTHUR, *Belfer Graduate School of Science, Yeshiva University*

KONEFSKY, SAMUEL J., *Author of* The Legacy of Holmes and Brandeis

KONNER, MELVIN, *Samuel Candler Dobbs Professor of Anthropology and Professor of Psychiatry, Emory University*

KONZELMANN, FRANK W., MD, *Director of the Laboratory, Mercy Hospital, Sea Isle City, N.J.*

KONZO, SEICHI, *Professor of Mechanical Engineering, University of Illinois; Coauthor of* Opportunities in Mechanical Engineering

KOO, SHOU-ENG, *Associate Professor of Economics, Indiana University; Fellow, Ford Foundation Faculty Research Seminar*

KOOPMAN, KARL F., *Department of Mammalogy, American Museum of Natural History*

KOPF, DOLORES, *Librarian, Oak Lawn Public Library*

KOPPELMAN, GEORGE, *IBM Research Center, IBM Corporation, Yorktown Heights, N.Y.*

KORF, ARTHUR J., DDS, *Member, American Prosthodontic Society and New York Academy of Dentistry*

KORFF, SERGE A., *Professor of Physics, New York University*

KORNBERG, ARTHUR, *Nobel Prize Winner in Physiology or Medicine, 1959; Head, Department of Biochemistry, Stanford University*

KORNBLUM, ZVI C., *Associate Professor of Chemistry, School of Engineering, Cooper Union for the Advancement of Science and Art*

KORNHAUSER, DAVID H., *Chairman, East Asian Studies, Asian Studies Program, University of Hawaii; Author of* Japan: Geographic Foundations of Urban-Industrial Development

KORTENDICK, JAMES J., SS, *Head of the Department of Library Science, Catholic University of America; Author of* The Library in the Catholic Theological Seminary in the United States

KOSAK, ALVIN I., *Professor of Chemistry, New York University*

KOSSOFF, FLORENCE S., *Staff Member, Frick Collection, New York City*

KOTSHER, B. J., *Editorial Director, Palmerton Publishing Co., Inc.*

KOVRIG, BENNETT, *Professor of Political Science, University of Toronto; Author of* Communism in Hungary from Kun to Kadar

KRADJIAN, ROBERT M., MD, *Surgeon, Mary's Help Hospital, Daly City, Calif.; Author of* Breast Lumps; *Coauthor of* Renal Carcinoma

KRAEHE, ENNO E., *Professor of History, University of Virginia*

KRAEHENBUEHL, JOHN O., *Author of* Electric Illumination

KRAELING, EMIL G., *Professor of Old Testament, Union Theological Seminary; Instructor and Visiting Professor of Semitic Languages, Columbia University; Author of* Rand McNally Bible Atlas

KRAEMER, JOEL L., *Department of History of the Middle East and Africa, Tel Aviv University; Editor of* Jerusalem: Problems and Prospects

KRAFT, CHARLES F., *Professor of Old Testament Interpretation, Garrett Biblical Institute*

KRAFT, IRVIN A., MD, *Medical Director, Texas Institute of Family Psychiatry; Associate Professor of Psychiatry and Pediatrics, Baylor College of Medicine; Clinical Professor of Mental Health, University of Texas School of Public Health*

KRAILSHEIMER, ALBAN, *Tutor in French, Christ Church College, Oxford University; Translator of Pascal's* Pensees *and* Provincial Letters

KRAKEL, DEAN F., *Director, National Cowboy Hall of Fame and Western Heritage Center, Oklahoma City*

KRAKOFF, IRWIN H., MD, *Professor of Medicine and Pharmacology, M. D. Anderson Cancer Center, University of Texas*

KRAMER, SAMUEL NOAH, *Author of* The Sumerians *and* History Begins at Sumer

KRAMRISCH, STELLA, *Professor of South Asian Art, University of Pennsylvania; Curator, Indian Section, Philadelphia Museum of Art; Author of* The Art of India *and other books*

KRANTZ, JOHN C., JR., MD, *Scope Director, U.S. Pharmacopeia, Huntington Research Center, Towson, Md.*

KRAPP, GEORGE P., *Editor of* Paris Psalter and Meters of Boethius

KRAUS, JON, *Professor of Political Science, State University of New York at Fredonia*

KRAUS, MICHAEL, *Professor of History, City College of New York; Author of* The Writing of American History

KRAUSE, DOROTHEA M., *Wausau Public Library*

KRAVITT, EDWARD F., *Chairman, Department of Music, Herbert H. Lehman College of the City University of New York*

KREIDER, LAWRENCE E., *Executive Vice President, Conference of State Bank Supervisors*

KRENKEL, JOHN H., *Professor of History, Arizona State University*

KREPS, CLIFTON H., JR., *Wachovia Professor of Banking, University of North Carolina; Author of* Money, Banking, and Monetary Policy

KRETCHMER, NORMAN, MD, *Former Director National Institute of Child Health and Human Development; Professor, Department of Nutritional Sciences, University of California at Berkeley*

KRIEGER, LEONARD, *Professor of History, University of Chicago*

KRIM, MATHILDE E., MD, *Head, Interferon Laboratory, Memorial Sloan-Kettering Cancer Center, New York City*

KRISTOF, LADIS K. D., *Associate Professor of Political Science, Portland State University*

KRITCHEVSKY, DAVID, *Wistar Institute of Anatomy and Biology, Philadelphia*

KRIZ, MIROSLAV A., *Vice President and Senior Economist, First National City Bank of New York*

KROEBER, KARL, *Professor of English, Columbia University; Author of* Backgrounds to British Romantic Literature

KROGMAN, WILTON MARION, *Professor and Chairman, Department of Physical Anthropology, Graduate School of Medicine, University of Pennsylvania*

KRONE, GLADYS L., *Librarian, Carnegie City Library, Fort Smith, Ark.*

KRONENBERG, BERNARD, MD, *Associate Clinical Professor of Ophthalmology, New York Medical College; Associate Clinical Professor of Ophthalmology, New York University Medical Center*

KROOSS, HERMAN E., *Author of* American Economic Development; *Coauthor of* Financial History of the United States

KROSBY, H. PETER, *Professor and Chairman, Department of History, State University of New York at Albany*

KRUG, RICHARD E., *City Librarian, Milwaukee Public Library*

KRÜGER, MARLIS, *Department of Sociology and Anthropology, City College of New York*

KRUGMAN, SAUL, *Chairman of Department and Professor of Pediatrics, New York University College of Medicine; Coauthor of* Infectious Diseases of Children

KRUTCH, JOSEPH WOOD, *Author of* Samuel Johnson *and* Edgar Allan Poe

KRYTHE, MAYMIE R., *Author of* All About the Months

KUBLIN, HYMAN, *Professor of History, Brooklyn College; Author of* Asian Revolutionary: The Life of Sen Katayama

KUBRIN, DAVID, *Assistant Professor of History, Dartmouth College*

KUEHL, WARREN F., *Professor of History, University of Akron; Director, Center for Peace Studies; Author of* Seeking World Order: The United States and International Organization to 1920; *Editor of the* Biographical Dictionary of Internationalists

KUEHNAST, KATHLEEN, *Department of Anthropology, University of Minnesota*

KUGLER, RICHARD C., *Director, Old Dartmouth Historical Society Whaling Museum, New Bedford, Mass.*

KUHN, HOWARD A., *Associate Professor of Metallurgical Engineering, Drexel Institute of Technology*

KUKLICK, BRUCE, *Professor of History, University of Pennsylvania; Author of* The Rise of American Philosophy

KULISEK, LARRY L., *Professor of History, University of Windsor, Ontario, Canada; Author of* Windsor: An Illustrated History

KUNKLE, E. CHARLES, MD, *Maine Medical Center; Professor of Neurology, Duke University Medical School*

KUNZ, F. A., *Associate Professor of Political Science, McGill University, Canada*

KUPERBERG, MARK, *Associate Professor of Economics, Swarthmore College*

KUPERMAN, ALBERT S., *Field Staff Member, Rockefeller Foundation*

KURATH, GERTRUDE P., *Coordinator, Dance Research Center, Ann Arbor, Mich.; Dance Editor,* Ethnomusicology; *Author of* Michigan Indian Festivals

KURLAND, PHILIP B., *Professor of Law, Law School, University of Chicago*

KURTZ, HAROLD, *Author of* The Trial of Marshal Ney

KURTZ, MARY, *Head Librarian, Ephrata Public Library, Ephrata, Pa.*

KURTZ, PAUL, *Professor Emeritus of Philosophy, State University of New York at Buffalo*

KURTZ, RUSSELL H., *Editor of* Social Work

KURTZ, STEPHEN G., *Dean of Wabash College*

KUSCH, POLYKARP, *Nobel Prize Winner in Physics, 1955; Eugene McDermott Professor of Physics, University of Texas at Dallas*

KUYKENDALL, MABEL M., *Columnist,* The Taos News

LABAREE, BENJAMIN W., *Professor of History, Williams College; Author of* Patriots and Partisans *and* The Boston Tea Party

LA BELLE, THOMAS J., *Professor, Graduate School of Education, University of California at Los Angeles; Author of* Nonformal Education and Social Change in Latin America; *Editor of* Education and Development: Latin America and the Caribbean *and* Educational Alternatives in Latin America

LACHS, JOHN, *Centennial Professor of Philosophy, Vanderbilt University; Author of* Mind and Philosophers *and* George Santayana

LACKEY, JAMES, *Botanist, U.S. Department of Agriculture, Hyattsville, Md.*

LACKNER, ELMER C., SM, *Vice President, Department of Public Relations, University of Dayton*

LACOSTE, PAUL, *Rector, University of Montreal, Canada*

LA DUE, WADE W., *Director, Public Relations and Publications, Veterans of Foreign Wars of the United States*

LA FARGE, OLIVER, *Author of* A Pictorial History of the American Indian

LAFFERTY, J. M., *Manager, General Physics Laboratory, Research and Development Center, General Electric Company*

LaFOLLETTE, Mrs. RUSSELL O., *Acting Librarian, Handley Library, Winchester, Va.*

LAFUENTE-FERRARI, ENRIQUE, *Author of* Breve historia de la pintura española

LA GRANGE, WALTER E., DVM, *University of Pennsylvania*

LAI, DAVID CHUENYAN, *Professor of Geography, University of Victoria, Canada*

LAIDLER, K. J., *Professor of Chemistry, University of Ottawa, Canada; Author of* The Chemical Elements

LAITMAN, CYNTHIA J., *Researcher, Department of Preventive Medicine, University of Wisconsin Medical School; Fellow, American Medical Writers Association; Editor of* World Health

LAM, TRUONG BUU, *History Department, University of Hawaii*

LAMB, HAROLD, *Author of* Alexander of Macedon: Journey to the World's End *and* New Found World

LAMB, I. MACKENZIE, *Director, Farlow Library and Herbarium, Harvard University; Coauthor of* Benthic Marine Algae of the Antarctic Peninsula

LAMB, ROBERT C., *Professor of Pomology, New York State Agricultural Experiment Station*

LAMBERT, RICHARD D., *Chairman, South Asia Regional Studies Department, University of Pennsylvania; President, American Academy of Political and Social Science; Author of* Factories, Workers and Social Change in India

LAMLEY, HARRY J., *Associate Professor of History, University of Hawaii*

LAMONT, BRIDGET LATER, *Director, Illinois State Library*

LAND, ROBERT H., *Chief, General Reference and Bibliography Division, Library of Congress*

LANDENBERGER, DONALD E., *Assistant Professor of Zoology, University of California at Los Angeles*

LANDER, E. M., JR., *Alumni Professor of History, Clemson University; Author of* A History of South Carolina, 1865–1960

LANDER, MAMIE, *Right Worthy Grand Secretary, Order of the Eastern Star*

LANDES, EDYTHE, *Librarian, Freehold Public Library*

LANDIS, PAUL H., *Professor of Sociology, Washington State University; Author of* Making the Most of Marriage *and* Your Marriage and Family Living

LANDREAU, ANTHONY N., *Curator of Education, Museum of Art, Carnegie Institute; Author of* America Underfoot: A History of Floor Coverings From Colonial Times to the Present; *Coauthor of* From the Bosporus to Samarkand: Flat-woven Rugs *and* Rugs Around the World

LANE, FERDINAND C., *Author of* The Story of Mountains, Earth's Grandest Rivers *and* World's Great Lakes

LANE, ROBERT F., *Librarian, Copiague (N.Y.) Memorial Public Library*

LANG, CECIL Y., *Professor of English, University of Virginia; Editor of* The Swinburne Letters

LANGBEIN, WALTER B., *Hydrologist, United States Geological Survey*

LANGDON, GEORGE D., JR., *Assistant Provost, Yale University; Author of* Pilgrim Colony: A History of New Plymouth, 1620–1691

LANGE, VICTOR, *Chairman, Department of Germanic Languages and Literatures, Princeton University; Author of* Modern German Literature

LANGENBACH, MICHAEL, *Assistant Professor, College of Education, University of Oklahoma*

LANGENHEIM, R. L., JR., *Professor of Geology, University of Illinois at Urbana*

LANGSTON, LAURA C., *Librarian, Centralia Public Library*

LANHAM, FRANK B., *Professor and Head, Department of Agricultural Engineering, University of Illinois*

LANSON, LUCIENNE, MD, *Author of* From Woman to Woman—A Gynecologist Answers Questions about You and Your Body

LANTOLF, JAMES P., *Associate Chair and Coordinator of Language Instruction, Department of Modern Languages and Linguistics, Cornell University; Author of* Vygotskyan Approaches to Second-Language Research; *Coeditor,* Journal of Applied Linguistics

LAPIDUS, IRA M., *Associate Professor of History, University of California at Berkeley*

LaPIERRE, WALTER, *Chief of Engineering Services, Diehl Division, Singer Company*

LaPLANTE, ALBERT A., JR., *Extension Entomologist, University of Hawaii*

LARDY, NICHOLAS R., *Professor of International Studies, Henry M. Jackson School of International Studies, University of Washington*

LARGE, DAVID C., *Warden and Lecturer in Geography, University of Reading, England*

LARIMORE, R. WELDON, *Aquatic Biologist, Illinois Natural History Survey*

LARNER, JOHN, *Director of Public Relations, Boston College*

LaROCCA, JOHN J., SJ, *Fordham University*

LARRICK, NANCY, *Author of* A Parent's Guide to Children's Reading

LARSEN, CARL W., *Director, Office of Public Relations, University of Chicago*

LARSEN, CHARLES E., *Professor of History, Mills College; Author of* The Good Fight: The Life and Times of Ben B. Lindsey

LARSEN, WILLIAM, *Professor of History, Radford College*

LARSON, ORVIN, *Chairman, Department of Speech and Theater, Brooklyn College; Author of* American Infidel: Robert G. Ingersoll

LARSON, RUSSELL G., *Editor of* Model Railroader Magazine

LARSON, T. A., *William R. Coe Distinguished Professor of American Studies, University of Wyoming; Author of* Wyoming's War Years: 1941–1945

LASH, JOSEPH P., *Author of* Eleanor and Franklin, Eleanor—The Years Alone, *and* Helen and Teacher: The Story of Helen Keller and Anne Sullivan Macy

LASLEY, M. M., *Associate Professor of Spanish, University of Florida*

LATHAM, J. G., *Chief Justice, High Court of Australia*

LATTIMORE, RICHMOND, *Professor of Greek, Department of Greek, Bryn Mawr College; Author of* Greek Lyrics

LATTIS, JAMES M., *University of Wisconsin at Madison*

LAUDAN, LAURENS L., *Director, Program in History and Philosophy of Science, University of Pittsburgh*

LAUN, H. CHARLES, *Assistant Professor of Biology, Stephens College*

LAURITIS, J. A., CSSP, *Duquesne University*

LAUVER, MAXINE, *Buchanan Public Library*

LAVER, JAMES, *Keeper of Prints and Drawings, Victoria and Albert Museum, London; Author of* Taste and Fashion *and* Costume in the Theatre

LAVERDURE, J. F. PAUL, *Research Associate, Faculty of Religious Studies, McGill University*

LAWNICZAK, LEROY J., *Librarian, Cicero Public Library*

LAWRENCE, GEORGE H., *Director, Hunt Botanical Library, Carnegie Institute of Technology; Author of* Introduction to Plant Taxonomy

LAWRENCE, NATHANIEL, *Massachusetts Professor of Philosophy, Williams College*

LAWRENCE, WILLIAM WITHERLE, *Author of* Medieval Story and the Beginnings of the Social Ideas of English-Speaking People

LAWREY, ROBERTA, *Librarian, Grand Island Public Library, Grand Island, Nebr.*

LAWSON, LT. COL. H. A. B., MVO, OSTJ, *Rothesay* Herald, *Scotland*

LAWSON, JAMES R., *Carillonneur, Riverside Church, New York City*

LAYTON, MARJORIE N., *Director, Long Branch Public Library, Long Branch, N.J.*

LEACOCK, ELEANOR, *Professor, Department of Anthropology, City College of New York, and Graduate Center, City University of New York; Author of* Teaching and Learning in City Schools; *Editor of* Culture and Poverty; *Coeditor of* North American Indians in Historical Perspective

LEAGANS, J. PAUL, *Professor of Extension Education, College of Agriculture, Cornell University*

LEAHEY, JOSEPH R., *Assistant Professor, Mercy College*

LEARMONTH, AGNES M., *Author of* Monsoon Asia *and Coauthor of* The Eastern Lands

LEARMONTH, ANDREW THOMAS AMOS, *Professor of Geography, Open University, England; Chairman, International Geographical Union Commission on Medical Geography; Coauthor of* India and Pakistan *and* The Eastern Lands

LEARNED, A. M., *Hobart and William Smith Colleges*

LEARY, LEWIS, *Kenan Professor of English, University of North Carolina; Author of* That Rascal Freneau

LEATHERS, JAMES A., *Director of Libraries, Mid-Continent Public Library Service, Independence, Mo.*

LEAVITT, JUDITH WALZER, *Associate Professor, Department of the History of Medicine, University of Wisconsin Center for Health Sciences, University of Wisconsin at Madison*

LEBEL, MAURICE, *Professor of Classical Greek; Former Dean, Faculty of the Humanities, Laval University, Canada*

LEBOEUF, MARCEL, *Public Relations Department, Laval University, Canada*

LEBRA, JOYCE C., *Professor of History, University of Colorado*

LE BUTT, KATHERINE, *Regional Librarian, York Regional Library, Fredericton, New Brunswick*

LECHEVALIER, HUBERT A., *Professor of Microbiology, Waksman Institute of Microbiology, Rutgers University; Coauthor of* Three Centuries of Microbiology; *Coeditor of* Handbook of Microbiology *and* The Microbes

LECKIE, WILLIAM H., *Vice President for Academic Affairs and Professor of History, University of Toledo; Author of* The Military Conquest of the Southwest Plains

LE CORBEILLER, CLARE, *Department of European Sculpture and Decorative Arts, Metropolitan Museum of Art*

LEDER, LAWRENCE H., *Professor of History, Lehigh University; Author of* The Glorious Revolution in America *and* Robert Livingston, 1654–1728, and the Politics of Colonial New York

LEDERBERG, JOSHUA, *President, The Rockefeller University; Nobel Prize Winner in Physiology or Medicine, 1958*

LEDERER, JEROME, *Adjunct Professor, Safety Institute, University of Southern California*

LEDERER, SUSAN E., *Department of the History of Science, University of Wisconsin at Madison*

LEE, DOROTHY C., *General Foods Kitchen*

LEE, THOMAS F., *Professor, Biology Department, St. Anselm College; Author of* Gene Future: The Promise and Perils of the New Biology

LEE, WEI-KUO, *Associate Professor of History, Georgetown University*

LEECH, CLIFFORD, *Professor of English, University College, University of Toronto, Canada; Author of* John Webster: A Critical Study *and* Webster: The Duchess of Malfi; *Editor of* Marlowe: A Collection of Critical Essays

LEEPER, G. W., *Associate Professor, School of Agricultural Chemistry, University of Melbourne, Australia*

LEEPSON, MARC, *Staff Writer, Editorial Research Reports*

LEES, JOSEPHINE T., *Coauthor of* Field Hockey

LEET, L. DON, *Chairman, Division of Geological Sciences, Harvard University; Author of* Earthquake Discoveries in Seismology

LEFFEL, ROBERT C., *Crops Research Division, U.S. Department of Agriculture*

LEFLER, HUGH T., *Kenan Professor of History, University of North Carolina; Author of* History of North Carolina

LEFTWICH, RICHARD H., *Regents Professor of Economics, Oklahoma State University; Author of* An Introduction to Economic Thinking

LEGAULT, ADRIAN R., *Chairman, Department of Civil Engineering, University of Nebraska*

LeGEAR, CLARA E., *Honorary Consultant in Historical Cartography, Geography and Map Division, Library of Congress*

LEHMANN, WINFRED P., *Ashbel Smith Professor and Chairman, Department of Linguistics, University of Texas; Author of* Historical Linguistics: An Introduction *and* Proto-Indo-European Phonology

LEHMANN-HAUPT, HELLMUT E., *Author of* The Life of the Book *and* Book in America

LEHRER, HENRY R., *Professor of Aeronautical Science, Embry-Riddle Aeronautical University*

LEICESTER, HENRY M., *Professor of Chemistry, University of the Pacific*

LEIDEN, CARL, *Professor of Government, University of Texas at Austin; Editor of* Conflict of Traditionalism and Modernism in the Muslim Middle East

LEIDTKE, WALTER, *Curator of European Paintings, Metropolitan Museum of Art*

LEIGHTON, ALBERT C., *Department of History, State University of New York, College at Oswego; Author of* Transportation and Communication in Early Medieval Europe

LEINBACH, THOMAS R., *Professor of Geography, University of Kentucky; Coauthor of* Development and Environment in Peninsular Malaysia

LEIREN, TERJE I., *Assistant Professor of Scandinavian Studies, University of Washington*

LEISER, ANDREW T., *Associate Professor of Environmental Horticulture, University of California at Davis*

LEISH, KENNETH, *Author of* The White House

LEITE, LAWRENCE A., *Professor of Art, George Washington University*

LEITH, EMMETT N., *Professor of Electrical Engineering, University of Michigan*

LEITH, JOHN H., *Pemberton Professor of Theology, Union Theological Seminary in Virginia; Author of* An Introduction to the Reformed Tradition

LELLINGER, DAVID B., *Associate Curator, Division of Ferns, U.S. National Museum, Smithsonian Institution*

LE MAISTRE, CHARLES A., MD, *President, University of Texas System Cancer Center*

LEMARCHAND, RENÉ, *Professor of Political Science, University of Florida; Author of* Rwanda and Burundi

LEMCO, JONATHAN, *Director, Canadian-American Committee, National Planning Association; Author of* Turmoil in the Peaceable Kingdom: The Quebec Sovereignty Movement and Its Implications for Canada and the United States; *Managing Editor,* Canada–U.S. Outlook

LEMMON, RICHARD M., *Associate Director, Laboratory of Chemical Biodynamics, Lawrence Berkeley Laboratory, Berkeley, Calif.*

LEMMON, SARAH M., *Professor of History and Political Science, Meredith College*

LEMON, CLYDE D., *President, National Greyhound Association*

LeNEVEU, ALLAN H., *Chief, Census Analysis Section, Statistics Canada*

LENZER, GERTRUD, *Associate Professor of Sociology, Brooklyn College*

LEONARD, BILL J., *Professor and Chair, Department of Religious Philosophy, Samford University; Author of* God's Last and Only Hope: The Fragmentation of the Southern Baptist Convention

LEONARD, LEROY E., *Alaskan Dog Mushers Association*

LEONHARD, PHILIP J., *Lecturer in Sociology, City College of New York*

LERCHE, CHARLES O., JR., *Author of* Foreign Policy of the American People

LERNER, M. E., *Editor,* Rubber Age

LESKO, LEONARD H., *Professor of Egyptology, University of California at Berkeley; Author of* The Ancient Egyptian Book of Two Ways, Glossary of the Late Ramesside Letters, *and* King Tut's Wine Cellar

LESSA, WILLIAM A., *Professor of Anthropology, University of California at Los Angeles; Author of* Ulithian Personality *and* Tales From Ulithi Atoll; *Coauthor of* Reader in Comparative Religion

LE TOURNEAU, ROGER, *Author of* Fez in the Age of the Marinides

LEVACK, A. PAUL, *Professor of History, Fordham University; Coauthor of* Burke's Politics *and* A History of the United States

LEVERING, MARY BERGHAUS, *Executive Director, Federal Library and Information Center Committee*

LE VINE, VICTOR T., *Professor of Political Science, Washington University, St. Louis, Mo.; Author of* Generational Conflict and Elites in French-Speaking Africa, The Cameroons from Mandate to Independence, *and* The Cameroon Federal Republic

LEVIN, NATHAN R., *Assistant Librarian, Chicago Public Library*

LEVIN, NORTON M., DO, *Director of Laboratories, Metropolitan Hospital, Central Division, Philadelphia, Pa.*

LEVINE, ALAN H., *Staff Counsel, New York Civil Liberties Union*

LEVINE, ERWIN L., *Professor of Government, Skidmore College; Author of* Theodore Francis Green: The Rhode Island Years, 1906–1936

LEVINE, LOUIS, *Professor of Biology, City College of New York; Author of* Biology of the Gene *and* Biology for a Modern Society

LEVINE, RUTH R., *Division of Medical and Dental Sciences, Boston University School of Medicine*

LEVITT, I. M., *Director, Fels Planetarium, Philadelphia, Pa.*

LEVITT, MORTON P., *Author of* The Cretan Glance: The World and Art of Nikos Kazantzakis

LEVY, MATTHYS, *Associate Professor, Department of Architecture, Columbia University*

LEVY, ROBERT I., MD, *Dean, School of Medicine, Tufts University*

LEWINE, MILTON, *Professor of Art History, Columbia University*

LEWIS, ANTHONY, *New York Times; Author of* Gideon's Trumpet

LEWIS, DOUGLAS, *Curator of Sculpture, National Gallery of Art, Washington, D.C.; Author of* The Villa Cornaro at Piombino *(Volume 9 of* Corpus Palladianum *series)*

LEWIS, FRANK M., *Professor of Political Science, University of Toledo*

LEWIS, GEOFFREY L., *Faculty Fellow of St. Antony's College, University of Oxford; Author of* Modern Turkey *and* The Atatürk I Knew

LEWIS, JOHN D., *Professor of Government, Oberlin College; Author of* Against the Tyrant: Tradition and Theory of Tyrannicide

LEWIS, LLOYD H., JR., *Reporter, Norfolk* Ledger-Star

LEWIS, MYRON E., JR., *Associate Director, Industrial Arts Education Division, State University College at Buffalo*

LEWIS, NORMAN, *Chairman, U.S. Olympic Fencing Committee; Captain, USA Olympic Team, 1968; Former President, Amateur Fencers League of America*

LEWIS, OSCAR, *Author of* San Francisco: A History *and* San Francisco: From Mission to Metropolis

LEWIS, PAUL H., *Professor of History, Newcomb College, Tulane University; Author of* Paraguay Under Stroessner *and* The Politics of Exile: Paraguay's Febrerista Party

LEWIS, WALKER, *Member of the Maryland Bar; Author of* Without Fear or Favor: A Biography of Chief Justice Roger Brooke Taney

LEWIS, WAYNE C., *U.S. Department of Agriculture, Forest Products Laboratory, Madison, Wis.*

LEWONTIN, R. C., *Alexander Agassiz Professor of Zoology and Professor of Biology, Harvard University*

LEWTHWAITE, GORDON R., *Professor of Geography, San Fernando Valley State University at Northridge*

LEYHAUSEN, PAUL, *Director of Research, Wuppertal Branch, Max-Planck-Institut für Verhaltensphysiologie; Author of* Verhaltensstudien an Katzen

LEYS, COLIN T., *Professor of Politics, University of Sussex, England; Coauthor of* A New Deal in Central Africa

LIANG SSU-CHOENG, *Fellow, Academia Sinica, Peking*

LIBBY, VIOLET K., *Author of* Henry Dunant

LIBRACH, JAN, *Author of* The Rise of the Soviet Empire

LICHINE, ALEXIS, *Author of* Encyclopedia of Wines and Spirits

LICHTENWANGER, WILLIAM, *Head, Reference Section, Music Division, Library of Congress*

LIDDELL HART, B. H., *Author of* The British Way in Warfare

LIDDICOAT, RICHARD T., JR., *Director, Gemological Institute of America*

LIDTKE, VERNON L., *Professor of History, Johns Hopkins University*

LIEB, FREDERICK G., *Author of* The Story of the World Series

LIEBENOW, J. GUS, *Professor and Chairman of African Studies, Indiana University; Author of* Liberia: The Evolution of Privilege

LIEBESKIND, HERBERT, *Professor of Chemistry, Cooper Union*

LIEDTKE, WALTER, *Curator of European Paintings, Metropolitan Museum of Art*

LIEGL, BERYL R., *Librarian, Emporia Public Library, Emporia, Kans.*

LIER, FRANK G., *Professor of Botany, Columbia University*

LIGHT, ALBERT, *Professor, Department of Chemistry, Purdue University; Author of* Proteins: Structure and Function

LIGHTBOWN, R. W., *Assistant Keeper, Department of Metalwork, Victoria and Albert Museum, London*

LILLEHOJ, ELIZABETH, *Assistant Professor of Art History, DePaul University*

LILLYMAN, WILLIAM J., *Professor of German, University of California at Irvine; Author of* Otto Ludwig's Zwischen Himmel und Erde: A Study of Its Artistic Structure

LINCOLN, C. ERIC, *Adjunct Professor of Religion, Vanderbilt University; President, Black Academy of Arts and Letters; Author of* Black Muslims in America, My Face is Black, *and* Is Anybody Listening to Black America?

LINCOLN, PHILIP A., *Technical Information Department, Research Laboratories, General Motors Corp.*

LINDAHL, MAC, *Associate Editor, Swedish North Star*

LINDBERG, DAVID C., *Evjue-Bascom Professor of the History of Science, University of Wisconsin at Madison; Author of* John Pecham and the Science of Optics

LINDBERG, ROY A., *Professor, Department of Mechanical Engineering, University of Wisconsin; Author of* Processes and Materials of Manufacture

LINDER, GEORGE R., *Director, Durham City-County Public Library*

LINDEROTH, RUTH W., *Librarian, Woodbury Public Library*

LINDGREN, RAYMOND E., *Professor of History and Dean of College, California State College at Long Beach; Author of* Norway-Sweden: Union, Disunion, and Scandinavian Integration

LINDSAY, R. BRUCE, *Professor of Physics, Brown University; Author of* The Role of Science in Civilization *and* Basic Concepts of Physics

LINDSEY, DAVID, *Professor of History, California State University at Los Angeles; Author of* 'Sunset Cox,' Irrepressible Democrat

LINFORD, HENRY B., *Professor of Chemical Engineering, Columbia University*

LINGG, ANN M., *Author of* Mozart, Genius of Harmony *and* Mephisto Waltz: The Story of Franz Liszt

LINGLE, JOHN C., *Supervisor, Biological Science Research Center, Shell Development Co.*

LINK, ARTHUR S., *Edwards Professor of History and Director of the Woodrow Wilson Papers, Princeton University; Author of* Woodrow Wilson

LINTON, GEORGE E., *Author of* Applied Basic Textiles

LINZ, SUSAN J., *Associate Professor of Economics, Michigan State University*

LIPINSKY, LINO S., *Curator of History, John Jay Homestead, Katonah, N.Y.*

LIPPITT, CHARLES WARREN, *President-General, Society of the Cincinnati*

LIPSCOMB, STEPHANIE, *Research Associate, Art Institute of Chicago, and Contributor to* Julia Margaret Cameron's Women

LIPTON, LAWRENCE, *Professor of Comparative Literature, American College in Jerusalem; Author of* The Holy Barbarians

LIPTZIN, SOL, *Author of* The Flowering of Yiddish Literature, A Historical Survey of German Literature, *and* Arthur Schnitzler

LISKER, LEIGH, *Professor of Linguistics, University of Pennsylvania; Author of* Introduction to Spoken Telugu

LISTER, EUGENE C., *Chief Electrical Engineer, Stanley Consultants, Inc.*

LITTLE, ELBERT L., JR., *Dendrologist, Forest Service, U.S. Department of Agriculture*

LITTLE, LEILA H., *Assistant Manager of Public Relations, Dictaphone Corporation*

LITTLE, MICHAEL A., *Professor of Anthropology, State University of New York at Binghamton; Coeditor of* Human Population Biology *and* Man in the Andes

LITWACK, LEON, *Professor of History, University of California at Berkeley; Author of* North of Slavery: The Negro in the Free States, 1790–1860

LIU, JAMES T. C., *Professor of Oriental Studies and History, Princeton University; Author of* Reform in Sung China

LIVINGOOD, JAMES W., *Distinguished University Professor, University of Tennessee at Chattanooga; Coauthor of* The Chattanooga Country: From Tomahawks to TVA

LIVINGSTON, WILLIAM S., *Professor of Government, University of Texas; Author of* Federalism and Constitutional Change

LIVINGSTONE, WILLIAM, *Editor, Stereo Review*

LLOYD, CHARLES W., MD, *Professor of Clinical Psychiatry and Codirector of the Center for the Study of Human Sexual Behavior, University of Pittsburgh*

LO, LORENZO, *Director, Board of Directors, St. John's University, Shanghai*

LOACH, JENNIFER, *Research Fellow, Somerville College, Oxford University*

LOADES, DAVID M., *Reader in History, University of Durham; Author of* The Reign of Mary Tudor, Politics and the Nation, The Oxford Martyrs, *and* The Tudor Conspiracies; *Editor of* The Papers of George Wyatt

LO BUE, VELIA, *Acting Head Librarian, Chicago Heights Free Public Library*

LOCHHEAD, JOHN H., *Professor of Zoology, University of Vermont; Coauthor of* Selected Invertebrate Types *and* The Physiology of Crustacea

LOCKHART, HELEN D., *Director, Shiloh Regional Library Center, Tenn.*

LOCKHART, L. W., *Assistant Director, Orthological Institute; Author of* The Basic Teacher

LOCKSPEISER, EDWARD, *Author of* Debussy: His Life and Mind

LOETSCHER, LEFFERTS A., *Author of* A Brief History of the Presbyterians

LOEW, FRANKLIN M., DVM, *Henry and Lois Foster Professor of Comparative Medicine and Dean, Tufts University School of Veterinary Medicine*

LOFTNESS, ROBERT L., *Director, Washington Office, Electric Power Research Institute; Author of* Nuclear Power Plants; Design, Operating Experience and Economics

LOGAN, BYRON E., *Associate Professor of Geography, Miami University, Ohio*

LOGAN, RAYFORD W., *Professor of History, Howard University; Author of* Haiti and the Dominican Republic *and* The Negro in the United States

LOGAN, WILLIAM B., *President, Webber College; Coauthor of* Vocational Education in Rural America

LOGSDON, JOSEPH, *Associate Professor of History, Louisiana State University at New Orleans*

LOMASK, MILTON, *Author of* Andrew Johnson: President on Trial

LOMAX, ALAN, *Coeditor and Compiler,* American Ballads and Folk Songs, Negro Folk Songs, *and* Our Singing Country

LONG, CHARLES H., *William Rand Kenan, Jr., Professor of History of Religions, University of North Carolina at Chapel Hill; Author of* Alpha, the Myths of Creation

LONG, CYRIL N. H., *Sterling Professor of Physiology and Chairman of the Department of Physiology, School of Medicine, Yale University*

LONG, DONALD, *Honeywell Corporate Research Center, Author of* Energy Bands in Semiconductors

LONG, E. B., *Director of Research, Bruce Catton's Centennial History of the Civil War*

LONG, HAROLD M., *Trustee, Crandall Library, Glens Falls, N.Y.; Coauthor of* Improving the Teaching of World Affairs: The Glens Falls Story

LONG, JOHN C., *Staff Writer and Saturday City Editor, Courier-Journal, Louisville, Ky.*

LONGENECKER, HERBERT E., *President, Tulane University of Louisiana*

LONGLEY, LAWRENCE D., *Assistant Professor of Government, Lawrence University*

LONGRIGG, STEPHEN H., *Author of* Four Centuries of Modern Iraq *and* The Middle East: A Social Geography

LOOFBOUROW, JOHN W., *Author of* Thackeray and the Form of Fiction

LOOKATCH, RICHARD P., *Instructional Designer, Agency for Instructional Technology, Bloomington, Ind.*

LOOMIS, LOUISE, *Beaumont Library Commission*

LOOMIS, TED A., MD, *Professor of Pharmacology and State Toxicologist, University of Washington; Author of Essentials of Toxicology*

LÓPES-DE-SILANES, FLORENCIO, *Assistant Professor of Public Policy, John F. Kennedy School of Government, Harvard University*

LOPEZ, ROBERT S., *Sterling Professor Emeritus of History, Yale University*

LORANT, STEFAN, *Author of The Presidency, a Pictorial History of Presidential Elections from Washington to Truman*

LORDI, GEORGE M., MD, *Professor of Medicine, University of Medicine and Dentistry of New Jersey*

LORINCZ, ALLAN L., MD, *Professor of Dermatology, University of Chicago*

LORWIN, LEWIS L., *Research Consultant to the New School for Social Research*

LOSS, LOUIS, *William Nelson Cromwell Professor of Law, Harvard University; Author of Securities Regulation*

LOTEN, H. STANLEY, *Member, Royal Architectural Institute of Canada*

LOVELL, SIR A. C. BERNARD, *Professor of Radio Astronomy, University of Manchester; Director of the Nuffield Radio Astronomy Laboratories, Jodrell Bank, England*

LOVEMAN, BRIAN, *Department of Political Science, San Diego State University; Author of Chile: The Legacy of Hispanic Capitalism*

LOVESEY, JOHN, *Sports Features Editor, Sunday Times, London*

LOW, CURTIS R., *Major General, Assistant Chief of Staff for Reserve Forces, U.S. Air Force*

LOW, DAVID, *Author of British Cartoonists*

LOWELL, CHRISTINE, *Librarian, Walker Memorial Library, Westbrook, Maine*

LOWENHAUPT, WARREN H., *Curator of Bookplates, Yale University Library*

LOWENHEIM, FREDERICK A., *Technical Editor, Plating (Journal of the American Electroplaters' Society); Consultant*

LOWENSTEIN, EDITH, *Attorney at Law; American Council for Nationalities Services; Director of the Study, The Alien and the Immigration Law*

LOWENTHAL, DAVID, *Wheaton College, Mass.*

LOWENTHAL, RUDOLF, *Author of Turkic Language and Literature of Central Asia*

LOWITT, BRUCE, *Coauthor of A Century of Champions*

LOWRANCE, E. W., *Professor of Anatomy, School of Medicine, University of Missouri*

LUBBOCK, F. J., *Pye TVT Limited, Cambridge, England*

LUBEROFF, BENJAMIN J., *Editor, Chemtech*

LUBIC, RUTH WATSON, *General Director, Maternity Center Association, New York City; Author of Nurse-Midwifery in Context*

LUBOWE, IRWIN I., *Clinical Professor of Dermatology, New York Medical College, Metropolitan Hospital Center*

LUBRANO, LINDA L., *Associate Professor, School of International Service, The American University; Author of Soviet Sociology of Science*

LUCAS, CHARLES E., *Public Affairs Officer, Department of Veterans Affairs*

LUCIE-SMITH, EDWARD, *Author of Late Modern: The Visual Arts Since 1945 and A Concise History of French Painting*

LUCK, GEORG, *Professor Emeritus of Classics, Johns Hopkins University*

LUCKENBACH, EDGAR F., JR., *President and Chairman of the Board, Luckenbach Steamship Co., Inc., New York City*

LUDLUM, DAVID, *Historian, American Meterological Society; Author of History of American Weather and County Journal New England Weather Book*

LUDWIG, RICHARD M., *Professor of English, Princeton University; Coeditor of Guide to American Literature Since 1890 and Literary History of the United States*

LUEBKE, FREDERICK C., *Charles Mach Professor of History, University of Nebraska at Lincoln*

LUFBURROW, ROBERT A., *Associate Professor of Physics, St. Lawrence University*

LUFT, JOHN N., *Manager, Federal Crop Insurance Corporation, U.S. Department of Agriculture*

LULING, VIRGINIA, *Author of A Somali Sultanate*

LUNAN, KENNETH D., *Senior Research Scientist, Stanford Research Institute, Menlo Park, Calif.*

LUND, PATRICIA, *Department of Biochemistry, Oxford University*

LUNN, GEORGIA M., *Librarian, Waverly Free Library*

LUNT, JAMES D., *Major-General, British Army; Author of Charge to Glory and Scarlet Lancer*

LURCH, E. NORMAN, *Associate Professor of Electronics, State University of New York Agricultural and Technical College at Farmingdale*

LURIE, MELVIN, *Professor of Economics, University of Wisconsin at Milwaukee*

LUSHINGTON, NOLAN, *Director, Greenwich Library*

LUSKY, LOUIS, *Professor of Law, Columbia University*

LUSTENBERGER, ANITA, *Secretary, Gordon Setter Club of America, Inc.*

LUTHER, KENNETH A., *Professor of Persian Studies, University of Michigan*

LUTHIN, JAMES N., *Professor of Water Science and Civil Engineering, University of California at Davis; Author of Drainage Engineering; Editor of Drainage of Agricultural Lands*

LUTIN, MARK, *Manager, Public Relations, Boys Club of America*

LUTZ, ALMA, *Author of Emma Willard: Pioneer Educator of American Women*

LUTZ, ELLEN L., *Adjunct Associate Professor of Law, Fletcher School of Law and Diplomacy, Tufts University*

LUXTON, HILARIE LYNNE, EdD, *Consultant in Rehabilitation and Independent Living; Rehabilitation Teacher of Blind Adults*

LUYKX, PETER, *Associate Professor of Cytology, University of Miami at Coral Gables*

LYELL, WILLIAM A., *Department of Asian Languages, Stanford University; Author of L. U. Hsun's Vision of Reality; Translator of Lao She's Mao-ch'eng chi (Cat Country)*

LYNCH, CYPRIAN J., OFM, *Assistant Professor of History, Siena College*

LYNCH, DONALD F., *Professor of Geography, University of Alaska at Fairbanks*

LYNCH, EDWARD W., *Librarian, Waukesha Public Library*

LYNCH, JOHN E., CSP, *Professor of Medieval History and the History of Canon Law, Catholic University of America*

LYNE, A. G., *Principal Research Scientist, Commonwealth Scientific and Industrial Research Organization, Australia; Author of Marsupials and Monotremes of Australia*

LYNN, ROBERT W., *Professor of Religious Education, Union Theological Seminary*

LYON, BRYCE, *Barnaby Conrad and Mary Critchfield Keeney Professor of History, Brown University*

LYON, DOROTHY, *Head Librarian, St. Lucie-Okeechobee Regional Library, Fort Pierce, Fla.*

LYON, E. WILSON, *President, Pomona College; Author of Louisiana in French Diplomacy, 1759–1804 and The Man Who Sold Louisiana; The Life of François Barbé-Marbois*

LYONS, DEBORAH, *Senior Editor, Practical Horseman Magazine*

LYSTAD, ROBERT A., *Professor of African Studies, School of Advanced International Studies, Johns Hopkins University; Author of The Ashanti: A Proud People and The African World: A Survey of Social Research*

MAARENEN, STEVEN A., *Assistant Professor of Political Science, Claremont Men's College*

MAC ADAM, ALFRED, *Professor of Latin American Literature, Barnard College–Columbia University*

MacAODHA, BREANDÁN S., *Professor of Geography, University College, Galway, Ireland*

MACARTNEY, C. A., *Author of Hungary: A Short History*

MACAULAY, NEILL, *Professor of History, University of Florida; Author of The Sandino Affair, A Rebel in Cuba, and The Prestes Column*

MACBETH, DANIELLE, *Department of Philosophy, Haverford College*

MAC CANA, PROINSIAS, *Professor of Early Irish Language and Literature, University College, Dublin*

MacCOLLUM, DONALD W., MD, *Assistant Professor of Surgery, Harvard Medical School; Senior Surgeon, Children's Medical Center, Boston*

MacDONALD, CHARLES B., *Deputy Chief Historian, Department of the Army; Author of* The Siegfried Line Campaign, The Last Offensive, *and* The Mighty Endeavor

MacDONALD, H. A., *Professor of Agronomy, Cornell University*

MacDONALD, JAMES C., *Editor,* The Blade, *Toledo, Ohio*

MacDONALD, SEBASTIAN, CP, *Vice Provincial, Passionist Provincial Office, Holy Cross Province*

MacFARLAND, LOIS, *Acting Assistant Director of University Relations, City University of New York*

MacGREGOR, GEDDES, *Distinguished Professor of Philosophy, University of Southern California; Author of* The Tichborne Impostor

MACHOVER, MAURICE, *Associate Professor of Mathematics, St. John's University*

MacINTYRE, ANGUS D., *Tutor in Modern History, Magdalen College, Oxford University*

MACIOR, LAZARUS W., *Professor of Biology, University of Akron*

MACK, JAMES D., *Director of Libraries, Lehigh University; Author of* Matthew Flinders, 1774–1814

MACK, MARY PETER, *Author of* Jeremy Bentham: An Odyssey of Ideas

MACK SMITH, D., *Senior Research Fellow of All Souls College, Oxford University; Author of* Mussolini *and* Mussolini's Roman Empire

MACKALL, LAWTON, *Author of* Knife and Fork in New York *and Coauthor of* The Restaurateur's Handbook

MACKAY-SMITH, A., *Editor of* The Chronicle of the Horse; *Author of* The American Foxhound

MacKENNA, R. O., *University Librarian and Keeper of the Hunterian Books and Manuscripts, University of Glasgow, Scotland*

MacKENZIE, DAVID, *Professor of History, University of North Carolina at Greensboro*

MacKENZIE, R. A. F., SJ, *Regis College, Canada*

MACKERNESS, ERIC D., *Reader in English Literature, University of Sheffield, England; Author of* A Social History of English Music

MacKINNEY, LOREN C., *Author of* The Medieval World

MacKINNON, FRANK, *Professor of Political Science, University of Calgary, Alberta, Canada; Author of* The Government of Prince Edward Island

MacLEAN, R. A., *Chairman, Department of History, St. Francis Xavier University, Antigonish, Canada*

MacLENNAN, CAROL A., *Professor of Political Science and Technology, Michigan Technological University; Coeditor of* The State and Democracy: Revitalizing America's Government

MACLINN, WALTER A., *Director, New Jersey Agricultural Experiment Station and Professor of Food Science, Rutgers University*

MacMASTERS, MAJEL M., *Professor of Flour and Feed Milling Industries, Kansas State University*

MacMILLAN, DOUGALD, *Kenan Professor of English, University of North Carolina; Coeditor of* Plays of the Restoration and Eighteenth Century

MacMILLAN, KEITH, *Executive Secretary, Canadian Music Centre; Editor of* MUSICANADA

MacNUTT, W. S., *Professor of History, University of New Brunswick, Canada; Author of* New Brunswick: A History

MACQUARRIE, JOHN, *Lady Margaret Professor of Divinity, Oxford University*

MACQUEEN, JAMES G., *Lecturer in Classics, University of Bristol, England; Author of* Babylon

MacRAE, DESMOND, *Lecturer, Frick Collection, New York*

MADDEN, RICHARD, *Professor, San Diego State College; Coauthor of the Stanford Achievement Test*

MADDEN, WILLIAM A., *Professor of English, University of Minnesota*

MADES, LEONARD, *Professor of Romance Languages, Hunter College; Author of* The Armor and the Brocade: A Study of Don Quixote and The Courtier

MADISON, CHARLES A., *Author of* Book Publishing in America

MADISON, KENNETH G., *Assistant Professor of History, Iowa State University*

MAGALONI, ANA MARÍA, *Director General of Libraries, Mexico*

MAGARSHACK, DAVID, *Author of* Chekhov: A Life *and* Dostoevsky

MAGNARELLI, SHARON D., *Professor of Spanish and Chair, Department of Foreign Languages, Albertus Magnus College; Author of* Understanding José Donoso

MAGNUS, SIR PHILIP, *Author of* Gladstone: A Biography

MAGNUS, RALPH, *Assistant Professor of Political Science, California State University at Northridge*

MAGUIRE, ROBERT A., *Professor of Russian Literature and Chairman, Department of Slavic Languages, Columbia University; Author of* Red Virgin Soil: Soviet Literature in the 1920's

MAHENDRA, BENI CHARAN, *President, Academy of Zoology; Director, Institute of Zoology, Agra, India*

MAHON, KATHARINE A., *Public Relations Director, Girls Clubs of America*

MAHONEY, MICHAEL S., *Professor of History, Princeton University*

MAIER, CHARLES S., *Lecturer on History, Harvard University; Author of* The Thirteenth of May: The Advent of de Gaulle's Republic

MAIURI, AMEDEO, *Director of Excavations at Pompeii; Author of* Pompeiian Wall Paintings *and* Pompeii

MAJCHRZAK, COLMAN J., OFM, *Professor of Philosophy, Holy Redeemer College, Wis.; Author of* A Brief History of Bonaventurianism

MAJDALANY, FRED, *Author of* The Battle of El Alamein

MAJUMDAR, R. C., *Vice-Chancellor, University of Dacca, Bangladesh; General Editor of* History and Culture of the Indian People; *Coauthor of* An Advanced History of India

MAKSIMOVICH, BOZIDAR Z., *Yugoslav Cabinet Minister of Education*

MALCOLM, LYDIA S., *Librarian, Henderson Public Library*

MALEFAKIS, EDWARD E., *Professor of History, Columbia University; Author of* Agrarian Reform and Peasant Revolution in Spain: Origins of the Civil War

MALEFIJT, ANNEMARIE DE WAAL, *Professor of Anthropology, Hunter College*

MALINO, JEROME R., *Rabbi Emeritus, United Jewish Center, Danbury, Conn.*

MALINOWSKI, ZENON S., *Professor of Industrial Administration, University of Connecticut*

MALIVER, BRUCE L., *Postgraduate Center for Mental Health, New York City*

MALLAMUD, JONATHAN, *Assistant Professor, Rutgers University School of Law*

MALLORY, J. R., *Professor of Political Science and Chairman, Department of Economics and Political Science, McGill University, Canada*

MALMSTRÖM, VINCENT H., *Professor of Geography, Dartmouth College; Author of* Geography of Europe: A Regional Analysis

MALONE, DUMAS, *Author of* Jefferson and His Time

MALONEY, FRANK E., *Professor of Law, University of Florida; Coauthor of* Materials on the Legal Profession and Legal Ethics

MALONEY, GEORGE A., SJ, *Associate Professor of Theology, John XXIII Center, Fordham University; Author of* Image and Likeness of God in Man

MANCHESTER, DOROTHY A., *Librarian, Bristol Public Library*

MANCHESTER, LORNE, *Associate Editor of* The Legionary

MANDEL, LUDWIG, *Member of the New York Bar*

MANDELBAUM, BERNARD, *Professor of English, Bronx Community College*

MANN, ROBERT, *First Violinist, Juilliard Quartet*

MANN, VIVIAN B., *Curator of Judaica, Jewish Museum, New York City*

MANNER, GEORGE, *Associate Professor, Department of Political Science, University of Illinois*

MANNHEIM, L. A., *Author of* How to Use Your Exposure Meter

MANNING, BAYLESS, *Dean, Stanford University School of Law; Author of* Conflict of Interest and Federal Service *and* Federal Conflict of Interest Law

MANNING, KATHRYN, *Director, Irving Municipal Library*

MANNING, RAYMOND, *Curator, Division of Crustacea, Smithsonian Institution*

MANNING, THOMAS, *Department of History, Texas Tech University; Author of* Government in Science: The U.S. Geological Survey, 1867–1894

MANORE, JEAN L., *History Department, University of Ottawa*

MANSCHRECK, CLYDE L., *Author of* Melanchthon: The Quiet Reformer

MANSFIELD, HARVEY C., JR., *Professor of Government, Harvard University*

MANSON, D. VINCENT, *Assistant Curator of Mineralogy, American Museum of Natural History*

MANVELL, ROGER, *Author of* The Animated Film, This Age of Communication, *and* The Film and the Public

MAPP, ERWIN, *Director, Jackson Municipal Library*

MARAMOROSCH, KARL, *Professor of Microbiology, Rutgers University*

MARCH, ANDREW L., *Visiting Assistant Professor of Geography and China Humanities, University of Denver*

MARCHAM, FREDERICK G., *Professor of English History, Cornell University; Author of* History of England

MARCHAND, LESLIE A., *Professor of English, Rutgers University; Author of* Byron: A Biography

MARCHANT, ALEXANDER, *Professor of History, Vanderbilt University*

MARCO, GUY A., *Senior Fellow and Adjunct Professor, Graduate School of Library and Information Science, Rosary College*

MARCOPOULOS, GEORGE J., *Associate Professor of History, Tufts University*

MARCUM, JOHN A., *Professor of Politics, University of California at Santa Cruz; Author of* The Angolan Revolution

MARCUS, EDWARD, *Professor of Economics, Brooklyn College; Coauthor of* Investment and Development Possibilities in Tropical Africa

MARCUS, GEOFFREY J., *Naval Historian; Author of* The Maiden Voyage *and* The Age of Nelson

MARCUS, GEORGE E., *Professor and Chair, Department of Anthropology, Rice University; Coauthor of* Anthropology as Cultural Critique

MARCUS, HAROLD G., *Associate Professor of History, Michigan State University; Author of* The Life and Times of Menilek II of Ethiopia

MARCUS, JOSEPH, *Billiards Editor, New York* Post

MARCUS, MILDRED RENDL, *Professor of Economics, Manhattan Community College; Coauthor of* Investment and Development Possibilities in Tropical Africa

MARCUSE, HERBERT, *Professor of Philosophy, University of California at San Diego*

MARDER, ELISSA, *Professor of French, George Washington University*

MARDER, PHILL, *Managing Editor,* The Ring *magazine*

MARGOLIS, OTTO, *Executive Secretary, National Association of Colleges of Mortuary Science, and Dean, American Academy McAllister Institute of Funeral Service*

MARION, JERRY B., *Professor of Physics, University of Maryland*

MARK, CARSON, *Former Division Leader, Theoretical Division, Los Alamos Scientific Laboratory, Los Alamos, N.Mex.*

MARKE, JULIUS J., *Professor of Law, Law Librarian, New York University; Author of* Vignettes of Legal History

MARKHAM, ROBERT P., *Special Secretary, Translations Department, American Bible Society; Coauthor of* An Introduction to the Bible Societies' Greek New Testament

MARKOW, JACK, *Author of* Cartoonist's and Gag Writer's Handbook

MARKOWITZ, WILLIAM, *Adjunct Professor, Nova University; Editor of* Geophysical Survey

MARKS, ELAINE, *Associate Professor of French, University of Wisconsin; Author of* Colette

MARKS, JONATHAN, *Literary Manager, Yale Repertory Theatre; Department of Drama, Yale University*

MARKS, ROBERT J., *Director, Lebanon Community Library, Lebanon, Pa.*

MARLOWE, DEREK, *Author of* A Dandy in Aspic

MARPLE, WESLEY W., JR., *Professor of Business Administration, Northeastern University*

MARQUIS, ROLLIN P., *City Librarian, Dearborn, Mich.*

MARR, WARREN, II, *American Missionary Association*

MARRARO, HOWARD R., *Author of* American Opinion on Unification of Italy, 1846–1861

MARROCCO, W. THOMAS, *Professor of Music, University of California at Los Angeles; Coauthor of* Music in the United States

MARSAK, LEONARD M., *Professor of History, University of California at Santa Barbara; Author of* Bernard Fontenelle: The Idea of Science in the French Enlightenment

MARSDEN, BRIAN G., *Astronomer, Smithsonian Astrophysical Observatory*

MARSH, ROBERT C., *Author of* Toscanini and the Art of Orchestral Performance

MARSHALL, HAROLD G., *U.S. Department of Agriculture*

MARSHALL, JOHN DAVID, *University Librarian, Middle Tennessee State University; Editor of* Books-Libraries-Librarians

MARSHALL, P. J., *Lecturer in History, Kings College, London; Author of* The Impeachment of Warren Hastings

MARSHALL, RODERICK, *Professor of English, Brooklyn College; Author of* Passage to More Than India

MARSTON, EDWIN H., *Associate Professor of Physics, Queens College*

MARTELL, EDWARD, *National Center for Atmospheric Research*

MARTIN, ALBRO, *Lecturer in Business History, Harvard University; Editor of* Business History Review; *Author of* James J. Hill and the Opening of the Northwest *and* Enterprise Denied: Origins of the Decline of American Railroads, 1897–1917

MARTIN, CHARLES E., *Professor of International Law and Political Science, Director of the Institute of International Affairs, University of Washington; Author of* Regionalism in International Law and Organization

MARTIN, J. E., *Tassel Reader in Economic Geography, London School of Economics and Political Science, University of London*

MARTIN, JAY, *Professor of English and Comparative Culture, University of California at Irvine; Author of* Robert Lowell

MARTIN, JOSEPH B., *Assistant in the Office of the President, Duke University*

MARTIN, LAURENCE W., *Author of* Diplomacy in Modern European History

MARTÍN, MIGUEL A., *Author of* España entre Inglaterra y Francia *and* Civilización

MARTIN, NIALL, *Department of the History and Philosophy of Science, University College, London*

MARTIN, RICHARD, *Curator, Costume Institute, Metropolitan Museum of Art*

MARTIN, ROBERT E., *Professor of Political Science and Associate Dean, College of Liberal Arts, Howard University; Author of* Negro Disenfranchisement in Virginia

MARTIN, S. WALTER, *President, Valdosta State College; Author of* Florida During the Territorial Days *and* Florida's Flagler

MARTY, MARTIN E., *Fairfax M. Cone Distinguished Service Professor of the History of Modern Christianity, Divinity School, University of Chicago*

MARTZ, JOHN D., *Professor of Political Science and Associate Director of Institute of Latin American Studies, University of North Carolina; Author of* Columbia: A Contemporary Political Survey

MARVIN, JAMES C., *Librarian, Topeka Public Library*

MARVIN, JOHN T., *Judge, American Kennel Club; Author of* The Book of All Terriers

MASON, ALPHEUS T., *McCormick Professor of Jurisprudence, Princeton University; Author of* Brandeis: A Free Man's Life

MASON, BRIAN H., *Department of Mineral Sciences, Smithsonian Institution; Coauthor of* Elements of Mineralogy

MASON, PHILIP P., *Professor of History, Wayne State University; Author of* Detroit, Fort Lernoult, and the American Revolution

MASSARO, DOMINIC R., *National Deputy, Order Sons of Italy in America*

MAST, ROBERT F., *President, ABAM Engineers Incorporated, Tacoma, Wash.*

MASTERS, KELLY R., *Author (under pseudonym Zachary Ball)* of Tent Show *and* Keelboat Journey

MASTNY, VOJTECH, *Associate Professor of History, Columbia University; Author of* The Czechs under Nazi Rule

MATENKO, PERCY, *Professor of German, Brooklyn College*

MATES, JULIAN, *Dean, School of the Arts, C.W. Post Center of Long Island University; Author of* The American Musical Stage Before 1800; *Coauthor of* Renaissance Culture

MATHEWS, JOSEPH J., *Professor of History, Emory University; Author of* Reporting the Wars

MATHEWS, THOMAS G., *Secretary General, Association of Caribbean Universities and Research Institutes*

MATLAW, MYRON, *Professor of English, Queens College; Author of* Modern World Drama; *Editor of* The Black Crook and Other 19th-Century American Plays

MATSCH, L. W., *Professor of Electrical Engineering, University of Arizona; Author of* Electromagnetic and Electromechanical Machines

MATSUDA, TOMO, *Director of Libraries, University of Tokyo*

MATSUOKA, JUDY CHIYO, *Instructor, Department of Rehabilitation, University of Arkansas at Little Rock; Coauthor of* HIV/AIDS Prevention: A Guide for Working with People Who Are Blind or Visually Impaired

MATTHEISEN, PAUL F., *Associate Professor of English, State University of New York at Binghamton*

MATTHEWS, EDITH S., *Director, J. Lewis Crozer Library, Chester, Pa.*

MATTHEWS, GLENN E., *Technical Editor, Kodak Research Laboratories, Rochester, N.Y.*

MATTHEWS, LAWRENCE D., *Senior Editor, Editorial Services, National Cash Register Company*

MATTHEWS, WILLIAM, *Professor of English and Director of the Center for Medieval and Renaissance Studies, University of California at Los Angeles; Editor of* The Diary of Samuel Pepys

MATTHEWS, WILLIAM H., III, *Professor of Geology, Lamar University; Author of* Fossils: An Introduction to Prehistoric Life, Exploring the World of Fossils, *and* Wonders of Fossils

MATTINGLY, GARRETT, *Author of* Renaissance Diplomacy

MATZKE, EDWIN B., *Professor of Botany, Columbia University*

MATZKIN, MYRON A., *Senior Editor of* Modern Photography

MAULDIN, JOYCE, *Librarian, Oklahoma* Journal

MAULITZ, RUSSELL C., *Duke University School of Medicine*

MAURER, DAVID W., *Professor of Linguistics, University of Louisville; Author of* The Big Con: The Story of the Confidence Man and the Confidence Game

MAURER, WALTER HARDING, *Professor of Sanskrit, University of Hawaii at Manoa; Author of* The Sugamānvayā of Vrtti, a Late Commentary in Jaina Sanskrit on Kālidāsa's Meghadūta; *Translator of* 100 hymns from the Rgveda

MAURICE, J. B., *English Setter Club, Marlborough, Wilts, England*

MAXWELL, HENRY J., *Professor of Spanish and Portuguese, Texas Tech University*

MAY, ARTHUR J., *Author of* The Hapsburg Monarchy, 1867–1914

MAY, ERNEST R., *Professor of History, Harvard University; Author of* The Making of the Monroe Doctrine

MAYER, GEORGE H., *Professor of American History, University of South Florida; Author of* The Republican Party 1854–1964

MAYER, RALPH, *Director, Artists Technical Research Institute; Author of the* Artist's Handbook of Materials and Techniques

MAYER, ROBERT, *Branch Librarian, Chatsworth Branch Library*

MAYHALL, TEMPLE R., *Assistant to the Director of Education, American Institute of Baking*

MAYNARD, JOHN K., *Senior Keeper, San Diego Wild Animal Park, San Pasqual, Calif.*

MAYR, ERNST, *Director, Museum of Comparative Zoology, Harvard University; Author of* Principles of Systematic Zoology *and* Populations, Species, and Evolution

MAYS, DAVID JOHN, *Author of* Edmund Pendleton, 1721–1803

MAZO, JOSEPH H., *Author of* Prime Movers: The Makers of Modern Dance in America

MAZZOLA, JOHN W., *Managing Director, Lincoln Center for the Performing Arts, New York City*

McALEER, JOHN J., *Professor of English, Boston College*

McAVOY, THOMAS T., CSC, *Professor of History, University of Notre Dame; Author of* The Great Crisis in American Catholic History, 1895–1900

McCAFFREY, LAWRENCE J., *Professor of History, Loyola University, Chicago; Author of* Irish Federalism in the 1870's: A Study in Conservative Nationalism *and* The Irish Question, 1800–1922

McCAIN, JOHN S., JR., *Admiral, U.S. Navy, Commander in Chief, Pacific*

McCALLUM, FRANCES T., *Coauthor of* The Wire That Fenced the West

McCALLUM, HENRY D., *Coauthor of* The Wire That Fenced the West

McCANDLESS, PERRY G., *Professor and Head, Department of History, Central Missouri State University*

McCARTHY, DENNIS J., SJ, *Professor of Old Testament Exegesis, Pontifical Biblical Institute, Rome*

McCARTHY, JOHN F., *Associate Professor of English, Boston College*

McCARTHY, KATHLEEN D., *Consultant, National Endowment for the Humanities; Author of* Noblesse Oblige: Charity and Cultural Philanthropy in Chicago, 1849–1929

McCLEAN, MARTIN, *University of London Institute of Education*

McCLESKY, CLIFTON, *Professor of Government, University of Texas at Austin; Author of* The Government and Politics of Texas

McCLINTOCK, MICHAEL, *Radio Standards Physics Division, National Bureau of Standards*

McCLINTON, EUGENIA, *Reference Librarian, Public Library, East St. Louis, Ill.*

McCLOSKEY, ROBERT G., *Jonathan Trumbull Professor of American History and Government, Harvard University; Author of* American Supreme Court

McCOLLUM, JOHN I., *Professor and Chairman, Department of English, University of Miami; Editor of* The Age of Elizabeth

McCOLLUM, JOHN P., *Coauthor of* Raising Vegetables and Producing Vegetable Crops

McCOMB, ARTHUR K., *Editor of* Selected Letters of Verrocchio

McCORMICK, BARNES W., *Boeing Professor Emeritus of Aerospace Engineering, Pennsylvania State University*

McCORMICK, JACK, *Curator and Chairman, Department of Ecology, Academy of Natural Sciences of Philadelphia; President, Jack McCormick & Associates*

McCORMICK, ROBERT J., *Editor, Associated Features, Inc.*

McCOUBREY, ARTHUR O., *Associate Director for Measurement Services, National Measurement Laboratory, National Bureau of Standards, U.S. Department of Commerce*

McCOY, DONALD R., *Professor of History, University of Kansas; Author of* Calvin Coolidge: The Quiet President

McCOY, J. J., *Author of* The Complete Book of Dog Training and Care

McCOY, OLIVE B., *Librarian, Wellington Public Library*

McCRACKEN, HAROLD, *Director, Whitney Museum of Western Art and Buffalo Bill Historical Center, Cody, Wyo.; Author of* Frederic Remington—Artist of the Old West *and* The Charles M. Russell Book

McCRACKEN, JANET M., *Professor of Early Childhood Education, Gamma College, University of West Florida*

McCREA, NELSON G., *Professor of Latin, Columbia University*

McCULLEN, J. T., JR., *Professor of English, Texas Tech University*

McCULLEY, PATRICIA W., *Senior Library Assistant, Bridgeton Free Public Library*

McDERMOTT, JOHN FRANCIS, *Research Professor of Humanities, Southern Illinois University*

McDONALD, DAVID L., *Admiral, U.S. Navy (Retired), Chief of Naval Operations*

McDONALD, FORREST, *Professor of History, Wayne State University; Author of* Insull

McDONALD, JAMES R., *Professor of Geography, Eastern Michigan University*

McDONALD, LEE C., *Professor of Government, Pomona College and the Claremont Graduate School; Author of* Western Political Theory: The Modern Age *and* Western Political Theory: From the Origins to the Present

McDONALD, R. THOMAS, *Associate Professor of History, Fairleigh Dickinson University*

McDONOUGH, PATRICK J., *Author of* Official Bowling Guide

McDOWELL, JOHN, *Executive Director, National Federation of Settlements and Neighborhood Centers; Former Dean of School of Social Work, Boston University*

McDOWELL, SAMUEL, *American Museum of Natural History*

McDUFFIE, BRUCE, *Laboratory for Trace Methods and Environmental Analysis, Department of Chemistry, State University of New York at Binghamton*

McELROY, WILLIAM D., *Chancellor, University of California at San Diego; Former Chairman, Department of Biology, Johns Hopkins University*

McELWEE, WILLIAM L., *Head, Department of Modern Subjects, Royal Military Academy, England; Author of* The Story of England

McENEANEY, KEVIN T., *Adjunct Professor of English, Marist College*

McFARLAND, DANIEL MILES, *Professor of History, James Madison University, Harrisonburg, Va.; Author of* Historical Dictionary of Upper Volta

McFARLAND, DAVID, *Chairman of Graduate Studies in Economics and Associate Professor of Economics, Graduate School of Business Administration, University of North Carolina*

McGAW, CHARLES, *Dean, Goodman School of Drama, Art Institute, Chicago; Author of* Acting Is Believing

McGILL, RALPH, *Publisher of* The Atlanta Constitution

McGILL, THOMAS E., *Hales Professor of Psychology, Williams College*

McGRATH, ALICE, *Coauthor of* Self-Defense for Women *and* Self-Defense for Your Child

McGRATTAN, SUZANNE M., *Member of the New York Bar*

McGRAW, HELEN COYNE, *Library Director, Irondequoit Public Library*

McGREW, CLAIRE, *Head Librarian, Burien Library*

McGUIRE, MARTIN R. P., *Professor of Greek, Latin, and Ancient History, Catholic University of America; Author of* Introduction to Mediaeval Latin Studies

McHENRY, HENRY M., MD, *Professor of Anthropology, University of California at Davis*

McINTYRE, ROBERT J., *Professor of Economics, Smith College; Author of* Bulgaria: Politics, Economy, and Society

McKAY, WILLIAM A., *Tutor, Scarboro College, University of Toronto, Canada*

McKELVEY, JAMES L., *Associate Professor of History, University of Connecticut at Storrs; Author of* George III and Lord Bute: The Leicester House Years

McKENNA, JOHN W., *W.D. and E.M. Scull Associate Professor of English Constitutional History, Haverford College; Author of* Henry VI of England and the Dual Monarchy

McKENNA, JOSEPH P., *Professor of Economics, University of Missouri at St. Louis; Author of* Aggregate Economic Analysis

McKENNA, MALCOLM C., *Frick Curator of Vertebrate Paleontology, American Museum of Natural History*

McKENZIE, HOWARD L., *Entomologist, College of Agriculture, University of California at Davis*

McKENZIE, JOHN L., *Author of* Two-edged Sword

McKENZIE, ROD C., *Chairman and Assistant Professor of Geography, University of Southern California*

McLANE, EUGENE G., *Director, Fond du Lac Public Library, Fond du Lac, Wis.*

McLAREN, MALCOLM G., *Professor of Ceramics, Rutgers University*

McLAREN, SYLVIA, *News Bureau, Idaho State University*

McLEAN, DONALD M., *Public Information Representative, Sperry Gyroscope Company*

McLEAN, HUGH, *Chairman, Department of Slavic Languages and Literatures, University of Chicago; Coeditor of* Harvard Slavic Studies

McLELLAN, DAVID S., *Professor of Political Theory, University of Kent, England; Author of* The Young Hegelians and Karl Marx, Marx Before Marxism, The Thought of Karl Marx, *and* Karl Marx: His Life and Thought

McLELLAN, DAVID S., *Department of Political Science, Miami University, Ohio; Author of* Dean Acheson: The State Department Years

McLELLAN, G. W., *Technical Lecturer, Corning Glass Works*

McLINTOCK, GORDON, *Vice Admiral, U.S. Maritime Service; Superintendent of the U.S. Merchant Marine Academy*

McLOUGHLIN, PAUL V. A., *Author of* The Orders of Knighthood, Decorations, and Awards of Honour of All Nations

McMAHON, JAMES E., *Deputy Director, Information Division, Agricultural Stabilization and Conservation Service*

McMANNERS, JOHN, *Regius Professor of Ecclesiastical History, Oxford University*

McMANUS, CHRISTOPHER, SJ, *Fordham University*

McMILLAN, EDWIN M., *Nobel Prize Winner in Chemistry, 1951; Director, Lawrence Radiation Laboratory, University of California at Berkeley*

McMILLAN, RUTH De CAMP, *Editor of* Grit and Steel

McMURRY, RICHARD M., *Department of History, North Carolina State University; Author of* John Bell Hood and the War for Southern Independence

McNALLY, ROBERT E., SJ, *Professor of Historical Theology, Fordham University*

McNASPY, CLEMENT J., SJ, *Professor of Music, Loyola University, New Orleans, La.; Board of Directors, National Liturgical Conference; Associate Editor,* Catholic Mind; *Author of* A Guide to Christian Europe

McNEILL, JOHN T., *Auburn Professor of Church History, Union Theological Seminary; Author of* Makers of the Christian Tradition

McNEILL, WILLIAM H., *Professor of History, University of Chicago; Author of* The Rise of the West

McNICKLE, GEORGE, *Sports Staff, New York Times*

McNICOLL, ROBERT E., *Director, Institute of Inter-American Studies, University of Miami, Coral Gables; Author of* Latin-American Panorama

McPHERSON, KENNETH F., *Director, Bloomfield Public Library*

McWHINEY, GRADY, *Professor and Chairman, Department of History, University of Alabama*

McWHORTER, EUGENE W., *Author of* Understanding Digital Electronics *and Coauthor of* Understanding Solid-State Electronics

MEADE, MARGARET, *Brockton Public Library*

MEADOWS, JOHN C., *Professor of Sociology, University of Georgia; Author of* Modern Georgia

MEALING, STANLEY R., *Professor of History, Carleton University, Canada*

MEARNS, BARBARA A., *Library Director, Clifton Public Library*

MECKLENBURG, VIRGINIA M., *Chief Curator, National Museum of American Art, Smithsonian Institution*

MEGAW, HELEN D., *Fellow of Girton College, Cambridge University; Author of* Ferroelectricity in Crystals

MEGAW, J. V. S., *Professor, Department of Archaeology, University of Leicester, England; Author of* Art of the European Iron Age; *Coauthor of* The Dawn of Man

MEGENITY, JACK, *College of Education, Georgia State University*

MEGLITSCH, PAUL A., *Professor of Biology, Drake University; Author of* Invertebrate Zoology

MEI, Y. P., *Author of* The Ethical and Political Philosophy of Motse *and* Motse, The Neglected Rival of Confucius

MEIJER, ROELOF F., *N.V. Philips Research Laboratories, Eindhoven, Netherlands*

MEININGER, ROBERT A., *Professor of Romance Languages, Nebraska Wesleyan University*

MEIROSE, LEO H., *Librarian, Fort Lauderdale Public Library, Fort Lauderdale, Fla.*

MELAVEN, A. D., *Professor of Chemistry, University of Tennessee*

MELCHER, EDITH, *Professor of French, Wellesley College; Author of* The Life and Times of Henry Monnier

MELDER, KEITH E., *Consultant, Old Sturbridge Village; Former Curator, Division of Political History, Smithsonian Institution*

MELENDY, H. BRETT, *Professor of History, University of Hawaii; Coauthor of* The Governors of California

MELENEY, FRANK L., MD, *Professor, College of Physicians and Surgeons, Columbia University; Author of* Treatise on Surgical Infections

MELINA, LOIS RUSKAI, *Author of* Raising Adopted Children *and* Making Sense of Adoption

MELLER, NORMAN, *Professor of Political Science, University of Hawaii*

MELLON, STANLEY, *Professor of History, University of Illinois at Chicago Circle; Author of* The Political Uses of History *and* François Guizot

MELTON, HELEN BOND, *Director, Carlsbad Public Library*

MEMMING, PATRICIA W., *University Relations, State University of New York at Buffalo*

MENCKEN, H. L., *Author of* The American Language *and other books*

MENDELSON, WALLACE, *Professor of Government, University of Texas; Author of* Justice Blacks and Frankfurter

MENDENHALL, THOMAS CORWIN II, *President, Smith College*

MENDOZA, E., *Professor of Physics, University College of North Wales, Bangor; Editor of* Carnot's Reflections on the Motive Power of Time

MENNIN, PETER, *Former President, Juilliard School*

MENZE, ERNEST, *Department of History, Iona College*

MENZIES, ELIZABETH G. C., *Author of* Before the Waters: The Upper Delaware Valley

MERCER, NORMAN A., *State Education Department, University of the State of New York*

MERCHANT, DONALD J., *Professor of Microbiology and Cell Biology, Eastern Virginia Medical School; Coauthor of* Handbook of Cell and Organ Culture

MERIAM, PHILIP W., *Director, Dedham Public Library*

MERMEL, T. W., *Chairman, World Register of Dams, International Commission on Large Dams*

MERRILL, JOHN C., *Director, School of Journalism, Louisiana State University; Coauthor of* The World's Great Dailies: Profiles of Fifty Newspapers

MERRILL, REED, *Coauthor of* Arthur Koestler: An International Bibliography

MERSEREAU, JOHN, JR., *Professor of Slavic Languages and Literatures, University of Michigan; Author of* Mikhail Lermontov

MERTZ, BARBARA G., *Author of* Temples, Tombs, and Hieroglyphs *and* Red Land, Black Land

MESERVE, BRUCE E., *Professor of Mathematics, University of Vermont*

MESSENGER, JOHN C., *Professor of Anthropology, Ohio State University*

MESSER, THOMAS M., *Director, Solomon R. Guggenheim Museum*

METTER, DEAN E., *Associate Professor of Zoology, University of Missouri*

METTLER, FREDERICK A., *Author of* Medical Source Book

METZGER, J. E., *Chairman of the Board, Dannon Milk Products*

MEWS, SIEGFRIED, *Professor of German, University of North Carolina.*

MEYER, B. ROBERT, MD, *Chief, Division of Clinical Pharmacology, North Shore University Hospital; Professor of Medicine and Pharmacology, Cornell University*

MEYER, BERNARD S., *Professor of Botany, Ohio State University*

MEYER, HENRY CORD, *Chairman, Department of History, University of California at Irvine*

MEYER, MICHAEL C., *Professor of History and Director of the Latin American Center, University of Arizona; Author of* Mexican Rebel: Pascual Orozco and the Mexican Revolution, 1910–1915 *and* Huerta: A Political Portrait; *Coauthor of* The Course of Mexican History

MEYER, ROBERT T., *Professor of Celtic, Catholic University of America; Author of* Merugud Uilix maic Leirtis

MEYER, ROGER E., MD, *Professor and Chairman, Department of Psychiatry, University of Connecticut School of Medicine*

MEYERRIECKS, ANDREW J., *Associate Professor of Zoology, University of South Florida at Tampa; Author of* Comparative Breeding Behavior of Four Species of North American Herons

MIAO, RONALD C., *Associate Professor of Oriental Studies, University of Arizona*

MICHAELIS, PATRICIA A., *Curator of Manuscripts, Kansas State Historical Society*

MICHALOPOULOS, ANDRÉ, *Professor of Classical Literature and Civilization, Fairleigh Dickinson University; Author of* Homer

MICHELSON, PAUL E., *Distinguished Professor of History, Huntington College*

MICKIEWICZ, ELLEN, *Professor of Political Science, Michigan State University; Author of* Handbook of Soviet Social Science Data *and* Soviet Political Schools

MICKLE, D. GRANT, *President, Highway Users Federation for Safety and Mobility, Washington, D.C.; Coauthor of* Highway Engineering Handbook

MIDDLEKAUFF, ROBERT, *Professor of History, University of California at Berkeley*

MIDDLETON, JOHN, *Chairman, Department of Anthropology, New York University; Author of* The Kikuyu and Kamba of Kenya, *and* The Lugbara of Uganda; *Editor of* Witchcraft, Magic and Curing *and* Gods and Rituals

MIDDLETON, JOHN T., *University of California at Riverside*

MIERS, EARL SCHENCK, *Author of* The General Who Marched to Hell

MIESEL, VICTOR H., *Professor of History of Art, University of Michigan; Author of* Voices of German Expressionism

MIGEOTTE, M., *Professor, Institut d'Astrophysique, University of Liège, Belgium*

MIHAILOVICH, VASA D., *Professor of Slavic Literature, University of North Carolina*

MIKKELSON, GERALD E., *Associate Professor of Slavic Languages and Literatures, University of Kansas*

MILES, E. P., JR., *Director, Computing Center, and Professor of Mathematics, Florida State University*

MILES, EDWARD J., *Professor and Chairman, Department of Geography, University of Vermont*

MILES, EDWIN A., *Professor of History, University of Houston; Author of* Jacksonian Democracy in the United States

MILL, EDWARD W., *Author of* The Conduct of Philippine Foreign Relations

MILLAR, JAMES R., *Director, Institute for Sino-Soviet Relations, George Washington University; Author of* The ABCs of Soviet Socialism *and* The Soviet Economic Experiment

MILLER, ALAN W., *Rabbi, Society for the Advancement of Judaism, New York City; Author of* God of Daniel S.: In Search of the American Jew

MILLER, Brigadier ANDREW S., *National Information Director, Salvation Army*

MILLER, BANNER I., *Research Meteorologist, National Hurricane Research Laboratory, Miami, Fla.; Coauthor of* Atlantic Hurricanes

MILLER, BEATRICE D., *Anthropologist*

MILLER, DAVID B., *Professor of History and Chairman, Department of History, Roosevelt University*

MILLER, ERNEST I., *Librarian, Public Library of Cincinnati*

MILLER, FRANK BLACK, MD, *Clinical Associate, Duke University Hospital, Durham, N.C.*

MILLER, FRANK C., *Professor of Anthropology, University of Minnesota; Author of* Old Villages and a New Town: Industrialization in Mexico

MILLER, FRANK W., *James Carr Professor of Criminal Jurisprudence, School of Law, Washington University; Author of* Prosecution: The Decision to Charge

MILLER, HALLIE, *Librarian, Temple Public Library*

MILLER, JAMES E., *Professor of Meteorology and Oceanography, College of Engineering, New York University*

MILLER, JOHN C., *Professor of History, Stanford University*

MILLER, LUTHER S., *Editor of* Railway Age

MILLER, M. CHARLES, *Library Director, Binghamton Public Library*

MILLER, MARTIN W., *Department of Food Science and Technology, College of Agriculture, University of California at Davis*

MILLER, MEL, *Curator, Ringling Museum of the Circus*

MILLER, NATHAN, *Professor of History, University of Wisconsin at Milwaukee; Author of* The Enterprise of a Free People: Aspects of Economic Development in New York State During the Canal Period, 1792–1838

MILLER, PATRICK D., JR., *Professor of Biblical Studies, Union Theological Seminary in Virginia; Author of* The Divine Warrior in Early Israel *and* Sin and Judgment in the Prophets

MILLER, RALPH L., *Senior Resident Geologist, U.S. Geological Survey*

MILLER, ROBERT J., *Professor of Anthropology and Indian Studies, University of Wisconsin*

MILLER, ROY ANDREW, *Professor of Asian Languages and Literature, University of Washington; Author of* The Japanese Language

MILLER, RUTH C., *Librarian, Downey City Library*

MILLER, SAMUEL J., *Professor of History, Boston College*

MILLER, SIDNEY I., *Professor of Chemistry, Illinois Institute of Technology*

MILLER, WILLIAM, *Author of* A New History of the United States *and* Men in Business

MILLETT, RICHARD L., *Associate Professor of History, Southern Illinois University at Edwardsville*

MILLIGAN, JOHN D., *Professor of History, State University of New York at Buffalo; Author of* Gunboats Down the Mississippi

MILLIGAN, W. O., *Distinguished Research Professor of Chemistry, Baylor University*

MILLING, CHAPMAN J., JR., *Librarian, Sumter County Library*

MILLON, HENRY A., *Author of* Key Monuments in the History of Architecture

MILLON, ROBERT P., *Author of* Mexican Marxist—Vicente Lombardo Toledano

MILLS, JOY, *President, Theosophical Society in America; Author of* Theosophy and Psychology *and* An Approach to the Study of the Secret Doctrines

MILNER, HENRY, *Associate Professor, Department of Political Science, Université Laval; Professor of Political Science, Vanier College*

MILOSZ, CZESLAW, *Nobel Prize Winner in Literature, 1980; Professor of Slavic Languages and Literatures, University of California at Berkeley; Author of* The History of Polish Literature

MILUNSKY, AUBREY, MD, *Director, Genetics Unit, Eunice Kennedy Shriver Center, Waltham, Mass.; Director, Genetics Clinic, Massachusetts General Hospital; Assistant Professor of Pediatrics, Harvard University Medical School*

MIMS, EDWIN, *Author of* Southern Prose and Poetry

MINADEO, RICHARD W., *Associate Professor of Classics, Wayne State University; Author of* The Lyre of Science: Form and Meaning in Lucretius' De Rerum Natura

MINER, ELLIS D., *Voyager Assistant Project Scientist, Jet Propulsion Laboratory, California Institute of Technology*

MINER, ROBERT F., *Boy Scouts of America Editorial Service*

MINGAY, G. E., *Professor of Agrarian History, University of Kent at Canterbury, England; Author of* The Agrarian Revolution, 1750–1880, English Landed Society in the 18th Century, *and* Rural Life in Victorian England

MINKIN, LEWIS, *Senior Lecturer in Government, Victoria University of Manchester, England; Author of* The Labour Party Conference

MINNICH, S. H., *General Electric Research and Development Center*

MINOGUE, K. R., *Senior Lecturer in Political Science, London School of Economics; Author of* The Liberal Mind

MINSKY, HYMAN P., *Professor of Economics, Washington University, St. Louis, Mo.; Author of* John Maynard Keynes

MINTON, SHERMAN A., JR., MD, *Professor of Microbiology, Indiana University at Indianapolis*

MIRANDA, CARLOS R., *University of Connecticut; Author of* The Stroessner Era: Authoritarian Rule in Paraguay

MIRON, ISSACHAR, *Department of Public Relations, American Friends of the Hebrew University, New York City*

MIRSKY, JEANNETTE, *Author of* Houses of God

MITCHELL, DENISE, *National Headquarters, Girl Scouts of the USA*

MITCHELL, GARY, *Associate Professor of Physics, North Carolina State University at Raleigh*

MITCHELL, GEORGE F., *Head, Tea Department, General Foods Corporation*

MITCHELL, JOSEPH B., *Lieutenant Colonel, U.S. Army; Chief, Historical Division, American Battle Monuments Commission; Author of* Decisive Battles of the Civil War

MITCHELL, NATHAN, OSB, *St. Meinrad School of Theology*

MITCHELL, R. JUDSON, *Professor of Political Science, University of New Orleans*

MITCHELL, RICHARD E., *Professor of History, University of Illinois*

MITCHELL, STEPHEN, *Lecturer in Classics, University College of Swansea, Wales; Editor of* Armies and Frontiers in Roman and Byzantine Anatolia

MITCHELL, WILLIAM C., *University of Oregon; Author of* The American Polity, Sociological Analysis and Politics: The Theories of Talcott Parsons, Political Analysis and Public Policy, *and* Anatomy of Public Failure

MITCHELL, WILLIAM J., *Professor of Music, State University of New York at Binghamton; Author of* Elementary Harmony

MITCHENER, R. D., *Assistant Director, Education Support Branch, Canadian Department of the Secretary of State*

MITGANG, HERBERT, *Editorial Board, New York Times; Author of* The Man Who Rode the Tiger

MITNICK, BARRY M., *Associate Professor of Business Administration, University of Pittsburgh; Author of* The Political Economy of Regulation

MITTAG, LAURENCE, *Fellow, Yale University*

MOCKMORE, CORA, *Librarian, Huerfano County Library, Walsenburg, Colo.*

MOEHRING, HORST R., *Professor of Religious Studies, Brown University*

MOES, ROBERT, *Curator of Oriental Art, Denver Art Museum*

MOGABGAB, WILLIAM J., MD, *Professor of Medicine, Section of Infectious Disease, Tulane University School of Medicine*

MOGER, ALLEN W., *Professor of History, Washington and Lee University*

MOHAN, ANAND, *Lecturer, Queens College; Author of* Indira Gandhi: A Personal and Political Biography

MOHLER, DONALD J., *Director of Technical Photography, General Electric Company*

MOHR, CHARLES E., *Executive Director, Delaware Nature Education Center; Coauthor of* The Life of the Cave

MOHR, J. P., MD, *Sciarra Professor of Clinical Neurology, New York Neurological Institute, Columbia-Presbyterian Medical Center*

MOIR, JOHN S., *Professor of History, University of Toronto (Scarborough College), Canada; Coauthor of* Changing Perspectives in Canadian History

MOLDENKE, HAROLD N., *Author of* Plants of the Bible

MOLEY, RAYMOND, JR., *Author of* The American Legion Story

MOLHO, ANTHONY, *Professor of History, Brown University*

MOLL, J. C., *Dean, Faculty of Arts, University of the Orange Free State (South Africa)*

MOLLAND, A. GEORGE, *Department of History and Philosophy of Science, King's College, University of Aberdeen, Scotland*

MOLLEMA, HELEN M., *Librarian, Owosso Public Library*

MONEY, JOHN, *Professor of Medical Psychology and Associate Professor of Pediatrics, Johns Hopkins University; Author of* Sex Errors of the Body; *Coauthor of* Transsexualism and Sex Reassignment

MONGAN, AGNES, *Curator of Drawings, Fogg Museum of Art, Harvard University; Author of* Andrew Wyeth: Dry Brush and Pencil Drawings

MONGAN, MARY ANN, *Librarian, Kenton County Public Library, Covington, Ky.*

MONKHOUSE, F. J., *Author of* A Regional Geography of Western Europe

MONTAGU, ASHLEY, *Author of* Introduction to Physical Anthropology

MONTAGU, JENNIFER, *Assistant Curator, Photographic Collection, Warburg Institute, London; Author of* Bronzes

MONTGOMERY, MARGARET, *Reference Librarian, Beverly Hills Public Library*

MOODY, B. E., *Head of Packaging Research, United Glass Limited*

MOODY, LINDA ALDEN, *Legal Advisor, Police Department, Oakland, Calif.*

MOORE, DEBORAH DASH, *Temple Sholom, Riveredge, N.J.*

MOORE, DORIS LANGLEY, *Author of* The Late Lord Byron

MOORE, E. L., *Assistant Chief, Tobacco and Sugar Crops Research Branch, Crops Research Division, U.S. Department of Agriculture.*

MOORE, ELIZABETH V., *Member, Edenton Historical Commission*

MOORE, GLOVER, *Professor of History, Mississippi State University; Author of* The Missouri Controversy, 1819–1821

MOORE, HARRY T., *Research Professor, Southern Illinois University; Author of* Age of the Modern *and Other Literary Essays*

MOORE, JOHN A., *Professor of Biology, University of California at Riverside*

MOORE, JOSEPH CURTIS, *Department of Ecology and Systematics, Florida Southern College*

MOORE, LILLIAN, *Author of* Images of the Dance

MOORE, TERRIS, *Professor of the University (Hon.), University of Alaska; Author of* Mt. McKinley; The Pioneer Climbs

MOORE, WILBERT E., *Professor of Sociology and Law, University of Denver*

MOOS, MALCOLM, *President, Fund for the Republic; Former President, University of Minnesota*

MORAES, FRANK R., *Author of* Jawaharlal Nehru

MORALES-CARRIÓN, ARTURO, *Director, Department of Information and Public Affairs, Pan American Union*

MORANDINI, GIUSEPPE, *Professor of Geography, Università degli Studi, Padua, Italy*

MORDDEN, ETHAN C., *Author of* Better Foot Forward: The History of American Musical Theatre

MORE, PAUL ELMER, *Critic and Philosopher; Author of* Platonism *and* The Religion of Plato

MOREHOUSE, LAURENCE E., *Professor of Kinesiology, University of California at Los Angeles*

MORELLI, WILLIAM J., sj, *Fordham University*

MORFORD, MARK PERCY OWEN, *Professor of Classics, Ohio State University; Author of* The Poet Lucan

MORGAN, BRIAN L. G., *Institute of Human Nutrition, Columbia University College of Physicians and Surgeons*

MORGAN, CHARLES HILL, *Mean Professor of Fine Arts, Amherst College; Author of* The Life of Michelangelo

MORGAN, DEWI, *Rector of St. Bride's Church, London; Author of* Seeds of Peace

MORGAN, EDMUND S., *Professor of History, Yale University*

MORGAN, H. WAYNE, *Professor of History, University of Oklahoma; Author of* William McKinley and His America

MORGAN, HELEN N., *Director, North Shore Branch, New England Conservatory*

MORGAN, ROBERT J., *Professor of Government and Foreign Affairs, University of Virginia; Author of* A Whig Embattled: The Presidency Under John Tyler

MORGAN, W. KEITH, MD, *Professor of Medicine, West Virginia University; Author of* Occupational Lung Diseases

MORGENSTIERNE, GEORG, *Professor of Indian Language and Literature, University of Oslo, Norway*

MORIN, ELLEN I., *Librarian, Fulton Public Library*

MORIN, RICHARD W., *Librarian, Baker Library, Dartmouth College*

MORK, GORDON R., *Associate Professor of History, Purdue University*

MORLEY, CHARLES, *Professor of History, Ohio State University*

MOROWITZ, HAROLD J., *Professor of Molecular Biology and Biochemistry, Yale University*

MORPHY, HOWARD, *Lecturer at the Pitt Rivers Museum and Senior Tutor in Linacre College, University of Oxford*

MORRAH, DERMOT, *The Times, London*

MORRIS, CLARENCE, *Professor of Law, University of Pennsylvania; Author of* Morris on Torts

MORRIS, DESMOND, *Curator of Mammals, Zoological Society, Regents Park, London; Author of* The Naked Ape *and* The Human Zoo

MORRIS, HENRY M., *Professor and Chairman, Department of Civil Engineering, Virginia Polytechnic Institute; Author of* Applied Hydraulics in Engineering

MORRIS, JACQUELINE G., *Manager, Learning Resources, Indiana Department of Education*

MORRIS, JAMES, *Author of* The World of Venice *and* The Presence of Spain

MORRIS, LEONARD L., *Professor of Vegetable Crops, Department of Vegetable Crops, University of California at Davis*

MORRIS, MARGARET, *Librarian, Galesburg Public Library*

MORRIS, RICHARD B., *Gouverneur Morris Professor of History, Columbia University; Author of* Alexander Hamilton and the Founding of the Nation

MORRISON, JOSEPH L., *Professor, University of North Carolina School of Journalism; Author of* Josephus Daniels: The Small-d Democrat

MORRISON, KARL F., *Professor of Medieval History, University of Chicago*

MORRISON, KENNETH D., *Director, Mountain Lake Sanctuary, Lake Wales, Fla.*

MORRISON, MILDRED E., *Librarian, Dover Public Library*

MORRISON, NEIL M., *Cosecretary, Royal Commission on Bilingualism and Biculturalism, Ottawa, Canada*

MORSE, EDWARD E., MD, *Director of Hematology Division of Laboratory Medicine, University of Connecticut Health Center*

MORSE, MARTHA, *Head Librarian, Herrick Memorial Library, Wellington, Ohio*

MORTON, COURTNAY KING, *Librarian, Ticonderoga (N.Y.) Public Library*

MORTON, LOUIS, *Author of* War in the Pacific: Strategy and Command

MORTON, MAURICE, *Regents Professor Emeritus of Polymer Chemistry, University of Akron; Author of* Rubber Technology

MORTON, W. L., *Chancellor, Trent University, Canada*

MOSBY, DEWEY F., *Director, Picker Art Gallery, Colgate University; Author of* Henry Ossawa Tanner

MOSCONA, AARON, *Professor of Biology and Director, Developmental Biology Training Center, University of Chicago*

MOSER, KENNETH J., *Professor of Mechanical Engineering, Stevens Institute of Technology*

MOSES, JOEL CHARLES, *Professor, Iowa State University; Author of* Regional Party Leadership and Policy-Making in the USSR

MOSES, WILSON J., *Professor of History, Pennsylvania State University*

MOSKOWITZ, SAUL, *NASA, Electronics Research Center*

MOSSNER, ERNEST CAMPBELL, *Professor of English, University of Texas; Author of* The Life of David Hume

MOTT, SIR NEVILL, *Cavendish Professor of Experimental Physics, Cambridge University*

MOULTON, VERNA, *Associate Professor, Clothing and Textiles, School of Home Economics, University of Connecticut; Coauthor of* Clothing Selection

MOURELATOS, ALEXANDER, *Professor of Philosophy, University of Texas at Austin; Author of* The Route of Parmenides: A Study of Word, Image, and Argument in the Fragments

MOWER, PAULINE G., *Director of Information, Future Homemakers of America*

MOYER, ALBERT E., *Assistant Professor, Department of History, Virginia Polytechnic Institute and State University*

MOYER, JANE S., *Librarian, Easton Public Library*

MOZINGO, HUGH N., *Professor of Botany, University of Nevada, Reno*

MUELLER, GEORGE E., *Chairman and President, System Development Corporation*

MUHRER, MERLE, *Professor of Biochemistry, University of Missouri*

MUILENBURG, JAMES, *Graduate Theological Union, Berkeley, Calif.*

MUIR, KENNETH, *King Alfred Professor of English Literature, University of Liverpool, England; Author of* An Introduction to Elizabethan Literature *and* Shakespeare as Collaborator

MUISE, DELPHIN A., *Professor of History, Carleton University, Canada*

MULHERN, PHILIP F., OP, *Author of* The Early Dominican Laybrother *and* Poor in Christ

MULLER, OTTO H., *Professor of Physiology, State University of New York, Upstate Medical Center*

MULLER, PRISCILLA E., *Curator of the Museum, Hispanic Society of America, New York City*

MULLER, STEVEN, *Vice President for Public Affairs, Cornell University*

MULLIN, DONALD C., *Professor of Drama, University of Guelph, Canada; Author of* The Development of the Playhouse

MULLINER, K., *Assistant to the Director of Libraries, Ohio University Libraries; Coeditor of* Southeast Asia: An Emerging Center of World Influence? Malaysian Studies II

MULVEY, T., *Professor of Electron Physics, University of Aston, Birmingham, England*

MUNDT, WHITNEY R., *Associate Professor and Director of Graduate Studies and Research, School of Journalism, Louisiana State University*

MUNGER, EDWIN S., *Professor of Geography, California Institute of Technology*

MUNITZ, MILTON K., *Author of* Theories of the Universe: From Babylonian Myth to Modern Science

MUNROE, JOHN A., *Chairman, Department of History, and H. Rodney Sharp Professor of History, University of Delaware; Author of* Federalist Delaware, 1775–1815

MUNSCH, ROBERT, SJ, *Fordham University*

MUNSTERBERG, HUGO, *Author of* The Arts of Japan, The Folk Arts of Japan, *and* Dictionary of Chinese and Japanese Art

MUNZ, PETER, *Professor of History, Victoria University of Wellington, New Zealand; Author of* The Place of Hooker in the History of Thought *and* Problems of Religious Knowledge

MURASKIN, WILLIAM, *Assistant Professor, Department of Urban Studies, Queens College*

MURDOCK, KENNETH B., *Professor of English Literature, Harvard University; Author of* Literature and Theology in Colonial New England

MURDY, LOUISE B., *Author of* Sound and Sense in Dylan Thomas's Poetry

MURPHEY, RHOADS, *Professor of History and Director, Center for South and Southeast Asia, University of Michigan; Author of* An Introduction to Geography

MURPHY, CHARLES S., *Chairman, Civil Aeronautics Board*

MURPHY, ELEANOR ECKFORD, *Director, Huntsville Public Library, Huntsville, Ala.*

MURPHY, FRANCIS X., CSSR, *Accademia Alfonsiana, Rome*

MURPHY, GORDON J., *Professor of Electrical Engineering and Computer Science, Northwestern University; Author of* Basic Automatic Control Theory

MURPHY, JAMES E., *Director of Public Information, University of Notre Dame*

MURPHY, JO ANNE, *Information Specialist, American Foundation for the Blind*

MURPHY, JOHN F., *Attorney at Law*

MURPHY, JOHN G., *Fordham University*

MURPHY, JOHN L., *Professor of Dogmatic Theology, St. Francis Seminary, Milwaukee, Wis.*

MURPHY, PAUL L., *Professor of History and American Studies, University of Minnesota; Author of* Liberty and Justice: A Historical Record of American Constitutional Development

MURPHY, RAYMOND E., *Professor of Economic Geography, Clark University*

MURPHY, ROLAND E., OC, *Professor of Old Testament, Catholic University of America*

MURPHY, WILLIAM PARRY, MD, *Lecturer on Medicine, Harvard Medical School*

MURRAY, MALCOLM A., *Professor of Geography, Georgia State University*

MURRAY, MARIA D., *Author of* The Art of Tray Painting

MURRAY, ROBERT D., JR., *Associate Professor of Classics, Princeton University*

MUSGRAVE, ALLAN E., *London School of Economics and Political Science*

MUSGRAVE, ROBERT B., *Professor of Agronomy, Cornell University*

MUSSEN, PAUL, *Professor of Psychology and Director of the Institute of Human Development, University of California at Berkeley; Author of* The Psychological Development of the Child; *Coauthor of* Child Development and Personality *and* Psychology: An Introduction

MYERS, CURTICE G., *Akron Public Library*

MYERS, JOYCE L., *Research Associate, U.S. Naval Academy*

MYERS, MARGARET G., *Professor of Economics, Vassar College; Author of* Origins and Development of the New York Money Market to 1913

MYERS, MITZI, *Lecturer, English and Writing Programs, University of California at Los Angeles*

MYERS, OLIVER T., *Professor and Chairman, Department of Spanish and Portuguese, University of Wisconsin at Milwaukee*

MYERS, ROBERT M., *American Radio Relay League, Inc., Newington, Conn.*

NADLER, ALLAN, *Director of Research, Yivo Institute for Jewish Research*

NADLER, PAUL S., *Professor of Finance, Rutgers University; Author of* Commercial Banking in the Economy

NAGY, ELEMER J., *Professor of Classics, California State University at Fresno*

NAKAMURA, HAJIME, *Professor of Indian and Buddhist Philosophy, University of Tokyo; Author of* Ways of Thinking of Eastern Peoples

NAKAMURA, KIKUO, *Professor of Political History, Keio University, Tokyo; Author of* Ito Hirobumi *and* Japanese Political Parties

NANKIVELL, J. E., *Professor of Mechanical Technology, Staten Island Community College*

NANNEY, HERBERT, *Professor of Music, Stanford University*

NAPARSTEK, IDA K., *Librarian, Ayer Junior-Senior High School*

NAPIER, JOHN R., *Director of Primate Biology Program, U.S. National Museum, Smithsonian Institution; Coauthor of* A Handbook of Living Primates

NARDINI, WILLIAM, *Commissioner of Correction, State of Delaware*

NASATIR, ABRAHAM P., *Author of* Before Lewis and Clark

NASH, GERALD D., *Professor of History, University of New Mexico; Author of* Issues in American Economic History *and* History of 20th Century America

NASON, ARTHUR H., *Author of* James Shirley, Dramatist

NATHAN, ANDREW J., *Professor of Political Science, Columbia University*

NATHAN, HANS, *Author of* Dan Emmett and Early American Negro Ministrelsy

NAYLON, JOHN, *Senior Lecturer in Geography, University of Keele, England*

NAYLOR, PHILLIP C., *Professor of History and Director of the Western Civilization Program, Marquette University*

NEARY, ANNA, *Bedlington Terrier Club of America*

NEARY, PETER, *Department of History, University of Western Ontario, Canada; Editor of* The Political Economy of Newfoundland, 1929–1972; *Coeditor of* By Great Waters: A Newfoundland and Labrador Anthology

NEBLETTE, C. B., *Rochester Institute of Technology; Author of* Photography, Its Materials and Processes

NEEDHAM, WESLEY E., *Adviser in Tibetan Literature, Yale University Library*

NEEDLER, MARTIN C., *Dean, School of International Studies, University of the Pacific*

NEFF, CARROLL F., *Technical Consultant*

NEFT, DAVID S., *Director of Research, Information Concepts Incorporated, New York City; Author of* Statistical Analysis for Areal Distributions

NEHRT, LEE C., *Professor of International Business, Indiana University; Author of* International Finance for Multinational Business

NEILSON, KATHARINE B., *Author of* Filippino Lippi: A Critical Study

NELSON, COL. C. EMIL, *National Chief Secretary, Salvation Army*

NELSON, CORDNER, *Founding Editor, Track & Field News; Author of* The Jim Ryun Story *and* Track's Greatest Champions

NELSON, DONALD F., *Bell Telephone Laboratories, Inc.*

NELSON, GLENN C., *Author of* Ceramics: A Potter's Handbook

NELSON, JAMES B., *Director, Cabell County Public Library, Huntington, W.Va.*

NELSON, JAMES H., *Chief of Geomagnetism Division, U.S. Coast and Geodetic Survey; Coauthor of* Magnetism of the Earth

NELSON, JOHN CHARLES, *Chairman, Department of Italian, Columbia University; Author of* Renaissance Theory of Love

NELSON, WILLIAM, *Professor of English, Columbia University; Author of* Edmund Spenser: A Study

NEMIAH, JOHN C., MD, *Psychiatrist-in-Chief, Beth Israel Hospital, Boston; Professor of Psychiatry, Harvard Medical School; Author of* Foundations of Psychopathology

NESHEIM, MALDEN C., *Professor of Animal Nutrition, Department of Poultry Science, Cornell University*

NETTELS, CURTIS P., *Professor of American History, Cornell University; Author of* George Washington and American Independence

NETTL, BRUNO, *Professor of Music and Anthropology, University of Illinois; Author of* Introduction to Folk Music in the United States *and* Folk and Traditional Music of the Western Continents

NEUBAUER, J. R., *Manager, Engineering Projects-Defense Communications System Division, RCA Corporation*

NEUMEYER, ALFRED, *Author of* Cézanne's Drawings *and* The Search for Meaning in Modern Art

NEVINS, ALBERT J., MM, *Editor,* Maryknoll Magazine, *Maryknoll, N.Y.; Director, World Horizon Films*

NEWBAUER, JOHN, *Editor in Chief,* Aerospace America

NEWELL, FRANK W., MD, *Professor and Chairman, Section of Ophthalmology, University of Chicago; Author of* Ophthalmology Principles and Concepts

NEWELL, I. M., *Professor of Zoology, University of California at Riverside*

NEWHALL, BEAUMONT, *Director, George Eastman House, Rochester, N.Y.*

NEWMAN, EDWIN S., *Attorney at Law; Author of* Civil Liberties and Civil Rights

NEWMAN, GUSTAVE, MD, *Center for the Study of Aging, Duke University*

NEWMAN, LOUIS E., *Director, Institute of Government Research, Louisiana State University*

NEWMAN, MURRAY A., *Director, Vancouver Public Aquarium*

NEWMAN, THOMAS L., *Former Executive Director, American Youth Hostels, Inc., Washington, D.C.*

NEWMAN, WILLIAM H., *Samuel Bronfman Professor of Democratic Business Enterprise, Columbia University; Coauthor of* The Process of Management

NEWSTEAD, GORDON, *Professor of Engineering Physics, Australian National University*

NICHOL, JOHN THOMAS, *Dean and Professor of History, Bentley College; Author of* Pentecostalism

NICHOLAS, H. G., *Fellow, New College, Oxford University*

NICHOLS, FREDERCK D., *Cary Langhorne Professor of Architecture, University of Virginia*

NICHOLS, WILLIAM C., *Consulting Psychologist and Marriage Counselor; Founding Editor of* Journal of Marriage and Family Counseling

NICHOLSON, IRENE, *Correspondent in Mexico of* The Times, *London; Author of* Conquest of Mexico

NICHOLSON, MARGARET, *Author of* A Dictionary of American-English Usage

NICHOLSON, THOMAS D., *Director, American Museum of Natural History—Hayden Planetarium*

NICKELSBURG, GEORGE W. E., *Professor, School of Religion, University of Iowa; Author of* Resurrection, Immortality, and Eternal Life in Intertestamental Judaism

NICKERSON, DOROTHY, *Color Technologist, U.S. Department of Agriculture*

NICKERSON, REV. J. RUSSELL, *Oblate College, Washington, D.C.*

NICOL, DONALD M., *Koraës Professor of Modern Greek and Byzantine History, Language and Literature, King's College, University of London*

NICOLA, SISTER M. ANN, SBS, *St. Elizabeth's Convent, Cornwells Heights, Pa.*

NICOLL, ALLARDYCE, *Author of* Dryden and His Poetry

NICOLSON, MARJORIE H., *Institute for Advanced Study, Princeton, N.J.; Author of* John Milton: A Reader's Guide to His Poetry

NIDIFFER, JANA, *Coauthor of* Beating the Odds: How the Poor Get to College

NIEBEL, B. W., *Head, Department of Industrial Engineering, Pennsylvania State University*

NIEDERHOFFER, ARTHUR, *Professor of Sociology, John Jay College of Criminal Justice; Author of* Behind the Shield: the Police in Urban Society

NIEMEYER, ROBERT F., *Editor and General Manager,* Greyhound Racing Record

NIGAM, ANURAG K., FRCS, *Research Fellow, Department of Surgery, Rayne Institute, University College, London*

NIGRO, PETER D., *Dean and Associate Professor of Business, Staten Island Community College*

NIHART, F. BROOK, *Colonel, U.S. Marine Corps (Retired); Deputy Director for Marine Corps Museums; Managing Editor and Senior Editor of* Armed Forces Journal *(1970–1973)*

NIKHILANANDA, SWAMI, *Editor and Translator of* The Bhagavad Gita

NISSMAN, DAVID B., *President, Turkic Information Center; Author of* The Soviet Union and Iranian Azerbaijan: The Use of Nationalism for Political Penetration

NITZ, OTTO W., *Head of Chemistry Department, Stout State University; Author of* Introductory Chemistry

NIXON, ELLIOTT B., *Member of the New York Bar; Editor,* American Maritime Cases

NOBLE, DAVID F., *Editorial Director, Que Corporation, Indianapolis, Ind.*

NOBLIN, STUART, *Professor of History, North Carolina State University at Raleigh; Author of* The Grange in North Carolina, 1929–1954

NOETHER, DORIT L., *Associate Editor,* Chemtech

NOETHER, EMILIANA P., *Professor of History, University of Connecticut; Author of* Seeds of Italian Nationalism

NOGEE, JOSEPH L., *Professor of Political Science, University of Houston; Coauthor of* Soviet Foreign Policy since World War II *and* Soviet Policy toward International Control of Atomic Energy

NOLAND, AARON, *Professor of History, City College of New York*

NOLLER, CARL R., *Professor of Chemistry, Stanford University*

NOLTE, ANN E., *Associate Director, School Health Education Study, Washington, D.C.; Author of* Health Education: A Conceptual Approach to Curriculum Design

NOLTING, ORIN F., *Executive Director, International City Managers' Association*

NORBECK, EDWARD, *Professor and Chairman, Department of Anthropology and Sociology, Rice University*

NOREN, STEPHEN J., *Associate Professor of Philosophy, California State University at Long Beach*

NORGAARD, MARGARET LIMA, *Coauthor of* Children's Reading

NORLAND, JIM, *Assistant Director, Office of Public Relations, University of Denver*

NORMAN, A. V. B., *Assistant to the Director, Wallace Collection, London, England; Author of* History of War and Weapons, 449–1660

NORMAN, JOHN, *Professor of History and Government, Pace University; Author of* Labor and Politics in Libya and Arab Africa

NORRIS, JOHN L., *Chairman, General Service Board of Alcoholics Anonymous*

NORRIS, KENNETH S., *Professor of Natural History, University of California at Santa Cruz; Editor of* Whales, Dolphins and Porpoises

NORRIS, RICHARD A., JR., *Professor of Dogmatic Theology, General Theological Seminary, New York City*

NORTH, DOUGLASS C., *Chairman, Department of Economics, University of Washington; Author of* Growth and Welfare in the American Past *and* The Economic Growth of the United States, 1790 to 1860

NORTH, JOHN D., *Oxford University; Author of* The Measure of the Universe

NORTON, BRYAN G., *Professor of Philosophy of Science and Technology, School of Public Policy, Georgia Institute of Technology; Author of* Toward Unity among Environmentalists *and* Why Preserve Natural Variety

NORTON, H. W., III, *Professor of Statistical Design and Analysis, College of Agriculture, University of Illinois*

NORWOOD, PERCY V., *Professor of Church History, Seabury-Western Theological Seminary*

NOSSAL, G. J. V., *Director, Walter and Eliza Hall Institute of Medical Research, Melbourne, Australia; Author of* Antibodies and Immunity

NOTTER, LUCILLE E., *Coeditor of* Cardiovascular Nursing; *Director, Open Curriculum Conferences, National League for Nursing*

PARTIAL LIST OF CONTRIBUTORS

NOURSE, EDWARD E., *Professor of Biblical Theology, Hartford Theological Seminary*

NOVACK, SAUL, *Professor of Music, Chair, Department of Music, Queens College*

NOVAK, ALFRED, *Chairman, Division of Allied Health, Stephens College*

NOVAK, MAXIMILLIAN E., *Professor of English, University of California at Los Angeles; Author of* Defoe and the Nature of Man; Realism, Myth, and History in Defoe's Fiction; *and* Eighteenth-Century English Literature

NOVAK, MILAN V., *Lecturer, Internal Medicine, University of Arizona*

NOWELL, CHARLES E., *Professor of History, University of Illinois; Author of* Great Discoveries and the First Colonial Empires

NOWLAN, JAMES D., *Member, Illinois Legislature*

NULSEN, ROBERT H., *President, Trail-R-Club of America; Author of* How to Buy Trailers *and* Travel Trailer Manual

NUMBERS, JANET S., *University of Wisconsin at Madison*

NUMBERS, RONALD L., *Professor and Chairman, Department of the History of Medicine, Center for Health Sciences, University of Wisconsin at Madison*

NUNIS, DOYCE B., JR., *Professor of History, University of Southern California; Author of* Andrew Sublette, Rocky Mountain Prince, 1803–1853

NUQUIST, ANDREW E., *Professor of Political Science, University of Vermont; Author of* Town Government in Vermont

NURNEY, GERALDINE L., *City Librarian, San Jose Public Library*

NYCE, BEN M., *Professor of Literature and Film, University of San Diego; Author of* Satyajit Ray

NYE, MARY JO, *Department of the History of Science, University of Oklahoma*

OAKLEY, STEWART, *School of Modern Languages and European History, University of East Anglia, Norwich, England*

OBER, JOSIAH, *Assistant Professor of History, Montana State University*

OBERSCHMIDT, LEO E., *Managing Editor, Brick and Clay Record*

O'BRIEN, DONALD M., *General Manager, International Association of Fire Chiefs*

O'BRIEN, ROMAEUS, OC, JCD, *Former Dean, School of Canon Law, Catholic University of America; Consultor to Preparatory Commission on Religion for Vatican Council II; Canonist, Diocese of Phoenix, Ariz.; Author of* The Provincial Religious Superior

O'BRIEN, THOMAS D., *Dean of Graduate School, University of Nevada*

O'CALLAGHAN, JOSEPH F., *Professor of Medieval History, Fordham University; Author of* A History of Medieval Spain

OCHOA, SEVERO, MD, *Nobel Prize Winner in Physiology or Medicine, 1959; Professor of Biochemistry, New York University School of Medicine*

OCHS, SIDNEY, *Professor of Physiology, Indiana University Medical Center; Author of* Elements of Neurophysiology

OCHSENSCHLAGER, EDWARD L., *Associate Professor of Classics, Brooklyn College*

OCHSENWALD, WILLIAM, *Professor of History, Virginia Polytechnic Institute and State University; Author of* The Middle East: A History

O'CONNELL, KATHY, *Founding Member, Connecticut Society of Film Critics*

ODAJNYK, WALTER, *Professor of Political Science, Columbia University; Author of* Marxism and Existentialism

O'DEA, THOMAS F., *Author of* The Mormons

O'DOHERTY, BRIAN, *Editor of* Art in America; *Author of* Object and Idea

OESPER, PETER, *Professor and Chairman, Chemistry Department, St. Lawrence University*

OFFNER, WALTER W., *Professional Engineer*

OGILVIE, MARILYN B., *Professor of the History of Science, University of Oklahoma*

OGILVIE, ROBERT S., *Author of* Basic Ice Skating Skills

OH, JOHN K. C., *Marquette University; Author of* Korea: Democracy on Trial

O'HARRA, DOWNING P., *Librarian, Ablah Library, Wichita State University*

OHL, DONALD G., *Associate Professor of Mathematics, Bucknell University*

O'KEEFE, PETER P., *Department of History, Marist College, Poughkeepsie, N.Y.*

OKUN, BARBARA S., *Office of Population Research, Princeton University*

OKUN, BERNARD, *Professor of Economics, Brooklyn College; Author of* Trends in Birth Rates Since 1870

OKUN, DANIEL A., *Professor of Environmental Engineering and Head, Department of Environmental Sciences and Engineering, School of Public Health, University of North Carolina; Coauthor of* Water and Wastewater Engineering

OLANOFF, SAMUEL, *Professor of Physics, Dutchess Community College, Poughkeepsie, N.Y.*

OLCOTT, MARTHA BRILL, *Professor of Political Science, Colgate University*

OLDROYD, HAROLD, *Senior Principal Scientific Officer, British Museum (Natural History), London; Author of* Collecting, Preserving and Studying Insects, Insects and Their World, *and* Elements of Entomology

O'LEARY, WILLIAM R., SJ, *Fordham University*

OLECK, HOWARD L., *Professor of Law, Wake Forest University; Author of* Damages to Persons and Property

OLIPHANT, J. ORIN, *Professor of History, Bucknell University*

OLIVE, LINDSAY S., *Professor of Botany, University of North Carolina*

OLIVER, DAVID B., *Secretary, Carnegie Hero Fund Commission*

OLIVER, JAMES A., *Director, Aquarium of the City of New York*

OLIVER, JOHN A., *Assistant Director, Flint Public Library*

OLIVIER, CHARLES P., *Director, Flower and Cook Astronomical Observatories, University of Pennsylvania*

OLOUGHLIN, J. L. N., *Coeditor of* Odhams Dictionary of the English Language

OLSEN, GLENN WARREN, *Associate Professor of History, University of Utah*

OLSON, EARL E., *Assistant Church Historian, Church of Jesus Christ of Latter-day Saints*

OLSON, KEITH W., *Associate Professor of History, University of Maryland*

OLSON, ROBERT W., *Professor of History, University of Kentucky*

O'MALLEY, C. D., *Professor of Medical History, School of Medicine, University of California at Los Angeles; Editor of* The History of Medical Education

O'MALLEY, JOHN W., SJ, *Professor of Church History, Weston School of Theology; Author of* Giles of Viterbo on Church and Reform

OMAN, CAROLA, *Author of* Lord Nelson

OMAN, CHARLES C., *Keeper, Department of Metalwork, Victoria and Albert Museum, London; Author of* English Church Plate *and* English Domestic Silver

O'MEARA, J. W., *Office of Saline Water, U.S. Department of the Interior*

O'MEARA, PATRICK, *Director, African Studies Program, Indiana University; Professor, Department of Political Science; Professor of Public and Environmental Affairs; Coeditor of* Southern Africa: The Continuing Crisis *and* International Politics in Southern Africa

O'NEIL, CHARLES J., *Professor of Philosophy, Villanova University*

O'NEIL, EDWARD N., *Chairman, Classics Department, University of Southern California*

O'NEILL, CHARLES L., *Assistant Professor of Humanities, St. Thomas Aquinas College*

O NUALLÁIN, LABHRÁS, *Professor of Applied Economics, University College, Galway, Ireland*

OOST, STEWART IRVIN, *Professor of Ancient History, University of Chicago*

OOSTING, HENRY J., *Professor of Botany, Duke University; Author of* The Study of Plant Communities

OPPENHEIMER, JANE, *Professor of the History of Science, Bryn Mawr College*

ORDWAY, FREDERICK I., III, *Coauthor of* Applied Astronautics, History of Rocketry and Space Travel, *and* Episodes in Rocketry

ORE, OYSTEIN, *Sterling Professor of Mathematics, Yale University; Author of* Cardano: The Gambling Scholar

ORMOND, CLYDE, *Author of* The Complete Book of Hunting

ORMSBEE, THOMAS H., *Author of* English China and Its Marks *and* Field Guide to Early American Furniture

ORNE, MARTIN, MD, *The Institute of Pennsylvania Hospital and University of Pennsylvania; Coeditor of* The Nature of Hypnosis *and* Psychiatry: Areas of Promise and Advancement; *Editor of* International Journal of Clinical and Experimental Hypnosis

ORR, DOUGLAS W., MD, *Member of the Los Angeles Psychoanalytical Society and Institute and the Southern California Psychoanalytic Institute; Author of* Professional Counseling on Human Behavior

ORREGO-SALAS, JUAN, *Professor of Music and Director of Latin American Music Center, School of Music, Indiana University*

OSBORN, ROBERT J., *Professor of Political Science, Temple University; Author of* Evolution of Soviet Politics *and* Soviet Social Policies

OSBORNE, JOHN T., *Hempstead Public Library, Hempstead, N.Y.*

OSBORNE, JOHN W., *Professor of History, Rutgers University*

OSBORNE, MICHAEL A., *University of Wisconsin at Madison*

OSBORNE, RAYMOND L., MD, *Adjunct Neurologist, Mt. Sinai Hospital, New York City; Author of* Diagnosis and Treatment of Nervous Diseases

OSBORNE, ROBERT E., *Professor of Spanish, Department of Foreign Languages, University of Connecticut; Coauthor of* Voces y Vistas: Active Spanish for Beginners

OSER, JACOB, *Professor of Economics, Utica College, Syracuse University; Author of* The Evolution of Economic Thought

O'SHAUGHNESSY, JAMES J., *Longines-Wittnauer Watch Company, Inc.*

O'SHEA, H. WILLIAM, *Director, Wake County Public Library, Raleigh, N.C.*

O'SHEA, WILLIAM J., *Professor of Sacramental Theology, Catholic University of America; Author of* Sacraments of Initiation

OSHIRO, KENJI K., *Professor of Geography, Wright State University*

OSLIN, GEORGE P., *Publicity Director, Western Union Telegraph Company*

OSNESS, WAYNE H., *Chairman, Department of Health, Physical Education, and Recreation, University of Kansas*

ÖSTENBERG, CARL ERIC, *Director, Swedish Institute for Classical Studies in Rome*

OSTER, GERALD, *Professor of Biophysics, Mt. Sinai School of Medicine, New York City*

OSTROFF, EUGENE, *Curator of Photography, National Museum of History and Technology, Smithsonian Institution*

OSTROM, JOHN H., *Professor of Geology, Division of Vertebrate Paleontology, Peabody Museum of Natural History, Yale University; Author of* The Strange World of Dinosaurs *and* Marsh's Dinosaurs

OSTROMECKI, JULIUS, *Director, Johnston Public Library, Hackensack, N.J.*

OSWALD, IAN, MD, *Department of Psychiatry, Royal Edinburgh Hospital, Edinburgh, Scotland*

OSWALD, ROBERT M., *National Director of Safety Programs, American National Red Cross*

OTTENBERG, MIRIAM, *Investigative Reporter,* Evening Star, *Washington D.C.; Winner of the Pulitzer Prize for Journalism, 1960; Author of* The Federal Investigators

OTTO, DAVID ARTHUR, *Professor of Biology, Stephens College*

O'TUAMA, SEAN, *Professor of Irish Language and Literature, University College, Cork, Ireland*

OUELLET, FERNAND, *Professor of History, University of Ottawa, Canada*

OUTLER, ALBERT C., *Professor, Perkins School of Theology, Southern Methodist University*

OVERTON, LEONARD C., *Yale University*

OVERTON, MICHAEL L., *Professor of Computer Science, Courant Institute of Mathematical Science, New York University*

OWEN, DOROTHY, *Librarian, Drake Public Library*

OZBUN, JIM L., *Assistant Director, Agricultural Experiment Station, Cornell University*

PACEY, DESMOND, *Author of* Creative Writing in Canada *and* Ten Canadian Poets

PACHNER, JOAN H., *Education Consultant, Storm King Art Center; Author of* Tony Smith: Architecture into Sculpture *in* Tony Smith: Sculpture and Drawings, 1961–1969

PACIFICI, SERGIO, *Professor of Italian, Queens College; Author of* A Guide to Contemporary Italian Literature *and* The Modern Italian Novel

PACKARD, ROBERT L., *Professor of Biology, Texas Tech University*

PAESANI, JUDITH B., *Assistant Director, Center for Real Estate and Urban Economic Studies, University of Connecticut*

PAGE, DENNIS R., *Director, Grand Forks Public Library, Grand Forks, N.Dak.*

PAGE, DON N., *Fellow, Canadian Institute for Advanced Research Cosmology Program; Professor of Physics, University of Alberta, Canada*

PAGE, LEROY E., *Associate Professor, Division of Natural Sciences, Monteith College, Wayne State University*

PAGE, THORNTON, *Astrophysicist, National Aeronautics and Space Administration; Author of* Neighbors of the Earth *and* Origin of the Solar System

PAGEL, WALTER, MD, *Author of* Introduction to Philosophical Medicine in the Era of the Renaissance

PAIGE, DOUGLASS, *Editor of* The Letters of Ezra Pound, 1907–1941

PAINTER, NELL IRVIN, *Professor of History, University of North Carolina at Chapel Hill; Author of* Exodusters: Black Migration to Kansas after Reconstruction *and* The Narrative of Hosea Hudson: His Life as a Negro Communist in the South

PAINTER, SIDNEY, *Author of* History of the Middle Ages *and* Rise of Feudal Monarchies

PALAIMA, T. G., *Dickson Centennial Professor of Classics and Director of the Program in Aegean Scripts and Prehistory, University of Texas at Austin*

PALISCA, CLAUDE V., *Chairman, Department of Music, Yale University; Author of* Baroque Music; *Coauthor of* Musicology

PALLISTER, JOHN C., *Research Associate, Department of Entomology, American Museum of Natural History*

PALLOTTINO, MASSIMO, *Professor of Etruscology and Italic Archaeology, University of Rome; Author of* The Etruscans

PALMER, E. LAURENCE, *Professor, Cornell University*

PALMER, H. BRUCE, *President, National Industrial Conference Board, Incorporated*

PALMER, HOWARD, *Professor of History, University of Calgary, Canada*

PALMER, NORMAN D., *Professor Emeritus of Political Science and Asian Studies, University of Pennsylvania*

PANAGOPOULOS, E. P., *Professor of History, San Jose State University*

PANELLA, DONALD A., *Professor of Old Testament, St. Joseph's Seminary, New York City*

PANO, NICHOLAS C., *Professor of History, Western Illinois University*

PAPADAKI, STAMO, *Professor of Architecture and Planning, Brooklyn College; Editor of* The Work of Oscar Niemeyer; *Author of* Le Corbusier

PAPP, JOSEPH, *Founder of the Joseph Papp Yiddish Theater*

PARADOWSKI, ROBERT J., *Associate Professor of the History of Science, Rochester Institute of Technology*

PARASCANDOLA, JOHN, *Professor of History of Pharmacy and History of Science, University of Wisconsin Center for Health Sciences, University of Wisconsin at Madison*

PARDES, HERBERT, MD, *Director, National Institutes of Mental Health*

PARDUE, DUNCAN, *Brooklyn College*

PARDUE, PETER A., *Associate Professor of Religious Studies, Indiana University*

PARHAM, PAUL, *University Librarian, Texas Christian University*

PARK, CHARLES F., JR., *Professor of Geology, Department of Applied Earth Sciences, Stanford University; Author of* Affluence in Jeopardy *and* Earthbound: Minerals, Energy, and Man's Future; *Coauthor of* Ore Deposits

PARK, DAVID, *Barclay Jermain Professor of Natural Philosophy, Williams College*

PARKER, D. VERDELLE, *Associate Professor of Physical Education, Purdue University*

PARKER, FRANKLIN D., *Professor of History, University of North Carolina at Greensboro; Author of* The Central American Republics

PARKER, HAROLD E., *Brigadier General, U.S. Army; Assistant Judge Advocate General for Military Law, Department of the Army*

PARKER, IAN C., *Associate Professor of Economics, Scarborough College, University of Toronto, Canada*

PARKER, J. H., *Professor of Italian and Hispanic Studies, University of Toronto, Canada; Author of* Gil Vicente

PARKER, MILTON E., *Director and Professor, Food Engineering, Technology Center, Illinois Institute of Technology*

PARKER, RICHARD A., *Wilbour Professor of Egyptology, Emeritus, Brown University*

PARKER, W. REN, *Professor of Scene Design and Technical Production, Department of Drama, Carnegie-Mellon University; Coauthor of* Scene Design and Stage Lighting

PARKES, HENRY B., *Professor of History, New York University; Author of* The American Experience

PARKES, JOSEPH P., SJ, *Fordham University*

PARKINSON, THOMAS F., *Professor of English, University of California at Berkeley; Editor of* A Casebook of the Beat

PARKS, JANET, *Curator of Drawings, Avery Library, Columbia University*

PARR, CAROLINE S., *Head, Central Children's Room, Arlington County (Va.) Department of Libraries*

PARRISH, FRED K., *Associate Professor of Biology, Georgia State University*

PARRISH, MICHAEL E., *Associate Professor of Modern American History, University of California at San Diego; Author of* Securities Regulation and the New Deal

PARRISH, WILLIAM, *Research Staff, IBM Corporation*

PARRY, JOHN H., *Gardiner Professor of Oceanic History and Affairs, Harvard University; Author of* The Age of Reconnaissance *and* The Spanish Seaborne Empire

PARRY, ROBERT W., *Professor of Chemistry, University of Utah; Author of* Chemistry: Experimental Foundations

PARSONS, MERRIBELL, *Bernard Berenson Fellow, Institute of Fine Arts, New York University*

PARSONS, TALCOTT, *Professor of Sociology, Harvard University; Author of* Politics and Social Structure *and* Systems of Modern Societies

PARTRIDGE, ERIC, *Author of* A Dictionary of Slang and Unconventional English *and* A Dictionary of Clichés

PASCHALL, DAVIS Y., *Former President, College of William and Mary*

PASQUIER, ROGER F., *World Wildlife Fund*

PASSMORE, JOHN A., *Professor of Philosophy, Institute of Advanced Studies, Australian National University, Canberra; Author of* Hume's Intentions *and* A Hundred Years of Philosophy

PATAI, RAPHAEL, *Author of* On Jewish Folklore *and* The Jewish Mind; *Editor of* Encyclopedia of Zionism and Israel

PATERSON, JOHN H., *Professor of Geography, Leicester University; Author of* North America *and* Land, Work, and Resources

PATRICK, REMBERT W., *Author of* Jefferson Davis and His Cabinet *and* The Reconstruction of the Nation

PATTERSON, JAMES T., *Professor of History, Brown University; Author of* Mr. Republican: A Biography of Robert A. Taft *and* The New Deal and the States

PATTERSON, MAUREEN L. P., *University of Chicago; Author of* Caste and Political Leadership in Maharashtra

PATTERSON, ROBERT LEET, *Professor of Philosophy, Duke University; Author of* The Philosophy of William Ellery Channing

PATTERSON, SAMUEL C., *Department of Political Science, Ohio State University; Editor of* Parliamentary Institutions in a Changing World

PATTERSON, YOLANDA ASTARITA, *Associate Professor of Foreign Languages, California State College at Hayward*

PATTISON, I. H., *Head of Pathology Department, Agricultural Research Council, Institute for Research on Animal Diseases, England*

PATTON, DONALD J., *Director of Publications, Carnegie Institution of Washington*

PAUCK, WILHELM, *Author of* The Heritage of the Reformation

PAUL, BARNABAS, FSC, *Brothers of the Christian Schools, New York City*

PAUL, JOHN, *Director, Beatson Institute for Cancer Research, Glasgow, Scotland; Author of* Cell Biology

PAUL, LESLIE, *Fellow of the Royal Society of Literature; Author of* The English Philosophers

PAUL, RODMAN W., *Edward S. Harkness Professor of History, California Institute of Technology; Author of* Mining Frontiers of the Far West, 1848–1880

PAULSEN, MONRAD G., *John B. Minor Professor of Law and Dean, Law School, University of Virginia*

PAULSON, GLENN L., *Assistant Commissioner, New Jersey Department of Environmental Protection*

PAULY, IRA B., *Professor of Psychiatry, University of Oregon Medical School*

PAYNE, DAVID A., *Professor of Educational Psychology and Director of Test Scoring and Reporting Services, University of Georgia*

PAYNE, ROBERT, *Author of* Mao Tse-tung, Chinese Diaries, *and other books; Editor of* The White Pony, an Anthology of Chinese Poetry

PEACH, BERNARD, *Professor of Philosophy, Duke University*

PEACOCK, JAMES L., *Kenan Professor of Anthropology, University of North Carolina at Chapel Hill; President, American Anthropological Association, 1993–1995*

PEACOCK, LESLIE C., *President, Crocker National Bank, San Francisco*

PEACOCK, LUCILLE, *Evans Memorial Library, Aberdeen, Miss.*

PEARL, RICHARD M., *Professor of Geology, Colorado College; Author of* How to Know the Minerals and Rocks *and* American Gem Trails

PEARL, VALERIE, *Former President, New Hall College, Cambridge University; Fellow, Royal Historical Society; Author of* London and the Outbreak of the Civil War

PEARSON, NORMAN HOLMES, *Professor of English and American Studies, Yale University; Coeditor of* The Oxford Anthology of American Literature

PEARSON, ROSS N., *Professor of Geography, Eastern Michigan University; Author of* Physical Geography

PECK, CAROLINE NESTMANN, *Teaching Associate, Department of Egyptology, Brown University*

PECK, PAULA, *Author of* The Art of Good Cooking

PECK, WILLIAM H., *Curator of Ancient Art, Detroit Institute of Arts*

PECKHAM, HOWARD H., *Director, William L. Clements Library and Professor of American History, University of Michigan; Author of* The Making of the University of Michigan, 1817–1967, *and* The War for Independence

PEDDLE, MICHAEL T., *Professor of Economics, College of the Holy Cross*

PEDEN, WILLIAM, *Professor of English, University of Missouri; Author of* The American Short Story

PEDERSON, CARL S., *State University of New York Agricultural Experiment Station at Geneva, N.Y.*

PEDERSON, LELAND R., *Professor of Geography, University of Arizona*

PEDICORD, HARRY WILLIAM, *Chairman, American Society for Theatre Research; Author of* The Theatrical Public in the Time of Garrick

PEDLEY, JOHN GRIFFITHS, *Professor of Classical Archaeology and Greek, University of Michigan; Director of the Kelsey Museum of Ancient and Mediaeval Archaeology, University of Michigan; Author of* Sardis in the Age of Croesus

PEERSON, ETHEL, *Director, Muscle Shoals Regional Library, Florence, Ala.*

PEGEL, JANE W., *Director, National Iceboat Authority; Secretary, International Skeeter Association; International DN Ice Yacht Champion*

PEGG, CARL H., *Professor of Modern European History, University of North Carolina; Author of* Contemporary Europe in World Focus

PEGUES, FRANKLIN J., *Professor of History, Ohio State University; Author of* The Lawyers of the Last Capetians

PEI, MARIO A., *Professor of Romance Philology, Columbia University; Author of* Language Today, The Story of Language, *and* Getting Along in Italian

PEIRCE, JOSEPHINE H., *Author of* Fire on the Hearth

PEIRCE, NEAL R., *Author of* The People's President

PEIXOTO, JOSÉ ROBERTO DE M., *I.G.B.E. Foundation, University of Wisconsin at Milwaukee*

PELOSO, VINCENT C., *Assistant Professor of History, Howard University*

PENNER, LOUIS A., *Department of Psychology, University of South Florida; Author of* Social Psychology: A Contemporary Approach

PENNIMAN, CLARA *Professor of Political Science and Director of the Center for Public Policy and Administration, University of Wisconsin*

PENNIMAN, HOWARD, *Professor of Government, Georgetown University; Author of* The American Political Process

PENTON, M. JAMES, *Professor Emeritus of History, University of Lethbridge, England; Author of* Apocalypse Delayed: The Story of Jehovah's Witnesses

PEPPER, ELEANOR, *Design Consultant; Professor of Interior Design, Pratt Institute*

PEPPER, JON V., *Head, Department of Mathematics, North East London Polytechnic*

PEPPERELL, PHYLLIS A., *Librarian, Castro Valley Branch Library*

PERDUE, ROBERT E., JR., *Botanist, Crops Research Division, U.S. Department of Agriculture*

PERETZ, DON, *Professor of Political Science, State University of New York at Binghamton*

PERICOT, LUIS, *Author of* La Espana primitiva

PERKINS, DEXTER, *Author of* The Evolution of American Foreign Policy *and* A History of the Monroe Doctrine

PERKINS, DWIGHT HEALD, *Professor of Economics, Harvard University; Author of* Market Control and Planning in Communist China

PERKINS, FRANK K., *Games Columnist, Boston* Herald

PERKINS, JOHN W., *City Librarian, Inglewood, Calif.*

PERKINS, WILLIAM L., SJ, *Fordham University*

PERLES, JULIA, *Chairman, Special Committee on Matrimonial Law, New York County Lawyers Association*

PERLIN, GEORGE C., *Assistant Professor, Department of Political Studies, Queen's University, Canada*

PERRIN, NANCY J., *Director, Corning Public Library*

PERRIN, ROBERT H., *Member, American Musicological Society*

PERROT, PAUL N., *Director, Corning Museum of Glass, Corning, N.Y.*

PERRY, E. CASWELL, *City Librarian, Burbank Public Library*

PERRY, JAMES M., *The National Observer; Author of* The New Politics: The Expanding Technology of Political Manipulation

PERUTZ, MAX F., *Nobel Prize Winner in Chemistry, 1962; Chairman, Medical Research Council Laboratory of Molecular Biology, Cambridge University*

PERVIN, LAWRENCE A., *Professor of Psychology, Rutgers University; Author of* Personality: Theory and Research *and* Current Controversies and Issues in Personality

PETER, CARL J., STD, *Dean, School of Religious Studies, Catholic University of America*

PETER, VAL J., JCD, STD, *Executive Director, Boys Town*

PETERS, RITA PUTINS, *Fellow, Russian Research Center, Harvard University; Lecturer, Department of Political Science, University of Massachusetts at Boston*

PETERSEN, WILLIAM J., *Superintendent and Editor Emeritus, State Historical Society of Iowa; Author of* Steamboating on the Upper Mississippi, Towboating on the Mississippi, *and* Mississippi River Panorama

PETERSON, A. D. C., *Director, Department of Education, Oxford University; Author of* 100 Years of Education *and* Educating Our Rulers

PETERSON, HAROLD, Sports Illustrated

PETERSON, RANDOLPH L., *Curator, Mammal Department, Royal Ontario Museum, University of Toronto, Canada*

PETERSON, SHOREY, *Professor of Economics, University of Michigan*

PETRIE, SIR CHARLES, *Fellow of the Royal Historical Society; Author of* The Edwardians *and* The Victorians

PETROPULOS, JOHN A., *Professor of History, Amherst College; Author of* Politics and Statecraft in the Kingdom of Greece, 1833–43

PETTER, FRANCIS, *Sous-Directeur, Laboratoire de Zoologie des Mammifères, Muséum National d'Histoire Naturelle, Paris; Author of* Les Mammifères

PETTYJOHN, TIMOTHY A., *Department of Anthropology, University of North Carolina at Chapel Hill*

PÉWÉ, TROY L., *Professor of Geology, Arizona State University*

PEYRE, HENRI, *Sterling Professor of French, Yale University; Author of* French Novelists of Today

PFAUTZ, HAROLD W., *Professor of Sociology, Brown University*

PFEFFER, LEO, *Professor of Constitutional Law, Long Island University; Author of* Church, State, and Freedom *and* This Honorable Court

PFEIFER, DANIEL, *Professor of Japanese, Georgia State University*

PFEIFFER, ROBERT H., *Author of* Introduction to the Old Testament

PFENNING, CHRISTINE, *Assistant Librarian, Fletcher Free Library, Burlington, Vt.*

PFLANZE, OTTO P., *Professor of History, University of Minnesota; Author of* Bismarck and the Development of Germany: The Period of Unification 1815–1871 *and* A History of the Western World: Modern Times

PHELPS, DAWSON A., *Historian, National Park Service*

PHELPS, MARY POWELL, *Director, Lexington Public Library, Lexington, Ky.*

PHELPS BROWN, E. H., *Professor of the Economics of Labour, University of London; Author of* The Growth of British Industrial Relations

PHILLIPS, ANTHONY V., *Assistant Professor of Mathematics, State University of New York at Stony Brook*

PHILLIPS, CHARLES FRANKLIN, *President, Bates College*

PHILLIPS, CHARLES J., *Professor of Ceramics, Rutgers University*

PHILLIPS, R. HART, *Correspondent, New York* Times; *Author of* Cuba: Island of Paradox

PHILLIPS, WALTER S., *Professor of Botany, University of Arizona; Author of* Vegetation of the Northern Great Plains

PHIPPS, J. B., *Professor of Plant Sciences, University of Western Ontario*

PHIPPS, MICHAEL, *Director, Cattermole Memorial Library, Fort Madison, Iowa*

PICCARD, JACQUES ERNEST, *Bureau Jacques Piccard, Lausanne, Switzerland*

PICKERING, JAMES H., *Director, Warder Public Library, Springfield, Ohio*

PICKERSGILL, JOHN W., *President, Canadian Transport Commission, Ottawa, Canada; Author of* The Liberal Party

PICKETT, BARZILLAI S., *Head, Department of Horticulture, University of Tennessee*

PICKETT, GEORGE E., MD, *Coauthor of* Public Health: Administration and Practice

PICKRELL, KENNETH L., MD, *Professor of Plastic and Maxillofacial Surgery, Duke University Medical Center*

PIERCE, CALVIN R., *Department of the History of Science, University of Wisconsin at Madison*

PIERCE, E. LOWE, *Professor of Zoology, University of Florida*

PIERCE, RICHARD A., *Professor of Russian History, Queen's University, Canada*

PIERI, PIERO, *Dean, Faculty of Pedagogy, University of Turin, Italy*

PIERSON, PETER, *Associate Professor of History, University of Santa Clara; Author of* Philip II of Spain

PIERSON, ROBERT H., *President, Seventh-day Adventists, Washington, D.C.*

PIGNATELLI, MASSIMO N., MD, *Senior Lecturer and Honorary Consultant in Histopathology, Royal Postgraduate Medical School, University of London*

PIKE, FREDRICK B., *Professor of History, University of Notre Dame; Author of* Chile and the United States, 1880–1962

PILEGGI, JOSEPH, *National Marine Fishery Service*

PILLION, GEORGE L., *Head Librarian, Fall River Public Library, Fall River, Mass.*

PIPER, MARIAN L., *Librarian, Acton Memorial Library*

PIPKIN, MICHAEL B., *Charles H. Taylor Memorial Library, Hampton, Va.*

PIRIE, PETER, *Director, Pacific Island Program and Associate Professor of Geography, University of Hawaii*

PIRNIE, HARRIETTE M., *Head Librarian, Exeter Public Library, Exeter, N.H.*

PISTON, WALTER, *Composer; Professor of Music, Harvard University; Author of* Counterpoint

PITKIN, ROBERT B., *Managing Editor,* American Legion Magazine

PITT, MALCOLM, *Professor of South Asia Studies, Hartford Seminary Foundation; Author of* Introducing Hinduism

PITTARO, ERNEST, *Author of* TV and Film Production Data Book; *Editor of* Photo-Lab-Index

PITTENGER, W. NORMAN, *Lecturer, Divinity Faculty, Cambridge University; Author of* Theology and Reality *and* Process Thought and Christian Faith

PLANK, JOHN N., *Professor of Political Science, University of Connecticut*

PLATT, RUTHERFORD, *Author of* This Green World *and* American Trees

PLECK, ELIZABETH H., *Research Associate, Center for Research on Women, Wellesley College; Author of* Domestic Tyranny: The Making of Social Policy against Family Violence

PLETCHER, DAVID M., *Professor of History, Indiana University; Author of* Rails, Mines, and Progress *and* The Awkward Years: American Foreign Relations Under Garfield and Arthur

PLETCHER, ELDON, *Editorial Cartoonist, Times-Picayune, New Orleans*

PLISCHKE, ELMER, *Professor of Government and Politics, University of Maryland*

PLUMB, J. H., *Professor of Modern English History, Cambridge University; Author of* In the Light of History

POBBI-ASARE, NICHOLAS, *Lecturer, Political Science and African Studies, State University of New York College at New Paltz*

PODELL, RICHARD N., MD, MPH, *Overlook Hospital, Summit, N.J.*

POGUE, FORREST C., *Author of* The Supreme Command

POHL, FREDERICK J., *Author of* Amerigo Vespucci, Pilot Major

POKORNY, JULIUS, *Author of* Historical Reader of Old Irish

POLDERVAART, ARIE, *Professor of Petrology, Columbia University*

POLITZER, HEINZ, *Professor of German, University of California at Berkeley; Coauthor of* German: A Comprehensive Course

POLIVKA, EMILY, *Librarian, Berwyn Public Library*

POLK, WILLIAM R., *Professor of History and Director, Center for Middle Eastern Studies, University of Chicago*

POLLACK, JAMES B., *Research Scientist, Theoretical and Planetary Studies Branch, National Aeronautics and Space Administration—Ames Research Center*

POLLARD, ERNEST C., *Chairman, Department of Biophysics, Pennsylvania State University; Coauthor of* Physics: An Introduction

POLLARD, SIDNEY, *Professor of Economic History, University of Bielefeld, Germany*

POLLOCK, DAVID, *Visiting Lecturer in Government, Harvard University; Author of* The Politics of Pressure: American Arms and Israeli Policy Since the Six Day War

POLLOCK, H. E. D., *Curator of Maya Archaeology, Harvard University; Author of* Round Structures of Aboriginal Middle America

POLOMÉ, EDGAR C., *Professor of Oriental and African Languages and Literatures, University of Texas at Austin; Author of* Swahili Language Handbook

POMEROY, KENNETH B., *Chief Forester, American Forestry Association*

POMPER, GERALD M., *Professor of Political Science, Livingston College, Rutgers University; Author of* Nominating the President

PONTIUS, MARJORIE A., *Librarian, Deadwood Carnegie Public Library*

POOLE, PETER A., *Author of* The Vietnamese in Thailand *and* Eight Presidents and Indochina

POPE, CLIFFORD H., *Author of* The Reptile World

POPENOE, JOHN, *Director, Fairchild Tropical Garden, Miami, Fla.*

POPKIN, HENRY, *Professor of English, State University of New York at Buffalo; Editor of* Concise Encyclopedia of Modern Drama

POPP, HELEN M., *Lecturer and Research Associate in Education, Graduate School of Education, Harvard University*

POPPER, EVA, *Assistant to the President, Carnegie Endowment for International Peace*

PORTER, H. TEULON, *Member of the Société Jersiaise*

PORTER, THEODORE M., *Division of Humanities and Social Sciences, California Institute of Technology*

POSNER, ERNST, *Professor, History and Archives Administration, American University, Washington, D.C.; Author of* American State Archives

POST, GAINES, *Professor of History, Princeton University; Author of* Studies in Medieval Legal Thought

POSTAL, BERNARD, *Director of Public Information, National Jewish Welfare Board, New York City*

POSTLETHWAIT, R. W., MD, *Chief of Staff, Veterans Administration Hospital, Durham, N.C.*

POSTOL, THEODORE A., *Center for International Security and Arms Control, Stanford University*

POTT, CLARENCE K., *Professor of German, University of Michigan*

POTTER, ELMER B., *Professor of Naval History, U.S. Naval Academy; Author of* The Naval Academy Illustrated History of the United States Navy; *Coauthor of* American Sea Power since 1775; *Coeditor (with Chester W. Nimitz) of* Sea Power: A Naval History

POTTLE, FREDERICK A., *Sterling Professor of English, Yale University; Coeditor of* The Yale Editions of the Private Papers of James Boswell

POUGH, FREDERICK H., *Consulting Mineralogist; Author of* The Story of Gems and Semi-Precious Stones

POUND, LOUISE, *Author of* American Ballads and Songs

POUNDS, NORMAN J. G., *University Professor of History and Geography, Indiana University*

POWELL, C. F., *Professor of Physics and Director of the H.H. Wills Physics Laboratory, University of Bristol, England; Nobel Prize Winner in Physics, 1950; Coauthor of* Nuclear Physics in Photographs *and* The Study of Elementary Particles by the Photographic Method

POWELL, HERBERT MARCUS, *Chemical Crystallography Laboratory, England*

POWELL, T. G. E., *Author of* The Celts and Prehistoric Art

POWER, DAVID N., OMI, *Associate Professor of Systematic Theology, Catholic University of America*

POWERS, CHARLES F., *Research Aquatic Biologist*

POWERS, JOSEPH M., SJ, *Associate Professor of Systematic Theology, Jesuit School of Theology, Berkeley, Calif.*

POWILLS, DOROTHY L., *Director-Editor, Chicago Playing Card Collectors, Inc.*

POYNTER, DANIEL F., *Author of* Hang Gliding

PRADEL, PIERRE, *Inspecteur-Général du Musée du Louvre*

PRALL, STUART E., *Professor of History, Queens College*

PRANG, MARGARET, *Professor of History, University of British Columbia, Canada*

PRASAD, BIMLA, *Author of* The Origins of Indian Foreign Policy

PRASAD, NARMADESHWAR, *University Professor of Sociology, Patna University, India; Author of* The Myth of the Caste System

PRATLEY, GERALD, *Film Critic and Commentator, Canadian Broadcasting Corporation*

PRATT, JULIUS W., *Author of* Expansionists of 1812

PRATT, ROBERTSON, *Professor of Pharmacognosy and Antibiotics, School of Pharmacy, San Francisco Medical Center, University of California*

PRESCHEL, TOVIA, *Professor of Talmud, Jewish Theological Seminary of America*

PRESS, EDWARD, MD, MPH, *Clinical Professor of Pediatrics and Clinical Professor of Preventive Medicine and Public Health, School of Medicine, University of Oregon*

PREUETT, STEPHEN B., *Assistant Professor, Department of Biology, Garner-Webb College, Boiling Springs, N.C.*

PREUSS, HARRY G., MD, *Professor of Medicine and Pathology, Georgetown University Medical Center*

PRICE, CHARLES, *Author of* The World of Golf

PRICE, HOMER, *Professor of Geology and Geography, Hunter College*

PRICE, MARTIN, *Thomas E. Donnelley Professor of English, Yale University; Author of* Swift's Rhetorical Art

PRICE, RICHARD W., MD, *Department of Neurology, Memorial Sloan-Kettering Cancer Center and Cornell University Medical College, New York City*

PRINCE, VIVIAN, *Associate Professor of Library Science, University of Southern California*

PRINGLE, EUGENE A., *Director, Warner Library, The Tarrytowns, N.Y.*

PRINGLE, HENRY F., *Author of* The Life and Times of William Howard Taft

PRITCHARD, JAMES S., *Department of History, Queen's University, Canada*

PRITCHETT, C. HERMAN, *Professor of Political Science, University of California at Santa Barbara; Author of* The American Constitution

PROCTOR, BETTY C., *Librarian, New Providence (N.J.) Memorial Library*

PROCTOR, SAMUEL, *Professor of History and Social Sciences, University of Florida; Editor of* Florida Historical Quarterly

PRODRICK, R. G., *Assistant Chief Librarian, University of Toronto, Canada*

PROJECTOR, THEODORE H., *Consulting Engineer, Kensington, Md.*

PROKHOROV, VADIM, *Author of* Russian Folk Songs

PROPER, DAVID R., *Librarian, Memorial Libraries, Deerfield, Mass.*

PROWN, JULES D., *Professor of History of Art, Yale University; Author of* John Singleton Copley

PUDNEY, JOHN, *Author of* The Thomas Cook Story

PUESCHEL, SIEGFRIED M., MD, PHD, *Professor of Pediatrics, Brown University School of Medicine*

PUGH, SAMUEL F., *Editor of* World Call

PULGRAM, ERNST, *Professor of Romance and Classical Linguistics, University of Michigan; Author of* The Tongues of Italy: Prehistory and History *and* Introduction to the Spectrography of Speech

PUNNETT, THOMAS R., JR., *Professor of Biology, Temple University*

PURDY, ALEXANDER C., *Author of* The Reality of God

PURVES, WILLIAM K., *Professor Emeritus of Biology, Harvey Mudd College; Coauthor of* Life: The Science of Biology, 4th ed.

PURVIS, DOUGLAS D., *Professor of Economics and Director, John Deutsch Institute for the Study of Economic Policy, Queen's University, Ontario, Canada*

PUSEY, MERLO J., *Author of the Pulitzer Prize-Winning Biography,* Charles Evans Hughes

PUSTAY, JOHN S., *Lieutenant Colonel, Headquarters, U.S. Air Force, Washington, D.C.; Author of* Counterinsurgency Warfare

PUTMAN, BRYAN, *Director of Advertising and Public Relations, Hallmark Cards, Inc.*

PUTNAM, D. F., *Professor of Geography, University of Toronto, Canada*

PUTNAM, PAUL A., *Chief, Beef Cattle Research Branch, Agricultural Research Service*

QUASHNOCK, JOSEPH M., MD, *U.S. Air Force School of Aerospace Medicine*

QUENNELL, PETER, *Author of* John Ruskin

QUIGG, CHRIS, *Head of Theoretical Physics Department, Fermi National Accelerator Laboratory*

QUINLAN, MAURICE J., *Professor of English, Boston College*

QUINN, ALONZO DeF., *Consulting Engineer; Author of* Design and Construction of Ports and Marine Structures

QUINN, MATTHEW J., *Director of Public Relations, College of the Holy Cross*

QUINN, MICHAEL, *Sports Staff,* Newsday

QUINN, ROBERT M., *Professor of Art History, University of Arizona; Author of* Mexican Colonial Art and Architecture

QUINTANA, RICARDO, *Professor of English, University of Wisconsin; Coeditor of* English Poetry of the Mid and Late Eighteenth Century

QUINTON, ANTHONY, *President, Trinity College, Oxford University*

QUIRK, HOWARD E., *Assistant to the Dean, New York State Veterinary College, Cornell University*

QUIRK, WILLIAM H., *Editorial Director, Engineering and Construction World*

RABASSA, GREGORY, *Professor of Romance Languages, Queens College*

RABE, WILMER T., *Director of Public Information, University of Detroit*

RABENECK, NICOLAI, *Linguist and Writer on European Nations and Cultures*

RABINOWICZ, ERNEST, *Professor of Mechanical Engineering, Massachusetts Institute of Technology; Author of* Friction and Wear of Materials

RABINOWITCH, ALEXANDER, *Professor, Department of History, Indiana University; Director, Russian and East European Institute, Indiana University; Author of* The Bolsheviks Come to Power: The Revolution of 1917 in Petrograd *and* Prelude to Revolution: The Petrograd Bolsheviks and the July 1917 Uprising

RABINOWITZ, HOWARD N., *Professor of History, University of New Mexico; Author of* Race, Ethnicity, and Urbanization *and* The First New South, 1865–1920

RACHELS, JAMES, *Professor of Philosophy, University of Miami; Editor of* Moral Problems: A Collection of Philosophical Essays

RADEST, HOWARD B., *Associate Professor of Philosophy, Ramapo College; Author of* Toward a Common Ground Of Life and Meaning Understanding Ethical Culture

RADIN, BEATRICE H., *New York Academy of Sciences*

RAE, WESLEY D., *Dean of the College of Arts and Sciences, University of Michigan at Flint; Author of* Thomas Lodge

RAFFEL, SIDNEY, *Professor, Active Department of Dermatology, Stanford University School of Medicine*

RAGOSINE, VICTOR E., *Manager, Research Department, Ampex Corporation*

RAHN, JOAN E., *Author of* Experiments in Science

RAINS, A. J. HARDING, *Professor of Surgery, Charing Cross Hospital Medical School, University of London; Author of* Gallstones; *Editor of* Treatment of Cancer in Clinical Practice

RAMBERG, EDWARD G., *Fellow, Technical Staff, RCA Laboratories*

RAMEY, MARY R., *Library Director, Danville Public Library*

RAMMELKAMP, CHARLES H., MD, *Professor of Medicine, Case Western Reserve University*

RAMSDELL, LEWIS S., *Professor of Mineralogy, University of Michigan*

RAMSEY, JACK, *Chief Librarian, City of Glendale*

RAMSEY, MARJORIE E., *Head, Division of Education, Georgia Southwestern College*

RAMSEY, WILLIAM, *Professor of Music, Stanford University*

RAMSTAD, ROBERT J., *National Park Service*

RANDALL, FRANCIS B., *Professor of History, Sarah Lawrence College; Author of* Stalin's Russia: An Historical Consideration

RANDALL, ROBERT H., JR., *U.S. Naval Oceanographic Office, Suitland, Md.; Author of* United States Surveys in the Pacific, 1900–1960

RANDALL, THEODORE A., *Professor of Ceramics, Alfred University*

RANDI, JAMES, *Magician and Author*

RANKIN, HUGH F., *Department of History, Tulane University; Author of* Rebels and Redcoats, The American Revolution, Theater in Colonial America, The Golden Age of Piracy, The North Carolina Continentals, *and* Francis Marion: The Swamp Fox

RANSOM, HARRY HOWE, *Professor of Political Science, Vanderbilt University; Author of* Central Intelligence and National Security *and* An American Foreign Policy Reader

RANSONE, COLEMAN B., JR., *Professor of Political Science, University of Alabama; Author of* The Office of Governor in the United States

RAPAPORT, FELIX T., MD, *Professor of Surgery and Pathology (Immunology), School of Medicine, State University of New York at Stony Brook; Coeditor of* Human Transplantation

RAPHAEL, MARC LEE, *Nathan and Sophie Gumenick Professor of Judaic Studies, College of William and Mary; Coeditor,* American Jewish History

RAPP, ROBERT, DDS, *Professor and Head, Department of Pedodontics, School of Dental Medicine, University of Pittsburgh*

RAPPAPORT, PAUL, *Associate Laboratory Director, RCA Laboratories, Princeton, N.J.*

RASMUSSEN, JORGEN S., *Professor of Political Science, Iowa State University; Author of* Retrenchment and Revival: A Study of the Contemporary British Liberal Party *and* The Process of Politics: A Comparative Approach

RATH, CHARLES E., MD, *Professor of Medicine and Director of Hematology, Georgetown University*

RATHBONE, CHARLES, *Associate Professor of Teacher Education, University of Vermont; Author of* Multiage Portraits: Teaching and Learning in Mixed-Age Classrooms

RATHBONE, PERRY T., *Director, Museum of Fine Arts, Boston*

RATIGAN, WILLIAM, *Author of* The Adventures of Paul Bunyan and Babe

RATNER, JANE FAUX, *Head of Technical Services, Willard Public Library, Battle Creek, Mich.*

RATTANSI, P. M., *Fellow, King's College, Cambridge University*

RATTEE, IAN D., *Professor and Head of Department of Colour Chemistry, University of Leeds, England*

RAUCH, LAWRENCE L., *Professor of Instrumentation, College of Engineering, University of Michigan*

RAVETZ, JEROME R., *Senior Lecturer in the History and Philosophy of Science, University of Leeds, England; Author of* Astronomy and Cosmology in the Achievement of Nikolaus Copernicus

RAVITCH, MARK M., MD, *Professor of Surgery, University of Pittsburgh*

RAY, CARLETON, *Associate Professor of Biology, Johns Hopkins University*

RAY, GORDON N., *President, John Simon Guggenheim Memorial Foundation; Author of* The Letters and Private Papers of William Makepeace Thackeray, Thackeray: The Uses of Adversity, 1811–1846, Thackeray: The Age of Wisdom, 1847–1863, Henry James and H.G. Wells, *and* H.G. Wells and Rebecca West

RAYBACK, JOSEPH G., *Professor of History, Temple University; Author of* A History of American Labor

RAYMOND, AGNES G., *Associate Professor of French, University of Massachusetts; Author of* Jean Giraudoux: The Theatre of Victory and Defeat

RAYMOND, ELLSWORTH, *Professor, Department of Politics, New York University; Author of* The Soviet State

RAYMOND, GEORGE M., *Professor of Planning and Chairman, Department of City and Regional Planning, Pratt Institute*

RAYMOND, PETER H., *Editor,* Oarsman *magazine*

READ, ALLEN WALKER, *Professor of English, Columbia University*

READ, DAVID H. C., *Minister, Madison Avenue Presbyterian Church, New York City*

READ, WILLIAM T., *Chemical Adviser, U.S. Department of the Army*

REAVIS, THETIS, *Director of Public Information, Foreign Policy Association*

REBAY, LUCIANO, *Professor of Italian, Columbia University; Author of* Alberto Moravia

RECK, ANDREW J., *Professor and Chairman, Department of Philosophy, Tulane University; Author of* Recent American Philosophy, Introduction to William James, New American Philosophers, *and* Speculative Philosophy

RECK, W. EMERSON, *Author of* College Publicity Manual

REDDIN, MICHAEL J., *Assistant Lecturer in Social Administration, London School of Economics*

REDFIELD, MARC, *Professor of English, Claremont Graduate School*

REDINGER, RUBY V., *Professor of English, Baldwin-Wallace College; Author of* George Eliot: The Emergent Self

REDMAN, BEN RAY, *Author of* The Oxford University Press

REED, HOWARD A., *Department of History, University of Connecticut*

REED, JOHN R., *Professor of English, Wayne State University; Author of* Victorian Conventions

REED, JOHN W., *Professor of Law, University of Michigan; Coauthor of* Pleading and Joinder: Cases and Statutes

REED, THOMAS HARRISON, *Municipal Government Counselor, Connecticut Public Expenditure Council*

REES, MINA, *Professor of Mathematics and Dean of Faculty, Hunter College*

REES, WILLIAM, *Professor, University of Wales; Author of* Cardiff: A History of the City

REESE, GUSTAVE, *Professor, Graduate School of Arts and Sciences, New York University; Author of* Music in the Renaissance

REESOR, MARGARET E., *Professor, Department of Classics, Queens University, Canada; Author of* The Political Theory of the Old and Middle Stoa

REEVE, F. A., *County Councillor, Cambridge, England; Author of* Cambridge

REEVE, FRANKLIN D., *Author of* Aleksandr Blok: Between Image and Idea *and* The Russian Novel

REEVE, RICHARD M., *Associate Professor of Spanish, University of California at Los Angeles; Author of numerous books and articles on Mexican and Latin American literature*

REEVES, JAMES, *Author of* A Short History of English Poetry *and* English Fables and Fairy Stories

REGAN, CHARLES L., *Associate Professor of English, Boston College*

REICH, MELVYN L., *Professor Emeritus of Educational Psychology, University of Connecticut at Storrs*

REID, JAMES M., *Author of* Scotland, Past and Present

REID, MARGARET G., *Libarian, Pikes Peak Regional District Library*

REIFF, ROBERT F., *Professor of Art, Middlebury College; Author of* Renoir

REILLY, ALICE F., *Librarian, Fresno County Free Library*

REIMAN, DONALD H., *Editor of* Shelley and His Circle

REIMER, BETH L., MD, *Author of* The Menopausal Years *and* Hysterectomy

REIMER, CHARLES W., *Curator, Department of Limnology, Academy of Natural Sciences of Philadelphia; Coauthor of* Diatoms of the United States

REMER, VICTOR, *Executive Director, Children's Aid Society*

REMINGTON, ROBIN ALISON, *Professor of Political Science, University of Missouri at Columbia; Author of* The Warsaw Pact: Case Studies in Communist Conflict Resolution

RENNER, RICHARD R., *Professor of Education, University of Florida*

RENOIR, ALAIN, *Professor of English and Comparative Literature, University of California at Berkeley; Author of* The Poetry of John Lydgate

RENTELN, PAUL A., *Professor, Department of Physics, California State University at San Bernardino*

RENTZ, GEORGE, *Stanford University; Editor and Coauthor of* Oman and the Southern Shores of the Persian Gulf

RENWICK, W. L., *Author of* Edmund Spenser: An Essay on Renaissance Poetry

RESCHER, NICHOLAS, *University Professor of Philosophy, University of Pittsburgh; Author of* The Philosophy of Leibniz

RESIS, ALBERT, *Associate Professor, Department of History, Northern Illinois University*

REUWEE, A. DANIEL, *Director of Information, Future Farmers of America*

REVELLE, ROGER R., *Richard Saltonstall Professor of Population Policy and Director of the Center for Population Studies, Harvard University*

REVELLI, WILLIAM D., *Professor of Music and Director of Bands, University of Michigan*

REXROTH, KENNETH, *Author of* Classics Revisited

REYES-GUERRA, DAVID R., *Executive Secretary, Engineers' Council for Professional Development*

REYNOLDS, FRANK C., *Trustees, Goodwin Memorial Library; Member, Hadley Historical Committee*

REYNOLDS, FRED J., *Director of Fort Wayne (Ind.) Public Library*

REYNOLDS, GRAHAM, *Keeper of Paintings, Prints, and Drawings, Victoria and Albert Museum, London; Author of* English Portrait Miniatures *and* Nicholas Hilliard and Isaac Oliver

REYNOLDS, HELEN, *Professor of Business Education, School of Education, New York University*

REYNOLDS, MARTHA L., *Director, Frederick County Public Libraries*

REYNOLDS, NANCY, *Author of* George Balanchine: A Catalogue of Works *and* Dance Classics

REYNOLDS, REGINALD, *Author of* Cleanliness and Godliness *and* Beds

REYNOLDS, TERRY S., *Director, Program in Science, Technology, and Society, Michigan Technological University; Author of* Stronger Than a Hundred Men: A History of the Vertical Water Wheel

REZA, FAZLOLLAH, *Chancellor, University of Teheran, Iran*

RHINE, JOSEPH BANKS, *Director, Parapsychology Laboratory, Duke University; Coauthor of* Parapsychology Today

RIAD, HENRY, *Chief Curator, Egyptian Museum, Cairo*

RIASANOVSKY, NICHOLAS V., *Professor of History, Center for Slavic and East European Studies, University of California at Berkeley*

RICE, DALE W., *Biologist, U.S. Fish and Wildlife Service, Seattle, Wash.*

RICE, H. DUSTIN, *Professor of Art History, Columbia University*

RICE, TAMARA TALBOT, *Author of* Elizabeth, Empress of Russia *and* A Concise History of Russian Art

RICH, ELAINE, *Coauthor of* Artificial Intelligence, 2d ed.

RICHARD, OSCAR, *Director of Information Services, Louisiana State University*

RICHARDI, JANIS, *Coauthor of* The American Novel through Henry James: A Bibliography

RICHARDS, J. MORRIS, *Coauthor of* A Brief History of Joseph City

RICHARDSON, DEUEL, *Public Relations Director, National Fire Protection Association, Boston, Mass.*

RICHARDSON, DON, *President, New York Orchid Society*

RICHARDSON, FRANCIS L., *Visiting Assistant Professor of Art, Vassar College*

RICHARDSON, GLEN A., *Director, Department of Electrical Engineering and Physics, Rose-Hulman Institute; Coauthor of* Principles of Radio

RICHARDSON, H. E., *Author of* Tibet and Its History; *Coauthor of* A Cultural History of Tibet

RICHARDSON, H. GERALD, *Author of* Parliaments and Great Councils of Mediaeval England *and* The Governance of Mediaeval England

RICHARDSON, HARRY V., *President, Interdenominational Theological Center, Atlanta, Ga.*

RICHARDSON, HAZEL ADAMS, *Librarian, Bryan Carnegie Library*

RICHARDSON, LYON, *Professor of English, Case Western Reserve University; Author of* Henry James

RICHARDSON, RALPH A., *Technical Information Department, Research Laboratories, General Motors Corp.*

RICHELSON, JEFFREY T., *National Security Archive, George Washington University*

RICHIE, DONALD, *Curator of Films, Museum of Modern Art; Author of* The Films of Akira Kurosawa

RICHMOND, H. M., *Professor of English, University of California at Berkeley*

RICKARDS, E., *Cocker Spaniel Breed Council, England*

RICKARDS, JOSEPH, *Joseph Rickards Gallery, New York City*

RIDDLE, MAXWELL, *Dog and Pets Editor, Cleveland Press Pet Columnist, Ledger Syndicate; Associate Editor, Dog World; American Kennel Club Judge; Author of* The Complete Book of Puppy Training and Care *and* You and Your Show Dog

RIESENBERG, PETER, *Professor of Medieval History, Washington University, St. Louis, Mo.*

RIESENFELD, STEFAN A., *Professor of Law, University of California at Berkeley; Author of* Creditors' Remedies and Debtors' Protection

RIGA, PETER J., *Professor of Theology, St. Mary's College, Calif.*

RIGG, ROBERT B., *Colonel, U.S. Army (Retired); Author of* Realistic Combat Training

RIGGS, LORRIN A., *Edgar J. Marston Professor of Psychology, Brown University*

RILEY, VIRGINIA P., *Librarian, Albany Carnegie Library*

RIMER, J. THOMAS, *Chair, Department of Hebrew and East Asian Languages, University of Maryland; Author of* Traditions in Modern Japanese Fiction

RIMLAND, BERNARD, *Institute for Child Behavior Research, San Diego, Calif.; Author of* Infantile Autism

RINDLER, WOLFGANG, *Professor of Mathematics, University of Texas at Dallas; Author of* Essential Relativity and Special Relativity

RINEHART, SHEILA, *Research Associate, Busch-Reisinger Museum, Harvard University*

RING, ALFRED A., *Professor of Real Estate, University of Florida; Author of* Real Estate Principles and Practices

RINGROSE, DAVID R., *Associate Professor of History, Rutgers University*

RINKER, JAMES W., *E.I. du Pont de Nemours & Company, Inc.*

RINN, FAUNEIL J., *Professor of Political Science, San José State University*

RIOPELLE, ARTHUR J., *Director, Tulane University Delta Regional Primate Research Center*

RIPLEY, RANDALL B., *Chairman, Department of Political Science, Ohio State University; Author of* Party Leaders in the House of Representatives *and* American National Government and Public Policy

RIPPA, S. ALEXANDER, *Professor of Education, University of Vermont; Author of* Education in a Free Society: An American History

RIQUER, MARTÍN DE, *Facultad de Filosofia y Letras, Universidad de Barcelona, Spain; Author of* Resumen de literatura catalana

RISCHIN, MOSES, *Professor of History, San Francisco State University*

RISER, NATHAN W., *Professor of Biology and Director of Marine Science Institute, Northwestern University; Coauthor of* The Biology of the Turbellaria

RISSE, GUENTER B., MD, *Department of the History of Medicine, University of Wisconsin; Editor and Contributor,* Modern China and Traditional Chinese Medicine; *Editor and Translator of* History of Physiology *by K.E. Roth-Schuh; Coeditor of* Medicine without Doctors: Home Health Care in American History

RIST, MARTIN, *Author of* Book of Revelation *in* The Interpreter's Dictionary of the Bible

RITCHIE, J. MURDOCH, *Professor of Pharmacology, Yale University School of Medicine*

RITTER, LEO J., JR., *Senior Editor, Engineering News-Record*

RIVIERE, WILLIAM A., *Author of* The Complete Guide to Family Camping *and* The Family Campers Cookbook

RIZZA, ROBERT A., MD, *Professor of Medicine, Endocrine Research Unit, Mayo Clinic*

ROBARD, SIMON, MD, *Director, Department of Cardiology, City of Hope Medical Center, Duarte, Calif.*

ROBB, DAVID M., *Professor of the History of Art, University of Pennsylvania; Author of* The Arts of the Middle Ages

ROBBINS, CHANDLER S., *Chief, Section of Migratory Non-Game Bird Studies, Division of Wildlife Research, U.S. Fish and Wildlife Service; Author of* Birds of North America

ROBBINS, JOHN E., *President, Brandon University, Canada*

ROBERTS, BRYNLEY F., *Senior Lecturer, Department of Welsh Language and Literature, University College of Wales*

ROBERTS, CALVIN A., *Coauthor of* New Mexico *and* A History of New Mexico

ROBERTS, LESLIE, *Coauthor of* Canada in Color

ROBERTS, NATHAN L., *Public Relations Associate, American Jewish Congress*

ROBERTS, SUSAN A., *Coauthor of* New Mexico *and* A History of New Mexico

ROBERTSON, DAVID A., JR., *McIntosh Professor of English, Barnard College; Author of* George Mallory; *Former Coeditor, American Alpine Journal*

ROBERTSON, DONALD, *Professor of Art, Newcomb College, Tulane University; Author of* Pre-Columbian Architecture

ROBERTSON, JAMES I., JR., *Chairman, Department of History, Virginia Polytechnic Institute and State University; Former Executive Director, U.S. Civil War Centennial Commission; Author of* The Stonewall Brigade *and* Civil War Books: A Critical Bibliography

ROBERTSON, S. D. T., *Professor of Electrical Engineering, University of Toronto, Canada*

ROBERTSON, WILLIAM, *Editor, Thoroughbred Record*

ROBINSON, BILL, *Editor of* Yachting Magazine; *Author of* New Boat *and* Bill Robinson's Book of Expert Sailing

ROBINSON, CHARLES A., JR., *David Benedict Professor of Classics, Brown University; Author of* Ancient History: From Prehistoric Times to the Death of Justinian

ROBINSON, CHARLES W., *Director, Baltimore County Public Library*

ROBINSON, DAVID, *Associate Professor of History, Michigan State University; Author of* Chiefs and Clerics; *Coauthor of* Sources of the African Past

ROBINSON, JAMES A., *President, University of West Florida; Author of* Congress and Foreign Policy Making *and* House Rules Committee

ROBINSON, LEIF J., *Editor of* Sky & Telescope; *Author of* Outdoor Optics

ROBINSON, ROSALIND F., *Library Director, Islip Public Library*

ROBINSON, TREVOR, *Associate Professor of Biochemistry, University of Massachusetts*

ROBINSON, W. STITT, *Professor of History, University of Kansas*

ROBINSON, WILLIAM A., *Bell Telephone Laboratories*

ROCK, IRVIN, *Institute for Cognitive Studies, Rutgers University*

ROCK, JOHN A., MD, *Professor and Chair, Department of Gynecology and Obstetrics, Emory University School of Medicine*

ROCKE, A. J., *Assistant Professor, Department of the History of Science, Case Western Reserve University*

ROCKWELL, FORD A., *Head Librarian, Wichita Public Library, Wichita, Kans.*

RODDMAN, PHILIP, *Associate Professor of English, Pratt Institute*

RODGERS, CARL T., *Specialist in Education, Braille, and Tactual Aids, American Foundation for the Blind*

RODIN, ROBERT J., *Professor, Biological Sciences Department, California State Polytechnic University at San Luis Obispo*

RODMAN, PETER S., *Department of Anthropology, University of California at Davis*

ROE, DAPHNE A., MD, *Professor of Nutrition, Cornell University; Author of* A Plague of Corn: The Social History of Pellagra

ROEDERER, JUAN G., *Director, Geophysical Institute, University of Alaska; Author of* Dynamics of Geomagnetically Trapped Radiation

ROEMER, ELIZABETH, *Professor of Astronomy, University of Arizona*

ROGEL, CAROLE, *Professor Emeritus of History, Ohio State University*

ROGERS, CHARLES A., DDS, FAGD, *Former Clinical Instructor, Columbia University School of Dental and Oral Surgery*

ROGERS, CHARLES H., *Museum of Zoology, Princeton University*

ROGERS, GEORGE C., JR., *Professor of History, University of South Carolina; Co-editor of* The Papers of Henry Laurens

ROGERS, L. R., *Head of the Faculty of Three Dimensional Design, Loughborough College of Art and Design, England; Author of* Sculpture

ROGERS, ROSEMARIE, *Professor of International Politics and Director of the Program in International and U.S. Refugee Policy, Fletcher School of Law and Diplomacy, Tufts University*

ROGERS, STEPHEN H., MD, *Senior Attending Surgeon, New York Eye and Ear Infirmary*

ROHLF, ROBERT H., *Director, Hennepin County Library, Minneapolis*

ROLAND, CHARLES P., *Professor of History, University of Kentucky; Author of* Albert Sidney Johnston: Soldier of Three Republics *and* A History of the South

ROLLE, ANDREW, *Cleland Professor of History, Occidental College; Author of* California: A History *and* Los Angeles: From Pueblo to City of the Future

ROLLIN, BERNARD E., *Professor of Philosophy and Physiology, Director of Bioethical Planning, Department of Philosophy, Colorado State University*

ROLO, P. J. V., *Professor of History, University of Keele, England; Author of* George Canning

ROMANO, CLARE, *Artist; Instructor in Printmaking, Pratt Institute*

ROMER, ALFRED S., *Professor of Zoology, Harvard College; Author of* The Vertebrate Body

ROMER, CARL W., *Editor and Publisher, Dairy Goat Year Book; Director at Large and Publications Chairman, American Goat Society, Inc.*

RONBERG, GARY M., *Sports Illustrated*

RONNE, EDITH M., *Specialist on Antarctic Affairs; Member of the Ronne Expedition*

RONNE, FINN, *Captain (Retired), U.S. Naval Reserve; Antarctic Explorer*

ROOHAN, JAMES EDMUND, *Yale University; Author of* American Catholics and the Social Question, 1865–1900

ROOT, E. R., *A.I. Root Company, Medina, Ohio*

ROOT, MARGARET COOL, *Assistant Professor, Department of the History of Art, University of Michigan; Assistant Curator, Kelsey Museum of Archaeology, University of Michigan; Author of* The King and Kingship in Achaemenid Art: Essays on the Creation of an Iconography of Empire

ROPER, DONALD M., *Associate Professor of History, State University of New York College at New Paltz*

ROPER, ELMO, *Public Opinion Analyst; Author of* You and Your Leaders

ROPP, THEODORE, *Professor of History, Duke University*

RORTY, RICHARD, *Professor of Philosophy, Princeton University; Author of* Philosophy and the Mirror of Nature

ROSAND, DAVID, *Professor of Art History, Columbia University*

ROSAND, ELLEN, *Professor of Music, Yale University; Author of* Opera in Seventeenth-Century Venice: The Creation of a Genre

ROSBERG, CARL G., *Professor of Political Science; Director, Institute of International Studies; University of California at Berkeley; Author of* Personal Rule in Black Africa: Prince, Autocrat, Prophet, Tyrant

ROSE, ERNST, *Professor, New York University; Author of* A History of German Literature

ROSE, JEANNE, *Reference Supervisor, Arlington County Library*

ROSE, JEROME G., *Associate Professor of Urban Planning, Rutgers University; Author of* The Legal Adviser on Home Ownership

ROSE, JOHN C., MD, *Vice-Chancellor, Medical Center, Georgetown University*

ROSE, LEO E., *Lecturer, Political Science, University of California at Berkeley; Associate Editor, Asian Affairs; Author of* Himalayan Battleground, Buffer State Strategy, *and* The Politics of Nepal

ROSEBERRY, C. R., *Author of* The Challenging Skies

ROSEBOOM, EUGENE H., *Professor of History, Ohio State University*

ROSEN, EDWARD, *Author of* Three Copernican Treatises *and* Kepler's Conversation with Galileo's Sidereal Messenger

ROSEN, GEORGE, *Deputy Director, Economic and Technical Assistance Department, Asian Development Bank, Manila; Author of* Democracy and Economic Change in India *and other books*

ROSEN, GEORGE, MD, *Professor of the History of Medicine, Epidemiology, and Public Health, Yale University School of Medicine*

ROSEN, HAROLD, MD, *Associate Professor of Psychiatry, Johns Hopkins University School of Medicine*

ROSEN, SAMUEL, MD, *Professor of Otolaryngology, Mount Sinai School of Medicine, New York City; Consulting Otologist, New York Eye and Ear Infirmary, New York City*

ROSEN, STEPHEN L., *Professor of Chemical Engineering, Carnegie-Mellon University; Author of* Fundamental Principles of Polymeric Materials

ROSENBERG, WILLIAM G., *Professor of History, University of Michigan; Author of* Liberals in the Russian Revolution

ROSENBERGER, HOMER T., *Columbia Historical Society, Washington, D.C.*

ROSENBLUM, LEONARD A., *Professor of Psychiatry, State University of New York, Downstate Medical Center; Co-editor of* The Squirrel Monkey

ROSENBLUTH, MARSHALL N., *Director, Institute for Fusion Studies, University of Texas at Austin*

ROSENFELD, LEON, *Professor, Nordic Institute for Theoretical Atomic Physics, Copenhagen; Author of* Nuclear Forces *and* Essay on Niels Bohr

ROSENFIELD, M. C., *Department of History, Southeastern Massachusetts University; Research Fellow, University of London*

ROSENTHAL, HAROLD, *Editor of* Opera Magazine; *Author of* Great Singers of Today; *Editor of* The Opera Bedside Book; *Coauthor of* The Concise Oxford Dictionary of Opera

ROSI, FRED D., *Director, Materials Research Laboratory, RCA Laboratories*

ROSKAM, JAN, *President, DARCorp.; Author of* Airplane Aerodynamics and Performance, Airplane Design, *and* Airplane Flight Dynamics and Automatic Flight Controls

ROSS, HERBERT H., *Professor, Department of Entomology, University of Goergia*

ROSS, MARION DEAN, *Professor of Architecture, University of Oregon*

ROSS, RUSSELL M., *Professor of Political Science, University of Iowa; Author of* Government and Administration of Iowa

ROSS, STANLEY R., *Professor of History and Director, Institute of Latin American Studies; University of Texas at Austin; Editor of* Is the Mexican Revolution Dead?

ROSS, WALTER S., *Author of* The Last Hero: Charles A. Lindbergh

ROSS, WALTER W., III, *President, Beta Sigma Phi International*

ROSSABI, MORRIS, *Professor of History, Case Western Reserve University; Author of* Khubilai Khan *and* China and Inner Asia

ROSSEL, SEYMOUR, *Author of* Journey Through Jewish History *and* Israel: Covenant People, Covenant Land

ROSSI, PETER H., *Stuart A. Rice Professor of Sociology, University of Massachusetts; Acting Director, Social and Demographic Research Institute, University of Massachusetts; Author of* Without Shelter: Homelessness in the 1980s *and* Down and Out in America: The Origins of Homelessness

ROSSITER, MARGARET W., *American Academy of Arts and Sciences*

ROTBERG, ROBERT I., *Professor of Political Science, Massachusetts Institute of Technology; Author of* A Political History of Tropical Africa *and* Joseph Thomson and the Exploration of Africa

ROTHBARD, MURRAY N., *Professor of Economics, Polytechnic Institute of New York; Author of* Man, Economy and State

ROTHENBERG, GUNTHER E., *Professor of History, Purdue University*

ROTHENBERG, MICHAEL G., *Adjunct Assistant Professor, Department of School Services, City College of New York*

ROTHENBERG, STANLEY, *Member of the New York Bar; Vice President, Copyright Society of the U.S.A.; Author of* Legal Protection of Literature, Art and Music

ROTHKRUG, LIONEL, *Professor of History, Concordia University, Canada*

ROTHNEY, G. O., *Author of* Canada in One World

ROTHSCHILD, JACQUARD H., *Brigadier General, U.S. Army (Retired); Commanding General, U.S. Army Chemical Corps Research and Development Command; Author of* Tomorrow's Weapons—Chemical and Biological

ROTHSCHILD, LINCOLN, *Author of* Sculpture through the Ages *and* Style in Art

ROUSE, IRVING, *Professor and Chairman, Department of Anthropology, Yale University*

ROUTLEY, ERIK, *Minister of the Congregational Church in England and Wales; Author of* Hymns and Human Life

ROWAN, ROBERT L., MD, FACS, *Assistant Professor of Clinical Urology, New York University School of Medicine; Coauthor of* Your Prostate; *Author of* Bed Wetting: A Guide for Parents

ROWE, JOHN G., *Professor of History and Dean of Arts, University of Western Ontario, Canada*

ROWE, JOHN HOWLAND, *Professor of Anthropology, University of California at Berkeley*

ROWELL, L. S., *President, Board of Trustees, University of Vermont and State Agricultural College*

ROWELL, MARGIT, *Curator of Special Exhibitions, Solomon R. Guggenheim Museum; Author of* Joan Miró, Mondrian, and Dubuffet

ROWEN, HERBERT H., *Professor of History, Rutgers University*

ROWLAND, LEWIS P., *Henry and Lucy Moses Professor and Chairman, Department of Neurology, College of Physicians and Surgeons, Columbia University; Director, Neurology Service, Neurological Institute of the Presbyterian Hospital, New York City*

ROWLEY, DIANA, *Editor, Special Publications, Arctic Institute of North America, Ontario, Canada*

ROWLEY, GRAHAM W., *Coordinator, Northern Coordination and Research Division, Department of Indian Affairs and Northern Development, Ottawa, Canada*

ROWSE, A. L., *Fellow of All Souls College, Oxford University (1925–1974); Author of* The Churchills; From the Death of Marlborough to the Present, The England of Elizabeth I, *and* The Expansion of Elizabethan England

ROXBOROUGH, HENRY H., *Author of* Great Days in Canadian Sport *and* The Stanley Cup Story

ROY, ARCHIBALD E., *Professor of Astronomy, Glasgow University, Scotland*

ROY, EMIL, *Professor of English, University of Tennessee at Martin; Author of* Christopher Fry

ROYSE, L. E., *Methods Engineer, American Telegraph and Telephone Company*

ROYSTER, VERMONT, *Editor and Vice President*, Wall Street Journal

ROZELL, MARK J., *Professor of Political Science, Mary Washington College; Author of* The Press and the Ford Presidency

RUDD, ROBERT L., *Professor of Zoology, University of California at Davis; Author of* Pesticides and the Living Landscape; *Coauthor of* Pesticides: Their Use and Toxicity in Relation to Wildlife

RUDDY, T. MICHAEL, *Professor of History, St. Louis University; Author of* The Cautious Diplomat: Charles E. Bohlen and the Soviet Union

RUDÉ, GEORGE, *Professor of History, Concordia University, Montreal, Canada; Author of* The Crowd in the French Revolution *and* Robespierre

RUDIN, HARRY R., *Colgate Professor of History, Yale University; Author of* The Germans in the Cameroons, 1884–1914

RUDWICK, M., *University Lecturer in History of Science, Cambridge University*

RUGGLES, ELEANOR, *Author of* The West-Going Heart: A Life of Vachel Lindsay

RULE, VIRGINIA, *Librarian, Carson City-Ormsby County Library*

RUMBAUGH, DUANE M., *Chairman and Professor of Psychology, Georgia State University; Department of Primate Behavior, Yerkes Regional Primate Research Center, Emory University*

RUNNELS, LYNN K., *Professor of Chemistry, Louisiana State University*

RUOFF, ARTHUR L., *Professor of Engineering, Cornell University; Author of* Materials Science *and* Introduction to Materials Science

RUPEN, ROBERT A., *Professor of Political Science, University of North Carolina*

RUSH, ALFRED C., CSSR, *Professor of Ecclesiastical History and Positive Theology, Catholic University of America; Author of* Death and Burial in Christian Antiquity

RUSSELL, COLIN A., *Principal Lecturer in Organic Chemistry, Harris College, Preston, England; Author of* A History of Valency

RUSSELL, DON, *Author of* Lives and Legends of Buffalo Bill *and* The Wild West

RUSSELL, FRANCIS, *Author of* The Shadow of Blooming Grove: Warren G. Harding in His Times

RUSSELL, T. RANDOLPH, *American Road and Transportation Builders Association*

RUSSO, ROBERT G., *Lecturer in Classical and Oriental Languages, City University of New York*

RUTLAND, ROBERT A., *Editor in Chief of the Papers of James Madison, Alderman Library, University of Virginia; Author of* George Mason, Reluctant Statesman, Birth of the Bill of Rights, Ordeal of the Constitution, The Newsmongers, *and* The Democrats from Jefferson to Carter; *Editor of* The Papers of George Mason

RUZICIC, GOJKO, *Professor of Serbo Croatian Language and Literature, Columbia University*

RYALS, CLYDE DE L., *Professor of English, Duke University; Author of* Theme and Symbol in Tennyson's Poetry to 1850

RYAN, A. N., *Senior Lecturer in Modern History; Director of Combined Studies, University of Liverpool, England*

RYAN, MSGR. JOHN K., *Professor of Philosophy, Catholic University of America*

RYAN, JOHN T., SJ, *Fordham University*

RYBCZYNSKI, WITOLD, *Martin and Margy Meyerson Professor of Urbanism, Graduate School of Fine Arts, and Professor, Department of Real Estate, Wharton School, University of Pennsylvania*

RYMER, OSCAR E., *Librarian, Gadsden Public Library*

RYZNAR, ELISKA, *Librarian and Head, Catalog Department, Stanford University Law Library; Coauthor of* Books in Czechoslovakia, Past and Present

SABERSKY, JANE, *Christie's of London*

SABINE, GEORGE H., *Author of* A History of Political Theory

SABLOFF, JEREMY A., *Professor of Anthropology, University of New Mexico; Coauthor of* A History of American Archaeology, *and* Ancient Civilizations: The Near East and Mesoamerica

SABRA, A. I., *Professor of the History of Arabic Science, Harvard University*

SACCIO, PETER, *Associate Professor of English, Dartmouth College; Author of* The Court Comedies of John Lyly: A Study in Allegorical Dramaturgy

SACHS, WILLIAM L., *Assistant Rector, St. Stephen's Church, Richmond, Va.; Author of* The Transformation of Anglicanism

SACK, R. BRADLEY, MD, *Johns Hopkins University School of Medicine*

SADDLER, JANE, *Professor of Textiles and Clothing, Iowa State University; Coauthor of* Textiles

SADOCK, BENJAMIN J., MD, *Professor of Psychiatry, New York University School of Medicine; Coeditor of* Comprehensive Textbook of Psychiatry *and* The Sexual Experience

SADOCK, VIRGINIA A., MD, *Associate Clinical Professor of Psychiatry, New York University School of Medicine; Assistant to the Editor,* Comprehensive Textbook of Psychiatry

SAFRAN, NADAV, *Professor of Government, Center for Middle Eastern Studies, Harvard University; Author of* Israel: The Embattled Ally

SAGAN, CARL, *Laboratory for Planetary Studies, Cornell University; Author of* The Cosmic Connection

SAGARIN, EDWARD, *Associate Professor of Sociology and Anthropology, City College of New York*

SAGE, LETITIA L., *Associate Editor,* Beauty Fashion *Magazine*

SAGER, DONALD J., *Director, Elyria Public Library, Elyria, Ohio*

SAGGS, HENRY W. F., *Professor of Semitic Languages, University College Cardiff, University of Wales; Author of* The Greatness that Was Babylon

SAGRIS, HARRY, *Director, Ipswich Public Library*

SAICH, TONY J., *Sinologisch Institute, Leiden; Author of* Discourse and Power: The Revolutionary Process in Mao's China

ST. JOHN-STEVAS, NORMAN, *Political Correspondent of* The Economist; *Visiting Fellow, The Yale Law School*

SALIBI, KAMAL S., *Professor of History, American University of Beirut, Lebanon; Author of* The Modern History of Lebanon

SALINGER, MARGARETTA M., *Curator of European Painting, Metropolitan Museum of Art*

SALKELD, ROBERT J., *System Development Corporation*

SALMON, J. H. M., *Professor of History, Bryn Mawr College*

SALMON, WESLEY C., *Professor of Philosophy, University of Arizona*

SALOMONE, A. WILLIAM, *Wilson Professor of European History, University of Rochester*

SALTHE, STANLEY N., *Professor, Department of Biology, Brooklyn College*

SALTI, DANIELLE, *Department of Languages and Literature, Livingston College, Rutgers University*

SALTMARSH, JOHN, *Fellow and Sometime Vice-Provost, King's College, Cambridge University; University Lecturer in History, Cambridge University; Author of* King's College and Its Chapel

SALTZER, ARTHUR M., *Librarian, Freeport Public Library*

SALVADORI, MAX, *Dwight W. Morrow Professor of History, Smith College; Author of* A Pictorial History of the Italian People

SALVATORELLI, LUIGI, *Author of* A Concise History of Italy

SALZBERG, H. K., *Consultant, Borden Chemical Company*

SALZMANN, J. A., DDS, *Clinical Professor of Dentistry, Mount Sinai School of Medicine, New York City; Author of* Practice of Orthodontics; *Former Editor of* New York Journal of Dentistry

SANDAGE, ALLAN R., *Astronomer, Hale Observatories*

SANDERLIN, WALTER S., *Professor of History, Washington and Jefferson College*

SANDERS, J. A., *President, Columbia Christian College*

SANDERS, JACQUELYN SEEVAK, *Director, Sonia Shankman Orthogenic School; Sr. Lecturer, Department of Education, University of Chicago; Author of* A Greenhouse for the Mind

SANDERSON, IVAN T., *Administrative Director, Society for the Investigation of the Unexplained; Author of* More Things *and* Abominable Snowmen

SANDFORT, JOHN F., *Professor and Head, Mechanical Engineering Department, South Dakota State University*

SANDROW, EDWARD T., *Author of* Judaism and Psychiatry

SANDS, C. DALLAS, *Professor of Law, University of Alabama*

SANFORD, J. P., *Professor of Internal Medicine, University of Texas Medical School at Dallas*

SANGEORGE, ROBERT, *Vice President, Public Affairs, National Audubon Society*

SANSOM, SIR GEORGE B., *Author of* Japan: A Short Cultural History

SARGEANT, WINTHROP, *Music Critic,* New Yorker; *Author of* Listening to Music

SARGENT, CHARLES S., *Associate Professor, Department of Geography, Arizona State University; Author of* The Spatial Evolution of Greater Buenos Aires, Argentina, 1870–1930; *Editor of* Urban Dynamics . . . the Changing Face of America's Cities *and* A Geography of Latin America

SARGENT, LYMAN TOWER, *Professor of Political Science, University of Missouri at St. Louis*

SARKISSIAN, A. O., *Library of Congress*

SARTON, GEORGE, *Author of* History of Science, *and* Ancient Science and Modern Civilization

SATER, JOHN E., *Research Coordinator, Arctic Institute of North America*

SAUER, WOLFGANG, *Professor of History, University of California at Berkeley*

SAUNDERS, E. DALE, *Professor of Japanese, University of Pennsylvania; Author of* Buddhism in Japan; with an Outline of Its Origins in India

SAUNDERS, J. B. DE C. M., *Professor of Anatomy, Regents Professor of Medical History, University of California, San Francisco Medical Center; Author of* Leonardo da Vinci on the Human Body *and* Vesalius: Illustrations from His Work

SAUNDERS, JOHN J., *Reader in History, University of Canterbury, Christchurch, New Zealand; Author of* Aspects of the Crusades

SAUNDERS, R. STEPHEN, *Senior Research Scientist, Jet Propulsion Laboratory; Magellan Project Scientist, California Institute of Technology*

SAVAGE, GEORGE, *Author of* Porcelain Through the Ages *and* Pottery Through the Ages

SAVAGE-RUMBAUGH, SUE, *Department of Psychology, Georgia State University; Department of Primate Behavior, Yerkes Regional Primate Research Center, Emory University*

SAVANT, C. J., JR., *Board Chairman, MCA Technology, Inc.*

SAVELLE, MAX, *Professor of History, University of Washington; Author of* Foundations of American Civilization

SAVETH, EDWARD N., *Distinguished Professor of History, State University of New York College at Fredonia*

SAVILLE, THORNDIKE, JR., *Chief, Research Division, U.S. Army Coastal Engineering Research Center*

SAVITZ, LEONARD D., *Professor of Sociology, Temple University*

SAVORY, ROGER M., *Associate Chairman, Department of Islamic Studies, University of Toronto, Canada*

SAWIN, MARTICA R., *Department of Art History, Parsons School of Design, New York City*

SAWKINS, SISTER ALPHONSUS MARIE, *Associate Professor of History, Marygrove College, Detroit*

SAWYER, RONALD C., *Department of the History of Science, University of Wisconsin at Madison*

SAX, JOSEPH L., *Professor of Law, University of Michigan Law School; Author of* Defending the Environment

SAXON, A. H., *Circus Historian; Author of* P. T. Barnum: The Legend and the Man

SAYEED, KHALID BIN, *Professor, Department of Political Studies, Queen's University, Ontario, Canada; Author of* The Political System of Pakistan, Pakistan: The Formative Phase, 1857–1948, *and* Politics in Pakistan: The Nature and Direction of Change

SAYERS, GEORGE, *Professor and Director, Department of Physiology, School of Medicine, Case Western Reserve University*

SAYLES, FRANKLIN N., *Art Director, Young People's Publications, Grolier Incorporated*

SAYLES, G. O., *Fellow, Institute of Advanced Legal Studies, University of London; Author of* The Medieval Foundations of England *and* Law and Legislation in Medieval England

SAYRE, A. NELSON, *Consultant and Groundwater Geologist, Behre Dolbear and Company*

SAYWELL, JOHN T., *Dean of Arts and Science, Professor of History, York University, Canada*

SCAMEHORN, LEE, *Professor of History, University of Colorado*

SCARISBRICK, JOHN J., *Lecturer in History, Queen Mary College, University of London; Author of* Henry VIII

SCHAAP, PHIL, *Curator and Archivist, WKCR, New York City; Author of* Dizzy Gillespie *(discography)*

SCHABERT, BARBARA, *Librarian, Glendale Public Library*

SCHACHT, RICHARD, *Professor of Philosophy, University of Illinois at Urbana-Champaign; Author of* Alienation

SCHAEFER, MARILYN L., *Associate Professor of Art, New York City Technical College, City University of New York*

SCHAEFER, MARY M., *Assistant Professor of Christian Worship and Spirituality Studies, Atlantic School of Theology, Halifax, Nova Scotia, Canada*

SCHAFER, JAMES E., *Librarian, Lincoln Park Library, Lincoln Park, Mich.*

SCHAFFER, HENRY M., *Assistant in History, Washington University, St. Louis, Mo.*

SCHAFFNER, KENNETH F., *Professor of Philosophy and the History and Philosophy of Science, University of Pittsburgh; Author of* Nineteenth-Century Aether Theories

SCHALLER, GEORGE B., *Research Associate, New York Zoological Society; Author of* Mountain Gorilla *and* Year of the Gorilla

SCHANTZ, KATHERINE, *Librarian, Wayne County Public Library, Wooster, Ohio*

SCHEARER, S. BRUCE, *Executive Director, Synergos Foundation*

SCHEFFER, VICTOR B., *Biologist, U.S. Fish and Wildlife Service; Author of* Seals, Sea Lions and Walruses

SCHEIDE, WILLIAM H., *Director, Bach Aria Group*

SCHEIN, EDGAR H., *Professor of Industrial Management, Sloan School of Management, Massachusetts Institute of Technology; Coauthor of* Coercive Persuasion

SCHERY, ROBERT W., *Director, Lawn Institute; Author of* Plants for Man

SCHESSLER, PATRICIA C., *Staff, Franklin News-Herald*

SCHIER, MARY JANE, *Research Associate, University of Texas System Cancer Center*

SCHIFF, ALVIN I., *Executive Vice President, Board of Jewish Education of Greater New York*

SCHIFF, LEONARD I., *Professor of Physics, Stanford University; Author of* Quantum Mechanics

SCHIFFERES, JUSTUS J., *Health Education Council, Livingston, N.J.*

SCHILLER, FRANCIS, MD, *Associate Clinical Professor of Neurology, University of California at San Francisco Medical Center; Author of* Founders of Neurology

SCHIMMEL, ANNEMARIE, *Lecturer on Indo-Muslim Culture, Middle East Center, Harvard University; Author of* Gabriel's Wing: A Study into the Religious Ideas of Sir Muhammad Iqbal

SCHINDLER, JOHN F., *Chief Scientist and Environmental Engineer, Alaskan Resource Science Corporation.*

SCHLEIFER, RONALD, *Professor of English, University of Oklahoma; Author of* Rhetoric and Death: The Language of Modernism and Postmodern Discourse Theory; *Editor of* Genre

SCHLESINGER, ARTHUR M., JR., *Schweitzer Professor of Humanities, City University of New York*

SCHLESINGER, LEE I., *University of North Carolina*

SCHMALSTIEG, WILLIAM R., *Professor of Slavic Languages, Pennsylvania State University; Coauthor of* An Introduction to Modern Lithuanian

SCHMECKEBIER, LAURENCE, *Professor, School of Art, Syracuse University; Author of* John Stewart Curry's Pageant of America

SCHMEIDLER, GERTRUDE, *Professor of Psychology, City College of New York; Editor of* Extrasensory Perception

SCHMERLING, ERWIN R., *Chief, Space Plasma Physics, National Aeronautics and Space Administration Headquarters*

SCHMIDMAN, JOHN, *Department of Labor Studies, Pennsylvania State University; Author of* Unions in Postindustrial Society *and* British Unions and Economic Policy

SCHMIDT, KARL P., *Chief Curator of Zoology, Chicago Natural History Museum*

SCHMIT, DOROTHEA F., *Librarian in Charge, Bensenville Community Public Library*

SCHMITT, BARTON D., *Assistant Professor of Pediatrics, University of Colorado Medical Center*

SCHMITT, BERNADOTTE E., *Professor of Modern History, University of Chicago; Author of* The Coming of War, 1914

SCHMITT, CHARLES B., *Research Fellow, Department of Philosophy, University of Leeds, England*

SCHMITT, HANS A., *Professor of History, University of Virginia*

SCHMITT, KARL M., *Professor of Government, University of Texas at Austin; Coauthor of* Evolution or Chaos: Dynamics of Latin American Government and Politics

SCHNEER, CECIL J., *Professor of Geology, University of New Hampshire*

SCHNEER, HENRY, *Associate Professor of Psychiatry, State University of New York, Downstate Medical Center*

SCHNEEWIND, JEROME B., *Professor of Philosophy and Provost, Hunter College; Editor of* Mill's Ethical Writings

SCHNEIDER-LEYER, ERICH, *Author of* Dogs of the World

SCHNETZLER, CHARLES C., *Scientist, Goddard Space Flight Center, National Aeronautics and Space Administration*

SCHOEDEL, ALAN E., *The Journal of Commerce*

SCHOENHEIM, URSULA, *Associate Professor of Classical Languages, Queens College*

SCHOEPFLIN, R. B., *Department of the History of Science, University of Wisconsin at Madison*

SCHOFIELD, BRIAN BETHAM, *Vice Admiral (Retired), Royal Navy; Author of* British Sea Power *and* The Russian Convoys

SCHOLZ, ROY O., MD, *Wilmer Institute, Johns Hopkins Hospital, Baltimore, Md.*

SCHONHORN, HAROLD, *Supervisor, Surface Chemistry Research, Bell Telephone Laboratories, Inc.*

SCHORER, MARK, *Professor of English, University of California at Berkeley; Author of* Sinclair Lewis: An American Life

SCHOTT, MARY F., *Librarian, Fort Scott Public Library, Fort Scott, Kans.*

SCHOU, AUGUST, *Director, Norwegian Nobel Institute (1946–1974)*

SCHRATZ, PAUL R., *Advanced Research Scholar, Naval War College, Newport, R.I.*

SCHREIBER, PAUL, *Professor of Social Work, Hunter College School of Social Work; Associate Editor of* The Encyclopedia of Social Work; *Coeditor of* Handbook of Counseling Techniques

SCHROEDER, M. R., *Professor of Applied Physics, University of Gsttingen*

SCHROEDER, OLIVER, JR., *Professor of Law and Director, Law-Medicine Center, Case Western Reserve University; Author of* Medical Facts for Legal Truth

SCHROEDER, RICHARD C., *Author of* The Politics of Drugs

SCHULL, JOSEPH, *Author of* Laurier: The First Canadian

SCHULLER, GUNTHER, *Composer; Author of* Early Jazz: Its Roots and Musical Development

SCHULTZ, LEONARD P., *Senior Zoologist, Smithsonian Institution*

SCHULTZ, SUSAN, *Thomas Edison Papers, Edison National Historic Site*

SCHUON, KARL, *Managing Editor,* Leatherneck *Magazine; Author of* The Leathernecks *and* Marine Corps Biographical Dictionary

SCHUR, EDWIN M., *Professor of Sociology, New York University; Author of* The Americanization of Sex

SCHUSTER, RUDOLF M., *Professor of Botany, University of Massachusetts; Author of* Boreal Hepaticae: A Manual of Liverworts of Minnesota and Adjacent Regions

SCHUTZ, JOHN A., *Professor of History, University of Southern California; Coeditor of* The Spur of Fame: Dialogues of John Adams and Benjamin Rush, 1805–1813

SCHWAB, PETER, *Assistant Professor, Department of Political Studies, State University of New York College at Purchase*

SCHWARTZ, ANTHONY M., *Principal Staff Scientist, Gillette Research Institute, Washington, D.C.*

SCHWARTZ, BENJAMIN, MD, *Meningitis and Special Pathogens Branch, Centers for Disease Control, Atlanta, Ga.*

SCHWARTZ, BERNARD, *Professor of Law, New York University; Editor of* The Code Napoleon and the Common-Law World; *Author of* French Administrative Law and the Common-Law World *and* American Constitutional Law

SCHWARTZ, BRIAN B., *Professor of Physics, Brooklyn College; Education Officer, American Physical Society; Coauthor of* Amorphous Semiconductors; *Coeditor of* Superconductor Applications: Squids and Machines, Solids and Plasmas in High Magnetic Fields, *and* Superconductor Materials Science: Metallurgy, Fabrication and Applications

SCHWARTZ, VICTOR E., *Professor of Law, Washington College of Law, American University; Chairman, U.S. Department of Commerce Task Force on Product Liability and Accident Compensation; Coauthor of* Cases and Materials on Torts; *Author of* Comparative Negligence

SCHWARTZBERG, JOSEPH E., *Professor of Geography, University of Minnesota; Editor of* A Historical Atlas of South Asia

SCHWARZ, ALFRED, *Professor of English, Wayne State University; Editor and Translator of* Hugo von Hofmannsthal: Three Plays

SCHWARZMANN, JOHN U., MD, *Senior Attending Physician, Hospital Center, Washington, D.C.*

SCHWARZSCHILD, STUART, *Professor of Insurance, Georgia State University; Author of* Principles of Life Insurance

SCHWEITZER, CHRISTOPH E., *Professor of Germanic Languages, University of North Carolina at Chapel Hill*

SCHWENDEMAN, JOSEPH R., *Distinguished Professor of Geography, Eastern Kentucky University*

SCHWENGEL, FRED, *President, U.S. Capitol Historical Society*

SCHYTT, VALTER, *Professor of Physical Geography, University of Stockholm*

SCIAMA, D. W., *Professor of Applied Mathematics and Theoretical Physics, Cambridge University; Author of* The Unity of the Universe *and* The Physical Foundations of General Relativity

SCOBIE, JAMES R., *Professor of History, Indiana University*

SCORER, R. S., *Professor of Theoretical Mechanics, Imperial College of Science and Technology, London; Author of* Weather *and* Cloud Study

SCOTT, ANTHONY W., *Author of* Rugby: An American Game Reborn

SCOTT, E. L., *Author of* Dalton and William Henry *in* John Dalton and the Progress of Science

SCOTT, FRANKLIN D., *Professor of History, Northwestern University; Author of* Emigration and Immigration

SCOTT, GAIL R., *Assistant Curator, Modern Art, Los Angeles County Museum of Art*

SCOTT, HENRY E., JR., *Professor of Art, University of Missouri at Kansas City; Author of* Historical Outline of the Fine Arts

SCOTT, JOHN D., *Author of* Life in Britain

SCOTT, PETER, *Professor of Geography, University of Tasmania, Australia*

SCOTT, ROBERT L., *Brigadier General, U.S. Air Force (Retired); Author of* Flying Tiger: Chennault of China *and* God Is Still My Co-Pilot

SCOTT, ROY V., *Professor of History, Mississippi State University; Author of* The Agrarian Movement in Illinois, 1880–1896

SCOTT, VERNE H., *Chairman, Department of Water Science and Engineering, University of California at Davis*

SCOTT, W. B., *Curator, Department of Ichthyology and Herpetology, Royal Ontario Museum, University of Toronto, Canada; Author of* Fishes of the Atlantic Coast of Canada

SCRIVEN, MICHAEL J., *Professor of Philosophy, University of California at Berkeley; Author of* Primary Philosophy

SEABORG, GLENN T., *Nobel Prize Winner in Chemistry, 1951; Chairman, U.S. Atomic Energy Commission*

SEABROOK, CHARLES, *Science Editor, Atlanta* Journal

SEARLE, HUMPHREY, *Composer; Author of* Twentieth-Century Counterpoint *and* Ballet Music

SEARLE, CAPT. W. F., JR., *Supervisor of Salvage, U.S. Navy*

SEARS, PAUL B., *Professor of Conservation, Osborn Botanical Laboratory, Yale University*

SEASTRUNK, CLIFF L., *School of Textiles, North Carolina State University*

SEBERA, DONALD K., *Professor of Chemistry, State University of New York Cooperstown Graduate Programs; Author of* Electronic Structure and Chemical Bonding

SEBRELL, WILLIAM H., JR., *Director, Institute of Nutrition Sciences, Columbia University*

SECORD, RALPH C., *Director of Libraries, East Hartford Public Library*

SEDGWICK, JOHN P., JR., *Coauthor of* Highlights: An Illustrated Handbook of Art History *and* Art Appreciation Made Simple

SEDGWICK, R. R., *Editor of* History of Parliament, 1715–1754

SEELE, KEITH C., *Director, Oriental Institute Nubian Expedition; Coauthor of* When Egypt Ruled the East

SEGAL, CHARLES P., *Professor of Classics, Brown University; Author of* Landscape in Ovid's Metamorphoses

SEGAL, JACK, *Director of Planning, Eureka, Calif.*

SEGEL, HAROLD B., *Professor, Department of Slavic Languages, Columbia University*

SEGRÈ, EMILIO G., *Nobel Prize Winner in Physics, 1959; Professor of Physics, University of California at Berkeley*

SEIDEL, ARTHUR H., *Member of the Pennsylvania Bar; Coauthor of* Trademarks: Law and Practice

SEIDENBERG, RICHARD L., *Manager, Optical Design, Scientific Optical Products Division, Bausch & Lomb, Inc.*

SEIDENSTICKER, EDWARD, *Professor of Japanese, University of Michigan; Author of* Kafu the Scribbler; *Translator of* Yasunari Kawabata's Thousand Cranes *and* Tanizaki Junichiro's Some Prefer Nettles

SEITZ, FREDERICK, *President, Rockefeller University; Author of* The Modern Theory of Solids

SEITZ, WILLIAM C., *Director, Poses Institute of Fine Arts, Rose Art Museum, Brandeis University; Author of* The Art of Assemblage

SELENKOW, HERBERT A., MD, *Associate Professor of Medicine, Harvard Medical School; Coauthor of* Diseases of the Thyroid *in* Principles of Internal Medicine

SELF, MARGARET CABELL, *Author of* The Horseman's Encyclopedia, *and* The American Horse Show

SELIGMAN, BEN B., *Author of* Main Currents in Modern Economics: Economic Thought Since 1870

SELLERS, CHARLES G., *Professor of History, University of California at Berkeley; Author of* James K. Polk, Jacksonian *and* James K. Polk, Continentalist

SENGERS, J. M. H. LEVELT, *Heat Division, National Bureau of Standards*

SENIOR, CLARENCE, *Professor of Sociology, Brooklyn College*

SENKEWICZ, ROBERT M., SJ, *Fordham University*

SENN, ALFRED E., *Professor of History, University of Wisconsin at Madison*

SENTER, RICHARD, JR., *Assistant Professor of Sociology, Oakland University*

SERBER, ROBERT, *Professor of Physics, Columbia University*

SERGEANT, DAVID E., *Canadian Fisheries Research Board*

SERMET, JEAN, *Professor of Geography of Spain and Hispanic Countries, University of Toulouse, France*

SERR, E. F., *Pomologist, University of California at Davis*

SERVEN, JAMES E., *Author of* Colt Firearms *and* The Collecting of Guns

SETO, JAMES B., *Special Projects, Fairchild Space & Defense Systems*

SEVCENKO, IHOR, *Professor of History, Harvard University*

SEVERSON, JOHN H., *Editor of* Surfer Magazine; *Author of* Modern Surfing *and* Great Surfing

SHABAD, THEODORE, *Author of* Geography of the USSR *and* China's Changing Map; *Correspondent in Moscow, New York Times; Editor, Soviet Geography Magazine*

SHACKELFORD, JOLE, *Department of the History of Science, University of Wisconsin*

SHAFFER, ARTHUR H., *Associate Professor of History, University of Missouri at St. Louis*

SHALE, MARK, *Department of the History of Science, University of Wisconsin at Madison*

SHAMBERGER, HAROLD J., *Director of University Relations, West Virginia University*

SHAPIRO, ARTHUR K., MD, *Clinical Professor of Psychiatry, Mount Sinai School of Medicine, New York City*

SHAPIRO, ELAINE, *Associate Clinical Professor of Psychiatry, Mount Sinai School of Medicine, New York City*

SHARBAUGH, A. H., *General Electric Research and Development Center*

SHARLET, ROBERT, *Professor of Political Science, Union College*

SHARP, A. J., *Professor of Botany, University of Tennessee*

SHARP, CAROLYN, *Senior Cataloger, Library Association of Portland, Oreg.*

SHARP, JAMES ROGER, *Department of History, Syracuse University*

SHARP, W. MALCOLM, *Instructor, Structures Department, Southern Alberta Institute of Technology*

SHATTUCK, ROGER, *Commonwealth Professor of French Literature, University of Virginia; Author of* The Banquet Years *and* Proust's Binoculars

SHAW, EARL B., *Professor of Geography, Assumption College, Worcester, Mass.*

SHAW, J. HOWARD, *Executive Secretary, Advent Christian General Conference*

SHAW, RONALD E., *Professor of History, Miami University, Ohio; Author of* Erie Water West

SHAW, THURSTAN, *President, Prehistoric Society, Cambridge, England; Author of* Nigeria: Its Archaeology and Early History

SHAW, WILLIAM W., *Director, Urban Studies Center, and Professor of Political Science, Tulane University*

SHEA, DONALD R., *Professor of Political Science; Dean of International Studies and Programs, University of Wisconsin at Milwaukee; Author of* The Calvo Clause: A Problem of Inter-American and International Law and Diplomacy

SHEAFFER, LOUIS, *Author of* O'Neill, Son and Playwright; *Winner of the Pulitzer Prize for Biography, 1974*

SHEARMAN, HUGH, *Author of* Ulster *and* Modern Ireland

SHEARMAN, JOHN, *Lecturer in History of Art, Courtauld Institute of Art, University of London*

SHEATS, PAUL D., *Professor of English, University of California at Los Angeles; Editor of* The Poetical Works of John Keats

SHEATSLEY, PAUL, *Director of the Survey Research Service, National Opinion Research Center*

SHEEDY, CHARLES E., CSC, *Dean, College of Arts and Letters, University of Notre Dame; Author of* The Christian Virtues

SHEEHAN, BERNARD W., *Associate Professor, Department of History, Indiana University; Author of* Seeds of Extinction: Jeffersonian Philanthropy and the American Indian

SHEEHAN, T. J., *Ornamental Horticulturist and Professor, University of Florida*

SHEFFIELD, EDWARD F., *Professor of Higher Education, Massey College, University of Toronto, Canada*

SHEFFIELD, MARVIN J., DVM, *Mamaroneck, N.Y.*

SHELDON, JOHN M., *Director, Department of Postgraduate Medicine, University of Michigan; Author of* A Laboratory Manual on Allergy

SHELLEY, BRUCE L., *Professor of Church History, Conservative Baptist Theological Seminary; Author of* Evangelicism in America

SHENTON, ROBERT E., *Recording Engineer, National Broadcasting Company, Washington, D.C.*

SHENTON, WALTER F., *Professor of Mathematics, American University*

SHEPARD, RICHMOND, *Author of* Mime: The Technique of Silence

SHEPHERD, D. G., *Professor of Mechanical Engineering and Director of the Sibley School of Mechanical Engineering, Cornell University; Author of* Introduction to the Gas Turbine

SHEPHERD, JACK, *Author of* The Forest Killers: The Destruction of the American Wilderness

SHEPHERD, JOHN T., MD, *Chairman, Section of Physiology, Mayo Clinic*

SHEPPE, WALTER A., JR., *Curator of Zoology, University of Zambia; Research Associate, California Academy of Sciences; Department of Biology, University of Akron*

SHERBURNE, FRANCES, *Associate Director of Education, Massachusetts Audubon Society*

SHERCLIFF, W. H., *Author of* Manchester: A Short History of Its Development

SHERIDAN, ROBERT N., *Director, Levittown Public Library, Levittown, N.Y.*

SHERMAN, WILLIAM B., MD, *Director, Institute of Allergy, Roosevelt Hospital, New York City; Clinical Professor of Medicine, Columbia University College of Physicians and Surgeons; Coauthor of* Allergy in Pediatric Practice

SHERMAN, WILLIAM L., *Professor of History, University of Nebraska, Lincoln; Author of* Forced Native Labor in Sixteenth Century Central America; *Coauthor of* The Course of Mexican History

SHERWOOD, SAMUEL R., *Post Librarian, Aberdeen (Md.) Proving Ground*

SHIELDS, JAMES, SJ, *Fordham University*

SHIELDS, LAURENCE L., *Program in the History of Science, Princeton University*

SHIFF, RICHARD, *Associate Professor of Art, University of North Carolina at Chapel Hill*

SHIGLEY, JOSEPH E., *Professor of Mechanical Engineering, University of Michigan; Author of* Machine Design

SHIMER, JOHN A., *Professor of Geology, Brooklyn College*

SHINN, ROGER L., *Reinhold Niebuhr Professor of Social Ethics, Union Theological Seminary; Adjunct Professor of Religion, Columbia University*

SHIPPS, JAN, *Professor Emeritus of Religious Studies and History, Indiana University-Purdue University, Indianapolis*

SHIRLEY, JAMES R., *Associate Professor of History, Northern Illinois University*

SHIVELY, GEORGE C., *Member of the New York Bar*

SHOOKHOFF, HOWARD B., MD, *Adjunct Professor of Tropical Medicine, Columbia University of College of Physicians and Surgeons, and Chief, Division of Tropical Diseases, Department of Health, City of New York*

SHORE, BRADD, *Professor and Chair, Department of Anthropology, Emory University; Author of* Sala'ilua: A Samoan Mystery *and* Culture in Mind: Meaning Construction and Cultural Cognition

SHORE, HERBERT, *Playwright and Theater Director; Professor, Division of Drama, University of Southern California*

SHOTWELL, J. A., *Director, Museum of Natural History, University of Oregon*

SHUE, DOROTHY E., *Director, Cumberland County Public Library, Fayetteville, N.C.*

SHULL, BERNARD, *Professor of Economics, Hunter College, City University of New York*

SHULMAN, COLETTE, *Research Associate, School of International Affairs, Columbia University; Editor of* We the Russians

SHUMWAY, FLOYD M., *Columbia University*

SHUMWAY, GEORGE, *Author of* Conestoga Wagon, 1750–1850

SHUTTLESWORTH, DOROTHY E., *Author of* The Story of Ants

SHY, JOHN, *Professor of History, University of Michigan*

SIBLEY, CHARLES G., *Professor of Biology and Director, Division of Vertebrate Zoology, Yale University*

SICKELS, EDMUND D., *Editor of* Wire and Wire Products

SIDEL, VICTOR W., MD, *Chairman, Department of Social Medicine, Montefiore Hospital and Medical Center, Albert Einstein College of Medicine; Coauthor of* Serve the People: Observations on Medicine in the People's Republic of China

SIEBER, ROY, *Professor of Fine Arts, Indiana University*

SIEGAL, HARVEY A., *Professor, Department of Sociology, City College of New York; Coauthor of* Crime: Emerging Issues

SIEGEL, ARTHUR, *Sports Illustrated*

SIEGEL, DANIEL M., *Associate Professor, Department of the History of Science, University of Wisconsin at Madison*

SIEGFRIED, ROBERT, *Professor of History of Science, University of Wisconsin at Madison*

SIEVERS, HARRY J., SJ, *Dean of Arts and Sciences, Fordham University*

SIEWIOREK, DANIEL P., *Director, Engineering Design Research Center and Buhl Professor of Electrical and Computer Engineering and Computer Science, Carnegie-Mellon University*

SIGWORTH, VAN, *News Advertising Manager, National Institute of Dry Cleaning*

SIHLER, EMMA, *Head Librarian, Adrian Public Library*

SILBEY, JOEL H., *Professor of American History, Cornell University; Author of* The Shrine of Party, Voters, Parties, and Elections, *and* The Transformation of American Politics

SILK, JOSEPH I., *Professor, Departments of Astronomy and Physics, University of California at Berkeley*

SILVER, HAROLD, *Coauthor of* A Social History of Education in England

SILVER, STEPHEN EURIC, MD, *Attending Dermatologist, Lawrence and Memorial Hospital, New London, Conn.; Clinical Instructor, Yale University*

SILVERMAN, SYDEL, *Professor of Anthropology, Ph.D. Program in Anthropology, Graduate School, City University of New York; Author of* Three Bells of Civilization: The Life of an Italian Hill Town; *Editor of* Totems and Teachers: Perspectives in the History of Anthropology

SILVERSTEIN, JOSEF, *Professor of Political Science, Rutgers University; Author of* Burmese Politics: The Dilemma of National Unity

SILVERT, FRIEDA, *Department of Sociology and Anthropology, City College of New York*

SILZ, WALTER, *Author of* Early German Romanticism

SIMMONDS, GEORGE W., *Author of* Soviet Leaders

SIMMONS, EDWIN H., *Brigadier General, U.S. Marine Corps (Retired); Director of Marine Corps History and Museums; Author of* The United States Marines, 1775–1975

SIMMONS, ERNEST J., *Author of* Russian Fiction and Soviet Ideology, Introduction to Russian Realism, *and* Leo Tolstoy

SIMMONS, MARC, *Department of History, University of New Mexico, Author of* Spanish Government in New Mexico

SIMON, ALBERT, *Professor of Mechanical and Aerospace Sciences, University of Rochester*

SIMON, NOEL, *Compiler,* Red Data Book *volume* Mammalia

SIMON, W. M., *Professor and Head of the Department of History, University of Keele, England; Author of* Germany: A Brief History

SIMONS, ELWYN L., *Professor of Geology, Yale University; Director, Division of Vertebrate Paleontology, Yale Peabody Museum*

SIMONS, SAVILLA MILLIS, *Director, National Travelers Aid Association*

SIMPKINS, JULIET, *Press Officer, Madame Tussaud's*

SIMPSON, ROBERT W., *Director, Flight Transportation Laboratory, Massachusetts Institute of Technology*

SINCLAIR, DAVID, *Professor of Anatomy, University of Aberdeen, Scotland; Author of* A Student's Guide to Anatomy, Cutaneous Sensation, *and* Human Growth After Birth

SINCLAIR, KEITH, *Professor of History, University of Auckland; Author of* The Origins of the Maori Wars, A History of New Zealand, *and* Walter Nash

SINEATH, TIMOTHY W., *Professor and Dean Emeritus, College of Library and Information Science, University of Kentucky*

SINGER, WALTER, *New York Botanical Garden, Bronx, N.Y.*

SINGH, KHUSHWANT, *Author of* Ranjit Singh, Maharajah of the Punjab

SINGLETON, CHARLES S., *Professor of Humanistic Studies, Johns Hopkins University; Editor of* The Decameron: A Diplomatic Edition

SINNEN, JEANNE, *Editor, University Press, University of Minnesota*

SINNOTT, EDMUND W., *Author of* Plant Morphogenesis; *Coauthor of* Botany

SINSHEIMER, ROBERT L., *Chancellor, University of California at Santa Cruz*

SIRLUCK, ERNEST, *President, University of Manitoba, Canada; Coeditor of* The Complete Prose Works of John Milton

SISTARE, SANFORD R., *Director, Press Office, Boston Symphony Orchestra*

SIVERTZ, B. G., *Director, Northern Administration and Lands Branch, Department of Northern Affairs and National Resources, Canada*

SIVIN, NATHAN, *Professor of Chinese Culture and of the History of Science, University of Pennsylvania*

SIZER, THEODORE, *Author of* The Works of Colonel John Trumbull, Artist of the American Revolution

SKALWEIT, STEPHEN, *Director of History Seminars, University of Bonn, Germany*

SKELTON, R. A., *Sometime Superintendent of Map Room, British Museum*

SKELTON, ROBERT W., *Assistant Keeper, Indian Section, Victoria and Albert Museum, London; Author of* Indian Miniatures from the 15th to 19th Centuries

SKEMP, SHEILA L., *Assistant Professor of History, University of Mississippi; Author of* Foundations of American Nationalism

SKINNER, B. F., *Edgar Pierce Professor of Psychology, Harvard University; Author of* Technology of Teaching *and* Beyond Freedom and Dignity

SKOURA, SOPHIA, *Author of* The Greek Cook Book

SLACK, A. V., *Chief, Applied Research Branch, Division of Chemical Development, Tennessee Valley Authority; Author of* Fertilizer Developments and Trends

SLAWSON, C. B., *Coauthor of* Gems and Gem Materials

SLIWA, STEVEN M., *President, Embry-Riddle Aeronautical University*

SLOAN, WILLIAM DAVID, *Professor of Journalism, University of Alabama; Author of* The Best of Pulitzer Prize News Writing

SLOANE, JOSEPH C., *Chairman, Department of Art, University of North Carolina; Author of* French Painting Between the Past and the Present

SLONIM, MARC, *Author of* Outline of Russian Literature

SLONIMSKY, NICOLAS, *Composer and Conductor; Author of* Music Since 1900

SLOTTEN, RALPH, *Associate Professor of Religion, Dickinson College*

SLOTTMAN, WILLIAM, *Professor of History, University of California at Berkeley*

SLY, JOHN FAIRFIELD, *Professor of Politics, Princeton University*

SMALL, MIRIAM R., *Author of* Oliver Wendell Holmes

SMART, JAMES D., *Jessup Professor of Biblical Interpretation, Union Theological Seminary; Author of* The Interpretation of Scripture

SMART, NINIAN, *Professor of Religious Studies, University of Lancaster, England; Author of* The Long Search, The Religious Experience of Mankind, *and* World Religions

SMEATON, W. A., *Reader in the History and Philosophy of Science, University College, London*

SMILEY, DAVID L., *Professor of History, Wake Forest University; Author of* Lion of White Hall; *Coauthor of* The South in American History

SMIT, JACOB W., *Queen Wilhelmina Professor of the History, Language, and Literature of the Low Countries, Columbia University*

SMITH, ALBERT B., *Associate Professor of French, University of Florida; Author of* Ideal and Reality in the Fictional Narratives of Théophile Gautier

SMITH, AUSTIN, MD, *Editor of* Journal of the American Medical Society

SMITH, BRADFORD A., *Associate Professor, Department of Planetary Sciences, University of Arizona*

SMITH, DALE C., *Section of Medical History, Uniformed Services University of the Health Sciences, Bethesda, Md.*

SMITH, DEAN, *Arizona State University, Tempe*

SMITH, ELVIN, *Department of Physiology and Biophysics, University of Mississippi Medical Center*

SMITH, F. DOW, *Vice President and Corporate Scientist, Itek Corporation*

SMITH, GARY W., *School of Textiles, North Carolina State University*

SMITH, GENE, *Financial Writer, New York Times*

SMITH, GEOFFREY, *Associate Professor of History, Queens University at Kingston, Canada*

SMITH, GERALD, *Director of Public Relations, Christian and Missionary Alliance*

SMITH, GOLDWIN, *Professor of History, Wayne State University; Author of* The Treaty of Washington

SMITH, GRAHAM, *Associate Professor of the History of Art, University of Michigan*

SMITH, H. D., *Scientific Consultant and Member of the Board of Governors, Nova Scotia Research Foundation*

SMITH, HALLETT, *Professor of English, California Institute of Technology; Author of* Elizabethan Poetry *and* Shakespeare's Romances: A Study of Some Ways of the Imagination

SMITH, HARRY HAWKINS, *Curator, Goshen Library and Historical Society, Goshen, N.Y.*

SMITH, HOBART M., *Professor of Biology, University of Colorado*

SMITH, HOWARD W., *Professor and Chairman, Department of History, Christopher Newport College, College of William and Mary*

SMITH, J. PERCY, *Vice-President Academic, University of Guelph, Ontario, Canada; Author of* The Unrepentant Pilgrim: A Study of the Development of Bernard Shaw

SMITH, J. W., *Secretary, American Fox Terrier Club*

SMITH, JACK, *Associate Editor,* Yachting Magazine

SMITH, JACK E., *Chief, Research and Cultural Resource Management, Mesa Verde National Park, Colo.*

SMITH, JILL, *Member of the Massachusetts Bar*

SMITH, JOHN B., *Director of Libraries, Texas A&M University (1969–1974)*

SMITH, JOHN WAYNE, *Director of Libraries, El Paso Public Library, El Paso, Texas*

SMITH, JOSEPH H., *George Welwood Murray Professor of Legal History, Columbia University*

SMITH, KENT, *Executive Director, Spina Bifida Association*

SMITH, MARIAN W., *London School of Economics and Political Science, University of London*

SMITH, MAXWELL A., *Professor of Modern Languages, Florida State University; Author of* A Short History of French Literature *and* Jean Giono

SMITH, MILDRED, *Village Historian of Garden City, N.Y.; Author of* History of Garden City

SMITH, MORTON, *Professor of History, Columbia University; Author of* Jesus the Magician

SMITH, NORMAN A. F., *Research Fellow at Imperial College of Science and Technology, London*

SMITH, PETER J., *Professor of Geography, University of Alberta*

SMITH, R. B., *School of Oriental and African Studies, University of London*

SMITH, ROBERT E., *Instructor in Film History, University of Connecticut; Visiting Instructor, Wesleyan University*

SMITH, ROBERT FREEMAN, *Professor of History, University of Toledo; Author of* The United States and Cuba: Business and Diplomacy, 1917–1960

SMITH, ROLLIN, *American Guild of Organists*

SMITH, SARAH C., *Anderson County Librarian*

SMITH, SWEETMAN R., *Fashion Institute of Technology, State University of New York; Coauthor of* The Dictionary of Retailing *and* The Dictionary of Marketing

SMITH, T. B., *Professor of Civil Law, University of Edinburgh, Scotland*

SMITH, WARREN H., *Associate Editor,* The Yale Edition of Horace Walpole's Correspondence

SMITH, WHITNEY, *Director, Flag Research Center, Winchester, Mass.; Editor,* Flag Bulletin

SMOCK, MILDRED, *Librarian, Council Bluffs Free Public Library*

SMOCK, RAYMOND W., *Coeditor of* The Booker T. Washington Papers

SMULLYAN, ARTHUR F., *Professor and Chairman of the Department of Philosophy, Rutgers University; Author of* Fundamentals of Logic; *Coeditor of* Introduction to Philosophy

SMYLIE, JAMES H., *Professor of American Church History, Union Theological Seminary in Virginia*

SMYTH, HENRY D., *United States Representative to International Atomic Energy Agency (1961–1970)*

SMYTH, THOMAS, JR., *Professor of Entomology, Pennsylvania State University*

SNAVELY, WILLIAM P., *Head, Department of Economics, University of Connecticut; Coauthor of* Intermediate Economic Analysis

SNELGROVE, C. P., *Librarian, Tennessee Technological University*

SNELL, JOHN L., *Professor of History, Tulane University; Author of* The Diplomacy of Global War, 1939–1945

SNIDER, DELBERT A., *Professor of Economics, Miami University, Ohio; Author of* International Monetary Relations *and* Introduction to International Economics

SNOOK, JOHN B., *Assistant Professor, Department of Religion, Barnard College, Columbia University*

SNYDER, EMILE, *Professor in African Studies Program, Indiana University*

SNYDER, EVELYN J., *Librarian, Cairo Public Library*

SNYDER, HENRY L., *Professor of History and Dean of Research and Graduate Studies, University of Kansas; Editor of* The Marlborough-Godolphin Correspondence

SNYDER, JAMES, *Professor of Art History, Bryn Mawr College*

SNYDER, LOUIS L., *Professor of History, City College of New York*

SNYDER, PAUL H. H., *Coauthor of* Knots and Lines Illustrated

SNYDER, ROBERT, *Director, Joint Graduate Program in Toxicology, Rutgers University, College of Pharmacy, Busch Campus, Piscataway, N.J.*

SNYDERMAN, GEORGE S., *Temple University*

SOBEL, MICHAEL, DMD, MDS, *Department of Pedodontics, School of Dental Medicine, University of Pittsburgh*

SOBEL, RONALD B., *Rabbi, Temple Emanu-El, New York City*

SOBIESZEK, ROBERT, *Associate Curator, Photography, International Museum of Photography, George Eastman House; Coeditor of* The Literature of Photography

SODERSTROM, THOMAS R., *Associate Curator, Division of Grasses, Department of Botany, Smithsonian Institution*

SOLLORS, WERNER, *Henry B. and Anne M. Cabot Professor of English Literature, Harvard University; Author of* Beyond Ethnicity

SOLNITZKY, OTHMAR, MD, *Professor of Anatomy, Georgetown University School of Medicine*

SOLOMON, IRVING, MD, *Assistant Clinical Professor of Medicine, Mt. Sinai School of Medicine, New York City*

SOLOTOROVSKY, MORRIS, *Professor of Bacteriology, Rutgers University; Coauthor of* Three Centuries of Microbiology

SOLOW, ROBERT M., *Professor of Economics, Massachusetts Institute of Technology; Author of* Growth Theory *and* Capital Theory and the Rate of Return

SOMERS, GERALD A., *Director, Brown County Library*

SOMERVILLE, JOHN, *Professor of Philosophy, Hunter College; Author of* The Philosophy of Marxism

SOPER, JOSEPH, *Department of Ophthalmology, Baylor University College of Medicine*

SORELL, WALTER, *Author of* The Dance through the Ages; *Editor of* The Dance Has Many Faces

SORICH, RICHARD, *China Bibliographer, East Asian Institute, Columbia University*

SOUCEK, PRISCILLA, *Professor, Institute of Fine Arts, New York University*

SOUKUP, MIROSLAV, *Union of Czechoslovak Classical Scholars*

SOUTHERN, SIR RICHARD, *President, St. John's College, Oxford University; Author of* The Making of the Middle Ages

SOUTHWORTH, FRANKLIN C., *Associate Professor of Modern Indo-Aryan Languages, Department of South Asia Regional Studies, University of Pennsylvania; Author of* Spoken Marathi *and* Transformational Structure of Nepali

SPACKS, PATRICIA M., *Professor of English, Wellesley College; Author of* The Poetry of Vision: Five Eighteenth-Century Poets *and* The Female Imagination, *winner of the National Book Award*

SPALEK, JOHN M., *Chairman, Department of Germanic and Slavic Languages, State University of New York at Albany; Author of* Ernst Toller and His Critics

SPANIER, JOHN W., *Professor of Political Science, University of Florida; Author of* American Foreign Policy Since World War II *and* World Politics in an Age of Revolution

SPAR, JEROME, *Professor of Meteorology, New York University*

SPARKS, SHIRLEY, *Assistant Director, Special Services, South Dakota School of Mines and Technology*

SPARLING, VIRGINIA V., *President, National Congress of Parents and Teachers*

SPAULDING, KENNETH A., *Chairman, Department of English, University of Wisconsin at Eau Claire; Author of* On the Oregon Trail

SPAULDING, ROBERT M., *Professor of East Asian History, Oklahoma State University; Author of* Imperial Japan's Higher Civil Service Examinations

SPEAIGHT, ROBERT W., *Author of* William Poel and the Elizabethan Revival

SPECTOR, JOHANNA, *Seminary Professor of Musicology and Director of the Ethnomusicology Department, Jewish Theological Seminary of America, New York City*

SPELLMAN, ROSALIE, *Aberdeen Public Library*

SPENCE, RAYMOND E., *Deputy Chief Engineer, Federal Communications Commission*

SPENCER, A. M., *Research Assistant, Geological Society of London*

SPENCER, DICK, III, *Publisher,* The Western Horseman; *Author of* Beginning Western Horsemanship

SPENCER, DOROTHY M., *Visiting Lecturer in Anthropology, South Asia Regional Studies Department, University of Pennsylvania; Author of* Indian Fiction in English, An Annotated Bibliography

SPENCER, HAROLD, *Professor of Art, University of Connecticut*

SPENCER, JEAN E., *Vice President for Policy and Planning, University of Maryland; Author of* Contemporary Local Government in Maryland

SPENCER, KATHERINE, *Librarian, Garden Grove Regional Branch, Orange County Public Library*

SPERONI, CHARLES, *Professor of Italian, University of California at Los Angeles*

SPIER, LESLIE, *Professor of Anthropology, University of New Mexico; Author of* Yuman Tribes of the Gila River

SPIER, ROBERT F. G., *Professor of Anthropology, University of Missouri at Columbia; Author of* From the Hand of Man

SPILLERS, ROGER E., *Librarian, Helena Public Library*

SPINKA, MATTHEW, *Author of* History of Christianity in the Balkans

SPIVACK, CHARLOTTE K., *Professor of English, University of Massachusetts*

SPOFFORD, SALLY HOYT, *Research Collaborator, Laboratory of Ornithology, Cornell University*

SPOHR, D. A., *Consulting Physicist, U.S. Naval Research Laboratory*

SPRAGUE, G. F., *Professor of Agronomy, University of Illinois*

SPRINGER, STEWART, *Fishery Biologist, Fish and Wildlife Service, U.S. Department of the Interior*

SPURLING, SIR STANLEY, *Member of Legislative Council, Bermuda*

SQUIRE, LARRY R., *Professor of Psychiatry and Neurosciences, School of Medicine, University of California at San Diego; Research Career Scientist, San Diego Veterans Affairs Medical Center*

SQUIRES, DICK, *Author of* The Other Racquet Sports

STACE, WALTER T., *Author of* Mysticism and Philosophy

STACKPOLE, EDOUARD A., *President, Nantucket Historical Association, Nantucket, Mass.; Author of* The Sea Hunters—Two Centuries of American Whaling *and* The Charles W. Morgan, Last of the Whaleships

STAFFORD, EDWARD P., *Commander, U.S. Navy (Retired); Author of* The Far and the Deep

STAFLEU, FRANS, *Professor of Systematic Botany, University of Utrecht, Netherlands*

STAGER, KENNETH E., *Senior Curator of Ornithology, Los Angeles County Museum of Natural History*

STAHL, WILLIAM H., *Chairman, Department of Classics and World Literature, Brooklyn College; Author of* Roman Science

STALLMAN, R. W., *Editor of* The Art of Joseph Conrad: A Critical Symposium

STALTER, NEIL J., *E.I. du Pont de Nemours & Company*

STAMLER, JEREMIAH, MD, *Professor of Community Health and Preventive Medicine, Northwestern University Medical School*

STANDAERT, FRANK G., MD, *National Institutes of Mental Health*

STANDEN, EDITH A., *Associate Curator, Textiles, Metropolitan Museum of Art*

STANIFORTH, SYDNEY D., *Professor of Agricultural Economics, University of Wisconsin at Madison*

STANILAND, KAY, *Assistant Keeper, Gallery of English Costume, Platt Hall, Manchester, England*

STANLEY, GEORGE F. G., *Dean of Arts; Head of the Department of History, Royal Military College of Canada; Author of* The Birth of Western Canada

STANNARD, JERRY, *Professor of History of Science, University of Kansas*

STANSELL, GARY, *St. Olaf College*

STANSFIELD, CHARLES A., JR., *Professor of Geography, Rowan College of New Jersey; Author of* New Jersey: A Geography

STANSKY, PETER, *Department of History, Stanford University; Coauthor of* The Unknown Orwell *and* Orwell: The Transformation

STARKE, EDGAR A., JR., *Director, Fracture and Fatigue Research Laboratory, Georgia Institute of Technology*

STARKIE, WALTER, *Author of* Road to Santiago *and* Writers, Modern Spain

STARKMAN, ERNEST, *Chairman of the Department of Thermal Systems, University of California at Berkeley; Environmental Activities Staff, General Motors Technical Center*

STARN, RANDOLPH, *Associate Professor of History, University of California at Berkeley; Author of* Donato Giannotti and His Epistolae

STARR, CHESTER G., *Professor of Ancient History, University of Michigan; Author of* History of the Ancient World

STARR, HOMER, *Assistant Managing Editor,* Chemical Week

STARR, JOHN BRYAN, *Executive Director, Yale-China Association; Author of* Continuing the Revolution: The Political Thought of Mao

STAVRIDI, MARGARET, *Author of* The History of Costume

STAYTON, KEVIN, *Assistant Curator of Decorative Arts, Brooklyn Museum*

STEAD, EUGENE ANSON, JR., *Florence McAlister Professor of Medicine, Department of Medicine, Duke University*

STEARN, WILLIAM T., *Department of Botany, British Museum, London*

STEARNS, PETER, *Heinz Professor of History, Carnegie-Mellon University; Editor of* Journal of Social History; *Author of* 1848: The Revolutionary Tide in Europe

STEEFEL, LAWRENCE D., *Professor of History, University of Minnesota*

STEEL, ROBERT W., *Professor of Geography, University of Liverpool, England; Coeditor of* Geographies and the Tropics; *Coauthor of* Africa; *Coeditor and Contributor to* Geographical Essays on British Tropical Lands

STEELE, WILLIAM O., *Author of* The True Stories of Six Pioneers *and* The Far Frontier

STEER, ALFRED G., JR., *Professor and Chairman of Department of Germanic and Slavic Languages, University of Georgia*

STEERE, EDWARD, *Author of* Wilderness Campaign

STEIN, M. L, *Professor of Journalism, California State University at Long Beach*

STEIN, PETER, *Regius Professor of Civil Law, University of Cambridge; Author of* Fault in the Formation of Contract in Roman Law and Scots Law, Regulae Iuris: From Juristic Rules to Legal Maxims, Legal Values in Western Societies, *and* Legal Evolution

STEINDL-RAST, DAVID F. K., OSB, *Monk of Mount Savior Monastery, Pine City, N.Y.; Chairman of the Center for Spiritual Studies; Contributor to* Exploring Inner Space, Crisis and New Vision, Cross Currents, *and* East-West Review

STEINMETZ, SOL, *Author of* Yiddish and English: A Century of Yiddish in America

STELLWAGEN, ALAN, *Assistant Professor of Geography, University of Colorado*

STEPHENS, H. MALCOLM, *Contributing Editor,* Dogs in Canada

STEPHENS, LAWRENCE J., *Professor of Chemistry, Elmira College; Coauthor of* Chemistry and the Living Organism, 6th ed.

STERLING, DAVID L., *Associate Professor of History, University of Cincinnati*

STERN, CHAIM, *Rabbi; Author of* The Gates of Prayer

STERN, CURT, *Professor of Zoology and Genetics, University of California at Berkeley; Author of* Principles of Human Genetics

STERN, IRWIN, *Senior Lecturer, Department of Spanish and Portuguese, Columbia University*

STERN, JEROME H., *Associate Professor of English, Florida State University*

STERNBERG, ERNEST, *Professor of Urban Planning, Department of Planning and Design, State University of New York at Buffalo*

STERRETT, DELBERT E., *Assistant Professor of Music, University of Florida*

STEVENS, RICHARD P., *Chairman, Political Science Department, and Director, African Studies Program, Lincoln University, Pa.; Author of* Lesotho, Botswana, *and* Swaziland *and* A Historical Dictionary of Botswana

STEVENS, ROBERT, *Professor of International Business, Graduate School of Business, Indiana University Northwest; Author of* Primer on Balance of Payments and International Monetary Reform

STEVENS, S. S., *Professor of Psychophysics, Harvard University; Author of* Hearing: Its Psychology and Physiology; *Coauthor of* Sound and Hearing; *Editor of* Handbook of Experimental Psychology

STEVENSON, CHARLES E., *Professor of Law, College of Law, University of Cincinnati*

STEVENSON, LIONEL, *James B. Duke Professor of English, Duke University; Author of* The English Novel: A Panorama

STEWARD, H. J., *Research Associate, American Geographical Society*

STEWART, ALBERT B., *Professor of Physics, Antioch College*

STEWART, EDGAR I., *Distinguished Professor of History, Eastern Washington State College; Author of* Custer's Luck

STEWART, FRANK, *Editor,* American Contract Bridge League Bulletin

STEWART, IAN G., *Professor of Economics, University of Edinburgh*

STEWART, MARK A., *Ida P. Haller Professor of Child Psychiatry, University of Iowa; Coauthor of* Raising a Hyperactive Child

STEWART, R. K., *Canadian Education Association*

STEWART-ROBINSON, J., *Professor of Turkish Studies, University of Michigan*

STILLWELL, PAUL, *Editor,* U.S. Naval Review, *U.S. Naval Institute*

STIMPSON, CATHARINE R., *Assistant Professor of English, Barnard College; Author of* J.R.R. Tolkien

STIMSON, ALLEN, *Author of* Photometry and Radiometry for Engineers

STIMSON, ERMINA, *Fashion Editor,* Women's Wear Daily

STIMSON, GEORGE W., *Author of* Introduction to Airborne Radar

STOCKENSTRÖM, GÖRAN, *Professor of Scandinavian, University of Minnesota*

STOCKSTILL, PATRICK, *Academy Historian, Academy of Motion Picture Arts and Sciences*

STODDARD, CHARLES H., *Author of* Essentials of Forestry Practice

STOEVER, HERMAN J., *School of Technology, Southern Illinois University*

STOKES, H. GORDON, *Author of* English Place-Names

STOKES, J. BUROUGHS, *Manager, Committees on Publication, First Church of Christ, Scientist*

STOKES, RALPH C., *Technical Adviser, Bureau of Yards and Docks*

STOKES, WILLIAM E., JR., *Coauthor of* The Papers of Randolph of Roanoke

STOKES, WILLIAM LEE, *Professor of Geology, University of Utah; Author of* Essentials of Earth History; *Coauthor of* Introduction to Geology

STONE, GEORGE WINCHESTER, JR., *Dean, Graduate School of Arts and Sciences, New York University; Author of* The London Stage, 1747–1776

STONE, OLIVE M., *Reader in Law to the University of London at the London School of Economics and Political Science*

STONE, ROBERT G., *Meteorologist, Air Weather Service, U.S. Air Force*

STONE, THELMA, *Librarian, Abington Public Library*

STONER, GEORGE E., JR., *Chairman, Geography Division, Bradley University*

STOPP, FREDERICK, *Gonville and Caius College, Cambridge University*

STOPPEL, WILLIAM A., *Librarian, Reeves Memorial Library, Westminster College, Mo.*

STORCK, JOHN N., *Director, Lima Public Library, Lima, Ohio*

STORER, TRACY I., *Professor of Zoology, University of California at Davis; Coauthor of* General Zoology

STOREY, ROBIN L., *Reader in History, University of Nottingham, England; Author of* The End of the House of Lancaster *and* The Reign of Henry VII

STORM, FAYETTA HALL, *Head Librarian, Lee County Library Headquarters, Fort Myers, Fla.*

STOUDEMIRE, ROBERT H., *Associate Professor of Political Science and Associate Director, Bureau of Governmental Research, University of South Carolina; Coauthor of* Municipal Government in South Carolina

STOUT, EVELYN E., *Professor of Design and Environmental Analysis, New York State College of Human Ecology, Cornell University*

STOUT, JAMES J., *Chief, Division of River Basins, Federal Power Commission*

STOVALL, JAMES C., *Professor of Geology, University of Oregon*

STOVER, JOHN F., *Professor Emeritus of History, Purdue University; Author of* Railroads of the South, American Railroads, A History of American Railroads, *and* Turnpikes, Canals, and Steamboats

STOW, CHARLES E., *Librarian, Greenville County (S.C.) Library*

STRAILE, WILLIAM E., *Grants Associate, Division of Research Grants, National Institutes of Health*

STRAINCHAMPS, EDMOND, *Department of Music, State University of New York at Buffalo*

STRAKOSCH, GEORGE, *Manager, Elevators, Otis Elevator Company*

STRASBERG, LEE, *Artistic Director, Actors Studio*

STRATTON, EUDOCIA, *Librarian, Jackson County Library*

STRAUS, W. L., JR., *Author of* Forerunners of Darwin

STRAUSBAUGH, PERRY D., *Professor of Botany, West Virginia University*

STRAUSS, GERALD, *Professor of History, Indiana University*

STRAW, RICHARD M., *Professor of Biology, California State College at Los Angeles*

STRAZDON, MAUREEN E., *Reference Department, Free Public Library of Elizabeth, Elizabeth, N.J.*

STREET, JAMES H., *Professor of Economics, Rutgers University*

STREETER, VICTOR L., *Professor of Hydraulics, Department of Civil Engineering, University of Michigan*

STRICKLAND, W. EARL, *President, Wesleyan College*

STROM, GORDON H., *Professor of Aerospace Engineering, Polytechnic Institute of New York*

STROMDAHL, JUDITH E., *Head Librarian, Robbins Library*

STRONG, LAURENCE E., *Professor of Chemistry, Earlham College*

STROTHER, DEAN C., *General, U.S. Air Force*

STROUD, ELAINE CONDOURIS, *Department of the History of Science, University of Wisconsin at Madison*

STROUD, WILLIAM G., *Chief, Advanced Plans Staff, NASA/Goddard Space Flight Center, Greenbelt, Md.*

STRUIK, DIRK JAN, *Professor of Mathematics, Massachusetts Institute of Technology; Author of* Concise History of Mathematics

STRUMIA, MAX M., MD, *Bryn Mawr Hospital, Bryn Mawr, Pa.*

STRUNING, WILLIAM C., *Professor of Quantitative Analysis, Seton Hall University*

STRUPP, HANS H., *Professor of Psychology, Vanderbilt University; Author of* Psychotherapists in Action *and* Psychotherapy

STUART, ALASTAIR M., *Associate Professor of Zoology, University of Massachusetts; Coauthor of* Biology of Termites

STUBBS, STANLEY, *Museum of New Mexico, Santa Fe*

STUCKEY, LILLIE M., *Coauthor of* The Spice Cookbook

STUERWALD, JOHN E., *President, International Association of Arson Investigators*

STUEWER, ROGER H., *Associate Professor of History of Physics and Physics, University of Minnesota; Editor of* Minnesota Studies in the Philosophy of Science

STRUHLINGER, ERNST, *Associate Director for Science, George C. Marshall Space Flight Center*

STURGEON, THEODORE, *Writer of Science Fiction; Author of* More Than Human

STURM, ALBERT L., *Professor of Government, Virginia Polytechnic Institute*

SUBER, HOWARD, *Chairman, Critical Studies Program and Director, Film Archive, Motion Picture Division, Department of Theater Arts, University of California at Los Angeles*

SUGARMAN, SALLY, *Professor of Childhood Studies and Education, Bennington College*

SUGGS, ROBERT CARL, *Senior Scientist, Kaman Systems Center, Bethesda, Md.; Author of* Survival Handbook *and* Archaeology of New York

SUKLOFF, HYMAN, *Author of* Small Property Owner's Legal Guide

SULLIVAN, BESSIE M., *Chairman, Book Committee, Ida Public Library, Belvidere*

SULLIVAN, EDWARD D., *Chairman, Council of the Humanities, Princeton University; Author of* Maupassant the Novelist *and* Maupassant: The Short Stories

SULLIVAN, FRANCIS A., SJ, *Professor of Theology, Gregorian University, Rome; Author of* The Christology of Theodore of Mopsuestia

SULLIVAN, JAMES B., *Senior Editor, Engineering News-Record*

SULLIVAN, MICHAEL, *Professor of Oriental Art, Stanford University; Author of* Chinese Art in the Twentieth Century

SULLIVAN, PEGGY, *Executive Director, American Library Association*

SULLIVAN, RICHARD C., *National Public Relations Director, AMVETS*

SULLIVAN, RICHARD E., *Dean, College of Arts and Letters, Michigan State University; Author of* A Short History of Western Civilization *and* Critical Issues in European History

SUMMERS, F. P., *Professor of History, West Virginia University; Author of* West Virginia: The Mountain State

SUMMERSELL, CHARLES GRAYSON, *Professor and Head, Department of History, University of Alabama*

SUNDERLAND, JEANNETTE, *Librarian, Danbury Library*

SURREY, ALEXANDER B., *Vice President for Research and Development, Sterling-Winthrop Research Institute*

SUSSMAN, MAURICE, *Professor and Chairman, Life Sciences Department, University of Pittsburgh*

SUTCLIFFE, ANTHONY, *Research Fellow, School of History, the University of Birmingham, England*

SUTHERLAND, ARTHUR E., *Bussey Professor of Law, Harvard Law School; Author of* Constitutionalism in America

SUTHERLAND, JAMES, *Lord Northcliffe Professor of Modern English Literature, University of London; Author of* Wordsworth and Pope

SUTTON, H. ELDON, *Director of the Genetics Institute and Ashbel Smith Professor of Zoology, University of Texas at Austin*

SUTTON, HORACE, *Associate Editor, Saturday Review; Author of* Aloha, Hawaii

SUTTON, WALTER, *Author of* Modern American Criticism

SUTTON-SMITH, BRIAN, *Professor of Psychology and Education, Teachers College, Columbia University; Author of* The Folkgames of Children *and* How to Play With Your Children: And When Not to

SUZUKI, MacGREGOR, *Department of Physics, Queens College*

SVENDSEN, LOUISE AVERILL, *Senior Curator, Solomon R. Guggenheim Museum, New York City; Editor of* Klee at the Guggenheim Museum

SWADESH, FRANCES LEON, *Curator of Ethnology, Museum of New Mexico; Author of* Los Primeros Pobladores: Hispanic Americans of the Ute Frontier

SWAN, ROY C., *Professor of Anatomy, Cornell Medical College*

SWANBERG, W. A., *Biographer and Historian; Author of* Citizen Hearst

SWANN, JOHN PATRICK, *School of Pharmacy, University of Wisconsin at Madison*

SWANSON, TOD D., *Associate Professor of Religious Studies, Arizona State University*

SWARTZ, CLIFFORD E., *Professor of Physics, State University of New York at Stony Brook*

SWEENEY, BEATRICE M., *Professor of Biology, University of California at Santa Barbara*

SWEENEY, LEO, SJ, *Professor of Philosophy, Creighton University*

SWEET, FREDERICK A., *Curator of American Painting and Sculpture, Art Institute of Chicago; Author of* Miss Mary Cassatt *and* The Hudson River School

SWEITZER, RAYMOND M., SJ, *Fordham University*

SWENSON, G. R., *Art and Artists Magazine; Author of* The Other Tradition

SWENSON, LOYD S., *Professor of History, University of Houston; Coauthor of* This New Ocean: A History of Project Mercury; *Author of* The Ethereal Aether: A History of the Michelson-Morley-Miller Aether-Drift Experiments, 1880–1930

SWEZEY, KENNETH M., *Author of* Nikola Tesla, in Science, *and* Science and Magic

SWIFT, HOWARD W., *Assistant Director, Garden Center of Greater Cleveland; Author of* Wonderful World of Plants and Flowers

SWIFT, MICHAEL D., *Archivist, Public Archives of Canada, Ottawa*

SWIHART, JOHN M., *President, Swihart Consulting, Inc.*

SWINDLER, WILLIAM F., *Professor of Marshall-Wythe School of Law, College of William and Mary; Author of* Magna Carta: Legend and Legacy

SWINTON, WILLIAM E., *Senior Fellow, Massey College, and Professor, University of Toronto; Author of* The Dinosaurs *and* Digging for Dinosaurs

SWISHER, CARL B., *Author of* The Supreme Court in Modern Role

SWITZER, GEORGE S., *Curator, Department of Mineral Sciences, Smithsonian Institution*

SYDER, EDWARD C., *Secretary, Golden Retriever Club of America, Inc.*

SYED, ANWAR, *Professor of Government, University of Massachusetts; Author of* Walter Lippmann's Philosophy of International Politics

SYKES, RICHARD B., *Vice President, Biological Sciences, Squibb Institute for Medical Research, Princeton, N.J.*

SYLVERS, MALCOLM, *Assistant Professor of History, Chico State College*

SYLVESTER, LORNA LUTES, *Associate Editor, Indiana Magazine of History*

SYNGE, R. L. M., *Nobel Prize Winner in Chemistry, 1952; Head of Protein Chemistry Department, Rowett Research Institute, Scotland*

SYNNESTVEDT, SIG, *Chairman, Department of History, State University of New York at Brockport*

SZAJKOWSKI, BOGDAN, *Senior Lecturer in Politics, University of Exeter; Editor of* Marxist Regimes: Politics, Economics, and Society

SZALAY, FREDERICK S., *City University of New York; Department of Vertebrate Paleontology, American Museum of Natural History*

SZATHMARY, ARTHUR, *Professor of Philosophy, Princeton University*

SZYKOWSKI, MATHIS, *Associate Professor of French, Oberlin College*

SZYPULA, GEORGE, *Gymnastics Coach, Michigan State University; Author of* Beginning Trampolining

TABER, RICHARD D., *Professor, College of Forest Resources, University of Washington*

TABORSKY, EDWARD, *Professor of Government, University of Texas at Austin; Author of* Communism in Czechoslovakia, 1948–1960 *and* Communist Penetration of the Third World

TAEUSCH, H. WILLIAM, MD, *Professor of Pediatrics, Charles R. Drew University of Medicine and Science; Professor of Pediatrics, University of California at Los Angeles*

TAFT, PHILIP, *Author of* Organized Labor in American History

TAFT, WILLIAM H., *Professor of Journalism, University of Missouri*

TAKUWA, SHINJI, *Professor, General Education Department, Kyushu University, Japan; Editor of* American Literature

TALBERT, CHARLES G., *Associate Professor of History, University of Kentucky; Author of* Benjamin Logan

TAN, CHESTER C., *Professor of History, New York University; Author of* Chinese Political Thought in the 20th Century

TANNER, J.M., MD, *Professor and Head, Department of Growth and Development, Institute of Child Health, University of London*

TAPPER, COLIN, *Fellow and Tutor in Law, Magdalen College, Oxford University*

TARASCIO, VINCENT J., *Professor of Economics, University of North Carolina at Chapel Hill; Author of* Pareto's Methodological Approach to Economics

TARTAR, VANCE, *Professor of Zoology, University of Washington*

TATA, S. N., *Editor, Indian Council of Agricultural Research, New Delhi*

TATE, GEORGE H. H., *American Museum of Natural History*

TATUM, EDWARD L., *Nobel Prize Winner in Physiology or Medicine, 1958; Professor, Rockefeller University*

TAUB, MIRIAM C., *Director, Zionist Public Relations Department of Hadassah, the Women's Zionist Organization of America, Inc.*

TAUBENFELD, HOWARD J., *Professor of Law and Director, Institute of Aerospace Law, Southern Methodist University; Coauthor of* The Law Relating to the Activities of Man in Space

TAUBER, MAURICE F., *Melvil Dewey Professor of Library Science, Columbia University*

TAYLOR, A. J. P., *Fellow of Magdalen College, Oxford University; Author of* English History, 1914–1945

TAYLOR, GEORGE V., *Professor of History, University of North Carolina*

TAYLOR, JOHN H., *Professor of History, Carleton University, Canada; Author of* Bytown Land Quarrels *and* Cities of the Depression; *Coeditor of* Urban History Review

TAYLOR, JOSEPH R., *Managing Editor, American Bar Association Journal*

TAYLOR, PAUL N., *Professor of Economics, University of Connecticut*

TAYLOR, ROBERT E., *Professor of French, University of Massachusetts*

TAYLOR, TALBOT J., *Louise G. T. Cooley Professor of English and Linguistics, College of William and Mary; Author of* Mutual Misunderstanding: Scepticism and the Theorizing of Language and Interpretation; *Coauthor of* Analysing Conversation

TAYLOR, ZACK, *Boats Editor,* Sports Afield

TEAL, J. DAVID, *Assistant Professor of Physics, Tougaloo College*

TEAL, JOHN M., *Senior Scientist, Woods Hole Oceanographic Institution*

TEALE, EDWIN WAY, *Editor of* The Insect World of J. Henri Fabre

TEBBEL, JOHN, *Professor of Journalism, New York University; Author of* American Dynasty: The Story of the McCormicks, Medills, and Pattersons *and* The American Magazine: A Compact History

TEDFORD, WILLIAM H., JR., *Department of Psychology, Southern Methodist University*

TEGNER, BRUCE, *Author of* Bruce Tegner's Complete Book of Self Defense *and* Karate

TELLER, EDWARD, *Professor of Physics-at-Large, University of California at Berkeley; Coauthor of* Our Nuclear Future

TEMPLEMAN, WILLIAM DARBY, *Professor of English, University of Southern California; Author of* On Writing Well

TENG, LEE C., *Fermi National Accelerator Laboratory*

TePASKE, JOHN J., *Professor of History, Duke University; Author of* Three American Empires *and* Explosive Forces in Latin America

TERADA, REI M., *Professor of English Language and Literature, University of Michigan; Author of* Derek Walcott's Poetry: American Mimicry

TERRIEN, SAMUEL, *Davenport Professor of Hebrew and Cognate Languages, Union Theological Seminary*

TERRILL, CLAIR E., *Staff Scientist, National Programs Staff, Agricultural Research Service, U.S. Department of Agriculture*

TERRY, WALTER, *Author of* The Dance in America, Ballet: A New Guide to the Liveliest Art, *and* The Ballet Companion

TETEL, MARCEL, *Professor of Romance Languages, Duke University; Author of* Rabelais

TETHER, J. EDWARD, MD, *Associate Professor of Neurology, Indiana University Medical Center; Coauthor of* Modern Health *and* Human Physiology

TEXTER, E. CLINTON, JR., MD, *Professor of Medical Physiology and Biophysics, University of Arkansas at Little Rock; Author of* The Physiology of the Digestive Tract

TEYLER, TIMOTHY J., *Professor of Neurobiology, Northeastern Ohio Universities College of Medicine*

THACKER, M. S., *Member, Planning Commission, Government of India*

THAPAR, ROMILA, *Professor of Ancient Indian History, Centre of Historical Studies, Jawaharlal Nehru University, New Delhi; Author of* Asoka and the Decline of the Mauryas *and* History of India *(Vol. I)*

THAYER, THEODORE, *Professor of History, Rutgers University; Author of* Pennsylvania Politics and the Growth of Democracy, 1740–1776

THEISEN, CHARLES W., *Detroit News*

THIEME, PAUL, *Professor of Indology and Comparative Religion, Tübingen University, West Germany*

THIERET, JOHN W., *Professor of Biology and Chairman, Department of Biological Sciences, Northern Kentucky University*

THODY, PHILIP, *Professor of French Literature, University of Leeds, England; Author of* Jean-Paul Sartre: A Literary and Political Study

THOLEN, DAVID J., *Professor of Astronomy, Institute for Astronomy, University of Hawaii*

THOMAS, ALEXANDER F., CFC, *Librarian, Ryan Library, Iona College*

THOMAS, BENJAMIN E., *Professor of Geography, University of California at Los Angeles; Author of* Transportation and Physical Geography in West Africa

THOMAS, BENJAMIN P., *Author of* Abraham Lincoln: A Biography

THOMAS, CHRISTOPHER A., *Assistant Professor, Department of History in Art, University of Victoria*

THOMAS, HAROLD E., *Research Hydrologist, Water Resources Division, U.S. Geological Survey*

THOMAS, JAMES B., *Associate Professor of Anatomy and Human Development, Michigan State University; Author of* Introduction to Human Embryology

THOMAS, LEWIS G., *Professor of History, University of Alberta, Canada; Author of* The Liberal Party in Alberta

THOMAS, M. K., *Director, Meteorological Applications Branch, Atmospheric Environment Service, Ontario; Author of* Climatological Atlas of Canada

THOMAS, ROBERT J., *Director, Holyoke Public Library, Holyoke, Mass.*

THOMAS, R. MURRAY, *Professor Emeritus, University of California at Santa Barbara*

THOMPSON, A. PAUL, *Director of Research, Chemical Division, Eagle-Picher Company*

THOMPSON, ELSA SMITH, *Library Director, Albuquerque Public Library*

THOMPSON, ERNEST F., *Former Curator, Bingham Oceanographic Laboratory, Yale University*

THOMPSON, JOHN, *Professor of History, Indiana University; Author of* Russia, Bolshevism, and the Versailles Peace; *and* Order and Reform: The Dilemma of the Tsarist Government in 1905–06

THOMPSON, KENNETH W., *Vice President, Rockefeller Foundation; Author of* The Moral Issue in Statecraft

THOMPSON, LEONARD M., *Professor of African History, Yale University; Author of* Politics in the Republic of South Africa; *Editor of* The Oxford History of South Africa

THOMPSON, STANLEY G., *Lawrence Radiation Laboratory*

THOMPSON, WILLIAM Y., *Professor of History, Louisiana Polytechnic Institute; Author of* Robert Toombs of Georgia

THOMSON, DAVID, *Master of Sidney Sussex College, Cambridge University; Author of* England in the Nineteenth Century *and* England in the Twentieth Century

THOMSON, KEITH S., *Associate Curator of Vertebrate Zoology, Peabody Museum of Natural History; Associate Professor of Biology, Yale University*

THOMSON, THERESA E., *Treasurer and Public Relations Officer, Canadian Writers Foundation, Incorporated*

THOREN, VICTOR E., *Associate Professor, Department of History and Philosophy of Science, Indiana University*

THORKELSON, H. JOHN, *Professor of Economics, University of Connecticut*

THORN, LINTON S., *Adjunct Assistant Professor of History, Hofstra College*

THORNBURY, WILLIAM D., *Professor of Geology, Indiana University; Author of* Principles of Geomorphology *and* Regional Geomorphology of the United States

THORNDIKE, ASHLEY H., *Author of* The Influence of Beaumont and Fletcher on Shakespeare

THORNE, MARCO G., *City Librarian, San Diego Public Library*

THORNE, ROLAND, *Editor, History of Parliament (1790–1820)*

THORNING, JOSEPH F., *Author of* Miranda: World Citizen

THREEFOOT, SAM A., *Dean, Professor of Medicine, Medical College of Georgia; Chief of Staff, Veterans Administration Hospital, Augusta, Ga.*

THROCKMORTON, JOHN L., *General, U.S. Army; Commander in Chief, U.S. Strike Command, Office of Reserve Components, Department of the Army*

TIEN, H. YUAN, *Professor of Sociology, Ohio State University*

TIERNEY, BRIAN, *Professor of Medieval History, Cornell University*

TIFFANY, CURRAN C., *Member of the New York Bar*

TIFFANY, STEPHEN T., *University of Wisconsin at Madison*

TIGER, LIONEL, *Professor of Anthropology, Rutgers University; Author of* Men in Groups

TIGNOR, ROBERT L., *Associate Professor of History, Princeton University; Author of* Modernization and British Colonial Rule in Egypt, 1882–1914; *Coauthor of* Egypt and the Sudan

TILLETT, ANNE S., *Associate Professor of Romance Languages, Wake Forest University*

TILLEY, NANNIE M., *Author of* The Bright-Tobacco Industry, 1860–1929

TILLMAN, C. G., *Department of Geological Sciences, Virginia Polytechnic Institute*

TIMKO, MICHAEL, *Professor of English, Queens College*

TINKER, HUGH, *Fellow, Institute of Commonwealth Studies, University of London; Author of* The Union of Burma

TINKLE, DONALD W., *Professor of Zoology, University of Michigan*

TINKLEPAUGH, JAMES R., *Associate Professor and Director of Technical Services, State University of New York, College of Ceramics at Alfred University*

TIPPETTE, GILES, *Author of* The Brave Men

TISO, FRANCIS, *Department of Religion and Philosophy, Mercy College, Dobbs Ferry, N.Y.*

TISON, JAMES C., JR., *Director, Coast and Geodetic Survey*

TITMUSS, RICHARD M., *Professor of Social Administration, University of London; Author of* Commitment to Welfare

TOBIAS, RICHARD, *Professor of English, University of Pittsburgh; Author of* The Art of James Thurber

TOBIN, JAMES G., *Chief, General Research and Humanities Division, New York Public Library*

TODD, MALCOLM, *Professor of Archaeology, University of Nottingham*

TOLAND, JOHN, *Author of* The Dillinger Days

TOLLES, FREDERICK B., *Jenkins Professor of Quaker History and Research, Swarthmore College; Coeditor of* The Witness of William Penn

TOMALIN, CLAIRE, *Literary Editor, London Sunday Times; Author of* Shelley and His World

TOMASEK, ROBERT D., *Professor of Political Science, University of Kansas; Editor of* Latin American Politics: 24 Studies of the Contemporary Scene

TOMASIC, D. A., *Professor of Sociology, Indiana University*

TOMPKINS, EDGAR, *Director of Libraries, Albany Public Library*

TOMPSETT, RALPH, MD, *Department of Internal Medicine, Southwestern Medical School, Dallas, Texas*

TONE, DONALD R., *Mining Engineering Magazine*

TONG, TE-KONG, *Professor of Asian Studies, City College of New York; Author of* United States Diplomacy in China, 1844–1860

TONKIN, HUMPHREY, *Associate Professor of English, University of Pennsylvania; Author of* Research Bibliography on Esperanto and Language Problems

TONNE, HERBERT A., *Professor of Business Education, State University of New York at Albany; Author of* Principles of Business Education

TONNELAT, MARIE ANTOINETTE, *Professor, Faculty of Sciences, University of Paris; Author of* Louis de Broglie *and* The Principles of Electromagnetic Theory and of Relativity

TORREY, J. G., *Professor of Botany, Maria Moors Cabot Foundation for Botanical Research; Author of* Development in Flowering Plants; *Coauthor of* Plants in Action *and* The Development and Function of Roots

TOSCH, ROBERT L., *Electronic Engineer, Federal Communications Commission*

TOULOUSE, MARK G., *Associate Dean and Professor of the History of Christianity, Brite Divinity School, Texas Christian University; Author of* Joined in Discipleship: The Maturing of an American Religious Movement

TOYE, CLIVE, *Former President, North American Soccer League; Author of* Soccer

TREADGOLD, DONALD W., *Professor of Russian History, University of Washington; Author of* Twentieth-Century Russia *and* Lenin and His Rivals

TREGLE, JOSEPH G., JR., *Professor of History, Louisiana State University in New Orleans*

TRELEASE, ALLEN W., *Professor of History, University of North Carolina at Greensboro; Author of* White Terror: The Ku Klux Klan Conspiracy and Southern Reconstruction *and* Reconstruction: The Great Experiment

TREMBLAY, RODRIGUE, *Professor of Economics, Université de Montréal; Author of* Modern Macroeconomics

TRESCOTT, PAUL B., *Professor of Economics, Southern Illinois University; Author of* Money, Banking, and Economic Welfare

TRESIDDER, ARGUS JOHN, *Author of* Ceylon, an Introduction to the Resplendent Land

TREXLER, PAT, *Author of* Knit and Crochet Ideas

TRIAY, PAULETTE, *Reference Librarian, Fullerton Public Library*

TRISCO, ROBERT, *Associate Professor of Church History, Catholic University of America; Editor of the* Catholic Historical Review

TROTT, BARBARA M., *Librarian, Witherle Memorial Library*

TROTT, CHRISTOPHER, *Department of Sociology and Anthropology, Concordia University*

TROTTA, GERI, *Travel Editor,* Harper's Bazaar

TROWBRIDGE, HOYT, *Professor of English, University of New Mexico; Author of* From Dryden to Jane Austen: Essays on English Criticism and Writers, 1660–1816

TRUEX, PHILIP E., *Coauthor of* The City Gardener

TRUITT, PENELOPE, *Museum of Fine Arts, Boston*

TRUMAN, EDWIN M., *Associate Professor of Economics, Yale University*

TRUMBULL, ROBERT, *Author of* The Scrutable East; *Chief, Tokyo Bureau, New York Times (1954–1961, 1964–1968)*

TSEVAT, MATITIAHU, *Professor of Bible, Hebrew Union College; Author of* A Study of the Language of Biblical Psalms

TUCHMAN, ARLEEN, *Department of the History of Science, University of Wisconsin at Madison*

TUCKER, GENE M., *Candler School of Theology, Emory University*

TUCKER, GLENN, *Author of* Poltroons and Patriots: The War of 1812

TUCKER, TERRY, *Author of* Bermuda's Story

TUITE, JAMES J., *Sports Editor, New York Times; Author of* Snowmobiles and Snowmobiling

TUKEY, HAROLD B., JR., *Professor, Department of Floriculture and Ornamental Horticulture, Cornell University*

TULL, CHARLES J., *Professor of History, Indiana University at South Bend; Author of* American History Since 1865

TULLY, JOHN, *Director of Public Relations, Drexel Institute of Technology*

TUNIS, EDWIN, *Author of* Oars, Sails, and Steam *and* Weapons

TUPPER, R. W., *American Automobile Association*

TURAN, SAIT, *Secretary General, University of Istanbul, Turkey*

TUREKIAN, KARL K., *Professor of Geology and Geophysics, Yale University; Author of* Oceans

TURK, EDWARD BARON, *Massachusetts Institute of Technology*

TURLEY, THOMAS P., *Fordham University*

TURNBULL, HERBERT W., *Author of* Great Mathematicians

TURNBULL, PATRICK, *Author of* The Foreign Legion

TURNBULL, ROBERT, *Travel Editor,* The Globe and Mail, *Toronto*

TURNER, ALLAN R., *Provincial Archivist, Saskatchewan Archives Board, University of Saskatchewan, Canada*

TURNER, C. DONNELL, *Professor of Biological Sciences, Duquesne University*

TURNER, G. L'E., *Assistant Curator, Museum of the History of Science, Oxford University*

TURNER, ROBERT A., *Colonel, United States Army (Retired)*

TURNER, RUFUS P., *Author of* Basic Electricity

TURNER, THOMAS E., *Professor of Political Science, Wheeling College; Coauthor of* The Rise and Decline of the Zairian State

TURTON, BRIAN, *Senior Lecturer in Geography, University of Keele, Staffordshire, England*

TUSSING, A. DALE, *Professor of Economics, Syracuse University; Author of* Poverty in a Dual Economy

TUTTLE, P. CARL, *German Shorthaired Pointer Club of America*

TYLER, JAMES C., *Associate Curator, Department of Ichthyology, Academy of Natural Sciences of Philadelphia*

TYLER, LEONA E., *Dean of the Graduate School, University of Oregon*

TYLER, MARY S., *Professor of Zoology, University of Maine; Author of* Developmental Biology: A Guide for Experimental Study

TYLER, VARRO E., *Dean, School of Pharmacy and Pharmacal Sciences, Purdue University*

TYSON, DAVID N., *Instructor, Department of Uralic and Altaic Studies, Indiana University*

UBBELOHDE, A. R., *Professor and Head of Department of Chemical Engineering and Chemical Technology, Imperial College, London*

UBBELOHDE, CARL, *Professor of History, Case Western Reserve University*

UDEN, GRANT, *Author of* The Knight and the Merchant

UDRY, J. RICHARD, *Carolina Population Center, University of North Carolina; Author of* The Social Context of Marriage

UEDA, MAKOTO, *Professor of Japanese, Stanford University; Author of* Matsuo Basho *and* Modern Japanese Writers and the Nature of Literature

UEDA, TOSHIO, *Professor of Tokyo University; Author of* An Introduction to Far Eastern Diplomatic History

UGENT, DONALD, *Associate Professor of Botany, Southern Illinois University*

ULEMAN, JAMES S., *Associate Professor of Psychology, New York University*

ULLMANN, JOHN E., *Professor of Management, Hofstra University; Author of* The Improvement of Productivity

ULRICH, HOMER, *Author of* Music: A Design for Listening; *Coauthor of* A History of Music and Musical Styles

UNDERWOOD, DALE, *Professor of English, University of New Hampshire; Author of* Etherege and the Seventeenth-Century Comedy of Manners

UNGER, LEONARD, *Professor of English, University of Minnesota; Editor of* T.S. Eliot: A Selected Critique *and* Seven Modern American Poets: An Introduction

UNGER, LEONARD, *Professor of Diplomacy, Fletcher School of Law and Diplomacy, Tufts University; U.S. Ambassador (Retired) to Laos, Thailand, and the Republic of China*

UNGURU, SABETAI, *The Institute for the History and Philosophy of Science and Ideas, Tel Aviv University; Author of* Witelonis Perspectivae Liber Primus

UNSTEAD, R. J., *Author of* A History of the World, Looking at History, A Dictionary of History, A History of the English-Speaking World, *and* Greece and Rome

UPJOHN, EVERARD M., *Professor of Art History, Columbia University; Coauthor of* History of World Art

UPTON, MILLER, *President, Beloit College*

URE, ROLAND W., JR., *Professor, College of Engineering, University of Utah*

URICK, ROBERT J., *Senior Research Physicist, Naval Ordnance Laboratory, Silver Spring, Md.; Author of* Principles of Underwater Sound

URRY, WILLIAM, *Canterbury Cathedral and City Archivist; Author of* Canterbury Under the Angevin Kings

USHER, ABBOTT PAYSON, *Author of* A History of Mechanical Inventions

USSACHEVSKY, VLADIMIR, *Composer; Professor of Music, University of Utah*

USSHER, ARLAND, *President of the Irish Academy of Letters; Author and Critic*

UTLEY, FRANCIS LEE, *Professor of English, Ohio State University*

UTLEY, ROBERT, *National Park Service; Author of* The Last Days of the Sioux Nation

UTZ, JOHN P., MD, *Professor of Medicine, Georgetown University*

VAILLANT, ALDRIGE A., *Professor, Department of Educational Leadership, Central Connecticut State University*

VADAKIN, JAMES C., *Professor of Economics, University of Miami; Author of* Family Allowances: An Analysis of Their Development and Implications

VAJDA, STEVEN, *Professor of Operational Research, University of Birmingham, England; Author of* The Theory of Games and Linear Programming *and* Mathematical Programming

VALENCY, MAURICE, *Brander Matthews Professor of Dramatic Literature, Columbia University; Author of* The Breaking String: The Plays of Anton Chekhov *and* The Flower and the Castle: An Introduction to Modern Drama

VALENTE, MARIO, MD, *Adjunct Associate Professor of Child Psychiatry, UCLA Neuropsychiatric Institute, Los Angeles, Calif.*

VALENTI, RAYMOND F., *Professor of Finance and Insurance, College of Business Administration, Syracuse University*

VALENTINE, DAVID H., *Professor of Botany, University of Manchester, England*

VANCE, ARLO M., *Entomologist, U.S. Department of Agriculture*

VAN CLEVE, JOHN VICKREY, *Professor and Chairman, Department of History, Gallaudet University; Editor in Chief of the* Gallaudet Encyclopedia of Deaf People and Deafness; *Coauthor of* A Place of Their Own: Creating the Deaf Community in America

VANDERHEYDEN, MARK A., *Assistant Professor of History, Rider College*

VANDERKAM, JAMES C., *Professor of Theology, University of Notre Dame; Author of Textual and Historical Studies in the Book of Jubilees*

VAN DER KEMP, GERALD, *Conservateur en Chef du Musée National de Versailles et des Trianons*

VAN DER KLOOT, WILLIAM G., *Professor of Physiology and Biophysics and Chairman of the Department of Physiology and Biophysics, State University of New York at Stony Brook*

VAN DER KROEF, JUSTUS M., *Dana Professor and Chairman, Department of Political Science, University of Bridgeport, Conn.; Author of* Indonesia in the Modern World, Indonesia after Sukarno, *and* Communism in Southeast Asia

VANDERPIJPEN, WILLY, *Director, Koninglijke Bibliotheek Albert I, Brussels; Lecturer, Universiteit van Antwerpen*

VANDER VELDE, LEWIS G., *Director, Michigan Historical Collections, University of Michigan; Editor of* Michigan and the Cleveland Era

VAN DEUSEN, GLYNDON G., *Research Professor of History, University of Rochester; Author of* Horace Greeley, Nineteenth-Century Crusader

VANDIVER, FRANK E., *Provost and Vice President, Rice University*

VAN DONGEN, IRENE S., *Associate Professor of Geography, California State College, Pa.; Author of* British East African Transport Complex

VAN DOREN, CARL, *Author of* The American Novel, Benjamin Franklin, *and* What Is American Literature?

VAN DUSEN, ALBERT E., *Professor of History, University of Connecticut; State Historian of Connecticut*

VAN EVERY, KERMIT E., *Aerospace Engineering, General Dynamics Corporation*

VAN GELDER, RICHARD G., *Department of Mammals, American Museum of Natural History*

VAN HANDEL, RALPH A., *Director, Gary Public Library*

VAN HEIJENOORT, JEAN, *Professor of Philosophy, Brandeis University*

VAN HOOK, ANDREW, *Professor of Physical Chemistry, College of the Holy Cross*

VAN JAARSVELD, F. A., *Professor of History, Rand Afrikaans University, Johannesburg, South Africa; Author of* The Awakening of Afrikaner Nationalism

VAN LOON, JON C., *Associate Professor of Geology, University of Toronto, Canada*

VAN RIPER, PAUL P., *Professor of Political Science, Texas A&M University; Author of* History of the United States Civil Service

VAN VALEN, LEIGH, *Associate Professor of Anatomy and Evolutionary Biology, University of Chicago*

VARDY, STEVEN BELA, *Professor of History, Duquesne University; Author of* Modern Hungarian Historiography

VARG, PAUL A., *Author of* Open Door Diplomat: The Life of William Woodkille Rockhill

VARIAN, HAL R., *Professor of Economics, University of Michigan*

VARLEY, H. PAUL, *Professor of Japanese History, Columbia University; Author of* The Onin War, The Samurai, Imperial Restoration in Medieval Japan, Japanese Culture: A Short History, *and* A Chronicle of Gods and Sovereigns

VARMA, BAIDYA NATH, *Associate Professor of Sociology and Anthropology, City College of New York; Author of* A New Survey of the Social Sciences *and* Contemporary India

VARNER, JOHN GRIER, *Professor of English, University of Texas; Author of* El Inca: The Life and Times of Garcilaso de la Vega

VARNEY, RONALD, *Vice President, Sotheby's*

VAUGHAN, ALDEN T., *Professor of History, Columbia University; Author of* New England Frontier: Puritans and Indians, 1620–1675

VAUGHAN, DAVID L., *Director, Greensboro Public Library*

VAUGHAN, J. A., *Ministry of Agriculture, Fisheries and Food, Agricultural Science Service, Worplesdon Laboratory*

VAUGHAN, TERRY A., *Department of Biological Sciences, Northern Arizona University*

VAUGHN, REESE H., *Professor of Food Science and Technology, University of California at Davis*

VAURIE, CHARLES, *Formerly, Department of Ornithology, American Museum of Natural History; Author of* The Birds of the Palearctic Fauna: Non-Passeriformes

VAWTER, BRUCE, *Professor of Scripture, Department of Theology, DePaul University; Author of* A Path through Genesis *and* New Paths Through the Bible

VAZ, EDUARDO, *Instituto Butantan, Sao Paulo, Brazil*

VECSEY, CHRISTOPHER, *Professor of Religion, Colgate University; Author of* Imagine Ourselves Richly: Mythic Narratives of North American Indians

VEIS, GEORGE, *Professor of Surveying, National Technical University of Athens, Greece; Research Associate, Smithsonian Astrophysical Observatory; Author of* The Determination of Absolute Direction in Space, Optical Tracking of Artificial Satellites, *and* The Use of Artificial Satellites for Geodesy

VELIMIROVIC, MILOS, *Professor of Music, University of Virginia*

VENCLOVA, TOMAS A., *Professor of Slavic Languages and Literatures, Yale University*

VENNESLAND, BIRGIT, *Director, Vennesland Research Division, Max-Planck Society, Berlin*

VERGARA, ISABEL R., *Professor of Spanish, George Washington University; Author of* El Mundo Satirico de Gabriel García Márquez

VERGARA, LISA, *Assistant Professor of Art, Hunter College*

VERTEY, HUGUETTE, *Assistant Librarian, Bibliothèque des Trois-Rivières, Quebec*

VESEY-FITZGERALD, BRIAN, *Author of* The Book of the Dog, The Domestic Dog, *and* The Dog Owner's Encyclopedia

VETTES, W. G., *Professor of History, University of Wisconsin at La Crosse*

VIAL, FERNAND, *Professor of French, State University of New York at Albany*

VICKERS, WILLIAM W., *Institute of Polar Studies, Ohio State University*

VICKERY, WALTER N., *Professor of Slavic Languages, University of North Carolina at Chapel Hill; Author of* Alexander Pushkin

VICKREY, ROBERT, *Painter*

VICKREY, WILLIAM, *Ford Research Professor, Department of Economics, Columbia University*

VICTOR, MAURICE, MD, *Professor of Neurology, Case Western Reserve University School of Medicine; Chief, Neurology Service, Cleveland Metropolitan General Hospital*

VICTOREEN, JOHN A., *Victoreen Laboratory of Orlando, Maitland, Fla.*

VIDAL, ELIE R., *Professor of French, California State College at Hayward*

VIGNESS, DAVID M., *Professor and Head, Department of History, Texas Tech University*

VILLICA,A, EUGENIO C., *Associate Professor of English, Columbia University*

VINCENT, CLARE, *Assistant Curator, Western Arts, Metropolitan Museum of Art*

VINCENT, JEAN ANNE, *Author of* History of Art

VIOLA, JEROME, *Assistant Professor of Art, Brooklyn College*

VIPPERMAN, CARL, *Assistant Professor of History, University of Georgia*

VIROLA, JUHARI, *Engineer*

VOGT, EVON Z., *Professor of Social Anthropology, Harvard University*

VOLD, MARJORIE J., *Adjunct Professor of Chemistry, University of Southern California*

VOLD, ROBERT D., *Professor of Chemistry, University of Southern California*

VOLLMANN, THOMAS E., *Professor of Management Science, University of Rhode Island; Author of* Operations Management

VOLLUZ, RAYMOND J., *Missiles and Space Division, Lockheed Aircraft Corporation*

VON BRAUN, WERNHER, *Coauthor of* History of Rocketry and Space Travel *and* Episodes in Rocketry

VON LAUE, THEODORE H., *Professor of History, Clark University*

VON MEHREN, ARTHUR T., *Professor of Law, Harvard University; Author of* The Civil Law System

VONNEGUT, BERNARD, *Professor, Department of Atmospheric Science, and Senior Scientist, Atmospheric Sciences Research Center, State University of New York at Albany*

VON OETTINGEN, W. F., MD, *Consultant, National Institutes of Health*

VORHAUS, LOUIS J., MD, *Assistant Professor of Medicine, Cornell University Medical College*

VOSS, GILBERT L., *Chairman, Division of Biological Sciences, Institute of Marine Sciences, University of Miami*

VOWLES, RICHARD B., *Professor of Scandinavian Studies and Comparative Literature, University of Wisconsin at Madison*

VRYONIS, SPEROS, JR., *Professor of Byzantine History, University of California at Los Angeles; Author of* Byzantium and Europe

VUCINICH, WAYNE S., *Professor of History, Stanford University*

WADDINGTON, RICHARD C., *Librarian, Fargo Public Library*

WADE, ARTHUR P., *Colonel, U.S. Army; Professor of Military Science, Boston University*

WADE, GERALD E., *Professor of Romance Languages and Literatures, University of Tennessee*

WADE, GORDON S., *Director, Carroll Public Library, Carroll, Iowa; Contributor,* The How-To-Do-It Manual for Small Libraries

WADE, MASON, *Professor of History, University of Western Ontario, Canada; Author of* Francis Parkman: Heroic Historian

WAGGONER, HYATT H., *Professor of English, Brown University; Author of* American Poets, From the Puritans to the Present

WAGNER, HENRY N., JR., MD, *Professor of Medicine, Radiology and Environmental Health Sciences, Divisions of Nuclear Medicine and Radiation Health Sciences, Johns Hopkins Medical Institutions*

WAGNER, PETER, *Chemistry Department, Michigan State University*

WAGNER, PHILIP M., *Boordy Vineyards, Ridgewood, Md.; Author of* Grapes into Wine, A Winegrower's Guide, *and* American Wines and Winemaking; *Coeditor of* Turner on Wine

WAGNER, ROBERT W., *Professor and Chairman, Department of Photography, Ohio State University*

WAHLKE, JOHN C., *Professor Emeritus of Political Science, University of Arizona; Coauthor of* Politics of Representation: Continuities in Theory and Research

WALD, ROBERT M., *Associate Professor, Department of Physics and Enrico Fermi Institute, University of Chicago; Author of* Space, Time, and Gravity: The Theory of the Big Bang and Black Holes *and* General Relativity

WALEY, PAUL, *Author of* Tokyo Now and Then

WALKER, DONALD S., *Senior Geography Master, Dame Allan's School, Newcastle upon Tyne, England*

WALKER, ERIC A., *Vere Harmsworth Professor of Imperial and Naval History, Cambridge University; Author of* The British Empire

WALKER, J. INGRAM, MD, *Assistant Professor of Psychiatry, Duke University Medical Center; Author of* Clinical Psychiatry in Primary Care

WALKER, JEROME H., JR., *Associate Editor, Editor and Publisher*

WALKER, JERRY T., *Associate Professor of Plant Pathology, University of Georgia*

WALKER, PHILIP D., *Professor of French, University of California at Santa Barbara*

WALKER, RUSSELL E., *Library Administrator, Altoona Public Library*

WALLACE, BIRGITTA L., *Research Associate, Section of Man, Carnegie Museum, Pittsburgh, Pa.*

WALLACE, CRAIG K., MD, *Commanding Officer, U.S. Naval Medical Reserve Unit, Ethiopia*

WALLACE, DAN, *Director, Canadian Government Travel Bureau*

WALLACE, ELISABETH, *Associate Professor of Political Science, Department of Political Economy, University of Toronto, Canada*

WALLACE, LAWRENCE G., *Associate Professor of Law, Duke University*

WALLACE-HADRILL, J. M., *Professor of Modern History, Oxford University*

WALLER, MICHAEL, *Senior Lecturer in Government, University of Manchester; Author of* The End of the Communist Power Monopoly

WALLERSTEIN, EDWARD, *Author of* Circumcision: An American Health Fallacy

WALLINGTON, G. GRANTLY, *Author and Editor*

WALLIS, EARL L., *Coauthor of* Figure Improvement and Body Conditioning Through Exercise

WALSH, CAROLINE P., *Librarian, Fairfield Public Library, Fairfield, Conn.*

WALSH, EDWARD A., *Chairman, Department of Journalism, Fordham University*

WALSH, JAMES J., *Author of* Catholic Churchmen in Science

WALSH, JOHN R., *Head of Department of Turkish Studies, University of Edinburgh*

WALSH, MARY G., *Director, Allegany County Libraries*

WALSH, RICHARD, *Professor of History, Georgetown University; Coauthor of* Maryland: A History *and* The Mind and Spirit of Early America

WALSWORTH, MARGARET W., *Librarian, Vermilion Parish Library*

WALTER, INGO, *Charles Simon Professor of Applied Financial Economics, New York University; Author of* Secret Money, Investment Banking in Europe, Global Financial Services, *and* Universal Banking in the United States

WALTERS, RAYMOND, JR., *Associate Editor,* New York Times Book Review; *Author of* Alexander James Dallas: Lawyer, Politician, Financier

WALTON, E. T. S., *Erasmus Smith's Professor of Natural and Experimental Philosophy, University of Dublin, Ireland; Nobel Prize Winner in Physics, 1951*

WALTON, GUY E., *Associate Professor of Fine Arts, New York University*

WALTON, HAROLD F., *Professor of Chemistry, University of Colorado*

WALTZ, SUSAN, *Associate Professor of International Relations, Florida International University*

WALZ, ROBERT B., *Professor of History, Southern State College*

WAN, CHIA-PAO, *Dramatist and Teacher*

WANDYCZ, PIOTR S., *Professor of History, Yale University*

WANGERIN, RUTH, *Graduate Center, City University of New York*

WARD, CECIL C., *Project Coordinator, Bartlesville Petroleum Research Center, U.S. Bureau of Mines*

WARD, F. A. B., *Keeper, Department of Physics, and Officer-in-Charge, Time Measurement Section, Science Museum, London; Author of* Time Measurement *and* Timekeepers

WARD, HARRY M., *Professor of History, University of Richmond (Va.); Author of* Richmond During the Revolution: 1775–1783

WARD, JOHN W., *President, Amherst College; Author of* Red, White, and Blue: Men, Books, and Ideas in American Culture

WARD, NORMAN, *Professor of Political Science, University of Saskatchewan, Canada*

WARD, PRISCILLA C., *Scientific Assistant in Anthropology, American Museum of Natural History*

WARD, RICHARD A., *Professor of Economics, University of Southern California; Author of* International Finance *and* Economics of Health Resources

WARD, ROBERT E., *Professor of Political Science, Stanford University; Coauthor of* Political Development in Modern Japan

WARDLE, RALPH M., *Jefferis Professor of English Literature, University of Nebraska at Omaha; Author of* Oliver Goldsmith

WARDROP, JAMES, *Deputy-Keeper of the Library, Victoria and Albert Museum, London*

WARDWELL, ALLEN, *Senior Consultant, Department of Tribal Art, Christie's, New York City*

WARNKE, FRANK J., *Professor and Head, Comparative Literature Department, University of Georgia; Editor of* John Donne, Poetry and Prose *and* European Metaphysical Poetry

WARNOCK, G. J., *Author of* Berkeley

WARREN, HARRIS G., *Professor of History, Miami University, Ohio; Author of* Paraguay: an Informal History

WARREN, JAMES F., *National Association for Mental Health, Incorporated*

WARREN, JOEL, *Life Science Center, Nova University*

WARREN, PETER M., *Professor of Ancient History and Classical Archaeology, University of Bristol, United Kingdom; Chairman, British School at Athens; Director of Excavations, Knossos, from 1978; Author of* Minoan Stone Vases, Myrtos: An Early Bronze Age Settlement in Crete, *and* The Aegean Civilizations

WARRENDER, HOWARD, *Professor and Head, Political Science Department, Queen's University, Belfast, Northern Ireland; Author of* The Political Philosophy of Hobbes

WARTH, ROBERT DOUGLAS, *Professor of History, University of Kentucky; Author of* Soviet Russia in World Politics

WASHER, FRANCIS E., *Chief, Refractometry Section, National Bureau of Standards*

WASHINGTON, BRIAN H., *Reader in Ancient History, University of Bristol, England; Author of* The North African Provinces From Diocletian to the Vandal Conquest, Carthage, *and* Nero—Reality and Legend

WASMUTH, CARL E., MD, *Chairman, Board of Governors, the Cleveland Clinic Foundation; Adjunct Professor of Law, Cleveland-Marshall College of Law; Author of* Law for the Physician *and* Law and the Practice of Anesthesia

WASON, BETTY, *Author of* A Salute to Cheeses

WASSER, HENRY, *Professor of English and Dean of the Faculties, Richmond College, New York City; Author of* The Scientific Thought of Henry Adams

WATERHOUSE, EDWARD J., *Director, Perkins School for the Blind*

WATERS, FRANK, *Author of* The Colorado

WATERS, JOHN M., JR., *Captain, U.S. Coast Guard; Author of* Rescue at Sea *and* Bloody Winter

WATKINS, FREDERICK M., *Professor of Political Science, Yale University; Author of* The Political Tradition of the West

WATSON, C. J., MD, *Regents' Professor of Medicine and Director of the University of Minnesota Unit for Teaching and Research in Internal Medicine, Northwestern Hospital of Minneapolis*

WATSON, GEORGE E., *Chairman, Department of Vertebrate Zoology, Smithsonian Institution*

WATSON, GEORGE F., *Bell Telephone Laboratories*

WATSON, J. D., *Nobel Prize Winner in Physiology or Medicine, 1962; Professor of Biology, Harvard University; Head of Cold Springs Harbor Laboratory of Quantitative Biology; Author of* The Double Helix

WATSON, RICHARD L., JR., *Professor of History, Duke University*

WATT, W. MONTGOMERY, *Professor of Arabic and Islamic Studies, University of Edinburgh, Scotland; Author of* Islamic Philosophy and Theology

WATTERSON, RAY L., *Professor of Zoology, University of Illinois; Author of* Endocrines in Development

WAX, MURRAY L., *Professor and Chairman, Department of Sociology, Washington University, St. Louis, Mo.*

WAYMAN, ALEX, *Professor of Sanskrit, Columbia University; Author of Analysis of the Sravakabhumi Manuscript*

WAYT, KEITH, *Professor and Head, Department of Veterinary Medicine, Louisiana State University*

WEAKLAND, REMBERT G., OSB, *Archbishop of Milwaukee*

WEATHERWAX, PAUL, *Professor of Botany, Indiana University*

WEAVER, ANTHONY JOHN, *Head of Modern Languages, St. Wilfrid's Comprehensive School, Sussex, England*

WEAVER, GLENN, *Professor of History, Trinity College, Hartford, Conn.; Author of Jonathan Trumbull, Connecticut's Merchant Magistrate*

WEBB, BERNARD L., *Associate Professor of Insurance and Actuarial Science, Georgia State University*

WEBB, KEMPTON E., *Professor of Geography and Director of Institute of Latin American Studies, Columbia University; Author of Latin America and Brazil*

WEBB, RICHARD E., *Director, Reference and Library Division, British Information Services*

WEBB, STEPHEN SAUNDERS, *Professor of History, Syracuse University; Author of The Governors General*

WEBBER, E. LELAND, *Director, Field Museum of Natural History, Chicago*

WEBBER, LAWRENCE, *Director, Fort Collins Public Library*

WEBER, J. SHERWOOD, *Chairman, Department of English and Humanities, Pratt Institute*

WEBER, JOSEPH, *Professor of Physics, University of Maryland; Author of General Relativity and Gravitational Waves*

WEBSTER, WILLIAM G., *Hayward City Librarian*

WECHSBERG, JOSEPH, *Author of* Blue Trout and Black Truffles

WECKSTEIN, RICHARD S., *Professor of Economics, Brandeis University; Author of* The Growth of World Trade and the Expansion of National Economies

WEDIN, WALTER, *Department of Agronomy, Iowa State University*

WEEDING, DOROTHY, *Director, Covina Public Library*

WEEKS, EDWARD, *Consultant and Senior Editor, Atlantic Monthly Press; Author of The Lowells and Their Institute*

WEICHERT, CHARLES K., *Professor of Zoology, University of Cincinnati; Author of* Anatomy of the Chordates

WEIGEL, GUSTAVE, SJ, *Professor of Ecclesiology, Woodstock College*

WEIL, ANDRÉ, *Professor, Institute for Advanced Study, Princeton, N.J.; Author of Foundations of Algebraic Geometry*

WEILER, ROYAL W., *Professor, Department of Near and Middle East Languages, Columbia University*

WEIMER, ARTHUR M., *Special Assistant to the President, Indiana University; Author of Business Administration*

WEINBERG, LOUIS, *Professor, Department of Electrical Engineering, City College and Graduate School, City University of New York; Author of* Network Analysis and Synthesis

WEINBERGER, MYRON H., MD, *Professor of Medicine, Director, Hypertension Research Center, Indiana University School of Medicine*

WEINER, MYRON, *Professor of Political Science and Senior Staff Member of the Center for International Studies, Massachusetts Institute of Technology; Author of* Party Politics in India *and other books*

WEINER, PAUL, *Professor of Economics, University of Connecticut*

WEINER, SEYMOUR, *Head, Applied Physics Department, Barnes Engineering Company*

WEINLICK, JOHN, *Dean, Moravian Theological Seminary*

WEINSHEIMER, JOEL, *Professor of English, University of Minnesota; Author of Gadamer's Hermeneutics, Philosophical Hermeneutics and Literary Theory, and Eighteenth-Century Hermeneutics*

WEINSHENKER, ANNE BETTY, *Art Historian*

WEINSTEIN, LOUIS, MD, *Professor of Medicine, Tufts University School of Medicine; Chief of the Infectious Disease Service, New England Medical Center Hospitals*

WEINSTOCK, HERBERT, *Coauthor of* Men of Music

WEISENBURGER, FRANCIS P., *Professor of History, Ohio State University; Coauthor of* A History of Ohio

WEISHEIPL, JAMES A., OP, *Director, Leonine Commission, Yale University, and Associate Professor of Philosophy, University of Toronto, Canada; Author of* Development of Physical Theory in the Middle Ages

WEISS, GERALD, *Associate Professor of Anthropology, Florida Atlantic University*

WEISS, THOMAS, G., *Executive Director, Academic Council on the United Nations, Watson Institute, Brown University*

WEISSTEIN, ULRICH, *Professor of German and Comparative Literature, Indiana University; Author of* Max Frisch

WEISZ, JUDITH, *Staff Scientist and Assistant Director, Training Program in the Physiology of Reproduction, Worcester Foundation for Experimental Biology*

WEISZ, PAUL B., *Professor of Biology, Brown University*

WELBORN, DAVID, *Professor of Political Science, University of Tennessee*

WELCH, CLAUDE, *Dean and President, Graduate Theological Union, Berkeley, Calif.*

WELCH, CLAUDE E., JR., *Distinguished Service Professor, State University of New York at Buffalo; Editor of* Human Rights and Development in Africa

WELLER, MILTON W., *Professor of Entomology, University of Minnesota at St. Paul*

WELLIN, EDWARD, *Professor of Anthropology, University of Wisconsin at Milwaukee*

WELLINGTON, HARRY H., *Sterling Professor of Law, Yale University*

WELLINGTON, RICHARD, *Professor, New York State Agricultural Experiment Station, Cornell University*

WELLS, COLIN M. T., *Frank Murchison Distinguished Professor of Classical Studies, Trinity University; Author of* The German Policy of Augustus *and* The Roman Empire

WELLS, JAMES M., *Vice President, The Newberry Library, Chicago, Ill.*

WELLS, RONALD A., *History Department, Calvin College*

WELTY, CARL, *Professor of Biology, Beloit College; Author of* The Life of Birds

WELU, JAMES A., *Director, Worcester Art Museum*

WENGER, JOHN C., *Mennonite Bishop; Author of* Glimpses of Mennonite History and Doctrine *and* Separated Unto God

WENIG, JEFFREY, *Section Head, Inflammation and Cardiovascular Research and Development, ENDO Laboratories*

WENTZ, RICHARD E., *Educational Director, Office of Religious Affairs; Assistant Professor of Religious Studies, Pennsylvania State University*

WENZLAU, THOMAS E., *President, Ohio Wesleyan University*

WERKMEISTER, W. H., *Author of* Philosophy of Science

WERLICH, DAVID P., *Associate Professor of History, Southern Illinois University; Author of* Peru: A Short History

WERNSTEDT, FREDERICK L., *Professor of Geography, Pennsylvania State University*

WESLAGER, C. A., *Author of* The Log Cabin in America

WESSMAN, ALDEN E., *Associate Professor of Psychology, City College of New York; Author of* Mood and Personality

WESSON, LAURENCE G., JR., MD, *Professor of Medicine and Head, Division of Nephrology, Jefferson Medical College, Philadelphia, Pa.; Author of* Physiology of the Human Kidney

WEST, EDWARD N., *Sub-Dean, Cathedral of St. John the Divine, New York City*

WEST, RICHARD S., JR., *Author of* Gideon Welles: Lincoln's Navy Department

WEST, RUSSELL J., *City Librarian, Torrance Public Library*

WESTCOTT, CYNTHIA, *Author of* Anyone Can Grow Roses *and* Gardener's Bug Book

WESTFALL, MINTER J., JR., *Professor of Biological Science, Department of Zoology, University of Florida; Coauthor of* A Manual of the Dragonflies of North America

WESTFALL, RICHARD S., *Professor of History and Philosophy of Science, Indiana University; Author of* Science and Religion in 17th Century England

WESTIN, ALAN F., *Professor of Public Law and Government, Columbia University; Author of* Privacy and Freedom

WESTMAN, JAMES, *Professor of Environmental Resources, Rutgers University*

WESTON, LOUISE C., *Assistant Professor of Sociology, Rider College*

WESTRUP, SIR JACK A., *Heather Professor of Music, Oxford University*

WESTWOOD, M. N., *Professor of Horticulture, Oregon State University*

WETMORE, WARREN C., *Engineering Editor, Aviation Week & Space Technology*

WETZEL, RALPH MARTIN, *Professor of Zoology, Department of Systematic and Evolutionary Biology, Biological Sciences Group, University of Connecticut; Coauthor of* Behavior Modification in the Natural Environment

WEVER, ERNEST GLEN, *Professor of Psychology, Princeton University*

WHALEN, MARGARET A., *Research Librarian, Maine State Library*

WHATMOUGH, JOSHUA, *Chairman, Department of Linguistics, Harvard University*

WHEATON, WILLIAM L. C., *Dean, College of Environmental Design, University of California at Berkeley; Coauthor of* Housing, People, and Cities

WHEELER, DOUGLAS L., *Associate Professor of History, University of New Hampshire*

WHEELER, GEORGE E., *Professor of Biology, Brooklyn College*

WHEELER, SIR MORTIMER, *Secretary, British Academy*

WHELIHAN, KATHARINE BUDD, *Assistant Secretary, Bryn Mawr College*

WHERLEY, MARILYN C., *Senior Librarian, Los Angeles Public Library*

WHITCOMB, MICHAEL E., MD, *Professor of Medicine and Director, Program for Health Policy and Health Services Research, Office of the Vice President for Health Services, Ohio State University*

WHITE, BARBARA C., *Editor,* Physical Therapy: Journal of the American Physical Therapy Association

WHITE, CHARLES E., *Professor of Chemistry, University of Maryland*

WHITE, CHARLES, SJ, *Professor of Philosophy and Religion, American University*

WHITE, DAVID MANNING, *Professor of Mass Communication, Virginia Commonwealth University; Coeditor of* The Funnies: An American Idiom

WHITE, DENIS M., *Faculty of Economics and Politics, Monash University, Clayton, Victoria, Australia*

WHITE, EDWARD E., *President, Spencer, White and Prentis, Incorporated*

WHITE, GEORGE W., *Research Professor of Geology, University of Illinois*

WHITE, HARRY J., *Professor of Applied Science, Portland State University*

WHITE, JOHN H., JR., *Chairman, Department of Industries, Smithsonian Institution*

WHITE, LESLIE A., *Professor of Anthropology, University of Michigan; Author of* The Concept of Cultural Systems

WHITE, MARJORIE LONGENECKER, *Birmingham Historical Society; Author of* The Birmingham District: An Industrial History and Guide

WHITE, MICHAEL, JD, *Professor of Genetics, University of Melbourne, Australia; Author of* The Chromosomes and Animal Cytology and Evolution

WHITE, PAUL DUDLEY, MD, *Professor, Harvard University Medical School; President, International Cardiology Foundation; Author of* Heart Disease

WHITE, PHILIP R., *Senior Staff Scientist, Jackson Laboratory, Bar Harbor, Maine; Author of* A Handbook of Plant Tissue Culture

WHITE, RICHARD J., *Vice President, Infectious Disease Research, Bristol-Myers Company*

WHITE, RONALD C., *Research Scholar, Huntington Library; Lecturer in History, University of California at Los Angeles; Author of* An Unsettled Arena: Religion and the Bill of Rights

WHITE, RONALD C., JR., *Princeton Theological Seminary*

WHITE, RUTH MORRIS, *Author of* Yankee From Sweden; *Coauthor with William Chapman White of* Tin Can on a Shingle

WHITE, STEPHEN W., *Senior Technical Staff Member, RISC System/6000 Division, IBM*

WHITE, T. D., *University of California at Berkeley*

WHITEHEAD, W. T., *Manager, Public Relations, Bell & Howell Business Equipment Group*

WHITEHILL, WALTER MUIR, *Director and Librarian, Boston Athenaeum; Author of* Massachusetts: From the Berkshires to the Cape

WHITEHOUSE, PETER J., MD, *Assistant Professor of Neurology and Neuroscience, Johns Hopkins University; Sloan Fellow; McKnight Fellow; Commonwealth Fellow*

WHITELOCK, DOROTHY, CBE, *Professor of Anglo-Saxon, Cambridge University; Author of* Anglo-Saxon Wills

WHITESIDE, DEREK T., *Research Associate, Whipple Science Museum, Cambridge, England*

WHITROW, GERALD JAMES, *Reader in Applied Mathematics, Imperial College of Science and Technology, University of London; Author of* The Natural Philosophy of Time, Structure and Evolution of the Universe, *and* Einstein— The Man and His Achievement; *Coauthor of* Atoms and the Universe

WHITTAKER, HERBERT, *Drama Critic,* Toronto Globe and Mail

WHITWORTH, FRED E., *Director, Canadian Council for Research in Education*

WICKENS, GEORGE MICHAEL, *Professor and Chairman of Islamic Studies, University of Toronto, Canada*

WICKS, JARED, SJ, *Bellarmine School of Theology, North Aurora, Ill.*

WIDMOYER, FRED B., *Professor and Head, Department of Horticulture, College of Agriculture and Home Economics, New Mexico State University*

WIENER, NORBERT, *Author of* Cybernetics, or Control and Communication in the Animal and the Machine

WIENPAHL, PAUL, *Professor of Philosophy, University of California at Santa Barbara; Author of* The Matter of Zen

WIENS, HEROLD J., *Professor of Geography, University of Hawaii and University of Illinois; Author of* Han-Chinese Expansion in South China *and* Mongolia

WIEWIOROWSKI, T. K., *Superintendent, Chemical Research and Development, Freeport Minerals Company*

WIGGINS, JOHN H., JR., *J.H. Wiggins Company; Author of* Effects of Sonic Boom

WIGGINS, ROBERT A., *Professor of English, University of California at Davis; Author of* Ambrose Bierce

WILBER, DONALD NEWTON, *Author of* Afghanistan: Its People, Its Society, Its Culture *and* Pakistan Yesterday and Today; *Coauthor of* United Arab Republic—Egypt: Its People, Its Society, Its Culture *and* Iran Past and Present

WILCOX, WAYNE AYRES, *Chairman, Department of Political Science, Columbia University; Author of* Asia and U.S. Policy

WILCOX, BRIG. GEN. WILLIAM W., USAF, *National Commander, Civil Air Patrol*

WILDE, RICHARD H., *Dean of the School of Letters and Science, California State University at Long Beach*

WILEY, E. O., *Associate Curator of Fishes, Museum of Natural History, University of Kansas*

WILKINSON, CHARLES K., *Curator of Near Eastern Art, Metropolitan Museum of Art*

WILL, GRINTON I., *Director, Yonkers (N.Y.) Public Library*

WILLARDSON, LYMAN S., *Professor of Soil and Water Resources, Utah State University*

WILLCOX, DONALD J., *Author of* Modern Leather Design

WILLEY, GORDON R., *Bowditch Professor of Central American and Mexican Archaeology and Ethnology and Curator of Middle American Archaeology, Peabody Museum, Harvard University; Author of* Introduction to American Archaeology

WILLEY, PATSY GAVEN, *Director, North Star Borough Library, Fairbanks, Alaska*

WILLIAM, ARTHUR J., *Registrar, University of Western Australia*

WILLIAMS, A. O., JR., *Professor and Chairman, Department of Physics, Brown University*

WILLIAMS, C. E., *President, Bates Manufacturing Company*

WILLIAMS, D. ALAN, *Professor of History, University of Virginia*

WILLIAMS, DAN A., *Director, Public Library of Des Moines, Iowa*

WILLIAMS, DANIEL D., *Roosevelt Professor of Systematic Theology, Union Theological Seminary; Author of* The Shaping of American Religion

WILLIAMS, DAVID, *Author of* A History of Modern Wales

WILLIAMS, DONALD C., *Author of* Ground of Induction *and* Principles of Empirical Realism

WILLIAMS, FORMAN A., *Professor, Department of Aerospace and Mechanical Engineering Sciences, University of California at San Diego*

WILLIAMS, FREDERICK D., *Professor of History, Michigan State University; Coeditor of* The Diary of James A. Garfield

WILLIAMS, GEORGE H., *Hollis Professor of Divinity, Harvard University*

WILLIAMS, HERMANN W., JR., *Director, Corcoran Gallery of Art*

WILLIAMS, JOHN A., *Associate Professor, Department of History, State University of New York at Stony Brook; Author of* Politics of the New Zealand Maori: Protest and Cooperation, 1891–1909

WILLIAMS, JOHN M., JR., *Member of the New York Bar*

WILLIAMS, L. PEARCE, *Codirector of the Program in the History and Philosophy of Science and Technology, Cornell University*

WILLIAMS, MARTHA E., *Professor of Information Science, Coordinated Science Laboratory, University of Illinois at Urbana-Champaign*

WILLIAMS, MARTIN T., *Author of* Where's the Melody? A Listener's Introduction to Jazz *and* The Jazz Tradition

WILLIAMS, R. E., *Editor of* A Century of Punch Cartoons

WILLIAMS, RAYMOND E., *Director of McIntire Public Library*

WILLIAMS, ROGER L., *Professor of History, University of Wyoming; Author of* Gaslight and Shadow: The World of Napoleon III *and* The Mortal Napoleon III

WILLIAMS, STEPHEN, *Peabody Professor of American Archaeology and Ethnology and Curator of North American Archaeology, Peabody Museum, Harvard University*

WILLIAMS, T. DAVID, *Lecturer, Department of Economics, University of Strathclyde; Author of* Malawi: The Politics of Despair

WILLIAMS, T. HARRY, *Boyd Professor of History, Louisiana State University; Author of* Romance and Realism in Southern Politics, Lincoln and His Generals, *and* Huey Long

WILLIAMS, THOMAS R., *Professor of Anthropology and Chairman, Department of Anthropology, Ohio State University; Author of* The Dusun: A North Borneo Society *and* Borneo Childhood: Education in a Dusun Village

WILLIAMSON, EDWARD, *Hollis Professor of Romance Languages and Literatures, Wesleyan University; Author of* Bernardo Tasso

WILLIS, F. ROY, *Professor of History, University of California at Davis; Author of* The French in Germany, 1945–1949

WILLIS, J. H., JR., *Professor of English, College of William and Mary; Author of* William Empson

WILLNOW, RONALD D., *News Editor, St. Louis* Post-Dispatch

WILLOUGHBY, STEPHEN S., *Professor of Mathematics and Mathematics Education and Chairman of Mathematics Education, New York University; Author of* Probability and Statistics

WILLOUGHBY, WILLIAM R., *Professor of History and Government, St. Lawrence University*

WILLS, BEVERLEY J., *Research Scientist, Department of Astronomy, University of Texas at Austin*

WILLSON, RICHARD E., *Director, Lorain Public Library, Lorain, Ohio*

WILMER, FLORENCE C., *Director of Library Services, Catonsville Community College*

WILMOT, SEAMUS, *Registrar, National University of Ireland, Dublin*

WILSON, ARTHUR M., *Daniel Webster Professor, Dartmouth College; Author of* Diderot: The Testing Years, 1713–1759

WILSON, CONSTANCE M., *Assistant Professor of Southeast Asian History, Northern Illinois University*

WILSON, ISABEL, *Supervisor of Public Affairs, Canadian Association for Adult Education*

WILSON, J. TUZO, *Director General, Ontario Science Centre; Coauthor of* Physics and Geology

WILSON, J. WALTER, *Professor of Biology, Brown University*

WILSON, JOE PETE, *Lake Placid Bobsled Club; Member U.S. World Bobsled Team; Coauthor of* Complete Cross-Country Skiing and Ski Touring

WILSON, LOGAN, *President, American Council on Education; Editor of* Emerging Patterns in American Higher Education

WILSON, LOIS, *Author of* Miniature Flower Arrangements and Plantings

WILSON, MARY S., *Librarian, Adams County Public Library, Gettysburg, Pa.*

WILSON, RICHARD F., *Professor of Animal Science, Ohio State University*

WILSON, RUTH SMITH, *Director, Free Public Library*

WILTBANK, WILLIAM J., *Associate Professor, Department of Fruit Crops, University of Florida*

WILTSE, CHARLES M., *Professor of History, Dartmouth College; Editor of* The Daniel Webster Papers

WILZ, JOHN E., *Professor of History, Indiana University; Author of* From Isolation to War, 1931–1941 *and* The Search for Identity: Modern American History

WIMHURST, C. G. E., *Author of* Complete Book of Toy Dogs *and* Dictionary of Dogs

WIMSATT, W. K., *Professor of English, Yale University; Author of* The Portraits of Alexander Pope

WINCHESTER, ALICE, *Editor of* Antiques *Magazine; Author of* How to Know American Antiques; *Coauthor of* The Flowering of American Folk Art, 1776–1876; *Editor of* Living with Antiques

WINCHESTER, CALEB, T., *Author of* A Group of English Essayists

WINCHESTER, GEORGE, *Professor of Physics, Rutgers University*

WINCHESTER, N. BRIAN, *African Studies Program, Indiana University*

WINDER, R. BAYLY, *Dean of Arts and Sciences, New York University*

WINFREY, DORMAN H., *Director and Librarian, Texas State Library*

WINGER, HOWARD W., *Professor, Graduate Library School, University of Chicago*

WINGERT, PAUL S., *Professor of Art History and Archaeology, Columbia University; Author of* Primitive Art: Its Traditions and Styles

WINGFIELD, JOSIEPHINE B., *Head Librarian, Jones Memorial Library, Lynchburg, Va.*

WINKLER, HENRY R., *President, University of Cincinnati; Former Professor of History, Rutgers University*

WINKLER, MICHAEL, *Assistant Professor of Germanics, Rice University*

WINKS, ROBIN W., *Professor of History, Yale University; Author of* British Imperialism *and* The Age of Imperialism

WINNINGTON-INGRAM, R. P., *Professor of Greek Language and Literature, King's College, University of London; Author of* Mode in Ancient Greek Music

WINSHIP, THEODORE, MD, *Senior Attending Pathologist, Washington Hospital Center*

WINSLOW, OLA ELIZABETH, *Author of* John Bunyan; *Winner of the Pulitzer Prize for Biography*

WINSTON, DAVID K., *Dow Chemical Company*

WINSTON, MICHAEL R., *Instructor in History, Howard University; Coauthor of* Ordeal of Democracy: The Negro in the United States, 1945–1970

WINTER, FRANK H., *Curator, Rocketry, National Air and Space Museum, Smithsonian Institution; Author of* Prelude to the Space Age: The Rocket Societies, 1924–1940

WINTER, JOHN, *Research Associate in the Museum, Applied Science Center for Archaeology, University of Pennsylvania*

WINTERS, ROBERT K., *Editor,* Fifty Years of Forestry in the U.S.A.

WINTERS, WENDELL D., *President, Aloe Research Foundation; Fellow, American Academy of Microbiology*

WINTHER, OSCAR O., *University Professor of History, Indiana University; Author of* The Old Oregon Country *and* The Great Northwest

WIPPER, KIRK A. W., *Director, Camp Kandalore, Minden, Ontario; Professor of Physical and Health Education, University of Toronto, Canada*

WISE, CHARLES S., MD, *Director of Physical Medicine, George Washington Hospital, and Professor of Physical Medicine and Rehabilitation, George Washington University School of Medicine*

WISEMAN, JAMES R., *Professor of Classics, Boston University*

WISLOCKI, FLORENCE CLOTHIER, *Assistant to the President, Vassar College*

WITHINGTON, WILLIAM A., *Department of Geography, University of Kentucky*

WITKOVSKY, PAUL, *Professor of Anatomical Science, State University of New York at Stony Brook*

WITTWER, SYLVAN, *Professor of Horticulture and Director, Michigan Agricultural Experiment Station, Michigan State University College of Agriculture and Natural Resources; Author of Greenhouse Tomatoes*

WITZLING, LAWRENCE PHILIP, *Associate Professor, School of Architecture and Urban Planning, University of Wisconsin at Milwaukee; Author of Physical Planning (Chapter 8 of Introduction to Urban Planning, by Catanese and Snyder)*

WOHL, HELLMUT, *Chairman, Department of Fine Arts, Boston University; Author of Leonardo da Vinci; Editor of The Life of Michelangelo by Ascanio Condivi*

WOIDECK, CARL, *Instructor of Music, University of Oregon; Instructor of Music, Lane Community College, Eugene, Oregon*

WOLCOTT, MERLIN D., *Librarian, Canton Public Library*

WOLF, A. V., MD, *Professor and Head, Department of Physiology, University of Illinois College of Medicine; Author of Thirst: Physiology of the Urge to Drink and Problems of Water Lack*

WOLF, JOHN B., *Professor of History, University of Illinois; Author of Emergence of European Civilization*

WOLFF, LARRY, *Associate Professor of History, Boston College; Author of The Vatican and Poland in the Age of the Partitions*

WOLFF, ROBERT PAUL, *Professor of Philosophy, University of Massachusetts; Author of Kant's Theory of Mental Activity*

WOLFLE, DAEL, *Executive Officer, American Association for the Advancement of Science*

WOLFSKILL, GEORGE, *Professor of History, University of Texas at Arlington; Author of The Revolt of the Conservatives*

WOLITZ, SETH L., *Gale Professor of Jewish Studies, University of Texas at Austin*

WOLOCH, ISSER, *Associate Professor of History, Columbia University*

WOLPE, BRUCE C., *The Wexler Group; Author of Lobbying Congress*

WOLPERT, STANLEY, *Professor of History, University of California at Los Angeles; Author of Nine Hours to Rama and other books*

WOLPOFF, MILFORD H., *Professor of Anthropology, University of Michigan*

WOOD, CHRISTOPHER S., *Assistant Professor of the History of Art, Yale University*

WOOD, DENNIS P., SJ, *Fordham University*

WOOD, FERGUS J., *National Oceanic and Atmospheric Administration*

WOOD, L. E., *Systems Engineer, Bendix Corporation*

WOOD, LEDGER, *McCosh Professor of Philosophy, Princeton University; Author of The Analysis of Knowledge*

WOOD, PAUL E., JR., *Honeywell Information Science Center, Cambridge, Mass.*

WOOD, RICHARD G., *Director, Vermont Historical Society*

WOODBRIDGE, KATE, *Editorial Assistant, Carnegie Corporation of New York*

WOODBURY, ROBERT S., *Professor of History of Technology, Georgia Institute of Technology; Author of Studies in the History of Machine Tools*

WOODFORD, FRANK B., *City of Detroit Historiographer; Author of Lewis Cass, the Last Jeffersonian*

WOODWARD, C. VANN, *Sterling Professor of History, Emeritus, Yale University; Author of Origins of the New South, Mary Chesnut's Civil War, and The Old World's New World*

WOODWARD, RALPH L., *Tulane University; Author of Central America: A Nation Divided, Central America: Historical Perspectives on the Contemporary Crises, Positivism in Latin America, 1850–1900 and El Salvador*

WOODWARD, ROBERT C., *Librarian, Bangor Public Library*

WOODWARD, THEODORE E., MD, *Professor and Chairman, Department of Medicine, University of Maryland School of Medicine and Hospital; Physician-in-Chief, University of Maryland Hospital, Baltimore*

WOODWORTH, G. WALLACE, *Professor of Music, Harvard University; Author of The World of Music*

WOOLDRIDGE, JEFFREY M., *Associate Professor of Economics, Michigan State University*

WOOLRYCH, AUSTIN H., *Professor of History, University of Lancaster, England; Author of Battles of the English Civil War and Oliver Cromwell*

WORK, HENRY H., *Chief, Professional Services, and Executive Secretary, Institutes on Hospital and Community Psychiatry, American Psychiatric Association; Author of chapter Sociopathic Personality Disorders. II: Sexual Deviations in Comprehensive Textbook of Psychiatry*

WORKMAN, JOHN ROWE, *Professor of Classics, Brown University; Author of A Term of College Latin*

WORRALL, DENIS J., *Professor and Director, Institute for Social and Economic Research, Rhodes University*

WORTIS, SAM BERNARD, MD, *Professor and Chairman, Department of Psychiatry and Neurology, New York University School of Medicine; Coeditor of Psychiatric Treatment*

WORTMAN, DORIS NASH, *Author of Kingsley Double-Crostic Puzzles*

WRENN, CHARLES L., *Professor of Anglo-Saxon, Oxford University; Author of A Study of Old English Literature*

WRIGHT, BARBARA E., *Director, Boston Biomedical Research Institute; Author of Control Mechanisms in Respiration and Fermentation*

WRIGHT, DONALD E., *Librarian, Evanston Public Library, Evanston, Ill.*

WRIGHT, DUNCAN G., *President of the Great Pyrenees Club of Michigan*

WRIGHT, G. ERNEST, *Parkman Professor of Divinity, Divinity School, Harvard University; Author of The Old Testament and Theology*

WRIGHT, GORDON, *Professor of History, Stanford University*

WRIGHT, H. E., *Professor of Geology and Director, Limnological Research Center, University of Minnesota*

WRIGHT, HARRISON M., *Professor of History, Swarthmore College*

WRIGHT, J. ROBERT, *Professor of Church History, General Theological Seminary, New York City*

WRIGHT, (JOHN) MICHAEL, *Barrister at Law, Lincoln's Inn, London*

WRIGHT, KATHRYN, *Sunday Editor, Billings Gazette*

WRIGHT, MURIEL H., *Editor, Chronicles of Oklahoma, Oklahoma Historical Society*

WRIGHT, QUINCY, *Author of A Study of War and The Role of International Law in the Elimination of War*

WRIGHT, ROBERTS J., *Editor, American Journal of Correction; Member, Board of Parole, State of New York*

WRONG, GEORGE M., *Professor of History, University of Toronto, Canada*

WROTH, LAWRENCE C., *Research Professor of American History, Brown University*

WU, CHENGTSU, *Associate Professor of Geography, Hunter College*

WYATT-BROWN, BERTRAM, *Professor of History, Case Western Reserve University; Author of Lewis Tappan and the Evangelical War Against Slavery*

WYLIE, C. RAY, *Professor of Mathematics, Furman University*

WYLIE, HAROLD A., *Assistant Professor of Romance Languages, University of Texas at Austin*

WYLLIE, IRVIN G., *Professor of History, University of Wisconsin; Author of The Self-Made Man in America*

WYLLIE, JOHN COOK, *Librarian, Alderman Library, University of Virginia*

WYMAN, DONALD, *Horticulturist, Arnold Arboretum, Harvard University*

WYNN, GRAEME, *Professor of Geography and Associate Dean of Arts, University of British Columbia; Coauthor of Vancouver and Its Region; Author of Timber Colony: An Historical Geography of Early Nineteenth-Century New Brunswick*

WYNOT, EDWARD D., JR., *Professor of History, Florida State University; Author of Warsaw between the World Wars, 1918–1939 and Polish Politics in Transition, 1935–1939*

WYRTKI, KLAUS, *Professor of Oceanography, University of Hawaii; Author of* Oceanographic Atlas of the International Indian Ocean Expedition

WYSCHOGROD, MICHAEL, *Professor of Philosophy, Bernard M. Baruch College, City University of New York*

WYSHAK, GRACE, *Associate Professor, Yale University School of Medicine*

YABLONSKY, LEWIS, *Professor of Sociology, California State University at Northridge; Author of* The Violent Gang *and* The Hippie Trip

YADIN, YIGAEL, *Author of* The Art of Warfare in Biblical Lands *and* Masada

YAHR, MELVIN, MD, *Professor and Chairman, Department of Neurology, Mt. Sinai School of Medicine, City University of New York*

YALEM, RONALD J., *Associate Professor of Political Science, University of Alabama; Author of* Regionalism and World Order

YANG, CHEN NING, *Nobel Prize Winner in Physics, 1957; Director, Institute of Theoretical Physics, State University of New York at Stony Brook*

YAPP, M. E., *Lecturer in the History of the Near and Middle East, School of Oriental and African Studies, University of London; Coauthor of* War, Technology, and Society in the Middle East

YARMOLINSKY, AVRAHM, *Author of* Dostoevsky

YASSO, WARREN E., *Associate Professor of Science Education, Teachers College, Columbia University; Author of* Oceanography

YATES, JACK E., *Executive Assistant to the President, United Church of Christ*

YEATON, KELLY, *Professor of Theatre Arts, Pennsylvania State University*

YERKES, ROYDEN KEITH, *Author of* Sacrifice in Greek and Roman Religions and Early Judaism

YOHE, G. R., *Chemist and Head, Section of Coal Chemistry, Illinois State Geological Survey*

YOKLEY, PETE, *Tennessee Walking Horse Breeders Association of America*

YOLEN, WILL, *Author of* The Complete Book of Kites and Kite Flying

YOLTON, JOHN W., *Professor of Philosophy, York University, Canada; Author of* Locke and Education

YOORS, JAN, *Author of* The Gypsies

YORK, J. LYNDAL, *Associate Professor, Biochemistry Department, University of Arkansas College of Medicine; Author of* The Porphyrias

YOUNG, ARTHUR C., *Professor of English, Russell Sage College*

YOUNG, CHARLOTTE, *Professor of Nutrition, Cornell University*

YOUNG, DONALD, *Chair, Atlantic Chapter, Sierra Club; Coauthor of* The Sierra Club Book of Our National Parks; *Author of* American Roulette: The History and Dilemma of the Vice Presidency

YOUNG, FRANK W., *Professor of Rural Sociology and Anthropology, Cornell University; Author of* Initiation Ceremonies: A Cross-Cultural Study of Status Dramatization

YOUNG, HARLAND H., *President, Research Advisory Service, Inc.*

YOUNG, J. CROMWELL, *General Editorial Adviser,* Encyclopedia Canadiana

YOUNG, JAMES A., *Assistant Professor of Range Science, University of Nevada; U.S. Department of Agriculture*

YOUNG, PHILIP, *Research Professor of English, Pennsylvania State University; Author of* Ernest Hemingway: A Reconsideration

YOUNG, ROBERT A., *Professor of Physics, York University*

YOUNG, STARK, *Member, Editorial Staff,* The New Republic; *Author of* Glamour: Essays on the Art of the Theatre

YOUNG, T. CUYLER, *Horatio Whitridge Garrett Professor of Persian Language and History, Princeton University*

YOUNGDALE, JAMES M., *American Studies Program, University of Minnesota; Author of* Third Party Footprints *and* Populism: A Psycho-historical Perspective

YOUNGER, R. M., *Author of* Australia and the Australians *and* The Changing World of Australia

YU, PING-KUEN, *Director, Center for Chinese Research Materials, Association of Research Libraries, Washington, D.C.*

YUN, HUNKI, *Associate Editor,* Golf Digest

YUNKER, CONRAD, *Senior Scientist, The National Institute of Allergy and Infectious Diseases, Rocky Mountain Laboratory, U.S. Public Health Service*

ZABEL, MORTON DAUWEN, *Editor of* The Portable Conrad

ZABEL, ORVILLE H., *Professor of History, Creighton University*

ZACEK, JOSEPH F., *Professor of History, State University of New York at Albany*

ZAHL, PAUL A., *Senior Natural Scientist, National Geographic Society, Washington, D.C.*

ZAHNISER, MARVIN R., *Professor of History, Ohio State University*

ZAIDE, GREGORIO F., *Author of* Philippine Political and Cultural History

ZANGER, JACK L., *Author of* Major League Baseball 1969 *and* Pro Football 1969

ZANINI, RICHARD J., *Superintendent of Schools Emeritus, Wethersfield, Conn.*

ZAPOLSKY, HAROLD S., *Professor and Chairman, Department of Physics, Rutgers University*

ZARCHY, HARRY, *Author of* Creative Hobbies, Model Railroading, *and* Building with Electronics

ZARTMAN, I. WILLIAM, *Professor, Department of Politics, New York University; Author of* Government and Politics in Northern Africa

ZASLOW, MORRIS, *Professor of History, University of Western Ontario; Author of* The Opening of the Canadian North

ZELLIOT, ELEANOR, *Professor of History, Carleton College*

ZEIGER, HERBERT J., *Lincoln Laboratory, Massachusetts Institute of Technology*

ZEMANSKY, MARK W., *Professor of Physics, City College of New York*

ZEOLI, HAROLD W., *Professor of Mathematics, Central Michigan University*

ZETLER, BERNARD D., *Research Oceanographer, Institute of Geophysical and Planetary Physics, University of California at San Diego*

ZEYDEL, EDWIN H., *Editor of* Sebastian Brant's Ship of Fools; *Author of* Ludwig Tieck and England *and* Goethe The Lyrist

ZIADEH, NICOLA A., *Professor of Arab History, American University of Beirut, Lebanon*

ZIEGLER, KARL, *Nobel Prize Winner in Chemistry, 1963; Professor of Chemistry and Director, Max Planck Institute for Coal Research*

ZIEGLER, LOUIS W., *Professor of Fruit Crops, University of Florida; Coauthor of* Citrus Growing in Florida

ZIENTY, FERDINAND B., *Chemical Consultant*

ZIMDARS, BENJAMIN F., *Associate Professor of History, Mary Washington College of the University of Virginia*

ZIMMER, WILLIAM, *Art Critic,* New York Times

ZIMMERMAN, FRANKLIN B., *Professor of Music, University of Pennsylvania; Author of* Henry Purcell: His Life and Times

ZIMMERMAN, JOHN J., *Professor of History, Kansas State Teachers College*

ZIMMERMAN, MARY T., *Director, Bexley Public Library*

ZIMMERS, EMORY, *Professor of Industrial Engineering and Director, Computer-Integrated Manufacturing Laboratory, Lehigh University; Coauthor of* CAD-CAM: Computer-Aided Design and Manufacturing

ZIMSKIND, NATHANIEL H., *Rabbi, Temple Israel, Uniontown, Pa.*

ZINSER, JANICE CHIVILLE, *Assistant Professor of French, Oberlin College*

ZIRKLE, CONWAY, *Professor of Botany, University of Pennsylvania*

ZOETHOUT, CARLA, *Senior Lecturer, Center for Constitutional Law, Erasmus University, Rotterdam, The Netherlands*

ZOLLO, RICHARD P., *Danvers Historical Society*

ZOLTVANY, YVES, *Associate Professor of History, University of Western Ontario, Canada; Author of* The French Tradition in America

ZORNOW, WILLIAM FRANK, *Professor of History, Kent State University*

ZUCKER, ADOLF E., *Professor of Modern Languages, University of Maryland*

ZUK, WILLIAM, *Professor of Architecture and Past Professor of Civil Engineering, University of Virginia*

ZUMWALT, DONALD D., *Curator of John G. Shedd Aquarium, Chicago*

ZVELEBIL, KAMIL, *Professor, South Asian Department, University of Chicago; Author of* Introduction to the Historical Grammar of Tamil *and* Comparative Dravidian Phonology

ZWEIFEL, RICHARD G., *Curator, Department of Herpetology, American Museum of Natural History*

ZWERMAN, PAUL J., *Professor of Soil Conservation, New York State College of Agriculture, Cornell University*

ZWIEP, DONALD N., *Professor and Head, Department of Mechanical Engineering, Worcester Polytechnic Institute*

Pronunciation Key

a, ă	add, hat, grass
ā, â	ape, bait, may, chaotic
ä	arc, father, balm
â	fare, air, heir, there
à	French *amie*
b	bat, ball, cub
ch	chin, question, catch
d	dot, day, bed
e, ĕ	ell, bury, said
ē	eve, greet, beat, yield, body
ę	here, deer
ê	event, befall
ẽ	perform, maker
f	for, safe, graph
g	gum, ghost, bag
h	hit, who, hush
hw	what, why, where
i, ĭ	it, cyst, event
ī	ivy, aisle, eye
j	jot, age, wedge
k	keep, back, come
KH, K	(small capitals) German *ach*, Scottish *loch*
l	last, able, deal
m	man, hem, wisdom
n	no, lessen, know
N	(small capital) French *vin, champ*
ng	bang, ink, uncle
o, ŏ	odd, hot, was
ō, ô	ode, note, beau, obey
ô, ǒ	organ, loft, all, saw, author
oi	oil, coin, boy
ŏŏ	foot, bull, took
ōō	boot, group, shoe, true
ou	our, cow, bout
p	pot, pat, cup
r	raid, deer, heard
s	say, cease, race
sh	shot, action, machine
t	tap, bet, cat
th	thin, thigh, bath
th̶	thy, bathe, either
u, ŭ	up, cud, undo, onion
ū, û	unit, due, beauty, unite, dew
û	urn, earn, myrtle, dirt, hermit; also German *schön,* French *feu*
ü	French *une;* German *grün*
v	vat, view, save
w	we, wet, awake
y	yes, union, hallelujah
z	zeal, applause, raise
zh	azure, measure, rouge
ə	(schwa) unstressed vowels as in china, taken, futile, connect, circus
ˏ	slurred vowels as in pardon, futile, and French *notre*
′	indicates principal syllable stress
-	used between unstressed syllables
[°]	pronunciation is unattested English-language equivalent of non-English word

Abbreviations

Abbreviations used in articles are listed below.

A

Å	(angstrom unit)
A$	(Australian dollars)
A.B.	(bachelor of arts)
ac	(alternating current)
Acad.	(Academic)
A.D.	(*anno Domini,* in the year of the Lord)
Adj.	(Adjutant)
Adm.	(Admiral)
AIDS	(acquired immune deficiency syndrome)
Ala.	(Alabama)
AM	(amplitude modulation)
A.M.	(master of arts)
A.M.	(ante meridiem, before noon)
Am.	(American)
Amb.	(Ambassador)
amp	(ampere)
Ariz.	(Arizona)
Ark.	(Arkansas)
art.; arts.	(article; articles)
Assn.	(Association)
Assoc.; Assocs.	(Associate; Associates)
ASSR	(Autonomous Soviet Socialist Republic)
ATP	(adenosine triphosphate)
at wt	(atomic weight)
Aug.	(August)
Aus.	(Austrian; Austria)
Aust.	(Australian; Australia)
A.V.	(Authorized Version)

B

b.	(born)
B.A.	(bachelor of arts)
bap.	(baptized)
BBC	(British Broadcasting Corporation)
bbl	(barrel; barrels)
B.C.	(before Christ)
B.C.E.	(before the common era)
Bé	(Baumé)
B.F.A.	(bachelor of fine arts)
bhp	(brake horsepower)
Bks.	(Books)
bp	(boiling point)
B.P.	(before the present)
Brig.	(Brigadier)
B.S.	(bachelor of science)
Btu	(British thermal unit)
bu	(bushel)

C

C	(Celsius; centigrade)
c.	(circa, about)
Calif.	(California)
Can.	(Canadian; Canada)
Can$	(Canadian dollars)
Capt.	(Captain)
C.B.E.	(Commander of the British Empire)
cc	(cubic centimeter)
CD-ROM	(compact-disc, read-only-memory)
C.E.	(common era)
cfm	(cubic feet per minute)
cfs	(cubic feet per second)
cg	(centigram)
cgs	(centimeter-gram-second)
chap.; chaps.	(chapter; chapters)
Chin.	(Chinese; China)
CIS	(Commonwealth of Independent States)
cm	(centimeter)
cm/sec^2	(centimeters per second per second)
Co.	(Company)
Col.	(Colonel)
col.; cols.	(column; columns)
Colo.	(Colorado)
Comdr.	(Commander)
comp.	(compiler; compiled)
Conn.	(Connecticut)
Corp.	(Corporation)
cos	(cosine)
cp	(candlepower)
Cpl.	(Corporal)
csc	(cosecant)
CST	(Central Standard Time)
Ctr.	(Center)
cu	(cubic)
cwt	(hundredweight)

D

d.	(died; pence)
D.B.E.	(Dame Commander of the British Empire)
dc	(direct current)
D.C.	(District of Columbia)
D.D.	(doctor of divinity)
D.D.S.	(doctor of dental surgery)
Dec.	(December)
Del.	(Delaware)
Dept.	(Department)
diss.	(dissertation)
dist.	(distributor; distributed)
Div.	(Division)
D.Litt.	(doctor of literature)
D.M.D.	(doctor of medical dentistry)
D.Mus.	(doctor of music)
DNA	(deoxyribonucleic acid)
Dr.	(Doctor)
DST	(daylight saving time)
D.V.M.	(doctor of veterinary medicine)

E

E	(east)
EC	(Economic Community)
ed.; eds.	(edition, editor; editions, editors)
Edns.	(Editions)
Educ.	(Education: Educational)
EEC	(European Economic Community)
EEG	(electroencephalogram)
EKG	(electrocardiogram)
emf	(electromotive force)
Eng.	(English)
enl. ed.	(enlarged edition)
erg-sec	(erg-second)
EST	(Eastern Standard Time)
est.	(estimate)
et al.	(*et alia,* and others)
EU	(European Union)
exp.	(expanded)

F

F	(Fahrenheit)
f.	(and following, singular)
fbm	(board feet or feet board measure)
Feb.	(February)
ff.	(and following, plural)
fig.; figs.	(figure; figures)
fl.	(flourished)
Fla.	(Florida)
FM	(frequency modulation)
Fnd.	(Foundation)
Fr.	(French; France)
F.S.C.	(Brothers of the Christian Schools)
ft	(foot)
ft/sec	(feet per second)

G

g	(gram; gravity)
Ga.	(Georgia)
gal	(gallon)
GDP	(gross domestic product)
Gen.	(General)
Ger.	(German; Germany)
GeV	(billion electron volts)
GHQ	(general headquarters)
GHz	(gigahertz)
GMT	(Greenwich Mean Time)
GNP	(gross national product)
Gov.	(Governor)
GPO	(Government Printing Office)

H

ha	(hectare)
Hist.	(Historical)
hms	(hours, minutes, seconds)
H.M.S.	(His, or Her, Majesty's Service, Ship, or Steamer)
hp	(horsepower)
Hung.	(Hungarian; Hungary)
Hz	(hertz)

I

ibid.	(*ibidem,* in the same place)
id.	(*idem,* the same author)
ihp	(indicated horsepower)
Ill.	(Illinois)
in	(inch)
Inc.	(Incorporated)
Ind.	(Indiana)
in/sec	(inches per second)
Inst.	(Institute; Institution)
Intl.	(International)
IQ	(intelligence quotient)
Ital.	(Italian; Italy)

J

J	(joule)
Jan.	(January)
Jap.	(Japanese; Japan)
Jr.	(Junior)

K

K	(Kelvin scale)
Kans.	(Kansas)
K.B.E.	(Knight of the British Empire)
kc	(kilocycle)
K.C.B.	(Knight Commander of the Bath)
KeV	(thousand electron volts)
kg	(kilogram)
K.G.	(Knight of the Garter)
KGB	(Committee for State Security)
kHz	(kilohertz)
km	(kilometer)
km/sec	(kilometers per second)
kPa	(kilopascal)
kph	(kilometers per hour)
kv	(kilovolt)
kva	(kilovolt-ampere)
kvar	(kilovar)
kw	(kilowatt)
kwh	(kilowatt-hour)
Ky.	(Kentucky)

L

£	(libra, pound)
L	(liter)
l.; ll.	(line; lines)
La.	(Louisiana)
Lab.; Labs.	(Laboratory; Laboratories)
lb	(pound)
lb/sq ft	(pounds per square foot)
L.I.	(Long Island)

Lib.; Libs.	(Library; Libraries)
Linn.	(Linnaeus; Linnaean)
Litt.D.	(doctor of literature)
LL.B.	(bachelor of laws)
LL.D.	(doctor of laws)
log	(logarithm)
LSD	(d-lysergic acid diethylamide tartarate)
Lt.	(Lieutenant)
Ltd.	(Limited)
Lt. Gen.	(Lieutenant General)

M

M	(magnitude)
M.	(Monsieur)
m	(meter)
ma	(milliampere)
M.A.	(master of arts)
Maj.	(Major)
Maj. Gen.	(Major General)
Mass.	(Massachusetts)
M.B.A.	(master of business administration)
mc	(megacycle)
Md.	(Maryland)
M.D.	(doctor of medicine)
Me.	(Maine)
MeV	(million electron volts)
Mex$	(Mexican dollars)
mf	(microfarad)
M.F.A.	(master of fine arts)
mg	(milligram)
MHz	(megahertz)
mi	(mile)
Mich.	(Michigan)
min	(minute)
Minn.	(Minnesota)
Miss.	(Mississippi)
MIT	(Massachusetts Institute of Technology)
ml	(milliliter)
MLA	(Modern Language Association)
Mlle	(Mademoiselle)
mm	(millimeter)
Mme	(Madame)
mol	(molecule)
MP	(military police)
mp	(melting point)
M.P.	(member of Parliament)
mph	(miles per hour)
Mo.	(Missouri)
Mont.	(Montana)
Mr.	(Mister)
Mrs.	(Mistress)
MS.; MSS.	(manuscript; manuscripts)
Ms.	(alternative for *Miss* or *Mrs.*)
M.S.	(master of science)
Msgr.	(Monsignor)
MST	(Mountain Standard Time)
Mt.	(Mount)
Mus.	(Museum)

Mv	(million volts)
Mw	(megawatt)

N

N	(north)
N.A.; n.a.	(not applicable; not available)
Natl.	(National)
N.C.	(North Carolina)
NCO	(noncommissioned officer)
n.d.	(no date)
N.Dak.	(North Dakota)
NE	(northeast)
Nebr.	(Nebraska)
Nev.	(Nevada)
N.H.	(New Hampshire)
N.J.	(New Jersey)
NKVD	(Russian secret police)
N.Mex.	(New Mexico)
no.; nos.	(number; numbers)
Nov.	(November)
n.p.	(no publisher)
N.S.	(New Style)
NW	(northwest)
N.Y.	(New York)
N.Y.C.	(New York City)

O

O.B.E.	(Officer of the British Empire)
Oct.	(October)
O.F.M.	(Order of Friars Minor)
Okla.	(Oklahoma)
Oreg.	(Oregon)
O.S.	(Old Style)
O.S.B.	(Order of St. Benedict)
oz	(ounce)

P

p.; pp.	(page; pages)
Pa	(Pascal)
Pa.	(Pennsylvania)
par.; pars.	(paragraph; paragraphs)
Pfc.	(Private First Class)
Ph.D.	(doctor of philosophy)
P.M.	(post meridiem, after noon)
Pol.	(Polish; Poland)
pop.	(population)
Port.	(Portuguese; Portugal)
ppm	(parts per million)
Pres.	(President)
psi	(pounds per square inch)
PST	(Pacific Standard Time)
PT boat	(patrol torpedo boat)
Pub.; Pubs.	(Publishing, Publisher; Publishers)
Publ.; Publs.	(Publisher; Publishers)
Pubn.; Pubns.	(Publication; Publications)
Pvt.	(Private)

Q

qq.v.	(*quae vide,* which see, plural)
qt	(quart)
q.v.	(*quod vide,* which see, singular)

R

r.	(reigned)
Rep.	(Representative)
Repr.	(Reprint)
Res.	(Research)
Rev.	(Reverend)
rev. ed.	(revised edition)
Rh factor	(Rhesus factor)
R.I.	(Rhode Island)
RNA	(ribonucleic acid)
Rom.	(Romanian; Romania)
ROTC	(Reserve Officers Training Corps)
rpm	(revolutions per minute)
rps	(revolutions per second)
R.R.	(Railroad)
RSV	(Revised Standard Version)
R.S.V.P.	(répondez s'il vous plaît)
Rt. Rev.	(Right Reverend)
Russ.	(Russian; Russia)
R.V.	(Revised Version)

S

S	(south)
s	(second)
s.	(shilling)
S.C.	(South Carolina)
S.Dak.	(South Dakota)
SE	(southeast)
sec	(second)
sect.; sects.	(section; sections)
sel.	(selected; selections)
Sen.	(Senator)
Sept.	(September)
Serv.; Servs.	(Service; Services)
Ser.	(Series)
SFSR	(Soviet Federated Socialist Republic)
Sgt.	(Sergeant)
sin	(sine)
S.J.	(Society of Jesus; Jesuit)
Soc.	(Society)
SOS	(distress signal)
Sp.	(Spanish; Spain)
sp gr	(specific gravity)
sp ht	(specific heat)
sq	(square)
Sr.	(Senior)
ssp.	(subspecies)
SSR	(Soviet Socialist Republic)
St; Ste	(French, Saint; Sainte)
St.	(Saint)
supp.	(supplement)
SW	(southwest)

T

tan	(tangent)
TASS	(Soviet news agency)
Tenn.	(Tennessee)
Tex.	(Texas)
tr.; trs.	(translated; translator; translators; translation; translations)
trans.	(translated; translator)
TV	(television)

U

UAR	(United Arab Republic)
UFO	(unidentified flying object)
UHF	(ultrahigh frequency)
U.K.	(United Kingdom)
UN	(United Nations)
Univ.	(University)
U.S.	(United States)
US$	(United States dollars)
USA	(United States Army)
USAF	(United States Air Force)
USCG	(United States Coast Guard)
USGPO	(United States Government Printing Office)
USMA	(United States Military Academy)
USMC	(United States Marine Corps)
USN	(United States Navy)
USNA	(United States Naval Academy)
USNR	(United States Naval Reserve)
U.S.S.	(United States Ship, or Steamer)
USSR	(Union of Soviet Socialist Republics)

V

v.	(versus)
Va.	(Virginia)
var.	(variety)
VD	(venereal disease)
VHF	(very high frequency)
Vice Pres.	(Vice President)
vol.; vols.	(volume; volumes)
VOR	(very high frequency omnirange)
Vt.	(Vermont)

W

W	(watt; west)
Wash.	(Washington)
Wis.	(Wisconsin)
W.Va.	(West Virginia)
Wyo.	(Wyoming)

	Early North Semitic	Phoenician	Early Hebrew (Gezer)	Early Greek	Classical Greek	Etruscan		Early Latin	Classical Latin
						Early	Classical		
A	K	⦣	⦣	A	A	A	A	A	A

Cursive Majuscule (Roman)	Cursive Minuscule (Roman)	Anglo-Irish Majuscule	Caroline Minuscule	Venetian Minuscule (Italic)	N. Italian Minuscule (Roman)
λ	u	a	a	a	a

The top row shows the evolution of the majuscule (capital, or uppercase) A; the bottom row shows that of the minuscule (small, or lowercase) letter.

A, the first letter of the English alphabet and of many other alphabets. It has headed the alphabet all during its history—some 3,500 years. The letter is derived through Latin and Etruscan from the Greek *alpha* (based on the Semitic *'aleph*). The modern name *a* is of Etruscan origin.

Development. The Greeks borrowed their alphabet from the North Semitic writing system. In the latter, *A* was not a vowel but a consonant, namely, the glottal stop as is heard in English between two consecutive, separate vowels (as in *aorta*), represented in pronunciation by the schwa—[ə]. The Greek *alpha*, which provides the first part of the word *alphabet,* has no meaning in Greek; it is based on the Semitic *'aleph.* *'Aleph* may have meant "ox," but the popular notion of the form of the letter itself as originally representing an ox is incorrect. In fact, the name *aleph* is a purely mnemonic device (like "*a* for apple").

The 12th- or 11th-century-B.C. Aḥiram inscription discovered in Byblos, northern Syria, in 1923 is a relatively trustworthy starting point for the history of the alphabet. The North Semitic *aleph,* which appeared in this inscription, developed by 1000 B.C. into the Phoenician and Early Hebrew *aleph.* Over the next thousand years of the letter's development, through the Greek, Etruscan, and Latin alphabets, there were relatively few changes. At the beginning of the Christian era, it became the classical Latin *A.* Subsequently this letter remained unchanged; it corresponds to the capital, or majuscule, *A* of the English alphabet.

The minuscule *a,* also known as lowercase *a,* is of Roman origin. In Rome the capital, or monumental (also known as "lapidary"), style was employed for writing on stone and, for literary purposes, on papyrus. A modification of this style was the cursive hand used for more utilitarian purposes and for writing on perishable surfaces.

Varieties and Styles. Because the writing surfaces used during Roman times were so perishable, few early examples of this cursive writing have survived. There are enough, however, to indicate that distinctive cursive varieties already existed in the first two centuries A.D., including majuscule cursive, minuscule cursive, and semicursive minuscule. Intermediate between the monumental and cursive Latin scripts were various other forms, including the early semiuncial, uncial, and later semiuncial. (See PALEOGRAPHY.)

About the time of the dissolution of the Roman empire (5th century A.D.), several ways of writing the cursive minuscule script appeared in various regions of western Europe. These included the semicursive minuscule in Italy, Merovingian script in France, Visigothic script in Spain, and Insular or Anglo-Irish semiuncial style (also known as

Anglo-Saxon majuscule) in Britain. In the 9th and 10th centuries, the Caroline minuscule *a* was already similar to the present-day lowercase letter. The Caroline script became the principal book hand (the handwriting used before the invention of printing) of western Europe and was responsible for the blending of majuscules and minuscules in west European scripts. In the 15th century in Venice, the humanistic or Renaissance style developed from the Caroline script. Two varieties of script emerged: the Venetian minuscule known as italics, and the roman hand. The "a" assumed the form *a* in the italic hand. Both styles spread, first over Europe and then over the whole world. All the typefaces ordinarily used by printers in the West developed from these two forms.

Pronunciation. In Greek, Etruscan, and Latin, the letter *A* represented the cardinal vowel [a] as in Northern English *back,* that is, the front, open, unrounded vowel very common in most of the European languages (except English). In English the letter *a* (which, as a letter, is pronounced [eɪ], except in a technical linguistic context, in which it is pronounced as the cardinal vowel [a]) has a wide gamut of phonetic realizations. These range from front half-close vowels over the central ("mute") vowel [ə] to back low vowels; compare the values of the letter *a* in the words *many* ([meni] or, with a more open vowel, [mɛni]), *name* ([neɪm]), *care* ([keər]), *add* ([æd] or [æˀd]), and *cat* ([kæt]), all with front vowels; *husband* ([hʌzbənd]) and *career* ([kəriər]), with the central vowel [ə]; *sofa* (American English [soʊfɐ], with the central vowel [ɐ], but British English [soʊfə]; and *all* [ɔːl] and *wash* (British [wɒʃ]), with back vowels.

The letter *a* also occurs in combinations of vowel signs, namely *aa* (only in names or words of foreign origin, such as *Spaak, aardvark,* and *kraal*), *ae* (in words of foreign origin), *ai, ao, au,* and *ay.* Such combinations may have various phonetic values. For example, *au* is pronounced [ɒ] or [ɔː] in *austere;* [ɑː]—or, in the United States, [æ]—in *aunt;* [ɔː] in *gaunt;* and [eɪ] in *gauge.* The combination *ae* has a different realization in words containing the element *aer-* (*aerial, aerodynamics, aerospace*), in which *ae* is pronounced [eə], and in words allowing the alternation with the simple vowel sign *e,* such as *aetiology/etiology* or *encyclopaedia/encyclopedia,* in which *ae* (or simple *e*) is pronounced [iː]. In combinations of vowel signs in which *a* is the second letter, the function of the *a* is to mark the length of the vowel corresponding to the first vowel sign, as in *cease* ([siːs]), or to constitute a specific glide together with the preceding element, as in *boat* ([bəʊt]).

See also ALPHABET.

DAVID DIRINGER*, *Author of "The Alphabet"*

1

A, ā, in general, the first term of any series. It frequently denotes excellence of performance, as in school grades, or high quality, as in the grading of food.

In music, A is the sixth note in the scale of C major and the root of the related minor (A minor). As a fixed tone, á (440 vibrations per second) is the standard by which all instruments are tuned. In key notation, A is the keynote of A major or A minor.

In logic, in categorical propositions, A is used to designate the subject of the proposition or the universal affirmative proposition itself (All A is B). In algebra, the first letters of the alphabet, *a*, *b*, *c*, and so on, are used to denote known quantities, while the last, down to *z*, denote the unknown—*a* and *x* being used first in all cases, the others being added according to need. In geometry, and in mechanical diagrams, the capitals A, B, C, and so on, are used to mark off points, lines, angles, and figures.

A PRIORI, ä prē-ôr′ē (Latin, "from what is prior"), a term in philosophy applied to knowledge not derived from or justified by sense experience. The concept is contrasted with a posteriori, or empirical, knowledge. What counts as a priori is one of the central debates in the history of philosophy. It is often noted that sense experience, with its variable and contingent content, presupposes concepts or judgments without which experience is not conceivable. Such assumptions, being not falsifiable, are necessarily true. Principles of logic ("Something cannot be both X and not X at the same time and in the same respect") and the metaphysical principle of causality ("Every event has a cause") have often been adduced as a priori.

Aristotle saw philosophic inquiry as an ascent from experience ("first for us") to such necessary presuppositions ("first in nature"), followed by deductive descent from these highest grounds to experiential truths. The demonstrative descent was called a priori in Scholastic philosophy. While doubting the senses, René Descartes (1596–1650) argued that the first principles of all sciences are to be found by reflecting on intuitive certainties (innate ideas) of the thinking "I," thus initiating the modern approach of viewing the human subject as the source of a priori truths. "First for us" and "first in nature" became, in a way, the same.

A major debate in modern philosophy has focused on the distinction between analytic and synthetic a priori. Certain propositions, termed analytic, are considered a priori, thus necessarily true, owing simply to the meaning of the linguistic expressions contained in them ("All unmarried men are bachelors"). The term *synthetic a priori* has been applied to propositions that are informative about experience (in contrast to analytic) while also necessarily true. David Hume (1711–1776) claimed that there are no a priori truths other than relations among ideas constructed by the human mind, in which he included mathematics. Thus all a priori truths are analytic; cause and effect are only an a posteriori synthesis of impressions customarily associated in experience.

In opposition to Hume, Immanuel Kant (1724–1804), the pivotal figure in modern thought on the a priori, argued that the principle of causality and mathematical propositions are instances of the synthetic a priori. Indeed, Kant reasoned that the possibility of all human experience rests on synthetic a priori judgments; the task of philosophy as "critical" or "transcendental" is to show how such judgments are possible. His account employed a priori "forms" of cognition (space and time as "pure intuitions" and pure categories), through which the human subject orders the given "matter" of sensation. This gave a new role to the human subject's free or spontaneous activity. Many of Kant's claims (notably on mathematics) have come under sharp attack.

Twentieth-century logical positivists rejected the synthetic a priori. W. V. O. Quine (1908–2000) denied the validity of the analytic-synthetic distinction and all a priori justification. Centrality was accorded the a priori by the phenomenologist Edmund Husserl (1859–1938) and others.

RICHARD VELKLEY
Catholic University of America

Bibliography: Bonjour, Lawrence, *In Defense of Pure Reason* (Cambridge 1998); Moser, Paul K., ed., *A Priori Knowledge* (Oxford 1987); Sumner, L. W., and John Woods, eds., *Necessary Truth* (Random House 1969); Tugendhat, Ernst, *Traditional and Analytic Philosophy*, tr. by P. A. Gorner (Cambridge 1982).

AA, ä, the name of some 40 streams in Europe. The most important of these streams are a river in northern France flowing to the Strait of Dover, two rivers in Latvia flowing to the Gulf of Rīga, one in the Swiss cantons of Lucerne and Aargau, and two in Germany.

The name *Aa* stems from an Indo-European word meaning "water," surviving in the German *ach* or *aach* (Aachen, Biberach) and the Scandinavian å or *aa* (Aarhus, Aalborg). It is cognate to the Latin *aqua* (French *Aix* in compounds).

AACHEN, ä′KHən, a city in Germany, in the state of North Rhine–Westphalia, on the Belgian border, 38 miles (61 km) west-southwest of Cologne. It is a chief point of entry into Germany from the west. It is known in French by its medieval name, Aix-la-Chapelle.

Situated in a coal-mining district, Aachen is a steel center and has large textile and electrical

Aachen's Gothic Town Hall (*Rathaus*) was built in the 14th century on the foundation of Charlemagne's palace.

equipment factories. The city has an engineering institute and is the seat of a Roman Catholic bishop.

Aachen's outstanding architectural attraction is its cathedral, which was commissioned by Charlemagne and begun, probably in 796, by Odo of Metz. After being partially destroyed by the Northmen in 881, it was restored in 983. Gothic additions were built in the 14th and 15th centuries. A tomb believed to be Charlemagne's is located within the cathedral.

Aachen was originally famed as a spa, and its sulfur springs still attract tourists. The Romans, who called the place Aquae Grani or Aquisgranum, established baths there in the 1st century A.D. The city increased in importance during the reign of Charlemagne, king of the Franks (768–814) and emperor of the West (800–814). He made it his capital north of the Alps and a center of learning, culture, and commerce.

Aachen was the coronation city for German emperors from 814 to 1531. During the Middle Ages, as an imperial city, it was a direct vassal of the emperor of the Holy Roman Empire, a status that gave it political and commercial advantages enjoyed by only a few other European cities. Aachen was also the scene of many imperial diets and of important church councils, including the council of 836, which dealt with ecclesiastical discipline, and the council of 1166, a schismatic council convened by the antipope Paschal III, which canonized Charlemagne. The treaties of Aix-la-Chapelle of 1668 and of 1748, ending, respectively, the War of Devolution and the War of the Austrian Succession, were signed there.

The French occupied the city from 1794 until they surrendered it to Prussia in 1815 after the Congress of Vienna. It was a Prussian military base in the Franco-Prussian War (1870–1871) and a German air force base in World War I. After Germany's defeat, the Allies occupied the city from 1918 until 1930.

As an important industrial center, Aachen was heavily bombed in World War II. It was the first major German city to fall to the Allies, on Oct. 20, 1944, after a ten-day battle in which a number of medieval churches were destroyed, including St. Foillan's (12th century), St. Nicholas's (14th century), and St. Paul's (15th century). The Aachen cathedral fortunately was only slightly damaged. Although 85% of the city was severely damaged by the time the war ended, Aachen made a rapid recovery in the postwar years. Population: 249,200 (2004 est.).

AAGESEN, Svend, ô'gə-sən, Danish historian who lived in the latter half of the 1100s. Aagesen compiled the *Compendiosa historia regum Daniae,* the first continuous history of Denmark. It covered the period 300–1185, from King Skjold to King Canute VI.

AAHMES. See AHMES.

AAKJÆR, Jeppe, ôk'yer (1866–1930), Danish poet and novelist whose lyrical verse about life and nature in his native Jutland has been called "the very voice of Denmark." He was born near Skive, Jutland, Denmark, on Sept. 9, 1866. As a young man he went to Copenhagen, where he earned a living as a proofreader and journalist. Returning to Jutland in 1907, he settled on his farm, Jenle, where he died on April 22, 1930.

Henry George, the American economist, influenced Aakjær's early novels in which he pleaded the cause of the farm laborer. As literature, however, Aakjær's fiction is of little value. More satisfying is his verse, influenced by the Scottish poet Robert Burns. Written in a melodious, lyrical vein, it is more conservative in feeling than the novels, but still reflects Aakjær's social consciousness. His volumes of poetry include *Rugens Sange* (1906; *Songs of the Rye*), *Den Sommer og den Eng* (1910; *That Summer and That Field*), and *Under Aftenstjernen* (1927; *Under the Evening Star*).

HALLBERG HALLMUNDSSON, *Editor*
"An Anthology of Scandinavian Literature"

AALBORG, ôl'bôrg, a seaport and railroad center in Denmark, in northern Jutland. It lies on the south bank of the Lim Fjord, a channel joining the Kattegat and the North Sea. The name is officially spelled Ålborg. The city is the seat of Aalborg amt (county) and of a bishop. The cathedral dates from about 1500. Other old buildings include a restored town house built in 1624 in Dutch Renaissance style, a castle, and a monastery. Among the newer buildings is a civic hall (1949), seating more than 3,000. Aalborg produces aquavit, cement, chemicals, and textiles.

Known in earliest times as Alburgum, Aalborg is one of Denmark's oldest cities. By the 1600s it was an important trade center, and by 1870 industry was emerging. In World War II it was used as an air base for the German attack on Norway. Population: 115,200 (1992 est.).

AALST, älst, a city in Belgium, in East Flanders province, on the Dender River, 15 miles (24 km) northwest of Brussels. The French form of the name is Alost. The city is a railroad junction and has brewing and textile industries.

Founded in the 800s, Aalst came under the control of the counts of Flanders in 1056. From then until 1830, when Belgium became independent, Aalst passed from one great European power to another. The French, Germans, Spanish, and Dutch occupied the city at different times. In World Wars I and II, the Germans held Aalst.

Landmarks include the unfinished Gothic church of St. Martin, begun toward the end of the 1400s. The church contains Rubens's *Saint Roch Interceding for the Plague-Stricken*, painted about 1623. The town hall, the oldest in Belgium, dates from the early 1200s. There is a statue of Thierry Martens, a native of Aalst, who established at Aalst in 1473 the first Belgian printing press. Population: 76,382 (1991 census).

AALTO, Alvar Henrik, äl'to (1898–1976), Finnish architect who was one of the most influential proponents of functional design. Aalto's early work was strictly functional, but in later designs he integrated his buildings with their environment through the use of natural materials and free-flowing volumes and spaces.

Hugo Alvar Henrik Aalto was born in Kuortane, Finland, on Feb. 3, 1898. He graduated from the Polytechnic School in Helsinki in 1921 and three years later married fellow student Aino Marsio (1894–1949), who collaborated in all his designs until her death. Their first office was in Jyväskylä. In 1927 they moved to Turku, and in 1933 they relocated to Helsinki. In 1952 he married Elissa Mäkiniemi, who became a partner in his office, and after 1955 they lived in or near Helsinki.

Alvar Aalto's Paimio table and chair (c. 1932–1933) take their name from the Finnish tuberculosis sanatorium designed by the architect. The Iittala glassware, designed in 1932 by his wife Aino Aalto, continues to be produced.

Aalto died in Helsinki on May 11, 1976.

Aalto's fame spread beyond Finland with early functional designs such as the block of buildings in Turku that includes the Finnish Theater (1927–1928); a tuberculosis sanatorium in Paimo (1929–1933); and his own home near Helsinki (1935–1936). For the sanatorium he designed some of the first bent-plywood furnishings, which were later mass-produced in a factory he set up near Helsinki. In 1933 Finmar was set up to import and sell Aalto furniture in Britain, and two years later the Artek company was founded to produce and distribute Aalto furniture and glassware.

From the late 1930s through the 1940s, Aalto divided his time between Finland and the United States. He also became active in city planning, an interest that grew out of his designs for industrial communities such as the Toppila Sulfate Mill at Oulu (1930). In 1944 he was put in charge of redesigning war-damaged cities in Finland. His most notable contribution to city planning was the idea of constructing basic housing units designed to be expanded over a period of years.

Aalto's departure from the severely functional in architecture was already evident in his Finnish pavilions for the Paris Exposition of 1937 and the New York World's Fair of 1939. Abandoning the starkly functional cube, he turned to more organic design. Wood, stone, and brick are prominent in his later work, in which the volumes, as well as the materials of the building, are closely integrated with the surrounding landscape. The serpentine shape of his dormitory for the Massachusetts Institute of Technology (1947) is an example of the greater freedom of form in Aalto's later designs. Other outstanding examples of this period are the Finnish Institute of Technology at Otaniemi (1949), the civic center on the island of Säynätsalo (1949–1952), and the cultural center at Wolfsburg, Germany (1963).

Bibliography: Reed, Peter, ed., *Alvar Aalto: Between Humanism and Materialism* (Abrams 1998); **Schildt, Göran,** *Alvar Aalto: The Complete Catalogue of Architecture, Design, and Art,* tr. by Timothy Binham (Rizzoli Intl. Pubns. 1994); **Schildt, Göran,** ed., *Alvar Aalto in His Own Words,* tr. by Timothy Binham (Rizzoli Intl. Pubns. 1998); **Weston, Richard,** *Alvar Aalto* (1995; reprint, Phaidon 1997).

AARAU, ä'rou, a city in Switzerland on the Aare River, 23 miles (37 km) west of Zürich. It is situated in a fertile plain, 1,100 feet (335 meters) above sea level, just south of the Jura Mountains. It is the capital of Aargau canton.

Aarau was founded in the 1200s. In 1415 the city of Bern took it from the Habsburgs. Aarau became the capital of the Helvetic Republic in 1798 and in 1803 joined the Swiss Confederation.

Aarau has a medieval castle, a library rich in records of Swiss history, and scientific, ethnographic, and historic museums. The city is particularly noted for its bell manufacturing. Scientific instruments and cotton textiles are also important among the manufactures of Aarau. Population: 16,481 (1990 census).

AARDVARK, ärd'värk, an insect-eating mammal native to Africa south of the Sahara and Sudan. The aardvark (*Orycteropus afer*) is the sole member of Orycteropodidae, the single family of the order Tubulidentata.

Physical Characteristics and Habitat. The aardvark has a combined head-and-body length of 3 to 5 feet (100 to 158 cm) and a thick muscular tail that is 17 to 28 inches (44 to 71 cm) long. It weighs from 110 to 154 pounds (50 to 70 kg) and is characterized by an elongated head, large ears, a piglike snout, and a massive body covered with a thick skin and sandy-colored, bristly hair. The aardvark's legs are short and powerful; its feet have blunt claws that are used to burrow and to open ant and termite hills.

O. afer is found in a wide range of habitats, including savannas, woodlands, grassy plains, and bush country. It tends to be particularly attracted to sandy soil.

Reproduction and Development. The aardvark's breeding season appears to vary according to location; for example, aardvarks in the Democratic Republic of the Congo (in Equatorial Africa) give birth in October or November, while those in South Africa do so between May and July, and species members in Botswana, also in southern Africa, give birth from May to August. The animal's gestation period is about seven months and typically culminates in the birth of a single offspring. The newborn weighs close to 4½ pounds (2 kg).

The offspring emerges from the burrow after about two weeks. Over the next several months the young aardvark and its mother will live in a number of different burrows, with the juvenile accompanying its parent until the next mating season. *O. afer* appears to reach sexual maturity by two years of age. Research indicates that females may give birth approximately once a year or less.

The aardvark (*Orycteropus afer*) forages with its snout to the ground, gathering insects with its tongue.

© NIGEL J. DENNIS/PHOTO RESEARCHERS, INC.

Behavior and Diet. The aardvark usually sleeps during the day and hunts at night. It is a rapid digger, constructing burrows about 10 feet (3 meters) long. A shy and slow-moving animal with extremely acute hearing, it seeks its burrow at the least provocation. Aardvarks consistently bury their feces, behavior that may somehow help them to either attract or avoid other aardvarks or animals of other species.

O. afer is normally solitary except during breeding season or those periods when a mother is accompanied by her offspring. Although females tend to remain in one area, males are generally more nomadic. The aardvark feeds primarily on ants and termites. The animal's long slimy tongue is used to gather the insects, which the aardvark finds by foraging with its snout to the ground, by digging into nests, or by attacking large armies of insects that have left the nest. Aardvarks feed on termites mainly during the wet season and on ants chiefly in the dry season, probably because termites tend to be inactive, and therefore less accessible, during the dry season. *O. afer* also consumes a species of wild cucumber, perhaps to obtain water during the dry season.

Economic Impact. The aardvark is eaten by some African tribes, and its hide is used to make bracelets and other articles. Because aardvark burrows can cause damage to farming equipment and earthen dams, there have been efforts to reduce the species' population in regions where this damage may occur. However, the elimination of insectivorous animals from an agricultural area can result in heavy insect-related crop damage.

Bibliography: Nowak, Ronald M., *Walker's Mammals of the World*, 5th ed., vols. 1 and 2 (Johns Hopkins Univ. Press 1991); Shoshani, Jeheskel, et al., "Orycteropus afer," *Mammalian Species*, no. 300 (Jan. 15, 1988); Wilson, Don E., and DeeAnn M. Reeder, eds., *Mammal Species of the World: A Taxonomic and Geographic Reference*, 2d ed. (Smithsonian Inst. Press 1993).

AARDWOLF, ärd'wŏŏlf, a hyenalike mammal found in southern and eastern Africa. The aardwolf (*Proteles cristatus*) belongs to the family Hyaenidae, in the order Carnivora, class Mammalia.

Physical Characteristics and Habitat. The aardwolf has a combined head-and-body length of about 22 to 31.5 inches (55 to 80 cm) and a shoulder height of around 27.6 to 36 inches (70 to 91.5 cm). The black-tipped, bushy tail is 8 to 12 inches (20 to 30 cm) long. The animal weighs between 20 and 31 pounds (9 to 14 kg), and its body fur is a coarse, black-striped, yellow gray, with a strip of hair running along the back that can be erected as a crest. The coat's underfur is long and loose. *P. cristatus* has sharp canines, but its jaws are weak and its cheek teeth are vestigial.

The aardwolf is found in a number of countries on the African continent, including Egypt, Tanzania, South Africa, and Zambia. It tends to inhabit plains and bush country.

Reproduction, Development, and Longevity. Limited data are available on aardwolf reproduction and development. Gestation may be 90 to 110 days long. In most of southern Africa females give birth in November and December, although they seem to be capable of breeding at various times of the year. Litter size appears to vary, with two or three offspring with each birth common in some areas but two to four being usual in southern Africa.

Males help to protect the young by guarding the den against black-backed jackals, possibly the aardwolf's greatest natural enemy. Cubs leave the den when they are about one month old and are weaned by the age of four months. Until they reach seven months of age, however, the offspring may still be accompanied by a parent while foraging, although just for a short period during the night, after which they will look for food by themselves. By the time the next year's litter is born, it is usual for young aardwolves to have left parental territory. Captive aardwolves have been known to live for more than 14 years.

Behavior and Diet. *P. cristatus* is primarily nocturnal and may live in the abandoned burrows of other animals, such as the aardvark, porcupine, and springhare, although it has been reported that in some cases it will dig its own burrow. Although aardwolves are usually solitary, individuals are seen with their mate. In winter several aardwolves may form a loose group.

P. cristatus is a territorial animal, marking its range with secretions from its anal glands. The aardwolf also defends itself by ejecting fluid from its anal glands as well as by using its sharp canine teeth and, to create the illusion of increased size, by making the crest on its back stand up. Because of its weak skull and jaws, the aardwolf feeds mainly on termites and insect larvae, which it digs out of the ground.

Environmental Status. Despite human encroachment into aardwolf habitats, the wild population

An 11-week-old female aardwolf (*Proteles cristatus*). Cubs leave the den at about one month of age.

© ROD WILLIAMS/BRUCE COLEMAN INC.

does not appear to have suffered a sharp decline. At one time the species was thought to be at some risk of becoming endangered, possibly because the animal's nocturnal habits and large territorial range made the aardwolf seem more scarce than it really is. Some farmers will shoot aardwolves in the belief that the species preys on lambs, although evidence indicates that the animals do not attack livestock. Aardwolves are also killed by packs of dogs that are used to hunt jackals and foxes.

Bibliography: Koehler, C. E., and P. R. K. Richardson, "*Proteles Cristatus,*" *Mammalian Species,* no. 363 (Oct. 23, 1990); Nowak, Ronald M., *Walker's Mammals of the World,* 5th ed., vols. 1 and 2 (Johns Hopkins Univ. Press 1991); Wilson, Don E., and DeeAnn M. Reeder, eds., *Mammal Species of the World: A Taxonomic and Geographic Reference,* 2d ed. (Smithsonian Inst. Press 1993).

AARE RIVER, ä′rə, in central and north Switzerland, a tributary of the Rhine. It is also known as the Aar. Formed by Bernese Alps glaciers, it flows northwest through the valley of Hasli over Handegg Falls (150 feet, or 46 meters, high) and passes through the Gorge of the Aare. It expands into Lake Brienz and then into Lake Thun. Navigable from the city of Thun, it flows through the capital city of Bern and turns north, then northeast along the southern slopes of the Jura past the towns of Solothurn and Aarau. After breaking through the mountain ridge, it empties into the Rhine opposite Waldshut, Germany. Its total length is 175 miles (282 km).

AARGAU, är′gou, a canton of Switzerland, in the extreme north of the country, on the German border west of Zürich canton. It is called *Argovie* in French. Its area of 542 square miles (1,404 sq km) consists mainly of spurs of the Alps and the Jura Mountains and numerous fertile valleys. Timber is plentiful, and fruit, vegetables, and vines are cultivated. The capital is Aarau.

The area was conquered by the Franks in the 5th century. It was a Habsburg fief from 1173 to 1415, when it was divided between Bern and Lucerne. It became a member of the Swiss Confederation in 1803. The suppression of Aargau's monasteries by reformers in 1841 led to the formation of the Sonderbund, or Secession League, of Catholic cantons in 1846. The subsequent defeat of the Sonderbund enabled Switzerland to create a more centralized state in 1848. Population: 523,114 (1995 est.).

AARHUS, ôr′hoōs, the second largest city in Denmark. Situated in east Jutland on a bay of the Kattegat, it is the chief port for the Jutland peninsula and the seat of Aarhus amt (county). Aarhus (Århus) has been a bishopric since 948. Its cathedral, begun about 1200, is among Denmark's finest. Other points of interest include Old Town, with its many old buildings, and the functionally styled town hall. There are shipbuilding yards, iron foundries, and textile mills. The University of Aarhus was founded in 1928. Population: 619,232 (1995 est.).

AARON, âr′ən, a figure in Hebrew history first mentioned in the Bible in connection with Moses and the Exodus. He is a more important figure in later than in earlier biblical writings. In the earlier sections of the Old Testament he is the brother of Moses (Exodus 4:14) and Miriam (Exodus 15:20). In Egypt he is spokesman for Moses, accomplishing mysterious acts before Pharaoh and bringing plagues upon the land to persuade Pharaoh to release the Hebrews from servitude. Aaron, however, has no power apart from Moses; he is simply the latter's mouthpiece (Exodus 4–11).

On the other hand, sections of the Old Testament written after the Exile of the Hebrews in Babylon (6th century B.C.) describe Aaron as a leader only slightly inferior to Moses himself. Like Moses, he can receive laws from God directly (Numbers 18). With Moses, he takes a census of the people (Numbers 1). Israel murmurs against two leaders, Moses and Aaron (Exodus 10:2). With Moses, Aaron disobeys God at Meribah and is punished by having his life end before the nation reaches Canaan (Numbers 20:24). Aaron is presented as the ancestor of all legitimate priests, having been consecrated high priest by Moses (Exodus 29:4–9; 30:30). Aaron alone is permitted to enter the Holy of Holies on the Day of Atonement (Leviticus 16). He represents the tribe of Levi, and only his descendants in this tribe are rightful priests.

In contrast, portions of the Old Testament written at earlier dates make no such claim for Aaron's importance. Ezekiel traces the origin of Jerusalem's priesthood only to Zadok (Ezekiel 40:46; 44:16), a priest who helped guard the Ark of the Covenant during Absalom's rebellion against David (2 Samuel 15:24–29). In the earliest accounts of the Exodus, religious rites are under the direction of Joshua (Exodus 24:13), and Moses alone is the high priest.

AARON, Henry Louis, âr′ən (1934–   ), American baseball player who in 1974 eclipsed Babe Ruth's lifetime record of 714 major league home runs. Hank Aaron was born in Mobile, Ala., on Feb. 5, 1934. In 1952, after a few weeks with a

Hank Aaron broke Babe Ruth's home run record in 1974.

barnstorming black baseball team, he joined Eau Claire (Wis.) of the Northern League as an infielder. He spent the 1953 season with Jacksonville (Fla.) of the Sally League and in 1954 was elevated to the major leagues, breaking into the Milwaukee Braves's starting lineup as a right fielder. Aaron moved with the Braves to Atlanta in 1966.

A right-handed hitter with unusually powerful wrists, Aaron produced line drives as well as home runs, winning the National League's batting championship in 1956 and 1959 and its Most Valuable Player award in 1957. He led the league four times in home runs (1957, 1963, 1966, 1967) and runs batted in (1957, 1960, 1963, 1966), and he received the Golden Glove Award for fielding in 1958, 1959, and 1960. His career batting average was .305. He earned the nickname "Hammerin' Hank" for his remarkable ability.

Lacking the flamboyance of a Babe Ruth or a Willie Mays, Aaron was seldom given his due as a hitter until it became evident that his extraordinary consistency was carrying him close to many lifetime marks, particularly Ruth's record of 714 home runs. Aaron tied that record on April 4, 1974, in Cincinnati. In a night game in Atlanta on April 8, he drove number 715—a fast ball thrown by Al Downing of the Los Angeles Dodgers—over the left-centerfield wall.

Aaron retired at the end of the 1976 season with a record of 3,771 hits, 2,297 runs batted in, and 755 home runs. He was inducted into the baseball Hall of Fame on Aug. 1, 1982. Aaron became one of the first blacks in major league baseball to move into an upper-level management position when he became Atlanta's vice president of player development.

BILL BRADDOCK
"New York Times"

Bibliography: Aaron, Hank, and Lonnie Wheeler, I Had a Hammer: The Hank Aaron Story (HarperCollins 1991); Tolan, Sandy, Me and Hank: A Boy and His Hero, Twenty-five Years Later (Free Press 2000).

ABABDA, ə-bab'də, an Arabic-speaking tribe, inhabiting the hilly area of northeastern Sudan and southeastern Egypt. The most northerly of the modern Beja, the Ababda number approximately 20,000. They are mainly pastoral nomads, but an increasing number are adopting a sedentary way of life. The religion they practice is Islam. The Ababda are the traditional guardians of the trade route across the Nubian Desert from the Sudan to Egypt.

ABACA. See CORDAGE; HEMP.

ABACO AND CAYS, ab'ə-kō, kāz, the northernmost district of the Bahama Islands. It consists of two long narrow islands, collectively called Abaco, and the nearby islets or cays. The two main islands—Great Abaco (about 100 miles long) and Little Abaco (about 30) to the northwest—are separated by a narrow channel. The area of the district is 776 square miles.

Most of the present inhabitants make their living from farming, fishing, boatbuilding, and tourism. The resort areas are mainly on the cays just east of Great Abaco.

Abaco was settled by Loyalists from the United States after the Revolutionary War. Population: 10,003 (1990 census).

ABACUS, ab'ə-kəs, a device used to perform arithmetic operations such as addition, subtraction, multiplication, and division. In its most widely used form, the abacus is a rectangular wooden frame with several parallel rods running across the width of the frame. Beads are strung on the rods and are used as counters. In a decimal system of numeration, the separate rods, beginning at the right, represent units, tens, hundreds, thousands, and so on. On such an abacus there are usually ten beads on each rod, so that each bead stands for a unit of place value. Thus, each bead on the units rod represents 1, each bead on the tens rod represents 10, and each bead on the hundreds rod stands for 100, and so on.

Operating the Abacus. Arithmetic operations are performed on the abacus by moving the beads from one side of the frame to the other. Thus to set up the number 23, three beads on the units rod would be moved to one side of the frame and two beads on the tens rod would be moved to the same side.

Addition. To add the number 14 to the number 23 already set up on the abacus, four beads on the units rod and one bead on the tens rod are moved to join the existing beads at one side of the frame. The abacus will then have three beads on the tens rod and seven beads on the units rod grouped together and thus produce the sum (37).

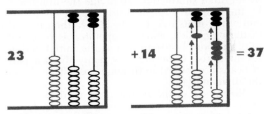

Abacus addition, such as 23+14, is performed by moving beads up the rods. Two beads on the tens rod and three beads on the units rod are initially moved to one side of the frame. The movement in the same direction of one bead on the tens rod and four beads on the units rod produces the sum (37).

Subtraction. To subtract the number 16 from the number 37 (already set up on the abacus as a result of the operation described above), six beads are moved from the group of seven on the units rod and one bead is moved away from the group of three beads on the tens rod. These operations will leave one bead on the units rod and

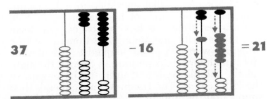

Abacus subtraction, such as 37−16, is performed by moving beads down each rod. Three beads on the tens rod and seven beads on the units rod are initially moved to one side of the frame. Moving down one bead on the tens rod and six beads on the units rod produces the difference (21).

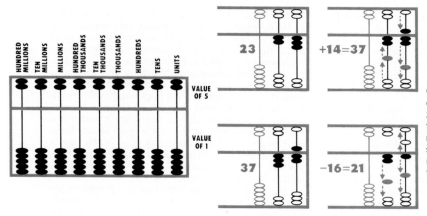

On a Chinese abacus (*far left*), each bead moved above the horizontal bar represents five times the place value of each vertical rod. Addition (*upper right*) and subtraction (*lower right*) require moving the beads toward or away from the horizontal bar.

two beads on the tens rod on one side of the abacus and thus produce the difference (21).

Multiplication. Multiplication is performed on the abacus by repeated addition. To multiply the number *12* by the number *4*, two beads are moved to an end of the units rod and one bead is moved to the same end of the tens rod. Performing this operation a total of four times will group eight beads at the end of the units rod and four beads at the end of the tens rod and thus produce the product (48).

Division. Division is performed on the abacus by repeated subtraction. To divide the number *8* by the number *2*, eight beads are set up at one end of the units rod. Two beads are then moved to the other side, and this operated is repeated until no more beads are left at the initial end of the units rod. Counting how many times a pair of beads are moved until none are left produces the dividend (4).

History. The abacus has been used for thousands of years and has appeared in various forms in different countries. The name, from the Semitic word *abq*, meaning "dust," comes from the primitive form of the abacus, a board covered with fine dust. Among the Hindus it was a wooden tablet covered with pipe clay, on which was sprinkled purple sand, the numerals being written with a stylus. This form was used by the ancient Greeks; Iamblichus asserts that Pythagoras taught geometry as well as arithmetic on an abacus. Its use among the Romans of the classical period also is well attested.

The most common ancient form of the abacus, which Herodotus tells us was used by the Egyptians and the Greeks and which has many modifications, is a board with beads sliding in grooves or on rods in a frame. Another form of abacus was a ruled table, on which counters were placed, somewhat like checkers on a backgammon board; the game of backgammon, in fact, was derived from this type of abacus. This form was the favorite one among the Romans, whose numerals were not at all adapted to calculation, and it maintained its position in Europe throughout the Middle Ages and until the latter part of the 16th century. The Hindu-Arabic numerals then supplanted the Roman numerals, and the abacus as an aid to calculation was thought superfluous in western Europe.

Small merchants in many countries still use the abacus to figure their accounts. It is widely used in India and appears in the form of the *suan pan* in China, the *soroban* in Japan, and the *tschoty* in Russia. The Chinese abacus has a separate division horizontally across the frame, below which units are counted up to five; the fives are transferred to the upper section, where each bead stands for five units. In the United States and many other countries, arithmetic teachers often use an abacus to give young students a better understanding of place value in the decimal system of numeration.

Bibliography

Dilson, Jesse, *The Abacus* (St. Martin's 1994).
Kojima Takashi, *The Japanese Abacus: Its Use and Theory* (Charles E. Tuttle 1954).
Moon, Parry Hiram, *The Abacus: Its History, Its Design, Its Possibilities in the Modern World* (Gordon & Breach 1971).
Nihon Shoko Kaigisho, *Soroban, the Japanese Abacus: Its Use and Practice* (Charles E. Tuttle 1967).
Yoshino Yozo, *The Japanese Abacus Explained* (1937; reprint, Dover 1963).

ABADAN, ä-bä-dän′, formerly one of Iran's largest cities. During the Iran-Iraq war the city was leveled by Iraqi aerial and artillery bombardments. Prior to that period, the city had been one of the major petroleum-refining centers of the world. A port city, Abadan is at the northern end of Abadan Island, on the left bank of the Shatt al-Arab, a short river formed by the confluence of the Tigris and the Euphrates rivers. The city is situated in Khuzistan province, about 30 miles (48 km) east-southeast of Basra, Iraq, and 30 miles north of the Persian Gulf. The climate is extremely hot and humid for over half the year.

Abadan developed as a town after oil was discovered in the area in 1908. The Anglo-Persian Oil Company (later known as the Anglo-Iranian Oil Company) established the first refinery there in 1909 and at the same time made the city the terminus of a series of pipelines from the rich oil fields to the east and northeast. By 1950 Abadan was the world's largest refining center, having grown from a small village to one of Iran's largest and most important industrial cities in less than 40 years. By 1960 the refinery had a capacity of about 185 million barrels a day.

Prior to the Iran-Iraq war (1980–1988), Abadan was a very busy port, possessing deepwater jetties for loading tankers and freighters. The city's chief industries, after oil refining, were port handling and construction. The war, however, destroyed the facilities and reduced the city's population by some 90%. After the war, reconstruction began and oil production resumed although on a smaller scale. The port was reopened in 1993. Population: 206,073 (1996 census).

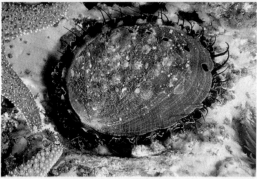

© NORBERT WU/PETER ARNOLD, INC.

A row of holes in the abalone's shell is used to discharge waste respiratory water as well as eggs or sperm.

ABALONE, ab-ə-lō'nē, any of a group of soft-bodied, one-shelled invertebrates found in warm seas throughout the world. The upper part of the abalone shell is broadly flattened and often ear-shaped in outline. A curving row of holes pierces the left side of the shell, and gill filaments extend through the holes, which also serve for the discharge of waste respiratory water and of sexual products. The older holes become closed with a chalky deposit, and new holes are formed as the shell grows; but the number of holes is not constant and does not indicate the age of the animal. The shell's outer surface is rough and dull, but the main substance and inner surface of the shell are a brilliant mother-of-pearl used in the jewelry and novelty trades. The fleshy foot, or body, of the abalone has two feelers, a pair of stalked eyes, and a central snout.

Abalones, also known as earshells or sea-ears, are gastropod mollusks belonging to the family Haliotidae, in the order Archaeogastropoda, class Gastropoda. The name *abalone* formerly was restricted to those members of the genus *Haliotis* inhabiting Californian waters but is now more widely applied. Abalone is harvested for its edible meat, which has been particularly popular in Asia and in California.

Bibliography: Bevelander, Gerrit, *Abalone: Gross and Fine Structure* (Boxwood Press 1988); **Hahn, Kirk O.,** ed., *Handbook of Culture of Abalone and Other Marine Gastropods* (CRC Press 1989); **Leighton, David L.,** *The Biology and Culture of the California Abalones* (Dorrance 2000); **Raloff, J.,** "A First: Scientists Oust a Marine Invader," *Science News* 156 (Sept. 4, 1999):151; **Spotts, Peter N.,** "Seashells Yield Tough Secrets," *Christian Science Monitor* 89 (Aug. 19, 1997):12.

ABANDONMENT, ə-ban'dən-mənt, a legal term that has a variety of meanings depending on the subject matter to which it refers. Besides tangible property, some things that can be abandoned are persons and personal relations, lawsuits and other legal proceedings, public offices, contracts, trusts, copyrights, patents, and trademarks.

As applied to property, abandonment means the unqualified relinquishment of possession and ownership without transferring it to any other person. It is roughly the equivalent of throwing property away. Since no one owns abandoned property, it can be appropriated by the first person who takes possession of it.

Abandonment, as distinguished from loss, must be voluntary and accompanied by an intention to part with ownership permanently. It also differs from dereliction (in maritime law) and from dedication to public use, but the distinctions are somewhat technical.

Personal property, whether it is a tangible thing, such as a ship, or an intangible thing, such as a claim against a bank for money deposited, can be the subject of abandonment. The same is true for incorporeal rights in land, such as franchises, easements, water rights, and mining claims. Real property cannot be abandoned, as a general rule.

As applied to marine or fire insurance, abandonment is a technical term meaning the act by which the insured's interest in property is relinquished to the insurer after "constructive total loss." There is constructive total loss where "actual total loss" (that is, complete destruction) appears unavoidable or where the cost of saving the ship or goods would exceed their value when preserved or repaired. As applied to relations between husband and wife, abandonment means desertion. As applied to the relation of parent to child, it means neglect or failure to support, which is generally punishable as a criminal offense.

In bankruptcy, abandonment means the turnover of a piece of the debtor's property to a creditor. This usually occurs when the creditor holds a "perfected security interest" (the property is collateral for a loan) in the property and "the amount of the security interest" (amount due on the loan) is more than the property is worth.

RICHARD L. HIRSHBERG*
Attorney at Law

ABASCAL, José Fernando, ä-bäs-käl' (1743–1821), Spanish statesman and soldier. Born in Oviedo, he entered the Spanish army in 1762, rising to the rank of brigadier general during the campaigns against Napoleon. He became governor of Cuba in 1796. In 1804 he was appointed viceroy of Peru, where he successfully suppressed local uprisings by the Creoles. He also led campaigns against rebels in Ecuador, Bolivia, Argentina, and Chile. For his efforts he was created Marquess de la Concordia in 1812. In 1816 he was recalled to Spain, where he died five years later in Madrid.

ABATE, Nicolò dell', ä-bä'te (between 1509 and 1512–1571), Italian painter whose work is in the Mannerist style of the school of Bologna. Although not considered a major Mannerist painter, Nicolò (or Niccolò) dell'Abate, a member of the first Fontainebleau school, exerted considerable influence in France, where he is credited with helping to introduce landscape painting. His surname is also spelled *Abati, Abbate,* or *Abbato.*

Born in Modena between 1509 and 1512, dell'Abate probably first studied with his father, a stuccoist. In the early 1540s, for the Boiardo family castle near Modena, he executed frescoes of the *Aeneid* that depicted battles, landscapes, and portraits of music-making family members. In 1547 he went to Bologna, where he saw works by, among others, Giorgio Vasari and Parmigianino, the latter of whose influence, along with that of Correggio, had earlier shown itself in dell'Abate's art. Among his early extant works are friezes (c. 1550) in the Palazzo Poggi, now part of the University of Bologna.

Armed with decorating skills acquired in Bologna, dell'Abate went to France sometime before 1552. He assisted Francesco Primaticcio of Bologna painting frescoes for the royal palace at Fontainebleau for Francis I and Henry II. These

The Continence of Scipio (c. 1555; Louvre) is by Nicolò dell'Abate, a painter in Fontainebleau for some 20 years.

works—among them the decoration of the Galerie d'Ulysse and the musical-themed Galerie Henri II—were influential in popularizing the Italian style of painting. Dell'Abate also produced easel paintings, largely of mythological subjects whose elegant figures inhabit idyllic landscapes, as in *The Death of Eurydice* (c. 1552–1571; National Gallery, London). His *Continence of Scipio* (c. 1555; Louvre, Paris) depicts a group of dignified figures. Dell'Abate, whose paintings presaged the works of Claude Lorrain and Nicolas Poussin, died in 1571, probably in Fontainebleau.

ABATEMENT, ə-bāt'mənt, legal term meaning discontinuation, cessation, destruction, or elimination. The term may be used in different contexts.

Abatement of an action refers to the cessation of a particular judicial proceeding because of some fact not affecting the merits of the controversy. The most common grounds for abatement are the pendency of another suit or the death of a party. To abate a later suit, the pending suit must be in the same jurisdiction with the same parties and legal issues. At common law, death of a party abated an action but did not necessarily extinguish the legal right on which it depended. Statutes in most U.S. states now provide that the action survives if the legal right survives. Other grounds for abatement of actions are defects of the parties (such as misnomer or incapacity); lack of jurisdiction of the court; dissolution of a corporation; premature commencement of an action; and transfer of a party's interest in the lawsuit. In a court of equity the abatement of a cause of action results in a suspension of the proceeding. Unlike a common-law abatement, which permanently extinguishes the suit, the abatement of a suit in equity may be revived.

Abatement of legacies means the destruction or reduction of certain bequests, by operation of law, where an estate's assets are insufficient.

Abatement of a nuisance means the elimination, whether by the party injured or through suit instituted by the party, of that which endangers life or health, gives offense to the senses, violates the laws of decency, or obstructs reasonable and comfortable use of property. The law allows an injured party to remove or destroy the nuisance personally, providing it is done without unnecessary destruction or breach of the peace.

RICHARD L. HIRSHBERG
Attorney at Law

ABAUZIT, Firmin, à-bō-zēt' (1679–1767), French scholar and scientist, praised for his learning by such figures as Rousseau, Voltaire, and Isaac Newton. Except for a few visits to the Netherlands and England, he spent most of his life in Geneva, Switzerland, where he served as city librarian.

Abauzit was born of Protestant parents in Uzès, France, on Nov. 11, 1679. In 1685, after the revocation of the Edict of Nantes canceled the civil and religious liberties previously enjoyed by Protestants, he emigrated with his mother and elder brother to Geneva. Educated in Geneva, Abauzit showed great proficiency in languages, theology, and science. He traveled in the Netherlands, where he met the philosopher-critic Pierre Bayle. On a trip to England he met Isaac Newton and made valuable corrections in his *Principia Mathematica*. King William III of England offered to be his patron, but Abauzit declined in favor of returning to Geneva. There he accepted a life position as city librarian, which afforded him leisure for his scholarly interests. He died in Geneva on March 20, 1767.

A scholar of wide-ranging interests and vast erudition, Abauzit assisted in translating the New Testament into French and wrote a number of theological and archaeological papers. He also edited and contributed to a history of the city of Geneva, and wrote articles for Rousseau's dictionary of music. It is said that when a visitor told Voltaire that he had come to see a genius, Voltaire inquired whether he had ever met Abauzit.

ABBA, à'-bà, Swedish pop music quartet that experienced huge global success from 1974 through 1982. Its infectious songs, almost always rendered in English and marked by a complex production sound, had catchy melodies, memorable harmonies, and often overdramatic lyrics. Among the first popular musicians to make promotional videos, the group featured in *ABBA: The Movie* (1977), an early example of the rock-film genre.

ABBA is an acronym for the first names of members Anni-Frid ("Frida") Lyngstad (born on Nov. 15, 1945, in Ballangen, Norway), Björn Ulvaeus (April 25, 1945, Göteborg, Sweden), Benny Andersson (Dec. 16, 1946, Stockholm), and Agnetha Fältskog (April 5, 1950, Jönköping, Sweden). By 1969 musicians Ulvaeus and Andersson were writing and recording songs, fostered by record company owner, and future ABBA manager, Stikkan "Stig" Anderson. Ulvaeus later married solo artist Fältskog (1971), and Andersson wed singer Lyngstad (1978); both couples later divorced.

In the early 1970s the four recorded their first album, placed third in Sweden's preliminary Eurovision Song Contest, and took the name *ABBA*. In 1974 they won the Eurovision competition with their jaunty love song *Waterloo*, which made the top ten on pop charts around the world. Later successful singles included *Fernando* (1976), *Dancing Queen* (1976), and *Take a Chance on Me* (1978). Among their hit albums were *ABBA* (1975) and *Arrival* (1976). ABBA was one of the world's most successful pop groups from the mid-1970s until their split in 1982, after which the four continued to work in the music industry; among other endeavors, the women made solo albums and the men collaborated with Tim Rice on the musical *Chess* (London, 1986; New York, 1988). Although ABBA no longer existed, their music remained popular in many countries. Two 1994 Australian films featuring ABBA songs, *Muriel's Wedding* and *The Adventures of Priscilla, Queen of the Desert*, helped spur an ABBA revival around the world, whose apex was arguably *Mamma Mia!*, a musical made up of ABBA songs woven around a frothy love story; it premiered in London in 1999 and on Broadway in 2001 and toured extensively.

ABBA MARI, ab'bä mä'rē, a French rabbi and scholar of the late 13th and early 14th centuries who was one of the leaders of the Jewish community of Montpellier in France. His full name was Abba Mari ben Moses Ha-Yarhi; he was also known as Don Astruc of Lunel. A strong opponent of Maimonides and his rationalistic philosophy, Abba Mari persuaded Solomon ben Adret of Barcelona, one of the greatest rabbinical authorities of his day, to issue a ban in 1305 against secular and philosophical studies by students under the age of 30. A counterban was then issued by Jacob ben Makhir ibn Tibbon, a leading astronomer, mathematician, and translator of scholarly and philosophical works from Arabic into Hebrew, who also lived in Montpellier. The dispute was ended, still unresolved, by the expulsion of the Jews from France in 1306. Abba Mari went to Arles and thence to Perpignan, where he compiled the story of the controversy in a book entitled *Minhat Kenaot (Offering of Zeal)*.

RAPHAEL PATAI
Theodor Herzl Institute

ABBADID, ab'ə-did, a Muslim Arab dynasty that ruled southwest Spain for most of the 11th century. It was the greatest of the minor Muslim dynasties (in Spanish called *taifas*) that inherited the domains of the Umayyad caliphate in Spain. From their capital, Seville, the Abbadids gradually absorbed the territories of their fellow taifas until, under Mutamid (reigned 1069–1091), they ruled most of the Iberian Peninsula south of the Guadiana River.

Expansion brought the Abbadids face to face with the growing power of Christian Spain. After the Spaniards under Alfonso VI of Castile and León captured Toledo in 1085, the taifas were forced to appeal for help from the Almoravid dynasty in Morocco. In 1086 the Almoravids crushed Alfonso at Sagrajas and later returned to conquer the Abbadids themselves. Abbadid rule ended with Mutamid's exile in 1091.

J. F. P. HOPKINS
Cambridge University

ABBADO, Claudio, ä-bä'dō (1933–   ), Italian conductor who was known for his broad repertory and analytical conducting style. Abbado was born in Milan on June 26, 1933. His father was a concert violinist, teacher, and musicologist; his mother, a children's writer and pianist. He studied piano with his father from the age of 8, and when he was 16, he entered the Milan Conservatory, studying conducting and graduating in 1955. Later he furthered his conducting studies at the Accademia Chigiano, Siena, and with Hans Swarowsky at the Vienna Academy of Music, where he was

© CLIVE BARDA/PAL/TOPHAM/THE IMAGE WORKS

Claudio Abbado rehearses the Gustav Mahler Jugendorchester (which he cofounded) in Edinburgh in 1999.

first exposed to the Austro-German repertory that figured largely in his later career.

In 1958, while studying in Massachusetts at the Berkshire Music Center at Tanglewood, summer home of the Boston Symphony Orchestra, Abbado won the Center's Koussevitzky Prize for outstanding student conductor. After returning to Italy, he made his symphonic and operatic debuts in Trieste and became an instructor in chamber music at the Parma Conservatory. In 1963 he won the first Mitropoulos International Competition in New York City, which included a season's assistantship with Leonard Bernstein at the New York Philharmonic. He made his Vienna Philharmonic Orchestra debut in 1965 and conducted both the London Symphony and Berlin Philharmonic orchestras for the first time the following year.

Abbado began his long, productive association with La Scala, Milan, in 1960, serving as its music director from 1968 to 1986. While in Milan he conducted not only the traditional Italian repertory but also contemporary opera. Concurrent with some of his La Scala years were his positions as guest conductor of the Vienna Philharmonic Orchestra, begun in 1971, and music director of the London Symphony Orchestra (1979–1988). He left La Scala for the Vienna State Opera, where he was music director until 1991. In 1987 he was named *Generalmusikdirektor* of the city of Vienna, and from 1989 to 2002 he was principal conductor and music director of the Berlin Philharmonic Orchestra. Interested in furthering young musical talent, Abbado was a founder of the European Community Youth Orchestra (1978) and the Gustav Mahler Jugendorchester (1986). In 1994 he became artistic director of the Salzburg Easter Festival, whose scope he broadened to include prizes for literature and art as well as music.

Abbado's conducting style was characterized by rhythmic firmness—which, as some music critics noted, could border on rigidity—as well as detailed analysis of texture, although refinement and subtlety of interpretation sometimes eluded him. From the late 20th century he was praised for inspired and imaginative performances of both the Austro-German and modern repertory.

VADIM PROKHOROV
Author of "Russian Folk Songs"

ABBAS, ab-bäs' (566–653), the paternal uncle of the prophet Mohammed who was the founder of Islam. He was also the great-grandfather of Abu'l-Abbas as-Saffah, founder of the Abbasid dynasty, which was named for Abbas. His full Arabic name was al-Abbas Ibn Abd al-Muttalib.

Abbas was a rich merchant in Mecca, and at first opposed his nephew Mohammed's innovations. Fighting against Mohammed in the Battle of Badr in 624, he was taken prisoner, but was later released. He subsequently became a convert and an important supporter of Islam. He joined Mohammed in his march on Mecca in 630, and participated in the Battle of Hunayn shortly afterward. At Hunayn he is said to have turned the tide in favor of the Muslim forces by shouting loudly at a crucial moment. Abbas later settled in Medina, where he died in 653.

ABBAS I, ab-bäs' (1813–1854), a pasha of Egypt who during his brief reign undid much of the progress achieved by his grandfather, Mohammed Ali. He succeeded his uncle Ibrahim Pasha as regent of Egypt in 1848. A year later, following Mohammed Ali's death, he became pasha. Opposed to the modernizing reforms instituted by Mohammed Ali, Abbas closed schools and factories and limited governmental activities. He also abolished trade monopolies and reduced the strength of the standing army by one half. He distrusted European, especially French, ideas and influence and dismissed most of his grandfather's foreign advisers. With one exception, he forbade European concessions. In 1851 a British firm was authorized to construct the first railroad between Alexandria and Cairo.

In 1853, during the Crimean War, Abbas demonstrated his loyalty to the Ottoman empire by sending 15,000 men and his fleet to assist the Turks. Shortly thereafter, Abbas, who had isolated himself in his palace in Benha, was strangled to death by two of his slaves.

ABBAS II, ab-bäs' (1874–1944), the last khedive of Egypt, deposed by the British. Also called Abbas Hilmi Pasha, he was a descendant of Mohammed Ali. He was educated in Vienna and succeeded his father, Mohammed Tewfik Pasha, as khedive of Egypt on Jan. 8, 1892.

Although nominally under Turkish suzerainty, Egypt had been occupied by Britain since 1882. The pro-Turkish Abbas was suspicious of British policy in Egypt. He resented the control exercised by the British consuls general, including Lord Cromer and Lord Kitchener, with whom he often came into conflict.

At the outbreak of World War I, Abbas was in Constantinople (now Istanbul) as a guest of the sultan of Turkey. He was recovering from wounds inflicted several months before by a would-be assassin. After Britain declared war on Turkey on Nov. 5, 1914, Abbas, who remained in Constantinople, was suspected of plotting against the British. On December 18, Britain made Egypt a British protectorate and terminated Turkish suzerainty. The following day Abbas was deposed in favor of his uncle Hussein Kamil, the eldest living descendant of Mohammed Ali. The title of khedive was abolished for that of sultan, which was replaced by the title of king in 1922.

During the war, Abbas lived in Constantinople and Vienna. After the war he remained in exile, chiefly in Switzerland. When Egypt became independent in 1922, his property was liquidated, and he was forbidden to enter Egypt. Abbas was excluded from succession to the throne, although the rights of his direct male descendants were

not affected. He published *A Few Words on the Anglo-Egyptian Settlement* in 1930. Abbas died in Geneva, Switzerland, on Dec. 21, 1944.

ABBAS I, ab-bäs' (1571–1629), shah of Persia from 1587 to 1629. Called *Abbas the Great*, he was an administrative genius and a superb military strategist who brought his nation more land, power, and riches than it ever again attained.

The son and successor of Shah Muhammad Khudabanda of the Safavid dynasty, Abbas was born on Jan. 27, 1571. In 1581 he was made nominal governor of Khurasan and was proclaimed shah of Persia when his father was deposed. He died in Mazanderan on Jan. 21, 1629.

Military Conquests. At the beginning of Abbas's reign, Persia was menaced from the east by the Uzbeks and from the west by the Ottoman Turks, who had annexed Persia's western provinces. Recognizing the Turks as the more formidable opponents, Abbas negotiated a treaty with them in 1590 confirming their conquests. He incorporated Gilan into his empire in 1592. He then concentrated his forces against the Uzbeks, whom he surprised and routed near Herat in 1598. He conquered Mazanderan and most of Afghanistan.

In 1602, after 15 years of preparation, Abbas marched westward to regain his lost provinces from the Turks. At Basra in 1605, with 60,000 men, he defeated a Turkish army of nearly twice as many troops. In 1618 Abbas routed the combined Turkish and Tatar armies and concluded a peace treaty restoring all the lost territory to Persia. He took Hormuz from the Portuguese in 1622 and broke his truce with the Turks in 1623, when he took from them both Baghdad and Diyarbakir. Abbas then ruled an empire that extended from the Tigris to the Indus rivers.

Domestic Policies. Inheriting his throne at a time of civil war and near anarchy, Abbas restored security and order throughout Persia. He introduced necessary laws, encouraged commerce, and built bridges, causeways, and way stations for trading caravans. He sought to unify his people by stressing their common Islamic heritage and once went on foot on an 800-mile pilgrimage to Meshed. He was also, however, tolerant toward Christians and receptive to foreign ideas. He established his capital at Isfahan and made it a magnificent, world-famous cultural center.

ABBAS, Ferhat, ab-bäs' (1899–1985), president of Algeria's first elected legislature after the nation gained independence in 1962. Born on Aug. 24, 1899, in Taher, Algeria, the son of a Muslim civil servant of the French colonial administration, Abbas attended French schools in Philippeville (later, Skikda) and Constantine, and then studied at the University of Algiers. He briefly served in the French Army before working as a pharmacist in Sétif.

Abbas first became actively involved in politics in 1938, when he helped organize the Algerian People's Union (Union Populaire Algérienne), which advocated equal rights for the Algerians and French under French colonial rule together with the maintenance of Algerian language and culture. Seeking to achieve Algerian independence by parliamentary means, he published the *Manifesto of the Algerian People* (1943), which called for an autonomous Algerian state as part of federative France. In the following year he cofounded the movement Friends of the Manifesto and Liberty (Amis du Manifeste et de la Liberté), which soon counted about 500,000 members. In 1946 he established and led the Democratic Union of the Algerian Manifesto (Union Democratique du Manifeste Algérien). For the next nine years Abbas, as a member of the French Constituent Assembly and the Algerian Assembly, attempted to cooperate with the French in setting up an Algerian state. In 1956, despairing of any progress, Abbas joined the revolutionary National Liberation Front (Front de Libération Nationale, or FLN), hoping to secure Algerian independence by revolution. He was elected president of the provisional government of the Algerian republic (based in Tunisia) in 1958.

When Algeria finally gained independence, in September 1962, after a bitter struggle with France, a constitutional assembly of the Algerian republic was formed with powers to draft a constitution. Abbas became its president, and Ahmed Ben Bella its premier. Once in power, Ben Bella outlawed opposition political parties except for the FLN; by the constitution of 1963 he created a presidential republic. As a symbolic protest against Ben Bella's authoritarianism, Abbas resigned from the presidency of the assembly. He was expelled from the FLN and, before being exiled, was held in detention by Ben Bella. Abbas was released in 1965, shortly before Houari Boumediene overthrew Ben Bella. Abbas, who died in Algiers on Dec. 24, 1985, was the author of several books, including *Le Jeune Algérien* (1931), *La Nuit coloniale* (1963), and *Autopsie d'une guerre* (1980).

Bibliography: Bennoune, Mahfoud, *Making of Contemporary Algeria, 1830–1987: Colonial Upheavals and Post-Independence Development* (Cambridge 1988); Horne, Alistair, *Savage War of Peace: Algeria, 1954–1962* (Viking Penguin 1987); Le Sueur, James D., *Uncivil War: Intellectuals and Identity Politics during the Decolonization of Algeria* (Univ. of Pa. Press 2001); Stone, Martin, *The Agony of Algeria* (Columbia Univ. Press 1997).

ABBASID, ab'ə-sid, a dynasty of 37 caliphs who were the titular rulers of the Islamic empire from 750 to 1258 A.D. The Abbasids were the second, the longest-lived, and the most renowned dynasty in Islam. The name of the dynasty comes from *al-Abbas,* the name of the uncle of the Prophet Muḥammad, through whom the Abbasids laid claim to the caliphate in opposition to their Umayyad predecessors in Damascus.

The rise of the Abbasids marked a fundamental change in Islamic civilization. Under the preceding Umayyad dynasty, the empire had been ruled from Syria by Arabs under the influence of Byzantine Syria and by Yemeni Arabs long domiciled in the area. The Abbasids reigned from Iraq, maintained standing armies, and based their culture to an ever-increasing degree on the highly developed Persian civilization.

Beginnings of the Dynasty. The Abbasids came to power by putting themselves, before the mid-700s, at the head of a coalition made up of Persians, Iraqis, members of the Shīī branch of Islam, and others who hoped to undermine the Umayyad regime. In 750, at the decisive battle of the Great Zab (a tributary of the Tigris River), the Umayyad Army was crushed. The Umayyad caliph, Marwan II, fled to Egypt, where he was slaughtered. Members of the Umayyad family were ruthlessly dealt with, but one of them, the youthful Abd ar-Rahman, escaped in disguise and reached Spain, where he established himself in 756 as an independent ruler. He laid the basis for a rival caliphate, the Umayyads of Córdoba.

Early Abbasid Caliphs. Abu'l-Abbas (reigned 750–754), the first Abbasid caliph, transferred the capital from Syria to Iraq. He assumed the title of as-Saffah ("the Bloodshedder") because he intended to rule with an iron hand.

Abu'l-Abbas was succeeded by his brother al-Mansur (reigned 754–775), who firmly established the new dynasty, chastised the Shīī, who expected a lion's share from the Umayyad heritage, and built a strongly fortified capital at Baghdad. The Persians, on whose military shoulders the Abbasids had climbed to the caliphate, also had to be removed. Al-Mansur, therefore, invited their leader, Abu Muslim al-Khurasani, to an interview and had him murdered.

Golden Age. The Abbasid empire reached its zenith under the fifth caliph, Harun ar-Rashid (reigned 786–809), who as a crown prince had attacked the Byzantine empire and exacted tribute from the regent, Irene. Harun exchanged embassies with Charlemagne, patronized learning, and maintained such a splendid court that his name has lived in legend and history as the unsurpassed Islamic monarch. During his reign and that of his son and successor, al-Mamun (reigned 813–833), translations were made from Syriac, Persian, and Greek writings, which for the first time brought Muslims into close contact with the scientific and philosophic thought of the day. Scientific works translated into Arabic included writings by Euclid, Ptolemy, Hippocrates, and Galen. In philosophy, Aristotle and Plato were accorded the highest place. The dean of translators was a Syrian Christian, Hunayn Ibn Ishaq (in Latin, Johannitius; 809–873), who presided over the House of Wisdom—a fusion of academy, library, and bureau of translation, established by al-Mamun.

Decline of the Abbasids. After the death of al-Mamun, the power of the Abbasids started to deteriorate. Al-Mamun's brother and successor, al-Mutasim (reigned 833–842), began the practice of using a bodyguard of Turkish slaves. The bodyguard became so unpopular with the people of Baghdad that the caliph had to move his capital to Samarra, 100 miles (160 km) up the Tigris River, which remained the capital for 56 years, during the reigns of eight successive caliphs. The caliphs were soon at the mercy of the Turkish soldiers, and the caliphate became a plaything to be disposed of at the pleasure of the commanding general. For about 200 years, caliphs continued to occupy the throne with little or no real power.

While the capital was at Samarra, there was a rebellion of slaves who had been imported from East Africa to work the saltpeter mines on the lower Euphrates River. One army after another was sent to put down the uprising, only to be cut to pieces. The rebellion lasted for about 13 years (870–883), taxing the government's resources to the utmost and contributing to the general disorder.

Various provinces meanwhile took advantage of the confusion to renounce their allegiance in part or in full to the central government. The Aghlabids of Tunisia had begun the process in 800. The more powerful Fatimids, who later ruled from Cairo, gave further impetus to the disintegration of the Abbasid empire when they established themselves as an independent dynasty in Tunisia in 909. The Fatimid caliphate belonged to the Shīī branch of Islam. It threatened the unity of Islam by challenging the Sunnī caliphate of the Abbasids in Baghdad.

Another but smaller Shīī state, the Hamdanid, arose in northern Syria with its capital at Aleppo. The most notable Hamdanid ruler was Sayf al-Dawlah (reigned 944–967), who patronized scientists, poets, and musicians, and developed a court that almost vied in grandeur with that of Baghdad in its heyday. Among those who enjoyed his patronage were the renowned poet al-Mutanabbi and the great musician al-Farabi. The Hamdanid armies clashed with the Byzantines several times, giving a foretaste of the warfare that was to follow during the Crusades.

Among the dynasties ruling new states east of Baghdad, the most important were the Persian Samanid dynasty of Transoxiana and Persia (874–999) and the Turkish Ghaznavid dynasty of Afghanistan and the Punjab (962–1186). Another Persian dynasty, the Buwayhid, arose in the center of the caliphate in 945 and held the Abbasid caliphs under its control for more than a century. The Buwayhids were Shīī and claimed descent from the Sassanids, whom the Arabs had displaced at the rise of Islam.

The Buwayhids were supplanted by the Seljuk Turks, who entered Baghdad in 1055. During the reigns of the first three Seljuk sultans, the political unity of Muslim western Asia was restored under the nominal leadership of the Abbasid caliph in Baghdad. However, as the Seljuk realm expanded, it became more fragmented.

In 1071, Alp Arslan, the second Seljuk sultan, won a decisive battle over the Byzantine forces at Manzikert, Armenia. He took the Byzantine emperor prisoner and opened the way for the influx of Turks, originally a Central Asian people, into Asia Minor. It was these Seljuk Turks with whom the Crusaders had to contend as they made their way from Constantinople to the Holy Land.

Last Abbasid Caliphs. Among the last caliphs, only an-Nasir (reigned 1180–1225) regained some of the temporal power that was associated with his high office. But the gain was only temporary. The empire continued to decline until the Mongol Hulagu, grandson of Genghis Khan, delivered the final blow in 1258. Hulagu captured and burned Baghdad, and executed the last caliph, al-Mustaasim.

See also CALIPHATE.

PHILIP K. HITTI
Princeton University

Bibliography

Brockelmann, Carl, *History of the Islamic Peoples* (Routledge 1980).
Cobb, Paul M., *White Banners: Contention in Abbasid Syria* (State Univ. of N.Y. Press 2001).
Hitti, Philip K., *History of the Arabs*, 10th rev. ed. (Palgrave Macmillan 2002).
Sourdel, Dominique, *Medieval Islam* (Methuen 1983).
Young, M. J. L., et al., eds., *Religion, Learning, and Science in the Abbasid Period* (Cambridge 1991).

ABBE, Cleveland, ab'ē (1838–1916), American meteorologist and astronomer who issued the first daily weather forecasts in the United States. Born in New York City on Dec. 3, 1838, Abbe earned a B.A. degree in 1857 and a master's degree in 1860 from the New York Free Academy (later, the College of the City of New York). He worked as a tutor of mathematics at Trinity Latin School in New York (1857–1858), an assistant professor of engineering at the Michigan State Agricultural College (1859), and a tutor in engineering at the University of Michigan (1859–1860), where he first became interested in astronomy. After assisting (1861–1864) the astronomer Benjamin Gould with telegraphic longitude determinations for the U.S. Coast and Geodetic Survey, he studied astronomy (1864–1866) under Otto Struve at the Imperial Observatory in Pulkovo, Russia, and served as a computer and assistant observer (1866–1868) at the U.S. Naval Observatory in Washington, D.C.

Appointed director of the Cincinnati Observatory in Ohio, Abbe on Sept. 1, 1869, began publishing daily weather bulletins, based on weather maps that he drew from telegraphed reports of weather conditions in other areas. These were the first scientific daily forecasts made public, although the Smithsonian Institution had earlier prepared similar reports for specialists. The popularity of Abbe's forecasts caused Congress in 1870 to establish the Weather Service within the U.S. Army Signal Office (later, Signal Corps). Abbe became its meteorologist in 1871 and began to distribute, nationwide, regular forecasts three times a day. His forecasts of "probable" storms earned him the nickname "Old Probabilities." When the service was reorganized as the U.S. Weather Bureau within the Department of Agriculture in 1891, he again was appointed meteorologist and remained until his retirement in 1916.

Abbe's *Report on Standard Time* (1879) helped bring about uniform standard time zones for the entire world. He was an adjunct professor of meteorology (1886–1905) at Columbian College (later, George Washington University) and a lecturer in meteorology (1896–1914) at Johns Hopkins University. Abbe died in Chevy Chase, Md., on Oct. 28, 1916. A brother, Robert Abbe, was a noted surgeon.

Bibliography: Abbe, Truman, *Professor Abbe and the Isobars: The Story of Cleveland Abbe, America's First Weatherman* (Vantage 1965); **Bartky, Ian R.,** *Selling the True Time: Nineteenth-Century Timekeeping in America* (Stanford Univ. Press 2000); **Humphreys, William J.,** "Biographical Memoir of Cleveland Abbe, 1838–1916," in *Biographical Memoirs/National Academy of Sciences* 8 (1919):469–508.

ABBE, Ernst, äb'ə (1840–1905), German physicist and industrialist who was a leader in the field of optics. Born in Eisenach in the grand duchy of Saxe-Weimar-Eisenach (later, part of Germany), on Jan. 23, 1840, Abbe studied physics at the universities of Göttingen and Jena, receiving his doctorate from the latter in 1861. He became a lecturer at Jena in 1863 and was appointed a professor of physics and mathematics there in 1870. Abbe began working for the Carl Zeiss optical firm in 1866 and became wealthy after accepting a partnership in the company in 1876. He became the sole owner of the firm after Zeiss died in 1888 and reorganized it as a business cooperative in 1896. Abbe died in Jena on Jan. 14, 1905.

Abbe in 1868 invented an apochromatic lens system that eliminated both the primary and secondary color distortion of microscopes and in 1870 used a condenser to give a high-powered even illumination in the field of view of microscopes. In 1874 he invented what became known as the Abbe refractometer, which measures the refractive index of substances. Abbe developed a clearer theoretical understanding of the limits to optical magnification and discovered what was later named the Abbe sine condition, which defines how a lens can form a sharp image without the defects of coma and spherical aberration.

ABBE, Robert, ab'ē (1851–1928), American surgeon who originated several surgical techniques and is credited as the founder of radiation cancer treatment in the United States. A brother of the meteorologist Cleveland Abbe, Robert was born in New York City on April 13, 1851. After earning his medical degree at Columbia University's College of Physicians and Surgeons, in 1874, Abbe began practicing general medicine in New York City. Within a few years he had also assumed surgical posts at New York's leading hospitals. He spent some time in Paris with the French physicists Marie and Pierre Curie, Nobel laureates renowned for their groundbreaking work in radiation. Abbe later became the first American surgeon to employ radium against cancer.

He was also a pioneer in the use of X rays for detecting kidney stones, in the use of catgut for sewing up surgical wounds, and in the practice of cutting nerve roots of the spinal cord to relieve pain. In addition, Abbe invented a device (Abbe's rings) used in surgery to join two parts of the intestine and devised another apparatus to treat constriction of the esophagus. He was also well-known for his work in plastic surgery, including in the correction of cleft lip. Abbe retired from active practice and teaching in 1923. He died in New York City on March 7, 1928.

ABBÉ, à-bā', the French title of respect for a member of the secular clergy, who is addressed formally as *Monsieur l'Abbé*. Originally, the term denoted an abbot of a monastery, but later it came to apply to any man entitled to wear secular clerical dress. By a concordat in 1516 between Pope Leo X and King Francis I, the French king gained the power to nominate secular clerics for the office of *abbé in commendum* (in trust), by which the holder would receive the benefice of a religious house. Sometimes this office went to nonclerics, who were expected to take holy orders unless exempted by a dispensation. In practice, however, they seldom took higher than minor orders, and often served as chaplains or tutors in noble households, or engaged in literary work. Until the French Revolution, *abbés* were an influential class in society, distinguished by their short violet robes.

ABBESS, ab'əs, the female superior of a community of nuns in certain orders of the Roman Catholic Church, such as the Benedictines, Cistercians, or Poor Clares. She is elected by her community and consecrated by the bishop of the diocese. She does not have the spiritual authority conferred on an abbot, and her jurisdiction is limited to administering the rule of her order and giving religious counsel. To become an abbess, a nun must be at least 40 years old and have been professed for 10 years.

ABBEVILLE, àb-vĕl', a town in France, in the department of the Somme and the region of Picardy, 25 miles (40 km) northwest of Amiens. It is situated on both banks of the Somme River, 12 miles (19 km) from its mouth, at the head of navigation. Located in an agricultural section, the town has a refinery to process sugar beets grown in the region. It is also noted for its textiles.

Abbeville has 17th-century fortifications built under the direction of the French military strategist Vauban. The Church of St-Vulfran, begun about 1488 during the reign of Louis XII, is a

The Church of St. Wolfram (St-Vulfran) in Abbeville, France, by the 19th-century English artist Samuel Prout.

good example of late Gothic architecture. The area around Abbeville is famous for its fossils and relics of primitive humans. The Abbevillian culture of the Lower Paleolithic Period takes its name from the town.

The ancient name of the town was *Abbatis villa.* In the 9th century it was dependent on the abbey of St-Riquier. It became the capital of the medieval region of Ponthieu and in 1184 received a commercial charter. With the marriage of Edward I of England to Eleanor of Castile in 1272, the city became part of English territory. Subsequently it was under alternate English and French rule until 1477, when the French took permanent control. It was an Allied base in World War I. In World War II the Germans held the town from 1940 until September 1944. Population: 25,439 (1999 census).

ABBEVILLE, ab'ē-vil, a city in Louisiana, and the seat of Vermilion parish. It is situated on Vermilion Bayou, 65 miles (105 km) southwest of Baton Rouge. The city has access to the Gulf Intracoastal Waterway. Abbeville is a trading and processing center for agricultural goods, including dairy products, rice, and sugar. There are oil wells, fisheries, and light industries in the vicinity. The city has an Acadian history museum and a community theater.

In 1843 a French priest bought land in this parish and planned the town in the French manner. Government is by mayor and council. Population: 11,187.

MARGARET W. WALSWORTH*
Vermilion Parish Library

ABBEVILLE, ab'ē-vil, a city in South Carolina, 65 miles (105 km) by road northwest of Augusta, Ga. It is the seat of Abbeville county and a center of light industry. Abbeville is the so-called "cradle and the grave of the Confederacy." Possibly the first organized meeting on South Carolina's secession from the Union took place there on Nov. 22, 1860, and Jefferson Davis held his last full cabinet meeting in the town on May 2, 1865. Settled in the 1700s, Abbeville was incorporated as a city in 1895. Population: 5,840.

ABBEVILLIAN, ab-vil′ē-ən, in archaeology, an epoch in the Lower Paleolithic period, or Early Old Stone Age. It corresponds to the first interglacial period in geology (approximately 540,000–480,000 B.C.). Characteristic of this epoch was the flint ax, one of the earliest tools shaped by man. Classified as a core implement, the ax was generally pear-shaped with a cutting edge around the tapered end. The epoch takes its name from Abbeville, a town in northern France, where such artifacts were discovered. The epoch was originally known as *Chellean.* The present name was adopted at the suggestion of Abbé Henri Breuil, French archaeologist, in 1932.

ABBEY, Edward, ab′ē (1927–1989), American essayist and novelist who wrote eloquently about the endangered landscape of the American Southwest. Abbey thought the landscape would ultimately recover from human depredations but that the price humankind would pay for being out of balance with the earth would be the loss of spirituality and the dignity of freedom. Much of his prose is not easily classifiable; he wrote in the tradition of the anarchist gadfly, raising questions rather than providing answers. Writing with passion and the desire "to make a difference," he despised writers who simply wrote for a market.

Born on Jan. 29, 1927, in Home, Pa., the eldest of five children, Abbey saw the childhood landscape he loved destroyed by mining and industrial pollution. In the summer of 1944, before entering his senior year of high school, he traveled around the American Southwest. After finishing high school he was drafted into the army and was stationed in Italy. In 1947, using his GI benefits, Abbey entered the University of New Mexico; he graduated in 1951 with a degree in philosophy and English and subsequently won a Fulbright fellowship, which he spent at the University of Edinburgh in Scotland.

Abbey's first novel, *Jonathan Troy* (1954), was followed up with *The Brave Cowboy* (1956); the actor Kirk Douglas so admired the outlandish plot of this modern Western and its antihero that he had it made into the movie *Lonely Are the Brave* (1962). In 1956 Abbey completed a master's degree in philosophy at the University of New Mexico, writing a thesis on the history of anarchism that examined the work of Proudhon and Kropotkin. (See PROUDHON, PIERRE JOSEPH; KROPOTKIN, PETER ALEKSEYEVICH.)

Thereafter Abbey worked at assorted jobs, including welfare counselor, seasonal park ranger, and fire lookout. From his summer notebooks he distilled meditative essays about the wilderness; these were published as *Desert Solitaire* (1968), the provocative book that allowed him to become a full-time writer. His novel *Black Sun* (1971) tenderly evoked the loss of a beloved. *The Monkey Wrench Gang* (1975), a novel, boisterously depicted a small band of ecological activists who oppose unthinking destruction of nature; *Hayduke Lives!* (1989) supplies the neo-Luddite sequel. (Some of Abbey's friends took up the ideas he expressed in the first of these works, founding the radical action movement Earth First! in 1980.) *Good News*

© SUZI MOORE/WOODFIN CAMP & ASSOCIATES
Edward Abbey expresses his deep distrust of encroaching technology with characteristic brio.

(1980), perhaps the first recorded science fiction Western, dramatizes the conflict between city and country in a post-American world. *The Fool's Progress* (1988), which Abbey began writing in the 1950s under the direction of Wallace Stegner (while on a creative writing fellowship at Stanford University), presents a Dionysian, picaresque hero who tries to escape the conformity of consumer society. (See also STEGNER, WALLACE EARLE.)

Abbey compiled numerous collections of his essays, including *The Journey Home* (1977), *Abbey's Road* (1979), *Down the River* (1982), *Beyond the Wall* (1984), and *One Life at a Time, Please* (1987). His prose displays an irreverent wit, an aesthetic sense of rhythm, satiric paradox, superb list making, and graphic autobiographical authenticity (even in his works of fiction). William Godwin, Henry David Thoreau, and D. H. Lawrence provided important influences on Abbey's writings, which he wrote in pencil and then banged out on a manual typewriter. (See GODWIN, WILLIAM; THOREAU, HENRY DAVID; LAWRENCE, DAVID HERBERT.)

In the 1980s Abbey taught at the University of Arizona. He was awarded a Guggenheim Fellowship in fiction writing (1974) and the Creative Achievement Award of the American Academy and Institute of Arts and Letters (1987), which he declined. Two of his five marriages were happy; his marriages produced five children. Terminally ill in a Tucson, Ariz., hospital, he disconnected his support tubes with the help of some friends and fled to the desert, where he died, in Oracle, Ariz., on March 14, 1989. He was buried secretly and illegally in the wilderness he loved.

KEVIN T. MCENEANEY
Marist College

Bibliography
Selections from Abbey's writings appear in *Confessions of a Barbarian: Selections from the Journals of Edward Abbey,* ed. by David Petersen (Little, Brown 1994), and *The Serpents of Paradise: A Reader,* ed. by John Macrae (H. Holt 1995), among other volumes. His poetry was collected by David Petersen and published as *Earth Apples: The Poetry of Edward Abbey* (1994; reprint, St. Martin's 1995).
Bishop, James, Jr., *Epitaph for a Desert Anarchist: The Life and Legacy of Edward Abbey* (Atheneum 1994).

Cahalan, James M., *Edward Abbey; A Life* (Univ. of Ariz. Press 2001).
Hepworth, James R., and Gregory McNamee, *Resist Much, Obey Little: Remembering Edward Abbey* (Sierra Club Bks. 1996).
Loeffler, Jack, *Adventures with Ed: A Portrait of Abbey* (Univ. of N.Mex. Press 2002) [a memoir].
Quigley, Peter, ed., *The Coyote in the Maze* (Univ. of Utah Press 1998).
Ronald, Ann, *The New West of Edward Abbey*, 2d ed. (Univ. of Nev. Press 2000).

ABBEY, Edwin Austin, ab'ē (1852–1911), American illustrator and painter who specialized in depicting scenes from English history and literature, mostly of the 17th and 18th centuries. Born in Philadelphia on April 1, 1852, Abbey studied at the Pennsylvania Academy of the Fine Arts. In 1870 he began a long but irregular association with New York City publisher Harper & Brothers, providing illustrations for *Harper's Weekly* and other publications. In 1878 Harper's sent him to England, where he soon settled. Abbey died in London on Aug. 1, 1911.

Abbey's first major assignment for Harper's was to illustrate *Selections from the Poetry of Robert Herrick*, which, when it appeared in 1882, was hailed as the finest illustrated book published in the United States up to that time. *Old Songs*, a volume of 17th- and 18th-century English songs, appeared in 1889; it was a joint project with the English painter Alfred Parsons (1847–1920), a collaborator and companion of Abbey, the latter of whose various artistic influences included the Pre-Raphaelites and contemporary English theater.

In 1886 Abbey received a commission from *Harper's Weekly* to illustrate Shakespeare's plays. The comedies appeared in four volumes in 1896; his illustrations for the tragedies and histories appeared periodically in *Harper's* until his death. From 1889 Abbey concentrated on oil paintings

Edwin Austin Abbey's Shakespearean-themed works include the 1895 pastel-on-paperboard *Queen in "Hamlet."*

and murals, most with Arthurian, Renaissance, Shakespearean, or allegorical themes. An early important oil painting, *May Day Morning* (1890; Yale University Art Gallery, New Haven), based on an earlier illustration of a Herrick poem, was warmly received at the Royal Academy summer exhibition of 1890. Abbey also designed costumes for the stage, including for Henry Irving's *Richard II* in 1898, the year the artist was elected a member of the Royal Academy.

On a visit to the United States in 1890, Abbey was commissioned to paint a mural for the Boston Public Library; the 15-panel *Quest of the Holy Grail* was finished in 1901. The next year he received a royal commission to paint *The Coronation of Edward VII* (1902–1904; Royal Collection, Buckingham Palace, London). Abbey's allegorical mural for the Pennsylvania State Capitol in Harrisburg, started in 1902 and incomplete at the time of his death, was finished by his friend and fellow American expatriate, John Singer Sargent.

Bibliography: Foster, Kathleen A., and Michael Quick, *Edwin Austin Abbey* (Yale Univ. Art Gallery 1973); Lucas, E. V., *Edwin Austin Abbey, Royal Academician: The Record of His Life and Work*, 2 vols. (Scribner 1921); Oakley, Lucy, *Unfaded Pageant: Edwin Austin Abbey's Shakespearean Subjects* (Wallach Art Gallery, Columbia Univ. 1994).

ABBEY, Henry Eugene, ab'ē (1846–1896), American theatrical and operatic manager who became the first manager of the Metropolitan Opera House in New York City. Born in Akron, Ohio, on June 27, 1846, Abbey managed the opera house there and in 1870 began to manage touring opera companies. In 1877 he went to New York City, where he managed a succession of theaters and represented such actors as Henry Irving, Edwin Booth, and Coquelin (the French actor).

Abbey went to Europe in 1880 and arranged for Sarah Bernhardt to appear in the United States. The success of her tour led to Abbey's appointment in 1883 as manager of the new Metropolitan Opera House, which he managed alone or with others intermittently until 1896. He secured the greatest European singers for his productions. He died in New York City on Oct. 17, 1896.

ABBEY, ab'ē, a monastery in which reside 12 or more religious headed by an abbot or abbess. As now constituted, abbeys must conform to a pattern established by canon law and be approved by the bishop in whose diocese they lie, although they retain autonomy within their community. Small monasteries are sometimes called priories, particularly in England. In these the authority held by the abbot in a larger community is vested in the local bishop. In the Middle Ages, abbeys were among the chief centers of learning in Europe and England. Some of the most famous abbeys were those at Cluny and Clairvaux in France, St. Gall in Switzerland, Fulda in Germany, and Westminster and St. Mary of York in England.

Origins. In the early Eastern and Western churches, a monastery was the simple habitation of a holy man, usually set far from the life of the city. Disciples often followed the solitary ascetic and lived in cells clustered around his cave or hut. Their crude dwellings were built with the materials at hand. The followers patterned their lives on that of their preceptor and accepted his guidance in all matters. As such communities grew, they adopted rules of conduct and sometimes appointed one hermit as their head.

© SCALA/ART RESOURCE, NY

Above, Church of the Katholikon, Hosios Loukas Monastery, Phocis, Greece (c. 1020). Like contemporary Benedictine abbeys, this Byzantine monastery was built on a mountainside. *Right,* A view of the nave and chevet of the church at Fontenay, a Cistercian abbey in Burgundy, France, established at this site in 1130. The abbey has three ranges of buildings surrounding the central cloister as well as a gatehouse and a forge. Fontenay was the second daughter-house of Bernard of Clairvaux's abbey of Clairvaux.

© PIERRE BOULAT/WOODFIN CAMP & ASSOCIATES

The first such community organization was formed in the East by Pachomius (c. 292—c. 346) at Tabennisi (near Dendera), Egypt. In the West monasticism received its impetus from Benedict of Nursia (c. 480—c. 547), who established his first abbey at Monte Cassino in Italy about 529 and laid down his rule for communal monasticism. This rule required each monk to observe celibacy, poverty, and obedience to the abbot and to engage in prayer and manual labor. To these Cassiodorus (c. 485/490–c. 580) in founding his own monastery added scholarly activities such as copying and translating learned works.

The increased religious fervor of the 11th century brought the foundation of ascetic orders, such as the Carthusians and Cistercians, which generally followed the rule of St. Benedict. The Franciscan, Dominican, and Carmelite orders that arose

Rendering of a 1774 renovation plan for the Augustinian abbey (1136) of Klosterneuburg, near Vienna. Like most abbeys, it was extensively rebuilt over its long history.

BRIDGEMAN ART LIBRARY

CANONIACLAVSTRONEOBVRG   ENSISVIGEATAMBROSIODEVOTA

in the 13th century maintained the monastic way of life but under rules of their own.

Form. St. Benedict and others who established abbeys in his era set up their communities in existing buildings, as, for example, at Monte Casino. When no suitable accommodations were available, houses were built in the prevailing style. Once St. Benedict's list of the essential components of each abbey under his rule was widely circulated (about the 9th century), abbeys were designed in a set pattern. According to the rule they had to include an oratory, a dormitory, a refectory, a kitchen, workshops, cellars, an infirmary, a novitiate, guesthouses, and a common meeting room. With only minor modifications to suit local conditions, all Benedictine abbeys are therefore basically similar. The principal buildings center on an arcaded cloister or quadrangle, with the church usually to the north. Carthusian abbeys differ in that all communal buildings are on one side of the quadrangle, and cottages, each for two or three residents, are on the remaining three sides. Many abbeys are enclosed by a high wall.

Since most abbeys include many more religious than the required 12, their monastic functions are usually delegated to assistants. First in rank in men's monasteries are the prior and subprior, who enforce the rule of the abbot. Others are the precentor, or choirmaster, who may also be the librarian; the sacristan, responsible for the care of the church; the cellarer, or housekeeper; the refectorian, who supervises the common room; the kitchener; the infirmarian; the almoner, who distributes alms to the poor and the sick; the guestmaster; the novicemaster; and the hebdomadarian, or celebrant of the week's religious rites. Under such organization the abbey is enabled to function as a smoothly running community. The body of religious are free to devote themselves fully to the contemplative, missionary, or scholarly life.

See also MONASTICISM; ABBOT.

PATRICK J. ASPELL* and J. RUSSELL NICKERSON*
Oblate College, Washington, D.C.

18

Bibliography

Benedict of Nursia, *The Rule of St. Benedict in English*, ed. by Timothy H. Fry et al. (Vintage Bks. 1998).

Fergusson, Peter, *Architecture of Solitude; Cistercian Abbeys in Twelfth-Century England* (Princeton Univ. Press 1984).

Fergusson, Peter, et al., *Rievaulx Abbey: Community, Architecture, Memory* (Yale Univ. Press 1999).

Hiscock, Nigel, *The Wise Master Builder: Platonic Geometry in Plans of Medieval Abbeys and Cathedrals* (Ashgate 1999).

Horn, Walter, and Ernest Born, *The Plan of St. Gall: A Study of the Architecture and Economy of and Life in a Paradigmatic Carolingian Monastery*, 3 vols. (Univ. of Calif. Press 1979).

Robinson, David, et al., *The Cistercian Abbeys of Britain: Far from the Concourse of Men* (Batsford 1998).

ABBEY THEATRE, ab'ē, a professional theatrical company in Dublin, Ireland, that resulted from the merger of the Irish Literary Theatre, W. G. Fay's Irish National Dramatic Company, and the Irish National Theatre Society. The Abbey, which is Ireland's national theater company, opened on Dec. 27, 1904, after a history of mergers dating to 1899. The brothers Frank and William Fay were responsible for assembling the company and producing the plays; administration was mainly in the charge of William Butler Yeats, Lady Gregory, and John Millington Synge, all of whom were also dramatists who contributed notably to the theater's repertoire. The money for equipping the theater was supplied almost entirely by Annie Horniman, an Englishwoman who had been Yeats's amanuensis in London. After the establishment of the Irish Free State in 1922, the Abbey became the first government-subsidized theater in any English-speaking country. (See YEATS, WILLIAM BUTLER; GREGORY, LADY; SYNGE, JOHN MILLINGTON.)

For a number of years the Abbey had considerable influence on the theater throughout the world. It trained many actors and actresses, including Sara Allgood, Barry Fitzgerald, Siobhan McKenna, and Cyril Cusack, who later became well known in London, on Broadway, or in Hollywood. The Abbey also provided an example of the way in which a small theater could be organized and run. Theater historian Dawson Byrne wrote in 1929 that the little theater movement in the United States sprang from the Abbey, and he listed several hundred companies that might not have existed but for the example set by the Abbey. Its influence declined somewhat after World War II for lack of important new dramatists to write for it, but it was still one of the world's most important theatrical companies.

At first the Abbey was permitted to present only Irish plays, but gradually changes in its constitution allowed it to mount other productions. Its current mission is threefold: to present new works by Irish writers and to stage classics both Irish and international.

The original Abbey Theatre on Lower Abbey Street held just over 500 people and had a small, cramped stage. In July 1951 fire gutted the theater, and, although the outer walls remained, it was abandoned. After appearing for a short time in a hall at the Guinness Brewery, the Abbey's theatrical company moved into Queen's Theatre. In 1964 the foundation stone was laid for the new Abbey Theatre on roughly the site of the original structure. The 628-seat theater, an austere gray-brick building, opened on July 18, 1966; it was designed by Irish architect Michael Scott in consultation with Pierre Sonrel, a specialist in theater design. As an architectural monument it has found few supporters, but it incorporates the most modern ideas in theater architecture, and the company has prospered in its new home. In 1967 the Peacock, a smaller theater for experimental works, opened at the Abbey.

Among the great plays first presented at the Abbey were Synge's *Playboy of the Western World* (1907), Yeats's *Land of Heart's Desire* (1911), Sean O'Casey's *Shadow of a Gunman* (1923) and *Plough and the Stars* (1926), and Paul Vincent Carroll's *Shadow and Substance* (1937). More recently, the works of modern Irish playwrights Brian Friel, Hugh Leonard, Frank McGuinness, and Jimmy Murphy have premiered at the Abbey, and some of these have found success as well in London's West End and on Broadway.

GERARD FAY*
Author of "Abbey Theatre: Cradle of Genius"

Bibliography: Hunt, Hugh, *The Abbey, Ireland's National Theatre, 1904–1978* (Columbia Univ. Press 1979); Saddlemyer, Anne, ed., *Theatre Business: The Correspondence of the First Abbey Theatre Directors, William Butler Yeats, Lady Gregory and J. M. Synge* (Pa. State Univ. Press 1982); Welch, Robert, *The Abbey Theatre, 1899–1999: Form and Pressure* (Oxford 1999).

ABBOT, Charles Greeley, ab'ət (1872–1973), American astrophysicist who studied solar radiation and its absorption by the earth's atmosphere. Born in Wilton, N.H., on May 31, 1872, Abbot graduated from the Massachusetts Institute of Technology (MIT) in 1894. A year later he was appointed an assistant at the Smithsonian Astrophysical Observatory (SAO; then located in Washington, D.C.) and worked under Samuel P. Langley, with whom he mapped the sun's infrared spectrum. He later served as the second director of the SAO (1907–1944) and the fifth secretary of the Smithsonian Institution (1928–1944). Abbot died in Washington on Dec. 17, 1973.

Abbot established a value for the solar constant, the average amount of radiant solar energy received by the earth's atmosphere. He believed that variations in the solar radiation affected terrestrial weather. Abbot improved the accuracy of Langley's bolometer and galvanometer. His books include *The Sun* (1911), *Everyday Mysteries: Secrets of Science in the Home* (1923), *The Earth and the Stars* (1925), *The Sun and the Welfare of Man* (1929), *Great Inventions* (1932), and the autobiographical *Adventures in the World of Science* (1958).

ABBOT, George, ab'ət (1562–1633), English clergyman, archbishop of Canterbury under the first two Stuart kings of England. Abbot was born into a rigorously Protestant worker's family in Guildford, Surrey, England, on Oct. 29, 1562. He studied at Balliol College, Oxford; became master of University College in 1597; and three times was vice-chancellor of the university.

Abbot met King James I in 1608. Within two years Abbot was appointed successively bishop of Lichfield and Coventry, bishop of London, and archbishop of Canterbury. Abbot adhered to the king and the Church of England as faithfully as his Puritan conscience would allow. His persistent advocacy of Protestant causes in foreign policy and his encouragement of Puritan elements in Commons often placed him in opposition to the king, but they were never permanently estranged. Abbot's influence was, nevertheless, greatly diminished by Charles I. Charles briefly denied him all authority (1627–1628) and thereafter held him in firm rein. Abbot died in semiretirement in Croydon on Aug. 4, 1633.

ABBOT, ab'ət, the superior of a monastery housing a fixed community of monks, usually numbering at least 12. The name, derived from the Aramaic *abba*, meaning "father," was first used in the Western church in the 5th century. It was given official status by Benedict of Nursia when he founded his first monastery, at Monte Cassino, Italy (about 529). The title now is used by several religious orders, particularly those in the Roman Catholic Church that follow the Rule of St. Benedict. The corresponding titles in the Eastern churches are *hegumenos* ("leader") and *archimandrite* ("ruler of the fold").

The first abbots were the founders of individual monasteries. Later, abbots were elected by their communities or appointed by the local bishop. Lay rulers exerted increasing influence, and, in time, appointments became the prerogative of the sovereign, giving rise to many abuses. To remedy this situation, the Council of Trent (1543–1563) decreed that an abbot should be elected under rules prescribed by canon law; he would be chosen for life in free and secret election by professed members of his own community. The election was then to be validated, usually by the Holy See.

Specific qualifications for abbots are now at the discretion of the individual foundations. On election the abbot assumes the title of abbot regular and has the status of a church prelate. He exercises complete control over the spiritual and temporal life of his community, subject to the limitations prescribed by his order's rules. In some cases the abbot's authority may extend to all religious and lay members of the church within a prescribed district of an episcopal see; in others it may be exerted over large areas that lie outside a bishop's province.

Superiors of certain long-established houses may bear the title of archabbot, and the presiding abbot of a group of monasteries within an order is often known as the abbot president or abbot general. Since 1893, when it was reorganized as a single unit, the Benedictine Order has had an abbot primate, who ranks above the order's abbots regular. There are also titular abbots, who hold title, as a mark of honor, to abbeys no longer in existence. Secular abbots are members of the secular (diocesan) clergy who receive benefices and honors that reverted to local churches from disbanded or suppressed abbeys. (See also ABBEY.)

ABBOTT, Benjamin Vaughan, ab'ət (1830–1890), American lawyer whose numerous treatises, digests, and reports of cases place him in the first rank of 19th-century legal authorities.

Born in Boston on June 4, 1830, the eldest son of the author Jacob Abbott, Benjamin Abbott was educated by his father before entering New York University in 1846. After his graduation in 1850, he attended Harvard Law School and in 1852 began to practice in New York City in partnership with his brother Austin. (See ABBOTT, JACOB.)

The Abbott brothers collaborated on 35 volumes of New York state case reports, covering the years 1854–1876. In 1860 they published their 5-volume *Digest of New York Statutes and Reports,* and its entirely original form became the accepted one for all later legal digests. They also produced more than a hundred other law books.

In 1870 Abbott was commissioned to revise the U.S. Statutes. He is credited with authorship of the single octavo that replaced 16 volumes of statutes. Between 1873 and 1879 he wrote a new *United States Digest* in 14 volumes. He also published several fiction and nonfiction books. Abbott died in Brooklyn, N.Y., on Feb. 17, 1890.

ABBOTT, Berenice, ab'ət (1898–1991), American photographer who was noted for her portraits of Paris's artistic and literary vanguard in the 1920s, her comprehensive documentation of New York City in the 1930s, and her eloquent espousal of a realistic, objective approach to photography during the first half of the 20th century. At one time a darkroom assistant to the surrealist artist Man Ray, she also uncovered the prints and negatives of the French photographer Eugène Atget, bringing him out of obscurity and promoting his work through various articles and exhibitions. (See also RAY, MAN; ATGET, JEAN-EUGÈNE-AUGUSTE.)

Abbott was born on July 17, 1898, in Springfield, Ohio, and she attended public schools in Columbus, Ohio, until 1916. Wishing to become a journalist, she studied briefly at Ohio State University and then moved to New York City, where she lived for three years. In 1921 Abbott moved to Paris, where she studied drawing and sculpture with Émile Bourdelle. In 1923 she attended Berlin's prestigious Kunstschule. When her money ran out, she returned to Paris and worked as Man Ray's assistant until 1925. During this time she was introduced to the work of Atget and, struck by his straightforward photographic style, purchased some of his prints and acquired his archives, which she maintained and promoted until it was purchased in 1968 by the Museum of Modern Art in New York City. Abbott also operated her own portrait studio in Paris from 1926 to 1929, photographing important Paris literary figures such as André Gide, Jean Cocteau, and James Joyce. (See also BOURDELLE, ÉMILE-ANTOINE.)

Flatiron Building, a silver gelatin print of circa 1930, is an iconic New York City photograph by Berenice Abbott.

In 1929 Abbott returned to New York City. Mindful of the rapid changes taking place there and compelled to document the city before it changed completely, she carefully began to record an urban landscape increasingly marked by architectural and industrial growth. Eventually subsidized by the Federal Arts Project of the Works Progress Administration, Abbott's efforts spanned the next decade and resulted in her first book, *Changing New York*, published in 1939 (reissued as *New York in the Thirties* in 1973). In these images Abbott focused on the physical structure of the city and employed modernist photographic devices—dynamic compositions; extreme, high angles; flattened pictorial space; and great detail—to reveal its energy and pulse.

Abbott's interest in the technical aspects of photography led her to write two technical books, *A Guide to Better Photography* (1941) and *The View Camera Made Simple* (1948), as well as several articles dispensing practical advice and suggestions for improvements to photographic equipment and supplies. She taught photography at the New School for Social Research in New York City from 1935 to 1958, and from 1958 to 1960 she worked in Boston for the Physical Science Study Commission of Educational Services, Inc., where she pursued a long-standing interest in exploring scientific problems photographically.

In 1968 Abbott moved to Maine, where she lived until her death, in Monson, on Dec. 10, 1991. She had by this time exhibited widely around the United States as well as abroad and actively encouraged more women to enter the field of photography. Abbott's clean, straightforward style, unfettered by sentiment or illusionism, matched her committed support of photography's development as a descriptive medium and her own passion for realism.

STEPHANIE LIPSCOMB, *Art Institute of Chicago*

Bibliography

Berenice Abbott: A View of the 20th Century (1994, Ishtar Films), Martha Wheeler's and Kay Weaver's hour-long documentary surveying Abbott's long, productive career, includes over 200 of her black-and-white photographs as well as interviews with Abbott and commentary from photography curators and critics. Books by Abbott include *New York in the Thirties*, 1973; *The World of Atget*, 1979; *Berenice Abbott*, 1988; *Berenice Abbott/Photographs*, 1990.

O'Neal, Hank, *Berenice Abbott, American Photographer* (McGraw-Hill 1982).

Yochelson, Bonnie, *Berenice Abbott: Changing New York* (Mus. of the City of N.Y./New Press 1997).

ABBOTT, Bud, and **COSTELLO, Lou,** a'bət, kos-tel'ō (1896–1974 and 1906–1959), American comedy duo who became a huge box-office draw in a series of agreeably low-brow movies in the 1940s and 1950s. From their 1940 film debut in *One Night in the Tropics* through their 1956 effort *Dance with Me, Henry*, Abbott and Costello appeared together in 35 raucous comedies as well as a popular television series.

William Alexander "Bud" Abbott was born in Asbury Park, N.J., on Oct. 2, 1896. The son of a circus family (his father was an advance man, his mother a bareback rider), he left school early and entered show business from the management side, working as treasurer and manager of numerous theaters across the United States. He also organized "tab shows," small troupes of comics and singers who toured burlesque houses. By the late 1920s Abbott was appearing onstage as well, playing straight man to various vaudeville comics.

PHOTOFEST

In a 1951 shot from their TV series, a hammer-handed Abbott and a hapless Costello strike an archetypical pose.

Costello was born Lewis Francis Cristillo in Paterson, N.J., on March 6, 1906. His father ran a silk mill and wanted his son to go into medicine, but the boy began working in vaudeville right after graduating high school. By 1931 Abbott was working as an assistant cashier at Brooklyn's Casino Theater, where the renamed Lou Costello was half of a double act. One day Costello's straight man failed to show, and Abbott filled in; the two hit it off instantly.

The duo struggled through most of the 1930s, playing burlesque houses and lesser vaudeville theaters throughout the country, honing their act. A break came in 1938, when the singer Kate Smith booked them for her popular radio show, which led to an appearance in the hit Broadway revue *Streets of Paris* (1939). A scout for Universal film studios spotted them and signed them to a one-picture deal, as comic relief in the musical *One Night in the Tropics* (1940). They were such a hit that Universal signed them to long-term contracts. The first five Abbott and Costello star vehicles were directed by Arthur Lubin, who later recalled, simply but fondly, "I loved the boys so much and enjoyed working with them so much." Their first film with Lubin, *Buck Privates* (1941), featured the pair as unwitting enlistees; the film grossed an amazing $10 million. The team made 13 films between their debut and the end of World War II, all of them cheaply produced and highly profitable for Universal, and they reached number-one box-office status by 1942. Among their early hits were *In the Navy* (1941), with the Andrews Sisters; *Pardon My Sarong* (1942); *It Ain't Hay* (1943); *Lost in a Harem* and *In Society* (both 1944); and *Here Come the Co-eds* and *The Naughty Nineties* (both 1945). Their films offered little in the way of plot variation or expensive costars; mostly, the "Everymen" Bud and Lou were thrust into promising situations with great comic potential, be it the military, college, or the Wild West.

Abbott and Costello rarely appealed to the intellectual fans of the Marx Brothers, and they lacked the inherent sweetness of Laurel and Hardy; the style of the two was more akin to that of boisterous, roughhousing comics such as the Ritz Brothers and the Three Stooges, who also numbered among their biggest fans adolescent boys and bumptious GIs. Their humor sprang from the roots of burlesque, from Weber and Fields: broad characterizations (the impatient Abbott, the nervous Costello), puns and wordplay, slapstick, and pretty young women in distress. "The great success of Abbott and Costello was attributed by the critics to their old-fashioned knock-about style, combined with a modern toughness of talk," said the New York Times upon Costello's death.

Their most famous routine was "Who's on First?," a fast-paced masterpiece of double-talk and crossed signals involving a baseball team ("Who's on first, What's on second, I Don't Know's on third . . . "), with Costello working himself into a rage of sputtering confusion (their recording of this renowned bit gained them an entry into the National Baseball Hall of Fame in Cooperstown, N.Y., in 1956, the first non-ball-playing celebrity inductees). They also revived and rejuvenated the classic vaudeville routine "Slowly I Turned" ("Step by step . . . inch by inch . . . "). Costello also successfully milked his two catch phrases, "Heeeey, Abbott!" and "I'm a baaaad boy."

With the end of World War II, the team ventured into comic, mostly horror tales: first The Time of Their Lives (1946), then a series of Abbott and Costello Meet . . . movies, wherein they encountered, among others, Frankenstein's monster (1948); the Killer (1949), played by Boris Karloff; the Invisible Man (1950); Dr. Jekyll and Mr. Hyde (1953); and the Mummy (1955). By this time their productions were distinctly low-budget, made to play the second half of double-bill matinees. The adult double entendres were a thing of the past, and their 1950s nonhorror films were essentially kids' shows: Comin' round the Mountain (1951), Lost in Alaska (1952), Jack and the Beanstalk (1952), Abbott and Costello Go to Mars (1953), and their last film together, the self-produced Dance with Me, Henry (1956). In 1952–1953 they starred in The Abbott and Costello Show on the Columbia Broadcasting System (CBS) television network, portraying unemployed actors who were living in a boardinghouse.

Their personal relationship was sometimes fractious, and the pair parted company several times, finally, during a nightclub engagement in 1957. Following their breakup Costello made his only solo film, a comedy called The 30 Foot Bride of Candy Rock (1959). Before its release, he died of a heart attack in Los Angeles on March 3, 1959. Abbott made occasional appearances on TV and stage following Costello's death but never anything approaching a "comeback." He died of cancer in Woodland Hills, Calif., on April 24, 1974.

"The Boys" and their childish but good, clean, latter-day brand of humor have remained very popular and even been influential, and their films still appear on television and are widely available for video rental. Look-alikes show up on TV commercials, Hanna-Barbera used them in a 1966 animated series, and comedian Jerry Seinfeld, a devoted fan, hosted a 1994 TV special, Abbott and Costello Meet Seinfeld.

EVE GOLDEN, Author of
"Anna Held and the Birth of Ziegfeld's Broadway"

Bibliography

Anobile, Richard J., ed., Who's on First? Verbal and Visual Gems from the Films of Abbott and Costello (Darien House 1972).
Costello, Chris, with Raymond Strait, Lou's on First: A Biography of Lou Costello (1981; reprint, Cooper Square Press 2000).
Cox, Stephen, and John Lofflin, The Abbott and Costello Story: 60 Years of "Who's on First?" (Cumberland House 1997) [originally published in 1990 as The Official Abbott and Costello Scrapbook].
Furmanek, Bob, and Ron Palumbo, Abbott and Costello in Hollywood (Putnam 1991).
Miller, Jeffrey S., The Horror Spoofs of Abbott and Costello: A Critical Assessment of the Comedy Team's Monster Films (McFarland 2000).
Mulholland, Jim, The Abbott and Costello Book (1975; reprint, Popular Lib. 1977).
Thomas, Bob, Bud and Lou: The Abbott and Costello Story (Lippincott 1977).

ABBOTT, George Francis, ab'ət (1887–1995), American director, producer, and playwright noted for his productions of fast-moving farces and musical comedies. Abbott was the author or coauthor, as well as the producer-director, of many of the American theater's biggest hits, many of which were revived one or more times—often with Abbott's help—during his long, illustrious career.

Abbott was born in Forestville, N.Y., on June 25, 1887. He graduated from the University of Rochester in 1911, spent the next year as a student in George Pierce Baker's playwriting class at Harvard University, and began his professional career in 1913 as an actor. As a playwright he had his first major hit in 1926, when he collaborated with Philip Dunning on Broadway.

Abbott's first directorial successes came with Three Men on a Horse, a 1935 farce by Abbott and John Cecil Holm, and On Your Toes, a 1936 musical on which he collaborated with Richard Rodgers and Lorenz Hart. After directing Brother Rat (1936) and Room Service (1937), he resumed his association with Rodgers and Hart in The Boys from Syracuse (1938) and other hits. In 1959 he directed Fiorello!, for which, as coauthor, he won the 1959 Pulitzer Prize for drama. (See also RODGERS, RICHARD; HART, LORENZ.)

Among the other shows Abbott staged were Chicago (1926), Twentieth Century (1932), Pal Joey (1940), Best Foot Forward (1941), Where's Charley? (1948), Wonderful Town (1953), Damn Yankees (1955), Never Too Late (1962), and A Funny Thing Happened on the Way to the Forum (1967). He reworked On Your Toes for its 1983 Broadway revival—it went on to win a Tony Award—and directed his melodrama Broadway when it returned to the stage in 1987. He was also involved with the Broadway revival of Damn Yankees in 1994, phoning and faxing script changes to the director during rehearsals.

Abbott wrote, produced, or directed (or sometimes all three) a number of movies as well, including the screen versions of his musical comedies The Pajama Game (1957) and Damn Yankees (1958), which he codirected with Stanley Donen. Mister Abbott, his autobiography, was published in 1963; he also wrote a novel, Tryout (1979). He was the recipient of numerous distinguished awards and honors, including the Handel Medallion of the City of New York (1976), the Kennedy Center Honors (1983), a career achievement Tony (1976) and a special Tony (1987), and the National Arts medal of the National Endowment for the Arts (1990). In 1966 New York's Adelphi theater was renamed the George Abbott Theater in his honor. Abbott died in Miami Beach, Fla., on Jan. 31, 1995.

ABBOTT, Grace, ab'ət (1878–1939), American social worker who devoted her life to the protection of immigrants and children. Abbott was born in Grand Island, Nebr., on Nov. 17, 1878. In 1908 she joined Jane Addams's Hull House in Chicago. As director of the Immigrant's Protective League, she sought to help new immigrants to that city. (See also ADDAMS, JANE.)

In 1917 Abbott went to Washington to administer the first federal Child Labor Act and helped prevent the exploitation of children in wartime industries. From 1921 to 1934 she headed the United States Children's Bureau and administered a program to improve the health of mothers and infants, fighting unsuccessfully for a constitutional amendment against child labor. She lectured and wrote frequently on social problems, sometimes with her sister Edith, also a social worker. Grace Abbott died in Chicago on June 19, 1939.

ALLEN F. DAVIS
University of Missouri

Bibliography: Costin, Lela B., *Two Sisters for Social Justice: A Biography of Grace and Edith Abbott* (Univ. of Ill. Press 1983).

ABBOTT, Jacob, ab'ət (1803–1879), American educator and prolific writer of children's books. Born in Hallowell, Maine, on Nov. 14, 1803, Abbott attended Bowdoin College (B.A., 1820; M.A., 1823). He later studied at the Andover Theological Seminary and was ordained a Congregational minister. From 1825 to 1829 he was professor of mathematics and theology at Amherst College, where he helped introduce a modern curriculum. Abbott established the Mount Vernon School for girls in

Title page of an 1859 edition of Jacob Abbott's Jonas stories. Abbott popularized children's fiction series books.

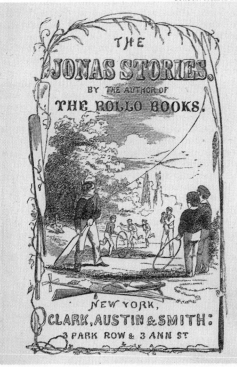

Boston in 1829, serving as its principal until 1834. His first notable book, *The Young Christian* (1832), consisted of lectures he gave there. After a year as a minister in Roxbury, Mass., he moved to Farmington, Me., devoting himself to literary activities until 1843, when he joined two of his brothers in founding the Abbott Institute in New York City. Jacob Abbott ran the institute until 1851.

Abbott's children's books reflected his innovative pedagogical activities. The most famous of his many works were the "Rollo" stories, 28 volumes published beginning in 1834, following Rollo on his worldwide travels. He also wrote the "Cousin Lucy" and "Franconia" series, among others. Abbott died in Farmington on Oct. 31, 1879.

ABBOTT, John Joseph Caldwell, ab'ət (1821–1893), statesman, businessman, educator, and prime minister of Canada. He was born in St. Andrew's, Lower Canada (now Quebec), on March 12, 1821. Upon his graduation from McGill University, he studied law and was admitted to the bar in 1847. He taught for a number of years at McGill, first as a lecturer and later as a professor of commercial and criminal law. He eventually became dean of the faculty, a title he retained until 1880.

Together with his father and brother, a railway engineer, Abbott was deeply involved in the promotion, financing, and expansion of the Canadian railway system. In fact, his role in the Canadian Pacific Railway Scandal, which tied him to an agreement to finance the election campaign of Conservative George Étienne Cartier in return for a contract to build the railway, caused the collapse of John Macdonald's Conservative government in 1874. (See MACDONALD, JOHN; CARTIER, GEORGE ÉTIENNE.)

Abbott's interests in railways brought him to politics, a field he entered in 1857 when he first served in the Legislative Assembly as a Conservative. He served successively in the Assembly and House of Commons until 1874. Returning to the House in 1880, he remained there until his appointment to the Senate in 1887.

When Macdonald resumed the prime ministership, Abbott joined the cabinet as minister without portfolio. He succeeded Macdonald in 1891 as a compromise candidate of warring Conservative factions, governing until ill health forced him to retire in 1892. In recognition of his public service, he was created a Knight Commander of the Order of St. Michael and St. George on May 25, 1892. He died in Montreal on Oct. 30, 1893.

ABBOTT, Lyman, ab'ət (1835–1922), American clergyman, editor, and author. Born in Roxbury, Mass., on Dec. 18, 1835, the son of the author Jacob Abbott, he graduated from New York University in 1853 and became a lawyer. Inspired by Henry Ward Beecher, he began private study for the ministry and was ordained by a Congregational council in Maine. He served a church in Terre Haute, Ind., from 1860 to 1865 and then returned to New York to direct the American Freedmen's Union Commission. In 1876 Abbott took up Beecher's invitation to help edit the *Christian Union*, quickly becoming its central figure. Renamed the *Outlook* in 1893, the paper became highly influential and remained a channel of Abbott's progressive views until the end of his long life. He was also a nationally known platform and pulpit figure and was Beecher's successor (1887–1899) at Brooklyn's Plymouth Congregational Church.

Abbott became a major spokesman for the social gospel and an articulate champion of the "New Theology," a liberal interpretation of evangelical faith. In many of his nearly 40 books, he sought to mediate between orthodox religious views and current scientific thought, as in *The Theology of an Evolutionist* (1897). He wrote his *Reminiscences* (1915) as well as *What Christianity Means to Me; A Spiritual Autobiography* (1921). Abbott died in New York City on Oct. 22, 1922.

ROBERT T. HANDY*, *Author of "A History of the Churches in the United States and Canada"*

Bibliography: Brown, Ira V., *Lyman Abbott, Christian Evolutionist* (1953; reprint, Greenwood Press 1970); Hopkins, Charles H., *The Rise of the Social Gospel in American Protestantism, 1865–1915* (1940; reprint, AMS Press 1982).

ABBOTT, Robert Sengstacke, ab'ət (1868–1940), American newspaper publisher and crusader for black civil rights. Robert Abbott was born on Nov. 28, 1868, to Thomas Abbott and Flora Butler Abbott, freed slaves, in Fort Frederica on St. Simons Island, Ga. After her husband's death in 1869, Abbott's mother moved with her son to Savannah. There she met John H. H. Sengstacke. They were married in 1874. The boy was known as Robert Sengstacke until 1897, when he entered law school as Robert Sengstacke Abbott. He briefly attended Beach Institute and Claflin University. In 1889 he enrolled at Hampton Institute, where he trained as a printer and earned a bachelor's degree in 1896.

Abbott moved to Chicago in 1897, earned a law degree at the Kent College of Law (1899), and attempted unsuccessfully to practice law in the Midwest. He returned to Chicago in 1905 to publish his own newspaper, which he called the *Chicago Defender*. Early on, Abbott's paper combined a bent for sensational news stories and vivid graphics with devotion to the crusade for black civil rights. The *Defender*'s signal achievement was its campaign, launched in 1917, to persuade its readers in southern states to move north in search of better opportunities. The "Great Northern Drive" was so successful that several southern states banned the paper's distribution. By 1920 the *Defender* boasted a paid circulation of 230,000 (and reached many more people as copies were passed around); two-thirds of its readership lived outside Chicago. The *Defender* was a pioneer in

THE GRANGER COLLECTION

Robert S. Abbott compiled, produced, and distributed his *Chicago Defender* on his own in its early years.

unionizing and was the first national paper to integrate, the immediate occasion being Abbott's need for a printing crew trained to operate the high-speed rotary press he used from May 1921.

Having begun the *Defender* with an investment of 25 cents, Abbott became one of the first African American millionaires. Ill in his last years, he passed control of the paper to his nephew, John H. Sengstacke. Abbott died in Chicago on Feb. 29, 1940.

ABBOTT AND COSTELLO.   See ABBOTT, BUD, AND LOU COSTELLO.

ABBREVIATIONS, ə-brē-vē-ā'shənz, letter symbols or contractions used as shortened forms of words and phrases to facilitate writing and save space. The practice of abbreviating goes back to antiquity and was often used by the Greeks and Romans. Early examples have survived on coins and in inscriptions, where lack of space made the shortening of words necessary. As writing spread, abbreviations were adopted by copyists to save labor. In the West, as the European vernaculars developed from Latin and assumed written form, the practice of abbreviating was retained and extended, and after the development of the mechanical printing press, various means of abbreviating words made their way into printed text as well.

Given the long reign of classical languages in the West as the medium of scholarship and science, it is not surprising that a whole host of abbreviations commonly found in English are abbreviated forms of Latin words, among them *e.g.* (*exempli gratia*, "for the sake of example"); *i.e.* (*id est*, "that is"); *q.v.* (*quod vide*, "which see"); and *viz.* (*videlicet*, "namely"). In modern times the rapid growth of the sciences, technology, and business and the increase in the number of governmental and supranational agencies produced a vastly increased vocabulary of abbreviations for use in specialized as well as general communication. Some abbreviations, and in the 20th century especially acronyms, became so common that the original words or phrases for which they stood were virtually forgotten. *Radar* (*radio detection and ranging*) and *AIDS* (*acquired immune deficiency syndrome*) supply cases in point.

Letter abbreviations may be written in uppercase or mixed upper- and lowercase letters with points (*B.A., Bachelor of Arts*) or without points (*MoMA, Museum of Modern Art; Ba, barium*); in punctuated lowercase letters (*mi., miles*); or in unpunctuated lowercase letters indistinguishable in form from an unabbreviated word (*laser, light amplification by stimulated emission of radiation*). Especially since the proliferation of computers, the tendency has been to minimize the use of points, as when, with the advent of ZIP (*zone improvement plan*) codes, the U.S. Postal Service moved from its standard abbreviations for state names to two-letter, uppercased, unpunctuated renderings: *Mass.* became *MA*, for example. An abbreviation consisting of the initial letters of a name or title or of some combination of initial and interior letters, spelled and pronounced as a word (such as *UNESCO, United Nations Educational, Scientific and Cultural Organization*, or *sitcom, situation comedy*), is called an acronym.

Standard dictionaries generally contain comprehensive lists of abbreviations, including acronyms. Full dictionaries of specialized and general abbreviations also are available.

ABC POWERS, a term applied collectively to Argentina, Brazil, and Chile, the three leading nations of South America. It is primarily connected with two events: the attempted ABC mediation of a dispute between the United States and Mexico in 1915 and the ABC alliance.

The movement towards an association of the three countries began in 1906, when a border dispute between Argentina and Chile threatened war. Sentiment for a tariff union and nonaggression pact was especially strong in Buenos Aires. The first opportunity to form a working association appeared in April 1915, when the United States became entangled in Mexican factional struggles. On April 25, four days after the United States landed marines at Veracruz, Mexico, the representatives of the ABC powers at Washington offered their services as mediators to the governments of Mexico and the United States. A conference held soon after at Niagara Falls, Canada, produced no settlement.

The informal cooperation of the mediating powers led to a closer association, and, on May 25, 1915, they signed at Buenos Aires a treaty (never ratified) providing for five years of peace. Each party undertook to refrain from attacking the others until the cause of the dispute could be investigated by an impartial committee. Later in 1915 other South American countries were drawn into the association. The movement for ABC guarantees waned thereafter until 1933, when Argentina signed antiwar treaties with Chile and Brazil.

ABD, äbd, is a word element in Arabic, meaning "slave" or "servant." It is frequently used in personal names, usually followed by Allah (God) or one of Allah's 99 divine attributes; for example, Abd al-Majid (Slave of the Glorious).

ABD AL-AZIZ IV (1881?–1943), əb-dōol'a-zēz', sultan of Morocco, who succeeded his father, al-Hasan III, in 1894. Eager to modernize the country, he surrounded himself with European advisers. His actions aroused the resentment of the conservative nobles, and his indulgence in expensive hobbies increased the antagonism against him. In 1902, Bu Hamara, claiming to be a brother of the sultan, headed a formidable revolt that was suppressed only with French assistance. The Anglo-French agreement of 1904 and the Algeciras Conference (1906) were further exemplifications of the extent of European influence in Morocco. Abd al-Aziz was unable to end the growing anarchy and discontent. In 1907 his brother, Abd al-Hafiz, led a successful revolt. The sultan made a vain attempt to regain his power, but on Aug. 21, 1908, abdicated in favor of his brother. He died in Tangier on June 10, 1943.

ABD AL-MALIK (646/647–705), əb-dōol' mə-lik', was the fifth caliph of the Umayyad dynasty. He came to power in 685 in the midst of the second Arab civil war. The legitimacy of the Umayyad house was being challenged by an anticaliph, Ibn al-Zubayr, who represented claims to leadership of the Muslim community put forth by the former companions of the prophet Mohammed in Mecca and Medina. Ibn al-Zubayr was widely supported in Iraq, where grievances over Umayyad administration and tensions generated by the forced settlement of Bedouins in garrison cities had caused rebellion and tribal warfare among the Arabs. In Syria the Arab tribes were equally divided in their allegiance. Abd al-Malik defeated the Qays tribes in Syria in 691, and a year later he regained control of Iraq and defeated his Meccan opponents.

These prolonged struggles made it necessary to introduce new policies to consolidate the supremacy of the caliphate over the Arab peoples. In 701 a garrison of Syrian forces was established at al-Wasit to police the dissidents in Iraq. With al-Hajjaj, the viceroy of Iraq, Abd al-Malik centralized the administration by tax reform and by translating the account registers from Greek and Persian into Arabic. He also took other measures to win and ensure the loyalty of the Arabs. He bolstered the caliphate's prestige by resuming the Arab campaigns in North Africa, central Asia, and Anatolia, by issuing a new, purely Arabic-Muslim coinage to supersede Byzantine and Sassanian money, and by constructing the monumental Dome of the Rock Mosque in Jerusalem.

IRA M. LAPIDUS
University of California at Berkeley

ABD AL-MUMIN (1094?–1163), əb-dōol' moo'-min, Muslim leader of North Africa, who founded the Almohad dynasty. He was a close friend and disciple of Ibn Tumart, founder of an Islamic reform movement known as the Almohad sect. Following Ibn Tumart's death in 1130, Abd al-Mumin was chosen as leader of the Almohads and proclaimed himself a caliph. He destroyed the Almoravid dynasty, which enabled him to organize his empire in North Africa. Later he crossed over into Spain and conquered Córdoba in 1148, Almería in 1151, Granada in 1154, and Seville in 1157. At his death in 1163, he ruled an empire that included North Africa as far east as Tunisia and most of Muslim Spain.

ABD AL-RAHMAN, əb-dōol' ra-män', a common Arabo-Islamic name. Its variants include Abdul Rahman, Abd er-Rahman, Abdurrahman, Abd ur-Rahman.

ABD AR-RAHMAN I (731–788), əb-dōor' ra-män', was a Muslim emir who founded an Umayyad dynasty at Córdoba (Cordova), Spain. Born in Damascus, he was a grandson of Hisham, the 10th Umayyad caliph there. In 750 he fled to Africa to escape the massacre of his family by Abul-Abbas as-Saffah, who was attempting to establish the Abbasid caliphate (see ABBASID; UMAYYAD). Abd ar-Rahman wandered for several years in North Africa, seeking refuge with the Berbers and other tribes. In 755 he decided to intervene between the rival Muslim factions in Spain. After a year, forces under his leadership prevailed, and he was proclaimed emir of Andalusia in May 756.

Abd ar-Rahman ruled in Córdoba for 33 years but spent most of the first 20 years at war. The deposed Abbasid emir, Yusuf al-Fihri, laid siege to Córdoba in 758 and continued to resist Umayyad rule until he was killed near Toledo in 759. Abd ar-Rahman suppressed rebellions led by other Arab and Berber chieftains in the 760's.

In the last 10 years of his reign, Abd ar-Rahman was able to devote himself to consolidating his empire and beautifying his cities, especially Córdoba, his capital. He built a great palace called the Munyat ar-Rusafah on the outskirts of the city, and began construction of a mosque, which was completed by his successors. It became a Roman Catholic cathedral when Córdoba was taken in 1236 by Ferdinand III, king of Castile and León. Abd ar-Rahman also built an aqueduct to supply pure water to Córdoba, and fortified the city with a wall. He encouraged intellectual life. By the end of his reign, Córdoba began to rival Baghdad and Constantinople as a cultural center. He also developed forms of administrative and military organization, modeled on Syrian lines, which his successors adhered to for several centuries. He died at Córdoba on Sept. 30, 788.

ABD AR-RAHMAN III (889–961), əb-dŏŏr-ra-män', Muslim caliph in Spain, was the 8th Umayyad ruler of Córdoba (Cordova). He was the greatest of the Cordovan caliphs and one of the ablest rulers in history. When he acceded to the throne in 912, at the age of 23, most of the provincial governors had thrown off allegiance to the Umayyads. The country was in a state of civil war and anarchy caused by racial, religious, and factional quarrels between Arabs and Moors. Córdoba was surrounded by independent, hostile states that were waiting for it to disintegrate. To the south, the Fatimid dynasty had established a great empire in Africa and was anticipating a speedy and bloodless conquest of Spain. To the north, the new Christian states of León and Navarre were growing rapidly.

Abd ar-Rahman first put down the worst internal revolt, instigated by Ibn Hafsun of Andalusia. This victory eventually gained for Córdoba the cities of Seville, Carmona, Elvira, Bobastro, and Toledo. He then checked the Fatimids by subsidizing the native African princes who were willing to hold out against them.

The most serious danger was from the north. In 920, Abd ar-Rahman collected and equipped a splendid army which gained a victory over the combined forces of León and Navarre. He then undertook several campaigns in which he penetrated to Pamplona, capital of Navarre. The victory at Pamplona enabled him to strike successfully against the Basques and to secure his land boundaries for several years. He suffered only one severe defeat, at Salamanca in 939.

In North Africa, Abd ar-Rahman captured several strongholds, most important of which was Ceuta, taken in 931. His navy, the most powerful in the world at the time, fought several successful battles with the Fatimid navy for control of the western Mediterranean Sea.

In 929, Abd ar-Rahman adopted the title of caliph and the name al-Khalifa an-Nasir li-Din Allah (Caliph-Defender of the Religion of God). At his death, in Córdoba on Oct. 15, 961, he left a consolidated kingdom, a full treasury, internal order maintained by a vigilant police, flourishing agriculture based on scientific irrigation, and prosperous industry and commerce.

ABD AR-RAHMAN (died 732), əb-dŏŏr-ra-män', was a Muslim emir of Andalusia, Spain, from 730 until his death. He is remembered chiefly for an expedition into Frankish lands to capture the basilica of St. Martin at Tours. Near Poitiers, at the Battle of Tours in 732, his army was defeated by the Frankish forces of Charles Martel. This defeat marked the end of the Muslim threat to France, although Moorish raids into France continued for several years.

ABD AR-RAHMAN KHAN. See ABDUR RAHMAN KHAN.

ABD EL-KADER (1808–1883), əb-dŏŏl-kä'dir, was an Algerian national leader, who led the Arab resistance movement against the French in Algeria. A devout Muslim, he made a pilgrimage to Mecca when he was about 20. In 1832 he was proclaimed sultan of the Arabs, replacing his father as leader of the Arab resistance movement that had begun in 1830 after France occupied Algiers. His forces were defeated in 1833, but the French commander, Gen. Louis A. Desmichels, was obliged to recognize Abd el-Kader as ruler of the Arabs.

After consolidating his power, Abd el-Kader continued to fight the French. Although his forces met with little success, they prevented the French from winning a decisive victory. The Treaty of Tafna, signed on May 30, 1837, was very favorable to Abd el-Kader. His authority was extended to new territory, including the province of Oran and part of the province of Algiers.

In 1839 he accused France of breaking the treaty and renewed the war. He was driven into Morocco by General Bugeaud in 1843. With the support of the Moroccan sultan, Abd ar-Rahman, he declared a holy war against France. Their armies were defeated by the French at the Battle of Isly on Aug. 14, 1844 and thereafter the sultan refused him any further support.

Abd el-Kader continued his opposition to the French until he was captured by them in 1847. He was taken to France and imprisoned for five years. While in prison, he wrote a religious book, which in 1858 was translated into French under the title *Rappel à l'intelligent: Avis à l'indifférent.*

On Oct. 16, 1852, he was released by Napoleon III. He settled in Damascus, Syria in 1855 and was awarded the Grand Cross of the Legion of Honor by Napoleon III in 1860 for his part in saving thousands of Christians from a crowd of rioting Muslims. Abd el-Kader spent his last years in Damascus on a French pension. He died there the night of May 25–26, 1883.

ABDALLAH (545?–?570), əb-dŏŏl-lä', was the father of the prophet Mohammed, founder of the Islamic religion. His full Arabic name is *Abd Allah Ibn Abd al-Muttalib.* Abdallah died either just before or just after the birth of Mohammed, and the child was brought up first by Abdallah's father, Abd al-Muttalib, and then by his brother, abu-Talib. Abdallah's wife, Aminah, died when Mohammed was about six.

ABDALLAH IBN ZUBAIR (624–692), əb-dŏŏl-lä' ib'ən zŏŏ-bĭr', was an Arab leader who proclaimed himself caliph of Islam. His grandfather was Abu Bakr, father-in-law of the prophet Mohammed. His father was Zubair, a brother-in-law of Mohammed's wife Aisha. Abdallah began to recruit followers of his own shortly after the death of the first Umayyad caliph, Muawiya I. The new caliph, Yazid I, sent an army to arrest him, but its leader was taken prisoner and killed. After Yazid's death in 683, Abdallah proclaimed himself caliph. The opponents of the Umayyads in Egypt, Syria, and southern Arabia recognized him as their ruler, but he never had real authority. In 692, the fifth Umayyad caliph, Abd al-Malik, attacked Abdallah's forces at Mecca and killed him.

ABDALLATIF (1162/1163–1231/1232), äb-däl-lä-tēf′, was an Iraqi physician and scholar. His name in Arabic is *Abd al-Latif al-Baghdadi*. After his early studies in Baghdad, Abdallatif went to Mosul and then to Damascus for further study. In 1191 he joined the group of learned men gathered at Akka (Acre) by the sultan Saladin. He then journeyed to Egypt, where he became acquainted with Maimonides, the great Jewish philosopher. In Cairo he became a teacher of medicine and philosophy.

Of the many works that Abdallatif is supposed to have written, only one is generally known—his *Account of Egypt*, preserved in manuscript at Oxford University in England.

ABDALWADID, äb-däl-wä′did, was a dynasty of Berber rulers in western Algeria from 1236 to 1550. They are sometimes referred to as the *Banu Zayyan*.

The first king, Yaghmurasan Ben Zayyan, was originally the leader of the Abdalwadid tribe of nomads. He founded a kingdom at Tlemcen that eventually extended from the present Moroccan border to Bougie, east of Algiers. The dynasty came to an end when Tlemcen was conquered by the Turks.

ABDERA, ab-dir′ə, was an ancient Greek city on the Thracian coast, east of the mouth of the Nestus River and almost opposite the island of Thasos. Originally founded about 650 B.C. (according to Greek legend, by Hercules), it was rebuilt about 500 B.C. and became one of the richest cities on the Aegean Sea. Although Abdera was the birthplace of the philosophers Democritus and Protagoras, Abderites were proverbially regarded as stupid by other Greeks.

ABDICATION, ab-di-kā′shən, is the renunciation of a throne, high office, dignity, or function. The term is most frequently applied to the action of sovereign rulers.

Abdication may be compulsory, in which case the ruler does not really abdicate but is deposed; or it may be voluntary. Abdication may be forced by foreign conquest; by command of a foreign ruler when the king is a puppet, as when Napoleon shifted his brothers from throne to throne; by command of *de facto* controllers of the state, as with the puppet Roman emperors under the barbarian commanders in chief of the army; or by popular or factional insurrections. Voluntary abdication may result from a desire to let constitutional machinery have a fair chance to work alone, as with the Roman emperor Diocletian; from weariness with royal burdens, as with Murad II of Turkey; from physical ailments and discouragement, as with Emperor Charles V of the Holy Roman Empire; from shame at the results of a bad policy, as with William I of the Netherlands; or from unwillingness to retain a throne against the popular will, as with Louis Philippe of France. Edward VIII of Britain abdicated when the nation would not accept as its queen the woman he had chosen to marry.

Usually a sovereign may abdicate at will. But in Britain, the sovereign may abdicate only with the consent of Parliament. This parliamentary prerogative can lead to a forced abdication, as in the case of James II, who had no intention of abdicating. Parliament, by declaring in 1689 that James had "abdicated the government," in fact deposed the king.

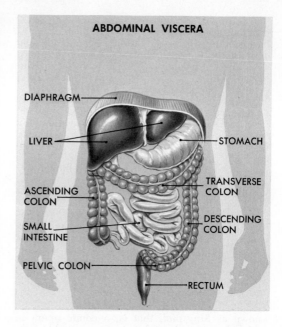

ABDOMINAL VISCERA

DIAPHRAGM

LIVER

STOMACH

ASCENDING COLON

TRANSVERSE COLON

SMALL INTESTINE

DESCENDING COLON

PELVIC COLON

RECTUM

ABDOMEN, ab′də-mən, the region of the human body trunk located between the chest region (thorax) and the lower part of the pelvis. It contains the abdominal cavity and the abdominal viscera, including most of the digestive organs. The abdominal cavity is bordered at the top and part of the back by the diaphragm, at the bottom by the rim of the lower part of the pelvis, at the back by the vertebral column and two muscles (psoas and quadratus lumborum) running along each side of the vertebrae, and at the front by several muscles, including the recti, transversus, and obliques.

The abdominal cavity is part of the coelomic cavity of the body. It is lined with peritoneum, a closed sac of serous membrane that also covers the viscera of the abdomen. Parts of the peritoneum form the mesenteries, omenta, ligaments, and bands that support and connect the abdominal organs.

When the abdominal cavity is opened, the abdominal viscera, or organs, are exposed as shown in the accompanying illustration. Other organs contained in the abdominal region, but not exposed initially, are the spleen, pancreas, gall bladder, kidneys, ureters, bladder, and, in the female, the uterus.

The abdomen is important in diagnosis. Such disturbances as acute appendicitis, perforated peptic ulcer, peritonitis, ectopic pregnancy, and acute pancreatitis can be recognized by abdominal signs.

"Abdomen" also is a descriptive term applied to the posterior portion of the body of arthropods. In some arthropods, such as the lobster, the abdomen bears appendages, while in higher arthropod forms, such as insects, it bears only egg-depositing structures or modified appendages. In many arthropods the abdominal section contains most of the internal organs.

ABDUCTION, ab-duk′shən, in criminal law, means the taking away of a wife, child, or ward (usually female) by fraud or persuasion or by open violence, for the purpose of marriage, sexual intercourse, concubinage, or prostitution.

Although the offense is variously defined in different states of the United States, most states have statutes that specify the taking and carrying away, detention, or harboring of a woman under a certain age (usually 16 or 18), with or without her consent.

If a statute forbids taking or detaining a woman against her will, the consent of her husband is no defense. The consent of a parent or guardian is a defense under some statutes. Unless the statute provides that awareness of a woman's age is an element of the offense, it makes no difference whether the person who is accused of abduction knew her age or may have believed her to be over the age limit.

ABDUCTION FROM THE SERAGLIO, sə-ral'yō, was Wolfgang Amadeus Mozart's first important German opera. Titled *Die Entführung aus dem Serail* in German, it was commissioned by Emperor Joseph II in 1781, but its premiere performance at the Vienna Burgtheater did not take place until the following year, on July 16, 1782. The libretto is an adaptation by Gottlieb Stephanie of a play by Christoph F. Bretzner.

The Abduction belongs to a class of opera known as *Singspiel*, that is, a comic opera in which the musical numbers are separated by spoken dialogue. Historically, *Singspiel* was English ballad opera (for example, John Gay's *Beggar's Opera*, 1728) transplanted to the German stage. *The Abduction* is the earliest example of it still regularly performed.

The plot of *The Abduction from the Seraglio* revolves around the efforts of Belmonte (tenor) and his servant Pedrillo (tenor) to rescue Constanze (soprano) and her maid Blöndchen (soprano) from the hands of Selim Bassa, a Turkish pasha (speaking part). The pasha's overseer, Osmin (bass), nearly foils the determined efforts of the rescuers, but at the last moment the good-hearted Selim relents and grants the two pairs of lovers their freedom.

The principal musical numbers of the opera include the overture; Constanze's staggeringly difficult aria, *Marten aller Arten;* Osmin's formidable "triumph" aria; the florid songs of Blöndchen; Belmonte's *Ich baue ganz;* and the Janissaries' chorus.

Although *The Abduction from the Seraglio* contains much fine music, it is not performed as frequently as Mozart's Italian operas. A complex work, it requires that the voices of the singers have great range and flexibility. In addition, *The Abduction* is an intimate opera that tends to be dwarfed in large theaters.

WILLIAM ASHBROOK, *Author of "Donizetti"*

ABDUL-AZIZ (1830–1876), äb'dōōl ä-zēz', was the 32d sultan of Turkey. A son of Mahmud II, he succeeded his brother Abdul-Medjid I on June 20, 1861. His reign was chiefly notable for the growth of Western influence in Turkey. He obtained loans from abroad, constructed railroads, reorganized the armed forces, and modernized and expanded public education.

The sultan's government had great difficulties to contend with in the Cretan insurrection of 1866. He was the first Turkish sultan to travel abroad. In 1874, because of inefficient administration, foreign debt, and royal extravagance, the government declared itself bankrupt. Abdul-Aziz was deposed on May 30, 1876, and committed suicide on June 4.

ABDUL-BAHA (1844–1921), äb'dōōl bä-hä', was the foremost exponent of the Bahai faith. Born *Abbas Effendi* in Shiraz, Iran, on May 23, 1844, he was the eldest son of Bahaullah, one of the founders of the faith. The date of Abdul-Baha's birth coincided with the revelation of the mission of Babism, from which the Bahai faith derived (see BABISM; BAHAULLAH).

Just before his death in 1892, Bahaullah designated Abdul-Baha as leader of the Bahais. Although he was vigorously opposed by his brothers, Abdul-Baha assumed the powers of interpretation and revelation in the Bahai faith. His doctrine of spiritual unity of all peoples allowed for no racial or religious prejudice. He was a strong crusader for international peace and advocated disarmament as a first step toward achieving this goal. His views attracted people from Asia and the Middle East.

The Bahais had been forced by Persian authorities to move from Baghdad to Acre, Palestine, where the Turkish government kept them in confinement for almost 40 years. As a result of the Young Turk movement in 1908, they were released. Abdul-Baha chose, however, to remain at Acre, maintaining that city as the center of the Bahai faith.

In 1910 he went to Egypt in the first of three great missionary journeys. From 1911 to 1913 he traveled through Europe and the United States, winning many converts to the Bahai faith. He was knighted by the British government in 1920. Abdul-Baha died in Acre on Nov. 28, 1921. His tomb is in the Bahai shrine on Mount Carmel, Haifa, Israel. See also BAHAI FAITH.

ABDUL-HAMID I (1725–1789), äb'dōōl hä-mēd', was a sultan of Turkey. The son of Ahmed III, he was born on March 20, 1725, and succeeded his brother, Mustafa III, on Jan. 21, 1774. The chief events of his reign were two wars with Russia, both of which were disastrous for Turkey.

When Abdul-Hamid acceded to the throne, Turkey was involved in a war with Russia that had begun in 1768. During the first year of his reign, Turkey suffered two devastating defeats by Russian troops and was forced to agree to the humiliating Treaty of Kuchuk Kainarji, by which Russia acquired large areas of land from Turkey and gained navigational rights on the Black Sea and through the Straits to the Mediterranean. Another important provision of the treaty set up the Crimea as an independent state.

Turkey was further humiliated in 1775, when Austria, taking advantage of Turkey's weakness, seized the province of Bukovina, and Persia invaded Kurdistan, touching off another war. Ottoman forces sent to Baghdad were badly defeated, and Basra fell to the Persians in 1776.

Another war with Russia began in 1787, in response to the annexation of the Crimea by Catherine the Great in 1783 and her encouragement of nationalists in Greece, then part of the Ottoman Empire. Abdul-Hamid died on April 7, 1789, after receiving news of a severe defeat of his forces by the Russians.

ABDUL-HAMID II (1842–1918), äb'dōōl hä-mēd', was the 34th ruler of the Ottoman empire. The son of Abdul-Mejid I and Tirimujgan, a Circassian, he was born on Sept. 21, 1842. He came to the throne during one of the most critical periods in the later history of the empire. The *Tanzimat* (reorganization) reform edicts, proclaimed first

ABDUL-HAMID II, autocratic sultan of the Ottoman Empire until 1909, when he was deposed by the Young Turks.

in 1839 and expanded in 1856, had prepared the ground for constitutional change and liberalization of the state. A group of ministers, including the constitutionalist Midhat Pasha, deposed Abdul-Aziz in May 1876 and placed his nephew Murad V on the throne. Murad's deranged mind necessitated his removal from the throne. Abdul-Hamid had declared himself in favor of constitutional government, and the fact that he had been associated with the liberal Society of New Ottomans won the confidence of the liberals, who placed him on the throne on Sept. 1, 1876.

Repression. To fulfill guarantees he had made before his accession, Abdul-Hamid proclaimed the first Ottoman constitution on Dec. 23, 1876. The constitution provided for a bicameral parliament, which met for the first time on March 17, 1877. It survived less than a year; Abdul-Hamid used a disastrous war with Russia as a pretext for closing it on Feb. 13, 1878.

The Treaty of Berlin (July 13, 1878), which ended the Russo-Turkish War, reduced Ottoman territory and led to increased national agitation among the sultan's non-Muslim subjects. Abdul-Hamid spent the next few years consolidating his position. In 1881, Midhat Pasha and several of his supporters were tried for the alleged murder of Abdul-Aziz. Midhat was convicted and banished to Arabia, where he was murdered in 1883, apparently on the sultan's orders. His disappearance reduced the activities of the sultan's foes. Many took refuge in Europe or went underground, keeping alive the desire to return to constitutional government. Both the inability of the liberals to agree on a course of action and the efficiency of Abdul-Hamid's secret police allowed him to stay in power.

Reform. Despite his bitter hostility to constitutional and liberal ideas, Abdul-Hamid accept-

ed some Westernization and reform in certain areas. Many administrative, legal, and educational reforms begun in earlier reigns were continued and actually speeded up during his reign. His greatest achievements were in education. He increased the number of secular schools training badly needed technicians and civil servants, and he established the University of Istanbul (1900).

Although he was less successful in reforming the empire's legal and fiscal systems, Abdul-Hamid effected great advances in communications as part of his attempt to centralize power in his own hands. He personally presided over the improvement and expansion of rail and telegraph services. In 1888, Hungary was linked with Istanbul and Ankara as part of the Baghdad Railroad project. In keeping with his pan-Islamic policy of uniting all Muslims around himself as caliph, Abdul-Hamid also sponsored the Hejaz Railway to the holy places in Arabia. The railway was built by popular subscription. The press, although greatly restricted by state censorship, developed swiftly and contributed significantly to the literacy and political awareness of the public. At the same time the output of books was almost doubled, chiefly in the fields of literature and education.

Rebellion. Meanwhile, dissatisfaction with Abdul-Hamid's rule continued to grow. Westerners called him "Abdul the Damned" and "Bloody Abdul." The Young Turk movement, an outgrowth of the earlier Society of New Ottomans, hoped to reinstate the constitution of 1876. Although hampered in their activities by factional dissensions and official repression, the Young Turks achieved some degree of unity when they succeeded in organizing the Committee of Union and Progress in 1907. Finally, on July 24, 1908, a revolt precipitated by the fear that the empire would lose more European provinces through the machinations of the great powers forced Abdul-Hamid to restore the suspended constitution of 1876. He remained on the throne but was suspected of intriguing with reactionary elements that staged an unsuccessful counterrevolution. This led to his deposition on April 28, 1909. The last of the strong sultans, he died in Istanbul on Feb. 10, 1918.

J. STEWART-ROBINSON
University of Michigan

ABDUL-JABBAR, ab'dōōl jə-bär', **Kareem** (1947–), American basketball player, a 7′2″ (218-cm) center who, at his retirement, had played more years (20), scored more points (38,387), and blocked more shots (3,189) than any other National Basketball Association (NBA) player. He perfected the "sky hook," using his long arms and finesse to swoop in over hapless defenders.

Jabbar, whose given name was Ferdinand Lewis Alcindor, was born in New York City on April 16, 1947, and grew up in Harlem. He led Power Memorial High School's basketball team to a 95-6 winning record. He went on to play for the University of California, Los Angeles. The Bruins won NCAA championships in 1967, 1968, and 1969, and he was named NCAA Tournament Outstanding Player each of those years. On converting to Islam in 1968, he took the name Kareem Abdul-Jabbar and changed his name legally in 1971.

First pick in the 1969 NBA draft, Jabbar quickly became a force with the Milwaukee

KAREEM ABDUL-JABBAR, playing for the Lakers, displays his famous "sky hook" in a game with the Celtics.

Bucks. He was rookie of the year and finished second in his league in scoring. Jabbar and guard Oscar Robertson together made Milwaukee unstoppable. The team closed the 1971 regular season with an .805 winning percentage and an NBA championship. Jabbar led the league in scoring, averaging 31.7 points per game, and won the first of his record six most valuable player (MVP) awards.

Four years and two MVP's later, prior to the 1975–1976 season, Jabbar was traded to the Los Angeles Lakers. He again gained MVP honors in his first two years with the Lakers. Point guard Earvin "Magic" Johnson's arrival in 1979 seemed to spark Jabbar, as had Robertson's with the Bucks. The Lakers won the 1980 NBA championship, and Jabbar received his sixth MVP.

The Lakers and Jabbar won four more championships in the 1980's. At the "grandfatherly" (for basketball) age of 41, Jabbar led his team to his final championship in 1988. He retired following the 1989 season.

HARVEY FROMMER, Coauthor of "Red on Red:
The Autobiography of Red Holzman"

ABDUL-MEJID I, äb'dōōl me-jēd'. (1823–1861), was a Turkish sultan of the Ottoman empire. Born on April 25, 1823, he succeeded his father, Mahmud II, as sultan on July 1, 1839. He was a liberal, refined, and humane ruler who was very receptive to Western ideas, but he lacked the strength necessary to put into effect the reforms he so earnestly desired. He died on June 25, 1861, leaving the empire in the throes of a financial crisis brought about largely by his unsound fiscal policies.

Abdul-Mejid (or *Abdul-Medjid*) came to the throne when the Ottoman armies had just suffered a humiliating defeat at the hands of Muhammad Ali, the rebellious governor of Egypt. To gain the support of the European powers, Abdul-Mejid promulgated on Nov. 3, 1839, the *Hatt-i Sherif of Gülhane* (Noble Rescript of the Rose Chamber). This document ended the internal war and inaugurated the era of the *Tanzimat* (Reorganization) reform.

Abdul-Mejid hoped, through rescripts, to continue the reforms begun by his father and to demonstrate to the Europeans that the Turks were capable of instituting a modern liberal state. A clause designed to reassure the European powers, who were concerned about the empire's non-Muslim population, promised to guarantee the liberty, life, and property of all subjects of the sultan. The decree also provided for modernization of the state with a view to regularizing recruitment into the armed forces, collection of taxes, and the judicial processes. Edicts implementing these innovations were issued, but only a few bore lasting results.

J. STEWART-ROBINSON
University of Michigan

ABDUL RAHMAN, äb'dōōl rä'män, **Tunku** (1903–1990), the first prime minister of Malaysia. His title "Tunku" means "prince."

Yang Teramat Mulia Tunku Abdul Rahman Putra al-Haj, the seventh son of Abdul Hamid Halim Shah, sultan of Kedah, was born in Alor Star, Kedah, Malaya, on Feb. 8, 1903. He graduated from St. Catherine's College, Cambridge, in 1925. For five years he read law at the Inner Temple in London but failed the bar examinations. In 1931 he returned to Malaya and became a district officer in civil service.

Until the Japanese occupation during World War II, when he came into contact with the Malayan independence movement, Abdul Rahman showed little capacity for serious work. After the war, determined to pursue a government career, he returned to London and passed the bar in 1949. His interest in politics was heightened by the postwar turmoil in Malaya, and on his return he became associated with the United Malay National Organization (UMNO). After serving in the federal government as a prosecutor and a judge, he was elected president of UMNO in 1951.

As leader of UMNO he brought about an alliance between his party and the Malayan-Chinese Association in 1952, thus forming the coalition known as the Alliance party, which became the dominant party in Malaya. Elected chief minister of Malaya in 1955, he continued to press for independence, and in 1957 he became prime minister of the new nation.

Abdul Rahman was the central figure in negotiating the union of Malaya with Singapore, North Borneo (now Sabah), and Sarawak in 1963. He guided the resulting federation of Malaysia as its prime minister. However, in 1965 he reluctantly asked Singapore to withdraw from Malaysia because of political problems. In 1969 tensions between Malays and Chinese erupted into violence, and Abdul Rahman suspended the constitution. Under attack for having placated the Chinese, allegedly to the neglect of Malay advancement, he resigned in 1970. He died on Dec. 6, 1990, in Kuala Lumpur.

JAMES R. SHIRLEY, *Northern Illinois University*

ABDULLAH, äb-dōōl'ä, **Sheikh Mohammed** (1905–1982), Kashmiri political leader, known as "The Lion of Kashmir." Born in Soura, Kashmir, on Dec. 5, 1905, he became active in political reform movements in his student days at Lahore University. The first of his nine imprisonments came in 1931, when he founded the Kashmir Muslim Conference, urging self-rule in Kashmir. As a noncommunal Muslim, he worked with Mohandas K. Gandhi and Jawaharlal Nehru in the Indian National Congress. In 1947 he gained control of the Kashmir government by a coup and became chief minister in 1948. Through his leadership a special position for Kashmir was worked out under the Indian constitution. In 1953 he denounced India's treatment of Kashmir and demanded self-determination. He was deposed and spent much of the next 20 years in "preventive detention" or in exile. Released in 1973, he expressed more moderate views and served again as chief minister of Kashmir from 1975 until his death in Srinagar on Sept. 8, 1982.

JAMES R. SHIRLEY, *Northern Illinois University*

ABDULLAH IBN HUSEIN (1882–1951), əb-dōōl-lä' ib'ən hōō-sän', was the first king of the Hashemite Kingdom of Jordan. He was born in Mecca, Arabia, the son of Husein Ibn Ali, king of the Hejaz. His early years were spent in Constantinople (now Istanbul) at the court of the Turkish sultan, Abdul-Hamid II. He sat in the Turkish parliament in 1908–1914, representing the Hejaz, then part of the Ottoman empire.

Abdullah participated in 1914 in the negotiations with Lord Kitchener, British consul general in Egypt, that led to the Arab revolt against Turkish rule during World War I. After the war, in 1920, the Arabs proclaimed Abdullah's younger brother Faisal (1885–1933) king of Syria and Abdullah king of Iraq, but France, the mandatory power for Syria, refused to recognize the arrangement. Faisal became king of Iraq, and the British government persuaded Abdullah to take the title of emir of Transjordan, at that time part of the British-mandated territory of Palestine.

With British financial and military air, Abdullah administered Transjordan successfully. During World War II he remained a steadfast ally of Britain, opposing the pro-Nazi mufti of Jerusalem. When the mandate was ended in 1946, Britain granted independence to Transjordan, and Abdullah assumed the title of king.

In the Palestine crisis that followed establishment of the state of Israel in 1948, Abdullah resisted United Nations truce efforts, led Arab troops across the Israeli border, and seized a long strip of territory on the west bank of the Jordan River and along the Red Sea coast. After the fighting ended, he refused to recognize a government for the Arab-controlled sections of Palestine that had been arranged by the Arab League. Instead, in 1950, he formally incorporated these areas of Palestine into his realm, which then became the Hashemite Kingdom of Jordan. The annexed area included the Old City portion of Jerusalem, within which lies the Mosque of Umar. Abdullah was assassinated as he entered the mosque for prayer on July 20, 1951. He was succeeded by his eldest son, Talal.

ABDUR RAHMAN KHAN (1844?–1901), äb'dər-ru-män' KHän, was an amir of Afghanistan, who took the throne with the aid of the British. He was the son of Afzul Khan and the grandson of Dost Mohammed Khan. Dost Mohammed Khan, before his death in 1853, named his third son, Shir Ali, as his successor. Upon Shir Ali's accession to the throne, his older brothers, Afzul Khan and Azam Khan, rose in revolt. They were supported by Abdur Rahman Khan in a civil war that lasted for five years. Shir Ali was finally victorious and Abdur Rahman Khan was forced to flee. He took refuge in Samarkand, under the protection of Gen. Konstantin Kaufmann.

During the Second British-Afghan War, Shir Ali died, his son was deported, and Abdur Rahman Khan was recognized as amir by the British. In return he granted Britain control of Afghanistan's foreign relations. He established a strong national army and instituted effective tax collection. In 1893 he accepted the Durand line as the Afghan-Indian boundary.

ABE LINCOLN IN ILLINOIS is a Pulitzer Prize-winning play by Robert E. Sherwood, first produced in 1938. The 12 scenes of the play are set in New Salem and Springfield, Ill., between 1831 and 1861. Based on historical events, the play traces Lincoln's career from unsuccessful storekeeper to president-elect of the United States. Lincoln changes from a melancholy and apathetic youth to a man of grave and responsible determination. The people who affect his life include Mentor Graham, the New Salem schoolmaster; Ann Rutledge, Lincoln's early love; William Herndon, his law clerk; Ninian Edwards, his brother-in-law; Mary Todd Lincoln, his wife; and Seth Gale, a friend whose difficulties in reaching Oregon symbolize for Lincoln the problems facing the nation. In the final scene Lincoln delivers his farewell address at the Springfield train station before leaving for Washington, D.C.

À BECKETT, ə bek'it, a family of English writers associated with the early days of the British humor magazine *Punch.*

GILBERT ABBOTT À BECKETT, born in London on Jan. 9, 1811, was a lawyer before becoming a writer. In 1831 he founded the magazine *Figaro in London,* and in 1841 joined the original staff of *Punch.* His most successful comic character was a lawyer, Mr. Briefless, who appeared in many of his stories in *Punch.* À Beckett wrote more than 60 plays and a number of humorous works, including *Comic Blackstone* (1846) and *Comic History of England* (1847). He died at Boulogne, France, on Aug. 30, 1856.

GILBERT ARTHUR À BECKETT, his son, was born in London on April 7, 1837. He also turned from law to writing, and became a well-known contributor to *Punch,* whose staff he joined in 1879. He was primarily a dramatist and librettist. His most popular work, written with William S. Gilbert, was *The Happy Land* (1873), a burlesque of Gilbert's *Wicked World.* He died in London on Oct. 15, 1891.

ARTHUR WILLIAM À BECKETT, another son of Gilbert Abbott, was born in London on Oct. 25, 1844. A precocious writer of satire and humor, he was assistant editor of the *Glowworm* by the time he was 20. He covered the Franco-Prussian War as a special correspondent for the London *Standard* and the *Globe.* From 1875 to 1902 he was on the staff of *Punch.* His books include *The À Becketts of "Punch"* (1903) and *Recollections of a Humourist* (1907). He died in London on Jan. 14, 1909.

ABEL, ā'bəl (from the Hebraic *Hebhel,* meaning "vapor" or "breath"), was the second son of Adam and Eve. Their first son was Cain. Abel became a keeper of sheep and Cain a tiller of the soil, and both offered the Lord sacrifices of the first fruits of their labor. For a cause not disclosed in the Old Testament narrative, Abel's sacrifice proved acceptable, while Cain's was rejected. Cain, out of jealousy, killed Abel, bringing down upon himself the curse of God. The Bible story is in Genesis 4:2–16.

Abel is mentioned in the New Testament (Matthew 23:35) as the first of the "righteous" who died for their faith. However, some Bible students interpret the story of Cain and Abel as telescoping a long period of time between man's first appearance and the emergence of animal husbandry and agriculture. Some identify it with a belief among early nomadic tribes that animal herding (their principal occupation) was more pleasing to the gods than agriculture. Hebrews 11:4 and 12:24 also give some insight into the meaning of Abel's death.

ABEL, ā'bəl, **John Jacob** (1857–1938), American physician and physiological chemist, whose major successes included the isolation of insulin in crystalline form and the isolation of adrenalin. He was also an authority on the chemistry of the ductless glands.

Abel was born at Cleveland, Ohio, on May 19, 1857. After receiving the Ph.B degree from the University of Michigan in 1883, he took advanced work in physiology at Johns Hopkins University for a year and then went abroad for seven years to study medicine and chemistry at the universities of Leipzig, Heidelberg, Vienna, Bern, Würzburg, and Strasbourg, receiving his M.D. degree at Strasbourg in 1888.

He served the Medical School of Johns Hopkins University as professor of pharmacology from 1893 to 1932, as emeritus thereafter, and as director of the Laboratory for Endocrine Research until his death. He made numerous discoveries concerning the chemical composition of animal tissues and fluids and the toxic and therapeutical action of many substances. Abel died at Baltimore, Md., on May 26, 1938.

ABEL, ä'bəl, **Karl Friedrich** (1723–1787), German musician and composer, who was the last great virtuoso player of the viola da gamba, a bass viol having a range of about that of the cello. There is a tradition that he studied with Johann Sebastian Bach at St. Thomas' School in Leipzig, but it is of doubtful authenticity.

Abel was born at Köthen, Germany, on Dec. 22, 1723. He studied music with his father, a musician in the court chapel at Köthen. From 1748 to 1758 he was a member of the Dresden Royal Polish Band. In 1759 he went to London, where he soon acquired fame as a player of the viola da gamba, the harpsichord, and other instruments. From 1765 he confined himself to the viola da gamba. He was appointed chamber musician to Queen Charlotte of England in 1765.

Beginning in 1765, Abel and Johann Christian Bach, a son of Johann Sebastian Bach, conducted a series of subscription concerts in London, at which the symphonies of Franz Joseph Haydn received their first British performances. After Bach's death in 1782, Abel occasionally produced other, though less successful, concert series. He died in London on June 20, 1787.

Abel wrote symphonies, overtures, sonatas, chamber music, and music for the viola da gamba. He also wrote two operas, *Love in a Village* (1760) and *Berenice* (1764). He was an exceptionally knowledgeable composer, and modern critics consider his music tasteful and melodic, if somewhat deficient in imagination.

ABEL, ä'bəl, **Niels Henrik** (1802–1829), Norwegian mathematician, who made important contributions to the development of mathematics. He was born on Aug. 5, 1802 on the island of Finnøy, Norway. At the age of 13, Niels Henrik entered the Cathedral School in Oslo. He was a mediocre student until a new teacher, B.M. Holmboe, discovered his unusual mathematical talent. Holmboe rapidly guided him through the principal mathematical works. Before graduating from high school, Abel was well on the path to independent research. His father died in 1820 and left a widow and five children destitute. From then on, Abel lived on fellowships and with the support of his university professors. He entered the University of Oslo in 1821.

Abel's first mathematical studies concerned a burning mathematical problem of the time: Can the solutions of an algebraic equation of fifth degree be expressed by radicals, that is, by successive extractions of roots? It had been known for centuries that solutions of equations of second, third, and fourth degree could be expressed by radicals. At first Abel believed he had found a solution to the problem, but he discovered his error. Then he turned the problem around and proved that there is no general radical solution for fifth degree and higher degree equations. He published his result in 1824 in a pamphlet that went unnoticed at the time.

In 1825, Abel received a government fellowship for foreign travel. In Berlin, he met A.L. Crelle, who was planning the publication of the first German mathematical journal. The first volumes of Crelle's journal (Journal for Pure and Applied Mathematics) contain a series of Abel's papers on equation theory, function theory, and power series—all with new results presented with a degree of mathematical stringency previously unattained.

From Berlin, Abel went to Paris, where he presented a now famous theorem on integrals of algebraic functions. The paper was disregarded by the referee, A.L. Cauchy, and it was not printed until long after Abel's death.

In 1827, Abel returned to Oslo; he was out of funds and sick with tuberculosis. Nevertheless, he managed to write a series of papers on elliptic functions, a new theory generalizing the trigonometric functions. Abel was spurred on by a paper by the German mathematician K.G.J. Jacobi, who seemed to be on the same path.

Abel's economic situation improved a little after he was appointed to a substitute position at the University of Oslo. At Christmas, 1828, he suffered a lung hemorrhage while visiting his fiancée in the country. He died at Froland on April 6, 1829, at the age of 26.

Abel's work had a profound influence on mathematics in the 19th century. A number of results and concepts in modern mathematics carry his name. His complete works were published at Oslo, in two volumes, in 1881.

OYSTEIN ORE, *Author of*
"Niels Henrik Abel,
Mathematician Extraordinary"

ABELARD, ab′ə-lärd, **Peter** (1079–1142), French philosopher and theologian, who was a brilliant teacher and dialectician and a leading figure in medieval Scholasticism. The French form of his name is *Pierre Abélard* or *Abailard;* the Latin form, *Petrus Abaelardus.*

Rise to Prominence. Abelard was born at Le Pallet, near Nantes, in northwestern France, the eldest son of the village lord. He studied logic at Loches, under Roscellinus, and at the Cathedral School in Paris under William of Champeaux. Dissatisfied with William's teaching, Abelard established his own school, first in 1102 at Melun, next at Corbeil, and later at Paris, where he engaged in a dispute with William, forcing the latter to change his views on the nature of universal ideas. Abelard then turned his attention to theology, attending the lectures of Anselm of Laon. However, his criticism of the renowned theologian led to his expulsion from Laon and his return to Paris.

His Calamities. Because of his growing reputation as a rhetorician and theologian, Abelard was granted an honorary canonship and offered the chair of philosophy and theology at Notre Dame Cathedral School in Paris. While this appointment marked the climax of his career, it was also the beginning of his serious troubles— difficulties he describes in his autobiographical notes *Historia calamitatum mearum.* Students from many lands, including future bishops, cardinals, and even a pope (Celestine II) were attracted by the brilliance of his mind and the warmth of his personality. At this time he became involved in the much romanticized episode with Héloïse, niece of Canon Fulbert. This affair resulted in the birth of a child and their subsequent secret marriage. Héloïse's uncle took revenge on Abelard by having him emasculated. After this cruel punishment, Abelard retired to the Abbey of St. Denis. Héloïse meanwhile had joined the Benedictine nuns at Argenteuil.

Abelard resumed his teaching at St. Denis, but his efforts to reform the monastic discipline there brought him into disfavor. The stituation was further complicated by publication of his treatise *De unitate et trinitate divina,* which was condemned in 1121 by the Council of Soissons. There followed a period of enforced retirement at the Monastery of St. Médard, after which he returned to St. Denis. Further difficulties with his superiors at St. Denis led to Abelard's flight from the abbey and his establishment of an oratory of the Paraclete near Nogent-sur-Seine. Here he lectured to a large student following until 1125, when he was elected abbot of St. Gildas de Rhuys in Brittany. After several years of unsuccessful effort to impose a stricter rule, Abelard left the abbey and returned to the Paraclete, where Héloïse had become superior of the convent he had founded. It is thought that the famous letters between Abelard and Héloïse were exchanged at this time.

In 1136, Abelard was again in Paris, teaching at Ste. Geneviève. Here new charges of heresy were leveled against him by Bernard of Clairvaux, causing Abelard to be condemned by the Council of Sens in 1141. He set out for Rome to plead his case before Pope Innocent II but learned that the pope had confirmed his condemnation and enjoined him from teaching.

Abelard was befriended by the abbot of Cluny, Peter the Venerable, and through Peter's good offices Abelard regained Bernard's friendship and retracted his theological errors. Abelard died at the Priory of St. Marcel, near Chalon-sur-Saône, on April 21, 1142. His body was taken to the Paraclete and later transferred to the cemetery of Père Lachaise in Paris.

Contributions to Philosophy and Theology. Abelard wrote a number of philosophical and theological works. They include several commentaries on the *logica vetus* (the logic known to him from Boethius' interpretation of Aristotle); *Dialectica,* his own elaboration of the logical doctrines; *Theologia Christiana,* an enlargement of his *De unitate; Theologia*—a further expansion of the *De unitate*—of which the only extant section is *Introductio ad theologiam; Sic et non,* a collection of conflicting patristic texts; *Scito teipsum,* a moral treatise; and *Dialogus inter philosophum, iudaeum et christianum,* a defense of Christian doctrine.

Abelard was a leading figure in early Scholasticism, known principally for his part in the controversy on universals. In this dispute he took a position between Roscellinus' nominalism and William of Champeaux's realism. Accepting Aristotle's definition of a universal as something that can be predicated of many things—"man" is predicated of all human beings—Abelard asked himself whether universals exist in reality or only in thought. His answer was that universals are not real things, since each real thing is individual. On the other hand, universals are not mere words since they express a common reality that exists in things and serves as a basis for logical predication. Universals are concepts formed by abstraction in such a way that the nature of a thing is freed, as it were, from all individuality, with no special relation to any particular individual of the species. Thus Abelard avoided attributing to a universal a reality of its own or downgrading it to a verbal entity with no conceptual import. His position was close to the later concept of moderate realism.

Abelard also applied his dialectic to theology. He argued that faith and reason are as distinct and different as the theology and philosophy on which they rest, respectively. Yet theology needs philosophy, and especially dialectic, to establish its status as a science. As proof he tried to show in his *Sic et non* that the proper solution of a theological issue can be obtained only by an objective study of all divergent texts on the subject. In his *Introductio ad theologiam* he also made the attempt—first of its kind in the history of Scholasticism—to coordinate and treat systematically all current theological issues. He seems, however, to have carried his dialectic too far by exaggerating the power of human reason in matters of faith and rationalizing even the mysteries of Christian doctrine.

BERNARDINO M. BONANSEA, O.F.M.
The Catholic University of America

Bibliography
Editions of Abelard's works include *Abaelardiana inedita* (Edizioni di Storia e letteratura 1958): *Ethics,* ed. by D. E. Luscombe (Oxford 1971); and *The Cruel Tragedy of My Life: The Autobiography of Peter Abelard* (Found Class Reprints 1985).
McCabe, Joseph, *Peter Abelard* (1901; reprint, B. Franklin 1972).
McCallum, James R., *Abelard's Christian Theology* (Oxford 1949).
Moncrieff, C. K. Scott, *The Letters of Abelard and Heloise* (Cooper Square 1974).
Smits, Edme R., *Peter Abelard, Letters IX–XIV* (Benjamins North Am 1983).
Starnes, Kathleen M., *Peter Abelard: His Place in History* (Univ. Press of Am. 1981).

ABELL, ä′bəl, **Kjeld** (1901–1961), Danish dramatist, whose plays combine sparkling, sophisticated wit with a socialistic message. He was born at Ribe, Jutland, Denmark, on Aug. 25, 1901. Although he earned a degree in political science, he turned to the theater, working for some years as a stage designer in London and Paris.

Abell achieved his first success as a playwright with *Melodien, der blev væk* (1935; Eng. tr., *The Melody That Got Lost*, 1939). His best work, however, is *Anna Sophie Hedvig* (1939; Eng. tr., 1944), in which a provincial schoolteacher is driven to commit murder. The play is essentially a study of contemporary dictatorship. Among his other works are *Dage paa en Sky* (1947; *Days on a Cloud*) and *Skriget* (1961; *The Scream*). Abell died at Copenhagen on March 5, 1961.

HALLBERG HALLMUNDSSON
Editor, "An Anthology of Scandinavian Literature"

ABERCROMBIE, ab′ər-krom-bē, **Lascelles** (1881–1938), English poet and critic, who became a leader of the Georgian poets, a group of pre-World War I poets that included Rupert Brooke, John Drinkwater, Wilfrid Gibson, and Walter de la Mare. Abercrombie was born at Ashton-upon-Mersey, England, on Jan. 9, 1881. In 1902 he left the University of Manchester to begin writing. His early books of verse included *Interludes and Poems* (1908), *Mary and the Bramble* (1910), and *Emblems of Love* (1912). He gave up writing during World War I when he worked as a munitions inspector. After the war he taught at the University of Liverpool (1919–1922), Leeds University (1922–1929), and the University of London (1929–1935). From 1935 he was Goldsmith's reader in English at Oxford. He died in London on Oct. 27, 1938.

Abercrombie has been called an "ivory tower" poet. Although his verse was praised by the critics of his day, it is difficult and unemotional, and it was never well known to the general public. His poetry often expresses disenchantment with the industrially orientated civilization of the 20th century, and unfailingly follows complex and irregular structural patterns that are highly suggestive of the poetic forms of classical antiquity.

Abercrombie's critical works include *Thomas Hardy: A Critical Study* (1912), *The Theory of Poetry* (1924), and *The Idea of Great Poetry* (1924). The latter two books develop a poetic philosophy in which the main function of poetry is to be an expression rather than an imitation of life. *The Sale of St. Thomas*, a verse drama that Abercrombie considered his best work, was published in 1930, the year in which his collected poems also appeared.

His brother, Patrick Abercrombie (q.v.), was the foremost British town planner of his day.

ABERCROMBIE, ab′ər-krom-bē, **Sir Patrick** (1879–1957), British town planner and architect, who was the foremost civic planner of his day. Born in Ashton-upon-Mersey, England, Leslie Patrick Abercrombie studied at schools in Locker's Park and Uppingham and gained practical experience with architectural firms in Manchester and Liverpool. He was professor of civic design at the University of Liverpool from 1915 to 1935 and professor of town planning at University College, London, from 1935 to 1946.

Abercrombie developed replanning projects for a number of English cities, including one for the preservation of Stratford-on-Avon (with his brother, the poet Lascelles Abercrombie). After World War II, he was active in planning the rebuilding of London, Plymouth, Bath, and other bomb-damaged English cities. In his most important book, *County of London Plan* (1943), written in collaboration with J.H. Forshaw, he envisioned the decentralization of London through a series of self-contained "satellite" communities near the urban center. At the time of his death, some of these "new towns" were well on their way to completion. His other writings include *Town and Country Planning* (1933).

Abercrombie was knighted in 1945. He died at Aston Tirrold, Berkshire, on March 23, 1957.

ABERCROMBY, ab′ər-krom-bē, **James** (1706–1781), British general whose forces were routed in 1758 at Ticonderoga, N.Y., during the French and Indian War. Made commander in chief of British forces in North America in March 1758, he advanced on the French at Fort Carillon (renamed Fort Ticonderoga the next year), performing a remarkable logistic feat in moving 15,000 fully equipped and supplied troops through the wilderness. His defeat, on July 8, was due in part to the loss of his troop commander but also to his own tactical ineptitude and his unwillingness to take advice from colonials. In repeated and prolonged frontal assaults, without artillery, against 5,000 entrenched soldiers, his army took frightful casualties until it panicked and fled. In the fall, Abercromby was recalled to England, where he died on April 28, 1781.

HARRISON BIRD
Author of "Battle for a Continent"

ABERCROMBY, ab′ər-krom-bē, **Sir Ralph** (1734–1801), British general, who was one of a group of able British officers whose fame has been overshadowed by the later achievements of the duke of Wellington.

Abercromby was born in Menstry, Scotland in October 1734. He entered the army in 1756, and from 1758 to the end of the Seven Years' War (1763) he served in Germany under Prince Ferdinand of Brunswick. These years of experience under a first-class commander taught Abercromby much. His Whig principles prevented his participation in the American Revolution, but he distinguished himself in the opening campaigns against France in 1793–1795 and gained an independent command in the West Indies in 1796, where he captured St. Lucia and Demerara. He returned to be commander in chief in Ireland in 1797, but preferred to resign rather than withdraw a general order condemning, with more truth than tact, the Irish army's ill discipline. The only successes in Britain's Dutch campaign of late 1799—the opposed landing at the Helder and the capture of the Dutch fleet—were due to Abercromby. In 1800 he went to the Mediterranean as commander in chief and on March 21, 1801, was mortally wounded while defeating the French outside Alexandria.

Integrity, firmness, consideration for his troops, thoroughness, and a clear intelligence were his great qualities. Of particular interest are his care for the health of his men in the West Indies and for training them in landing operations in the Mediterranean.

RICHARD G. GLOVER, National Museum of Canada

ABERDEEN, 4th Earl of, ab-ər-dēn′ (1784—1860), prime minister of Britain during much of the Crimean War. He was born George Hamilton Gordon at Edinburgh, Scotland, on Jan. 28, 1784. His father died when he was seven, and his mother died four years later; his guardians were William Pitt and Lord Melville. He succeeded to the Scottish earldom of Aberdeen on the death of his grandfather in 1801. Before his graduation from St. John's College, Cambridge, in 1804, travels on the Continent and in Greece had furthered his classical leanings and made him an ardent Hellenist. Between 1806 and 1812 he was three times elected a Scottish representative peer in the House of Lords.

Family connections and his own ability favored a political career. In 1813 he was sent to persuade the Austrian emperor, Francis I, to enter the coalition against Napoleon and then was made ambassador to Vienna. He signed the treaty of alliance with Austria at Töplitz, served as a British representative at the Congress of Chàtillon in 1814, and later in that year helped negotiate the Treaty of Paris. He then returned home to be created a peer of the United Kingdom and to enjoy a temporary retirement.

Aberdeen returned to prominence in 1828 in the duke of Wellington's short-lived cabinet, became foreign secretary, and was influential in negotiating the protocols of 1829 and 1830, granting Greece its independence and fixing its boundaries. He resigned with Wellington in 1830 and in 1834 took office as colonial secretary during Sir Robert Peel's brief ministry.

Aberdeen came into his own as foreign secretary (1841—1846) in Peel's second cabinet. He strove to reestablish friendly relations with France and settled the boundary differences with the United States by the Webster-Ashburton and Oregon treaties of 1842 and 1846.

On Peel's death in 1850, Aberdeen became leader of the Peelites (or liberal conservatives). In 1852 he founded a coalition ministry with the Whigs and became prime minister. Although his cabinet was united on domestic policy, it split over the negotiations preceding the Crimean War. Aberdeen's policy of maintaining peace by evolving a formula acceptable to all the great powers and by restraining Turkey was opposed by several associates.

To avoid the fall of his cabinet, the prime minister consented to a compromise, on which the war party capitalized. The outcome was that Turkey was able to force England to assist it. The consequent blunders, military disasters, and mounting casualty lists, as well as the cabinet's irresolute policy, deprived the government of support, and it was defeated in January 1855 on a motion to inquire into the conduct of the war. Aberdeen interpreted this as a vote of no confidence and resigned, leaving to Viscount Palmerston, his successor, the task of terminating the war and to the earl of Clarendon the duty of concluding the treaty of peace.

Aberdeen married his first wife, Lady Catherine Elizabeth Hamilton, in 1805. None of the four children produced by this marriage lived into adulthood. When Lady Elizabeth died of consumption in 1812, Aberdeen wore mourning for the rest of his life. In 1815 he married Harriet, widow of Viscount Hamilton. Aberdeen had five children by his second wife. She died in 1833. Aberdeen died in London on December 14, 1860.

ABERDEEN, ab′ər-dēn, a town in Maryland, in Harford county near Chesapeake Bay, 26 miles (42 km) northeast of Baltimore. It is a residential and light-industrial area with some agriculture. The military installation, Aberdeen Proving Ground, is situated 2 miles (3 km) from the town. Aberdeen was settled about 1800 and named after Aberdeen, Scotland. The town was incorporated in 1892. Population: 13,842.

SAMUEL R. SHERWOOD
Post Librarian, Aberdeen Proving Ground

ABERDEEN, ab′ər-dēn, a city in Mississippi. It is an agricultural and manufacturing center and the seat of Monroe county. The city is situated 30 miles (50 km) by road northwest of Columbus, on the Tombigbee River near the head of navigation. The surrounding region has natural gas fields. Aberdeen has several fine houses built before the Civil War. Among its residents have been Robert Paine (1799–1882), an organizer and bishop of the Methodist Episcopal Church, South, and William A. Evans (1865–1948), author of the first American syndicated health column.

Founded by Robert Gordon of Aberdeen, Scotland, the city was first called Dundee and was chartered in 1837. Population: 6,415.

LUCILLE PEACOCK
Evans Memorial Library, Aberdeen

ABERDEEN, ab-ər-dēn′, until 1975 a county in Scotland; it was also called Aberdeenshire. It was bounded on the north and east by the North Sea; on the south by the counties of Kincardine, Angus, and Perth; and on the west by the counties of Banff and Inverness. Buchan peninsula formed the eastern section, and the Cairngorm Mountains, rising to an elevation of 4,296 feet (1,309 meters) at the summit of Ben Macdhui, were found in the west and the south. Aberdeen had an area of 1,957 square miles (5,068 sq km), and the main relief regions were (1) the southernmost of the eastern Scottish Highlands, which reach the sea between Aberdeen and Stonehaven in Kincardineshire; (2) the western Uplands, a foothill region cut through by rivers rising in the Highlands; and (3) the Buchan platform, the rolling lower eastern region at an elevation of 400 to 600 feet (120 to 180 meters), reaching to the coast. The northwestern and southeastern extremities of the lower county had easy connections with the Moray Firth region by way of Banff and with the Scottish Lowlands by way of Stonehaven, the latter route commanded by the ancient city of Aberdeen, the former county seat.

The land that constituted Aberdeen has a geology consisting of a series of metamorphic and sedimentary rocks, folded and faulted with a general south by southwest to north by northeast trend, and massive intrusive granites. The whole area has been much dissected by river erosion and is heavily glaciated. Glacial erosion during the Pleistocene period has left many upland corries, or basins, and the deep glens of the rivers Dee and Don are glacial troughs. The northern coast is cliffed, while the eastern coast has sand dunes.

The region's climate is generally equable, with rainfall averaging 30 inches (75 cm) a year, varying according to exposure. The highlands benefit from prolonged winter snow cover, and there are quasi-permanent snow patches in the Cairngorm Mountains.

St. Machar's Cathedral in Aberdeen.

ABERDEEN, ab-ər-dēn', a city in Scotland with the status of a royal burgh. County seat of former Aberdeen county, it is a busy port, commercial center, and market city in northern Scotland.

Aberdeen is situated on the estuaries of the rivers Dee and Don on the North Sea, about 125 miles (200 km) by road northeast of Edinburgh. The lower Don follows a steep course, the ravines providing water-power sites, but it has a shallow estuary. The lower Dee valley is wider, with flat terraces and a gentle fall, and has been developed as the harbor. The suburbs now extend across both river barriers. There is a 13-foot (4-meter) tide, and harbor installations include stone piers to protect the exposed mouth of the Dee. The persistent sandbars are regularly dredged.

The largest regional distributive trade center for Scotland north of the Lowland, Aberdeen is also a principal supply port for the Orkneys and Shetland Islands. Granite quarrying (especially gray granite at Rubislaw) and polishing (using some imported colored stone) are carried on in the burgh, which is known as the "Granite City." It is a major fishing port and a ship-repair center. Whitefish landings, shipped south by rail from the fish auctions, are important, but herrings have declined. Boxes are made for fish packing, using local wood. There is a large paper-making industry, employing imported pulp and esparto grass, and some specialized textile manufacturing. Aberdeen regional airport is located at Dyce, a suburb 6 miles (10 km) to the northwest.

Little is known about Aberdeen between the time of its founding, in the 8th century or earlier, and the settling of the Flemish, about 1130. Old Aberdeen on the Don, originally Kirktown of Seaton, grew up around St. Machar's Cathedral, the bishopric being inaugurated in 1137. New Aberdeen became a local trade center by virtue of a succession of royal charters, the first dated about 1178. The two settlements grew separately, though the cathedral was only 1½ miles (2½ km) from the center of the new market town, and only in 1891 were they united administratively. Aberdeen University was chartered in 1860, by the union of King's College, founded in 1495 as St. Mary's College, and Marischal College, a Protestant university founded in 1593.

Trade grew following the building of the Bridge of Balgownie across the Don to the north in 1320, and of the Bridge of Dee to the south, completed in 1530. In the early 17th century, Flemish weavers founded woolen and stocking manufacture. Linen was manufactured from the 18th century, though textile making declined following 19th-century development of textile factories in areas closer to coalfields. The harbor improvement acts (from 1780), the coming of the railway (1850), and the introduction of steam trawling (from 1882) combined to promote the growth of a major fishing industry and the expansion of granite production.

Aberdeen's position on the coast and its pleasant climate, excellent golf links, and handsome architecture have brought a summer resort trade and many retired people to the city. St. Machar's Cathedral, a fine granite structure, and St. Nicholas, the burgh church, were once complete Norman buildings. Some traces of the Norman period remain in the church, but none in the cathedral, the rebuilding of which was completed in 1520. Population: 219,100 (1995 est.).

DAVID C. LARGE*, *University of Reading*

Farming, except for hill sheep grazing, in the area is largely confined to the Lowlands. Stock rearing and fattening are the main activities, with the Aberdeen Angus and Aberdeen Shorthorn for beef. Oats, turnips, and hay are the chief crops, and barley is of limited importance.

Climbers and winter ski parties take accommodations in villages in the upper glens and use the barren and generally depopulated moorlands of the Highlands. The Cairngorm National Nature Reserve (60 square mi, or 160 sq km) contains red deer, ptarmigan, mountain hare, foxes, and wildcats. Some of the grouse moors of the lower hill country, owned or rented for shooting, are giving way to forest plantations, principally of fast-growing coniferous species. Roe deer are found in these woods, and there is excellent salmon fishing in the rivers, especially the Don and the Dee.

Royal Deeside is a popular tourist area, centering on Balmoral Castle, a royal residence built in the 1850s for Queen Victoria. Ballater, at the head of the Deeside railway, is a summer resort, and Braemar is a climbing center. Other small settlements are minor fishing ports or marketing centers, but the city of Aberdeen is increasingly functioning as the port and commercial center for the whole region.

The area was originally inhabited by Picts. While little evidence exists of Roman occupation, there are numerous crannogs, or lake dwellings. Vikings and Danes raided the coast, and in the 12th century the Saxons, Scandinavians, and Flemish arrived. Beginning in this period the great families arose, and Anglo-Scottish rivalry became prevalent. Subsequent history is to a large extent the history of the city of Aberdeen. (See ABERDEEN [city].)

DAVID C. LARGE*, *University of Reading*

ABERDEEN, ab'ər-dēn, a city in South Dakota, is the seat of Brown County. Situated in the James River valley, 82 miles north of Huron, it serves as a wholesale and retail marketing center for the towns and farms of a rich 14-county agricultural area in which livestock and cereals are raised. Local industries include automotive tools, oxygen and acetylene gas, wood products, farm implements, machine shops, and a multimillion-dollar dairy industry. Transportation is furnished by commercial airline, bus, and railroad. Aberdeen's educational facilities include Northern State College; Presentation Junior College and School of Nursing; the School of the Blind; St. Luke's Schools of Technology, X-Ray Technology, and Anaesthesia; and the Aberdeen School of Commerce. Alexander Mitchell Library and the Brown County Regional Library are the public libraries.

Named for the birthplace of one of its founders, Alexander Mitchell, a Scotsman, the city was settled in 1881 and incorporated in 1882. Population: 24,658.

HELEN GLAU
Alexander Mitchell Library

ABERDEEN, ab'ər-dēn, is a city in Washington, in Grays Harbor County. It is the largest urban center and principal seaport in southwest Washington, and is important as a trading center and as a gateway to the 890,000-acre Olympic National Park. Aberdeen is situated on Grays Harbor, at the confluence of the Wishkah and Chehalis rivers, 18 miles east of the Pacific Ocean. The city is adjacent to Hoquiam to the west and lies 46 miles by road west of Olympia. Lumbering is Aberdeen's leading industry, with fishing second; in addition, metal products, dairy products, pulp, paper, and fisheries byproducts are produced. Rainfall exceeds 50 inches in most years, and the average temperature is 49.8° F.

The city's Community Center contains an art gallery, and the Grays Harbor Historical Association has a museum with local historical items. Schools include Grays Harbor College (a two-year college) and Grays Harbor Business College. The Aberdeen Public Library has an outstanding collection of local Americana.

First settled in 1867 by Samuel Benn, Aberdeen was incorporated as a city in 1890. Population: 16,461.

ROSALIE N. SPELLMAN
Aberdeen Public Library

ABERDEEN, University of, ab-ər-dēn', a coeducational institution in Aberdeen, Scotland, formed from the union of two universities, King's College in Old Aberdeen and Marischal College in New Aberdeen.

The modern university traces its origin to the founding of a university in 1494–1495 by William Elphinstone, bishop of Aberdeen, under a bull of 1494 issued by Pope Alexander VI at the request of King James IV of Scotland. It was called the College of St. Mary when it opened in 1505, and later King's College. It was chartered to include faculties of arts, law, theology, and medicine, and was the first university in Britain to offer a course in medicine. Elphinstone was its chancellor, and the historian Hector Boece (Boethius) was its first principal.

A second university, Marischal College, was founded in 1583, about a mile from King's, by George Keith, 5th Earl Marischal, under a char-

ter approved by the Scottish Parliament. Of the many attempts to unite it with King's College, the most notable was that of King Charles I, who issued a charter in 1641 incorporating the two schools as a single university. They separated, however, after the Restoration and remained apart until 1860 when, under the Universities (Scottish) Act of 1858, they were united as the University of Aberdeen.

The university has faculties in arts, law, medicine, divinity, and science, the latter including pure science, forestry, engineering, and agriculture. Associated schools are the North of Scotland College of Agriculture and Robert Gordon's Technical College. The university library includes a fine series of early manuscripts and works on classical antiquity and Celtic history.

W.S. ANGUS
University of Aberdeen

ABERDEEN AND TEMAIR, ab-ər-dēn', tə-mâr', **1st Marquess of** (1847–1934), British political leader. He was born *John Campbell Gordon,* at Edinburgh, Scotland, on Aug. 3, 1847. A grandson of the 4th earl of Aberdeen, he succeeded his brother as 7th earl in 1870. He was active in the House of Lords and served as lord lieutenant of Ireland (1886, 1906–1915) and as governor general of Canada (1893–1898). His work in these posts was highly regarded; and he was created marquess in 1916. He died in Aberdeenshire, Scotland, on March 7, 1934.

Ishbel Maria, Marchioness of Aberdeen and Temair (1857–1939), his wife, was active in social and political work. She became a leader of the feminist movement in Britain, founded the Victorian Order of Nurses in Canada, and was for many years president of the International Council of Women.

ABERDEEN PROVING GROUND, ab'ər-dēn, in Maryland, is a major research and testing installation of the United States Army Materiel Command. Located northeast of Baltimore on the western shores of upper Chesapeake Bay, it comprises approximately 75,000 acres.

Its commands include the Headquarters, United States Army Test and Evaluation Command; the Army Materiel Command Board; and Headquarters, Aberdeen Proving Ground. Its subordinate activities include Development and Proof Services and the Foreign Technical Intelligence Office. Also located on the installation are the United States Army Ordnance Center and School; United States Army Ordnance Combat Development Agency; Limited War Laboratory; Ballistic Research Laboratories; Human Engineering Laboratories; and Coating and Chemical Laboratory.

The main operations consist of research, development, and testing of arms, ammunition, tanks, and transport vehicles. Further, the Ordnance School trains officers and enlisted men in the supply and maintenance of ordnance materiel. The installation's facilities include a supersonic wind tunnel, scientific laboratories, firing ranges, and courses for testing combat vehicles.

ABERHART, a'bər-härt, **William** (1878–1943), Canadian political leader, who founded the Social Credit party of Alberta. He was born near Seaforth, Ontario, on Dec. 30, 1878, and was raised in a staunchly Baptist, agrarian environment. He attended business school and a normal college before obtaining, through correspondence courses

38

and summer sessions, a B.A. degree from Queen's University, Kingston, Ontario. In 1910 he moved to Calgary, Alberta, to teach, and from 1915 to 1935 he was principal of a Calgary high school. Simultaneously, he served as dean of the Calgary Prophetic Bible Institute.

Under the impact of the economic depression, Aberhart adopted and advocated the radical creed of Clifford Hugh Douglas, a British exponent of social security through direct money payments to all citizens. Aberhart organized the Social Credit party, campaigned for a $25 monthly payment to every man, woman, and child in Alberta, and swept into the prime ministership of Alberta in the general elections of 1935. In office the party failed to fulfill its promise. At odds with the national government and opposed by the courts, it gradually shed its radicalism. Aberhart remained Social Credit prime minister of Alberta until his death in Vancouver, British Columbia, on May 22, 1943.

ABERRATION, Optical, ab-ə-rā'shən, the image-impairing factors inherent in a lens. Optical aberrations reduce the quality of definition and alter the positions of given image points from their ideal position. The principal optical aberrations are: distortion, curvature of field, astigmatism, longitudinal spherical aberration, coma, and chromatic aberration. Each of these aberrations must be reduced to tolerable values.

Distortion is the failure of a lens to reproduce accurately in the image plane the space relationships of objects in the object space. It arises from a change in scale factor or focal length with angular separation from the axis. In consequence, the image of a straight line lying near the edge of the object plane is curved. If the image line is concave toward the center of the image, the lens has negative, or barrel, distortion; if the line is concave outward, the lens has positive, or pincushion, distortion.

Curvature of field is a lens aberration that causes the lens to image a plane object on a curved surface rather than a plane surface. The lens is affected by *astigmatism* when the plane of best definition for lines radiating outward from the point of intersection of object plane and lens axis differs from the plane of best definition for circles concentric with the lens axis and lying in the same object plane.

Longitudinal spherical aberration is the variation in focal length with zone radius of the light-transmitting area of a lens. When the magnitude of this aberration is appreciable compared to the focal length, there is no clear-cut plane of best axial focus because of the superposition of out-of-focus images from other lens zones.

Coma arises from inequality of magnification for different concentric zones of the entrant light-transmitting area of a lens. In the presence of coma a nonaxial object point is imaged as a comet-shaped blur.

Chromatic aberration in lenses arises from the change in the refractive index, n, of the lens glass with wavelength, λ. This change causes the dispersion of light. Lateral chromatic aberration produces an image size change that depends on the color (or wavelength) of the light incident on the lens. Longitudinal chromatic aberration produces a change in focal length for different colors (measured on the optical axis).

FRANCIS E. WASHER
National Bureau of Standards

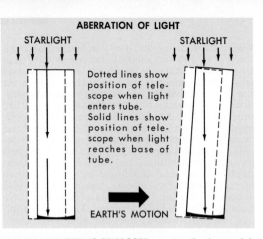

ABERRATION OF LIGHT

STARLIGHT STARLIGHT

Dotted lines show position of telescope when light enters tube. Solid lines show position of telescope when light reaches base of tube.

EARTH'S MOTION

LIGHT RAY ENTERING TELESCOPE on axis strikes base to left of center, because telescope is moved to right by earth's motion around the sun. When the telescope is tilted slightly, the incoming axial light ray strikes the center of the base.

ABERRATION OF LIGHT, ab-ə-rā'shən, in astronomy, is the displacement of the line of sight from the true direction to a star. When a man looks at a star, he does not sight directly along the line joining him and the true position of the star; he sights the apparent position, which is in a direction at a small angle with respect to this line. This displacement of the line of sight from the true direction results from the combined effect of the velocity of earth and the finite velocity of light.

As shown in the figure, the telescope must be tilted in the direction of its motion so that the starlight will pass down its axis. The maximum aberration, which occurs when the earth is moving at right angles to the line to the true position of the star, is 20.47 seconds of arc, or about $\frac{1}{180}$ degree.

Stellar aberration was discovered in the early 1700's by James Bradley in an attempt to account for the day-to-day changing declination of the star γ-Draconis. Bradley observed that this star was farthest to the south when it was observed (nearly overhead at London) at sunrise and farthest to the north half a year later when it was observed at sunset. From this and many other observations, Bradley realized that the displacement always was in the direction of the earth's motion past the star. He gave the correct explanation (stellar aberration) in 1729. From the known velocity of the earth about the sun and the observed aberration, Bradley computed the velocity of light more precisely than anyone had done previously. Bradley's evidence for the motion of the earth about the sun was the final blow to geocentrism.

During the 19th century, aberration was considered to be direct evidence that the earth is in motion through an all-pervading ether. However, the Michelson-Morley experiment in 1887 established that if there is an ether, it moves with the earth. The dilemma posed by these two contradictory ideas about the ether was resolved by the special theory of relativity. The observed aberration is in good agreement with that predicted by the relativity theory.

Stellar parallax results from the changed position of the earth relative to a (close) star. Stellar aberration results from the velocity of the earth as it moves past the star. See also PARALLAX.

ALBERT B. STEWART, *Antioch College*

ABERYSTWYTH, ab-ər-ist'with, a town in Dyfed county, Wales. It is situated on Cardigan Bay of the Irish Sea, at the mouths of the Rheidol and Ystwyth rivers, 35 miles (55 km) northeast of Cardigan, in west-central Wales. Aberystwyth is a seaside resort and a commercial center. Its chief industry is leather tanning. Two major institutions of learning, the University College of Wales, founded in 1872, and the National Library of Wales, opened in 1937, are situated here.

During the Middle Ages Aberystwyth was a fortified town that sprang up near an English castle built in 1277. The Welsh destroyed the castle in 1282, but it was rebuilt by King Edward I of England in 1284. In the early 1400s it was used as a fortress by the Welsh chieftain Owen Glendower. The castle was razed a second time, in 1646, by the Parliamentarians during the Civil War in England. Population: 8,666 (1981 census).

ABHORRERS, əb-hôr'ərz, in English history, persons who "abhorred" the agitation in 1679–1680 for persuading Charles II to assemble Parliament. They feared Parliament would oppose the succession of James, duke of York, afterward James II. Those seeking parliamentary action to bar James from the throne are called Petitioners.

The political division between Petitioners and Abhorrers led to the British party system of Whigs and Tories—the Whigs favoring a more limited monarchy; the Tories, a strong monarchy.

ABIB. See AVIV.

ABIDJAN, ab-i-jän', the largest city in Côte d'Ivoire. It is situated on the north shore of Ébrié Lagoon, which is separated from the Atlantic Ocean by a sandbar. The city is the chief port and the commercial hub of the country. In addition, it is a financial center for the nations of former French West Africa. Among its industries are food processing, textile milling, sawmilling, iron and steel making, motor-vehicle assembly, petroleum refining, and the manufacture of clothing, paper, and tobacco products. Its deepwater port, which includes container-handling facilities, is one of the best in West Africa, serving Burkina and Mali as well as Côte d'Ivoire. The international airport handles traffic for some 20 airlines. Abidjan is also the educational and cultural center of Côte d'Ivoire. It is the home of the Université Nationale Côte d'Ivoire, more than half a dozen specialized colleges, the Musée de la Côte d'Ivoire, and various libraries and research institutes.

Abidjan was a village in 1903 when it was chosen as the starting point of a railroad that eventually reached Ouagadougou in Burkina. In 1935 the French colonial capital of Côte d'Ivoire was moved to Abidjan from Bingerville. The port was opened to ocean shipping in 1950 with the completion of the Vridi Canal through the sandbar. Its deepwater harbor was completed in 1954 and later much improved. The economic and population booms experienced by Côte d'Ivoire after independence in 1960 were reflected in Abidjan's rapid growth and rising skyline. Within three decades the population had increased to almost 3 million. Although in 1983 the national capital was formally transferred inland from Abidjan to Yamoussoukro, the birthplace of the first Ivorian president, Félix Houphouët-Boigny, Abidjan remained the legislative and defacto capital of Côte d'Ivoire. Population: 2,797,000 (1995 est.).

ABIE'S IRISH ROSE, a three-act comedy by the American author Anne Nichols. It opened at the Fulton Theatre in New York City on May 23, 1922, and set a new record for the number of consecutive performances—2,327, over a period of five years. A sentimental mixture of Irish and Jewish jokes, the play became a favorite of theater groups throughout the United States.

The play is set on New York's East Side. It concerns the marriage of a Jewish boy, Abie, and an Irish girl, Rosemary. The marriage, performed by a Methodist minister, a rabbi, and a Catholic priest, starts a family feud that is ended only when twins—Rebecca and Patrick Joseph—are born to the couple.

ABIGAIL, ab'ə-gāl, in the Old Testament, the wife of Nabal, a wealthy sheep raiser. While David was in hiding from King Saul, he requested provisions from Nabal, to whom he had given protection. Nabal refused, and David organized a march against him. When Abigail learned of this, she intercepted David's forces and appeased them with gifts. Nabal died ten days later, and David married Abigail. Abigail was carried off during a raid by the Amalekites, but David rescued her. She bore David a son named Chileab, or Daniel. Her story is told in I Samuel 25.

Another Abigail, David's sister, married Jether, the Ishmaelite. She was the mother of Amasa, a supporter of the disloyal Absalom.

ABIJAH, ə-bī'jə, in the Old Testament, the second king of Judah, succeeding his father Rehoboam, who was a son of Solomon. He is also called Abijam and, in the Douay Bible, Abia or Abiam. His reign is estimated to have been two to three years. The greatest event of Abijah's reign was his victory over Jeroboam, king of Israel. According to II Chronicles 13, the two armies met in the hills of Ephraim, Abijah's numbering 400,000 and Jeroboam's 800,000. When the battle ended, 500,000 men of Israel had been slain. Biblical historians regard these figures as exaggerations by the chronicler.

ABILA, ab'ə-lə, in ancient geography, one of the Pillars of Hercules, flanking the eastern entrance to the Strait of Gibraltar, at the western end of the Mediterranean Sea. The other "pillar" is Gibraltar (ancient Calpe). Abila (also spelled *Abyla*) is identified with both modern Mount Acho and Jebel Musa near Ceuta, a Spanish possession on the North African coast.

ABILENE, ab'ə-lēn, in northern Kansas, a city on the Smoky Hill River, 90 miles (145 km) by road west of Topeka. It is the seat of Dickinson county. Abilene has light agricultural industries, which include the shipping of grain.

Abilene was settled in 1856 and from 1867 to 1871 was the railhead for the cattle-raising region to the Southwest. A monument marks the end of the Chisholm Trail, over which cattle were driven from Texas. Places of interest include the Eisenhower Center, which includes the boyhood home of Dwight D. Eisenhower; a museum housing his mementos, trophies, and medals; and the Dwight D. Eisenhower Library. Old Abilene Town, a reconstruction of the town's old Texas Street, is also of interest. Abilene was incorporated in 1869. Population: 6,543.

CLARA A. HANSON, *Abilene Public Library*

ABILENE, ab'ə-lēn, a city in west central Texas, is a financial, commercial and educational center, and the seat of Taylor County. Situated 152 highway miles southwest of Fort Worth, in a ranching, farming, and oil region, it has diversified manufacturing, processing, and service industries. Abilene s industrial products include wearing apparel, food, watches, brick and tile, concrete, feed, cottonseed products, structural steel, machine-shop products, musical instruments, and electrical appliances. The chief agricultural products of the city's trading area are beef cattle, wheat and feed grains, cotton, peanuts, and pecans. About 200 oil-industry firms operating in the west central Texas oil and gas district have offices in Abilene. A commercial airport serves the city.

The city has three centers of higher learning: Abilene Christian College, Hardin-Simmons University, and McMurry College. The community supports the Abilene Fine Arts Museum, ACT (Abilene Community Theatre), and the Abilene Philharmonic Orchestra. The Abilene Public Library moved into a new building in 1960. Near the city is Dyess Air Force Base, a permanent installation of the Strategic Air Command.

The frontier village of Buffalo Gap, first seat of Taylor County, is 12 miles south-southwest of Abilene, and nearby is Abilene State Park. The city is the site of the West Texas Fair, the Abilene Fat Stock Show, and the West Texas Hereford Cattle Show and Sale.

Founded as the terminus of the Texas & Pacific Railroad in 1881 and incorporated in 1882, the city was named for Abilene, Kans., to which cattle herds from the area had been driven. Population: 110,442.

THELMA ANDREWS*
Abilene Public Library

ABILENE CHRISTIAN COLLEGE is a private coeducational institution in Abilene, Texas, sponsored by the Church of Christ. It was chartered in 1906 as Childers Classical Institute and renamed in 1912. College-level instruction began in 1914; graduate studies, in 1953. Special studies are offered in agriculture, the Bible, and industrial education. Enrollment rose from 711 in 1940 to almost 3,000 in the mid-1960's.

ABILITY, ə-bil'ə-tē, is a general term used to refer to any characteristic of a person that makes it possible for him to carry out some sort of activity successfully. The term covers broad traits such as intelligence as well as narrow traits such as manual dexterity. It refers to learned skills such as reading proficiency as well as to talents or aptitudes presumed to exist prior to learning. Psychologists have worked out tests for measuring many different abilities. When any of these tests is administered to a group of persons, individual differences become apparent.

Abilities are determined in complex ways. Heredity always plays a part, but practice and training usually seem to be involved as well. The structure and condition of various parts of the body help to determine the level of functioning of some abilities, but mental qualities are even more important. For example, an individual's brain is more influential than his eye muscles in determining his level of reading ability. Up to some usually unattained physiological limit, any ability can be increased through training.

LEONA TYLER, *University of Oregon*

ABIMELECH, ə-bim'ə-lek, was the name of two figures in the Old Testament. One was king of the city-state of Gerar in Palestine. During his reign, the Hebrew patriarch Abraham sojourned in Gerar, as related in the 20th chapter of Genesis. Abimelech later encountered Isaac (Genesis 26).

The other Abimelech was one of the sons of the Israelite leader Gideon. After Gideon's death, Abimelech killed all but one of his brothers and persuaded the people of Shechem to crown him king. He ruled Israel for three years and then was killed in a rebellion (Judges 9).

ABINGTON, ab'ing-tən, is a town in Massachusetts, in Plymouth County, 19 miles southeast of Boston by road. It is mainly residential but has a small business complex of printing and machine shops. Government is by town meeting.

The town was first settled in 1665 and was incorporated in 1712. Peregrine White, the first person born in New England of English parentage, held a land grant in Abington. It became the Peregrine White Bird Sanctuary and is now included in Ames Nowell State Park.

The first cannon made in the United States were cast at the Abington foundry of Aaron Hobart, and from this foundry Paul Revere of Boston learned to cast bells. The rare Benner redware pottery was made for the first time in the town in 1765.

From 1846 to 1865 Abington was a center of abolitionist activities and served as a major station on the Underground Railroad. In Island Grove Park, known then as Abolition Grove, William Lloyd Garrison, Wendell Phillips, Theodore Parker, and Lucy Stone denounced slavery before great crowds. During the Civil War the town was a major center of boot and shoe manufacturing. Population: 14,605.

THELMA STONE, *Abington Public Library*

ABINGTON, ab'ing-tən, is an urban township in southeastern Pennsylvania. Situated in Montgomery County, it is a northern suburb of Philadelphia and is chiefly residential. The 15-square mile township includes the communities of Abington, Ardsley, Crestmont, Glenside, McKinley, Noble, North Hills, Roslyn, and Roychester. It is governed by a commission.

What is now Abington Township was turned over to William Penn in 1683 by the Delaware Indian chief Tamenend (Tammany) for wampum, guns, and other goods. The area was first settled in 1696. During the Revolutionary War the Battle of Edge Hill (1777) was fought there. Population: 56,103.

ABIOGENESIS, ab-ē-ō-jen'ə-sis, is the spontaneous generation of life. It is the converse of biogenesis. See BIOGENESIS.

ABITIBI, Lake, ab-ə-tib'ē, in Canada, on the Ontario-Quebec boundary in Cochrane County, Ontario, and Abitibi County, Quebec. The name is derived from the Abitibi Indians inhabiting the region. Lake Abitibi lies at an elevation of 868 feet and has an area of 350 square miles.

The 340-mile-long *Abitibi River* rises from the lake and flows west through the Abitibi Game Refuge and then north to the Moose River, which empties into James Bay. Several hydroelectric dams and stations have been built along the Abitibi River.

ABKHAZIA, äb-кнá′zē-u,[*] an administrative division within the Republic of Georgia; from 1930 until 1991 the region constituted the Abkhaz Autonomous Soviet Socialist Republic. Abkhazia covers 3,320 square miles (8,600 sq km) between the Black Sea and the crest of the Caucasus Mountains. Its capital is Sokhumi, a Black Sea port.

The Abkhaz people, a branch of the Georgians, speak Abkhaz, a Caucasian language. They are Muslims, whereas most ethnic Georgians are Christians. The Abkhaz make up less than a fifth of their republic's population.

The Abkhaz, known to the ancient Greeks and Romans as Absagians, were converted to Christianity in the 6th century. The kingdom of Absagia was founded at the end of the 8th century. In 1008 Absagia and Kartli were united to form the kingdom of Georgia, which broke up in the mid-15th century. After Abkhazia came under Turkish domination in the 16th century, Islam slowly displaced Christianity. Russia occupied what is now known as Sokhumi in 1810 and annexed Abkhazia in 1864. Abkhazia became a Soviet republic in 1921 and was made part of the Georgian republic in 1930. In July 1992 Abkhazia declared itself a sovereign state, and Georgia sent in troops to regain control. By September 1993, however, the Abkhazians had driven the Georgian forces from the region. United Nations-sponsored peace talks followed, only to be suspended in November 1994 when Abkhazia adopted its new constitution and declared itself a sovereign state. Population: 250,000 (2000 est.).

ABLATIVE, ab′lə-tiv, a case in grammar, especially in Latin, Sanskrit, Finnish, and Hungarian. In English, prepositional phrases serve the same functions as ablative constructions in other languages.

In Latin the ablative expresses various relationships that fall within three groups: the "from" ablative (*suis finibus,* "from their territory"), the "with" ablative (*omnibus suis copiis,* "with all his forces"), and the "in" ablative (*aestate,* "in summer"). In certain constructions the ablative takes the prepositions *ab, cum, de, ex, prae, pro,* and *sine,* and sometimes *in* and *sub.*

The ablative absolute is a noun in the ablative, together with an adjective, other noun, or participle, that has no grammatical connection with another word in the sentence, as in *Servo accusato, dominus discessit* ("The slave having been accused, the master departed").

ABLAUT, äb′lout, in linguistics, the vowel change in the root form of a word, with a corresponding alteration in meaning. The term was originally used by the German philologist Jacob Grimm to designate the process by which certain verbs form the past tense (*ring, rang, rung; finden, fand, gefunden*), as opposed to the process of adding *d* or *t* to the root form of the verb (*arrive, arrived; burn, burnt*).

ABLUTION, ə-bloo′shən, the practice of ceremonial washing, especially as a rite of religious purification. Rites to remove religious impurity have been observed in many of the world's religious traditions.

In Jewish Mosaic law, ablution had four purposes: (1) to cleanse in preparation for initiation into a higher position or office, as when Aaron and his sons, having been chosen for the priesthood, were washed with water before they were invested with their priestly robes; (2) to cleanse to make oneself fit to perform special acts of religious ceremony, as when the priests were required, under the penalty of death, to wash their hands and feet before approaching the altar; (3) to cleanse from uncleanness brought about by certain acts or circumstances in everyday life, of which the law recognized no fewer than 11 kinds; and (4) to cleanse to free oneself of possible guilt of an unsolved crime—for example, in the case of a murder the perpetrator of which is unknown, the elders of the village washed their hands over a slaughtered heifer, saying, "Our hands have not shed this blood, neither have our eyes seen it" (Deuteronomy 21). Similar rites were common among the Greeks and Romans. It is undoubtedly in accordance with such practice that Pilate in Matthew 27:24 calls for water and washes his hands to signify that he holds himself innocent of the blood of Jesus.

Egyptian priests carried the practice of ablution before the performance of sacred ceremonies to such lengths that they shaved their entire bodies every third day and washed themselves in cold water twice daily and twice nightly so that no particle of filth might rest upon them. These acts corresponded somewhat to the simpler *wuḍū'* of the Muslims, a ceremonial washing performed five times a day, before the recital of prayers. The latter practice, however, is only one of the formal acts of cleansing required by Islamic law. The ablution required by Mosaic law for defilement has its counterpart in the Muslim rite of *ghusl,* a washing of the entire body in ceremonially pure water. Islamic law, however, specifies the kinds of defilement in greater detail, greatly exceeding in number those recognized by the ancient Hebrews. Islamic law is so strict on this point that when water cannot be obtained, the devout Muslim performs the ritual with something that represents water: the act of purification is performed by rubbing the hands and face with dust. This form of ritual cleansing is called *tayammum.*

The ceremony of ablution at Communion was adopted by the early Christian Church and has been retained in churches celebrating the Eucharist along traditional lines. In these churches ablution is a liturgical term denoting the twofold act of cleansing performed during the service, though it may also be performed afterward: the ablution of the chalice to disengage any particles that may be left in the vessel and the concomitant ablution of the priest's fingers. In the Eastern Orthodox Church, ablution denotes the ceremony performed seven days after baptism, when the anointment of the chrism (olive oil and balsam) is formally washed off.

ABNAKI, ab-nä′kē, a federation of Algonkians, including the Passamaquoddy, the Penobscot, and other peoples, formerly centered in Maine and southern New Brunswick. The word *Abnaki* means "east" or "easterners." In the colonial period the Abnaki, many of whom were converted to Christianity by Jesuit missionaries, allied themselves with the French against the English. The English destroyed one of their principal towns at Norridgewock in 1724; thereafter most of the Abnaki moved to Quebec, where several hundred of their descendants still live. Some of the Penobscot made peace with the English, and their few remaining descendants now live in Old Town, Maine.

LET THE NORTH AWAKE!

T. B. M'CORMICK

Will Discuss the Immorality, Illegality and Unconstitutionality of

AMERICAN SLAVERY,

And the Duty and Power of the General Government to Abolish it.

IN *illur Hall* __

AT *1 & P.M. war 5 %*

Mr. M'CORMICK is the Clergyman for whom the Governor of Kentucky made a Requisition upon the Governor of Indiana, charging him with aiding in the escape of Fugitive Slaves. The Warrant was issued and Mr M'Cormick is thereby exiled from his home. All are respectfully invited to attend.

CAUTION!!
COLORED PEOPLE
OF BOSTON, ONE & ALL,

You are hereby respectfully CAUTIONED and advised, to avoid conversing with the

Watchmen and Police Officers of Boston,

For since the recent ORDER OF THE MAYOR & ALDERMEN, they are empowered to act as

KIDNAPPERS
AND
Slave Catchers,

And they have already been actually employed in KIDNAPPING, CATCHING, AND KEEPING SLAVES. Therefore, if you value your LIBERTY, and the Welfare of the Fugitives among you, Shun them in every possible manner, as so many HOUNDS on the track of the most unfortunate of your race.

Keep a Sharp Look Out for KIDNAPPERS, and have TOP EYE open.

APRIL 24, 1851.

CULVER PICTURES, INC.

THE OHIO HISTORICAL SOCIETY

BETTMANN ARCHIVE

ABOLITIONIST William Lloyd Garrison (*left*) helped turn antislavery into a crusade. The movement's moralistic tone is reflected in a handbill (*center*) and a placard (*right*) attacking the Fugitive Slave Act of 1850.

ABNEY, ab'nē, **Sir William de Wiveleslie** (1843–1920), English physicist. Born in Derby, England, on July 24, 1843, he graduated from the military academy at Woolwich in 1861 and served in the Royal Engineers. He was elected to the Royal Society in 1876. From 1893 to 1895 he was president of the Royal Astronomical Society and then, for two years, president of the Physical Society of London. Abney was knighted in 1900. In 1903 he became adviser to the science and art department of the Board of Education, and also a member of the advisory council for education at the War Office. He died in Folkestone on Dec. 3, 1920.

Abney's reputation rests largely on his researches in photographic chemistry, stellar photometry, color photography, and spectroscopy. He particularly is noted for the development of a photographic emulsion used to map the solar spectrum into the infrared. His books include *Instruction in Photography* (1870), *Instantaneous Photography* (1895), and *Researches in Color Vision and the Trichromatic Theory* (1913).

ABOLITIONISTS, members of the radical wing of the antislavery movement in the United States before and during the Civil War. They advocated that slavery be abolished immediately, regardless of political consequences or of constitutional guarantees to the slaveholders. The term "abolitionist" came into use about 1835.

From the foundation of the American republic, many Northerners and Southerners favored the gradual abolition of the institution of slavery, and there was no prejudice against the freest expression of opinion on the subject. But Eli Whitney's cotton gin, invented in 1794, quickly made the slave system enormously profitable. After the Missouri Compromise (1820), the South insisted that states be admitted to the United States only in pairs, one slave and one free. The new zeal of the South in upholding, extending, and justifying the slave system was met by a new intensity in the North in opposing it, though for a long time such opposition was confined to a small band of agitators.

The abolitionist movement took formal shape in 1833, when William Lloyd Garrison, Arthur and Lewis Tappan, and a group of businessmen formed the American Anti-Slavery Society in Philadelphia. Two years earlier, Garrison had founded the *Liberator,* a weekly that he continued to publish until 1865. From the beginning it denounced the slave system and all persons connected with that system. In addition to the *Liberator,* a brilliant group of orators, philanthropists, and political leaders kept the slavery issue before the people. Among them were Wendell Phillips, Charles Sumner, Gerrit Smith, and Lucretia Mott, all of whom worked to mobilize public opinion for the fight against slavery.

The abolitionists looked upon the fugitive slave laws as "a covenant with death and an agreement with hell." They defied these laws systematically by assisting in the escape of runaway slaves through the machinery known as the Underground Railroad, concealing the slaves from pursuit and forwarding them from stage to stage until they reached Canada. But in 1840 the abolitionists divided on the question of the formation of a political antislavery party, some moderates forming the Liberal Party. The two wings remained active on separate lines to the end.

It was largely due to the abolitionists that the Civil War was regarded by the North chiefly as an antislavery conflict. The abolitionists considered the Emancipation Proclamation a vindication of this view.

Abolitionist literature began to appear about 1820 and increased in volume until the Civil War. The antislavery press published newspapers and periodicals, sermons and addresses, reports of abolitionist societies, correspondence, and the memoirs of runaway slaves.

Of the many abolitionist poems and novels, *Uncle Tom's Cabin,* a novel by Harriet Beecher Stowe, had by far the widest impact.

ABOMINABLE SNOWMAN, a legendary creature of the Himalaya mountain region. It is reported to live in forested regions near the snow line. The creature is also called yeti as well as other local names.

The "abominable snowman" is reputed to walk upright and to have the general appearance of half-man, half-ape. It is said to have long, fine hair and the facial features of an ape. Many of the stories and descriptions of abominable snowmen are based on the finding of large, formerly unidentifiable prints in the snow around the Himalaya. The first and second toes of the creature are said to be large and widely opposed, while the third, fourth, and fifth toes are small and close together.

Various expeditions have been undertaken to ascertain the truth behind the abominable snowman legends. There was a great deal of interest in the subject during the 1950s, especially about the time of the conquest of Mt. Everest in 1953 by Sir Edmund Hillary and Tenzing Norkay. In 1960, Hillary led an expedition that did much to disprove the legend. Today, the abominable snowman is believed to be a bear or other Himalayan mountain animal. The prints used to support the legends are thought to be either the prints of a bear or markings left by drifting snow and falling rocks.

The legend of the abominable snowman has been kept alive largely by the Sherpa, a people of Nepal who live in the high valleys of the Himalaya. In addition, the abominable snowman has a religious significance to peoples of some Himalayan countries. For these peoples the creature is an awesome figure to be feared and protected.

There is no real evidence for the existence of abominable snowmen, and most scientists are reluctant to consider the matter seriously. The idea that these Himalayan creatures might be relics of Neanderthal peoples was advanced for a while but was later discarded.

No creature called an abominable snowman is known to have been examined scientifically or reliably described. However, there were reports that Chinese and Soviet scientists captured abominable snowmen in southern China and in the Caucasus. Similar creatures are reported from other parts of the world, notably the bigfoot, or Sasquatch, from northwestern North America. (See also BIGFOOT.)

ABORIGINES, ab-ə-rij′ə-nēz, the earliest known inhabitants of a region. Derived from Latin *ab origine,* meaning "from the beginning," the term first was applied by Roman writers to the tribes that became known as Latins and gave their name to Latium, the territory on which Rome developed. The term is more widely employed in English-language writings than its equivalent of Greek origin, autochthons.

The San are described as the aborigines of South Africa because they occupied the land before Bantu-speaking Negroid peoples and European settlers. The tribal peoples who occupied Australia before the coming of the Europeans, and who in the 19th century often were referred to as "blackfellows," now are regularly known as Australian Aborigines (Aboriginals), to distinguish them from Australians of European origin. (See AUSTRALIAN ABORIGINALS; SAN.)

ELIZABETH BACON, *Michigan State University*

ABORTION, ə-bôr′shən, the termination of a pregnancy by loss or destruction of a fertilized egg, embryo, or fetus before birth. A spontaneous abortion, commonly called a miscarriage, occurs naturally. Usually, however, the term refers to induced abortion—intentional termination of pregnancy prior to the time when the fetus attains viability, or capacity for life outside the uterus. (The timing and conditions of viability cannot currently be generalized, since they are affected by advances in, and availability of, sophisticated neonatal medical care.) (See also EMBRYOLOGY; HUMAN REPRODUCTION; WOMEN'S HEALTH; POPULATION CONTROL.)

1. Attitudes toward Abortion

At all times and in all societies, women (themselves or with the assistance of others) have, for a wide range of reasons, sought to terminate pregnancies. While efforts at self-induced abortion often entail serious physical risk to the woman, today the inducement of abortion in the early weeks of pregnancy by a trained practitioner and under proper conditions usually is a relatively simple and safe medical procedure. Social attitudes toward the practice, however, continue to vary greatly.

Formation of Attitudes in the West. For most societies, past or present, there has been no single source from which one can reliably infer a single dominant attitude toward abortion. On the contrary, there usually is a complex mix of indicators that reveals a diversity of views. These indicators include the extent of women's recourse to abortion, social and legal responses to the practice, and the stated views of concerned specialists, such as philosophers, theologians, legal thinkers, and physicians. To these factors can be added the results of public-opinion surveys and the positions adopted by relevant professional associations and by organized interest groups.

Abortion was prevalent in the world of ancient Greece and Rome. Some commentators believe that its specific proscription in the Hippocratic Oath may have been atypical of the prevailing attitudes at that time. The Greek philosophers Plato and Aristotle discussed abortion approvingly as a useful means of population control. Under Roman law, regulation of abortion primarily reflected family rule by the husband, who on the one hand could order an abortion and on the other could punish or divorce his wife if she ended a pregnancy without his consent.

With the advent of Christianity abortion became more widely condemned. Early church doctrine considered abortion as murder only after the point at which the rational soul became instilled or "animated," usually said to be 40 days after conception. This doctrine held sway until 1588, when it was abrogated by Pope Sixtus V. From then on, despite some subsequent fluctuations in church doctrine, the overall trend within the Roman Catholic Church has been toward the present position, which is that the fetus is infused with a soul from the time of conception, making any termination of pregnancy a violation of the sanctity of life.

Under present Roman Catholic doctrine, strongly reasserted by Pope Pius XI in 1930, even if the life of the mother is threatened by giving birth, abortion is unjustified. The only exception to the abortion prohibition that the church has considered to be morally acceptable has been the destruction of the fetus as an indirect consequence of other surgery that is deemed necessary.

Roman Catholic doctrine has been a major force affecting attitudes toward abortion. The Eastern Orthodox churches also oppose abortion, as do some Protestant denominations. The doctrines of ancient and modern Judaism have not produced a consistent viewpoint.

20th-Century Developments. Insofar as they reflected attitudes toward abortion, public policies during the 20th century indicated considerable diversity. In the former Soviet Union abortion was legalized after the 1917 revolution, restricted during the 1930s (mainly because of population concerns), and legalized again in the mid-1950s. Sweden allowed abortion on broadly stated grounds but coupled this with social services in support of childbearing. Various eastern European countries legalized abortion, including several in which the Roman Catholic Church maintained considerable strength. Abortion was officially encouraged in post–World War II Japan and, under the policy of one child per couple established in 1979, in the People's Republic of China.

Even in countries with restrictive legislation, the demand for abortion has remained widespread. Women seeking abortions in these countries have obtained them from illegal practitioners, under sordid conditions and at substantial risk of physical injury or even death. This criticism led in the 1950s to a movement for legal reform that sought broadened indications for so-called therapeutic abortions, such as those based on eugenic or humanitarian grounds or that are required to preserve the mother's health. A strong and worldwide feminist movement during the 1960s heightened the pressure to legalize abortion. In the United States this trend culminated in a 1973 Supreme Court ruling in *Roe* v. *Wade* that in effect legalized abortion during the early months of pregnancy. Similar developments occurred in other countries, such as Italy, which, despite having a large Roman Catholic population, legalized abortion in 1978.

Abortion in the United States. In the American colonies that were to become the United States, abortions were permitted. It was not until the mid-1800s that abortion became the subject of a campaign led by physicians seeking to maintain professional control over the practice, leading to its strict legal regulation. For almost 100 years thereafter, in most U.S. jurisdictions, abortion was illegal unless performed by a physician to preserve the mother's life.

The *Roe* v. *Wade* decision allowed states to pass regulations affecting second-trimester abortions and to prohibit third-trimester abortions entirely. Further regulation at the state level was permitted by the Supreme Court's 1989 *Webster* v. *Reproductive Services* decision, which upheld a Missouri law prohibiting the performance of abortions by public employees or in taxpayer-supported facilities. Subsequent Court decisions likewise tended to erode the protections of *Roe* v. *Wade*. The Court's 1991 decision in *Rust* v. *Sullivan* upheld federal regulations forbidding abortion counseling in federally funded clinics.

Advocates as well as opponents of abortion rights support their arguments with what they consider to be basic moral principles and pragmatic considerations. "Pro-choice" advocates declare that a woman has a right to bodily self-determination and deny the "personhood" of the fetus. Additionally, they stress the importance of a woman's quality of life and deplore the situation of the "unwanted" child. These individuals point out also that abortions would take place even if the procedure was made illegal and that criminalization of it would lead to unsafe abortion practices, particularly among the poor. Few advocates consider abortion a social good, however, but rather see its availability as a necessity.

Abortion-rights opponents commonly perceive abortion as murder and a violation of the fetus's "right to live." Some believe that the acceptance of abortion will lead to the acceptance of infanticide and ultimately to a disregard for human life in general. A number of "right-to-life" advocates contend also that the acceptance of abortion encourages sexual immorality.

The Partial-Birth Abortion Act of 1997 was introduced to the U.S. Congress in an attempt to outlaw abortions in late pregnancy. The bill defined partial-birth abortion as the partial vaginal delivery of a living fetus, which is then killed before delivery is completed. As of 1998, however, a ban on the procedure had failed to become federal law.

The abortion question has given rise to a powerful, and at times violent, conflict between opposing social movements. In the 1990s several workers in U.S. abortion clinics were wounded or killed by bombs or gunfire.

EDWIN M. SCHUR*, *New York University*

2. Medical Aspects of Abortion

As indicated earlier, abortion refers to the loss or destruction of an embryo or fetus before birth. It may be spontaneous or induced.

Spontaneous Abortion. Abortions that occur without medical or other intervention are known as spontaneous abortions, or miscarriages. Probably about 25% of all pregnancies result in miscarriage. As a general rule the chance of miscarriage is highest for women older than 35 or younger than 17 years of age, for couples who have difficulty in achieving pregnancy, and for women who have had at least two previous miscarriages.

Although the causes of miscarriage are not completely understood, it is likely that many result from non-inherited genetic defects of the embryo. Among the most common of these defects is the presence of an abnormal number of chromosomes, as a result of faulty cell division. The occurrence of a miscarriage owing to this defect does not increase the chance that a following pregnancy will terminate in miscarriage. In rare cases, however, miscarriage may be caused by an inherited chromosomal defect. The nature of a chromosomal abnormality can be detected by a microscopic examination of cells from the fetus and the parents. In the case of an inherited chromosomal defect, the doctor may be able to predict how likely it is that the same defect will cause subsequent abortions.

About 90% of miscarriages occur during a pregnancy's first trimester (the first 12 weeks). In many cases the miscarriage takes place before a woman realizes that she is pregnant, and she may not even realize that she has aborted. A typical 10th-week miscarriage resembles a very heavy menstrual period. There may be several days of bleeding and cramps before the contents of the uterus are expelled, followed by a short period of bleeding while the lining of the uterus heals. A miscarriage after the 12th week may resemble a mild version of the labor of childbirth, with strong contractions that dilate the cervix and expel the fetus. Miscarriages during the second trimester (the 13th to 24th week) most often result from faulty attachment of the placenta to the wall of the uterus or from a weak cervix that dilates too soon.

Ultrasound imaging may demonstrate that the gestational sac is empty and that there is no embryo or fetus. This is called a blighted ovum. If the patient waits for the onset of spontaneous contractions, such activity will resemble a very shortened period of labor.

The various stages of actual or possible miscarriages have been given medical names. In a so-called threatened abortion, the patient usually experiences vaginal bleeding with some cramps, and the cervix is closed. Bed rest is generally the only treatment needed. In a few cases the symptoms disappear and the rest of the pregnancy is normal. But if the bleeding continues and becomes heavy, it typically means that the cervix is dilating and the contents of the uterus are being expelled. This is called an inevitable abortion.

If all of the contents are expelled, the abortion is called a complete abortion, and no treatment other than rest is usually needed. All of the expelled tissue should be saved for examination by a doctor to make sure that the abortion is complete. Also, a laboratory examination of the tissue may determine the cause of the abortion. If the uterus retains part or all of the placenta, the abortion is called incomplete. Hemorrhaging may occur if part of the placenta adheres to the uterine wall and the uterus does not contract to seal the large blood vessels that feed the placenta. The usual treatment is a drug that induces labor by stimulating uterine contractions.

In a missed abortion the fetus is retained in the uterus more than six weeks after its death. A missed abortion is ordinarily indicated by the disappearance of the signs of pregnancy except for the continued absence of menstrual periods. Missed abortions are usually treated by induction of labor or by dilation and curettage (D & C), a procedure described below.

Induced Abortion. In an induced abortion drugs or instruments are used to stop the normal course of pregnancy. Since most women can be brought safely through pregnancy even with serious medical problems, few abortions need to be performed to protect the mother's health.

There are four main techniques for performing abortions. Regardless of the method used, however, abortions performed by unqualified persons are extremely dangerous.

Menstrual Extraction, Suction Curettage, and RU-486. Menstrual extraction, which is also called vacuum suction, is used for most abortions that are carried out during the first trimester. It is performed by suctioning out the lining of the uterus (endometrium), often through a thin, flexible tube inserted through the opening of the undilated cervix. The procedure is used after a woman has just missed a period or anytime thereafter up to about the eighth week of pregnancy. It can be done safely in a doctor's office and has a very low rate of mortality. If performed after a positive test for pregnancy, it is sometimes called very early abortion or early uterine evacuation.

An abortion-inducing drug known as RU-486, or mifepristone, causes the uterus to shed its lining and expel the fertilized egg. The hormone-like substance prostaglandin is usually administered with the drug to increase the latter's effectiveness. RU-486 can be used only until about the 47th day after the last menstrual period and can produce serious side effects in some women.

A technique known as suction curettage can be used late in the first trimester and early in the second trimester. The cervix is first dilated, sometimes utilizing a series of rods inserted into the opening following the administration of a local anesthetic. Laminaria, a type of seaweed, also can be used to dilate the cervix. Inserted into the patient in dry form, laminaria expands as it absorbs moisture.

Following dilation a rigid suction tube is employed to remove the contents of the uterus, using a more powerful suction than that required in menstrual extraction. Next the physician may use a narrow metal loop, called a curette, to gently scrape the uterine walls in order to ensure that all of the placental tissue has been removed.

Dilation and Curettage (D & C) and Dilation and Evacuation (D & E). Another abortion technique that is sometimes used during the first trimester is the D & C. In this the curette, rather than suction, is employed throughout the procedure. After the 12th week of pregnancy, abortions are commonly performed using dilation and evacuation (D & E), a method that requires the use of suction and curettage, with special forceps possibly required to help remove the fetal parts. The mortality rate for the D & C and D & E is approximately 3 per 100,000 abortions.

Prostaglandin or Saline Administration. For late abortions (at 15 to 24 weeks), many physicians prefer to induce labor rather than perform a surgical procedure. Labor can be triggered by injecting prostaglandin through the uterine wall and into the amniotic sac, which holds the fetus. This procedure is intended to result in the delivery of a nonviable fetus, but serious ethical and legal problems can arise if the fetus is born alive.

Hypertonic saline and urea have also been used to induce labor, but these tend to have higher complication rates. The overall maternal mortality rate for second-trimester abortions performed by prostaglandin or saline administration is approximately 20 per 100,000 abortions.

Hysterotomy. A major abdominal operation that is essentially a cesarean section, hysterotomy is usually performed only when other abortion methods have failed repeatedly. The fetus is often born alive. The maternal mortality rate is approximately 200 per 100,000 abortions.

DENIS CAVANAGH*, M.D., *Professor of Obstetrics and Gynecology, University of South Florida*

Bibliography

Baird, David T., et al., eds., *Modern Methods of Inducing Abortion* (Blackwell 1995).

Grossmann, Atina, *Reforming Sex: The German Movement for Birth Control and Abortion Reform, 1920–1950* (Oxford 1995).

Hadley, Janet, *Abortion: Between Freedom and Necessity* (Temple Univ. Press 1997).

Morowitz, Harold J., and James S. Trefil, *The Facts of Life: Science and the Abortion Controversy* (Oxford 1992).

Riddle, John M., *Contraception and Abortion from the Ancient World to the Renaissance* (Harvard Univ. Press 1992).

Shapiro, Ian, ed., *Abortion: The Supreme Court Decisions* (Hackett 1995).

Solinger, Rickie, *The Abortionist: A Woman against the Law* (Univ. of Calif. Press 1996).

Tribe, Laurence H., *Abortion: The Clash of Absolutes* (Norton 1992).

World Health Organization, *Complications of Abortion: Technical and Managerial Guidelines for Prevention and Treatment* (1995).

ABRAHAM, ā′brə-ham (originally ABRAM), Biblical patriarch, was the traditional progenitor of the Hebrews, Ishmaelites (Arabs), and a number of other tribes. He lived in about the 19th century B. C. The historical background of the Biblical Abraham stories is the Mesopotamian and Canaanite society of that time. They reflect the social order that left its traces in the documents of Mari and Nuzi and in the Babylonian Code of Hammurabi. Also a count of generations back from the Exodus, or from King David, points to the same period.

Biblical Narrative—To Birth of Ishmael. The Biblical narrative (Genesis 11:27–25:10), combining historical traditions with legendary motifs, derives Abraham's genealogy from Sem (Shem), oldest son of Noah. Abram marries his half-sister, Sarai (Sarah). Their father, Terah, migrates with them from his native Ur of the Chaldees in Mesopotamia to Haran, and dies there. Abram, upon God's command, goes on from Haran to the land of Canaan, together with Lot, the son of his deceased brother Haran. Before his departure, God promises to make him a great nation, and upon his arrival to give the land of Canaan to his seed. Abram, whom the Biblical story describes as a tent-dwelling, sheep- and goat-breeding nomadic chieftain, gradually moves down to southern Palestine, building altars to God wherever he sojourns. Driven by a famine, he crosses over into grain-rich Egypt. Fearing that the Egyptians might kill him in order to obtain the beautiful Sarai for themselves, Abram passes her off as his sister, not his wife. When Sarai is, in fact, taken into the pharaoh's harem, God visits plagues upon the ruler and his house. Pharaoh thereupon restores Sarai to Abram and orders them out of Egypt.

Back in Canaan, a typical nomadic quarrel breaks out between Abram and his nephew Lot over grazing land. The kin group thereupon splits up, Lot moving into the southern Jordan Valley and Abram pitching his tents around Hebron in the uplands. The bonds of kinship, however, are not severed as a result of this separation; and when Lot is captured in the course of an armed conflict, Abram hurries to his rescue with his servant army of 318 men. Abram's exemplary conduct in this victorious campaign brings him the blessings of Melchizedek, king of Salem, referred to as "priest of the most high God" (Genesis 14:18).

Abram, who is getting on in years, becomes worried that if he dies childless, his servant Eliezer of Damascus would inherit all his property. But God repeats His promise and, in a fiery night vision, discloses to Abram what is to happen to his progeny—four centuries of servitude in an alien land, and thereafter dominion over Canaan.

To provide an heir for Abram, Sarai gives him her handmaid Hagar as a concubine. The son born of this union, Ishmael, is destined to become the progenitor of the Ishmaelites (later identified by Arab tradition with the North Arabian tribes).

Abraham and Isaac. Years later, God changes Abram's name to Abraham and that of Sarai to Sarah, commands Abraham to carry out the rite of circumcision as a mark of the Covenant, and again promises him that his seed will have the land of Canaan as an everlasting possession. Soon thereafter, God, appearing in the shape of three men, announces to Abraham that his wife Sarah will bear him a son within a year. After the departure of the men, God informs Abraham that he intends to destroy the sinful cities of Sodom and Gomorrah. Abraham pleads and bargains with God to have pity on the cities; but since not even 10 righteous men are to be found in them, they are destroyed. Only Lot and his two daughters escape. Eventually the long-awaited true heir, Isaac, is born to Sarah. He is circumcised when eight days old. Upon God's instructions, Abraham complies with Sarah's demand and sends off Hagar and Ishmael into the desert. The greatest trial of Abraham's faith and obedience is yet to come. When Isaac grows up to be a young lad, God commands Abraham to sacrifice him as a burnt offering. Ready to obey, Abraham is about to slaughter his son, but God's angel stops him, and Abraham sacrifices a ram instead. As a reward, God repeats, more emphatically than on previous occasions, his blessings and promises to Abraham.

Sarah dies at the age of 127, and Abraham purchases from Ephron the Hittite the Cave of Machpelah as a family grave. Following the burial of Sarah, he sends his steward Eliezer to get a wife for Isaac from among his kinsfolk in Mesopotamia, and he himself marries Keturah and has children by her, as well as by a number of concubines. At the age of 175, Abraham dies, and his sons Isaac and Ishmael bury him in the Cave of Machpelah.

Character and Religion. Abraham's character emerges from the Biblical episodes as composed of traits still regarded as ideal by the Middle Eastern nomads of our own day. He is shrewd and not above lying when lying is required by self-interest. He is loyal to his kin, brave in war, desirous of numerous offspring, extremely hospitable, just, a hard bargainer, and an unquestioning believer in God.

Abraham's religion, according to the Bible, was the first monotheistic faith. God revealed Himself to Abraham and blessed him, and Abraham, in turn, obeyed God and served Him; he built altars, sacrificed, and "called on the name of the Lord" (Genesis 13:4). The Covenant entered into by God and Abraham perpetuated this relationship; Abraham's seed had to be circumcised, and the "God of Abraham" became their protector. The God of Abraham did not yet have the attributes of Yahweh in His later Mosaic and prophetic revelations. But he was the almighty and eternal God whose blessing meant prosperity, progeny, and long life. He did not yet have special sanctuaries, rituals, or holidays, but appeared to Abraham in many places, conversed with him, and demanded of him only the fulfillment of an occasional command. He was more man's divine friend than a God who circumscribed life by innumerable laws.

Later Legends. Abraham became the subject of many legends in the later rabbinical and Muslim traditions, in which he broke the idols in his father's house and opposed the Chaldean astrologers. When, according to legend, Nimrod cast him into a fiery furnace, Abraham's faith caused the fire to cool and become a rose garden. Mohammed accepted Abraham as the founder of the Muslim religion. The "standing place of Abraham" (Koran, sura 3:91) is marked by a shrine at Mecca, the Makam Ibrahim, which encloses the stone on which Abraham was believed to have stood while he built the Kaaba, Isl m's holiest temple.

RAPHAEL PATAI
Author of "The Jewish Mind"

Further Reading: Van Seter, John, *Abraham in History and Tradition* (Yale Univ. Press 1987).

ABRAHAM IBN DAUD HA-LEVI (c. 1100–1180), ā'brə-ham ib'ən dä-wōōd' hä-lā-vē, Jewish historian and philosopher. Born in Córdoba, Spain, he may be identical with Avendauth, translator of Avicenna's works into Latin. Anticipating Maimonides, Ibn Daud waged a vigorous battle against Jewish Neoplatonism, formulating the first systematic synthesis of Judaism along medieval Aristotelian lines. He was martyred in Toledo.

Ibn Daud's exposition of Jewish philosophy, *al-'Aqīda al-Rafī'a* (1168), has survived only in a Hebrew translation, *ha-Emunah ha-Ramah* (late 14th century; *The Exalted Faith*, 1986). His chief historical work, *Sefer ha-Qabbalah* (1161; *A Critical Edition . . . of the Book of Tradition [Sefer ha-qabbalah]*, 1969), traces rabbinic authority from earliest times to his day. No longer universally considered entirely reliable as history, it is still an important source for the study of early Jewish culture in Spain.

GERSON D. COHEN*
Jewish Theological Seminary of America

ABRAHAM LINCOLN BRIGADE, a force of 2,800 American volunteers who fought on the side of the Spanish republic during the Spanish Civil War (1936–1939). The Lincoln Brigade (technically, a battalion), together with some 50 other international volunteer units, was organized by the Comintern (Communist International) as a means of assisting the popular army of the republic against the military revolt led by Gen. Francisco Franco and supported by Hitler and Mussolini. Many of the Lincoln volunteers were young unemployed persons or students who, under the dispiriting conditions of the Great Depression, had joined the U.S. Communist party or other left-wing organizations. The rise of domestic fascist groups intensified their interest in stopping international fascism.

The first Lincoln troops arrived on the Iberian Peninsula in January 1937. The battalion's efforts centered primarily on the defense of Madrid. Hastily trained, inadequately armed, and organized along nontraditional lines (some officers, for example, were "elected"), they nevertheless managed to hold off Franco's forces long enough to allow the Republican Army to build itself up. Losses were high, however, with over 750 men (27%) losing their lives. When, in November 1938, Spanish prime minister Juan Negrin ordered all international brigades out of the country in an attempt to pressure Hitler and Mussolini to do the same, the Lincoln Brigaders returned to the United States. They were received as popular heroes, but no official recognition was given them by the government. During the anticommunist investigations of the 1950s led by Sen. Joseph McCarthy, many Lincoln Brigade veterans were called before the Subversive Activities Control Board as "premature antifascists," investigated by the Federal Bureau of Investigation, or otherwise harassed.

Bibliography: Carroll, Peter N., *The Odyssey of the Abraham Lincoln Brigade: Americans in the Spanish Civil War* (Stanford Univ. Press 1994); **Nelson, Cary, and Jefferson Hendricks,** eds., *Madrid 1937: Letters of the Abraham Lincoln Brigade from the Spanish Civil War* (Routledge 1996).

ABRAHAMITES, ā'brə-ham-īts, the name of two religious sects. The first, a 9th-century sect of Syrian deists who denied the divinity of Christ, was founded by Abraham of Antioch. The second sect to bear this name was a group of Bohemian deists of the late 18th century. They identified themselves as followers of Jan Hus, but accepted no religious doctrine beyond the unity of God, and nothing of the Bible but the Ten Commandments and the Lord's Prayer. In 1782 Emperor Joseph II promised them toleration if they would accept either the Jewish or Christian faiths. When they refused, he expelled them from Bohemia the next year and scattered them through Hungary, Transylvania, and Slavonia, where they lost their identity as a sect.

MINNESOTA MINING & MANUFACTURING CO.

Garnet paper and other coated abrasive papers are dried in long rooms during the manufacturing process.

ABRASIVES, ə-brā'sivz, natural and synthetic substances that are used to remove material from workpieces made of metal, wood, plastic, ceramic, or glass. The material is removed by a fracturing or shearing action. Removal of chips by shear or fracture is attained by forcing hard abrasive particles through a softer workpiece layer or by causing abrasive particles to strike the workpiece. Efficient chip removal requires a proper application and selection of abrasives to obtain high material removal rates, achieve precise dimensional and geometrical accuracy, and produce controlled finishes. In theory the sharp cutting edges of the abrasive must be presented to the workpiece material in a definite orientation. Abrasive particle orientation is accomplished by producing grinding wheels and sticks, coated abrasive belts and paper, and loose abrasive particles.

Effective abrasive manufacturing operations can be achieved when a processed abrasive is used in conjunction with hand methods or machine tools. Common abrasive manufacturing operations are surface and cylindrical grinding, impact grinding, honing, lapping, superfinishing, polishing, buffing, sanding, and tumbling. Abrasive manufacturing operations play a key role in the manufacture of products for home, business, and industry. Abrasives are used directly in the manufacture of products or in the building of machines and tools used to make products.

History. The development of abrasives parallels man's progress in technology. Until the 20th century, man's technological progress was slow. A contributing factor was a lack of adequate abrasive materials to take advantage of advances in metallurgy, machine design, and manufacturing ideas and techniques. Without abrasives of good fracture strength, hardness, and wear resistance, toolmakers and machinists had great difficulty in producing spindles, bearings, bearing surfaces, machine ways, and other structural elements of machine tools. Early machine tools could not meet the high speed, heavy cutting, and mass production requirements of modern methods.

Archaeological evidence indicates that sand polishing and stone rubbing of weapons and utensils were attempted between 25,000 and 15,000 B.C. In the Iron Age, man fashioned implements by rubbing stone against iron and bronze.

Thousands of years later other natural abrasives were discovered. Diamonds, which have better hardness and wear properties than sandstone or sand, were mined first in India about 700 B.C. Emery was probably first used as an abrasive about 100 A.D., but it may have been used hundreds of years earlier.

During the Middle Ages, scholars recorded that naturally bonded grinding wheels of quartz and flint were used and that gemstones were lapped with natural abrasives between metal plates.

Corundum was discovered in India about 1825. Of all natural abrasives, corundum is closest to diamonds in hardness. About this time, the first use of an artificially bonded, natural-abrasive grinding wheel was reported in India. It contained corundum bonded with gum resin.

Advances in engineering material sciences and manufacturing process applications led to a need for improved abrasives. In 1891, Edward G. Acheson commercially produced silicon-carbide crystals (carborundum). These crystals are second only to diamonds in hardness. Synthetically produced silicon-carbide crystals are superior to emery and corundum in hardness, toughness, and fracture strength. The use of general-purpose, artificially bonded grinding wheels and loose abrasive grains of silicon carbide led to great improvements in abrasive manufacturing operations.

In 1900, Charles Jacobs manufactured aluminum oxide from bauxite and developed a tempering technique that provided a synthetic abrasive with hardness and strength suitable for abrasive processes.

Man-made diamonds, which became available to industry in 1955, are widely used as abrasive grains bonded in thin layers to metal or resinoid wheels. The cost of natural and man-made diamonds still is a serious limitation. Silicon carbide, aluminum oxide, and natural and man-made diamonds are the major abrasives used by modern industry.

Physical Description. Each abrasive has definite hardness, toughness, and fracture characteristics. The abrading performance of synthetic and natural diamond abrasives is predictable. This is not true of other natural abrasives because impurities are present. Diamonds are the hardest abrasive material; silicon carbide is second in hardness; and aluminum oxide is third. The hardness property permits penetration into workpiece material. Diamonds are used to measure the hardness (scratch resistance) of other abrasive materials. Silicon carbide generally has less body strength (toughness) and more friability. These properties provide less resistance to grain fracture. Aluminum oxide, which generally has more body strength and less friability, resists dulling when it is applied to tough, high-tensile-strength materials.

Body strength and friability properties vary, depending on grain size, grain shape, and crystal structure. Natural abrasive grains such as emery, crocus, or pumice, do not have high hardness, high strength of grain cutting edge, or high body strength. In use, they progressively break down. However, these abrasives are well suited for buffing and polishing under light load pressures.

Grain size is of utmost importance for rapid removal rates or finish. Grain sizes range from 10 mesh size for fast material removal to 600 and 1,000 mesh size for lapping and polishing. Abrasive grain size is determined by screening grains through a series of sieves of progressively smaller hole size. The lower the grain size number, the coarser is the abrasive grain.

Abrasive Forms. Abrasive grain bonding secures the grain in a desirable shape, as in wheels, stones, sticks, or endless belts. The bonding material permits the release of dull grains and permits grain fracture to expose new sharp cutting edges to the workpiece. Grinding wheels commonly have a vitrified, rubber, or resinoid bonded construction. In coated abrasive belts, discs, and papers, the abrasive is applied to a backing surface in a thin layer and is bonded to the surface. Loose abrasive grains carried in air, water, or oil media are examples of a non-bonded form. In all abrasive forms, abrasive grain size and type are important in achieving a desired result from abrasive processes.

Synthetic Abrasives—Silicon Carbide. A compound of silicon and carbon has hard, friable properties suitable for grinding dense, hard, or brittle workpieces made of cast-iron, ceramic, carbide, nonmetallic, or nonferrous materials. A variety of abrasive forms can be used to produce flat surfaces, accurately sized external and internal diameters, and fine finishes by any of the common abrasive manufacturing operations.

Aluminum Oxide. Aluminum oxide (alumina) is less hard and more tough than silicon carbide. Because of its desirable grain-fracture characteristics, aluminum oxide is suitable for grinding tough, high-strength materials, such as alloy and tool steels. This abrasive is suitable for obtaining fine finishes and for removing small amounts of material by lapping, honing, superfinishing, polishing, or buffing.

Man-made Diamonds. Synthetically produced diamonds, which are nearly pure carbon, are very hard. Major applications for synthetic diamond abrasives are wheel grinding and honing of tungsten-carbide and aluminum-oxide cutting tools and truing of silicon-carbide and aluminum-oxide grinding wheels.

Applications for Synthetic Abrasives. Silicon carbide, aluminum oxide, and synthetic diamonds are used in a variety of forms to manufacture crankshafts, cutting tools, bearings, and functional surfaces of machines and workpiece holding devices. Honing of cylinder-block bore diameters to improve roundness, straightness, and taper is an example of a corrective operation. Cutoff and snag grinding with tough, bonded abrasive wheels are important preparatory operations on cast, welded, and forged parts. Lapping with loose abrasives suspended in oil can provide extremely accurate dimensions, correct shape imperfections, refine finish, and produce close fits.

Miscellaneous Abrasives. Abrasive materials are available as steel wool, steel shot, and glass pellets. Steel wool is used to remove corrosion and to smooth metal workpieces. Steel shot and glass pellets are used to change surface characteristics by striking the workpiece surface.

Natural Abrasives. *Silica*, which is silicon dioxide, occurs in the form of quartz, flint, and agate. This abrasive may be used loose or bonded to paper, fabric drums, or belts.

Emery, which chiefly consists of aluminum oxide and iron oxide, is used to polish and buff. It usually is bonded to fabric, coated on rolls, or compounded into solid bars or liquid. Emery is placed on fabric, on sheepskin, on fiber discs, and on fiber wheels.

Tripoli is an amorphous silica that contains iron compounds. Die castings, aluminum, copper, and brass are buffed with tripoli. It is not used on ferrous metals because it is too soft for them.

Rouge is a ferric oxide material used to obtain a high coloring on gold, copper, and brass. It also is used to polish and buff other metals.

Crocus consists chiefly of iron oxide in a less refined form than rouge. It is used in buffing and polishing cutlery. Crocus cloth is available for light metal removal and polishing.

Pumice is a porous, spongy form of volcanic glass. In loose or block forms it is used for polishing and buffing plastics, glass, and wood.

Garnet is a hard, glasslike mineral that consists of calcium, iron, and magnesium silicates. Garnet paper, disc, and roll forms are used to sand wood products.

Diamonds, which are nearly 100 percent carbon, are mined as gemstone and bort. Bort, which is low-quality, flawed diamond stones and fragments, is crushed to graded grain sizes for grinding and honing applications. Mounted diamond fragments and flawed stones are used for truing grinding wheels. As cutting tools, they are used for material removal processes. Bonded diamond wheels are used to saw stone, granite, and concrete for highways and aircraft runways.

Industrial Uses. Synthetic abrasives and natural abrasives, such as emery, tripoli, pumice, and rouge, are used to brighten and improve a workpiece surface before plating or painting. Die-cast plumbing fixtures, automobile hardware, molded plastic products, and finish conditioning of industrial tools are important applications. Endless belts and buffing wheels are widely used. Impact grinding, blasting, and tumbling operations are performed with synthetic or natural abrasives. Silica and granite stones are used where abrasive loss is high, as in masonry building cleaning and in blasting cast parts to remove scale and oxides.

Home Uses. Sandpaper, a common abrasive, primarily is used in finishing wood products. A graded silica is coated on paper or fabric to form sheets, belts, and discs. Similar but more expensive abrasives, such as emery, garnet, or crocus, are available in paper, belt, or cloth form. Steel wool can be used in finishing wood products and cleaning metal implements. Pumice is used to refine the finish of cabinetry in the home workshop. Silicon-carbide sticks, aluminum-oxide sticks, and small grinding wheels are essential for maintaining sharp cutting edges on the home craftsman's tools.

THEODORE W. JUDSON, *General Motors Institute*

Further Reading: Coes, L., *Abrasives* (Springer-Verlag 1971); Collie, M. J., ed, *Industrial Abrasive Materials and Compositions* (Noyes 1981); McKee, Richard L., *Machining with Abrasives* (Van Nostrand Reinhold 1981); Pinkstone, William G., *The Abrasive Ages* (Sutter House 1975); Society of Manufacturing Engineers, *Tool and Manufacturing Engineers Handbook*, vol. 3 (1985).

ABRAXAS, ə-brak'səs, was a term used by the Basilidians, an early Gnostic sect, to designate emanations from the Supreme Power (see GNOSTICISM). Probably derived from Hebrew, it was applied by the Basilidians not to the highest deity himself but to the spirits of the world collectively. Written in Greek, the letters of *abraxas*, computed numerically, have the value of 365, the mystic number often inscribed on the stones used by the sect. These stones were cut in different forms and bore a variety of capricious symbols, most often a human body with a fowl's or lion's head and snakes for limbs.

Gnostic symbols were later adopted by all sects given to magic and alchemy; therefore it is probable that most of the abraxas stones containing cabalistic forms were made in the Middle Ages as talismans.

Further Reading: Walker, Benjamin, *Gnosticism: Its History and Influence* (Borgo Press 1986).

ABREU, ə-brâ'ōō, **Casimiro de** (1837–1860), Brazilian poet, who was one of the most popular writers of Brazil's romantic movement. He was born in Barra de São João, Rio de Janeiro, on Jan. 9, 1837. Much against the young man's wishes, his father sent him to Lisbon, Portugal, in 1853 to pursue a business career. Casimiro remained there for four years, and then returned to Brazil, where he died at Nova Friburgo on Oct. 18, 1860.

Abreu's best poetry expresses a kind of nostalgia known as *sausade*, a Portuguese word meaning "longing." Abreu's particular longing was for his homeland. His versification is conventionally correct, and his poetic style is frequently simple and naïve. But in his masterpiece, *As primaveras* (1859; *Springtimes*), a volume of lyrics that was begun in 1855 while he was still living abroad in Portugal, the verses are characterized by a poetic honesty and moving sadness.

ABREU, ə-brâ'ōō, **João Capistrano de** (1853–1927), Brazilian historian and philologist, who was the father of modern Brazilian historical writing. He was born at Maranguape, Ceará province, and taught at the University of Brazil in Rio de Janeiro from 1883 to 1899. He died at Rio de Janeiro on Aug. 13, 1927.

His book, *Caminhos antigos e povoamento do Brasil* (1899), is the authoritative study of Brazil's early years and had a lasting influence on Brazilian historiography. Other important historical works by Abreu include *O Brasil no século XVI* (1880), *O descobrimento do Brasil* (1883), and *Capitulo de historia colonial* (1907).

ABROGATION, ab-rə-gā'shən, a term derived from canon and Roman law, means the complete repeal or annulment of an authoritative decree. Abrogation may be effected either by the enactment of a new law that expressly declares the abolishment of an older one, or simply by the acceptance of another law whose provisions contradict a previous law. The latter form is called *implied abrogation*.

In common law, the abrogation of a law reestablishes preexisting statutes which, in turn, had been abrogated by that law. A legal act involving only a partial repeal is called *derogation*, while the term abrogation denotes total annulment.

ABRUZZI, ä-broo'tsē, **Duke of the** (1873–1933), Italian naval officer, mountain climber, and explorer. He was born in Madrid, Spain, on Jan. 29, 1873. His father, Prince Amedeo of Savoy, duke of Aosta, was king of Spain from 1870 to 1873. Two weeks after the birth of the child, who was named *Luigi Amedeo of Savoy,* the king abdicated and left Spain.

The duke was trained for a career in the Italian navy and completed his studies at the naval academy in Livorno. Off duty he practiced mountain climbing in the Alps. In 1897 he led the first successful expedition to the summit of Mount St. Elias (18,008 feet) in the Alaskan-Canadian Rockies. Two years later he sailed on the *Stella Polare* as commander of an expedition to the North Pole. Although he failed to reach the pole, he mapped the northern coast of Franz Josef Land.

In 1906, Abruzzi led a party of explorers to the Ruwenzori Mountains on the Congo-Uganda border. They mapped the entire range, measuring and climbing the highest peaks, including Mount Stanley (16,795 feet). In the Himalayas, in 1909, Abruzzi reached an altitude of 22,650 feet on K^2 (Mount Godwin Austen) but failed to conquer the summit.

In World War I the duke commanded the Italian fleet and Allied naval units in the Adriatic, rescuing the defeated Serbian army and evacuating it to Corfu. He resigned in 1917 because of disagreements with his chief of staff. After the war he went to Italian Somaliland, where he founded an agricultural colony, Villaggio Duca degli Abruzzi (now Giofer, Somalia). In 1928 he explored the upper Shebeli River, in Ethiopia. He died on March 18, 1933, in the Somaliland settlement he had founded.

ABRUZZI, ä-broot'tsē, is a region of central Italy, extending from the Apennine Mountains to the Adriatic Sea. It also is spelled *Abruzzo.* Neighboring Molise constituted one region with Abruzzi until it became a separate entity in 1963. Abruzzi's area of 4,168 square miles comprises the provinces of Sulmona, Teramo, and L'Aquila. The city of L'Aquila is the regional capital.

Abruzzi is one of the less-developed and more sparsely populated areas of Italy. The limited productiveness of its soil, its mountainous terrain, frequent earthquakes, scarcity of good roads, and absence of harbors have hampered progress. Sheep raising, once the backbone of the economy, has declined in importance. Several ski resorts cater to winter visitors, mostly from Rome.

Abruzzi comprises two distinct geographic areas. One is a mountain region in the western and central section, noted for its savage beauty and its long and cold winters. The region is crossed by ranges of the Apennines that reach their highest point in Monte Corno (9,560 feet, or 2,914 meters), in the Gran Sasso d'Italia massif. Except for cultivated plateaus and high valleys and the reclaimed area of Lake Fucino, this mountain region is rocky and unproductive. The second geographic region consists of hills and narrow valleys sloping eastward to the Adriatic. Cereals, olives, and grapes are produced here. Population: 1,262,392 (2001 census).

ABSALOM, ab'sə-ləm, in the Old Testament, was the third son of King David. His story is told in II Samuel 13–19. The Bible presents him as a handsome and charming prince. He avenged his half brother Amnon's rape of his sister Tamar by killing Amnon, and was banished from his father's court for five years. Aided by the shrewd Ahithophel, he organized a rebellion against his father, which forced David to flee east of the Jordan. David, however, succeeded in collecting a new army, and his veteran captain, Joab, routed Absalom's forces. Absalom, trying to escape, was caught by his long hair in the branches of a tree under which he was riding. Although David had ordered that his son's life be spared, Joab killed Absalom with his spear. David was greatly grieved by Absalom's death and ordered public mourning.

ABSALOM, ABSALOM!, ab'sə-ləm, is a novel by the American writer William Faulkner (q.v.), published in 1936. It is regarded by some critics as his best work. The story centers around Thomas Sutpen, a West Virginia mountaineer, who goes to Jefferson, Miss., in 1833, determined to become a Southern aristocrat. His first wife had been a woman of mixed white and black lineage. His second wife is a white woman. The son of the second marriage murders the son of the first, and Sutpen himself is later murdered by the grandfather of a girl whom he had seduced. Sutpen's dream of establishing a dynasty ends with his great mansion burnt to the ground and his only surviving descendant a moronic grandson.

The story is told by three people—Rosa Coldfield, who relates it to a young friend, Quentin Compson, on the eve of his departure for Harvard in 1910; Quentin's father, who, over a period of years, supplements Rosa's account and completes the story in a letter to Quentin; and, finally, Quentin himself, who retells the story, adding his own interpretation, to his Harvard roommate. As Quentin interprets the tale, the chronicle of Thomas Sutpen becomes the story of the 19th century American South, with its deep and conflicting passions, its tragedy, ruin, and decay.

In *Absalom, Absalom!* Faulkner continued his experimentation with interior monologue, a literary device through which the narrator reveals his own personality. In this case, with three narrators, Faulkner projects three sets of attitudes toward the Sutpen story.

ABSALOM AND ACHITOPHEL, ab'sə-ləm, ə-kit'-ə-fel, is a satire in heroic couplets, written in 1681 by John Dryden, who was then poet laureate, to defend the king's party in England. It refers in allegorical form to the plan of Lord Shaftesbury (Achitophel) to install the duke of Monmouth (Absalom), the illegitimate son of King Charles II (David), on the throne, instead of the king's reputedly Roman Catholic brother, James, duke of York. The satire stands out for its brilliant characterization, cogent political reasoning, and mastery of form. It succeeded brilliantly in exposing the characters and motives of the king's opponents, and thus helped to kill the Bill of Exclusion by strengthening James' succession.

Taking a part of the story of Absalom's rebellion against his father David (II Samuel 15–18), Dryden ingeniously adapts it to contemporary characters and conditions. The story of *Absalom and Achitophel* is slight and unimportant, but for this defect the characterization and political reasoning amply atone. The characters are neither merely impersonal types, nor, like most of Pope's, are they too sharply individualized. Furthermore, they seemingly are drawn without personal animus, and the satirist has the air of pronouncing judgment like an Olympian. The portraits of Achitophel, Zimri (Buckingham), and Shemei (Slingsby Bethel) deserve their place in the picture gallery of great satire.

Scarcely less remarkable is the political philosophy of the poem, which mingles the specious with the profound. In the mouth of Achitophel, whose reasoning he seems to condemn, the poet puts arguments that are now generally accepted as valid. It is hard to tell just what Dryden really believed. The verse shows mastery of the heroic couplet, which Dryden perfected and which is, all things considered, the best vehicle that English satire has discovered.

A second part of *Absalom and Achitophel* was written by Nahum Tate. To this Dryden contributed only 200 lines (lines 310–509) on the poets Shadwell and Settle. They are in Dryden's best vein and form the only readable portion of the poem.

MARION TUCKER
Polytechnic Institute of Brooklyn

ABSALON (c. 1128–1201), àp'sà-lon, Danish bishop, statesman, and soldier. He was born about 1128 near Ringsted in Sjælland. A member of a powerful family, Absalon became bishop of Roskilde in 1158 after aiding his foster brother Waldemar I in his successful struggle for the Danish throne. As a general and counselor to Waldemar I and to his son and successor Canute (Knud) VI, he worked for the stabilization of the realm, then ravaged by Wendish pirates from Pomerania and Rügen. He personally led numerous military expeditions against the Wends and in 1167 fortified the village of Havn, which later became Copenhagen. By 1169 he had conquered the Wendish stronghold on Rügen, baptized the pirates, and incorporated the island into the Danish kingdom. Only after his naval victory in 1184 over the duke of Pomerania, however, did the Wendish threat finally subside.

Absalon became archbishop of Lund in 1177 but retained his diocese of Roskilde. As a church leader he enforced discipline and celibacy among the clergy and, with the king's help, crushed a peasant's rebellion against tithes in Skåne.

Absalon's promotion of cultural endeavors probably influenced Saxo Grammaticus, his secretary, to write the monumental *Gesta Danorum*, a history of Denmark from legendary times. Absalon died at Sorø in 1201.

HALLBERG HALLMUNDSSON, *Editor,*
"An Anthology of Scandinavian Literature"

ABSCESS, ab'ses, a localized collection of pus caused by bacteria, fungi, or parasites that have gained access to solid tissue.

Cause. Most abscesses are caused by pus-forming (pyogenic) bacteria. These bacteria include staphylococci, streptococci, gonococci, and meningococci. They liberate toxins that destroy cells, increase the local acidity, and cause the capillaries to dilate. White blood cells (leukocytes) then can pass through the dilated capillary walls. These white cells liquefy dead tissue, resulting in a cavity containing pus. Pus consists of living and dead bacteria, fragments of destroyed tissue, some white cells, and fluid given off from cells. When an abscess occurs, monocytes (certain white cells) are mobilized to eliminate the dead cells and bacteria by a process known as phagocytosis. Other cells combine with newly formed capillaries and other elements to form a wall to delimit the abscess. The size of the abscess is determined by the number and virulence of the bacteria and also by the resistance of the host.

Symptoms. The chief signs of an abscess are swelling, pain, heat, and redness. Swelling is the result of the accumulation of fluid, serum, and other substances given off by the cells. Pain is attributed to increased tension that exerts pressure on local sensory nerve endings. Heat and redness are due to the engorgement of blood vessels. When the pain is severe, a fifth sign may appear: interference with the normal functioning of the organ or organism. Fever and a general feeling of malaise may also occur. Other complaints vary with the location of the abscess.

Types of Abscesses. Various names are applied to abscesses according to the causal agent and the location of the abscess.

Brain abscesses may result from different types of bacteria carried from an original site of infection in the ear, nasal passages, lung, or heart. The majority of brain abscesses come from middle ear infections and occur in the area of the cerebellum. However, an abscess may develop in any part of the brain.

An abscess around the tonsil (peritonsillar abscess) sometimes develops as a complication of streptococcal tonsillitis. Also known as quinsy sore throat, it may produce pus that spreads to form another abscess behind the pharynx (retropharyngeal abscess).

A lung abscess is usually caused by the aspiration of infected material. This may follow surgery in which a general anesthesia has been used, or it may result from an infected blood clot or from some types of bacterial pneumonia. When the abscess erodes a major part of the bronchial tube, the patient coughs up large amounts of pus. If the abscess remains untreated, pus may develop in the cavity around the lungs (pleural cavity), causing empyema.

Abscesses of the kidney are usually the result of infections spreading up from the bladder; they may also result from bacteria carried in the blood from a carbuncle or from an inflammation of the lining of the heart (endocarditis).

Abscesses of the liver may be caused by bacteria in the veins, arteries, and ducts entering the liver. The portal vein, which drains the intestinal tract and goes to the liver, is responsible for most abscesses of the liver. An example is the amoebic abscess, a common complication of amoebic dysentery.

Ovarian abscesses often are associated with an infection of the fallopian tube on the same side. In such a case, the term "tubo-ovarian abscess" is employed.

Treatment. The general treatment for an abscess is the surgical evacuation and drainage of the abscess and the administration of antimicrobial drugs to combat infection. Small abscesses may undergo complete resolution without drainage, while larger abscesses may continue to accumulate pus until the abscess breaks.

When uncontrolled, bacteria from abscesses may get into the blood stream and cause abscesses to appear in distant organs.

THEODORE WINSHIP, M.D.
Washington Hospital Center

ABSENTEE OWNERSHIP, ab′sən-tē′ ō-nər-ship, is the total or partial ownership of property by persons remote from the location of the property or the control of its use. The term applies both to land ownership and to ownership of productive processes by individuals or by corporations. In any case, the owners have claims on income from the use of the property received in the form of rent, interest, profits, or dividends.

In its original sense, absentee ownership meant land ownership without owner residence on the property. Because the absentee owners of landed estates received income from them but did not cultivate or manage them directly, they were frequently accused of exploiting their tenants. The latifundia, or great landed estates of the Roman empire, were often worked by slave labor while the owners lived in Rome. In prerevolutionary France, many of the nobility lived at Versailles, leaving managers to handle their estates. In the 20th century some governments have confiscated absentee-owned lands and redistributed them for the use of peasants on the ground that land reform was needed to correct economic and social abuses.

In the United States, from the 1870's until the 1930's, the problem of farm tenantry on absentee-owned lands received considerable attention. Although that problem is no longer important, a certain amount of absentee land ownership exists among professionals and business executives, who hold the land primarily for recreational use or as a place for retirement.

Absentee ownership in the United States is more interesting in its application to business, where corporate ownership is highly diversified through the device of stocks and other financial arrangements. The control of companies is left to salaried employees often referred to as the "managerial class," who may or may not own stock in the companies. Early in the 20th century the economist Thorstein Veblen maintained that a few powerful investors—absentee owners—could control industrial prices and output although they did not participate in the productive processes. Beginning with the 1930's, increased governmental regulation and control of the economy has offset this danger.

Kathleen Edith Dunlop, *East Carolina College*

ABSENTEE VOTING, ab-sən-tē′ vōt′ing, is the practice of casting ballots elsewhere than at the polls. The privilege is extended by state or national laws in most democratic countries to authorized voters who are unable by reason of illness or absence from home to vote at the polls in person on election day.

In the United States, absentee ballots were used in colonial times as early as the 17th century. Their first extensive use in the states was for soldiers in the field during the Civil War. Beginning in 1896 certain states granted the privilege by statutes to civilians compelled to be away from their homes on election day. In World War II the federal government adopted the "soldier ballot" and assigned election duties to certain officers. Since the war the states also have permitted absentee ballots for servicemen and their wives and for civilian personnel accompanying the armed forces.

Several states have added sickness and physical disability to the reasons for absentee voting. College students away from home are eligible in some states. California and a few other states allow absent voting for persons living 10 miles or more from the nearest voting precinct. In the mid-1960's only New Mexico permitted no form of absentee voting in state or local elections.

Absentee ballots may be cast by proxy or by mail. In Virginia, for instance, the voter may vote by proxy by appearing at the office of the registrar of elections until five days before the election and fill out a ballot. The ballot is placed in a sealed envelope and certified. If the voter applies for the privilege of voting by mail, the clerk mails the ballot, a certificate to be notarized, a ballot envelope, and an outside envelope to be returned by registered mail. In either case the clerk verifies the voter's eligibility and forwards the material to the precinct judges to be counted on election day.

Spencer D. Albright, *University of Richmond*

ABSIL, àb-sēl′, **Jean** (1893–1974), Belgian composer, who was a major influence on 20th century Belgian music. Born at Peruwelz on Oct. 23, 1893, he studied at the Brussels Conservatory and with the composer Paul Gilson. His early work won a number of prizes, including the Prix de Rome (1922). In 1923 he was named head of the Music Academy at Etterbeek, which under his direction became one of the outstanding music schools in Belgium. From 1931 he also was a professor of harmony at the Brussels Conservatory. He helped found the *Revue internationale de musique* in 1938.

In the late 1920's Absil repudiated many of his early traditional works and began to evolve a new, personal style, unfettered by academic harmonies and meters. His compositions include symphonies, concertos, chamber music, and songs. He died in Brussels on Feb. 2, 1974.

ABSINTHE, ab′sinth, is a liquor obtained by adding the essential oils of wormwood (*Artemisia absinthium*), anise, fennel, and coriander seed to high-strength neutral spirits. The liquor is of Swiss origin but was first made and distributed on a large scale by the French firm of Pernod at the beginning of the 1800's. The approved method of drinking absinthe was to put a small quantity in a tumbler and very slowly pour in a generous measure of iced water over a perforated silver strainer containing a lump of sugar. The weakening of the alcohol caused the essential oils of the herbs to precipitate so that the liquor, at first green, became attractively opalescent, with a taste predominantly of aniseed.

Absinthe was marketed at nearly twice the strength of spirits such as whiskey. Its highly intoxicating effect caused it to be banned in Switzerland in 1908 and in France six years later. In 1912 the United States forbade its importation, and its sale is now widely restricted or forbidden. Much-modified forms of absinthe, such as the French pernod and the Greek ouzo, remain popular.

Walter James
Author of "Wine, a Brief Encyclopedia"

ABSOLUTE, ab′sə-lōot, **Sir Anthony,** a character in Richard Brinsley Sheridan's comedy *The Rivals* (1775). He is a fiery-tempered, strong-willed, generous old man, always in a towering passion, even while he commends his own mildness of manner. The father of Captain Jack Absolute, the hero of the play, Sir Anthony insists that his son marry the woman Sir Anthony chooses.

ABSOLUTE, ab'sǝ-loot, in philosophy, the concept of that which is complete in itself and includes everything within itself—the unconditioned, ultimate reality. The absolute is reducible or referable to nothing other than itself, and all things are manifestations or determinations of it.

Absolute also denotes a primary principle in certain special branches of philosophy. In ethics, for example, the categorical imperative is seen by Kant as an absolute that is binding on all rational beings. In epistemology the Cartesian principle of the thinking ego is claimed as the ultimate basis for all certainty.

The term "absolute" as denoting the ultimate reality came into prominence with post-Kantian German idealism, particularly in the philosophy of Hegel, and also was used by certain neo-Hegelians and idealists of the late 19th century. However, the problem that gave rise to the concept of a metaphysical absolute goes back to the origins of philosophical inquiry in Western civilization.

Philosophers do not agree either on an absolute as ultimate reality or on absolutes as primary principles of the special branches of philosophy. Ethical relativists, for example, maintain that moral obligation is not an absolute since it does not derive from any unconditional imperative but is relative to time, place, and circumstance. In metaphysics, those who conceive of an ultimate reality often differ among themselves about the nature of such a reality. Some philosophers hold that there is an absolute reality but deny that it is knowable by man, and many view as nonsensical the very quest of an ultimate reality, whose verification, they claim, is impossible in principle.

Ancient Philosophy. Parmenides (early 5th century B.C.), the chief figure of the Eleatic School, challenged the concepts of reality put forward by other schools of philosophy by showing that they could not account for change and plurality without contradicting the meaning of "to be." Disregarding the testimony of the senses and relying solely on abstract reasoning, Parmenides offered the first philosophical absolute: what "is" is an eternal, full, immutable, undifferentiated One.

Such a concept of reality seemed impossible to accept and impossible to refute logically. Subsequent philosophers, including Plato and Aristotle, undoubtedly offered far richer and more satisfying concepts of reality than the sterile monism of Parmenides. Yet in Plato the *chorismos* (separation) of the transient particularities and the eternal forms, and in Aristotle the obscurity of the relation between the unmoved mover and the world of motion may be seen as instances of a failure to meet the Parmenidean demands. To the Stoic philosophers of about 300 B.C. reality consisted of forms of the one divine logos, an absolute whose being is material (fire).

In the metaphysic of Plotinus (3d century A.D.) the absolute is conceived as the ineffable and transcendent One. It is not like the One of Parmenides, however, for from the One of Plotinus emanate the eternal Nous (mind or intelligence) and realm of forms, which in turn produce the twofold World Soul, particular beings, and matter.

Modern Philosophy. In Christian thought the absolute is immaterial spirit: the eternal almighty God, creator and sustainer of the world and all things therein. This doctrine and the ancient concepts of an absolute were challenged by 17th century rationalists such as Spinoza, who charged in his *Ethics* (1674) that the Christian concept of a creation in time contradicted the concept of the eternal perfection of God. Any bridging of the gap between immaterial and material substance through creation *ex nihilo* (from nothing) or emanation was rejected by Spinoza as self-contradictory. Hence Spinoza put forward a concept of the absolute as infinite eternal substance that includes in its essence the attributes of both immateriality and materiality (thought and extension). The physical universe is God under the attribute of extension (space). Leibniz's monadology, with its principle of the preestablished harmony, was another absolute system of the period of early modern science.

Kant considered the Spinozist and Leibnizian visions of an ultimate reality as extensions of human knowledge beyond the realm of possible experience and therefore illegitimate. However, by demonstrating that the a priori ground of all human knowledge is the unifying activity of the thinking consciousness, Kant provided the germinating idea for the systems of absolutes of Fichte, Schelling, and Hegel.

For Fichte the Kantian concept of the transcendental subjectivity becomes a metaphysical absolute in the form of an infinite spiritual life. For Schelling the absolute is the unity of the real and the ideal, nature and thought. Schelling's absolute of "identity" or "indifference" is neither subjectivity nor objectivity, yet is the source of both.

It is in Hegel that the concept of the absolute as *Geist* (mind or spirit) assumes its most compelling form. According to Hegel's *Phenomenology of the Mind* (1807), the unity of the temporal and the eternal, the one and the many, subject and object can be realized only as spirit. Abstract being—the immutable and undifferentiated One of Parmenides—is the same as nothing. But differentiation that preserves unity must be inner or self-differentiation, the self-distinguishing of mind that remains one with itself in its distinguishing. This is the life of *Geist*.

Hegel's system did not withstand the advancing positivism and empiricism of the time. In England the introduction of Kant and German idealism modified somewhat the empiricist influence of Hume. Nevertheless, for Scottish philosopher Sir William Hamilton the absolute as the "unconditioned" remained inaccessible to human thought, as did the "unknowable" of Herbert Spencer and the absolute of Francis Herbert Bradley.

In the United States, Josiah Royce, especially in the "Supplementary Essay" to *The World and the Individual* (1901), conceived the absolute as an infinite self-consciousness whose "knowing" and "willing" embraced all of time past, present, and future at once. Royce sought to clarify this conception by analogy with the "actual infinite" developed by the German mathematician Richard Dedekind. Few would say, however, that Royce and other philosophers of the absolute have succeeded in resolving those basic questions of time and eternity, freedom and individuality, evil and contingency, that had been left problematic in all previous endeavors to conceive an absolute.

MURRAY GREENE, *New School for Social Research*

Further Reading: Copleston Frederick C., *History of Philosophy*, 9 vols. (Paulist Press 1976).

ABSOLUTE MUSIC, ab′sə-lо̄о̄t mū′zik, is music that refers to nothing outside itself and makes no attempt to convey specific emotions, visual images, or ideas related to the objective world. It is contrasted with *program music.*

The meaning of absolute music lies in its structure alone. It does not imitate the sounds of nature, tell a story, or illustrate a text. It is almost exclusively instrumental, the exceptions being the rare cases in which the voice is used purely as a wordless instrument, as in Villa-Lobos' *Bachianas brasileiras No. 5,* for voice and eight cellos.

The concertos and suites of Bach, the symphonies of Beethoven (with the exceptions of the *Pastoral Symphony* and the choral finale of the Ninth Symphony), and the chamber music of Brahms fall into the category of absolute music, as do most of the instrumental works in the standard concert repertory. In certain instances even music associated with the theater can stand independently as absolute music. For example, the overture to Mozart's *The Marriage of Figaro* is a composition in sonata form and needs no operatic reference to complete its meaning.

Many works that cannot be defined strictly as "absolute" are nevertheless structurally complete without a "program." The first movement of Beethoven's *Pastoral Symphony,* for example, is among the most tightly knit and economical of classical compositions; if it were not for the fact that Beethoven himself supplied a "story," the piece could justifiably be classified as absolute music.

SHIRLEY FLEMING, *"Musical America"*

ABSOLUTE ZERO, ab′sə-lо̄о̄t zē′rо̄, or *zero degrees absolute,* is the lowest temperature on the Kelvin thermometric scale (absolute thermodynamic scale of temperature), $-273.16°$ C, or $-459.69°$ F. It is the temperature that matter would have if all heat were removed from it, and is therefore the lowest possible temperature.

The planets far from the sun are so remote from any heat source that their temperatures are thought to be near zero degrees absolute. Earth is much warmer. To cool an object to temperatures near absolute zero on this planet, it must be subjected to a fairly complicated refrigeration process. A temperature of zero degrees absolute can never be realized, but only approached. A few millionths of a degree above absolute zero is the lowest temperature ever attained in the laboratory.

The thermal energy of matter is viewed as the rapid random motion of its molecules, and this energy is proportional to temperature. As the temperature of an object is reduced, therefore, the disordered motions of its molecules become less agitated. In the classical view of nature, molecular motion ceases altogether at absolute zero.

With the advent of quantum mechanics, this classical view required modification. Matter is now thought to retain a zero-point energy of random molecular motion at absolute zero. (See ZERO-POINT ENERGY.)

MICHAEL MCCLINTOCK
University of Colorado

ABSOLUTION, ab-sə-lо̄о̄′shən, in the ecclesiastical sense, implies a remission of sin or its penalties. In the Roman Catholic Church the power to absolve is vested in the priest. Basis for the doctrine is found in Christ's commission to the Apostles (John 20:22–23), the traditions of the church, and teachings of councils and synods. The power is universal and all-inclusive since there is no limitation on the number and kinds of sins to which it extends. From Christ's words "whose sins you shall retain," it is deduced that the power is of a juridical nature; that is, it requires an act of judgment. This presupposes the knowledge of sins committed and evidence that the penitent is properly disposed to receive forgiveness. Acts required of the penitent receiving absolution are confession, contrition with amendment, and the acceptance of a penance to make reparation for his sins.

In circumstances where the penitent cannot make an auricular confession—when too ill to speak, for example—absolution can be given on the grounds that the penitent has a desire to fulfill the conditions when he is able.

Absolution in the church has a twofold reference—to the sins themselves or to penalties, such as excommunications, incurred in connection with sins. In the Western church the indicative form, "I absolve you . . . ." is used; in the Eastern church the form, "May Christ absolve you . . ." is employed. The term "absolution" is also used to designate a prayer to implore, for departed souls, remission of punishment due to sin. See also CONFESSION, SACRAMENTAL; PENANCE.

RAYMOND HAIN
Catholic University of America

ABSOLUTISM, in philosophy. See ABSOLUTE.

ABSOLUTISM, ab′sə-lо̄о̄t-iz-əm, is the political theory and political system under which the ruler or rulers govern a community without clearly defined restraints of law and morality. In the ancient world, the Babylonian, Assyrian, and Egyptian empires were governed by the political principles and institutions of absolutism; by contrast, the Greeks and Romans knew periodic dictatorships, but they never developed a full-fledged theory or practice of absolutism. The spirit of individualism, restlessness, and inquiry that characterized the Greek and Roman civilizations stood as a bulwark of defense against the spread of Asian absolutism and uniformity into Europe; and the struggle between these two conflicting ways of life has remained one of the recurrent major themes of Western civilization and of world history. In the ancient Jewish heritage, too, there was little room for the concept or practice of political absolutism. Monotheism, with its belief in one God, led to the idea of the brotherhood of men, equal before God, thus eliminating the possibility of an absolute ruler. Moreover, the Biblical conception of a higher law, a "law behind the law," was a constant reminder to earthly rulers that over and above political government there was the higher law of God.

In the Middle Ages, the strong sense of custom and immemorial law obstructed the growth of absolutism as a political theory or system of government. Feudalism, the most characteristic institution of the medieval period, was social and economic in its origins, but it also had important political implications. While the vassal owed loyalty, obedience, and respect to his feudal lord, the lord, in turn, owed protection, justice, and aid to his vassal. Whereas in the typical relationship of absolutism the ruler has only rights and privileges and the ruled only duties and obligations, the medieval relationship of feudalism was characterized by reciprocity of rights and duties for both the rulers and the ruled.

From the 16th century onward absolutism became a more powerful reality in the Western world. The modern national state was born in struggles against the claims of church and empire to universal authority, as well as against the divisive tendencies of minor princes. As a result, the doctrine of the absolute authority of the monarch, derived from the theory of royal sovereignty or supreme power, served to consolidate and unify the national state as the new type of political organization. The Tudors and Stuarts in England and Louis XIV of France are famous examples of absolute rulers. Louis XIV's famous dictum *"L'état c'est moi"* ("I am the State") perfectly expressed the royalist mood of classic absolutism.

In the 18th century, absolutism was challenged by the American and French revolutions—a century after the Puritan revolution had freed England from royalist absolutism. In the 19th century, absolutism seemed on the way out, as constitutional government (in form at least, if not always in substance) spread throughout the world, even in ancient bastions of absolutism, such as Germany, Russia, and Japan. The 20th century witnessed the revival of absolutism in the form of the totalitarian system of fascism. Whereas absolutism is confined mainly to politics and government, totalitarianism seeks to dominate all aspects of human life. Absolutism is also closely related to the concept of authoritarianism, the rule of a person or group of persons who arrogate to themselves all political power in the state.

See also AUTHORITARIANISM.

WILLIAM EBENSTEIN, *Princeton University*

ABSORPTION, əb-sôrp′shən, the taking up of matter or energy by penetration into an absorbing medium, so that the absorbed matter or energy apparently disappears.

In chemical processes, absorption refers to the solution of a gas in a liquid, the solution being obtained by the washing, or intimate contacting (scrubbing), of a gas mixture with the liquid. In the ideal situation an equilibrium is attained, and there is a definite relationship between the concentrations of the gas phase and the liquid phase of the absorbed component.

Gas scrubbing is an important process for the recovery of products and the removal of pollution. For example, when coke-oven gas is scrubbed with water, ammonia is absorbed in the water. It is recovered as a useful by-product of the destructive distillation of coal. Sulfur dioxide can be removed as an air pollutant by scrubbing combustion-reaction products with water.

Absorption of substances may be either a physical process or a chemical process. The driving forces behind physical absorption are the solubility of the absorbed substance and the equilibrium vapor-pressure relationships of the substances. In chemical absorption, driving forces are more complex, and absorbed gas reacts chemically with the liquid.

Gas-liquid absorption (physical or chemical) usually is accomplished in vertical countercurrent flow patterns through packed, plate, or spray towers. The packed tower is a shell filled with specifically shaped packing materials. Plate towers contain plates at various heights within the tower. In spray towers the liquid surface is increased by forcing it through spray nozzles, forming many tiny droplets that fall through the rising gas stream.

In the absorption of light, specific wavelengths are absorbed by the material through which the light travels. The ultraviolet wavelengths of sunlight are absorbed by glass, warming it slightly by the conversion of light to heat. Transparent liquids often are identified and analyzed by passing light through them and measuring the absorption of the incident light.

HERBERT LIEBESKIND
Cooper Union

ABSTRACT ART, a type of art referring to images based on nonrepresentational forms that do not imitate the viewed world. The roots of modern abstract art can be traced to 19th-century neoclassicism, which saw beauty in the Platonic solids, and Romanticism, which glorified the objectivity of the artist's individual interpretation. Since the mid-1870s onset of impressionism, many artists used looser brushstrokes, creating rhythms on the canvas independent of the subject depicted. Symbolist images based on interior visions also fostered the trend toward abstraction. Paul Cézanne's paintings, structured in a personal, nonscientific manner, influenced other artists to use underlying abstract shapes in nature as their subject.

Abstract art, first developed in Europe between 1910 and 1919, falls into two general categories: images that take as their starting point objects in the visible world, never completely eliminating recognizable details, such as the cubist art of Picasso and Braque, and nonobjective art, pioneered in the wake of cubism, which intentionally bears no relationship to visible reality.

By the 1920s, biomorphic abstraction—paintings that comprise irregular, cell-like shapes emulating forms from the biological world—emerged together with surrealism and its emphasis on art generated spontaneously from the unconscious. Geometric abstraction—regular, crisply painted shapes with hard edges—is often associated with the rational world of humankind, but it was also used to evoke spiritual aspects of nature.

Following World War II American abstract expressionists, including Jackson Pollock, Mark Rothko, and Barnett Newman, synthesized earlier innovations and enlarged their abstract canvases to mural size, reflecting expanded ambitions for nonobjective art to communicate a wide range of emotional content. In the 1960s minimalists Robert Morris and Donald Judd took the abstract cube to a different extreme, insisting on its presence as a pure object and emptying it of the meaning imposed on it by the previous generation. Artists in the later 1960s and the 1970s, who subsequently reinvested cubic forms with meaning, are often referred to as postminimalists. Since 1980, postmodern artists have appropriated abstract styles developed earlier in the century as their subject matter, forcing a reevaluation of the claims made on behalf of early modernism.

JOAN H. PACHNER
Storm King Art Center
Mountainville, N.Y.

Bibliography: Krauss, Rosalind E., *The Originality of the Avant-Garde and Other Modernist Myths* (MIT Press 1985); Rosenblum, Robert, *Cubism and Twentieth Century Art*, rev. ed. (Prentice-Hall 1976); Wheeler, Daniel, *Art since Mid-Century: 1945 to the Present* (Vendome Press 1991).

Abstract expressionist Jackson Pollock (1912–1956) executes one of his famous "drip" paintings.

ABSTRACT EXPRESSIONISM, a mid-20th-century art movement, centered in New York City, that encompassed a range of nonrepresentational painting styles, some revolutionary in technique and most emphasizing the expressive qualities of paint and other media. The term first appeared in 1929 and was used to describe the paintings of Wassily Kandinsky. Its initial use germane to its most widely accepted definition dates from 1946, when *New Yorker* art critic Robert Coates applied it to new paintings by Mark Rothko, Adolph Gottlieb, and Jackson Pollock that could not be categorized as cubist, expressionist, or surrealist.

Origins and Influences. The abstract expressionists—sometimes called the New York School—were a loosely affiliated group of artists whose mural-sized abstractions used line and color alone as emotional vehicles. Their paintings ranged in style from object-oriented works by Arshile Gorky and Willem de Kooning; to gestural abstractions by Pollock, Robert Motherwell, and Lee Krasner; to broad expanses of undifferentiated color by Clyfford Still and Barnett Newman. Sculptors David Smith, Theodore Roszak, David Hare, and Tony Smith were also affected by these developments.

The New York artistic community coalesced initially in the 1930s, largely through the government-sponsored Works Progress Administration (WPA) art programs. Artists exchanged ideas in casual settings such as the Cedar Bar in Greenwich Village. They sought to intensify human experience through introspective art, communicating transcendental, universal values to the viewer.

The evolution of this romantic style was influenced by various factors, including existentialism and Jung's theory of the collective unconscious. Most important to the style's development was the emigration of major European artists to New York City beginning in the 1930s, including Max Ernst, Yves Tanguy, and Piet Mondrian. The surrealists' use of irregular, biomorphic shapes, and their emphasis on automatic techniques—that is, exploiting chance elements and using the hand to draw freely and spontaneously—to generate new subject matter from the unconscious, offered a liberating alternative to representational styles and to geometric abstraction.

Major Exponents. During World War II the nascent abstract expressionists explored the potential of mythic and "primitive" subject matter, often rendered in a loosely expressive, automatic style. But by 1950 recognizable subject matter was basically eliminated from their paintings.

In late 1947 Pollock radically altered the creative process of art, as he began to paint by setting a large canvas on the floor and, using a stick, freely dripping and splattering sinuous lines of paint onto it. Pollock revolutionized painting by creating an all-over image without a single focus, inventing an alternative to spatial and compositional hierarchies that had dominated since the Renaissance. By 1951 he was painting in black and white on raw, unprimed canvas; recognizable images began to reemerge in the paintings. Pollock's work was satirized in the popular press and defended by the art critic Harold Rosenberg, who in 1952 coined the term *action painting*, calling the canvas "an arena in which to act."

De Kooning's abstract style, based on jagged, overlaid forms set into a shallow space, culminated in the near-white painting *Excavation* (1950; Art Institute of Chicago). But almost at once he took on a new challenge: to reintegrate the figure into art. He succeeded with *Woman I* (1950–1952; Museum of Modern Art, New York City).

At the same time that Pollock and de Kooning exploded gestural abstraction, Rothko, Newman, and Still evolved a style minimizing gesture and emphasizing large expanses of pure, unmodulated color. Works such as Rothko's mural series at the St. Thomas University chapel in Houston, Tex. (1964–1967), reflected these artists' ambitions for nonobjective art to convey a wide range of emotional content, especially the sublime and the spiritual. Clement Greenberg, arguably the most influential postwar art critic, championed these color-field (or abstract-imagist) paintings as the logical conclusion of modern art's evolution.

Abstract expressionism was enshrined as the epitome of postwar American culture in a show organized by the Museum of Modern Art in New York City. It toured Europe in 1958–1959, by which time a new generation of painters had emerged, including Joan Mitchell, Alfred Leslie, and Grace Hartigan, who continued exploring the concerns and techniques of abstract expressionism.

JOAN H. PACHNER
Storm King Art Center, Mountainville, N.Y.

Bibliography: Anfam, D., *Abstract Expressionism* (Thames & Hudson 1990); Polcari, S., *Abstract Expressionism and the Modern Experience* (Cambridge 1991); Sandler, I., *The Triumph of American Painting* (1970; reprint, HarperCollins 1976).

ABSTRACT OF TITLE is a summary of legal documents and facts which appear on the public records that affect title to land. An abstract consists of concise statements of the contents of all recorded conveyances, wills, mortgages, judgments, and other matters on which the title depends, or which might impair the title. Since the purpose of an abstract is to aid prospective purchasers, it should furnish a complete and accurate picture of the state of the record title. It should contain all pertinent data, including valid instruments and doubtful matters, and must be prepared from the public records. Abstracts formerly were made by public officers, such as county clerks, but now are usually prepared by private individuals or corporations.

ABSTRACTION, ab-strak'shən, in philosophy, is the act of forming general ideas (universals). Examples of general ideas are the ideas of "horse," "tree," "redness," which cannot be directly perceived, as contrasted with such ideas as "this horse," "this tree," "this red," which can be directly present to sense perception. Because communication and knowledge are virtually impossible without general ideas or universals, philosophers have speculated about the nature of such ideas, what they stand for, and how the mind acquires them.

Plato conceived universals as eternal forms that are more real than the transient particulars of sense experience. For Plato our knowledge of such universals as beauty or justice does not arise from sense experience but from the recollection (anamnesis) of what is already latently present in the soul. Some later philosophers, such as Descartes, held somewhat similar views, maintaining that certain universal ideas come from a clear and distinct intuition by reason rather than from sense experience, though sense experience may occasion the intuition.

The term "abstraction" is perhaps more suited to the empiricist doctrines of general ideas than to Platonic recollection or Cartesian intuition. According to Locke's *An Essay Concerning Human Understanding* (1690), things exist only as particulars, but the mind frames a general idea when it "abstracts" the qualities wherein particular things differ, and "retains" the qualities wherein they agree. According to Berkeley's introduction to his *Principles of Human Knowledge* (1710), men have only sensuous particular ideas and no abstract general ideas, but they can make a particular idea "represent" or "stand for" all other particular ideas of the same "sort." Hume, in a *Treatise of Human Nature* (1739), accepts much of Berkeley's view but tries to show how, through associative and customary connections, a particular idea can come to serve a representative function. In *An Examination of Sir William Hamilton's Philosophy* (1865), John Stuart Mill also holds that men have no "general concepts," but by focusing attention on certain parts of a concrete idea and allowing those parts to determine by association the train of thought, they are able to reason about them as if they could conceive of them in abstraction from the rest.

The "associationism" of the British empiricists was sharply criticized by the German phenomenologist Edmund Husserl, who held that abstraction and abstract ideas have their own "evidential" and logical character that cannot be reduced to the mere association of particulars.

MURRAY GREENE, *New School for Social Research*

ABSURD is a term used originally to describe a violation of the rules of logic. It has acquired wide and diverse connotations in modern theology, philosophy, and the arts, in which it expresses the failure of traditional values to fulfill man's spiritual and emotional needs.

Philosophy. The term "absurd" was first used with its modern implications in the work of the Danish philosopher Søren Kierkegaard. He described Christianity as absurd because no man could comprehend or justify it according to rational principles. The concept of the absurd recurred in the work of the French and German existentialists. It was used by Martin Heidegger to describe Christian faith; by Jean-Paul Sartre to characterize the apparent pointlessness of life and the terrors of "nonbeing"; by Albert Camus to express the disparity between "man's intention and the reality he encounters"; by Karl Jaspers as an indication of the manner in which reality repeatedly "checkmates" the individual; and by Gabriel Marcel as a symbol of the "fundamental mystery" of life.

Theater. In the "theater of the absurd," human experience is seen as fragmented and purposeless. The search for truth characteristic of romantic drama is rejected. The movement has affinities with the work of Nikolai Gogol and Bertolt Brecht and with the techniques and philosophies of Dadaism and surrealism in art.

Alfred Jarry's grotesque *Ubu Roi* (1888) anticipated the movement in the French theater, and Jarry is credited with originating some of the concepts on which it rests. Samuel Beckett, Eugène Ionesco, and Jean Genet are among the foremost European adherents. In Beckett's plays, life itself seems to have come to a halt, and his characters typically engage in fruitless and repetitive actions that underscore the meaninglessness of their existence. The surface of Ionesco's plays is often more overtly comic, but he also emphasizes man's inability to control and order experience and repeatedly shows man as the victim of modern technology and bourgeois values. In Genet's work, illusion and reality are often violently and erotically fused to suggest the painful absurdity of contemporary life. In the English-language theater, John Osborne presents a similar vision of society, although in form his plays are more conventionally realistic. Both Harold Pinter and Edward Albee reveal the inversion and corruption of conventional patterns of friendship, love, and family allegiance and the terrifying process whereby language becomes a barrier rather than an aid to communication.

Novel. Novels of the absurd have major antecedents in the work of Rabelais, Laurence Sterne, and James Joyce. However, Camus' *The Stranger* (1942) was one of the first conscious attempts to illustrate absurd metaphysics in fiction. Greater departures from conventional tone were made by Beckett and most of the American novelists who adopted the preposterous, antirealistic methods of absurd literature. The latter include the generation of "black humorists" who came to prominence in America after World War II—most notably John Barth, Thomas Pynchon, Joseph Heller, and James Purdy. A far more pessimistic tone characterizes the work of William Burroughs, who also demonstrates the major hazard of absurd literature—its tendency toward overembellishment and incoherence.

DAVID D. GALLOWAY
Author of "The Absurd Hero"

ABU SIMBEL TEMPLES were moved from this site, now flooded by the lake created by the Aswan High Dam.

GUNTER REITZ, FROM PIX

ABU BAKR (c. 573–634), ə-boo' bak'ər, was the first caliph (ruler) of the state founded by Mohammed at Medina. Born in Mecca about 573 A.D., he became a merchant there. When Mohammed began to preach the new religion of Islam, about 610, Abu Bakr is said to have been the first male to accept it. He became Mohammed's close friend and adviser and accompanied him on his migration to Medina in 622. Abu Bakr's special position among the Muslims was marked by Mohammed's marriage to his daughter Aisha. During Mohammed's lifetime Abu Bakr kept in the background, but his expert knowledge of the genealogies and intrigues of the Arab tribes must have been of great value to Mohammed in his dealings with them.

After Mohammed's death on June 8, 632, Abu Bakr was accepted as head of the Islamic state. He was given the title of "caliph [successor or deputy] of the Messenger of God." His two-year reign was occupied mostly with quelling revolts. He sent the first expeditions into Iraq and Syria. He died on Aug. 23, 634.

W. MONTGOMERY WATT
University of Edinburgh, Scotland

ABU DHABI, a'boo dub'ē, an emirate on the southern shore of the Persian Gulf. It is the southernmost and largest emirate in the United Arab Emirates. Saudi Arabia borders it on the west and south; Oman on the east; and Dubai, another of the emirates, on the northeast. The capital is the city of Abu Dhabi.

The emirate was founded in the 18th century by the Al Bu Falah family, members of which have ruled there to the present. Abu Dhabi concluded its first treaty with Britain in 1820 and joined the First Maritime Truce imposed by Britain in 1835. In 1892 the Trucial States, as the emirates were then known, signed an exclusive agreement with Britain that in effect made them protectorates of Britain. In 1971, Abu Dhabi and the other emirates became independent of Britain and joined together to form the United Arab Emirates. The sheikh of Abu Dhabi was the first president of the union.

Oil was discovered offshore of Abu Dhabi in 1958 and on the mainland in 1960. Production began two years later. The fields are unusually rich and produce a "sweet" petroleum—that is, one low in sulfur pollutants. Abu Dhabi's wealth resulting from the oil boom that began in 1973 has given the sheikhdom one of the highest per capita incomes in the world. Proved oil reserves are about 31 billion barrels. Population: 798,000 (1991 est.).

GEORGE RENTZ*
Hoover Institution, Stanford University

ABU SIMBEL, a'boo sim'bel, situated in Egypt on the west bank of the Nile River about 762 miles (1,227 km) south of Cairo, was the site of two temples commissioned by the pharaoh Rameses II about 1250 B.C. and hewn in the sandstone cliffs overlooking the water. Behind rock-cut terraces the façades resembled temple gates and were provided with colossi arranged symmetrically around a central doorway. Inside the cliff were the essential rooms of an Egyptian temple, adorned with ritual and battle scenes. The small temple was dedicated to Hathor and the deified queen Nefertari. The larger contained cult statues of Ptah, Amon-Re, King Rameses II himself, and Re-Harakhti, but it was dedicated chiefly to Re-Harakhti, god of the rising sun. His disk-crowned figure in a niche above the doorway received the first rays of the sun as it rose.

In the 1960's the United Nations Educational, Scientific and Cultural Organization (UNESCO) sought to save the monuments of Lower Nubia from flooding by the High Dam at Aswan. The temples at Abu Simbel were included in the project and given priority. Eventually, 51 countries contributed funds to the undertaking. The work was planned and executed by an "International Joint Venture" of German, French, Egyptian, Italian, and Swedish firms. The method of salvage consisted in removing the hill around each temple, leaving about 2½ feet (0.80 meters) of stone as roof and walls, then cutting the structures into some 950 blocks and reassembling them 210 feet (64 meters) higher and 590 feet (180 meters) farther inland. Work was completed in 1966.

CAROLINE N. PECK, *Brown University*

ABUKIR, ab-oo-kir', is a village in Egypt, 13 miles northeast of Alexandria. The name is also spelled *Aboukir.* The village is situated on Abukir Bay, a Mediterranean inlet, on the approximate site of ancient Canopus. Napoleon's army of occupation in Egypt crushed a Turkish force under Mustafa Pasha at the battle of Abukir on July 25, 1799. See also CANOPUS.

ABU'L-ABBAS AL-SAFFAH (died 754), ə-bool' ab-bäs' al-saf-fäch', was the first caliph of the Abbasid dynasty, which ruled the Islamic empire from 750 to 1258. He came to power in Kufa, Iraq, in 749, after several decades of clandestine political and religious opposition to the reigning Umayyad dynasty. In one year he succeeded in destroying the Umayyads, winning the name al-Saffah, "the bloodletter," for his ruthlessness. Other rivals for the barely established authority of the Abbasid caliphate were also put down. The tasks of establishing the legitimacy of the dynasty and a stable and effective administration were left to future caliphs.

IRA M. LAPIDUS
University of California at Berkeley

ABUTILON, ə-bū'tə-lon, is a genus of tropical and subtropical plants used for commercial fibers and for ornamental purposes. Commonly called *flowering maple* and *Chinese bellflower,* the genus is characterized by a distinctive column of stamens, lobed leaves, and single, bell-shaped flowers.

Abutilon belongs to the mallow family (Malvaceae), in the order Malvales. The most common of its 100 species is *A. theophrastus,* also called *Indian mallow* or *velvetleaf. A. theophrastus* is a tall annual with velvety leaves and yellow flowers. The species yields a long, strong fiber, which is used as China jute and in rugmaking. It is also found widespread as a weed in southern Europe and in Asia.

ABYDOS, ə-bī'dəs, was an ancient city in Asia Minor. Settled by Greeks from Miletus, it was situated at the narrowest point of the Dardanelles (Hellespont).

In the ancient legend of Hero and Leander, Leander swam the Hellespont nightly from Abydos to visit his love, Hero, at Sestos across the strait. Xerxes I of Persia led his armies into Greece in 480 B.C. over a bridge of boats from Abydos to Sestos.

ABYDOS, ə-bī'dəs, was a city of ancient Egypt. It was situated about 320 miles south of Cairo, near the site of the modern town of Araba el Madfuna. Abydos was the chief town of the 8th province of the 1st dynasty kings of Upper Egypt. According to legend, the head of Osiris, god of the underworld, was buried here. The importance of the town increased as the cult of Osiris grew. A famous temple of Osiris, built by Rameses II (reigned 1290–1223 B.C.), was erected at Abydos on the foundations of another temple some 2,000 years older.

Abydos was the burial place of kings from the 1st to the 30th dynasties (c. 3100–341 B.C.). The royal tombs have yielded such treasures as the funerary stela (commemorative slab) of the serpent king (Iti, Djet, or Uadji) of the 1st dynasty, and an ivory figurine, perhaps of the pharaoh Khufu (Cheops), of the 4th dynasty.

Probably the most celebrated discovery at Abydos is the temple of Seti I (reigned 1303–1290 B.C.), father of Rameses II. This temple, with its unusually well-preserved ceilings, doorways, and decorations, contains the mural *Tablet of Abydos,* a stone-carved list of kings of the principal dynasties. A similar register from the temple of Osiris is in the British Museum at London. These lists have been invaluable in reconstructing the succession of Egyptian pharaohs.

ABYSSAL ANIMALS, ə-bis'əl, are organisms that live at depths of 6,500 feet to 19,500 feet in the world's oceans, below the limit of light penetration. The environment in this region is extreme: pressure is about 1,000 atmospheres, temperature is as low as 41° to 30° F (5° to −1° C), and there is total darkness. As a result, abyssal animals are almost all blind and colorless. Bioluminescence (q.v.) is also a common characteristic of these animals.

Examples of abyssal animals are *squids, sea anemones, bristle worms, bivalve mollusks,* and *sea cucumbers.*

Since the absence of light precludes the manufacture of organic material by plants in the region inhabited by abyssal animals, they depend for food on organic matter that falls from the higher levels of the ocean. The ecological balance of the abyssal regions is relatively stable because of the high degree of specialization that animals living at these depths must acquire. Thus there is little competition from new forms, as only animals adapted to the extreme pressure can survive in the abyss.

ABYSSINIA. See ETHIOPIA.

ACACIA, ə-kā'shə, is a genus of flowering tropical and subtropical trees and shrubs. Its individual flowers are small, but usually occur in dense, globular heads or elongated spikes. They are characteristically yellow, although sometimes white. The flowers usually have five sepals and petals, many stamens, and a single pistil. The almost countless stamens give the flower clusters a soft, fuzzy, golden appearance and make the plant an attractive ornamental.

The leaves of the acacia are either pinnate (small leaflets along both sides of the leafstalk) or reduced to a leafstalk with no blades, as in many of the Australian and Pacific forms. In these forms, the leafstalk and leaf axis are flat vertically, the leaflets are partially or completely absent, and the basal portion of the leafstalk often develops into thorns.

Species. Acacia is classified in the pea family (Leguminosae) and in the mimosa subfamily. There are some 500 species, about 300 of them found in Australia and on the islands of the Pacific. The rest are widely distributed in the tropics and warmer parts of the temperate zones. They are especially numerous in the bush veldt of South Africa. About 70 of the species are American, nearly half of them native to Mexico. A few occur in the drier areas of the central and southwestern United States.

Numerous species of acacia are cultivated in greenhouses, and in warmer areas they are grown outdoors as ornamentals. *Acacia armata,* the kan-

THE ACACIA (below, *A. decurrens*) is identified by its fuzzy golden flower heads and its feather-like leaves.

ROCHE

ACADEMIC STYLE of painting is exemplified by Alma-Tadema's *Reading from Homer* (1885).

garoo thorn of Australia, is grown for Easter displays. This spreading shrub also serves as a hedge plant and as a plant cover for sand dunes. Leafstalks in this species are about 1 inch long and ¼ inch wide. The yellow flower heads are about ¼ inch in diameter.

Species cultivated in California are *A. baileyana*, a shrub or small tree with exceedingly fine gray-green leaflets; *A. decurrens*, the green or tan wattle, a striking tree native to southeastern Australia and Tasmania; *A. farnesiana*, a shrub with richly scented, deep-yellow flower heads, widely grown in the tropics; *A. pycnantha*, the golden wattle of Australia, a tree with conspicuous leafstalks and abundant flower heads; and *A. melanoxylon*, the pyramidal blackwood acacia of southeastern Australia, used as a street tree in California.

Uses. Acacia is important economically. Gum arabic is derived mainly from *A. senegal*, found in the Anglo-Egyptian Sudan and in the northern Sahara; other species yield inferior gum arabics. (Gum arabic has been in use for over 2,000 years in paints and watercolors. It also is used in confections, medicines, calico printing, dyeing, and in the making of silk, paper, and cosmetics.)

The bark of many species of acacia is rich in tannin, with some species (*A. decurrens mollis* and *A. pycnantha*) containing almost 50 percent tannin. Many of the Australian species are important to the tanning of leather.

Acacia also furnishes good lumber. *A. melanoxylon*, for example, is used for furniture, cabinetmaking, oars, tools, and gunstocks.

In the deserts of Asia and Africa, goats and camels browse on leaves and young shoots of acacias, and in Australia other species serve as forage for cattle and sheep. In Africa, California, and elsewhere, certain species of acacia have been used as binders for the shifting sands of the seacoasts. Some of the species provide food and shelter for insects, such as the stinging ant and the lac insect of India.

The following plants are incorrectly called acacias: the plume albizzia (*Albizzia distachya*); the silk tree (*Albizzia julibrissin*); the three-thorned acacia, or honey locust (*Gleditsia triacanthos*); and the false acacia, or black locust (*Robinia pseudoacacia*).

EDWIN MATZKE, *Columbia University*

ACADEMIC ART, ak-ə-dem'ik ärt, is a style of painting and sculpture, particularly the style sanctioned by the French Académie des Beaux-Arts in the 19th century. Although the French Academy was then the dominant arbiter of artistic taste, it had influential counterparts in other nations, particularly the Royal Academy in England. The annual exhibitions, or salons, of the national academies featured the work of members and other work selected by a jury. Most salon art reflected the taste of the new bourgeoisie, which was often sentimental and literary, with cultural pretensions.

Academic art was characterized by a respect for classical antiquity, faithful transcription of nature, illusionistic space, minute detail, and eclectic borrowing from the past. It was basically retrogressive, with an emphasis on traditionalism, and usually lacked originality. It was against the canons of academic art that the progressive artists of the 19th century constantly battled, and their reaction against it led to the rise of styles that were diametrically opposed to the academic.

The birth of impressionism in the 1870's brought the dominance of academic art to an end. In the 20th century, when the intense opposition to academic art had diminished, some merits were found in it as a reflection of its time and for its sound technique.

WILLIAM GERDTS, *University of Maryland*

ACADEMIC COSTUME. See COSTUME, ACADEMIC.

ACADEMIC DEGREES. See DEGREE.

ACADEMIC FREEDOM, ak-ə-dem'ik frēd'əm, is the right of a teacher to teach and of a learner to study without unreasonable interference or restraint. Academic freedom ranks with freedom of speech, freedom of the press, and freedom of worship as an essential characteristic of democratic society.

Essentials of Academic Freedom. For the teacher, academic freedom has three sides. He must be at liberty to pursue scholarly inquiry to any honest conclusion. He must be free to present to his students his findings and judgments about his field of specialization. Finally, he must be free to publish the results of his research and reflection so that his colleagues and the general public can benefit by and criticize his work. To the extent that a scholar must slant his investigations or twist or suppress his conclusions, the progress of knowledge is slowed. By the mid-20th century, teachers in the United States, Canada, Britain, and many other countries had won recognition of the principle of academic freedom. Debate continued over the application of the principle.

For the student, academic freedom includes the right to have honest instruction, the right to form his own conclusions on the basis of his studies, the right to hear and express opinions, and the right to a reasonable voice in deciding what he is to study. College students in the 20th century have considerable liberty to choose courses and have some voice in college affairs through student governments. Following World War II, students in the United States and various countries in Europe and Latin America began to demand a much larger share in making and administering university rules and in planning the curriculum. Such student movements enlarged the meaning of student academic freedom.

Neither students nor teachers can expect academic freedom to be unlimited. The right to exercise any liberty implies the duty to use freedom responsibly. Justice Oliver Wendell Holmes of the U.S. Supreme Court stated that freedom of speech does not imply the right to raise a false alarm of fire in a theater. By the same reasoning, freedom to teach does not give a professor a right to present his views in such a way as to delude his students or colleagues. Freedom used without responsibility becomes license and interferes with the academic freedom of others.

In addition to the limits set by individual responsibility, there are specific checks imposed on academic freedom by society. For example, the laws that regulate speech and publication restrict what a teacher can say or publish. Faculties and institutions make rules to govern the behavior of their members. In general, the rules are much more restrictive in elementary and secondary schools than they are in colleges and universities. Society and the authorities in charge of the schools have taken the attitude that younger, less mature learners need more protection against possibly dangerous teaching than do college students. Also, school teachers have enjoyed less prestige than college professors, who are usually more extensively trained. Students are granted more autonomy as they advance to higher levels of study.

One of the most difficult issues related to academic freedom is the question of limiting out-of-school activities by teachers and students. The issue is illustrated by the long-standing custom that American public school teachers stayed out of politics. They did not run for office or take any part in political campaigns. Even college teachers felt pressures to avoid public controversies. In the 20th century, teachers established their right to act as normal citizens in their communities. However, this right is hedged in practice by the expectation that a teacher will always act with awareness of his responsibility as a guide to younger persons. Larger communities usually grant teachers more freedom to live their own lives than do small towns. Another factor is the temper of the times. During a national or international crisis, teachers and students are subject to unusual pressures and restrictions, both in and out of school.

Early History. The debate on barriers to academic freedom is a theme that can be traced through the history of education from ancient times onward. Much of the debate has involved conflict between the liberal views of teachers and students and the conservatism of established authorities. In antiquity, for example, Socrates was put to death by the Athenian authorities because they believed that his teachings corrupted the minds of youth. In the Middle Ages such noted scholars as Peter Abelard and Marsilius of Padua found themselves in conflict with the church. Some of Abelard's teachings were condemned as heretical. Suspicion of heresy drove Marsilius, once rector of the University of Paris, to seek refuge in Germany. The Reformation created new sources of conflict. Martin Luther was one of the scholars of this period who became famous for maintaining his own convictions in spite of opposition from the authorities. Pioneers in science also found that their investigations were not welcomed. One of Galileo's books was banned by the Inquisition. Such repressions did not prevent teachers and students from working—although they might have attained greater heights if they had had more freedom.

The Modern Concept. The beginning of the modern attitude toward academic freedom—that is, the belief in maximum opportunities for teachers and students—can be traced to the founding of the University of Leiden in Holland in 1575. This institution did not grant complete academic freedom, but the religious and political restrictions on faculty and students were at a minimum. Unfortunately, the record of this university as a center of free inquiry was dimmed by religious restrictions imposed by Calvinist church authorities early in the 17th century.

In the second half of the 17th century the movement toward academic freedom accelerated. In 1667, for example, a model for a free university was proposed in Germany. Baron Bengt Skytte, a Swede, persuaded Frederick William, the Great Elector of Brandenburg, to sponsor an institution for research and instruction of a most liberal design. The faculty was to be interethnic, interreligious, and international and was to work with no restrictions except a ban on proselytizing for any religious faith. The university was never established, but the plan served as a guide for later educators.

Another pioneer was Christian Thomasius, who in 1687 introduced the practice of lecturing in German rather than Latin at the University of Leipzig. This innovation, plus his opposition to superstition and to witchcraft trials, led to his hasty departure from the university. However, Thomasius and other dissidents were invited to the liberal university of Halle, founded in 1694.

During the 18th century, academic freedom in Germany became firmly established at the University of Göttingen (founded in 1737). Another milestone for European education was a report issued in 1792 by the marquis de Condorcet, a French scholar. He was inspired by the atmosphere of the French Revolution to demand that education be free from controls by the government, church, and all other outside forces, including public opinion. France, however, did not put these ideas into effect. Napoleon introduced centralization in higher education and other policies that restricted academic freedom.

As one counter to the power of Napoleon, Prussia founded the University of Berlin in 1811.

Here the principles of *Lehrfreiheit und Lernfreiheit* (freedom of teaching and studying) were both formulated and practiced. The classic summation of these principles was made by the rector, Johann Gottlieb Fichte. According to the famous philosopher, a university can achieve its intellectual aims only if it has "complete external freedom, academic freedom in the widest sense."

Another statement of the ideals behind academic freedom was made by Thomas Jefferson in 1819 when the University of Virginia was founded. He pledged that the new institution would be based "upon the illimitable freedom of the human mind."

The history of academic freedom in the 19th and 20th centuries is a record of problems and progress. Forces as varied as nationalism, clericalism, conservatism, and radicalism exerted pressures on schools and universities. The effects of such pressures can be shown by a few examples. In Germany, two distinguished linguists and folklorists, Jacob and Wilhelm Grimm, were dismissed from the faculty of the University of Göttingen in 1837 because they opposed the abrogation of the constitution by the king of Hannover. In England, religious qualifications for students at the universities of Oxford and Cambridge were not removed until 1871. In England, the United States, and other countries, scholars who supported Darwin's theory of evolution faced ridicule and even loss of their positions. Far into the 20th century, barriers to teaching Darwinian biology persisted. The famous Scopes trial in 1925 failed to upset a Tennessee law forbidding the teaching of the concept of evolution in the public schools.

In spite of resistance, the campaign for academic freedom progressed. In the United States the growth of secularism, the example of German universities, and a broadening of social and intellectual outlooks helped the cause of freedom in education. The founding of such organizations as the National Education Association (1857), the American Association of University Professors (1915), the American Federation of Teachers (1916), and the American Civil Liberties Union (1920) gave teachers new aids in establishing and keeping their rights and privileges.

The Loyalty Issue. International and ideological tensions have stirred up major battles over academic freedom in the 20th century. During World War I some teachers were harassed or even dismissed from their jobs because they were suspected of being disloyal to their countries. During the depression of the 1930's, when Communism gained some ground in intellectual circles, many state legislatures in the United States passed laws requiring that teachers take loyalty oaths. The National Defense Education Act of 1958 specified loyalty oaths as a condition for federal aid to students. The same condition applied to aid from the National Science Foundation.

Concern for national security in a time of chronic international crisis brought the U.S. Supreme Court into the debate on academic freedom. In *Adler* v. *Board of Education of New York* (1952) the court upheld the constitutionality of a law barring public school teachers from advocating the overthrow of the government by unlawful means. The majority of the justices held that no denial of freedom of speech was involved. Justice William O. Douglas, however, wrote a dissenting opinion stating that "when suspicion fills the air and holds scholars in line for fear of their jobs, there can be no exercise of the free intellect."

Another Supreme Court decision affecting academic freedom was handed down in the case of *Sweezy* v. *New Hampshire* (1957). The court reversed a contempt conviction in a state court of a professor who refused to answer questions about his association with the Progressive party and his lectures at the state university. In *Beilan* v. *Board of Education of Philadelphia* (1958) the Supreme Court upheld the right of a public school system to discharge as incompetent a teacher who refused to answer questions about charges of earlier Communist activities. In *Barenblatt* v. *United States* (1959) the court ruled that the House Committee on Un-American Activities had the legal power to investigate possibly subversive activities in education. The majority opinion insisted that the court "will always be on the alert against intrusion by Congress into this constitutionally protected domain," namely, "academic teaching-freedom and its corollary learning-freedom, so essential to the well-being of the Nation." Some coercion seems to be involved in a congressional inquiry into the activities of teachers and students, but the court held that the public interest superseded individual and academic immunity.

Student Involvement. Freedom to learn has always been a major part of academic freedom. For centuries, however, major issues in this area involved teachers more than students. Typical conflicts were fought out between faculty and administration, president and trustees, or faculty and state or national government. In the second half of the 20th century, students became increasingly involved in movements that extended the meaning of academic freedom and complicated the problem of defining the bounds of this freedom. In the United States, Latin America, and other countries, students showed that they expected to have a voice in university policy. Some, for example, asked to be allowed to evaluate faculty performance. Many demanded almost complete freedom in social behavior and political action. These demands were backed up by activist tactics, such as sit-in demonstrations and strikes. As a result of student efforts, the scope of student academic freedom expanded enormously in less than a decade.

WILLIAM W. BRICKMAN
University of Pennsylvania

Bibliography

American Civil Liberties Union, *Academic Freedom and Civil Liberties of Students in Colleges and Universities,* rev. ed. (1971).

Bok, Derek C., *Beyond the Ivory Tower* (Harvard Univ. Press 1982).

Fenichel, A., and Mandel, D., *Academic Corporation—Justice, Freedom and the University* (Black Rose Bks. 1987).

Hofstadter, Richard, and Metzger, Walter P., *The Development of Academic Freedom in the United States* (Columbia Univ. Press 1955).

Kirk, Russell, *Academic Freedom* (1955; reprint, Greenwood Press 1977).

Pincoffs, Edmund L., ed., *The Concept of Academic Freedom* (Univ. of Texas Press 1975).

Robbins, L. C., *Of Academic Freedom* (Longwood 1986).

ACADEMIC PAINTING. See ACADEMIC ART.

ACADÉMIE DES BEAUX ARTS. See INSTITUT DE FRANCE.

ACADÉMIE FRANÇAISE. See INSTITUT DE FRANCE.

ACADEMY, ə-kad′ə-mē, Plato's school in ancient Athens. The name later was adopted by similar schools and still later, in a more general sense, by other institutions. The name "academy" now is applied to any of the following: a school above the primary level, usually a private high school or college; a school in which special subjects or skills are taught, such as military training, riding, or dancing; or a learned society devoted to the promotion of art, science, or literature.

Ancient Schools. The first academy was a voluntary association ostensibly devoted to worship of the Muses but actually a school of philosophy. Plato founded it in 387 B.C. He met with his pupils and friends in a public garden northwest of Athens, not far from the city. The garden was said to have belonged long before to a man called Academos, a local hero of the Trojan War. In the 5th century B.C. the house and garden were the property of Cimon, who not only improved the place with walks and fountains but opened it to the public, bequeathing it to the city at his death. Here Socrates delivered orations and Plato taught philosophy, his followers being known as *Academists* and his school as the *Academia.*

The schools that subsequently were opened by Plato's followers were known by the same name and modeled on the original group in Academos' garden. They survived in similar form for almost nine centuries, until Justinian abolished the academies and confiscated their property in 529 A.D. Cicero, a devotee of Greek learning, named his villa near Puteoli "The Academy," and it was there that he wrote his *Academic Questions* and other dialogues based on discussions between the members of the groups of learned guests whom he entertained there.

The academies of antiquity are considered to fall into three distinct categories—(1) the Old, Plato's original foundation, which was continued by Speusippus, Xenocrates of Chalcedon, Polemon of Athens, and Crates; (2) the Middle, founded by Arcesilaus (316–241 B.C.), Crantor's pupil, who broke away from the older group; and (3) the New, a short-lived group formed by Carneades (214?–129 B.C.).

Medieval Associations. The academy in the sense of an association for the protection or advancement of knowledge emerged as Greek civilization declined. At the beginning of the 3d century B.C., Ptolemy I founded the Museum at Alexandria, the first association of its kind. The Museum was devoted to the encouragement and cultivation of letters and science, and to it came scholars of outstanding brilliance; its valuable collections of books and treasures were the germ of the great library of Alexandria. Establishments for the preservation and encouragement of learning were founded by the Arabs from Córdoba to Samarkand, following the example of the Christian and Hebrew foundations that had been laid in Babylonia, Palestine, and Armenia.

In 782 A.D., Charlemagne, influenced by the Anglo-Saxon churchman Alcuin, started an academy in his palace; it was a meeting-place of learned men who came there to discuss and to teach. An institution for the advancement of science was started at Constantinople by Caesar Bardas in the 9th century. At the end of the 13th and the beginning of the 14th century, many academic societies were established in southern France and in Italy, mostly devoted to the cultivation of poetry.

One of the most famous of the medieval academies was the Académie des Jeux Floraux (Academy of Floral Games), started by troubadours in May 1323. It was devoted to literature and the arts, and after the reading of the works by their authors a prize of a golden violet was awarded to the work judged the best. In 1500 it was firmly established, and its permanence was secured by private patronage; in 1694 it was incorporated as an academy by letters patent of Louis XIV.

Renaissance Societies. The downfall of the Byzantine empire in the 15th century brought Greek scholars and a revival of Greek literature to Western Europe, and from this time on many new academies sprang up, first in Italy and shortly afterward all over the continent. The Accademia Pontaniana (named after Pontano, its principal benefactor) was established in Naples in 1433, and soon after 1438 the Accademia Platonica was founded in Florence by Cosimo de' Medici, whose grandson Lorenzo (1449–1492) continued to patronize it. It was in Lorenzo's palace in Florence or his villa in Fiesole that the members met, modeling their discussions on Plato's *Symposium.* The academy expired in about 1499 but was revived twice, the second time in 1540, for the purpose of studying the Italian language.

All over Italy similar academies were coming into existence, many of them with curious names, such as Academy of the Dead, of the Smokers, of the Hidden, of the Fantastic, of the Humorists. Most of them were endowed by wealthy patrons, and the most famous of them was the Accademia dei Lincei (the Lynx-eyed), which was founded in Rome in 1603 by Prince Federico Cesi. Closed at his death, it later was revived and is in existence today.

Another early Italian academy was the one formed by a group of scholars under the patronage of Alfonso V of Aragon in Naples, mainly for the consideration of literary style. Another was founded in Venice by Aldus Manutius. It counted Erasmus among its members and was largely concerned with the printing of the classical texts produced by Manutius.

By 1725 more than 600 Italian academies were in existence. Of these the most influential and the longest-lived was the Accademia della Crusca (chaff), which, with the aim of purifying the national language, was founded by the poet Grazzini in Florence in 1582. His dictionary, first published in 1612, still is considered the authority for the Italian language. The academy still survives under its own name, although it became incorporated with two others. As a general rule the academies of the Renaissance differed from those of modern times in that they did not devote themselves to the publication of memoirs or transactions that would make permanent their contributions to learning but they were remarkable rather for the scholarship of their individual members and their encouragement of learning.

National Academies. Between the 16th and 18th centuries a change took place in the basis of the academies. Gradually they became societies of men of learning who came together for the exchange of opinions and for the fostering of knowledge, rather than groups gathered under the patronage of some wealthy individual. One of the most famous and important of these is the Académie Française. It was founded in 1635 to develop a national French language and safeguard its use. This academy and four others now make up the Institut de France.

In England the Royal Society was suggested originally as "King James, his Academie or College of Honour," then as "The British Academy." It finally was chartered under its present name in 1661. The Royal Society always has been devoted primarily to expanding knowledge in the sciences. Consequently, in 1901 the British Academy was founded to provide for history, philosophy, and the arts. The Royal Society for the Encouragement of Arts, Manufactures, and Commerce (now the Royal Society of Arts) was founded in 1754. It is the only society in Britain that does not concern itself with special aspects of knowledge, although by now it has somewhat narrowed its original extremely broad fields of interest.

The Preussische Akademie der Wissenschaften in Berlin (Prussian Academy of Sciences until 1946; afterward, the Deutsche Akademie) was established by Frederick I in Berlin in 1700. The Real Academia Española was founded in 1713 by the Duke of Escalona to protect the Spanish national tongue. Like the Crusca in Italy, it published the great national dictionary and also a grammar of the Spanish language. In Sweden a private society started by Linnaeus and a few other scientists in 1739 became, two years later, the Kungl. Svenska Vetenskapsakademien (Royal Swedish Academy of Science). In the Netherlands the Academia Lugduno-Batava, now the University of Leiden, was established in 1575 through the generosity of William of Orange. The Akademiya Nauk, SSSR (Academy of Sciences of the USSR) was founded in 1724 as the Imperial Academy of Sciences. It is affiliated with a large number of dependent institutions, with branches in many parts of the Soviet Union. The Akademiya Nauk, SSSR, issues a wide range of publications.

American Societies. The first learned society in America was founded in 1743, when Benjamin Franklin published "A Proposal for Promoting Useful Knowledge among the British Plantations in America." This led to the establishment, in the same year, of the American Philosophical Society. Franklin was its first secretary and held office as president from 1769 until his death in 1790. The society has published its *Transactions* since 1771, and its *Proceedings* since 1838. In 1780 the American Academy of Arts and Sciences was founded in Boston. Its main interests are the antiquities and natural history of America, and it has published its *Transactions* since 1785.

The Academy of Natural Sciences of Philadelphia was founded in 1812 for "the acquirement, increase, simplification and diffusion of natural knowledge." It maintains a museum of natural history and furnishes papers and periodicals on scientific subjects.

The New York Academy of Sciences was founded in 1817 as the Lyceum of Natural History (the present name dates from 1876) for the advancement of science.

The American Association for the Advancement of Science originated in a society called the Association of American Geologists and Naturalists, resolving itself into the present organization in 1848. Its general aims are to further the work of scientists, facilitate cooperation among them, and improve the effectiveness of science in the

promotion of human welfare. It publishes *Science,* a weekly.

The National Academy of Sciences was chartered by Congress in 1863 to investigate and report on scientific questions. Its library now is combined with that of the National Research Council.

Other scientific societies include the Franklin Institute in Philadelphia, founded in 1824 to advance learning and public education in science and industry, and the Academy of Science of St. Louis, organized in 1856 for the promotion of science. The latter has a library of about 70,000 volumes, chiefly scientific periodicals, and publishes *Transactions.*

The National Institute of Arts and Letters was founded in 1898 to further the interests of literature and the fine arts in the United States. In 1904 the American Academy of Arts and Letters was founded, and in 1916 it was incorporated by Congress.

In other special fields there are such foundations as the American Academy of Political and Social Science, founded in 1889, and the Pennsylvania Academy of the Fine Arts, established in 1805, which has a school for the study of the fine arts. The Pennsylvania Academy sponsors annual exhibitions.

The New York Academy of Medicine, founded in 1847 and incorporated in 1851, has 12 sections, each concerned with a special branch of medicine or surgery. Its general aims are the promotion of the science and art of medicine, the maintenance of a public medical library, and the promotion of public health and medical education.

Canadian Societies. The Royal Society of Canada, modeled on the Royal Society of London and on the French Academy, was founded in 1882. One of its purposes was to counterbalance the emphasis likely to be placed by a pioneer country on material things. The society also hoped to achieve the completion of national collections in various fields. Since geology already was well represented, the society was to pay particular attention to archives, paintings, and objects illustrating ethnology and all branches of natural history. The National Museum, the National Archives, and the National Gallery, owe their foundation in a large measure to the efforts of the Royal Society.

The Association Canadienne-Française pour l'Avancement des Sciences, in Montreal, was founded in 1925 and chartered in 1931 for the promotion of science and scientific education. A federation of 51 societies, it grants funds for special studies and for the publication of scientific memoirs in French.

See also separate entries on major individual academies and societies.

OLIVE A. JOHNSON
University of Auckland Library, New Zealand

Bibliography
Hall, Marie B., *All Scientists Now* (Cambridge 1985).
Kaupert, Walter, ed., *International Directory of Arts* (Deutsche Zentral Druckerei, biennially).
Oleson, Alexandra, and Brown, Sanborn C., eds., *American Scientific and Learned Societies from Colonial Times to the Civil War* (Johns Hopkins Univ. Press 1976).
Regis, Ed., *Who Got Einstein's Office?: Eccentricity and Genius at the Institute for Advanced Study* (Addison-Wesley 1987).
Verrel, Barbara, and Opitz, Helmut, eds., *World Guide to Scientific Associations and Learned Societies* (K. G. Saur 1984).
Vucinich, Alexander, *Empire of Knowledge: Academy of Sciences of the U. S. S. R., 1917–1970* (Univ. of Calif. Press 1984).

THE ACADEMY OF MOTION PICTURES ARTS AND SCIENCES

The Oscar has been awarded annually since 1929 for distinguished achievement in film acting and production.

ACADEMY AWARD, an award given by the Academy of Motion Picture Arts and Sciences. An Academy Award can take the form of a trophy, plaque, or certificate, but the name most commonly is used to refer to the gold statuette, known as the Oscar, given annually for outstanding individual or collective efforts in about 25 categories of film acting and production. The first Academy Awards were presented on May 16, 1929, for the 1927–1928 film year. Among the first winners were Emil Jannings (best actor), Janet Gaynor (best actress), Frank Borzage (best director), and *Wings* (best film).

The Academy of Motion Picture Arts and Sciences was founded in Hollywood, Calif., in May 1927. Its specific aims are to foster cooperation for cultural, educational, and technological progress in the industry; to recognize outstanding achievements in the industry; and to provide a common forum for the various branches and crafts of the motion picture industry.

Membership in the academy is by invitation of the board of governors through a process of peer sponsorship—that is, film editors sponsor film editors, directors sponsor directors, actors (male or female) sponsor actors (male or female), and so on—based on screen credits. Active members pay annual dues; retired members pay half the annual dues (but have no voting privileges); life members (those appointed by the board) pay no dues but have all the privileges of membership.

The academy and its educational wing, the Academy Foundation, present programs, seminars, and exhibits, open to the general public, on film history or filmmaking techniques; award Student Academy Awards and the Nicholl Fellowship in Screenwriting; and support the Center for Motion Picture Study, which includes the Margaret Herrick Library and the Academy Film Archive.

The presentation of the Academy Awards is the best known of the organization's activities. Balloting for nominations for the awards is restricted in each award category to members of the academy branch concerned—that is, actors (male or female) nominate actors (male or female), film editors nominate film editors. The foreign language film (first presented in 1948), makeup (1981), and documentary (1941) award categories are nominated by committees made up of members from all branches, and the best picture nominations are voted by all academy members. Ten of the 13 branches make 5 nominations each in their fields, and the entire academy membership of more than 5,000 persons votes to determine the winner. Balloting is done anonymously and in secret. Results are tabulated by an impartial auditing firm, which keeps the results secret until "the envelope" is opened at the awards ceremony.

Categories (other than the ones listed above) in which awards are or have been presented are as follows: art direction, assistant director, cinematography, costume design, dance direction, documentary short subject, engineering effects, film editing, music scoring, original song, animated and live action short films, sound, sound effects, special effects, unique and artistic picture, visual effects, and writing.

Other awards, voted by the board of governors (made up of three members from each branch) are the scientific and technical awards; the Irving G. Thalberg Memorial Award, established in 1937 upon the death of Thalberg, who was MGM's head of production, and given to "creative producers whose bodies of work reflect a consistently high quality of motion picture production"; the Jean Hersholt Humanitarian Award, named after the actor and former academy president and first given in 1956 to a person "whose humanitarian efforts have brought credit to the industry"; the Gordon E. Sawyer Award, named after the late head of the Warner Bros. Studio sound department and first given in 1981 for "technological contributions"; and various special and honorary awards given to individuals or organizations.

The prize itself, called an Oscar, is a gold-plated statuette designed and first cast in late 1928 by sculptor George Stanley, under the supervision of MGM art director Cedric Gibbons. Many stories are told about how the Oscar got its nickname. The earliest (but least documented) supposedly happened in 1931, when Margaret Herrick, later executive director of the Academy, saw it for the first time and remarked, "It looks like my Uncle Oscar." The actress Bette Davis also claimed the dubbing of the nickname, upon winning the best actress award for *Dangerous* on March 5, 1936, when she said it looked like her husband, Harman Oscar Nelson, from the rear. The first known incidence of the name Oscar appearing in print is in Sidney Skolsky's syndicated Hollywood gossip column, datelined "Palm Springs, Cal., March 18 [1934]," in which he wrote, "Katharine Hepburn wasn't present to receive her Oscar."

PATRICK STOCKSTILL, *Academy Historian*
Academy of Motion Picture Arts and Sciences

Bibliography: Fischer, Erika J., *The Inauguration of "Oscar": Sketches and Documents from the Early Years* (K. G. Saur, Munich 1988); Osborne, Robert A., *65 Years of the Oscar: The Official History of the Academy Awards,* 2d ed. (Abbeville Press 1994); Wiley, Mason, and Damien Bona, *Inside Oscar: The Unofficial History of the Academy Awards,* 10th anniv. ed. (Ballantine Bks. 1996).

ACADEMY AWARD WINNERS

1927—28: Picture: *Wings;* Actor: **Emil Jannings** (*The Last Command* and *The Way of All Flesh*); Actress: **Janet Gaynor** (*Seventh Heaven, Street Angel,* and *Sunrise*); Director: **Lewis Milestone** (*Two Arabian Knights*) and **Frank Borzage** (*Seventh Heaven*)

1928—29: Picture: *Broadway Melody;* Actor: **Warner Baxter** (*In Old Arizona*); Actress: **Mary Pickford** (*Coquette*); Director: **Frank Lloyd** (*The Divine Lady*)

All Quiet on the Western Front.

PHOTOFEST

1929—30: Picture: *All Quiet on the Western Front;* Actor: **George Arliss** (*Disraeli*); Actress: **Norma Shearer** (*The Divorcee*); Director: **Lewis Milestone** (*All Quiet on the Western Front*)

1930—31: Picture: *Cimarron;* Actor: **Lionel Barrymore** (*A Free Soul*); Actress: **Marie Dressler** (*Min and Bill*); Director: **Norman Taurog** (*Skippy*)

1931—32: Picture: *Grand Hotel;* Actor: **Wallace Beery** (*The Champ*) and **Fredric March** (*Dr. Jekyll and Mr. Hyde*); Actress: **Helen Hayes** (*The Sin of Madelon Claudet*); Director: **Frank Borzage** (*Bad Girl*)

1932—33: Picture: *Cavalcade;* Actor: **Charles Laughton** (*The Private Life of Henry VIII*); Actress: **Katharine Hepburn** (*Morning Glory*); Director: **Frank Lloyd** (*Cavalcade*)

1934: Picture: *It Happened One Night;* Actor: **Clark Gable** (*It Happened One Night*); Actress: **Claudette Colbert** (*It Happened One Night*); Director: **Frank Capra** (*It Happened One Night*)

1935: Picture: *Mutiny on the Bounty;* Actor: **Victor McLaglen** (*The Informer*); Actress: **Bette Davis** (*Dangerous*); Director: **John Ford** (*The Informer*)

1936: Picture: *The Great Ziegfeld;* Actor: **Paul Muni** (*The Story of Louis Pasteur*); Actress: **Luise Rainer** (*The Great Ziegfeld*); Director: **Frank Capra** (*Mr. Deeds Goes to Town*); Supporting Actor: **Walter Brennan** (*Come and Get It*); Supporting Actress: **Gale Sondergaard** (*Anthony Adverse*)

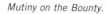

Mutiny on the Bounty.

SPRINGER/BETTMANN FILM ARCHIVE

The Great Ziegfeld.

PHOTOFEST

1937: Picture: *The Life of Emile Zola;* Actor: **Spencer Tracy** (*Captains Courageous*); Actress: **Luise Rainer** (*The Good Earth*); Director: **Leo McCarey** (*The Awful Truth*); Supporting Actor: **Joseph Schildkraut** (*The Life of Emile Zola*); Supporting Actress: **Alice Brady** (*In Old Chicago*)

1938: Picture: *You Can't Take It with You;* Actor: **Spencer Tracy** (*Boys Town*); Actress: **Bette Davis** (*Jezebel*); Director: **Frank Capra** (*You Can't Take It with You*); Supporting Actor: **Walter Brennan** (*Kentucky*); Supporting Actress: **Fay Bainter** (*Jezebel*)

Gone with the Wind.

PHOTOFEST

1939: Picture: *Gone with the Wind;* Actor: **Robert Donat** (*Goodbye, Mr. Chips*); Actress: **Vivien Leigh** (*Gone with the Wind*); Director: **Victor Fleming** (*Gone with the Wind*); Supporting Actor: **Thomas Mitchell** (*Stagecoach*); Supporting Actress: **Hattie McDaniel** (*Gone with the Wind*)

1940: Picture: *Rebecca;* Actor: **James Stewart** (*The Philadelphia Story*); Actress: **Ginger Rogers** (*Kitty Foyle*); Director: **John Ford** (*The Grapes of Wrath*); Supporting Actor: **Walter Brennan** (*The Westerner*); Supporting Actress: **Jane Darwell** (*The Grapes of Wrath*)

1941: Picture: *How Green Was My Valley;* Actor: **Gary Cooper** (*Sergeant York*); Actress: **Joan Fontaine** (*Suspicion*); Director: **John Ford** (*How Green Was My Valley*); Supporting Actor: **Donald Crisp** (*How Green Was My Valley*); Supporting Actress: **Mary Astor** (*The Great Lie*)

1942: Picture: *Mrs. Miniver;* Actor: **James Cagney** (*Yankee Doodle Dandy*); Actress: **Greer Garson** (*Mrs. Miniver*); Director: **William Wyler** (*Mrs. Miniver*); Supporting Actor: **Van Heflin** (*Johnny Eager*); Supporting Actress: **Teresa Wright** (*Mrs. Miniver*)

Casablanca.

All about Eve.

1943: Picture: *Casablanca;* Actor: **Paul Lukas** (*Watch on the Rhine*); Actress: **Jennifer Jones** (*The Song of Bernadette*); Director: **Michael Curtiz** (*Casablanca*); Supporting Actor: **Charles Coburn** (*The More the Merrier*); Supporting Actress: **Katina Paxinou** (*For Whom the Bell Tolls*)

1944: Picture: *Going My Way;* Actor: **Bing Crosby** (*Going My Way*); Actress: **Ingrid Bergman** (*Gaslight*); Director: **Leo McCarey** (*Going My Way*); Supporting Actor: **Barry Fitzgerald** (*Going My Way*); Supporting Actress: **Ethel Barrymore** (*None But the Lonely Heart*)

1945: Picture: *The Lost Weekend;* Actor: **Ray Milland** (*The Lost Weekend*); Actress: **Joan Crawford** (*Mildred Pierce*); Director: **Billy Wilder** (*The Lost Weekend*); Supporting Actor: **James Dunn** (*A Tree Grows in Brooklyn*); Supporting Actress: **Anne Revere** (*National Velvet*)

1946: Picture: *The Best Years of Our Lives;* Actor: **Fredric March** (*The Best Years of Our Lives*); Actress: **Olivia de Havilland** (*To Each His Own*); Director: **William Wyler** (*The Best Years of Our Lives*); Supporting Actor: **Harold Russell** (*The Best Years of Our Lives*); Supporting Actress: **Anne Baxter** (*The Razor's Edge*)

1947: Picture: *Gentleman's Agreement;* Actor: **Ronald Colman** (*A Double Life*); Actress: **Loretta Young** (*The Farmer's Daughter*); Director: **Elia Kazan** (*Gentleman's Agreement*); Supporting Actor: **Edmund Gwenn** (*Miracle on 34th Street*); Supporting Actress: **Celeste Holm** (*Gentleman's Agreement*)

1948: Picture: *Hamlet;* Actor: **Laurence Olivier** (*Hamlet*); Actress: **Jane Wyman** (*Johnny Belinda*); Director: **John Huston** (*The Treasure of Sierra Madre*); Supporting Actor: **Walter Huston** (*The Treasure of Sierra Madre*); Supporting Actress: **Claire Trevor** (*Key Largo*); Foreign Language Film: *Monsieur Vincent* (France)

1949: Picture: *All the King's Men;* Actor: **Broderick Crawford** (*All the King's Men*); Actress: **Olivia de Havilland** (*The Heiress*); Director: **Joseph L. Mankiewicz** (*A Letter to Three Wives*); Supporting Actor: **Dean Jagger** (*Twelve O'Clock High*); Supporting Actress: **Mercedes McCambridge** (*All the King's Men*); Foreign Language Film: *Ladri di biciclette/The Bicycle Thief* (Italy)

1950: Picture: *All about Eve;* Actor: **Jose Ferrer** (*Cyrano de Bergerac*); Actress: **Judy Holliday** (*Born Yesterday*); Director: **Joseph L. Mankiewicz** (*All about Eve*); Supporting Actor:

George Sanders (*All about Eve*); Supporting Actress: **Josephine Hull** (*Harvey*); Foreign Language Film: *Au delà des grilles/The Walls of Malapaga* (France/Italy)

1951: Picture: *An American in Paris;* Actor: **Humphrey Bogart** (*The African Queen*); Actress: **Vivien Leigh** (*A Streetcar Named Desire*); Director: **George Stevens** (*A Place in the Sun*); Supporting Actor: **Karl Malden** (*A Streetcar Named Desire*); Supporting Actress: **Kim Hunter** (*A Streetcar Named Desire*); Foreign Language Film: *Rashomon* (Japan)

1952: Picture: *The Greatest Show on Earth;* Actor: **Gary Cooper** (*High Noon*); Actress: **Shirley Booth** (*Come Back, Little Sheba*); Director: **John Ford** (*The Quiet Man*); Supporting Actor: **Anthony Quinn** (*Viva Zapata!*); Supporting Actress: **Gloria Grahame** (*The Bad and the Beautiful*); Foreign Language Film: *Jeux Interdits/Forbidden Games* (France)

1953: Picture: *From Here to Eternity;* Actor: **William Holden** (*Stalag 17*); Actress: **Audrey Hepburn** (*Roman Holiday*); Director: **Fred Zinnemann** (*From Here to Eternity*); Supporting Actor: **Frank Sinatra** (*From Here to Eternity*); Supporting Actress: **Donna Reed** (*From Here to Eternity*); Foreign Language Film: Not awarded

1954: Picture: *On the Waterfront;* Actor: **Marlon Brando** (*On the Waterfront*); Actress: **Grace Kelly** (*The Country Girl*); Director: **Elia Kazan** (*On the Waterfront*); Supporting Actor: **Edmond O'Brien** (*The Barefoot Contessa*); Supporting Actress: **Eva Marie Saint** (*On the Waterfront*); Foreign Language Film: *Jigokumon/Gate of Hell* (Japan)

1955: Picture: *Marty;* Actor: **Ernest Borgnine** (*Marty*); Actress: **Anna Magnani** (*The Rose Tattoo*); Director: **Delbert Mann** (*Marty*); Supporting Actor: **Jack Lemmon** (*Mister Roberts*); Supporting Actress: **Jo Van Fleet** (*East of Eden*); Foreign Language Film: *Myamoto Musashi/Samurai, The Legend of Musashi* (Japan)

1956: Picture: *Around the World in 80 Days;* Actor: **Yul Brynner** (*The King and I*); Actress: **Ingrid Bergman** (*Anastasia*); Director: **George Stevens** (*Giant*); Supporting Actor: **Anthony Quinn** (*Lust for Life*); Supporting Actress: **Dorothy Malone** (*Written on the Wind*); Foreign Language Film: *La Strada* (Italy)

1957: Picture: *The Bridge on the River Kwai;* Actor: **Alec Guinness** (*The Bridge on the River Kwai*); Actress: **Joanne**

The Best Years of Our Lives.

The Bridge on the River Kwai.

Ben-Hur.

My Fair Lady.

Woodward (*The Three Faces of Eve*); Director: **David Lean** (*The Bridge on the River Kwai*); Supporting Actor: **Red Buttons** (*Sayonara*); Supporting Actress: **Miyoshi Umeki** (*Sayonara*); Foreign Language Film: **Le Notti di Cabiria/The Nights of Cabiria** (Italy)

1958: Picture: *Gigi;* Actor: **David Niven** (*Separate Tables*); Actress: **Susan Hayward** (*I Want to Live*); Director: **Vincente Minnelli** (*Gigi*); Supporting Actor: **Burl Ives** (*The Big Country*); Supporting Actress: **Wendy Hiller** (*Separate Tables*); Foreign Language Film: **Mon oncle/My Uncle** (France)

1959: Picture: *Ben-Hur;* Actor: **Charlton Heston** (*Ben-Hur*); Actress: **Simone Signoret** (*Room at the Top*); Director: **William Wyler** (*Ben-Hur*); Supporting Actor: **Hugh Griffith** (*Ben-Hur*); Supporting Actress: **Shelley Winters** (*The Diary of Anne Frank*); Foreign Language Film: **Orfeu negro/Black Orpheus** (France)

1960: Picture: *The Apartment;* Actor: **Burt Lancaster** (*Elmer Gantry*); Actress: **Elizabeth Taylor** (*Butterfield 8*); Director: **Billy Wilder** (*The Apartment*); Supporting Actor: **Peter Ustinov** (*Spartacus*); Supporting Actress: **Shirley Jones** (*Elmer Gantry*); Foreign Language Film: **Jungfru källan/The Virgin Spring** (Sweden)

1961: Picture: *West Side Story;* Actor: **Maximilian Schell** (*Judgment at Nuremberg*); Actress: **Sophia Loren** (*Two Women*); Director: **Jerome Robbins, Robert Wise** (*West Side Story*); Supporting Actor: **George Chakiris** (*West Side Story*); Supporting Actress: **Rita Moreno** (*West Side Story*); Foreign Language Film: **Såsom i en spegel/Through a Glass, Darkly** (Sweden)

1962: Picture: *Lawrence of Arabia;* Actor: **Gregory Peck** (*To Kill a Mockingbird*); Actress: **Anne Bancroft** (*The Miracle Worker*); Director: **David Lean** (*Lawrence of Arabia*); Supporting Actor: **Ed Begley** (*Sweet Bird of Youth*); Supporting Actress: **Patty Duke** (*The Miracle Worker*); Foreign Language Film: **Cybèle ou les dimanches de ville d'Avray/Sundays and Cybele** (France)

1963: Picture: *Tom Jones;* Actor: **Sidney Poitier** (*Lilies of the Field*); Actress: Patricia Neal (*Hud*); Director: **Tony Richardson** (*Tom Jones*); Supporting Actor: **Melvyn Douglas** (*Hud*); Supporting Actress: **Margaret Rutherford** (*The V.I.P.'s*); Foreign Language Film: **Otto e mezzo/8 ½** (**Italy**)

1964: Picture: *My Fair Lady;* Actor: **Rex Harrison** (*My Fair Lady*); Actress: **Julie Andrews** (*Mary Poppins*); Director: **George Cukor** (*My Fair Lady*); Supporting Actor: **Peter Ustinov** (*Topkapi*); Supporting Actress: **Lila Kedrova** (*Zorba the Greek*); Foreign Language Film: **Ieri, oggi, domani/Yesterday, Today and Tomorrow** (Italy)

1965: Picture: *The Sound of Music;* Actor: **Lee Marvin** (*Cat Ballou*); Actress: **Julie Christie** (*Darling*); Director: **Robert Wise** (*The Sound of Music*); Supporting Actor: **Martin Balsam** (*A Thousand Clowns*); Supporting Actress: **Shelley Winters** (*A Patch of Blue*); Foreign Language Film: **Obchod od na korze/The Shop on Main Street** (Czechoslovakia)

1966: Picture: *A Man for All Seasons;* Actor: **Paul Scofield** (*A Man for All Seasons*); Actress: **Elizabeth Taylor** (*Who's Afraid of Virginia Woolf?*); Director: **Fred Zinnemann** (*A Man for All Seasons*); Supporting Actor: **Walter Matthau** (*The Fortune Cookie*); Supporting Actress: **Sandy Dennis** (*Who's Afraid of Virginia Woolf?*); Foreign Language Film: **Un Homme et une femme/A Man and a Woman** (France)

1967: Picture: *In the Heat of the Night;* Actor: **Rod Steiger** (*In the Heat of the Night*); Actress: **Katharine Hepburn** (*Guess Who's Coming to Dinner?*); Director: **Mike Nichols** (*The Graduate*); Supporting Actor: **George Kennedy** (*Cool Hand Luke*); Supporting Actress: **Estelle Parsons** (*Bonnie and Clyde*); Foreign Language Film: **Ostře sledované vlaky/Closely Watched Trains** (Czechoslovakia)

Lawrence of Arabia.

In the Heat of the Night.

1968: Picture: *Oliver!;* Actor: **Cliff Robertson** *(Charly)*; Actress: **Katharine Hepburn** *(The Lion in Winter)*; and **Barbra Streisand** *(Funny Girl)*; Director: **Sir Carol Reed** *(Oliver!)*; Supporting Actor: **Jack Albertson** *(The Subject Was Roses)*; Supporting Actress: **Ruth Gordon** *(Rosemary's Baby)*; Foreign Language Film: *Voina i mir/War and Peace* (USSR)

1969: Picture: *Midnight Cowboy;* Actor: **John Wayne** *(True Grit)*; Actress: **Maggie Smith** *(The Prime of Miss Jean Brodie)*; Director: **John Schlesinger** *(Midnight Cowboy)*; Supporting Actor: **Gig Young** *(They Shoot Horses, Don't They?)*; Supporting Actress: **Goldie Hawn** *(Cactus Flower)*; Foreign Language Film: *Z* (Algeria)

1970: Picture: *Patton;* Actor: **George C. Scott** *(Patton)*; Actress: **Glenda Jackson** *(Women in Love)*; Director: **Franklin Schaffner** *(Patton)*; Supporting Actor: **John Mills** *(Ryan's Daughter)*; Supporting Actress: **Helen Hayes** *(Airport)*; Foreign Language Film: *Indagine su un cittadino al di sopra di ogni sospetto/Investigation of a Citizen above Suspicion* (Italy)

1971: Picture: *The French Connection;* Actor: **Gene Hackman** *(The French Connection)*; Actress: **Jane Fonda** *(Klute)*; Director: **William Friedkin** *(The French Connection)*; Supporting Actor: **Ben Johnson** *(The Last Picture Show)*; Supporting Actress: **Cloris Leachman** *(The Last Picture Show)*; Foreign Language Film: *Il Giardino dei Finzi-Continis/The Garden of the Finzi-Continis* (Italy)

SPRINGER/BETTMANN FILM ARCHIVE

The Godfather.

1972: Picture: *The Godfather;* Actor: **Marlon Brando** *(The Godfather)*; Actress: **Liza Minnelli** *(Cabaret)*; Director: **Bob Fosse** *(Cabaret)*; Supporting Actor: **Joel Grey** *(Cabaret)*; Supporting Actress: **Eileen Heckart** *(Butterflies Are Free)*; Foreign Language Film: *Le Charme discret de la bourgeoisie/The Discreet Charm of the Bourgeoisie* (France)

1973: Picture: *The Sting;* Actor: **Jack Lemmon** *(Save the Tiger)*; Actress: **Glenda Jackson** *(A Touch of Class)*; Director: **George Roy Hill** *(The Sting)*; Supporting Actor: **John Houseman** *(The Paper Chase)*; Supporting Actress: **Tatum O'Neal** *(Paper Moon)*; Foreign Language Film: *La Nuit américaine/Day for Night* (France)

1974: Picture: *The Godfather, Part II;* Actor: **Art Carney** *(Harry and Tonto)*; Actress: **Ellyn Burstyn** *(Alice Doesn't Live Here Anymore)*; Director: **Francis Ford Coppola** *(The Godfather, Part II)*; Supporting Actor: **Robert DeNiro** *(The Godfather, Part II)*; Supporting Actress: **Ingrid Bergman** *(Murder on the Orient Express)*; Foreign Language Film: *Amarcord* (Italy)

1975: Picture: *One Flew over the Cuckoo's Nest;* Actor: **Jack Nicholson** *(One Flew over the Cuckoo's Nest)*; Actress: **Louise Fletcher** *(One Flew over the Cuckoo's Nest)*; Director: **Milos Forman** *(One Flew over the Cuckoo's Nest)*; Supporting Actor: **George Burns** *(The Sunshine Boys)*; Supporting Actress: **Lee Grant** *(Shampoo)*; Foreign Language Film: *Dersu Uzala* (USSR)

1976: Picture: *Rocky;* Actor: **Peter Finch** *(Network)*; Actress: **Faye Dunaway** *(Network)*; Director: **John G. Avildsen** *(Rocky)*; Supporting Actor: **Jason Robards** *(All the President's Men)*;

Supporting Actress: **Beatrice Straight** *(Network)*; Foreign Language Film: *La Victoire en chantant/Black and White in Color* (Ivory Coast)

1977: Picture: *Annie Hall;* Actor: **Richard Dreyfuss** *(The Goodbye Girl)*; Actress: **Diane Keaton** *(Annie Hall)*; Director: **Woody Allen** *(Annie Hall)*; Supporting Actor: **Jason Robards** *(Julia)*; Supporting Actress: **Vanessa Redgrave** *(Julia)*; Foreign Language Film: *La Vie devant soi/Madame Rosa* (France)

1978: Picture: *The Deer Hunter;* Actor: **Jon Voight** *(Coming Home)*; Actress: **Jane Fonda** *(Coming Home)*; Director: **Michael Cimino** *(The Deer Hunter)*; Supporting Actor: **Christopher Walken** *(The Deer Hunter)*; Supporting Actress: **Maggie Smith** *(California Suite)*; Foreign Language Film: *Préparez vos mouchoirs/Get out Your Handkerchiefs* (France)

1979: Picture: *Kramer vs. Kramer;* Actor: **Dustin Hoffman** *(Kramer vs. Kramer)*; Actress: **Sally Field** *(Norma Rae)*; Director: **Robert Benton** *(Kramer vs. Kramer)*; Supporting Actor: **Melvyn Douglas** *(Being There)*; Supporting Actress: **Meryl Streep** *(Kramer vs. Kramer)*; Foreign Language Film: *Die Blechtrommel/The Tin Drum* (West Germany)

1980: Picture: *Ordinary People;* Actor: **Robert DeNiro** *(Raging Bull)*; Actress: **Sissy Spacek** *(Coal Miner's Daughter)*; Director: **Robert Redford** *(Ordinary People)*; Supporting Actor: **Timothy Hutton** *(Ordinary People)*; Supporting Actress: **Mary Steenburgen** *(Melvin and Howard)*; Foreign Language Film: *Moskava slezam ne verit/Moscow Does Not Believe in Tears* (USSR)

1981: Picture: *Chariots of Fire;* Actor: **Henry Fonda** *(On Golden Pond)*; Actress: **Katharine Hepburn** *(On Golden Pond)*; Director: **Warren Beatty** *(Reds)*; Supporting Actor: **John Gielgud** *(Arthur)*; Supporting Actress: **Maureen Stapleton** *(Reds)*; Foreign Language Film: *Mephisto* (Hungary)

1982: Picture: *Gandhi;* Actor: **Ben Kingsley** *(Gandhi)*; Actress: **Meryl Streep** *(Sophie's Choice)*; Director: **Sir Richard Attenborough** *(Gandhi)*; Supporting Actor: **Louis Gossett, Jr.** *(An Officer and a Gentleman)*; Supporting Actress: **Jessica Lange** *(Tootsie)*; Foreign Language Film: *Volver a empezar/To Begin Again* (Spain)

1983: Picture: *Terms of Endearment;* Actor: **Robert Duvall** *(Tender Mercies)*; Actress: **Shirley MacLaine** *(Terms of Endearment)*; Director: **James L. Brooks** *(Terms of Endearment)*; Supporting Actor: **Jack Nicholson** *(Terms of Endearment)*; Supporting Actress: **Linda Hunt** *(The Year of Living Dangerously)*; Foreign Language Film: *Fanny och Alexander/Fanny and Alexander* (Sweden)

1984: Picture: *Amadeus;* Actor: **F. Murray Abraham** *(Amadeus)*; Actress: **Sally Field** *(Places in the Heart)*; Director: **Milos Forman** *(Amadeus)*; Supporting Actor: **Haing S. Ngor** *(The Killing Fields)*; Supporting Actress: **Dame Peggy Ashcroft** *(A Passage to India)*; Foreign Language Film: *La Diagonale du fou/Dangerous Moves* (Switzerland)

1985: Picture: *Out of Africa;* Actor: **William Hurt** *(Kiss of the Spider Woman)*; Actress: **Geraldine Page** *(The Trip to Bountiful)*; Director: **Sydney Pollack** *(Out of Africa)*; Supporting Actor: **Don Ameche** *(Cocoon)*; Supporting Actress: **Anjelica Huston** *(Prizzi's Honor)*; Foreign Language Film: *La Historia official/The Official Story* (Argentina)

1986: Picture: *Platoon;* Actor: **Paul Newman** *(The Color of Money)*; Actress: **Marlee Matlin** *(Children of a Lesser God)*; Director: **Oliver Stone** *(Platoon)*; Supporting Actor: **Michael Caine** *(Hannah and Her Sisters)*; Supporting Actress: **Dianne Wiest** *(Hannah and Her Sisters)*; Foreign Language Film: *De Aanslag/The Assault* (The Netherlands)

1987: Picture: *The Last Emperor;* Actor: **Michael Douglas** *(Wall Street)*; Actress: **Cher** *(Moonstruck)*; Director: **Bernardo Bertolucci** *(The Last Emperor)*; Supporting Actor: **Sean Connery** *(The Untouchables)*; Supporting Actress: **Olympia Dukakis** *(Moonstruck)*; Foreign Language Film: *Babettes gaestebud/Babette's Feast* (Denmark)

1988: Picture: *Rain Man;* Actor: **Dustin Hoffman** *(Rain Man)*; Actress: **Jodie Foster** *(The Accused)*; Director: **Barry Levinson** *(Rain Man)*; Supporting Actor: **Kevin Kline** *(A Fish Called Wanda)*; Supporting Actress: **Geena Davis** *(The Accidental Tourist)*; Foreign Language Film: *Pelle Erobreren/Pelle the Conqueror* (Denmark)

1989: Picture: *Driving Miss Daisy;* Actor: **Daniel Day-Lewis** *(My Left Foot)*; Actress: **Jessica Tandy** *(Driving Miss Daisy)*; Director: **Oliver Stone** *(Born on the Fourth of July)*; Supporting Actor: **Denzel Washington** *(Glory)*; Supporting Actress: **Brenda Fricker** *(My Left Foot)*; Foreign Language Film: *Nuovo Cinema Paradiso/Cinema Paradiso* (Italy)

1990: Picture: *Dances with Wolves;* Actor: **Jeremy Irons** *(Reversal of Fortune)*; Actress: **Kathy Bates** *(Misery)*; Director:

A Beautiful Mind.

Chicago.

Kevin Costner (*Dances with Wolves*); Supporting Actor: Joe Pesci (*Goodfellas*); Supporting Actress: Whoopi Goldberg (*Ghost*); Foreign Language Film: *Reise der Hoffnung/Journey of Hope* (Switzerland)

1991: Picture: *The Silence of the Lambs;* Actor: Anthony Hopkins (*The Silence of the Lambs*); Actress: Jodie Foster (*The Silence of the Lambs*); Director: Jonathan Demme (*The Silence of the Lambs*); Supporting Actor: Jack Palance (*City Slickers*); Supporting Actress: Mercedes Ruehl (*The Fisher King*); Foreign Language Film: *Mediterraneo* (Italy)

1992: Picture: *Unforgiven;* Actor: Al Pacino (*Scent of a Woman*); Actress: Emma Thompson (*Howards End*); Director: Clint Eastwood (*Unforgiven*); Supporting Actor: Gene Hackman (*Unforgiven*); Supporting Actress: Marisa Tomei (*My Cousin Vinny*); Foreign Language Film: *Indochine* (France)

1993: Picture: *Schindler's List;* Actor: Tom Hanks (*Philadelphia*); Actress: Holly Hunter (*The Piano*); Director: Steven Spielberg (*Schindler's List*); Supporting Actor: Tommy Lee Jones (*The Fugitive*); Supporting Actress: Anna Paquin (*The Piano*); Foreign Language Film: *Belle Epoque* (Spain)

1994: Picture: *Forrest Gump;* Actor: Tom Hanks (*Forrest Gump*); Actress: Jessica Lange (*Blue Sky*); Director: Robert Zemeckis (*Forrest Gump*); Supporting Actor: Martin Landau (*Ed Wood*); Supporting Actress: Dianne Wiest (*Bullets over Broadway*); Foreign Language Film: *Utomlénie sólntsem/Burnt by the Sun* (Russia)

1995: Picture: *Braveheart;* Actor: Nicolas Cage (*Leaving Las Vegas*); Actress: Susan Sarandon (*Dead Man Walking*); Director: Mel Gibson (*Braveheart*); Supporting Actor: Kevin Spacey (*The Usual Suspects*); Supporting Actress: Mira Sorvino (*Mighty Aphrodite*); Foreign Language Film: *Antonia/Antonia's Line* (The Netherlands)

1996: Picture: *The English Patient;* Actor: Geoffrey Rush (*Shine*); Actress: Frances McDormand (*Fargo*); Director: Anthony Minghella (*The English Patient*); Supporting Actor: Cuba Gooding, Jr. (*Jerry Maguire*); Supporting Actress: Juliette Binoche (*The English Patient*); Foreign Language Film: *Kolya* (Czech Republic)

1997: Picture: *Titanic;* Actor: Jack Nicholson (*As Good as It Gets*); Actress: Helen Hunt (*As Good as It Gets*); Director: James Cameron (*Titanic*); Supporting Actor: Robin Williams (*Good Will Hunting*); Supporting Actress: Kim Basinger (*L.A. Confidential*); Foreign Language Film: *Karakter/Character* (The Netherlands)

1998: Picture: *Shakespeare in Love;* Actor: Roberto Benigni (*La vita è bella/Life Is Beautiful*); Actress: Gwyneth Paltrow (*Shakespeare in Love*); Director: Steven Spielberg (*Saving Private Ryan*); Supporting Actor: James Coburn (*Affliction*); Supporting Actress: Judi Dench (*Shakespeare in Love*); Foreign Language Film: *La vita è bella/Life Is Beautiful* (Italy)

1999: Picture: *American Beauty;* Actor: Kevin Spacey (*American Beauty*); Actress: Hilary Swank (*Boys Don't Cry*); Director: Sam Mendes (*American Beauty*); Supporting Actor: Michael Caine (*The Cider House Rules*); Supporting Actress: Angelina Jolie (*Girl, Interrupted*); Foreign Language Film: *Todo sobre mi madre/All about My Mother* (Spain)

2000: Picture: *Gladiator;* Actor: Russell Crowe (*Gladiator*); Actress: Julia Roberts (*Erin Brockovich*); Director: Steven Soderbergh (*Traffic*); Supporting Actor: Benicio Del Toro (*Traffic*); Supporting Actress: Marcia Gay Harden (*Pollock*); Foreign Language Film: *Wo hu zang long/Crouching Tiger, Hidden Dragon* (Taiwan)

2001: Picture: *A Beautiful Mind;* Actor: Denzel Washington (*Training Day*); Actress: Halle Berry (*Monster's Ball*); Director: Ron Howard (*A Beautiful Mind*); Supporting Actor: Jim Broadbent (*Iris*); Supporting Actress: Jennifer Connelly (*A Beautiful Mind*); Foreign Language Film: *Nikogarsnja zemlja/No Man's Land* (Bosnia and Herzegovina)

2002: Picture: *Chicago;* Actor: Adrien Brody (*The Pianist*); Actress: Nicole Kidman (*The Hours*); Director: Roman Polanski (*The Pianist*); Supporting Actor: Chris Cooper (*Adaptation*); Supporting Actress: Catherine Zeta-Jones (*Chicago*); Foreign Language Film: *Nirgendwo in Afrika/Nowhere in Africa* (Germany)

2003: Picture: *The Lord of the Rings: The Return of the King;* Actor: Sean Penn (*Mystic River*); Actress: Charlize Theron (*Monster*); Director: Peter Jackson (*The Lord of the Rings: The Return of the King*); Supporting Actor: Tim Robbins (*Mystic River*); Supporting Actress: Renée Zellweger (*Cold Mountain*); Foreign Language Film: *Les Invasions barbares/The Barbarian Invasions* (Canada)

2004: Picture: *Million Dollar Baby;* Actor: Jamie Foxx (*Ray*); Actress: Hilary Swank (*Million Dollar Baby*); Director: Clint Eastwood (*Million Dollar Baby*); Supporting Actor: Morgan Freeman (*Million Dollar Baby*); Supporting Actress: Cate Blanchett (*The Aviator*); Foreign Language Film: *Mar adentro/The Sea Inside* (Spain)

The Lord of the Rings: The Return of the King.

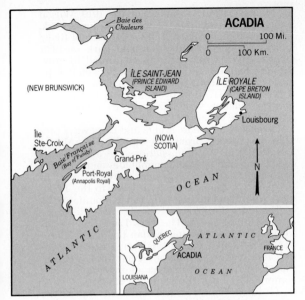

ACADIA

0   100 Mi.
0   100 Km.

Baie des Chaleurs

ÎLE SAINT-JEAN
(PRINCE EDWARD ISLAND)

ÎLE ROYALE
(CAPE BRETON ISLAND)

(NEW BRUNSWICK)

Louisbourg

Île Ste-Croix

(NOVA SCOTIA)

Baie Française
(Bay of Fundy)

Grand-Pré

N

Port-Royal
(Annapolis Royal)

OCEAN

ATLANTIC

QUEBEC   ATLANTIC

Acadie   ACADIA   FRANCE

LOUISIANA   OCEAN

ACADIA, ə-kā′dē-ə, the name applied by France to its Atlantic coastal possessions in North America, which in the 17th century comprised the territory between the Atlantic Ocean and the lower river and gulf of St. Lawrence. The name in French is *Acadie.* The name, Acadia, appears in a commission, which was issued in 1603 to Pierre Du Gua de Monts by the French government.

De Monts's colony was originally established at Île Ste-Croix (near present-day Calais, Maine) in 1604 but was transferred to Port-Royal (now Annapolis Royal, Nova Scotia) in 1605. The colony was abandoned in 1607 following the cancellation of his charter. Port-Royal was revived in 1610 by Jean de Biencourt de Poutrincourt, one of de Monts's associates. But he was forced to return to France to secure financial aid, and during his absence the infant settlement was plundered and burned by the English adventurer Samuel Argall in 1613.

In 1614 Poutrincourt, returning and finding Port-Royal in ruins, took the majority of the colonists back to France. After his death in 1615 his son and successor, Charles de Biencourt, neglected the settlement and made his living off the fur trade. When Biencourt died in 1623 or 1624, Charles de St. Étienne de La Tour became the colony's leader.

Meanwhile, in 1621, Sir William Alexander had been given a grant of Nova Scotia by James I of England. Encouraged by Sir David Kirke's capture of Quebec, Alexander besieged Cap de Sable in 1629. Charles de La Tour refused to surrender it. Port-Royal, which was captured by Alexander's son Sir William in 1629, was returned to France in 1632.

Perturbed by Alexander's incursions, France then made its first real effort to aid the Acadians. It sent out an able and energetic lieutenant governor, Isaac de Razilly, under whom the colonists made substantial progress in the cultivation of the soil as well as in the shore fishery and the fur trade. Following Razilly's death in 1635, a feud developed between his successors, Charles de La Tour and Charles de Menou d'Aulnay. The latter gained the upper hand and secured appointment as governor of all Acadia in 1641. Under d'Aulnay's capable administration the colony prospered until his death in 1650.

Four years of confusion ensued, marked by bitter rivalry between Charles de La Tour, who was appointed governor in 1651, and Emmanuel Le Borgne, one of d'Aulnay's creditors, who took over d'Aulnay's properties in Port-Royal.

The New England colonists quickly took advantage of this dissension. An expedition from Boston led by Robert Sedgwick overran Acadia in 1654. An English garrison was placed in Port-Royal, and the area remained in English hands until Charles II restored Acadia to France by the Treaty of Breda (1667).

France failed to strengthen the colony's defenses, and in 1690 Port-Royal fell an easy prey to a New England force under the leadership of Sir William Phips in King William's War. Restored again to France in 1697, Port-Royal was retaken by the New Englanders in 1710. The colony was renamed Annapolis Royal when, with the rest of Acadia, it was ceded to Britain by the Treaty of Utrecht (1713).

Stung by the loss of Acadia, the French built a fort at Louisbourg on Île Royale (Cape Breton Island), which lay outside the ceded territory. Louisbourg was captured in 1745 by the American colonial troops in King George's War, but it was returned to the French by the Treaty of Aix-la-Chapelle (1748). Thereupon the British founded Halifax and demanded a binding oath of loyalty from the Acadians, with the option of withdrawing into French territory. Their refusal to accept either alternative caused the British to comply with repeated New England requests for the expulsion of the Acadians.

The expulsion of the Acadians in 1755 has been defended as an act of military and political necessity, but it undoubtedly caused great hardship and suffering among those who were ousted from their homeland. Approximately 6,000 Acadians, out of a total of 10,000, were expelled during this period. Of those who survived this hardship, many returned later to reestablish themselves in Acadia, or, more commonly, in northern New Brunswick and in pockets of the other Maritimes. Approximately 2,000 of the exiles decided to return and, together with those who had not been evicted, were peacefully assimilated into the population of Nova Scotia. A number of the refugees eventually settled in Louisiana, where their descendents, known as Cajuns, still preserve a distinct culture. (The Acadians' plight was movingly described by Henry Wadsworth Longfellow in his celebrated poem *Evangeline.*) Historians say responsibility for the tragedy rests mainly with the French officials and the priests, who had convinced the Acadians that they still owed allegiance to France.

ALLAN M. FRASER
Archivist, Province of Newfoundland

ACADIA NATIONAL PARK, ə-kā′dē-ə, a scenic section of the coast of Maine, about 37 miles (60 km) southeast of Bangor. The park occupies approximately one-third of Mount Desert Island, which is about 14 miles (23 km) long and 12 miles (19 km) wide. All or part of several smaller islands and a portion of the mainland, on Schoodic Peninsula, are included in the park.

Granite dominates the eastern part of Mount Desert Island and forms the major mountains in the western half. These mountains, clothed in evergreen and deciduous forests, descend to the sea.

Within the past few million years, approximately 20 to 30 glaciers crushed New England, further reshaping the land. The last glacier, up to 9,000 feet (2,750 meters) thick, retreated from Acadia a scant 13,000 years ago, leaving deep valleys in which lakes formed. On the northern slopes of newly carved mountains, the glacier polished and rounded the surfaces, but the southern slopes were left torn and precipitous. Relieved of the weight of the ice, the land became elevated. The sea, flooded with melted ice, also rose, intruding onto the land and turning small hills close to the ocean into islands. Somes Sound, a fjord that just about cuts the island in two, is actually a flooded valley.

Plants and Animals. Pink lady's slipper, trailing arbutus, painted trillium, fringed polygala, bluet, and wood lily are among the many wildflowers found in the park. Red spruce is the dominant tree, but the evergreen forest also includes black and white spruces, balsam fir, and several species of pine. The island's tree cover changed radically after 1947. In the fall of that year, which was unusually dry, a fire burned for nearly a month, destroying 17,000 acres (6,900 ha), including 10,000 acres (4,000 ha) in the park. Aspen, birch, maples, and other deciduous trees, heretofore limited in number, moved in to fill the void left by the destroyed evergreens, a shift in variety that has resulted in brilliant displays of fall foliage.

Among land mammals the red fox is common, but the bobcat and black bear are both quite rare. The diverse bird life includes many species of warbler.

The intertidal zones are defined by the proportion of time that each is above water as tides rise and fall. In the spray zone, above high tide, periwinkles (marine snails) graze on a blue-green alga that has stained the rocks black. Acorn barnacles by the millions cling to the rocks in the barnacle zone, resisting heavy pounding by the waves. Next lower, rockweed (in the rockweed zone), also firmly anchored to rock, lies prostrate when exposed at low tide but floats upright when underwater. In the Irish moss zone, which is above water only twice a month, Irish moss provides sanctuary for various marine species. Kelp grows in the laminarian zone, uncovered only twice a year. Lobsters, seals, and porpoises flourish in shallow waters beyond the tidal zones.

History. Native Americans, most recently the Abnakis, camped on the island for approximately 6,000 years. The French explorer Samuel de Champlain, noting the treeless summits in 1604, named the place Île des Monts Déserts ("Island of Barren Mountains"). A French Jesuit mission, established in 1613, was destroyed by the English. England's victory over France in North America in 1763 opened the way to English colonization of the area. By the early 19th century settlers were farming, lumbering, fishing, and building ships on the island.

Artists and journalists spread word of the island's natural beauty, and wealthy Americans bought land and built summer estates on it. One wealthy resident, George Dorr, devoted much of his life to preserving the landscape for the benefit of all. He persuaded a number of residents to donate land to the government, and in 1913 Pres. Woodrow Wilson proclaimed the creation of Sieur

de Monts National Monument. In 1919 Wilson signed an act creating Lafayette National Park, the first national park east of the Mississippi River. It was renamed Acadia National Park in 1929. Over the years the park has continued to grow through bequests of land. John D. Rockefeller, Jr., alone donated 11,000 acres (4,500 ha). Tragic though it was, the 1947 fire, by destroying 67 summer estates, somehow symbolized the arrival of a new era of public access.

Recreation. A short bridge and causeways provide easy access from the mainland to Mount Desert Island. Accommodations are available at Bar Harbor and in other communities on the island. Auto routes provide excellent views of most of the park's features. One drive leads to the 1,530-foot (470-meter) summit of Cadillac Mountain, the highest elevation located on the Atlantic Coast of the United States. The Park Loop Road leads to Sieur de Monts Spring, Jordan Pond, and Thunder Hole—a spot where tidal zones can be studied and where thunderous explosions are produced by the phenomenon of incoming water compressing air at the back of a cavern.

Cadillac Mountain also represents one of the most challenging hikes in the park. Altogether there are more than 50 trails. Between 1915 and 1933 John D. Rockefeller, Jr., constructed 57 miles (92 km) of carriage paths so that residents could

Bass Harbor Head Light, on the southern shore of Mount Desert, was built to mark an entrance to Blue Hill Bay.

escape the growing presence of the automobile. Today most of these routes are open to hikers, cyclists, horseback riders, and cross-country skiers. Fishing on the island has been described as fair to poor.

Schoodic Peninsula, the mainland portion of the park, may be explored by car on a route affording fine views of the windswept coast. The remote Isle au Haut, which is about one-half parkland, is not accessible by car. Hikers and campers may travel to the island by mailboat.

See also MOUNT DESERT ISLAND.

DONALD YOUNG, *Coeditor*
Sierra Club Guides to the National Parks

ACANTHOCEPHALA, ə-kan-thə-sef'ə-lə, a phylum of spiny-headed worms that live in large numbers as parasites in the intestines of vertebrates. Over 500 species are found worldwide. They have a high reproductive capacity.

Classification. Acanthocephala has been classified only recently as a separate phylum. Although the worms' bodies appear flattened while they are in the host intestines, they become cylindrical when placed in water. Thus some scientists grouped these worms under phylum Nemathelminthes (roundworms); others grouped them in phylum Platyhelminthes (flatworms). But because of distinctive features of their anatomy and life cycle, they are in a separate phylum.

Anatomy. Acanthocephalans range in size from less than 1 to 15 inches (2.5–38 cm). The larger species are found in mammals. Although naturally translucent or white, the worms usually are colored by the intestinal matter of their hosts. Some of the species appear to have segmented bodies, but the segments involve only the surface structures of the worm. Spines are found on the body trunk of some species. The sexes are separate. A small group of nerve cells serves as a brain.

Life Cycle. The eggs of the species are ejected by the female into the intestinal tract of the host, and they then are passed out by the host's body. An intermediate host—usually an arthropod— ingests the eggs. The eggs hatch in the body of the intermediate host and begin to develop into infectious larvae. The arthropod containing the larvae then is ingested by another vertebrate host. The worms free themselves, attach themselves to the walls of the vertebrate's intestines, grow to sexual maturity, and repeat the cycle.

ACANTHUS, ə-kan'thəs, a group of thorny perennial herbs or small shrubs, found in the Mediterranean area and in Asia and Africa. Most of the species live in dry places. About 3 to 4 feet (0.9–1.2 meters) tall, the plants are characterized by thistlelike leaves 1 to 2 feet (0.3–0.6 meter) long and showy flowers clustered in erect spikes 1 to 1.5 feet (0.3–0.45 meter) long. The flowers are dull white to rose or purplish in color and consist of a short tube with a 3- to 5-lobed expanded lip. The four stamens of the flower are prominent. The fruit of the acanthus is a capsule that opens elastically; the seeds are thrown out by rodlike growths.

Acanthus, also commonly known as bear's-breech, is a genus in the family Acanthaceae, a plant grouping that contains some 200 genera in the tropical regions of the world. *Acanthus* contains about 20 species. Common among them are *A. spinosus*, which served as the pattern for the decoration of the capitals of ancient Corinthian columns; *A. montanus*, which is the species usually grown as an ornamental; and *A. mollis*, a species with nonspiny leaves.

A CAPPELLA, äk-ə-pel'ə, a musical term that now refers to singing performed without accompaniment. An *a cappella* choir or chorus, therefore, is one that specializes in unaccompanied singing. The term is an Italian phrase meaning literally "as in a chapel."

Originally the term was applied to church music for voices only or, if the voices were accompanied, to music in which the instruments merely duplicated the voices. The music of Giovanni Pierluigi da Palestrina (1525–1594) is generally considered the best model of *a cappella* composition.

ACAPULCO, ä-kä-pōōl'kō, a resort city on the Pacific coast of southern Mexico, in the state of Guerrero, 260 miles (420 km) by road south of Mexico City. It is situated on an oval bay, backed by steep, green mountains and lined with

ROCHE   W. H. HODGE

Acanthus (left, *A. mollis*) is a weedy plant found in southern Europe. For centuries the design of acanthus leaves has been used in decorative motifs, as on the columns at the Temple of Zeus, Athens (detail at right).

The luxury hotels of Mexico's world-famous resort of Acapulco front on a crescent beach fringing the bay.

palm-fringed beaches, luxurious houses, and modern hotels. Acapulco's year-round climate is warm.

Acapulco offers visitors a wide choice of activities within the city and in the surrounding area. Besides swimming and sunbathing, there is excellent deep-sea fishing. Sports, such as waterskiing, skin diving, canoeing, golf, and duck hunting, are popular. Entertainment includes bullfights, jai alai matches, and discothèques. Visitors can take tours in glass-bottom boats or moonlight cruises on ships with music and dancing. One of the best-known spectacles is provided by boys who plunge at night from La Quebrada Cliffs into the ocean, carrying flares as they dive.

Acapulco was settled by the Spanish in the 1530s, and by 1600 it was an important link in the trade route between the Far East and Spain. The port declined when this trade dried up in the early 1800s. The city's modern development dates from the late 1930s. In time it became one of the world's great resorts. Population: 722,499 (2000 census).

ACARINA, ak-ə-rī'nə, a group of arachnids commonly known as ticks and mites. They inhabit almost all types of environments and are parasitic to both plants and animals. They also carry such diseases as Rocky Mountain spotted fever, tularemia, and Texas cattle fever.

Small in size—mites are less than 0.04 inch (0.10 cm) long, and ticks are about 0.79 inch (2 cm) long—the acarinoid body is divided into two regions. The anterior part is called the cephalothorax; the posterior part is called the abdomen. There is no distinct division between the cephalothorax and abdomen. Ticks and mites have four pairs of jointed legs but lack antennae.

Most species of Acarina lay eggs, although a few bear their young alive. Development usually follows the pattern of egg, larva, nymph, and metamorphosis to adult.

Some common types of Acarina are the harvest mites (chiggers or redbugs), which attack man; water mites, which are parasitic to fish and crabs; and the orbatid mites, which are important in maintaining soil fertility and also serve as an intermediate host for sheep and cattle tapeworms.

Acarina constitute an order in the class Arachnida, phylum Arthropoda. The order is divided into five suborders, one containing the ticks and the other four the mites. There are over 20,000 known species.

ACARNANIA, ak-ər-nā'nē-ə, a largely mountainous region in west central Greece bordering the Ionian Sea. The region is politically part of the *nomos* (department) of Aetolia and Acarnania.

In ancient times, Acarnania was bounded on the north by the Ambracian Gulf. The Achelous River separated it from Aetolia, which lay to the east. Isolated geographically, its residents, the semibarbarous Acarnanians, made few contributions to Greek civilization. During the 5th century B.C. they were allied with Athens, with whose help they maintained their independence against Corinth and Sparta. The area, however, came under Spartan control for a time in the next century.

In 314 B.C. the Acarnanians formed a new city league around Stratus, their chief city. It existed until 30 B.C., when Acarnania was included in the Roman province of Achaea.

Acarnania was subsequently part of the Byzantine and Ottoman empires. It became part of independent Greece in 1832.

Acarina are carriers of disease. This small tick *(Dermacentor andersoni)* carries Rocky Mountain spotted fever.

ACCELERATION, ak-sel-ə-rā′shən, is the rate at which a velocity changes. There are two principal types of acceleration, linear acceleration and angular acceleration.

Linear Acceleration. A linear velocity, measured for example in miles per hour (mph) or meters per second (m/sec), can change in amount or magnitude, or it can change in direction. Either of these changes in linear velocity produces a linear acceleration, measured for example in meters per second per second (m/sec²). Thus, an automobile travelling in a given direction experiences a linear acceleration whenever it speeds up or slows down. The same automobile, when driven around a curve, also experiences a linear acceleration by virtue of the change in its direction of motion.

Angular Acceleration. When a phonograph record revolves about a vertical axis, its rotational speed is usually measured in revolutions per minute (rpm) or revolutions per second (rev/sec). A line drawn from the center of the rotating disk to any other point on the disk rotates along with the disk, sweeping out an ever-increasing angle as it turns. After one revolution, it has swept out an angle of 360° or 2π radians (rad); after two revolutions, 720° or 4π rad; and so forth. The angular speed of the rotating disk is the angle swept through by the rotating line per unit time, and is usually measured in degrees per second or in radians per second. Angular speed in radians per second is always equal to the constant 2π times the rotational speed in revolutions per second.

Angular velocity is a vector quantity; that is, it has both magnitude and direction. For any rotating body, the size or magnitude of its angular velocity is simply its angular speed. The direction of its angular velocity is taken by convention as pointing along its axis of rotation. Angular acceleration is the rate of change of angular velocity. Thus, a top experiences angular acceleration when it is "whipped" into motion, when it slows down, and when its axis of rotation exhibits a wobble.

Linear and angular acceleration can be illustrated by considering an object whirling at the end of a string around a fixed center. The string connecting the object to the center sweeps out some angle in a unit time as the object traverses a corresponding distance along the arc of the circle. Thus, the angular speed of the object in radians per second is proportional to the linear speed of the object. If the object moves in the circle at constant speed, its angular acceleration

is zero, although it continually undergoes a linear acceleration because it is continually changing its direction of motion toward the center of the circle. Such a linear acceleration is called a *centripetal acceleration.* If the object moves on the circle with changing speed, it experiences an additional acceleration along the line of its motion, called a *tangential acceleration;* for a given length of string, the body's angular acceleration is proportional to its tangential acceleration.

For a discussion of the relationship of acceleration to force and of the acceleration caused by the attraction of one mass for another, see FORCE; GRAVITY.

SAMUEL OLANOFF
Bard College

ACCELERATOR. See PARTICLE ACCELERATOR.

ACCELEROMETER, ak-sel-ə-rom′ət-ər, an instrument or device that measures acceleration. An accelerometer for measuring linear acceleration usually consists of a mass attached to a restraining spring, and free to move only in the direction of the spring's axis, which is called the sensitive axis of the accelerometer. The tension of the spring and the mass are adjusted so that the displacement of the spring due to a force acting on the mass along the sensitive axis is directly proportional to the force and thus to the acceleration resulting from the force. This follows Newton's second law of motion, $F = ma$, where F is the force, m the mass, and a the acceleration. An indicator operated by the mass enables the magnitude of the acceleration to be read off directly.

An angular accelerometer is similar in principle to a linear accelerometer. The mass in this case is usually a disk attached to a spiral spring, and the rotation of the mass caused by an angular acceleration is again used to operate an indicator from which the acceleration can be read off.

In testing automobiles, accelerometers are clamped to the dashboard in order to study the various vertical accelerations to which the vehicles are subjected. The pickup and braking power of automobiles, the side load on tires, and various other vibrations are also studied with this instrument. Accelerometers have been used to measure the vibrations of the hulls of ships as well.

In seismology, a recording instrument called the *accelerograph*, which consists of several accelerometers, is used for measuring the acceleration, period of vibrations, and duration of the shock during an earthquake.

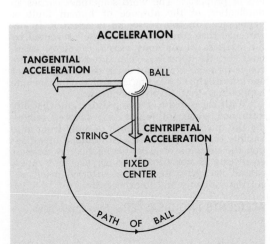

ACCELERATION

TANGENTIAL ACCELERATION

BALL

STRING

CENTRIPETAL ACCELERATION

FIXED CENTER

PATH OF BALL

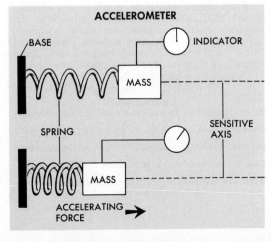

ACCELEROMETER

BASE

INDICATOR

MASS

SPRING

MASS

SENSITIVE AXIS

ACCELERATING FORCE

ACCENT, ak'sent, the general term in phonetics and linguistics for the sound qualities in speech that give more prominence to one syllable than to others in a word, or more emphasis to one part of a group of words. Accent may be the only difference in sound that signals a difference in meaning between two similar utterances. For example, in English the words *pérmit* (certificate of permission) and *permít* (to allow) are differentiated only by accent.

The Three Voice-Qualities. Accent may be carried by one or more of three voice-qualities: loudness, pitch, and duration of sound. Accent by voice-loudness is usually called *stress;* accent by voice-pitch is called *tone;* and accent by the relative length of sound is called *quantity.* To some extent, every language has all three of these qualities. English and the other Germanic languages characteristically use a very strong stress accent. Chinese, Thai, and most African languages use primarily a pitch accent to distinguish similar words or the grammatical functions of words; as a consequence, they are called *tone languages.* Quantity is not prominent in any particular language or group of languages, but Italian, Swedish, and Ojibwa, among others, have vowel length as one differentiating element.

Development of Accent. Indo-European, the language from which the speech of Europe, much of the Middle East, and much of India is descended, had a pitch accent that could occupy various places in a word. In the development of the subfamilies of Indo-European the movable pitch accent was replaced by a fixed stress accent. This process was fundamental in bringing about the immense differences between such languages as Norwegian and Armenian, for example. Both are Indo-European languages, but it is almost impossible for anyone but a linguist to demonstrate the kinship between them. A cardinal achievement of 19th century linguistics was the demonstration by the Danish philologist Karl Verner that certain confusions in the history of the Germanic languages could be clarified by showing the position of the accents in the Indo-European roots (see also VERNER'S LAW).

As far back as the English language can be traced, it has had four levels of stress—primary (´), secondary (^), tertiary (`), and weak (˘). In speech a one-syllable word by itself has primary stress (*cár*), two-syllable words usually have primary and weak (*ăbóve, ángĕl*), and multisyllable words have primary, tertiary, and weak (*célĕbràte*). Secondary stress almost never occurs in single words, but it is used to differentiate between similar pairs, such as *róttenstòne* and *rótten stóne.*

Pitch accent on single words is not characteristic of English, but pitch is crucial in expressions where intonation determines meaning. For example, the difference between "John!" and "John?" and between "Am I happy!" and "Am I happy?" is signaled chiefly by pitch.

See also LINGUISTICS.

ROBERT L. CHAPMAN, *Drew University*

Bibliography
Calvert, Donald R., *Descriptive Phonetics,* 2d ed. (Thieme, Inc. 1986).
Gussmann, Edmund, *Studies in Abstract Phonology* (MIT Press 1981).
Herbert, Robert K., *Language Universals* (Mouton Pub. 1986).
Lass, R., and Anderson, J. M., *Studies in Old English Phonology* (Cambridge 1975).
Weitzman, Raymond S., *Studies in the Phonology of Asian Languages* (Scholarly Press. 1970).

ACCESSION, ak-sesh'ən, in international law, the formal act by which a state becomes a party to a treaty already in force among the original signatories. Treaties often provide for the accession of all or specified other states before a fixed date or in the indefinite future. The Kellogg-Briand Pact, signed by 15 states in 1928, provided for accession by all states, and 63 eventually became parties.

The term *adhesion* is sometimes used with the same meaning as accession but more properly with the implication that the adhering state accepts the principles of the treaty without becoming a party bound by its detailed obligations and entitled to its rights. Adhesion, therefore, implies less than accession but more than *approval,* which means that the approving state makes no objection to the conclusion of the treaty by the signatory and acceding states.

QUINCY WRIGHT
University of Virginia

ACCESSORY, ak-ses'ər-ē, in law, a person who was not the chief participant in an offense or was not present at its commission, but still is connected with it in some way. One may be an accessory before or after the fact. The English jurist Sir Matthew Hale (1609–1676) defined an accessory *before the fact* as one who, although absent at the time of the crime, did yet procure, counsel, or command another to commit it. If the procurer is present when the crime is committed, that person is not an accessory but a principal. An accessory *after the fact* is one who, knowing a felony to have been committed, receives, relieves, comforts, or assists the felon.

In high treason, there are no accessories; all are principals. In petit treason, murder, and felonies, there may be accessories, except in offenses which, by judgment of law, are sudden and unpremeditated, such as manslaughter, and cannot have any accessories before the fact. Also, in petit larceny and in all crimes under the degree of felony, there are no accessories either before or after the fact; all persons concerned therein, if guilty at all, are principals.

ACCHO. See ACRE, ISRAEL.

ACCIDENT, ak'sə-dənt, in law, a casualty or unforeseen event, usually characterized by suddenness and external force or violence. The term has no settled legal interpretation. It is applied most frequently to an unfortunate happening that causes death or personal injury or damage to or loss of property. The word sometimes carries an implication of the absence of human fault or negligence. In this sense, an accident is an occurrence that could not have been prevented by the exercise of ordinary care. In many cases, however, the term has been interpreted by the courts to mean simply an event occurring without one's foresight or expectation and thus to include happenings that involve negligence.

With the spread of compulsory auto liability insurance, some authorities have favored removing the question of negligence entirely from auto liability cases and reserving for criminal investigation the question of gross negligence. A sickness or disease is not considered an accident unless caused or aggravated by an external event occurring suddenly and unexpectedly.

ACCIDENTS AND DISASTERS. See DISASTERS.

ACCIPITER, ak-sip'ə-tər, is a genus of small and medium-sized hawks, including *Cooper's hawk,* which preys on poultry. In its plural form, Accipitres, the term is often used as a synonym for Falconiformes, an order of birds of prey that includes eagles, falcons, and vultures.

ACCIUS, ak'shi-əs, **Lucius** (c. 170 B.C.–c. 90 B.C.), was a Roman dramatist and prose writer. Also known as *Attius,* he was born in Pisaurum (Umbria). During his life he was considered one of the greatest writers of tragedies. He mainly adapted Greek dramas, but also wrote some original plays that have a Roman setting. Only fragments of his work have been preserved.

ACCLAMATION, ak-lə-mā'shən, is approval or disapproval shouted by an assembly as an expression of its judgment. Although Cicero used the word *acclamatio* to mean either approval or disapproval, in classical times the term usually connoted group applause at private or public occasions, such as marriages, theater or circus performances, or triumphs. This complimentary significance has carried over to the English and French words derived from the Latin.

The expression of applause among the Romans was often as formal as the rehearsed cheers of college undergraduates at football games, with the words similarly fixed and combined in chanting utterance. The emperor and his family on appearing at the circus, theater, or Senate were greeted with a conventional rhythmic *acclamatio.* The Augustiani, Nero's corps of young nobles, were trained in Oriental forms of acclamation under the direction of a professional music master. Acclamations might be accompanied by handkerchief waving or tossing of flowers. A victorious army gave its commander the title of *imperator* with shouts of *"Io triumphe!"* Magistrates, after their election by the Senate, were accorded popular acclamations. At Roman weddings, following the Greek custom, the bride and groom were escorted to the nuptial chamber by a torchlit procession of flute players and singers, with a chorus of youths and maidens chanting the marriage song, *"Hymen, O Hymenaee, Hymen,"* and, as the husband carried his bride over the threshold, the wedding guests shouted *"Talassio!"* (Both Hymen and Talassio were marriage deities.)

In modern political life, decisions of legislative bodies and political conventions are often ratified by acclamation. This occurs, however, only if there is no opposition, or the opposing minority is so small that it prefers to forego its privilege of putting the question to a counted vote. A vote by acclamation may come as a first vote or as the last of a series of votes in which the opposition has progressively dwindled to negligible proportions.

The handclapping applause of a theater audience, no matter how enthusiastic and prolonged, is not, strictly speaking, an acclamation, although it is often so termed. However, if applause is accompanied by spontaneous outbursts of "bravo," "hurrah," and similar words, it becomes an acclamation.

ACCLIMATIZATION, ə-klī'mə-tə-zā'shən, is the process by which an organism adjusts itself to living under climatic conditions differing from those of its native area. Acclimatization may involve only one part or function of the organism, or it may concern all of its parts and cover its entire life cycle. A plant or animal established in a foreign area, where it is able not only to develop but also to reproduce and maintain itself, generation after generation, is said to be "naturalized." This would seem to be the ultimate, though relatively rare, step in acclimatization.

Preacclimatization. It can be said that plants and animals are more or less efficiently adapted to meteorological elements at the intensities, fluctuations, frequencies, and times at which they occur within their spontaneous range of dispersal (see ADAPTATION). If conditions are closely duplicated in remote parts of the world, an organism would seem to stand a good chance of thriving under one of these climatic equivalents. Such is, indeed, the case of western European trees (for example, Norway maple and Scotch pine), so commonly planted along eastern North American highways or city streets. Some of these plants tend to leaf out earlier in the year and to retain their foliage almost as late as they would in their country of origin. They suffer little injury from the slightly different climate. However, although they leaf, flower, and fruit quite abundantly, they hardly ever manage to propagate themselves spontaneously. By contrast, reproduction in foreign surroundings is achieved widely not only by roadside herbs like mustard, noxious insects like the corn borer, and mammals like rats, but also by less injurious invaders of relatively undisturbed habitats. The North American muskrat (*Ondatra zibethica*), introduced to Czechoslovakia, is now diffused all over central Europe.

Climatic equivalence or near-equivalence, however, in no way ensures acclimatization (very much less, naturalization), and attempts at transplantation and domestication have often proved unsuccessful. The unpredictability of an organism's capacity to acclimatize to a new location is another factor to be recorded in the case of organisms excellently acclimatized, and even naturalized, under a foreign climate quite different from their native one. Thus, the success of the California coastal Monterey pine (*Pinus radiata*) and of the European deer and rabbit in New Zealand reveal the great capacity of these organisms to adjust to and thrive in another climate. The rabbit, in fact, has a much wider climatic tolerance than to the climates of Europe and New Zealand, as witnessed by its spectacular invasion of even dry and hot regions of Australia.

Directed Acclimatization. Man has utilized these relative tolerances of plants and animals in two ways: he has established them usefully under new climatic conditions by affording them protection against adverse periods or seasons, and he has bred them consciously for the purpose of achieving greater tolerance. Thus, cereals, most of them of tropical or subtropical origin, generally are stored in the form of seed and do not undergo the rigors of winter, whereas perennial pasture grasses and orchard trees have been genetically improved with respect to cold-resistance. Similarly, domestic cattle and pigs are sheltered in man-made constructions. Many races of fowl have been bred for the particularly trying conditions of both cold and tropical regions.

Evolution and Acclimatization. Response to climatic factors is only one of the many complex, interrelated features of adaptation; and it is not always readily separable from other responses. For instance, an animal may have to adapt in response to a change in climate over a period of time. But an animal may also have to adapt to a new location if it has migrated. Many species have become extinct in the face of such changes, but others have responded successfully and have maintained themselves. Viewed on a broad geological time scale, the species of oak have developed the deciduous habit in the moist-cool and cold-temperate regions, and have much reduced the size of their evergreen leaves in the dry and warm regions.

As for man, his acclimatization to the extremely dry, warm, or cold parts of the earth has been achieved through some hereditary shifts in metabolic activity and through the development of proper cultural habits of clothing and food. Studies of these habits in the Eskimo and the high Andean Indians have revealed the biological and cultural nature of the acclimatization of these groups.

PIERRE DANSEREAU, *New York Botanical Gardens*

Bibliography

Alscher, Ruth G., and Jonathan R. Cumming, eds., *Stress Responses in Plants: Adaptation and Acclimation Mechanisms*, vol. 12 of *Plant Biology* (Wiley-Liss 1990).

Heath, Donald, and David Reid Williams, *High-Altitude Medicine and Pathology*, 4th ed. (Oxford 1995).

Houston, Charles S., *High Altitude: Illness and Wellness* (ICS Bks. 1993).

Rivolier, J., et al., eds., *High Altitude Deterioration*, vol. 19 of *Medicine and Sport Science* (Karger 1985).

Ward, Michael P., et al., *High Altitude Medicine and Physiology* (Arnold/Oxford 2000).

West, John B., and Sukhamay Lahiri, eds., *High Altitude and Man* (Am. Physiological Soc. 1984).

ACCOLTI, äk-kôl′tē, **Benedetto** (1415–1464), called the Elder, Italian judge and writer. He was born into a distinguished Tuscan family in Arezzo, Italy, and became professor of jurisprudence at the University of Florence. After the death of Chancellor Giovanni Poggio Bracciolini in 1458, Accolti became chancellor of the Florentine republic. He held the post until his death in 1464.

Accolti wrote, probably with his brother Leonardo, a 3-volume history in Latin of the First Crusade. The work, published in 1532, is said to have inspired Torquato Tasso's epic poem *Jerusalem Delivered*. Accolti also wrote biographical sketches of contemporaries.

ACCOLTI, äk-kôl′tē, **Benedetto** (1497–1549), called the Younger, was an Italian ecclesiastic. A grandson of Benedetto Accolti the Elder, he succeeded his uncle Pietro as archbishop of Ravenna. Pope Clement VII, who had named him his secretary, made him a cardinal in 1527. Later accused of misgovernment, Accolti was tried and jailed by Pope Paul III, but escaped, gaining the protection of Emperor Charles V.

ACCOLTI, äk-kôl′tē, **Bernardo** (1458–1535), Italian poet and ecclesiastic. Born at Arezzo, Italy, on Sept. 11, 1458, he was the son of Benedetto Accolti the Elder. He was greatly admired as an improvisatore. Whenever he announced that he would recite his verses, shops were closed and people flocked to hear him. Eminent churchmen were always with him, and he was accompanied by a body of Swiss troops. Pope Leo X, who esteemed him highly, made him apostolic secretary, cardinal, and papal legate at Ancona. In his own day he was known as *Unico Aretino* (The Only One of Arezzo), but the fame of his works perished with him.

The style of his verses is hard, his images are forced, and his taste is marred by affectation. Best known is his comedy, *Virginia,* first performed in 1493. His other published works include some lyric poetry, epigrams, octaves, and verses in *terza rima*. He died at Rome on March 1, 1535.

ACCOLTI, äk-kôl′tē, **Francesco** (c. 1416–c. 1484), was an Italian jurist. A brother of Benedetto Accolti the Elder, he was born at Arezzo, Italy, about 1416. A distinguished lecturer on civil and common law at the University of Siena, he was a renowned humanist and a friend of Lorenzo de' Medici. He also did some verse translations, and wrote several biographies.

ACCOLTI, äk-kôl′tē, **Pietro** (1455–1532), was an Italian cardinal. He was born at Florence, Italy, in 1455. A son of Benedetto Accolti the Elder, he was appointed bishop of Ancona by Pope Julius II. In 1511 he became a cardinal, and later served as archbishop of Ravenna. He is credited with writing the famous bull, *Exsurge, Domine* (July 15, 1520), against Martin Luther. He died at Rome, Italy, on Dec. 12, 1532.

ACCOMMODATION, ə-kom-ə-dā′shən, is the process by which something is brought into adjustment with its surroundings or functions.

In biology, it is the process by which an organism becomes adapted to its environment.

In commerce, it usually denotes temporary financial assistance rendered by one merchant or bank to another. Accommodation paper includes notes or bills of exchange made, accepted, or endorsed without any consideration. While in the hands of the party to whom it is made, or for whose benefit the accommodation is given, such paper is open to the defense of lack of consideration, but when received by third parties in the usual course of business, it is governed by the same rules as other paper.

In physiology, the accommodation of the eye is the function by which objects, near or distant, may be seen distinctly. It is accomplished by the relaxing or contracting of the ciliary muscle.

In theology, in precise usage, it is the presentation of a truth not absolutely, but with some modification to suit it either to some other truth or to the person addressed. Accommodation is distinguished as *formal* and *material,* the former relating to the method of teaching, and the latter to what is taught. Formal accommodation includes teaching by parables or symbols or by progressive stages graduated to the capacity of the learner. It also commonly means the forcing of texts away from their obvious meaning to make them conform to theories derived from other sources. Material accommodation, as commonly used, means the theory that Christ and the writers of Scripture modified the truth to accommodate it to the limited understandings or to the prejudices of persons in their times.

ACCOMPANIMENT, ə-kump′ə-nē-mənt, in music, is the part of a composition that supports and is subservient to a predominating melody part. The accompaniment is often played by a secondary instrument to supply harmonic underpinning for a solo voice or instrument, although it may also contribute to the character of a musical composition as a whole.

Accompanied song can be traced as far back as the trouvères and troubadours of the 12th and

13th centuries. Accompaniment became more important in 1600, when Jacopo Peri (q.v.) and his colleagues in Rome wrote the first opera, employing vocal recitative supported by figured bass—that is, by a keyboard part in single notes, in which the harmony (indicated by numbers) was supplied by the performer.

With the development of the art song, a genre that reached its peak in the 19th century with Schubert, Schumann, Brahms, and Wolf, the accompaniment took on new significance. Schubert, in particular, drew the piano part into the drama of the song, and since then, sophisticated writers of song have tended to treat the accompaniment as an integral part of the composition.

For many years the accompanist was music's stepchild, but by the mid-20th century this attitude had changed, and schools of music taught accompanying as an independent art. The good accompanist, in addition to commanding a large repertoire, must be able to adjust to each artist with whom he works, setting the mood of a piece in the introduction, balancing his tone with the soloist, making subtle shifts in tempo when necessary, anticipating when a singer may breathe, and maintaining a steady and vital rhythm. He must, in short, engage in a solid and reliable partnership with the solo performer.

SHIRLEY FLEMING
"Musical America"

ACCOMPLICE, ə-kom′plis, one who aids or participates in the commission of a crime. The term has no universally recognized definition in law, being used in various contexts as synonymous with "accessory," "aider and abettor," or "joint principal." The word is most commonly used to describe the relationship of a witness to a defendant in criminal cases involving questions as to the weight or admissibility of evidence. For example, an accused cannot be convicted on the uncorroborated testimony of an accomplice. In order to be an accomplice, a person must himself be liable to indictment for the same offense, according to the rule generally accepted by the weight of judicial authority. The mere presence at, acquiescence in, or concealment of knowledge of the commission of a crime is not sufficient to make a person an accomplice in the eyes of the law.

ACCORAMBONI, äk-kō-räm-bô′nē, **Vittoria** (1557–1585), an Italian lady famous for her beauty. She was born at Gubbio, Italy, on Feb. 15, 1557. Her contemporaries thought of her as one of the most fascinating Italian women of the time. Paolo Giordano Orsini, duke of Bracciano, who was believed to have murdered his wife, sought to marry Vittoria, but her father gave her to Francesco Peretti, nephew of Cardinal Montalto. Peretti was assassinated, and Vittoria fled to Bracciano, whom she married secretly in 1581 and publicly in 1583.

When Montalto became pope as Sixtus V in 1585, the couple took refuge in Venetian territory. After a few months' residence at Salo on Lake Garda, the duke died, leaving Vittoria almost all his great fortune. An incensed relative of his, Ludovico Orsini, had her murdered on Dec. 22, 1585, at Padua, where she had moved.

The commonly accepted facts of Vittoria's life are related in Domenico Gnoli's *Vittoria Accoramboni* (Florence 1870). This account places her on the level of other passionate, unscrupulous women of the Renaissance. Countess Evelyn Martinengo-Cesaresco reexamined the evidence in "Vittoria Accoramboni," published in *Lombard Studies* (London 1902) and found her innocent of complicity in crime. Her story has been used in literature, including John Webster's play *The White Devil or Vittoria Corombona* (1612) and Ludwig Tieck's *Vittoria Accoramboni* (1840).

ACCORD AND SATISFACTION, a means of discharging a debt or other legal obligation, such as a tort claim, by the payment of money or the delivery of property, in accordance with terms other than those originally agreed upon by the parties to a transaction. This method of satisfying a debt is approximately equivalent to the settlement of a claim by *compromise;* but technically the two can be differentiated, because a compromise must be based on a claim which is disputed, while an accord and satisfaction may arise out of an undisputed claim. The *accord* involved in an accord and satisfaction is an agreement between the parties, and the *satisfaction* is the carrying out of this agreement. The two elements often occur as part of the same transaction; for example, the cashing or deposit by a creditor of his debtor's check inscribed "in full payment." When an amount is thus tendered with the clear expression of an intention to make payment in full, the payee, as a general rule, must either reject it entirely or accept it subject to the stated condition. He cannot, without the consent of the debtor, accept such a conditional tender and apply it in part payment.

ACCORDION, ə-kord′ē-ən, a portable musical instrument of the reed-wind variety. It is box-shaped and consists of a bellows with a framework attached to each end. At the player's right is the frame that supports the melody keyboard, with from 5 to 50 keys. At his left is the frame that has the grip for operating the bellows and also has the keys for playing bass notes and full chords. As the player works the bellows, he depresses the keys to open the valves and admit air to the free reeds.

Some bass keyboards now have as many as 120 buttons, complexly arranged. When a piano keyboard is substituted for buttons on the right, the instrument is known as a *piano accordion.*

The principle of the accordion was long known in China, but the earliest accordions in the Western world were made by C. Friedrich Buschmann in Berlin (1822) and Cyril Demian in Vienna (1829). See CONCERTINA.

Student Accordion

M. HOHNER, INC.

Treble Part
(Melody, Right Hand)

Bass Part
(Chords, Left Hand)

Bellows

Piano Keys

Button Keys

ACCOUNTANTS rely on complex data-processing and storage systems in collecting, interpreting, and controlling data.

INTERNATIONAL BUSINESS MACHINES CORP.

ACCOUNTING AND BOOKKEEPING, ə-kount′ing, book′kē-ping.

Accounting is the art of analyzing and interpreting economic data. Knowingly or unknowingly, every business and every individual uses accounting in some form. Both must evaluate financial information—for example, is the bank account large enough to meet next month's needs?—and communicate the result to others. In business, accounting pervades every activity and serves as an indispensable management tool.

Accounting is generally agreed to be an art rather than a science. However, it is usually conceded that many scientific methods are, and should be, used in accounting. In contrast, bookkeeping is limited to the recording, classifying, and summarizing of financial data according to an established plan.

Accounting covers a broader area than bookkeeping, but no sharp line of distinction can be drawn between the two. Both cover recording, classifying, and summarizing functions, but accounting also involves the analysis and interpretation of data. Bookkeeping is limited to dealing with transactions having a financial aspect. Under a broad definition, accounting may become involved in transactions having no immediate financial aspect.

Accounting Defined. Probably the most authoritative and widely used definition of accounting is that formulated in 1941 by the American Institute of Accountants, now the American Institute of Certified Public Accountants (AICPA). Published in Accounting Terminology Bulletin No. 1, it reads: "Accounting is the art of record-

ing, classifying, and summarizing in a significant manner and in terms of money, transactions and events which are, in part at least, of a financial character, and interpreting the results thereof."

Because the concept of the area of accounting has widened since the 1940's, another definition has become widespread: Accounting is the determination, analysis, interpretation, and communication of economic data.

Mechanically, accounting involves the development of methods of recording (systems and procedures), internal control, and testing methods, as well as reporting.

Bookkeeping Defined. Bookkeeping is the act or method of recording business transactions of a financial nature in a systematic and convenient form. The purpose of bookkeeping is not only to provide a record of a transaction at the time when it occurred and the amount involved in terms of money, but also to record all financial transactions of a firm in such a manner that its financial position at a given time and the amount of profit or loss for a stated period can be determined.

The distinction between accounting and bookkeeping may be considered to be one of degree, with some overlap, rather than one of complete difference of activity. For example, both accountants and bookkeepers may record transactions in a convenient and systematic manner, and both may set up simple accounting systems. However, it is generally held that the establishment of an accounting system is an accounting function and that the recording of transactions in accordance with an established system is a bookkeeping function. This suggests that the accountant, using professional knowledge and theory, determines how transactions should be recorded; and that the bookkeeper follows the accountant's instructions and records routine transactions mechanically. The following distinctions are often drawn: (1) the accountant determines how and what should be done, the bookkeeper does it; and (2) accounting begins where bookkeeping leaves off.

Society confers higher status to the profession of accounting than to bookkeeping. For this reason, many persons performing bookkeeping functions are granted the title of accountant.

Modern Concept of Accounting. Accounting is an art, not a science in the same sense as the physical sciences. Accounting is concerned with business transactions brought about by human beings. Because all human beings do not react to a given stimulus in the same way, accounting "laws" cannot be established with the same degree of inflexibility as can laws of physics or chemistry. Scientific methods developed in mathematics and statistics certainly may be used in analyzing and evaluating economic data. Nevertheless, "art" is important in determining which alternative methods or procedures to apply, and in the effective interpretation and presentation of facts.

Accounting often is referred to as a tool of management. A tool may be ignored at the discretion of the user, but the accounting function cannot be ignored, for it pervades all business activity. It is better, therefore, for management to consider accounting as a business control device that will aid in making better decisions.

1. Accounting as a Control Device

Understanding is a prerequisite of the ability to control a situation. It is in this respect that accounting is important as a control device. Accounting provides the basis for making wise decisions through the understanding that is brought about by the proper recording, summarizing, analyzing, and interpreting of relevant economic data.

The primary function of accounting is to serve society. Accounting accomplishes this by arraying and evaluating economic data and by communicating the results to the appropriate groups. Two basic questions asked by society are: (1) What is the financial position of the firm under consideration? (2) How much profit or loss did the firm have during a particular period? These questions can be answered by the preparation of general-purpose statements, such as balance sheets and income statements. However, various groups desire additional or more detailed information, or want especially prepared information. Such information may be provided through special-purpose statements, such as inventory analyses and analyses of receivables; or, perhaps, only after special studies have been made by the accountant.

From the point of view of accounting, society can be broken down into three major groups: management, public, and government.

Management. Management is composed of all persons in a firm who are charged with the responsibility of administering the firm's activities. Management needs to have readily available great masses of detailed information, in addition to general-purpose statements that are prepared periodically.

Public. From the point of view of a business concern, the "public" consists of employees, creditors (and potential creditors), and investors (and potential investors). The public does not need the detailed information required by management, because it does not have to make the decisions that confront management. Employee groups do not need to know such details as which items were most profitable, which were least profitable, or why some activities were profitable while others were not, for employees do not decide which items to produce or how to produce or market them. However, so that employees can judge the fairness of their wages or negotiate new wage scales intelligently, they must have accounting information on the profitableness of the firm. The general-purpose

statement will usually provide adequate information for this purpose.

Creditors and potential creditors are interested in the safety of advances or loans and the promptness with which repayments may be expected. This can be determined only by recourse to accounting data. In addition to the general-purpose statements, or instead of them, this group may require special-purpose reports providing more detailed accounting information on such things as the state and composition of inventories, the adequacy of working capital, the use to which funds will be placed, the quality of security provided, or the ability to repay on schedule.

Investors are the owners or potential owners of a firm. They are induced to invest their funds because of expected profitable returns in the form of dividends or a future profitable sale of their holdings. Only through intelligent use of accounting data can wise investment decisions be made. This group is interested in a firm's financial stability and long-run profitableness.

Government. Many different branches of government at the federal, state, and local levels are interested in the activities of a firm. Broadly speaking, government interest in a business stems from the needs for revenue and control. Revenue may be raised by taxes levied on income, property, sales, or transactions. However, before any taxes can be paid, the tax base must be developed from accounting data.

Governmental control is exercised for the benefit of society as a whole. Control may take the form of requiring certain acts—for example, compelling a public utility to provide service to all subscribers according to an established rate schedule; or it may prohibit certain acts, such as the sale of liquor to minors. To exercise control over business firms, governmental divisions and agencies need detailed information about them. Often this information must be provided in a form prescribed by law or custom, as in special reports required by the Internal Revenue Service, the Interstate Commerce Commission, or the Securities and Exchange Commission.

At one time a firm caused suspicion if it kept two sets of records. Today it is quite common and proper for a firm to have two sets of records so that its profits and financial position may be established according to generally accepted accounting principles and, at the same time, data may be provided in the manner requested by governmental agencies. For example, for reasons of equity and practicality the rules for establishing taxable income for federal income tax may vary substantially from those for establishing accounting income.

2. Bases of Accounting

One of the prerequisites of a profession is that it have an established body of knowledge and basic and guiding tenets. This is true of accounting. It has a vast number of such tenets, referred to by such terms as concepts, principles, conventions, and standards. Unfortunately, the distinctions or similarities are not always clear.

Concepts. Concepts are general ideas that help to standardize a function. Concepts are basic to the development of accounting theory, since they are necessary assumptions or conditions upon which accounting principles are based. They may be referred to also as *axioms* or *postulates*. The validity of concepts is considered to be self-evident, or assumed, even though they may not be provable. Thus, with certain facts or conditions taken for granted, the groundwork is laid for further development of accounting theory within preestablished limits. Concepts provide a basis on which to develop principles.

Principles. Principles are propositions that are deemed to be controlling in a particular situation. To be effective, they must have the approval and acceptance of the professional group (accountants). A principle is assumed to be the best choice of alternative courses leading to desired ends. If a principle is accepted without proof, it takes on the characteristics of a concept.

Accounting principles are laws or rules controlling the handling of economic data. The laws are man-made and thus may be changed when a generally recognized need arises. For example, the principle of retirement accounting for fixed assets has given way to depreciation accounting for them, and the principle of pricing inventory on a first-in, first-out basis has lost ground to the principle of pricing inventories on a last-in, first-out basis.

Conventions. Conventions are general guides to procedure based on custom or agreement. A convention is a rule that, by common consent of the group involved (accountants), may be used to reach an acceptable solution to a given situation or problem. Alternate conventions may exist side by side. For example, there are a number of equally logical and equally valid ways of taking depreciation.

Standards. Standards are measures, models, or goals. A standard may be established by custom or consent, by scientific or. professional groups, or by law, usually after research and experimentation. Standards may be changed from time to time as warranted by changes in conditions or in the body of knowledge.

3. Basic Concepts

Accountants agree that for the growth and development of accounting theory it is necessary to have a basic framework on which to build. This foundation is the group of concepts or postulates generally accepted at face value. There is some lack of agreement as to whether some statements are concepts to be accepted without proof, or conventions to be used as general guides, or principles offering the best of alternate choices under specific circumstances. It is agreed that concepts are more basic in the development of accounting theory than are conventions and principles. However, the difference is not so great that the lack of agreement will cause great harm. The development of accounting theory is not seriously hindered because some accountants consider consistency and conservatism to be conventions while others consider them to be concepts.

Because of the lack of agreement as to the classification of some statements, it would be impractical to list all accounting concepts. However, four of the more generally recognized concepts are: "going concern," "business entity," "dollar as a unit of measure," and "stability of the dollar."

Going Concern. It is assumed that the economic unit under consideration will ·continue indefinitely. Therefore, in preparing the usual accounting statements for a firm, no consideration is given to possible liquidation values of assets or the effect that such consideration might have on profits. Under this concept, only such portions of costs as are allocable to current activities are charged against current income. This is often referred to as the continuity concept.

Business Entity. Before an accounting system can be developed for a particular firm, the scope and identity of the firm must be established. If such limits or boundaries were not established, the resulting confusion would make it impossible to establish a usable accounting system. Are the owners to be considered a part of the business? Questions such as this must be answered before an accounting system can be established.

The firm is generally considered to be an entity in its own right, separate and distinct from the owners or those who provide the funds for it. In some cases, a single proprietor separates his personal activities from his business activities; in other cases, he considers them as a single unit. In corporations it is common to find consideration given to the business or economic entity concept, in that a corporation owning one or more subsidiaries which are separate legal entities prepares consolidated statements for the entire group as if all formed a single entity. Also, a corporation is considered to be a business unit entirely separate from its owners.

Dollar as a Unit of Measure. This broad concept encompasses several other equally important but more limited concepts such as *cost concept, costs attach concept,* and the *matching of expenses and revenue concept.*

When accounting was defined in such a way as to restrict it to business transactions having a financial aspect, it was correct to state that the only common unit of measure was a unit of money—in the United States, the dollar. With the broadened concept of accounting have come measures available for special purposes, such as man-hours or units of material, although the most common measure is still the dollar. For financial accounting, the dollar remains the only acceptable measure.

Accountants are still firmly committed to a cost basis. Under the *cost concept* assets are valued at their original cost less proper deductions, rather than evaluated on arbitrary bases. The cost basis has the advantage of being objective and impersonal, whereas other methods, such as appraisals, tend to be subjective.

The *costs attach concept* is a further development of the cost concept. The cost of various units may be combined or merged to obtain the cost of a larger or more complex unit. This is especially evident in the production of inventory items where costs of various items of raw material, semi-finished parts or components, direct labor, and overhead are combined to establish the cost of the unit of finished goods.

The *matching of expenses and revenue concept* (often referred to as matching of costs and revenue) is basic to the periodic determination of income for a going concern. The determination of periodic income is being granted increased importance in accounting and financial circles. It is indicated by the shift in emphasis from the balance sheet to the income statement. The determination of the profitability of a firm is of utmost importance to creditors, owners, and management; and profit can be determined fairly only by the proper matching of periodic expenses with periodic revenue. The problem of matching expenses and revenue is basically one of discovering suitable bases of association. Which costs should be considered to have expired in the current period and which should be carried forward to be "expensed" in future periods? Which revenues should be considered actually earned in the current period and which should be deferred and recognized as earned in future periods?

Stability of the Dollar. The dollar is the generally accepted unit of measure in accounting. To be useful, a unit of measure must be constant. This is true whether measures refer to weight, length, or value. Accounting follows the basic concept that the value of a dollar remains constant while other things may change in value in relation to a dollar. Accountants recognize that in times of inflation the reverse may be true; that is, the value of nonmoney items may remain constant while the value of a dollar changes. However, the accounting profession generally feels that although there are evident imperfections in the stability of the dollar concept, it is so much better than any suggested alternative that it should be maintained.

In times of inflation or deflation, pressures increase for the adjustment of historical cost to reflect changes in the price level. The American Institute of Certified Public Accountants and the American Accounting Association do not recommend departure from the cost basis of accounting. However, they suggest the use of supplementary data to show the effect of price-level changes.

4. Types of Accounting

The term "accounting" encompasses many different types of accounting based on the group or groups served.

Private or Industrial Accounting. Accounting activity confined to a single firm is called private or industrial accounting. A private accountant makes his skills and services available to a single employer for a salary on an employer-employee basis. Where the employer-employee basis exists, the accounting service and the accountant are termed private, even though the employer is a public corporation.

Public Accounting. Accounting service offered to the general public by a public accountant is called public accounting. An accountant is said to be public rather than private when there is a practitioner-client relationship rather than an employer-employee relationship. Public accounting usually is considered to be more professional than private accounting, and the public accounting done by a certified public accountant (CPA) is considered to be of the highest professional caliber.

Public accounting services are provided by noncertified as well as certified accountants, by single practitioners, and by partnerships ranging in size from two to many hundreds of members. The firms may be local, national, or international in scope. Firms that are international in scope, however, also are referred to as "national."

Governmental Accounting. Accounting for a branch or unit of government at any level, such as federal, state, or local, is called governmental accounting. The object of the government units is to provide services rather than to make prof-

NATIONAL CASH REGISTER CO.

ELECTRONIC COMPUTER systems are designed so that more data-processing units can be added as required.

its. Governmental accounting has much in common with conventional accounting methods: both use the double-entry system of accounting; both use journals and ledgers. Because the profit motive is absent in typical government units and hence is not available as a means of measuring efficiency, other controls must be developed. Thus, special fund accounting is used in order to enhance control. Some divisions or agencies tend to adopt conventional accounting methods, especially for cost determination purposes. Just as a business entity may use the services of both private and public accountants, so may a governmental unit.

Fiduciary Accounting. Fiduciary has been defined as a position of trust or confidence. Fiduciary accounting therefore is the keeping of records and the preparation of reports by a trustee, adminstrator, executor, or anyone in a position of trust. This may be done by authorization of, or under the jurisdiction of, a court of law. It is necessary for a fiduciary accountant to seek out and to control all property subject to the estate or trust. The laws of the particular state having jurisdiction must be followed. The courts having jurisdiction of estates and trusts are referred to in various states as orphan's courts, probate courts, or surrogate's courts. In fiduciary accounting, the concept of proprietorship that is common in the usual types of accounting is absent or greatly modified. The proprietary function is replaced by authority and responsibility delegated to a third party.

National Income Accounting. What is known as either national income accounting or social accounting is a special type using an economic or social concept in establishing the accounting unit rather than the usual business entity concept. It provides an estimate of the nation's annual purchasing power. A related term is "gross national product," which covers the total market value of all production within the nation for a given period of time, usually a calendar year. Because of an increasing interest on the part of the United States government in the welfare of its citizens, the Department of Commerce has been preparing reports on national production since 1932.

BANK COMPUTERS process immense amounts of data. This system handles work from nearly 100 branch offices.

Integrated Data Processing (IDP). IDP is a broad term cutting across many types of accounting business and economic activities. It has come into prominence because of the widespread use of electronic computers that collect, analyze, and disseminate great masses of information in an amazingly short time. Although electronic computers are used by scientists, engineers, economists, and others, as well as by accountants, a discussion of accounting requires some mention of electronic computers. The term "electronic data processing" (EDP) refers to the act of processing data by electronic computers. Thus EDP is similar to, although not identical with, IDP. Most of the integration of large amounts of data is now being done electronically.

5. Areas of Accounting

Financial or General Accounting. Financial or general accounting, which sometimes is called *administrative accounting*, is the accounting for assets, liabilities, and ownership interest, as well as for revenues and expenses. One end toward which financial accounting is directed is the preparation of financial statements—the balance sheet, the income statement, perhaps a statement of retained earnings, and, more recently, a funds statement or a cash flow statement. These are prepared in general terms suitable for presentation to owners (stockholders), creditors, and the general public. They are also of interest to management, although management needs more detailed and more frequent information that can only be obtained from special reports. Some special reports may be prepared by the general accountants; others may be prepared by accountants in specialized areas such as cost or taxes.

Cost Accounting. Cost accounting deals with the recording, classifying, summarizing, allocating, analyzing, and reporting of costs in a meaningful manner. The systems and procedures of cost accounting must be coordinated closely with the financial accounting systems and procedures. In many ways cost accounting is an extension or refinement of financial accounting. Matters dealt with in general terms in financial accounting are analyzed in detail in cost accounting so that cost determination, identification, and control can be improved. Some cost systems are not "tied in" with the financial accounting system; however, to be most effective they should be so handled.

It is sometimes said that an effective financial accounting system is a prerequisite to a good cost system. However, there is some interdependence between these systems in that financial accounting often relies on cost accounting for certain important data. The total amount of costs must be the same whether costs are reported as financial accounting data or as cost accounting data. Usually the detailed and analytical information presented by the cost accounting department is given only in summary form by the financial accounting department. Financial accounting deals with totals. Cost accounting analyzes costs by nature of the components, such as direct material, direct labor, and overhead, or on the basis of cost accumulation by territory, salesman, nature of sale, branch, department, cost center, or unit.

In contrast to financial accounting, which is designed primarily to meet the needs of groups outside the particular firm, cost accounting is designed primarily to meet the needs of groups inside the firm—that is, management. The primary functions of cost accounting are to provide bases for inventory valuations, budgets, and special cost investigations, and for cost analysis, cost comparisons, cost planning, and cost control.

Managerial Accounting. Sometimes referred to as *management accounting*, managerial accounting is a term used to encompass that broad functional aspect of accounting designed to aid management in making wise decisions. Managerial accounting cuts across such areas as cost accounting, budgeting, internal auditing, and financial accounting to provide the various levels of management with pertinent data. An important function of management accounting is to provide frequent, repetitive reports dealing with performance and efficiency. Such reports are often expressed in quantities as well as in dollars. Managerial accounting is a broader concept than cost accounting. It not only reports costs but also uses them—as well as data from various economic and statistical sources—to assist management in planning possible alternate courses of action.

Auditing. Auditing deals with the independent examination of original business documents to establish their authenticity and accuracy, as well as the independent review of accounting systems and procedures required to pass judgment on the fairness of the records or statements.

When an audit is conducted by a professional public accountant—a third party—it is said to be an external audit. Such an audit is made primarily for the benefit of stockholders, creditors, and the general public. When an audit is conducted by employees of the firm, it is said to be an internal audit. To be of value, such an audit must be conducted as an independent staff function. Internal audits are done primarily to assist management.

Both the external and internal auditors are

interested in the accuracy of documents. The external auditor primarily is interested in operating procedures only to the extent necessary to be assured of the fairness of the statement on which an opinion is to be issued. However, the internal auditor is interested in determining how closely company polices have been followed. The internal auditor should be alert to detect weaknesses in the system and should suggest possible improvements when he discovers such weaknesses.

Historically, auditing was the main function of public accountants, and it still is. But in recent times other areas—such as systems work, tax work, and, most recently, management services—are claiming greater portions of the public accountant's time and efforts.

Systems. The design and installation of systems was a separate area of accounting at one time. Now it is a part of management services in many large firms. Systems work involves the designing and installation of accounting forms, including journals and ledgers and a chart of accounts, as well as methods of internal check and control. An indication of the type, form, and frequency of reports is also a part of the complete system design.

Taxes. Taxes are compulsory assessments levied by the government against the income or wealth, real or personal, of a person or business for the benefit of the government. Taxes should not be confused with license charges or other similar assessments for special privileges or benefits. Taxes take many different forms, but by far the most important and complex is the tax on income. It is in this area that the tax accountant is most important.

An income tax is self-assessed—that is, the taxpayer (or someone on his behalf) establishes the tax base, applies the proper rate or rates, and determines the amount of tax. Income determination is an accounting problem, and even though the calculation of "accounting" income and "taxable" income are not always the same, it is well to start with "accounting" income and make the necessary adjustments to this conventional income figure in arriving at the "taxable" income.

Budgeting. Budgeting involves a plan of operations. For general purposes, a brief but useful definition is that a budget is a plan of action, a "blueprint." For accounting purposes, a budget is a formalized written plan setting forth, in financial terms, the projected activities of the firm for a definite period of time. Historically, a budget was a document prepared in financial terms for a governmental unit or agency in which anticipated revenues were matched against anticipated expenditures of a given fiscal period.

The term "budget" may refer to the complete or over-all plan for the entity, in effect a master budget, or it may refer to subsidiary or partial budgets such as for sales or for materials. In the final analysis the various subsidiary budgets and the master budget may be expressed in common terms—money. However, for some purposes, the budgets also may be expressed in other terms. For example, an operating foreman is more concerned about the quantity of material consumed and the number of hours of labor used than in the costs incurred, because he is responsible for quantities and time used rather than prices and rates paid. The foreman would like a budget prepared in such a way as to show budgeted quantities of material and time. Budgeting involves three functions: planning, coordinating, and controlling. To obtain the greatest benefit, all three must be used. By definition, a plan need not be in writing; however, for the sake of clarity and analysis, as well as permanence, it is essential to reduce the budget to written form.

Management Services. The management services area, also referred to by such terms as administrative services and specialized services, is probably the fastest growing among the many activities carried on by public accountants. Most large accounting firms now have a separate department specializing in managerial activities, just as they have an audit department and a tax department.

Although public accounting was well established in the United States at a much earlier date, it was not until after World War I that public accountants were encouraged to offer management consulting services. It is a logical development, however, for no other outsider would be as intimately acquainted with a firm's problems as its accountants. After World War II the management services departments developed at a rapid rate. This was due in large measure to greater pressures on business because of the increased size and complexity of the business operation, the "profit squeeze" and, especially, the advent of the electronic computer.

The management services department of a large public accounting firm should have on its staff many different kinds of specialists, such as industrial engineers, electrical engineers, industrial psychologists, and mathematicians. In many cases these men are not certified public accountants.

An important and glamorous activity of such a department is operations research ("OR"), or management science. This is a generic term and as such involves the operations of the firm as a whole. OR involves the determination of the best possible uses of labor, material, and plant. Usually OR programs are conducted by the use of models, especially mathematical models. Linear programming may also be used. Many complex mathematical problems can be solved efficiently only by use of electronic computers. Thus the need arises for programmers, mathematicians, and engineers.

6. Accounting Terminology

The professions of medicine and law have developed professional vocabularies by creating special terms with special meanings. This has not been the case with accounting. Accounting has taken general terms and assigned to them special or restricted meanings. This has caused considerable confusion for nonaccountants in the reading of accounting reports. A few of the terms which most frequently cause trouble are discussed in this section.

Reserve. In a general nonaccounting definition, a reserve is a supply held for future use, or something set apart for a special purpose. In accounting the term has been used in several different ways: to indicate a deduction from an asset (a contra asset account); a liability, the exact amount of which is undetermined; or an earmarked portion of retained earnings. Sometimes it even indicates a separate group of accounts on the balance sheet. In an effort to reduce confusion, the AICPA recommends that the term "reserve" be restricted to net worth accounts.

Surplus. Surplus is defined in a general non-accounting sense as an excess of what is needed, an overflow. In accounting it refers to the stockholders' equity in a corporation in excess of the par or stated value of the capital stock. This equity may represent value paid into the corporation by the stockholder (paid-in surplus); earnings retained in the corporation (earned surplus); or any increase in asset values resulting from an appraisal (appraisal surplus). The AICPA has recommended that the use of the term "surplus" be discontinued, and the recommendation is now generally followed. "Retained earnings" or similar terms have replaced earned surplus. "Paid-in surplus" has become "contributed capital." And "appraisal surplus" has been dropped in favor of "appreciation of fixed assets."

Cash Basis. The cash basis of keeping accounts is one whereby revenue is recognized when received and expenses are recognized when paid and are recorded as such, regardless of when the revenue was earned or when the expenses were incurred. The greatest advantage of the cash basis of accounting is its simplicity.

Accrual Accounting. The accrual accounting basis is one in which revenue is recognized and recorded when earned rather than when received, and in which expenses are recognized when incurred rather than when they are paid or the liability for payment is established. This basis provides for a more accurate matching of revenue and expense, period by period. It is the basis generally used by all but the smallest of business firms.

Real Account. A real account is one of that group of ledger accounts that is balanced rather than closed at the end of each fiscal period. The balance is carried forward to the succeeding period. This practice gives a particular account the characteristic of continuing through a series of periods, and for this reason it is often referred to as a "permanent account." Real accounts are often defined as balance sheet accounts, since only accounts from this group appear on the balance sheet. Asset, liability, and net worth accounts, as well as the contra (opposed) accounts to each of the three groups, are real accounts.

Nominal Account. A nominal account is one of that group of accounts which are regularly closed rather than balanced at the end of each fiscal period. To close such an account, the difference between the debits and credits must be determined. That amount is then added to the smaller side of the account and to the opposite side of another nominal account, "Income and Expense Summary," which in turn is closed into a real account, "Retained Earnings." Nominal accounts are so designated because they are opened by the accountant at the beginning of each fiscal period and closed by him at the end of each period for his convenience; therefore, they are said to exist in name only. A more descriptive—though less frequently used—name for this group of accounts is "Temporary Accounts," in that such accounts exist only for one period, although they may be reopened each period. These are revenue and expense accounts, and they appear on the income statement.

Contra Account. As the general definition of the term "contra" implies, a contra account is one that is opposite to, or opposed to, another account. Thus, under the concept of debits and credits, the balance of the contra (or secondary) account is deducted from the main (or primary) account.

Book Value. Book value is the amount at which an item is carried on the books of account. The term may be applied to assets, liabilities, and net worth. The book value of an asset is the cost price, or amount paid, plus additional costs incurred in putting the asset in usable condition, less such recognized decreases in value as accumulated depreciation in the case of tangible fixed assets, or allowance for loss on bad debts in the case of accounts receivable. Book value is cost oriented and should not be confused with market value or price-level-adjusted values. The book value of capital stock is determined by dividing the net worth applicable to a given class of stock by the number of shares of that class outstanding. In cases where there is only one class of stock outstanding, the book value can be determined by dividing net assets (assets minus liabilities) by the number of shares that are outstanding.

Capital Stock. Capital stock represents units of residual ownership in a corporation. To understand the accounting concept of the term, the general meaning of the two words should be considered. While there are many definitions of each word, the one closest to accounting concepts may be as follows: *Capital* is funds or wealth available in a firm for use in producing more wealth. *Stock* is a store or supply which may be drawn upon freely or at will. Thus, in nontechnical language, capital stock is a supply of wealth that may be used freely by the owners of the firm in the production of more wealth. In technical terms, capital stock does not represent the supply of wealth itself, but rather the undivided ownership of the wealth. The division of the ownership is made possible by issuing "shares" of capital stock.

There are two major classes of capital stock: *common* and *preferred*. Preferred stock is like common stock, except that it may have been granted certain privileges over the common in return for surrendering certain rights. One of the privileges most frequently granted preferred stock is a preference as to dividends—that is, preferred stock receives a stipulated dividend before the common stock receives any. One of the rights most frequently surrendered by preferred stock is the right to share in management—that is, the right to vote.

Stock may have a par value, a value set forth on its face. If no such amount is shown, the stock is said to be no par. Stated value stock is no-par stock to which a value has been assigned.

Inventory. In general terms, an inventory is an itemized list or schedule of goods owned, together with an indication of their value, such as the inventory of goods in an estate or trust. In accounting, the usual use of the term is more restrictive: not all goods owned are included, but only certain types of goods reserved for certain use. Items not yet expensed or capitalized are includable in the inventory. Goods classified as current assets, ultimately to be consumed or sold in the regular operations of the business, are included in the inventory. In accounting, inventory refers both to the list of items and to the items themselves. Typical classifications of inventory items are: raw material, work in process, finished goods, and supplies, in a manufacturing firm; and merchandise, in a sales organization.

Cost vs. Expense. These terms often are used interchangeably, sometimes because the differences are not recognized and sometimes through carelessness or custom.

Cost may be defined, for general purposes, as the amount paid or to be paid for anything, an outlay. For accounting purposes, cost and its measurement must be delimited more precisely. Cost is the "forgoing," the sacrifice, or the giving of one thing for something else. It is the exchange of cash or other assets or services or capital stock, or the incurrence of a liability in exchange for an asset, a service, or the reduction of a liability, each being measured by a market value in monetary terms.

Expense can be defined most accurately and briefly as an expired cost. However, the value of goods or merchandise sold is referred to universally as a "cost" rather than an "expense." Strictly speaking, a cost was incurred when the goods were acquired, and it became an expense when they were sold. It is common also to speak of "matching revenue and costs"; technically, it would be better to refer to "matching revenue and expenses." The amount paid or agreed to be paid for a fixed asset represents its cost. The amount of depreciation charged off period by period represents an expense.

Expenditure. An expenditure is the disbursement of cash, the transfer of other property, the incurring of a liability, or the issuing of capital stock to acquire other goods or services or to settle a loss.

An expenditure occurs when goods are bought; an expense is incurred when the goods are consumed or sold.

7. Development of Accounting

Accounting is often referred to as one of the oldest professions; equally often it is referred to as one of the newest and most rapidly growing professions. This difference stems largely from the fact that there are broad and narrow definitions and concepts of accounting.

When accounting is considered in broad general terms as the recording and communication of financial or economic data, it is indeed as old as civilization. When accounting is considered in a truly professional sense, as a highly developed and systematized method of collecting, interpreting, and controlling economic data by members of a recognized profession, then it is very new.

Early History. There is historical evidence that taxes were levied and collected in the Babylonian Empire as early as 4500 B.C. Clay tablets were used for recording temple receipts and disbursements as early as 2300 B.C. An improved method of record keeping was developed in Egypt by 400 B.C. with the discovery of papyrus (paper) and *calamus* (pen).

A major step forward in numeration occurred in 850 A.D. with the development of the decimal system by the Arabs. The earliest known use of a complete double-entry bookkeeping system was in Genoa in 1340.

Accounting as it exists today may well have had its beginnings in Italy in the early part of the 15th century. As early as 1431 the Medici family used a complex set of books consisting of a cash book, a stock book, a wage book, and a book of income and outgo.

In 1494, Luca Pacioli, an Italian mathematician and Franciscan monk, published *Summa de arithmetica, geometria, proportioni et proportionalità,* a treatise containing a section on record keeping. It is the first printed book on accounting. For the next 100 to 200 years European writers followed or perhaps paraphrased Pacioli's writing. In 1543 an English bookkeeper, Hugh Oldcastle, wrote a treatise on accounting, and in 1581 the first accounting association was formed in Italy. It appears that double-entry bookkeeping originated in Italy during the Renaissance, which included an awakening of an interest in trade. The expanding trade, especially through joint ventures involving long sea voyages, required large investments. Investors insisted on records being kept of their investments in these enterprises.

The Industrial Revolution and the resulting complexities of business and finance gave impetus to accounting in the British Isles as well as in Europe. Late in the 18th century a directory of Edinburgh listed seven "accountants." The first professional restriction on the public practice of accounting occurred in Italy in 1790 when the government recognized "chartered" accountants as the only accountants qualified to act as public accountants.

In the middle of the 19th century Scotland recognized "chartered accountants." England recognized the title by 1880, and the first qualifying examination in England was given in 1882. New York was the first state in the United States to regulate public accounting. In 1896 the state legislature provided for the granting of the title "Certified Public Accountant" (CPA) upon the accountant's passing a professional examination administered by New York University. Pennsylvania, in 1899, became the second state to regulate accounting. By 1923 all 48 states and the District of Columbia had laws providing for the control of public accounting and the issuing of CPA certificates.

Recent History and Growth. The constantly increasing size of business firms has been accompanied by an increased need on the part of government, creditors, investors, employees, and even the general public, for increased economic data properly summarized and interpreted. This has created a growing need for accountants. The passage of the federal income tax law in 1913 gave a great stimulus to accounting in the United States. War contracts during two world wars, as well as during various peacekeeping periods, created a need for profit and cost control for the protection of the public. This required the services of skilled accountants.

In 1900 there were fewer than 300 CPA's in the United States. In 1955 there were 52,600 CPA's, and by the mid–1960's the number had increased to 92,000.

The growth of a profession must be measured not only by the number of its members but also by the scope and quality of professional activities. Since the mid–19th century the accounting function has grown from the simple reporting of history to complex advising on all types of business decisions. Accountants are now active in preparing budgets. They are consulted by business executives on tax and financial matters. They are also consulted on problems which as recently as 1958 were considered to be outside the province of accounting, such as production planning and control and personnel problems.

8. Accounting as a Profession

A profession may be defined briefly as an occupation that requires a liberal education and places emphasis on mental rather than manual activity. The "three learned professions" have been, historically, theology, medicine, and law. More recently, engineering has qualified as a learned profession. The latest contender for such status is accounting.

There are at least four characteristics essential to a true profession. They are: a recognized body of knowledge, an established code of ethics, certification or organized control of the group by itself, and professional schools.

A look at the vast amount of accounting literature or a review of the many college curriculums in accounting verifies the existence of an adequate body of accounting knowledge. The American Institute of Certified Public Accountants for many years has been active in formulating a code of ethics, and in enforcing adherence to the code by its members. All certified public accountants are controlled by the group, in that the group is instrumental in having each state pass laws regulating the practice of public accounting.

It is in the area of professional schools that accounting's claim to professional status is weakest. There are no separate professional schools of accounting as there are of theology, medicine, law, and engineering. However, the accounting department is typically one of the larger departments in collegiate schools of business. There is now some pressure for the formation of separate schools of accounting at the college level.

As yet, there are no such schools. However, some business schools are granting special degrees in accounting, such as Bachelor of Accounting and Master of Accounting, instead of the usual Bachelor or Master of Business Administration. It is important to note that the Bachelor and Master of Accounting degrees are conferred by business schools, not by professional schools of accounting. A step toward achieving greater professional status would be to establish professional schools of accounting.

Accounting Groups. A profession may be judged by the number, size, quality, and perhaps the age of its professional groups or organizations. A few of the many accounting organizations are:

American Accounting Association. The AAA was organized in Columbus, Ohio, in 1916 as the American Association of University Instructors in Accounting. As the original name implies, the association's charter members were educators. Although educators still constitute the largest part of the total, membership is open also to practicing accountants and others interested in accounting. Because of this growing diversity in membership, the association's name was changed to its present one in 1936. Annual meetings are held in late August or early September. The AAA publishes the *Accounting Review*, a quarterly of special interest to students and teachers.

American Institute of Certified Public Accountants. The organization was chartered in 1887 in New York State as the American Association of Public Accountants. In 1916 the name was changed to the American Institute of Accountants and in 1956 to its present one. This last change was made to bring the name in line with the group's long-established practice of restricting membership to certified public accountants. An

U.S. ACCOUNTING GROUPS, 1935–1965

Group	1935	1945	1955	1965
National Association of Accountants	5,161	18,506	36,500	55,258
American Institute of Certified Public Accountants	4,557[1]	8,980	26,073	53,528
American Accounting Association	477	1,527	6,247	10,255
Financial Executives Institute	461	2,725	4,513	6,019
Institute of Internal Auditors	0	821	3,203	5,993

[1] 1936 figure, to reflect merger of American Society of Certified Public Accountants with AICPA.

annual meeting is held each fall. The AICPA publishes the *Journal of Accountancy*, of interest to public accountants, and also many books and pronouncements resulting from research.

National Association of Accountants. The NAA was called the National Association of Cost Accountants when the group was formed in Buffalo, N.Y., in 1919. At the time the organization was founded its membership was supposed to be restricted to cost accountants; however, with the broadening concepts of accounting, membership was opened to anyone interested in accounting. Because of this shift in membership, the name was changed to its present one in 1957. The group's annual meeting is held in June. It publishes the *NAA Management Accounting* monthly for members only, a magazine consisting of general-interest articles and association notes.

Institute of Internal Auditors. Founded in New York in 1940, the Institute of Internal Auditors has always restricted full-membership status to practicing internal auditors. However, the group accepts educators and public accountants on an associate- or limited-membership basis. The group holds its annual meeting in May or June. Its quarterly, the *Internal Auditor*, is of interest to those in the field of internal auditing.

Financial Executives Institute. Founded in New York in 1931 as the Controllers' Institute the group changed its name to the present one in 1962 because persons other than controllers were being admitted to membership. The broadening of membership came about because of the changing concepts and the interrelationships of the functions of accounting, controlling, and financing. To qualify for active membership in the FEI, an applicant must be an executive officer carrying out the controllership or treasureship function in an eligible enterprise. To be considered eligible, the enterprise must meet requirements as to size. A limited number of associate memberships are granted on an individual basis to educators. An international conference is held each fall. The group has an active research foundation to further the arts and sciences of controllership and treasureship. Its monthly publication, *Financial Executive*, contains articles of special interest to accountants in administrative or managerial positions.

9. Careers in Accounting

Educational and Other Requirements. Accounting has long been recognized as a profession, but not quite on an equal footing with medicine and law. However, that gap seems to be closing. This is due in part to the increase in educational requirements that must be met by candidates for the profession.

Each state and the District of Columbia has established by law the minimum educational and experience requirements which must be met by an applicant before he can sit for the CPA examination. Originally, most states required only that the applicant be able to read and write or at most that he have a high school education. But an increasing emphasis has been placed on education, with the result that most states now require the applicant to have a college degree. Some even specify that the applicant have a major in accounting. Nearly every state requires that the applicant have some experience in working for a CPA or in equivalent work before he is granted a certificate. Experience required ranges from as little as one year to as much as five years. Three years appears to be the most common period required, but some states deduct one year from the three if the applicant has a master's degree. Almost all states require that the applicant be a citizen of the United States; that he be a resident of or maintain an office in the state in which he applies to take the examination; and that he be of good moral character.

Noncertified accountants are not regulated by law as to qualifications as are certified accountants. However, because employers feel that accountants are professional people, young men and women expecting to succeed as accountants today must have a college degree.

Outlook for Employment. A constant and growing demand exists for accountants in industry, government, public practice, and teaching. (For summaries of positions and the nature of the work, see section *4. Types of Accounting* and section 5. *Areas of Accounting.*)

Because of the interrelationship of industry, government, taxpayers, employers, investors, and creditors, there is a constant need for internal auditors, external auditors, and government auditors. Because of increased interest in efficiency and the periodic "profit squeezes," there is a growing demand for the services of accountants trained in such management services areas as operations research. Because of the heavy tax burden, there is a great need for tax accountants —accountants who because of their knowledge of accounting and tax law can help their clients reduce their taxes by expert planning. Because of the complexities of modern production and distribution, there is constant need for cost accountants. In addition, accountants are in great demand for the analysis and interpretation of all types of economic data, including credit analysis.

Many accountants are hired by the Federal Bureau of Investigation and other government agencies. For instance, the U.S. General Accounting Office increased its employment of professional accountants from 1,217 in 1955 to 2,272 in 1965.

Earnings and Advancement. Pay and prospects for the young accountant are becoming comparable to those for young persons going into medicine and law. Accounting majors usually receive slightly higher starting salaries than other business school graduates. Top executives of many of the world's larger corporations have risen from the rank of accountants.

10. Accounting Bibliography

Anthony, Robert N., and Graham-Walker, Ross, *Essentials of Accounting: A Reference Guide* (Addison-Wesley 1985).

Arnold, J., and others, eds., *Topics in Management Accounting* (Humanities Press 1981).

Batty, J., *Designing and Presenting Financial Information* (Gower Pub. 1988).

Carey, John L., and Skousen, K. Fred, *Getting Acquainted with Accounting*, 2d ed. (Houghton 1977).

Cherrington, J. Owen, *Accounting Basics* (Kent 1981).

Hendricksen, Eldon S., *Accounting Theory* 4th ed. (Irwin 1982).

Hobbs, James, and Moore, Carl L., *Financial Accounting: Concepts, Valuation, and Analysis* 3d ed. (SW Sci. Pub. 1984).

Hughes, Hugh P., *Goodwill in Accounting: A History of the Issues and Problems* (Ga. State Univ. Pubs. 1982).

Jensen, Daniel L., and others, *Advanced Accounting* (Random House 1988).

Kohler, Eric L., *A Dictionary for Accountants*, 3d ed. (Prentice-Hall 1965).

Levy, Morton, *Accounting Goes Public* (Univ. of Pa. Press 1977).

Littleton, A. C., and Yamey, Basil S., eds., *Studies in the History of Accounting* (1956; reprint, Ayer 1978).

BOOKKEEPING

Bookkeeping is the act of recording, classifying, and summarizing financial data according to an established plan. It provides a basis for the interpretation of data and the preparation of financial statements. The establishment of recording systems, whether they be referred to as accounting systems or bookkeeping systems, is a function reserved for the accountant, as is also the art of interpreting the data and the preparation of financial statements. A bookkeeper is one who keeps books—that is, makes entries as instructed by an accountant. The bookkeeper is skilled in the technique of making entries. The accountant supervises the bookkeeping function, determines what system shall be used, and interprets the results. Bookkeeping is mechanical; accounting is interpretative and artful. In small firms, however, one person may function as both accountant and bookkeeper.

11. Bookkeeping or Accounting Equation

Debit and Credit. "Debit," used as a verb, means to enter or post an amount on the left side of an account. Used as a noun, debit refers to the normal balance of an asset, expense, or contra credit account.

"Credit," used as a verb, means to enter or post an amount on the right side of an account. Used as a noun, credit means the normal balance of a liability, net worth, income, or contra debit account.

A debit to an account does not necessarily represent an increase, nor does a credit always represent a decrease, as often is believed erroneously. There are five broad classes of accounts, two of which debit to increase and three of which credit to increase. Asset and expense accounts debit to increase and credit to decrease. Income, liability and net worth accounts credit to increase and debit to decrease. This is indicated in the following diagrams:

INCREASES	
Debit	Credit
Assets	Liabilities
Expenses	Net worth
	Income

DECREASES	
Debit	Credit
Liabilities	Assets
Net worth	Expenses
Income	

Such a theory of debits and credits is utilized in the development of the accounting equation.

Accounting Equation. Developed to its fullest under the double-entry system, the accounting equation is a simple statement:

Assets = Liabilities + Net Worth.

An increase in an asset account represented by a debit to an asset account (an entry to the left side of the equation) may be offset by a credit of an equal amount to a liability account, or a net worth account (on the right side of the equation), thus leaving the equation in balance. Following the theory of debits and credits under which every account has two sides, one represents increases and the other, decreases. There is no direct subtraction; rather, an entry is made on the opposite or decreasing side. For example, if an asset account balance is to be decreased $100, the bookkeeper adds $100 to the credit or decreasing side instead of substracting $100 on the debit side. If a liability account balance is to be decreased $100, the bookkeeper adds $100 on the debit side instead of subtracting $100 on the credit side.

If a gift of $100 is received, it results in an increase of $100 in assets and an increase of the same amount in net worth. According to the rules of debit and credit, asset increases are recorded as debits, and net worth increases are recorded as credits. Therefore, $100 would be debited to the proper asset account, and a credit of $100 would be entered in the proper net worth account. If a $100 asset is lost, there is a decrease in assets and a decrease in net worth. Thus, following the same debit and credit rules, the decreases are recorded as a credit to the proper asset account and a debit to the appropriate net worth account.

12. Bookkeeping or Accounting Systems

System. As generally defined, system is an orderly arrangement or combination of parts into the whole; it is also a method of codification or classification. In accounting, system may be defined as the proper codification and classification of accounts together with the opening of adequate journals and ledgers, and the establishment of proper procedures and controls over assets, liabilities, revenues, and expenses, so that adequate data can be provided all interested parties. A system may be defined also as any combination of integrated procedures established to provide for the recording and controlling of all, or a significant portion, of a firm's activities.

Procedure. Procedure may be defined as all the steps necessary to perform the acts required to carry out a given system. A procedure is clerical and routine. The establishing of an accounting system is an accounting function. The carrying out of the system's procedures is a bookkeeping function.

Single-Entry System. By today's standards, a single-entry bookkeeping system is really a partial or incomplete double-entry system, even though the double-entry system was developed later than the single-entry system and is a refinement of it. Any transaction involves at least two accounts, but in a single-entry system only a partial set of accounts—usually a cash account and personal accounts—is used. Thus only one part of the total transaction is recorded. There is no detailed record of losses or profits, and when statements are prepared, they must be constructed from fragmentary material. Because of these inadequacies of the single-entry system, the double-entry system was evolved.

Double-Entry System. A double-entry bookkeeping system is the type of system now used almost universally except in very small businesses. This method gives full recognition to the fact that every business transaction involves two elements of equal amounts, but of opposite character as to debits and credits. Each transaction may be said to represent both a giving and a receiving of something of value.

For example, cash is given in exchange for supplies received. Following the theory of the bookkeeping equation, the asset account entitled "Supplies" increases by the value of the goods received and therefore is debited for that amount; meanwhile the asset account entitled "Cash" decreases by the same amount and is credited for the specified amount. The theory works equally well if the supplies are bought on account. Under such conditions, there would be a debit (an increase) to the asset account "Supplies," and an offsetting credit (an increase) for the same amount to a liability account, "Accounts Payable."

"Double entry" does not mean, as is often thought, that a given transaction is entered twice, but rather that each of two elements is entered once. In comparison with the single-entry system, the double-entry system increases accuracy of recording and control over financial data. Although single-entry bookkeeping employs only a partial set of real accounts, double-entry bookkeeping employs a full set of accounts, both real and nominal.

13. Basic "Books"

There are only two basic types of books in a modern accounting system—a journal, or book of original entry, and a ledger, or book of secondary entry. It is possible for a firm to record all of its accounting data in only two books, a general journal and a general ledger. However, to save time, labor, and space, as well as to add to the divisibility of work, variations of the general books may be added in the form of special journals and subsidiary ledgers.

Journal. "Journal" is taken from the French word that means "diary" or "daybook." Transactions are recorded in the journal on a daily or chronological basis, with due regard being given to the need for maintaining an equality of debits and credits. The act of making entries in a journal is referred to as *journalizing*.

There are possible minor variations in the form of a general journal. Here is the most common form:

General Journal					Page 1
Date	Item	LP	Debit		Credit
1968 Jan. 1	Office Supplies		200 00		
	Cash	1			200 00
	Purchased office supplies				
12	Cash	1	1,500 00		
	Sales				1,500 00
	Sold merchandise for cash				
30	Rent		400 00		
	Cash	1			400 00
	Paid rent				

The typical journal has a pair of columns at the left for the date, a wide space in the center for items or account titles and explanation, followed by a narrow column for the posting reference, and two money columns at the extreme right. The inner money column (the one to the left) is to receive the debit amounts and the outer one (the one to the right) is to receive the credit amounts.

The following transactions are journalized as examples:

On January 1 the company bought $200 worth of office supplies for cash.

On January 12 the company sold $1,500 worth of merchandise for cash.

On January 30 the company paid rent of $400.

The number of the year appears only once on each page and so does the name of month, unless there is a change of months. The day of the month is indicated on the first line of each entry. The account or accounts to be debited are entered first and brought out to the left margin of the item space. The account or accounts to be credited are recorded last and indented about one half inch from the margin.

Ledger. A ledger is a book or collection of accounts. Historically, the ledger was a bound volume, but because of the desirability of keeping the accounts in a predetermined sequence, such as alphabetically or according to a chart of accounts, this was long ago replaced by a loose-leaf volume. In many cases, the loose-leaf volume has been replaced in turn by "ledger cards" kept in a predetermined order in a file cabinet. Some firms have adopted "ledgerless" bookkeeping in which no ledger, in the usual sense, is kept, but the information is stored mechanically, as on tape or memory drums.

In conventional accounting systems, data are entered first in the journal and then in the proper accounts of the book of secondary entry, the ledger. No item is placed in the ledger unless it has already been entered in the journal. The act of making entries in the ledger is referred to as *posting*.

Each account in the ledger contains data pertinent to a particular person, thing, or item. In the journal, the unit is the whole transaction; in the ledger, the unit is a part of the transaction as it affects a particular account.

The conventional form of the ledger account gives consideration to the theory of debits and credits in that the page is divided into two equal and identical parts, the left side being the debit side, and the right side being the credit side.

The three entries in the journal may be used to illustrate posting to the ledger. Since only a "Cash" account is illustrated, only those parts of each entry affecting cash can be posted, but the same principles would be involved in posting other accounts.

The credits to cash in the first and third journal entries are recorded on the credit side of the "Cash" account on the date of each transaction, and a brief explanation is given. The entry on January 12 indicates a cash debit, and that debit is posted to the "Cash" account on January 12.

The journal has a posting reference column headed "LP" (ledger page) adjacent to the money columns, and each half of the "Cash" account has a posting reference column entitled "JP" (journal page) next to the money column. These columns are used for cross referencing data between the books and to indicate which amounts in the journal have been posted. The illustration involves only the first page of each book; therefore, the number "1" is used in all cases. Where loose-leaf books are used, the numbering of pages is impractical. In such cases, a check (√) mark may be used to indicate in the journal the amounts which have been posted.

At the end of each accounting period the real accounts may be balanced as a matter of convenience for preparing statements and utilizing the information in the account during the next period. This is done, as in the ledger illustration, by adding a sufficient amount to the smaller side to make it equal to the larger one and then showing the same amount on the opposite side below the balancing totals. The credit item of $900 required to equate the debits and credits is dated as of the end of the month under consideration (Jan. 31), and the offsetting debit is dated as of the first of the next month (Feb. 1). This balancing procedure does not require a journal entry.

14. Bookkeeping or Accounting Cycle

The accounting cycle begins with the journalizing of daily transactions and ends with the drawing off of a post-closing trial balance, which provides evidence that the books are ready to receive entries for the new period. During a bookkeeping cycle, a number of steps occur. Daily transactions are journalized and posted. At the end of the period a trial balance is prepared, necessary adjustments are determined, a work sheet is prepared, the balance sheet and income statement are prepared, adjusting and closing entries are journalized and posted, and finally, a post-closing trial balance is taken.

Real accounts (balance sheet accounts) are balanced; *nominal accounts* (income and expense statement accounts) are not balanced, but are "closed to" the income and expense account at the end of each period. The closing of nominal accounts is done by adding enough to the smaller side of the account to make it equal to the other side; a like amount is then added to the op-

An account in the general ledger   Cash

Date		Item	JP	Debit		Date		Item	JP	Credit	
1968						1968					
Jan.	12	Sales	1	1,500	00	Jan.	1	Supplies	1	200	00
							30	Rent	1	400	00
							31	Balance		900	00
				1,500	00					1,500	00
Feb.	1	Balance		900	00						

posite side of the income and expense account. For example, if an expense account, "Rent," has total debits of $600 and total credits of $200 at the end of the period, the account will be closed by debiting "Income and Expense" for $400 and by crediting "Rent" for $400. A "closing entry" is required in the journal to support the closing of a nominal account in the ledger.

be to an asset account, "Prepaid Rent." By the end of January, the account would still show a balance of $6,000, but only the unused portion of $5,000 is still an asset and the used portion of $1,000 has become an expense which belongs in a nominal account. The expense portion is transferred to a nominal account by an adjusting entry debiting "Rent Expense" for $1,000 and crediting

An account in the journal   Rent

Date		Item	JP	Debit		Date		Item	JP	Credit	
Jan.	1	Rent paid	1	200	00	Jan.	20	Rent refund		200	00
Jan.	15	Rent paid	1	400	00	Jan.	31	To income and ex- pense		400	00
				600	00					600	00

This "income and expense" account represents the summarization of all the nominal accounts for the period and must be closed in turn to a "real account," such as "retained earnings" in the case of a corporation.

Besides real and nominal accounts, there is a third type, known as *mixed accounts*, which contain elements of both real and nominal accounts. In the accounting cycle, mixed accounts must be treated before real accounts are balanced and nominal accounts are closed. To determine the profit or loss for the period, as well as to be able to prepare the balance sheet (using real accounts) and the statement of income and expense (using nominal accounts), the bookkeeper must separate the mixed accounts into real-account elements and nominal-account elements. This is done by analyzing the accounts and making the necessary "adjusting entries." For example, assume that on January 1 the company paid $6,000 in advance for six months' rent. The debit would

"Prepaid Rent" for $1,000.

The first procedural step at the end of the period is to prepare a trial balance containing both debit and credit columns. The trial balance is a listing of all the ledger accounts with their balances recorded in the proper debit or credit columns. If the postings have been made correctly, the total of the debits will equal the total of the credits. The trial balance will be useful as the first part of a work sheet on which adjustments will be made as the basis for adjusting entries, and for the preparation of the balance sheet and the income statement.

After the adjusting and closing entries have been posted, a post-closing trial balance may be drawn off. If the books have been closed correctly, this trial balance will contain only real accounts, because the nominal accounts have no balances immediately after closing.

15. Statements

The two most important accounting statements are the *balance sheet* and the *income statement*. Historically, the balance sheet was considered the more important, but currently the income statement is considered the more important. The change came about because the ability to repay based on the earning power of the borrower is now a major factor in the granting of credit. Formerly credit was granted largely on the basis of security provided by the value of assets owned by the borrower.

Another important statement is the *statement of earned surplus*, now often called the *statement of retained earnings*. The *funds-flow statement* has also gained considerable importance.

Balance Sheet. The most common title given to the formal statement of the assets, liabilities, and net worth of a firm is "balance sheet." This statement also is referred to as the *statement of financial condition*, the *statement of financial position*, or simply the *statement of position*. The balance sheet indicates the financial position of the firm as of a moment of time. There are various forms of balance sheets, but the most commonly used is the "account form," illustrated for a mythical ABC Company.

Income Statement. The preferred title for a firm's formal statement summarizing its revenues and expenses for a period is "income statement." Other titles for this are *profit and loss statement*, *statement of profit and loss*, *profit statement*, and

CARD PUNCH AND VERIFIER enter and check data on cards which then go to a computer for processing.

INTERNATIONAL BUSINESS MACHINES CORP.

ABC COMPANY
BALANCE SHEET
December 31, 1968

Assets				Liabilities and net worth		
				Liabilities		
Current assets:				Current liabilities:		
Cash		$ 1,100		Accounts payable		$ 1,000
Inventory—at cost		15,000		Dividends payable		4,000
Accounts Receivable	$ 5,000					
Less: Allowance for loss				Total current liabilities		$ 5,000
on bad debts	100	4,900		Non-current liabilities:		
Prepaid expenses:				Bonds payable		100,000
Insurance	400			Total liabilities		$105,000
Supplies	600	1,000				
Total current assets		$ 22,000				
				Net Worth		
Fixed assets:						
Land		$ 60,000		Capital stock, par value $100		
Building	$200,000			1000 shares issued	$100,000	
Less: Allowance for				Retained earnings	50,000	
depreciation	27,000	173,000		Total net worth		150,000
Total fixed assets		$233,000				
Total assets		$255,000		Total liabilities and net worth		$255,000

statement of income. There is a great variety of income statement forms. A common form is illustrated for the XYZ Company.

The balance sheet is a statement of static condition. The income statement is a statement of activity.

Statement of Retained Earnings. The currently recommended title for the statement that shows changes in retained earnings for a period between two balance sheet dates is "statement of retained earnings." This title substantially has replaced "statement of earned surplus," popular in the early part of the 20th century. "Retained earnings" are increased by current profits and are decreased by current losses, dividend distributions, and transfers to other net worth accounts.

Funds-Flow Statement. The funds-flow statement is also referred to as *funds statement,*
statement of source and application of funds, statement of application of funds, statement of resources provided and applied, and the *"where-got, where-gone" statement.* A balance sheet summarizes the financial condition of a firm; an income statement and retained earnings statement summarize the activities that brought about changes in net worth during the period; but it is left to the funds flow statement to summarize the increasingly important function of the utilization of scarce financial resources during the period.

Such a statement answers two important questions: (1) Where did funds come from? (2) How were the funds used?

XYZ COMPANY
INCOME STATEMENT

For the Year Ended December 31, 1968

Gross sales			$100,000
Less: Sales returns and allowances	$ 2,000		
Sales discounts	1,000	3,000	
Net sales			97,000
Cost of goods sold:			
Inventory—Jan. 1, 1968	$10,000		
Purchases—net	50,000		
Total available for sale	$60,000		
Less: Inventory—Dec. 31, 1968	15,000		
Cost of goods sold		45,000	
Gross profit		52,000	
Operating expenses:			
Selling expenses:			
Sales salaries	$16,000		
Depreciation of store	2,000	$18,000	
Administrative expenses:			
Officers' salaries	$20,000		
Miscellaneous administrative expenses	1,000	21,000	
Total operating expenses		39,000	
Net operating income		$ 13,000	
Other revenue and expense:			
Interest expense		3,000	
Net income before income taxes		$ 10,000	
Income taxes		5,000	
Net profit after taxes		$ 5,000	

ABC COMPANY
FUNDS-FLOW STATEMENT

For the Year Ended Dec. 31, 1968

Funds were provided by:	
Decrease in working capital	$ 10,000
Profit from operations	5,000
Depreciation	2,000
Sale of equipment	63,000
Issuance of stock	50,000
Total funds provided	$130,000
Funds were applied to:	
Purchase of equipment	$ 80,000
Retirement of bonds	40,000
Payment of dividends	10,000
Total funds applied	$130,000

16. Machine Bookkeeping

Machine bookkeeping includes any system of keeping accounting records by mechanical means. Systems may be so simple that they use uncomplicated machines to make recordings in modified journals and ledgers; or they may be highly complex and use electronic computers. Increasingly, journals and ledgers, if they exist at all, are kept in the form of cards. Even without a computerized system a general ledger may be operated by storing information on punched cards—or on tape, or in memory drums—and then "printing out" information when needed.

W. ASQUITH HOWE, *Temple University*

The University of Ghana, founded in 1948, is located in Accra's northern suburb of Legon.

© MARC RIBOUD/MAGNUM

ACCRA, ə-krä′, the capital and largest city of Ghana, in West Africa. Situated on the coast of the Gulf of Guinea, it is an important commercial center. Accra is connected by railroad with the cocoa-growing regions and chief towns of southern Ghana. The industrial town of Tema, 16 miles (26 km) to the east, which has an artificial deepwater harbor, serves as the capital's seaport. Power for the industries of the metropolitan area—including aluminum smelting, oil refining, and motor-vehicle assembly—is supplied by the Akosombo Dam on the Volta River. Accra's airport serves both foreign and domestic flights.

Accra is a spacious city with broad avenues, public gardens, and sandy beaches. Multistoried government and commercial buildings rise in the central business district. Other large structures have been erected in well-planned housing estates. Despite its modern buildings and squares, Accra retains its tropical atmosphere, with fruit trees growing in profusion.

The city is the educational center for a wide area of Ghana. It is the headquarters of the national academy of arts and sciences and the site of the national museum, which houses archaeological and ethnological exhibits from Ghana and other parts of West Africa. The University of Ghana, founded in 1948, is in the northern suburb of Legon.

Accra grew up around three fortified posts built in the 17th century during the height of the slave trade—James Fort (English), Crèvecoeur (Dutch), and Christiansborg Castle (Danish). In the 19th century these forts came under British control, and, in 1876, Accra was made the capital of the British colony of the Gold Coast. James Fort and Crèvecoeur (renamed Ussher Fort) now serve as prisons, and Christiansborg Castle is the official residence of the president of Ghana. Population: metropolitan area, 1,781,100 (1990 est.).

NICHOLAS POBBI-ASARE
State University of New York
College at New Paltz

ACCREDITATION OF SCHOOLS AND COLLEGES, in the United States, the recognition given to institutions that meet certain standards. Accreditation is the closest American equivalent to the practice followed in many other countries of having the central government establish standards for education. Under the United States Constitution the federal government has no direct responsibility for regulating education. Legal control of education is largely the responsibility of the 50 states. Because state standards for schools and colleges differ, nationwide criteria are established by voluntary accrediting agencies.

Although accrediting agencies have no legal control, annual lists of accredited institutions generally are accepted as the best available measure of quality. The lists are used widely by students in selecting colleges and by college admissions officers. Many colleges will not accept course credits from nonaccredited institutions, and licenses to practice in many professions are granted only to graduates of accredited programs. For a list of accrediting agencies, see COLLEGES AND UNIVERSITIES—*Accreditation.*

Further Reading: Accreditation Procedures Manual (American Association for Counseling and Development 1982); Young, Kenneth E., and others, *Understanding Accreditation* (Jossey-Bass 1983).

ACCUSATIVE CASE, ə-kū′zə-tiv, in grammar, a form used in highly inflected Indo-European languages, such as Greek, Latin, and German, to denote the direct object of a verb or the object of certain specified prepositions. The accusative corresponds with the objective case in English, except that the objective case is used for the objects of all prepositions. See also CASE.

ACEROLA, as-ə-rō′lə, a subtropical evergreen shrub of the family Malpighiaceae whose tart cherrylike fruits are high in vitamin C. The shrub (*Malpighia glabra*) grows to about 10 feet (3 meters) high. Its range extends from southern Texas to northern South America and throughout the West Indies. It has dark green wedge-shaped leaves up to 4 inches (10 cm) long and bears clusters (umbels) of small rose or red flowers.

The best-known variety is the so-called Barbados, Puerto Rican, or West Indian cherry, which may be a hybrid between *M. glabra* and the similar shrub *M. punicifolia.* Its fruit is the most concentrated natural source of vitamin C.

ACETAL RESIN, as'ə-təl rez'in, any of a group of thermoplastic materials produced under several tradenames, including Celcon and Delrin in the United States.

Acetals are polymers of formaldehyde (CH_2O) in which the basic formaldehyde unit is repeated 10,000 to 40,000 times. They are hard, rigid, tough, milky-white, slippery materials that are resistant to most chemicals. These characteristics make them useful as small mechanical and electrical parts such as gears and insulating switch parts. In the home they are most frequently encountered in aerosol valves. Well over 50 million pounds (22.7 million kg) per year are used in the United States.

BENJAMIN J. LUBEROFF, *Editor, "CHEMTECH"*

ACETALDEHYDE, as-ət-al'də-hīd, a volatile, reactive, clear, and pungent liquid, CH_3CHO, that is an important natural flavor constituent of fruits and wines. The CHO group in its molecular formula places it in the class of compounds called aldehydes. In the chemical industry, acetaldehyde is an intermediate for making other chemicals, of which acetic acid was by far the most important until the 1970's. Over 2 million tons of acetaldehyde per year are produced worldwide.

The history of the acetaldehyde industry is an object lesson in the development of chemical technology. Originally the compound was made from ethyl alcohol, which in turn was made by fermentation of agricultural products. Later acetaldehyde was made from acetylene derived from coal, but since the mid-1950's it has been made from ethylene by a process that uses a solution of palladium salts as a catalyst. That process is so efficient that in the 1960's it replaced well over 80% of the world manufacturing capacity for acetaldehyde.

In the 1970's, however, a process was introduced for making acetic acid from carbon monoxide and hydrogen, which in turn can be obtained from coal, oil, or natural gas. Since the new acetic-acid process is cheaper than the one utilizing acetaldehyde, much of the acetaldehyde manufacturing capacity installed in prior years was shut down.

BENJAMIN J. LUBEROFF
Editor, "CHEMTECH"

ACETAMINOPHEN, ə-sē-tə-min'ə-fən, a drug widely used to reduce pain and fever. It is available over-the-counter under the trade names Tylenol and Panadol and is also an ingredient in stronger prescription painkillers, such as Percocet and Darvocet.

Acetaminophen is a popular alternative to aspirin because it is often just as effective for pain and fever but has fewer objectionable side effects. It does not cause stomach irritation or intestinal bleeding, and individuals who are allergic to aspirin can take acetaminophen safely. Unlike aspirin, acetaminophen does not reduce inflammation such as that associated with rheumatic diseases, nor does it inhibit blood clotting.

While acetaminophen is extremely safe in normal doses, an overdose can cause serious liver injury and even death. If the overdose is diagnosed promptly, administration of N-acetylcysteine will prevent serious liver injury.

B. ROBERT MEYER, M.D.
Cornell University Medical College

ACETATE, as'ə-tāt, a salt or ester of acetic acid, CH_3COOH. When acetic acid reacts with a metal oxide (M_2O) or a metal hydroxide (MOH), a salt called an acetate is produced, in which the acidic hydrogen ion, H^+, is replaced by the metal ion, M^+. Thus,

$$CH_3COOH + MOH — CH_3COO^- M^+ + H_2O$$

| Acetic acid | Metal hydroxide | Metal acetate | Water |

In sodium acetate, for example, M is Na, giving $CH_3COO^- Na^+$.

The term acetate also refers to esters of acetic acid, with the general formula CH_3COOR, in which a hydrocarbon group, R, has replaced the acidic hydrogen. Cellulose acetate—encountered daily in fibers, fabrics, and photographic films—belongs to this structural class and is commonly referred to simply as acetate.

BENJAMIN J. LUBEROFF, *Editor, "CHEMTECH"*

ACETIC ACID, ə-sē'tik, a weak acid, CH_3COOH, best known in the form of vinegar, which is a water solution containing about 5% acetic acid and small amounts of other flavoring ingredients. Vinegar, made by fermenting fruit beyond the wine stage, is one of the earliest acids known.

Although food-grade acetic acid is still made by fermentation, much of the 2 billion pounds used each year in the United States is made from carbon monoxide and hydrogen derived from coal, oil, or natural gas, by a process introduced in the 1970's. In this process, methyl alcohol, CH_3OH, is synthesized from carbon monoxide and hydrogen, and the methyl alcohol is then reacted with more carbon monoxide to yield acetic acid. This process has largely displaced the older industrial process based on oxidation of acetaldehyde, CH_3CHO.

The main use of acetic acid is to make its ester, vinylacetate, a precursor of the polymers from which water-based paints, adhesives, and thickeners are made. A great deal of acetic acid is used for making cellulose acetate for fabrics. It is also a raw material or process solvent (often in the form of its esters) for dyes, drugs (aspirin is *acetyl*salicylic acid), and other products.

Pure acetic acid is a water-clear, corrosive liquid with a biting odor. Less volatile than water, it boils at 244°F (118°C) and freezes at 63°F (17°C). Its high freezing point underlies the method formerly used to separate acetic acid from its water solutions. If such solutions were sufficiently concentrated, chilling them caused pure acetic acid to crystallize. This is the origin of the term "glacial acetic acid," which is still used for the pure acid. Today separation is done by distillation—a more energy-efficient process—in large fractionating towers.

BENJAMIN J. LUBEROFF, *Editor, "CHEMTECH"*

ACETONE, as'ə-tōn, a volatile, clear, colorless industrial solvent, CH_3COCH_3, with a sweetish odor. It is most often encountered in the home in the form of nail-polish remover. In the human body acetone is a product of protein metabolism. It may occur at near toxic levels in diabetics and in people on severe weight-loss diets that are low in carbohydrates and high in protein.

More than 1 billion pounds (450 million kg) of acetone is made each year in the United States. About 15% is used in industry as a solvent for paints and other surface coatings, but steps to reduce air pollution have resulted in lessened use of such volatile solvents as acetone for this purpose. This has not affected acetone's use as a solvent in closed systems, in which the solvent is continually recycled and not released to the atmosphere. Acetone is also used to make other chemicals, including less volatile solvents. The largest single use—about one third of total production—is for conversion to polymethylmethacrylate plastics, which are sold under several tradenames, including Plexiglas and Lucite.

Acetone, also called dimethyl ketone, is the simplest of the ketones, which are characterized by the group:

$$\begin{array}{c} O \\ \parallel \\ C-C-C \end{array}$$

It is most simply made by removing two hydrogens from isopropyl alcohol, $CH_3CHOHCH_3$, but only about a quarter of the acetone is made in that way today. Instead, most acetone is generated as a coproduct of phenol via the oxidation of cumene (isopropylbenzene) by the following reactions:

$$\underset{\text{Cumene}}{\overset{\overset{\displaystyle CH_3}{\vert}}{\underset{\underset{\displaystyle CH_3}{\vert}}{C_6H_5CH}}} + O_2 \longrightarrow \underset{\text{Cumene hydroperoxide}}{\overset{\overset{\displaystyle CH_3}{\vert}}{\underset{\underset{\displaystyle CH_3}{\vert}}{C_6H_5-C-OOH}}} \overset{H+}{\longrightarrow} \underset{\text{Phenol}}{C_6H_5OH}$$

$$+ \underset{\text{Acetone}}{CH_3-\overset{\overset{\displaystyle O}{\parallel}}{C}-CH_3}$$

This is the only good route to phenol, although acetone can be made from isopropyl alcohol, as described above. Thus phenol is the higher-priced product, and acetone is sometimes a glut on the market.

During World War I, acetone was a critical material for producing the gunpowder cordite. To fill a shortage of acetone, which had previously been imported from Germany, Chaim Weizmann, a British Zionist leader, developed a process for making acetone from agricultural products. This vital contribution to the British war effort played a key role in gaining British support for the creation of a Jewish homeland in Palestine, which subsequently became the State of Israel with Weizmann as its first president.

BENJAMIN J. LUBEROFF, Editor, "CHEMTECH"

ACETOPHENETIDIN. See PHENACETIN.

ACETYLCHOLINE, ə-sēt-əl-kō′lēn, a chemical compound that functions as a transmitter in nerve and muscle activity. In vertebrates and other animals it plays a major role in the transmission of nerve impulses across the narrow gap—known as the synapse—between adjacent nerve cells, and it also triggers the contraction of muscle cells by nerve impulses. Both impulses and contractions are electrochemical phenomena in which electrically charged atoms, called ions, flow across the membrane that encloses the nerve or muscle cell. In a nerve impulse, for example, the region of ion flow moves along the length of a nerve fiber until it reaches a synapse. There the nerve impulse apparently stimulates the release of a transmitter such as acetylcholine, which is stored in small sacs or vesicles in nerve cells. The acetylcholine diffuses across the synapse and binds to the membrane of the adjacent fiber. There it may trigger an exchange of sodium and potassium ions across the cell membrane, initiating an impulse in the second nerve cell. See also MUSCLE—*Skeletal Muscle.*

The mechanism that causes the release of acetylcholine is unknown. Soon after its release, it is neutralized by the enzyme cholinesterase, and the synapse is restored to its resting condition—ready to transmit another impulse. If acetylcholine were not neutralized by cholinesterase or a similar enzyme, a single nerve impulse would be tremendously amplified within a synapse and the nervous system would run out of control, resulting in nervous storms similar to those caused by injection of acetylcholine or of cholinesterase inhibitors.

Many insecticides, including the widely used organophosphate Malathion, work by inhibiting the enzyme cholinesterase that hydrolyzes acetylcholine in the nervous system of insects. They are therefore classified as neurological poisons.

Most organophosphates used as insecticides are relatively unstable and are broken down in the livers of mammals. For this reason they are much less toxic to man and other mammals than to insects. More stable organophosphates, which are not readily destroyed by the liver, are used for the military nerve gases known as binary weapons. These gases result from the reaction of two nonpoisonous chemical precursors, which are kept separate in the gas projectile until after the projectile has been fired. Up to this time, the nonpoisonous precursors can be stored or disposed of with little risk.

ACETYLENE, ə-set′əl-ən, a colorless gas, $HC \equiv CH$, that produces extremely hot flames when burned in air or oxygen. The temperature of an oxyacetylene flame, about 6000°F or 3300°C, is higher than that produced by any other mixture of combustible gases. This is the basis for the wide use of oxyacetylene torches for welding and cutting steel and other metals.

Acetylene gives off a bright white light when burned. Before compact electric batteries were available, acetylene lamps were widely used on cars and in mines, buoys, and other applications requiring a source of bright light. The acetylene was produced by a reaction between water and calcium carbide in a simple gas generator in which water was dripped onto a calcium carbide tablet.

Acetylene was formerly used on a large scale as a chemical intermediate in processes for making vinyl chloride, vinyl acetate, acetic acid, and acrylonitrile. However, these chemicals can now be made by less costly processes based on ethylene, propylene, or carbon monoxide.

For many years most acetylene was produced by the chemical reaction between water and calcium carbide. The calcium carbide, in turn, was made from coal and limestone in electric-arc furnaces. Most acetylene now is manufactured by a process based on the thermal cracking of hydrocarbons such as methane and ethane. Among the largest producers of acetylene are chemical plants that make ethylene as a primary product and acetylene as an unavoidable by-product.

Acetylene is a useful storehouse for much of the energy used in its manufacture. Its high energy content accounts both for the high temperature of its flames and for its great chemical reactivity. Unfortunately, because it is also thermodynamically unstable, it can decompose spontaneously to the elements carbon and hydrogen, giving off sufficient heat to cause a violent explosion if the heat is not dissipated quickly enough. That is why pipes for carrying compressed acetylene have a tiny bore or are packed with heat-conducting material. Both of these designs dissipate heat quickly and thus prevent a temperature rise that might set off an explosion. Acetylene is stored under pressure in a specially designed cylinder containing acetone, in which acetylene is extremely soluble. To prevent formation of large voids where an explosion could start, the cylinder is packed with porous clay, on which the acetylene-acetone solution is adsorbed.

BENJAMIN J. LUBEROFF, *Editor, "CHEMTECH"*

ACETYLSALICYLIC ACID. See ASPIRIN.

ACHAEA, ə-kē′ə, a region of ancient Greece on the north coast of the Peloponnesus, bounded on the landward side by Elis, Arcadia, and Sicyon. The modern Greek *nomos* (department) of Achaea (Akhaia) occupies almost the same area.

In the 5th century B.C., 12 cities of Achaea were joined in a loose confederation out of which developed the renowned Achaean League of the 3d and 2d centuries B.C. The name Achaea was later applied to a Roman province that included all of Greece south of Thessaly, and in the Middle Ages it was applied to a French principality comprising most of the Peloponnesus. Achaea Phthiotis was in ancient times a district of southern Thessaly.

ACHAEAN LEAGUE, ə-kē′ən, a confederation of cities in Achaea and other places in the Peloponnesus in ancient Greece. An early league, composed of 12 cities, flourished in Achaea during the time of Herodotus (5th century B.C.) and endured through the 4th century B.C. when the Peloponnesus came under Macedonian control. In 280 B.C., while Macedonia was torn by internal struggles, the Achaean cities of Patrae, Dyme, Tritaea, and Pharae formed an alliance, afterward joined by the other Achaean cities, and the second Achaean League, which was to give south central Greece more than a century of efficient government, was begun.

The government of this second league was perhaps the nearest approach to representative government in ancient Greece. The league was a federal union of absolutely independent states, each having equal power in a council that met at least twice a year—at first at the Temple of Zeus Amarios in Aegium, but later in each of the league cities in rotation. Each city maintained a strict local autonomy, but all questions of foreign policy, the army, federal taxes, or offenses against the league were referred to the league council. Votes were cast by the cities as a unit, not by elected delegates. Any citizen over 30 years of age had a right to attend and to vote. The chief executive was the commander in chief of the army, who served a one-year term and was eligible for reelection every other year. Other officers included a secretary, a treasurer, an admiral, and 10 *demiourgoi* (assistants).

The league began to expand after 251 B.C. when Aratus of Sicyon, having joined his city to the league, became the league's commander in chief and served thereafter in alternate years for some 30 years. In 243 B.C. he seized the Macedonian citadel at Corinth as a first step in ridding the Peloponnesus of Antigonus II Gonatas of Macedon and the tyrants he supported. Aratus won over city after city until, by 228 B.C., the league comprised almost all of the Peloponnesus.

But for Sparta, the league might have continued to be the leading power in the Peloponnesus. In 227 B.C., Cleomenes III of Sparta attacked the league, subduing Corinth and Argos. Aratus was forced to appeal to his old enemies, the Macedonians, and with the help of Antigonus III Doson of Macedon, he defeated Cleomenes in 222 B.C. Sparta, however, then became a Macedonian ally, and Corinth was restored as a Macedonian fortress.

In 198 B.C. the Achaean League allied with Rome against Philip V of Macedon and thus avoided any interference from Rome as the league again expanded throughout the Peloponnesus. Under Philopoemen of Megalopolis, the league repeatedly defeated Sparta and finally drafted that city into the league in 192 B.C. Rome, however, suspected hostility to its expansionist designs and, as a measure for future security, deported a thousand leading Achaeans to Italy (among them, the historian Polybius) to be kept as hostages. When Sparta sought to secede from the league, Rome attempted to mediate. War resulted between the league and Rome in 146 B.C. The league was totally defeated at Corinth by the Roman general Mummius and was dissolved in that year. Thereafter the Peloponnesus and parts of central Greece were incorporated into a Roman province called Achaea.

ACHAEANS, ə-kē′ənz, one of the principal peoples of ancient Greece. Their original home is uncertain, but by the 14th century B.C. they had begun a migration southward into the Aegean area. They settled first in southern Thessaly, where even as late as the time of Herodotus (5th century B.C.) a district—Achaea Phthiotis—was still known by their name.

Before the mid-13th century B.C. the Achaeans moved into the Peloponnesus. They quickly dominated the cities of the Argolis peninsula, whose inhabitants adopted their language, while they themselves absorbed the culture of their Mycenaean predecessors. About 1250 B.C. they sacked Troy. Their prior siege of that city was later celebrated by Homer in the *Iliad*. Invasions from the north by Dorian tribes, beginning perhaps as early as the 12th century B.C., drove some of the Achaeans east of the Aegean and others to a region of the northern Peloponnesus known in classical times as Achaea.

ACHAEMENIDS, ə-kem′ə-nidz, the ruling dynasty of the first Persian Empire (hence also called the Achaemenid Empire). Under them, Persian rule reached from the Nile to the Danube and eastward to the Indus.

The empire was founded by Cyrus the Great (reigned 549–530 B.C.), and the dynasty was named for his ancestor Achaemenes. Cyrus' son Cambyses (reigned 530–522) added Egypt to its territory. He was succeeded by Darius I (reigned 522–486), who built Persepolis and began the long struggle with the Greeks. Darius' son Xerxes I (reigned 486–465) won the Battle of Thermopylae and burned Athens. Darius III (reigned 336–330), the last Achaemenid ruler, was defeated by Alexander the Great.

ACHEBE, ə-chä′bä, **Chinua** (1930–   ), Nigerian novelist, who is considered one of the most accomplished African authors writing in English. A member of the Ibo people, he was born in Ogidi, in southeastern Nigeria, on Nov. 16, 1930. After attending a Church Missionary Society school, where his father was a teacher, he went to a government secondary school in Umuahia from 1944 to 1947 and then to University College in Ibadan from 1948 to 1953.

In 1954, Achebe joined the Nigerian Broadcasting Corporation and from 1961 to 1966 served as director of the Voice of Nigeria, the foreign-broadcasting service. During the civil strife that beset Nigeria in the late 1960's, Achebe worked for Biafran independence, including touring the United States to raise funds for the rebellious state. After the collapse of Biafra in 1970 he was a research fellow at the University of Nigeria, where he became professor of English in 1973. Also, beginning in 1971, he was editor of *Okike,* a journal devoted to publishing the work of new Nigerian writers.

Things Fall Apart (1958), Achebe's first novel and widely regarded as his best, deals with the clash between native African and English-imposed cultures. The impact of colonialism, with its destructive, often tragic, consequences, is the theme of later novels: *No Longer at Ease* (1960), a sequel to *Things Fall Apart; Arrow of God* (1964); and *A Man of the People* (1966). In commenting on these works, critics noted especially Achebe's ability to give English the tones and rhythms of African speech—a quality particularly apparent in his translations of Ibo proverbs, which impart a sense of universality to the narrative.

In addition to long works of fiction, Achebe wrote short stories, poetry, books for children, and essays.

ACHERON, ak′ə-ron, in Greek mythology, one of the five rivers in Hades that the souls of the dead had to cross. It was known as the river of woe and had murky, foul waters. The souls were conducted across the river by the ferryman Charon, whose fee was a piece of money previously deposited under the tongue of the deceased. A living person would be taken across only if he showed Charon a golden bough obtained from the Cumaean Sibyl.

Acheron is also the name of an actual river in Greece. In ancient times this Acheron was connected with legends of the lower world. The river is located in the Thesprotia region of Epirus and flows into the Ionian sea. The ancient Greeks believed this region to be the end of the world in the west and the entrance to the lower world. As this region became better known, the Greeks placed the river farther away and finally in the lower world itself.

ACHESON, ach′ə-sən, **Dean Gooderham** (1893–1971), American diplomat, who was U.S. secretary of state under President Truman. During his term of office (1949–1953) the program to contain communism through foreign aid was expanded, and the U.S. faced crucial tests in Asia.

Born in Middletown, Conn., on April 11, 1893, Acheson attended Groton School and Yale University, graduating in 1915. He received a degree from Harvard Law School in 1918, after serving briefly as a naval ensign during World War I. Acheson then served two years in Washington, D.C., as private secretary to Louis D. Brandeis, associate justice of the Supreme Court. In 1921 he joined a Washington law firm, specializing in corporation and international law.

Appointed undersecretary of the treasury by Franklin D. Roosevelt in 1933, Acheson resigned after only six months in office and resumed his law practice. He returned to full-time government service as assistant secretary of state (1941–1945) and in 1943 was appointed a U.S. member of the council of the United Nations Relief and Rehabilitation Administration. He advanced to the post of undersecretary of state in August 1945, serving until July 1, 1947, six months after George C. Marshall became secretary of state.

Secretary Marshall relied heavily on Acheson for policy formulation and implementation, recognizing in him a keen student of foreign affairs and an expeditious administrator. Both men agreed that the only effective counter to expanding Soviet power was the judicious use of American power. When Greece and Turkey appeared to be drifting toward internal anarchy and possible Soviet domination early in 1947, Acheson and Marshall proposed aid. The result was the Truman Doctrine, announced March 12, 1947. Acheson also played a part in formulating the Marshall Plan (1948).

After a short time in private law practice again, Acheson was appointed secretary of state by President Truman in January 1949. With his Europe-first orientation, Acheson worked to maintain an Atlantic coalition capable of meeting Soviet challenges. He strongly supported creation of the North Atlantic Treaty Organization. Although militantly anti-Communist, he came under heavy attack by the Republican party for what it contended was his contribution to the collapse of the Chinese Nationalist regime on the mainland in 1949. Frustrations arising from the Korean War stalemate prompted these charges, and Acheson was attacked because of policy failures in East Asia.

Acheson played a key role in 1951 in arranging the final World War II peace settlement with Japan. After resigning as secretary of state in January 1953, Acheson was an adviser to presidents. He died in Sandy Spring, Md., on Oct. 12, 1971.

Acheson's books include *Power and Diplomacy* (1958), *Morning and Noon* (1965), *Private Thoughts on Public Affairs* (1967), and *Present at the Creation* (1969). The last-named won the 1970 Pulitzer Prize for history.

MARVIN ZAHNISER
The Ohio State University

ACHEULIAN, ə-shoo′lē-ən, in archaeology, a tool culture of the Paleolithic period, or Old Stone Age. In Europe it corresponds to the second to third interglacial periods in geology (690,000–125,000 years ago).

Essentially a continuation of the Abbevillian tool culture, the Acheulian was characterized by a refinement in the production of hand axes and other stone implements of the core type, with many associated flake tools. The culture takes its name from St. Acheul, a locality in northern France along the Somme River where artifacts of this tradition were first found. Discoveries from Acheulian cultures have also been made at archaeological sites in Western Europe, North Africa and sub-Saharan Africa, the Near East, and India.

ACHIEVEMENT TEST, a set of questions or problems designed to determine how much an individual knows about some subject area. Broadly speaking, the term would cover the examinations that schoolteachers prepare and use as a basis for assigning grades, the bar examinations that lawyers must pass before they are permitted to practice, the oral examination that Ph.D. candidates must pass, and many other testing situations. Ordinarily, however, the term achievement test is limited to standardized, published instruments designed and constructed by specialists in measurement techniques. Such tests are given in arithmetic, English grammar, biology, history, and many other school subjects.

The development of an achievement test involves several steps. The first is to delineate the area the test is intended to cover. The usual practice is to assemble a committee of outstanding teachers of the subject. They outline the topics about which questions are to be written and determine what proportion of the questions should be focused on each topic.

The second step is to write the questions or problems. They should be written in such a way that only accurate knowledge and an appropriate thinking process will produce correct answers. It has proved possible to involve many kinds of reasoning processes in objective test items such as true-false and multiple-choice questions. Thus achievement tests are not limited to measuring simple factual knowledge but can assess such complex mental skills as judgment, application of principles, and organization of ideas.

The third step is statistical. The test under construction is administered to a trial group similar to the one for which it is intended, and an item analysis is made. All the answers given by the members of the trial group are tabulated. From these tabulations indices are obtained showing how difficult each item is for the group in question and how well the items discriminate between good and poor students of the subject. Various kinds of errors and ambiguities in the items also become apparent at this stage. Often it is necessary to rewrite the test and repeat the item analysis. This trial stage makes it possible to determine the overall reliability or accuracy of the test.

The fourth step is to administer the revised test to a large group chosen in such a way as to be representative of the people on whom the test is to be used. From the scores of this group, norms are developed—age norms, grade norms, percentile scores, standard scores, or some combination of these. How well an individual performs on the test can be judged by comparing his score with one or more of the norms.

In evaluating an achievement test, the main consideration is content validity. This depends on the competence of the persons who made the initial decisions about the makeup of the test and on the skill with which the educational objectives were incorporated in the test items.

Achievement tests are used for many purposes such as educational research, educational planning, placement of individuals in special classes and sections, and selection of students for college admission and for scholarships and awards. At the same time they also serve as a basis for a person's own analysis of his potentialities and handicaps.

LEONA TYLER
University of Oregon

ACHILLES, ə-kil′ēz, a legendary Greek warrior, the hero of Homer's *Iliad*. Homer describes him as the handsomest and bravest of the Greeks who fought at Troy. Achilles' destructive wrath is the subject of Homer's epic.

In Greek legend, Achilles was the son of Peleus, king of Phthiotis, and of Thetis, a Nereid (sea nymph). According to Homer, he was educated by Phoenix, who taught him to be both an eloquent speaker and a man of action, and by Chiron, the centaur, who taught him the art of healing. Homer also tells of the choice with which Achilles was faced, between a long, inglorious life and a short, glorious one. He chose the glorious life, and though there are times in the course of the Trojan War when he questions the wisdom of dying for glory, his ultimate choice symbolizes his belief in the heroic code.

As depicted by Homer, Achilles is a complex character, intense in his love as well as in his hate, intelligent, courageous, and capable of both great cruelty and great kindness. In the *Iliad*, Agamemnon inspires Achilles' anger by demanding Briseis, a young woman whom Achilles had captured, to replace his own captive Chryseis, whom Agamemnon must return to her father. Unjustly deprived of his "prize," Achilles withdraws from the battle and summons his mother, Thetis, asking her to persuade Zeus to aid the Trojans, to indicate to the Greeks how much they need Achilles and make them aware of Agamemnon's injustice to him. Zeus promises to help her. As a result of the god's intervention, the Greeks suffer many defeats. Despite Agamemnon's offer to return Briseis to Achilles and to give him many presents, Achilles refuses to rejoin the Greeks in battle. His wrath has become so obsessive that he does not respond to the pleas of the Greek leaders, Odysseus and Diomedes, or of his own teacher, Phoenix.

Only after his beloved friend Patroclus is killed by Hector, the Trojan leader, does Achilles return to battle. His wrath is now turned against Hector, whom he pursues three times around Troy and then kills. Achilles then ties Hector's body to his chariot by the feet and drives the chariot around the walls of Troy. Finally, persuaded by Thetis, at Zeus' command, Achilles returns Hector's body to Priam. The scene in which Hector's old father comes to Achilles to ask for his son's body is one of the most moving episodes in the *Iliad*.

In the *Iliad*, as Hector is dying, he prophesies that Achilles will be killed by Paris and Apollo at the Scaean Gate, and the prophecy is fulfilled. The mourning for Achilles is described in the *Odyssey*, and in this epic he appears as a shade in the Underworld.

According to post-Homeric legends, Thetis attempted to make the infant Achilles immortal by dipping him in the river Styx. Because she held him by the heel, he remained vulnerable in that part. The story is told for the first time in Statius' epic poem *Achilleid*. Other post-Homeric legends relate that Peleus or Thetis attempted to prevent Achilles' participation in the Trojan War, where they knew he would die, by sending him disguised as a girl to the court of King Lycomedes, on the island of Scyros. Here Deidameia, one of the daughters of Lycomedes, bore Achilles a son, Neoptolemus. When the prophet Calchas warned the Greek leaders that they could not defeat the Trojans without Achilles, Odysseus and Diomedes went to Scyros and revealed Achilles' true identity. He then accompanied them to Troy.

Achilles also is an important character in Euripides' *Iphigenia in Aulis*. See also ILIAD.

LILLIAN FEDER
Queens College, New York

ACHILLES TENDON, ə-kil'ēz ten'dən, a tendon that extends from the calf muscles to the back of the heel bone (calcaneus). Known anatomically as the tendo calcaneus, it is about 6 inches (15 cm) long. When the calf muscles are contracted, the tendon pulls up the back of the heel. This makes the foot pivot at the ankle and extend downward, as when standing on tiptoe.

ACHROMYCIN. See under TETRACYCLINE.

ACID RAIN, the common term for rain or other precipitation of higher than normal acidity. In extreme cases the acidity may reach a pH of 3.2—nearly as acid as a carbonated beverage. In some regions, especially parts of northeastern North America and western Europe, acid rain has been associated with the decline of forests and with the destruction of fish and other waterlife. The existence of acid rain was first documented in 1852 by Robert A. Smith, a British chemist.

Cause. Manmade increases in the acidity of precipitation are traced mainly to the burning of coal, oil, and gas by heavy industry and electrical utilities. Burning these fuels releases sulfur and nitrogen oxides (SO_x and NO_x) to the atmosphere, where they combine with water vapor to produce sulfuric acid (H_2SO_4) and nitric acid (HNO_3). The acids in the atmosphere are carried downwind—sometimes for great distances—and deposited on the earth's surface in rain, snow, and other precipitation.

Distribution. The most severe effects of acid rain occur in southeastern Canada, northeastern United States, and western Europe. These regions are downwind of large industrial complexes such as those in the Ohio Valley in the United States and the Ruhr Valley in West Germany. Less severe acid rain is much more widespread.

Possible Effects. Acid rain has been associated with death of fish in ponds and lakes, death of forest trees, and with changes in soil chemistry. It also has been linked with the deterioration of exposed surfaces of buildings, monuments, and statues, with the deterioration of fabrics, and even with human disease.

In many of these cases, it is not clear to what extent acid rain is responsible for the observed effects—either because the effects are indirect or because other possible causes are involved. However, experimental acidification of a small Canadian lake irreversibly changed the balance of phytoplankton species, wiped out bottom-living crustaceans, and stopped fish reproduction. This experiment tends to support the contention that similar changes in lakes in the Adirondacks, southeastern Canada, and Scandinavia were caused by acidification.

Some effects ascribed to acid rain may be secondary effects caused by aluminum, which is abundant in most soils and is in certain forms toxic to many organisms. If soil acidity is increased by acid rain, the aluminum becomes more soluble and washes into streams and ponds, where it can injure exposed organisms.

In the eastern United States and western Europe, acid rain (along with other forms of air pollution) has been blamed for causing needle loss, leaf yellowing, branch and crown dieback, and eventual death of trees in coniferous and deciduous forests. However, these effects may be only indirectly related to acid rain. Other factors may be responsible for much—if not all—of the damage. For example, widespread drought in the eastern United States in the mid-1960's may have been a more significant factor than acid rain in slowing tree growth. On the other hand, in West Germany, where components of acid rain are present in a concentration nearly twice that in eastern North America, some studies reached tentative conclusions that acid rain causes the decline of forests.

No precise effects of acid rain have been demonstrated for agricultural crops. The sulfur and nitrogen in acid rain may act as fertilizers in some soils.

Control. The equipment for removing sulfur and nitrogen from flue gases is so expensive to install and operate that most countries—including the United States—have been reluctant to mandate its use. Less expensive measures may include more reliance on nuclear energy, hydroelectric power, and fossil fuels low in sulfur, such as Western coal in the United States.

ROBERT L. BURGESS, *SUNY College of Environmental Science and Forestry*

Bibliography: Alm, Leslie R., *Crossing Borders, Crossing Boundaries: The Role of Scientists in the U.S. Acid Rain Debate* (Praeger 2000); Kennedy, I. R., *Acid Soil and Acid Rain*, 2d ed. (Wiley 1992); Somerville, Richard C. J., *The Forgiving Air: Understanding Environmental Change* (Univ. of Calif. Press 1996).

ACIDOSIS AND ALKALOSIS, as-ə-dō'sis, al-kə-lō'sis, excess acidity or alkalinity of the blood and other body fluids. Normally the acidity (pH) of blood is close to 7.4. In severe acidosis the pH may fall below 7.0, and in severe alkalosis it may rise above 7.5. Acidosis and the much less common alkalosis both are symptoms of various diseases and disorders.

The acidity of body fluids is regulated by three mechanisms. The first mechanism is provided by the blood, whose proteins act as a buffer that limits changes in acidity. The second mechanism is provided by the lungs, which give off carbon dioxide and thus prevent accumulation of carbonic acid. The third mechanism is provided by the kidneys, which can adjust acidity by excreting or retaining acids and bases, and which can reduce acidity by manufacturing bicarbonate ions.

Causes. Acidosis and alkalosis have many causes. Diseases such as emphysema or kidney failure reduce the effectiveness of the lungs or kidneys, and thus interfere with their ability to regulate acidity. Diseases characterized by severe diarrhea may cause alkalosis through excessive loss of basic fluids. Starvation and uncontrolled diabetes may cause acidosis because of excessive acid produced by metabolism of large amounts of body fat. Acidosis or alkalosis can result from ingestion of large amounts of acidic or basic substances. In addition, alkalosis may be caused by loss of carbonic acid through too-rapid breathing or by loss of stomach acids from excessive vomiting.

Treatment. In both acidosis and alkalosis the underlying disorder should be corrected, if possible. In acute cases acidic or basic fluids may be administered orally or intravenously.

ACIDS AND BASES, two related types of chemical compounds that are virtually omnipresent in nature, industry, and everyday life. For example, biochemical processes are almost always associated with acid-base reactions in the cell or in the entire organism. The proper acidity or alkalinity of soil and water are essential for plant growth, and animal life depends on keeping the acidity of blood and other body fluids within a narrow range. In industry, acids and bases are reactants or catalysts in countless processes. In the home, a variety of acids and bases—including vinegar and lye—are used in cooking and cleaning.

Acids were traditionally characterized as compounds that have a sour taste, turn the blue litmus dye red, and corrode some metals. Bases (or alkalis) were characterized as compounds that have a bitter taste, are slippery or soapy to the touch, and are able to change red litmus to blue. In addition, it was known that when an acid and a base react, they neutralize each other and form a salt. With advances in chemistry these characterizations have largely been replaced by precise theories that have extended and deepened the concepts of acids and bases.

History. Such acidic and basic substances as vinegar and lime probably were used in prehistoric times. The discovery of vinegar (in the form of sour wine) doubtless came soon after the discovery of wine.

In historical times, an early reference to vinegar occurs in the Bible (Numbers 6:13). At an early date lime (calcium oxide, CaO), a base, was prepared by roasting limestone (calcium carbonate, $CaCO_3$). Calcium carbonate is a salt that yields an alkaline solution when dissolved in water. The bases sodium (NaOH) and potassium hydroxide (KOH) were prepared by the reaction of slaked lime (calcium hydroxide, $Ca(OH)_2$) in water with sodium and potassium carbonate, Na_2CO_3 and K_2CO_3, respectively. The latter two compounds are salts and have basic properties in aqueous solution.

The body of knowledge concerning acids and bases was slowly expanded by medieval physicians and alchemists. During the 8th century, the Arabic alchemist Jabir Ibn Hayyan (Geber) discovered nitric acid and the mixture of nitric and hydrochloric acids, which was called *aqua regia,* "kingly water," because of its ability to dissolve the noble metal gold. Sulfuric acid was discovered in the 10th century.

In the 17th century, atomists tried to explain chemical properties and reactions in terms of the shapes postulated for the atomic particles. For example, the French physician Bertrand conjectured that acids were sour because they consist of pointed or spiky particles that prick the tongue. Neutralization was postulated to occur when the spikes of acid particles fit into the pores of alkaline particles, locking them together.

Oxygen Theory of Acids. In 1777 the French chemist A. L. Lavoisier proposed that all acids must contain the element oxygen. Because of this error, he coined the element's name "oxygen" from two Greek words meaning "acid-producing."

Hydrogen Theory of Acids. At the beginning of the 19th century, investigations of hydrochloric acid by Sir Humphry Davy in Britain and J. L. Gay-Lussac and L. J. Thénard in France showed that hydrogen, and not oxygen, was the acid-producing element.

In 1838 the German chemist Justus von Liebig provided the first satisfactory definition of an acid. He proposed that an acid is a compound that contains hydrogen in a form that can be replaced by a metal, but bases were still defined only by their ability to neutralize acids.

Integrated Theories of Acids and Bases. The fact that acids and bases are capable of neutralizing each other indicates the existence of an underlying structural relationship. Attempts to explain this relationship met with little success until 1887, when the Swedish chemist S. A. Arrhenius proposed the ionic theory, which extended the simple hydrogen theory of acids proposed by Davy and Liebig some 50 years previously.

IONIC THEORY

Hydrogen and Hydroxide Ions. The ionic theory of Arrhenius stated that acids and bases, in aqueous solution, ionize to some extent. That is, they break up into electrically charged particles known as ions. The theory defined an acid as a substance that ionizes in water to yield hydrogen ions (H^+), and a base as one that ionizes in water to produce hydroxide ions (OH^-).

Examples of these definitions can be provided by the following reactions involving nitric acid (HNO_3) and the base sodium hydroxide (NaOH):

$$HNO_3 \text{ (aq)} \rightarrow H^+ + NO_3^-$$
$$NaOH \text{ (aq)} \rightarrow Na^+ + OH^-$$

(The symbol "aq" indicates that the substance is in *aqueous* solution.) Acidic or basic properties are thus ascribed to the presence of H^+ ions or to OH^- ions, respectively.

Acid-Base Strengths. The strength of a particular acid or base was explained in terms of the degree of ionization of the acid or base. Accordingly, a strong acid is one that supplies a relatively high concentration of H^+ ions, whereas a weak acid is only slightly ionized and thus produces a low concentration of H^+ ions. A substance that contains hydrogen but does not ionize in water is not considered an acid. An example is methane (CH_4), which is essentially nonacidic.

Electrolytic Dissociation Theory. The ionic theory of acids and bases originated from the electrolytic dissociation theory conceived in the 1880's by Arrhenius and the German chemist Wilhelm Ostwald. The theory states that certain compounds, called electrolytes, dissociate into their component ions when dissolved in water. Arrhenius surmised that acids are electrolytes that give rise to hydrogen ions and bases are electrolytes that yield hydroxide ions.

The electrolytic dissociation theory provides a quantitative measure of the acidity or alkalinity of a solution and hence a measure of the strength of the acid or base. This is obtained by evaluating the ability of the solution to carry an electric current. The electrical conductivity of the solution is a measure of the concentration of the ions in solution and hence a measure of the concentration of the hydrogen of hydroxide ions.

Neutralization. Arrhenius' theory provided a simple explanation of the neutralization of acids by bases: the hydrogen ions from the acid react with the hydroxide ions from the base to yield neutral water:

$$H^+ + OH^- \rightarrow H_2O.$$

Limitations of the Arrhenius Definition. The Arrhenius definition of acids and bases in aqueous solution was generally accepted for about 35 years. It was then realized that a definition was required that explained the behavior of acids and bases in solvents other than water.

Also, according to the Arrhenius concept, an acid that was dissolved in water should produce H^+ ions in solution. The H^+ ions are simply protons—the nuclei of hydrogen atoms that have lost their one electron. However, electrical conductivity measurements and other experiments show that the protons do not exist free in solution. Instead, there is much evidence that the proton (H^+) is intimately attached to a solvent molecule. In water, for example, the H^+ is attached to an H_2O molecule to form the hydronium (or oxonium) ion, H_3O^+. If liquid methanol (CH_3OH) is the solvent, the proton is attached to a solvent molecule and exists as $CH_3OH_2^+$ (methyloxonium ion). In the solvent ammonia (NH_3), the H^+ is attached to an NH_3 molecule and exists as NH_4^+ (the ammonium ion).

Furthermore, several ambiguities arose regarding the possible classification of certain compounds as bases even though they do not contain a hydroxide as part of their structure. For example, ammonia in combination with water produces hydroxide ions.

PROTON-TRANSFER THEORY

A generalization of the Arrhenius concept of acids and bases was provided in 1923 by the Danish chemist J. N. Brønsted and independently by the English chemist T. M. Lowry.

Proton Donor/Acceptor. The Brønsted-Lowry definition states that any proton donor is an acid and any proton acceptor is a base. This definition has a number of advantages over the simple hydrogen ion–hydroxide ion theory. First, the new definition is independent of the particular solvent in which the acid or base is dissolved. Second, the acidic or basic species could be an anion (a negative ion) or a cation (a positive ion) and not just a neutral molecule.

The Brønsted-Lowry concept can be summarized by the following reaction involving a hypothetical acid *HX* and a hypothetical base *B:*

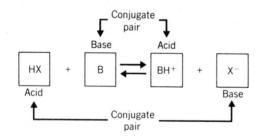

The above generalized acid-base reaction is a proton-transfer reaction, whereby the acid HX donates a proton (H^+) to the base B. The base becomes BH^+ whereas the acid becomes X^-. The original reactants can be reformed by the reverse reaction between the products BH^+ and X^-. In the reverse reaction, the BH^+ species acts as an acid by donating a proton, whereas the X^- species acts as a base by accepting a proton. (Chemists use the term species to refer to a particular kind of molecule, atom, or ion.)

Conjugate Acid-Base Pairs. The acid on one side of the reaction is paired with its complementary base on the other side of the equation. Hence,

HX and X^- make up a conjugate acid-base pair, and similarly BH^+ is the conjugate acid of the base B. Within a conjugate pair, the acid differs from its base counterpart by a proton (H^+); the acid has the extra proton.

The charges that are indicated on the species of the above reaction need not be the actual charges on the species. These charges are relative and simply signify that an acid has one more positive (or one less negative) charge than its conjugate base. Hence, besides neutral molecular acids and bases, there also exist ionic acids and bases. For instance, the ammonium cation NH_4^+ reacts as an acid and the acetate anion $C_2H_3O_2^-$ has basic properties.

Proton-Transfer Reactions. The following examples illustrate Brønsted-Lowry acid-base reactions in water and in methanol.

Ionization of an Acid in Water

$$HC_2H_3O_2 \quad + \quad H_2O \rightleftarrows C_2H_3O_2^- + H_3O^+$$
$$\text{(acetic acid)} \qquad\qquad \text{(acetate ion)}$$
$$\text{Acid} \qquad\qquad \text{Base}$$

Ionization of a Base in Water

$$NH_3 \qquad + H_2O \rightleftarrows NH_4^+ + OH^-$$
$$\text{(ammonia)} \qquad\qquad \text{(ammonium ion)}$$
$$\text{Base} \qquad \text{Acid}$$

Ionization of an Acid in a Nonaqueous Solvent

$$HC_2H_3O_2 + \quad CH_3OH \quad \rightleftarrows CH_3OH_2^+ + C_2H_3O_2^-$$
$$\text{(methanol)} \qquad \text{(methyloxonium ion)}$$
$$\text{Acid} \qquad\quad \text{Base}$$

Ionization of a Base in a Nonaqueous Solvent

$$NH_3 + \quad CH_3OH \quad \rightleftarrows CH_3O^- + NH_4^+$$
$$\text{(methanol)} \quad \text{(methoxide ion)}$$
$$\text{Base} \qquad\quad \text{Acid}$$

Neutralization of a Strong Acid by a Strong Base in Aqueous Solution. In aqueous solution, a strong acid such as HCl (hydrochloric acid) supplies H_3O^+ ions, and a strong base, such as NaOH (sodium hydroxide) provides OH^- ions:

$$HCl + H_2O \rightarrow Cl^- + H_3O^+$$
$$NaOH \rightarrow Na^+ + OH^-.$$

In the actual reaction, the hydronium (the proton donor) and the hydroxide (the proton acceptor) ions combine to yield neutral water:

$$H_3O^+ + OH^- \rightarrow 2H_2O.$$

In the above example, the sodium (Na^+) and chloride (Cl^-) ions from the salt sodium chloride (NaCl) are present in the solution.

Hydrolysis of Salts. When NaCl, which results from the reaction between NaOH and HCl, is dissolved in water, it will not alter the neutrality of the solution. However, if a salt is not derived from the reaction of a strong acid with a strong base, its aqueous solution may have either acidic or basic properties. Thus, an aqueous solution of a salt such as sodium acetate ($NaC_2H_3O_2$), which is derived from a weak acid ($HC_2H_3O_2$) and a strong base (NaOH), will yield a basic solution. The action of water—hydrolysis—on the anion ($C_2H_3O_2^-$) of the salt yields OH^-:

$$NaC_2H_3O_2 \text{ (aq.)} \qquad \rightleftarrows Na^+ + C_2H_3O_2^-;$$
$$C_2H_3O_2^- \quad + \quad H_2O \rightleftarrows HC_2H_3O_2 + OH^-.$$

Similarly, an aqueous solution of a salt such as ammonium chloride (NH_4Cl), which is produced from the reaction between hydrochloric acid (HCl), a strong acid, and ammonia (NH_3), a weak base, will result in an acidic solution. The hydrolysis of the cation (NH_4^+) of the salt yields hydronium ions:

$$NH_4Cl(aq) \rightleftarrows NH_4^+ + Cl^-$$
$$NH_4^+ + H_2O \rightleftarrows NH_3 + H_3O^+.$$

The Hydronium Ion. As noted previously, the hydronium ion (H_3O^+) is a hydrated proton—that is, an H^+ that is attached to an H_2O molecule. However, a number of experiments have demonstrated that in aqueous solution even the hydronium ion is hydrated by attachment of additional water molecules. The actual structure of the hydrated hydronium ion has not been definitely determined. However, it is believed that three water molecules are attached to the H_3O^+ ion to form the $H_9O_4^+$ species, as illustrated below.

The structure of $H_9O_4^+$ shown here in two dimensions, is actually three-dimensional.

The structure of the hydrated hydronium ion indicates that each hydrogen of the H_3O^+ species is attached to an oxygen of water. The hydrogen atom has a slight positive charge, whereas the oxygen has a slight negative charge. The attraction between these oppositely charged parts results in a bond between a hydrogen of one unit and the oxygen of another unit. This bond, known as a hydrogen bond, is represented by the dots between the atoms.

Polyprotic Acids and Polybases. Acids that can ionize in water to yield more than one proton per molecule are called polyprotic acids. A monoprotic acid, such as HCl (hydrochloric acid), yields one proton. Diprotic and triprotic acids, such as H_2SO_4 (sulfuric acid) and H_3PO_4 (phosphoric acid) yield two and three protons, respectively. For example, the sequential release of the three protons from phosphoric acid is represented by the following scheme:

$$H_3PO_4 + H_2O \rightleftarrows H_3O^+ + H_2PO_4^-$$
$$H_2PO_4^- + H_2O \rightleftarrows H_3O^+ + HPO_4^{2-}$$
$$HPO_4^{2-} + H_2O \rightleftarrows H_3O^+ + PO_4^{3-}$$

A series of three salts can be formed from a triprotic acid. For example, NaH_2PO_4 (sodium dihydrogen phosphate), Na_2HPO_4 (sodium monohydrogen phosphate), and Na_3PO_4 (sodium phosphate).

Bases that can ionize to form more than one hydroxide ion per molecule are called polybases. For example, $Ba(OH)_2$ (barium hydroxide) in aqueous solution can provide two hydroxide ions per molecule.

Amphoteric Species. A molecular or ionic species that has both acidic and basic properties is said to be amphoteric. Amphoteric species include the neutral molecules H_2O and NH_3, as illustrated by the following reactions:

autoionization of water:
$$2H_2O \rightleftarrows H_3O^+ + OH^-$$
autoionization of ammonia:
$$2NH_3 \rightleftarrows NH_4^+ + NH_2^-.$$

In each of these ionizations, one molecule acts as an acid, the other as a base. Thus, even in pure water, both hydronium and hydroxide ions are present. In pure water, the concentrations of the hydrogen and hydroxide ions are the same and equal to 1.00×10^{-7} mole/liter at 25°C. (One mole is one gram molecular weight of the species in question.) Other neutral amphoteric molecules include methanol (CH_3OH), which ionizes to $CH_3OH_2^+$ and CH_3O^-, and ethanol (C_2H_5OH), which ionizes to $C_2H_5OH_2^+$ and $C_2H_5O^-$.

Amphoteric species also include the anions of polyprotic acids. For example, in aqueous solution, each of the two anions of H_3PO_4, $H_2PO_4^-$ and HPO_4^{2-}, can act either as an acid or as a base, as demonstrated by the following hydrolysis reactions for $H_2PO_4^-$:

$$H_2PO_4^- + H_2O \rightleftarrows H_3O^+ + HPO_4^{2-}$$
Acid   Base

$$H_2PO_4^- + H_2O \rightleftarrows OH^- + H_3PO_4.$$
Base   Acid

The amphoteric properties of H_2O are also displayed in the above reactions. Other amphoteric anionic species include the bisulfate ion (HSO_4^-) and the bicarbonate ion (HCO_3^-).

Nomenclature of Protic Acids. The names that are given to Brønsted-Lowry acids follow a systematic pattern. An acid with the general symbol HX consists of a proton, H^+, and the anion X^-. The name of this acid depends on the suffix of the anion name. In general, anions have any one of three suffixes. Monatomic anions, which consist of one atom, have the -ide suffix. Oxyanions (those that contain one or more oxygen atoms) have either the -ate suffix or, if there is one less oxygen atom than in an -ate anion, the -ite suffix. The following rules will supply the appropriate acid name:

(1) -ide anion → hydro (anion name, less suffix) ic acid.

(2) -ate anion → (anion name, less suffix) ic acid.

(3) -ite anion → (anion name, less suffix) ous acid.

Examples: The acid HCl, which contains the cloride anion (Cl^-), is called "hydrochloric" acid according to rule (1). The acid HNO_3, which contains the nitrate anion (NO_3^-), becomes "nitric" acid according to rule (2). Similarly, HNO_2, which contains the nitrite anion (NO_2^-), is called "nitrous" acid according to rule (3).

ELECTRON-PAIR SHARING

In 1923, the same year that Brønsted and Lowry independently devised their proton definition of acids and bases, the U.S. chemist G. N. Lewis presented a further expansion of the concept of acids and bases.

According to the Lewis definition, an acid is any species that accepts and attaches itself to an unshared pair of electrons in another species; a base is any species that donates a lone pair of electrons to be shared by another species—the acid. This definition was suggested by the fact that an acidic hydrogen atom attaches itself to a free pair of electrons in the basic molecule during a Brønsted-Lowry proton-transfer reaction. According to Lewis, any species that acts in this fashion, even if it does not contain any hydrogen atoms, should be considered an acid. This Lew-

RELATIVE STRENGTHS OF SELECTED ACIDS AND BASES IN AQUEOUS SOLUTION
(Grouped in conjugate pairs)

	Acid		Base		
very strong	$HClO_4$	perchloric	ClO_4^-	chlorate ion	extremely weak
	HI	hydriodic	I^-	iodide ion	
	HBr	hydrobromic	Br^-	bromide ion	
	H_2SO_4	sulfuric	HSO_4^-	bisulfate ion	
	HCl	hydrochloric	Cl^-	chloride ion	
	HNO_3	nitric	NO_3^-	nitrate ion	
strong	H_3O^+	hydronium ion	H_2O	water	very weak
weak	H_2SO_3	sulfurous	HSO_3^-	bisulfite ion	weak
	HSO_4^-	hydrogen sulfate (or bisulfate) ion	SO_4^{2-}	sulfate ion	
	HF	hydrofluoric	F^-	fluoride ion	
	$HC_2H_3O_2$	acetic	$C_2H_3O_2^-$	acetate ion	
	$C_5H_5NH^+$	pyridinium ion	C_5H_5N	pyridine	
	HSO_3^-	hydrogen sulfite (or bisulfite) ion	SO_3^{2-}	sulfite ion	
	H_2S	hydrosulfuric	HS^-	bisulfide ion	
	NH_4^+	ammonium ion	NH_3	ammonia	
	HCO_3^-	hydrogen carbonate (or bicarbonate) ion	CO_3^{2-}	carbonate ion	
	$CH_3NH_3^+$	methylammonium ion	CH_3NH_2	methylamine	
very weak	H_2O	water	OH^-	hydroxide ion	strong
extremely weak	C_2H_5OH	ethanol	$C_2H_5O^-$	ethoxide ion	very strong
	NH_3	ammonia	NH_2^-	amide ion	
	H_2	hydrogen	H^-	hydride ion	
	OH^-	hydroxide ion	O^{2-}	oxide ion	

is definition is based on the valence theory of bonding. Thus, a Lewis acid is any species that accepts an electron pair from a base to form a coordinate covalent bond, and a Lewis base is any species that donates an electron pair to form such a bond. See BOND.

Lewis Acid-Base Reactions. The reaction between a Lewis acid and base results in an *addition* prod*uct*—an adduct. This compound consists of the two reacting species united by a coordinate covalent bond.

Neutral (or Uncharged) Molecules. The reaction between boron trifluoride (BF_3) and ammonia (NH_3) results in the following adduct (the pair of heavy dots represents the pair of electrons to be used in a coordinate covalent bond):

Acid	Base		Adduct

The BF_3 acts as an acid by accepting an electron-pair from NH_3, the base, which donates the pair, to form the coordinate covalent bond between the two species.

Charged Species. The reaction between silver ion (Ag^+) and ammonia results in the diammine-silver(I) ion complex, $[Ag(NH_3)_2]^+$, according to the following acid-base reaction:

Acid	Base	Adduct

Similarly, the reaction between BF_3 and the hydroxide ion, OH^-, yields the adduct $[BF_3(OH)]^-$, according to:

Acid	Base	Adduct

Other Lewis acids that are not covered by the Brønsted-Lowry definition include $AlCl_3$ (aluminum chloride), $ZnCl_2$ (zinc chloride), and $TiCl_4$ (titanium chloride).

ACID-BASE STRENGTHS

Qualitative Considerations. In the Brønsted-Lowry proton-transfer theory, any acid or base that ionizes or dissociates nearly completely in a solvent to form ionic products is called a *strong* acid or base in that particular solvent. If only a small fraction of the species molecules break up, it is considered to be *weak* in that solvent.

As examples, the ionizations of hydrochloric (HCl) and acetic ($HC_2H_3O_2$) acids in aqueous solutions will be considered. The ionization of HCl is nearly complete, as can be illustrated by use of large forward arrow:

$$HCl + H_2O \rightleftharpoons H_3O^+ + Cl^-.$$
$$Acid_1 \quad Base_2 \quad Acid_2 \quad Base_1$$

Hence, HCl is a strong acid in water. However, acetic acid is a relatively weak acid. Its ionization could be written with a large reverse arrow, which indicates that the ionic products can readily combine to revert to the un-ionized molecules of acetic acid:

108

$$HC_2H_3O_2 + H_2O \rightleftarrows H_3O^+ + C_2H_3O_2^-$$
$$\text{Acid}_1 \quad\quad \text{Base}_2 \quad\quad \text{Acid}_2 \quad\quad \text{Base}_1$$

In each of the above two reactions, an acid and a base are on each side of the reaction. The relative strengths of the two acids or of the two bases in a particular solvent can be determined if the extent of the ionization of one of the acids is known. In the HCl example, the reaction proceeds almost completely to the right. This indicates that HCl, the acid on the left side of the reaction, is a stronger acid than is H_3O^+, the acid on the right side. Similarly, H_2O as a base is stronger than Cl^-. In the second reaction, the acetic acid ionization proceeds only slightly to the right. Thus, $HC_2H_3O_2$ is a weaker acid than H_3O^+, and H_2O is a weaker base than $C_2H_3O_2$.

By the study of other ionizations in aqueous solution, the accompanying table can be constructed. Note the placement of the three acids and the three bases that were just discussed. Acid strengths decrease in the order $HCl > H_3O^+ > HC_2H_3O_2$, whereas base strengths increase according to $Cl^- < H_2O < C_2H_3O^-_2$.

This table shows that if an acid is strong, its conjugate base is weak. Similarly, a strong base has a weak conjugate acid. Thus, if HCl is relatively strong, then Cl^- is weak.

pH. The degree of acidity or alkalinity of an aqueous solution can be quantitatively described by its pH, which is defined as the negative logarithm of the hydrogen-ion concentration—or, more accurately, of the hydronium-ion concentration. At 25° C, an acidic solution has a pH value less than 7; a basic solution has a pH greater than 7; and a neutral aqueous solution has a pH equal to 7. See also PH.

Buffer Solutions. Buffered aqueous solutions resist drastic changes in their pH, despite the addition of a strong acid or a strong base. Buffered solutions are composed of a weak acid and its salt (the conjugate base) or of a weak base and its salt (the conjugate acid). The particular pH of a buffer solution is dependent on the relative strength of the weak acid or of the weak base.

STRUCTURAL CLASSIFICATION OF ACIDS AND BASES

Acids and bases are classified as either organic, if the species contains carbon, or inorganic.

Organic acids are further subdivided according to the type of structural group that contains the ionizable hydrogen: (1) carboxylic acids have the —COOH (carboxyl) group; (2) alcohols and phenols have the —OH (hydroxyl) group, where, in a phenol, the —OH group is attached to a benzene ring, $\bigcirc$; (3) sulfonic acids are organic derivatives of sulfuric acid; and many other types. Organic bases usually include the amines, compounds that are closely related to ammonia.

Inorganic bases include metal hydroxides—such as the very strong bases LiOH, NaOH, KOH, RbOH, CsOH, $Ca(OH)_2$, $Sr(OH)_2$, and $Ba(OH)_2$—as well as ammonia and its related hydroxides.

ZVI C. KORNBLUM
Cooper Union

Bibliography

Boikess, R. S., and E. Edelson, *Chemical Principles*, 3d ed. (Harper 1985).
Cohen, Jordan J., and Jerome P. Kassiver, *Acid-Base* (Little 1982).
Hand, Clifford W., *Acid-Base Chemistry* (Macmillan 1986).
Heisler, N., ed., *Acid-Base Regulation in Animals* (Elsevier Pub. Co. 1986).
Turchot, J. P., *Comparative Aspects of Extracellular Acid-Base Balance* (Springer-Verlag 1987).

ACKNOWLEDGMENT, in law, the formal act of declaring the execution of a legal instrument before an appropriate public official. The word is also applied to the written evidence, or certificate, of such an act. Deeds, mortgages, leases, and powers of attorney affecting land are the kinds of instruments most commonly requiring an acknowledgment, but in some U.S. states other documents, such as articles of incorporation, also must be acknowledged.

Acknowledgment is a statutory requirement, the provisions varying from one U.S. state to another. Its purposes are to entitle the deed or other instrument to be recorded and to authenticate the instrument so that it can be admitted in evidence. Acknowledgment must be made by the person who executed the instrument or, in limited circumstances, by his or her agent. The statutes authorize various officers, such as judges, justices of the peace, clerks of courts, and public notaries, to take acknowledgments. The formal execution of a certificate by the officer taking the acknowledgment is ordinarily required. This writing may appear on the paper containing the acknowledged instrument or may be attached to it, depending on the particular statute. Under some statutes, lack of acknowledgment makes an instrument void.

RICHARD L. HIRSHBERG, *Attorney at Law*

ACNE, ak'nē, an inherited disorder of the skin's hair-and-oil follicles, resulting in blemishes or pimples on the face, chest, and upper back. The common form of acne, acne vulgaris, is seen in most adolescent boys and girls. Although it may begin in earliest puberty—between the ages of eight and ten—it is most common in the midteens. Acne often clears spontaneously in late adolescence or early adulthood, but many people are plagued with it throughout life.

The first stage of acne vulgaris is usually marked by blackheads and whiteheads (comedones). Thereafter, during preadolescence, red, inflamed blemishes may appear with different degrees of severity. Most superficial red blemishes heal by themselves within a week, but deeper cysts may require several weeks before disappearing. Some deep acne cysts may be painful and result in permanent scarring.

Another form of acne, which develops in middle age, is termed acne rosacea. It causes the central part of the face to erupt in red patches, red blemishes, and occasionally pustules. Acne rosacea is most common in women but is often more severe in men. A severe variant, rhynophyma, may result in a bulbous nose.

Cause. Acne vulgaris is caused by the effect of androgen hormones on the hair follicle and its sebaceous (oil) gland. Blackheads and whiteheads result from the accumulation of skin fragments (scales) and a fatty substance (sebum) in hair follicles. Pigment, not dirt, residing in the follicles causes the black color of blackheads. Certain bacteria (*Proprionobacterium acnes*) appear to be important in promoting the evolution of blackheads and whiteheads into red, inflamed pimples, pustules, and cysts. These bacteria incite inflammation by attracting the body's white blood cells into the area of the follicle.

Contributing Factors. The tendency to develop acne vulgaris is inherited. Among individuals who are genetically predisposed to the condition, periods of stress and tension may bring about flare-ups of acne. Abrasive skin cleansing frequently worsens existing cases. Also, certain creams, lotions, and cosmetics encourage formation of blackheads and whiteheads (and possibly may lead to more severe acne).

Although a few individuals can correlate specific items such as sweets or oily foods with new eruptions, diet generally plays no significant role in the cause or treatment of acne. Even chocolate causes little trouble for most people.

Hygienic Treatment. Acne is not related to dirt or ineffective cleansing. In fact, it may be worsened by overzealous cleansing and abrasive scrubbing. Gentle washing of the face and other involved areas once or twice a day with mild soap or skin cleanser is generally all that is necessary. Astringents and alcohol can reduce oiliness on the skin surface but do very little to treat acne.

Medical Treatment. Great advances in acne treatment have been made since the early 1970's in both medications applied directly to the skin and internal medications taken by mouth.

Topical Medications. Because acne lesions begin as comedones, most topical treatment is designed to loosen and dissolve the plugs in the blocked follicles. Regular application of tretinoin (retinic acid, a derivative of Vitamin A) in the form of a cream, liquid, or gel over a period of a few months often helps dissolve most of the plugs. Benzoyl peroxide gels help both to dissolve comedones and to kill skin bacteria. Salicylic acid creams and gels and sulfur creams also may tend to dissolve comedones. Other topical lotions are designed to reduce the numbers of bacteria—specifically *Proprionobacterium acnes*—in the follicles. These lotions usually contain an antibiotic such as tetracycline.

Internal Medications. Two basic forms of internal medication generally are of great help in treating inflamed blemishes and cysts in acne. Antibiotic pills have been used for this purpose for several years. These antibiotics also reduce the bacteria present in the follicles. It may be necessary to continue the treatment for months or years, but with careful monitoring by a physician antibiotics have few side effects and are remarkably safe.

A retinoid drug taken by mouth—13-cis-retinoic acid—has a profound effect on severe cystic acne and is now widely used for this devastating disease. The therapeutic effects of this drug—unlike those of antibiotics—continue long after it is discontinued. Thus treatment may be required for only four to five months.

Vitamins and trace-metal supplements such as zinc have not been found useful in acne treatment.

Physical Agents. Because ultraviolet light in the form of moderate exposure to summer sunlight is helpful for most acne sufferers, acne tends to improve in the summer months. However, summer heat and humidity may increase the development of inflamed red lesions. For this reason, acne may be very severe in the humid tropics. Artificial ultraviolet light in the form of sunlamps should be avoided, for severe sunburns have resulted from their injudicious use. Excessive exposure to ultraviolet light from any source may lead to premature wrinkling and skin cancer.

X-ray treatment is not recommended, because it, too, may tend to induce cancer.

Hormone therapy with estrogen or cortisone-like hormones is considered only in severe cases, when more conservative treatment has not been effective, because of undesirable side effects. However, injecting a dilute cortisone solution into deep inflamed cysts is a routine procedure that is both safe and helpful.

Acne surgery sometimes is used to extract comedones and to open pustules and cysts. Chemical peeling of the skin with mild acids or thermal peeling by the controlled application of cold in the form of liquid nitrogen or a slush of dry ice may have superficially similar effects.

Psychosocial Effects. During the formative adolescent years disfigurement resulting from acne may have a profound emotional effect. The social development during the teenage years can be severely and permanently impaired by low self-esteem and a poor self-image resulting from severe acne. For this reason it is especially important that young persons with acne receive treatment. It is equally important that psychosocial counseling be part of the treatment.

BARRY S. GOLDBERG, M.D., *Yale University*

Further Reading: Cullen, S. I., ed., *Focus on Acne Vulgaris* (Longwood 1985); Fulton, James E., and Black, Elizabeth, *Dr. Fulton's Step-by-Step Program for Clearing Acne* (Harper 1983).

ACOMA, ak'ō-mô, an Indian pueblo (village) in Valencia county, New Mexico, about 55 miles (88 km) west of Albuquerque. Archaeological studies indicate that it was established by 1100 A.D., making it the oldest continuously occupied village in the United States.

The pueblo is situated on a steep-sided sandstone mesa 357 feet (108 meters) high, called Acoma Rock. The Acoma population in 1990 was 2,590, but except for special occasions, few Acoma people remain on the Rock. Most of them inhabit the farming communities of Acomita and McCartys in the surrounding Acoma Indian Reservation (245,672 acres, or 99,420 hectares) or work elsewhere in the Southwest.

Ancestors of the Acomas probably inhabited the region before the 1st century A.D. Their legends, like those of many Southwest Indians, tell of a migration from the north. These may refer to peoples who arrived about 1300 A.D. Documentary history begins in 1540 with the visit of Hernando de Alvarado of the Coronado expedition. In 1599, Vicente de Zaldívar destroyed much of the pueblo. Father Juan Ramirez may have built the first church here in 1629. Acoma took part in the Pueblo Rebellion of 1680, but the Spanish regained control in 1692.

Keresan is the native Acoma language, but almost everyone speaks English or Spanish. Social organization is based on clan affiliation with matrilineal descent. Kinship partly controls membership in the important medicine societies and *katchina* groups. The philosophy of these groups is that people are a part of nature and that ceremonies help in the succession of the seasons, the fertility of plants and animals, and the coming of rain.

The Acomas are subject to United States laws, but local government rests with the *caciques*, who control all religion and ceremonialism. They also appoint the secular officers of the pueblo, including the governor, two lieutenant governors, the sheriff, ten councilmen, and several lesser officials. Visitors are welcomed at the pueblo.

ALFRED E. DITTERT, JR., *Museum of New Mexico*

TOM HOLLYMAN, FROM PHOTO RESEARCHERS

Aconcagua, highest peak in the Western Hemisphere.

ACONCAGUA, ä-kông-kä′gwä, the highest mountain in the Western Hemisphere. A peak of the Andes system, it is located in west central Argentina near the Chilean border. A toothlike eminence, Aconcagua rises from precipitous ridges to an elevation of 22,831 feet (6,959 meters). Although it is in the heart of the Andes, where much volcanic action has occurred, it is not considered a volcano.

The summit of Aconcagua was first reached on Jan. 14, 1897, by the Swiss Alpinist Mattias Zurbriggen, who was a member of a mountain-climbing expedition led by Edward A. Fitzgerald.

ACONITE, ak′ə-nīt, is a showy herbaceous flowering perennial, commonly known as monkshood or wolfsbane. It is found in the temperate and cooler parts of the northern temperate zones. Aconites contain a poisonous alkaloid, aconitin, which causes respiratory paralysis if ingested.

About 2 to 7 feet (0.6–2.1 meters) tall, depending on species, aconites have hooded flowers that are usually blue or purple, but sometimes white or yellow. The flowers have five petal-like sepals, one of which is enlarged to form a hood over the rest of the flower. Two of the upper petals are hooded also but are concealed. The leaves are lobed in a handlike fashion, and the roots are tuberous or thickened.

The genus *Aconitum* belongs to the buttercup family (Ranunculaceae). There are about 100 species. Leaves and roots of the species *A. napellus*, grown in England and continental Europe, yield aconite, a drug formerly used as a sedative. *A. uncinatum* is the species found in the eastern United States.

ACORN. See under OAK.

ACORN WORM. See HEMICHORDATE.

ACOUSTICS, ə-kōō′stiks, a branch of physics that deals with the production, propagation, reception, and use of sound. It is one of the oldest of the physical sciences. Its historical roots go back to the ancient Greeks and earlier cultures. The term acoustics comes from the Greek word *akoustikos,* meaning "related to hearing."

The design of Greek and Roman amphitheaters attests to the acoustical insights of builders and scientists of ancient times. For centuries, man has used sounds to make music, which depends on relationships between sounds. One of the best-known musical scales is the Pythagorean, named after its reputed inventor, Pythagoras, the Greek philosopher and mathematician, who lived in the 6th century B.C. During the Middle Ages, acoustics, like most other sciences, was dormant. It was revived in the upsurge of science following the Renaissance.

Modern Acoustics. Acoustics now comprises a wide variety of fields: physical acoustics and ultrasonics (the study of matter by using sound waves); architectural acoustics (the study of sound waves in auditoriums and concert halls); psychoacoustics and physiological acoustics (the study of hearing); speech communication (the study of the human speaking apparatus and verbal communication); underwater sound; noise control; mechanical vibrations and shock waves; and many other disciplines.

Acoustics can be divided roughly into two large areas of study: the interaction of sound waves with physical matter, and the interaction of sound waves with living organisms. Another useful distinction is between information-bearing sound waves (such as human speech and birdcalls) and noise, sometimes loosely called "unwanted sound."

The science of acoustics has progressed on many fronts, most of which are related to important needs of human society. The design of concert halls and auditoriums with better listening conditions and the specification of office and apartment buildings with better sound insulation are well-known examples of acoustics research that affect the well-being of many persons. Noise control, for example of takeoff noise at airports, is important in transportation.

Communications between persons and between persons and machines are areas of rapidly increasing importance in which acoustics plays a decisive role. Computer-controlled speech synthesizers will have many applications, including automatic answering and information services for weather, stock prices, inventory data, and the like, and automatic book-readers for the blind. While further research and development is needed before such applications are routine, the basic technology is well understood. Computerized speech synthesis is already used by telephone information services to provide callers with telephone numbers.

The development of computer programs that can reliably recognize human speech is a more difficult task. Such programs will make it possible to design machines that can both recognize individual speech patterns and execute verbal instructions. Speaker recognition will be useful in applications such as banking transactions, where verification of identity is crucial.

Sound waves of extremely high frequencies are an important tool in probing basic properties of matter and in gaining a better understanding of important physical phenomena, such as thermal vibrations and superconductivity. The frequencies of the sound waves that are used for such purposes often exceed the audible range (ultrasound) and may be as high as several billion cycles per second (hypersound). At such high frequencies, sound, like light, is transmitted in little packets of energy called phonons. The study of the interaction of phonons and electrons is giving new insights into the structure of metals and other materials, including superconductors.

Inaudible, extremely low-frequency sound waves stemming from earthquakes and underground explosions are useful for studying the composition of the earth's mantle. Nuclear explosions above ground generate low-frequency sound waves of such high intensity that they still can be detected after they have traveled around the entire globe.

In more practical applications, ultrasonic waves are used to locate faults in component parts used in construction, such as spacecraft, where the utmost reliability is required. Ultrasonic waves also are used to facilitate chemical reactions and to clean, dye, and mix different substances. In medicine, ultrasonic waves have found wide application for therapeutic purposes. Strongly focused ultrasonic pulses can be used to guide the blind. Waterborne sound waves of lower frequency are used to guide and locate ships, including submarines.

A particularly important area of acoustics research is the exploration of structural vibrations and fatigue of metals and other materials used in designing aircraft and rockets.

These applications and a myriad other applications serve to emphasize the importance of sound to man in his modern world.

Physics of Sound. Sound waves are the regular movements of atoms and molecules superimposed on their irregular thermal movements.

In the case of sound waves in solid materials, the sound waves can be interpreted in terms of the model shown in the drawing below. The individual atoms are represented by the identical masses, M. The forces between the atoms are represented by the identical springs, F, which connect adjacent masses. If the masses are equidistant, then no net forces are exerted by the springs on the masses. In the uppermost diagram (represented by time t_0) the masses are in their rest positions. This condition corresponds to the absence of sound in a solid material. If the end

SOUND WAVE in a solid material is represented by a mechanical model, as explained in the accompanying text. The masses, M, represent the individual atoms. The springs, F, represent the forces between the atoms.

mass begins to be displaced in an oscillatory fashion about its rest position, then the spring that is attached to it exerts a force on the neighboring mass. This force, in turn, is exerted by the connecting spring on the next mass, and the effect propagates down the chain. The action is shown for several successive instants in time (t_1, t_2, . . . t_6) in Fig. 1. After a delay, which is determined by the size of the masses, the spring stiffness, and the distance along the chain, each mass will begin to perform an oscillatory motion about its rest position. The maximum displacement is called the *amplitude* of the motion. The time of the maximum displacement determines the *phase* of the motion.

Waves in which the particles move along the line of the direction of wave propagation are called *longitudinal waves.* In solids and certain liquids the particles also can move at right angles to the direction of wave propagation. Such waves are called *transversal,* or *shear, waves.*

In gases the forces between atoms and molecules cannot easily be represented by springs because the forces are caused by collisions between the individual particles. The forces resulting from these collisions are called *gas pressure.* Because pressure is a longitudinal force, only longitudinal waves can exist in gases.

The number of oscillations per second is called the *frequency,* which is measured in cycles per second or Hertz (Hz). The shortest distance between particles oscillating in equal phase is called the *wavelength* of the wave. The product of frequency and wavelength equals the *velocity* with which the wave propagates.

For an observer who moves with respect to the source of the waves, the apparent frequency differs from the frequency for a stationary observer.

If observer and source move toward each other, the apparent frequency is increased. If observer and source move away from each other, the apparent frequency is decreased. This phenomenon is called the Doppler effect. It can be heard, for example, as a sudden drop in frequency, or *pitch,* when a whistling train passes an observer at high speed.

When two waves of different frequencies are perceived simultaneously, a pitch corresponding to the difference of the two frequencies is sometimes heard. This pitch is known as a *beat note.*

When two waves of equal frequency and equal amplitude travel in opposite directions, they produce a *standing wave.* In a standing wave all particles move in equal or opposite phase; that is, they reach their extreme amplitudes at identical times. Standing waves are very common. For example, the air in an organ pipe or the string of a violin moves as a standing wave.

Sound Transmission. Sound propagates as waves. In contrast to light, which can travel through empty space, sound waves require some kind of elastic matter for their propagation. The propagation medium can be a gas, such as air; a liquid, such as water; or a solid, such as the walls of a building. The sounds we hear reach our ears by way of the air surrounding us. Fish "listen" to sound waves propagating in water. The vibrations of the walls of a noisy building are called "solid-borne" sound.

The speed of sound is determined by the pressure, temperature, and other properties of the material through which it travels. The speed of sound in air, at a temperature of 77° F (25° C) and at normal atmospheric pressure, is 1,055 feet (322 meters) per second. Thus, a sound wave requires almost one second to traverse a distance of 1,000 feet (305 meters). A light wave travels the same distance in less than a millionth of a second. It is because of this large difference between the velocities of sound and light that we hear thunder after we see the lightning.

The velocity of sound in liquids and solids usually is considerably greater than in gases. This is so because the atoms and molecules in liquids and solids are much closer to each other than in gases, and the forces between them are much greater. At 70° F (21° C), the velocity of sound in pure water is 5,100 feet (1,555 meters) per second; in steel it is 17,200 feet (5,243 meters) per second.

The transmission of sound always is accompanied by an attenuation of its intensity. In homogeneous and isotropic media, sound spreads in spherical waves. This spreading causes a progressive decrease in the intensity of sound as it travels farther and farther from its source. This behavior is much like circular water waves on the surface of a pond; the waves become weaker and weaker with increasing distance from their origin. The intensity of a spherical wave is reduced fourfold for every doubling of distance because the same total energy is spread over four times the original areas ($A = \pi r^2$).

Relative sound intensity often is expressed in *decibels*. The decibel is defined as "10 times the logarithm to the base 10 of the ratio of intensities." In mathematical form, the definition of the decibel looks as follows: attenuation in decibels $= 10 \log_{10}\left(\dfrac{I_o}{I}\right)$, where I is the later intensity of the sound, and I_o is the original intensity. For a doubling of distance, $\dfrac{I_o}{I} = 4$. In this case, the attenuation of a spherical wave is:

$$10 \log_{10}(4) = 6 \text{ decibels.}$$

Because the intensity of a sound wave is proportional to the *square of the sound pressure amplitude* associated with the wave, the definition of a decibel also can be rendered in the following form:

$$\text{attenuation in decibels} =$$
$$10 \log_{10}\left(\frac{p_o{}^2}{p^2}\right) = 20 \log_{10}\left(\frac{p_o}{p}\right),$$

where p is the actual sound pressure amplitude, and p_o is the reference sound pressure amplitude.

SOUND WAVES radiating from a telephone receiver are made visible by a special photographic technique.

The attenuation of sound waves due to spreading can be avoided by confining the waves to a narrow region. In the case of airborne and liquid-borne sound, this confinement can be accomplished by using hollow tubes. In the case of solid-borne sound, the spreading can be avoided, for example, by transmitting the sound through thin rods.

In addition to attenuation caused by spreading, sound is attenuated by the internal friction that occurs between the atoms and molecules in a viscous medium. This kind of attenuation is called sound absorption. However, the energy of the sound wave is not completely lost. As in all friction processes, energy is converted into heat. The heat generated may be imperceptibly small, but it may represent a substantial fraction of the energy of the sound wave.

In general, there is more friction in gases and liquids than in hard solids, especially metals and certain crystals. At normal temperatures and pressures the attenuation of audible sound waves in steel is about 100 times smaller than in air. The low sound absorption of steel, together with the lack of spreading, accounts for the fact that one can hear a distant railroad train by putting an ear to the track, even though the airborne sound is much too weak to be heard.

In general, sound absorption increases with frequency. Quartz is a material that has particu-

VOICES, like fingerprints, apparently are unique for each individual. Voiceprints, which are sound spectrograms, present a picture of speech. This contour voice print shows a female voice saying "This is a voiceprint."

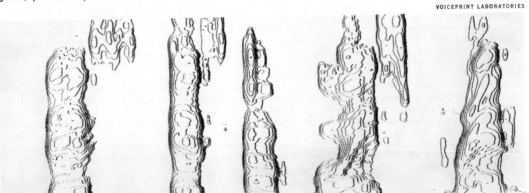

larly low sound absorption, even at very high frequencies. Therefore, quartz crystals are used in many industrial applications when sound has to be transmitted with a minimum of loss. Because nature's supply of quartz is insufficient, quartz crystals now are grown artificially in many laboratories.

Sound Sources: The Human Voice. An important source of sound is the human voice. From the elemental sounds that the respiratory and oral systems can produce, humans have developed a highly sophisticated tool: speech. Although human speech is weak in physical energy, it is a most powerful means of communicating. It can be informative, persuasive, edifying, destructive, boring, or simply unintelligible.

All speech sounds are generated by the air escaping from the lungs. There are two kinds of speech sounds: *voiced,* and *unvoiced.* For voiced speech sounds, such as the vowels and diphthongs ($\ddot{a}, \ddot{e}, \overline{oo}, a, i, o$), the air stream from the lungs is chopped into short pulses of air by the vocal cords. The rate at which this chopping occurs determines the fundamental frequency, or pitch, of the voice. The pitch is low for males (about 100 pulses per second), higher for female voices (about 200 pulses per second), and higher still for children. The pulses of air enter the space within the vocal tract. Like any hollow pipe, the space has resonances that impart a characteristic tone quality, or *timbre,* to the air pulses. Each speech sound is distinguished by a different timbre. The resonance frequencies, and therefore the timbre, depend on the position and shape of the articulators (the tongue, the lips, the palate). By varying the position and shape of the articulators, one produces continuous speech.

For unvoiced speech sounds the vocal cords remain inactive. For these speech sounds, the audible sound is generated by sudden release of pressure (pops) or by turbulence caused by friction of the air stream in narrow passages. Examples of *plosive* speech sounds are p, t, and k. Examples of fricative sounds are f, s, and th (as in thin). Some speech sounds, like z and v, are neither purely voiced nor purely unvoiced. They are called *voiced fricatives.* For other speech sounds (m, n, ng) the air escapes from the nostrils. These sounds are *nasals.* (See also VOICE.)

Many questions concerning the production and perception of speech by humans are still unanswered. Much research is devoted to these problems both for the sake of a better basic understanding of these processes and because of the many applications that would become possible as a result of such an understanding. Among the applications are automatic speech recognizers and speaking machines that produce intelligible speech from written text. Automatic speech recognizers for a small number of carefully pronounced words have been developed. Speaking machines that produce synthetic speech from a phonetic symbol input have been simulated on digital computers, but the artificial "computer speech" does not yet sound very human.

An important application of synthetic speech for communication is the *vocoder* (a word coined from *voice* and *coder*). Vocoders analyze speech into its individual frequency components. After transmission, vocoders resynthesize artificial speech at some distant receiving point. Information concerning the frequency components of *several* speech signals can be transmitted over a single telephone circuit. Thus, long-distance communication will become more economical when the artificial speech of a vocoder can be made to sound natural.

Sound Sources: Musical Instruments. Musical instruments are another important class of sound sources. Musical instruments produce their sounds by a variety of physical mechanisms. Some instruments, such as the violin, the cello, the double bass, the guitar, and the harp, produce their sounds by vibrating strings, which are set into motion by plucking or bowing. Other instruments, such as the accordion, use vibrating reeds. Many musical instruments use a combination of mechanisms, such as vibrating reeds and resonating air columns. The clarinet, the bassoon, and the saxophone are in this class. For some musical instruments the performer's lips play the role of the reed. Well-known examples are the bugle, the trumpet, the trombone, and the tuba. In organ pipes, flutes, and recorders the resonating air column is set into motion by an air reed that periodically interrupts the flow of air.

Drums of all kinds use vibrating membranes to produce sound. In bells, chimes, and glockenspiels the sound is generated by the impact of hammers on variously shaped resonating metal bodies.

In contrast to these purely mechanical instruments, loudspeakers convert a given electrical signal into a corresponding acoustical wave. Loudspeakers play an increasing role for the generation of sounds of all kinds. A loudspeaker can reproduce, with more or less fidelity, the sounds of other musical instruments. When coupled to an electric organ or other music synthesizer, the loudspeaker becomes an integral part of the instrument.

Sound Receivers: The Human Ear. Among the many receivers for sound the human ear, in many respects, is the most sophisticated and capable.

Unlike human vision, which is limited to a frequency ratio of 2 to 1, or one octave, normal human hearing spans more than 10 octaves: from 16 cycles per second to more than 16,000 cycles per second. In this frequency range, humans are able to distinguish a virtually unlimited variety of sounds—the spoken word of a fellow human, the roar of a modern jet, the humming of an insect, and the crescendo sound of a symphony orchestra are examples.

In addition to its great range in frequency the human ear has an almost unbelievable range in sound intensity. For the faintest sounds that the ear can detect, the ear drum moves by less than a billionth of an inch—about the diameter of a hydrogen atom. The loudest sounds that the human ear can tolerate without pain have an intensity of 1,000 billion times greater than the faintest. The frequency sensitivity of the ear is remarkable too. At 1,000 cycles per second the human ear can detect a frequency difference of only a few cycles, that is, a few parts in 1,000.

One of the astonishing properties of binaural (two-eared) hearing is the capability to localize where the sound comes from. Not only can we distinguish left from right, front from back, and many intermediate directions, but we can also "focus" on a particular source of sound surrounded by other sources. This amazing ability of human hearing sometimes is called the "cocktail party effect." Without it we would be unable to extract and understand the speech of a single speaker from the surrounding babble. The cocktail party effect is related to the "precedence effect"—the ear can concentrate on the first arriving sound wave and reject later arriving echoes of the same sound wave. Without this ability it would be very difficult or even impossible to understand speech in reverberant rooms. In fact, an echo that arrives 0.01 second later can be 10 times as intense as the original sound before it becomes distracting. This extension of the precedence effect is known as the "Haas effect." The Haas effect is utilized in modern sound reinforcement systems. The amplified sound from the loudspeakers is delayed by approximately 0.01 second with respect to the direct sound from the original source. In this manner an acoustic illusion is created—all the sound seems to be coming from the original source rather than from the loudspeaker.

The complicated interactions that take place in binaural hearing are not yet fully understood, but they are being investigated by scientists in many laboratories. Concurrent with this research, attempts are being made to duplicate binaural interaction by using electronic circuits. When this duplication is accomplished, it may become much easier to hold conferences between large groups of people by telephone, thereby eliminating much unnecessary traveling.

The Human Hearing Mechanism. The human hearing mechanism may be divided into three parts: the outer ear, the middle ear, and the inner ear. The outer ear consists of the external ear (pinna) and the ear canal, which is terminated in the eardrum (tympanic membrane). Behind the eardrum is the middle ear, a small cavity in which three bones—the hammer, the anvil, and the stirrup—form the elements of a lever system for transmitting vibrations from the eardrum to an aperture (the oval window) of the inner ear.

The inner ear (cochlea) has a form resembling a snail shell. It is divided along its length by a wedge-shaped tunnel, or partition, composed of two membranes: the basilar membrane and Reissner's membrane. A viscous fluid (endolymph) fills the partition, and a different fluid (perilymph) fills the outer canals (scalas). Inside the partition and situated on the basilar membrane is the organ of Corti, which contains the auditory nerve endings and hair cells. There are about 30,000 nerve fibers running from the cochlea to the brain. Each nerve fiber is enclosed in a sheath like that of an insulated wire. The 30,000 nerve fibers form a single cable, which is a little more than one millimeter in diameter. The cable of nerves passes through the temporal bone to the base of the brain.

When a sound wave enters the ear canal, it impinges on the eardrum. The eardrum vibrates with a motion corresponding to the undulations in the sound wave. The motion of the eardrum is transmitted to the oval window of the cochlea by the lever system of the middle ear. The vibrations of the oval window are transmitted into the fluid of the cochlea back of the oval window. The sound waves in the cochlea cause a relative motion between the basilar membrane and another membrane (the tectorial membrane) located inside the cochlea partition. This motion causes the hair cells to stimulate the endings of the auditory nerve.

The cochlea is a frequency-selective mechanism. The portion of the cochlea nearest the oval window is most sensitive to high frequencies; the midportion of the cochlea is excited predominant-

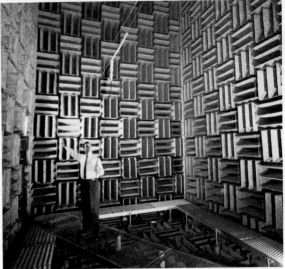

ECHOLESS room for testing sound insulation materials for flight craft has walls made of glass fiber wedges.

ly by medium frequencies; and the portion farthest from the oval window is excited by low frequencies. The various frequencies in a complex sound wave are sorted out by the frequency-selective properties of the cochlea. Thus, the cochlea is, in effect, a sound analyzer.

The nerve fibers transmit short electrical impulses. The intensity of the sound determines the number of impulses that are transmitted along a nerve fiber in one second. The greater the intensity, the greater is the excitation of the hair cells, and a correspondingly greater number of nerve impulses are sent to the brain.

Loudspeakers and Microphones. Because signals, such as speech and music, can be transmitted effectively as electrical signals, the transformation of sound waves into corresponding electrical signals and vice versa is of great practical importance. Devices that accomplish these transformations are called electromechanical transducers. The best known examples of electromechanical transducers are loudspeakers, which convert electrical energy into sound, and microphones, which convert sound into electrical energy.

In the electrodynamic loudspeaker, the most common type, an electrical current that is proportional to the signal is sent through a coil attached to a paper membrane. The coil moves inside a permanent magnet; the magnetic field exerts a force on the coil that is proportional to the electrical current. The resulting movement of the coil and the attached membrane sets up sound waves in the surrounding air.

The most common microphone is the carbon-button microphone, which is used in most telephone handsets. In a carbon-button microphone the sound wave impinging on the microphone membrane varies the electrical resistance between the small carbon granules enclosed in a space behind the membrane. If a voltage is applied to the electrical terminals of the microphone, the resulting current varies in proportion to the amplitude of the second wave.

Recording of Sound. Since Thomas Edison's invention of the phonograph, the recording of sound for later playback has made great strides. The modern long-playing record can store almost the entire frequency range of audible sound with

U.S. GYPSUM COMPANY

LINCOLN CENTER FOR THE PERFORMING ARTS

UNITED PRESS INTERNATIONAL

(Above) METROPOLITAN OPERA HOUSE in Lincoln Center, New York, has a ceiling suspended on springs to improve the acoustical properties of the hall. Circular stepped coffers around the chandelier scatter sounds in all directions for more equal distribution of volume.

(Upper left) ACOUSTICAL PLASTER ceiling material, applied to a honeycomb ceiling design, provides a quiet, attractive dining room in Holy Cross Hospital, Chicago.

(Left) OUTDOOR CONCERTS at Hollywood Bowl can be heard by an audience of 20,000 persons seated along the slopes of a steep hill which forms a natural amphitheater with excellent acoustical properties. The semicircular shell in the foreground houses the orchestra.

little distortion. In many cases the quality of the reproduced sound is very similar to that of the original signal. By modulating both edges of the disc groove, stereophonic sound signals can be stored in a single groove and picked up separately by a stereophonic cartridge, which is a special kind of electromechanical transducer. The resulting two electrical signals are amplified separately and are reproduced by two or more loudspeakers. From a good stereophonic recording, the reproduced sound can be heard in any direction between the loudspeakers.

Recording of sound on magnetic tape provides even higher fidelity than disc recordings. On a magnetic tape the sound signal is stored as a variable spot of magnetization that is detected by a magnetic playback head and reconverted into an electrical signal.

Architectural Acoustics. An important branch of acoustics deals with the transmission of sound waves inside reverberant rooms, such as auditoriums, theaters, and concert halls. In a reverberant room the sound reaches a listener's ears not only directly (in a straight line from the source) but also by way of reflections from the ceiling, the floor, and the walls. If these reflections are sufficiently strong and arrive after a delay greater than 0.05 second, they are heard as echoes. Otherwise, they are heard as reverberation. The time interval in which the reverberation is attenuated to one millionth of its original intensity is called the reverberation time. Typically, living rooms have reverberation times of 0.5 second or less. Lecture halls have reverberation times of approximately one second. Good concert halls have reverberation times of about two seconds. Large churches, railroad stations, and indoor swimming pools can have reverberation times as long as 10 seconds or more.

The acoustical quality of a concert hall is de-

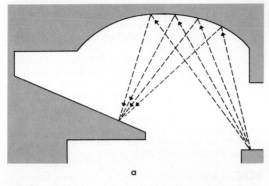

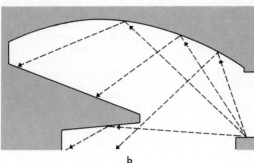

(*Above*) ARCHITECTURAL ACOUSTICS involves analysis of the shape of an auditorium and the paths of the sound waves in it. In top drawing, sound waves are poorly distributed throughout the auditorium. In bottom drawing, redesigned ceiling distributes sound waves more evenly for reception in the entire auditorium.

(*Upper right*) PHILHARMONIC HALL in New York City as originally designed, with overhead acoustical panels arranged low near the stage, and generally flat walls.

(*Right*) Reconstructed for a second time to correct acoustical problems, Avery Fisher Hall (formerly called Philharmonic Hall) in New York's Lincoln Center was reopened in October 1976 with a completely new interior.

termined in part by its reverberation time. But there are many other factors that influence acoustical quality. Many of these factors are not yet fully understood, and much basic research is required to elucidate the complex problems of sound transmission and perception in reverberant spaces.

A related subject is the study of sound transmission in buildings and through walls. Ordinarily, the sound insulating efficiency of a wall is proportional to its mass per unit area. An important practical problem is to obtain good sound insulation for lightweight construction, which is particularly important for better sound insulation in apartment buildings and airplanes. Much progress has been made by using a sandwich type of construction in which a sound-absorbing material is inserted between the two surfaces of the wall.

M.R. SCHROEDER, *Bell Telephone Laboratories*

Bibliography

Beranek, Leo, *Concert Halls and Opera Houses: Music, Acoustics, and Architecture*, 2d ed. (Springer-Verlag 2003).

Everest, F. Alton, *Master Handbook of Acoustics*, 4th ed. (McGraw-Hill/TAB Bks. 2000).

Filippi, Paul, et al., *Acoustics: Basic Physics Theory and Methods* (Acad. Press 1999).

Jordan, V. L., *Acoustical Design of Concert Halls and Theatres* (Elsevier Pub. Co. 1980).

Kinsler, L. E., and Austin R. Frey, *Fundamentals of Acoustics*, 4th ed. (Wiley 1999).

Lord, Peter, and Duncan Templeton, *Detailing for Acoustics*, 3d ed. (Routledge 1996).

Morse, Philip M., and K. Uno Ingard, *Theoretical Acoustics* (1986; reprint, Princeton Univ. Press 1987).

Olson, Harry Ferdinand, *Acoustical Engineering* (1957; reprint, Professional Audio Journals 1991).

Parker, Sybil P., ed., *Acoustics Source Book* (McGraw-Hill 1988).

Ristic, Velimir M., *Principles of Acoustic Devices* (Wiley 1983).

Roederer, Juan G., *The Physics and Psychophysics of Music: An Introduction*, 3d ed. (Springer-Verlag 2001).

Thompson, Emily, *The Soundscape of Modernity: Architectural Acoustics and the Culture of Listening in America, 1900–1933* (MIT Press 2002).

ACQUI, äk'kwē, a town in northern Italy, in Alessandria province. It is situated in the Piedmont region, 37 miles (60 km) northwest of Genoa. The official name is *Acqui Terme.*

Acqui has been a health resort since Roman times because of its natural hot sulfur springs. The sulfurous waters bubble up under a pavilion in the center of town. There are four arches that are left from a Roman aqueduct and the ruins of earlier baths. The town has a Romanesque cathedral that was consecrated in 1067 and a number of castles built in the 1300s and 1400s. Modern Acqui produces wine, bricks, macaroni, glassware, clothing, and metal goods. Population: 19,184 (2001 census).

ACQUIRED IMMUNE DEFICIENCY SYNDROME. See AIDS.

ACQUISITION, ak-wə-zish'ən, primarily the act of procuring property. It also means property that has been acquired. Property may be acquired by inheritance, by purchase, by gift, through the operation of natural causes, or by its incorporation into other property. Property that has never belonged to anyone or that has been abandoned and has no rightful owner may be acquired by occupancy or by finding.

ACQUITTAL, ə-kwit'əl, in criminal law, the judicial discharge of a person accused of a crime. The accused may be acquitted by a jury's verdict of "not guilty," by a judge's ruling, or by simple operation of law, as in the case of an accessory when the principal is acquitted. Acquittal discharges a person from guilt, pardon only from punishment.

In the United States, acquittal may be the result of some technical defects in the proceedings. A second trial of the case may then be instituted. But if the accused is acquitted as the result of a verdict in his or her favor on the merits of the case, the acquittal bars further prosecution for the same offense. This protection is guaranteed by a provision of the U.S. Constitution that "no person shall be twice put in jeopardy for the same offense."

In civil law, acquittal is the judicial release of a person from the terms of a contract, debt, or other obligation. In feudal law, acquittal was the obligation of a mesne lord to protect his tenants from claims by higher lords resulting from his own debts to the higher lords.

ACRANIA, ā-krā'nē-ə, the lower chordate animals, including species making up the subphylum Tunicata (the tunicates) or the class Cephalochordata (the lancelets). Small marine animals, acrania have no skulls, jaws, vertebrae, or paired appendages. In Greek the word *acrania* literally means "without skulls."

Acrania are members of the animal phylum Chordata, which also includes the vertebrates (Vertebrata). The latter species, which possess skulls, are known as craniata. Some zoologists apply the name *acrania* to only the lancelets.

Bibliography: Frick, J. E., and E. E. Ruppert, "Primordial Germ Cells and Oocytes of *Brachiostoma virginiae* (Cephalochordata, Acrania) Are Flagellated Epithelial Cells: Relationship between Epithelial and Primary Egg Polarity," *Zygote* 5 (1997):139–151; Pechenik, Jan A., *Biology of the Invertebrates,* 3d ed. (Brown, W. C. 1996); Salvini-Plawen, L., "The Urochordate Larva and Archicordate Organization," *Journal of Zoological Systematics and Evolutionary Research* 36 (1998):129–145.

ACRE, ä'kre, a state of Brazil. It is situated southwest of the state of Amazonas and borders northernmost Bolivia and southeastern Peru. Its capital is Rio Branco.

Acre formerly belonged to Bolivia, and within its 58,915 square miles (152,589 sq km) contained fabulous wealth in wild rubber trees. Brazilian traders encroached upon the territory. In a dispute that arose between Bolivia and Brazil, Acre declared itself independent in 1899. The territory was annexed by Brazil in 1903, after an indemnity of $10,000,000 was paid to Bolivia. Population: 455,200 (1995 est.).

ACRE, ä'kər, a historic city in northern Israel. It is situated on the Bay of Acre, an arm of the Mediterranean Sea, 10 miles (16 km) north of Haifa. Once an important commercial center and fortress, Acre is now mainly a fishing port and industrial city. It has a steel-rolling mill built by the Israelis. Acre is also the center of the Bahai religion. The Bahai leader Abdul-Baha died at Acre in 1921 and is buried there.

Acre has been known by a number of names since ancient times. In the Old Testament it is called *Accho.* One of its Greek names was *Ptolemais.* The Arabs gave Acre the name *Akka.* During the Crusades the city became known to the Western world by its French name, *St. Jean d'Acre* or *Acre.* In the modern Hebrew of Israel it is called *Akko.*

From ancient times until about 1900, Acre was an important shipping center on one of the main trade and travel routes between Europe and Asia. Its trade came by sea over the Mediterranean and by land over camel caravan routes from various parts of the Middle East. Haifa, now the chief

The seawall at Acre, an Israeli port on a bay of the Mediterranean, was built by the Crusaders about 1100, after they took the city from the Muslims.

ISRAEL GOVERNMENT TOURIST OFFICE

port of Israel, outstripped Acre in size and commercial importance after 1900 because of Haifa's superior harbor and railroad communications. A railroad built by the British during World War II linked Acre with Haifa and with Beirut, the capital of Lebanon, but the Lebanese-Israeli border was closed in 1948.

History. Acre is first mentioned in Egyptian inscriptions of about 1450 B.C. During the following centuries, it was included in the empires of Egypt, Assyria, Persia, and Macedonia.

After the Macedonian empire of Alexander the Great broke up in the late 300s B.C., Acre again came under Egyptian control. In the early 200s B.C. it was named *Ptolemais* for the line of Macedonian kings of Egypt that began with Ptolemy Soter. The city subsequently became part of the Seleucid empire of Syria, and was later acquired and colonized by the Romans. In the early years of the Roman empire, Acre was a city of great importance. Ancient granite and marble pillars still exist today as reminders of its grandeur.

In 638 A.D. the Muslim forces of Khalid and Abud Ubayda captured both Acre and Damascus. The city was then seized successively by the Egyptian caliphs (969), the Seljuk Turks (1079), the Crusaders (1099), King Baldwin I of Jerusalem (1104), and Saladin, sultan of Egypt and Syria (1187). After a two-year siege that cost hundreds of thousands of lives, Richard the Lion-Hearted and Philip Augustus of France took the city in 1191. They made it a bishopric and gave it to the Order of St. John.

During the next century, despite continual assaults, Acre became a large, rich, and powerful city. After the beginning of the 1200s it was the chief center of Christian power in Palestine. But in 1291 the Mamluk ruler of Egypt, al-Malik al-Ashraf, took Acre after a bloody siege that completely destroyed the town.

In 1517 Acre fell into the hands of the Turks, and by the beginning of the 18th century it was a vast scene of ruin, relieved only by a few cottages, a mosque, and houses that were inhabited by French merchants. In the mid-1700s the city revived under the Bedouin sheikh of Palestine, Zahir al-Umar, who made Acre the capital of his kingdom, and in general ignored Turkish overrule. Al-Umar was succeeded by Ahmad al-Jazzar, a Turkish governor who continued to improve the city.

Al-Jazzar successfully defended the city against the French armies of Napoleon Bonaparte in 1799. After a 61-day siege, Napoleon was forced to retreat when English soldiers and marines under the command of Sir William Sydney Smith came to the rescue of al-Jazzar.

Acre continued to prosper, despite the rigors of Turkish rule, until the winter of 1831–1832, when Egyptian and Lebanese troops besieged it, destroying the majority of its buildings. After capturing the city, the Egyptians repaired it and improved its fortifications. It was laid in ruins once again by the bombardment of a combined British-Austrian-Turkish fleet in 1840. From 1841 it was under Turkish rule once more, until the British captured it, virtually unopposed, in 1918. Acre was placed under a British mandate at the end of World War I.

In 1948 Acre fell to Israeli troops. A year later the city became part of the new state of Israel. Population: 37,400 (1990 est.).

LAND-AREA MEASURES STILL COMMONLY USED[1]

Country	Unit	Size (in acres)
Argentina	cuadra	4.17
Austria	joch	1.42
Brazil	cuadra	0.92
Canary Islands	fanegada	1.30
Chile	cuadra	3.88
Mainland China	gong qing	2.47
Costa Rica	manzana	1.73
Czech and Slovak Republics	jitro	1.42
Denmark	tondeland	1.32
Dutch East Indies	bouw	1.75
Egypt	feddan	1.04
Estonia	lofstelle	0.46
Finland	tunnland	1.22
France	arpent[2]	0.85
Greece, ancient	plethron	0.235
Hungary	joch	1.07
Iraq	mishara	0.62
Ireland	acre	1.62
Italy	quadrato	1.25
Japan	cho	2.45
Latvia	lofstelle	0.92
Mexico	fanega	8.81
Netherlands	mud	2.47
Paraguay	cuadra	1.85
Peru	topo	0.67
Rome, ancient	jugerum	0.62
Russia	dessiatine	2.70
Scotland	acre	1.27
Spain	aranzada	0.94
	fanegada	1.35
Venezuela	fanegada	1.73
Wales	cover	0.67

[1]The benchmark is the acre, the unit of measure used in Canada, England, and the United States. [2]Unit is used in surveying.

ACRE, ā′kər, a unit of measure of land area. Originally the word meant a piece of tilled land, a field, or a pasture. Later it was used for a rough measure of size, representing approximately what one person could plow in a day. In England it was reckoned as the amount of land a yoke of oxen could plow daily.

In the 13th century and later, English law fixed a definite measurement for the acre. The statute acre, now a standard unit of area in England, the United States, and Canada, is a square measuring about 208 feet 8 ½ inches on a side. It equals 43,560 square feet, or 4,840 square yards, or 160 square rods or perches, or 4 roods. In Scotland, Ireland, Wales, and several English counties, older land-area measures for the acre, all different, are still used.

The most common land-area measure in continental Europe is the hectare, or square hectometer. Part of the metric system, it is equal to 100 ares, or square dekameters, or 10,000 square meters, and is equivalent to 2.47 acres.

See also MEASURES AND MEASURING SYSTEMS.

Bibliography: Johnstone, William D., *For Good Measure: The Most Complete Guide to Weights and Measures and Their Metric Equivalents* (NTC Publ. Group 1998).

ACRE RIVER, ä′krē, a South American stream about 400 miles long, mostly in Brazil. It is part of the Amazon system. The Acre rises on the Peruvian-Brazilian border and flows eastward, forming part of the boundary between Bolivia and Brazil. Turning northeast into Brazil, it becomes navigable for small steamers at Xapuri, continues past Rio Branco, the capital of Acre Territory, and empties into the Purus River at Bôca do Acre. The river is the chief artery of a potentially valuable rubber forest district.

ACRIDINE, ak-rə-dēn, is an organic compound that is used in drugs and dyes. It was discovered in 1871 by Karl Graebe and Heinrich Caro, who extracted it from anthracene (C_6H_4-$(CH)_2$—C_6H_4). The molecular structure of acridine (C_6H_4 — CH — N — C_6H_4) consists of two benzene rings that are linked by a pyridine ring (C_5H_5N).

Several valuable drug products are derived from acridine. Atabrine was useful in suppressing malaria during World War II. Acriflavine was used as a wound antiseptic in World War I. Rivanol is effective against amebic dysentery.

Important dyes derived from acridine, such as acridine orange and benzoflavine, are used for dyeing leather, cotton, silk, and wool. Other derivatives of acridine provide the most valuable and fastest vat dyes and vat-dye pigments for dyeing cotton goods and for coloring plastics.

CURT BAMBERGER, *Patent Chems, Inc.*

ACROLEIN, ə-krō'lē-ən, or *propenal,* is a member of the class of organic compounds that are called unsaturated aldehydes. (An unsaturated molecule can add on other atoms before saturation is reached.) The molecular formula of acrolein is CH_2=$CHCHO$. A colorless liquid, it boils at 126° F(52° C) and melts at −126° F (−88° C). On standing, it becomes a white solid called disacryl. Acrolein can make the eyes produce tears. Its pungent odor is largely responsible for the disagreeable smell of overheated fats.

There are three industrial methods for manufacturing acrolein. One way is to use air and a catalyst to oxidize propylene. A second way is to use the aldol reaction between formaldehyde and acetaldehyde. A third way is to dehydrate (remove water from) glycerol.

Acrolein is an intermediate in the manufacture of other organic compounds. It has been used in military poison gas mixtures, in the manufacture of metal colloids, and as a warning agent in refrigerants.

ALVIN I. KOSAK, *New York University*

ACROMEGALY, ak-ro-meg'ə-le, is a chronic disease occurring in middle life. It is characterized by increased secretion of growth hormone by the front region of the pituitary gland and enlargement of parts of the head, hands, and feet.

Cause and Characteristics. The pituitary gland (q.v.) contains several kinds of cells that secrete different hormones. In acromegaly there is an increase in the number of growth hormone-secreting cells. This increase in cell number usually produces a pituitary tumor, which may press on the optic nerves and interfere with vision.

The excessive secretion of growth hormone causes many abnormalities. The most obvious changes are in certain soft tissues, cartilage, and bones. These changes give a characteristic burly, large-jawed appearance to patients with the disease. The skin of the face is puffy, and the facial lines are exaggerated. The nose and ears enlarge; the larynx is big, and the voice is husky. The jawbone lengthens and protrudes forward. Because the rib cartilages lengthen, the chest cage becomes barrel-like. Bony overgrowth in the spine causes difficulty in bending forward and also causes arthritis. Less obvious abnormalities are increased hairiness, sweating, enlargement of the thyroid gland, diabetes, and sometimes high blood pressure.

Symptoms. Acromegaly is usually benign and lasts many years. (Rarely, there is bleeding into the pituitary tumor, which requires quick surgical intervention.) Patients sometimes have bothersome symptoms in various areas: severe headaches; tingling and numbness in hands and feet; back, hip, or knee pain due to arthritis; or severe weakness and wasting of muscles. Except for the change in appearance, most patients tolerate the disease well and are relatively healthy. The major complications are due to diabetes or high blood pressure, when they exist. Occasionally, remaining pituitary tissue is destroyed by the tumor, causing failure of the glands that are dependent upon the pituitary.

Treatment. X-ray treatment of the pituitary region is the most commonly used method. In most cases, this treatment stops the growth of the tumor and, in some cases, reduces the excessive growth hormone secretion. If visual damage is sudden or great, surgery may be necessary to remove the tumor. Newer, experimental methods are destruction of the pituitary tumor by liquid nitrogen or direct insertion of radioactive materials into the pituitary gland.

NICHOLAS P. CHRISTY, M.D.
Roosevelt Hospital, New York

ACRONYM, ak'rənim, a word formed from the initial letter or letters of the words that make up a name or phrase; for example, *radar* (from *r*adio *d*etecting *a*nd *r*anging). The term derives from the Greek *akros* (top) and *onyma* (name) and apparently was first used in *American Notes and Queries* in the issue of February 1943. An acronym differs from an ordinary abbreviation in that it is pronounced as a single word and not as a series of separate letters. For example, *AWOL* (Absent Without Leave) was an abbreviation in World War I, since all four initials were pronounced as separate letters, but it became an acronym in World War II, when it was pronounced "ā'wôl."

The use of words formed of initials is very old. Some of the great medieval Jewish scholars are known mainly by their acronyms: *Rashi* (*Rabbi Shelomo ben Yitzhak*, 1040–1105), a famous commentator on the Bible, and *Rambam* (*Rabbi Moses bar Maimon*, 1135–1204), known also as Maimonides, who was the greatest Jewish philosopher of the Middle Ages.

Acronyms have long been employed by business firms (*Texaco, Socony*). Most acronyms in common use, however, were coined during and after World War II. One of the first, invented by American soldiers, was *snafu* (*s*ituation *n*ormal—*a*ll *f*ouled *u*p). Others include technical names, such as *radar* and *sonar* (*so*und *na*vigation *a*nd *r*anging). In the late 1950's came *maser* (*m*icrowave *a*mplification by *s*timulated *e*mission of *r*adiation), and in the early 1960's, *laser* (*l*ight *a*mplification by *s*timulated *e*mission of *r*adiation). Acronymic abbreviations also came into use for the names of political units, such as *NATO* (North Atlantic Treaty Organization) and *UNESCO* (United Nations Educational, Scientific, and Cultural Organization). In some cases the name or phrase seems to have been invented to fit the acronym, as *VISTA* for Volunteers in Service to America. In other cases a play on words results accidentally, as in AIDS (Acquired Immune Deficiency Syndrome).

DAVID DIRINGER
Author of "The Alphabet"

THE ACROPOLIS OF ATHENS dominates the city. It is crowned by the ruins of the Parthenon, one of the great masterpieces of ancient Greek architecture. A forested preserve covers the near slopes of the hill.

ACROPOLIS, ə-krop'ə-lis, the high part of an ancient Greek city, usually an elevation overlooking the city, and frequently its citadel. Notable among such citadels were the acropolises of Argos, Messene, Thebes, and Corinth, but the most eminent of them all was Acropolis of Athens, to which the name is now chiefly applied.

The Athenian Acropolis was the site of the original city and, later, of the upper city as distinguished from the lower. It was built upon an isolated butte, or hill, of the Hymettus, a mountain ridge east of the present-day city. This mass of rock rises sharply to a height of 500 feet above sea level. An uneven plateau about 500 feet wide and 1,000 feet long forms the summit. Remarkable specimens of architectural art were reared on this height, chiefly in the days of Pericles (died 429 B.C.).

At the western end, where there was a zigzag road for chariots, stands the massive, columned gateway to the Acropolis—the Propylaea—still in excellent condition. Entering this way, the visitor immediately sees the northwest corner of the Parthenon, the temple dedicated to Athena, tutelary deity of Athens. North of the Parthenon is the Erechtheum, famous for its portico upheld by six caryatids. The Erechtheum housed the cults of many lesser deities. Between these principal buildings stood the huge statue of Athene Promachos by Phidias, the helmet and spear of which were the first objects visible from the sea. About these centerpieces, and extending down the steep slopes, were lesser temples, statues, theaters, and odeums (music halls). The more noted included the Theater of Dionysus, the Odeum of Pericles, the small, perfect temple of Athena Nike, and the Odeum of Herodes Atticus.

The ravages of time, accident, war, and Athenian marble merchants have largely destroyed these classic works, but archaeologists have preserved important remains of the Acropolis. Some are in the National Museum at Athens; others, in collections throughout Europe. Notable among the latter are the portions of the Parthenon in the British Museum in London, brought to England by the Earl of Elgin, early in the 19th century. See also ATHENS; ELGIN MARBLES.

ACROSTIC, ə-krôs'tik, a word composition, usually a poem, in which the initial, middle, or final letters of the lines, taken in order, spell out something besides the meaning of the text. The 119th Psalm, the initial letters of whose stanzas follow the order of the Hebrew alphabet, is the earliest known example. Acrostical religious verses and love poems were common in Europe for many years until the 19th century, when criticism made the form unfashionable.

The acrostic is most frequently used today in word puzzles. The best known is probably Elizabeth S. Kingsley's invention, the *Double-Crostic,* introduced in the *Saturday Review* in 1934. The words to be discovered in this puzzle form a quotation. The definitions are arranged in acrostical order so that the initials of the unknown words spell the name of the author and the work from which the quotation is taken. A variation of the *Double-Crostic* uses both the initial and the final letters (the telestich) to disclose the author's name and title, respectively.

The acrostic principle is further extended in the *Syllabic Acrostical Enigma,* a word puzzle in verse introduced by the National Puzzlers' League. In this puzzle, the successive syllables of a key word—not just its single letters—are used to begin groups of verses. Each unknown syllable combines with the word following it, or the first part of that word, in order to complete the sense of the verses. In the following example composed by the author, each syllable to be guessed is printed as a capitalized tag (ONE, TWO, and so on). The tag represents either the unknown syllable or an unknown word beginning with that syllable. The tag "ALL" represents the key word.

ONE million in White Sea's reflection
Suggests U.S.S.R.'s complexion: (*vermillion*)

TWO derived from flames tossed high
Brings sudden pain to many an eye.   (*cinder*)

THREE tingles in the miser's heart,
For acquisition is his art.   (*getting*)

FOUR bit off more than one could chew:
A long way round for me and you!   (*orbit*)

FIVE Ionic king so fine,
Who did his hopeless love resign,
Still turns and turns, yet comes up nine.   (*Ixion*)

Triumphant Caesar, home from Gaul,
Led captives many, blond, and tall,
Who paved the way for General ALL.
    (*Vercingetorix*)

DORIS NASH WORTMAN
Author of "Kingsley Double-Crostic" Puzzles

ACRYLIC RESIN. See Plastics.

ACT OF GOD, in law, is an accident that arises from a cause operating without interference or aid from man. Sir William Jones (1746–1794) proposed adopting "inevitable accident" instead of "act of God," but other authorities have held that the two terms are not equivalent. Except under special contract, a person cannot be held liable for damage resulting from an act of God.

ACTA DIURNA, ak'tə dī-ûrn'ə, official written accounts of daily events in ancient Rome. The term means "daily acts" in Latin. The *Acta Diurna* were also known as *Acta Populi* (*Acts of the People*), *Acta Publica* (*Public Acts*), or *Acta Urbana* (*Municipal Acts*). News was collected by reporters (*actuarii*) employed by the state, who then posted the *Acta* on a whitened board (*album*) so that anyone might read or copy the reports. After a time the originals were taken down and filed in the state archives as a record. The news contained a miscellany of everything that might interest the citizen: the latest war news; abstracts of the best speeches in the Senate, the Forum, or the courts; and the most important legal decisions or political events (probably even interviews). Unusual omens or prodigies (*lusus naturae*) were also reported, as well as less important events—births, marriages, divorces, deaths, murders, and accidents.

The *Acta* seem to have taken the place of the discontinued *Annales* some time after 131 B.C. The *Annales* were yearly chronicles that reported only the more important occurrences. They were published too infrequently for the later, more active republic. The *Acta* were in use in the time of Julius Caesar (100–44 B.C.) and may have been instituted by him.

ACTAEON, ak-tē'ən, in Greek mythology, was a celebrated hunter who was trained to the art by the centaur Chiron. His parents were Aristaeus, son of Apollo and Cyrene, and Autonoë, daughter of Cadmus. According to Ovid, Actaeon, while hunting, chanced to see Artemis (Diana) and her nymphs bathing. The chaste goddess, deeply offended at having been seen, changed Actaeon into a stag. In this form he was set upon and torn to pieces by his own dogs. Other versions of the myth relate that his offense consisted of boasting that he was superior to the goddess in the hunt.

ACTH is a hormone produced by the front part of the pituitary gland. The letters stand for *adrenocorticotropic hormone*. Its principal function is to maintain and regulate secretion of many of the cortical steroid hormones (such as cortisol and corticosterone) produced by the adrenal cortex, the outer layer of the adrenal gland (q.v.).

In normal physiological conditions, the secretion of ACTH is regulated by the blood levels of certain adrenocortical hormones. When the blood level of adrenal cortical steroids is low, the pituitary compensates for this by releasing a greater quantity of ACTH. Increased release of ACTH continues until the level of cortical steroids in the blood is elevated to a point at which it depresses further ACTH secretion.

Action of ACTH, Direct and Indirect. The adrenal cortex is the main target organ on which ACTH has a direct effect. However, it also exerts a direct effect on other systems.

Direct effects of ACTH include stimulation of cortisol and corticosterone secretion, increase in weight of adrenals, and depletion of ascorbic acid (vitamin C) and cholesterol in the adrenal cortex. Its direct effects on other systems are the stimulation of melanocytes (pigment cells) and the promotion of an increase in the concentration of nonesterified fatty acids in blood plasma, thus affecting adipose tissue. (Similarities in structure between the ACTH molecule and MSH [melanophore stimulating hormone] molecule account for the MSH activity of ACTH.)

ACTH also has an indirect effect on many biological systems. Most of its indirect effects probably occur as a result of secretion and action of adrenocortical steroids.

Secretion of ACTH. The mechanisms regulating ACTH secretion and release are complex. This is not surprising, since the release of ACTH from the pituitary may be evoked by any kind of physiological or psychological stress and by a variety of external stimuli. The actual release, however, is mediated through the central nervous system by way of neurohumoral substances originating in the hypothalamus, a regulatory area of the brain. These substances, called corticotropin-releasing factors (CRF), pass from the hypothalamus to the pituitary and in some way stimulate the pituitary to secrete and release corticotropin.

Chemistry of ACTH. More work has been done on isolating, identifying, and explaining the mechanism of action of ACTH than on any other pituitary hormone. Highly purified preparations of ACTH have been made from sheep, pig, beef, and human pituitaries, and their molecular weights and structures have been established.

Pig, sheep, beef, and human corticotropins are straight-chain polypeptides (proteins containing many amino acids) composed of 39 amino acid residues. The molecular weight of purified corticotropin is approximately 4,500. Complete synthesis of the molecule has been accomplished.

Importance of ACTH. ACTH is essential for normal production of adrenal steroids. These steroids enable the organism to make whatever adjustments are needed to maintain metabolic equilibrium. They are essential for life, whereas ACTH is not. In the absence of ACTH, the adrenals may continue to secrete steroids, but at a subnormal level.

ACTH in Clinical Use. Long-acting ACTH has been prepared and tested clinically in the treatment of various diseases. It is particularly effective in treating such diseases as rheumatoid arthritis and asthma. Favorable results have been obtained with ACTH treatment of the following diseases: multiple sclerosis, lymphatic leukemia, inflammatory disease of the eyes, inflammation of the colon or thyroid gland, rheumatic fever, and acute leukemia. ACTH is also effective, for a time, in relieving the pain and discomfort of patients suffering with severe burns.

The beneficial effects of ACTH in therapy are most likely due to an indirect action that involves stimulation of the secretion of adrenal cortical steroids. This is particularly so in inflammatory conditions, since certain adrenal steroids have anti-inflammatory actions.

THOMAS F. HOPKINS
Worcester Foundation for Experimental Biology

ACTORS begin rehearsing by reading the play on a bare stage, without make-up, costumes, lighting, or scenery.

ACTING is the art of portraying a character in the theater, films, or other media. However, it is a complex art, and there is no really satisfactory simple definition. Success in acting is achieved only by the relatively few persons who combine natural talent with well-developed techniques, dedication, and self-discipline. Even the greatest actors are frequently aware of how limitations of talent or technique keep them from realizing the full possibilities of the roles they play. In motion pictures, stardom is sometimes achieved through a combination of a high degree of personal magnetism and physical attractiveness. These are rare gifts to be exploited by skillful directors and cameramen, but such stars seldom achieve true greatness unless they develop their craft through arduous training and long experience.

Acting and Children's Games. Acting is often compared to children's make-believe games. To some extent the comparison is apt, and to a degree it is helpful in understanding what an actor does when he is creating and performing a role. With his kings and queens, his cowboys and Indians, or his spacemen, the child projects himself into a make-believe world. From his imagination—triggered by his own experience, limited though it may be—he provides circumstances of time, place, and relationships between the characters. He then proceeds to behave, that is, to speak and to perform physical actions, in a manner that he believes is appropriate to these circumstances. If the game is to prove interesting, these circumstances must provide a reason for carrying out the actions. He has to rescue the princess from the enchanted castle, or rid the town of dangerous bandits, or get his spaceship into orbit without being detected by the enemy.. A child with imagination can become involved in such a game to the extent that it has for him a degree of reality, and he may become resentful of adults who intrude into his make-believe world.

Playing this kind of game is similar in many ways to acting. The playwright provides the basic circumstances of time, place, and character relationships; he gives the actors lines to speak, suggests physical actions, and certainly implies (although he may not specifically state) the purpose behind each character's behavior. Like the child's, the actor's imagination is triggered by these circumstances, and he proceeds to accomplish his purpose by speaking the lines and carrying out the actions in the way he believes is most suitable. Like the child, he may become so involved in what he is doing that the imaginary world displaces the real world to some extent. The ability to achieve such involvement is an important part of an actor's technique because it enables him to concentrate his attention on his stage tasks and consequently to draw the attention of the audience. For both actor and child there is nothing mystic or hypnotic about this involvement. It is similar to the experience all people have had of becoming so absorbed in an activity that they lose some degree of consciousness of the world around them.

But acting is much more than becoming involved in an imaginary world. It is different from, or perhaps it is better to say that it extends, the game of make-believe in several ways. One of these ways has already been suggested by the statement that the imaginary circumstances, including the words to be spoken and many of the physical actions to be performed, are given to the actor by the playwright. The actor must be able to say the words and perform the actions spontaneously, as if he had thought them up himself. He must be able to do this in front of others and whenever he is called upon to perform. In the professional theater he must effectively repeat his performance eight times a week and often for a period of many months. Furthermore, his ultimate aim is to induce an

PICTORIAL PARADE

PICTORIAL PARADE

PICTORIAL PARADE

Hamlet

Henry V

The Entertainer

Sir Laurence Olivier, one of the most versatile actors of the 20th century, in six of his roles.

CULVER PICTURES

PICTORIAL PARADE

BLACK STAR

Othello

Beckett

Titus Andronicus

audience, not himself, to believe in the imaginary world of the stage.

Acting Techniques. To accomplish his purpose, the actor develops two kinds of techniques. They are interdependent, but distinct enough to be discussed separately. They can be designated as the *outer* and *inner*, or the *external* and *internal*, techniques. The accomplished actor is well trained in both and uses both as fully as possible.

External Techniques. A most important part of the outer technique is the training of the body and the voice so that the actor's physical equipment becomes an effective instrument. A musician plays on a violin, a piano, or a trumpet, but the actor's instrument is his own body. He must learn to move with the greatest possible efficiency. He must train his body so that it can assume the appearance of a hunchbacked beggar or a mighty king. He must learn to speak so he can be heard clearly and understood easily without unintentional provincialisms. He must be able to speak blank verse and rhymed couplets. He must train his voice so he can speak like a guttersnipe or a grandee. Even more, he must develop both his voice and body so that they respond immediately and instinctively to subtle changes of thought and feeling. This training requires determination and self-discipline. It must be carried on over an extended period of time (a lifetime, in fact, for a true artist never ceases to study) and under the direction of competent teachers.

Other outer techniques include skill at makeup, which enables the actor to change the appearance of his face and hair to suit the character he is playing and the period of the play, and the ability to wear costumes and use costume accessories (fans, swords, walking sticks, snuffboxes) of any historical period. It is quite possible that a young actress engaged by a summer stock company might have to play a medieval princess, a Renaissance lady-in-waiting, an 18th century scullery maid, a Victorian governess, and a modern working girl—all within a few weeks' time. If she is well trained, she will have a knowledge of the speech and manners of the periods, and social classes involved.

Until about 1940 all training for actors and all writing about the process of acting were concerned almost exclusively with the development of an external technique. During the 19th century, actors (and would-be actors) studied elocution and deportment. It was always recognized that the outer techniques alone did not make an actor, but it was assumed that whatever else was necessary was a matter of natural talent, which could not be consciously trained.

Internal Techniques. The man responsible for

ON STAGE, Judith Anderson (*left*) as the tragic heroine in Robinson Jeffers' adaptation of Euripides' *Medea*; Anne Bancroft (*right*) as a nun in John Whiting's *The Devils.*

ON SCREEN, Sophia Loren (*left*), kneeling, with Eleanora Brown, in *Two Women*; Elizabeth Taylor (*right*) in the film of Edward Albee's *Who's Afraid of Virginia Woolf?*

finding ways of developing an inner technique was Stanislavsky. An actor and a cofounder in 1898 of the famed Moscow Art Theatre, Stanislavsky spent a great part of his life exploring the creative process of acting. He divided the process into three principal parts and published the results of his work in three important books —*An Actor Prepares* (Eng. tr, 1936), *Building a Character* (Eng. tr., 1949), and *Creating a Role* (Eng. tr., 1961).

The first book is concerned with the development of the actor's "inner resources." It recognizes that he must learn to relax under the pressure of having to perform before an audience, so that no excessive muscular strain interferes with concentrating his attention on carrying out his tasks. It emphasizes the necessity of an actor's having an objective or intention, that is, of his knowing what the character he is playing wants to accomplish, scene by scene and in the play as a whole. Stanislavsky called this objective the "motivating force" behind the character's behavior and stressed that everything the actor does and says throughout his performance should serve in some way toward accomplishing his objective. The book maintains that actors must carefully observe both themselves and the world around them, so that their behavior on stage will be truthful. It describes exercises in

improvisation (similar to children's make-believe games) to help the actor respond freely to imaginary circumstances. It helps the actor to discover ways of inducing sensory and emotional responses without forcing them.

The key ideas in the above paragraph—relaxation, concentration, objectives, motivating force, observation, improvisation, imaginary circumstances, and sensory and emotional responses —are some of Stanislavsky's principal concepts for developing "inner resources." They point the way to an internal technique by which the actor learns to use his mind, his senses, and his feelings as effectively as he learns to use his body and voice. This approach to acting has become known as the "Stanislavsky system." Anyone seriously interested in acting will profit by studying Stanislavsky's books with great care and can gain further understanding from some of the materials that have been published about his theories.

While *An Actor Prepares* primarily concerns the actor's work on himself and his "inner development," Stanislavsky's other two books consider the way an actor develops a character given him by a dramatist, the way he brings the character into existence on the stage, and the way he uses his performance to communicate the playwright's meaning to an audience. *Building*

Stanislavsky

The Moscow Art Theatre production of Maxim Gorky's *The Lower Depths*, staged in 1902, with Stanislavsky (*center*) playing the role of Satine.

a Character discusses the effective use of the body and voice, making clear Stanislavsky's belief that the actor must use both internal and external techniques if he is to realize fully the possibilities of his art.

Stanislavsky did not invent a system of acting. He discovered what the world's finest stage performers have always done, then set down a series of principles and exercises that permit talented young actors to learn to do what formerly was accomplished either through trial and error or through intuition. There are accounts of actors as long ago as the classic period in Greece who used inner techniques identical with Stanislavsky's principles.

Stanislavsky has had great influence on the art of acting, especially in the United States. His methods have been disseminated by both actors and teachers who worked and studied with him, as well as by those who became acquainted with his ideas through his writings. In the 1950's a fascination with the inner technique caused some American actors to neglect the training of the voice and body and to underestimate its importance. At the same time, British and Continental actors tended to favor the development of externals. In the 1960's the necessity of a more balanced approach began to be widely recognized.

Acting as a Career. Anyone considering acting as a career should realistically assess his potential and carefully plan his training. It is a highly competitive profession, providing satisfactory rewards only to those with abundant talent and fully developed skills. The number of stage productions in New York and the number of touring companies decrease each year, with a corresponding decrease in actor employment. Even when work is obtained in New York's commercial theater, the actor may find his future by no means secure, since many productions close after only a few performances.

This picture is somewhat brightened by the increasing number of resident repertory companies being established throughout the United States, such as the Minnesota Theatre Company at the Tyrone Guthrie Theatre in St. Paul, Minn.; the Arena Stage in Washington, D.C.; the Alley Theatre in Houston, Texas; and the Actors' Workshop in San Francisco, Calif. These groups operate throughout most of the year, giving members of their companies some semblance of the security and permanence provided by the state-supported theaters of Europe. Some are housed in splendidly equipped buildings, and they present a wide repertory of classic and modern plays. These companies doubtless offer the serious young actor his best opportunity, but they require that he come to them with a considerable amount of training. The demands are great because plays of many different styles and periods may be included in a single season of performances.

Other outlets of the trained actor's talents are films and television. Both these media stress intimacy of performance but use basically the same techniques as those employed in stage acting.

Training. Where does an aspiring actor get his training? Fifty years ago he attached himself to one of the stock companies that existed in every American city. There he learned his art and craft in a school of sometimes very hard knocks. If he was talented and determined, he might in time graduate (without benefit of degree or diploma) to the "big time" of Broadway. Today these stock companies are nonexistent, and he must find some other way of preparing for his career.

He will have to make a choice between a college of liberal arts that offers a substantial curriculum in theater (many colleges and universities do) and a specialized professional school. The choice is not easy, and the results are not readily predictable, since students from both types of institution have achieved success. Both offer work in acting and voice and speech along with courses in the liberal arts. In a college offering a substantial major in drama, the offerings are approximately three to one in favor of cultural subjects. In a professional school the ratio is reversed; the work in acting and speech is both more extensive and more intensive. It is augmented by courses in physical training, usually including body building, acrobatics, fencing, and various forms of period and modern dancing. Both colleges and professional schools are likely to offer courses in the history of theater and in dramatic literature and to provide the opportunity to develop practical performance skills through participation in an extensive production program.

See also DRAMA; MAKEUP; MOTION PICTURE; THEATER.

CHARLES McGAW, *Author of "Acting Is Believing"*

Bibliography

Adler, Stella, *The Technique of Acting* (1988; reprint, Bantam 1990).
Benedetti, Robert L., *The Actor at Work*, 9th ed. (Allyn 2004).
Brustein, Michael, *Letters to a Young Actor: A Universal Guide to Performance* (Basic Bks. 2005).
Gordon, Mel, *The Stanislavsky Technique: Russia: A Workbook for Actors* (1987; reprint, Applause Bks. 2000).
Hagen, Uta, and Haskel Frankel, *Respect for Acting* (Wiley 1973).
Hagen, Uta, *Challenge for the Actor* (Scribner 1991).
Kahan, Stanley, *Introduction to Acting*, 4th ed. (Allyn 1997).
Mamet, David, *True and False: Heresy and Common Sense for the Actor* (1997; reprint, Heritage 1999).
Meisner, Sanford, and Dennis Longwell, *Sanford Meisner on Acting* (Vintage 1987).
Moss, Larry, *The Intent to Live: Achieving Your True Potential as an Actor* (Bantam 2004).
Shurtleff, Michael, *Audition: Everything an Actor Needs to Know to Get the Part* (1978; reprint, Bantam 1980).
Stanislavsky, Konstantin, *Stanislavsky on the Art of the Stage*, tr. and ed. by David Magarshack (1967; reprint, Faber 1988).
Strasberg, Lee, *A Dream of Passion: The Development of the Method* (1987; reprint, Plume Bks. 1990).

ACTINIDE SERIES

ACTINIDE SERIES, ak′tə-nīd, the group of elements, all with similar properties, beginning with actinium (atomic number 89) and ending with lawrencium (atomic number 103). The first four members of the series—actinium, thorium, protactinium, and uranium—occur naturally. The transuranium elements in the actinide series (atomic numbers 93 to 103) are not found in nature but are produced artificially. All of the elements of the actinide series are radioactive; they decay by emitting alpha particles. In some isotopes of these elements, however, electron capture, spontaneous fission, or emission of beta particles is the predominant mode of decay.

Two isotopes of uranium, ^{233}U and ^{235}U, and an isotope of plutonium, ^{239}Pu, undergo fission when they capture slow neutrons. These isotopes are fuels for nuclear reactors. The much more abundant ^{232}Th and ^{238}U are not used directly as nuclear fuels, but ^{232}Th can be converted to ^{233}U, and ^{238}U can be converted to ^{239}Pu. All elements in the actinide series, except uranium and thorium, are so radioactive that special handling precautions are required to avoid health hazards.

Danish physicist Niels Bohr was the first to propose that the transuranium elements might resemble the lanthanide series of elements. He suggested that electrons fill into the inner 5f subshell of the transuranium elements in a fashion similar to the filling of the inner 4f subshell in elements of the lanthanide series. In 1944 the American chemist Glenn T. Seaborg suggested that actinium was the first member of a series that included the transuranium elements. This series is now called the actinide series.

All elements of the lanthanide series and all transplutonium elements of the actinide series form a +3 ion when in an aqueous solution. For this reason, the transplutonium elements closely resemble the lanthanide elements in their chemistry. However, other members of the actinide series form ions of a different charge than +3. Thorium forms a +4 ion, and protactinium, uranium, neptunium, and plutonium exhibit a variety of ionic charges. This variation in the behavior of these early members of the actinide series is attributable to the relatively small difference in the energy levels of the electrons in the 5f and 6d subshells of these elements.

GREGORY R. CHOPPIN, *Florida State University*

ACTINIUM

ACTINIUM, ak-tin′ē-əm, a very rare radioactive element, symbol Ac. Its atomic number is 89, and its atomic weight is 227.028. Actinium occurs as 1 part in 7 billion in uranium minerals. A silvery-white metal, it glows slightly in the dark and oxidizes rapidly in moist air to form a coating of white actinium oxide. In compounds, it is colorless and trivalent. Actinium's melting point is 1051° C (1924° F), it has a face-centered cubic structure, and its standard oxidation potential of about 2.6 volts indicates its highly electropositive character. Actinium is in Group IIIB of the periodic table. It was discovered in 1899 by André-Louis Debierne, a colleague of Marie Curie. (See also METAL; TRANSITION ELEMENTS.)

The only isotope of actinium with a long half-life (about 22 years) is ^{227}Ac, in the decay chain originating with ^{235}U. Isotopes with mass numbers from ^{210}Ac to ^{232}Ac are known. Decaying to ^{228}Th by beta emission, actinium-228 often is used in tracer level studies of actinium chemistry.

Actinium is similar to yttrium and lanthanum in both electronic structure and chemistry. Because the crystal radius of Ac^{+3} (1.11 Å) is slightly larger than that of La^{+3} (1.06 Å), Ac^{+3} has greater basicity, causing differences in chemical properties sufficient to separate actinium from lanthanum and the lanthanide ions by ion exchange and solvent extraction techniques.

Cation exchange resins with nitric acid or citrate solutions separate actinium from Ra^{+2}, Th^{+4}, La^{+3}, and the trivalent lanthanides. Thenoyltrifluoroacetone solutions in benzene separate actinium from these elements by solvent extraction. In aqueous solution Ac^{+3} forms weak complex compounds with halides and nitrate and sulfate anions. It forms stronger complex compounds with organic anions such as acetate, glycolate, citrate, and ethylenediaminetetraacetate.

The fluoride, hydroxide, carbonate, phosphate, and oxalate compounds are insoluble and are used in purification. As a separation method, tracer concentrations of Ac^{+3} are coprecipitated with lanthanum fluoride or oxalate. Iron hydroxide, aluminum hydroxide, barium sulfate, and zirconium iodate also can be used to coprecipitate tracer concentrations of Ac^{+3} under proper conditions. Actinium is produced by the reduction of actinium fluoride or chloride with lithium or potassium vapor. It has no commercial uses.

GREGORY R. CHOPPIN, *Florida State University*

Bibliography: Emsley, John, *The Elements,* 2d ed. (Oxford 1991); Greenwood, N. N., and A. Earnshaw, *Chemistry of the Elements* (Pergamon 1984); Lide, David R., ed., *CRC Handbook of Chemistry and Physics,* 75th ed. (CRC Press 1994).

ACTINOMETER

ACTINOMETER, ak-tə-nom′ə-tər, an instrument for measuring the intensity of radiation, usually light, by using photochemically active substances. Silver bromide emulsions, a solution of oxalic acid and uranyl sulfate in water, and a mixture of hydrogen and chlorine gases are examples of such substances. Radiation falling on the substances is absorbed and causes a chemical reaction. The intensity of the absorbed radiation can be determined by measurement and computation.

The actinometer has been replaced by other instruments in measuring the intensity of sunlight and as a photographic instrument for measuring exposure. It remains useful in photochemistry to provide information about the mechanism, amount, and rate of chemical reactions.

ACTINOMYCETES

ACTINOMYCETES, ak-tə-nō-mī′sēts, the common name for an order of organisms that are transitional forms between true bacteria and mold fungi, characterized by elongated filamentous cells, or hyphae, 0.5 to 0.8 microns in diameter. The hyphae spiral and branch to form a true mycelium (a mass of interwoven filaments) on solid culture mediums; they may segment to form rod-shaped bodies morphologically indistinguishable from bacteria. Most actinomycetes contain pigments.

Actinomycetes can grow on all types of natural substrates in a temperature range of 68° to 86° F (20° to 30° C). Most of the members of the order are aerobic (requiring oxygen), but some pathogenic forms are either nonaerobic or grow best at a low oxygen pressure. They reproduce by spores or fission.

Actinomycetes are important because they bring about the decomposition of plant and animal residues and liberate carbon and nitrogen for plant growth. They also inhibit the growth of

Actinomycetin, used to treat infecting colon bacilli, is derived from one of the actinomycetes (shown above).

other bacteria and fungi and thus serve as a source for most antibiotics. Two known diseases—actinomycosis, which affects cattle, and narcodosis, which affects humans—are caused by actinomycetes.

Actinomycetes belong to the order Actinomycetales, class Schizomycetes.

ACTINOMYCETIN, ak-tə-nō-mī-sē′tən, an antibiotic produced in beef-bouillon cultures by the ray fungus *Streptomyces albus.* It acts by dissolving the cell walls of certain dead bacteria, such as the colon bacilli that cause infection of urinary and intestinal tracts, and of living organisms in water solution, such as *Staphylococcus aureus*, which causes infection of skin, bones, lungs, and blood.

Composed of a proteinlike substance that speeds chemical reactions and a fatty acid that kills bacteria, actinomycetin can be dissolved in water and can be caused to precipitate by acetone, alcohol, or ammonium sulfate. Strong acid destroys it, and increasing heat reduces its activity. A temperature of 140° to 158° F (60° to 70° C) causes it to become completely inactive. It was described in 1941 but has not been widely used.

ACTINOMYCOSIS, ak-tə-nō-mī-kō′səs, an infectious disease affecting cattle and humans, more often men. Characterized by skin lesions and abscesses that may drain pus through long tracts (sinuses) and by woody swellings, the disease usually affects the face and neck, chest, or abdomen.

Description. Actinomycosis in the face and neck, also called cervicofacial actinomycosis, accounts for about 60 percent of all cases of the disease. The gums, mouth, tongue, pharynx, larynx, and neck may become discolored, swollen, and uneven. The appearance of the disease is sometimes known and well-described as "lumpy jaw." It is the least severe form of the disease, although in some cases it may affect the brain and the membranes surrounding the brain.

Actinomycosis in the chest, the most serious form of the disease, usually begins at the bronchial root of the lung and extends to the esophagus and to the membranes enveloping the lungs and heart. Often mistaken for tuberculosis, actinomycosis of the chest accounts for about 25 percent of all the cases of this infection. A cough, bloody sputum, pain in the chest that becomes worse with breathing, and a draining skin lesion are the chief symptoms.

Actinomycosis in the abdomen often begins in the appendix and spreads to the liver and spleen. Inflammation of the kidneys, bladder, and rectum can also occur. Abdominal pain, a palpable mass in the abdomen, and a draining skin lesion are the common symptoms.

In all forms of actinomycosis, fever, night sweats, chills, weight loss, pallor, and weakness may occur.

Cause. In cattle, actinomycosis is caused by the fungus *Actinomyces bovis;* in humans, by *A. israeli.* The fungus may be present normally in the mouth, tonsils, and gastrointestinal tract and cause disease only when it invades nearby tissue in persons with low resistance. The fungus is found in the pus and tissue of the abscesses as small, yellowish granules, termed "sulfur granules."

Treatment. Actinomycosis is treated by the incision and drainage of the lesions and abscesses and the administration of antimicrobial drugs. Penicillin has been found to be the most effective drug. Almost all treated patients survive.

JOHN P. UTZ, M.D.
Medical College of Virginia

ACTINOZOA. See ANTHOZOA.

ACTION, ak′shən, in law, a proceeding or demand for the enforcement or protection of a right, the redress or prevention of a wrong, or the punishment of a public offense.

At common law, actions were subject to highly technical differentiations. It was therefore necessary to make a factual situation conform exactly to rigid categories—called *forms of action*—in order to invoke the jurisdiction of a court. Under modern procedural rules, however, actions are usually classified only as *civil* or *criminal* for purposes of pleading. A concise statement of facts and a request for damages or other appropriate remedy provide a sufficient basis for judicial relief.

In addition to their broad designation as civil actions, private (or noncriminal) actions are classified in various ways denoting the nature of their origin, their effect upon parties and property, and other legal consequences. Characterized with respect to its object, an action may be *in personam* or *in rem.* The purpose of an action *in personam* is to gain a judgment against an individual, while the purpose of an action *in rem* is to determine the status of property or of individuals in their relationships to others. Whether a suit is *in personam* or *in rem* is primarily of importance in connection with the adequacy of service of process and the jurisdiction of courts.

A distinction is also made between real actions, for the determination of rights in land, and personal actions, for damages or for other redress unrelated to rights in real property. Under modern law, the chief significance of this classification is in determining where an action may properly be brought. In general, actions relating to real estate are local and must be brought where the property is located, while other kinds of actions are transitory and can be brought wherever the defendant is found.

Civil actions are also classified as *ex contractu* and *ex delicto*, the former arising from breach of contract and the latter comprising torts, or wrongs to person or property originating in breaches of noncontractual duties. The abolition of forms of actions made this distinction less important.

ACTION FRANÇAISE, ȧk-syôN′ frȧN-sâz′, was a reactionary political group in France, formed in 1898 by the writer Charles Maurras (q.v.). Maurras' political program combined support of monarchy and Roman Catholicism with violent anti-Semitism. Its protofascist doctrines gained notoriety after the establishment of the movement's daily newspaper, *L'action française,* in 1908.

Pope Pius XI condemned the Action Française in 1926 for its opposition to the standards of Catholic faith and morality.

During the 1930's the Action Française lost some of its members to other extremist groups, like the Croix de Feu, a veterans' organization. After the fall of France in 1940, Maurras gave his support to the Vichy regime. His cooperation alienated many of his followers and contributed to the disintegration of the movement.

ACTIUM, Battle of, ak′shē-əm, a crucial naval battle between Mark Antony and Octavian, who at the time of the battle ruled the Roman world, Antony in the east and Octavian in the west. By the battle of Actium, Octavian (later Emperor Augustus) won the mastery of the Roman world. It took place on Sept. 2, 31 B.C., in the Ionian Sea, off Actium. Actium is a promontory of Acarnania on the west coast of Greece, at the entrance to the Ambracian Gulf.

Antony advanced his army in September to Actium, where he established winter quarters on the flat, sandy headland. His fleet of 400 large vessels was anchored offshore. It included one squadron that belonged to Cleopatra, queen of Egypt and Antony's paramour. Octavian had moved his army across the Ionian Sea and occupied a position on the Epirote coast, just north of Actium.

Agrippa, who commanded Octavian's fleet of about 400 small but capable ships, cut off Antony's supply communications to the south. Antony's forces were besieged on two sides by the enemy and weakened by many desertions. Acting largely under Cleopatra's influence, he rejected proposals to withdraw his army into Macedonia and decided on a naval battle.

Antony deployed his fleet in three formations to face Octavian's fleet, also in three formations. Cleopatra's squadron was to the rear of Antony's forces, supposedly supporting them. When the wind shifted, both sides attempted an outer flanking movement. In the fighting that followed, Octavian's smaller ships were able to outmaneuver Antony's cumbersome fleet. Antony's center and left backwatered, and portions of his immediate command raised their oars in a token of surrender. Left with no alternative but flight, Cleopatra's squadron broke through the front ranks and sailed for Egypt. Antony followed, leaving the rest of his command to its fate. Octavian captured about 300 ships, many of which he burned. A week later Antony's land army surrendered.

In commemoration of his triumph, Octavian enlarged the temple of Apollo at Actium, which dated from the 5th century B.C., and there dedicated his newly won war trophies. He instituted games (held every five years) at Actium and built Nicopolis ("City of Victory") on the site of his army's camp near present-day Preveza.

ACTON, ak′tən, **1st Baron** (1834–1902), English historian. *John Emerich Edward Dalberg-Acton* was born in Naples, Italy, on Jan. 10, 1834, the son of Sir Richard Acton and the grandson of Sir Francis Edward Acton (q.v.). His mother was the daughter of Duke Emmerich Joseph de Dalberg. The family was Roman Catholic. Acton was educated at Oscott College, England, and at the University of Munich, Germany, under Johann Joseph Ignaz von Döllinger, whose friend and adherent he remained throughout his life.

Acton was a member of the House of Commons for Carlow from 1859 to 1865, and became a trusted supporter of William Ewart Gladstone, who secured a peerage for him in 1869. A strong Liberal in politics and religion, in 1859 he became editor of the *Rambler,* a Roman Catholic periodical; he merged this into the *Home and Foreign Review* in 1862, and continued to edit it until 1864. At the Ecumenical Council in Rome in 1870 he vigorously opposed the dogma of papal infallibility. From 1895 until his death at Tegernsee, Bavaria, on June 19, 1902, he was regius professor of modern history at Cambridge University.

Acton was a scholar of wide and vast erudition, but his passion for acquiring knowledge seemed to act as a check on his productive powers. Few modern men of such great abilities have left so few literary productions. Between 1868 and 1890 he gave to the press a few historical essays and anonymous letters; and in 1895 he published a *Lecture on the Study of History,* which was his first address on taking the professorial chair at Cambridge. In 1882 he planned a comprehensive history of liberty, but this design he never carried out. As editor, he planned the great *Cambridge Modern History,* but he did not live to see its publication. His *Lectures on Modern History* (1906), which were edited by J.N. Figgis and R.V. Laurence, are models of both form and content.

Of the many aphorisms coined by Lord Acton, the best known is "Power tends to corrupt; absolute power corrupts absolutely."

ACTON, ak′tən, **Sir John Francis Edward** (1736–1811), English officer in the service of Tuscany and Naples. Born at Besançon, France, he entered the Tuscany navy, and in 1775 commanded a frigate in the operations of Tuscany and Spain against Algiers. His exploits in covering the withdrawal of the fleet attracted the notice of Maria Carolina, queen consort of Naples and the Two Sicilies. In 1779 she persuaded her brother, Grand Duke Leopold I of Tuscany, to lend Acton to her to reorganize the Neapolitan navy. Becoming her prime favorite, he was given command of both the navy and the army, and was minister of finance and, eventually, prime minister.

In 1793 he collaborated with Sir William Hamilton, British ambassador to Naples, in securing Austrian and British help for Naples in preference to help from Spain. This move aroused the opposition of France, and after the French victories in 1798 he was forced to flee with the royal family to Sicily. Five months later, following the downfall of the Parthenopean republic set up by the French in Naples, Acton and the royal family returned. Acton instituted a reign of terror, sending many to prison or the block. At French demand, he was temporarily removed from office in 1804; and when the French entered Naples in 1806 he once more took refuge in Sicily. He died at Palermo, Sicily, on Aug. 12, 1811.

ACTON, ak'tən, a residential town located in eastern Massachusetts, in Middlesex county, 22 miles (35 km) northwest of Boston. The town was founded in 1735 and was originally a part of Concord, known as "The Village." Acton was the birthplace of Capt. Isaac Davis, a Minuteman, who died in the Battle of Concord on April 19, 1775. A monument honoring him and others who fell in this battle stands in the center of the town. Population: 20,331.

MARIAN L. PIPER
Acton Memorial Library

ACTON, ak'tən, a former industrial town in southern Ontario, Canada, situated in an agricultural area 35 miles (56 km) west of Toronto. Its manufactures included electrical equipment, plastics, leather and knitted goods, dairy foods, and farm equipment. Acton was named for a suburb of London, England. Settled about 1820, it was incorporated as a village in 1873 and as a town in 1950. In 1974 it became part of Halton Hills.

ACTON VALE, ak'tən vāl, an industrial town located in southern Quebec, Canada, 50 miles (80 km) east of Montreal. Its industries produce shoe, rubber, and woolen products. The town was formerly a copper-mining center. Acton Vale was founded in 1859 and was named for Acton, a suburb of London, England. It was incorporated as a town in 1908. Population: 7,299.

ACTORS STUDIO, a theater workshop in New York City, with a branch in Los Angeles, serving professional actors concerned with their growth as craftsmen. It was founded in 1947 by Cheryl Crawford, Elia Kazan, and Robert Lewis, all former members of the Group Theatre. In 1948, when Lewis resigned, Lee Strasberg, who also had been in the Group Theatre, joined the organization and became its artistic director.

The Actors Studio is recognized as the home of "Method" acting, although the studio does not insist that every member subscribe to this approach. The Method, a version of the system formulated by Stanislavsky, places great emphasis on stimulating the actor's imagination and stresses control of physical energy through relaxation and concentration. It encourages the actor to create a character in the context of a specific situation and therefore is basic to good acting in any period or style.

An actor becomes a member of the studio through a series of auditions. Membership is permanent, and there are no fees. From the original membership, actors who have attained great prominence include Marlon Brando, Eli Wallach, and Julie Harris. Later members were James Dean, Anne Bancroft, Ben Gazzara, Kim Stanley, Paul Newman, and Susan Strasberg. Plays produced professionally by the studio include *Strange Interlude* (1963), *Marathon* (1963), *Baby Want a Kiss* (1964), *Blues for Mister Charlie* (1964), and *The Three Sisters* (1964).

LEE STRASBERG, *The Actors Studio*

ACTS OF THE APOSTLES is the fifth book in the New Testament. It follows the four Gospels and precedes the Epistles of Paul. The opening lines refer to a "first book" (the Gospel of Luke). Both books were written by the same man. Both also were dedicated to Theophilus, perhaps a Roman magistrate who tried Christians.

Purpose. Acts is a historical sketch of the earliest period in church history, from the resurrection of Jesus (with which the Gospel ends) to the arrival of Paul in Rome, approximately the 30 years from 30 to 60 A.D. The material was selected and edited to serve the author's purpose, which was to prove that Christianity was not a threat to law and order; that Jesus had not been a revolutionist, though put to death by a Roman procurator on a charge of insurrection; that Jesus' followers were law-abiding and loyal, many of them representative or influential citizens or even Roman officials; and that the disturbances accompanying the spread of Christianity resulted from the persecutions stirred up by rivals or enemies, chiefly the unbelieving (non-Christian) Jews. The whole work was also designed to show how the new faith moved steadily from Jerusalem to Rome.

Point of View. Since Acts is the only surviving account of the spread of the early church, it is a priceless record. Careful examination of its contents and probable sources confirms its general reliability. Only a few dates, names of persons, and descriptions of the Jewish or Gentile background have been questioned, and these do not affect the main features of the work.

Luke, the author, was much less biased against Judaism than some of the other New Testament writers were. In fact, Luke describes early Christianity as a "way," a sect or school, not a party, and therefore entitled to the same protection and privileges at law enjoyed by all Jews since the reign (37–4 B.C.) of Herod the Great. As a movement within Judaism, the Christians were permitted to worship the God of their fathers without molestation or the requirement to do reverence to pagan deities. As the Jewish Sanhedrin sat in Jerusalem, so the Apostolic Council (chapter 15) assembled there and issued a decree binding upon Christians elsewhere. The decree was based upon the ancient Hebrew law of the *gērim* (resident aliens). Gentiles who became Christians were not to be required to be circumcised and observe the whole Law of Moses, but to observe only the rules laid down long before for such strangers (Leviticus 17, 18). Jesus and his immediate followers and all the apostles, including Paul, had been devout Jews, carefully observing the sacred law. Even in Rome, the Jewish leaders had assumed Paul to be innocent and his converts harmless, despite contrary reports (Acts 28:21).

Date. The author's view of Jewish-Christian relationships helps date the work (perhaps 85 or 90 A.D., but possibly somewhat earlier). Surely it was not possible to claim that Christians were really Jews much later than the persecution under Nero (in 64), though some Christians assumed it even late in the 2d century. Nor could the great mark of division be longer ignored, even by Romans: it was the Christian identification of Jesus with the Jewish Messiah. Persecution was the test, and it forced the Christians out into the open. It was then clear that Jews and Christians did not think and believe alike on some of the crucial convictions in their common faith. Luke's argument for the identity of Christians and Jews, valid at the beginning of the church's history, could not be maintained much later than a generation following the death of Nero and the fall of Jerusalem (70 A.D.).

Structure. The arrangement of the book is simple and clear, the main sections often ending with a brief summary or suggestion of what the next section will be. After an introduction (Acts 1:1–5) connecting the two parts of "Luke-Acts" (as the Gospel and its sequel are now called), the first main section (1:6 to 5:42) describes the early church in Jerusalem in the days immediately following the death and resurrection of Jesus. This section is based on very old tradition, some of it reinterpreted by Luke to provide a program for the whole story of Christian missionary expansion (the account of Pentecost, 2:1–42). The incidents are primitive and reflect local color and the atmosphere of the early days in Judaea.

The second section (6:1 to 12:24) describes the spread of the church throughout Palestine, beginning with the martyrdom of Stephen and the "scattering" of the apostles, and recounts the great events of Paul's conversion (9:1–31), Peter's pastoral ministry, and the beginning of the church at Antioch in Syria. A third section (12:25 to 15:35) explains how Christianity spread from Antioch to Cyprus and thence to Galatia in central Asia Minor, and describes the Council held at Jerusalem to decide the terms of admission of Gentiles.

The fourth section (15:36 to 18:22) relates the second journey of Paul to central Asia Minor and his further advance to Macedonia and Achaia —all the way to Athens and Corinth and back again to Antioch. The fifth section (18:23 to 21:16) pictures the more settled ministry of Paul in Ephesus and Corinth, with visits to other cities and regions, and his final return to Jerusalem, his arrest there, and his imprisonment at Caesarea.

The sixth and final section (21:17 to 28:31) recounts Paul's imprisonment and successive trials, his appeal to Caesar, the thrilling story of his journey to Rome, with the shipwreck at Malta, and his residence under "house arrest" for two years awaiting trial in Rome. There the story ends. The Gospel had come to Rome. But what happened after the two years were over, no one knows—though many have guessed. It may be that Luke did not wish to end his story of the triumphal advance of Christianity with an account of martyrdom, especially the death of both Peter and Paul and of the humble converts who had gathered about them in Rome and who died in Nero's gardens for their faith and loyalty.

Sources. The author of Luke and Acts (see Luke 1:1–4, which covers both books) was evidently familiar not only with the Christian tradition but also with other writings that embodied it. He did careful research, as he claims; and as the Gospel shows, he made use of various sources. Modern scholars have attempted to reconstruct these sources, not only in the Gospel but also in Acts, assigning them to various places of origin, such as Jerusalem and Antioch (especially in chapters 1 to 15). The task of reconstruction is easier in the Gospel than in Acts, as the Gospel has parallel accounts in Matthew and Mark (see LUKE, THE GOSPEL ACCORDING TO SAINT), whereas for Acts there are no surviving parallels. But it is probable that the opening chapters of Acts contain material from more than one source, some of them originally in Aramaic; that a long speech like Stephen's in Chapter 7 may originally have been an independent document; and that the account of Peter's journeys in Judaea may have come from still another traditional source. In no case does the evidence amount to proof.

In the latter half of Acts (chapters 12 to 28),

which recounts the missionary work of St. Paul, we come upon the famous "we passages." Here the style changes abruptly, and "he" and "they" give way to "we" (16:10–17; 20:4–16; 21:1–17; 27:1 to 28:16). These passages suggest that the author was using a document of his own, a diary, a letter, or some kind of "travel document" written by one of Paul's companions—probably Luke himself. Whether this was the Luke referred to in Philemon 24 is uncertain. Perhaps the best explanation is that the passages came from Luke's own "notebook." And since we know Luke chiefly as he is reflected in his writings (the Gospel and Acts), it does not greatly matter how we identify the Luke whose "notebook" it was. If the author was not the Luke referred to elsewhere in the New Testament, it must have been another man by the same name. Although he did not name himself in either volume, neither work has ever been attributed to anyone else, either in ancient manuscripts, tradition, or serious speculation. The "we passages" begin with Paul's crossing over from Troas to Macedonia—from Asia to Europe—and it is not unlikely that Luke was a native, or at least a resident, of this area in northwest Asia Minor (though a 2d century tradition says that he came from Antioch). It is generally agreed by modern scholars that Luke made no use of Paul's letters as a source; perhaps they had not yet been collected into a body ("corpus").

Criticism. The chief criticism of Luke-Acts has concerned the author's uncertain chronology (despite the efforts evident in Luke 1:1–4; 1:5; 2:1–2; 3:1–2). Theudas is misplaced in Acts 5:36ff., and there are other errors. His chronology in the latter half of Acts is far more reliable. With this part of the story he was personally familiar, though when a choice is necessary scholars prefer the firsthand testimony of Paul's letters to the secondary authority of Acts. The difficulties faced by ancient authors in using traditional material are hard to realize today, when every library has historical works containing or based upon exact dates. No such writings were generally accessible in ancient times. Luke did the best he could with the available resources.

Another criticism concerns the gaps in his narrative. But, again, he was writing down traditional material, not all of it yet in written form. Moreover, he was selecting incidents, compiling speeches, and narrating the general course of the spread of Christianity in such a way as to win favorable consideration for the new faith. Above all, he was an artist, if not with brush and paint as later legend related, certainly with well-chosen words—chiefly Old Testament, many classical— and his material was arranged for literary effect and persuasion. His "second book" is on a par with his first, which Ernest Renan called "the most beautiful book in the world."

See also BIBLE; GOSPELS; LUKE, SAINT.

FREDERICK C. GRANT
Union Theological Seminary

Bibliography

Alexander, Joseph, *Commentary on the Acts of the Apostles* (Klock & Klock 1979).
Gloag, Paton J., *A Critical and Exegetical Commentary on the Acts of the Apostles* (Klock & Klock 1979).
Grant, Frederick C., *Nelson's Bible Commentary*, vol. 6 (Macmillan 1962).
Joyce, Jon L., *Acts of the Apostles* (CSS of Ohio 1972).
Krodel, Gerhard A., *Augsburg Commentary on the New Testament: Acts* (Augsburg 1986).
Schmidt, Elizabeth, *Do We Hear the Song of This Joy? Meditations on the Acts of the Apostles* (Pilgrim Press 1983).

ACUPUNCTURE, ak′yoō-pungk-chər, is an Oriental medical therapy in which small, solid needles, usually made of stainless steel, are inserted into specific body points in order to relieve pain or improve health.

History and Theory. Records of acupuncture practice and related therapy go back more than 2,500 years. Needle therapy was an outgrowth of an ancient Oriental philosophy that considered man as a microcosmic image of the universe, subject to the same tensions and disruptions as nature itself. The immutable course of nature, the Tao, was thought to act through two component forces, Yin and Yang, which were constantly struggling with each other. Yin represented that which was cold, passive, dark, and feminine and Yang that which was hot, active, bright, and male. The ancient Chinese thought that a balance of Yin and Yang was essential to health.

The human body was thought to consist of 12 physiological, or functional, systems, each associated with a major visceral organ and a pathway, or meridian, of energy flow in the body. Through each meridian flowed a vital life force termed the *chi*, which was thought to circulate according to a circadian, or daily, rhythm. Disturbances in the flow of the vital life-force resulted from disharmonies in the natural forces within the individual. Such disturbances, if not corrected, would eventually lead to a disease state affecting either the organ associated with the meridian in which the blockage of the *chi* occurred or at some point along that pathway. Acupuncture therapy was intended to correct blockages, excesses, or imbalances in the flow of the vital life-force. More than 365 points were located on the meridians for treatment by needle therapy, and ancient acupuncture specified exacting procedures for needle insertion and manipulation and duration of treatment.

Modern Practice and Theories. Many variations on classical acupuncture have been developed. In Japan, physicians tap needles into place using guide tubes and then apply electric current to the needles. In China, acupuncture methods are combined with Western medical techniques to prevent the pain normally associated with surgery. Many, but not all, of the classical points are used for acupuncture anesthesia, and a number of new points have been added, but the theory of Yin and Yang is no longer cited.

There is no satisfactory, and probably no single, explanation for the phenomena associated with acupuncture. Some Japanese acupuncturists contend that needle therapy affects the autonomic nervous system. In China, physicians contend that acupuncture works by means of nerve impulses and some mechanism that they are unable to specify. In the West, scientists have speculated that such factors as counterirritation, psychological set (emotions and attitudes), or the control of pain by higher processes in the brain are responsible for the effects of acupuncture. Some Western physicians explain acupuncture therapy and anesthesia on the basis of the "gate control" theory of pain, which holds that minor irritations that stimulate the senses of touch and heat can selectively act on the transmission of nerve messages in the spinal cord and other parts of the central nervous system by closing a neurological gate, thus preventing pain impulses from reaching the brain.

Value. Because emotional and other factors play such a major role in pain and disease, re-

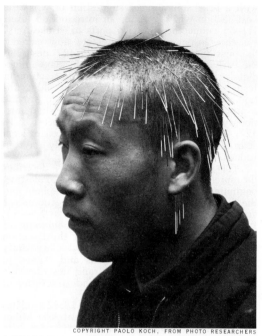

ACUPUNCTURE, a traditional form of Oriental medicine, involves the insertion of small solid needles into specific body points to relieve pain and improve health.

searchers have been unable to determine whether acupuncture is truly effective as an analgesic or medical therapy. If, in fact, needle treatment has reliable physiological therapeutic qualities, it would be of great value to Western medical practice. It is an inexpensive treatment that, in some cases, provides an excellent alternative to therapy involving drugs.

While acupuncture is essentially a harmless procedure, it must be practiced by a skilled, medically trained therapist in order to be safe. Serious accidents have occurred when acupuncture needles have pierced the heart or the lungs, and hepatitis, local infection, and similar complications may occur when unsterilized needles are used. An additional risk is that some patients who seek this form of therapy as an alternative to medical examination and treatment may have important symptoms of major diseases that could go undetected.

C. RICHARD CHAPMAN, PH. D.
JOHN J. BONICA, M. D.
Anesthesia Research Center
University of Washington School of Medicine

ADA, ā′də, a city located in south-central Oklahoma, 85 miles (137 km) southeast of Oklahoma City. It is the seat of Pontotoc county and the home of East Central University. The city has some light industry.

The community was settled in 1889 and named for Ada Reed, the daughter of its first postmaster. The railroad arrived in 1900 and Ada became a marketing and trade center for cattle and grain. The town quickly gained a reputation for violence, but a mass lynching by irate citizens in 1909 led to tighter law enforcement throughout the region. The discovery of oil in the area contributed to the town's growth. Ada was incorporated in 1910. Population: 15,691.

ADAK, ä′däk, a barren island in the center of the Andreanof Islands, part of the Aleutian Islands of Alaska. It is about 30 miles (48 km) long, 3 to 20 miles (5–32 km) wide, and rises to an altitude of 3,900 feet (1,189 meters) at Mt. Moffat. A U.S. naval station is there.

Adak was discovered in 1741 by the Vitus Bering exploration party. Fur traders subsequently killed off most of the island's wildlife. In World War II the United States carried out military operations from Adak against the Japanese on Kiska and Attu islands in the western Aleutians. The military bases were closed in 1995.

ADALBERT, ä′däl-bert, **Saint** (c. 956–997), Christian missionary and martyr, who was known as the *Apostle of the Prussians.* He was born near Prague, the son of a noble Bohemian family of Vojtech. Educated in a monastery at Magdeburg, he received his teacher's name, Adalbert, at his confirmation.

Adalbert was appointed bishop of Prague in 982. Discouraged, however, by the religious apathy and political opposition of the local rulers in Bohemia, he retired to a monastery in Italy in 900. He returned to Prague in 993, after receiving assurances of civil support, but left again for Italy because of political difficulties. While he was in Italy, his missionary ideas impressed Emperor Otto III.

In 996 he made his final journey to Bohemia and allegedly baptized Saint Stephen, later king of Hungary, during the trip. Because the rulers of Prague refused to let Adalbert enter the city, he and two companions undertook missionary work in Poland and in the Baltic lands occupied by Germans. Although warmly welcomed in Poland by King Boleslav I, he was suspected by the Germans of being a Polish spy and was murdered on April 23, 997, near the present city of Kaliningrad. Boleslav recovered his body and buried it at Gniezno, Poland, where it remained until its transfer to Prague in 1039.

Adalbert was involved in the political struggles of central Europe, yet he remained a friend of both Otto III and Boleslav I, who opposed Otto's efforts to expand the Holy Roman Empire eastward.

ADALBERT, ä′däl-bert (c. 1000–1072), was a German prince-bishop and imperial adviser, who exercised extraordinary political power. He was born in Thuringia, a member of a noble family, and attended the cathedral school at Halberstadt. In 1043, Emperor Henry III of the Holy Roman Empire named Adalbert, who was a favored friend and a trusted adviser, archbishop of Bremen-Hamburg. Adalbert intensified missionary efforts in Scandinavia, which was part of his see, and hoped to establish a "patriarchate of the north." In 1046, Henry offered to make Adalbert pope, but Adalbert refused. Pope Leo IX made Adalbert papal legate and then vicar in northern Europe in 1053. As papal agent, Adalbert had the mission of evangelizing the area. He was never granted the larger "patriarchate" that he desired.

During the minority of Emperor Henry IV, Adalbert of Bremen gained a great deal of influence as a guardian and tutor of the young monarch. By 1064, Adalbert had virtually taken over the administration of the empire in the emperor's name. Rival German princes accomplished Adalbert's removal from Henry's court in 1066. Henry IV summoned his capable–and very ambitious–adviser back to court in 1069, but Adalbert never regained his political dominance. He died in Goslar on March 16, 1072. Adalbert was buried in the cathedral of Bremen, the city whose very active commerce at that time was, in large measure, due to his efforts.

ADAM, à-däɴ′, **Adolphe Charles** (1803–1856), French composer, who is best remembered for his ballet *Giselle* (1841), a standard work of the dance repertoire, and for his Christmas song *Cantique de Noël* (*O Holy Night*). He was also renowned during his lifetime as a composer of comic operas, notably *Le Postillon de Longjumeau* (1836), as well as *Si j'étais roi* (1852), whose overture is a popular modern concert piece. In addition, Adam composed several grand operas, such as *Richard en Palestine* (1844), which are rarely heard today.

Adam was born in Paris on July 24, 1803. He entered the Paris Conservatory in 1817 and later studied with François Boieldieu, a celebrated opera composer. Adam's first work was a one-act opera, *Pierre et Catherine* (1829). His career was launched in 1830 with the success of his three-act opera *Danilowa*. He became professor of composition at the Paris Conservatory in 1849. Adam died in Paris on May 3, 1856.

ADAM, Robert. See ADAM STYLE.

ADAM AND EVE, according to the Judeo-Christian tradition and the Muslim tradition derived from it, were the parents of the human race. The Bible tells that they were created in the image of God and placed in the Garden of Eden, where they were responsible for the care of the earth and its inhabitants. When they ate the fruit of a single forbidden tree, they were expelled from Eden by God and cursed with frustration in work and with death.

The Biblical story of Adam and Eve is the Hebrew version of an account of origins that is very ancient in the Middle East. Most peoples, when they have reached a certain cultural level, manifest an urge to speculate about the origins of things and thus produce their tales about the beginnings of human life. The Greeks, for instance, told of Deucalion and Pyrrha; the ancient Indians, of Yama and Yami; the Iranians, of Mashya and Mashyoi; the Norsemen, of Askr and Embla; and the Andaman islanders tell of Tomo, the first ancestor, and Puluga, his wife.

The names "Adam" and "Eve" themselves are symbolic, and although they came to be used as personal names ("Eve" is always a proper name in the Bible), they were not necessarily such in the first instance. *Adam* is the Hebrew word for "man" or "mankind." The derivation of both names is uncertain, but the most probable suggestion is that *Adam* meant "reddish" and *Eve,* "living one."

The Account in Genesis. In Genesis 1 to 5, two distinct accounts of the first human pair have been woven together. The older (Genesis 2:4b to 4:26) is that of the J document (so called because of its use of the name "Jahweh"–or Yahweh–for God). It tells how God formed a man out of the dust of the ground, gave him life by breathing the breath of life into his nostrils, and set him in the garden that he was to cultivate but of whose tree of knowledge he was not to eat. The animals were created for man's companionship; but when it became evident that their companionship was inadequate for man, woman was created from one of the man's ribs to be a helpmeet for him. But the serpent persuaded the woman to eat of the forbidden fruit, and she shared it with her husband. As a result of this action, they gained knowledge, became conscious sexually, and could distinguish good and evil. They were driven out of the garden, however, had to labor to survive, became subject to pain and death, and were at enmity with the serpent.

Cain and Abel were born to them, but Cain, the tiller of the soil, killed Abel, the keeper of flocks. Another son, named Seth, was born to them to replace Abel, and the two human stems, the Cainites and the Sethites, descended from these two sons.

The later tradition (Genesis 1:1 to 2:4a; 5:1 ff) is that of the P document (Priestly Code). It tells that after God created the vegetation and animals, he created mankind, male and female, in his own image, to rule over the animal creation and have the vegetation for their subsistence. God bade the first pair to increase and multiply, and consequently Seth was born to them as the first of numerous sons and daughters from whom the races of mankind are descended.

In both of these accounts there are details that are shared with even more ancient Middle Eastern traditions about the beginnings of things (see CREATION). The Biblical writers purified these accounts from all polytheism and crudity and by means of this adaptation used these traditions as a vehicle to express their own theology about human origins. Man, according to these Biblical writers, is in a peculiar sense the work of God, and God provides for his welfare, plans his way of life, instructs him, places him under Divine law with its punishment for sin, and even after man has sinned, still makes it possible for there to be communication between man and God.

Later Accounts. In later times pious imagination embroidered the Adam and Eve story with a great variety of fanciful legends. We are told, for instance, of Adam's enormous size, which was reduced because of his sin, and of how the various classes of matter contributed material for his body, which, as it left the hands of God, was a microcosm reflecting in small the macrocosm in which his life was set. We are told that the angels were bidden to do him obeisance, that Satan refused and for his disobedience was cast out of heaven with the hosts who followed him, and that in revenge for this, Satan used the serpent to deceive Eve and cause Adam in his turn to be cast out. Adam, however, is given a revelation of God's will for mankind with the promise that the ideal life that had been lost by his sin would be restored by the coming of the Second Adam.

The New Testament incorporates the idea of this Second Adam (Romans 5:12–21; I Corinthians 15:20–23, 45–49), whom it identifies with the Christ. As early as the Jewish philosopher Philo (1st century B.C.–1st century A.D.) there were attempts to allegorize the Biblical stories of Adam and Eve and treat them as representations in story form of philosophical realities. Thus Adam figures prominently in the speculations of Gnostic groups, in Manichaeism and Mandaism, and later in the Jewish Qabbala (or Cabala). A number of apocryphal Books of Adam circulated during the early centuries of the Christian era.

ARTHUR JEFFERY, *Columbia University*

ADAM BEDE, ad'əm bēd, the first long novel of George Eliot, published in 1859. The action takes place in Hayslope, an English village, where the hero, Adam, a simple carpenter of sterling worth, pursues his trade. Very different from Adam is his brother Seth, a gentle and loving person, whose religious emotions have been strongly engaged by a Methodist revival of the time. Seth is devotedly in love with Dinah Morris, the leading exponent of the sect in the community, but she is consecrated to her work of evangelical preaching and refuses to think of him except with sisterly and religious affection.

Adam loves Hetty Sorrel, a beautiful but vain and shallow country girl, who encourages him but secretly hopes to make a loftier marriage. When Arthur Donnithorne, the village squire's son, falls in love with her, both her passion and her ambition are stirred. Arthur, who is kind-hearted but weak willed, tries to resist his infatuation but finally yields to it, with tragic consequences for all of the major characters.

The subject of Hetty's and Arthur's sin is handled with delicacy, and Hetty's wretched journey in search of Arthur after she learns that she is pregnant is one of the most poignant incidents of fiction. The characters are portrayed with unusual distinctness, and their appeal is direct and powerful. The analysis of Hetty's character is particularly vivid. In the midst of pity for her fate, the reader is never allowed to forget the girl's shallowness and selfishness. Yet Adam, iron-willed and morally uncompromising, remains the dominant character. The theme of the inevitable consequences of wrongdoing, ever present in Eliot's novels, is strongly emphasized.

JAMES H. HANFORD*, *Newberry Library, Chicago*

ADAM DE LA HALLE, à-dän' dä là àl' (c. 1240–1287), French dramatist, poet, and musician, nicknamed *Adam the Hunchback.* He was one of the most distinguished of the poet-musicians known as *trouvères,* who helped form the French language in the 1100s and 1200s.

Born at Arras, France, he was educated at the Abbey of Vauxcelles, near Cambrai, but left the abbey to marry. After separating from his wife, he studied in Paris. In 1282 he went to Italy as a poet in the service of Count Robert II of Artois, who belonged to the court of Duke Charles of Anjou at Naples. Adam died at Naples in 1287.

Adam wrote two historically important dramatic works. *Le jeu de la feuillée,* a distant ancestor of the French revue, has been called the first French comedy. The characters in the play represented well-known residents of Arras who make coarse but good-natured fun of one another. The musical refrains that Adam wrote for this work have been lost. *Le jeu de Robin et Marion* was written for the French court at Naples. A pastoral play with airs, couplets, and duets for alternating voices, it was a forerunner of the *opéra comique* (opera with spoken dialogue). Of the many songs that Adam composed to his own lyrics, a group of rondeaux survives.

ADAM STYLE, ad'əm stīl, a neoclassical revival in late-18th-century architecture and design, chiefly associated with the works of Robert Adam (1728–1792), Scottish architect and designer of decorations and furniture. His brothers John, James, and William were at various times associated with him in architectural projects.

The bold and handsome palette characterizing the Adam style of decoration can be seen in Robert Adam's drawing room (1762–1768), removed from Lansdowne House, London, and installed in the Philadelphia Museum of Art in 1943. With its painted decoration of classical scenes and decorative devices, the room is considered one of the finest and best-preserved 18th-century interiors in a U.S. museum. In the mid-1980s the drawing room was cleaned, regilded, and restored to its original splendor.

PHILADELPHIA MUSEUM OF ART: GIVEN IN MEMORY OF GEORGE HORACE LORIMER BY GRAEME LORIMER AND SARAH MOSS LORIMER

Balance and symmetry were characteristic of Robert Adam's work. His chief aim was to establish complete harmony between exterior and interior architecture. In addition he strove for unity between interior architectural decoration and the contents of a room. The classical elements that he incorporated into his work included paterae, shell ornaments, palm leaves, honeysuckle, and festoons of husks or bellflowers.

Adam's designs for furniture were borrowed, expanded, and widely disseminated by George Hepplewhite and Thomas Sheraton. The Adam style had considerable effect on architecture on the Continent and in the United States. (See HEPPLEWHITE; SHERATON, THOMAS.)

Robert Adam was born in Kirkcaldy, Scotland, on July 3, 1728, the son of the architect William Adam (1689–1748). He was educated at Edinburgh University and studied in Italy from 1754 to 1758, when he settled in London. He was much impressed by Roman architecture, especially by the detail that was used on the walls and ceilings of small private apartments. He also studied the works of Raphael and found inspiration in the decorative elements the artist derived from Roman sources. In July 1757 Adam journeyed to Spalato in Dalmatia, where he studied and measured the remains of the palace of Roman Emperor Diocletian. He published the results of his research in *The Ruins of the Palace of Diocletian* (1764), a book that established his reputation in England.

Adam served as architect to King George III from 1762 to 1768. During the first phase of his career, from about 1760 to 1770, when he worked mainly at remodeling English country homes, his style was extremely bold. His major commissions during this period were Croome Court for Lord Coventry, Bowood for Lord Shelburne, Kedleston for Sir Nathaniel Curzon, and Syon for the duke of Northumberland.

During the second phase of his career, Adam's style became more refined and precise, prompting later critics to call it effeminate. The progression from the early to late style is seen best in the rooms he designed for Osterley Park, Middlesex, rebuilt between 1761 and 1780. Adam was chiefly occupied during this period with building and decorating London town houses. His most famous projects include the Admiralty Screen in Whitehall; No. 20 St. James Square; Home House on Portman Square; and Apsley House, Piccadilly. Adam died in London on March 3, 1792.

JOSEPH T. BUTLER*
Historic Hudson Valley, Tarrytown, N.Y.

Bibliography: Bolton, Arthur T., *The Architecture of Robert and James Adam*, 2 vols. (1922; reprint, Antique Collectors' Club 1984); **King, David**, *The Complete Works of Robert and James Adam* (Butterworth-Heinemann 1991); **Parissien, Steven**, *Adam Style* (Preservation Press 1992); **Rykwert, Joseph, and Anne Rykwert**, *Robert and James Adam: The Men and the Style* (Rizzoli Intl. Pubns. 1985); **Tait, A. A.**, *Robert Adam: Drawings and Imagination* (Cambridge 1993).

ADAMIC, Louis, ad'ə-mik (1899–1951), Slovene American author. He was born on March 23, 1899, at Blato, Slovenia (then part of Austria-Hungary), the son of peasant parents. After studying at the gymnasium in Ljubljana, Slovenia, he emigrated to the United States in 1913. He became an American citizen in 1918.

In the early 1920s Adamic began translating Slovenian, Croatian, and Serbian stories into English, primarily for the magazine *Living Age*. In 1932 he returned briefly to Yugoslavia, where he gathered material for *The Native's Return* (1934). This book, about life in that country, made his reputation. Previously he had published *Dynamite: The Story of Class Violence in America* (1931; rev. ed., 1934) and *Laughing in the Jungle* (1932), an autobiographical volume.

Adamic explored the life of immigrants in America in the novels *Grandsons* (1935) and *Cradle of Life* (1936); a second autobiographical volume, *My America, 1928–1938* (1938); and *From Many Lands* (1940). His conception of America's potential influence on Europe was expressed in *Two-Way Passage* (1941). In *My Native Land* (1943) he supported Marshal Tito's faction of the Yugoslav underground movement, and his last book *The Eagle and the Roots* (published posthumously, 1952) was largely a biography of Tito. Adamic died at Riegelsville, N.J., on Sept. 4, 1951.

ADAMITES, ad′əm-īts, several Christian sects which, at various periods, advocated return to the extreme simplicity and innocence attributed to Adam. The first of these sects, mentioned by St. Epiphanius and St. Augustine, was located in northern Africa during the 2d and 3d centuries A.D. Data on the sect are obscure, but it apparently combined Gnostic and ascetic doctrines. To symbolize the state of primitive innocence, its members appeared naked at religious gatherings. The Adamites called their meetings "paradises" and denounced marriage because Adam and Eve had not been married. (See GNOSTICISM.)

Similar sects arose in Europe among the Waldenses in the 14th century and the Anabaptists in the 16th century, but were suppressed. Other groups appeared in Austria and Russia in the middle of the 19th century.

ADAMNAN, ad′əm-nan (c. 624–704), Irish monk, writer, and saint. He was born in Drumhome, County Donegal, Ireland. Also known as *Eunan,* he was abbot of the monastery at Iona, Scotland, from 679 until his death on Sept. 23, 704. His feast day is celebrated on Sept. 23.

After a visit to England in 688, he adopted the Roman date for celebrating Easter. Though he secured its acceptance throughout Ireland, he was unable to do so in his own monastery. In 697 the Synod of Tara adopted his rule that women and children should not be taken prisoner in warfare, later known as the *Canon of Adamnan.*

His most important work was the *Vita Columbae,* a life of Saint Columba, founder of the Iona monastery. It is regarded as the best of early religious biographies. His *De locis sanctis* is an account of holy places in Palestine and other Eastern countries, based on a pilgrim's report.

ADAMOV, Arthur, àd-à-môf′ (1908–1970), French Russian playwright, one of the leading exponents of the avant-garde theater in France. He was born in Kislovodsk, Russia, on Aug. 23, 1908. He was brought up in France and was schooled in Switzerland and Germany. In 1924 he settled in Paris, and following World War II he became editor of a Paris literary review, *L'heure nouvelle.*

Adamov began to write for the stage in the mid-1940s, and most of his works were produced in France in the next decade. His earlier plays, which include *La parodie, L'invasion, Le professeur Taranne,* and *Le ping-pong,* are classified as works of the Theater of the Absurd, for they are imbued with the sense of the futility and absurdity of life. With *Paolo Paoli* (1957), however, Adamov changed course. This work is an epic drama in the tradition of Bertolt Brecht.

Adamov also is noted as a translator and adapter of foreign works for the French stage, including Christopher Marlowe's *Edward II.* He died in Paris on March 16, 1970.

ADAMS, ad′əmz, a Massachusetts family that for four generations had a unique influence on the course of U.S. political and intellectual history. Passing suddenly from village obscurity into international fame in the late 18th century, the family became aristocratic in the best possible sense, producing—despite some personal limitations and failures—outstanding individuals for generations.

The family's founder in the United States was Henry Adams, who married Edith Squire about 1609 and in 1636 emigrated from England to Braintree, Mass. Of the next three generations of Adamses, none displayed particular distinction in the larger life of Massachusetts; all did their private and public duty in their narrow village sphere.

With the fourth generation, in the person of John Adams (1735–1826), the family achieved national and international position. The son of John Adams (1691–1760) and Susanna Boylston Adams (1699–1797) and the second cousin of the revolutionary patriot Samuel Adams (1722–1803), John Adams generally is remembered for his rather unhappy tenure as 2d president of the United States. Of more enduring significance, however, was the leading role he played in the struggle against Britain and in the establishment of the conservative political tradition in America. His wife, Abigail Smith Adams (1744–1818), was a celebrated letter writer; in fact, both John and Abigail wrote voluminously.

John Quincy Adams (1767–1848), their son, had a public career remarkably parallel to that of his father. He, too, made many notable contributions beyond serving as president. As secretary of state in James Monroe's cabinet, he was principally responsible for the acquisition of Florida, the enunciation of the Monroe Doctrine, and the formation of an expansionist national spirit. President John Quincy Adams did not retire to private life after being engulfed by the Jacksonian democratic tide of 1828; he returned to public affairs in the U.S. House of Representatives as an uncompromising voice of national conscience against slavery.

This tradition remained alive in the next generation. Charles Francis Adams (1807–1886), the son of John Quincy Adams, was extremely active both in the battle of words preceding the Civil War and in wartime diplomacy. He served in Congress and in the 1840s was a leader of the abortive Free-Soil Party. During the Civil War he was minister to Great Britain; his courageous diplomacy was a principal factor in the maintenance of British neutrality.

The sons of Charles Francis Adams—John Quincy Adams 2d (1833–1894), Charles Francis Adams 2d (1835–1915), Henry Adams (1838–1918), and Brooks Adams (1848–1927)—made their contributions generally outside public office. John Quincy Adams 2d did enter the Massachusetts House of Representatives, and his son, Charles Francis Adams 3d (1866–1954), was a prominent lawyer, financier, and U.S. secretary of the navy. Charles Francis Adams 2d became a distinguished railroad expert, civic leader, and historian. Henry Adams and Brooks Adams were important historians and keen observers of the American scene.

In one way or another, the experience of the Civil War had caused the four sons of the first Charles Francis Adams to break away from the ancestral pattern of entering politics. But the family culture was far more than a habitual calling to law and politics, being grounded in a set of concepts or supporting ideas. These, amply evident in the writings of this generation of Adamses, were a belief in the rational as opposed to the emotional approach to public issues, the need for an educated national leadership, and the need for continual national self-analysis.

Other Adams descendants include Alvin Adams (1804–1877), a pioneer in the express business; Charles Baker Adams (1814–1853), the naturalist; William Claflin (1818–1905), Massachusetts merchant and governor, whose mother was an Adams; William Taylor Adams (1822–1897), author of fiction for young readers under the pseudonym *Oliver Optic;* and Herbert Baxter Adams (1850–1901), a historian.

WENDELL D. GARRETT*, *Associate Editor of "Adams Family Correspondence"*

Bibliography: The Adams Papers series, ed. by Lyman H. Butterfield et al. (Belknap Press/Harvard Univ. Press 1961–   ), will encompass some 100 volumes of diaries, correspondence, and state papers. See also **Brookhiser, Richard,** *America's First Dynasty: The Adamses, 1735–1918* (Free Press 2002); **Nagel, Paul C.,** *Descent from Glory: Four Generations of the John Adams Family* (1983; reprint, Harvard Univ. Press 1999); **Shepherd, Jack,** *The Adams Chronicles* (Little, Brown 1975).

ADAMS, Abigail, ad'əmz (1744–1818), wife of John Adams, 2d president of the United States, and mother of John Quincy Adams, 6th president. Her husband's confidante during his long public career, Adams was the mother of the most important family dynasty in U.S. public life. She was a gifted letter writer, and the volume, continuity, and literary quality of her writings are unsurpassed by those of any other American woman of her era.

Born Abigail Smith, in Weymouth, Mass., on Nov. 11, 1744, the second of four children of the Rev. William Smith and Elizabeth Quincy Smith, she was delicate in health. The greatest influence on her character and education was that of her maternal grandmother, Mrs. John Quincy, with whom she spent much of her youth at Mount Wollaston. She married John Adams, a young Braintree, Mass., lawyer, in 1764, when she was 20, and bore five children: two daughters, one of whom died as an infant, and three sons—John Quincy, Charles, and Thomas Boylston.

After 10 years of happy married life, Adams found her household broken up by the onset of the American Revolution. For the next 10 years she had to attend not only to the care of four children but also to the upkeep of the farm at Braintree, for public business frequently kept her husband away. In 1784 she finally joined him in Europe, where he was engaged on diplomatic missions, spending eight months in Paris and then 3 years in London. In 1788 the Adamses returned to the United States. During the 12 years of her husband's terms as vice president and president, she divided her time between the capital and Quincy (formerly part of Braintree).

Despite attacks of serious illness, Adams seems to have been of cheerful disposition. Her letters, full of references to current politics, are often tart and partisan, for she was an ardent Federalist. After 1801, happily resuming her "operations of a dairy-woman," she lived in Quincy, where she died on Oct. 28, 1818, of typhoid fever.

WENDELL D. GARRETT, *Associate Editor "Adams Family Correspondence"*

Bibliography: Adams's correspondence is included in *The Adams Papers,* ed. in 6 vols. by Lyman H. Butterfield et al. (Belknap Press/Harvard Univ. Press 1963–1993). Volumes of selections include *The Book of Abigail and John; Selected Letters of the Adams Family, 1762–1784,* ed. by Lyman H. Butterfield et al. (Harvard Univ. Press 1975). See also **Akers, Charles,** *Abigail Adams: An American Woman,* 2d ed. (Longman 2000); **Gelles, Edith Belle,** *Portia: The World of Abigail Adams* (Ind. Univ. Press 1992); **Levin, Phyllis Lee,** *Abigail Adams* (St. Martin's 1987); **Nagel, Paul C.,** *The Adams Women; Abigail and Louisa Adams, Their Sisters and Daughters* (1987; reprint, Harvard Univ. Press 1999).

ADAMS, Alvin, ad'əmz (1804–1877), American businessman and pioneer in express delivery service. Born at Andover, Vt., on June 16, 1804, he entered the express business in 1840 by carrying parcels and valuables between New York City and Boston. In 1849, after acquiring the express business of William F. Harnden (1812–1845) in the East, Adams extended his service to California, where he eventually lost out to Wells Fargo. Following further consolidations, he capitalized the Adams Express Company at $10 million in 1854. It was a leading firm until 1918, when it was merged into the American Railway Express Company. Adams died at Watertown, Mass., on Sept. 1, 1877.

ADAMS, Ansel, ad'əmz (1902–1984), American photographer whose majestic black-and-white landscapes of the American West and impeccable craftsmanship made him the most widely exhibited and recognized photographer of his generation. An ardent conservationist and environmentalist, Adams incorporated his sense of the redemptive beauty of the wilderness into a meticulous art form that conveyed both the innate grandeur of America's wild areas and the fragility of their preservation.

Ansel Easton Adams was born in San Francisco on Feb. 20, 1902. He took an early interest in music and became a self-taught pianist. In 1916 Adams took a trip to California's Yosemite National Park and made his first pictures with a Kodak Brownie camera. From that time on, the park, nature, and the High Sierras were among his major interests. He studied photo processing for a short time in San Francisco and returned to Yosemite every year to explore and to photograph. In 1920 Adams decided to become a professional musician, giving concerts and piano lessons until 1927, when the publication of his first portfolio of pictures earned him wide critical acclaim.

In 1930 Adams decided to become a professional photographer. He studied diligently and became as proficient in photography as he was in music. In 1932 he was accomplished enough in the medium to be given a one-man show at San Francisco's M. H. de Young Museum. That same year he joined Imogen Cunningham, Edward Weston, and others in forming the short-lived Group *f*/64 (the name signifying the aperture setting on the camera lens that produces the most sharply defined image), an association of West Coast photographers who, in reaction to the conventional soft-focus, pictorialist style of the day, espoused clarity of definition and purity of form in photography.

Over the course of his 50-year career, Adams's favorite photographic subjects continued to be the wilds of his native West, and his eloquent photographs of western scenes won him wide recognition as a poet-photographer of nature. His involvement with the Sierra Club (serving as its director from 1934 to 1971) and its efforts at environmental protection gave his art a social function of profound effect. As both a practitioner and teacher of photography, Adams played a central role in the acceptance of the medium as a fine art. He began to teach in the 1930s, founding the photography department at the California School of Fine Arts (now the San Francisco Art Institute) in 1946 and teaching his renowned Ansel Adams Workshop in Yosemite every summer from 1946 until 1981, when he transferred it to the Monterey Peninsula in California. In 1935 he published *Making a Photograph,* the first of his many manuals on technique. By 1939 he had devised the Zone System, a method of exposure

Ansel Adams's striking photograph *Winterstorm 1944* (c. 1944) captures the austere grandeur of California's Yosemite National Park.

ANSEL ADAMS

and development that allows a photographer to control the tones of black-and-white prints.

In 1936 the well-known photographer Alfred Stieglitz arranged a one-man show for Adams at his New York City gallery, An American Place. Adams and the curator and historian Beaumont Newhall helped establish, in 1940, the photography department at the Museum of Modern Art in New York City. In 1967 Adams founded the San Francisco–based Friends of Photography, one of the country's leading organizations for the appreciation and promotion of the art of photography. He received Guggenheim Fellowships in 1946, 1948, and 1958 and was awarded the Presidential Medal of Freedom in 1980. Adams died in Monterey, Calif., on April 22, 1984. His archives of 20,000 negatives and over 2,000 master prints are housed at the University of Arizona's Center for Creative Photography in Tucson, which he helped found in 1975.

STEPHANIE LIPSCOMB
Art Institute of Chicago

Bibliography: Adams, Ansel, *The Portfolios of Ansel Adams* (Bulfinch Press 1981); Callahan, Harry M., ed., *Ansel Adams in Color* (Little, Brown 1993); Dawson, Robert, *Ansel Adams, New Light: Essays on His Legacy and Legend* (Univ. of N.Mex. Press 1994); Spaulding, Jonathan, *Ansel Adams and the American Landscape* (Univ. of Calif. Press 1995); Turnage, William A., and Andrea G. Stillman, eds., *Ansel Adams: Our National Parks* (Bulfinch Press 1992).

ADAMS, Brooks, ad'əmz (1848–1927), American historian. The son of Charles Francis Adams (died 1886), he was born in Quincy, Mass., on June 24, 1848. He was graduated from Harvard in 1870 and turned to politics and law, but forsook both for lecturing, freelance writing, and travel. Attempting to solve the major problems of human civilization by applying scientific methods to the study of history, he became the intellectual partner of his brother, Henry Adams, and an adviser to Theodore Roosevelt. Although Adams often missed the mark, he was the first American to write a history of Western civilization based systematically on economic evidence.

The Emancipation of Massachusetts (1887), Adams's first book, utilizing social Darwinian theory, pictures the development of society in well-marked stages resulting from the struggle among humans for the survival of the fittest. It takes the theo-cratic stage of Massachusetts history as an example. *The Law of Civilization and Decay* (1895) elaborates on the earlier book. It postulates that as centralization of government is achieved, the currency narrows because bankers manipulate prices and wages until intense competition among businessmen and the inability of workingmen to command adequate salaries sap the energy of the nation. Society decays; a cycle of history concludes.

In a series of letters, Adams persuaded his brother Henry that a cycle of history would end by 1980. America's one chance to survive the coming Darwinian struggle between Europe and Asia would be to centralize government and industry to achieve absolute economic efficiency and become the center of the world's financial exchanges.

America's Economic Supremacy (1900) forecast the dissolution of Britain's empire, and *The New Empire* (1902) predicted France's decline. In his final work, Adams complained that he could not change the course of history. His introduction to Henry Adams's *The Degradation of the Democratic Dogma* (1919) insists that the graph of history leads to futility. America must fall, and with it the last hopes of Western civilization.

Brooks Adams, who died in Boston on Feb. 13, 1927, misunderstood the role of science. He sought an infallible picture of the world, whereas science can discover only data with which the historian must wrestle in endless experiment.

ARTHUR F. BERINGAUSE
Bronx Community College

ADAMS, Charles Follen, ad'əmz (1842–1918), American poet known for his dialect verse. Of New England stock, Adams was born in Dorchester, Mass., on April 21, 1842. He enlisted for Civil War service in 1862 with the 13th Massachusetts Infantry and was wounded and taken prisoner at Gettysburg. After the war he established himself in the dry goods business.

Following the example of Charles Godfrey Leland, whose humorously satirical "Hans Breitmann" ballads were immensely popular, Adams wrote poems in the Pennsylvania Dutch "scrapple" dialect. *The Puzzled Dutchman* appeared in 1872 and *Leedle Yawcob Strauss*, which established his reputation, in 1876. His complete poems were published as *Yawcob Strauss and Other Poems* (1910). Adams died in Roxbury, Mass., on March 8, 1918.

ADAMS, Charles Francis, ad'əmz (1807–1886), American diplomat whose statesmanship was in the tradition of his father, Pres. John Quincy Adams, and his grandfather, Pres. John Adams. Born in Boston on Aug. 18, 1807, he was raised in Russia, France, and England until age ten. He graduated from Harvard College in 1825. After reading law in the office of Daniel Webster, he was admitted to practice in 1829. That year he married Abigail Brooks, a daughter of Peter Chardon Brooks, a Boston insurance tycoon. Relieved of financial worry, Adams turned to journalism and politics. After five years as a Whig legislator in Massachusetts (1840–1845), he became an antislavery "Conscience Whig" and, in 1848, was the unsuccessful Free Soil candidate for vice president. Thereafter he edited John Adams's papers and wrote a biography of him. He was elected to Congress as a Republican in 1858 and 1860.

It was as a diplomat, however, that Adams excelled. In 1861 President Lincoln appointed him minister to the Court of St. James's in London. His primary task was to hold Britain to a strict neutrality during the U.S. Civil War. Adams succeeded in preventing the British government from receiving Southern agents as official ministers of an independent state, but he had great difficulty preventing British shipbuilders from building a Confederate navy, in violation of British neutrality. The *Alabama* and other Confederate cruisers built in British shipyards were escaping the government's surveillance. As soon as the vessels reached the open sea, they raised the Confederate flag and thereafter ravaged the Union's merchant marine. A crisis developed in 1863, when the "Laird rams," a pair of ironclads equipped to break the Northern blockade of the Southern coast, were ready to leave British waters. Adams's energetic protests finally rose to the pitch of his official statement: should the warships put to sea, "It would be superfluous for me to point out to your lordship [the British foreign secretary, Lord Russell] that this is war." The necessity of this warning is still disputed, for the British government had already decided not to allow the vessels to depart. A major problem confronting Adams was to prevent Britain—perhaps jointly with France—from intervening diplomatically in the struggle between North and South, a course advocated by Confederate sympathizers in Britain. Adams dealt with the problem ably, but it was really the Union victories at Antietam (September 1862) and at Gettysburg and Vicksburg (July 1863) that convinced the British government to desist.

Adams resigned his post in 1868 and ended his public career in 1872 as U.S. commissioner on the board that arbitrated the *Alabama* claims. (See ALABAMA CLAIMS.) At home in Massachusetts he was active in local civic affairs, did historical writing, and prepared for publication voluminous portions of his father's famous diary, *Memoirs of John Quincy Adams* (12 vols., 1874–1877). Adams died in Boston on Nov. 1, 1886.

SAMUEL FLAGG BEMIS, *Yale University*

Bibliography: Adams's writings, notably his diary (ed. by Aïda DiPace Donald and David Donald in 8 vols., Belknap Press/ Harvard Univ. Press 1964–1986), are included in the volumes of the Adams Papers series, ed. by Lyman H. Butterfield et al. (Belknap Press/Harvard Univ. Press 1961–   ). See also **Brookhiser, Richard,** *America's First Dynasty: The Adamses, 1735–1918* (Free Press 2002). **Duberman, Martin B.,** *Charles Francis Adams, 1807–1886* (1960; reprint, Stanford Univ. Press 1968); **Shepherd, Jack,** *The Adams Chronicles* (Little, Brown 1975).

ADAMS, Charles Francis, ad'əmz (1835–1915), American railroad official and historian noted for his advocacy of railroad reform. Adams was born in Boston, Mass., on May 27, 1835, the son of the diplomat and historian Charles Francis Adams, the grandson of Pres. John Quincy Adams, and the brother of the historians Henry Adams and Brooks Adams. Adams graduated from Harvard College in 1856 and was admitted to the bar in Massachusetts in 1858, but he soon gave up the practice of law. He served as a cavalry officer during the Civil War, fighting at the battles of Antietam and Gettysburg and rising from first lieutenant to brigadier general.

After the war Adams wrote a series of essays that advocated regulation of the railroads. In particular he attacked the practices of the speculator Jay Gould and the businessman Cornelius Vanderbilt in their fight for control of the Erie Railroad. He was elected one of three members of Massachusetts's board of railroad commissioners in 1869 and served as its chairman from 1872 to 1879. He served as president of the Union Pacific Railroad Company from 1884 until 1890, when Gould regained control of the firm.

The author of numerous biographies and books on history, Adams was elected a member of the Massachusetts Historical Society in 1872 and served as its president from 1895 to 1915. He was a member of the Board of Overseers of Harvard University (1882–1906) and president of the American Historical Association (1901). Adams died in Washington, D.C., on March 20, 1915.

ADAMS, Franklin Pierce, ad'əmz (1881–1960), American journalist and humorist, and a leading newspaper columnist. Born in Chicago, Ill., on Nov. 15, 1881, he studied at the University of Michigan (1899–1900). In 1903 he began to write a daily feature for the Chicago *Journal*, and later went to New York City, where he wrote a column for the *Evening Mail*. In 1913 he joined the New York *Tribune*, and his column took the name by which it became famous, "The Conning Tower." It appeared in the *Tribune* until 1922, in the *World* until 1931, in the *Herald-Tribune* until 1937, and in the *Evening Post* from 1938 to 1941. From 1938 to 1948, Adams also was a panel member on the "Information Please" quiz program on radio.

In "The Conning Tower," FPA (as he was commonly known) displayed his talent for humorous verse and prose, crusty wit, and wide-ranging erudition, and provided an outlet for some of the brightest writing of the time. Contributors to his column included such contemporary wits as Dorothy Parker and Ring Lardner. Much of his work was reprinted in book form, including *Tobogganing on Parnassus* (1910), *By and Large* (1914), *So There!* (1923), *Christopher Columbus* (1931), *The Diary of Our Own Samuel Pepys* (1935), and *Nods and Becks* (1944). He died in New York City on March 23, 1960.

ADAMS, Gerry, ad'əmz (1948–   ), president of Sinn Fein, an Irish nationalist movement (in effect the political arm of the terrorist Irish Republican Army, or IRA) that advocates the unification of Ireland. Gerard Adams was born on Oct. 6, 1948, in the Roman Catholic ghetto of West Belfast, Northern Ireland, the oldest of ten surviving children in a working-class family.

Adams joined Sinn Fein as a student. He was a founding member of the Northern Ireland Civil

Rights Association, which campaigned for equal political and economic rights for Catholics. While Adams never admitted to being a member of the IRA (which is illegal in both Northern Ireland and the Irish Republic), it is believed that he led the IRA's Belfast brigade in the early 1970s. He was interned without trial for several years during the 1970s, and he spent much of the decade in jail or on the run.

Adams was elected vice president of the provisional wing of Sinn Fein in 1978 and its president in 1983. In 1982 the British government lifted its ban on home parliamentary rule in Northern Ireland and Adams was elected to a seat in the Northern Ireland (Ulster) Assembly. In 1983 he was also elected as a member of the British Parliament from West Belfast. Adams refused to take his seat in the House of Commons because of the compulsory oath of allegiance to the crown of England. He was severely wounded in a 1984 assassination attempt. Adams lost his seat in the House of Commons in 1992 but regained it in 1997 and was reelected in 2001, still refusing to sit in the British Parliament.

While defending the IRA's use of violence to achieve its goals, Adams was one of the chief architects of Sinn Fein's shift to a policy of seeking a peaceful settlement to sectarian violence in Northern Ireland. He worked on an Irish peace initiative in the early 1990s, helping to pave the way for a cease-fire signed in August 1994 between the IRA and Protestant militias. However, the peace process was put in jeopardy by renewed violence on the part of the IRA in 1996. Because of this, negotiations begun in June 1996 did not include Sinn Fein. Following a renewed cease-fire in July 1997, peace talks began in September of that year. These efforts culminated in the historic Good Friday peace agreement for Northern Ireland of April 10, 1998, which provided for an end to the violence between the IRA and Unionist militants and for the political restructuring in the province that would allow Protestants and Catholics to govern jointly in a democratically elected Assembly.

In September 1998 Adams met for the first time with Unionist leader David Trimble to discuss the disarming of the paramilitaries and the formation of a Northern Ireland government. Members of Sinn Fein were elected to the Assembly and participated in the province's government. Home rule was suspended (from February to May 2000) when the IRA refused to agree to disarm, but it later agreed to inspections of its arms dumps.

Adams is the author of numerous articles and several books. His 1990 autobiography, *Cage Eleven: Writings from Prison*, drew heavily on his experience as an internee and prisoner.

ADAMS, Henry, ad′əmz (1838–1918), American historian and man of letters. Henry Brooks Adams was born in Boston, Mass., on Feb. 16, 1838, the son of Charles Francis Adams (1807–1886) and Abigail Brown Books Adams and the grandson of Pres. John Quincy Adams. He graduated from Harvard University in 1858 and spent the next two years in Europe, studying law in Germany and traveling in Italy and France. He then became private secretary (1861–1868) to his father, the U.S. minister in London.

From 1870 to 1877 Adams taught medieval history at Harvard, where he introduced the graduate seminar to America. During most of this time

BETTMANN ARCHIVE

Henry Adams, as a professor of history at Harvard.

(1870–1876) he was also editor of the distinguished *North American Review*. He married Marian Hooper of Boston in 1872; they had no children. After 1877 he lived in Washington, D.C., devoting himself to writing. In later years he traveled widely, as far as Japan and the Pacific Islands. Adams died in Washington on March 27, 1918.

Adams's first major historical work was the *Life of Albert Gallatin* (1879), a model biography in which quotation and paraphrase from Gallatin's writings are skillfully fused with careful, objective interpretation. In the novel *Democracy*, published under a pseudonym in 1880, politics in Washington are despairingly held up to scorn. His biography *John Randolph* (1882) shows some of the bias of his presidential ancestors toward the controversial Virginian. The conflict between science and religion is the theme of the novel *Esther* (1884), also published pseudonymously.

After his wife's suicide in 1885, Adams stoically completed the monumental *A History of the United States during the Administrations of Jefferson and Madison* (9 vols., 1889–1891) and collected his essays on economic and political history in *Historical Essays* (1891). *Mont-Saint-Michel and Chartres* (privately printed, 1904) and *The Education of Henry Adams* (privately printed, 1907) were conceived as an artistic whole—*Chartres* as a "study in 13th Century unity" and the *Education* as a "study of 20th Century multiplicity." *Chartres* has been valued as a perceptive account of medieval culture. On its public printing (1918), the *Education* was recognized as a classic.

For the instruction of his fellow historians in the importance for history of the revolutionary developments in the physical sciences, Adams published *A Letter to American Teachers of History* in 1910. This essay was republished posthumously in *The Degradation of the Democratic Dogma* (1919), along with his most ambitious effort to generalize history in terms of the laws of contemporary science ("The Rule of Phase Applied to History") and a memoir by his brother Brooks. Adams was also a fine letter writer.

See also EDUCATION OF HENRY ADAMS.

HENRY WASSER, *City College of New York*

Bibliography

A selection of Adams's writings appears in *A Henry Adams Reader*, ed. by Elizabeth Stevenson (1958; reprint, P. Smith 1968). His correspondence is collected in the 6-vol. *Letters of Henry Adams* (1982–1988) and its 2-vol. *Supplement* (1989), ed. by Jacob C. Levinson et al. (Belknap Press/Harvard Univ. Press).

Chalfant, Edward, *Both Sides of the Ocean: A Biography of Henry Adams; His First Life, 1838–1862* (Archon 1982).

Chalfant, Edward, *Better in Darkness: A Biography of Henry Adams; His Second Life, 1862–1891* (Archon 1994).

Chalfant, Edward, *Improvement of the World: A Biography of Henry Adams; His Last Life, 1891–1918* (Archon 2000).

Contosta, David R., and Robert Muccigrosso, eds., *Henry Adams and His World* (Am. Philosophical Soc. 1993).

Decker, William M., *The Literary Vocation of Henry Adams* (Univ. of N.C. Press 1990).

Dusenberre, William, *Henry Adams and the Myth of Failure* (Univ. Press of Va. 1980).

Harbert, Earl N., *Henry Adams: A Reference Guide* (G. K. Hall 1978).

Samuels, Ernest, *Henry Adams* (Belknap Press/Harvard Univ. Press 1989) [abridgment of Samuels's Pulitzer Prize–winning 3-vol. biography, incorporating new research].

Simpson, Brooks D., *The Political Education of Henry Adams* (Univ. of S.C. Press 1996).

Young, James P., *Henry Adams: The Historian as Political Theorist* (Univ. Press of Kans. 2001).

ADAMS, Henry Carter, ad'əmz (1851–1921), American economist and social philosopher who pioneered in the fields of public finance and the relation of government to industry. In both areas he was an influential practitioner as well as a scholar. His views on federal intervention in industry, formed prior to its serious advent, were considered radical when advanced but are now common doctrine.

Adams was born in Davenport, Iowa, on Dec. 31, 1851, the son of missionaries. He graduated from Iowa (renamed Grinnell) College and attended Andover Theological Seminary but turned to economics and in 1878 received one of the first Johns Hopkins doctorates. He taught from 1879 at Cornell, Johns Hopkins, and the University of Michigan, where he was a professor of political economy from 1887 to 1920.

From 1887 to 1911 Adams was associated with the Interstate Commerce Commission, developing the system of accounts and statistics that provided the factual basis for railroad regulation. Later he performed a similar service for the Chinese Republic. Adams was a founder and early president of the American Economic Association and president of the American Statistical Association. He died in Ann Arbor, Mich., on Aug. 11, 1921. (See AMERICAN ECONOMIC ASSOCIATION.)

SHOREY PETERSON
University of Michigan

ADAMS, Herbert, ad'əmz (1858–1945), American sculptor who was noted for his medallions and other works in relief, and for his portrait busts of women. Adams was born in Concord, Vt., on Jan. 28, 1858, and studied in Paris from 1885 until 1890 under Antonin Mercié, the noted French sculptor. Returning to the United States, he was elected a member of the National Academy of Design in 1899 and subsequently served as its president. He founded the National Sculpture Society and was its president for three terms.

In his refined realism and great technical skill in marble cutting, Adams closely approached the early Renaissance style. He used polychromed marble in a bust called *Portrait of a Young Lady* (1894; Detroit Institute of Arts) and white marble in a relief portrait called *Singing Boys* (1894; location not known). He died in New York City on May 21, 1945.

ADAMS, Herbert Baxter, ad'əmz (1850–1901), American historian, who was a founder (1884) and secretary (1884–1900) of the American Historical Society. He was born in Shutesbury, Mass., on April 16, 1850. Graduating from Amherst College in 1872, he took a Ph.D. at Heidelberg in 1876 and joined the faculty of Johns Hopkins University as a fellow in history. In 1880 he became professor of history at Johns Hopkins, where he taught until his death in Amherst, Mass., on July 30, 1901.

His writings include *Methods of Historical Study* (1884), *Maryland's Influence upon Land Cessions to the United States* (1885), and *Life and Writings of Jared Sparks* (2 vols., 1893).

ADAMS, Isaac, ad'əmz (1802–1883), American inventor, who improved the printing press. He was born in Rochester, N.H., on Aug. 16, 1802. At the age of 22 he went to work in a machine shop in Boston, Mass. In 1828 he invented the Adams power press, which rapidly displaced hand presses that were being used at the time. The Adams power press was the primary machine for book printing until the end of the 19th century, when it was displaced by the more rapid cylinder press. From his invention Adams made a fortune of more than $1 million. He died in Sandwich, N.H., on July 19, 1883.

ADAMS, James Truslow, ad'əmz (1878–1949), American historian, who wrote scholarly, readable books on many subjects. His style, marked by brilliant syntheses of research materials, was widely praised, although some critics regarded him as an amiable popularizer.

Born in Brooklyn, N.Y., on Oct. 18, 1878, Adams attended the Polytechnic Institute of Brooklyn (B.A., 1898) and Yale University (M.A., 1900). He was associated with a New York Stock Exchange firm from 1900 to 1912 and then turned to writing. *The Founding of New England* (1921), his first book to attract wide attention, won the Pulitzer Prize for history. He then published *Revolutionary New England, 1691–1776* (1923) and *New England in the Republic, 1776–1850* (1926). The trilogy was acclaimed as a masterpiece of scholarship. Next came *Provincial Society, 1690–1763* (1927), *Hamiltonian Principles* (1928), *Jeffersonian Principles* (1928), and *Our Business Civilization* (1929). Although not a Massachusetts Adams, he wrote *The Adams Family* (1930) and *Henry Adams* (1933).

By mid-career, Adams concluded that "the ripest fruit of knowledge is to *interpret* facts, to try to find out how they are related and how they influence one another."*The Epic of America* (1931) reflected that spirit; this broad-stroked historical survey was popular in the United States and won an audience elsewhere through translations. Subsequent books included *America's Tragedy* (1933), *Building the British Empire* (1938), *Empire on the Seven Seas* (1940), *The American* (1943), and *Big Business in a Democracy* (1945). *The Living Jefferson* (1936) criticized the New Deal. An economic conservative, Adams often called for a return to what he regarded as the old-fashioned virtues.

In the last decade of his life, Adams edited three valuable reference works: *Dictionary of American History* (6 vols., 1940); *Atlas of American History* (1943); and *Album of American History* (4 vols., 1944–48). He died in Westport, Conn., on May 18, 1949.

2d President of the United States 1797–1801

Birth—Oct. 30, 1735, in Braintree (Quincy), Mass.
Higher Education—Harvard College (B.A., 1755).
Religion—Unitarian.
Occupation—Lawyer.
Marriage—Oct. 25, 1764, to Abigail Smith (1744–1818).
Children—Abigail Amelia (1765–1813); John Quincy (1767–1848); Susanna (1768–1770); Charles (1770–1800); Thomas Boylston (1772–1832).
Nickname—"Atlas of Independence."
Political Party—Federalist.
Position When Elected—Vice President.
Administration: Major Events—Establishment of the Department of the Navy (April 30, 1798); Alien and Sedition Acts passed (June-July 1798); conclusion of treaty with France (Sept. 30, 1800), which averted war.
Principal Writings—*The Life and Works of John Adams*, 10 vols., ed. by Charles F. Adams (1856); *The Diary and Autobiography of John Adams*, 4 vols., ed. by Lyman H. Butterfield and others (1961)
Death—July 4, 1826, in Quincy, Mass., at age 90.
Burial Place—First Unitarian Church, Quincy, Mass.

NATIONAL GALLERY OF ART, GIFT OF MRS. ROBERT HOMANS, 1954

(Left) JOHN ADAMS was pleased by this Gilbert Stuart portrait, for it "actually took a likeness to the face."

ADAMS, ad'əmz, **John** (1735–1826), 2d president of the United States. He devoted his life to politics, participating with distinction first in the revolutionary activities of Boston and Philadelphia and later in the founding of the republic. He served as a Massachusetts delegate to the Continental Congress, as a diplomat in the struggle to win European recognition of American independence, and as vice president and president of the United States during its critical, formative years.

Adams' diaries, letters, and books provide invaluable information about the politics of his time. His writings reveal the mind of an astute observer and philosopher—a very human one whose warmth, wit, and playfulness captivate the reader. His reputation as an intelligent and courageous statesman endures; but his name has been overshadowed by others—perhaps because he was not uniquely connected with any single great event.

Boyhood and Education. Adams was born in the village of Braintree (Quincy), Mass., on Oct. 30 (Old Style, Oct. 19), 1735. His parents and ancestors had been honored members of the community since its founding. His father, John Adams, was influential in town business, serving as selectman and officer of the militia; his mother, Susanna Boylston Adams, was known for her devotion to family and church. The Adams clan had arrived from England about 1640 and settled on land that their descendants were still tilling in John's boyhood.

Besides receiving the informal instruction of village life, Adams attended dame and Latin school. In spite of his inclination to be a farmer, his schooling prepared him for college and a career in the ministry. With some special tutoring in Latin from Joseph Marsh, a local scholar, John passed his entrance examinations for Harvard College in 1751 and began four absorbing years of study that excited his imagination. "I

was a mighty metaphysician, at least I thought myself such"; he was a mighty scientist, debater, and orator, too. As he examined career possibilities, the ministry soon appeared less interesting to him than law, medicine, and public service. At graduation in 1755 he was still undecided, and he accepted a teaching position in Worcester while he contemplated the future.

Early Public Career. The career of a schoolmaster was most unsatisfying for Adams. His pupils were "little runtlings" who barely knew their ABC's, and his students noted that he was preoccupied with other matters. His position, however, enabled him to meet the intellectuals of Worcester, including James Putnam, its most distinguished lawyer. Adams finally decided to make a career of the law and apprenticed himself to Putnam. Since the intense young man was not interested in being a country lawyer, he returned as soon as possible (in 1758) to Braintree, where family connections could win him introductions to the Boston bar.

Lawyer Adams began his career in Braintree writing wills and deeds and taking an interest in town affairs. Although local matters were important to him, his law practice began to take him farther and farther from Braintree. On his way to and from Plymouth he would stop at Weymouth to visit Abigail, the young daughter of the Reverend Mr. William Smith. John and Abigail were married on Oct. 25, 1764, and he loved her deeply throughout their long marriage.

Adams' legal practice often took him to Boston, where he became well acquainted with James Otis, Jr., and his distant cousin Samuel Adams. With them he attended the clubs of tradesmen and joined the "Sodalitas" as a founding member. This group of Boston lawyers mixed scholarly discussions of law with debates on the legality of the Stamp Act of 1765. Out of these meetings came Adams' anonymous articles for the Boston *Gazette*, later reprinted as

A Dissertation on Canon and Feudal Law. In these he traced the origin and rise of freedom. The rights of Englishmen, he wrote, were derived from God, not from king or Parliament, and would be secured by the study of history, law, and tradition.

Adams expressed these views in political form when he drew up for Braintree a protest against the Stamp Act that became a model for similar remonstrations elsewhere in New England. He assailed the stamp tax as an unnecessary burden upon the people and an unconstitutional levy— "no free man can be separated from his property but by his own act or fault." These ideas gave him much prominence in Massachusetts. Braintree recognized him now as a leading townsman by electing him a selectman, but legal work kept him in Boston, so he gave up his post as selectman and moved there in 1768.

Though Adams was always ready to speak out for liberty, he maintained his political independence and offered his talents to anyone in trouble. His most dramatic case occurred in 1770 when he and Josiah Quincy defended the British soldiers accused of murder in the Boston Massacre. It was an incident of justice versus unlawful authority, but the culprit this time was the Boston mob that provoked the incident. For taking the case Adams was sharply rebuked in the patriot newspapers, yet he was privately congratulated on winning this case for liberty.

Since May 1770, Adams had been a Boston representative in the legislature (General Court). Associating daily with men deeply concerned about liberty, he was troubled by the issues confronting the colonies. These preyed upon his mind, and he decided in 1771 to leave public life. After 16 months of semiretirement, partly taken up in travel and bathing in the mineral springs of Stafford, Conn., and partly in farming, he returned to Boston.

Rise to Leadership. The radicals were happy to have Adams available for consultation and as a writer for the newspapers. They elected him to the Governor's Council in May 1773, only to have him ejected by the governor for his partisanism. He was, indeed, involved in patriotic maneuvers, and he rejoiced when Bostonians dumped the hated tea into the harbor in the Boston Tea Party of 1773. Britain's retaliation drew him into full partnership with the radicals, and he became a delegate to the First Continental Congress in 1774.

During the next three years in Philadelphia, Adams pushed Congress into decisive action that was to separate the colonies from Britain. He urged successfully the appointment of George Washington as commander in chief of colonial forces and the creation of a naval force to challenge Britain's supremacy of the seas. In committee and on the floor of Congress, he laid down principles of foreign policy, helped write the resolutions of May 10, 1776, that declared America independent, and defended the Declaration of Independence during debate in Congress.

As chairman of the Board of War and Ordnance for nearly a year (1776–1777), Adams attempted to equip the army. Important to the revolutionary cause also were his extensive correspondence and his published writings. His *Novanglus* papers (1774–75) and his *Thoughts on Government* (1776) outlined principles of liberty and order for the Americans.

ABIGAIL ADAMS, as portrayed by Gilbert Stuart.

In Diplomatic Service. In 1778, Adams was sent to replace Silas Deane, one of the American diplomatic agents in Paris negotiating a commercial and military alliance with France. Before he arrived, however, the American commissioners there had successfully concluded the negotiations. Adams returned to Braintree in time to be chosen a member of the Massachusetts constitutional convention; he composed most of the articles of the state constitution accepted by the convention in 1780.

Adams' work on the state charter was barely completed when he was appointed a minister plenipotentiary in anticipation of peace negotiations with Britain. In Paris, while awaiting the start of negotiations, he was expected to be patient and inconspicuous—a role unsuited to his nervous, passionate temperament. With blunt advice for all parties, Adams irritated the French officials by meddling in policy matters, and he angered Benjamin Franklin by comments on his behavior. Finally giving way to their hostility, he withdrew to the Netherlands where he secured recognition of American independence and negotiated a loan and treaty of amity and commerce.

Returning to Paris in October 1782, Adams joined John Jay and Franklin in the peace discussions. In these proceedings Adams particularly, and successfully, insisted on the rights of the United States to fish off the Canadian coast, and he also was interested in extending American territory as far west as possible. The Treaty of Paris, ending the War of Independence, was concluded on Sept. 3, 1783.

While the peace treaty was being ratified by Congress, Adams and his son, John Quincy Adams, toured England. In 1783–1784, Adams negotiated loans for the United States in the Netherlands and commercial treaties in France. In 1785 he was appointed first U.S. minister to Britain. His three years in London were fruitless in winning trade concessions or putting Anglo-American relations on a friendly basis. Adams used his time to good purpose, however, by getting well acquainted with Thomas Jefferson, U.S. minister to France, and writing *A Defence of the Constitutions of Government of the United States*

(3 vols., 1787). Like Adams' other writings, this work was unpolished and somewhat polemical, but it contained a wealth of information on constitutional theory and was often cited in the Constitutional Convention of 1787. Adams strongly approved of balanced government and praised the British parliamentary system as the "most stupendous fabric of human invention."

While Adams favored states' rights and reform of the Articles of Confederation, he had worried about the continuing weakness of the national government. In 1788 he welcomed the proposed Constitution as "admirably calculated to preserve the Union." As his thoughts turned homeward, he resigned his unproductive London post and returned to Braintree to study, write, and garden. Within the year, in the first election held under the Constitution, he was chosen vice president of the United States, confirming his national position as second only to President Washington.

The First Vice President. As in all of his positions, Adams, who was reelected in 1792, accepted the responsibilities of the vice presidency with energy and seriousness. He presided over the U.S. Senate and cast the deciding vote frequently, often for measures that would increase generally the powers of the national government or specifically those of the presidency. Always ready to offer opinions, Adams lectured the Senate on its duties. He also published a series of essays, *Discourses on Davila* (1791), which commented broadly on civil disorders, with special reference to the French Revolution.

As Washington's "heir apparent," Adams discovered that even the presidency was being reduced to the level of human passions and party objectives. According to his philosophy, the position should seek the man, and knowledge as well as virtue should qualify the man, without regard to partisanship. Unlike Washington, Adams had rivals for the presidency, and he should have been more flexible. Instead, he permitted Alexander Hamilton to assume leadership of the Federalist party, while he tried to remove himself from partisan politics by associating even with his party's critics.

Hamilton was angry over this conduct and sought another candidate to represent the Federalist party. But the party was embroiled with the Jeffersonian Republicans in fierce contests over the direction of foreign affairs. This division centered on the war between England and France, with the Federalists favoring the English, and the Republicans, the French. The climax came during the ratification of Jay's Treaty with Britain in 1794 (see JAY'S TREATY). Its pro-English character offended both the French government and the pro-French Republicans who carried on a scurrilous newspaper campaign against Jay and the administration., The bitterness, however, brought a reaction in favor of the moderates and many leaders, wishing to avoid excess, rallied to Adams, who had managed to stay out of the dispute.

Hamilton, who had greatly influenced the treaty negotiations, was helpless but not reconciled to the choice of Adams as Federalist candidate for president. During the presidential campaign of 1796 he secretly tried to substitute Thomas Pinckney for Adams and thus divided the party. As a result, the election was extremely close: Adams won the presidency by three electoral votes (71–68) over the Republican Jefferson, who, under the electoral system then in use, became the vice president.

The Presidency. Adams entered office on March 4, 1797. Fully aware of his slender victory, he sought political harmony. His inaugural address, tracing the progress of the nation, declared his faith in republicanism and called upon the people to end partisan politics. He tried to reach an accord with Jefferson, conciliate the Hamiltonians, and steer a peaceful course through the controversy with France over Jay's Treaty. But he encountered supreme difficulties.

As the first president to succeed another, Adams had no guidelines to follow on cabinet appointments, patronage, and policy enunciations. He decided to keep Washington's mediocre cabinet, partly because he wanted to reconcile the Federalists and partly because he knew how difficult is was to get good men to serve. The cabinet was Federalist—and more, Hamiltonian—in loyalty. Adams did not fully realize the inherent dangers of this situation until 1799, when the cabinet violated its trust by working against his policies.

With Federalists about him, Adams found partisan politics impossible to avoid, though he favored Republicans Benjamin Rush and Elbridge Gerry with appointments. As relations with France worsened, he had to recommend preparations for defensive warfare while negotiations for peace continued. These measures irritated the Republicans, but Adams was not deterred. He held to his policy of peace and preparedness even after the French Directory insulted American envoys (see XYZ CORRESPONDENCE) and began detaining American vessels. In January 1798 he proposed the creation of a navy department and asked for funds to put the military on a war footing.

Four bills to control subversion, the Alien and Sedition Acts of 1798, were also passed. One of the acts imposed severe penalties on those who criticized the government. These harsh measures, formulated in a time of fright, were approved by Adams. Although a score of journalists were punished for their attacks on the administration, the laws were not ruthlessly applied. The opposition, however, made them appear cruel and turned them into symbols of Federalism.

Adams' reprisals against French seizures of American shipping were popular for a time, and the Federalists won the 1798 congressional elections. Though Congress did not declare war, Adams pushed ahead with military preparations, selecting Washington, Henry Knox, Charles C. Pinckney, and Hamilton, in that order, to be the ranking generals of the army. But while Adams was visiting in Quincy (which had been set off from Braintree in 1792), the cabinet secured Washington's backing to move Hamilton ahead of his colleagues and make him second in command (actually, commander since Washington was not expected to take the field). Adams grasped the significance of this maneuver. He saw lawful control of the army shifted to Hamilton and, more, the naked specter of militarism. Hamilton and the cabinet wanted to prolong the crisis with France and use the opportunity to consolidate the Federalist party and spread the war into Spanish America.

By the time Adams fully realized what was happening, he had advice from Europe that France would resume negotiations. In February

1799 he abruptly nominated William Vans Murray as a special envoy, to the amazement of the Hamiltonians. Debate over the action was bitter, and Adams compromised by agreeing to name a commission instead of a single delegate, but he withstood the pressure of Hamilton, the British minister, and some members of his cabinet. The commission finally concluded a treaty with France on Sept. 30, 1800. Thus Adams succeeded in preventing a war with France and preserving his country's neutrality.

The treaty negotiations had split the party, and the Federalists now openly considered the effect of this division on the 1800 election. When two cabinet members, Secretary of State Pickering and Secretary of War McHenry, revealed their disloyalty to Adams, he forced their resignations without any political finesse. His abrasive action infuriated the Hamiltonians, who vented their feelings in public, matching the president's undiplomatic conduct. The Republicans, led by Jefferson and Aaron Burr, enjoyed the Federalist predicament. Adams was temperamentally unable to assume the responsibilities of a party boss or to dramatize the achievements of his administration. The election results reflected this weakness. The Federalists lost the presidency to Jefferson and the Republicans by eight electoral votes (73 to 65) and also lost Congress.

Later Years. Adams left the presidency in 1801 for private life in Quincy. He remained bitter toward Hamilton and the Federalists, yet he regained his sense of humor and served his country in a different way, becoming president of the Massachusetts Society of Arts and Sciences, the Massachusetts Society for Promoting Agriculture, and other societies. He also wrote articles for the Boston *Patriot* reviewing events of his administration, and he corresponded with many people in the spirit of Cicero's *Letters*. His correspondence on politics, history, national affairs, religion, and philosophy was designed to guide posterity in maintaining the principles of 1776. His letters to Jefferson and Benjamin Rush are monuments of erudition, revealing a charming personality that could be crusty, petty, and lovable within the space of dozen lively lines.

Adams died in Quincy, Mass., on July 4, 1826, the 50th anniversary of the Declaration of Independence. Jefferson died the same day.

See also ADAMS (FAMILY); UNITED STATES—*The Founding of the Nation, 1763–1815.*

JOHN A. SCHULTZ, *University of Southern California*

Bibliography

Adams's writings are included in *The Adams Papers*, ed. by Lyman H. Butterfield et al. (Belknap Press/Harvard Univ. Press 1961–), a projected 100-vol. edition in several series of Adams family documents—diaries, correspondence, and state papers—in the custody of the Massachusetts Historical Society. Series include *The Papers of John Adams*, ed. by Robert J. Taylor et al., 10 vols. through 1996 (1977–); *The Diary and Autobiography of John Adams*, ed. by Lyman H. Butterfield, 4 vols. (1961), and its supplement, *The Earliest Diary of John Adams*, ed. by Lyman H. Butterfield et al. (1966); and *The Legal Papers of John Adams*, 3 vols., ed. by L. Kinvin Wroth and H. B. Zobel (1966). Adams's correspondence has been gathered in several editions, notably *The Adams-Jefferson Letters*, ed. in 2 vols. by Lester J. Cappon (1959; reprint, Inst. of Early Am. Hist. and Culture/Univ. of N.C. Press 1988), and *The Book of Abigail and John; Selected Letters of the Adams Family, 1762–1784*, ed. by Lyman H. Butterfield et al. (Harvard Univ. Press 1975).

Brookhiser, Richard, *America's First Dynasty: The Adamses, 1735–1918* (Free Press 2002).

Brown, Walt, *John Adams and the American Press: Politics and Journalism at the Birth of the Republic* (McFarland & Co. 1995).

Ellis, Joseph J., *Passionate Sage: The Character and Legacy of John Adams* (Norton 1993).

Ferling, John E., *John Adams: A Life* (1992; reprint, H. Holt 1996).

Ferling, John E., *John Adams: A Bibliography* (Greenwood Press 1994).

Hutson, James H., *John Adams and the Diplomacy of the American Revolution* (Univ. Press of Ky. 1980).

McCullough, David G., *John Adams* (Simon & Schuster 2001).

Peterson, Merrill D., *Adams and Jefferson: A Revolutionary Dialogue* (1976; reprint, Oxford 1978).

Ryerson, Richard A., ed., *John Adams and the Founding of the Republic* (Mass. Hist. Soc. 2001).

Shaw, Peter, *The Character of John Adams* (Norton 1977).

Smith, Page, *John Adams*, 2 vols. (1962, 1963; reprint, Greenwood Press 1969).

Weisberger, Bernard A., *America Afire: Jefferson, Adams, and the Revolutionary Election of 1800* (Morrow 2000).

ADAMS, John Couch, ad'əmz (1819–1892), English mathematician best known for his role in the discovery of the planet Neptune. Born in Laneast, Cornwall, England, on June 5, 1819, Adams won a scholarship to the University of Cambridge, where he graduated first in his class in mathematics in 1843 and remained afterward as a tutor. He later served as professor of mathematics at the University of St. Andrews (1858–1859) and Lowndean Professor of Astronomy at Cambridge (1859–1892). He was elected president of the Royal Astronomical Society for the 1851–1853 and 1874–1876 terms and became director of the Cambridge Observatory in 1861. Adams, who declined a knighthood offered by Queen Victoria in 1847, died in Cambridge on Jan. 21, 1892.

In 1841, while still an undergraduate, Adams began an investigation of the irregularities in the motion of the planet Uranus around the sun, and by September 1845 he had concluded that an unknown planet beyond the orbit of Uranus was perturbing its motion and he predicted a position for it. Because the hypothetical planet was not at that time in a favorable position for viewing, a search was not immediately undertaken. After the French mathematician Urbain Le Verrier published results that were similar to Adams's in June 1846, however, George Airy, the astronomer royal, asked Cambridge Observatory's director, James Challis, to undertake a search for the new planet. While the latter was doing so during that summer, Le Verrier sent the results he had obtained to the German astronomer Johann Galle in Berlin, who on Sept. 23, 1846, observed an object near Le Verrier's predicted position that was not on a recently printed star chart. Challis had actually observed the same object on Aug. 4 and 12, 1846, but had not immediately realized this. Not only did his observatory lack a similar chart for the area being surveyed, but also he did not have the time to compare his observations. Le Verrier and Adams are now both credited with correctly predicting the existence and position of the new planet, subsequently named Neptune.

Adams also studied terrestrial magnetism and the motions of the moon and determined that the Leonid swarm of meteors follows a cometlike orbit. The Adams Prize, awarded biannually for the best student essay in astronomy, mathematics, or physics, was founded in 1848 at the University of Cambridge in his honor.

Bibliography: Grosser, Morton, *The Discovery of Neptune* (Harvard Univ. Press 1962); Harrison, H. M., *Voyager in Time and Space: The Life of John Couch Adams*, Cambridge Astronomer (Book Guild 1994); Standage, Tom, *The Neptune File: A Story of Astronomical Rivalry and the Pioneers of Planet Hunting* (Walker & Co. 2000).

CULVER PICTURES, INC.

John Quincy Adams

6th President of the United States (1825–1829)

Born—July 11, 1767, in Braintree (Quincy), Mass.
Higher Education—Harvard College (B.A., 1787).
Religion—Unitarian.
Occupation—Lawyer.
Marriage—July 26, 1797, to Louisa Catherine Johnson (1775–1852).
Children—George Washington Adams (1801–1829); John Adams (1803–1834); Charles Francis Adams (1807–1886); Louisa Catherine Adams (1811–1812).
Nickname—"Old Man Eloquent."
Political Party Affiliations—Federalist; Democratic-Republican; Whig.
Position When Elected President—Secretary of State.
Principal Published Writings—*Memoirs*, 12 vols. (1874–77); *Writings of John Quincy Adams*, 7 vols. (1913–17).
Died—Feb. 23, 1848, Washington, D.C., at age 80.
Burial Place—First Unitarian Church, Quincy, Mass.

JOHN QUINCY ADAMS, during the first year of his presidency, from a portrait painted by Thomas Sully.

ADAMS, ad′əmz, **John Quincy** (1767–1848), 6th president of the United States. He was the son of John Adams, 2d president. Independence and Union were the watchwords of his career; a Union of the United States of North America to grow by the destiny of Providence and nature to become a continental republic of free men stretching from ocean to ocean and from Gulf to Arctic.

"The Second Adams" was the only son of a president to become president; in fact, his parents actually trained him for highest office. His mother told the boy that some day the state would rest upon his shoulder. As he grew up with the new nation, he had during his long lifetime two notable careers, separated by a strange interlude. The first career was as an American diplomat who rose to become secretary of state. The second career was as a member of the House of Representatives and opponent of slavery. The strange interlude was as president of the United States; for four years the state did indeed rest, uneasily, upon his shoulder. Never publicly popular, often reviled by his political enemies, he nevertheless ended his life in the sunshine of national esteem.

Early Life. John Quincy Adams was born in Braintree, Mass., on July 11, 1767. During the first years of the American Revolution, he received his education principally by instruction from his distinguished father and gifted mother, the incomparable Abigail. As a boy of ten he accompanied his father on diplomatic missions to Europe. There he learned French fluently in a private school at Paris; next he studied at the University of Leiden. In 1782–1783 he accompanied Francis Dana, as secretary and interpreter of French (then the language of the Russian court), on a journey through the German states to St. Petersburg, returning to Holland by way of Scandinavia and Hannover.

Adams was already extraordinarily well versed in classical languages, history, and mathematics when he returned to the United States in 1785 to finish his formal education at Harvard (class of 1787). After studying law at Newburyport, Mass., under the tutelage of Theophilus Parsons, he settled down to practice at Boston in 1790.

Diplomatic Career. The young lawyer came particularly to George Washington's attention because of articles he published in Boston newspapers defending the president's policy of neutrality against the diplomatic incursions of Citizen Genêt, the new French Republic's minister to the United States. As a result Washington appointed Adams as U.S. minister to the Netherlands, where he served from 1794 to 1797. At The Hague, Adams found himself at the principal listening post of a great cycle of European revolutions and wars, which he continued to report faithfully to his government both from the Netherlands and from his later post as minister to Berlin in 1797–1801. While on a subsidiary mission to England, connected with the exchange of ratifications of Jay's Treaty, he married on July 26, 1797, Louisa Catherine Johnson, one of the seven daughters of Joshua Johnson of Maryland, U.S. consul at London.

President John Adams relieved his son of the post at Berlin immediately after Jefferson's election in 1801. Returning to Boston, John Quincy Adams resumed the practice of law but was soon elected in 1803 as a Federalist to the U.S. Senate. His independent course as a senator dismayed the Federalist leaders of Massachusetts, particularly the Essex Junto. When he voted for Jefferson's embargo, they in effect recalled him by electing a successor two years ahead of time. Adams was then also serving as Boylston professor of oratory and rhetoric at Harvard (1806–1809). He had once more turned to the law when President Madison appointed him as the first minister of the United States to Russia, where he served from 1809 to 1814.

At the court of Alexander I, Adams again was diplomatic reporter extraordinary of the great events of Europe, including Napoleon's invasion of Russia and his subsequent retreat and downfall. Meanwhile the War of 1812 had broken out between Britain and the United States. After Alexander's abortive attempts at mediation, Adams was called to the peace negotiations at Ghent, where he was technically chief of the American mission. He next served as minister of the United States to England from 1815 to 1817.

As a diplomat John Quincy Adams had made very few mistakes, influenced many people, and made many friends for his country, including particularly Czar Alexander I. His vast European experience made him a vigorous supporter of Washington's policy of isolation from the ordinary vicissitudes and the ordinary combinations and wars of European politics.

Secretary of State. President James Monroe recalled Adams from England to become secretary of state in 1817. He held the office throughout Monroe's two administrations, until 1825. As secretary, Adams, under Monroe's direction and responsibility, pursued the policies and guiding principles that he had practiced in Europe. More than any other man he helped to crystallize and perfect the foundations of American foreign policy, including the Monroe Doctrine, which, however, appropriately bears the name of the president who assumed official responsibility for it and proclaimed it to the world.

Adams' greatest diplomatic achievement as secretary of state was undoubtedly the Transcontinental Treaty with Spain, signed on Feb. 22, 1819 (ratified Feb. 22, 1821). By this treaty Spain acknowledged East Florida and West Florida to be a part of the United States and agreed to a frontier line running from the Gulf of Mexico to the Rocky Mountains and thence along the parallel of 42° to the Pacific Ocean. In this negotiation, Adams took skillful advantage of Andrew Jackson's military incursions into Florida and of Spain's embarrassment in the revolutions of her American colonies. Over the opposition of Henry Clay, ambitious speaker of the House of Representatives, Adams deferred recognition of the independence of the new states of Spanish America until the Transcontinental Treaty was safely ratified. Immediately afterward President Monroe recognized Colombia, Mexico, Chile, the United Provinces of the Río de la Plata, and later Brazil and the Confederation of Central America. Peru remained to be recognized by Adams as Monroe's successor. The idea of drawing the frontier line through to the other ocean in the Spanish treaty was Adams' own inspiration. It has been called "the greatest diplomatic victory ever won by a single individual in the history of the United States."

At the same time Secretary Adams defended the northeastern frontier against proposed British "rectifications" and held the line of 49° in the Oregon country. Except for an overcontentious wrangle on commercial reciprocity with the British West Indies, his term as secretary of state, in the aftermath of Waterloo, was marked by unvarying successes, including the Treaty of 1824 with Russia. He was perhaps the greatest secretary of state in American history.

Presidency. John Quincy Adams may have been the greatest U.S. secretary of state, but he was not one of the greatest presidents. He was really a minority president, chosen by the House of Representatives in preference to Andrew Jackson and William H. Crawford following the inconclusive one-party election of 1824. In the popular contest Jackson had received the greatest number of votes both at the polls and in the state electoral colleges, but lacked a constitutional majority. Henry Clay, one of the four candidates in 1824, threw his support to Adams in the House in February 1825, after secret conferences between the two, thus electing Adams on the first ballot. The supporters of Jackson and Crawford

GEORGE M. CUSHING, JR.

LOUISA CATHERINE ADAMS, wife of John Quincy Adams, from a Gilbert Stuart portrait.

immediately cried "corrupt bargain": Clay had put Adams into the White House in order to become his secretary of state and successor. The judgment of historians is that there was an implicit bargain but no corruption.

President Adams believed that liberty had already been won—at least for white people—by the American Revolution and that this liberty was guaranteed by the Constitution of the United States. His policy was to exert national power to make freedom more fruitful for the people. Accordingly he called for strong national policies under executive leadership: the Bank of the United States as an instrument of the national fiscal authority; a national tariff to protect domestic industries; national administration of the public lands for their methodical and controlled disposal and settlement; national protection of the Indian tribes and lands against encroachments by the states; a broad national program of internal physical improvements—highways, canals, and railways; and national direction in the field of education, the development of science, and geographical discoveries. He preferred the word "national" to "federal." His outlook anticipated by nearly a century the "New Nationalism" of Theodore Roosevelt and (by a strange reversal in Democratic party policy) of Franklin D. Roosevelt.

Adams as president was too far in advance of his times. The loose democracy of the day wanted the least government possible. And the South feared that his program of national power for internal improvements, physical and moral, under a consolidated federal government might pave the way for the abolition of slavery. He had no real party to back him up. The opposition, with Andrew Jackson as its figurehead and "bargain and corruption" as its battle cry, combined to defeat him for reelection in 1828.

Congressman. In November 1830, more than a year and a half after Adams left the White House, the voters of the 12th (Plymouth) District of Massachusetts elected him to Congress. He accepted the office of congressman eagerly, feeling himself not a party man but, as ex-president, a representative of the whole nation. As a member of Congress the elderly Adams entered the most spectacular phase of his long career of public service. He preached a strong nationalism against the states' rights and pro-slavery dialectics of John C. Calhoun. Never an outright abolitionist, he deemed himself "bonded" by the Constitution and its political compromises always to work for universal emancipation within its framework. He frustrated the Southern desire to annex Texas in 1836–1838 and in 1843 helped defeat Pres. John Tyler's annexation treaty, only to see Texas incorporated into the United States by joint resolution of Congress in 1845, after the election of James K. Polk over Henry Clay in 1844.

Adams tried in 1839 to introduce resolutions in Congress for constitutional amendments declaring that no one could be born a slave in the United States after 1845, but the "gag rule" prevented the discussion of anything relating to slavery. "Old Man Eloquent," as Adams was nicknamed, staunchly defended the right of petition and eventually overthrew the gag in 1844. An abolitionist at heart but not in practice, he tried to postpone the sectional issue over slavery until the North was strong enough and sufficiently united in determination to preserve the Union and abolish slavery, if necessary by martial law.

The Adams Legacy. A man of gruff exterior and coolness of manner, Adams was given to ulcerous judgments of his political adversaries but bound friends to himself with hoops of steel. He was, before Woodrow Wilson, the most illustrious example of the scholar in politics. His constituents regularly elected him to Congress from 1830 on. He died in the House of Representatives on Feb. 23, 1848: "This is the last of earth. I am content."

Of Adams's three sons, only one, the youngest, Charles Francis Adams, minister to Britain during Abraham Lincoln's presidency, survived him. Charles Francis Adams edited for publication substantial portions of his father's monumental diary, which traverses more than 60 years of his extraordinary life.

SAMUEL FLAGG BEMIS, *Yale University*

Bibliography

Adams's writings are included in *The Adams Papers*, ed. by Lyman H. Butterfield et al. (Belknap Press/Harvard Univ. Press 1961–), a projected 100-vol. edition of family documents in the custody of the Massachusetts Historical Society. Among these vols. is the *Diary of John Quincy Adams*, ed. by David Grayson Allen (Harvard Univ. Press 1981). One-vol. selected editions of Adams's works include *The Selected Writings of John and John Quincy Adams*, ed. by Adrienne Koch and William Peden (1946; reprint, Greenwood Press 1981), and *John Quincy Adams and American Continental Empire: Letters, Papers, and Speeches*, ed. by Walter LaFeber (Quadrangle Bks. 1965).

Bemis, Samuel Flagg, *John Quincy Adams and the Foundations of American Foreign Policy* (1949; reprint, Greenwood Press 1981).

Bemis, Samuel Flagg, *John Quincy Adams and the Union* (1965; reprint, Greenwood Press 1980).

Brookhiser, Richard, *America's First Dynasty: The Adamses, 1735–1918* (Free Press 2002).

Hargreaves, Mary W. M., *The Presidency of John Quincy Adams* (Univ. Press of Kans. 1985).

Hecht, Marie B., *John Quincy Adams: A Personal History of an Independent Man* (1972; reprint, Am. Political Biography Press 1995).

Jones, Kenneth V., *John Quincy Adams, 1767–1848; Chronology, Documents, Bibliographical Aids* (Oceana Pubs. 1970).

Nagel, Paul C., *John Quincy Adams: A Public Life, a Private Life* (Knopf 1997).

Parsons, Lynn Hudson, *John Quincy Adams: A Bibliography* (Greenwood Press 1993).

Richards, Leonard L., *The Life and Times of Congressman John Quincy Adams* (Oxford 1986).

Russell, Greg, *John Quincy Adams and the Public Virtues of Diplomacy* (Univ. of Mo. Press 1995).

ADAMS, Maude, ad'əmz (1872–1953), American actress who was a great stage star in the early 20th century. She projected an elfin quality that was especially suited to the plays of James M. Barrie, including *The Little Minister* (1897, 1905, 1916), *Quality Street* (1902), and *What Every Woman Knows* (1908). She is best remembered, however, for her performance in Barrie's *Peter Pan*, which she first played in 1906.

She was born in Salt Lake City, Utah, on Nov. 11, 1872, the daughter of a leading lady in a stock company. As Maude Adams (her family name was Kiskadden, but she used her mother's maiden name), she first appeared on the stage as a child. At 16 she joined the E.H. Sothern Company in New York City. Later she became the leading lady of the Charles Frohman Stock Company.

After 13 years in retirement, she appeared as Portia in *The Merchant of Venice* (1931) and as Maria in *Twelfth Night* (1934). She headed the drama department at Stephens College from 1937 to 1943, and then taught part-time at the college. She died in Tannersville, N.Y., on July 17, 1953.

ADAMS, Samuel, ad'əmz (1722–1803), American patriot who was the leading publicist of the American Revolution. An effective polemicist, he was single-mindedly devoted to preserving the liberties guaranteed to Americans by their charters. Perhaps more than anyone else, Adams stirred up anti-British passions during the stormy years preceding the Revolution.

Early Life. Adams was born in Boston on Sept. 27, 1722, the son of Samuel Adams, a prosperous businessman, and Mary Fifield Adams. Like his second cousin John Adams, the 2d president of the United States, Samuel was descended from Henry Adams, who emigrated from England to Massachusetts in the 1630s. At age 14 Samuel Adams entered Harvard College, where his mind was fired by John Locke's treatise *Of Civil Government*. Adams later was to become a principal American proponent of Locke's doctrine that every citizen was endowed with "natural rights" of life, liberty, and property; that a ruler could not take property from his subjects—tax them—without their consent. Adams insisted that the taxing power rested with the provincial assembly.

Adams graduated from Harvard in 1740 and earned a master's degree there in 1743. His father tried to make a merchant of him, but he had no head for business; politics was his passion. His early political offices in Boston included that of tax collector (1756–1765), an experience that proved nearly disastrous. He fell greatly in arrears in his collections because of poor business sense and a provincewide financial depression. In this period Adams was married twice: in 1749 to Elizabeth Checkley, who died in 1757, leaving him with two small children; and in 1764 to Elizabeth ("Betsy") Wells, who bore no children.

Stamp Act Agitation. By 1763 Adams was a member of the secret, powerful Caucus Club, through which a small group of Boston's leaders controlled the decisions of the Town Meeting. In 1764 he was charged with the task of writing instructions to Boston's representatives in the Assembly. At this point, shifting British policy brought about Adams's emergence as a leading patriot. Since their founding, the colonies had lived under virtual home rule. The Massachusetts legislature voted the salaries of crown officials and judges and levied taxes. Parliament fixed duties on imports but had never otherwise tried to tax the Americans. In 1765, however, the Stamp Act was passed, requiring the purchase of "stamped paper" for every business and legal transaction. Samuel Adams led the outcry in Massachusetts against this form of taxation. Boston rioted, and Adams instructed the representatives to ignore the act.

In September 1765 Adams was elected to the Massachusetts House of Representatives. From the outset he drafted state papers and thus came into conflict with Gov. Francis Bernard, an Englishman, and with Lt. Gov. Thomas Hutchinson, who was American-born but a staunch Tory. In 1766 Adams helped the radical patriots win a majority in the House; the radicals excluded five conservatives from the Council, Hutchinson among them. Adams himself was reelected to the House that year and represented Boston continuously until 1774, serving also as clerk of the House. During these years of radical ascendancy, he was the chief radical spokesman.

Townshend Acts Struggle. Parliament repealed the Stamp Act in 1766 but the next year passed the Townshend Acts, which established import duties on paint, paper, glass, and tea. Again Adams led the opposition. He helped organize the merchants in the Nonimportation Association and wrote the "Circular Letter" to other colonial assemblies, attacking British policy. British troops were sent to Boston in 1768 to maintain peace. Adams's fiery protests enkindled popular hatred of the troops in Boston. Periodic clashes occurred, and on the night of March 5, 1770, a mob baited soldiers on duty at the customhouse. At length the soldiers fired, killing three men and wounding others, two of whom later died. This "Boston Massacre" had one much-desired effect: Adams led a delegation to Hutchinson, demanding that the troops be removed. Reluctantly Hutchinson gave the order.

The Townshend duties were soon repealed, although the tax on tea was retained. The colonists' resentment of British policies abated, but Adams wrote inflammatory newspaper articles warning his compatriots that their liberties were being imperiled. By keeping the controversy alive, he made a signal contribution to the coming revolution. In 1772 he learned that crown officers and judges were to receive salaries from customs revenues. This, he insisted, was unconstitutional. He prevailed on the Boston Town Meeting to appoint a "committee of correspondence" to formulate the colonists' rights and to communicate them "to the several towns and to the world."

Boston Tea Party. Parliament exacerbated the situation in May 1773 by giving the faltering East India Company a monopoly of the American tea trade and the right to use its own consignees instead of regular merchants. When three ships carrying tea arrived in Boston, Hutchinson (now governor) refused to order them to return to England, as Adams and his followers demanded. Late in the afternoon of December 16, as Adams presided over a mass meeting, word arrived of Hutchinson's refusal. Adams announced, "This meeting can do nothing more to save the country." At this signal, 50 to 100 men, thinly disguised as Indians, boarded the ships and dumped the tea into the harbor—the famous Boston Tea Party.

Britain's answer was the Intolerable (or Coercive) Acts (1774), the first of which closed the Boston port. Troops were sent, and the provincial capital was removed to Salem. When the Assembly met there in June 1774, Adams kept the

COURTESY OF THE CITY OF BOSTON

Samuel Adams points to the Massachusetts Charter in this famous Copley portrait in the Boston Museum.

chamber locked to prevent the governor from dissolving the legislature before representatives could be elected to the First Continental Congress. Adams was among those chosen.

Independence and After. In September 1774 Adams highly approved the adoption of the Suffolk Resolves, which placed Massachusetts in virtual rebellion. He helped win endorsement of these resolutions by the Continental Congress. Elected to the Second Continental Congress, he avoided arrest by British troops and returned to Philadelphia (May 1775). He voted for and signed the Declaration of Independence.

Adams sat in Congress until 1781, when he returned to Boston to take his place in the state Senate. While he remained active in politics for many years, his influence diminished; the great goal of his life had been accomplished in July 1776. Adams was a delegate to the Massachusetts constitutional convention (1779–1780). He ran for Congress in 1788 but was defeated. As a member that year of the convention called to ratify the federal Constitution, he initially stood in opposition but ultimately lent his support. In 1789, as John Hancock's running mate, he was elected lieutenant governor of Massachusetts. He became governor in 1793 on Hancock's death and was subsequently elected to the post in his own right. He served until 1797, when he retired from public life. Adams died in Boston on Oct. 2, 1803.

STEWART BEACH, *Author of*
"Samuel Adams: The Fateful Years, 1764–1776"

Bibliography: Adams's works are gathered in *The Writings of Samuel Adams,* ed. in 4 vols. by Harry A. Cushing (1904–1908; reprint, Octagon 1968). *Samuel Adams; Selections from His Writings* was edited by Elizabeth Lawson (Intl. Pubs. 1946). See also **Alexander, John K.,** *Samuel Adams: America's Revolutionary Politician* (Rowman & Littlefield 2002); **Fowler, William,** *Samuel Adams: Radical Puritan,* ed. by Oscar Handlin (Longman 1997); **Maier, Pauline,** *The Old Revolutionaries: Political Lives in the Age of Samuel Adams* (1980; reprint, Vintage Bks. 1982); **Wells, William,** *The Life and Public Services of Samuel Adams,* 2d ed., 3 vols. (1888; reprint, Books for Libs. 1969).

ADAMS, ad'əmz, **Samuel Hopkins** (1871–1958), American author and journalist, who was best known for his numerous works of light fiction. He was born at Dunkirk, N.Y., on Jan. 26, 1871. After graduating from Hamilton College, he became a special writer and reporter on the New York *Sun* (1891–1900), managing editor of McClure's Syndicate (1900–1901), and a member of the staff of *McClure's Magazine* (1903–1905). As a magazine writer, he exposed various social evils, and his articles for *Collier's* on patent medicines were responsible in part for the enactment of the federal pure food and drug acts.

Adams, who sometimes used the pseudonym *Warner Fabian*, was a prolific writer of fiction. His early novels include *The Clarion* (1914), a newspaper story, and *Revelry* (1926), a novel based on the scandals of the Harding administration. The award-winning motion picture *It Happened One Night* (1934) was based on his novelette *Night Bus*, and his novels *The Gorgeous Hussy* (1934) and *The Harvey Girls* (1942) were also film successes. Adams' *Tenderloin* (1959) was made into a Broadway musical of the same name in 1960. In *Grandfather Stories* (1955), he wrote of the early days of the Erie Canal.

Adams also wrote biographies, including *The Incredible Era: The Life and Times of Warren Gamaliel Harding* (1939) and *Alexander Woollcott: His Life and His World* (1945). He died at Beaufort, S.C., on Nov. 15, 1958.

ADAMS, ad'əmz, **Sherman** (1899–1986), American political leader, who was the chief executive assistant to President Dwight D. Eisenhower from 1953 to 1958. He had a major role in handling routine duties of the executive office for the president, in reviewing matters of presidential concern during Eisenhower's illnesses, and in advising the president on matters of national policy.

Adams was born in East Dover, Vt., on Jan. 8, 1899. His father, a grocer, moved to Providence, R.I., where Adams attended public schools. After brief service with the Marines in World War I, Adams entered Dartmouth College and was graduated in 1920. Later he became manager of a paper and lumber business in New Hampshire.

Adams made his entrance into politics in 1940. After four years in the state house of representatives and an unsuccessful bid for the governorship of New Hampshire, he was elected to the U.S. House of Representatives in 1944. Four years later he won the governorship, to which he was reelected in 1950. He provided the state with an efficient, businesslike administration in which he reorganized many state agencies.

Adams early declared his support of Eisenhower for the Republican presidential nomination in 1952. He served as Eisenhower's floor manager at the Republican national convention and then as his campaign chief.

After he was elected, Eisenhower named Adams assistant to the president, a post that he filled with quiet efficiency. Adams soon came to be widely regarded as one of the most powerful members of the administration.

In mid-1958 it was revealed that Adams had accepted gifts from his friend, Bernard Goldfine, a Boston manufacturer. Testimony established that Adams had made routine inquiries of federal officials about the industrialist's difficulties with federal agencies. Adams conceded that he may have been "imprudent" in his actions but denied any wrongdoing. Supported by Eisenhower, who stated "I need him," Adams for a time resisted pressures for his resignation. He finally retired from public life on Sept. 22, 1958. He wrote a memoir, *Firsthand Report: The Story of the Eisenhower Administration* (1961). Adams died in Hanover, N.H., on Oct. 27, 1986.

ADAMS, ad'əmz, **William Taylor** (1822–1897), American author, who wrote popular books and stories for boys under the pen name *Oliver Optic*. His heroes were noted for clean living, patriotism, and a taste for travel and adventure, and their virtues were unfailingly rewarded.

Adams was born in Bellingham, Mass., on July 30, 1822. From 1845 to 1865 he taught in Dorchester (now part of Boston) and Boston schools. Thereafter he devoted his time to writing. He died in Dorchester on March 27, 1897.

Adams wrote more than 1,000 stories and 116 full-length books for boys. Most of them appeared in series, including the *Boat Club* series (1854), the *Woodville* series (1861–67), the *Army and Navy* series (1865–94), the *Starry Flag* series (1867–69), the *Onward and Upward* series (1870), and the *Great Western* series (1875–82). He founded and edited *Oliver Optic's Magazine for Boys and Girls* (1867–1875), and later edited *Our Little Ones* and *Student and Schoolmate* magazines.

ADAMS, ad'əmz, a town located in northwestern Massachusetts, in Berkshire county, that contains the villages of Adams (formerly South Adams), Maple Grove, Renfrew, and Zylonite. The town is on the Hoosic (Hoosac) River, which is 15 miles (24 km) north of Pittsfield and immediately south of North Adams, which was set off from Adams in 1878. The area of Adams is 21 square miles (54 sq km). Within its limits is Mt. Greylock, the highest point in Massachusetts (3,491 feet, or 1,064 meters), with a state War Memorial beacon on its summit.

Founded in 1749 as East Hoosuck, the town was renamed for Samuel Adams in 1778, when it was incorporated. The leading industries are the manufacture of cotton goods, paper, and lime. Notable among the chief buildings in the town is the Friends meetinghouse, built in 1784. Susan B. Anthony, the suffragette, was born there in 1820. Population: 8,809.

ADAMS, Mount, ad'əmz, a peak in northern New Hampshire, in the Presidential Range of the White Mountains. Situated in southern Coos County, it is part of a resort section noted for its timber and wildlife. Mount Adams, with an altitude of 5,798 feet, is the second-highest peak in the Presidential Range. Mount Washington, the highest, is 4 miles south of it.

ADAMS, Mount, ad'əmz, an extinct volcano in the southwestern part of the state of Washington, in the Cascade Range. Its altitude is 12,307 feet. It is situated in southwestern Yakima County, about 45 miles south of Mount Rainier.

ADAM'S APPLE, ad'əmz ap'əl, a protuberance on the forepart of the throat, formed by the thyroid cartilage. It is prominent in men, but scarcely noticeable in women. The name is believed to have arisen from the popular notion that a portion of the forbidden fruit, assumed to have been an apple, stuck in Adam's throat when he attempted to swallow it. See also LARYNX.

ADAM'S NEEDLE, ad'əmz nē-dəl, the common name for several yucca plants native to the southeastern and central United States. The plant forms a rosette of leaves that are two to three feet (60 to 90 cm) long, pointed at the tips, and have filamentous threads along their edges. In June or July, it produces a branching flower cluster, about four to six feet (1.2 to 1.8 m) high, of bell-shaped, fragrant, white flowers. Also known as bear-grass, Adam's needle belongs to the genus *Yucca;* the most common example is *Y. filamentosa.*

Pollination of Adam's needle is carried out entirely by the yucca moth, *Pronuba yuccasella.* The moth first lays its eggs in the flower ovulary (seed receptacle) and then packs the pollen collected from another flower into the flower pistil. After the moth eggs hatch, some of the developing yucca seeds provide food for the larvae.

DEREK BURCH
Missouri Botanical Garden

ADAMSON, Robert.   See HILL, DAVID OCTAVIUS.

ADANA, ä-dä-nä', the fourth-largest city in Turkey and a commercial and industrial center 240 miles (390 km) south-southeast of Ankara. It is in the province of Seyhan in Asia Minor, on the Seyhan River, 30 miles (50 km) from the river's mouth on the Mediterranean Sea. The fertile plain surrounding Adana is irrigated by the Seyhan River Dam. The city trades in cotton, wheat, and oats and manufactures cotton goods, tobacco products, and farm machinery.

Originally a Lydian settlement, Adana was rebuilt in the 1st century B.C. by Pompey the Great after it had been destroyed by war. It developed as a Roman military post and vied with Tarsus as a commercial center for the area. After a period of decline, its prosperity was restored by Harun al-Rashid in the 700s A.D. The city's great mosques date from the 15th and 16th centuries, after Adana became part of the Ottoman empire. Population: 1,066,544 (1995 census).

ADAPTATION, a shift in function or form, or both, that ensures fitness in a certain environment. On the part of living organisms, it supposes an adjustment of requirements and tolerances and the achievement of a certain efficiency. The case of humans is hardly different, even though social and psychological requirements may have precedence over climatic and physiological ones.

In biology, adaptation is the state of an organism or of one of its parts that enables it to cope with the total conditions of its environment or with one such condition in particular. A fish is adapted to life in the water because of its gill-breathing mechanisms, its tactile sensitivity, and its streamlined body, which is easily propelled by its mobile fins. An amphibian has some of these characteristics, but it also is capable of life on land because its skin does not dry too readily, it has limbs that allow both swimming and either walking or leaping, and it has lungs that take oxygen directly from the air. Cacti, which grow in desert areas, have no actively functioning leaves—these are reduced to spines—and have compactly built stems with a thick skin often covered by flowers. The stems transpire very little and hold large quantities of water. Pitcher plants have leaves that hold rainwater and can drown and digest invertebrate animals. Primarily, therefore, adaptation is an external and internal process that involves adjustment to environmental changes.

Adaptation may be achieved in similar ways by different organisms; that is, the organisms all may adapt to the same environmental condition by evolving organs or body parts that are similar in function but that are different in structure and origin. Thus insects, birds, and mammals have achieved adaptation to flight, but each animal has achieved this adaptation in a different way. Plant seeds, likewise, can become airborne, by using wings or silky appendages on the seed.

In a sense all plants and animals that are found to exist and to perpetuate themselves through several generations in any one environment or habitat must be adapted to that environment. Some, however, are narrowly confined to a niche in nature; others are widely distributed. This variation is called amplitude or plasticity. In addition, the capacity of the organism to exploit the environment operates at many levels of efficiency. Some features are temporary and concern one organ, one function, or one set of responses. Others show considerable duration and involvement. Modifications of function and form arise and maintain themselves in a variety of ways not always obviously connected with the challenge of the surroundings. The origin and evolution of such modifications follow a roundabout course.

Amplitude.   Any organism that can withstand both a high and a low intensity of one or more elements in its environment shows great amplitude. This may find expression in geographical distribution. Thus the black spruce tree is found from the lower reaches of the Canadian Arctic south to New England and the Great Lakes states. It has a broad climatic extension, as has the Virginia deer, whose various races are present from the Gulf of St. Lawrence to the Florida keys. Even more widely distributed are the bracken fern and the brown rat, which occur over the major part of most continents, the rat having achieved this distribution with the help of humans. In contrast, some organisms are narrowly restricted—for instance, the cedars of Lebanon, on one mountain range in Asia Minor, and the tuatara lizard, on a small island in New Zealand.

Amplitude also may be detected in habitat range, quite irrespective of geographical breadth. Thus the widely distributed mangrove tree is present on either side of the Atlantic Ocean but ecologically is limited to tropical, intertidal flats of mostly very fine sediments. On the other hand, New Zealand flax, although it does not occur outside New Zealand, occupies positions in swamps, on dry hillsides, and in open scrub and cleared forests, as well as on sand dunes.

Geographical range and ecological range show only the upper and lower limits of tolerance of a species to a deficiency or excess of a certain factor. For instance, among the organisms cited above, black spruce, bracken, and Virginia deer show their tolerance of low to high temperatures, whereas the cedar of Lebanon and the tuatara lizard exist only within a narrow heat range; New Zealand flax is found on some of the wettest and on some of the driest soils, whereas the mangrove tree requires a finely textured, constantly saturated salt soil.

Efficiency.   Somewhere between tolerable extremes an organism must find an optimum condition under which it will grow better, reproduce more freely, and build up larger populations. The organism will not respond uniformly in different parts of its geographical or ecological range, but it will show degrees of efficiency as a transformer of environmental resources and as a colonizer of its habitat. Thus New Zealand flax grows more leaves, produces sturdier plants, flowers more profusely, and has more individuals per unit-area in the well-lighted, not-too-dry and not-too-wet sites. The black spruce forms dense stands on many different sites and over hundreds of square miles in the median part of its range where it also has maximum ecological amplitude; it is a straggling shrub at its northern border where it occupies only the most protected places; it is a slow-growing tree on the edges of the infrequent bogs on its southern edge.

Duration. Adaptations to stress may differ in intensity and in kind in the same species in early and late stages and at different seasons. For instance, some aquatic plants, such as the dwarf spike rush (*Eleocharis acicularis*), produce stems, runners, and leaves in abundance when submerged but never flower until the water recedes to soil level. Many herbs in the deciduous forest flower in the full light of spring and produce leaves in the deepening shade of summer. Toads normally live on land but require ponds to reproduce. Salmon live in salt water, which they leave to ascend freshwater streams at spawning time, whereas eels follow the reverse course. All these examples illustrate apparently contradictory requirements in organisms whose functions are geared to a different intensity or quantity of an environmental factor.

It is important to mention the capacity of some organisms to make an immediate adjustment to an environmental stimulus. Thus, on many forest trees, the leaves of the crown, exposed to full sunlight, usually are thicker, more deeply cut, and smaller than the shade leaves. The same is true of bog shrubs, for instance, Labrador tea, growing out in the open and in the shade of the forest. On the other hand, many plants have developed genetically stable coastal and alpine races that, when transplanted inland from the coast and down to sea level, retain their maritime and alpine characteristics. Such is the case of the yarrow in California.

Origin and Evolution. Adaptations presumably arise as a result of the pressure of natural selection, which tends to conserve in a population the features that are most advantageous. Mutations do not arise in response to external agents but, instead, at random. Those features that have adaptive value stand the best chance of transmission to further generations and can in time spread to entire populations. The operation of these new features may increase through other hereditary changes, such as multiplication of the chromosomes or cross-fertilization with other units. The patterning of heredity, although not directly caused by environment, is restricted to certain channels by habitat conditions.

It is therefore not surprising to find similar traits in unrelated organisms that share the same habitat: the small leaves of desert shrubs, the thin ones of temperate forest herbs, the thick fur of northern mammals, the pale color of shore animals, and so on. However, the form cannot unfailingly reveal the function, nor, conversely, does the performance always elicit a structural response—the spiny fruits of the cocklebur probably are disseminated just as often by water as by animals; many shade-loving shrubs of the New

Zealand forest have small, hard leaves instead of broad, thin ones; many small Arctic mammals have long, thin, seemingly vulnerable extremities. What these examples show is that some adaptations may persist in a line of descent beyond their period of usefulness and that all organisms physiologically fit have not developed morphological, or structural, features of response. Vanishing or regressing species, often the victims of genetic weaknesses, usually do not display a lack of harmony with their surroundings. Such is the case of the redwoods in California and the dawn redwood of China, now so restricted in comparison with their former domain, or the Canadian elk and the Australian dingo, all seemingly well-equipped species, whose range has narrowed.

The complexity of the total adjustment of plants and animals to all the elements of their habitat leads to this ultimate paradox: no species encounters in any one environment optimum conditions for each and every phase of its life cycle. Thus, many forest trees make much better growth in open fields, and some of them cannot reproduce in their own shade. If the supply of optimum living conditions is to meet their demands, well-adapted species move from one environment to another (the salmon from salt to fresh water) or else adjust their cycle to the variability of the environment, as with the spring-flowering herbs of deciduous forests.

PIERRE DANSEREAU, *New York Botanical Garden*

Bibliography

Brooks, Daniel R., and Deborah A. McLennan, *The Nature of Diversity: An Evolutionary Voyage of Discovery* (Univ. of Chicago Press 2002).

Costa, Giovanni, *Behavioural Adaptations of Desert Animals* (Springer-Verlag 1995).

Dejours, P., ed., *Adaptations to Extreme Environments* (Karger 1987).

Hoffmann, Ary A., and Peter A. Parsons, *Extreme Environmental Change and Evolution* (Cambridge 1997).

Orzack, Steven Hecht, and Elliott Sober, eds., *Adaptationism and Optimality* (Cambridge 2001).

Stearns, Stephen C., ed., *Evolution in Health and Disease* (Oxford 1999).

ADAR, ä-där', is the 12th month of the Jewish calender, falling in February-March of the Gregorian calendar. The feast of Purim is celebrated on the 14th of Adar, except in leap years, when it is celebrated on the 14th day of the 13th month, called *Second Adar,* which is added to the calender following Adar.

ADDAMS, ad'əmz, **Charles Samuel** (1912-1988), American cartoonist, whose macabre humor made him one of America's most popular and successful cartoonists. He was born in Westfield, N.J., on Jan. 7, 1912. He began drawing at an early age, and studied at Colgate University, the University of Pennsylvania, and at the Grand Central School of Art in New York City. In 1935 he sold a cartoon to *The New Yorker,* where his work appeared regularly thereafter. He died in New York City on Sept. 29, 1988.

Addams' cartoons are noted for their witty sense of the macabre. His characters are caught up in a fantastic, goblin world. One of his favorite settings is a dilapidated Victorian mansion inhabited by a family of ghouls.

Addams' drawings have been exhibited at Harvard University's Fogg Art Museum and at the Metropolitan Museum of Art, New York City. Published collections of his cartoons include *Drawn and Quartered* (1942), *Home Bodies* (1954), *My Crowd* (1970), and *Creature Comforts* (1981).

ADDAMS, ad'əmz, **Jane** (1860–1935), American social worker who founded the Chicago social welfare center known as Hull House. She was born in Cedarville, Ill., on Sept. 6, 1860, the daughter of a prosperous merchant. She graduated from Rockford College (then Rockford Seminary) in 1881. Traveling in Europe, she was stirred by the social reform movement in England and especially by a visit to Toynbee Hall, the first university settlement. In 1889, with her college classmate Ellen Gates Starr, she founded Hull House in the slums of Chicago.

Hull House grew rapidly and soon became the most famous settlement house in America. Many reformers came there, not so much to serve as to learn. Jane Addams was the leader and dominant personality. Hull House pioneered in child labor reform and in the fight for better housing, parks, and playgrounds. It initiated steps toward progressive education and attempts to acclimatize immigrants to America.

Jane Addams was a practical idealist and an activist. She favored prohibition and woman suffrage, and she campaigned for the Progressive party in 1912. She went beyond politics, however, for politics to her was part of a larger movement to humanize the industrial city.

She had always been a pacifist, and when World War I broke out in 1914, she became chairman of the Woman's Peace party and president of the International Congress of Women. In 1915 she visited many countries in Europe, urging the end of the war through mediation. She remained a pacifist when the United States entered the war in 1917, and as a result she was denounced by many Americans. In 1931 she was awarded the Nobel Peace Prize (sharing the award with Nicholas Murray Butler).

Jane Addams continued to be in the vanguard of social reform movements until her death in Chicago on May 21, 1935. She wrote ten books (including her famous *Twenty Years at Hull House*) and more than 400 articles. The influence that had begun at Hull House continued to spread around the world.

ALLEN F. DAVIS
University of Missouri

ADDAX, ad'aks, a North African antelope related to the oryx, and like the oryx in its habits. Its large hoofs enable it to travel on loose sand. It has a short tail and spirally twisted horns two to three feet in length. The animal measures about three feet in height at the shoulder. In color it is nearly white underneath, shading to brown on the head and the front of the body. The hoofs are black, and there is a dark brown shaggy marking on the forehead above a white blaze on the nose.

The addax is classified technically as *Addax nasomaculatus.*

ADDER, ad'ər, the most widely distributed venomous snake of Europe. Often known as the common European adder or *viper*, it is found farther north in Europe than any other snake. Its range crosses the Arctic Circle in Finland and Scandinavia and extends across Europe and the heart of Asia to the Pacific coast.

The color pattern of the adder is complex, and males have more strongly contrasted colors than females. Adult females often are a little more than two feet (60 centimeters) in length. Males are noticeably shorter than the females.

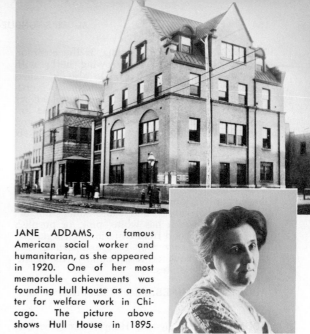

JANE ADDAMS, a famous American social worker and humanitarian, as she appeared in 1920. One of her most memorable achievements was founding Hull House as a center for welfare work in Chicago. The picture above shows Hull House in 1895.

BROWN BROS. PHOTOS

The adder lives in many types of habitats and is active during the day and night. Its choice of habitat and time of activity depends to a large measure on the food supply. Lizards and small mammals are favorite prey, and bird eggs and nestlings as well as amphibians and various invertebrates also are eaten. Adders have a highly toxic venom that is used for killing prey and also for defense. The bite often is fatal to domestic animals but rarely to man. The adder hibernates during the winter.

Adder reproduction is different from that of most snakes because the female adders have placentae; the placentae are, however, a primitive type. The gestation period is a little over two months. From 6 to 20 young are born each year in the late summer, except in the extreme north, where a brood may be born every other year.

The adder's technical name is *Vipera berus;* it belongs to the family Viperidae.

CLIFFORD H. POPE, *Author, "The Reptile World"*

ADDER, or common European viper (*Vipera berus*), occurs from the British Isles to Eurasia.

JOHN MARKHAM

ADDER'S-TONGUE, ad'ərz tung, is the common name for a group of low-growing herbs with bulblike underground stems. It also is called *fawn lily* and *trout lily.* It is found in North America, with one species in Eurasia. About six inches to two feet in height, adder's-tongue has two broad, almost basal leaves and large, nodding flowers. The flowers are six-parted, with six stamens and a nectar-bearing groove.

Adder's-tongue belongs to the genus *Erythronium* in the lily family, Liliaceae; there are 16 species. Among the species are the common adder's-tongue, *E. americanum,* which has yellow flowers and is found from eastern Canada to Florida and Arkansas; and white adder's-tongue, *E. albidium,* which has white, pink, or purplish flowers and is found from Ontario to Georgia and Texas. The *glacier lily, E. grandiflorum,* is a golden-yellow flowered form found in the north-western United States.

ADDING MACHINES. See CALCULATING MACHINES.

ADDINGTON, ad'ing-tən, **Henry,** 1ST VISCOUNT SIDMOUTH (1757–1844), prime minister of Britain, whose brief Tory administration between the two Tory administrations of William Pitt the Younger was occasioned by a split in party ranks.

Born in London on May 30, 1757, he was the son of George III's personal physician. He studied at Winchester and Brasenose College, Oxford, and briefly practiced law. In 1784, under Prime Minister Pitt's aegis, he entered the House of Commons as a Tory, and, as house speaker from 1789 to 1801, won grudging respect for his reliability and common sense. Pitt meanwhile was increasingly criticized for his vigorous but costly prosecution of the war with revolutionary France. In 1801, to avoid further criticism from Tories opposed to administration plans to lift the ban against Roman Catholics in public office, Pitt yielded power to Addington.

The Addington ministry was foreseeably brief. Tory front benchers declined to serve in Addington's cabinet, and Pitt remained the hope of war-weary Britain. In 1804, after three years of consolidation and a year's fragile peace, Addington voluntarily stepped aside, and Pitt returned to prosecute the renewed war against Napoleon I. Thereafter, Addington became increasingly conservative. He was created a peer in 1805. As home secretary from 1812 to 1821, he harshly repressed working class agitation brought on by economic hardships. He resigned from the government in 1824. He died at Richmond on Feb. 15, 1844.

ADDINSELL, ad'ən-sel, **Richard Stuart** (1904–1977), English composer, noted for his incidental music for the stage and films. He was born in London on Jan. 13, 1904. He was educated privately and also studied at Oxford, at the Royal College of Music, and in Berlin and Vienna. His first success was his musical setting for Clemence Dane's play *Adam's Opera* (1928).

In 1933, Addinsell visited the United States and worked in New York and Hollywood. During World War II he contributed musical scores for over 20 government documentary films. His most popular work was the *Warsaw Concerto,* which he composed for the film *Dangerous Moonlight* (1941). Among his other film scores were *Goodbye, Mr. Chips* (1939), *Blithe Spirit* (1945), and *The Roman Spring of Mrs. Stone* (1961). He also composed for radio and television and wrote many light songs for English revues. He died in London on Nov. 14, 1977.

ADDIS ABABA, ad'is ab'ə-bə, is the capital and largest city of Ethiopia. It is situated in Shoa province, on hilly terrain about 8,000 feet (2,438 meters) above sea level. It is surrounded by mountains and has a pleasant climate with warm, sunny days and cool nights. Major highways radiate from Addis Ababa to all the provinces of Ethiopia. A modern international airport is located nearby, and the city is connected by railroad with the port of Djibouti in French Somaliland. Its chief industries include tanneries, cement works, breweries, and textile mills.

The city is the permanent headquarters of the United Nations Economic Commission for Africa and the temporary home of the Organization for African Unity. The emperor's palace and Ethiopia's parliament building are situated in the city.

Addis Ababa is the site of the country's only university—Haile Selassie I University, which was founded in 1950. There are also technical schools and teacher-training colleges in the city. The National Library, founded in 1944, contains some 60,000 volumes, and the university library is known for its collection of rare books.

Addis Ababa was founded in 1887 by Menelik II, who was then king of Shoa. Two years later he made it the capital of Ethiopia. In 1896 the peace treaty in which Italy recognized Ethiopia's independence was signed at Addis Ababa. The city was occupied by Italy in 1936 and was the capital of Italian East Africa until it was liberated by British forces in 1941. Population: 2,112,737 (1994 census).

NICHOLAS POBBI-ASARE
State University College of New York at New Paltz

ADDIS ABABA'S LIBERTY SQUARE. The monument in the center commemorates Ethiopia's liberation from Italy.

ADDISON, ad′ə-sən, **Joseph** (1672–1719), English essayist, who was a major influence on English public opinion in the 18th century. He was a man of fine intellect, lofty character, considerate and distinguished manners, and great personal charm. His fame rests almost exclusively on his contributions to two papers, the *Tatler* and the *Spectator,* which published nearly all he had to say of permanent value. Socially, he tried to improve English life and manners and inculcate virtue. Intellectually, he attempted to elevate the taste of his generation. Through his unprecedented skill in drawing realistic human characters, particularly those of Sir Roger de Coverley and other members of the Spectator Club, Addison contributed to the art of novel writing and prepared the way for Samuel Richardson and Henry Fielding.

ART REFERENCE BUREAU

JOSEPH ADDISON, from a portrait painted by Godfrey Kneller, in the National Portrait Gallery, London.

As a stylist, Addison had no superior in the writing of inoffensive social satire and gentle humor. The famous pronouncement by Samuel Johnson remains largely true: "Whoever writes to attain an English style, familiar but not coarse, and elegant but not ostentatious, must give his days and nights to the volumes of Addison." Addison brought English prose to a degree of finish and accessibility that had been wanting before. Even his great predecessor Dryden, one of the most flexible and easy of prose writers, did not have quite the sense of audience possessed by Addison.

Early Life. Addison was born at Milston, Wiltshire, England, on May 1, 1672, first son of a Royalist clergyman, Lancelot Addison. After the Restoration, Lancelot was chaplain of the garrisons at Dunkirk and Tangier, and at the time of the birth of Joseph he was rector of Milston. Later (1683) he was made dean of Lichfield. He was a man of character, attainment and considerable literary gift, which found its most interesting expression in *Revolutions of the Kingdoms of Fez and Morocco,* a lively historical sketch. Addison's mother was Jane Gulston, daughter of Dr. Nathaniel Gulston and sister of William Gulston, bishop of Bristol.

Addison was brought up in a family of admirable manners; his home life is described by Richard Steele as delightful. He went to schools in the neighborhood of Milston and to the Charterhouse School, London, where he acquired some knowledge of Greek and a considerable familiarity with Latin literature.

In 1687 he entered Queen's College, Oxford, but after two years transferred to Magdalen College. The change was the result of some excellent Latin verses written in 1689 in honor of King William, which attracted the admiration of Addison's preceptor and won him a scholarship. At Magdalen he lived a quiet, studious life, and his scholarly reputation is said to have extended to London during his years at Oxford.

Early Works. Addison's first published work was an *Account of the Greatest English Poets* (1693), interesting today chiefly because of the low plane which, following the taste of the times, he accorded to the great Elizabethans. Complimentary verses to John Dryden the same year won him Dryden's favor. He next experimented with translation, rendering the fourth book of the *Georgics,* two books of Herodotus, and the second book of Ovid's *Metamorphoses.* This last task, though a distasteful one, had a marked effect on his taste in that it taught him to avoid extravagance of style.

By this time he had made a fair reputation as a writer and had attracted the notice of the ministers Charles Montague (afterward Lord Halifax) and John Somers. They may have induced him to write a perfunctory *Address to King William* (1695), and they probably persuaded him to enter civil rather than ecclesiastical life. At all events, Halifax and Somers obtained for him, in 1699, a pension of £300 a year for foreign travel.

In the summer of 1699, Addison set out for France, where he remained a year and a half, chiefly at Blois, studying the language. From December 1700 to December 1701 he toured Italy. From Italy he went to Switzerland and, in the autumn of 1702, to Vienna. He also visited parts of Germany and reached the Netherlands in the spring of 1703. In the fall, on receipt of news of the death of his father, he returned to England. Some time previous to his return he had been deprived of his pension, for the death of William III in 1702 led to the dismissal of Addison's patron, Halifax, and Addison was accordingly out of employment.

The literary result of his travels was a *Letter from Italy,* in verse, and his prose *Remarks on Italy.* Italy was interesting to Addison chiefly as the source of classical poetry, and his pleasure in it was almost wholly literary. His judgments, too, on the taste of the medieval church builders were made from a narrow classical point of view. During the journey, Addison wrote his *Dialogue on Medals* (1702) and the first four acts of *Cato.*

In 1704, on the recommendation of Halifax, Addison was asked by the earl of Godolphin to write a poem on Marlborough's victory at Blenheim. Accordingly, in that year, he produced *The Campaign,* a panegyric narrative in heroic couplets. The poem was of such aid to the Whig party that Addison at once gained preferment and was, in 1706, made undersecretary of state. His political duties did not keep him wholly from literature. In 1705 he helped Steele with *The Tender Husband,* a drama. On April 2, 1706, Addison's opera *Rosamund* was presented. It failed on the stage but had some success when printed.

On the loss of his political office in 1708, Addison was almost immediately made secretary to the lord lieutenant of Ireland, Lord Wharton, and the same year, through Wharton's influence, he was elected a member of Parliament for Malmesbury, a position that he held until his death. From the Irish appointment dated his friendship with Jonathan Swift. It suffered some strain

155

when, in 1710, at the fall of the Whig ministry, the two writers found themselves arrayed on opposite sides in a struggle between the Whigs and the Tories. Addison wrote five numbers of the *Whig Examiner* (up to October 8) in opposition to the *Examiner* of the Tories, of which Swift took charge in November. Addison lost most of his offices when the Tories came to power, and thus was freed to pursue the course on which his fame rests.

"Tatler" and "Spectator." Steele had issued the first number of the *Tatler* on April 12, 1709. It appeared three times a week and was first issued as a newspaper, with political, social, and literary news purporting to come from different quarters of London. The paper, however, was not long in losing these distinctions and soon became chiefly moral. For this change, Addison, who entered at the 18th number and wrote 42 of the total of 271 numbers, may have been largely responsible.

Coming to an end on Jan. 2, 1711, the *Tatler* was followed, on March 1 of the same year, by the *Spectator*. While modeled on the *Tatler*, the *Spectator* was an improvement on it in all ways. It appeared daily and was more essaylike in form, more varied in subject, and more satirical in tone. It addressed a wider range of readers, particularly women, in the belief that improvement in manners must begin with them. Its place, as a form of literature, had been carefully prepared by the rise of the daily press and, as an organ of education, by the growing reaction against the dissoluteness of Restoration manners and literature. Consequently, it had marked success. Its circulation is estimated to have been 10,000 copies toward the close of its career on Dec. 6, 1712 (a continuation, issued three times a week, came to an end in 1714), and the sale of completed volumes was equally great. Addison contributed 274 papers to 236 by Steele; Addison's are nearly all signed by one of the letters C.L.I.O.

Plays. On April 13, 1713, Addison's play *Cato* was produced. Built on severely classical and unromantic principles, it was wholly different from the popular plays of the time, but it had great success and was acted for 35 nights, an unprecedented run. This was largely due to the political situation—the eve of the fall of Tory power and of Whig success—and Addison was a man of such political eminence that his play was naturally to be regarded as of uncommon importance. Abroad, the play was well received. It was twice translated into Italian, twice into French, and once into Latin. Voltaire praised it highly and regarded it as much superior to preceding English plays. Later critics have called it a poem of noble sentiments rather than a dramatic play. In 1715, Addison wrote *The Drummer*, which was coldly received at the Drury Lane Theatre.

Political Advancement. In 1714, on the ascendancy of the Whig party, Addison was made chief secretary to the lord lieutenant of Ireland, the duke of Shrewsbury, an office he held until August 1715. From December 23 of that year until June 9, 1716, he wrote the *Freeholder*, a semiweekly of 55 numbers altogether, designed to prove to the freemen of England the justice of the Whig cause and the need of the Protestant succession. In 1716 he was made a commissioner for trade and the colonies.

Also in 1716, Addison married Charlotte, countess dowager of Warwick, to whom he is said to have been long attached. The marriage has been called unhappy, and there is a long-established tradition to that effect. In Alexander Pope's innuendo, he "married discord with a noble wife." For the tradition there is, however, no good evidence. The couple had one daughter, Charlotte, who died unmarried in 1797.

Addison's marriage coincided with the height of his political career. In 1717 he was made secretary of state, an office he resigned in March of the following year. His health was failing, and he had never been an effective public speaker.

Famous Quarrels. The last five years of Addison's life were somewhat embittered by two famous literary quarrels. The first, with Pope, in 1715, was due, generally, to the fact that the two were essentially incompatible. In particular, Pope felt aggrieved because Addison had warmly praised a rival translation of the *Iliad* by Tickell, and even went so far as to suspect Addison of being the real author. Addison's acquaintance with Pope began with a favorable comment in the *Spectator* on Pope's *Essay on Criticism*, but thereafter he never spoke of Pope so highly. Addison may have advised Pope against adding to *The Rape of the Lock* the brilliant and charming machinery of the fairies, and Pope is said to have tried to dissuade Addison from presenting *Cato* on the stage. Neither piece of counsel was likely to increase the mutual respect of the two authors. The result was that long after Addison's death, Pope published, in his *Epistle to Arbuthnot*, his famous satire on Addison, already written during the latter's life, and then defended his course by the publication of a somewhat doctored correspondence.

In 1719, Addison and Steele found themselves on opposite sides of a bill for limiting the number of peers. Steele, though a Whig, opposed the party measure in a pamphlet called *The Plebeian* (March 14), and was answered by Addison five days later in *The Old Whig*. The contest ended with Steele's making some cutting personal remarks about Addison. Before a reconciliation could take place, Addison died in London on June 17, 1719.

WILLIAM T. BREWSTER
Coauthor, *"Introduction to the English Classics"*

Bibliography

Editions of Addison's writings include *The Works of the Right Honourable Joseph Addison*, with notes by Richard Hurd, in Bohn's British Classics, 6 vols. (Oxford 1856); *Letters*, ed. by Walter Graham (Macmillan 1941); *The Freeholder: Or, Political Essays* (1716; reprint, Am. Biog. Ser. 1985); and *Essays in Criticism and Literary Theory*, ed. by John Loftis (Harlan Davidson 1975).

Aiken, Lucy, *Life of Joseph Addison* (Oxford 1843).

Beljame, Alexandre, *Men of Letters and the English Public in the Eighteenth Century, 1660–1744; Dryden, Addison, and Pope*, ed. by Bonamy Dobree and tr. by E. O. Lorimer (1948; reprint, Scholarly Press 1971).

Bloom, Edward A., and Bloom, Lillian D., *Addison and Steele: The Critical Heritage* (Methuen 1980).

Bloom, Edward A., and Bloom, Lillian D., *Joseph Addison's Social Animal: In the Marketplace, on the Hustings, in the Pulpit* (Univ. Press of New England 1981).

Courthope, John William, *Addison*, ed. by John Morley (1889; reprint, AMS Press 1968).

Humphreys, Arthur Raleigh, *Steele, Addison, and Their Periodical Essays* (British Bk. Centre 1959).

Johnson, Samuel, *The Lives of the English Poets* (1905; reprint, Adler's Foreign Bks. 1968).

Ketcham, Michael G., *Transparent Designs: Reading, Performance and Form in the Spectator Papers* (Univ. of Ga. Press 1985).

Lannering, J., *Studies in the Prose Style of Joseph Addison* (1951; reprint, Kraus 1981).

Otten, Robert, *Joseph Addison* (G. K. Hall 1982).

Smithers, Peter, *Life of Joseph Addison*, 2d ed. (Oxford 1968).

Thackeray, William M., *The English Humorists* (1912; reprint, Biblio. Dist. 1968).

ADDISON, ad'ə-sən, a village located in northeastern Illinois, in Du Page county, 18 miles (29 km) west of the center of Chicago. It is a residential suburb of Chicago. O'Hare International Airport is 6 miles (10 km) to the northeast. Addison is governed by a mayor and council. Population: 35,914.

ADDISON'S DISEASE, ad'ə-sənz diz-ez', a relatively rare disease caused by a decreased activity of the adrenal glands. The disease was first described by the English physician Thomas Addison in 1855. Addison's disease is usually caused either by tuberculosis of the adrenal glands or by the atrophy, or wasting away, of the outer layer (cortex) of the gland. It may also be caused by cancer, by some fungus infections, or by the surgical removal of the glands.

The most characteristic symptom of Addison's disease is a gradual tanning or bronzelike coloring of the skin, often accentuated at points of pressure, such as the knees, elbows, and waistline. Other symptoms include weakness, anemia, weight loss, abdominal pain, blue-black spots inside the mouth, dark freckling, and various digestive disorders, such as diarrhea, vomiting, and nausea. The patient may also undergo mental changes, becoming irritable, nervous, and emotionally unstable. Under physical stress, such as surgery, infection, or trauma, an acute crisis of the disease may occur, characterized by a worsening of all symptoms, fever, shock, and even death.

Addison's disease is treated by the oral administration of cortisone or hydrocortisone, two very similar hormones normally produced by the adrenal cortex. Sometimes it is necessary to place the patient on a high-salt diet and to administer salt-retaining hormones. Although Addison's disease was once considered to be fatal, modern therapy now allows patients to lead practically normal lives.

IRVING SOLOMON, M.D.
Mount Sinai Hospital, New York City

ADDITION, ə-dish'ən, is a basic operation of arithmetic. The symbol for the operation of addition is the plus sign (+). Addition is a binary operation; that is, two numbers (a + b) are added at a time. The rules for addition and multiplication operations are part of the fundamental assumptions formulated by mathematicians for governing all arithmetic procedures.

The study of addition is begun by considering the formation of a new set of objects from two given sets. For example, a child may be asked to form one set of blocks by combining a set of 3 red blocks and a set of 5 black blocks. In set language this task is equivalent to forming the union of two disjoint sets. The union of two sets contains all the objects (elements) in the sets. Two sets are disjoint if they have no common elements. The union of two sets is indicated symbolically by AUB, where A and B represent the two disjoint sets and U is the symbol for union. In this example, set A contains 3 red blocks, and set B contains 5 black blocks.

Sets and Numbers. Addition is a mental process that directly involves abstract ideas of numbers and only indirectly involves blocks or any other concrete objects. The numbers referred to are the so-called cardinal numbers that the child has abstracted from much experience with numerous sets of equivalent sets that contain concrete objects or other elements. For example, the two-

ness property of numerous equivalent sets is shown by sets C, D, E, and F:

C = {1, 2} (two numerals)
D = {0, □} (two geometric drawings)
E = {John, Henry} (two names of boys)
F = {bird, dog} (two animals).

The idea of the number 2 is an abstraction from the twoness property. The threeness property of numerous equivalent sets is shown by set G:

G = {a, b, c} (three letters of the alphabet).

Likewise, we have the idea of the number 3 as an abstraction of the threeness property of three objects in a set of type G, and similarly for the ideas of the numbers 4, 5, 6, and so on. This number property of a set of equivalent sets is called the cardinality of the set. The cardinal number of the set is the number of elements in the set. In the case of the equivalent sets C, D, E, and F, the number property was twoness. We denote each of the sets C, D, E, and F by the cardinal number 2. Likewise, we denote set G by the cardinal number 3.

The set of counting numbers is used to set up a *mapping*, or a *one-to-one correspondence*, between the counting numbers and the elements of sets to determine the cardinal number of any set. Consider sets H and I, where H is a set of counting numbers and I is a set of stars:

$$H = \{ 1, \quad 2, \quad 3, \quad 4, \quad 5, \quad 6, \quad 7, \quad 8\}$$
$$\updownarrow \quad \updownarrow \quad \updownarrow \quad \updownarrow \quad \updownarrow \quad \updownarrow \quad \updownarrow \quad \updownarrow$$
$$I = \{\star \quad \star \quad \star \quad \star \quad \star \quad \star \quad \star \quad \star\}.$$

Each counting number is paired with one and only one star, and each star is paired with one and only one counting number. The last counting number that is used to set up the one-to-one correspondence with this set of stars is eight. Therefore, we can say that the cardinal number of the set of stars, I, is 8. Symbolically, for any set X, $n(X)$ represents the cardinal number for set X. In forming the new set of blocks, $n(A)$ is the cardinal number of the set of red blocks, $n(B)$ is the cardinal number of the set of black blocks, and $n(A) + n(B) = n(AUB) = 3 + 5 = 8$. Summarizing, the cardinal numbers 3 and 5 are added to get the sum, 8.

The same total number of blocks are formed whether the black blocks are brought to the red blocks or the red blocks are brought to the black blocks. Symbolically, $AUB = BUA$, $n(A) + n(B) = n(B) + n(A) = n(A + B) = n(B + A)$, and $3 + 5 = 5 + 3$. Similarly, $(AUB)UI = AU(BUI)$, and $(3 + 5) + 8 = 3 + (5 + 8)$. The empty set, Ø, has no elements. Thus, $AUØ = A$, and $3 + 0 = 3$.

Basic Rules. By using sets, the child gains experience with all the basic addition facts, such as $7 + 8$, $3 + 5$, $9 + 2$, $2 + 9$, and $7 + 0$. He notices that addition is a binary operation—it applies to just two set cardinal numbers at a time. He also learns that three or more numbers may be added by adding by twos successively as follows: $4 + 5 + 6 = (4 + 5) + 6 = 9 + 6 = 15$, and $3 + 2 + 1 + 7 = (3 + 2) + 1 + 7 = (5 + 1) + 7 = 6 + 7 = 13$. From experiences of this type he learns the five basic assumptions (also called laws) that govern the operation of addition. These assumptions, where a, b, and c represent *any real numbers*, are as follows:

(1) Closure assumption for addition: $(a + b) = c$. (The sum of any two real numbers always equals a real number.)

(2) Commutative assumption for addition: $a + b = b + a$. (The two numbers can be added in either order.)

(3) Associative assumption for addition: $(a + b) + c = a + (b + c)$. (The numbers can be grouped in any pairs for addition; the results are the same.)

(4) Additive identity for addition, zero: $a + 0 = a$. (When zero is added to a number, the number is unchanged.)

(5) Distributive assumption for multiplication and addition: $a(b + c) = ab + ac$. (multiplication is distributive with respect to addition.).

Addition Example. After using these five assumptions and the knowledge of place value in our decimal system of writing numbers, the addition procedure is shifted from thinking in terms of sets to thinking in terms of arithmetic. This shift permits the student to work easily with large as well as small numbers. As an example, suppose the problem is to add 43 and 25. The solution is as follows:

$43 = 4 \cdot 10^1 + 3 \cdot 10^0$ } (Expanded form of a numeral
$25 = 2 \cdot 10^1 + 5 \cdot 10^0$ } in decimal notation)

$43 + 25 = (4 \cdot 10^1 + 3 \cdot 10^0) + (2 \cdot 10^1 + 5 \cdot 10^0)$
(Addition)

$43 + 25 = \{4 \cdot 10^1 + (3 \cdot 10^0 + 2 \cdot 10^1)\} + 5 \cdot 10^0$
(Associative assumption)

$43 + 25 = \{4 \cdot 10^1 + (2 \cdot 10^1 + 3 \cdot 10^0)\} + 5 \cdot 10^0$
(Commutative assumption)

$43 + 25 = (4 \cdot 10^1 + 2 \cdot 10^1) + (3 \cdot 10^0 + 5 \cdot 10^0)$
(Associative assumption)

$43 + 25 = (4 + 2)(10^1) + (3 + 5)(10^0)$
(Distributive assumption)

$43 + 25 = 60 + 8$ (Contracted form)
$43 + 25 = 68$ (Addition)

Addition Algorithm. All of the foregoing theory of addition can be incorporated into the following neat and easily performed addition algorithm. For example, the student is to add 356, 894, and 107. He follows this pattern:

(1) Set the addends underneath each other, being careful to keep the ones, tens, and hundreds numerals in vertical columns.

(2) Draw a line beneath the lower addend.

(3) Add the numbers represented by the ones numerals $(6 + 4 + 7 = 17)$, set the 7 in the ones column of the sum underneath the horizontal line, and carry (regroup) the 1 to the tens column. Carried numerals need not be written.

(4) Add the numbers represented by the tens numerals $(1 + 5 + 9 + 0 = 15)$, set the 5 in the tens place in the sum, and carry the 1 to the hundreds column.

(5) Add the numbers represented by the hundreds numerals $(1 + 3 + 8 + 1 = 13)$, set the 3 in the hundreds place in the sum, and set the 1 in the thousands place in the sum. The result is:

```
  11   (carry numerals)
 356   (addend)
 894   (addend)
 107   (addend)
1357   (sum).
```

LEE E. BOYER
Harrisburg Area Community College

ADDRESS, Forms of, ə-dres'. In writing to persons with titles, there are certain conventional forms to use in addresses and salutations. When a person holds two or more titles but only one is used, the highest is preferred. For example, a professor who is also a nobleman should be addressed by his title of nobility, which takes precedence over his professional title.

A selected list of the most commonly used forms of address follows. The written salutation is usually an adaptation of the spoken form of address. For example, when an individual writes to an ambassador of another country, the proper salutation in English is either "My Dear Mr. Ambassador" or "Excellency"; but when speaking, he may address him as "Mr. Ambassador," "Mr. Jones," or "Excellency." In many instances, the spoken and written forms are identical.

FORMS OF ADDRESS

(The envelope address is given first and is printed in roman type; the salutation follows and is printed in italics.)

Abbot: The Right Reverend _____, (followed by the initials of his order), Abbot of _____; The Right Rev. Abbot _____.
Right Reverend Abbot; Dear Father Abbot; My dear Father _____

Ambassador (American): The Honorable _____ _____, American Ambassador.
Sir; My dear Mr. Ambassador.

Ambassador (foreign): His Excellency, The Ambassador of _____.
Excellency; My dear Mr. Ambassador.

Apostolic Delegate: His Excellency, The Most Reverend _____, The Apostolic Delegate.
Your Excellency.

Archbishop (Church of England): The Most Reverend His Grace the Lord Archbishop of _____.
My Lord Archbishop; Your Grace.

Archbishop (Eastern Orthodox): The Most Reverend _____, Archbishop of _____.
Your Eminence; My dear Archbishop _____

Archbishop (Roman Catholic): His Excellency, The Most Reverend _____ _____, Archbishop of _____.
Your Excellency; My dear Archbishop _____

Army Officers: General _____, Chief of Staff, United States Army (or other general rank and official position or command); Colonel _____, U.S.A.; (U.S.A. is not used for retired officers of any rank.)
Sir; My dear General _____; *Dear General* _____

Assemblyman: The Honorable _____, Member of the Assembly; Assemblyman _____ _____.
Sir; My dear Mr. _____.

Associate Justice: The Honorable _____, United States Supreme Court; Mr. Justice _____, The Supreme Court.
Sir; My dear Mr. Justice; Dear Justice _____.

Baron: The Right Honourable the Lord _____; The Lord _____.
Sir; Dear Lord _____.

Baroness: (if a baroness in her own right) The Right Honourable the Baroness _____; (if not in her own right) The Right Honourable the Lady _____.
Madam; Dear Baroness _____;

Dear Lady _____.

Baronet: Sir _____ _____, Bart.
Dear Sir; Dear Sir _____ (given name).

Bishop (Church of England): The Right Reverend the Lord Bishop of _____; The Lord Bishop of _____.
My Lord Bishop; My Lord.

Bishop (Eastern Orthodox): The Right Reverend _____, Bishop of _____.
Right Reverend Sir; My dear Bishop _____.

Bishop (Methodist): The Reverend _____, Methodist Bishop; Reverend Bishop _____.
Reverend Sir; My dear Bishop _____.

Bishop (Protestant Episcopal): The Right Reverend _____, Bishop of _____; (if a presiding bishop) The Most Reverend _____, Presiding Bishop.
Right Reverend Sir; Most Reverend Sir; My dear Bishop _____.

Bishop (Roman Catholic): His Excellency, The Most Reverend _____, Bishop of _____.
Your Excellency; My dear Bishop _____

Cabinet Officers: The Honorable ———, ————, Secretary of ————; The Honorable ————, Attorney General.
Sir; My dear
Mr. Secretary; My dear Mr. Attorney General (or *Postmaster General*)

Cardinal: His Eminence ———— (given name) Cardinal ———— (last name).
Your Eminence; My dear Cardinal ————.

Chief Justice (Canada): The Honourable ————, Chief Justice of Canada.
Sir.

Chief Justice (United States): The Chief Justice of the United States; The Chief Justice.
Sir; My dear Mr. Chief Justice.

Clergyman (Protestant): The Reverend ————; (if a doctor of divinity) The Reverend ————, D.D.
My dear Sir; My dear Mr. ————; *My dear Dr.* ————.

Commissioner of a Bureau: The Honorable ————, Commissioner of the Bureau of ————.
Sir; My dear Mr. ————.

Congressman: The Honorable ————, House of Representatives.
————; *My dear Dr.* ————.

Dame: Dame ————, (followed by the initials of the order).
Madam.

Dean (Protestant Episcopal): The Very Reverend ————, Dean of ———— Cathedral.
Very Reverend Sir; My dear Dean ————.

Dean (Roman Catholic): The Very Reverend ————, V.F. (abbr. for "vicar forane").
Very Reverend Father.

Doctor of Medicine: ————, M.D.
My dear Dr. ————.

Domestic Prelate: The Right Reverend Monsignor ————, Domestic Prelate (or D.P.).
Right Reverend Monsignor; My dear Monsignor ————.

Duchess (nonroyal): Her Grace the Duchess of ————; The Most Noble the Duchess of ————.
Madam; Your Grace.

Duchess (royal): Her Royal Highness the Duchess of ————.
Madam.

Duke (nonroyal): His Grace the Duke of ————; The Most Noble the Duke of ————.
Sir; My Lord Duke; Your Grace.

Duke (royal): His Royal Highness the Duke of ————.
Sir.

Earl: The Right Honourable the Earl of ————; The Earl of ————.
Sir; Dear Lord ————.

Governor: The Honorable ————, Governor of ————.
Sir; My dear Governor ————.

Governor General of Canada: His Excellency the Right Honourable ————, (followed by rank or title, if any).
My Lord, or *Sir* (according to rank).

Judge (Canada): (if of a superior court) The Honourable Mr. Justice ————; (if of a lower court) His Honour Judge ————.
Sir.

Judge (United States): The Honorable ————, Judge of ————.
Sir; My dear Judge ————.

Justice: see *Associate Justice; Chief Justice; Judge.*

King: His Majesty the King. *Sir; Your Majesty.*

Lady: Lady ————.
Madam; My Lady; Your Ladyship. (See also *Baroness; Viscountess; Countess; Marchioness.*)

Lawyer: Mr. ————, ————, Attorney-at-Law.
Sir; My dear Mr. ————.

Lord: see *Baron; Viscount; Earl; Marquess.*

Marchioness: The Most Honourable the Marchioness of ————; The Marchioness of ————.
Madam; Dear Lady ————.

Marquess: The Most Honourable the Marquess of ————; The Marquess of ————.
Sir; Dear Lord ————.

Mayor (Canada): His Worship, The Mayor of ————.
Sir.

Mayor (United States): The Honorable ————, Mayor of ————.
Sir; Dear Mr. Mayor; My dear Mayor ————.

Minister (American): The Honorable ————, American Minister to ————.
Sir; My dear Mr. Minister.

Minister (foreign): The Honorable ————, Minister of ————.
Sir; My dear Mr. Minister.

Mother Superior of a Religious Order: The Reverend Mother Superior, Convent of ————; Reverend Mother ————, (followed by the initials of her order).
Reverend Mother; My dear Reverend Mother.

Naval Officers: Admiral ————, ————, United States Navy; Captain ————, U.S.N.
Sir; My dear Admiral ————; *Dear Captain* ————; (for officers below the rank of commander) *Dear Mr.* ————.

Papal Chamberlain: The Very Reverend Monsignor ————.
Very Reverend Monsignor; My dear Monsignor ————.

Pope: His Holiness Pope ————.
Most Holy Father; Your Holiness.

Premier of a Canadian Province: The Honourable ————, Premier of the Province of ————.
Sir.

President of a Canadian Legislative Council: The Honourable ————, The President of the Legislative Council.
Sir.

President of a College or University: ————, (followed by the initials of his highest degrees), President of ———— University.
Dear Sir; Dear President ————; *My dear Dr.* ————.

President of the Senate of the United States: The Honorable ————, President of the Senate.
Sir.

President of the United States: The President, The White House.
Mr. President; My dear Mr. President.

Priest (Eastern Orthodox): The Very Reverend ————.
My dear Father ————.

Priest (Roman Catholic): The Reverend ————; (if a member of a religious order) Reverend ————, (followed by the initials of his order).
Reverend Father; Dear Father ————.

Prime Minister (Canada): The Right Honourable ————, P.C., Prime Minister of Canada.
Sir; Dear Mr. ————.

Prime Minister (United Kingdom): The Right Honourable ————, P.C., M.P., Prime Minister.
Sir; Dear Mr. Prime Minister; Dear Mr. ————.

Prince: His Royal Highness Prince ———— (given name).
Sir; Your Royal Highness.

Prince Consort: His Royal Highness the Prince Consort.
Sir; Your Royal Highness.

Princess: Her Royal Highness the Princess ———— (given name).
Madam.

Prior: The Very Reverend the Prior of ————; The Very Reverend Father ————, (followed by the initials of his order), Prior of ————.
Very Reverend Father; Dear Father Prior.

Prioress: The Very Reverend the Prioress of ————; The Very Reverend Mother ————, (followed by the initials of her order), Prioress of ————.
Very Reverend Mother; Dear Reverend Mother.

Professor in a College or University: Professor ————, ————, (followed by the initials of his highest degrees), Professor of ————.
Dear Sir; Dear Professor ————; *My dear Professor; My dear Dr.* ————.

Queen: Her Majesty the Queen.
Madam; Your Majesty.

Queen Mother: Her Gracious Majesty Queen ————.
Madam; Your Majesty.

Rabbi: Rabbi ————; The Reverend ———— (these forms may be followed by the initials of his academic degree).
Sir; My dear Rabbi ————; *My dear Dr.* ————.

Secretary General of the United Nations: His Excellency ————, Secretary General of the United Nations.
Excellency; My dear Mr. Secretary General.

Senator (Canada): The Honourable ————.

Senator (United States): The Honorable ————, The United States Senate.
Dear Sir; Dear Senator ————. *Sir; My dear Senator* ————.

Sister of a Religious Order: Sister ————, (followed by the initials of her order).
Dear Sister; My dear Sister ————.

Speaker of the House of Commons (Canada): The Honourable ————, The Speaker of the House of Commons.
Dear Mr. Speaker.

Speaker of the House of Representatives (United States): The Honorable ————, The Speaker of the House of Representatives.
Sir; My dear Mr. Speaker; My dear Mr. ————.

Speaker of the Senate (Canada): The Honourable ————, Speaker of the Senate.
Dear Mr. Speaker.

State Senator: The Honorable ————.
Sir; My dear Senator; My dear Mr. ————.

Undersecretary in United States Cabinet: The Honorable ————, Undersecretary of ————. *Sir; My dear Mr. Undersecretary.*

United States Representative to the United Nations: The Honorable ————, United States Representative to the United Nations.
Sir; My dear Mr. Ambassador.

Vicar General: The Right Reverend Monsignor ————, V.G.
Right Reverend Monsignor; Dear Monsignor ————.

Vice President of the United States: The Vice President, the United States Senate.
Mr. Vice President.

Viscount: The Right Honourable the Viscount ————, The Viscount ————.
Sir; Dear Lord ————.

ADE, George, ād (1866–1944), American journalist and author who was best known for his *Fables in Slang* and for several plays, including *The County Chairman* (1903) and *The College Widow* (1904). He was born in Kentland, Ind., on Feb. 9, 1866. After receiving a B.S. degree from Purdue University in 1887, he worked on newspapers in Lafayette, Ind., until 1890, when he joined the staff of the Chicago *Morning News* (later the *Record*). In his column in the *Record*, begun in 1893, he tried to portray realistically the city dwellers of the period and introduced the slangy, wisecracking characters who figured in his first books: *Artie* (1896), *Pink Marsh* (1897), *Doc Horne* (1899), and *Fables in Slang* (1900). In the *Fables*, his most successful work, he employed the form of *Aesop's Fables*, full of wit and ending with a flip moral. Much of its success resulted from the fact that many Americans were then leaving the farms for lives in the city and could be identified with Ade's yokels-turned-city-slickers.

Ade gave up newspaper work in 1900 and took a trip to the Orient. A meeting with Hadji Mohammed Jamului Ki-ram, sultan of the Sulu Islands, provided the inspiration for his first venture in writing for the stage—*The Sultan of Sulu* (1902), a comic opera that enjoyed a long Broadway run. Other plays include *Just Out of College* (1905) and *The Fair Co-Ed* (1908). Among his other writings are *Ade's Fables* (1914), *Hand-Made Fables* (1920), and *Thirty Fables in Slang* (1933). He died in Brook, Ind., on May 16, 1944.

ADELAIDE (931–999), ad'ə-lād, queen of Italy and empress of the Holy Roman Empire. Known in German as Adelheid, she was the daughter of Rudolf II of Burgundy. In 947 she married Lothair II, king of Italy. After his death in 950, Adelaide was imprisoned until 951, when Otto I, king of Germany and later emperor, rescued and married her.

After her marriage to Otto, she helped shape the policies of the Holy Roman Empire, especially during the reign (973–983) of her son, Emperor Otto II, and the minority (983–996) of her grandson, Emperor Otto III. Adelaide was noted for her piety. She died in Seltz, Alsace, on Dec. 16, 999, at one of the many monasteries she had established.

ADELAIDE, ad'əl-ād, a city in Australia and the capital of the state of South Australia. Situated 6 miles (10 km) east of Gulf St. Vincent, an inlet of the Indian Ocean, the city is also the commercial and cultural center of the state. It was named in honor of Queen Adelaide, consort of King William IV, the reigning monarch of Britain when the city was founded in 1836.

Plan of the City. Adelaide stands on a fertile plain, which slopes gently from the Mount Lofty Ranges in the east to the shore of Gulf St. Vincent. The Torrens River flows through the city from east to west, dividing it into South Adelaide, the business district, and North Adelaide, the residential area. An extensive belt of parklands, covering 1,700 acres (690 ha), completely surrounds the city, separating it from the sprawling suburbs. Port Adelaide is in the suburban area, 7 miles (11 km) from the heart of the city.

Designed by Col. William Light, who surveyed it early in 1837, Adelaide is a well-planned city, with wide streets, set at right angles to each other, and numerous city squares. King William Street,

Adelaide, divided by the Torrens River (*center*) into business and residential areas, has vast park areas.

the main thoroughfare, runs north and south, passing through Victoria Square, a small park in the center of the city. South Adelaide is bounded by four main avenues, known as North, South, East, and West terraces.

Points of Interest. Adelaide is the site of the main cultural institutions and government buildings of South Australia. The State Library of South Australia, the Art Gallery of South Australia, and the South Australia Museum, a natural history museum, are located on North Terrace. The state Parliament House, a classical building of native marble and gray granite, and the state Government House also are on North Terrace. The city has several excellent institutions of higher learning, including the University of Adelaide, incorporated in 1874, and the University of South Australia, founded in 1991. Adelaide is often called the city of churches because of its many houses of worship, which include two cathedrals—St. Peter's (Anglican) and St. Francis Xavier (Roman Catholic).

Adelaide's pleasant climate and fine location, between the sea and the hills, combine to make the city a recreational center. Portions of the parklands have been made available for sports arenas, including the Adelaide Oval, for cricket and football; the Memorial Drive Tennis Courts, scene of the Davis Cup challenge rounds; and the Victoria Park Race Course. The shore of Gulf St. Vincent provides long stretches of safe, sandy bathing beaches. In 1960 the biennial Adelaide Festival of Arts was inaugurated. It is held for 2–3 weeks in March and includes a variety of musical entertainment ranging from classical recitals to jazz and rock concerts. The Adelaide Festival Centre, a performing arts center, has been the world premiere venue for several notable ballets.

Economy. Adelaide is the chief port and marketplace for South Australia. It is connected by railroad with Port Adelaide and with the outer harbor, which services oceangoing liners. Wheat, wool, hides, fruit, and wine are exported from the port.

Industrial growth was very rapid in the city in the middle of the 20th century. Large factories produce automotive parts, machinery, chemicals, and textiles as well as refined petroleum. The city also functions as the processing center for the region's agricultural produce and dairy products.

History. Before settlement by Europeans the Adelaide area was occupied by Kaurna Aborigines. Early English explorers included Matthew Flinders, who surveyed the coastline in 1801–1802, and Capt. Collet Barker, who, in 1831, was the first European to view the future site of the city. Adelaide was founded on Dec. 31, 1836, by Col. William Light, who chose the site despite much opposition from various rivals. In 1840 Adelaide became the first Australian municipality to be incorporated. Three years later, however, the colonial government took control of the city's affairs, and the city corporation was not revived until 1852. Adelaide is the fifth largest metropolitan area in Australia. Population: metropolitan area, 1,002,127 (2001 census).

G. L. FISHER*
Public Library of South Australia

ADELAIDE, University of, ad′əl-ād, a coeducational institution in Adelaide, South Australia, established in 1874 by the South Australian legislature and opened in 1876. There are six academic divisions: agricultural and natural resource sciences; engineering and mathematical sciences; health sciences; humanities and social sciences; performing arts, law, architecture, urban design, economics, and commerce; and science. Specialized units of the university are the Elder Conservatorium of Music and Waite Agricultural Research Institute. Affiliated schools are St. Mark's, St. Ann's, Aquinas, and Lincoln colleges, South Australian Institute of Technology, and Roseworthy Agricultural College. The University of Adelaide's libraries holdings exceed 1.5 million volumes. The Barr Smith Library, where the main collection is stored, first opened in 1932 and has been expanded repeatedly to meet growing needs.

ADÉLIE COAST, ä-dā-lē′, the coast of Antarctica between 136°12′ and 142°02′ east longitude, approximately 2,000 miles (3,000 km) south of eastern Australia. The French name *Terre Adélie (Adélie Land)* denotes both the coast and the entire Antarctic sector between 136°20′ and 142°20′, claimed by France since 1934. (This claim is not recognized by the United States.) In 1955, France combined Adélie Land with several islands in the Indian Ocean to form the French Southern and Antarctic Territories.

The ice-covered Adélie Coast is one of the windiest, most forbidding regions in the world, but emperor and Adélie penguins are found there. It was discovered in 1840 by the French navigator Capt. Jules Dumont d'Urville, who named it for his wife.

In 1950 the French established a scientific base on the coast at Port Martin. Destroyed by fire in 1952, the installation was replaced four years later by the permanent Dumont d'Urville base farther to the west.

ADÉLIE PENGUIN.   See PENGUIN.

ADELPHI, ə-del′fi, the last of six comedies by the Roman playwright Terence. Adapted from Menander's *Adelphoe*, the play was performed in Rome in 160 B.C. The title means "The Brothers." It is perhaps Terence's best work and, unlike most other Roman comedies, contains a lesson.

The play deals with two conflicting methods of education for youths, restraint versus excessive leniency. Micio adopts Aeschinus, the son of his brother Demea, and rears him with leniency. Demea rears his other son, Ctesipho, with severity. The play chronicles the compromising love affairs of the two youths and the effects of the affairs upon the fathers. Both fathers and sons become involved in a series of misunderstandings. The conflicts are resolved when Demea, upon Micio's advice, understandingly accepts Ctesipho's romantic involvement. Demea realizes that Micio's popularity with the two youths rests upon Micio's excessive leniency and generosity. Demea changes his attitude and wins the affections of both his sons by his generosity. Terence obviously felt that the "golden mean," which avoids extremes of both severity and excessive leniency, was to be favored in education as in all things.

Among later dramas influenced by *Adelphi* were Molière's *L'École des maris* (1661), Thomas Shadwell's *The Squire of Alsatia* (1688), Barthélémy Fagan's *La Pupille* (1734), David Garrick's *The Guardian* (1759), and Richard Cumberland's *The Choleric Man* (1774).

ADELPHI UNIVERSITY, ə-del′fi, a privately endowed, coeducational, and nonsectarian institution located in Garden City, N.Y. It was chartered in 1896 as Adelphi College, with its campus in Brooklyn. The college was moved to Garden City in 1929 and became a university in 1963. Adelphi was the first degree-granting institution on Long Island. Originally coeducational, Adelphi became a college for women only after 1912. In 1946 it again became coeducational to accommodate World War II veterans. A division, Adelphi Suffolk College, was established in 1959 at Sayville, N.Y., and moved to Oakdale, N.Y., in 1963.

The university offers bachelor's degrees in arts, science, business administration, nursing, arts and sciences, and social work. Doctoral degrees are offered from the School of Nursing, the School of Social Work, and the Institute of Advanced Psychological Studies. Adelphi University also offers seven-year joint programs in dentistry with Georgetown University and in optometry with the State University of New York College of Optometry. New buildings include the School of Social Work completed in 1984 and the Hy Weinberg Center completed in 1986.

ADELUNG, Johann Christoph, ä′də-lŏong (1732–1806), German philologist, grammarian, lexicographer, and librarian who was influential in standardizing the German language. He was born in Spantekow, Pomerania, on Aug. 8, 1732.

Adelung's chief works include *Grammatisch-kritisches Wörterbuch der hochdeutschen Mundart* (5 vols., 1774–86), *Über den Ursprung der Sprache und den Bau der Wörter* (1781), *Deutsche Sprachlehre für Schulen* (1781), *Über den deutschen Stil* (3 vols., 1785), and *Mithridates, oder Allgemeine Sprachenkunde*. Only one volume of the latter was completed at the time of Adelung's death, on Sept. 10, 1806, in Dresden. Two more volumes were added by Johann Severin Vater.

Aden is a port of the People's Republic of Yemen.

ADEN, ād'n, äd'n, a city in the Yemeni Republic, in the southwest corner of the Arabian Peninsula. The city and port of Aden are situated on the Gulf of Aden approximately 100 miles (160 km) east of the mouth of the Red Sea.

An important station on the traditional sea route from Europe to the Indian Ocean and the Far East, Aden was, until the closing of the Suez Canal in 1967–1975, one of the world's busiest bunkering ports. Persian Gulf oil for bunkering was refined at Little Aden, west of the main city. As a free port, Aden used to handle many of the imports for the neighboring regions, but in the mid-1960's, Djibouti (then in French Somaliland) took away some of its trade because of disturbances in Aden. When, in the 1960's, the Soviet Union built a port at Hodeida in the Yemen Arab Republic, the latter became less dependent on Aden as an entry point for goods.

The oldest part of Aden town is Crater, which lies in an extinct volcano. On the same peninsula as Crater are the newer quarters of Steamer Point, Tawahi, and Maala. North of the peninsula is the civil and military airport of Khormaksar. Population: 400,783 (1993 est.).

The People's Republic of Yemen. Aden was the capital of the People's Democratic Republic of Yemen until 1990, when that country and the Yemen Arab Republic united as the Yemeni Republic. Known as South Yemen before 1970, the Democratic Republic consisted of Aden and surroundings and the former British Protectorate of South Arabia (earlier called the Aden Protectorate). It extended along the coast of Arabia for some 700 miles (1,125 km) and in places reached about 200 miles (320 km) inland, giving a total area of roughly 100,000 square miles (259,000 sq km). Barren mountains dominated the landscape, but many valleys had green patches of cultivation. The people of the republic were almost all Muslim Arabs. The city of Aden once had large settlements of foreigners, but troubles in the mid-1960's forced many to leave. Arab immigrants from the Yemen Arab Republic outnumbered the native-born Adenese Arabs.

The British protectorate included over 20 sultanates, amirates, and sheikdoms, each one semi-independent and linked to Britain by a protectorate treaty. Determined to wipe out the antiquated tribal system on which the political structure of the British protectorate was based, the republican government divided up the country into six governorates. One of these embraced the islands belonging to the republic: Perim, at the mouth of the Red Sea; Kamaran, off the coast of the Yemen Arab Republic; and Socotra, some 200 miles (320 km) off the southern Arabian coast. In 1967, Britain ceded to Oman the nearby Kuria Muria Islands, which had been administered from Aden, but the People's Democratic Republic of Yemen challenged the legality of the cession.

History. In ancient times Aden was a port for the incense and spice trade between East and West. It is probably the merchant city of Eden mentioned in the Bible (Ezekiel 27:23). Control of the East-West traffic originally lay in the hands of the people of southwest Arabia, who developed the Sabaean civilization. Their monopoly was broken by Greek sailors who crossed the Arabian Sea to India.

A Christian church was built in Aden in the 4th century. Two centuries later the Persians occupied southwest Arabia for a brief period, but they were supplanted in the 7th century by the new Arab power of Islam. At times Aden was subject to the rulers of Yemen, as when it was given as a dowry to Queen Sayyida in the 11th century. The Portuguese tried to capture Aden in the 16th century but failed. Later the Ottoman Turks succeeded in taking it. In 1735, Aden was annexed by the sultan of the nearby oasis of Lahej. The British seized Aden in 1839 and made it a British colony to guard the route to India.

Under British sponsorship, six states in the Protectorate of South Arabia in 1959 formed a federation, which three years later became the Federation of South Arabia. At British urging, Aden adhered to the federation in 1963 in return for special status. Although membership in the federation eventually reached 17, the large sultanates in the eastern part of the protectorate steadfastly refused to join. A basic weakness of the federation was the discrepancy between the cosmopolitan society and vigorous economy of Aden and the tribal society and meager existence of the protectorate states.

When the British government decided to grant independence to Aden and the protectorate, it hoped that the federation would become the successor state. Anti-British leaders, however, formed rival organizations, the most effective of which proved to be the National Liberation Front (NLF). In 1967 the NLF undermined the federation, overthrew many of the rulers in the protectorate, and decisively defeated the rival anti-British organizations. Britain was compelled to negotiate with the NLF for the transfer of power. Independence came at the end of November 1967, accompanied by British evacuation of the strong naval base of Aden.

Although favoring the ultimate union of the two Yemens, the new regime did not take steps immediately to bring this about. Before the end of 1967, the republic joined the Arab League as its 14th member. While proclaiming a policy of nonalignment, the republic sought close relations with the Soviet Union and other Communist states. After the reopening of the Suez Canal in 1975, Aden failed to recover its prosperity because fewer ships needed to stop there for refueling. However, the city's future brightened when Aden became the chief port and economic center of the united Yemens in 1990.

GEORGE RENTZ*, *Stanford University*

ADEN, Gulf of, äd'ən, an arm of the Indian Ocean between the southern coast of Arabia and the northern coast of Somalia, Africa. Its length is about 550 miles (880 km), its greatest width about 200 miles (320 km). It connects the Red Sea with the Arabian Sea by the Bab el-Mandeb Strait. The gulf port of Aden is the chief port of the Republic of Yemen. Djibouti and Berbera are also important gulf port cities.

ADENAUER, ä'də-nou-ər, **Konrad** (1876–1967), German statesman. He was born in Cologne on Jan. 5, 1876. Adenauer studied law and economics before becoming assistant judge in the district court at Cologne. In 1906 he was elected deputy mayor of Cologne and was lord mayor from 1917 to 1933. A devout Roman Catholic, Adenauer served on the executive committee of the Catholic Center party and was active in Prussian politics until 1933. He also served in the Provincial Diet of the Rhineland.

Upon his dismissal by the Nazis from all public offices in 1933, Adenauer withdrew to the village of Rhöndorf, where he remained until the end of the war. Constantly harassed by the Gestapo, he was imprisoned for four months in 1944. When the Americans occupied Cologne, they reinstated Adenauer as lord mayor. However, he irritated the British military government and was dismissed in October 1945 and forbidden to pursue any political activity.

Nonetheless, Adenauer soon became active in the new Christian Democratic Union (CDU). Elected the president of the CDU in the British zone in 1946, he became party whip in the North Rhine-Westphalia Diet. He was chosen president of the parliamentary council created in 1948 to draft a Basic Law for West Germany. In September 1949, Adenauer became chancellor of the new Federal Republic, a position he held until his retirement in October 1963. He was also foreign minister from 1951 to 1955 and president of the CDU from 1950 to 1966.

Governmental Policies. Adenauer's administration was characterized by a deep personal commitment to the establishment of close ties with the democratic Christian West. He recognized that little could be done to bring about the reunification of Germany in the foreseeable future. Under his leadership West Germany achieved full independence in May 1955, and its economic recovery was so complete that it is still referred to as the "Economic Miracle." Adenauer was instrumental in bringing about West Germany's membership in many organizations, including the North Atlantic Treaty Organization and the European Economic Community.

Adenauer's desire for a rapprochement with France reached fruition in the signing of a "Reconciliation Treaty" in January 1963, calling for regular consultations between the two governments. After his retirement, Adenauer remained constant in this policy and criticized his successor, Ludwig Erhard, for what he considered a drift away from Franco-German cooperation.

Adenauer's administration was primarily a one-man affair, yet his regime established an environment favorable to the success of democratic processes. Adenauer regarded the Nazi treatment of the Jews as a monstrous national crime, and he therefore undertook symbolic retribution payments to Israel. One of his first public acts as a private individual was a visit to Israel in the spring of 1966.

EDO LONIG FROM BLACK STAR

KONRAD ADENAUER was host to France's President de Gaulle in 1962, in one of several exchange visits.

Adenauer had seven children, three by his first wife, Emma Weyer (died 1916), and four by his second, Auguste Zinsser (died 1948). Known as *"Der Alte,"* Adenauer in retirement remained an influential figure in West Germany. He died in Rhöndorf, near Bonn, on April 19, 1967.

PAUL C. HELMREICH
Wheaton College

ADENET LE ROI, àd-ne' lə rwä', a French trouvère of the 13th century, was born in Brabant about 1240. He was also known as *Adam, Adans, Adenès,* and *Adenez le Roi.* He was attached to the court of Henry III, duke of Brabant, until 1269, when he entered the service of Guy de Dampierre, later count of Flanders. In 1270 he accompanied the latter in the crusade which ended disastrously at Tunis with the death of King Louis IX of France.

Adenet's chief work was *Cléomadès,* a long chanson de geste based on Moorish and Spanish traditions, which was published in a two-volume edition in Brussels in 1863–1866. His other poems included *Les enfances Ogier, Berte aus grans piés,* and *Bueves de Commarchis.*

ADENITIS, ad-ə-nī'təs, is an inflammation of a gland or lymph node. (The lymph nodes manufacture white blood corpuscles.) Enlargement of the regional lymph nodes occurs as a result of infections and inflammations of the neighboring lymphatic channels.

Adenitis of the neck, called *cervical adenitis,* is the most common form. It may arise from a great variety of acute inflammations that involve the mouth, throat, and ears. *Adenitis of the groin* may be caused by venereal disease. Chronic enlargement of the lymph glands is observed in tuberculosis, leukemia, and syphilis.

Constitutional symptoms are generally present in acute forms. These symptoms are rise in temperature, localized pain, and swelling. Treatment consists of penicillin, rest, and if pus is present, incision into the gland. The treatment of chronic adenitis depends upon the nature of the cause and whether it can be removed.

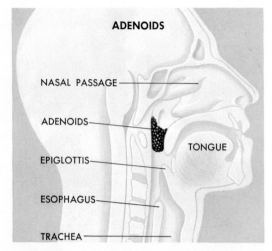

ADENOIDS

NASAL PASSAGE

ADENOIDS

TONGUE

EPIGLOTTIS

ESOPHAGUS

TRACHEA

ADENOIDS, ad'ən-oidz, are folds of tissue, similar to tonsils, located in the nasopharynx, the area in which the nose leads to the back of the throat. Composed of lymphatic tissue covered with ciliated epithelial cells, they are present in early life but tend to shrink or atrophy in adulthood. Their purpose is uncertain, but they do participate in the formation of lymphocytes (a white blood cell type).

Infection. Like the tonsils, adenoids are a frequent source of bacterial infection, particularly in young children. When infected, the adenoids become enlarged and drain pus and mucus into the throat, blocking the normal airway through the nose. This respiratory blockage gives rise to the so-called "adenoid facies," a facial expression in which the person affected has a staring, vacant look and keeps the mouth open in order to breathe. Infection from adenoids can spread to the opening of the Eustachian tubes of the ear or into the tonsils below the adenoids.

Treatment. Since they infect each other, diseased tonsils and adenoids usually are removed together by surgery, unless the individual is beyond adolescence and the adenoids have atrophied. Adenoids are removed surgically by inserting a curette (a scoop-, loop-, or ringshaped instrument) behind the soft palate and scraping the adenoids off close to the posterior wall of the pharynx. Adenoid tissue around the Eustachian tubes is curetted similarly. Recovery occurs in five to six days, once residual hemorrhage and suctioning of secretions have been accomplished. After adenoidectomy, a child may "talk through his nose" (nasal speech) for three or four weeks until he learns how to bring his soft palate and the back of the throat together.

Complications. The most serious complication of adenoid infection, if allowed to go untreated, is the obstruction of the opening of the Eustachian tube from the ears. This allows pus to back up into the middle ear from the oral cavity and may lead to ear drum perforation, hearing loss, and even mastoiditis.

Also, lymphoid tissue may grow back in the area where adenoids are removed, especially where allergic conditions exist. In rare cases, additional surgery may be needed.

REAUMUR S. DONNALLY
Washington Hospital Center

ADENOSINE TRIPHOSPHATE. See ATP.

ADEODATUS I, ä-dē-od'ə-təs, **Saint** (died 618), pope from 615 to 618. He is known also as *Deusdedit.* Little is known of his life except that he was a Roman, the son of a subdeacon named Stephen. As pope, he was distinguished chiefly for his affectionate concern for the secular clergy. His reign was troubled by political disturbances in Italy, notably between the empire and the Lombards. Adeodatus' feast day is November 8.

MSGR. FLORENCE D. COHALAN, *Cathedral College*

ADEODATUS II, ä-dē-od'ə-təs, **Saint** (died 676), pope from 672 to 676. He was a Roman, the son of Jovinian, and was a monk of the Abbey of St. Erasmus on the Coelian Hill. The few surviving records describe him as affable and hospitable. He was probably the first pope to date his letters from the year of his pontificate. He died of the plague and was buried in St. Peter's.

MSGR. FLORENCE D. COHALAN, *Cathedral College*

ADHESION, ad-hē'zhən, is the force of attraction between molecules in the surface of one material and molecules in the surface of another material when the surfaces are in contact with each other. There is no chemical reaction between the two materials; that is, the adhering particles remain unchanged. The two different materials can be two solids, a liquid and a solid, or two liquids. Examples of adhesion are chalk particles adhering to a blackboard, glue holding together pieces of an object, solder joining metals together, and water adhering to glass.

The force of adhesion depends on the materials in contact, the cleanliness of their surfaces, the temperature, and the pressure on the materials. The adhesion force acting at an interface tends to bind the surfaces together, and therefore force is required to separate the materials. By measuring this force, the force of adhesion can be estimated.

The force of adhesion is similar to another molecular force, the force of cohesion. Adhesion, however, is the attractive force between unlike molecules, whereas cohesion is the attractive force between like molecules. Also, the force of adhesion acts at the surface of two different materials, whereas the force of cohesion acts among the molecules throughout a single material.

Perhaps adhesion can be understood best by considering examples of liquid-solid interfaces in capillary tubes. In these examples, the force of adhesion is compared with the force of cohesion.

The angle between the vertical tube wall and the liquid surface next to the tube is called the angle of contact. This angle indicates the relative values of the forces of adhesion and cohesion. When the liquid surface near the glass curves upward, the force of adhesion is greater than the force of cohesion. For example, a water surface near the glass curves upward because the adhesive force between water and glass is greater than the cohesive force of water. When the liquid surface near the glass curves downward, the cohesive force is greater than the adhesive force. For example, a mercury surface near the glass curves downward because the cohesive force of mercury is greater than the adhesive force between mercury and glass.

When the adhesive force is greater than the cohesive force, a liquid spreads out on a solid. When the cohesive force is greater, the liquid does not spread out. See also COHESION.

ADHESIVES, ad-hē'sivz, are materials used for joining objects. They include binders, cements, glues, mucilages, gummed tapes, and pressure-sensitive tapes. The process of joining consists of applying the adhesive to the component materials, assembling the joint, and then allowing the adhesive to harden under pressure. Adhesive bonding differs from other joining techniques because no structural contrivances, such as bolts, rivets, screws, or staples, are used to hold the components together.

Adhesives hold components, commonly called *adherends* or *substrates,* by both mechanical and chemical adhesion. *Mechanical adhesion* is the portion of the adhesive strength given by mechanical interlocking of the adhesive in the pores of the adherend. *Chemical adhesion* is the remaining portion of the adhesive strength. It is given by a chemical reaction between the adhesive and the adherend or by intermolecular electrical forces that cause mutual attraction between the adherend and the adhesive.

Types of Adhesives. Adhesives are compounded from one of two basic types of materials: *thermoplastic* and *thermosetting.* Thermoplastic materials soften under heat and are soluble in selected solvents. Natural adhesives are predominantly thermoplastic. Thermosetting materials harden (cure) under the action of heat or catalysts. Once hardened, they do not melt, and they are insoluble. Thermoplastic and thermosetting adhesives are supplied as air-drying material, fusible material, pressure-sensitive tape, and chemically reactive material.

Air-drying adhesives usually are thermoplastics. They are converted to the solid state by evaporation of the solvent. They bond by mechanical adhesion and mutual attraction. The adhesive is applied to the cleaned substrates and, if necessary, is baked or air dried for a short time to remove residual solvent before assembling the joint. After assembly, pressure is applied on the components.

Fusible adhesives are mainly thermoplastics, such as animal glue or sulfur. They are converted to the solid state by cooling previously melted adhesive material. They bond by mechanical adhesion and mutual attraction. The adhesive is melted and applied to the cleaned adherends. Then the joint is assembled, and the adhesive is allowed to solidify under pressure.

Pressure-sensitive adhesives are predominantly thermoplastics. They are supplied in tape form on a paper, plastic, or similar backing. Some tapes require no moisture, heat, or other treatment before or after application. Other tapes are activated with water or solvent before application. Pressure-sensitive tapes bond by mechanical adhesion and mutual attraction.

Chemically reactive adhesives are predominantly thermosetting materials. They are converted to the solid state by catalysts or heat. They bond primarily by chemical reaction and secondarily by mechanical adhesion and mutual attraction. The adhesive is activated and applied to the cleaned substrates. Then the joint is assembled and cured under pressure at room or high temperature.

Uses for Adhesives. Adhesives have been used for thousands of years for joining paper and, to a lesser extent, wood. Hydraulic-setting cements and natural asphalt have been used as structural adhesives since ancient times. It was not until the late 1930's, when synthetic resins were introduced, that adhesives were developed for joining a great variety of materials. These synthetic resins, unlike natural counterparts, such as animal glue or starch, have high strength and give long service. Adhesives now have many applications. They are used in dentistry, medicine, electrical applications, metal joining, optics, and packaging and bonding paper. Adhesives also are used to bond plastics, rubber, and wood.

Plastics Adhesives. Thermoplastic plastics, because of their sensitivity to heat and solvents, can be joined by heat-welding or solvent-welding techniques as well as by conventional adhesive-bonding techniques. Thermosetting plastics can be joined only by adhesive bonding.

Adhesive bonding of thermoplastics is best achieved with adhesives that have a composition similar to that of the adherend. Thus, cellulose nitrate is bonded with cellulose nitrate base adhesives, acrylics with acrylic-base cements, and so on. Thermoset plastics can be bonded with adhesives that do not have a composition similar to that of the adherend. Phenolic, resorcinol, melamine, furane, epoxy, synthetic rubber, and isocyanate base adhesives are used.

Rubber Adhesives. Rubber materials generally are bonded with rubber-base adhesives in order to retain elasticity. The best bonds are achieved with adhesives formulated from the same rubber as the adherend. Available adhesives include those based on natural, butyl, polysulfide, urethane, neoprene, silicone, and nitrile rubbers.

Wood Adhesives. Wood can be bonded with interior, semidurable, and weatherproof adhesives. Interior adhesives are used for assemblies subject to normal indoor temperature conditions where relative humidities are not high and do not fluctuate widely. Animal glue and vinyl are suitable for these applications.

Semidurable adhesives are used for assemblies subject to severe conditions for limited periods. These bonding agents deteriorate slowly and ultimately fail completely. Urea and casein are suitable for these conditions.

Weatherproof adhesives are used for marine service and other applications where there are severe conditions for protracted periods. These adhesives are more durable than wood and are virtually indestructible by weather, mold, and heat. Phenolic, resorcinol, melamine, furane, and epoxy adhesives are commonly used.

Markets for Adhesives. Approximately two billion pounds of adhesives are being used each year in practically every segment of home and industrial activity. In a television set, adhesives insulate electronic components and hold them together. Packaging adhesives help to put a tube of toothpaste in the consumer's hand. An adhesive will hold the bandage in place over a scratch. When a space vehicle is launched, dozens of adhesives are holding it together. Highway departments are restoring roads with adhesive materials, and builders are substituting adhesives for mortar in constructing houses and fences. The transportation, building trade, toy, and capital goods industries all use adhesives—some even for prime structural purposes. In the future, new uses for adhesives will be found.

Irving Katz, *North American Aviation, Inc.*

Further Reading: Ash, M., and Ash, I., *Formulary of Adhesives and Sealants* (Chemical Pub. 1986); Katz, Irving, *Adhesive Materials, Their Properties and Usage* (Libraries Unlimited 1964); Kinloch, A. J., *Adhesion and Adhesives: Science and Technology* (Methuen 1987).

ADIABENE, ad-ē-ə-bē′nē, was an ancient kingdom, lying between the Tigris River and two of its tributaries, the Great and the Little Zab. At one time it included all of Assyria proper and the Mesopotamian province of Nisibis (modern Nusaybin) and the district of Ecbatana (modern Hamadan).

In 116 A.D. the country was conquered by Trajan, who made it a Roman province under the name of Assyria. Hadrian, however, allowed it to resume its autonomy under Parthian suzerainty. The capital of the kingdom was Arbela (Erbil).

ADI-BUDDHA, ä-dē-bōōd′ə, the Primordial Buddha, represented as self-existent and omniscient. This concept of Buddha, due probably to the influence of Christianity, came into vogue among the northern Buddhists about the middle of the 10th century.

ADIGE RIVER, ä′dē-jä, in northern Italy, the second-largest river of Italy, with a length of 255 miles. It rises in three small lakes in the Italian Alps north of Bressanone and south of the Brenner Pass, which connects Austria and Italy. It flows first in a southwesterly direction through Trento and Rovereto, passing about six miles east of Lake Garda. In its lower course, through the region of Veneto, it flows generally southeast, passing through Verona and near Rovigo, and empties into the Adriatic Sea five miles south of Chioggia. On its way to the sea it receives the Noce, Isarco, and Avisio rivers.

Although it is navigable in its lower course, the Adige is used chiefly for irrigation and hydroelectric power.

ADIGRANTH, ä′di-grunt, the sacred scriptures of the Sikhs. It is also called *Granth*. It was compiled mainly by the guru (spiritual guide) Arjan Mal (1581–1606), fifth successor of the founder Nanak. He gathered up the poetical pieces of his four predecessors and fragments from other great teachers, including Ramananda, Kabir, and Namadeva, and added compositions of his own. The tenth and last Sikh guru, Govind Singh (1675–1708), made additions to it and composed a supplementary Granth, the "Granth of the Tenth Reign." The language of the Granths is chiefly Punjabi and Hindi. The Granths, with the biographies of gurus and saints and instructions for ritual and discipline, comprise the Sikh sacred books.

ADIPOSE TISSUE, ad′ə-pōs tish′ōō, is loose connective tissue in which fat cells have accumulated in such great numbers that they have excluded all other cells. Such tissue, which is used to store neutral fat in the body, is most often found under the skin, in the kidney region, and in the mesenteries (the membranes that surround and connect the intestines).

Adipose tissue is divided into two types— *unilocular* and *multilocular.* Unilocular adipose tissue, which is most common in humans, is white or yellow fat in which the cells each have a single large fat vacuole. White or yellow fat is lost or accumulated according to the nutritional condition of the body. Multilocular adipose tissue is brown fat that occurs in hibernating animals and contains a light brown pigment. Many small fat droplets appear in the cytoplasm of brown fat cells. Brown fat seems to be affected by endocrine rather than by nutritional changes.

ADIRONDACK MOUNTAINS, ad-ə-ron′dak, a region of varied natural beauty in northern New York, bounded by Lake Champlain on the east and by the valleys of the Mohawk (south), Black (west), and St. Lawrence (north) rivers. Although the region is within a day's drive from home for 35 million people, its remotest woods, peaks, and waters are among the most primitive in the eastern United States. Twelve wilderness areas in the mountains are accessible only on foot or by canoe. But large numbers of tourists are accommodated in villages and resorts and at state campsites near highways. Adirondack Park, comprising private and public lands totaling 5.7 million acres (2.3 million hectares), is larger than Massachusetts. Public lands in the park make up the bulk of New York State's Forest Preserve. The private holdings are part of the park but not of the preserve. The state continues to acquire land and now owns 2.3 million acres (931,500 hectares) of forest preserve within park boundaries, an area larger than any national park.

Approximately 2,000 peaks are prominent enough to be called "mountains" by residents of the region. Of greatest interest to mountaineers are the high peaks, concentrated in a circular area in the northeast quarter. As seen in summer from Mount Marcy (5,344 feet, or 1,628.8 meters), the highest point in New York State, the high peaks drop away in blue-green billows accented by outcroppings of gray rock. Forty-four of the peaks range between 4,000 and 5,114 feet

MONKMEYER PRESS PHOTO

ADIRONDACK MOUNTAINS show sharp peaks, long ridges. Whiteface Mountain (foreground) is climbed by Memorial Highway.

(1,219 and 1,558.7 meters). Twelve rise above the timberline and are snowcapped through May. Some are isolated; most are in groups joined by densely forested ridges. Whiteface Mountain, an isolated peak with a celebrated view, is ascended by a toll highway. Others can be scaled only on foot. Passes and gorges with cliffs rising over 1,000 feet (300 meters) challenge the climber.

Geology and Geography. The Adirondacks are a southeasterly arm of the Canadian Shield. Their rock tells of complex geologic change. The oldest goes back more than a billion years (the Precambrian era) to lofty mountains thrust upward from a sea once covering New York State. It has been much altered by repeated cycles of erosion to sea level, resubmergence, sedimentation, pressure, and upheaval. The last era of mountain building occurred about 25 million years ago. The only major geologic influence since then, the ice age ending about 9,000 years ago, rounded off peaks and ridges, gouged U-shaped valleys, and deposited glacial debris to form lake and swamp basins, drumlins, eskers, and other features. In arrangement and sculpturing, the Adirondacks are relatively new mountains, but the ancient underlying rock, an anorthosite, makes them among the oldest in the world.

The principal river systems are the Sacandaga, Black, Oswegatchie, Grass, Raquette, St. Regis, Saranac, and Ausable. Numberless brooks cascade down mountain slopes and cliffs. Drainage on the east, north, and west of the region is into the St. Lawrence and, on the south, into the Hudson. About 2,200 lakes and ponds hang like pendants on a chain from stream systems or are enfolded by hills. The lonely Lake Tear of the Clouds, highest pond source of the Hudson, lies in a pocket of Mount Marcy at 4,320 feet (1,316.7 meters). More hospitable to bathers are the sand beaches and birch groves of the Fish Creek ponds and other public campsites. Some of the large lakes with both public and private shores are George, Placid, the Saranacs, Long, Raquette, the Fulton chain, Indian, and Tupper.

Forests and Conservation. The forest covers all but a minor fraction of the land and is extremely varied. It gives a distinctive color pattern to every season. Most of it had been cut or burned at least once before protective measures were taken, but in the Forest Preserve natural growth is making a strong recovery. Throughout the park are remnants of a climax forest of northern hardwoods, hemlock, and white pine; at higher elevations, spruce and balsam. In the northwest quarter is a tract of 50,000 acres (20,250 hectares) that never has been logged.

The Forest Preserve of the Adirondacks and Catskills was created in 1885 and the Adirondack Park in 1892. In 1894 a constitutional amendment provided that forest preserve lands then owned and thereafter acquired should be kept forever as wild forest lands; this is still the basic conservation law of the state.

The Forest Preserve is administered by the State Conservation Department, which encourages hiking, hunting, water sports, and nature study. More than a million people enjoy its trails, leantos, and tent-and-trailer camps each year. Its educational programs have improved the public's use and appreciation of this region.

Efforts to preserve wildlife have had mixed results. Heavy stocking of waters that once teemed with native trout and salmon lags behind use. Elk, moose, panther, and timber wolf have disappeared except for strays, but deer are abundant, and black bear and small game hold their own. Coyotes are recent immigrants. Beaver, trapped out by 1850, have returned in force.

Climate. Altitude and Canadian air temper summer heat. Daytime temperatures rarely reach 95° F (35° C), and nights are cool. In winter the coldest days (−35° F, or −37° C, is fairly common) usually are accompanied by dry air, clear skies, and little wind. For 80 years the climate was recommended for treatment of pulmonary diseases, but modern therapeutic methods have reduced the need for sanatoriums.

Resources and Tourism. Lumbering, once the major industry, continues on a reduced scale on private lands. Several magnetic iron-ore deposits are worked. The Benson mine near Star Lake is one of the world's largest open-pit magnetite mines. The MacIntyre development at Tahawus is the largest source of titanium in the United States. Other mineral products are granite, marble, and a high grade of garnet for abrasives.

The major resource for the 109,000 residents of the area is the tourist trade. A growing number of ski slopes has helped to lengthen the season. Most local people recognize the importance of scenic and recreational values and cooperate with state authorities to preserve them.

History. The eastern border of the Adirondacks occupied an important position in American history. For centuries the corridor formed by Lake George and Lake Champlain was the only easy route to Canada, though exposed to hostile attacks. First a warpath for Indian tribes, it later became a path of empire in the French and Indian War and of strategic military importance in the American Revolution and the War of 1812. The heroic names associated with this corridor in two centuries of wilderness conflict—Champlain, Father Isaac Jogues, Sir William Johnson, Maj. Robert Rogers, Mohawk Chief Hendrick, Montcalm, Ethan Allen, Benedict Arnold, General Burgoyne—turned history into romance. The story is retold graphically in the museum and restorations at Fort Ticonderoga and in the Adirondack Museum at Blue Mountain Lake.

The interior of the Adirondacks has a shorter history. Indians had no permanent settlements in it. The Mohawks of the Six Nations and the Algonkians of Canada were rival claimants but used it only as a hunting ground. It was without a generally accepted name until 1838, when a state surveyor proposed "Adirondacks," usually translated as "tree-eaters"—an insulting name used by the provident Iroquois for their backwoods neighbors north of the mountains. Some lasting white settlements were founded on the fringes of the region shortly after the Revolution, and the interior was thinly settled 30 to 70 years later. Early settlers were mostly Vermonters. Irish immigrants from Canada and French Canadians were drawn by the logging camps.

The report of the first ascent of Mount Marcy in 1837 drew a trickle of tourists that swelled to great numbers by 1875. The unregulated traffic of tourists and developers threatened to spoil the woods and deplete the wildlife. An alliance of conservationists gathered "to save the Adirondacks." It has remained vigilant. Designated a national historical monument in 1964, the Adirondacks are a link with America's past as well as a vast playground.

PAUL F. JAMIESON
Editor of "The Adirondack Reader"

ADJECTIVE, aj'ik-tiv, the name in grammar for a word used chiefly to modify a noun. The word derives from the Latin *adjectivus* ("added," "supplemental"). The adjective has been a feature of English and of all related languages as far back as they can be traced or reconstructed, but grammarians disagree about how the term should be defined and which words are adjectives.

Traditional Grammar. Traditional grammar, even that used for the analysis of English, is largely based on classical Latin. In "school grammar," the simplified version of traditional grammar, the adjective is usually defined as "a word used to modify (that is, to qualify, limit, or restrict) a noun or pronoun." An adjective that qualifies a noun usually occurs either in the predicative position, where it follows a linking verb of which the noun is the subject (That hat is *green.* Those men seem *jolly.*), or in the attributive position, where it stands next to and usually before the noun (the *green* hat; a *jolly* fellow). It can qualify a pronoun only in the predicative position (We are *sleepy.*). In this position it is called a predicate adjective and is a type of subjective complement.

Adjectives that qualify nouns and pronouns in these ways are called descriptive adjectives, answering the question "What kind?" Adjectives that limit or restrict form a much smaller group, called limiting adjectives; they answer the questions "How many?" "Which ones?" "Whose?" and "How much?" They are chiefly the articles *a, an,* and *the;* the possessives, such as *my* and *your;* the relatives, such as *which* in "I know *which* road to take" and *what* in "I know *what* kind it is"; the interrogatives, such as *what* in "*What* time is it?" and *which* in "*Which* man did it?"; and the indefinites, such as *all* and *any.*

Most adjectives can be "compared," that is, used with the suffixes *-(e)r* and *-(e)st* or with *more* and *most* to form the comparative and superlative degrees. The suffixes are used with one-syllable and some two-syllable adjectives; *more* and *most* are used with some two-syllable adjectives and with all longer adjectives. The words *less* and *least* are used in "reverse comparison." Some adjectives have completely different forms when compared (*good, better, best*), and some cannot be compared because their qualities cannot be thought of in amounts and degrees (*dead, unique*).

Since the definition of the adjective in traditional grammar is based on function, words like *boat* in *boat license, up* in *the up staircase,* and *stop* in *stop sign* are called adjectives, even though they behave unlike the kinds of adjectives discussed thus far. Most school grammars ignore such nonadjective modifiers, while others ignore their own functional definitions and call them "nouns (or adverbs or verbs) used as adjectives."

Structural Grammar. In the 1930s defects in traditional grammar led a number of U.S. linguistic scientists to devise a kind of analysis called structural grammar. Structural linguists define the parts of speech, or "form classes," according to the regular differences of form among types of words. In this grammar, adjectives are words that have the regular pattern of change (inflectional pattern) exemplified by *high, higher, highest.* Since some adverbs also have this pattern, the adjective class must be further limited to such words that can also form adverbs with the suffix *-ly* and nouns with the suffix *-ness.* Thus, the word *soon,* although it may take the comparative and superlative suffixes (soon*er,* soon*est*), is not an adjective because there are no words *soonly* or *soonness.* Other adjectives are definitely identified by special suffixes such as *-less* (*hopeless*), *-ary* (*solitary*), *-ial* (*bestial*), *-ous* (*dangerous*), and *-ile* (*fragile*). Yet such a strict morphological definition excludes most of the words traditionally called adjectives, the hundreds of words such as *absurd, candid, earnest,* and *proper* that are compared using *more* and *most,* lack the characteristic adjective suffixes and yet are undeniably related to the pure adjectives in their modifying function.

Structuralists generally account for these words in one of two ways. Some use a purely positional (syntactic) definition, setting up "test frames":

a —— door;
The door seems ——;
This door is very ——.

Any word (such as *small*) that fits all the blanks is an adjective. Other structuralists adhere to the strict morphological definition, calling all other words that fit such test frames "adjectivals."

Finally, in structural grammar the modifying of nouns is not a role limited to adjectives, nor is this function used to define them. *Boat* in *boat license* is a noun; *up* in *the up staircase* is an adverb; and *stop* in *stop sign* is a verb—all so designated by their form-class characteristics.

Generative Grammar. In this school of grammar, the adjective is "defined" by listing words that can replace the symbol *Adj* in a string of symbols representing the structure of every grammatically normal sentence. In clarifying the processes underlying noun modification, some interesting subclasses of adjectives have been revealed. For example, adjectives that describe inherent properties differ from those describing temporary states not only in meaning but syntactically; the latter cannot be followed by adverbs of place.

ROBERT L. CHAPMAN*, *Drew University*

Bibliography: Chomsky, Noam Avram, *The Logical Structure of Linguistic Theory* (1975; reprint, Univ. of Chicago Press 1985); **Ferris, D. Connor,** *The Meaning of Syntax : A Study in the Adjectives of English* (Longman 1993); **Rusiecki, Jan,** *Adjectives and Comparison in English: A Semantic Study* (Longman 1985).

ADJOINING LANDOWNERS, ə-join'ing lan'dō-nərz, a term used in law. Adjoining landowners owe certain duties to each other. In general, they are required by law to use their land reasonably in order to avoid injury to each other. Keeping on one's own side of the boundary line is one of the more obvious duties. Encroachment by buildings or other structures is a legal wrong, which in some cases must be compensated for by damages and in others can be remedied by injunction to compel removal, or by removal without legal proceedings. (See ABATEMENT.) Landowners do not usually incur liability for the escape of various substances, such as water, from their land onto their neighbor's unless they have been negligent.

A landowner must refrain from removing earth to such an extent as to cause shifting of a neighbor's soil in its natural state. This is known as the duty to give "lateral support." There is no absolute duty to supply support when the lateral pressure has been increased by buildings, but only a duty to excavate with reasonable care.

The owner of underlying strata of the earth or of the lower floors of a building owes an absolute duty of "subjacent support" to the owner of the surface or of the upper floors. Since the duty is absolute, the absence of negligence will not excuse its violation.

RICHARD L. HIRSHBERG, *Attorney at Law*

ADJOURNMENT, ə-jûrn′mənt, a suspension of the business of a court or legislative body for a specified or an indefinite time. A term of court is the period of time prescribed by statute or authorized by a public official for holding sessions of the court. The act by which a term is ended is referred to as final adjournment. A "temporary adjournment" is an intermission from one day to another day within the same term. The latter type of adjournment may serve either as a mere recess in the sessions of the court or as a device for extending the term for the completion of unfinished business.

ADJUDICATION, ə-jōōd-i-kā′shən, in law, the rendering of judgment or determination in a judicial proceeding. It is a conclusion of law reached by a court or administrative agency after hearing the arguments and receiving the evidence submitted by interested parties on the factual issues involved. The term is applied also to the entry of a decree by a court in respect to the parties in a case. In federal administrative procedure, adjudication means the process used by an administrative agency for the formulation of an order. In bankruptcy law, adjudication means a decree that a person is a bankrupt.

ADJUSTMENT, ə-just′mənt, in insurance, a settlement or arrangement that ascertains the amount of a loss covered by insurance, as in a fire. An adjustment also may be the apportioning of a loss among those liable to pay for it. For an adjustment to be binding it must be intended and understood by the parties to be absolute and final. If an adjustment is made through the fraudulent conduct of one party, it will not bind the other party. Likewise, if one party is led into a material mistake of fact by fault of the other, the adjustment will not bind him or her.

ADJUTANT, aj′ə-tənt, the common name for a species of stork (*Leptoptilos dubius*) found from northern India to Java and Borneo. Also known as the greater adjutant stork, it is about 5 to 7 feet (1.5 to 2.1 meters) in height and is identified by a head and neck bare of feathers; a large bill; dirty black, gray, and white plumage; and a 15-inch (38-cm) air pouch hanging from its cheek. The greater adjutant stork's name is a reference to its military-like gait.

The adjutant stork is common in northern India in the summer, where it lives singly or in flocks on the outskirts of villages. It feeds on carrion and on small aquatic animals, such as frogs, fish, and reptiles. Its flight is heavy and noisy, but it lacks a voice. Its nest is a very large structure built on either a pinnacle or a lofty tree. Generally in the period between October and December, the female lays three or four white eggs.

The adjutant stork is a member of the stork family, Ciconiidae, in the order Ciconiiformes, class Aves. The lesser adjutant stork (*L. javanicus*) is smaller and lacks the cheek pouch. It is found in wooded areas from central India to south China.

ADJUTANT, aj′ə-tənt, a military staff officer, the right-hand man to the commanding officer of a brigade, battalion, post, camp, or station. He or she usually holds the rank of lieutenant or captain, but a post adjutant is often a major. Most routine contact with the commanding officer is made through the adjutant. The adjutant is responsible for administration of personnel, supervision of quarters, and preparation, distribution, and posting of all official correspondence, orders, reports, and records. The adjutant of a brigade or battalion is assisted by an officer directly responsible for personnel and administration.

ADJUTANT GENERAL, aj′ə-tənt, an army staff officer, primarily responsible for the administration of personnel and other records, for the authentication, publication, and distribution of orders, and for providing general administrative services.

The office of adjutant general in the U.S. Army had its origin in a resolution of the Continental Congress, adopted on June 16, 1775. Today, the adjutant general is the chief of the Adjutant General's Corps—the administrative service of the army—and in this capacity is both a member of the army staff in the Department of the Army and the commander of troops, activities, and installations assigned to his or her command. In assistance are a number of adjutants general who are officers of the Adjutant General's Corps.

The adjutant general provides military personnel management and administrative services for the army. Among the adjutant general's duties are the procurement, classification, career management, assignment, promotion, and retirement and separation of military personnel; casualty reporting; personnel research; disciplinary custody; statistical and strength accounting; and special services (recreational) activities. He or she also provides administrative services for the Department of Defense and for the navy and air forces, as assigned.

ADLER, Alfred, äd′lər (1870–1937), Austrian psychiatrist who was the founder of what became known as individual psychology. Born in Vienna on Feb. 7, 1870, he began his medical career as an ophthalmologist but turned to psychiatry. Sigmund Freud appointed him chairman of the group of psychoanalysts in Vienna, but Adler broke away in 1911 to found the Society for Free Psychoanalytic Research, later renamed the Society of Individual Psychology.

His secession incurred the anger of Freud, but Adler was successful in establishing points of view that attracted an increasing amount of attention. He disagreed with the great emphasis that Freud placed on sexual conflicts as a cause of mental illness and instead emphasized the role of organ inferiorities as determinants of the structure of personality. In his view, an attitude of inferiority develops when an individual feels deficient in comparison with others. Adler postulated a basic striving for superiority or self-assertion, which leads one who feels inferior to seek to compensate.

For some years Adler was a popular lecturer and teacher in the United States, where his views were applied in education and social work. He died in Aberdeen, Scotland, on May 28, 1937.

Adler's writings include *The Neurotic Constitution* (1912; Eng. trans. 1917); *The Practice and Theory of Individual Psychology* (1920; Eng. trans. 1927); *Understanding Human Nature* (1927; Eng. trans. 1927); and *Social Interest* (1933; Eng. trans. 1938). (See also INDIVIDUAL PSYCHOLOGY.)

PHILIP L. HARRIMAN*, *Susquehanna University*

ADLER, Cyrus, ad′lər (1863–1940), American educator prominent in Jewish cultural affairs. He was born in Van Buren, Ark., on Sept. 13, 1863. Educated at the University of Pennsylvania and Johns Hopkins University, he later taught at Johns Hopkins and served as librarian of the Smithsonian Institution.

Adler edited the *American Jewish Year Book* (1899–1906), served on the editorial board of the *Jewish Encyclopedia* (1899–1905), and (until 1916 with Solomon Schechter) edited the *Jewish Quarterly Review* (1910–1940). He was a founder (1892) and president (1898–1922) of the American Jewish Historical Society. He directed a translation of the Old Testament into English.

Adler was president of Dropsie College in Philadelphia (1908–1940) and succeeded Schechter as president of the Jewish Theological Seminary in New York (1924–1940). He was a founder (1906) and president (1929–1940) of the American Jewish Committee. A religious Conservative, Adler served as president of the United Synagogue of America (1914–1918). He died in Philadelphia on April 7, 1940.

ADLER, Felix, ad′lər (1851–1933), German-born American educator, reformer, author, and founder of the Ethical Culture movement. Born in Alzey, Germany, on Aug. 13, 1851, he emigrated with his family to the United States in 1857. He graduated from Columbia College in 1870. Adler went to Germany to study for the rabbinate but abandoned theology for secular philosophy, taking a Ph.D. at Heidelberg in 1873. After teaching Hebrew and Oriental literature at Cornell University, he moved to New York City, where in 1876 he founded the Society for Ethical Culture.

Under his direction, the society emphasized "deed rather than creed" and applied itself to education and social reform. Adler set up the first free kindergarten in New York, founded the Child Study Association, and was chairman of the National Child Labor Committee (1904–1921). After 1902 he was professor of ethics at Columbia. He died in New York on April 24, 1933. Adler's most noted books include *The Essentials of Spirituality* (1905), *An Ethical Philosophy of Life* (1918), and *The Reconstruction of the Spiritual Ideal* (1924).

ADLER, Friedrich, äd′lər (1827–1908), German architect who was an authority on ancient and medieval architecture and took part in the excavations at Olympia, Greece. He was born in Berlin on Oct. 15, 1827, and studied at the Berlin Architectural Academy, after which he began to travel extensively. In 1863 he was appointed professor at the Berlin Academy, and from 1877 until he retired in 1903 he was consulting architect to the Prussian minister of public works. He died in Berlin on Sept. 15, 1908.

ADLER, George J., ad′lər (1821–1868), German-born American philologist. Adler was born in Leipzig, Germany, in 1821 and went to New York City in 1833. He graduated from New York University in 1844, where from 1846 until 1854 he was professor of German. Adler's *German-English Dictionary,* notable for its careful discrimination of synonyms, appeared in 1848, followed by *German Grammar* and *Wilhelm von Humboldt's Linguistic Studies* in 1868. Adler translated Claude Fauriel's *Histoire de la poésie provençale* (1846)

as *History of Provençal Poetry* (1860). Adler died in New York City on Aug. 24, 1868.

ADLER, Hermann, ad′lər (1839–1911), Jewish religious leader in England. Adler was born in Hannover (now in Germany) on May 30, 1839. In 1891 he succeeded his father, Nathan Marcus Adler, as Britain's chief rabbi, representing his own Orthodox community but also Reform and Sephardic Jews. A supporter of the nonpolitical Ḥovevei Zion movement, he opposed Theodor Herzl's political Zionism. He died in London on July 18, 1911.

ADLER, Julius Ochs, ad′lər (1892–1955), American newspaper executive. Born in Chattanooga, Tenn., on Dec. 3, 1892, he was a nephew of Adolph Ochs, publisher of the *New York Times* and the *Chattanooga Times.* Adler joined the staff of the *New York Times* in 1914, after graduating from Princeton University, and managed the paper's business affairs from 1919 to 1935. From 1935 he was general manager of the *New York Times* and publisher of the *Chattanooga Times.*

Adler served in the U.S. Army during World Wars I and II, attaining brigadier general rank in 1941 and major general (in the reserve) in 1948. He died in New York City on Oct. 3, 1955.

ADLER, Larry, ad′lər (1914–2001), American instrumentalist who raised the harmonica to the level of a concert instrument. Lawrence Cecil Adler was born in Baltimore on Feb. 10, 1914. After briefly studying piano at Baltimore's Peabody Conservatory of Music, he left home at the age of 14. He played harmonica on the streets of New York City and soon found work performing there.

In 1934 Adler made his film debut in *Many Happy Returns,* and a performance that year at New York's Paramount theater led to a role in the London production *Streamline.* Despite becoming a star in Britain, he returned home to appear in clubs and films. In 1941 he and dancer Paul Draper began giving joint recitals, and in 1948 the two, who had supported the Hollywood writers called before the House Un-American Activities Committee, were blacklisted as communist sympathizers. Unable to find work at home, by the early 1950s Adler had settled in London.

Adler's playing was marked by superb musicianship, sensitivity, and richness of tonal coloring. In 1939 he debuted as a soloist with the Symphony Orchestra of Sydney, later appearing with the world's major orchestras. He also provided the sound track music for several films. In 1959 he returned to the United States to perform and thereafter concertized regularly there. The author of several books, including *It Ain't Necessarily So: An Autobiography* (1984; 1st U.S. ed., 1987), Adler died in London on Aug. 6, 2001.

ADLER, Mortimer Jerome, ad′lər (1902–2001), American philosopher, editor, educator, and best-known spokesman for a liberal education chiefly founded in the reading and discussion of the classics of the Western tradition. To this end, under the auspices of the *Encyclopedia Britannica* and in association with Robert Maynard Hutchins, he helped edit and publish the 54-volume *Great Books of the Western World* (1952). Later he extended his prescriptions for education from the college and adult level to that of the secondary and even primary school in two books, *The Paideia Proposal* (1982) and *The Paideia Program: An Educa-*

tional Syllabus (1984). The author of works on ethics, politics, metaphysics, theology, and law as well as education, he described himself as an "enlightened Aristotelian."

Born on Dec. 29, 1902, in New York City, Adler attended Columbia University (Ph.D., 1928). In 1930 he became associate professor of philosophy at the University of Chicago and joined Hutchins, the university's new president, in an ambitious reorganization of undergraduate education. His *Dialectic* (1927), an approach to reading great philosophers of the past as though they were contemporaries, and *The Nature of Judicial Proof; An Inquiry into the Logical, Legal, and Empirical Aspects of the Law of Evidence* (1931), written with Jerome Michael, display the parameters of his intellectual life. In 1952 Adler became director of the Institute for Philosophical Research, first in San Francisco and then in Chicago. Adler and Hutchins edited *Gateway to the Great Books* in ten volumes (1963). In 1969 Adler became director of planning for *Encyclopedia Britannica*'s 15th edition; he chaired the *Britannica*'s board of editors from 1974 until 1995. Adler died in San Mateo, Calif., on June 28, 2001. The fullest working out of his views on liberal education exists in the four-year Great Books program at St. John's College, in Annapolis, Md., and Santa Fe, N.Mex.

Bibliography: Smith, Winfree, *A Search for the Liberal College: The Beginnings of the St. John's Program* (St. John's College Press 1983).

ADLER, Stella, ad′lər (1901–1992), American actress, director, and teacher of acting whose disciplined, demanding training inspired several generations of actors. Adler was born in Manhattan, N.Y., on Feb. 10, 1901, to Jacob and Sarah Adler, Russian-immigrant tragedians preeminent in Yiddish theater. All six Adler children became actors, with Stella debuting in 1906 in her father's production of *Broken Hearts*. She appeared in nearly 200 plays at home and abroad, including *The House of Connelly* (1931), *Success Story* (1932), and Clifford Odets's *Awake and Sing!* (1935). She directed many stage productions, notably an acclaimed European tour of Odets's *Golden Boy* in 1938–1939, and she acted in three films (her 1938 debut, *Love on Toast*, billed her as "Stella Ardler").

In the mid-1920s Adler studied at the American Laboratory Theatre school, where she was first exposed to the revolutionary Stanislavsky system of acting. In 1931 she joined the Group Theatre, two of whose founders were Harold Clurman (second of her three husbands) and Lee Strasberg, later a rival teacher. In 1934 Adler studied with Konstantin Stanislavsky in Paris, and on her return home she advocated—and advanced, through teaching—the Russian master's revised technique, wherein imagination, not emotion memory, was the key to successful acting. Adler advised students not to use their "conscious past" to create a character but their creative imagination to "create" a past belonging to that character. She emphasized more externalized methods, such as physical and vocal techniques, dependence on a playwright's text, and knowledge of historical periods, and decried Strasberg's "Method," which stressed emotion and "affective memory."

A tall, passionate woman of aristocratic mien and guarded praise, Adler was a scholarly, dedicated teacher. In 1949 she founded the Stella Adler Theatre School, later the Stella Adler Conservatory of Acting, in Manhattan, whose students have included Marlon Brando and Robert De Niro. She also taught at the New School for Social Research, Yale University, and New York University. In 1988 her book, *The Technique of Acting*, was published. Adler died in Los Angeles on Dec. 21, 1992.

Bibliography: Kissel, Howard, ed., *Stella Adler: The Art of Acting* (Applause Bks. 2000); Paris, Barry, ed., *Stella Adler on Ibsen, Strindberg, and Chekhov* (Knopf 1999).

ADMINISTRATION, əd-min-ə-strā′shən, the management of executive affairs. The term also denotes the group of managers and the period of their management.

In law, administration is the management, under the jurisdiction of a court, of the estate of anyone dying intestate or without an executor. The administrator is empowered to make an inventory of the estate, collect accounts due, pay all debts, and distribute the remainder of the estate to the heirs.

In its broadest sense, as synonymous with management, administration conveys the idea of group cooperation under executive direction, seeking fulfillment of goals through planning and organization. Developing nations often suffer more from a lack of management skills than from a scarcity of raw materials.

In the United States, scientific management began in the early 1900s. As it developed, it gave rise to professional specializations in such fields as organization and efficiency, budgeting and planning, personnel management, cybernetics, and decision making. More recently it has been extended to include long-range business and public policymaking concerned with the structure and growth of the entire economy.

As society becomes more and more institutionalized, management and executive leadership play an increasing role. Hence the frequent use of such terms as *administered society, administrative state,* and *administered prices.* In business, government, hospitals, universities, and even ecclesiastical affairs, administration is a professional occupation with specialized training and codes of ethics. Standards are set by groups such as the American Management Association and the American Society of Public Administration and by organizations specific to certain professions. The need for these organizations becomes especially clear as professionals in their respective disicplines become administrators without adequate prior training in the art and science of administration.

Comparative administration seeks to find what is universal and basic in diverse fields of management. As corporate size and technology increase, business management and public administration tend progressively to resemble each other. The distinction virtually disappears in such new fields as administration of government corporations.

In recent years, administration, as a profession and social resource, has grown rapidly both in the public and private sectors. At the same time, there is a danger that administration will become too mechanical and neglect human needs. If consumer freedom, democratic participation, and individual enterprise are to be protected within institutions, management will have to combine the insight of the philosopher and humanist with the highest degree of technical competence.

MARSHALL E. DIMOCK
Professor Emeritus, New York University

ADMINISTRATIVE LAW, əd-min′ə-strāt-iv lô, is the branch of law that limits government officials and agencies in their relationships with private persons and groups. The term is customarily restricted to laws delimiting the powers of officials and agencies and is not applied to the mass of particular technical rules and regulations that are issued by agencies such as the Federal Communications Commission in the United States.

Origins and Development. The term came into general use in the United States only in the 1930's, although administrative law itself is concerned with ancient legal problems. Establishing limits on the powers of government officials has been a pervasive concern of Anglo-American law since the time of Magna Carta. Nevertheless, a strong tradition has opposed classifying the rules governing officialdom into a separate category, and this is why the term "administrative law" is often thought of as a 20th century improvisation.

Opposition to the "administrative law" label both in England and in the United States is explainable in terms of two historical phenomena. The legislative triumph over the monarchy that ended the constitutional struggles of 17th century England had the effect of putting the crown "under the law" and consequently of generating the notion that all were alike under the law—commoner, nobleman, and official. To suggest that the law relating to government officials was in any way different from ordinary law was to imply opposition to the hard-won limitations on the royal prerogatives.

In the second place, 19th century France, in contrast to Britain and the United States, had developed a special body of rules and principles to govern its officials (*droit administratif*). Some eminent Anglo-American scholars, examining the French experience, found the Anglo-American approach to control of public officials to be superior. Although these criticisms of the French *droit administratif* were misleading and unjustified, they were so widely circulated and influential that the term "administrative law" came to be regarded with deep suspicion in both Britain and the United States.

Nevertheless, as far back as 1893 the pressing claims for recognition of the field were noted in the United States by Frank Goodnow's perceptive book *Comparative Administrative Law.* Other scholars followed Goodnow's lead, and the legitimacy of their concern was amply fulfilled in the first quarter of the 20th century. Land-use controls, utility and transportation regulation, banking regulation, and regulation of business practices—all by administrative agencies—had become established and accepted. However, the terms "administrative law" and "administrative agency" did not come in general use in the United States until the 1930's. The heated national debate over administrative law generated by the New Deal provided valuable reports and studies and laid the foundation for the Federal Administrative Procedure Act of 1946.

Following World War II, opposition in the United States and Britain to the concept of "administrative law" abated, and by 1950 almost every law school offered it as a regular course. During this same period the standard legal encyclopedias and digests began to list administrative law as a special subject or digest topic.

Functions and Safeguards. The best-known United States administrative agencies are the in-

dependent regulatory commissions created by Congress at different times: Interstate Commerce Commission (1887); Federal Trade Commission (1915); Federal Power Commission (1920); Federal Communications Commission (1934); Securities and Exchange Commission (1934); National Labor Relations Board (1935); Civil Aeronautics Board (1938); and Atomic Energy Commission (1946). Typical state agencies are public utilities commissions, workmen's compensation boards, tax commissions, and zoning boards.

Almost all of these agencies get their powers from a statute. For example, the U.S. Congress cannot fairly determine once and for all just who is entitled to operate broadcasting facilities. It had to create the Federal Communications Commission to do this. The extent of power granted by legislation creating such administrative bodies, and the implicit limitations on such power, form a part of administrative law. During the 1930's the U.S. Supreme Court invalidated two New Deal programs on the ground that Congress had delegated power to the point of abdication. However, this is not likely to recur if the congressional delegation of power appears necessary to secure congressional objectives.

Most of the objections to the administrative action today relate to improper procedures, as when a public utilities commission uses improper evidence. Both federal and state constitutions have been interpreted as imposing minimum procedural requirements on administrative agencies, but additional safeguards have been imposed through administrative procedure acts.

While courts are the principal checks on administrative agencies, the courts regard their functions as limited. The propriety of judicial intervention depends upon the type of administrative action involved, the legislative intention as to the scope of review, and whether the irregularity is within the judicial competence.

Other checks and balances can be found in the congressional power of the purse or committee investigation and, in Britain, through parliamentary questioning of the responsible minister. Special commissions—such as the Hoover Commission and the Attorney General's Committee in the United States, and the Lord Chancellor's Commission and the Franks Committee in Britain —have invoked the restraint of publicity.

Serious consideration has been given to the establishment of institutional checks and balances apart from the courts. The idea of a permanent "watchdog," modeled on the Swedish *ombudsman,* who would be charged with handling complaints about the administrative process, has aroused some enthusiasm. The U.S. Congress established an administrative conference, with a permanent chairman, to develop new procedures and methods that will better secure private rights without impairing the efficiency of administrative agencies.

All observers agree that the United States has turned a corner and that the administrative agency is a permanent feature of government. Administrative law not only has been accepted as a special field of law, but also shows signs that it may be becoming the most important branch of the law.

FREDERICK DAVIS, *University of Missouri*

Further Reading: Cane, Peter, *An Introduction to Administrative Law* (Oxford 1986); Harlowe, Carole, and Rawlings, Richard, *Law and Administration* (Rothman 1984); Modjeska, Lee, *Administrative Law: Practice and Procedure* (Lawyers Co-op 1982).

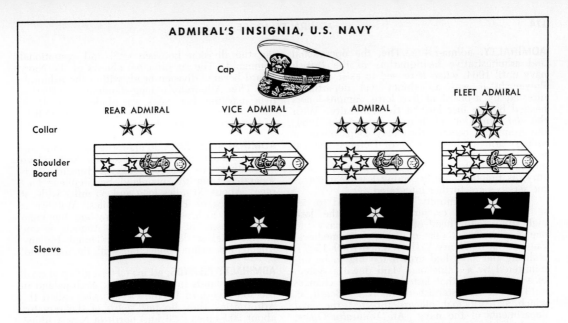

ADMIRAL'S INSIGNIA, U.S. NAVY

Cap

	REAR ADMIRAL	VICE ADMIRAL	ADMIRAL	FLEET ADMIRAL
Collar	★★	★★★	★★★★	

Shoulder Board

Sleeve

ADMIRAL, ad'mə-rəl, is the collective term designating naval officers who command fleets or their major subdivisions. The regular grades in most navies are *rear admiral, vice admiral,* and *admiral,* corresponding to *major general, lieutenant general,* and *general* in most armies. Admirals generally command task fleets; vice admirals, task forces; and rear admirals, task groups or units.

Rank in most navies is symbolized by gold stripes on the sleeves of blue uniforms. A rear admiral wears a two-inch stripe and a single half-inch stripe; another half-inch stripe is added for each higher grade. In the United States the terms *two-, three-,* and *four-star admiral* refer to the number of silver stars on the shoulder boards or pin-on insignia. A rear admiral wears two stars.

Admirals are also known as *flag officers,* because an admiral's presence is indicated by a personal flag from a mast of the ship in which he is embarked, or from some similarly suitable place if his duty is ashore. The flag of a line officer bears two to four white stars on a blue field; the flag of a staff corps officer bears blue stars on a white field.

History. The word "admiral" is Arabic in derivation. It was first used in the West, to denote a naval commander, about 1300, by the Knights of St. John (later, Knights of Malta). The Knights introduced the rank when they began forming a navy on Cyprus, after being driven from the Holy Land. Until the 16th century, admirals were high officials under kings, and were charged with protecting the realm from sea attack. They held political as well as military jurisdiction over coasts and contiguous seas.

The sailing warship mounting broadside guns caused a revolution in warfare in the late 16th century, creating both the professional navy and the modern concept of sea power. In the 1600's and 1700's and the early 1800's, fleets composed of ships of the line were employed for battle in column ("line ahead"), the formation in which the guns were most effective and in which admirals could maintain control of the action. The commanding admiral normally placed his flagship near the center; the vice admiral, second in command, took position in the lead; while the rear admiral sailed at the end of the line where he could discourage straggling and be in the lead should course be reversed, a frequent maneuver in naval warfare.

United States. Because of early American prejudice against monarchic forms, no admirals of any grade were commissioned until 1862. Captains commanding squadrons had the honorary title of commodore. John Paul Jones, the best known American naval officer in the Revolutionary War, was never an admiral in the Continental Navy, but after the war he was an admiral in the Russian Navy.

The law of July 16, 1862, authorized nine rear admirals. David G. Farragut was the senior. In 1864 he was promoted to vice admiral and in 1866 to admiral, with David D. Porter becoming vice admiral. On Farragut's death in 1870, Porter was made admiral and Stephen C. Rowan vice admiral. Both offices were abolished with the death of these men. Franklin Buchanan was the only Confederate admiral. After the Spanish-American War the grade of *admiral of the navy* was created by special act of Congress to honor George Dewey.

During World War II, four U.S. (5-star) *fleet admirals* were commissioned: William D. Leahy, Ernest J. King, Chester W. Nimitz, and William F. Halsey. This step was taken not only to recognize their services and responsibilities, but also for protocol, since the corresponding British rank was *admiral of the fleet.*

Great Britain. Britain's most renowned admiral was Horatio Nelson, who defeated Napoleon's fleets at the battles of the Nile (1798) and Trafalger (1805). Also famous was Sir Francis Drake, although against the Spanish Armada in 1588 he was vice admiral under Charles, Lord Howard of Effingham, Lord High Admiral. Another notable British admiral was Edward Hawke, who defeated a French invasion fleet at Quiberon Bay (1759) in the Seven Years' War.

Britain's first admiral was Robert Blake (1599–1657), one of Oliver Cromwell's generals who did not board a warship until he was 50 years old. Blake in large measure created the naval profession, independent of soldier and mariner but a combination of both. He also initiated modern naval strategy, having been the first to undertake extended overseas campaigns and close-in blockade.

JOHN D. HAYES, *Rear Admiral, U.S. Navy, Retired*

ADMIRALTY, ad′mə-rəl-tē, **The,** the operational and administrative headquarters of the British navy until 1964, when it ceased to exist as such. Previously it was a cabinet-level department directed by a board of five lords commissioners headed by the first lord of the admiralty. With the reorganization of British defense in 1964, the Admiralty became the Navy Department, a military arm of the Ministry of Defence coequal with the Army and Air departments. Although an Admiralty Board still exists within the ministry, its functions are becoming less clear cut as the services are further integrated.

The term "admiralty" was first used to describe the office, or jurisdiction, of the lord high admiral, the head of the English navy and one of nine "great officers of state" in medieval England. King Henry VIII (reigned 1509–1547), realizing the navy had grown too big to be administered by a single man, laid down a system of administration that lasted with minor changes until 1964. He established the *Navy Board,* in which six principal officers directed the civil departments of the navy. An *Admiralty Office,* to which the Navy Board was answerable, was set up under the lord high admiral's control.

Under King Charles I (reigned 1625–1649), the Admiralty Office became an independent department of state. Charles placed the office of the lord high admiral in the hands of five lords commissioners appointed by the crown and called the *Board of Admiralty.* As the board developed, its members were given specific responsibilities, although they never were strictly heads of departments. They were jointly and coequally lords commissioners, subject to the authority of the first lord, who was directly responsible to the sovereign and Parliament. Only once after 1709, in 1827–1828, was the office not in commission.

In 1832 the first lord, Sir James Graham, brought the Navy Board into the Admiralty, ending the division between civil and operational command. The six principal officers of the Navy Board became division heads within the Admiralty. The Admiralty's long-standing jurisdiction over maritime law cases was abolished in 1873.

P.K. KEMP, O.B.E.
Lieutenant Commander, Royal Navy (Retired)

ADMIRALTY ISLAND, ad′mə-rəl-tē, is a mountainous forested island in the Alexander Archipelago of southeastern Alaska, south of Juneau. It is separated from the mainland by Stephens Passage. About 90 miles long and 35 miles wide, it has an area of 1,664 square miles. Wildlife is abundant. Fishing and lumbering are the main occupations. The largest town, Angoon, is one of the chief settlements of the Tlingit Indians. Angoon has airline connections with the mainland.

ADMIRALTY ISLANDS, ad′mə-rəl-tē, a group of small volcanic islands in the Bismarck Archipelago in the southwestern Pacific Ocean. Also called the Admiralties, they lie just south of the equator, about 200 miles (320 km) north of New Guinea, and are part of the Manus district of the Independent State of Papua. The total area of the islands is about 800 square miles (2,070 sq km). The chief products are copra and pearls.

Manus, the only large island, is about 50 miles (80 km) long and 20 miles (30 km) wide, with an area of about 600 square miles (1,555 sq km). The island is surrounded by approximately 16 smaller islands and a number of low, sandy coral atolls. Manus is largely covered with jungle, with mountains rising to 3,000 feet (915 meters). It has small but serviceable harbors. Lorengau, on the east coast, is the main town and administrative center of the islands.

The islands were discovered by a Dutch navigator, Willem Schouten, in 1616, but Englishmen were the first Europeans to land. In 1884 the island group was annexed by Germany, remaining a German protectorate until occupied by Australia in 1914. Following World War I, Australia administered the islands for the League of Nations as part of the mandated Territory of New Guinea. Japan seized the islands in 1942. Retaken by the Allies in 1944, they served as a strategic air and naval base for the duration of World War II.

After the war the Admiralty Islands reverted to Australia under a United Nations trusteeship. Papua New Guinea gained independence in 1975.

ADMIRALTY LAW. See MARITIME LAW.

ADOBE, ə-dō′bē, is sun-dried brick made from native clays, especially those made in the arid southwestern region of the United States, in Mexico, and in Central America. The clay is mixed with grass or straw, molded, and dried in the sun for a week or two. A mortar of the same material is used in construction. The word "adobe" comes from the Spanish *adobar,* meaning "to plaster."

Adobe was the earliest building material in Assyria and Egypt, and it is still used in Japan and China. Adobe houses may last for centuries if they have dry stone foundations and wide eaves, since moisture absorbed from the ground or from a defective roof is the chief cause of the crumbling of adobe walls.

Adobe clays are plastic when wet but too hard to cultivate when dry. They are lightened by plowing in sand or sandy loam.

ADOBE BRICKS, formed and sun-dried at the building site, are being built into walls at Guadalajara, Mexico.

COLVIN FROM MONKMEYER

ADOLESCENCE has many sides. One of these is growth toward an adult level of interest in world affairs. Here delegates to a conference of teenage leaders discuss "Protest: A Right and a Responsibility" at Williamsburg, Virginia.

ADOLESCENCE, ad-ə-les′əns, is that period of life during which the growing individual makes the transition from childhood to adulthood. The period is marked by what anthropologists call rites of passage. These are ceremonies or customs at major transitions, such as birth, puberty, marriage, and death. Virtually all cultures have some way of observing adolescence. For example, Australian aborigines, the Masai of Africa, and various South American Indian tribes put adolescents through an initiation that may involve fasting or other ordeals and periods of instruction in hunting and ritual. The Australian aborigines and some African peoples circumcise adolescents, and in the South Pacific tattooing has a similar significance. Among some of the Indian tribes of South America, changes in clothing and hair style mark the passage to adult rank.

In simple cultures the periods of initiation are usually short. Young men and women are needed to do adult work; hence pubescent youths are admitted to the adult world as soon as they can begin to do the work of grownups. In more complex societies, however, the period of apprenticeship between childhood and adulthood may last for years rather than months.

The American anthropologist Margaret Mead has pointed out the contrast between adolescence in the United States and in the far simpler culture of the Pacific islands. Coming of age in Samoa, as she observed it, was relatively short and simple. Samoans had one religion, followed an uncomplicated moral code with few restrictions on behavior, and put little emphasis on personal prestige and material success. The Samoan did not experience a jarring change between childhood and adulthood. Youth in the United States, on the other hand, found adult standards and demands confusing; the stresses of adolescence sometimes led to maladjustment.

The great majority of young people in complex societies grow up without becoming neurotic. Yet adolescence is a period of some stress, and the experiences of adolescence influence adult life. Hence the period has been studied intensively by psychologists, sociologists, and educators, especially in such countries as the United States, Canada, and Britain. This article summarizes some of their findings.

Duration. In complex societies, adolescence usually is said to last from the age of 12 or 13 to 21 or 22. No precise limits can be set, however, because adolescence is measured by many factors. Physically it begins at the onset of puberty, the time of life during which the reproductive organs become capable of functioning, and ends when an individual has matured sexually and has reached his full height. In terms of education and work, adolescence corresponds to the years of high school and college, high school and military service, or high school and starting a job. An individual enters adolescence as a child, still dependent on his parents for financial support and personal and social guidance. He can be called an adult when he can earn a living for himself and can make his own decisions about work, money, and social behavior. Legally a young adolescent is an infant; at 21 a person becomes a full adult in the eyes of the law.

The legal definition of adulthood illustrates the fact that society has held confusing views of adolescence. Until 1971 young men and women under the age of 21 were not eligible to vote in most states in the United States. Yet young men could be conscripted for military service at 18, and young men and women could marry and start raising families at 18 or earlier. Adults frequently exhort young people to grow up. To help students mature, educators have introduced high school subjects in the elementary and middle grades. Parents give children more freedom than was allowed to earlier generations. Thus children may enter educational and social adolescence before they are 12, and there are some pressures to hurry them to grown-up status. On the other hand, there are pressures to extend adolescence well into the 20's. Some educators advise that compulsory schooling continue through 14 grades. Many students have to stay in college for 5, 7, or more years before they are equipped to start their careers.

Because of such factors, the length and the nature of adolescence vary for different individuals and different circumstances. For example, children of poor families may have to start adult-level jobs while they are still in their teens. Children of more prosperous families tend to stay in school and college longer. In time of war, boys of 17 are considered fit to work and fight as men. In peacetime, 17-year-olds are told that their place is in school.

As these examples suggest, there is no standard pattern for adolescence, even within one country. However, certain changes take place in all adolescents, and certain problems interest most adolescents and their parents and teachers.

Physical Changes. All adolescents experience physical changes. In fact, puberty is used to define the start of adolescence. In the male it is difficult to determine the onset of puberty, but roughly this is the time when the boy begins to need an occasional shave, his voice begins to deepen, and the sex organs mature. On the average, such characteristics develop in boys at about 14½ years of age. However, these changes may appear over a range from about 12 years to about 18 years.

Boys tend to have a spurt in growth at about age 13. Again there are great individual differences, the ages ranging from 10 to 14. Those boys in whom the spurt occurs late often feel a serious, though unwarranted, anxiety that they will never be real men. Boys who have an early growth spurt and sexual development do have the temporary social advantage of maturing at about the same time as girls of their age.

Usually the menarche (the start of menstruation) is considered as indicating the onset of puberty in girls. On the average, the menarche occurs at 13, but the age may range from 10 to 18. Enlargement of the breasts is one of the earliest criteria of maturation in girls. In most girls this development begins before the first menstrual period.

In girls there tends to be a spurt in growth at about 11. However, within the normal range this spurt may occur as early as the latter part of the 8th year or as late as the latter part of the 11th year. From the age of 11 to 13 or 14, girls are often taller and heavier than boys of their age. This is a normal condition, but it may cause unhappiness for the girl.

Intellectual Changes. Physical growth is the most obvious sign of adolescence, but intellectual development is also a major factor. Psychologists have developed various tests to measure general intellectual ability. This kind of ability, as reflected by scores on such tests, continues to increase until about age 20 or slightly older. The rate of change tends to slow down as the individual approaches the close of the adolescent period. This does not mean that a person grinds to an intellectual standstill as he reaches adulthood. The reason for the slowdown is that most tests, as used in schools, are not adequate for measuring adult intellectual activities.

During early adolescence, girls show a slight superiority over boys in terms of intelligence test scores. This is to be understood partly in terms of their earlier maturation and partly in terms of the fact that most tests are highly verbal in content. Girls make consistently higher scores on test items that measure knowledge and skills in such areas as vocabulary, language usage, and analogies, whereas boys tend to be superior in items involving spatial relations and mechanical abilities.

Intelligence tests are of great value to the trained counselor. Unfortunately, they can be a source of worry to adolescents and their parents, who often place more faith in a single test score than is justified. If an adolescent suspects that he has a rather low score he may feel that he will not be able to succeed in adult life. He will have less cause to worry if he remembers that many jobs require abilities other than those measured by the usual intelligence tests. The boy or girl with high scores on such tests may well plan for college and graduate school training and for executive or professional life work. Curiously enough, adolescents who are exceptionally capable often feel inferior because they compare themselves only with others who are exceptionally capable or with an almost unattainable ideal.

In addition to the increase in general intellectual ability, the adolescent years bring changes in breadth of knowledge, understanding, and judgment. There is a marked improvement in the ability to think not only in terms of the past but also in terms of the future. The adolescent becomes capable of thinking about highly complex technical processes and about national and world problems. His vocabulary increases until he can hold his own not only with his peers but also in communication with adults.

Many educators believe that high school students are capable of doing more advanced work than the traditional curriculum requires. In the 1950's and 1960's many schools introduced honors courses to challenge superior students, and colleges began the practice of admitting students with advanced standing.

Emotional Changes. Emotions are, of course, important throughout life, but during adolescence some emotional states seem to reach a new intensity. Affection, aggression, and fear are especially likely to cause problems.

Such emotions are to be understood partly in terms of changing body chemistry and partly in terms of social conditions. For example, the sex hormones influence the nature and intensity of affectional behavior, but cultural factors are also at work. Television programs, movies, books, magazines, and conversations remind the adolescent of the importance of friendships and the desirability of "falling in love." To love and be loved become extremely important.

Close friendships with those of the same sex often precede, or at least are apparent before, the development of heterosexual love. Because of his feelings of uncertainty and social insecurity, the younger adolescent often derives a great deal of satisfaction from such friendships. The adolescent who has had close friendships with those of the same sex is likely to be well prepared for heterosexual friendships.

Ways of expressing anger tend to change during adolescence. The young child may show his anger by kicking, biting, hitting, or screaming. However, such behavior usually is punished, and by the time he reaches adolescence the individual may not give such direct expression to his anger. The young child is likely to become angry at objects or persons that inflict pain on him, and he probably gives immediate vent to his anger. Rather than giving immediate expression to his anger, the adolescent may "boil inside" for hours after an offending event. He then may vent on his parents and siblings the anger that actually was generated by some happening at school.

The adolescent is especially likely to be angered by what he considers unfairness and lack of consideration. Teasing often arouses anger, and the adolescent may, in turn, express his anger by teasing others. Boys often express anger through swearing, whereas girls are more likely to express anger by crying, which is socially approved for females. Anger may be expressed indirectly through violent arguing or openly by joining some group bent on destruction of property or other antisocial behavior, often called "delinquency." About two thirds of those who are delinquents in adolescence begin their undesirable behavior in preadolescence. Delinquency tends to increase during the teen years, rather slowly up to about age 15 and then rapidly up to age 19. After this there continues to be an increase in the rate of delinquent behavior, although at a slower rate, up to age 25.

The adolescent may express his rebellion by turning to drugs that give him some kind of temporary satisfaction. The use of drugs often begins in the same spirit of recklessness that characterizes the automobile driving of some adolescents. For many young people the use of drugs is only a temporary or "experimental" phase of development. There is a risk, however, that young people will be preyed on by narcotics pushers and that they will become addicts.

Anger and fear are closely related. If the individual feels that angry retaliation is useless or even dangerous to himself, he becomes fearful. Young children express fear of such things as animals, giants, robbers, kidnapers, the dark, and death. By adolescence, fears of specific physical hazards, or of real or imagined persons, have declined and tend to be replaced by worries, which are a form of fear. Adolescents worry about school work, social problems, war conditions, popularity, relations with the other sex, personal limitations, moral standards, and about preparing for and getting a job.

The small child often is "shamed" if he says he is afraid. Thus it is no wonder that by adolescence, expression of fear often is disguised. Fears may be expressed in the form of anger, as in the case of the adolescent who becomes very angry at some teacher because, basically, he is afraid of the teacher. On the other hand, fear may be expressed in the form of submissiveness and conformity. Such behavior protects the individual from social disapproval, which he fears.

Increasing Sex Interests. Some of the most discussed problems of adolescence are those that involve dating and other signs of growing sex interests. Young people worry about how to get dates and about how to behave while dating. Their parents worry about how to control adolescent behavior on dates. Dating, it may be noted, is particularly a problem in countries, such as the United States, that grant the adolescent great freedom. In many other societies courtship is regulated strictly by adult rules. Young people have less freedom—and other sources of worry.

It often is assumed that all adolescents have and enjoy dates. Statistics vary with social groups and over the years, but there is some evidence that only about half of high school freshmen and only a little over 80 percent of seniors participate in dating. Many adolescents think of a first date with shyness and even fear. Some begin dating in order to conform to group pressures rather than because they really enjoy dating. Because of their earlier biological and social maturity, girls become interested in dancing and dating before boys of their own age develop such interests. Girls, or their parents, arrange social events to which it is almost necessary to drag the boys of the same age.

During the adolescent years most individuals "fall in love" several times, although later in life they may refer to temporary affairs as infatuations rather than the "real thing." Some start at a rather early age to "go steady." "Going steady" is not a recent phenomenon, although in earlier days a different term may have been used; for example, the girl may have spoken of her "beau" rather than of her "steady." For some adolescents, going steady may be almost as serious as being engaged. For others it may mean little

THREE LIONS

MUSIC, DANCING, AND DATING are among the strong interests of adolescents, such as these young Americans.

more than a temporary agreement that dating will be limited to one person.

Biological drives obviously are significant in dating. Yet it is important to recognize that the adolescent's developing heterosexual love involves more than sexual desire. There is often a tendency to idealize the loved one. There is an almost desperate desire to be in the company of the beloved. From the point of view of an adult—but not from the point of view of the adolescent—there is often an almost ridiculous expression of tenderness and a desire to comfort and protect. There is likely to be an almost unlimited wish to share with the other party.

Increasing Independence from Parents. As the adolescent grows and his interests expand, he normally wants and gets more freedom from parental control. Psychologists use the term "emancipation" to refer to the process of outgrowing family domination. This process may be painful both for the adolescent and for the parents, although not necessarily so. It is difficult for parents to admit that they are no longer young adults with babies and that they must now relinquish some of their loving care for their offspring. It is difficult for the adolescent, with all his energy and enthusiasm, to realize that he is not completely capable of standing on his own feet.

From their point of view, adolescents have more problems with their mothers than with their fathers, and girls have more problems with both parents than do boys. On the other hand, reports indicate that both boys and girls often find that they can confide in their mothers more easily than they can confide in their fathers.

When asked what complaints they have about their parents, adolescents list such topics as the following: Parents limit our use of the car; they hound us about school marks; they pester us about table manners and other forms of etiquette; they don't like our boy or girl friends or tease us about them; they insist on checking on where parties are to be held and what is to go on at them; they make us account for money spent; they hold a brother or sister up as a model.

When parents are asked about problems related to their adolescent children, they produce lists of their own. They say, for example, that customs have changed since they were young. Economic conditions have changed so much that it is difficult to understand current spending habits. Parents worry about accidents (vital statistics and automobile insurance rates indicate that such concern is not without justification). Parents are fearful about adolescent sex behavior (statistics on illegitimate births, forced marriages, and divorces indicate that such concern may be realistic). Some parents have feelings of failure because children are not living up to the standards set for them. Parents sometimes feel rejected by their children.

As part of the process of emancipation the adolescent may experience homesickness. The young adolescent is likely to make visits and the older boy or girl may go off to college or to the armed forces. If there has been a normal and desirable emotional attachment to the home, going away may cause homesickness. This nostalgia is not in itself an indication of weakness or basic lack of independence. At least, the adolescent who leaves home and feels homesick is in better emotional health than the one who refuses to leave home for fear of homesickness. Many times, what seems to be homesickness is really an expression of dissatisfaction with the new living conditions rather than a yearning for the home that has been left behind.

Increasing Responsibility in School and College. As young people grow up, they sometimes demand—and sometimes are forced to take—more responsibility for their education. In the great majority of elementary schools the children learn to play a role that is basically submissive to adult authority. In spite of the fact that they are approaching social maturity, adolescents often find that they must continue to play the submissive role in the teacher-dominated high school. Real enthusiasm often is limited to extracurricular activities. Adolescents who are teacher-dominated throughout high school may have difficulty in adjusting to the much greater freedom they are allowed in colleges. Fortunately, many of the better high schools have a cooperative arrangement in which students and teachers share in planning the program and making the rules.

Career Planning. In some cultures everyone, child and adult, works as hard as he can. In the United States, the work of the child is usually limited to part-time help around the house, in the store, or on the farm. Yet the adult is expected to devote a large part of his time to his job and to earn enough to keep up a proper standard of living for himself and his family. In this respect, as in many others, the American adolescent has to make a transition from one pattern of life to another.

Because a job is one of the centers of an adult's life, selecting a field of work is a major decision. In the modern world this applies to girls as well as to boys. Traditionally, girls became homemakers like their mothers. It has become common, however, for married women to work. Thus vocational planning is important to all adolescents.

One problem in career planning is that a young person may believe he wants to enter a certain field but actually may have no more than a superficial interest in that kind of work. It is not easy to assess interests. Psychologists have developed tests in an attempt to measure basic vocational interests and aptitudes. Such measuring devices are valuable when used by a trained counselor. For example, test results might give a counselor grounds for suggesting areas of work to consider or to avoid. A boy who shows evidence of interest in science and of dislike for outdoor work might be advised to consider laboratory research rather than petroleum geology. No test, however, can tell the adolescent what field to enter. He has to make his own choice, using all the available evidence about himself. He can get clues from his school record, from experience in part-time work, and through study of job descriptions.

He also can get help from adults. Parents have more influence than any other individuals on the job choices of their children. The advice and example of parents can be useful guides. On the other hand, parents may set unrealistic goals for their children, perhaps insisting on a professional career because of its prestige. Parents and young people may fail to realize that qualifying for a profession may demand 7 to 10 years of undergraduate and graduate training.

Young people often are urged to make career plans early in their high school years so that they can pick their courses to fit their future jobs. However, many students change their plans after they have started college. During late adolescence and early adulthood about two thirds of Americans make some change in their career plans. Counselors advise that young people keep their plans flexible and prepare for a group of related jobs rather than for one specific occupation. Thus they will be able to adjust their goals if they find their interests have changed. Moreover, they will be able to shift to a new job if technological change makes their present skills obsolete.

All career planning for men has to allow for the possibility of military service. Changing draft quotas and reconsideration of deferment policies make it necessary for an individual to be alert to the likelihood that his education or work will have to be adjusted to fit around a period in the armed forces.

Adolescents face many problems as they take on more and more responsibility for their own education, jobs, and social behavior. Some studies of adolescence stress the problems so much that the period seems to be a series of crises. Yet it is a mistake to treat adolescence as a time of particular difficulty. The adolescent years are part of a lifelong process of change, and problems can arise at any stage of this process from the rites of passage that mark birth to those at death.

T.L. ENGLE, *Indiana University*

Bibliography

Ausubel, David P., and others, *Theory and Problems of Adolescent Development* (Prentice-Hall 1983).

Coleman, James S., and others, *The Adolescent Society: The Social Life of the Teenager and Its Impact on Education* (1961; reprint, Greenwood 1981).

Forisha, Barbara, *Experience of Adolescence: Development in Context* (Scott Foresman 1983).

Gross, Leonard H., ed., *The Parent's Guide to Teenagers* (Macmillan 1981).

Jersild, Arthur T., *Psychology of Adolescence*, 3d ed. (Macmillan 1978).

Kaplan, Louise, *Adolescence: The Farewell to Childhood* (1984; reprint, Simon & Schuster 1986).

Mahoney, Harold J., and Engle, T. L., *Points for Decision—A Guide to Help Youth Solve Their Problems* (Harcourt 1961).

Malmquist, Carl, ed., *Handbook or Adolescence* (J. Aronson 1985).

Muuss, Rolf E., *Theories of Adolescence*, 5th ed. (Random House 1988).

Sprinthall, Norman, and Collins, W. Andrew, *Development in Adolescence*, 2d ed. (Random House 1988).

ADONAIS, ad-ə-nā′is, an elegiac poem by Percy Bysshe Shelley, written in 1821 to commemorate the death of John Keats. Many critics rank it with Milton's *Lycidas* as among the best elegies in the English language. Shelley, usually a severe critic of his own work, said that *Adonais* was a "highly wrought piece of art" and the "least imperfect of my compositions."

The poem was begun in May 1821 and was finished in June, four months after Keats' death and about a year before Shelley's own death. It was first published in Pisa, Italy, in July 1821.

Adonais is written in 55 Spenserian stanzas. The first portion follows the classical lament in tone, particularly two famous Greek elegies, Bion's *Lament for Adonis* and Moschus' *Lament for Bion*. The latter portion is original in imagery and thought, and is Shelley's most eloquent expression of his philosophy of life and death.

ADONIS, ə-don′əs, in classical legend, a young man famed for his beauty and loved by Aphrodite (Venus), the goddess of love. He was born of the incestuous love of Myrrha for her father, Cinyras, king of Cyprus. An avid hunter, Adonis was killed by a wild boar. When Aphrodite pleaded for his life, Zeus agreed to allow Adonis to spend half a year in Hades and the other half on earth with her.

The legend is one version of the myth of death in winter and rebirth in spring or summer, and is the basis of fertility rites, such as the Greek women's festival Adonia, commemorating the life and death of Adonis. The Babylonian legend of Tammuz, the sun god, and the goddess Ishtar is an earlier form. Tammuz among Semitic peoples was addressed as Adonai (my lord), from which the Greek word *Adonis* is derived.

ADONIS, ə-don′əs, a genus of small annual and perennial plants found in the Mediterranean region and western Asia. It is commonly known as pheasant's eye. The adonis is an erect plant about 1 to 2 feet (0.30–0.60 meters) high, with alternately arranged leaves. The flowers, which are yellow or red, are solitary and have 5 to 16 petals; the fruits are arranged in globular or elongated heads. The common species of *Adonis* are *A. vernalis,* the yellow spring adonis; the crimson-flowered *A. aestivalis,* or summer adonis of central Europe; and *A. annua,* the autumn adonis, a deep-red flower found from central Europe to western Asia. The adonis is a member of the buttercup family, Ranunculaceae.

YELLOW SPRING ADONIS (A. vernalis)

ROCHE

ADOPTION, the practice of forming a family by bringing together children and parents who are genetically unrelated. Parents and children in adoptive families have the same rights and responsibilities as in families formed by birth, including the right to inheritance. The relationship is validated by a legal process.

Historical Practice. Adoption has historically served various cultural needs. In ancient Rome and in Asia, for example, the purpose of adoption was primarily to provide a male heir for a childless couple or individual. Sometimes adults were adopted for this purpose. Adoption was also used to provide a family with additional laborers or to provide new church members.

Informal adoption, sometimes called "kinship fostering," has been practiced throughout the world among extended family and in some relatively small societies in which some members take personal responsibility for the welfare of others in the community. The purpose is usually to provide parents for a child whose biological parents are unable to raise the child themselves. The ties to the biological parents are never legally severed. The child may have contact with the biological parents but is treated as a full and equal member of the adoptive family. In some places, such as Oceania, kinship fostering approaches the modern Western practice of adoption, including the granting to adoptees of the right of inheritance.

Adoption became institutionalized in many Western countries at the end of the 19th century. As industrialization led to urbanization and individuals moved away from their familial and community supports, there was no mechanism to provide for children who could not be cared for by their biological parents. Modern adoption laws grew out of the efforts of 19th-century reformers to assure the welfare of these children. This was the beginning of the current emphasis on putting the interests of the children first.

In Western industrialized countries in the late 20th century, infertility rose and the number of infants available for adoption declined, as a result of legalized abortion and greater acceptance of single parenthood. Western adopters increasingly looked for children to adopt from Third World countries, where more children were available for adoption, in part because the adoption of nonrelatives was not practiced extensively. As Third World countries became industrialized, however, many experienced the same problems Western countries had experienced at the end of the 19th century and took up Western practices of legalized adoption to solve them.

As the number of infants available for adoption declined, social service agencies began encouraging parents to adopt children previously thought "hard to place" owing to age, behavior, or disabilities. The number of children with "special needs" who were adopted increased, but many more remained in foster care.

Legal Aspects. Because the purpose of modern adoption is to serve the best interests of the children, governments have set up objective criteria for prospective adoptive parents. These commonly include age, marital status, length of time married, and residency but may also include income, health, sexual preference, or other factors. Adopters may also be restricted or prohibited from adopting a child of a different race. Governments often require adopters to meet subjective criteria as well, such as satisfactory parenting ability and psychological stability. In addition to legal requirements for prospective adopters, social service agencies or intermediaries may have their own criteria, such as religious requirements. Some countries have limits on the age of the child being adopted.

Laws differ as to the birth parents' right to change their minds after placing a child for adoption, the length of time after placement before the adoption can be finalized through the courts, and the procedures for adopting a child living in a different legal jurisdiction.

Laws also vary on who can assist in an adoption. Public or private social-service agencies are often involved in adoption, since they are often the first to become aware of a child in need of care. But in some places, birth parents themselves make arrangements with the adoptive parents, either directly or indirectly through a lawyer, physician, or other intermediary.

"Open" Adoption. As adoption became formalized, it became common to keep the identity of the birth family from the adoptee. Sometimes adoptees were even raised to believe they had been born into their adoptive families. Such secrecy was sometimes thought necessary to lessen the stigma associated with illegitimacy for the child and the birth mother. But it also reflects a suspicion that the legal process could not supplant children's ties to their biological parents.

The need for and desirability of secrecy in adoption began to be questioned during the 1960s as an outgrowth of the movement for women's and minorities' rights. Adoptees maintained they had both a need for and a right to information about their biological origins. Some governments responded by simplifying the procedure to open adoption records. In some places the practice of formal adoption gradually began to change to resemble that of informal adoption, with birth parents and adoptive families having ongoing contact with each other. The adoptee remains the legal child of the adoptive parents.

Sociological Issues. Adoptive families face issues that families connected genetically do not face, particularly in societies in which adoption is unusual. Although adoptive families generally feel as deeply attached to each other as genetically related families, they may also feel a sense of loss because of not being genetically related. Adoptees may also feel grief over the loss of their birth families and have questions, as they mature, about their identity. Adoptive parents may feel pressure to demonstrate that their families are not inferior to other families.

Social scientists who have studied adoptive families have arrived at a variety of conclusions about the long-term outcome of adoption. It would appear that adoptive families, because of the losses they have experienced, are at greater risk for interpersonal or psychological problems than genetically related families. Nevertheless, it appears that when adoption is discussed openly, when adoptees and adoptive parents recognize and express their feelings about it and the losses connected with it, and when there are no other negative factors, such as a dysfunctional family environment, adoption is successful.

LOIS RUSKAI MELINA
Author of "Making Sense of Adoption"

Further Reading: Benet, Mary Kathleen, *The Politics of Adoption* (Free Press 1976); Gilman, Lois, *The Adoption Resource Book*, rev. ed. (HarperCollins 1992); Melina, Lois Ruskai, *Raising Adopted Children* (Harper 1986).

ADRENAL GLANDS, u-drēn′əl glandz, compound paired structures in mammals, situated on either side of the abdomen immediately above, or anterior to, the upper pole of the kidney. They are also called *suprarenals.* They consist of an outer portion, the cortex, and an inner portion, the medulla. The entire gland is enclosed in a dense capsule of connective tissue. In lower vertebrates, tissues homologous with the cortex and medulla may be separate.

The cortex is mesodermal in origin, whereas the medulla is of ectodermal origin. Cells of the mammalian cortex are arranged in such a manner that, when viewed with a microscope, three zones may be defined: the zona glomerulosa—the outermost layer; the zona fasciculata—the middle layer; and the zona reticularis—the innermost layer.

The adrenal medulla is composed primarily of chromaffin cells (cells that have granules that stain black or brown with chromic acid) and sympathetic ganglion cells that may be interspersed among the chromaffin cells. Small cells that resemble lymphocytes also are present. Medullary hormones are produced by the chromaffin cells.

Adrenal Cortex. The adrenal cortex is essential for life. Surgical removal (adrenalectomy) or functional failure due to disease or injury of the adrenal cortex results in death within a week or two. Death can be prevented by replacement therapy such as the administration of cortical steroids. Life also may be prolonged by administering sodium chloride.

Cortical Steroids. Hormones produced by the adrenal cortex belong to a class of chemical substances that are known as steroids, all of which make important contributions to the metabolic status of the organism. They may be categorized into three different groups: glucocorticoids (hydrocortisone, or cortisol, and corticosterone); mineralocorticoids (aldosterone and 11-desoxycorticosterone); and the androgens. Cortisol is produced by the zona fasciculata. Corticosterone, which is about half as potent as cortisol, is produced by the fasciculata and the glomerulosa. Aldosterone, which is the main mineralocorticoid, is produced by the zona glomerulosa.

Adrenal cortical steroids are synthesized from lipids (mainly cholesterol) that are stored in the cortex. The rates of synthesis and secretion are determined by the physiological needs at the time and are stimulated by ACTH (adrenocorticotropic hormone), which is released by the front part of the pituitary.

Steroid Activities. The glucocorticoids have some effect on electrolyte balance, but they are not as effective as aldosterone. They cause a retention of sodium and chloride and an excretion of potassium. Among other processes influenced by glucocorticoids are conversion of protein to glucose, antagonism to insulin action, reabsorption of phosphates, and fat deposition.

Aldosterone is by far the most potent of the mineralocorticoids. Its primary effect is on the regulation of sodium and potassium excretion by the kidney, but it also has an effect on the concentration of electrolytes in sweat and saliva. Aldosterone (and desoxycorticosterone) causes reabsorption and retention of sodium and chloride and excretion of potassium, thus maintaining a normal electrolyte concentration and fluid volume in the body. Aldosterone secretion is maintained at a normal rate even in the absence of the pi-

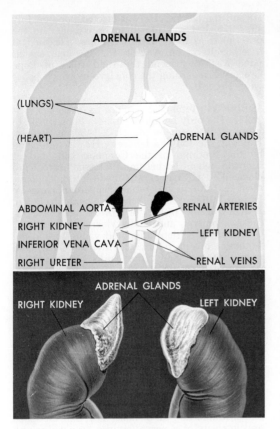

ADRENAL GLANDS

(LUNGS)

(HEART)

ADRENAL GLANDS

ABDOMINAL AORTA

RENAL ARTERIES

RIGHT KIDNEY

LEFT KIDNEY

INFERIOR VENA CAVA

RIGHT URETER

RENAL VEINS

ADRENAL GLANDS

RIGHT KIDNEY

LEFT KIDNEY

does produce hormones that elicit important physiological effects.

The principal hormones produced by the adrenal medulla are adrenalin and noradrenalin (epinephrine and norepinephrine). They are produced by the chromaffin cells of the adrenal medulla and also are referred to as catecholamines. Adrenalin and noradrenalin also are secreted by nerve endings of the sympathetic nervous system where they serve as transmitter substances. At these sites, noradrenalin is produced in greater quantities than adrenalin; whereas adrenalin is present in medullary tissue in a much greater concentration than noradrenalin.

Adrenalin administered in sufficient quantities causes increased cardiac output, increased pulse pressure, increased heart rate, and peripheral vasodilatation. Noradrenalin produces peripheral vasoconstriction, a decrease or no effect on cardiac output and heart rate, and a rise in blood pressure.

Both adrenalin and noradrenalin cause hypertension, but the mechanisms by which they raise the blood pressure are different. Also, when administered in sufficient quantities, adrenalin and noradrenalin will produce hyperglycemia (increased blood sugar). Adrenalin is more effective than noradrenalin. The increased blood sugar evoked by adrenalin causes an increase in insulin secretion by the pancreas.

Release of ACTH and thyrotropin by the pituitary is elicited by adrenalin. Adrenalin and noradrenalin increase plasma levels of nonesterified fatty acids. In man, an increased release of adrenalin occurs in most cases of stress, whereas secretion of noradrenalin is negligible or decreased.

THOMAS F. HOPKINS
Worcester Foundation for Experimental Biology

ADRENALIN. See ADRENAL GLANDS.

ADRENOCORTICOTROPHIC HORMONE. See ACTH.

ADRIAN, Roman emperor. See HADRIAN.

ADRIAN I (died 795), ā´drē-ən, pope from 772 to 795. He is described as a firm, skillful, and tactful ruler. The effective founder of the Papal States, he made papal temporal power a reality and freed the church from much outside political interference. On the other hand, he was greatly dependent on Charlemagne, King of the Franks, who extended his power into Italy in 774 in response to Adrian's appeal for help against the Lombards.

During Adrian's reign the controversy over the veneration of images was ended at the Second Council of Nicaea in 787, and the use of the canon law of the Church of Rome began to spread throughout the Frankish empire. Adrian died at Rome on Dec. 25, 795.

MSGR. FLORENCE D. COHALAN
Cathedral College, New York

ADRIAN II (c. 792–872), ā´drē-ən, pope from 867 to 872. A Roman, he was made a cardinal by Pope Gregory IV in 842. Having refused the papacy in 855 and 858, he accepted it reluctantly in 867. He lacked the firmness of his predecessor Nicholas I (reigned 858–867). Therefore, he suffered much, including the murder of his wife and daughter, at the hands of the Roman nobles,

tuitary, and ACTH is not essential for aldosterone secretion from the zona glomerulosa. Although aldosterone secretion may be stimulated by conditions such as dehydration, low sodium intake, or other conditions that reduce the fluid volume of the body, the hormone(s) responsible for secretion of aldosterone is yet to be identified.

The adrenal androgens are not of as much importance as the other steroids produced by the cortex. At puberty, the adrenals secrete an increased amount of androgens.

Cortical Diseases and Conditions. Diseases and conditions causing abnormal (decreased or increased) adrenal function have been studied extensively. Decreased adrenal function might result from pituitary failure to secrete ACTH (Simmonds' disease) or from destruction of, or failure of, the adrenal cortical tissue, as in Addison's disease. In cases of complete adrenal failure or of adrenalectomy, death is imminent unless adrenal cortical therapy is instituted.

Increased adrenal cortical function occurs in pathological and nonpathological conditions. Some of the conditions that cause an increase in adrenal cortical function are heat, cold, muscular fatigue, infections, nervous strain, shock, burns, surgery, and fear. Increased adrenal cortical function also is associated with pathological conditions such as Cushing's syndrome, adrenogenital syndrome, and hyperaldosteronism (Conn's syndrome).

Adrenal Medulla. The adrenal medulla is not essential for life. Evidence that it is not indispensable is seen in patients suffering from Addison's disease and in adrenalectomized animals in which life is maintained by hormones of the adrenal cortex. However, the adrenal medulla

who resisted papal claims to temporal power. Adrian managed, however, to keep on friendly terms with the Germans and the French.

One of his lasting achievements was approval of the Slavonic liturgy of Saints Cyril and Methodius, missionaries from the Church of Rome to the southern Slavs in Moravia and Pannonia. Another was his convening of the Second Council of Constantinople. Adrian died on Dec. 14, 872.

MSGR. FLORENCE D. COHALAN
Cathedral College

ADRIAN III, ā′drē-ən, **Saint** (died 885), pope in 884–885. Little is known of him except that he was a Roman and was elected to the papacy on May 17, 884. In his short reign he dealt severely with the factious Roman nobility. Invited to Worms by Emperor Charles the Fat to help settle the question of imperial succession, Adrian fell ill and died. He was buried in the monastery of Nonantola, near Modena, Italy. His feast day is September 7.

ADRIAN IV (c. 1100–1159) ā′drē-ən, pope from 1154 to 1159. The only Englishman to ascend to the papacy, he was born *Nicholas Breakspear* near St. Albans, England. He entered the monastery of St. Rufus near Arles, France, and became its abbot in 1137. Bitter complaints from his subjects brought him to the attention of the Holy See, but he was vindicated by Pope Eugenius III. The pope then tactfully removed Nicholas by making him cardinal bishop of Albano.

As papal legate to Scandinavia in 1152–1154, he reorganized the diocesan structure in Norway and Sweden and introduced the collection of Peter's pence. On his return to Rome, Nicholas was hailed as the Apostle of the North.

He was unanimously elected pope on Dec. 4, 1154, taking the name Adrian IV. He almost immediately became involved in disputes with the Romans and Emperor Frederick Barbarossa. The Romans were temporarily subdued by being placed under interdict (the first in their history) until they exiled Arnold of Brescia, a religious reformer and foe of the temporal power of the papacy. Frederick was crowned emperor on June 18, 1155, after rendering the homage he previously had refused to the pope. His relations with the pope remained strained, however. The coronation precipitated a Roman rising, which drove Adrian from Rome until November 1156.

In 1155, Henry II of England asked the pope's permission for a planned invasion of Ireland. A bull called "Laudabiliter," granting permission, was attributed to Adrian but has been proved a forgery. Yet, Adrian did give carefully qualified approval to Henry's plan. This permission was not used during Adrian's life but was renewed by Pope Alexander III in 1172.

Charitable and industrious, Adrian was a strong supporter of the clergy and a man of irreproachable personal and public life. He died at Anagni, near Rome, on Sept. 1, 1159, and was bured in Rome in St. Peter's.

MSGR. FLORENCE D. COHALAN
Cathedral College

ADRIAN V (died 1276), ā′drē-ən, pope for one month in 1276. He was born *Ottobono Fieschi* into a noble Genoese family. His uncle, Pope Innocent IV, made him a cardinal in 1252. As legate to England from 1265 to 1268, Ottobono successfully mediated the struggle between Henry

III and the barons. He was elected pope on July 11, 1276, but was too ill to be ordained to the priesthood or to be crowned pope. He died at Viterbo, Italy, on August 18. His one act as pope was to suspend the rigid rules of Pope Gregory X regarding the conclave by which popes were elected.

ADRIAN VI (1459–1523), ā′drē-ən, pope in 1522–1523. The only Dutch pope, he was born Adrian Florensz Boeyens on March 2, 1459, in Utrecht, Holland, the son of a laborer. He was educated by the Brethren of the Common Life and at Louvain, where he became professor, rector, and chancellor. His career was made by his appointment as tutor to the future Emperor Charles V (reigned 1519–1556). Sent by Charles to Spain, Adrian became bishop of Tortosa, cardinal, inquisitor general, and finally viceroy of Spain.

As pope, Adrian attempted vainly to end the Lutheran revolt, reform the Roman Curia, and unite Europe against the Turks. His untimely death was welcomed in Rome, where he was despised as a reformer and detested as a foreigner. He was learned, devout, and reserved and was scrupulously conscientious in the matter of conferring benefices.

MSGR. FLORENCE D. COHALAN, *Cathedral College*

ADRIAN, ā′drē-ən, **Edgar Douglas** (1889–1977), English physiologist and co-recipient (with Sir Charles Scott Sherrington) of the 1932 Nobel Prize in physiology and medicine. Adrian's work was concerned primarily with the functions of nerve cells. While working with Keith Lucas, he demonstrated the "all-or-none" law, that the speed and intensity of a nerve impulse do not diminish as the impulse travels along the nerve. By isolating a single sensory nerve fiber and connecting it to a sensitive electrical amplifier vacuum tube, Adrian was able to amplify and record its discharge of impulses. Using this technique, he found that the rhythmic discharge of impulses was related in rate and duration to the nature and intensity of the stimulus. Various kinds of sensory stimuli were studied, and Adrian also recorded and studied impulses of single motor nerve fibers. For these and other discoveries he was awarded a share of the Nobel Prize.

Shortly after receiving the Nobel Prize, Adrian began studying the electrical activity of the brain and gave support to the work of Hans Berger. Berger was an Austrian psychiatrist who devised the electroencephalograph and differentiated between different kinds of brain waves. Adrian, in his research on the ganglia and brains of insects, fish, and mammals, helped show the practical value of encephalograms of the human brain.

Life. Adrian was born on Nov. 30, 1889, in London, England, and was educated at Trinity College, Cambridge. From 1920 to 1929 he was a lecturer at Cambridge and later was appointed a professor at both the Royal Society and Cambridge. In 1955 he was created *Baron Adrian of Cambridge.* He was vice chancellor (1957–1959) and chancellor (1968–1975) of Cambridge University, and a trustee of Rockefeller Institute (now Rockefeller University) in New York. Lord Adrian died in London on Aug. 4, 1977.

Lord Adrian's published books include *The Basis of Sensation* (1928), *The Mechanism of Nervous Action* (1932), and *The Physical Basis of Perception* (1947).

SIDNEY OCHS, *Indiana University Medical Center*

ADRIAN, ā′drē-ən, a city in southeastern Michigan, is the seat of Lenawee County and is situated 70 miles southwest of Detroit. It is a trading center for an agricultural county that raises dairy cattle and other livestock, wheat, and corn. The city's more than 40 diversified industries make automobile and aircraft parts, silicones and other chemicals, paper and metal goods, garden and farm gates, and dairy products. The city is the home of Adrian College, Siena Heights College, and Saint Joseph Academy. The Dominican Mother House is situated in Adrian.

Within a radius of 25 miles are more than 35 lakes with recreational facilities. The Irish Hills region, directly north of Adrian, was so named because its landscape of hills, lakes, and woods resembles Ireland. In this area are Walter J. Hayes State Park and St. Joseph Wayside Chapel, with its outdoor Stations of the Cross.

Adrian was founded by Addison J. Comstock in 1825 and received a city charter in 1853. First called Logan, it was renamed by the founder's wife for the Roman emperor Hadrian. The theatrical and industrial designer Norman Bel Geddes was born in the city in 1893. Adrian has a commission-administrator plan of government, adopted in 1957, consisting of a mayor and six commissioners. Population: 21,574.

EMMA SIHLER, *Adrian Public Library*

ADRIANOPLE, ā-drē-ə-nō′pəl, was the historic name of the present city of *Edirne*, Turkey. It was originally named *Hadrianopolis*, for the Roman Emperor Hadrian, who built it in 125 A.D. on the site of the ancient city of Uskudama. The form *Adrianople* is derived from this. In the 14th century it fell to the Turks, who renamed it Edirne. (See also EDIRNE.)

The city is located in Thrace, in European Turkey, about 130 miles northwest of Istanbul, on the Greek border. It is near the western end of the Thracian plain, at the confluence of the Meriç (Maritsa), Tundzha, and Arda rivers. This strategic location has made it a place of great importance since ancient times.

When the Romans lost Adrianople to the Visigoths in 378, Greece lay open to invasion by the barbarians. Adrianople was subsequently taken by the Avars, by the Bulgarians, and by the Crusaders. The Turks under Murad I captured the city in 1361 and made it the residence of their sultans until they won Constantinople in 1453. Adrianople remained in Turkish hands until it fell to Russia briefly in 1829 and again in 1878. Bulgaria took the city in 1912. By the Treaty of Sèvres in 1920, it was awarded to Greece. The Treaty of Lausanne, however, restored Adrianople to Turkish rule in 1922.

Little remains of Adrianople's early magnificence except several mosques, including those of Bayezid II (1488) and Selim (1574–1575).

ADRIANOPLE, Battle of, ā-drē-ə-nō′pəl, a battle between the Romans and the Goths, which took place on Aug. 9, 378 A.D. The Roman army, which was all but destroyed at this battle, had not suffered such a defeat since Hannibal's victory over it at Cannae in 216 B.C.

Pushed southward by the Huns, the Goths had asked permission of the Romans, who ruled the area, to settle in the lands south of the Danube River. This request was granted on condition that they come unarmed and leave the children of their leading families in Roman hands as hostages. When the Goths complied, the Roman officers who were to supply them with food forced them to pay exorbitant prices for it, and sold or kept many of the girls as concubines.

The enraged Goths retaliated by invading and plundering Thrace. They were driven back for a time, but returned in the spring of 378, reinforced by Huns and Alans, and advanced to a point near Constantinople (now Istanbul). Roman Emperor Valens was jealous of his brilliant nephew Gratian, who had just won a great victory over the Western barbarians. Eager to fight before Gratian could join him and receive credit for a fresh victory, Valens made a long march on a hot day and attacked the Goths with his tired troops. The Roman legions were practically exterminated by the Gothic cavalry in the ensuing battle, and Valens was never seen alive again. As a result of their victory, the Goths obtained possession of the plains south of the Danube.

ADRIANOPLE, Treaty of, ā-drē-ə-nō′pəl, the treaty that ended the Russo-Turkish War of 1828–1829. According to its provisions, Russia acquired the strategic mouth of the Danube River and part of the Black Sea coast; navigational rights on the Black Sea and through the Straits joining the Black Sea to the Mediterranean; and protective custody of Moldavia and Wallachia (now part of Rumania). Turkey was obliged to withdraw its troops from the Danube and from Moldavia and Wallachia, and to pay Russia an indemnity.

ADRIATIC SEA, ā-drē-at′ik, an arm of the Mediterranean Sea, extending northwest to southeast for a length of about 500 miles (800 km) from the gulfs of Trieste and Venice in the north to the Strait of Otranto in the south. It is bordered by Italy on the north and west and by Croatia, Slovenia, Yugoslavia, and Albania on the east. The Adriatic is a shallow sea, reaching a maximum depth of about 4,000 feet (1,220 meters) in the southernmost of its two deepest troughs. Its width varies from 60 to 140 miles (95 to 225 km).

The most important coastal features are the Istrian Peninsula, which juts out from the Croatian coast, and the promontory of Monte Gargano on the Italian side. The Italian coast is generally low and straight, except between Trieste and Ravenna, where it is interrupted by marshes, lagoons, and sandspits. The eastern shore is high and rocky, fringed with islands and inlets.

The most important ports are Trieste, Venice, Bari, and Brindisi in Italy; Rijeka, Split, and Dubrovnik in Croatia; and Durrës and Vlonë in Albania. Fishing is an important activity, particularly along the eastern coast, where lobsters and sardines are plentiful. The mild climate, blue waters, and striking landscape have made of the Adriatic, and especially its Croatian coast.

The Adriatic was named after *Adria*, southwest of Venice. Adria once was a flourishing port, but the port has been closed by siltage at the delta of the Po River. During the Roman period the Adriatic had little commercial importance, but it was important militarily: Aquileia was a strategic military center, and Classis, the port of Ravenna, a great naval base. With the rise of the republic of Venice during the Middle Ages, the Adriatic became the chief trade route between central Europe and the Orient. It declined in importance with the fall of Constantinople in 1453 and still further with the opening of the Suez Canal in 1869.

ADULT CLASSES serve a wide range of ages and interests. This is a beginners' course in guitar playing.

ADSORPTION, ad-sȯrp'shən, is the taking up of a gas, vapor, or liquid by a surface or interface. This term, rather than "absorption," is used when no surface penetration occurs. When doubt exists as to whether adsorption or absorption takes place, the term "sorption" is used.

Adsorption results from unbalanced forces associated with surface molecules of a solid or liquid. The high potential energy of these molecules is reduced by the attraction of foreign substances. The adsorbed substances show increased reactivity.

Solids that have large surface areas compared with their bulk volumes are *adsorbents* on which molecules of gas, vapor, or liquid (*adsorbate*) are adsorbed. A large surface-to-volume ratio is found either in finely divided solids or in large bodies that contain a network of pores.

In physical adsorption, the bonding between adsorbent and adsorbate is caused by Van der Waal forces. Chemical adsorption, or *chemisorption*, is characterized by exchange or sharing of electrons between adsorbent and adsorbate.

Adsorption on a liquid surface occurs when the adsorbate dissolves in the liquid. If the substance dissolved in the liquid is more concentrated at the surface than in the bulk of the liquid, the surface tension of the liquid is lowered. Such solutes are called *surface-active agents*.

Solid adsorbents can be *polar* or *nonpolar*. Ion-dipole or dipole-dipole interactions between the solid and adsorbate predominate on polar surfaces, such as alumina, barium sulfate, calcium carbonate, glass, ion-exchange resins, silica gel, and zeolites. Dispersion forces predominate on nonpolar surfaces, such as carbon black, graphite, charcoal, organic resins, plastics, paraffin, and talc.

The amount of adsorption depends on the surface area, the adsorbent, the adsorbate, and the temperature. The adsorption can be very great: one volume of boxwood charcoal adsorbs 90 volumes of ammonia. Gas-mask canisters contain layers of charcoal that remove toxic gases by adsorption. Charcoal also is used to purify water and to decolorize sugar solutions.

Trace materials can be separated from biological samples by taking advantage of the different effect of powdered adsorbent on each component of the mixture. This method of separation is called *adsorption chromatography*.

HERBERT LIEBESKIND, *The Cooper Union*

ADULT EDUCATION, ə-dult' ej-ə-ka'shən, in its broadest meaning, includes all experiences that help mature men and women acquire new knowledge, understandings, skills, attitudes, interests, or values. In this sense it encompasses practically all life experiences, individual or group, that result in learning. Thus it includes reading books, listening to music, talking with people, and even learning from the daily experiences of family life and work. In a more technical sense, the phrase "adult education" is used to denote planned or organized activities carried on by adults for the purpose of self-improvement. In this restricted meaning it encompasses organized classes, study groups, lecture series, planned reading programs, systematic discussions, conferences, institutes, and similar activities.

In more recent years, the term *continuing education* has been widely used. While it is often used interchangeably with "adult education," there is a difference in emphasis. Adult education is the more comprehensive term, including kinds of educational activity that are primarily remedial (literacy education, for example), as well as continuing education, which suggests formal educational activity that could not be carried on at an earlier age. For example, part-time courses in business methods for office workers come under the heading of continuing education. Students in such courses have probably completed high school or other training.

SCOPE OF THE ADULT EDUCATION MOVEMENT

In the broad sense then, adult education includes the activity of people learning together, the process by which individuals learn systematically from daily experiences, and a popular movement that combines all these activities and processes. The movement is dedicated to the improvement of the adult learning process, the extension of opportunities for adults to learn, and the development of ways to raise the general cultural level.

Forces Promoting Adult Education. As one of the fastest-growing movements in modern society, adult education might be called the educational frontier of the 20th century. Several forces have worked together to make adult education a significant factor in modern social progress. Perhaps the foremost is the increased pace of change. Changes in technological processes, in communications, in knowledge, in social organization, and in patterns of living are so frequent and continuous that modern man must constantly learn new ideas, new facts, new skills, and new attitudes in order to keep up with the progress of society.

Another force in the advancement of adult education is the rising proportion of older people in the population. In 1850, for example, youths under 20 accounted for over half the population of the United States, but in 1930 they constituted under two fifths of the total. By 1980 they will probably represent about a quarter of the population. The percentage of people over 45 more than doubled between 1850 and 1950. In 1965 one out of every 11 Americans was over 65 years of age. These older people have time for informal and formal study, and many of them are interested in learning new skills and meeting new ideas.

A third force is the shortened work week, which provides leisure hours in which adults below retirement age can pursue cultural interests. Still another force is what has been called the "third communications revolution," exemplified in radio, television, inexpensive newspapers, paperback books, weekly magazines, and other media that bring world events and great ideas into the common man's living room. There are, perhaps, other forces as well, but underneath them all is the drive for self-betterment that has flowered in this century as a basic ingredient of life.

National Patterns. The origin of the adult education movement can be traced to ancient times. Many of the great teachers of the past—Confucius, Isaiah, Socrates, Plato, Aristotle, Jesus—were teachers of mature men and women more than of children. Not until the 19th century, however, did adult education begin to take shape as a formal, organized movement in many nations of the world.

The movement has taken different forms in different countries. In Denmark it has been largely institutionalized in the folk high schools. These schools—sometimes called "people's colleges"—were devised specifically to refashion the national culture by giving courses to young adults. In Sweden it has been essentially a working-class movement spearheaded by labor unions, cooperative associations, temperance societies, and the Social Democratic party. To generalize about western Europe, the principal institutional forms of adult education include the folk high school, the residential college, the tutorial class, and the study circle.

The adult education movement in Britain has been characterized by a drive for further education of the working class, sponsored by labor unions, voluntary associations, local education authorities, and universities. Since 1944, adult education in Britain has had the liberal support of the government.

In Communist countries, the government-sponsored movement largely involves political indoctrination. The governments of most developing nations of Asia and Africa sponsor adult education programs to raise the literacy rate and to coordinate and extend opportunities for broadening education. As was the case after the establishment of the United States, there is a need in these countries to create through education a politically responsive citizenry, able to cope with the problems of self-government.

In Argentina, Guatemala, and other Latin American countries, the *universidad popular* (popular university) is an adult education center, not connected with the formal university structure, that offers noncredit educational opportunities in a variety of fields. The Mexican government has brought the museum to a high level of excellence as an educational institution. *Unidades* (unions or associations), operated by the Institute of Social Security, offer adult education opportunities and other services for thousands of people in and around the large cities of the country.

International Bodies. International organizations for adult education have developed steadily since the founding of UNESCO in 1945. This movement was spurred by two UNESCO international conferences on adult education—the first in Elsinore, Denmark, in 1949, and the second in Montreal, Canada, in 1960. UNESCO's International Committee on Adult Education has focused attention on the need for adult education by helping to stimulate pilot projects in literacy and the development of national and regional associations for adult education in the developing nations of Asia, Africa, and Latin America. The International Congress of University Adult Education and the Adult Education Committee of the World Confederation of the Organizations of the Teaching Profession provide communication and help to promote cooperation and effective planning among the institutions affiliated with them.

ADULT EDUCATION IN THE UNITED STATES

In the United States, adult education has become a diversified movement, carried on by a wide variety of agencies for many different purposes. A process of adult education, perhaps one of the most important in the history of the United States, was going on during the colonial period, when the colonists were learning, through participation in town meetings, colonial legislatures, and other governmental activities, to use the tools of liberty and self-government.

Probably no undertaking of any society ever staked more on the ability of adults to learn than did the founding of the American republic. For the new United States could survive only if it succeeded in transforming an entire people from subjects of a monarchy to active citizens of a republic, from a people used to being governed by an aristocracy to a people able to govern themselves. The means by which this gigantic adult education task was accomplished were informal, and in a sense unplanned. They included town meetings, cracker-barrel discussions, committees of correspondence, pamphlets, editorials, books, speeches, poems, and plays, which explored the issues and ideas of democracy. The American Revolution was thus a social and intellectual revolution, as well as a political one.

Growth of the Movement—Early 19th Century. One important development that fostered adult education in the United States, as elsewhere, was the progress of the age of science. Between the American Revolution and the Civil War there was a vast upsurge of secular thought and of interest in the natural sciences that produced an eager quest for knowledge. This urge for the diffusion of knowledge was expressed in many ways.

Numerous institutions were founded, including the American Academy of Arts and Sciences, in 1780; the Pennsylvania Academy of Fine Arts, in 1791; the Boston Mechanics Institute, in 1826; the Franklin Institute, in New Haven, in 1828;

the first library supported by public taxation, in Peterborough, New Hampshire, in 1833 (the first legislation enabling a municipality to establish and maintain a public library was passed by the Massachusetts legislature in 1848, in reference to Boston); the Lowell Institute, in Boston, in 1836; the Smithsonian Institution, in Washington, in 1846; the Young Men's Christian Association, in 1851 (transplanted from England); Cooper Union, in New York City, in 1859; the land grant colleges (provided for in the Morrill Act of 1862); and the first women's club, in 1866.

The American Lyceum, the first and one of the most famous adult education programs, was initiated in 1826 by Josiah Holbrook of Massachusetts. The lyceum flourished as a center of discussion and study. Its three basic principles were the advancement of the public school system, organization of libraries and museums, and the formation of lecture courses and discussion sessions for adults. By 1835 there were some 3,000 town lyceums presenting lecture discussions at weekly meetings "for the mutual improvement of their members and the common benefit of society." By the 1840's the lyceum had fulfilled its mission as a national movement, but it stayed alive for many years as a medium of local adult education. The lecture-discussion form it had developed was adopted and extended by its successors including the Chautauqua Movement and the university extension and public forum movements. See also LYCEUM.

Civil War to World War I. Between the Civil War and World War I a great number of organizations devoted to adult education were established throughout the United States. The American penchant for "joining," which Alexis de Tocqueville had observed in the 1830's, reached its peak in this period, and most of the institutions providing educational opportunities for adults trace their origins to this era.

One of the notable of these was the Chautauqua Institution. Established in 1874 in Chautauqua, N.Y., as a summer school for Sunday school teachers, this organization rapidly broadened its program to include literature, science, history, and other subjects of general culture. Its Literary and Scientific Circle, founded in 1878, grew into a nationwide system of home study connected with local reading circles, and popularized a new adult education form—the correspondence course. For many years the traveling Chautauquas, inspired but not sponsored by the Institution, carried cultural stimulation into American towns and villages. See also CHAUTAUQUA MOVEMENT.

The years between the Civil War and World War I also witnessed the founding of large numbers of welfare agencies, including settlement houses, the Salvation Army, and family welfare societies; youth agencies such as the Young Women's Christian Association, the Young Men's and Young Women's Hebrew associations, the Boy Scouts, Girl Scouts, and Campfire Girls; service organizations such as Rotary, Kiwanis, Altrusa, and the Lions; and health agencies such as the National Tuberculosis Association, the American Social Hygiene Association, and the American Red Cross. All of these are concerned with the education of adults as volunteers, members, or clients.

During this period there was also a phenomenal growth of large-scale voluntary associations with primarily adult educational purposes. These included the National Congress of Parents and Teachers, the General Federation of Women's Clubs, the American Association of University Women, the National Council of Jewish Women, B'nai B'rith, and many others. Labor unions, manufacturers' associations, trade associations, and other groups were organized around economic interests to promote the education of their members and of the public. A small but vital movement of independent adult schools, following the lead of Cooper Union, was stimulated by the founding of the Watkins Institute, in Nashville, Tenn., in 1855.

One of the most popular and far-reaching innovations of this era was the idea of systematic learning by correspondence. Pioneered by Chautauqua, the idea was rapidly developed by private correspondence schools and correspondence divisions in the universities. Standards and practices of private correspondence schools have been improved and systematized by the National Home Study Council, a national accrediting agency established in 1926. Privately operated trade and technical schools also have established a national organization for this purpose. Millions of Americans have received further education through correspondence.

The established educational institutions—the public schools, colleges, and universities—developed extensive adult education programs. Evening classes for adults had been instituted in a few scattered communities before the Civil War; but the evening school did not become a set part of the public school program until later in the century, when massive waves of immigration created a serious problem of Americanization. In 1889 an appropriation of $15,000 for evening lectures in the city schools was included for the first time in the regular New York City budget. By the beginning of World War I some of the states were initiating the establishment of state-wide systems of evening schools, with continuous state assistance.

The idea that a university has a responsibility for the education of the adult citizens of its community culminated around the turn of the century in the establishment of university extension courses. The University of the State of New York received the first state appropriation for university extension in 1891, and the first national conference on university extension was held the same year. When the University of Chicago opened in 1892, university extension was included as a formal, permanent division of the university.

The modern model of university extension was created at the University of Wisconsin in 1906. There, emphasis was shifted from academic and cultural subjects to a broad program covering all areas concerned with the problems of the people and the state—agriculture, industry, politics, social problems, and moral problems. Following the broad pattern set at Wisconsin, extension divisions have been organized in the majority of colleges and universities of the United States.

Another development began in this period that has greatly affected the character of the adult education movement in the United States. Agencies and leaders of adult education began to form associations according to type of institution, occupational interest, or type of subject matter, for the purpose of promoting the advancement of their particular interests. Examples of these early associations are the American Public Health Association, the American Library Association, the Association of Land Grant Colleges and Universities, the National University Extension Association, and the American Home Economics Association. Although most of these associations were not concerned exclusively with adult education, and they did not call it by that name, the concept was an important phase of their work.

Two significant facts about this early pattern of organization of the adult education movement stand out: (1) adult education developed as an adjunct of some other kind of activity, rather than as a distinct activity with independent character; and (2) individuals and agencies concerned with the education of adults developed intercommunication and loyalties around specialized interests before there was any consciousness of general national aims. The emerging pattern of the adult education movement thus took the form of a designless mosaic, rich in diversity but devoid of unity.

Federal Aid. The modern era of adult education began during World War I, when new forces diversifying the movement were introduced. One of the most powerful of these forces was the entrance of the federal government into the direct support of certain phases of adult education. The initial move was made in 1914 with the passage of the Smith-Lever Act, providing federal funds to supplement state funds in establishing and operating a cooperative agricultural extension service.

The program of federal aid has become one of the largest single enterprises in adult education, and its impact on American society and culture has been massive. By the mid-1960's there were at least 16,000 county agents, home demonstration agents, and subject-matter specialists influencing millions of farm families by some phase of extension work. Since its inception, the federal program of extension and vocational courses and community farm organizations has been an integral part of the revolutionary modernization of rural life, brought about by vast technological improvements.

The federal government also responded to the need for skilled industrial workers in war industries during World War I. The Smith-Hughes Act of 1917 made federal funds available to augment state and local appropriations for the expansion of vocational education in agriculture and the mechanical arts, principally through the public schools. These funds were augmented further during the depression of the 1930's with the passage of the George-Deen Act. Also during the depression, the federal government supported a wide variety of adult educational activities by the Works Progress Administration, the National Youth Administration, and the Civilian Conservation Corps. The government also provided one of the most dramatic examples of community adult education through the work of the Tennessee Valley Authority.

Since World War II, and especially since 1960, the role of the federal government has grown so enormously that it is transforming the entire picture of adult education in the United States. Beginning with the GI Bill of Rights for veterans of World War II, Congress has consistently extended educational opportunities for veterans of the military services. Apart from its combat training program, the Department of Defense operates one of the largest national pro-

ADULT CONTINUATION SCHOOL in Sweden has an enrollment with an average age of 67. The oldest is 77.

grams of adult or continuing education in the country. The department cooperates with universities, schools, and other nonprofit agencies through tuition subsidies and other financial assistance programs. According to a directory of federal government agencies supporting or engaged in adult education, released by the Adult Education Association of the U.S.A., by the mid-1960's almost 100 federal agencies were collectively spending well over a billion dollars a year for adult or continuing education.

This rapid growth stems both from the acceptance of adult education by federal agencies as essential to their programs and from the spate of new legislation passed in the 1960's. One of the outstanding pieces of legislation was the Manpower Act of 1965 (amending the Manpower Development and Training Act of 1962). Aimed chiefly at school dropouts under 22 years of age, the 1965 act provided training allowances for people in approved training programs and provided support for job programs as well as research and experimental programs. Private training facilities were to be used extensively, and considerable attention was given to counseling and placement, foreshadowing another probable major development in structured adult education programs. In 1966 eligibility for these benefits was extended to men over 45.

The Economic Opportunity Act of 1964 (amended in subsequent years) was largely an experimental crash program to uplift the poverty-stricken through urban and rural training centers and educational programs closely allied to social services. Separate funds for adult basic education in public schools were made available in 1964 through this act and in 1966 through the Elementary and Secondary Education Act. Title I of the Higher Education Act of 1965 authorized funds for public and private institutions of higher education for use in programs designed to help solve community problems. The National Endowments for the Arts and Humanities, established in 1965, provides funds for adult and other educational activities. The International Education Act of 1966 was designed chiefly to establish university centers to improve teaching about international affairs. The act also set up a program of fellowships and demonstration grants directed toward making adult educational activity more effective.

While more time must pass before the full

LITERACY is a major objective of adult education. This class is part of a government program in Nigeria.

impact of the massive growth of federal involvement in adult education can be accurately assessed, some trends are apparent. Aside from funds for facilities (particularly for libraries, universities, and television stations), the bulk of federal funds are being channeled through state systems or established institutions. A smaller portion (rarely as much as 20 percent) for demonstration purposes or training programs is awarded directly by the federal agency involved. The rapid growth of adult education further supports the conviction that education will be the top "growth industry" in the United States for the rest of the 20th century, and that the nation's economic prosperity will to a large extent depend on the continuing success of the adult education movement.

Agencies Promoting Adult Education. Another force influencing modern adult education is the pressure toward national coordination of activities. Until 1924 the term "adult education" was almost unknown. Agencies in the field were unrelated and had no common name for their work. In 1924, however, Frederick P. Keppel, president of the Carnegie Corporation of New York, initiated a drive toward an integrated movement in the United States, patterned after similar movements in Europe. Under Keppel's leadership, conferences were held with leaders of various agencies, resulting in the formation of the American Association for Adult Education in 1926. During its 25 years of existence, the association was a national clearinghouse for information about adult education. It conducted annual conferences, published the quarterly *Journal of Adult Education* (1929–1950), sponsored many studies, and published many books. Its most notable publications were the series "Studies in the Social Significance of Adult Education." The association, comprised of about 3,000 members, was generously financed by the Carnegie Corporation for most of its existence.

In 1921, five years before the founding of the American Association for Adult Education, a Department of Immigrant Education was established in the National Education Association.

Originally composed of administrators and teachers engaged in educating immigrants, the department broadened its scope and in 1924 became the Department of Adult Education. For several years the department's members were drawn exclusively from the public school field, but in 1927 it was expanded to include personnel from both public and private programs.

Because of extensive overlapping, the Department of Adult Education and the American Association for Adult Education merged to form the Adult Education Association of the U.S.A., in Columbus, Ohio, on May 14, 1951. This association acts through annual and regional conferences to stimulate research and support improved professional programs for the training of adult educators. The AEA also publishes numerous books and pamphlets as well as three periodicals—the monthly *Adult Leadership* and two quarterlies, *Adult Education* and *Washington Newsletter*. The AEA works to develop communication and coordination among the major organizations serving different areas of the field.

Two other organizations, with limited membership, were established at the same time as the AEA. The first, the National Association for Public School Adult Education, includes persons directly employed in or related to public school programs of adult education. The second, the Council of National Organizations for Adult Education, derives most of its members from national voluntary organizations. The entry of the American Council on Education and the American Association of Junior Colleges into the adult education field in the mid-1960's further underscored the growing concern for such programs evinced by long-established formal educational institutions.

The impulse toward coordination and cooperation is expressed at the local level by general-purpose adult education associations in most of the states and many larger cities. The growth of regional associations was formerly sporadic, but they now seem certain to increase steadily in size and influence. In 1965 the AEA created the Council of State Associations to enable these units to work closely together in planning and carrying out their programs.

The community development movement has been closely allied with adult education. Immediately after World War II this program sought to raise cultural levels by community action on pressing problems. It sought to broaden individual development through community development. While this is still an important program in Kentucky, Illinois, Missouri, and other states with many relatively small, impoverished communities, the movement has shifted much of its attention to the urban scene in line with the modern trend toward rapid urbanization.

One of the most widespread forms of urban community development is the program of community self-help. Adopted by the Community Action Program of the Office of Economic Opportunity, this program encourages citizens of depressed neighborhoods to band together in self-help projects for the improvement of ghettos and other poverty-blighted areas. Several large religious organizations have also adopted this type of program. As part of an effort by the United Nations and its affiliated agencies to provide means for an international exchange of experiences, UNESCO has established a Regional Community Development Training Center for Latin

America at Pátzcuaro, Mexico. Moreover, the Adult Education Association has convened several national and inter-American conferences on community development.

Support from Foundations. Private foundations also have given large-scale support to adult education. This movement was initiated by the Carnegie Corporation of New York, which had contributed greatly to the American Association for Adult Education, especially to the writing and publication of literature on adult education. The Kellogg Foundation has also given active support to special projects, particularly to centers for continuing education at Michigan State University, the universities of Georgia, Oklahoma, and Nebraska, and the University of Chicago. A trend toward regional cooperation in university work was begun by a Kellogg grant to the University of New Hampshire for the establishment of the New England Center for Continuing Education. The New England Center is designed to bring about cooperation and coordinate plans for the continuing education programs of the six New England state universities.

For a time, the Ford Foundation exercised a major influence on adult education through its Fund for Adult Education, established in 1951. Separate grants to most of Ford's independent organizations (such as this fund) were discontinued in the late 1950's, and Ford today has no strong program of direct support for adult education. During its existence the Fund for Adult Education championed liberal education, study-discussion programs, and educational television, helping to secure the allocation of many TV channels for educational and community purposes. Perhaps its major legacy was the establishment of National Educational Television (NET) as a programming and production center for the growing complex of noncommercial stations. In 1966 the Ford Foundation announced plans to spend $10 million on linking noncommercial television channels in the United States via satellites, coaxial cables, and microwave relays, thus creating an additional national network.

State Aid. Another force at work since World War I has been state aid for public school adult education in the form of tax funds and service bureaus. By the mid-1960's each of the 50 states had a special unit or individual assigned to providing services for public school adult education. While much of the funding of this program has come from the Adult Basic Education Program included in the Economic Opportunity Act of 1964, the growing trend is toward more increased state support for a broader range of offerings in the public school program. Expenditures for public school adult education approached the billion dollar mark in the late 1960's.

Methods and Programs. Extensive experimentation and research into the problems of adult education have added much to the knowledge of this field. In 1928, Edward L. Thorndike of Columbia University published *Adult Learning*, a report of research proving that the ability of adults to learn declined very little with age. The success of this endeavor evoked a flurry of studies in the 1930's, sponsored by the American Association for Adult Education. Following World War II, the focus of research shifted to studies of the process of learning in groups. Out of this came a large body of literature on "group dynamics." A wide variety of new methods of teaching adults resulted from these studies. Lectures have

been largely replaced by group discussions, field trips, motion pictures, and other audiovisual aids, including recordings. Learning tends to be keyed to problems, experiences, and common daily needs, rather than to abstract subject matter.

Technological developments applied to education constitute another force working for change. The widespread use of television in connection with discussion groups, adaptation of "open line" radio broadcasts for educational purposes, long-distance telephone conferences (telectures), programmed learning systems, and study carrels (library areas for individual study) are introducing flexibility and variety into the field of adult education as they are in other areas.

Perhaps the most visible characteristic of the modern era in adult education is its expansion in institutions outside the formal educational system. Churches and synagogues have developed adult study groups in their Sunday Schools and established week-night programs of general studies that command a regular attendance of millions of people. Labor unions have broadened their concern for the education of members beyond that required for union membership alone and have multiplied participation in union adult education activities. The health and welfare agencies see adult education as a major means of achieving their purposes, as do business and industry. Adult education is rapidly expanding into other sectors of American life through such agencies as the American Hospital Association, the National Council of Churches, the American Medical Association, the National Life Underwriters Association, and others seeking to provide extensive programs for the continuing education of professional people.

From the perspective of history, the character of the adult education movement has been greatly influenced by the changing needs of society. The process of adult education, even when not known by that name, has been a principal instrument for meeting these needs—the need for developing citizen-rulers, for increasing industrial skills, for Americanizing waves of immigrants, for constructively using leisure time, and for readjusting and reintegrating alienated sectors of society into American life. In former times adult education grew mainly during periods of crisis, but after World War II its growth was both rapid and continuous.

Numbers Participating. To measure the scope of adult education statistically, it is necessary to limit its definition to continuous (as against sporadic) experiences organized specifically for adult learning. Even with this limited definition, however, it is practically impossible to obtain reliable statistics. Attendance rosters are kept by relatively few adult education organizations, and no systematic method for reporting enrollment exists.

Fairly meaningful estimates have been made by projecting from samples of adult educational groupings, as well as by analyzing actual enrollment reports. These estimates do not take into account the fact that some individuals may participate in more than one type of activity. Even so, they indicate that the number of persons involved in adult education in the United States increased from nearly 15 million in 1924 to over 49 million in 1955. In general, the major portion of the total in these years came from enrollment in agricultural extension programs. The significant increase from the mid-1930's to the mid-1950's, however, came from the vastly increased activity of religious institutions in the adult education arena.

According to a study by the National Opinion Research Center, a considerably smaller figure of approximately 25 million persons in adult education was established for 1961. The difference between this later study and the earlier ones lies primarily in the definitions used and in the methods of collecting data. Therefore, these studies are not really comparable. The older studies indicated that probably more than one third of all adult citizens participated in some form of organized educational activity in 1955. With the dramatic upsurge of participation in adult education that resulted from continuing prosperity, massive tax support, and the "War on Poverty," it is certain that current participation is considerably higher than the most optimistic of the earlier figures.

Another index of the scope of adult education is the number of persons engaged as administrators, supervisors, or part-time and volunteer leaders and teachers in providing educational opportunities for adults. Reliable estimates are available for only a relatively few adult education agencies, but these suggest that adult educators constitute an emerging corps of considerable importance.

In the late 1960's there were approximately 16,000 full-time and 2,000,000 part-time workers involved in agricultural extension, 4,000 full-time and 150,000 part-time in public school adult education programs, and 1,500 full-time and 50,000 part-time in university extension and evening college programs. (Corresponding figures for the mid-1950's were approximately 12,000 full-time and 1,150,000 part-time in agricultural extension programs, 2,500 full-time and 83,500 part-time in public school adult education programs, and 1,000 full-time and 35,000 part-time in university extension and evening college programs.) Reliable estimates of the number of persons involved in providing adult education services through libraries, educational radio and television, and national health and welfare agencies were not available.

Available figures for programs of all kinds in the mid-1950's showed a total of about 48,600 full-time workers and 2,789,500 part-time workers. At that time it was assumed that an equal number were employed in programs for which figures were not available, bringing the actual total to about 100,000 full-time and over 5 million part-time workers. Total estimates for the late 1960's, based on the same assumption, came to about 150,000 full-time workers and 6 million part-time workers.

Trends. The most noticeable trend in adult education in the second half of the 20th century is expansion. Projecting the curve of growth of the second quarter of the century into the third quarter, it can be anticipated that by 1975 over one half of all adults in the United States will be participating in some form of organized learning activity. It is becoming accepted in the national culture that it is as normal—and essential—for adults to keep learning as it is for children to go to school.

There is, further, a trend toward the professionalization of adult education. The notion is spreading that there are special skills and knowledge involved in teaching adults and that special training is required to produce successful adult educators. Whereas in 1935 only one United States university offered a doctoral degree in adult education, in the mid-1960's 21 universities offered such degrees, and many others offered special courses or maintained special institutes. In addition, many adult educational agencies have evolved intensive in-service training programs for part-time and volunteer leaders and teachers.

Increasing attention is being given to research in the field of adult education. The social sciences are conducting action-research in community organization, group behavior, and education for the aging. Knowledge about adult learning and social change is accumulating rapidly, but the surface has as yet only been scratched.

There is a growing concern, as well, for the development of common aims and a social philosophy that will reconcile such apparent differences as those between "individual-centered" and "social-centered" education, or "content vs. method" or "liberal vs. vocational" adult education. Through the process of exploring such issues as these, the goals of adult education are becoming clarified.

Finally, the basic conception of adult education is broadening. Adult education is extending out of the classroom into the marketplace. Evidences of this trend can be found in the rapid expansion of adult education as a major undertaking of noneducational institutions. It is also apparent in the shift of emphasis away from academic subjects toward life problems, and in the greater emphasis being given by the universities and public schools to off-campus community services.

See also EXTENSION EDUCATION; JUNIOR COLLEGE; VOCATIONAL EDUCATION.

MALCOLM S. KNOWLES
Boston University
EUGENE I. JOHNSON
Adult Education Association of the U.S.A.

Bibliography

Axford, Robert W., *Adult Education: The Open Door to Lifelong Learning* (Halldin Pub. 1980).
Biddle, William, *The Cultivation of Community Leaders* (Arco 1953).
Boone, Edgar J., *Developing Programs in Adult Education* (Prentice-Hall 1985).
Collins, Michael, *Competence in Adult Education: A New Perspective* (Univ. Press of Am. 1987).
Cook, Wanda D., *Adult Literacy Education in the United States* (Intl. Reading Assn. 1977).
Fraser, Bryna S., *The Structure of Adult Learning Education and Training Opportunity in the United States* (National Inst. for Work & Learning 1980).
Grattan, Clinton H., ed., *American Ideas about Adult Education, 1710–1951* (Teacher's College Press 1959).
Grattan, Clinton H., *In Quest of Knowledge: A Historical Perspective on Adult Education* (1955; reprint, Ayer 1971).
Griffin, Colin, *Adult Education and Social Policy,* ed. by Peter Jarvis (Longwood 1987).
Griffin, Colin, *Curriculum Theory in Adult and Lifelong Education* (Nichols 1982).
Jones, R. Kenneth, *The Sociology of Adult Education* (Gower Pub. 1984).
Knowles, Malcolm S., *Adult Education Movement in the U. S.* (1962; reprint, Krieger 1977).
Knowles, Malcolm S., ed., *The Handbook of Adult Education* (Dent 1960).
Knowles, Malcolm S., *Informal Adult Education* (1950; reprint, Gulf 1984).
Leirman, Walter, and Kulich, Jindra, eds., *Adult Education and the Challenges of the 1990's* (Methuen 1987).
Mohrman, Kathryn, *Adult Students and the Humanities* (Assn. of Am. Colleges 1983).
Rivera, William M., *Planning Adult Learning: Issues, Practices and Directions* (Methuen 1987).
Roger, Alan, *Teaching Adults* (Taylor & Francis 1986).
Smith, Robert, *Learning How to Learn* (Cambridge 1982).
Stewart, David W., *Adult Learning in America* (Krieger 1987).

ADULTERATION, ə-dul-tə-rā′shən, is the partial substitution of one product for another one. Some form of adulteration occurs in almost every product on the market, including foods, drugs, cosmetics, clothing fabrics, plant seed, fertilizers, chemicals, and building materials. Generally the substance used for adulteration, called the *adulterant,* is inferior to the original product and may sometimes even be harmful. The addition of harmless materials to improve the quality of a mixed product is an approved practice if the product is properly labeled. However, any additions that adversely affect the consumer's health or lower the economic value of the product are not approved. In the United States there are many federal, state, and local laws to protect public health and prevent fraud in the sale of adulterated foods and other products. Similar laws exist in other countries.

Foods. Foods may be adulterated in a variety of ways. Mineral oil is sometimes substituted for vegetable oil, and saccharine is sometimes used in place of sugar. Powdered cocoa is sometimes extended with starch, just as butter may be extended with margarine. One of the most common food adulterants is water, which also serves to lower the value of the food. Water is often added to milk to reduce the concentrations of butterfat and milk solids to the minimum standards set by law. Other products that naturally contain water are also subject to this form of adulteration.

With the beginning of the atomic age, a new kind of food adulterant appeared. Every time an atomic device was exploded in the atmosphere, it released molecules of radioactive strontium-90. In some regions, the accumulations of strontium-90 on the ground became great enough to cause considerable danger. If the contaminated grass and fodder grown in these areas is eaten by dairy cows, strontium-90 will be present in the milk they produce. Once a person drinks the contaminated milk, the strontium-90 becomes incorporated with the calcium of his bones and soon begins bombarding the surrounding tissues and organs with beta-ray emissions. In addition to strontium-90, other radioactive chemicals are finding their way into food and water supplies through similar routes.

Some substances are added to foods as preservatives, and these substances should not be confused with adulterants. For example, small amounts of sodium benzoate are often added to bread and other foods to retard the growth of mold. Another commonly used preservative is sulfur dioxide, which is used in bleaching and preserving dried fruit.

Drugs and Chemicals. Adulteration in drugs is less common than in foods. However, it does occur when impure sources are used. For example, the plants from which a drug is obtained may be mixed with straw or the roots of other plants. This added plant material is not harmful, but it does add substances that reduce the concentration of the drug.

The accidental contamination of drugs is generally more common than adulteration. This sometimes happens when the same piece of equipment is used in the processing of different compounds without being thoroughly cleaned after each use. In one case the equipment used for mixing a synthetic female hormone into feed for steers (male cattle) was later used for mixing feed for cows (female cattle). The equipment was not carefully washed after the first batch was mixed, and some of the hormone was accidentally mixed in with the second batch. As a result, the cows that were fed the contaminated batch suffered serious harmful effects.

Agricultural chemicals are also often subject to adulteration, sometimes resulting in serious consequences. In the late 1950's in the United States it was found that a certain weed killer used for cranberries had been adulterated with aminotriazole, a chemical that was known to produce cancer in laboratory animals. When this was discovered, the Food and Drug Administration stopped the sale of all cranberries that had been treated with the particular weed killer.

Public Protection. Protection of the public against adulteration is provided in the United States by the Federal Food, Drug, and Cosmetic Act. This act, which was passed in 1938, bars from sale all impure foods, drugs, and cosmetics. Congress also extended the power of the Federal Trade Commission to forbid false advertising in the sale of these products. Products are considered impure if they contain unclean or spoiled substances or anything that is a known health hazard. Food is also considered impure if any valuable part is removed or if anything is added to decrease its value. In addition, food may not be colored to conceal defects or poor quality.

In subsequent years the Food and Drug Administration was given additional power in regulating the sale of drugs. One of the issues that led to this regulation was the use of the drug thalidomide by pregnant women. Thalidomide had been widely used as a tranquilizer and was considered safe until it was found that when given to women during early stages of pregnancy, it produced congenital malformations in their babies. Shortly after this was discovered, Congress passed a drug amendment. According to this law, new drugs cannot be introduced into interstate commerce without proper government approval. In addition, a drug that has been approved may be suspended immediately by the secretary of health, education, and welfare if the drug is found to be a hazard to public health. Other regulations require the approval of the secretary on advertisements for prescription drugs.

The Food and Drug Administration also regulates the use of pesticides and other agricultural chemicals. Prior to 1966 the Food and Drug Administration approved the use of certain pesticides on a "no residue" basis. This meant that if residues of these chemicals became incorporated into the plant tissues and were later found in food products, the foods would be condemned. A major problem that developed from this ruling was that instruments and techniques had been devised to detect even the slightest traces of residues, amounts that could in no way be harmful. As a result, minute traces of residues were found in large quantities of foods, especially milk, and these foods had to be destroyed.

A new ruling, stemming from recommendations of the National Academy of Sciences, was announced early in 1966 by the Department of Agriculture and the Department of Health, Education, and Welfare. This ruling replaced the "no residue" policy with regulations based on the individual tolerance levels of each chemical. Starting in 1968, all new pesticide registrations would be accompanied by tolerance and analytical data.

MERLE MUHRER, *University of Missouri*

ADULTERY, ə-dul'trē, voluntary sexual intercourse by a married person with a partner outside the marriage. Throughout history most societies have been concerned with adultery, treating it variously as a crime, a moral wrong, a private matter, an infringement of the husband's rights, or a threat to family stability and orderly succession.

Legal Restraints. Almost all societies for which data are available have established guidelines for sexual behavior. In addition to incest taboos prohibiting coitus between certain blood relatives, most groups provide restraints for extramarital intercourse. Under Muslim law a wife who engages in the act of adultery may be killed with impunity by her husband, and mere suspicion of adultery is acceptable grounds for divorce. In Western society women traditionally have been treated more severely than men for infidelity; both the Mosaic code and Roman law defined adultery as a criminal offense only when committed by a married woman. English common law loosely followed this definition in that it held only the woman culpable but, except for a brief period during Cromwell's reign, did not regard adultery as a crime. English ecclesiastical law, however, has exacted punishment for adultery, holding men as well as women accountable.

In the United States there are wide variations in laws and attitudes relating to adultery. These differences stem partly from the mixed heritage of English common law and ecclesiastical tradition. In the early days of the Massachusetts Bay Colony, Puritans attempted to confine sexual intercourse to monogamous marriage. Statutes provided the death penalty for adultery, though it was rarely inflicted. Other colonies imposed fines, brandings, whippings, and imprisonment as means to curtail adultery.

Actual prosecution for adultery is now rare in the United States, even though adultery remains on the books as a crime in a number of states. Although state laws set forth a broad array of criminal sanctions against adultery, legal experts agree that there is little reason to believe that these sanctions still serve as much of a deterrent. The American Civil Liberties Union argues that many of these statutes should be declared unconstitutional because they violate the right to sexual privacy among consenting adults. Federal courts have generally agreed that private sexual conduct among heterosexuals is protected from state prescription.

Varying Social Standards. Attitudes toward adultery vary widely within different cultures and over time. In societies in which monogamous marriage and fidelity are not considered so important, adultery may not be viewed as immoral or as a threat to marital or family stability. In other societies, a distinction frequently is made between extramarital coitus with an unrelated individual and with certain relatives, such as a brother- or sister-in-law. Adultery with such relatives by marriage or with cross-cousins is permitted in many societies. Some societies, such as the Australian Arunta, sanction considerable extramarital intercourse for both husbands and wives. Since marriage does not imply exclusive sexual privileges for the mates, sexual freedom may be allowed them during a major ceremony or on a similar special occasion.

In general women are much less at liberty to engage in adultery than are men. This fact can be illustrated by the patterns anthropologists have found among Bantu peoples of Africa. Adultery by a wife constituted an offense against her husband's rights. Adultery by the husband was not regarded as a violation of his responsibilities. In some societies a husband's privileges may extend to lending his wife to a visitor. This rare custom exists among certain Inuit and other groups. However, should his wife act on her own initiative, the Inuit husband has the right to punish the wife and her partner.

Many other societies have taken the attitude that adultery is to be expected and have left control and punishment to the offended parties and their families. Among the Cheyenne of North America, for example, the rare case of adultery was considered a private matter. The offended husband not only had a right to chastise his wife and to secure reparations from the male, but was forced to do so by group opinion.

WILLIAM C. NICHOLS, JR.*, *Merrill-Palmer Institute*

ADVAITA, əd-vīt'ə, the monistic Vedānta philosophical school of India, systematized by Saṅkara (Shankara), who wrote at the beginning of the 9th century A.D. Advaita (from Sanskrit words meaning "not two") holds that the only reality in the universe is Brahman, the universal principle, and that the human soul is identical with Brahman. The dualism positing a division between the self and the world and between spirit and matter is a result of illusion or ignorance.

See also VEDANTA; SHANKARA.

ADVENT, ad'vent, in Christian tradition, a season of preparation observed for four to six weeks before Christmas. Although fasting is no longer required, the Advent season is a time of penance. In the Roman Catholic, Lutheran, Anglican, and Protestant Episcopal churches, Advent lasts four weeks, beginning on the Sunday following November 26, or on the Sunday nearest St. Andrew's Day (November 30). In the Greek Church, however, Advent lasts six weeks, beginning on November 11 (St. Martin's Day).

Advent was first noted at the Synod of Lerida (524); two surviving sermons indicate that by 542 it was generally observed. Also in the 6th century, the Eastern and Western churches, following the Nestorians, made Advent the beginning of the ecclesiastical year instead of Easter. Advent's four Sundays are thought to have been introduced into the calendar by Pope Gregory I (reigned 590–604) to signify the fourfold coming of Christ: in the flesh, at the hour of death, at the fall of Jerusalem, and at the Day of Judgment.

Bibliography: Adam, Adolf, *The Liturgical Year: Its History and Its Meaning after the Reform of the Liturgy,* tr. by Matthew J. O'Connell (Liturgical Press 1981); **Cowley, Patrick,** *Advent: Its Liturgical Significance* (Faith Press 1960).

ADVENT, Second.   See MILLENNIUM.

ADVENTISM, ad'ven-tiz-əm, a religious movement characterized by belief in the imminent, cataclysmic second coming of Jesus Christ. Adventists place special emphasis on this belief, based on their reading of apocalyptic scriptures in the biblical books of Daniel and Revelation. For them, Adventism implies a belief in the bleakness of the human condition in the face of a declining age. The corollary of such pessimism, however, is the Adventist expectation that with Christ's return the wicked world will be destroyed, and a new heaven and new earth will replace it.

Though some form of Adventist doctrine has been in evidence over the history of Christian teaching, Adventism as a religious movement grew out of an "awakening" of belief in the second advent that spread primarily throughout Great Britain and the northeastern United States in the early 19th century. William Miller (1782—1849), a Baptist farmer and lay preacher from Low Hampton, N.Y., established himself as the movement's leader with public lectures predicting the end of the world between March 1843 and March 1844. His intrachurch movement of Methodists, Baptists, Christians, Presbyterians, and Congregationalists, who became known as "Millerites," numbered from 50,000 to 100,000 adherents at its peak in 1844. After a series of disappointments over Miller's failed calculations, however, including the notorious "Great Disappointment" following a final prediction of Oct. 22, 1844, as the date of Christ's return, Millerism declined dramatically in membership. (See MILLER, WILLIAM.)

Despite the Millerite debacle Adventism survived among several small religious groups, which eventually formed church organizations. The four denominational descendants of the Millerite movement still extant are the Advent Christian Church, headquartered in Atlanta, Ga., with 49,000 members in 9 countries; the Church of God of Abrahamic Faith, based in Oregon, Ill., with 4,000 members in the United States and Canada; the Seventh-day Adventist Church, which has a general conference headquarters in Washington, D.C., serving 8 million members in 200 countries; and the Church of God (Seventh Day), centered in Denver, Colo., with 6,000 members in North America and more than 100,000 around the world.

In addition to believing in an imminent second coming, all four contemporary Adventist groups embrace the doctrine of baptism by immersion. They also believe in the doctrine of conditional immortality, which rejects the notion of natural immortality and asserts that eternal life is gained only through the resurrection based on a relationship with Jesus Christ. All four groups also publish religious periodicals and support worldwide missionary organizations. They have founded educational institutions as well. The Advent Christians have a college and a university; the Church of God of Abrahamic Faith has a Bible College; the Church of God (Seventh Day) has a seminary; and the Seventh-day Adventists have five universities and ten liberal arts colleges in North America alone. The Advent Christians and the Church of God of Abrahamic Faith observe Sunday as a day of worship, while the Seventh-day Adventists and the Church of God (Seventh Day) keep Sabbath on Saturday.

The Seventh-day Adventists have far surpassed the other Adventist bodies in membership, despite—or because of—their distinctive teachings. In addition to the Saturday Sabbath, Seventh-day Adventists adhere to Levitical dietary proscriptions. Further, they accept the 19th-century visionary Ellen White (who, with her husband James White and others, helped organize the church) as a prophet. Ellen White's more than 80 books and hundreds of periodicals are taken as directly inspired by God.

JONATHAN M. BUTLER, *Coeditor of "The Disappointed: Millerism and Millenarianism in the Nineteenth Century"*

Bibliography

Hewitt, Clyde I., *Midnight and Morning* (Venture Bks. 1983).
Land, Gary, ed., *Adventism in America: A History* (Eerdmans 1985).
Numbers, Ronald L., and Jonathan M. Butler, eds., *The Disappointed: Millerism and Millenarianism in the Nineteenth Century* (Univ. of Tenn. Press 1993).
Schwarz, Richard W., *Light Bearers to the Remnant* (Pacific Press Pub. Assn. 1979).

ADVENTURES OF AUGIE MARCH, a novel by the American author Saul Bellow. It received the National Book Award as the "most distinguished work of fiction published in 1953." It was Bellow's third novel, following *Dangling Man* (1944) and *The Victim* (1947).

Augie March draws on the traditions of the picaresque novel and the *bildungsroman*. The plot is structured chronologically, following the seemingly unconnected experiences that mold the hero's character. Written in the first person, the novel gives an account of the youth of Augie March, one of three sons of a poor Jewish woman living on Chicago's West Side during the late 1920s and the 1930s. The style is realistic, vividly conjuring up the scenes of Augie's adventures and the varied characters in his life. The novel takes him through family problems, various jobs, love affairs, crime, college, travel, and slum life. Augie's ebullient, conversational prose is richly humorous.

See also BELLOW, SAUL.

ADVENTURES OF BARON MUNCHAUSEN, mun' chou-zən, a collection of fabulous stories allegedly based on the adventures of Baron Karl Friedrich Hieronymus von Münchhausen, known in England as Baron Munchausen. The original stories were written in English by Rudolf Erich Raspe and were published anonymously as *Baron Munchausen's Narrative of His Marvelous Travels and Campaigns in Russia* (1785). An edition enlarged by other anonymous contributors appeared the following year as *Gulliver Reviv'd: the Singular Travels, Voyages, and Adventures of Baron Munchausen*. Numerous other editions were published with spurious additions written mostly by publishers' hacks. A German translation by Gottfried August Bürger, *Des Freiherrn von Münchhausen wunderbare Reisen und Abenteuer* (1786), was also popular.

Although the book was influenced by Jonathan Swift's *Gulliver's Travels* (1726), it made use of the popular reputation of Baron von Münchhausen as a notorious fabricator of travel stories. Von Münchhausen had apparently enjoyed an adventurous life as an officer in the Russian campaign against the Turks in 1737—1739, and after returning to his German estate, he gained a popular reputation as a storyteller.

Raspe had met the famous raconteur before leaving Germany to live in England, but most of the stories actually have counterparts in earlier literature, and Raspe undoubtedly used such sources as Heinrich Bebel's *Facetiae Bebelianae* (1508) and J. P. Lange's *Deliciae academicae* (1665).

ADVENTURES OF HUCKLEBERRY FINN. See HUCKLEBERRY FINN, ADVENTURES OF.

ADVENTURES OF ROBINSON CRUSOE. See ROBINSON CRUSOE.

ADVENTURES OF TOM SAWYER. See TOM SAWYER, ADVENTURES OF.

ADVERB, ad'vûrb, is the name in grammar for a word used chiefly to modify a verb. The word derives from the Latin *ad-verbium,* meaning "(added) to the verb," and early grammarians defined it as an indeclinable part of speech (that is, one having only a single form) whose meaning is added to that of the verb. Modern grammarians disagree about the definition of "adverb" and about which words are adverbs.

Historically, in both English and the other Indo-European tongues, most adverbs and the word endings associated with them have been derived from other parts of speech. This may suggest that the adverb is not one of the most ancient and primary features of language.

Traditional Grammar. Traditional grammar, even that used for the analysis of English, is based largely on classical Latin. It has been taught in British and American schools in about the same form since the late 1700's.

In "school grammar," the most simplified version of traditional grammar, the adverb is ordinarily defined as "a word that modifies a verb, an adjective, or another adverb." It makes the meaning of the modified word more explicit by specifying time and answering the question "When?" (He will come *soon.* We stopped *immediately.*); by specifying place and answering the question "Where?" (The car is *outside.* Hold it *up.*); by specifying manner and answering the question "How?" (They walked *slowly.* The door swung *creakily* open.); or by specifying degree and answering the question "To what extent?" (*very* tired; *fairly* quickly). These general kinds of modification can be subdivided. Certain adverbs of time, for example, can be called adverbs of frequency; certain adverbs of place are more precisely adverbs of direction.

All these are the adverbs closest in function to the historical class and the meaning of *adverbium,* but traditional English grammar also describes at least five special kinds of adverbs: (1) the interrogatives (*When* can we start? *How* does this work?); (2) the relatives (Tell me *when* you can come. I don't know *where* she is.); (3) the correlatives (He is *as* tall *as* I am. *When* he jumps, *then* I'll jump.); (4) the independents (You have it, *then? Now,* don't be a fool!); and (5) the transitionals (*However,* he knows best. I won; *therefore,* I get the prize.).

Most adverbs in English, including nearly all newly formed adverbs, have the ending *-ly,* which derives from an adjective ending in Old English. Many adverbs, however, including most of the special kinds, are uninflected forms without the *-ly* ending. One small but troublesome group of adverbs is identical in form with related adjectives (*bright, deep, fair, hard, slow,* and others). Most had distinctive endings in Old English but lost them in Middle English.

Like adjectives, most adverbs may be "compared," that is, used with the suffix *-(e)r* or with *more* to show a relatively higher degree, and with the suffix *-(e)st* or with *most* to show the relatively highest degree. The suffixes are used with the small group of adverbs that function as modifiers and do not end in *-ly* (*bright, brighter, brightest; fast, faster, fastest*), while *more* and *most* are used with the many adverbs ending in *-ly* (*sweetly, more sweetly, most sweetly*). *Less* and *least* are used in "reverse comparison."

Adverbs that cannot be compared include all five special kinds and those that have an absolute meaning—*there, now, not, abroad,* and others. Some adverbs have irregular comparison—*little, less, least; much, more, most,* and others.

The adverbs in traditional grammar form a large, diverse, and not very satisfactory class. They include words as dissimilar as *yes, arbitrarily,* and *notwithstanding.* Their functions are so various that one authority doubts that there is anything an adverb may not at one time or another be found to modify (in *junior year abroad* and *the up escalator,* for example, they modify nouns). Some grammarians helplessly define the adverb by elimination, as any modifier that is not an adjective or a noun. Others frankly classify words as adverbs "because we have to put them somewhere."

Structural Grammar. It was such defects as these in traditional grammar that prompted a group of American linguistic scientists, beginning in the 1930's, to work out the kind of grammatical analysis called structural grammar. In order to exclude meaning entirely as a basis for determining grammatical class, the structuralists set up "form classes" and "positional classes." The form classes are usually named after the traditional parts of speech, and the related positional classes have the same name plus the suffix *-al* or *-ial* (adverb and adverb*ial;* adjective and adjec*tival;* noun and noun*al* or nomin*al*).

The form class "adverb" is restricted to words (like *roughly*) that consist of an adjective plus *-ly* and that cannot receive the additional suffixes *-(e)r* and *-(e)st;* and words (like *crabwise*) that consist of a noun plus *-wise.* The form class takes care of most adverbs because most end in *-ly,* but it does not account for the many uninflected modifiers called adverbs in traditional grammar. Some of these are located, along with true adverbs, in the positional class "adverbials." Adverbials are words that can occupy the sentence positions or test-frame positions that adverbs regularly occupy. This has not been entirely satisfactory, since the English adverb can occupy a bewildering number of positions.

The other uninflected modifiers traditionally called adverbs are excluded from the class in structural grammar. They are generally called "function words" and subclassified under names that vary according to the grammarian consulted. Typically, *not* is called "the negator"; words like *very* are called "intensifiers"; words like *when, where,* and *why* are called "interrogators"; words like *nevertheless* and *therefore* are called "connectors"; words like *well, oh,* and *now* are called "attention signals"; and *yes* and *no* are called "responses."

The new and very active school of transformational or generative grammar has followed structural grammar in rejecting the catchall traditional class of adverbs and has revealed how the newer classification has its logical basis in the step-by-step processes by which grammatically normal sentences are constructed.

ROBERT L. CHAPMAN, *Drew University*

Bibliography

Bartsch, R., *Grammar of Adverbials* (Elsevier Pub. Co. 1976).
Chomsky, Noam, *The Logical Structure of Linguistic Theory* (Plenum Pub. 1975).
Dik, S., *Functional Grammar,* 3d ed. (Foris Pub. 1983).
Huang, Shuan-Fan, *A Study of Adverbs* (Mouton Pubs. 1975).
McCawley, James D., *Adverbs, Vowels and Other Objects of Wonder* (Univ. of Chicago Press 1985).
McKay, S. L., ed., *Teaching Grammar* (Pergamon 1985).
Taylor, Barry, *Modes of Occurrence: Verbs, Adverbs and Events* (Basil Blackwell 1986).

ADVERTISING

ADVERTISING DISPLAY IN TIMES SQUARE, NEW YORK (PHOTO BY A. DEVANEY, INC.)

ADVERTISING, ad′vər-tīz-ing, is any paid form of nonpersonal presentation and promotion of products, services, or ideas by an identifiable individual or organization.

The products advertised may be as varied as toothpaste and automobiles, and the services may range from laundries to travel agencies. The ideas advertised may involve contributing to a mental health agency, voting for a certain candidate, or going to church on Sunday. In each case the advertising points out the qualities of the product, the service, or the idea that would make it attractive to the persons the advertiser wishes to influence.

A single advertisement is usually only part of a total advertising *campaign.* Although the purpose of the campaign is to stimulate people to thought and action, this does not imply that the goal of all advertising is to make a sale. Instead, the goal of advertising is to awaken or produce predispositions to buy the advertised product or service.

This may be illustrated by the following three categories of advertising (in which, however, there is some overlapping):

(1) *Immediate Action.* The primary purpose of some advertising is to induce immediate action. In this category is most newspaper advertising—especially for bargain-priced products, special deals, coupon offers, foods, and department-store items—as well as mail-order advertising.

(2) *Awareness.* Some advertising primarily creates an awareness on the part of the listener, viewer, or reader. This category includes announcements of a new product or model, improvements in a known product, a change in price, or a change in package design.

(3) *Image.* Some advertising seeks principally to create, reinforce, or change an image of a product or service (or organization) in the minds of those to whom the advertising is directed. Usually it is expected that the desired change of attitude will take place gradually over a period of time.

About three fourths of the dollars spent for advertising messages are invested in six media—

newspapers, television, direct mail, magazines, radio, and outdoor, in that order. Advertising provides the principal source of revenue for these media, which cost consumers relatively little.

Many persons object to advertising because some of it seems silly to them. They then conclude erroneously that most advertising is deceptive. Yet actual untruths are rare in most advertising. In the United States, this is especially true of products and services advertised on a nationwide basis. For example, it would be hard to find anything misleading in national advertising for insurance, shirts, soups, television sets, or pens.

One difficulty is that advertising tends to have a special language of its own. Most persons do not use such phrases as "cold, crisp taste," "fast, long-lasting, safe relief," or "volcano of fashion culture." Also, in many families more time is spent watching television than any other activity, and just looking at a great number of TV commercials over a long period of time leads many people to be critical of all advertising.

Some people who want new products and buy them make advertising the scapegoat by claiming that they were duped or forced into buying something they did not need. Yet the most far-reaching advertising campaign cannot force someone to buy something he does not want.

The consumer is still king (or queen) as to what he does with his money. The consumer is free to save or to spend his money in any way he wishes.

Advertising flourishes mainly in free-market, profit-oriented countries. It is one of the most important factors in accelerating the distribution of products and in helping to raise the standard of living.

The first sections of this article deal with advertising in the United States. In Canada, advertising practices are similar to those in the United States, except that in the province of Quebec advertising often is presented in both English and French. (For a brief summary of advertising outside the United States, see section 9.)

1. The Role of Advertising in the United States

Influence of Advertising. Advertising has an important role in informing and influencing consumers. Virtually every individual in the United States is exposed to advertising. It has become one of the most important economic and social forces in society. Partly because of the influence of advertising, people have learned to want ever better products and services, to take better care of their health, and to improve their way of living.

Advertising cannot turn a poor product or service into a good one. What advertising can do—and does—is to create an awareness about both old and new products and services. It stimulates wants, indicates the differences among various products (and services), and shows how various needs and wants can be satisfied. Increasingly, advertising performs one of the main functions of a salesman, by providing some advance information about products and services to consumers before they reach the place of purchase.

Advertising is one of the most important techniques of modern business enterprise. A company's decisions about advertising affect its product development, packaging, pricing, distribution, and retailing. In turn, each of these activities affects advertising. Most important of all, a company's advertising affects consumers' decisions as to what to buy or not to buy.

Advertising is especially important in product development. In a competitive market, each manufacturer attempts to improve his products and to introduce new products to gain a sales advantage. Advertising enables a business firm to tell consumers about such improvements.

Magnitude of Advertising. Of some 4.4 million business firms in the United States, practically all do some advertising. Over 3,800 advertising agencies are listed in the *Standard Directory of Advertising Agencies*. They render special services to many business firms as well as to governmental agencies and nonprofit organizations.

ADVERTISING VOLUME IN THE UNITED STATES

Advertising medium	1955	1960	1955
		(in thousands)	
Newspapers	$3,087,800	$3,702,800	$4,435,000
Radio	539,300	668,000	889,300
Magazines	729,400	940,800	1,197,700
Farm papers	33,800	34,500	33,500
Direct mail	1,298,900	1,830,200	2,271,400
Business papers	446,200	609,300	678,500
Outdoor	192,400	203,300	180,000
Television	1,025,300	1,605,000	2,497,000
Miscellaneous, including transit advertising	1,841,300	2,337,800	2,937,600
	$9,914,400	$11,931,700	$15,120,000

Source: *Printers' Ink.*

The great majority of smaller business firms do not use an advertising agency, but almost all large firms do. The advertising agency plans, prepares, and places advertising for advertisers. However, advertising agencies account for only about 25 percent of all dollars invested in advertising in a given year.

The total dollar amount of all advertising nearly tripled in a 15-year period, rising from $5.7 billion in 1950 to $15.1 billion in 1965. Of this amount, national advertising—for products and services throughout the United States—accounted for about two thirds of the total.

2. Advertising Objectives and Communication

Advertising is essentially persuasive communication. Thus, the goals set for advertising are communications tasks: to reach a defined audience, to a given extent, and during a given time period.

Consumers do not often change suddenly from uninterested individuals to convinced purchasers. In many cases they go through several steps before buying a product. In general, they move from unawareness of the product or service to awareness and then to knowledge, liking, preference, acceptance (or conviction), and then to purchase of the product or service.

Objectives of Advertising. The above steps in persuasive communication indicate three major objectives of advertising: (1) to produce awareness and knowledge about the product or service; (2) to create liking and preference for it; and (3) to stimulate thought and action about it.

These objectives vary with the maturity or life cycle of the product or service. As the product is introduced to the market, the major goal of advertising might be informational. Later, as the product progresses to rapid growth, emphasis might be placed on competitive appeals. Later, as the product passes into a period of maturity, advertising might be aimed at keeping the name of the product or service before consumers.

In a sense, therefore, advertising management is a process of varying the advertising objectives for each product or service in accord with the specific goals of the advertiser. It is especially important for the advertiser to set clearly defined written objectives prior to the development of advertising campaigns. Only in this way can the promotional techniques employed be directly relevant to the objectives sought. Only in this way can the effectiveness of the campaign be determined.

Mail-order advertising provides a measure of effectiveness in terms of number of replies. But direct effects on sales of other types of advertising are difficult to separate from other sales determinants, such as product design, price, and personal selling. That is why a goal such as "to increase sales" or "to increase profits" is not a measurable goal for advertising.

Functions of an Advertising Manager. The advertising activities of a company usually are headed by an advertising manager, and sometimes by a brand manager or product manager. The number of persons working for him depends on the size of the company, the importance of advertising to the company, and the company's sales goals.

Although the advertising manager's (or brand manager's) job differs from company to company, usually he has the following responsibilities:

(1) determining basic advertising policy; (2) establishing advertising objectives; (3) representing the company with its advertising agency or agencies; (4) planning the advertising program to meet the requirements of the product (or service), of consumers, and of distribution methods; (5) originating various advertising ideas; (6) establishing the advertising budget, working with both company management and with the advertising agency; (7) controlling the spending of advertising funds; (8) organizing and supervising all elements of the advertising program; (9) evaluating the results of advertising; and (10) integrating and coordinating the advertising with the company's other departments and functions, such as direct selling, sales promotion, and public relations.

3. Advertisers

Kinds of Advertising. Advertising can be classified according to who advertises what to whom and where in order to bring about what response. Although they are not all-inclusive and there is some overlap, the following eight classifications of advertising provide an overall view of the kinds of advertising:

(1) *National Advertising.* Branded consumer products and services are closely identified with the firm's name; producers advertise nationally —although sometimes differently in different geographical regions—to consumers. The message is: "Buy *our* brand (or service)." Examples: Maytag and United Air Lines, in *Life* magazine.

(2) *Retail Advertising.* The advertisers are consumer outlets, such as department stores, supermarkets, and drug stores; and service institutions, such as dry cleaners, laundries, and banks. Their items and services are advertised to consumers within a geographical market area. The message is: "Do business with *us*." Examples: the Marshall Field department store and the Continental Illinois Bank, in the *Chicago Tribune*.

(3) *Industrial Advertising.* The advertisers make such products as office equipment, machinery, and computers—items and services that are used in manufacturing or that aid the operation of a business or institution. These items and services are advertised to industrial buyers, either nationally or regionally. The message is: "Use *our* product or service in your operation." Examples: Clark lift trucks and IBM computers, in *Business Week* magazine.

(4) *Trade Advertising.* Producers and distributors have both branded and nonbranded consumer products ready for consumption that are bought for resale to someone else. These products are advertised to retailers and to wholesalers, through whom the products are sold to consumers. The message is: "Stock and promote the sale of *our* product." Example: Dial soap in *Progressive Grocer* magazine.

(5) *Professional Advertising.* Certain producers and distributors depend largely on professional people to recommend, prescribe, or specify their products to buyers. Items strongly influenced by a professional person are advertised with the message: "Recommend, prescribe, or specify *our* product." Example: Abbott Laboratories drugs, in the *Journal of the American Medical Association*.

(6) *Farm Advertising.* The farm is a consuming unit—and some advertising features consumer products that appeal to farm families as house-

RETAIL ADVERTISING invites consumers to do business with a specific department store or other firm.

hold units. But the farm is also a producing unit, and other advertising is directed to greater farm efficiency. The message is: "Buy *our* product or service." Example: John Deere farm equipment in the *Farm Journal*.

(7) *Nonproduct or "Idea" Advertising.* Churches, political parties, individuals, and groups (fraternal, trade, and social) advertise. Institutions, ideologies, and social betterment are nationally and locally advertised to citizens and community leaders. The messages are: "Accept *our* idea," "Vote for *our* candidate," or "Help *our* cause." Examples: Republican party and Red Cross, on radio and television.

(8) *Classified Advertising.* Most of the "want ads" (classified advertising) in newspapers and in some magazines are short statements, one column wide, set in small type. Some of the ads, however, are of the display variety—that is, a bit larger and presenting more white space, various kinds of type, and sometimes illustrations to attract special attention. Classified advertisements are grouped according to products and services. The message is: "Get in touch with *me* for what you want." Example: "Help Wanted."

Leading Advertisers. The heaviest U.S. advertisers are those who sell food products, drugs and cosmetics, soaps and cleansers, automobiles, and tobacco. In a typical year in the mid-1960's, the 125 leading U.S. advertisers invested over $4 billion in advertising, thus accounting for over one fourth of the nation's total advertising.

ADVERTISING EXPENDITURES BY 5 INDUSTRIES REPRESENTING 63 OF THE 125 LEADING U.S. ADVERTISERS—1965

Industry	Number of Companies	Expenditures
Foods	22	$691,000,000
Drugs and cosmetics	23	631,000,000
Soaps and cleansers	5	466,000,000
Automobiles	5	409,000,000
Tobacco	8	313,000,000

Source: *Advertising Age.*

Advertising expenditures differ among industries because of many variables, such as the nature of the product, the nature of the market, and the nature of the competition. Heavily advertised convenience goods such as cosmetics, soaps, and tobacco are inexpensive, frequently purchased, and require little thought by the buyer in his decision to purchase. By contrast, most companies that produce appliances and other durable goods use relatively little advertising. These products are expensive, infrequently purchased, and require a substantial amount of thought before purchase.

Company Advertising Departments. Basically, there are two ways of organizing an advertising department—with a general advertising manager or with brand managers (or product managers).

In a general advertising department, functions range all the way from developing and placing all advertising to delegating this work to an advertising agency or agencies. This department generally acts as an aid to the sales department. Companies such as International Business Machines and U.S. Steel have general advertising departments.

A different organizational concept is used by many consumer-goods manufacturers. Individuals known as brand managers (or product managers) are assigned to one or more of the company's products. They are responsible for all advertising, promotion, and profit (or loss) for a specific brand. Introduced by such companies as Procter & Gamble and General Electric, the brand-management concept has been adopted by many other companies.

4. Advertising Agencies

Services. The basic function of an advertising agency is to interpret to the public, or to that part of the public which the client (the advertiser) desires to reach, the advantages of a given product, service, or idea. Some agencies specialize—for example, in industrial advertising or fashion advertising.

An advertising agency must understand the client's advertising objectives, products or services, and the market for these products or services. To formulate an effective advertising plan, the advertising agency may conduct research as to effective appeals for the advertising messages and as to appropriate media through which to communicate these advertising messages.

After the client has approved the advertising

CREATIVE TECHNIQUES in making an advertisement include shaping a type block to fit a certain design.

The HEEL, said Christopher Marlowe, was invented by a woman who was always being kissed on the forehead. Undeniably, it raises her stature, giving her footing and elevation. This is done not by inches alone, but with a sizable measure of savoir faire. A DELMAN heel is a trompe-l'oeil par excellence. It abbreviates the foot, lengthens the body, lightens the carriage, takes inches off the hips, and gives the costume altogether new dimension. She who walks in beauty, walks in DELMAN heels.

BERGDORF GOODMAN
FIFTH AVENUE AT 58TH STREET

ADVERTISING AS PERCENT OF SALES AMONG SELECTED LEADING ADVERTISERS—1965

Rank[1]	Company	Industry	Advertising (millions)	Percent of sales
1	Procter & Gamble	Soaps, cleansers	$245.0	10.9
2	General Motors	Automobiles	173.0	0.8
3	General Foods	Foods	120.0	8.7
5	Bristol-Myers	Drugs, cosmetics	108.0	27.6
12	American Tobacco	Tobacco	71.0	5.8
29	Goodyear	Tires	40.0	1.8
36	Jos. Schlitz	Beer	35.0	10.8
53	Standard Oil (Ind.)	Petroleum products	23.5	0.8
63	Wm. Wrigley, Jr.	Gum, candy	21.0	16.3

[1] Position among all advertisers in total annual advertising expenditures. Source: *Advertising Age.*

plans, the agency prepares the advertising and places it in various media. Some agencies provide information and counsel on product development, product design, package design, display material, and sales methods. Others consider such services outside their scope.

Organizational Structure. Agencies vary greatly in size—from only one or two persons up to several thousand. In the one-man agency, an individual handles copy, media, art, merchandising, or whatever else is necessary. In what might be called a multiple agency, a group of persons handles the contact, planning, and creative work for one or more clients; another group does the same for one or more other clients; and so on. In a sense, a multiple agency consists of several one-man agencies, each man handling his own group of accounts.

The most common type is the functionalized agency, in which the creative, media, research, and other functions are departmentalized. In this way every department serves all clients.

Account Management. Once an "account"—that is, an advertiser—has selected an agency, policies and procedures must be established to make certain that the advertiser will be satisfied with the services rendered by the agency, and also that the agency will find it profitable to handle the work. The account supervisor or account executive acts as liaison between the agency and the client and works in planning the advertising program and in obtaining client approval.

Creative Department. A number of creative functions are involved in developing an advertisement. These include writing copy, preparing art work, and laying out the format of the finished advertisement in many alternative advertising appeals and treatments, from which the final advertising approach is selected.

Media Department. The planning and buying of print space and broadcast time are the functions of the media department. The goal is to choose the advertising medium or combination of media that will do the most effective job of exposing the advertisements to prospective purchasers of the product or service. Decisions must be made as to the kinds of media (for example, magazines compared with newspapers); the individual vehicles (for example, *Time* compared with *Newsweek*) that will carry the advertising message; and when and how many advertisements are to be placed.

Research Department. A few of the many specialized functions of the research department include the gathering of factual information about the product or service, the present and potential market, and the effectiveness of specific advertisements or campaigns. Such information provides assistance in creating, preparing, and placing advertising messages.

Other Functions. An agency's organizational structure also includes the important departments or functions of mechanical production, broadcast production, traffic, merchandising, personnel, and accounting, as well as business management of the agency.

The plans board or review committee develops and reviews the advertising plans for a client or group of clients. A plans board is characteristic of the larger agencies and usually comprises representatives from major departments of the agency—who, of course, have other regular duties.

At least three types of ability are needed to run an advertising agency: creativity, sales ability, and business management. Sometimes the head of an agency provides all three, but more often two or more management persons join in supplying the needed abilities.

Numerous outside service organizations perform specialized tasks, such as finished art work, photoengraving, production of television commercials, and supplying information on television ratings.

Compensation. Advertising agencies receive their operating revenue from three main sources: from commissions allowed by media; from agencies' own percentage charges on the cost of materials and services purchased for clients; and from fees from advertisers. However, media commissions predominate, and provide approximately three fourths of the entire income of the agency business in the United States.

Most of the large agencies receive the great bulk of their income in the form of commissions, whereas most small agencies receive a higher percentage of their income from percentage charges and fees.

Commissions. The medium compensates the agency by allowing it to deduct an agency commission. Generally, commissions amount to 15 percent of the price quoted by the medium in which space or time is purchased. The amount of money for this purchase of media space or time represents billings of the agency.

This works in the following way: Client A contracts with Agency X to develop an advertising campaign for the company. Agency X then contracts with several media for $450,000 worth of space. The media then bill Agency X for $450,000 less the 15 percent commission, or a net bill of $382,500. Agency X pays this net amount, and bills Client A for $450,000, thus leaving the agency $67,500 for services rendered.

Percentage Charges. Agencies almost always buy materials (such as typography and printing plates) and services (such as research data) from suppliers on behalf of clients. When they do, most add a percentage to the supplier's invoice. This percentage is agreed upon with each client and may vary from agency to agency, but most agencies add 17.65 percent to the net cost of the material or service purchased—the equivalent of 15 percent of the total cost to the client (17.65 percent of $85 equals 15 percent of $100).

Fees. Various methods are used for charging advertisers the fees for materials or services: net cost to the agency; cost plus 15 percent flat hourly fee; and "profit-target fee," designed to net the agency 1.5 to 2.5 percent of billings after taxes (that is, 1.5 to 2.5 percent of the dollar amount of all advertising placed by the agency).

to be Jewish

to love Levy's
real Jewish Rye

DOYLE DANE BERNBACH, INC.

CAR CARDS, such as this one directed to bus and subway riders, rely on short text and strong impact.

Size and Location of Major U.S. Agencies. In the mid-1960's, about 400 U.S. advertising agencies had billings exceeding $1 million. The breakdown, as reported by *Advertising Age,* was: over $25 million, 46 agencies; $10–25 million, 60 agencies; $5–10 million, 60 agencies; and $1–5 million, 231 agencies.

New York has the greatest number of advertising agencies, Chicago is second, and Los Angeles third. Philadelphia, San Francisco, Detroit, and St. Louis follow in that order. Advertising agencies are situated in both large and small communities all over the United States.

5. Creating the Advertisement

Development of Advertisements. The development of an advertisement is a creative process, involving copy, art, and production.

Copy consists of all written material (or all words) in the advertisement.

Art work involves anything that is primarily seen rather than read. Art work includes pictures, photographs, drawings, illustrations, the layout of the advertisement for print advertising, and television story boards (the drawings of the scenes of a TV commercial, usually accompanied by the copy and scene-by-scene directions).

Production consists of all efforts directed to putting the ideas for copy and art work into final form. It includes television direction (getting the commercial completed and on the air); preparing in final form the newspaper advertisement or magazine advertisement; getting the art work made into engravings; or having outdoor posters printed.

Generally, the creation of an advertisement is a group process. Those in copywriting, layout, art, and other assignments work together to produce the final advertisement. These creative people develop from many facts and opinions a copy rationale or *copy platform* and then try to

199

create advertising that is informative and persuasive.

For a specific advertisement, the copywriter may provide most of the creative thought, but in another instance the artist may contribute many ideas. These two work together as a team.

The Total Advertisement. The creative group considers every detail of the advertisement. However, the advertisement is not likely to be perceived by the advertiser's audience strictly in terms of its individual parts. The total impact of an advertisement depends, among other things, on attention-getting, simplicity, realism, sincerity, and surprise. An effective advertisement for one set of conditions is not necessarily a good advertisement for another. As the product (or service), the market, and competition vary, the advertisement also varies.

Basic Considerations. Many basic considerations arise in developing advertising. First, ideas for advertisements develop not only from opinions but from facts. Fact-gathering continues throughout the various stages of planning.

Second, the purpose or objective of the advertisement must always be determined. The creative group must know what the advertisement is to accomplish. Who is to be influenced to do what, and when, and where?

A third consideration is the assembling of the ideas and materials that might possibly be included in the advertisement.

A fourth factor is the organizing of the advertising materials. Which idea or ideas will receive the greatest emphasis?

Selection of the dominant appeal is a fifth consideration. To create an effective advertisement, an appeal must be selected that will tend to persuade the consumer that the product or service will satisfy his wants and needs better than any competing product or service.

Visualizing various ways of presenting the advertisement is another essential step. This is a problem of coordinating and integrating physical elements, such as headline, text, and illustration. A number of "rough" layouts or visualizations of the advertisement may be developed, taking into account the dominant appeal or main theme.

Pretesting of the advertisement is desirable, to determine whether it attracts attention, has a dominant appeal, is persuasive, and so on. Finally, many revisions and refinements of the advertisements may take place. Every detail must be reevaluated. Additions, deletions, and replacements may be necessary to get the advertisement in finished form.

6. Selecting the Media

Reaching the Audience. *Media*—the plural of the word "medium"—is the term used to denote the various ways an advertiser can expose his advertising message to people, such as through newspapers, magazines, television, and radio. The following definitions show the considerations involved in selecting media.

Vehicle. An individual advertising medium; for example, a magazine or radio station.

Circulation. The number of copies of a print vehicle sold or distributed; the number of radio sets or television sets possessed by families within the range of a station signal; or the number of people passing an outdoor advertisement who have a reasonable opportunity to see it.

Exposure. Contact of an individual with an advertising medium or advertisement.

Audience. Persons who have an opportunity to listen to, view, or read an advertising message in an advertising vehicle.

Audience Composition. The makeup in terms of age, sex, and other demographic characteristics of the people who have an opportunity to listen to, view, or read an advertising message.

Coverage The number of individuals or homes exposed to (or capable of being exposed to) a vehicle within a specified period of time.

Penetration. The number of people in a given market or market segment who can be exposed to an advertising message or advertising campaign.

Reach (or Cumulative Audience). The net unduplicated audience—that is, the total audience a medium can cover, or does cover, during a given period of time, counting only once each person exposed to the medium.

Frequency. The average number of repeated advertising messages being delivered to the members of an audience over a given period of time.

Continuity. The advertising of a single theme or selling proposition over a period of time.

Rate. The unit cost of time or space for advertising in a specific vehicle. (The rates can be reduced by volume discounts.)

Cost per Thousand. A dollar figure to evaluate the relative cost of various media or media vehicles within a selected audience criterion—such as cost per thousand circulation, cost per thousand families, and cost per thousand homes.

Objectives. The advertiser's objectives are to select media that will, within certain cost limitations: (1) pinpoint and attract the largest possible audience of potential customers; (2) lead people who listen to, view, or read the medium to have a high probability of exposure to the

BILLBOARDS enable an advertiser to display a sales message to motorists as they travel near retail outlets.

TELEVISION ADVERTISING appeals to eye and ear. Eydie Gorme and Vic Damone (*right*) in an extravaganza. Bill Cullen (*above*) tapes a commercial.

advertising itself; and (3) generate as much perception of the advertising itself as possible.

Merits and Rates of Various Media. Each medium offers special advantages to the advertisers, and media rates fit a broad range of budgets.

Newspapers. Newspapers offer the advertiser universal appeal, timeliness of message, frequent publication, localized circulation, high reader interest, and penetration into all socioeconomic groups. Rates vary according to many factors, including whether the advertising appears in a daily or Sunday edition. As an example, the rate per agate line (1/14 inch high and one column wide) in the Chicago *Tribune* is over $2.00 daily and over $3.00 Sunday.

Consumer Magazines. These provide the advertiser with prestige, selectivity (special kinds of readers), national or regional distribution, relative permanence of advertising compared with other media, large secondary circulation, and good mechanical reproduction. The national advertising rate for a one-time insertion of a full-page four-color advertisement in *Look* costs more than $50,000.

Business Papers and Magazines. The business press includes industrial publications, edited primarily for those in business; institutional publications, edited for hotels, hospitals, schools, and other institutions; professional publications, edited for physicians, lawyers, and similar groups; and merchandising publications (the so-called "trade papers"), edited for retailers, jobbers, and wholesalers. As a specific instance, a one-time insertion of a full-page black-and-white advertisement in *American Machinist* cost more than $1,000.

Farm Magazines. These provide advertising vehicles for manufacturers of products for the farm to advertise to a farm audience. The rate for a one-time insertion of a full-page black-and-white advertisement in the *Farm Journal* is approximately $14,000.

Radio. The radio advertiser is offered entertainment value, persuasiveness of the human voice, penetration into all socioeconomic groups, and flexibility in techniques of presentation. Rates for radio commercials depend on the length of message, time of day, and size of audience. For example, a 30-second daytime commercial on WGN (Chicago) costs more than twice as much during morning and evening traffic rush hours (over $150 compared to over $70) because of the greater number of automobile radios in use.

Television. This medium offers the entertainment, persuasiveness, penetration, and flexibility of radio, plus even more personalized selling through visual messages and frequent use of product demonstrations. The rates vary greatly with the length of the message, the time of day, and other factors. An evening, one-minute message aired once on WGN-TV (Chicago) costs from less than $1,000 to more than $3,000. The rate covers time only; a commercial that is broadcast during a program involves production costs of the show itself. The total cost of a one-minute commercial during an evening network program averages more than $30,000.

Outdoor Advertising. Posters (or "billboards") and bulletins painted on buildings are tailored for a short message. Advertising is sold in packages or "showings" of, say, a 100 percent coverage (theoretically) of a geographical market. For Chicago, a 100-showing—that is, over 250 posters—costs more than $22,000 per month. Outdoor advertising provides the advertiser with large illustrations of product and trademark, constant repetition of the sales message, flexibility of coverage, and presentation of the message on highways and near retail outlets.

Direct Mail. Sent to the home, office, and school, direct mail provides the advertiser with effective timing of message, a method of selling directly to prospects, and diversity of types of advertising. Depending on many factors, direct mail might cost 15 to 30 cents per prospect for a one-page letter.

Other Media. These include films, catalogs, trade-show exhibits, transit advertising, dealer displays, counter displays, store signs, electric displays, posters in public conveyances, package inserts, matchbook covers, directories, and skywriting. The cost might range from $2 for a cardboard counter display to $3,000 (or many times that amount) for a trade-show exhibit.

7. Research in Advertising

Objectives and Techniques. A variety of fact-finding techniques used to plan and evaluate advertisements is grouped under "advertising research." However, unless there are clear-cut goals or objectives for the advertising, there can be no clear-cut objectives for the research.

The research can be carried out in dozens of ways. There is no single best way to test advertising effectiveness, but rather many combinations of ways. Measurements of readership of print advertisements by Daniel Starch & Staff, ratings of the size of television audiences by the A.C. Nielsen Company, and scores of other methods give information that helps to determine the extent to which advertising has communicated the

Think small.

Our little car isn't so much of a novelty any more. | flivver don't even think 32 miles to the gallon is going any great guns. | some of our economies, you don't even think about them any more.
A couple of dozen college kids don't try to squeeze inside it. | Or using five pints of oil instead of five quarts. | Except when you squeeze into a small parking spot. Or renew your small insurance. Or pay a small repair bill.
The guy at the gas station doesn't ask where the gas goes. | Or never needing anti-freeze. | Or racking up 40,000 miles on a set of tires. | Or trade in your old VW for a new one.
Nobody even stares at our shape. | | Think it over.
In fact, some people who drive our little | That's because once you get used to |

DOYLE DANE BERNBACH, INC.

NATIONAL ADVERTISING makes prospects in many regions aware of a branded product or special service.

intended message through the advertising medium or media.

The basic job of research in advertising is to provide information that will help in evaluating various executions of the advertising messages, and the effectiveness of the medium or media of communications.

The two primary areas of advertising research are *message research* and *media research*.

Message Research. Research on the advertising message includes background information for development of the message, and techniques for testing the effectiveness of the message. Background information includes product analysis, consumer research, and market analysis. Product analysis provides insights into the want-satisfying characteristics of the product or service. Consumer research reveals some information about consumer motivations and attitudes as a basis for message appeals. Market analysis provides information about the people with purchasing power who, it is hoped, will buy the product or service.

The effectiveness of the advertising message may be tested before the message is in final form (pretesting) and after the advertisement has circulated (posttesting). The advertisement may be tested in totality, or various aspects may be tested, such as theme, format, headline, or copy. The major techniques of measurement are summarized as:

Recognition Tests. These are the most widely used method. Individuals are asked to look at an advertisement and state if they have seen it before.

Recall and Association Tests. These are the second most frequently used method. Individuals are asked to tell, without having the advertisement or commercial before them, those features they remember having heard, read, or seen.

Opinion and Attitude Ratings. These call for personal reactions to a given advertisement.

Projective or Clinical Methods. Such methods make up a large part of what popularly is called "motivation research"—using such psychological techniques as word-associations, sentence-completions, and role-playing.

Laboratory Tests. Special devices and instruments that measure reactions of the eyes and ears to advertisements, as well as other physical indicators of "emotional" responses, are used in laboratory tests.

Content Analysis. Such analysis consists of identification and classification of advertising copy to permit quantitative statements about it.

Inquiries Received and Sales Results. These measures become possible only after the circulation of advertisements.

One of the largest advertising agencies, the Leo Burnett Company of Chicago, has divided its research program for advertising campaigns into six steps. Prior to the development of the advertising, there are (1) *preliminary research*, analysis of the market and market size, and (2) *theme research*, determining the relevance and meaning of various appeals and ideas. During development of the advertising itself, there are (3) *developmental research*, evaluation of the advertising in its very early stages, and (4) *pretesting*, research on an advertisement or commercial before it runs. After the commercial or advertisement has run, there are opportunities for (5) *posttesting* and (6) *campaign research*, studies of the campaign and those of competitors, to determine changes in awareness, attitudes, and preferences. For different campaigns, some steps are followed more completely than others; and sometimes certain steps are omitted.

Media Research. Many techniques are available for determining audiences of different advertising media, exposure of advertisements, audience composition, attitudes of audiences, and extent of audience accumulation. Ideally, media research can be approached in the following six stages:

(1) *Vehicle Distribution.* The number of physical units of a medium can be counted and audited to determine the number that could possibly transmit the advertising message.

(2) *Vehicle Exposure, or Total Audience Potential.* In broadcasting, the commercial audience potential can be measured by whether sets are turned on, and in print media, by determining total readership of each medium, including "pass-along" readers.

(3) *Advertising Exposure.* The number of prospects reached by the advertising message is estimated by auditing the number of sets tuned to a specific channel at the time of a broadcast, or by analyzing records in diaries of viewing habits; or by calculating the number of people exposed to a print advertisement.

(4) *Advertising Perception.* Some awareness of the message stimulus causes some degree of remembering. This stage is concerned with measuring either recognition or recall, or both, of a given message.

(5) *Advertising Communication.* Depth of recall, attitude change, and emotional involvement are tested.

(6) *Sales Response.* To the extent that the advertising affects predispositions to purchase the product or service, this would be the ideal measure in media research. The exact methodology, however, has not been perfected for most advertising.

Value of Research. Research is not a substitute for creativity, but research provides facts upon which creativity can go to work. No research finding really tells the advertiser or advertising agency exactly what to do. But what the findings do provide is information that can be helpful in making a judgment or decision about the advertising messages and media. Results of research can sometimes be more helpful in indicating what not to do than what to do.

8. Regulation of Advertising

Self-Regulation. Although many people react to various advertisements and campaigns with dislike and then claim that most advertising is deceptive, usually they are thinking of puffery or bragging in the advertisements. The majority of advertising is not deceptive. Virtually all advertisers, advertising agencies, and media are well aware of both their ethical and legal responsibilities. Self-regulation is their watchword.

To stay in business, it is essential for a company to follow policies that will lead to satisfied customers. This means trying to make its products or services more satisfactory than those of competitors and using advertising that people can trust. If consumers think an advertisement is deceptive, the advertiser has not succeeded in being persuasive. The greatest protection of consumers against deceptive and misleading advertising is the competitive struggle of all advertisers for their favor.

The various media maintain standards as to what specific claims are or are not acceptable. In addition, there is the Creative Code of the American Association of Advertising Agencies, endorsed also by the Association of National Advertisers and by the Advertising Federation of America. And the advertising publications, especially *Advertising Age* and *Printers' Ink*, have vigorously endorsed the highest principles in advertising.

Nationally and locally, the Better Business Bureaus are supported by business firms that want to eliminate unfair practices. If an individual or a business firm complains to a Better Business Bureau about an advertisement, the advertiser may be asked to prove his claim and, if he cannot, to change his advertising. Media are also informed of the misleading nature of the advertising and advised not to accept it. If the advertiser does not improve his practices, the complaint may be taken to a government agency.

Government Regulation. The involvement of federal, state, and local government in activities affecting consumer interests is substantial. A model statute aimed at curbing deceptive advertising was drafted in 1911 by *Printers' Ink,* and this has become the basis of legislation enacted by 44 states and the District of Columbia.

Almost 300 federal departments and agencies participate in consumer-protection and consumer-interest activities. Of special interest are the Federal Trade Commission, the Food and Drug Administration, the Federal Communications Commission, and the Post Office.

Federal Trade Commission. Probably the government agency most active in regulating advertising is the FTC. Its task is to "prevent persons, partnerships, or corporations . . . from using unfair methods of competition in commerce." This directive is interpreted to include false and misleading advertising. The FTC's power was strengthened in 1938 by the Wheeler-Lea Amendment to the FTC act, forbidding "unfair or deceptive acts or practices in commerce."

When the FTC receives a complaint about false advertising, it investigates, and if the advertising is found to be misleading, the FTC issues a cease-and-desist order against the offending advertiser. The advertiser may appeal to a U.S. Court of Appeals.

In a typical year the FTC considers over a million advertisements in all media but issues only about 500 cease-and-desist orders—about $\frac{5}{100}$ths of 1 percent of all advertisements examined. About 425 of these 500 orders are settled without further legal discussion. Only about 75 advertisements end in litigation—less than $\frac{8}{1,000}$ths of 1 percent of all advertisements.

Food and Drug Administration. Since 1940 the FDA has been part of the Department of Health, Education, and Welfare, with the duty of administering the Federal Food, Drug and Cosmetics Act of 1938. The FDA enforces federal laws affecting product misrepresentation and false labeling. Regulations provide for identifying the quality and composition of packaged goods, as well as for safeguarding against the misuse of dangerous drugs.

Federal Communications Commission. The FCC was formed in 1934 to regulate interstate and foreign communications by wire, radio, and television. It also is responsible for licensing and regulating radio and television stations. To receive licenses, stations must agree to operate in the public interest. The FCC sets standards for modulation of commercials and for program content.

Post Office. Any direct-mail advertisers whose claims defraud the public are subject to prosecution by the U.S. Postal Service in a U.S. district court.

Other Federal Controls. Several other federal laws apply to advertising. Among other things, the Robinson-Patman Act of 1936 prohibits manufacturers from discriminating among retailers when granting advertising allowances. The Wool Products Labeling Act, the Fur Products Labeling Act, and the Textile Fiber Products Identification Act provide standards for labeling and advertising textiles and apparel. The Lanham Act provides for registration and protection of trademarks.

State and Local Regulations. Several thousand rules and regulations have been enacted in the states and various municipalities to limit various advertising practices. State legislation is exemplified in a model law that prohibits advertising "which contains any assertion, representation, or statement of facts which is untrue, deceptive, or misleading."

Private Organizations. Consumers Union, with headquarters in Mount Vernon, N.Y., and Consumers' Research, Inc., Washington, N.J., are nonprofit organizations devoted to testing and evaluating consumer products. Through their publications and through other activities, they influence consumers and thus advertisers as to truth in advertising.

9. Advertising Outside the United States

Advertising has developed much greater volume in the United States than elsewhere, but the principles and techniques of advertising are important in many nations, and they can be applied wherever there are facilities for mass communications.

Votre salade de fruits... avec

FRENCH INTEREST in tasteful concoctions is dramatized by an orange in a chef's cap. The advertisement promotes the use of an orange liqueur for fruit salad.

BRITISH HUMOR enlivens a color poster. This may be classified as an "image" advertisement, in that it makes no call for immediate buying action.

BATTEN, BARTON, DURSTINE & OSBORN, LTD.

LEADING NATIONS IN ANNUAL VOLUME OF ADVERTISING—1965	
United States	$15,300,000,000
Britain	1,558,000,000
West Germany	1,500,000,000
Japan	956,000,000
Canada	685,000,000
France	545,000,000
Italy	450,000,000
Australia	299,000,000
Sweden	250,000,000
Netherlands	220,000,000
Switzerland	180,000,000
Mexico	160,000,000

Source: *Advertising Age.*

The growth of advertising is closely related to the level of a nation's economic development. Thus Japan spends 10 times as much on advertising per capita as most other Asian countries, and its advertising techniques are very similar to those in the United States. In the underdeveloped and developing countries, advertising is limited or almost nil.

Britain. British advertising differs somewhat from that of the European continent in three major aspects:

1. A commercial television network has gained importance as an advertising medium.

2. There are a few newspapers that offer national coverage.

3. Considerable emphasis is placed on self-regulation through advertising associations.

Continental Europe. Advertising in western Europe is growing rapidly. The Scandinavian countries spend twice as much on advertising per capita as France and four times as much as Italy.

In general, advertising methods on the Continent differ from those in the United States and Britain as follows: (1) a number of advertising agencies control space-selling rights; (2) there is no uniform billing commission system; (3) television commercials either are nonexistent or in their infancy; and (4) governments impose relatively few controls.

10. History of Advertising

Beginnings. In a sense, advertising began around 3200 B.C. when the Egyptians stenciled inscriptions of the names of kings on the temples being built. Later they wrote runaway-slave announcements on papyrus. Signboards were placed outside doors in Greece and Egypt around 1500 B.C.

Perhaps the most important event in history for advertising was the printing of the Gutenberg Bible, about 1450 to 1455—the first time that Western man used the principle of movable type. In about 1477 in London, the first printed advertisement in English announced a prayerbook sale. The first newspaper advertisement appeared on the back page of a London newspaper in 1625. The early town crier was also a "medium" of advertising.

Early U.S. Advertising. It was not until 1704 that paid advertisements were printed in the United States. Later, Benjamin Franklin made advertisements more readable by using large headlines and by surrounding the advertisements with considerable white space. By 1771 there were 31 newspapers in the colonies, and all carried advertising.

The development of a national transportation system during the last half of the 19th century increased the number of readers who could be reached and led to expansion in newspaper and magazine circulation.

AN 1899 ADVERTISEMENT made the public aware of a specific kind of horseless carriage (the Locomobile), named its price ($600), and detailed its merits.

PEARS' SOAP became one of the foremost advertisers of the late 19th century. Soap and cleanser companies rank among the heaviest advertisers of the modern era.

At first, service to advertisers was provided by newsdealers who accepted advertisements for any U.S. newspaper. This gave rise to advertising agents who obtained information about publishers—their locations, rates, and susceptibility to bargaining. By 1860 these agents were bargaining effectively by holding out until the publisher's deadline, causing him to lower his rates to get advertising. The agents usually received 30 percent in commissions.

The first modern advertising agency was N.W. Ayer & Son, Inc., founded in Philadelphia, Pa., in 1869. Ayer introduced the commission system in the 1870's by convincing newspapers to give discounts; the agency then charged the client full price for the space used. This same concept later spread to magazines, radio, and television. (See above, *4. Advertising Agencies—Compensation—Commissions.*)

At the turn of the 20th century, J. Walter Thompson Company, Lord & Thomas, N.W. Ayer & Son, and Pettengill & Company pioneered in the preparation of advertising material. Previously, advertising agencies had been basically media selectors, and only occasionally prepared advertising. Agencies then began adding a 15 percent commission rate to the cost of material and services used in preparing advertisements, in addition to receiving their discounts on the media used.

Radio. Commercial radio dates only from about 1920, when Westinghouse began to utilize the vast investment it had made in radio research and in the manufacture of radio equipment during World War I. On November 2 of that year Westinghouse's station KDKA in Pittsburgh, Pa.,

initiated program service by broadcasting the presidential election returns. The growth of radio usage was fast. By 1926 the foundation had been laid for national networks, resulting in much greater use than ever before of radio as a major advertising medium. From modest beginnings radio has grown to vast proportions. In 1965 there were over 198 million radios in the United States, or 3.2 per home. By that year the nation had 3,972 AM radio stations and 1,270 FM stations on the air.

Television. Experimentation in the "radio transmission of faces and pictures" took place in the late 1920's. Progress in commercial television slowed up during World War II. However, by 1949 there were 75 stations operating commercially in the United States, and more than 200 advertising agencies had television departments.

By 1965 there were 726 television stations—598 commercial and 128 noncommercial. Over nine out of ten homes had television sets, and over 30 percent of these could receive at least four stations.

11. Advertising as a Career

Careers in advertising may involve working for advertisers, media, advertising agencies, or suppliers and special services. At most, only 35 colleges and universities in the United States have effective programs of advertising education. Fewer than 10 offer any truly significant amount of graduate work in advertising. However, advertising draws people from a variety of educational backgrounds.

Advertisers. Most companies that advertise extensively have advertising managers, or brand managers. Because these people help to coordinate the company's advertising program with its sales program and with the company's advertising agency, they must have aptitudes for both advertising and management.

Media. All media use salesmen to sell advertising space or broadcasting time. Media salesmen must be knowledgeable about business and skilled in salesmanship.

Advertising Agencies. A variety of specialists is required in an advertising agency because it develops advertising programs, prepares advertisements, and places them in media. Those interested in advertising research and fact gathering should know both statistics and consumer psychology. Competence in media planning and evaluation is essential for a career in media. The media buyer must identify and determine the most effective media in which to expose the advertising messages, and purchase space or time in these media.

Copywriting requires creative writing skills and ability to visualize ideas. The copywriter is a developer of advertising ideas and messages.

Layout, typography, and visualization are essential for those in art, both for print advertising and for television commercials. Print-production specialists must know printing, photoengraving, and typography.

Experience in "show business," dramatics, photography, music, playwriting, and allied fields are excellent backgrounds for the television producer. Those in traffic activities are involved in coordinating. Orderliness and conscientiousness are requisites.

As the agency's contact with the advertiser, the account executive needs the aptitudes of a salesman and a manager. He works with the client to determine the advertising objectives and to obtain final approval of a campaign. He also works with the agency's personnel to develop advertising messages, media, and fact finding to implement these objectives.

Suppliers and Special Services. Positions similar to some of those already described are offered by the following services that support advertising: marketing research organizations, television and radio producers, film producers, art studios, photographers, producers of display materials, typographers, photoengravers, and product and package designers.

Job Prospects. Some 200,000 people, about $\frac{1}{10}$ of 1 percent of the U.S. population, work in advertising, but their numbers are expected to grow rapidly. Opportunities for rapid advancement are generally greater in advertising than in most other industries. How rapidly a person moves up in responsibilities and pay is based largely on his own efforts, more than on age or length of employment. For women, opportunities in advertising—at least in advertising agencies and in retailing—tend to be greater than in most other business enterprises.

The rate of pay for advertising practitioners varies with the kind and size of organization, geography, size of city, and the worker's skills. In general, the compensation is comparable to that of business executives and professional men, such as physicians and lawyers in the same community.

STEUART HENDERSON BRITT
School of Business
Northwestern University

Bibliography

Berkman, Harold, and Gilson, Christopher, *Advertising: Concepts and Strategies*, 2d ed. (Random House 1986).

Fox, Stephen, *The Mirror Makers: A History of Twentieth Century American Advertising* (Morrow 1984).

Sandage, C. H., and Fryburger, Vernon, *Advertising: Theory and Practice*, 11th ed. (Irwin 1983).

Wright, John S., and Warner, Daniel S., *Advertising*, 5th ed. (McGraw 1982).

For Specialized Study

Baker, Stephen, *The Systematic Approach to Advertising Creativity* (McGraw 1983).

Bellavance, Diane, *Advertising and Public Relations for a Small Business* (DBA Bks. 1987).

Keeler, Floyd Y., and Haase, Albert E., *The Advertising Agency, Procedure and Practice* (Garland 1985).

Lucas, Darrell Blaine, and Britt, Steuart Henderson, *Measuring Advertising Effectiveness*, ed. by Henry Assel and Samuel Craig (Garland 1985).

Olson, Jerry, and Sentis, Keith, eds., *Advertising and Consumer Psychology*, vol. 3 (Praeger 1986).

ADVERTISING SYMBOLS change to reflect new ways. The original White Rock girl (*left*) dates from a painting exhibited at the World's Columbian Exposition in 1893. Now she has a new hairdo and a new background.

ADVOCATE, ad'və-kət, in law, a term sometimes used for a lawyer, counsel, or attorney.

In ancient Rome an *advocatus* was one who was called in to help another in a legal process—hence, a pleader. The *advocatus fisci* was one chosen to argue the emperor's cause in questions affecting his revenue.

In continental Europe during the Middle Ages, the term *advocatus* was applied to secular lords who acted as legal representatives of abbeys in lay affairs. In time this function became one of actively protecting church rights and seeing that they fulfilled their secular obligations to the feudal state. In medieval England the *advocatus* was a pleader in common-law courts, but the term also applied to one who enjoyed the hereditary right of naming the parson of a church. This right of *advocatio* of the patron became known in English law as an *advowson*.

In modern England *advocate* has not been used in the general sense of an attorney or counselor, as it often is in the United States and to some extent in France (*avocat*). This is because in England the advisory and trial functions of members of the legal profession have been differentiated and allocated, respectively, to the solicitor and the barrister. From the 16th to the 19th century the word was chiefly used in England to denote those who practiced in the courts of civil and canon law and who were generally members of Doctors' Commons, a society of ecclesiastical lawyers in London. In a more special sense, the term was applied to the king's advocate, otherwise known as his majesty's advocate-general, an important official acting for the Crown in questions of ecclesiastical and international law, and to whom all orders in council were submitted for approval. The office has been obsolete, however, since the 19th century.

In Scotland an advocate is a member of the bar of Scotland, and the Faculty of Advocates is the collective membership of the bar. The lord advocate is the principal Scottish law officer of the crown. (See also ADVOCATUS DIABOLI.)

G. L. HASKINS
University of Pennsylvania

ADVOCATUS DIABOLI, ad-və-kā'təs dī-ab'ə-lī, in English translation from the Latin, "devil's advocate," a name once popularly given to the *promotor fidei* ("promoter of the faith"), one of the most important officials in the Roman Catholic Church's process of beatification and canonization. Before the promulgation of Pope John Paul II's apostolic constitution *Divinus perfectionis magister* ("Divine Teacher and Model of Perfection") in January 1983, the duty of the promoter of the faith was to examine critically the evidence offered during the proceedings by the *postulator causae* ("postulator [or advocate] of the cause") attesting to the candidate's sanctity and practice of the theological and cardinal virtues to a heroic degree.

The term *devil's advocate*, never adequate as an expression of the duties of the *promotor fidei*, entirely lost its traditional religious application when, in accordance with the apostolic constitution, the functions of *postulator causae* and *promotor fidei* were, in effect, merged. The critical function of the so-called devil's advocate was given over to the *promotor justitiae* ("promoter of justice"), a priest who, before a case is submitted to the Congregation for the Causes of Saints, tests the case's merits in the diocese in which the subject died. (See PROMOTER OF THE FAITH; BEATIFICATION; CANONIZATION.)

The term *devil's advocate* is also applied to one who pleads a point of view chiefly to initiate or stimulate argument.

ADY, Endre, o'di (1877–1919), Hungarian poet. Ady was born in Érmindszent, Transylvania, Austria-Hungary (later, Ady Endre, Romania), on Nov. 22, 1877. After studying law and working as a journalist in Hungary, he traveled to the Riviera and to Paris, where he came under the influence of the French symbolist movement.

Ady's first volume of poems, *Új versek* (1906; "New Poems"), written in an unconventional, modern idiom, made a powerful impression, and he became a noted figure in Hungarian letters. Characterized by violent and tormented imagery, his poems are variously on national, social, erotic, and religious themes. He came to be recognized as Hungary's greatest lyric poet of the 20th century.

Ady also wrote short stories and numerous articles for progressive journals, notably *Nyugat* ("West"), often attacking the conservative government and the materialism of the Hungarian upper classes. He died in Budapest on Jan. 27, 1919.

Bibliography: Balakian, Anna, ed., *The Symbolist Movement in the Literature of European Languages,* (Akadémiai Kiadó 1982); Reményi, Joseph, *Hungarian Writers and Literature,* ed. by August J. Molnar (Rutgers Univ. Press 1964); Stade, George, ed., *Pío Baroja to Franz Kafka,* vol. 9 of *European Writers: The Twentieth Century,* ed. by W. T. H. Jackson et al. (Scribner 1989).

ADYGEYA, à-dē-gyā'yə (also, Adygea), an administrative subdivision of the Russian Federation; formerly the Adyge autonomous oblast. It is situated in the northern foothills of the Caucasus Mountains, about 80 miles (130 km) east of the Black Sea. Its area of 2,930 square miles (7,600 sq km) is mostly farmland. About 70% of the people live in rural areas and work at lumbering or at farming, chiefly corn and tobacco. The capital and industrial center of Adygeya is Maikop. Its main industries are food and timber processing.

In 1830–1864 the independent principalities occupying the land that now makes up Adygeya were gradually taken over by czarist Russia. In 1922 the Soviet government set up the Adyge autonomous region as the homeland of the Adyge people, who speak Circassian. But immigration of Russians soon made the Adyge a minority, and they now account for less than 25% of the total population. Population: 447,109 (2002 census).

THEODORE SHABAD*
Editor of "Soviet Geography" Magazine

ADZHARIA, à-jàr'ę-yə (also, Ajaria), an administrative subdivision of the Republic of Georgia. Formerly known as the Adzhar Autonomous Soviet Socialist Republic, it is situated in southwestern Georgia, bordering the Black Sea and Turkey. The republic's area is 1,160 square miles (3,000 sq km). Its capital is Bat'umi.

More than half of the people earn their living by farming or livestock raising. The coastal lowland has a subtropical climate and produces tea and citrus fruits. The villages usually consist of widely separated houses, each surrounded by vineyards and orchards. Manufacturing is concentrated in Bat'umi. The chief industries are oil refining and sawmilling.

In the 600s and 500s B.C., Greek merchants established colonies in Adzharia. The Romans ruled it for several centuries, but by the 800s A.D. independent principalities had sprung up throughout the area. Turkish armies occupied the region in the 1500s and 1600s as they attempted to capture Bat'umi, which finally fell to the Turks at the start of the 1700s. In 1878, at the end of the Russo-Turkish War, Russia acquired Adzharia. In 1921 it became an autonomous republic in Georgia. Population: 376,016 (2002 census).

ELLSWORTH RAYMOND*
New York University

Æ, AE, or A.E. See RUSSELL, GEORGE WILLIAM.

AEDILE, ē'dīl, the title of an ancient Roman magistrate. According to tradition, the aedileship, which ranked above the quaestorship and below the praetorship in political importance, was created in 494 B.C., when two plebeians were elected aediles. In 367 B.C. two patricians were added to the office. The latter were called *curule aediles,* since they sat in an official chair (*sella curulis*), and the former were known as *plebeian aediles,* with no distinctive mark of office.

About 45 B.C. the aedileship reached a membership of six (probably one patrician and one plebeian were added). The aedileship disappeared before 235 A.D., by which time imperial officials had assumed aedilician duties. Aediles also acted as minor administrators in Roman municipalities and colonies and in guilds.

Urban aediles exercised jurisdiction in minor offenses. This duty evolved from their care of the city, since they supervised the maintenance of public works (streets, baths, temples, markets, aqueducts, sewers, bridges, theaters, amphitheaters, colonnades, monuments, cemeteries, public buildings), and superintended public celebrations (parades, games, shows, festivals, funerals, thanksgivings). They also regulated traffic, procured and distributed grain, controlled mercantile transactions, inspected weights and measures, stored public archives, and licensed prostitutes. As officers of the markets, they introduced important features into the laws governing sales and administered punishment, particularly of persons selling slaves and domesticated animals under false pretenses.

Their custom of providing elaborate spectacles as a bid for future popular support of their political careers was an expensive drain on the aediles.

P. R. COLEMAN-NORTON
Princeton University

AEDUI, ed'ū-ī, an ancient people of central Gaul, now east-central France. The Aedui were protected by Rome from 121 B.C. and appealed to Rome for assistance about 60 B.C. when they were invaded by neighboring tribes. Although they aided Julius Caesar in his subsequent conquest of Gaul (58—51 B.C.), they nevertheless joined in the final Gallic resistance to Rome (52 B.C.). Under the Emperor Augustus (reigned 27 B.C.—14 A.D.), the tribe became a federated state of Rome, and its capital was removed from Bibracte to Augustodunum (modern Autun).

Despite their participation in a revolt against Rome in 21 A.D., the Aedui became in 48 A.D. the first Gallic tribe to be granted privileges in the Roman Senate.

P. R. COLEMAN-NORTON
Princeton University

AEGEAN CIVILIZATION, i-jē'-ən, a term applied to the Bronze Age civilizations of the lands bordering the Aegean Sea (Greece, Macedonia, Thrace, and the Aegean coast of Asia Minor) and the islands of that sea (Crete, Rhodes, Cyclades, Sporades, and others). It generally refers to the period from about 2800 B.C. to about 1100 B.C. but sometimes is loosely extended to include the preceding Stone Age cultures of the area.

Greek Legends and Epics. Greeks of the classical period (about 850—323 B.C.) had only a vague understanding of earlier cultures. A few preclassical architectural remains existed, most notably the fortification walls of Mycenae, Tiryns, and Athens, in massive masonry, which classical Greeks believed had been raised by superhumans or Cyclopes (hence the term *cyclopean masonry*), and the tholos (beehive) tombs, of which the most impressive example is the Treasury of Atreus at Mycenae. If any written records of the Bronze Age survived, the Greeks were unable to decipher them. They knew, or preserved, legends of peoples who were not of Greek stock (such as the Pelasgians and the Eteocretans), but they failed to recognize them as evidence of populations that had been absorbed on their arrival in Greece. In some states where the official doctrine was that the Greek populace was autochthonous (sprung from the soil), speculation about a pre-Greek stratum was not encouraged. No systematic history emerged.

Both the Greek states and prominent families preserved legends of the deeds of their predecessors, such as the Voyage of the Argonauts, the War of the Seven against Thebes, the war between the Achaeans (also known as the Argives or the Danaï) of the Greek mainland and the inhabitants of a city in Asia Minor known as Ilium or Troy, the exploits of Heracles (Hercules) and of Theseus, and the Return of the Heraclidae. Families kept genealogies that professed to record continuous lines of descent from ancestors who had traveled to Colchis with Jason or who had taken part in the fighting at Troy. From these, minstrels composed the long narrative poems called epics. The names and synopses of 15 or so survive, and two, the *Iliad* and the *Odyssey,* survive in their entirety.

The epics passed among the Greeks as the history of primitive Greece. They even ventured to assign dates to the fall of Troy; Eratosthenes gave a date corresponding to about 1183 B.C., and the Parian marble, on which events in Greek history were inscribed, gives about 1209 B.C.

In the early days of classical scholarship, however, it was assumed that the epics were fiction. The internal evidence of the *Odyssey,* with its supernatural monsters, sorceresses, visit to Hell, and repeated divine intervention, furnishes little to refute the charge. The *Iliad,* on the other hand, appears to fix within close geographical limits the scene of a certain military operation, near the Dardanelles, and to contain circumstantial references to coastlines, streams, fortification walls and gates, the view from the heights, the palace of the ruling prince, and other data for locating or identifying a site.

ARCHAEOLOGY

The liberal movement of the 19th century, by clearing away some of the theological obstacles to archaeological research, made it possible for the scientific study of European prehistory to

A FRESCO FROM THE PALACE OF MINOS at Knossos depicts the acrobatic bullfighters of ancient Crete. This restored wall painting dates from the Middle Bronze Age.

begin. By 1870 the sequence of Old Stone (Paleolithic) Age, New Stone (Neolithic) Age, Bronze Age, and Iron Age cultures had been established; the foundations of a relative chronology were laid; and the way was paved for Charles Darwin's *The Descent of Man* (1871). Man was shown to have inhabited central and western Europe for many thousands of years, and a search for evidence of prehistoric civilizations in Greece and the Aegean might therefore be successful. It is against this background that the work of Heinrich Schliemann (1822–1890) must be understood.

Schliemann. A German by birth, a naturalized United States citizen, a successful businessman, and a gifted linguist, Schliemann was convinced that the *Iliad* portrayed events of an actual war and that it contained internal evidence by which the site of Troy could be located and identified. After he retired from business, he went to northwestern Asia Minor in 1870. Investigating a mound known locally as Hissarlik, which seemed to fit the topographical requirements of the *Iliad*, he found a number of successive occupation levels, later known as Schliemann's Seven Cities of Troy. Only the latest of them contained coins, inscriptions, and ceramics of historical types, so that all levels below it must have been prehistoric. In one of the lowest levels he found a splendid gold treasure and declared that he had found the treasure of Priam, hidden at the sack of Troy. As an amateur he encountered skepticism and outright rejection, until he uncovered the prehistoric circle graves of Mycenae and linked Tiryns and the tholos tomb of Orchomenos to the same culture. His claim that he had identified the remains of the Troy sacked by the Achaeans and the citadel and graves of the Achaean leaders themselves at Mycenae then was heard with increasing respect. Modern scholarship has modified his conclusions. The Troy that fell before the Achaeans was not level II, as Schliemann held, or level VI as his assistant and successor, Wilhelm Dörpfeld, said, but level VIIa. The burials of the circle graves at Mycenae now are thought to have taken place many generations before the time of Agamemnon and Aegisthus. However, the study of the prehistory of Greece, and the effort to classify and date the material remains of preclassical Greece and relate them to the legends, began with Schliemann.

Evans. In 1900 an English archaeologist, Sir Arthur Evans (1851–1941), began excavations at Knossos, traditionally the capital of the Cretan maritime empire, and uncovered the ruins of a vast, many-storied structure, the "Palace of Minos." Within and beneath it he found successive deposits of a Cretan Bronze Age civilization extending over 1,500 years. He named it the Minoan civilization after the legendary king Minos. The deposits contained artifacts related to finds on the Greek mainland and to datable finds from Egypt. In the absence of intelligible written records, these elements were essential to the establishment of relative and absolute chronologies for the area. He also found seals and other objects inscribed in two unknown hieroglyphic scripts, which he called Hieroglyphic A and B, and more than 3,000 clay tablets inscribed in two unknown linear scripts, which he named Linear A and B.

Later Excavations. Further excavations were made on Crete (at Phaistos, Hagia Triada, Gournia, Mochlos, and elsewhere), in the islands of the Aegean (at Melos, Thera, Mytilene, and elsewhere), and on the Greek mainland (at Mycenae, Tiryns, Asine, Vaphio, Zygouries, Korakou, Corinth, Athens, Haghios Kosmas, Eleusis, Eutresis, Pylos, and Nemea, to name only a few), as well as at Troy itself. They have furnished new or amplified evidence about the Bronze Age cultures of the Aegean area, contributing to the refinement of the classification of the artifacts and to the clarification of the chronology. But for many questions of detail only inadequate or provisional answers could be attempted.

Terminology. *Aegean* is the inclusive term, covering the Bronze Age cultures of the Greek mainland, the Aegean Islands, Crete, and Troy. *Helladic* refers to the Bronze Age cultures of Hellas, the Greek mainland. Local divisions, such as *Thessalian* and *Macedonian*, are used as needed. Early investigators believed they detected three periods marked by improved techniques or new artistic motifs, resulting from the arrival of fresh populations. Accordingly they divided the Bronze Age of the mainland into Early, Middle, and Late Helladic periods, each in its turn divided into two or more subperiods. The term *Mycenaean* is synonymous with the Late Helladic period. Although modern research has shown that the Middle and Late Helladic periods are continuous, and that on the mainland only two major periods, Early Helladic and Late Helladic, are to be distinguished, the threefold division is so firmly embedded in the literature that any effort to supplant it would undoubtedly lead to chaos.

Cycladic refers to the Bronze Age cultures of the islands of the Aegean Sea, not only the Cyclades but also the other islands, except Crete.

Minoan refers to the Bronze Age cultures of Crete, named for Minos, according to legend the greatest of the Cretan sea kings. Probably Minos was a title rather than an individual's name.

AEGEAN PREHISTORY

The prehistory of the Aegean area as revealed by the surviving monuments and artifacts may be summarized briefly as follows.

Old Stone Age. Evidence of Paleolithic industry in Greece has been so meager as to permit no conclusions regarding the orgin, ethnic or linguistic affinities, or movements of their makers. Implements of the Aurignacian type, found near Larisa in Thessaly, gave promise of more to come.

New Stone Age. Efforts to identify premetallic horizons in Greece have been rewarded by the discovery of extensive Neolithic deposits in Macedonia, Thessaly, Boeotia, Attica, the Peloponnesus, Crete, and some of the smaller islands. These deposits are characterized by small settlements with crude housings. They give evidence of agriculture and husbandry and contain excellent pottery, but no metal. At first they were divided into two groups, Neolithic A and B, distinguishable with some precision by the typology of the pottery and apparently reflecting successive waves of invasion. An important discovery in Thessaly of prepottery Neolithic requires further refinement of this classification. There existed in Crete, at the end of the fourth millennium B.C., a Neolithic culture contemporary with the later phases of the Neolithic B of the mainland, but no typological connection between the two has been established.

Early Bronze Age. Somewhat later than 3000 B.C. a new wave of migrants, a hostile invasion to judge from the evidence of burning of the older settlements, appeared on the mainland. Scraps of bronze and, occasionally, gold have been found. Pottery fabrics indicate contemporaneity with the Early Bronze cultures of neighboring areas, and some vase forms show derivation from metal prototypes. However, evidence of native metallurgy is lacking, and it appears that the only bronze used was obtained in trade from bronze-producing areas to the east. Polished stone implements of familiar Neolithic types, as well as tools and weapons of bone, horn, obsidian, and other materials, continued in use everywhere. For these reasons some archaeologists reject the term "Early Bronze Age," preferring one that suggests the close link with the Neolithic period, such as "Subneolithic," "Chalcolithic" ("bronze-stone") or "Aeneolithic" ("bronze-stone"). Even the term "Bronze Age" is under fire, since the metal in general use was not the intentional alloy of copper with tin implied by the term "bronze," but copper contaminated by traces of silver, gold, arsenic, tin, and other elements, which primitive metallurgists were able to refine. We should perhaps substitute the term "Copper Age," and for the Early Copper Age the alternative "Cuprolithic" ("copper-stone"), even at some risk of confusion.

Middle and Late Bronze Ages. Whereas the culture of the Early Bronze (or Chalcolithic or Cuprolithic) period was relatively static, showing little progress from the Neolithic, the Middle and late Bronze ages were an era of ferment, characterized by rapid and vigorous advances in the arts, architecture, communications, and political organization, indicating a rising standard of living. In Crete a maritime empire was established at the beginning of the Middle Bronze Age and reached its period of greatest prosperity between 1600 and 1400 B.C. A vast and well-appointed palace, known as the Labyrinth or Palace of Minos, was built at Knossos. Sophisticated mural paintings and superb pottery (the Palace Style and the polychrome Kamares ware) were developed, and written records were introduced. The Late Bronze Age began in Crete shortly after 1600 B.C. with signs of destruction and cultural reorientation. It is not clear whether this was caused by social movements within the island or a raid from the outside. The appearance on the mainland during this period of artifacts showing artistic influences from Crete led some scholars to postulate Minoan political, as well as cultural, domination of the mainland, a view that later became untenable. Michael Ventris, an English architect, ascertained in 1952 that the language of more than 3,000 inscribed clay tablets found at Knossos is Greek. The only explanation of this would be a prolonged occupation of the Cretan capital by Greeks from the mainland.

On the mainland, the first Greeks appear shortly before 2000 B.C., their arrival accompanied by broad destruction of the Early Bronze Age settlements and the effective submergence of the pre-Greek populations. From that time the development of Hellenic culture was continuous. From the Middle of the Late Bronze Age there was no important cultural break. With the Greeks came increased use of metal and the typical Middle Helladic pottery wares, Gray Minyan and Yellow Minyan, the distinction resulting from a technological improvement in the kiln that raised the firing temperature. The pottery of Late Helladic 1 is Yellow Minyan ware to which painted decoration has been added. Polished stone implements of Neolithic types continued in use. The rising standard of living is evidenced by the increasing size of the settlements, indicating a growing population; the increase in both types and the quantities of artifacts of all kinds; and the development of architecture, with housing of more solid construction, improved appearance, and more rooms. To the 17th century B.C. (or Middle Helladic 2) is ascribed the rise of a powerful aristocracy, whose wealth was revealed at Mycenae by the rich contents of the Second Grave Circle, discovered in 1951. Their descendants constructed, perhaps before 1500 B.C., the Schliemann Grave Circle and the nucleus of the Mycenae palace. Scholars do not agree as to the date of the fortification walls of Mycenae, with the famous Lioness (commonly called Lion) Gate, and of Tiryns and Athens, but the evidence indicates that throughout the 15th and 14th centuries B.C. the citadel palaces were unfortified, except for their own walls and guarded entrances. The construction of stout siege defenses came with the threat of invasion or social unrest in the 13th century B.C. The Treasury of Atreus and other tholos tombs at Mycenae, Vaphio, Dendra, and Orchomenos may belong to the same century. The tombs of the Grave Circles and chamber tombs at widely separated sites have yielded goldwork of exquisite beauty and refinement of taste, gold cups, inlaid dagger blades, jewelry, and death masks. The most famous objects of Late Helladic or Mycenaean art are the gold cups found beneath the floor of a plundered tholos tomb at Vaphio, a suburb of Sparta, ascribed to the 13th century B.C. It became apparent that great care and skill were lavished on small sculptures, cosmetic jars, and furniture inlays in delicately carved ivory when improved techniques of excavation and conservation made their recovery possible. Like the Palace of Minos at Knossos, the public rooms of the mainland palaces were decorated with gay mural paintings, the best of them approaching in freshness and charm the Knossos murals.

Some scholars ascribe the walls, palace, or tombs of Mycenae to the period of Perseus, legendary founder and first king of Mycenae, or his successors, or to the period of Pelops and the Pelopidae (Atreus, Thyestes, and Agamemnon). This ascription should be regarded as premature, pending refinement of the chronology. Many are inclined to agree, however, that the scholars of the University of Cincinnati, under Carl W. Blegen, who excavated the important Mycenaean palace of Epano Englianos, near Pylos, in southwestern Greece, have correctly identified this with the palace of King Nestor, who plays an important part in both the *Iliad* and the *Odyssey*. Nearly all scholars now are agreed that there is a firm basis of truth in the legend of the Trojan War, in which a king of Mycenae or of nearby Argos led a long-remembered amphibious expedition to lay siege to Troy, ending with the destruction of Troy and subsequent disaster to nearly all the Achaean chieftains. Whether the real cause was the seduction by a Trojan princeling of the Mycenaean king's brother's wife, or Troy's stranglehold on the Black Sea trade via Hellespont, is not known. A firm date for the destruction of Troy would aid in fixing the otherwise floating chronologies of the Late Helladic period. Schliemann's identification of Troy II, and Dörpfeld's of Troy VI, as the Troy of legend were overthrown by the re-exploration of the site by the University of Cincinnati expedition under Blegen from 1932 to 1938. The most significant result was Blegen's demonstration that Troy VI's destruction had been caused around 1300 B.C. by an earthquake, whereas Troy VIIa showed the general burning associated with a successful assault, dated by

Blegen at around 1260 B.C., which is in fair agreement with the estimates of the Greek chronographers.

In the ruins of the Mycenaean palace at Thebes in Boeotia, founded according to legend in the remotest past by the exiled Phoenician prince Cadmus, a deep sounding has yielded a number of inscribed cylinder seals of Mesopotamian origin and Late Bronze Age date. Although scholars cannot accept the legend that it was Cadmus who introduced the alphabet into Greece, the discovery that the stronghold associated with the name of Cadmus had direct commercial relations with the Semitic East before 1250 B.C. is of exceptional interest.

Another significant find was made by the Greek archaeologist Platon at Kato Zakro on the eastern end of Crete: a Minoan palace containing an extraordinary quantity of domestic art that rivaled in taste, execution, and variety comparable artifacts from Knossos and Phaistos.

WRITING

Evans found in Crete two series of hieroglyphic scripts and texts in two linear scripts, which he named Linear Scripts A and B. As long as these scripts could not be read the Aegean cultures remained in the province of prehistory and required the application of the principles of prehistoric research. Sporadic finds of pottery with scratched or painted symbols were not sufficient to prove even the knowledge of writing on the mainland, since these inscriptions could have been made by Minoan potters or at the command of Minoan patrons. New avenues of attack were opened with Blegen's discovery in 1939 of 600 clay tablets in the Palace of Nestor inscribed in Linear Script B, and with further Linear B discoveries after World War II at Pylos and Mycenae. Since Prince Nestor was a Greek, rather than a Minoan, it was conceivable that his palace accounts would be kept in Greek. In 1952, Ventris transliterated a number of Linear B sign groups on tablets from both Pylos and Knossos as Greek words and familiar proper names. After his report of this brilliant discovery, formally announced in 1953, progress in decipherment proceeded rapidly. The phonetic values of some symbols have not been established and few tablets have been translated in full, but hundreds of Greek words have been identified, and a provisional glossary of the Achaean dialect, which was the language of the Late Bronze Age

PROVISIONAL TABLE OF RELATIVE CHRONOLOGIES

	Crete	Aegean Islands	Greek mainland	Troy
Early Bronze Age	Early Minoan c. 2800–c. 2100 B.C.	Early Cycladic	Early Helladic c. 2500–c. 1950 B.C.	Troy I–IV
				Troy V
Middle Bronze Age	Middle Minoan 1 c. 2000–c. 1850 B.C. Middle Minoan 2 c. 1850–c. 1700 B.C. Middle Minoan 3 c. 1700–c. 1580 B.C.	Middle Cycladic	Middle Helladic 1 c. 1950–c. 1700 B.C. Middle Helladic 2 c. 1700–c. 1580 B.C.	Troy VI
Late Bronze Age	Late Minoan 1 c. 1580–c. 1450 B.C.	Late Cycladic 1	Late Helladic 1 (Mycenaean 1) c. 1580–c. 1500 B.C.	
	Late Minoan 2 c. 1450–c. 1400 B.C.	Late Cycladic 2	Late Helladic 2 (Mycenaean 2) c. 1500–c. 1400 B.C.	
	Late Minoan 3 c. 1400–c. 1100 B.C.	Late Cycladic 3	Late Helladic 3 (Mycenaean 3) c. 1400–c. 1100 B.C.	Troy VIIa

Greeks who conquered Troy, has been compiled. That the language of the Linear B tablets from Knossos is also Greek came to many scholars as a grave shock, forcing the acknowledgment, contrary to earlier doctrine, that as of about 1450 B.C., Achaean forces from the mainland had overthrown the Minoan sea-king dynasty, organized the island under their own control, and kept records in their own language and script.

No less revolutionary was the picture of the Achaean civilization revealed by the reconstructed vocabulary, largely names of commodities and occupations. Instead of a feudal system that held a politically and economically inert populace in bondage for the profit of a few overlords and their palace coteries, the texts revealed a highly organized society in which men and women were assigned to specific service on behalf of the community as a whole. The discovery by Alan J. B. Wace of Linear B tablets in the residences of merchants, in the lower town of Mycenae, additionally supports the radically new view of a society in which private citizens could engage in trade for their own gain. When fully evaluated, these discoveries will require a complete rewriting of Aegean, or Minoan-Mycenaean, political, economic, social, and cultural history.

The decipherment of Linear Script B and the establishment of the phonetic values of over 70 of its approximately 88 symbols have spurred scholars to new efforts to decipher Linear A. There is no evidence, however, that Linear A will prove to be the still mysterious Minoan language; on the contrary, Cyrus Gordon, an American scholar, has proposed reading the language of Linear Script A as Semitic, a kind of waterfront Akkadian. In 1959 another American, Benjamin Schwartz, offered a tentative Greek transliteration and translation of the hieroglyphic syllabary of the famous Phaistos Disk, found at Phaistos in Crete by Luigi Pernier in 1908. These proposals are regarded by most scholars as controversial.

JOTHAM JOHNSON, *New York University*

Bibliography

Barber, R. L., *The Cyclades in the Bronze Age* (Univ. of Iowa Press 1987).
Blegen, Carl W., *The Palace of Nestor at Pylos in Western Messenia,* vol. 1 (Books on Demand 1966).
Burn, Andrew R., *Minoans, Philistines, and Greeks B.C. 1400–900* (1930; reprint, Shoe String 1968).
Evans, Arthur John, *The Palace of Minos,* 4 vols. (Biblio. Dist. 1921–36).
Finley, M. I., *Schliemann's Troy: 100 Years After* (Longwood 1974).
Jones, Allen H., *Bronze Age Civilization* (Pub. Aff. Press 1975).
Rapp, George, and Gifford, John A., eds., *Troy: The Archaeological Geology* (Princeton Univ. Press 1982).
Schuchardt, Karl, *Schliemann's Excavations,* tr. by E. Sellers (1891; reprint, Ayer 1975).
Taylour, W., and French, E., eds., *Well Built Mycenae: The Helleno-British Excavations Within the Citadel at Mycenae, 1959–1969* (Humanities Press 1982).
Ventris, Michael, and Chadwick, John, *Documents in Mycenaean Greek,* 2d ed. (Cambridge 1973).
Wood, Michael, *In Search of the Trojan War* (Facts on File 1986).

AEGEAN ISLANDS, i-jē'ən, in Greece, in the Aegean Sea, between mainland Greece and Turkey. They include the Cyclades, Dodecanese, and Sporades groups. The total land area is about 5,600 square miles. Island farmers raise grains, olives, fruits, nuts, and tobacco, and fishermen gather fish, coral, and sponges.

Colonized by Greeks from about 1000 to 700 B.C., most of the islands were successively part of the Athenian, Macedonian, Roman, and Byzantine empires. During the Middle Ages, Venetian and

LARGEST AEGEAN ISLANDS

Island	Area (sq mi)	Island	Area (sq mi)
Evvoia (Euboea)	1,457	İmroz	108
Lesvos (Lesbos)	632	Skiros (Scyros)	81
Rodhos (Rhodes)	542	Paros	77
Khios (Chios)	321	Tinos (Tenos)	74
Samos	194	Samothraki (Samothrace)	71
Thasos	170		
Naxos	169	Milos (Melos)	61
Andros	145	Kea	60
Kos (Cos)	111	Amorgos	44
Karpathos (Carpathos)	111	Ios	43
		Kalimnos	41

Genoese merchants controlled some of them. They were gradually taken by the Turks and remained part of the Ottoman empire until the 1820's. By the Treaty of Adrianople (1829), which recognized Greek independence, most of the islands were awarded to Greece. Italy, however, held the Dodecanese group from 1923 to 1947.

P.R. COLEMAN-NORTON, *Princeton University*

AEGEAN SEA, i-jē'ən, an arm of the Mediterranean Sea, bounded on the north and west by Greece, on the east by Turkey, and on the south by Crete. About 400 miles long and 200 miles wide, it is connected by the Dardanelles with the Sea of Marmara and the Black Sea. In places it reaches a depth of 7,500 feet. The Aegean is studded with islands (the word *archipelago* originally was applied exclusively to it). Its chief ports are Piraeus and Salonika in Greece, and İzmir in Turkey.

The ancient Greeks divided the Aegean into the Thracian Sea in the north, the Myrtoan Sea in the west, the Sea of Crete in the south, and the Icarian Sea in the east. Its name has variously been said to derive from: (1) Aegeus, a mythological king of Athens and the father of Theseus; (2) Aegea, queen of the Amazons, who, according to legend, drowned in it; and (3) the ancient city of Aegae (modern Limne) in Euboea.

AEGEUS, ē'jē-əs, in Greek legend, was a king of Athens. His son, Theseus, went to Crete, where he slew the Minotaur, to which Athens had been giving human sacrifice as tribute to the Cretan king Minos. On his return, Theseus used a black sail (signifying mourning) on his ship instead of a white sail (signifying victory). Watching for his son's return, Aegeus saw the black sail and committed suicide by leaping into the sea, which is now called the Aegean Sea.

P.R. COLEMAN-NORTON, *Princeton University*

AEGINA, i-jī'nə, is an island in Greece, located in the Saronic Gulf about 17 miles southwest of Athens. The name is spelled *Aíyina* in modern Greek. A triangularly shaped island, about 32 square miles in area, it forms part of the *nomos* (department) of Attica and Boeotia.

The terrain is generally unproductive because of inland gorges and coastal cliffs, except in the western part, where there is a well-cultivated plain. Grain, figs, olives, grapes, and nuts (pistachio and almond) are grown.

The island's main industries are fishing, tourism, and trade with the mainland, to which it exports sponges, nuts, and pottery. The town of Aegina, on the west coast, is the principal port.

Near the northeast corner of the island are the ruins of the Doric temple of Athena-Aphaea, built about 500 B.C. on the ruins of an earlier temple dedicated to Aphaea alone, probably a local goddess of fertility. Portions of the pediment are preserved in the Glyptothek in Munich, Germany.

History. According to the ancient myth, the island was named for Aegina, a nymph carried there by Zeus. Archaeological evidence indicates that Aegina was inhabited from late Neolithic times ((about 4000 B.C.) and was in contact with Minoan and Mycenaean civilization (1400–1200 B.C.). About 1000 B.C. it was conquered by the Dorians. The Argive tyrant Pheidon seized the island early in the 7th century B.C. and is said to have minted there the first "Aeginetan tortoises"—silver coins which, by the 5th century B.C., were employed throughout the Aegean area. Aegina became second only to Athens as a mercantile power, but because of the island's alliance with Sparta, it was subdued by Athens and forced into the Delian League (458 B.C.). In 431 B.C., at the onset of the Peloponnesian War, the islanders were expelled and replaced by Athenian colonists. They were recalled during Sparta's supremacy (about 405 B.C.), but the island never regained its former greatness.

Aegina subsequently was part of the Roman, Byzantine, and Ottoman empires. In the late 1820s it was the temporary capital of Greece. Population: 12,430 (1991 census).

P. R. COLEMAN-NORTON, *Princeton University*

AEGIR, ag'ər, in Norse mythology, was the god of the sea. He sumptuously entertained the other gods. His wife, Ran, sank ships in storms and then cared for the drowned sailors. Their nine daughters personified aspects of the sea.

AEGIS, ē'jəs, in classical mythology, a goatskin worn on the shoulders like a short cloak or over the left arm like a shield. It was originally made by Hephaestus (Vulcan) for Zeus (Jupiter) and Athena (Minerva). In later times, it became associated more with Athena, and took the form of a shield covered with goatskin and bordered with snakes, with the head of the Gorgon Medusa in the center. It was both an instrument of defense and a symbol of divine protection. See also GORGON.

AEGISTHUS, ē-jis'thəs, in Greek legend, was the son of Thyestes and his daughter Pelopia. Exposed to the elements to die because of his incestuous birth, he was saved by shepherds and reared by Atreus, his father's brother. Atreus and Thyestes had been vying for control of the kingdom of Mycenae. Atreus eventually inherited the kingdom from Eurystheus, its king, and to safeguard it, he tried to induce Aegisthus to kill his father. But Thyestes recognized his son, persuaded him to kill Atreus instead, and took over Mycenae.

While Agamemnon, Atreus' son, was away from Mycenae during the Trojan War, his wife, Clytemnestra, became Aegisthus' lover. When Agamemnon returned, he was killed—either by Aegisthus or by Clytemnestra, or by both. After a seven-year reign, Aegisthus and Clytemnestra were killed by Orestes, Agamemnon's son. The tale of Aegisthus has been told in various ways by ancient authors, especially the tragedians Aeschylus, Sophocles, and Euripides.

P.R. COLEMAN-NORTON, *Princeton University*

AEGOSPOTAMI, ē-gəs-pot'ə-mī, was the name of a town and small river in ancient Greece. It was situated on the peninsula of ancient Thrace called the Chersonese (now called the Gallipoli Peninsula of Turkey in Europe). Off the river's outlet into the Hellespont (now the Dardanelles), the Spartans under Lysander won a decisive naval victory in 405 B.C. over the Athenians, which led, in the following year, to the end of the Peloponnesian War.

P.R. COLEMAN-NORTON, *Princeton University*

AEHRENTHAL, â'rən-täl, **Count von** (1854–1912), Austro-Hungarian statesman who was responsible for much of his country's expansionist policy in the Balkans immediately prior to World War I. Alois Lexa, count von Aehrenthal, was born at Gross-Skal, Bohemia, on Sept. 27, 1854. After studying law at Prague and Bonn, he entered the diplomatic corps in 1877 and was ambassador to Rumania (from 1895) and to Russia (from 1899). In 1906 he succeeded Count Agenor von Goluchowski as foreign minister of Austria-Hungary.

Aehrenthal's concern with the Balkans became apparent in 1908 when he announced plans for a railroad through the Novi Pazar district in southwestern Serbia. The railway would have joined a proposed Turkish line from Salonika, Greece, and would have increased Austrian influence in the Balkans.

Aehrenthal abandoned his plans for the railroad as a result of a meeting with Aleksandr Izvolsky, the Russian foreign minister, in September 1908. Aehrenthal agreed that Austria-Hungary would not oppose Russian efforts to gain free access for its navy to the Mediterranean from the Black Sea, and Izvolsky agreed that Russia would not oppose Austria-Hungary's annexation of Bosnia and Hercegovina.

When Austria-Hungary annexed Bosnia and Hercegovina in October 1908, the Balkans were brought close to war. Izvolsky denied having agreed to the annexation. But Germany, Austria's ally, forced Russia to withdraw its support of Serbia and Montenegro, which had opposed Austria's move. The annexation aggravated relations between Russia and Austria-Hungary and added to the tensions that later erupted in World War I. Aehrenthal died at Vienna on Feb. 17, 1912.

ÆLFRIC (c. 955–c. 1020), al'frik, was an Anglo-Saxon writer and churchman. After being educated at Winchester, he served as monk and mass priest at Cerne (Cerne Abbas), Dorsetshire, from 987 until 1005, when he became abbot of Eynsham, Oxfordshire. Inspired by his teacher Æthelwold, bishop of Winchester and one of the leaders of the Benedictine reform in England, Ælfric devoted the remainder of his life to educating members of the clergy in the fundamentals of church doctrine.

Ælfric's writings reflect not only a practical educational program to meet the needs of the time, but also a mastery of effective and graceful prose. No other writer of the Old English period, not even his more illustrious contemporary, Archbishop Wulfstan, can match the variety of his style, which ranges from seemingly artless simplicity to polished and sophisticated rhetoric, strongly marked by alliteration and rhythm. Read and imitated by later devotional writers, Ælfric is acknowledged as a major figure in the development of English prose.

His greatest works are *Catholic Homilies* (ed. by B. Thorpe, 1844–46), a course of sermons for the church year originally issued in two sets, the first (989) containing 40 sermons, and the second

(992), 45; and *Lives of the Saints* (993–998; ed. by W.W. Skeat, 1881–1900), containing about 40 reading pieces, not sermons, commemorating various saints. In both, Ælfric drew freely on Gregory the Great, Bede, and other Latin writers, but he never permitted himself to translate them slavishly.

His *Grammar and Glossary* (ed. by J. Zupitza, 1880) and *Colloquy* (ed. by G.N. Garmonsway, 2d ed., 1947) constitute an elementary course in Latin taught by the direct method. The *Colloquy*, an amusing Latin dialogue between teacher and pupils, has an interlinear translation which almost certainly Ælfric did not write. The *Grammar* is a translation and simplification of Priscian, and the *Glossary* is a topically arranged list of Latin words with English equivalents to be used for learning vocabulary. The *Grammar and Glossary* was written soon after the *Catholic Homilies*, probably about 993, and the *Colloquy* not much later.

The Heptateuch (ed. by S.J. Crawford, 1922) cannot be precisely dated. Some of it (notably *Genesis*) was written about the time of the *Grammar*, but various additions were made at later dates. This English version of selected portions of the first seven books of the Bible is only partly Ælfric's. His concern that the Old Testament should be properly understood and his doubts about the wisdom of translating it are expressed in the preface.

Besides the major works cited above, Ælfric prepared English versions of Bede's *De Temporibus* (ed. by H. Henel, 1942) and Alcuin's *Interrogationes Sigewulfi in Genesin* (ed. by G.E. MacLean, 1883), and wrote a Latin life of his teacher Æthelwold (ed. by J. Stevenson, 1858) and various homilies and letters.

Norman E. Eliason, *University of North Carolina*

AELIAN, ē'lē-ən, was a Greek military tactician of the early 2d century A.D. He was known as *Aelianus Tacticus*. From earlier authors he compiled a treatise on Graeco-Macedonian military tactics, entitled *Taktike theoria* and dedicated to Roman Emperor Trajan (reigned 98–117). Though outmoded even in Trajan's time, the tactics he described seem to have influenced the military organization and tactics of Greeks and Arabs in the Middle Ages and of Spaniards and Netherlanders during the 16th and 17th centuries.

The best Greek text is by Hermann A.T. Köchly and Wilhelm Friedrich. Rüstow, *Griechische Kriegsschriftsteller* (1855). An English translation, by Viscount Dillon, was published in 1814.

AEMILIAN (c. 206–253 A.D.), ē-mil'iən, Roman emperor for three months in 253. *Marcus Aemilius Aemilianus* was born in the Mauretanian region of North Africa. In 252, while governor of Moesia in the Balkans, he was saluted emperor by his troops after repelling a Gothic invasion. In 253 he invaded Italy. When Emperor Gallus was murdered by his own troops, Aemilian was accepted in Rome as emperor. It was soon learned, however, that Valerian, Gallus' emissary in Raetia (now a part of Austria) had also been proclaimed emperor, and Aemilian was assassinated by his soldiers near Spoletium (now Spoleto, Italy).

P.R. Coleman-Norton, *Princeton University*

AEMILIAN WAY, ē-mil'iən, an ancient Roman state road built by the consul Marcus Aemilius Lepidus in 187 B.C. It was primarily a military road to connect Rome with her new possessions in Cisalpine Gaul (Lombardy).

About 175 miles long, the Aemilian Way began at Ariminum (Rimini) on the Adriatic, where the Flaminian Way from Rome ended; traversed Bononia (Bologna), Mutina (Modena), and Parma; crossed the Padus (Po) River; and ended at Placentia (Piacenza).

AENEAS, i-nē'əs, in Greek and Roman legend, was a Trojan prince, the son of Anchises and the goddess Aphrodite (Venus). In the *Iliad*, Homer describes Aeneas as second in valor only to his kinsman Hector among the Trojan warriors. During the Trojan War the gods saved Aeneas from danger because, as Poseidon prophesied, he was fated to rule over the Trojans who survived the fall of Troy. There is no hint in the *Iliad* that Aeneas and his followers emigrated from the region of Troy.

According to the legend as told by later Greek writers (apparently as early as Stesichorus and Sophocles), Aeneas led the Trojans westward and founded various cities on islands in the Mediterranean, especially Sicily. By the middle of the 3d century B.C., the story of Aeneas' arrival in Italy seems to have been well established, and soon afterward Rome claimed a political relationship with Troy on the basis of the descent of the Romans from Aeneas and the Trojans.

Virgil (70–19 B.C.) made Aeneas the hero of his great national epic, the *Aeneid*, likewise connecting him with the origin of Rome. In the poem, Aeneas tells Queen Dido of Carthage the story of the fall of Troy, his escape with his father Anchises and his son Ascanius, the loss of his wife Creusa, and his subsequent journey with the surviving Trojans to Thrace, Delos, Crete, Epirus, and Sicily. The main themes of the poem are Aeneas' love affair with Dido, her suicide upon his departure, and the arrival of the Trojans in Italy, where they war with the Latins and Rutulians and finally win victory, with the aid of Greeks and Etruscans. The *Aeneid* ends with Aeneas' victory over his rival, Turnus, king of the Rutulians. See also Aeneid, The.

Other Roman writers relate that Aeneas married Lavinia, daughter of King Latinus, and founded Lavinium, later the chief city of the Latin League. Upon his death Aeneas was considered a god with the title *Indiges*.

George E. Duckworth, *Princeton University*

AENEAS SYLVIUS. See Pius II.

AENEAS TACTICUS, i-nē'əs tak'ti-kəs, was a Greek military tactician who lived about 350 B.C. He wrote several treatises on military tactics, of which the only one extant is *Peri tou pos chre poliorkoumenous antechein* (*On How Besieged Persons Should Make Their Defense*). Considered the best ancient work on the subject of sieges, it is valuable for its large stock of technical terms connected with siegecraft, and also for its information on political and social conditions in Greece during the early 4th century B.C. In the latter respect it is quite modern, because Aeneas, whose identity is still disputed, repeatedly calls attention to the persistent peril of the "fifth column" to the defenders of besieged cities. Later tacticians borrowed extensively from Aeneas' works.

P.R. Coleman-Norton, *Princeton University*

AENEID, i-nē'id, the finest epic of ancient Rome and one of the great poems of world literature. It was composed in Latin by Virgil in 30–19 B.C. and left without the final revision. Virgil before his death wished the work destroyed, but it was published by his friends Lucius Varius Rufus and Plotius Tucca at the request of Emperor Augustus.

The *Aeneid* is filled with mythology, history, and archaeology; it is rich in patriotism, religious feeling, and pathos; it contains adventure and romance. It is not only a national epic but an epic of human life with the universal significance characteristic of the greatest works of literary art, and in this respect Virgil's masterpiece ranks with those of Homer, Dante, and John Milton. His superb poetic power, as seen in his imagery, his sound effects, and the melody and rhythm of his verse, adds immeasurably to the splendor of the epic.

The Story. The *Aeneid* contains 12 books. The first six describe the wanderings of Aeneas and the band of Trojans who, after the capture of Troy by the Greeks, journey westward to Sicily; to Africa, where they are welcomed by Dido, queen of Carthage; and finally to Italy, where, at Cumae, Aeneas descends to the underworld and receives from his father Anchises a prophetic vision of Roman history and the new era of peace brought to the Roman world by Augustus. The second six books relate the adventures of the Trojans upon their arrival in Latium; their unwilling conflict with the native Latins and Rutulians; their alliance with the Greeks of Pallanteum (a settlement on the Palatine Hill) and the Etruscans of Caere; the tragic deaths of heroes on each side; and Aeneas' ultimate victory over Turnus, king of the Rutulians, his chief opponent and his rival for the hand of the princess Lavinia, daughter of King Latinus.

Sources. The sources of the *Aeneid* are many and varied; they include much of the best of earlier Greek and Roman poetry. Virgil's indebtedness to the *Iliad* and *Odyssey* of Homer is very great, but it is wrong to look upon the *Aeneid* as an "Odyssey" of wanderings followed by an "Iliad" of battles; such a view does little justice to the richness and the unity of the poem.

It is equally wrong to view Virgil as an inspired imitator lacking in originality; the Homeric material is absorbed and utilized to create something new—a poem that celebrates the greatness, under divine sanction, of Roman achievement and Roman purpose. Among other sources may be cited the Cyclic epics, the *Argonautica* of Apollonius of Rhodes, Greek tragedy, Quintus Ennius' *Annales*, and the *De rerum natura* of Lucretius. Perhaps the most important after Homer were the tragedies of Euripides, from whom Virgil derived many specific details (for example, the tragic episode of Nisus and Euryalus in the *Aeneid*, book 9, is indebted to the *Rhesus* as well as to the *Iliad*, book 10) and also much of his tragic conception of character.

Structure. Structure and content in the *Aeneid* are inextricably interwoven, with three discernible structural patterns:

(1) The even-numbered books are the more significant and tragic ones (book 2, the fall of Troy; book 4, the death of Dido; book 6, trip to the underworld; book 8, visit to the site of Rome; book 10, the great battle; book 12, the victory over Turnus). The odd-numbered books are of a lighter nature, serving to relieve the tension.

(2) The corresponding books in each half are linked by numerous parallels and contrasts. For example, in book 1, Juno causes the storm at sea, and the arrival and welcome in Carthage are described; in book 7, the arrival and welcome in Latium are related, and Juno causes the war on land. In book 2, the fall of Troy is described, and at the end Aeneas carries on his shoulder from the burning city his aged father, a symbol of the past; in book 8, the picture of early Rome is drawn, and at the end Aeneas lifts to his shoulder the shield with historic scenes culminating in the victories and triumphs of Augustus. In book 4, the tragedy of love is delineated (death of Dido); in book 10, the tragedy of war (deaths of Pallas, Lausus, and Mezentius).

Finally, (3) the poem may be viewed as a trilogy composed of three sections of four books each, with the central portion (books 5–8) containing the most historical, patriotic, and Augustan passages; here long Homeric episodes (games from the *Iliad*, book 23; underworld scene from the *Odyssey*, book 11; catalog from the *Iliad*, book 2; shield from the *Iliad*, book 18) are reworked for the portrayal of ancient Italy, the glorification of Rome and its history, and the praise of Augustus. This central portion is framed by books 1–4, in which the main theme is the tragedy of Dido, and by books 9–12, which deal primarily with the tragedy of Turnus. In this manner also Virgil avoids too sharp a break into an "Odyssey" of wanderings and an "Iliad" of battles.

Historical Symbolism. The *Aeneid* is not merely the story of Aeneas and the Trojans, but the story of Rome and Augustus as well. Jupiter's speech in book 1, the revelations of Anchises in book 6, and the scenes on the shield in book 8 give by means of prophecy and foreshadowing much of the history of Rome from its founding to Virgil's own day. The epic is rich in symbolism—historical, political, and religious. As the death of Dido in book 4 symbolizes the later fall of Carthage, so the union of Latins and Trojans at the end of the epic depicts the formation of the Roman people. The earlier alliance of the Trojans with both Greeks and Etruscans is Virgil's way of accounting for the presence of so many Greek and Etruscan elements in Roman life and culture. The virtues of Aeneas—*clementia, iustitia,* and above all, *pietas* (the sense of duty toward his gods, his people, and his family)—are likewise the virtues attributed to Augustus; and as Augustus, in Virgil's day, had erected a great temple to Apollo, so Aeneas in book 6 promises to build such a temple. The simplicity of Evander's life on the Palatine Hill foreshadows the unpretentious home where Augustus himself lived.

Character Portrayal. Divine machinery was a necessary part of a mythological epic such as the *Aeneid*, but Virgil's interest in human emotions and the psychology of his characters made it impossible for him to explain human action entirely by the working of fate or divine intervention. What the god or goddess usually does is merely to accentuate or inflame a state of mind already eager to do what the deity wishes.

There are many tragic deaths—Dido, Nisus and Euryalus, Pallas, Lausus, Mezentius, Turnus—and Virgil stresses the effect of the death on the one who is near and dear. The laments of Anna, of Euryalus' mother, of Mezentius, of Aeneas, and of Evander are among the most emotional and the most magnificent scenes in the poem. These deaths are tragic, however, in another sense; they result from the action or wrongdoing of the character himself. The characters have freedom of will; they make their own decisions and suffer the consequences. Dido, for instance, sins by being unfaithful to the memory of her husband Sychaeus; Nisus and Euryalus are misled by wrong motives and bring disaster upon themselves; and Turnus, the most complex character of all, had a basic weakness, an inability to live up to his own ideals and a reluctance to face Aeneas. Many characters, both divine and human, fail in part because they stand for the irrational forces of darkness and disorder as opposed to world order and justice represented by Jupiter, the supreme deity, and symbolized by Aeneas on the human level.

The character of Aeneas himself has been misunderstood and criticized. He is not a weak person or a puppet in the hands of fate, but a worthy hero of the epic that bears his name. There is no lack of strong emotion in Aeneas, but he gradually subordinates his feelings to fate and the will of Jupiter. As an instrument of a divine plan he is victorious, but at the cost of personal happiness. His tragedy is on a higher plane than the tragedies of the other characters and arises from his sorrow and pity at the unnecessary suffering and death caused by the war that he is forced to wage. From this and from Virgil's own hatred of war comes the sense of "melancholy" that has been considered a characteristic feature of the poem.

See also AENEAS; VIRGIL.

GEORGE E. DUCKWORTH, *Princeton University*

Bibliography

Bernardus, Silvestris, *Commentary on the First Six Books of Virgil's "Aeneid,"* tr. by E. G. Schreiber and Thomas E. Maresca (Univ. of Neb. Press 1980).
Garrison, Daniel H., *The Language of Virgil: An Introduction to the Poetry of the Aeneid* (P. Lang 1984).
Hardie, Philip, *Virgil's Aeneid: Cosmos and Imperium* (Oxford 1986).
Lee, M. O., *Fathers and Sons in Virgil's Aeneid* (State Univ. of N.Y. Press 1979).
Mackail, John William, *Virgil and His Meaning to the World of To-day* (1930; reprint, Cooper Square 1963).
Pöschl, Viktor, *Art of Virgil: Image and Symbol in the "Aeneid,"* tr. by Gerda Seligman (1962; reprint, Greenwood Press 1986).
Prescott, Henry W., *The Development of Virgil's Art* (1927; reprint, Russell & Russell 1963).
Proutfoot, L., *Dryden's Aeneid and Its Seventeenth Century Predecessors* (1960; reprint, R. West 1980).
Williams, Gordon, *Technique and Ideas in the Aeneid* (Yale Univ. Press 1985).

AENESIDEMUS, ē-nes-ə-dē′məs, was a Greek philosopher of the 1st century B.C. Born at Knossos, Crete, he taught skepticism in Alexandria, Egypt. His writings, which are lost, included *Kata sophias* (*Against Wisdom*), *Peri zeteseos* (*On Inquiry*), and *Prote eisagoge* (*First Introduction*).

Ten well-known arguments asserting the impossibility of knowledge are attributed to Aenesidemus. These arguments, called *tropoi tes epoches* (tropes of suspense of judgment), contain only a few distinct ideas, since some of them express the same thought in different ways. They are: (1) sensations and perceptions differ; (2) mental and physical differences among individuals make things appear differently to them; (3) different senses produce different impressions; (4) perceptions depend upon an individual's mental and physical condition at the time of perception; (5) things appear different in different positions and at different distances; (6) perception is never direct, but always through a medium; (7) things appear different according to variations in their color, motion, quantity, and temperature; (8) degrees of familiarity cause differences in perception; (9) all supposed knowledge is based on predication; and (10) opinions and customs differ in different countries.

AEOLIAN HARP, ē-ō′lē-ən, a musical instrument played by the wind. It consists of a box in which several strings are stretched across two bridges. The strings, all stretched to produce the same pitch, vary in thickness. When the instrument is hung so that currents of air pass through it, the strings vibrate variously and produce a fundamental tone with many harmonic overtones. These vary constantly with varying pressure of air. The name is taken from Aeolus (Aiolus), god of the winds in classical Greek mythology.

In its modern form, the Aeolian harp appears to date from about the middle of the 17th century, but in ancient times an instrument of the same nature undoubtedly existed. The German poet Eduard Mörike (1804–1875) wrote a poem, *Die Aeolsharfe*, which sets forth the romantics' attitude toward this "mysterious" instrument; both Hugo Wolf and Johannes Brahms set this poem as a song. Attempts to tame the Aeolian harp with a keyboard and artificially produced currents of air have proved unsatisfactory, and it remains rather a sounding ornament than a true musical instrument.

HERBERT WEINSTOCK, *Music Writer and Critic*

AEOLIAN ISLANDS. See LIPARI ISLANDS.

AEOLIANS, ē-ō′lē-ənz, were one of the four major groups of ancient Greeks. In prehistoric Hellas they were more numerous and more powerful than the Achaeans, Ionians, or Dorians, the three other Hellenic groups. Supposedly descendants of the legendary Aeolus (q.v.), son of Helen of Troy, the Aeolians came from the north before 1000 B.C. and settled first in Thessaly. They then spread southward into Boeotia and, later, westward into Phocis, Locris, and Aetolia. Eventually they crossed the Corinthian Gulf and descended the western Peloponnesus into Elis and Messenia. So many Aeolians, however, also emigrated eastward from Thessaly into northwestern Asia Minor that a region there was called Aeolis (q.v.). En route to Asia they occupied several of the Aegean Islands, notably Lesbos, where their Aeolic dialect of Greek became perfected in the Lesbian school of lyric poetry.

P.R. COLEMAN-NORTON, *Princeton University*

AEOLIS, ē′ō-lis, was an ancient district on the western coast of Asia Minor. It extended along the Aegean Sea from the entrance of the Hellespont (now the Dardanelles) south to the Hermus River (now the Gediz River). It was named for the Aeolians (q.v.), some of whom migrated there from Greece before 1000 B.C. Aeolis was, however, an ethnological and linguistic enclave rather than a geographical unit. The district often was considered part of the larger northwest region of Mysia.

By the 8th century B.C., 12 of the southern Aeolian city-states were grouped together in a league. The most celebrated of the cities was Smyrna (modern İzmir, Turkey), but in 699 B.C., Smyrna became part of an Ionian confederacy. The remaining cities were conquered by Croesus, king of Lydia (reigned 560–546 B.C.). Later they were held successively by the Persians, Macedonians, Seleucids, and Pergamenes. Attalus III, the last king of Pergamum, bequeathed Aeolis to Rome in 133 B.C. Shortly afterward, it was made part of the Roman province of Asia. At the partition of the Roman empire (395 A.D.), Aeolis was assigned to the East Roman (Byzantine) empire and remained under Byzantine rule until the early 1400's, when the Ottoman Turks occupied the area.

P.R. COLEMAN-NORTON, *Princeton University*

AEOLUS, ē′ə-ləs, in classical mythology, was a king in the Aeolian (Lipari) Islands off Sicily. Zeus (Jupiter) made him ruler of the winds, which he kept in caves or in bags and released either at his own discretion or at the will of the gods. He gave Odysseus (Ulysses), who was on his way home to Ithaca, a bag containing all the stormy winds to carry on his ship. Within sight of home a sailor opened the bag, and the sudden release of the winds forced the ship back toward the islands.

Aeolus had six sons and six daughters, who intermarried. The most famous of them were Sisyphus and Canace.

In Greek legend there was another Aeolus, son of Hellen, after whom the Hellenes (Greeks) were named. He was a king in Thessaly, in east-central Greece, and was the reputed ancestor of the Aeolians.

AEQUI, ē′kwī, an ancient Italic tribe that originally occupied the mountainous area in central Italy watered by the tributaries of the Avens River (modern Velino River). Their origin is unknown, but they probably spoke Oscan and may have been related to the Volscians, with whom they often were allied.

About 500 B.C. the Aequi began to expand westward to the sea. They soon occupied the hills behind Tibur (modern Tivoli) and Praeneste (modern Palestrina), and advanced as far as the Alban Hills southeast of Rome. According to tradition, the Roman dictator Lucius (Titus) Quinctius Cincinnatus checked their advance in 458 B.C. They were finally dislodged from the Alban Hills in 431 B.C. by the dictator Aulus Postumius Tubertus and were forced back to their original home.

Continued warfare with Rome almost annihilated the Aequi, but in 304 B.C. Rome established the colony of Carsioli in their region (through which the Via Valeria was extended), and conferred limited Roman citizenship on the tribe. Thereafter the Aequi rapidly became Romanized and by the 1st century B.C. enjoyed full Roman citizenship.

P.R. COLEMAN-NORTON
Princeton University

AERATOR, âr′ā-tər, an apparatus by means of which oxygen in the air is introduced into water, and dissolved in it, for the purpose of destroying bacteria. In city reservoirs, aeration is accomplished by spraying water into the air from fountains, by bubbling compressed air through the water, or by flowing the water over a series of cascades. In addition to oxidizing organic matter in the water, aeration removes sulfur and other gases that cause an unpleasant odor or taste. It is one of a combination of methods, including filtration and chlorination, used to purify municipal water supplies.

In dairies, milk is aerated to remove animal and barn odors. The usual method is to run the milk in a thin layer over an exposed surface immediately after milking. Most dairy aerators are cooled with ice, ice water, or spring water, to remove animal heat as well.

AERENCHYMA, ar-eng′kə-mə, a loose, spongy tissue in plants, especially in water plants. It is believed to facilitate aeration. Typically, the tissue is composed of radially arranged arms of thin-walled cells enclosing large air spaces.

U.S. AIR FORCE

AERIAL PHOTOGRAPH reveals an antiaircraft emplacement as a bombing mission target in North Vietnam.

AERIAL PHOTOGRAPHY, âr′ē-əl fə-tog′rə-fē, is the photographing of the earth's surface by means of cameras mounted in aircraft. The pictures thus obtained are used in the preparation of maps and surveys and for the identification of objects on or near the ground.

In the early days of aerial photography, the camera was airborne by means of kites and, later, captive balloons. With the advent of the airplane and the needs of World War I, aerial photography became an important reconnaissance tool and the development of aerial camera equipment advanced rapidly. This trend continued. Thus, during World War I thousands of aerial photographs were taken every day, but during World War II millions of photographs were taken daily. In World War II, and later during the Korean War, 80 percent of military intelligence was derived from aerial photographs.

Uses. Undoubtedly, the chief role that aerial photography plays is in *military reconnaissance.* It provides a permanent record which can be studied, put away, and reevaluated at a future date, or cross checked with other available data. Military forces use aerial reconnaissance to chart and map enemy positions, activities, and equipment, and to confirm intelligence data secured by other means. Aerial photography is used to identify targets for bombing missions and for later assessment of bomb damage. Furthermore, with the aid of good aerial photographs, water depths can be measured, underwater objects can be located, heights of buildings and structures can be determined, types and quantities of vehicles and aircraft can be identified, and the general deployment of troops can be recorded.

There are several types of military reconnaissance missions. The search reconnaissance mission is used to obtain initial information about an area. In such a mission, maximum area coverage

THIS PANORAMIC AERIAL VIEW of the New York City area (*across both pages, above*) was taken at an altitude of 30,000 feet (9,000 meters) and runs from the tip of Manhattan (*far right*) across the Upper Bay and Staten Island, and well into New Jersey. At left, the enlarged detail of the strip (*indicated by the white square above*) illustrates to some degree the amount of information that can be gained from aerial photographs. A trained photo interpreter could estimate the size, height, and nature of individual structures appearing in these photographs.

is desired along the entire flight path. For this reason, small-scale cameras are used and are continuously operated along the line of flight. The number and rate of exposures are generally controlled so that each succeeding exposure will cover some of the area covered in the previous photograph. This overlap is usually set at about 10 percent (or 60 percent when stereoscopic viewing is desired).

Specific objective reconnaissance differs from search reconnaissance in that it provides large-scale photography of selected targets. Prestrike reconnaissance missions serve to obtain current information about a given target, to confirm previous information, or to form the basis for revising the strike plan. Strike photo reconnaissance is used to evaluate the impact of bombs and other weapons. Poststrike reconnaisance permits a complete evaluation of the effectiveness of a bombing mission, and may serve as the prestrike photography of a later mission.

In *civilian use*, aerial photography has been applied to such diverse activities as mapping, archaeology, geology, meteorology, urban planning, road planning, traffic analysis, and agricultural and forestry surveys. Perhaps second in over-all importance to military applications is government mapping, which makes extensive

use of aerial photography. Virtually all major mapping activities are dependent on aerial photographs for charting new areas as well as the revision and updating of old maps. The speed and ease with which aerial photography covering large areas can be converted to accurate maps cannot be matched by ground survey techniques.

Equipment. There are two basic types of cameras used in aerial photography. The *frame* camera is used mostly in mapping and search missions whereas the *panoramic* camera is used extensively in prestrike and poststrike missions.

The frame camera is similar in principle of operation to cameras widely used by amateurs and professionals. The panoramic camera, however, relies upon scanning optics to achieve a wide angular field of view. Photographic scan angles range up to 180° (a half circle) in one exposure.

Some of the special features that can be found in aerial cameras include automatic exposure control, automatic focusing, image motion compensation devices, film flattening by vacuum, in-flight processing, and auxiliary data recording. Shutter mechanisms are grouped into three basic types: between-the-lens, focal plane, and louver. All modern aerial cameras are motor driven and electrically controlled.

Associated with the development of the aerial camera has been the development of high-performance optics. This has been particularly true in recent years with the advent of the high-speed electronic computer, which has enabled the lens designer to make a lens design rapidly and evaluate its performance without the need to build the actual lens. Present-day lenses used in aerial cameras range from short focal-length units of 1½ inches (3.75 centimeters) to units with focal-lengths of 48 inches (122 centimeters) and more.

Photographic emulsions that couple high resolution performance with high speed have been developed especially for aerial photography. In these applications, roll film is used almost exclusively. Film widths range up to 20 inches (50 centimeters); the commonly used widths are 70 millimeters (3 inches), 5 inches (12½ centimeters), and 9½ inches (24 centimeters). Film lengths range from 15 feet (4.5 meters) up to thousands of feet or meters.

Installations for aerial cameras range from the very simple to the very complex. In a simple installation, the camera is merely bolted to a structural part of the aircraft. Vibration isolation trusses are sometimes interposed between the camera and the aircraft. For critical installations such as mapping cameras and very long focal-length camera systems, 3-axis stabilized platforms are often used. In virtually all installations, electrical hookups of varying complexity are required for pilot control and operation as well as for the recording of pertinent mission data. The cameras are mounted with a line of sight that may be vertical, pointing forward, pointing sideward, or pointing backward; the first two are the most common positions.

Future Developments. Intensive efforts are being devoted to furthering the effectiveness of airborne camera systems. In-flight processing (with subsequent photo transmission to ground stations) is being refined. Systems capable of photography under extremely low light-level conditions are rapidly approaching reality. Perhaps the area of greatest need lies in the data-processing field, where photographic interpretation still depends heavily on manual study of the film. Automatic data-reduction equipment has helped to alleviate this condition, but a great deal more needs to be done. Correlation and recognition systems are under development that will drastically cut data-reduction time. As more automatic data-handling equipment is developed, aerial photography will find new applications that will further increase its importance. See also PHOTOGRAPHY.

JAMES B. SETO
Fairchild Camera and Instrument Corporation

AËRIANS, ā-ir′ē-ənz, a Christian sect of the 4th century in Pontus, Asia Minor. They were followers of Aërius, a presbyter of Sebaste in Pontus (modern Sivas, Turkey), who regarded many practices and traditions of the Christian church as excessive. The sect took the position that presbyters had the same sacred character and authority as bishops. They also rejected fasting and abstinence, opposed prayers for the dead, and urged the nonobservance of Easter. Some modern scholars view the efforts of Aërius and his followers as a forerunner of the Protestant Reformation. Others have seen the sect specifically as an early form of Presbyterianism.

AEROBATICS. See Aviation and Soaring and Gliding.

AERODYNAMICS, âr-ō-dī-nam′iks, the study of the behavior of air in motion, especially the effect air has on bodies that move through it and on stationary objects. Thus it may be more generally stated that aerodynamics is the study of air in relative motion. An aerodynamicist is normally concerned with the effect of air on an aircraft such as an airplane, a helicopter, or an airship. (See Airplane.) Aerodynamics also treats the aerodynamic forces exerted on ground vehicles and high-speed trains; on ballistic missiles, spacecraft, and projectiles; and on stationary structures, such as bridges, chimney stacks, and buildings. The collapse of the Tacoma Narrows Bridge in Tacoma, Wash., on Nov. 7, 1940, owing to aerodynamic forces, demonstrated the importance of aerodynamics in structural design.

Properties of the Atmosphere. To understand the source and nature of aerodynamic forces, one must realize that air, though normally invisible, has mass. In fact, the typical weight of a cubic foot of air at sea level is approximately 0.0766 pound (0.0347 kg). A layer of air at a given altitude must exert a static pressure to support the air above it. Being a gas, air is compressible, and thus its density (weight per unit volume) increases as it is subjected to higher pressure.

Conversely, air density and static pressure decrease as altitude increases. Also, the temperature of the atmosphere generally decreases with increasing altitude; the rate at which temperature drops with altitude is nearly constant up to an altitude of 36,000 feet (11 km). Above this altitude, the temperature remains constant up to an altitude of 82,000 feet (25 km). Standard atmosphere is defined as air at a temperature of 60° F (15° C), exerting a pressure equivalent to 29.9 inches (76 cm) of mercury. An aerodynamicist works with the mass density of air rather than the density defined by the weight. Because the atmosphere constitutes only a thin layer of gas relative to the entire earth, one can assume that the acceleration due to gravity on earthbound vehicles is constant.

Dimensionless Coefficients. The aerodynamic forces of major concern on an aircraft are lift and drag. Lift is defined as the aerodynamic force perpendicular to the aircraft's velocity vector; drag is the force parallel to the velocity vector but in the opposite direction. In level flight the lift is the force directed upward, which balances the aircraft's weight. The drag is the force directed to the rear, which must be balanced by the thrust from some kind of engine. An aircraft in flight with all forces and moments in balance and under control is said to be "in trim."

A wing placed at an angle to the velocity vector with the front, or leading, edge upward will produce a lift. This angle is referred to as the angle of attack. Aerodynamicists generally work with forces and moments expressed as dimensionless coefficients (converting results to real values later). This means that the quantity has no units such as feet, pounds, or seconds. Using dimensional analysis, it can be shown that any aerodynamic force produced by a body having a fixed geometric shape varies directly with the square of the airspeed, the area of the body, and the air-mass density. For example, the lift, L, and the drag, D, of a particular wing shape at a

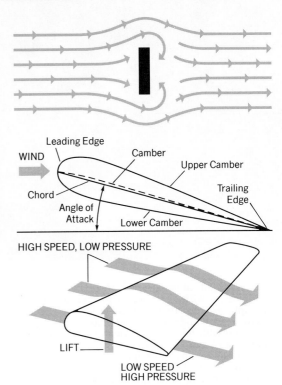

Figure 1. The aerodynamic principle. An upright plate in an airstream experiences complex forces from the air current and the rearward eddies (*top*). When air flows over an airfoil, the pressure differential between the upper and lower surfaces creates a lifting force (*bottom*). At high speeds, the intricacies of aerodynamic forces at various locations on the wing become significant factors.

particular angle of attack can be expressed in terms of dimensionless quantities called the lift coefficient, C_L, and the drag coefficient, C_D, defined by the following equations:

$$L = C_L \, \tfrac{1}{2} \, (\rho \, V^2) \, S; \text{ and } D = C_D \, \tfrac{1}{2} \, (\rho \, V^2) \, S$$

The Greek letter rho, ρ, represents the value of the air-mass density, while V is the airspeed. The quantity $\tfrac{1}{2} \, (\rho \, V^2)$ is referred to as the dynamic pressure and is usually denoted by the letter q in publications on aerodynamics. S is the projected, or planform, area of the wing when viewed from above or below. Since the lift and drag coefficients are dimensionless, they will not change in going from the English to the SI system of units. The advantage of using these coefficients is that once they are determined, the actual forces can then be determined for any size of wing, airspeed, and altitude.

The aerodynamic forces on a wing result from the pressure distribution over the wing's upper and lower surfaces. Simply put, the pressure on the bottom pushes upward while the pressure on the top pushes downward. If the pressure on the bottom is greater than that on the top, then a lift is produced on the wing.

Streamlines. A streamline is defined as an imaginary line such that the velocity of air is everywhere tangent to the line. A streamline presents a picture of the flow of air around an object. Since at every point on the body surface the normal (or perpendicular) component of the velocity must vanish (since the air cannot penetrate the surface), it follows that the body itself is defined by a surface of streamlines. A collection of streamlines gives a picture of the total airflow around an object. Bodies that permit moving air to flow around them with a minimum of resistance are said to be streamlined.

The wind tunnel is the principal aerodynamic experimental tool. A closed-circuit tunnel is a structural loop in which the air circulates continuously around the tunnel pushed by a powered fan. Most large wind tunnels are of this type. Smaller tunnels are frequently of the single-pass type, where the air enters a nozzle inlet from the outside, passes through the test section, and then is diffused and exits. The wind tunnel used by the Wright brothers was of the single-pass type. (See WIND TUNNEL.)

Lift and Drag. One has only to blow across the top of a sheet of paper held only at one end, with the other end allowed to dangle, in order to observe the lift effect of moving air. The dangling end of the sheet rises, lifted by the greater pressure of the stationary air underneath. This basic application of Bernoulli's principle may be enough to explain aircraft flight at low velocity, but with increased speed, altitude, size, and weight, more complex mechanisms come into play.

Calculation of Lift. The cross section of a wing is referred to as an airfoil. An airfoil is generally rounded at the front, or leading, edge and pointed at the rear, or trailing, edge. The upper surface is usually curved outward; the lower surface is flatter and sometimes even curved inward. A line drawn through points midway between the upper and lower surfaces from the leading edge to the trailing edge is the camber line. The chord line is a straight line connecting the leading and trailing edges of the camber line. The pointed trailing edge is necessary to ensure that the flow leaves in the direction of the edge in order to produce lift. The leading edge is rounded to ensure that the flow follows around the surface and does not separate from it. The angle of attack of an airfoil, usually denoted by α (alpha), is measured relative to the chord line.

A symmetrical airfoil is one in which the camber is zero, that is, the camber line is a straight line. At zero angle of attack, the lift coefficient of a symmetrical airfoil is zero. A cambered airfoil at zero angle of attack, however, will produce a lift coefficient that is given approximately by $C_{Lo} = 4\pi z$, where z is the ratio of the maximum camber to the chord. This ratio is normally small—typically 0.05 or less. Because this lift coefficient is for two-dimensional flow, it is defined as the lift per unit length of span divided by the dynamic pressure and the chord.

For a symmetrical airfoil at zero angle of attack ($\alpha = 0$), the lift is zero. As the angle of attack is increased or decreased, the C_L will increase or decrease in direct proportion to alpha at a rate, theoretically, of 2π per radian, or 0.110 per degree. This rate is known as the slope of the lift curve. (In practice, the value is usually less than the theoretical value by about 5%.) As the angle of attack continues to increase, a value is reached where the air is no longer able to follow the contour of the airfoil. If the angle of attack is increased beyond this value, the flow will separate from the upper surface with an accompanying loss in lift, and the airfoil is said to be stalled. The highest value of C_L attainable by an airfoil is known as the maximum lift coefficient, C_{Lmax}. Since the airfoil is symmetrical, there is no preference with regard to angle of attack, so that the magnitude of the negative C_{Lmax} is the same as that for a positive angle.

Camber has practically no effect on the slope of the lift curve; however, owing to the fact that C_L is not zero at a zero angle of attack, the lift coefficient for a cambered airfoil will be higher than for its symmetrical counterpart at the same angle of attack. Also, C_{Lmax} will be somewhat higher for a cambered airfoil.

A graph of the drag coefficient, C_D, of an airfoil versus its lift coefficient is parabolic in shape. The bottom of the parabola, where the drag is a minimum, occurs at a C_L of zero for a symmetrical airfoil. For a cambered airfoil, the minimum drag occurs at a small, positive lift coefficient. Thus camber increases the maximum lift coefficient and produces the minimum drag coefficient at a small lift coefficient. In general, for a given lift coefficient, the drag coefficient will be less if the lift is obtained from camber rather than from angle of attack.

The lift and drag coefficients below stall, C_L and C_D, can be determined from equations of the form

$$C_L = C_{L\alpha}\,\alpha + C_{Lo}$$
$$C_D = C_{Dmin} + k(C_L - C_{Lopt})^2$$

where C_{Dmin} is the minimum value of the drag coefficient corresponding to a lift coefficient of C_{Lopt}. The value of k is a constant, and $C_{L\alpha}$ is the lift curve slope. Typically, k and C_{Dmin} equal approximately 0.008. (Experimental wind-tunnel results are necessary for predicting the lift and drag of specific airfoils.)

The maximum lift coefficient of an airfoil can be increased appreciably by lowering a flap at the trailing edge. There are many different types of flaps, and a well-designed double-slotted flap with a leading-edge flap, comparable to the high-lift system found on modern jet transports, can almost triple the maximum lift coefficient of the unflapped airfoil.

Drag of Nonlifting Bodies. The calculation of the drag of a given body shape is something of an art. Either a model is built and tested in a wind

Schlieren analysis (using oil droplets) in wind-tunnel tests of the SST Concorde reveal that at supersonic speeds significant air vortices form over the wings.

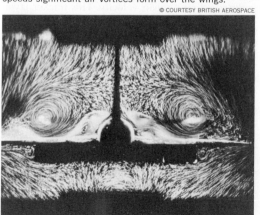

tunnel, or one must search the literature for drag coefficients that have been measured for similar shapes. Educated guesses or approximate analytical techniques are then used to correct the data.

An understanding of the origin of drag is essential to its estimation. Consider two extremes; a flat plate normal to the flow and a flat plate parallel to the flow. In the first instance, the flow impacts on the plate, spreads outward, and separates from the edges, leaving a large wake of turbulent air behind the plate. The static pressure in front of the plate is considerably higher than the pressure behind the plate, which causes a high "form," or pressure, drag.

In the case where the plate is parallel to the flow, the flow does not have to go around an obstacle and so there is no pressure drag. However, air is viscous, so that the viscous shearing of the air as it makes contact with the surface of the plate causes viscous, or skin-friction, drag. The layer of air immediately in contact with the surface comes to rest and slows the adjacent layers of air away from the plate through viscous shearing action.

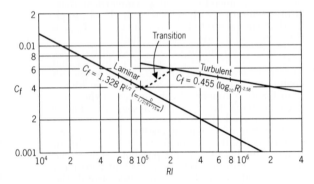

Skin-Friction Coefficient vs. Reynolds Number

This thin layer of slower-moving air, which thickens toward the rear of the plate, is known as the boundary layer. In general, the drag of a body shape will be composed of both pressure and skin-friction drag. If the body is streamlined, most of the drag will be skin friction, but as the shape becomes progressively blunter, pressure drag becomes a greater percentage of the total drag.

Scale Effects. Though it is true in many instances that dimensionless aerodynamic force and moment coefficients depend only on the particular geometric shape and not on the size of the body or the velocity of the air, this is not true in general. Lift and drag coefficients depend, in particular, on two dimensionless parameters known as the Mach number (after Ernst Mach, 1838–1916) and the Reynolds number (after Osborne Reynolds, 1842–1912). The Mach number is the ratio of the airspeed to the speed of sound. At sea level and at a temperature of 60° F (15° C), the speed of sound is 1,116 feet (340 meters) per second, or 760 miles (1,225 km) per hour. The Reynolds number is proportional to the ratio of the viscous shearing forces on a surface to the dynamic pressure. The Reynolds number, R, is defined as $R = Vl\mu/\rho$, where V is the airspeed, l is a characteristic length of the body, μ is the viscosity of air, and ρ is the mass density. For an airfoil, l is usually taken to be the chord length.

(For other shapes, l will be determined by another parameter.)

Separation and viscous drag are the two aerodynamic properties primarily affected by an object's Reynolds number. If a body shape is bluff, with sharp corners at which the flow will separate under any condition, then the drag coefficient for the shape will be a constant almost independent of Reynolds number. Conversely, if the shape has rounded corners the flow may not separate at low values of R. Generally, depending on the shape, the flow over such a body will still separate if the Reynolds number is sufficiently high. Thus at a critical Reynolds number, the drag coefficient can suddenly decrease as the Reynolds number increases because of a reduction in the pressure drag.

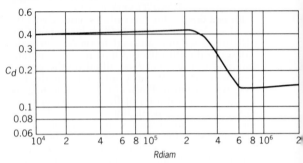

Drag Coefficient for Sphere vs. Reynolds Number as a Function of Diameter

Reynolds number will have the opposite effect on a body that is highly streamlined and for which the drag is caused mostly by skin friction. The drag coefficient resulting from viscous shear is given the symbol C_f, with the reference area being the wetted, or surface, area in contact with the air. In this form C_d is called the skin-friction coefficient. Near the front of a streamlined shape, the flow in the boundary layer is ordered and smooth, with the air particles moving in laminae (sheets), hence the term laminar boundary layer. The layer thickens as the flow moves toward the rear, until a point is reached where small disturbances in the boundary become unstable and grow rapidly, causing the boundary layer to thicken rapidly. This part of the boundary layer is called a turbulent boundary layer and is characterized by a random velocity superimposed on a mean velocity. This thicker layer has a much higher skin-friction coefficient than the laminar layer. Thus it is desirable to keep the transition point between laminar and turbulent flow far back on a streamlined body.

For entirely laminar or entirely turbulent flow, C_f will decrease as the Reynolds number increases. But since the transition point for a given geometric shape moves forward as the Reynolds number is increased, the skin-friction drag of a shape over which the flow is both laminar and turbulent will increase. A great deal of research has been done on increasing the extent of laminar flow on the wings of airplanes. The problem is complicated by the fact that small ripples in the surface, dirt or smashed bugs, or any other surface roughness can cause a transition from a laminar boundary to a turbulent one.

Mach number effects on lift and drag are

very pronounced as the speed of a body moving through the air approaches the speed of sound. Even if the Mach number of the body is less than 1, the flow over the body locally at some point can exceed the speed of sound, producing a shock wave. This will cause the boundary layer to suddenly thicken or even separate, resulting in a large increase of drag coefficient. Such a mixture of subsonic and supersonic flow is called transonic flow. As the Mach number exceeds 1, the entire flow over the body can become supersonic, which drastically changes the flow pattern over the body. The occurrence of oblique shock waves attached to and traveling with the body causes an additional drag known as wave drag. The pressure distribution over a body is drastically different for supersonic flow as compared with subsonic flow. Hence all of the dimensionless coefficients are strongly dependent on Mach numbers near or in excess of 1.

Airplane Aerodynamics. The seeming ease with which a huge jet aircraft takes off from a runway can easily mislead one into believing that the interactions between the natural forces and an aircraft's mechanisms are relatively simple and all clearly understood. In fact, however, there is much in the field of aerodynamics and aircraft design that is still not completely understood. The complex interactions between the gaseous molecules of the atmosphere, the surfaces of wings and fuselage, and the control and propulsion systems of an aircraft, all magnified with ever-increasing parameters of performance, are still being explored and tested on the blackboard, on the computer screen, and in the wind tunnel. And the skills required to pilot aircraft are several orders of magnitude greater than those needed to drive a ground vehicle. For a discussion of aircraft design and systems, and for information on flight procedures, see AIRPLANE.

Airplane Lift and Drag. The flow over an airplane wing is three-dimensional, since air can flow from the high-pressure region under the wing around the wing tips to the low pressure on top. This gives rise to swirling air trailing from each wing tip, called a tip vortex. The rolling moment produced by one of the vortices from a large jet on a small airplane that penetrates the axis of the vortex can significantly exceed the roll control of the smaller airplane. This hazard to a smaller airplane posed by the wake from a larger one is known as wake turbulence and is one of the main factors that determine separation distance regulations between airplanes.

The vortex wake from a wing causes a downward flow, or downwash, that effectively reduces the geometric angle of attack of each airfoil section of the wing. This induced angle of attack is given approximately by $\alpha_i = C_L^2/\pi[AR]$, where $[AR]$ is the wing's aspect ratio, B/C, B being the span of the wing and C the average chord (equal to the wing planform area divided by the span). Because of this induced angle, the slope of a wing's lift curve is less than that of the airfoil that forms the wing. To a close approximation, the slope of the wing's lift curve is equal to the slope of the airfoil lift curve multiplied by the factor $[AR]/([AR] + 2)$. Thus, for example, an airfoil at a 10° angle of attack will produce a lift coefficient of about 1.0. But if this airfoil shape is incorporated into a wing having an aspect ratio of 6, the wing will produce a lift coefficient of only 0.75 at the same angle of attack.

In the first analysis, it is fair to assume that the lift of an airfoil is perpendicular to the velocity. As part of a wing, the airfoil experiences a flow that is directed downward from the direction of the freestream velocity. This, in turn, causes the lift force to be tilted backward, giving rise to yet another source of drag, known as induced drag. The minimum value of the induced drag coefficient of a wing is related theoretically to its lift coefficient by $C_{Di} = C_L^2/\{\pi[AR]e\}$.

The factor e is an empirical correction factor giving an effective $[AR]$. It varies from approximately 0.6 for low-wings to 0.8 for high-wings. The total drag of an airplane is the sum of this drag, the drag of the airfoils from wind-tunnel measurements, and the drag of the rest of the airplane components.

The total drag minus the induced drag is known as the parasite drag. It can be estimated by estimating the drag of each component of the airplane—fuselage, tail surfaces, landing gear, and antennae—and then summing the results. This procedure is known as a drag breakdown. An easier way to accomplish this, and possibly just as accurate, is to use a skin-friction coefficient based on the total wetted area of the airplane. The value of C_f is chosen to be equal to that for an airplane with a similar degree of streamlining.

TYPICAL DRAG COEFFICIENTS OF VARIOUS AIRPLANES

C_F	Airplane Designation	Description
0.0100	Cessna 150	Single prop, high wing, fixed gear
0.0095	PA-28	Single prop, low wing, fixed gear
0.0070	B-17	Four props, World War II bomber
0.0066	C-47	Twin props, low wing, rectractable gear
0.0060	P-40	Single prop, World War II fighter
0.0060	F-4C	Jet fighter, engines internal
0.0059	B-29	Four props, World War II bomber
0.0054	P-38	Twin props, twin-tail booms, World War II fighter
0.0050	Cessna 310	Twin props, low wing, rectractable gear
0.0049	Beech V35	Single prop, low wing, retractable gear
0.0042	Learjet 25	Twin jets, pod-mounted on fuselage, tip tanks
0.0038	P-51F	Single prop, World War II fighter
0.0038	C-5A	Four jets, pod-mounted under wing, jumbo jet
0.0036	747	Four jets, pod-mounted under wing, jumbo jet
0.0033	P-80	Jet fighter, engines internal, tip tanks, low-wing
0.0032	F-104	Jet fighter, engines internal, midwing
0.0031	A-7A	Jet fighter, engines internal, high wing

As an example, consider a light, four-place, single-engine, propeller-driven airplane having a gross weight of around 2,500 pounds and a fixed landing gear. Such an airplane is somewhat aerodynamically inefficient and can be expected to have a relatively high value of C_f, say, of approximately 0.0095. The wing has a span of 30 feet and a constant chord of 5 feet. A reasonable value for the total wetted area of such an airplane would be around 600 square feet. Thus the total drag of this airplane can be calculated from $D = \frac{1}{2}\rho V^2(SC_{Di} + S_W C_f)$.

At sea level, at a speed of 100 mph, the following final numbers are obtained: $V = 146.7$ feet per second; $q = 25.6$ psf; $C_L = 0.651$; $C_{Di} = 0.0225$; and the drag is 232.3 pounds.

The Area Rule. In the late 1940s, attempts to reach speeds at or above the speed of sound were frustrated in spite of dramatic improvements in propulsion systems. Aerodynamicist Richard T. Whitcomb conducted extensive wind-tunnel tests at the Langley Memorial Laboratory and, using Schlieren optical analysis, discovered that, in the transonic flow regime (between Mach 0.8 and 1.2), the shock-wave development and drag rise were similar for wing-body combinations to those for an isolated body with the same axial distribution of cross-sectional area. Thus to decrease the transonic drag rise of a wing-body combination, he argued, the cross-sectional area of the fuselage should be decreased where the wing is attached. This gave rise to the so-called Coke-bottle design of transonic aircraft. This meant that the fuselage had to be narrowed where the wing section began and that the nose section had to be enlarged so that the total cross-sectional area of the airplane varied in a smooth, continuous curve—the "area rule." In wind-tunnel tests, and later in the altered design of the Convair F-102, drag was reduced significantly and aircraft speed was increased an astounding 20% over the conventional fuselage design.

Airplane Performance. The total drag of an airplane is seen to be composed of two parts, the induced drag, which varies inversely with the square of the speed, and the parasite drag, which varies directly with the speed. It is interesting to note that at the speed for minimum drag, the induced drag and parasite drag are equal and their sum is a constant, independent of altitude.

The work done in moving an airplane a unit distance through the air is equal to the drag. The time to do this work is equal to the inverse of the velocity. Power is the rate of doing work, or the work divided by the time. It follows, therefore, that the power required to overcome the drag of an airplane is equal to the product of the drag and the velocity at which the drag occurs. In the above example, the power equals 34,078 foot-pounds per second, which is equivalent to 62.0 horsepower (hp).

In the case of an engine-propeller combination, the power must be delivered to the air through the propeller, hence the propeller efficiency must be taken into account in calculating the required engine power. A well-designed propeller will have an efficiency of 85% or higher. Assuming an 85% efficiency for the example results in a required engine power of 72.9 hp. If the installed engine power is greater than this value, then the airplane can go faster. The maximum speed in level flight will be the speed at which the required power is equal to the available power. In the case of a jet-propelled airplane, the maximum speed will be that at which the maximum thrust from the engines is equal to the drag of the airplane.

If an airplane is flying at some speed below its maximum in level flight, the pilot can use the excess power to increase the kinetic energy (speed) or the potential energy (altitude) of the airplane, or a combination of both. Suppose that the pilot advances the throttle so as to keep the airspeed constant. The excess power will then cause the airplane to climb at a rate denoted by R/C. Since the power required to raise the weight, W, of the airplane at the rate of climb is equal to the product of the weight and the rate of climb, it follows that R/C is equal to the excess power divided by the weight, or:

$$R/C = (T - D)/W.$$

In the previous example, suppose that the installed engine power is equal to 180 hp and

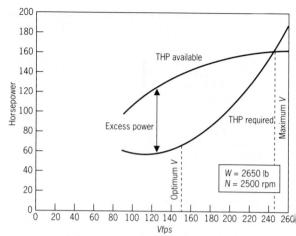

Required and Available Power vs. Velocity for a Typical Light, Low-wing Airplane

the propeller efficiency is again 85%. Since 180 hp is equivalent to 99,000 foot-pounds per second, the rate of climb is calculated to be: $R/C = [(99,000)(0.85) - 34,078]/2,500 = 20.0$ feet per second.

It is customary to express R/C for an airplane in feet per minute, so that for this example one would estimate a final rate of climb of 1,200 feet per minute, a value typical of light, general aviation airplanes.

As the speed of the airplane decreases, the required power will decrease to a speed at which the power required by the induced drag, the induced power, begins to exceed the parasite power. Below this speed, the pilot is flying on the back side of the power curve, where it actually takes more power to fly slower.

Regardless of power, there is a minimum speed below which an airplane cannot fly. This is the stalling speed, which is determined by the C_{Lmax} of the wing. Although the angle of attack to cause stall is higher for a wing than for the airfoil that forms the wing, the maximum lift coefficient of the wing is close to that for this airfoil. The exception to this is the case in which flaps extend over only part of the wing's span. In this case, C_{Lmax} of the wing will be less than the flapped airfoil but higher than that of the unflapped portion of the wing.

Control and Stability of Airplanes. The motion of an airplane is normally analyzed with respect to body axes, x, y, and z, which are fixed with respect to the airplane. (As the airplane moves, the axes move with it—the x-axis is directed forward, y to the right, and z downward.) Linear velocities along these axes are denoted by U, V, and W, while angular velocities are designated by P, Q, and R. Angular motion about the x-axis is referred to as rolling, about the y-axis as pitching, and about the z-axis as yawing. Forces along the three axes are represented by x, y, and z coordinates and by moments L, M, and N. An airplane is normally symmetrical about a vertical plane through its centerline. Motion in this plane (U, W, and Q components) is known as longitudinal motion, while motion of this plane (V, P, and R components) is referred to as lateral-directional motion. Having the possibility of linear and angular motions along three axes, an airplane is said to possess six degrees of freedom.

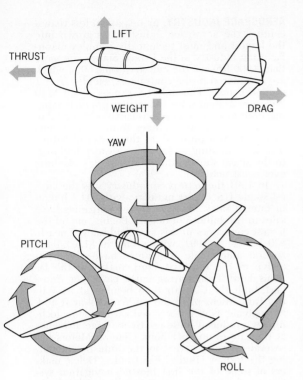

THRUST

LIFT

WEIGHT

DRAG

YAW

PITCH

ROLL

Figure 2. Forces on an airplane. An aircraft is "in trim" when all forces, both transverse and rotational, are balanced as the aircraft is in flight.

(By contrast, a ground vehicle possesses only three degrees of freedom.)

Control. The horizontal tail provides pitch control by means of a movable control surface known as an elevator. The horizontal tail is in effect a small wing, and the elevator corresponds to a flap on this wing. When the elevator moves up, a negative lift is exerted on the tail that produces a positive rotation (tail-down, nose-up) about the pitch axis. Moving the elevator down will produce an opposite effect. The fixed part of the horizontal tail ahead of the elevator is known as the horizontal stabilizer.

Similarly, the vertical tail is composed of a vertical stabilizer and a movable rudder, similar to a rudder on a ship. When the rudder moves to the right, a force is exerted on the vertical tail to the left. This in turn produces a yawing moment about the craft's center of gravity (CG) to move the nose to the right.

The wing has two movable surfaces just outboard of the flap that can move not only down like the flap but up as well. These surfaces, known as ailerons, move oppositely as the pilot turns the control wheel. If the aileron on the right wing moves up, the one on the left wing will move down, causing a rolling moment about the x-axis, which will bank the airplane to the right.

Stability. An airplane in trim can suddenly be subject to a disturbance (a gust of wind, for example) that causes changes in the lift and pressure distribution over the aircraft. If the airplane noses, or pitches, upward, then the angle of attack of the airplane will tend to increase. The airplane is then said to be longitudinally, statically unstable. If, however, this increase in the angle of attack produces a negative pitching mo-

ment about the CG, such a moment will tend to restore the airplane to its trimmed position, and the airplane is then said to be longitudinally, statically stable. Similarly, an airplane is directionally stable if the aerodynamic yawing moments generated by a gust of wind from the side tend to yaw the airplane into the wind—this is sometimes called weathercock stability.

Aircraft Instability. An airplane can be statically stable yet dynamically unstable if, when perturbed, the restoring force pushes the aircraft beyond the trim point. An airplane, like any dynamic system, exhibits motions that are the superposition (mathematical combination) of longitudinal and lateral-directional components, known as the normal modes. In the longitudinal case, an airplane typically exhibits two normal modes: the short-period mode and the phugoid (long-period) mode.

If an airplane in trim pitches up and is then returned to its original position, its inertia and aerodynamic forces may carry it beyond the original trimmed position to a nose-down orientation at a higher airspeed. The pitch angle and airspeed will then oscillate up and down, almost directly out of phase. This oscillatory motion is initially composed of both the short-period mode and the phugoid mode, but the short-period mode (so named because its period is usually a second or two) is heavily damped. The phugoid motion has a period of approximately 30 seconds, with the time to damp to half amplitude about the same. For some airplanes, the phugoid mode does not damp out unless the pilot or a stability augmentation system (SAS) moves to do so.

There are three normal modes associated with lateral directional motion: the Dutch-Roll mode, in which the airplane bobs and weaves (like a Dutch ice skater), oscillating in roll, yaw, and sideslip; the roll mode, which is a nonoscillatory, pure rolling motion in which the roll rate, but not the roll angle, converges to zero (the craft remains neutrally stable with regard to the angle; there are no moments produced to either increase or decrease the roll angle); and the spiral mode, for most airplanes a diverging, unstable motion. The spiral mode presents a real hazard to the inexperienced pilot, who may suddenly encounter conditions where a visual reference to the horizon is lost. Unless corrected, this unstable mode will cause the airplane to bank and turn, resulting in an ever-tightening downward spiral, during which the inertial forces may cause the pilot to believe that the plane is level.

Neither an unstable phugoid mode nor the spiral divergent mode is dangerous if proper piloting is done. Many pilots do not even aware of these unstable modes and provide an instinctive light touch to the controls to oppose these motions. An airplane can actually be more responsive if it is slightly unstable. These instabilities, it should be noted, are expected in the course of flight and are allowed by the regulating agencies that certifies the airworthiness of airplanes.

BARNES W. McCORMICK
Dept. of Aerospace Engineering
Pennsylvania State University

Bibliography: Allen, John E., *Aerodynamics: The Science of Fluid in Motion*, 2d ed. (McGraw 1982); Anderson, John D., Jr., *Fundamentals of Aerodynamics* (McGraw 1984); McCormick, Barnes W., *Aerodynamics, Aeronautics, and Flight Mechanics* (Wiley 1979); Smith, Hubert C., *The Illustrated Guide to Aerodynamics* (TAB Bks. 1986).

AERONAUTICAL ENGINEERING. See AEROSPACE INDUSTRY; AIRPLANE; AVIATION.

AERONAUTICS, âr-ə-nôt′iks. Originally thought of as the science of operating aircraft, the term has since been expanded to include all branches of science, engineering, business, and industry pertaining to the design, manufacture, and operation of aircraft.

Although sometimes used interchangeably with *aviation, aeronautics* applies to both lighter-than-air craft and heavier-than-air craft, while aviation usually applies only to heavier-than-air craft. As understanding of the mechanisms at work in the atmosphere deepens, aeronautics expands to include the effects of complex atmospheric conditions on aircraft, ground vehicles, and even stationary structures.

Aeronautical principles are critical in the design of ballistic missiles, rockets, and spacecraft. For this reason alone, the designation of the U.S. space agency as the National Aeronautics and Space Administration would be entirely appropriate. In addition, however, NASA conducts a great deal of research in aeronautics.

The basic physical principles used in aeronautics are found in AERODYNAMICS; ROCKET; and WIND TUNNEL. The most direct applications of aeronautical principles are found in AIRCRAFT; AIRPLANE; and AIRSHIP. The history of the development of aeronautics is presented in AEROSPACE INDUSTRY; AIR TRANSPORTATION; and AVIATION. Related material can be found in AIR SAFETY; BALLOON; BALLOONING; and SOARING AND GLIDING.

AEROSOL, âr′ə-sol, a suspension of small liquid or solid particles in a gaseous medium, such as air. There are many natural and artificial aerosols, including fog, mist, dust, and smog.

Aerosols can occur when bulk matter is pulverized or atomized. Examples are atmospheric dust resulting from volcanic eruption, and a nasal spray produced by atomization of a liquid stream forced through a fine nozzle at a high speed. Aerosols also can occur when a supersaturated vapor condenses on particles, as with air that cools and condenses to form a cloud or fog.

Liquid aerosol particles are spherical. Solid aerosol particles vary in shape. The diameter of the particles ranges from less than a millionth of an inch to several thousandths of an inch. Particles larger than these will settle out of a medium because of the force of gravity. Aerosol particles have random movements. When they collide, they aggregate, or coagulate. The more concentrated the aerosol is, the more rapidly the aggregation proceeds. The concentrations in nature range from those of smoke, which contains billions of particles per cubic inch, to those of dust clouds in interstellar space, which contain only a few particles per cubic mile.

Aerosols have interesting optical properties. In a smoke-filled room or a foggy atmosphere, a light beam shows clearly because of the intense scattering of the light by aerosol particles. The blue of the sky and the red of the setting sun are due primarily to the scattering of light by air molecules. But scattering of light by atmospheric aerosols also contributes to these effects, and the more brilliant aspects of twilights and sunsets are due to aerosols.

MILTON KERKER
Clarkson College of Technology

AEROSPACE INDUSTRY, âr′ō-spās. In less than a century the aerospace industry has grown into the largest and most technically complex manufacturing industry in the United States. The more than 4,000 firms of the industry (some 60 of which are considered prime contractors) employ over 1 million people. The industry grosses about $140 billion in annual sales and makes products ranging from laser gyroscopes to earth-orbiting laboratories. Product size ranges from microcircuits smaller than a pinhead; to the powerful Saturn 5 rocket, standing as tall as a 36-story building; to the space shuttle, the most complex machine ever constructed.

In 1991 the aerospace industry was the largest single U.S. export industry, with $41.7 billion in foreign sales. Many of these companies have sales in the billions of dollars. Boeing, one of the largest companies in this area, had sales of nearly $30 billion in 1991, with profits of $1.6 billion. Several automobile companies have also been active in the industry. Ford, maker of the famous Ford Trimotor, an early passenger transport, built the Convair B-24 bomber at its Willow Run, Mich., plant during World War II and, by applying its well-developed assembly-line techniques, produced these relatively large airplanes at the rate of one per hour. General Motors has several divisions active in the industry, including the former Hughes Electronics; Delco, makers of some of the first inertial navigation systems; and Allison, an engine maker. Other large corporations involved primarily in other enterprises have a significant involvement in aerospace—a notable example being General Electric, an important manufacturer of jet engines.

The term *aerospace* was first used by the U.S. Air Force in connection with Project Farside, a 1955 program involving the high-altitude launch of balloon-borne research rockets. The term became widely accepted when the Aircraft Industries Association changed its name to the Aerospace Industries Association on Jan. 1, 1959. Today the term refers generally to industries involved in aviation, rocketry, and space technology.

History. It is generally believed that the Wright brothers of Dayton, Ohio, made the first powered flights in a heavier-than-air machine. That the Wright brothers, with no formal education as engineers, were able to reason out the essential elements of control of flight was indeed remarkable. The Wright brothers not only discovered that control was the key to success, they made aerodynamic research in a wind tunnel of their own construction a central element of their program. They tested hundreds of airfoils and applied their findings to both wing and propeller design. They built their own engines, using bicycle drive chains to turn their craft's counter-rotating propellers.

From those brilliant manufacturing and research efforts, culminating in the first flight of a heavier-than-air craft on Dec. 17, 1903, at Kitty Hawk, N.C., has grown one of the major industries of the 20th century. The Wright brothers were greeted with disinterest and skepticism in the United States, but in Europe they had caused excitement and a flurry of activity. In France they were received with great praise and adulation. The Wrights sold the patents to their airplane in 1908 to the French Astra syndicate, thus marking the first significant business transaction of the new industry. A flying school was set up in Pau, France, and Wilbur Wright personally trained its first three students.

The advance of the aerospace industry is closely tied to the major conflicts of this century and to the attempts by nations, even in peacetime, to exploit the war-making capabilities of aircraft. Fortunately, much of this development has been adaptable to commercial use.

World War I. The Wrights were so influential that when World War I started each European country already had advanced models of reconnaissance, fighter, and bomber designs in production. The early airplane manufacturers in Europe included Henri Farman, Louis Blériot, the Voisin brothers, and Leon Levavasseur, all in France; Hugo Junkers in Germany; Thomas Sopwith in England; and Igor Sikorsky in Russia.

The U.S. industry, partly as a result of extended litigation between the Wright brothers and Glenn L. Curtiss, was not able to furnish a single combat aircraft for the U.S. Expeditionary Forces in Europe. The U.S. government belatedly realized the potential of aircraft in warfare and created the National Advisory Committee for Aeronautics (NACA) in 1915. The first NACA wind tunnels were built at the Langley Memorial Aeronautical Laboratory at Langley Field, Hampton, Va., in 1917. The Langley Research Center made significant contributions to the several technological revolutions that have caused the industry to advance so rapidly.

Several companies, led by visionaries who believed strongly in the future of the airplane, not only as a military fighting machine but as a peacetime vehicle with great potential in carrying passengers and freight, survived the economic collapse following the war. Some of these determined individuals (and the companies they founded) were William E. Boeing (The Boeing Company), Glenn L. Martin (Martin Marietta Corp.), Donald W. Douglas, Sr. (Douglas Aircraft Company), Robert and Courtland Gross (Lockheed Corp.), J. H. "Dutch" Kindelberger (North American Aviation, Inc.), John K. Northrop (Northrop Corp.), Larry Bell (Bell Aerosystems, Inc.), Vincent J. Bendix (Bendix Aviation Corp.), Reuben Fleet (Convair-General Dynamics), Frederick Rentschler (United Aircraft Corporation), and later J. S. McDonnell (McDonnell Aircraft Co., now merged to form the McDonnell-Douglas Corp.). These companies, founded in World War I and early in the period between the wars, still exist as individual firms or as divisions of merged companies.

Between the World Wars. Until the mid-1920s, airplanes were made of wood spars and ribs, cloth skin (stitched together by hand on the production floor), and sometimes steel trusses. The discovery that aluminum skin could carry substantial loads at light weight led, by the early 1930s, to the construction of aluminum spars, ribs, frames, and skin. The use of wind tunnel expanded rapidly in this period, and aerodynamicists found ways to dramatically reduce drag.

As a result of the reduction of drag and the increases in engine horsepower in the 1930s, speeds of both military aircraft and the first practical transport aircraft increased rapidly. The Boeing 247 and the Douglas DC-1 and DC-2, introduced to the market in the early 1930s, took full advantage of the low-drag engine cowlings developed at the NACA Langley Laboratory. These transports inaugurated the civilian aircraft industry as we know it today. Douglas soon followed its original models with the famous DC-3 in 1936. This airplane was to become the workhorse of the U.S. air forces in World War II, and Douglas built more than 10,000 of them.

It was also during this period that the German government began to build a formidable aircraft industry to produce fighting airplanes. This in turn gave impetus to many countries, but especially Britain, to greatly improve the quality and quantity of their airplanes. Speed and efficiency were the most sought after elements, and in the late 1930s Sir Frank Whittle in Britain and Hans von O'Hain in Germany simultaneously invented the gas turbine, or "jet" engine. It was a relatively simple device, consisting basically of a compressor, a combustion chamber, and a turbine wheel, but it was to revolutionize the airplane industry.

When World War II began in September 1939, U.S. aircraft manufacturers were building a few military aircraft that were definitely inferior to the frontline machines of the Germans; however, they did have designs on the drawing boards and a few prototypes of machines that would match the German airplanes. The British and the French, who had lagged behind the Germans, swamped the U.S. industry with orders for both existing and new designs, starting the industry on a growth curve that, except for brief periods, has continued into the 1990s.

World War II. By the time the United States was attacked at Pearl Harbor on Dec. 7, 1941, the orders previously placed by the British and French had already stimulated substantial expansion. The fear of attack on the East Coast from the Germans and on the West Coast from the Japanese caused the companies to locate plants in the interior. Plants were built in Kansas, Nebraska, Oklahoma, Georgia, Tennessee, Ohio, Illinois, and Michigan.

The combination of new training programs, the conversion of some of the auto industry to aircraft production, and the new facilities helped the industry produce an astounding 275,245 aircraft during World War II. President Franklin D. Roosevelt had asked the industry to produce 50,000 planes per year by 1944, and the industry responded by producing 95,272 aircraft in 1944. The intense efforts during the war at the services research centers such as Wright Field and at NACA's research laboratories at Langley Field, Moffett Field, and the Lewis Center at Cleveland, produced amazing increases in engine power and reductions in airplane drag. From 1935 to 1945 the average speed increased from just over 100 to nearly 500 miles (160–800 km) per hour. The Messerschmitt 262 fighter combined the turbine engine with the low drag of a wing with sweepback on the leading edge to achieve speeds approaching the speed of sound. The jet engine revolution, however, was just beginning as the war came to a close.

The United States demobilized after World War II in much the same haphazard manner as it had following World War I, and in the immediate postwar years production declined to less than 10% of wartime levels. Some visionaries in industry, government, and academia saw the developing efforts from the war as a new horizon. George Schairer of Boeing had been on the strategic bombing survey after Germany's defeat and saw immediately the potential of the swept wing and the jet engine for a revolutionary new bomber.

The Boeing B-47, a six-engine swept-wing bomber, made its first flight on Dec. 17, 1947, and Boeing and Lockheed went on to produce more than 2,000 of them. John Stack of Langley saw the potential for supersonic flight and received the Collier Trophy, along with Lawrence Bell, for the conception of the Bell X-1. This pioneering experimental airplane was the first to exceed the speed of sound, during a flight in October 1947, initiating the X-series of aircraft. The series culminated in the X-15, which established speed records of over 4,000 miles (6,500 km) per hour. Dr. Theodore von Karman of the California Institute of Technology, Gen. H. H. Arnold, chief of the Army Air Forces, and Dr. George Lewis, chairman of NACA, were each instrumental in advancing the frontiers of these new technical capabilities.

The Cold War Period. The Cold War between the United States and the Soviet Union, beginning in earnest with the Berlin airlift in 1947, spurred each country to incorporate these new technical capabilities into fighting machines. Once again, U.S. industry and NACA, acting in concert, accelerated research into supersonic flight. John Stack was to win a second Collier Trophy for his discovery that a wind tunnel with a ventilated (slotted) test section could record data accurately at speeds from about 0.8 of the speed of sound through and beyond the speed of sound.

The industry and research centers embarked on an intensive design and development program for supersonic fighters and bombers and for new subsonic bombers and transports. The Century series fighters, from the F-100 through the F-111, were all developed in the decade from 1950 to 1960. The B-52 bombers, as well as the supersonic B-58 bombers, were all being produced by the industry in the 1950s. This intense effort to build a new fighting force in the event of conflict with the Soviet Union laid the groundwork for the swept-wing turbine-engine transport, which would greatly expand the world's air transportation system.

Boeing built a prototype of a four-engine jet transport in 1954; Douglas followed with the DC-8. The competition between these two companies was intense during this period. The introduction of airplanes that carried twice the number of passengers at twice the speed of the propeller-driven transports then in service caused air traffic growth to nearly triple in the early part of the 1960s. Boeing also received a U.S. Air Force contract to make a jet tanker version of its transport prototype, to be used to refuel bombers and fighters in flight; by the early 1960s over 800 units had been built. Lockheed became the prime producer of military transports with the C-130 and C-141. This rapid expansion of the prime industry also led to the development of supporting second- and third-tier industries.

Industry involvement in rocketry and space exploration dates back to the early support of Robert Goddard's work by Charles Lindbergh and the Guggenheim Foundation for Aeronautical Research. Though the V-2 rocket used by the Germans in World War II had a very strong aerodynamical component (and was often described by the military as "a bomb that could fly itself"), it was not until after the war, when it was realized how devastating a missile carrying a nuclear bomb could be, that intense industry involvement in the design and produc-

tion of intercontinental ballistic missiles (ICBMs) began. With the Soviet launch of Sputnik in October 1957, a significant portion of the aircraft manufacturers' resources worldwide became devoted to missile and space technology.

Dr. Wernher Von Braun, one of the developers of the V-2 missile and then head of the U.S. space program, recognized that the launching of an earth satellite was only a step in the process of building a system that would escape earth's gravity and allow flight to the moon and beyond. U.S. president John F. Kennedy called on the industry to build a system that would land a man on the moon before the end of the 1960s. The industry, with its new knowledge from the ICBM research, coupled with the research activities of the National Aeronautics and Space Administration, or NASA (NACA's new name as of 1958), developed the 36-story Saturn-Apollo moon rocket system. This system combined the talents of almost the entire industry and resulted in the landing of American astronaut Neil Armstrong on the moon in July 1969. The total system integration required for the successful moon landings represented another technological advance that moved the industry from mere airplane building toward its present size and diversity.

Industry Structure and Systems. The aerospace industry can be divided into three major areas: aircraft, avionics, and rocketry and space. Aircraft is the leading product of the industry, accounting for 54% of annual sales, with civil transport aircraft sales slightly larger than military sales. Space programs represent 22%, missiles 9.5%, and related products 14.5% of industry activity. During most of its development, the industry has found that the requirements of its systems have been so far beyond those in other industries that it has had to create entire companies and fields of research to address its needs.

Aircraft. While efforts to upgrade rail transportation continue, flying remains the most efficient means of long-distance transportation when all factors (cost, time, wear and tear) are taken into account. As a result, the demand for civil air transports is up in the 1990s, despite international turmoil in eastern Europe and the Middle East and economic hard times worldwide. The soaring civil transport market dominated aircraft sales in the early 1990s. The demand is great enough to add an airline the size of United Airlines to the world fleet each year. The 1960s saw the addition of jets small enough to serve regional markets (Boeing 737, Douglas DC-9, and British Aircraft BAC-111), and in January 1970 the first wide-body aircraft (having two or more aisles), the Boeing 747, with 360 seats to meet the increasing demand on long international routes, was introduced.

In 1966 Douglas introduced three "stretched" versions of the DC-8, to compete in the short-, medium-, and long-range markets. Douglas and Lockheed also introduced wide-body jets, the three-engine DC-10 and the L-1011. The market appeared large enough that the French, German, British, Dutch, and Spanish governments started a consortium called Airbus Industries; their first product was a wide-body twin jet, the A-300, to compete with the DC-10 and the L-1011. The British and French collaboration on a small supersonic transport resulted in the 100-seat Concorde being introduced into transatlantic service in 1976. The Tupolev Tu-144 supersonic transport was nearly the same size as the Concorde; however, one of the two models produced suffered a serious crash and the other was never put into international service.

In the late 1970s Boeing and Airbus introduced smaller twin-engine wide-body transports called the 767 and the A-310, respectively. Boeing also introduced a 186-seat twin jet called the 757 to replace the older 727s; in 1992 nearly 2,000 flights per month were being made by twin-engine jet transports over the North Atlantic. Douglas, Boeing, and Airbus were all introducing new models to accommodate growth and replacement of the older models. Boeing was constructing the model 777 (purported to be the most electronically advanced air transport ever built); Douglas introduced the MD-11 and was designing the MD-12; and Airbus expanded its family to the A-330 twin and the A-340 four-engine aircraft. At nearly 600 passengers, the MD-12 is the first serious competition to the latest model of the Boeing 747-400, currently the dominant aircraft in its class. As a result of the traffic growth in the Pacific Rim, there is once again a serious study of the economic and technical possibilities of a second-generation long-range supersonic transport.

Avionics. Avionics (a contraction of *aviation* and *electronics*) systems are an outgrowth of a number of devices used in World War II, the first conflict in which electronics played a significant role. Such innovations as autopilot, radio, radar, and remote guidance demonstrated the importance of sophisticated instrumentation in flight and weapons. This became even more clear in the design of intercontinental ballistic missiles, where proper navigation and guidance were critical to performance.

As these electronic components became smaller and more reliable, they found applications in more and more devices. The B-29 bomber of World War II contained a few thousand; the B-52 used 50,000; ICBMs use hundreds of thousands; and the modern commercial transport has hundreds of microprocessors that contain millions of components, making them virtually flying computers. The development of these miniature electronic devices has brought many new companies into the aerospace industry, and some former subcontractors to the prime manufacturers have become prime manufacturers in their own right.

The power of computers has advanced to the point where it is possible to calculate completely the flows about airplanes and missiles for all speed ranges, thereby vastly reducing the dependence on wind tunnels to obtain the data necessary for safe operation. In addition, these devices allow the transmittal of digital electronic data sets and computer data instructions on a worldwide basis. Avionics including sensors such as infrared, millimeter-wave radars, inertial navigation systems, satellite navigation systems, and television guidance have greatly increased the accuracy of weapons delivery by both missiles and crewed aircraft. Flight control systems for military aircraft now use digital electronics for stabilization and control, and control cables, pulleys, and tighteners have been eliminated.

Avionics is also a central component of airborne weapons systems. The development of night vision devices and so-called smart bombs has played an important role in recent conflicts, but the most significant achievement of avionics has been in the development of "stealth" technology, making aircraft invisible to adversary radar. Stealth aircraft use a combination of "low-observable" (LO) materials and contours and highly sophisticated radar signal jamming and diversion. The Lockheed F-117A fighter and the B-2 bomber are the first examples of this type of aircraft.

Rocketry and Space. The ICBM force assembled in the 1960s to deter the Soviet Union from engaging in a nuclear war (a line of reasoning shared during this period by the Soviet Union), consisting of land-based solid-fuel rockets (Minuteman I, II, and III), was supplemented by submarine-based solid-fuel missiles (Poseidon) in the 1970s. Further developments in the 1980s were the Trident missiles placed on submarines; air-launched cruise missiles, capable of navigating by computer recognition of adversary terrain; and the MX land-based missiles with multiple, independently targeted warheads (MIRVs) and extremely accurate inertial navigation systems. The development of these very accurate navigation systems, coupled with very precise radar and infrared sensors, led to the production of a variety of missile systems, such as the Sidewinder, Pershing, Tomahawk, and Patriot missiles.

Aerospace industries have played a pivotal role in the exploration and utilization of space, not only because of the relationship between aerial flight and spaceflight but also because the technical expertise, tight quality controls, and large-scale management required for space projects are routinely applied in the industry.

Business Organization. The history of the aerospace industry is replete with examples of boom and bust periods. The industry nearly collapsed after World War I and again following World War II; only the dogged determination of its pioneers kept it alive. The resurgence at the start of the Cold War, followed almost immediately by the Korean War, caused a typical boom period, when the industry could not hire engineers or factory workers fast enough. Except for brief periods, the industry generally enjoyed substantial growth through the mid-1980s.

During the latter half of the 1980s there was a consolidation in the industry, and it is estimated that it will shrink by 30% by 1995. There has already been considerable consortium activity to allow firms to pool their resources to bid for the shrinking amount of government business. Examples of this include Lockheed, General Dynamics, and Boeing as equal partners on the F-22 fighter; Bell and Boeing on the V-22 tilt-rotor transport; General Dynamics and McDonnell Douglas on the A-12; and Sikorsky and Boeing on the Comanche helicopter. In general, industry attempts to diversify into fields outside its prime area of expertise have met with failure, but as the world enters a period of reduced military expenditure by the major powers, these industries may have little choice but to reallocate their resources to other areas of production.

Internationalization. The aerospace industry, like the automobile and electronics industries, is becoming international in scope. Aircraft engines are made in Great Britain, France, Germany, Japan, China, Russia, and the United States. Teams from the United States, Britain, Germany, Italy, and Japan produce a power plant used on commercial aircraft made by both Airbus Industries and Douglas. Another team, from General Electric in the United States and Snecma in France, builds engines used by Boeing and Airbus.

Aircraft typically contain parts produced in many places around the world, and second- and third-tier suppliers from many countries are in constant competition for business from the prime manufacturers. Many countries—Indonesia and Singapore, for example—have fledgling aerospace industries. Indonesia, in cooperation with the Spanish industry CASA, produces the CN-225, a small commuter transport. Countries such as these want the technical knowledge associated with aerospace development, and hence in many contracts it is necessary to place some work with the buyer's industries in order to make a sale.

Aerospace Careers. The early engineers employed by the industry were trained as mechanical engineers with some knowledge of fluid flows. In the late 1920s Daniel and Florence Guggenheim created a foundation to build aeronautical engineering schools in the United States, including those at New York University and Georgia Institute of Technology. As the speed and complexity of the airplanes and, later, missiles increased, more of the industry work force came to be made up of engineers, scientists, and technicians with specialties in electronics and electrical, mechanical, chemical, industrial, nuclear, aeronautical, and aerospace engineering. Many aeronautical engineering schools added *aerospace* to their names in the late 1950s to reflect the inclusion of aerospace subjects in the curriculum.

A college degree, preferably at the master's level, is the normal requirement for the industry. Some specialist positions require a doctorate in the field. Management positions today are increasingly being awarded to holders of an M.B.A. or LL.D., in addition to engineering degrees. Electrical, electronics, and laboratory technicians as well as drafters, technical writers, and communications specialists are also required. The advent of the high-speed computer and the sophisticated workstation have increased the need for computer-literate personnel with computational science degrees, and the modeling capabilities of computers are eliminating the need for large numbers of drafters.

The emphasis on "Total Quality Management" and "Continuous Quality Improvement," coupled with the need to bring all elements of the vehicle design together simultaneously, has brought down barriers that once separated engineers and production workers. In the current industrial environment, the tool designer and the industrial engineer must sit with and be a part of the design-build team as it generates the three-dimensional digital data set from which the vehicle will be built. As a consequence, production work is no longer relegated to those with less than college educations. There is still the need for skilled sheet metal, machining, and assembly workers and especially for electrical and avionics installers. The industry is still concentrated near the West Coast of the United States, with nearly half of all aerospace jobs in the country located in the states of California, Washington, and Arizona.

See also AIR TRAFFIC CONTROL; AIR TRANSPORTATION; AIRPLANE; AIRPORT; AVIATION.

JOHN M. SWIHART, *Swihart Consulting, Inc.*

AEROSPACE MEDICINE. See SPACE EXPLORATION—*Man in Space.*

AERSCHOT, ar'sĸʜôt, or Aarschot, a town in Belgium, in Brabant province, on the Demer River, 23 miles (37 km) northeast of Brussels. It became well known in the early days of World War I, when the Germans shot 150 civilians there on Aug. 19, 1914, the first such mass slaughter in the war. Population: 26,020 (1980 census).

AERTSEN, àrt'sən, **Pieter** (c. 1508–1575), Dutch painter. His name also is spelled Aertzen. One of the first genre painters, he often drew his subject matter from the daily life of peasants. He made an important contribution to the development of still-life painting and also painted biblical and historical subjects. Though influenced by Italian painting, Aertsen adhered to a traditionally Dutch style. His work influenced 17th-century painters in Italy and Spain, especially Caravaggio and Velázquez.

Aertsen was born in Amsterdam in 1508 or 1509. He studied with the Flemish painter Jan Mandijn and settled in Antwerp in 1535. His best-known work of this period is a Crucifixion triptych (1546). Aertsen returned to Amsterdam permanently about 1555. His later works include *The Egg Dance* (1557), *Christ in the House of Mary and Martha* (1559), and *The Cook* (1559).

AESCHINES, es'kə-nēz (389–c. 314 B.C.), Athenian orator, the rival of Demosthenes. Aeschines was a clerk and an actor before entering public life. He concentrated on a powerful delivery rather than literary perfection in his speeches and was an outstanding extemporaneous speaker. In 348 he was sent as envoy to the Peloponnesus to organize resistance to Philip of Macedon, but he soon advocated a negotiated peace instead. This was accomplished in 346 after two missions to Macedon in which Aeschines was joined by Demosthenes. In 345 Demosthenes persuaded Timarchus to impeach Aeschines, who, Demosthenes felt, had betrayed Athens in the negotiations. Aeschines retaliated by successfully prosecuting Timarchus on charges of immorality. In 343 Demosthenes again failed to indict Aeschines.

In 337 Aeschines impeached Ctesiphon for proposing a crown for Demosthenes. When the case was heard in 330, the jury accepted Demosthenes' brilliant defense ("On the Crown"). Forced to leave Athens, Aeschines retired to Asia Minor. He is said to have taught rhetoric until his death about 314.

AESCHYLUS, es'kə-ləs (524?–456 B.C.), Greek dramatist, the first of the three great ancient Athenian writers of tragedy, considered to be its true creator. (Sophocles and Euripides were his younger contemporaries.) Before his time there was only one actor (always the poet himself) in the play. This actor might change his mask and costume and hence assume more than one role, but he could conduct dialogue only with the Chorus. Aeschylus introduced a second actor. He also made innovations in dramatic costume. Most important, as suggested by the fact that he is the earliest playwright whose works have been preserved, he must have been the first to give plots a truly artistic shape and to capture in them a genuinely tragic spirit. Of some 90 Aeschylean plays only 7 survive in complete form.

Aeschylus was born of an aristocratic family at Eleusis near Athens. In 499 B.C., some 30 years after the reputed invention of tragedy by Thespis, he made his writing debut, entering a group of tragedies in the contest of the annual festival of Dionysus. His fellow contestants were Choerilus and Pratinas, the leading dramatic poets of the day. In the Persian wars Aeschylus served as a foot soldier, helping to repel the Persian invasion at Marathon (490) and at Salamis (480). In 484 he received the highest award in the playwriting contest. At some time in his career he was tried for impiety and acquitted, having been charged with divulging secrets of the great mysteries of Demeter. He made several trips to Sicily under the patronage of Hiero I, tyrant of Syracuse, and retired there. He died at Gela, Sicily, about 456. His verse epitaph, which he wrote himself, says nothing of his plays, mentioning only his service in the Persian wars.

Early Plays. Aeschylus's earliest tragedy, *The Persians,* was the second play of a tetralogy (a trilogy of three tragedies, followed by a satyr play) produced in March 472. Apparently this trilogy was spurious rather than genuine—there was no connected plot sequence from play to play and no unifying theme. The date of the action is 480. A chorus of Persian elders waits in the council hall for news of King Xerxes' expedition against Greece. The forebodings of all are confirmed when a messenger delivers a vivid description of the disastrous naval defeat at Salamis. The ghost of the former king, Darius, is raised up; he pronounces the Persian reverse to be the direct result of Xerxes' folly and impiety. The play ends with the entrance of Xerxes himself, disgraced and broken-spirited. The drama is remarkable in that it is one of the few instances in which a Greek playwright dealt with history rather than mythology. It also shows a rare magnanimity, celebrating Greek patriotism while avoiding unseemly triumph over a chastened foe.

The Seven against Thebes, his next play, was the third tragedy in a tetralogy based on the misfortunes that resulted from the misdeeds of Laius, his son Oedipus, and the rest of the Theban royal family. The tetralogy, produced in 468 or 467, exhibited a developing plot throughout and a unified theme; hence it was an example of a genuine tetralogy, a class of works particularly associated with Aeschylus. The central character is Eteocles, one of Oedipus's two sons, who is defending Thebes against the assault of six chieftains, led by Oedipus's other son, Polynices. At the end a messenger relates how the brothers killed each other, thus bringing to logical culmination the disorder set in motion by the impious deeds of the Theban royal line.

For a long time scholars thought that Aeschylus's *The Suppliants* was the oldest extant Greek play. This seemed to confirm the ancient theory that drama grew out of the Chorus, since in this play the 50 daughters of Danaus, singing together, take the leading role. But a papyrus published in the 1950s showed conclusively that the Danaid tetralogy, of which *The Suppliants* was the first part, must be dated late in Aeschylus's career, probably in 463. In the extant play, Danaus and his daughters have fled to Argos in Greece to forestall a forced marriage with their cousins, the sons of Aegyptus. In the subsequent lost plays, the marriage was carried through, but all but one of the Danaïdes executed their father's order to murder their husbands on their wedding night. The theme was undoubtedly violent lust in juxtaposition with true love and domestic affection. Aphrodite appeared at the end to celebrate love as the mainspring of nature and human society.

The Oresteian Trilogy. Three plays, *Agamemnon, Choephori (The Libation-Bearers),* and *Eumenides,* compose the *Oresteia,* the only Greek tragic trilogy extant. The trilogy won the first prize in the drama contest of 458. The first play tells how King Agamemnon, commander of the Greek forces in the Trojan War, returns triumphantly to Argos, only to be murdered with his concubine, the Trojan prophetess Cassandra. The murderers, Agamemnon's wife Clytemnestra and her lover Aegisthus, then take over the rule of Argos. The second play, constructed as a strict counterpart to the first, shows how, some 20 years later, Clytemnestra and Aegisthus are slain by her son Orestes, urged on by his sister Electra. But Orestes acts only on divine command, and his reluctance to commit the deed is contrasted with Clytemnestra's earlier eagerness for revenge for Agamemnon's sacrifice of their daughter Iphigenia. Orestes' mental torment after this murder is contrasted with Clytemnestra's gloating joy. At the end of this play Orestes flees in madness, pursued by the Erinyes (Furies), spirits of retributive justice. The climactic play, which may be considered a synthesis of the thesis and antithesis of the first two, shows how Orestes goes to Athens at the bidding of the Delphic oracle to stand trial for matricide, with Apollo as his defender and the Furies as his accusers. He is acquitted by the vote of Athena, who then appeases the Furies, converting them into Eumenides (Kindly Ones) by welcoming them to Athens and assuring them that their function of retributive justice is to be the state's foundation.

The *Oresteia* is generally acknowledged to be the most impressive monument in all dramatic literature—for its scope and complexity, for the careful elaboration of its symbolic myth, for its reinforcement by an unusually rich system of imagery, and for its weighty ethical and theological themes. It broaches for the first time in the history of human thought such themes as the meaning of suffering (*Pathei mathos,* "Man learns by suffering," is a persistent sentiment), the necessity for a unified conception of god ("Zeus, whoever you are—by that name I shall call you—for you are all I have to call upon," the Chorus sings near the beginning), and the mystery of justice, involving as it does the penetration of human reality by the divine.

"Prometheus Bound." This play, the only remaining part of the trilogy *Prometheia,* has provoked endless controversy about its meaning, its date—most assign it to his last years—and its authenticity. Its interpretation depends entirely on the reconstruction of the missing plays. The extant play presumably was the first of the three. It represents the punishment of the Titan Prometheus for defying Zeus and stealing fire from heaven out of friendship for humankind. For this he is chained to a mountain crag. His lamentations and protests are echoed by the Chorus, the Daughters of Ocean. He commiserates with Io, another apparent victim of divine oppression, and is finally plunged beneath the earth for his continued rebellion. All agree that the trilogy ended with a reconciliation between Zeus and Prometheus, between God and humanity, but the nature of this reconciliation is the source of much disagreement. *Prometheus Bound* has exerted more in-

© SCALA/ART RESOURCE

Orestes' killing of Clytemnestra in retribution for the murder of Agamemnon, recounted in *Choephori (The Libation-Bearers)*.

fluence than any of Aeschylus's other works. The Romantic age took up Prometheus as a symbol of heroic revolt against tyranny, reaching its high point in Shelley's *Prometheus Unbound* (1820).

Lost Plays. Among the lost tragedies of Aeschylus, *The Aetnaeans*, a festival play written for the poet's patron, Hiero I of Syracuse, was remarkable for a Greek drama because it had several changes of scene. In *Niobe* a mourning mother, all her children slain by the gods, sits silently on stage through much of the play. Particularly regrettable is the loss of all the satyr plays, but in the 20th century enough fragments of two satyr plays, *The Isthmiasts* and *The Net Pullers*, have been recovered to give some ideas of their plots. In *The Isthmiasts*, satyrs are represented as athletes in the Isthmian games. *The Net Pullers* shows how satyrs help a fisherman retrieve a chest from the sea; they discover in it Danaë and her infant son Perseus, who had been put there by her wicked father.

Critical Appraisal. The first critical estimate of Aeschylus is to be found in Aristophanes' *Frogs*, produced 50 years after Aeschylus's death, in which Aristophanes considers Aeschylus to be a source of moral improvement for Athenians. In the 4th century B.C., when revivals became the custom, Aeschylean plays were produced much less often than those of Sophocles and Euripides. Nevertheless, Aeschylus was acknowledged to rank with them, and his statue was accordingly erected in the Theater of Dionysus. Among the Romans, also, he won admiration and respect rather than popularity or affection.

Since the Renaissance, evaluation of Aeschylus has not greatly changed. In the 18th and 19th centuries the suggestiveness of his Prometheus character had more influence on thought and literature than did his actual plays. (Marx even chose Prometheus as a symbol for the communist movement.) But the 20th century, more than any other, has appreciated Aeschylus for his profundity of religious thought, largeness of dramatic structure, and mastery of poetic imagery.

RICHMOND Y. HATHORN
Author of "Tragedy, Myth, and Mystery"

Bibliography

Herington, John, *Aeschylus* (Yale Univ. Press 1986).
Murray, Gilbert, *Aeschylus, the Creator of Tragedy* (1940; reprint, Greenwood Press 1978).
Rosenmeyer, Thomas G., *The Art of Aeschylus* (Univ. of Calif. Press 1982).
Smyth, Herbert W., *Aeschylean Tragedy* (1924; reprint, Biblio. Dist. 1969).
Spatz, Lois, *Aeschylus* (G. K. Hall 1982).
Tucker, T. G., *The "Supplices" of Aeschylus*, ed. by Leonardo Taran (Garland 1987).

AESCULAPIUS, es-kyōō-lā′pē-əs, in Roman mythology, the god of medicine, known to the Greeks as Asclepius (Asklepios). In the *Iliad*, Homer calls him the "peerless physician" and identifies him as the father of Podaleirius and Machaon, physicians to the Greeks in the Trojan War. Later he was considered the father of Hygieia, Panaceia, and Iaso, personifications of health. Post-Homeric poets described him as a son of Apollo and the nymph Coronis. When Coronis was unfaithful to Apollo, either he or Artemis killed her. Her unborn child, Asclepius, was saved by Apollo or Hermes and reared by the centaur Chiron, who taught him the art of healing.

Asclepius was worshiped in many areas, but the best-known center of his cult was Epidaurus. Great temples were erected in his honor, where patients seeking the god's help slept, their dreams sometimes providing a clue to their cure. The staff and the snake (a symbol of renewal) were the chief attributes of Asclepius. It is thought that the worship of this god was brought to Rome—where he was called Aesculapius—from Epidaurus in 293 B.C. by order of the Sibylline Books or in the hope of ridding the city of a plague.

LILLIAN FEDER
Queens College, The City University of New York

AESCULUS, es′kyə-ləs, a genus of about 25 trees and shrubs in the family Aesculaceae. They are found in the temperate regions of North America and in East Asia, the Himalayas, and the Balkan Peninsula.

Several species of *Aesculus* are widely used as street and roadside trees. The best known is *A. hippocastanum*, the horse chestnut, popular in the United States, Canada, and Europe as an ornamental tree. The tree, which attains a height of 60–80 feet (18–24 meters), grows leaves early in the spring and provides a dense shade. (See also BUCKEYE; HORSE CHESTNUT.)

AESIR, a′sir, in Scandinavian mythology, the name given either to all the gods collectively or to a pantheon of the most powerful gods. They lived in Åsgard, at the mansion called Gladsheim, and were presided over by Odin. Although accounts differ as to their number, most authorities specify 12, namely, Thor, Baldr, Freyr, Týr, Bragi, Hodr, Heimdallr, Vithar, Vali, Ullr, Vé, and Forseti. Many of these gods were worshiped in Teutonic mythology, and some of their names were given to days of the week. At one time, the Aesir warred with the Vanir, a rival race of gods, but later assimilated with them.

AESOP (620?–?560 B.C.), ē'sop, was a semilegendary Greek writer, the reputed author of hundreds of fables. Late in the 5th century B.C., collections of fables passing as his work seem to have been current, and the custom had already grown up of ascribing to him almost any fable of whatever origin. In some ancient sources, events of his life are linked with famous people of his supposed time—King Croesus of Lydia, the courtesan Rhodopis, Solon the Athenian lawgiver, and the Seven Wise Men—but such connections are extremely dubious. There was approximate agreement on only a few details: that Aesop was a slave from Phrygia, that he suffered a long servitude on the island of Samos, that he was eventually freed and traveled extensively, and that he came to his death by a mishap at Delphi.

This last story contains elements of folk tale and even of myth. Aesop was said to have insulted the Delphians by alleging that they lived off the rest of mankind, thanks to their famous oracle. For revenge, they planted a sacred golden bowl in his luggage and detained him when he was departing. He was judged a thief and thrown off a cliff, after which Delphi labored for some time under a curse.

Aesop's very existence has been in doubt among scholars since the Renaissance. The Greeks were so inclined to assign every art, artifact, technique, pastime, custom, literary type, city-state, race—in short, any human product or activity—to a specific founder or inventor that if an inventor were unknown, they did not hesitate to create one. Thus the ancient *Life of Aesop*, which has come down in several similar versions, though interesting in itself, is of no historical value. It consists of a string of anecdotes and fables in which Aesop appears as a buffoon whose native wit and homely common sense confound the book learning of philosophers, royal councillors, and other professional wise men.

The writing is plain, and the tone is anti-intellectual and even anti-Greek; the whole piece is valuable as a rare specimen of popular literature but not for any light it throws on its subject. The personality of Aesop portrayed here was probably much influenced by the treatment of him as a character in comedy (Alexis, a Greek comic playwright, wrote an *Aesop*, now lost, in the 4th century B.C.). More remotely, it exhibits the usual traits of the mythical trickster-hero.

Manuscripts of the Fables. Whether referring to a real person or not, Aesop's name very early became a convenient label to attach to traditional stories and bits of folk wisdom, many of which must actually have come down from prehistoric times. Even collections of proverbs were assigned to him. In spite of the great age of this lore, there is no evidence that it was systematically written down before the time of Demetrius Phalereus, about 300 B.C. When Herodotus, composing his history more than a century before this, refers to Aesop as a well-known figure, and when Herodotus' younger contemporary Aristophanes makes glancing reference to Aesop in comedy, both were probably thinking of familiar stories transmitted by word of mouth. Likewise, Socrates, who was represented by Plato in the *Phaedo* as beguiling the time until his execution by versifying Aesop's fables, was probably working not from a book, but from memory.

Actually, the earliest examples of classical fable extant are the Latin verse stories of Phaedrus (q.v.), dating from the beginning of the

---

A Fable by Aesop . . .

THE TWO FELLOWS AND THE BEAR

Two fellows were travelling together through a wood, when a bear rushed out upon them. One of the travellers happened to be in front, and he seized hold of the branch of a tree, and hid himself among the leaves. The other, seeing no help for it, threw himself flat down upon the ground, with his face in the dust. The bear, coming up to him, put his muzzle close to his ear, and sniffed and sniffed. But at last with a growl he shook his head and slouched off, for bears will not touch dead meat. Then the fellow in the tree came down to his comrade, and, laughing, said "What was it that Master Bruin whispered to you?"

"He told me," said the other, "NEVER TRUST A FRIEND WHO DESERTS YOU AT A PINCH."

Christian era. The collections in Greek prose that pass as "Aesop's Fables" were assembled in the 2d or 3d century A.D., but the bulk of the material must have taken shape several centuries earlier. Extant manuscripts represent about four different collections, largely overlapping one another. The stories are arranged alphabetically according to the first word, so that, for example, all fables beginning "A fox . . ." may be found together. There were attempts in antiquity to differentiate the Aesopic fable proper from other kinds, mainly on the basis of characters, but those now ascribed to Aesop show all kinds of relationships among beasts, men, and gods.

Some of them, like the stories involving Hermes the Trickster, even verge on mythical narrative. There were also attempts at classification according to place of origin, listing them under various lands in the Middle East, Africa, and the Mediterranean world. Modern scholars, however, have been most interested in parallels and possible prototypes from ancient India and Sumer.

The Morals. Each story now ends with an explicit moral. There is dispute as to when these morals were appended, but the question is unimportant for two reasons. In the first place, since no Greek or Roman would have collected fables purely out of enthusiasm for folklore, the Aesopic corpus obviously came into being for educational and rhetorical purposes. Schoolboys used the fables as themes for exercises in composition and declamation, and orators used them to illustrate a point (Aristotle divides arguments from example into those examples drawn from history and those drawn from fable); for either use the explicit moral would be convenient.

In the second place, because the very reason for the fable's existence was to serve as a commentary on human behavior, the moral was implicit from the beginning. In the hands of Phaedrus, the fable often concealed social and political satire in its naïve story and polished verse. This tradition of the verse fable as a vehicle for satire was reinforced by the medieval *fabliau* and found expression in such fabulists as La Fontaine in France, Christian Gellert and Gotthold Lessing in Germany, and Ivan Krylov in Russia.

See also FABLE; FABLIAU.

RICHMOND Y. HATHORN
Author of "Tragedy, Myth, and Mystery"

Further Reading: Anand, M. R., *Aesop's Fables* (Apt. Bks. 1987); Perry, B. E., *Studies in the Text History of the Life and Fables of Aesop* (Scholars Press 1981).

AESTHETICS, es-thet'iks, has traditionally been conceived of as the branch of philosophy concerned with beauty and the beautiful in nature and art. However, this definition is too narrow for present-day purposes. Alexander Baumgarten (1714–1762), a minor German philosopher, gave the name "aesthetics" (from the Greek *aisthesis*, meaning "sense perception") to what earlier philosophers had called either the theory of beauty or the philosophy of taste. Baumgarten chose "aesthetics" because he wished to emphasize the experience of art as a means of knowing. Aesthetics, a not very tidy intellectual discipline, is a heterogeneous collection of problems that concern the arts primarily but also relate to nature.

Many problems revolve around the arts or relate to nature. The important questions are: which of these problems belong to aesthetics, and by virtue of what characteristics are they assigned to it? To isolate the problems of aesthetics, three different kinds or levels of statements and questions may be distinguished. First, there are the critical statements that describe, interpret, or evaluate particular works of art. Second, there are more general statements that are made by literary, musical, or art theorists to describe the characteristic features of artistic genres: for example, tragedy, the sonata form, or abstract painting. Third, there are those questions that are not always easily distinguished from the questions implied in the second category; they ask: "What is beauty?" "Is art an imitation?" "Should art be subordinated to morality?" "Does art exist for its own sake?" "Can the concept of tragedy or the concept of art itself be defined?" "Is form the only important aspect of art?" "What is the nature of aesthetic experience?" Philosophers, even though they disagree about how aesthetics should be defined, agree that these are some of the questions that constitute the subject matter of aesthetics.

Many of the activities that go on under the name "aesthetics" are psychological rather than philosophical in nature. Consequently, philosophical or analytic aesthetics must be distinguished from psychological or scientific aesthetics. Philosophical aesthetics is concerned with the meaning and the conditions for determining the truth of statements about art and aesthetic experience, although not every statement that can be made about a work of art or an aesthetic experience is its concern. Philosophical aesthetics performs an analytical task, as distinguished from an empirical or scientific one. On the other hand, psychological aesthetics is concerned with such empirical questions as "What causal factors are involved in artistic creation?" and "What kinds of shapes and colors do people find pleasing?"

PHILOSOPHICAL AESTHETICS

Aesthetics is conceived of by some philosophers as the analysis of the concepts employed by critics when they make statements about the arts. In this approach, called *metacriticism*, critical statements are considered the basic subject matter of aesthetics. Metacriticism, because it takes the description, interpretation, and evaluation of the arts as its subject matter, concerns itself not with the creation of art but with such questions as "What is meant by 'representational' in the term 'representational painting'?" "What does 'symbolic' mean when critics speak of the symbolic meaning of a poem or some

image in a poem?" and "What is meant by such evaluative terms as 'good,' 'fine,' 'valid,' when they are applied to works of art?" While earlier philosophers were much concerned with the beauty and sublimity of aspects of nature, metacriticism has tended to ignore nature and to make aesthetics a philosophy of art criticism. The most complete statement and defense of metacriticism is by the American scholar Monroe C. Beardsley (1915–   ) in *Aesthetics: Problems in the Philosophy of Criticism* (1958).

Attitude Theory. Whereas metacriticism takes the criticism of art as its subject matter, and thereby gives the adjective "aesthetic" whatever meaning it has for metacriticism, other philosophies hold that "aesthetic" refers to an identifiable attitude. This attitude is a nonpractical one that can be taken toward any object and is contrasted with such practical attitudes as the moral, the economic, the intellectual, and the personal. An early proponent of the aesthetic attitude was Edward Bullough (1880–1934) of Britain. His theory of *psychical distance* assumes a psychological state that a spectator either puts himself into or is induced into by attending to some object. An object is an aesthetic object as a result of the spectator's state of mind; it is by virtue of its being psychically distanced that an object is an aesthetic object, aesthetically enjoyed by the spectator. Bullough's theory involves a special psychological state, but another version conceives of the aesthetic attitude as involving an ordinary action done in a particular way. *Disinterested perception* is the key concept of this theory, and the aesthetic is virtually identified with disinterestedness. A great many philosophers, including the American Eliseo Vivas (1901–   ), have adopted some version of the aesthetic attitude theory.

Although metacriticism and the attitude theory compete, they are not mutually exclusive. Attitude theorists make critical analyses in the light of their understanding of the aesthetic attitude. They think of the field as divided into aesthetics and the philosophy of art criticism. Proponents of metacriticism find that the theory of aesthetic attitude is uninformative and offers no guidance in the analysis of concepts, and that the basic notion of disinterested perception is particularly confused. Consequently, they simply identify aesthetics with the philosophy of art criticism.

Intentionalistic Criticism. Some critics use the concept of the artist's intention to maintain that a painting is good because the artist realized his intention, or that an obscure passage in a play must be understood in a certain way because the author has declared elsewhere that he so intended it, or that a piece of music ought to be performed in a specified manner because the composer intended it to be so performed. Is it legitimate to make use of the intention of the artist? Some philosophers support intentionalistic criticism, arguing that an artist occupies a privileged position in respect to the performance, interpretation, or evaluation of his own work. Intentionalistic critics typically think of a work of art as a vehicle for expression by an artist and of the experience of a work as a communication between artist and appreciator. For example, the Italian philosopher Benedetto Croce (1866–1952) contended that the real work of art exists in the mind of the artist and that a statue or a painting is a device to help the appreciator to recreate what the artist intended.

Other philosophers speak of "the intentional fallacy," arguing that works of art are independent of their creators' intentions and must stand on their own. They contend that if literary scholars had to know the artist's intentions, they would be unable, for example, to interpret or evaluate Shakespeare's plays, not knowing what Shakespeare intended. But even if all artists' intentions were known, the anti-intentionistic philosophers would argue that intentions are clearly irrelevant to evaluation: the intention and the work are distinct entities. A work of art is independent of its creator's intention and must be evaluated for what it is. Also, the intention may have been very modest or even corrupt. Simply because an artist has realized his intention is no reason to judge his work good. The anti-intentionists make a similar argument with regard to interpretation of meaning. A poem, for example, means what it says quite apart from the poet's intention. If a line of poetry cannot be understood unless the reader brings to it outside knowledge of the poet's intention, then the line may be legitimately criticized for obscurity or ambiguity. Anti-intentionists develop parallel arguments with respect to performance.

Evaluative Theories. Dispute over evaluations has always been of great interest to philosophers. They have worked out a variety of theories of evaluative concepts, such as good, bad, beautiful, ugly, intrinsically valuable, and instrumentally valuable, which have frequently, although not always, closely paralleled theories of ethical concepts. There are several important contemporary evaluative theories: (1) *Intuitionism* holds that evaluative terms such as "good" refer to an object's nonempirical qualities that must be intuited. Because it is difficult to characterize intuition positively, it is usually defined negatively as a mode of knowing something that cannot be known by ordinary sense perception. Plato's theory of beauty is an early version of intuitionism. (2) *Subjectivism* holds that "good" is to be defined with reference to states of mind. In one version of subjectivism, "good" means "I like it" or perhaps "I approved it"; in another, "good" means "it is approved by a particular group of persons" (the group may be specified in a variety of ways: the majority of cultured people in my community, informed critics, and the like). Although subjectivism is probably widely adhered to, it is rarely, if ever, put forth by a philosopher as his explicit view. (3) *Emotivism*, a view widely held in the recent past, and defended by A.J. Ayer (1910–   ) and Charles Stevenson (1908–), maintains that evaluative terms do not refer to anything at all. "Good," "bad," and the like serve to express or evince the feelings of the speaker who uses them. Emotivism is sometimes confused with the "I like" version of subjectivism but it is a distinct theory. The theory that beauty is in the eye of the beholder may be associated with either emotivism or subjectivism. (4) *Instrumentalism* avoids the problem of defining evaluative terms used in aesthetic judgments. Instead, it characterizes a good work of art as one that produces in a spectator a good or valuable aesthetic experience. It is assumed that a certain kind of experience can be identified as aesthetic and is good. "Good" appears in both the expression characterized ("good work of art") and in the expression used to characterize it ("produces a good aesthetic experience"). Hence, "good" is not defined by instrumentalism

but is assumed as given. Beardsley develops this theory explicitly, drawing on the work of John Dewey (1859–1952).

The relation of aesthetics to criticism is clear: criticism in one way or another is the subject matter of aesthetics, and from the point of view of criticism, aesthetics clarifies critical concepts and thereby makes criticism more clearheaded. But what of aesthetics and appreciation? The appreciation of art can be greatly enhanced by good criticism, for, simply put, criticism is an aid to understanding particular works of art. The way to get the most enjoyment from a work of art is to experience it in the light of good criticism, and the way to separate good criticism from bad is on the basis of sound principles of aesthetics.

Classical Aesthetics. Questions that may be regarded as problems of aesthetics occur in several of Plato's dialogues: *Ion, Symposium, Republic, Phaedrus, Sophist,* and *Laws.* Plato views the practice of art as a craft (*technē*) that produces something, but he does not place arts now regarded as "fine" in a class apart. According to Plato's theory, the art product is an imitation (*mimesis*)—the painter reproduces (imitates) his subject on canvas and the dramatist depicts (imitates) the actions of men in his plays. Because he conceives of works of art in the light of his theory of reality, Plato regards them as deficient in a manner that may strike the modern reader as odd. Works of art are imitations of such things as chairs, apples, and the just acts of men; but the chairs, apples, and just acts are themselves imitations of ideal forms of chairness, appleness, and justice. These forms are not experienced with the senses but are known intuitively by reason. Plato regards them as the real and the objects of ordinary sense experience as unreal. Because works of art imitate the unreal, sensible world, they are twice removed from reality. In saying that art is imitation, Plato set a precedent that many philosophers follow even today in such theories as "art is expression," "art is wish fulfillment," and "art is play." An assumption of Plato, and of those who agree with him on this point, is that there is some single characteristic (imitation, expression, or the like) that is the form or essence of art and that is present in every work of art.

Plato's greatest concern was the proper organization of the state, and the most important question about art for him was the role it ought to play in the life of the citizen. He objected to art not only because it is doubly unreal but also because it is of doubtful moral value. He objected to the use of the epic poems as moral guides because they frequently provided bad models—the heroes and the gods were guilty of immoral acts, for example. Many plays presented characters in overwrought emotional states, and Plato thought this inflamed the passions of the spectator and weakened his reason.

Plato discusses various philosophical problems raised by the possession of beauty. In keeping with his general metaphysical theory, he maintains that objects are beautiful to the degree that they exemplify the timeless and nonspatial form of beauty. In the *Symposium* he maintains that a person comes to know the form of beauty by first experiencing a series of beautiful things, progressing from objects of physical beauty to beautiful institutions (the ideal state) and then passing on to the contemplation of beauty itself.

Plato probably thought of beauty as a simple property that must be directly experienced and therefore is unanalyzable and indefinable. For Plato, an object, to be beautiful, must possess order and proportion. But order and proportion do not define "beauty"; they are simply the conditions for the occurrence of beauty.

Aristotle. The main basis for the discussion of Aristotle's views on aesthetics is the *Poetics,* which is primarily a contribution to literary theory rather than to aesthetic theory. However, in his treatment of epic poetry and tragedy, he does raise questions of a broader philosophical kind. Aristotle follows Plato in concluding that art is a productive process that imitates its various subject matters; poetry, for example, imitates with words the actions of men. Whereas Plato raises questions about art as a subordinate matter within the context of a larger discussion (of politics, for example), Aristotle is concerned simply with examining poetry and determining its nature, devoting himself to specifying the characteristics that distinguish the various kinds of art from each other. His famous definition of "tragedy" in the *Poetics* is a good example of his concern for careful and exact classification (see POETICS OF ARISTOTLE).

In a famous remark, Aristotle says that poetry is more philosophical than history. (By history Aristotle means the mere chronicle of events, and by philosophy the study of forms.) In epic poetry and tragedy something more than the mere chronicle of events occurs, for events and actions follow one another in a necessary or probable way, revealing essential aspects of human nature. Aristotle thus attributes a cognitive value to poetry, and by implication to art in general, a value that Plato wished to deny.

Aristotle apparently developed his theory of catharsis as a counterattack to what he considered Plato's misunderstanding of the effect of art on its audience. As it is usually understood, catharsis is the purging, or alleged purging, of an audience's emotions of pity and fear as the direct result of their having viewed pitiful and fearful events on the stage. The theory of catharsis, if valid, is a partial answer to Plato's excessive fears about the effects of art.

Medieval Aesthetics. Because art was thought of as dealing with earthly rather than heavenly matters and was associated with pagan Greece and Rome, the early Christian church was hostile toward art and discouraged philosophical reflection on the subject. St. Augustine (354–430), however, was interested in the arts and in the discussion of them. He developed a kind of Christianized Platonism in which the Platonic forms exist in the mind of God. Beauty is one of the forms, and the beautiful in art and nature is thus related to religion. St. Augustine thought of beauty as derived from the unity that varies with the order and proportion of the object. Essentially, he followed Plato's theory of beauty, but because animals imitate but are not capable of art, he rejected the Greek notion of art as imitation. St. Augustine also was interested in the nature of fiction and distinguished between the "lies" of literary works, which do not intend to deceive, and real lies, which do.

Whereas St. Augustine discussed problems of aesthetics from within a Platonic framework, which held that the forms (the real) transcended the visible world, St. Thomas Aquinas (1225?–1274) adopted an Aristotelian metaphysic, which held that the forms were immanent in the empirical world. Aquinas thought that goodness and beauty were basically the same, both being derived from a form or species. The good, which all seek, is what calms desire, but the beautiful calms desire and pleases simply by being seen or known. The experience of the beautiful is a matter of recognizing the form in an individual thing. Something is beautiful if it is an unimpaired example of its form or species, is proportional or harmonious, and is bright or clear. Aquinas' Aristotelian viewpoint furnishes a more hospitable environment for philosophy of art than does Augustine's Platonism. Art assumes a greater importance if beauty exists in the visible world rather than as an abstract quality that transcends empirical nature.

Renaissance Aesthetics. The Renaissance was a time of great innovation and advance in the arts. For the most part, however, 15th and 16th century philosophers, such as Marsilio Ficino and Giordano Bruno, put forth theories that were versions or revisions of Platonism, Neoplatonism, or Aristotelianism. For example, drawing on Plato's theory of the soul, Ficino developed a view of contemplation in which the soul withdraws from the body and its earthly concerns.

However, the painting, musical, and literary theorists developed new and bold ideas. Leon Battista Alberti (1404–1472), who also wrote treatises on sculpture and architecture, advocated painting what the eye sees. He conceived of a painting as a three-dimensional representation in contrast to the flat two-dimensional paintings of medieval times. He also stressed the faithful and consistent depiction of the dramatic subject of a painting and recommended that artists study human anatomy. He contended that there is a special sense with which beauty is immediately perceived. Arguing that painting and sculpture are difficult and require special talent, a liberal education, and a comprehension of scientific laws, Alberti advocated distinguishing them from mere crafts. Leonardo da Vinci (1452–1519) and other theorists of the visual arts advanced similar ideas, and Renaissance musical and literary theorists developed comparable themes.

Early Modern Aesthetics. Anthony Ashley Cooper, the 3d earl of Shaftesbury (1671–1713), posed many of the questions discussed by later thinkers. He developed a Neoplatonistic metaphysic that envisioned a harmonious world created by God. Aspects of this harmonious nature in men included a moral sense that judges the actions of men, and a sense of beauty that judges and appreciates art and nature. By a "sense" he meant a judgment, similar to taste, not mediated by reasoning. In arguing against the egoism of Thomas Hobbes (1588–1679), Shaftesbury concluded that aesthetic contemplation is disinterested, and this disinterestedness is a source of his theory of the aesthetic attitude. Perhaps because of his broad metaphysical interest in nature, he pointed out that the sublime, like beauty, is an important aesthetic category. Shaftesbury's ideas, originally rather diffusely presented, were systematized and made more precise by the Scottish philosopher Francis Hutcheson (1694–1746).

Although David Hume (1711–1776) owed much to Shaftesbury and Hutcheson, he went considerably beyond their views. He held that beauty is not an objective quality of objects but exists in the mind. Man takes a disinterested pleasure in certain structures and calls them beautiful; he takes a similar pleasure in the utility of certain things. Hume, like Hutcheson, contended that what people think is beautiful is determined by the primary constitution of human nature, adding that custom and individual preference also enter into the determination. This addition, as well as the observable diversity of taste, raises for Hume the question of the possibility of a justified standard of taste. Hume concluded that although there is no absolute standard, taste may be corrected by extensive experience, the avoidance of prejudice, careful attention, and sensitivity to the qualities of things.

Immanuel Kant (1724–1804), like Hume, held that beauty is not an objective quality of objects, but that an object is called beautiful when its form causes a harmonious interplay between the imagination and the understanding. Judgments of taste are, therefore, subjective in this sense. Ordinary judgments, such as "The painting is three feet high," affirm a concept ("three feet high") of an object, but judgments of taste, such as "The painting is beautiful," cannot affirm a concept since "beautiful" does not refer to any property of the painting. However, if judgments of taste are subjective and conceptless, they are saved from being sheer expressions of individual caprice because they involve cognitive faculties (imagination and understanding) that all men possess. Judgments of taste are thereby capable of being universal and necessary, that is, they can hold for all men. Judgments of sublimity, unlike those of beauty, have objects that are boundless (without form), and the interplay of the imagination and the understanding caused by the awesome object is not harmonious. Kant also maintained that aesthetic judgments are disinterested.

Contemporary Aesthetics. Croce worked out his aesthetic theory within a philosophical system of idealism (a metaphysical theory that maintains that everything is ideal, that is, everything is the activity of mind). The activities of mind divide into the theoretical and the practical: the practical consists of economics and ethics, and the theoretical consists of two kinds of knowledge—logic and aesthetics. For Croce aesthetics is the domain of intuitive knowledge (or intuition), as distinguished from logical knowledge (including scientific knowledge). An intuition is an image that exists in the mind. Croce's theory of art equates art and intuition, and this entails the thesis that art is a kind of knowledge. He also developed the novel thesis that art exists in the mind of the artist, so that the physical things artists produce are not art. The physical product is simply an aid to help in the re-creation of art in the mind of the appreciator. Croce also equates intuition and expression, so that art is expression. What is expressed is the artist's emotion. Croce's view gives to the concept of art the single defining essence that philosophers who follow Plato's precedent feel is so important. But, paradoxically, it denies to paintings, statues, and the like the status of art. Robin G. Collingwood (1889–1943), an influential English philosopher, followed Crocean principles in developing an important aesthetic theory.

The American philosopher George Santayana (1863–1952), who called himself a materialist, developed a naturalistic aesthetics. The hedonistic account of aesthetics in his influential book *The Sense of Beauty* (1896) is something of a landmark, coming as it did in a period when idealism dominated the philosophical scene. Like Hume and Kant, Santayana denies that beauty is an objective property of things. Beauty is identical with the pleasure that is experienced when certain objects are perceived. It had been mistakenly thought, Santayana maintains, that beauty is a property of objects because the pleasure felt is objectified in (projected into) the perceived object. The pleasure felt is experienced as a quality of the object and is called beauty. Santayana also gave considerable importance to the physiological and psychological factors involved in the experience of beauty.

Dominating the pragmatism of another American philosopher, John Dewey, are his insistence on continuity and his attack on dualisms of any kind (the Cartesian contention that mind and body are two distinct substances is an example of philosophical dualism). Dewey attempts to show that art is part of ordinary life and that it is a mistake to separate it from the rest of life. Another important theme is Dewey's instrumentalism, which, as set forth in *Art as Experience* (1934), views knowledge and the objects of perception as, basically, instruments in the life and experience of an organism interacting with its environment. Although Dewey stresses the importance of instrumentalities and means, he conceives of aesthetic experience as consummatory. The experience that results from the appreciation of art is unified and complete.

Clive Bell (1851–1964), whose views are provocative though no longer influential, and Roger Fry (1866–1934) introduced the paintings of Paul Cézanne and other modern artists to the English public. In defending these painters, they used and made popular the notions of "significant form" and "aesthetic emotion." Significant form is allegedly the property that makes certain works of art valuable. Aesthetic emotion is distinct from the ordinary emotions and occurs only when someone is aware of significant form.

SCIENTIFIC AESTHETICS

Scientific aesthetics deals with questions that can be answered by the empirical methods of science. Most of the work in this area falls into four categories: experimental psychology, introspective psychology, Gestalt psychology, and psychoanalysis.

Charles Darwin's attempt to give an evolutionary explanation for the presence of brightly colored markings on some birds is an early example of scientific aesthetics. Darwin speculated that some female birds have an aesthetic preference for bright markings on males and that, therefore, the more brightly marked males will produce more progeny and perpetuate their own characteristics. However, Darwin's speculations about the aesthetic preferences of birds were not tested by experimental methods.

Experimental Aesthetics. Gustav Fechner (1801–1887) is considered the originator of experimental aesthetics, that is, of the attempt to solve aesthetic problems with laboratory methods. Fechner used the colorful expression "aesthetics from below" to characterize his empirical approach and to distinguish it from the "aesthetics from above" of the philosophers. Experimental aesthetics, as it has developed, typically deals with such things as (1) the discovery of preferred colors, shapes, sounds, and the like, and the establishing of preference orders among them, and (2) attempts to deal experimentally with meanings.

In preference experiments, subjects may be presented with two or more shapes and asked to indicate which they prefer. "Meaning" experiments are of several kinds, one of which involves asking a group of subjects the question, "Does music have meaning?" and telling them to answer yes or no and to comment. Another kind of "meaning" experiment presents a selected group of nonobjective paintings or musical passages to a group of subjects and asks the subjects to choose from a list of adjectives the one that best describes the work of art. The results are analyzed to see what percentage of the subjects' selections match the selections of expert judges, or to see to what extent the subjects' selections agree. How (or even whether) such experiments are relevant to the kinds of problems philosophical aestheticians deal with is still a matter of debate.

Aesthetics and Psychology. Although I.A. Richards (1893–1979) did not perform experiments, his *Principles of Literary Criticism* (1924) is an interesting example of the influence of a theory of experimental psychology on aesthetics. Richards attempted to understand aesthetic experience in terms of behavioristic psychology. He characterized aesthetic experience as a balancing of impulses caused by the experiencing of a work of art.

Gestalt psychologists, who are interested in the properties of wholes that are not simply the sums of their parts, have been influential in aesthetic theory. Melody is an example of a Gestalt property. The Gestalt notion of "requireness" has obvious application to works of art. Requireness is the demand that elements in a perceptual field make on other elements in the field. For example, a given sequence of tones seems to demand a certain concluding tone, and certain lines demand a further line or shaded area.

Introspective psychologists have made a number of important contributions to aesthetics. Edward Bullough, cited earlier in connection with attitude theory, put forth his theory of psychical distance as an introspective discovery. Bullough described his task as an investigation of aesthetic consciousness. Theodor Lipps (1851–1914), another introspectionist, developed a theory about the nature of certain qualities of perceived objects in which the key concept was empathy (an alleged projection of human feelings into a perceived object). George Santayana's view that beauty is pleasure objectified is closely akin to Lipps' theory.

Psychoanalytic theory has been applied to art in a variety of ways. A number of psychoanalytic studies of artists have been carried out in an attempt to throw light on the nature of artistic creation, asking, for example, whether artistic creativity is related to neurosis. Psychoanalytic explanations have been given as to why a writer created a particular work, or as to how an event or character functions as a symbol with an underlying psychoanalytic meaning. Archetypal patterns that occur repeatedly in literature may be explained in terms of a racial unconscious by critics influenced by Jungian psychoanalytic theories. Psychoanalytic theories have been used to try to explain the behavior of characters in literary works, especially when the behavior is as complicated and obscure as, for example, Hamlet's.

GEORGE T. DICKIE
University of Illinois at Chicago Circle

Bibliography

Anderson, Mary R., *Art in a Desacralized World: 19th-Century France and England* (Univ. Press of Am. 1984).
Beardsley, Monroe C., *Aesthetics*, 2d ed. (Hackett 1981).
Beardsley, M. C., *Aesthetics from Classical Greece to the Present* (1966; reprint, Univ. of Ala. Press 1975).
Bell, Clive, *Art* (1914; reprint, Putnam 1959).
Bosanquet, B., *History of Aesthetics* (1982; reprint, Ibis Pub. 1986).
Bullough, Edward, *Aesthetics: Lectures and Essays*, ed. by Elizabeth M. Wilkinson (1957; reprint, Greenwood Press 1977).
Bungay, Stephen, *Beauty and Truth: A Study of Hegel's Aesthetics* (Oxford 1987).
Butcher, Samuel H., *Aristotle's Theory of Poetry and Fine Art*, 4th ed. (Dover 1955).
Carritt, Edgar F., *The Theory of Beauty* (1914; reprint, Folcroft 1977).
Chandler, Albert R., *Beauty and Human Nature* (1934; reprint, AMS Press 1976).
Chandrasekhar, S., *Truth and Beauty: Aesthetics and Motivations in Science* (Univ. of Chicago Press 1987).
Cohen, Ralph, ed., *Studies in 18th-Century British Art and Aesthetics* (Univ. of Calif. Press 1985).
Cooper, Lane, *The Poetics of Aristotle* (1923; reprint, Cooper Square 1963).
Croce, Benedetto, *Aesthetics*, tr. by Douglas Ainslie (1922; reprint, Godine 1978).
Danto, Arthur C., *The Philosophical Disenfranchisement of Art* (Columbia Univ. Press 1986).
Dewey, John, *Art as Experience* (1934; reprint, Putnam 1958).
Dickie, George T., *Art and the Aesthetic: An Institutional Analysis* (Cornell Univ. Press 1974).
Dufrenne, Mikel, *In the Presence of the Sensuous* (Humanities Press 1987).
Eco, Umberto, *Art and Beauty in the Middle Ages*, tr. by Hugh Bredin (Yale Univ. Press 1986).
Gilbert, Katherine E., and Kuhn, Helmut, *A History of Esthetics*, rev. ed. (1934, reprint, Greenwood Press 1972).
Greene, Theodore M., *The Arts and the Art of Criticism* (1940; reprint, Gordian Press 1973).
Hutcheon, Linda, *A Theory of Parody: The Teachings of 20th-Century Art Forms* (Methuen 1985).
Kain, Philip J., *Schiller, Hegel, and Marx: State, Society and the Aesthetic Ideal of Ancient Greece* (McGill-Queen's Univ. Press 1982).
Kant, Immanuel, *Critique of Judgment*, tr. by J. H. Bernard, 2d ed. (Hafner 1914).
Kennick, William E., ed., *Art and Philosophy*, 2d ed. (St. Martin's Press 1979).
Knox, I., *The Aesthetic Theories of Kant, Hegel, and Schopenhauer* (1938; reprint, Humanities Press, 1958).
Kristeller, Paul O., *The Philosophy of Marsilio Ficino*, tr. by Virginia Conant (P. Smith 1943).
Langer, Susanne K., *Feeling and Form* (1953; reprint, Macmillan 1977).
Langer, Susanne K., *Philosophy in a New Key*, 3d ed. (Harvard Univ. Press 1957).
Listowel, William F. H., *A Critical History of Modern Aesthetics* (Gordon Press 1933).
Margolis, Joseph, ed., *Philosophy Looks at the Arts;* 3d ed. (Temple Univ. Press 1987).
Maritain, Jacques, *Art and Scholasticism*, tr. by J. F. Scanlan (1930; reprint, Ayer 1970).
Mauron, Charles, *Aesthetics and Psychology* (1935; reprint, Kennikat 1970).
Meynell, Hugo A., *The Nature of Aesthetic Value* (State Univ. of N.Y. Press 1986).
Morris, Bertram, *The Aesthetic Process* (1943; reprint, AMS Press 1975).
Mothersill, Mary, *Beauty Restored* (Oxford 1987).
Naylor, G., *The Bauhaus Reassessed* (Van Nostrand Reinhold 1986).
Philipson, Morris, and Gudel, Paul, eds. *Aesthetics Today*, rev. ed. (P. Smith 1986).
Plato, *The Republic*, tr. by Francis M. Cornford (Oxford 1945).
Rader, Melvin, ed., *A Modern Book of Esthetics*, 5th ed. (Holt 1979).
Santayana, George, *Reason in Art* (1903; reprint, Dover 1982).
Santayana, George, *The Sense of Beauty* (Dover 1896).
Savile, Anthony, *The Test of Time: An Essay on Philosophical Aesthetics* (Oxford 1982).
Sheppard, Anne, *Aesthetics* (Oxford 1987).
Sparshott, Francis, *The Structure of Aesthetics* (Univ. of Toronto Press 1963).
Stevenson, Charles L., *Facts and Values* (1963; reprint, Greenwood Press 1975).
Wellbery, David E., *Lessing's Laocoon: Semiotics and Aesthetics in the Age of Reason* (Cambridge 1984).
Wellek, René, and Warren, Austin, *Theory of Literature*, rev. ed. (Harcourt 1956).
Wolff, Janet, *Aesthetics and the Sociology of Art* (Allen & Unwin 1982).

AETA. See NEGRITOS.

ÆTHELBALD (died 757), ath'əl-bôld, was king of Mercia, England, from 716 until his death. His name is also spelled *Ethelbald*. By 731 he succeeded in conquering the region south of the Humber River. He later conquered Wessex (733), Northumbria (740), and Wales (743), but lost Wessex at the Battle of Burford in 752.

ÆTHELBALD (died 860), ath'əl-bôld, was king of Wessex, England. The name is also spelled *Ethelbald*. He seized the throne in 856, while his father, King Æthelwulf, was on a pilgrimage to Rome. On his return, Æthelwulf relinquished the throne to avoid civil war.

ÆTHELBERHT, a'thəl-berкнt, **Saint** (died 794), king of East Anglia (now part of England). He also was called *Ethelbert* or *Albert*. He was murdered by order of King Offa of Mercia, whose daughter he had sought to marry. His feast day is May 20. Hereford Cathedral and several other Anglican churches are dedicated to him.

ÆTHELBERT, ath'əl-bert, **Saint** (c. 552–616), king of Kent from 560 to 616. His name is often spelled *Ethelbert*. He married Bertha, a Frankish princess who was a devout Christian, and in 597 he was converted to Christianity by St. Augustine of Canterbury, thus becoming the first Christian king to rule in England. St. Æthelbert promulgated (about 600) the first written code of British laws. His feast day is February 25.

ÆTHELBERT (died 866), ath'əl-bûrt, was king of Kent and Wessex, in England. His name is also spelled *Ethelbert*. On the death of his father, King Æthelwulf, in 858, he became king of Kent, and in 860 he succeeded his brother Æthelbald, as king of Wessex. His reign was disturbed by Danish and Gallic pirate raids.

ÆTHELFLAED (died 918/919), ath'əl-flâd, was a Saxon princess, daughter of King Alfred the Great. Known also as *Ælfled* or *Ethelfleda*, she married Æthelred, earl of Mercia, about 880. After her husband's death in 912, she was called the *Lady of the Mercians*. By raising armies and erecting fortresses, she helped defend England against Scandinavian invaders. She died at Tamworth, England.

ÆTHELHEARD (died 805), ath'əl-ha-ərd, was archbishop of Canterbury during the period when the church in southern England was divided briefly into two metropolitan sees. Shortly before Æthelheard's election in 791, Lichfield had been created as a competing see at the instigation of King Offa of Mercia. Kent resented Mercian interference in its church, and the feeling was reinforced by the election of Æthelheard, who was an adherent of Mercian authority. The supremacy of Canterbury was not reasserted until 802. His name also appears at *Ethelhard, Adelard,* and *Edelred.*

ÆTHELRED, a'thəl-rād, **Saint** (c. 1109–1166), English monk and historian. His name is sometimes spelled *Ethelred*, and he also was called *Ailred* or *Aelred*. He was abbot of the Cistercian monasteries at Revesby, Lincolnshire (1142–1146) and at Rievaulx, Yorkshire, for the rest of his life. His theological works led scholars to call him the "English St. Bernard." He wrote a biography of St. Edward the Confessor, king of England (1043–1066). His feast day is March 3.

ÆTHELRED I, ath'əl-red, was king of Wessex and Kent, in England, from 866 until his death on April 23, 871. He was the third reigning son of Æthelwulf and the elder brother of Alfred the Great, who succeeded him as king. His reign was marked by repeated wars with Danish invaders, who sought unsuccessfully to overthrow him. His name is also spelled *Ethelred*.

ÆTHELRED II (c. 968–1016), ath'əl-red, king of England from 978 to 1016. He was known as Æthelred (Ethelred) the Unready ("redeless") because he lacked sound "rede" or counsel.

His reign began in an atmosphere of suspicion following the treacherous murder of his brother, King Edward the Martyr. An ineffective, weak ruler during a period of Danish incursions and ascendancy in England, Æthelred instituted (991) the practice of paying tribute to the Danish invaders to obtain peace (see DANEGELD). In 1013, when Sweyn the Dane was declared king of England, Æthelred fled to Normandy. After Sweyn's death in 1014, however, he returned by invitation of the Saxon witan, promising to rule more justly—the first recorded pact between an English king and his subjects. Sweyn's son, Canute, withdrew, but gained the throne after Æthelred died, at London, on April 23, 1016. Emma, his widow and mother of Edward the Confessor, married Canute.

ÆTHELTHRYTH, ath-əl-thrith', **Saint** (c. 630–679), queen of Northumbria and founding abbess of Ely, who was one of four sainted daughters of Anna, king of the East Angles.

Her reputation for asceticism and chastity, despite two marriages, secured her a high place in the canon of saints. After the death of her first husband, Tonbert, prince of the fen countrymen of South Cambridgeshire, she married Egfrid, the 14-year-old heir to the throne of Northumbria. Following his accession she fled to Ely to avoid a consummation of the marriage. She became a nun about 672 and founded a monastery for monks and nuns at Ely in 673. The cathedral there was built over her grave.

Her name also appears as *Ætheldreda, Etheldreda, Ætheldrythe,* and *Audry.* From a contraction of her name, *St. Audry,* the word *tawdry* is derived. This denoted a type of lace worn as a neckband by women, and also referred to cheap finery sold at St. Audry's fair. Her feast day is the day of her death, June 23.

ÆTHELWEARD (died ?998) a'thəl-wa-ərd, was an English chronicler who translated the *Anglo-Saxon Chronicle* from the vernacular into Latin. Based on a lost version of the chronicle, the translation is very valuable as a source of English history before 973. His name is also spelled *Ethelwerd.*

ÆTHELWOLD, a'thəl-wōld, **Saint** (c. 908–984), English prelate, also called *Ethelwold*. He was abbot of Abingdon and then bishop of Winchester, where he built a cathedral. With St. Dunstan and St. Oswald he worked to reform the English church and to revive monastic life, which had declined during the Danish wars. His feast day is August 1.

ÆTHELWULF, ath'əl-woolf, king of the West Saxons from 839 to 858. He inherited from his father, Egbert, the most extensive realm in England up to that time. He and his father are regarded by some historians as the first two kings of all Anglo-Saxon England. Although politically unambitious, Æthelwulf preserved the monarchy that foreshadowed the eventual unification of England. During his reign, Berkshire was annexed, the militant Britons of Wales were contained, and a Danish army of conquest was defeated. Alfred the Great was one of his four sons who succeeded as king. Æthelwulf's name also appears as Adelwulf, Athulf, and Ethelwulf.

AËTIUS, Flavius, ā-ē'shē-əs (c. 396–454), Roman general. He was born at Durostorum (now Silistra, Bulgaria). After Emperor Honorius's death in 423, Aëtius supported the usurper Joannes against the empress regent, Galla Placidia, and brought an army of 60,000 Huns to Joannes's aid. After Joannes was defeated and the Huns departed, Aëtius was reconciled with the empress and became count of Italy, commander of the army, and chief adviser to Galla Placidia and her children.

From 433 to 450, Aëtius was the ruling spirit in the Western Empire. In 450 the Huns under Attila invaded Gaul. On Sept. 20, 451, Aëtius defeated Attila in the Battle of Châlons, the Western Empire's last victory and one of the world's decisive engagements. Attila died in 453, dissolving the Hun coalition. Emperor Valentinian III, Placidia's son, who had submitted to Aëtius's power only from fear of Attila, stabbed Aëtius to death in Rome in 454.

AETOLIA, ē-tō'lē-ə, a mountainous region in central Greece forming the northern coast of the Gulf of Patrai (Patras). It makes up the largest part of the modern Greek nomos (department) of Aetolia and Acarnania, the administrative center of which is Mesolongion (Missolonghi). The Aetolia and Acarnania nomos is primarily a farming and grazing area. Tobacco, wheat, oats, and grapes are cultivated on the plain of the Akheloös (Achelous) River and on the level tracts around Lakes Trikhonis and Lisimakhia, two large communicating lakes north of Mesolongion. The rest of the region is largely mountainous.

In ancient times Aetolia was a separate district bounded by Epirus on the north and Locris on the east. The Akheloös River divided the region from Acarnania on the west. The early Aetolians long remained a congeries of independent tribes, devoted mostly to piracy, but they were sufficiently organized to repel an Athenian invasion in 426 B.C. In the 4th century B.C. they formed the Aetolian League, which endured until the 2d century B.C., when Aetolia was conquered by Rome and made part of the province of Achaea. It fell to the Turks in 1450 and then became part of independent Greece in 1832.

AETOLIAN LEAGUE, ē-tō'lē-ən, a federation of cities in Aetolia in ancient Greece. At its height, the federation stretched across central Greece from the Ionian to the Aegean Sea.

The league is known to have existed by 367 B.C. Presumably it was formed sometime earlier in the 4th century B.C. from the loose tribal organization of the Aetolians that had existed previously. Its center was at Thermum. The government of the league provided for a popular assembly that met twice yearly and included all citizens of Aetolia. The assembly determined foreign policy for the league, but each member of the league enjoyed internal autonomy. A federal council ruled in the interim between assembly meetings.

The league was headed by a general, who was elected annually, and other officials. Later, as the league expanded and government by mass meeting became unwieldy, an inner council was set up. It sat permanently with the officials and, in effect, governed the league.

During the 3d century B.C. the league enlarged its territory substantially, encompassing eventually all or parts of Acarnania, Locris, Phocis, Boeotia, and Thessaly. Full Aetolian citizenship (with assembly voting rights) was granted to the citizens of the added areas. In addition, the league controlled the island of Cephallenia and various cities in the Peloponnesus, Thrace, and Asia Minor.

Further Aetolian expansion led to a general war in 220 B.C. with Philip V of Macedon. In 211 B.C. the Aetolians allied themselves with Rome against Philip. Although peace was made in 205 B.C., warfare resumed five years later. In 197 B.C. Philip was defeated at Cynoscephalae, largely with the help of Aetolian cavalry. The Aetolians, resentful that their former Thessalian possessions were not restored, allied themselves with Antiochus III of Syria against Rome. But the defeat of Antiochus by the Romans in 189 B.C. compelled the Aetolians to surrender. In 167 B.C., Rome dissolved the Aetolian League, and later in the century, it incorporated Aetolia into the province of Achaea.

AFARS, ä'färz, a Hamitic people of northeast Africa, who live in the arid Danakil region of Ethiopia and in southeastern Eritrea and northern Djibouti. Also known as the Danakil, they speak a Cushitic language. Their religion is Islam, but most do not practice it actively.

The Afars, who number about 110,000, are divided into two classes—the nobles, or "red men," and the commoners, or "white men." Pastoral nomads, they wander the desert with herds of camels, sheep, goats, and donkeys. They also mine salt, which is exported in the form of bars.

AFARS AND ISSAS.   See DJIBOUTI.

AFFENPINSCHER, af'ən-pin-chər, a toy dog popular in Europe since the 16th century but not standardized until the 19th century, in Germany. It stands no more than 10.25 inches (25.6 cm) at the shoulder and should weigh at most 8 pounds (3.6 kg) but preferably 7 pounds (3.15 kg). The Affenpinscher has cropped ears and a docked tail, and it has a shortish, uneven, wiry coat.

Too fragile and a bit too highstrung for children, the breed is well suited to adults who want a lively little dog that seeks attention and barks at all strange noises. It was a forebear of the more widely known Brussels griffon. Both breeds may be hard to housebreak.

JOHN HOWE
Author of "Choosing the Right Dog"

AFFIDAVIT, af-ə-dā'vit, a written or printed statement or declaration of facts made voluntarily, under oath or by affirmation, before an officer, such as a notary public. It is used in applying for a license or passport and also in legal proceedings, where the purpose is submission of facts to a court or an official agency. In the latter instance an affidavit is an ex parte statement (that is, made by, and for the benefit of, one side only) without notice to the opposing party and with no cross-examination.

AFFIRMATIVE ACTION, a series of steps, procedures, policies, and programs designed to overcome the present effects of past discrimination on members of minority groups. Age, race, religion, national origin, and sex are the principal classifications in the United States. In the latter part of the 20th century, affirmative action programs in government, educational institutions, and businesses were the subject of serious controversy.

After the U.S. Congress passed the Civil Rights Act in 1964, it became apparent that certain accepted policies and procedures, such as seniority status and aptitude tests,. were, in effect, barriers against full equality in employment. Realizing the need for remedial action, Pres. Lyndon B. Johnson issued an executive order on Sept. 24, 1965, that required federal contractors "to take affirmative action to ensure that applicants are employed . . . without regard to their race, creed, color, or national origin." This first step was followed by a series of court cases amplifying the principle of affirmative action, as in the U.S. Supreme Court decision in *Griggs* v. *Duke Power Company* (1971), which invalidated intelligence tests and other criteria as indeterminate measures that tended to restrict minority employment.

The Civil Rights Act of 1964 did not cover educational institutions. The Equal Employment Act of 1972, however, recognized educational opportunities to be as significant as those relating to employment. Consequently, colleges and universities came under increasing pressure to admit members of minorities in greater numbers, especially in professional and graduate schools.

The most serious court challenge to affirmative action was the Supreme Court case *Regents of the University of California* v. *Bakke.* Allan Bakke, who had been denied admission to the medical school of the University of California at Davis because of its quota system, contended that he, as a non-minority student, was a victim of reverse discrimination and that his right to equal protection under the law had been violated. In 1978 the Supreme Court ruled that such special admissions programs were unconstitutional, and Bakke was admitted. The court also ruled, however, that race-conscious programs that did not rely on rigid preference systems remained constitutional. (See BAKKE CASE.)

Although a number of lower courts later challenged the validity of *Bakke,* as of the year 2000 it remained binding (albeit controversial) as precedent. At the same time several states (most notably, California) began experimenting with statewide policies banning race as a factor in all public university admissions. These controversial policies have survived all legal and constitutional challenges to date.

In another landmark case Brian F. Weber, a white man, sued his employer for denying him a place in a training program, although two black workers with less seniority were admitted. The Supreme Court in *United Steelworkers of America* v. *Weber* (1979) ruled that employers could establish voluntary programs to aid minorities and women in employment. In 1980 the court, in *Ful-*

lilove v. *Klutznick,* upheld the constitutionality of federal public works legislation providing that 10% of the work be reserved for minority contractors.

Beginning in the late 1980s, however, a more conservative Supreme Court began to invalidate affirmative action programs that were deemed unjustifiable on the measure of whether a clear showing of past discrimination was present. In its 1989 decision in *Richmond* v. *J. A. Croson,* the court struck down a 30% quota for minority contractors that was otherwise patterned exactly like the program upheld in *Fullilove.* In 1995 the court, in *Adarand Constructors* v. *Peña,* applied strict scrutiny to a federal affirmative action program in contracting, mandating that all such programs be narrowly tailored to serve a compelling government interest.

DAVID A. YALOF, *University of Connecticut*

Bibliography

Beckwith, Francis J., and Todd E. Jones, eds., *Affirmative Action: Social Justice or Racial Discrimination?* (Prometheus Bks. 1997);
Bowen, William G., and Derek Bok, *The Shape of the River: Long-Term Consequences of Considering Race in College and University Admissions* (Princeton Univ. Press 1998);
Chavez, Lydia, *The Color Blind: California's Battle to End Affirmative Action* (Univ. of Calif. Press 1998);
Curry, George E., ed., *The Affirmative Action Debate* (Addison-Wesley 1996);
Rosenfeld, Michael, *Affirmative Action and Justice: A Philosophical and Constitutional Inquiry* (Yale Univ. Press 1991).

AFGHAN HOUND, af'gan, a tall, long-haired dog breed in the hound group. Noted for speed, strength, and endurance, it is a sight, or gaze, hound used for hunting fleet-footed animals, such as the gazelle and hare. The Afghan is characterized by a silky coat, curved tail, and topknot on the skull. All colors are allowed by breed standards, but white markings are undesirable. The standard height is 27 inches (67.5 cm) for males and 25 inches (62.5 cm) for females; weights range from 50 to 60 pounds (22.5 to 27 kg).

The Afghan is one of the oldest breeds. It may have originated in Egypt and later became established in Afghanistan. It was not introduced into the United States until 1926.

J. J. McCoy, *Author of "The Complete Book of Dog Training and Care"*

The Afghan hound is a strong and aristocratic hunting breed developed in the mountains of Afghanistan.

EVELYN M. SHAFER

© CLARO CORTES IV/REUTERS/LANDOV

The Blue Mosque in Mazar-i Sharif houses the tomb of Ali, who is venerated by Shī'ī Muslims.

AFGHANISTAN, af-gan'ə-stan, a mountainous, land-locked country in Central Asia. With an area of 250,775 square miles (649,507 sq km), it is bordered on the north by Turkmenistan, Uzbekistan, and Tajikistan, all formerly republics of the Soviet Union; on the northeast briefly by China; on the east and south by Pakistan; and on the west by Iran.

Both Afghanistan's name (Afghānistān) and its borders have been determined by outsiders, and its diverse population is the result of repeated migrations and invasions stretching from the second millennium B.C. to the late 20th century. Variants of the word *Afghān* were first used in the neighboring civilizations of Iran and India about 2,000 years ago. The name always referred to the Pashtu-speaking peoples, who in the early 21st century are the most numerous ethnic group in eastern and south-central Afghanistan. Pashtu, or in its variant pronunciation, Paktu, is an eastern Iranian or Indo-European language, linguistically part of the same family as Persian and Sanskrit. The name *Afghānistān*, the country of the Afghans, has historically designated the territory dominated numerically, and since the mid-18th century politically, by Pashtu-speaking tribes. For millennia, this territory has also been home to numerous other linguistic or ethnic groups.

Following the 1973 coup by Muhammad Daud (Muḥammad Dā'ūd) against his cousin Zahir Shah (Ẓāhir Shāh), the last Pashtun king, Afghanistan spiraled into political and economic chaos. The most destructive period occurred after the 1979 invasion by the Soviet Union, which triggered more than two decades of warfare. By the time the Soviets withdrew in 1989, the Afghan state had ceased to exist. The internecine struggle that followed the Soviet withdrawal culminated in the victory of the fundamentalist Taliban regime in 1996 and the rise of the al-Qaeda (al-Qā'ida) terrorist organization as a semiautonomous power within Afghan territory. By the fall of 2001, when the United States intervened in response to the al-Qaeda destruction of the World Trade Center in New York City, the educational system was moribund, libraries and museums had been either closed or destroyed, irrigation systems had collapsed, millions of land mines obstructed travel and agriculture, and much of the national infrastructure had ceased to exist. At least 10% of the estimated population of nearly 28 million lived in exile in Iran, Pakistan, Central Asia, Europe, and the United States. When reconstruction began in 2002, no reliable figures existed for any aspect of the economy, the educational and health systems, or the demographic characteristics of the population.

INFORMATION HIGHLIGHTS

Total Area: (land and inland water) 251,759 square miles (652,225 sq km).
Boundaries: *North,* Turkmenistan, Uzbekistan, Tajikistan; *east,* China, Pakistan; *south,* Pakistan; *west,* Iran.
Population: 27,755,775 (2002 est.).
Capital and Largest City: Kabul.
Major Languages: Pashtu and Dari (Afghan Persian), both official.
Major Religions: Sunnī and Shī'ī Islam.

For Afghanistan's flag, see FLAG, both illustration and text.

1. The Land

The climate and geography of Afghanistan explain a great deal about its economy, its history, and the location of its ethnic groups. Situated between the historic civilizations of Iran, India, and Central Asia, Afghanistan is about the same size as the combined area of California and Nevada. It is similar to the latter two states in climate and topography. The country has a largely arid, continental climate with three distinct regional variants: the central mountains, the steppe-like terrain on the periphery of these mountains, and the extreme desert in the southwest. Rainfall in all of these areas is sparse, with the greatest amount, sometimes as much as 16 inches (406 mm), falling in the Hindu Kush mountains, which dominate the center of the country, and in the Jalalabad region east of Kabul. Agriculture depends largely on the rivers and small irrigation canals that are fed by melting winter snows in these mountains. The principal exception to this weather pattern is the monsoon shadow region of eastern Afghanistan, which receives rain from the southwest monsoons. This occurs mainly in July and early August, as some rain-laden clouds that strike the Himalayas are diverted to the west and northwest, producing the forested regions of Gardez and Nuristan and the subcontinental climate of Jalalabad.

The Hindu Kush (literally, "Hindu-killer") mountain system is not only the principal source of water for the agricultural economy, but it is also a geographical feature influencing the region's settlement patterns, military and political history, distribution of ethnic groups, and patterns of trade. These mountains are an extension of the Himalayan and Pamir mountain system, formed when plate tectonics brought the present Indian subcontinent into collision with the Eurasian landmass. As part of this system, these ranges are prone to the earthquakes that plague regions along major plate fault lines. The Hindu Kush mountains spread in a fan-shaped pattern from the Pamirs in the extreme northeastern corner of the country, a sliver of territory known as the Wakhan corridor. The Pamirs themselves signify the same thing as the European Alps, that is, high mountain valleys, which in Afghanistan have traditionally been the home of such nomadic and semi-nomadic people as the Turkic Kirghiz. In the Wakhan corridor the mountains rise to between 9,800 and 19,600 feet (3,000–6,000 meters), and they are only slightly lower in the Badakhshan and Nuristan regions to the immediate west and south.

Due west of Kabul the central part of the Hindu Kush range is also known as the Hazarajat, named after the Hazarah population that inhabits much of this mountainous territory. There the highest peaks are between 13,000 and 16,000 feet (4,000–5,000 meters). A number of passes traverse these mountains from south to north, but most are closed by snow in the winter. Only in 1964 was the all-weather Salang Tunnel constructed to allow motorized traffic to pass from Kabul to the northern cities throughout the year. West and southwest of the Hazarajat, the Hindu Kush steadily declines in height as the mountains fan out in a series of smaller local ranges with broader valleys. These ranges include the Sefid Kuh, or Paropamisus, which extends nearly to the Iranian border just north of Herat, and the smaller Shah Maqsud range just above Qandahar in the southwest.

The five principal cities of 21st-century Afghanistan are all located on rivers fed by mountain snows that flow out of the Hindu Kush range to the south, southwest, west and north. All five are built above or near prehistoric, ancient, and medieval human settlements. In modern times, but not always historically, Kabul has been the most populous of these cities. It is located on the Kabul River, which flows eastward into the Indus River and thus into the Arabian Sea; however, the size of Kabul in modern times is not entirely determined by its riverside location, for the city is situated in relatively mountainous terrain with a very modest agricultural hinterland. Two other factors behind the city's growth are its location on trade routes linking India, Iran, and Central Asia and its role as the political capital of the country since the mid-19th century. The latter factor was especially important in the 20th century, for as the capital Kabul also became the industrial and educational center of the country.

Two other Afghan cities are located in far more favorable agricultural regions, and historically they rivaled Kabul in importance and population. These are Qandahar in the southwest and Herat in the far west. Both cities are located in relatively fertile river valleys, Qandahar in the Arghandab-Helmand watershed and Herat in the Hari Rud valley. Both cities are also located on major trade routes linking India with Iran and, in the case of Herat, connecting Iran with Central Asia. After the Mongol invasions of the 13th century and prior to the formation of the first Afghan state in 1747, Herat was one of the most important artistic, literary, and religious centers in the eastern Islamic world and certainly the most important city within the territory of modern Afghanistan. All three of these cities, Kabul, Qandahar, and Herat, now dwarf the principal northern cities of Mazar-i Sharif and Qunduz, which are also located on rivers flowing out of the Hindu Kush. Before the Mongol invasions, however, the city of Balkh, near present-day Mazar-i Sharif, was known as the "mother of cities" because of its size, economic importance as a trading link with Central Asia, and role as a major center of Islamic learning.

2. The People

The population of Afghanistan was estimated in 2003 to be 27,755,775. Nearly all Afghans are Muslims, and the overwhelming majority belong to the Sunni division of the faith, which is the dominant form in the Islamic world. Most Sunni Muslim Afghans are, in turn, adherents of the Hanafi legal school, which is also the most prevalent school in Central Asia, India, Pakistan, and Turkey. The major Afghan religious minority is the Shīī Hazarah population of the Hindu Kush, whose faith links them with the predominantly Shīī Iranian population to the west. Within the majority Sunni population an undetermined number of people are also sufis (ṣūfis), that is, they belong to one of several Muslim devotional or mystical religious orders. The most important of these are the Qādirīyah, the Naqshbandīyah, and the Chishtīyah. During the Taliban period sufi orders were banned, particularly as some utilize music in their devotions, which the puritanical religious students (ṭalibān) believed to be contrary to Islam. Most of the rural Afghan popula-

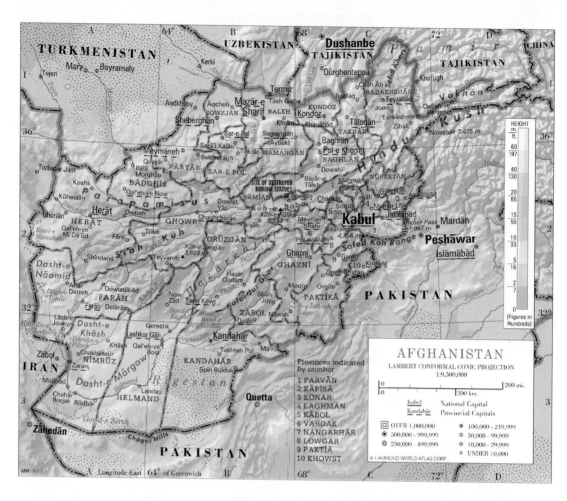

AFGHANISTAN

tion have contact only with mullahs, poorly educated members of the *'ulamā'* (those learned in Islamic faith and practice). Most of these men know only the Qur'ān (Quran, Koran) and a few other religious texts; the majority of them are both religiously and socially conservative. They often equate tribal custom with Islamic doctrine,

and historically they and tribal leaders have led the opposition to modernization and social change.

Afghanistan is not now a theological or educational center in the larger Islamic world, and during the last several centuries most Afghans who have had formal religious training beyond the elementary level have found it in South Asia or Egypt. Most of the Taliban, for example, were educated in poorly staffed religious schools in Pakistan. Only after the establishment of Kabul University in 1946 did significant numbers of Afghan 'ulamā' receive advanced theological training within the country. Despite Sunnī-Shīʿī differences and the relatively poor level of religious education, most political leaders of Afghanistan have regarded Islam as a force that can be used to unify Afghanistan's diverse ethnic and linguistic groups. Sometimes, particularly during conflicts with such non-Muslim foreign powers as Britain and the Soviet Union, Islam has at least temporarily had this effect. Historically members of the Afghan 'ulamā' have not exercised political power at the national level, but their role was greatly magnified during the ten years of Soviet occupation, and members of the clerical class dominated the country during the Taliban period, 1996–2001.

The internecine struggle that followed the Soviet withdrawal in 1989 sharpened the ethnic divisions of the groups that make up the Afghan population. The identity of these groups provides an important key to phases of Afghan history during the Islamic period. The phrase *ethnic group* refers to a population that shares a common identity, whether that identity is determined primarily by language, fundamental values, descent from a common ancestor, or simply the belief that the population in question is and should remain separate from its neighbors. The largest single ethnic group in 21st-century Afghanistan is that of the Pashtuns (also called Pushtuns, Pakhtuns, Pathans), who have dominated Afghan politics since the first Afghan state was formed in 1747. At the beginning of the 21st century, they comprised an estimated 38% of the Afghan population. The Pashtuns are not a tribe but an ethnic group composed of numerous tribes, many of whom have historically been bitter enemies. Most adhere to one of two large tribal confederations, the Durranis and the Ghiljis. These confederations inhabit a belt of territory stretching from the eastern Afghan border southwest to Qandahar and beyond. Since the late 19th century small numbers of Ghilji Pashtuns have also lived in northern Afghanistan, where the Durrani government in Kabul

forcibly resettled them both to weaken their influence in the south and to Pashtunize the north. An equal or greater number of Pashtuns live in Pakistan, a fact of major importance in Afghan-Pakistani relations and the rise of the Taliban.

Pashtun ethnicity is usually associated with three principal criteria: a belief in descent from a common ancestor, the Pashtu language itself, and a social code usually identified as *pashtūnwalī*. All Pashtuns trace their descent from Qais, reputed to have been a contemporary of the prophet Muḥammad. Some believe him to have been a descendant of Saul and a member of the Beni Israel tribe that settled in Ghur, the mountainous region in west-central Afghanistan. He is said to have left Ghur to join the Prophet in Mecca, where he converted to Islam, and then returned to his Afghan home, where his descendants generated all the later Pashtun tribes and clans. As was indicated above, Pashtun has historically been equated with the term Afghan, and Durranis such as the Sadozai and Muhammadzai have always been the political and military leaders of the governments formed since 1747.

After the Pashtuns, Persian speakers, who comprise perhaps 25%–30% of the population, constitute the next largest linguistic group in the country. In Afghanistan their language (with Pashtu one of two official Afghan languages) is known as Dari, signifying ancient or "original" Persian. Many individual Afghans refer to the language as either Farsi, the historic Iranian name for the language, or Tajik, the name used to identify the Persian speakers in Central Asia. Unlike Pashtuns, Persian speakers do not constitute a single ethnic group in Afghanistan, even an internally divided one. Rather, there are a number of different Persian-speaking communities. Prior to the Soviet invasion and subsequent civil war, there were seven identifiable Persian-speaking populations in Afghanistan, four of which were not as distinct from one another as they were from other ethnic groups. These four are: the Persian speakers of Herat in western Afghanistan; the Farsiwan, or Persian speakers, of the northeast; Persian-speaking nomads of the same region; and the so-called "mountain Tajiks" of the extreme northeast.

The Salang Pass, 13,370 feet (4,075 meters) above sea level, has long provided travelers, traders, and invaders with access through the Hindu Kush.

Many of the Persian speakers of Herat are virtually indistinguishable from their Iranian neighbors, just as the Tajiks are part of the larger community in Tajikistan immediately to their north.

The Hazarahs comprise the fifth, and most distinct, Persian-speaking group in Afghanistan. At the beginning of the 21st century, they comprised about 19% of the Afghan population. The Hazarahs illustrate the fact that shared language does not necessarily mean a common community or shared ethnicity. Their distinctiveness is partly a factor of their physical isolation and partly a result of the Turkic or Mongoloid features of some members of the population, although many Hazarahs are racially indistinguishable from the Farsiwan or other Persian speakers. However, it is mainly due to the fact that the Hazarahs are Shīī Muslims, whereas nearly all of the rest of the population are Sunnīs.

A sixth Persian-speaking community, and also a distinct ethnic group, is the Afghan-Arabs of northern Afghanistan, a small community whose separate identity is based almost entirely on a consciousness of distinct descent. They trace their origin either to the original Arab Muslim conquerors of this region in the 7th and 8th centuries A.D. or to those who were forcibly resettled in northern Afghanistan and Central Asia by the Central Asian conqueror Timur in the 14th century. None of them now speak Arabic; a few speak Uzbek in addition to Persian. A population estimated at 100,000 in 1975, they are settled primarily in the region between Maimana and Qunduz in the northeast, although a small number also live in the Jalalabad region.

The seventh, last, and numerically smallest Persian-speaking population is the Qizilbash, who are Shīīs. The Iranian invader Nadir Shah Afshar (Nādir Shāh Afshār) left the ancestors of the Qizilbash in Kabul to garrison and administer the city as he passed through on his way to invade India in 1739. The Qizilbash community has been an influential minority in Kabul ever since. While they consider themselves a separate ethnic group, members of the community regularly intermarry with other Persian speakers and Pashtuns.

The next category is Turkic speakers, the Uzbeks and the Turkmen, whose languages are completely unrelated to Pashtu or Persian. They are descended from the Turkic tribes that conquered western Central Asia and northern Afghanistan in the late 15th and the early 16th century, but they do not constitute a single ethnic group any more than do the Persian speakers. Most of them live in north-central and northwestern Afghanistan, respectively. Like the mountain Tajiks, both the Uzbeks and the Turkmen are part of larger populations, the majority of whom live across the border in the Central Asian republics of Uzbekistan and Turkmenistan. The Uzbeks and the predominantly nomadic Turkmen, who together constitute about 10% of the Afghan population, marry across ethnic boundaries less frequently than do Pashtuns and Persian speakers.

A number of much smaller communities make up the remaining 8% of the population. These are the Kafirs, the Baluchis, and the Hindu, Sikh, and Jewish communities. The Kafirs, located in isolated valleys just northeast of Kabul, are a population of small-scale agriculturalists who were non-Muslims until forcibly converted in the late 19th century. The Kafirs are still a distinct ethnic group, even though they are now entirely converted to

© ARKO DATTA/REUTERS/LANDOV

After the fall of the Taliban, some, but not all, Afghan girls and women began to shed the enveloping *burqah*.

Islam. The Baluchis are largely concentrated in the desert areas of the south and southwest and extending into Iran and Pakistan. Speaking an Iranian language, they constitute a group of extremely poor nomadic or seminomadic tribes who have adapted to the exceptionally harsh environment of their homeland.

The non-Muslim populations of Hindus, Sikhs, and Jews have formed a tiny part of the Afghan population but have performed historically important economic functions. Hindu commercial castes from northwestern India, such as the Panjabi Khattris, have been active in Afghan, Central Asian, and Iranian trade at least since the 16th century. Later the Sikhs joined them in Afghanistan and Iran as merchants, craftsmen, and more recently technicians of various kinds. Both Hindus and Sikhs have been present in Afghanistan in far larger numbers than the very small numbers of Jews, who were part of a commercial diaspora extending into Central Asia and China. Most substantial villages and towns in eastern Afghanistan have a Hindu or Sikh family acting as shopkeepers or moneylenders, whereas Jews resided only in Kabul and the larger cities. By the early 21st century no Jewish families remained in the country; Kabul had only one impoverished synagogue with a single Jewish caretaker.

In Afghanistan, as in other societies, clothing is a superficial marker of ethnic difference. Among the Afghans it is mainly headgear that distinguishes one group from others. Most men in villages and small towns normally have a long cotton shirt over baggy trousers and often a sleeveless vest. Women in these areas normally wear long shirts over baggy trousers or long skirts and some kind of shawl or *chadar* but rarely the enveloping head-to-foot garments commonly seen in cities, known to outsiders as *burqahs* and to Afghans as *chadaris*. Some men, such as the Nuristanis, wear distinctive clothing, but what normally distinguishes pastoral nomadic groups from the sedentary population is the garb of the women. Afghan nomad women often wear brightly colored clothing. Turkmen women, in particular, are famous for the tall pointed caps worn during marriage ceremonies and other festivals, a tradition that can be traced back to the 15th century.

Music also has ethnic connotations at the local level, where people of all ethnicities perform linguistically and musically distinct songs. An example is a small ethnic group known as the Pashai. A population of little more than 100,000 agriculturalists living in the mountains north of Jalalabad, the Pashai speak an Indo-European language with no written form and have a musical tradition with no stringed instruments. They use two different kinds of drums, an oboe known as the *surna*, and a *pinuri*, or flute. The Pashai men play most of their music at weddings and festivals. They usually accompany the singing of poems devoted to profane or sacred love, heroic epics, or simple themes related to everyday life, many of them adaptations of Persian verse known to all Afghan ethnic groups. At the provincial and national level, the influence of Persian literature and instrumental traditions in music is very strong. This is especially true in the Iranian-dominated Persian cultural center of Herat. In the east, the influence of Indian classical and film music is equally pervasive, having gained wide popularity after Radio Kabul began broadcasting regularly in the 1950s.

3. The Economy

The dry climate and mountainous geography of Afghanistan sharply limit the possibility of intensive agriculture; only about 10% of the land is arable. However, the semiarid regions historically offered a habitat for significant numbers of pastoral nomads, many of whom also functioned as long-distance traders prior to the mid-20th century. Agriculture, pastoralism and trade were the three principal sources of wealth in Afghanistan until the mid-20th century. The overwhelming majority of Afghans have always been farmers who have grown wheat, barley, and other cereal grains and a wide variety of fruits and nuts, such as melons, pomegranates, grapes, almonds, and pistachios. These fruits have been a staple Afghan export to South Asia for centuries. Subsistence agricultural villages are scattered throughout the country wherever sufficient water exists, but intensive agriculture was and is possible only in the principal river valleys, where agricultural productivity has provided the surplus to support cities. In these regions water is brought to the fields by surface canals or by the famous underground channels, known as *kārīzes* or *qanāts*, that are used on the southern slope of the Hindu Kush. Irrigation from wells is largely confined to the exceptionally arid regions of the southwest. In the post–World War II period, irrigation was expanded as the United States and the Soviet Union financed and gave technical help to restore old dams and build new large earthen-filled dams in the Arghandab-Helmand Basin and near Kabul and Jalalabad. Some of these dams, such as Jabal al-Siraj, near Kabul, also supplied badly needed electricity to urban areas. Afghan pastoralists of various ethnicities make their livelihoods largely by raising sheep and goats and through their trading activities. Sheep produce wool for carpets and the famous karakul caps, and both sheep and goats are the principal source of meat in the Afghan diet. Most pastoralists also engage in trade, although their commercial importance declined dramatically in the late 20th century.

Trade has been an important source of income for Afghanistan's cities in historic times. Kabul, in particular, historically functioned as an entrepôt through which goods were shipped east to India, north to Central Asia, or west to Iran. Kabul, probably more than any other Afghan city, derived a high if undetermined percentage of its revenues from taxes on trade before the mid-20th century. Much of the Afghan agricultural produce and Indian cotton and silk cloth that comprised the bulk of this trade was carried to the city by pastoral nomads who migrated yearly between their summer pastures in the eastern Hindu Kush and the lowlands in the Indus River Valley. Some of these tribesmen also brought horses and other Central Asian goods to both Afghanistan and India. In this eastern region a group of Pashtun tribes known generally as *powindahs* and composed of Nuharni or Luharni tribes, dominated this trade. Some of them became professional merchants and used their transport animals to carry goods from Bengal in eastern India to Bukhara in Central Asia or Isfahan in Iran. As late as the early 20th century, some of these Afghan merchants traveled as far east as Calcutta, where the Bengali writer Rabindranath Tagore described them in his charming story "The Kabuli Walla." Others settled and became substantial merchants in cities. Indians

© BAKUKI MUHAMMAD/REUTERS/LANDOV

Mounted tribesmen vie for possession of the headless carcass of a goat in the ancient Afghan game *buzkashi*.

© SCALA/ART RESOURCE

A 175-foot (53-meter) statue, destroyed by the Taliban in 2001, bore witness to Afghanistan's Buddhist past.

also played an important part in this trade for many centuries as both financiers and merchants.

Only in the 20th century did significant manufacturing and a modern banking system develop in Afghanistan. Before then the principal Afghan manufactures were carpets, and until the 1930s manufacturing was largely confined to government workshops. At that point entrepreneurs began large-scale cotton cultivation in the north and established a textile factory in Qunduz, which sold most of its output to the Soviet Union. Some of the same businessmen also began exporting karakul lambskins to western Europe, and these sales grew to become a principal source of hard currency for the country for the next four decades. These men also founded the first investment bank in the country in 1932. Later called the Banki-i Melli, or "National Bank," it funded much of the industrial development in northern and eastern Afghanistan after World War II. After 1945 manufacturing grew substantially, partly aided by Soviet-American Cold War competition for influence. These governments funded infrastructure projects such as roads, airports, and communications facilities. During the postwar decades textile manufacturing grew along with the processing of sugarcane and the production of fertilizer and cement. With the exception of cotton, nearly all of these manufactures supplied internal demand. By the late 1960s a pipeline had been constructed to carry gas from northern Afghan fields to Soviet Central Asia. Gas exports immediately became the third most valuable export after fruit and nuts and karakul skins.

Nevertheless, probably fewer than 100,000 Afghans worked in industry in the pre-1979 period, and the economic development that occurred between 1945 and 1979 was halted and then reversed by the Soviet invasion and the factional

fighting that followed the Soviet withdrawal. This made a poor country even more impoverished. Even before the cataclysm of 1979–2001, Afghanistan was one of the world's poorest countries, with a per capita income of less than that of India, infant mortality as high as 20%, and perhaps 80% illiteracy. The country was also wracked by drought from 1998 to 2002, leading to further economic decline and starvation in the mountainous rural areas. Only massive amounts of food aid prevented large-scale humanitarian disaster in winter 2001–2002. By winter and spring of 2002 the most profitable economic activities in the country were probably opium production, gem mining, and smuggling.

4. History and Government

The popularity of Persian and Indian music in Afghanistan reflects the historic influence of those cultures and civilizations in the region both before and after the first Afghan state was founded in 1747. These cultures are in turn regional derivatives of the Aryan or Indo-European peoples who settled these areas between the 4th and the 2d millennium B.C. Pashtu, like Persian and Sanskrit, is an Indo-European language distantly related to Greek and Latin. Unlike the Indo-Europeans who settled Iran and India, however, those who remained in Afghanistan did not develop an urban civilization and literary culture of their own until modern times. In fact, prior to the 15th and 16th centuries, virtually nothing is known of the Pashtu-speaking people, other than brief references in geographic works. Before that time the territory of modern Afghanistan was usually dominated either by Iranians or by Indians or was temporarily overrun by invaders such as Alexander the Great in the 4th century B.C., the Mongols in the 13th century A.D., and Timur (Tamerlane) in the 14th century A.D. Persian dominance was the norm in both pre-Islamic and Islamic times, and the legacy of that domination can be seen most of all in the use of Persian as the principal literary and governmental language of Afghanistan and in the presence of many Persian-speaking communities. Indian influence was less pervasive. It was symbolized by the Buddhist statues in the Bamian Valley, built in the 4th century A.D. and destroyed by the Taliban in 2001. In modern times Indian influence is present in the form of Indian merchants, Indian music, and in eastern Afghanistan Indian cuisine.

The Prenational Islamic Period. The Islamic period in Afghan history begins with the Arab-Muslim campaigns that destroyed the Iranian Sassanian empire in 642 A.D. It was many years after that victory, however, before Muslims occupied Afghan territories. The Chinese Buddhist pilgrim Hsüan-tsang (Xuanzang) did not mention the presence of Muslims when he visited eastern Afghanistan in 644, but his visit is important for dating the relative decline of Buddhism and the resurgence of Indian Brahmanical influence in this eastern Afghan region. Muslim armies raided western and northern Afghanistan in the middle of the 7th century and established permanent bases in Central Asia by the latter part of that century. Only in the following century did Muslim rulers from Iran, the Saffarids, occupy Kabul. When they took the city in around 870 A.D., they displaced the Indian Hindu Shahi dynasty, whose rulers then retreated east into the Panjab. With the beginnings of Muslim occupation and the historical and geographical texts produced by Muslim scholars, the first references to Afghans were recorded. The 11th-century Greco-Islamic scientist al-Biruni (Abū Rayhām al-Bīrūnī) mentioned them, as did an anonymous geographical text from the same period, the *Ḥudūd al-'Ālam*. In both cases the term Afghan apparently referred to the Pashtun tribes inhabiting the mountainous regions of southeastern Afghanistan. In roughly the same period, Firdausi (Firdawsī) produced the great Persianlanguage epic poem *Shāh-nāmah* in Ghazni, whose rulers had also brought al-Biruni and other Muslim intellectuals and writers to their capital. From that time down to the 20th century, Persian written in the Arabic script remained the principal language of government and literature throughout Afghanistan, with Arabic the language of science, as it was for al-Biruni and the rest of the Islamic world.

From the time of the Ghaznavids (reigned 977–1186), who eventually controlled virtually all of Afghanistan, northeastern Iran, and northwestern India, the Afghan region was controlled by a series of Muslim dynasties. Many of these dynasties were based in Iran or Central Asia and were ethnically Turks or Mongols, although once they entered Iran and Afghanistan, nearly all adopted Persian language and culture. The Ghaznavids themselves were in origin Turkic military slaves, and their successors in eastern Iran and western Afghanistan, the Saljuqs, were a branch of the Turkic Oghuz pastoral nomadic tribal confederation. One of the few exceptions to this pattern of "foreign" rulers was the Ghurids, a hill people from the west-central Hindu Kush region. After destroying the remnants of Ghaznavid rule in eastern Afghanistan in the late 12th century, they pushed eastward into India, where they laid the foundations of Muslim rule in Delhi. In the early 13th century Afghanistan suffered from the Mongol invasion, during which Herat was virtually destroyed. Mongols continued to operate in the region throughout most of the century, even sending armies and raiding parties into India. In Iran they established a separate Mongol dynasty, the Ilkhans, who became Muslims in the late 13th century, having already begun to absorb the Persian culture of the indigenous administrative class. The ethnic Mongol populations near present-day Herat are undoubtedly a legacy of this period, and the obvious Mongol traits of some Hazarahs probably date to the 13th century as well. In the 14th century Afghanistan was subjugated by yet another Central Asian conqueror, Timur (Tamerlane), as he advanced from Iran to Delhi.

Following Timur's death in 1405 his descendants, collectively known as the Timurids, ruled nearly all of Afghanistan for the next century. The period of Timurid rule is important for later Afghan historical consciousness because literate Afghans claim the Perso-Islamic cultural florescence that occurred in Herat as part of their own national heritage. Especially during the reign of the Timurid sultan Husain Baiqara (Ḥusayn Bāyqarā, reigned 1486–1506), Herat became the most important center of Perso-Islamic culture in the Islamic world. Husain Baiqara and others at his court lavishly patronized poetry, music, and miniature painting. The most impressive artifacts of Perso-Islamic religious architecture in Afghanistan date to the Timurid period. These include the cathedral-like mosque in Herat and the Ali shrine in Mazar-i Sharif. The city was also home

to distinguished Muslim theologians. The most famous miniature painter of the age, Bihzad (Bihzād), worked in Herat. Perhaps the best-known example of a literary figure claimed by both Iranians and Afghans is Abd al-Rahman Jami ('Abd al-Raḥmān Jāmī; 1419–1492), widely regarded as the last great classical Persian poet. Jami was also a Naqshbandi sufi, one of the most important devotional-mystical Muslim orders in Afghanistan, even in the 21st century. While Turki, the native language of the Timurids, was also used in Herat, Pashtu was never mentioned in any literary or historical source as either a spoken or literary language at that time. Not until the early 20th century did Pashtu publications appear in Afghanistan in any significant number.

The earliest record of Afghans as a ruling class dates to the 15th century. A coalition of Pashtun tribes led by the Ludis established a tribal oligarchy in northwestern and northern India. Ruling from 1451 to 1526, the Ludi dynasty was overthrown by the descendant of Timur, Zahir al-Din Muhammad Babur (Ẓāhir al-Dīn Muḥammad Bābur), who in his memoirs gives the first detailed account of Pashtun tribes in the Kabul region. Babur identified characteristics of the Kabul region and the Pashtu tribes that characterized the city and the region in later centuries. These are: ethnic and linguistic complexity, tribal autonomy, and a relatively primitive level of cultural and political development. Between the time of Babur's death in 1530 and the founding of the Afghan state in 1747, Afghans once again became a subject population, dominated by Babur's successors, the Mughals in Kabul and eastern Afghanistan, and by the Iranian Safavid state in the west. Both states were culturally Persian; their rulers spoke Persian and used the language in their administration. The Safavids, however, were Shī'ī Muslims, and it may have been during their rule that the Hazarahs embraced this form of Islam.

During this period the first Afghan voice was recorded in the poetry of the 17th-century Pashtun chieftain Khushal Khan Khattak (Khushḥāl Khān Khaṭak; 1616–1689). His verse is important in Afghan history because it articulated Pashtun warrior ideology; described these tribes' continuous, bloody intratribal warfare; and has been seen by modern Afghans as expressing a kind of protonationalist ideology because of the poet's conflicts with the Mughals and his glorification both of Pashtu as a literary language and of his homeland in the mountains of eastern Afghanistan.

The Afghan State: 1747–1933. Despite Khushal Khan's posthumous prestige, it was only in the retrospective view of 19th- and 20th-century Afghans that his poetry was seen as an expression of Pashtun nationalism. His verse played no known role in the foundation of the first independent Pashtun state in Afghanistan, which began with anti-Safavid rebellions by two major Pashtun tribal confederations, the Ghilji and the Abdali. First, in 1709 Mir Wais (Mīr Ways) of the Ghilzai confederation led a rebellion against the Safavid governor of Qandahar. Seven years later, as Safavid power was weakening in western Afghanistan, members of the Abdali confederation expelled Safavid officials from Herat. Six years after that Mir Wais's son Shah Mahmud (Shāh Maḥmūd) and his lightly armed tribal force defeated the Safavid army defending the Iranian capital, Isfahan. During the next seven years, Shah Mahmud was the de facto successor to the Safavids as the ruler

Delegates from throughout Afghanistan attended a *loya jirga*, which is a traditional assembly of tribes, in June 2002 to pick an interim government for the country.

of Iran and south-central and southwestern Afghanistan. This nascent Afghan state, however, was itself overthrown in 1729 by the Iranian tribal leader Nadir Shah Afshar (Nādir Shāh Afshār; reigned 1688–1747), who also captured Herat from the Abdalis. Eight years later, in 1737, Nadir Shah allied himself with the Abdalis in an attack on Ghilji-controlled Qandahar. This intensified the traditional hostility between the two tribal confederations, which persisted throughout the history of the Afghan state. Following his victory, Nadir Shah transferred land from the Ghiljis to the Abdalis before he continued eastward to invade India, sacking Delhi in 1739 and essentially destroying the already weakened Mughal empire. This series of events explains why in 1747, when Nadir Shah was assassinated, the Abdalis were able to fill the power vacuum created by the collapse of both Iran and India as major powers, and create the first true Pashtun, or Afghan state, with Qandahar as its first capital.

Ahmad Shah Durrani (Aḥmad Shāh Durrānī; reigned 1747–1773) was the leader of the Sadozai branch of the Populzai tribe of the Abdali tribal confederation. He renamed the Abdali confederation Durrani, from his royal title Durr-i Durān ("Pearl of Pearls"). Ahmad Shah quickly exploited the simultaneous power vacuums in Iran and India to conquer territory in both regions. By the time of his death, the kingdom was a major territorial power in the eastern Islamic world, controlling most of Afghanistan and wealthy provinces in northeastern Iran and northwestern India.

The Durrani kingdom, however, remained virtually throughout its history a tribal oligarchy rather than a centralized bureaucratic state. While it established the precedent for Pashtun rule, it was plagued by dissension within the Durrani confederation as well as between the Durranis, the Ghiljis, and other ethnic groups. The power of the Pashtun tribes was represented by the *jirga*, the tribal council, which elected the early Durrani monarchs and often vetoed or abrogated government policies. (Similarly, a national council of tribes, or *loya jirga*, legitimized the post-Taliban Afghan government in 2002.) One of the most persistent themes in Afghan history since 1747 has been the attempt of Afghan monarchs to centralize power by weakening the Pashtun tribes. In this effort most Afghans monarchs have failed. A second important constant in Afghan history is the economic poverty of the state, for by the early 19th century Ahmad Shah's successors had lost his most valuable territorial conquests in Iran

and India. The deficiency of arable land and natural resources has meant that even strong Afghan monarchs have lacked the wherewithal to modernize the state.

The third major theme in the history of the Afghan state has been the interference and intervention of outside powers. In the 19th and the early 20th century, it resulted primarily from the competition of Britain and Russia for influence in the region. Operating from their Indian territories, the British invaded the country three times: in 1839, 1878, and 1919. While Russian influence with the Afghan governments in Kabul was the principal reason for the first two invasions, the British also resented the independence of the dynamic, modernizing Durrani rulers in power at those times. These were Dust Muhammad Khan (Dūst Muḥammad Khān, reigned 1826–1838 and 1842–1863) and Shir Ali (Shīr ʿAlī, reigned 1868–1878). Following the second British invasion the Afghans had to cede control of their foreign policy to London. Suspicion and hostility toward foreigners became a characteristic trait of Afghan monarchs and commoners alike. These were evident in the rule of Abd al-Rahman (ʿAbd al-Raḥmān, reigned 1880–1902), who set about centralizing power and unifying the country with a ferocity unequaled in Afghan history in the hope of building a strong, independent state. Early in his reign he experienced British imperial coercion himself, when he was forced in 1893 to recognize the Durand Line as the boundary between British India and Afghanistan, although it divided the Pashtun-populated lands widely known as Pashtunistan. Symptomatic of his policies were his draconian assault on Pashtun tribes in the Kabul region, the creation of the nucleus of a modern army, and the political and economic isolation of the state from outside powers.

Abd al-Rahman fell short of his goal of a strong, independent Afghan state. His successors pursued the same policies, also with varying degrees of success, always limited by the acute lack of resources, the autonomy of most tribes, and the threat of outside interference. His son, Habibullah (Ḥabīb Allāh, reigned 1902–1919) initiated policies that had long-term consequences in Afghan history. He established the first secular educational institution, the Habibiya College, in 1903. Hitherto education in the country had been almost completely controlled by the ʿulamāʾ, the socially and intellectually conservative Islamic religious class. The Habibiya created the early nucleus of an Afghan bureaucratic and professional class. Encouraging Habibullah in these modernizing policies was Mahmud Tarzi (Maḥmūd Ṭarzī), the son of a Pashtu poet and a member of the ruling elite. A cosmopolitan intellectual influenced by Western ideas while in the Ottoman empire, Tarzi stimulated the development of a new generation of "Young Afghans" who shared his goals of modernism, nationalism, and pan-Islamic unity.

A constant struggle between modernizing rulers and their small coterie of Westernized supporters, on the one hand, and the autonomous Pashtun tribes and their natural allies the 'ulamā', on the other, characterized the history of Afghanistan in the early 20th century. As Afghan rulers became convinced that modernization could be achieved only through systematic educational and social reform, they increasingly came into conflict with the tribes, who jealously guarded their independent, conservative way of life, and the 'ulamā' who saw their influence threatened. These conflicts first came to a head in the reign of Amanullah (Amān Allāh; reigned 1919–1929), a disciple of Tarzi who was forced to abdicate in 1929 because of the outcry against his radical modernizing policies. Amanullah is also remembered for ending British control over Afghan foreign policy by launching the monthlong Third Anglo-Afghan War in 1919, taking advantage of Britain's weakened condition after World War I.

Amanullah's successor, Nadir Shah (Nādir Shāh, reigned 1929–1933), canceled most of his radical and divisive measures while cautiously continuing some modernization, such as the founding of the first medical college in Kabul in 1932. His successor, Zahir Shah (Zāhir Shāh, reigned 1933–1973), however, presided over a golden age of relative stability, economic progress, educational reform, and social modernization.

Zahir Shah and Daud: Nationalism, Marxism, and Islam. Following Nadir Shah's assassination his son Zahir Shah came to the throne peacefully at age 19. His reign can be divided into three periods: 1933–1953, 1953–1963, and 1963–1973. During the first two decades it was not he but three of his uncles who effectively ran the state. They presided over a period of cautious neutrality in World War II, although prior to the outbreak of war Germany had become the most influential foreign nation in Afghanistan. Economic development was modest until after the war, which left Afghanistan with an unusual surplus of hard currency. Utilizing these funds in 1946, the government contracted with the American engineering firm Morrison-Knudsen to develop the Arghandab-Helmand basin with dams and irrigation works. While this project was plagued with innumerable problems, many caused by the lack of social planning, dams on the Arghandab and Helmand rivers were completed by the early 1950s and an additional part of the project continued until 1959. Also during this period Kabul University was established in 1947, completing the development of the secular educational system begun with the foundation of Habibiya College in 1903. Persian was the language of instruction at the university, with the exception of certain technical subjects, such as engineering, which was taught in English.

In 1953 Muhammad Daud (Muḥammad Dā'ūd), a cousin of the king and commander of the Afghan armed forces in Kabul, staged a coup against his uncle, who was also the king's uncle, with the widespread support of the royal family. Zahir Shah continued as king, but Daud took control

of the government and quickly intensified the pace of economic development and social change. Influenced by the example of Turkey, Daud believed in using the state to develop the country, and he quickly turned to the Soviet Union for aid. In 1956 he signed an agreement for a long-term development loan, and in the following years the Soviet Union and its Eastern European satellites built hydroelectric plants; irrigation systems; roads, including the Salang Tunnel; Bagram airport, north of Kabul; and a fertilizer factory. Failing to obtain military aid from the United States early in the Eisenhower administration, Daud also turned to the Soviet Union for arms and the development of military airfields in the north of the country. As important as any of these projects for the political future was the Soviet training of the Afghan officer corps. Not only did the army become the most modern institution in the country but also many of its members became sympathetic to the Soviet Union and members of the Afghan Communist Party. They were instrumental in Daud's second coup, in 1973. In the middle 1950s American involvement was still largely limited to the Helmand project and a grandiose international airport built in Qandahar in 1956. By the late 1950s, however, Soviet aid began to attract increasing amounts of American aid, demonstrating the success of Daud's policy of nonalignment, which welcomed assistance from both of the Cold War antagonists. By the early 1960s Americans were constructing commercial airports near the Soviet-built military airports in northern Afghanistan.

Muḥammad Daud did not limit himself to economic development but hoped to modernize society as well. Like Amanullah, Daud regarded the customs of *purdah*, or female seclusion and veiling, as anachronistic artifacts not actually required by the two fundamental sources of the Islamic faith, the Qur'ān, God's revelation to Muḥammad, and the *ḥadīth*, the reported sayings and actions of the Prophet. In Afghanistan, as in most Islamic countries, such restrictions on women were primarily urban customs, for the physical labor required of both peasant and nomad women made the restrictions impractical. Consulting with Afghan scholars educated both in Islamic theology and jurisprudence and in Western secular law, Daud was told that neither source clearly prescribed women's seclusion and public veiling. Proceeding with far greater care than the impatient Amanullah, Daud nevertheless allowed women to work in public offices and factories without being veiled. Then, in August 1959, at the national festival that commemorated the realization of full Afghan independence in 1919, Daud and other members of the ruling family and high-ranking officers appeared on the reviewing stand with their wives and daughters unveiled. The predictable reaction of conservative clerics was met first with Daud's challenge to prove that Islam required *purdah*. When these men failed to do so and then began agitating against the regime, they were charged with treason and heresy and briefly imprisoned. The regime easily survived both this challenge and another later in the year when religious and tribal leaders in Qandahar revolted over attempts to collect taxes.

Four years after these events, when Daud resigned under pressure from Zahir Shah, neither his economic nor his social policies were at issue. Rather it was due to the consequences of his unrelenting nationalist confrontation with Pakistan over the Pashtunistan issue. This was a legacy of the 1893 Durand Line, which the Afghans, unlike the Pakistani authorities, had never recognized as a fixed international boundary. There had been tension between the two countries over the issue since Pakistan's creation in 1947, and violence erupted sporadically in the Pashtun tribal areas.

When Pakistan began reorganizing its provincial governments in 1961, many Afghans interpreted the change as the beginning of an attempt to integrate the Pashtun borderlands into Pakistan. Daud had long supported Pashtunistan and advocated a plebiscite for both Afghan and Pakistani Pashtuns to decide the issue. On September 6, 1961, he closed the border despite the threat it posed to the valuable Afghan trade with Pakistan and India. The Soviet Union, which had supported Afghanistan on the Pashtunistan issue since 1956, relieved some of the economic pressure by importing large quantities of fruit by air. Fruit was also shipped by the new Ariana Afghan airlines to India. Nonetheless, the economic loss to both Afghanistan and Pakistan during the 16-month closure was substantial. Apart from the direct economic losses to both countries, considerable amounts of materials destined for Afghan foreign aid projects remained in Pakistani warehouses while the standoff continued, irritating the American and German governments that had provided them. The confrontation ended with the Pashtunistan issue unresolved when Daud resigned.

The third phase of Zahir Shah's monarchy began when his new ministers shelved the unresolved Pashtunistan issue in order to reestablish diplomatic relations and normal trade and aid flows. During the next decade the country continued to benefit substantially from both Soviet and Western aid projects. By 1973 the infrastructure of Afghanistan had been successfully modernized, even if the economy was still primarily agricultural and the population still largely illiterate. Indeed, the scale of these road, irrigation, power, communications, and air transportation projects masked the essential poverty of the country. During this period foreign aid accounted for over 40% of the annual budget whereas taxes on farmland and livestock amounted to little more than 2%.

Politically, the greatest change during this period was the introduction of the first truly representative constitution. Initially drafted by Daud before his resignation, the constitution was written by reform-minded ministers, explained publicly by the government-controlled press, and then presented to a representative *loya jirga* in September 1964. Approved after vigorous debate but with remarkably little trouble, the document established a constitutional monarchy with a bicameral legislature. It had three particularly important aspects: it included all citizens of the country in its definition of Afghans, it gave precedence to secular law over Islamic religious law (*Shari'ah*), and it guaranteed freedom of the press. The greatest pressure for these changes had come from the very small and essentially unrepresentative group of Westernized intellectuals in Kabul, as was reflected in the first elections when relatively few people voted in rural areas. Women voted in significant numbers only in the larger cities.

The 1964 Afghan constitution was an enlightened, progressive document written by dedicated reformers under the direction of a king who was committed to a constitutional monarchy, although it still guaranteed Pashtun dominance. But during the short period that it was in force, the political life of the capital was chaotic, and by the early 1970s the entire system seemed on the verge of collapse. In retrospect it is easy to identify the problems—a parliamentary system with no recognized political parties and no ministerial responsibility, sudden press freedom, and, at Kabul University, a vocal student minority capable of exercising disproportionate influence in the city. The lack of cohesive political parties and the inability of parliamentarians to select the cabinet, which was presented to them for approval by the king's chosen prime minister, produced both frustration and irresponsible behavior. These tensions within parliament were exacerbated by the proliferation of newspapers and the repeated disturbances at the university, which often became politicized.

In this situation influence accrued to the most highly ideological political parties with the most external support, the Marxist People's Democratic

© JOSEF POLLEROSS/THE IMAGE WORKS

The United States and others supplied the *mujāhidīn* with arms to fight Soviet occupation forces in 1979–1989.

Party of Afghanistan (PDPA) and the Islamic Association. These groups had entirely new visions of an Afghan state based on their respective universalist ideologies. Their rise to political prominence presaged the bitter conflicts of the late 1970s and the decade of Soviet occupation. In this context Muhammad Daud, who had resigned with seemingly remarkable calm and grace in 1963, staged a coup in 1973 while the king was in Italy. In his return to power, Daud had the critical support of the pro-Soviet Parcham faction of the PDPA, setting the stage for the Marxist coup of 1978 and the Soviet invasion that followed a year later.

With Daud's coup the political and press liberties of the constitutional decade evaporated. Some political leaders were arrested, including members of the Islamic Association. Daud's PDPA allies also pressured him to pursue his Pashtunistan policy, which would have led to greater dependence on the Soviet Union. By the mid-1970s, however, Daud's disenchantment with his Marxist colleagues and a rebellion by Muslim conservatives led him to alter his political alliances and external policies. He dismissed PDPA members from his government and passed a criminal code intended to restrict their activities. Externally, he now sought financial support in Iran and among Arab countries, abandoned his confrontational Pashtunistan policy, and began to distance himself from the Soviet Union, whose leaders criticized him for accepting Western aid projects. In 1977 and 1978 new conflicts between Muslim conservatives and Marxists prompted him to arrest many PDPA members; however, one, Hafizullah Amin (Ḥāfiẓ Allāh Amīn), remained free long enough to organize PDPA members among the officer corps, who launched a coup in late April 1978 after Amin himself had been imprisoned. After his release he directed an uprising in which Daud and a number of his family members and ministers were killed. Durrani rule ended, although Pashtun dominance in the form of the PDPA leadership endured.

Descent into Chaos. The first leader of the new regime was not Amin but Nur Muhammad Taraki (Nūr Muḥammad Tarahkī; 1917–1979), the elder statesman of the PDPA and one of its founders in 1965. A poorly educated, unsophisticated man who had briefly served as a press attaché in the Afghan embassy in Washington, Taraki was a Ghilji Pashtun from the Ghazni region. Well read in Marxist literature, including Persian-language works of the Iranian Marxist Tudeh Party, Taraki established a single-party dictatorship and immediately began to implement socialist programs. His policies almost immediately triggered resistance. In Herat thousands of people, including Russian officers, advisers, and their wives and families, were massacred. Taraki, an indecisive man, relied almost entirely on the Soviet Union and actually requested Soviet troops to help suppress the Herat outbreak. The unrest his policies provoked in the country were matched by the political conflicts within his government and between the two factions of the PDPA, his Khalq group and the Kabul-based Parcham, whose leader, Babrak Karmal (1929–1996), had helped bring Daud to power. Karmal and other Parcham members were exiled to European ambassadorships and later stripped of their Afghan citizenship.

Conflict also plagued Taraki's own Khalq faction, and in September 1979 Amin overthrew his longtime mentor, Taraki, and shortly afterward had him killed. Amin favored more measured social policies and greater independence from their Soviet allies, but by this time Soviet advisers had penetrated most organs of the Afghan state. When Amin moved to distance himself from the Soviets by dismissing PDPA members from his cabinet and introducing Western-trained bureaucrats and Muslim conservatives into the government, the Soviets began to search for alternatives. Sometime in 1979 they decided to occupy the country to achieve their objective. As early as July Soviet troops began arriving at Bagram air base, which they had built north of Kabul. In December they occupied the capital, killed Amin, and installed Karmal in his place. Thus began the tragedy of modern Afghanistan.

During the next decade Karmal and his successor, Najibullah (Najīb Allāh; 1947–1996), functioned as agents of the Soviet Union, unable to establish themselves as legitimate Afghan rulers. From the outset Karmal had to face organized opposition and armed resistance. Islamic groups came to dominate the opposition; some of these were Muslims from traditional backgrounds, while others belonged to politicized Islamic movements with origins in Pakistan, Muslim India, and Egypt. These groups overshadowed traditional tribal leaders and more secular nationalists, partly because of the aid given them by Pakistan or later by the United States through Pakistan.

As in 19th-century conflicts with Britain, the Afghans defined their conflict with the Soviets as a *jihād*, a struggle for the faith. At first the resistance was entirely localized, and to a large extent it retained this character to the end. To eliminate local support for the fighters, all of whom came to be called *mujāhidīn*, or warriors for the faith, the occupying Soviet forces responded to attacks with unrestrained brutality, often annihilating entire villages. Throughout the Soviet period, secular nationalists and traditional tribal leaders were marginalized. First, leaders of various Muslim exile groups in Pakistan became the de facto spokesmen for the *mujāhidīn* in general. Second, the Pakistani government, eager to defuse the Pashtunistan issue, gave preference to Islamic rather than nationalist groups, magnifying the importance of religious leaders. Finally, as Afghans showed they were capable of successfully resisting the Soviets, the United States became an arms supplier to the *mujāhidīn*, most importantly supplying them with Stinger antiaircraft missiles to negate Soviet air power. These arms were distributed through the Pakistani military intelligence department, the Inter-Services Intelligence agency (ISI), enabling the ISI to direct them to their chosen Muslim resistance parties.

By 1985, when Mikhail S. Gorbachev came to power in the Soviet Union, a bloody stalemate existed in Afghanistan. In 1986 Soviet leaders decided to withdraw from the country, which they eventually did in 1989. To bolster the Afghan regime, they established a new Communist-dominated government led by Najibullah, the former head of the Khad (secret police), who was "elected" as party secretary at a Soviet-controlled meeting in Kabul in May 1986. As the Soviets prepared their withdrawal between 1986 and 1989, Najibullah attempted to modify the autocratic Marxist regime. In late 1987 he presided over a handpicked *loya jirga*, which adopted a new, outwardly democratic constitution, in an attempt to legiti-

Kabul, relatively untouched by the decadelong war against Soviet occupation, sustained heavy damage between 1993 and 1996 as the victorious factions fought one another for control.

mize his rule by attracting support from traditional elements in Afghan society. He also reversed Soviet-era policy by presenting himself as a pious Muslim, both through religious rhetoric and through the ostentatious support of Muslim institutions. In fact, the state continued to function as an autocratic regime and maintained itself in Kabul largely because of its superior military capabilities and the divisions among the *mujāhidīn* factions opposing it. The *mujāhidīn* groups continued the armed struggle in 1989 and 1990, but their frontal assault on Jalalabad in 1989 demonstrated their inability to function as a regular army. An attack a year later by the radical Islamist Gulbuddin Hekmatyar also failed miserably.

Gradually, however, conflict within Najibullah's government, defections from his military, continued military pressure from the *mujāhidīn*, and international negotiations that produced a cutoff of foreign military aid to both sides in 1992 produced a situation in which Najibullah was forced to step down. Hekmatyar, from his base in Pakistan, and the Tajik *mujāhidīn* leader Ahmad Shah Masud (Aḥmad Shāh Masʿūd), from his Panjshir base north of Kabul, converged on the city and then fought for control. After Masud emerged victorious, the exiled religious leaders arrived and attempted to form a new government.

This sequence of events compounded the tragedy begun with Daud's 1973 coup and the Soviet invasion of 1979. By 1992 the Soviet Union had collapsed and, consequently, official American interest in the fate of Afghanistan evaporated. Various Afghan factions contended for power. Regional leaders seized their respective home bases, such as Ismail Khan (Ismāʿīl Khān) in Herat and Gen. Abdul Rashid Dostum (ʿAbd al-Rashīd Dūstam), an Uzbek, in Mazar-i Sharif. Burhanuddin Rabbani and Masud, both Tajiks, and Gulbuddin Hekmatyar, a Pashtun, continued to vie for power in Kabul. Masud had been the single most successful *mujāhidīn* commander, while Hekmatyar had spent most of the Soviet period in exile in Pakistan, where he had received substantial Pakistani aid for his Islamic political faction. These men failed to find common ground, and as their infighting continued during the next three years, conditions in the country continued to deteriorate. Between 1992 and 1995, leaders changed sides

with bewildering rapidity, many people died, and much of Kabul was destroyed as Hekmatyar shelled the city because of his exclusion from the government. This chaotic situation allowed the Taliban to emerge in 1994 and 1995, and then swiftly take over most of the country.

The Taliban were a phenomenon born of three principal factors: the destructive infighting among the *mujāhidīn* factions, a fundamentalist group of Afghan and Pakistani Muslims eager to end the chaos, and and the active, ongoing support of this group by Pakistan's ISI. Most Taliban leaders were Afghan or Pakistani Pashtuns whose education was limited to experience in war or a basic Muslim religious education in one of the hundreds of religious schools in Pakistan. These schools taught the fundamentals of the Qurʾān and *ḥadīth* but little else, about either Afghan history or the modern world. The *ṭalibān*, or students of Islam, and the *mujāhidīn* who joined them were motivated by a desire to end the suffering of the people of Afghanistan and to establish an Islamic state. Implicitly, their movement also represented a resurgence of the Pashtuns at a time when Kabul and the north were held by Tajiks and Uzbeks. Many of the Taliban were idealists in every sense of the word, but they were idealists who were brought to power with the determined support of Pakistan, which armed, supplied, and trained them. What is remarkable about their success is that initially it came at very small human cost. Many *mujāhidīn* leaders either simply changed sides or were bribed to do so. By April 1996 the Taliban controlled Herat, Qandahar, and part of the southeast, and Mullah Muhammad Omar (Mullāh Muḥammad ʿUmar), their enigmatic, reclusive chief, proclaimed himself the *amīr al-muʾminīn*, or commander of the faithful. Several Afghan monarchs had used this title, but in this case it invoked the memory of the Prophet Muḥammad and signaled the establishment of a Muslim state, later titled the Emirate of Afghanistan. After shelling Kabul throughout much of 1996 and killing hundreds if not thousands of civilians, the Taliban suddenly captured the eastern Afghan provinces in the late summer. They overwhelmed the capital in September 1996 as Masud's outnumbered forces evacuated the city. Immediately on their arrival, the Taliban executed Najibullah and imposed the harshest form of Islamic rule known anywhere in the world.

Initially welcomed by many Afghans for bringing an end to the chaos, destruction, and corruption of the post-Soviet era, the Taliban quickly turned Afghanistan into their vision of a pure Islamic state. In its early phases the Taliban governed through a *shūrā*, a council of religious leaders reminiscent of the early Islamic period, but Taliban rule evolved into a secretive, autocratic regime directed by the reclusive Mullah Omar. Justifying their actions in terms of Islam, the Taliban represented the most conservative instincts and traditions of the rural Pashtuns. Kabul, especially, was treated as a occupied city by these conservative Durranis. Music, television, soccer, chess, kite flying, and virtually any other forms of entertainment were outlawed; Islamic punishments of stoning and amputation were instituted. Women suffered most of all. Forbidden from working or leaving their homes without a male relative, they became domestic prisoners. Married women seen walking with men who were not relatives were subject to execution for "adultery"; single women would be flogged. Thousands of war widows were reduced to begging for food. Young girls were forbidden to be educated beyond the primary level, one of many injunctions more consistent with Pashtun tribal values than with Islam. The Taliban saw to the operation of the religious police in Kabul and other cities, but they took almost no interest in the effective administration of large urban areas or in the revival of the economy. While Taliban forces continued to expand their territorial control in 1997 and 1998, both the economy and the internal coherence of the Taliban movement deteriorated. In 2001 the Taliban government was destroyed as a result of the activities of Osama bin Laden (Usāmah bin Lādin).

Bin Laden, the son of a millionaire Saudi contractor, had fought with the *mujāhidīn* against the Soviets, with hundreds of Arabs and other Muslims who had joined the *jihād*. After returning home in 1990 bin Laden was further radicalized by the Gulf War and the continuing presence of American troops in Saudi Arabia. He returned to Afghanistan in 1996. There the Taliban offered him sanctuary as one who had fought with the *mujāhidīn* and who was willing to share at least some of his wealth with the Taliban. From Afghanistan, bin Laden and his group, al-Qaeda (al-Qā'ida), began planning their worldwide assault on the United States and, rhetorically at least, Christian and Jewish civilization. Training camps were established, Islamic cells set up throughout the world, and attacks planned on American targets. The destroyer U.S.S. *Cole* was attacked, American embassies in Kenya and Tanzania were bombed, and then, on Sept. 11, 2001, a suicide mission damaged the Pentagon and destroyed the World Trade Center in New York City, killing nearly 3,000 people in all.

Apparently as a carefully coordinated part of that attack, a suicide bomber had killed Masud two days earlier, on Sept. 9, 2001. Masud was then the leader of the Northern Alliance, the last coherent military force in Afghanistan still fighting the Taliban regime. He had been the most charismatic and effective commander during the Soviet years, but the Pashtuns had never accepted him as a national leader because he was a Tajik. He was probably assassinated because his was the only indigenous force capable of resisting the Tali-

ban. In response to the attacks of September 11, the United States began bombing Afghanistan on October 7. The Northern Alliance recovered from Masud's death and, supported by the U.S. air assaults on Taliban forces, entered Kabul on Nov. 13, 2001. The Taliban had withdrawn or been expelled from all Afghanistan's major cities by the end of December, and reconstruction of the country slowly began. Neither Mullah Omar nor Osama bin Laden, however, was captured.

Rebuilding Afghanistan. On Dec. 22, 2001, an interim government was established in Kabul. Although headed by Hamid Karzai, an Indian-educated Qandahari Pashtun, it was otherwise dominated by the Tajiks of the Northern Alliance. The government, installed with U.S. and European support, controlled little more than Kabul, the Panjshir homeland of Masud, and some northeastern areas. Regional leaders resumed control of the remainder of the country. Aided by a foreign military presence in the capital and continued U.S. attacks on suspected Taliban and al-Qaeda targets, the interim government stabilized the situation in Kabul and prepared for the *loya jirga* that was to select a transitional government.

The former king, Zahir Shah, now 89, returned to preside over the *loya jirga*, which was held in Kabul on June 11–16, 2002; but under U.S. pressure, he rejected any role for himself in the new government. Karzai was selected to lead a cabinet that brought together representatives of the Northern Alliance, various ethnic factions, local power brokers, and a few technocrats. This transitional government began the painful process of rebuilding and reunifying the country, but it faced the same fundamental issues that had plagued Afghan rulers since 1747: foreign interference, ethnic and tribal independence and conflict, a conservative religious class, poverty, and a lack of state resources, institutions, or authority.

A new constitution was ratified on Jan. 4, 2004, but the government extended its authority only gradually beyond Kabul. In October 2003 NATO agreed to help maintain security outside the capital, but it had difficulty finding troops. Elections were delayed, and attacks by the Taliban became more frequent.

Karzai, ruling by consensus, sought to accommodate contending forces, including the regional leaders now ensconced as governors. But in July 2004 he warned that the regional militias were becoming a greater threat than the Taliban.

A presidential election was held, after some delay, on Oct. 9, 2004. Although the Taliban had threatened to disrupt the process, it proceeded without incident.

STEPHEN FREDERIC DALE, *Ohio State University*

Bibliography

Borovik, Artyom, *The Hidden War* (Atlantic Monthly Press 1990).
Doubleday, Veronica, *Three Women of Herat* (Univ. of Tex. Press 1990).
Dupree, Louis, *Afghanistan* (1973; reprint, Oxford 1997).
Gregorian, Vartan, *The Emergence of Modern Afghanistan* (Stanford Univ. Press 1969).
Kakar, M. Hasan, *Government and Society in Afghanistan: The Reign of Amir 'Abd al-Rahman Khan* (Univ. of Tex. Press 1979).
Kakar, M. Hasan, *Afghanistan: The Soviet Invasion and the Afghan Response, 1979–1982* (Univ. of Calif. Press 1995).
MacKenzie, D. N., ed. and tr., *Poems from the Divan of Khushal Khan Khattak* (Allen & Unwin 1965).
Rashid, Ahmed, *Taliban: Militant Islam, Oil, and Fundamentalism in Central Asia*, rev. ed. (Tauris 2002).
Rubin, Barnett R., *The Fragmentation of Afghanistan*, 2d ed. (Yale Univ. Press 2002).

AFRICA

Eastern Africa—the probable cradle of humanity.

AFRICA, af'ri-kə, the world's second-largest continent in area, after Asia, and the third-largest in population, after Asia and Europe (including the western Soviet Union). Africa is the central continent of the global "land hemisphere," whose water counterpart is the Pacific Ocean. No continent lies as close to all the others as Africa does. Northward, across the Mediterranean Sea, is Europe. To the northeast, just over the Suez Canal and the Red Sea, begins Asia. The Indian Ocean separates eastern Africa from Australia and southern Africa from Antarctica. On the west, beyond the Atlantic Ocean, stretch the two Americas.

A notable feature of the African landmass is the regularity of its coastline. The continent lacks prominent inlets and peninsulas, and even good natural harbors. Moreover, it has no extensive continental shelves, the ocean floor falling steeply close offshore. In many places the rise of the land from the coast also is abrupt, with the result that Africa has few broad coastal plains. Africa is the only continent bisected by the equator, extending about an equal distance north and south of that line. Contrary to common perceptions, its western bulge and eastern hornlike projection make Africa as broad as it is long.

The continent falls into two distinct major divisions—Northern Africa, which is geologically, climatically, culturally, and historically a part of the Mediterranean world, and the region south of the Sahara, or Black Africa, which includes the whole of tropical Africa as well as all those areas that were separated from Europe until relatively recent times. This separation was caused partly by the great desert barrier of the Sahara, but environmental characteristics of sub-Saharan Africa also were responsible for discouraging European penetration of the interior.

Africa, including the large offshore island of Madagascar and small islands, contains 20% of the world's land area but little more than half that percentage of the global population. However, the continent's rate of natural increase is higher than that of the rest of the world, and by the beginning of the 21st century Africa is expected to have more inhabitants than Europe and more than North and South America combined.

Perhaps no region in the world presents such a diversity of peoples and cultures as those indigenous to Africa. The modern political units, however, are the artificial creations of European colonial powers that partitioned the continent among themselves in the 19th century. Thus

present frontiers cut across ethnic lines, placing some peoples under the authority of more than one central government and grouping others, often uncomfortably, under a common national administration.

From a group of political and economic appendages of Europe, Africa has emerged as a community of independent states and a new force in world affairs. In the wake of World War II, nationalism swept through the continent, bringing political emancipation to all but the southernmost area. With political sovereignty came social and economic changes that have profoundly affected the daily lives of virtually all Africans.

The modern African revolution has been the more striking because of the outside world's relative ignorance of the continent. The 20th century British historian Arnold Toynbee, for example, in identifying about two dozen "civilizations" since the beginning of the world's history, did not recognize a single one in sub-Saharan Africa. Because of the lack of written records, little was known about the African past. Contemporary research, in many fields and much of it by Africans themselves, is providing new information—about the African origins of human beings, the great migrations of early peoples, and the rise and fall of trading emporiums, kingdoms, empires, and civilizations. The recovery of the past is a vital part of the struggle of Africans to understand their present and to chart the course of their future.

INFORMATION HIGHLIGHTS

Area: 11,700,000 square miles (30,300,000 sq km).

Northernmost Mainland Point: Ras al-Ghiran (Ras Ben Sekka), near Cap Blanc (Ras al-Abiadh), Tunisia — 37°21' N.

Southernmost Mainland Point: Cape Agulhas, South Africa — 34°50' S.

Easternmost Mainland Point: Ras Hafun, Somalia — 51°24' E.

Westernmost Mainland Point: Pointe des Almadies, on the Cape Verde (Cap Vert) Peninsula, Senegal — 17°32' W.

Highest Elevation: Kilimanjaro, Tanzania — 19,340 feet (5,895 meters).

Lowest Elevation: Lake Assal, Djibouti — 512 feet (156 meters) below sea level.

Population: (1985) 555,000,000.

© DIANE RAWSON/PHOTO RESEARCHERS

The Blue Nile plunges over Tesissat Falls after emerging from Lake Tana in the Ethiopian Highlands.

GEOGRAPHY

The whole African continent, except for the linear fold mountains of the extreme northwest (the Atlas chain) and the extreme south (the Cape Ranges), consists of one great rigid block of ancient rocks that has changed little in its essential geology for perhaps 200 million years. Geologists believe that Africa formed the core of a former continent called Gondwana, to which other old blocks in Southwest Asia, India, Antarctica, and South America also belonged before the various sections drifted apart. See also CONTINENT—*Continental Drift.*

1. Physical Features

A striking feature of the African landscape is the vast extent of flat or gently rolling terrain. The continent is essentially a vast plateau, with resistant rock masses standing above the general level of the worn surface. The plateau is lower in the north and west ("Low Africa") than in the east and south ("High Africa"), where it also falls more abruptly to the coast in the steep face known as the Great Escarpment. Low Africa has average elevations of 500 to 2,000 feet (150–600 meters), whereas High Africa rises generally above 3,000 feet (900 meters). Relatively little of the continent is less than 500 feet above sea level. On the other hand, while lacking broad coastal plains along most of its circumference, Africa has few interior areas higher than 7,500 feet (2,300 meters).

Rift Valleys and Mountains. The African plateau was formed by long cycles of erosion without

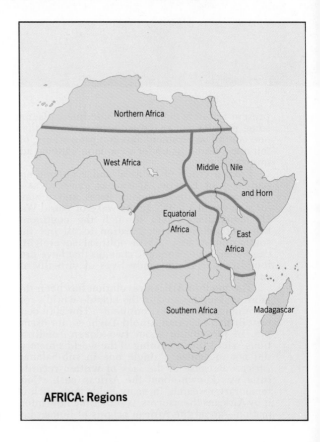

AFRICA: Regions

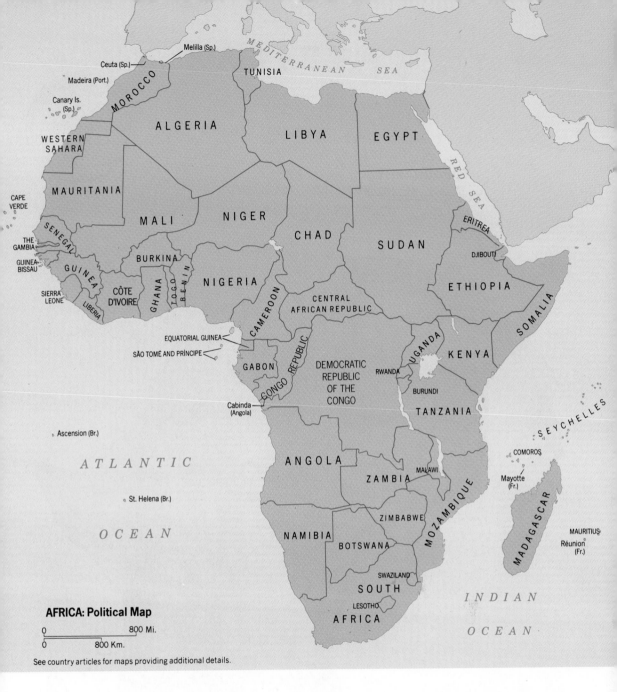

AFRICA: Political Map

0   800 Mi.

0   800 Km.

See country articles for maps providing additional details.

extensive folding, followed by elevation of the continental block. Afterward fracturing took place, especially in the east, where it created the Great Rift Valley. This system of troughs can be traced from the Red Sea through the Horn, or eastern projection of the continent, and into East Africa; from there a branch of the rift extends to the valley of the Shire River in Southern Africa. The troughs are partly occupied today by deep lakes, such as Rudolf (Turkana), Albert, Edward, Kivu, Tanganyika, and Nyasa (Malawi).

Associated with the fracturing that formed the rift valleys was volcanic activity, which was responsible for the lava flows of the Ethiopian Highlands and the volcanoes of East Africa, notably Kilimanjaro, Meru, Kenya, Elgon, and the Virunga group. On the other side of the continent, volca-

nism created the Ahaggar and Tibesti mountain masses of the Sahara as well as Cameroon Mountain, a series of peaks stretching from the Guinea Coast into the sea, where they appear as islands.

Thus despite Africa's great expanses of tableland, its surface is not as uniform and monotonous as it has sometimes been characterized. The continent does not lack mountainous terrain; what distinguishes it topographically from other continents is the absence of a mountainous backbone— a great linear system of ranges comparable to the Himalaya, the Alps, the Rockies, and the Andes. The Drakensberg, in the southeast, is not a mountain range but part of the Great Escarpment. Only the Atlas and Cape Ranges are mountains with a linear structure, and they are confined to corners of the African landmass.

AFRICA

TOPOGRAPHY

Madeira

CANARY IS.

ER RIF

C. Bon

ATLAS MOUNTAINS

Toubkal
13,665

Gt. Western Erg

Gt. Eastern Erg

Gulf of
Sidra

Nile
Delta

Suez Canal

Sinai
Pen.

Qattara
Depr.

Libyan

Desert

AHAGGAR
Tahat 9,850

TIBESTI

Emi Koussi
11,204

L.
Nasser

C. Blanc

S   a   h   a   r   a

Arabian Desert

Nile

Nubian
Desert

AIR
(AZBINE)

C. Verde

Niger

Bani

L.
Chad

Shari

Jeb. Marra
10,130

Ras Dashan
15,157

C. Guardafui

FUTA
JALLON

S   u   d   a   n

Benue

ADAMAWA
MASSIF

Sanaga

Volta

Niger

Ubangi

Uele

Sudd

Blue Nile

Atbara

White Nile

ETHIOPIAN
HIGHLANDS

OGADEN

Wabi
Shebelle

C. Palmas

Cameroon
13,350

Congo

Margherita
16,795

Kenya
17,058

Gulf of Guinea

C. Lopez

Ogooué

Congo

Lualaba

L.
Rudolf

L.
Victoria

Kilimanjaro

Zanzibar

Kwango

Kasai

Lake
Tanganyika

Rufiji

Ruvuma

C. Delgado

COMORO
IS.

C. Amber

BIHÉ
PLATEAU

MITUMBA RANGE

Lake
Nyasa

Maromokotro
9,450

Cunene

Cubango

Zambezi

Zambezi

Victoria
Falls

Mozambique Channel

Madagascar

Namib Desert

Kalahari
Desert

Limpopo

Save

Orange

Vaal

DRAKENSBERG

C. Ste-Marie

GT. KARROO

C. of Good Hope

C. Aguihas

| 5,000 m. | 2,000 m. | 1,000 m. | 500 m. | 200 m. | 100 m. | Sea | |
| 16,404 ft. | 6,562 ft. | 3,281 ft. | 1,640 ft. | 656 ft. | 328 ft. | Level | Below |

259a

AVERAGE JANUARY TEMPERATURE

AVERAGE JULY TEMPERATURE

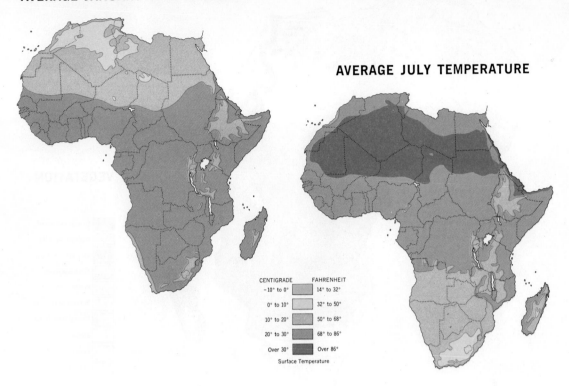

CENTIGRADE	FAHRENHEIT
-10° to 0°	14° to 32°
0° to 10°	32° to 50°
10° to 20°	50° to 68°
20° to 30°	68° to 86°
Over 30°	Over 86°

Surface Temperature

AVERAGE ANNUAL PRECIPITATION

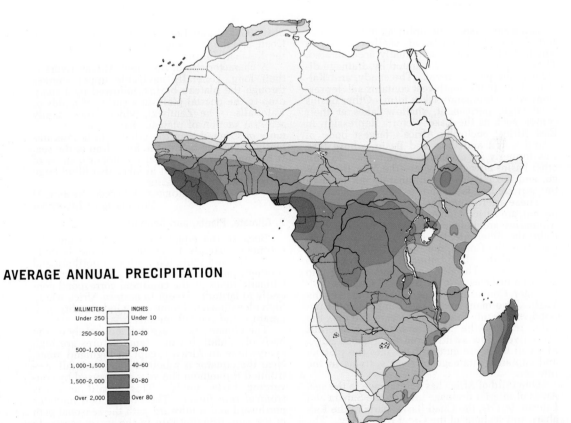

MILLIMETERS	INCHES
Under 250	Under 10
250-500	10-20
500-1,000	20-40
1,000-1,500	40-60
1,500-2,000	60-80
Over 2,000	Over 80

259b

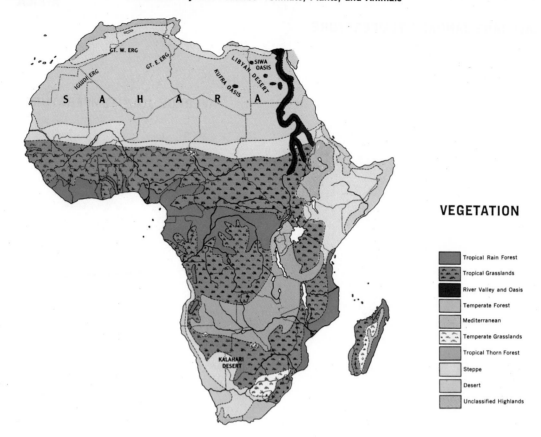

VEGETATION

- ▨ Tropical Rain Forest
- ▨ Tropical Grasslands
- ▨ River Valley and Oasis
- ▨ Temperate Forest
- ▨ Mediterranean
- ▨ Temperate Grasslands
- ▨ Tropical Thorn Forest
- ▨ Steppe
- ▨ Desert
- ▨ Unclassified Highlands

Basins and Rivers. The uplifting of the plateau surface also produced broad, shallow basins in which thick sediments eventually accumulated. These depressions are separated by drainage divides at the plateau level. The sandy, arid Kalahari Basin in the southwest contains subdepressions where temporary lakes form. Other basins have large, permanent, shallow lakes at their center, such as the Lake Victoria depression in East Africa, enclosing Africa's largest body of inland water, and the Chad Basin, whose lake was formerly an extensive inland sea. In still other basins flow great rivers—the Nile, the Congo, and the Niger—that ultimately cut through the surrounding tableland to reach the sea.

These arteries and the Zambezi, in the order named, are Africa's longest rivers. Some of their tributaries are long or important in their own right: the Blue Nile, the Ubangi and Kasai confluents of the Congo, the Benue tributary of the Niger, and the Shire outlet of Lake Nyasa into the Zambezi. The principal rivers flowing into the Atlantic Ocean are the Senegal, Gambia, Volta, Niger, Congo, and Orange (which receives the Vaal). Two main rivers, the Zambezi and Limpopo, empty into the Indian Ocean; and one, the Nile, reaches the Mediterranean. Numerous short rivers flow swiftly from the plateau edge. Many of these are cutting back into the plateau and capturing drainage of river systems in the interior.

One third of Africa has no drainage to the sea. Areas of interior drainage include the Sahara and Libyan deserts, the Chad Basin, parts of the Kalahari, and sections of the Great Rift Valley. The

Shari (Chari) and Logone rivers flow into Lake Chad, and the Okavango empties into a swamp in the Kalahari Basin.

A characteristic of the great African rivers is their long, generally navigable upper courses through the plateau basins, followed by a sharp drop to the coastal plain in a series of rapids or waterfalls. The Zambezi, which flows mainly across a section of plateau that has no basin, is more obstructed than the others but is intermittently navigable before the final drop to the sea. It has been suggested that the upper courses of these rivers once ended in lakes that filled large parts of the interior basins.

ROBERT W. STEEL (Section 1)
University of Liverpool

2. Climate, Plants, and Animals

Because the equator crosses Africa and the continent extends to about the same latitude north (37°) and south (35°), Africa's northern and southern portions have similar climatic patterns. Climatic zones on the continent correspond generally to latitude, except in eastern Africa where high elevations and monsoon winds modify temperature and rainfall regimes.

The climatic types are defined mainly on the basis of rainfall, because temperatures are high everywhere in Africa except in highland areas. Near the equator is a belt of heavy rainfall, distributed throughout the year and caused by converging trade winds. This humid area has *tropical rain forest*. The rainfall belt migrates northward and southward with the seasonal path of the sun, bringing rain in the warm season to savanna and tropical steppe zones bordering the forests; the cooler season is dry. Monsoon winds along the east coast of Africa also bring rainfall seasonally, causing additional areas of savanna and steppe. These grasslands merge into the *tropical desert zone* of the Sahara in the north and the Namib and Kalahari in the south. The deserts have little rain because they lie in belts (20° to 30° north latitude and 20° to 30° south latitude) where air masses tend to descend.

Along the Mediterranean Sea in the north and near Cape Town in the south the edges of the continent come under the influence of westerly winds, which have intermittent cyclonic storms. The storms bring rain only during the winter seasons of the respective areas, causing a *Mediterranean zone* of mild climate with dry summers and wet winters. A *subtropical grassland zone* occurs in Southern Africa because of the tempering effects of elevation and also distance from the equator.

Within the aforementioned areas, high plateaus and mountains form *highland zones* with cooler climates and modified vegetation.

Tropical Rain Forest. The tropical rain forest climate and vegetation prevail on the equator and for about 10° to the north and south. Because of high elevations and monsoon winds in eastern Africa, however, tropical rain forest is restricted mainly to the western areas, particularly the Congo (Zaire) Basin and the Guinea Coast.

Climate. Temperatures are high, often over 80°F (27°C), with little range from month to month or from day to night. They rarely rise as high as 100°F (38°C) or go much lower than 70°F (21°C) at night or during the cooler rainy seasons. The high humidity (often 80%) and the monotonously high temperatures make the climate unpleasant for people from cooler regions.

On the coasts some relief is provided by sea breezes, and in West Africa sometimes by dry winds from the Sahara. Rainfall is usually highest following the equinoxes (March and September) when the sun is over the equator, giving two rainy seasons separated by drier periods. Total annual rainfall is usually from 50 to 70 inches (1,270–1,780 mm). But where moisture-laden winds ascend steep slopes, the total rises to more than 200 inches (5,080 mm).

Vegetation. The tropical rain forest extends over the regions where it is always warm, where severe drought does not occur, and where drainage and soils are suitable for forest growth. The tree cover is dense, with many species, varying from moderate to great height. Often there are several stories of trees, with crowns that prevent sunlight from reaching the forest floor. As a result, undergrowth is not as abundant as in jungle areas, but there are usually many vines. Some trees have prop roots, or buttressed trunks.

Many species of trees in the rain forest are economically useful. The oil palm furnishes oil from its fruit and palm wine from its sap, as well as fiber for building material. Timber is obtained from the African mahogany, sapele, niangon, teak, and other trees, including several types of ebony, but a major economic problem is the scattered occurrence of these useful trees. Pure stands are rare; the useful types are mixed with trees for which there is no ready timber market. Cola nuts, raffia, copal (a resin), robusta coffee, and rubber are other products from the rain forest.

One of several types of African grasslands, this parklike environment in East Africa is called a tree savanna.
© LAWRENCE SCHILLER/PHOTO RESEARCHERS

Marginal Areas. The dense evergreen rain forest gives way to a semideciduous type of forest in areas that have a short dry season. Contrary to popular opinion, jungle—a mixture with few large trees but almost impenetrable undergrowth—is comparatively rare in Africa. It occurs on slopes that are too steep for rain forest, and along rivers and in swamps where poor drainage discourages the growth of many tropical trees.

Mangrove forest grows on tidal flats and coastal deltas invaded by salt water from the ocean, but not in freshwater areas. Mangrove swamps occur on the delta of the Niger River and along poorly drained coasts of the tropical forest, and also into the coastal areas of savanna regions. On the Atlantic side of the continent, mangrove forest extends, with interruptions, along the coasts of West and Equatorial Africa. On the eastern side, it can be found in areas from the Somali coast southward and along the coasts of Madagascar. The trees and their roots form a tangle of vegetation from 25 to 75 feet (8–23 meters) high. The bark of the mangrove, used for tanning, and boles used for construction are important products from coastal eastern Africa, but the West African mangrove species are less useful. Sandy coastal areas often have coconut palms, which are lacking in the poorly drained mangrove swamps.

Wildlife. Some mammals of the rain forest, such as the chimpanzees and the okapi, a small relative of the giraffe, are not found in other parts of Africa. The gorilla lives only in two areas: a western area along the coast of Equatorial Africa and an eastern area in the Congo Basin and adjoining montane forests. Buffaloes, antelopes, and wild pigs inhabit parts of the rain forest, but they are rarely seen. More obvious are the many species of monkeys, as well as squirrels and bats.

Birds are numerous, including pheasants, doves, kingfishers, hornbills, owls, and parrots. The reptiles and amphibians are represented by crocodiles, snakes, lizards, chameleons, toads, and frogs. The rock python is the largest snake of Africa, reaching a length of 25 feet (8 meters). The Goliath frog of western Equatorial Africa is the largest frog in the world, weighing up to 7 pounds (3 kg) or more. Although the cobra, vipers, and black mamba are poisonous, the African rain forest does not have a large number of venomous snakes, and deaths from snakebite are rare. As in other tropical areas, there are many insects. The *Anopheles* mosquito carries malaria, and the *Aëdes aegypti* mosquito, yellow fever. Tsetse flies spread African sleeping sickness among humans, and fatal forms of it among domesticated animals.

Savanna and Tropical Steppe Zones. The savanna and steppe zones south of the Sahara, in eastern Africa, and in south-central Africa form an almost continuous belt enclosing the tropical rain forest on the north, east, and south. Savanna and steppe cover more than a third of the continent's surface.

Climate. In the north and south these zones are transitional between the equatorial forests and the deserts. Rainfall usually occurs in the warmer months. It is abundant on the forest margins but decreases toward the deserts until, in the steppe areas, it is very light and irregular. Winters are generally without rainfall.

Along much of the Indian Ocean coast there are two rainy seasons, caused by monsoon winds that blow from the southwest toward Asia during the Northern Hemisphere summer and from the northeast during the winter. A major cause of the monsoons is the change from great heat and low atmospheric pressure in interior Asia in summer to cold and high pressure in winter. The changing pressure system alternately attracts and repels air masses from eastern Africa.

Temperatures in the drier parts of the northern savanna-steppe zone are very high, reaching well over 100°F (38°C) during March, April, and May, just before the summer rains. The rainy period has slightly lower temperatures, and in the winter temperatures are commonly in the 70°–90°F range (21°–32°C). Because of elevation and marine influences from the ocean, the eastern and southern zones are less hot. Many plateaus with savanna in East Africa have average temperatures in the 70's F (21°–26°C). Average temperatures in the southern savannas are intermediate between those of the north and those of the east.

Average annual rainfall in the savanna and steppe zones ranges from more than 40 inches (1,020 mm) on the forest margins but to about 10 inches (250 mm) near the deserts, but it is often highly variable from year to year. The rainy season in the northern savannas occurs usually in June, July, and August, and in the Southern Hemisphere savannas in December, January, and February.

Vegetation. Savanna grasslands near the rain forest have a luxuriant growth, with patches of forest. These combined forest and grassland areas, or tree savannas, occur where rainfall is between 35 and 50 inches (890–1,070 mm) and the dry season lasts three months or less. One band, about 500 miles (800 km) in width, extends across the northern savanna zone. Within this band is a gradation from dense to lighter growth as the length of the dry season increases northward. The vegetation varies also with slope, drainage, and soil types. In the south, much of another broad band has open stands of trees, so that it is often called woodland instead of savanna. Part of this open woodland and savanna has replaced the original forest as a result of burning, cutting, and cultivation. In East Africa are patches of tree savanna varying from grassland with scattered trees and a parklike appearance to scrubby areas with mixed palms and acacias and wooded areas with grasses and low shrubs. Several useful trees occur in these savanna areas. Oil palms grow in moister regions of West and Equatorial Africa. Some trees yield rubber, and the iroko and African ebony are used for timber. The kernels of the shea tree provide a solid white fat (shea butter), and the fruits of some trees are edible.

Less humid savanna areas, where the average annual rainfall drops to 35 or 25 inches (890–635 mm) and the drought period extends from three to six months, have fewer trees and many of these are small and flat-topped. Thorn trees and shrubs occur in patches. There is much grass cover during the rainy season, but during long periods of drought the dry grass and thorn bushes give many areas a semidesert appearance. The baobab, the largest tree, grows at lower elevations. The people use its fruit for food and, in some places store water in the large trunk as an emergency supply for the dry season. The branching and strange-looking doom palm has

Lofty Kilimanjaro, though only 200 miles (320 km) from the equator, is mantled with snow.

nuts (vegetable ivory) from which buttons are made.

A still drier savanna zone, with 15 to 25 inches (380–635 mm) of rainfall per year, has drought-resistant scrubby acacias, thorn bushes, and desert grasses. Except for periods of rain it has a dry and almost steppelike appearance. This dry savanna occurs in a belt south of the Sahara, in parts of the Eastern Horn region, and on the west coast of Southern Africa, where it widens toward the south. Gum arabic is obtained from the *Acacia senegal* in the north. In many places the grasses provide grazing for cattle and sheep, and goats browse on some of the shrubs. The low rainfall, hot summers, and sparse vegetation discourage tsetse flies. Whereas the dry savanna has many domesticated grazing animals, the tree savannas, because of tsetse flies, have almost none.

The dry savanna merges into a steppe zone, with about 10 inches (250 mm) of rainfall, as it nears the Sahara, the Somali desert in the Eastern Horn, and the Namib desert along the southwest coast. After periods of rain, grass and shrub growth is sufficient for the animals of nomadic peoples. The northern dry savanna lies within the marginal region known as the Sahel, receiving between 4 and 24 inches (100–600 mm) of rainfall a year.

Wildlife. The savannas of Africa have a greater variety of large animals than any other part of the world. The grasslands provide forage for antelopes of many kinds, ranging in size from the giant eland to the tiny duikers and dik-diks. Large herds of hartebeests, wildebeests (or gnus), gazelles, oribis, kobs, waterbucks, and reedbucks once roamed the savannas, but now they are restricted largely to less-inhabited areas and to game reserves. Other herbivorous animals are the giraffe, zebra, and rhinoceros. Elephants and the African buffalo have adapted to both forest and grassland areas, and the crocodile and hippopotamus inhabit riverine areas. Warthogs, baboons, porcupines, anteaters, and rats and other small rodents add to the variety of animal life. Some of the herbivores provide food for the well-known carnivorous animals—lions, leopards, several types of smaller cats, wild dogs, hyenas, and jackals. The hunting of elephants for ivory and of big game for food and trophies, as well as the killing of animals that are destructive to crops, has greatly reduced the numbers of large wild animals; in many settled farming areas they are now rare.

Most of Africa's 2,300 species of birds can be found in some part of the savanna and steppe zone. Ducks and geese, herons, rollers, bulbuls, warblers, sunbirds, weaverbirds, hawks, and owls have a wide range. Open grasslands have hunting birds such as the secretary bird, kites, eagles, bustards, and falcons, which are easily observed; but quails, hemipodes, pheasants, and francolins usually hide until disturbed. Vultures gather around the bodies of dead animals. Lakes and swamps attract cranes, ibises, snake birds, spoonbills, cormorants, storks, flamingos, and pelicans. Guinea fowls live in both grassland and wooded areas. The ostrich, now comparatively rare, formerly ranged in dry grassy areas from the northern Sahara to Southern Africa.

Tropical Desert Zone—Sahara. The Sahara, extending for 1,000 miles (1,600 km) from north to south, and for more than 3,000 miles (4,800 km) from east to west, is the world's largest desert. It is also one of the driest. Almost all parts of the Sahara receive less than 10 inches (250 mm) of rainfall per year, and the most barren areas less than one inch (25 mm). The southern margins

Africa's dwindling elephant herds are protected in havens such as the Amboseli Game Reserve in Kenya.

receive light summer rainfall from occasional storms that enter from the savanna zone, and the northern edges receive light winter rains from the adjoining Mediterranean zone. The center is almost rainless.

Temperatures are exceedingly high in summer because of the lack of clouds and humidity and the northern position of the sun. Azizia, south of Tripoli, recorded a temperature of 136.4°F (58°C) in the shade, and daytime summer temperatures of over 100°F (38°C) are common in many areas. The nights are cooler because of the rapid radiation of heat after sundown. Winter daytime temperatures are often pleasant, ranging in the 70's and 80's F (21°–32°C) with cool to chilly nights. The northern Sahara has occasional winter nights when the temperature drops to freezing; but the southern Sahara, like the adjoining steppe and savanna, is frostless.

Winds from the Sahara sometimes carry sand and dust across the Mediterranean to Europe. But the harmattan winds from the desert bring periods of drier weather to West Africa, making the otherwise hot and humid climate more bearable. Sea breezes, combined with the cool Canary Current, lower the temperatures where the Sahara meets the Atlantic Ocean.

Other Desert Areas. In Southern Africa, the west-coast Namib desert is extremely dry because winds there usually blow from the land to the sea. But the nearby cool ocean, plus frequent periods of fog, make the Namib less hot than the Sahara. Inland, the Kalahari, often called a desert, is mostly a semidesert or steppe area, with many sections receiving more than 15 inches (380 mm) of rain per year. The sandy

soils and lack of surface water, rather than extremely low rainfall, account for its barrenness. In the Eastern Horn, the driest spots have a desert climate, but steppe and savanna areas are more extensive.

Vegetation and Wildlife. Most desert areas have shrubs that can survive the drought, as well as grasses, weeds, and flowers that spring up after the rare periods of rain. Only a few areas, such as the gravel desert of the Tanezrouft in the central Sahara, are without vegetation. The northern parts of the Sahara have sufficient rainfall in the winter so that nomads migrate into the desert with their herds at this season. The southern margins have summer rains, attracting summer migrants from the savanna to the south. In the central Sahara the Ahaggar and Tibesti mountains have shrubs and grass that support a light pastoral population.

In the Kalahari the tsama melon (a watermelon) furnishes both food and drink, and shrubs and grass provide forage for domestic animals. The most important food plants of the African desert are the many varieties of date palms that grow in the oases of the northern Sahara. The date palm also supplies timber, and palm fronds are used for roofing and mats.

Through specialization, the desert mammals are able to cope with high temperatures, low water supply, and lack of shade trees. These mammals include gazelles, foxes, jerboas, rabbits, and hedgehogs. Sand grouse and coursers are restricted largely to the deserts, but oases often have many kinds of small birds as well as some larger ones that halt temporarily on their migrations.

The Mediterranean Zone—Northwestern Africa.
Coastal areas of northwestern Africa are influenced in winter by rain-bearing westerly winds that come from the Atlantic Ocean. Rainfall varies with the exposure of slopes to the winds and with distance from the coasts. Tangier receives 32 inches (810 mm) of rainfall per year; Algiers, 30 inches (760 mm); and other lowland places farther east and south, less than 20 inches (500 mm). The Atlas Mountains, however, receive heavier rain and, at higher elevations, snowfall. The whole region is dry in the summer, when the westerly winds and accompanying rains shift to the north. There are also periods in summer when dry winds blow from the Sahara. Hot spells may bring temperatures of more than 90°F (32°C). Casablanca and other cities on the western coast have cooler summers than Algiers and Tunis on the Mediterranean because of sea breezes and the cool Canary ocean current. In the winter, coastal areas have a cool climate, with temperatures in the 50's and 60's F (10°–21°C). The sunshine and the mild winters, together with coastal and mountain scenery, make the Mediterranean area attractive to visitors.

Cape of Good Hope. Cape Town and an adjoining coastal area in the extreme southwest of Africa also have a Mediterranean climate and also attract tourists. Winter, and the rainy season, come in June, July, and August in this Southern Hemisphere region. Rainfall is about 25 inches (635 mm) per year. Nearness to the ocean modifies the summer heat, but the interior Cape region is not as cool as the Atlantic coast of northwestern Africa.

Vegetation and Wildlife. Vegetation in the northern Mediterranean climatic area varies from an evergreen forest in the more humid areas to a thick growth of bushes and small trees (chaparral) and a scattered growth of shrubs and grass near the desert margins. The trees are similar to those of southern Europe. The olive and fig trees provide fruit, and cork is obtained from the cork oak. Showy bulbous plants include the narcissus, crocus, madonna lily, oleander, and chrysanthemum. On the dry high plateaus, alfa (esparto) grass is grown to make paper.

The small area of Mediterranean climate near the Cape of Good Hope has a wide range of vegetation types from the humid to the dry areas. The chaparral and scrubby forests are similar in appearance to those of Northern Africa, but there are no dense forests comparable to those of the Atlas Mountains. Ironwood, yellow wood laurel, kamassi, white pear, and clanwilliam cedar are the principal forest trees.

The Mediterranean region of Northern Africa has an animal life similar to that of Europe and Southwest Asia. The Barbary sheep, the Barbary ape, African red deer, ibex, and the jerboa (a rodent), are found north of the Sahara but not south of it. The southern Cape area, however, has animals of the same type as the nearby grasslands and forests.

Subtropical Grassland Zone. The High Veld of southernmost Africa is a zone of middle latitude steppe climate with subtropical grassland. The climate is the result of elevation, distance from the equator, dry cold winters, and light to moderate rainfall occurring mostly in the summer months. Summers (November, December, and January) are warm, with average temperatures above 70°F (21°C). Winters are cool to moderately cold, with occasional frosts during a three to six month period, depending on elevation. Flurries of snow occur at times. Because of the moderating effect of the nearby Indian Ocean, both winters and summers are milder than in the

A caravan skirts hills of sand in the Sahara. Camels were introduced from Arabia about the 1st century A.D.

© TOR EIGFLAND/BLACK STAR

In the Ruwenzori and other East African mountain areas, settlement occurs up to 7,000 feet (2,150 meters).

steppes of Asia and North America. Annual precipitation varies from about 40 inches (1,015 mm) in the higher and more humid east to about 15 inches (380 mm) on the margins of the Kalahari.

Typical vegetation in the more humid areas is tall grass, about 3 feet (90 cm) high, with no trees, but the growth is less dense and shorter in the subhumid areas. As the transition is made to the Kalahari on the west, the grassland gives way to areas of desert scrub.

Highland Zones. In the Horn and East Africa the mountains are within the tropics, but their elevation so reduces the temperatures that the climates and vegetation are not tropical in type. The daily averages of temperatures drop to 60° to 70°F (16°–21°C) on the high plateaus, giving them a perpetual springlike quality and making possible the cultivation of crops similar to those of temperate realms. Wheat and maize (corn) in East Africa and indigenous grains in the Ethiopian Highlands are examples of the crops cultivated. In East Africa, the tallest peaks of the Ruwenzori range and high volcanoes like Kilimanjaro have permanent snowfields. The highest peaks of the Ethiopian Highlands normally have no snowfall, but the mountains rise above the tree line and have alpine meadows.

Temperate rain forest occurs at high elevations where rainfall is from 40 to 80 inches (1,015–2,030 meters) per year, and there is no severe dry period. Growth is luxuriant, with a great variety of trees and a lower growth of banana plants, vines, ferns, and mosses. Highland (Arabica) coffee is native to the Ethiopian Highlands. Some of the indigenous trees used for timber are yellow woods, juniper, African camphor, olive, and African mahogany. Often there is a level of mountain bamboo before the higher grasslands are reached. The Ruwenzori

and other moist, high mountains have a series of vegetation zones corresponding to the changes in climate at different levels.

In Northern Africa the Atlas Mountains rise above the level of oak and chaparral to forests of pine and fir. In Southern Africa the Drakensberg also has temperate forests.

Madagascar. The island of Madagascar off the southeastern coast of continental Africa, has more savanna vegetation than other types because the large interior plateau receives only seasonal rainfall. But the wet coasts have tropical forest and swamp vegetation; the dry southwest, steppe and semidesert scrub; and the highest parts of the island, temperate forest.

Madagascar has been separated from the mainland of Africa for long geological ages and has developed a distinctive animal life. It has no monkeys, but many varieties of lemurs. The only large mammals are the hippopotamus and imported domesticated animals. Madagascar has no poisonous snakes. Other reptiles are abundant, however, as are birds, insects, and small mammals. Some of these are related to the animal types of Southeast Asia rather than of Africa.

BENJAMIN E. THOMAS
University of California, Los Angeles

3. Environmental Concerns

Africa is often described as a continent of low population density and abundant land resources. However, this assessment is mistaken, because it ignores the fact that much of the environment is so unfavorable to agriculture that it can support few people. The Sahara alone covers a quarter of the continent's surface. In large areas where average rainfall is more ample it is unreliable, and soils in general are poor. Certain parts of the continent do have enormous water resources;

these, linked to the best soils—as they are in parts of the Nile Valley—could greatly increase food supplies. Instead, because of too rapid population growth, declines in food production, and environmental degradation, famine has become endemic.

Population and Food Supply. The rate of population increase in Africa is the highest of any continent, ranging from 2% to as much as 4% a year in all but a few countries. Moreover, the average rate for the whole continent increased after the 1960's, in contrast to the global trend. Better nutrition and improved health care for many Africans, as well as increased fertility, contributed to this growth.

Meanwhile, however, agricultural output declined by 25%. Nearly every country in Black Africa, self-sufficient before independence, became a food importer. By 1975 production had fallen below the annual 140 kilograms (64 pounds) of cereals per capita determined by the Food and Agriculture Organization of the United Nations as the minimum for a healthy diet. Afterward, sub-Saharan output slipped below 100 kilograms (45 pounds).

Owing to natural limitations and demographic increase, over a dozen countries, with half the population of Black Africa, do not have enough usable agricultural land to sustain themselves. Millions of pastoralists have pressed into marginal farmland, and farmers into forests. Overgrazing and excessive tree cutting and bushfire clearing have caused widespread soil erosion as well as displacement of wildlife.

Drought, War, and Famine. Much of Africa's shortfall in food production has been attributed to chronic drought. But prolonged deficiencies of rainfall can be caused or intensified by dehumidification due to destruction of grasslands and forests. Moreover, where erosion is severe the resumption of rainfall may bring further erosion, rather than a renewal of the land's productive capacity.

Drought has been particularly calamitous in the Sahel, the southern margin of the Sahara, turning large areas of grazing land into desert. In this region an unfortunate combination of natural disaster and human pressure on the land has placed 30 million people at risk and maybe beyond the possibility of ever feeding themselves again.

The worst famines of recent times have been associated with wars, such as the global conflicts of the first half of the 20th century, and it is war that has been consuming three fourths of World Food Program relief in Africa. Civil unrest—affecting simultaneously as many as a third of the states of Black Africa, creating millions of refugees and disrupting the lives of scores of millions less direly affected—has exacerbated existing economic problems and consumed large chunks of limited import budgets. In Angola, for example, decades of strife beginning in the early 1960's reversed the country's food surpluses and

Refugees from drought in northeastern Africa shelter on a bleak plain that supports only a few hardy trees.

© TOM HARTWELL/BLACK STAR

destroyed its iron, diamond, and coffee industries. At various times since 1960, the Democratic Republic of the Congo (formerly, Zaire), Uganda, Chad, Mozambique, and others have fared little better under the curse of war.

Wilderness and Marine Resources. Humankind's enemies—population explosion, natural disasters, war, and unrestrained greed—have been ruthless with Africa's wilderness resources. Of particular concern to the world has been the depletion of the continent's animal life. The black rhinoceros is nearly extinct; the mountain gorilla is in great peril; and even the elephant, though still a million strong, is insecure. Meanwhile, Madagascar's treasure of unique species, such as the lemurs, is diminishing daily.

The human need for wood as well as agricultural land and stock pasturage is narrowing the range of many kinds of animals and plants. In Africa, wood and charcoal are still the prime source of heating and cooking energy for 90% of the people. For vegetation and wildlife the problem of habitat destruction is nowhere greater than in tropical forests, because of their density of species. Extensive African woodlands, as in Madagascar, have been cleared for farming or cut for lumber and firewood. Worldwide, tropical forests with an aggregate area the size of England and Wales are lost each year.

With the spread of pollutants, seas adjacent to Africa are becoming unviable. Industrial growth along the Red Sea coast, fueled by oil revenue, has put that body of water in danger. Offshore oil wells between the Niger Delta and the mouth of the Congo pollute the Gulf of Guinea, whose waters are also contaminated by untreated human sewage spewed out from expanding coastal centers and thousands of tons of pesticides reaching the sea because of largely unrestricted use inland. In addition, high-pollution petrochemical and other industries may be expected to develop in that area, further staining the ocean for many miles. Few of the safeguards common in Western industrial nations are employed in Africa to limit the effects of these polluters.

Protecting the Future. Of Africa's many environmental concerns, those related to food production are the most dangerous and persistent. Unrestrained population increase and human degradation of the environment, along with governmental neglect of agriculture or policies that actually discourage food production, seem only to abet a grim natural process. Insects, for example, may destroy an entire country's grain harvest. Locusts have struck hardest in the drought-ridden Sahel, where in one year four species of these grasshoppers attacked crops simultaneously.

Insufficient food production has greatly increased the financial burdens of African countries. Slim resources for national development are increasingly pared down by food imports and debt payments. Imported grain is feeding a fourth of the continent's population. A third of the foreign-exchange earnings of African states that do not export oil is spent on debt service, and international lending agencies have had to reschedule most of it.

Yet despite this gloomy picture Africa can draw encouragement from Third World models, including its own. India and China, for example, in the face of grievous economic obstacles succeeded in growing enough food to supply populations greater than that of all Africa. Botswana launched

a famine relief program that worked. Zimbabwe, aided by rain and strong leadership, reversed its food production decline. Meanwhile, the states of Northern Africa have been working in unison to create a green belt from the Nile to the Atlantic.

Modern cooking stoves that reduce wood use by 500% can save whole forests. Tourist industry revenues, if not international goodwill, can rescue East Africa's wildlife preserves, and debt relief contingent on wilderness protection can help preserve vast forests and grasslands. Primary health care, clean water, and population control are achievable goals. Even the problem of famine, which generally is due to a breakdown in the system of food distribution, rather than of food production, can be made to yield to political and technical solutions.

The obstacles to overcoming Africa's environmental problems are formidable, but many leaders are finally linking economic decline with environmental degradation. This is the important first step toward the proper management of resources. Africa's wealth in oil, minerals, and many agricultural commodities is its promise for the future. The world's need for these assets will keep Africa a vital part of the global village.

LATHARDUS GOGGINS, *University of Akron*

THE ECONOMY

Africa is rich in mineral wealth and energy resources and possesses much potentially good arable land. But for historical reasons, and because of its climate and geography, the continent has been slow to develop the kind of modern industrial economy and the resulting commercial relations that operate in most of the world.

In the international economic system, Africa for centuries was primarily a resource reservoir on the one hand, and a market on the other, for the far more developed countries of Europe and North America. With the transformation of most of the African colonial territories into independent states by the early 1960s, the governments of the new nations sought to achieve economic as well as political independence and to raise the living standards of their people by creating urban-industrial societies of their own. Meanwhile, their economies continued to function on two levels: traditional subsistence production of goods for self-consumption; and modern exchange production of goods for sale to others. Many Africans participate in both sectors, for example, as subsistence farmers who sell a small surplus locally, or as city wage earners whose families grow food for themselves at home in the countryside.

The primary source of wealth for Africa has remained the output of agricultural and mineral products. Manufacturing industries have been developed, but slowly and on a small scale. The emphasis on extractive activity for export earnings has meant that Africa depends heavily on world demand for its raw materials and thus favorable prices for these commodities, but price levels fluctuate widely. Perhaps the most volatile prices are those of agricultural products such as coffee and cocoa. For these commodities the basic problem often is large and uncontrolled surpluses. African nations have joined with other primary producers, notably in the United Nations Conference on Trade and Development (UNCTAD), to pressure the richer states for price-support programs.

4. Traditional Land Use

The use made of the land by the peoples of Africa depends largely on topographical, climatic, vegetational, and soil conditions. The widely different ways in which land is used are further explained by differences in accessibility and in commercial opportunities, and by the varied cultural characteristics of the people.

Most of Africa's peoples occasionally hunt and gather wild plant food. However, this is a permanent mode of life for only a decreasing few. The Pygmies of the Congo forests hunt and trade part of their catch with their farming neighbors. San (Bushmen) who still preserve their traditional ways, subsist on what they hunt and collect in the semiarid Kalahari. Several peoples along the west coast live primarily by fishing, as do communities along the upper Niger River, the Congo and Uele rivers, near some of the Great Lakes, and in swamp areas.

Agriculture, in the broad sense that includes livestock raising, is nearly everywhere the principal occupation and the basis of livelihood. It would be an undue simplification to divide farmers into cultivators and pastoralists, since many Africans combine the growing of crops with the rearing of livestock. Nevertheless some justification does exist for such a division. People who are primarily pastoralists must move in search of food and water as the needs of their animals require; they may, therefore, be forced to wander over extensive areas, especially where the dry season is long and intense. Cultivators, by contrast, are directly dependent on the climatic and soil conditions of their farmlands, though within limits they may modify their production environment by such methods as manuring, crop rotation, and irrigation.

Crop Cultivation. Over large parts of tropical Africa shifting cultivation, or "bush fallowing," prevails. A plot is cleared of the natural vegetation and farmed for one or two seasons; it is then abandoned when soil fertility has declined or when the growth of crops is checked by the growth of weeds. This simple, if primitive, system is adequate provided that land is plentiful and not too many people are competing for it. Where soils are more fertile, or where animal manure is available for the fields, more permanent and intensive cultivation is possible.

In the drier areas, cultivation is restricted to those districts with available water. Farming is intensive in the oases of the desert and in some parts of the valleys of rivers like the Nile and the Orange. Intensive horticulture is practiced in the northwest and near the Cape of Good Hope. Commercial mixed farming (crops and livestock) of an extensive nature is practiced in the grassland areas of Southern Africa and in the highlands of East Africa. But in nearly all parts of Africa farmers have to face many special difficulties, such as unreliable rainfall and swarming locusts. Crop cultivation therefore often proves hazardous.

Throughout the grain-producing areas of Africa the mode of agriculture and the nature of the diet are similar. The chief agricultural implements are the hoe—short-handled in most places but long-handled in some areas—and the long knife, called a *matchet* in West Africa and a *panga* in the east. Use of the plow pulled by oxen is less common. In a few places the digging stick, with or without a metal tip, is still found.

In most areas the heavy work of clearing the land is done by men, who also prepare the fields and may even do the planting. The women then take over the tasks of weeding, harvesting, and carrying the grain to the homestead or to the drying platforms. The harvest is stored in granaries that generally resemble small houses, usually built on platforms to give some protection from rats and other pests.

Except for rice, which is cooked whole, grain in Africa is ground, traditionally by hand on rectangular millstones but today often by hand-operated mills or even by power mills at the village

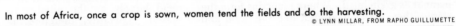

In most of Africa, once a crop is sown, women tend the fields and do the harvesting.
© LYNN MILLAR, FROM RAPHO GUILLUMETTE

Fulani pause with humpbacked cattle in search of forage.   Pastoralism is a way of life for many African peoples.

center. The flour is cooked into a thick porridge that provides most of the calories of African diets in the grain belt. The porridge is served with a sauce prepared of oils, meats (usually chicken, goat, or fish), and vegetables.

Where subsistence is based on root crops, their culture may impose additional work on the men of the community, who must, in shallow soil, make 2-foot (0.6-meter) mounds in which to grow yams or smaller mounds for other roots. The roots are either cooked and mashed or dried and made into flour that is treated in the same manner as grain meal. Where plantains form the staple, they are cooked and, like the grain and roots, made into porridge and eaten with a sauce.

Livestock Raising. Pastoralism is common throughout Africa, despite the widespread incidence of animal diseases. Tsetse flies, for example, which infest the wet-forest regions except at higher elevations, cause fatal forms of animal African sleeping sickness in cattle and horses.

Thus pastoralism is especially characteristic of the drier parts of the continent, where tsetse flies are absent and where animals often can survive even though crops cannot be grown. If necessary the animals can be driven over great distances in search of fodder and water. The migrations of livestock often follow definite routes and take place within strictly defined districts. They play an important part in the social as well as economic life of predominantly pastoral peoples such as the Masai of East Africa, the Fulani of West Africa, and the Bedouin of the Sahara.

Relatively few Africans depend on their cattle for food. Although some pastoralists tap blood from the neck veins of their cattle and mix it with sour milk for consumption, studies by food economists, dietitians, and geographers indicate that blood can supply at most a few hundred calories

a week. Milk and butter are much more important in the diet of these herders, who seldom slaughter their animals for meat.

In many African societies the possession of animals is regarded as an indication of wealth, and the exchange of beasts is an essential part of various transactions, including the payment of "bride wealth" by the family of the groom to that of the bride. Cattle also are often surrounded by religious and magical beliefs and practices, and are to be slaughtered only on ceremonial occasions. An individual's status in society may depend largely on the number of animals possessed. Quantity, therefore, is preferred to quality, and little attention is given to improved breeding. Thus in many areas the land has to support far more livestock than it should, and overgrazing, soil erosion, and the diminution of water supplies due to falling water tables are evident in the most heavily overstocked districts. The cattle often are emaciated, especially toward the end of the dry season when supplies of water and fodder are at a minimum. Under such circumstances they are particularly susceptible to diseases.

However, the livestock picture has its brighter side. Some Africans show a particular appreciation of improved methods of stock rearing, while increased markets for meat and milk, as well as hides and skins, have encouraged a more commercial attitude toward the raising of livestock. The most successful commercial stock raising is, nevertheless, in the hands of whites. The contrast between overgrazed African rangelands and the well-maintained, lush pastures of white ranches and dairy farms is striking in some sub-Saharan countries where European farmers remain.

Forest Use. About 13% of the land surface of Africa is wooded. Nearly half of this area is dense equatorial forest and the remainder is more open savanna woodland, together with the limited forests of the Mediterranean zone and the temperate forests of the higher parts of East and Southern Africa. Forests are important as a source of wood fuel as well as timber and other products; and trees help bind the soil together, checking erosion.

The shifting-cultivation system of farming over much of tropical Africa is an expensive use of forestlands. The new vegetation that grows after the farmer has cleared trees, planted crops for a few years, and then moved on is of poor quality compared with the original. Consequently, the loss of thousands of square miles of virgin forest annually to temporary cultivation is extremely serious. Although many governments try to maintain an adequate forest cover by appropriate legislation and by the establishment of forest reserves, this policy becomes increasingly difficult to implement as population continues to grow and intensifies pressure on the land available for cultivation.

See also the section "Health" in this article.

ROBERT W. STEEL
University of Liverpool

5. The Emergence of Modern Economic Systems

Modern economic systems have had a short history in Africa. South of the Sahara before 1880 there were four main points of contact with the outside world: the ancient trans-Saharan trade between the Western Sudan and Mediterranean Africa; European trading posts on the west coast; Arab settlements on the east coast; and European colonization at the southern tip of the continent. Foreign goods and ideas came into sub-Saharan Africa for centuries from these points of entry, but except for the introduction of new crops, especially root crops from the Americas, they made little impact on the means by which most people gained their livelihood. Africa remained primarily a continent of subsistence production.

The three centuries of European dealings with sub-Saharan Africa had not required movement into the interior, for contact had been based mainly on the coastal trade in slaves. When Europe carved up Africa in the latter part of the 19th century, it found economic systems unchanged for as long as people could remember. In most of the continent modern economic development began only after 1900.

Colonial Development. It is commonly believed that economic development was slow in most of Africa before World War II. That is not true. The rate of economic change from 1900 to 1930 was extraordinarily rapid in most territories, especially during the 1920s. The depression of the 1930s slowed it temporarily, but the record over the whole period from 1900 to 1960 is one of impressive achievement. Many of the newly independent countries started with a good base for subsequent development.

It is hard to measure long-term rates of economic growth in Africa because of inadequate statistics. Figures for national income over a long period exist in only a few countries. However, in the case of South Africa, between 1911 and the mid-1950s the national output grew at a rate of about 4.5% a year. In the Belgian Congo (Democratic Republic of the Congo) from 1920 to the mid-1950s, the annual figure was about 4%. These are among the highest growth rates in the world for that period. Export statistics, a much less reliable indicator of economic growth, are the only available means of measuring long-term performance in the rest of Africa. They also tell a story of rapid expansion in many African countries. In the decade before World War I the value of exports more than quadrupled in the Gold Coast (Ghana), Kenya, and Tanganyika; it rose more than sixfold in Nyasaland (Malawi) and more than tenfold in Uganda. During the 1920s export values at least doubled everywhere. They tripled in Northern Rhodesia (Zambia), Uganda, and Tanganyika, quadrupled in Kenya, increased fivefold in French Equatorial Africa and the Belgian Congo, rose by a factor of 8 in French West Africa, and jumped by over 15 in Nigeria.

After a sharp contraction in the 1930s, the rhythm of growth was recaptured and surpassed in the years after World War II. The most rapid development occurred during the years 1949–1954, but boom conditions persisted through most of the 1950s. More Africans came into the money economy, either as wage earners or cash crop growers; numbers in paid employment doubled in many countries. Export earnings climbed to new heights. In many African countries, exports were between 10 and 15 times greater in value in the late 1950s than they had been in the late 1930s, whereas general price levels had risen by only about 3 times over the same period. Increases in investment were also greater than ever before. In French Africa, for example, more public capital assistance was received from France between 1947 and 1958 than in the previous 50 years of French rule.

African economic performance during these years was on the whole better than that in most other underdeveloped areas. Rates of gross capital formation, the proportion of national income invested in fixed capital, exceeded 40% in the Rhodesias (Zambia and Zimbabwe) during some years, were in the neighborhood of 30% in the Belgian Congo in the early 1950s, and were less than 15% in only a few countries. These are respectable rates of capital formation, higher than are commonly found in countries in early stages of economic development.

The pace of expansion slowed after 1958. Prices of coffee, cocoa, and some other major African exports fell sharply on world markets. Political independence or turbulence led to hesitancy among private investors, and in some cases to a large-scale flight of capital. A mass outflow of capital occurred in the Belgian Congo in 1959–1960 and in South Africa in 1959. Less severe loss of capital took place elsewhere. The result was some slowdown of economic activity, although continued increases in the volume of exports in most countries offset price declines and maintained the level of export earnings. Considering the unfavorable price picture for African exports during the years 1958–1962, and the fact that this period witnessed political transformations without parallel, it is remarkable that the economic transition was as smooth as it was.

The Two Money Economies. The process of economic development in Africa involved either the activation of idle resources or the transfer of resources out of subsistence agriculture into money-earning activity. Despite much diversity, two types of modern exchange economies arose in the colonial period: those that were based on mining, expatriate agricultural production, or both; and those that were based on peasant African pro-

© MARK BOULTON/PHOTO RESEARCHERS

Mechanized agriculture is slowly taking hold in Africa. The seed-hungry birds in this rice field are a major pest.

duction of cash crops. Typical of the countries in the first group were those in Northern and Southern Africa. Most of West Africa fell into the second category.

The two contrasting types of economies are simplified models, however, into which not all countries can easily be fitted. French Guinea, for example, had a mineral export sector based on foreign investment; its main export crop, coffee, was produced by African peasants, but its bananas were grown for export by expatriate planters. Nonetheless, the broad distinction between mining–expatriate agriculture economies and peasant-producer systems is useful. The differences can be seen in several indices.

(1) The number of Europeans tended to be much greater in the first type. Thus the ratio of Europeans to Africans was 1 to 3 in South Africa and 1 to 10 in Southern Rhodesia (Zimbabwe), whereas it was insignificant in the second type: 15,000 Europeans and about 36 million Africans in Nigeria, 7,000 Europeans and nearly 7 million Africans in Ghana, 9,000 Europeans and 2.8 million Africans in Nyasaland.

(2) Most capital investment in the colonial period was concentrated in the mining–expatriate agriculture economies. South Africa received 42% of the total foreign investment in sub-Saharan Africa between 1880 and 1936, the two Rhodesias another 18%, and the Belgian Congo 11%. The Gold Coast and the French West African areas received less than 3% each.

(3) With regard to the numbers of wage earners, the same divisions are seen. In South Africa and Southern Rhodesia over one fourth of the African population was in "modern" paid employment; in Kenya, Northern Rhodesia, and the Congo the proportion was about 10%. In most of the rest of the continent it was below 5%.

(4) The clearest indicator of the essential differences between the two groups of economies is national income distribution. In South Africa, Northern Rhodesia, Kenya, and the Congo, less than one third of the total money income generated was African income. In the peasant-producer countries of West Africa and in Uganda, African incomes were about two thirds of total money income. At the same time, in the mining–expatriate agriculture economies, between 65% and 90% of all money income accruing to Africans came from wage earning. In Uganda, on the other hand, only about 25% of African money income was derived from wages, and in the Gold Coast probably less than 20%.

These differences are significant. The economies resting on a mining or expatriate agricultural base were generally richer and more industrialized. But the peasant-producer countries had a more even distribution of incomes, wider participation of Africans in economic decision-making, and more political experience. These economies were more resilient, at least in being less exposed to withdrawal of foreign skill and capital.

ELLIOT J. BERG
Georgetown University

6. Development in the Independence Era

In the great majority of African countries, per capita and personal income is low and the livelihood of most of the people derives from agriculture—farming and herding. About half of the agriculturalists have little contact with the money economy. Because African leaders have expressed concern about improving average living standards, they must induce the people to change traditional ways of living and working as rapidly as possible in order to meet increased expectations with regard to education, housing, and diet.

From the 1960's on, many more Africans did in fact enter the money economy, both by growing cash crops and by working for pay in extractive and related processing industries, in commerce and services, and in government. However, African countries have remained short of highly trained people in almost every endeavor. More teachers are needed, as are specialists in agriculture, business management, and government economic planning and implementation. In fact, many countries have been unable to utilize significant increases in capital because of insufficient skilled personnel, both technical and administrative.

Government assistance has been needed to help small farmers increase production and to develop the means of transporting produce to market. The tradition-bound agricultural economies have lacked personnel and experience to diversify or to discover new business opportunities. It has been difficult to get such economies moving, since the rate of increase in agricultural output has been slow to increase—insufficient in many cases to meet the rising demands of ever-larger populations. Moreover, the effects of the production lag have been made worse by inefficient food distribution and marketing systems. As a result, strong inflationary pressures have arisen in some African countries, especially where large imports of food have been required because of population increases or poor harvests. If the government also follows a policy of economic expansion by increasing expenditures while the growth of its revenues is slow, there is still more inflationary pressure. The resulting budget deficits and money-supply expansion produce inflated domestic demand, increased imports, and declining foreign-exchange reserves, particularly if export receipts are stagnant.

The problem of budget deficits is not easily solved. In countries whose entire economies depend on one or two export crops, efforts have been made to diversify, but this is not always an easy task. For example, Egypt, which depended on cotton exports for revenue and needed alternative export products, was limited by a lack of raw materials and energy supplies. In some countries in a similar predicament, agricultural production can be increased, but for certain crops greater output only reduces world prices because of a relatively inelastic demand.

Many countries attempt to industrialize in order to offset the need for foreign imports and thus equalize the balance of trade. This was tried, for example, in Egypt, which from about 1960 emphasized factory construction. Despite this effort, Egypt, which had to import food and raw materials, still experienced deficits in its balance of trade. Interestingly, a more equitable land distribution did not materially increase productivity, although politically the program was popular. But the redistribution of land noticeably increased the earnings of the poor peasant class, and this will ultimately increase the size of the market. Expansion of the domestic market is of extreme importance, since a major obstacle to the growth of industry is a market restricted by low purchasing power.

Industrialization of underdeveloped countries does not, however, always produce significant progress toward an exchange economy. For even though the introduction of modern industries in such countries will raise wage levels, overall employment may not increase markedly.

© BLAIR SEITZ/PHOTO RESEARCHERS

Farmers winnow teff, an Ethiopian millet. The first sub-Saharan grain growers domesticated native grasses.

Agriculture. Despite rapid industrialization after the early 1960's, some 70% of the African population still is rural, and three fourths of the rural workers are cultivators. About two thirds of the cultivated land is devoted to subsistence production of grains, roots, and fruits. Cattle are raised mainly outside the money economy as well.

Africa's soil is therefore its most important natural resource, yet it does not compare favorably in fertility with the soils of other continents. With notable exceptions, such as the Nile Valley, the alluvial soils of the continent are not so rich and extensive as such soils are elsewhere. Nor are the tropical savanna and steppe soils comparable in quality to similar soils in the middle latitudes. African soils must be enriched and conserved if the key agricultural sectors of the continent's struggling economies are to flourish and expand.

Subsistence Agriculture. At the subsistence level, agriculture in Africa forms several broad patterns. The patterns of pastoral activity and crop cultivation overlap.

Camels are raised throughout the inhabited Sahara and its fringes, both north and south, and in the Eastern Horn as well. A cattle belt, or corridor, extending across the widest part of the continent from the Atlantic Ocean to the Nile between the desert and the forests, turns south along the Nile; from Lake Victoria it runs both east and south, eventually swinging back to the Atlantic between the forests of the Congo region on the north and the Kalahari "thirstland" on the south. In much of the cattle area, however, the herds do not actually form the subsistence base, but rather the basis of prestige and wealth. These pastoralists are reluctant to kill their animals but may exchange their dairy products for grain. Some starchy staple enters the diet of almost all African herders.

The grain belt forms a crescent overlapping the herding areas. Along the Mediterranean are grown Eurasian grains—wheat and barley—but south of the Sahara the cereals are primarily African in origin. A native rice, only partly replaced by the preferred Asian rice, is cultivated in the high-rainfall region of West Africa. Eastward from the Senegambia area, rice gives way as a staple crop to sorghum and millet. Still father east, in the southern Nilotic Sudan and the Eastern Horn, the primary grains are eleusine, teff, and fonio. As one turns south, east of Lake Victoria, maize (corn) and sorghum become the staples and, except for pearl millet in the southern Congo region and a few other places, they remain the basic food all the way to the southern end of the continent. The staple of Madagascar is rice.

The subsistence area based on roots forms a rough circle in the Congo region and includes a strip extending along the Guinea coast. In these regions the crops are yams, cassava (manioc), taro, sweet potatoes, and other tubers.

In parts of the Sahara dates are a staple. In sections of East Africa, in a zone across Equatorial Africa, and in a few spots on the west coast, plantain bananas are the basic food.

In order to improve the living standards of subsistence farmers, African governments are trying to show them new techniques of cultivation, including the use of fertilizers and machines. Farmers are sometimes regrouped and resettled on better soil, and crop rotation and mixed farming have been introduced to maintain soil fertility.

In addition, there is much interest in cooperative techniques in farming, such as the communal use of machines and services, and also in marketing. The aim of many of the agricultural segments of national development plans and programs is to increase such cooperation. This, it is hoped, will bring about a modest but steady increase in the cash incomes of individual farmers and make it possible to improve health, education, and other social services in the villages.

Export Crops. Where the agricultural sector is not completely given over to subsistence food production or stock raising, most countries have tended to concentrate on one or two crops for export. In many countries emphasis in agricultural expansion has been on export crops rather than on higher production of food for local consumption.

The value of agricultural exports determines to a large extent the economic growth of most African countries. They rely to an overwhelming degree on the returns from these exports for funds to finance their imports and their economic development plans. Not only do world prices of these products fluctuate widely—particularly for cocoa and coffee, though for sugar, rubber, and cotton as well—but also some of the consumer countries have aggravated the problem by imposing high excise taxes on commodities like coffee, thus decreasing the demand.

Many attempts have been made to assist the producer countries. The International Coffee Organization (ICO), for example, has set world quotas for producers in order to stabilize prices. The United Nations has been seeking methods that would ensure stable export earnings either through agreements on prices, quotas, and buffer stocks or through some kind of financial arrangements that would guarantee minimum annual incomes from commodity exports.

In order to retain their share of the market at favorable price levels, almost all African coun-

Large yams and other tubers, rather than grains, are dietary staples in most of Africa's wet-forest zone.

© WILLIAM CAMPBELL/SYGMA

Tea carpets a plantation in East Africa. It was introduced by the British, who still buy much of the crop.

tries have become associated with the European Economic Community (EEC), or Common Market. Under the Lomé Conventions, first signed in 1975, most of their agricultural export commodities were given duty-free entry to the EEC.

Among the more important cash crops, Africa produces more than half the world's cocoa, which is especially important to West Africa; more than a fifth of the coffee (grown mostly in East Africa and the Horn); about a fifth of the peanuts (West and Equatorial Africa) and palm oil (West Africa), and a tenth of the tea (East Africa). Kenya alone supplies four fifths of the world's pyrethrum, an ingredient of insecticides. In addition Africa is a leading producer of cashews, cloves, sesame seed, and sisal.

Some products for which Africa does not account for much of the total world output are nonetheless important, even dominant, in regional or national economies. Among these are coconuts (on the east coast), cotton (Nile Valley), rubber (West Africa), and sugarcane (Southern Africa, the Nile Valley, and the Mascarene Islands—Mauritius and Réunion). Although Africa produces only about 5% of the world's maize, that grain is a major commercial as well as subsistence crop in large parts of the continent.

Livestock. Animals are raised everywhere in the inhabited parts of Africa. The most common livestock are cattle, sheep, goats, and poultry. Pigs are important only in non-Islamic areas, because Muslims do not eat pork.

The distribution of cattle is restricted by the prevalence of tsetse flies in the rain forest and wetter savanna lands. The cattle are mainly of two kinds: the indigenous breeds, frequently humped and common in tropical Africa; and introduced varieties, characteristic of Northern and Southern Africa. Settled cultivators may keep cattle as a supplementary investment of land, labor, and food, because the animals can be quickly converted to meat or cash when needed. Commercial cattle ranching is practiced chiefly in Southern Africa.

Sheep are more widely distributed than cattle because they can tolerate drier conditions. They are particularly numerous in the drier parts of the Atlas Mountains in the northwest and in the savanna areas of tropical Africa. In the southern grasslands European breeds, including the merino, were introduced and have given rise to an important wool trade. Goats are raised generally in the same areas as sheep but are especially characteristic of the region near the Mediterranean Sea.

In the Sahara, the camel is not only the beast of burden but also a supplier of milk, hair, and skin. The relative scarcity of horses in Africa impeded European penetration of the interior before the age of railroads.

Forestry. Many of the less-developed tropical African countries have stressed the necessity of surveying forest resources and determining the potentials for sawn timber, plywood, and paper and pulp industries. In many areas the forests are inland, however, and significant exploitation would require expansion of transport facilities.

Exporting sawn timber or plywood rather than unconverted logs, is economically advantageous, for the waste products of the sawmills can be used as fuel in making steam or electricity, which can be utilized in factories. Conversion of the logs into sawn timber also saves shipping space and makes the wood easier to grade.

African forests have been greatly reduced in size through the years. Their replacement by farms has reduced the water supply and the fertility of the soil besides depleting some valuable timber species. Although exploitation is still

261

To procure logs of this size from the rain forest involves selective tree felling, often with low yields.

Fishermen mending nets, before setting out to sea. Fish is a valuable supplement to protein-poor diets in Africa.

proceeding at a faster pace than replacement, government leaders are now aware of the need to expand forest reserve areas, to use sustained-yield schemes, and to maintain competent forestry departments.

Much of Africa's tree cover is not suitable for lumbering—for example, in the savanna belt below the Sahara and north of the coastal areas in West Africa. However, wood in Africa is used principally for fuel, and trees everywhere are cut for that purpose.

The more southerly areas of West Africa and the coastal areas of Equatorial Africa are rich in softwoods—chiefly okoumé—that are exploited for lumber and plywood. Tropical hardwood production in Africa is mainly in those areas as well, with cabinet varieties (mahogany, ebony, rosewood, and satinwood) the chief exports. Although much of the southern part of the continent is poor in natural forest resources, extensive plantings of pine, eucalyptus, and other species have made South Africa relatively self-sufficient in timber for construction, furniture, pulp, and paper.

African forests yield many products other than wood. One of the most important trees is the oil palm, which is found wild in groves besides being cultivated on plantations. Oil from the pulp is used locally for cooking and is exported as an ingredient of margarine and other foods. The kernel oil is used in Africa and overseas for soapmaking. The sap from the trunk ferments by itself into palm wine, a popular intoxicating beverage in parts of the continent. Rubber trees, both wild and cultivated, are tapped for the export trade, and African forests produces various gums for which demand is limited outside the continent. In the northwest, cork is stripped from the cork oak. In addition, certain cultivated trees such as the cacao grow best in cleared areas within the forest.

Fisheries. Africans engage in ocean, lake, and river fishing to supply local needs. However, only limited amounts of fish and related products

Oil flows across Saharan lands once thought to be useless.   Excess gas burns off wells in the distance.

are processed, and large population groups inland rely on imports. Although coastal fishing resources are extensive, they are not used intensively by Africans because of the limited number of larger fishing vessels available and the lack of storage and processing facilities in much of tropical Africa. Much of the ocean fishing is done by foreign fleets, and in some areas marine resources are in danger of depletion.

Fisheries are best developed off the southeastern coast. The catch is of high quality and is exported to all parts of the world. Rock lobster products, canned pilchards, and fish meal and oil head the list of exports.

A second major area of marine fishing is the coast of West Africa. Some West African countries also have established internal fishing industries and fish farms along lakes, in which tilapias, in particular, are raised.

Emphasis in tropical Africa has been placed on the need to popularize such unfamiliar protein-rich processed products as fish flour. This emphasis is needed because of a growing need for protein foods and the technical and economic problems in preserving and transporting fish.

Energy. Accessibility, at moderate cost, of the energy needed for industrial development is essential to the growth of Africa's economy. The continent measures very low in utilized energy per capita, although overseas countries and international agencies have provided funds to remedy this situation.

Although Africa possesses waterpower resources estimated at 40% of the world's total, it was not until the 1950's and 1960's that the building of major hydroelectric projects was undertaken to any great extent. But the projects completed from then onward form only a small percentage of the world output of hydroelectric energy. Moreover, huge dams such as the Aswan on the Nile River, the Akosombo on the Volta, the Inga on the lower Congo, and the Kariba and Cabora Bassa on the Zambezi are economically justified only when sufficient demand exists for irrigation or for the use of electric power in industrial development or mining. Thus Kariba, for example, supplies energy for large-scale copper mining.

Much of Africa's electricity is generated by hydroelectric power stations, because most of the known coal deposits on the continent are of poor quality. The generation of thermal power for electricity is most extensive in South Africa, which has sufficient and cheap coal resources for it. Some high-quality coal is found elsewhere in Southern Africa, and inferior-quality reserves in West, Equatorial, and Northern Africa.

The Sahara contains major areas of petroleum and natural-gas production. Output also is substantial off the coasts of several countries from the Niger Delta to the mouth of the Congo. Exploration in many areas, especially along the coasts, continues. However, much of Africa is basement rock, where petroleum is not likely to be found.

Fissionable raw materials of significant amounts exist in Southern Africa, Equatorial Africa, and the Sahara. These resources are not important now for energy production but may be so in the future.

Africa produces less than 10% of the world's oil, but in the major producing countries crude petroleum and its products are the leading export. South Africa accounts for almost all of the continent's coal production and is a leading international source of uranium.

Mining. Although some African countries rely on their nonenergy minerals for nearly all of their income and some are world leaders in the minerals they produce, in fact only a few countries account for a high percentage of Africa's total value of mineral production. In some countries no mineral resources of consequence have been found, and in others they are minor. Thus it is wise, when considering the continent as a whole, not to overestimate the importance of such mineral resources. Much long-range study and exploration are needed to determine more

Copper, Africa's "red gold," is mined chiefly on the Congo-Zambezi watershed.

completely the nature and amounts of available nonenergy mineral reserves so that they can be properly utilized for the maximum benefit of the economies of which they are a part.

Countries in Northern and East Africa are generally poor in these resources, whereas most in Southern Africa are exceptionally well endowed. South Africa, for example, mines about half of the world's gold, nearly seven eighths of the platinum produced by non-Communist countries, and a substantial proportion of the international supply of platinum, chromium ore, antimony, and manganese, besides being the leading source of gem diamonds.

Africa accounts for about two thirds of the world output of natural diamonds, with the Congo Basin the continent's primary source of industrial stones. Several West African countries are important diamond producers, as are others in Southern Africa besides South Africa itself. About two fifths of the world's cobalt comes from Africa, chiefly the Congo-Zambezi watershed. The cobalt is associated with copper produced in the same area, accounting for the greater part of Africa's one sixth of world copper production. The continent is the source of three tenths or more of manganese and chromium ores, with major production in western Equatorial Africa for manganese and in the highlands between the Zambezi and Limpopo rivers for chromium, both secondary to South Africa's output. West Africa is rich in bauxite, the source of aluminum, and provides one sixth of the world demand. Northern Africa's chief mineral, other than petroleum, is phosphate, and that region produces more than half of the continent's quarter share of global production. With the exception of South Africa, most of the African output of nonenergy minerals is exported overseas after the primary processing stage, rather than being consumed by domestic industry.

An important spur to economic development in many underdeveloped areas of the world is an iron and steel industry. This industry exists in South Africa and Zimbabwe, which have significant deposits of iron ore and the coal required for smelting it. Some of Africa's iron-ore reserves, as in West Africa, are of a high grade and contribute substantially to the producing countries' exports, but not to local manufacturing. Vast iron-ore deposits are unworked for lack of capital, transportation, and overseas markets.

Manufacturing. Capital is in very short supply in African countries. The major foreign investments made in the past were in the exploitation and export of raw materials and were of limited value to the development of domestic industry. Little has gone into domestic manufacturing and commercial enterprise, which could develop the Africans' economic and technical capacity. The main exception has been the significant foreign private investment in the industry of South Africa, already a developed country.

Part of the hesitancy of foreign investors has been due to the hostile attitude of some African countries to private foreign investment, part to fear of expropriation, and part to the world economic environment. Many industrial projects in Africa are not so profitable as alternative investment either in the industrialized world or in other areas of the less-developed world.

The markets for some products are very small, since the African economies have a large subsistence sector. Production of consumer goods to replace imports is costly, because the scale of output is less than optimal. Thus survival would depend on the imposition of very high tariffs to protect the infant industries. This, of course, would raise the prices for the Africans and further limit the size of the market. Another reason for the high costs of producing consumer goods is the low productivity of the inadequately trained labor force. Still another is the high cost of capital because of relative scarcity. As a consequence, African manufacturers could not compete in world markets. The same problems that pertain to the development of light industries in Africa also hinder the growth of the continent's heavy industries.

A suggested answer is economic integration —regional common markets within an African common market—for the purpose of centralized production with wide distribution. For example, radios could be manufactured in Tanzania for its own market and also to supply Kenya, Uganda, Malawi, and others. Or Zambia could refine copper for export to the entire African market instead of shipping only partly processed copper abroad for further processing in Europe.

Excluding South Africa, where manufacturing is well developed, industry in Africa represents only about 1% of the world total as measured in value added by manufacturing. Even that small share is concentrated in a few countries of Northern and West Africa.

About 60% of the value added comes from light industries, such as food, beverage, and tobacco processing and the manufacture of textiles, apparel, and small household necessities. Heavy industry consists chiefly of oil refining, mineral processing, and the manufacture of chemicals, metal and rubber products, and cement.

In many countries, small and medium-sized enterprises producing basic consumer goods and agricultural inputs have been neglected in favor of prestige projects or the output of luxury items for the urban elite. Often large-scale projects such as steel mills operate far below capacity. Moreover, the production of expensive consumer durables such as refrigerators and automobiles has meant that a substantial portion of industry may be devoted to the final processing or assembly of imported manufactures, requiring considerable expenditures of foreign exchange without adding significantly to value added or industrial employment.

Transportation. A major reason for the relatively low level of economic development in Africa has been the inadequacy of roads, railways, and waterways. The network of transportation facilities is not set up for an integrated development of the continent. Rather, the transportation system—especially the railroads, which often are the most important means of moving goods—reflects the emphasis on the export of primary products. As a result, many networks serve areas of primary (particularly mineral) production without linking key centers of population. This lack of coordination has slowed economic growth.

Since the major part of Africa's resources are inland, their development cannot be accomplished until railroads exist. For example, iron ore in western Equatorial Africa cannot be conveyed to port for overseas shipment unless rail facilities are completed. Railroad builders in Africa are faced with problems of climate and topography unlike those on other continents. The mountains and escarpments and the high temperatures and humidity in tropical areas often require special equipment that can negotiate steep gradients and withstand the climate. Because of these difficulties and high costs, Africa, with the exception of the far south, is one of the few parts of the world with an inadequate rail system.

Roads, too, are poorly developed. In many instances they are either trails or dirt tracks, which are impassable in the rainy season. Such

© GEORGE HOLTON/PHOTO RESEARCHERS

Hides soaking in these Moroccan tanning vats may become leather coats sold in Paris, London, or New York.

conditions make vehicle repairs expensive and road-maintenance costs high. One aim has been to spend less money and manpower on maintaining dirt roads and more on roads of tarmac, concrete, or other material that is less costly in the long run. Another goal has been to develop the network of feeder roads in order to end rural isolation.

The inland waterways are not very useful. Since Africa has a plateau landscape, with scarps typically falling away sharply near the coasts, the rivers have many rapids and waterfalls far downstream. This, together with fluctuations in water levels caused by varied rainfall, limits the value of even the largest waterways.

The harbors in Africa are considerably better than the inland transportation system. Some of the best are in Southern Africa, notably Lobito on the west coast and Maputo on the east coast. Lobito has rail connections with Africa's major centers of copper and cobalt mining inland, and Maputo is linked as well with the industrial area around Johannesburg. The southern coast, between Maputo and Cape Town, has limited natural harbor facilities, and expansion of ports (as at Richards Bay, for coal exports) has required huge capital outlays, especially in building large breakwaters. West and East Africa have some good natural harbors, but other ports in those regions have had to be artificially constructed at great expense—for example, Takoradi, Abidjan, and Monrovia. African ports in general are not sufficiently developed for a significant increase in trade. Many have become acutely congested, with resulting costly delays in the transportation of goods. New facilities require either outside borrowing or assistance from foreign governments and international agencies as well as considerable technical aid.

The airline and airport network was developed at the same time as in the rest of the world and was expanded after World War II. In many countries this system of transportation helps compensate for deficiencies in the planning, maintenance, and security of the rail and road systems.

Pipelines transport petroleum products at lower costs than would be possible by rail or road. However, their use is restricted largely to the petroleum producing countries because of large initial capital expenditures.

Trade. At the local level women play an important part in trade, as they do in agriculture. Usually they control at least a portion of the crops they raise, and where they engage actively in trade they may be more prosperous than their husbands.

Africa has two types of traditional local trading places: daily markets and periodic markets. Daily markets usually developed in towns and led to the creation of permanent shopping areas. They sell imported as well as local goods, including produce and craft wares from the rural areas. Periodic markets are most common in the countryside. Besides distributing rural products to the urban areas, they depend on the town markets and shops for domestic and imported consumer manufactures. A small area may have a periodic market in each of its villages operating on successive days, until each market has had its turn and the cycle resumes.

Because of generally small national populations and low purchasing power, cooperation to promote intra-African trade is imperative. This requires comprehensive development planning, not only by each country but also among the regional partners in common-market arrangements. A problem here, however, is that countries that might logically cooperate in one area—for example, power development—might not be suited to agricultural or industrial integration. In addition, old colonial divisions or current political or economic antagonisms might impede groupings that were otherwise complementary.

The Council of the Entente, founded in 1959 by several countries of French West Africa just before their independence, developed into a customs union with free trade among its members and a common external tariff. A similar organization, the Economic and Customs Union of Central Africa (UDEAC in French) was established in 1964 by states of former French Equatorial Africa.

The West African Economic Community (CEAO in French) was created in 1974, overlapping the Council of the Entente. It took in more former French West African countries but offered free trade only in raw materials. The even more comprehensive Economic Community of West African States (ECOWAS), which included English-speaking countries, came into being in 1976 with the aim of eventually forming a full customs union among its members.

The Southern African Development Coordination Conference (SADCC), first held in 1979, sought to harmonize the planning of its members and to reduce their economic dependence on South Africa. It included countries that continued to maintain a customs union with South Africa.

For Africa as a whole, the structure of both exports and imports in overseas trade changed after the independence era began in the early 1960's. Exports of primary products remained dominant, but with petroleum taking a two-thirds share formerly accounted for by agricultural products. Only a few African countries, however, are major sources of oil. At independence, Africa imported more consumer goods than capital goods, but afterward such products as machinery and transportation equipment assumed the

Although railroads are important to Africa, much of the rolling stock is antiquated. Most lines are one track.

© ADRIEN GALLO/BLACK STAR

Tourists flock to see Northern Africa's ancient monuments, injecting foreign currency into local economies.

greater importance as the economies developed. On the other hand, many countries that were formerly self-sufficient or nearly so in food have had to import substantial quantities of grain because of recurrent droughts and a neglect of agriculture.

Prospects for Economic Growth. The growth potential of Africa is excellent if its rich natural resources can be developed. This necessitates large capital investments and the intensified use of resources. Long-range growth requires that there should be no pausing once a beginning is made. Growth can bring more growth, particularly when many of the early stumbling blocks have been removed. These include, primarily, management and organizational deficiencies. Such deficiencies have retarded the economic development and growth of agriculture, industry, and mining. Because of them, mineral resources have gone untapped and potentially rich agricultural and forest areas have had no access to markets. This situation is being remedied through the development of better transportation and communications networks and sources of power supply.

Besides basic facilities, such as power stations, railways, roads, and ports, Africa's economic growth requires increasing numbers of educated and skilled people who can help the continent in its economic transformation. Technological and managerial skills can push forward the long-term economic growth. Here, however, the population problem must be taken into account. Africa's rate of population increase expanded rapidly during the independence period. The less optimistic believe that the present and prospective rates of population growth on the continent mean that there are few prospects for substantial increases in living standards over the

next few decades. Others believe that the African countries can slow their rates of population growth enough to raise living standards to a significant degree. This conflict of opinions plays a part in international debates on the allocation of foreign aid.

Various world and national organizations, public and private, make surveys of countries and offer assistance in planning resource development and allocation. Such planning is of great importance to African nations. Generally these countries are in economic and financial difficulties, if not crisis. They tend to run constant budget deficits, which affect financial stability and lead to inflationary pressures. They also tend to have balance-of-payments deficits, which are financed, first, by drawing down reserves and then by more foreign aid or borrowing. The interest charges for the latter have created additional deficits. Other results of balance-of-payments shortfalls are import restrictions and controls. Domestically this can cause shortages of essential foods, raw materials for industry, or spare parts for machinery, with the result that domestic economic development is curtailed.

Ways are needed to finance industrial development and especially to mobilize domestic savings for local investment through savings institutions. There is also a need to create strong industrial development banks and corporations that will not only obtain the necessary financing but will also be equipped to help the countries translate plans into working projects. In some instances the government must use its policy-making powers to promote fiscal and monetary responsibility, encourage savings, and improve the tax systems.

Applications for aid must be backed by statements of the areas intended for expenditure—

Farming in Africa ranges from hoe cultivation to agribusiness using equipment such as motorized sprinklers.

that is, specific plans and projects—so that the assisting countries and international agencies will not regard their help as a mere waste of funds. Most countries have some type of periodic plan that sets income, production, industrial, and diversification goals. Open-door policies toward private foreign investment are important, as even avowedly Marxist governments have begun to recognize.

For many countries, economic growth rates depend greatly on variations in export earnings. African countries have begun forming broader customs unions that would remove internal duties and have common external tariffs—for example, ECOWAS. Coordinated development of the members states is necessary, however, before viable economic communities can be created.

The reasoning that demands a regional or all-African approach to economic problems stems from the Africans' belief that world economic conditions are not in their favor—that the terms of trade are to their disadvantage, that the developed countries are not sufficiently committed to aid underdeveloped countries, and that interest charges and installments on the debts they have accumulated in many instances are becoming too much of a burden. Many African countries are saddled with debts that are so large that more than half of the foreign exchange earned from exports must be used for interest and amortization payments.

In reply to criticism of the West for compounding Africa's dilemmas, economic and political analysts overseas have cited the failures of African governments in tackling basic economic and social problems. Rather than accept an impasse, however, the leaders of African nations, industrialized countries, and international financial organizations have sought agreement on new, more resilient responses to the issues of African development.

EDWARD AND MILDRED RENDL MARCUS*
Authors of "Investment and Development Possibilities in Tropical Africa"

THE PEOPLE

Little is known about the demography of Africa prior to modern times, and even now the census data are not reliable for more than a few countries. Traditional African peoples undoubtedly had high birth and death rates, with infant mortality rates at or above 50% and life expectancy at or below 30 years. Rates of natural increase changed rapidly during the 20th century, resulting in a large increase in population.

One estimate places the population of the entire continent at about 55 million in 1600, after which (despite the overseas slave trade) it rose gradually to about 80 million in 1850. From then on the population is known to have increased rapidly, reaching perhaps 100 million before 1900, more reliably 200 million before 1950, and probably 385 million by 1975. The 20th century growth was exponential: 27% in the first quarter of the century, 46% in the second quarter, and 88% in the third. After the 1960's the rate of natural increase rose to 3% a year, or about 75% above the world average. At that rate the population would reach 900 million by about the year 2000.

The distribution of Africa's population is highly uneven. About 30% of the continent is sparsely inhabited desert, whereas certain areas—notably the lower Nile Valley, the vicinity of Lake Victoria, and the central Guinea Coast—have long supported large numbers of people per square mile. On the other hand, few large urban concentrations have developed south of the Sahara and north of the Limpopo River. Two parts of West Africa—the bend of the Niger River and Yorubaland on the Guinea Coast—have traditions of dense urban settlement that predate the arrival of Europeans by several centuries, but elsewhere the great movement of people to the cities is a recent phenomenon. Traditional Africa is composed primarily of rural dwellers settled in small villages or dispersed hamlets and of nomadic or seminomadic peoples.

Africa's overall population density, a little over half the world average, suggests that the continent is not overpeopled. However, generally poor soils and, in many areas, unreliable rainfall have limited the land's ability to withstand more than gradual population increases accompanied by greater productivity. In the 20th century ecological brakes failed to prevent spiraling population growth, which after the 1960's began to outstrip food production. Indications of mass poverty included infant mortality (40% above the world figure), life expectancy (still only 50 years), and per capita product (hardly more than a fourth the value for the world as a whole). Unchecked population growth, at a rate that would double the number of Africans every quarter-century, threatened the continent with unparalleled impoverishment and instability unless offset by seemingly impossible rates of economic investment.

7. African Peoples

A great variety of peoples, languages, and cultures are found on the continent of Africa. Thus the word "African" is misleading if it suggests much more than the persons called African identifying themselves with that continent rather than with another. Many types of classifications could be used to differentiate certain African peoples from others. Those most frequently employed are based on racial, linguistic, and cultural criteria.

Racial Groups. Racial criteria are the least satisfactory means of classification, since they are based on observations of relatively few physical characteristics, which cannot be precisely measured because their historical and genetic origins are relatively unknown. Some characteristics do not belong exclusively to one population but are found in several and, furthermore, are subject to considerable variation within any one population. In addition, the peoples of Africa have been quite mobile, and there has been widespread mixing among populations, with a consequent sharing and blending of physical features.

However, it is possible to recognize some general physical differences among several more or less distinctive groups. The most numerous and the most widely distributed of these groups are the "true," or Forest, Negroids, who inhabit most of sub-Saharan Africa. They have brown to dark brown skin color, kinky or woolly black hair, broad and rather flat noses, and everted lips. Their height varies greatly, but all are over 5 feet (150 cm) tall. Often classed as a variation of the Forest Negroids are the Nilotics, who tend to be taller and more slender, with narrower noses and less everted lips. They live primarily in the Great Lakes and eastern Sudan regions and have frequently mixed with neighboring populations of Forest Negroids. Also dwelling among Forest Negroid populations in the forested areas of Equatorial Africa are the Pygmies. They differ from the Forest Negroids primarily by their height, which averages under 5 feet.

Another racial group are the Bushmanoids (Capoids), small populations of whom live in southwestern Africa. They are represented by the San (Bushmen) and Khoikhoi (Hottentots). Bushmanoids average a little over 5 feet in height, and their skin, which tends to wrinkle, is more yellow-brown in color than that of Negroids. Their short black hair is tightly spiraled,

© CARL FRANK/PHOTO RESEARCHERS

Berbers live in the mountains and deserts of northwestern Africa. They were the region's pre-Arab inhabitants.

and many of them, especially females, have fatty deposits on the buttocks, a feature called steatopygia.

Most people in Northern Africa belong to the Caucasoid physical type. The Caucasoids in sub-Saharan Africa arrived in comparatively recent times from Europe and Asia, and cannot yet be regarded as indigenous there.

Finally, there are numerous populations, such as the Fulani in the regions just south of the Sahara in West Africa and many of the Somali, who appear to have acquired their characteristics from both Negroid and Caucasoid ancestors. These peoples may be most properly regarded as "mixed."

Linguistic Groups. Maps of linguistic areas of Africa can be drawn with a greater degree of precision than can racial maps. Even the simplified color map "Languages" accompanying this text suggests a linguistic situation of considerable complexity, for the few categories indicated on the map include at least 1,000 different and mutually unintelligible languages spoken on the continent. Speakers of a very few of these languages number in the millions, some only in the hundreds, while the great majority are spoken by far less than 100,000 people each.

A widely accepted classification lists four major language families, none of which bears any more similarity to any of the others than do the Indo-European languages to Chinese. The languages belonging to one of these families, the Congo-Kordofanian, are spoken by most of the people in sub-Saharan Africa. Within this great

269

LANGUAGES

Modified from Greenberg, *The Languages of Africa*.

I   CONGO-KORDOFANIAN
   I A   Niger-Congo
   I B   Kordofanian

II   NILO-SAHARAN
   II A   Songhai
   II B   Saharan
   II C   Maban
   II D   Fur
   II E   Chari–Nile
   II F   Koman

III   AFRO-ASIATIC
   III A   Semitic
   III B   Egyptian (extinct)
   III C   Berber
   III D   Cushitic
   III E   Chad

IV   KHOISAN
   IV A   South African Khoisan
   IV B   Sandawe
   IV C   Hatsa

V   INDO-EUROPEAN
   V A   Germanic
   V B   Romance

VI   MALAY-POLYNESIAN
   VI A   Indonesian
       (Malagasy)

family are 11 subfamilies of languages. Each consists of a number of languages more closely resembling one another in the use of sounds and meanings than they resemble the members of the other subfamilies. They are similar to one another in the way that the Germanic languages are similar to the Romance or Slavic languages within the Indo-European family. Within the subfamilies the languages resemble one another in the way that English resembles German. This situation, of course, has hindered communication between separate African societies, since people living only a few miles apart may speak languages that are mutually unintelligible.

One of the best known of the Congo-Kordofanian subfamilies is the Bantu, on the accompanying map called Benue-Congo. It is composed of several hundred languages spoken by the peoples of most of Equatorial, East, and Southern Africa.

The three other major language families—the Nilo-Saharan, the Khoisan, and the Afro-Asiatic —are also divisible into subfamilies. Each subfamily, in turn, is divisible into smaller subclassifications, each indicating a still closer degree of relationship that never reaches the point of mutual intelligibility until the specific language is reached. Among the best known of the Afro-Asiatic subfamilies are the Semitic and Cushitic, which contain languages spoken by many peoples in Northern Africa and the Middle Nile and Horn region.

Before English, French, and, to a lesser degree, Portuguese came to be spoken as second languages by large numbers of Africans, certain African languages had gained usage outside their native areas. Known as "lingua francas," each of these consisted basically of one African language that became useful for trade and other communi-

cation in a large region. One of these is Swahili, a Congo-Kordofanian language of the Bantu subfamily, which over a period of time acquired a large additional vocabulary from Arabic, brought by Arab traders to Zanzibar and the adjacent coast. Its utility in commerce was recognized by many other Africans, so that today one or another dialect of Swahili is current in many parts of East Africa. Elsewhere such languages as Bemba, Ngala, and Kongo (Bantu languages of Equatorial Africa), Hausa (a member of the Chadic subfamily of the Afro-Asiatic family, spoken in West Africa), and Mandingo (a member of the Mande subfamily of the Congo-Kordofanian family, also spoken in West Africa) have become lingua francas of their regions.

Cultural Groups. Just as racial "boundaries" do not correspond to linguistic boundaries, neither corresponds precisely to cultural or ethnic boundaries. One attempt to summarize certain general differences among styles of life in various regions of sub-Saharan Africa is that by Melville J. Herskovits. In *The Human Factor in Changing Africa*, he recognized seven culture areas south of the Sahara, in each of which most of the inhabitants share a particular combination of social and cultural characteristics that makes them distinguishable from the peoples of any other area.

The Khoisan area of southwestern Africa is inhabited by the Khoikhoi and San peoples, both essentially nomads living in small bands with relatively simple political and religious institutions. The San make their livelihood by hunting and by gathering wild plants, and the Khoikhoi primarily by raising cattle.

The East African cattle area stretches from southernmost Africa to the region of Lake Victoria, then northward in a narrowing band through the Nilotic Sudan to Egypt. Distinctive of most of the peoples of this area is their dependence on rather simple agriculture or gardening for their subsistence and on cattle both as a means of subsistence and as a measurement of relative wealth and prestige. Cattle are exchanged between individuals and groups as a symbol and reinforcement of their interdependence and mutual interests. Characteristic of this area is the manner in which males of approximately the same age are grouped together to provide services to the various communities and families from which they are drawn. As the members of each group grow to an older age, the functions of the group change, and its members acquire more power in their communities. They regulate the politics of the peoples and, through their common membership, help reduce the friction between their respective communities and defend them against threats from the outside. Within this area the peoples farther south tended to form rather large, complex political units or states, of which the Zulu is one of the best known. In the northern reaches, politics and government were more simply organized along the lines that have led some observers to refer to the groups as "tribes without rulers."

A third culture area, called the Eastern Sudan, reaches from the Nile River to Lake Chad. The common characteristics of this area are difficult to describe because of the lack of extensive knowledge and the great heterogeneity in styles of life. Cattle are of predominant importance to the people living closer to the Nile, but their place is taken by camels in the regions to the west, where the horse also becomes a more useful animal. Throughout the area are other peoples who are more dependent on agriculture for their livelihood and who are poor herdsmen. Islam is the religion dominant in the lives of most of the peoples. Politically the area was fragmented into small groups, each conscious of its own separateness and individuality, each unwilling to unite into a political network with others to form anything like the states of the south or of the Guinea Coast area.

The area called the Eastern Horn, named for the eastward projection of continent south of Arabia, has closer cultural affinities with Egypt and the Asian Middle East than with the remainder of Africa. It is also marked by considerable internal heterogeneity, although Islam is a unifying force.

In the Congo Basin the Pygmies' simple life, based on hunting and gathering, contrasts greatly with the more complex arrangements of most of the other peoples of the area. The Congo ethnic groups depend heavily on agriculture of a more intensive, skilled, and productive sort than that of the East Africa area. On the other hand, they do not raise any of the larger domesticated animals. Their craft specializations in weaving, woodcarving, and iron working, are distinctive. Trade involving the use of money is widespread. Some of the peoples, such as the Kongo, Kuba, and Lunda, created large, complicated political states through conquest or federation. Most ethnic groups, however, lived in small, relatively stateless societies, dependent solely on the village or a cluster of related villages as the major political unit.

Stretching westward from the Congo area in a relatively narrow, forested belt is the Guinea Coast area. The peoples of this zone have a relatively high population density supported by agriculture that surpasses that of most of the non-industrialized world in its productivity. Particularly in the central part of the region, such peoples as the Ashanti, Dahomeans, Bini, and Yoruba developed complex and comparatively

Masai dancers. The Masai, who live in East Africa, are Negroids of the tall, slender Nilotic type.

© JEANETTA BAKER/FPG

© TIM GIBSON/PHOTO RESEARCHERS

Medieval ancestors of this West African ruled over savanna civilizations supported by long-distance trade.

influence on how people make their living, on their degree of economic productivity, and on the sizes of populations and elaborations of cultures they can afford to support.

When such criteria are used, Africans can be classified as primarily hunters and gatherers (Khoisan and Pygmies); fishers (located along the coasts or rivers); herders (found throughout the great continental crescent that swings from Southern Africa through East Africa and westward north of the forest to the Atlantic coast); and farmers. The farmers engage in different types of agriculture, depending in large part on their geographic environment. Farmers in the forested regions of western and central Africa grow root crops, such as yams and cassava, and tree crops, such as bananas and other fruits. Those outside the forest zone are predominantly growers of grains, such as millet, maize, and rice. In all the areas, hunting and food gathering supplement the more staple food supplies.

ROBERT A. LYSTAD
Johns Hopkins University

8. Traditional Social and Political Organization

The largest social unit with which traditional Africans identify themselves is the ethnic group, or tribe. These terms can be used with respect to traditional African societies only in the most general way, as any group of people who think of themselves as different in various ways from all others and who have a distinctive name for themselves. The members of the group feel a greater sense of identity with one another than with "outsiders."

Cultural Differentiation. Although most groups resemble one another in some respects, these similarities are only of a general sort, and it is the differences between them that are more crucial. In size, for example, there is great disparity. Some groups number only a few hundred, as in the Khoisan area, while perhaps 20 number more than a million members each. The great majority have fewer than 250,000 people, and most have fewer than 100,000. Nearly all of them occupy a territory, more or less well defined, that they regard as their own. However, migrations have overrun many such boundaries, resulting in the joint settlement of a territory by many groups. Also, the settlement of small groups within the territory of a larger one frequently has reduced the exclusiveness of the established society, which nevertheless tends to regard immigrants as outsiders or "strangers" for several generations before incorporating them more fully into its ranks.

What the "inside" members of the group share is a common culture, a common way of life. Perhaps the most important aspect of this shared culture is the language, which makes possible easy communication and learning, and if one criterion were to be used for determining the boundaries of a tribal group the most useful would be the language. Even this criterion is not ideal, however, for people who speak dialects of a single language may nonetheless identify with different ethnic groups. Furthermore, some groups that speak one language may live great distances apart and have so little to do with one another that they cannot really be regarded as a single society.

Among the other aspects of culture that help to unify members of a single group are their social institutions, such as family, marriage, and

wealthy states. They evolved complicated market and trading networks, using controlled currencies and professional tradesmen, and developed a relatively high degree of labor specialization. In politics the authority centralized in chiefs and elders tended to be balanced by more democratic organizations of commoners. The traditional religions of this area are rich in ritual and intricate in theology. The region's sculpture, music, and dance have become well known and even influential in the Western world.

The Western Sudan, which lies in the savanna zone north of the Guinea Coast area and south of the Sahara, is marked by great cultural diversity. With respect to its high population density, the specialization of labor and trading enterprises, its complex political units, and its artistic production, it resembles the Guinea Coast. But its people are far more dependent on cattle, which are absent in the forest zone; styles of clothing and housing differ from those to the south; and Islam is the dominant religion of the ruling classes and in the cities. In its earlier history, prior to the 18th century, it was probably the most elaborately developed of all the sub-Saharan culture areas. It gave rise to a succession of empires, such as Ghana, Mali, Songhai, Kanem-Bornu, and the Fulani-Hausa, beginning about the 5th century A.D. and ending only with the advent of intensive European colonialism in the 19th century.

Such a classification of culture areas cannot do justice to the richness and diversity of the variations either within or between areas. However, it does serve to point up the inadequacy of such general terms as "African" or "tribal."

Ecological Groups. It is also possible to outline certain groupings of African peoples by reference to ecological factors. These exert a great

In traditional Africa, a family in need of more living space can simply add a dwelling to the compound.

other patterns of kinship. All members of the group are likely to subscribe to the same rules governing relationships among family members and determining the heads of families and the nature of their authority. The children are likely to be reared in approximately the same way and educated to understand all the social roles that must be played by members of the cooperative group. They learn the proper ways of making a living and of sharing their labor, production, and wealth. Members of the group thus come to share an outlook on the organization of social life and to accept a common system of values and attitudes toward right conduct and its goals.

Reinforcing such common features as these are the religious beliefs affirmed by nearly all members of a group and the ceremonies and rituals in which they participate. They learn a common body of myths, legends, traditions, and explanations for events that occur in the world. Through learning the styles of their traditional music and dance and of their plastic and verbal arts, they often associate aesthetic activities with religious beliefs and rituals. The members of the group come to appreciate their own traditions as distinctive and usually as "better" than those of other groups.

Material objects also frequently have features unique to a group. Variations in the design, materials, construction, and decoration of tools and of houses and other buildings are found between even neighboring groups. Styles of clothing and cosmetics and modes of marking the body vary too, as do the kinds of food preferred and the methods of preparing them.

Another aspect of traditional life that distinguishes one group from another is the political. Members of a single group recognize as their own a certain system of organizing and controlling communal activity. This does not mean that all members necessarily recognize a single person or body of individuals as having authority over them, for many African societies possess no such central authority, no single unified public administration. But in every subdivision that makes up such a "stateless" society is an awareness that the others have a political system that can link up with theirs when necessary. They all speak the same language and share patterns of culture, and they are, therefore, members of the same society.

Group differences do not necessarily foster enmity or conflict. There have been places and times in which intergroup warfare has been frequent and fierce, others in which little or no interaction has existed. Nonetheless, the majority of African peoples have lived in some degree of cooperation or peaceful coexistence, trading with one another, intermarrying, or aligning with one another in mutual defense against a common enemy. Some groups, previously independent, have even voluntarily joined together under a common political administration.

Not all groups, of course, differ greatly from all others. Some are very similar to one another in all cultural aspects, while nonetheless retaining a sense of distinctiveness. The concept of the culture area suggests how groups in proximity tend to resemble one another, and another concept, that of "culture clusters," has been used to show how these similarities are frequently more intense in relatively small districts within a region. Still, proximity is not necessarily the crucial factor, for a distance of only a few miles may separate groups with only vaguely similar cultures.

Types of Kinship and Community. African societies traditionally have placed greater emphasis on heavy and lasting responsibilities to the individual's social groups than on the personal right to associate with or dissociate from them. Although individuality is not lost in group life, people are less than free to conduct their own affairs at their own discretion. The principal groups that limit such freedom are based on two kinds of kinship: those into which one is born (descent groups) and those one enters through marriage (affinal groups). Both determine the people, from among all others, on whom individuals may depend most heavily and who, reciprocally, depend on them.

Descent Groups. Nearly all African societies have acquired patterns of descent that are called unilineal; that is, a person belongs to a kinship group all of whose members trace their ancestry back through only one parent rather than through both. Most African societies are patrilineal: a person belongs to a kin group composed of all those people descended from a common male ancestor through males only. A large minority, however, are matrilineal: a person belongs to a kin group composed of all those people descended from a common female ancestor through females only. In a small minority of societies, the person belongs to two separate, about equally balanced, and complementary kin groups, one traced through the father, the other through the mother. Unilineal descent groups do not ignore the other parent. Both parents have well-defined obligations to their children in the elementary family they compose, but the unilineal group is dominant for most purposes over the kin of the other parent throughout the entire life of the individual.

Whether patrilineal or matrilineal in nature, the largest kinship grouping is the clan, or sib, whose members claim descent from a common ancestor. The original ancestor and many of the intervening ancestors may not actually be known, and the original may even be thought of as some kind of mythological creature or natural phenomenon, such as an animal or topographic feature, that remains as a symbol of clan membership.

Frequently the thousands or even millions of clan members have become dispersed, and many may have little or nothing to do with most of the others. The kinship unit that is more effective than the clan in the lives of most Africans, therefore, is the lineage, whose members share a common known ancestor of a more recent generation. It is the lineage that is likely to control the property, especially the land, that individuals have the right merely to use; it may own the house in which they live; it is likely to own and manage the religious shrines and conduct the rituals in which its members participate; and it is likely to exert great influence in the selection of marriage partners for its members. Leadership and authority are usually in the hands of the older males, who carry the responsibility of maintaining order and discipline, of punishing miscreants, and of protecting the rights of the members in their relations with other kinship groups. The lineage usually has claim to specific political offices in the larger community as well, posts held by one or more of the qualified older men, who thereby represent their lineage in community affairs. In cases of dispute between individuals from different lineages, each lineage gives full support to its own members. Some segments of a lineage, tracing themselves back to a specific generation or particular ancestor, often have specific services that they perform for the others, such as providing the lineage chief. From time to time some segments may decide to move away, become more autonomous, or initiate new traditions. But the principles of organization

and of the subordination of the individual to the group tend to remain the same in any case.

The lineage varies greatly in size with the vicissitudes of history and circumstance, but it is likely to include at least several dozen people and may include several hundred. Since each is pledged to the social, economic, and political support of the others, the individual has a great number of people to depend on. While relinquishing much personal freedom to their control, a person finds physical and psychological security in remaining one with them.

Affinal Groups. Nearly all African societies recognize marriage more as a union between two lineage groups than as a union between two individuals. The creation of such an alliance is usually recognized by an exchange of wealth between the contracting lineages. Since the greater wealth usually goes from the groom's lineage to the bride's, the payment is referred to as bridewealth, and it constitutes at least a partial compensation for the services her lineage is losing. It may also serve as a deterrent to divorce, because each lineage brings pressure to bear on its members to fulfill the obligations they have incurred in marriage. Thus affinal kinship extends the network of joint dependency outside the African's own lineage into that of the spouse.

Marriage also includes certain sexual rights, not necessarily exclusive, and certain mutual economic obligations and family-rearing responsibilities. Polygyny (one husband with two or more wives) is the traditional ideal in Africa, although the majority of married African men have only one wife. Where there is more than one wife, each cowife and her children are usually housed separately, whether widely apart or within the same household, and the proper relationships between them, whether as equals or as dominant and subordinate, are made clear. Polygyny is clearly a source of tension in traditional African households, but in general it is not despised by African women, who may well receive benefits of heightened prestige and reduced labor as a consequence.

Most African societies regulate marriage in several other ways. Nearly all forbid marriage or extramarital sexual relations between members of the same lineage or clan or between close relatives on the side of the other parents. Many of them prescribe or, at least, encourage marriage between persons standing in a certain relationship to each other, as in "cross-cousin" marriage, whereby a man marries the daughter of his father's sister or mother's brother. In many societies the sister (or cousin) of a wife who dies or fails to bear children may be given in marriage to the husband. It is also common for a widow to become the wife of her deceased husband's brother or of some other heir in her husband's lineage who assumes an obligation for her continued well-being.

Extended Families. These and many other rules and customs are consistent with the widespread African view that the principal purposes of marriage are procreation, the formation and replenishment of the many human relationships necessary to the lineage and the general welfare, and the provision of mutual economic and social security services. In a particular community these are effected through the establishment of households and of extended families, which characteristically consist of the people of several lineages

Recess at a girls' school in Libya. Fewer African girls are educated than boys, but the gap is narrowing.

who live together and who share common ec-
nomic and child-rearing obligations.

Joined together in these units are usually an
elder male, who is the head of the group, his
wives, their children or nieces and nephews, and
their appropriate grandchildren, grandnieces,
and grandnephews. A girl in most societies
moves into the household of her husband, who
remains with or near the head household of his
descent group. It is not uncommon, however,
for a groom to live with and work for his wife's
lineage or father. The composition of the household changes from time to time as new spouses
marry into it or as children marry and move into
other households or as elders die and have their
places taken by those next in line for authority.
However, the continuity of the household ideally
is maintained from one generation to the next,
providing the basic security for which it was
originally established.

Nonkinship Groups. Kinship groups, such as
the lineages, affinal groups, and extended families, are linked within a community and between
communities through several possible types of
nonkinship groupings or associations. Important
among these, especially in the East African area,
are associations based on age, in which persons,
usually males, of approximately the same age
have an identity and leadership and group life of
their own, which they retain as they grow older.
Members come from all the kinship groups and
even from the various communities that compose
the society. Age groups thus tend to provide a
balance to relationships that might become ten-
dentious if the individual's only close ties were
with a kinship group or community. They also
play a part in the educational system, defense,
and government of the community. Occupational guilds and secret societies, particularly in

parts of West Africa and the Congo Basin, play
similar roles.

The communities themselves assume widely
different forms, depending on the nature of the
physical surroundings, the technology used in
exploiting the environment, relations with
neighboring societies, and personal relations
within the society itself. Some peoples, such as
the hunting-and-gathering Khoisan and Pygmies,
live in small nomadic bands. Those of the Khoisan stay near water holes during the dry season
and range over much larger territory at other
times. The Pygmy bands simply encamp near
game. Some nomadic cattle herders, such as the
Fulani of the Western Sudan culture area, move
about with the seasons. They negotiate rights to
graze their cattle with local landowners and never establish permanent settlements of their own.
Other herders, such as the Masai of East Africa,
have permanent villages on their own lands and
move between them seasonally.

Some agriculturalists merely exploit the land
until its nutrients have been depleted and then
shift to another area of cultivation a few miles
away. Most, however, are sedentary, remaining
at a fixed site while practicing crop rotation, irrigation, fertilization, and other devices for maintaining soil productivity. The Yoruba people of
the Guinea Coast have clustered in large cities
while engaged primarily in farming both within
and beyond the outskirts of the city. Even within such cities there is a strong tendency for the
members of a single lineage or clan to live in
the same neighborhood and to find their main
support in their own close groupings. For most
Africans, though, it is the small village or a few
related villages, with their limited number of
lineages and their friends and companions, that
shelter and satisfy throughout life.

Politics and Government. Whenever people claim territory as their own and whenever there is a need to regulate relations within a group, someone must be given power to see that their claims and regulations are enforced. This is the nature of politics and government. Africans have worked out two basic systems for solving these problems, although with many variations. One is the state system, in which a bureaucracy is empowered to make, administer, and enforce rules and to defend or aggress against outsiders. The other is a stateless system, in which a commonly accepted body of rules is enforced either by the extended families and lineages or by agreement between two power groups of relatively equal strength within the society.

States have been created in many parts of Africa where large numbers of people enjoyed a relative superiority in technology and economic production. Most of these states have had kings, assisted and even held in check by councils representing various lineage groups and regions within the state. The kings and lesser chiefs, now generally subordinate to the modern central government, are thought to be either sacred themselves or entitled to own the sacred symbols of their offices. Thus the political office is also a religious office, and the king normally represents his people before the gods and ancestors and represents the divinities before the people.

Usually the king, by traditional custom, delegates much of his authority to the lesser chiefs, who hold a sacred post in their own jurisdiction similar to that of the king at the higher level. Many such successively lower spheres of authority are defined down to the level of the village. Although numerous methods of selecting chiefs have been devised, nearly all of them make use of the lineage principle. One lineage, designated as royal within its jurisdiction in legendary times, is alone eligible to provide the occupant of a particular office. Not all regulatory powers are vested in the central authority, however, and many matters of life and death and of property remain in the hands of lineages and local authorities—though always subject to the customary rules that are shared by all the members of the society.

The simplest of the stateless societies, dependent for authority only on extended families, are found among such groups as the Khoisan peoples and the Pygmies. In the more complex stateless systems a balance of power is struck between the sublineages or lineages of which the disputants are members. It will be recalled that fellow members of a kinship group rally as one to the support of a lineage brother. Once a dispute is settled, however, both kinship groups recognize their co-membership in another, more encompassing group, and the peaceful balance between them is reestablished. In such a system there are no officeholders, no decision makers, no judges to affirm the law, and no enforcement agencies. There are only leaders of unified groups, representatives of their respective kin who, backed by the power of their lineages, work out compromise solutions to problems, based on their mutual acceptance of the common cultural code. Once their specific task of conciliation is complete, they become simply members of the group without any particular authority or rights to permanent office.

ROBERT A. LYSTAD
Johns Hopkins University

9. Religions

The varieties of indigenous African religious expression are even more numerous than the languages spoken on the continent. Each traditional society developed its own system of faith and ritual intimately related to its distinctive culture and not deliberately exportable to others. In many areas, however, these systems have given way to the two great proselytizing religions of Middle Eastern origin—Islam and Christianity.

Traditional Beliefs and Practices. Despite the local variations that make each indigenous religion distinctive, certain features are widespread throughout sub-Saharan Africa. Among these is the view that the universe is a unity of being, not a combination somehow of the physical and the spiritual, of the body and the soul. Although distinctions are made between forces and persons that are visible and those that are invisible, between the corporeal and the incorporeal, these are not separate realms of being that occasionally affect each other. They are a single, completely integrated phenomenon.

This viewpoint becomes especially clear when it is realized that a lineage consists not only of the living members but of the invisible ancestors as well. Though not normally seen, the ancestors are influential in the affairs of the lineage, which therefore may be thought of as a religious group. The land controlled by the lineage is regarded as ancestral property held in trust for the invisible ancestors whose pleasure, welfare, and goodwill are also dependent on its proper disposition and use. Rights to political office and leadership in most societies are also derived from the ancestors who held them before and who continue to serve in decision-making,

Muslims pray five times each day. Islam has millions of followers in Africa on both sides of the Sahara.

© JOHN LEWIS STAGE/LENSGROUP

© VICTOR ENGLEBERT

Ethiopian Christian priests lead a holy day procession. King Ezana brought Christianity to Aksum in about 350.

administrative, and enforcement capacities. A chief, in this way, is primarily a representative and symbol of the ancestors.

Because of this integrated view of the world, distinctions between the secular and the sacred tend to be far less sharp than in Western cultures. The sources of disease, death, and poverty, for example, are not to be found solely in physical materials or events; they exist in the invisible forces of which the physical causes are merely visible manifestations. The cures for trouble lie in the restoration of proper relationships between the visible and the invisible as well as in the commonsense relief of the observable symptoms of disorder.

A second widespread feature of the religions of Africa is the belief in a Creator of all things, who gave the world its order, and who infused it with ongoing energy. It is the purpose of human beings to do their part in directing this energy into beneficial channels and to divert it from harmful paths. Humans therefore have a considerable responsibility; because the Creator is a rather aloof and distant being, not normally given to interference in earthly affairs. The Creator, however, has provided a large number of lesser, intermediate gods and hosts of local spirits whose interest and assistance must be solicited by humans. This is done through the performance of rituals, prayers, and sacrifices, which are the means of communicating with the invisible world, maintaining proper ties with it, and restoring broken ties after human fallibility or selfishness has disrupted the smooth beneficent flow of energy. Even more important than the rituals, however, is the living of a proper life in the society. Antisocial acts are one and the same with anticosmic acts and are thus to be avoided because of their repercussions on the lineage, the community, and possibly the whole society.

Since religion so permeates the life of the community and people and is so much a part of daily activity, few societies have any organization resembling a church. Full-time professional clergymen or a priestly class are similarly rare. Priests, diviners of the future, rainmakers, curers, and other wonderworkers are usually just members of the lineage or community who have acquired special religious skills. In some societies they may be the king or chief; in others, different persons whose ritual services are necessary to the proper performance of the task.

The Spread of Nonindigenous Religions. Both Islam and Christianity have long histories in Africa. By the 4th century, Christianity had gained a dominant position in the religious life of Mediterranean Africa as far west as Carthage. Beginning in the 7th century, however, its influence was largely swept away. Ethiopian Christianity, established in the 4th century but not widely propagated among the people until the 6th century, survived in isolation.

Christianity had not advanced across the desert to the Western Sudan, and many centuries were to elapse before Europeans introduced it to sub-Saharan Africa. Meanwhile, entire societies were converted to Islam throughout Mediterranean Africa, the Sahara, and southward nearly to the forest zone of the Guinea culture area. On the eastern side of the continent, the coastal peoples as far south as the Limpopo River became Muslims.

In modern times Islam has won many additional converts across a broad front in West Africa. Its influence in some sections of that region's forest zone has been increased by intensified southerly migration of Muslims from the Western Sudan.

European Christianity did not begin to have a major impact in sub-Saharan Africa until about the middle of the 19th century. The Portuguese in the 16th century had established missions along some of the more southerly coasts and at several points on the West African littoral, but it remained for the great liberal movements of 19th century Europe to foster any significant mission enterprise. The only exception was the Calvinism brought to Southern Africa by Dutch settlers in the 17th and 18th centuries. By 1860 both European and American Protestant and Roman Catholic missionaries had begun their work at many points along the West and Equatorial African coasts and in several parts of East Africa. Afterward their efforts expanded to virtually all areas south of the Sahara. Only in regions long dominated by Islam—Northern Africa and portions of West and East Africa—was Christianity unable to gain large numbers of converts.

A phenomenon of the 20th century was the rise and growth of independent African Christian churches such as the Kimbanguist (Church of Jesus Christ on Earth Through the Prophet Simon Kimbangu), which has several million adherents in the Congo Basin. The new churches accommodate Christian teaching with traditional African beliefs and practices that are deeply rooted in everyday life.

Estimates of religious affiliation in Africa are only rough approximations, because various denominations employ different methods of counting members and the data convey little information about the depth of religious commitment. By the turn of the 21st century, it was estimated that about 46.6% of the population was Christian, 40.3% was Muslim, and 11.5% adhered to "tribal" religions. Within any one region or country, though, the proportions are likely to be quite different from those of the continent as a whole. For example, countries north of the Guinea Coast area are apt to be 80% to 100% Muslim. In the Guinea Coast states, Muslims are found primarily in the northerly areas, and in East Africa, along the coast. Christians are most numerous in the remainder of the continent, which was not heavily Islamized.

Of the three major religious traditions, Islam appears to have an advantage because it requires a less drastic revision of the traditional outlook on life. It has been carried, furthermore, by African peoples, whereas mainstream Christianity has had difficulty changing its image as a "European religion" closely associated with colonialism. On the other hand, Christianity's expansion has occurred predominantly through the schools, a potent force. It was the churches that founded, administered, staffed, and financed modern education until fairly recently, when independent African governments assumed those roles. Many sub-Saharan African political leaders and other influential persons were educated in Christian schools and identify themselves as Christian. In any event, the religious tradition most likely to wane is the indigenous, which in many respects seems less suited to the changing conditions of modern life.

ROBERT A. LYSTAD
Johns Hopkins University

10. Traditional African Values

It is manifestly impossible to label any system of values as typical of the peoples of a continent as heterogeneous as Africa. Each society has its basic values, which in many ways are as distinctive as are the languages, political styles, and other features of the cultures. On a very general level, however, certain observations can be made about similarities in outlook on a few crucial matters, particularly if one does not attempt to relate them to any specific society or even to any particular individuals or groups within a society.

Traditional Africans tend to view human nature as neither inherently good nor evil; it is morally neutral. Human beings, nonetheless, are capable of error. They are also only relatively weak or strong and can become weaker or stronger. Because of their failings, they may become what other people judge to be good or evil, generous or selfish, depending on the social results of their actions. If they do wrong, their reaction is that of shame at weakness rather than guilt at the commission of sin. The wrong can be righted by just compensation of the wronged and by ritual strengthening of the weak character. This restores the wrongdoers to their proper position in the society and universe, which is the desired condition of the good person.

In a world in which humanity, nature, and the supernatural are part of one totality, it is the purpose of men and women to live in harmony with the other two aspects. The Creator has prepared an orderly universe in which what is already known is about as much as can be known. Scientific experimentation and inquiry into the mystery of the universe in order to alter it and become its master are not consistent with the traditional view of the world. The physical world is given, and humans best serve themselves and their fellows by adapting to it as it is. The invisible world of spirit is similarly given, and mortals must adapt themselves to what they have been taught is its nature.

The basic adaptations to nature and the supernatural have been discovered by past generations and are stored in the accumulated culture inherited by each generation. Thus, it is in precedent—in tradition, legend, and folk wisdom—that traditional Africans seek solutions to present problems. It is not characteristic of them to devote much thought or planning to the creation of a radically changed and improved future. Even the common view of life beyond the "mortal life" is that it is lived in a society patterned quite like the present one; indeed, it is an indivisible, though invisible, part of this life. Thus it is the understanding of the past, embodied in the ancestors and what they have done and continue to do, that directs present actions far more than does a conception of a better future.

Consistent with such views is the belief that a life lived in spontaneous enjoyment of what exists is the most satisfying. This hedonism, however, is not indulged in at the expense of the fulfillment of social obligations, for in their relationships with others traditional Africans are fundamentally humanitarian. They share their property and services with those who are close and expect them to reciprocate. Individuals see themselves not as free to engage in their private pursuits but as members of groups whose mutual well-being depends on each person's actions. What one gives up in personal freedom is more than compensated by the security gained from coordinating one's own affairs with those of others.

The groups to which the individual feels this sense of obligation are the extended family, the lineage, the community, and, if necessary, the society as a whole. The world outside these, however, recedes rather quickly from view, and Africans may give the appearance of callousness toward human life that is not closely linked with their own. Nor are all people, even some within one's own community, necessarily equal or equally deserving, and one may exhibit indifference toward some of them. The universe has been so created that some people are born, or fall, into inferior positions; others are born into, or achieve, superior positions. Individuals must accept, and adapt themselves to, their status, fully exploiting its inherent advantages but also recognizing its limitations.

These values and the other features of traditional African life are undergoing rapid change.

Young Africans, bound for business or pleasure, book airline flights at a computerized ticket counter. Modern transportation technology, beginning with railroads, helped to bring interior Africa into the network of world interdependence.

© SALGADO/MAGNUM

Many Africans, nevertheless, continue to find them satisfying. Traditional values are so resilient and so susceptible to variation and moderate degrees of change that they are likely to influence the styles of life in sub-Saharan Africa for many decades to come.

ROBERT A. LYSTAD
Johns Hopkins University

11. Modernization and Social Change

The African revolution that has brought political independence to the former colonies since the 1950's has been accompanied by social and economic changes that have affected the life of virtually every person on the continent. This process of bringing traditional societies into the world of contemporary technology has become known as "modernization." The wide implications of the process have begun to be understood by both Africans and by the non-African world, but so closely interconnected are the parts that make up the structure of African societies that the full effects of modernization will not be realized for many generations to come.

Urbanization. As in other areas of the world, citizens of African nations have been flocking to towns and cities, participating in the powerful trend toward urbanization. Often the locales of the political unrest that led to decolonialization, African cities also have been the settings for the important social changes that have been taking place since independence. The mushrooming urban centers, with their presidential palaces, ministerial buildings, office blocks, and housing estates—and their shantytowns, traffic jams, and air pollution—are perhaps the most striking material evidence of the ongoing transformation of African society.

Education. Basic to all modernization is education, not only within the formal system of the schools but also at the level of adult literacy and specialized extension work in agriculture and public health. The popular demand has been such that no African government would have been able to resist rapid expansion of educational facilities even if it had desired to do so. One problem has been to maintain a balance between economic growth and educational advance. Where young people who are the products of the new education do not find that their talents and skills can be immediately utilized, their dissatisfaction is likely to be reflected in political instability.

Social Control. Modernization has had a profound influence on institutional forms of social control. Just as the authority of the traditional chiefs has been subordinated to the powers of central governments, the constraints exercised by family heads are being reduced by the loosening of domestic ties. The solidarity of the extended family unit is being weakened by the movement to the cities, where the disruptive influences of modern communications media can be more keenly felt. Within the urban areas different ways of life must be learned by the newcomers. They are dependent on an employer for their livelihood, and unless they retain their traditional links with kinfolk they can no longer rely on the family group as a form of social security. Ethnic-based urban voluntary associations help fill the gap, however. In most African states, governmental security plans are only in a rudimentary state of development.

New Legal Codes. An important aspect of social transformation has been the creation and adoption of new legal codes. The regulation of society by local law and custom has given way to rule by national law under central governments. Traditional law has not been eliminated, however. On the contrary, governments have sought to incorporate into new legal codes those aspects of traditional law that they deem still applicable and desirable, while at the same time providing for the use of norms based on non-African legal systems. The process of producing compromises between the traditional and the modern often has been delicate and difficult. Too rapid change could easily undermine popular respect for, and

The suburban way of life is becoming increasingly common among African business and professional families.

faith in, the fairness of the judicial system. If, on the other hand, the changes in the law were not made quickly enough, the court system could not adequately meet the needs of the modernizing sectors of society.

Foreign Aid. It has been evident to most African leaders that fundamental changes in African societies cannot be accomplished without outside assistance. Financial help for economic development has been forthcoming from many sources, as has technological aid supplied by foreign specialists. While the need for these specialists has been widely understood, their presence has become an irritating factor in an already tense situation of major social adjustment. Inevitably they have been open to the accusation of interference in the internal affairs of African countries because of the vital nature of the tasks they perform. If they are citizens of the former colonial country, they are doubly under suspicion as agents of neocolonialism.

The occasional outbursts of resentment against foreign financial and technical assistance are a reflection of the intense strains to which African societies have been subject during a period of social revolution. They illustrate, too, the essential dualism in young educated Africans, who are aware of the necessity for technical advice but react against outside influences that seem to be directing their lives. The insecurity that affects Africans today is a product of the search for touchstones of permanence in a world that appears to be totally in flux. The old and trusted framework of family and lineage is being eroded by irresistible forces that are creating the new societies, but it may take individuals many years to find their places in the new social order.

Protest Literature. The strains of the postindependence period have been mirrored in the work of contemporary African writers. Such novels as Chinua Achebe's *Things Fall Apart* and much of the poetry of French-speaking African authors are in part an expression of protest against personal insecurities in the world about them. The theme of the desire to return to a golden age of Africa before the European period and to recover the essential values of African life lost in the colonial era contrasts sharply with the African's search for identity in a modern world.

New Interest Groups. With the weakening of the traditional structures of African society new groups have formed, based on needs created by modern economic life. In the cities, where ethnic identification increasingly plays a secondary role to association with craft or business interests, professional groups and labor unions have in some degree begun to form the bases of the new societies. But for the rural areas, where modernization has only begun to appear, the old loyalties still retain their power.

L. GRAY COWAN, *Author of* *"The Dilemmas of African Independence"*

12. The African City

Compared with other continents, Africa's level of urbanization remains low. Among the chief reasons for the generally rural location of Africans are their largely subsistence economies and the consequent lack of work opportunities for urbanites. Young men and women trained for urban jobs by the expanding school systems often find that suitable employment is unavailable in the towns.

Nonetheless, about a third of all Africans live in cities and towns. It is of great political and social significance that Africans have been exposed, through mass media and the presence of foreigners, to the patterns of life and the extent of affluence of the industrialized nations. Unlike, for example, the societies of Eastern Europe, which inhibited contacts of their citizens with wealthier communities during the period of construction and reconstruction following World War II, Africa in its period of economic construction has been wide open to foreign influence. What has been called the "international demonstration effect" has created demands that migrants expect Africa's cities to meet—demands that the cities frequently cannot meet because of national poverty, adverse trade balances, difficulties of administration, and other problems characteristic of developing regions. Consequently, cities have become arenas within which the dissatisfactions of being poor can be expressed and acted on.

Urban-Rural Social Patterns. While urbanization may be a somewhat stressful feature of African social change, the way many Africans organize their urban lives affords them genuine continuity between rural and urban experience. The voluntary associations formed in towns by migrants from particular rural areas provide financial and psychological support for newcomers, permit the migrants some articulated public influence, and maintain the social pressures appropriate to rural life. Thus many urban Africans retain close contact with rural communities and perpetuate traditional customs with regard to marriage, morals, and economic and political obligations. Furthermore, the maintenance of kinship and geographical ties mitigates the estrangement many feel in city living.

In some areas, particularly, in Southern Africa, men may work in cities or mining areas and remit money to their rural families. Their wives and children operate the family farms, and the men return if urban employment becomes unavailable. Even among the relatively urbanized Yoruba of West Africa it is common for families to maintain plots of land close to the city so that they may enjoy urban amenities while practicing rural skills. In this way involvement is possible in both the potentially affluent urban money economy and the more familiar and secure agricultural subsistence economy.

There are other, less desirable consequences of the African pattern of rural-urban migration. While the transfer of money from men employed in the cities or mines to their rural families helps distribute wealth, it also slows the growth of urban capital funds that could become a source of investment and economic expansion. Also, the maintenance of kin associations tends to keep alive ethnic loyalties and antipathies, hindering the development of an impartiality toward other people that fosters a modern urbanized economy.

In some communities, ethnic affiliations are expressed by voluntary spatial segregation. For example, Hausa people in Accra, West Africa, have tended to cluster in a certain homogeneous area. The most extreme instances of ethnic and racial segregation have been in the urban areas of white-ruled Southern African countries, where problems normally associated with urban life have been exacerbated by social attitudes requiring duplication of facilities, complex legislation, and elaborate supervision of residence and even physical movement.

Development of Cities. Before the 1960's, African cities were relatively few, small, and poor. Such urban concentrations as existed were clustered close to the Mediterranean Sea and in the industrialized areas of Southern Africa. The Yoruba, on the Guinea Coast, had the only major urban formation in tropical Africa.

As countries became independent, their new governments promoted the expansion and adornment of urban centers, especially the capitals, conscious of the city as a symbol of progress and modernity. Concern with economic development tended to focus on urban projects, often to the neglect of rural efficiency.

Contact with foreigners has been extremely important in determining the form of African cities. Often, even after independence, principles of city planning developed in Europe and North America and appropriate to their climates and social systems were applied to drastically different African conditions. Some cities, such as Cairo, in Northern Africa, and Kano, in West Africa, have sections that reflect indigenous traditions, but because most African nations are without a strong urban tradition the general pattern has been to create city forms approximating those of Europe and America.

African cities experienced phenomenal growth after the 1950's; the population of metropolitan Cairo, for example, easily passed the 10 million mark. In most countries the urban population is concentrated in one or two cities, either the capital alone or the capital and the chief port or commercial-industrial center. In many countries the largest city or urban agglomeration has a population of more than a million. Both the rapidity and volume of this growth have created problems of unemployment, inadequate housing, and strained municipal services that newcomers usually are well aware of. The rural migrants keep coming because they are willing to take their chances on improving their lot in an urban environment.

An oasis town in Egypt. Northern Africa is one of the few areas of the continent that have an urban tradition.

Although Luanda is an old Angolan city, like most sub-Saharan capitals it has developed along Western lines.

Several nations have built or planned new capitals. Two did so simply because the seat of the colonial administration lay outside the national territories. In other cases, the decision to move the capital was based partly on its congestion and partly on such considerations as economic decentralization, a geographically or ethnically more central location, or even the honoring of the president's birthplace.

LIONEL TIGER
Rutgers University

13. Health

Health in Africa is affected by a broad range of both infectious and noninfectious diseases and by a large number of social and environmental determinants. Among these determinants are living standards, food supplies, personal hygiene and communal sanitation, traditional attitudes toward illness, fluctuations in climate, and armed conflict. Many diseases found in Africa—including malaria, onchocerciasis (river blindness), cholera, and yellow fever—occur elsewhere, as in tropical America or Asia. Their pattern of spread, however, often is modified by specific local African conditions. African trypanosomiasis (African sleeping sickness), on the other hand, is unique to Africa. Measles, which in North America and Europe is a relatively benign childhood illness, is a major killer of African children because it is often superimposed on other infections, such as malaria, or on malnutrition or marginal nutrition.

Environmental Factors. Both regional and seasonal differences may affect the occurrence of diseases. In the rain forests—in coastal West Africa, the Congo Basin, and eastern Madagascar—rainfall, humidity, and temperatures are high the year long, facilitating the survival of insect vectors such as the anopheles mosquito, which transmits malaria. Although farmers can plant throughout the year, they primarily grow low-protein root crops. Moreover, cattle are not raised because of the presence of species of the tsetse fly that transmit fatal forms of animal African trypanosomiasis. Thus, because the diet is poor in protein from both animal and vegetable sources, malnutrition is widespread. Various microorganisms and parasites also thrive in this hot, humid climate, and diseases such as hookworm are prevalent.

The savanna that covers much of sub-Saharan Africa is characterized by seasonal farming and the cyclical movement of herds of livestock by nomadic populations in search of water and forage. Farmers in the savanna produce not only protein-rich grains but also cash crops such as cotton and peanuts, which in many areas have increasingly replaced cereals. In contrast to rain-forest dwellers, people in the savanna are only seasonally exposed to insect vectors such as the anopheles mosquito, and thus malaria tends to be mainly a rainy-season disease. Because both protein-rich grains and cattle are found in the savanna, protein malnutrition should be rare. However, unreliable rains and frequent droughts put savanna dwellers at high risk of crop failure, and the reluctance of herdsmen to part with their symbols of wealth greatly reduces the availability of meat. Adequate nutritional levels in the savanna are further compromised by the shift from food to cash crops and by government marketing strategies that discourage farmers from producing above their own needs. Often, government marketing boards pay little to farmers for cereals in order to sell to increasing numbers of urban dwellers at artificially low prices. The net effect is a marked decline in annual food production.

In both the rain forest and the savanna, traditional methods of slash-and-burn shifting agriculture are unable to cope with ever-increasing needs for food due to rapid population growth. This, coupled with civil strife as well as periodic fluctuations in rainfall, rural-urban population movements that reduce the supply of farm labor, and agricultural policies that create production disincentives, leads to regular cycles of mass malnutrition and starvation. Those people who are pushed into the shadow of marginal nutrition are more vulnerable to the ravages of infectious diseases.

The seasonal harvests of the savanna produce seasonal variations in nutritional levels. Young children, whose nutritional needs are great for normal growth and development, are particularly vulnerable to the preplanting scarcities that regularly occur when the previous year's harvest begins to run out. It is during this hot, dry season that they tend to be most vulnerable to measles as well. Human movement is greatest in the savanna during the hot, dry season when farming is not done. This facilitates the spread of measles because of increased human contact at a time when children's nutritional levels are usually at their lowest. Poor nutritional levels reduce individual resistance to disease, often leading to concurrent infections.

Because water is scarce in the savanna during the dry seasons, people use wells. Concentrated use of these reduced water sources makes them susceptible to contamination with a variety of microorganisms, among which are those that cause typhoid fever, cholera, and other intestinal diseases. Diarrhea caused by various microorganisms is especially serious in young children and, together with malaria and measles, is responsible for most of the infant mortality in tropical Africa.

The desert and semidesert areas of Africa support sparse populations whose health is extremely vulnerable to fluctuations in the little rainfall that does fall. The grazing and water requirements of their herds of goats, sheep, and camels require cyclical movement. However, overgrazing due to uncontrolled herd size, periodic droughts, and the cutting of shrub cover for firewood lead to progressive environmental degradation, reducing the ability of nomads to survive in these marginal lands. Droughts have had especially adverse affects not only on the economic basis of nomadic life but also on the health of nomads.

Social Determinants. The major social transformations that continue throughout tropical Africa have a significant impact on health. Progressive urbanization does not alleviate malnutrition or the transmission of malaria, but it often gives people access to potable water supplies and easier access to medical care services. This gain is frequently offset, however, by crowding and poor levels of environmental sanitation.

Sexually transmitted diseases are major problems in African urban centers, replacing some of the vector-borne diseases such as river blindness and African sleeping sickness found in the countryside. Acquired Immune Deficiency Syndrome (AIDS) has been particularly alarming. The transmission pattern of AIDS in Africa is primarily heterosexual, in contrast to the pattern

An Angolan medical facility. A big health problem in Africa is to reduce risks of reinfection after treatment.

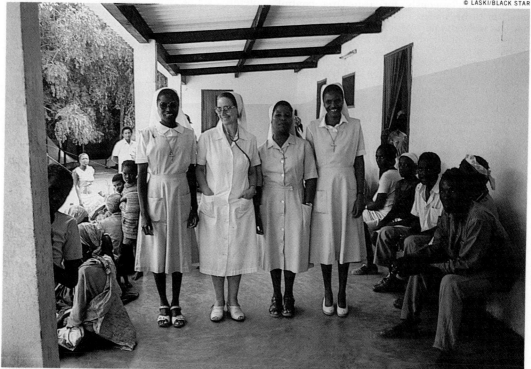

seen in Europe and North America, for reasons not fully understood. Therefore a rapid dissemination of the disease throughout Africa in the absence of any effective cure would make it increasingly a leading cause of morbidity and mortality on the continent.

Education raises levels of knowledge about the causation and prevention of diseases and modifies traditional attitudes and beliefs about disease. Yet many African countries officially promote traditional medicine, seeing it as a resource that can be mustered to supplement modern medical care. Traditional medical attitudes often worsen the course of diseases. Children with measles, for example, are frequently not given water and protein—two elements they desperately need—in the mistaken belief that these impede the development of the rash. Traditional attitudes of this kind, which once greatly hindered major disease prevention and control programs, are slowly disappearing as education spreads.

The Conquest of Disease. Mass immunization and environmental health programs have had great impact on the health of tropical Africa. These have demonstrated that diseases such as measles, tetanus, diphtheria, and whooping cough can be prevented in individuals and controlled in large populations. Programs aimed at the vectors of certain diseases, such as malaria and river blindness, have had to be more complex, employing a variety of strategies to ensure success. In the case of malaria, stagnant water sources where mosquito larvae breed are drained, chemicals known as larvicides are placed in stagnant water, and spray insecticides are used to kill adult mosquitoes. In addition, people are given drugs to suppress the malaria parasites and are advised to screen their dwellings, use mosquito nets, and wear protective clothing. All of these measures must be implemented simultaneously for a malaria control program to be successful. However, economic barriers prevent many African states from implementing any or all of them in most areas where there is a need. The emergence of strains of malaria parasites resistant to the drugs that have long been used for suppression and treatment is a major challenge. This form of malaria is particularly dangerous to outside visitors to Africa who possess no immunity to the parasites.

In general, great progress has been made in producing medicines effective against the major infectious diseases in Africa. Among outstanding examples are the oral drugs oxamniquine, praziquantel, and metrifonate, for the treatment of the parasitic worm infection schistosomiasis. Highly effective, easy to use, and with few side effects, such drugs represent a great leap beyond the toxic injection drugs that once had to be given over several weeks. However, modern medicinal cures are often expensive and thus unaffordable for many in Africa. In addition they have limited value in helping those who are constantly exposed to reinfection.

The conquest of disease in Africa must take place on several fronts. People must be treated, but their risk of reinfection must also be eliminated. This can be achieved only through improvements in sanitation, immunization programs, control of insect vectors of disease, raising levels of nutrition, and altering human habits.

PASCAL JAMES IMPERATO, M.D.
Author of "A Wind in Africa"

THE ARTS

The arts of Africa are fully understandable only in their cultural contexts. The usual museum exhibit of the "naked" object, stripped of its associated features, is a pitiful fragment of the object in all its panoply. To begin to understand an African mask, for example—not merely to appreciate its form—one must clothe it again in its contextual accompaniments: the costume, movements, gestures, music or sound effects, staging, and even lighting of the masquerade presentation. All of these aspects of the masquerade would have been immediately comprehensible to the onlookers, for whom the "arts" were an integral part of their daily lives.

Thus the cultural context of an African sculpture, dance, or folktale includes not only its immediate surroundings but the entire ethnographic environment in which it appeared and functioned. Although Africa is as diverse in peoples, languages, and cultures as Europe is, certain broad features of the role that the arts played in traditional societies can be distinguished. Whether promoting agricultural or human fertility, spiritual or physical health, leadership, peacekeeping, or other forms of social control, the arts served the well-being of the people and the individual. Certainly they had aesthetic or entertainment value besides, but these were subordinate to validating and reinforcing the beliefs, institutions, and customs of the community.

In addition, the cultural context of African arts has a historical dimension, which is not as well understood as its anthropological framework. The arts did not exist in a cultural timelessness, but changed along with their societies. However, the art historian has the same problems as any historian in recovering the African past, notably a lack of written documentation for which oral tradition and archaeology cannot completely compensate. Part of this process of change can be discerned in the influence of Islamic and Western forms and modes of expression. The most dynamic interplay of traditional and outside artistic currents is in modern African performing arts, where new, multidisciplinary forms such as the Yoruba "folk opera" have been created.

African arts have in turn influenced Western culture. American jazz rhythms, fundamentally African in origin, are an obvious example of this cross-cultural fertilization. Modern European painters and sculptors discovered African art in the first decade of the 20th century and undoubtedly drew inspiration from it, especially the Fauvists and Cubists.

14. The Visual Arts of Black Africa

This article discusses the art and architecture of Black Africa, the portion of the continent lying south of the Sahara. The visual arts of Northern Africa, except for the remnants of ancient civilizations, belong primarily to the Arab world and the Islamic cultural tradition. See also EGYPT, ANCIENT—*Architecture and Art;* ISLAMIC ART AND ARCHITECTURE.

The Study of African Art. Early historical references to the visual arts of Black Africa are rare. Although Muslim and European travelers occasionally noticed the arts, their reports contain little useful data for the historian. For example, although a mask caught the attention of a visitor at the court of Mali in the 14th century and Benin

(Left) The Luba of the Congo Basin made wooden carvings of female figures whose upraised hands supported seats or bowls. *(Right)* Benin specialized in bronze casting for objects such as plaques depicting the *oba* (king).

bronze plaques were observed in the mid-17th century, the descriptions fail to give a clear picture of the styles of the objects.

At times the early travelers returned with examples of art. These, often destined for the collections of European aristocrats, were treated as curiosities rather than as art objects. Some fortunately found their way into museums, and at times it is possible through such collections to fit more recent art into a historical context. However, many traditions cannot be reconstructed, not only because of the absence of data but also because of the perishability of the major media of African artists and artisans. Further, oral traditions that record the introduction or invention of art forms usually are not sufficiently complete or detailed to serve as documentary evidence. Archaeological explorations, such as those at Nok and Ife in West Africa, have revealed figurative art traditions. In fact, many relatively imperishable art forms in terra cotta and metal are known, but study of their histories has barely begun. Much depends on the future findings of archaeologists, coordinated with further investigation of more recent forms and traditions.

Too often, studies of African art have been limited to styles and types and to analyses of methods of production—in short, to the works of art themselves. The behavioral aspects of art have been inadequately reported. Information is therefore still scant on aesthetic responses, the role and status of the artist, and other sociological and psychological aspects of art and the artists themselves.

No clear division between the fine and applied arts nor between the artist and artisan can be made. It is not known whether a hierarchy of the arts existed or, if it did, whether painting and sculpture, for example, were rated higher than ceramics and weaving, as they are in the Western world.

The artist-artisan was a specialist, usually having served an apprenticeship with a master in order to acquire a particular skill. But the specialization was usually practiced only part-time. Like most members of the culture, the artist was intensively involved in subsistence agriculture or other modes of basic survival. Skills and craft specializations were usually based on the sex of the specialist; generally women were potters, and men were wood-carvers and metalworkers. In West Africa both practiced weaving, but on different types of looms. Where evidence exists, it would seem to indicate that artists were assigned a special status, usually low on the social scale. At the same time their products were esteemed as materially or socially essential.

Sculpture. Perhaps the best-known sub-Saharan art form is sculpture. The first major influx of African art into Europe was the famous bronzes of Benin, a city and kingdom in the Guinea Coast area of West Africa. Several thousand of these objects were brought to Britain following its defeat of Benin in 1897. They were immediately thought to be European-inspired on the assumption that "savages" were incapable of developing such forms and techniques. Later, a pre-European origin was established for the art of Benin and for the earlier but more recently discovered bronzes of nearby Ife. Unfortunately, scholars seem to have taken one of two sharply opposed positions: some held that African sculpture was heavily dependent on outside (and "higher") cultures, while others thought they were totally indigenous.

Among the earliest known sculptures from sub-Saharan Africa are those of the Nok culture, which flourished in the Western Sudan as early as the 5th century B.C. The style is clearly African. The head-body ratio of the Nok figurines, approximately 1:3 or 1:4, is widespread and may be considered a basic style criterion for sub-Saharan Africa that has existed for over two millennia.

At the same time, outside influences are evident in some metalworking techniques. For ex-

African masks, forming part of ceremonial or festive costumes, are made of a variety of materials, including wood (Kuba, *left*), bronze (Benin, *center*), and combinations (Senufo tent mask, *right*).

ample, the forms and decorations of brass casting among the Ashanti of the Guinea Coast are clearly Islamic in origin. Further, clothing and architectural styles have been influenced by Islamic, particularly northwestern African, forms. In sum, it is impossible to assume either a totally derived or a totally local base for African art.

The wood carvings of West and Equatorial Africa are the most numerous and best-known forms of African art. With few exceptions, the pieces are of recent date, for wood cannot long survive the climate and insects. Wooden figu-

An ivory armlet from Benin. The city was one of the few places in Africa that excelled in ivory carving.

rines have served a broad range of uses, including funerary, ancestral, commemorative, healing, and fertility functions.

Clay sculptures, fired or unfired, also appear frequently. In addition to the Nok culture pieces, terra-cotta figurines, at times associated with pottery forms, occur on the Guinea Coast among the Akan as funerary pieces and among the Yoruba as shrine objects. They have been found extensively in the Western Sudan as well. Unfired clay (or mud) sculpture is widespread.

Stone, ivory, and bone have also been used for African sculpture. Hard stone figures are rare, occurring, for example, at Ife and neighboring areas. Soft stone figures—usually soapstone or steatite—are more widespread. Ivory and bone are more easily worked than stone, although they are harder than wood. Notable among sculptures in these media are works produced in Benin and by the Warega of the northern Congo Basin.

Forged ironwork includes some figurative sculpture from the Congo Basin and West Africa, and elaborate and often highly decorated weapons over most of the subcontinent. The bronze and brass figurative works of Ife, Benin, Ashanti, and other areas of the Guinea Coast represent a tradition of copper-alloy casting that dates from as early as the 9th century at Igbo Ukwu on the lower Niger River. From that site come chased copper objects and leaded bronze castings of elaborately decorated ceremonial vessels. Afterward, Ife smiths even cast unalloyed copper.

Gold, particularly in West Africa, is usually associated with leadership. Cast or repoussé (hammered relief) objects as well as wood carvings covered with gold leaf serve as symbols of rule among the Akan peoples. Silver is used to make leadership objects among the Akan and the neighboring Fon.

Masks. Associated with sculpture are masks, which may be made of wood or other hard material but also of fiber or even painted directly on the face. Often they are linked with social controls. They may be part of the paraphernalia used in the initiation of boys into adulthood, as are the Poro masks of West Africa and the masks of the Bayaka and Bapende of Equatorial Africa. Masks may be used in funerary rites and have played a part in the structure of government, as in the higher grades of the Poro secret society. At times they are used for entertainment, often to make devastating comments on social conditions or values.

Wooden masks range in type from simple face coverings to casques, horizontal caplike structures, crests, and headdresses. They may be painted or have attached a variety of fibers, feathers, beads, and shells. Masks often are worn with elaborate costumes and have special songs and dances associated with them.

Painting and Architecture. Freely movable paintings did not exist traditionally. Prehistoric rock paintings and engravings are found over most of Africa, although those of Southern Africa and the Sahara are best known. Decorative painting on houses is widespread, but because the surface is mud or unfired clay, it is quite unsubstantial. It is usually done by women, and there seems to be a great diversity of styles, although the painting within a given geographical and ethnic area often falls into a single style complex.

A wide range of architectural forms exists: from round mud huts with conical thatched roofs to rectangular, flat-topped, mud houses with buttressed walls; from casual hemispherical structures of saplings and leaves to the exceptional stone edifices of medieval Zimbabwe. Again, imperishable forms are rare, and it will prove difficult to reconstruct a history of traditional African architecture. Architectural decoration may appear in the form of painting, low mud reliefs (painted or unpainted), and carved or otherwise embellished lintels.

Decorative Arts. Body decoration by painting, tattooing, and scarification is widespread. Such marks may serve for ethnic or family identification, or be associated with prestige or particular religious cults or societies, or be cosmetic.

Jewelry includes necklaces, bracelets, anklets, and rings. Almost any substance that lends itself to decorative or prestige use as jewelry is worked, from gold and semiprecious stones to elephant tail hairs for bracelets.

Utilitarian objects are often decorated. Thus,

Ancient traditions of Christian art survive in Ethiopia. A monastery fresco depicts St. George slaying the dragon.

wooden stools, wooden or calabash bowls and spoons, and basketry containers may be ornamented either in the process of construction or additively. Baskets may be made of several colors of fibers woven into patterns. Wooden spoons, stools, and heddle pulleys for looms may contain geometric or figurative carved forms. Wooden or calabash containers may be decorated with chip carving or pyrograved designs.

The Contemporary Scene. African antiquities are much in world demand among private collectors and museum directors. Some African countries have, in addition to art museums, open-air displays of the nation's regional architectures.

Ashanti is noted for its goldwork. At right are a tiny shield, a scorpion, and bells. Such objects often were made for counterbalances in weighing gold dust.

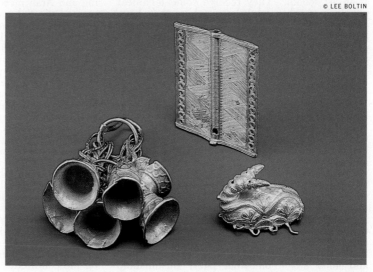

The Tuareg, a Saharan people, make fine jewelry: at left and right, earrings; center, a pendant.

Within the traditional community itself the need for new ceremonial objects persists, if only because the old ones may have deteriorated or been stolen. Many artists with traditional training also work for the tourist trade.

Increasingly, African artists have been trained not in their native communities but abroad or at African universities. Exposed to Western influences and unrestricted by local conventions, some of them have turned to new materials such as oil paint, cement, and aluminum and have incorporated subjects of foreign origin such as Christianity. Often they interpret African themes in a nontraditional, highly personal manner.

Artists of another type have emerged as well, untrained either in the traditional community or at an art school. They receive some technical guidance at urban workshops, where they have an opportunity to display and sell their works. Both the school-trained and "popular," or "folk," practitioners have enriched African art with innovative forms and modes of expression.

ROY SIEBER*, *Indiana University*

15. Music and Dance

Whenever music is played in Africa, it is usually accompanied by dancing. Likewise, as in cultures the world over, there is seldom dancing without some type of music, the dancers often making percussive and other sounds that support and elaborate the rhythmic structure of the music. Even when music is made for itself alone, the players often resort to bodily movements, while those who happen to overhear the music may break into impromptu dancing.

History. Early records of African music and dance are extremely sketchy. Dancers and an animal-horn player are depicted in Saharan rock paintings probably dating from between 6000 and 4000 B.C. Somewhat later, Bushmanoid peoples south of the equator used rock art techniques to paint and engrave what seem to be ceremonial dances, with men dancing in animal disguises and women clapping. Paintings in Egyptian royal tombs of the Old Kingdom (about 2664–2180 B.C.) depict music and dancing—arched harps, flutes, and double clarinets played in ensemble with singers, and dancers performing in stately stylized patterns. Dancers of the New Kingdom (about 1554–1075 B.C.) employ metal rattles (sistrums), wooden clappers, and hand drums as they perform; musicians play instruments such as long-necked lutes and double oboes—perhaps imported from Asia.

However, these records are almost exclusively from Northern Africa. Only centuries later, when the great West African states were flourishing and Arab merchants, travelers, and scholars crossed the Sahara to visit them, were detailed descriptions of musical practices south of the desert carried to the outside world.

Abu Ubaid al-Bakri reported the use of drums in the court ceremonies of 11th century Ghana, and Ibn Battuta witnessed royal musicians (two-stringed-lute players, drummers, and trumpeters) in 14th century Mali. Cast bronze plaques from 16th century Benin depict musicians playing ivory horns, metal gongs, calabash rattles, and wooden slit-gongs.

With the eventual control of Africa by European powers, ever-increasing amounts of information appeared regarding Africa's music and dance. But only the refinement of sound recording and photographic equipment in the 20th century brought detailed knowledge of this aspect of African culture to the rest of the world.

Musical Styles. Africa's music is as diverse as its peoples and its languages. Nevertheless, three basic styles—one of Middle Eastern origin and two indigenous to Africa—can be identified on the continent.

Arab music, found throughout the Sahara and northward to the Mediterranean, lies within the musical tradition of Middle Eastern populations. Its most striking characteristics are: (1) a rather tight-throated, nasal singing voice, commonly pitched quite high; (2) highly embellished melodic lines, often involving pitches of less than a standard European semitone; (3) melismatic relationship of text to music—that is, several notes to one syllable or word; (4) a generally monophonic (one-line) conception, though the single-melody line may appear simultaneously in variant forms (heterophony) when singers or instrumentalists perform together (there may also be a drone accompaniment to the principal melody or, with certain stringed instruments, a parallel line at the interval of a fourth or fifth; and (5) rhythmic and metric structures fairly straightforward and unilinear in design.

The typical music indigenous to Africa is more difficult to delimit geographically, since it is by no means as homogeneous a style as the other two. For general purposes, it may be said to cover most of the continent south of the Sudan, the savanna belt just below the Sahara. Its main characteristics are (1) an open, full-throated singing voice, often with a rasping quality; (2) a general lack of embellishment of melody lines; (3) syllabic relationship of words to music—that is, one note to one syllable, often delivered at a fast rate of speed; (4) polyphonic conception, harmony in two parts being perhaps the most common texture, with some ethnic groups singing by preference in parallel thirds, others in fourths and fifths, and still others in a mixture of intervals; and (5) sophisticated rhythm structures, consisting of several patterns (usually simple individually) overlaid to form a multilinear, polyrhythmic complex (see musical quotation). This last characteristic is by far the most distinctive.

Another kind of music is found among the hunting-and-gathering peoples of the Kalahari region of Southern Africa and in some parts of the equatorial forest. Its characteristics are (1) yodeling as a systematic technique for constructing the musical lines, with alternation of "head" and "chest" registers of the voice (elements such as vocal quality, melodic embellishment, and text-music relationship are subject to the peculiar restrictions of the yodeling technique—for example, vocables are used more frequently than

are actual words); (2) highly polyphonic conception, more contrapuntal than harmonic in texture, with several melodies sounding together to form the overall complex; and (3) polyrhythmic frameworks constructed generally of fewer simultaneous patterns than in the more common Black African style.

Most African musical practices fall within one of the first two styles. However, in Sudanic Africa, in the Great Lakes region, and on the eastern coast the two basic styles have interacted strongly to produce composite patterns.

Musical Scales. It is difficult to generalize about the tone systems, or scales, used by Africans. Pentatonic (five-tone) systems are commonly encountered, but hexatonic and heptatonic (six-tone and seven-tone) systems also occur. African seven-tone systems are more often akin to the earlier "modal" systems of European music than to the more recent major and minor scales. For example, Mixolydian and Dorian modes are common in African songs.

Musical Instruments. Among Africa's musical instruments, the drums have received by far the most attention in the past; however, many other instruments play important roles in the musics of the continent. Various gourd-resonated xylophones, often called by some form of the name "marimba," are distributed widely south of the Sahara. Distributed perhaps more densely within roughly the same area is the renowned African "hand-piano," commonly called *mbira*, which consists of series of metal or bamboo strips of varying lengths that are plucked with thumbs or fingers, the sound being amplified by resonators (often gourds).

Stringed instruments (cordophones), from the simplest musical bows to sophisticated harps, lyres, and zithers, are common—the former distributed widely in sub-Saharan Africa, the latter found mostly north of the equator and in East Africa. Arab long-necked lutes are found in those areas where Arab style is predominant. Wind instruments (aerophones) are perhaps the least developed of African instruments; nevertheless, animal-horn trumpets, reed flutes, and whistles abound all over the continent.

Percussive sounds, however, occupy the preeminent position in much of Africa's music. When no percussive instrument is in use, handclapping by singers and dancers supplies this element; but there are usually idiophones (instruments whose materials vibrate to make the sound) to accentuate the rhythm of the music—metal and wooden gongs, calabash rattles, scrapers, and others. Of particular interest are the slit-gongs of Equatorial Africa. Sections of logs are hollowed out through a slit in one surface; the lips of the slit are varied in thickness so that striking them at different points will provide different pitches. Consequently, slit-gongs are one of the most important forms of the famous "talking drums" of Africa; their varying pitches are used to simulate the speech tones that are essential elements of many African languages.

Besides the slit-gongs, several types of drums (membranophones, or hollow vessels with coverings of animal hide) are used for "talking," particularly the tension drums of West Africa because of their variable-pitch capabilities. Two drumheads, one at either end of an hourglass-shaped wooden vessel, are laced together around their edges by means of leather strings. Controlling the tension of these laces by pressure from

ATSIA RHYTHM PATTERNS

The relative tones and pitches of the drums and the techniques for playing have not been indicated except for the following:

1) Arrows indicate direction of the Axatse, up or down.
2) ✖ = beats in which the drum head is stopped with the stick.
3) > = beats that allow the head to vibrate free and loudly.

Atsimevu, the largest drum, is not noted here; on it the master drummer would be playing intricate variations of the rhythmic patterns given above.

A musician from the Central African Republic displays an 11-string arched harp with decorative carving. Stringed instruments in Africa, called cordophones, range from simple musical bows to sophisticated harps, lyres, and zithers.

Dancers in sub-Saharan Africa may adorn their bodies with paint to make their movements more expressive.

the arm or hand, the player can change the pitch of the drumheads and imitate the language tones. Master dummers of orchestral ensembles in Black Africa often "talk" in this manner to the dancers and spectators while the music is in progress. Membranophones frequently dominate the musical scene in Black Africa; together with the idiophones, they usually create the rhythmic complex from which the singers and dancers draw their song and their patterns of movement.

Such a complex of rhythm patterns is the atsia dance-song rhythm of the Ewe people of West Africa (see quotation). Rhythm complexes similar to this one may be encountered widely among Bantu-speaking and West African Negroid peoples. It should be noted, however, that the iron-gong (gankogui) pattern within this complex is widespread in Black Africa as a whole.

With all its various instruments, however, African music is largely vocal at basis, or potentially so. When instruments are played, usually a soloist or a chorus sings along; indeed, there are few occasions for music when singing would not be appropriate. Thus, in a sense, Africa's most important musical instrument is the human voice.

Dance. The important events in African life are always accompanied by music and dance, sometimes to the exclusion of other kinds of expression. Religious rituals, court functions, initiation ceremonies, and funerals all have their appropriate repertories. There are highly individualistic solo dances such as those of the West African fetishists and other medicine men throughout Africa, who dance to gain entree to the supernatural world. On the other hand, there are regimented, strictly choreographed dances such as the bobongo suites of the Ekonda (Equatorial Africa). Contrasting with the violent leaping dances of the Turkana (East Africa) are the earthbound, restrained dances of Yoruba women (West Africa). High on stilts, dancers of the Toma people (West Africa) perform breathtaking gyrations; down on their knees and with arms sweeping from side to side and upward,

Basotho girls (Southern Africa) perform the mokhibo dance.

Round dancing is virtually all-African. The dancers sometimes circle shoulder to shoulder, as do Chokwe women (Southern Africa) around their drummers. Sometimes African dancers move in single-file formation like Venda boys and girls (Southern Africa) in the tight, snakelike python dance that they must perform as part of their initiation rites.

On the other hand, line dances also abound, with performers abreast in long lines like those of the Chopi (Southern Africa) when they dance their elaborately arranged ngodo with its several movements (including solo and duet dances), accompanied by orchestras of many timbilas (marimbas). Formation dancing is common in eastern Africa south of the equator, some of it apparently inspired by the close-order drill practice of European military personnel of the 19th century. An example is the malipenga dance, of the Lake Nyasa area, in which men dance in platoons while humming their own musical accompaniment into kazoos made of gourds.

Patterns of Change. Male-female couple dancing, as in Western cultures, has never figured in Africa's dance traditions, and any manifestations of the practice today are the results of European influence. The "highlife" of West Africa is one of the striking examples of a basically non-African style (it is from the Americas) taken over by Africans to make a new and very popular form of music and dance for entertainment. The kwela of Southern Africa is a similar phenomenon.

However, it is not only the impact of cultures outside African continental limits that has brought about change in music and dance practices. The movements of laborers within Africa during the 20th century contributed to an interchange of African traditions, and emerging national alignments in the mid-20th century fostered an amalgamation of the music and dance traditions of ethnic groups within each nation.

Africans, however, are turning more and more to the preservation in pure form of their traditional music and dance. Although change is inevitable, there can be no doubt that the traditional music and dance practices are of hardy stock and will long remain strong and distinctive.

NICHOLAS M. ENGLAND
California Institute of the Arts

16. Black African Literature

Modern black African literature flows from the confluence of many streams—its own diverse local traditions, the impact of the Islamic and Arab worlds, and the pervasive influence of European colonialism and Christianity. Africans have been remarkably productive in the decades since World War II. Using French, English, Portuguese, and more than 40 distinctive African languages, they have written poetry, fiction, and drama and created forms for which the European world has no names. Their works portray modern social and political realities, examine both African and non-African value systems, and at the same time base themselves on indigenous traditions and distinctly African world views.

Long before the coming of the Europeans, even before the development of writing itself, the peoples of sub-Saharan Africa gave artistic expression to their deepest thoughts, feelings, and concerns in myths and legends, allegories, parables and tales, songs and chants, poetry, proverbs, riddles, and theater. Traditional forms of oral literature have continued to the present day, and new forms are still being created. They treat contemporary themes and subjects as well as those of the past. Their styles are influenced from the outside and cross-culturally from within Africa. They have adjusted to modern influences and are themselves influencing the various modes of contemporary writing. Traditional literatures suggest models for new structures, new techniques, and new styles that transcend the fixed literary patterns imposed by Europe.

HERBERT SHORE
University of Southern California

Playing drums, Kikuyu in ceremonial costume perform a traditional dance in celebration of Kenyan independence.
©FREDERICK AYER III/PHOTO RESEARCHERS

ORAL TRADITION

The African tradition of oral literature is as rich in content and variety as that of any other major cultural area, folk or civilized, past or present. This tradition is less well known to the Western world than is African art, for it has not been studied extensively and has received little publicity. Prose narratives—myths, legends, folktales, anecdotes, and jokes—are the most collected form of African oral literature, but of equal importance in African society are proverbs, riddles, song and drama texts, poetry, praise names, and tongue twisters. These forms possess a basic homogeneity and a remarkable vitality, even among urban dwellers, who are experiencing rapid cultural change. In fact, the governments of some nations have employed traditional literature to serve the nationalistic ends of identity and esprit de corps. The works of many contemporary writers display the influence of the oral legacy, in subject matter, style, and spirit.

It has been estimated that there exist in Africa over a quarter million myths, legends, and folktales. Most of the prose narratives share types (plots) and motifs (incidents, characters, and objects) with those found in other culture areas of the Old World, indicating a unity brought about by diffusion. Each African society, however, has refashioned these elements in its separate literature according to its own cultural dispositions.

Myths and legends are seldom differentiated from history in indigenous classifications but are regarded as true historical narratives distinct from folktales, which are held to be fictitious. Animal trickster folktales, featuring the tortoise, hare, rabbit, chevrotain, or spider, are the best-known African narratives. Human and divine tricksters, kings and commoners, twins, hunters, ogres, and the "little people," among many other characters, also figure prominently in African folktales.

Proverbs are employed frequently to give point and add color to conversation, and their skillful use is a mark of erudition and elegance of speech in African societies. Many proverbs are subtle and can be understood only by those who are familiar with the culture of the user. Examination of a body of proverbs will provide significant insight into a culture's basic values.

Riddles have been studied far less in Africa then proverbs, because they are told mostly by children. Ordinarily they are couched in the form of a statement rather than a question, and the connection between query and reply can be subtle and require deep understanding of the cultural matrix for comprehension. Both tone-riddles (statements linked only through tonal similarity) and proverb-riddles (adages that are meaningfully linked but may be used independently) are reported from Africa. Sometimes riddles are recited not to puzzle the audience but as a form of social interaction in which the answers are known by all and are recited in unison. In most African societies the store of riddles is stable and is known to most of the group.

Storytelling is a fine art in Africa and is professionalized in some societies. Folktales usually are told at night during the dry season, and the interplay between narrator and audience has a highly dramatic quality. The expert storyteller is a skilled actor, employing voice, hands, and body to best effect while mimicking the antics of the trickster or the stalking of the hunter. Riddling often precedes storytelling, and the folktale is punctuated with music and song, with participation by the listeners. A question posed by the narrator may be answered by the audience, or the audience may act as a chorus answering solo songs. As the story unfolds, the audience will interpolate its assent from time to time, and on occasion it may criticize the narrator for some deficiency in performance.

The genres of oral literature serve many functions in African society. In addition to providing amusement, these forms are used to educate the young, to validate ritual and belief, to promote conformity to cultural norms, and to provide psychological release in an institutionalized manner. Often a terse statement of proper behavior is appended to a folktale told to children in order to emphasize its moral implications. Riddles serve to sharpen the wits of young people, just as dilemma folktales, which have no correct answers, do for their elders. Myths are regarded as an authority on questions of supernatural belief and ritual practice and are called on to justify land ownership, social position, and political authority. Proverbs may be used in ordinary conversation to guide, to encourage, to praise, to admonish, and to reprove. They may be cited in court as precedents in developing a case or used as rhetorical devices to sway the judges. Drama associations among the Ibibio-speaking peoples use satirical plays acted by humans and puppets to exert social control over persons and groups failing to conform to cultural precepts. Finally, distortions of cultural reality in folktales may represent wish fulfillment. The characters in a narrative often act as the people wish they could but cannot because of social restrictions; thus the telling of the folktale has a cathartic effect.

JOHN C. MESSENGER
Ohio State University

WRITTEN LITERATURE

The streams of written literature, like those of oral literature, trace their course far back into the past. Antar (Antara ibn Shaddad al-Absi), an Afro-Arab warrior-poet who died in in 615 A.D. before the advent of Islam, is the subject of a celebrated epic entitled *Sirat Antara (The Antar Romance)*. Portions of this prototype of the Arabic romance of chivalry were written by Antar himself. Its narrators created a style of their own and were called "Antarists" (*Antariyya*). Some of Antar's verse and many other poems in the long *Romance* refer to his African origins, and this was the first classical work concerned with color prejudice. The black poet Abu Dulama ibn al-Jaun, who died in 777, wrote witty verse for the Abbasid court in Baghdad. Ziryab (Abul Hasan Ali ibn Nafi), an Afro-Persian known as the "Black Nightingale," went in 822 to Spain, where he made an enormous contribution to the evolution of Andalusian poetry, music, and singing.

All of these poets were born slaves. Other displaced African writers emerged in various parts of Europe, and afterward in the Americas. Among them were Juan Latino (born in Guinea), who wrote in Latin, and Afonso Alvares, the first to write in a European language (Portuguese). The experience of being a slave and then a freedman inspired what must be the first African account of exile written in a European language: *The Interesting Narrative of the Life of Olaudah*

Equiano or Gustavus Vassa the African, Written by Himself (1789). In this autobiography Equiano describes his boyhood in Nigeria, his kidnapping, his life as a slave in the American South and the Caribbean, and ultimately his life as a freedman in England.

Literature written in Africa can be traced back at least to the 18th century. The earliest extant Swahili manuscript, *Utenzi wa Tambuka (The Narrative Poem of Tambuka)* dates from 1728. The 19th century produced the poetry of Joaquim Dias Cordeiro da Matta (Angola) and Caetano da Costa Alegre (São Tomé), as well as works by several Xhosa South Africans: the poems and both fictional and autobiographical narratives of Samuel E. K. Mqhayi; the poems and hymns of Kobe Ntsikana; the didactic poetry of William W. Gqoba; and the protest writings of Hadi Waseluhlangani, who was called "the Harp of the People."

20th Century Pioneers. Among those authors who pioneered modern black African literature prior to 1945, four figures stand out. All but one wrote in African languages.

The continent's first modern novelist to achieve international recognition, Thomas Mofolo (South Africa), wrote three important works of fiction in Southern Sotho: *Moeti oa bochabela (Traveler to the East),* an allegorical account of African life in ancient days and the conversion of Africans to Christianity; *Pitseng (To the Pot)* a village love story centering on the education and courtship of two young people; and the most famous of the three, *Chaka,* a biographical novel of the great hero-figure from the Zulu past, first published in 1925 and translated into many European languages. All three novels reflect Mofolo's Christianity but at the same time reveal a deep identification with his own people and his own cultural traditions.

Jean-Joseph Rabéarivelo (Madagascar) is a tragic example of the impact of colonialism on a sensitive imagination. Rabéarivelo taught himself French and dreamed of meeting the French poets he admired from afar. His country became for him a physical, moral, and intellectual prison, driving him to despair and finally to suicide. Although his influences were the poets of France, he assimilated into his work the quality of the traditional Malagasy *hain-teny* oral poetic form and developed the technique of the extended image. His poetry became his substitute for the freedom that he believed he would never know. —Four volumes make up the body of his work—*Sylves, Volumes, Presque-songes,* and *Traduit de la nuit.*

Shaaban Robert (Tanzania) was the first Swahili African writer to write in a variety of genres, drawn from English as well as Swahili models. He was a master of traditional techniques but wrote to be read rather than sung. Shaaban was among the first to advocate acceptance of Swahili as the principal language for all of East Africa, and he wrote short stories and poetry for people like himself who had received no higher education. His essays, on many subjects, are collected in *Kielezo cha Insha (Model Essays)* and his other works in the multi-volume *Diwani ya Shaaban.*

Modern prose fiction in Yoruba had its genuine beginnings in 1938, when Olorunfemi Fagunwa (Nigeria) produced *Ogboju Ode Ninu Igbo Irunmale,* translated by Wole Soyinka as *The Forest of a Thousand Daemons.* An old hunter recounts his adventures in the thick forest. Many of the stories he tells are folktales, illustrating Yoruba beliefs about spirits, ghosts, and the strange incidents that can take place in the forest. At the same time, the book deals with ordinary problems in the daily lives of traditional households. Interspersed are moral and ethical observations. Each of Fagunwa's next three novels—*Igbo Olodumare (The Jungle of the Almighty), Ireke Onibudo (The Cane of the Guardian),* and *(Irinkerindo Ninu Igbo Elegbeje (Irinkerindo the Hunter in the Town of Igbo Elegbeje)*—is a similar quest story. His last, *Adiitu Olodumare (God's Mystery-Knot)* is less fantasy filled and more realistic. Fagunwa demonstrated how folk materials could be used in modern prose fiction, raised the consciousness of literate Yoruba to the value of their traditional legacy, and was an important influence on other Nigerian writers.

Modern Fiction. Following Fagunwa's lead and frequently using the same material, Amos Tutuola (Nigeria) wrote six books of fiction that received worldwide attention: *The Palm Wine Drinkard, My Life in the Bush of Ghosts, Simbi and the Satyr of the Dark Jungle, The Brave African Huntress, Feather Woman of the Jungle,* and *Ajayi and His Inherited Poverty.* All are stories of mythical quest, romances using Yoruba tales and legends and a style in English akin to the folk idiom, but making abundant use of modern references—X ray, electric wires, the motor horn, and the "ghost with television sets for hands."

The publication in 1958 of *Things Fall Apart* by Chinua Achebe marked the rise of the modern black African novel in English. He brought an integrated African world into fiction, and his style is indebted to oral tradition in idiom, use of proverbs, rhythm, and tenor of speech. *Things Fall Apart* tells the story of the disorientation of a well-organized, tightly knit community in Nigeria when the first missionaries and colonial officials persuade some to give up their traditional beliefs. *No Longer at Ease* is a sequel, dramatizing its conflict in a young man returning to his village from university studies in England full of European aspirations. *Arrow of God* shows Christianity as a divisive force in African society. The struggle among the gods has been placed squarely in the political arena.

By the 1960's, writers of fiction in English had turned their attention more to contemporary problems. In *A Man of the People,* Achebe used satire to criticize corrupt government and machine politics. *The Interpreters,* by Wole Soyinka (Nigeria), is a kaleidoscopic view of African urban life, told through the simultaneous misadventures of five different "heroes." His *A Season of Anomy* is an allegory of Nigeria's experiences under authoritarian civilian and military governments. The novels of Ayi Kwei Armah (Ghana)—*Two Thousand Seasons, Fragments,* and *The Beautyful Ones Are Not Yet Born*—offer a visionary reconstruction and evaluation of the past and, at the same time, a vivid impression of corruption and moral decay in independent Africa. The allegorical novel *This Earth, My Brother . . .,* by Kofi Awoonor (Ghana), describes a young man's mental breakdown in the midst of moral confusion.

Black African fiction in French dealt with the struggle against colonialism, the search for identity, and conflicts with tyranny after independence. Mongo Beti (Cameroon) attempted to destroy pretenders to political, cultural, and spiritual superiority. His novels are masterly erosions of both Christian and colonial myths. *Ville cruelle* deals with the experiences of rural Africans in a European-owned logging industry. *Le Pauvre Christ de Bomba, Mission terminée*, and *Le Roi miraculé* are satirical studies of the idiocies and cruelties of colonial rule. *Remember Ruben* (the title is in English) and *Perpétue et l'habitude du malheur* concern the struggle just before independence and the impact on individuals of authoritarian rule. *La Ruine presque cocasse d'un polichinelle* carries these same themes into the period of independence.

Ferdinand Oyono (Cameroon) wrote with a conscious and purposeful realism, biting humor, and a gift of merciless observation in his principal novels, *Une Vie de Boy, Le Vieux Nègre et la médaille*, and *Chemins d'Europe*. The imaginative recreation of an authentic African reality and world view permeates the writing of Camara Laye (Guinea), both in a movingly poetic, autobiographical work, *L'Enfant noir*, and in *Le Regard du roi*, a complex allegory of the interplay of African and European values.

Sembène Ousmane (Senegal) achieved international renown both as a filmmaker and novelist. His novels *Le Docker noir, Ô Pays, mon beau peuple!, Les Bouts de bois de Dieu, L'Harmattan*, and *Le Dernier de l'empire* are epic in scope and conception, combining revolutionary fervor with a distinctly humanist vision, reaching beyond realistic narrative in their delineation of human strengths and weaknesses, heroism, and communal solidarity.

Ngugi wa Thiong'o (Kenya) became East Africa's major modern novelist. His first three books deal with Africans under colonial rule. *Weep Not, Child* is a story of hardship and suffering during his country's war for independence. *The River Between* is set during the founding of the Kikuyu Independent Schools Movement, an attempt to provide an alternative to missionary education. *A Grain of Wheat* tells a complex and powerful story of betrayal and suffering in the aftermath of independence. Ngugi's central themes were political power and the movement of history; his major fictional symbol was the land. *Petals of Blood* and *Caitaani Mutharabaini* (written in Kikuyu and translated as *Devil on the Cross*) were penetrating critiques of independent Kenya.

South Africa has a rich tradition of fiction in African languages, most notably in the works of A. C. Jordan and Jordan K. Ngubane. A. C. Jordan's novel *Ingqumbo Yeminyanya* (*The Wrath of the Ancestors*) is a classic of modern Xhosa fiction. Ngubane's novel *Uvalo Lwezinhlonzi* (*His Frowns Struck Terror*), written in Zulu, was followed by *Ushamba* in English, a work that was banned in South Africa.

The first black South African novel in English to attract international attention was *Mine Boy*, by Peter Abrahams. His works, written mostly while he lived in Ghana, England, and Jamaica, also include *A Wreath for Udomo, Wild Conquest, The Path of Thunder*, and the autobiographical *Tell Freedom* and *Return to Goli*.

Alex La Guma's short novels offer an intense delineation of the particularized realities of South African life under apartheid, but they move beyond the limits of naturalism and provide profound and disturbing insights into humanity. *A Walk in the Night* and *And a Threefold Cord* deal with life in a Cape Town ghetto. *The Stone Country* draws graphically on his own experiences of imprisonment. *In the Fog of the Season's End* is a novel about the activist struggle in South Africa, and *Time of the Butcherbird* deals with the forced removal of black Africans to territorially segregated "homelands." Bessie Head, although South African by birth, spent most of her life in Botswana. The themes of exile and alienation are central to her novels— *When Rainclouds Gather, Maru*, and *A Question of Power.*

Es'kia Mphahlele became the most widely known of the black South African writers in English. His *Down Second Avenue* is a masterpiece of autobiographical writing, and it was followed by a second book in the same genre, *Afrika My Music*. He also wrote essays in literary criticism—*Voices in the Whirlwind* and *The African Image*. In two novels he treated the theme of exile: *The Wanderers* draws extensively on his own exile experience; and *Chirundu*, set in Zambia, is in part concerned with two black South African exiles, one of whom concludes that a return to police custody and torture is preferable to remaining abroad.

The short story form produced a rich harvest of writing in South Africa. Mphahlele's short stories were collected in *Man Must Live* and *The Living and the Dead*. Nat Nakasa, Can Themba, Arthur Maimane, Bloke Modisane, Richard Rive, and Alex La Guma, among others, produced small masterpieces in this genre.

Writing in Portuguese, Bernardo Honwana of Mozambique gained prominence for his short stories. In Angola, José Luandino Vieira came to the fore with his *Luuanda*, three long tales that captured the language and life of the urban poor.

Modern Poetry. African poetry in French had its modern birth outside the continent, among poets who attempted to rediscover an African identity, to reassert a lost sense of dignity, and to proclaim the heritage of African history and culture to a European-dominated world that had denied its existence. In his famous *Cahier d'un retour au pays natal*, the Caribbean poet Aimé Césaire gave the name *négritude* to that assertion of African identity. For Leopold Sédar Senghor (Senegal) the concept became an aesthetic, a mystique, and a theme. In his essay *L'Esthétique négro-africain* he attempted to define *négritude*, which he illustrated in his *Anthologie de la nouvelle poésie noire et malgache de langue française*. With these and his own volumes of poetry, *Chants d'ombre, Éthiopiques*, and *Nocturnes*, he became the voice of the movement. *Négritude* was reflected in the poetry of three other West Africans: Birago Diop, David Diop, and Bernard Dadié. The poem *Souffles* by Birago Diop is often quoted as an illustration of *négritude*. Tchicaya U Tam'si (Congo) interwove the influences of surrealism, Césaire, French symbolism, Roman Catholic imagery, the Congo landscape, and the anguish of exile to produce five powerful books of poetry—*Feu de brousse, À Triche-Coeur, Épitomé, Le Vente*, and *Arc musical*.

African poetry in English treated similar themes and subjects. Often it added a dimension of humor, sometimes bitter and sardonic, at other times warm and genuinely comic.

Christopher Okigbo (Nigeria), seemed to escape the alienation and frustration of the earlier generation. His best known works, *Heavensgate* (in four parts) and *Limits*, are about ordeal, agony, and cleansing. Two collections, *Idanre and Other Poems* and *A Shuttle in the Crypt* marked Wole Soyinka as a major Nigerian poet. Kofi Awoonor's impressive collection *The House By the Sea* includes a group of powerful poems written during the year he was imprisoned by a military government.

South African poetry in English is filled with the passion of protest and the poignancy of exile. Dennis Brutus produced collections—*Sirens, Knuckles and Boots, Letters to Martha and Other Poems from a South African Prison, Thoughts Abroad, A Simple Lust, Strains,* and *Stubborn Hope*—that deal with imprisonment, revolution, and liberation, and with the experience of exile. Arthur Nortje, described by Brutus as "perhaps the best South African poet of our time," was forced into exile and committed suicide in 1970. His poetry is collected in *Dead Roots.* Like Brutus, other major poets left South Africa and wrote in exile: Mongana Serote's writings include an important volume of poetry, *Tsetlo,* and a novel, *To Every Birth Its Blood;* among Keorapetse Kgositsile's collections are *Spirits Unchained, For Melba, My Name Is Afrika, The Present Is a Dangerous Place to Live In,* and *Herzspuren* (published in Germany); Mazisi Kunene, a poet and a scholar of Zulu literature who wrote in both Zulu and English, attempted in two large-scale epic poems—*Emperor Shaka the Great* and *Anthem of the Decades*—to capture the spirit, the substance, and the techniques of Zulu oral tradition.

The number of African poets writing in Portuguese grew dramatically in the 20th century. Leading among them in the years prior to World War II were Eugénio Tavares and Jorge Barbosa of Cape Verde, the blind poet and folklorist Óscar Ribas from Angola, Rui de Noronha of Mozambique, and Francisco José Tenreiro from São Tomé. The bridge to the modern period is found in the work of Mário da Andrade (Angola), not only in his own poetry, but in his seminal collection *Literatura africana de expressão portuguesa.* Contemporary poetry in Portuguese includes the work of Agostinho Neto (the first president of Angola), Valente Malangantana and José Craveirinha of Mozambique, and António Cardoso of Angola.

Theater. Although theater flourishes in modern Africa, drama, in the form of published literary texts, seems sparse. From an African perspective, there is no contradiction. Theater is a highly complex, multidisciplinary *performing* art, tracing its development far back into black African traditions. The *ntsomi* was a Xhosa performing art, as were the masquerades of Nigeria. The Zulu performance *Umxakazawakogingqwayo* was written down from an oral performance in the late 19th century. The folktale, the praise song, and certain rituals and ceremonies, among others, were themselves forms of theater. They combined song, music, mime, the spoken word, dance, and other forms of symbolic action, together with costume, props, and masks, while providing all the elements of plot, characters, and action, as well as spectacle, that make theater. They have continued to the present day, incorporating contemporary material and often absorbing external influences into their modes and techniques of presentation.

These traditions have also given rise to new modern forms, such as the "concert party" in Ghana and Yoruba "folk opera" in Nigeria, that do not lend themselves readily to the publication of meaningful printed texts.

African performing arts flourished also in the form of biblical plays in which the Scriptures were handled freely, often with ribald humor, and African music and songs played an important role. In the 1940's and 1950's, Hubert Ogunde (Nigeria) secularized this type of theater, turning it first to popular entertainment and then to shrewd, humorous, and effective social criticism. Ogunde, followed by Kola Ogunmola (Nigeria) working in the same vein, created the genre that came to be known as Yoruba folk opera. Ogunmola's masterwork was an operatic version of Amos Tutuola's *The Palm Wine Drinkard.* Duro Ladipo's *Oba koso (The King Does Not Hang)* is one of the few folk operas that were published in their original language, and his *Three Yoruba Plays,* including *Oba koso* and *Oba waja (The King Is Dead)* were published in English versions. These works, drawn from Yoruba history, myth, and legend, are best appreciated in performance. The dialogue is minimal. The language is filled with proverbs, allusions, and imagery. The themes are austere and tragic, and a major part of the impact lies in the music, drumming, and ceremonial dances.

J. P. Clark (Nigeria) wrote several important works in English for the stage: *Song of a Goat,* a moving drama set in an Ijaw fishing village on the Niger Delta; *The Masquerade; The Raft;* and *Ozidi,* a reworking of an Ijaw ceremony for the modern stage. But by far the most significant African dramatist to emerge was Wole Soyinka (Nigeria). Confronting the artistic task of African self-apprehension, rooting himself in the mythical and cosmological world of the Yoruba, and at the same time dealing with contemporary subjects relevant not only to Nigeria but to all of Africa, Soyinka created penetratingly powerful, yet often satirically comic stage works. African in their idiom, they are universal in their perceptions and impact.

Soyinka's *A Dance of the Forest,* commissioned to celebrate Nigerian independence but banned from performance, is a complex work, textured in Yoruba myth, of a nation forced to look clearly at its own history, its illusions about itself, and the choices confronting its people. *The Lion and the Jewel* and *The Trials of Brother Jero* are comic satires on village and urban life and the veneer of Europeanism. *The Strong Breed* and *The Swamp Dwellers* are poignant dramas of village life. *Kongi's Harvest* portrays an African dictator and the personality cult that surrounds him. *The Road, Death and the King's Horseman,* and *Madman and Specialist* are complex philosophical dramas. These represent only a portion of Soyinka's output for the theater, which made him, indeed, the most prolific dramatist on the continent.

For his achievements in drama, poetry, and fiction, as well as criticism and theory (*Myth, Literature and the African World*), Wole Soyinka in 1986 was awarded the Nobel Prize for literature. The first black African writer to receive that honor, Soyinka accepted it not for himself alone but as a recognition of the literary achievements of all of Africa.

HERBERT SHORE
University of Southern California

HISTORY

At the end of World War II, as African independence approached reality, Africans exhibited an accelerating interest in their history. There was need to discover a past that could support and nourish future freedom, adding self-respect to self-determination, banishing the prejudice of colonial masters who had seen Africa's history solely in terms of European occupation. The independence years, therefore, witnessed a vigorous growth of historical scholarship by individuals and by departments of history in the new national universities. New works appeared, written by Africans, examining Africa's past from an African perspective and looking far back into the period before modern European contact.

17. African Historical Writing

The recovery of Africa's past presented problems of methodology. Most African peoples were preliterate, and extant written sources were by necessity foreign—Arab, European; Muslim, Christian—dealing with an alien bias and an accidental, partial time span. African historical research, therefore, had to go beyond the written word, to utilize sources scarcely recognized by conventional methods. The need was great and African historians responded with resourcefulness. Analysis of modern African languages was utilized to trace ancient movements of peoples, such as the vast migration of Bantu speakers across subequatorial Africa in the two millennia of the Christian era. Archaeology was diverted from the study of monuments to the humbler but essential analysis of village sites, markets, and middens, the better to know the social and economic character of early African societies. Study of genetic changes in animals and plants yielded further information regarding the origins and nature of early peoples. Perhaps most striking was the use of oral evidence, in the form of traditions that had survived by word of mouth through the exertions of either amateurs or professional linguistic specialists. Such devices, however, had their limitations: oral evidence, for example, could sustain a time depth of only a few hundred years. But the new sources were invaluable supplements to available written documentation.

African historians also sought to break away from the conventions of Western historical research: to ask different questions of their material and to turn from the "ancient," "medieval," and "modern" divisions of European historiography. These many efforts had their successes, from the revolutionary historical theses of the Senegalese scholar Cheikh Anta Diop to systematic teaching and research by numerous university history departments. By the mid-1960's historical studies in Africa had achieved impressive results in the training of specialists and publication of their research. Afterward, however, faltering economic and political progress across the continent brought growing doubt and disillusion concerning the efficacy of historical studies that seemed to be only romantic appeals to a useless past. African historians nevertheless remained undaunted, secure in the knowledge that new contemporary needs would ultimately arise to ask new questions of the African past, a past that would again be an essential means to an understanding of the African present.

ROBERT W. JULY
Author of "A History of the African People"

18. Prehistory

African prehistory encompasses the vast span of time before the practice of making written records began in Africa. Thus the greater part of the continent's history can be reconstructed only through archaeology, historical linguistics, related disciplines, and reliable oral traditions.

Early Hominid Evolution in Africa. A particular area may produce an unusually large number of fossils merely because it has been more thoroughly investigated than others. However, a rich distribution of finds may reflect a genuine pattern from the past. In regard to the early hominids of eastern Africa—humans and near humans—the latter explanation seems to be valid. Good grounds exist for believing that in this area, and no other, hominids evolved from a common ancestor shared with the apes.

About 10 million years ago, wide areas of African forest began to become savanna or grassland. Between 8 and 4 million years ago, although the fossil record is sparse, it seems that early ancestors of human beings developed a habitual upright posture and striding two-footed (bipedal) gait, adaptations suitable to open country. By about 3 million years ago, the changed environmental conditions sparked a burst of evolutionary activity, and contemporaneous remains of bipedal hominids have been discovered in eastern Africa at many sites.

These upright-moving hominids eventually included several species of near-human australopithecines (members of the genus *Australopithecus*), as well as a being commonly called *Homo habilis* and thereby recognized as human. Scientists disagree, however, about the taxonomic status of *H. habilis* and as to which, if any, of the australopithecines could have been in the direct line of human ancestry. Also unclear is which early hominids were toolmakers as well as tool users, since more than one type of hominid has been found in the deposits yielding the earliest recognizable stone artifacts, dated about 2 million years ago.

The Early Stone Age. The earliest hominid tools must have been of perishable materials, such as wood. The earliest known stone tools are called Oldowan, after the type site Olduvai (Oldowai) Gorge, in Tanzania. With some overlap they were succeeded, about 1 million years ago, by tools of a more developed type, among which the biface is characteristic. Bifaces are oval or pointed-oval stones carefully chipped over both faces to set and regular patterns. Some have a straight chisellike cutting edge at one end and are known as cleavers. Collections of biface stone tools are called Acheulian after St. Acheul, France, where they were first recognized, although the African finds are older.

Acheulian tools are commonly associated with a more advanced type of hominid, *Homo erectus*, although in some areas the species seems to have maintained the chopping-tool tradition. *H. erectus* had a brain about twice the size of the australopithecines' but only two thirds that of modern humans. This early human being spread Acheulian tools over southern Eurasia as well as widespread parts of Africa, including areas of what is now the Sahara desert but was then better watered.

The Middle Stone Age. The Acheulian tool kit persisted for a long time, until 100,000 to 50,000 years ago. Thereafter, regional specializations were developed, first into the tool industries called Fauresmith in Southern Africa and Sangoan in Equatorial and West Africa, and then into those of the African Middle Stone Age, or in Northern Africa, the Aterian culture (about 40,000–25,000 years ago). Initially the human type was comparable to the Neandertal of Eurasia.

As different groups of the increasing population adapted their way of life to a greater variety of ecological niches, more and more specialized tool kits were developed. Hunting, fishing, and gathering wild products were the basic way of life, as before, but a greater range of strategies was employed in exploiting the resources of particular environments. Whereas the Acheulians had wooden thrusting spears, later made more lethal with a stone point, many of the Middle Stone Age peoples had light stone-tipped throwing spears.

The Late Stone Age. By the beginning of the Late Stone Age, the human type throughout Africa was the modern species, *Homo sapiens*, who used the bow and arrow and made composite tools of wood, stone, and bone. The main racial divisions of the continent were then evolving.

Certain physical characteristics of African Negroids are evolutionary responses to a hot climate but with differing conditions of humidity. Dark skin pigmentation is a protection against ultraviolet radiation under open, cloudless skies, while an elongated body form is a response to extreme heat. Wide nostrils are an adaptation to a humid atmosphere; narrow ones, to aridity. Thus, apart from breaks in the general pattern due to past migrations, there tends to be a general cline, or gradient, within the African Negroids—from the tall, narrow-nosed types in the north and east of the Negroid area to the broader-nosed, squatter types in the west and center. The Pygmies probably represent a highly specialized bodily adaptation to dense forests.

The Capoid physical type of the extreme southwest is characterized by low stature, reddish-yellow skin, peppercorn (tightly spiraled) hair, and female steatopygia (enlarged buttocks). This is the physical type of the Khoikhoi (Hottentots) and San (Bushmen). Now confined almost entirely to the Kalahari arid zone, Capoids were formerly more widespread. Their genetic history remains obscure, but they are believed to be less distinct from the Negroids than was at one time thought and to be another specialized development from what was originally a common stock. Most of the peoples of the Sahara and Mediterranean Africa belong to the Caucasoid physical type. A fourth racial strain, the Mongoloid, was introduced into Madagascar from Indonesia, probably during the first millennium A.D.

In northwestern Africa the Aterian tool culture was succeeded by the Iberomaurusian (about 20,000–7,000 B.C.) and the Capsian (about 7,000–4,000 B.C.), while south of the Sahara the Late Stone Age seems to have begun at dates ranging from 40,000 to 10,000 B.C. in different areas. For all these communities hunting was an important economic (and probably social) activity, to judge by the small, shaped stone artifacts known as microliths, some forms of which were slotted into arrow shafts as points and barbs. The gathering of wild products was also important, although it commonly leaves less obvious traces in the archaeological record.

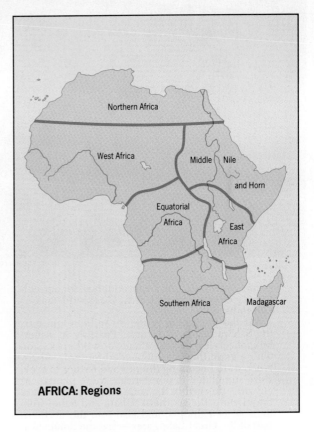

AFRICA: Regions

As population increased, different communities exploited an even greater range of environments and devised more specialized techniques for the purpose. Seasonal movement was often involved, and from Nubia and certain areas near the Nile Valley in Egypt comes evidence of the intensive collection of wild grain. By 10,000 B.C. cemeteries with bodies pierced by stone arrow points suggest intercommunity warfare, perhaps occasioned by population growth outstripping local resources. During the 6th to the 4th millennia B.C. the southern Sahara and adjacent semiarid Sahel were still considerably wetter than at present, supporting communities that derived much of their subsistence from fishing in the lakes and streams. This way of life also stretched down into the northern part of the Great Lakes area of East Africa. Dependence on such aquatic resources would seem to imply at least a semisedentary type of existence. The central Sahara was also wetter than now, and its highlands in particular were the home of large numbers of cattle pastoralists. The cattle, widely portrayed in Saharan rock art, may have been derived from an indigenous domestication of the wild North African ox or from cattle introduced via Tunisia or Egypt.

By the 5th millennium B.C. people in the lower Nile Valley were able to adopt cereal agriculture, despite the lack of rainfall. They used the annual Nile floodwaters to irrigate their crops of wheat and barley, whose domestication earlier had been pioneered in winter rainfall areas of Southwest Asia. Sub-Saharan Africa, however, where natural irrigation is generally unavailable, lies in the summer rainfall zone and it is impossible to grow wheat and barley there by dry-

Prehistoric rock paintings in the Sahara date from perhaps the 9th millennium to the 2d millennium B.C. The Sahara formerly was much better watered than it is today, and the central highlands supported numerous cattle pastoralists. The region began to dry up about 3000 B.C.

© GEORGE HOLTON/PHOTO RESEARCHERS

farming methods. As a consequence, for agriculture to develop in that area, local wild grasses had to be domesticated.

At the beginning of the 3d millennium B.C., the Sahara began to dry up. Possibly its fisherfolk, observing that the stands of wild grasses on whose grain they also depended for their subsistence were becoming thinner and farther to seek, were stimulated to domesticate these plants. At any rate, it is just in the zone across Africa where they lived—the southern Sahara and Sahel from Senegal to Ethiopia, and also into the northern part of the Great Lakes area—that the domestication took place. The local wild grasses formed the African tropical grain crops known today: millets—Guinea corn (sorghum), pearl (bullrush) millet, and finger millet—African rice, fonio ("hungry rice"), chindumba ("jungle rice"), and the tiny Ethiopian grain called teff. Goats and sheep (as well as pigs, but less important) must have been spread from the northeastern corner of Africa into the rest of the continent.

The Iron Age. Most of sub-Saharan Africa missed out on a Copper or Bronze Age and passed directly, at widely different times in different areas, from the Stone Age into the Iron Age. Only in Mauritania and Niger was copper exploited before the advent of an iron technology. At Akjoujt, Mauritania, copper ores were worked in the 5th century B.C.; arrowheads and other weapons and tools made of copper have been found in the surrounding area. Native copper was exploited even earlier in the Agadès region of Niger, but ores were not smelted. It is uncertain whether the metallurgy practiced at Akjoujt and in Niger gave rise to an iron technology in sub-Saharan West Africa or whether ironworking was introduced there from the area of Mediterranean Africa influenced by Carthage.

Carthage was probably founded, toward the end of the 8th century B.C., by settlers from the Levant, an area in which iron had become common for tools and weapons before it did in Egypt (after 600 B.C.). Iron smelting was practiced on a large scale in Meroe, on the middle Nile, from the 5th century B.C. onward, and it has been suggested (though it now seems less likely) that it was from Meroe that ironworking penetrated the Lake Victoria area of East Africa by the 5th or 4th century B.C. Iron-smelting furnaces of about the same date are known from West Africa, associated with the remarkable terra-cotta figurines of the Nok culture in Nigeria.

Long-established cereal-farming communities existed in the savanna lands of West Africa, probably at least from the 3d millennium B.C., but in the forests of the eastern part of that region food production had been established on the basis of yams and other tuberous crops and oil-palm products. The acquisition of iron must have made forest farming more efficient and may have helped to build up population pressures. In the central part of eastern Nigeria and in adjacent Cameroon, people speaking a language ancestral to the Bantu linguistic group began a movement eastward through the savanna lands and northern forest margins of Equatorial Africa until they reached the northeast angle of the rain forest, where they turned southward. What generated this movement is not known; data to demonstrate population pressure as the stimulus are insufficient, although this is the most commonly offered explanation. Another group from the same homeland seems to have reached the savanna lands south of the equatorial rain forest either coastally or along tributaries of the Congo (Zaire) River at a somewhat later date.

These eastern and western streams of Bantu migrants interacted to form complex movements of dispersal over the rest of subequatorial Africa, having reached the Transvaal and Natal by the middle of the 1st millennium A.D. Much of the southwest corner of Africa had been inhabited by hunting-and-gathering Capoid peoples. In some areas they survived and were able to maintain their way of life alongside the Negroid farmers; in others they were driven out or absorbed. In some parts of Africa a stone technology appears to have remained in use for more than a thousand years after iron was first employed elsewhere south of the Sahara.

Where a population of settled peasants is established in an area over a long period, ultimately towns tend to arise or other kinds of centralized institutions to develop, or both. The stimulus for this development is not the same in all areas, and there are a number of potentially conducive factors, sometimes working together, sometimes in isolation, differing in different areas. It may be a matter of historical or geographical accident whether this kind of development takes place sooner or later.

298

Two factors combined to delay the process in sub-Saharan Africa: first, the need to domesticate indigenous cereals, because unlike Egypt and Europe, tropical Africa could not for climatic reasons just take over those domesticated in Southwest Asia; and second, the desiccation that in the 3d millennium B.C. changed the Sahara from a broad corridor into a barrier, just when the Nile Valley civilization was in its youthful stage in Egypt.

Despite these factors, urbanized communities and centralized government did develop south of the Sahara in widely separated places before the Arab conquest of Mediterranean Africa in the 7th century A.D. The Arabs hastened this process after they began probing across the desert, using camels and digging wells, in order to obtain gold, ivory, and tropical products. The injection of long-distance trading demands into localized exchange networks stimulated urban growth and the rise of kingly courts.

THURSTAN SHAW
Cambridge University

19. Ancient Civilizations in the North

The process by which African peoples developed agriculture, domesticated animals, and laid the foundations of settled life began in the lower Nile Valley as early as the 5th millennium B.C. There the ancient Egyptians evolved institutions of centralized government, probably because harnessing the annual floodwaters of the Nile for irrigation required the organization of a mass cooperative effort.

Egypt. A transition from small independent communities to increasingly large territorial units took place in Egypt over many centuries. It ended toward the close of the 4th millennium

B.C. when, according to Egyptian tradition, two kingdoms had emerged and were united under a ruler named Menes, who instituted the first of a long series of royal dynasties.

During the period of the first three dynasties (about 3110–2615 B.C.) Egyptian statecraft was not fully elaborated. Nonetheless, certain characteristic features of the mature Egyptian civilization and government were already evident. Arithmetic, geometry, surveying, and astronomy were known, and a 365-day calendar was devised. A native system of writing was developed. The king (pharaoh) was regarded as a god incarnate, and magnificent royal tombs were built, at first in brick but by the 3d dynasty in stone. These and also predynastic burials contained food, furniture, jewelry, and weapons for the deceased, indicating early Egyptian belief in an afterlife resembling the life on earth. The growing use of stone—for fine vases and increasingly well-proportioned sculptures in the round, as well as tombs, temples, and wall reliefs—was paralleled by advances in metallurgy. At this stage, though, the technology was based on copper, as before, rather than iron. Meanwhile, long-distance trade flourished by land, river, and sea.

This sustained growth reached its zenith under the 4th dynasty (about 2614–2502 B.C.), a period unmatched in the wealth, power, and splendor of the Egyptian state for more than a thousand years afterward. A complex system of royal officials administered the details of government at the capital and in each province. The king kept tight control of the bureaucracy by granting high offices in this period only to members of his own family. The centralized and absolutist rule of the divine pharaoh is epito-

Civilization in Africa began in Egypt, where the three Great Pyramids were built in the 26th century B.C.
© STEVE VIDLER/LEO DE WYS

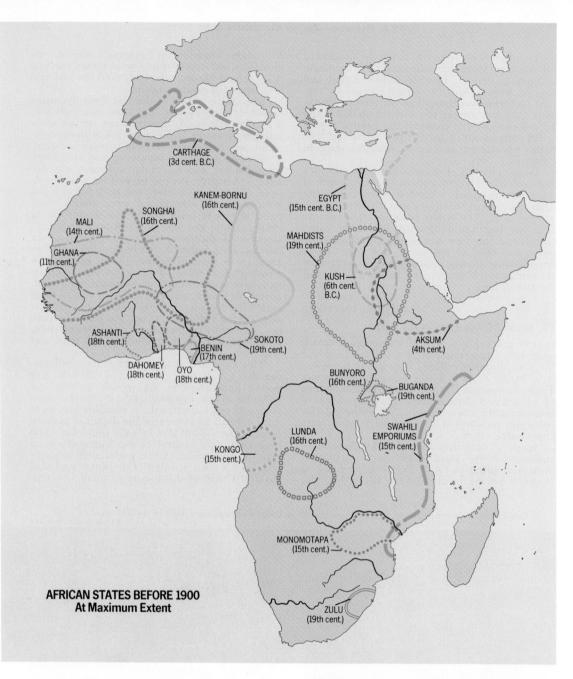

AFRICAN STATES BEFORE 1900
At Maximum Extent

Map labels:
CARTHAGE (3d cent. B.C.)
KANEM-BORNU (16th cent.)
EGYPT (15th cent. B.C.)
MAHDISTS (19th cent.)
SONGHAI (16th cent.)
MALI (14th cent.)
GHANA (11th cent.)
KUSH (6th cent. B.C.)
ASHANTI (18th cent.)
BENIN (17th cent.)
SOKOTO (19th cent.)
AKSUM (4th cent.)
DAHOMEY (18th cent.)
OYO (18th cent.)
BUNYORO (16th cent.)
BUGANDA (19th cent.)
LUNDA (16th cent.)
SWAHILI EMPORIUMS (15th cent.)
KONGO (15th cent.)
MONOMOTAPA (15th cent.)
ZULU (19th cent.)

mized by the tomb of Khufu (Cheops): the largest of the three Great Pyramids at Giza, it is surrounded by lesser tombs for his queens, children, and courtiers. In statuary and relief sculpture, a level of excellence was reached that continued into the 5th dynasty but was never surpassed.

After the 5th dynasty, which ended in the 24th century B.C., Pharaonic Egypt experienced two major periods of decline followed by two of recovery. The particularly resplendent 18th dynasty (about 1554–1304 B.C.) foreshadowed a final waning of the empire's creative energies a century and a half later. It was under the 18th dynasty, whose wealth is barely suggested by the tomb treasures of a minor ruler, Tutankhamen, that Egypt became a great military power, extending its dominion into Asia as far as the borders of Mesopotamia. The last great

warrior-pharaoh, Ramses III of the 19th dynasty, repelled a mass onslaught of migrating "Sea Peoples"; but from the close of his reign (about 1158 B.C.) the empire was confined to the Nile Valley. Exhausted by incessant wars the civilization of Egypt lapsed into stagnation, though it survived in mummified grandeur for many centuries to come.

Carthage. Egypt, lacking timber resources, had long traded with port cities on the eastern side of the Mediterranean for wood from the famed cedars of Lebanon, ancient Phoenicia. As early as the mid-8th century B.C. the seafaring, trade-minded Phoenicians began sending out colonists to the western Mediterranean, where their most important foundation was Carthage. Situated on the African coast facing Sicily, at the narrowest point of the great inland sea, Carthage controlled communications between the eastern and western Mediterranean, enabling the Phoenicians to command trade through the connecting passage. Inland from their port cities, which extended eastward to the Gulf of Sidra and westward as far as the Atlantic, the Phoenicians showed little interest in permanent settlement. The African hinterland was left to its indigenous Berber inhabitants.

Isolated from their homeland by the Assyrian conquest of Phoenicia and Egypt in the 7th century B.C., the western Phoenicians rallied around Carthage against the expanding Greeks. Thus Carthage came to dominate the other Phoenician settlements in the west, creating a commercial empire in which foreigners could trade only with Carthage itself. The city exchanged locally produced textiles, olive oil, and wine, together with luxury items from Greece and Italy, for gold, silver, tin, and iron, which it obtained through its far-flung satellites. Monopolizing the export of these metals from its mercantile domain to the eastern Mediterranean, Carthage grew rich and powerful.

The Greeks. Although the thrust of Greek expansion toward the Carthaginian sphere was directed at Sicily and the Italian peninsula, the Greeks founded important colonies in the coastal area of Africa east of Carthage, between the Gulf of Sidra and Egypt. Their chief settlement was Cyrene, which from the late 7th century B.C. prospered as an exporter of grain, wool, dates, and especially "silphium," a medicinal herb that sold for its weight in silver. The city was a seat of learning, as well, noted for its medical school and philosophers.

Greeks helped Egypt regain its independence from Assyria under the 26th dynasty (664–525 B.C.), and the new rulers encouraged Hellenic settlement. In the Nile Delta the Greeks founded the city of Naucratis, which became the center of trade and cultural exchange between Egypt and the Aegean region.

Egypt, and also the Cyrenaic cities, submitted to the Persians in 525 B.C. As a result, when Alexander the Great of Macedon conquered the Persian Empire in 334–330 B.C., Egypt entered the orbit of Hellenism. The country was governed for Alexander and his legitimate successors by one of the conqueror's generals, Ptolemy, who afterward ruled Egypt as the first king of the Ptolemaic dynasty (305–30 B.C.). The city of Alexandria, founded by Alexander in 332 B.C., replaced Naucratis in trade and influence, emerging as the focal point of Greek cultural penetration of Egypt and a leading intellectual center of the Mediterranean world.

Kush. Along the middle Nile on Egypt's southern flank was the land of Kush (Cush), or Nubia. At times this region was at least partly under Egyptian control, and its native culture acquired a strong Egyptian overlay. The pharaohs' interest in Kush was economic as well as military, for the country exported to Egypt much gold, along with ivory, ebony, hides, and aromatic oils.

In the 8th century B.C., having reasserted their independence some time before, the Kushites conquered Egypt; their ruler, Piankhi, became the first king of Egypt's 25th dynasty (736–657 B.C.). Although expelled from Egypt

Leptis Magna was the largest Roman city in Africa after Alexandria and Carthage. The ruins are in Libya.

by the Assyrians in the 7th century B.C., the Kushite kings continued to rule in Nubia, first at Napata and from the 6th century B.C. at Meroe, farther south.

Despite Egyptian influence, which is most evident in tombs and other architecture, Kush retained its own gods and language and developed its own script. Meroe was a major center of ironworking, and East Africa may have acquired iron technology from that source.

The Romans. The Carthaginians and Greeks had fought a long series of inconclusive wars, mainly over Sicily, that ended only with the appearance of a third major power on the scene. The new contender for supremacy in the Mediterranean was Rome, which defeated Carthage in the Punic Wars (264–146 B.C.) despite severe setbacks of its own when the Carthaginians invaded Italy under Hannibal. The city of Carthage was destroyed, and its territory was made the Roman province of Africa. With the absorption of Cyrenaica in 96 B.C., Egypt in 30 B.C., and Mauretania (west of Carthage) about 42 A.D., all of Mediterranean Africa belonged to Rome.

With the decline of Roman power in the western half of the empire, northwestern Africa was overrun by the Vandals early in the 5th century. The Vandals were expelled from Carthage and adjacent areas about 100 years later by the Eastern Roman general Belisarius, but Mauretania was not regained and passed into several centuries of obscurity.

Aksum, in ancient Ethiopia, had many commemorative monoliths, some carved to resemble multistoried buildings.

MARC & EVELYNE BERNHEIM, FROM RAPHO GUILLUMETTE

Egypt was part of the Eastern Roman (Byzantine) Empire from the beginning, though lost to Persia briefly in the 7th century. In 642, soon after its restoration, it was conquered by an Arab army under the banner of Islam. The Arabs continued westward clear across northern Africa, and from Mauretania in 711 invaded Spain. The peoples of Mediterranean Africa, who largely had become Christian, were for the most part gradually converted to the Muslim faith.

Aksum. The Arab conquest of Egypt cut off from the Mediterranean world the mercantile kingdom of Aksum (Axum), which had arisen centuries before in the highlands adjacent to the southwestern shore of the Red Sea. The Aksumites were a genetic and cultural blend of Africans related to the Kushites and of immigrants from southern Arabia. The kingdom maintained close relations with Egypt, and through its Red Sea port of Adulis and interior caravan routes it had a prominent place in the commercial network linking the Mediterranean lands, eastern Africa, and India. Aksum exchanged local spices, gums, and tortoiseshell—together with imported gold dust, ivory, rhinoceros horn, and animal hides—for Egyptian metals and manufactured goods. The kingdom reached the height of its power, prosperity, and cosmopolitanism in the mid-4th century under its ruler Ezana, who in his greatest military campaign crushed the state of Kush. Ezana had adopted Christianity, and slowly the people of Aksum followed his example.

The troubles that after Ezana's time beset Rome and the Middle East disrupted the trade on which Aksum depended and severed its contacts with other Christian countries. Moreover, the kingdom lost its seacoast to the Arabs and could no longer prevent incursions of Beja nomads from the north. External pressures soon were coupled with a decline of central authority and with warfare among the nobles. By degrees the Aksumites moved southward into the interior of the plateau and its mountain fastnesses. There they mixed with related peoples to whom they introduced their Semitic language, Ge'ez, and their Monophysite Christianity, foundation stones of an Ethiopian civilization that embodies the longest-independent state in Africa.

For the exploration of Africa in ancient times, see under EXPLORATION AND DISCOVERY. For the history of Northern Africa from the Arab conquest to the 19th century, see under EGYPT and NORTH AFRICA.

20. Sub-Saharan Societies to 1800

When the Sahara began drying up some three millennia before Christ, its inhabitants were pushed outward in many directions—notably southward, to people the western savanna and forest. By the time of Christ the southward movement had resumed its impetus in the great Bantu dispersion that covered almost all of subequatorial Africa, in the process displacing indigenous hunter-gatherer nomads. Meanwhile, other peoples emerged from the Ethiopian highlands to dispute the eastern high plains with the Bantu. By 1800 A.D., many states had risen from these movements—some already defunct, such as Kongo; others flourishing, such as Buganda; and still others in decay, such as the Swahili coastal emporiums. As the migrations continued through the 19th century more states were to arise.

© GEORG GERSTER/PHOTO RESEARCHERS

Djenné, in West Africa, adopted Islam about 1300. Its mosque has permanent scaffolding prongs for easy repair.

With the fall of Rome the Mediterranean world lost sight of Africa for many centuries; much more aware were the Arabs, whose long and intimate mercantile contact with the coast of East Africa was expanded in the 7th and 8th centuries as Islam swept across Northern Africa and began to move southward, both up the Nile Valley and across the Sahara. What the Arabs found were established African powers: the kingdom of Ghana in the west and the Christian states of Nubia, Maqurra, and Alwa, where Kush had once held sway, along the Nile.

Ghana. The western savanna kingdom of Ghana (not to be confused with modern Ghana to the southeast) was already thriving when it came to the notice of Arab commentators late in the 8th century. Significantly it was first mentioned as the "land of gold," the wealth of its black Soninke kings squarely based on a trans-Saharan trade that sent merchandise such as animal hides, ivory, ebony, and slaves to the Maghrib (Northern Africa west of Egypt), but chiefly gold dust or ingots destined for the bullion-hungry markets of Europe and the Middle East. In return the southerners received fine cloth, steel, perfumes, cowries, and glass beads, but it was the salt brought south from the mid-Saharan mine at Taghaza that was most eagerly sought in the saline-starved West African savanna.

Taghaza lay in the open desert, a cheerless site of brackish water and sand flies. Its only permanent inhabitants were the slaves who mined the salt from open pits, cutting out 200-pound (90-kg) blocks that were loaded on camelback and marched several hundred miles south to the savanna. If the caravans were late in returning with provisions, the miners could starve; many of them already suffered from blindness caused by the severe sandstorms of the region. At Taghaza the plentiful salt was utilized as a building material for the houses of the inhabitants. By the time it reached the savanna markets, however, it had become so precious that it was said to be worth its weight in gold. Bro-

ken into smaller pieces, it was spread widely throughout West Africa, serving not only as a necessity for health but as a form of currency as well.

The gold mines lay to the south of Ghana in a region known as Wangara. This term was loosely applied, for the exact location of the mines was kept secret by their workers and, in fact, involved several sites. The gold-bearing areas were primarily alluvial plains that had been honeycombed with narrow underground galleries, dark and awash with seepage, where gravels were extracted by children or young girls because of their small stature. The gravel was floated to a central point in baskets and then washed in calabashes to separate the precious particles. When ready, the gold was marketed by means of the celebrated "silent trade," whereby seller and buyer assembled at an appointed site, offering alternately and without speech what they were willing to exchange until an agreement was struck.

Although the Ghana kings did not control the gold mines, their surveillance of the trade was sufficient to ensure their wealth and power. They amassed their wealth simply by taxing the gold on its way north, the king confiscating the nuggets while letting the gold dust pass. This practice was both a tariff and an economic necessity designed to forestall oversupply in distant markets and a ruinous devaluation.

The mid-11th century marked Ghana's apogee. At that time the king was described holding court amidst a splendor that featured royal animals and retainers caparisoned in gold, the royal horse tethered by a heavy gold nugget. But in 1076 the Ghana capital of Kumbi Saleh was sacked by Sanhaja Berbers from the city of Awdaghost to the northwest. The Sanhaja were led by a puritanical Muslim sect, the Almoravids, and their attack on the pagan Soninke people marked the beginning of Ghana's decline. Its strength ebbing and its trade disrupted, Ghana survived until the early 13th century when it was overrun by a minor state and onetime vassal. By then, however, the locus of savanna power was already tilting eastward toward the burgeoning state of Mali.

Mali. As with Ghana, the Mali kings relied for their wealth on the Saharan trade and its market cities such as Timbuktu, which had been founded about 1100 by Tuareg nomads. Situated at the top of the Niger bend, Timbuktu grew as a major southern port of call for caravans reaching the Sahel, as the Arabs called the southern "shore" of the Saharan "sea." Like Kumbi Saleh and later caravan terminals such as Gao and Kano, Timbuktu was a cosmopolitan city and a religious center featuring a fine mosque doubling as a university in the Muslim tradition, along with large libraries that attracted the learned and scholarly. An early 16th century traveler, Leo Africanus, reported the fine homes and busy shops in the Muslim quarter; the lively trade in copper, spices, ivory, ostrich feathers, and slaves, along with the gold and salt; the sweet-water supply brought from the Niger by canal to support an abundant dairy and grain production; and the lavish display of wealth by the governor, whose gold-bedecked court was reminiscent of the glory days of Ghana. A city of some 25,000 when visited by Leo, Timbuktu had a chiefly Mandinka (Malinke, Mandingo) population noted for its gentle and cheerful disposition, and its fondness for public celebrations that featured singing and dancing far into the night.

Savanna cities like Timbuktu were an exotic growth nurtured primarily by the desert commerce. Beyond the towns lay the timeless Africa of small farming villages where families worked their fields with the short-handled hoe, cultivating sorghum and millet along with beans, squash, melons, and citrus fruits. To be sure, such villages were part of the savanna trading network, for salt and other goods arriving at the Sahel emporiums were quickly diffused throughout the region. Occasional travelers and provincial traders like the Dyula and Hausa visited village markets where they exchanged salt, cowries, or cloth for chickens, millet, sour milk, and other farm products. Basically, however, these farming hamlets were self-sufficient, surviving in an area of uncertain rainfall and varying land fertility. The people put much stock in the mutual support of clan and lineage, and were governed by chiefs and elders whose local authority remained largely independent of the princes of the realm.

Village and kingdom were linked, however, for the rulers of Mali had sprung originally from local clans, spreading their fiat as much by the mutual obligation of lineage ties as by military exploits. Tradition names Sundiata as the founder of Mali during the first half of the 13th century. He and his successors quickly expanded their realm at the expense of other powers like Tekrur to the west and the Songhai in the east. Sundiata was a pagan, but by the reign of *Mansa* (King) Musa a hundred years later, the royal line had been converted to Islam. Muslim historians described Musa's pilgrimage to Mecca in 1324, remarkable for its lavish bounty that astonished the outside world and for a time depressed the value of gold on the Cairo exchange.

Mali continued to thrive until the end of the 14th century when complications of royal succession and outside pressures precipitated decline.

By 1450 the subject state Macina had gained its independence, the Tuareg and Mossi were crowding in from the north and south respectively, while Songhai, led by its great chieftain *Sunni* Ali, was expanding from its base at Gao on the Niger bend. Timbuktu fell to Ali's armies in 1468 as Songhai began a century-long domination of the upper Niger country and its trade northward across the desert from the marts of Gao and Timbuktu.

Songhai. Like *Mansa* Musa, the Songhai rulers from *Sunni* Ali onward were nominal Muslims. But they also followed traditional religion and custom, for the savanna population remained resolutely devoted to its time-honored practices, and royal authority rested as much on customary as Islamic sanction. The power of the Songhai was essentially military. Ali's energetic campaigning carved out the bulk of the state, largely at the expense of Mali, and after his death in 1492 the renowned *Askia* (King) Muhammad Toure consolidated and extended Ali's work.

Muhammad's successors proved ineffectual, however, complicating succession and encouraging hostile neighbors. In 1591 an army was able to cross the desert from Morocco, defeating Songhai at the Niger River and blotting out the kingdom.

Ethiopia and the Middle Nile States. The Moroccan conquest put an end to empire in the western Sudan; in the east Muslim-inspired pressures had long tried resident states. The Ethiopians, cut off from the Hellenistic world by the 7th century expansion of Islam, were forced to stand by powerless in their mountain fastness as a ring of Muslim states formed on their southern and eastern frontiers. During the early 16th century the Muslims united to attack the Ethiopians, overrunning and laying waste much of the country, and converting large numbers to Islam. With great difficulty the invaders were finally repulsed, their defeat effected with aid of the Portuguese, who had only recently arrived in eastern Africa.

Ethiopia's ability to survive did not extend to those other Christian states—Nubia, Maqurra, and Alwa—located in the Nile Valley. They had stood firm during the Arab occupation of Egypt in the 7th century, but coexistence of Muslim Egypt and the Christian south was shattered by Egypt's aggressive new Mamluk rulers in the 13th century. Military campaigns and large-scale Arab immigration eventually toppled the southern kingdoms. Their populations were absorbed by the Arabs and became Muslim. Their territory was devastated and eventually occupied by a new power, the Funj, of obscure origin and recent conversion to Islam. The Funj sultanate, which had appeared suddenly along the Blue Nile early in the 16th century, maintained hegemony over the eastern Sudan for 300 years.

Kanem-Bornu. Across the savanna in the central Sudan, just east of Lake Chad, the Kanuri people were also reaching the height of their powers. Their origins went back many centuries, their Saifawa dynasty dating probably from the 800's. By the 11th century the Saifawa *mais*, or kings, appear to have been converted to Islam, and Kanem dominated the central Saharan trade routes, spreading its influence northward to the Fezzan.

Ensuing political and military reversals forced the Kanuri to migrate to Bornu, on the western side of Lake Chad, where they reestab-

© HARRISON FORMAN

The stone ruins of Zimbabwe date from the 14th century and earlier. Zimbabwe became the seat of the Rozwi kings.

lished themselves late in the 14th century and slowly regained their strength. During the reign of *Mai* Idris Alooma (1571–1603) the Kanuri once again dominated the central Sudan. Alooma reconquered Kanem, defeated the Tuareg and Teda on his northern frontier, and secured Hausaland to the west. Military strength was combined with an administrative efficiency, based in Islamic law, that prompted a contemporary tribute to his greatness: "So he wiped away the disgrace, and the face of the age was blank with astonishment."

The Hausa States. Alooma's successes in Hausaland were due as much to Hausa disunity as to Kanuri military prowess. Situated between Songhai and Kanem-Bornu, the Hausa states—Gobir, Daura, Katsina, Zaria, Kano, Rano, and Biram—claimed a common tradition of northern origin. But unity ended there, for the Hausa spent much of their strength in internecine warfare, failing to join forces even against outside aggression.

Typical savanna farmers, the Hausa raised barley, rice, and cotton in fields surrounding their walled trading cities, especially Kano and Katsina, that catered to the trans-Saharan commerce. Islamic culture and religion arrived gradually via these urban centers, conversion probably coming from Bornu, although Hausa tradition claims Songhai. Orthodoxy touched the Hausa lightly, however, and their political dissension was intensified by religious differences that reflected the long-standing confrontation between the orthodoxy of Islam and the strength of traditional religious practice.

The Swahili Emporiums. The juxtaposition of Islamic and traditional African culture was also apparent among the Swahili emporiums of the East African coast. Like the kingdoms of the savanna, these city-states had long antedated Islam in the region, sharing an ancient Indian Ocean trade that joined India, southern Arabia, Egypt, and East Africa. The traders were mostly Arabs, many of whom settled on the East African coast, giving rise to a mixed population that came to be named Swahili. Islam took hold later, probably during the 13th century, adding its character to the cultural mixture of Swahili civilization. The term Swahili meant many things—

a people, a culture, and a language, all mixtures of diverse elements. The language, for example, is a combination of Bantu and Arabic.

Each year the traders came from the north, from southern Arabia, or in earlier times even starting from Egypt. Before the expansion of Islam they might have stopped at Adulis, the port city of Aksum. From there the trip took them around the Eastern Horn of Africa and down the Somali coast to Mogadishu, the northernmost of the Swahili ports. The ships brought foodstuffs, crafted glass, pottery, and cloth. In return the traders received animal products such as tortoiseshell, leopard skins, and particularly ivory. The skins were favored in Arabia, where they were made into saddles. Ivory in quantity went to India and China for use as decorative objects such as sword handles, the palanquins of Chinese nobility, and ceremonial bangles used in Hindu marriages. Some specialization was also apparent. Mogadishu, for example, produced a cloth popular in Egypt, both Malindi and Mombasa to the south exported worked-iron goods, while Kilwa and Sofala farther down the coast came to be known for their special trade in gold.

The coastal emporiums usually were sited on islands for defensive purposes, though unlike offshore Zanzibar most were separated from the mainland only by tidal creeks. Judging from surviving accounts the Swahili were prosperous and comfortable. The renowned Berber traveler Ibn Battuta, visiting the coast in the 14th century, reported lavish dress and domestic arrangements at Mogadishu as well as heavy meals of rice with ghee and side dishes of stewed meats, fish, and vegetables. Later, Portuguese explorers noted the riches of Kilwa, prominently displayed by ladies bedecked in gold and silver jewelry. Today the ghost town of Gedi, just south of Malindi, is a graveyard of fine stone structures—houses, a palace, and a mosque—bespeaking a mercantile community that thrived from the 14th to the 16th century.

Monomotapa. Although the Swahili emporiums were oriented outward as part of an Indian Ocean commerce, they had important mercantile contacts with the African interior. Excavations far inland have yielded quantities of coastal seashells, Indian beads, and Chinese porcelain; moreover, the gold of Sofala and Kilwa came from a country that lay between the Limpopo and Zambezi rivers, a land called Monomotapa by the Portuguese after the praise name *Mwene Mutapa* of its *mambos,* or kings. Monomotapa was celebrated not just for its gold but also for its great citadel of Zimbabwe. Besides attracting the Swahili coastal trade, the country's fame and gold lured Portuguese expeditions that arrived on the coast early in the 16th century.

Migrating Bantu peoples were probably in the land between the Zambezi and Limpopo rivers well before the end of the 1st millennium after Christ. By the early 2d millennium, the latest of successive waves had occupied the site of Zimbabwe. At first consisting of rough walls, the stone construction at Zimbabwe grew in complexity and refinement until the mid-14th century, which marked the acme of the Zimbabwean architecture. The construction, of close-fitted but unmortared dressed stone, is unique in design: its purpose was to house the king in an elaborate kraal more imposing than the simple mud-and-wattle architecture of the average village. A state also took shape, elaborated in the 15th century under the direction of the *mambos* Mutota and his son Matope of the Rozwi dynasty. Their warmaking earned them the praise name *Mwene Mutapa,* or Master Pillager, and pushed the nation's frontiers to their farthest extent, from the Indian Ocean westward to the Kalahari Basin.

The substantial production of gold, presided over by these forerunners of the Shona and shipped down the Zambezi to the ports of Kilwa and Sofala, was mined from open shafts. Gold mining appears to have been a royal monopoly, but the trade was dominated by coastal merchants traveling upcountry, dealing in ivory as well as gold. Matope died about 1480, after which strained communications and court intrigue among an increasingly heterogeneous population led to an eventual breakup of the realm. The southern provinces seceded to form the Changamire kingdom, while the reigning *mambo* moved his court northward near the Zambezi.

States in Equatorial Africa. The realm of the *Mwene Mutapa* was only one, though the most illustrious, of the numerous states created by the Bantu expansion. The kingdom of Kongo, for example, took shape during the 14th century south of the lower Congo River, as a confederation that extended about 200 miles (320 km) along the Atlantic coast and inland almost to the Congo's Kwango tributary. The king, or *manikongo,* ruled through provincial and district officials, who held their posts at his pleasure, collecting taxes and directing trade. As in the western savanna, however, the basic unit was the village with its locally chosen head.

Another state, the small principality of Ndongo, lay south of Kongo. Its affairs were directed by the ruling *ngola,* although for a time, during the 16th century, the *ngola* acknowledged the paramountcy of the *manikongo.* From *ngola* came the modern name Angola.

Kongo and Ndongo were to fall afoul of Portuguese aggression, but farther inland other Bantu states prospered, untouched by external interference. Along the upper reaches of the Kasai River, east of Kongo, the Lunda people created a powerful kingdom beginning about 1600, its

cultural and political influence blanketing the Congo-Zambezi watershed.

West African Forest States. Historical linguists hypothesize that the Bantu originated in an area near the Benue tributary of the Niger River. In this event, Bantu languages are an offshoot of the large West African Niger-Congo family stretching from Senegal to Cameroon and beyond. Indeed, the early Bantu speakers left a vast region of thriving communities that gave eventual rise not only to major kingdoms of the savanna but also to important states in the West African forest zone.

Many West Africans have traditions of eastern and northern origins—for example, the Yoruba of western Nigeria. Yoruba legend suggests the possibility that strangers settled at the site of Ife during the first millennium after Christ, mixing with the indigenous population and eventually founding the Oyo empire, even taking a hand in the development of the nearby non-Yoruba kingdom of Benin. These states were probably founded during the early years of the 2d millennium, and by the late 15th century the ubiquitous Portuguese encountered in Benin a well-administered and stable power. Oyo was also developing in strength, but the spiritual and artistic center of Yorubaland remained at the shrine city of Ife.

Ife became the center of an unusually creative artistic outburst, chiefly in ceramic and metal figures of remarkable beauty and craftsmanship that rank among the world's sculptural masterpieces. Many were naturalistic portraits of royalty and their attendants, the earlier pieces of terra cotta and later examples cast by the lost-wax method in copper or brass. These works have been dated between the 11th or 12th and the 14th centuries. The center of casting then shifted to Benin, producing another flowering of magnificent metal sculpture work down into the 19th century. Benin bronzes were a product of the same lost-wax techniques but were much more stylized than their realistic Yoruba forerunners, although they too were devoted primarily to celebrating the persons and exploits of royal patrons.

Metal casting was not limited to Ife and Benin, however. To the west, the Akan-speaking Ashanti were noted for the inventiveness and humor of their cast gold-weight figurines, used as counterbalances in weighing gold dust. Ashanti political and military talents gave rise to an empire that took shape in the 17th century and came to dominate the Gold Coast area until the advent of European colonialism in the mid-19th century.

Ashanti beginnings were modest. Probably between the 11th and 13th centuries they had moved south into the Kumasi area, where their village communities were unified by 1700 largely through the exertions of Osei Tutu, an early *asantehene,* or king. Osei Tutu established the spiritual unity of Ashanti through the sacred Golden Stool, which was said to have descended from the heavens "in a black cloud . . . amidst rumblings." (See also GOLDEN STOOL.) Tutu's successor, Opoku Ware, campaigned east and west, also extending the Ashanti hegemony south to the coast and far into the gold-producing regions of the north. Subsequent *asantehenes* developed a remarkable bureaucratic administration that transcended and replaced clan loyalties and held the Ashanti confederacy intact until

A Yoruba *oni*, or king *(left)*, was portrayed in bronze at Ife before the Portuguese reached the area in the 15th century. A Portuguese musketeer *(right)* was depicted in bronze at nearby Benin.

beset by British military action on the eve of the European scramble for Africa. Although the Ashanti were subsistence farmers, the state gained much of its wealth from trade, not only in gold but also in slaves, which its rampaging armies gathered in the course of systematic raiding.

The Great Lakes Region. Concurrently, far to the east, the important kingdom of Buganda established itself along the northwestern shore of Lake Victoria. It, too, based much of its wealth on a profitable slave trade, in this case with the Swahili merchants of the East African coast.

The migrations that gave birth to Buganda were complex, involving not only Bantu but also Nilotic peoples and others. The Rift Valley and its adjacent highlands originally had been the habitat of Bushmanoid hunters, who were infiltrated first by peoples from the southern Ethiopian highlands, perhaps as far back as the 2d millennium before Christ, then by the Bantu expansion. Into this region also came pastoralists, Hima and Tutsi, the latter moving to the highlands east of Lake Kivu and Lake Tanganyika. About the end of the 15th century A.D., the Hima were supplanted by Nilotic Luo from the Bahr al-Ghazal tributary of the White Nile. The Luo founded Bunyoro, a monarchy that maintained its cohesion through clan loyalty surrounding the person of the ruling *mukama*. A ring of tributary principalities was established, Buganda included, but Bunyoro continued to hold the stage in this part of Africa during the 16th and early 17th centuries.

In time Buganda gained its freedom, expanding largely at the expense of its former Nyoro master, developing strength through a bureaucratic administration directed by its *kabaka*, or king. His control of long-distance trade fed the royal treasury and made possible a military strength that not only protected commercial enterprise but ensured unswerving loyalty to the crown.

The Shape of Things to Come. Like Ashanti, Buganda eventually fell victim to late 19th century colonialism, but by that time other events had taken place that brought profound changes to the map of Africa. In the western savanna, for example, while Kanem-Bornu settled into a rigid middle-aged complacency, the Hausa states bickered among themselves, their divisiveness and political impotence setting the stage for the great Fulani jihads of the 19th century. In Egypt, Muhammad Ali, an Ottoman mercenary, fought in the power vacuum caused by the departure of Napoleon's occupying forces, and awaited his moment. In Southern Africa the last stages of the Bantu expansion were to create Shaka's militant Zulu state, while on the West African coast European missionaries began the portentous process of modernization and Westernization of the continent. See Section 22—*Africa on the Eve of European Partition.*

ROBERT W. JULY (Section 20)
Author of "A History of the African People"

21. European Intrusion and the Slave Trade

During the 15th century, Portuguese mariners sailed around the southern end of the African continent searching both for a sea passage to the East and a linkage with the mythical Prester John, who, they thought, would help in a latter-day Christian crusade to recapture the Holy Land. What Prince Henry of Portugal began with his initial explorations along the West African coast, culminated at century's end in the voyages of Bartholomeu Dias and Vasco da Gama, the latter reaching India via Southern and East Africa in 1498.

European Commercial Penetration. Although intent on the Eastern trade, the Portuguese did not neglect African commerce, for they also sought gold both in West and East Africa. They therefore founded commercial colonies such as São Jorge da Mina (Elmina) on the Gold Coast of West Africa and another in the Kongo kingdom near the mouth of the Congo River, and they occupied ports such as Luanda farther south and the Swahili east coast emporiums of Sofala, Kilwa, and Zanzibar.

While the Spaniards turned westward in search of the East, others followed the Portuguese to Africa: English, French, Danes, Brandenburgers, and Swedes, but most notably the Dutch. Slaves were not a major consideration at first. More important was bullion, greatly

Fortified Gorée Island, in Senegal, was a major port for transporting slaves to America in the 18th century.

needed in the expanding money markets of Europe, although other products found favor, such as skins, ivory, and spices, exchanged for cloth, steel swords, and cowries and eventually for firearms and alcoholic spirits. Initial Portuguese contacts also contained a religious and political element. At the urging of Afonso, the Christian-convert *manikongo* (king) of Kongo, Portugal in 1512 offered to propagate the Christian faith in the kingdom and to introduce Portuguese custom and law, in return for trading advantages in ivory, copper, and slaves. Whether altruistic or self-serving, this substantially accepted early scheme for assimilation failed. Kongo could not quickly absorb such vast cultural innovations, and the Portuguese commercial exploitation and missionary zeal placed severe strains on the African state. With Afonso's death in 1545, Kongo began to disintegrate, its demise accelerated by a steadily rising slave traffic and the traumatic attacks of the militant and cannibalistic Jaga, who overran the kingdom during the late 1560's.

Overextended and with slender resources, Portugal was unable to maintain control over its African interests. In East Africa the Portuguese were eventually limited to the Mozambique coast, while their Atlantic posts foundered or were disputed by others. A promising commercial liaison with the kingdom of Benin did not survive the 16th century. The Dutch supplanted the Portuguese on the Gold Coast and for a time held Luanda, while the French established themselves on the Senegalese coast and British captains became widely active in West African waters. Drawn by a lucrative trade, these interlopers concentrated increasingly on the commerce in slaves, which was driven by the vast need for manpower generated in the New World colonies, especially the labor-intensive plantations of Brazil and the sugar islands.

The Slave Trade. The Atlantic slave trade started slowly. Estimates are highly diverse, but the most reliable figures suggest approximately 275,000 slaves imported into the Americas between 1450 and 1600, a jump to about 1.3 million during the 17th century, a dramatic increase to 6 million during the 18th century, and a decline to less than 2 million until the trade came to an end about 1870. The total of over 9.5 million does not include losses suffered en route during the infamous Atlantic Middle Passage or the decimation of populations in Africa in the course of slave raiding. Shipboard losses showed a great range, depending on such factors as length of voyage and quality of care at sea. Losses appear to have declined with the passage of time: the range recorded chiefly in the 18th and 19th centuries, from necessarily scattered samples, fell to between 10% and 25%.

African responses to the slave trade varied. The Ashanti and the Aro, an Ibo subgroup, pursued slaving with vigor and profit. For a time the kingdom of Dahomey based its economy chiefly on the trade. The Yoruba and others utilized the slave trade as a means for the disposal of war captives. Fishing villages on the Niger delta were transformed into mercantile city-states ruled by powerful families, or "houses," that accumulated large numbers of slaves to man war canoes engaged in the slave traffic. In many communities chattel slavery was substituted for traditional forms of criminal punishment.

In general, the smaller, less well-organized communities suffered as victims. In any given locale the effects could be devastating and everywhere weighed disproportionately on the younger, healthier segments of society. Nevertheless, during the period of the slave trade, there appears to have been little important demographic impoverishment. African populations seem to have sustained themselves. For example, major states like Oyo and Ashanti remained strong, and Iboland, from which many slaves were drawn, apparently suffered no serious population loss.

The European Impact on Africa. The European trade in slaves and other commodities affected Africa in many diverse ways, however. New products like firearms, spirits, and tobacco were introduced along with crops such as cassava (manioc), sweet potatoes, and maize (corn). What overall impact these imports had is difficult to assess, as is the effect of disease strains such as the smallpox that bore heavily on the Southern African Khoikhoi.

Europeans also brought fateful changes in the form of permanent settlements. Mixed Eurafrican communities appeared at Gorée and Saint-Louis in Senegal and along the windward coast of West Africa. At Freetown, Monrovia, and Libreville colonies of former slaves grew through the exertions of the European antislavery naval squadrons. Most of all, the Dutch colony at Cape Town had profound implications for the subsequent history of Southern Africa.

In 1652 the Dutch established a provisioning station at the site of Cape Town to supply ships on their way to and from the East Indies. The Cape colony soon became a permanent settlement wherein were established racial attitudes toward the resident Khoikhoi, San, and Bantu that would eventually form the basis for the system of white supremacy known as apartheid. European farmers ("Boers") trekked eastward during the 17th and 18th centuries, staking out huge ranches for their cattle, pushing the indigenous peoples aside or absorbing them as landless labor. The early Dutch settlers regarded African customs as barbaric; hence attitudes of social superiority and then racial superiority came to be marked by skin color. Chattel slavery and a local variety of serfdom soon appeared, as did an early attempt at physical racial separation when the Dutch colony was screened from the Khoikhoi by a fortified restraining hedge.

During the 19th century the Great Trek inextricably bound Boer and Bantu into an indivisible but unequal social, economic, and political union that spread from the Cape to the Transvaal. British colonial rule, first introduced in 1795 and abandoned with the creation of the Union of South Africa in 1910, had no essential impact on the unequal development of the races in South Africa. The system of apartheid, made official in 1948, had long been in effective operation as an established fact.

ROBERT W. JULY
Author of "A History of the African People"

22. Africa on the Eve of European Partition

For Africa the 19th century was an era of revolutionary change. As the century opened, a way of life held sway that had changed only by slow degrees for hundreds of years. By century's end, a modern Africa had been born.

Muhammad Ali and Egypt. The forces of modernization appeared first in Egypt and West Africa, driven by French revolutionary expansion and the British antislavery movement. Napoleon's brief occupation of Egypt (1798–1801) had brought resistance from the Ottoman Turks. Muhammad Ali, who had arrived as a Turkish mercenary, remained to wield virtually absolute power in the country for almost half a century

until his death in 1848. He seized and retained power through political and military means, but to sustain an up-to-date Westernized army he moved to modernize Egypt's inefficient subsistence economy and to introduce Western technology and scientific education. Schools were founded that taught military tactics along with appropriate scientific subjects, an attempt was made to introduce domestic industry, and traditional agriculture was transformed into an efficient cash-crop production. An effective state capitalism controlled the economy through nationalization of land as well as through pricing and production monopolies. Peasants were heavily taxed and were obliged to contribute labor for public works and for military service in Muhammad Ali's rejuvenated armies.

Egypt became the dominant military power in the Middle East, with a vibrant economy based chiefly on the export of high-quality cotton, and a society combining Western-style education, a bureaucratic government, and a dawning sense of nationalism. Such innovations soon ran afoul of British imperial expansionism and clashed with traditional Islamic tenets and institutions in ways that cast a long shadow forward, anticipating problems of Muslim leadership and modernization in the Middle East today.

Modernization in West Africa. Although less dramatic than Muhammad Ali's reforms, modernization in West Africa in the long run may have been more influential throughout the African continent. In Sierra Leone the British antislavery movement had founded Freetown in 1787 as a rehabilitation center for slaves liberated by the British navy, while at Saint-Louis and Gorée on the Senegal coast the ideals of the French Revolution found sympathetic response among the local population.

In either case there emerged small but significant numbers of Africans persuaded that European culture had important advantages in its Christianity, its technical superiority and mercantile sophistication, its antislavery principles, and its political establishments. Urged by European missionaries and government officials, Africans began to adapt to Western ideas and institutions: cash-crop agriculture along with modern technology, capitalism hand in hand with Christianity, Western education combined with Western dress. Much of traditional Africa remained, but a new leadership emerged. Churchmen, merchants, and public officials espoused revolutionary social and economic concepts that, surviving colonialism, would eventually lead toward economic modernization and to the realization of African independence.

Muslim Revolution in the Western Sudan. In the 19th century revolution also came from within. Across the West African savanna, and especially in Hausaland, complex social and economic forces gathered to nourish a growing conviction among Muslims that they were the persecuted victims of unorthodox taxation and other practices unsanctioned by Islamic law. Fulani settlers in Hausaland, primarily pastoralists, were particularly exercised by what they regarded as tyrannical and irreligious governments led by rulers of essentially unsympathetic agricultural communities. A charismatic Fulani religious leader, Usuman dan Fodio—called the *Shehu* (chief) by his followers—arose to initiate in 1804 a jihad that eventually overthrew the Hausa states. It created in their stead the vast Sokoto caliphate, which extended from the desert to the forest.

Other jihads followed. While Kanem-Bornu survived as a Muslim nation, the state of Macina appeared about 1818 on the Niger bend, to be followed during the 1850's by the Tokolor empire of the great leader al-Hajj Umar, who eventually absorbed Macina and established his rule from the Sokoto frontier as far as the French posts in Senegal. During the 1870's a Mandinka conqueror, Samori Toure, fashioned his own Muslim state across the upper Niger Basin south of the Tokolor. On the eve of the European scramble for Africa, the western Sudan had been united in Islam from Lake Chad to the Senegal River.

Upheaval in Southern Africa. Far to the south another African revolution created both unity and diversity. By the 18th century, Bantu peoples migrating across the subequatorial continent had reached deep into Southern Africa, on the eastern coast probing well beyond the Kei River. Pressed into a narrow corridor between the Indian Ocean and the Drakensberg ranges, these southern Bantu may have suffered population pressures that overtaxed the land. At any rate, early in the 19th century peaceful migration led to increasingly violent conflict, which saw the rise of an unusually gifted military leader, the Zulu prince Shaka (Chaka). Shaka revolutionized regional warfare, utilizing coordinated fighting tactics and carefully planned strategies carried out by well-drilled, strongly armed regiments, or *impis.* He redesigned the traditional *assegai,* or spear, converting the light throwing javelin into a short heavy stabbing sword that was used by massed phalanxes advancing behind a wall of large cowhide shields. An undisciplined, lightly armed foe, however brave, stood little chance against such forces.

During the 1820's, Shaka carved out a Zulu kingdom in northern Natal that absorbed many disparate groups and sent others fleeing north and west, refugees from conquest but simultaneously conquerors, preying on others who had not yet absorbed the Shakan fighting tactics. Called the *Mfecane,* or "Crushing," the Zulu expansion marked a time of great chaos, of vast migrations, of stateless refugees, and of famine, even cannibalism; but from the whirlpool of war other new states took shape. In addition to the Zulu kingdom, the Sotho and Swazi nations emerged; the Ndebele broke from Shaka, founding their own state, first in the Transvaal and later beyond the Limpopo at Bulawayo. Similarly the Ngoni fled Shaka to embark on a long migration that paused to destroy the remnants of the Zimbabwe civilization and then split into several segments that established warlike states across the eastern plains almost as far as Lake Victoria. In southernmost Africa the newly formed Bantu communities eventually were obliged to struggle against Afrikaner (Boer) expansionism signaled by the Great Trek beginning about 1836. There the Sotho kingdom was preserved by its remarkable monarch Moshesh I.

East Africa: The Omani and Buganda. Farther north, where powerful Ngoni terrorized local populations, systematic slave-catching expeditions were undertaken largely under the direction of Sayyid Said, prince of Muscat and Oman and suzerain over much of the Eastern African coast. As slaving enterprise prospered, Sayyid consolidated his grip on the Swahili coast, sub-

duing the virtually independent Mazrui governors of Mombasa in 1837 and three years later transferring the seat of government from his native Arabia to Zanzibar.

In the interior of East Africa, on Lake Victoria, Arab traders in 1844 encountered the well-organized kingdom of Buganda. The Arabs could not extend their slaving into Buganda because, under its *kabakas* (kings) Suna and Mutesa, it was too strong. Thus legitimate trade and religious proselytization was substituted.

The Mahdist State in the Eastern Sudan. The widening wave of Islamic revivalism that had engulfed the western Sudan climaxed to the east in the career of Muhammad Ahmad, who proclaimed himself the expected Mahdi in 1881. Islamic doctrine asserts that the Mahdi, or God-guided one, will come with the end of the temporal world in cataclysm and the triumph of God's true faith. Here was a doctrine that appealed to frustrated and poverty-stricken peasants along the Sudanese Nile, uneasy over Egyptian rule and its Westernizing tendencies, and they quickly rallied behind the Mahdi as he performed the traditional *hijra* (withdrawal) and jihad that resulted in a Muslim theocratic rule spread throughout the Nilotic Sudan.

With the fall of Khartoum in 1885, Egyptian power was broken in the south and the Mahdist state came into being. Though the Mahdi died shortly thereafter, his government survived until 1898 when it fell before a British force led by Gen. H. H. Kitchener.

The Birth of Modern Africa. Kitchener's victory came late in the era of Europe's scramble for Africa. By century's end virtually the whole African continent had been encumbered by colonialism, while Western social and economic influences vied with traditional ways to create a new synthesis of both indigenous and foreign character. In the case of Islam in West Africa, a similar process was already well under way. Political unification in the savanna had been accompanied by mass conversions that had affected all levels of the population, also penetrating deep into the West African forest region to touch such peoples as the Yoruba.

While tradition remained strong in the sub-Saharan countryside, with its villages, subsistence agriculture, and social life based on family, the lineage, the clan, and the age grade, important changes were introduced as a result of European influences. Christianity brought literacy and Western education, the beginning of cities, a shift toward market agriculture, an emphasis on new crops (such as rubber, peanuts, maize, and cassava), the influence of an international price structure, large-scale networks of transportation and communication, and the practice of wage labor. In the 20th century, territories created in the council chambers of 19th century Europe slowly became national entities as Africans moved increasingly between town and country, and became aware of themselves in terms of national rather than local origins.

With colonialism also came repression, the desire for independence, and the consequent rise of politicians who sought both to share in the perquisites of power, as in the French colonies, or govern independently, as in the British. Colonialism also introduced Western medical and public-health reforms that began to control disease and increase life expectancy but would eventually contribute to enormous population increases. Perhaps most of all, the 19th century bore heavily on the minds and spirits of Africans. By challenging their traditional institutions and values and by introducing inexorable changes in their ways of life, it forced them to straddle the two worlds of Europe and traditional Africa.

ROBERT W. JULY
Author of "A History of the African People"

23. The Opening Up of Africa

Most of the Europeans attracted to sub-Saharan Africa before the late 18th century had been content to remain on the coasts near the forts that protected them while slaves, gold, and ivory were brought in by coastal peoples, who acquired such goods in the interior. The first serious move in the systematic exploration of the interior of the continent came with the founding of the African Association by British scientists and businessmen in 1788.

West Africa. The African Association sent explorers into West Africa, particularly to determine the origin, course, and outlet of the Niger River. The most successful was a Scot, Mungo Park, who from a base on the Gambia River reached the upper Niger in 1796, discovering that it flowed northeastward. Park was killed, however, before he could trace the river to its mouth.

In 1822 a British expedition started from Tripoli, on the Mediterranean, and crossed the Sahara. It discovered Lake Chad. Hugh Clapperton, who headed the expedition after the death of its first leader, explored Hausaland where he visited the city of Kano. After a brief trip back to Europe he returned to West Africa and entered the interior from the neighborhood of Lagos, on the Guinea Coast. Reaching Sokoto, he found Sultan Muhammad Bello ruling over a Fulani kingdom created by his father, Usuman dan Fodio, after the overthrow of several Hausa emirates. When Clapperton died in 1827, two English brothers, Richard and John Lander, carried on his work and became the first Europeans to solve the riddle of the Niger. They discovered its mouth to be the wide delta on the Guinea Coast that had long been known to white traders as the Oil Rivers. The Niger reaches that outlet after making a great curve from northeast to southeast on the edge of the Sahara.

In 1826 a Scot, Alexander Gordon Laing, reached the fabled city of Timbuktu, at the top of the Niger bend, after crossing the Sahara from Tripoli. But he was murdered before he could report his discovery to Europe. The first European to visit Timbuktu and return was a Frenchman, René Caillié, who had made his way to the city in 1828 disguised as an Arab.

The most significant explorations in West Africa were those of Heinrich Barth, a German who started from Tripoli in 1850. For four arduous years he traveled in territories along the Niger and near Lake Chad, collecting accurate information on the region's geography, peoples, natural resources, and economic production, and discovering early Arabic texts of great historical importance.

The Mystery of the Nile. The riddle of the sources of the Nile fascinated Europe as it had the ancient world. James Bruce, a Scot exploring Ethiopia, established in 1770 that the Blue Nile originated there in Lake Tana. He did not know, however, that the Portuguese had made the same discovery more than 150 years earlier.

The source of the White Nile, the river's longer branch, was to elude Europeans until the late 19th century.

Muhammad Ali, the ruler of Egypt as the nominal Turkish viceroy, sponsored expeditions up the White Nile that got beyond the *sudd*—masses of floating vegetation that obstruct the river's flow. His explorers mapped the river as far as the rapids above Gondokoro, which was reached in 1840. If they had gone a few hundred miles beyond they would have found the source of the Nile, but no further progress was made in this southerly direction.

More successful were the explorers who trekked from the coast of East Africa into the Great Lakes region, where the Nile begins. Information about three large lakes in the far interior had come to Europeans from Arab traders on the coast, whose quest for slaves had taken them to Ujiji on Lake Tanganyika and by 1844 to the royal court of Buganda overlooking the shore of Lake Victoria. However, on the basis of reports by two German missionaries, Ludwig Krapf and Johann Rebmann, as well as African accounts, the local Europeans tended to believe that these lakes and Nyasa to the south formed one great inland "Sea of Ujiji."

Richard Francis Burton, already famous for his exploits in Arabia, explored Somaliland with John Hanning Speke in 1854. The Royal Geographical Society, which had taken over the work of the African Association, then sponsored an expedition of the two Englishmen to determine the limits of the "Sea of Ujiji," to gather economic and anthropological data, to find the "Mountains of the Moon" mentioned in ancient geography, and if possible to locate the source of the Nile. In 1858 they discovered Lake Tanganyika, and later that year Speke on his own discovered and named Lake Victoria.

To prove his thesis that Lake Victoria was the ultimate source of the Nile, Speke, accompanied by a Scot, James Augustus Grant, went around the lake to Buganda on its northern side. There, in 1862, Speke found the falls over which the waters of the Nile drop out of Lake Victoria for their long journey northward. In the following year the two explorers went down the Nile toward Lake Albert. But local warfare forced them to leave the river valley and proceed directly to Gondokoro, where they met Samuel White Baker, an Englishman who had journeyed south along the Nile. Information supplied by Speke enabled Baker in 1864 to discover Lake Albert, which the Nile flows into and out of. One stretch of the river between Lakes Albert and Victoria remained unexplored, however, and Speke's belief that he had found the main source of the Nile was not proven until later in the 19th century.

Southern Africa and the Congo Basin. The explorer whose achievements stirred the greatest interest was the Scottish missionary David Livingstone, who arrived in Southern Africa in 1841 to work for the London Missionary Society. In 1849 he discovered Lake Ngami while crossing the Kalahari. From the upper Zambezi River in 1853 he made his way to Luanda, on the Atlantic Ocean, which he reached the following year. Returning east, he followed the course of the Zambezi, discovering Victoria Falls in November 1855, and the following May he was on the shores of the Indian Ocean at Quelimane. Thus he became the first white to cross tropical Africa,

The historic meeting of Henry M. Stanley *(left)* and David Livingstone *(right)*, at Ujiji on Lake Tanganyika in 1871, as portrayed in a contemporary engraving. Stanley wrote that the engraving, "for which I supplied the materials . . . is as correct as if the scene had been photographed."

although he had been preceded on a similar route by two mixed-race slave traders, Amaro José and Pedro João Baptista, between 1802 and 1814. After a hero's reception in England he severed connections with the London Missionary Society and returned as explorer, commissioned by the British government. John Kirk, a fellow Scot, accompanied him. The two explored the Shire River and reached Lake Nyasa (Lake Malawi) in September 1859. The exploration of Lake Nyasa showed that no river connected it to Lake Tanganyika.

After another trip to England, Livingstone returned to Africa in 1866 for his third and last expedition into the heart of the continent. Going into the interior from Zanzibar, on the east coast, he discovered lakes Mweru and Bangweulu and a river he believed to be the source of the Nile but later found to be a branch of the upper Congo. When a long time had passed with no word from Livingstone, the journalist Henry Morton Stanley was sent out by the New York *Herald* to find him. The two men finally met in November 1871 at Ujiji on Lake Tanganyika. Together they explored the northern end of Lake Tanganyika, but they found no river flowing out of it, presumably into the Nile. When he died in 1873 on the shores of Lake Bangweulu, Livingstone was still engaged in the search for the Nile's sources, later discovered to be nominally headstreams of the Kagera River, which flows into Lake Victoria.

Stanley completed the large-scale exploration of subequatorial Africa by his journey (1874–1877) across the continent from east to west, on which he followed the Congo to its mouth. In 1888 he discovered south of Lake Albert the towering Ruwenzori range, commonly identified with the mysterious "Mountains of the Moon."

The Impact of European Exploration. These many pathfinders were followed by Roman Catholic and Protestant missionaries, who learned African languages, reduced them to writing, preached the Gospel, and built schools. At the same time the missionaries helped propagate in Europe the idea that Western influence would benefit Africa. Commercial interests followed as well, and trading outposts expanded into enclaves ruled by Europeans. Minor wars with the surrounding Africans gradually led to an unanticipated growth of these toeholds and finally to the partition of almost all of Africa into European colonies or dependencies.

HARRY R. RUDIN
Yale University

24. The Scramble for Africa

Some European countries had been in possession of African territories long before the rush to participate in the continent's final partition occurred in the late 1870's. Portugal and Britain controlled most of the territory in European possession.

Early Spheres of Influence. Portugal had ancient and undefined claims to Portuguese Guinea, Angola (Portuguese West Africa), and Mozambique (Portuguese East Africa), besides controlling various islands—Madeira, the Cape Verde group, São Tomé, and Príncipe. Spain had established itself in the Canary Islands and the Gulf of Guinea, while maintaining outposts on the coasts of Morocco.

France, which had lost its early African possessions in wars with Britain, revived its interest in Africa with the restoration of Senegal in 1817. During 1830–1847 it conquered Algeria. In 1849 it established a home for emancipated slaves at Libreville in Gabon, as the British had done at Freetown in Sierra Leone in 1787, and the Americans in Liberia in 1822. Britain had gained footholds in West Africa at Lagos, in Sierra Leone, on the Gambia River, and on the Gold Coast. In Southern Africa, Cape Colony became a British possession in 1814. Natal was acquired in 1843, and Griqualand West in 1871 after the discovery of diamonds in the area. By two treaties in the 1850's the British renounced interference in the Afrikaner Transvaal and Orange Free State, which became independent, as Liberia had been from 1847. The British grew interested in the French-constructed Suez Canal, opened to navigation in 1869, and in Egypt, from which 44% of the canal shares were purchased in 1875 and over whose financial affairs dual control with France was established in 1876.

Traders of many countries were busy at numerous posts in West and East Africa. During the middle of the 19th century, the French, Italians, and British were drawn to Tunisia, competing for concessions from the bey of Tunis. As European countries became industrialized, competition for trade increased along the coasts of Africa, and in the 1850's and 1860's traders frequently turned to home governments for support. This rivalry burst into the open in the 1870's, when depression set in because of the inability of European countries to find markets for their growing surpluses.

The Congo and the Berlin Settlement. Leopold II, king of Belgium, had been dreaming of colonies for his small country, more for prestige than for other reasons. To carry out his purposes, he summoned a conference to Brussels in September 1876. The nations that participated organized the International Association for the Exploration and Civilization of Central Africa. Then, in 1878, Leopold formed the Committee for the Study of the Upper Congo. He succeeded in getting the services of Henry Morton Stanley, who had just returned from exploring the Congo River. Soon after Stanley had set out secretly for Africa to begin his labors for Leopold, the French government sent Pierre Savorgnan de Brazza into the Gabon area. While it could be made to appear that both men were working for the international association of 1876, the fact is that they were rivals, working for Belgium and France. The scramble for Africa had now begun.

Alarmed by this threat to ancient claims to the Congo growing out of the "right" of discovery, Portugal sought the aid of its old ally, Britain. The two nations signed a treaty on Feb. 26, 1884, defining Portuguese territory at the mouth of the Congo and providing for the two to regulate navigation on the river. This defiance of the interests of other nations and of a growing body of opinion favoring international control of the Congo and the Niger rivers led to such wide protest that within four months Britain abandoned the treaty. Meanwhile, overproduction in European industrial countries, the consequent depression,

and the pressing need for overseas markets had accelerated the European powers' advance into Africa and Asia. The French established themselves on the Ivory Coast, in Guinea, and in Dahomey, and they expanded eastward from Senegal along the Niger toward Lake Chad. In 1881, France proclaimed a protectorate over Tunisia. Worried about the Suez Canal, the French sought to internationalize its operation, but in the 1888 Convention of Constantinople they obtained only the very minimium of international control.

The British expanded into the hinterland of their trading posts—up the Gambia River and into the interiors of Sierra Leone, the Gold Coast, and Nigeria. In 1882 they occupied Egypt, ending the dual financial control of that country.

Europe was taken by surprise when the German chancellor, Prince Otto von Bismarck, long an opponent of overseas possessions for Germany, suddenly decided in 1884 to occupy African territory. Only under the pressure of a commercial crisis did Bismarck consent to the occupation of Togo, the Cameroons, and South West Africa in that year.

Many colonial rivalries were under way when 14 countries, including the United States, met in Berlin on Nov. 15, 1884, in the Conference on African Affairs, called to consider questions raised by the Anglo-Portuguese Treaty of February 26. That treaty, however, was no longer an issue, the British government having refused to have it ratified by Parliament. On Feb. 26, 1885, the conference agreed to a treaty providing for international control of navigation on the Congo, establishing the principle that occupation of African territory must be effective to be legal and assuring equal trading rights to all nations in a carefully defined Congo Basin. The treaty also offered signatory countries an occasion to proclaim opposition to slavery and the sale of liquor and firearms to Africans and to support Christian missionary activities. Instead of international control of the Niger, the conference accepted a pledge of the British to administer navigation on

© HISTORICAL PICTURES SERVICE

Africans, including Menelik II of Ethiopia *(center)*, resisted the European partition of the continent in the 19th century. Menelik defeated Italian invaders in 1896, enabling his country to preserve its independence continuously except from 1936 to 1941.

that river in accordance with the principles governing the Congo.

In the meantime, Leopold had created the Congo Free State, which he presented to the world as a federation of African tribes, with himself as their European representative. Charges of ruthless exploitation of Africans and their resources led in 1908 to the assumption of control by the Belgian government.

Cape to Cairo. Outside West Africa the chief vector of British interest ran north and south, one of the objectives being to link the Cape Colony with Cairo by rail and telegraph, a dream cherished by the empire builder Cecil Rhodes. In 1885, Bechuanaland was occupied. This move barred German expansion eastward from South West Africa and cleared the way for the railroad northward from the Cape. A treaty of debated validity with the Ndebele king Lobengula in 1889 enabled whites to settle in what became known as Rhodesia and defeated plans of both Afrikaners and Portuguese to occupy the territory. Nyasaland became a British protectorate in 1891. Because of the German seizure of Tanganyika (made formal in 1890) no continuous land connection could be obtained with the British protectorates of Uganda (1894) and Kenya (1895) until Germany lost all African possessions in World War I and Tanganyika became a British mandate under the League of Nations.

North of Uganda the British had faced difficulties in the Nilotic Sudan, from which they and the Egyptians had been expelled by the forces of the Mahdi in 1885. By encouraging Italian ambitions in Ethiopia through treaties in 1891 and 1894 that defined respective spheres of influence in Ethiopia and the Nilotic Sudan, Britain assured itself of a right-of-way up the Nile. At the same time, the Italians were given an opportunity to link the protectorate of Eritrea (1882) with that of Somaliland (1889) by the conquest of Ethiopia. Thus the British hoped to thwart French plans for a trans-African empire from the French Congo across the middle Nile to French Somaliland, a protectorate since 1884. The victory of the Ethiopians over the Italians at Aduwa on March 1, 1896, compelled the British to block French advances toward the Nile. As a result, Lord Kitchener, in command of a British-Egyptian force, advanced to meet Capt. Jean Baptiste Marchand of France at Fashoda (now Kodok) in September 1898. War between the traditional enemies was narrowly averted, and a treaty in 1899 delimited territories to the satisfaction of both parties.

The crisis over the Sudan did not end too soon for the British, who found themselves at war later that year with the Afrikaners of the Transvaal and Orange Free State. The discovery of gold in 1886 had resulted in a rush of hated Britishers into the Transvaal. Difficulties arose between the new settlers and the Afrikaners that negotiation could not settle. The grievances remained after the failure of Rhodes and Leander Starr Jameson to overthrow the Afrikaner government by a raid into the Transvaal in December 1895. War broke out in October 1899 and lasted until May 1902. Defeated, the Afrikaners had to cede their two states to the British, who promised self-government to the vanquished. That promise was fulfilled in 1910 by the creation of the Union of South Africa, formed by joining the two former Afrikaner states with Cape Colony and Natal.

Northern Africa. The détente in Anglo-French relations after the Sudan affair in 1899 led eventually to the Entente Cordiale of April 8, 1904, when France allowed Britain a free hand in Egypt in return for the same in Morocco. The British insisted that Spain be assigned that part of Morocco nearest to Spanish territory, an arrangement to keep a strong France from getting too close to Gibraltar. When France proclaimed its protectorate over Morocco in 1912, Spain moved into its sphere, and a special regime was set up for Tangier. France made territorial concessions to Germany in Equatorial Africa. Britain waited until 1914 before proclaiming a protectorate over Egypt.

The Italians, who had feared for Libya ever since France occupied Tunisia in 1881, decided in 1911 to undertake the conquest of that area after asking and getting assurances of diplomatic support from the major European powers. Libya was invaded, but the actual conquest was not completed until 1931. A new opportunity to conquer Ethiopia came in 1935–1936, when Benito Mussolini invaded, defeated, and annexed the country. Only Liberia was never a European colonial possession.

HARRY R. RUDIN, *Yale University*

25. Colonial Administrations and the Struggle for Independence

The period from 1914 to 1939 saw the full flower and the beginning of the decline of the colonial system in Africa. The administrations established by the major colonial powers before 1914 had three primary goals: to preserve law and order, to erect an administrative structure designed for effective government at a minimum cost, and to promote forms of economic development that would provide raw materials demanded by markets in the home country.

The political and administrative institutions that the Europeans created in their African colonies were modeled on those they knew best— their own. Often there was little regard for the fact that these institutions had been developed for European countries, whose histories, social backgrounds, and administrative needs bore little if any relationship to those of Africa. For the most part during the colonial period, little consistent thought was given by European administrators to the long-range development of the colonies toward independence. Moreover, some administrations forced Africans to work under deplorable conditions or to plant export crops instead of staple food crops. It was only through the gradual spread of education and the consequent emergence of political awareness among a small segment of the African population that demand arose for a share in political power. From this small group of nationalist leaders came the popular movements that finally swept the colonial administrations out of existence.

Colonial Government. In the case of Britain, the theory of "indirect rule" was the basis of administration. British officers governed through the traditional chiefs, seeking to preserve as far as possible the power and prestige of those leaders while adapting the customary methods of rule to meet the needs of modern society. It was hoped in this way to ease the impact of the transition from traditional to modern government. By 1939, however, it was becoming clear that indirect rule was unsatisfactory; the chiefs could not always be adapted to new ways, and the system

AFRICA IN 1914

Belgian · British · French · German · Italian · Portuguese · Spanish

TANGIER (neutral zone)
SPANISH MOROCCO
Madeira (Port.)
Canary Is. (Sp.)
INFI (Sp.)
MOROCCO
RIO DE ORO
CAPE VERDE (Port.)
ALGERIA
TUNISIA
LIBYA
EGYPT (Br. occupation)
FRENCH WEST AFRICA
GAMBIA
PORTUGUESE GUINEA
SIERRA LEONE
LIBERIA
GOLD COAST
TOGOLAND
NIGERIA
KAMERUN
SPANISH GUINEA
SÃO TOMÉ AND PRÍNCIPE (Port.)
FRENCH EQUATORIAL AFRICA
Cabinda
BELGIAN CONGO
ANGOLA
ANGLO-EGYPTIAN SUDAN (condominium)
ERITREA
FRENCH SOMALILAND
BRITISH SOMALILAND
ETHIOPIA
ITALIAN SOMALILAND
UGANDA
BRITISH EAST AFRICA
GERMAN EAST AFRICA
ZANZIBAR (Br.)
SEYCHELLES (Br.)
NYASALAND
NORTHERN RHODESIA
SOUTHERN RHODESIA
MOZAMBIQUE
Comoro Is. (Fr.)
MADAGASCAR
MAURITIUS (Br.)
RÉUNION (Fr.)
ASCENSION (Br.)
ST. HELENA (Br.)
SOUTH WEST AFRICA
Walvis Bay (U. of S. Afr.)
BECHUANALAND
SWAZILAND
UNION OF SOUTH AFRICA (Br. Dominion)
BASUTOLAND

left no place for the young, educated Africans to share in local administration. Gradually, in the years after World War II, elected local councils were substituted for the "native authorities" (the chiefs and their councils). These new councils became the testing ground for nationalist political parties.

France, in its African colonies, pursued a policy of assimilation and direct rule. The objective was to acquaint its African subjects as fully as possible with French institutions, language, and culture, the ultimate goal being complete assimilation of the colonies to the home country. For this reason little effort was made until after World War II to create representative political institutions in the colonies, and the traditional chiefs were largely subordinated to the French administrations. In the long run, French assimilation was no more successful than British indi-

rect rule. For the comparatively small number of Africans who were able to enjoy the full benefits of the French educational system, assimilation was complete. Most Africans, however, were only superficially exposed to the French way of life and proved unwilling to give up their traditional cultures, particularly in the Muslim areas, where religion became a block to full acceptance of France. Beginning in 1946, therefore, efforts were made to create territorial assemblies, or local parliaments, in each colony.

Portuguese policy, to a greater degree than that of France, was based on full assimilation. Administratively the colonies were regarded as overseas provinces of Portugal. But Portuguese rule was characterized by abuse of authority, a low level of African education, and (except in Angola after World War II) severe limitations on economic development. In part this restrictive

Mozambicans celebrate their country's independence in 1975 after a decade of armed struggle under the Liberation Front of Mozambique (FRELIMO). The new leadership intended to build Africa's first truly Marxist state.

policy could be accounted for by the poverty of Portugal itself; yet it was also a reaction to the spread of nationalism elsewhere in Africa. Portuguese resistance to the trend toward independence resulted in the outbreak of revolution in its territories in the early 1960's. Only after a military coup deposed Portugal's conservative government in 1974 did that country become reconciled to the end of its colonial empire.

In the Belgian Congo, the home country pursued a policy of strong paternalism. Africans were prepared by widespread primary education for technical positions, but virtually no attempt was made to create African political representation, nor were political parties organized. In consequence, when Belgium decided in 1960 to grant immediate independence, the colony was unprepared for self-rule and chaos ensued.

Two colonial powers, Germany and Italy, disappeared from Africa between 1918 and 1943. Following World War I the German colonies were separately placed under the administration of Belgium, Britain, France, and South Africa—at first under the overall supervision of the Mandates Commission of the League of Nations, and after 1945 under the Trusteeship Council of the United Nations in preparation for their independence. Italy lost all its colonies during World War II. Ethiopia regained full sovereignty in 1941 after less than five years of Italian rule, and after the war the Italian colony of Eritrea was joined to Ethiopia. The other two Italian possessions became independent.

Although the colonial system was showing signs of decline by 1939, what shattered the old order was World War II. The war exposed the weakness of the major colonial powers and had profound effects on all dependent territories in Africa. The European belligerents, hard pressed

by their war effort, made exceptionally heavy demands on their African subjects. Because of the shortage of officials, the colonial administrations were forced to grant Africans a degree of responsibility that would hitherto have been impossible. African leaders showed that they were capable of holding the reins of government. In turn, they encouraged and organized the popular demand for autonomy that forced the colonial powers to give way, first in local government and later at the level of central administration. As new institutions for popular representation were created, the stage was set for the transformation to self-government and finally, by the mid-1950's, to full independence.

The Independence Movement. Although World War II accelerated the growth of African nationalism, the seeds of independence had been sown in most parts of the continent before the war. In Egypt, for example, what prompted British occupation in 1882 was a nationalist movement expressing popular discontent with international control of the country.

In tropical Africa, the earliest nationalist parties were founded shortly after World War I by professional men in two British colonies: the Gold Coast (afterward Ghana) and Nigeria. Seeking a greater share in the decisions made by the colonial administrations, these parties were not concerned with mass participation in government but with obtaining a share in decision-making for their own small, well-educated elites.

One of the first mass nationalist parties, the National Council of Nigeria and the Cameroons, was founded in 1944, and beginning in 1946 similar mass parties sprang up in the French territories of West Africa. In the Gold Coast it was not until 1950 that the Convention People's Party, headed by Kwame Nkrumah, became the focus for mass nationalist demonstrations in favor of independence. Thereafter the spread of nationalist sentiment was rapid throughout Africa.

During the early postwar years the colonial administrations fought against the organization and growth of political parties. The trade union movement, however, represented an alternative source for experience in organization and mass discipline, which younger nationalists put to good use. Particularly in French Africa, where the union movement was dominated by the French General Confederation of Labor, the newly formed unions provided training in political party organization.

The rapid influx of young men from the rural areas to the mushrooming cities contributed substantial numbers of recruits for the growing political parties, which promised the new urban dwellers all the advantages of modernization that presumably would come with independence. Most of the recent arrivals in the cities retained close connections with their villages and became the chief avenue through which political nationalism was spread.

The nationalist parties were organized with a tightly disciplined, hierarchical type of leadership that stretched in an unbroken line from the single leader at the top to the hundreds of village party groups scattered throughout the country. This network of communication made it possible to mobilize mass public opinion in favor of independence and, when the time came, to arouse the people to active resistance to the colonial administrations. Faced with such popular action, the colonial powers could do little but attempt to slow down, through constitutional negotiations, the transfer of power from European hands. The small group of educated leaders at the top of the nationalist parties, themselves often the product of schools run by European missionaries, were to become the new rulers of the African states.

L. GRAY COWAN, *Author of*
"The Dilemmas of African Independence"

26. Independent Africa

The political transformation of Africa brought into existence some 50 new national states after the early 1950s. All of them were the products of successful nationalist movements, and all had behind them a colonial heritage from which developed a bewildering variety of political institutions and forms of government.

Political Leadership. On their departure the European powers left to their African territories much of the framework of Western constitutional democracy. The basic political forms—parliaments, cabinets, ministries, and local councils—were established in many areas, the Democratic Republic of the Congo (formerly, the Belgian Congo) being the most notable exception. It was anticipated that on this foundation the new African states would begin to build their political futures, with the prospect that, in time, they would become reasonable facsimiles of the European models. But to the disappointment of their mentors the institutions inherited from Europe often failed to flourish. Parliaments with majority and minority parties withered and were replaced by elective bodies in which one party dominated; or, in other cases, all traces of formal opposition were snuffed out. Elections in most countries became a matter of marshaling popular support for policy decisions already made by the nationalist party leadership rather than a presentation of meaningful choices to the voters.

The growth of political systems dominated by a single party, with a supreme leader to whom charismatic qualities were attributed, became the hallmark of postindependence political development in Africa. In most cases these were the same parties that had organized the nationalist resistance to colonial rule and had established efficient networks of local branches at the village level. The success of the leadership in rallying popular support for independence had brought the party to power with widespread electoral strength. In fact, opposition to the nationalist party often had meant being branded as a traitor or a supporter of colonialism. In consequence there was frequently little place for an opposition in the preindependence years, and its role as a critic of the government later was often regarded by the party in power as an unnecessary interference in the pressing tasks of development and modernization.

As the moment of independence receded into the past, the popular enthusiasm that accompanied it abated. The new government was faced with the increasingly complex problems of economic transformation and social change. To reach its goals of industrialization and higher living standards, the party leadership had to make unpopular decisions, particularly in taxation and control of imported goods. Thus it alienated in some measure its former followers. The desire to remain in power, coupled with the mounting frustrations in projected economic development, created tensions within the ruling group that frequently led to harsh measures of repression against those who, rightly or wrongly, were accused of opposing the government's aims. Within the governing party, ideological splits created further pressures.

The growing discontent with the failure of the political leaders to produce the expected results from independence, combined with economic hardship and dictatorial rule, brought about a series of military revolts in the mid-1960s and afterward. These uprisings forced the politicians out of power and replaced them with military leaders who ruled as the new strongmen until their own ouster in the next coup. The result was, in many of the African countries, continued political instability as a concomitant to the profound changes being created by the modernizing revolution.

Economic Development. For a period after independence the attention of the leaders was primarily attracted to internal politics and the creation of the international image of their countries. To their cost, they either neglected or glossed over the hard facts of economic necessity, so that the promises made at independence of a better life for all were seldom fulfilled. The colonial economies had been designed to produce primary materials for Europe and to consume the manufactured goods of the industrialized West. One of the first goals of the African governments was to assert their economic, as well as political, independence from Europe. To do so meant creating at home the facilities for manufacturing the goods that hitherto came from abroad.

But in their drive to establish an urban-industrial base on the Western model the fledgling governments were often faced with seemingly insurmountable barriers, at least in the short run.

Taken as a whole, the African continent has vast untapped natural resources, particularly in potential hydroelectric power. However, the uneven distribution of these resources creates immense problems for development. In some areas, such as Equatorial Africa, mineral wealth of all types abounds; elsewhere the absence of minerals means that some countries must depend on improved agricultural production for increased prosperity. Whatever the resource base of the country may be, its development depends on the availability of capital and technical knowledge. With rare exceptions, the African states could produce only a fraction of the needed capital from domestic savings, and they continued therefore to be dependent on outside sources. While the educational systems turned out increasing numbers of technically qualified young people, the demand for trained personnel far exceeded the supply, particularly in positions requiring a high degree of professional competence. For this aspect of development, too, the African states continued to depend on foreign assistance.

The inability to provide the basic requirements for their own development created an ambivalence to foreign aid that was partially a reflection of nationalism and partially a result of ideological commitment. African leaders acknowledged their need for help from all possible sources, yet always in the background lurked the perceived threat of "neocolonialism." By this term the African leaders meant the desire on the part of the donors, particularly if they were former colonial powers, to control the new African states by continued economic pressure when direct political control was no longer possible. Fear of conditions that might be attached to economic aid accounted in part for the public stance of neutralism adopted generally by African governments.

Whatever its stage of economic progress, every African state evinced a desire for a greater or lesser degree of economic planning. The existence of a plan provided a basis for orderly development and for assigning priorities to certain sectors of the economy in order to provide balanced growth. To an extent, also, planning was a reflection of the ideological position of the party leadership. Most ruling parties favored, in some measure, a form of socialist economic organization, which varied from country to country and which, under the name of African socialism, might depart widely from the doctrines of Marxian socialism.

Most African leaders were prepared to rely on Western markets for some years to come, but they also felt the need for intra-African economic cooperation to develop wider markets and more rationalized planning. Provision of an economic basis for the unification of the African community came to the forefront of much African thinking, and various regional or common-language organizations were formed, as well as the African Development Bank. Several of these—such as the East African Community and the Organisation Commune Africaine et Mauricienne (OCAM), whose objectives were a common market of member states—disintegrated under political or other pressures. However, some progress was made toward regional economic integration, notably in West Africa. There, 15 countries in 1975 formed the Economic Community of West African States (ECOWAS), with one of its objectives the creation of a customs union among the members.

African Unity. The unification of Africa has been an abiding theme in the continent's politics and was a major preoccupation of some leaders such as Kwame Nkrumah, the first president of Ghana. The arguments advanced for more than limited, regional unification in Africa have stemmed from both cultural and practical considerations. African history shows that large political units existed prior to the coming of the Europeans, and the memory of these states is still green in parts of the continent. The more practical arguments for unity arise from considerations of external security, economic necessity, and the prevention of further "balkanization" of the continent into small, weak states. But one of the most cogent reasons advanced for unification is the feeling of brotherhood engendered by the common experience of the struggle for independence.

Despite these motivations, there has been no general agreement on the degree of unity desired or on the form that the ultimate union should take. Some theories call for full political union, in which national sovereignty would be surrendered to a United States of Africa along the lines of union established in North America. The other extreme is a loose confederation in which each state would retain its full sovereign powers. Between these two ends of the spectrum various compromises have been suggested involving larger or smaller regional units based on the particular advantages of greater local cooperation. The Organization of African Unity represents the state of commitment to unity on which common agreement has been reached.

Obstacles to unification involve problems of directing and controlling the unifying body as well as determining its structure. There are vested interests in national sovereignty, and the leaders are not likely to accept the preeminence of one of their number as speaker for the whole African community. Moreover, they differ ideologically, and it would be difficult for any union of African states to adopt an ideological stand that was anything more than a series of vague compromises. See also ORGANIZATION OF AFRICAN UNITY and PAN-AFRICANISM.

The African Community in World Affairs. Although the African states are most directly concerned with issues of foreign policy related to their own continent, they have sought to establish for themselves a place in world affairs, particularly through their membership in the United Nations. They regard their position in that international body as especially important because it is the forum through which they can express their views to a world audience and in which they can play a substantial role in determining action on issues of global concern.

On specific foreign-policy questions the views of African states vary according to their individual national interests. But on one point—neutralism, or professed nonalignment in the conflict between East and West—they have endeavored to present a common front. The African leaders have sought to stand aside from the ideological struggle, not because they are uninterested in the outcome but rather because they feel that in any conflict that might arise from it their countries are bound to be losers. A position of nonalignment, they argue, affords an opportunity to decide particular issues on their

Delegates from 30 independent African countries founded the Organization of African Unity (OAU) in 1963.

merits and in the light of African interests at the time.

Perhaps the most delicate area in which the African states have been called upon to act in the world community is their relations with the former colonial states. Many leaders were educated in England or in France and retain personal and sentimental ties to Europe. But as national political figures they are required to prove the independence of their states by clearly breaking the former colonial ties. At the same time, they are aware of the continuing dependence of Africa on European technical skills and financial help. Further, the military weakness of the African states forces an unwanted reliance on Europe for national security, both against external foes and against internal subversion. Africa's major markets remain in Europe, and the advantages gained by association with the European Economic Community continue to be a factor in African development plans.

In their relations with the world community the African states are faced with an ever-present dilemma. The desire for independence and freedom to choose the course of action that seems best to them is constantly countered by the fact of dependence for their existence on forces over which they have no control and which they suspect of seeking to undermine their hard-won sovereignty.

L. GRAY COWAN, *Author of*
"The Dilemmas of African Independence"

27. Contemporary Problems in Africa

African independence has not fulfilled the great expectations that accompanied it. Instead, after a promising start, the years since the 1960's have been characterized by widespread economic decline and political instability. In part this deterioration has been due to reciprocally reinforcing crises of poverty, illiteracy, divisive religious and ethnic differences, and underdevelopment. Responding to such crises, many African leaders have eliminated formal parliamentary opposition and tried to create consensus through the adoption of more authoritarian systems. Democratic institutions such as the press, political parties, and trade unions have suffered as a result. Single-party regimes, however, seem not to have been any more successful at governing than the multiparty systems that they replaced, and many, in turn, have themselves been replaced by military regimes. Since independence, most African states have experienced at least one successful coup d'état, and over half of them, more than one.

In response to a hostile environment, problems inherited from the colonial past, international economic pressures, and internal mismanagement and corruption, Africa's politicians, soldier-politicians, and public administrators have directed uncertain political and institutional experimentation. The years of experimentation are reflected in the range of regime ideologies, from doctrinaire Marxism-Leninism to foreign-dominated corporate capitalism, and from multiparty to single-party regimes to military rule.

Economic Decline and Conditionality. After modest economic growth in the first years following independence, economic and financial conditions in Africa began to decline, reaching near-crisis proportions by the 1980's. Two thirds of the world's 50 poorest countries are located in Africa, and the gap separating them from the rest of the developing world has widened. Responsibility for the decline can be attributed to various factors, including a prolonged drought of historic dimensions that ultimately affected nearly half of the countries on the continent, a drop in commodity prices and worsening terms of trade with the industrialized nations, and the devastating long-run effects of OPEC oil price increases.

The World Bank, on the other hand, laid much of the blame on Africans themselves. It saw the deterioration as in part the result of inappropriate policies and programs, including the erosion of incentives in agriculture, overexpansion of the public sector at the expense of the private sector, and inefficient marketing, transportation, financial, and other support services. Substantial bank loans from international lenders hid the severity of Africa's economic crisis for several years until by the 1980's African recipients were unable to meet even interest payments on their loans. In response, the International Monetary Fund (IMF) and other international lending agencies imposed new conditions before subsequent loans would be granted. This new "conditionality," which required drastic changes in domestic monetary and fiscal policies, created severe economic and political strains on a number of regimes.

Drought and Famine. Between 1968 and 1985, Africa experienced two of the worst droughts of the century, the latter affecting an estimated 150 million people living in 24 countries. These natural disasters were aggravated by civil strife, mismanagement, corruption, poor land conservation, and encouragement to produce export crops rather than basic foods. Mauritania, Senegal, Mali, and Niger on the edge of the Sahara desert were hard hit by drought, as were Kenya and Ethiopia in the east. Mozambique, Angola, and other parts of Southern Africa also suffered. The impact of drought and consequent famine led to widespread starvation despite massive international aid.

Examples of Political and Social Conflict. The limits and possibilities confronting African nations are vividly evident in a comparison of Sudan and Nigeria. Both had to face regional, ethnic, sectarian, and administrative crises, but because of the disparity in the resources available to them, they differed in their ability to respond and in their success in doing so.

Sudan, the largest country in Africa, reflected many of the continent's postindependence problems. Even before Sudan's independence in January 1956, Sudanese economic and political stability had been undermined by conflict between the dominant Arab-Muslim north and the black African Christian and animist south. Southern secessionist ambitions, which continued as a low-intensity civil war for 17 years, were followed by an uneasy truce throughout the 1970's, only to erupt once again into open hostilities in 1984 as a result of renewed southern fears of domination. The intensity of this conflict was exacerbated by a devastating drought-induced famine and the influx of over a million refugees fleeing from civil strife in neighboring Ethiopia, Chad, Uganda, and Zaire (later, Democratic Republic of the Congo). A state of emergency, declared in 1984 to control the rebellion in the south, led to further hostilities and public resentment and then ultimately to the end of the 15-year regime of Pres. Gafaar al-Nemeiry in a bloodless coup d'état in April 1985. The Transitional Military Council that took control acted as a caretaker government for one year and voluntarily relinquished power to civilian rule after multiparty elections were held in April 1986 for the presidency and for the national assembly. However, as the civil war in the south had prevented large numbers of southerners from participating in the election, continued resentment and hostility seemed assured.

If Sudan's predicament epitomized Africa's despair, Nigeria for all of its problems remained one of the continent's best hopes. Despite a series of successful coups d'état since independence as well as a debt-ridden economy, Nigerians remained committed to the restoration of participatory democracy and to freedom of the press.

Nigeria, the most populous country in Africa, became independent in 1960 as a federation of three regions. From the very beginning it experienced serious ethnic, regional, and religious tensions, which were further reinforced by economic and educational inequities between the north and south. In 1967 the intensity of these divisions culminated in the secession of the Eastern Region (southeastern Nigeria) and a wrenching three-year civil war that ended in 1970 with the defeat of the self-proclaimed Republic of Biafra.

Nigeria demonstrated its resilience with a surprisingly easy and rapid reconciliation, which allowed the country to turn its attention to the task of national reconstruction and development. The end of the civil war permitted a significant increase in the daily production of oil, coinciding with dramatic increases in the price of oil worldwide. For Nigeria this combination of events meant a spectacular rise in foreign-exchange earnings, which led to a period of unprecedented growth and expansion. In 1979, during this period, the military relinquished power and restored civilian rule; northerner Shehu Shagari was elected president. Shagari was reelected in August 1983, only to be overthrown by the military on December 31. The coup appears to have been a direct result of economic mismanagement, widespread corruption, and allegations of election fraud. Much of the country's economic malaise was in fact due to drastically dwindling foreign-exchange earnings as a result of the sharp decline in oil prices beginning in 1980.

Nigeria's sixth military regime since independence seized power in August 1985 and moved quickly to reestablish press freedoms and to release political prisoners; it made a public commitment to human rights and a return to democratic government as soon as possible. Although problems remained, long-needed economic reforms, if sustained, promised to return Nigeria to economic stability.

Crisis and Change in South Africa. After 1948, while most of the African continent was moving away from colonial rule toward self-determination, white-controlled South Africa, in contrast, was reinforcing and extending white power through new statutes governing an elaborate system of social, economic, and political privilege and discrimination. In this context, such fundamental rights as freedom of movement and of political expression, protection from search without warrant, and immunity from detention without hearing or trial were severely circumscribed. From 1948 onward the National Party, representing predominantly the interests of the white Afrikaner population, governed multiracial South Africa. The centerpiece of its policy was apartheid ("separateness"), which it promoted as a program for the separate development of the races. In fact, however, apartheid was and remained a doctrine of white supremacy that permeated nearly all aspects of South African life. Apartheid legislation determined where people could live, what schools and churches they could attend, what jobs they could hold, and whom they could marry—all on the basis of race.

South Africa's system of white supremacy, known as apartheid, was backed by the full coercive powers of the state.

Of necessity the economy remained racially integrated because of its dependence on black labor. Despite the implementation of numerous race-inspired labor laws governing, among other things, job security, wages, unionization, and unemployment compensation, black labor emerged as a potent political force. Blacks gained some concessions in wages and entrance to more skilled positions, and black unions were able to exert increasing pressures through strikes and boycotts.

Black opposition, which had been peaceful and lawful for many years, became increasingly disobedient and violent in response to white intransigence to legitimate black demands for justice and equality. By the mid-1980's South Africa was in the midst of an internal crisis of unprecedented magnitude, with the cycle of black violence and officially sanctioned state counterviolence escalating. The banned African National Congress (ANC), which had been founded in 1912 and whose leader, Nelson Mandela, remained imprisoned for more than 20 years, was a primary source of black opposition. Its guerrilla fighters were responsible for acts of sabotage and bombings that occurred with increasing frequency in different parts of the country. South Africa's imposition of draconian states of emergency, despite intense international financial and diplomatic pressure, demonstrated that whites were still firmly in control and unlikely to surrender their power and privileges easily.

With the ascension of F. W. de Klerk to the presidency in September 1989, however, political change began to occur at a rapid rate. Faced with a deepening economic crisis and continuing political violence, de Klerk moved to create an atmosphere in which negotiations between the white government and legitimate black leaders could take place. The subsequent legalization of multiracial antiapartheid demonstrations, the desegregation of select public facilities and urban neighborhoods, and the release of prominent black political prisoners, including Mandela, led to an opening up of the political process, culminating in the March 1992 whites-only referendum, which gave de Klerk an overwhelming mandate to continue the reform process. Democratic, nonracial elections followed, with the formerly banned ANC garnering 63% of the vote. It will take many years, however, to redress the legacy of apartheid.

Africa's Positive Achievements. The popular image of Africa is of a continent beset by poverty and economic decline, political instability, and authoritarian rule. Unfortunately, the postindependence accomplishments of many African nations have been lost in the more dramatic accounts of drought and famine and of military intervention in civilian politics. While authoritarian systems have become more common than democratic states, not all military regimes have proved to be repressive and not all single-party states undemocratic. Some military regimes voluntarily have relinquished power to civilian rule, and orderly constitutional transfers of power in sub-Saharan Africa have taken place since the late 1970's. Such transfers occurred, for example, after the deaths of Jomo Kenyatta of Kenya and Sir Seretse Khama of Botswana, and as leaders in Senegal, Cameroon, Nigeria, and Tanzania voluntarily stepped down in favor of younger successors. Perhaps most instructive was the 1979 negotiated settlement of the protracted guerrilla war in Zimbabwe between the politically dominant white minority and the oppressed black majority, followed by a democratic election in 1980.

One or two generations is not a very long time for newly independent countries as disadvantaged as most of those in Africa to have developed effective and responsive political and economic institutions. What does Africa's immediate future hold? Ethnic, religious, and ideological hostilities will not disappear, nor will economic problems be easily resolved. There is room for optimism, however, as African and international leaders begin to deal more realistically with the continent's economic and political problems.

PATRICK O'MEARA* and N. BRIAN WINCHESTER
African Studies Program, Indiana University

28. Bibliography

General Works. *Africa South of the Sahara* (Europa Pubs., annually). AZEVEDO, MARIO, and PRATER, GWENDOLYN, *Africa and Its People* (Kendall-Hunt 1982). BEST, ALAN C., and DE BLIJ, HARM J., *African Survey* (Wiley 1977). BOATENG, E. A., *A Political Geography of Africa* (Cambridge 1978). GROVE, ALFRED T., *Africa*, 3d ed. (Oxford 1978). HANCE, WILLIAM A., *The Geography of Modern Africa*, 2d ed. (Columbia Univ. Press 1975). KNIGHT, C. GREGORY, and NEWMAN, J. L., *Contemporary Africa: Geography and Change* (Prentice-Hall 1976). LEGUM, COLIN, ed., *Africa Contemporary Record* (Africana, annually). LIPSCHUTZ, MARK R., and RASMUSSEN, R. KENT, *Dictionary of African Historical Biography*, 2d ed. (Univ. of Calif. Press 1986). MARTIN, PHYLLIS M., and O'MEARA, PATRICK, eds., *Africa* (Ind. Univ. Press 1978). MURRAY, JOCELYN, ed., *Cultural Atlas of Africa* (Facts on File 1981). O'CONNOR, ANTHONY M., *The Geography of Tropical African Development*, 2d ed. (Pergamon 1978). OLIVER, ROLAND, and CROWDER, MICHAEL, eds., *The Cambridge Encyclopedia of Africa* (Cambridge 1981). PROTHERO, R. MANSELL, ed., *A Geography of Africa*, rev. ed. (Routledge 1973). STAMP, L. DUDLEY, *Africa: A Study in Tropical Development*, 3d ed. (1972; reprint, Bks. Demand UMI, n.d.). THOMAS, BENJAMIN E., and others, *Africa*, rev. ed. (Fideler 1986). UDO, REUBEN K., *The Human Geography of Tropical Africa* (Heinemann 1982). VAN CHI-BONNARDEL, REGINE, ed., *The Atlas of Africa* (Free Press 1974).

Geography and Economy

Physical Environment. DORST, JEAN, and DANDELOT, PIERRE, *A Field Guide to the Larger Mammals of Africa*, 2d ed. (1972; reprint, Greene 1985). GRIFFITHS, J. F., *The Climates of Africa* (Elsevier 1972). LUARD, NICHOLAS, *The Wildlife Parks of Africa* (Merrimack 1986). McKELVEY, JOHN, JR., *Man Against Tsetse: Struggle for Africa* (Cornell Univ. Press 1973). MOREAU, R. E., *The Bird Faunas of Africa and Its Islands* (Acad. Press 1967). Moss, R. P., ed., *The Soil Resources of Tropical Africa* (Cambridge 1968). NISSEN-PETERSEN, E., *Rain Catchment and Water Supply in Rural Africa* (Hodder & Stoughton 1983). SKAIFE, S. H., *African Insect Life*, rev. ed. (Struik 1979). TECHNICAL CONFERENCE ON CLIMATE—AFRICA, *Proceedings, Arusha, United Republic of Tanzania, 25–30 Jan., 1982* (Unipub. 1982). THOMPSON, B. W., *Africa: The Climatic Background* (Oxford 1975). TIMBERLAKE, LLOYD, *Africa in Crisis: The Causes, the Cures of Environmental Bankruptcy* (Earthscan 1985). TREWARTHA, GLENN T., *The Earth's Problem Climates*, 2d ed. (Univ. of Wis. Press 1981). UNITED NATIONS ENVIRONMENTAL PROGRAM, *Ecology and Development in Africa* (Pergamon 1981). VAN ANDEL, TJEERD H., *New Views of an Old Planet: Continental Drift and the History of Earth* (Cambridge 1985).

Economic Development. ADEDEJI, ADEBAYO, and SHAW, TIMOTHY, eds., *Economic Crisis in Africa: African Perspectives on Development Problems and Potentials* (Lynne Rienner 1985). ASANTE, S. K. B., *The Political Economy of Regionalism in Africa* (Praeger 1985). BATES, ROBERT H., *Essays on the Political Economy of Rural Africa* (Cambridge 1983) and *Markets and States in Tropical Africa: The Political Basis of Agricultural Policies* (Univ. of Calif. Press 1981). BERG, ROBERT J., and WHITAKER, JENNIFER S., eds., *Strategies for African Development* (Univ. of Calif. Press 1986). COMMINS, STEPHEN K., AND OTHERS, eds., *Africa's Agrarian Crisis: The Roots of Famine* (Lynne Rienner 1986). CRUMMEY, DONALD, and STEWART, C. G., eds., *Modes of Production in Africa: The Precolonial Era* (Sage 1981). DAVIDSON, BASIL, *Can Africa Survive? Arguments Against Growth Without Development* (Little 1974). DOMMEN, S., ed., *Agriculture and the New Technology in Tropical Africa* (Geneva 1977). FIELDHOUSE, D. K., *Black Africa, 1945–1980: Decolonization and Arrested Development* (Allen & Unwin 1986). FRANSMAN, MARTIN, ed., *Industry and Accumulation in Africa* (Heinemann 1982). GHAI, DHARAM, AND OTHERS, eds., *Agrarian Policies and Rural Poverty in Africa* (Holmes & Meier 1983). GUTKIND, PETER, and WALLERSTEIN, IMMANUEL, *The Political Economy of Contemporary Africa*, 2d ed. (Sage 1985). HYDÉN, GORAN, *No Shortcuts to Progress: African Development Management in Perspective* (Univ. of Calif. Press 1983). ILIFFE, JOHN, *The Emergence of African Capitalism* (Univ. of Minn. Press 1984). ODETOLA, T. O., *Military Regimes and Development* (Allen & Unwin 1982). ONWUKA, RALPH I., and ALUKO, OLAJIDE, eds., *The Future of Africa and the International Economic Order* (St. Martin's 1986). RICHARDS, PAUL, *Indigenous Agricultural Revolution: Ecology and Food Production in West Africa* (Westview 1985). ROSE, TORE, *Crisis and Recovery in Sub-Saharan Africa: Realities and Complexities* (OECD Development Center 1985). SANDBROOK, RICHARD, *The Politics of Basic Needs: Urban Aspects of Assaulting Poverty in Africa* (Heinemann 1982). SHAW, TIMOTHY M., *Towards a Political Economy for Africa: The Dialectics of Independence* (St. Martin's 1985). THOMAS, M. F., and WHITTINGTON, G. W., eds., *Environment and Land Use in Africa* (Methuen 1969). TWOSE, NIGEL, and GOLDWATER, MICHAEL, *African Famine: Search for Change* (Inst. for Food and Development Policy 1985). WORLD

BANK, *Accelerated Development in Sub-Saharan Africa: An Agenda for Action* (Intl. Bank for Reconstruction and Development 1982) and *Towards a Sustained Development in Sub-Saharan Africa: A Joint Program of Action* (Intl. Bank for Reconstruction and Development 1984). YOUNG, CRAWFORD, *Ideology and Development in Africa* (Yale Univ. Press 1982).

The People

Population. CLARKE, JOHN I., AND OTHERS, eds., *Population and Development: Projects in Africa* (Cambridge 1985). CLARK, JOHN I., and KOSINSKI, LESZEK A., *Redistribution of Population in Africa* (Heinemann 1982). WORLD BANK, *Population Growth and Policies in Sub-Saharan Africa* (Intl. Bank for Reconstruction and Development 1980).

Peoples and Cultures. BIGGERS, JOHN, *Ananse: The Web of Life in Africa* (1962; reprint, Univ. of Tex. Press 1979). BOHANNAN, PAUL, and CURTIN, PHILIP, *Africa and the Africans*, rev. ed. (Natural Hist. Press 1971). DU TOIT, BRIAN M., ed., *Ethnicity in Modern Africa* (Westview 1978). GIBBS, JAMES L., ed., *Peoples of Africa*, abr. ed., (Holt 1978). GLUCKMAN, MAX, *African Traditional Law in Historical Perspective* (Longwood 1976). GROVE, ALFRED T., and KLEIN, F., *Rural Africa* (Cambridge 1979). HERSKOVITS, MELVILLE J., *The Human Factor in Changing Africa* (Knopf 1962). JEFFERSON, MARGO, and SKINNER, ELLIOTT P., *Roots of Time: A Portrait of African Life and Culture* (Doubleday 1974). KOPYTOFF, IGOR, ed., *The African Frontier: The Reproduction of Traditional African Societies* (Ind. Univ. Press 1986). MURDOCK, GEORGE P., *Africa: Its Peoples and Their Culture History* (McGraw 1959). ONWUEJEOGWU, M. ANGULU, *The Social Anthropology of Africa* (Humanities 1975). SCHNEIDER, H., *The Africans: An Ethnological Account* (Prentice-Hall 1981). TURNBULL, COLIN M., *Man in Africa* (Doubleday 1976) and *The Mbuti Pygmies* (Holt 1983). VAN DER POST, LAURENS, *The Lost World of the Kalahari* (Harcourt 1977).

Languages. ALEXANDRE, PIERRE, *An Introduction to Languages and Language in Africa* (Heinemann 1972). DALBY, DAVID, *Language Map of Africa and the Adjacent Islands* (Intl. African Inst., London, 1977). DALBY, DAVID, ed., *Language and History in Africa* (Cass 1970). GREENBERG, JOSEPH H., *The Languages of Africa*, 3d ed. (Ind. Univ. Press 1970). MANN, MICHAEL, and DALBY, DAVID, eds., *A Thesaurus of African Languages* (K. G. Saur 1986).

Religions. BOND, GEORGE, AND OTHERS, eds., *African Christianity: Patterns of Religious Continuity* (Acad. Press 1979). BRAVMANN, RENÉ A., *African Islam* (Smithsonian 1983). FASHOLÉ-LUKE, EDWARD, AND OTHERS, eds., *Christianity in Independent Africa* (Ind. Univ. Press 1978). HASTINGS, ADRIAN, *A History of African Christianity: 1950–1975* (Cambridge 1979). HEUSCH, LUC DE, *Sacrifice in Africa: A Structuralist Approach* (Ind. Univ. Press 1985). JULES-ROSETTE, BENNETTA, ed., *The New Religions of Africa* (Ablex 1979). LAWSON, E. THOMAS, *Religions of Africa: Traditions in Transformation* (Harper 1984). LEWIS, I. M., ed., *Islam in Tropical Africa* (Ind. Univ. Press 1980). MBITI, JOHN S., *Introduction to African Religion* (Heinemann 1975). PARRINDER, E. G., *African Mythology* (Bedrick 1986) and *African Traditional Religion*, 3d ed. (Greenwood 1976). PEEL, J. D. Y., and STEWART, C. C., *Popular Islam: South of the Sahara* (Manchester Univ. Press 1986). SHORTER, AYLWARD, *African Christian Theology—Adaptation or Incarnation?* (Orbis 1977). VAN BINSBERGEN, WIM, and SCHOFFELEERS, MATTHEW, eds., *Theoretical Explorations in African Religion* (Kegan Paul 1985). ZUESSE, EVAN M., *Ritual Cosmos: The Sanctification of Life in African Religions* (Ohio Univ. Press 1979).

Social Change. COWAN, L. GRAY, *Black Africa: The Growing Pains of Independence* (Foreign Policy 1972). GUGLER, JOSEF, and FLANAGAN, WILLIAM G., *Urbanization and Social Change in West Africa* (Cambridge 1978). HAY, MARGARET J., and STICHTER, SHARON, *African Women South of the Sahara* (Longman 1984). KASFIR, NELSON, ed., *State and Class in Africa* (Cass 1984). KAYONKO-MALE, D., and ONYANGO, P., *Sociology of the African Family* (Longman 1984). MARKOWITZ, IRVING L., *Power and Class in Africa* (Prentice-Hall 1977). OBUDHO, R. A., and EL SHAKHS, SALAH S., eds., *Development of Urban Systems in Africa* (Praeger 1979). O'CONNOR, ANTHONY M., *The African City* (Africana 1983). OPPONG, CHRISTINE, *Middle Class African Marriage* (Allen & Unwin 1982). PEIL, MARGARET, *Consensus and Conflict in African Societies* (Longman 1977). REGIONAL MEETING ON YOUTH IN AFRICA, *Youth, Tradition, and Development in Africa* (Unipub. 1981). ROBERTSON, PEARL, and SKINNER, ELLIOTT P., eds., *Transformation and Resiliency in Africa* (Howard Univ. Press 1982). SHACK, WILLIAM A., and SKINNER, ELLIOTT P., eds., *Strangers in African Societies* (Univ. of Calif. Press 1979).

Health. AZEVEDO, MARIO J., AND OTHERS, eds., *Disease in African History* (Ohio Univ. Press 1978). BECK, ANN, *Medicine, Tradition, and Development in Kenya and Tanzania, 1920–1970* (Crossroads Press 1981). IMPERATO, PASCAL J., *African Folk Medicine: Practices and Beliefs of the Bambara and Other Peoples* (York Press 1977) and *A Wind in Africa: A Story of Modern Medicine in Mali* (Warren H. Green 1975). MAY, JACQUES M., *The Ecology of Malnutri-*

tion in the French-Speaking Countries of West Africa and Madagascar (Haffner 1968) and The Ecology of Malnutrition in Northern Africa (Haffner 1967). PARRY, E. H. O., ed., Principles of Medicine in Africa, 2d ed. (Oxford 1984). PATTERSON, K. DAVID, Infectious Diseases in Twentieth-Century Africa: A Bibliography of Their Distribution and Consequences (Crossroads 1979).

The Arts

Visual Arts. ANDERSON, KAJ B., African Traditional Architecture (Oxford 1977). D'AZEVEDO, WARREN L., ed., The Traditional Artist in African Societies (Bks. Demand UMI 1973). BASCOM, WILLIAM, African Art in Cultural Perspective (Norton 1973). BRAIN, ROBERT, Art and Society in Africa (Longman 1980). BRAVMANN, RENÉ A., Islam and Tribal Art in West Africa (Cambridge 1980). COLE, HERBERT M., ed., I Am Not Myself: The Art of African Masquerade (UCLA Mus. of Hist. 1985). DELANGE, JACQUELINE, The Art and Peoples of Black Africa (Dutton 1974). DENYER, SUSAN, African Traditional Architecture (Holmes & Meier 1978). FISHER, ANGELA, Africa Adorned (Abrams 1984). FRASER, DOUGLAS, and COLE, HERBERT M., eds., African Art and Leadership (Bks. Demand UMI 1972). GILLON, WERNER, A Short History of African Art (Facts on File 1984). LAUDE, JEAN, The Arts of Black Africa (Univ. of Calif. Press 1971). LEUZINGER, ELSY, The Art of Black Africa (Rizzoli Intl. 1979). MOUNT, MARSHALL, African Art: The Years Since 1920 (Ind. Univ. Press 1973). SIEBER, ROY, African Furniture and Household Objects (Ind. Univ. Press 1980) and African Textiles and Decorative Arts (Mus. of Modern Art 1972). VANSINA, JAN, Art History in Africa (Longman 1984). VOGEL, SUSAN, and N'DIAYE, FRANCINE, African Masterpieces from the Musée de l'Homme (Abrams 1985). WILCOX, A. R., The Rock Art of Africa (Holmes & Meier 1984). WILLETT, FRANK, African Art: An Introduction (Thames & Hudson 1985).

Music and Dance. BEBEY, FRANCIS, African Music: A People's Art (L. Hill 1975). BLACKING, JOHN, How Musical Is Man? (Univ. of Wash. Press 1973). CHERNOFF, JOHN MILLER, African Rhythm and African Sensibility: Aesthetics and Social Action in African Musical Idioms (Univ. of Chicago Press 1980). HUET, MICHEL, The Dance, Art, and Ritual of Africa (Pantheon 1978). JONES, A. M., Studies in African Music, 2 vols. (Oxford 1959). MERRIAM, ALAN P., African Music in Perspective (Garland 1982). NKETIA, J. H. KWABENA, The Music of Africa (Norton 1974). NKETIA, J. H. KWABENA, and DJE DJE, JACQUELINE C., eds., Selected Reports in Ethnomusicology, vol. 5 (Program in Ethnomusicology, UCLA Dept. of Music, 1984). WACHSMANN, KLAUS P., ed., Essays on Music and History in Africa (Bks. Demand UMI 1971).

Black African Literature. ABRAHAMS, ROGER D., ed., African Folktales: Traditional Stories of the Black World (Pantheon 1983). ACHEBE, CHINUA, and INNES, C. L., eds., African Short Stories (1985). ANDRZEJEWSKI, B. W., AND OTHERS, Literature in African Languages: Theoretical Issues and Sample Surveys (Cambridge 1985). AWOONOR, KOFI, The Breast of the Earth: A Survey of the History, Culture, and Literature of Africa South of the Sahara (NOK 1983). BANHAM, MARTIN, African Theatre Today (Wesleyan Univ. Press 1977). DATHORNE, O. R., African Literature in the Twentieth Century (Univ. of Minn. Press 1976). ETHERTON, MICHAEL, The Development of African Drama (Holmes & Meier 1983). GÉRARD, ALBERT S., African Language Literatures (Three Continents 1981) and European Language Writing in Sub-Saharan Africa, 2 vols. (Humanities 1986). GLEASON, JUDITH, ed., Leaf and Bone: African Praise-Poems, an Anthology (Viking 1980). GRAHAM-WHITE, ANTHONY, The Drama of Black Africa (French 1974). MOORE, GERALD, and BEIER, ULLI, eds., The Penguin Book of Modern African Poetry, 3d ed. (Penguin 1984). NKOSI, LEWIS, Tasks and Masks: Themes and Styles of African Literature (Longman 1981). OKEPWHO, ISIDORE, The Epic in Africa (Columbia Univ. Press 1979) and Myth in Africa: A Study of Its Aesthetic and Cultural Relevance (Cambridge 1983). SOYINKA, WOLE, Myth, Literature, and the African World (Cambridge 1975). SOYINKA, WOLE, ed., Poems of Black Africa (Hill & Wang 1975). WAUTHIER, CLAUDE, The Literature and Thought of Modern Africa, 2d ed. (Three Continents 1979). ZELL, HANS M., AND OTHERS, eds., A New Reader's Guide to African Literature, 2d ed. (Africana 1983).

History

General Works. AJALA, ADEKUNLE, Pan-Africanism (St. Martin's 1975). AJAYI, J. F., and CROWDER, MICHAEL, eds., Historical Atlas of Africa (Cambridge 1985). BENNETT, NORMAN R., Africa and Europe: From Roman Times to National Independence, 2d ed. (Holmes & Meier 1975). The Cambridge History of Africa, 8 vols. (Cambridge 1975–86). DAVIDSON, BASIL, The African Genius: An Introduction to African Cultural and Social History (Little 1970). EHRET, CHRISTOPHER, and POSNANSKY, MERRICK, Archaeological and Linguistic Reconstruction of African History (Univ. of Calif. Press 1982). FAGE, J. D., A History of Africa (Knopf 1978). FREEMAN-GRENVILLE, G. S. P., Chronology of African History (Oxford 1973). FREUND, BILL, The Making of Contemporary Africa: The Development of

African Society Since 1800 (Ind. Univ. Press 1984). GAILEY, HARRY A., History of Africa, ref. ed., 2 vols. (Krieger 1981) and The History of Africa in Maps (Denoyer 1979). GEISS, IMANUEL, The Pan-African Movement (Methuen 1974). JULY, ROBERT W., A History of the African People, 3d ed. (Macmillan 1980). KONCZACKI, Z. A. and J. M., eds., An Economic History of Tropical Africa, vols. 1 and 2 (Cass 1977). MAQUET, JACQUES, Civilizations of Black Africa, rev. ed. (Oxford 1972). MAZRUI, ALI A., The Africans: A Triple Heritage (Little 1986). McEVEDY, COLIN, The Penguin Atlas of African History (Penguin 1980). OLIVER, ROLAND, and FAGAN, BRIAN, Africa Since 1800, 3d ed. (Cambridge 1981). OLIVER, ROLAND, and FAGE, J. D., A Short History of Africa, 5th ed. (Penguin 1975). UNITED NATIONS EDUCATIONAL, SCIENTIFIC, AND CULTURAL ORGANIZATION, General History of Africa, 8 vols. (Unipub. 1981–). VANSINA, JAN, Oral Tradition as History (Univ. of Wis. Press 1985). WICKENS, PETER, An Economic History of Africa (Oxford 1981). WILLIS, JOHN RALPH, Studies in West African Islamic History (Cass 1979).

Prehistory and Archaeology. ANQUANDAH, JAMES, Rediscovering Ghana's Past (Longman 1982). INNSKEEP, R. R., The Peopling of Southern Africa (D. Philip 1978). LEAKEY, RICHARD E., and LEWIN, ROGER, Origins (Dutton 1982). OLIVER, ROLAND, and FAGAN, BRIAN M., Africa in the Iron Age (Cambridge 1975). PHILLIPSON, D. W., African Archaeology (Cambridge 1983) and The Later Prehistory of Eastern and Southern Africa (Heinemann 1977). SHAW, THURSTAN, Filling Gaps in Africa Maps: Fifty Years of Archaeology in Africa (Indiana Africa 1975) and Nigeria: Its Archaeology and Early History (Thames & Hudson 1978).

Precolonial Period. BOVILL, EDWARD, and HALLETT, ROBIN, Golden Trade of the Moors (Oxford 1968). CHITTICK, H. MELVILLE, and ROTBERG, ROBERT I., eds., East Africa and the Orient: Cultural Synthesis in Precolonial Times (Holmes & Meier 1975). DAVIDSON, BASIL, The African Slave Trade, rev. ed. (Little 1981) and The Lost Cities of Africa, rev. ed. (Little 1970). DIOP, CHEIKH A., Precolonial Black Africa (L. Hill 1986). HULL, RICHARD W., African Cities and Towns Before the European Conquest (Norton 1977). LEVTZION, NEHEMIA, Ancient Ghana and Mali (Holmes & Meier 1980). MAIR, LUCY, African Kingdoms (Oxford 1977). OLIVER, ROLAND, and ATMORE, ANTHONY, The African Middle Ages: 1400–1800 (Cambridge 1981).

Colonial Period. BETTS, RAYMOND D., Uncertain Dimensions: Western Overseas Empires in the Twentieth Century (Univ. of Minn. Press 1985). DUIGNAN, PETER, and GANN, L. H., eds., Colonialism in Africa, 1870–1960, 5 vols. (Cambridge 1970–75). GIFFORD, PROSSER, and LOUIS, WILLIAM ROGER, eds., The Transfer of Power in Africa, 1940–1960 (Yale Univ. Press 1982). MUNRO, J. FORBES, Africa and the International Economy, 1800–1960 (Rowman & Littlefield 1976). PEARCE, R. D., The Turning Point in Africa: British Colonial Policy, 1938–48 (Cass 1982). ROTBERG, ROBERT I., Africa and Its Explorers: Motives, Methods, and Impact (Harvard Univ. Press 1970). VAN ORMAN, RICHARD A., The Explorers: Nineteenth Century Expeditions in Africa and the American West (Univ. of N. Mex. Press 1984). WILSON, HENRY S., The Imperial Experience in Sub-Saharan Africa (Univ. of Minn. Press 1979).

Contemporary Period. AUSTIN, DENNIS, Politics in Africa (Univ. Press of New England 1978). CARTER, GWENDOLEN, and O'MEARA, PATRICK, eds., African Independence: The First Twenty-Five Years (Ind. Univ. Press 1985). COKER, CHRISTOPHER, NATO, the Warsaw Pact, and Africa (St. Martin's 1985). COLLIER, RUTH BERINS, Regimes in Tropical Africa: Changing Forms of Supremacy, 1945–1975 (Univ. of Calif. Press 1982). DAVIDSON, BASIL, Let Freedom Come (Little 1978). DIOP, CHEIKH A., Black Africa: Economic and Cultural Basis for a Federated State (L. Hill 1984). FOLTZ, WILLIAM J., and BIENEN, HENRY S., eds., Arms and the African: Military Influences on Africa's International Relations (Yale Univ. Press 1985). GAILEY, HARRY A., Africa, Troubled Continent: A Problem Approach (Krieger 1983). HENRIKSEN, THOMAS H., ed., Communist Powers and Sub-Saharan Africa (Hoover Inst. 1982). JACKSON, ROBERT H., AND ROSBERG, CARL G., Personal Rule in Black Africa (Univ. of Calif. Press 1982). KASFIR, NELSON, The Shrinking Political Arena: Participation and Ethnicity in African Politics (Univ. of Calif. Press 1976). LEVINE, VICTOR T., and LUKE, TIMOTHY W., The Arab-African Connection (Westview 1979). MAZRUI, ALI A., The African Condition (Westview 1980) and Africa's International Relations (Westview 1977). MAZRUI, ALI A., and TIDY, MICHAEL, Nationalism and New States in Africa (Heinemann 1984). SHAW, TIMOTHY, and HEARD, KENNETH A., eds., The Politics of Africa: Dependence and Development (Dalhousie Univ. Press 1979). SMITH, ANTHONY D., State and Nation in the Third World: The Western State and African Nationalism (St. Martin's 1983). TORDOFF, WILLIAM, Government and Politics in Africa (Ind. Univ. Press 1984). UNGAR, SANFORD J., Africa: The People and Politics of an Emerging Continent (Simon & Schuster 1985).

Consult also periodicals such as Africa Report (Transaction, bimonthly) and Journal of Modern African Studies (Cambridge, quarterly). These sources are especially important for information on recent events that have not yet been covered in book form.

© MICHAEL HOLFORD

A Carthaginian, or Punic, votive stela, which is housed in the British Museum.

AFRICA, Roman, the territories of the Roman empire in North Africa. After the Third Punic War, ending in 146 B.C., Rome established a province (Africa Vetus) in North Africa in the fertile region behind the ruined city of Carthage, in what is now Tunisia. The province was later extended along the Tripolitan coast (of modern Libya), and in 46 B.C. Numidia (modern northeastern Algeria) was added, first as a separate province (Africa Nova). The emperor Augustus united the two provinces as Africa Proconsularis in 25 B.C. In 42 A.D. the emperor Claudius formed two new provinces in Mauretania (now northwestern Algeria and northern Morocco).

Roman Africa prospered greatly and became the granary of Rome. Overrun by the Vandals in the 5th century, it was reconquered by the Eastern empire in the 6th century but finally fell to the Arabs late in the 7th century.

AFRICAN-AMERICAN RELIGIONS. Like other religions, African-American religions manifest themselves in both historical and transhistorical configurations. On the one hand (as organizations, ideas, rituals, artistic expressions), they evince chronological order. On the other (as systems of beliefs or agents of group consciousness), they reveal a timelessness. For all their similarities to other religions, African-American religions are unique in that they appear to have developed in the context of racial stigmatization of African-Americans in the Americas, especially North America.

Although this article is chiefly concerned with African-American religions in the United States, it begins with a discussion of Africans' adaptations of their religious traditions to the conditions they faced in their American enslavement. These adaptations originated—and are still deeply rooted in—the Caribbean, where most of the first waves of enslaved Africans were concentrated. The article goes on to discuss African-American religions, using a four-part chronological typology. Each part has a conceptual title so as to characterize the transhistorical qualities of the religions within it. Each part, moreover, is marked historically by a beginning and an ending event. Thus "Religions of Enslavement" originate with a missionary pledge and end with a slave revolt, defining mutually exclusive visions of Christianity. "Religions of Group Separatism" emerge out of free African-Americans' initial attempts to form small prayer groups and culminate in the formation of a nationwide denomination. In response to the virulent racism of the first half of the 20th century, "Religions of Racial Identification" appear, beginning with claims to an Afro-Judaism and climaxing with a "raceless" man-god figure. Espousing a universal African essence, "Religions of Africanity" reference themselves at first by "blackening" Christian icons and later africanize rites, liturgies, and, ultimately, theologies.

Survivals of African Religions. Enslaved Africans who were brought to the Americas came primarily from the coastal sub-Saharan area that ranges from Senegambia in the north to Angola in the south. They brought with them two major religious traditions. The most pervasive was the folk-based, or indigenous, religion. The other tradition, Islam, could be traced to the ancient kingdoms of Ghana, Mali, and Songhay, each of which had trade, political, and cultural ties with northern African Islamic countries.

Indigenous African traditions survived in two ways, each of which illustrates an aspect of the interplay between the historical—the reality of captivity—and the transhistorical—the systems of beliefs constructed to survive captivity. The first is found among enslaved Africans of the Caribbean, who embraced Christianity (mostly of the Roman Catholic sort) but also africanized it by blending in elements of their former religions. Formal religions such as candomblé in Brazil, santería in Cuba, shango in Trinidad, cumina in Jamaica, and vaudou in Haiti can trace their origins to the religions of one or more of the three groups of West African enslaved peoples: the Fon-speaking groups of Dahomey, the Yoruba of Nigeria, and the Akan of Ghana. The blending process (syncretism) evolved out of a demonstrable correlation between the structures and rituals of African religious traditions and Catholicism. The second way that African traditional religions survived was through fragments of beliefs and rituals, known collectively as religious Africanisms. These bits and pieces of African traditional religions are distributed among African religious groups throughout South America and the Caribbean, and they survive in folk beliefs and thought throughout North America.

Religions of Enslavement, 1701–1831. In 1701 the Society for the Propagation of the Gospel in Foreign Parts (SPG) was established by the Anglican Church, with "conversion of the Negroes" as one of its stated goals and England's American colonies as its chief focus. In 1831 Nat Turner led a group of rebels in the most famous slave uprising in U.S. history. A devout Christian, Turner claimed that God had charged him with overthrowing the enslavement of Africans: . . ."the Spirit instantly appeared to me . . . and [said] that I should . . . fight against the Serpent, for the time was fast approaching when the first should be last and the last should be first."

To the extent that their religious outlook was shaped by enslavement, African-Americans adopted a Christianity more resonant with Turner's than with that presented by the SPG and slave owners. By 1709 Francis Le Jau, one of the first SPG missionaries, required each "Adult Slave" baptismal candidate to declare publicly "that you do not aske for the holy baptism out of any design to ffree yourself from the Duty and Obedience you owe to your Master." In 1837 a slave owner advised fellow owners of the "excellent effect" of church attendance: "at such places" the enslaved learned "the reasons which sanction the master to exact of him his respective duties."

Efforts to convert the enslaved were clearly successful if measured by the formation of slave churches and the numbers of enslaved added to the rolls of white churches. By the late 1700s the first mission churches appeared, among them the Bluestone African Baptist Church on the Byrd plantation in Mecklenburg, Va. (1758) and the Silver Bluff (S.C.) Baptist Church (1773). These were followed in 1776, 1780, and 1785 by churches in Petersburg, Richmond, and Williamsburg, Va., respectively. Between 1835 and 1865 more than 200,000 enslaved Africans were placed on the rolls of white Methodist churches and comparable numbers for white Baptist churches.

To no small degree, these efforts at harnessing the enslaved in Christianity came in response to the persistence of non-Christian African religions among the enslaved. As late as 1831, the year of Turner's insurrection, African Islam was evident. Omar ibn Seid of South Carolina wrote in Arabic script and quoted the Koran. Biographical narratives of African Muslims and many accounts of Islamic practices among the enslaved have survived. In North America traditional African religions survived solely as remnants, such as conjuring and voodoo, strewn among folk religions. New Orleans voodoo devotees, among them the widely respected mother-daughter priestesses Marie and Marie Laveau, regularly called on the Dahomean *loa* (god) Damballa, even assigning the *loa* a more localized name, Li Grand Zombi. Henry Bibb, a slave in Kentucky in the early 19th century, found what he called "hoodoo" practiced among the "great masses of southern slaves."

Though slaves joined the white slave owners' churches, they developed a distinctive Christianity alongside their conjuring and in defiance of their owners' version. All along, the enslaved had disdain for the missionary's stock sermon text, "Slaves obey your masters." Beverly Jones remembered that the reward for such obedience was "to go to heaven." But he noted that the sermon never promised freedom there: "You see, they didn' want slaves to start thinkin' 'bout freedom, even in Heaven." But the enslaved appropriated Christianity for its millennialist messages. Jesus was a messiah, a liberator who would establish a kingdom: "King Jesus is de captain, captain, captain," goes the spiritual, "And she's makin for de Promise Land." Enslavement religion recast the biblical millennium into a collective cataclysmic deliverance of God's chosen from their wretchedness. He would rescue them so they could live in a paradise: "Just let me in the Kingdom when the world ketch a-fire!" "Gonna put on my shoes and walk all over God's heaven."

These messages prompted Christianized resistance of two sorts. The secret meeting in the "brush harbor" was the most common of the two. Mary Reynolds recalled such a meeting from her childhood enslavement in Louisiana, during which a preacher drove home the deliverance message:

© CHESTER HIGGINS, JR.

Spirit possession in an Akan ritual held in New York City. Traditional West African religions survived in the Americas in occult form but have been revived from African sources.

"A day am coming when niggers only be slaves of God." Turner's rebellion exemplifies prophetic Christian violent resistance, the second sort. In the wake of the deaths of 55 whites during Turner's messianic war, the South Carolina legislature acknowledged the potency of enslavement Christianity by passing a law forbidding independent meetings among the enslaved "for the purpose of mental instruction or religious worship."

Religions of Group Separatism, 1786–1895. In 1786, African-American members of the mostly white St. George's Methodist Episcopal Church in Philadelphia began holding their own prayer meetings. They were led by Richard Allen, a former slave, now a Methodist "exhorter." After one 5 A.M. Sunday service, he made the observation, "A few souls were awakened." In 1895 a group of African-American Baptist leaders met to vote on whether to establish a nationwide convention of African-American Baptist congregations or to remain members in a white-dominated organization of Baptist missionary groups. The "separatists" prevailed over "cooperationists," voting to establish what became the largest Christian African-American organization, the National Baptist Convention.

From the gathering of the prayer band in Philadelphia to formation of the Baptist Convention, black churches were prompted into being by religious group separatism—the compelling desire of African-Americans for worship and fellowship among themselves. Indeed, this movement marks the emergence of the Black Church (the generic name for Protestant African-American religious bodies). The separatist spirit can best be understood in terms of the nonreligious mutual aid societies that African-Americans formed in northern cities during the last two decades of the 18th century. These societies provided members with burial insurance, legal aid, and protection against sudden impoverishment. They also functioned as religious associations, providing alternative sites for devotional meetings. Such organizations existed

A small group of African-American Pentecostal Christians holding an open-air prayer meeting. Racially separate congregations of mainstream denominations began to form by the end of the 18th century; new African-American denominations were a later development.

© CHESTER HIGGINS, JR.

in Boston (1776, African Lodge No. 1), in Newport, R.I. (1780, African Union Society), in Philadelphia (1786, Free African Society), and in many other cities along the eastern seaboard. The trend to organize these associations became pronounced as free, northern, urban African-Americans began to respond in common to the menace of racial bigotry. In 1787, Prince Hall, one of the founders of Boston's society, petitioned the Massachusetts legislature for a school for African-American children, who were prohibited from attending the "free schools"; when the legislature refused, Hall and the society set up a private school.

In 1787, less than a year after he had begun meeting with the prayer band, Allen and the other African-American congregants walked out of St. George's in disgust after an usher attempted to force several of them up from prayer and into segregated seats at the rear of the building. This incident furnished the prayer group with a racial stimulus to organize itself, not just into the Free African Society with bylaws and financial rules, but ultimately, in 1794, into the first two African Methodist churches, St. Thomas' African Episcopal Church and Bethel Church of Philadelphia. Throughout the Middle Atlantic states, similar separatist groups gathered themselves into societies and Methodist congregations. In 1816 five of the churches met together to found the African Methodist Episcopal (AME) denomination. They elected Allen as their bishop. Five years later a set of similarly situated separatist societies and churches in New York formed the African Methodist Episcopal Zion (AMEZ) denomination.

The separatist church movement constitutes the first recognizable racialization of Christianity by African-Americans. Because each Baptist congregation was independent, African-American Baptists could organize themselves into individual, racially separate congregations relatively easily. But that same independence caused difficulties when Baptist churches attempted to unite into regional and national bodies. The earliest African-American Baptist associations began forming in the sparsely settled West, perhaps because in this vast region their bonding together did little to limit the freedom and authority of the individual churches. Between 1834 and and 1841 the first groupings appeared in Ohio, Illinois, and Amherstburg (in Upper Canada, later Ontario). There were three failed attempts at nationwide associations, of which the largest, with more than a million members, was the American National Baptist Convention (1886).

Thus the 1895 meeting establishing the National Baptist Convention was destined to become the ultimate merger. Urged on by their experiences as second-class bureaucrats in white missionary Baptist associations, the separatists acknowledged their new racial solidarity: "We must either do something worthy of our numbers or be relegated to a back seat." The black church in its several guises won, or as Allen might have put it, "awakened" a few souls.

Religions of Racial Identification, 1896–1946. In 1896, preaching that African-Americans were the heirs of the ten lost tribes of Israel (while Caucasian Jews were not), William S. Crowdy founded the Church of God and Saints of Christ. Fifty years later, Major J. (Father) Divine secretly married Sweet Angel, a 21-year-old white Canadian, announcing later that the marriage was not physical; it "consummated the union of GOD and man." Common to both of these incidents is the effort to reconfigure 20th-century black identity. While Crowdy altered the black heritage, Divine announced that he had ceased to be black: "I AM NOT an N and I AM NOT representing any such thing as the N or C race; but I AM REPRESENTING THE TRUE AND LIVING GOD INFINITELY."

African-American religions of racial identification emerged during a period when racism became legally and systematically codified. The same year Crowdy first began to preach his message, the U.S. Supreme Court declared in *Plessy* v. *Ferguson* that racial segregation was legal as long as it was "equal." A month before Divine's marriage, five African-American men—among them a veteran recently returned from World War II—were lynched in Georgia in retaliation for an unexpectedly high African-American voter turnout. A sign plastered on the door of a church read: "First nigger to vote will never vote again."

There were secular versions of the choices that Crowdy and Divine made. From revised labels (such as Alain Locke's "New Negro") to prominent advertisements in African-American newspapers for agents to straighten hair and lighten skin, African-Americans sought out ways to become less racially marked.

Given the historical circumstances in which they evolved, African-American religions of racial identification are by nature racially reactionary. They share a common resistance to the notion—whether benign or racist—of "Negro," especially as a genetically determined character and destiny. Perhaps this causes them to be classified often as sects or cults in the most deviant sense. But their diversity of expression and thought defy categorization in such terms.

By World War I, in New York City alone, at least eight African-American religions espousing Judaism as belief or ritual or as bloodline or culture were active. Some were isolated and orthodox, such as Rabbi Leon Richlieu's Moorish Zionist Temple. Others courted mainstream movements. "Ethiopian Hebrew" Arnold J. Ford tried in vain to have his Beth B'nai Abraham congregation and its emigrationist ideology declared the official religion of Marcus Garvey's back-to-Africa Universal Negro Improvement Association (UNIA).

This same breadth of diversity characterizes African-American Muslim religions. In 1913 Noble Drew Ali forbade members of his Moorish Science Temple, generally acknowledged as the first African-American Muslim group in the United States, to refer to themselves as "Negroes," "Colored Folks," "Black People," or "Ethiopians," all "slaveholder names." Proudly wearing fezzes and brandishing wallet-sized cards, these followers became "descendants of the ancient Moabites," now "Asiatics." For their part, members of the Lost-Found Nation of Islam in the Wilderness of North America (later the Nation of Islam, or Black Muslim movement) learned from Elijah Muhammad in the late 1930s that Islam was not only a religion but a lineage descending from the "Tribe of Shabazz."

African-American Muslim movements developed a strain of racial identification religion that can be classified as racial nationalism. Whereas some African-American racial religions can be viewed as escapist (that is, as advocating abandoning race for the identity and ancestry of some other religious heritage), racial nationalists appropriated a religion and then used it to redefine their race. Under its first leaders, Wallace Fard and Elijah Muhammad; under its most popular adherent, Malcolm X; and, later, under its most charismatic thinker, Minister Louis Farrakhan, the Nation of Islam has taught that every "Black Man under the sun is born a Muslim by nature."

For all their variety, religions of racial identification still seem epitomized by Father Divine. He lived and espoused racelessness, a religion that resisted being bound atavistically to Islam or Judaism or even Africanity. Having transcended race, he quite logically could assume divinity, becoming Father Divine, "GOD."

Religions of Africanity, 1924–1990. As chaplain-general of Garvey's UNIA, the Rev. George Alexander McGuire prodded Garveyites at their 1924 convention to call "an international day when all the negroes of the world should tear the pictures of a white Madonna and a white Christ out of their homes and make a bonfire of them." In 1990 a visitor to Imani Temple of the African-American Catholic Congregation in Washington, D.C., remarked, "I've been a Catholic for almost 50 years. I didn't feel like I had been fed. [Imani] is both the religion and the culture." She had just attended a service beginning with a procession of musicians and clergy in African vestments

© BETH BLOCK/BROOKLYN IMAGE GROUP

An African-American Muslim mosque. Racially nationalistic American Muslim movements grew rapidly in the late 20th century.

and including a traditional African call to the ancestors; inspirational readings from the likes of Harriet Tubman, W. E. B. Du Bois, and James Weldon Johnson; and a powerfully nationalistic sermon preached by Imani's founder, the Rev. George Augustus Stallings, Jr.

Unlike religions of racial identification, with their emphasis on the acquisition of new traditions and ancestry, religions of Africanity conceive of themselves as africanizing conventional religions—almost always Christianity or Islam—and in so doing reorienting these religions to address African-Americans' struggle for equality. They differ from one another in the extent of this reorientation. From the beginning of his Pentecostal mission, Bishop Charles Harrison Mason—founder in 1907 of The Church of God in Christ, the largest African-American Pentecostal denomination—concluded, "If I want Him to baptize me I will have to let the people's rights and wrongs all alone." On the other hand, Elder Lucy Smith, another Pentecostal leader—pastor of her own socially activist All Nations Pentecostal Church in Chicago during the 1930s—did not "care much for those folks who are stuck up and live separated from the common people."

Most mainline Protestant churches saw racial welfare as part of the Christian mission, but not to the extent of embracing the African-American peoples' struggle of a McGuire or Stallings or even of a Martin Luther King, Jr. In 1962, at the first rumblings of civil rights unrest, the Rev. Joseph H. Jackson, president of the National Baptist Convention, admonished the church: "Protest is not enough"; furthermore, "a theology that substitutes pigmentation for divine principle is not sufficient to save any race." That same year King and a number of former top leaders left the Convention to organize the more activist Progressive

National Baptist Convention, with the motto "Unity, Service, Fellowship, Peace."

The same struggle between this-worldly and otherworldly outlooks split the Nation of Islam. Shortly after the death of his father, Elijah Muhammad, Wallace D. Muhammad founded the World Community of al-Islam in the West (later the American Muslim Mission; dissolved in 1985). It represented a shift away from the racially utilitarian Islamic Africanity of the Black Muslim movement to orthodox—some would say, Sunni—Islam.

Ultimately the alignment of Christianity with the North American—African diaspora's vision of social justice hinged on a new interpretation of Christianity. Prompted by the Black Power movement and a sense that African-Americans were becoming disillusioned with Christianity, African-American theologians (notably James H. Cone) derived Black Theology, based on the black experience in North America. From Nat Turner's messianic revolt to Martin Luther King, Jr.'s nonviolent protests, black Christianity has followed a "theology of liberation" that is, in Cone's words, "accountable to a black church that has always been involved in our historical fight for justice."

Armed with a theology, Africanity advocates developed religions that manifested themselves either as independent, black Christian churches— such as the Black Christian Nationalist Church—or as alternatives to existing Christian churches— such as Stallings's African-American Catholic Congregation. The members of the independent Black Christian Nationalist Church (a denomination of several midwestern churches founded by Albert Cleage in 1972) belong to Shrines of the Black Madonna and subscribe to the creed, "I Believe that Jesus, the Black Messiah, was a revolutionary leader, sent by God to rebuild the Black Nation, Israel." Stallings's Imani Temple exemplifies the other manifestation of Africanity. Given the Roman Catholic Church's longstanding encouragement of indigenous rites, Stallings's African-American liturgy alone might not have prompted his excommunication. But beyond African symbolism, the religions of Africanity articulate a theology of black community uplift. In addition to the African drums and black history readings, Stallings's Africanity required a school and provision for the homeless. More radically, it demanded communion for the baptized of other denominations, ordination of women, and community-derived positions on abortion, marriage and divorce, and homosexuality. Stallings insists that his church is Catholic, "just not Roman Catholic."

Toward a Unified African-American Religion. In terms of their transhistorical concepts, African-American religions defy the discreteness that the historical typology above suggests. The accommodationism-resistance of enslavement religions, the separatism of early churches, the racialism of the 20th-century movements, and the Afrocentrism of contemporary institutions are interwoven in the African-American experience. Only the relative prominence of each manifestation at some historical moment serves to distinguish the divisions. Indeed, those concepts intermingle so constantly as to appear to create, over time, one African-American religion.

Perhaps the clear emergence of such a single religion will mark the next phase of African-American religious expression. Signs of a unified religion are becoming more pronounced as African-Americans face the 21st century, some having fulfilled their aspirations, others in despair over the futility of their efforts to subsist. Modern-day religious outlooks draw on an African-American religion that has endured over time as the link between the experience and the destiny of being African in America.

MICHAEL W. HARRIS, *University of Iowa*

Bibliography

Austin, Allan D., ed., *African Muslims in Antebellum America: A Sourcebook* (Garland 1984).

Baer, Hans A., and Merrill Singer, eds., *African-American Religion in the Twentieth Century* (Univ. of Tenn. Press 1992).

Barrett, Leonard, *Soul-Force: African Heritage in Afro-American Religion* (Anchor/Doubleday 1974).

Boles, John B., ed., *Masters and Slaves in the House of the Lord: Race and Religion in the American South, 1740–1870* (Univ. of Ky. Press 1988).

Cone, James H., *For My People: Black Theology and the Black Church* (Orbis 1984).

Davis, Cyprian, *The History of Black Catholics in the United States* (Crossroad 1990).

Epstein, Dena J., *Sinful Tunes and Spirituals: Black Folk Music to the Civil War* (Univ. of Ill. Press 1977).

Fitts, Leroy, *A History of Black Baptists* (Broadman 1985).

Harris, Michael W., *The Rise of Gospel Blues: The Music of Thomas Andrew Dorsey in the Urban Church* (Oxford 1992).

Higginbotham, Evelyn B., *Righteous Discontent: The Women's Movement in the Black Baptist Church, 1880–1920* (Harvard Univ. Press 1993).

Lincoln, C. Eric, *The Black Muslims in America* (Beacon 1973).

Lincoln, C. Eric, and Lawrence H. Mamiya, *The Black Church in the African-American Experience* (Duke Univ. Press 1990).

Marsh, C. E., *From Black Muslims to Muslims: The Transition from Separatism to Islam, 1930–1980* (Scarecrow Press 1984).

Raboteau, Albert J., *Slave Religion: The "Invisible Institution" in the Antebellum South* (Oxford 1978).

Simpson, George E., *Black Religions in the New World* (Columbia Univ. Press 1978).

Washington, James M., *Frustrated Fellowship: The Black Baptist Quest for Social Power* (Mercer Univ. Press 1986).

Watts, Jill, *God, Harlem U. S. A.: The Father Divine Story* (Univ. of Calif. Press 1992).

AFRICAN HUNTING DOG, a large wild dog found throughout most of sub-Saharan Africa. It somewhat resembles the hyena, to which it is not related. The head and body are about 40 inches (100 cm) long, and the tail about 18 inches (46 cm). The mottled black, white, and orange color of the body is variable in pattern. The ears are large and erect.

The African hunting dog can have litters of 2 to 16 offspring, but the average is about 7.

© HELMUT ALBRECHT/BRUCE COLEMAN LIMITED

African hunting dogs live in packs, usually of about a dozen animals, and hunt at any hour of the day or night. They pursue even the larger kinds of antelope. The dogs do not bark but utter a variety of high-pitched, birdlike sounds.

The single species, *Lycaon pictus,* belongs to the family Canidae, order Carnivora.

JOSEPH A. DAVIS, JR.
New York Zoological Society

AFRICAN NATIONAL CONGRESS, a multiracial resistance movement in South Africa. After the consolidation of European political power in South Africa in 1910, an organization was founded in 1912 to ensure by constitutional means equal rights for blacks. At first called the South African Native National Congress, it became the African National Congress (ANC) in 1923. In the late 1920s the leadership divided over its role and whether to affiliate with the Communist party. With conservatives in control, the ANC faded in the 1930s.

In 1940 Alfred Xuma revived the organization. He broadened its membership base and accommodated African intellectuals such as Oliver Tambo, Walter Sisulu, and Nelson Mandela in its new Youth League in 1944. These activists displaced the ANC's moderate leadership in 1949. Membership swelled to nearly 100,000 following the nonviolent Defiance Campaign of 1952 against the government. Under Albert Luthuli, the ANC in 1955 joined with groups representing Coloureds, Asians, and whites to form the Congress of the People, whose Freedom Charter called for multiracial democracy. Luthuli received the Nobel Peace Prize in 1960 in recognition of his commitment to nonviolence.

The shooting of unarmed demonstrators by police at Sharpeville in 1960 and the outlawing of the ANC the following year forced the ANC to review its nonviolent strategy. In 1961 it formed a military wing, Umkhonto we Sizwe (Spear of the Nation), with Mandela at its head and committed to carrying out selective acts of sabotage. In 1963 Mandela and seven other Umkhonto leaders were indicted for treason, found guilty, and sentenced to life in prison. With Tambo as its leader in exile, the ANC continued the struggle, conducting raids from its bases in the neighboring "frontline" states.

Not until 1989, under Pres. F. W. de Klerk, did the South African government agree to seek a political settlement with blacks. The ANC became the chief bargaining voice of the black opposition. The release of Sisulu and others was followed early in 1990 by the legalization of the ANC and the freeing of Mandela, who was elected its deputy president. Mandela led the ANC in negotiating with de Klerk on the shape of a new constitution that would give blacks the vote. These events changed the political climate in South Africa and ushered in the dismantling of the apartheid system. Mandela and de Klerk shared the Nobel Peace Prize in 1993, because of their joint efforts to bring about a peaceful transition to a nonracial democracy.

After the assassination of its leader Chris Hani in April 1993, the ANC managed to contain protests. In the fall, after the National Party agreed to share power, the ANC played an active role in the multiracial transition council that would oversee preparations for the very first universal-suffrage elections scheduled for April 1994. Once these plans were under way, the ANC also appealed to the international community to end all remaining sanctions against South Africa.

By the end of 1997 Mandela was ready to "pass on the baton" to a new generation of leaders, and Thabo Mbeki, the nation's deputy president (and eventual president), was unanimously elected to head the ANC.

VIRGINIA CURTIN KNIGHT*, *"Current History"*

Bibliography: Frederikse, Julie, *The Unbreakable Thread: Non-Racialism in South Africa* (Indiana Univ. Press 1990); Holland, Heidi, *The Struggle: A History of the African National Congress* (G. Braziller 1990); Mkhondo, Rich, *Reporting South Africa* (Heinemann 1993); Rantete, Johannes, *The African National Congress and the Negotiated Settlement in South Africa* (J. L. van Schaik Academic 1998).

AFRICAN SLEEPING SICKNESS. See TRYPANOSO-MIASIS.

AFRICAN VIOLET, a stemless, perennial, herbaceous plant native to coastal eastern Africa. The African violet has long-stemmed, fleshy leaves clustered around its base. About 1.5 to 3 inches (3.8 to 7.6 cm) long, the leaves are usually purple or light green on the underside and deep green on the upper side, which is covered with soft hair. The flowers are usually violet and occur in loose clusters of one to six. The flower tube, which is about 1 inch (2.5 cm) across, has five unequal lobes and two stamens.

The African violet belongs to the Gesneria family, Gesneriaceae. The most widely cultivated species is *Saintpaulia ionantha.* One variety, *grandiflora,* has large, intensely violet flowers.

AFRIKAANS, af-ri-käns', one of the two official languages (with English) of South Africa. It is spoken as a first language by several million people, nearly half of whom are of mixed race (Cape Coloureds), and as a second language by about as many people, most of whom are blacks. Derived from Dutch, the language of the early white settlers, it had evolved as a distinct form of speech by 1800, when its written use began. Following movements for its recognition begun in the late 19th century, it received official status in 1925.

Afrikaans is basically Germanic in structure and vocabulary. It has been influenced by borrowings from the Khoisan and Bantu languages of South Africa and from the Portuguese and Malay dialects that were spoken by household slaves and servants. The language of the majority of white and mixed-race South Africans, it is regarded by Afrikaners as fundamental to their group identity. A literature in Afrikaans has developed since about 1870.

AFRIKANER, af-ri-kän'ər, a member of one of the major cultural groups in South Africa. Afrikaners are a people of European descent who speak the Afrikaans language. The group is made up of descendants of the original 17th-century Dutch, German, French Huguenot, and other non-British European settlers in South Africa, and of later immigrants and their descendants who identify themselves with this group, sharing its cultural heritage and language. Once a predominantly rural group, Afrikaners began to migrate into the cities after World War I, and, between 1948 and 1994, were the predominant political force in South Africa. Afrikaners constitute up to two-thirds of the white population of South Africa, thus less than a 12th of the total population.

The meaning of the term *Afrikaner* has changed through the centuries. In the 17th-century *Africaander* described the indigenous people. In the early 18th century it referred to white colonists born in South Africa, as distinguished from immigrants born in Europe. In the 19th century *Afrikaner* denoted people of Dutch descent living throughout South Africa, while *Boer* (Dutch, "farmer") was reserved for Afrikaners of the "Boer republics"—the Orange Free State and the South African Republic (Transvaal). In the 20th century, as a large proportion of the people came to live in the cities and towns, *Boer* became merely historical and yielded to *Afrikaner*.

Evolution of the Afrikaner People. The Afrikaner people were molded as a group during the years that the Dutch East India Company ruled Cape Province (1652–1795). During this period it is estimated that the Netherlanders were joined in Cape Province by Germans, French Huguenots, and other nationalities in the proportions of 50:27:17:6. The remoteness of the home countries, the isolation of the advancing frontier, and the virtual cessation of immigration after 1707 were instrumental in uniting the various elements that accepted South Africa as a fatherland. Although the Cape Province prospered, a glut in its agricultural market motivated the Afrikaners to move into the interior and pursue a more self-sufficient way of life. This migration dates from the beginning of the 18th century—the era of the *trekboer*, or pioneer stock-farmer. During this period Afrikaners fought frequent range wars with the indigenous African population and were hostile to attempts made by the Cape Province to hinder their movements or to control their commerce.

Afrikaner Identity. Politically the Afrikaners were and still are republicans. Their Dutch Calvinist faith, which emphasized the sovereignty of God, the concept of the "Chosen People," and other Old Testament ideas, has influenced them spiritually and socially. More than three-quarters of the modern Afrikaners belong to the Dutch Reformed Church.

From the beginning the Calvinist Afrikaners distinguished between "Christian" and "heathen," and during the second half of the 18th century, there was an increasing tendency to equate these classifications with "white" and "nonwhite." Most Afrikaners rejected interracial relationships and equalization of the races, and they were supportive of the policies of differentiation and segregation later known as apartheid. These policies were practiced in the Boer republics from the days of the "Great Trek," the northward migration of the *voortrekkers* (pioneers).

Afrikaner Nationalism. The Cape Province came under British control at the end of the Napoleonic Wars. Alienated by many of the new British policies, such as the emancipation of slaves, more than 10,000 Afrikaners left on the Great Trek, which began in 1835. Heading for southern Natal and the high veld, they eventually established the South African Republic (1852) and the Orange Free State (1854) and, consequently, polarized South Africa into a republican north and a colonial south. Attempts by the British to confederate the republics and colonies by force led to the first Anglo-Boer war (1880). The continuing struggle for supremacy between Boer and Briton, which coincided with the discovery of gold in the Transvaal and the international scramble for Africa, resulted in the second Anglo-Boer war (South African War,

1899–1902) and the British conquest of the two republics.

Afrikaner nationalism was intensified by the British victory. The death in exile in 1904 of Paul Kruger, the president of the South African Republic, magnified Afrikaner nationalism and became the rallying point for republican feeling in later years. The Great Trek became the great national epic; it and the Anglo-Boer wars were the foundation stones of the national tradition and national consciousness that permeated the cultural revival of the Afrikaners in the 20th century.

Afrikaner Politics. When South Africa was unified in 1910, Afrikaners formed their own political party, the South African Party (SAP), under Generals Louis Botha, Jan Smuts, and James Hertzog. However, Hertzog broke away in 1913 and established the National Party (NP), which rejected the coalition with the British and revived republican ideals. The struggle for supremacy between Boer and Briton continued along party lines, and in 1924 Hertzog became prime minister. Fusion between Smuts's SAP and Hertzog's NP occurred in 1934, but in 1939 they parted, and Smuts became prime minister (1939–1948).

Beginning in 1948, under Prime Minister D. F. Malan and his successors, the NP followed a policy of apartheid, or "separate development," for the country's ethnic groups. In 1961 the party achieved its long-standing goal of turning South Africa into a republic, which withdrew from the Commonwealth of Nations. Although the Afrikaners had composed the core of the right-wing opposition to the abolition of apartheid, a majority of them supported the reforms that were outlined in the 1992 referendum. Some hoped to establish a separate Afrikaner homeland within the new South Africa. (See also AFRIKAANS; APARTHEID; GREAT TREK; ORANGE FREE STATE; SOUTH AFRICA; SOUTH AFRICAN WAR; TRANSVAAL.)

F. A. VAN JAARSVELD*, *Author of*
"The Awakening of Afrikaner Nationalism"

Bibliography: February, Vernon A., *The Afrikaners of South Africa* (Columbia Univ. Press 1991); Goodwin, June, and Ben Schiff, *Heart of Whiteness: Afrikaners Face Black Rule in the New South Africa* (Scribner 1995); Le May, G. H. L., *The Afrikaners: An Historical Interpretation* (Blackwell 1995).

AFTERIMAGE, a luminous sensation experienced after a light stimulus is removed. If one stares at a bright light for a few seconds and then shuts it off, one retains an image—the afterimage—of the light. A single flash from a photographic flash lamp provides an even more effective example. For a few moments in the dark the image will look bright—the positive afterimage. However, when the image is viewed against a white background, it will appear dark—the negative afterimage. The negative afterimage, sometimes tinged with color, can be revived by blinking the eyes.

Afterimages appear to have the character of a photographic imprint on the retina. Thus, if the eye is temporarily blinded by pressure on the eyeball, the light stimulus that is received during the blind period is retained as an afterimage when the eye is returned to its normal state. A further indication that the afterimage is an imprint on the retina is that when the eye moves, the afterimage follows.

The negative afterimage is ascribed either to a local fatigue of the nerve connections at the retina or to a local depletion there of photosensitive pigment (visual purple). Fatigue of the retinal elements is shown in successive contrasts of color. If a disk of colored paper is placed on a well-lighted sheet of white paper and looked at fixedly, when the disk is taken away, that part of the paper previously covered by the disk appears in the complementary color. Consequently, if the disk is red, the afterimage will be green.

The apparent size of the afterimage changes with the appearance of the background image on which it is superimposed. The larger the background image, the smaller the afterimage.

The sequence of afterimages after exposure to a brief flash of light can be quite complicated. In the dark, the initial positive afterimage is followed by a longer negative phase, then a still longer positive phase, then a much longer negative phase, and so on.

GERALD OSTER*
Polytechnic Institute of Brooklyn

AGA KHAN, ä'gə KHän, the title (Āghā Khān) of the imām, or spiritual leader, of the Nizārī Ismāʿīlī sect of Shiʿa Islam, which has been estimated to have 20 million adherents in Africa and Asia. The title is hereditary, based on a claim of direct descent from Muḥammad's daughter Fāṭimah, through the Fāṭimid caliphs of Egypt. It was first given to the 46th imām, Ḥasan ʿAlī Shāh, in 1817 by the Qajar shah of Iran.

AGA KHAN I. Ḥasan ʿAlī Shāh (1800–1881) married a daughter of Fatḥ ʿAlī Shāh, who granted him the title Aga Khan after Ḥasan's father, Khalīl Allāh, was murdered. Ḥasan rebelled against the shah's successor, Muḥammad Shāh, in 1838, was defeated, and fled to Sind in 1840. He tried unsuccessfully to reestablish himself in Persia and eventually settled in Bombay. There his title was confirmed by the British in 1866, after an internal struggle among his Khōja followers. The British in turn enjoyed his support. He died in April 1881.

AGA KHAN III. After the short rule of Ḥasan's son ʿAlī Shāh (died 1885) as Aga Khan II, the title passed to Sulṭān Sir Muḥammad Shāh (1877–1957), then only eight years old. Born in Karachi on Nov. 2, 1877, Aga Khan III received both a traditional Muslim education and a modern European one. His background in both the Asian and European worlds prompted him, among others of similar upbringing, to seek to bridge the gap between them. As a result, he was instrumental in raising the level of Muslim education and in introducing reforms in the treatment of Muslim women. He also participated in Indian politics, serving in the viceroy's legislative council (1902–1904). In 1906 he led a delegation to the viceroy asking for separate representation for Muslims. This principle of granting separate electorates to minorities stemmed from the Muslims' concern for their future in a Hindu-dominated India. The delegation also established the Muslim League, which carried the seeds of Muslim separatism and eventually was instrumental in the creation of Pakistan.

In World War I the Aga Khan supported the British. Afterward he was an intermediary in Indian politics, supporting neither anti-British agitation nor Muslim communalism. In 1929 he was president of the All-India Muslim Conference in Delhi, and in 1930–1931 chairman of the British-Indian section of the round-table conference in London. In 1932 and from 1934 to 1937 he represented India at the League of Nations, serving as Assembly president in 1937. During World War II he lived in Switzerland. Thereafter he was active in attempts to raise the material well-being of his followers, and he advocated the creation of cooperative enterprises by Ismāʿīlī Muslims. He died in Versoix, Switzerland, on July 11, 1957.

AGA KHAN IV. In selecting his successor, Aga Khan III had passed over his two sons, Aly (1911–1960) and Sadruddin (born 1933), in favor of Aly's son Shāh Karīm al-Ḥusaynī. Aga Khan IV was born in Geneva on Dec. 13, 1937, and was educated in Switzerland. After a tour of Ismāʿīlī communities in East Africa, he enrolled at Harvard to study engineering but instead pursued Arabic and Asian history. He was invested as Aga Khan IV on July 13, 1957, and after another tour of Ismāʿīlī communities he returned to Harvard, where he received a B.A. degree in 1959. Aga Khan IV was a notably successful real estate developer and, like his grandfather, became well known for his interest in thoroughbred breeding and racing. He continued his grandfather's tradition of promoting his followers' welfare, establishing a development bank in Damascus, a health service in Karachi, and the Aga Khan Foundation in Geneva, which supports numerous health, education, and development projects.

JAMES R. SHIRLEY*, *Northern Illinois University*

Bibliography: Edwards, Anne, *Throne of Gold: The Lives of the Aga Khans* (Morrow 1995); Frischauer, Willi, *The Aga Khans* (Bodley Head 1970).

AGADE. See AKKAD.

AGADIR, ä-gə-dir', a city in Morocco, on the Atlantic Ocean, 5 miles (8 km) north of the mouth of the Sous River and 75 miles (121 km) south of Mogador, with which it is united by highway. Agadir is the shipping center for an area raising early fruits and vegetables and has canneries and factories producing metal goods and building materials. Overlooking its natural harbor is a citadel surmounting a rock 720 feet high (219 meters).

Agadir, a port city in Morocco.

© ANDREA PISTOLESI/THE IMAGE BANK

Agadir was developed by the Portuguese, who occupied it from 1505 to 1541. Later, in 1765, the Moroccans closed it to general commerce. In 1911, Agadir was the scene of a serious international incident, when Germany sent the warship *Panther* to the port. The crisis was resolved on November 4 of that year, when agreements were signed recognizing the right of France to establish a protectorate over Morocco. The port was open to commerce in 1930. (See also MOROCCO— *History: Establishment of the Protectorate.*)

After World War II the city grew rapidly. It flourished as a winter resort, and improvements in its harbor facilities increased its importance as a port. On Feb. 29, 1960, a devastating earthquake occurred, followed shortly by a tidal wave and another less severe tremor. The first quake was the most violent ever recorded in Morocco; from 10,000 to 12,000 persons were killed, and a large part of the city was destroyed. The city has been rebuilt. Population: 137,000 (1993 est.).

AGAG, ā'gag, in the Hebrew Scriptures, a king of the Amalekites. Against Samuel's orders, Agag was spared by Saul when the Amalekites were slain, precipitating a final rupture between Samuel and Saul. Later, Agag was hacked to pieces by Samuel in Gilgal (I Samuel 15). According to the Haggadah, Haman was a descendant of Agag.

AGALMATOLITE, ag-əl-mat'ə-līt, a soft, massive stone, generally grayish or greenish, but sometimes yellow, brown, or red, or streaked with these colors. It is soft enough to be cut with a knife and takes a good polish. Because of its use by the Chinese in carving small pagodas and sculptured figures, it is also known as either pagodite or figure stone. Its hardness varies from 1 to 2, and its specific gravity is 2.5 to 2.8. Agalmatolite belongs to the pinite, pyrophyllite, or steatite (soapstone) groups.

AGAM, Yaacov, ä-gäm' (1928–   ), Israeli multimedia artist who was one of the founders of kinetic art. The son of an orthodox rabbi, he was born Yaacov Gipstein in Rishon-le-Zion, Palestine (now Israel), on May 11, 1928.

Agam studied art with Mordecai Ardon at the Bezalel School of Arts and Crafts, Jerusalem (1947–1948), and architecture with Siegfried Giedion at the Kunstgewerbeschule, Zurich (1949). In 1951 he settled in Paris, where his first one-man show, featuring kinetic and transformable paintings, was held in 1953 at Galerie Craven. In 1955 Agam participated in Le Mouvement—considered the definitive exhibition of kinetic art—at Galerie Denise René, Paris.

His artistic oeuvre can be divided into three categories. The contrapuntal or "polyphonic" paintings are op art images in which a number of individual themes lose their identity entirely, changing color and form as the work is viewed from different standpoints; this genre is exemplified in *Double Metamorphosis II* (1964; Museum of Modern Art, New York City). Transformable objects, such as *Beating Heart* (1971; private collection, London), are stainless-steel sculptures with spiral-shaped rods that can be manipulated by the viewer to form different shapes. Works aspiring to envelop the environment include tactile constructions that vibrate, emitting light, water, and/or sound; an example is the 1972 room installation at the Palais de l'Élysée, Paris, which encompassed the ceilings, walls, and floor. Agam incorporated aspects of all three types in some later pieces, and he also expanded his repertoire to include both environmental and electronic telekinetic elements.

Agam strove to demonstrate the principle of reality as a continuous becoming rather than as a circumscribed statement, and he was deeply influenced by the Judaic concept that reality cannot be represented in a graven image and that what is seen consists of fragmented images that cannot be grasped as a whole. This led him to create works that could not be viewed completely at any one time. Historic symbols of Judaism such as the menorah and the Star of David often appear in his work, as do geometric figures such as the circle, square, ellipse, cylinder, and cube.

In addition to painting and sculpture, Agam's creative output encompassed theater, architecture, film, writing, and typography. Essentially, all his artistic endeavors were involved with the concept of time, change, and movement. His kinetic art provided a means for illustrating the ever-changing nature of the universe, manifesting his fundamental interests in the nature of reality based on a Jewish view of life and art, rooted in the Talmud and in Cabala.

Agam took part in group exhibitions around the world and was the subject of many solo shows, including a retrospective at the National Museum of Modern Art, Paris, which also toured Amsterdam, Düsseldorf, and Tel Aviv (1972–1973), and "Beyond the Visible" (1980), at the Guggenheim Museum, New York City. Among his international honors were the Chevalier de l'Ordre des Arts et Lettres (1974), an honorary doctorate from Tel Aviv University (1975), and the Medal of the Council of Europe (1977).

SUSAN TUMARKIN GOODMAN
Chief Curator, Jewish Museum

Bibliography: Kaniel, Paul, *Yaacov Agam: Selected Suites* (Jewish Museum 1975); Popper, Frank, *Agam*, 3d ed. (Abrams 1989).

AGAMEMNON, ag-ə-mem'non, in Greek legend, the king of Mycenae and leader of the Greeks in the Trojan War. Accounts of him include those in Homer's *Iliad*, in Aeschylus's *Oresteia*, and in plays by Euripides. Agamemnon may have been a historical figure. He was the object of hero cults in historical times.

Agamemnon was a son of Atreus and the brother of Menelaus, king of Sparta. After Atreus was murdered by his nephew Aegisthus, Atreus's brother Thyestes seized the throne of Mycenae, and Agamemnon and Menelaus fled to Sparta. There Agamemnon married Clytemnestra, daughter of King Tyndareus, who bore him a son, Orestes, and three daughters, Iphigenia (Iphianassa), Electra (Laodice), and Chrysomethis. Menelaus became king of Sparta and married Clytemnestra's sister Helen. When King Priam of Troy refused to order Helen's return after her abduction by Paris, the Greeks declared war on Troy and chose Agamemnon as their leader. The Greek fleet was held up at Aulis by adverse winds sent by the goddess Artemis because Agamemnon had offended her. To appease Artemis and secure a favorable change of wind, Agamemnon agreed to sacrifice his eldest daughter, Iphigenia. At the last moment Artemis spared her.

Among the prisoners taken by the Greeks in their victories over Troy were two young women,

© MICHAEL HOLFORD

A Greek vase painting of the 5th century B.C. depicts Agamemnon with Hecuba, the wife of Priam, to his left.

Chryseis, who was given to Agamemnon, and Briseis, who was given to Achilles. Chryseis was the daughter of a priest of Apollo. When Agamemnon refused to release her for ransom, Apollo visited a plague on the Greek camp. Forced to give her up, Agamemnon seized Briseis in her place. Achilles, infuriated, withdrew from the battle at Troy. Achilles and Agamemnon were reconciled only after the death of Patroclus.

After the final victory over Troy, Agamemnon received Cassandra, daughter of Priam, as part of his spoils. Cassandra, a prophetess, warned Agamemnon not to return to Mycenae. He ignored her advice and on his first day home was murdered by his cousin, Aegisthus, who had become Clytemnestra's lover. Seven years later Orestes, aided by Electra, avenged his father's death by killing both Aegisthus and Clytemnestra.

AGAMIDAE. See Lizard.

AGAÑA, ä-gä'nyä, the capital of the U.S. territory of Guam in the western Pacific Ocean. In 1998 its name was changed from Agaña to Hagåtña. Located at the mouth of a river on the central-west coast of Guam, the town is about 5 miles (8 km) north of Apra Harbor, the island's chief port. It is a political, administrative, and commercial center with relatively few residents.

Hagåtña was developed by Spain in the 16th century and served as the administrative center of its Pacific island holdings. The island of Guam was ceded to the United States at the close of the Spanish-American War of 1898, and a naval base was established in Apra Harbor. In 1941 the Japanese took possession of Hagåtña, and it was severely bombed before its recapture by the United States in 1944. The area was rebuilt in a modern style after the war and remains a U.S. naval center. Excluding U.S. military personnel, the population is mainly Chamorro and Filipino.

Points of interest include the cathedral, known as Dulce Nombre de María, which was built by the Spanish in 1669 on the site of Guam's first

Catholic church. Also of interest is the Latte Stone Park, whose latte stone pillars, which date from about 500 B.C., are believed to be house pillars used by the ancient Chamorro people in the construction of their homes. Population: 1,100.

AGAPE, ä-gä'pä, charity or philanthropy, a word used by the New Testament writers to refer to the love of God or the love of Christians for one another. The Greek word *agapē*, in this sense often translated as "love feast," also designates a religious meal held in the evening by the early Christians to promote fellowship and benefit the poor.

In the earliest Christian times the Eucharist was celebrated at a meal, and Paul called both celebration and meal "the Lord's supper" (I Corinthians 11:20). By the 2d century, however, the Eucharist had been separated from the meal, which became known as the agape (Jude 12). Each person at the agape received from the bishop, who had to be present, a piece of blessed bread (called "eulogy," not "eucharist"), and the participants took and blessed their own cups of wine. Both agape and Eucharist inherited these elements from the Jewish meal. After the official recognition of Christianity by Rome in 313, the love feasts began to lose their religious character and were suppressed. They were last officially referred to at the Trullan Synod held in Constantinople in 692.

AGAPETUS I, ag-ə-pē'təs (died 536), pope in 535–536. His name also is spelled *Agapitus*. Agapetus spent most of his reign in Constantinople, where he tried in vain to persuade the Byzantine emperor Justinian to call off the invasion of Italy by Belisarius. He succeeded, however, in persuading Justinian that Anthimus, the Monophysite patriarch, should be removed for heresy. Agapetus personally deposed Anthimus and proceeded to consecrate Mennas as his successor. Justinian then wrote a declaration of faith, which the pope accepted. Agapetus's feast day in the Western Church is September 20; the feast day in the Eastern Church is April 22.

AGAPETUS II, ag-ə-pē'təs (died 955), pope from 946 to 955. His name is also spelled *Agapitus*. During his reign, Rome was ruled by the prince and senator Alberic II, and the temporal power of the papacy was greatly diminished. Agapetus was known as a saintly and resolute man, highly respected throughout the Christian world. He worked to restore ecclesiastical discipline, supported Emperor Otto the Great in his plans to convert the heathen of northern Europe, and persuaded him to invade Italy to restore order.

AGAR, äg'är, a complex mixture of polysaccharides obtained from marine red algae. Also called agar-agar, it is prepared from a mixture of up to seven different washed and dried algae, mostly species of *Gelidium*. The agar is extracted from the algae with boiling water. As the hot-water extract cools, the agar forms a gel, which is dried and shredded. Agar is used as an emulsion stabilizer in foods, as a size for fabrics, and as a solid substrate for the laboratory culture of microorganisms. Agar contains D-galactose; 3,6-anhydro-L-galactose; and some L-galactose 6 sulfate.

Agar is relatively insoluble in water. It dissolves at 199° F (93° C) and forms a gel at 100° F (38° C). (Highly purified agar will form a gel even at a concentration of 0.9%.) It is not toxic and will not precipitate in the presence of the salts and nutrients used in the culture of microorganisms. In addition, agar is not degraded by most microorganisms. For these reasons it is used for the culture of microorganisms almost to the exclusion of gelatin and all other solid supporting media.

THOMAS R. PUNNETT, JR., *Temple University*

AGARIC, ag′ə-rik, any fungus of the mushroom or gill fungi family, Agaricaceae. The group includes all mushrooms, both edible and poisonous. The name is also applied to the dried fruit body of the mushroom.

Members of the family Agaricaceae grow in soil that is rich in organic matter or on rotting logs or tree stumps. Agarics typically have a stalk (stipe) topped by an umbrella-shaped fleshy cap (pileus). On the undersurface of the cap are gills, which are radially arranged plates of tissue active in the production of spores and in the absorption of food. Most agarics are classified as saprophytes because, unlike green plants, they cannot synthesize their own food.

AGASSI, Andre, ag′ə-sē (1970–   ), American tennis player and charismatic showman who overcame a reputation for being cavalier about his profession when he won the Wimbledon Championships in 1992, the U.S. Open in 1994, and the Australian Open in 1995. An inordinately aggressive baseline stylist, Agassi developed a mighty forehand with startling pace and precision and a superb two-handed backhand, which many players believed was the best in the game. Above all, his incomparable return of serve off both sides made him a champion and enabled him to seize control of matches against stronger rivals with wider shotmaking arsenals.

Andre Kirk Agassi was born in Las Vegas, Nevada, on April 29, 1970. His father Mike, a former boxer from Iran, helped him get started. It was apparent from the outset that Agassi had extraordinary hand-eye coordination and an excellent sense of anticipation. For nearly a decade he was guided by the expert motivator and coach Nick Bolletieri and swiftly ascended to number three in the world at age 18 in 1988. In the next three years Agassi gave disappointing accounts of himself and lost his first three Grand Slam finals—the 1990 French and U.S. Open title matches and the 1991 French Open championship match.

Gradually Agassi altered his self-image and raised his ambitions, helped to a large extent by his coach Brad Gilbert. At the end of 1993, wrist surgery threatened to end his career, but he returned in the spring of 1994 determined to exploit his considerable potential. Agassi started to take every tournament seriously, and his strategic court sense improved dramatically. The realignment of his attitude led to markedly more consistent play in 1994 and 1995. In April 1995, he became only the 12th player since the inception of the official Association of Tennis Professionals (ATP) rankings were first released 22 years earlier to earn the number one world ranking. In 1996 he performed erratically but managed to capture the gold medal at the Olympic games in Atlanta. In 1999 Agassi began a dramatic comeback and ultimately amassed seven Grand Slam titles. He was ranked as one of the top ten players in the world going into the 21st century.

STEVE FLINK*
Senior Correspondent Tennis Week

AGASSIZ, Elizabeth Cary, ag′ə-sē (1822–1907), first president of Radcliffe College and a natural history writer whose works made scientific theory accessible to the general public. Elizabeth Cary was born in Boston on Dec. 5, 1822, to Mary Ann (Perkins) and Thomas Cary. In frail health as a child, she did not attend school but was instead tutored at home in subjects such as languages, drawing, and music.

By the late 1840s Elizabeth had been introduced to Boston intellectual society by her sister Mary, who was married to Cornelius C. Felton, a professor of Greek at Harvard University. Through the Feltons Elizabeth met Louis Agassiz, a widower with children who had formerly served as a professor at the University of Neuchâtel, in Switzerland, and now taught natural history at Harvard's Lawrence Scientific School. She married Agassiz in 1850. (See AGASSIZ, LOUIS.)

Throughout their marriage the Agassizes collaborated or worked in association with one another on different projects. In 1856 financial need compelled the couple to open a girls' school, which they ran for seven years. In 1865 Elizabeth accompanied her husband on a trip to Brazil to study the region's fauna. Serving as the expedition's clerk, she kept a detailed journal of their voyage.

In 1871 Elizabeth joined Louis on a deep-sea dredging expedition along the Atlantic and Pacific coasts of the Americas aboard the coast survey vessel *Hassler.* She again took exacting notes of the journey. The next year the couple participated in their final project together, the planning and administration of the coeducational Anderson School of Natural History. Functioning as both a summer school and a marine laboratory, the facility began operation in 1873.

After Louis's death, that same year, Elizabeth devoted herself to caring for her stepson Alexander's three children (his wife had died eight days after Louis) and writing a biography of her husband. She later returned to her interest in education, helping in 1879 to open the Harvard Annex, an educational facility for women. The school was subsequently incorporated as the Society for the Collegiate Instruction of Women, with Agassiz serving as its first president, from 1882 to 1899. In 1894 the institution was renamed Radcliffe College and was authorized by Massachusetts to grant degrees. Agassiz died in Arlington Heights, Mass., on June 27, 1907. (See RADCLIFFE COLLEGE.)

Although Agassiz lacked formal science training, her work with Louis gave her a grounding in natural history. She consequently played an important role in preserving and popularizing his ideas. Writing her first book, *A First Lesson in Natural History* (1859), under Louis's direction, she put out a revised version, *Seaside Studies in Natural History,* six years later, in collaboration with Alexander, a marine biologist. A popular marine biology textbook and field guide, *Seaside Studies* included drawings of marine animals and accounts of their geographical distribution, a discussion of echinoderm embryology, and a general description of radiate animals.

In collaboration with Louis, Agassiz also published *A Journey in Brazil* (1867), an account of the couple's Brazilian expedition. Her two-volume biography of her husband, *Louis Agassiz: His Life and Correspondence,* was published in 1885.

MARILYN B. OGILVIE
University of Oklahoma

Bibliography

Hawkins, Hugh, "Agassiz, Elizabeth Cabot Cary," in *Notable American Women, 1607–1950: A Biographical Dictionary*, vol. 1, ed. by Edward T. James (Belknap Press 1973).

Ogilvie, Marilyn Bailey, *Women in Science: Antiquity through the Nineteenth Century* (MIT Press 1986).

Paton, Lucy Allen, *Elizabeth Cary Agassiz: A Biography* (1919; reprint, Arno Press 1974).

AGASSIZ, Louis, ag′ə-sē (1807–1873), Swiss American naturalist who made significant studies on the classification of animals, especially fossil forms, and on the movement and distribution of glaciers and prehistoric ice ages. Although he was a staunch antievolutionist who believed that animal life was constructed according to a divine plan, much of his work provided evidence for the theory of natural selection, put foward by 19th-century British naturalist Charles Darwin. As a lecturer and teacher, Agassiz worked to bring science, especially natural history, to the public. (See DARWIN, CHARLES ROBERT.)

Jean Louis Rodolphe Agassiz was born on May 28, 1807, at Môtier en-Vully, Canton Fribourg, Switzerland. The son of a minister, he attended the universities of Zürich and Heidelberg and then took his medical degree at the University of Munich in 1830. His real interest, however, was natural history, so he went to Paris where he worked under Georges Cuvier, the famous French paleontologist and anatomist, until 1832. While in Paris, he also attracted the interest of Alexander Humboldt, one of the founders of scientific geography. After Cuvier's death, Humboldt's recommendation helped obtain for Agassiz the post of professor of natural history at the University of Neuchâtel in 1832. (See CUVIER, GEORGES.)

Zoological and Glacial Studies. While still in Munich, Agassiz had the opportunity to work on a collection of fish brought back from the Amazon River. His careful classification of these (*Selecta genera et species piscium*) was published in 1829. He subsequently began work on a monumental classification of fossil fish (*Recherches sur les poissons fossiles*, 5 vols., 1833–1844).

Agassiz went on to a meticulous consideration of zoological classification in general (*Nomenclator zoologicus*, 1842–1846), and his work in this field had two profound effects. First, he aroused interest in the study of fossils. Second, he introduced order into the zoological jungle of the past and present, making it easier to work out a rational theory of evolution, which Darwin was attempting to do.

Still more spectacular was Agassiz's work on glaciers. As a native of Switzerland, he was particularly aware of glaciers and therefore interested in reports that the northern European plains were dotted with boulders that might have been brought there by glaciers. The question, however, was whether glaciers could have made the necessary advance and retreat.

Agassiz spent his vacations in 1836 and 1837 exploring glaciers. He convinced himself that glaciers did move, that the accumulations of rocks and debris at the ends and sides of glaciers were the product of motion, and that these rocks had been scoured and grooved by the passage of glaciers (and their embedded rocks and pebbles) over them. In 1839 he proved these assumptions with experiments at a glacier.

Since it was now established that glaciers did move, it was possible to suggest that they had once spread out over wide areas. Agassiz decided

ARCHIVES, MUSEUM OF COMPARATIVE ZOOLOGY LIBRARY, HARVARD UNIVERSITY

Louis Agassiz, eminent 19th-century naturalist, is shown teaching a class in natural history at Harvard.

that grooved and scoured rocks that appeared in areas now free of glaciers might indicate the previous presence of glaciers. In 1840 he was able to detect these signs of glaciation in the British Isles.

Agassiz published his *Études sur les glaciers* in 1840. In it he postulated an ice age, a period long eons ago in which huge ice sheets covered most of northern Europe. This dramatic work provided a picture of slow but extensive environmental changes, which would help supply the motive force for natural selection in Darwin's theory of evolution. Agassiz never accepted Darwin's ideas, and he was the most prominent antievolution scientist in the United States. Indeed, he believed that throughout the earth's history, divine intervention had been responsible for perhaps 20 separate instances of creation and that each time this occurred, plants and animals were produced bearing no relationship to those that already existed.

Agassiz in America. Agassiz was an excellent lecturer, and on the recommendation of Charles Lyell, the famous British geologist, he was invited to Boston in 1846 to give a series of lectures. Agassiz was a great success. Tall and handsome, with an excellent platform manner, he spoke to large and enthusiastic audiences. With his lectures and later his scientific essays for popular magazines, he became one of the great 19th-century scientists who brought science to the general public.

Agassiz fell in love with America and decided to remain permanently in the United States. He accepted a post as professor of natural history at Harvard University in 1848 and soon became a successful and beloved teacher. His first wife had died in Europe, and in 1850 he married Elizabeth Cary of Boston. In 1861 he became an American citizen. (See AGASSIZ, ELIZABETH CARY.)

Agassiz continued his work at classification, now with animal species of the New World. His *Journey to Brazil* (1868), written in collaboration with his wife, was a successful popularization of natural history. Too, he found signs of ancient glaciation in North America, indicating that it, like Europe, had undergone an ice age.

In 1858 Agassiz founded the Museum of Comparative Zoology (now named in his honor) at Harvard, and he served as its curator in the final decade of his life. He also founded the Anderson School of Natural History on Penikese Island, located off the coast of Massachusetts. This facility served as both a summer school for marine research and a marine biological station. Although the school did not survive his death, it served as the model for other such schools.

Agassiz died in Cambridge, Mass., on Dec. 14, 1873. He was succeeded as curator of the Museum of Comparative Zoology by his son, Alexander Emanuel Agassiz, who carried on his father's interests in natural history.

ISAAC ASIMOV*
Author of "Asimov's Biographical Encyclopedia of Science and Technology"

Bibliography: Agassiz, Louis, *Geological Sketches* (1885; reprint, Ayer 1985); Lurie, Edward, *Louis Agassiz: A Life in Science* (Univ. of Chicago Press 1967).

AGASSIZ, Lake, ag'ə-sē, a large shallow lake that existed in North America during the Pleistocene Period. About 110,000 square miles (285,000 sq km) in area, it covered most of what are now southern Manitoba and parts of Saskatchewan, Ontario, North Dakota, and Minnesota.

As the continental ice sheet retreated, its melting waters formed Lake Agassiz, which found its outlet to the south because the normal northward drainage of the region was blocked by ice. When the ice melted completely, the lake drained away to the north. Lakes Winnipeg, Manitoba, and Winnipegosis and Lake of the Woods are remnants of Lake Agassiz, a large part of whose bed is now the fertile wheatland valley of the Red River of the North.

The lake was named in 1879 for the Swiss-American naturalist Louis Agassiz, who had demonstrated that much of North America was covered by a vast glacier during the geologic epoch preceding the present one.

AGATE, ag'ət, a special type of chalcedony, a quartz mineral. It has a characteristic banded or layered structure and is used chiefly as a gemstone. Agate is formed in rock cavities by the deposition of layers of chalcedony on the walls of the cavity. The layers may fill the cavity completely or leave an opening, often lined with projecting quartz crystals, in the center. Agate is cryptocrystalline; that is, its crystals are so fine that they are not visible through a microscope.

According to Theophrastus and Pliny, agates were so named because they were found along the Achates River in Sicily, now known as the Acate or Dirillo. Agate is mentioned in Exodus 28:19 as one of the stones in the high priest's breastplate, but the actual character of the original stone is not known, because in antiquity gem names were often applied to substances now known to be different mineral species.

Although agates are found in both igneous and sedimentary rocks, those of good quality are taken chiefly from igneous rocks of basaltic character. They vary in size from that of a pea to two or more feet in diameter. Because the quartz of which they are composed is more resistant to weathering than the rocks in which they occur, agate masses may be found loose on the ground or in stream or beach deposits.

Originally the agate material was in the form of a silica gel; that is, somewhat like a coarse and very porous sand. The impurities in the material separate and then harden in successive bands. The bands are closely spaced, and each of them

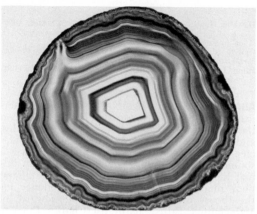

© SINCLAIR STAMMERS/PHOTO RESEARCHERS

Agate, a quartz mineral, displays colored bands in a variety of patterns.

consists of multitudes of minute quartz crystals. In exceptional cases the bands are evenly spaced. In most agates, however, the banding is not pronounced, and practically all gem agates of commerce are artificially colored. This is possible because the agate layers, although they appear compact to the eye, have varying degrees of porosity.

Dyeing. The commercial dyeing of agates began on a large scale about 1820 in the Idar-Oberstein district of western Germany. Because of the occurrence of a fine grade of agate in this area, an agate-cutting industry had developed there as early as the 16th century. The original dyeing process consisted of drying the agate thoroughly and then immersing it in a honey solution for several days until the solution had penetrated the stone. The agate was then boiled in concentrated sulfuric acid, which charred the honey to carbon, the carbon being precipitated in the interstices of the apparently solid agate. Some nonporous layers remained white while others varied from light brown to black, depending on the porosity of the agate. Most of the acid was then removed by washing and the remainder by heating the agate for several days. Sugar solutions and sulfuric acid are now more commonly used.

A wide range of color can be produced. The dried agate is first placed in a solution of an iron, chromium, or cobalt salt. The saturated agate is then placed in a second solution that causes an insoluble compound to precipitate in the stone. An iron salt followed by ammonia precipitates iron hydroxide, which is converted into reddish or black iron oxide on heating. Using potassium thiocyanate instead of ammonia produces a red color, while potassium ferrocyanide produces Prussian blue. Aniline and other organic dyes have also been used. The depth of color produced depends on the porosity of the layers of agate.

Cutting. The Idar-Oberstein district has also been the world's most important cutting center for semiprecious stones. Before World War I the industry was strung out along the Idar Valley, and each little cutting plant, employing 4 to 20 workmen, was supplied with power from its own waterwheel. The cutting was done on a sandstone wheel 5 feet in diameter and 1½ feet thick, mounted on a horizontal shaft at or near floor level. To cut the larger agates the workman lay face down on a crude wooden framework pivoted at the floor, with his feet braced on a floor cleat to the rear. The agate was forced against the rotating wheel by a stout stick that ran from near the base of the pivoted framework on which the cutter lay. This crude device multiplied by leverage not only the leg thrust of the workman but also the forward thrust exerted by his body weight. Smaller pieces of agate were cut by a workman sitting on a stool in front of the wheel, holding the stone in one hand and forcing it against the wheel by a wooden stick held in the other hand.

Gem engraving, the cutting of cameos and intaglios, is a specialized branch of the industry calling for considerable artistic talent. Pieces of dyed agate with two sharply differentiated colored layers, usually black and white or red and white, are cut into rough blanks of ring size. A figure is cut into one layer, while the other layer forms the background for the design. In cameos the design is in relief. In the early years of the 20th century many ornamental objects were cut from agate, but the demand for them did not revive after World War I.

With the economic recovery of Germany after World War I, electric power began to displace water power, and the cutting equipment was modernized. Smaller silicon carbide grinding wheels rotating at much higher speeds displaced the cumbersome sandstone wheels. The cutting and faceting of semiprecious stones began to outrank agate cutting in importance, and some diamond cutting was also done in the district. The local sources of agate had long since been exhausted, and most of the stones still being cut were imported from Uruguay and Brazil. A major factor in the decline of the agate industry, however, was the loss of popularity in the jewelry markets.

Amateur Lapidaries. Although agate cutting has declined as a commercial industry, a large group of amateur lapidaries has grown up in the United States. Because agate is one of the most plentiful gem stones and is comparatively easy to work, it has been by far the most popular for amateurs to cut. While much agate is imported, the American lapidary is usually a collector who prefers to obtain his or her own material in the field. This activity has resulted in the discovery of many new sources of supply, especially in Oregon, California, Washington, and Montana, to supplement the older known localities in the Lake Superior district.

Because of its mode of formation, the colored bands within the agate take on a great variety of patterns. These patterns have inspired descriptive names such as moss agate, eye agate, carnelian agate, and iris agate. Moss agate acquires its name from the beautiful patterns of black and red treelike or dendritic growths it exhibits. These occur when salts of manganese and iron infiltrate the translucent chalcedony pebbles. Eye agate contains nodules exhibiting strongly contrasting color; when cut across and polished, they show circular patterns. Carnelian agate forms when the agate has been infused by solutions bearing iron salts, causing a red oxide precipitate. Iris agate is indistinguishable from common chalcedony and often mistaken for it. However, a thin, polished slice of iris agate becomes flushed with pure and vivid rainbow colors as it is held before light. Geologists speculate that its many successive growth bands interfere with the normal functions of light, causing the light to splinter into its spec-

tral colors. Agates of these types are the most highly prized by lapidaries. Although many lapidaries in the United States cut and polish small pieces for mounting in jewelry, it is a more common practice to saw the agate into sections and impart a high polish to the flat surfaces.

Industrial Uses. Those dense, compact varieties of agate that are not readily susceptible to artificial coloring find an important use in industry. Because large pieces of uniform texture are readily available, and since agate is harder than most other materials, it has long been the best material for mortars and pestles. It takes a fine edge and does not tarnish or corrode, and so is used for knife edges and for the flat fulcrums on which the edges rest in precision balances.

C. B. SLAWSON
University of Michigan

Bibliography

Arem, Joel E., *Color Encyclopedia of Gemstones*, 2d ed. (Van Nostrand Reinhold 1987).
Metz, Rudolph, *The Face of Precious Stones: Minerals and Crystals*, 2d ed. (1964; reprint, Kraus 1978).
O'Donoghue, M. J., *Quartz* (Butterworths 1986).
Sinkankas, John, *Gem Cutting*, 3d ed. (Van Nostrand Reinhold 1984).
Vargas, Glenn, and Martha Vargas, *Description of Gem Materials*, 3d ed. (Glenn Vargas 1985).

AGATHA, ag'ə-thə (died c. 251), a Christian martyr born in Catania, or Palermo, Sicily. Agatha was martyred in the city of Catania. It is believed that she was a virgin who suffered martyrdom because she rejected the attentions of a Roman official, although only the fact of her martyrdom has been authenticated.

Veneration of the saint, whose feast day is February 5 (the date of her death), has flourished since the 5th century. Her intercession is invoked against fire and lightning and she is the patron saint of bell founders.

AGATHARCHIDES, ag-ə-thär'ki-dēz, a Greek historian and geographer of the 2d century B.C. He is also known as Agatharchus. A native of Cnidus, he wrote treatises on Europe, Asia, and the Red Sea. Extracts from the treatise on the Red Sea (which he called the Erythraean Sea) survive in the *Myriobiblion* of Photius.

AGATHIAS, ə-gā'thē-əs (c. 536–582), Greek poet and historian, surnamed Scholasticus. He was born in Aeolis, in Asia Minor. After studying law at Alexandria and Constantinople, he practiced in Constantinople until his death. He wrote love poems and epigrams, which he included in a collection of his own works and the works of others. About 100 of his epigrams survive, as well as his history, *The Reign of Justinian*, in five books. He died in Constantinople in 582.

AGATHO, ag'ə-thō (died 681), pope from 678 to 681 and saint of the Roman Catholic Church. He was born in Sicily and is said to have been more than 100 years old when he was elected. He was known as *Thaumaturgus* ("Wonder-worker") because of the miracles he is supposed to have performed. The greatest event of his reign was the Sixth Ecumenical Council, held in Constantinople in 680. His legates presided and condemned the Monothelites, who by this time posited that Jesus had "one will" rather than both divine and human nature. Agatho's feast day is January 10.

AGATHOCLES, ə-gath′ōklēz (361 B.C.–289 B.C.), a tyrant of Syracuse, Sicily. Born at Thermae Himerenses, Sicily, the son of a potter, he became a soldier and an opponent of the oligarchic party of Syracuse. By 316 he had become tyrant of the city and ruler of most of Sicily. Defeated by the Carthaginians in 311, he carried the war to Africa (310–306) and on his return assumed the title of king. Later he also invaded southern Italy.

Although he was cruel, he was generally popular with the poorer classes of Syracuse, which enjoyed some prosperity under his rule. He died at Syracuse in 289, perhaps as a result of poisoning by his grandson, Archagathus. His son-in-law, King Pyrrhus of Epirus, inherited his influence in Sicily and southern Italy.

AGATHON, ag′ə-thon (448 B.C.–402 B.C.), Greek tragic poet. He was a close friend of Euripides and Plato. The *Symposium* of Plato immortalizes the banquet given on the occasion of Agathon's winning a competition in drama in 416 B.C. About 40 lines of his poetry survive.

AGAVE, ə-gā′vē, in Greek legend, the daughter of Cadmus and Harmonia and the wife of Echion. Her son, Pentheus, who succeeded Cadmus as king of Thebes, opposed the introduction of worship of the god Dionysus. Dionysus changed Pentheus into a wild beast, and Agave and two of her sisters tore him to pieces in the frenzy of a Dionysian revel.

AGAVE, ə-gā′vē, a genus of American desert plants. The best known is *Agave americana*, the century plant, erroneously called American aloe. In Mexico it is called the maguey.

From the high, dry Mexican tablelands, agaves extend south through Central America to Colombia, east through the West Indies, and north to Arizona, Utah, and, in the eastern United States, to Maryland. The plants were introduced into Europe very early and were recorded in Spain and elsewhere in the latter part of the 16th century. *A. americana* now grows in southern Europe, northern and southern Africa, Sri Lanka, and India.

In most species of agave, the leaves are clustered near the base of the short stem. The flower stalk, which may be 3 feet (1 meter) or more high, ultimately develops from the center of the leaf cluster. In *A. americana* the thick, leathery, gray-green leaves are 3 to 7 feet (1–2 meters) long and 6 to 8 inches (15–20 cm) wide, with one short, curved terminal spine and numerous marginal spines. Varieties with white or yellow margins or stripes occur.

Agaves bloom infrequently, some species requiring 7 to 10 years. *A. americana* usually takes somewhat longer, while *A. attenuata* apparently needs 20 to 30 years to flower. Under unfavorable conditions, agaves may grow 50 years or more without blooming. In many species, including *A. americana*, the plant dies after fruiting, although suckers are retained to produce new plants. Other species may blossom repeatedly.

The flower cluster is a striking pyramid shape or spike; in the century plant it is candelabralike and sometimes reaches 40 feet. Flowering, accompanied by a shrinking of the leaves, may continue for five months in some species. In the century plant the yellowish green flowers, nearly 3 inches (8 cm) wide, have a many-seeded ovary. Bees are attracted by the abundant nectar.

In warm regions, agave is exceedingly important. Sisal hemp is derived from the leaves of *A. sisalana*, a plant probably native to Yucatán but grown extensively in the Bahamas, Africa, Java, Sumatra, and India. Henequen is a fiber obtained from the leaves of *A. fourcroydes*, native to Yucatán and largely grown there. These fibers are used for binder twine, small ropes, and other cordage. (See CORDAGE.) Pita fiber comes especially from the leaves of *A. americana*.

Agave is the source of several important Mexican drinks. In the preparation of pulque, the bud of the flower cluster, especially of *A. atrovirens*, is removed, and the sugary liquid exuding is collected and fermented. A vigorous plant is said to yield approximately 250 gallons (950 liters) of sap. A distilled drink, mescal, is obtained from other species. Some agaves furnish soap, and others have been used medicinally. Century plants are widely grown as ornamentals.

EDWIN B. MATZKE
Columbia University

The American desert plant *Agave americana*, the century plant, is a source of pita fiber.

© HAROLD W. HOFFMAN/PHOTO RESEARCHERS

AGAWAM, ag′ə-wom, a town in southern Massachusetts, in Hampden county, 3 miles (5 km) southwest of Springfield, of which it is a residential suburb. It includes the village of Feeding Hills. The Agawam and Westfield rivers flow through the town. Before the expansion of the Springfield urban complex, Agawam was an agricultural community. There are dairy and poultry farms in Feeding Hills, and tobacco, fruit, and vegetables are grown. The town was settled in 1636 and named from an Algonkian word meaning "crooked river." After becoming part of West Springfield, it was incorporated as a separate town in 1885. Population: 28,144.

AGEE, ā′jē, **James** (1909–1955), American writer of journalism, poetry, novels, short stories, and screenplays. While Agee was admired during his lifetime primarily for film reviews in *The Nation*

CULVER PICTURES

James Agee, early in his career, around the time *Let Us Now Praise Famous Men* was published.

and *Time* magazine and for his screenplay *The African Queen* (1952), his literary reputation soared after his posthumously published autobiographical novel *A Death in the Family* won the Pulitzer Prize for fiction in 1958. Agee's forgotten journalistic masterpiece *Let Us Now Praise Famous Men*, written during the Great Depression in collaboration with the photographer Walker Evans and first published in 1941, was then reissued to great acclaim in 1960. *All the Way Home*, Tad Mosel's stage adaptation of *A Death in the Family*, won a Pulitzer Prize for drama in 1961 and was filmed in 1963, sustaining interest in Agee's work. The successive publications of *Agee on Film: Reviews and Comments* (1958), *Agee on Film: Five Film Scripts by James Agee* (1960), and *The Letters of James Agee to Father Flye* (1962) further enhanced his literary reputation. These were followed by *The Collected Poems of James Agee* and *The Collected Short Prose of James Agee* (both 1968) and *James Agee: Selected Journalism* (1985).

James Rufus Agee was born in Knoxville, Tenn., on Nov. 27, 1909. Shortly after his father's death in an automobile accident, an event that haunted him throughout his life, he was enrolled at St. Andrew's School near Sewanee, Tenn. The school was run by the Order of the Holy Cross, an Episcopal monastic order. There Agee came under the influence of Father James Flye, who became his lifelong friend and confidant. St. Andrew's School was the setting for Agee's short lyrical novel *The Morning Watch* (1951). After returning briefly to Knoxville, Agee attended Phillips Exeter Academy and was graduated in 1932 from Harvard University, where he edited the *Harvard Advocate*. A collection of his early poetry, *Permit Me Voyage*, was published in 1934.

Agee became a staff writer at *Fortune* magazine. His dissatisfaction with conventional journalism led to *Let Us Now Praise Famous Men*, which grew out of an assigned article that *Fortune* had declined to publish. This brooding manifesto, Agee's greatest work and a singular document of American letters, questions not only the social responsibility of journalism but also the democratic and moral values of American society and New Deal reforms. The book is structurally complex and seems inspired by numerous sources, including the Anglican liturgy, Shakespeare's *King Lear*, and the prophetic books of the Bible. Agee continued to write for magazines before turning to the cinema. In addition to *The African Queen*, his screenplays include *The Night of the Hunter* (1955) and *Noa Noa*, a biography of Paul Gauguin (never produced). He also wrote television scripts, notably *Abraham Lincoln—The Early Years* (1952). Agee died in New York City on May 16, 1955.

Some critics have suggested that Agee wrote too much journalism and not enough poetry and fiction to gain a lasting place in American literature. Yet his eclectic interests, his enthusiasm for the cinema as a serious art form, and his willingness to probe new forms of writing and reporting continue to attract a devoted popular and critical following. Infusing all his best writing is a sense of compassion for the human condition and a spiritual reverence for the dignity of life, expressed most eloquently and directly in his letters to Father Flye.

PAUL G. ASHDOWN
University of Tennessee
Editor of "James Agee: Selected Journalism"

Bibliography: Bergreen, Laurence, *James Agee: A Life* (Dutton 1984); Kramer, Victor, *James Agee* (G. K. Hall 1975); Lofaro, Michael, ed., *James Agee: Reconsiderations* (Univ. of Tenn. Press 1992); Moreau, Geneviève, *The Restless Journey of James Agee* (Morrow 1977).

AGELADAS, aj-ə-lā′dəs, a Greek sculptor of the late 6th and early 5th centuries B.C. His name also is rendered as *Hageladas*. A member of the Argive school, Ageladas was known especially for his statues of Greek gods and Olympic heroes. Most of his work, none of which is extant, was done in bronze.

Ageladas's most famous works were two statues of Zeus. One, representing the god as a boy, was made for Aegium, and was pictured on the coins of that city. The other, at Ithome, represented the god striding forward and hurling a thunderbolt, with an eagle perched on his left hand. According to Pausanias, this statue originally was made for the Messenian settlers at Naupactus. Ageladas also is known to have made statues of the victors of the Olympic games of 520, 516, and 508 B.C.

The tradition that he was the teacher of the sculptors Phidias, Myron, and Polyclitus has been discredited.

AGEN, à-zhäN′, a city in France, the capital of the department of Lot-et-Garonne. It lies along the Garonne River, 74 miles (118 km) southeast of Bordeaux. Its interesting structures include a fine stone bridge of 11 arches and the aqueduct bridge of the Canal Latéral. Known as Aginnum in ancient times, the city has been an episcopal see since the reign of Clovis (481–511), prior to which it was a Roman station. It has a sizable agricultural trade, owing to its position between Bordeaux and Toulouse, and is a textile-manufacturing center. Population: 32,180 (1999 census).

AGENCY, ā′jən-sē, in law, the relationship that exists when two persons agree that one is to act on behalf of the other and be subject to the latter's control. The relatively recent branch of the law involving this relationship developed out of the old law of master and servant about the middle of the 18th century. It reached its highest expression in 1958 in the *Restatement of Agency* (2d ed.) by the American Law Institute. Because the law of agency in great part has been left to the courts for development, agency is a part of the common law of each state.

Principal and Agent. Agency, in brief, is concerned with doing through others. Just as a person may use a tool to accomplish a purpose, so he or she may use a second person, who becomes an extension of his or her personality. The first person, for whom another acts, is called a principal; the second person, who acts for the first person, is called an agent. All employees are agents, as are also brokers and auctioneers for buyers and sellers of property, lawyers for their clients, and factors of goods. The manifestation presented to agents by principals to show that the agents are to act for them creates in the agents the necessary power to act. Just as principals are responsible for their words and actions, so they are responsible for their controlled use of their agents' conduct. Therefore, the principal is liable for the agent's conduct while the agent acts within the scope of his or her authority. (In certain instances, however, public policy also imposes liability upon principals for their agents' unauthorized conduct.)

The extent of the agent's authority is determined by what the agent reasonably can understand the principal's manifestation to him to mean. That part of it that expressly specifies what the agent is to do is called express authority. What the agent reasonably can understand from the principal's indication of what he or she is to do in order to carry out what was expressly stated is called implied or inferred authority.

A person may ratify previous unauthorized conduct by another. For ratification to occur, generally a person must manifest consent—expressly or in a manner implied by his conduct—to a second person's unauthorized act, not binding on the first person, done by one who claimed to act as his agent and on his behalf.

The term *servant* is used only to describe an agent who is to render services and over whose physical conduct or acts the principal, or master, has control. Since a principal is liable only for what she has the right to control, she is not liable for wrongful physical harm caused by an agent unless the latter is a servant.

Other terms important to agency are *subagent* and *independent contractor*. A subagent is a person appointed by an agent to act for the principal and for whose conduct the agent agrees, with the principal, to be primarily liable. An independent contractor is a person who contracts to produce an end result but who does not act on behalf of another and is not subject to the other's control. Plumbers, lawyers, engineers, doctors, builders, and brokers are examples of independent contractors. When an independent contractor is employed and his conduct is subject to the employer's control, he then becomes an agent for that particular employment.

An agent authorized to perform a single transaction is known as a special agent. An agent authorized to perform a series of transactions embodying a continuity of service is called a general agent. (Most general agents are also servants.) A factor of goods is a special agent, but if she receives additional compensation for guaranteeing payment by the buyer of goods to her principal, she is known as a *del credere* agent.

The Third Person. While it is essential to agency and authority that the principal's manifestation, or delegation, of authority be made to the agent, the principal's telling a third person that a named person is her agent does not thereby create agency or authority. However, if this disclosure causes the third person reasonably to believe that the second person is an agent with authority, then the latter is known as an apparent agent, with apparent authority. The scope of such apparent authority is determined by what the third person reasonably may understand from the apparent principal's manifestation.

Agency, in working practice, affects three persons—the principal, the agent, and the third person. As between the principal and the third person, if the principal's identity is known, he is a disclosed principal, while if the agency is unknown to the third person, he is an undisclosed principal. Unless otherwise agreed between the agent and the third person, the parties to the transaction are only the disclosed principal and the third person. Generally, if a written contract specifically excludes the principal as a party, or if the contract is a negotiable instrument (check, note, draft, certificate of deposit) in which the principal's name does not appear, the contract is then only between the agent and the third person. When the principal is undisclosed, the parties to the contract are the agent and the third person and, by law, also the undisclosed principal.

Termination. Termination of authority ends agency, and termination of apparent authority ends apparent agency. Termination of one does not of itself terminate the other. Inasmuch as the legal relationship of agency is agreed to by a principal and an agent, if either withdraws consent, the relationship ceases.

To terminate agency, each must manifest to the other the desire to terminate, and the other must actually receive such manifestation. Death of the principal or agent or the loss or destruction of the subject matter or of the principal's interest therein terminates authority and apparent authority without notice.

Liability. As between the principal and the agent, each has contractual obligations to the other. Unless otherwise agreed, principals are to compensate, reimburse, and indemnify their agents. Agents are to be loyal to and obey their principals, exercise reasonable care, and account to their principals. Workmen's compensation acts in the various states generally impose liability without fault upon an employer for harm sustained by an employee while acting within the scope of that employee's authority.

Any person acting as an agent warrants, expressly or by implication, that he or she has authority to so act and is liable to third persons for breach of such warranty. An agent is legally liable to third persons also for misfeasance (misdoing or active misconduct) and in some instances for nonfeasance (not doing or failure to act), irrespective of his or her agency status.

JOSEPH L. FRASCONA
University of Colorado

Bibliography: Klein, William A., et al., *Business Associations: Agency, Partnerships, and Corporations* (Foundation Press 1999); Mnookin, Robert H., et al., eds., *Negotiating on Behalf of Others* (Sage Pubns. 1999).

AGENCY FOR INTERNATIONAL DEVELOPMENT, United States

AGENCY FOR INTERNATIONAL DEVELOPMENT, United States (USAID), an independent agency of the U.S. government responsible for foreign development programs. USAID (originally, AID) was established in 1961 within the Department of State to administer foreign nonmilitary economic assistance under the Foreign Assistance Act of that year. In 1979 the agency became a component of the U.S. International Development Cooperation Agency (IDCA), but by 1988 the latter was no longer in operation and USAID was functioning on its own.

USAID attempts to direct American development aid toward solving the most severe economic problems in developing countries, particularly in such fields as health, agriculture, population planning, education, and energy. It also administers funds aimed at promoting economic and political stability in areas where the United States has special interests or where economic aid may be useful in securing peace or averting crises. Increasingly, it has awarded work to private contractors to achieve its goals.

USAID assists U.S. nonprofit organizations that sponsor American schools and hospitals abroad, coordinates international disaster assistance, helps lower-income families in developing countries to finance housing, and helps administer the Food for Peace program. The agency has been criticized for following arguably effective economic development models and for mixing politics and capitalism with humanitarian goals. Its defenders, on the other hand, say that USAID has done much good in the world and that its policies and programs are both pragmatic and apolitical.

Bibliography: Cooper, Frederick, and Randall Packard, eds., *International Development and the Social Sciences* (Univ. of Calif. Press 1998); Porter, David, *U.S. Economic Foreign Aid: A Case Study of the United States Agency for International Development* (Garland 1990).

AGERATUM, aj-ə-rā′təm, a genus of annual and perennial herbs and shrubs generally native to the American tropics. The plants, from 1 to 2 feet (30 to 60 cm) high, have a cluster of tassel-like flowers that are white, blue, or pink in color and remain for long periods. The leaves are stalked, located oppositely, and egg shaped in outline, with scalloped or saw-toothed edges.

Ageratum belongs to the family Asteraceae, in the order Asterales, class Magnoliopsida. There are 45 species. *A. houstonianum* and *A. conyzoides* are often used as edging for gardens.

AGES OF THE WORLD, a concept of history, widespread among the cultures of the world, according to which the world, considered as an organism, has stages of development that are comparable in some way to those of a human individual. The concept may take many forms but is usually cast in terms of world periods, or ages; of myths of recurrence; or of a system of cosmic eras. It may comprehend the cosmos, just the earth, or human history alone.

The ancient Indo-Iranian idea of a succession of periods from creation to destruction apparently influenced Greco-Roman, Jewish, and later Christian patterns. The early Iranian tradition laid out in relatively late Pahlavi formulations is reflected in earlier literature. The elements of a primordial golden age, of a savior figure, and of future transformation are present very early. Later cosmogonies posited three periods, the first two of

GOTTSCHO-SCHLEISNER

Ageratum species include popular garden plants.

which extended for three millennia and the last of which was a golden age. In its later elaboration in the *Bundahishn* ("Book of Primordial Creation," 9th century, but containing material from much earlier), the three periods became four three-thousand-year periods, each having its savior, until, in the last trimillennium, there is a final judgment and transformation to an immortal world.

Passages in the Book of Daniel detailing a system of four empires followed by a divine reign owe a great deal to formulations of the Iranian material; no such indigenous Jewish tradition has been identified. Other Jewish texts vary the number of periods and cast them differently, often in multiples of seven, such as the seven millennia of the Testament of Abraham. The early Christians adopted from the Jewish rabbinic tradition a binary emphasis on "this time" versus "the time to come," but later Christians extrapolated more complex systems from the biblical account of the seven "days" of Creation. Augustine's 5th-century A.D. *De Civitate Dei* ("City of God") contains such a scheme, ending, however, with an eighth age, eternity. Later Christian theorists modeled their own systems on Augustine's.

Greco-Roman conceptions of history probably borrowed ideas of recurrence from the Babylonian notion of a cosmic "great year." Hesiod's 8th-century B.C. *Works and Days* divides human history into five ages—the Golden, Silver, Brazen, Heroic, and Iron ages—over the course of which evil gradually increases. Hesiod had little hope of human progress and regarded the Iron Age as both the present and future of humanity. In this respect his ideas have some congruence with those asserting an endless succession of identical worlds, each destroyed by fire at particular planetary conjunctions and out of fire born again.

The most complex conceptions of the ages of the world combine successive periods with ideas of eternal recurrence. Parts of the dense scheme developed in India's epic and Puranic literature evidences contact with Hellenic and West Asian traditions. Complete cosmic cycles (*mahāyugas*), divided into four *yugas*, or ages, of varied proportions, figure in vast cycles of creation and destruction determined by cosmic numerology. Aztec myth, too, posits unending cosmic creations and destructions but superimposes on the cycles five "suns," or ages, culminating in the fifth age (the present age), which transforms the cycle.

AGGRESSINS, ə-gres′ənz, nontoxic substances that are assumed to be present in disease-causing bacteria. Aggressins enable the infecting bacteria to invade and infect the host more rapidly by overwhelming the defense mechanisms of the host.

A well-known aggressin is that of *Bacillus anthracis,* the anthrax bacterium. Its aggressin presumably inactivates both the defensive white blood corpuscles and the blood-serum-immune bodies that are responsible for neutralizing the anthrax toxin.

Similar to the aggressins are the virulens, bacterial substances responsible for the intensity of an infection after it has been established in the host. Virulens appear only during active infection. Tetanus toxin, for instance, does not appear until the aggressins have enabled the infecting bacteria to invade and infect the host.

MILAN V. NOVAK
College of Medicine
University of Illinois

AGGRESSION, ə-gresh'ən, in international law, an illegal use of force in international relations. One of the purposes of the United Nations, as stated in its Charter, is "to take effective collective measures for the prevention and removal of threats to the peace, and for the suppression of acts of aggression or other breaches of the peace" (Article 1). In pursuance of this purpose the Charter provides that "All Members shall refrain in their international relations from the threat or use of force against the territorial integrity or political independence of any state" (Article 2, par. 4) and that "The Security Council shall determine the existence of any threat to the peace, breach of the peace, or act of aggression and shall make recommendations, or decide what measures shall be taken ... to maintain or restore international peace and security" (Article 39). The only provisions set forth in the UN Charter that expressly permit states to use force are those that require them to assist the United Nations in collective security operations (Article 2, par. 5; Article 25; and Chapter VII) and those that permit "individual or collective self-defense" against armed attack (Article 51).

Definition of Aggression. The United Nations, like the League of Nations that preceded it, frequently has found it necessary to deal with situations of international hostility and to determine whether any of the states involved has committed aggression. To make such activity more effective, it has been continuously engaged in efforts to formulate a precise definition of the term *aggression* and to develop more adequate procedures to prevent or suppress actual aggressions. Despite such efforts, however, no general agreement on these matters has been achieved, and the three following major questions remain.

Does aggression refer only to the illegal use of armed force, or may other types of coercive action, such as economic pressure, propaganda, and intervention to subvert a government by bribery, infiltration, or support of revolutionaries, constitute aggression? Usage of the term *aggression* in treaties and diplomacy prior to the UN Charter seemed to limit it to military action, and the Charter itself limits it to "breaches of the peace." However, the Rio treaty among the American states refers to "an aggression which is not an armed attack" (Article 6), and such terms as *economic aggression, psychological aggression,* and *indirect aggression* are used in UN debates.

What uses of armed force in international relations are permissible and consequently do not constitute aggression? Apart from the express permissions of the UN Charter, it has been suggested that the ancient right of reprisal exists if a state cannot gain a remedy for injuries by peaceful means. It also has been argued that authorization by a regional organization such as the OAS may justify military action, although the UN Charter explicitly provides that "no enforcement action shall be taken under regional arrangements or by regional agencies without the authorization of the Security Council" (Article 53). These express and implied exceptions have raised issues concerning the capacity of the UN General Assembly and the Security Council to justify military action by recommending enforcement measures. They have also raised issues concerning the meaning of armed attack that justifies self-defense, concerning the need for an express invitation to a third state or a regional agency by the state alleged to have been attacked to justify collective self-defense, and concerning the capacity of regional agencies to authorize military preventive or defensive action without Security Council authorization.

Is a state guilty of aggression before it has been so found by a competent international procedure? Must a state be deemed innocent until proved guilty? The Harvard Research in International Law, in a proposed codification of the law of aggression in 1939, defined aggression as "a resort to armed force by a state when such resort has been duly determined, by a means which that state is bound to accept, to constitute a violation of an obligation." Accepting this concept, the question has been raised whether general recognition of aggression establishes it as a fact, as well as a determination of aggression by a council or tribunal whose authority has been accepted by the states involved. General recognition has been the means to determine the existence of states, governments, and belligerency. The Nuremberg Tribunal attached weight to the general recognition that the Axis powers had violated their obligations under the Kellogg-Briand Pact of 1928 in determining that these states had engaged in wars of aggression.

Findings of Aggression. In practice both the League of Nations and the United Nations have been sparing in finding states guilty of aggression. Although 46 instances of hostility of considerable magnitude occurred from 1920 to 1966, the League and the United Nations, together, made findings of aggression on only nine occasions during that time period. The League found aggression in six instances—Greece in 1926 for invading Bulgaria, Japan in 1932 for invading Manchuria and in 1937 for invading Shanghai, Italy in 1935 for invading Ethiopia, Paraguay in 1936 for violating the cease-fire in the Chaco area, and the Soviet Union in 1939 for invading Finland. The United Nations found aggression in only three cases—North Korea and Communist China in 1950 for invading South Korea, and the Soviet Union in 1956 for invading Hungary. In three other cases it found a "threat to the peace"—Spain in 1946 for having supported Hitler and South Africa in 1963 for its apartheid laws and for violation of its South West Africa mandate.

Both the League and the United Nations have preferred to call upon conflicting states to observe a cease-fire, equally applicable to both, and to make a finding of aggression only if a party refuses to accept the cease-fire order or subsequently violates it. In some cases no action was taken because the hostilities were considered civil strife, within the domestic jurisdiction of a state, or were referred to a regional agency, or because of strong political opposition to UN action in the situation.

The United Nations sought to maintain peace by conciliation, provisional orders, and the dispatch of peace-keeping forces—as in Suez (1956), Congo (1960), and Cyprus (1964)—under Chapter VI and Article 40 of its Charter, reserving for extreme emergencies the collective security action set forth in Chapter VII, which calls for a determination of aggression.

QUINCY WRIGHT, *University of Virginia*

Bibliography: Custance, Reginald, *Study of War* (1924; reprint, Assoc. Faculty Press 1970); Ferencz, Benjamin B., *Defining International Aggression*, 2 vols. (Oceana Pub. 1975); Goodwin, G. L., *New Dimensions of World Politics* (Longwood 1975); Stone, Julius, *Conflict through Consensus* (Johns Hopkins Univ. Press 1977); Wright, Q., *A Study of War* (Univ. of Chicago Press 1983).

AGGRESSION, ə-gresh'ən, in psychology, a disorganizing emotional response that is elicited by intense frustrations and leads to hostile, destructive behavior. Though in popular usage the term has a wide connotation, in psychological and psychiatric literature it usually denotes an unreasoning hostility that may be directed against the individual's environment, toward some aspect of his or her general situation, or even toward him- or herself. It also denotes the presence of underlying frustrations in the person who is aggressive.

Senseless acts of vandalism, physical injury to defenseless persons, wanton destruction, self-injury, and crimes that are easily detectable by police officers are conceived to be the aggressive behavior of frustrated individuals motivated by unreasoning rage or hate.

Young children normally respond to frustrating circumstances by having a fit of temper. An essential part of their socialization consists of teaching them how to inhibit overt expressions of rage over frustrations. As they become adults, they will be expected to develop many psychological resources for dealing with frustrations. If an adult utilizes childish outlets for aggressive impulses, a diagnosis of social immaturity may be indicated. The most familiar pattern of aggressive outburst is the tantrum. This may take the form of destructive behavior, or it may be expressed verbally. Aggressions may be "displaced"—that is, directed toward outlets in no way related to the frustrations that initially elicited them.

In dealing with aggressive tendencies, a person is faced with interesting problems. If these tendencies are pent up, grave personality difficulties may ensue. If, on the other hand, they are expressed, rejection may occur, a career may be ruined, or a friendship destroyed.

Western culture is said to be unduly severe in its demands upon individuals and to impose inescapable frustrations. Hence if a person is not to become aggressive, it seems necessary to find compensatory outlets that have social and ethical sanction.

PHILLIP L. HARRIMAN
Editor of "Encyclopedia of Psychology"

AGINCOURT, Battle of, à-zhaN-kōōr', one of the decisive battles of the Hundred Years' War (1337–1453). At Agincourt, a French village that is now in the Pas-de-Calais department, an army led by King Henry V of England defeated the chivalry

A 15th-century artist's rendition of the Battle of Agincourt found in *St. Albans Chronicle.*

of King Charles VI of France on Oct. 25, 1415.

Reviving the claims of his ancestors to the French throne, Henry invaded Normandy in August 1415 and laid siege to Harfleur. The town fell on September 22; but by then the English army had been seriously weakened by dysentery as well as by battle casualties. Of the 11,000 men who had sailed from England, fewer than 5,000 archers and 1,000 men-at-arms survived to march north to Calais.

The English troops' path was blocked at Agincourt by a French force of 20,000 to 30,000 men—most of them knights in heavy armor and on horseback—concentrated in the cramped space between two woods. Henry drew up his troops in order of battle, placing his archers in wedge-shaped groups on each side of three blocks of dismounted men-at-arms and in wings at either extremity of his 900-yard-long line. Then he led the army forward to within bowshot range, where the archers let fly a stream of arrows to provoke the enemy to charge.

Stung into action, the undisciplined French knights galloped through the mud into a fresh hail of arrows and onto sharp-pointed stakes that the English archers had stuck into the ground in front of them. A second attack, by dismounted men-at-arms, was initially successful. But as more and more knights entered the battle, they became so densely packed that there was scarcely room to strike a blow. Thousands of them were hacked to the ground by the less encumbered English. Thousands more were taken prisoner, until Henry ordered that these too should be killed for fear they might rejoin the battle. In all, between 7,000 and 10,000 Frenchmen were left dead. The English losses were less than 450.

Henry's early death in 1422, however, rendered his triumph an empty one. His son and successor, Henry VI, lacked the father's leadership and had to contend with the rising force of French national pride and its inspired epitome, Joan of Arc. He was to lose all that Henry V had fought for.

CHRISTOPHER HIBBERT
Author of "Agincourt"

Agni, his head wreathed in fire, depicted in a sandstone sculpture (Rajasthan, 12th–13th century). Agni mediates between the human realm and the divine. He has both a benevolent and a destructive aspect. In the latter he is closely affiliated with Rudra, a precursor of Síva.

DENVER ART MUSEUM,
HAROLD P. AND JANE F. ULLMAN COLLECTION

AGING. See Geriatrics; Gerontology; Senility.

AGNES, ag′nes (died c. 304), Christian saint and virgin martyr in Rome who was condemned to be burned at the stake for refusing to renounce her faith and marry the prefect's son. When the flames would not burn her, she was beheaded. Every year on her feast day (January 21) the wool of two lambs is blessed in the Church of St. Agnes in Rome. The wool is made into the pallia worn by the pope, patriarchs, and archbishops.

In art, Agnes is represented with a lamb, as a symbol of purity. John Keats's poem *The Eve of St. Agnes* is based on the legend that a girl might dream of her lover if she fasted and observed the proper rituals on St. Agnes's Eve.

AGNEW, Spiro Theodore, ag′noō (1918–1996), 39th vice president of the United States (1969–1973). Spiro Agnew was born in Baltimore, Md., on Nov. 9, 1918, the son of a Greek immigrant whose name originally was Anagnostopoulos. An army officer during World War II, he attended the University of Baltimore law school, receiving his degree in 1947.

In 1962, as a Republican reformer, he was elected chief executive of preponderantly Democratic Baltimore county. Democrats also helped elect him governor of Maryland in 1966. As governor, he backed tax and judicial reforms. Republican presidential candidate Richard M. Nixon chose him as his running mate in 1968.

Vice President. As vice president, Agnew soon gained wider attention with a number of controversial speeches. He charged that opponents of the Vietnam War were encouraged by "an effete corps of impudent snobs." While opposing violent dissent, he supported peaceful protest. He said that some newspapers and magazines critical of the administration were often unfair and inaccurate and contended that "a small and unelected elite," unrepresentative of the American people and often biased, controlled television news programs.

It was assumed that in general Agnew reflected President Nixon's views. Though many people deplored Agnew's attacks as vague and inflammatory, he was popular among political conservatives and at Republican fund-raisers.

During the 1970 congressional campaign, Agnew was his party's major speaker. His severe criticism of Democrats, many of whom he called "radical liberals," was not very effective. When running successfully for reelection with Nixon in 1972, Agnew was more restrained.

Resignation. Agnew came under investigation by the U.S. attorney in Baltimore for allegedly receiving payoffs from engineers seeking contracts when Agnew was Baltimore county executive and governor of Maryland. Agnew asserted his innocence, but he then resigned on Oct. 10, 1973, and pleaded nolo contendere, or no contest, to a single charge that he had failed to report $29,500 of income received in 1967. He was fined $10,000 and placed on three years' probation. After his resignation he started a successful business career as an international broker. Agnew died on Sept. 17, 1996, in Berlin, Md.

AGNI, ug′nē, one of the chief deities in Vedic mythology, the Hindu god of fire. Agni encompasses the domestic hearth (earthly fire), moon (atmospheric fire), and sun (heavenly fire) in a tripartite cosmos. He is associated especially with the marriage and funeral rituals and presides at every sacrifice. His manifestations (Vaiśvānara, Jātavedas, Apām Napāt) are characteristically transformative or mediating.

AGNON, Shmuel Yosef, äg′nōn (1888–1970), Israeli author. A leading figure of 20th-century Hebrew literature, he shared (with Nelly Sachs) the Nobel Prize for literature in 1966.

Samuel Josef Czaczkes was born in Buczacz, Galicia, on July 17, 1888. He was educated privately and studied Hasidic literature in the synagogue of the Chortkov Ḥasidim. He wrote in both Yiddish and Hebrew until he went to Palestine (now Israel) in 1908; thereafter he wrote only in Hebrew. He lived in Jaffa and Jerusalem, supporting himself by a variety of clerical, tutoring, and literary jobs.

Moving to Germany in 1913, he was an editor for *Juedischer Verlag* and continued tutoring. His stories were published (in German translation) in Martin Buber's *Der Jude*, and the two began a collection of Hasidic folklore. After most of his books and manuscripts were destroyed by fire in 1924 he returned to Palestine, settling in Jerusalem. From his youth his work had been published both under his own name and under a variety of pseudonyms; he signed "Agunot" (1908, "Forsaken Wives"), the first story he published in Palestine, with the pseudonym Agnon and in 1924 made Agnon his legal name. Agnon lived in Jerusalem until his death, in Rehovot, Israel, on Feb. 17, 1970.

Agnon is noted for his mystical, introspective novels and short stories of Jewish life in both his native Galicia and Palestine (now Israel). Much of his writing starkly depicts the effects of modern society on the Ḥasidim. His works include the novels *Hakhnasat kallah* (1922; *The Bridal Canopy*, 1937), based on a Hebrew folk epic; *Ore'ah natah lalun* (1945; *A Guest for the Night*, 1968); the highly regarded *Temol shilsholm* (1947; "Only Yesterday"), and the unfinished, posthumously published *Shirah* (1971; *Shira*, 1989), which is considered by many critics to be his masterwork.

AGNOSTICISM, ag-nos′tə-siz-əm, is a form of skepticism that maintains that the human mind lacks the information or rational capacity to make judgments about ultimate reality, and in particular about the existence or nature of God. The word was coined by T.H. Huxley about 1869 from the Greek negative prefix *a* and the verb *gignoskein* (to know). Unlike atheism, agnosticism does not deny the reality of God or offer any alternative to theism. It suspends judgment, maintaining that man does not know.

Actually the agnostic tradition precedes by many centuries the origin of the word. Some of the pre-Socratic philosophers, as well as the Sophists in the time of Plato, raised the basic agnostic questions. The ancient Skeptics—including especially Pyrrho (c. 360–c. 270 B.C.) and Sextus Empiricus (3d century A.D.)—denied the possibility of any certain knowledge and formulated most of the specific doubts and questions that modern agnostics were to use.

Modern agnosticism became a self-conscious movement in the 18th and 19th centuries. David Hume, the great Scottish skeptic, seeking to trace all knowledge to sense impressions, denied the validity of any metaphysics. In particular he rejected the adequacy of evidence for belief in God, miracles, and immortality. Consistent with his method, Hume avoided any claim to prove that there is no God. Proving the negative case would require as much evidence as proving the positive case. Apparently with tongue in cheek, Hume suggested that faith might be maintained independently of empirical evidence. Hume's own advice was to suspend judgment on all beliefs that could not be empirically grounded. But the obvious effect of his argument upon such beliefs was negative, insofar as he insisted that they were not and could not be verified.

19th Century Agnosticism. England in the latter half of the 19th century was the scene of the great agnostic crusade. Herbert Spencer, the influential philosopher of evolution, developed an elaborate metaphysic, contrary to Hume's skepticism. Spencer, however, rejected the traditional doctrines of God and referred everything in the last analysis to "the Unknowable." He held that "the power which the Universe manifests to us is utterly inscrutable" (*First Principles*, 1862). Although he maintained a kind of religious piety toward the Unknowable, more radical agnostics were quick to point out that there was little point in talking about any power that is completely unknowable.

Thus the time was ripe for Huxley to invent the word "agnosticism" and to argue its case. First introducing the word in conversations, then developing its implications in writings, Huxley argued strenuously against accepting any beliefs without adequate evidence. Huxley insisted that his position was not a dogmatic denial of any belief. In fact, his "scientific Naturalism" was avowedly open to the possibility that an omnipresent, practically omniscient intellect might exert indefinably great power within the universe. But he saw no evidence to verify such a conjecture, so he answered all ultimate questions with the confession of ignorance. To the assertions of conventional believers he opposed the agnostic motto, "not proven."

Major Roots. The agnostic case has two major roots. The first is epistemological, involving an appeal to science as the model of all knowledge. Here the standard is an intellectual method that proceeds by the examination of evidence and suspends judgment on all propositions for which adequate evidence is lacking.

The second root is moral. The agnostic, who in his moral judgments is often as passionate as any believer, considers it immoral to hold convictions that are not adequately supported by evidence. Huxley, insisting that his case was "as much ethical as intellectual," said: "it is wrong for a man to say that he is certain of the objective truth of any proposition unless he can produce evidence which logically justifies that certainty" (*Essays upon Controverted Questions*, 1892). W.K. Clifford, one of the most militant of the agnostics, wrote: "It is wrong always, everywhere, and for anyone, to believe anything upon insufficient evidence" ("The Ethics of Belief," 1879). Such a belief, even if it should be true, is "sinful," said Clifford.

In its moral aspects agnosticism tends to depart from its original position of suspended judgment. On metaphysical questions it moves from a tentative position ("we deny nothing; we simply say we do not know") to what amounts to a practical negation ("we do not know; but it is immoral to believe"). In its ethical judgments it abandons the skepticism of Hume for the moral certainty that Huxley called an "absolute faith" in the agnostic principle.

William James, the American psychologist and philosopher, pointed out this discrepancy between the tentative theoretical stance of agnosticism and its practical certitude. He held that the agnostic moral faith rested upon a passional rather than a scientific decision. Challenging Clifford's position, James argued for a willingness to risk error rather than to give up the aspiration for truth. And he held that religious belief was more akin to the moral decision than to scientific inquiry (*The Will to Believe*, 1897).

The 20th Century. In the 20th century, agnosticism remains a widely held position. Its adherents have less fervor than its 19th century partisans, but agnosticism is more diffused. Some of its skepticism has been taken up by logical positivism, which even more emphatically denies the possibility of metaphysical knowledge. But whereas agnosticism holds that the metaphysical questions are real, even though we cannot know the answers, logical positivism maintains that they are pseudoquestions, which analysis shows to be meaningless.

Meanwhile, religious thinkers often incorporate a considerable element of agnosticism within their thought. They are less likely than in many periods of the past to take science as a model for religious thought and verification. They are more modest than many of their forebears in elaborating metaphysical systems. And they draw upon those elements of the religious traditions that always have insisted that the believer, confronting the divine mystery, will be both wise and reverent if he frequently says "I do not know," even as he makes his confession of faith and his commitment.

ROGER L. SHINN, *Union Theological Seminary*

Further Reading: Armstrong, Richard A., *Agnosticism and Theism in the 19th Century* (Gordon Press 1977); Huxley, Thomas H., *Science and Christian Tradition* (1894; reprint, Century 1981); James, William, *The Will to Believe* (1897; reprint, Harvard Univ. Press 1979); Lightman, Bernard, *The Origins of Agnosticism* (Johns Hopkins Univ. Press 1987).

AGNUS DEI, äg'nŏŏs dā'ē, is Latin for *Lamb of God,* a name given to Jesus, commemorating his sacrifice for mankind. John the Baptist twice referred to Jesus by this name (John 1:29, 36). In the Roman Catholic and Greek churches the figure of a lamb surmounted by a halo and bearing a cross or banner came to be used as an emblem of Jesus Christ, and it often is embroidered on vestments and altar cloths. The figure appears frequently in religious art.

Among Roman Catholics the name is given to a sacramental, consisting of a wax medallion stamped with the figure of a lamb, which is blessed by the pope in the first year of his reign and every seventh year thereafter. See also Sacramentals.

In the Roman Catholic Church a prayer beginning with the words "Agnus Dei" or the vernacular equivalent is recited before communion at Mass. In the Anglican Communion an anthem beginning "O Lamb of God" is chanted.

AGORA, ag'ə-rə, is a Greek word that originally (8th century B.C.) referred to an assembly of the people; later it was used to designate the place where this assembly met. By the 7th and, more particularly, the 6th century, the word had come to mean "marketplace." The agora became the center of economic, political, social, and, to a large extent, religious activity in the Greek *polis,* or city-state.

Every Greek city possessed an agora, and some, such as Athens and Thebes, possessed two. Usually the agora was located on a level or gently sloping area near the base of the city's acropolis. Wherever possible, the agora was centrally located and easily accessible from the major roadways of the city, which in some cases passed directly through it.

Prior to the 4th century the agoras were not carefully planned. Generally, however, an agora was partially enclosed by long buildings called *stoai,* which ran along two or more of its sides. Within the agora itself were located nearly all the public buildings, including temples and altars to the gods and goddesses of the city, law courts, assembly halls, state archives, libraries, and offices of city officials. Inscriptions of public interest were set up there, as were statues of local heroes. Commercial activity was carried on either in temporary stalls set up for the purpose or in large *stoai,* such as the Stoa of Attalus, which has been reconstructed on its original foundations along the eastern border of the Athenian agora. These *stoai* housed small shops and stores, which dispensed a wide variety of goods and services.

The agora was especially important as a center of social activity, since ancient Greeks spent much of their time outdoors. The shaded porches of the *stoai* provided the citizens with an excellent place to meet and converse with their friends. The open area in the center of the agora was considered sacred ground, and certain persons, such as those charged with murder, were not allowed entrance. Games and festivals were held in this open area, and public lectures were sometimes delivered there. It was in the open area of the Athenian agora that votes were cast for ostracism, and here too any citizen could suggest a law by writing it down on a board set up for this purpose.

Thomas Kelly
University of Alberta

AGORACRITUS, ag-o-rak'ri-təs, was a Greek sculptor of the 5th century B.C. Born at Paros, he was the favorite pupil of Phidias. His chief work, attributed by some to his master, was the colossal statue of Nemesis at Rhamnus. The head of this statue is in the British Museum, and fragments of its pedestal reliefs are in the museum at Athens.

AGORAPHOBIA, fear of open spaces. See under Phobia.

AGOSTA. See Augusta, Italy.

AGOSTINO AND AGNOLO, ä-gō-stē'nō, ä-nyō'lō, Italian sculptors who were active in the late 13th and early 14th centuries. Their full names are *Agostino di Giovanni* and *Agnolo di Ventura.* They studied together under Giovanni Pisano and in 1317 were jointly appointed to serve as architects for their native city, Siena.

Their most important surviving work is the tomb (1330) of Bishop Guido Tarlati, in the cathedral at Arezzo. The tomb includes an effigy of the bishop set within a high Gothic tabernacle, with bands of sculptured reliefs at the base depicting scenes from his life. The reliefs are in a style similar to the monumental mode established in painting by Giotto in Florence and formerly were believed to have been designed by Giotto himself.

Works in Siena attributed to Agostino and Agnolo, or to their famous workshop, include a number of statues in the Opera del Duomo. The wall tomb (1286) of Pope Gregory X, in the cathedral at Arezzo is believed to be their work, as are the tomb (1337) of Cino de' Sinibaldi and that of Bishop Ricciardi (died 1343) in the cathedral at Pistoia and the tomb of Gastone della Torre in the cloister of Santa Croce, Florence.

AGOSTINO DI DUCCIO, ä-gō-stē'nō dē dŏŏt' chō (1418–?1481), Italian sculptor and architect, who developed a very personal, lyrical style of sculpture, marked by its linear quality. He was born in Florence and apparently received his early training there. His earliest known work is a series of reliefs for the cathedral at Modena (1442). In 1446 he was forced to leave Florence because he had been accused of theft. After a sojourn in Venice he went to Rimini, where he worked from about 1449 to 1454 with Matteo de' Pasti on the decorations for the façade of the Tempio Malatestiano, designed by Leon Battista Alberti. The reliefs, an allegory in praise of Sigismondo Malatesta, lord of Rimini, incorporate pagan muses, sibyls, and other figures from classical art.

Agostino's next important work, usually considered his masterpiece, is the design of the façade of the Oratory of San Bernardino in Perugia (1457–1461). Derived from Alberti's Tempio, the design contains sculptured reliefs on the typanum and door jambs, showing the final refinement of Alberti's linear style. Agostino worked briefly in Florence and Bologna, then returned to Perugia. No mention of him after 1481 has been found.

Reliefs of a Madonna and Child attributed to Agostino are in the Louvre, Paris, and the National Gallery of Art, Washington, D.C.

James Snyder
Bryn Mawr College

AGOULT, à-gōō′, **Countess d'** (1805–1876), French writer, who is best known for her liaison with the composer and pianist Franz Liszt. She was born *Marie Catherine Sophie de Flavigny* in Frankfurt am Main, Germany, on Dec. 31, 1805. In 1827 she married Charles, Count d'Agoult. After several years of marriage she separated from him to live and travel with Franz Liszt, by whom she had three children. One of them, her daughter Cosima, was the wife of pianist Hans Guido von Bülow and, after divorcing him, of composer Richard Wagner.

Countess d'Agoult left Liszt in 1839 and went to Paris, where, using the pseudonym *Daniel Stern*, she began to write. Her novel *Nélida* (1846) is largely an autobiographical account of her liaison with Liszt. She was a good friend of novelist George Sand and figures as "Arabella" in Sand's *Lettres d'un voyageur*. Countess d'Agoult was well known in the 1840's for her Paris salon, which was a gathering place for the leading thinkers, writers, and musicians of the day. She died in Paris on March 5, 1876.

She wrote on history, politics, and philosophy. Her works included *Lettres républicaines* (1848), *Esquisses morales et politiques* (1849), and *Histoire de la révolution de 1848* (3 vols., 1850–53). Her *Mes souvenirs 1806–1833* (1877) and *Mémoires 1833–1854* (1927) provide a view of French social circles of the period.

AGOUTI, ə-gōō′tē, a rodent that inhabits the tropical American mainland from southern Mexico to Paraguay, and also the Lesser Antilles. Although agoutis resemble and are about the size of large rabbits, they are much more closely related to such rodents as guinea pigs and porcupines. They also differ from rabbits in having short ears and rather hooflike claws (four and a greatly reduced fifth on each forefoot, three on each hind foot), and they run rather than hop. Their color is a speckled gray or brown, sometimes with a contrastingly colored reddish rump. A number of forms have been described, but all may actually constitute one species. They feed on fruit and other soft vegetable matter. Agoutis belong to the genus *Dasyprocta*.

AGRA, ä′grə, is a city in India, in western Uttar Pradesh state, on the south bank of the Jumna River, 110 air miles (177 km) southeast of Delhi. Chosen as capital by the Mughul (Mogul) emperor Akbar (1542–1605) about 1560, Agra is now famous chiefly for its fine examples of Mughul architecture, which include the Taj Mahal. It is also important as a rail junction and center of education and light industry.

Like most cities of former British India, Agra is composed of Indian and "European" sections, the latter consisting of a cantonment, or area where troops were stationed, and a civil station. The cantonment area, on the south, is spacious and contains parks, parade grounds, and most of Agra's hotels. To the northwest, in the former civil station, are schools, churches, and hospitals; most date from the 19th century.

The old city, facing the Jumna, lies between these two areas and includes Agra Fort, one of the great monuments of the Mughul era and a major attraction of the city. Much more than an ordinary fortification, Agra Fort, built about 1566, was the capital of the Mughul emperors Akbar, Jahangir (1569–1627), and Shah Jahan (c. 1592–1666). Within its walls, which are 70

TAJ MAHAL AT AGRA, built by Emperor Shah Jahan as a mausoleum for his wife, is on the Jumna River.

feet (21 meters) high, are mosques, palaces, audience halls, and other buildings of great beauty and magnificence.

A little over a mile (1½ km) east of the fort, on the right bank of the Jumna, stands the exquisite Taj Mahal, completed in 1648 as the mausoleum and memorial to Shah Jahan's favorite wife, Mumtaz Mahal. Elsewhere in Agra and its neighborhood are other examples of Mughul architecture, typically constructed of red sandstone and white marble, including the tomb of Akbar at Sikandra.

Among Agra's educational institutions are Agra University, St. Peter's College (Roman Catholic), and St. John's College (Church Missionary Society). The army paratroopers' training school is nearby.

Agra's manufactures include glass, leather and shoes, cotton goods, steel pipe, and cut stone. Tourism is important. The city has long been important as the gateway to a major trade route between the Ganges plains and central India—a function that it maintains today as a railroad junction. Population: 1,259,979 (2001 census).

JOEL M. ANDRESS
Central Washington State College

AGRA UNIVERSITY, ä′grə, in Agra, Uttar Pradesh, India, is a coordinating institution for over 100 centers of higher education. It was formed in 1926 to assume jurisdiction over colleges formerly affiliated with the University of Allahabad. The university proper comprises two institutes: social studies and Hindi studies. Affiliated colleges teach engineering, law, medicine, science, technology, veterinary science, and animal husbandry. Almost half of the affiliates confer master's degrees, but doctoral studies are under university jurisdiction. By the 1960's, the total enrollment of the university proper and its affiliated colleges had grown to about 40,000 full-time and 16,000 part-time students.

AGRAMONTE, ä-grä-môn′tä, **Aristides** (1869–1931), Cuban physician and bacteriologist. He was born in Camagüey, Cuba, on June 3, 1869, and was brought to the United States while still a child. During 1885–1887 he attended the College of the City of New York and then entered the College of Physicians and Surgeons of Columbia University, from which he graduated in 1892. He practiced in New York City until the outbreak of the Spanish-American War when he became an assistant surgeon in the U.S. Army.

Agramonte's major contributions were in the field of tropical medicine. In 1900 he was appointed, with Walter Reed, James Carroll, and Jesse William Lazear, to the United States Army Yellow Fever Commission. This group, often referred to as the Reed Commission, studied and eliminated many of the conflicting theories that had been advanced to explain the transmission of yellow fever and proved that under specific conditions some mosquitoes could carry the disease. See also YELLOW FEVER.

For many years Agramonte was professor of bacteriology and experimental pathology at the University of Havana. He later organized the department of tropical diseases at Louisiana State University Medical School and served as its head until his death in New Orleans on Aug. 17, 1931.

AGRAMONTE, ä-grä-môn′tä, **Ignacio** (1841–1873), Cuban soldier who commanded a revolutionary army in the Ten Years' War against Spain. Born at Puerto Príncipe (now Camagüey), he studied law at the University of Havana and in 1867 was admitted to the bar.

In 1868 he became a supporter of Carlos Manuel de Céspedes in the struggle against Spain and was made secretary of the provisional government set up by the revolutionists. Resigning this post because of a disagreement with Céspedes, he was given command of the forces in the Camagüey district. After the retirement of other leaders he acted for some time as commander in chief of the revolutionists. He was killed at the Battle of Jimaguayu. See also CUBA —History.

AGRAPHA, ag′rə-fə, sayings ascribed to Jesus but not recorded in the New Testament. They are found in the manuscripts of early Christian writers and in other sources. Among early examples of the sayings are: "That which is weak shall be saved by that which is strong"; "Wrath destroyeth even wise men"; "A man is unapproved if he be untempted"; "Jesus on whom be peace has said: The world is merely a bridge; you are to pass over it, and not to build your dwellings upon it." This last saying was found inscribed on the gateway of a mosque at Fatehpur Sikri, near Agra, India, by Alexander Duff, a 19th century missionary.

The most important sayings were found in 1897 and 1903 by Bernard Pyne Grenfell and Arthur Surridge Hunt at Bahnasa (ancient Oxyrhynchus) in Egypt. Among these, which all begin "Jesus saith," are the following: "Jesus saith, I stood in the midst of the world, and in the flesh was I seen of them, and I found all men drunken and none found I athirst among them, and my soul grieved over the sons of men, because they are blind in their heart and see not"; "Jesus saith, Wherever there are two they are not without God, and wherever there is one alone, I say I am with him. Raise the stone, and there thou shalt find me; cleave the wood and there am I."

An important collection of Gnostic "sayings of Jesus" was found near Nag Hammadi in Egypt in 1945. Some of them show how the Gnostics erected a bridge between their faith and that of the Christian church. See GNOSTICISM.

AGRARIAN LAWS, ə-grâr′ē-ən, enactments framed at different times by the Romans to regulate the public domain. They were designed to control uses of public property for private profit and to extend such uses to more Roman citizens.

In the first epoch of the growth of Rome, before the city extended beyond the Palatine Hill, all of the territory of the state was undivided public property. Each citizen received a share of the territory for his private use. In the course of time, descendants of the original citizens transformed these primitive concessions into an absolute right, called in the Roman law *de jure quiritio*. Persons to whom the right was extended were called *patricians*.

As conquest increased the public domain, a class of *plebeians*, not descended from founders of the state, was formed. Plebeians were entitled to an interest in the public property as private property on condition that they paid a tribute and undertook other public services. Patricians, however, continued to receive by right, for their indefinite use, portions of the public domain. From the earliest period of Roman history, privileges thus held could pass by inheritance or sale, although the state always reserved the power to repossess the land.

Spurius Cassius, a patrician who became a consul in the early period of the republic, was responsible for the first agrarian law. Enacted in 486 B.C., the law required that some portion of the public lands occupied by the nobles should be surrendered to the state and assigned to needy citizens. The law proved ineffectual, however, because of the resistance of the patricians, who not only prevented any new division of the public lands but by violence and usury acquired landholdings of the plebeians.

Eventually large herds of cattle owned by the patricians nearly ruined the common pasture lands and virtually excluded small farmers from them. This caused the publication, in 367 B.C., of the Licinian law, so called from Licinius Calvus Stolo, its author.

The Licinian law called for reforms at the expense of the patricians. Neglected for nearly 200 years, it was resurrected by Tiberius Sempronius Gracchus with certain conditions and modifications favoring the patricians. Attempts to put the law into effect resulted in Tiberius' death in 133 B.C. See GRACCHUS.

Probably none of the agrarian laws were ever executed, although a leveling and confiscatory function was often attributed to them by historians. Authorities believe that the laws never aimed at dividing real estate owned by individuals in their own right, or intended any limitation on the ownership of land. On the contrary, their effect appears to have been only to limit the abuses to which public lands were subjected.

AGRARIAN MOVEMENTS. See CANADA—*Agrarian Movement;* GREENBACK PARTY; PEOPLE'S PARTY; UNITED STATES—*Agriculture.*

AGREEMENT. See CONTRACT.

AGRICOLA, ä-grē′kō-lä, **Georgius** (1494–1555), German scholar, who has been called the "father of mineralogy" and the "forefather of geology." He was one of the first natural scientists to recognize that research and observation rather than metaphysical speculation are the foundation on which science is built.

He was born in Glachau, Saxony, on March 24, 1494. ("Georgius Agricola" is the Latin form of his original name, *Georg Bauer.*) In 1517 he graduated with the degree of B.A. from the University of Leipzig, and in 1518 he began to teach Greek and Latin at the municipal school in Zwickau. After two years as a lecturer at the University of Leipzig he resumed his studies of natural history, medicine, and philosophy in 1524, attending various Italian universities, which were at that time the centers of enlightened thinking. Agricola then returned to Saxony and in 1527 was chosen town physician at Joachimsthal, Bohemia. Retiring from this position in 1530, he spent three years traveling and visiting mines.

Agricola became city physician at Chemnitz in 1533. At the age of 52 he entered public life as a burgher. He then became burgomaster of Chemnitz, and he later served as a diplomat for Duke Maurice of Saxony. He died in Chemnitz on Nov. 21, 1555.

Agricola's treatise on mineralogy, *De natura fossilium,* which appeared in 1546, was the first original textbook of mineralogy written in the 1,500 years since Pliny's *Natural History.* Agricola's 10-volume work identifies some 20 previously undescribed minerals, presents the first systematic classification of minerals, and describes the physical properties and occurrence of some 800 minerals. Originally written in Latin, it has been translated several times—most recently into English, when it was published by the Geological Society of America in 1955. *De ortu et causis subterraneorum,* which also appeared in 1546, consists of five volumes on geology.

Of greatest general interest is Agricola's major work, *De re metallica,* which consists of 12 volumes covering mining, metallurgy, and geology. Published the year after his death, the work served as a textbook and guide for miners and metallurgists for the next 200 years. An English translation published in 1912 in the *Mining Magazine* of London is an invaluable source of information about Agricola and his work. The translation was made by American mining engineer Herbert Hoover (later president of the United States) with the assistance of his wife.

D. VINCENT MANSON
American Museum of Natural History

AGRICOLA, ə-grik′ə-lə, **Gnaeus Julius** (40–93 A.D.), general and governor of Roman Britain. His career, typical for a competent administrator of imperial Rome, was eulogized by his son-in-law, the historian Tacitus, in the *Agricola.* Agricola was born in Forum Julii, now Fréjus, in Provence, France. Thus he typified imperial provincials, rising to high posts. Through his ability and connections he became a quaestor in Asia, senator, tribune of the plebs, praetor, consul, pontifex, and legate (governor) of Aquitania. In each office he showed intelligence, integrity, and political common sense.

His career centered mainly in Britain, however. In 61, Agricola, as *tribunus militum* (staff officer), joined a victorious attack on the Druid stronghold on Mona (Anglesey) and then faced a widespread revolt led by Queen Boadicea (Boudicca). Though the Romans had to withdraw from the cities, their disciplined legions annihilated 80,000 Britons. The victory broke the anti-Roman confederacy but turned Roman policy for a decade from expansion to consolidation.

In the civil wars of 68–69, Agricola declared for Vespasian, and from 71 to 73 he was legate of the XX Legion in Britain. Vespasian had reactivated the aggressive policy in Britain, and Agricola proved his generalship in hard fighting against the powerful Brigantes. From 78 to 84 he was legate of Britain. Like other able legates before him he made great strides in Romanizing conquered Britain, building cities, schools, and roads and cultivating Roman ways. He crushed a revolt in Wales and Mona and established permanent order in the mountainous region. He next secured Britain's west coast with a strategically engineered chain of forts and roads. The emperor Domitian then authorized campaigns in the Scottish Highlands. At Mons Graupius, in 84, Agricola defeated the Scots, who retreated to the Highlands. Total conquest of Scotland seemed possible; but Domitian, awarding Agricola high honors, recalled him to Rome and withdrew legionnaires from Britain to fight on the Rhine. This ended the Flavian advance in Britain. Agricola's forts were gradually abandoned and north Britain remained independent. He left a legacy of military security, conscientious administration, and Romanization that drew Britain more firmly into the empire.

ELEANOR HUZAR, *Michigan State University*

AGRICOLA, ä-grē′kō-lä, **Johannes** (1494–1566), German religious reformer and an active supporter of Martin Luther. He was born at Eisleben, Germany, on April 20, 1494. His real name was *Johannes Sneider* (later *Schnitter*); he also was called *Magister Islebius.*

Agricola studied at Wittenberg and was afterward rector and preacher in Frankfurt, Eisleben, Wittenberg, and Berlin. In 1526, at the Diet of Spires, he was chaplain of the Elector John of Saxony. He later took part in the delivery of the Augsburg Confession and in the signing of the Articles of Schmalkalden. While professor at Wittenberg, where he went in 1536, he stirred up a controversy with Luther and Melanchthon by temporarily supporting Antinomianism.

In addition to his theological works, Agricola wrote *Deutscher Sprichwörter* (1528; enlarged 1529; 1548), explaining the common German proverbs. Its patriotic spirit, strict morality, and pithy style place it among the leading German prose compositions of the time, ranking with Luther's translation of the Bible. Agricola died at Berlin on Sept. 22, 1566.

AGRICOLA, ä-grē′kō-lä, **Martin** (1486–1566), the Latinized pen name of the German writer on music theory *Martin Sohr,* or *Sore.* He proposed a new, improved tablature for the lute, and his writings are an important source of information on the evolution of modern musical notation. His most famous work is *Musica instrumentalis deudsch* (1528), written in rhymed verse in a simple, powerful German vernacular style.

Agricola was born in Schwiebus, Brandenburg, in 1486. From 1524 until his death he was a teacher and cantor in the first Protestant school at Magdeburg.

AGRICOLA, à-grē′kō-là, **Rodolphus** (1443–1485), Latinized pen name of the Dutch scholar *Roelof Huysman,* who is called the "father of German humanism." Through his writings and his teaching at German universities, he helped to break down the rigid dogmatism of scholastic philosophy and bring about the revival of classical studies. These developments were of primary importance in kindling the intellectual renaissance that took place in 16th century Germany.

Agricola was born in 1443 at Baflo, near Groningen, the Netherlands. After graduating as a master of arts at Louvain, he studied in Paris and then in Italy, where from 1473 to 1480 he attended the lectures of some of the most celebrated men of his age, including lectures on the Greek language by Teodoro Gaza. At Ferrara he entered into a close friendship with Johann von Dalberg, who later became bishop of Worms. In 1482, at the invitation of the bishop, Agricola became a professor of Greek and Roman literature at the University of Heidelberg. For the following three years he lectured alternately at Heidelberg and Worms. He opposed many of the tenets of the scholastic philosophy of the day, calling for the freedom of reason from dogma and for greater emphasis on the study of classical, pre-Christian thought. His ideas were praised by Erasmus, Melanchthon, Hegius, and other scholars of the northern European Renaissance. He died at Heidelberg, Germany, on Oct. 28, 1485.

Agricola's most important work is *De inventione dialectica* (1479), in which he criticizes and attempts to reform the methods of scholastic philosophy. He also wrote a treatise on education, *De formando studio* (1484); a biography of Petrarch (1477); and occasional verse; and he made translations from the Greek. Most of his writings were published in two volumes in 1539 by Alard of Amsterdam.

AGRICULTURAL ADJUSTMENT ADMINISTRATION,

an agency of the United States government, established in 1933 to help farmers recover from the economic depression. It was created under the Agricultural Adjustment Act of 1933, which provided for a program of soil conservation, storage of surplus farm products, and control of the production of farm goods.

The basic purpose of the AAA was to reduce and control crop surpluses, thereby raising prices and stabilizing farmers' incomes. The act empowered the secretary of agriculture to fix marketing quotas for farm products; take surplus products off the market; cut the production of staple crops, including corn and wheat, by offering farmers benefit payments for reducing production of these commodities; and impose high taxes on cotton and tobacco to discourage farmers from raising these crops.

In 1936 the Supreme Court declared the act unconstitutional on the ground that giving cash benefits to farmers cooperating in a program of crop reductions constituted an act of coercion. The court also invalidated vital sections of the act that infringed on powers of the states, declaring that the regulation of agriculture was a state function (*United States* v. *Butler,* 297 U.S. 1 [1936]). Congress then, in February 1936, enacted the Soil Conservation and Domestic Allotment Act. It authorized payments to farmers who participated in soil conservation by raising soil-building, rather than staple grain, crops. De-

spite this measure, farm prices fell in 1937. Congress then passed the Agricultural Adjustment Administration Act of 1938. Special "parity" payments made under this act were intended to balance the difference between prices farmers received for their products and prices they had to pay for labor, equipment, and necessary living costs. Basic crops were allotted certain fixed acreages; marketing quotas were set up in years of extra large harvests; and farmers were offered insurance against loss in wheat yields. Systematic government storage of surplus farm products was introduced.

During World War II, the nature of the AAA was changed to meet wartime needs. Under the new title of *Agricultural Adjustment Agency,* it became concerned with means of increasing production of food and purchasing surplus food products to give to relief groups. The AAA was superseded in 1946 by the Production and Marketing Administration of the U.S. Department of Agriculture.

AGRICULTURAL COOPERATIVE. See COOPERATIVE MOVEMENT.

AGRICULTURAL EDUCATION,

ag-ri-kulch′ər-əl ej-ə-ka′shən, trains people to produce, process, and distribute food or fiber, and spreads scientific and technical information related to all phases of such work. It strives to help the people of the world improve the quantity and quality of products indispensable to human life.

Agricultural education is concerned with one of the oldest and largest areas of work. In many countries of Latin America, Asia, and Africa, from 50 to 80 percent of the working force is employed in farming. These countries face the need to multiply the productivity of their farms if their increasing populations are to escape undernourishment or outright famine. In the highly industrialized nations the proportion of the labor force engaged in farming may be relatively small, perhaps 10 percent, but agriculture continues to be a major industry. In such countries it takes in far more than the work done on the traditional family farm—not only raising crops and livestock, processing them, and marketing them but also providing many of the goods and services that farmers use. Agriculture must continually increase its productivity in the industrial countries also, so that they can feed their own expanding populations, provide raw materials for the textile, plastics, and other industries, and ship surpluses abroad.

Agricultural education takes many forms, from children's classes in village schools to graduate study in university laboratories. Much of it goes on outside of school. Some of the most useful training is given by men and women who work directly with farmers to demonstrate new crops, techniques, and machines. All forms of agricultural education can be illustrated by descriptions of programs in the United States. Hence these programs will be described first, with notes on other countries following.

UNITED STATES PROGRAMS

The United States is one of the highly industrialized nations in which farmers are a relatively small group. The comparatively small number of farmers in the nation represents a great change from the middle of the 19th century, when about 85 persons lived on the land for

AGRICULTURAL EDUCATION takes many forms. Here young farmers in Klamath County, Oregon, get pointers on livestock raising at a cattle judging session organized by the local 4-H Club.

every 15 who lived in cities. In the course of a century these figures were reversed, and only about one seventh of the total labor force remained in agriculture. But while people moved away from the farms, the productivity of agricultural labor increased by more than 600 percent between 1870 and the mid-1960's. Four fifths of this increase occurred after 1945.

The number of farmers in the United States has decreased at each census while the total population has increased. For these reasons, agricultural workers have needed to acquire the technical skills and scientific knowledge that would enable them to meet the rapidly expanding demand for their products. Agricultural education has grown rapidly to meet this need.

Developments Before 1862. In the United States, organized agricultural education began toward the end of the 18th century. The Philadelphia Society for the Promotion of Agriculture was organized in 1785, with George Washington and Benjamin Franklin as members. Similar societies were established in South Carolina (1785), Maine (1787), New York (1791), Massachusetts (1792), and Connecticut (1794). In addition to publishing bulletins and encouraging the establishment of agricultural fairs and exhibitions, these societies furthered agricultural instruction in the common schools. The Philadelphia Society, for example, in 1794 prepared a plan to promote agricultural instruction through the University of Pennsylvania and, at a lower level, through the common school system of that state.

The earliest specialized school of agriculture in the United States was the Gardiner Lyceum, founded at Gardiner, Me., in 1821. In 1823 the state legislature appropriated $1,000 for the maintenance of the school, in what was probably the first instance of state aid for agricultural education. By 1840, agricultural instruction in the schools was being encouraged in Maine, Massachusetts, Connecticut, New York, and Michigan. In the domain of higher education there was considerable agitation early in the 19th century for the establishment of state colleges of agriculture. In 1818, Governor De Witt Clinton of New York recommended that the state legislature take steps "by which means a complete course of agricultural education would be taught." By the time of the American Civil War some states already had created colleges of agriculture. The state constitution adopted in 1850 by Michi-

gan required that a college of agriculture be established and maintained. The Michigan Agricultural College (now Michigan State University) was dedicated on May 13, 1857. In Pennsylvania the Farmers' High School was founded in 1855 and became, in 1862, the Agricultural College of Pennsylvania (now Pennsylvania State University). The Maryland Agricultural College was chartered in 1856 and became part of the University of Maryland in 1920.

The constantly growing interest in agricultural education prior to 1862 influenced later developments in this field of learning. One influence arose from the work of Philipp Emanuel von Fellenberg (1771–1844), the founder of an agricultural school at Hofwyl, near Bern, Switzerland, in 1799. The Fellenberg system encouraged agricultural education by stressing the combination of manual labor and schooling. A more direct impetus was provided by Charles L. Fleischmann, a graduate of the Royal Agricultural School of Bavaria, in Germany. In 1838 he presented a memorial to the United States Congress, in which he pointed out that the European schools of agriculture were based on the study of chemistry and the other natural sciences and on experimental research. His ideas became a part of the guiding philosophy of many state agricultural societies and found their way into the growing demand for the establishment of institutions of higher education for the farmer, which culminated in the passage of the Morrill Act (1862).

The Stimulus of Federal Aid. The year 1862 was a milestone in the development of agricultural education in the United States. On May 15, 1862, Congress created the Department of Agriculture. Among other functions, the department was "to acquire and diffuse among the people of the United States useful information on subjects connected with agriculture . . . ." On July 2, 1862, President Abraham Lincoln signed the Land-Grant College Act, called the Morrill Act after its original sponsor, Justin S. Morrill. Under the provisions of the act, each state was offered 30,000 acres of public land (or its equivalent in scrip) for each of its senators and representatives who were then in Congress. Proceeds from the sale of these lands were to be used for the establishment of at least one college "where the leading objects shall be . . . to teach such branches of learning as are related to agriculture and the mechanic arts . . . ." By this act, higher education was placed within the reach of the growing number of youths from all walks of life who sought training in scientific, agricultural, and industrial pursuits.

Subsequent legislation provided for related institutions of agricultural education. The first agricultural experiment station was established in Connecticut at the privately operated Wesleyan University in 1875. In 1887 Congress passed the Hatch Act to establish such stations at all the land-grant institutions. Several additional congressional acts increased the appropriations for the land-grant colleges and the experiment stations and widened the scope of their work. Most important of these were the Second Morrill Act of 1890 and the Smith-Lever Agricultural Extension Act of 1914. The latter measure established the Cooperative Agricultural Extension Service to aid in diffusing "useful and practical information, on subjects relating to agriculture and home economics and to encourage the application of the same."

Secondary Schools. Following the American Civil War, vocational subjects entered the secondary schools as well as the colleges. By 1900, for example, Minnesota had at least 10 publicly supported agricultural high schools. In many other states the number of agricultural high schools or general high schools offering some courses in agriculture increased rapidly as a result of state subsidies. By 1913 about 2,300 high schools were offering some work in agriculture. In 1917, President Woodrow Wilson signed the Smith-Hughes Act "to provide for cooperation with the states in the promotion of such vocational education in agriculture and the trades and industries" on the secondary school level. The Smith-Hughes Act of 1917 (supplemented in 1946 by the George-Barden Act) gave great encouragement to the growth of vocational agricultural education on the secondary level. The Vocational Education Act of 1963 provided funds to expand vocational education to include any subject involving knowledge and skills in agriculture. Enrollment in high school agricultural training rose from about 15,000 students in 1918 to more than 800,000 in the mid-1960's.

Under the provisions of the Smith-Hughes, George-Barden, and 1963 Vocational Education acts, funds for secondary vocational education are allocated by the Department of Health, Education, and Welfare through the Division of Vocational and Technical Education. The actual control of the school programs remains in the hands of the state and local boards of education. These acts provide for yearly appropriations to the states to help pay for agricultural education, trade and industrial education, home economics education, and the training of teachers in these fields. The acts generally require that federal grants be matched by state appropriations.

High school vocational education programs in agriculture are designed to meet the needs of three groups: in-school youth; out-of-school young farmers (ages 16 to 30), and adult farmers and others in agricultural occupations. The full-time vocational agricultural high school course normally lasts four years; some schools, however, offer three-year or even two-year courses. In any course, specialization in vocational agriculture takes only a portion of the student's time. The program includes classroom study of voca-

tional and general subjects, laboratory investigations, and supervised farm work.

An important current development in vocational agricultural education is the increase of enrollment in classes for adults and out-of-school youth. These groups represent nearly half the enrollment in vocational agriculture in more than 10,000 high schools that have such departments. Programs for adults are planned to help established farmers and other agricultural workers to improve their skills. Organized on a seasonal basis, these programs extend over a period of weeks. Classes for young farmers (out-of-school youth) are designed to help men and women in this group establish themselves in farming. Young farmers are taught by the vocational agriculture teachers. Classes usually meet on a part-time basis throughout the year.

Land-Grant Colleges. The land-grant colleges and universities created with the help of the Morrill Act are in a central position in agricultural education. They offer a threefold program of resident instruction, research, and extension education service. Moreover, the curricula of these institutions have greatly influenced the development of farming in the 50 states. Federal aid for land-grant colleges and universities is administered, for resident instruction, by the U.S. Office of Education and, for research and extension, by the Department of Agriculture. This aid, however, represents only a small proportion of the total institutional expenditures. State and local governments contribute more than twice as much as the federal government.

Resident Instruction. The main purpose of the land-grant colleges was, originally, to train for general farming. It was realized in the 19th century that rapid advances in science and technology demanded that the average farmer receive training beyond the secondary level—training that could be obtained best through resident instruction at the college level. In the 20th century, however, resident instruction in land-grant schools has concentrated increasingly on research, training for extension work, preparation of vocational agricultural teachers, and the development of specialists for aspects of the agricultural industry, such as soil testing, pest control, and improvement of stock breeding. The fields of service open to graduates in agriculture include —in addition to farming—agricultural business and industry, public agricultural service, research, college or high school teaching, and extension work.

By the mid-1960's, more than 50,000 students were enrolled for bachelor's degrees in agriculture. About 40,000 of these were studying in 65 land-grant institutions. There were about 15,000 graduate students enrolled in agriculture, mostly in the land-grant colleges. Bachelor's degrees earned in agricultural curricula numbered about 10,000 yearly; master's degrees, close to 2,500; and doctor's degrees, nearly 1,000.

Experiment Stations. The agricultural experiment stations, established with the help of the Hatch Act of 1887 and expanded by subsequent legislation, have become major features of the land-grant institutions. These stations serve a twofold purpose: they solve particular problems for the farmers of a region through research, and they train future research personnel.

Research in the experiment stations of the land-grant colleges has been a major contributor to the "technological revolution" that has characterized the American agricultural industry since World War II.

Extension Service. Another function of the land-grant colleges is to help operate one of the largest adult education agencies in the world, the Cooperative Agricultural Extension Service. The purpose of the Extension Service is to disseminate useful information, including the results of research in agriculture, home economics, and related subjects. Also, through its educational programs, the service helps families to apply this information on the farm, in the home, and to community problems. The American agricultural industry is so complex that agriculture can no longer be equated with farm production alone. Accordingly, the Extension Service has expanded its efforts to cover a wide range of problem areas, including marketing, consumer economics, resource development, and public issues of many kinds. In the 1960's the Extension Service began to work in towns and cities, offering nonfarm people help on such topics as health, gardening, and consumer economics.

The service is organized on four levels, which function cooperatively. On the federal level the program is handled by the Department of Agriculture and is operated by a small staff, headed by the administrator of extension work. On the state level, each of the 50 states has an extension director, with a staff of supervisors and subject matter specialists. Staff members, mostly connected with land-grant colleges, work with the third level. This third level comprises the county personnel, commonly referred to as county agricultural agents, home-demonstration agents, and Four-H Club agents. At the fourth level there are local volunteer leaders whose aid is indispensable in planning and executing extension programs. Volunteers, for example, help instruct more than 2 million boys and girls in Four-H Clubs.

The Extension Service has a nationwide professional staff of nearly 15,000 workers. Of these, more than 10,000 are on the county staff, close to 4,000 in the state headquarters and land-grant colleges, and about 100 in the federal extension office.

The county extension staffs employ several methods of instruction, usually in various combinations. These methods include demonstrations, office calls, farm and home visits, letters, bulletins, telephone calls, tours, group meetings, and short courses. Education also is carried on through mass media, such as radio, television, newspapers, and films.

Private Agencies. Nonpublic organizations play an important part in nonacademic agricultural education, both through research and through publication of information. Among these agencies are private research laboratories, seed companies, manufacturers of farm machinery, and distributors of such commodities as fertilizer and feed. The Department of Rural Education of the National Education Association distributes information on farm topics. The American Association of Land-Grant Colleges and State Universities concerns itself not only with those institutions but also with agricultural policy in general. In addition, many philanthropic foundations promote agricultural research and education in the United States and other parts of the world.

PROGRAMS AROUND THE WORLD

The worldwide scope of agricultural educa-

UNITED NATIONS veterinarians give farmers in the Democratic Republic of Congo advice on cattle raising.

tion can be shown by brief descriptions of programs in representative countries and regions.

Canada. Agricultural education in Canada was introduced into Methodist mission schools for Indians as early as 1826. Instruction in agriculture was begun in 1847 in the public schools of Upper Canada (corresponding roughly to present-day southern Ontario). Work on the college level began when a chair of agriculture was established at the University of Toronto in 1851. The first agricultural college, St. Anne's Agricultural School (now affiliated with Laval University), was opened at Ste. Anne de la Pocatière, Quebec, in 1859. The first institution that succeeded in taking agricultural education to the farmer through extension work was the Ontario Agricultural College, founded at Guelph in 1874. The success of this school led to the establishment of similar schools throughout the Dominion. By the 1960's each province except Newfoundland provided agricultural education in at least one college or university.

The rise of college-level agricultural schools led to the widespread introduction of agricultural education into the secondary schools, and by the 1960's most high schools offered such training. The Dominion Department of Agriculture provides supplementary agricultural education. It distributes agricultural publications, including audio-visual materials, maintains information services at experimental farms, and stages exhibitions.

Britain. It is a policy in Britain not to introduce vocational education directly into the secondary schools. However, many schools, particularly in rural areas, teach agriculture as part of the basic curriculum, often using the farm and the garden as practical aids to instruction. Boys and girls who leave school at 15 years of age may study farming techniques in continuation classes. Formal training is supplemented by Young Farmers' Clubs (similar to American Four-H Clubs), farm institutes, and county advisory services. In higher education, faculties of agriculture were first established at Edinburgh University in 1790 and at Oxford University in 1796. Agricultural faculties exist in many other leading universities.

In order to pursue one of the recognized careers in agriculture, graduates of all institutions giving agricultural instruction must qualify for national diplomas in agriculture. To win such diploma, a student must live on a farm for at least one year, in addition to passing an examination given by the National Agricultural Examinations Board.

West Germany. West German students who have successfully completed the *Gymnasium*, or classical language school, may work toward a degree in agriculture at one of the leading universities, such as Bonn, Göttingen, or Kiel. Certain technical universities also offer agricultural curricula but grant a diploma instead of a degree.

For students who have not completed the *Gymnasium* but who show an aptitude for agriculture, there are lower-level schools called *Ackerbauschulen*. These offer two- or three-year courses, including more practical experience during school terms than is given at the universities. Students who have completed only elementary school and wish to study agriculture may attend either part-time vocational schools or full-time agricultural schools.

France. In France, students who have completed elementary school at the age of 14, and who take up farming as a vocation, are required to follow an agricultural curriculum on an extension basis until they reach 17 years of age. There are seasonal schools of agriculture, usually open from November to March. Urban children can study agriculture in public or private agricultural apprenticeship schools.

On the middle level, children between the ages of 14 and 18 may attend practical or specialized vocational schools of agriculture. Instruction in the practical schools includes experimental work as well as farm experience. On the college level there are a number of national schools of agriculture. These institutions specialize in the relationship of the physical, biological, and economic sciences to agriculture. The course of study, which is both practical and experimental, lasts three years.

Africa. In Africa, as in Latin America and Asia, population growth has caused governments to give increasing emphasis to agricultural education. The pattern varies by countries, but three types of programs are widely offered. First, vocational agricultural training is provided in village schools, and in special schools of varying types, for young boys who may take up farming as a career. Second, schools of agriculture at less than college grade are operated to train high school graduates in technical agriculture. These graduates usually serve as extension agents, working with farmers to help them improve their crops. Third, colleges of agriculture exist in almost all African countries. Extensive efforts now are being made by these institutions to strengthen their professional staffs, expand physical facilities, widen the scope of research, enlarge student enrollments, and otherwise improve training for rural development.

India. By the mid-1960's India's population was nearly a half billion, and increasing food production became the country's most acute problem. Hence, developing higher levels of competence among farmers is a top priority interest of the government.

The Indian Council of Agricultural Education, founded in 1952, has made a great contribution to developing and systematizing agricultural education. Nine agricultural universities patterned after U.S. land-grant colleges and 31 agricultural colleges, together enrolling about 6,000 new students annually, have been established. To supplement basic courses, students are trained to work with farmers on experimental farms attached to the colleges. Below the college level, agriculture is taught in vocational agricultural schools and as one subject in multipurpose higher secondary schools. Moreover, the national extension service, with a staff of more than 50,000 workers, reaches all parts of the country. This staff is trained in the colleges of agriculture and in 126 extension training centers.

Latin America. Almost all Latin American countries offer agricultural education at the primary, secondary, and university levels. Most countries have university faculties in agricultural sciences, for example, at the University of San Simón in Bolivia and at the universities of Buenos Aires and La Plata in Argentina. The intermediate agricultural school is a common pattern at this level. Many countries have special programs in rural schools to give young people knowledge and skills they will need to work on the land. Each country has an extension service, patterned after the U.S. system, to offer agricultural education to country people.

International Programs. Since World War II, many public and private agencies have promoted agricultural education on an international scale. The Food and Agricultural Organization of the United Nations, the United States Agency for International Development, and the Foreign Agricultural Service of the United States Department of Agriculture engage in worldwide educational activities. For example, they promote the exchange of agricultural students, farm workers, and rural youth to encourage the interchange of ideas and techniques between countries. Much of the work of the American volunteers in the Peace Corps is closely related to agricultural education. In the mid-1960's the Peace Corps had 12,000 volunteers serving in 47 countries. Religious organizations aid international agricultural education by sending funds and teachers to agricultural schools in many countries. The Ford Foundation, the Rockefeller Foundation, and the Kellogg Foundation have made major contributions to agricultural education by supporting research, professional training, and consultant services and by building new schools.

See also AGRICULTURAL ENGINEERING; AGRICULTURAL EXPERIMENT STATION; AGRICULTURE, DEPARTMENT OF; COLLEGES, LAND-GRANT; FARMS AND FARMING; FEDERAL AID TO EDUCATION IN THE UNITED STATES; VOCATIONAL EDUCATION.

J. PAUL LEAGANS, *Cornell University*

Bibliography

Board on Agriculture and Natural Resources, *Sustainable Agriculture Research and Education in the Field: A Proceedings* (Natl. Academy Press 1991).

Blum, Abraham, *Teaching and Learning in Agriculture: A Guide for Agricultural Educators* (Food and Agric. Organization of the U.N. 1996).

Bor, Wout van den, et al., *Rethinking Rural Human Resource Management: The Impact of Globalisation and Rural Restructuring on Rural Education and Training in Western Europe* (Mansholt Inst. 1997).

Kunkel, H. O., and C. L. Skaggs, eds., *Revolutionizing Higher Education in Agriculture: Framework, Principles, and Agenda for Action* (Iowa State Univ. Press 2001).

Marcus, Alan I., *Agricultural Science and the Quest for Legitimacy: Farmers, Agricultural Colleges, and Experimental Stations, 1870–1890* (Iowa State Univ. Press 1985).

Price, David P., ed., *Modern Agriculture: Science, Finance, Production, and Economics* (SWI Pub. 1989).

Rao, A. N., ed., *Food, Agriculture, and Education* (Pergamon 1987).

Rogers, Alan, and Peter Taylor, *Participatory Curriculum Development in Agricultural Education: A Training Guide* (Food and Agric. Organization of the U.N. 1998).

Seevers, Brenda, et al., *Education through Cooperative Extension* (Delmar Pubs. 1997).

Spedding, C. R. W., ed., *The Human Food Chain* (Elsevier Pub. Co. 1989).

AGRICULTURAL ENGINEERING,

AGRICULTURAL ENGINEERING, ag-ri-kul'chə-rəl en-jə-nēr ing, is a specialized branch of engineering that is concerned with the design, development, and application of agricultural machinery, farm structures, farm power, and soil and water control. It is a profession that, in the broadest sense, had its beginning with man's first need and his struggle for existence.

The history of agricultural engineering begins with the cave, lean-to, or other crude shelter where early man housed his few domesticated animals, and it comes up to the modern mechanical milk-production plant. It also includes developments from the back-breaking toil of harvesting grain with the hand sickle and flail to harvesting grain with the self-propelled combine, which cuts, threshes, and cleans wheat at a rate undreamed of years ago. But its history does not stop with present-day developments, for the most fascinating chapters lie ahead and are yet to be filled with advances from the teams of soil physicists, agronomists, horticulturists, plant pathologists, animal scientists, farmers, and agricultural engineers working in agricultural technology.

In the solution of a given problem, it is very often necessary for the agricultural engineer to contribute as a member of a team. For example, in a problem of mechanizing the harvest of a given crop, the basic solution may not lie in the area of machine design or redesign, but in cooperation with the botanist or plant breeder in developing a new variety of plant that is better adapted to presently available machines. Once a solution is found, the team is dependent on the agricultural engineer, perhaps more than on any other member, to translate and carry the process or development into practical usage.

In view of the increasing emphasis in feeding and clothing the people of the world, the horizons of the practicing agricultural engineer are becoming international in character. The demand is great for service in overseas projects sponsored by land-grant colleges and universities, in federally supported programs, and with private industries as they expand their domestic operations to international proportions.

Professional Training. Young people interested in choosing agricultural engineering as a career should consider at first only the broad over-all engineering profession, which involves forces, materials, power applications, machine design and layouts, and the organization and management of human resources in relation to these fields. Later, the selection of a particular branch of engineering, such as agricultural engineering, may be considered. A liking for, and ability in, secondary school general science, chemistry, physics, and mathematics are excellent indicators for later success in engineering training.

Other factors that might lead the prospective engineer to select agricultural engineering include a rural or small-town background, which may result in an appreciation of rural life, including both its compensations and problems; an interest in the growing of plants and animals; an interest in problems involving food, including the better feeding of the peoples of the world; a desire to be a part of an improved engineering service to the oldest and still most basic of our industries; and a desire to help solve the multitude of engineering problems associated with the industry.

Also, since agriculture is a composite of some 5 million relatively small operations, the agricul-

AGRICULTURAL ENGINEERING

AGRICULTURAL ENGINEERS overcame the problem of frost damage to crops by designing this wind machine.

tural production unit is closely interrelated with the farmer's home. Thus an understanding of economic principles and their application is of particular importance for the agricultural engineer. Most often, he is faced with the need to solve engineering problems with a minimal capital outlay.

From an engineering standpoint, he is confronted with definite challenges, which include the weather, biological variables, and widely varying soils and soil conditions. These conditions point to the first basic requirement of the agricultural engineer—a thorough grounding in engineering fundamentals. In recognition of this requirement, many engineering colleges have developed a common program for all freshmen engineering students, with continuing similarity of studies during the second and part of the third year. Such a program appropriately provides for thorough grounding in mathematics, chemistry, physics, theoretical and applied mechanics, hydrology, hydraulics, electricity and magnetism, and other elements of the basic engineering curriculum.

There are approximately 47 professional agricultural engineering curriculums in the land-grant colleges and universities of the United States, and several educational institutions in Canada offer a program leading to a professional degree. During the past 25 years, engineering education has become dynamic, and curriculum builders, including those in agricultural engineering, have made real efforts to keep abreast of developments in technology. Accreditation standards, established by the Engineering Council for Professional Development (the recognized agency for the engineering profession), have been met by agricultural engineering curriculums at about 35 American colleges and universities. Many curriculums allow for some specialization, roughly corresponding to the areas of application in which agricultural engineers normally engage. These include farm power and machinery, farm structures, soil and water control, and electric power and processing. There is also an increasing appreciation of and demand for the agricultural engineer who is qualified to provide an integrated engineering service for a given agricultural operation that might include several or perhaps all of these areas.

Fields of Specialization. *Farm power and machinery* is the field in which the majority of agricultural engineers express a primary technical interest and find employment. Assignments in the field vary widely, but include design, research and development of experimental and prototype machines, testing, and sales. Such engineers may be employed not only with the so-called full-line farm machinery companies, but with manufacturers of component parts. Producers of petroleum products, manufacturers of crop-drying equipment, and a great number of other industries making products for the agricultural industry regularly employ agricultural engineers. Industrialists often consider them to be the best-qualified individuals to translate the needs of the farm operator to the manufacturer in language understandable to the latter.

Farms have become larger in size but fewer in number, while machines and mechanization are, in many instances, replacing the "hired man." American farmers have invested millions of dollars in farm machinery; for example, a farm tractor costing $7,000, and a self-propelling combine priced at twice this figure, are among the machinery that is used on many modern farms. Thus farming, as a way of life, is giving way to farming as a business. Competition among manufacturers of farm equipment has become as keen as in any other major line of business. Farmers also are becoming increasingly conscious of equipment costs and operating cost differentials, the efficiencies of machines, comfort factors, and built-in safety features. Agricultural engineers who are employed by manufacturers of farm machinery and equipment are offered ample challenge in this field to stimulate the development of the highest professional standards.

In the 1940's, the major interest of agricultural engineers was in getting electrical energy to the farm. This task has been essentially completed. The task ahead is to place electrical energy to work as a productive servant of agriculture, for there are a great multitude of farm tasks which an electric motor of fractional horsepower can perform at a cost of only pennies per day. Agricultural engineers who are specialists in the field of *electric power and processing* are busy at this assignment, working with power suppliers, manufacturers of electrical equipment, and distributors and retailers of electrical equipment. One phase that is receiving much attention in this field is the mechanical handling of materials where enormous volumes and weights are involved. For example, the amount of manure that is handled on American farms in a given

year is equivalent, in tonnage, to the annual steel production of the United States.

The trend toward fewer farms and larger operational units has resulted in larger animal population per farm. This trend brings about challenging problems in devising electrical equipment for environmental control measures, materials-handling methods and systems, and waste-disposal techniques. For example, electrical energy is applied on the farm in such machinery as the powered barn cleaner, which in a matter of minutes accomplishes one of the most disagreeable tasks of the dairy farmer. It is also applied in the mechanical handling of silage, including the unloading of frozen silage; in the pneumatic conveyance of grains and feeds, including the transport of materials in both low and high pressure air streams; in new mechanical and automatic systems of feeding livestock; in new concepts in the drying of grain to include both heat and refrigeration; and through automatic and simultaneous selection of eggs, according to their weight and color. Application of electrical energy as a power source in agriculture has only begun, and these are but a few areas in which research is being carried out.

In the field of *farm structures*, the agricultural engineer may be concerned with the design and construction of buildings that can withstand the pressure of a wide variety of farm goods, as for example silage, wheat, or pelletized feeds. Others in the field may be engaged in the design, manufacture, marketing, and erection of buildings for drying grain and hay, for the conditioning of other feeds, and for the processing of agricultural products. Their primary technical interest may be the application of new building materials and an improved application of old materials. The agricultural engineer is confronted with a major task in helping the farmer maintain, replace, and keep his buildings abreast of technological progress, for the farmer has more than one fifth of his total capital outlay invested in farm buildings.

Challenging problems are associated with farm buildings. It is generally true that the mechanization of field operations has surpassed similar modernizing developments in and around the buildings. However, the proportion of the time spent by the farmer in doing chores about the farmstead varies from as much as 80 percent in poultry and dairy farming to a low of 2 percent for cash grain farming. A striking illustration of this proportion is given in a report, made by the U.S. Department of Agriculture: The average number of man-hours of labor used to produce an acre of corn in a Midwestern state was reduced from 19.5 in 1910–1914 to 10.3 in 1938–1942, and to 7 in 1965. Top Midwestern farmers report figures of 2 and even less. It was estimated that 80 percent of the California tomato crop was harvested mechanically in 1966. In contrast, no change was reported in the man-hours required in the production of beef cattle and egg-laying hens, while a 5 percent increase was noted in the labor associated with dairying.

Crop mechanization extends to qualitative as well as quantitative aspects. A mechanical lettuce harvester, for example, has been developed that selects mature, salable heads and allows the immature heads to remain for further growth and subsequent harvest.

The agricultural engineer still has much to contribute, not only in the design of equipment

ENGINEERING principles were used to develop this high-velocity air blast sprayer for fruit trees.

for handling crops, but also in improved designs and layouts of buildings that will accommodate such equipment with a maximum of efficiency. In recent years, agricultural engineers have worked toward making farm buildings more flexible in the uses to which they may readily be adapted. The useful life of a farm building is considered to be from 40 to 50 years. However, the average tenure period for all farm operators in the United States is slightly more than 12 years; for tenant-operated farms, the tenure is not quite half this period. Thus, the design of the farm building may be based only on the requirements of one specific enterprise. Such a design is unrealistic from at least two standpoints. During its lifetime, the building will serve from 4 to 10 different operators, all of whom will have varying likes, dislikes, and capabilities in farming. Also, at a later time, price fluctuations, demand factors, and technological developments may indicate the desirability, or may even dictate the necessity, of changing the enterprise or abandoning it altogether in view of the inflexibility of the buildings. Because of the difficulties in extending planning horizons intelligently over the expected life span of a farm building, and the attendant inflexibility of its use, farm buildings sometimes have been considered as mere attachments to the land, with little tangible, productive worth. On many farms, it is not uncommon to find that buildings that have been built for a specific purpose are being used for miscellaneous storage.

In the field of *soil and water control*, agricultural engineers are usually employed and are most active in upper watershed development, which includes gully control, small retention dams, retaining walls, lined and unlined ditches, terraces, and other engineering aspects of soil and water control practices. Irrigation—until recently thought of in terms of arid regions only

—today is finding increased application in humid areas, particularly on high-value-per-acre crops. Surface and subsurface drainage—with the latter representing an annual investment of approximately $3 million by the farmers of a single Midwestern state—continues to present challenging problems. Agricultural drainage problems associated with highway and airfield developments are also of increasing concern to agricultural engineers. In the soil and water field, some of the problems facing engineers are the use of simple, yet reasonably accurate, means of determining when to irrigate; determination of the amount of surface flow from a watershed, the basic hydraulic nature of the flow, and the mechanics of soil erosion and subsequently its control; the use of plastics and other new materials in irrigation and drainage; the depth and spacing of drains; the movement of soil moisture; and waterplant growth relationships.

Such problems as these are attacked by civil engineers, soil physicists, agronomists, and other highly trained scientists. In the area of soil and water problems the agricultural engineer most often works as a member of a team, and the results of such work depend on the quality of the team effort.

Teaching and Research. Many agricultural engineers are employed by land-grant colleges and universities for teaching, research, and other public service responsibilities. The U.S. Department of Agriculture and other major departments and divisions of the federal government regularly employ agricultural engineers. In an increasing number of employment situations, the demand is for professional training that goes beyond the bachelor of science degree. Many leading colleges and universities now offer graduate programs leading to the master of science and the doctor of philosophy degrees. The success of agricultural engineers in private practice at-

349

tests to the demand that exists for comprehensive engineering services, particularly for some of the larger farming operations.

Professional Organization. Although the work of agricultural engineers is quite diverse, unity is provided through a continuing interest in engineering applications to agriculture and a professional society, the American Society of Agricultural Engineers. Founded in 1907 at the University of Wisconsin, the society now numbers over 6,000 throughout the world. Four technical divisions—one each for power and machinery, farm structures, electric power and processing, and soil and water—along with an education and research division, constitute the framework on which the program of the society is built. Six full-time members staff the national headquarters of the society, at St. Joseph, Mich. Cooperative relations with the American Society for Engineering Education, the Engineers' Council for Professional Development, the American Association for the Advancement of Science, and the Engineers' Joint Council help maintain the professional consciousness of the organization at a high level. More than 100 committees are actively engaged in widely varying professional and society activities. A student program is fostered by the parent society, and organized student branches are maintained at 44 American colleges and universities, three Canadian universities, and the Indian Institute of Technology at Kharagpur, India. The society has the important function of promoting and making available the literature of the profession. This is done mainly by a monthly journal, *Agricultural Engineering*, the yearly *Transactions of ASAE*, and the *Agricultural Engineers Yearbook*.

A problem that has hampered the advance of the profession since its inception is the shortage of trained manpower. This shortage is especially acute today. To cope with this problem, the society established the A.S.A.E. Personnel Service several years ago to facilitate contacts between agricultural engineers and their employers and generally to facilitate placement. The heavy demand for and relatively short supply of engineers still exist and are of continuing concern. An active program is under way to acquaint high school youth with the nature of this young and rapidly growing profession and the opportunities it offers. This program is sponsored by and participated in by the American Society of Agricultural Engineers, the departments of agricultural engineering in land-grant colleges and universities, industry, and other groups, and is aimed at increasing the enrollment in professional agricultural engineering curriculums. Through the national headquarters of the A.S.A.E., as well as through most departments of agricultural engineering, a motion picture is available. The film is entitled *Agricultural Engineering—The Profession With A Future.*

FRANK B. LANHAM, *University of Illinois*

Bibliography

Christianson, L. L., and Roger P. Rohrbach, *Design in Agricultural Engineering* (Am. Soc. of Agric. Engineers 1986).
Hall, Carl W., and Wallace C. Olsen, eds., *The Literature of Agricultural Engineering* (Cornell Univ. Press 1992).
Haygarth, P. M., and S. Jarvis, eds., *Agriculture, Hydrology and Water Quality* (C.A.B. Intl. 2002).
Roth, Lawrence O., and Harry L. Field, *Introduction to Agricultural Engineering: A Problem-Solving Approach*, 2d ed. (Van Nostrand Reinhold 1991).
Tollner, Ernest W., *Natural Resources Engineering* (Iowa State Univ. Press 2002).

AGRICULTURAL EXPERIMENT STATION, an institution in which systematic research is carried on to enlarge the body of scientific knowledge applicable to agriculture. In the United States this designation generally applies to the state agricultural experiment stations. Their purpose is to find answers to problems that farmers cannot solve by themselves.

History. The need for public sponsorship of institutions that would bring agricultural development through research and education was recognized early in United States history. In his last message to Congress on Dec. 7, 1796, President George Washington urged the establishment of public boards charged with collecting and diffusing information that would lead to a spirit of discovery and improvement. The idea was first written into law when the U.S. Congress passed "An Act to Establish a Department of Agriculture," signed by President Abraham Lincoln on May 15, 1862. On July 2, 1862, President Lincoln also signed an act "donating public lands to the several States and Territories which may provide colleges for agriculture and mechanic arts." These two acts, followed by the Hatch Act of 1887, signed by President Grover Cleveland on March 2 of that year, and the Smith-Lever Act of May 8, 1914, signed by President Woodrow Wilson, are the principal laws under which the U.S. Department of Agriculture and the state land-grant colleges and universities cooperate in "collecting and diffusing" scientific information for the farmers and the general public in the United States.

The modern type of agricultural experiment station, which combines laboratory study and field trials, came into being in Europe during the 1840's and 1850's. This was followed in the United States by the first agricultural experiment station, which was organized in 1875 in Connecticut. Between 1877 and 1888, agricultural experiment stations known as such were created in 14 states. In 13 other states the land-grant agricultural colleges carried on systematic research in laboratories and field experimental plots. The Hatch Act of 1887 authorized annual appropriations for payments to each state that would establish an agricultural experiment station for engaging in systematic, scientific research that would answer problems related to the agricultural economy of the state. Later laws that authorized additional federal-grant payments for research in the states were the Adams Act of 1906, the Purnell Act of 1925, the Bankhead-Jones Act of June 29, 1935, and title I, section 9 of the amendment of 1946 to the Bankhead-Jones Act. In separate legislation Congress also extended the authorizations for federal-grant research payments to Alaska, Hawaii, and Puerto Rico. In 1955 the Hatch Act of 1887 was amended to combine the separate authorizing acts into one, under Public Law 352. It was approved by President Dwight D. Eisenhower on Aug. 11, 1955.

The present-day purpose of the agricultural experiment stations is summarized in section 2, Public Law 352, as follows:

It is further the policy of the Congress to promote the efficient production, marketing, distribution, and utilization of products of the farm as essential to the health and welfare of our peoples and to promote a sound and prosperous agriculture and rural life as indispensable to the maintenance of maximum employment and national prosperity and security. It is also the intent of Congress to assure agriculture a position in research equal to that of industry, which will aid in maintaining an equitable balance between agriculture and other segments of our economy. It shall be the object and duty of the state agricultural experiment stations through the expenditure of the appropriations hereinafter authorized to conduct original and other researches, investigations, and experiments bearing directly on and contributing to the establishment and maintenance of a permanent and effective agricultural industry of the United States, including researches basic to the problems of agriculture in its broadest aspects, and such investigations as have for their purpose the development and improvement of the rural home and rural life and the maximum contribution by agriculture to the welfare of the consumer, as may be deemed advisable, having due regard to the varying conditions and needs of the respective States.

On July 22, 1963, President John F. Kennedy signed Public Law 88–74 to assist the states in providing the buildings, laboratories, and other capital facilities necessary to conduct the research of the agricultural experiment stations.

Organization. The agricultural experiment stations are the official bodies charged in their respective states with carrying on the publicly supported agricultural research of their institutions. In each case, a director is the official in charge. He is responsible only to his state authorities. There are 53 main agricultural experiment stations—two each in Connecticut and New York and one in each of the other states and Puerto Rico. All except the Connecticut Agricultural Experiment Station at New Haven and the Ohio Agricultural Research and Development Center at Wooster are responsible to the land-grant college or university in the state. The two named have separate governing boards.

The close relationship between the station and the land-grant college or university must be recognized in order to understand the continuing research operations. In addition to training undergraduate students in agriculture (many of them preparing to go into farming), the agricultural colleges train graduate students, the majority of whom become research workers or extension agents or enter a specialty in agriculture, veterinary science, or specialized fields of work in private business. Many graduate students carry on research for the experimental stations. While the experiment stations are concerned primarily with scientific research, and the extension services with farmer education, there is a close working relationship between the two on the land-grant college campus. Research and extension specialists frequently have offices together or near each other. Some specialists, especially heads of such departments as animal husbandry and agronomy, are responsible for leadership in both research and agricultural extension programs.

The agricultural experiment stations are responsible for scientific operations at about 500 centers, including the main stations, branch or substations, and outlying laboratories and farms. When the centers operated by the Department of Agriculture under special legislation are added to these, the publicly financed national establishments engaged in agricultural research total about 600. The need for such a widely dispersed activity is inherent in the geography of the area that comprises the United States and the territories. It presents a great variety of climatic factors, variations in soil types, and a great range of adaptable vegetative growth. There are five distinct climatic belts between east and west, and from north to south the range is from arctic to subtropic. A minimum of 514 type-of-farming areas have been identified, and soil scientists have described at least 5,500 soil series, with the num-

CROSS-BREEDING produces a new and better onion.

ber growing as a result of new surveys. In many states, farmers likewise are confronted with special crop problems arising from different soil types and climatic differences and with a variety of marketing and distribution problems, which explains the need for separate research locations that are directed from the main station.

Finance. Since 1887 the U.S. Congress has annually appropriated federal-grant funds for state experiment station research. These sums serve as an incentive to the states to seek additional public and private support of research that is directed toward solution of problems of agricultural production, marketing, and rural living in the states. The federal funds are of two principal types, those supporting specific projects at individual experiment stations and those supporting regional programs in which two or more state experiment stations join in the scientific study of regional problems. Scientists of the U.S. Department of Agriculture take part in the technical discussions of most regional committees, and the department is an active research participant in some of the regional projects. The amount of federal aid and the proportion to moneys expended,

LOGS are examined for damage by wood-boring insects.

AGRICULTURAL EXPERIMENT STATION scientists take X-ray photographs of an injured calf.

COLORADO A & M COLLEGE

from public or private sources within states have varied through the decades. However, since 1904, expenditures of nonfederal funds for conduct of research at the state agricultural experiment stations have exceeded expenditures from federal-grant funds. As present, the ratio of nonfederal to federal grant expenditures is approximately 3 to 1. The ratios for the 4-year period 1962–1965 were as follows:

RATIO OF NONFEDERAL TO FEDERAL GRANTS TO STATE AGRICULTURAL EXPERIMENT STATIONS

Fiscal year	Federal grants	Nonfederal	Ratio nonfederal to federal
1962	$34,700,000	$126,154,000	3.64
1963	36,670,000	135,980,000	3.71
1964	39,130,000	147,950,000	3.78
1965	45,925,000	158,299,000	3.45

Organizational machinery has been provided for a close coordination of research programs at the various levels. Since the state stations are autonomous institutions, the state-federal coordinative machinery has to be primarily on a cooperative basis. Devices for coordination include regional organization of state experiment station directors, who are affiliated closely with a national committee of experiment station directors; the national committee consists of nine persons who are authorized, under Public Law 352, to recommend use of regional research funds for cooperative regional projects, technical committees, and professional organizations in related disciplines through which there is a great deal of scientific collaboration on an informal basis. There is a minimum of supervision of federal funds that have been allotted to experiment stations. The director of each experiment station has primary responsibility but acts with the advice and counsel of a small technical and administrative staff in the department, which also is responsible for coordinating state and federal research to avoid unnecessary duplication. Since passage of the Hatch Act of 1887 the secretary of agriculture has been charged by law with certain specific responsibilities in the administration of federal-grant funds in the states. For many years the department maintained a small technical and administrative staff known as the Office of Experiment Stations. In 1942, when the Agricultural Research Administration was created, the Office of Experiment Stations became a part of that agency. Under a departmentwide reorganization undertaken in 1953 the Agricultural

Research Administration was renamed the Agricultural Research Service, and the office was renamed the State Experiment Stations Division. In subsequent reorganizations the division was renamed the Cooperative State Experiment Station Service in 1961 and the Cooperative State Research Service in 1963. Its administrator was made responsible to the secretary of agriculture for the administration of federal-grant payments. Administrative and technical staff members who are directly concerned with the payment-to-states program visit each station and review, with the individual scientists and department heads, all research conducted under earmarked federal-grant and related projects. They also take part in meetings of technical committees that have been assigned to a total of 200 cooperative projects carried on with regional research funds. Lines of communication also are maintained by administrative letters and publications.

Achievements. In the 1964–1965 fiscal year the state experiment stations issued a total of 741 periodicals; 906 bulletins, circulars, and reports; 9,295 articles in scientific journals; and 656 miscellaneous publications. In addition, 862 popular and 1,314 technical reports, bulletins, and circulars were processed by the stations. The research personnel of the state experiment stations in 1965 included 3,466 staff members devoting full time to station research. There were an additional 6,629 who divided their hours between research and teaching or extension work.

Agricultural research—as carried on in the dual system of publicly sponsored research in the United States, in close cooperation with the agricultural extension services and with wholehearted cooperation from farmers, scientific bodies, and private industry—has made many major contributions toward a rapidly advancing farm technology. During World War I, American farmers produced needed food and fibers with 13½ million workers; during World War II they met the all-out requirements with 10½ million workers; and in 1965, only 6 million workers were needed to produce crops in abundance. In 1965 one farm worker was able to produce all the food and fiber necessary for himself and 30 other persons. Productivity of the American farmworker in the 1950's increased by 5.4 percent a year. Such productivity generally is recognized in other countries as a major achievement in history.

E.C. ELTING, *Agricultural Research Service*

Egyptian wall painting from the Tomb of Menena in Thebes, dating from about 1415 B.C., shows a harvest scene.

AGRICULTURE, History of,

AGRICULTURE, History of, ag'ri-kul-chər. Agriculture is the systematic raising of useful plants by human management. Food production is the main reason for agriculture, but cultivated plants also furnish substances useful as textile fibers, dyestuffs, medicines, and ornaments. Gathering wild plants for food or other purposes is not agriculture. The crucial innovation that separated wild plant gathering from true agriculture was the deliberate planting of seeds and other plant material. Cultivation, harvesting, and processing were byproducts of this innovation.

In a broad sense, "agriculture" often includes animal husbandry, which is closely associated with plant raising. On the other hand, "agriculture" can be used in a limited technical sense to refer only to raising field crops; in this usage it is differentiated from horticulture (gardening) and arboriculture (orcharding). The present article deals with plant cultivation of all kinds—field, garden, and orchard—from the viewpoint of the history of human culture.

Other articles provide information on other aspects of agriculture. The origins of animal husbandry are described in ANIMALS, DOMESTICATION OF. Modern agriculture is covered in FARMS AND FARMING and in articles on specific animals and crops such as CATTLE and WHEAT and on special topics such as IRRIGATION.

Man has lived by farming for only a short time. For most of his existence—now believed to extend to protohuman forms as much as 2 million years old—man lived as a wild plant gatherer and as a hunter. Deliberate plant raising began only about 10,000 years ago. In this relatively brief period, farming has made possible revolutionary changes in human life. Human population has greatly increased, partly because more people could be fed. Moreover, agriculture has been a major factor in transforming human societies from small, primitive local bands into huge, technologically advanced nations. Agriculture does not by itself create civilization, but without agriculture civilization cannot develop.

THE NEOLITHIC REVOLUTION

Hunting and wild plant gathering were sufficient for the world's small human population until the close of the Pleistocene period, 12,000 to 10,000 years ago. The melting of the continental ice sheets of the last glaciation brought a return of milder climates and led to rises in sea level and major shifts in both plant and ani-

mal life. Several important game animals became extinct, and the growing scarcity of game appears to have caused a shift to more intensive harvesting of wild seeds and roots. Improved seed-collecting methods, storage baskets, and seed grinders developed near the beginning of what archaeologists call the Neolithic, or New Stone Age. Evidence of a stage between wild plant gathering and systematic agriculture comes from Owens Valley in eastern California, occupied by the Paiute Indians. The Paiutes increased the yield of wild grasses by building rock and earth checkdams to slow the runoff of water and by harvesting seeds. The fundamental difference between this and true agriculture is that the grass was not planted, but seeded itself.

The first real cultivation was probably incidental and casual, begun by people having no notion that they were embarking on a momentous phase of cultural evolution. It was during the Neolithic period that the actual change from hunting and gathering to food production, the so-called "Neolithic revolution," occurred. This "food-producing revolution"—the incipient phase and the interval between the achievement of agriculture and the advent of urban life—lasted almost 4,000 years. The establishment of permanent agricultural villages had (and still has) certain disadvantages: Farming peoples who are overly dependent on a single starch staple often suffer from nutritional deficencies. Closely built villages promote communicable diseases. Stored surpluses invite enemy attack, and growing crops are subject to destruction by storms, floods, or insect ravages in ways that wild resources are not. Cleared tropical forests spread malaria. Irrigation farming in tropical areas favors transmission of liver flukes from snails to barefoot farmers. Because of such factors it is probable that the development of agriculture brought about significant biological changes in man, apart from its effect in promoting population expansion.

Wild plant gathering did not cease with the advent of farming. Nuts, berries, various greens, fruit, and mushrooms are still gathered wild even in the most advanced agricultural countries. Moreover, most of the world's wood products still come from wild forest growth, although replanting (or "tree farming") is increasing.

Evidences of Early Farming. There are no written records of the actual beginnings of agriculture, but it is clear from archaeological findings that the earliest agriculture, in the Middle East and in the New World, preceded pottery making, one of man's ancient crafts. The carbonized remains of clearly domesticated plant forms have been unearthed in early sites. Finds of farming tools are another line of evidence, although early stone or wooden implements may also have been used by nonfarming food collectors. In later times hoe blades were made of polished stone, bone, or shell. Plows, unambiguous evidence of farming, appeared no earlier than about 3000 B.C. in the Middle East. In some areas traces of old field patterns exist, but the best evidence of farming is found around the buildings where crops were stored and processed.

Botanical evidence, based on studies of the distribution range of plants, indicates fairly conclusively that wheat, barley, and rice originated in the Old World and that maize, potatoes, and manioc came from the Americas. With the advent of writing, records became important evidence. Certain ancient peoples left well-illustrated documents, the earliest of which come from Egypt and Mesopotamia. Many crops and farming methods are described in the Old Testament. The ancient Greeks and later Romans compiled treatises on plant life. A handbook written by the Carthaginian Mago was captured by the Romans and used as a source book for Roman agriculture. A history of Chinese agriculture was written about the 5th century A.D. Medieval Persian, Arabic, and European writings on farming are numerous.

Despite the variety of archaeological and historical evidence, however, it is difficult to trace the geographical diffusion of early cultivated plants. Conclusions about dates and routes by which plants were spread in ancient times remain conjectural. Only in recent times have precise records become available. For example, a recent instance of plant diffusion involving the Brazilian rubber plant is well documented. The seeds of the rubber plant were smuggled from Brazil to the Royal Botanical Gardens at Kew, near London, in the 1870's. From there they were taken to Ceylon and the East Indies.

CENTERS OF EARLY AGRICULTURE

Archaeologists have determined that there were a number of centers in which farming developed. It has also been possible to trace, within broad limits, the spread of many crop plants and farming techniques around the world.

Southwestern Asia. From the archaeological evidence, southwestern Asia—including most of what is now called the Middle East—seems to have been the earliest agricultural focus. This region was the homeland of wheat and barley and of the chief Old World domestic animals and the site of the invention of the plow. Influence from this ancient center spread into Europe, Africa, across the rest of Asia to Malaysia and Indonesia, and after 1500 A.D. to almost all inhabited parts of the world.

In addition to wheat and barley, the Middle Eastern area furnished rye, peas, lentils, broadbeans, onions, garlic, carrots, grapes, olives, dates, apples, pears, cherries, flax, and a great many other plants. At the lowest level excavated at Jericho in Jordan, agricultural artifacts have been found dating from 9500 B.C.; at this time hunting and gathering were still important. By around 8000 B.C. emmer wheat and barley were being grown by villagers in a wide zone, extending from Asia Minor to western Iran and south

into Israel and Jordan. Neolithic sites, with evidences of agricultural beginnings, have been discovered in Iraq, Jordan, Turkey, and Cyprus.

The widespread Mesopotamian Halaf Culture, which appeared by 4500–4300 B.C., introduced the use of flax, and the Ubaid Culture in southern Iraq initiated irrigation on the lower Tigris-Euphrates plain. Eventually, with its greater farming efficiency, Ubaid-type culture spread into the Halaf area to the north. Prior to this movement farmers relied on rainfall and natural flooding, with varying success. As irrigation systems grew, rules for water usage and coordination of planning and labor to keep the systems in repair helped achieve legal and political integration over larger areas. Some areas that are now desert were converted by irrigation into productive farm regions in ancient times. The Negev in southern Israel and part of southwestern Arabia, where a dam was built in 600 B.C. at Marib, are examples of this transformation.

With the appearance of city-states, writing developed in connection with keeping records of grain and other tribute payments and of land management. By 3000 B.C., plows pulled by oxen were in use in Iraq and Egypt. This use of oxen for plowing was one of many ways in which agriculture and animal husbandry became interdependent. Special crops such as alfalfa and sweet clover, both probably from Iran, were grown for forage. Animal dung was used to fertilize fields, and stock were grazed on stubble. Oxen sometimes were used to tread out grain on threshing floors or to drag flint-studded sledges over harvested grain ears. With the invention of the wheel, animal labor could be used in irrigation and in milling or to haul farm produce into market towns.

The first wheat grown was emmer, little different from its wild ancestor, which was probably native to the Syria-Palestine area. However, einkorn wheat also was cultivated. Emmer predominated in Iraq and Egypt until Graeco-Roman times. Einkorn spread from Asia Minor into southeastern Europe. Today's bread wheats are hybrids of emmer and einkorn.

Egypt. The basic ideas of agriculture spread into Egypt from southwestern Asia sometime before 4500 B.C. The water from the usually dependable Nile flood made farming along the river extremely productive, and the annually replenished silt made fertilizer unnecessary. Many of the plants and grains from southwestern Asia and the Middle East were readily adapted to Egyptian soil. In addition to the vegetables and fruits from the southwest Asian area, the Egyptians grew date and doum palms, flax, lotus, ornamental shrubs, and some papyrus, although this was usually gathered wild. Cotton was being grown in the Sudan by 300 B.C., but linen remained the standard Egyptian textile. Cotton did not replace flax until the Arab period of the 7th century A.D. By the time of the Ptolemies (323–30 B.C.) water wheels were being used to raise irrigation water from the Nile. Egypt became a major wheat source for Rome.

Europe. The basic pattern of plant domestication in Europe was imported from Asia Minor prior to 6000 B.C., as shown by sites at Nea Nikomedeia (6220 B.C.) and Argissa in Greece. From there farming spread to the rest of the Balkan Peninsula, up the Danube Valley into Europe, and eastward to the Ukraine. The main crops were einkorn wheat and barley.

By 4500 B.C. farming was replacing hunting and gathering in the Rhineland, Belgium, and Holland and in Poland. Fields were tilled with the digging stick. Heavy forest soils were avoided, and farming spread mainly into areas of easily worked light, sandy soils. Incipient agriculture based partly on local "weeds" like the ribwort plantain reached Denmark between 4000 and 3000 B.C. By the latter date farming was under way in most of Spain and Portugal, France, Italy, Switzerland, and central and southwestern Europe and had even penetrated to England. By 2500 B.C. all but the coldest parts of Europe were at least semiagricultural.

The Lake-Dweller villages of late Neolithic and Bronze Age Switzerland and Scandinavia furnish valuable data on early crops, showing gradual forest clearing and increasing plant cultivation. In the Aegean and in southeastern Europe farmers equipped with bronze tools and the plow developed trade in olive oil and wine about this time. Olives and grapes were well suited to the eastern Mediterranean area, and they spread westward from there. In general, however, bronze was too expensive for common farm tools, and implements continued to be of wood and stone. Remains of English field patterns showing cross-plowing have been dated not long before 1000 B.C.

European plant domesticates included oats, woad used as a dye, white goosefoot for coarse porridge and bread, certain apples, cherries, plums, figs, and carob—the last two possibly originating in North Africa. Cabbage resembling kale was grown in Bronze Age Europe. During the Iron Age, beginning around 1000 B.C., the climate of northern Europe grew colder, forcing greater reliance on rye, oats, and various so-called "weeds" that are no longer cultivated. Rye and oats were originally weeds that intruded into wheat and barley fields. However, since they were hardier than wheat or barley, they came to be planted along with the latter and could be saved if cold weather destroyed the other crops.

By 400 B.C. cheap iron permitted a much wider use of metal plowshares and iron colters for cutting the sod in England. Milling was improved by the use of rotary stones, which were depended on by Roman legionary bakers. In Rome, farming efficiency declined as Roman power and wealth increased. This was partly because the very large estates (latifundia) were worked by the apathetic slave labor that replaced Roman freedmen farmers. During this period Celtic and Germanic tribesmen introduced well-made farm wagons and exceedingly large plows. Also about this time water power was first applied to grain milling somewhere between Rome and China. Numerous improvements followed, indicating the close relationship between agriculture and mechanical invention. About the 6th century A.D. the invading Anglo-Saxons introduced heavy plows to England along with a method of farming in long, narrow strips. Between the 7th and 10th centuries A.D. the Persians invented windmills that were carried west in the wave of Arab conquest. By the 12th century, windmills were being built in England, although water mills were far more common.

The Muslims who first invaded Spain and Portugal in the 8th century brought several crops, including alfalfa, rice, and sugarcane, along with their windmills. Rice and sugarcane had come to the Arabs from farther east. Farming in north-ern Europe was meanwhile pushed to its northernmost limits with the crops available. However, these crops did not yet include the potato.

The breakup of Roman administration and economic organization was followed by the rise of feudalism. At the same time trade declined and the cities lost population. Self-sufficient manorial estates spread over much of Europe, managed by stewards and worked with serf labor, commonly on a three-field system. This method involved long narrow fields plowed by ox teams and rotated from winter wheat to barley, oats, or broadbeans, or left fallow. Under the English feudal system, flax was raised extensively, although wool also was important, and hay and leaves were harvested for forage. Long-handled scythes replaced sickles in northern Europe, especially for haying.

Africa. In the Mediterranean coastlands of Africa, farming was not greatly different from that of southern Europe. Africa south of this coastal strip received its earliest crops by diffusion along the Nile; farming had reached the Sudan near Khartoum around 3500–3000 B.C. The Sahara, though less a desert and more a grassy steppe at this period, could support farming only in a few oases, and was a major barrier to the southward diffusion of Mediterranean agriculture.

The Niger Basin was a significant early focus of African agriculture. It has been estimated that farming started in the basin about 4500 B.C., with many distinctively African crops including fonio (a native grain), pearl millet, Guinea corn, an African rice independent of the Asian species, and the oil palm. It is possible that sesame and cotton also were first cultivated in the Upper Niger Basin.

The Upper Nile Valley obtained wheat, dates, and probably certain millets, as well as cattle and the plow, from Egypt and, in the case of Ethiopia, probably also from southern Arabia. Although Ethiopia has been considered a notable focus of early agriculture, the only important crop unquestionably originating from the Ethiopian highlands is coffee.

Around 1 A.D. various southern and eastern Asian crops were brought by sea to the Somalia coast. From there they were diffused westward into central Africa along a corridor south of the grasslands. These crops included bananas, taro, yams, and sugarcane. Migrant farmers and herders with iron tools and weapons moved into the Congo forests and beyond, where their farming and cattle raising obliterated several hunting populations. Other farming peoples moved south into the Lake Victoria area, where the chief crops were millet and, in forested areas, bananas and yams. Between 200 B.C. and 500 A.D. vast areas of south central Africa became agricultural or pastoral or both. The farming was plowless, with women doing most of the hoeing and harvesting, as had been the case in the earliest agricultural communities. Beer was a major end product of grain production. A few sub-Saharan Africans practiced irrigation and constructed terraces, but labor-saving devices generally were lacking. Persian and Arab traders who settled on the East African coast in the latter part of the first millennium A.D. introduced Asian rice, betel pepper and areca palm (for chewing), mangoes, coconuts, and other plants. But they left local farming to African slaves and did little to improve it.

Southern Asia. About 3000 B.C. the first crops

spread overland from Iraq and Iran into southern Asia. By 2500 B.C. a flourishing civilization began to arise in the Indus Valley. Crops were bread wheat, barley, dates, cotton, and perhaps rice. At the time much of the rest of the Indian subcontinent was probably without agriculture, although India may be the homeland of rice, sugarcane, jute, and other plants.

The Indus civilization collapsed around 1500–1300 B.C., about the time that Indo-European or Aryan-speaking barbarians invaded from the northwest. The newcomers brought no new crops or farm techniques of importance and allowed the existing irrigation systems to deteriorate. A long "dark age" ensued, although farming spread slowly over much of the Indian subcontinent. The northwest (West Pakistan and the Punjab) remained primarily a wheat region. Elsewhere, the staples were millet or rice. Oil seeds also were important. Bananas, mangoes, and other fruits, and coconuts and various spices and dyestuffs grew in southern India. Around the beginning of the Christian era the spice trade of southern India and Ceylon became important to Roman and Persian markets. Eastward extensions of this trade established links with Indonesia and southeast Asia and served as a transmission belt for various agricultural crops and techniques. In southern India and Ceylon large earth-walled irrigation reservoirs, or "tanks," were constructed in this period.

Central Asia. The same wheat- and barley-farming pattern was established in central Asia as in northwestern India. These crops spread overland through Iran into what is now Soviet Turkestan. Other crops included millet, rye, rice, grapes, peaches and apricots, and various melons. Irrigated farming replaced hunting and fishing in the marshy areas around the shores of the Aral Sea, and a chain of farming oases spread gradually eastward into Chinese Turkestan (Sinkiang). Western archaeologists believe that Neolithic agriculture reached the North Chinese by this route. Siberia played a marginal role in the growth of world agriculture. What farming there was in Late Neolithic or Bronze Age times south of Lake Baikal, eastern Manchuria, and the Vladivostok area came from North China.

Eastern Asia. This area also benefited from the overland diffusion of the southwest Asian wheat complex. Root and rhizome (rootstock) crops such as yams, taro, and bamboo, along with bananas, lotus, local millets and sorghums, soybeans, and rice are native to the subtropical Far Eastern region. About 2500 B.C. the Neolithic North Chinese grew two kinds of millet, kaoliang sorghum, dry rice, hemp, wheat, and probably mulberry. Irrigation was present by about 1500–1050 B.C., but wet rice was not cultivated until a later date. The Chinese population grew at the expense of tribal "Southern Barbarians," some of whom migrated farther south into the Indochina peninsula. By this time the migrants also had wet-rice farming and metal tools and weapons, enabling them to displace in turn still more backward tribes.

Plowing in China did not begin until sometime before the Han dynasty (202 B.C.–220 A.D.). Horses began to be used for plowing around 100 B.C., after the invention of the horse collar by the Chinese. Over several centuries the use of horses for plowing spread westward. By way of the central Asian land route that served the thriving silk trade the Chinese acquired wine grapes, apri-

cots, peaches, and other plants from Persia. Hemp and ramie were the common fiber plants until cotton came into China over the Silk Road during the Sung dynasty (10th–13th centuries A.D.). Buddhist monks in China began to drink tea around 300–500 A.D., and in the course of several centuries tea growing increased in southeast China and was introduced to Japan in the 12th century. Chinese tea was traded into central Asia, Siberia, and eventually to Russia by caravan routes. Tea drinking was later adopted by the British, who established tea plantations in India and Ceylon, breaking the Chinese monopoly in the 19th century.

Feudalism ended in China during the Han dynasty (202 B.C.–220 A.D.). But in contrast to the situation in Europe, the end of feudalism was not followed by a revolution in agriculture. Drastic modernization of Chinese agriculture is a recent phenomenon. However, Chinese farmers have long been receptive to new plants and have invented or adopted ingenious methods of irrigation, cultivation, and processing.

Other areas of eastern Asia benefited from the Chinese experience. Korea received its agricultural pattern from China during the first millennium B.C. Japan adopted rice farming from China by way of Korea a few centuries B.C. but northern Japan remained a hunting and fishing area for several hundred years. Wheat and barley are still grown in Korea and Japan, but whereas Japan adopted the tea plant, tea growing never became important to the Korean economy.

Southeast Asia. Vietnamese agriculture is largely of the Chinese type, since northern Vietnam was a Chinese province for nearly 1,000 years. In the rest of Southeast Asia, agriculture is a mixture of the possibly older root-crop pattern indigenous to the area and diffusions from China (spread by southward migrating ethnic groups), from India, and, since the 16th century, from the Americas. The more backward hill tribesmen (who are often called Montagnards) living on the Southeast Asian mainland and the Indonesian and Philippine archipelagoes exhibit a generally plowless agriculture. These mountain tribesmen grow dry upland rice, yams, and, in the last few centuries, sweet potatoes and maize. Wet-rice farming in the river valleys, coastal plains, and deltas is believed to have spread southward around 500 B.C., stimulating population expansion in this area. Around the beginning of the Christian era Indian merchants established trading centers on the mainland of southeast Asia and in Indonesia for tropical spices and similar products. The resultant interchange of crop plants makes it difficult to determine whether a given plant originated in the India-Ceylon area or the Southeast Asia-Indonesia-Philippine region. Migrating peoples spread the betel pepper vine and the areca palm, now found from East Africa, over much of south and Southeast Asia and Indonesia, far into Melanesia. The wide distribution of turmeric, saffron, spices, flavorings, and food dyes in the same area is also attributed to migrating tribes.

Oceania. Agriculture in New Guinea and the Pacific islands remained somewhat primitive until modern times. Australian aborigines developed no indigenous agriculture. Perhaps no more than 2,500 years ago southeast Asian root crops were diffused to New Guinea and the rest of Melanesia by canoe migrants. Micronesia and Polynesia received their first settlers and agriculture around the same period. The main Oceanian crops are taro, yams, coconuts, bananas, sugarcane, bread-fruit, mangoes, bottle gourds, arrowroot, and melons. Many interior New Guinea tribes have only a limited agriculture.

The Americas. North and South American agriculture stems from the domestication of indigenous American plants. The few possible pre-Columbian diffusions from the Old World are of minor significance. Hunters and gatherers migrated to the Americas from Siberia by way of the Bering Strait and spread out over the Americas. By 7000–6000 B.C. some local plants were cultivated by Indians in southern Mexico, initiating a process similar to that under way only slightly earlier in the Old World, but with strikingly different botanical resources. Possibly around the same time Indians in the forests of eastern North America began to experiment with plant cultivation, although definite evidence is not available. With the deterioration of big-game hunting, wild seeds were collected and milled on stone slabs. The pace of American agriculture was slower than in the Middle East, perhaps because of a dearth of domesticable animals. Eventually, the llama and alpaca were domesticated in Peru and Bolivia. Neither the plow nor the wheel was invented in the New World, and nearly all laborsaving devices were lacking. In contrast to the Old World there were few if any long-distance contacts by sea. Despite these limitations New World native farming exhibited several noteworthy accomplishments.

Southern Mexico is considered the first center of New World agriculture. Hunting and gathering persisted as the backbone of the economy from about 6000 B.C. to 1500 B.C. The first crops were chile peppers and avocados. Findings in caves of northeastern Mexico show bottle gourds, peppers, and pumpkins to be the earliest cultivated plants there. Maize (Indian corn) first appeared as a cultigen around 5000 B.C. in Coxcatlan Cave in the Tehuacán Valley. Conversion of maize into a dietary staple was slow. Later, maize was diffused with beans and squash, which were often planted together. Squash appeared in the Tehuacán Valley about 5000 B.C. and beans about 3000 B.C. This crop complex spread into northwest Mexico by 2500 B.C. Irrigation was established in the Puebla region by 900 B.C., although really large-scale irrigation was not undertaken. Manioc and some potato varieties entered from South America. Other crops included grain amaranths, cotton, agave, cactuses, tobacco, and cacao. Cacao pods were used as a medium of exchange. Altogether, the Middle American Indians cultivated over 100 plant species, in which they carried a brisk regional trade. Although Old World crops were introduced by the Spanish, the basic pre-European crops are still extremely important. See also ARCHAEOLOGY.

Maize came into the area that is now the United States from northwestern Mexico about 2000 B.C. Bat Cave, New Mexico, is the earliest known site of maize in the United States. Simple ditch irrigation to aid the cultivation of maize, beans, and squash began around 1 A.D. in southwestern Arizona. Improved varieties of maize and cotton were planted between 500 and 800 A.D. The Hohokam Culture in southwestern Arizona developed canal irrigation. On the Lower Colorado River crops could be irrigated by natural flooding, as had been done along the Nile. Farming was a male task, as it had become in Mexico, since hunting was no longer profitable.

The Southwestern Indians still carry on the essentials of their farming tradition, although some crops and tools were adopted from the Spanish.

In what is now the eastern United States signs of incipient agriculture appear after 1000 B.C. The first crops of Mexican origin to reach the area were gourds and squashes. The Atlantic coastal tribes continued to subsist by hunting, fishing, and gathering, as did most of the peoples in the southeast, until a few centuries B.C. By 700-1000 A.D. more effective farming spread out from the middle Mississippi region, with improved maize, sweet corn, beans, sunflowers, pumpkins, and tobacco. Most farming in eastern North America was women's work, although in parts of the southeast, men tilled the fields. Most of the eastern forest area was uncleared, and farm plots were confined to the light river-bottom soils. This farming pattern spread into the Great Plains along rivers. Tribes farther to the west and northwest raised only tobacco.

South America was a focal area for some major plant domestications, although its first agriculture appeared somewhat later than in Mexico. The oldest prepottery coastal farm villages of Peru, dating from 4700 to 3000 B.C., have yielded chile peppers, squash, beans, and various roots and tubers. Cotton was grown in Peru earlier than in Mexico and was somehow hybridized with an Asian species around 2500 B.C. About 1500 B.C. maize entered South America from Central America and seems to have encouraged population growth and cultural advancement. The peanut, originating in Brazil, spread across the Andes to the Pacific coast. By 800 B.C. the lower coastal valleys were being intensively farmed. New forms of maize, avocados, sweet manioc, kidney beans, and other crops were added. Both the sweet and white potato and various cultigens still confined to western South America were being grown by the early centuries A.D. Canal irrigation began on the north Peruvian coast by 200 A.D. Settlement expanded into the high Andean valleys, the peoples relying chiefly on potato and quinoa. By the time of the Spanish conquest of Peru in the 16th century over 100 varieties of potato alone were present. As in Middle America, plowless agriculture, unaided by labor-saving devices and with only llamas for transport, provided the basis for a populous empire at a Bronze Age level of technology.

Less is known of early farming in Ecuador and Colombia. Cultural expansion was associated with maize farming, which may have started in Colombia by 3000 B.C. In Chile most of the Andean crops were grown, although potatoes were the staple crop. Sweet potatoes and sweet manioc apparently originated on the eastern Andean slopes—as did the narcotic coca.

The tropical forest lowlands of South America developed an agriculture based on root crops such as manioc, the cultivation of which may go back to 1000 B.C. Other crops were sweet potatoes, peanuts, gourds, chile peppers, pineapples, beans, a native tobacco, dyestuffs, and cotton. Modern Indians of the tropical forests also grow yams, sugarcane, and citrus fruits, obtained through contact with European cultures.

DEVELOPMENTS SINCE 1500

After the time of Columbus, world agriculture exhibited a rapid interchange of crop plants and farm techniques as a result of overseas exploration and colonization. As contacts multiplied, world agriculture was transformed. Maize, potatoes, better species of beans, tobacco, chile peppers, pumpkins and squashes, new cotton strains, tomatoes, and manioc were some of the crops brought from the New World in exchange for sugarcane, bananas, yams, okra, wheat, oats, barley, alfalfa, wine grapes, citrus fruits, and other Old World tropical or Asian crops. Numerous domestic animals were introduced to the New World by the colonizers, who also brought the plow, such wheeled devices as water- and millwheels, and iron metallurgy. Certain crops, such as bananas, were introduced specifically to feed slaves. White potatoes were brought from western South America to Europe about 1565 and are said to have reached Ireland by 1580. They were not grown in New England, however, until the early 18th century. By the early 19th century, potatoes were becoming the mainstay of north and central European peasants.

Commercial sugarcane production came to center in the West Indies. Tea, coffee, and chocolate became habitual beverages. The coffee center moved first from Ethiopia and western Arabia to Java, Malaya, and India, and then to Brazil in the late 19th century. Cacao is now produced mainly in West Africa. Cotton overtook older fibers such as flax and wool to become the world's chief clothing material. Cotton growing in the United States modified the agricultural landscape of much of the southeastern area. In modern times cotton growing expanded in Egypt, India, the Sudan, Soviet Central Asia, and China. Specialty crops previously grown on a small scale became prominent during this era of expanding international commerce. The many new plant species available after 1500 stimulated botanical studies.

Four principal agricultural developments have taken place since about 1500: (1) a gradual enrichment of local subsistence farming with new crops and methods but without a drastic break with the past—typical of much of Asia, Africa, and the remoter parts of Latin America and Oceania; (2) persistence of native peasant farming with new crops and methods but with control of land and marketing largely by an alien elite—characteristic of much of Latin America until quite recently; (3) development of a plantation system involving concentration on a single crop and cheap imported labor in regions of previously scanty population and low or nonexistent agriculture; and (4) virtual replacement of the native population by colonists with new crops and methods, common to agriculture in the United States, Canada, Australia, parts of Latin America, and southern Africa, where there was initially small population and little agriculture.

These developments were long-term processes. In Europe the medieval manorial system was abandoned gradually. Serfdom persisted in the Russian empire, and agriculture in much of eastern and southern Europe languished under oppressive semifeudal conditions. Economic thinking shifted from the mercantilist theories of maintaining a favorable trade balance at all costs to the ideas of the 18th century Enlightenment, which stressed the importance of agriculture or exaggerated farming as the sole creative occupation. Later, increasing population and trade volume and the application of technology to farming led to agricultural improvements. In Britain and elsewhere there were advocates of farm reform, including, in the United States, Benjamin Franklin and Thomas Jefferson.

Progress in industry and transportation helped raise the level of agricultural efficiency and the processing and distribution of farm output. The leading countries in the modernization of agriculture were the United States, Canada, Australia, New Zealand, and Britain and other northwest European countries. Governments began to take an active part in agricultural promotion, setting up colleges, organizing land surveys and rural settlement programs, and mapping soils. Most of the more advanced countries established ministries or departments of agriculture, centralizing many of these functions, and today nearly every country has a similar department. Problems of the economic welfare of farmers stimulated political movements, and sporadic peasant uprisings that had been a feature of European history began to assume a coordinated pattern.

Modernization has not been limited to peoples of European origin. In Asia, most notably in Japan, great strides have been made. Mainland China has made tremendous efforts with varying success to overcome numerous difficulties brought on by an expanding population. India, Pakistan, and much of the rest of southeast and southern Asia are making slow agricultural headway. Sub-Sahara Africa, apart from a few favorable areas, is, however, occupied by poor farmers and herders. Much of Latin America suffers from agrarian poverty, although it is generally less extreme than in Asia or Africa. The Middle East, homeland of agricultural beginnings, today presents a somewhat unfavorable agricultural picture. The gap between modern farmers in the United States, Canada, western Europe, Australia, and New Zealand and the subsistence farmers of India, Pakistan, or African tribal areas is enormous.

The outlook is hardly optimistic, despite the rate of improvement in the most advanced countries. Growing food shortages in large underdeveloped countries have evoked concern over the increasing population explosion. A related problem is environmental pollution, the effects of which go far beyond crop damage. Waterways and soils are being polluted with sewage, industrial waste, garbage, and insecticides, and the atmosphere is being seriously modified by contaminants. In the rapidly growing urban and industrial areas of the world, fine farmland is being built over thoughtlessly.

Although man has depended increasingly on agriculture for a period of 10,000 years, he has been applying science to its problems systematically for less than 200 years. If agriculture is to continue to support mankind's expanding billions, rapid and far-reaching changes will be required in the backward, traditional, and poverty-stricken areas that comprise two thirds of the world's farming communities.

GORDON W. HEWES, *University of Colorado*

Bibliography

Atak, Jeremy, and Bateman, Fred, *To Their Own Soil* (Iowa State Univ. Press 1987).
Carter, Vernon G., and Dale, Tom, *Topsoil and Civilization*, rev. ed. (Univ. of Okla. Press 1981).
Cohen, Mark N., *The Food Crisis in Prehistory: Over Population and the Origins of Agriculture* (Yale Univ. Press 1979).
Gompertz, M., *Corn from Egypt: The Beginning of Agriculture* (1928; reprint, Arden Library 1979).
Gras, Norman S., *History of Agriculture in Europe and America* (Johnson Reprint 1968).
Mellaart, James, *Earliest Civilizations in the Near East* (Thames and Hudson 1965).

AGRICULTURE, U.S. Department of, ag'ri-kul-chər, an executive department of the U.S. government. USDA, as the department is commonly called, is divided into five areas of public policy: farm commodity and international programs, product marketing and inspection services, natural resources and the environment, food and consumer services, and rural community development. Those five areas show the complexity and the range of tasks assigned to USDA. The department's jurisdiction extends far beyond farm policy and the growing of food. Only about one-fifth of the department's budget and personnel were allocated to farm and ranch problems in the early 1990s. That allocation of resources represents the most significant change in the history of USDA.

Founded in 1862, USDA originally was a small science agency devoted to the development and distribution of better seed and plant stocks. The department started with fewer than 10 employees who, despite their small numbers, were given a very broad charge. Today USDA employs more than 110 thousand full-time workers and spends approximately $65 billion annually, depending on economic conditions and resulting subsidy payments. These expenditures make USDA the fourth largest cabinet-level department. Another indicator of USDA size is the scope of its responsibilities. The farms, components of the food and fiber industrial system, wholesalers and retailers, and forests under USDA jurisdiction encompass about 15% of gross domestic product (GDP).

USDA and the Agricultural Policy Revolution. USDA's very founding was a matter of considerable controversy. As early as 1776, advocates within the federal government had argued for such an organization, but they encountered two persistent obstacles that prevented the creation of the agency, even when Pres. George Washington proposed the idea again in 1796. The general political belief in a constitutionally limited government, one that worked under laissez-faire principles, led to considerable resistance to new agencies and policies of government, including agriculture with its vast social importance in a largely rural nation where 40% of the population farmed. The second obstacle stemmed from regional disagreements within the United States. While the North and the expanding West were populated by small independent farms and ranches that often existed at subsistence levels, agriculture in the South was dominated by large plantation owners. Their tenants and even existing small landowners counted for little. This North-South division played into conflicts over a limited versus a more active federal government. Small-scale northern agriculture faced problems of national importance: continued farm failures, low farm incomes, and the inability to move from subsistence to commercially successful agriculture.

Advocates for a department of agriculture believed that agriculture could become a viable economic sector if the government promoted the modernization and commercialization of farm practices. These advocates emphasized the need for better science and production management as the means to an improved farm economy. They identified three strategic components considered essential to accomplish these goals: improved research and development of superior production methods, education to improve the farming and technical skills of producers, and outreach from government to distribute scientific advances locally to those producers who needed assistance. Despite the seemingly innocuous contribution of those three strategies, the South and its representatives in government refused to accept them.

Southern plantation agriculture, with its emphasis on cotton and tobacco and its dependence on slave labor, was already commercially successful. Education and outreach to small southern farmers and tenants, moreover, was thought to be undesirable to plantation operations. A knowledge-based and economically successful small-scale agriculture in the South, it was feared, would change the social and economic class structures of that region. Furthermore, successful development of the West would hurt the cause of slavery. The South for years quite logically blocked the creation of USDA as well as other plans for agricultural development through government intervention.

The Civil War changed that successful resistance, only because southern state congressional delegations went home from Washington upon secession from the Union. Congress and the Lincoln administration acted promptly to found the long-desired national agriculture agencies and to put into effect other parts of science and development plans.

The Act of Establishment for the new department, which was not given cabinet status until 1889, was only one of four pieces of federal legislation that marked the unusual departure of government away from a limited economic role into one of conscious activism and sector development. Science and development needs also led to the 1862 passage of the Homestead Act, which opened up less-prime western land to promote the westward expansion of agriculture; the Morrill Land Grant College Act, which transferred federal lands to the states for building agricultural and industrial colleges; and the Transcontinental Railroad Act, which hastened westward expansion by creating access for farmers, ranchers, their products, and supplies. Government, through agriculture and USDA, was well on its way to a significantly expanded role in public service. The exit of the South from the Union not only produced the Civil War, it also created a modest revolution in the way U.S. government dealt with the domestic economy.

USDA and the Agricultural Establishment. USDA, after that modest revolution, was only the cornerstone for agricultural modernization and commercial development in the United States. Many organizations came to be included in government's "agricultural establishment." As the land-grant colleges developed in each of the states, they became prime vehicles for reaching producers and disseminating information. The land grants, as state institutions that worked closely with state government departments of agriculture, were joined by federally mandated and supported experiment stations under 1887 legislation. Those research stations were set up in each of the states, usually sharing facilities and space with college employees. From cooperative efforts between the states and USDA emerged a complex partnership arrangement for both governing and promoting agriculture. The most significant act of cooperation was the development of a system of outreach efforts by agricultural professionals to bring science directly to farm families. Early cooperation proved so successful that, in 1914, this outreach arrangement was given legal status with the creation of the Extension Service within USDA. (See also AGRICULTURAL EDUCATION and AGRICULTURAL EXPERIMENT STATION.)

While USDA's Extension Service coordinated farm outreach activities, the actual operation of programs in each state fell to the land-grant colleges. The experiment stations and state departments of agriculture frequently became at least informally involved as well, by sponsoring research and mandating new programs. USDA, with this cooperation in place, extended its involvement in farm practices far beyond the policy planning circles of Washington, D.C. As problems of chronic farm surplus and low prices continued in the 20th century, USDA programs grew to encompass farm commodity price supports, soil conservation efforts, disease controls, and farm and rural housing loans. Each of these programs as well as the Extension Service were administered locally in nearly every county within the nation. This resulted in more than 15,000 local USDA offices, many of whose thousands of employees were hired by boards and officials. Matters became so organizationally complex and interdependent that former USDA secretary Edward R. Madigan frequently observed in the 1990s that he was never able to get an accurate count of how many employees actually worked for USDA and how much money they spent.

Despite the logistical difficulties of cooperation and accountability, this extended agricultural establishment grew and managed the single biggest domestic policy venture in U.S. history. While USDA was a critical participant, particularly in planning and policy development, the works of the land grants, experiment stations, state departments, and local county offices were no less instrumental to the national effort to modernize and commercialize the nation's farm sector. USDA continues to make much of its impact on American agriculture through cooperation with these other establishment organizations.

A New USDA. As the farm population contracted from 40% of the U.S. population to less than 2%, USDA and agricultural policy in general faced extensive criticism. Consumer, welfare, environmental, and other public interest groups who became intense critics of USDA complained about spending large amounts on programs that were designed primarily for farmers and about the relative neglect of the food and fiber interests of the rest of society. The Nixon administration proposed eliminating USDA entirely, while the Carter administration wished to transfer many of its food programs to other federal agencies, such as the Food and Drug Administration. The Clinton administration did, however, close and consolidate many field offices in 1994, striving to save $3.6 billion.

Two circumstances have kept USDA vital and largely intact. First, the department has always enjoyed strong support from its farm clientele. These clients, often through farm and agribusiness interest groups, have considerable political influence within Congress. This has kept USDA's budget growing rather than contracting. Second, USDA became a leader in cultivating new clients beyond its traditional farmer base. These efforts began in the 1970s as USDA agencies were added or expanded to provide services in areas such as food stamps, infant nutrition, world food needs, international trade, food safety, environmental protection, animal welfare, and numerous other social and economic causes popular with the public and the news media. USDA not only reallocated farm program budgets to support those efforts, it also encouraged other components of the agricultural establishment to serve the new clientele.

The expansive mission statement developed in 1862 made these moves possible. The overall result has been a new USDA, one that has significantly expanded its emphasis on agricultural development. It is often argued that there are really two USDAs at the beginning of the 21st century: the national leader of efforts to improve the agricultural economy and a socially concerned public agency that extensively regulates agriculture's relationship with the rest of society.

WILLIAM P. BROWNE
Central Michigan University

SECRETARIES OF AGRICULTURE

Name	Term	Under president
Norman J. Colman	1889	Cleveland
Jeremiah M. Rusk	1889–1893	Harrison
J. Sterling Morton	1893–1897	Cleveland
James Wilson	1897–1913	McKinley, T. Roosevelt, Taft
David F. Houston	1913–1920	Wilson
Edwin T. Meredith	1920–1921	Wilson
Henry C. Wallace	1921–1924	Harding, Coolidge
Howard M. Gore	1924–1925	Coolidge
William M. Jardine	1925–1929	Coolidge
Arthur M. Hyde	1929–1933	Hoover
Henry A. Wallace	1933–1940	F. D. Roosevelt
Claude R. Wickard	1940–1945	F. D. Roosevelt
Clinton P. Anderson	1945–1948	Truman
Charles F. Brannan	1948–1953	Truman
Ezra T. Benson	1953–1961	Eisenhower
Orville L. Freeman	1961–1969	Kennedy, Johnson
Clifford M. Hardin	1969–1971	Nixon
Earl L. Butz	1971–1976	Nixon, Ford
John Knebel	1976–1977	Ford
Bob Bergland	1977–1981	Carter
John R. Block	1981–1986	Reagan
Richard E. Lyng	1986–1989	Reagan
Clayton K. Yeutter	1989–1991	G. H. W. Bush
Edward R. Madigan	1991–1993	G. H. W. Bush
Mike Espy	1993–1994	Clinton
Daniel R. Glickman	1995–2001	Clinton
Ann M. Veneman	2001–2005	G. W. Bush
Mike Johanns	2005–	G. W. Bush

Bibliography

Baker, G. L., *The County Agent* (Univ. of Chicago Press 1939).
Benedict, M. R., *Farm Policies of the United States, 1790–1950* (Twentieth Century Fund 1950).
Browne, W. P., *Cultivating Congress* (Univ. Press of Kans. 1995).
Hadwiger, D. F., "The Old, the New, and the Emerging United States Department of Agriculture," *Public Administration Review* 36 (1976):155–165.
Hamilton, D. E., *From New Day to New Deal* (Univ. of N.C. Press 1991).
Hansen, J. M., *Gaining Access* (Univ. of Chicago Press 1991).
Hurt, R. Douglas, *The Department of Agriculture* (Chelsea House 1987).
Rasmussen, W. D., and G. L. Baker, *The Department of Agriculture* (Praeger 1972).

AGRIGENTO, ä-grē-jen'tô, a city in Italy, in southwestern Sicily. It is 57 miles (92 km) southeast of Palermo and about 3 miles (5 km) from the sea. Until 1927 it was called Girgenti.

Agrigento is the capital of Agrigento province, a hilly area whose highest point is Mount Cammarata (5,239 feet, or 1,597 meters). The two main rivers of the province are the Platani and the Salso. Olives, almonds, grapes, and wheat are the major agricultural products. Local fisheries yield tunny, coral, and sponge. In the eastern part of the province, sulfur and rock salt are mined. The sulfur industry is chiefly concentrated around Agrigento, Porto Empedocle, and Licata. Porto Empedocle is the province's principal port.

The city of Agrigento, known in ancient times as Agrigentum or Acragas, was founded about 582 B.C. by Dorians from the Greek colony at Gela. Favorably situated for commerce with Carthage, it became one of the most important Sicilian cities of the day. It was ruled from about 570 to 554 B.C. by the tyrant Phalaris, who reportedly roasted his victims in a brazen bull until he was put to death in the same manner. The city prospered until 406 B.C., when it was captured and plundered by the Carthaginians. Although it never fully regained its former power and wealth, it enjoyed a lively trade in agricultural products, textiles, and sulfur after it was taken by the Romans in 210 B.C.

Remains of a remarkable group of Greek temples are located on the site of the ancient city. Among them are two temples incorrectly attributed to Hera and Concordia and the gigantic Temple of Zeus, with a 25-foot (7.5-meter) reconstructed figure of a telamon (a male figure used as a supporting column). Population: 54,619 (2001 census).

AGRIMONY, ag'rə-mō-nē, the common name for a genus of plants with five-petaled, yellow flowers containing notched petals and 7 to 20 stamens. The elongated end of the stem that bears the flower is covered with hooks and encloses a small, dry, one-seeded fruit. Agrimony belongs to the family Rosaceae. Its genus, *Agrimonia*, has 10 species, found in the northern temperate zone, Brazil, and South Africa.

AGRIPPA, Marcus Vipsanius, ə-grip'ə (63–12 B.C.), Roman statesman and general, who was the most trusted and able of the friends of Emperor Augustus. He fought at Augustus's side in many military expeditions. In 31 B.C. he commanded the fleet at Actium that defeated the forces of Antony and Cleopatra.

Augustus bestowed various honors on Agrippa. He was consul three times and governed several important provinces. After he married the emperor's daughter Julia, he became the heir designate of Augustus, sharing with him the tribunician power and the *imperium maius*, which gave him command over other provincial governors. Agrippa built many public works in Rome, including the original Pantheon (built 27–25 B.C.).

On his death in 12 B.C. in southern Italy, Agrippa's body was carried to Rome, where Augustus himself delivered the funeral oration. The body was interred in the mausoleum of Augustus.

ARTHER FERRILL
University of Washington

AGRIPPA I and II. See HEROD AGRIPPA I; HEROD AGRIPPA II.

AGRIPPINA, ag-rə-pī'nə, the name of two notable Roman women. Vipsania Agrippina (c. 13 B.C.–33 A.D.), called Agrippina Major, was the daughter of Marcus Agrippa and Julia, daughter of Emperor Augustus. About 5 A.D. she married the popular prince Germanicus, the heir-designate of Emperor Tiberius. She accompanied her husband on many military expeditions. When Germanicus died unexpectedly in Antioch in 19 A.D., she returned to Rome convinced that Tiberius had had a hand in his death. Her animosity resulted in ruthless court intrigue, until finally in 29 A.D. Tiberius banished her to Pandateria, where she starved to death. She bore nine children, including the emperor Gaius, known also as Caligula, and Julia Agrippina.

Julia Agrippina (c. 15–59 A.D.), called Agrippina Minor, was first married to Domitius Ahenobarbus. Their child Nero later became emperor. During the reign of her brother Caligula (37–41 A.D.) she became involved in a conspiracy against him and was banished from Rome. She was allowed to return when her uncle Claudius became emperor following Caligula's assassination. In 48 A.D. the emperor's wife Messalina was executed for adultery and treason. Agrippina courted her uncle until he agreed to marry her. Even though Claudius had a son, Britannicus, by his previous marriage, Agrippina induced him to name Nero as heir-designate. She had taken every step to prepare Nero for the throne, including the appointment of the Stoic philosopher Seneca as his tutor.

In 54 A.D., Claudius died—some believe he was poisoned by Agrippina—and Nero was proclaimed emperor. From the beginning of Nero's reign, Agrippina quarreled with her son and interfered in affairs of state until Nero ordered her murder in 59 A.D.

ARTHER FERRILL, *University of Washington*

AGUADILLA, ä-gwä-thē'yä, a seaport town on the northwest coast of Puerto Rico, 70 miles (115 km) west of San Juan. The University of Puerto Rico and the Inter American University of Puerto Rico have branches there. Aguadilla is a trading center for an agricultural district that produces sugarcane, coffee, tobacco, and fruit. Straw hats and cigars are manufactured in the town, and sugar is refined there. Aguadilla was founded in 1775. Population: 16,776; municipio, 64,685.

AGUASCALIENTES, ä-gwäs-kä-lyän'täs, a small inland state of Mexico, bounded on the south by Jalisco state and on the other sides by Zacatecas. It has an area of 2,158 square miles (5,589 sq km) and is part of the central Mexican plateau. Elevations in the state average 6,000 feet (1,830 meters). The climate varies from subtropical in the southwest to cool in the north, mainly because of differences in altitude. Numerous streams compensate for a light rainfall. The state, whose name means "hot waters," has many mineral springs, the most popular of which are near the city of Aguascalientes, the capital.

Primarily agricultural, Aguascalientes produces excellent cattle, mules, sheep, and horses. Its crops include corn, chick-peas, grains, fruit, vegetables, sugarcane, and tobacco. There are extensive forests. The state has silver, gold, lead, and copper mines, but its mineral wealth is not extensively developed. Manufacturing is concentrated in the capital city. Population: 944,285 (2000 census).

AGUASCALIENTES, ä-gwäs-kä-lyen'täs, a city in central Mexico and the capital and industrial center of Aguascalientes state. The city is situated on a plateau about 6,180 feet (1,880 meters) above sea level, roughly 265 miles (426 km) northwest of Mexico City. It was named Aguascalientes, which means "hot waters," after the many hot mineral springs that dot the area.

The city is built over a labyrinth of tunnels, presumably dug by prehistoric Indians for unknown reasons. Chief points of interest include the Municipal Palace, the churches of San Marcos and San Antonio, and San Marcos Garden.

The Spanish conquerors of Mexico first reached the site of Aguascalientes in 1522, when Hernán Cortés sent an expedition under Pedro de Alvarado against the Chichimec Indians. The Spaniards established a military base on the site in 1575, and for many years it remained a small outpost in a hostile wilderness. It became important in the early 1800s, when silver was discovered nearby, and was made the capital of Aguascalientes state in 1835. The city is famous in modern Mexican history as the site of the Convention of Aguascalientes (1914), an unsuccessful attempt to settle differences among the rival revolutionary leaders Pancho Villa, Emiliano Zapata, and Venustiano Carranza. Population: 643,419 (2000 census).

AGUESSEAU, Henri François d', à-ge-sō′ (1668–1751), French chancellor. He was born in Limoges on Nov. 27, 1668. As procurator-general of France from 1700 to 1717, he opposed interference by the Holy See in the affairs of the French church. When Pope Clement XI, in the bull *Unigenitus* (1713), condemned Pasquier Quesnel's commentary on the New Testament, d'Aguesseau resisted publication of the bull in France.

Under Louis XV, d'Aguesseau was three times chancellor of France (1717–1718, 1720–1722, and 1727–1750). In this office he effected important reforms in the administration of justice but failed in his attempt to produce a unified legal code. He died in Paris on Feb. 9, 1751.

AGUILAR, Grace, ä-gē-lär′ (1816–1847), Anglo-Hebrew author, who wrote religious books and novels. Born in London on June 2, 1816, she was the daughter of a Sephardic (Spanish) Jewish merchant. She began writing at an early age. Her first books, including *The Spirit of Judaism* (1842), *The Women of Israel* (1845), and *The Jewish Faith* (1846), concern the religion and history of the Jews. In these she emphasized spiritual and moral values and deprecated formalism.

She was better known, however, for her fiction, which won her a wide following in the second half of the 19th century. *Home Influence* (1847) was her only novel published during her lifetime. The others were edited by her mother and published posthumously. They include *The Vale of Cedars* (1850), *A Mother's Recompense* (1850), *Woman's Friendship* (1851), and *The Days of Bruce* (1852). Her novels are sentimental, domestic, and pious but have a certain charm. She died in Frankfurt am Main, Germany, on Sept. 16, 1847, and was buried in a Jewish cemetery there.

AGUINALDO, Emilio, ä-gē-näl′dō (1869–1964), Philippine revolutionary general and president. Emilio Aguinaldo was born on March 22, 1869, in Kawit, Cavite province. He briefly attended Letran College in Manila but left to help his family manage their extensive lands.

In 1895 Aguinaldo became Kawit's municipal captain (mayor). That year he was inducted into the secret Katipunan revolutionary society. On Aug. 31, 1896, shortly after the Katipunan was exposed, he disarmed the Spanish *guardia civil* in Kawit and the next day captured nearby Imus.

Among the victories that followed, his greatest was his defeat of Spanish regulars in the Battle of Binakayan, on Nov. 10, 1896.

On March 22, 1897, the Tejeros Convention chose Aguinaldo president of the revolutionary government. When Andres Bonifacio disputed the election, he was tried and executed for treason. In November, Aguinaldo's constituent assembly approved a republican constitution, but a military impasse between the Spaniards and the guerrillas produced a truce in December. Aguinaldo went into exile in return for a general amnesty, Philippine representation in the Spanish Cortes (parliament), and full civil rights for Filipinos.

Shortly after the outbreak of the Spanish-American War in April 1898, Aguinaldo returned after U.S. Comdr. George Dewey had defeated the Spanish fleet in Manila Bay on May 1. When asked to let his troops be replaced by newly arrived U.S. forces, Aguinaldo withdrew to Malolos, where, on June 12, national independence was proclaimed. The first republic, with Aguinaldo as president, was inaugurated on Jan. 23, 1899.

This act defied the Treaty of Paris, by which Spain had ceded the Philippines to the United States; as a result, the Philippine-American War broke out on Feb. 4, 1899. Though ill-equipped for guerrilla warfare in the tropics, U.S. troops eventually triumphed. Aguinaldo, driven into the mountains of Isabela province, was betrayed by Macabebe scouts from Pampanga and was captured on March 23, 1901. On April 1 he swore allegiance to the United States, although other Filipino generals fought on for another year.

Aguinaldo retired to Kawit until 1935, when he ran unsuccessfully for the presidency against Manuel Quezon. His threat to raise 60,000 veterans to prevent the inauguration of Quezon, who he feared would be dictatorial, was peaceably deflected. In his seventies during the Japanese occupation, he was required to read ghost-written radio appeals to the defenders of Corregidor, urging them to save Filipino lives by surrendering. But he adamantly refused to join his own ex-general, Artemio Ricarte, who wanted to lead Japanese troops against the Americans. Aguinaldo died in Quezon City on Feb. 6, 1964.

GRETCHEN CASPER
University of Michigan

AGULHAS, Cape, ə-gul′əs, the southernmost point of Africa, about 100 miles (160 km) east-southeast of the Cape of Good Hope. The Portuguese named it Agulhas (meaning "needles") because of the saw-edged reefs and sunken rocks that extend from the shore and make navigation dangerous. The meridian of Cape Agulhas (20° E) marks the dividing line between the Atlantic and Indian oceans. The Agulhas Banks are excellent trawling grounds.

AHAB, ā′hab, king of Israel from about 875 to about 853 B.C. He was the son and successor of Omri. The biblical account of the reign of Ahab is found in I Kings 16:29 to 22:53, recording that he succeeded his father and reigned for 22 years. He did evil in the sight of the Lord, principally by marrying Jezebel, the daughter of the king of Tyre, and by building places of worship to her god Baal. Moreover, Ahab permitted her to obtain for him a vineyard he wished to have, by causing its owner, Naboth, to be falsely accused of cursing God and the king and then stoned. Jezebel also caused a number of priests of Yahweh, the God of Israel, to be slaughtered.Israel was subjected to divine punishment in the form of a serious drought, as foretold by the prophet Elijah.

Ahab, with Obadiah, the governor of his house, tried to take measures to alleviate the drought. Elijah arranged a dramatic contest between himself, as the prophet of Yahweh, and the prophets of Baal on Mount Carmel. Elijah prayed to his God, and the prophets of Baal to their gods. Elijah's prayer was answered when God set fire to an offering on an altar; thus Elijah was victorious. He had the priests of Baal slaughtered, which earned him the enmity of Jezebel. The end of the drought followed.

Elijah prophesied the death of Ahab and the end of his dynasty because of the Naboth incident. The story related in I Kings concludes with an account of Ahab's alliance with Jehoshaphat, the king of Judah, and their battle against Ben-hadad, the king of Syria, to regain Ramoth-Gilead. Ahab was killed in this battle.

This biblical narrative about the reign of Ahab combines two opposed views of the king. According to popular tradition, Ahab was a brave, capable, and popular king. In the priestly view, on the other hand, he was an ungodly ruler. As finally written down, the narrative appears intended to emphasize monotheism and high ethical standards, and most of it is unfavorable to Ahab. Its context and other sources, however, show that politically and militarily Ahab was a prince of great energy and resource.

An inscription on the Moabite Stone, an ancient record found in Jordan, indicates that Ahab crushed an insurrection on the part of the Moabites. (See MOAB.) He made the kingdom of Judah an ally and perhaps a vassal. By his marriage to Jezebel he gained the neutrality and perhaps some resources of the kingdom of Tyre.

The fact that 400 priests of Yahweh prophesied before him previous to his last campaign indicates that he did not desert Yahweh. Ahab felt, rather, that his first duty to his country and its religion was to prevent absorption by Syria. Conquest would have ended both the Kingdom of Israel and the maintenance of its religion.

AHASUERUS, ə-haz-ū-ē′rəs, in the Old Testament, a king of Persia, identified by some scholars as Xerxes I. He banished his first wife, Vashti, and married Esther, a beautiful Jewish maiden who was the niece of Mordecai, a court official. Esther succeeded in having Ahasuerus spare the Jews from extermination, as threatened by Haman, the king's minister, who hated Mordecai. The festival of Purim commemorates this deliverance of the Jews. See also ESTHER, BOOK OF.

Another Ahasuerus in the Old Testament is identified with Cambyses II, son and successor of King Cyrus the Great of Persia (Ezra 4:6). A third Ahasuerus is referred to in Daniel 9:1 as the father of Darius the Mede.

AHAZ, ā′haz, in the Old Testament, a king of Judah, succeeding his father, Jotham, about 735 B.C. During his reign (recounted in II Kings 16 and II Chronicles 28) he introduced the worship of Syrian idols, for which he was censured by the prophet Isaiah. When Pekah, king of Israel, and Rezin, king of Syria, allied against Assyria, they invaded Judah to force Ahaz to join them. Against the advice of Isaiah, Ahaz appealed for help to Tiglath-pileser, king of Assyria, to whom he sent Temple treasures. Assyria defeated Syria and ravaged northern Israel, but Judah became its vassal, and Assyrian deities were introduced into the Temple at Jerusalem.

AHAZIAH, ā-hə-zī′ə, the name of two kings in the Old Testament. The first was a king of Israel. After the death of Ahaziah's father, King Ahab, the Moabites rebelled against paying tribute to Israel. Before Ahaziah could take action against them, he died of injuries from a fall through a window of his palace, as related in the Second Book of Kings, chapter I.

The second Ahaziah was a king of Judah. With an uncle, Jehoram, king of Israel, he served in the campaign against Hazael, king of Syria. After a reign of one year, Ahaziah was slain, along with Jehoram, while trying to suppress a revolt led by Jehu under the guidance of the prophet Elisha (II Kings 9:27).

AHENOBARBUS, ə-hē-nō-bär′bəs, the name of a Roman plebeian family. Its members included Gnaeus Domitius Ahenobarbus, who served as a tribune about 104 B.C., as pontifex maximus in 103, as consul in 93, and as censor in 94. Lucius Domitius Ahenobarbus, his son, was consul in 54 and succeeded Caesar as governor of Gaul in 49. He supported Pompey in the civil wars and was killed after the Battle of Pharsala in 48. Gnaeus Domitius Ahenobarbus, son of Lucius Domitius, was governor of Bithynia in 40 and consul in 32. He deserted Mark Antony for Octavian at Actium in 31 and died shortly thereafter. He is the character Enobarbus in Shakespeare's *Anthony and Cleopatra.*

AHIDJO, Ahmadou, ä-ē-jō′ (1924–1989), first president of independent Cameroon. He was born on Aug. 24, 1924, the son of a Fulani chief, in Garoua in the northern region of French Cameroun and received his secondary education in Yaoundé. Ahidjo worked in the post office and became leader of the Young Muslims movement, working particularly to improve understanding between the northern and southern parts of the country. In 1947 he was elected to the newly created Territorial Assembly and was reelected in 1952. In 1953 he was elected to the Assembly of the French Union in Paris and became its vice president in 1956. In the same year he was reelected to the Territorial Assembly.

Ahidjo was vice premier and minister of the interior in the first African cabinet in French Cameroun, formed in 1957. Unable to agree with the premier, he founded his own party, the Union Camerounaise, and became premier in 1958. Ahidjo was elected president of the republic after independence in 1960 and retired from office in 1982. Accused in 1983 of plotting a coup, he left the country and was sentenced to be executed. He died in Dakar, Senegal, on Nov. 30, 1989.

AHIMSA, ə-him′sä, a Sanskrit term for the ethical principle of noninjury to living creatures. As practiced in its most extreme form by the Jains of India, and to a lesser extent by Buddhists and Hindus, *ahimsa* requires people to avoid bringing injury to any living organism. It is a fundamental principle of yoga. Gandhi's principles of nonviolence were based on *ahimsa*. See also HINDUISM—*Beliefs and Practices*; JAINISM.

AHMAD SHAH DURRANI, ä'məd shä dōōr-rä'nē (1724–1773), the first amir of Afghanistan. A chief of the Abdali tribe, he extended his sway over the other Afghan chieftains during a period of Persian dominion over the Afghans. In 1747, on the assassination of Nadir Shah of Persia, the Afghan chiefs declared themselves independent and elected Ahmad as their shah. Ahmad then changed the name of the Abdali tribe to Durrani (Pearl) and took Durrani as part of his title. In a series of attacks on the weakened Mughul empire of India, he captured Lahore and Kashmir in 1748 and sacked Delhi in 1756.

AHMADABAD, ä'məd-ə-bäd, the principal city of Gujarat state in western India and one of the largest cities in the country. Presently the state's industrial and cultural center, Ahmadabad (also spelled *Ahmedabad*) was temporarily its capital (1960–1969) until replaced by Gandhinagar. The city is on the Sabarmati River about 280 miles (450 km) north of Bombay and 500 miles (800 km) southwest of Delhi. It is noted for its cotton mills and exquisite architecture.

The city is one of the busiest industrial centers in India and is well served by airlines and railroads. More than a quarter of Gujarat's factories are located here, and, with Bombay, it is one of India's two great cotton-milling centers. Other manufactures include tobacco, glass, silk brocades, carpets, and ivory and copper crafts.

Ahmadabad is rich in beautiful mosques, tombs, and gateways built in the 15th, 16th, and 17th centuries, some of which combine Muslim and Hindu styles. The Jami Masjid, or "Great Mosque" (1423), is a fine example of such a mixture.

Ahmadabad was founded in 1411 by Sultan Ahmad Shah I of Gujarat (reigned 1411–1443), and in the time of the early Mughul (Mogul) kings (15th and 16th centuries) was one of the great cities of India. It has known periods of decline and growth but generally has prospered since 1818. Population: 3,515,361 (2001 census).

JOEL M. ANDRESS
Central Washington State College

AHMED, ä-met', the name of three Ottoman sultans of Turkey.

AHMED I (1590–1617), the son of Mohammed III, succeeded his father on Jan. 22, 1603. The first part of his reign was efficient, and he introduced much-needed administrative reforms. But a series of revolts that broke out in various parts of the empire during the early years of his reign weakened Ahmed's government, and in 1606 he was forced to sign the Treaty of Sitvatorok, ending 13 years of war with Austria. The treaty gave the Turks a large indemnity but canceled an annual tribute from Austria.

AHMED II (1643–1695) succeeded his brother Suleiman II on June 23, 1691. During his reign the Ottoman armies were defeated by the Austrians at Slankamen and pushed out of Hungary, and the Venetians were able to take Chios in the Aegean Sea and Gabella in Dalmatia.

AHMED III (1673–1736) succeeded his brother Mustafa II on Aug. 21, 1703, when Mustafa was forced by a revolt to abdicate. During his reign Ottoman armies defeated a Russian force along the Pruth (Prut) River. The resulting Treaty of Pruth in 1711 was advantageous to Turkey. But the army suffered disastrous defeats by the Persians in the 1720s. Ahmed was overthrown in 1730.

AHMED SHAH, ä-mad'shä (1898–1930), shah of Persia from 1909 to 1925. He was born Ahmed Mirza in Tabriz in 1898. When his father, Mohammed Ali, was deposed on July 16, 1909, Ahmed succeeded to the throne and ruled under a regency until he was crowned in 1914. He went to Paris to live in 1923 and, refusing to return to Persia, was deposed on Oct. 31, 1925. He died in Paris on Feb. 27, 1930.

AHMES, ä'mes, Egyptian scribe, who wrote (about 1650 B.C.) a mathematical work that apparently was a compilation from earlier scripts. His name also is spelled "Aahmes." The Ahmes (or Rhind) papyrus, in the British Museum, and the Golenishchev (or Moscow) papyrus, in Moscow, are the two main original sources on Egyptian mathematics. The older Golenishchev papyrus dates from about 1900 B.C.

Ahmes shows mathematical procedures for solving simple practical problems of addition, subtraction, multiplication, and division concerning numbers of loaves of bread and jars of beer. One of his more difficult problems is "What number, added to its fifth, gives 21?" His solution is cumbersome but correct—the answer is 17½.

The area of a circle is given as the square of 8/9 of the diameter, which gives a value of 3⅙ for π. Division is a complicated process of solving equations in which a fraction with a numerator of 2 or more is equal to the sum of fractions in which the numerator is always 1. Ahmes gives a table of fractions with 2 as the numerator. He uses a special symbol for the fraction ⅔.

AHMOSE I, ä'mōs, an Egyptian king who reigned about 1554–1529 B.C. and founded the 18th dynasty, the first of the New Kingdom. Ahmose finally liberated Egypt from the Hyksos, the nomads from Asia who had conquered the land a century or two earlier. Finishing a task begun by other Egyptian kings, Ahmose captured the last Hyksos fortress, Avaris; expelled the invaders from Egypt; and followed them into southern Palestine, where he besieged their army for five years and finally destroyed it. He then subjugated most of Palestine and the eastern Mediterranean seaboard. After returning to Egypt he recovered Nubia. He was succeeded by his son, Amenhotep I.

AHMOSE II. See AMASIS.

AHURA MAZDA. See ZOROASTRIANISM.

AHWAZ, ä-wäz', a town in southwestern Iran, on the Karun River. Formerly called Nasiri, the town is situated about 80 miles (130 km) northeast of Khorramshahr, on the Trans-Iranian Railway. It is an important oil center, connected by pipeline with Abadan's refineries.

During the 12th and 13th centuries the town, then known as Agines, was a trade center for sugar, rice, and silk. Little remains of the ancient town, over which the modern town has been built. Population: 804,980 (1996 census).

AIDA, ä-ē'dä, a grand opera in four acts by Giuseppe Verdi, with an Italian libretto by Antonio Ghislanzoni. The opera was a huge success at its premiere in Cairo on Christmas Eve, 1871, and remains an international favorite. The music is melodious and has a spontaneous, torrential vigor, and the orchestration is richly expressive.

The opera was originally commissioned by Ismail Pasha, khedive of Egypt, for the opening of the Italian Theater in Cairo in 1869, as part of the dedication ceremonies for the Suez Canal. The production, however, was delayed—first because Verdi twice refused the commission, and then because the outbreak of the Franco-Prussian War made it impossible to get the sets and costumes out of France.

The story takes place in ancient Egypt. Aida, a captive Ethiopian princess, is the slave of Amneris, daughter of the king of Egypt. Both women are in love with Radames, leader of an Egyptian campaign against Ethiopian forces under Amonasro, Aida's father. Radames loves Aida but is awarded the hand of the princess Amneris. Torn between love for her country and an apparently hopeless love for Radames, Aida finally entices from Radames the secret of Egypt's plan against Ethiopia. Radames is entombed alive as a traitor. Aida conceals herself in the tomb before he enters and there joins him in death.

AIDAN, ā′dən (died 651), saint of the Roman Catholic Church; an Irish monk known as the "apostle of Northumbria." In 635, at the request of King Oswald of Northumbria, Aidan and his missionaries left their monastery on Iona, off the Scottish coast, to establish schools and monasteries at Lindisfarne (Holy Island) in Northumbria, England. Aidan was named the first bishop of the diocese established there, and by the time of his death on Aug. 31, 651, he had effected a firm Christian revival in northern England.

AIDOO, Ama Ata, ā′dōō (1942–   ), Ghanaian author. She was born in Abeadzi Kyiakor, Ghana, and graduated from the University of Ghana. Afterward she studied at Stanford University in California and became a professor of English at the University of Cape Coast, Ghana.

In her fiction and plays Aidoo deals with the conflicts between the traditional and modern in African society. Typically, one of her protagonists is a "been-to" (an African educated abroad) or a woman with feminist ideas. Her novel *Our Sister Killjoy* (1976) is semiautobiographical. *No Sweetness Here* (1970) is a collection of stories. In Aidoo's first play, *The Dilemma of a Ghost* (1965), a "been-to" returns home with a black American wife and watches as bitter quarrels develop between the Western wife and her African in-laws. In the play *Anowa* (1970), which is set in the 19th century, a woman marries a man whom her parents consider worthless, but through her resourcefulness and ambition she makes him into a prosperous trader. However, the feminist wife and the conventional husband cannot live together happily. In *The Dilemma of a Ghost* the dilemma is resolved through the triumph of a traditional African value, hospitality. In *Anowa* no such resolution is obtainable, and both the wife and her husband commit suicide. Aidoo's most recent work is a collection of poems, *Talking to Someone* (1985), in which she continues to explore the clash of cultures.

AIDS, the acronym for acquired immune deficiency syndrome, a progressive, degenerative disease of several major organ systems, including the immune system and central nervous system. The disease is caused by a virus, the human immunodeficiency virus type 1 (HIV-1).

1. AIDS: Physiology of AIDS

The initial symptoms of HIV-1 infection often resemble influenza or mononucleosis and appear within a few days or weeks after exposure. These symptoms usually disappear after several weeks. A prolonged disease-free period may last ten or more years after initial infection; more commonly, eight to ten years elapse before the onset of serious disease symptoms. During this latter phase the HIV-infected (or HIV-positive) patient is said to have AIDS.

Long-term studies have revealed that all or almost all of those infected with HIV-1 eventually develop progressive immune deficiency. Death often results from infections that occur once the immune system fails or else from destruction of the brain, from wasting, or from cancers that frequently appear in AIDS patients. These conditions are termed opportunistic because they gain a foothold in the body by taking advantage of the individual's depressed immune system. All or almost all of those infected with HIV-1 will ultimately die of an opportunistic disease or from damage to the central nervous system or intestinal tract caused by the AIDS virus itself.

The types of symptoms that occur as a result of HIV-1 damage to the immune system vary according to such diverse factors as an individual's gender and geographic location as well as the prevalence of specific infectious diseases in his or her community. In the United States, as in most industrialized nations, persistent yeast and fungal infections of the oral cavity are typical early signs that the immune system has been depleted. In women pelvic inflammatory disease is also a common early symptom.

In developed nations pneumonia caused by the organism *Pneumocystis carinii* is often one of the first life-threatening illnesses to appear in AIDS patients. This is not the case in poorer countries, where many other infectious diseases threaten the population. In areas with a high rate of tuberculosis, for example, TB is often the first threat to an individual's shrinking immune defenses.

Kaposi's sarcoma, a tumorlike disease of the blood vessels, is prevalent in male homosexuals with AIDS. There is a strong suspicion that Kaposi's sarcoma is itself transmitted sexually and that in the gay community, where a large share of individuals have engaged in sexual relations with numerous partners, a greater risk of infection has existed. People with AIDS also suffer from a high rate of B-cell lymphomas.

Defining AIDS, as opposed to HIV infection, has been difficult because in many instances it is the opportunistic diseases, and not HIV-1 itself, that prove fatal. For a number of years AIDS was defined as the stage of an HIV-1 infection when certain conditions, including *Pneumocystis carinii* pneumonia and Kaposi's sarcoma, first occur. In 1993, however, the U.S. Centers for Disease Control and Prevention (CDC) expanded the definition, so that a diagnosis of AIDS could also be based on levels of a type of immune system cell, the $CD4^+$ T helper lymphocyte, in the bloodstream. According to the revised definition, if an infected individual's $CD4^+$ T lymphocyte count drops to 200 or less per microliter or if the percentage of these cells is less than 14% of all lymphocytes in the bloodstream, the patient is diagnosed with AIDS. In addition, pulmonary tuberculosis, recurrent pneumonia, and invasive cervical cancer were included in the list of secondary conditions that signal the onset of AIDS.

Transmission. HIV-1 can be transmitted throughout the course of an individual's infection, even if that person exhibits no symptoms. There is some evidence indicating that the longer an individual is infected, the more readily he or she can transmit the virus through sexual contact. This may be due to an increase in the levels of the AIDS virus later in the infection.

The virus can be transmitted through vaginal or anal intercourse from men to women, from women to men, and from men to men. Evidence also suggests that it is possible for the virus to be transmitted between two women during sexual contact. During a long-term sexual relationship, the chance that an uninfected male or female will become infected with HIV-1 through vaginal intercourse with an infected partner is greater than 50% over a two-year period. Use of condoms reduces the frequency of heterosexual transmission by about 90%.

Research indicates that during sexual intercourse the virus need not enter the bloodstream directly but can instead pass into the body and establish infection across intact sexual mucous membranes in the cervix, vagina, and penis. There is no evidence that the virus enters the body through intact skin, however.

One-fifth to one-third of all children born to a mother infected with HIV-1 will also become infected with the AIDS virus. Infection of infants generally occurs either during delivery, as a consequence of the birth trauma, or later through breast feeding.

Infection in infants can follow two courses. About one-half of children infected at birth fail to thrive, experience severe multiple infections during the first several months of life, and die within the first year. In the second outcome an infected infant will initially exhibit only minor symptoms of infection and may survive for six to ten years or more.

In addition to the routes described above, the AIDS virus can be transmitted by way of a transfusion with infected blood. Although screening tests for infected blood have dramatically reduced the chances of contracting the virus through a transfusion, the risk has not been entirely eliminated. There is a period of between four weeks and six months following the initial infection when the presence of the virus cannot be detected in a donor's blood. However, it is estimated that in the United States and western Europe, the risk of contracting HIV-1 through a transfusion is less than 1 in 300,000.

The AIDS virus can also be passed on through transplanted organs containing infected blood or live, infected tissue. Many countries test organ donors for evidence of HIV-1, dramatically reducing the risk of transplant-related transmission. Another route for HIV-1 infection is through shared needles or syringes containing fresh blood or, in some cases, dried blood, in which HIV-1 may remain active for several weeks. Intravenous (IV) drug abuse is a common means of spreading the virus. In the United States, for example, it was found that in 1995, almost one-third of the people, both heterosexuals and homosexuals, with AIDS had also been intravenous drug abusers. For the majority of American women with AIDS, HIV-1 infection can be tied either directly or indirectly to intravenous drug abuse, with injection drug use being the direct cause in 32% of U.S. women diagnosed with AIDS in 1997.

The transmission of AIDS through the blood has also been a concern for hemophiliacs, who are often treated with blood-clotting factors culled from human plasma. It was not until 1984 that the blood products required for these patients were submitted to heat or chemical treatments to kill the AIDS virus. This means that numerous hemophiliacs treated prior to this period were infected with HIV-1.

The virus is rarely, if ever, transmitted by means other than those described above. There are several reports of HIV-1 infections transmitted through exchange of saliva during deep kissing, but the risk appears to be low.

Monitoring. The progress of an HIV-1 infection is most reliably determined by measurement of the number of CD4$^+$ T lymphocytes in the bloodstream. This immune cell plays a central role in disease prevention. For most adults infected with HIV-1, however, the level of these lymphocytes declines steadily from the time of initial infection. When the level drops to less than 20% of the normal count, the immune system fails to control many types of infection. When the level falls below 10%, life-threatening infections are frequent.

An HIV-1 infection's progress can also be monitored by measuring the level of the virus in the patient's bloodstream. Within the first four to six weeks following infection, the virus level is very high. It then drops sharply as the immune system begins to remove HIV-1 from the circulatory system and to eliminate infected cells. The virus cannot be completely eliminated, however, although the level remains low during the disease's long, asymptomatic period. Eventually, as the individual's immune system begins to fail, the concentration of HIV-1 in the tissues and bloodstream rises again, reaching high levels in patients with AIDS.

Testing. Testing for the presence of the AIDS virus is a multistep process. Infection is commonly diagnosed through detection of an immune reaction to HIV-1, that is, by testing for the antibodies produced against the virus. Antibodies to HIV-1 often appear within six weeks of infection, although a very small number of infected people remain free of antiviral antibodies for more than six months.

The ELISA (enzyme-linked immunosorbent assay) test, which is commonly used to screen for the virus, is very sensitive and detects almost all patients who have developed antibodies to HIV-1. A negative result in the initial screening test is interpreted to mean that an individual is not infected. A positive result is followed by a confirmatory test, the more specific Western blot. The latter test may indicate either that the results from the initial screening were correct or that the ELISA test detected the presence of antibodies that were not related to HIV-1 infection. Although the combination of the ELISA and Western blot tests is normally conclusive, in a small fraction of cases the tests are indeterminate and retesting is necessary at a later time.

The AIDS Virus. The causative agent of AIDS, HIV-1, belongs to a family of viruses called retroviruses. Upon infection, these small viruses, composed of ribonucleic acid (RNA), convert their genetic information into deoxyribonucleic acid (DNA). A protein produced by the virus, RNA-dependent DNA polymerase, is required for this process. Retroviruses insert the newly made DNA into the chromosomes of the host cell—a process called integration—with the help of integrase, another enzyme manufactured by the virus. The virus-derived DNA cannot be removed from the chromosomes of the host cell. Consequently, a person infected with HIV-1 remains so for life.

Using the inserted DNA, HIV-1 replicates by directing the construction of proteins used as the building blocks for the virus particles. It also manufactures proteins involved in guiding the reproduction process. The rate at which the virus replicates depends on some of these latter proteins and on the type of cell the virus has invaded. HIV-1 multiplies very slowly in some cells and rapidly in others. The physiological state of the cell also can play a role in reproduction. For example, in some cells the virus can replicate only when the cell is dividing.

Once a cell is infected, it can make hundreds of new virus particles. Some white blood cells, including the CD4$^+$ T lymphocytes, are killed during this process. Other types of white blood cells, including monocytes and circulating dendritic cells, can produce HIV-1 particles without being destroyed, which means they serve as reservoirs of infection. The AIDS virus is unusual in the broad range of blood and other cell types that it can infect, as well as in the variety of factors that influence reproduction of the virus.

Other Immunodeficiency Viruses. Although HIV-1 is the principal immunodeficiency concern among Western nations, a second AIDS-like virus, the human immunodeficiency virus type 2 (HIV-2), occurs frequently in some West African countries. The virus differs from HIV-1 somewhat in structure and in the proteins used to regulate replication. It is considered rare outside of West Africa, although some cases have been found in Europe and North America, including in the United States. Disease symptoms appear more slowly in people infected with HIV-2 than they do in those infected with HIV-1, and it is possible that HIV-2 does not induce disease in all people infected with this virus.

Treatment. Treatments for AIDS and HIV infection include the use of antiviral drugs to slow the rate of replication of the HIV-1 virus. Other treatments are designed to prevent or to fight opportunistic infections and cancers that result from the breakdown of the immune system. Nucleoside analogue drugs (medications based on the structure of DNA components) have been used with some success against HIV-1. They include azidothymidine (AZT), dideoxyinosine (ddI), and dideoxycytosine (ddC), all of which inhibit viral DNA polymerase. These drugs are licensed for use in the United States and other countries for the treatment of AIDS.

Unfortunately, AZT, ddI, and ddC can have serious toxic side effects when used for prolonged periods. Adverse reactions include depletion of red blood cells, blood-clotting disorders, and nerve damage to the hands and feet. The intensity of the side effects varies among patients, but they are often so severe that treatment with the AIDS drug must be terminated.

Development of drug-resistant strains of the AIDS virus is another major problem limiting treatment with antiviral drugs. HIV-1 spontaneously changes as it replicates, so that viral DNA polymerase is altered and the virus is no longer sensitive to medications targeting that enzyme. Resistance to AZT occurs in almost all patients who take the drug for prolonged periods. Resistance to ddI also occurs in many patients using this medication. The problem of drug resistance has prevented large-scale testing of several new treatments that had appeared promising.

New antiviral drugs directed against specific viral proteins are currently being evaluated for their ability to slow damage to the immune system. One of these, saquinavir, became the first *protease inhibitor* to receive the U.S. Food and Drug Administration's approval for the treatment of HIV infection. The compound disables a protease enzyme that HIV-1 needs to mature and become infective.

The use of combinations of drugs in HIV therapy has greatly changed medicine's approach to the treatment of HIV. Initially, in the mid-1990s, research indicated that it was more effective to treat HIV-1 infection by administering AZT in combination with either ddI or ddC than by using AZT alone. Soon afterwards it was found that a multidrug regimen in which patients were treated with a protease inhibitor and at least two other HIV medications was particularly successful in drastically reducing the concentration of HIV in the bloodstream. Although the virus can quickly mutate and become resistant to a single drug, it is far less likely to mutate quickly enough to resist three or more medications at the same time. While effective, however, this therapy did not appear to offer an actual cure. The feasibility of gene therapy, in which genes that inhibit virus replication are inserted into normal cells, has been another area of study.

Vaccine Research. Some experimental AIDS vaccines have contained killed virus particles or virus components. Others have been composed of live organisms, such as vaccinia virus, adenovirus, and the salmonella bacteria, that have been altered to carry part of the AIDS virus.

The ability of a vaccine to protect against HIV-1 infection in humans has not been extensively evaluated, however, and it may prove difficult to create an effective AIDS vaccine. This is because vaccines traditionally work by "educating" the immune system to recognize a foreign substance. When the invader is again encountered, the immune system can respond swiftly and eliminate the foreign material before it causes damage. To be effective, however, an AIDS vaccine must recognize all variants of HIV-1, and the number of strains appears to be very large. Experiments with chimpanzees and monkeys show that vaccines that protect animals against infection by one strain of virus may not be protective against another strain.

The life cycle of the AIDS virus also poses serious difficulties for vaccine researchers. Once HIV-1 has established itself in the immune cells, the body is unable to rely on its natural defenses to clear the infection, a characteristic that makes the AIDS virus different from many other infectious agents. Therefore, an effective AIDS vaccine may have to prevent the infection from starting in the first place. Unfortunately, this task is considerably more difficult for the immune system than is the elimination of an invading organism after infection has begun.

Another complication in the effort to develop a vaccine is the route of infection taken by the AIDS virus. It is estimated that 80% to 90% of infections worldwide result from heterosexual contact. During sexual intercourse the virus may enter the body by way of mucosal surfaces, regions that are less well protected by the immune system than is the circulatory system. Moreover, the invading virus particles are sometimes transported into the body inside infected cells present in vaginal or seminal fluid.

History. AIDS was first recognized in 1981 as a cluster of related symptoms in a group of male homosexuals with profoundly depressed immune function. Patients with similar symptoms were later found among intravenous drug abusers, hemophiliacs, transfusion recipients, female and male sex partners of people with AIDS, and infants of infected mothers. The AIDS virus was isolated at the Pasteur Institute in France in 1983. A diagnostic test, suitable for the screening of blood and organ donors, was developed in the United States at the National Institutes of Health in 1984 and was rapidly adopted in North America and most European countries. Blood-screening tests are now used in most nations.

Worldwide Prevalence. Occurrences of HIV-1 infection have been reported in almost every nation. In North America, the Caribbean, and Europe, HIV-1 initially spread most rapidly in homosexual male and intravenous-drug-abusing populations. Over time that pattern changed. In these regions HIV-1 is now spreading most rapidly through sexually active young women. According to the CDC adult and adolescent females accounted for 19% of newly reported AIDS cases in 1995, compared with 7% a decade earlier. In Africa and Asia HIV-1 infection has been and remains a heterosexual disease, infecting both sexes in equal numbers.

Because AIDS was initially recognized in the male homosexual population, a false impression was created that heterosexual men and women were not at risk for infection. Despite studies that have demonstrated unequivocally that the AIDS virus can be transmitted between heterosexual partners during vaginal intercourse, the perception remains for many that heterosexuals remain at low risk for infection. Statistics show that in certain countries the rate of infection in young, heterosexual adults is greater than it was at the peak of the epidemic among male homosexuals in the United States.

There appear to be a variety of reasons for the particularly strong inroads that AIDS has made within many African countries, including Uganda, Rwanda, Malawi, and Tanzania. One factor is the tendency among men engaged in jobs far from home to have multiple sex partners; the necessity of living far from wives and other female intimates can lead to frequent sexual encounters with prostitutes. The prevalence of other types of venereal diseases—which can cause open lesions, making the AIDS virus easier to transmit—also may contribute to the rapid spread of HIV-1. Another factor is the low incidence of male circumcision among the African population. When an individual is circumcised, much, though not all, of the mucous membrane on the penis hardens and becomes less vulnerable to infection. The World Health Organization (WHO) and the Joint United Nations Programme on HIV/AIDS (UNAIDS) estimated that globally more than 30 million people were living with HIV infection or AIDS by the end of 1997.

Prevention and Education. Infection with HIV-1 can be prevented by avoiding sex with an infected person, by not using contaminated needles and syringes, and by testing blood and organ donors for HIV-1 infection. As previously mentioned, the use of condoms during sex greatly reduces, but does not eliminate, the risk of infection. Transmission of the AIDS virus has been reported between regular sex partners who claimed to use condoms during every sexual contact.

In the United States the incidence of sexually transmitted diseases and the number of pregnancies among teenagers rose dramatically in the years 1986 to 1992. This indicates that risky sexual behavior by teens increased rather than decreased during that period, despite a proliferation of AIDS education efforts directed by state and private organizations. A 1990 U.S. government study indicated that 19% of American high school students had engaged in sexual relations with at least four partners. The figure for males was about 27%, and for black males, 60%. Moreover, of those students surveyed who had engaged in sexual intercourse within the previous three months, less than half had used a condom during the most recent encounter.

However, two 1995 federal government surveys found a decline in the percentage of teenagers between the ages of 15 and 19 who had engaged in sexual intercourse at least once, the first such recorded drop within this group since the 1970s. The reduction includes a 5% decrease between 1990 and 1995 among female teens and another 5% decline between 1988 and 1995 among never-married males in this age group.

Additionally, there has been some success in encouraging the use of safer sexual practices in the homosexual population of the United States. This is evidenced by a significant decrease in the rate of new HIV infections among gay males. Unfortunately, many young homosexual males have developed the dangerous perception that AIDS presents a risk only to older men.

Intravenous drug abuse continues to be a significant problem in many urban areas worldwide. Research suggests, however, that offering sterile needles and syringes may help curb the spread of HIV-1 among intravenous drug abusers. In Canada, where needle-exchange programs began in 1989, a study found the percentage of IV drug abusers in Toronto infected with the AIDS virus to be among the world's lowest.

The availability of treatment and supportive care required by AIDS patients varies dramatically from country to country. Patients in those nations that offer well-developed, state-supported health-care systems generally receive more consistent, higher-quality care than do individuals in countries providing health-care and insurance systems that combine public and private services, such as the United States. Very little treatment or care is available to AIDS patients in many developing nations.

WILLIAM A. HASELTINE*, PH.D.
Harvard Medical School

Bibliography

Dolin, Raphael, et al., *AIDS Therapy*, 2d ed. (Churchill Livingstone 2003).

Fan, Hung, et al., *Biology of AIDS*, 4th ed. (Jones & Bartlett 2000).

Feigal, Ellen G., et al., eds., *AIDS-Related Cancers and Their Treatment* (Dekker 2000).

Goudsmit, Jaap, *Viral Sex: The Nature of AIDS* (Oxford 1997).

Huber, Jeffrey T., and Mary L. Gillaspy, *Encyclopedic Dictionary of AIDS-Related Terminology* (Haworth Info. Press 2000).

Mandell, Gerald L., ed., *Atlas of AIDS*, 3d ed. (Current Medicine 2001).

Montagnier, Luc, and Marie-Lise Gougeon, *New Concepts in AIDS Pathogenesis* (Dekker 1993).

Schoub, Barry D., *AIDS and HIV in Perspective: A Guide to Understanding the Virus and Its Consequences*, 2d ed. (Cambridge 1999).

Schuitemaker, Hanneke, and Frank Miedema, eds., *AIDS Pathogenesis* (Kluwer Acad. Pubs. 2000).

Stine, Gerald J., *Acquired Immune Deficiency Syndrome*, 3d ed. (Prentice Hall 1998).

Wormser, Gary P., ed., *AIDS and Other Manifestations of HIV Infection*, 3d ed. (Lippincott-Raven 1998).

2. AIDS: Social Issues

The history of epidemic disease is one of fear, stigma, repression, and social conflict. For centuries physicians were all but powerless to prevent epidemics, such as the outbreak of bubonic plague that devastated 14th-century Europe, killing perhaps a quarter of the population. Consequently, individuals with an infectious disease were commonly either quarantined or expelled from the community.

Over the course of the 19th and 20th centuries, with the rapid advance of scientific medicine and dramatic changes in the living conditions of the populations of Europe and North America, the threat of epidemics receded. Thus it came as a profound shock when, after the first cases of acquired immune deficiency syndrome (AIDS) emerged in the early 1980s, the global extent of the disease became known. Uncertainty about the causes of AIDS in the very first years of the epidemic, along with its association with gay and bisexual men as well as intravenous drug users, provoked great social anxiety. When it became clear that the disease could also be transmitted through blood transfusions, the sense of alarm intensified.

With the identification of the human immunodeficiency virus (HIV) as the cause of AIDS and with careful studies of the social distribution of the new epidemic, it became evident by 1984 that the disease could not be casually transmitted; it was instead found to be contracted through specific activities, including heterosexual or homosexual intercourse, the sharing of injection equipment by illicit drug users, blood transfusions, or, on rare occasions, exposure of open wounds to infected blood. It can also be passed from an infected mother to her fetus. Such knowledge led public health officials around the world, including those at the World Health Organization (WHO), to argue that no justification exists for discriminating in school, the workplace, or public accommodations against persons with AIDS or against asymptomatic individuals infected with HIV. In the United States many local antidiscrimination statutes related to HIV were enacted, while legal interpretations of civil rights statutes and regulations extended protection to people with AIDS. The Americans with Disabilities Act, enacted in 1991, included HIV infection among conditions that could not legally be used as a basis for discrimination.

Despite such efforts, however, a number of AIDS-related issues have proved difficult to resolve. Questions remain, for example, as to whether physicians and dentists who are themselves infected with HIV should be permitted to perform invasive procedures, even if the risk of exposing patients to the virus is extremely small. In addition, the issue of insurance discrimination has not been resolved. AIDS activists have insisted that any discrimination with regard to health insurance is unacceptable, while insurers have asserted the right to employ underwriting principles in order to determine coverage eligibility for people with HIV infection. Another issue concerns HIV-related immigration restrictions instituted by a number of nations, including the United States.

Public Health versus Private Rights. With the spread of AIDS the threat of a lethal viral infection has become associated with intimate behaviors that typically occur in private settings. Consequently, every economically advanced, democratic society has had to confront the problem of protecting public health while safeguarding the right to privacy. Resolution of this tension has been made more difficult by feelings of suspicion and fear toward government agencies, particularly among drug abusers and within the homosexual community, groups that have borne the burden of HIV.

A central question asked by all nations in the early 1980s was whether AIDS should be treated like other infectious or communicable diseases. To understand the significance of this debate, it is necessary to recall that conventional approaches to public health threats, typically codified in the late 19th and the early 20th century, generally entailed provisions for mandatory screening and the abrogation of patient confidentiality; they also established conditions under which those who posed a risk to public health could be confined and isolated.

Owing to changing patterns of morbidity and mortality and the emergence of medical alternatives to isolation, these provisions were rarely employed during the latter half of the 20th century and came to be viewed, in fact, as a threat to civil liberties. Public health traditionalists, many of whom have been associated with the conservative end of the political spectrum, have argued that since AIDS is both infectious and sexually transmitted, any disease response should be influenced by laws pertaining to these types of illness.

In contrast, many public health officials, clinicians, gay rights leaders, and civil libertarians have insisted that AIDS policies must differ from those conventionally applied to public health threats. They maintain that because AIDS is incurable, requires difficult modifications of the most intimate behaviors, and afflicts populations that have a historically rooted distrust of government, preventive measures must avoid the trappings of coercion and control that had once been associated with public health efforts. This alternative approach, HIV exceptionalism, has become standard public health policy in democratic nations.

Under this philosophy mandatory or quasi-mandatory routine screening has been almost universally rejected. HIV testing has instead been undertaken only with a patient's specific consent and in association with counseling about the risks and benefits of screening. Blood donation screenings have been the only type of mandatory tests to be universally embraced. Preventive education, often by publicly supported, community-based groups, has become integral to the campaign against AIDS, and confidentiality of HIV-related records has been emphasized to secure the privacy of those who were tested and diagnosed.

AIDS-prevention strategies have thus reflected the proposition that the defense of public health is not dependent on the abrogation of civil liberties and privacy but is, rather, linked to their protection. At the same time, the exigencies of the AIDS epidemic have compelled a number of nations, including the United States, to undertake radical departures in public policy in order to stem the spread of HIV. Some of these measures—including the distribution of condoms to high school students and the provision of sterile injection equipment to illicit drug users—have provoked sharp public controversy.

By the early 1990s preventive efforts had met with some international success, so that striking increases in HIV infection in the United States and western Europe had stopped. These achievements were nonetheless mitigated by the wide transmission of the virus at the outset of the epidemic, in the early to mid-1980s.

Epidemiological and Social Burdens. The true burden of the AIDS epidemic cannot be measured strictly by studying people who have been diagnosed with the full-blown disease. It must instead be understood in terms of the overall distribution of HIV because virus carriers may require assistance, both social and medical, even if they do not yet have AIDS. More important, the prevalence of infection as well as the rate at which the virus is spreading indicate the extent to which the disease will exist in the future.

By the end of 1997 approximately 641,000 U.S. AIDS cases had been reported to the U.S. Centers for Disease Control and Prevention (CDC). As previously mentioned, HIV infection has occurred predominantly among several groups, including gay or bisexual men and intravenous drug abusers. High infection rates have also been found among the sexual partners of drug abusers and among individuals who, prior to the start of extensive virus screening in 1985, either received clotting factor for hemophilia or were given blood transfusions. By the end of June 1995, among adults and adolescents, more than 3,000 individuals with hemophilia/coagulation disorder and more than 7,100 people who had received blood transfusions had been reported to have AIDS. (These figures include only those people with a single known risk factor, as opposed to individuals who may have become infected through one of several routes.) By the mid-1990s as many as 50% of all gay men in San Francisco carried HIV, and within this and other gay communities entire friendship networks had succumbed to AIDS, profoundly affecting a generation of young and middle-aged gay men. Sixty percent of intravenous drug abusers in the northeastern United States were infected as well, but lower figures prevailed in other parts of the nation.

African Americans and Latinos have together made up the largest share of the infected population. Of all U.S. AIDS cases reported in 1997, 45% were among blacks, 33% among whites, and 21% among Hispanics. As a result many minority children have been orphaned by the disease and the greatest proportion of HIV-infected American children are minorities.

The distribution of AIDS in Africa, Asia, and Latin America has been far different from that in Western industrial nations. In Africa the AIDS epidemic has been rooted primarily in heterosexual transmission. By the mid-1990s, according to one estimate, the rate of infection in at least ten capital cities exceeded 10%. In several other cities the rate was over 30%, and in one severely affected region of Uganda, 12% of all children below age 15 had lost a mother or father to AIDS. It was also estimated that by the mid-1990s more

than 2 million African children had been infected, wiping out achievements in child health and mortality that had been made in the two previous decades. Estimates of the ultimate demographic impact of AIDS vary and have been the subject of sharp controversy, but there has been some indication that the disease will cause the rate of population growth in parts of Africa to decline dramatically and even reverse itself.

WHO and the Joint United Nations Programme on HIV/AIDS (UNAIDS) estimated that by the end of 1997 there were 20.8 million persons living with HIV infection and AIDS in sub-Saharan Africa, 6 million in South and Southeast Asia, and 1.6 million in Latin America and the Caribbean. The total worldwide figure was estimated at over 30 million, with approximately 16,000 new infections occurring per day and more than 90% of infected individuals residing in developing nations.

However, it is still uncertain how severe the societal effects of HIV may be. Since AIDS strikes sexually active men and women during their productive years, it was believed that the impact on the economic well-being of the hardest-hit African nations would be marked. Yet some research suggests that countries that have suffered particularly high AIDS-related losses, such as Tanzania and Malawi, have not been severely affected in terms of per capita income growth. This seems to be at least partially related to the fact that a large surplus of labor exists in these nations, as well as because the more highly educated workers have apparently been taking precautionary measures against HIV infection.

Care and Its Cost. The desperation engendered by medical science's inability to find a cure for AIDS spawned two important social responses. Dissatisfied with AIDS-related governmental efforts, community-based organizations in the United States and other nations developed an extraordinary array of services for those in need. In cities in North America, western Europe, and Australia, it was the gay community in particular that pioneered volunteer programs offering services such as home visits, individual counseling, group therapy, and assistance in seeking access to social welfare services.

In addition to establishing supportive services, AIDS activists—again, most notably, those in the gay community—helped pressure the U.S. government to increase its commitment to treatment research and to speed access to new drugs. In the decades immediately preceding the AIDS epidemic, a stringent set of regulations emerged that governed the conduct of medical research and drug testing. These rules were designed to protect research subjects from exploitation.

The lethal nature of AIDS forced a reconsideration of these standards, with AIDS activists demanding a loosening of protective regulations in order to allow more extensive participation of AIDS patients in treatment studies. Activists also won the right for AIDS patients to gain access to therapeutic agents before the efficacy of these treatments was firmly established.

Partially because of the cost of new therapeutic agents, but also because of the complexity of the care required by people with AIDS, the cost of treatment emerged early in the epidemic as a matter of great concern. Indeed, even before the development of AIDS-related drugs, speculation arose that the disease would represent the single most expensive illness to treat. In 1986, federal researchers suggested that each case could cost as much as $147,000. Many health services researchers later came to believe that early cost estimates were grossly exaggerated (estimating that the total cost of care administered following a diagnosis of AIDS was about $33,000 per patient in the mid-1980s), but such figures led the health insurance industry to raise the specter of financial disaster. By the early 1990s, as the life expectancy of AIDS patients increased, the cost of treating each patient also increased and was believed to be approximately $69,000.

Multidrug treatments introduced in the late 1990s and employing medications known as protease inhibitors have proved expensive, with estimated annual costs ranging from $9,000 to $18,000 per person. By the late 1990s, according to the CDC, the total treatment costs for a person infected with HIV were estimated at about $154,000 to $195,000 and the expense incurred by the United States through lost productivity was $500,000 per infected individual.

As with its distribution, the financial impact of AIDS in the poorer nations of Africa, Asia, and Latin America varies greatly from its effect on industrialized countries. Costly antiviral drugs, such as azidothymidine (AZT), are beyond the reach of developing nations, as are other treatment expenses. Even as new treatments for AIDS and HIV infection become available, such economic limitations will continue to be keenly felt.

RONALD BAYER*, PH.D.
Columbia University School of Public Health

Bibliography

Barnett, Tony, and Alan Whiteside, *AIDS in the Twenty-First Century: Disease and Globalization* (Palgrave Macmillan 2002).

Bayer, Ronald, *Private Acts, Social Consequences: AIDS and the Politics of Public Health* (Rutgers Univ. Press 1991).

Bond, George C., et al., eds., *AIDS in Africa and the Caribbean* (Westview Press 1997).

Farmer, Paul, *AIDS and Accusation: Haiti and the Geography of Blame* (Univ. of Calif. Press 1992).

Fee, Elizabeth, and Daniel M. Fox, eds., *AIDS: The Burdens of History* (Univ. of Calif. Press 1988).

Global AIDS Policy Coalition, *AIDS in the World II: Global Dimensions, Social Roots, and Responses*, ed. by Jonathan M. Mann, and Daniel J. M. Tarantola (Oxford 1996).

Goss, David, and Derek Adam-Smith, *Organizing AIDS: Workplace and Organizational Responses to the HIV-AIDS Epidemic* (Taylor & Francis 1995).

Gostin, Lawrence O., *The AIDS Pandemic: Complacency, Injustice, and Unfulfilled Expectations* (Univ. of N.C. Press 2003).

National Research Council, *The Social Impact of AIDS in the United States* (National Academy Press 1993).

Reamer, Frederick G., ed., *AIDS and Ethics* (Columbia Univ. Press 1991).

Shilts, Randy, *And the Band Played On: Politics, People, and the AIDS Epidemic* (St. Martin's 1993).

Willinger, Barbara I., and Alan Rice, eds., *A History of AIDS Social Work in Hospitals: A Daring Response to an Epidemic* (Haworth Press 2003).

AIKEN, Conrad Potter, ā′kən (1889–1973), American poet. Aiken also achieved a distinguished reputation as a novelist, short-story writer, and literary critic. His themes centered on spiritual disillusionment and defeat. A student of Freudian psychology, Aiken was one of the first American writers to employ the technique known as stream-of-consciousness.

Aiken was born in Savannah, Ga., on Aug. 5, 1889. When Aiken was ten, his father killed his mother and then committed suicide. The boy was sent to live with relatives in New England. He attended Harvard University, from which he graduated in 1911. Aiken began publishing poetry in 1914 and became a leading figure in the "new poetry" movement of the imagists and symbolists. From 1917 to 1919 he was a contributing editor on the magazine *Dial*. From 1950 to 1952 he held the poetry chair at the Library of Congress.

Aiken won the 1930 Pulitzer Prize for *Selected Poems* (1929), the 1954 National Book Award for *Collected Poems* (1953), and the 1956 Bollingen Prize in poetry for *A Letter from Li Po, and Other Poems* (1955). Other volumes of his poetry include *The House of Dust* (1920), *Senlin* (1925), *Brownstone Eclogues* (1942), *Sheepfold Hills* (1957), *The Morning Song of Lord Zero* (1963), and *A Seizure of Limericks* (1964). His prose works include the novels *Blue Voyage* (1927), *Great Circle* (1933), and *Conversation* (1940) as well as the autobiographical *Ushant: An Essay* (1952). *The Collected Short Stories of Conrad Aiken* appeared in 1960. In 1969 Aiken was awarded the prestigious National Medal for Literature. He died in Savannah on Aug. 17, 1973.

AIKEN, Howard Hathaway, ā′kən (1900–1973), American mathematician who designed the first operational program-controlled computer in the United States. Aiken was born in Hoboken, N.J., on March 8, 1900. He was raised in Indianapolis, Ind., and was educated at the University of Wisconsin. He studied physics at Harvard University, where he received a Ph.D. in 1939.

In 1937 Aiken devised a plan for an automatic computer. He got backing from the International Business Machines Corporation (IBM) and the U.S. Navy. In 1944 Aiken and a group of IBM engineers headed by Clair D. Lake completed the Mark I, an electromechanical computer programmed by punch tape and able to carry out any sequence of five arithmetical operations automatically. Although the Mark I was 100 times faster than the usual manual devices, it was soon made obsolete by all-electronic computers such as ENIAC (1946).

Aiken served as head of Harvard's Computation Laboratory from 1947 to 1961. Under him Harvard's laboratory trained many of America's early computer designers and introduced numerous design methods, including the use of logical algebra in switching circuits. Aiken died in St. Louis, Mo., on March 14, 1973.

TERRY S. REYNOLDS
Michigan Technological University

AIKIDO, ī-kē-dō (Japanese, *aikidō*), a Japanese method of hand-to-hand fighting. It is a modification of a jujitsu system of holds and locks, combined with a spiritual principle.

The principal physical techniques of aikido are bending and twisting actions applied mainly to the wrist, elbow, and shoulder joints of the adversary. Although these twists and holds would not necessarily throw an opponent, the partners practice safety falls resembling judo and wrestling falls, and they respond to the aikido techniques by taking rolling and leaping falls. This aspect of aikido makes it a beautiful and graceful exercise. Aikido is practiced primarily in *kata*, or "forms," which are prearranged and rehearsed series of attack and defense actions in which the students alternate the roles of *uke*, the assailant, and *nage*, the person who is assaulted. The latter applies the holds and then throws the assailant. In addition to the principal weaponless techniques, there are also stick-fighting variations.

The practice hall or arena is called a *dōjō*, as it is in judo. The uniform worn for aikido practice consists of a cotton kimono-style jacket and the *hakama*, a pleated, ankle-length garment that is either like a skirt or split like trousers.

Colored belts indicate proficiency in *kata*. There are no universal standards of grading or requirements for promotion from one proficiency level to the next. Typically, however, the novice wears a white belt. Intermediate levels are indicated by a variety of color schemes, including a progression from orange through green and blue to brown. Expert level is indicated by a black belt. Aikido instructors may promote a student at their discretion. The student is expected to spend many years in training and practice in order to become proficient in aikido techniques.

Aikido was developed in Japan by Ueshiba Morihei as a result of a moment of enlightenment that he reportedly experienced in 1925; previously Ueshiba had studied jujitsu systems with the aim of becoming a superior fighter. After 1925 he worked out his system of aikido based on a quasireligious, mystical concept of a universal cosmic power called *ki* (Chinese, *ch'i*), which could be tapped for mental and physical control of an adversary as well as for spiritual uplift and purification and for bodily health. Aikido is translated as "the way (*dō*) of union with (*ai*) the life force of the universe (*ki*)."

Practice of aikido is linked to concentration on the "single spot" and the resulting pouring forth of *ki*. Students are instructed to concentrate on a spot just below the navel and to think of it as the center of the mind. Diligent practice is said to give the individual an understanding of the true laws of nature, make him or her impervious to assault and indifferent to fatigue, endow the person with a sixth sense of events about to occur, and make daily life free of anxiety.

BRUCE TEGNER
Author of "Aikido and Bokata"

AILANTHUS, ā-lan′thəs, a genus of trees that is native to eastern and southern Asia and northern Australia. The trees are also naturalized in subtropical and temperate regions elsewhere. The name is Moluccan for "tree of heaven."

A smooth-barked, rapidly growing tree, the ailanthus has large, ferny leaves with one dozen to three dozen leaflets identified by solitary pimplelike glands on the largest notches of the leaf margins. The flowers are borne in clusters on the upper branches. Male trees have small malodorous flowers; the flowers of the female trees ripen into grayish masses of papery wings and persist until the wind scatters their seeds widely. In hot weather, ailanthus seedlings develop rapidly. If hoed out, they sprout back. Old trees may sprout when cut down, forming thickets. Though frequently a nuisance, ailanthus trees withstand industrial pollution, and they are valued in the parks and zoos of large cities.

The genus *Ailanthus* belongs to the quassia family, Simaroubaceae. *A. glandulosa* is the common variety. *A. erythrocarpa*, which possesses brilliant red seed clusters, is rare in the Western Hemisphere except in parts of California.

EDGAR ANDERSON*, *Missouri Botanical Garden*

AILEY, Alvin, ā′lē (1931–1989), African American dancer and choreographer who was instrumental in bringing black traditions into the mainstream of American dance. The muscular, intense style of dancing and the highly theatrical productions he favored helped win new audiences for dance during the 1960s and 1970s and made his company immensely popular both in the United States and abroad. Ailey frequently worked to scores by major jazz musicians, and his choreography blended elements of Afro-Caribbean traditions, ballet, American modern dance, and American jazz dance. (See MODERN DANCE.)

Ailey was born on Jan. 5, 1931, in Rogers, Tex. At the age of 12 he moved with his mother to Los Angeles, where, inspired by the work of Katherine Dunham, he began his dance training at the studio of Lester Horton, a modern-dance choreographer who operated one of the first multiracial dance companies in the United States. (See DUNHAM, KATHERINE.)

While attending the University of California at Los Angeles and other colleges in the area, Ailey continued to study and perform with Horton's troupe; he took over the direction of the company on its founder's death in 1953. The following year Ailey moved to New York City, where he performed as both an actor and a dancer in off-Broadway plays and Broadway musicals. He formed his company, the Alvin Ailey American Dance Theater, in 1958 and at its first concert presented the premiere of *Blues Suite*, a theatrical, humorous dance to traditional music inspired by the life of the black community near the choreographer's birthplace. Two years later Ailey produced his most famous work, *Revelations*, a choreographed tribute to the African American religious heritage.

In 1962 the Ailey troupe, now a multiracial company, embarked on the first of several foreign tours sponsored by the U.S. State Department. The following year Ailey retired from performing in order to concentrate on choreography. Besides his eponymous company, he also founded the Alvin Ailey American Dance Center, a school in New York City, in 1971.

Ailey's lifetime output as a choreographer exceeded 70 works. Among the many notable dances he created were those to Samuel Barber's *Antony and Cleopatra*, with which the new Metropolitan Opera House opened in 1966, and to Leonard Bernstein's *Mass*, the inaugural work at the Kennedy Center for the Performing Arts in Washington, D.C., in 1972. He created pieces for several important dance companies besides his own, including *The River* (1981) for American Ballet Theatre. Among the dances he made for his own troupe were *Masekela Langage* (1969), *Cry* (1971), *The Lark Ascending* (1972), *Night Creature* (1974), *Memoria* (1979), and *Witness* (1986).

Ailey was the recipient of numerous awards and degrees, including Kennedy Center Honors in 1988 and honorary doctorates from Bard College and Princeton and Adelphi universities. He died on Dec. 1, 1989, in New York City. He was succeeded as artistic director of the company by the celebrated dancer Judith Jamison, a former company member, who maintained the traditions established by Ailey while also introducing contemporary, innovative choreography into the repertory.

JOSEPH H. MAZO, *Author of "Prime Movers"*

Bibliography

Alvin Ailey and/or his dance troupe appear in the videos *Ailey Dances* (Kultur 1982), *An Evening with the Alvin Ailey Amer-*

ican Dance Theater (RMArts 1986), and Tribute to Alvin Ailey (RMArts 1990).

Ailey, Alvin, and A. Paul Bailey, Revelations: The Autobiography of Alvin Ailey (Carol Pub. Group 1995).

Cook, Susan, and Joseph H. Mazo, The Alvin Ailey Dance Theater (Morrow 1978).

Emery, Lynne F., Black Dance in the United States: From 1619 to Today, 2d rev. ed. (Ayer 1988).

Long, Richard A., The Black Tradition in American Dance (Rizzoli Intl. Pubns. 1989).

Mazo, Joseph H., Prime Movers: The Makers of Modern Dance in America (Morrow 1977).

AILLY, Pierre d', à-yē′ (1350–1420), French cardinal, theologian, and philosopher. He was born in Compiègne and studied at the College of Navarre, in Paris. In 1381 he became a doctor of theology, and in 1389 he was appointed chancellor of the University of Paris. Subsequently he was named bishop of Puy (1395) and of Cambrai (1397) and in 1411 was made a cardinal.

D'Ailly took an active part in the Council of Constance (1414–1418). The council ended the Great Schism of the West, which had split the church into factions supporting rival claimants to the papacy. Cardinal d'Ailly defended the conciliar theory—the belief that an ecumenical council should be superior to the pope.

As a philosopher, d'Ailly followed the teaching of William of Occam and promoted his system at the University of Paris. As a church leader, he contributed to the Gregorian reform of the calendar. As a writer, he influenced Columbus through his teaching that the Indies could be reached by sailing west. A copy of his Image of the World, now in the Columbian Library at Seville, contains many marginal notes in Columbus's handwriting.

BERNARDINO M. BONANSEA
Catholic University of America

AINTAB. See GAZIANTEP.

AINU, ī′noō, aborigines of the North Pacific, inhabiting Sakhalin Island and Hokkaido, the northernmost island of Japan. As the Ainu are fair-skinned, round-eyed, and hirsute, they were, until the 20th century, believed to be a Caucasoid people; however, there is no physical evidence to support this theory.

Although their specific origins are unknown, the Ainu are regarded as descendants of a people who once occupied northeastern Honshu, an area possessing many Ainu place names. The origin of their language is also unknown. Of the three known Ainu dialects—Hokkaido, Sakhalin, and Kurile—only Hokkaido and Sakhalin have survived, and they are mutually unintelligible. There is no written language, but there is a rich oral tradition, which is dominated by the yukar, the epic poetry of the Ainu.

Traditional Ainu beliefs stress the importance of the soul in all sentient beings. This belief is expressed in Ainu burial rites and the bear ceremony, which is essentially a funeral ritual for the bear. One purpose of the ceremony is to ensure the animal's reincarnation as a bear so that it may return to the Ainu with gifts of meat and fur. Thus the bear ceremony is seen as a means of ensuring the existence of future game.

Owing to Japanese assimilation, few Ainu continue to follow the traditional occupations of hunting, gathering, and fishing. Education has become compulsory, and Japanese is the prevalent language among the young.

AIR, the mixture of gases that composes the atmosphere of the earth. At altitudes below 100 kilometers (62 miles) the predominant gases in the mixture are molecular nitrogen and oxygen. After water vapor has been removed from the air, nitrogen and oxygen constitute 78% and 21% (by volume) of the air, respectively. The remaining 1% of this dry air consists principally of argon. In addition, carbon dioxide and small quantities of neon, helium, krypton, xenon, hydrogen, methane, and nitrous oxide (N_2O) are found as constant components of the air.

Water vapor, one of the variable constituents of air, constitutes less than 3% of even the most humid air. Nevertheless, water vapor is essential for life as we know it. Another variable component of air necessary for life is ozone (O_3). Its concentration, which is less than 0.07 part per million parts of air near sea level, rises to a maximum of only 10 parts per million in the ozone layer at 30 kilometers (18.6 miles) above sea level. This layer absorbs most of the ultraviolet radiation from the sun and thus shields the earth from harmful radiation. Other variable components of air include sulfur dioxide, nitrogen dioxide, and traces of ammonia, carbon monoxide, and iodine.

The first atmosphere of the earth probably consisted of water vapor, ammonia, hydrogen, and methane. Oxygen appeared later, partly by photolysis of water vapor but largely by exhalations from plants. Other gases, such as argon, resulted from the decay of radioactive elements in the earth. Most of the lighter gases, such as hydrogen, in the first atmosphere escaped from the earth long ago. The first atmosphere was replaced by subsequent exhalations from the earth and from plants and by by-products of photodissociation (the breakup of complex molecules by sunlight).

Air constantly cycles through the system of living organisms (the biosphere). It has been estimated that the entire oxygen content of the atmosphere passes through the biosphere every 3,000 years and that the entire carbon dioxide content of the air is consumed and replaced by the biosphere every 10 years.

Oxygen, Nitrogen, and Argon. Among the first to recognize that air is a mixture of gases was John Mayow, in the 17th century, who separated the part of air that supports combustion and life (later named oxygen) from the inert part that does not. In the 18th century the inert part was called nephitic (poisonous) air by Daniel Rutherford; Lavoisier called it azote (lifeless). It received its present name, nitrogen, in 1823. Scientific historians grant equal credit for the discovery of oxygen (1773–1774) to Carl Wilhelm Scheele and Joseph Priestley. In 1756 Mikhail V. Lomonosov recognized that rusting of iron was due to the action of air. In 1794 Lavoisier showed that oxygen was the responsible agent.

In 1784 Henry Cavendish published the first accurate determination of the composition of air: 79.16% nitrogen and 20.84% oxygen (by volume). These values are remarkably close to the currently accepted values (78.084 and 20.948). Later Cavendish found that an inert gas was left over after all the nitrogen and oxygen had been removed. This gas was identified as argon by Lord Rayleigh and Sir William Ramsay in 1894.

Carbon Dioxide. The first atmospheric constituent to be identified was carbon dioxide, which was recognized in the 17th century by Jan Baptista van Helmont and described by Joseph Black in 1755. Like water vapor, carbon dioxide is an effective absorber of infrared radiation from the earth, and thus this gas plays an important role in the atmospheric heat balance. Carbon dioxide enters the atmosphere by exhalations of animals and plants, by bacterial action on decaying organic matter, and by the burning of carboniferous fuels. The burning of fuel may be gradually raising the carbon dioxide content of the atmosphere and possibly changing the climate. Carbon dioxide leaves the air largely by absorption by plants and the sea.

Radioactive Gases. Small quantities of radioactive gases are found in the air as a result of bombardment by cosmic rays and the disintegration of radioactive earth materials, such as radon, thoron, and actinon. These three materials have short half-lives. The earth exhales about 6,000 curies of radon each second, but its biological effects are believed to be small. In the upper atmosphere, the bombardment of nitrogen by cosmic ray-produced neutrons produces radioactive carbon (the isotope carbon-14). Radioactive carbon dioxide, which results from the combination of carbon-14 and oxygen, is absorbed by plants. Its long half-life (5,600 years) makes it useful for determining the age of dead organic material. Radiocarbon dating, based on the ratio of carbon-14 to the normal carbon-12 found in wood, bones, and other organic remains, is widely used in geology and archaeology. Since 1945, humans have added new radioactive contaminants to the air by atomic explosions. A portion of this artificial radioactivity falls to earth fairly quickly after an atomic explosion, and some of it remains in the air for several months before it reaches the ground.

Aerosols. Many small solid and liquid particles, called aerosols, are suspended in the air. These particles generally have a diameter less than 0.001 millimeter. Aerosols fall so slowly, owing to the frictional drag of the air, that they are airborne and move like the air itself. Sources of aerosols include volcanoes, soil, sea spray (salt), pollen, spores, smoke, automobile exhaust, and meteors. Aerosol concentration is very variable, ranging from nearly zero over some ocean areas to as much as one million per cubic centimeter over some cities. The concentration decreases with altitude. At 5 kilometers (3.1 miles) above the earth, there are fewer than 0.05% of the number of aerosols found per unit volume near the ground. Hygroscopic aerosols (on which water vapor condenses readily), such as salt and sulfur dioxide, are called condensation nuclei. They play an important role in the formation of clouds and precipitation.

Air Pollution. Pollution results from numerous human activities, notably the burning of waste materials and fossil fuels. (See AIR POLLUTION.)

Water Vapor. Water is found in the air in three phases: solid (ice crystals in clouds, snowflakes, sleet, hail), liquid (cloud water droplets, drizzle, rain), and vapor. Like the constant constituents of air, water vapor is an invisible gas.

Air at High Altitudes. At altitudes above 50 kilometers (31 miles) the air contains relatively high concentrations of electrically charged particles (ions and free electrons). The highest concentrations are found in the D, E, and F layers of the ionosphere, which absorb and reflect radio waves and have an important effect on long-range radio communications.

The chemical composition of clean, dry air is nearly constant up to about 80 kilometers (49.7 miles) above sea level. Above that level, the relative abundance of atomic oxygen increases, and above 130 kilometers (90.8 miles) most of the oxygen is atomic. Atomic oxygen is produced by the dissociation of molecular oxygen by ultraviolet solar radiation. Nitrogen, which is not so easily dissociated by ultraviolet radiation, is present in molecular form even at very high altitudes.

The Atmosphere. For information on atmospheric variations in the composition and properties of air, including variations in the temperature, pressure, and density as a function of the altitude, see ATMOSPHERE. See also AIR PRESSURE; METEOROLOGY; WEATHER.

Bibliography: Brimblecombe, P., *Air Composition and Chemistry* (Cambridge 1986); Fleagle, Robert G., and J. A. Businger, *An Introduction to Atmospheric Physics*, 2d ed. (Academic Press 1980); Frei, R. W., and J. Albaiges, eds., *Air and Water Analysis* (Gordon & Breach 1986); Wiin-Nielsen, A., ed., *Compendium of Meteorology for Use by Class I and Class II Meteorological Personnel*, 2 vols. (Unipub 1973–1979).

AIR, a melody for voice or musical instrument. Accompaniment may be provided by other voices or instruments. English musicians of the Elizabethan period, notably John Dowland in 1597, defined the air as a simple tune or song, and the spelling *ayre*, frequently used in writings of the period, has been retained in modern usage to distinguish these songs from later compositions referred to as *airs*. During the 17th century the air became increasingly popular as an instrumental form, and by the 18th century it was widely used by composers in their instrumental suites. In Italian vocal music, especially opera, the air developed as a more elaborate form in the 17th and 18th centuries, so that the cognate Italian term *aria* now refers to operatic and oratorio solos only.

AIR BRAKE, a mechanical device that utilizes air pressure to slow down or stop the motion of a vehicle. The air-operated mechanical brake was invented by George Westinghouse in 1868. This automatic air brake became standard equipment on railroad cars about 1872. For the first time, it gave the engineer in the locomotive cab full control in stopping the train. Previously, brakemen had set mechanical brakes manually after a whistle signal by the engineer. This method was ineffective, and train wrecks were almost commonplace. The Westinghouse air brake was a milestone in providing safe railway transportation. Air brakes, with some modifications of the original air brake that was patented by Westinghouse, are used on passenger and freight trains, trucks, buses, and streetcars.

In a typical railroad train installation, an air compressor is located on the locomotive. From the compressor the air goes to a brake valve controlled by the engineer. The air then goes through pipes on the cars and flexible rubber hoses connecting car to car to reach a control valve on each car. The car control valve responds to pressure changes in the line and adjusts the brake cylinder pressure, which then sets or releases the brakes by applying a force between the brake shoe and wheel. The engineer controls these pressure changes with the brake valve. Usual pressures are between 50 and 100 pounds per square inch (3.5 to 7 kg per sq cm).

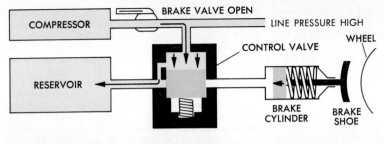

BRAKE VALVE OPEN
COMPRESSOR
LINE PRESSURE HIGH
CONTROL VALVE
WHEEL
RESERVOIR
BRAKE CYLINDER
BRAKE SHOE

Brake is released when brake valve is open and line pressure is high. Control valve cuts off reservoir air from cylinder, and a spring holds brake shoe free of wheel.

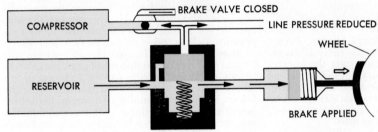

BRAKE VALVE CLOSED
COMPRESSOR
LINE PRESSURE REDUCED
WHEEL
RESERVOIR
BRAKE APPLIED

Brake is applied when brake valve is closed and line pressure is reduced. Control valve admits compressed air to cylinder, and piston forces shoe against the wheel.

Two principal advantages of the air brake are its inherent safety features and its simplicity of operation. Each brake has two high-pressure air reservoirs, one for regular use and one for emergencies. If the pressure in the air pipe drops, the reservoir pressure actuates the brake cylinder and forces the brake shoe against the wheel. Hence if any car should break loose from a train, the car's own brake quickly and automatically brings it to a stop because the air line is cut.

Improvements in the air brake since the first brake was made by Westinghouse enable much larger trains to be handled, and freight trains of more than 150 cars are not uncommon. Also, improved brakes have increased the ability to handle high-speed passenger trains. Speeds of 100 miles (160 km) per hour are not unusual, and some trains have been developed to run at more than 150 miles (240 km) per hour. In general the air brakes on trains, streetcars, buses, and trucks have increased the operator's control of the vehicle, improved the operational capacity by permitting larger loads and higher speeds, and provided high safety standards.

The economics of vehicle operation also have been helped by use of the air brake. The improved quality of air brake equipment has virtually eliminated mechanical failures and has provided improved efficiency in stopping, slowing, and starting a vehicle.

Another type of air brake is used on high-speed commercial and military aircraft during flight maneuvers. This air brake is a movable, flat surface. When the flat surface is protruded into the air flow over the wing or some part of the fuselage, the drag forces on the aircraft are increased. Typical maneuvers in which high-speed aircraft use air brakes include reducing aircraft speed to the speed required in a traffic pattern, increasing the rate of descent, slowing the aircraft during rough weather, and flying in formation.

A special type of air brake, used almost exclusively for high-performance military aircraft, is the parachute brake. It is customarily deployed by the pilot just after the plane makes contact with the ground.

DONALD N. ZWIEP
Worcester Polytechnic Institute

AIR CONDITIONING, the technique of regulating the condition of air in order to provide a comfortable environment for people or a favorable environment for making industrial products. Air conditioning usually involves control of four physical properties of air: its temperature, its relative humidity, its motion or circulation, and the dust particles in it. Some control of these four properties is important in air conditioning for human comfort. In certain industrial environments these properties are even more precisely controlled, and there may be control of other properties, such as odors and air pressure.

Air conditioning in its broadest sense includes any treatment of air to some desired quality level. In common usage air conditioning is considered the same as air cooling, but this is too narrow a concept. Control of the temperature of the air includes both heating and cooling processes. In general, air conditioning involves more than cooling the air.

Air conditioning has many applications. Air conditioning for the home is useful in regions where outdoor air temperature and moisture content vary widely or suddenly. Stores, restaurants, and theaters have found it necessary to have air-conditioned premises to attract customers on hot or humid days. Air-conditioned buses, trains, aircraft, and passenger cars are a feature of modern transportation. Many industrial plants need close control of temperature and humidity conditions during manufacturing operations to provide a high-quality product. In addition, industrial air conditioning for the comfort of workers can thus provide more efficient operation of the plant.

History. Air conditioning may be considered to have started when the first fire was used to warm human habitations. Subsequent development of temperature control of the environment can be traced through the development of open fireplaces, hearths, ceramic stoves, Franklin stoves, coal-fired furnaces, and central heating. The first straw-thatched hut kept out the sunlight and permitted the air to seep through. This design provided indoor temperature control and cooling by air motion. The use of palms as fans was a forerunner of the slow-speed propeller fans that were installed in ceilings during the early 20th century.

At some early date it was found that dry desert air was cooled when it passed through a wetted cloth surface. This type of process now is called evaporative cooling.

The birth of modern air conditioning has been attributed to Willis H. Carrier (1876–1950). The physical components of an air-conditioning system had been in existence for many years, but Carrier described the energy relationships that existed in an air and water-vapor mixture, and he proposed some simplifying steps that enabled engineering designers to predict the performance of the component parts more accurately.

Summer air conditioning can be considered to have started about 1920, along with the advent of reliable refrigeration machinery. Studies of residential cooling were made in the early 1930s at the University of Illinois. In one study the hourly cooling load of a large two-story house was determined accurately by measuring the melting rate of ice. The sight of twenty 200-pound (90-kg) cakes of ice melting on a hot day was dramatic evidence of the size of the cooling load.

Both winter and summer air conditioning were largely an American development, in which improvements in automatic controls, automatically fired furnaces and boilers, refrigeration compressors, and thermal insulation played a large role.

The pioneering research work in home cooling in the 1930s was more than 15 years ahead of the times because Depression conditions prevented the acceptance of a relatively expensive addition to the living standard. In the late 1940s the demand for home cooling units became strong, and industry was ready with mass-production facilities. In the 1950s and 1960s many homes were equipped for air conditioning.

Temperature Control in Winter. Control equipment operates the heating system automatically to maintain a desired room air temperature. The room thermostat in the control equipment acts as a constant watchdog over the room air temperature and gives commands whenever the temperature rises above or falls below a desired level.

During the winter, warm air is circulated through the ducts to registers, which admit the warm air into the room. The warm air temperature does not remain constant but varies with the demand. When the room thermostat demands heat, the burner in the furnace starts generating heat, and the air outside the furnace becomes heated. When this air temperature rises to about 120° F (49° C), a blower starts circulating this warm air through the ducts to the registers. The warm air delivered to the rooms displaces the cooler room air, and the room air temperature begins to rise. When the room air temperature reaches the value at which the room thermostat is set, the burner is shut off, and the furnace begins to cool. The blower continues to introduce warm air into the room, but the circulating air temperature gradually drops and so does the room temperature. Eventually the room thermostat demands heat again, and the process is repeated dozens of times each day. In a well-insulated home provided with a well-installed heating system, the temperature can be maintained within 1° F (about 0.5° C) of the desired setting. The components of the heating system are so ruggedly built that a system will function for years with minimum servicing.

Temperature Control in Summer. In a central cooling system the room air temperature is controlled by a room thermostat. In this case a rise in room air temperature causes the thermostat switch to close and the compressor to start operating. A flow of a cooled refrigerant fluid through the inside of the cooling coil then takes place. A fan circulates the room air over the outside of the coil. The contact of the room air with the cold surface of the coil cools the air. Also, part of the moisture in the air is condensed on the coil and drained away from the house. The cool, dry air introduced into the room through the registers replaces the warm, humid air, and both the room air temperature and relative humidity gradually are lowered. On a hot day the compressor may operate for several hours before the room temperature is lowered even one or two degrees.

Humidity Control. In cold climates where prolonged subfreezing temperatures can prevail, the indoor relative humidity can be reduced to low levels. Leakage of outdoor air into the structure lowers the indoor humidity. However, household activities, such as bathing, cooking, and laundering, increase the indoor humidity. In leaky houses the indoor humidity can fall below 20% in extremely cold weather. A reduction of air leakage or the addition of water vapor into the air may be required. The quantity of water required to maintain a constant relative humidity will vary with the weather; more water is needed in very cold weather than in warmer weather.

When the outdoor temperature rises to about 60° F (16° C), the relative humidity may rise above the 30% to 40% level that some consider to be desirable. If excessive moisture release occurs inside a house, the relative humidity may remain at levels higher than desired, especially in mild weather. The indoor moisture level can be reduced by opening windows and doors and allowing drier outdoor air to replace the moist indoor air. When the outdoor air temperature is between 60° F and 80° F (16° C and 27° C), this ventilation process may fail because the moisture content of the outdoor air may be as high as that of the indoor air. Some humidity control can be provided by an air cooling unit.

In arid lands the indoor relative humidity may remain comfortable in the summer. In moister areas in the summer the reduction of indoor relative humidity below about 60% is as important as the reduction in indoor air temperature.

Air Circulation Control. The register in a room discharges air into the room in a controlled direction and with a desired pattern of air distribution without incurring large pressure losses or air noise. In the northern United States the best location of registers for year-round air conditioning is at room perimeters (under windows). The air is discharged upward from a register located in the floor or at the baseboard to counteract the cool downdrafts from cold window surfaces in the winter. In the summer the register air (now cooler than room air) is discharged toward the ceiling. It falls slowly into the lower parts of the room. This same perimeter system works effectively in warmer parts of the country.

A single-story residence with a large roof surface will have a relatively large heat gain through the ceiling. However, larger amounts of circulating air for summer cooling can readily be sent through the same ducts used for winter heating. In a two-story or split-level house the heat gain through the ceiling may not be unusually large, but the relative amounts of circulating air for the upper and lower parts of the house change from winter to summer. Studies indicate that warm air introduced into the lower story in winter tends to rise through the open stairways to the upper stories. In summer the cool air introduced upstairs tends to roll down the stairs. If the duct system has been adjusted to provide for balanced heating on both stories, an extra supply of cool air will be needed for second-story rooms in the summer. The extra air can be provided by adjusting the dampers in the duct system to reduce the supply of cool air to the downstairs.

The return-air grille returns the room air to the furnace or the cooling coil. The grille should not offer undue resistance to air flow nor create an air noise. The location of the return-air grille is relatively unimportant because the suction effect of the opening does not extend more than a few inches from the grille. However, the air motion within a room is affected by the location of the supply air register. The designer of the system should consider the best location for the supply air register and be sure of the proper size of the return-air grille.

Dust and Lint Control. The air we breathe contains dust, lint particles, smoke, spores, pollen, and bacteria. The most common air filter is a screen or mat composed of crossed fibers impregnated with an adhesive material that holds the dust particles that come in contact with the fibers. In an electrostatic precipitation air filter the dust particles are electrically charged at the entry to the filter and are then collected on plates of the opposite electrical charge at a downstream location.

The throwaway fiber filter is used until the dust concentration greatly reduces the air flow. Lint accumulation forms a matting on the top surface of the filter and throttles the air flow. In window room coolers the reduction in air flow may cause the surface temperature of the cooling coil to drop below the freezing point. At this stage ice forms on the coil and causes a further decrease in air flow. The cure is to shut off the unit, defrost the coil, and replace the air filter before starting the unit. If filter clogging occurs in a warm-air furnace system, the air flow is steadily reduced. The usual remedy is to replace the filter.

Although the fiber filter is designed to trap small dust particles, extremely fine particles, such as in cigarette smoke, will evade capture. The precipitation type of filter screens these small particles from the circulating air. However, any air filter can screen only the air that passes through the device.

Room Air Conditioner. The lowest-cost cooling device is the room air conditioner. The indoor portion of the unit consists of an air filter, a fan, and a cooling coil. The warm, humid indoor air is drawn through the filter and into the fan. The fan blows the warm, humid air over the cooling coil, which cools and dehumidifies the air before it is blown into the room.

The cooling coil contains a refrigerant fluid. The refrigerant fluid changes from a liquid state to a gas state because heat from the warm air passing over the coil causes evaporation of the refrigerant fluid. This process takes heat from the warm, humid room air.

The outdoor portion of the unit consists of a compressor, a fan, and a condenser. The compressor receives low-temperature, low-pressure refrigerant gas from the cooling coil. The compressor delivers high-temperature, high-pressure refrigerant gas to the condenser. The fan blows outdoor air over the condenser. Inside the condenser the high-temperature, high-pressure refrigerant gas is converted to refrigerant liquid. The cooler outdoor air passing over the condenser takes heat from the hotter refrigerant gas. This causes the refrigerant gas to change to the liquid state. The refrigerant liquid then is delivered to the cooling coil.

The refrigerant fluid constantly circulates in a closed path through the cooling coil, the compressor, and the condenser. The fan for cooling the condenser sucks in relatively cool outdoor air, passes the air over the condenser, and blows the hotter air back outdoors.

In the room air conditioner the compressor and the two fans are driven by electric motors. Smaller units use 110-volt-line supplies, and larger units use 220-volt-line supplies. Some room air conditioners have sufficient capacity to cool an entire small residence.

Most room units can provide only widely fluctuating room air temperatures. Also, it is difficult to obtain quiet operation of the equipment and even distribution of cooling air. For these reasons the more expensive central cooling system eventually may replace the room air-conditioning units. A central cooling system can be obtained by modifications and additions to an existing home warm-air heating system.

Central Cooling System. The central cooling system commonly is divided into two units; one unit is inside the home, and the other unit is located outdoors. The internal unit consists of a filter, a fan, and a cooling coil. The filter and fan are part of the heating system. Only the cooling coil has to be added. It usually is placed in the bonnet above the furnace. A drain pan to collect condensation and a drain line also need to be installed.

The external unit consists of a motor-driven compressor, a fan for the condenser, and a condenser. These components are enclosed in a cabinet that is mounted outdoors. Originally, water-cooled condensers were common, but many communities have restricted water use for condensers.

Most home cooling systems provide humidity reduction but only rather limited humidity control. The reduction in moisture content depends on the length of compressor operation. For example, on a hot day when the compressor operates continuously for several hours, the indoor humidity can reach a low value of about 40%. However, as soon as the compressor stops operating, the water drops on the cooling coil tend to evaporate. The jump in indoor humidity during the off period of the compressor may occur much more quickly than the decrease in humidity during the on period, and large fluctuations in humidity can occur during the day. This limited humidity control has been acceptable to homeowners.

In some industrial operations, humidity control may be as important as temperature control. By the addition of equipment the circulating air is cooled below the desired temperature until the moisture content of the air is reduced to the desired value. Then the dry air is heated to the desired temperature. However, it costs more to obtain full humidity control. If humidity acceptance standards of homeowners reach higher lev-

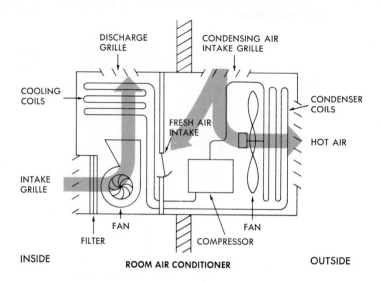

A room air-conditioning unit is installed in a window or wall space. In the indoor portion of the unit, the fan sucks in warm room air and passes it over the cooling coils. The chilled air is blown into the room. In the outdoor portion, the compressor and condenser provide refrigerant fluid for the cooling coils. The fan blows outdoor air over the condenser to extract heat.

els, they may provide their homes with equipment for full humidity control.

Winter Heating System. The three general types of central heating systems for winter air conditioning of the home are warm-air, hot-water, and steam systems. The warm-air system is most readily adapted to year-round air conditioning because the duct system, the fan, the filter, the register, and the return-air grille are used in both the warm-air heating system for winter and the central cooling system for summer.

It is more difficult to convert hot-water and steam systems to year-round air conditioning. In homes heated with hot water or steam, the summer cooling system commonly is a separate system. Research is in progress on the possibility of providing a home air-conditioning system that uses a water piping system for hot water in winter and chilled water in summer.

Selection of Equipment. The selection of equipment for a building is made from load calculations under specified conditions. For example, the heating load of a home is determined by calculating the hourly rate of heat flow that occurs when indoor air leaks through the walls, doors, windows, and ceiling or the outdoor air leaks into the home. This hourly load calculation is based on a temperature about 10° F to 15° F (about −12° C to −9° C) warmer than the coldest temperature experienced in the region. Equipment so selected has sufficient capacity for any cold day that may occur. For calculating summer cooling loads, the design outdoor temperature is about 5° F to 15° F (about −15° C to −9° C) less than the highest value recorded for the locality. The capacity of the cooling equipment so selected should be adequate for any hot day.

The equipment ratings are stated in terms of BTUs (British thermal units) per hour or in terms of tons of refrigeration capacity. A unit rated at 12,000 BTUs per hour is equivalent to one that is rated at a one-ton refrigeration capacity. One ton of refrigeration capacity is equivalent to the cooling capacity of 2,000 pounds (900 kg) of ice when it melts from a solid to a liquid during a 24-hour period. In order to maintain uniformity within the industry, the units are rated under precise laboratory conditions.

Human Comfort and Health. Proof that people will live longer or stay in better health as a result of a controlled indoor climate is not available. The main argument for using home cooling is that the occupants can be made more comfortable even on hot and humid days. The reduction in relative humidity and the removal of visible sweating is as important to the occupants as the reduction in air temperature.

Few systems installed in homes completely meet the four basic requirements of air conditioning because complete control of relative humidity is not obtained in winter and summer.

Design of the Home for Air Conditioning. Although homes are not designed around the air-conditioning system, provisions can be made to reduce heat losses in winter, reduce heat gains in summer, and protect against high relative humidity.

A study of cooling loads on buildings that have large roof expanses and large window areas on east and west exposures indicates that good cooling design includes proper treatment of the solar load. For example, the rate of solar energy entering a south window can be reduced by the use of roof overhangs over windows. On the east and west windows, roof overhangs are not so effective, but other measures can be taken to minimize solar heat gains. These include providing smaller windows on the east and west or orienting the building so that large glass areas are on the north and south; providing heat-absorbing glass; using shade screens, inside venetian blinds, or outside blinds or awnings; and providing an attic space that can be ventilated. A two-story building has a smaller roof area than a one-story building with the same total cooling load. Black tarred roofs absorb more heat than do whitewashed roofs.

Many houses are not properly built for indoor relative humidities in excess of about 30% in extremely cold weather. Condensation and frost will form on single-pane windows, and ice may form inside the studding space of a frame wall. Condensation on windows can be prevented by using storm sash or double-paned windows. A moisture-resistant material (vapor barrier) should be installed just below the inside wall surface to prevent water vapor from passing through the wall surface.

Air Conditioning for Office Buildings and Schools. In most parts of the United States no modern office building can afford to omit summer air conditioning. Unlike home cooling, the office system can provide full control of temperature, humidity, dust, and air distribution. Basically, the office air conditioner resembles the room air conditioner. There is a cooling coil through which the refrigerant passes, and there is a separate unit where refrigeration occurs.

In the larger units required for a multistory office building, water-cooled condensers are used because air-cooled condensers seldom are feasible. To conserve water, water-cooled condenser installations usually include a separate cooling tower in which the condenser water is cooled by evaporation into outdoor air.

One of the trends in office air conditioning is temperature control for sections of the building with different demands. By using one duct that carries cool air and another duct that carries warm air, the air entering a space can be mixed to the desired temperature indicated by the thermostat setting. In order to conserve space, duct systems have been developed in which air velocities and air pressures are considerably higher than those used for home systems.

Schools have been provided with cooling equipment. This trend will continue, especially if year-round operation of the school becomes necessary. Many one-story schools have large glass exposures to the east and west and large solar heat gains through the roof and windows. Such schools require cooling even during the normal school year. With air conditioning, more effective teaching and learning can be expected during late spring and early fall.

Although some evidence exists that the use of air conditioning in an office or school results in a decrease in respiratory ailments, the evidence is far from conclusive. A correlation between the use of air conditioning and a decrease in absenteeism in hot weather has been shown.

Industrial Applications. Air conditioning for industrial applications reached a peak of development before comfort cooling because the dollars saved by quality control or increased production could be related to the investment cost of the air-conditioning system. The benefits include reduction of shrinkage or expansion of paper in a printing plant, improved electrical resistance of dry components of a cable, increased reliability of a device made in a dust-free atmosphere, and reduction of surface rusting of parts touched by wet hands. Also, comfort cooling of workers can result in fewer shutdowns and more effective production.

Commercial Applications. The first air-cooled store in any community forced other stores to follow suit or face failure. In the early days of cooling, glaring signs advertised that it was "20 degrees cooler inside." Numerous stories were spread about people collapsing on entry or exit from the premises or catching colds and pneumonia the next day. But people of normal health have not been adversely affected. Stores, restaurants, theaters, and hotels are common commercial enterprises in which air conditioning has proved to be useful for summer business.

Increased Needs for Air Conditioning. Changes are taking place in the living habits of people, in the air environments of the cities, in the requirements for industrial production, and in many other facets of modern society. These changes make it necessary to give more attention to air-conditioning requirements.

The outdoor air in cities will continue to contain large amounts of undesirable foreign matter, such as dust, pollen, smoke, automobile exhaust gases, chemical fumes, and odors. Extensive use of air-conditioning equipment will be one factor in providing a desirable air environment for urban dwellers. With the trend toward urban living, there will be greater concentrations of people in smaller areas and more apartments. Air conditioning will help to provide a comfortable environment in apartments.

By using air conditioning, industries can move to regions with unfavorable climates but having desirable raw materials, labor supplies, or trans-

A central cooling system for the home is provided by using many parts of an installed forced-air heating system and adding a cooling coil, a compressor, and a condenser. The duct system, the fan, the filter, the register, and the return-air grille are used in both the heating system and the cooling system. This installation provides a central air-conditioning system for year-round use.

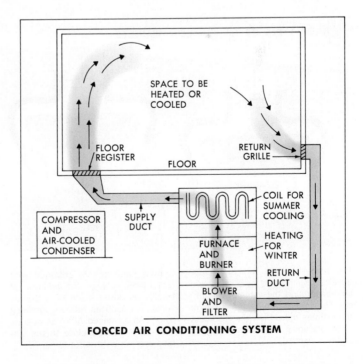

FORCED AIR CONDITIONING SYSTEM

portation. Weather limitations that formerly were considered to be too formidable for employees can be ignored.

The demand for manufactured goods of consistent quality can be met by close control of the environment. For example, a high-speed printing press must position overlapping colors precisely on a moving sheet of paper. This operation requires close control of the humidity to avoid expansion and contraction of the paper as it moves along the press.

Modern architecture tends to use large amounts of exposed glass and large, flat roof surfaces. These practices accentuate the building heat gains from the sun and make air conditioning more necessary. Also, as air pollution becomes more widespread, the air introduced into buildings must be treated to purify the air.

S. KONZO*
University of Illinois

AIR CUSHION VEHICLE, a form of surface transportation that can travel over water, ice, snow, land, marsh, or any dense surface. The terms *ground effect machine* (GEM), *hovercraft*, and *hydroskimmer* are also used for such vehicles. As the name implies, an air cushion vehicle (ACV) travels on a cushion of air that is trapped and maintained beneath the craft. The air cushion is usually kept at 40 to 80 pounds per square foot (200 to 400 kg per sq meter) above atmospheric pressure.

The original design of the ACV, with a large air clearance between vehicle and surface (the "peripheral jet"), required too much power. It has been superseded by a skirted or trunked ACV, in which almost all the clearance is provided by the flexibility of a tough nylon skirt, covered with an elastic substance such as nitrile rubber. A fan pumps air into the air cushion to counteract the constant leakage under the lower edge of the nylon skirt. Propulsion is provided by one or more variable-pitch propellers.

Another form is the "side-wall" ACV (sometimes referred to as the CAB, or captured air bubble), which has sides extending into the water. It may be used when low speeds are needed and when the operation is not amphibious or not in shallow water.

The first ACV was operated in 1959. Development since then has been very rapid. A typical small ACV weighs about 8 tons and can carry 15 passengers or 3½ tons of cargo. It may speed along at 60 miles (100 km) per hour and maintain this speed in waves 3 feet (1 meter) high or may operate at reduced speeds in waves 8 feet (2.5 meters) high. Other plans for ACVs include surface effect ships (SES) of 5,000 to 30,000 tons, capable of crossing the oceans at speeds ranging from 70 to 115 miles (110 to 180 km) per hour.

JOHN B. CHAPLIN, *Bell Aerosystems Company*

AIR FORCE, United States Department of the, one of the three major divisions of the U.S. Department of Defense. Its primary responsibility is the maintenance of the nation's air power at strength sufficient to deter potential aggressors, while projecting military power abroad and providing for the country's air defense in wartime and periods of crisis.

The department was created by the National Security Act of 1947. It began operations as an autonomous military service on Sept. 18, 1947. The same act established the U.S. Air Force within the U.S. Department of the Air Force by transferring to it the facilities and personnel of the Army Air Forces. The act was amended by Congress in 1949, and the department was made a military division within the Department of Defense, equal in status to the army and navy departments. Its frontline strength includes 500 intercontinental ballistic missiles (ICBMs) and over 4,700 jet and propeller-driven aircraft in various combat, refueling, reconnaissance, and transport configurations. An additional 1,900 aircraft are operated by Air

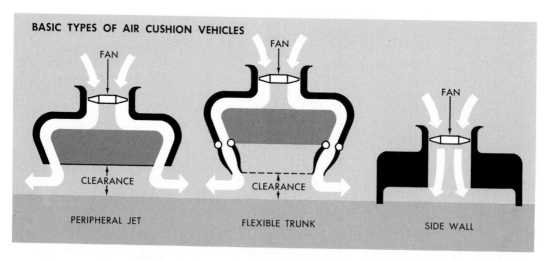

BASIC TYPES OF AIR CUSHION VEHICLES

FAN   FAN   FAN

CLEARANCE   CLEARANCE

PERIPHERAL JET   FLEXIBLE TRUNK   SIDE WALL

The air cushion over which the ACV travels is maintained by a downward air flow around the vehicle's periphery. The clearance obtained is two or three times more than the thickness of the escaping air stream, but great power is needed.

Similar clearance is obtained with less power through the addition of trunks, or skirts, made of a flexible substance such as rubber-containing nylon. An advanced ACV can operate with the skirt very close to the surface over which it is traveling.

A side-wall ACV may be used for travel at low speeds over water that is sufficiently deep. The sides of the vehicle extend slightly below the surface of the water, so that the vehicle rides on a bubble of air—the CAB (captured air bubble) concept.

Force Reserve and Air National Guard elements.

Organization and Functions. The department is headed by the secretary of the air force, a civilian appointed by the president and subordinate to the secretary of defense. The secretary of the air force is assisted by an undersecretary, also a civilian, and a supervisory staff of five special secretaries for manpower: reserve affairs, installations, and environment; financial management; acquisition; space; and general counsel. In addition, the secretary has assistance for specialized areas. These positions and offices include the inspector general, a civilian administrative assistant, the auditor general, the Office of Legislative Liaison, and the Office of Public Affairs.

Supervision of the air force is vested in military air staff responsible to the secretary. The air staff consists of a chief of staff, vice chief of staff, not more than five deputy chiefs, and military and civilian assistants. Also, several independent offices in the air staff report directly to the chief of staff. The chief of staff furnishes professional assistance to the secretary, is principal adviser on air force activities, and serves on the National Security Council and the Joint Chiefs of Staff.

History. The Department of the Air Force is descended from several earlier organizations. The first appeared on Aug. 1, 1907, when the Aeronautical Division of the Army Signal Corps was established. Staffed only by an officer and two enlisted men, it was assigned to study possible military uses of airplanes. The aerial service was not built up until World War I. In April 1917 the Aviation Section numbered 1,200 officers, who had no knowledge of the air war in Europe. The section had 740 airplanes, most manufactured in Europe, and 45 squadrons. Few of these aircraft were used in service on the front, but those units actually committed to combat distinguished themselves.

In May 1918 Congress created the Air Service, still under army administration. On July 2, 1926, after an unsuccessful battle for autonomy in the defense establishment, the Air Service was renamed the Air Corps. In 1935 the General Headquarters Air Force was organized. It became the Air Force Combat Command in June 1941 and, subsequently, during World War II, the Army Air Forces.

Experience in global war convinced U.S. military and political leaders that a separate organization for the air corps should be established. Enabling legislation was adopted in the National Security Act of 1947, and the U.S. Department of the Air Force, with the U.S. Air Force as its primary component, came into existence.

The first major air commands were established during the next three years. After the Korean War ended in 1953, another phase in the development of the service began when the first steps were taken toward a mixed force concept. The department became the prime agency for developing missile systems. On Nov. 26, 1956, it was assigned sole responsibility for all land-based intermediate and intercontinental ballistic missile systems. These forces, in concert with land-based nuclear bombers and submarine-based nuclear missiles, formed the third leg of the so-called triad strategy, the mainstay of American nuclear deterrence throughout the Cold War. By 1965 the U.S. Air Force was fully responsible for research and development of satellites, boosters, space probes, and associated systems used by the National Aeronautics and Space Administration (NASA). Air force personnel were assigned to cooperate with NASA teams on the spaceflights related to Project Apollo, the U.S. manned lunar exploration program.

Being perhaps the most technologically oriented of the three services, the air force conducts active scientific research programs for weapons research, which has resulted in new and effective stealth (invisible to radar) aircraft like the F-22 Raptor interceptor, the B-1 Lancer and B-2 Spirit bombers, and multi-mission designs such as the C-17 Globemaster II transport. More conventional mainstays such as the F-15 Eagle, the F-16 Fighting Falcon, and the venerable B-52 Stratofortress are continually updated with new avionics and engines to keep abreast of developments elsewhere. Space-based technology also is a priority, especially for satellite reconnaissance and global communication "eavesdropping" intelligence functions.

Owing to the maturation of modern air power through increasingly sophisticated technology, the U.S. Air Force played a significant role in the Vietnam War. Its tactical forces were used in missions over North Vietnam and southern Laos. Tanker aircraft were also used in operations over Cambodia. By 1972 giant B-52 bombers, reassigned from nuclear responsibilities, also played a role in strategic bombing campaigns, primarily against the Hanoi-Haiphong area (Operations Linebacker I and Linebacker II) with destructive effects. This conflict also witnessed the rise of the first precision-guided munitions (PGM), which enjoyed good success rates against difficult targets. But perhaps the biggest lesson learned from Vietnam was a lessening of reliance on missiles for air combat and the reintroduction of classic fighter tactics through exercises like "Red Flag." Though the U.S. Air Force was heavily involved in Vietnam, most operations were conducted under the control of theater commanders rather than a single air force agency.

During the Persian Gulf War (1990–1991), more than 55,000 air force personnel were deployed and participated actively in allied offensive operations against Iraq. Air Force Reserve and National Guard members also were deployed, and they maintained aircraft for their various operations in the war. A monthlong bombardment of Iraqi command and control structures, utilizing new and highly effective PGMs, decapitated the enemy's ability to control and maneuver units in the field.

The end of the Cold War in 1991 also signaled a new flexibility for the air force in terms of deployment, principally in United Nations–sponsored missions against Bosnia (1995) and Kosovo (1999). There short but exceedingly intense periods of aerial bombardment against Serbian forces led to their speedy withdrawal from the Muslim-occupied enclaves. Following terrorist attacks on the World Trade Center and the Pentagon in September 2001, air force units began a strategic bombardment campaign directed against the terrorist-harboring Taliban regime of Afghanistan, driving them from power in only a month—one of history's most impressive applications of air power. Strategic airlift units then deployed thousands of U.S. and NATO forces to the region while also continually providing logistic support.

In March 2003, when Operation Iraqi Freedom commenced, air force units departed from their usual task of long-term bombardment in favor of a short campaign of devastating close-air support for rapidly moving ground forces. This was also the first conflict to witness wide-scale deployment of new satellite guided munitions, which could speedily apply accurate firepower in concert with real time reconnaissance. Despite intense fighting, these improved munitions greatly reduced collateral damage to civilians. As in the first Gulf War, U.S. aerial assets completely demolished all organized opposition with scant loss.

Principal Commands. The U.S. Department of the Air Force has about 375,000 officers, cadets, and enlisted personnel on active duty. Additional personnel includes about 155,000 civilians and about 260,000 guard and reserve personnel. The department maintains nine major air commands and 35 additional operating field commands. The major air commands and their missions are as follows:

Air Combat Command (ACC) operates, organizes, supplies, and equips the U.S. Air Force combat aircraft and associated equipment.

Air Education and Training Command (AETC) recruits and trains all pilots, air crews, and technicians for the air force.

Air Force Materiel Command (AFMC) manages integrated research, development, test, and acquisition of weapons systems. It also operates the U.S. Air Force School of Aerospace Medicine and U.S. Air Force Test Pilot School.

Air Force Reserve Command (AFRC) adjudicates and oversees staffing levels and policies for reserve forces and their deployment abroad in times of crisis.

Air Force Space Command (AFSPC) operates and tests U.S. Air Force Intercontinental Ballistic Missile forces for the U.S. Strategic Command. It also operates and monitors missile warning radars and space launch facilities.

Air Force Special Operations Command (AFSOC) serves as the U.S. Air Force component of the U.S. Special Operations Command, deploys specialized air power, and provides unconventional direct action and associated support.

Air Mobility Command (AMC) provides rapid, global airlift and aerial refueling for U.S. armed forces.

Pacific Air Forces (PACAF) plans, conducts, and coordinates offensive and defensive air operations in Pacific and Asian theaters. It also organizes, trains, and maintains resources to conduct air operations.

U.S. Air Forces in Europe (USAFE) plans, conducts, coordinates, and supports air and space operations to implement U.S. and NATO objectives, based on tasks assigned by the commander in chief of the U.S. European Command.

In addition to the nine major commands, the U.S. Air Force supports 35 separate operating agencies, each with its own distinct mission. Thus situated, the air force enjoys unprecedented technical superiority and global reach.

See also AIR FORCE RESERVES; UNITED STATES—Armed Forces.

JOHN C. FREDRIKSEN, *Author of "America's Military Adversaries: From Colonial Times to the Present"*

Bibliography

Arnold, David C., *Spying from Space: Constructing America's Satellite Command and Control Systems* (Tex. A&M Univ. Press 2005).

Controvich, James T., *United States Air Force and Its Antecedents* (Scarecrow 2004).

Frankum, Ronald B., *Like Rolling Thunder: The Air War in Vietnam, 1964–1975* (Rowan & Littlefield 2005).

Meilinger, Phillip S., *Airpower: Myths and Facts* (Air University Press 2003).

Putney, Diane T., *Airpower Advantage: Planning the Gulf Air War Campaign, 1989–1991* (Air Force Hist. and Mus. Program 2004).

Thompson, Thomas W., *The Fifty-Year Role of the United States Air Force in Advancing Information Technology* (Mellen 2004).

Wolk, Herman S., *Fulcrum of Power: Essays on the United States Air Force and National Security* (Air Force Hist. and Mus. Program 2003).

AIR FORCE, United States. See AIR FORCE, UNITED STATES DEPARTMENT OF THE.

AIR FORCE ACADEMY. See UNITED STATES AIR FORCE ACADEMY.

AIR FORCE RESERVES. The reserves of the U.S. Air Force, officially called the Air Reserve Forces, consist of two components—the Air National Guard and the Air Force Reserve. As such they are not considered major commands, but rather field operating agencies taking orders directly from Air Force Headquarters. The Air Force Reserve, established in 1948, is composed of the 4th, 10th, and 22d air forces, being principally concerned with military airlift operations; however, two space operations squadrons also are extant and share satellite control responsibilities with their active Air Force counterparts. Both the Air Force Reserve and the Air National Guard are drawn from three basic elements: the Ready Reserve, the Standby Reserve, and the Retired Reserve.

Approximately 260,000 Ready Reserve (Air Guard and Air Force Reserve) members may be ordered to active duty immediately on declaration of a national emergency by the president or Congress. Of this number, about 75,000 troops are combat-ready Selected Reserves who train regularly and are paid for their participation in unit or individual programs. The remainder are members of the Individual Ready Reserve; they have a service obligation, are subject to recall but do not have a training component, and are not paid. Approximately 60% of the Ready reservists have had active duty, primarily in the air force.

Standby Reserve members include reservists who hold civilian jobs that are considered vital to the national defense or are on standby because of a temporary disability or personal hardship. In 2003 they numbered 23,000 individuals. They may be ordered to active duty only by Congress. Retired Reserve members may be called on by Congress only after all other reservists have been activated. Standby and Retired reservists belong to the Air Force Reserve. Most of them are former Ready reservists from either the Air National Guard or the Air Force Reserve. They do not belong to units, are not in training, and have no mobilization assignments. An exception is the Non-Affiliated Reserve Section (NARS) of the Standby, whose members may train for retirement points in order to qualify for a pension at age 60. Transfer from Ready to Standby occurs at the end of the individual's obligated service unless he or she voluntarily remains in the Ready Reserve. The Retired Reserve (590,000 members) consists of older personnel, to be mobilized as a last resort.

Air National Guard. The first National Guard air unit was organized back in 1915, and the present organization was enacted by Congress through the National Security Act of 1947. Consisting entirely of Ready Reserve men and women assigned to flying units or nonflying support units, the Air National Guard is organized on a state-by-state basis in each of the 50 states of the Union and Puerto Rico, with the respective governors commanding during peacetime. The District of Columbia unit is commanded by the commanding general of the D.C. National Guard; however, each or all may be called up and assigned a military mission by an act of Congress or the president. In 2003 the tally of workforce assets was 108,000 individuals.

The Air National Guard receives policy direction and support from Air Force Regulations and National Guard Regulations (most of which are similar), applied through the National Guard Bureau in the Pentagon near Washington, D.C. Since 1954 the Air National Guard has provided a major part of the nation's aerospace defense force on a full-time, around-the-clock basis, with air crews continuously on active-duty runway alert. As such they are the primary force behind all facets of continental aerospace defense. A number of squadrons of various types are assigned to this duty, intercepting and identifying unidentified aircraft entering airspace in the United States. In times of disaster or civil disturbance, the Air National Guard may fly hundreds of missions on either federal or state duty. Other units are tasked with specialized missions pertaining to aerial refueling (a critical strategic function), reconnaissance, and tactical ground support.

Air National Guard officers receive commissions from their state, and both Air National Guard and Air Force Reserve officers are commissioned in the reserve of the air force.

Air Force Reserve. Despite their secondary status, compared with regular military commissions, reserve units are often called on to fly first-line equipment such as the B-1 Spirit bomber, the F-15C Eagle, and F-16C Fighting Falcon. (The A-10 Thunderbolt II, a highly armored and effective ground support jet aircraft, is presently being phased out and replaced by modified F-16s.)

Ready reservists, serving as members of reserve units, or individually, and all Standby and Retired reservists compose the Air Force Reserve. Those with individual mobilization, or "M-Day," orders are assigned to specific jobs with major air force commands or operating agencies to which they may be recalled in a national emergency. All other Air Force Reserve personnel are directed and supported by the Air Force Reserve Command. The command's subsidiary, the Air Reserve Personnel Center, maintains all the records on all members of the Air Force Reserve.

Besides serving full time when recalled, Air Force Reserve units since 1954 have provided assistance to the air force on a regular basis in air transport and rescue services. Troop carrier units help the Air Combat Command by combining training with airlift of personnel and supplies. Each year they drop more than 100,000 paratroopers to aid army airborne training. They help with the cargo and passenger flights of the Air Mobility Command and assist the Air Force Special Operations Command in escorting distressed aircraft and providing rescue service for downed aircraft. The Air Force Reserve units also take an active part in counternarcotics efforts, providing specialized training, reconnaissance, and a variety of unique capabilities to law enforcement officials at all levels. In the wake of the destruction of the World Trade Center and part of the Pentagon on Sept. 11, 2001, Air National Guard units also witnessed a manifold increase in patrolling and protecting national air space, principally from the threat of hijacked domestic airliners. This service has placed considerable strain on manpower and equipment but has otherwise functioned admirably.

Technician Program. Certain Air National guardsmen and Air Force reservists, often called technicians, are reservists but at the same time are permanently employed in a civilian capacity at their military jobs. They provide continuity for their units through full-time service in high-skill positions, administration, planning, recruiting, and supervision of training.

History. Several National Guard aviation units were formed before World War I. In World War II, 29 National Guard Observation Squadrons as well as 700 flying officers of the Army Air Corps Reserve were mobilized. In the Korean War, 45,000 Air National guardsmen and 141,000 Air Force reservists were called to fight. During the Cold War these reserve forces were also important in the Berlin crisis (1961), the Cuban missile crisis (1962), the peacekeeping operations in the Dominican Republic (1966), the war in Vietnam (1964–1973), and the first Persian Gulf War (1991), where 23,500 reservists and 12,500 guardsmen were deployed.

The fall of the Soviet Union in 1991 saw no lessening of overseas deployment for Air Force Reserve and Air National Guard personnel, many of whom were tapped to support peacekeeping efforts in Somalia (1992), Bosnia (1995), and Kosovo (1995). The buildup to Operation Iraqi Freedom in fall 2002 also witnessed widespread mobilization of reserve personnel, as has the occupation of that country (2003–2004). Presently, thousands of individuals remain in theater to augment the regular forces already committed there. The reserve components of the U.S. Air Force have never been as professionally trained nor equipped with such superlative, up-to-date equipment as of late, and they will continue as a vital factor in the American military equation for years to come.

CURTIS R. LOW, *Major General, USAF*
Revised by JOHN C. FREDRIKSEN
Author of "America's Military Adversaries: From Colonial Times to the Present"

AIR LAW. See AVIATION LAW.

AIR LOCK, a two-door, airtight chamber in which the air pressure can be regulated to permit transfer of personnel or material from one environment to another.

In tunneling operations, the air lock separates the normal outside air pressure from the tunnel environment, in which compressed air is used to prevent water entry. Before going into the tunnel, the personnel enter the air lock, where the pressure gradually is raised to equal the pressure in the tunnel. On leaving the tunnel, the personnel enter the air lock, where the pressure slowly is reduced to that of the outside air. Slow decompression in the air lock prevents the bends (aeroembolism), which can occur when there is a rapid decrease of pressure on the body.

JEROME SPAR, *New York University*

AIR MASS, âr mas, a broad mass of air with small variations of temperature and moisture on the horizontal direction. An air mass extends over an area 1,000 miles (1,600 km) or more in diameter. Its individual characteristics are observed up to an altitude of 2 to 4 miles (3 to 6 km). An example is the polar continental air mass that forms in air resting over the snow-covered surface of Canada in winter. Polar continental air is cold and dry. Its temperature increases upward for 1,000 to 2,000 feet (300 to 600 meters) above the earth's surface. It remains constant until a height of about 10,000 feet (3,000 meters) is reached and then starts to decrease. These changes in temperature in the air mass are distinctly different from the normal consistent decrease of temperature with altitude.

Source Regions. Air masses obtain their characteristic properties from the surface of the earth underlying them. A region of fairly uniform surface properties, such as the wintertime snow surface of Canada, is an air mass source region. When a large body of air remains over a source region for several days, it becomes uniformly warm or cold, moist or dry, according to the nature of the source region. Besides Canada, other source regions are the oceans, the deserts, Siberia, central Africa, the Arctic, and Antarctica.

The formation of polar continental air is an interesting example of the way in which a source region determines the properties of the air mass. A snow surface reflects most of the sunshine falling on it while radiating heat energy outward. The surface receives and absorbs some infrared energy from the air lying over it, but in the Canadian winter this energy is not sufficient to make up for the surface heat loss—not, at least, until the temperature of the snow is $-40°$ F ($-40°$ C) or lower. At the same time, the lowest layer of the atmosphere cools, and its temperature at the earth's surface becomes approximately equal to the very low temperature of the snow. Thus, an air mass with the characteristics described above evolves, with temperature increasing upward, becoming nearly constant with height, then decreasing at altitudes where the energy interaction with the snow surface becomes negligible. The cooling air becomes saturated with water vapor, and moisture is deposited on the snow. Another characteristic of polar continental air is, therefore, low moisture content.

Transition Regions. In contrast to air mass source regions, many areas of the earth do not have uniform properties and hence are incapable of producing a true air mass. These areas of varying surface properties (especially temperature) are called transition regions. When an air mass leaves its source region and passes over a transition region, it is modified from below. The modifications are rapid if the transition region is warmer or moister than the source region and less rapid if the transition region is colder or less moist than the source region.

When polar continental air sweeps southward across the United States, the forward edge of the air mass is more moist and considerably more warm than the trailing edge. The temperature may vary from $0°$ F ($-18°$ C) on the Canadian border to $50°$ F ($10°$ C) in the southern United States. Although the mass of air is no longer homogeneous, as it was in the source region, it still is referred to as polar continental air, with the understanding that it is in a transitional state.

A tropical air mass from the Gulf of Mexico or the subtropical Atlantic Ocean is cooled by the earth's surface as it moves northward or northeastward across the United States in winter. The cooling leads to the formation of low stratus clouds and sometimes fog and drizzle. On the other hand,

a tropical air mass in summer usually is heated by the land surface, because the temperature of the land exceeds the temperature of the water in the source region.

One of the anomalies of weather is that invasion of the United States by polar continental air in summer may result in a temperature rise instead of a temperature fall. The physical reason for this is that the cold air mass usually is preceded by cloudy, rainy weather, with moderate temperatures, and followed by sunny skies with rapid heating of the originally cold polar air. Despite the rise in temperature, however, the polar continental air brings significantly lower moisture content and a change from warm and muggy to warmer but much drier weather.

Air Mass Classifications. There are four main air mass classifications: Equatorial (E), Tropical (T), Polar (P), and Arctic (A). These are divided into subclasses according to whether the source region is continental (c) or maritime (m).

Equatorial Air. Equatorial air masses are formed principally over the oceans near the equator. In this zone the northeast trade winds collide with the southeast trade winds coming from the Southern Hemisphere. The warmth of the ocean surface and the lifting of the air caused by the collision of the trade winds combine to form a very warm, moist, deep air mass in which showers and thundersqualls are common.

Tropical Air. Tropical maritime air is warm and moist at the surface of the earth. Its temperature and moisture content decrease rapidly upward to an altitude of about 1 mile (1.6 km). At this altitude—especially in winter—there often is found an increase of temperature and an abrupt decrease of moisture in a layer about 1,000 feet (300 meters) thick. This inversion of temperature results from the sinking and warming of the atmosphere in the vast weather systems known as subtropical anticyclones. Above the temperature inversion region, the temperature in tropical maritime air resumes its rapid decrease. Tropical continental air differs from the maritime variety in its extreme dryness.

Polar Air. Polar continental air is cold and dry, while polar maritime air is cool and moist. Also, the marked increase of temperature with altitude in the lowest layer of polar continental air is not found in polar maritime air.

Arctic Air. Arctic air is a more extreme version of polar air, not always distinguishable from it. There are times, however, when an outbreak of air from the north is so unusually cold that it can be reasonably identified as arctic.

Air Masses and Weather. Weather changes almost always are associated with a change from one kind of air mass to another. For example, the change to cool, clean air often observed following a shower appears to be a result of the shower's cooling and washing of the air. It is, however, actually a replacement of unstable, partially polluted tropical air by fresh polar air.

In spring the clash of polar continental air with tropical maritime air in the midwestern region of the United States produces a spectacular combination of squall lines, severe thunderstorms, and tornadoes. The tropical air tends to move northward from the Gulf of Mexico along a low-level air current, or jet, in which the air is very warm and moist. The polar air sometimes spills over the lower tropical air in a strong jetstream from the west. This combination of cold air over warm, moist air is unstable. It needs only a nudge to start a turbulent boiling of warm air upward, replaced by cold air that is sinking. When the instability is great enough, tornadoes are spawned. Though small in extent compared to other weather systems, these are the most violent storms in weather's repertoire. Twisting along a path 1 to 3 city blocks wide, the tornadoes, with winds of more than 300 miles (480 km) per hour and with an almost instantaneous pressure drop, devastate everything in their path.

The transformation of polar maritime air moving eastward from the Pacific Ocean is so great that the air mass becomes practically unrecognizable. When the moist air strikes the Cascade Range and the Sierra Nevada in the western United States, it is forced to rise and grow cooler. It becomes saturated, since warm air can hold more water vapor than cool air, and the water is precipitated as heavy rain or snow on the windward slopes of the mountains. The polar maritime air, continuing eastward across the Rocky Mountains, loses more and more of its moisture.

At the same time, it gains heat from the condensation of the water vapor. Then, when it descends the eastern slopes of the mountains, the air mass is heated by compression. It now appears as a very warm, dry wind, quite different from its characteristics in the source region. This wind is known locally as the "chinook" and generally as the *foehn*. It occurs in many different parts of the world and is of further interest in that it is said to cause nervous depression among susceptible persons. The chinook may raise the local temperatures as much as 50° F (28° C) in less than an hour. In winter it frequently causes rapid disappearance of ground snow.

Fronts and Frontal Zones. When the boundary zone between two contrasting air masses is sharply defined, it is called a frontal zone. The edge of the frontal zone that is next to the warmer air is called the front. A front is, in fact, a sloping surface of air. The colder, heavier air lies in the shape of a thin wedge beneath the warmer air. The slope rises at the rate of about 1 mile (1.6 km) vertically for every 100 or 200 miles (160 or

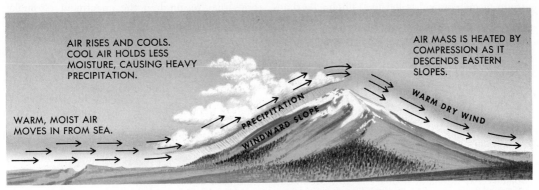

MODIFICATION OF AIR MASSES BY LAND STRUCTURES

Air masses cannot be formed above transition regions of the surface of the earth, but are modified by passing over such regions. Above, an example is the transfor-

mation of a warm, moist air mass moving inland from the Pacific Ocean across the western United States. After crossing the mountains it has become a warm, dry wind.

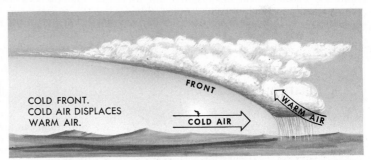

COLD FRONT

Cold fronts are formed as a mass of cool air displaces a mass of warmer air. The cool air wedges its way beneath the warm air as it advances because cool air is denser and therefore is heavier than warm air.

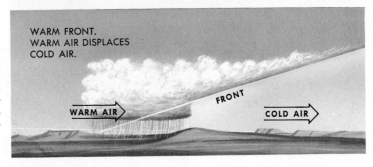

WARM FRONT

In contrast to a cold front, a warm front is formed when a mass of warm air displaces a mass of cooler air. The warm air moves up over the retreating wedge of the cool air mass, usually producing a line of storms.

320 km) horizontally. The process by which two air masses converge and produce a frontal zone is called *frontogenesis.*

Fronts are identified by their direction of motion. When colder air displaces warmer air, the front is referred to as a *cold front.* When warmer air advances, it is called a *warm front.* When neither air mass displaces the other, it is called a *stationary front.* The *occluded front,* a more complicated system, results from the overtaking of a warm front by a cold front.

The Study of Air Masses. Humankind has long recognized the existence of distinctive air masses. A local wind of particular properties was identified by a name, such as the direction from which the wind came. For example, the *sirocco,* a hot, dry, dusty wind blowing over the northern portions of Africa from the south or southeast, derives its name from an Arabic word implying the wind's eastern origin. Actually, the sirocco is tropical continental air from the Sahara.

The poorly understood concepts of air masses and fronts were organized into a well-defined science of weather analysis and forecasting by a group of meteorologists led by Vilhelm Bjerknes in Norway during World War I. The group defined the various types of air masses and fronts and showed their relationships to the development and movements of weather systems. For 20 years the science of air mass and frontal analysis dominated the practical, day-to-day work of the weather analyst and forecaster. Even today this branch of meteorology is quite useful, and no forecaster can ignore the principles that were advanced by Bjerknes's group.

Late in World War II, however, came the development of electronic calculators that were fast enough to make weather predictions based on a variety of atmospheric data. The possibility of the objective, mathematical analysis and prediction of weather drew many meteorologists away from their traditional methods and attracted physicists and mathematicians who felt the challenge of the opening field of electronic weather prediction. This field has become extremely sophisticated, and the mathematical models that are used in computers have made possible remarkably accurate forecasts of air circulation.

See also ATMOSPHERE; CLIMATE; METEOROLOGY; WEATHER FORECASTING.

JAMES E. MILLER
New York University

AIR NAVIGATION. See NAVIGATION.

AIR PLANT. See EPIPHYTE.

AIR POCKET, in aviation, an inaccurate but colorful term to describe what happens when an airplane encounters a sudden downward stream of air during flight. To the passengers aboard it seems as though the airplane has dropped into a "pocket" in the air.

A downward gust of air has simply reduced the angle at which the wings of the plane meet the air, so that there is a loss of lift. The plane drops until it passes through the turbulence. Similarly, an upward stream of air gives the airplane a "bump" or sudden upward lift.

AIR POLLUTION, the contamination of air by unwanted gases, smoke particles, and other substances. Although generally considered a relatively recent

phenomenon, pollution of the air, particularly by smoke, has plagued many communities since the beginning of the Industrial Revolution. By the late 19th century there was considerable agitation by citizens' groups in London who protested the smoke-laden air of the city, but their protests were drowned out by the clamor for industrial development. Complaints against air pollution were registered elsewhere in Europe as well as in the United States. Laws on air quality were adopted as early as 1815 in Pittsburgh. Chicago and Cincinnati followed with smoke-control measures in 1881. By 1912, 23 of the 28 American cities with populations over 200,000 had smoke-abatement ordinances.

From the 1930s to the 1950s, when smoke pollution was at its worst in the United States, air pollution was still regarded as a nuisance worthy of only local attention. During that period, in a number of eastern and midwestern industrial cities, the smoke was so thick, particularly during the winter, that at noon it was sometimes nearly as dark as at midnight. Finally, the sheer soiling nuisance of the problem provoked public outcries that resulted in the enactment of smoke-control legislation, its partial enforcement, and visible improvement in the atmosphere of a number of industrial cities.

These efforts were focused primarily on reducing smoke from fossil fuels, particularly coal, by regulating the types of coal that could be burned, by improving combustion practices, and in some cases by using special devices to control emissions of particles into the air. The replacement of steam locomotives by diesel engines and the increased use of gas for heating also contributed greatly to the reduction of air pollution.

In the 1940s a new type of air-pollution problem emerged. When the residents of Los Angeles complained of smog, few people suspected that smoke pollution and general air pollution were not the same problem. Los Angeles used virtually none of the fuels primarily responsible for the smoke problems of other cities, and yet its smog problem became worse. It was discovered that the Los Angeles smog was not due primarily to smoke in the air but to the action of sunlight on gases emitted by car exhausts and certain industrial processes.

The experience of Los Angeles in the 1940s revealed a general pattern of air-pollution problems that developed in the 1950s and 1960s in cities elsewhere in the United States and in other parts of the world. This pattern, characterized by rapid industrial growth, development of metropolitan areas with their associated urban centers and suburban satellites, and dependence on motor vehicles, creates new gaseous and particulate emissions that complement, interact with, and further complicate the action of the more common pollutants.

Urban development, increased use of motor vehicles, industrial expansion, construction and operation of large facilities using fossil fuels for generating electricity, production of iron and steel, petrochemicals, and petroleum refining gave rise to regional air-quality problems in many areas of the United States. They are manifest as seasonal episodes of unhealthy air quality in the Los Angeles south-coastal basin and the Baltimore to Boston urban corridor, and as regional hazes and poor visibility in the western Great Basin, Appalachia, and Adirondacks. Another manifestation is the acid-rain phenomenon in several parts of the United States and Canada.

These contemporary air quality problems are due to a combination of factors—the physical nature of urban and industrial developments, the spatial density of emissions, land and weather features that affect diffusion, dispersion, and transport of pollutants, and the chemical and physical transformation of the plumes of pollution that hang over cities and industrial centers. A wide range of pollutants currently pose an ecological threat in cities all over the United States and in other industrialized countries. (See also CONSERVATION; ENVIRONMENT.)

COSTS OF AIR POLLUTION

The total costs of air pollution in the United States and the economic benefits from its control are difficult to estimate because of incomplete, uneven, and uncertain assessment and accounting methods. Business and industry bear the direct costs of compliance with air-pollution-control regulations. These costs—investments and capital outlays for process change and for the operation and maintenance of control systems—vary with the type of industry, its location, age, production process, and prescribed level of emission control and time for compliance.

The costs for air-pollution-control systems vary widely. When compared with the total annual investment made by U.S. industry in new plants and equipment, the share allocated to air-pollution-control systems initially peaked at 4.2% in 1975 and then rose sharply again in the 1980s and 1990s.

TYPES OF POLLUTANTS AND CONTROLS

The six principal classes of air pollutants are carbon monoxide, particulate matter, sulfur oxides, gaseous hydrocarbons, nitrogen oxides, and ozone. Billions of metric tons are discharged into the air worldwide each year. A seventh class of pollutants includes the hazardous toxic substances that are discharged into the air from particular sources.

Carbon Monoxide. A colorless, odorless, poisonous gas that is slightly lighter than air, carbon monoxide is produced by the incomplete burning of carbon fuels. Carbon monoxide comes largely from motor vehicles, with lesser amounts from nonautomotive engines, open fires, and industrial processes. The supply of air, combustion-chamber design, flame temperature, and other factors determine whether combustion is complete and carbon monoxide emissions are minimized.

The control of carbon-monoxide emissions is more easily accomplished by large industrial and utility plants than by smaller sources, such as automobile engines. Since carbon monoxide represents a loss of unused fuel, there are economic incentives for large plant and utility operators to reduce carbon monoxide output. In some industries, such as iron and steel plants and petroleum refineries, the concentrated streams of carbon monoxide gas are collected and used in waste-heat recovery systems. Control of carbon monoxide emissions from automobile engines is a complicated problem requiring control of hydrocarbons and nitrogen oxides as well as the attainment of optimum combustion performance coupled with exhaust-gas thermal controls or catalytic afterburners. (See also CARBON MONOXIDE.)

Suspended Particulate Matter. Also known as particulates, suspended particulate matter (SPM) includes particles of solids or liquids ranging in size from those that are visible as soot and smoke to those that are so minuscule they can be seen only through an electron microscope. Such small particles can remain suspended for long periods and can be carried great distances by winds. Fuel combustion in stationary sources—heating and power plants—produces most of the visible particulates, a large part of the fine particles, and substantial amounts of invisible gases that may be transformed into aerosol particles. The sand, stone, and cement industries emit considerable quantities of large particles that create local problems but are not suspended and carried for long distances.

Techniques for controlling particulate emissions from boiler stacks or waste-air streams include filtering, washing, centrifugal separation, and electrostatic precipitation. These processes work well for most particles, but removal of very fine particles is both difficult and costly.

The emission of lead particles from car exhausts has been significantly decreased by the phasing out of leaded gasoline. Control of diesel smoke can be controlled by improved engine design, upgraded engine maintenance, use of engines rated for specific load requirements, and adoption of proper operating procedures.

Sulfur Oxides. Consisting of a mixture of sulfur-containing materials—the chief ones being sulfur dioxide, sulfuric acid, and various sulfate compounds—sulfur oxides are produced when sulfur-containing fuel is burned and ores are smelted. Sulfur oxide emissions in the United States are primarily from electric generating plants. Copper and lead smelters and industrial plants using sulfur-containing coal and oil also produce significant amounts.

The burning of coal produces most of the sulfur oxide emissions, but industrial processes that use sulfur produce small amounts of sulfur oxides as a result of inefficiencies. Most sulfur oxides in the United States are emitted in areas where industries and populations are concentrated. However, large individual sources of sulfur oxides, such as smelters and power plants, may be present in rural areas.

Sulfur oxide emissions can be reduced by switching to fuels that naturally contain less than 1% sulfur, removing sulfur from the fuels, or removing the sulfur oxides from the combustion gases. Switching fuels is feasible only when an alternate, low-sulfur fuel is readily available. In the United States most coal that is available near centers of high population and power demand is high in sulfur. Coal that is low in sulfur not only has to be transported long distances but is often more expensive because of demand by foreign and domestic steelmakers who use it for coke. Low-sulfur oil is available in limited quantities from northern and western Africa, Venezuela, Indonesia, and other areas. The economics of fuel utilization encourages increased use of coal and discourages use of low-sulfur or desulfurized oil. Although natural gas has an insignificant sulfur content, its suitability for specialized industrial, commercial, and domestic purposes tends to preclude its use for power generation.

Sulfur can be removed from coal and oil, but it adds to the cost. Crushing and cleaning can remove mineral sulfur from some soft coal, but sulfur in its organic form cannot be removed without gasifying or liquefying the coal into high-

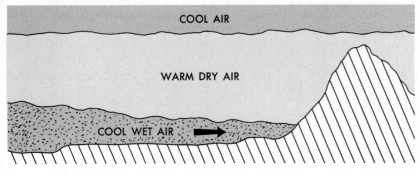

Thermal Inversion, a common factor in smog formation in Los Angeles, is illustrated in this schematic diagram. Cool, wet air from the ocean becomes trapped below warm, dry air, remaining stationary until the warm air rises and lets the cool sea air, laden with pollutants, escape over the nearby mountains.

grade hydrocarbon fuels. Desulfurization of some petroleum stocks is done by coking and specialized catalytic processes at added fuel cost.

Methods are available to remove sulfur from stack gases after fuel is burned. Fluidized-bed combustion systems make use of the controlled combustion of pulverized coal in a bed of granular dolomite or limestone. The sulfur oxides are absorbed by the alkaline mineral, preventing their release to the stack. Flue-gas desulfurization systems chemically scrub the stack gases given off by burning coal or oil. The entrained sulfur wastes are either removed as a waste product and discarded or the converted sulfur waste is recovered, treated, and marketed as liquid sulfur dioxide, sulfuric acid, or elemental sulfur. (See also SULFUR.)

Hydrocarbons. Like carbon monoxide, the gaseous hydrocarbons in air represent unburned, wasted fuel. Unlike carbon monoxide, hydrocarbons at concentrations normally found in the atmosphere are not toxic. But they are a major pollutant because of their role in the formation of ozone and associated photochemical oxidants.

The major portion of airborne hydrocarbons comes from transportation and industrial processes, with substantially lesser amounts produced by fires and wasted solvents. Most hydrocarbon emissions occur in urban areas, where metal-finishing plants, paint factories, printing shops, gasoline and diesel-fuel distribution stations, machine shops, and cleaning establishments are located. In addition, urban areas have more automobiles than rural areas do, and the resulting traffic con-

ditions increase hydrocarbon emissions.

Reduction of hydrocarbon emissions from car exhaust requires controls such as those for carbon monoxide, while separate controls are used for the crankcase, gas tank, and carburetor. Control of industrial emissions is achieved by vapor-recovery systems, improved manufacturing processes, and use of waste hydrocarbons as a supplemental energy source. (See also HYDROCARBON.)

Nitrogen Oxides. During the combustion process, when nitrogen in fuel and air combines with oxygen in high-temperature flames, nitrogen oxides are formed. Transportation vehicles, power plants, and other sources of combustion together account for more than 90% of the nitrogen oxides emitted into the atmosphere. Nitric oxide is the principal pollutant emitted, although a substantial portion is converted to nitrogen dioxide, in a chemical reaction promoted by sunlight.

The control of nitrogen oxides from stationary sources is complicated and difficult. Partial control is achieved through combustion-chamber design and controlled firing. Developments are under way to remove nitrogen from liquid fuels by chemical means, to reduce nitrogen oxide formation from coal by staged combustion, and to remove nitrogen oxides by treatment of the combustion flue gas.

Control of nitrogen oxides in automobile exhaust may be partially achieved by improved engines, but controls using reduced cylinder-flame temperatures result in penalties in fuel consumption. Development of three-way catalytic exhaust converters eliminates nitrogen oxides by causing

MAJOR AIR POLLUTANTS IN THE UNITED STATES

(Millions of metric tons per year)						
	CO	SOx	VO	SPM[1]	NOx	PB[2]
Transportation:						
Total	63.5	1.0	7.5	1.7	9.4	1.4
Road vehicles	50.2	0.7	5.5	1.4	6.8	1.3
Fuel combustion:						
Total	5.6	17.7	0.6	1.0	10.6	0.4
Electric utilities	0.3	14.4	nil	0.1	6.8	0.1
Industrial processes	4.6	1.9 ·	9.9	1.8	0.8	2.1
Solid waste disposal	1.5	nil	2.1	0.2	0.1	0.7
Misc. uncontrollable (forest fires, building fires, solvents, etc.)	3.9	nil	0.5	42.0	0.1	nil
TOTAL EMISSIONS	79.1	20.6	20.6	46.7	21.0	4.7

NOx = nitrogen oxides   SOx = sulfur oxides   CO = Carbon monoxide
SPM = suspended particulate matter   VO = volatile organic compounds   PB = Lead

Note: Metric ton = 1.1023 short ton.

[1]Particulates represent both PM-10 (particles with an aerodynamic diameter less than 10 μm) and PM-10 fugitive dust (which includes dust from sources such as wind erosion, unpaved roads, construction, mining, and quarrying). [2]In thousands of metric tons.

Source: United States Environmental Protection Agency, 1992 data.

nitric oxide to oxidize carbon monoxide and hydrocarbons, yielding inert nitrogen, carbon dioxide, and water. (See also NITROGEN COMPOUNDS.)

Ozone. An unstable, toxic form of oxygen, ozone is found in smog. It is produced from the reaction of nitrogen oxides with gaseous hydrocarbons, in the presence of sunlight. Ozone sources also include lightning storms and sporadic, upper-atmospheric downdrafts, neither of which contributes to the national smog problem. Control of ozone and other photochemical oxidants is dependent on effective control of both nitrogen oxides and gaseous hydrocarbons. (See also OZONE.)

Toxic Substances. Asbestos, beryllium, mercury, and vinyl chloride are recognized hazardous substances requiring special controls for their production, manufacture, and use. Arsenic, benzene, and some radionuclides are also identified as hazardous airborne materials, and ways to control them are being formulated.

EFFECTS OF AIR POLLUTION

Effects on Human Health. The worst episode of air pollution in modern times occurred in London in 1952. That infamous "killer smog" is believed to have been responsible for 4,000 deaths. In the United States a similar incident occurred in 1948 in Donora, an industrial town in the mountains of western Pennsylvania. Almost half of the town's 14,000 inhabitants became ill, and 20 people died during the five-day smog episode. A study indicated that many who survived the episode suffered permanent health impairment. Another serious episode took place in New York City in 1953, when 200 people died as a result of high levels of sulfur oxides and particulate matter. The London, Donora, and New York City episodes occurred when unusual weather conditions that lasted several days prevented dispersal of the pollutants.

However, the subtle, long-range effects on human health caused by prolonged exposure to low-level air pollution are more far-reaching than the consequences of major pollution-related disasters. Long-term exposure has been linked to reduced exercise performance by healthy children and adults, an increased incidence of emphysema and bronchitis, and greater mortality rates for other illnesses, including cancer and heart disease. For example, smokers who live in polluted cities have a much higher rate of lung cancer than do those in rural areas. Among children, air pollution has been shown to be associated with a high incidence of asthma, allergies, and acute respiratory infection. Such childhood disorders may lead to chronic disease in later life. Nonetheless, a variety of factors, including difficulty in measuring exposure rates to pollutants and a lack of research into the effects of such exposure, have made it difficult to make a precise assessment of pollution-related health problems.

Carbon Monoxide. When carbon monoxide is inhaled, it displaces the oxygen in the blood and reduces the amount of oxygen carried to the body's tissues. At levels commonly found in city air, carbon monoxide can affect the reactions of even the healthiest persons, making them more prone to accidents. It also imposes an extra burden on those already suffering from, for example, anemia, diseases of the heart and blood vessels, chronic lung disease, an overactive thyroid, or fever. Persons with angina pectoris (chest pain caused by a narrowing or closure of coronary arteries, owing to atherosclerosis) are at particular risk when exposed for one hour or more to 35 milligrams of carbon monoxide per cubic meter of air (35 mg/m^3), which amounts to 30 parts per million (30 ppm), or if exposed for eight hours to 10 mg/m^3 (9 ppm). Such exposure can cause angina attacks to occur earlier in life and with greater frequency. Exposure of healthy persons to short-term levels of about 35 mg/m^3 can affect their muscle- and nerve-reaction times and visual acuity and induce headaches. Such levels of carbon monoxide are commonly found in cities throughout the world. In heavy traffic, levels of 80 mg/m^3 (70 ppm), 91 mg/m^3 (80 ppm), and 114 mg/m^3 (100 ppm) are not uncommon.

Sulfur Oxides. The sulfur oxides can cause either temporary or permanent injury to the respiratory system. Sulfur dioxide gas alone can irritate the upper respiratory tract, but when sulfur oxides are inhaled along with particulate matter—the bits of carbon, ash, oil, grease, and metal that constitute much of the visible pollution of the air—health damage (including attacks of asthma) increases significantly. The air-pollution disasters of recent years have been due primarily to sharply increased levels of both sulfur oxides and particulates.

Chronic health effects are observed when annual levels of sulfur oxides exceed 120 μg (micrograms)/m^3 (0.04 ppm) in the presence of particulates. Asthmatic attacks are initiated and reversible changes in pulmonary function occur when sulfur oxides, measured as sulfur dioxide, are present for 24 hours at a level above 200 μg/m^3 (0.07 ppm) and are associated with particulates. Levels above 300 μg/m^3 (0.1 ppm) increase disease rates, while higher and recurring levels increase mortality—again, in association with particulates.

Sulfur oxide problems are no longer widespread in the United States. Nationwide, average annual levels of sulfur oxide are typically below 80 μg/m^3 (0.03 ppm). While the 24-hour levels are usually well below 300 μg/m^3 in most eastern and midwestern cities, levels exceed 400 μg/m^3 (0.14 ppm) in many western regions, particularly in the vicinity of smelters.

Particulates. The adverse health effects of particulates depend not only on their amounts but also on their chemical and physical properties. Particle size limits access to the lungs. Those reaching the lungs by mouth are usually less than 15 μm (micrometers) and by nose, less than 10 μm. Fine aerosol particles, 2 μm or smaller, ultimately reach the lung's fine structures, the individual alveoli. The effects produced depend on their chemical properties—toxicity, acidity, solubility—and physical structure. Larger particles have few health effects but may cause soiling and deterioration of materials and damage to some agricultural crops and vegetation.

It is not clear what health effects are caused by particles alone, because particles typically occur together with other airborne contaminants or may themselves transport absorbed or adhering deleterious substances. For example, the toxicity of particulates in association with sulfur oxides is clearly responsible for a wide variety of adverse health effects.

Some particulates present special health hazards. Beryllium, emitted from a few industrial sources and rocket fuels, can cause lesions in the lung, leading to serious respiratory damage and even death. Asbestos, long recognized as an occupational hazard, enters the atmosphere as a result of construction materials, brake linings, and other products, and as a result of the razing of buildings containing asbestos. Long exposure produces the lung-scarring disease asbestosis. Even without heavy or continued exposure, asbestos can produce mesothelioma—a type of lung cancer associated almost exclusively with asbestos.

A host of other particulates are of concern even though they may not constitute an immediate and direct threat. For example, lead levels in the blood and urine of urban residents—although below those associated with classic lead poisoning—may affect the ability of the body to produce red blood cells and may have unsuspected adverse effects, particularly in children. Decreased use of leaded gasoline lessens the threat of illness from breathing airborne lead.

Ozone. Eye irritation occurs whenever short-term ozone concentrations are 200 µg/m³ (200 micrograms per cubic meter, or 0.1 ppm) or higher. The causal agent is not ozone itself, but rather some associated compounds such as aldehydes and peroxyacyl nitrates (PAN). Ozone at levels of 200 µg/m³ and higher irritates the mucous membranes of the respiratory system, causes coughing, choking, and pulmonary edema, and aggravates chronic respiratory diseases. Reduced pulmonary function occurs upon short-term exposure to about 500 µg/m³ (0.25 ppm) and can impair physical performance of healthy children and adults. Ozone levels from 200 µg/m³ to 600 µg/m³ (0.3 ppm) are commonly observed in both the summer and fall in many metropolitan areas.

Nitrogen Oxides. Short-term exposure to nitrogen dioxide can impair adaptation of the human eye to darkness—at about 140 µg/m³ (0.07 ppm)—and affect odor perception—at 200 µg/m³ (0.1 ppm). Disturbed pulmonary function and lowered resis-

tance to lung infections from short-term exposures occur at a nitrogen dioxide concentration of about 940 µg/m³ (0.5 ppm) nitrogen dioxide. Perhaps the most important health effect of nitrogen dioxide is its contribution to the production of ozone and to the formation of a variety of airborne nitrates and aerosols.

Effects on Plant Life. Sulfur dioxide fumes from a large copper smelter set up after the Civil War in Copper Basin, Tenn., devastated some 17,000 acres (7,000 ha) of plants and damaged 30,000 more acres (12,000 ha) of surrounding timberland. Much of this originally forested mountain land is still barren. In the vicinity of a British Columbia smelter, which in 1929 emitted an average of 16,000 metric tons of sulfur pollutants a month, plant injury was observed as far as 52 miles (84 km) from the smelter. Douglas fir, ponderosa pine, and forest shrubs as far as 30 miles (50 km) from the smelter sustained damages of 60% to 100%. Fluorides from aluminum smelters have caused similar injuries to native vegetation in Oregon and Washington.

Damage to plant life from these chemicals is less dramatic now than it was in the days of unrestricted smelter operations. However, chronic injury to agricultural, forest, and ornamental vegetation by increasing quantities and varieties of air pollutants and their alterations to ecosystems now affects all sections of the country. Smog in the south coastal basin of California contributes to the decline in production of citrus fruits and grapes and damages trees in the San Bernardino National Forest 50 miles (80 km) from Los Angeles. Smog in the San Francisco Bay area damages commercial crops and native vegetation in the nine-county area and adds to the damaging air pollution in the agriculturally important Sacramento and San Joaquin valleys, over 100 miles (160 km) distant, and injures forests in the Sierra

Effects of pollution on white pines: The young tree on the left was grown in filtered air and is healthy. The one on the right was exposed to air pollution and shows signs of chlorotic dwarf disease.

foothills. In New Jersey, pollution injury to vegetation has been observed in every county, and damage has been reported to at least 36 commercial crops. Similar injury occurs in Maryland, Delaware, Pennsylvania, New York, and Connecticut.

Sulfur dioxide damage rarely occurs in cities and is less severe around remote industrial sources. Chronic injury from such low-level, long-term exposure is usually associated with decline in tree growth, accumulation of sulfate in leaves, changes in foliation, alterations in nutrient cycling, changes in lichen populations, and alterations in coniferous ecosystems.

Ozone is the most serious air-pollutant threat to leafy vegetables, field and forage crops, shrubs, and fruit and forest trees, particularly conifers. Ozone damage to eastern white pine occurs after only four hours of exposure to 120 μg/m³ (0.06 ppm), while western ponderosa pine is damaged at about twice that level. The foliation changes lead to the premature fall of needles, increases in pine-beetle infestation, increases in ground-cover and attendant fire hazards, and decreases in seedling germination and thus fewer adult trees. Some kinds of tobacco exposed to 60 μg/m³ (0.03 ppm) can be so severely damaged as to be unmarketable.

Effects on Buildings and Materials. Air pollutants are damaging to a wide variety of materials. Steel corrodes two to four times faster in urban and industrial areas than in rural areas. When particulate matter is also present in the air, the corrosion rates increase greatly. Sulfur oxides accelerate the erosion of statuary and buildings throughout the world, causing alarm for future integrity of ancient buildings such as the Acropolis in Athens. Works of art made of stone or bronze are often moved indoors to preserve them from deterioration caused by air pollution. Particulate matter not only accelerates the corrosive action of other pollutants but in itself is responsible for costly damage and soiling. Ozone damages textiles, discolors dyed materials, cracks rubber, and adds to the total cost of producing tires by requiring the addition of antioxidant chemicals.

Visibility. Decreased visibility caused by air pollution interferes with the safe operation of aircraft and automobiles and disrupts transportation schedules. Low visibility caused by smoke, haze, and dust has been cited as a cause of plane crashes in the United States.

Nitrogen dioxide from electric-power, steel, and fertilizer plants and from motor vehicles is responsible for the brown haze that stains the sky over many cities and country areas. The major villains in reducing visibility locally and causing large-scale regional hazes, however, are particulates. These include ash, carbon, dusts, and the aerosol particles formed in the photochemical smog reaction and from the conversion of gaseous sulfur dioxide and nitric oxide to particulate sulfates and nitrates.

Particles suspended in the air scatter and absorb light, reducing the contrast and altering the coloration between objects and their background. Particles with radii of 0.1 to 1.0 micrometers have the greatest effect on visibility. The effect of an increase or decrease in particulates on visibility depends on existing pollution levels. For example, the addition of 2 μg/m³ sulfate aerosol to air in an area with a visual range of about 62 miles (100 km) would reduce visibility by 12 miles (20 km), obliterating some vistas and altering others.

The same addition of aerosols to air with a visual range of about 16 miles (26 km) would reduce visibility by only 1 mile (2 km) and would result in little change in vista. For this reason, a little cleaning in clean air does a lot, while the same cleaning in dirty air does little.

Weather and Climate. One of the most intriguing aspects of air pollution is its effect on weather and climate. In some sections of the United States, emissions of particulates have affected patterns of precipitation. Suspended particulates act as condensation nuclei and affect cloud formation and precipitation. Particulate pollution in eight U.S. cities has increased precipitation 9% to 17% downwind from pollution sources. In Pittsburgh and Buffalo, for example, rainfall has generally been lower on Sundays, when industrial production and automobile use are lowest. In Toronto, Canada, snow patterns show a similar correlation with levels of particles in air. Particulates in the air also reduce the amount of sunlight penetrating the atmosphere and adversely affect agricultural crop production.

Possible changes in the quality of sunlight reaching the earth may result from the release of chlorofluorocarbons (CFCs), used as refrigerants in air-conditioners and other appliances and formerly used as propellants in household spray cans. Use of these compounds has been restricted, the result of evidence indicating that once they reach the upper atmosphere, CFCs are capable of damaging the earth's ozone layer. Because the ozone layer absorbs much of the sun's ultraviolet radiation, reductions in ozone may pose a health threat in the form of increased exposure to ultraviolet light and, as a consequence, a potential rise in cases of skin cancer and cataracts.

The effects of increasing concentrations of particulates and other air pollutants throughout the world are not well understood. Some experts believe that a cooling trend in regional and global climate may be associated with increased aerosols in the atmosphere. They warn that at some time in the future a further reduction in solar radiation, caused by high particulate levels, might bring on another ice age.

Other experts see a different danger. They note that by 1994, worldwide, carbon dioxide was being released into the atmosphere at a rate of almost 6 billion tons annually. Researchers also discovered that since 1958, when measurements were first taken, the concentration of carbon dioxide in the atmosphere had risen from 314 parts per million to 358 ppm. With no change in present trends of fuel use, cutting of forests, and growth of farm acreage, carbon dioxide levels may approximately double in the first half of the 21st century. As a result of the so-called greenhouse effect, this may cause a worldwide temperature increase of 2° to 3.5° C (3.6°–6.3° F). Experts warn that such a change might melt the polar ice caps, raise the level of the oceans, and inundate many coastal areas. (See also GREENHOUSE EFFECT.)

Increasing amounts of pollutant aerosols in the atmosphere also contribute to acid precipitation in the United States, Canada, and northern Europe. Rain is naturally somewhat acid, about pH 5.6, because of its reaction with atmospheric carbon dioxide and at times with pollutants from forest fires and volcanoes. Rain becomes more acid after reacting with sulfate and nitrate aerosols produced in the atmosphere by emissions from fossil-fuel combustion in stationary and mobile sources. Acid rain disturbs aquatic ecosystems, resulting in lakes without fish; alters some terrestrial ecosystems; and may damage agricultural crops and reduce the growth of forest trees. Acid rain in the western United States usually is higher in nitrates than in sulfates and usually has a pH of 5.5. to 5.0. Eastern acid rains are typically higher in sulfates and range mostly from pH 5.0 to 4.0.

Acid rain occurs in most states east of the Mississippi River. It is particularly prevalent in an area extending from southern Illinois to southern Maine, with the area of greatest impact in the Adirondack Mountains of New York. Internationally, emissions that result in acid rain are a source of friction between some countries. Many Canadian lakes have suffered fish kills as a result of acid rain originating in the United States. Similarly, the acid rains that fall in Scandinavian countries are caused by pollution originating in industrial centers of Britain, France, and Germany.

PROGRAMS FOR COMBATING POLLUTION

United States. In the United States a variety of federal, state, and local programs are aimed at combating air pollution. The first federal program was created in 1955. It provided for federal leadership, technical assistance, and financial support, but primary responsibility for dealing with community problems was vested in state and local governments. In 1963 Congress enacted the Clean Air Act, authorizing direct federal grants to state and local agencies to assist them in developing and improving air-pollution-control programs, and established a federal activity to abate interstate air pollution. The Clean Air Act was amended in 1965 to establish federal controls for motor-vehicle emissions. Amendments in 1967 provided a systematic basis for assuring protection of the public health from air pollution throughout the nation. The 1970 and 1977 amendments enunciated the role of state and local governments in meeting national air-quality goals, detailed a system for their achievement, established reinforcement procedures, and reserved responsibility for their compliance to the Environmental Protection Agency (EPA). The Clean Air Act of 1990 added some strength to the earlier bill, legislating the replacement of CFCs in industrial production and providing the EPA with new tools for attacking acid rain, smog, and airborne chemicals.

The chief goal of the federal program is to protect public health and welfare. National primary air-quality standards are established to safeguard health from damaging effects of carbon monoxide, lead, nitrogen dioxide, ozone, particulate matter, and sulfur oxides. National secondary air-quality standards are established to prevent damage to property, crops, and livestock, as well as undesirable effects on the environment, including acid precipitation and diminished visibility.

Federal air standards are expressed in terms of exposure to a specified amount of pollutant for a given period and a reference method for their measurement. The primary standards, designed to protect against adverse health effects and provide a margin of safety, are: carbon monoxide, a maximum of 40 mg/m^3 (35 ppm) for 1 hour or a maximum of 10 mg/m^3 (9 ppm) for 8 hours, measured by infrared spectroscopy; lead, not to exceed a three-month average of 1.5 µg/m^3, measured by atomic absorption spectroscopy; nitrogen dioxide, not to exceed an annual mean of 100 µg/m^3 (0.05 ppm), measured by chemiluminescence; ozone, a maximum daily average of 235 µg/m^3 (0.12 ppm) for 1 hour, measured by chemiluminescence; particulate matter, for particles less than 10 micrometers in diameter, an annual mean of 50 µg/m^3 or a maximum of 150 µg/m^3 for 24 hours; and sulfur oxides, a maximum of 365 µg/m^3 (0.14 ppm) for 24 hours, with an annual mean not to exceed 80 µg/m^3 (0.03 ppm), measured as sulfur dioxide by the pararosaniline method.

Each state is responsible for preparing an enforceable strategy, called a state implementation plan (SIP), to meet the national air-quality standards where air quality is poorer than standards specify, and it becomes effective following review and approval by EPA. This plan must show how air at least as clean as the standards require will be maintained. Each SIP presents inventories of the kinds and amounts of pollutants from stationary and mobile sources, specifies the emission limitations and compliance schedules for stationary sources, gives transportation-control measures and schedules to be used to reduce traffic and traffic-inducing development, and provides for an air-quality measurement network to monitor compliance with the air-quality standards.

National standards limiting emissions at sources of pollution are established for hazardous toxic substances, designated classes of industries, and motor vehicles. These performance standards prescribe only the allowable emissions and leave open the compliance technology to be used, thus providing opportunity for technical innovation and cost savings.

Nationally, four types of emission-control technologies are designated for use under varying demands of air-quality improvement. In areas where existing air quality is poorer than the national air-quality standards specify, new industrial sources may be required to use the control technology that produces the lowest achievable emission rate (LAER) rather than merely meeting federally specified new-source performance standards (NSPS). Existing industries in such areas may be obliged to install reasonable available control technology (RACT). In some clean air areas, new sources may be required to install best available control technology (BACT) in order to prevent significant deterioration of the air resource. In cases where pollution from existing plants causes poor visibility in areas of national interest, such as national parks and wilderness areas, the offending sources can be required to use the best available retrofit technology (BART). Enforcement of scheduled emission limits for major sources is by judicial action by the states or the EPA. Compliance may be enhanced by threat of penalties and by citizen suits against violators.

Progress in meeting the national air-quality goals established by the national air-quality standards is monitored by some 4,000 air-quality measuring stations throughout the nation. Measurements are made continuously and on a programmed intermittent schedule using EPA-approved methods. The information system is centralized and computerized, and reports are published summarizing the data by cities and regions and giving national trends.

Programs in Other Countries. Air pollution is a problem in most large urban centers and industrial communities throughout the world, especially those in areas with land and climates that prevent rapid diffusion and dispersion of pollutants. Member nations of the European Community rec-

EPG

Pollutants from midwestern power plants and factories cause acid rains in the U.S. Northeast and Canada.

ognize the importance of collective action, since air-pollution-control measures in one country affect air quality in another, both by the transport of pollution from stationary sources and by the international movement of polluting motor vehicles. Motor vehicles manufactured within the community since the early 1970s have been equipped with crank-case and exhaust emission controls. Stationary-source emissions have been variously controlled by national regulations applying reasonable available control technology. The benefits of emission controls have been greatly augmented by programs in land-use planning and management, which determine sites for industrial plants based on permissible emission densities, and by specific protection of residential and recreation areas.

Abatement and control of pollution in Australia, Brazil, Japan, and Mexico strongly focus on smog problems in metropolitan centers. Smog in Mexico City, for example, is particularly difficult to control because of the city's size, population, elevation, high actinic radiation, terrain, and weather conditions. These all favor seasonal accumulation of pollution and aggravate smog formation from emissions of the many motor vehicles and local industries. Motor vehicles in Australia and Japan are equipped with emission-control systems, and state and local governments inspect vehicles to ensure compliance. Brazil reduces transportation pollution by use of clean-burning sugarcane alcohol as a partial substitute for gasoline, as well as limits emissions from stationary sources. Japan requires very advanced control systems for industrial emissions in cities where land and weather conditions accentuate the health risk of air pollution.

An international treaty, the Geneva Convention on Long-Range Transboundary Air Pollution, was adopted in 1979 as a means of controlling the emission of air pollutants and discouraging their spread across national boundaries. Another international agreement, a nonbinding treaty resulting from the 1992 UN Conference on Environment and Development, also known as the Earth Summit, directs signatories to decrease their carbon dioxide emissions to 1990 levels by the year 2000. The 1990s also saw the majority of nations agreeing to a phaseout of chlorofluorocarbons before the end of the 20th century.

JOHN T. MIDDLETON*
University of California at Riverside

Bibliography

Carter, F. W., and D. Turnock, eds., *Environmental Problems in Eastern Europe* (Routledge 1993).
Council on Environmental Quality, *The Global 2000 Report to the President: Entering the 21st Century,* vol. 1 (Penguin 1982).
Dorfman, Robert, and Nancy S. Dorfman, *Economics of the Environment: Selected Readings,* 3d ed. (Norton 1993).
Dunnette, David A., and Robert J. O'Brien, eds., *The Science of Global Change: The Impact of Human Activities on the Environment* (American Chem. Society 1992).
Flagan, Richard C., and John H. Seinfeld, *Fundamentals of Air Pollution Engineering* (Prentice-Hall 1988).
Francis, B. Magnus, *Toxic Substances in the Environment* (Wiley 1994).
Moore, Curtis, and Alan Miller, *Green Gold: Japan, Germany, the United States, and the Race for Environmental Technology* (Beacon Press 1994).
Ney, Ronald E., *Fate and Transport of Organic Chemicals in the Environment,* 2d ed. (Government Insts. 1995).
Sullivan, T. F. P., ed., *United States Environmental Protection Agency Guidebook, 1984–85* (USGPO 1984).
Tillman, David A., *Trace Metals in Combustion Systems* (Academic Press 1994).
Wark, Kenneth, and Cecil F. Warner, *Air Pollution: Its Origin and Control,* 2d ed. (Harper 1981).

AIR POWER. See Air Warfare.

AIR PRESSURE, âr presh′ər, is the force per unit area exerted by the atmosphere. The atmosphere, or air, exerts a pressure because of its weight (gravitational force between the air and the earth). The fact that air has weight was first demonstrated in 1644 by the Italian scientist Evangelista Torricelli, who invented the mercury barometer to prove his point. At sea level, the pressure of the atmosphere is approximately equal to the weight per unit cross-sectional area of a column of mercury 76 centimeters high.

At any altitude, the weight of the air is proportional to the mass of air above the altitude. Therefore, air pressure, like air mass, decreases with increasing height. This fact, which was first proved by Blaise Pascal in 1648, is the basis for the pressure altimeter, an instrument that determines altitude by measuring pressure. Mercury barometers, aneroid barometers, and other types of barometers are used to measure air pressure.

Pressure often is expressed in inches, centimeters, or millimeters of mercury. However, the correct unit of pressure should have the dimensions of force divided by area. In meteorology, the unit of air pressure is the *millibar,* which is defined as 1,000 dynes per square centimeter. (The dyne is the unit of force in the cgs system.) At sea level, the air pressure is approximately equal to 1,000 millibars. At 6 kilometers above sea level the pressure is about 500 millibars. A pressure of 1,000 millibars corresponds to approximately 76 centimeters (30 inches) of mercury, which is equivalent to a pressure of about 14.5 pounds per square inch.

In high-altitude commercial airplanes, the pressure inside the plane is maintained at a value that is safe and comfortable for human activity. Without this pressurization the air pressure would be too low to provide sufficient oxygen for life, and the rapid pressure changes accompanying changes in altitude would produce serious physical discomfort as well as "bends" (aeroembolism). This condition is caused by the release of nitrogen bubbles into the blood when pressure drops too rapidly.

Air pressure varies in space and time. Local pressure variations are associated with changes in weather. Falling pressure usually is associated with deteriorating weather, and rising pressure with improving weather. This relationship can be understood in terms of a weather map on which the distribution of pressure over some region is shown. Lines of equal pressure on the map are called *isobars.* The isobars delineate areas of high and low pressure. The low pressure areas are called *lows;* the high pressure areas are called *highs.* In the Northern Hemisphere, the wind travels counterclockwise and inward around lows and clockwise and outward around highs. In the Southern Hemisphere, the direction of the air circulation is reversed. The lows frequently are regions of cloudiness and precipitation; the highs frequently are regions of clear weather. A low frequently brings poorer weather, and a high usually brings improving weather. See also Air; Barometer; Meteorology; Weather.

Air pressure is used in the operation of water pumps, vacuum cleaners, pressure cookers, and a myriad of other devices.

Jerome Spar, *New York University*

AIR PUMP. See Pumps; Vacuum Pumps.

AIR RESERVE FORCES. See Air Force Reserves.

AIR RIGHTS, âr rīts, in law, are the rights in that area or space above improved or unimproved real property. The term means especially those air rights that could be owned apart from the land itself.

The use of air rights permits the development of land to the highest degree. The former real estate doctrine recognized ownership of land as running from the center of the earth to the sky, with the inherent right to use of the air space above the property itself.

Since the beginning of the so-called population explosion after World War II, air rights have assumed significant importance. The unprecedented growth of cities, with the consequent scarcity of land for buildings, highways, and parking facilities, created such a problem in horizontal expansion that city planners focused their sights on vertical expansion; this has brought about legislation restricting and limiting property rights in the space above ground. The original use of air rights was limited to the building of structures over railroad tracks and rights of way, but with increasing demands new uses of air rights are constantly being conceived.

Several outstanding examples of air rights use in the United States are found in New York City. These include the towering buildings that have been erected over the New York Central Railroad tracks; an immense housing project built in air rights over part of the George Washington Bridge approach; and the Pan Am Building, which utilized air rights over the Grand Central Terminal (the upper floors being extended over a city roadway without interfering with traffic).

In 1966, New York Gov. Nelson A. Rockefeller signed a bill permitting New York City to build hundreds of millions of dollars' worth of schools with apartments or offices above them. An unusual fund plan authorized the city to transfer land, on which a public school was to be built, to a private developer. He would build a school on the site and use the air rights over the school (for which use he would pay the city) to construct apartments and office space.

Other notable uses of air rights include the huge Chicago Merchandise Mart, which stands over the Chicago and Northwestern Railroad tracks. A portion of the Cleveland Athletic Club is erected horizontally over the roof of a lower adjoining structure. Federal post offices have been constructed in air rights across the country, with additional air rights acquired over adjoining properties to ensure light and air. Hotels and office buildings have been built in the air rights over parking lots.

The increased use of air rights in the United States and elsewhere has given rise to new problems; for, like real property, air rights are bought, sold, mortgaged, leased, and otherwise dealt with. However, laws affecting air rights have been favorably and liberally construed. Air rights are taxed like real property.

Increasing use of air rights can be envisaged in the city of the future—a city of multi-decked streets and many-storied buildings, literally a city upon a city.

Hyman Sukloff
Author of "Small Property Owner's Legal Guide"

AIR SAFETY, or the safe operation of aircraft, is a goal that provides many challenges. Air flight involves a unique problem because aircraft must remain in motion in order to resist the force of gravity. Unlike trains, ships, or automobiles, aircraft cannot be stopped for an emergency. Helicopters and other vertical-lift aircraft can hover in flight, but they too depend on the continuing motion of rotors.

Besides those safety problems intrinsic to an aircraft's need for constant motion, there are many others that must be solved if air safety is to be achieved. Aircraft must be designed to provide stability and control, structural integrity, and reliability. They must be able to operate in emergencies and without visual reference to the earth. Their pilots have to meet high standards of skill and judgment. Adequate airports and reliable aids for navigation and communication are essential, and standard regulations for flight must be formulated and enforced. Natural hazards, such as dangerous terrain, violently turbulent air, loss of visual reference to the earth, and the formation of ice on the wings, must be dealt with as well. A more recent problem in air safety concerns terrorism and hijacking. The vulnerability of aircraft to these hazards has caused designers of aircraft and airports to adopt a total systems approach in designing for safety.

Accident Causes and Control. When catastrophic accidents (such as midair collisions or crash landings with fires possibly following the crash) take place, their causes are investigated intensively so that similar accidents can be prevented in the future. Causes of accidents include loss of control because of air turbulence, engine failure and disintegration, metal fatigue, and sabotage. In addition, pilots may become the victims of sensory illusions or may unwittingly or deliberately depart from safe flying practices. One of the primary objectives of air safety regulations is to eliminate as far as possible variations in vehicle design, procedures, and pilot performance that are common in other modes of transportation so that the causes of mishaps can be identified.

Collisions. Midair collisions are relatively rare, as the control of air traffic depends largely on rules stating that airplanes must maintain certain distances from each other. Thus planes flying in the same direction keep a horizontal distance between them equivalent to about 10 minutes of flying time. Planes traveling in different directions keep a vertical distance between them of about 1,000 feet (300 meters). At heights above 24,000 feet (7,200 meters) the vertical separation must be about 2,000 feet (600 meters). Aircraft are identified en route by position reports submitted to ground control units by the pilot or automatically by radar. Ground control supervises planes that are operating on approved flight plans. Flight plans are required for operation in poor-visibility weather when the pilot must fly by instruments. They are not mandatory in clear weather except above 24,000 feet. The separation between aircraft near busy airports is controlled by radar approach systems and the airport control tower. A collision-avoidance device that automatically separates aircraft on collision courses is used in large commercial aircraft and is available for use in general aviation.

Fires. The problem of fires following a crash is being attacked by experiments with improved, tougher fuel-tank material. Structures surrounding the tanks are designed to reduce the probability of their penetrating the tanks during a crash. Fire- or spark-producing sources are separated from flammable fluids where possible, and fuel lines are run inside other metal lines as a protective measure. The most promising avenues of research are the development of "thickened" fuels that will not burn explosively except within the engines, and the design of anticombustible foam systems that can be activated in the event of a crash.

Turbulence. Clear-air turbulence can occur in the lee of mountains, in the wake of aircraft, and in the upper reaches of the atmosphere. Devices to detect turbulence and wind shear (sudden severe downdrafts) have been installed at most major airports. Forecasting techniques also are being improved for the more precise prediction of such turbulence. The turbulence associated with storms usually can be discovered by radar. Furthermore, new piloting techniques enable pilots to retain better control of their craft when severe turbulence is encountered.

Unsafe Flying Procedures. All jet-powered transports must carry a flight recorder—the so-called black box—that registers speed, time, acceleration, heading, and altitude of the craft. Departures from safe flight practice can be detected, within the limits of the recorder, before they result in accidents.

Supersonic Flight. The supersonic transport (SST), capable of flight faster than the speed of sound, raises additional problems. The heat generated by friction between air and aircraft may reach 400° F (260° C), making reliable air conditioning an absolute requirement. The effects of radiation and ozone on passengers and on structural materials also must be considered. The thorough research that led to the development of supersonic military craft has been successfully applied to supersonic transports such as the Concorde.

Safety Regulations. Civil aviation is divided into two categories: air-carrier operations, both passenger and cargo, and nonair-carrier operations, or general aviation (for instance, instructional, pleasure, business, advertising, or law enforcement flight). Though air carriers are required to operate with the highest degree of care, nonair carriers are still expected to meet rigorous standards of safety so that the skies will be safe for all aircraft.

Both categories of civil aviation in the United States are subject to safety regulations issued by the Federal Aviation Administration (FAA). The FAA establishes and enforces standards of airworthiness and performance, air traffic rules, and standards governing the competence of fliers. The FAA builds, maintains, and operates the Air Traffic Control systems and supervises the airways. It also participates with the Weather Bureau in disseminating weather information.

The Bureau of Safety of the Civil Aeronautics Board (CAB) investigates accidents, prepares reports of their probable causes, and makes safety recommendations to the FAA. It also arbitrates when pilots accused of violating regulations or unable to satisfy the physical requirements set by the FAA wish to appeal for adjudication.

See also AIR NAVIGATION; AIRPLANE; CIVIL AERONAUTICS BOARD; FEDERAL AVIATION ADMINISTRATION.

JEROME F. LEDERER
Cornell-Guggenheim Aviation Safety Center

Personnel and equipment at the San Francisco International Airport air traffic control tower monitor and direct airspace movement and airport ground activity and coordinate air traffic with nearby Oakland International Airport.

AIR TRAFFIC CONTROL, the general network of radio and radar navigation systems used to control flights of aircraft from one airport to another. The continuing growth of air traffic around the world has placed increasing demands on flight management systems to ensure safety and orderly operations. This growth has also made it increasingly apparent that however limitless airspace may seem, it is in fact a finite resource.

Airspace Management and Control. The basic purpose of air traffic control (ATC) is the same as that for surface-vehicle traffic control—the avoidance of collisions. When a pilot's visibility is such that the pilot can "see and be seen" sufficiently to avoid a collision with other aircraft, few ATC restrictions are in effect once a flight plan has been filed. When visibility is poor, or when an aircraft is flying through "positive controlled airspace" (near congested airports, over restricted military areas, or at high altitudes), separation and guidance criteria must be provided by some external agency.

This separation is accomplished by assigning to each aircraft a definite unit of airspace, like a huge box or cube that moves along with the aircraft as it progresses. If an aircraft encounters traffic congestion, this box is enlarged to provide space for the aircraft to "hold" (fly in a descending oval pattern) while awaiting approval to proceed. Further, the sky is divided into highways for air travel, much like roads for ground transportation. These three-dimensional channels, known as airways or air lanes, are the means of organizing, directing, and regulating air traffic.

Typically, usable airspace has a ceiling of 75,000 feet (23,000 meters) and is usually divided into two levels: below 18,000 feet (6,400 meters) for small aircraft, and over 18,000 feet for large transports. (Military aircraft generally travel at still higher altitudes, over 50,000 feet, or 15,200 meters.) Aircraft traveling in opposite directions in the same airway are normally separated by 1,000 feet (300 meters) of altitude when below 24,000 feet (8,500 meters), and by twice that when above that height.

Federal Aviation Administration. On Aug. 23, 1958, the U.S. Congress passed the Federal Aviation Act establishing the Federal Aviation Administration (FAA). The FAA is responsible for setting, reviewing, and enforcing Visual Flight Rules (VFR) and Instrument Flight Rules (IFR) and for establishing the competency level required of pilots in order to abide by these rules. Piloting qualifications are designated by the pilots' Airline Transport Rating (ATR).

National Airspace System. In 1981 the FAA charted a comprehensive blueprint for modernization, the National Airspace System (NAS) plan, transforming air traffic control to a safer, more efficient airspace-management system, primarily through automation. A further improvement, the Capital Investment plan (CIP), has been instituted by the FAA.

Advanced Automation System. The NAS plan, revised annually through 1989, provided a solid base for the FAA development program. The backbone of the NAS plan is the Advanced Automation System (AAS), which was scheduled to begin operation in 1992 and is expected to meet all airspace-management operating needs through the year 2010.

The AAS serves as an air traffic controller's window to the outside world. All the information received by the controller is processed and displayed by the AAS, serving as a central clearinghouse for data on which decisions are based. For the first time, all primary air traffic controllers have real-time control over aircraft traveling under Instrument Flight Rules. The integrated, automated AAS is designed to control the airspace and be supportive of any future flight-management system.

Voice Switching and Control System. A critical part of the FAA's AAS implementation plan is the development of the Voice Switching and Control System (VSCS), which replaces the radio-communication switches at en route centers nationwide and interfaces with the new controller workstations. The VSCS provides computer-controlled voice switching for air-to-ground, interphone, and intercom communications, with controllers able to change communication channels from their workstations. The VSCS also assigns any frequency to any workstation, so that the airspace under a controller's command can be easily configured. The VSCS position equipment, located in the sector-suite consoles, is flexible and reconfigurable in a manner compatible with the evolving AAS.

Ground- and Space-based Systems. Supporting the air traffic control system is a network of ground-based and planned space-based communications, navigation, and radar systems. Navigation aids ("navaids") show a great deal of variation and development from country to country, pointing to the great need for a uniform and universal standard for air traffic control.

VHF Omnidirectional Radio Range System. The VHF Omnidirectional Radio Range (VOR) is currently approved by the International Civil Aviation Organization (ICAO) for ground-based, short-distance navigation, providing azimuth information.

Distance Measuring Equipment. Distance Measuring Equipment (DME) is a system combining ground-based and airborne equipment to measure the distance of an aircraft from the ground facility. DME is used primarily for fixing an aircraft's position, approaching an airport, avoiding protected airspace or ground space, holding at a given position, or figuring ground speeds. The DME ground station is usually located at the same site with other navigation systems.

DME ground stations are capable of handling approximately 100 aircraft interrogations at one time. If more than 100 aircraft interrogate the ground station, the station limits its sensitivity and replies to the strongest 100 interrogations. In poor signal areas it is possible that the airborne DME may not receive replies to all of its interrogations, so modern DMEs are designed to operate at a 50% reply efficiency, with little detriment to their operation.

The international standard civil navigation system used in the United States is a combination of VOR and DME, usually operating from one site. The VOR provides the aircraft azimuth information relative to the VOR/DME ground station, while the DME furnishes distance from the aircraft to that facility.

Depending on available facilities, VOR and DME navigation aids may be used in one of the following configurations: VOR only, VOR/DME, or DME/DME. The utilization of dual DMEs significantly improves position-determination accuracy in areas that have suitable dual DME coverage.

Tactical Air Navigation System. The Tactical Air Navigation System (TACAN), originally developed in the early 1950s for military use, was intended to provide the pilot with an automatic visual indication of azimuth bearing and distance measurements to or from a TACAN ground installation. The ground antenna pattern provides both bearing and distance information.

The distance-measuring function of the modern TACAN system operates in the same manner as the civil Distance Measuring Equipment. It is compatible with the international standard DME system and therefore accessible to all users possessing a DME interrogator. So that both civil and military aircraft can navigate using the same airways network, TACAN facilities are usually part of VOR facilities, the combination known as VORTAC.

LORAN System. LORAN, an acronym for *long-range navigation,* is an electronic means, developed for marine use during the early 1940s, for establishing position relative to three or more stations transmitting low-frequency radio signals from points as far away as 1,000 miles (1,600

© BRIAN PARKER/TOM STACK & ASSOCIATES

Controller at remote ATC site monitors storms (*left*). Screen at Aurora, Ill., shows direction, altitude, speed, and ID tail number for each aircraft, and air lanes and ATC sectors (*below*).

© CAMERAMANN INT'L, LTD.

km). The commercial development of the computer microchip in the 1960s opened the door to a vastly improved form of LORAN. A minicomputer coupled to the receiver is not only capable of calculating position but can also be programmed to give other vital information. The FAA has recognized LORAN-C as the standard for long-range, over-water navigation.

NAVSTAR/Global Positioning System. In recent years the pilot's ability to navigate worldwide has been further enhanced by the development of the space-based NAVSTAR/Global Positioning System (GPS). The GPS has potential accuracies of 52.5 feet (16 meters) in three dimensions, the correct time within one-millionth of a second, and the user's velocity to the nearest one-tenth of a meter per second. (By contrast, current oceanic systems commonly show navigation errors of 10 miles [18 km] or more when aircraft reach land.)

As designed, GPS consists of a network of 21 satellites (plus three operational spares) in six orbital planes, each broadcasting precise time and location information. The satellites operate in circular 12,500-mile (20,200-km) orbits at an inclined angle of 55° and with a 12-hour period, precisely arranged so that a minimum of five satellites will be in view at all times at any spot on the globe. If desired, the GPS signal could ultimately be used in an airborne collision-avoidance mode and in maritime hazard-avoidance systems. As the system gains worldwide acceptance by the military and civil sectors, more sophisticated uses are sure to be found.

GLONASS. The Global Orbiting Navigation Satellite System (GLONASS), primarily a military system developed by the former Soviet Union, was offered to the world's aviation community as a navigation source in 1988. The structure of the GLONASS signal is similar to that of GPS and enables the use of both signals in a single integrated-receiver design.

Precision Landing Systems. In the course of any flight the landing represents the most risk-laden operation. In earlier systems pilots relied on coded runway lights and on Ground-Controlled Approach (GCA), a "talk down" system in which a radar operator using Precision Approach Radar (PAR) guided the pilot in for a landing. With landings at major airports reaching a rate of one per minute, a more reliable system was required.

Instrument Landing System. For over 40 years the Instrument Landing System (ILS) has been the worldwide standard precision-instrument approach-and-landing system approved by the ICAO. It provides vertical and horizontal navigational information to aircraft during the critical period of the plane's approach to landing at an airport runway.

There have been many changes and improvements to ILS equipment in the aircraft since its inception. Although the ILS still remains the ICAO-approved precision landing system, the need for a replacement was identified as long ago as 1967. Given the system's serious limitations, the ICAO has recommended that a new Microwave Landing System (MLS) replace the ILS as the world's standard precision landing system.

Microwave Landing System. The Microwave Landing System (MLS) operates on the same basic principle as the ILS, in that the system provides a horizontal (or azimuth) signal and a glide angle (or elevation) signal, both of which are converted to a display in the cockpit, establishing a flight path for the landing approach. But unique features of the MLS provide distinct advantages over the ILS. MLS signals, in combination with on-board computers, also introduce a new element of flexibility in designing IFR curved and segmented approaches, using area navigation types of way points and straight-line segments. This allows adjusting the approach design for the lowest possible weather minimum without loss of safety. Additionally, it makes it possible to use an approach course for landing at nonaligned runways. Under IFR conditions, this could increase the capacity of some airports appreciably without further construction.

Surveillance Systems. Surveillance systems provide aircraft position information to air traffic management facilities. Such information may be derived from information available in the cockpit and transmitted automatically or manually to the ground facility, or it may be derived by independent means.

Mode S Secondary Radar and Datalink System. Future air traffic surveillance over much of the earth's surface will be obtained through the use of satellite links. With the advent of tighter spacing between aircraft because of anticipated air traffic growth, reliable communications are critical. This consideration is at the heart of the FAA's Capital Investment plan.

A portion of the CIP is devoted to the Mode S (for *Select*) Secondary Radar and Datalink System, which is expected to provide digital communication between FAA ground facilities and the aircraft. With Mode S there exists for the first time within the air traffic control system the capability to exchange information directly between the aircraft, ground-based weather, and air traffic control. A prime advantage of Mode S is that each aircraft equipped with a Mode S transponder is assigned a unique address, guaranteeing positive identification.

Automatic Dependent Surveillance. The concept of Automatic Dependent Surveillance (ADS), based on satellite-communication technology, represents a revolutionary new way air traffic control may be performed in the large oceanic areas that are beyond the coverage of land-based radar. For example, domestic air traffic control within the United States is based on the use of radar surveillance and VHF communications, both of which are line-of-sight systems. Oceanic air traffic control, however, usually begins where these systems are no longer applicable.

ADS is based on the concept of transferring aircraft-derived position reports via digital datalink from the aircraft to an air traffic control facility for display to the controller. In concept, the aircraft position reports are transmitted automatically at predetermined intervals without direct involvement of either the pilot or the controller. Combined with GPS, ADS could provide data nearly as accurate and current as ground-based radar surveillance used in domestic airspace.

See also AIR TRANSPORTATION; AIRPORT; AVIATION.

SAM FISHBEIN
National Air and Space Museum
Smithsonian Institution

Bibliography: Nolan, Michael S., *Fundamentals of Air Traffic Control* (Wadsworth 1990); **Obe, Arnold E.,** *International Air Traffic Control: Management of the World's Airspace,* 2d ed. (Pergamon 1985); **Turner, James E.,** *Air Traffic Controller* (Arco 1986).

The supersonic Concorde (*above*) and Pan American's Sikorsky S-42 flying boat ("China Clipper") of the mid-1930s, each the ultimate in air travel in its day.

AIR TRANSPORTATION. The transport of passengers by aircraft between the major cities of the world is one of the most remarkable developments of the 20th century. Ocean liners for intercontinental travel and railways and motorbuses for continental intercity passenger transportation have effectively been replaced by jet aircraft, typically traveling at 550 miles (885 km) per hour over nonstop distances up to one-third of the earth's circumference. From 1960 to 1990 U.S. air travel has grown tenfold, doubling its market share during that period from 45% to 91%; rail has declined by 66%; and bus transportation has risen by only 20%.

Air transport has helped to change the political world from a set of isolated, independent nation-states to a highly interdependent global community of nations, and the business world from firms with a single national identity to a world of multinational and international businesses. National leaders and businesspeople are able to visit any other country within hours for important face-to-face meetings with their counterparts. Goods manufactured in one country can be flown quickly to another to satisfy unexpected market demands. The United States has maintained a position of world leadership in the civil air transportation industry since the end of World War II despite many turbulent episodes.

Historical Factors. The development of air transport in this century has been marked by advances in aeronautical technology. Improvements in nonstop range, cruising speed, seating capacity, passenger comfort, and operational safety have been remarkable and have allowed a corresponding growth of international and domestic air transportation services.

These improvements in aircraft performance were achieved by the aircraft-manufacturing industries developed by the governments of all the industrialized nations of the world following World War I, when aircraft emerged as a major factor in military power. The civil air transportation industry is the by-product of military aviation development by governments around the world. Whereas the European aircraft industry was in a leading position at the end of World War I, the policies and actions of the U.S. government between the world wars, and the large aircraft-manufacturing role assigned by the Allies to the United States during World War II, placed the U.S. aircraft-manufacturing industry in a predominant position at the end of World War II.

The governments of the major nations of the world have also played a more direct role in promoting the development of civil air transportation services. While airlines may have begun as private ventures, they were generally unprofitable, and governments were easily persuaded that subsidizing air transportation was in their national interest, especially for colonial powers. National "flag" carriers were created and supported by most governments as an expression of national pride and the health of their economy. They were used mainly for the rapid carriage of mail, government officials, and businesspeople between nations. In the larger countries, such as the United States, Canada, and Australia, there were political reasons to subsidize the development of internal domestic services that would stimulate regional and national economic development. Public subsidization inevitably led each government to develop national policies and regulations to direct the administration of civil aviation in financial, economic, and safety matters.

As air transport expanded, the construction of larger civil airports and the provision of expanded air traffic control services became the responsibility of governments. At the end of World

War II the United States led the world in establishing an international body to promulgate international standards, recommend practices for air navigation, and assist poorer nations in establishing an aviation infrastructure that would ensure safety in international air transportation. This body, the International Civil Aviation Organization (ICAO), is now part of the United Nations, with a membership of 186 nations.

The original reasons for governmental support are fading as improvement in global telecommunications is reducing reliance on air travel, and a larger portion of air travel is now being done by private persons for personal pleasure in the form of global tourism, leisure vacations, and visits to friends and relatives. Yet it may very well turn out that increased electronic communication in business and government may actually increase the need and desire for in-person contact across the continents.

Impact of Technology on Transport Aircraft. In the early part of this century several well-known scientists predicted that engineers would never be able to design a practical transport aircraft. They were unable to foresee the amazing advances in aeronautical technologies ahead.

The early aircraft were limited in speed, range, and payload and were unable to fly in bad weather. Their reliability and safety were such that early aviators, like today's astronauts, were regarded as daredevils and heroes; early passengers were regarded as somewhat foolhardy for risking their lives. But the dream of fast transportation of mail and passengers by aircraft persisted. Private persons, newspapers, and aviation clubs sponsored well-publicized competitions with substantial monetary rewards to spur aircraft engineers and pilots to achieve such goals as building an aircraft capable of flying nonstop from New York to Paris. Governments, through their military agencies, set challenging performance specifications for new types of aircraft for manufacturers to produce.

In the mid-1930s several important technological advances occurred: the development of reliable, high-power, lightweight, radial, air-cooled piston engines, such as the Wright Whirlwind and Pratt & Whitney Wasp; the introduction of the variable-pitch metal propeller, which offered efficiencies at both takeoff and cruise; the development of the retractable undercarriage, which reduced cruise drag; the use of duralumin alloys to construct stiff, all-metal, lightweight shell structures for fuselages and wings; the invention of the electronic autopilot for cruise flight; and the use of wind tunnels for fuselage, wing, and engine design.

These technologies were all used on the Douglas DC-3, the first profitable passenger aircraft in U.S. domestic air transportation without airmail subsidies from the federal government. It rapidly became the predominant U.S. domestic transport aircraft, and in 1938 it carried 95% of all U.S. passengers. During World War II it became the ubiquitous military transport aircraft for the Allies when over 10,000 were constructed for all theaters of war. About half of these were converted to civil transports by the end of 1946, to become the initial transport aircraft for many airlines all around the world. Some 50 years later they are still in commercial service.

The DC-3 was powered by two 1,200-horsepower Pratt & Whitney engines and cruised at 180 miles (290 km) per hour at altitudes of up to 10,000 feet (3,000 meters). It had an unpressurized cabin, carrying 21 passengers over a nonstop distance of 700 miles (1,125 km). Its productivity was 3,780 seat-miles per hour, triple the productivity values of prior aircraft. Profitable domestic airfares dropped in 1938 to 52 cents per passenger mile (all dollar amounts are in terms of 1990 dollars). The remarkable increase in aircraft productivity owing to continuing technological advances over the next 40 years is the key factor in the corresponding reductions in airfares.

The pioneering aircraft for intercontinental air service, the S-42, also appeared in 1935. It was the first of the "Clipper" flying boats built for Pan American World Airways by the Sikorsky division of United Aircraft. In the years 1935–1938 it opened new long-distance routes to Bermuda, South America, and Europe and across the Pacific to China and New Zealand.

The Sikorsky S-42B had four 750-horsepower Pratt & Whitney Hornet engines and cruised at 155 miles (250 km) per hour over a range of 1,200 miles (1,930 km). It could carry 32 passengers in eight separate compartments that could be converted to provide 14 berths, since some of the flight stages were over 20 hours in length. The advantage of the flying boat was that by using existing harbors and lagoons it made unnecessary the building of new airports.

In 1939 Pan American initiated service on both the Pacific and Atlantic routes, using the largest aircraft built up to that time, the Boeing 314 flying boat. It had four 1,500-horsepower Wright Cyclone engines capable of carrying 74 passengers on two decks. It had 40 berths, a separate dining room capable of seating 15, and a honeymoon suite with private bath, and it cruised at 165 miles (265 km) per hour over a range of 3,100 miles (4,490 km). During World War II these aircraft provided long-distance transport for military and political leaders.

But the flying boat disappeared after the war, supplanted by pressurized long-range transports with four turbocharged piston engines. These aircraft operated from the many new airports with long, paved runways constructed all over the world during the war. They cruised at 15,000 to 25,000 feet (4,600 to 7,600 meters) at 270 to 300 miles (435 to 485 km) per hour. They could seat 60 to 90 and had a range of over 4,000 miles (6,500 km), allowing nonstop flights across the Unites States and the North Atlantic and one-stop flights across the Pacific.

Typical of these aircraft was the Lockheed Constellation (the "Connie"), which introduced nonstop transcontinental service in 1947. It cruised at 270 miles per hour at 22,000 feet (6,700 meters), using on-board weather radar to fly above and around bad weather. It carried 64 passengers over 3,000 miles (4,800 km), and its productivity was more than four times that of the DC-3. Average domestic yields were almost halved, dropping to 28 cents per passenger mile. In the 1950s a new class of service was introduced, called coach or economy class, which offered spartan cabin service and substantially reduced fares in order to attract the "nonbusiness" traveler.

In 1952 British Overseas Airline Corporation introduced the first jet transport aircraft, the de Havilland Comet, on the old "Imperial" routes to Egypt, South Africa, and India. This aircraft was a radical innovation, increasing speeds to

490 miles (790 km) per hour, cruising at 30,000 to 35,000 feet (9,100 to 10,700 meters), and carrying 36 passengers some 2,100 miles (3,375 km). Planned during the war, the Comet was the British answer to the U.S. aircraft manufacturers, but it suffered a series of tragic accidents traced later to catastrophic metal-fatigue failures of the thin skins of the pressurized cabin at cruising altitudes. The aircraft was grounded for over two years, and the hiatus in its program allowed Douglas and Boeing to offer the DC-8 and B-707 aircraft, respectively. These were to become the spearhead aircraft of the worldwide transition of air transportation into the jet age.

The technologies that allowed the radical jump from piston to jet aircraft were the subsonic aerodynamics of swept wings and the development of fuel-efficient jet engines that thrived on operating in the cold, thin air of the stratosphere. At a true airspeed of 550 miles (885 km) per hour at 40,000 feet (12,290 meters), the modern jet transport is indicating an airspeed of only 275 miles (443 km) per hour because of the reduced air density. This is the secret of high-speed subsonic air travel: the reward for climbing to reach the cold ($-58°$ F, or $-50°$ C), thin air (one-quarter sea level density) is that both drag and fuel consumption are reduced by one-quarter.

The Boeing 707 was the first of a long series of successful aircraft that have made the Boeing Commercial Aircraft Company of Seattle, Wash., the dominant manufacturer of jet transports since 1960. The company has consistently captured a 60% share of world production measured in sales volume. The initial versions of the B-707, introduced in the early 1960s, cruised at 35,000 feet at a speed of 550 miles per hour, carrying up to 180 passengers over 3,600 miles (5,800 km). Its productivity was 99,000 seat-miles per hour, quadrupling the values of the earlier piston transports. Average yield in the 1960s was reduced by 30% to roughly 20 cents per passenger mile, and the airlines began marketing air services to leisure travelers at a variety of discount fares.

Because of its cruising efficiencies, the jet transport was initially considered appropriate only for long-haul services, but in 1964 Boeing introduced a short- to medium-haul trijet, the B-727, which carried up to 150 passengers over ranges of 2,500 miles (4,000 km). The B-727-200 became the standard transport for all domestic airlines in the 1970s, allowing a complete transition to jet service on most routes. It introduced new aerodynamic technology in the form of leading and trailing edge wing flaps that produced very high lift for takeoff and landing and reduced the required length of runways, allowing it to operate from most of the smaller cities and airports around the United States. Another technological improvement that became increasingly apparent in the 1960s was the unusual reliability of the jet engine. There were significant decreases in the cost of maintaining jet engines by eliminating unnecessary preventive maintenance.

The next step in the evolution of jet transport aircraft came with the introduction of "wide-body" or "jumbo-jet" aircraft during the 1970s. Boeing built the four-engine B-747 aircraft for long-haul international service for Pan American. Douglas and Lockheed introduced the DC-10 and Lockheed L-1011, respectively, in response to a competition initiated by American Airlines. While the wide bodies were no faster, capacities and productivity were doubled. These craft, with their twin aisles and modern (if not luxurious) high-technology atmosphere (even in coach), did much to build public confidence and interest in flying.

The technology that made the wide bodies possible was the result of intense government research directed at producing the high-thrust, turbofan engine necessary for a very large military cargo aircraft, the C-5, that would allow the rapid deployment of troops and equipment from the United States to any point in the world. These "high-bypass ratio" fan engines are now the standard type of engine for all new subsonic jet transports, since they simultaneously provide much more thrust at takeoff with much less noise and significantly improve cruise fuel consumption. Improved materials technology was able to provide the high-temperature alloys required for the core of these engines.

The DC-10-10 is a typical wide-body jet transport in domestic service. It carries up to 350 passengers over 2,760 miles (4,440 km) at 550 miles per hour, doubling productivity and (by 1978) reducing the average domestic yield to 17 cents per passenger mile.

Having failed to achieve success in the subsonic jet transport market, the British and French governments joined forces in the 1960s to produce the world's first supersonic transport (SST), the Concorde. Although the U.S. Congress refused in 1974 to fund a similar SST project, the Concorde development continued, and the world's first SST service was introduced by the national airlines of Britain and France in 1976. The Concorde cruises at 60,000 feet (18,300 meters) at a speed of 1,300 miles (2,100 km) per hour (twice the speed of sound), carrying 100 passengers over the North Atlantic with a range of up to 3,800 miles (6,100 km). While it is deemed a technical and operational success, it has been (as predicted) an economic failure, carrying less than 1% of North Atlantic traffic even though its high fares are set to recover only its marginal operating costs.

In the 1990s the Boeing B-747-400 is the premier transport aircraft for all long-haul international routes. It has only two pilots, seats up to 450 passengers, and flies nonstop over 8,200 miles (13,200 km). Its productivity is 250,000 seat-miles per hour, and it has proved a very profitable aircraft. A single nonstop round-trip on the Los Angeles–Sydney route produces more than $1 million of revenue (in less than 36 hours) at an operating cost of less than $300,000.

While the advancement of aeronautical technologies created expanded air transportation around the world, the increase of jet operations also created severe noise and environmental problems for the communities near major airports. Airport noise became an important political issue in the 1970s, resulting in the closing of many airports to night operations. Strong opposition arose to the expansion of existing airports or the construction of new commercial airports anywhere near the cities they were intended to serve. As a result, many cities experienced shortages of airport capacity as well as congestion and delays during busy periods of the year.

A three-stage international program was instituted by the ICAO to limit the takeoff and landing noise of new jet aircraft and to phase out the older, noisier aircraft. Fortunately, the high-bypass turbofan engine was amenable to various noise suppression techniques, which allowed the noise "footprint" of newer and larger transport aircraft to be reduced significantly. Designing new airports that are environmentally sound is still a worldwide problem.

The Demand for Air Travel.   Air travelers fall into two distinctly different categories: those traveling for business reasons and those traveling for personal reasons. Business travelers must travel at specific times and to a specific destination. Timeliness is important to business travelers, and they cannot be persuaded to go at another time or to another destination. Personal travelers may have considerable latitude in the choice of destination and time, and a lower price may even persuade them to make a trip they had not been planning.

Analysis of the growth in business and personal air travel in various regions of the world shows that it is highly correlated with regional gross domestic product (GDP) and that personal air travel is also correlated with decreasing average yields. Air travel grew very rapidly in the United States in the 1938–1978 period and in Europe in the 1960–1980 period, and it is now growing very rapidly in Asia along the Pacific Rim. For example, in the period from 1938 to 1958, U.S. domestic air transport grew at an annual rate of 21% (doubling in less than five years), decreasing to 10% in the jet era (1958–1978) and to 5% in the wide-body era since 1978. Growth rates in Asia have been in the 10% to 15% range, corresponding to rapid growth in GDP in that area, and are expected to be at least 8% in the 1990s.

U.S. domestic air travel, which was 68% of the world market in 1945 declined to roughly 30% in the 1990s, but this was still higher than the 25% share of the world's economy that the U.S. GDP represents. In terms of revenue passenger miles (RPM) per capita, North Americans average 1,740 air miles per person annually, four times the European average and much more than that of other areas of the world. In 1960 fewer than 10% of U.S. adults had taken at least one flight within the year. In 1990 this value had risen to more than 31%.

The fear of flying by the traveling public, once a great concern of the airline industry, has virtually disappeared, as evidenced by the fact that U.S. travelers very rarely purchase flight life insurance, since the risks of death per boarding are now less than one in 10 million for U.S. domestic flights. (The risks for commercial flights in other parts of the world, while also improving, are ten times higher.)

The International Airline Industry.   International air transportation started after World War I, when the European nations began to organize national flag airlines to provide airmail and passenger service to their colonies. France flew across the Mediterranean to West Africa. The Netherlands, with an airline that is still known as KLM, started services to the Dutch East Indies, or Indonesia as it is known today. Britain started services along its Imperial Route through the Middle East to India, Singapore, and Hong Kong. Germany, interested in trade with countries in South America, initiated many domestic airlines there and operated services across the South Atlantic, using the Graf Zeppelins and a monstrous 12-engine flying boat called the Dornier DOX.

In the United States there was no such need, but there was a public aversion to government ownership of airlines. During the 1920s the financial lions of Wall Street were eager to make their fortunes in this new industry. Passengers, however, were not eager to buy air services at the prices of the day, and it seemed sensible to use air transport to upgrade domestic and international mail service while allowing air transportation to prove itself. Accordingly, the subsidy for initiating air service in the United States came in the guise of generous long-term contracts to airlines to carry mail along both domestic and international long-haul routes after a "competitive" award by the politically appointed postmaster general. The pioneering routes of Pan American to South America and across the Pacific were financed by lucrative U.S. airmail contracts, with revenue from cargo or passengers a welcome byproduct to be shared with the U.S. government.

Juan T. Trippe, the founder and president of Pan American, negotiated agreements between Pan American and foreign governments and bought out any foreign airlines that already possessed traffic rights in those countries in order to ensure that Pan American was the only bidder in the U.S. foreign airmail competitions. By 1939 the U.S. government had inserted itself into Pan American's negotiations with Great Britain on transatlantic service.

International Regulation.   Aviation law has established that every nation has sovereignty over the airspace above its territories. Civil aircraft of another nation cannot enter its airspace without permission. For noncommercial aircraft, the rights to fly over or visit another nation are usually made available by that nation's participation in the ICAO. For commercial aircraft of one nation, the right to perform air transportation in another nation is determined by a bilateral air agreement between the two nations. In 1944, at the meeting called to establish the ICAO, the United States attempted to create an "open skies" multilateral agreement, but since it was clear that when World War II was over the U.S. airlines and aircraft-manufacturing industries would dominate worldwide air transportation, it was rejected. Subsequently the United States and Great Britain met in Bermuda to reopen negotiations on North Atlantic air service between their countries and established an agreement on the exchange of commercial air rights that served as a model for hundreds of similar bilateral air agreements (referred to as Bermuda agreements) between countries.

These agreements are used to ensure that the airlines of each nation achieve a fair share of the international market, and they generally prohibit entry of foreign airlines into domestic markets. The Bermuda agreement avoided government involvement in setting fares by sanctioning the creation of a private commercial association of airlines called the International Airline Transportation Association (IATA). It provided a variety of commercial services that facilitated cooperation among the world's airlines, the most important of which was a mechanism for publishing airfares so that airlines and travel agents worldwide could sell tickets on behalf of a foreign airline. IATA's annual regional fare conferences produced a set of fares and services that, under the original Bermuda structure, would be reviewed and approved by the governments of the countries involved before taking effect. Since the 1970s this fare-approval mechanism has been radically modified by governments trying to allow some degree of freedom for individual airlines to set their own prices and in so doing introduce competition into international air travel.

In recent years governments of the larger nations have tended to divest themselves of their national airlines. In the 1980s there were various interairline cooperative marketing agreements and even exchanges of ownership shares by international airlines. If large multinational airlines emerge in the 1990s, it will confound the current intergovernmental regulatory structure, with its bilateral agreements on behalf of national flag airlines. A reversal of the historical ban on cabotage (the provision of domestic services by a foreign airline) is being openly discussed, so that perhaps in the future, foreign airlines will be able to offer their services inside the United States.

The World's International Airlines. In analyzing both domestic and international air transportation, it is apparent that U.S. airlines are dominant, carrying almost 40% of the world's air traffic, some 454 billion RPM. As expected, the leading industrialized nations carry their share (Great Britain and Japan with 5.3% each; France and Germany with 2.7% and 2.4%, respectively), but geographically larger nations, such as the former USSR (13%), Canada (3%), and Australia (2.1%), have higher ranking than expected because of the greater need for bridging vast distances. On the other hand, the outstanding performances of Singapore (1.7%) and the Netherlands (1.4%) are the result of aggressive marketing.

The world's largest airline had been Aeroflot, the national airline of the former USSR. Following the dissolution of the Soviet Union it broke up into a number of state and privately owned airlines of the new republics of the Commonwealth of Independent States. The U.S. airlines, owing to their large domestic market, dominate any ranking of airlines by size. American Airlines handled 76 million passengers in 1991; they traveled 82 billion passenger miles (132 billion km) for an average of 1,080 miles (1,740 km) per trip segment. American's revenues were $12 billion, so that the average cost per trip was $157, and its average yield was 14.5 cents per mile.

The largest non-U.S. airline in 1991 was British Airways, handling 23 million passengers who traveled 8.6 billion passenger miles (13.8 billion km) for an average of 1,695 miles (2,725 km) per trip segment. British Airways had revenues of $8.6 billion, with an average cost per trip of $373, or 22 cents per mile. In productivity terms, American Airlines produced 132 million passenger miles (212 million km) per aircraft from its fleet of 622 aircraft and $136,000 per employee from each of its 88,000 employees. British Airways did better, generating 169 million passenger miles (272 million km) from its 230 aircraft and $172,000 per employee from its 50,000 employees.

As a result of these fares and productivities, British Airways declared a profit in 1991 of $357 million, which greatly exceeded the $17 million declared by American Airlines. The U.S. passenger airlines have never ranked high in profitability, and it has been claimed that their losses in recent years have wiped out the aggregate of all the profits they have ever made.

Oddly enough, the most profitable U.S. airline in 1991 was Federal Express, which declared an operating profit of $320.6 million, but this derived from its small-package express air services and not from carrying passengers. The most profit-able world carriers in 1991 were Singapore Airlines, which claimed a profit of $659 million on revenues of only $3 billion, and Cathay Pacific of Hong Kong, which claimed $468 million on only $2.7 billion. These are relatively small airlines with high productivity measures. Singapore produced 20 billion passenger miles (32.2 billion km) with only 46 aircraft, for a productivity value of 434 million passenger miles (698 million km) per aircraft (more than three times the figure for American Airlines), and $236,000 for each of its 12,500 employees (almost twice that of American). Cathay Pacific produced $333 million per aircraft and $212,000 for each of its 12,700 employees. The average yield for Singapore Airlines in 1991 was 15 cents per passenger mile, not much different from that of American Airlines, and 18 cents per passenger mile for Cathay Pacific. The success of these two small airlines derives from their exclusively wide-body fleet, their low-cost labor force, and the currently strong growth of air travel in the Far East.

The U.S. Airline Industry. After the stock market crash of 1929, a new postmaster general, perceiving the need for fewer and financially stronger airlines, began to rationalize the industry into a system of trunk and feeder routes by forcing the combination of certain airlines. As a result, there emerged the "Big Four" longer-haul trunk airlines of United, American, TWA, and Eastern, along with many other smaller regional airlines. In the 1930s all modes of transportation in the United States were placed under much stronger regulation by the federal government, and in 1938 the Civil Aeronautics Act was passed. In 1940 the Civil Aeronautics Board (CAB) was created, with five independent members appointed by the president but responsible mainly to the Congress for the commercial development of the U.S. airline industry.

Regulation of the U.S. Airline Industry. The act gave the CAB explicit authority to develop competitive air transportation in the United States. This was accomplished through investigations and public hearings. After more than a year of such efforts, findings concerning fare levels and structures and the award of routes to new competitors were submitted to the CAB, which then dealt with the political interests in the matter and often reversed the findings. The Big Four were free of airmail subsidy shortly after World War II, and the CAB turned its attention to strengthening the smaller independent airlines (Delta, Western, Continental, Braniff, National, Northwest, Northeast) by allowing them to compete with the Big Four in the larger markets. By the late 1950s most of these airlines were free of subsidies.

In the 1960s the CAB's attention shifted down to the local service airlines, which acted as feeder airlines to the trunk airlines and which still received subsidies to furnish air service to the very small cities and low-density areas of the United States. This air service was considered essential to maintaining economic development in these cities, and politicians paid close attention to the activities of these airlines. These airlines (Allegheny, Bonanza, Central, Frontier, Mohawk, North Central, Ozark, Pacific, Piedmont, Reeve, Southern, Trans-Texas, West Coast, Wien Alaska, and others) upgraded from DC-3s to turboprop transports (Fokker F-27, Nihon YS-11, Nord 262, Convair 580) and finally in the 1960s to small jet transports (BAC-111, DC-9) as they were given routes vacated by the larger airlines.

The initiative in fare levels rested with the airlines, and a filing of a proposed fare change would go into effect in 30 days unless the CAB decided to intervene and call for a public hearing. In the interests of equity there was a distance-based national fare structure ensuring that the price for a 500-mile (800-km) trip at a given class of service was identical everywhere in the country. Twice the CAB instigated a general investigation of fares, and after the second ended in 1974, it enunciated a domestic fare structure based on a "fair rate of return on investment" that, after 36 years of regulation designed to introduce competition, resulted in the airline industry being treated by the CAB as though it were a public utility. Industry fare levels would depend on industry costs and investment. The reaction to this was a vociferous public debate on "deregulation" of the domestic airline industry that lasted for four years. In 1978 Congress passed the Airline Deregulation Act, which over the next five years phased out the CAB. The result of this was to eliminate completely the rules of competition for the industry. Domestic airlines were free to start and eliminate service anywhere and charge any price. New start-up airlines, providing minimal evidence of financial and operational viability, were given certificates freely. Lower fares in individual markets initiated by the newcomers caused instant declaration of matching fares by the incumbents. The major airlines invented computerized revenue-management systems that carefully controlled the actual availability of these low-fare seats, restricting them to the surplus seats on their flights with low load factors.

The result has been chaotic air travel markets in which consumers have difficulty in understanding the daily variations in prices and in keeping track of who is serving the market. Travel agents, once valued consultants for passengers seeking lower-priced seats, are biased in their advice by airlines that offer extra commission fees when initiating new competitive services.

The competition between the domestic airlines has produced unexpected results. Initially it was thought that it would be difficult for the smaller airlines to survive against the larger carriers. Instead, using their lower labor costs and their smaller jet aircraft (DC-9, B-737), they added longer-haul services out of their traditional hub airports, allowing passengers to go directly to destinations on their airline instead of connecting to the larger carriers. This caused considerable early expansion and success for regional airlines such as Allegheny (renamed USAir), Piedmont, Frontier, and Republic. The new "start-up" jet lines copied this service pattern of building a hub utilizing small jet transports (PeoplExpress at Newark, Texas Air at Houston, Midway Airlines at Midway Airport in Chicago, New York Air at Laguardia, America West at Phoenix, Ransome at Philadelphia), introducing cheaper "no frills" service and innovative management-labor ownership. However, the success of these smaller firms was transitory, and by 1991 they all had disappeared except for USAir and America West.

To respond to this challenge, the larger airlines reversed their long tradition of ordering larger and ever more productive aircraft and acquired very large fleets of these same smaller and less productive jet transports (MD-80, B-737), using them to build new competitive patterns of hub service from airports already within their route structures. They could then rapidly enter most of the larger and medium-sized markets of the United States, using indirect instead of their traditional nonstop services, and could control the traffic flows to aggregate loads at these hubs that filled their wide-body flights on existing services between the hub airports.

The airlines initiated "frequent flyer" plans that rebated free travel to customers based on mileage flown, but the attractiveness of vacation destinations on the larger airlines gave them an advantage over the smaller and newer airlines. To make travel planning even more complicated, airlines offered off-season sales in terms of reduced mileage requirements for rebated travel.

While spectacular travel bargains became available, the overall reduction in fares touted by proponents of deregulation has been disappointing when expressed in terms of average domestic yield. In the early years of regulation (1938–1958), when the introduction of more productive transport fleets matched annual domestic growth rates averaging 21%, the annual reduction in real domestic yield was 3.5%. In the era of jet introduction (1958–1978) the average annual reduction in domestic yield was reduced to 2.6%, and average domestic growth was 10.4%. In the 12 years after deregulation took place the average annual reduction in average real domestic yield has been only 1.1%, and average annual domestic growth only 5.5%. Fare reduction since deregulation has been less than one-half the annual reduction during the prior 12 years of domestic regulation.

The U.S. Domestic Airlines. In the 1990s there has been a significant reduction in the number of airline competitors and an increasing concentration of the top three airlines (American, United, and Delta). While new airlines entered the domestic market in the early 1980s as expected, the threat of leveraged buyouts and a desire to achieve expansion in domestic markets faster than potential rivals led the larger airlines to deplete their financial resources in buying smaller airlines during the mid-1980s. The consolidation of the domestic airline industry continued as some of the larger airlines ran into financial difficulties at the end of the decade, when the prolonged economic expansion faltered and domestic growth in air travel reversed into a decline. Bankrupt airlines sold off parts of their systems to the larger airlines and eventually stopped operations. By 1991 the 23 airlines operating at the start of deregulation had been reduced to 6 financially viable airlines (United, American, Delta, USAir, Northwest, and Southwest). The top three domestic U.S. airlines have transformed themselves into major international airlines.

There also has been a remarkable change in the makeup of the very small commuter or regional airlines. Before deregulation there were more than 250 such airlines, using 7- to 18-seat piston and turboprop aircraft that supplied air service from their very small cities to the nearest major airport. These privately owned, fiercely independent small entrepreneurs had a virtual monopoly on local services.

When deregulation allowed larger airlines to abandon money-losing, small-traffic markets, the manufacturers in several foreign nations foresaw a large potential U.S. market for short-haul turboprop transport aircraft of seating capacity from 30 to 50 seats. The resulting competition involved creative financing of the sales and leasing of these larger commuter aircraft to the more ambitious operators. Marketing alliances were forged between regional commuter and major airlines, and some major airlines bought commuter lines outright, in order to provide feeder traffic to hub airports. All of these regional airlines are now subject to the direction of a larger airline in establishing their schedules and have aircraft owned or financed by that airline and painted in its colors. To add to the confusion, schedules suggest that flights are operated by the larger airline.

The future development of the U.S. domestic airline industry is not clear. Instead of public hearings on fare levels and structures held by the CAB, the larger domestic airlines, in a manner characteristic of oligopolistic industries, now conduct an industry debate in the national media and undertake punishing short-term reprisals to initiatives taken by their competitors that they consider undesirable. The issues of reregulation of the industry and of allowing foreign ownership of U.S. airlines have arisen in Congress. It is no longer inconceivable that cabotage may be deemed necessary to maintain real competition in domestic markets. Thus as the industry moves into the 21st century, it can be expected to remain an enterprise that is dynamic, interesting, and full of surprises.

ROBERT W. SIMPSON
Flight Transportation Laboratory
Massachusetts Institute of Technology

AIR UNIVERSITY, one of the major commands of the U.S. Air Force (USAF), with headquarters at Maxwell Air Force Base, Montgomery, Ala. It was established in 1946 as a unified and integrated educational program designed to address the following needs: to provide career officers of the Air Force with the knowledge and capabilities required in command and staff positions; to assist in shaping and guiding future thought on air power; to develop an awareness of trends in the design, production, and use of new weapons; and to operate schools for the professional education of Air Force officers. A 15-member Board of Visitors, appointed to 3-year terms by the USAF chief of staff, oversees the operations of this command.

The Air University is also assigned the following functions: to conduct research in aeromedical and social science fields, to study continuously the entire system of training and education of the Air Force, to review and evaluate Air Force tactics and techniques, to prepare publications on basic Air Force doctrines, and to supervise the Air Force Reserve Officers' Training Corps (Air Force ROTC) program.

DEAN C. STROTHER, *United States Air Force*

AIR WARFARE, military operations that utilize the equipment and weapons of air power—airplanes, spacecraft, guided and ballistic missiles, bombs, and rockets. This power is projected through the aerospace, the earth's atmosphere and space beyond it. Air warfare takes on varying degrees of intensity, being responsive to controls determined by both political and military objectives, especially in those conflicts in which the distinction between war and peace is blurred.

Early Theorists of Air Warfare. The original theories of air warfare must be credited mainly to three theorists: Gen. Giulio Douhet of Italy, Gen. William ("Billy") Mitchell of the United States,

and Air Marshal Sir Hugh M. Trenchard of Great Britain. Often impatient and bluntly outspoken, these visionaries, between 1915 and 1925, formulated a new and fundamental body of thought on the roles and functions of air power in war. These aerial avatars shared the common belief that in future wars air power would emerge as the dominant military force and therefore should be a separate, autonomous service, enjoying comparable status to the army and navy.

Older theories of war held that elimination of an enemy's military might was the sole objective of war. In contrast, the early air theorists argued that the object of war was to destroy the enemy nation's will, as well as its ability to resist, and to impose one's own will on the enemy. To them, traditional naval and ground forces were simply a kind of barrier outside the vulnerable civil structure of the enemy's support base. With the introduction of the airplane, this barrier could be transcended and attacks mounted through the air to strike at the enemy's population or at the industry and economy supporting that population. No longer were air forces to be relegated to auxiliary functions, or to operate simply as extensions of the army and the navy, and restricted to observatory roles or furnishing longer-range delivery for ground artillery, as was true almost to the end of World War I. Such precepts evoked vigorous debate, but they irrevocably altered the classic approaches to warfare—and the role air power would play.

Developing Doctrine of Air Power. Each modern nation has an air doctrine governing the use of its air power in wartime. Such doctrines are influenced by many considerations: national policy objectives, the governmental and military structure, cultural background, geographical location, size and composition of armed forces, evaluation of the possible enemy threat, analysis of the lessons of past wars, and the capability of available weapon systems.

By today's standards most air action during World War I, 1914–1918, would be considered tactical air operations. Aircraft of the United States Air Service, for example, were initially employed by the American Expeditionary Force (AEF) for reconnaissance, to observe and adjust artillery fire, and to attack other aircraft. Both the British and the Germans followed the same pattern, although the Germans occasionally used dirigibles (large, lighter-than-air craft) and airplanes to bomb London and Paris. These sporadic raids were directed primarily at the morale of the civilian population, a step toward what later was termed strategic bombardment. Near the end of the war, the British, followed by the Americans, planned for intensive bombing of German cities in the Ruhr and Rhineland regions, transportation networks, factories, and troop concentrations deep inside Germany—which would have constituted strategic bombardment in the classic sense. And, as a harbinger of things to come, the Royal Air Force (RAF) became the world's first independent air arm in the spring of 1918.

Impetus behind rapidly developing air doctrines between the two world wars proceeded from several influences: rapid advances in technology; the views of leading military authorities; experience gained in small wars; and, in the United States, the organizational subordination of the Air Corps to the ground forces of the army, coupled with the tendency toward isolationism.

Throughout that period, army commanders in the United States evinced little confidence in aviation or its future; they looked on the airplane solely as a useful adjunct for traditional ground forces. Changes in the direct application of air power as reflected in national doctrine were therefore very slow. By 1935, however, adhering to the increasingly popular air-power tenants of Douhet, Mitchell, and Trenchard, the Army Air Corps induced the U.S. War Department to publish a training regulation recognizing air power's utility as an integrated force on the onset of hostilities, and long before enemy and allied surface forces met in combat. The main tasks of U.S. air forces would be to gain and maintain air superiority, conduct strategic bombardment of enemy industry and transportation, support ground and naval forces, and airlift troops, supplies, and the wounded—in sum, a quantum leap in terms of function compared with the ground-oriented tactics of World War I.

Despite these practices, however, the prevailing army concept for the employment of air power as the United States entered World War II was that air power was auxiliary to land power. By that definition its usefulness varied directly with the closeness of air strikes to the front lines and, also, all air effort had to further the ground battle through bombardment support and reconnaissance. Long-range bombardment of enemy war potential, while theoretically attractive, was still considered ineffective and unreliable.

This conservative approach to air doctrine was not shared by the second generation of Army Air Corps thinkers. Such men as Henry Arnold, Laurence Kuter, Claire Chennault, Carl Spaatz, George Kenney, and Ira Eaker believed that air power could play a more decisive role, especially with the kind of equipment made possible by advancing technology. On the civilian front, air power found in the former Russian ace Alexander De Seversky an articulate champion whose prophetic book, *Victory through Air Power* (1942), was an immediate best-seller. All these men saw in air power an inherent flexibility unmatched in any other force. Properly understood, organized, and directed, it could bring new dimensions and lethality to warfare—a new practicability to objectives, a greater degree and quality to surprise, a geometric enlargement to mobility, an increased potential to the principle of economy, and a new simplicity to problems of coordination.

Air Power in World War II. By 1940 the Battle of Britain was demonstrating the soundness of these emerging points of doctrine, both in bombing tactics and fighter defense. Its lessons were so transcendentally obvious that in 1941 the United States created and expanded the Army Air Forces (AAF). And in 1942, following American entry into World War II, army field manuals were beginning to suggest that air power could contribute significantly to the destruction of any enemy's ability to make war.

North Africa. The new doctrine of the proper uses of tactical aviation and of the importance of gaining early air superiority did not gain general acceptance until the North African campaign granted fledgling doctrine more practical experience under actual wartime conditions. Initially, and under the close supervision of army commanders, American air power in Tunisia in late 1942 and early 1943 was basically used to protect frontline troops and supply dumps. Air operations usually were restricted to the frontline areas, while aircraft were being parceled out—rather than concentrated—all over the theater. Thus the veteran but outnumbered German Luftwaffe retained air superiority longer than anticipated.

Events quickly changed once Air Vice Marshal Sir Arthur Coningham, RAF, commander in chief of the Northwest African Tactical Air Force, assumed command and operational control of all Allied tactical air forces in North Africa early in 1943. Coningham transformed air power's defensive role into a concentrated aerial offensive, frequently independent of land-based considerations. Fighter and bomber aircraft now struck at German airfields, and fighters began pressing attacks against enemy planes in the air. The Allies gained air superiority, their first objective, in a short time, and air sorties could then be diverted to interdiction of enemy movement on the battlefield, strikes against lines of communication, with heavy blows delivered against troops and matériel. The tide of battle turned the situation in North Africa from a possible defeat to an Allied victory, and U.S. air forces and ground forces had finally achieved parity on the battlefield and at the planning table.

The North African campaign thus highlighted the validity of command and employment concepts that had been held by air corps officers since the 1920s and resulted in acceptance of their concept in the doctrine published in July 1943, in War Department Field Manual 100-20. It promoted equal status between ground and air forces, harmonized their interaction, and promulgated doctrinal employment with a broad statement of missions listed according to priority. The principal objective of the AAF thus became gaining and maintaining air superiority, now accomplished by demolishing the enemy's aircraft factories and by destroying enemy planes in the air and on the ground. The former would be achieved by strategic bombardment and the latter by tactical air operations. Other tactical missions included isolation of the battlefield by interdicting enemy movement and direct, close air support for ground troops. These principles were instituted as standard air power procedures and closely followed for the rest of the war.

Europe. Victory in North Africa was followed by equally successful long-range air actions preceding the invasion of Sicily and Italy in 1943. These included intense aerial bombardment, which, alone and with no losses to Allied ground troops, forced the surrender of the island of Pantelleria. The growing successes of air operations against Germany and in the Pacific strengthened the Allies' belief in the value of strategic air power.

But it was over the skies of continental Europe that strategic bombardment wielded its greatest impact. The Allies demonstrated the practicality of deep penetrations of enemy territory by bomber aircraft, employing American daylight precision-bombing techniques accompanied by nighttime area-saturation bombing by the RAF. By 1944 such actions were accompanied by long-range fighter escort. They even became convinced that, with sufficient numbers of bombers, they could destroy Germany's industrial base and so weaken its ability to resist that an actual invasion by ground forces would prove unnecessary. While this theory was overly optimistic, conclusive evidence exists for the immense effectiveness of U.S. Air Force missions in Europe—in gaining and maintaining air superiority, reducing the enemy's

Strategic air power is exemplified by the B-52, which can drop over 10 tons of bombs 9,000 miles (14,500 km) from its base.

capacity to wage war, isolating the battlefield, and directly supporting troops. Aviation pundits continue debating whether or not air power was the single-most important factor in the overall equation of victory, but, regardless, it certainly was a major factor. Even so, the military strategy for winning the war in Europe remained essentially a surface strategy, and air power basically continued in a cooperating or supporting role, with no chance to demonstrate its effectiveness in a fully independent, strategic role.

Pacific Theater. Employment of carrier-based air power in the Pacific campaign during World War II again demonstrated new dimensions of warfare. Japanese naval aviation was extremely capable and delivered a devastating blow against American battleships and other naval assets at Pearl Harbor and elsewhere. But as the tide eventually turned, enemy airstrips were bombed and strafed, and Japanese planes were destroyed in the air, to ensure local air superiority prior to each island invasion. The doctrine established in July 1943 applied as well in the Pacific as in the European and North African theaters. The tactics, however, grew out of the grand strategy developed in the Pacific theater. General Douglas MacArthur conceived the strategy of "island hopping," whereby enemy strong points would be bypassed entirely and isolated through air power based on neighboring islands. Thus, until 1945, strategic and tactical air forces were employed primarily to prepare areas for invasion by amphibious forces or in direct support of troops after each invasion.

The arrival of the Boeing B-29 Superfortress long-range bombers in 1944 completely changed the tenor of air war in the Pacific. This giant craft made it possible to launch a major strategic bombing campaign against the Japanese mainland. The operations of the 20th Air Force struck decisive blows against poorly defended and highly combustible Japanese cities, industrial centers, and urban areas. The strategic offensive against Japan proved so effective that many air commanders believed that the nation would surrender without invasion—a theory that, fortunately, was never tested. Even though the two atomic bombs of early August 1945 provided the coup de grâce

that forced surrender, the effectiveness of the naval blockade, air superiority, tremendous destruction achieved by the B-29s, and the island-hopping advance of ground forces had already ensured an Allied victory.

Air Power to Aerospace Power. Since World War II, air-power doctrine has evolved through constant analysis and testing of military operations in the light of national objectives, the changing military environment, and unprecedented technological advances. The arrival of the thermonuclear age precipitated a new and more pressing milieu for developing new concepts for air warfare.

Previously limited to lower altitudes, air forces gradually achieved greater flexibility through concurrent advances in space technology. To accommodate this change, air-force doctrine refers to the expanse above the earth's surface within which it now operates as aerospace, a continuum that includes the atmosphere and vacuum of outer space above. According to the aerospace doctrine espoused in the late 1960s, aerospace forces, as a specialized element of national military power, are for use in coordination with national diplomatic, economic, and other instruments to assist in the achievement of basic national policy objectives. Yet air power remains the principal means of enacting these priorities.

Lacking the clear distinctions between war and peace that commonly existed prior to World War II, conflict today may appear in different forms and assume varying levels of intensity—cold war, limited war, or total war—requiring a wide range of responses by aerospace forces. The world of the early 21st century is beset by an onslaught of religious-based (largely Islamic) terrorism that has struck the United States, Russia, and other countries with deadly results. The Americans mounted the most aggressive counterstrokes against terrorists by invading Afghanistan in 2001 and Iraq in 2003, and in each instance air power played a prominent role.

Present aerospace weaponry provides unprecedented flexibility and lethality to national power. Advantages of aerospace in the military sense include range, mobility, responsiveness, and tactical versatility. Fundamentally important to a nation's deterrent posture, aerospace forces must be capable of surviving enemy attack and subsequently be capable of responding to that attack, as directed. Different kinds of military conflict create different operating conditions for aerospace forces. The various kinds of conflict include general war, tactical nuclear war, war with conventional weapons, and counterinsurgency.

As stated in air-force doctrinal manuals, the guiding principle in all conflict is to limit military force to those systems and intensities appropriate for the specific issues at stake. Military forces must be used in a manner that denies aggressors their objectives and yet destroys only those forces necessary to achieve satisfactory war termination. But it may be necessary to increase the intensity of conflict to prevent the success of aggression.

Air Power since World War II. The United States emerged from World War II as the most powerful nation in the world—politically, economically, and militarily. The strength of the newly established Strategic Air Command (SAC), Tactical Air Command (TAC), and Air Defense Command (ADC) gave the United States overwhelming aerial superiority over the Soviet Union, its anticipated adversary. The Americans also enjoyed an atomic monopoly coupled with strategic bombers capable of delivering atomic weapons to targets anywhere in the world. In 1949, however, the USSR broke that monopoly and, in 1953, achieved its first thermonuclear explosion. America's strategic monopoly was reduced to strategic superiority. After World War II the Soviet Union also developed a long-range bomber force, capable of striking targets in the United States with inflight refueling, but the Red Air Force reached neither the size nor the efficiency of SAC. One reason for this overall dominance was the person of Curtis LeMay, commander of SAC, 1948–1958, who finely honed human resources, machines, and missions to achieve the goals desired. Thereafter the Soviet Union apparently acknowledged its inferiority by concentrating on development and production of ballistic missiles. American missile development and production, initially behind that of the USSR, was stepped up considerably after 1954–1955 to overtake the Soviet advantage.

By early 1962, and despite several close calls in the international arena such as the Cuban missile crisis, it had become clear that the danger of general nuclear war was diminishing. The nuclear deterrent force of SAC bombers and missiles and U.S. Navy *Polaris* submarines was building up to a level considerably higher than that of the USSR, and would not be challenged until the 1980s. Those conflicts considered most likely to happen would be small-scale, nonnuclear wars of "national liberation," aided and abetted by the Soviet Union and Communist China. In 1961 the United States, while retaining and strengthening its nuclear deterrent force, also had general-purpose forces designed to deter or, if necessary, to defeat small-scale aggression at the lowest possible level of violence. This was not a new function for air warfare. During the Korean War (1950–1953), the first limited engagement of the so-called Cold War, the U.S. Air Force ensured air superiority, interdicted delivery of enemy supplies, and furnished air support to the ground forces, and in the last year of the war, it participated with other forces in a campaign designed to maintain military pressure on the Communists, thereby forcing them to accept United Nations terms for an armistice.

Given the preponderance of Chinese personnel assets on the ground, air power helped neutralize an advantage that might otherwise have proved decisive.

The Vietnam War became the first real test of air power in counterinsurgency, or classic guerrilla-style warfare. Initially, U.S. assistance to the government of South Vietnam was limited to training, supplies, and advisers, but, as the scale of fighting increased, air power was called on to carry out its traditional functions: reconnaissance, interdiction, support of ground forces, and maintenance of air superiority. Air power's supporting role soon grew into a major role, however, for air power was found to be so effective that its traditional functions were expanded to include, for example, aerial defoliation of brush and trees likely to hide guerrilla bands. New generations of jet aircraft were also developed that carried tons of cannon, bombs, rockets, and napalm, and made conventional forays by the North Vietnamese Army (NVA) prohibitively costly.

The war in Vietnam also witnessed a new form of technology, helicopters, come to the fore. With them, an entirely new concept of air transport has been developed. Called Air Line of Communications (ALOC), it delivers personnel, equipment, and supplies from the continental United States to units of battalion level and below in the combat zone. Strategic and tactical airlift has been greatly speeded and enlarged with gigantic craft such as the McDonnell-Douglas C-17 Globemaster III and Lockheed C-5A Galaxy , and, as larger and faster transport aircraft become available, a new rapidity of reaction by ground forces becomes a reality. Large military forces can now be deployed in hours or days to far-flung areas of the world and can be supplied by air for extended periods. The global reach long sought by air-power advocates is finally a reality.

Air power's versatility and flexibility were shown in the use of B-52 strategic bombers for the area bombing of Vietcong troop concentrations and facilities in South Vietnam. In February 1965, air operations were begun against targets in North Vietnam, to impede the flow of personnel and supplies to the Vietcong in the South. In December 1972 these same bombers reverted back to conventional strategic bombers during Operation Linebacker II, whose concentrated assaults on Hanoi and other strategic regions forced the Communist regime back to the Paris peace talks and secured a temporary negotiated settlement. Its use in strategic persuasion was a new role for air power, one that could resolve or prevent similar conflicts in the future.

Aerial warfare has also played a particularly significant role in several Middle East conflicts—between Israel and its neighboring Arab states, 1956–1973; between Iran and Iraq, 1980–1988; and between the U.S.-led forces and Iraq in the Persian Gulf War of 1991. Air power was also plied with deadly effect during the overthrow of dictator Saddam Hussein during Operation Iraqi Freedom in the spring of 2003. Armed and equipped with the latest satellite-directed ordnance, U.S. aircraft routinely performed pinpoint strikes against Islamic guerrillas with little risk of collateral damage to nearby civilians. Air power was and remains one of the most significant tools of power projection available to national policymakers.

JOHN W. CARPENTER III*, *Lieutenant General USAF Commander, Air University*

AIRCRAFT, any machine or device capable of atmospheric flight. Included in this category is a remarkable array of devices—airplanes of every conceivable design, gliders, all manner of autogyros and helicopters, dirigibles, and hot-air balloons. Though air cushion vehicles might be considered aircraft because they hover just over the surface, they are generally categorized as ground vehicles. The wing-in-ground (or WIG) aircraft, a close relative of the air cushion vehicle, is usually considered an aircraft even though it is confined to near-surface flight.

The development of aircraft has been one of the most dramatic aspects of the 20th century, involving great intellectual application and personal courage. Aircraft manufacture and air transportation are among the world's major industries; air superiority has become the critical military consideration in virtually every conflict since World War II; and air travel has brought people together from the farthest corners of the globe.

The physical principles of flight are found in AERODYNAMICS. The design, construction, and operation of airplanes is found in AIRPLANE. The development of the air travel and commerce is presented in AIR TRANSPORTATION and AIRPORT. A history of flight is presented in AVIATION and AIR WARFARE.

Types of Aircraft. Aircraft can be classified as fixed-wing, rotary-wing, flapping-wing, and lighter-than-air. The first three classes are heaver-than-air vehicles. Four forces act on a heaver-than-air vehicle in flight through the atmosphere: weight, aerodynamic lift, drag (a retarding force, also aerodynamically generated), and thrust (a propulsive force provided by an engine or engine-propeller combination of some sort). For lighter-than-air vehicles, the weight is balanced by an upward buoyancy force.

The evolution of aircraft is marked by advances and discoveries that changed one or more of the parameters of flight. Often a technological advance in an unrelated field was immediately applied to aircraft, with stunning results. The history of flight can be divided into five periods, as discussed below.

Pre-1903 Developments. The dream of human flight can be traced as far back as ancient mythology. The first concrete evidence of aircraft design comes from the notes of Leonardo da Vinci, the great Italian Renaissance painter, sculptor, scientist, and military engineer. Between 1486 and 1490, da Vinci designed scores of human-powered flying machines; more than 35,000 words and 500 sketches in his surviving manuscripts deal with flight. Most of these machines had flapping wings for both lift and propulsion, emulating bird flight. Such machines, called ornithopters, have thus far been unsuccessful, yet the human desire to fly like a bird has been strong enough to keep research in this area alive.

Human efforts to fly literally got off the ground for the first time in a sustained fashion on Nov. 21, 1783, when a hot-air balloon carried Pilâtre de Rozier and the marquis d'Aarlandes across Paris for 5 miles (8 km). Designed and built by two brothers, Joseph and Etienne Montgolfier, this balloon made no real technical contribution to the advancement of powered flight, but it captured public interest in flying and made people comfortable with the notion of flight.

A major breakthrough in aircraft design took place in 1799. In that year, Sir George Cayley, a moderately well-to-do baron from Yorkshire, England, conceived the idea of the modern airplane. He was the first to abandon the idea of flapping wings; instead, he separated the mechanisms of lift and propulsion, using a fixed wing inclined to the airflow for lift and a totally separate mechanism for propulsion. In 1804 he designed and flew the first modern-configuration airplane in history—a hand-launched glider made of wood and paper. This glider, 3.3 feet (1 meter) long, had a fixed wing, fuselage, and a tail with horizontal and vertical surfaces, just as conventional airplanes have today. A full-scale model of Cayley's glider is on display at the Science Museum in South Kensington, London.

During most of the 19th century, various experimenters and inventors tried to extend Cayley's ideas to a full-scale, crewed, powered machine, without sustained success. However, at the end of the century, major progress was made by Otto Lilienthal, a German mechanical engineer who designed and flew the first successful crewed gliders in history. Lilienthal carried out over 2,500 successful glider flights between 1891 and 1896. He crashed on Aug. 9, 1896, and died in the hospital the next day.

That year saw two other important aeronautical developments. First, Samuel Pierpont Langley, secretary of the Smithsonian Institution in Washington, D.C., successfully test-flew a steam-powered, uncrewed, heavier-than-air aircraft, which he called an aerodrome. It was an airplane with "tandem" wings, or one wing behind the other. Its success served as a graphic example of the technical feasibility of Cayley's ideas. Second, it was in 1896 that two brothers named Wright, inspired by Lilienthal's exploits, became acutely interested in powered flight.

All the aeronautical ideas and experiments of the 19th century culminated in the intense dedication and work of Wilbur and Orville Wright. Starting in 1896, they digested all the existing literature on flight. In 1900–1901 they built and attempted to fly full-scale gliders at Kitty Hawk, N.C., and later at Kill Devil Hills, 4 miles (6.4 km) south of Kitty Hawk. Their initial results were disappointing; their gliders' lifting power was half or less of what their calculations predicted. This prompted them to reject all existing data from earlier experimenters and generate their own aerodynamic results by building and using a wind tunnel in the winter of 1901–1902. With their new data, the Wrights built and flew a successful glider in 1902.

The Era of the Biplane. When the Wright brothers carried out the first successful, crewed, powered, heavier-than-air flight on Dec. 17, 1903, a new world was born. The 1903 Wright Flyer, a biplane (two wings, one above the other) with structural bracing achieved by a lattice of struts and wires between the wings, introduced the basic aircraft configuration for the next 25 years. These airplanes had strut-and-wire bracing that created an inordinate amount of aerodynamic drag. They also had short, stubby wings with low aspect ratios (the ratio of the wing span to the chord, or wing width). Low-aspect-ratio wings further increase the aerodynamic drag compared with high-aspect-ratio wings; hence the early biplanes were "high-drag" machines.

By the end of World War I, however, the aerodynamic consequence of low-aspect-ratio wings was finally appreciated through a series of experiments and wind tunnel tests carried out by the famed aerodynamicist Ludwig Prandtl at Göttingen University in Germany. Henceforth, airplane designers appreciated the aerodynamic advantages of high-aspect-ratio wings, but they always faced a compromise: such wings need extreme structural stiffening to avoid buckling of the wing under severe aerodynamic loading. (Modern airplane designers still wrestle with these same problems.) The increase of lift in the first period of flight was the product of careful wing design. Now the increase in thrust could be accommodated only with sturdier and more aerodynamically efficient designs.

Period of Mature Monoplanes. The next leap in airplane design and performance took place during an era that started about 1927, coincidentally the year of Charles Lindbergh's spectacular solo flight across the Atlantic. In this period, speed and altitude became the dominant factors in airplane design. It was an era of competitive air races, one of the most notable being the Schneider Cup Races. This competition—which actually started in 1913 with a streamlined French Deperdussin monoplane winning the race with a maximum speed of 46 miles per hour (74 km/hr) and ended in 1931 with a British Supermarine 5.6B winning the race with a maximum speed of 240 miles per hour (386 km/hr)—served as a major incentive for great leaps in airplane design.

Airplane speeds rapidly increased, mainly because of two technical developments: increases in engine power and decreases in aerodynamic drag. More powerful engines, such as the Pratt and Whitney Wasp, came on the scene, accompanied by major decreases in drag, brought about in part by the elimination of struts and wires and the decision to concentrate on the monoplane design.

Another major development was the NACA (National Advisory Committee for Aeronautics) cowling, a ring around a radial piston engine, almost totally enclosing the otherwise exposed cylinders and greatly decreasing the drag. First appearing in 1928, the NACA cowling in wind tunnel tests reduced drag by a stunning 60%. The Lockheed Vega, a fine example of a 1930-era monoplane, in the uncowled version had a maximum speed of 165 miles per hour (265 km/hr); with the NACA cowling, the speed jumped to 190 miles per hour (306 km/hr). For the next decade, and well into World War II, major increases in thrust and detailed attention to drag reduction brought about substantial increases in speed and altitude, resulting in period classics such as the venerable Douglas DC-3 transport and the North American P-51 Mustang fighter (top speed, 440 mph, or 708 km/hr).

It was during this period that planes began to look like the machines of today. Fuselages were enclosed, construction was sturdy, and careful attention was paid to streamlining and design efficiency, all of which was to set the stage for the next great advance in the development of flight: jet propulsion.

Period of Modern Jet Airplanes. On Aug. 28, 1939, the first successful flight of a jet-propelled airplane, a German Heinkel He 178, took place, opening a new world of atmospheric flight—flight at much higher velocities and altitudes. This massive increase in thrust provided by the jet engine, combined with further improvements in streamlining (such as the swept wing), increased the advantage of thrust over drag to previously unimagined values. Subsonic airplanes flew ever closer to the speed of sound, until Capt. Charles "Chuck" Yeager's historic flight in the Bell X-1 on Oct. 14, 1947, where a crewed aircraft flew faster than sound (supersonic) for the first time.

Yeager's flight marked the beginning of a long series of experimental "X-series" aircraft powered by rocket engines and built for the single purpose of exploring the unknown supersonic region of flight. From the 1950s to the present day, military fighter jets have been typically designed to fly two to three times the speed of sound (Mach 2 or 3).

A major aerodynamic event in the 1950s was the discovery of the *area rule*, which states that necking the fuselage area down in the vicinity of the wing (creating the so-called Coke bottle design) reduces drag near Mach 1 (transonic speeds) and allows conventional jet airplanes to fly faster than sound. This period also saw the advent of the jet-powered transport airplane, starting with the de Havilland Comet in Britain and the Boeing 707 in the United States, both in the 1950s, followed by their more modern offspring, such as the Boeing 747 jumbo-jet.

Flight's "Second Golden Age." The period between the world wars is sometimes referred to as aviation's "golden age" because of the many dramatic flights that took place. Despite the enormous proliferation of aircraft and the importance of air transportation in the modern world, the glamour of those exciting years was absent during the post—World War II period, when most headlines about flight dealt with accidents or downed spy planes. Space flight supplanted airplane flight as the seat of heroism in most minds.

Recent developments, however, have changed that state of affairs somewhat. The spirit of adventure has been rekindled through such flights as the nonstop round-the-world flight of the *Voyager* and the flights of human-powered and solar-powered aircraft. And military aircraft have reached a level of lethal sophistication that makes the "top gun" combat pilot once again the critical player in a conflict.

Only recently have we seen aircraft designers explore new configurations, materials, and propulsion systems. Development of the following technologies—all undertaken during a period of economic and political turmoil—bespeaks the advent of what might possibly be considered a "second golden age" of flight: rotary-wing machines (helicopters and autogyros); tilt-rotor aircraft, which can rotate either their wings and engines to allow vertical takeoff and landing (VTOL) or simply the engine exhaust, as in the British Harrier; wing-in-ground (WIG) aircraft, developed in Russia and resembling the "clipper" boatplanes of the 1930s; and integration of computer-controlled "fly-by-wire" technology. Significant research is even being done in lighter-than-air machines, so that we may yet see some form of the giant airship once again coursing silently across the skies.

Meanwhile, we can expect the airplane to be with us for as long as modern civilization exists and grows. More fuel efficient, environmentally sound aircraft with quieter engines are on the drawing boards, and research and development on new hypersonic aircraft, capable of flying at Mach numbers as high as 25, is in progress.

JOHN D. ANDERSON, JR., *University of Maryland*

The U.S.S. *Carl Vinson* is one of the U.S. Navy's Nimitz-class aircraft carriers. The ship is powered by two nuclear reactors and, functioning at a peacetime activity level, is expected to operate for 20 years without refueling.

© GEORGE HALL/WOODFIN CAMP

AIRCRAFT CARRIER, a ship containing a flight deck for aircraft takeoff and landing. The advantage of operating from ships was recognized shortly after the airplane was invented, and the development of the aircraft carrier followed only a generation later.

Mission. At the outset, naval aircraft were considered the eyes of the fleet and were flown from battleships, cruisers, and land bases. Their mission was essentially defensive and limited to searching for the enemy fleet. As aircraft developed, naval ships and naval tactics changed, and a new type of ship to operate wheeled aircraft—the aircraft carrier—was created.

Between World Wars I and II it became clear that carrier-based air power could play a significant role both in land battles and in naval battles. The end result was that aircraft carriers increasingly became instruments of offensive warfare. During World War II these carriers, with their combination of fighter, scout-bomber, and torpedo-bomber aircraft, demonstrated that they were not only capable of destroying enemy naval forces and shipping, but that they were ideal for carrying the war to the enemy.

After the development of nuclear weapons, the carrier, with its nuclear-capable aircraft, became a deterrent to nuclear conflict because of its mobility and relative invulnerability.

Advantages. The primary value of the modern aircraft carrier lies in its mobility, versatility, and flexibility. Conflicts since World War II have occurred in the Middle East, South Asia, Korea, Africa, Latin America, and Southeast Asia—usually in areas where airfields are lacking or inadequate. Often the carrier has been the only available airfield capable of supporting high-performance aircraft. As such, the carrier is much more than a floating airstrip. It provides maintenance facilities, spare parts, fuel, and ammunition for its embarked aircraft, as well as food and living quarters for personnel.

Another major advantage of the carrier is that it is, in effect, part of its nation's sovereign territory. It may cruise freely in international waters, which means that significant air power may be brought into useful range of potential targets at the sole discretion of the country the ship serves.

Types and Capabilities. Until the mid-1970s U.S. Navy carriers were designated CVA or CVS, with an *N* added when the carrier had nuclear propulsion. The *A* identified an attack carrier, one whose air wing was developed around aircraft capable of surface attack missions. The *S* designated an antisubmarine carrier, with aircraft capable of detecting and attacking submarines. As the number of carriers in active service was reduced, it became clear that it would be impossible to maintain separate groups of carriers for these two missions.

Operational exercises showed that both attack and antisubmarine aircraft could be operated together from modern carriers. When a carrier is outfitted to support both forces, its designation is changed to CV (CVN, when it has nuclear propulsion). A program begun in the mid-1970s eventually converted all attack carriers to the multipurpose CV configuration.

Air power aboard one of these carriers can be adjusted from one tailored to sea control missions with a high concentration of antisubmarine and fighter aircraft, through intermediate stages of moderate antisubmarine and increased attack strength, to one optimized for projection of tactical air power ashore. At the antisubmarine end of the capability spectrum is an air wing of antisubmarine warfare (ASW) fixed-wing aircraft and ASW helicopters (to detect and attack submarines), fighter aircraft (for defense against air reconnaissance and air attack), and a moderate number of attack aircraft (to defeat surface combatant ships). At the opposite end of this spectrum is the tactical air wing, strong in attack aircraft.

History. The first test launch of an aircraft from a ship occurred on Nov. 14, 1910, when a civilian pilot, Eugene Ely, flew off the U.S. cruiser *Birmingham* from a temporary wooden platform. The first landing aboard ship was demonstrated by Ely on Jan. 18, 1911, on a platform aboard the armored cruiser U.S.S. *Pennsylvania*.

In spite of Ely's success, the U.S. Navy set aside further development of aircraft operations from ships until 1919, preferring to concentrate on seaplanes. Meanwhile, the British developed and used carriers during World War I. In 1919 the U.S. Navy converted the collier U.S.S. *Jupiter* into an experimental aircraft carrier. This ship joined the U.S. fleet on March 20, 1922, as the U.S.S. *Langley.* Japan also developed carriers and commissioned the *Hosho* on Dec. 27, 1922. Although the British were the first to operate aircraft from a ship specifically designed for that purpose, the *Hosho* was the first ship built from the keel up as a carrier. The first true British carrier was the *Hermes*. The first true U.S. carrier, the *Ranger*, was commissioned in June 1934.

World War II. In terms of naval warfare, World War II was a carrier war. In the Atlantic, small escort carriers were effective against Germany's submarines, relieved the besieged island of Malta, and spearheaded the North African landings. In the Pacific, the surrender of Japan in 1945 was due in large part to the vast U.S. fleet built around the aircraft carrier.

At the outbreak of World War II the United States had 7 carriers, Britain 7, and Japan 8. Germany, the USSR, and France had 1 carrier each. By the end of the war the United States had 37 fleet (attack) carriers and 79 escort carriers, while the British Commonwealth had 14 fleet carriers and 42 escort carriers.

The United States built three types of carriers during the war: fleet carriers, light carriers, and escort carriers. Escort carriers were conversions built on hulls originally designed for merchant vessels. These carriers were used primarily against submarines in the Atlantic. They could make 18 knots (20.7 mph; 33.3 km/hr), carried 20 to 30 aircraft, had a 500- to 550-foot (152- to 168-meter) flight deck, and had catapults to launch aircraft. Light carriers were built on hulls originally intended for light cruisers and were capable of high speed.

The chief U.S. Navy carrier type in World War II was the Essex-class fleet carrier, of which 23 were commissioned during the period from 1942 to 1946. These 33-knot (38-mph; 61-km/hr) ships displaced 36,000 tons and had an overall length of 872 to 888 feet (266 to 271 meters).

Postwar Development. After World War II the Essex-class carriers underwent significant modification and modernization, which increased their length to 895 feet (273 meters) and their displacement to 42,500 tons. One major change was the addition of the deck-edge aircraft elevator to augment the two centerline elevators, which improved the handling of aircraft. Other improvements were the addition of an angled deck and the utilization of steam catapults instead of hydraulic catapults. The angled deck permits the simultaneous launching and landing of aircraft with a large degree of safety. This is achieved by angling the after portion of the flight deck an average of approximately 10° to port from the fore-and-aft axis of the ship. An aircraft that lands on this portion of the deck, and whose hook fails to engage an arresting wire, simply flies around for another landing attempt.

The steam catapult, used on all modern carriers, has a launching capacity of 70 million foot-pounds (9,681,000 kg-meters). This means that an 80,000-pound (36,288-kg) airplane can be accelerated to 140 knots (161 mph; 259 km/hr) from a standing start in a 315-foot (96-meter) distance.

Another important aircraft carrier development has been the Fresnel lens system, which uses a series of vertical lights on the carrier flight deck to let the pilot know whether the aircraft is at the proper level.

The *Lexington*, the last of the ships originally designated as Essex class, was eventually used as a training ship before being relieved of its duties in 1992.

U.S. Carriers. In the late 1960s the United States still had 16 Essex-class aircraft carriers, but by the mid-1970s there were only 2: the *Hancock* and the *Oriskany*. The *Hancock* was commissioned during World War II; the *Oriskany* was completed in 1950.

The Midway-class carrier, of which there were three, was designed during World War II but did not see action. After being modernized, these carriers had a length of 968 feet (295 meters), a displacement of approximately 62,700 tons, and a capacity for carrying about 80 high-performance aircraft.

During the period from 1955 to 1959 four aircraft carriers of the Forrestal class were completed. These vessels were approximately 1,047 feet (319 meters) in length, with displacements ranging from 76,000 to 80,700 tons, and were capable of steaming at speeds in excess of 30 knots (35 mph; 56 km/hr).

The *Enterprise*, which joined the U.S. fleet in 1961, was the first carrier to be propelled by nuclear power. Slightly larger than the Forrestal class, displacing 87,000 tons and having a length of 1,102 feet (336 meters), it carried about 100 aircraft.

A nuclear carrier has many advantages over carriers with conventional power: it can reach high speed quickly and maintain it indefinitely without refueling, and it utilizes part of the space required for fuel oil on other carriers to carry more ammunition and aviation fuel.

By the early 1990s there were 15 U.S. carriers. Six of these, in the Nimitz class, had a more advanced nuclear propulsion system than the *Enterprise*. The latter carrier was powered by eight nuclear reactors; the Nimitz class relied on two reactors operating at greater efficiency. Based on a peacetime activity level, nuclear-powered carriers are expected to run 20 years without refueling.

Other Countries. Countries other than the United States that have aircraft carriers of various types include the United Kingdom, France, Argentina, Brazil, and Spain. The U.K., with three aircraft carriers in the early 1990s, finished a modernization program for the *Invincible* in January 1989 and in August 1991 began a 2½-year program to modernize the *Illustrious*.

Also in the early 1990s, France had two aircraft carriers, both commissioned in the early 1960s. It was in the process of building a third, the nuclear-powered *Charles de Gaulle*, as a replacement for one of the older vessels.

Russia, which had five aircraft carriers in the early 1990s, also was building two more. By early 1992, however, it was uncertain whether one of the ships, the *Ulyanovsk*, would be completed. See also AVIATION.

DAVID L. McDONALD*
Admiral, U.S. Navy (Retired)
Former Chief of Naval Operations

Bibliography

Chesneau, Roger, *Aircraft Carriers of the World: 1914 to the Present* (Naval Inst. Press 1984).

Friedman, Norman, *U.S. Aircraft Carriers: An Illustrated Design History* (Naval Inst. Press 1983).

Garrison, Peter, *CV: Carrier Aviation*, 3d ed. (Presidio Press 1987).

Humble, Richard, *U.S. Fleet Carriers of World War II in Action* (Sterling 1984).

Jordan, John, *An Illustrated Guide to Modern Naval Aviation and Aircraft Carriers* (Arco 1983).

Messimer, Dwight R., *Pawns of War: The Loss of the U.S.S. Langley and the U.S.S. Pecos* (Naval Inst. Press 1983).

AIRCRAFT INDUSTRY.   See AEROSPACE INDUSTRY.

AIREDALE TERRIER, âr'dāl ter'e-ər, one of the largest of the terriers. It was developed from crossing the now-extinct old English terrier with the otterhound. The dog breed takes its name from the Aire valley in northern England.

An ideal Airedale is erect and squarely built, with a long head and powerful jaws. Its coat is hard, wavy, and wiry, and the fur is tan with black or grizzled markings on the sides and upper part of the body. Some Airedales have red in the sides and upper body markings. Certain strains also have a small white mark, or blaze, on the chest. Height varies from 22 to 23 inches (56 to 58 cm), and weight ranges from 40 to 50 pounds (18 to 23 kg).

While primarily developed for hunting otter, fox, badger, and rats, the Airedale also makes a loyal companion and aggressive watchdog. It was among the first breeds selected for police and guard work in Britain and Germany. The breed is used as a guide dog for the blind in some countries.

J. J. McCOY, *Author of*
"The Complete Book of Dog Training and Care"

AIRFLOW.   See AERODYNAMICS.

AIRFOIL.   See AERODYNAMICS.

AIRGLOW, âr'glō, a faint, natural glowing of the earth's upper atmosphere. The term *airglow* refers to both a barely perceptible light at night called the nightglow and a similar but more complex phenomenon that occurs during the day called the dayglow.

The energy for producing the nightglow, and in a more complex fashion the dayglow, comes originally from the sun. During the day, ultraviolet light from the sun breaks apart molecules of oxygen into separate oxygen atoms. At night the atoms come together again to form molecules. Energy is liberated in the process. Some of the energy is distributed to other gas molecules in the atmosphere, but some is released as light. Oxygen atoms also combine with oxygen molecules to form ozone, the triatomic form of oxygen. Reactions of ozone with small amounts of hydrogen in the atmosphere are known to produce light as well. Atomic oxygen reactions of one sort or another produce almost all of what we call the nightglow.

The nightglow is peculiar in that the wavelengths of which it is composed indicate that the light comes from excited molecules that ordinarily do not emit light. Such molecules are called metastable. Some of the nightglow—mostly from molecular and atomic oxygen—is emitted from a layer of the atmosphere about 6 miles (10 km) thick, at an altitude of about 60 miles (100 km). This is where atomic oxygen is most concentrated. Below this layer the amount of ozone increases, reaching a maximum concentration about 21 miles (35 km) above the earth. In this region ozone reacts with atomic hydrogen to yield excited hydroxyl (OH) radicals that emit infrared light. Above a height of 60 miles a very metastable form of excited atomic oxygen emits light. The brightness of the light increases with an increase in altitude.

ROBERT A. YOUNG*
Stanford Research Institute

AIRLANGGA, âr-läng'gä (1001–1049), Javanese king who built a powerful empire in 11th-century Java. He is regarded as a national hero in modern Indonesia.

Upon his succession to the throne in 1016 Airlangga held sway over only a fragment of the former East Javanese kingdom. His father-in-law and predecessor, Dharmavaṃsa, had lost most of his patrimony to the Sumatran kingdom of Śrīvijaya in 1006. But raids by the Cōlas of India about 1025 weakened Śrīvijaya, and Airlangga began to assert his authority over the local Javanese lords. In 1030 the king of Śrīvijaya recognized Java's independence and gave Airlangga a daughter in marriage.

Under Airlangga, Java exercised supremacy over the eastern part of the Malay archipelago, while Sumatra dominated the west. Local elites continued to wield considerable power, but Airlangga moved to centralize administrative authority at his court in Janggala. A lynchpin of his power was his development of the Brantas River delta, a project that controlled regional flooding and opened new bottom lands to cultivation. The resulting increase in rice production provided a valuable export commodity that could be traded through the deepwater port he had created at Surabaya as part of the Brantas River delta project. About 1045 Airlangga divided his domain between two sons and retired to a monastery.

Airlangga worked to forge a syncretic political, artistic, and literary culture based on Indian and Javanese models. Fashioning himself a Javanese Arjuna, one of the heros of the Indian epic *Mahābhārata*, he patronized both Hindu and Buddhist cults and was the subject of an allegorical interpretation of his life, the *Arjunavivāha* ("Marriage of Arjuna"), composed in his honor by the court poet Mpu Kanwa.

AIRPLANE, a heavier-than-air flying machine with fixed wings that use the pressures created by moving through the air to lift the craft and control its movement. Observing a large airliner gracefully take off and fly through the air can lead one to believe that flight is a simple and natural activity. In fact, however, airplane flight—and thus the designing of suitable aircraft—is a very

CONTENTS

complex affair. Whereas ground vehicles are constrained by the ground surface on which they move, an airplane moves laterally in three-dimensional space and routinely executes rotational motion around each of three axes in normal flight. This freedom complicates airplane flight enormously. In addition, the safety requirements for an aircraft must be very stringent, since any loss of control or system failure can have catastrophic consequences, not only for the passengers on the craft but for people on the ground.

The first sustained controlled flight of an airplane took place on Dec. 17, 1903. The aircraft, known then as the *Flyer*, was designed and built by Wilbur and Orville Wright of Dayton, Ohio, culminating a century of theory, design, and experimentation. Several earlier episodes could conceivably lay claim to launching the era of flight, but the modern design of airplanes and airplane systems, in all their complexity, subtlety, and technological sophistication, clearly began with the Wrights. The phenomenal growth of this technology, of air transportation, and all its associated industries are among the great achievements of the 20th century.

For related material on the science and technology of flight, see AERODYNAMICS; INTERNAL COMBUSTION ENGINE; JET ENGINE; PROPELLER; ROCKET; and WIND TUNNEL. Material on the history of flight can be found in AEROSPACE INDUSTRY; AIRCRAFT; and AVIATION. The practices and state of the air transportation industry can be found in AIR SAFETY; AIR TRAFFIC CONTROL; AIR TRANSPORTATION; AIRPORT; and AUTOMATIC PILOT. The technology of other aircraft is discussed in AIRSHIP; BALLOON; and HELICOPTER. Military applications of flight technology are discussed in AIR WARFARE and AIRCRAFT CARRIER. Related material may be found in AIR FORCE; KITE; SOARING AND GLIDING; SUPERSONIC TRANSPORT; and TECHNOLOGY.

1. Airplane Configuration Design

Airplane configuration refers to the manner in which the aerodynamic surfaces of the craft are designed and placed in relation to one another and to the other parts of the airplane (such as the fuselage and landing gear). The basic parts of an airplane (in this case, a conventional configuration) are depicted in figure 1.

In designing an airplane, some of the earliest design decisions involve choosing the basic airplane configuration that meets the purposes for which the craft will be used, or the craft's "mission profile." The requirements and limitations imposed by the craft's mission profile, the capabilities of materials and technology at hand, and the existing budgetary and regulatory restrictions will all play a role in the construction of any airplane, whether it is a "homebuilt," meaning a privately constructed aircraft, or a large passenger airliner.

Configuration Types. The variety of airplane configurations that have been developed is remarkable. (Many aircraft referred to in this article are depicted in figure 2; others are shown in the article AVIATION.) One reason for this is that, given a set of specific design parameters, there will often be several satisfactory configurations that appear to be quite different. A classic example is the case of the AVRO Vulcan B2 and the Boeing B–47 Stratojet (similar in configuration to the B-52H), produced by two design teams to meet very similar specifications.

The basic configuration types are tail-aft (also called conventional), such as the Boeing 747-200B; canard (also called tail-first), such as the Wrights' *Flyer* and the Miles M39B Libellula; three-surface, such as the Piaggio P-180; and the flying wing, such as the Northrop YB-49 (and the B2A Stealth Bomber).

In addition to the overall wing configuration of a plane (sometimes referred to as its "geometry"), wing position on the fuselage, wing shape, engine position relative to the craft's center of gravity, and landing gear type are used as configuration identifiers as described below.

Wing position on the fuselage can be low wing, mid-wing, and high wing; wings raised above the fuselage are known as parasol wings. The wings can lie flat, can tilt up on each side, in which case they are referred to as dihedral, or can tilt down on each side, in which case they are referred to as anhedral. (The F4U-1 Corsair fighter of World War II is an example of wing configuration that is both dihedral and anhedral.)

The wing planform can be rectangular, elliptical, tapered (toward the tips), delta, swept back or swept forward. Planes generally have single-wing, or monoplane, configurations (extending out on both sides of the fuselage). Planes can also be equipped with two (biplane) and three (triplane) wings for specific missions, such as agricultural aviation. Special mission requirements have given rise to variable-geometry designs, in which the craft is able to change its aerodynamic design in flight, such as the "swing wing" configuration of the F-14A Tomcat.

For the propeller or jet engine placement, a "tractor" configuration refers to placement in front of the center of gravity (CG); a "pusher" design places the engine behind the center of gravity. Engine (also referred to as the craft's "power plant") placement will have a significant effect on an aircraft's stability and maneuverability.

The landing gear can be a tricycle configuration, a tail-dragger (or tail-wheel) used for small aircraft such as the Schweizer G-164D, or a tandem (also called bicycle) arrangement, as used by the AV-8B Harrier. Several hybrid configurations have also evolved to meet specific needs. Though all the parameters of the aircraft are constantly being altered and tested, airplane designers are by nature conservative, so that the conventional tail-aft configuration has become a widely applied standard in airplane design.

Mission Parameters. The type of configuration selected by the designer depends on the type of mission the airplane is required to perform, safety requirements, and budgetary and environmental restrictions. The difference in all these areas between civil and military aviation is considerable, so that the first distinguishing feature of an aircraft is whether it is designed for civil or military use.

Examples of civil uses include personal transportation, recreation, passenger transportation, cargo shipment, business and utility transportation, search and rescue missions, agricultural use, and training. Typical military missions include personnel and equipment transportation; liaison and utility transportation; ground assault by cannon, missile fire, or bombing; plane-to-plane combat; search and rescue; ground and electronic air reconnaissance; jamming and electronic warfare; and training.

Differing mission profiles of military and civil aircraft, which translate into widely divergent performance parameters, become immediately apparent. Both begin with engine ignition and warm-up, but a military airplane may have to be flight-ready in a much shorter time. Both begin flight with a takeoff, but a civil airplane climbs as quickly as possible to clear the area around the airport, while a military airplane might have to become airborne more quickly and accelerate to high speeds at low altitudes before climbing in order to maintain radar secrecy. A typical range, or "block distance," for a civil airplane might be 500 to 6,000 nautical miles (900 to 11,100 km), while a military aircraft's "action radius" might be 500 nautical miles. In flight, most civil aircraft would probably not have to be very maneuverable. Military aircraft, on the other hand, may have to be capable of executing rapid 360° turns sustaining high g forces while quickly gaining altitude. A military aircraft has to be able to release bomb and missile loads and fire cannon while maintaining speed and stability. The landing of a civil transport aircraft is likely to require more runway and be softer. Military aircraft may also require a quicker turn-around time on the ground. In the history of aviation, care and diligence in defining mission parameters has often rewarded designers and nations with superior aircraft and air tactical advantages.

The performance elements that are designed in response to mission parameters include block distance; takeoff distance; descent, climb, glide or dive rates; landing distance; crew requirements; cruise speed and altitude ceiling; service and maintenance turn-around; and equipment and avionics requirements. Airworthiness performance and environmental aspects include takeoff and landing distances and speeds, maneuvering, noise and chemical pollution, turbulent-air penetration, communication and avionic equipment, minimum climb rate or gradient—with all engines operating and with one or more engines inoperative. Regulatory authorities usually specify the numerical requirements for many airworthiness parameters to ensure that airplanes meet minimum safety standards. For civil airplanes these safety standards are published in the Federal Air Regulations (FAR). For military airplanes corresponding safety standards are published in various military specifications.

The designer commences the configuration design process by examining the customer mission specification to identify whether or not any of the performance specifications are unusually severe. The Rutan Voyager and the K.U. High Altitude Reconnaissance airplanes are examples of configuration solutions designed to meet extreme range and endurance mission requirements.

Because the takeoff and landing requirements placed upon an airplane play a dominant role in its design, both civil and military missions can be classified into the following types:

1. conventional takeoff and landing (CTOL)
2. short takeoff and landing (STOL)
3. vertical takeoff and landing (VTOL)
4. hybrid missions, such as short takeoff and vertical landing (STOVL) and conventional takeoff and short landing (CTOSL).

Configuration Selection. Configuration choices are made on the basis of a number of design criteria. Among the most important are safety, performance, weight, cost, and complexity. Designers strive to get the best safety and performance for the least cost and complexity. Other criteria that play an important role in the design process are inspectability, serviceability and maintenance, and operating cost.

In many cases a "red-white-blue" team approach is used, in which two or more preliminary design teams are formed and instructed to design a total aircraft to meet given specifications. When reviewing these various designs, one or more configurations will usually stand out in terms of weight, cost, or complexity and will then be selected for further detailed design development.

Configurations other than conventional are referred to in the design community as "unusual" configurations. Yet one or more design requirements may be so severe that a conventional configuration is clearly not workable, or the weight, cost, or complexity of a conventional configuration can be shown to be significantly greater than that for one of the unusual configurations. Following are some of the considerations that would cause an aircraft designer to consider an unusual configuration.

Canard Configuration. Canard configurations have been used periodically ever since the Wright *Flyer*. Several recent designs have used the ca-

Figure 1. BASIC PARTS OF AN AIRPLANE

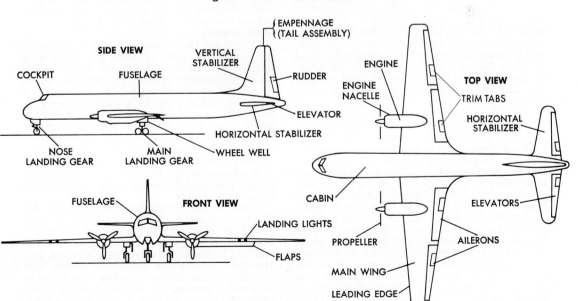

nard, including the Rutan Voyager, the Grumman forward-swept wing X-29 (actually a three-surface canard) and the Beech Starship. It is often incorrectly believed that an advantage of the canard configuration is that in trim (with all forces in balance during flight) it provides lift on both sides of the center of gravity and thus greater lift; whereas the tail-aft configuration generally requires a downward force on the tail section to balance the moments around the CG. The result is a greater downward force on the plane as a whole.

However, the canard also generates a wake that influences the aerodynamics of the wing. Canard-to-wing interference can be favorable or unfavorable, depending on flight conditions as well as on the relative placement of the canard to the wing and on the size of the canard in relation to the size of the wing. In certain situations it is possible to take advantage of the flow interference between a canard and a wing. (Such favorable interference was exploited on the SAAB JA 37 Viggen fighter.)

In a pure canard configuration, designers would limit engine noise in the cabin by moving the engine to the very rear of the plane. This makes a conventionally configured airplane difficult to balance but presents virtually no problem to the canard.

In low-altitude attack and high-speed attack airplanes, the ride qualities as experienced by the crew can become very marginal, particularly in airplanes with significant aeroelastic behavior. In that case the canard configuration offers a convenient solution: since the wing is located close to the cockpit, it can be used to deflect motion in such a way as to lower the vertical acceleration levels at the cockpit station. The XB-70 Valkyrie (an SST with a canard wing) and the B-1B bombers are examples of this design approach.

Three-Surface Configurations. Designers look to a three-surface configuration when there is a particular need for an improved trimmed lift-to-drag ratio over and beyond that provided by a conventional or pure canard type of configuration; when they wish to limit structural weight, which they achieve by integrating the rear pressure bulkhead, wing-fuselage carry-through structure, and main landing gear structure in one area, and by using an unswept high-aspect-ratio wing; or, when there is a need to provide a quiet ride, by moving the engines to the rear and out onto the wing. All these objectives were achieved on the P-180.

The three-surface is not without its difficulties, however. The canard wing interferes with access to and service of commercial aircraft.

Flying Wings. The first flying-wing glider flew in 1906, and Hugo Junkers was granted a patent for the flying wing in 1913. Several famous aircraft were nearly flying wings, including the Messerschmitt 163 Rocket Fighter and the de Havilland DH 108. But the name most closely associated with this design in the United States is Jack Northrop, the legendary designer and aviation pioneer who built several flying-wing bombers, such as the propeller-driven XB-35, between 1943 and 1947. Modern incarnations of the design include the Handley Page 126 Aerobus and the B2A Stealth Bomber. Despite the fact that the design was highly thought of in the 1940s, flying wings have not gained a foothold.

The advantages of the flying-wing configuration are aerodynamic efficiency, due to the absence of components such as fuselage, horizontal tail, and vertical tail (though this does not necessarily result in superior lift-to-drag ratios, as was once thought); efficient weight management, since all the payloads, systems, and structure are in the wing itself, thereby reducing the root-bending moment, which in turn reduces the wing weight; and very low observables, making a flying wing inherently more difficult to detect by optical means or by radar.

As might be expected, there are some disadvantages associated with flying wings, as illustrated by the following practical example. Envision a flying-wing passenger airplane for 150 passengers. These passengers are to fit inside the wing with the normal cabin amenities. Assume that an acceptable minimum internal cabin height (floor-to-ceiling) is 6.5 feet (2 meters). Allowing 1.5 feet (46 cm) for total structural depth below the floor and above the ceiling, the external thickness of the flying wing will thus be 8 feet (2.4 meters). In a subsonic airplane a typical airfoil-thickness ratio is about 12%. Therefore, the local chord length will be $8/0.12 = 66.7$ feet (20 meters). It is further assumed that this local chord is in fact the mean geometric chord of the wing, that the wing aspect ratio is 8 (typical of modern transports) and that the wing taper ratio is 0.4. The required wing area, S, is calculated: $S = 31,602$ ft^2 (2,939 m^2), which is a very large area indeed, especially when compared with a wing area of about 2,000 square feet (186 sq meters) for a conventional design with the same passenger requirements. Clearly a flying wing would not be a suitable configuration choice for a medium sized passenger airplane.

For a flying wing to be stable, its CG must be forward of the aerodynamic center (AC), the point around which rotational moments due to aerodynamic forces act. Since both the empty-weight CG and the loaded-weight CG must be located forward of the AC—in fact, forward of the quarter chord point, which is itself well forward—little room is available for fuel and payload. Moreover, there is much useless volume behind the quarter chord point and in the rear of the aircraft.

There are two solutions to this problem: either sweep the wing or make the flying wing inherently unstable and equip it with an automatic stabilization system. The second method is used by the Northrop B-2 bomber, but as a result the craft requires highly sophisticated electronics. The first method yields enough flexibility for a reasonable allocation of masses and volumes, but by sweeping the wing, the weight will increase because of the additional amount of torsion load the structure is supporting. In a high subsonic design, the wing needs to be swept in any case to keep compressibility drag from becoming too large.

Conventional airplanes use flaps for high lift, which often results in a large negative (nose down) pitching moment. Trimming out such a negative pitching moment without a tail is not practical because of the lack of a moment arm. Therefore, most flying wings use airfoils with very little camber (upper surface curvature) or even reflex camber. To achieve low speed the flying wing uses a large area and a very low wing loading (pressure experienced by the wing).

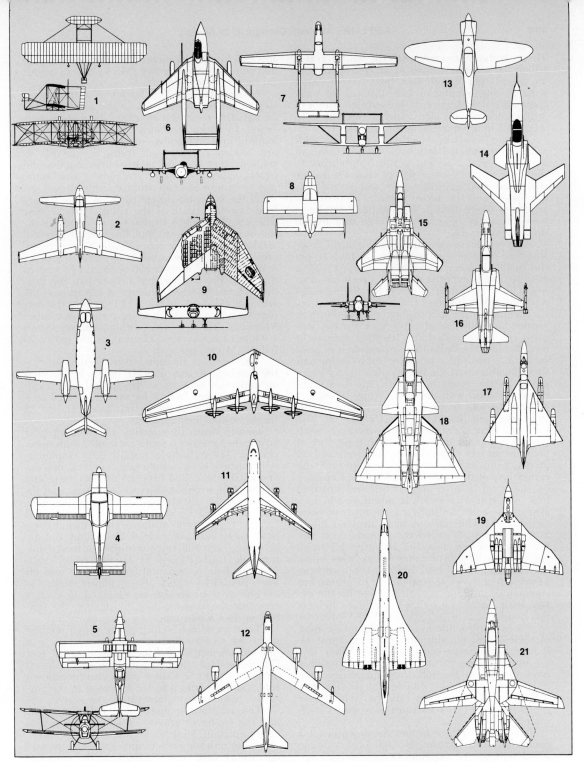

Figure 2. Airplane configurations (all planes facing upward): three-view of Wright *Flyer* (1); classic canard design, used in modern Miles M39B Libellula (2); Gates Piaggio GP-180 (3), a three-surface; Valmet L-70 (4), a conventional tail-aft; Schweizer AG-CAT (5, with front view), a modern biplane; two split-fuselage ("twin boom") designs: Hawker Siddeley Sea Vixen (6, with front view; note high stabilizer and off-center cockpit), and the WSK-Mielec M-15 (7, with front view; note double, tapered, high-aspect-ratio wing); typical "homebuilt" Piel C.P.500 (8); two flying wings: Handley Page 126 Aerobus (9, with front view; note passenger compartment), and Northrop YB-49 (10); Boeing 747-200B (11), low-wing conventional; Boeing B-52H (12), high-wing conventional; Isaacs Spitfire (13), with elliptical wing; Grumman X-29A (14), forward-swept, three-surface "fly-by-wire" fighter; McDonnell Douglas F-15C Eagle (15, with front view; see fig. 4); Northrop F-20 Tigershark (16, note dual intake ports and single exhaust); Convair B-58A Hustler (17), delta wing; SAAB JA 37 Viggen (18), combination canard and delta wings; AVRO Vulcan (19), almost a flying wing; Aerospatiale/BAC Concorde (20), with rudder but no rear stabilizer; Grumman F-14A Tomcat (21), three-surface canard wings sweep back into a delta configuration.

That is certainly the case with the Northrop B-2, which has a wing loading at takeoff of roughly 48 pounds per square foot (psf), as compared with a wing loading of 120–150 psf for most conventional jet transports, indicating a factor of 3 difference in wing size, which is equivalent to a factor 3 in a requirement for high lift.

A flying wing also experiences problems with a lack of directional stability. This problem can be addressed by adding vertical stabilizers to the wing tips of a swept flying wing. Of course, when that is done, extra weight and wetted area are added, and the added surfaces increase the airplane's observability. The vertical stabilizers would have to be relatively large due to the small moment arm.

That still leaves the directional control problem following an engine failure at takeoff. On the Stealth Bomber, and earlier on the YB-35, a so-called drag rudder is used for directional control. This drag rudder is somewhat like an aileron split into two halves that can be opened up. By opening up the split trailing edge of the drag rudder in a differential manner, a yawing moment can be generated, but the drag increase is considerable. The difficulties encountered in pressurizing a passenger cabin or cargo hold, and the difficulties that the design presents for evacuation in the event of a crash, are two additional problems with the flying-wing design.

Wing Layout. In most airplanes the wing is the component that carries most of the lift. The load on a wing is distributed spanwise and chordwise in a manner that depends on a number of flight parameters. Generally, the aerodynamic load increases toward the fuselage and toward the center line of the wing; the addition of engines on the wing helps decrease this load distribution. This is inertial relief. In addition, when an airplane maneuvers ("pulls g"), the loads increase significantly. The ratio of total airplane lift to airplane weight is called the airplane load factor. Airplanes are designed to carry 1.5 times their design limit load factor before they break up. The design limit load factor is obtained from so-called V-n (speed-to-load-factor) diagrams. For commercial airplanes a typical value for the design limit load factor is 2.5; for military fighters this number can be as high as 9.0.

The wing structure must be able to take most of these loads. In addition, the wing must be light and not create too much drag. When laying out the wing for an airplane, the designer must decide on the following quantities: area (S), sweep angle (Λ_{LE}), dihedral angle (Γ), span (b), taper ratio (λ), aspect ratio $(A = b^2/S)$, and the twist angle $(\varepsilon_T,$ a measure of a wing's stalling properties).

In addition to these factors, the designer must decide on such features as high or low wing, winglets, fixed or variable sweep, and folding wing tips. The wing is also used to attach the high-lift system (trailing and/or leading edge flaps) and the lateral (or roll) control surfaces. In airplanes where the wingspan is limited for reasons such as deck space or hangar space on an aircraft carrier or gate space at existing airports, folding tips or winglets are sometimes selected.

Wing aspect ratios range from 3 to 5 (for fighters) and 7 to 13 (for transports). Another important parameter is the wing loading: weight divided by wing area (W/S). Typical values for wing loading range from 10 pounds per square foot (4.5 kg/0.09 sq meter), for light airplanes, to 140 pounds per square foot (63.5 kg/0.09 sq meter), for jet transports.

Fuselage Layout. The layout of a fuselage is dependent on the mission of the airplane: civil or military, passenger or cargo, land- or water-based. In cargo airplanes, which require rapid loading and unloading, ramps and large doors are needed. In passenger transports, special attention must be paid to passenger ingress and egress, especially under emergency conditions, and to ease of baggage storage and retrieval.

A fundamental design decision in any fuselage layout is that of the cabin cross section. The size of this cross section has an obvious bearing on weight and on drag. For a small personal airplane like the Cessna Citation II, the entire cross section of the cabin is devoted to passengers, providing a space 56 inches (142 cm) in diameter. For a passenger airliner like the Boeing 727, the fuselage diameter of 128 inches (325 cm) is divided 44 inches (112 cm) from the bottom for a cargo hold, leaving a passenger cabin 84 inches (213 cm) high (with curved sides) and a width of 128 inches (325 cm), or just under 20 inches (51 cm) per seat.

The fuselage fineness ratio ("slenderness")—the fuselage length divided by its height—has an important bearing on weight and drag. Typical values range from 5 for small airplanes, to 8 for business jets, to 10 for transports, and to 22 for supersonic airplanes.

Landing Gear. In selecting the landing gear layout, the designer is again confronted with many choices. These include overall gear configuration (tailwheel or taildragger, tandem, or conventional—also called tricycle); number, type, and size of tires; number, disposition, length, and diameter of the struts; and fixed or retractable. The gear must be designed to take loads and transfer these to the airframe; these include vertical loads that are caused by taxiing and by dropping onto the runway during a hard landing, side loads caused by landing in a "crab" (runway hole or indentation), and fore and aft loads caused by wheel spin-up and braking.

The gear must also be designed in such a way that the airplane does not damage the runway surface when touching down or rolling.

The touchdown velocities for which landing gears are designed range from around 12 feet (3.7 meters) per second for transports to 25 feet (7.6 meters) per second for some carrier-based aircraft. A factor 2 change in vertical touchdown rate translates into a factor 4 change in the vertical kinetic energy absorbed by the gear.

The relationship between the landing gear and the center of gravity of an airplane is also very important. Most planes must meet "tip-over" criteria in order to prevent mishaps during ground operations. As a very general rule, the most forward and most aft location of a plane's center of gravity (CG) must be within 15° of the outermost landing support. There are also ground-clearance criteria that must be observed to prevent damage to nacelles or wing tips in case of tire or strut deflation, and to prevent rear assembly damage during takeoff rotation.

The structural integration of the landing gear into the airframe is another important aspect of airplane design. The gear is basically "deadweight" for most of the flight, so it is important to keep its weight as low as possible.

Empennage Layout. The airplane's empennage is the combined horizontal and vertical tail and in some instances the canard (also called forward wing) assembly. Tail and canard surfaces are normally added to airplanes to provide adequate control power and stability. Tails can be vertical, double vertical (as in the F-15 Eagle), T-tail (with the rear horizontal stabilizer placed at the top of the vertical stabilizer, as in the case of the Piaggio P-180), and V-tail (with two stabilizers radiating out from the tail section in the shape of a V, used in the design of the Lockheed F-117A Stealth fighter). In both the T-tail and V-tail configurations, additional structural requirements add weight, and control can be complicated and difficult. For this reason, unless there is a compelling reason (such as the additional lift on takeoff provided by the T-tail or the net decrease in empennage observability for the V-tail), most aircraft will utilize a conventional tail design.

In most airplanes, control power is obtained by adding moving control surfaces to the tail or to the canard. These surfaces include elevators, rudders, and canard-vators. The function of the control surfaces is to provide for trim, maneuverability, and stability augmentation. Many control surfaces are equipped with "trim tabs," small surfaces that are used to fine-tune aircraft trim.

JAN ROSKAM
*Ackers Distinguished Professor of Aerospace
Engineering, University of Kansas*

2. Airplane Propulsion

Airplanes are propelled forward as a result of the rearward acceleration of matter that, by the simple application of Newton's third law (for every action there is an equal and opposite reaction), provides a thrust to the engine and thence to the aircraft to which it is attached.

Thrust is generated in three ways: by propelling air backward through the action of a propeller that is turned by an engine; by burning an air and fuel combination and jettisoning the product rearward, causing the engine, and hence the airplane, to move forward; or by the burning of fuel by a rocket engine. In the first two cases it is the ambient air that is sent in the direction opposite the aircraft's motion; in the third, it is the product of the rocket fuel's combustion. In all three cases this rearward discharge propels the plane forward.

The engine that propels an airplane is referred to as the power plant. Many types of engine have been integrated into airframes (the term for the structural part of an airplane). Among them are piston engines (reciprocating or rotary) combined with a propeller; turbo-propeller engines; prop-fan engines; jet engines—with or without bypass, and with or without after-burning; ramjet engines; pulse-jet or pulse-detonation wave engines; rocket engines—solid or liquid; and electric motors with propellers.

The table indicates the approximate speed and altitude ranges over which these engines are typically applied. It can be seen that there is a significant amount of overlap in these ranges of applicability.

Power-Plant Requirements. The basic requirements of an airplane's power plant are that it be of sufficiently low weight, that it deliver sufficient thrust for the aircraft's mission profile, and that it do so efficiently, reliably, and economically.

An airplane's total weight is divided among the airframe, the propulsion system, the fuel, and the payload (crew, passengers, and cargo). The weight of the propulsion system must be a low enough percentage of the total weight of the aircraft to allow a sufficient payload to be carried an adequate distance. The engines on a long-range transport account for about one-tenth of the plane's total weight, while those on a military interceptor may account for one-third of the total weight.

The weight required of an engine on a particular airplane is determined by how much the plane weighs and how much force is required to propel it. A commercial transport flying at less than the speed of sound requires between 0.05 and 0.07 pounds (0.02–0.03 kg) of propulsion force for each pound of airframe. An airplane flying faster than the speed of sound may require several times as much force. Engine weight, then, depends on how much total force is required to propel the plane. In general, the engine should not weigh more than about 0.2 pounds (0.1 kg) for each pound of force produced.

Reliability is determined by the length of time an engine can run without major overhaul and by the relative occurrence of minor engine failures. A time interval of at least 800 hours between overhauls is desirable for piston engines, and about 3,000 to 5,000 hours for jet engines. An engine of a new model is required to pass an acceptance test before being put into use. This test generally requires about 150 hours of trouble-free operation on a test stand, with periods of acceleration, full throttle, partial throttle, and idling. The tested engine then is given a rating that indicates, say, that the engine can be operated for five minutes continuously at maximum thrust, 30 minutes continuously at a lower thrust, and without a time limitation (except for the length of the flight) at lowest thrust. This last value is called the continuous rating. The higher thrusts are required for takeoff, climb, emergencies, or, in the case of military airplanes, for combat.

Engine Types and Function. The types of propulsion systems are discussed here in the order in which they came into prominence. (See figure 3. See also INTERNAL COMBUSTION ENGINE; JET ENGINE; and ROCKET.) Steam engines were considered as possible airplane power plants in the late 19th century but proved to be much too heavy and inefficient. Human-powered flight is still at the early experimental stage despite the heroic accomplishments of Bryan Allen and his *Gossamer Albatross*. Nuclear-powered flight, while feasible, is so fraught with environmental hazards that it is not likely to be deployed even experimentally very soon. Hybrid combinations of many of these engines are also possible.

SPEED AND ALTITUDE RANGES FOR VARIOUS ENGINE TYPES

Engine type	Mach number range	Altitude range (ft)
Piston/Propeller	up to 0.4	up to 25,000
Turbopropeller	up to 0.7	up to 40,000
Prop-fan	up to 0.85	up to 50,000
Jet	up to 3.0	up to 75,000
Ramjet	0.4 to 25 or higher	up to 200,000
Rocket	no limit	no limit
Electric	up to 0.7	up to 40,000

Figure 3. PROPULSION SYSTEMS

Turboprop. Air is drawn into the engine, compressed, then heated by the burning of fuel. The expanding exhaust gases impart sufficient power to the turbine stages to drive both the compressor and a propeller.

Turbojet. In a turbojet, air is also compressed and heated, but expansion of the exhaust gases takes place in a nozzle that discharges directly to the rear. The resulting thrust propels the airplane.

Ramjet. At high airspeeds, the air entering a ramjet is sufficiently compressed to eliminate the need for a compressor and thus for a turbine. However, an auxiliary power source is required for takeoff.

Rocket Engine. Because it carries its own oxidant, a rocket engine can be used outside the atmosphere. The liquid-propellant type (*right*) provides more operational flexibility than does the solid-propellant type.

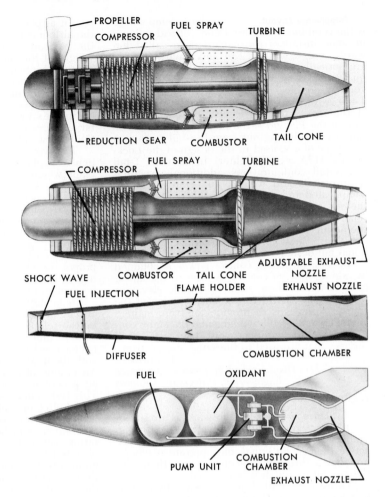

Piston with Propeller Engine. The output shaft of the piston engine drives a propeller (either directly or via a gearbox). Typical propeller rotational speeds range from 1,200 to 3,000 revolutions per minute (rpm) depending on the application. Piston engines are available in the horsepower range of around 20 to 3,000. In most current airplane installations the piston engines are air-cooled. Liquid-cooled engines tend to be more efficient, albeit heavier. Although they were extensively used in World War II, they were not used for some three decades, and only in the late 1980s were they again used.

In a turboprop engine (more accurately, a turbo-shaft engine driving a propeller via a gearbox), most of the energy generated by the engine is directed toward the propeller, which then provides the thrust.

Turbojet Engine. The jet engine, with its continuous combustion, provides an almost vibration-free environment, which is one reason for its popularity with airplane designers. Another is the fact that typical turbojet engines have fewer parts than do piston engines, so that their service life is much better, thereby reducing the cost to the operator. Finally, at high speeds the efficiency of the turbojet and its derivatives, the turbofan engines, exceeds that of other engine types. For extra thrust in military installations, afterburners are used.

Ramjet Engines. Ramjet engines have no moving parts and are therefore very simple. However, they require a fairly high speed (Mach 2) to become competitive with the turbojet engines. At very low speeds a ramjet does not produce sufficient thrust to be at all useful. Therefore, airplanes with ramjet power plants require another form of propulsion for takeoff, climb, and acceleration. Ramjets have yet to be applied with any regularity to airplanes, having found their greatest application in missiles and drones.

Pulse-Jet Engine. Pulse-jet engines are also very simple in operation. The German V-1 type pulse jet used moving inlet valve plates. The French acoustic pulse jet (SNECMA) has no moving parts. These pulse-jet engines develop thrust at zero speed and are very light. However, they are extremely noisy (the V-1 was known as the "buzz bomb" because the buzzing caused by its valves could be heard for miles) and have very high fuel consumption. These engines have not seen significant application in airplanes.

Rocket Engines. Rocket engines have not been used widely in airplanes because of their very high fuel consumption. However, they do have a relatively high thrust-to-weight ratio and for that reason have been used as auxiliary power plants for takeoff under high-weight or high-altitude conditions (as, for example, in the B-47 bomber). In such instances they are referred to as JATO (jet-assisted takeoff) or RATO (rocket-assisted takeoff) installations. These were used even in commercial airplanes in the 1950s, when jet engines had not yet developed to a high level of installed thrust-to-weight ratio.

Electric Motors Driving Propellers. A major advantage of the electric motor is its relatively low noise and vibration-free operation, coupled with high efficiency. Its two disadvantages are a high weight-to-power ratio and the still heavy and inefficient methods available for electric energy storage. With the advent of rare-earth materials (such as samarium-cobalt), the weight of electric motors has decreased significantly.

Engine-Airframe Integration. Engine-airframe integration is an important aspect of airplane design. Engines can be mounted on the fuselage, wings, tail, or on a pod mounted above the fuselage. Engines can either be "buried," meaning that they are integrated into the body of the plane, or "podded," meaning that they are attached to the plane but separated from its body.

The following considerations are particularly important in determining the type of engine-airframe integration to be used: the effect of the installation on installed thrust (or power) and on inlet efficiency; the effect of the installation on stability and control; structural factors; maintenance, accessibility, and servicing factors; safety; noise and environmental factors; and observability factors.

Internally mounted engines tend to cause less installation drag than externally mounted engines, but externally mounted engines are much easier to service, inspect, and maintain. Most civil and military jet transports use external mounting. In fighters and in stealth airplanes the internal mounting method is preferred to reduce both drag and observability. Most single-engine airplanes have internally mounted engines.

Inlet Efficiency, Stability, and Control. In any type of jet-engine installation, care must be taken not to ingest any surface boundary layers in the inlet, since doing so leads to significant loss of efficiency. Figure 4 shows the inlet design for the F-15 Eagle fighter plane. The intake ducts are placed on either side of the fuselage.

The location of the thrust line relative to the center of gravity of the airplane can have a major effect on stability and control. For example, propellers located forward of the center of gravity act in a destabilizing way, while propellers located behind the CG tend to behave in a stabilizing manner. Neither design is inherently superior to the other, but these effects must be accounted for in deciding engine layout. The effect on the aerodynamics of the airplane of any propeller slipstream (the air pushed back by the propeller) or engine exhaust must also be considered. Slipstream when directed over a lifting surface tends to augment lift.

Structural Considerations. Weight is of paramount importance in airplane design. Since lift on wings is also responsible for the bending moment of the wing structure, minimizing that bending moment is one tool the designer has to lower weight. By distributing engines along the wing, inertial forces cause bending moments that oppose the bending moment owing to lift, which allows for a lighter wing. Subtle but measurable elements of harmonic motions created by the relation between engine and wing structure (such as whirl-mode flutter and extension shaft vibrations) can be dangerous, even catastrophic, when not considered early in the design process.

Servicing Considerations. When ready access to engines is provided, the time required for service and maintenance is considerably reduced, which in turn lowers operating costs. The podded engine approach, as first used by Boeing on the B-47 bomber, has proved to be a very accessible installation. Many jet transports have adopted that design philosophy. Fuselage-mounted engines are more difficult to reach, particularly on larger airplanes.

Safety Considerations. Engines must be separated from fuel, from the crew, and from passengers by suitable means, such as "fire walls," which separate the engine compartment from the passenger compartment in light airplanes. A similar design feature is used in jet transports; the part of the wing directly behind a jet engine usually has a dry bay with no fuel, to help minimize the risk of a spreading fire in case the engine itself ignites. In transport airplanes, engine nacelle installations are designed to cleanly break away in the event of a crash. This is done with so-called fuse pins.

Noise and Observability. The technology that deals with airplane detection is referred to as low-observables (or "stealth") technology. Major improvements have been made in this area since the 1970s. The Lockheed F-117A Nighthawk and the Northrop B-2 bomber are recent unclassified examples of successful stealth aircraft. By a combination of external shaping, "hiding" the inlets, and radar-energy-absorbing materials, the radar observability (as determined by the radar cross section) of these airplanes is made very small. By hiding the exhausts and diffusing them over a large area, the infrared observability is lowered. Visual observability is diminished by lowering the frontal aspect of an airplane. Noise is lowered by sound-absorbing materials and by mixing cool air with the exhaust gases.

All civil airplanes are subject to strict noise regulations as set forth in FAR 36. To reduce noise levels, special care is taken in the design of propellers (for example, through the use of low tip Mach numbers to reduce shock-induced noise) and jet engines (by installing sound absorbing materials in the nacelles).

JAN ROSKAM
Ackers Distinguished Professor of Aerospace Engineering, University of Kansas

3. Airplane Systems

Some airplane systems are so important to the safe conduct of flight that they are called flight crucial. If a flight-crucial system fails, the safe continuation or termination of the flight may be seriously jeopardized. Examples of flight-crucial systems are the control and navigation system in jet transports. Other systems only present a nuisance when they fail and are thus called non–flight crucial.

For an airplane to carry out its mission requirements, a number of systems must work (often together) safely. The systems are designed so that failure of any one of them does not interfere with the safe operation of other systems, particularly the flight-crucial systems.

Typical flight-crucial systems on civil and military aircraft (except where noted) include flight control; navigation; propulsion control; hydraulic, fuel, and electrical systems; crew oxygen (in civil aircraft, when flying above 10,000 feet, or 3,000 meters); and de-icing or anti-icing systems. Typical non-flight-crucial systems include fire detection and extinguishing, potable water and wastewater containment (except in small civil planes and fighters), noncrew oxygen systems (in civil aircraft, when flying above 10,000 feet), emergency escape, and electronic warfare and weapons control (in military aircraft).

Control Systems. Airplanes, unlike surface vehicles, must be controlled in a three-dimensional space. The motion of an airplane is endowed with six degrees of freedom: linear displacement along each of three axes and angular rotation about each of three axes. The pilot (or autopilot) must be provided with the means to control speed and rotation along and about three axes simultaneously. (See AERODYNAMICS.)

There are two fundamentally different types of flight control systems used in airplanes: reversible and irreversible systems. In a reversible control system the control surfaces move in direct response to the movement of the cockpit controls, but the opposite is also true: any turbulence in the air that moves a control surface also moves the corresponding cockpit controls. In an irreversible system the cockpit controls merely send a command to a control surface actuator (usually hydraulic). Any effect of turbulence on the control surfaces is counteracted by the actuator, and there is no feedback to the cockpit controls.

Reversible systems are used mainly in low-cost, low-performance airplanes, such as general aviation, business, and small transport airplanes. Irreversible systems are used mainly in high-performance airplanes, such as large transports and nearly all military airplanes.

Most flight control systems provide the pilot with the following basic functions: primary flight control, secondary flight control, stability augmentation, and automatic flight control.

Primary Flight Controls. The function of the primary flight controls is to provide some form of direct moment control about the three axes of the aircraft: rolling-moment control about the x-axis; pitching-moment control about the y-axis; and yawing-moment control about the z-axis.

Various types of controls are used to generate these controlling moments. Generically, three types of controls are recognized: aerodynamic-surface controls, thrust-vectoring controls, and vortex controls. All these controls are activated from the cockpit with the help of a control wheel (or stick) and rudder pedals.

Aerodynamic-surface controls are effective only above a certain speed, since they depend on aerodynamic pressure forces that themselves vary with the square of airspeed. Rolling-moment controls typically consist of ailerons, roll-control spoilers, differential stabilizers, and various other roll-control devices. Light airplanes tend to use only aileron control surfaces. Jet transports tend to use a combination of ailerons and roll-control spoilers. In fighters, differentially controlled stabilizers are used in addition to ailerons and spoilers. Pitching-moment controls typically consist of elevators, all-moving horizontal tails (also called stabilizers), canard-vators, all-moving canards, and various other pitch-control devices. Yawing-moment controls typically consist of rudders, all-moving vertical tails, and a variety of other yaw controls.

Thrust controls are effective at any speed. However, at moderate to high airspeeds, aerodynamic controls tend to be more effective than thrust controls, when the system weight is taken into consideration. Therefore, thrust controls tend to be used mostly at low speeds. For VTOL airplanes, the thrust (or vernier) controls are the only effective controls.

Control of thrust magnitude is used primarily to control speed and climb. However, if the thrust lines are not pointing directly through the airplane center of gravity, thrust automatically becomes a means of creating moments about the center of gravity. In some advanced fighters these principles are carried to an extreme by adding the capability to rotate the line of thrust. This is called thrust vectoring.

Vortex controls are a recent development in the repertory of airplane controls. Vortices—the spiraling air currents produced at the surface junctures and tips of wings—can be used to alter the pressure distribution over any part of an airplane. By controlling the strength and location of a vortex, moment control can be achieved.

Secondary Flight Controls. Typical secondary flight controls include trim systems and high-lift systems. The function of trim systems is to allow the pilot to attain moment equilibrium without having to exert any forces on the cockpit controls—allowing for "hands-off" flight. The function of the high-lift system is to allow the pilot to fly the airplane at low speeds. High-lift systems are typically made up of a combination of wing-trailing-edge and wing-leading-edge flaps.

Stability Augmentation. All airplanes must have certain levels of natural stability, both static and dynamic. Static stability is the tendency for the airplane to develop forces or moments that tend to restore the airplane to its trim state. Dynamic stability is the tendency for perturbed airplane motions to damp out within a certain number of oscillations, or not to diverge rapidly from an initial trim state. Although stability is normally a desirable characteristic, too much stability makes airplanes difficult to maneuver and can also cause "trim drag." Stability in many airplanes is built in by assuring that the aerodynamic center is located behind the center of gravity. In most airplane configurations this condition is brought about with the help of stabilizing surfaces such as the horizontal tail for longitudinal stability and the vertical tail for directional stability.

Because these tail surfaces increase airplane weight and wetted area (which in turn increases drag), airplane designers constantly look for ways to minimize the size of these surfaces. In high-performance airplanes this reduction in surface area leads to marginal stability or even instability. A stability-augmentation system is used to provide the static or dynamic stability of a marginally stable or unstable airplane.

Automatic Flight Control. Airplanes are continually perturbed away from their intended flight path and attitude when flying through turbulent air. Controlling any airplane in such conditions increases the work load of the flight crew. Also, airplanes must be navigated according to a variety of operational and regulatory requirements. The purpose of automatic flight-control systems is to relieve the flight crew from such duties and to achieve a much more precise means of controlling the airplane than human crews can provide. Many automatic flight-control systems

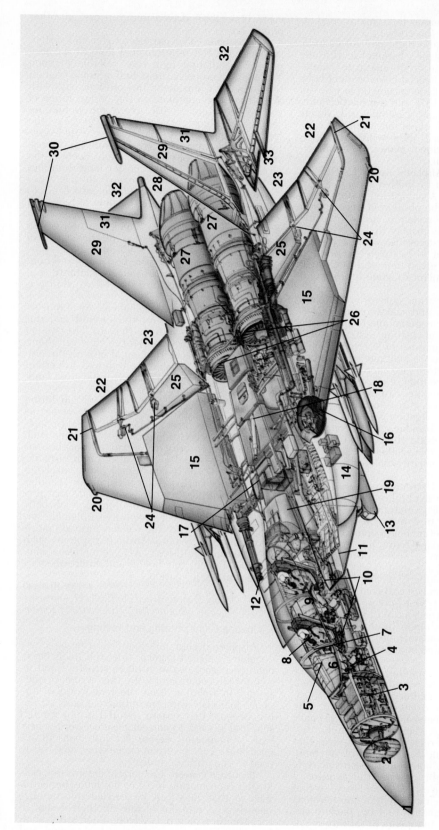

Figure 4. McDonnell Douglas F-15E Eagle flight systems. Fuel system in red; avionics in green; hydraulics and environmental control (ECS) in blue; propulsion in brown; weapons in yellow. (1) glassfibre radome; (2) Hughes APG-70 pulse-doppler radar scanner; (3) avionics equipment bay; (4) rudder pedals; (5) wide-field head-up display (HUD); (6) instrument panel shroud; (7) starboard-side control panel; (8) pilot in Aces II "zero-zero" ejection seat; (9) rear instrument (weapons systems) display console; (10) cockpit engine throttles; (11) swivel air-intake port; (12) M61A-1 Vulcan 20mm cannon; (13) Low Altitude Navigation and Targeting Infrared Night (LANTIRN) targeting pod; (14) forward conformal fuel tank; (15) wing-fuselage fuel tanks; (16) in-flight, boom-type refueling receptacle; (17) ammunition magazine (940 rounds); (18) air brake hydraulic jack (yellow) and center fuselage fuel tank (red); (19) air-conditioning system (blue) and forward fuselage fuel tank (red); (20) navigation light and forward ECM antenna; (21) fuel overflow jettison pipe; (22) outer ailerons; (23) inner control flaps; (24) control surface hydraulic actuators; (25) wing trailing-edge fuel tanks; (26) Pratt & Whitney F100-PW-220 afterburning turbofan engine; (27) afterburner ducts; (28) variable area afterburner exhaust nozzle; (29) twin rudders; (30) fin-tip ECM aerials; (31) swing rudder plane; (32) stabilizer with rear elevators; (33) stabilizer leading-edge "dog tooth."

allow some flight parameter to be maintained at a value preselected by the crew.

Examples of automatic flight control include altitude hold (the airplane's barometric altitude or height above ground is automatically maintained), Mach hold or airspeed hold, heading hold (the heading of the airplane—magnetic or true—is automatically maintained), and automatic landing and flare (the airplane is automatically flown along an invisible glide-slope line until the runway threshold is passed, after which an automatic flare and touchdown maneuver is initiated). (See AUTOMATIC PILOT.)

Navigation Systems. Airplanes are navigated from one point on the earth to another with the help of navigation systems. A navigation system automatically determines the position of the airplane relative to a reference system (the earth, for example) and can usually display that information to the crew. Such systems use signals from a known reference point to establish the position of the airplane at any given time and to forecast the position of the airplane at some future point in time.

Two types of navigation systems are in common use: autonomous and nonautonomous systems. An example of an autonomous navigation system is an inertial navigation system, which consists basically of a number of laser gyroscopes and a computer. For very-long-range applications, inertial systems need to be updated periodically because of the accumulation of error inherent in any gyroscope. Such updates can be achieved by feeding accurate position "fixes" to the computer.

Nonautonomous navigation systems rely on signals, such as radio or radar signals, coming to the airplane from outside the aircraft. Several types of nonautonomous navigation aids have been developed and are currently in operation. (See AIR TRAFFIC CONTROL.)

Hydraulic Systems. Hydraulic systems are typically used to provide hydraulic-fluid flow to an actuator. This actuator (which acts like a piston inside a cylinder) in turn moves a control surface, a landing-gear retraction system, or a steering lug on a nose gear. Hydraulic systems are used for such functions as moving primary flight-control surfaces, such as elevators, stabilizers, ailerons, spoilers, and rudders; moving high-lift devices, such as speed brakes; and controlling landing systems, such as wheel brakes, landing-gear steering, and thrust reversers. Most hydraulic systems consist of a hydraulic fluid reservoir, hydraulic pumps, accumulators, distribution valves, pressure regulators and nonreturn valves, and hydraulic lines.

Modern hydraulic systems operate at pressures of 2,500 to 3,500 pounds per square inch (psi), although some military systems use pressure levels of 5,000 to 8,000 psi. If the hydraulic system is the only means of moving the primary flight-control surfaces, then the hydraulic system becomes flight crucial, which requires that it have a catastrophic failure rate of no more than 1 per 10^9 flight hours. In the current state of the art of hydraulic systems, this requires a minimum of three levels of redundancy, so that three independent hydraulic systems are required. True redundancy demands that the backup systems be completely independent. Multiple systems that all rely on the electrical system of the aircraft are not considered redundant. Therefore, a number of airplanes use an independent ram-air-turbine (RAT)-driven pump in case all other pumps fail.

Fuel Systems. The purpose of the fuel system is to provide the required fuel flow to the propulsive installation in a safe, reliable manner. To function properly, most fuel systems contain the following components: fuel tanks or bays with a total volume adequate to the design range of the airplane along with any required fuel reserves; fuel lines and fuel pumps to carry the fuel from the tanks to the engines; a fuel-venting system to prevent excessive buildup of pressure inside the fuel tanks (as might occur if the airplane is parked in the sun for long duration) and to provide positive pressure in the tanks during flight; and a fuel-management system to allow the crew to regulate the flow of fuel from various tanks to the engines. This is especially important in airplanes in which the fuel is also used to manage the location of the center of gravity. In many modern civil and military airplanes, fuel is carried in the horizontal tail (and sometimes in the vertical tail) to facilitate center-of-gravity control. Fuel shut-off capability is required to cope with fires.

The fuel system must include a way of quickly refueling the airplane on the ground and (for military airplanes) also in the air. The system must also be designed so that the crew can dump fuel. Although an environmental hazard, the procedure may nevertheless be required in certain emergencies (such as landing with impaired landing gear).

Anti-Icing Systems. When ice forms on lifting surfaces, control surfaces, engine inlets, or in carburetors, it can present a hazard to safe operation by creating leading-edge distortions. Such distortions cause serious degradation of the performance and handling qualities of an airplane. To cope with such conditions, many airplanes are equipped with systems to eliminate ice after it has formed (de-icing) or with systems that prevent ice from forming (anti-icing), or with both. The leading-edge boot system uses inflatable surfaces to crack the ice after it has formed (and is thus a de-icing system). Anti-icing systems, such as the thermal anti-ice (TAI) system, use a combination of circulating hot air and antifreeze spray to prevent ice formation.

JAN ROSKAM
Ackers Distinguished Professor of Aerospace Engineering, University of Kansas

4. Airplane Manufacturing and Testing

Airplane design and manufacturing have undergone significant changes since the 1970s. Once, detailed design of the airplane structure and its systems was done largely by the "design organization" in isolation from the real world of airplane manufacturing, maintenance, and servicing. Because that system resulted in much redesign and rework to correct design errors, a new way of managing design activities was developed, known as concurrent engineering, now widely used in the airplane industry.

The Design Process. Concurrent engineering calls for the coordination of all of the following activities so that they can be carried out simultaneously and mindful of one another: design of the structure, materials selection and stress analysis, design for manufacturing sequencing and tooling, systems design and conflict analysis, system functional checks (such as landing gear and flap movement), check for ability to assemble, check for inspectability, check for ability to service, check for repairability, and check for ability to disassemble.

As part of these activities, experts from manufacturing, servicing, inspection, and repair divisions work together with the design and stress engineers to decide on the final release of any drawings. These "drawings" appear on paper only derivatively; their fundamental form is in fact an electronic database. Computer-aided design (CAD) and computer-aided manufacturing (CAM) hosted on mainframe computers and on workstations are the technologies that enable this level of integration. These CAD systems allow such a high degree of fidelity that the actions of human mechanics can be simulated to determine whether certain parts can be seen, reached, inspected, disassembled, and assembled again.

The design, testing, and manufacturing of airplanes has grown into an international business. Nearly all major airplane programs are the result of some form of international cooperation. Managing such international team efforts is a significant industry challenge.

The Construction Process. Although most airframes are still largely constructed from metallic materials (such as aluminum, titanium, and steel), a great variety of composite materials are finding their way into airframes of all types (carbon fiber, glass fiber, and boron fiber, to name a few). In addition, various hybrid materials (examples are Arall and Glare), which combine the properties of metals and composites, have been developed.

The fundamental forms used in the construction of most airframes remain those developed before and during World War II. These include the spar-rib-skin combination for lifting surfaces; the semimonocoque design—in which the skin, supported by frames and longerons, carries much of the load—for fuselages; and the truss, either welded steel tubes or boxlike spars with pin joints, for engine attachments.

Composite materials are increasingly being used in airframe structural applications. Advantages claimed for composites include greater strength per unit of weight, greater stiffness, and more resistance to fatigue and corrosion. Whether or not these claims can be realized depends on the application and on the certification standards applied. Thus far, composites have often turned out to be significantly more costly than metals, while saving relatively small amounts of weight.

Through the use of composites it has become possible in some instances to adopt the pure monocoque method, in which the skin bears all the loads. An example of the latter is the Beech Starship, in which frames and longerons used in typical semimonocoque structures are largely absent. Composites lend themselves more to bonding (such as with graphite epoxy) than to mechanical fasteners (such as rivets or bolts).

The Manufacturing Process. Airframes are manufactured with a wide variety of materials. These materials are formed and joined into subassemblies, components, and finally major assemblies by techniques such as riveting, bolting, welding, brazing, casting, forging, extrusion, powder metallurgy, cutting, machining, chemical bonding, diffusion bonding, resin-transfer molding, plastic forming, and super-plastic forming.

Aircraft components are finally assembled in so-called assembly jigs. In deciding which mate-

© DAVID SEARS/GAMMA LIAISON

Boeing aircraft test facility, Seattle, Wash. Each airplane undergoes a regimen of ground tests before being flight-tested and put into service.

rials and which manufacturing technique to use, the designer must weigh a multitude of factors, some of which conflict with one another. Typical of such factors are weight, cost, available labor skills, available facilities, and environmental concerns. Finally, the ultimate disposal of the airplane in an environmentally acceptable manner is becoming a factor in the design process.

The Testing Process. Before airplanes are given a certificate of airworthiness or a type certificate, a considerable amount of ground and flight testing must be performed. Ground tests normally consist of the following: functional testing of all flight-crucial airplane systems, to ensure that they perform according to their intended function; testing for structural strength and fatigue, during which the airplane is mounted in a special rig so that loads can be applied to the structure to ensure that the maximum design loads can be borne without loss in airworthiness; and testing the ability of the fuselage to withstand cabin pressurization loads, in which the fuselage is mounted underwater in a tank and repeatedly tested for leaks and cracks while alternate pressurization loads are applied.

Flight tests are carried out to make certain that all systems function safely and in accordance with civil or military regulations; to ensure that the airplane has handling qualities consistent with its mission requirements with all systems functioning, as well as with certain systems failed; to ensure that the airplane meets its intended performance requirements—mission as well as airworthiness performance requirements; and to determine the airplane "math model," as required for use in simulators.

Even with the most thorough testing, certain deficiencies may come to light only when an airplane enters service. Such deficiencies are communicated by the operators to the manufacturer (and to the airworthiness authorities, as warranted), after which flight testing aimed at eliminating the deficiencies is begun.

In military airplanes, depending on the specific role for which the airplane was designed, many flight tests must be conducted to ensure that the airplane will indeed be able to carry out its intended mission. In the case of testing for weapons compatibility, testing continues during the entire operational life of the airplane, because new and improved weapons continue to enter the military inventory.

JAN ROSKAM
Ackers Distinguished Professor of Aerospace Engineering, University of Kansas

5. Flight Training

Flying an airplane requires a combination of aeronautical skill and knowledge. Learning how to fly takes hours of intensive flight and ground instruction over a period of months. Teachers, called flight instructors, must be certified by the government. Student pilots must study materials selected by their flight instructors, attend ground-school lessons for one or more students, practice in flight simulators, receive one-on-one flight instruction in dual-equipped training aircraft, and accumulate flight time in solo flight, during which they can practice skills and maneuvers.

As pilot training progresses there are skills and knowledge that must be demonstrated at each step of the way, leading to certification as a private, commercial, or airline transport pilot. Private pilots may carry passengers, commercial pilots may fly passengers for hire, and airline transport pilot certificates are required for flying with a scheduled airline. Pilots can also receive ratings for flying during periods of decreased visibility using instruments only, for operating various classes and categories of aircraft, and for giving flight instruction themselves.

Proficiency as a pilot requires staying legally "current." Government regulations specify currency requirements in terms of a minimum number of takeoffs and landings, flight hours, and instrument approaches within a certain time period of a flight. Pilots also require special training, and sometimes recurrency training, for specific aircraft. Active pilots are therefore accustomed to a continuous process of training and retraining to maintain proficiency.

General Aviation Pilot Training. General aviation pilots are pilots other than those flying for the certificated air carriers or the military. Included in this population are student, private, and commercial pilots. In 1992 the General Aviation Manufacturers Association reported that there were nearly 300,000 private and nearly 150,000 commercial pilots in the United States. In addition, there were over 100,000 airline-transport-rated pilots, who could be employed by the certificated air carriers or in general aviation.

The flight training of all pilots is closely regulated by the Federal Aviation Administration (FAA) of the Department of Transportation. The specific eligibility requirements for each certificate or rating issued by the FAA—as well as the amount of aeronautical knowledge, flight proficiency, and minimum aeronautical experience

(flight hours) required—are contained in the Federal Aviation Regulations (FAR) issued by the FAA. For example, a private pilot must be familiar with the basic elements of navigation and standard flight procedures; a commercial pilot must be knowledgeable in complex airplane operations and skilled in precision flight maneuvers; an airline transport pilot must be conversant with all airplane system operations and capable of dealing effectively with abnormal and emergency situations.

The various certificates and ratings require a minimum number of hours flown and a flight test; often a written examination is required. The hours required consist of both "dual" (with an instructor in the airplane) and "solo" (with the trainee as the sole occupant of the airplane) flight. A private pilot requires 40 hours of flight for certification (35 hours if the certification is earned at an FAA-approved accelerated flight school); a commercial pilot requires 250 hours (190 at an FAA-approved school); and an airline transport pilot requires 1,500 hours of flight time.

Military Aviation Pilot Training. The military is one of the largest aviation training organizations in the country. All branches either have their own training facilities or share facilities with another branch. For example, the U.S. Coast Guard and the U.S. Marines are trained by the U.S. Navy. The U.S. Army, however, maintains its own facilities and focuses on preparing rotary-wing (helicopter) pilots, although a small number of fixed-wing pilots are trained.

Naval aviators begin their training with primary flight, which includes approximately 100 dual and solo flight hours. These hours are completed over a five- to six-month period. At this point the student aviators separate into three tracks: strike (an assignment leading to carrier-based airplanes), maritime (large, multi-engine, turboprop airplanes), and rotary wing. A few pilots are chosen to fly early-warning or logistics airplanes, which combine a strike and maritime syllabus and which require 200 to 250 hours of training in an aircraft and 50 to 150 hours in a simulator.

The preparation of U.S. Air Force pilots begins with undergraduate pilot training and includes both airplane and simulator training. This training consists of about 175 hours in airplanes and 65 hours in simulators. The Air Force is currently moving to a dual-track curriculum that will separate students after about 65 hours of airplane flying time; at this point the training will center around either tactical or transport operations.

Airline-Sponsored Pilot Training. The airlines (certificated air carriers) employ well over 70,000 pilots who fly over 5,500 aircraft. In several countries, the use of an *ab initio* ("from the beginning") training regime has been used by air carriers for several years. In such programs pilot candidates are carefully selected and begin their training with a sole focus on becoming future airline pilots. However, this training methodology has not received widespread acceptance.

The air carriers divide their training programs into six areas: initial, transition, upgrade, differences, programmed, and in-flight training. The FAR outlines the specific requirements for each. Initial training is for pilots who have not qualified on another airplane of the same group (propeller-driven or turbojet power), while individuals who have qualified in the same group require only transition training. Upgrade training is given to persons moving from flight engineer to first officer—second in command—or from first officer to captain—pilot in command; individuals who receive differences training are qualified for a specific airplane type but require, by FAA directive, specific instruction in a variant of that airplane. Programmed hours are those hours that may be reduced upon showing the FAA that circumstances merit a lesser amount. In-flight training refers to maneuvers, procedures, and functions that must be performed in an airplane.

The specific flight training that each air carrier engages in is solely at the discretion of that carrier, provided that the FAA approves the curriculum and record keeping, the training personnel, and the training equipment. Most air carriers train in excess of the minimum number of hours required by the FAA.

Flight Simulation. The use of simulators with both sophisticated visual and motion systems in flight training situations has become more important, first as a means of reducing cost, and second as a means of providing a more realistic environment in which specific training scenarios or procedures may be safely performed. Although simulators represent a large capital cost, from $100,000 for a nonmotion training device (less sophisticated training equipment) to several million dollars for a state-of-the-art system, the per-unit cost of training over time represents a significant savings of training costs. Simulators may be used anywhere, in any weather and at any time, and they do not disturb the environment.

The use of simulators or training devices has been widely accepted in both the military and air carrier flight training community. All branches of the armed services as well as all airlines either have their own simulator systems and support equipment or contract with others for such services. The general aviation community uses simulators as well, in that there are many flight schools that use simulators or training devices to deliver part of the training curriculum.

The FAA grants waivers for certain accelerated schools. The waivers allow a percentage of training to occur in simulators and other training devices; this percentage is based on approval of the device and on the specific phase of training involved. Additionally, several companies that specialize in advanced airplane type ratings utilize extremely sophisticated simulators as an integral part of the instructional program.

Certification. Pilot certificates and ratings, other than those for student and flight instructor, are issued without an expiration date. However, all certificates mandate recent flight experience for the pilot-in-command or any required flight-crew members. If the pilot does not maintain such currency, he or she will most likely require flight instruction. The FAR outlines the number of takeoffs and landings and specifies in which class (single or multiengine) or type airplane these operations are to be performed. Night takeoffs and landings are required if the pilot wishes to carry passengers during that period.

For instrument-rated pilots, the expectation of currency takes the form of the number of instrument-approach procedures and flight hours logged during the previous six months. Part of this requirement can be completed in a simulator or other training device or by completing an instrument-competency check with a certificated instrument-flight instructor, designated FAA inspector or check airman, or an authorized military check pilot.

The completion of a biennial flight review, consisting of a combination of selected flight maneuvers and a review of current general operating and flight rules, is required of all pilots every 24 months. Individuals who complete a proficiency check (given by an appropriately designated person) for a new pilot certificate, rating, or operating privilege are not required to complete the biennial flight review. However, each non-instrument-rated private pilot who has not completed at least 400 hours of flight as a pilot must complete a flight review every 12 months.

The certificated airlines have requirements for recency of experience. Pilots must complete takeoffs and landings under various conditions and with simulated power-plant failures. Proficiency checks or an approved simulator course must be completed every six months by all pilots in command and every 12 months by other pilots.

Numerous sources of information are available for those who would like to begin flight instruction. Among these sources are flight schools located at local airports; national organizations that promote flight training, such as the Airplane Owners and Pilots Association in Frederick, Md., and the General Aviation Manufacturers Association in Washington, D.C.; and colleges and universities that are actively involved in aeronautical education.

Several universities, such as Embry-Riddle Aeronautical University in Daytona Beach, Fla., and Prescott, Ariz.; Parks College of St. Louis University in Cahokia, Ill.; and the University of North Dakota in Grand Forks have very large flight-training programs. Additional information about college and university aviation programs can be secured from the University Aviation Association in Opelika, Ala.

Henry R. Lehrer
and Steven M. Sliwa
Embry-Riddle Aeronautical University

Bibliography

Bent, Ralph D., and James L. McKinley, *Aircraft Electricity and Electronics*, 3d rev. ed. (McGraw 1981).

Blakelock, J. H., *Automatic Control of Aircraft and Missiles* (Wiley 1991).

Bramson, Alan, *The Book of Flight Tests* (Arco 1984).

Federal Aviation Administration (FAA), *Federal Aviation Regulations* (U.S. Government Printing Office).

Herrington, R. M., P. E. Shoemacher, E. P. Bartlett, and E. W. Dunlap, *Flight Test Engineering Handbook* (AFFTC 1966).

Horne, D. F., *Aircraft Production Technology* (Cambridge 1986).

Mattingly, J. D., W. H. Heiser, and D. H. Daley, *Aircraft Engine Design* (AIAA 1987).

McCormick, Barnes W., *Aerodynamics, Aeronautics, and Flight Mechanics* (Wiley 1979).

McRuer, D., I. Ashkenas, and D. Graham, *Aircraft Dynamics and Automatic Control* (Princeton 1973).

Neese, W. A., *Aircraft Hydraulic Systems* (Krieger 1987).

Niu, M. C., *Airframe Structural Design* (Technical 1989).

Peery, David J., and J. J. Azar, *Aircraft Structures*, 2d ed. (McGraw 1982).

Raymer, D. P., *Aircraft Design: A Conceptual Approach* (AIAA 1989).

Rolfe, J. M., and K. J. Staples, *Flight Simulation* (Cambridge 1986).

Roskam, Jan, *Airplane Design, I-VIII*, (RAEC 1989).

Treager, Irwin, *Aircraft Gas Turbine Engine Technology*, 2d ed. (McGraw 1978).

The United Airlines terminal at Chicago O'Hare International Airport. The high traffic density at larger, "hub" airports requires that designers coordinate traffic patterns for passengers as well as for air and ground vehicles.

AIRPORT, an area of land (including buildings, installations, and equipment) intended to be used either wholly or in part for the takeoff, landing, and ground movement of aircraft. The size of an airport and the size and variety of its facilities depend on the character and volume of its flight activity, the volume of its air traffic (passengers, mail, express delivery, and freight), the number and types of aircraft that use it as a base, and the runway length and maintenance and protection areas required to accommodate the most demanding aircraft likely to use the airport.

· The small piston-engine aircraft of the early part of this century operated from "airfields," simple facilities consisting of a few hundred acres of level turf allowing takeoffs and landings in any direction depending on the wind. There was a single hangar to store aircraft, with a few mechanics who serviced and refueled them; the hanger also served as shelter for the several passengers who might show up for the next flight. For night operations there was a rotating, lighted aeronautical beacon, similar to a maritime lighthouse, that aided pilots in navigation. Even today, out of the more than 17,000 landing locations for civil aviation in the United States, only 8,000 have paved runways, and only 450 of those have air traffic control towers. Thus there are 9,000 airfields operating in the Unites States, used mainly by the more than 200,000 privately owned small aircraft and helicopters in the country's general aviation fleet.

The typical large modern commercial airport has grown to encompass more than 40,000 acres (16,200 ha) and employs 25,000 people in handling 1,000 aircraft and over 100,000 passengers per day. It usually has a few paved and lighted runways over 2 miles (3 km) in length, perhaps 10 miles (16 km) of taxiways, boarding gates, and aprons to park 100 or more aircraft. Passen-

gers and cargo are processed in one or more large complex terminal buildings that may be connected by an internal airport transit system, and they arrive and depart from the airport using various forms of road and rail ground transportation and parking garages that may accommodate over 150,000 cars. Such airports take over five years to build and may cost several billion dollars. The transformation of the early airfields into architecturally striking and technologically sophisticated airports has been an astounding feature of modern air transportation.

Management Arrangements. Around the world most airports are owned and operated by some agency of the national government as a public utility. The development of aviation in the 1930s spurred nations to invest in the construction of airports to match the growing needs of their civil airlines and military forces. During World War II many airports were built worldwide for military transport between the various theaters of war and were later converted by national governments to the civil airports needed by the rapid growth of international air transportation.

However, U.S. national policies put the responsibilities for the ownership and operation of civil airports on local or state governments. The federal government did own two airports near Washington, D.C., but in 1986 transferred these to Maryland and Virginia. For many large airports in the United States and Europe, where the task of operating the airport has grown beyond the capabilities of local governments and where there is a major source of revenue from the airlines, quasi-independent airport authorities have been established to operate the airport as a nonprofit public utility. Based on long-term lease agreements with airlines, these authorities have been able to borrow large amounts of private funds to finance the construction and expansion of these commercial airports. (Their quasi-government status also permits land acquisition by the power of eminent domain and protection of approach lanes by zoning authority.)

In the United States, airlines rent space and gates from the airport authorities and perform their own processing of aircraft, passengers, and bags. They also pay a small fee for each aircraft landing (based on aircraft weight), to pay for use of the "airside" facilities. In Europe and elsewhere the airport authority or the national airline may provide all airport services for foreign airlines with its own employees and recover its expenses with a much larger landing fee or a fee per passenger handled.

For smaller U.S. airports there may not be enough revenue from general aviation activities to cover all costs of owning and operating the airport. Local taxes may sustain the airport as a general benefit to the community in the form of local economic development and good access by air to the rest of the country. There has been a continuous program of federal aid to airports since 1946, when the first U.S. Federal Airport Act was passed. Federal taxes on airline tickets, freight waybills, and general aviation fuels and tires, and a departure tax on international passengers have been used to provide these funds.

On the international level, conventions on airport standards have been set forth by Annex 14 to the Convention on International Aviation.

The Airside Component of an Airport. The airport consists of three components: airside, landside, and terminal. Airside is the area where aircraft are operating on the ground and consists of the runways, taxiways, and parking aprons. There are often runways in two or three directions at older airports to overcome the crosswind problems associated with the slower landing speeds of piston-engine aircraft, but at new jet airports it is common to construct parallel runways in only one direction. The hourly capacity of the runways (measured in terms of takeoffs and landings per hour) is higher if two parallel streams of landing traffic can be safely established, especially in times of poor visibility.

The larger commercial airports have dual parallel runways—a pair of runways on each side of the terminal buildings, with one of the pair used only for takeoffs and the other only for landings. Some new airports have constructed three parallel runways and are planning to operate three parallel streams of landings as traffic continues to grow. Because at present it is necessary to have 0.8 mile (1.3 km) between the approaching streams to allow independence of actions by air traffic controllers, there is sufficient room between the runways to construct a major terminal building complex. This high-capacity layout (widely spaced parallel runways with center-field terminal complex) has become the standard layout for new airports in the 1980s.

In addition to hangars for servicing and quarantining aircraft (for international flights carrying produce), there must be facilities for the storage of various kinds of airplane fuel and means of fueling aircraft. Airports also typically have emergency rescue and fire-fighting services capable of reaching any part of the airport quickly in the event of a mishap.

The Landside Component of the Airport. The landside consists of the access roadways, the parking garages, and perhaps a subway or rail system used to deliver passengers and goods to the airport. At U.S. airports most of the passengers arrive by car, so that 75% to 80% of the ground vehicles are automobiles, and usually half of these are taxis. At some U.S. airports (Cleveland, Chicago, Atlanta, Boston, Philadelphia, Washington), the subway or local rail transit system extends out to the airport. In Europe most of the airports have access by the local metropolitan rail system, and some (Zurich, Amsterdam, Frankfurt, Paris) also have a major intercity rail station be-

Exterior of the United Airlines terminal at Chicago O'Hare International Airport. Automobile access is facilitated by separate vehicular levels for arriving and departing passengers and by adjacent parking structures.

Aerial views of Hartsfield Atlanta International Airport, Georgia (*top*), and John F. Kennedy International Airport, New York City (*right*), reveal contrasting designs in gate layout.

neath the airport terminal so that a passenger from another city (or town or country) may arrive by fast train and check in for the departing flight on the rail platform before going upstairs to board the airplane.

For roadway vehicles the interface with the terminal building is called the curbside and is often a point of congestion at peak times. Taxis and private cars stop briefly to unload bags and passengers just outside the check-in counters of their intended airline. Providing curbside, short-term, and long-term parking is a major design challenge for airports; travelers often encounter facilities in stark contrast to the efficient design of other airport operations. Parking is a major source of revenue for airports. The Port Authority of New York and New Jersey collects fees from more than 1 million cars per month in the summer peak at its three airports (John F. Kennedy International Airport, La Guardia Airport, and Newark International Airport) and from more than 10 million cars per year.

The Terminal Component of the Airport. The terminal is the component that connects the airside and the landside and has a flow of passengers and baggage (and their associated greeters and well-wishers) through a series of passenger-processing activities. For departing passengers there is the check-in process, which takes the baggage, "lifts" the tickets, assigns a seat, and issues a boarding pass. It is desirable to have the baggage check-in process as close to the curbside as possible, and it may actually be available outside the terminal on the curb. The other elements of the check-in process may be bypassed, since today many passengers will arrive having purchased a ticket from a travel agent who has already assigned a seat and issued the boarding pass using the airline's computer-reservation system. Such changing practices have a significant effect on the design and layout of terminal buildings. The departing passenger then proceeds to the aircraft for the boarding process, passing through a security process along the way. For arriving passengers there may be immigration, baggage pickup, and customs processes before transferring to ground transportation.

There are four major layouts for terminal buildings that have been used over the years. The earliest is called the central processor with piers.

It developed from an original single terminal building at the airport when long, thin piers or fingers were added to increase the number of aircraft-parking gates and to provide a covered walkway out to the gate for passengers. Later the piers became wider as waiting lounges were added to accommodate waiting passengers and greeters. As the piers became longer, some airports installed moving walkways to ease travel between the central building and aircraft gates. Examples of such layouts exist at Frankfurt, Chicago, San Francisco, and Miami.

The second layout is called the central processor with satellites, in which separate satellite buildings exist for the boarding process. Aircraft do not park at the central building used for check in, and to reduce the walking distances, an airport transit system carries passengers to and from the satellites. This more modern layout originated at Tampa, where four totally automated shuttle trains resembling a "horizontal elevator" transfer passengers on an elevated guideway to four separate satellites about 0.25 mile (0.40 km) away from the central building. In Seattle (two satellites) and Atlanta (five satellites), the transit system went underground below the gates and parked aircraft.

The third layout is called the gate arrival, in which the automobile curb is located relatively near the gates so that the passenger has only a short distance to travel from automobile to aircraft. It requires that all processing be available near the boarding gates distributed throughout the terminal, and unlike the finger piers, only one side of the terminal building is used to park aircraft, since the other side is used by ground vehicles. This requires a much longer, thinner building and creates longer walking distances for connecting passengers. Examples are Kansas City International Airport, Dallas–Fort Worth International Airport, and Roissy–Charles de Gaulle Airport outside Paris.

The fourth layout is called the mobile transporter. Special buses (or a "mobile lounge," a larger ground vehicle resembling the passenger waiting lounge that attaches itself to the central processor building) take passengers to the boarding satellites or directly to the aircraft by driving over the aircraft parking ramp area. Examples are Washington Dulles International Airport and King Abdul Aziz International Airport at Jeddah, Saudi Arabia.

Because many departing passengers arrive early, and connecting passengers often have to wait for their next flight, there is a large number of people with discretionary time waiting in the terminal buildings. Large airports provide a variety of commercial activities to keep them occupied. There are churches, barber and beauty shops, movie theaters, restaurants, children's nurseries with baby-sitters, aircraft museums with dozens of full-size antique aircraft, and luxury shopping malls (with duty-free stores for liquor and tobacco, and in the case of Frankfurt a store that sells fur coats for the forgetful traveler). In fact, the modern large airport has been compared to a small, self-contained city, since it also may have its own fire and police departments, snow-removal force, a hospital with full-time doctors, dentists, veterinarians, banks, convention centers, and a choice of hotels.

The Outlook for Commercial Airports. As operations by jet transport aircraft grew at major airports, their noise impact on the surrounding communities quickly became a problem. Severe political opposition to airport expansion or the construction of new airports prevented the adequate addition of airport capacity where it was needed around the world. Many airports were subjected to nighttime curfews. During the 1970s and 1980s the planning and approval processes were very difficult and often did not succeed. It required 28 years to build Munich's new Franz Josef Strauss ("Munich 2") Airport, from the initial planning to its opening in May 1992. It was sited on a large swampy area 35 miles (56 km) north of the city and proposed considerable improvements to the local urban area such as extending the local S-Bahn transit system to nearby towns and planting over 10,000 new trees, but it still was bitterly opposed. It has been described as the last new airport for Europe.

As a result, the international aviation industry adopted in the 1970s a noise program for the design, construction, and operation of quieter jet transport aircraft. By the year 2000, most of the early noisy jet transport aircraft will be replaced by the much quieter "stage 3" aircraft now being built. However, it remains to be seen if the noise contours around existing airports will actually shrink, since the number of daily operations continues to increase.

An expensive solution to the airport-siting problem has been found for the new airports now being constructed to meet the burgeoning demand for air travel in Asia. Airports are being constructed on artificial islands at Hong Kong, Macau, Osaka, and Seoul that are touted as 24-hour airports. The noise footprints of these airports are placed over harbor waters. As well as building the island, this requires the construction of an extensive road and rail access system involving a long bridge or causeway. The cost of the island and access approximately doubles the cost of such new airports. At Hong Kong the new airport is expected to cost over U.S.$14 billion, and the subway and roadway access system, requiring the construction of the longest suspension bridge in the world, will cost an additional U.S.$3 billion. However, the total project represents a major improvement of the urban environment for Hong Kong. It is not just a new airport project. There are two new urban towns, access to another large island, and a major improvement to the city's subway and roadway systems. The same may be said of the projects at Seoul and Osaka.

All of these cities are competing with one another to become the leading city of Asia. Singapore has recently completed the second phase of the successful expansion of its airport. Bangkok is planning a new commercial airport on a swampy area near the city. The importance of excellent air-transportation services to the economic development of the surrounding area is the underlying reason for this competition and the willingness to invest such large sums of money in new island airports and the associated urban improvements. Perhaps the 21st century will see the development of many more such island airports in Japan, Europe, and North America.

See also AIR TRAFFIC CONTROL; AIR TRANSPORTATION; AVIATION.

ROBERT W. SIMPSON
Flight Transportation Laboratory
Massachusetts Institute of Technology

DIFFERENT TYPES OF AIRSHIPS

RIGID AIRSHIP

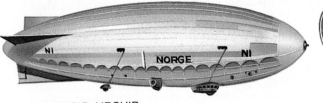

SEMIRIGID AIRSHIP

Cross section
through center

The three major types of airship are
distinguished by their structural design. Rigid airships, such as the
U.S. Navy's U.S.S. *Macon,* feature
an internal skeleton of rigid rings
and girders with compartments for
separate cells of lifting gas. Semirigid airships, such as the Italian
Norge, attach loads along a rigid keel
fastened to a single-compartment
fabric envelope. The nonrigid airship, or blimp, such as the U.S. Navy's "K" class, also features a fabric
envelope, but the car is supported
from the top of the envelope by internal cables and in some cases also
by external cables glued to load
patches on the side of the envelope.

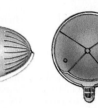

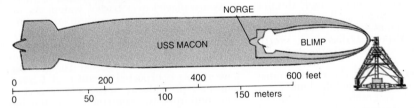

AIRSHIP, any of a range of lighter-than-air (LTA)
craft utilizing light gases occurring in nature as
a major component of their lift. LTA systems feature the use of light gases, such as helium or hot
air, to realize the benefits of basic physical principles. Because lighter fluids are buoyed up by
denser, heavier fluids, airships using light gases
are able to rise or fly in heavier air. The term
airship is relatively new to describe an LTA system. Vehicles invented over the years, such as
dirigibles, balloons, blimps, and air-buoyant vehicles, can be categorized as airships. *Dirigible*
for example, is French for "steerable" and was
applied in the early 1800s to distinguish LTA
vehicles with fixed and movable control surfaces
from balloon systems, which operated at the mercy
of prevailing air currents.

   History.   The advent of manned LTA systems
is credited to the Montgolfier brothers, Charles
and Robert, who in 1783 successfully launched
themselves airborne into the French countryside.
Their reception by the local populace, armed with
pitchforks and rakes to do battle with what they
thought was a visitation of the Devil, indicated
that innovation could be dangerous at that time.
After a hundred years of experiments, the next
major developmental step was prompted by the

investor and aeronaut Santos Dumont, who won
an aviation prize in Paris in 1901 for piloting his
semirigid airship over an 8-mile (13-km) measured
course around the Eiffel Tower. His machine was
already well known to Parisians because of his
habit of tethering his craft to Paris rooftops and
climbing down to dine with friends.

   During the years prior to the Industrial Revolution, the technologies for materials, structures,
and propulsion were just being invented. At this
exploratory stage, few if any practical applications could be identified. The idea for a kind of
airship other than the balloon occurred in the
mind of Count Ferdinand von Zeppelin. While
Zeppelin served as a German army observer with
the Union forces during the U.S. Civil War, he
was involved in balloon operations for observing
enemy troop movements. Convinced that travel
at an elevation (altitude) had military value, he
conceived the idea of harnessing the lift of multiple free balloons within the rigid structural framework of a single large vehicle.

   Prior to World War I, interest in airships was
growing in Britain and France as well as Germany. France purchased Schutte-Lanz (S-L) airships for aerial passenger service from Germany.
During the war German airships were originally

assigned to scouting duties. But to divert attention from the stalemate in the trenches and to attack British morale, the "zeppelins" were pressed into strategic bombardment roles. This tactic initially succeeded in reducing morale in London, though physical damage was minimal. The surveillance potential for airships was not lost on the British, who employed nearly 160 nonrigid envelopes, or "blimps," with airplane fuselages underneath to patrol the North Sea for Axis submarines.

Following the war, the Allies demanded as part of war reparations that Germany hand over airships along with their latest technology. In 1923 the U.S. Navy commissioned the first American rigid airship, the *Shenandoah* (ZR-1), whose design copied zeppelin techniques. While attempting to penetrate a storm in Ohio in 1925, violent updrafts caused the ship to break up and crash. (Airship designers, like the airplane designers of the day, lacked the numerical design techniques now taken for granted.)

In Italy a series of semirigid airships achieved fame by a flight to the North Pole in 1929. The American rigids, the *Akron* and *Macon*, built in 1931 and 1933, respectively, were more successful. These U.S. Navy airships were much larger and featured their own complement of airplanes, which, utilized for extensive scouting, were launched and recovered by the airship using a unique trapeze device. While many hours of safe flight were logged, each of these Navy airships was lost during storm conditions featuring violent updrafts. Despite early airship successes, the British suffered a somewhat similar fate with the loss of the R101 after a rush preparation for its inaugural flight to India. In contrast, the famous German rigids, the *Graf Zeppelin* and, subsequently, the *Hindenburg* were enjoying tremendous success plying the Atlantic commercial air trade from Germany to South America (Rio de Janiero) and the United States (Lakehurst, N.J.).

These successes were overshadowed, however, by the demise of the *Hindenburg* at Lakehurst in May 1937. Whether the *Hindenburg* was the victim of sabotage against the Nazi government or of a static electric discharge, the resulting fire of the ship's flammable hydrogen created an immense public outcry against airships, particularly since the disaster was reported live over radio by an announcer on the scene. Little notice was taken of the fact that two-thirds of the 93 people on board, including both passengers and crew, survived the crash—many walking away virtually unharmed.

The next advance in airships appeared in the form of nonrigids, or blimps. By 1942, World War II was in full swing. An Allied strategy of grouping shipping into convoys in the North Atlantic was failing miserably against "wolfpacks" of German submarines. Airplanes of the day could not provide sufficient airborne surveillance, owing to range and endurance limitations. As a last resort, instructions were given to mass-produce airships for anti-submarine warfare. By war's end in 1945, 15 squadrons had been fielded across three continents patrolling 3 million square miles (7.8 million sq km) of ocean. Military records show that no ships were lost from convoys that were escorted by airships. Furthermore, the airships operated in all weather conditions with an operational readiness of 87%.

Airships continued to be utilized for antisubmarine patrol after the war, and operations were

The *Hindenburg* disaster at Lakehurst, N.J., on May 6, 1937, ended commercial rigid-airship travel.

BROWN BROTHERS

expanded to include airborne early warning using the nonrigid ZPG-3W. Many improvements, such as new underway refueling techniques and mechanical ground handling equipment, were developed. This chapter of airship history ended in 1962, when the threat of enemy bombers gave way to the threat of enemy missiles, requiring a much quicker warning. With force levels dwindling, the overhead costs to train pilots and support personnel became unaffordable.

Technologies. A number of technologies play a major part in LTA systems. A brief discussion is provided here.

Aerostatics. The static lifting gas is the key ingredient for airships. Ten combinations of naturally occurring light gases are found to possess molecular weights less than that of air. These light gases are identified in the figure below, which shows the differences in lightness by indicating the ability for static lift of 1,000 cubic feet (28 cubic meters) of each gas at a purity of 100%. Note that while hydrogen is the most capable

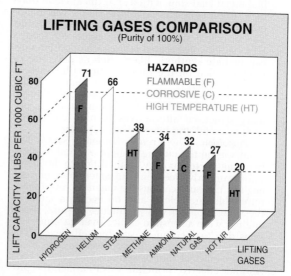

LIFTING GASES COMPARISON
(Purity of 100%)

LIFT CAPACITY IN LBS PER 1000 CUBIC FT

HAZARDS
FLAMMABLE (F)
CORROSIVE (C)
HIGH TEMPERATURE (HT)

HYDROGEN 71 F
HELIUM 66
STEAM 39 HT
METHANE 34 F
AMMONIA 32 C
NATURAL GAS 27 F
HOT AIR 20 HT

LIFTING GASES

© STEVE ROSS/LEO DE WYS

The Goodyear blimp, a nonrigid airship, is used extensively in company advertising.

gas, it is only 10% lighter than helium, which unlike hydrogen is nonflammable. At the beginning of LTA innovations, prior to discovery of the elements, hot air provided the mechanism for flight. In later years, the Germans led the world in the application of hydrogen, since it was more easily obtainable. Airships using helium of commercial grade (which is typically 94% pure) are capable of lifting 63.5 pounds per 1,000 cubic feet (1.02 kg per cubic meter) of gas.

Structures and Materials. Aviation material technology has evolved significantly over the past 200 years. The early balloonists had few choices of materials for gas containment. Fabrics such as silk or doped cotton were used. The problems of permeability or contamination of the gas became important only after hydrogen or helium came into use for extended flights. At that point methods of sealing the fabric with paraffin or, in the case of the large rigid airships, the intestines of oxen, known as "goldbeater's skin," were necessary. Airship designers first used wicker baskets for primary structural members, then turned to lightweight metal alloys. Duralumin, developed for use in the German rigids, was extensively used. In the 1920s the novel approach of a metal skin was attempted. The U.S. Navy's ZMC-2 was the first metal-clad ship, with a skin thickness of 0.008 inch (0.002 cm). The envelope shape was maintained by the pressure exerted by the gas inside. The principal structural components for today's LTAs still involve coated fabrics. Composition now can include synthetic fibers such as polyester or Kevlar sealed on the inside with a film such as saran or Mylar. A barrier coating such as Tedlar offers protection against ultraviolet radiation on the outside. In addition to aluminum alloys, primary structural alternatives include composites such as metal graphite or thermoplastic.

Propulsion. The French aeronaut Santos Dumont was on the cutting edge of internal combustion engine technology, but although he made significant advances in the conception of such engines, the early combustion engines proved noisy, unreliable, inefficient, and on occasion fatal. By the time Zeppelin was producing airships, diesel engines were a sensible choice over gasoline versions due to their increased fuel efficiency. The use of multiple smaller-horsepower engines made for more efficient throttle settings for slower speeds. Another effective principle was to attach the pro-

pellers as close to the ends of the airship as possible to aid in rapid steering changes. The engines were located closer to the crew and connected to the propellers by driveshafts through transmissions to facilitate in-flight repair. Modern technology has allowed airships to incorporate tilting, ducted fans for a similar purpose.

Aerodynamics. An airship is generally either a cylinder with rounded ends or an ellipsoid. Since the theory of aerodynamics did not exist when airships were first developed, each vehicle was designed from indirect observations of, for example, the flight of birds or the motions of fish. It was impossible to conduct valid tests prior to actual flight. Even through the 1930s, after universities had begun to conduct wind-tunnel analysis, key parameters relating the most important variables in aerodynamics were still being formulated. Practical applications of the Reynolds number, which relates size, speed, air density, and viscosity in a way that subscale testing in a wind tunnel can fairly accurately predict the behavior of the full-scale machine, began to be applied during this period. Now, nondimensional parameters for lift, drag, and pitching moment can be examined in extensive detail to predict the dynamics of the airship across a range of flight conditions. Once this is developed, the designer can incorporate the proper fixed and movable flight controls into the design to ensure steady and efficient flight.

Avionics. Electronic devices such as radar sensors enable safe and precise flight operations. While virtually nonexistent in aviation's early days, avionics are essential today. All aircraft are equipped with certain "core," or common, avionics to provide safe, basic flight plus additional subsystems and sensors, which vary depending on the aircraft and the mission. The large size of airships allows a spacious arrangement of cockpit, sensor operator stations, and crew berthing, making repair and maintenance possible while under way. The low vibration and low rate of acceleration of airships also provide a favorable environment for electronic equipment, greatly extending the time between failures of electronic systems.

Design Tools and Models. The design methods available today were not even imagined in the early days of airships. Modern numerical methods make possible extensive analysis over a wide range of parameter values. Computer-aided design (CAD) programs are available for most forms of aviation, including airships. For example, one airship code, the Naval Airship Program for Sizing and Performance (NAPSAP), combines fundamental geometric and weight estimation equations to develop preliminary airship designs for both nonrigid and rigid airships. These designs can then be "flown" on the computer through complicated missions over multiday endurances to calculate fuel, stores, and payload requirements.

Ground-Handling Equipment and Techniques. In the early 1900s, when the motions of airships were not fully understood, takeoff and landing were the riskiest parts of the flight. Hundreds of men on handling ropes were required to "manhandle" the ship away from and back to its moorings. During World War II the size of ground-handling parties dwindled from nearly 100 to about 50. By the time the U.S. Navy ended LTA operations in 1962, ground procedures for 400-plus-foot (120-plus-meters) airships were developed requiring ground crews of fewer than 20. For airships today the vectored thrust precision of tilt rotors, ducted fans, and lateral direction bow thrusters offers the prospect of virtually eliminating ground crews.

Controversial Issues. Airships come under criticism for two main reasons: vulnerability and weatherability. Though no form of aviation is indestructible, airships have been unfairly judged as being fragile as toy balloons. This is not the case. The internal pressure of an airship is very low. In fact, that pressure is virtually equal to the air pressure outside the ship. The resulting effect is that in the event of a leak—even a hole several feet in diameter—the loss of lifting gas is very gradual, allowing a graceful descent. This is very unlike an airplane, which falls rapidly when its wing-generated lift is interrupted by accident.

Weatherability, the degree of susceptibility to nature's elements, is also misrepresented. In conditions of low visibility the slow speed of the airship is a positive attribute; dense fog, for example, can be waited out for many hours. Trials conducted by the U.S. Navy in the North Atlantic in January 1957 proved this. For ten days a series of airships maintained a barrier station when no other forms of aviation were able to fly. Flight operations were conducted in conditions that included icing, snow, sleet, rain, fog, and winds of up to 60 knots (69 mph, or 111 kph).

Current Activities. Since the U.S. Navy's decommissioning of airships in 1962, there have been periodic flurries of interest in using airships for both civilian and military purposes. Several government agencies, led by the National Aeronautics and Space Administration (NASA), organized a workshop at the Naval Postgraduate School in Monterey, Calif., in 1974. And the American Institute of Aeronautics and Astronautics (AIAA) began holding international LTA technology conferences every two years starting in 1975. In 1979 a small British company, Aerospace Developments, Ltd., produced the first modern-technology nonrigid airship featuring a composite-structure gondola, tilting ducted fans, and a new single-ply polyester fabric skin. The U.S. Navy, together with the U.S. Coast Guard and NASA, in 1983 leased one of their airships, the AI-500/03, for a year of examination in the United States.

By 1985 many U.S. government agencies were giving LTAs serious consideration. The Customs Service, the Forestry Service, the navy, the Strategic Defense Initiative office, NASA, the air force, and the Coast Guard had programs under way. In 1985 the navy commissioned concept formulation studies to examine the airship for airborne early warning roles for surface battle group defense. The chief of naval operations and the secretary of the navy in 1987 approved a contract with Westinghouse and Airship Industries to produce an operational development model airship to demonstrate modern airship technology and to operate with fleet battle groups over the course of a four-year program. Air force studies preceded a feasibility flight demonstration in North Carolina using an Airship Industries AI-600 to quantify the ability for low-speed maneuverability. The former Goodyear Aerospace (now Loral Systems Group) produced and now operates a new generation of advertising airship with tilting, ducted propulsors, the GZ-22.

Future Outlook. LTA systems are now in their third century. Their capabilities have evolved from flights of fancy to meeting specific practical needs across a wide spectrum of applications. An increasing number of technologists and planners envision modern-technology LTA systems that capitalize on airships' inherent features of long endurance (or range), fuel efficiency, low 'costs for development and operation, and very low environmental effects.

DAVID B. BAILEY, *Naval Air Warfare Center*

Bibliography: Association of Airship and Balloon Constructors, eds., *Aerostation* (quarterly); Beaubois, Henry, *Airships: An Illustrated History* (Two Continents Pub. Group 1973).

The skeleton of the U.S.S. *Akron* was constructed using an aluminum alloy to make the ship as light and sturdy as possible.

COURTESY U.S. NAVY

AIRY, âr'ē, **George Biddell** (1801–1892), English astronomer. He was born in Alnwick, Northumberland, on July 27, 1801, and graduated from Trinity College, Cambridge, in 1823. After teaching mathematics there he became Plumian professor of astronomy and director of the Cambridge observatory in 1828. In 1835 he succeeded John Pond as astronomer royal (director of the Greenwich observatory), a position he held until 1881. Airy was knighted in 1872.

As director at Greenwich, Airy had modern equipment installed and won world renown for the observatory. He determined the density of the earth and made careful studies of the motions of the earth and Venus. Airy introduced regular observation of sunspots and of magnetic phenomena and invented instruments for lunar observations. Airy's spiral, an optical phenomenon visible in quartz, is named for him. Among his works are *Mathematical Tracts on Physical Astronomy* (1826) and *Popular Astronomy* (1849). His autobiography, edited by his son, was published in 1896. Airy died in London on Jan. 2, 1892.

'A'ISHA, ä'i-sha (c. 614–678), the third and favorite wife of the Prophet Muḥammad (Mohammed), founder of Islam. Her father, 'Abu Bakr, was Muḥammad's chief adviser. Born in Mecca about 614, she was taken to Medina in 622. She was betrothed to Muḥammad, who was then about 50 years old, and married him about 623. They had no children. In 627 an incident involving 'A'isha and a handsome young man led to serious political trouble when Muḥammad's opponents magnified the scandal and used it against him. But Muḥammad proved that any rumors of misconduct were unjustified.

'A'isha lived on good terms with Muḥammad's other wives, of whom there often were eight. Muḥammad was in the habit of spending a night in turn with each of his wives, but as death approached, he asked their permission to remain in 'A'isha's chamber. He died on June 8, 632, and was buried in her chamber.

'A'isha took no part in politics during the caliphates of her father (632–634) and 'Umar I (634–644). Following the murder of the third caliph, 'Uthmān, in 656, however, she opposed the succession of 'Ali and went to Basra with a thousand Meccans. After taking Basra the Meccans engaged in a battle with 'Ali's forces and were defeated. The episode is known as the Battle of the Camel because the worst fighting took place around the camel bearing 'A'isha's litter. Thereafter she lived quietly in Medina, where she died in 678.

W. MONTGOMERY WATT, *University of Edinburgh*

AISNE RIVER, ān, in France, rising near Vaubecourt in Meuse department. From the Argonne Forest it flows northwest and then west, for 165 miles (265 km), joining the Oise River above Compiègne. Its main tributaries are the Aire and the Vesle, and the Aisne is connected with the Oise and Marne rivers by canals.

The Aisne, which was known in ancient times as the Axona, runs through the departments of Meuse, Marne, Ardennes, Aisne, and Oise, and it passes the towns of Vouziers, Rethel, and Soissons. Near its source it flows through the low hills of Champagne, but after it turns west there is a long line of steep ridges on its north bank. The ridges range in height from 450 feet (140 meters) to 200 feet (60 meters).

During World War I, after the Germans were defeated on the Marne in September 1914, they dug in on the plateau above the Aisne. This area, known as the Chemin des Dames, became the scene of prolonged trench warfare until the Germans were finally driven out by French and American troops in October 1918. During World War II the river was crossed by the U.S. Army during its offensive of August 1944.

AITKEN, āt'kən, **Robert Ingersoll** (1878–1949), American sculptor. Born in San Francisco on May 8, 1878, he studied at Mark Hopkins Institute there and stayed on as professor of sculpture from 1901 to 1904. During this period he executed the William McKinley Monument (1903) in Golden Gate Park and the Hall McAllister Monument (1904).

After three years in Paris, Aitken worked in New York City, doing busts of Thomas Jefferson, Daniel Webster, Benjamin Franklin, and Henry Clay for the Hall of Fame at New York University. He also executed the Battle of Manila Bay memorial in San Francisco, created two sculptures for the San Francisco Panama-Pacific Exposition (1915), and designed the U.S. $50 gold piece issued at the time. The crowning achievements of his career, however, were the west pediment (completed in 1934) of the U.S. Supreme Court Building in Washington, D.C., and the 68-figure frieze (1937) on the Gallery of Fine Arts in Columbus, Ohio. Aitken died in New York City on Jan. 3, 1949.

AIX-EN-PROVENCE, eks-äN-prô-vaNs,' a town in southeastern France, in Bouches-du-Rhône department, 17 miles (27 km) north of Marseille. A trading center for wine, olives and olive oil, almonds, and fruit produced in the surrounding region, its industries include preserving and candying fruit and the manufacture of felt hats and carpets. The town's commercial life also depends on the tourists who visit its mineral waters and historical and cultural attractions. The law and philosophy divisions of Aix-Marseille University, founded in Aix in 1409, are located there. The Church of St. Jean de Malte dates from the middle of the 13th century, and parts of the Cathedral of St. Sauveur were built in the 11th, 12th, and 13th centuries. In 1705 new baths were constructed near the ruins of the ancient Roman ones.

The mineral springs at Aix attracted the Roman consul Gaius Sextius Calvinus, who made a camp there about 123 B.C. called Aquae Sextiae. In 102 B.C. the Roman general Marius inflicted a severe defeat upon the Teutons in the battle of Aquae Sextiae. By the 4th century A.D. it was the major town of the eastern part of the Roman province of Gallia Narbonensis. During much of the Middle Ages, Aix was the capital of Provence, and it became an important seat of learning.

Union of Provence with the French crown was formally accomplished in 1487, after a meeting of the estates of Provence, sitting at Aix. From 1501 to 1789 the city was the seat of a provincial parliament established by King Louis XII. Paul Cézanne was a native of Aix-en-Provence. Population: 137,067 (2001 census).

AIX-LA-CHAPELLE. See AACHEN.

AIX-LA-CHAPELLE, Congress of, eks-là-shà-pel'. Following the defeat of Napoleonic France by the Quadruple Alliance (Austria, Great Britain, Prussia, and Russia), the members of the alliance agreed to meet whenever necessary to settle problems arising from the settlements made at the Congress of Vienna (1814–1815) and the Second Peace of Paris (Nov. 20, 1815).

The powers held their first congress at Aix-la-Chapelle (Aachen, Germany) in September 1818 at the request of the government of King Louis XVIII of France. The congress decided that there was little value in continuing the military occupation of France because the growing hatred felt for the occupiers would soon make it impossible to reabsorb France into the circle of peaceful nations. The French cabinet believed that it could exist without further support of foreign arms, and the French parliament approved a plan to have private bankers advance the indemnity that had been imposed by the Allies. The representatives of the Allies were willing to show some trust in a Bourbon France.

The question of future relations with France brought out differences among the Allies over the objectives of the Quadruple Alliance. Czar Alexander I of Russia considered it an international union devoted to the aims of the Holy Alliance. The English government believed that it applied to relations with France alone. Prince Klemens von Metternich of Austria, the leading diplomat on the Continent, intended to use the alliance for a lasting conservative control of Europe. After long discussion the powers agreed not to bring France into the Quadruple Alliance but to invite France to join the others in a looser grouping known as the Quintuple Alliance for the maintenance of peace.

MINNA R. FALK, *New York University*

AIX-LA-CHAPELLE, Treaties of, eks-là-shà-pel'. The first Treaty of Aix-la-Chapelle (May 2, 1668) ended the War of Devolution, begun in 1667 by Louis XIV of France to enforce his claim to the Spanish Netherlands, in the name of his wife Marie Thérèse, daughter of the late King Philip IV of Spain. By this treaty, Louis received from his brother-in-law, Charles II of Spain, 11 towns in the Spanish Netherlands, including Tournai, Douai, Lille, Kortrijk, Oudenaarde, and Charleroi. Louis's willingness to accept such small gains may have been a result of the alliance that Holland had made in January 1668 with England and Sweden to curb the French. He may also have been influenced by the agreement he made with Emperor Leopold I to divide up the Spanish possessions on Charles's death.

A second Treaty of Aix-la-Chapelle (Oct. 18, 1748) concluded two simultaneous wars—the War of the Austrian Succession (1740–1748) in Europe and King George's War overseas. By the treaty, Frederick II of Prussia was guaranteed possession of Silesia, which he had occupied since the Treaty of Dresden (1745). Maria Theresa of Austria also gave up Parma, Piacenza, and adjacent territory to Don Philip, younger brother of Ferdinand VI of Spain. But the Pragmatic Sanction by which Maria Theresa held her lands was affirmed, and neither France, Saxony, nor Bavaria, which had also attacked her, was granted any territory.

King George's War, third of four duels between France and Britain, resulted in a return to the status quo. English colonists restored Louisburg (Nova Scotia) to the French, and Madras went back to the English East India Company. France's inability to win on the European continent, however, marked the country as a weakening power.

See also KING GEORGE'S WAR; SUCCESSION WARS.
MINNA R. FALK
New York University

AJACCIO, ä-yät'chō, a city in France on the island of Corsica in the Mediterranean Sea. It is situated on the island's west coast, on a tongue of land projecting into the Gulf of Ajaccio. It is also the capital of Corse-du-Sud department.

© PATRICK WARD/STOCK BOSTON

The rich Gupta-period ornamentation of the caves of Ajanta contrasts sharply with their stark surroundings.

A busy port and shipbuilding center, Ajaccio dates from the 7th century A.D. The Genoese settled the present site in 1492. In 1768 it passed to France. Population: 54,697 (1999 census).

AJANTA, ə-jun'tə, a village in India, in the northern part of Maharashtra state. The famous caves of Ajanta, 29 caves carved out of rock formations by followers of Gautama Buddha, are located about 5 miles (8 km) north of the village.

Hollowed into the side of a steep ravine, the caves consist of a series of monasteries (*viharas*) and halls of worship (*caityas*). The earliest date from the 2d century B.C. and the latest from about 650 A.D. They were abandoned to the jungle when Buddhism declined in India and were rediscovered by British soldiers in 1819. The walls and ceilings are decorated with frescoes depicting the life of ancient India. The caves provide an uninterrupted survey of the evolution of Indian Buddhist art.

AJAX, ā'jaks, in Greek legend, the name of two Greek chieftains in the Trojan War. The more important, known also as Telamonius (Greek, Aias Telamonides), was the son of Telamon, king of Salamis, and led the Salamian warriors in the siege of Troy. He is described in Homer's *Iliad* as a hero of great size, second only to Achilles as a warrior but of slow wit. He fought a duel with the Trojan leader Hector and, by a later account, rescued Achilles' body while Odysseus (Ulysses) held off the Trojans. When Achilles' armor was awarded to Odysseus, Ajax, mad with anger and disappointment, killed himself.

Ajax the Lesser was a minor Greek chieftain in the Trojan War. The son of Oïleus, chief of the Locrians, he is represented by Homer as brave and swift-footed but of ignoble character. According to post-Homeric writers, Ajax dragged the prophetess Cassandra from the temple of Athena in Troy and raped her. When Ajax boasted of saving himself after Poseidon (Neptune) had guided him to shore when he was shipwrecked on his way home from the war, Poseidon hurled him back into the sea, where he drowned.

433

AJAX, ā′jaks, a tragedy (c. 447 B.C.) by Sophocles and his earliest extant play. The play begins after Ajax loses the battle for Achilles' armor to Odysseus, following Achilles' death in combat. Insane with anger, he slaughters a flock of sheep, mistaking them for the Greek leaders who have unjustly denied him the armor. He kills himself in shame after recovering his reason.

Ajax's right to an honorable burial is seriously debated. Menelaus and Agamemnon regard Ajax as a traitor and try to prevent his burial. Odysseus persuades Agamemnon to allow the burial after praising Ajax as a great warrior.

AJMER, uj-mēr′, a city in Rajasthan state, India, 215 miles (346 km) southwest of New Delhi. It is a railroad junction and a trade and marketing center for an agricultural region.

Ajmer became the capital of the Cauhān dynasty of Rājpūts in the 12th century. The ruins of a mosque built at Ajmer by Quṭb-ud-Dīn Aybak (Qutb ud-Din Aibak), Muslim founder of the Slave dynasty of Delhi, still stand. Ajmer was a favorite headquarters of the Mughul (Mogul) emperors during the 16th and 17th centuries. Akbar built a palace that now serves as a museum. Marble pavilions built by Shāh Jahān are now maintained by the Indian government.

In 1616, at Ajmer, Jahāngīr received Sir Thomas Roe, the first British ambassador to the Mughul court. Under British rule Ajmer was capital of the province of Ajmer-Merwara. Capital of the state of Ajmer in 1950, it was incorporated into Rajasthan with the 1956 reorganization of states. Population: 485,197 (2001 census).

AKBAR, ak′bər (1542–1605), 3d Mughul emperor of India, regarded as the greatest emperor that this Muslim dynasty produced and as one of the 16th-century's most remarkable personalities.

He was born Abū-ul-Fatḥ Jalāl-ud-Dī Muḥammad, the son of Emperor Humāyūn. At the time of Akbar's birth in Umarkot, India (presently in Pakistan), in October or November 1542, Humāyūn was in flight from Shēr Shāh, the Afghan chief, who had defeated him.

Akbar was called to the throne at the age of 14, upon the death of his father, in 1556, only one year after Humāyūn had returned to India and regained possession of a small part of his kingdom. During the next two decades the young ruler, by a series of brilliant military campaigns, not only recovered the lost dominions but eventually extended his empire until it included the whole of north India, a strip of territory in the Deccan, and the northwestern frontier region to Kabul and Kandahar.

Akbar made excellent arrangements for the administration of this vast domain and for the assessment of land revenue on the basis of actual land measurements. His methods stood the test of time and served as the foundation on which the British built their administrative structure. He pursued a policy of religious toleration far in advance of his historic time period, conciliating his Hindu subjects by abolishing the hated poll tax called *jizya*, appointing Hindus to high civil and military posts, and establishing matrimonial relations with the Rajput royal families. Akbar assembled learned representatives of the principal religious sects, listened to their discourses, and actually practiced some of their religious injunctions. Finally, he went to the length of promulgating a new religion called Dīn-i-ilāhī, which was a compound of elements taken from the scriptures of various religious sects. Although Akbar probably was illiterate, his insatiable thirst for knowledge, combined with an excellent memory, enabled him to learn by ear much more than most could learn by reading. He assembled around him an illustrious group of talented persons, including Abū al-Faẓl ʿAllāmi, the court historian, and the great musician Tansen.

The last days of Akbar's reign were blighted by the rebellion of his son, Salīm. Shortly after the two were reconciled, Akbar died in Agra, India, on Oct. 17, 1605. He left as his legacy a prosperous empire that was broadly based on the affection and goodwill of the people. (See also under INDIA—*History.*)

R. C. MAJUMDAR
General Editor of
"History and Culture of the Indian People"

AKHENATON. See AMENHOTEP.

AKHMATOVA, äKH-mä′tō-və, **Anna** (1888–1966), a leading Russian poet of the 20th century. Anna Andreyevna Gorenko, who assumed the pseudonym "Akhmatova" when she began publishing poetry, was born in Odessa, Russia. In 1910 she married Nikolai Gumilev. She died in Moscow on March 5, 1966.

Gumilev founded the "acmeist" literary movement, which supported romanticism and advocated the theory of "art for art's sake." A coleader of the acmeists, Akhmatova published five volumes of poetry between 1912 and 1921. Her work, distinguished by its religious, mystical, and individualistic sentiments, aroused the official wrath of the Soviet government.

After 20 years of inactivity Akhmatova resumed publication in Leningrad magazines during World War II but was bitterly denounced by the Communist party in 1946. Her poems continue, however, to be very popular in the former Soviet Union. They are distinctive in their economy of words, in the creation of word pictures, and in the use of unusual rhythms.

The chief collections of Akhmatova's poetry are *Vecher* (1912, "Evening"), *Chyotki* (1913, "The Rosary"), *Belaya Staya* (1917, "The White Flock"), *Anno Domini MCMXXI* (1921, "A.D. 1921"), and *Iva* (1940, "The Willow"). Most of her works have been published in English translation.

ELLSWORTH RAYMOND, *New York University*

AKIBA BEN JOSEPH, à-kē′vä ben jō′zəf (c. 50 A.D.—c. 135), Palestinian Jewish sage or rabbi of humble origin. His name is also spelled *Akiva*. He began to study Hebrew law when he was 40 and soon rose to scholarly preeminence. Developing a method of his own in biblical interpretation, he attributed a special meaning to every word and even every letter of the scriptural text and was also interested in mystical speculations centering on the secrets of creation. He collected and arranged the entire Oral Law as taught by the leading sages of the period, a collection that later formed the basis of the Mishnah recorded by Rabbi Judah (Jehudah) ha-Nasi. Akiba was regarded as the greatest scholar of his age, and thousands of pupils flocked to his school in Bene Berak (the modern Bnei Braq, near Jaffa, Israel).

Akiba's activities included representing the interests of Palestinian Jews in a mission to Rome.

About 132 A.D. he supported the anti-Roman uprising of Bar Kokhba, whom, according to a Talmudic tradition, he believed to be the Messiah. He ignored the Roman prohibition against studying the law, was arrested as a rebel, and was tortured and executed by the Romans. According to Talmudic tradition, he was flayed alive. His fame and reputation remained great for many generations. A number of religious works were later attributed to him in order to invest the works with authority.

RAPHAEL PATAI
Author of "The Jewish Mind"

AKIHITO, ä-kē-hē-tō (1933–　　　), the 125th emperor of Japan. The elder son of Emperor Hirohito and Empress Nagako, he was born in Tokyo on Dec. 23, 1933, and was installed formally as crown prince in 1952. In his childhood he attended the Gakushuin (Peers' School) in Tokyo but was evacuated from the city during World War II. After the war he was tutored by Elizabeth Gray Vining, an American Quaker, whose principal task was to familiarize him with the ideals of democracy. In 1950 he returned to the Gakushuin and in 1956 graduated from its university. Like his father, he became an authority on marine biology.

Prince Akihito made the first of many state visits abroad in 1953, when he attended the coronation of Queen Elizabeth II in England. In 1959 he married Shoda Michiko, the first commoner to wed an heir apparent to the throne of Japan. The royal couple had three children: Prince Naruhito in 1960, Prince Fumihito in 1965, and Princess Sayako in 1969.

When Emperor Hirohito died on Jan. 7, 1989, Prince Akihito immediately succeeded him. The government recognized the new era as Heisei (Peace and Concord), which would be the emperor's reign name used posthumously.

HYMAN KUBLIN, *Brooklyn College*

AKITA, ä-kē-tä, a port city in Japan, in northwestern Honshū, at the entry of the Omono River into the Sea of Japan (East Sea). It is the capital of Akita prefecture. An industrial center, the city produces petrochemicals, machinery, fertilizer, wood pulp, and zinc. It is the seat of Akita and other universities and has a prefectural museum.

Akita began in 733 as a fortified outpost used in the defense of Japanese settlers against the tribal people of northern Honshū. During the Tokugawa period (1603–1867) it was the chief castle town of the Satake warrior family. Population: 317,625 (2000 census).

AKITA, ä-kē'tə, a handsome Japanese dog breed that has become an increasingly popular member of the American Kennel Club's Working Group. The breed has a short, dense coat that can be any color, often marked with white; a bushy, upturned tail that curls across its hind quarters; and prick ears. It weighs from 75 to 100 pounds (34–45 kg). Standard height for the males is 26 to 28 inches (66–71 cm); for the females, 24 to 26 inches (61–66 cm).

Powerful and strong-willed, the Akita is best suited to an owner who is experienced in teaching obedience to big dogs. Many Akitas attack other dogs and therefore should be walked only by someone who can control them. Properly trained and managed, however, the breed is an

© NELSON GROFFMAN/FPG
The Akita is a breed that must be properly trained.

exemplary pet, loyal, alert, protective, well behaved, and good with children if it has been brought up with them from early puppyhood. Aside from its tendency to develop hip dysplasia, it is generally healthy, and its coat, though it does shed, requires no more than a brisk combing twice a week.

Some breeders maintain that the Akita does not bite intruders but instead, like the mastiff, simply holds them at bay. Other breeders say the Akitas will bite hard. In either case they are likely to be suspicious of strangers. Like other big breeds, they require a lot of regular exercise.

JOHN HOWE
Author of "Choosing the Right Dog"

AKKAD, ak'ad, the northern division of ancient Babylonia, as distinguished from Sumer or southern Babylonia. The name is also spelled *Accad.* Akkad was well located commercially, and the nomadic Semitic peoples who came to the region during the 3000s and 2000s B.C. soon became prosperous through trade. Akkad reached its greatest height in the mid-2000s, when Sargon I united the several city-states of the area, conquered the Sumerian peoples, and extended his power from the mountains of Elam to the shores of the Mediterranean Sea and into Asia Minor, creating the first great empire in history.

After Sargon's conquests the Akkadians adopted a more settled mode of existence, taking over many aspects of Sumerian culture, such as the calendar, weights and measures, cuneiform script, numerals, business methods, sculpture, and crafts. Following the fall of Sargon's dynasty (c. 2180), a joint nation of Sumer and Akkad controlled the Babylonian region for a period of about three centuries. The Akkadian language, a Semitic tongue, was adopted as the spoken and written language.

The region of Akkad received its name from the royal city of Akkad, also known as Agade, which was still flourishing in the days of Nebuchadnezzar about 1125. The city is mentioned in Genesis 10:10. Its exact site was about 30 miles (50 km) north of Babylon.

AKKADIAN LANGUAGE.　See ASSYRIOLOGY.

AKMOLINSK.　See TSELINOGRAD.

435

AKRON, ak′rən, an industrial city in northeastern Ohio, situated on the Little Cuyahoga River, 35 miles (56 km) southeast of Cleveland. It is the seat of Summit county.

Akron is an important distribution point between the eastern seaboard and the Midwest. It is served by major railroads, airlines, and interstate highways and is one of the largest truck-terminal cities in the United States. Akron is the center of a metropolitan area with a population nearly three times that of the city itself.

The city became famous as the world's leading rubber-manufacturing center and still hosts the corporate headquarters of several rubber companies. With the closing of the last tire plant in 1982, however, emphasis shifted to polymers, including plastics. Akron was also a pioneer in making U.S. Navy dirigibles at a Goodyear plant in the early 1930s. Other industries include the manufacture of transportation equipment, machinery, electrical equipment, and fishing tackle.

Akron is the home of the University of Akron and the Akron Art Museum. There are also a symphony orchestra and chorus, community playhouses, and a civic theater. The house of the abolitionist John Brown is maintained as a museum.

The center of a lake district with many scenic attractions, fishing, and water sports, Akron is traversed by the old Portage Path, a Native American trail between the Cuyahoga and Tuscarawas rivers that for a time after 1785 formed a portion of the western U.S. boundary.

Middlebury, now a part of Akron, was settled in 1807; Akron proper was first settled in about 1818. Its real growth dates from 1825, when the village was platted by Simon Perkins along the projected Ohio and Erie Canal, which opened in Akron in 1827. Later Akron became the terminus of the Pennsylvania and Ohio Canal, built in 1840. Early prosperity was based largely on the development of native clay deposits; then water power from the canals led to the establishment of the Schumacher gristmills, manufacturing rolled oats. Population: 217,074.

CURTICE G. MYERS*, *Akron Public Library*

Bibliography: Love, Steve, and David Giffels, *Wheels of Fortune: The Story of Rubber in Akron* (Univ. of Akron Press 1998); McGovern, Frances, *Written on the Hills: The Making of the Akron Landscape* (Univ. of Akron Press 1996).

AKSAKOV, Sergei Timofeyevich, äk-sä′kəf (1791–1859), Russian writer of the realist school. He was born in Ufa, Russia, on Sept. 20, 1791. A member of the rural gentry, he at first served as a government official but after 1830 devoted himself to writing. He died in Moscow on April 30, 1859.

Aksakov's literary fame rests chiefly on four autobiographical books: *Zapiski ob uzhenii ryby* (1847, "Notes about Fishing"); *Zapiski ruzheinovo okhotnika Orenburgskoi gubernii* (1852, "Notes of a Hunter of Orenburg Province"); *Semeinaya khronika* (1856; *A Russian Gentleman,* 1917); and *Detskie gody Bagrova vnuka* (1858; *Years of Childhood,* 1916). His *Istoria moevo znakomstva s Gogolem* (1890, "Recollections of Gogol") is an excellent analysis of the writings of Nikolai Gogol, Aksakov's inspiration and friend.

KONSTANTIN SERGEYEVICH AKSAKOV (1817–1860), elder son of Sergei, poet, dramatist, and philologist. He was born in Nova-Aksakovo on April 10, 1817. He was a prominent member of the Slavophile movement, which sought Russia's salvation in the Orthodox religion and peasant democracy rather than in imitating Western cultural institutions. He died in Tzakynthos on Dec. 19, 1860.

His writings include *Lomonosov v istorii russkoi literatury i russkovo yazyka* (1846, "Lomonosov in the History of Russian Literature and Language") and *O vnutrennem sostoyanii Rossii* (1855, "On the Internal Situation in Russia").

IVAN SERGEYEVICH AKSAKOV (1823–1886), younger son of Sergei, poet, dramatist, and journalist. A leading figure in the Pan-Slav movement, he recruited Russian volunteers to fight for the liberation of the Balkans from Turkish rule and worked as a writer and editor of various Pan-Slav journals. His unfinished poem about peasant life, *The Tramp* (1852), was his most influential work.

ELLSWORTH RAYMOND, *New York University*

AKSUM, äk-sōōm′, a town in Tigre province, northern Ethiopia, situated 12 miles (20 km) west of Aduwa, at an altitude of about 7,000 feet (2,100 meters). The town is a market center for agricultural produce.

Aksum is a religious center of the Coptic Christians, who claim that the original Ark of the Covenant, brought to the town by a descendant of King Solomon and the Queen of Sheba, is in the local cathedral. Known in ancient times as Axumis, the town became the capital, in the 1st century A.D., of the Axumite (Auxumite) kingdom. For the next 500 years it was a major center of commerce between India, Arabia, Greece, and Rome. Among its surviving ancient monuments are a number of great stone obelisks. Population: 27,148 (1994 census).

AKTYUBINSK, ək-tyōō′bensk, a city in Kazakstan. Known as Aktyubinsk under the USSR, the city, after the 1991 independence of Kazakstan, adopted the Kazak form for its name, Aqtöbe. A railroad center on the Elek River, it is an important industrial and commercial city. Its industries include a ferroalloy plant, wool- and food-processing plants, and machinery factories.

Aqtöbe is the capital of Aqtöbe region, a productive farming and mining area. The region spreads over an area of about 115,000 square miles (297,900 sq km) in the Mugodzhar Hills. Most of the people are concentrated in the fertile agricultural area of the north. The semidesert area to the south has important chromite and nickel mines.

The city was founded in 1869 as a Russian fort and named Ak-Tyube ("White Hill"). In 1932 it was renamed Aktyubinsk and became the regional capital. Population: 253,100 (1999 census).

THEODORE SHABAD*
Author of "Geography of the USSR"

AKUREYRI, ä′kür-ā-rē, the second largest city in Iceland and the chief urban center of its northern region. It is located near the base of Eyja Fjord, an inlet of the Greenland Sea, about 150 miles (240 km) northeast of Reykjavík.

Akureyri is a leading fishing port and the center of many cooperatively owned textile mills, shoe factories, and freezing plants. The city has a technical college, a branch of the national university, an agricultural experiment station, and a circumpolar studies research institute. An impressive landmark is the modernistic twin-spired Lutheran church. Population: 15,102 (1998 census).

ALA. See AMERICAN LIBRARY ASSOCIATION.

ALABAMA

Great Seal of Alabama

ALABAMA, al-ə-bam'ə, is a southeastern state of the United States, situated east of the Mississippi River in the center of the far southern tier of states. Popularly, it has been called the "Heart of Dixie" because of its central location among the Southern states.

Alabama is also a Gulf state and an Appalachian state. The narrow panhandle of Florida separates Alabama from the Gulf of Mexico except in the southwest. There a section of the state, shaped somewhat like a boot heel, extends to the Gulf, giving Alabama a major seaport—the historic city of Mobile, founded by the French in 1711—miles of sandy beaches, and extensive saltwater fishing grounds.

Sections of the Appalachian Highlands, the dominant physical region of the eastern United States, reach into the northern half of Alabama, providing it with an important share of that region's scenic beauty and mineral wealth. Deposits of iron, coal, and limestone, located in close proximity, gave rise to the iron and steel industry at Birmingham, which came to be called the Pittsburgh of the South.

TENNESSEE VALLEY AUTHORITY

GUNTERSVILLE DAM, on the Tennessee River, is one of several dams that provide flood control, navigation, and power production—vital factors in Alabama's economy.

The Black Belt stretches through the center of the state. This section, so named because of its dark-colored soils, once was the heart of the Cotton Kingdom. Cotton still is grown there as elsewhere in Alabama, but the area rapidly is becoming a beef cattle and dairying region.

INFORMATION HIGHLIGHTS

Location: In east-south-central United States, bordered north by Tennessee, east by Georgia and Florida, south by Florida and the Gulf of Mexico, west by Mississippi.

Elevation: Sea level to 2,407 feet (734 meters).

Total Area: (land and inland water) 51,705 square miles (133,916 sq km); rank, 29th.

Resident Population: 4,447,100 (2000 census). Increase (1990–2000), 10.1%.

Climate: Long, hot summers; mild winters; generally abundant rainfall.

Statehood: Dec. 14, 1819; order of admission, 22d.

Capital: Montgomery.

Largest City: Birmingham.

Number of Counties: 67.

Principal Products: *Manufactures*—primary metals (especially rolled and finished steel), chemicals, textiles; *farm products*—cotton lint, chickens (broilers), cattle; *minerals*—coal, cement, stone, petroleum.

State Motto: We Dare Defend Our Rights.

State Song: *Alabama.*

Origin of the Name: From *Alabama,* meaning "I open [clear] the thicket," the name of a Native American tribe residing in the area.

State Nicknames: Heart of Dixie; Cotton State; Yellowhammer State.

State Bird: Yellowhammer (*Colaptes auratus*).

State Flower: Camellia.

State Tree: Southern pine (*Pinus palustris Mill*).

State Flag: A crimson cross of St. Andrew on a field of white. (See also FLAG.)

Bellingrath home, near Mobile, has famous gardens. Seasonal flowers beautify the patio.

The river systems of Alabama are of such significance that they are displayed on the Great Seal of the state. Once they were important principally for transportation. Today, with improved navigation channels, large dams and lakes, power stations, and an abundant flow of generally pure, soft water, the rivers are of major importance for industry, commerce, and recreation.

To add to its natural endowments Alabama has extensive tracts of pine woods, from which come lumber, naval stores, and wood pulp for the pulp and paper industries. Deposits of petroleum and salt supply the raw materials needed by the chemical industries. A generally mild climate and good soils enable Alabama to grow a great variety of field crops, vegetables, and fruits.

Alabama is confronted by various problems. The struggle of the state's large black population for full civil rights, the resistance in some quarters to changes in age-old patterns of thinking and living, educational standards below the national average, rural poverty affecting both whites and blacks—all have engaged national attention.

Progress in meeting these problems is being made through the efforts of business, community, and religious leaders working within the state. Schools in some areas, as well as public accommodations, have been desegregated without incident. With increasing frequency, major national companies are selecting industrial sites in Alabama, thus broadening both the economy and the outlook of the state. The large scientific community at the George C. Marshall Space Flight Center at Huntsville contributes to U.S. goals for conquest of outer space as well as to a new national, and even international, consciousness in Alabama.

1. The People

Most Alabamians are native-born. Many are descendants of settlers from states to the east and northeast who came to Alabama during the early decades of the 19th century. Many others are descendants of Africans brought in to supply labor on the cotton plantations that flourished in the central counties before the Civil War. African

Americans now make up 26% of the population.

At the time of earliest settlement, Alabama had one of the largest Native American populations in the country. The 2000 census enumerated only 22,430 Native Americans, mostly in small communities in the southern part of the state; but Creek, Choctaw, Chickasaw, and Cherokee have left their names on the land. The Spaniards, representatives of the first European country to hold sovereignty over what is now Alabama, left no permanent settlements, although a record of their explorations remains in place-names such as De Soto State Park. The French, who were next to hold sovereignty, came as colonists, bringing their customs and traditions, which still can be noted in the Mobile area.

Way of Life. Agrarian is the word most commonly used to describe the traditional way of life in Alabama. Yet emphasis on the farmer and his interests has diminished through the years. The increasing efficiency of farming methods has reduced agricultural employment, and farming has become more a strictly economic activity and less a distinctive pattern in the Alabama way of life. Through the years there has been a tendency for population to move from the rural areas to the towns and from the towns to the cities, but it was not until 1960 that the balance shifted from rural to urban. Then, for the first time, more Alabamians lived in urban than in rural areas.

RESIDENT POPULATION SINCE 1820

Year	Population	Year	Population
1820	127,901	1950	3,061,743
1840	590,756	1960	3,266,740
1860	964,201	1970	3,444,354
1880	1,262,505	1980	3,893,978
1900	1,828,697	1990	4,040,587
1920	2,348,174	2000	4,447,100
1940	2,832,961		

Gain, 1990–2000: 10.1% (U.S. gain, 13.2%). **Density,** 2000: 87.6 persons per sq mi of land area (U.S. density, 79.6).

URBAN-RURAL DISTRIBUTION

Year	Percent urban	Percent rural
1920	21.7 (U.S., 51.2)	78.3
1930	28.1 (U.S., 56.2)	71.9
1940	30.2 (U.S., 56.6)	69.8
1950	43.8 (U.S., 64.0)	56.2
1960	55.0 (U.S., 69.9)	45.0
1970	58.4 (U.S., 73.5)	41.6
1980	60.0 (U.S., 73.7)	40.0
1990	60.4 (U.S., 75.2)	39.6

LARGEST CENTERS OF POPULATION

City or metropolitan area	2000	1990	1980
Birmingham	242,820	265,968	284,413
Metropolitan area	921,106	907,810	847,487
Montgomery	201,568	187,106	177,857
Metropolitan area	333,055	292,517	272,687
Mobile	198,915	196,278	200,452
Metropolitan area	540,258	476,923	443,536
Huntsville	158,216	159,789	142,513
Metropolitan area	342,376	238,912	308,593
Tuscaloosa	77,906	77,759	75,211
Metropolitan area	164,875	150,522	137,541
Hoover	62,742	39,788	19,792
Dothan	57,737	53,589	48,750
Decatur	53,929	48,761	42,002
Auburn	42,987	33,830	28,471
Gadsden	38,978	42,523	47,565

ALABAMA

TOPOGRAPHY

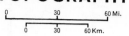

0   30   60 Mi.

0   30   60 Km.

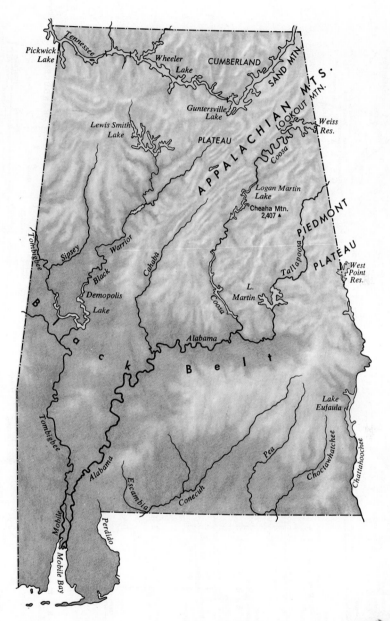

Pickwick
Lake

Tennessee

Wheeler
Lake

CUMBERLAND

SAND MTN.

Guntersville
Lake

LOOKOUT MTN.

Weiss
Res.

Lewis Smith
Lake

PLATEAU

Coosa

APPALACHIAN MTS.

Logan Martin
Lake

Cheaha Mtn.
2,407 ▲

PIEDMONT

Tombigbee

Sipsey

Warrior

Cahaba

Tallapoosa

PLATEAU

West
Point
Res.

Black

Demopolis
Lake

Coosa

L.
Martin

B   l   a   c   k

Alabama

B   e   l   t

Lake
Eufaula

Tombigbee

Pea

Choctawhatchee

Chattahoochee

Alabama

Escambia

Conecuh

Mobile

Perdido

Mobile Bay

| Below Sea Level | 100 m. 328 ft. | 200 m. 656 ft. | 500 m. 1,640 ft. | 1,000 m. 3,281 ft. | 2,000 m. 6,562 ft. | 5,000 m. 16,404 ft. |

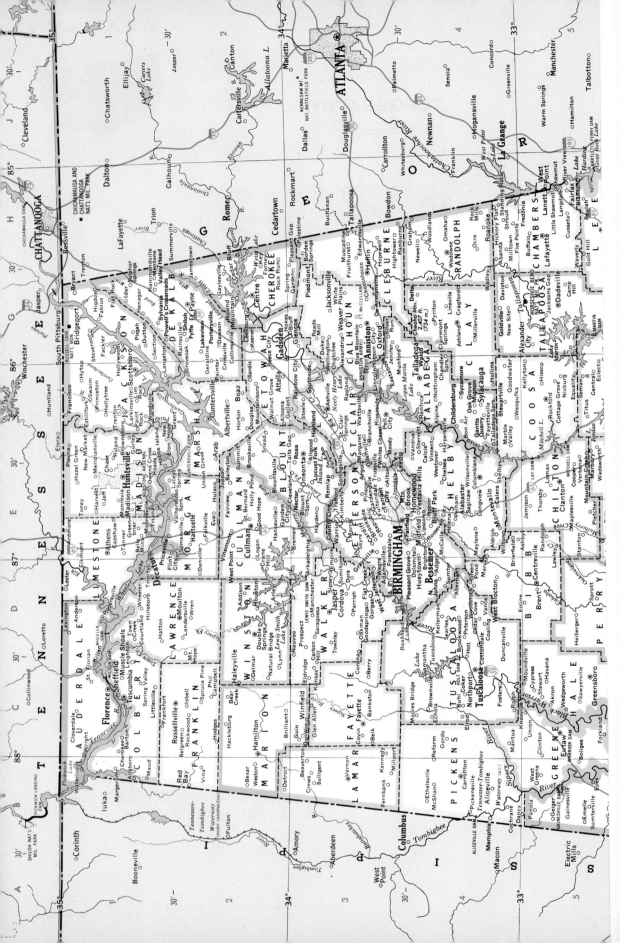

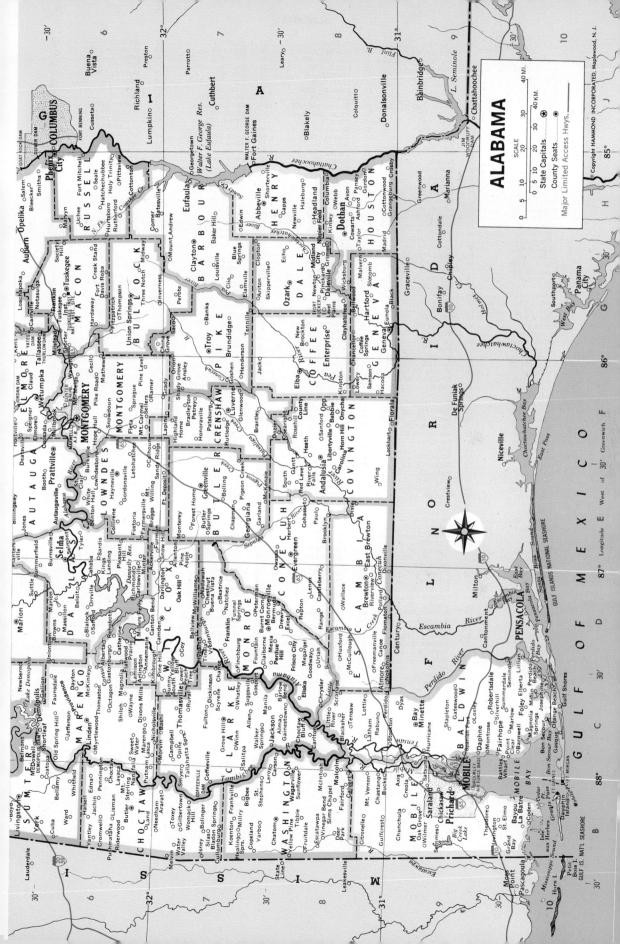

ALABAMA

SCALE

State Capitals ⊛
County Seats ⊙
Major Limited Access Hwys. ___

© Copyright HAMMOND INCORPORATED, Maplewood, N.J.

COUNTIES

Autauga 43,671 E5
Baldwin 140,415 C9
Barbour 29,038 H7
Bibb 20,826 D5
Blount 51,024 E2
Bullock 11,714 G6
Butler 21,399 E7
Calhoun 112,249 G3
Chambers 36,583 H5
Cherokee 23,988 G2
Chilton 39,593 E5
Choctaw 15,922 B6
Clarke 27,867 C7
Clay 14,254 G4
Cleburne 14,123 G3
Coffee 43,615 G8
Colbert 54,984 C1
Conecuh 14,089 E8
Coosa 12,202 F5
Covington 37,631 F8
Crenshaw 13,665 F7
Cullman 77,483 E2
Dale 49,129 G8
Dallas 46,365 D6
De Kalb 64,452 G2
Elmore 65,874 F5
Escambia 38,440 D8
Etowah 103,459 F2
Fayette 18,495 C3
Franklin 31,223 C2
Geneva 25,764 G8
Greene 9,974 C5
Hale 17,185 C5
Henry 16,310 H7
Houston 88,787 H8
Jackson 53,926 F1
Jefferson 662,047 E3
Lamar 15,904 B3
Lauderdale 87,966 C1
Lawrence 34,803 D1
Lee 115,092 H5
Limestone 65,676 E1
Lowndes 13,473 E6
Macon 24,105 G6
Madison 276,700 E1
Marengo 22,539 C6
Marion 31,214 C2
Marshall 82,231 F2
Mobile 399,843 B9
Monroe 24,324 D7
Montgomery 223,510 F6
Morgan 111,064 E2
Perry 11,861 D5
Pickens 20,949 B4
Pike 29,605 G7
Randolph 22,380 H4
Russell 49,756 H6
Saint Clair 64,742 F3
Shelby 143,293 E4
Sumter 14,798 B5
Talladega 80,321 F4
Tallapoosa 41,475 G5
Tuscaloosa 164,875 C4
Walker 70,713 D3
Washington 18,097 B8
Wilcox 13,183 D7
Winston 24,843 D2

CITIES and TOWNS

Abbeville▲ 2,987 H7
Abernant 405 D4
Ackerville 200 D6
Adamsville 4,965 D3
Addison 723 D2
Adger 400 D4
Akron 521 C5
Alabaster 22,619 E4
Alberta 100 D6
Albertville 17,247 F2
Aldrich 500 E4
Alexander City 15,008 G5
Alexandria 3,692 G3
Aliceville 2,567 B4
Allen 149 C7
Allgood 629 F3
Allsboro 300 B1
Alma 500 C8
Alpine 150 F4
Alton 150 E3
Altoona 984 F2
Andalusia▲ 8,794 E8
Anderson 354 D1
Annemanie 100 D6
Anniston▲ 24,276 G3
Arab 7,174 E2
Ardmore 1,034 E1
Argo 1,780 E3
Ariton 772 G7
Arkadelphia 150 E3
Arley 290 D2
Arlington 200 C6
Ashby 500 E4
Ashford 1,853 H8
Ashland▲ 1,965 G4
Ashville▲ 2,260 F3
Athens▲ 18,967 E1
Atmore 7,676 C8
Attalla 6,592 F2
Auburn 42,987 H5
Autaugaville 820 E6
Avon 466 H8
Axis 500 B9
Babbie 627 F8
Baileyton 684 E2
Baker Hill 300 H7
Banks 224 G7
Bankston 125 C3
Barlow Bend 300 C8
Barnwell 700 C10
Barton 150 C1
Bashi 225 C7
Batesville 100 H6
Battles Wharf 300 C10
Bay Minette▲ 224 C9
Bayou La Batre 2,313 B10
Bear Creek 1,053 C2
Beatrice 412 D7
Beaverton 226 B3
Belgreen 500 C2
Belk 214 C3
Bellamy 700 B6
Belle Mina 675 E1
Bellview 200 D7
Bellwood 400 G8
Beloit 100 D6
Bermuda 120 D8
Berry 1,238 C3
Bessemer 29,672 D4
Beulah 500 H5
Billingsley 116 E5
Birmingham▲ 242,820 D3
Black 202 G8
Blacksher 200 C8
Bladon Springs 125 B7
Blanton 100 H5
Bleecker 250 H5
Blountsville 1,768 E2
Blue Mountain 233 G3
Blue Springs 121 G7
Boaz 7,411 F2
Boligee 369 C5
Bolinger 175 B7
Bolling 100 E7
Bon Air 96 F4
Bon Secour 850 C10
Booth 200 E6
Boyd 100 B5
Braggs 180 E6
Branchville 825 F3
Brantley 920 F7
Bremen 125 E3
Brent 4,024 D5
Brewton▲ 5,498 D8
Bridgeport 2,728 G1
Brierfield 250 E4
Brighton 3,640 D4
Brilliant 762 C2
Brooklyn 300 E8
Brookside 1,393 E3
Brooksville 120 F2
Brookwood 1,483 D4
Browns 375 D6
Brownsboro 150 F1
Brownville 2,386 C4
Brundidge 2,341 G7
Bryant 300 G1
Bucks 201 B8
Buhl 100 C4
Burkville 250 E6
Burnsville 100 E6
Butler▲ 1,952 B6
Cahaba D6
Calcis 200 F4
Calera 3,158 E4
Calhoun 950 F6
Calvert 600 B8
Camden▲ 2,257 D7
Campbell 200 C7
Camp Hill 1,273 G5
Canoe 560 D8
Canton Bend 300 D6
Carbon Hill 2,071 D3
Cardiff 82 E3
Carlowville 100 D6
Carlton 275 C8
Carolina 248 E8
Carrollton▲ 987 B4
Carson 400 C8
Castleberry 590 D8
Catherine 250 D6
Cedar Bluff 1,467 G2
Cedar Cove 100 D4
Central 300 F5
Centre▲ 3,216 G2
Centreville▲ 2,466 D5
Chancellor 200 G8
Chandler Springs 100 F4
Chapman 300 E7
Chase 175 E1
Chastang 200 B8
Chatom▲ 1,193 B8
Chelsea 2,949 E4
Cherokee 1,237 C1
Chestnut 125 D7
Chickasaw 6,364 B9
Childersburg 4,927 F4
Choccolocco 500 G3
Choctaw 600 B6
Chrysler 400 C8
Chunchula 700 B9
Citronelle 3,659 B8
Claiborne 125 D7
Clanton▲ 7,800 E5
Clayhatchee 501 G8
Clayton▲ 1,475 G7
Cleveland 1,241 E3
Clinton 150 C5
Clio 2,206 G7
Cloverdale 100 C1
Coaling 1,115 D4
Coden 600 B10
Coffee Springs 251 G8
Coffeeville 360 B7
Coker 808 C4
Collinsville 1,644 G2
Collirene 100 E6
Columbia 804 H8
Columbiana▲ 3,316 E4
Cooper 250 E5
Coosada 1,382 F5
Copeland 160 B7
Cordova 2,423 D3
Corona 300 C3
Cottondale 500 D4
Cottonton 324 H6
Cottonwood 1,170 H8
County Line 257 E3
Courtland 769 D1
Cowarts 1,546 H8
Coy 950 D7
Crane Hill 355 D2
Creola 2,002 B9
Cromwell 650 B6
Crossville 1,431 G2
Cuba 363 B6
Cullman▲ 13,995 E2
Cullomburg 325 B7
Cusseta 650 H5
Cypress 300 C5
Dadeville▲ 3,212 G5
Daleville 4,653 G8
Dancy 116 B4
Danville 300 D2
Daphne 16,581 C9
Darlington 150 D7
Dauphin Island 1,371 B10
Daviston 267 G4
Dayton 60 C6
De Armanville 350 G3
Deatsville 340 F5
Decatur▲ 53,929 D1
Deer Park 300 B8
Delmar 200 C2
Delta 100 G4
Demopolis 7,540 C6
Detroit 247 B2
Dickinson 250 C7
Dixons Mills 100 C6
Dixonville 125 E8
Dora 2,413 D3
Dothan▲ 57,737 H8
Double Springs▲ 1,003 D2
Douglas 530 F2
Dozier 391 F7
Duke 250 G3
Duncanville 150 D4
Dutton 310 G1
Dyas 250 C9
Eastaboga 300 F3
East Brewton 2,496 E8
Echo 200 G8
Echola 300 C4
Eclectic 1,037 F5
Edwardsville 186 H3
Edwin 296 H7
Elamville 180 G7
Elba▲ 4,185 F8
Elberta 552 C10
Eldridge 184 C3
Eliska 200 C8
Elkmont 470 E1
Elmore 470 F5
Elon 125 F1
Elrod 746 C4
Emelle 31 B5
Empire 600 D3
Enterprise 21,178 G8
Epes 206 B5
Equality 125 F5
Estillfork 200 F1
Eufaula 13,908 H7
Eunola 182 G8
Eutaw▲ 1,878 C5
Eva 491 E2
Evergreen▲ 3,630 E8
Excel 582 D8
Fabius 150 G1
Fackler 250 G1
Fairfield 12,381 E4
Fairford 200 B8
Fairhope 12,480 C10
Fairview 522 E2
Falkville 1,202 E2
Farmersville 200 E6
Faunsdale 87 C6
Fayette▲ 4,922 C3
Fayetteville 200 F4
Finchburg 150 D7
Fitzpatrick 108 G6
Five Points 146 H4
Flat Rock 750 G1
Flatwood 300 C6
Flint City 1,033 D1
Flomaton 1,588 D8
Florala 1,964 F8
Florence▲ 36,264 C1
Foley 7,590 C10
Forestdale 10,509 E3
Forkland 629 C5
Forney 100 H2
Fort Davis 500 G6
Fort Deposit 1,270 E7
Fort Mitchell 900 H6
Fort Payne▲ 12,938 G2
Fosters 400 C4
Fostoria 200 E6
Frankfort 125 C1
Franklin 149 G6
Frankville 200 B7
Fredonia 300 H5
Freemanville 200 D8
Frisco City 1,460 D8
Fruitdale 500 B8
Fruithurst 270 G3
Fulton 308 C7
Fultondale 6,595 E3
Furman 200 E6
Fyffe 971 G2
Gadsden▲ 38,978 G2
Gainestown 300 C8
Gainesville 220 B5
Gallant 475 F2
Gallion 239 C6
Gantt 241 E8
Garden City 564 E2
Gardendale 11,626 E3
Garland 155 E7
Gasque 100 C10
Gateswood 200 C9
Gaylesville 140 G2
Geiger 161 B5
Geneva▲ 4,388 G8
Georgiana 1,737 E7
Geraldine 786 G2
Gilbertown 187 B7
Glen Allen 442 C3
Glencoe 5,152 G3
Glenwood 191 F7
Good Hope 1,966 E2
Goodsprings 360 D3
Goodwater 1,633 F4
Goodway 200 D8
Gordo 1,677 C4
Gordon 408 H8
Gordonsville 318 E6
Gorgas 500 D3
Goshen 300 F7
Gosport 500 C7
Graham 100 H4
Grand Bay 3,918 B10
Grant 665 F1
Graysville 2,344 D3
Greenbrier 100 E1
Green Pond 750 D4
Greensboro▲ 2,731 C5
Greenville▲ 7,228 E7
Grimes 459 H8
Grove Hill▲ 1,438 C7
Guin 2,389 C3
Gulf Crest 200 B8
Gulf Shores 5,044 C10
Guntersville▲ 7,395 F2
Gurley 876 F1
Gu-Win 204 C3
Hackleburg 1,527 C2
Haleburg 108 H8
Haleyville 4,182 C2
Halsell 250 B6
Hamilton▲ 6,786 C2
Hammondville 486 G1
Hanceville 2,951 E2
Hardaway 600 G6
Harpersville 1,620 F4
Hartford 2,369 G8
Hartselle 12,019 E2
Harvest 3,054 E1
Hatchechubbee 840 H6
Hatton 950 D1
Havana 150 C5
Hayden 470 E3
Hayneville▲ 1,177 E6
Hazel Green 3,805 E1
Headland 3,523 H8
Healing Springs 100 B7
Heath 249 F8
Heflin▲ 3,002 G3
Heiberger 310 D5
Helena 10,296 E4
Henagar 2,400 G1
Higdon 925 G1
Highland Home 150 F7
Highland Lake 408 F3
Hillsboro 608 D1
Hissop 250 F5
Hobbs Island 100 F1
Hobson City 878 G3
Hodges 261 C2
Hokes Bluff 4,149 G3
Hollins 500 F4
Holly Pond 645 E2
Hollywood 950 G1
Holt 4,103 C4
Holy Trinity 400 H6
Homewood 25,043 E4
Honoraville 200 F7
Hoover 62,742 E4
Hope Hull 975 F6
Horton 100 F2
Houston 100 D2
Hueytown 15,364 D4
Hulaco 225 E2
Huntsville▲ 158,216 E1
Hurricane 300 C9
Hurtsboro 592 H6
Huxford 141 D8
Hybart 200 D7
Hytop 315 F1
Ider 664 G1
Irondale 9,813 E3
Irvington 150 B9
Isbell 250 C2
Isney 145 B7
Jachin 150 B6
Jack F7
Jackson 5,419 C8
Jacksons Gap 761 G5
Jacksonville 8,404 G3
Jamestown 147 G2
Jasper▲ 14,052 D3
Jeff 150 E1
Jefferson 300 C6
Jemison 2,248 E5
Jenifer 300 G3
Jones 135 E5
Joppa 200 E2
Josephine 200 C10
Kansas 260 C3
Keener 125 G2
Kellerman 100 D4
Kellyton 375 F5
Kennedy 541 B3
Kent 180 G5
Key 400 G2
Killen 1,119 D1
Kimberly 1,801 E3
Kimbrough 150 C6
Kinsey 1,796 H8
Kinston 602 F8
Knoxville 200 C4
Laceys Spring 400 E1
Lafayette▲ 3,234 H5
Lakeview 163 G2
Lamison 200 C6
Landersville 150 D2
Lanett 7,897 H5
Langston 254 G1
Lapine 300 F7
Larkinsville 425 F1
Latham 133 C8
Lavaca 500 B6
Lawley 125 E5

▲ County seat.

ALABAMA

Leeds 10,455	E3
Leesburg 799	G2
Leighton 849	D1
Lenox 150	D8
Leroy 699	B8
Lester 107	D1
Letohatchee 250	E6
Level Plains 1,544	G8
Lexington 840	D1
Libertyville 106	F8
Lillian 350	D10
Lincoln 4,577	F3
Linden▲ 2,424	C6
Lineville 2,401	G4
Lipscomb 2,458	E4
Lisman 653	B6
Little River 400	C8
Littleville 978	C1
Livingston▲ 3,297	B5
Loachapoka 165	G5
Lockhart 548	F8
Locust Fork 1,016	E3
Logan 300	E2
Lomax 300	E5
Longview 475	E4
Lottie 150	C8
Louisville 612	G7
Lower Peach Tree 926	C7
Lowery 100	F6
Lowndesboro 140	E6
Loxley 1,348	C9
Luverne▲ 2,635	F7
Lynn 597	C2
Madison 29,329	E1
Madrid 303	H8
Magnolia 100	C6
Magnolia Springs 800	C10
Malcolm 300	B8
Malvern 1,215	G8
Manchester 400	D3
Manila 100	C7
Maplesville 672	E5
Marbury 300	E5
Margaret 1,169	F3
Margerum 250	B1
Marion▲ 3,511	D5
Marion Junction 400	D6
Marvel 100	D4
Marvyn 300	H6
Maud 150	B1
Maylene 500	E4
McCalla 657	E4
McCullough 500	D8
McIntosh 244	B8
McKenzie 644	E7
McKinley 100	C6
McShan 50	B4
McWilliams 305	D7
Megargel 240	D8
Melvin 300	B7
Mentone 451	G1
Meridianville 4,117	F1
Mexia 200	D8
Midfield 5,626	E4
Midland City 1,703	H8
Midway 457	H6
Miflin 150	C10
Mignon 1,348	
Millbrook 10,386	F6
Millers Ferry 300	D6
Millerville 345	G4
Millport 1,160	B3
Millry 615	B7
Milltown 125	H4
Milstead 150	G6
Minter 450	D6
Mobile▲ 198,915	B9
Monroeville▲ 6,862	D7
Monrovia 500	E1
Montevallo 4,825	E4
Montgomery (cap.)▲ 201,568	F6
Montrose 750	C9
Moody 8,053	F3
Morris 1,827	E3
Morvin 355	C7
Mosses 1,101	E6
Moulton▲ 3,260	D2
Moundville 1,809	C5
Mountainboro 338	F2
Mountain Brook 20,604	E4
Mountain Creek 300	E5
Mount Carmel 300	F6
Mount Hope 125	D2
Mount Meigs 150	F6
Mount Sterling 175	B6
Mount Vernon 844	B8
Mount Willing 300	E6
Munford 2,446	F3
Muscadine 105	H3
Muscle Shoals 11,924	C1
Myrtlewood 139	C6
Nanafalia 500	B6
Napier Field 404	H8
Natchez 135	D7
Natural Bridge 28	C2
Nauvoo 284	D3
Nectar 372	E3
Needham 97	B7
Newbern 231	C5
New Brockton 1,250	G8
New Hope 2,539	F1
New Market 1,864	F1
New Site 848	G4
Newton 1,708	G8
Newville 553	H8
Nicholsville 200	C6
Nixburg 150	F5
Nokomis 125	D8
North Johns 142	D4
Northport 19,435	C4
Notasulga 916	G5
Nottingham 175	F4
Oak Grove 436	B9
Oak Grove 457	F4
Oakman 944	D3
Ocre 180	H4
Octagon 150	C6
Odenville 1,131	F3
Ohatchee 1,215	G3
Oneonta▲ 5,576	E3
Onycha 208	F8
Opelika▲ 23,498	H5
Opine 101	C7
Opp 6,607	F8
Orange Beach 3,784	C10
Orrville 230	D6
Owassa 130	E8
Owens Cross Roads 1,124	E1
Oxford 14,592	G3
Ozark▲ 15,119	G8
Painter 265	F2
Paint Rock 185	F1
Panola 200	B5
Pansey 300	H8
Parrish 1,268	D3
Pelham 14,369	E4
Pell City▲ 9,565	F3
Pennington 353	B6
Perdido 500	C8
Perdido Beach 250	C10
Perdue Hill 225	C8
Peterman 600	D7
Phenix City▲ 28,265	H6
Phil Campbell 1,091	C2
Pickensville 662	B4
Piedmont 5,120	G3
Pigeon Creek 100	E7
Pike Road 310	F6
Pinckard 667	G8
Pine Apple 145	E7
Pine Hill 966	C7
Pine Level 200	F6
Pinson 5,033	E3
Pisgah 706	G1
Pittsview 300	H6
Plantersville 650	E5
Pleasant Grove 9,983	D4
Point Clear 1,876	C10
Pollard 120	D8
Portersville 100	G2
Powell's Crossroads 636	G1
Prairie 100	D6
Prattville▲ 24,303	E6
Priceville 1,631	E1
Prichard 28,633	B9
Princeton 300	F1
Providence 311	C6
Pushmataha 200	B6
Putnam 276	B6
Rabun 300	C8
Ragland 1,918	F3
Rainbow City 8,428	F3
Rainsville 4,499	G2
Ramer 680	F6
Ranburne 459	H3
Randolph 100	E5
Range 275	D8
Reads Mill 150	G3
Red Bay 3,374	B2
Red Level 556	E8
Reece City 634	G2
Reform 1,978	C4
Rehoboth 993	D6
Remlap 800	E3
Renfroe 400	F4
Repton 280	D8
Republic 500	E3
Richmond 100	D6
River Falls 616	E8
Riverside 1,564	F3
Riverview 99	D8
Roanoke 6,563	H4
Robertsdale 3,782	C9
Rockford▲ 428	F5
Rock Mills 676	H4
Rockwood 145	C2
Rogersville 1,199	D1
Roosevelt City 3,352	E4
Rosa 313	E3
Rosehill 132	F5
Russellville▲ 8,971	C2
Rutherford 232	H6
Rutledge 476	F7
Safford 150	D6
Saginaw 475	E4
Saint Clair 120	E6
Saint Clair Springs 300	F3
Saint Elmo 700	B10
Saint Florian 335	C1
Saint Stephens 700	B7
Salem 350	H5
Salitpa 550	C7
Samantha 400	C4
Samson 2,071	F8
Sandy Ridge 300	E6
Sanford 269	F8
Saragossa 200	D3
Saraland 12,288	B9
Sardis 1,438	E6
Sardis 883	D7
Satsuma 5,687	B9
Sawyerville 175	C5
Sayre 700	E3
Scottsboro▲ 14,762	F1
Scranage 150	C4
Scyrene 200	C7
Seale 350	H6
Section 769	G1
Sellers 200	F6
Selma▲ 20,512	E6
Selmont-West Selmont 3,502	E6
Seman 50	F5
Seminole 275	D10
Semmes 200	B9
Sheffield 9,652	C1
Shelby 500	E4
Shiloh 289	C2
Shorter 355	G6
Shorterville 400	H7
Shortleaf 253	C2
Silas 529	B7
Silverhill 616	C9
Silver Run 250	G3
Sims Chapel 232	B8
Sipsey 552	D3
Skipperville 100	G7
Slocomb 2,052	G8
Smiths 21,756	H5
Snead 748	F2
Snowdoun 250	F6
Society Hill 150	H6
Somerville 347	E2
Southside 7,036	F3
Spanish Fort 5,423	C9
Speigner 150	F6
Sprague 140	F6
Spring Garden 100	G3
Spring Valley 600	C1
Springville 2,521	E3
Spruce Pine 300	C2
Standing Rock 300	H4
Stanton 250	E5
Stapleton 975	C9
Steele 1,093	F3
Sterrett 350	F4
Stevenson 1,770	G1
Stewart 450	C5
Stewartville 250	F4
Stockton 500	C9
Stroud 100	H4
Suggsville 400	C7
Sulligent 2,151	B3
Sulphur Springs 150	G1
Sumiton 2,665	D3
Summerdale 655	C10
Summerfield 100	E5
Summit 120	F2
Sumter 150	D4
Sumterville 175	B5
Sunny South 350	C7
Swaim 125	F1
Sweet Water 234	C6
Sycamore 800	F4
Sylacauga 12,616	F4
Sylvania 1,186	G1
Taits Gap 150	F3
Talladega▲ 15,143	F4
Talladega Springs 124	F4
Tallahatta Springs 161	C7
Tallassee 4,934	G5
Tanner 600	E1
Tarrant 7,022	E3
Taylor 1,898	H8
Tensaw 200	C8
Theodore 6,811	B9
Thomaston 383	C6
Thomasville 4,649	C7
Thorsby 1,820	E5
Tibbie 675	B8
Titus 125	F5
Toney 200	E1
Town Creek 1,216	D1
Townley 500	D3
Toxey 152	B7
Trafford 523	E3
Trenton 200	F1
Triana 458	E1
Trinity 1,841	D1
Troy▲ 13,935	G7
Trussville 12,924	E3
Tunnel Springs 200	D7
Tuscaloosa▲ 77,906	C4
Tuscumbia▲ 7,856	C1
Tuskegee▲ 11,846	G6
Tyler 200	E6
Union 227	C5
Union Grove 94	E2
Union Springs▲ 3,670	G6
Uniontown 1,636	D6
Uriah 450	D8
Valhermoso Springs 500	E2
Valley 9,198	H5
Valley Head 611	G1
Vance 500	D4
Vandiver 700	F4
Verbena 500	E5
Vernon▲ 2,143	B3
Vestavia Hills 24,476	E4
Vina 400	B2
Vincent 1,853	F3
Vinegar Bend 200	B8
Vredenburg 327	D7
Wadley 640	G4
Wadsworth 500	E5
Wagarville 550	B8
Waldo 281	F4
Walker Springs 710	C7
Wallace 150	D8
Walnut Grove 710	F2
Ward 100	B6
Warrior 3,169	E3
Waterloo 208	B1
Wattsville 550	F3
Waugh 150	F6
Waverly 184	G5
Weaver 2,619	G3
Webb 1,298	H8
Wedgeworth 100	C5
Wedowee▲ 818	H4
Wellington 180	G3
Weogufka 500	F4
West Blocton 1,372	D4
West Jefferson 344	D3
Weston 384	B2
Westover 500	F4
West Point 295	D2
West Selmont	E6
Wetumpka▲ 5,726	F5
Whatley 800	C7
Wheeler 100	D1
White Hall 1,014	E6
White Plains 350	G3
Whites Chapel 336	F3
Whitfield 175	B6
Wicksburg 400	G8
Wilmer 494	B9
Wilsonville 1,551	E4
Wilton 520	E4
Winfield 4,540	C3
Wing 100	E8
Woodland 192	G4
Woodstock 340	D4
Woodville 761	F1
Wren 200	D2
Wright 180	C1
Yantley 500	B6
Yarbo 150	B7
Yellow Bluff 181	C7
Yellow Pine 350	B8
York 2,854	B5

OTHER FEATURES

Alabama (riv.)	C8
Aliceville (dam)	B4
Anniston Army Depot	F3
Bankhead (lake)	D4
Bartletts Ferry (dam)	H5
Big Canoe (creek)	F3
Big Creek (lake)	B9
Black Warrior (riv.)	C5
Bon Secour (bay)	C10
Buttahatchee (riv.)	B3
Cahaba (riv.)	D5
Cedar (pt.)	B10
Chattahoochee (riv.)	H8
Chattooga (riv.)	H2
Cheaha (mt.)	G4
Choctawhatchee (riv.)	H8
Coffeeville (dam)	B7
Conecuh (riv.)	D8
Coosa (riv.)	F4
Cowikee, North Fork (creek)	H6
Cumberland (plat.)	F1
Dannelly (res.)	D6
Demopolis (dam)	C5
Demopolis (lake)	C5
Elk (riv.)	D1
Escambia (creek)	D8
Escambia (riv.)	D9
Escatawpa (riv.)	B8
Eufaula (Walter F. George Res.) (lake)	H7
Fort Gaines	B10
Fort McClellan Military Reservation 4,128	G3
Fort Morgan	C10
Fort Rucker 6,052	G8
Gainesville (dam)	B5
Goat Rock (dam)	H5
Goat Rock (lake)	H5
Grants Pass (chan.)	B10
Gunter Air Force Base	F6
Guntersville (dam)	F2
Guntersville (lake)	F2
Harding (dam)	H5
Herbes (isl.)	B10
Holt (dam)	D4
Horseshoe Bend Nat'l Mil. Park	G5
Inland (lake)	E3
Jordan (dam)	F5
Jordan (lake)	F5
Lay (dam)	E5
Lewis Smith (dam)	D3
Lewis Smith (lake)	D2
Little (riv.)	G2
Little (riv.)	C8
Locust Fork (riv.)	E3
Logan Martin (lake)	F4
Lookout (mt.)	G2
Martin (dam)	G5
Martin (lake)	G5
Maxwell Air Force Base	F6
Mexico (gulf)	E10
Mississippi (sound)	B10
Mitchell (dam)	E5
Mitchell (lake)	F5
Mobile (bay)	B10
Mobile (pt.)	B10
Mobile (riv.)	C9
Mulberry (creek)	E5
Mulberry Fork (riv.)	E3
Neely Henry (lake)	F3
Oakmulgee (creek)	D5
Oliver (dam)	J5
Paint Rock (riv.)	F1
Patsaliga (creek)	F7
Pea (riv.)	F8
Perdido (bay)	D10
Perdido (riv.)	C9
Pickwick (lake)	B1
Pigeon (creek)	E7
Redstone Arsenal 2,365	E1
Russell Cave Nat'l Mon.	G1
Sand (mt.)	G1
Sandy (creek)	H7
Sepulga (riv.)	E7
Sipsey (riv.)	B4
Sipsey Fork (riv.)	D2
Tallapoosa (riv.)	G4
Tennessee (riv.)	C1
Tennessee-Tombigbee Waterway	B4
Tensaw (riv.)	C9
Thurlow (dam)	G6
Tombigbee (riv.)	B7
Town (creek)	C1
Tuscaloosa (lake)	D4
Tuskegee Institute Nat'l Hist. Site	G6
Walter F. George (dam)	H7
Walter F. George (res.)	H7
Warrior (dam)	C5
Weiss (lake)	G2
West Point (lake)	H4
Wheeler (dam)	D1
Wheeler (lake)	D1
Wilson (dam)	C1
Yates (dam)	G5

▲ County seat.

BELLINGRATH HOME, southwest of Mobile, houses the Bessie Morse Bellingrath collection of antique furniture, porcelain, crystal, rugs, and other works of art. House and surrounding gardens are one of Alabama's prime tourist attractions.

AUTHENTICATED NEWS INTERNATIONAL

BELLINGRATH GARDENS occupy over 60 acres of 800-acre estate. Trees draped with Spanish moss provide a lush background for handsome year-round displays of flowering plants, such as chrysanthemums, azaleas, camelias, and annuals.

AUTHENTICATED NEWS INTERNATIONAL

Largest Centers of Population. Alabama has eight centers of population classified as standard metropolitan statistical areas. These, in order of size, are Birmingham, Mobile, Huntsville, Montgomery, Tuscaloosa, Florence, Anniston, and Gadsden. The five largest have a central city of 50,000 or more inhabitants.

2. The Land

Alabama lies partly in the Gulf Coastal Plain and partly in the Appalachian Highlands. The fall line (line of demarcation between these two regions) curves from Phenix City, on the Alabama-Georgia border, to the northwestern corner of the state. South and west of this line the land is generally below 500 feet (152 meters) in elevation; north and east, above that elevation. The three sections of the Appalachian Highlands projecting into Alabama are the Piedmont Plateau, the Valley and Ridge Province, and the Cumberland Plateau.

Rivers, Lakes, and Coastal Waters. With the exception of the Tennessee River, which flows westward through northern Alabama and then northward to join the Ohio, the rivers of Alabama flow toward the Gulf of Mexico. The major drainage basin is formed by the Mobile River system. The Mobile River itself is formed by the confluence of the Alabama and Tombigbee rivers about 40 miles (64 km) north of Mobile. Both of these large rivers are fed by numerous tributaries. The most important are the Coosa and Tallapoosa rivers, which meet northeast of Montgomery to form the Alabama, and the Black Warrior River, chief tributary of the Tombigbee. The southeastern part of the state is drained by the Chattahoochee, which forms part of the Alabama-Georgia boundary, and by the Choctawhatchee, the Conecuh, and other small rivers and creeks. The Perdido River forms the boundary between Alabama's boot heel and the panhandle of Florida.

Government and private interests have spent millions of dollars to remove obstructions from river courses and build multiple-purpose dams for flood control, navigation, and the production of power. These dams, in turn, have created large lakes with thousands of miles of shoreline attractive to industrial and recreational development.

Perhaps the best known of the dams and lakes are those on the Tennessee River. The earliest of these, Wilson Dam, traces its origin to World War I, when the federal government built nitrate plants for munitions at Muscle Shoals (rapids in the Tennessee River, above Florence) and began construction of the dam. In 1933, when the Tennessee Valley Authority was created, the dam and other properties were transferred to the TVA (see TENNESSEE VALLEY AUTHORITY).

Alabama has about 50 miles (80 km) of coastline on the Gulf of Mexico. The total shoreline—including that of Mobile Bay, other bays and inlets, and offshore islands—is about 600 miles (966 km) long. Dauphin Island is the largest of the offshore islands.

Climate. Since elevations in Alabama are low to moderate, climatic differences largely reflect differences in latitude between the northern and southern extremities of the state. Climate varies gradually from one area to another, with midwinter readings showing more variation than midsummer readings. In July the average tem-

AUTHENTICATED NEWS INTERNATIONAL

BIRMINGHAM CITY HALL faces Woodrow Wilson Park in the business center of Alabama's largest city.

perature throughout the state is about 80° F (27° C). In January average temperatures vary from about 43° F (6° C), at Valley Head in the northeast, to 53° F (12° C) at Mobile in the southeast. Montgomery, in the central part of the state, has a January average of 49° F (9° C).

Alabama enjoys a very long growing season. At Valley Head the frost-free period averages 198 days, and at Mobile, 298 days.

Light snow falls every winter in northern Alabama and occasionally in the far south. In general, rainfall is abundant. The statewide average is 50 inches (127 cm) or more per year. Along the Gulf coast the average exceeds 65 inches (165 cm). Seasonal distribution varies more widely than annual rainfall. In northern Alabama the rainy seasons are winter and spring; along the coast the heaviest rainfall occurs in summer. Throughout the state, however, September, October, and November are the driest months.

Plant Life. It is estimated that when Europeans first arrived in Alabama, about 65 percent of the land was covered with trees—approximately the same percentage as today. The trees most commonly found in Alabama are the pines, of which the shortleaf and the loblolly are the most plentiful. The oak is the most abundant of the hardwoods.

Among the flowering trees are the magnolia and the dogwood. Palmetto groves are found in the south. In several areas pecan trees and tung trees are grown commercially. The seeds of the tung tree, which is native to China, yield an oil that is used chiefly in quick-drying varnishes and paints. Shrubs, mosses, wildflowers, vines, and grasses grow abundantly throughout the state.

Animal Life. Ornithologists have identified more than 300 species of birds in Alabama. Among the game birds are quail, duck, and dove. The state is noted for its fine quail hunting. Animals of the woods include deer, wildcat, bear, opossum, raccoon, red fox and gray fox, mink, beaver, nutria, rabbit, and squirrel.

Alabama abounds in fish of both freshwater and saltwater varieties. Bass, bream, and crappie are popular freshwater game fish. Among fish found in Alabama that spend part of their lives in fresh water and part in salt water are shad, striped bass, and sturgeon. The variety of saltwater fish is virtually endless; most im-

439

Pine seedlings in this nursery will be transplanted to cut-over forest areas to provide pulpwood.

portant commercially are the mullet and red snapper. The great game fish that migrates through coastal waters of Alabama each year is the tarpon. Other seasonal migrants are king mackerel, bluefish, bonita, redfish, dolphin, and pompano.

The shellfish—shrimp, crabs, and oysters—are more important commercially in Alabama than all other kinds of fish combined.

Minerals. Important minerals found in Alabama include limestone, lignite, petroleum, bauxite, salt, fuller's earth, ocher, manganese, mica, brick clay, graphite, marble, iron ore, coal, and dolomite. Some deposits are too small or inaccessible to be of value. Others have contributed materially to the state's industrial growth.

Coal is mined from several basins or fields, including the Warrior basin and the Cahaba field near Birmingham, the Plateau field extending north and northeast from the Warrior, and the Coosa basin in Shelby and St. Clair counties. The Birmingham district is unique in having the three chief components of steel manufacturing—coal, iron ore, and fluxing stone (dolomite and limestone)—all found in close proximity.

Some of the finest marble in the country is produced from the Sylacauga quarries in east central Alabama. The first successful oil well in the state was brought in at Gilbertown, Choctaw County, in 1944. At present there are several hundred producing wells, and crude oil has become a major factor in the economy.

Conservation. Important evidences of conservation in Alabama are the tree farms and pine plantations—established by state and federal agencies, farmers, and paper companies—that

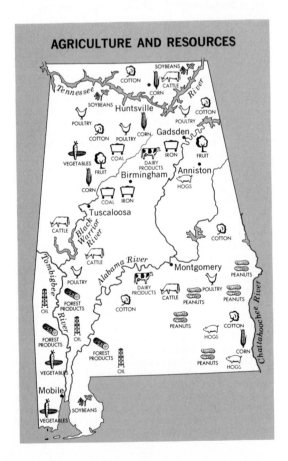

AGRICULTURE AND RESOURCES

reclaim eroded or worn-out croplands and ensure a continuing supply of timber. Conservation and management of water resources and wildlife are functions of both state and federal agencies. Refuges in the state include the Tennessee River, the Choctaw River, the Eufaula National Wildlife Refuge on the Chattahoochee River, and the Oakmulgee Wildlife Management Area located near Centreville.

3. The Economy

Alabama's early industries were chiefly small grain mills, sawmills, textile plants, and ironworks. The economy shifted to agriculture, specifically the raising of cotton, until the cotton fields were devastated by the boll weevil during the first quarter of the 20th century. Since that time Alabama has worked to balance agriculture with industry.

The leading industries in the state are mining and manufacturing, and the farmland once dominated by cotton supports a variety of crops and livestock. The "one-crop" economy began to change in the late 1930s, and manufacturing began to rise. By 1940 livestock and crops other than cotton were an important part of cash farm income. Industry now employs more people than does agriculture.

The economic picture in Alabama is further enhanced by U.S. government installations in a number of locations, particularly in Redstone Arsenal and the National Aeronautics and Space Administration's George C. Marshall Space Flight Center, both located in Huntsville.

Agriculture. Alabama is still a leading cotton producer, but the state's most valuable field crop is soybeans. Other crops include peanuts, corn, wheat, vegetables, and pecans. Most of the agricultural income comes from livestock and livestock products, especially chickens, eggs, beef cattle, hogs, and milk.

PERSONAL INCOME IN ALABAMA

Source	1980[1]	1990[1]	2000[1]
Farms	232	828	1,100
Mining	556	588	596
Construction	1,381	2,680	4,729
Manufacturing	6,182	10,500	13,748
Transportation and public utilities	1,617	3,061	4,741
Wholesale trade	1,357	2,504	4,225
Retail trade	2,155	4,016	6,606
Finance, insurance, and real estate	970	2,047	4,215
Services	3,283	8,948	17,350
Government and government enterprises	5,243	9,907	14,325
Other[3]	92	232	471
Per capita personal income[2]	7,892	15,826	23,460
Per capita income, U.S.[2]	10,183	19,572	29,451

[1]Millions of dollars. [2]Dollars. [3]Agricultural services, forestry, fishing, and other.

Source: U.S. Department of Commerce, Bureau of Economic Analysis.

The Black Belt, which is the heart of the old cotton-plantation system, has become a center of cattle and poultry production. Montgomery, still a great cotton market and has become a major cattle market as well. The land in that section of the state never was particularly well suited to growing cotton, and during the early 1900s the boll weevil so destroyed the cotton crops that farmers were forced to find other sources of agricultural income.

The majority of the agricultural income in Alabama comes from livestock and livestock products. The main products are chickens, eggs, beef cattle, hogs, and milk.

The southeastern part of the state is peanut country. Dothan holds an international peanut festival each autumn.

Truck farming, once localized in the Mobile area, is gaining in importance around all the large centers of population, as is dairying. Special

TVA steam plant on Guntersville Lake, with eight generating units, is one of the world's largest.

TENNESSEE VALLEY AUTHORITY

PAT PEACOCK/FARM AND HOME PHOTOGRAPHS

Cotton, Alabama's major crop, is harvested efficiently by large stripping and picking machines.

products include pecans and watermelons, grown in various parts of the state, and watercress.

Tree farming is another important activity in Alabama. Fast-growing species are harvested within five to seven years and provide a steady source of income for the owners.

In Alabama, as in other states, the average size of farms is increasing, and the number of farms is decreasing. Modern machinery and mechanization have cut the number of workers needed in agriculture. Many of the farmers supplement their farming income with full-time jobs in nearby factories.

Molten iron is charged into an open-hearth furnace to make steel, a major industrial product of Alabama.

UNITED STATES STEEL CORPORATION

Manufacturing. Alabama's early industries were chiefly small grain mills, sawmills, textile plants, and ironworks. The first major impetus to industrialization was the rise of the iron and steel industry in the late 1880's. The next was the installation of electric power facilities, which has proceeded at a rapid pace during the past two decades.

The primary metals industry, centered around Birmingham, ranks first among Alabama's industries in value added by manufacture, chiefly in rolled and finished steel. Since about 1960, industries manufacturing chemicals and chemical products have displaced the textile industry in second place. Anniston, Decatur, Mobile, and Sheffield are leading centers for chemicals. Textile mills tend to be concentrated in the east—at Alexander City, Huntsville, Opelika, Phenix City, and Talladega—but cities elsewhere in the state also have large textile plants.

Food processing is increasing. Communities throughout the state have plants that process meats, dairy products, grains, vegetables, and fruits. Lumber still is produced in quantity, although it has declined in relative importance. At the same time, the other wood-using industries— pulp and paper mills and factories that make paper products—have become more numerous.

Mobile is a major center of pulp and paper production, but its remarkably varied industries include shipbuilding, bauxite reduction, petroleum refining, steel fabricating, and food processing. Gadsden, third-ranking industrial city (after Birmingham and Mobile), has plants that produce steel, tires, and heavy machinery. Decatur, an important center of heavy industry in the Tennessee Valley, produces steel ships and barges and structural and ornamental iron.

Mining. Great reserves of iron ore, coal, and limestone support the steel industry in Alabama. The major mines are found in the Appalachian district, near Anniston, Selma, Coosa, and Warrior. The state is also one of the leading producers of bauxite. Natural gas, white marble, and oil are also found in the state. Other minerals include manganese, greenstone, copper, colomite, and asbestos.

Transportation. The chief transportation centers in Alabama are Birmingham, Montgomery, and Mobile. Railroad freight and passenger service are handled by 4,500 miles (7,240 km) of track, and about 180 airports in the state are served by five national airlines. Alabama's 87,000 miles (140,000 km) of highway and roads include several well-traveled state roads and national interstates.

Mobile is Alabama's only seaport. From the state docks and other docks on the Mobile River are shipped lumber, naval stores, cotton, and a wide variety of manufactured products; incoming vessels bring bauxite, iron ore, and varied commodities from Latin America and from United States ports. Both the federal and the state governments have spent large sums on the development of Mobile harbor and in widening and increasing the navigational length of the rivers for which it serves as the chief shipping outlet.

The dams and locks of the Black Warrior River system make it possible to ship Birmingham's products to Mobile. The Tombigbee River is navigable to Columbus, Miss., and the Alabama River is navigable to the junction of the Coosa and Tallapoosa rivers above Montgomery. The Coosa River is also navigable as far as

ALABAMA

Shrimp boats are moored at Bayou La Batre, on the Gulf coast. Early in the 19th century this fishing town provided a harbor for the famous privateer Jean Laffite.

Alabama's superb river system provides not only recreation—as for the young fishermen pictured above on the Alabama River—but also water for power and irrigation.

(Above) Birmingham's blast furnaces contribute a major share of Alabama's important steel industry. (Below) The Governor's Mansion in Montgomery exemplifies the charm and grace of the state's numerous antebellum mansions.

Wilson Dam, at Muscle Shoals on the Tennessee River, is the TVA's largest hydroelectric installation in Alabama.

Cathedral Caverns, southeast of Huntsville in northeastern Alabama, contains one of the world's largest stalagmite formations.

A beach resort on Dauphin Island, largest of Alabama's offshore islands, situated at the entrance to Mobile Bay.

Bellingrath Gardens, near Mobile, are noted for azaleas and camellias.

Modern port facilities are located in Mobile on the Mobile River north of the downtown city area.

Rome, Ga. In the north, the Tennessee Valley Authority has extended navigation on the Tennessee River as far as Knoxville, Tenn. Thus, the state's three major commercial centers—Birmingham, Mobile, and Montgomery—are well served by water transportation. These cities also have excellent communications by highway, airline, and railroad. Birmingham is a major rail junction.

4. Government and Politics

The present constitution of Alabama, the sixth in the history of the state, was adopted in 1901. It provides for an executive department headed by the governor and including the lieutenant governor, secretary of state, attorney general, auditor, treasurer, commissioner of agriculture, and superintendent of education. The governor appoints the directors of most state government departments. He may succeed himself but may not serve three terms in a row; he cannot be elected or appointed to any state office or to the U. S. Senate while governor or for a year after.

The legislative department consists of a Senate and a House of Representatives. The legislature is required to meet on the first Tuesday in May. A constitutional amendment approved in June 1975 provided for annual, rather than biennial, sessions of the legislature, beginning in 1976. Special sessions may be called by the governor as the need arises.

The judicial department consists of a supreme court with a chief justice and 6 associate justices; the Senate sitting as a court of impeachment; a court of appeals of 3 members; 33 circuit courts; county and juvenile courts; and various courts of limited jurisdiction. All judges, except for some juvenile court judges, are elected.

Public Finance. A state budget system introduced in 1921 requires the governor to submit a detailed budget to the legislature every second year. This budget, covering the two succeeding fiscal years, must be accompanied by recommendations for legislation to put it into effect.

Taxes account for about half the total receipts, and federal government payments for about one fourth. The sales tax; taxes on motor fuel, alcoholic beverages, and tobacco; the graduated income tax; and property levies provide the bulk of tax revenue. Other substantial income producers include licenses and franchises.

Social Services. The state health department is directed and controlled by a committee of 10 physicians (the governor serving as chairman) who elect the state health officer. County health departments are organized along similar lines. A new department of mental health was created by the state legislature in 1965. Public welfare is in the hands of county welfare departments, which are supervised by the state department of public welfare. They administer assistance from federal and state funds to the blind and handicapped, to dependent children, and to aged persons. Administration of the state unemployment insurance system, under the department of industrial relations, is supported by federal funds.

The prison system was reorganized after the abolition of the convict lease system in 1927, and able-bodied convicts now work on road con-

---

GOVERNMENT HIGHLIGHTS

Electoral Vote—9. **Representation in Congress**—U.S. senators, 2; U.S. representatives, 7. **State Legislature**—House of Representatives, 105 members; Senate, 35 members; all 4-year terms. **Governor**—4-year term; he may succeed himself only once. **Voting Qualifications**—Age, 18; residence in state, 1 year; in county, 6 months; in district, 3 months. **Elections**—Primary elections to select candidates, first Tuesday in May of even-numbered years; general and state elections, Tuesday after first Monday in November of even-numbered years.

The state capitol at Montgomery was the scene of the formation of the Confederate States of America in 1861.

struction or in industries at the various prisons. Income from the sale of products made by prisoners goes toward the cost of their maintenance.

Politics. Alabama has traditionally shown allegiance to the Democratic party. In the 1960s Alabama Democrats found themselves far to the right of the national Democratic party. George C. Wallace, a Democrat, elected governor of Alabama in 1962, stood on a firm states' rights platform and pledged "segregation forever." He refused to support Democratic presidential candidate Lyndon B. Johnson in 1964, and for the first time since Reconstruction, Alabama voted for a Republican presidential candidate. From 1986, alternation between the parties became common in gubernatorial elections.

GOVERNORS OF ALABAMA

Governors of Mississippi Territory (including Alabama)		
Winthrop Sargent	Federalist	1798–1801
William C. C. Claiborne	Democrat	1801–1805
Robert Williams	Democrat	1805–1809
David Holmes	Democrat	1809–1817
Alabama Territorial Governor		
William W. Bibb	Democrat	1817–1819
State Governors		
William W. Bibb	Democrat	1819–1820
Thomas Bibb	Democrat	1820–1821
Israel Pickens	Democrat	1821–1825
John Murphy	Democrat	1825–1829
Gabriel Moore	Democrat	1829–1831
Samuel B. Moore	Democrat	1831
John Gayle	Democrat	1831–1835
Clement C. Clay	Democrat	1835–1837
Hugh McVay	Democrat	1837
Arthur P. Bagby	Democrat	1837–1841
Benjamin Fitzpatrick	Democrat	1841–1845
Joshua L. Martin	Democrat	1845–1847
Reuben Chapman	Democrat	1847–1849
Henry W. Collier	Democrat	1849–1853
John A. Winston	Democrat	1853–1857
Andrew B. Moore	Democrat	1857–1861
John G. Shorter	Democrat	1861–1863
Thomas H. Watts	Democrat	1863–1865
Lewis E. Parsons (provisional governor)	Democrat	1865
Robert M. Patton	Republican	1865–1867
Wager Swayne	Military governor	1867–1868
William H. Smith	Republican	1868–1870
Robert B. Lindsay	Democrat	1870–1872
David P. Lewis	Republican	1872–1874
George S. Houston	Democrat	1874–1878
Rufus W. Cobb	Democrat	1878–1882
Edward A. O'Neal	Democrat	1882–1886
Thomas Seay	Democrat	1886–1890
Thomas G. Jones	Democrat	1890–1894
William C. Oates	Democrat	1894–1896
Joseph F. Johnston	Democrat	1896–1900
William J. Samford	Democrat	1900–1901
William D. Jelks	Democrat	1901–1907
Russell McW. Cunningham	Acting governor	1904–1905
Braxton B. Comer	Democrat	1907–1911
Emmett O'Neal	Democrat	1911–1915
Charles Henderson	Democrat	1915–1919
Thomas E. Kilby	Democrat	1919–1923
William W. Brandon	Democrat	1923–1927
Bibb Graves	Democrat	1927–1931
Benjamin M. Miller	Democrat	1931–1935
Bibb Graves	Democrat	1935–1939
Frank M. Dixon	Democrat	1939–1943
Chauncey M. Sparks	Democrat	1943–1947
James E. Folsom	Democrat	1947–1951
Gordon Persons	Democrat	1951–1955
James E. Folsom	Democrat	1955–1959
John Patterson	Democrat	1959–1963
George C. Wallace	Democrat	1963–1967
Lurleen Wallace	Democrat	1967–1968
Albert P. Brewer	Democrat	1968–1971
George C. Wallace	Democrat	1971–1979
Forrest James, Jr.	Democrat	1979–1983
George C. Wallace	Democrat	1983–1987
Guy Hunt	Republican	1987–1993
James E. Folsom, Jr.	Democrat	1993–1995
Fob James, Jr.	Republican	1995–1999
Donald D. Siegelman	Democrat	1999–2003
Robert R. Riley	Republican	2003–

5. Education and Culture

Alabama's public-school system, which maintained separate schools for blacks and whites, underwent a troublesome decade when desegregation was ordered by the U. S. Supreme Court in 1954. The changeover was a difficult one, as it represented a traumatic social eruption in the custom-bound heart of the Deep South, where time-honored styles do not change easily or fast. Within two decades, however, the great majority of Alabama's blacks attended integrated schools.

The low-key cultural atmosphere in Alabama is dominated by music, both classical and folk, against a traditional architectural background that reflects English, Spanish, French Colonial, and Creole influences. Many of the elegant plantation homes built between 1820 and 1850 in the Greek Revival style have been restored, maintained, or copied, to reflect and retain the charm and lifestyle of the antebellum society of the Old South.

Elementary and Secondary Education. The first school in Alabama was opened in 1799 near Mobile. A public-school system was established in 1854. Alabama schools were segregated until 1963 following the 1954 ruling of the U. S. Supreme Court that made segregation unconstitutional. The state's policy of separate public schools was challenged in court in 1956. At this time the voters approved a measure that would end the public-school system and permit the legislature to subsidize private schools if and when the federal government should compel desegregation. In 1958 a U. S. district court approved a law giving local school boards autonomy in pupil placement, and in 1959 the state legislature authorized the use of public funds for private schools. As a result of these measures, schools in Alabama remained segregated until 1963 when, under federal supervision, previously all-white schools enrolled their first black students.

Elementary and secondary education is under the supervision of the state superintendent of education, who is appointed by the state board of education. The nine-member board is elected for four-year terms. State law requires school attendance by all children between the ages of 7 and 15, inclusive.

Higher Education. The largest of the state-supported institutions are the University of Alabama, with its main campus in Tuscaloosa (University), other autonomous campuses in Birmingham and Huntsville, and extension centers in Montgomery, Gadsden, and Dothan; and Auburn University, with its main campus in Auburn and another in Montgomery.

Other public institutions of higher education include Alabama Agricultural and Mechanical University (in Normal), Alabama State University (Montgomery), Jacksonville State University (Jacksonville), Livingston University (Livingston), University of Montevallo (Montevallo), University of North Alabama (Florence), University of South Alabama (Mobile), and Troy State University, with a main campus at Troy.

Privately controlled institutions include Birmingham-Southern College (Birmingham), Huntingdon College (Montgomery), Judson College (Marion), Miles College (Birmingham), Mobile College (Mobile), Oakwood College (Huntsville), Samford University (Birmingham), Spring Hill College (Mobile), Stillman College (Tusca-

loosa), Talladega College (Talladega), and Tuskegee Institute (Tuskegee Institute), founded in 1881 by Booker T. Washington. The state also has several two-year colleges and technological trade schools.

The University of Alabama accepted its first black student, Autherine Lucy, in 1956 at the insistence of the courts. Her enrollment was of short duration, and no other black students enrolled until 1963. Of the two who entered the university that year, one remained to graduate in 1965. Since that time black students have been accepted in all previously all-white Alabama colleges and universities.

Libraries and Museums. Alabama's first major library, the State and Supreme Court Library, was established in Montgomery in 1828. The department of archives and history in Montgomery was established in 1901. Alabama has approximately 180 free public libraries, including municipal, county, and regional libraries. Bookmobiles operate in more than half of the 67 counties. The Birmingham Public Library, the largest in the state, has an art gallery with collections of prints and paintings and owns the Rucker Agee collection of rare maps and atlases. Special libraries with large or notable collections include the Amelia Gayle Gorgas Library at the University of Alabama in Tuscaloosa, one of the largest libraries in the South; and the Lawrence Reynolds Library at the University of Alabama Medical Center in Birmingham, which contains a collection of rare medical books.

The state's leading fine arts museums are the Birmingham Museum of Art, the Fine Arts Museum of the South in Mobile, and the Montgomery Museum of Fine Arts. The George Washington Carver Museum, which is part of the Tuskegee Institute National Historic Site, includes an art gallery with displays of African art and sculpture, paintings by American Negro artists, and dioramas depicting Negro contributions to civilization.

The Anniston Museum of Natural History, specializing in anthropology, features displays of birds and mounted animals in their natural habitats. The University of Alabama maintains two museums of natural history, one on the main campus, devoted chiefly to geology, and the other

The Montgomery Public Library is of modern design.

at Mound State Monument in Moundville, with exhibits of the mound builders' culture and artifacts. Another important natural history museum is maintained at Russell Cave National Monument, an archaeological site first excavated in 1953.

The Edith Nourse Rogers Museum, at the U. S. Women's Army Corps Center, Fort McClellan (near Anniston), is a military museum devoted to the history of the Women's Army Corps. A museum at Horseshoe Bend National Military Park near Dadeville has military weapons and Indian relics.

Other museums include the W. C. Handy Home and Museum in Florence, the birthplace of the composer of the *St. Louis Blues,* one of the most enduringly popular American songs; Burritt Museum in Huntsville, which displays historical items including antique furnishings, clothing, and accessories; the Museum of the City of Mobile, located in a restored 1872 townhouse and featuring documents and artifacts pertaining to the history of Mobile; the Phoenix Fire Museum in Mobile; the Army Aviation Museum at Fort Rucker, which houses an extensive collection of U. S. Army aircraft; and Sturdevant Hall Museum, a restored antebellum mansion in Selma, an outstanding example of neoclassic architecture containing period antiques.

Other Cultural Activities. Amateur musical groups flourished in the 1850's in Mobile, where the Clara Schumann Club was founded in 1894. Folk music is also an important part of the Alabama cultural scene, particularly Negro spirituals and blues. W. C. Handy, the "Father of the Blues," was born in Florence. Birmingham has a

professional symphony orchestra founded in 1933. Mobile, Huntsville, Montgomery, and Muscle Shoals have organizations that bring concert and ballet performances to each of these cities. Both Birmingham and Mobile have permanent opera companies.

Symphony orchestras are established at the University of Alabama and at Huntsville and Mobile. Art festivals are held annually in Birmingham and Tuscaloosa.

Alabama's contributions to the arts include artists Frederick Arthur Bridgman, Kelly Fitzpatrick, Roderick D. MacKenzie, and sculptor Giuseppe Moretti, who lived in Talladega and executed the statue of the god Vulcan overlooking Birmingham. Art festivals are held annually in Birmingham and Tuscaloosa. Alabama writers include Sidney Lanier; Booker T. Washington, the first Negro to gain worldwide literary attention; and Harper Lee, whose novel *To Kill a Mockingbird* earned the author a Pulitzer Prize in 1961.

Communications. Alabama's first newspaper was the *Mobile Sentinel,* which began publication at Fort Stoddert (Mount Vernon) on May 23, 1811. The oldest continuously published newspaper is the *Mobile Register,* founded as the *Gazette* in 1813. More than 20 daily newspapers are published in Alabama. The daily newspapers with the largest circulation are the Birmingham *News* and *Post-Herald;* the *Advertiser* and *Alabama Journal,* both published in Montgomery; and the *Mobile Register* and *Press.*

The state's first licensed radio station, WBRC, began broadcasting in Birmingham in 1925, and the first television stations were opened there in 1949. Alabama began operating one of the nation's first state-owned educational television networks in 1955.

6. Recreation

National Areas. Alabama has four national forests—the William B. Bankhead (formerly the Black Warrior) in the northwest; the Talladega in two sections, one between Tuscaloosa and Montgomery and the other near Talladega and Anniston; the Tuskegee, near Tuskegee; and the Conecuh on the southern border of the state, near Andalusia. Except for the very small Tuskegee National Forest, which is primarily a pine plantation, the national forests provide varied scenic attractions; hunting for turkey, deer, and small game; excellent fishing streams and lakes; and numerous camp and picnic sites.

The National Park Service administers three areas in Alabama. Horseshoe Bend National Military Park near Dadeville preserves the site on the Tallapoosa River where Gen. Andrew Jackson broke the power of the Creek Indian Confederacy on March 27, 1814, opening Alabama and other parts of the region to settlement. Russell Cave National Monument near Bridgeport preserves a large limestone cavern that contains an almost continuous archaeological record of human habitation from at least 6000 B. C. to about 1650 A. D. The Natchez Trace Parkway crosses the northwest corner of Alabama. See also Horseshoe Bend, Battle of; National Forest; National Park; Natchez Trace.

Fish abound in the lakes impounded by TVA dams. Bass and crappie are the most plentiful game fish in these waters.

SPACE ORIENTATION CENTER at the George C. Marshall Space Flight Center shows types of rockets for U.S. research programs.

State Areas. The state maintains a system of about 20 parks, forests, and monuments. The monuments include Mound State Monument near Moundville, Fort Toulouse near Wetumpka, and Fort Mims near Tensaw.

The forested mountain parks in the northern part of the state are notable for gorges, waterfalls, caves, and lookouts that afford sweeping views of the countryside. Cheaha State Park encompasses Cheaha Mountain, highest point in the state. De Soto State Park, on Lookout Mountain, includes De Soto Falls and Little River Canyon. Oak Mountain State Park, south of Birmingham, contains Peavine Falls and much rugged mountain country.

Gulf State Park includes excellent beaches on the Gulf of Mexico as well as freshwater lakes. Fort Morgan State Park, on Mobile Point, provides recreational facilities, although its chief purpose is preservation of Fort Morgan, one of the two historic guardians of the entrance to Mobile Bay; the other is Fort Gaines on Dauphin Island.

Other Points of Interest. Some natural attractions are Cathedral Caverns near Woodville, Natural Bridge near Haleyville, and Dismals Gardens near Hackleburg. Ave Maria Grotto, a shrine on the campus of St. Bernard College, St. Bernard, is a unique man-made attraction. It consists of scores of miniature representations of famous churches and other structures in many parts of the world.

Homes of famous Alabamians, now maintained as shrines, include Ivy Green, the birthplace and early home of Helen Keller in Tuscumbia; Magnolia Grove, home of Richmond Pearson Hobson in Greensboro; and the Gorgas House, home of the Gorgas family, on the main campus of the University of Alabama.

Notable antebellum mansions include Gaineswood near Demopolis and Rosemont near Boligee. Others may be seen in Huntsville, Selma, Eufaula, Greensboro, Mobile, Tuscaloosa, and several other towns and cities. The First White House of the Confederacy in Montgomery is so named because it was the home of Jefferson Davis when Montgomery served as the Confederate capital during the early months of the Civil War.

Attractions in the Mobile area include the magnificent Bellingrath Gardens and Home; the Azalea Trail, some 35 miles (56 km) long; and Oakleigh, the museum headquarters of the Historic Mobile Preservation Society. The U.S.S. *Alabama*, World War II battleship, is permanently moored as a memorial in Mobile Bay. Fairhope, a town on the east side of Mobile Bay, was founded in the late 1890's as a single-tax colony by followers of the economist Henry George (see SINGLE TAX).

The Space Orientation Center on the grounds of the George C. Marshall Space Flight Center at Huntsville attracts many visitors, as do the dams, lakes, and other installations in the Tennessee Valley area.

7. History

No one knows when or how man first came to the area now called Alabama. It is known that Russell Cave in the northeast corner of the state was a site of almost continuous human habitation from at least 6000 B.C. to early colonial times (about 1650 A.D.). This remarkable discovery was made during the years 1956–1958, when workers sponsored by the Smithsonian Institution and the National Geographic Society excavated the floor of the cave, layer by layer. The radiocarbon method of dating was used to check tools, weapons, bones, charcoal, and other remains found at the various levels. Other sites in Alabama, and elsewhere, have been dated earlier than Russell Cave, but few places in the United States have been found with a comparable record of long-continuing habitation.

European Exploration and Tenure. Alabama has a long history of European exploration. The outline of Mobile Bay appears in the Martin Waldseemüller map of 1507, the map that gave America its name. The Spanish explorers Alonso de Piñeda, Pánfilo de Narváez, and Hernando de Soto all explored the region. De Soto, with a well-armed band of soldiers, passed through its valleys in 1540 in search of gold. In October of that year he fought the Choctaw chieftain Tuscaloosa ("Black Warrior") at the chief's village, Mabila. Spaniards on the scene estimated that at least 2,500 Indians were killed.

In 1558, Guido de las Bazares, with three ships, explored the Alabama coast. The next year Spanish colonists under Tristán de Luna established a number of settlements in the Alabama area, but a series of violent storms, dissension, and hunger forced abandonment of the new communities.

The earliest permanent settlement was made by the French, who landed on Dauphin Island in 1701. The next year they founded Fort Louis de la Mobile at Twenty-seven-mile Bluff, north of present Mobile. As part of their great system of forts and trading stations that spread through Canada and Louisiana, the French established Fort Toulouse near the present city of Wetumpka in 1714 and Fort Tombecbé near the confluence of the Tombigbee and Black Warrior rivers in 1736. In 1711, floods and famine caused the colonists at Twenty-seven-Mile Bluff to move their settlement down the river to the permanent location at Mobile, which remained the capital of Louisiana Territory until 1722, when the seat of government was transferred to New Orleans.

Meanwhile, English traders and settlers had begun to move into northern Alabama, and the colony became involved in the series of wars fought between Great Britain and France in the years from 1689 to 1763. When this series of wars was ended by the Treaty of Paris (1763), France ceded present-day Alabama and other territories east of the Mississippi River to Great Britain. During the next 20 years the Mobile area and other parts of southern Alabama were administered as part of the colony of British West Florida.

Acquisition by the United States. Under the treaty (1783) ending the American Revolution, Britain ceded West Florida, along with East Florida, to Spain. The remainder of Alabama, to which Georgia laid claim, passed to the United States. The precise location of the boundary line dividing Georgia and the Floridas caused considerable friction between the United States and Spain. The dispute was settled in 1795 by the Treaty of San Lorenzo, which set the boundary at 31° N, a few miles north of Mobile. In the meantime, Georgia relinquished its claims to the land west of the

Chattahoochee, and in 1798 the Mississippi Territory, embracing northern Alabama and Mississippi, was created. Spain continued to control the Mobile area until the War of 1812, when Gen. James Wilkinson captured the city (April 15, 1813).

At that time the Indians still owned nine-tenths of the land of Alabama, and they feared the advance of white settlement. Tecumseh, the great Shawnee chief, had come south in 1811 to induce the Indians to unite with northern tribes against the white settlers. On Aug. 30, 1813, the Creeks (Red Sticks), led by William Weatherford (Red Eagle) and other chiefs, attacked Fort Mims and killed several hundred men, women, and children. This massacre was avenged by troops under Gen. Andrew Jackson in several battles, of which the most important was the Battle of Horseshoe Bend (March 27, 1814).

Defeat of the Creek Indians in the War of 1812 paved the way for removal of the Creeks and other tribes from Alabama. As a result of this removal, white settlers flooded into the area after the War of 1812.

Territorial Status and Statehood. In 1817 the Mississippi Territory was divided into the state of Mississippi and the Territory of Alabama, and two years later Alabama was admitted to the Union as the 22d state. Settlers cleared land for farms and built towns in the river valleys. Increasingly, farmers specialized in cotton, importing food and draft animals from other states. A plantation economy developed, and the state, especially in the Tennessee Valley and 15 Black Belt counties, prospered. Schools and colleges were established, newspapers were founded, and handsome public

---

PROMINENT PEOPLE IDENTIFIED WITH ALABAMA

Bankhead, John Hollis (1842–1920), U.S. representative and senator for 33 years; his sons, John Hollis Bankhead (1872–1946), U.S. senator (1930–1946), and William Brockman Bankhead (1874–1940), member of the U.S. House of Representatives (1917–1940) and speaker of the House (1936–1940).

Bankhead, Tallulah Brockman (1903–1968), actress, daughter of William Brockman Bankhead.

Bibb, William Wyatt (1781–1820), physician, politician, first territorial and state governor of Alabama.

Black, Hugo La Fayette (1886–1971), U.S. Supreme Court justice from 1937.

Campbell, John Archibald (1811–1889), lawyer, U.S. Supreme Court justice (1853–1861).

Carver, George Washington (1864–1943), agricultural chemist, educator at Tuskegee Institute from 1896.

Cohen, Octavus Roy (1891–1959), writer of detective fiction and stories about African Americans in Birmingham.

Cole, Nat King (1919–1966), born Nathaniel Adams Coles; jazz musician and actor.

Curry, Jabez Lamar Monroe (1825–1903), legislator, diplomat, and educator.

Denny, George Hutcheson (1870–1955), president and chancellor of the University of Alabama (1912–1955).

Evans (Wilson), Augusta Jane (1835–1909), novelist; known especially for the best-seller *St. Elmo* (1866).

Gorgas, Josiah (1818–1883), soldier, educator, president of the University of Alabama, (1878–1879); his wife, Amelia Gayle Gorgas, daughter of John Gayle (governor of Alabama, 1831–1835); their son, William Crawford Gorgas (1854–1920), army officer and sanitation expert.

Handy, William Christopher (1873–1958), composer of *St. Louis Blues* (1914) and other blues songs.

Hill, Luther L. (1862–1946), heart surgeon; his son, Lister Hill (1894–1984), U.S. senator (1938–1969).

Hobson, Richmond Pearson (1870–1937), naval hero of the Spanish-American War.

Keller, Helen Adams (1880–1968), blind and deaf author and lecturer; world famous for work on behalf of those with physical disabilities.

Kemp, (James) Hal (1905–1940), orchestra leader; known for popular recordings.

King, William Rufus DeVane (1786–1853), U.S. senator, minister to France, vice president of the United States.

Louis, Joe (1914–1981), born Joseph Louis Barrow; world heavyweight boxing champion.

McKinley, John (1780–1852), U.S. senator (1826–1831), U.S. Supreme Court justice (1837–1852).

Morgan, John Hunt (1825–1864), Confederate general; famous for cavalry raids.

Morgan, John Tyler (1824–1907), U.S. senator (1877–1907), arbiter in Bering Sea Controversy.

Murphy, Edgar Gardner (1869–1913), clergyman who worked for improved race relations and public education.

Owens, Jesse (1913–1980), track-and-field star, Olympic sprint and jump champion in 1936.

Pratt, Daniel (1799–1873), pioneer industrialist in Alabama, founder of Prattville.

Pugh, James Lawrence (1820–1907), soldier, U.S. representative and senator.

Semmes, Raphael (1809–1877), naval officer, captain of the Confederate raider *Alabama*.

Sibert, William Luther (1860–1935), soldier, engineer, builder of Gatun Locks and Dam of the Panama Canal.

Smith, Holland McTyeire (1882–1967), commander of the Fleet Marine Force in the Pacific (1944–1946).

Strode, Hudson (1892–1976), educator, lecturer, writer of travel books, poet, playwright.

Tutwiler, Julia Strudwick (1841–1916), educator and social reformer, author of Alabama's state song.

Underwood, Oscar Wilder (1862–1929), U.S. representative and senator (1895–1927).

Van de Graaff, Robert Jemison (1901–1967), nuclear physicist and inventor.

Washington, Booker Taliaferro (1856–1915), educator and social reformer, founder of Tuskegee Institute.

Wheeler, Joseph (1836–1906), known as "Fighting Joe"; Army officer, legislator, writer.

Williams, Hank (1923–1953), country singer and writer of popular songs.

Wyeth, John Allan (1845–1922), surgeon and medical educator.

Yancey, William Lowndes (1814–1863), political leader, advocate of states' rights.

Plantation houses reflected the gracious living of the early-19th-century years. Oakleigh, in Mobile, is an example of the classical style for which they were noted.

and private buildings were erected. By 1800 the state had a population of 964,201, of whom 55% were whites and 45% were blacks, mostly slaves.

The Civil War and Reconstruction. Despite the earlier opposition of many Alabamians to the drastic step of secession, the secession movement gained strength after the Republican victory in the presidential election of 1860. In December of that year a special election was held to choose delegates to a secession convention. This convention met at Montgomery on Jan. 7, 1861, and four days later it passed a secession ordinance by a vote of 61 to 39. On Feb. 4, 1861, delegates from seven Southern states met in the capitol at Montgomery to organize the Confederate States of America. Within four days a provisional constitution was adopted. Montgomery remained the capital of the Confederacy until May 1861, when the government moved to Richmond, Va.

The most important military action in Alabama was the Battle of Mobile Bay, on Aug. 5, 1864, in which a Union fleet commanded by Adm. David G. Farragut blockaded the entrance to the bay after successfully engaging the Confederate ram *Tennessee*, commanded by Adm. Franklin Buchanan. The city itself was not captured until the following year, which also witnessed an extensive Union raid in the central part of the state.

In April 1865 Alabama was occupied by Union troops, and in June Lewis E. Parsons was appointed provisional governor by Pres. Andrew Johnson. Parsons ordered an election of delegates to a constitutional convention to meet in Montgomery in September. This convention revoked the ordinance of secession, abolished slavery, and provided for the equality of the freedmen in the rights of person and property, but it restricted the electorate to white males. The state government set up by the new constitution was recognized by the president as soon as the legislature had ratified the 13th Amendment to the U.S. Constitution, and it went into effect in December, Robert M. Patton, a Republican, having been elected governor.

In the following year, however, the legislature refused to ratify the 14th Amendment. Alabama's representatives to the U.S. Congress were denied seats by that body, and in March 1867 the state was placed under military rule as part of the 3d Military District. General John Pope, commander of the district, ordered the election of delegates to a new constitutional convention.

Military rule ended in 1868, when Congress approved the constitution drawn up at the convention and the new state legislature ratified the 14th Amendment. Radical elements controlled the state government until 1870, when the Democrats succeeded in electing a governor and a majority in the House of Representatives, but in 1872 the radicals (as the Republicans were called in Alabama) again secured control of the state government. The carpetbag government issued large numbers of bonds for railway construction, increasing the debt to $32 million and bankrupting the state. With the election of George S. Houston, a Democrat, as governor in 1874, the Reconstruction period came to an end in Alabama.

State Reforms. A new constitution was drawn up in 1875; debt was reorganized, placing state finances on a sound basis. The Democratic party continued to win state elections by large majorities on a program of economy, efficiency, encouragement of industry, and white supremacy. In 1880 the first blast furnace began operating in Birmingham, and in 1888 the first steel in the state was rolled at Bessemer. But times were hard for the farmers, and conditions grew worse in the 1890s. The share-cropping system and the growing indebtedness of planters to merchants and banks made farming increasingly precarious. Accordingly, some reform groups—the Farmers' Alliance, Populists, and Jeffersonian Democrats—unsuccessfully backed Reuben F. Kolb, state commissioner of agriculture, for the governorship in 1890, 1892, and 1894. Later, however, many reform demands became law, and charges of corruption in the hard-fought campaigns and close elections led to adoption of a new constitution in 1901.

The Struggle for Civil Rights. Beginning in the mid-1950s, civil rights groups frequently tested federal antidiscrimination legislation and court decisions in Alabama. On several occasions in the early 1960s, racial tensions generated violence in various cities and towns. These events were brought to a climax with the inauguration of George C. Wallace as governor in January 1963.

Wallace, a professed segregationist and champion of state's rights, was a major figure in Alabama for nearly two decades, during which he also became prominent in national politics. He sought unsuccessfully to prevent racial integration of the University of Alabama and succeeded temporarily in stopping the integration of the state's public schools. Then the Alabama National Guard was federalized by order of Pres. John F. Kennedy, and U.S. Army troops were sent into the state to curb extremist segregationist elements. In March 1965 a five-day civil rights march from Selma to the state capitol in Montgomery, led by Dr. Martin Luther King, Jr., drew 25,000 demonstrators.

Alabama's universities and public schools gradually began desegregation efforts under a series of federal court orders, and the U.S. Civil Rights Act of 1964 brought a measure of desegregation in public accommodations. Congressional redistricting and the Voting Rights Act of 1965 increased the representation of African American citizens by ensuring and increasing their votes. Over the years Governor Wallace, who was seriously wounded in an assassination attempt in 1972 while campaigning for the Democratic presidential nomination, modified his views on segregation, even appointing many African Americans to state offices. That Wallace won his fourth term as governor (1983–1987) on a platform of working to better the lives of "all" of his state's residents was a significant indicator of the easing of tensions in the late 20th century.

CHARLES GRAYSON SUMMERSELL*
University of Alabama

Bibliography

Abernathy, Thomas P., *The Formative Years in Alabama, 1815–1828,* rev. ed. (Univ. of Ala. Press 1965).

Clayton, Lawrence A., and R. Reid Badger, *Alabama and the Borderlands: From Prehistory to Statehood* (Univ. of Ala. Press 1985).

Doster, James, and David C. Weaver, *Tenn-Tom Country: The Upper Tombigbee Valley* (Univ. of Ala. Press 1987).

Feldman, Lynne B., *A Sense of Place: Birmingham's Black Middle-Class Community, 1890–1930* (Univ. of Ala. Press 1999).

Gray, Daniel S., and J. Barton Starr, *Alabama: A Place, a People, a Point of View* (Kendall-Hunt 1977).

Hackney, Sheldon, *Populism to Progressivism in Alabama* (Princeton Univ. Press 1969).

HISTORICAL HIGHLIGHTS

1519 Spanish explorer Alonso Alvarez de Piñeda becomes first European to enter Mobile Bay.

1540 Hernando de Soto explores river valley in Alabama in search of gold.

1559 Spaniard Tristán de Luna, seeking gold, starts temporary settlement on Mobile Bay.

1702 French settlers led by Pierre Le Moyne, sieur d'Iberville, found Fort Louis de la Mobile on Mobile River.

1763 Treaty of Paris ends French and Indian War; France cedes land including present-day Alabama to Great Britain.

1783 Britain cedes much of Alabama area to United States and the Mobile region to Spain.

1798 Mississippi Territory, including present-day Alabama and Mississippi, created.

1802 Cotton gin invented and built near Montgomery.

1811 *Mobile Sentinel* published; first newspaper in what is now Alabama.

1813 United States seizes Mobile region from Spain (April 15); Creeks attack Fort Mims (August 30).

1814 Gen. Andrew Jackson defeats Creeks at the Battle of Horseshoe Bend; land surrendered to the United States.

1817 Alabama Territory created when Mississippi achieves statehood.

1819 Alabama admitted to Union as 22nd state (December 14).

1831 State's first railroad constructed, near the Tennessee River.

1846 Montgomery designated state capital.

1861 Alabama secedes from the Union (January 11); Montgomery serves as first capital of the Confederate States of America (February–May).

1868 Alabama readmitted to Union (June 25).

1881 Booker T. Washington establishes the Tuskegee Normal and Industrial Institute.

1933 Congress creates the Tennessee Valley Authority.

1954 Martin Luther King, Jr., becomes pastor of Dexter Avenue Baptist Church in Montgomery.

1955 Arrest of Rosa Parks for refusing to yield her seat on a public bus to a white man launches the Montgomery bus boycott, bringing Martin Luther King, Jr., to national prominence.

1956 U.S. Supreme Court declares state's bus segregation law unconstitutional. Autherine J. Lucy becomes first black student to enroll at the University of Alabama; she is barred from the campus within days and later expelled.

1961 Redstone rocket, developed in Huntsville, boosts first astronaut into outer space.

1963 George C. Wallace inaugurated as governor for the first of four terms.

1965 Martin Luther King, Jr., leads 25,000 followers from Selma to Montgomery to protest voter discrimination; the march leads to the passage of the Voting Rights Act of 1965.

1972 Campaigning for the U.S. presidency, Gov. George C. Wallace is seriously wounded in an assassination attempt in Laurel, Md.

1985 Tennessee-Tombigbee Waterway opens, linking Mobile with inland ports in other states.

1986 Guy Hunt becomes Alabama's first Republican governor since Reconstruction.

1993 Gov. Hunt is removed from office and indicted on charges of conspiracy and theft of campaign contributions.

1999 Alabama voters reject a state lottery proposal that was to have provided funds for improving education.

Hamilton, Virginia Van der Veer, *Alabama: A Bicentennial History* (Norton 1977).

Hamilton, Virginia Van der Veer, *Alabama: A History* (Norton 1984).

Hamilton, Virginia Van der Veer, and Jacqueline A. Matte, *Seeing Historic Alabama: Fifteen Guided Tours*, new ed. (Univ. of Ala. Press 1996).

Jackson, Harvey H., III, *Rivers of History: Life on the Coosa, Tallapoosa, Cahaba, and Alabama* (Univ. of Ala. Press 1995).

Jordan, Weymouth T., *Ante-Bellum Alabama: Town and Country* (Univ. of Ala. Press 1986).

Lofton, J. Mack, Jr., *Voices from Alabama: A Twentieth-Century Mosaic* (Univ. of Ala. Press 1993).

Martin, David L., *Alabama's State and Local Governments*, 2d ed. (Univ. of Ala. Press 1985).

McMillan, Malcolm C., *Constitutional Development in Alabama, 1798—1901* (1955; reprint, Reprint Co. 1978).

Owen, Thomas W., *History of Alabama and Dictionary of Alabama Biography*, 4 vols. (1921; reprint, Reprint Co. 1978).

Peirce, Neal R., *The Deep South States of America: People, Politics, and Power* (Norton 1974).

Thomas, M. M., *Riveting and Rationing in Dixie: Alabama Women and the Second World War* (Univ. of Ala. Press 1987).

Walker, Alyce B., and Harry Hansen, eds., *Alabama: A Guide to the Deep South* (Hastings 1975).

Wiener, Jonathan M., *Social Origins of the New South: Alabama, 1860—1885* (La. State Univ. Press 1978).

ALABAMA, University of, al-ə-bam′ə, a public, coeducational institution supported by the state of Alabama. Its main campus is in Tuscaloosa. This campus, along with those at Birmingham and Huntsville, is degree granting and autonomous. Extension centers are located in Gadsden, Dothan, and Montgomery.

Major university divisions include colleges of arts and sciences, commerce and business administration, education, and engineering; schools of communications, dentistry, home economics, law, medicine, nursing, public health, optometry, and social services; the New College; community health services; and a graduate school of library service. In total, more than 300 degree programs are offered.

In 1819 the U.S. Congress gave 46,000 acres (18,600 ha) of federal land in Alabama for a university, which was chartered in 1820 and opened to students in 1831. Most of the buildings were razed in the Civil War, and classes did not resume until 1869. The Birmingham campus was established as an extension center in 1936 and as a university in 1966, becoming autonomous in 1970; the Huntsville campus was founded in 1950 and became autonomous in 1969. Newer buildings include a continuing education and conference facility and an $8-million fine arts complex.

ALABAMA CLAIMS, al-ə-bam′ə, claims for indemnity made by the United States against Britain for damage to American shipping during the American Civil War. The damage was inflicted by the *Alabama* and ten other ships that were built or outfitted in British ports and sailed from them in the interest or service of the Confederate States. The claims were based on the alleged failure of Britain to observe the obligations imposed by international law on neutral nations.

The *Alabama*, built at Birkenhead, England, and equipped in the Azores with guns from two British vessels, captured between 65 and 70 United States ships, most of which it destroyed. Entering the Confederate service in 1862 under Capt. Raphael Semmes, the ship did not reach the end of its career until June 19, 1864, when it was sunk outside Cherbourg, France, by the U.S.S. *Kearsarge* under Capt. John Winslow.

The *Florida*, a companion ship also built at Birkenhead, cleared from there for the Mediterranean on March 22, 1862, but went instead to the Bahamas, where it took aboard guns and ammunition. Later, running the blockade, the ship entered Mobile Bay and lay there until 1863, when it escaped. After cruising for 20 months and destroying many vessels, the *Florida* was sunk by the U.S.S. *Wachusett* off Salvador, Brazil.

The *Shenandoah*, a British ship, was taken over by the Confederacy at Funchal, Madeira, in October 1864 and went to Melbourne, Australia, where it coaled, made repairs, and recruited men. It then proceeded to the Arctic regions, where it destroyed a number of United States whaling ships. On Nov. 6, 1865, the ship docked at Liverpool, surrendered to the British government, and was turned over to the United States.

During the war Charles F. Adams, minister to Britain, and other officials of the United States repeatedly protested to the British government against its failure to halt the building of the ships and against its other alleged violations of the neutrality laws. After the war, efforts to obtain reparations resulted in the Treaty of Washington (1871). A board of arbitrators, one each appointed by the United States, Britain, Italy, Switzerland, and Brazil, met at Geneva, Switzerland, on Dec. 15, 1871. On Sept. 14, 1872, the board awarded the United States $15,500,000 in gold for direct damages inflicted by the *Alabama* and two other Confederate vessels.

ALABAMA RIVER, al-ə-bam′ə, a stream in Alabama formed by the union of the Tallapoosa and Coosa rivers about 10 miles (16 km) northeast of Montgomery. Navigable throughout its course of 315 miles (507 km), it winds west to Selma and then southward. Its chief tributary, the Cahaba, rises near Birmingham and flows south into the Alabama about 17 miles (27 km) below Selma.

The Alabama River drains about 22,600 square miles (58,534 sq km). It joins the Tombigbee River 44 miles (77 km) above Mobile, to form the Mobile and Tensaw rivers.

ALABASTER, al′ə-bas-tər, a compact, fine-grained variety of gypsum, the most common sulfate mineral. (See also GYPSUM.) Chemically alabaster is hydrous (water-containing) calcium sulfate. Because of its white or delicately shaded color, it has long been used ornamentally. Many museums contain Roman vases and statuettes that were carved from this slightly translucent material, which resembles marble but is much softer.

Deposited from seawater or saline lakes by evaporation, gypsum has formed beds in the strata of most geologic periods but particularly in those of the Permian, which ended about 230 million years ago. The beds frequently are found underlying beds of rock salt. While gypsum is worldwide in occurrence, the alabaster variety is less common. The deposits occurring in Tuscany, Italy, are particularly notable. Other famous deposits occur in Derbyshire, England. In the United States, most alabaster deposits are found in Colorado.

The name *Oriental alabaster* is given to a variety of calcite also known as onyx marble. (See CALCITE.) It is harder than true alabaster and is used as a decorative building material.

Composition (true alabaster): $CaSO_4 \cdot H_2O$; hardness, 1.5 to 2.0; specific gravity, 2.3; crystal system, monoclinic.

D. VINCENT MANSON
American Museum of Natural History

ALACOQUE, á-lá-kôk', **Saint Margaret Mary** (1647–1690), French nun, who initiated public devotion to the Sacred Heart of Jesus. Christened *Marguerite Marie* at her birth in Lauthecour, France, on July 22, 1647, she joined the Visitation order at Paray-le-Monial in 1671 and became noted for her piety. She revealed to her confessor, Father Claude de la Colombière, that Christ had appeared to her in a vision urging special honor to His Sacred Heart on the first Friday of each month and on the feast of the Sacred Heart. Devotion to the Sacred Heart had been practiced since the 11th century, and St. Jean Eudes (1601–1680) had incorporated it in the liturgy. After Margaret Mary's revelations it became widespread, and Pope Pius IX raised the feast to major rank in 1856. Margaret Mary died at Paray-le-Monial on Oct. 17, 1690, and was canonized in 1920. Her feast day is October 17.

ALADDIN, OR THE WONDERFUL LAMP, ə-lad'-ən, is one of the stories in *The Arabian Nights' Entertainments.* Aladdin, the son of a poor widow, comes into possession of a magic ring and lamp, and thus becomes the master of the powerful jinns who are the slaves of the lamp and ring. With their aid he amasses great wealth and is made sultan. The magic lamp occurs in the folklore of nearly all Europe as well as that of India and China. See also ARABIAN NIGHTS.

ALAGOAS, ä-lə-go'əs, a small state of northeastern Brazil. It is bounded on the east by the Atlantic Ocean, on the north and west by the state of Pernambuco, and on the south by the São Francisco River, which separates Alagoas from the states of Bahia and Sergipe. The area is 10,676 square miles (27,650 sq km). Maceió is the state's capital, largest city, and principal seaport.

Alagoas is largely agricultural, producing sugarcane, cotton, rice, fruit, and tobacco. Part of it lies within the "drought polygon" of northeastern Brazil—an area of irregular and often deficient rainfall. Paulo Afonso Falls, where the São Francisco River drops 275 feet (84 meters), is the site of a major hydroelectric project.

When the Portuguese divided Brazil into *capitanias* or colonial grants in 1532, Alagoas formed part of the *capitania* of Pernambuco. During the Dutch occupation of northeastern Brazil (1630–1654), escaped black slaves from the Pernambuco sugar plantations founded the republic of Palmares in the interior of Alagoas. They preserved their independence from the Dutch and Portuguese until 1697. Alagoas separated from Pernambuco in 1817 and became a province of the independent empire of Brazil in 1823. It has been a state since the federal republic was established in 1889. Population: 2,633,251 (1996 census).

ALAIN-FOURNIER (1886–1914), á-laN' foor-nyá', was a French novelist of the pre–World War I period. His real name was *Henri Alain Fournier.* He was born in Chapelle-d'Angillon, France, on Oct. 3, 1886, and died in action early in World War I at Bois St. Remy on Sept. 22, 1914. His one complete work was the influential novel *Le grand Meaulnes* (1913; Eng. tr., *The Wanderer,* 1928), which blends a child's world of dream and reality. His posthumously published *Miracles* (1924) contains poems, essays, and a fragment of a novel, *Colombe Blanchet.* His *Correspondance* (1926–28), letters written from 1905 to 1914, reveals the evolution of *Le grand Meaulnes.*

ALAIS. See ALÈS.

ALAJUELA, ä-lä-hwä'lä, a city in Costa Rica and the capital of Alajuela province. It is on the Pan American Highway, 12 miles (19 km) northwest of San José. Because it is the westernmost city on Costa Rica's central plateau, it is a trading center for both the surrounding highlands and the adjacent lowlands. Large quantities of coffee, sugarcane, lumber, and cattle are marketed in the city. Alajuela is also a summer resort. It has a cathedral and a scientific research institute. Population: 178,484 (1997 est.).

ALAMÁN, ä-lä-män', **Lucas** (1792–1853), Mexican public official and historian. He was born in Guanajuato, Mexico, on Oct. 18, 1792. He went to Europe in 1814 and later served briefly as a Mexican deputy in the Spanish Cortes (parliament). Mexico was independent when Alamán returned in 1822, and for the next 30 years he was the national spokesman for Conservative interests. He was foreign minister in the government of Guadalupe Victoria (1824–1829) and then the powerful chief minister of Anastasio Bustamante (1829–1832). An opponent of the United States, Alamán contributed significantly to the bad relations between the countries during this period. He was instrumental in returning Antonio López de Santa Anna to power in 1853 and headed Santa Anna's cabinet. Before his ambitious economic development program could be instituted, however, Alamán died, on June 2, 1853. His historical works included *Disertaciones sobre la historia de la república mejicana,* 3 vols. (1844–49) and *Historia de Méjico . . .,* 5 vols. (1848–52).

ALAMANNI, al-ə-man'ī, a confederacy of several German tribes which, at the beginning of the 3d century A.D., came into conflict with the Roman imperial troops. The name is also spelled *Alemanni.* Caracalla first fought against them in 211, but did not conquer them; Severus was likewise unsuccessful. About 250 they began to move westward across the Rhine, and in 255 they overran Gaul along with the Franks. In 259 a body of the Alamanni was defeated in Italy at Milan, and in the following year they were driven out of Gaul by Postumus.

Notwithstanding their numerous defeats by Roman troops, the Alamanni continued their incursions. In the 4th century they crossed the Rhine and ravaged Gaul, but were severely defeated by the Emperor Julian and driven back. Subsequently they occupied territory on both sides of the Rhine. In 496 the Frankish leader Clovis broke their power and deprived them of a large portion of their possessions. Part of their territory was latterly formed into a duchy called *Alamannia* or *Swabia.* The latter derived from *Suevi,* the name that they gave themselves.

ALAMEDA, al-ə-mē'də, is a residential city in California, occupying two islands and part of a peninsula, on the east side of San Francisco Bay. It lies southwest of Oakland, across a narrow estuary that forms a deepwater harbor shared by the two cities. Bridges and tunnels connect Alameda, by way of Oakland, with other neighboring cities.

The main island—about 6 miles (9.7 km) long and 1.5 miles (2.4 km) wide—is largely residential, though industrial plants and many ship-service enterprises occupy the estuary shores, and the westernmost third of the island is the site of the Alameda Naval Air Station, one of the largest United States carrier bases. This island, originally a peninsula, was created about 1900, when a canal was cut from San Francisco Bay to San Leandro Bay to remove silt by tidal action.

The smaller island, situated in the estuary and known as Government Island, is a United States Coast Guard base. The southern part of the city occupies the tip of a peninsula, which is shared with Oakland and the Metropolitan Oakland International Airport. This part of Alameda, called Bay Farm Island, has been enlarged by filling operations to provide sites for homes and for commercial and educational areas.

Alameda long has been a recreational center. The estuary and San Leandro Bay are used for boating and fishing. A state beach park and municipal beaches are situated on San Francisco Bay. Alameda was incorporated as a city in 1854. It has a mayor and council form of government. Population: 72,259.

CARL W. HAMILTON, *Alameda Free Library*

ALAMEIN, El, al-ə-mān', a railway station 60 miles west of Alexandria, Egypt, near the coast of the Mediterranean Sea. Its name was given to two battles in World War II, fought on a defensive line established by the British Eighth Army south from El Alamein into the desert. In the first battle, in July 1942, the German-Italian army of Field Marshal Erwin Rommel was halted in its drive to the east. In the second, one of the decisive encounters of the war, the Eighth Army, commanded by Lt. Gen. Bernard L. Montgomery, attacking from October 23 to November 5, 1942, drove the Germans and Italians back into Libya. This drive began the offensive that, in conjunction with the Allied landings in Algeria and Morocco, cleared North Africa of German and Italian troops. See also WORLD WAR II—*Mediterranean Operations*.

ALAMO, al'ə-mō, a mission-fortress in San Antonio, Texas. Within its walls, during the Texas Revolution of 1836, a band of Texans made a heroic resistance against an overwhelming Mexican army. Known as the "Cradle of Texas Liberty," the Alamo has become a symbol of steadfast courage and sacrifice for honor.

The Alamo was founded originally in 1718 as the Franciscan mission of San Antonio de Valero. It was converted into a fort and military barracks after 1793. Its name was changed to "Alamo" either because a military company from Alamo del Parras, Coahuila State, once was stationed there or because of the cottonwood (*álamo*) trees that grew in the environs. At the time of the famous battle the site consisted of a courtyard enclosed by stone walls.

The Siege. The Alamo served as Mexican military headquarters in Texas when the revolution broke out against the rising dictatorship of Gen. Antonio López de Santa Anna. A force of Texans captured and occupied the fort in December 1835. When news came the next month of an impending invasion by a strong army under Santa Anna, Gen. Sam Houston ordered the Alamo abandoned and destroyed. Instead, the garrison chose to defend it.

The commanding officers of the fort were Colonels William Barret Travis and James Bowie. Incapacitated by illness, Bowie relinquished full command to the 26-year-old Travis early in the siege. David Crockett, recently arrived from Tennessee, was one of the well-known defenders, as was James Butler Bonham of South Carolina.

The tone for the battle was set early. The vanguard of Santa Anna's army entered San Antonio on Feb. 23, 1836, and the general demanded the immediate surrender of the Alamo. Travis answered with a cannon shot. The Mexican then ordered the red flag of "no quarter" hoisted on the tower of San Fernando Cathedral.

The next day Travis dispatched couriers to other parts of Texas, carrying ringing appeals

THE ALAMO as it appeared at the time of the siege and battle in 1836 is shown in this drawing of the overall mission. The shrine existing today is the small structure at the right (containing powder magazine).

ADAPTED FROM "A TIME TO STAND," BY WALTER LORD (HARPER & ROW)

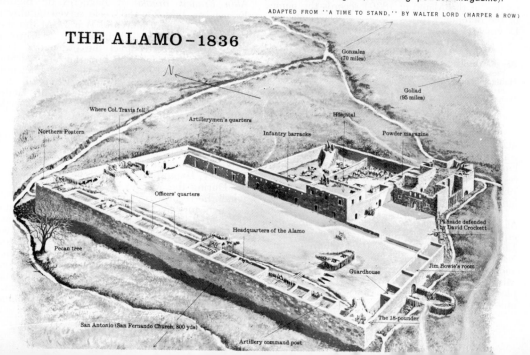

THE ALAMO - 1836

Gonzales (70 miles)

Goliad (95 miles)

Where Col. Travis fell

Artillerymen's quarters

Hospital

Powder magazine

Northern Postern

Infantry barracks

Officers' quarters

Palisade defended by David Crockett

Headquarters of the Alamo

Jim Bowie's room

Pecan tree

Guardhouse

The 18-pounder

San Antonio (San Fernando Church, 800 yds)

Artillery command post

for aid. Only 32 men made their way through enemy lines to reach the besieged Texans on March 1. The new arrivals brought the fighting force within the Alamo to 184 men. Meanwhile, Mexican troops continued to arrive, reaching a total estimated at 6,000.

A dramatic moment was reached on the evening of March 5 when Travis, realizing that the garrison was doomed, paraded his men in single file before him and described their plight. According to a popular account, he drew a line on the ground with his sword, challenging those who wished to remain to cross the line. All but one did so.

The Final Attack. Preparations for the final assault were completed by early dawn of Sunday, March 6. In near-freezing temperature, Santa Anna gave the order to attack. As regimental bands played a Moorish march called the *Degüello* (signifying "no quarter"), troops bearing scaling ladders and muskets assailed the fort from four sides. Although they suffered appalling losses, they finally carried the walls and overcame the desperate defenders in hand-to-hand fighting in the courtyard and in the buildings.

The 13-day siege ended with the deaths of all 183 defenders. Only about 15 persons, three of them Americans (a woman, her child, and a servant), were spared. The bodies of the fallen Texans were burned. The Mexicans suffered about 1,550 casualties; their dead were buried in the cemetery.

The Battle of the Alamo provided other Texans with precious time to rally their defenses. "Remember the Alamo" was the battle cry of Houston's forces when they decisively defeated Santa Anna's army at San Jacinto six weeks later.

Historic Shrine. Since the battle the Alamo has been claimed at various times by the state of Texas, the Roman Catholic Church, the Confederate States of America, and the U.S. government. Under a Texas legislative resolution of 1905 the Alamo was given to the Daughters of the Republic of Texas, which has maintained it as a historic site and museum. A cenotaph on Alamo Plaza fronting the chapel (the only remaining section of the Alamo of 1836) records the names of the defenders.

DAVID M. VIGNESS, *Texas Technological College*

Bibliography

Baugh, Virgil E., *Rendezvous at the Alamo* (Univ. of Neb. Press 1985).
Habig, Marian A., *The Alamo Mission* (Franciscan Herald Press 1977).
Huneycutt, C. D., *The Alamo: An In-Depth Study of the Battle* (Gold Star Press 1986).
Lord, Walter, *A Time to Stand* (1961; reprint, Univ. of Neb. Press 1978).

ALAMO HEIGHTS, al′ə-mō, a city located in south-central Texas, in Bexar county. It is 5 miles (8 km) northeast of San Antonio, of which it is a residential suburb. The city was incorporated in 1926. Government is by mayor and council. Population: 7,319.

ALAMOGORDO, al-ə-mə-gôr′dō, is a city in southern New Mexico, 85 miles by road northeast of El Paso, Tex. It is the seat of Otero County. Near Alamogordo are Holloman Air Force Base and missile development center and White Sands Missile Range. The first atomic bomb was exploded on the range at Trinity Site, about 60 miles northwest of the city, on July 16, 1945.

The city is a trading center and resort in a scenic area. To the southwest lies White Sands National Monument, a gypsum desert of shifting sand dunes that rise as high as 40 feet (12 meters). To the east is a large tract of Lincoln National Forest. Alamogordo was settled in 1889. It adopted the city manager form of government in 1950. Population: 35,582.

ALAMOSA, al-ə-mō′sə, a city located in southern Colorado, and the seat of Alamosa county. It is situated on the Rio Grande, 120 miles (190 km) southwest of Pueblo, Colo., at an altitude of 7,544 feet (2,299 meters). It is the commercial center of the San Luis Valley. Adams State College is in Alamosa. The city was incorporated in 1878 and adopted city manager government in 1952. Population: 7,960.

ALAN OF LILLE (c. 1128–1212), al′ən, lēl, was a French scholastic theologian and poet, often called *Doctor Universalis* for the breadth of his learning. His name is sometimes given in its Latin form, *Alanus de Insulis;* its French form is *Alain de Lille,* Lille being the town of his birth. He had great success as a teacher before retiring to the Cistercian abbey at Cîteaux, where he died.

As a theologian, Alan sought rational proofs for the "preambles of faith"—that is, truths paving the way to faith—and developed something like a geometrical method in philosophy. He was also concerned with heresies such as the Albigensian, and wrote works defending Catholicism against them. His other writings include two ethical poems, *Anticlaudianus* and *De planctu naturae (The Complaint of Nature),* both translated into English. His works show the influence of Neoplatonic thought.

ALANBROOKE, al′ən-brŏŏk, **1st Viscount** (1883–1963), British field marshal, who was the British army's outstanding staff officer in World War II.

A man behind the scenes, he was a military intellectual whose sober professionalism was a corrective to the sometimes wayward genius of Winston Churchill, especially when the prime minister's strategic ideas ran riot. He was born *Alan Francis Brooke* at Bagnères de Bigorre, France, on July 23, 1883. He served notably in the Royal Artillery in World War I. At the start of World War II he led the British 2d Corps in France and helped direct the evacuation from Dunkirk. As chief of the Imperial General Staff in London from 1941 to 1946, he was chief military adviser to Prime Minister Churchill and, with Gen. George C. Marshall of the United States, was a joint architect of the Anglo-American strategy that defeated Germany in the West.

Alanbrooke was made a field marshal in 1944 and was created *1st Viscount Alanbrooke of Brookeborough* in 1946. He died at Hartley Wintney, Hampshire, England, on June 17, 1963.

During the war he kept a personal diary in which he recorded his private thoughts. In 1957 a war history by Sir Arthur Bryant (*The Turn of the Tide*), based on this diary, caused a sensation by its intimate revelations of what it was like to work closely with Churchill. The tone was one of exasperated admiration. The human portrait of the prime minister shocked some readers; to others it was endearingly convincing.

FRED MAJDALANY
Author of "The Battle of El Alamein"

ÅLAND ISLANDS, ō'lånd, in Finland, a group of about 6,500 islands in the Baltic Sea at the entrance to the Gulf of Bothnia between Finland and Sweden. Åland is the Swedish name for the islands; the Finnish name is *Ahvenanmaa*. About 80 islands in the archipelago are inhabited. The group has an area of approximately 580 square miles and forms a province of Finland. The capital is Mariehamn, a port on the largest island, which is called Åland. Residents of the islands are almost entirely Swedish-speaking. Fishing and cattle raising are the chief industries, but the tourist trade is increasing.

The islands were colonized by Swedes in the 1100s and remained almost continuously under Swedish control until 1809, when Sweden surrendered Finland to Russia. After Finland became independent in 1917, a pro-Swedish secessionist movement in the islands led to a grant of internal autonomy in 1920, but Finland refused to allow the islands to secede. The resulting dispute between Finland and Sweden was settled in 1921 by the League of Nations, which confirmed Finnish sovereignty but guaranteed special rights to the islanders. Population: 25,008 (1993 est.).

ALANI, ə-lā'nī, one of the warlike tribes that migrated from Asia westward at the time of the decline of the Roman empire. The earliest historical record places them east of the Caucasus Mountains, where Pompey fought against them. From this center the Alani (or *Alans*) spread over the south of modern Russia to the confines of the Roman empire. They were at war with Rome in the time of Hadrian (reigned 117–138 A.D.), and were defeated. Marcus Aurelius (reigned 161–180) kept them out of the empire with difficulty, and Marcus Claudius Tacitus concluded a treaty with them in 275.

A century later, those on the banks of the lower Danube were conquered by the Huns, after which most of the Alani joined the Huns' ravaging expeditions. They accompanied Radagaisus (Radagais) on his march into Italy in 405. After his defeat, they settled on the Rhine and, about 411, moved to what is now Portugal, where they unsuccessfully fought the Visigoths. Soon they were absorbed by the Vandals and vanished from history as a distinct group.

ALAPAYEVSK, ə-lə-pī'əfsk, a city in Russia, in Sverdlovsk oblast, in the eastern foothills of the Ural Mountains. Situated amid pine and birch forests on the Neva River, Alapayevsk is the center of a lumbering and mining district. It has one of the oldest iron and steel works in the Urals, and it manufactures machine tools and wood products. The city is a railroad junction, linked with nearby iron ore and asbestos mines. The composer Peter Ilyich Tchaikovsky spent his childhood there. Population: 44,263 (2002 census).

THEODORE SHABAD
Author of "Geography of the USSR"

ALARCÓN, ä-lär-kôn', **Hernando de** (1466?–1540?), 16th century Spanish explorer in America. He was born in Trujillo, Spain. In 1540, when Francisco Vásquez de Coronado moved by land from Mexico to what is now the southwestern United States, Alarcón commanded two supporting ships. He explored the Gulf of California, proving that Lower California is a peninsula and not an island. Alarcón also discovered the Colorado River and explored its lower reaches.

ALARCÓN, ä-lär-kôn', **Pedro Antonio de** (1833–1891), Spanish novelist, whose works are among the outstanding examples of 19th century romantic regionalism in Spanish literature. His best-known work is the short novel *El sombrero de tres picos* (1874; Eng. tr., *The Three-Cornered Hat,* 1918), a bedroom farce. The ballet of the same name, with music by Manuel de Falla and first produced in its final form in 1919, is based on the story by Alarcón.

Alarcón was born in Guadix, Spain, on March 10, 1833. He abandoned law studies to work as a journalist in Cádiz. The success of an early novel, *El final de Norma* (1855), started him on a literary career. After his play *El hijo pródigo* was hissed off the stage in 1859, Alarcón, in disgust, joined the Spanish campaign in Morocco. His *Diario de un testigo de la guerra de África* (1859–60), is a masterpiece of war memoirs. Returning to Spain, he edited an antiroyalist journal, *El látigo.* Later he became a political conservative and served for a short time in the Spanish Cortes but finally abandoned politics. His other novels include *El escándalo* (1875), *El niño de la bola* (1880), and *La pródiga* (1882). He died in Madrid on July 20, 1891.

ALARCÓN Y MENDOZA, ä-lär-kôn' ē män-dō'sä, **Juan Ruiz de** (c. 1581–1639), Spanish dramatic poet, who was one of the great figures of the golden age of Spanish literature. He was born in Mexico about 1581, the son of a superintendent of mines from Cuenca, Spain. He studied canonical and civil law in Mexico, but moved to Spain in 1600. After taking two degrees at the University of Salamanca, he practiced law in Seville and then in Mexico City, and received a master's degree from the University of Mexico in 1609.

Returning to Spain in 1613, Ruiz de Alarcón settled permanently in Madrid. There his persistent efforts to secure a government post were finally rewarded in 1626 when he was appointed to the office of reporter of the Council of the Americas. He was never married but had an illegitimate daughter, Lorenza de Alarcón, by Angela Cervantes. He died in Madrid on Aug. 4, 1639.

Ruiz de Alarcón began to write for the stage around 1613. He was a hunchback, and the cruel jibes that he suffered on this account probably deepened in him the attitude of stoicism so often reflected in his plays. Composed within the formula of the drama established by Lope de Vega, most of his plays may be classified as comedies rather than tragedies. His most famous dramatic works, *La verdad sospechosa* (*The Suspected Truth*), which Corneille adapted in *Le menteur,* and *Las paredes oyen* (*The Walls Have Ears*), carry didactic or moral messages, much as in the works of the later 17th century French playwright Molière. Critical disputes have arisen among scholars over attempts to identify in Ruiz de Alarcón's plays the traits that are distinctively Mexican rather than Spanish.

Ruiz de Alarcón's dramas more closely approximate the classical spirit than do the plays of most of his contemporaries, but they are somewhat deficient in lyrical qualities. Carefully and slowly composed, they display an acute observation of people and customs, springing from a contemplative temperament and independence of judgment.

GERALD E. WADE, *The University of Tennessee*

ALARIC, al'ə-rik (370?–410), was king of the Visigoths and a conqueror of Rome. He was born on the island of Peuce, now in Rumania, at the mouth of the Danube River. In 390 A.D. he led a band of Visigoths south of the Danube. Checked by the Roman legions under Flavius Stilicho in 392, he later commanded the Gothic auxiliaries under the Roman emperor Theodosius I.

After the death of Theodosius in 395, Alaric left the Roman army and was elected king of the Visigoths, whom he led into Greece. He ravaged Greece until 397, when Theodosius' son Arcadius, emperor of the Eastern Empire, brought peace by making Alaric *magister militum* (master of the soldiers) in Illyricum, now in western Yugoslavia.

The empire was divided at this time by the rivalries of the supporters of Honorius and Arcadius, the two young sons and successors of Theodosius. Honorius, in the west, was influenced by his Vandal guardian, the general Stilicho. In the east, the weak Arcadius was in the hands of his ambitious advisers. Alaric was able to strengthen himself by forcing concessions from the rival imperial parties.

Alaric used his position as *magister militum* to equip his forces and then turned west, invading Italy in 401. He was defeated by Stilicho at Pollentia (the modern Pollenza) in 402 and at Verona in 403. Following his second defeat, Alaric was inactive until Stilicho was murdered in 408. After the murder, the Roman soldiers turned on their Gothic allies, who soon deserted to Alaric in large numbers. Since Stilicho had been the only general able to stop the barbarians, Alaric and his newly enlarged army were able to invade Italy without serious hindrance.

Alaric quickly laid siege to Rome, but lifted it twice to negotiate payments from the emperor and the Romans. When the emperor condoned an attack on Alaric's camp, the Visigoths laid siege to Rome for a third time in 410. Through treachery within the city, Alaric and the Visigoths entered Rome on Aug. 24, 410. Although there was considerable plundering, the Visigoths, perhaps because they were Christians, showed unexpected humanity to the citizens.

Alaric's capture of Rome was less significant for the city, which soon recovered physically, than for the Mediterranean civilization as a whole. Roman prestige declined among the barbarian tribes of the north, who became more confident of their strength. The fall of Rome indicated to many the end of law and order and symbolized the decline of the western Roman Empire. Thereafter Rome's prestige was to be based on the papacy rather than on the empire.

Alaric soon left Rome and moved to southern Italy, planning to invade Africa and find a home for his tribe. His invasion fleet was wrecked before leaving Italy, however, and Alaric died at Cosentia (the modern Cosenza) in 410. When he was buried near Cosentia, slaves diverted the Busento River and buried the body in the river's bed. The river was then returned to its course and the slaves were killed, so that the location of the body would remain secret.

Even when he campaigned against the Romans, Alaric's purpose was not to destroy the Roman Empire. He regarded the empire as a necessary institution in which he and his people had a rightful place. Although never completely successful in his relations with Rome, Alaric exerted great influence over the unruly Visigoths and tried to reconcile the barbarians and the empire.

ALARIC II, al'a-rik (died 507), was a king of the Visigoths. He succeeded his father, Euric (Evaric), in 484. At the outset of his reign, the dominions of the Visigoths were at their greatest extent, embracing most of what is now Spain and all of western Gaul (France) south of the Loire. Lacking the aggressive military character of his forebears, Alaric attempted to advance peaceful forms of government, but his behavior was interpreted as weakness by Clovis, king of the Franks, who invaded the Visigothic kingdom. In a battle at Vouglé, near Poitiers, in 507, Alaric was slain and his army completely defeated. The *Breviarum Alaricianum* (Breviary of Alaric), a code of laws largely derived from Roman sources and designed for the use of Alaric's Roman subjects, was compiled by a commission of jurists at his command.

ALARMS, Electric. See Burglar Alarm; Fire Alarm System.

ALAS, ä'läs, **Leopoldo,** Spanish author, who had a strong influence on the Spanish writers who matured in the late 19th and early 20th century. Born at Zamora, Spain, on April 25, 1852, he studied law at the universities of Oviedo and Madrid and later taught at the universities of Salamanca, Zaragoza (Saragossa), and Oviedo. Writing under the pseudonym *Clarín,* he first became known as a literary critic through his contributions to various periodicals. He was noted for his brilliant if somewhat caustic style and was both respected and feared for his erudition, wit, and keen insight. He died at Oviedo on June 13, 1901.

Although best known in his lifetime as a critic, Alas' reputation today rests on his novels and short stories, particularly the long novel *La regenta* (1884–85), a penetrating study and complex recreation of life in a provincial cathedral town. Some have called it one of the major 19th century novels in any language, and it has often been compared to Gustave Flaubert's *Madame Bovary.* The anticlerical tone of *La regenta* and some of Alas' other works provoked bitter critical attacks by orthodox writers. His later writings are considerably more mellow, lacking the anticlerical tone of the earlier criticism and fiction. Among his other major works are *Solos de Clarín* (1881–91); *El señor, y lo demás son cuentos* (1886); *Su unico hijo* (1890); *Folletos literarios* (1886–91); *Dona Berta, cuervo superchería* (1892); *Paliques* (1893); *Cuentos morales* (1896); and *El gallo de Socrates* (1900).

C. Lewis Morgan, Jr., *University of Miami*

ALAŞEHIR, ä-lä-shə-hĕr', is a town in Turkey, in Manisa vilayet (province). The name is sometimes spelled *Alashehir.* The town is a trade center for a farming region in western Asiatic Turkey, about 75 miles east of İzmir.

The town was founded in 150 B.C. by Attalus II Philadelphus, king of Pergamum, and was known in ancient times as *Philadelphia.* It was held for a time by the Byzantines and then was independent for several centuries. It was the last of the independent Greek cities in Asia Minor when it fell to the Turks in 1391. The Mongol conqueror Timur (Tamerlane) seized Alaşehir in 1402, but the town later reverted to Turkish rule under Murad II (reigned 1421–1451). Population: 29,484 (1985 est.).

© RICK McINTYRE/APERTURE PHOTOBANK & ALASKA PHOTO

A caribou stands at the foot of Mt. McKinley (Denali), the highest peak in Alaska and North America.

ALASKA

The State Seal

ALASKA, ə-las′kə, the largest and northernmost state in the United States of America. More than twice the size of Texas, it was purchased from Russia in 1867. After finally entering the Union as the 49th and least populous state in 1959, it attracted newcomers at a rapid rate, though of all the states it still has the fewest people per square mile.

INFORMATION HIGHLIGHTS

Location: In the northwestern part of North America, bordered on the north by the Beaufort Sea (Arctic Ocean), east by the Yukon Territory and British Columbia (Canada), south by the Gulf of Alaska and Pacific Ocean, and west by the Bering and Chukchi seas.

Elevation: *Highest point*—Mount McKinley, 20,320 feet (6,190 meters); *lowest point*—sea level; *approximate mean elevation*—1,900 feet (580 meters).

Total Area: (land and inland water) 591,004 square miles (1,530,700 sq km); rank, 1st.

Resident Population: 626,932 (2000 census). Increase (1990–2000), 14%.

Climate: Four major climatic regions—Arctic, continental, transitional, and maritime.

Statehood: Jan. 3, 1959; order of admission, 49th.

Origin of the Name: From an Aleut word, *alakshak,* meaning "the great land."

Capital: Juneau.

Largest City: Anchorage.

Political Divisions: Organized into one municipality and 15 boroughs covering approximately 30% of the state; the remainder, called the unorganized borough, basically administered by state government.

Principal Products: *Manufactures*—processed seafood (halibut, salmon, herring, shellfish), lumber and pulp; *farm products*—dairy, meat, fodder grains, barley; *minerals*—petroleum and natural gas, sand and gravel, gold, building stone, coal, tin.

State Motto: North to the Future.

State Song: *Alaska's Flag.*

State Nickname: Last Frontier (unofficial).

State Bird: Willow ptarmigan (*Lagopus lagopus alascensis* Swarth).

State Flower: Forget-me-not (*Myosotis alpestris Schmidt Boraginaceae*).

State Tree: Sitka spruce (*Picea sitchensis*).

State Flag: Eight gold stars (Big Dipper and North Star) on a field of blue. (See also FLAG.)

Alaska, whose name means "the Great Land," contains the highest mountain, the biggest glaciers, and the largest number of active volcanoes in the United States. Its fishing grounds are the richest in the country. Alaska is believed to hold just about every important mineral needed for modern industry except bauxite, the ore of aluminum. It probably possesses most of the nation's undiscovered oil and natural gas, and it has more coal and hydroelectric potential than any other state. Alaska also has most of the land owned directly by the federal government and accounts for one-fifth of all the petroleum produced in the United States.

1. The Land

Alaska occupies the large northwestern peninsula of the North American continent that extends close to Siberia. The western, maritime boundary with the Soviet Union runs from a point west of Attu Island through the Bering Sea and Bering Strait into the Arctic Ocean. Within the strait are two small islands, Big Diomede (Soviet) and Little Diomede (U.S.), which are separated by only 2 miles (3 km) of water. On the east, Alaska's boundary with Canada is longer than that of any other state. The northern coastline on the Beaufort Sea makes Alaska the only state touching the Arctic Ocean. On the south, Alaska lies along the Great Circle short sailing route of the Pacific, which connects the west coast of North America with Asia. The shortest airline routes linking Asia with the United States and northwestern Europe cross Alaska.

At its extremes, Alaska extends from about 72°N at Barrow to about 52°N on a small island near Adak, in the Aleutian group; and from 130°W clear across the 180th meridian to 172°E on Attu Island. Thus Alaska covers almost as many degrees of latitude as—and more degrees of longitude than—the 48 contiguous states of the Union, or what Alaskans call the "Lower 48." Technically the state has four time zones, but only two are used. Technically also, Alaska is not only the northernmost and westernmost state but also the easternmost, because the Aleutian Islands lie partly in the easternmost longitudes of the Eastern Hemisphere.

GENERAL PHYSIOGRAPHY

Alaska is crossed from east to west by three major mountain ranges—the Brooks, Alaska, and Coast Ranges—and by the Yukon River. The southern third of the state forms an arc centered on Mt. McKinley (Denali), 20,320 feet (6,194 meters) in elevation and capping the Alaska Range. The western leg of this arc curves through the Alaska Peninsula, continues through the Aleutian Islands, and has 57 active volcanoes. The eastern leg curves to Dixon Entrance, on the border with British Columbia. It includes the volcanic Wrangell Mountains, the heavily glaciated St. Elias Mountains, and mountainous Southeastern (the southeastern "panhandle" of Alaska). The northern third of the state forms a gentle arc along the crest of the Brooks Range. The middle third of Alaska consists of plains, plateaus, and rolling hills drained by the Yukon River system into the Bering Sea. Northern Alaska drains into the Arctic Ocean and southern Alaska into the Pacific.

Because of low temperatures, 80% of Alaska is underlain by permafrost, permanently frozen ground. To the south the Gulf of Alaska and the North Pacific are ice free. On the north the Beaufort Sea, with its shallow coastal shelf, is usually covered with ice; the shallow Chukchi and Bering seas to the west are ice covered during the winter.

NATURAL REGIONS

Alaska is divisible into four major natural regions: the Arctic, Western Alaska, Southern Alaska, and the Interior.

The Arctic. This region stretches from the 141st meridian, the boundary with the Yukon (Canada) on the east, to the Chukchi Sea on the west; and from the Beaufort Sea of the Arctic Ocean on the north to the crest of the Brooks Range and Kotzebue Sound on the south. Arctic Alaska includes the northern foothills of the Brooks Range, the Arctic Coastal Plain (or North Slope), and the coasts of the Chukchi Sea and Kotzebue Sound.

The region has a mean annual temperature of about 10°F (−12°C) and receives only about 10 inches (250 mm) of precipitation a year. The prevailing winds are from the east, the Polar Easterlies, but storms come usually from the south and west. Because the region lies north of the Arctic Circle, it has 24 hours of sunshine in the summer but no direct sunlight from mid-November to mid-January. Average monthly summer temperatures seldom exceed 50°F (10°C), and the ground is frozen. Because evaporation rates are low, the Arctic lowlands are wet and covered with lakes. The dominant vegetation is lichens, mosses, and other small plants, collectively called tundra.

Western Alaska. Consisting of the coastal areas and islands of the Bering Sea, Western Alaska is bounded on the east by the forests of the Interior region. It includes the volcanic Aleutian Islands, the northern side of the Alaska Peninsula, the Bristol Bay Lowland, the Yukon-Kuskokwim Lowland, and the Seward Peninsula. The region is dominated by the Bering Sea. The main ocean current flows from south to north along the coast, and storms come from the south or west. Because of the cooling effect of the Bering Sea, as well as cloud cover, average monthly summer temperatures are low, seldom exceeding 50°F (10°C), and wind speeds are often high. The principal vegetation is tundra.

The Aleutians are affected by two contrasting currents. On the Bering Sea side, the prevailing current is from Siberia to Alaska, while on the Pacific side the currents move from Alaska to Siberia. This contrast creates very foggy and wet conditions. In addition, the eastern Aleutians are the center of one of the world's major low-pressure systems, the Aleutian low. The combination of high winds and low to moderate summer temperatures is unfavorable to tree growth.

Southern Alaska. The Southern region extends from the Gulf of Alaska to the crests of the Alaska Range, the Wrangell Mountains, and the Boundary Range of Southeastern. Geologically the region is extremely active, with a history of volcanic eruptions and frequent powerful earthquakes and tsunamis.

The coastal portion of Southern Alaska has a mean annual temperature of about 40°F (4°C) in the lowlands. The area is dominated by an almost constant airstream from the North Pacific, bringing moisture-laden clouds. Annual precipitation is high, as much as 12 feet (3,650 mm),

ALASKA

COAST MTS.
ALEXANDER ARCH.
ST. ELIAS MTS.
WRANGELL MTS.
Gulf of Alaska
Montague I.
Yukon
Tanana
BROOKS RANGE
ALASKA RANGE
Mt. McKinley 20,320
Kenai Pen.
Cook Inlet
Kodiak I.
Koyukuk
Pt. Barrow
Colville
Iliamna L.
KUSKOKWIM MTS.
Yukon
Kuskokwim
Bristol Bay
ALEUTIAN RANGE
Alaska Pen.
Pt. Hope
Seward Pen.
Norton Sound
Kuskokwim Bay
Chukchi Sea
Bering Str.
Nunivak I.
St. Lawrence I.
St. Matthew I.
PRIBILOF IS.
Bering Sea
Unimak I.
Unalaska I.
Umnak I.
FOX IS.
ALEUTIAN ISLANDS
Atka I.
ANDREANOF IS.
Kiska I.
RAT IS.
Attu I.
NEAR IS.

TOPOGRAPHY

400 Mi.
400 Km.
200
200
0
0

5,000 m.
16,404 ft.
2,000 m.
6,562 ft.
1,000 m.
3,281 ft.
500 m.
1,640 ft.
200 m.
656 ft.
100 m.
328 ft.
Sea Level
Below

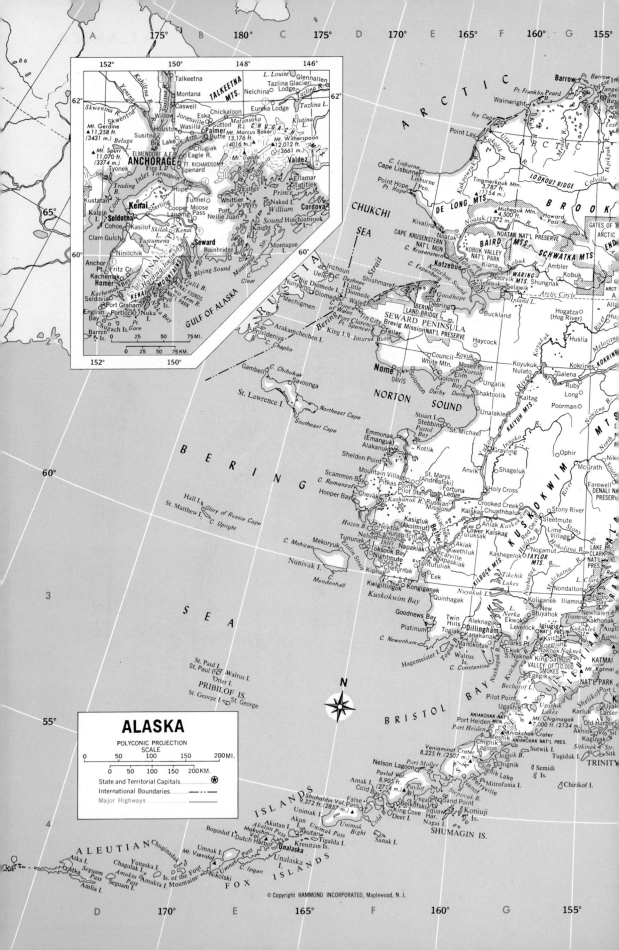

ALASKA

McBride Glacier confronts the sea in Glacier Bay National Park northwest of Juneau.

and snowfall is heavy. Coastal Southern Alaska is a land of glaciers, high mountains, fjords, and, particularly in Southeastern, lush forests.

The inland part of Southern Alaska is the broken lowland between the Coast Ranges—the Kodiak, Kenai, Chugach, and St. Elias mountains—and the crest of the Alaska Range. It is forested and was once heavily glaciated. Its mean annual temperature of about 30°F (−1°C) is critical for creating or destroying permafrost, so that some soils are frozen and others not. Precipitation declines to about 30 inches (750 mm), because the area is sheltered from storms by the Coast Ranges.

The Interior. The forested Interior region consists of the extensive lake-studded lowlands drained by the Yukon-Tanana River system, together with the hills and uplands that separate those two rivers. Summers are warm, because the region tends to be highly influenced by the long daylight hours rather than by oceanic factors, which are blocked or diminished by the sheltering mountains to the north and south and by distance from the Bering Sea to the west.

The farther east one goes along the Yukon, the higher the summer temperatures. Conversely, winter temperatures can be severe, with extremes as low as −75°F (−59°C) and commonly several weeks of −40°F (−40°C). Large parts of the interior contain permafrost, and only modest differences in elevation or other determinants of permafrost can mean that it either forms or melts.

RIVERS, LAKES, AND COASTS

Alaska's chief river, the Yukon, is the fourth longest in North America. The state's lakes are too numerous to count.

Rivers. The Yukon, which originates in Canada, receives the White, Chandalar, Tanana, and Koyukuk rivers, among other major tributaries. Both the White (flowing mainly in Canada) and the Tanana are fed by glaciers, and it is glacial meltwater that brings extensive silt into the parent stream, giving it a white or milky color. The Yukon generally freezes in October and thaws in May. Because of its latitudinal flow (in this case from east to west), the freezing and melting occur rather rapidly along its whole course. Even so, ice dams often form, causing extensive flooding. The river crosses the Yukon Flats, a large lowland that is also crossed by two tributaries, the Porcupine River and Birch Creek. Before entering the sea the Yukon forms a large delta, which oceangoing vessels cannot enter.

The lower Kuskokwim River flows through an extensive lowland, which it shares with the lower Yukon. Because the Kuskokwim carries less sediment than the Yukon, its delta is not as large and oceangoing vessels can reach the town of Bethel.

The area around Kotzebue, a town at the tip of the Baldwin Peninsula in the northwest, is drained by the Noatak, Kobuk, and Selawik Rivers. These are navigable by small craft, and their valleys make convenient routes in the winter. For this reason, Kotzebue has traditionally been a significant trading center.

Numerous rivers flow from the Brooks Range northward into the Beaufort Sea. The longest is the Colville, the headwaters of which can be reached by going up the Noatak. Others of importance are the Meade, Sagavanirktok, and Kongakut. The northward-flowing Arctic rivers are shallow and freeze in winter. They are natural transportation routes in winter and significant sources of fish in summer.

The Copper River and its main tributary, the Chitina, drain the Lake Louise Plateau, the Copper River Lowland, the Wrangell Mountains, the

Only in winter are Kotzebue and its roadless peninsula accessible by automotive vehicle, here a snowmobile.

southern slope of the Alaska Range, and the northern slope of the Coast Ranges. Because the Copper River is glacially fed and drains a former lake bed, it has an extremely high silt load. It forms a large delta and is not suitable for oceangoing vessels.

The Alsek, Taku, and Stikine rivers from Canada reach the sea through the southeastern extension of Alaska. They are glacially fed and carry high silt loads but were used by small boats in the 19th century.

For transportation the most important river system is the Susitna-Chulitna in Southern Alaska. The two rivers themselves are not navigable for seagoing vessels. However, their valleys provide the shortest and lowest route from the Gulf of Alaska to the Interior, which is reached through Broad Pass in the Alaska Range. From there the valley of the Nenana River leads to that of the Tanana. The route through the Susitna, Chulitna, and Nenana valleys is taken by the Alaska Railroad and the Parks Highway, which connect the seaport of Anchorage with Fairbanks, on the Chena tributary of the Tanana River. At the town of Nenana, goods brought by rail or truck are placed on barges that haul bulk cargoes to villages along the rivers of the Interior.

Lakes. In addition to large lakes of geological origin, Alaska has four basic types of lakes: glacially dammed, kettle, thaw, and oxbow. Each type was formed in a different way.

Alaska underwent two major periods of glaciation, with the first and more extensive covering half the area of the state. When the ice receded it left behind terminal moraines, large piles of rocks deposited at the former glacier edges. These moraines were often located at the heads of valleys and became natural dams behind which lakes formed. Such glacially dammed lakes are very common in the Coast Ranges, the Alaska Range, the Ahklun Mountains north of Bristol Bay, and the southern side of the Brooks Range.

At the conclusion of the last glacial period, about 8,000 to 10,000 years ago, the lower portions of the glaciers ceased to move and melted in place. In the process they left behind numerous lakes that are round and usually have steep banks. Known as kettle lakes because of their resemblance to the kitchen vessel, they are quite common in the Anchorage area.

Although glaciers covered the Brooks Range and the southern third of Alaska, the Arctic coast and much of the Interior remained free of ice. However, the extremely low winter temperatures caused the land to freeze and contract. The contraction created polygonic surfaces, much like the cracks in dried mud. The resulting polygonic surface cracks eventually filled with meltwater, which then refroze into large wedges of ice. Subsequently, many of these ice-wedge polygons melted and left what are called thaw lakes, which are very common in lowland areas. They are usually round and shallow, and sometimes have in the center an uplifted, conically shaped island called a pingo (an Eskimo word). In the Arctic, thaw lakes were usually distorted into rectangles by the wind action of the Polar Easterlies.

Other lakes developed when meandering rivers cut shorter courses, damming loops in their former channels, which were left as crescent-shaped "oxbow" lakes. Such lakes usually have well-drained banks, sites that are well suited to the growth of white spruce, the largest tree of the Interior.

Alaska's largest and best-known lake is Iliamna, at the base of the Alaska Peninsula. Situated close to Shelikof Strait but draining into Bristol Bay, it provides a natural passage between the two sides of the peninsula and also is popular for sportfishing and hunting. The large number of lakes feeding into Bristol Bay form the world's most important salmon-spawning area. The many lakes in the state's lowlands make excellent nesting grounds for waterfowl.

Coasts. The Arctic coast is exposed to winds and currents crossing the Arctic Ocean. The prevailing current is from the east-northeast, and in some areas it pushes ice through the shallow coastal waters and up against the shoreline. The ice acts as a bulldozer, excavating material that forms ridges. In some cases the ice overruns the shore itself, and in others it digs deep trenches into the beach. Under certain circumstances it can cause very rapid coastal erosion.

The western coast is shallow, and the northward-moving ocean currents have created numerous offshore bars and coastal spits. Because the spits are excellent places from which to observe and hunt whales and other sea mammals, they became the sites of numerous native settlements.

The southern coast is mostly deep, with soundings as great as 600 feet (180 meters) just offshore in many locations. Characteristic of most of the southern coastline are fjords—steep glaciated valleys that were drowned when the sea level rose about 10,000 years ago.

CLIMATE

Alaska can be divided into four climatic zones: continental, maritime, transitional, and Arctic. These zones are differentiated by the predominance or balance of land and sea influences. A large landmass gains and loses heat rapidly, while the seas show much less variation in temperature. This is the difference between the continental climate of the Interior and the maritime climate of coastal Southern Alaska and the Aleutians. Where the two zones meet the climate is called transitional, as in Western Alaska (except for the Aleutians) and the inland part of Southern Alaska. The Arctic climate of the North is influenced by the existence of sea ice throughout most of the year and by the darkness of the winter.

Weather Conditions. The main weather hazard in Arctic Alaska, which has winter temperatures somewhat higher than in the Interior, is not the cold but the wind. Even though snowfall is low, the easterly winds blow the snow, creating "white out." This condition causes drivers, airplane pilots, and people traveling on foot to lose all sense of the horizon and thus easily get lost.

The Interior has calm, cold winter weather, which is usually ideal for flying the aircraft that many people own. But during severe cold spells, frigid air drains down the valleys and creates temperature inversions. At very low temperatures, particularly around −40°F (−40°C) the air cannot absorb any moisture. As a result, water vapor quickly condenses into very fine ice particles that form "ice fog," which severely limits its visibility. On hot summer days, thunderstorms with high, gusty winds are common. Besides being a danger to aircraft, these storms produce lightning that sets off serious forest fires. On the average, 1 million acres (400,000 hectares) of forest burn each year in the Interior.

The maritime climate of Southern Alaska produces so much snow that as much as 81 feet (25 meters) have been measured in one winter. Avalanches are common, and snowstorms can close passes connecting the ports of Valdez and Haines with the Interior. The heavy snowfall also feeds Alaska's more than 1,700 square miles (4,400 sq km) of glaciers and sustains the huge ice sheets that support the Malaspina Glacier (the largest piedmont glacier in the United States), as well as large cirque and valley glaciers. The chief weather hazard in Western Alaska is the frequent high winds.

Storms in the Gulf of Alaska and the Bering Sea can be hazardous to shipping. For that reason, vessels plying Southeastern waters prefer to use the Inside Passage, a route lying close to the coast and sheltered by islands from the gulf.

The Inside Passage, seen at Ketchikan, shelters vessels from the open sea and provides a scenic cruise route.
© PORTERFIELD-CHICKERING/PHOTO RESEARCHERS

Changes of climate are of great importance in Alaska. A warming trend started perhaps 12,000 years ago, causing most glaciers to melt. It reached its peak about 5,000 years ago, when sea levels were higher than at present. Subsequently temperatures lowered, but over the last century they became warmer again. This change caused most of Alaska's glaciers to retreat, a fact carefully documented in Glacier Bay, in the southeast.

PLANT AND ANIMAL LIFE

Much of the southern and interior regions are covered by forests, whereas treeless Arctic and western Alaska support a tundra vegetation. The state is rich in large land mammals and in marine life, including sea mammals. Untold millions of migratory waterfowl breed every summer in the lowlands of interior, Arctic, and western Alaska.

Within the lush woodlands of southeastern Alaska the Sitka Spruce—Coastal Western Hemlock Forest is very dense. Its southernmost part also contains cedar, the basic tree used by the Native Tlingit and Haida peoples to build houses and canoes. The southeastern forests are home to brown bears, Sitka deer, and some moose. The abundant marine life includes salmon, herring, halibut, smelt, and numerous sea mammals. Among the birds are eagles and ravens.

Lowland parts of Kodiak Island support western hemlock and Sitka spruce. There is a wide assortment of wildlife in the Kodiak area.

Forests of western hemlock and Sitka spruce also are found in the Prince William Sound area and in sections of the Kenai Peninsula, particularly near Homer on Kachemak Bay and along parts of the western side of upper Cook Inlet. The Kenai Peninsula and the remainder of southern Alaska outside of Kodiak and the southeast have many moose. So many graze at Anchorage International Airport that they can cause the field to be closed. Black and brown bears are common in the southern region, and caribou have been introduced in the Kenai Peninsula.

The spruce, aspen, birch, and willow forests of the interior support moose, an important source of food for local people. Caribou herds decreased after the mid-20th century. Black, brown, and grizzly bears are common, as are wolves. Ravens are everywhere.

The tundra vegetation characteristic of the western region makes suitable grazing both for caribou, which are native to Alaska, and reindeer, which were introduced from Siberia and Lapland in the 1890's. The shallow coastal waters are one of the world's richest fisheries, famous for salmon and crab.

The caribou of the Arctic tundra roam in the hundreds of thousands. The Arctic also contains black and grizzly bears, lemmings, foxes, and wolves. The coasts are noted for whales, seals, walruses, fish, and polar bears.

NATURAL RESOURCES

Geologists study blocks of rocks that when similar in nature are called terranes. Numerous terranes have been identified in Alaska. The state has a very complex geology related to periods of intensive mountain building, faulting, and vulcanism. Geologic mapping, which is essential to modern, systematic mineral exploration, has covered only a small part of Alaska.

A large number of fault lines bend around the Gulf of Alaska. Large and small blocks of granite are common, the largest of which—called the Coast Range Batholith—underlies the Boundary Range in the southeast. The blocks of granite and the faults are associated with mineralized zones, which probably contain great amounts of metals, including lead, zinc, silver, gold, and copper. Such zones exist also along the southern edge of the Brooks Range and the Wrangell Mountains and in the uplands of the interior.

Alaska's lowlands and continental shelves are composed of sedimentary rocks that have accumulated to great depths. Much of the Alaska Range, the Coast Ranges, and Brooks Range consists of uplifted sedimentary rocks, though intruded with blocks of granite. The widespread sedimentary rocks contain huge quantities of coal, particularly in northwestern Alaska and the Cook Inlet area. Petroleum and natural gas are in the Yakutat-Katalla area, Cook Inlet and the Kenai Peninsula, and along the Arctic coast. Large reserves may exist in the sedimentary basins of the Chukchi, Bering, and Beaufort seas, and other areas.

ENVIRONMENTAL PROTECTION

Because so much of Alaska is federal land, the federal government is heavily involved in conservation and environmental protection. Fish and wildlife resources and state lands are managed by the state government.

2. The Economy

Alaska's economy relies on "basic industries," activities producing goods and services that cause money to flow in from the outside. In addition are local industries, which derive from the basic industries, and subsistence activities. Alaska's basic industries are defense, government, petroleum and other natural resources, and tourism.

Defense. As a basic industry, defense benefits Alaska by providing jobs in the construction and service sectors. It also produces income for Alaskans from spending by military personnel, civilian employees of the Department of Defense, and their dependents. The significance of Alaska's location along the Great Circle route connecting North America and Asia was clearly seen during World War II. As a result of Japan's attack on the Aleutians and the need to provide a route to send American aircraft to the Soviet Union, an enormous military construction program was undertaken and led to the establishment of major mil-

PERSONAL INCOME IN ALASKA

Source	1980[1]	1990[1]	2000[1]
Farms	4	8	16
Mining	359	848	983
Construction	614	709	1,035
Manufacturing	375	594	549
Transportation and public utilities	616	914	1,476
Wholesale trade	167	296	606
Retail trade	442	883	1,238
Finance, insurance, and real estate	197	317	606
Services	776	1,829	3,096
Government and government enterprises	1,968	3,732	4,495
Other[3]	103	314	198
Per capita personal income[4]	14,807	22,712	29,597
Per capita income, U.S.[4]	10,183	19,572	29,451

[1]Millions of dollars. [2]Not available. [3]Agricultural services, forestry, fishing, and other. [4]Dollars.

Source: U.S. Department of Commerce, Bureau of Economic Analysis.

itary bases at Shemya, Adak, Kodiak, Sitka, Anchorage, Fairbanks, Delta, and elsewhere. After the war military construction resumed to provide early warning of a possible hostile attack against the United States. Early-warning sites were built along Alaska's coasts and a ballistic missile early warning station at Clear. A later round of military construction occurred with the buildup of the U.S. Navy and the formation of light-equipment Army units to be based in Alaska but capable of deployment worldwide. While the actual number of military personnel on active duty in Alaska is normally small, less than 15,000, the military bases are large and are used to train regular and reserve units from the Lower 48 in periodic maneuvers. Numerous federal civilian employees of the Department of Defense are stationed in Alaska.

Government. If military personnel on active duty are included, government of all types is the largest employer in Alaska. Because the federal government is the largest landowner in the state, the management of this land creates many federal jobs for Alaskans. Various federal programs also send money to Alaska. Because of the state's long coastline and the need to protect its valuable fisheries from unauthorized use, the U.S. Coast Guard is a major presence and spender. Alaska built the institutions necessary for its own government after 1959. As a result, state and local government also became a major employer.

State spending based on oil revenues caused an economic boom in Alaska as the government invested money in new ports, harbors, roads, schools, subsidies for home mortgages, and loans for agricultural and small-business development. The boom attracted people to Alaska, and a dramatic increase in population further fueled the economy.

Petroleum. The reserves along the Arctic are extensive. Prudhoe Bay is the largest oil field in the United States and also contains enormous reserves of natural gas. Accounting for about 20% of the nation's crude oil output, the Prudhoe Bay field is on state-owned land. Alaska thus

© TED LODER/SHOSTAL

Alaskan king crab, a gourmet's delight, fetches fancy prices in markets and restaurants of the Lower 48.

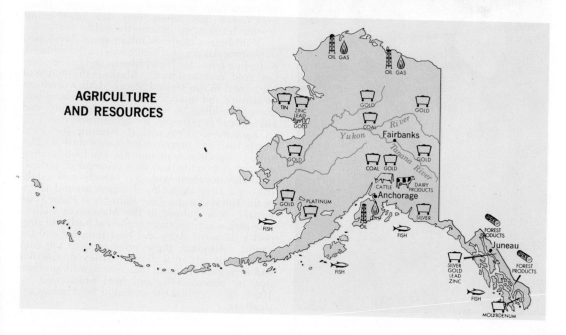

AGRICULTURE AND RESOURCES

(*Above*) Islets of timber float near a sawmill in the forest-rich Kachemak Bay area of south central Alaska. (*Below*) An Alaskan cabbage nurtured by long hours of summer sun is so large that it must be sawn off its stem.
© JOE RYCHETNIK/PHOTO RESEARCHERS

© JIM REARDON/ALASKA PHOTO

derives significant revenue from petroleum taxation, and before prices slumped the state optimistically estimated that its oil revenues would reach $8 billion a year. Looking at this huge potential income, the government eliminated income taxes, reduced local property taxes, and established a savings account known as the Alaska Permanent Fund. Part of the revenues earned by this multibillion-dollar fund was reinvested and the rest distributed to permanent residents of Alaska, each of whom received about $800 to $1,000 per year. The danger of such heavy reliance on a single industry became evident when oil prices unexpectedly declined. A precipitous fall in petroleum revenues curtailed state spending so much that economic depression set in and thousands left Alaska. But the value of the petroleum industry to Alaska's economy is more than just taxes. It is also employment, related services, and construction.

Other Natural Resources—*Fisheries.* Most of Alaska's fish and shellfish is exported, particularly to Japan. The fishing industry creates jobs for thousands of people and is a major consumer of local goods and services. Thus a significant portion of the income from fishing stays in Alaska. Because the fishing industry is so important, there are significant conflicts between the fishermen and the federal government when Washington seeks to foster petroleum exploration along Alaska's coasts. The spilling of 11 million gallons of crude oil into Prince William Sound when the tanker *Exxon Valdez* went aground in 1989 not only threatened the livelihoods of local salmon fishermen but also destroyed thousands of birds and sea mammals and polluted hundreds of miles of shoreline.

Mineral Industries. Coal became a significant element in Alaska's export economy when the mine at Healy began to export its low-sulfur coal to Korea and sent experimental shipments to Taiwan. Coal is the main fuel used in power plants in the Interior.

Meanwhile, gold mining, undertaken in the Interior for over a century, remained a significant contributor to the Alaskan economy. The industry was subject to a wide variety of environmental restrictions to control placer mining. However, some new mines were developed using arsenic leaching to remove the gold.

World-class hardrock mines were developed in postwar Alaska near Ketchikan (molybdenum), Kotzebue (zinc, lead, and silver), and Juneau (silver, gold, zinc, and lead). Alaska is the source of tin mined in the United States. Other products of mining and quarrying in Alaska are sand and gravel, building stone, platinum, antimony, and jade. Peat is extracted for agricultural use.

Agriculture. Commercial farming for local needs has been practiced for two centuries. Despite competition from non-Alaskan food producers, the state embarked on a program of agricultural development with the objective of establishing a large agricultural region around Delta in the Interior and a dairy industry at Point Mac-Kenzie, near Palmer in the Matanuska Valley. The idea was to produce sufficient barley to support a domestic dairy and beef industry and for export. Although these projects later ran into difficulties, within a decade barley production had increased by more than 300%, milk production by almost 50%, and beef production by 100%, thus proving the potential for Alaskan agriculture.

Reindeer have been raised in Alaska since 1892. During the 1920's, herds existed throughout Western Alaska and in parts of the Aleutians and the Arctic. In the 1930's, however, the size of the herds decreased dramatically, and afterward the industry was restricted largely to the Seward Peninsula. Reindeer are raised mostly for local markets, although some meat is exported. Reindeer antlers have a market in Asia, where they are used medicinally.

Large numbers of Alaskans have small gardens and raise livestock for their own use. This small-scale, noncommercial farming is popular because food is expensive in Alaska and because Alaskan-raised vegetables and some other products are superior in quality to imports. Potatoes, cabbages, and vegetables are widely grown, and many people are essentially self-supporting in food. Horses are raised for pleasure and for use as pack animals. Berry picking, especially for wild blueberries, is popular.

Forestry. Before whites settled in Alaska, the native peoples used the forests for construction materials, implements, and fuel. The Russians, who built sawmills and ships in Alaska, used wood for construction, fuel, and other purposes. The Americans did the same, but only for local needs.

The federal government established national forests covering most of Southern Alaska just prior to World War I and became the primary regulator and promoter of forestry. Commercial export forestry began during the war with shipments of Sitka spruce to Seattle for use in airplane manufacturing. After World War II the government fostered the development of pulp mills near Ketchikan and Sitka. Pulp and cut logs (called cants) became important exports from Southeastern. In some years, logs were exported from the Kenai Peninsula and from parts of the Interior. But the Interior spruce trees do not make good lumber because the wood warps easily, and some experts see a greater future for the birch trees, which have many potential uses. The issue of whether Alaska's forestry potential should be further developed is a matter of federal concern since the federal government owns the best forests in the state.

Alaska created state forests in the Interior and began to develop forestry for local needs. The University of Alaska, Fairbanks, has a school of forestry, which helps the state decide how best to manage its woodlands. In many parts of Alaska, people use the forests directly, for logs to build houses and for fuel. This use of the forests is a significant activity.

Tourism. Visitors come to Alaska not only from other states and Canada but from all over the world, particularly from Japan and West Germany. Tourism first developed in Alaska during the 1880's when cruise ships started to sail the Inside Passage. However, tourism did not become a major basic industry until nearly a century later. Cruise ships carry passengers through Southeastern to Skagway and Valdez. Tourists can travel by bus or car via Whitehorse and Dawson in Canada to Fairbanks and then take the train or Parks Highway to Denali National Park.

In addition, large numbers of people make airplane tours through Arctic Alaska, while others travel on their own. The numerous visitors coming to Alaska on sports hunting and fishing expeditions support many lodges and other facilities, particularly on the Alaskan Peninsula, along Bristol Bay, and in Southeastern. Floatplane trips to favored hunting and fishing spots are popular. Mountain climbing also is popular, and in the summer as many as 100 people may be on Mt. McKinley at the same time. The newer national parks in Alaska attract increasingly larger numbers of tourists.

Alaskan communities such as Anchorage, Fairbanks, Juneau, Sitka, and Valdez have developed convention centers. These cities promote both winter and summer tourism as well as business conferences.

Subsistence Activities. Perhaps 70,000 Alaskans, primarily natives, live in large part off the land by hunting, fishing, gathering wild plants or fruits, and trapping. Many other Alaskans augment their incomes by hunting and gathering, limited trapping, and small-scale placer mining. Most Alaskans have some salmon, moose, and blueberries in their freezers.

Manufacturing. Statistically, most manufacturing in Alaska is related to fish processing and canning, the largest single employer of people in the natural-resource sector. However, small manufacturing has been increasing for such local needs as construction materials, rebuilt trucks, automobile batteries, and specialty items. Alaska has refineries in the Kenai area and Fairbanks producing fuels for the local market. In addition, the Kenai exports urea, a fertilizer made from natural gas.

Labor. Statistics on wage and salary employment omit the self-employed, such as the owners and many crew members of fishing vessels and small-business proprietors. Active-duty military personnel and retired people are not counted. Many military personnel retire in Alaska but secure civilian employment.

Over the long run, Alaska has had a higher percentage of its total population employed than other states. However, short-term unemployment rates can be high, because of the seasonal nature of Alaska's construction and natural-resource industries and people coming to the state looking for work. The completion of major construction projects such as the pipeline from Prudhoe Bay and a downturn of world prices for Alaskan commodities such as oil also causes unemployment. Historically, Alaska has had a high percentage of women in its labor force.

Transportation. The Alaska Railroad, connecting Anchorage and Seward with Fairbanks, is a key element in Alaska's transportation system, particularly for hauling bulk cargoes such as sand and gravel, coal, petroleum, and construction materials. While Alaska's highway system is sparse in terms of the size of the state, it is constantly being improved. The main highway between Anchorage and Fairbanks follows the Alaska railroad. Fairbanks and the Delta-Tok-Tetlin Junction region are hubs for radial road systems. The Dalton Highway from Fairbanks is the main overland connection for goods going to Prudhoe Bay. Valdez is connected to Anchorage and Fairbanks by the Richardson and Glenn highways. Southeastern Alaska and Kodiak are tied into the state's road system by ferries, known as the Alaska Marine Highway.

The Interior is connected with the Lower 48 by the Alaska (Alcan) Highway, which passes through Canada. Branch routes of the highway run from the highway to Skagway and Haines in Southeastern.

© SHOSTAL

A commercial plane delivers supplies to Anaktuvuk Pass, a remote Eskimo village in the Arctic Alaskan interior.

Alaska is very dependent on air transportation to connect smaller communities with larger cities and with one another. Anchorage has emerged as the major hub of air travel not only within Alaska but also between Alaska and the Lower 48 and foreign countries. Numerous foreign airlines fly through Anchorage, particularly from East Asia and northwestern Europe, using the polar route.

Air transportation is gaining in significance because of the use of efficient, large cargo craft to carry high-value goods between Asia and the United States via Alaska. The state's airfields have been steadily improved by both the Alaskan and federal governments, creating more opportunities for local use of cargo planes.

The port of Valdez, the southern terminus of the Trans-Alaska Pipeline, is the major outlet for oil from Prudhoe Bay, which is shipped to California and Texas for refining. Dutch Harbor and Kodiak are centers for fishing boats and for vessels transiting between the North Pacific and the Bering Sea. American, Japanese, Chinese, Korean, Russian, Polish, and other ships can be seen in Dutch Harbor. Alaska's main imports come to the port of Anchorage on high-speed vessels from Seattle and Tacoma. The Good Friday 1964 earthquake caused the floor of Cook Inlet to drop, thus increasing the depth of water and allowing Anchorage to become an essentially year-round port. This led to a decline of Seward as the port for Anchorage, but it also decreased shipping costs.

3. The People

Alaska's Native peoples are diverse, and the immigrant American population represents a genuine cross-section of all the other states. Although most Alaskans are urban residents, numerous Alaskans live in rural areas on a subsistence basis.

Population rose dramatically after 1970 through immigration. The growth occurred principally in the suburbs of Anchorage, Fairbanks, and Juneau. Over 40% of all Alaskans live in Anchorage.

The Native Peoples. The preponderant population of western and Arctic Alaska and large parts

RESIDENT POPULATION SINCE 1890

Year	Population	Year	Population
1890	32,052	1960	226,167
1900	63,592	1970	302,583
1920	55,036	1980	401,851
1940	72,524	1990	550,043
1950	128,643	2000	626,932

Gain, 1990–2000: 14% (U.S. gain, 13.2%). **Density,** 2000: 1.1 persons per sq mi of land area (U.S. density, 79.6).

URBAN-RURAL DISTRIBUTION

Year	Percent urban	Percent rural
1960	37.9 (U.S., 69.9)	62.1
1970	56.9 (U.S., 73.6)	43.1
1980	64.3 (U.S., 73.7)	35.7
1990	67.5 (U.S., 75.2)	32.5

LARGEST CENTERS OF POPULATION

City	2000	1990	1980
Anchorage	260,283	226,338	174,431
Juneau	30,711	26,751	19,528
Fairbanks	30,224	30,843	22,645
Sitka	8,835	8,588	7,803
Ketchikan	7,922	8,263	7,198
Kenai	6,942	6,327	4,324
Kodiak	6,334	6,365	4,756
Bethel	5,471	4,674	3,576
Wasilla	5,469	4,028	1,559
Barrow	4,581	3,469	2,207

of the Interior and Southern Alaska is native. In fact, most of the actual land area of the state is inhabited primarily by natives: Inupik (Inupiaq) Inuit in the Arctic; Yupik and Pacific (Sugpiaq) Inuit in Western Alaska; Aleuts in the Aleutians and the Alaska Peninsula; Tlingit, Haida, and Tsimshian in Southeastern; and Athapascans, who speak almost a dozen different dialects, in the Interior.

The approximately 98,000 Natives can trace a heritage that goes back at least 10,000 years, to the end of the last ice age, when human beings left the first clear record of their settlement in Alaska. Inuit traditions derive in large part from the Thule sea-mammal hunting culture, which was developed in Alaska but named for a site in Greenland to which Inuit (Eskimos) had migrated. This way of life is threatened by government restrictions on hunting sea mammals, particularly whales. Traditional Athapascan culture is based largely on harvesting such game as caribou and moose and fishing for salmon. The southeastern salmon-fishing groups are famous for their war canoes and totem poles.

Large numbers of Aleuts were murdered by the Russians in the latter part of the 18th century, but in the early 19th century Aleuts joined the Russian Orthodox Church, learned Russian, and became exployees of the Russian America Company, a trading concern. Today many middle-aged Aleuts speak fluent English, Aleut, and Russian.

Many of the Inuit peoples of the Bristol Bay and lower Yukon areas also accepted the Russian Orthodox faith. But otherwise, until they began taking jobs in newly established fish canneries around Bristol Bay at the turn of the 20th century, they remained little affected by outside influences. The Inuit of the Seward Peninsula tradi-

tionally were great traders. Their way of life was altered by the turn-of-the-century gold rushes. They moved into such towns as Nome (where they are a majority today), secured employment in gold mining, and also suffered from imported diseases, particularly influenza and tuberculosis. The other Inuit, in Arctic Alaska, by and large remained culturally stable until the construction of military early-warning stations after World War II, when they took jobs on such defense projects. The construction work provided an economic basis for the development of towns, which led, for example, to an increase in the population of Barrow.

Similarly, the major economic impact on the natives of the Interior came first with the gold rushes and later with postwar military development. However, the earliest and perhaps most lasting influences derived from the Roman Catholic and Episcopal missionaries who entered the Interior down the Porcupine River and from the Hudson's Bay Company post established by British traders at the confluence of the Porcupine and Yukon in 1847. The peoples of Southeastern lived reasonably well with the Russians. The first real impact on them was the development of fish canneries in the 1880's and 1890's, together with the impress of Presbyterian missionaries who founded a college to educate the natives.

What the gold rushes left behind was not only mining operations and a developed river transportation system but also widespread infectious diseases that decimated the native population. Effective medical care, which became available to the Alaskan natives only in the 1950's, led to a doubling of the native population thereafter.

Despite involvement in the money economy, Alaskan natives to a great degree have main-

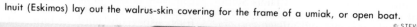

Inuit (Eskimos) lay out the walrus-skin covering for the frame of a umiak, or open boat.

© STEVE McCUTCHEON

For many residents of the state, the Alaskan way of life includes a personal aircraft as well as an automobile.

tained a subsistence life-style. Nor were they ever confined by the U.S. government to reservations. The issue of native land rights, preserved but deferred in the Organic Act of 1884, was not addressed until the Alaska Native Claims Settlement Act of 1971. Under this act, Alaska natives were divided into regional and village corporations. The corporations in turn were given a financial settlement of about $900 million and were to receive about 44 million acres (18 million hectares) of land. Individual natives became shareholders in one of the 200 villages and in one of the 13 regional corporations. Because they have remained in Alaska and constitute a stable element of the population, natives make up a significant percentage of older Alaskans. Moreover, their interest groups have more political power both within the state and with the federal government than native numerical strength might suggest.

Alaskan natives form the backbone of two significant organizations: the Eskimo Scouts, responsible for military reconnaissance of Alaska's coastlines; and the excellent firefighting crews that, when not occupied in Alaska, are sent to the Lower 48 to fight forest fires.

The Americanization of Alaska. Russian America was managed by 500 to 800 Russians who employed 1,500 to 2,000 Aleuts, many of whom headed small trading posts and served as explorers. The U.S. acquisition of Alaska in 1867 led to an influx of speculators to Sitka, the capital of Russian America. Most of them soon left, and by 1880 there were fewer Americans in Alaska than there had been Russians. The development of fish canning and gold mining in the 1880's and 1890's brought more Americans northward, but the majority of these Americans also left, which

explains the decline in Alaska's population between 1900 and 1920.

As late as 1940 almost half the population of Alaska was native. The American population consisted largely of people who had recently immigrated to the United States from other countries, especially northwestern Europe. World War II changed Alaska's demographic picture, and by 1950 a majority of people in Alaska were American-born and white.

By place of birth, the people who immigrate to Alaska represent the entire United States. Most, however, have moved first to another part of the country—typically the West Coast—before going to Alaska. Most come from urban areas, are highly skilled in the trades or well educated in the professions, and are in their 20's and 30's. The majority go to Anchorage, Fairbanks, and Juneau. Most, however, stay less than five years, a reflection of the turnover that is normal in federal, civilian, and military service, in construction, and in certain other fields.

The median age of Alaskans has been lower than the national average, reflecting the generally young age of Alaska's immigrant population. The median age has increased, however, in part because many older people preferred to retire in Alaska rather than move elsewhere.

Main Centers of Population. Anchorage was founded in 1914 by the U.S. Army Corps of Engineers as the site for the headquarters of the Alaska Railroad. The city has a central location in relation to the Interior, the Aleutians, and Southeastern, and its specific site provided more level, ice-free land than any other settlement in Alaska. As a major port and airline hub, it has become the state's leading center of commerce, banking, finance, medical care, and federal services. The city's relatively mild climate and attractive setting have bolstered the advantages of its general location and specific site.

Fairbanks, situated close to the geographic center of the Interior, started as a trading post in 1902. It became first the service center of gold-mining operations in the Interior and afterward of military activities in much of Alaska. Because of the rich agricultural and mineral potentials of the Interior, Fairbanks was selected as the site of the Alaska Agricultural College and School of Mines, formally founded in 1914. In the 1970's the city played a key role in the construction of the oil pipeline from Prudhoe Bay in the Arctic to the port of Valdez on the Gulf of Alaska and remained a nodal point for numerous construction and mining projects.

Juneau, the chief city in Southeastern, was founded in 1880 to promote the development of huge lode gold deposits. From 1905 it became successively the capital of the district, territory, and state of Alaska. Its administrative importance enabled it to survive the collapse of the Juneau–Douglas gold mines, which closed during World War II. Juneau is the center of air travel in Southeastern, a supply point for the development of new mining operations, and a destination for tourists.

Smaller towns in Alaska are Barrow in the Arctic; Kotzebue, Nome, Bethel, and Dillingham in the Western region; Unalaska in the Aleutians; Kodiak on Kodiak Island; and Sitka, Wrangell, Petersburg, and Ketchikan in Southeastern. Each is a locally important trading, service, and educational center.

4. Education and Culture

In much of Alaska until the 1950's, native education was conducted within the village and family. Education in hunting-and-gathering skills, village traditions, and oral history was quite effective, as evidenced by the survival of native cultures to the present day. For nearly a century after the U.S. acquisition of Alaska, the formal school system was limited and poorly funded. One of the many penalties Alaska suffered as a district and as a territory was the neglect of education. That situation changed dramatically after statehood.

Elementary and Secondary Education. Although the Russians had opened schools in Alaska in the 1820's, formal education in American Alaska was essentially ignored until Amanda McFarland opened a girls' school in Wrangell in 1877. This development attracted the attention of the Presbyterian Church and a missionary leader, Sheldon Jackson. Eventually with the support of the U.S. government, Jackson established a system of schools for natives in Southeastern and in Western Alaska. He actively encouraged different Protestant groups to set up missions in various parts of Alaska. Included among them were Moravians, who founded the town of Bethel, and Congregationalists, who founded a mission at Wales. This missionary effort sponsored not only the local school system but also the introduction of reindeer to Alaska. The U.S. government funded the schools, and the married missionary couples were, at one and the same time, missionaries, salaried U.S. government school

In Anchorage warm summer days bring a turnout to parks and even beaches.

© STEVE McCUTCHEON

teachers, and reindeer herders. The missionary teachers functioned as the informal representatives of the federal government throughout much of Western Alaska.

In the Interior the first formal schools were established by the Episcopal and Roman Catholic churches, for both natives and whites. The Catholics, under the Sisters of Mercy and Providence and the Society of Jesus (the Jesuits), had the greater resources and so the schools, orphanages, and hospitals they established were more significant. There was, however, no competition between the Catholic and Episcopal groups.

Although local communities established their own schools, a publicly supported school system did not truly develop until Alaska became a territory in 1912. Even then, the federal laws establishing the territorial government severely limited its power to levy taxes, required it to balance budgets, and denied it the right to incur indebtedness. These restrictions handicapped the territory's support of schools. The federal Bureau of Indian Affairs (BIA) took over the native schools and established at Mount Edgecombe near Sitka a boarding high school for natives from all over Alaska. Limited funds and a paternalistic attitude led to low levels of education in BIA schools, a legacy that persisted.

With the achievement of statehood, Alaska undertook to expand publicly supported education. Today most of the funds spent on education come from the state rather than local governments, and Alaska's urban areas have one of the best school systems in the nation. In the 1970's the state also became responsible for native education. The native peoples wanted rural high schools, because many wished their children to remain at home for high school. In response, the state built many secondary as well as primary schools in what is called "the bush." Local teachers, however, remained in short supply and often the rural schools relied on teachers brought in from the Lower 48. However, because of the high cost and difficulty of living in the bush, many teachers stayed only for a few years. As a result the state had to pay higher salaries to rural instructors than to urban ones.

Higher Education. In 1878, Sheldon Jackson established in Sitka the first college in Alaska. Sheldon Jackson College was dedicated to providing vocational and other types of education to Alaskan natives. It produced the first generation of modern Alaskan native leaders. The second school of higher education was the Alaska Agricultural College and School of Mines, which, although formally founded at Fairbanks in 1914, did not open its doors to students until 1923. This was the nucleus of the University of Alaska, which developed from 1935 onward.

After statehood, Alaska undertook a vigorous expansion of the university and created a statewide system of university campuses, junior colleges, extension centers, and research facilities.

PROMINENT PEOPLE IDENTIFIED WITH ALASKA

Baranov, Aleksandr Andreyevich (1747–1819), first general manager of the Russian America Co. (1799–1818); the Russian leader in Alaska.

Bartlett, Edward Lewis ("Bob") (1904–1968), considered the founding father of the state for the leading role he played in the fight for statehood.

Benson, Benny (1913–1972), creator of Alaska's flag (1926) in a competition among schoolchildren.

Cook, Capt. James B. (1728–1779), leader of first British expedition to accurately map the coast of Alaska, which led to development of Great Circle trading route between North America and Asia across the North Pacific.

Dall, William Healey (1845–1927), American explorer in Alaska, who was part of the Western Union Telegraph Expedition of 1867; author of *Alaska and Its Resources.*

Gruening, Ernest (1887–1974), territorial governor (1939–1953); state senator (1958–1969); with Bartlett, a leader in the fight for statehood.

Heintzleman, B. Frank (1888–1965), territorial governor (1953–1957); advanced economic development through promotion of Alaska's natural-resource enterprises.

Jackson, Sheldon (1834–1909), Presbyterian missionary and educator; founded Alaska's first college, at Sitka, 1878.

Juneau, Joe (c. 1826–1900), prospector and gold miner, for whom city of Juneau was named.

Shelikhov, Grigori Ivanovich (1747–1795), original organizer of the Russian America Co.

Veniaminov, Innokenty (1797–1879), first Russian Orthodox bishop for Alaska and Kamchatka; first ethnographer of the Aleuts; canonized in 1979.

Wickersham, James (1857–1939), federal judge, a founder of Fairbanks and delegate to U.S. Congress; introduced first Alaska statehood bill, 1916; founded Alaska Agricultural College and School of Mines (afterward University of Alaska), 1914.

The Fairbanks campus is the leading research center in the Free World for the study of scientific and engineering problems unique to the lands and seas of the Arctic and sub-Arctic.

In the 1950's the Methodist Church had founded in Anchorage a small, essentially liberal arts college for which it created a beautiful campus. The church withdrew its support in the 1970's, and after a reorganization the school became Alaska Pacific University, with programs not only in the liberal arts but also in business and in Pacific Rim and native studies.

The interdenominational Alaska Bible College in Glennallen was established to promote Christian education, and St. Herman's Theological School in Kodiak to train Orthodox priests, particularly natives. Both the Episcopal and Roman Catholic Churches created programs in Alaska for training deacons.

Responsibility for vocational-technical training was taken for the most party by the University of Alaska's community colleges. However, some local schools also undertook to support vocational training, as did several of the major construction unions in Alaska.

Libraries and Museums. The first real library in Alaska was established by the Russians in Sitka. In American Alaska, gold prospectors set up reading rooms in all their settlements. The prospectors as a group were quite literate—most self-educated, many highly educated—and they placed a high value on quality reading materials. This tradition is manifest in the libraries that are found all over the state. The principal research-oriented libraries are the State Library in Juneau and the Rasmusson Library of the University of Alaska, Fairbanks. Both have excellent collections on Alaska, and the Rasmusson's Alaska and

PARTIAL LIST OF UNIVERSITIES AND COLLEGES

Name	Location
Alaska Pacific University	Anchorage
Sheldon Jackson College	Sitka
University of Alaska, Anchorage	Anchorage
University of Alaska, Fairbanks	Fairbanks
University of Alaska, Juneau	Juneau

© BAROSH/SHOSTAL

Historic Sitka, now a fishing and pulp-milling center, was founded by the Russians in 1804 as New Archangel.

Polar Regions Collection is among the best of its kind in the world, attracting scholars from many nations.

Most Alaskan communities have good historical museums, often supported by a fraternal order, the Pioneers of Alaska. The Sheldon Jackson Museum in Sitka preserves Alaskan native materials, particularly from Southeastern, and is a center for native cultural studies. The State Museum in Juneau performs similar functions and has fine collections on the mining history of Alaska. The museum of the University of Alaska, Fairbanks, is a research institute as well as a museum, dedicated to the natural history, ethnology, and archaeology of Alaska and the North. The Baranof Museum in Kodiak preserves the History of the Russian America Company, as does St. Michael's Cathedral and Orphanage in Sitka. Palmer has a transportation museum.

Alaskans have long shown a great interest in art, music, and theater. Organizations sponsoring activities in these fields include the University of Alaska, the Alaska Council on the Humanities, local cultural societies, and special groups that arrange annual art and other festivals. A popular drama on the history of Russian America, *Cry of the Wild Ram,* is performed in Kodiak every August. Among the state's many other local performing groups are Russian dancers in Sitka and Kodiak, the Chilkoot Dancers, and the Athapascan fiddlers from the Fort Yukon area.

5. Recreation and Places of Interest

Alaska contains more national parks than any other state. It has an increasing number of officially designated historic sites, as well as colorful festivals.

National Parks. The state's national parks, monuments, and wildlife refuges cover an area one fourth again as large as the entire state of California. Many of these were created by the Alaska National Interest Lands Act of 1981. The state itself has created many parks and wildlife preserves. In addition are the national forests of Southern Alaska and federally owned land comprising most of Alaska north of the Brooks Range as well as the Aleutians. More of these areas are being opened for tourism.

Hardly a visitor comes to Alaska who does not spend time in Denali National Park and Preserve viewing wildlife and spectacular geology. Within the park is Mt. McKinley, the highest peak in North America. Formerly inaccessible Katmai National Park and Preserve, a region with active volcanoes and rich wildlife, is reached by air from Anchorage. Hunting, fishing, and backpacking areas are becoming increasingly available in the White Mountains north of Fairbanks and the Brooks Range. Many people hike the Chilkoot Trail from Dyea, close to Skagway.

Historic Sites and Monuments. In Sitka is the site of the oldest American military cemetery west of the Mississippi. The Baranof Museum in Kodiak is housed in a structure built in the time of Russian America. Sitka National Historical Park preserves the heritage of the Tlingit. Barrow's monument to Eskimo whalers is adjacent to a structure built by American explorers as part of the first geophysical year in the early 1880's. Sitka has a historic restored Russian Orthodox cathedral, and fine examples of Orthodox churches are preserved in Unalaska (in the Aleutians), St. Paul (in the Pribilof Islands), Kodiak, and elsewhere.

Annual Events. A year-round cycle of events in Alaska attracts tourists and Alaskans alike. In February and March are the Anchorage Fur Rendezvous and the two most grueling dogteam races in the world: the Iditarod from Anchorage to Nome and the Yukon Quest between Fairbanks and Whitehorse (in Canada). The Arctic Winter Games in March bring together native

469

The Russian Orthodox Church of the Holy Ascension dominates the town of Unalaska in the Aleutian Islands.

athletes from Alaska and from the Yukon, the Northwest Territories, and Nunavut, Canada. The Nenana Ice Classic, a lottery on the date and time the Tanana River ice breaks up, occurs in May, as do conventions of Alaska's numerous fraternal, service, and social organizations. Norwegian Independence Day, May 17, is celebrated magnificently in Petersburg, a largely Norwegian American community. The Fourth of July traditionally has been celebrated with parades and baseball games everywhere, and with a marathon race in Seward. The Eskimo-Indian Olympics are held during a festival that takes place in Fairbanks in July. Golden Days, celebrating the founding of Fairbanks, also occurs in July, and in

August state fairs are hosted by Palmer, Haines, and Fairbanks. Kodiak's Russian Festival in August features a popular historical drama, *The Cry of the Wild Ram.* Salmon derbies take place during the summer in Homer, Valdez, and Seward.

The most popular winter sports are basketball, hockey, cross-country and downhill skiing, snowmobiling, and ice fishing. Summer activities are baseball, fishing, hunting, hiking, camping, and boating. Many Alaskans own airplanes as well as cars and campers. Wheeled light aircraft are often kept at small airports and, when flown to remote areas, they land on sandbars in rivers. Float planes are used for landing on lakes and are often converted into ski planes in the winter.

The lead pair of dogs lunges from the starting point of a 30-mile (48-km) team race, one of several such winter events in Alaska.

6. Government and Politics

Alaska's constitution provides for separate executive, legislative, and judicial branches of government acting as checks and balances on one another so that no branch can become supreme. The state has no counties. In politics, most Alaskans regard themselves as independents.

State Government. The governor and lieutenant governor are chosen by popular vote in balloting that does not coincide with presidential elections. As a result, national elections have little direct effect on gubernatorial elections in Alaska. The governor has the right to reduce or eliminate any line item in the budget that is approved by the legislature. Members of the bicameral legislature are elected by popular vote, each representing a separate electoral district. The highest court is the Supreme Court.

The constitution stipulates that the citizens will be asked every 10 years whether they wish a new constitutional convention to be called. Particularly regarding the administration of justice, the management of land and resources, and the funding of education, the charter gives the state government more responsibility and authority than most of its counterparts have. The state administers the court system, which is unified under the Supreme Court. The governor appoints the attorney general, district attorneys throughout the state, and judges, although after stated periods judges must be approved and subsequently reconfirmed by the electorate. In anticipation of the time when Alaska would receive title to more than 100 million acres (40 million hectares) of federal land, the constitution directed the government to provide for the development, use, and conservation of land and resources belonging to the state. After 1981 significant amounts of land were, in fact, transferred from federal to state control and to native corporations, but detailed land surveys often were lacking. Until the federal Alaska National Interest Lands Conservation Act, Alaska had responsibility for most fish and game management in the state. However, for large areas the 1981 act transferred that responsibility to federal agencies. The Alaska constitution also mandates only one state-supported, accredited system of higher education, the University of Alaska.

Local Government. Settlements can request the type of local government they desire and can afford to support. Cities are in general responsible for police and fire protection, road construction and maintenance, sewerage, and water supply. Boroughs in general do not have these burdens but are responsible for planning and zoning, parks and recreation, tax collection, and, with state support, schools. In that two thirds of Alaska called the "unorganized borough," essentially all governmental functions are performed by the state. As Alaska's population grows and its economy develops, the characteristics and responsibilities of local governments change, a matter foreseen in the state constitution. Local government in Alaska is still evolving.

GOVERNMENT HIGHLIGHTS

Electoral Vote—3. **Representation in Congress**—U.S. senators, 2; U.S. representative, 1. **Legislature**—Senate, 20 members, 4-year terms; House of Representatives, 40 members, 2-year terms. **Governor**—4-year term; consecutive terms limited to two.

As a result of the Alaska Native Claims Settlement Act of 1971, which organized the native people into regional and village corporations, the regional corporations set up nonprofit organizations to receive federal grants and to provide services. Natives of Venetie, Tetlin, and Metlakatla have their own reservations. The native organizations perform many functions of local government. The federal government, as the largest single landholder in Alaska, performs numerous governmental functions on its lands, while the extensive military reservations report basically to the U.S. secretary of defense.

Politics. Because Alaskans are so heavily dependent on both the federal and state governments, which essentially control most land and jobs in the state, its citizens tend to have an intense interest in politics at all levels. Besides the Democratic and Republican parties, the Alaskan Independence and the Libertarian parties sometimes contend for offices. Party loyalties, however, are not strong in Alaska. While candidates run as party candidates, they largely rely on their personal organizations to get elected. Some politicians, such as Alaska's delegation in the U.S. Congress, are reelected for term after term. However, the role of parties is critical to the organization of the state legislature.

Finally, politics in Alaska involves the administrative problems of dealing with numerous federal and state agencies, particularly when an attempt is made to develop resources. In no other state does the issue of what can or cannot be done with land and resources involve so many governmental complexities.

7. History

The first human beings to settle the Americas may have reached Alaska from Siberia 25,000 to 40,000 years ago.

Native Settlement and Dispersal. The peoples that entered Alaska from Asia probably followed the ice-age mammals across the present Bering Strait at a time when the sea level was low enough to expose the continental shelf. They followed the Yukon and Tanana valleys upstream and settled the Interior, becoming the Athapascans. At the end of the last ice age some moved from the Interior across the Alaska and Coast Ranges to the Pacific coast. These peoples became the Tlingit, Haida, and Tsimshian peoples. Other groups probably moved from Asia following the coastline of the continental shelf and then retreated landward as the sea level rose. Developing strong cultures in the Aleutians, on Kodiak and St. Lawrence islands, and along the western edge of the Seward Peninsula, they became the Inuit (Eskimos) and Aleuts. Some migrated eastward into the Prince William Sound area and perhaps Southeastern. Aleuts settled the Aleutians from east to west.

From the Bering Strait, Eskimo groups that had developed the "Thule" sea-mammal hunting culture moved about 1,000 years ago across Arctic Alaska and Canada to Greenland where they encountered Viking settlers. By the mid-18th century, there were probably 70,000 native people in Alaska, about the same number as today. The Aleuts were driven out of most of the Aleutians in two phases: first by the Russians in the latter half of the 18th century, and later by the American military during World War II.

Russian Alaska. The Russian occupation of coastal Alaska was the final stage of an eastward movement that began during the reign of Ivan the Terrible in the mid-16th century. Russian explorers ventured in sometimes bloody fashion to the Pacific, which they reached in 1640.

Government-sponsored expeditions, notably those of Vitus Bering and Aleksei Chirikov in 1741, led to a half-century of brutal exploitation of the Aleuts. This was ended by the establishment of trading companies that in 1799 were placed under surveillance of the government with the formation of the Russian America Company. The leaders of this organization, most from the Russian Navy, by and large were talented and administered Alaska in a benign fashion.

British, French, Spanish, and American as well as Russian explorers charted the coast of Alaska in the late 18th and the early 19th century. The most important of these venturers was Capt. James Cook, whose British expedition (1778) led to the development of the Great Circle trading route in the North Pacific. During the early 19th century, American vessels that had entered the North Pacific became the dominant traders there. The Americans established close relationships with the Russians, carrying goods on consignment for the Russian America Company to Hawaii and Canton (Guangzhou), China. By the time the mid-century California Gold Rush had led to the formation of strong trading ties between San Francisco and Alaska, many American whaling vessels were already hunting along the coasts of western and Arctic Alaska. In the 1860s an American firm, the Collins Overland Telegraph Company, attempted to build a telegraph line down the Yukon across Alaska to connect North America to Russia and also sponsored explorations in Alaska under the auspices of the Smithsonian Institution.

By 1867 the U.S. government had accumulated an excellent body of knowledge about Alaska.

American Alaska: 1867–1912. Russia sold Alaska to the United States in 1867 as a consequence of the Crimean War, which had convinced the Czarist government that the area could not be defended in case of another war with Britain. The U.S. purchase, supported overwhelmingly by the Senate, was based on Alaska's strategic placement on the Great Circle trading route and knowledge of the region's fur, fishing, and probable mineral resources. Although the United States paid only $7.2 million for Alaska, critics of the purchase treaty negotiated by Secretary of State William H. Seward derided Alaska as "Seward's folly."

American governance in Alaska from 1867 to 1884—successively under the departments of the army, treasury, and navy—was extremely limited. An American company was given a monopoly over the significant fur-seal harvest on the Pribilof Islands, which had been colonized by Aleuts under Russian direction. American traders also opened a route along the entire Yukon River to Fort Reliance, near present Dawson, Canada, while prospectors searched for gold in southern Alaska, especially in the southeast.

Fish canneries established throughout southern Alaska in the 1880s and 1890s, brought in their own labor, took over the best fishing sites, and disrupted Native life. Gold prospecting led to a big lode discovery near Juneau in 1880. As a consequence of new economic development, the United States made Alaska a judicial district in 1884, with the basic purpose of applying mining laws so as to adjudicate disputes over land. At the same time, Congress deferred the issue of Native land claims.

HISTORICAL HIGHLIGHTS

c. 38,000–23,000 B.C. Paleo-Indians begin migrations across the Bering land bridge from Siberia into what is now Alaska.

c. 7,000–4,000 B.C. Eskimos and Aleuts migrate to Alaska from Siberia and Arctic Canada.

1728 Danish navigator Vitus Bering, commissioned by the Russian Navy, is the first European to discover St. Lawrence Island; he sails through the Bering Strait between Alaska and Siberia.

1741 Bering's expedition members, the first Europeans known to have walked on Alaskan soil, land on Kayak Island.

1784 Russian fur trader Grigori Shelikhov establishes Alaska's first permanent white settlement, on Kodiak Island.

1821 Russia forbids other countries from trading in Alaskan waters.

1825 Great Britain and Russia define their boundaries in northwestern America through a treaty with the United States; Alaska's southern boundary is set at 54°40′ latitude.

1847 Fort Yukon, first permanent English-speaking settlement in Alaska, is established by the Hudson's Bay Company, a British trading company.

1867 United States purchases Alaska from Russia for $7.2 million in gold.

1877 The Treasury Department assumes administration of Alaska, replacing the army.

1880 Richard Harris and Joseph Juneau make first major Alaskan gold strike, in Gastineau Channel.

1891 Siberian reindeer brought to provide food to Eskimos, who are threatened with starvation by near extinction of whales and walrus.

1892 Gold Rush begins (through 1910).

1912 Alaska becomes a U.S. territory (August 24); violent volcano eruption of Mt. Katmai.

1917 Mt. McKinley National Park established.

1922 Native voting rights established through courts.

1923 Federally owned, 470-mile (760-km) Alaska Railroad is completed.

1935 Hundreds of families are brought to Alaska by the federal government to farm the Matanuska Valley; Alaska Agricultural College and School of Mines becomes the University of Alaska.

1942 The 1,420-mile (2,280-km) Alcan Highway opens a route from Montana through Canada to Alaska (November 20); Japanese bomb Dutch Harbor in the Aleutian Islands and occupy Attu and Kiska islands.

1943 U.S. forces recapture occupied Alaskan Territory from Japanese.

1956 Alaska adopts its present constitution.

1959 Alaska becomes the 49th state (January 3).

1964 Most severe earthquake ever recorded in North America devastates south-central Alaska.

1971 The federal Alaska Native Claims Settlement Act grants peoples full title to some 40 million acres (16 million ha) and $962.5 million in cash.

1977 The $8 million, 798-mile (1,284-km) Trans-Alaska oil pipeline completed.

1979 Owing to high revenues from oil, Alaska's legislature abolishes state individual income tax.

1980 Alaska National Interest Lands Conservation Act assigns 104 million acres (42 million ha) to National Park System.

1989 Oil tanker *Exxon Valdez* runs aground in Prince William Sound, spilling 11 million gallons (42 million liters) of crude oil, the largest oil spill in U.S. history.

1994 Federal trial results in $5 billion verdict in the *Exxon Valdez* case.

1996 Congress lifts ban on exporting Alaskan crude oil.

1999 United States and Canada sign long-term Pacific Salmon Treaty tying annual catch limits to the strength of Pacific salmon stocks.

With a developed though modest transportation system along the Yukon and with American exploration of some of the major routes leading from southern to interior Alaska, gold prospecting exploded in the 1890s. One discovery after another culminated in the Klondike (1898) and Nome (1899) rushes. The gold miners who invaded Alaska moved from strike to strike in the great arc of the Yukon River basin. Skagway, in the southeast, was developed as a port for the Klondike field in Canada; other ports for mining operations were established at Valdez and Cordova; and interior settlements such as Fairbanks, Circle, and Rampart thrived as mining service centers.

The development of fish canneries, an extensive minerals industry, and the beginnings of agriculture required a more effective government than existed at the time. Thus, in 1912 Alaska became a territory but with limited political powers.

The Territory: 1912–1959. By 1920 mining for copper and gold was mostly under the control of large corporations able to afford the dredges needed for gold and the expensive facilities for underground operations at Kennicott and Juneau. While many of the dreams of early years, mainly regarding coal exports, were not realized, Alaska's economy between World Wars I and II was stable and slowly developing. Because the price of gold was fixed by the federal government, during the Great Depression gold mining was very profitable. Roads were improved, new communities were built, and the airplane and radio brought settlements closer together.

During World War II, especially because of the Japanese invasion of the Aleutians in 1942, about 200,000 American military personnel were sent to Alaska. Bases were built at Adak, Kodiak, Sitka, Anchorage, Fairbanks, and elsewhere, and the initial, pioneer Alaska (Alcan) Highway was completed. Until the end of the 1950s, with a few pauses, military construction was on a large

© STEVE MCCUTCHEON

The Trans-Alaska oil pipeline has earthquake-resistant features where it crosses a fault near Miller Creek.

scale and brought with it an influx of construction workers. Many military personnel stayed in Alaska after their tours of duty or retired there.

Contemporary Alaska. After statehood in 1959, oil development—first on the Kenai Peninsula and later at Prudhoe Bay—caused a new influx of construction workers to Alaska. They were followed by other people attracted by the economic expansion resulting from state government spending. Petroleum taxation built contemporary Alaska. Despite fluctuations in price, petroleum became a reasonably stable part of the economy, but by the mid-1980s the "boom" was over. For its future prosperity Alaska looked to tourism, further oil and gas development, metal mining, and trading opportunities in Asia, especially with Japan, South Korea, and Taiwan, areas deficient in the resources that Alaska has in abundance.

DONALD F. LYNCH*
University of Alaska at Fairbanks

GOVERNORS OF ALASKA

District		
John H. Kinkead		1884–1885
A. P. Swineford		1885–1889
Lyman E. Knapp		1889–1893
James Sheakley		1893–1897
John G. Brady		1897–1906
Wilford B. Hoggatt		1906–1909
Walter E. Clark		1909–1913
Territory		
John F. A. Strong		1913–1918
Thomas Riggs, Jr.		1918–1921
Scott C. Bone		1921–1925
George A. Parks		1925–1933
John W. Troy		1933–1939
Ernest Gruening		1939–1953
B. Frank Heintzleman		1953–1957
Michael A. Stepovich		1957–1958
Waino Hendrickson (acting governor)		1958–1959
State		
William A. Egan	Democrat	1959–1966
Walter J. Hickel	Republican	1966–1969
Keith H. Miller	Republican	1969–1970
William A. Egan	Democrat	1970–1974
Jay S. Hammond	Republican	1974–1982
William Sheffield	Democrat	1982–1986
Steve Cowper	Democrat	1986–1990
Walter J. Hickel	Independent	1990–1994
Tony Knowles	Democrat	1994–2002
Frank H. Murkowski	Republican	2002–

Bibliography

Bancroft, Hubert Howe, *History of Alaska, 1730–1885* (1890; reprint, Hafner Pub. Co. 1970).

Coates, Peter A., *The Trans-Alaska Pipeline Controversy: Technology, Conservation, and the Frontier* (Univ. of Alaska Press 1994).

Hedin, Robert, and Gary Holthaus, eds., *Alaska: Reflections on Land and Spirit* (Univ. of Ariz. Press 1994).

McBeath, Gerald A., and Thomas A. Morehouse, *Alaska Politics and Government* (Univ. of Nebr. Press 1994).

McPhee, John, *Coming into the Country* (1977; reprint, Noonday 1991).

Morehouse, Thomas A., et al., *Alaska's Urban and Rural Governments* (Univ. Press of Am. 1984).

Naske, Claus-M., and Herman E. Slotnick, *Alaska: A History of the 49th State*, 2d ed. (Univ of Okla. Press 1994).

Schorr, Alan E., ed., *Alaska Place Names*, 4th ed. (Denali Press 1991).

ALASKA, Gulf of, ə-las′kə, a wide inlet of the Pacific Ocean, off the southern coast of Alaska, between the Alaska Peninsula and the Alexander Archipelago. Much of the population of the state of Alaska is found along the coast of this gulf, which has numerous fine small harbors as well as the ports of Anchorage, Seward, Valdez, and Cordova. Kodiak, a large island in the western part of the gulf, is one of the most historic areas of Alaska. Salmon, shrimp, and crab fishing is conducted in the coastal waters.

ALASKA, University of, ə-las′-kə, a coeducational land-grant institution at College, near Fairbanks, Alaska. It was first projected by the U.S. Congress in 1915 as a territorial college of agriculture and school of mines, and was provided for on May 3, 1917, by the Alaska Territorial Legislature with a grant of $60,000. The legislature appropriated an additional $41,000 in 1921, and the college opened for classes in 1922 with an enrollment of six students served by six faculty members under the presidency of Charles E. Bunnell. In 1935 it was granted university status. By 1940 the student body numbered 270, and in 1950 it had risen to 330. The first community college affiliate, at Anchorage, was opened in 1953, and others were added later at Ketchikan, Juneau-Douglas, Palmer, Sitka, and Kenai, bringing the total enrollment in the early 1960's to over 3,000. There is also a Division of Statewide Services open to all Alaska residents.

The six faculties of the university are: arts and letters; behavioral sciences and education; biological sciences and renewable resources; business, economics, and government; earth sciences and mineral industry; and mathematics, physical sciences, and engineering. The university library of over 50,000 volumes contains special collections on Alaska and the Arctic.

ALASKA BOUNDARY DISPUTE, an international controversy involving the United States, Canada, and Britain. It arose in 1898, after the discovery of gold in the Klondike, a tributary of the Yukon River in the Yukon Territory, east of Alaska. The Canadian desire to control access to the Pacific to the goldfields induced the Canadian government to reexamine the Anglo-Russian Treaty of 1825, which delimited the boundary between Alaska and Canada. The United States had fallen heir to the Russian rights under the treaty when it purchased Alaska from Russia in 1867. Although the boundary had never been accurately surveyed, for 73 years the treaty had generally been interpreted as including within the Panhandle of Alaska a strip about 30 miles wide, measured from the low water mark, of inlets and estuaries that indented the coast, thus barring Canadian access to the sea.

Canadian Claims. The Treaty of 1825 provided that from a given point at the south end (54° 40′ N) "the line of demarcation shall follow the summit of the mountains situated parallel to the coast," except that if such summits "shall prove to be a distance of more than ten marine leagues from the ocean" the boundary "shall be formed by a line parallel to the windings of the coast, and which shall never exceed the distance of ten marine leagues therefrom." This provision seems to have been based on the observations of Capt. George Vancouver, who explored the coast in the latter part of the 18th century and reported that a range of mountains ran parallel to the coast, 25

or 30 miles from the sea. Actually there is neither a continuous range of mountains nor a well-defined watershed along much of this coast.

Canada contended, on the basis of the official French text of the treaty, that the range of mountains referred to consisted of peaks directly on the coast or, in some cases, on islands separated from the mainland by narrow channels, and that the boundary cut across such channels and deep inlets. It insisted, particularly, that certain islands at the mouth of the Portland channel (now called Portland Canal), at the south end of the Panhandle, were in Canadian territory, and that the same applied to the Lynn channel (Lynn Canal) in the northern part of the Panhandle. The latter claim was especially important since Lynn Canal gave access to the headwaters of the Yukon, which was navigable to the Klondike.

Appointment of Tribunal. A commission established by an Anglo-American conference in Washington during May 1898 to settle many outstanding disputes manifested "irreconcilable differences" on the Alaskan boundary, but an exchange of notes on Oct. 20, 1899, between Secretary of State John Hay and the British chargé d'affaires, Reginald Tower, provided a *modus vivendi* assuring access to both Canadians and Americans in the Lynn Canal area. United States interests criticized this agreement, and, by a convention signed on Jan. 24, 1903, it was agreed that the boundary question be arbitrated by a tribunal of six, three appointed by the United States and three by Britain, a majority vote being required for decision. Several specific questions were asked, four concerning the Portland channel and neighboring islands and three concerning the general interpretation of the treaty, particularly as to the designation of the range of mountains parallel to the coast, whose crests, if less than 10 marine leagues from the coast, should mark the boundary. This also called into question the interpretation of the term "coast," which could be applied either to the mainland shore, generally far removed from the open ocean, or to a line following the western beaches of the outlying islands, under which definition a boundary lying "ten marine leagues from the ocean" would not, in some sectors, even approach the mainland and would leave most of the disputed islands and inlets in Canadian hands.

To gain Senate approval of the treaty, President Theodore Roosevelt said that the United States might win but could not lose, implying that he would appoint arbitrators known to be committed to the American contentions. Such appointments would guarantee that the United States could not emerge the loser because, unlike most arbitral tribunals, no provision was made for an impartial umpire to assure decision if the arbitrators appointed by the parties should be equally divided.

President Roosevelt appointed to the tribunal Secretary of War Elihu Root, Senator Henry Cabot Lodge, and former Senator George Turner. The British government appointed Lord Alverstone (formerly Sir Richard Webster), chief justice of England, and two Canadians, Sir Louis Jetté and Allen B. Aylesworth. Former Secretary of State John Watson Foster was counsel for the United States, and Clifford Sifton for Britain.

Decision of Tribunal. The Alaska Tribunal (or Alaska Boundary Commission) convened in London on Sept. 3, 1903, and published its decision on October 20. It upheld the claims of the United States on most of the critical issues by votes of the three Americans and Lord Alverstone, to the discontent of the Canadian members of the tribunal, who wrote dissenting opinions. Lord Alverstone wrote a separate opinion agreeing with the British (or Canadian) contention that some of the narrow inlets, channels, and estuaries would not normally be regarded as parts of the Pacific Ocean, but also pointing out that neither the text of the Treaty of 1825 nor the records of its negotiation gave evidence that Britain had claimed any part of the shores of these inlets at the time, probably because the geography of the area and the possible importance of the inlets were unknown. The British contentions might, he thought, be grounds for urging a "just and equitable modification of the treaty," but they could not affect the construction of the treaty, which alone was before the tribunal and which supported the American contentions. The award resulted in a permanent settlement of the boundary dispute, but doubtless contributed to the Canadian demand, subsequently realized, for independence in the handling of international relations.

QUINCY WRIGHT, *University of Virginia*

Further Reading: Bailey, Thomas, *A Diplomatic History of the American People,* 10th ed. (Prentice-Hall 1980); Hulley, Clarence, *Alaska: Past and Present,* 3d ed. (1970; reprint, Greenwood Press 1981); Malloy, William, ed., *Treaties, Conventions, etc., Between the United States and Other Powers, 1776–1927,* vol. 1 (1901; reprint, Scholarly Press 1927); Starr, S. Frederick, *Russia's American Colony* (Duke Univ. Press 1987).

ALASKA HIGHWAY, ə-las'kə, a highway from Dawson Creek, British Columbia, to Fairbanks, Alaska, built by the United States Army Engineers and other government agencies during World War II. The road was constructed because of the military necessity of connecting army installations in Alaska with the United States by a protected land route. Construction started from Whitehorse, Yukon Territory, in April 1942, and from Dawson Creek in May. The road was completed in November of the same year at an estimated cost of $110 million.

Dawson Creek, on the eastern border of British Columbia, may be reached by two routes: via Edmonton, Alberta, and via Prince George, in central British Columbia. The route from Great Falls, Mont., to Dawson Creek via Edmonton is about 962 miles long. From Seattle, Wash., to Dawson Creek via Vancouver and Prince George the distance is 839 miles. From Dawson Creek, it is 918 miles to Whitehorse, 1,221 to the Alaska boundary, and 1,523 miles to Fairbanks.

The northern end of the Alaska Highway has several branches and connects with the Richardson Highway, the Denali Highway, and other parts of the Alaska highway system.

ALASKA PENINSULA, ə-las'kə, a mountainous peninsula of North America, extending in a southwesterly direction from the southern Alaskan mainland, between Bristol Bay of the Bering Sea and the Pacific Ocean. It is about 500 miles long. It is similar to the Aleutian Islands in its vegetation, which consists mostly of grasses, and its climate, which is cool and damp, with much fog. Its rugged mountain system, the Aleutian Range, contains many volcanic peaks and may be considered a northeastern extension of the Aleutian Island chain.

The peninsula is sparsely populated in the interior regions, but the Katmai National Monument in the northeast receives many visitors. There are fishing villages along both coasts.

ALASKA RANGE, ə-las'kə, a mountain range of southern Alaska. It extends about 400 miles in a quarter circle from the base of the Alaska Peninsula in the southwest to a point near the Tanana River valley in the northeast, and contains some of the loftiest mountains in North America, including the continent's highest peak, Mount McKinley (20,320 feet). Other important peaks are Mount Foraker (17,395 feet) and Mount Hunter (14,580 feet).

The range, a part of the Coast Mountain system, plays an important role in determining the climate of the state of Alaska. Mount McKinley National Park, in the northern part of the range, is a popular resort area, with some of the finest alpine scenery in the world.

ALASKAN BROWN BEAR. See BEAR.

ALASKAN MALAMUTE, mal'ə-mūt, the largest of the sled-dog breeds. According to the American Kennel Club (AKC) standard, the male should stand 25 inches (64 cm) high at the shoulder and weigh 85 pounds (39 kg); the female, 23 inches (58 cm) and 75 pounds (34 kg). With its dense, straight, longish coat of gray, black, or cinnamon, marked with white, the malamute resembles its smaller cousin, the Siberian husky, but never has blue eyes. Both breeds are heavy seasonal shedders.

A member of the AKC Working Dog group, the malamute has immense energy and endurance, qualities necessary in a sled dog but not in a pet puppy whose owner is training it to behave. Because it is very stubborn, the breed does not learn quickly. It may be hard to housebreak and is inclined to howl and to be destructive if left alone in the house. Although it quarrels with strange dogs, it is not a good watchdog or guard dog. Its beauty and playfulness, however, have made the malamute a popular pet.

JOHN HOWE
Author of "Choosing the Right Dog"

The Alaskan malamute, the largest of the sled dogs, is noted for its energy, strength, and endurance.

EVELYN SHAFER

AL-AZHAR, äl az′hər, a mosque-university in Cairo, Egypt, is the oldest seat of learning with a continuous history in the Islamic world. It was completed in 972 as the chief mosque of the Fatimid dynasty and disseminated the doctrines of the unorthodox Ismaili branch of Islam until Saladin destroyed the Fatimids in 1171. Since 1266, when the Mamluk sultan Baybars revived it as a seat of Muslim orthodox (Sunni) learning, al-Azhar has remained Cairo's leading mosque-school. As a result of centuries of Mamluk patronage, it is today a living museum of medieval architecture, although much of the original construction has been replaced or repaired.

Lavish endowments and the excellence of its scholarship made al-Azhar the Islamic world's leading university, especially after the Mongol destruction of eastern Islamic centers in the 13th century. In the 19th century it became the bastion of conservative religious scholars who opposed Egypt's growing secularization. Instruction centered almost solely on the memorization of the Koran and a syllabus of medieval religious materials. It was at once a mosque, a school system, and a theological college. A half century of spasmodic reform left it, in 1930, with the structural form of a Western university but with a medieval approach to education.

The government decreed a fundamental reform in 1961. Instruction at all levels was modernized, faculties of science were added, and a new campus was created. Under government auspices it annually sends hundreds of its teachers of Arabic and religion to other Islamic countries and accepts thousands of foreign students. It continues to be a leading center of religious thought and Islamic culture.

DANIEL N. CRECELIUS
California State College at Los Angeles

ALB, alb, a long robe of white linen, worn by Roman Catholic (and some Anglican) priests while conducting the Mass. It extends to the feet, has close-fitting sleeves, is bound around the waist by a cincture, and is often ornamented with an embroidered figure or panel near the bottom.

ALBA, Duke of. See ALVA, 3D DUKE OF.

ALBA, äl′bä, is a town in northern Italy, on the Tanaro River. It is situated about 30 miles southeast of Turin, in an important grape-growing section of the Piedmont. Alba is a market for agricultural products, raw silk, and livestock. It produces wine, automobile chassis, farm machinery, and bricks.

In Roman times, the town was known as Alba Pompeia. Alba has a cathedral built about 1500 and a museum with collections of rare ancient coins, manuscripts, and household utensils. Population: 29,910 (2001 census).

ALBA IULIA, äl′bä ū′lyä, is a city in Romania, on the Mureş River about 170 miles northwest of Bucharest. It is situated in the Hunedoara region of Transylvania.

The city is a rail junction and a distributing center for a farming region that produces wine, grain, poultry, and fruit. It has some light manufactures, including chiefly soap, furniture, and footwear.

As *Apulum,* the city was the capital of the Roman province of Dacia in the 100's and 200's A.D. Shortly after 1000 it came under Hungarian rule. Its name in Hungarian is *Gyulafehérvár.* The Hungarians made it the residence of a Roman Catholic bishop, and in the 1100s they built the cathedral, where the Hungarian hero János Hunyadi is buried. In the early 1700s, after the Austrian Habsburgs had conquered Translyvania, they constructed the citadel and named the city *Karlsburg* after Emperor Charles VI. The Romanians changed the name to Alba Iulia after World War I. Population: 71,254 (1992 census).

ALBA LONGA, al′bə lông′gə, was an ancient city in Italy, 12 miles southeast of Rome. It stood on the western side of Lake Albano, near what is now Castel Gandolfo, a summer residence of the popes.

Alba Longa was the oldest and at one time the most powerful city in Latium. Its traditional founder was Ascanius, the son of Aeneas. Ascanius is said to have built the city around 1150 B.C. Romulus, the mythical founder of Rome, was supposed to have been a grandson of a king of Alba Longa. The Romans destroyed the city about 600 B.C., and it was never rebuilt. All that remains of the city is a necropolis containing tombs more than 3,000 years old.

ALBACETE, äl-vä-thä′tä, is a city in Spain, 140 miles southeast of Madrid. It is the capital of Albacete province. The city lies in an irrigated section of the high, barren La Mancha plain. Albacete is noted for two products—saffron and knives. It also trades grain, wine, and cattle, and manufactures pottery, tiles, furniture, cement, chemicals, and food products.

Albacete is divided into an old upper town and an expanding new section below. The main points of interest are the archaeological museum, a church built in the 1500s, and the ruins of a much older wall of Moorish origin. Population: 148,934 (2001 census).

ALBACORE, al′bə-kôr, a tuna found in warm to temperate seas. It is most abundant in the Pacific Ocean, where it is caught commercially. Its white meat is the source of most canned tuna.

The albacore, about three feet long and weighing between 40 and 80 pounds, is the smallest of the tunas. It is identified by its long pectoral fins, which may be half as long as the fish. These fins fit into grooves along the side of the albacore. The tail fin is crescent-shaped and provides powerful propulsion. The albacore is blue above and yellow on the underside.

The albacore belongs to the order Perciformes, family Thunnidae (Scombridae). Its scientific name is *Thunnus (Germo) alalunga.*

ALBAN, ôl′bən, **Saint** (died about 304), the first British Christian martyr. He is said to have been a native of Verulamium (now St. Albans), in Hertfordshire. He suffered martyrdom under Roman Emperor Diocletian. Bede's *Ecclesiastical History* relates that Alban was converted to Christianity by a fugitive priest to whom he had given refuge and that later he was beheaded for contriving the cleric's escape. A chapel was erected at Alban's grave, and, in 793, King Offa of Mercia built a monastery in his honor. Pope Adrian IV (reigned 1154–1159) exempted the monastery from episcopal jurisdiction and named it England's leading abbey. Alban's feast is celebrated by Roman Catholics on June 22; by Anglicans, on June 17.

Vlorë lies just inland from its port. Albanian independence was proclaimed in this city in 1912.

© ZITA/SYGMA

ALBANIA, al-bā′nē-ə, a small country in south-eastern Europe. Situated in the western part of the Balkan Peninsula, it faces Italy across the Strait of Otranto, the entrance to the Adriatic Sea.

The Albanian people are descendants of the Illyrians, an Indo-European people who settled in the Balkan Peninsula during the first millennium B.C. The Illyrians were conquered in 167 B.C. by the Romans, who ruled the area for the next 500 years and left a considerable imprint on the Illyrian provinces. Those Illyrians who lived in the interior of what is now Albania were more resistant to Roman influences. These people were known as the *Albani* or the *Albanoi.* After the division of the Roman Empire in 395 A.D., Albania became part of the Eastern, or Byzantine, Empire.

In the last half of the 6th century A.D., groups of Slavic tribes began moving into the Balkan Peninsula and into the area of present-day Albania, imposing their culture on the already diluted Illyrian culture. As the Byzantine Empire began to decline, warring feudal lords took control of Albania. By the early 1400's, Turkey, by now the dominant power in the area, had taken advantage of the internal strife in Albania and had gained control of the region. With one brief intermission, Albania remained under Ottoman Turkish rule until 1912. The long period of Turkish domination left its mark on Albania's way of life, most notably its religion; by the end of the 17th century most Albanians had embraced the Islamic faith.

Albania became independent in 1912 but was occupied by foreign powers during World War I. Again independent after the war, Albania fell under the economic influence of Italy, and in April 1939, just before the beginning of World War II, Italy annexed Albania. Albanian partisans took control of the government in 1944.

1. The People

Albania is one of the most ethnically homogeneous states in the world. Approximately 98 percent of its inhabitants are Albanian in origin and speech. The only significant minority is a group of 60,000 Greeks in southern Albania. Several thousand Vlachs, Gypsies, Serbs, and Bulgarians live in the country.

The Albanian people are divided into two groups, the Ghegs in the north and the Tosks in the south, with the Shkumbi River forming a natural boundary between their territories. Despite slight differences between the groups, both regard themselves as Albanians.

The Ghegs, who lived primarily in the rugged, almost inaccessible mountainous regions of northern Albania, managed to preserve their ancient customs and traditions well into the 20th century. The Tosks, who lived mainly in the valleys and lowlands of southern Albania, worked as tenant farmers on the large estates of Albanian and foreign landlords. They were subjected to a greater degree of foreign influence than the Ghegs and therefore tended to be more liberal in their political and social views.

INFORMATION HIGHLIGHTS

Total Area: (land and inland water) 11,097 square miles (28,748 sq km).
Boundaries: *North,* Yugoslavia; *east,* Yugoslavia, Macedonia, Greece; *south,* Greece; *west,* Strait of Corfu, Strait of Otranto, Adriatic Sea, Yugoslavia.
Population: 3,500,000 (1999 est.).
Capital and Largest City: Tiranë.
Major Languages: Albanian (official), Greek.
Major Religions: Sunnī Islam, Albanian Orthodox Church, Roman Catholicism.

For Albania's flag, see under FLAG, both illustration and text.

Language. The Albanian language is an Indo-European language of Thraco-Illyrian origin. Owing to the poverty of the ancient Illyrian language and the many foreign conquests Albania has experienced, modern Albanian has been enriched by the addition of words and phrases of Latin, Greek, Turkish, Slavic, and Romance origin.

Two dialects, Gheg and Tosk, make up modern Albanian. The differences between them are superficial, and the two groups have little difficulty in understanding each other. In recent years linguists have attempted to standardize the spelling and grammar of Albanian and to expand its

vocabulary to meet modern requirements.

Religion. Another factor differentiating the Ghegs and Tosks was religion. An overwhelming majority of the Ghegs adhered to Sunnī Islam; the rest were Roman Catholics. Although most Tosks were Muslims, they were Sunnīs and Bektāshīs (Ṣūfīs) in almost equal numbers. The Tosk Christian minority belonged to the Albanian Orthodox Church. On the eve of World War II, 70 percent of the population was Muslim, 20 percent was Orthodox, and 10 percent was Roman Catholic.

The Communist takeover of the state in 1944 produced drastic changes in the nation's religious life. During the late 1940s and the early 1950s, the government brought all religious bodies under its control, purging the various denominations of their leaders and replacing them with individuals willing to follow official Communist dictates. From 1967 to 1990 the government prohibited religious services, with the result that religion lost its hold on a large segment of the Albanian population. In 1996 the proportion of the population actively practicing was 20 percent for Muslims, 6 percent for Orthodox Christians, and 3 percent for Roman Catholics.

Urbanization and Public Health. The policies of the Communist regime also affected other areas of Albanian life. The Communists tried to eradicate the distinctions between the Tosks and the Ghegs by encouraging migration and resettlement from one area of the country to another. By fostering industrialization, the Communist regime also promoted urbanization. Before World War II only 15 percent of the Albanian people lived in cities and towns, whereas by 2001 the figure had risen to more than 42 percent.

© C.S. HAMMOND & Co., Maplewood, N.J.

ALBANIA Map Index

Population: 3,413,904   Area: 11,100 square miles

CITIES and TOWNS

Berat, 40,500	A4
Bilisht, 4,000	B4
Borjë	B3
Burrel, 6,200	B3
Cërrik, 8,500	B3
Corovodë, 1,900	B4
Delvinë, 6,000	B5
Drenovë	B4
Durrës (Durazzo), 78,700	A3
Elbasan, 78,300	B3
Ersekë, 2,300	B4
Fier, 40,300	A4
Gjirokastër, 23,800	A4
Gramsh, 2,200	B4
Himarë	A4
Katjel	B3
Kavajë, 24,200	A3
Koplik	A2
Korçë, 61,500	B4
Krujë, 9,600	A3
Krumë	B2
Kuçovë, 12,300	B4
Kukës, 9,500	B2
Leskovik, 1,700	B4
Lezhë, 6,900	A3
Lushnjë, 26,900	A4
Maliq, 3,900	B4
Mborje	B4
Memaliaj, 4,000	B4
Memelisht	B4
Patos, 11,600	A4
Peqin, 3,800	A3
Përmet, 4,000	B4
Peshkopi, 5,500	B3
Pogradec, 13,100	B4
Pukë, 1,700	A2
Rrogozhinë, 3,500	A3
Rubik, 1,100	A3
Sarandë, 10,800	B5
Selenicë, 5,000	A4
Shëngjin, 1,000	A3
Shijak, 6,200	A3
Shkodër, 76,300	A2
Tepelenë, 2,500	A4
Tiranë (Tirana) (cap.), 239,381	A3
Vlorë (Vlonë), 67,700	A4

OTHER FEATURES

Adriatic (sea)	A3
Buenë (Bojanë) (river)	A3
Devoll (river)	B4
Drin (gulf)	A3
Drin (river)	B2
Drin i zi (river)	B3
Epirus (region)	B4
Erzen (river)	A3
Gramoz (mt.)	B4
Karaburun (pen.)	A4
Karavastas (lag.)	A4
Korab (mt.)	B3
Mat (river)	A3
North Albanian Alps	A2
Ohrid (lake)	B3
Osum (river)	B4
Otranto (str.)	A4
Pindus (mts.)	B4
Prespa (lake)	C4
Sazan (isl.)	A4
Seman (river)	A4
Shkodër (lake)	A2
Shkumbi (river)	B3
Vijosë (river)	B4
Vlorë (bay)	A4

Total Pop. - 1995 official estimate; cap. - 1989 final census; Other pops - 1979 final census, 1987 official estimate, 1964 off. est.

THE MOSQUE, like the church, fell into disrepair in Albania after the government banned religious worship.

A MARKET IN TIRANË draws peasants from the countryside to sell their produce to the capital's inhabitants.

The Communist regime did much to improve the health of the masses. Between 1938 and 1996 the life expectancy of the average Albanian at birth increased from 38 to 68 years of age, while the yearly death rate dropped from 18 to 5 persons per 1,000. Meanwhile, between 1950 and 1996 population growth declined from 3 percent to less than 1.34 percent.

2. The Land and Natural Resources

Albania is largely a mountainous country. Approximately 70 percent of its area lies 1,000 feet (300 meters) or more above sea level. The remaining 30 percent consists of a marshy coastal plain (in the process of being reclaimed), rolling hills, and mountain and river valleys. Only 22 percent of the land surface is arable.

There are three major lakes in Albania, Lake Shkodër in the northwest and Lake Ohrid and Lake Prespa in the east. Shkodër and Ohrid lie partly in Yugoslavia, and Prespa is at the junction of Albania, Greece, and Yugoslavia. The most important rivers are the Drin, Seman, Shkumbi, Vijosë, and Buenë; all empty into the Adriatic Sea.

Environment. Although Albania is a small nation, it has a diverse climate because of its varied topography. There are three main climatic zones in the country. The southern coastal lowlands enjoy a Mediterranean climate with mild, rainy winters and hot, arid summers. The most common kinds of vegetation in this region are Mediterranean-type fruit trees and scrub oak. In the lowlands of central and north Albania a moist continental climate prevails. Here more abundant rainfall makes possible a wider variety of vegetation. Various food crops and forests of willow, poplar, elm, pine, oak, and white beech are found in this region. The rugged highlands of northern and eastern Albania have an Alpine climate, characterized by cool, moist summers and severe winters. Large stands of beech and black pine are found here. Most Albanian wildlife—wolves, bears, wild boars, deer, and eagles and other mountain birds—is concentrated in this region.

Albania is subject to severe earthquakes. On the southwest coast, tsunamis may occur.

Natural Resources. Albania is relatively rich in mineral resources. Among the most important are petroleum, bitumen, lignite, chrome, copper, iron-nickel ore, clay, and limestone. The government has placed a high priority on the development of these resources.

Albania's rapid streams and waterfalls give the country a considerable potential for hydroelectric development.

3. The Economy

When Albania became independent in 1912, its chief components were primitive agriculture and livestock raising. There was no significant industry and little interregional or foreign trade. After World War I, Albania sought economic assistance from the League of Nations in the hope that it might be able to develop its economy without becoming dependent on a foreign power. When the League turned down its plea, Albania sought help from Italy.

Between 1925 and 1939, Albania became an economic dependency of Italy. On the eve of World War II, however, Italian aid had only slightly altered the character of the Albanian economy. In 1938 agriculture accounted for 92 percent of Albania's national income. When the Communists seized power in 1944, the Albanian economy was on the brink of collapse.

Coordinated economic planning in Albania began with a one-year plan in 1948. This was followed by a two-year plan and then a series of five-year plans. The goal of the five-year plans was to transform Albania from a backward agricultural state into a modern industrial-agricultural nation. While the plans were not completely successful, they expanded Albanian industrial production to the point where it accounted for almost half the national income. Still, Albania remained the poorest country in Europe, as it had been in 1912.

Agriculture. In 1945–1955 the government initiated a series of agricultural reforms that broke up the large estates and divided them among the peasants. The peasants resisted attempts to collectivize agriculture, and in 1956 the government abandoned its "conciliatory" policy toward the peasantry and used every means at its disposal to bring about collectivization. By 1973, all of Albania's agriculture had been collectivized.

The most significant change in agriculture, apart from collectivization, was increased production of industrial crops. Chief among these were sugar beets, cotton, and tobacco.

479

The Communists also stressed the mechanization of agriculture and tripled the arable land surface through an extensive reclamation program. While Albania's livestock population increased only slightly after World War II, the animals were of a higher quality.

Mining and Energy. Albania is an important producer of chrome, copper, and ferronickel. Although the country also produces petroleum and natural gas, most of its energy comes from hydroelectricity. Power potential was exploited on the Drin and other rivers, and rural electrification was substantially completed by 1970.

Industry. Between 1945 and 1947 the Communist regime quickly nationalized Albania's industry, which afterward was expanded rapidly. Production, which before World War II was limited largely to foodstuffs, cement, and cigarettes, was diversified to include textiles, footwear, fuel oil, fertilizer, machinery, copper products, and iron and steel.

Labor. One of the major problems confronting Albanian economic planners after 1945 was the shortage of skilled labor. To remedy this problem, a system of vocational and technical schools was established. Many industrial enterprises also provided specialized training for unskilled or semiskilled workers. Virtually all laborers were enrolled in the state-sponsored trade union movement.

Foreign Trade. The composition of Albanian foreign trade changed drastically after World War II. Before the war Albania imported mainly foodstuffs and consumer goods, while exporting animal and agricultural products. By the 1990's, Albania's exports consisted largely of minerals, finished or semifinished manufactured goods, and agricultural produce; imports, reflecting the drive for industrialization, consisted primarily of machinery and industrial raw materials.

At the time of the Soviet-Albanian break in the early 1960's, the USSR was Albania's main trading partner. By 1962, China had assumed that role. After the late 1970's, however, Albania expanded its range of trading partners and no single country dominated its foreign commerce.

Transportation and Communications. Albania's primitive transportation and communications systems contributed heavily to the country's

economic backwardness before World War II. Under the Communist regime the Albanian highway system increased from about 1,400 miles (2,250 km) to 4,200 miles (6,700 km). A railroad network was developed, chiefly linking the port of Durrës with Tiranë and other inland cities. The ports were modernized and enlarged, and oil and gas pipelines were built. The nation's communication systems also were improved.

4. Education

Albania had no national educational system when it became an independent state. Although during the 1920's and 1930's the government sought to expand educational facilities, in 1938 approximately 80 percent of the Albanian people were still illiterate. Education made great strides under the Communist regime. It should be stressed, however, that the Communists regarded education as a device to inculcate the people with socialist ideology and to develop their talents for the benefit of the state.

Between 1945 and 1990 the number of elementary school pupils in Albania rose from 54,000 to more than 540,000. Even more spectacular gains were made in secondary education, where enrollment increased from 2,500 in 1938 to nearly 200,000 in 1990.

After 1945 the Albanian government constructed from scratch a national system of higher education. Between 1945 and 1951 a number of "higher institutes" in such fields as agriculture, medicine, education, and technology were formed. The institutes were merged in 1957 to form the State University of Tiranë, Albania's first university. In addition to the university, the state established a conservatory of music and institutes of fine arts and drama.

An extensive program of adult education was undertaken. Although the Albanian government claimed to have wiped out illiteracy, by the 1990's possibly 25 percent of the people still could not read.

5. Cultural Life

The cultural development of Albania before the 20th century was greatly hindered by Turkish domination. Modern Albanian literature emerged only after the Albanian national revival of the late 19th and early 20th centuries. Most of the work produced in this era had strongly patriotic overtones.

From 1912 to 1939, Albanian literature became more sophisticated in style and more varied in content. In the 1930's, literature of social protest became popular among Albanian intellectuals. There was, however, little activity and interest displayed in the fields of art, drama, music (except folk music), and painting.

In the period after 1945 the Albanian government made a conscious effort to enrich the cultural life of the people. The state subsidized writers and artists and established theaters, libraries, museums, and cultural centers. Albania today has its own symphony orchestra, motion picture studio, and ballet and theater groups.

Albania's new culture, however, developed in accordance with the doctrines of socialist realism, which lent a drab quality to it. Most Albanian literature in this period dealt with such themes as the social injustice that existed under the pre-Communist regime, the heroic struggle of the Albanian partisans during World War II, and the building of socialism in Albania.

SARANDË, because of its fine natural harbor, became an Italian naval station during World War I.

EASTFOTO N.Y.

THE PEASANT BAZAAR continued to be an important market despite the communization of the economy.

AGRICULTURAL COOPERATIVES devoted to raising cotton and other crops became basic to the economy.

There were strong indications by the mid-1960's that many young talented writers and artists were protesting the strictures that had been placed on them, just as their counterparts in other Communist states had done. Literary output, however, continued to grow.

6. History and Government

The Illyrians, who settled in the Balkan Peninsula in the first millennium B.C., appear to have been a fairly advanced people economically and culturally. Politically they were at first divided into tribes and principalities, but between the 4th and the 2d centuries B.C. several strong and capable rulers united the tribes and formed the kingdom of Illyria. The Illyrian phase of Albanian history ended in 167 B.C. when the kingdom was conquered by the Romans.

Dilution of the Illyrian Heritage. During the period of Roman rule (167 B.C.–395 A.D.) the Illyrian provinces prospered, and most of the Illyrians became Romanized. At least six Roman emperors—Claudius, Marcus Aurelius, Probus, Diocletian, Constantine the Great, and Justinian—were of Illyrian descent. Some of the Illyrians, however, chiefly a group known as the Albani or Albanoi, living in what is now central Albania, strongly resisted Roman influence and preserved their culture.

Most inhabitants of the Roman Illyrian provinces had embraced Christianity by the end of the 4th century A.D. When the Roman empire was divided in 395 A.D., Albania became part of the Byzantine empire. The Albanian Church, however, remained subordinate to the Roman pope until 732, when it was placed under the control of the patriarch of Constantinople. In 1054, at the time of the schism between the Eastern and Western churches, northern Albania returned to the Roman fold, while southern Albania remained loyal to the patriarch.

The movement of the Bulgars, Serbs, and other Slavic peoples into the Balkan Peninsula was of even greater significance in the history of the Albanian people. These incursions, which began in the last half of the 6th century, diluted further the Illyrian heritage. Once again, only the Albanoi were able to preserve their identity in the face of an alien influence.

The external threat to Albania increased in the 1100's–1400's as the Byzantine empire began to decline. Bulgars, Normans, Angevins, Venetians, and Serbs each sought control of Albania, but none was able to dominate the country for any great length of time. By the time the power of the last of these groups, the Serbs, was broken in 1355, the Byzantine empire was too weak to reassert its authority in Albania.

At this point Albania broke up into a number of feudal states. Quarrels soon erupted among the leading noble families, and by the end of the 1300's one of the warring factions had turned to the Ottoman Turks for assistance. The Turks used this opportunity to enhance their own position in Albania. By the 1430's they had reduced most of Albania to the status of a Turkish satellite.

Ottoman Rule. Encouraged by the papacy and by Venice, the Albanians continued to resist the Turks. In 1443 the Albanian people found a capable leader in the person of Skanderbeg (1405–1468), whose exploits have made him Albania's national hero. Between 1444 and 1468, Skanderbeg's armies expelled the Turks from Albania and held them at bay. After his death in 1468, organized resistance to the Turks gradually collapsed. By the end of the 15th century all of Albania was once again under Turkish control. It remained under Turkish rule until 1912.

Most of the Albanians who did not emigrate had embraced Islam by the end of the 17th century. In about 1690 a large group of these Muslim converts were forced by the Turkish authorities to resettle in Kosovo, which became part of Yugoslavia. These Albanians were never assimilated by the Yugoslavs, and they formed the largest foreign minority in Yugoslavia.

From the 16th to the 18th century, Albania was divided into a number of military fiefs (*timars*). By the 18th century most of these fiefs had become hereditary estates (*cifliks*) controlled by native Albanian Muslim landlords and cultivated by tenant farmers. There was little economic or cultural progress in Albania during this period. Most ambitious and talented Albanians entered the Ottoman military or civil service. Many of these distinguished themselves in the employ of the Turks.

National Awakening. As the power of the Ottoman empire began to decline in the late 18th and early 19th centuries, Albania fell under the control of several native pashas who were in theory vassals of the Ottoman sultan but who were in fact independent of his control. The most important of these local rulers were Ali Pasha of Janina, who was master of southern and central Albania in 1788–1822, and the leaders of the Bushati clan, who dominated northern Albania in 1757–1831.

THE STATE UNIVERSITY OF TIRANË was formed in 1957 by merging several institutes of technology.

The destruction of the Bushatis' power in 1831 and the inauguration of a reform program in the Ottoman empire gave impetus to an Albanian national revival in the 19th century. Politically the national revival championed the creation of an autonomous Albanian state within the Ottoman empire; culturally it sought to make the Albanian people aware of their historical and literary heritage.

Unfortunately for the Albanians, their aspirations conflicted with those of their neighbors, the Greeks and the Serbs. Both these groups hoped to add territory inhabited by the Albanians to their own states. Furthermore, by the end of the 19th century, Austria-Hungary and Italy also began to take an active interest in Albanian affairs. It was not until September 1912, after repeated uprisings, that the Albanians were finally granted a large measure of autonomy by the Turkish government. A month later the First Balkan War (October 1912–May 1913) broke out when Bulgaria, Greece, Montenegro, and Serbia invaded the Balkan Ottoman provinces.

Independence. Threatened with partition among their neighbors, the Albanians declared their independence on Nov. 28, 1912. The European Powers formally recognized the independence of Albania in July 1913 and placed the new nation under their protection. Both Greece and Serbia had violently opposed the creation of an independent Albanian state. The Albanian nationalist leaders were bitterly disappointed over the fact that the large Albanian community in Kosovo was incorporated into Serbia. Greece claimed the southern provinces of Albania (Northern Epirus) on the grounds that the substantial Orthodox population inhabiting the area were Greeks, not Albanians. The Kosovo and Northern Epirus questions have been a constant source of friction between Albania and its neighbors since 1913. The strong national feeling that these two issues generate has been an important factor in the political life of the Albanian state.

The European Powers appointed an international control commission to advise the provisional government, headed by Ismail Qemal, and to choose a permanent ruler for Albania. Prince Wilhelm of Wied became king of Albania on March 7, 1914, but his reign was a short one. Unable to quell a series of uprisings that broke out in central and southern Albania, Wilhelm left the country on Sept. 3, 1914.

During World War I there was a complete breakdown of central authority in Albania, as the armies of first one and then another of the belligerents occupied the country. After the war, to combat more effectively attempts on the part of Greece, Italy, and Yugoslavia to partition Albania, a group of Albanian notables met at Lushnjë on Jan. 21, 1920, to draw up a new constitution. Under this constitution, between 1921 and 1924, the Albanian people enjoyed the greatest degree of political freedom in their history. But since neither the liberals nor the conservatives had the support of a majority of the electorate, governments rose and fell with alarming frequency. By 1923, Bishop Fan S. Noli had become the leading spokesman for the liberals, and Ahmet Zogu for the conservatives. Noli wanted to institute a sweeping program of economic and social reforms in Albania without delay. Zogu was not wholly unsympathetic to reform but wanted to proceed cautiously, so as not to arouse unduly the powerful conservative interests in the nation.

The conservatives gained control of the government in 1923, but they were overthrown by a revolution of the pro-Noli forces in June 1924. The Noli regime remained in power only six months. Its failure to carry out reforms alienated the Albanian masses, and its recognition of the Soviet Union aroused great concern in Yugoslavia. In December 1924, Zogu invaded Albania with the aid of the Yugoslavs and forced the Noli government into exile.

King Zog. Zogu ruled Albania from 1925 to 1939. Between 1925 and 1928, Albania was a republic under the presidency of Zogu. In September 1928, Zogu transformed Albania into a hereditary monarchy and assumed the title Zog I, King of the Albanians. During his reign Zog established a modern, well-trained police force; reformed Albania's legal system along Western lines; took preliminary steps to establish a national educational system; and started a modest public works program. Zog ruled, however, as a dictator. Although careful to preserve the appearance of constitutionality, he destroyed the political liberties of the Albanian people and reduced the Albanian parliament to a rubber stamp.

During Zog's reign Albania became an Italian satellite. In November 1926, Albania and Italy signed a treaty of friendship and a year later concluded a 20-year defensive alliance. Through these agreements Italy assumed the direction of Albanian military and foreign affairs. Italy also enjoyed a favored economic position in Albania at this time. Not content with this indirect control over Albania, Italy invaded and annexed Albania on April 7, 1939.

Foreign Rule. Between April 1939 and September 1943, Albania and Italy were joined in a personal union under King Victor Emmanuel III. Italy ruled Albania through a series of puppet governments that did not enjoy the support of the Albanian people. After the surrender of Italy in 1943, Germany assumed control of Albania. The Germans restored Albania's independence and set up a non-Communist government. The authority of this regime, however, was challenged by the Communists, who by 1944 were tightening their grip on Albania.

Communization. World War II, which paved the way for the Communist seizure of power, marks a major turning point in the history of Albania. Prior to the war the Albanian Communists were divided into a number of small and contending factions, and it was not until Nov. 8, 1941, that these dissident groups were brought together under Yugoslav auspices to form the Albanian Communist Party (called the Albanian Party of Labor after 1948). Enver Hoxha, a former teacher, was named first secretary of the party.

By taking a leading role in the Albanian resistance movement during World War II, the Communists were able to gain the confidence of a sizable portion of the Albanian people. In September 1942 they formed the National Liberation Movement, a coalition of all anti-Axis forces in Albania, behind which they carried on a civil revolution in Albania. By the spring of 1944 the Communists had discredited and defeated the only organized non-Communist resistance groups in the nation. When the last German troops were evacuated from Albanian soil in October 1944, the Communists seized power and named Hoxha as head of Albania's provisional government.

In 1944 and 1945 the Hoxha regime consolidated its position. The government moved to gain control over the economy, eliminate its internal opposition, and make preparations for the election of a constituent assembly. On Dec. 2, 1945, the Communist and pro-Communist candidates, running under the banner of the Democratic Front (the successor to the National Liberation Front), won an overwhelming majority of the seats in the constituent assembly. The assembly proclaimed Albania a "people's republic" on Jan. 11, 1946, and on March 14, 1946, it approved the new Albanian constitution, patterned after those of the Soviet Union and Yugoslavia.

The Yugoslav Threat. From 1944 to the spring of 1948, Soviet leader Joseph Stalin appears to have given Marshal Tito of Yugoslavia a free hand in dealing with Albania. During the late 1940s, Tito sought to isolate Albania from the outside world, to prepare the way for its incorporation into Yugoslavia. The 1946 Albanian-Yugoslav mutual assistance pact, followed by a series of economic agreements between the two nations, gave Yugoslavia a controlling interest in Albanian military and economic affairs. In addition, Tito sought to overthrow Hoxha and replace him with Koçi Xoxe, the pro-Yugoslav minister of the interior. By 1948, Xoxe appeared to be on the verge of toppling Hoxha from power. At this juncture both Hoxha and Albania were saved from extinction by the eruption of the Soviet-Yugoslav dispute. Hoxha's enthusiastic backing of the Soviet Union enabled him to reassert his authority and pose as the savior of the country. Thereafter, relations between Albania and Yugoslavia remained tense.

Soviet Domination. Having freed itself from Yugoslav domination, Albania became a full-fledged satellite of the Soviet Union and began to play a more active, though still limited, role in the affairs of the Communist world. In January 1949 Albania became a member of the Council for Mutual Economic Assistance (COMECON). In the 1950s the Soviet Union granted Albania increased economic and technical assistance.

The death of Stalin in March 1953 caused a wave of unrest in Albania. In accordance with the new Soviet policy of collective leadership, Hoxha relinquished his posts of foreign and defense minister, while retaining those of premier and party first secretary. In July 1954 he resigned as premier and appointed Mehmet Shehu to this post. Hoxha and Shehu were the dominant political personalities in Albania until the 1980s.

Until 1955 there was no evidence of serious conflict between Albania and the Soviet Union.

Backed by the USSR, Albania became a charter member of the Warsaw Pact and a member of the United Nations in 1955. However, differences arose between Moscow and Tiranë during the latter part of 1955, when the Soviet Union took steps to improve relations with Yugoslavia. The de-Stalinization campaign, which was announced at the 20th Congress of the Communist Party of the Soviet Union in February 1956, further strained relations between the USSR and Albania. Hoxha and Shehu felt that they could not endorse these new policies without endangering their positions of leadership.

Soviet Premier Nikita Khrushchev made a determined effort to reach an understanding with the Albanians between 1957 and 1959. He increased Soviet economic assistance to Albania and canceled its debt to the USSR. In 1959 Khrushchev visited Albania in a last unsuccessful effort to bring the Albanians into line.

China's Ally. By 1960, Soviet-Albanian relations had taken a new turn for the worse. Albania by this time had found a new ally in the People's Republic of China (PRC), which was also at odds with the Soviet Union. Albania and the PRC were united in their opposition to Khrushchev's policies of de-Stalinization, peaceful coexistence, and conciliation toward Yugoslavia. In June 1960, Albania publicly supported China on those issues, which had become points of contention between Moscow and Beijing.

During the summer of 1960 the Soviet government appears to have backed an abortive coup aimed at overthrowing Hoxha and Shehu. By the fall of 1960, Soviet economic and technical aid to Albania had been drastically curtailed. In November 1960, at an international meeting of Communist party leaders, Hoxha denounced Khrushchev. The Soviet government retaliated by withdrawing the credits it had promised to finance Albania's third five-year plan. In early 1961, however, China agreed to supply Albania with credits of $123 million to help underwrite the plan.

When the Albanians made it clear in 1961 that they had no intention of backing down in the face of Soviet pressure, the Russians recalled their technical advisers and terminated all aid programs in Albania. The Albanians in turn closed the Soviet submarine base at Vlorë and boycotted the activities of the Warsaw Pact and COMECON. In December 1961 the Soviet Union broke off diplomatic relations with Albania. China, plagued by internal problems, failed to keep its economic promises to Albania in the 1960s, and relations with Beijing cooled after China's accommodation with the United States in 1971–1972. In 1978, with Albania increasingly critical of China's post-Mao leadership, Beijing ended its assistance. Rejecting aid offered by the USSR, Albania cautiously began establishing trade contacts with other countries in Europe.

A new constitution in 1976 redefined Albania as a "people's socialist republic." It enhanced the dominant position of the Party of Labor and sought to ensure that Hoxha's Stalinist policies would be continued after his death. In 1981, Premier Shehu was "liquidated" for attempting to seize power. Hoxha himself died in 1985 and was succeeded as party first secretary by Ramiz Alia, who remained the head of state.

The End of Communism. Albania at first resisted the reforms that began to sweep Communist Eastern Europe at the end of the 1980s. In March

President Sali Berisha, Albania's first post-Communist leader, was forced to resign after civil unrest in 1997.

© GIRY-SITTLER/REA/SABA

1990, however, in order to defuse popular discontent, Alia announced a limited democratization. Prominent hard-liners were removed from government and party posts, and independent parties were authorized.

On March 31, 1991, in the first multiparty elections since World War II, the Communists retained power, although the opposition did extremely well in urban areas. The parliament elected Alia president of the "Republic of Albania." Civil unrest in May, however, led to the resignation of the Communist cabinet on June 4. Alia then formed a transitional government in which the Communists and the opposition had equal representation. New elections, held in March 1992, yielded a victory for the Democratic Party (DP), and Sali Berisha, president of the DP, was elected president of Albania on April 6.

Under Berisha, controls over the political system were loosened, pluralism was expanded, and the security forces were professionalized. Virtually all collectivized land was distributed, creating a new landowning class and spurring a recovery in agriculture. Soon, however, opposition figures and human rights organizations began to accuse Berisha of dictatorial tendencies, including the arbitrary imposition of a presidential system of government. The government grew less tolerant of criticism in the press, and journalists were arrested in the name of "state security." Leaders of the opposition Socialist Party (SP), the successor to the Party of Labor, were imprisoned on corruption and conspiracy charges they claimed were politically motivated. Critics of the president within the DP were dismissed.

In 1996 the DP won by substantial margins in elections that international monitors said were flawed by "serious irregularities." In February 1997, however, the country was rocked by rioting after the collapse of fraudulent investment schemes erased the life savings of half the population. Police and military forces rapidly disintegrated, and military arsenals were thrown open to the public. Order was restored only in April, when Italy led a multinational force into the country, but armed bands continued to permeate the country and many weapons were funneled to rebels in neighboring Kosovo.

Early elections, held in June, were won overwhelmingly by the SP. The DP, now in opposition, accused it of dictatorial tendencies and boycotted the parliament for months. In September 1998 the government accused Berisha of attempting to overthrow it by inciting renewed rioting after the assassination of a DP official.

Albania's relations with its neighbors were strained over the issues of Albanian refugees in Italy and Greece, the status of the Greek minority in Albania, and the status of the Albanian minorities in Macedonia and Kosovo, Serbia. Ethnic Albanian refugees and rebels from Kosovo used Albanian territory as a safe haven in 1998–1999, threatening to ensnare Albania in that region's civil war. NATO (North Atlantic Treaty Organization) then used Albania as a staging ground for its 1999 bombing campaign against Serbia to bring the Kosovo war to a end.

NICHOLAS C. PANO*, *Western Illinois University*

Bibliography

Jacques, Edwin E., *The Albanians: An Ethnic History from Prehistoric Times to the Present* (McFarland & Co. 1995).
O'Donnell, James, *A Coming of Age: Albania under Enver Hoxha* (East European Monographs 1999).
Vaughan-Whitehead, Daniel, *Albania in Crisis: The Predictable Fall of the Shining Star* (Edward Elgar 1999).
Vickers, Miranda, *The Albanians: A Modern History* (St. Martin's 1997).

ALBANY, Duke of, Scottish title held by members of the Stuart family. In 1881 it was bestowed as a United Kingdom title upon Leopold, son of Queen Victoria. (See STUART.)

ALBANY, äl′bə-nē, a residential city in California. It is situated in Alameda county, on the eastern shore of San Francisco Bay, just north of Berkeley. Settled in 1853, it was incorporated in 1908. Population: 16,444.

ALBANY, äl′bə-nē, a city in southwestern Georgia, and the seat of Dougherty county and its industrial and commercial center. Albany is located in a semitropical region at the head of navigation on the Flint River, 145 miles (233 km) south of Atlanta. The city is a trade center for a productive agricultural region and has developed a diversified industrial economy. Paper-shell pecans are among the city's important agricultural products. Albany is situated in the Plantation Trace region. The area is well known for quail hunting.

Albany State College, a liberal arts college, was established in 1903. Other educational institutions include Albany Junior College, Darton College, and the Albany Technical Institute. The cultural interests of Albany are served by the Albany Museum of Art and the Thronateeska Heritage Center, which includes the Wetherbee Planetarium and a natural history and space museum. Within Chehaw Park is the Chehaw Wild Animal Park. Lake Worth is a popular recreation site as well.

Originally inhabited by a tribe of Creek Indians who called the site Skywater, Albany was laid out in 1836 by Alexander Shotwell and was named after Albany, N.Y. Colonel Nelson Tift, a Connecticut Yankee, built the first house and store in Albany and later built the first bridge over the Flint River. The city was incorporated in 1841. Population: 76,939.

VIRGINIA P. RILEY*, *Albany Public Libraries*

The Nelson A. Rockefeller Empire State Plaza in Albany, N.Y., is dominated by the Tower Building (center).

ALBANY, ôl'bə-nē, the capital of New York state and the seat of Albany county. It is situated on a hill on the west bank of the Hudson River, in east central New York, 140 miles (225 km) north of New York City. Its distinctive skyline is most evident from the south and east. Crowning the hill are the state capitol, the Legislative Office Building, and the Nelson A. Rockefeller Empire State Plaza. The city's Dutch ancestry is apparent in the architecture of some of its older buildings. Downtown, the steep and narrow streets, winding up from the river, date from early settlement.

Albany began a program of urban rehabilitation in the third quarter of the 20th century. Ninety acres (36 hectares) in the substandard downtown section were condemned by the state and made the site for a great complex of state office buildings, housing, and recreational areas, including an amphitheater for outdoor events. This complex, the Nelson A. Rockefeller Empire State Plaza, has contributed greatly to the rejuvenation of the inner city and its commercial life. Other important new developments include housing units for low-income and older citizens, middle-income apartments, arterial highways to ring the city, and a new bridge across the Hudson.

Major Economic Activities. Albany is the trading center for a large agricultural and resort area. One of its major industries is manufacturing; the city produces machine tools, paper products, felt, softballs, aspirin, brake linings, cement, steel products, electrical equipment, dental products, and chemicals. Albany is served by airlines, Amtrak, and interstate bus lines. It is the focal point of the Albany-Schenectady-Troy greater metropolitan area.

Albany is also a deepwater port and a major transshipping point for railroads, trucks, barges, and oceangoing vessels. It is about 8 miles (13 km) south of the point at which the Mohawk River and the Erie Canal enter the Hudson. Thus it is an important stop on the barge canal system of New York, which reaches the Great Lakes via the Erie Canal and Lake Champlain via the Champlain Canal. The port has specialized petroleum installations and is one of the largest oil storage and distribution centers on the Atlantic seaboard. It also has molasses storage facilities and a grain elevator and flour mill. In 1960 the U.S. Congress authorized improvements for the port. After a pier collapsed in 1967, the state provided a $3 million loan to rehabilitate the pier and other port facilities.

Social and Cultural Institutions. The State University of New York at Albany, which absorbed the New York State College for Teachers (founded in 1844), occupies a handsome campus on land acquired in the 1960's for that purpose by the state. Other institutions of higher learning include the Albany Law School, Medical College, and College of Pharmacy, which are branches of Union University (main campus, Schenectady); the College of St. Rose and Siena College, both Roman Catholic institutions; and an evening college affiliated with Russell Sage College (main campus, Troy). The city also has a junior college, a business college, a school of nursing, and a secretarial school. Elementary and secondary enrollment is divided almost evenly between public and private or parochial schools.

Of great cultural and educational interest are the New York State Museum and the New York State Library, which are housed in the Cultural Education Center of the Empire State Plaza. Close by is the Albany Institute of History and Art, which has collections of regional art, silver, pewter, and furniture dating from Dutch settlement to the present. Other places of interest include the Schuyler Mansion (1762), now a museum depicting the life-style of a prominent 18th century family; Quackenbush Square (1730), the site of the oldest house in Albany, containing a museum, cafe, park, and gardens; and Cherry

485

Hill (1787), a preserved home occupied by the Van Rensselaer family for nearly 200 years.

Albany's most notable public buildings are the state capitol and the Nelson A. Rockefeller Empire State Plaza, which command an impressive view of the downtown section from the top of State Street Hill. Begun in 1868 and completed 30 years later, the capitol was designed by four architects and constructed in French Renaissance style. The Empire State Plaza, begun in 1962 and completed in 1978, is an 11-building complex that includes a convention center, a performing arts center, and a 44-story tower building with an observation deck. Other interesting buildings include City Hall, which is listed in the National Register of Historic Places; the Court of Appeals (1842); the governor's Executive Mansion; the First Church in Albany (Reformed), whose pulpit, carved in Holland in 1656, is the oldest in the United States; and St. Peter's Episcopal Church (1859), containing a silver Communion service that was donated by Queen Anne.

History. In 1609, Henry Hudson, the English navigator employed by the Dutch, arrived at what is now Albany and thus ended his exploration of the river that was to bear his name. In 1614, Dutch traders built Fort Nassau, which was short-lived; in 1624 they built Fort Orange in its place. Fort Orange was captured by the English in 1664 and renamed Albany after James, duke of York and Albany. It became the chief fur-trading center of the English colonies and in 1686 was chartered as a city by the provincial governor, Thomas Dongan. The British allowed the Dutch residents to keep their own language, customs, religion, and other institutions.

Before the American Revolution, British colonial officials and representatives of the Native American tribes used Albany as a meeting place to make treaties and settle differences. During the French and Indian War, in the mid-18th century, the city was a point of departure for colonial and British forces on their way west and north against the French. In 1754, at the Albany Congress, Benjamin Franklin presented his Plan of Union, a forerunner of the United States Constitution. Because of this, Albany has been known as the "Cradle of the Union." During the Revolution, the British campaign of 1777, aimed at splitting the colonies, made the capture of Albany its primary objective. This was prevented by the defeat of Gen. John Burgoyne at Saratoga.

Albany was made the capital of New York state in 1797. The first steamboat, the *Clermont*, reached the city in August 1807. With the opening of the Champlain Canal in 1822 and the completion of the Erie Canal in 1825, Albany became an important commercial city. From 1820 to 1830 its population doubled.

After the Civil War, increasing industrialization and immigration added to Albany's commercial importance. A number of large manufacturing plants were established in the 1860s and 1870s. The increasing prominence of New York state in national politics after 1900 enhanced the position of the capital city. The careers of several New York governors, Theodore Roosevelt, Charles Evans Hughes, Alfred E. Smith, Franklin Delano Roosevelt, Thomas E. Dewey, and Nelson A. Rockefeller, have continued to center national interest on Albany as well as New York state.

Albany was the birthplace of Gen. Philip Schuyler, Philip Livingston, Gen. Philip Sheridan, and Bret Harte. It was the home of such important figures as Aaron Burr, James Fenimore Cooper, Duncan Phyfe, Joseph Henry, Horace Greeley, Herman Melville, and William and Henry James. Presidents Martin Van Buren and Grover Cleveland lived in Albany as governors of New York—as did the two Roosevelts—and Chester A. Arthur is buried in the Albany Rural Cemetery. Population: 95,658.

EDGAR TOMPKINS*, *Albany Public Library*

ALBANY, äl′bə-nē, a city in western Oregon and the seat of Linn county, about 25 miles (40 km) south of Salem. Situated at the junction of the Willamette and Calapooia rivers, Albany is a wholesale and shipping center for lumber and agricultural products. Its other industries include the processing of rare metals and wood. Albany was settled in 1848 and incorporated in 1864. The city has a council-manager form of government. Population: 35,748.

ALBANY CONGRESS, an assembly of American colonial representatives held in Albany, N.Y., in June 1754. Their plan for a federal union of the colonies is regarded as a precursor of the U.S. Constitution. Called by the British crown to effect ways of improving the colonies' common defense on the eve of the French and Indian War, the congress also aimed to conciliate the Iroquois, with whom the French were actively seeking alliances. Commissioners from Massachusetts, New Hampshire, Rhode Island, Connecticut, New York, Pennsylvania, and Maryland met with representatives of the six nations of the Iroquois. Various agreements, mostly short-lived, were concluded.

The congress's importance lay in the delegates' advocacy of a colonial union, which they agreed was essential to the colonies' preservation. Benjamin Franklin, a delegate, drafted a model constitution, the Albany Plan of Union. This was a farseeing proposal to distribute power between a central colonial government and the governments of the member colonies. The central government was to consist of a president-general chosen by the crown and a congress chosen by the separate colonial assemblies. This government would deal with war and peace, taxation, defense, westward expansion, and trade, subject to a presidential veto. Representation was to be apportioned based on the size of each colony's contribution to the central treasury. Many of Franklin's ideas were later embodied in the Articles of Confederation and the federal Constitution. Yet the plan was too far in advance of its time; not one colony ratified it. The colonists thought it conceded too much power to the central government, and the crown regarded it as too democratic.

Bibliography: Shannon, Timothy J., *Indians and Colonists at the Crossroads of Empire: The Albany Congress of 1754* (Cornell Univ. Press/N.Y. State Hist. Assn. 2000).

ALBANY PLAN OF UNION. See ALBANY CONGRESS.

ALBANY REGENCY, the first U.S. political machine, a powerful group of New York state Democratic Party leaders who influenced state and national affairs from about 1820 to 1848. The group became known as the Albany Regency when its leader, Martin Van Buren, was serving in Washington, D.C. It dispersed after Van Buren's defeat in the 1848 presidential election. (See BARNBURNERS.)

FRANCISCO ERIZE/BRUCE COLEMAN, INC.

During courtship, the wandering albatross stretches its wings. Its huge wingspan makes it an excellent glider.

ALBATROSS, al'bə-trôs, any one of several large oceanic birds of unsurpassed powers of flight constituting a family in the petrel group. They are most common in the turbulent seas around Cape Horn and other far southern waters, where they ride out the roughest storms with ease. Sailors traditionally regarded the albatross with awe and veneration. When Coleridge's "ancient mariner" shot the fabled albatross, the bird was hung from his neck in penance, but this did not stay the hand of misfortune.

Appearance. Like petrels, albatrosses have three fully webbed toes, while the hind toe is either absent or represented by a claw. The bill of an albatross is 4 or more inches (10 cm) long and very thick and has a powerful hook at the tip. The nostrils open from round horizontal tubes, on each side of the base of the bill, instead of together on top as with the petrel. The wings are extremely long and pointed, and the tail is short and somewhat rounded. The feathers of the body form a coat thick enough to withstand both water and severe cold.

The albatross belongs to the family Diomedeidae, order Procellariiformes. The largest and best known of the 13 species is the wandering albatross (*Diomedea exulans*), an imposing white bird with a wingspread of nearly 12 feet (3.7 meters)—the longest of any living seabird.

Habits. The wandering albatross, like others of its family, usually nests on small islands. Courtship display consists of an elaborate, ritualized dance. A single egg is laid, which requires more than two months of incubation. After it has hatched, another four or five months pass before the chick reaches adult size. Even then it is still covered with fluffy down and is unable to fly. The young bird huddles in the nest, often covered with snow, and waits, sometimes for as long as three months, until its feathers are sufficiently grown to enable it to fly out to sea in search of food. During this stage the parents return to feed the young two or three times a week.

Although albatrosses are absent from the North Atlantic, two kinds nest on Midway and other islands of the Pacific, north of the equator. One Pacific species, the black-footed albatross (*D. nigripes*), wanders widely over the North Pacific. It often follows ships and gobbles down any greasy food waste thrown overboard. The chief food of albatrosses, however, is squid and other small marine creatures. (See also PETREL.)

DEAN AMADON, *University of Ornithology*
The American Museum of Natural History

ALBEE, Edward Franklin, ôl'bē (1928–   ), American playwright, one of the leading dramatists of his generation. His grimly humorous plays, usually categorized as "theater of the absurd," focus on humans' tendency to torment others and destroy themselves. Albee has acknowledged some autobiographical motifs in his work but has also observed that almost all of his plays "have been about our consciousness, how we live, how we perceive being conscious."

Albee was born in Washington, D.C., on March 12, 1928. When he was two weeks old, he was adopted by Reid Albee and his wife, Frances Cotter Albee. He grew up in New York City and the suburbs of Westchester county. Albee attended private schools in the East, graduating from Choate in 1946. After a year and a half at Trinity College in Hartford, Conn., he lost interest in formal education. Having inherited a trust fund from his grandmother, he settled in Greenwich Village in New York City, where he held various odd jobs during the 1950s.

Albee's first play, *The Zoo Story* (written in 1958), a one-act drama about a psychopathic homosexual who induces an innocent stranger to kill him, was produced first in 1959 in Berlin and then in 1960 at the Provincetown Playhouse in New York City; it won the 1960 Vernon Rice Award for outstanding achievement in an off-Broadway production. His next three works, also one-act plays, produced in 1960 and 1961, were *The Death of Bessie Smith*, depicting tensions between the races and the sexes in Memphis, Tenn., and *The Sandbox* and *The American Dream*, both ridiculing American middle-class values. Albee's first full-length play was *Who's Afraid of Virginia Woolf?* (1962), a savage but witty dissection of two marriages in an academic setting. The play was recommended by the panel of nominating jurors for a Pulitzer Prize in 1963, but the Pulitzer Prize board declined to bestow the award.

Albee's work became increasingly spare, experimental, and allusive. *Tiny Alice* (1964) and *A Delicate Balance* (1966) intrigued and puzzled critics, yet both were nominated for several Tony awards, and the latter was awarded a Pulitzer Prize for drama. His subsequent works, such as *Everything in the Garden* (1967), the paired plays *Box* and *Quotations from Chairman Mao Tse-Tung* (1968), *All Over* (1971), *The Lady from Dubuque* (1980), *Finding the Sun* (1982), and *Marriage Play* (1986–1987), largely dismissed dramatic narrative and were often met with incomprehension if not outright hostility. *Seascape* (1975) shared these works' theatrical experimentation, but the play's meditations on love, mortality, and human possibility are sharpened and given comic immediacy by the advent in the second act of two large sea lizards, curious about human ways. The play garnered Albee a second Pulitzer Prize in drama. In 1988 he was named distinguished professor of drama at the University of Houston, where he conducts workshops in playwriting.

Albee was playwright-in-residence for the 1993–1994 season at the Signature Theater in New York City, which mounted productions of *Marriage Play*, *Counting the Ways* (1976), *Listening* (1976),

Sand (consisting of *Box*, *The Sandbox*, and *Finding the Sun*), and *Fragments* (1993). *Three Tall Women* (1994), in a critically acclaimed off-Broadway production, earned Albee a rare third Pulitzer as well as a New York Drama Critics Circle Award for best play. Revolving around a 92-year-old woman looking back on her life, the play has autobiographical roots in Albee's perceptions of his adoptive mother. His subsequent plays include *The Play about the Baby* (1996) and *The Goat; or, Who Is Sylvia?* (2002), winner of the 2002 Tony Award for best play and a Pulitzer Prize nominee. In *Homelife* (2004) Albee provided a one-act companion play for *The Zoo Story*, set in the hours preceding the action of the earlier play; performed in sequence, the two plays compose a full-length drama, *Peter and Jerry*.

In 1996 Albee received the most prestigious U.S. arts award, Kennedy Center Honors for lifetime achievement. He was awarded the National Medal of Arts in 1997.

Bibliography: Gussow, Mel, *Edward Albee* (Simon & Schuster 1999); Horn, Barbara Lee, *Edward Albee: A Research and Production Sourcebook* (Praeger 2003); Mann, Bruce J., ed., *Edward Albee: A Casebook* (Routledge 2003).

ALBEMARLE SOUND, al′bə-märl, a narrow, shallow body of water on the North Carolina coast, extending inland for some 60 miles (97 km) west of the Atlantic Ocean, from which it is separated by a low sand barrier. On part of this long barrier is the Kill Devil Hill National Monument, commemorating the Wright brothers' flight in 1903.

Tides do not affect the water in the sound, which is generally fresh. The sound is the outlet for numerous streams, notably the Chowan and Roanoke rivers. Its maximum depth is about 18 feet (6 meters), except where channels have been dredged. The most important channels form links in the Atlantic Intracoastal Waterway.

ALBÉNIZ, Isaac Manuel Francisco, äl-bā′nēth (1860–1909), Spanish composer. Albéniz was born in Camprodón, Gerona province, on May 29, 1860. A child prodigy as a pianist, he early made concert tours in Europe and the Americas and later wrote many short piano pieces, although only a few of the more than 250 compositions from his youthful period retain their popularity.

In 1893 Albéniz settled in Paris, where he came under the influence of Vincent d'Indy and Claude Debussy. In Paris he wrote the works for which he is best remembered—the orchestral suite *Catalonia* (1899) and the 12 piano pieces that make up the suite *Iberia* (1906–1909). Depicting scenes from 12 parts of Spain, *Iberia* was later transcribed for orchestra by Enrique Fernández Arbós. Albéniz's most successful opera, *Pepita Jiménez*, was produced in Barcelona in 1896. He died in Cambo-les-Bains, France, on May 18, 1909.

ALBERDI, Juan Bautista, äl-ber′thē (1810–1884), Argentine political writer. Born in Tucumán, Argentina, on Aug. 29, 1810, Alberdi studied in Buenos Aires and in Montevideo, where in 1840 he received a law degree. He at first supported the dictatorship of Juan Manuel de Rosas but soon became Rosas's bitter enemy. A prominent member of the Generation of 1837, an influential group of young intellectuals formed in opposition to the government, Alberdi was forced into exile in 1838. After Rosas was defeated by Justo José de Urquiza in 1852, Alberdi was appointed minister plenipotentiary to arrange treaties in Madrid, Paris, London, and Washington. This was his only important government post, for in 1861 another of his adversaries, Bartolomé Mitre, overthrew the government, and Alberdi again went into exile.

Alberdi's *Bases y puntos de partida para la organización política de la república argentina* ("Bases and Starting Points for the Political Organization of the Argentine Republic"), a monument to democracy, social justice, and tolerance, was first published in Valparaíso, Chile, in 1852, the fruit of 20 years' thought. When the constitutional assembly of 1853 met in Santa Fe, the new constitution that it adopted was formulated largely on the basis of this work. In this, and in his insistence on the importance of immigration, Alberdi probably had a greater influence on the development of Argentine institutions than did any of his compatriots. He was also the author of short *costumbrismo* sketches on manners and customs, using the pseudonym Figarillo for such lighter works. Alberdi died in Paris on June 18, 1884.

ALBERS, Josef, äl′bûrs (1888–1976), German-born American artist who started out as a public school teacher and figurative artist and came to be known as a pioneering abstractionist, a renowned color theorist, and one of the most influential art teachers of the 20th century. Albers was born on March 19, 1888, in Bottrop, Germany. Although during his lifetime he kept his early work mostly secret, Albers the youthful artist was a portraitist and draftsman of considerable rigor and flair.

From 1908 to 1913 Albers worked as a schoolteacher in Bottrop. While studying art and art education in Berlin (1913–1915), he painted a series of oil-on-canvas still lifes that demonstrated his early interest in issues of spatial play, simultaneous symmetry and asymmetry, and the reversal of forms. He returned to teaching from 1916 to 1919 but also studied printmaking and began to create stained-glass windows. In 1919 he enrolled at the Munich Art Academy, taking a painting class with Franz von Stuck, the symbolist artist. There Albers produced a series of bold brush-and-ink studies of nudes and of Bavarian scenery.

In 1920 Albers entered the Bauhaus, the German art school, where he began to make glass assemblages, as well as design elegant, streamlined furniture. In 1923 he started conducting the school's preliminary course in material and design, and in 1925 he was the first student raised to Bauhaus master status. That year he married Annelise Fleischmann, a weaving student who later, as Anni Albers, became a world-renowned textile artist. Besides writing texts on visual experience and taking photographs of note, Albers at this time became an abstract artist of considerable bravura and originality. In his teaching, as in his own work, he was intrigued by the idea of deception in art and by the possibilities of pure form and color to create art that bore no characteristics of the time or place of its creation.

After the Nazis closed the Bauhaus in 1933, Albers went to the United States to head the art department at North Carolina's newly formed Black Mountain College, where art was deemed central to the curriculum. Albers began to teach and to continue his efforts at printmaking, resulting in woodcuts and linoleum cuts of original and rather playful abstract forms. His painting took off in new directions, with bold abstract oils that often used unmixed paint, straight from the tube, to create powerful biomorphic and anthropomorphic, yet nonrepresentative, forms.

Along with his wife, Albers in 1934 made his first trip (of 14) to Mexico, which exerted a great influence on his color sensibility and his interest in a vague spiritual presence in art. During this decade he continued his photography; gave lectures in Havana, at Harvard, and elsewhere; and, in 1939, became a U.S. citizen. He also began showing his work in leading U.S. museums and galleries. By the late 1940s Albers began some of his weightiest series of geometric abstraction, increasingly hard edged but always with hand-drawn lines: the *Biconjugates, Kinetics,* and *Variants,* the latter series demonstrating many of the points about color effects and mutability with which the artist was becoming ever more preoccupied.

In 1950 Albers became chair of the design department at Yale, where he held several important academic posts and exerted continued influence as a teacher. Also in 1950 he began the series for which he is best known and which he continued for the rest of his life, the *Homages to the Square.* For these oil-on-panel works, Albers developed precise arrangements of nested squares of solid colors, centered along the vertical axis but weighed downward along the horizontal axis. The paintings move in seemingly contradictory directions simultaneously and create a series of color effects. Albers, whose major color treatise, *Interaction of Color,* done in collaboration with his students, appeared in 1963 (rev. ed., 1978), died in New Haven, Conn., on March 25, 1976.

NICHOLAS FOX WEBER
Director, Josef and Anni Albers Foundation

Bibliography: Danilowitz, Brenda, *The Prints of Josef Albers: A Catalogue Raisonné, 1915–1976* (Hudson Hills Press 2001); **Licht, Fred, and Nicholas Fox Weber,** *Josef Albers: Glass, Color, and Light* (Guggenheim Mus. 1994); **Weber, Nicholas Fox, et al.,** *Josef Albers: A Retrospective* (Abrams 1988).

ALBERT I, al'bərt (1875–1934), king of the Belgians. Born in Brussels on April 8, 1875, he was the second son of Philippe, count of Flanders, and the nephew of King Leopold II. From 1893 to 1898 he was a member of the Belgian Senate. He traveled widely, visiting the United States in 1898 and the Belgian Congo in 1909. He succeeded his uncle on the throne in 1909.

As the threat of a European war increased, Albert tried to maintain Belgium's neutrality through appeals to neighboring states and by strengthening Belgium's armed forces. Emperor William II of Germany rejected his appeal, however, and in August 1914 demanded that German troops be given free passage through Belgium. Albert became an inspiration to his people when he refused the German ultimatum and took personal command of the Belgian armed forces during the costly Belgian retreat in the autumn. He made his headquarters for four years on the Belgian coast at De Panne, while the army held a small area around Ypres. At the start of the final Allied general offensive in September 1918, he commanded Belgian and French army groups and led them toward Brussels, which he entered on November 22. After the war he worked for his nation's economic restoration.

Albert married Elisabeth, daughter of Karl Theodor, duke of Bavaria, in 1900. Their elder son, who succeeded to the throne as Leopold III, abdicated in 1951. The other children were Charles

and Marie José. Albert lost his life in a fall while rock climbing at Marche-les-Dames, near Namur, on Feb. 17, 1934.

ALBERT, Prince, al'bərt (1819–1861), consort of Queen Victoria of Britain. Albert Francis Charles Augustus Emmanuel was born near Coburg, Germany, on Aug. 26, 1819, the younger son of Ernest I, duke of Saxe-Coburg-Gotha, and Louise, daughter of the duke of Saxe-Gotha-Altenburg. He was a delicate child but grew up into a healthy, handsome man. After attending the University of Bonn, he traveled through Italy with Baron Christian Friedrich von Stockmar, adviser to Queen Victoria. On Feb. 10, 1840, in London, Albert married Victoria, his first cousin, who at the age of 20 had already been queen for nearly three years.

Albert soon became Victoria's most trusted counselor. He learned to adapt himself and his advice to British constitutional conditions, although at first he was suspected of encouraging in his wife Continental ideas of the functions of royalty. Under other conditions he might have excelled as a statesman, but his statesmanship could only be exercised indirectly. Victoria gave him the title of Prince Consort in 1857.

Music, painting, literature, science, industry, and social improvement all came within the sphere of his interests and patronage. He was a principal organizer of the Great Exhibition of 1851. He also gave a great deal of time and energy to political affairs and often served as an intermediary between Victoria and her cabinet. His last official act was counseling restraint in Britain's protest to the United States over the Trent Affair.

Overwork contributed to Prince Albert's inability to resist an attack of typhoid fever. He died at Windsor Castle on Dec. 14, 1861, at the

Prince Albert, consort of Queen Victoria of Britain.

age of 42. His widow mourned him deeply for the remaining years of her long reign.

ALBERT, al'bərt, two kings of Germany who were rulers of the Holy Roman Empire but were not crowned emperor by the pope.

ALBERT I (1250?–1308), eldest son of Emperor Rudolf I of Habsburg, became duke of Austria in 1282. He failed to gain the German crown after his father's death in 1291, however, because of general distrust of the Habsburg's growing power and because of opposition at that time to hereditary succession to the throne.

The German crown went to Adolf of Nassau instead. But the nobles turned against Adolf when he tried to increase his family holdings through wars in Meissen and Thuringia, disputed areas in east and central Germany. Fearing that territorial acquisitions would give the king too much power, the nobles deposed him in 1298 and elected Albert in his place. Albert was crowned king of Germany at Aachen (Aix-la-Chapelle) later in the year.

Pope Boniface VIII forbade the German princes to obey Albert, hoping to force the king to make concessions to the papacy in Germany in return for papal support. Instead, Albert allied himself with the pope's foe, Philip IV of France. With the help of French troops and money, Albert succeeded in subduing the archbishops of Cologne, Mainz, and Trier by 1302. But his fear of the increasing French influence in Germany and his desire for peace with the papacy led Albert to break his alliance with Philip in 1302. In 1303 he swore an oath of obedience to the pope and promised to defend the papal interests in Italy.

Albert never succeeded in being crowned by the pope. But his peace with the pope allowed him to concentrate on increasing the Habsburg possessions. He became involved in wars in the Netherlands, Hungary, Bohemia, and Thuringia, but the rulers of these countries were strong enough to retain their independence. His last campaign was in Switzerland, where the Habsburgs held disputed title to various estates. When the Swiss forest cantons of Schwyz, Nidwalden (part of Unterwalden Canton), and Uri revolted, Albert welcomed the chance to subjugate all of Switzerland. At the same time, his nephew, John of Swabia (later known as John the Parricide), requested recognition of his Swabian inheritance, but Albert rejected these demands. In revenge, John had him assassinated along the Reuss River, near Brugg, Switzerland, on May 1, 1308.

ALBERT II (1397–1439) was born on Aug. 10, 1397, and succeeded his father Albert as duke of Austria in 1404. The young duke, known as Albert V of Austria, took control of the government when he was 14. He assisted Emperor Sigismund in his unsuccessful war in Bohemia, and in 1422 married the emperor's daughter Elizabeth.

After Sigismund's death in 1437, Albert was crowned king of Hungary on Jan. 1, 1438, and of Bohemia six months later. He was chosen king of Germany on March 18, 1438, but was never crowned emperor. Although he gave promise of being an able ruler during his short reign, he was chiefly occupied with suppressing an insurrection in Bohemia and defending Hungary against the Turks. He died from dysentery on Oct. 27, 1439, while campaigning against the Turks in Hungary. After his death, the German crown passed to his cousin, Frederick III. It remained in the Habsburg family thereafter, with only one interrup-

tion, until the Holy Roman Empire was dissolved in 1806.

ALBERT I, al'bərt (1100?–1170), first margrave of Brandenburg. Known as Albert the Bear , he was the son of Otto the Rich, count of Ballenstedt, whose Saxon estates he inherited in 1123. For helping Lothair, duke of Saxony, in his war with Bohemia, the ambitious Albert received the East Mark, an area between the Oder and Elbe rivers. After Lothair became Emperor Lothair II, he curbed Albert by depriving him of the East Mark in 1131. However, for his aid on an Italian expedition in 1134, Albert was given the North Mark (later part of Brandenburg).

Albert made several attempts to increase his territory in Saxony by supporting the emperors in their struggles with the strong Saxon dukes, Henry the Proud and his son, Henry the Lion. In 1138, Emperor Conrad III tried to weaken Henry the Proud by giving Saxony to Albert. Although Henry died in 1139, his family continued to hold Saxony. Albert renounced his claims to Saxony in 1142.

Unable to expand in Saxony, Albert directed his main energies eastward. Since western Europe's rising population had made land scarce and expensive there, Albert, like great lords of the more eastern parts of Europe, had little trouble in recruiting colonists by offering land with few feudal obligations. With the church's help, he colonized the area east of the Elbe with farmers from western Germany and the Netherlands. In 1150 Albert's eastern position was strengthened when he inherited Brandenburg from its last Wendish ruler and combined it with the North Mark.

Albert proceeded to consolidate his territory in Brandenburg. By treating the Slavs fairly, he won their acceptance and encountered less resistance to colonization than the Saxon dukes found further north. Continuing his allegiance to the emperors, he served under Emperor Frederick Barbarossa in Italy in 1162. In 1169 he divided his territories among his six sons and died the next year at Ballenstedt on November 13. Albert was the first of the Ascanian dynasty, which ruled Brandenburg until 1320.

ALBERT, al'bərt (1490–1568), first duke of Prussia. He was born in Ansbach, Germany, on May 16, 1490, the son of Frederick of Ansbach and grandson of Albert III (Achilles), elector of Brandenburg. In 1508 he took part in the operations against Venice under Emperor Maximilian I. Then, in 1511, the Teutonic Knights chose him to become grand master of their order. Because he was the son of Sophia, sister of Sigismund, king of Poland, and descended from one of the most powerful German families, the Knights hoped by this choice to be freed from the feudal overlordship of Poland and placed under the protection of the empire.

Recognized as grand master by Poland, Albert proceeded to Königsberg and assumed the government of the order's territories in 1512. He refused the oath of allegiance to Poland, which the previous grand master had evaded, and prepared for resistance. In 1520, after protracted negotiations, Sigismund attempted to enforce submission by an invasion of the lands of the order, but the contest was without decisive result and in the following year a truce of four years was agreed to at Thorn.

Albert appeared before the Imperial Diet at Nuremberg as a German prince of the empire to seek the aid of the other princes in his struggle against the Poles. Failing to obtain support, he soon after espoused the cause of the Reformation. To preserve his possessions from being taken over by Poland, Albert, on Martin Luther's advice, had himself proclaimed secular duke of Prussia and placed himself under the sovereignty of Sigismund. He earnestly sought to promote the welfare of his duchy, established the ducal library, founded the University of Königsberg in 1544, and gathered about his person many literary men. In 1527 he was married to Dorothea, the daughter of Frederick, king of Denmark.

The latter years of his reign were troubled with many intrigues, foreign and domestic. In 1532 he was put under the ban of the empire, but he succeeded in transmitting his succession to his son. Albert died in Tapiau (Gvardeisk, Kaliningrad oblast, Russia) on March 20, 1568.

ALBERT, al'bərt (1828–1902), king of Saxony. He was born in Dresden, Saxony, on April 23, 1828, the eldest son of King John of Saxony. His full name was Frederick Augustus Albert. He succeeded to the throne of Saxony in 1873, following his father's death. In 1871, the kingdom of Saxony had become part of the German Empire.

Before becoming king, Albert had a military career. He led the Saxon forces in the Seven Weeks' War (1866), in which Saxony, allied with Austria and other German states, was defeated by Prussia. After Prussia forced Saxony to join the North German Confederation, Albert loyally supported the alliance and received command of the Saxon troops of the North German army. During the Franco-Prussian War (1870–1871) he commanded the Prussian army of the Meuse. At the war's end he was promoted to field marshal. He died in Sybellenort, Silesia, on June 19, 1902.

ALBERT, al'bərt (1865–1939), duke of Württemberg. He was born in Vienna, Austria, on Dec. 23, 1865, the son of Philip, duke of Württemberg. Albert became an officer in the German army and rose to high command. At the outbreak of World War I in 1914, he was given command of the German Fourth Army in France. In 1916, having been promoted to field marshal, he became the commander in chief of the group of armies in Alsace-Lorraine.

Albert was heir presumptive to the crown of the kingdom of Württemberg. When the German Empire and its constituent kingdoms were abolished at the end of World War I, he retired to his estates in Württemberg. He died in Altshausen, Germany, on Oct. 29, 1939.

ALBERT, al'bərt (c. 1340–1412), king of Sweden. He was the nephew of King Magnus II of Sweden. In 1365 the Swedish council of nobles chose him to succeed his uncle, but he reigned as a figurehead and was deprived of power by the council in 1371. He became duke of Mecklenburg as well as king of Sweden in 1384, reigning in Mecklenburg as Albert III. In 1389 the forces of Queen Margaret of Denmark and Norway defeated him at the Battle of Falköping and took him prisoner. He renounced the throne of Sweden in 1395 and returned to Mecklenburg, where he ruled until his death, in Kloster Doberan, on April 1, 1412.

ALBERT, Count von Bollstädt. See ALBERTUS MAGNUS.

ALBERT, Carl Bert, (1908–2000), American political leader who rose to power in the U.S. House of Representatives. Albert was majority whip (1955–1961) and majority leader (1962–1970) before serving as speaker of the House (1971–1977).

The oldest of five children, Albert was born in McAlester, Okla., on May 10, 1908. He graduated from the University of Oklahoma, studied law at Oxford University under a Rhodes scholarship, and was admitted to the Oklahoma bar. During World War II he served with the judge advocate general's department and with the U.S. Army Air Force, attaining the rank of lieutenant colonel. He was elected to the U.S. House of Representatives in 1946 as a Democrat and served until his retirement in 1977.

Congressman Albert, a moderate, won the respect of his Democratic colleagues through hard work and party loyalty. Albert supported Pres. Lyndon Johnson's domestic programs and intervention in South Vietnam, but he criticized the economic policies of Pres. Richard Nixon. As Speaker, Albert exercised his leadership with restraint. When the vice presidency was vacant in 1973 and in 1974, he was next in line for the presidency. His autobiography, *Little Giant: The Life and Times of Speaker Carl Albert* (1990), describes his upbringing, the reforms in congressional rules and procedures, attacks on the seniority system, and efforts to strengthen the Democratic caucus that took place during his tenure in Congress. Albert returned to McAlester following his retirement. He died there on Feb. 4, 2000.

ALBERT, Eugen d'. See D'ALBERT, EUGEN.

ALBERT LAKE, al'bərt, a body of water in central Africa, between Uganda on the east and the Democratic Republic of the Congo on the west. It is also known as Lake Mobutu Sese Seko.

Albert Lake is part of the Great Rift Valley, a depression that extends southward to Lake Tanganyika and northward across the Red Sea basin into Asia. The lake is about 100 miles (160 km) long and 20 miles (30 km) wide, and has an area of 2,064 square miles (5,300 sq km). It lies within the basin of the Nile River, 2,200 feet (670 meters) above sea level. It has few natural harbors. At the southwestern end, it is fed by the Semliki River, which issues from Lake Edward. At the northeast end, it receives the Victoria Nile just below Murchison Falls. Albert Lake's outlet is the Albert Nile, known as Bahr el Jebel when it enters Sudan on its way north to form the White Nile.

The British explorers John Hanning Speke and James Augustus Grant traveled near Albert Lake in 1862, although they did not see it. Acting on their information, the English explorer Sir Samuel Baker found the lake in 1864. Baker named it for Prince Albert, consort of Queen Victoria.

ALBERT LEA, al'bərt lē, a city in southern Minnesota, about 100 miles (160 km) by road south of Minneapolis. The seat of Freeborn county, the city is a summer resort, a market center for an agricultural area, and an important manufacturing and distributing center.

The city was named for Albert M. Lea, who was the U.S. topographer for the region in 1835. It was chartered in 1878. Population: 18,356.

© H. DAMM/LEO DE WYS

Cradled by the Rocky Mountains, Maligne Lake nestles in a valley of Jasper National Park, western Alberta.

ALBERTA

The Provincial Coat of Arms

CONTENTS

ALBERTA, al-bûrt′ə, the most westerly of three Canadian provinces known as the Prairie Provinces (Manitoba, Saskatchewan, and Alberta). Alberta is completely landlocked, but the Columbia Ice Field, high in the Rocky Mountains on Alberta's southwestern boundary with British Columbia, is the source of rivers that drain eventually to the Pacific, the Arctic, and the Atlantic oceans.

The Rocky Mountains are the most striking scenic feature of the province. Much of the mountain area—with its majestic peaks, ice fields, beautiful lakes, forests, mineral hot springs, and abundant wildlife—has been preserved in national parks, which attract visitors from all over the world. Banff National Park, in the central Rockies, is the oldest and best known of Canada's national parks.

The crests of the Rockies in Alberta reach more than 12,000 feet (3,700 meters). To the east they fall away sharply into a band of foothills. The remainder of the province slopes to the north and east at a gentle gradient. The lowest point is in the extreme northeast along the Slave River, which drains Lake Athabasca to Great Slave Lake north of Alberta. The first permanent fur-trading post in present-day Alberta was established on the shores of the Athabasca River. From Fort Chipewyan on Lake Athabasca, Alexander Mackenzie in 1789 led a party of voyageurs and Indians down the Slave River to Great Slave Lake. He discovered the river outlet of that lake, and proceeded downstream along the river that now bears his name (the Mackenzie) to the Beaufort Sea of the Arctic Ocean.

Southern Alberta is well populated and highly developed. The largest areas of rich farmlands are in that half of the province, and the first significant discoveries of coal, petroleum, and natural gas were made there.

The forested northern half of the province is relatively unexplored and uninhabited except in the fertile Peace River district around Grande Prairie. Between the Peace and the Athabasca rivers, and north of Lesser Slave Lake, is a vast area in which the main industry until modern times was the trapping carried on by a few Indians and *métis* (descendants of European fur trappers and Indian women). Into this region have gone the geological and geophysical crews of companies searching, with notable success, for petroleum and natural gas.

Alberta is rich in agricultural lands, timber, and fossil fuels. Its resources are situated far from tidewater and from the major population centers of North America. Nevertheless, the evolution of new modes of transportation and an ever-increasing population help to overcome these disadvantages.

Alberta originally formed part of a large territory purchased by Canada in 1869 from the Hudson's Bay Company. It was incorporated as a province in 1905, thereafter passing from the fur-trapping era, through an almost solely agricultural era, to one characterized by a more urbanized, industrial, mining, and commercial economy.

1. The Land

The province extends more than 750 miles (1,200 km) from north to south, and about 400 miles (640 km) at the widest point from east to west. The distance along the international boundary in the south is about 180 miles (290 km).

Major Physical Divisions. Most of Alberta lies within the great central plains of North America, but the province includes a small share of the Rocky Mountain system, and of the Canadian Shield, a large region of generally low relief and shieldlike outline surrounding Hudson Bay on the east, south, and west.

The Rocky Mountains of Alberta are a part of the eastern system of the Canadian Cordillera. Their high, serrated ranges form a natural boundary more than 300 miles (480 km) long between Alberta and British Columbia. The foothills to the east vary in elevation from 6,000 to 4,000 feet (1,800 to 1,200 meters). Together, the mountains and foothills comprise a band averaging about 70 miles (110 km) in width.

The Canadian Shield covers only a small area in the northeast corner of the province. The shield, which is one of the few areas of the world never covered by seas, is composed of Precambrian rock. Lake Athabasca is typical of the large lakes that have been formed at the edge of the Canadian Shield.

The rest of Alberta is classified as plains, but it includes a variety of surface features. The major rivers have incised deep valleys, the floors of which may range to several hundred feet below the surrounding flat surface. Scattered groups of hills rise above the plains. The highest of these, with elevations of about 4,000 feet (1,200 meters), are the Cypress Hills in the southeast and the Swan Hills south of Lesser Slave Lake.

Dinosaur Provincial Park in southeastern Alberta contains abundant remains of ancient reptiles and amphibians.

© JOSE VIESTI

INFORMATION HIGHLIGHTS

Location: In western Canada, bordered west by British Columbia, north by Northwest Territories, east by Saskatchewan, south by Montana.

Elevation: Highest point—Mt. Columbia, 12,294 feet (3,747 meters), in the southwest; lowest—686 feet (209 meters), along the Slave River in the northeast.

Area: 255,285 sq mi (661,189 sq km), including 6,485 sq mi (16,796 sq km) of fresh water; rank among Canadian provinces, 4th.

Population: 2,974,807; rank, 4th.

Climate: Short, pleasant summers; cold winters, often relieved by chinooks (warm winds).

Made a Province: Sept. 1, 1905 (with Saskatchewan, as the 8th and 9th provinces).

Capital: Edmonton.

Principal Products: Petroleum and natural gas, petrochemicals, sulfur, coal, grains, livestock, processed foods.

Floral Emblem: (adopted 1930) Wild rose (*Rosa acicularis*).

Coat of Arms: (assigned by royal warrant, 1907) Displays Alberta's wheatlands, prairies, and hills, unfolding toward snow-covered mountains in the west—all surmounted by the cross of St. George.

© THOMAS KITCHIN/ VALAN PHOTOS

Bighorn sheep graze in foothills of the Miette Range of the Rockies in Jasper National Park.

Much of southern Alberta is rolling prairie, broken at intervals by tree- or shrub-covered hills and deeply eroded valleys. The Cypress Hills were never glaciated, and they retain some of the flora and fauna of pre-Ice Age eras. The Red Deer River valley is noted for its badlands and dinosaur fossils.

About 150 miles (240 km) north of the southern border begins a broad belt known as parkland (a transitional zone between the prairies and the northern forest belt). The soils of the parkland are particularly fertile, and trees set off the gently rolling landscape. Another section of parkland occurs in the Grande Prairie district.

Rivers and Lakes. Three major river systems drain the province. The Milk River, which rises in the United States, drains the extreme southern section. It is part of the Missouri-Mississippi system, flowing south to the Gulf of Mexico.

Southern and central Alberta are drained by the Saskatchewan River system, which flows generally eastward to Hudson Bay. The North Saskatchewan River rises in the Columbia Ice Field. The South Saskatchewan River is formed by the confluence of the Bow and the Oldman rivers in southern Alberta. It receives the Red Deer River in Saskatchewan and joins the North Saskatchewan River in that province to become the Saskatchewan proper.

Northern Alberta is in the Mackenzie River drainage basin. The Mackenzie River proper is not in Alberta (it issues from Great Slave Lake to the north of Alberta and flows northward to the Arctic Ocean), but most of its major headstreams are in the province. The Athabasca River rises in the Columbia Ice Field and follows a long northeasterly course to Lake Athabasca. The Peace River rises in northern British Columbia and flows east, then northeast, eventually joining the Slave River in northeastern Alberta. Other headstreams of the Mackenzie in Alberta are the Hay and the Slave rivers.

The main natural lakes are Lake Athabasca (shared by Alberta and Saskatchewan), Lake Claire, and Lesser Slave Lake. The area north and east of Edmonton is thickly studded with relatively small natural lakes. Lake Louise is one of the most beautiful of the Rocky Mountain lakes. In the south there are several artificial lakes, which were formed to provide reservoirs for the irrigation systems. The largest of these lakes are St. Mary Reservoir, Lake Newell, and Lake McGregor.

Climate. Summer days are desirably warm; nights are pleasantly cool. Occasionally the temperature drops to very low levels in winter, but the cold is alleviated by bright sunshine and low relative humidity. The mean January temperature at Edmonton is 7.7°F (−13.5°C); at Calgary, 15.8°F (−9°C). Both cities have a July mean of about 63°F (17°C). At Edmonton the highest temperature on record is 99°F (37.2°C); the lowest, −57°F (−49.4°C).

A particular feature of the climate of southern Alberta is the chinook, a warm, dry wind that blows eastward from the leeward side of the Rocky Mountains. It can raise midwinter temperatures from bitter cold to well above freezing within a few hours.

Precipitation is adequate for farming except in the southeast. Agriculture is favored by patterns of precipitation that bring half the rainfall during the growing season. Only about one fourth of the total annual precipitation falls as snow.

Throughout the grain-growing area, the average frost-free period ranges from 80 to 120 days. The period is longest near the southern border. Farther north, the longer daylight hours compensate for the shorter season.

Plant Life. Buffalo grass, or "prairie wool," is the chief type of natural vegetation in the prairie area. Along watercourses there are poplar bluffs and copses, as well as fruit-bearing shrubs such

ALBERTA

AGRICULTURE, INDUSTRY
and
RESOURCES

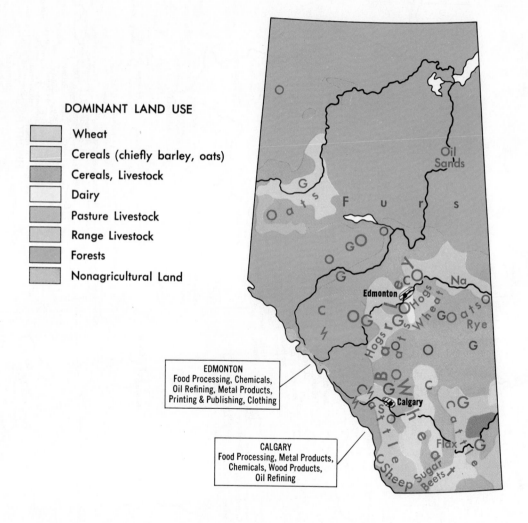

DOMINANT LAND USE

- Wheat
- Cereals (chiefly barley, oats)
- Cereals, Livestock
- Dairy
- Pasture Livestock
- Range Livestock
- Forests
- Nonagricultural Land

EDMONTON
Food Processing, Chemicals,
Oil Refining, Metal Products,
Printing & Publishing, Clothing

CALGARY
Food Processing, Metal Products,
Chemicals, Wood Products,
Oil Refining

MAJOR MINERAL OCCURRENCES

- C Coal
- G Natural Gas
- Na Salt
- O Petroleum
- S Sulfur
- ⚡ Water Power
-   Major Industrial Areas

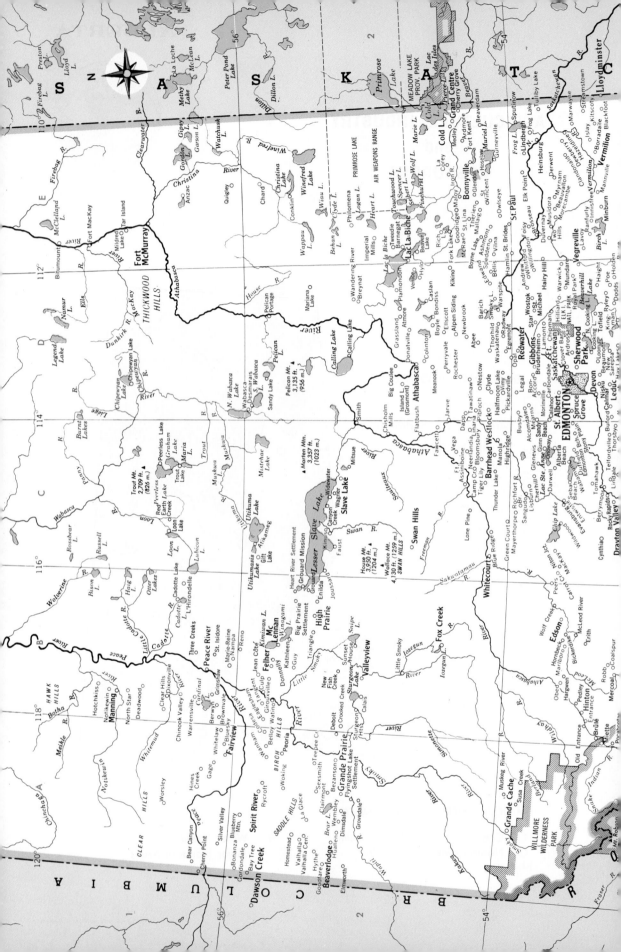

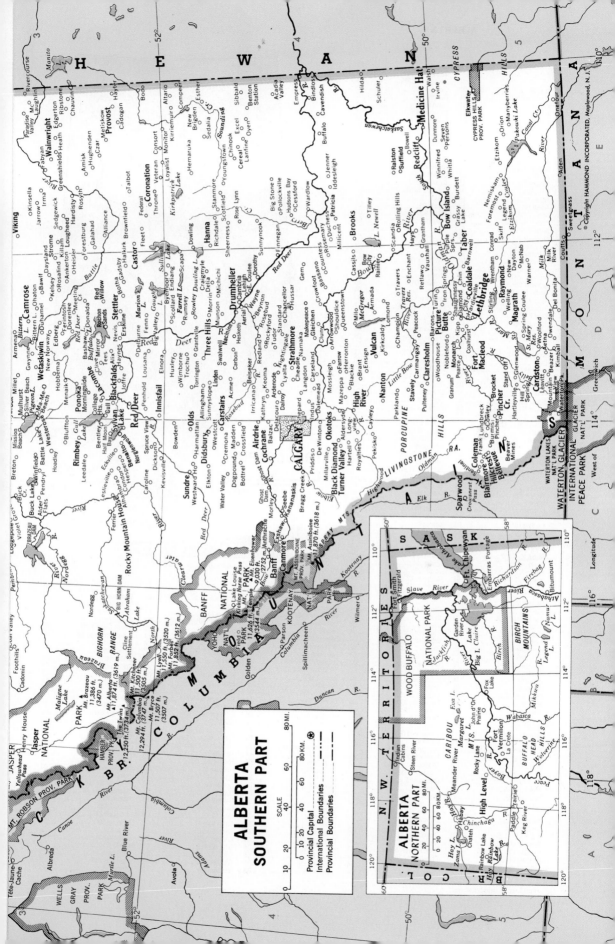

ALBERTA
SOUTHERN PART

SCALE
0   20   40   60   80 MI.
0 10 20 40 60 80 KM.

Provincial Capital ⊛
International Boundaries ⎯·⎯·⎯
Provincial Boundaries ⎯·⎯·⎯

ALBERTA
NORTHERN PART

SCALE
0 20 40 60 80 MI.
0 20 40 60 80KM.

ALBERTA

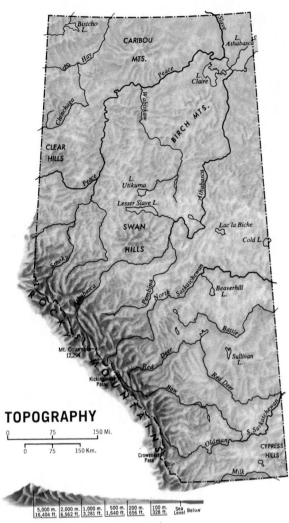

TOPOGRAPHY

0   75   150 Mi.

0   75   150 Km.

| 5,000 m. 16,404 ft. | 2,000 m. 6,562 ft. | 1,000 m. 3,281 ft. | 500 m. 1,640 ft. | 200 m. 656 ft. | 100 m. 328 ft. | Sea Level | Below |

ALBERTA

A coal train hauls one type of fossil fuel abundant in Alberta. Coal was mined there as early as 1870.

as wild raspberries, blueberries, and saskatoons. In the parkland region, sizable stands of aspen, pine, and spruce are common. The northern half of the province and the eastern slopes of the Rockies are mainly conifer-forested, although aspen and birch usually appear after forest fires.

Animal Life. The predominant type of land animals are hoofed. Deer, elk, moose, and caribou are found in all the forested areas and in some prairie coulees. Buffalo were numerous at one time, but only small herds are left in protected areas, notably Elk Island and Wood Buffalo national parks.

Of the carnivores, the coyote roams the prairie, and various species of bears inhabit the forest and mountain areas. Furbearers, such as beaver, muskrat, and ermine, flourish and are harvested in the north.

Bucket loaders excavate oil sands from the Athabasca deposits in northeastern Alberta.

Large grain farms dominate the Alberta prairie. Agriculture is the province's most visible economic activity.

Some ducks and geese remain in the lake areas of the province during the summer, but the greater number fly northward to nest and reproduce in the Arctic and subarctic. Good game fish are found in many of the mountain streams. The number and variety have been increased for the sports fisherman. Several commercial species—whitefish, jackfish, and goldeye—are found in the larger lakes.

Mineral Resources. Vast coalfields underlie most of southern Alberta. The varieties of coal range from anthracites, which occur close to the mountains, to lignites, farther to the east. Oil and gas pools are widely present, except in the Canadian Shield. Sulfur, dissolved as hydrogen sulfide, is associated with many of the natural-gas fields. Oil-sand deposits underlie 23,000 square miles (60,000 sq km) of northern and eastern Alberta. The four major deposits—Athabasca, Cold Lake, Wabasca, and Peace River—are estimated together to hold close to 260 billion cubic yards (200 billion cu meters) of bitumen.

The Rocky Mountains contain tremendous quantities of limestone. A major low-grade iron deposit is located in the central Peace River district. Vast salt beds, left by seas in past eras, lie under the east-central part of the province. Gypsum occurs in various places, notably along the Peace River west of Lake Athabasca and in the Fort McMurray area.

2. The Economy

The economy of the region has historically reflected dependence on a single primary natural resource, as well as reliance on external rather than domestic markets. From the late 18th through the late 19th century, the primary product was fur. Fur harvesting later gave way to cattle raising and then to grain farming.

Until the 1950's, agriculture was the major industry, accounting for more than half the net value of production. The agricultural sector, however, is always subject to wide fluctuations in availability of markets, prices of commodities, and weather. Diversification of crops and improved agricultural methods are of some benefit to farmers, but uncertain market demand and shifting prices always pose a problem.

The economic base began to change radically after the discovery of substantial oil deposits in the Turner Valley southwest of Calgary in the 1930's. (Oil had first been discovered there in 1914.) The production of petroleum and natural gas gained first place in the economy in the ensuing decades, followed by construction, manufacturing, and agriculture. Services grew in importance, reflecting increasing emphasis on commerce and industry.

Minerals and Mining. Alberta ranks first among the Canadian provinces in production of crude oil, natural gas and its products, and sulfur. The boom touched off by the Turner Valley find was accelerated by the discovery of the significantly larger Leduc oil field near Edmonton in 1947. Other major oil and gas fields were developed over the next two decades. In 1967 successful commercial development and production of the Athabasca oil sands began. A second major plant followed a decade later.

The movement of oil to other parts of Canada and to foreign markets required the construction, beginning in 1950, of an extensive system of pipelines. Oil and gas pipelines extended east to heavily populated markets in Ontario, Quebec, and the United States, and west to Vancouver, the Puget Sound area, and California.

Alberta is the world's largest producer of sulfur derived from hydrocarbon sources as a co-product of natural-gas processing. Extraction plants are scattered throughout the southwest and west-central areas wherever natural gas is produced.

Alberta's coal deposits represent a significant percentage of the total Canadian reserves of this fuel. Coal was mined in the Lethbridge area as early as 1870, and significant development occurred into the 1930's. Production increased again after the 1960's, more than trebling prewar volumes, owing to the construction of electric power plants in close proximity to coal deposits and to the development of significant export markets in Japan. Although petroleum production and reserves have received the most attention and publicity, the provincial coal reserves are, by a wide margin, more important in terms of fossil-fuel energy.

Manufacturing. The manufacturing industry in its early years was based on the satisfaction of local consumer needs in the basic areas of food and housing. Remoteness from the more heavily populated parts of Canada ruled out the development of products aimed at a wider market. The evolution of more sophisticated forms of manufacturing was limited by the high cost of rail freight, with the result that markets tended to be restricted to the four western provinces. Apart from production for local consumption, much of the focus was on upgrading basic natural resources for further processing elsewhere.

With the development of Alberta's extensive petroleum industry after World War II, equipment needed in the oil fields began to be manufactured increasingly within the province, stimulating expansion in metalworking and fabricating plants. Production of chemicals and petrochemicals increased rapidly because of the presence and low costs of basic raw materials. The fertilizer industry, based on abundant supplies of natural gas, developed into a major component of local manufacturing.

Agriculture. Although agriculture ceased to dominate the economy, it is still the most visible activity. On the open prairies, large grain farms predominate. Where moisture is inadequate for grains, cattle ranches are well established. A third type of agricultural activity—mixed grain and livestock farming—is practiced in the parkland regions.

Agricultural production, like mineral production, is heavily dependent on exports. After World War II, the traditional markets continued to be European, mainly British, but vast new markets subsequently opened in the Soviet Union and in China.

Historically, the total farm value of grains was far above that of livestock. In the years following World War II, however, a balance between livestock and grain production evolved, with cattle, hogs, and dairy and poultry products accounting for a larger share of annual farm cash income. Oilseed crops, especially rape and flax, were introduced.

The climate of southern Alberta is almost ideal for the production of vegetables of superior flavor and nutrient value. Sugar beets are grown under irrigation.

Forest Industries, Furs, and Fisheries. Logging and sawmilling are dependent on activity in the construction industry both locally and elsewhere in North America. Mills also produce wood pulp for paper.

Trapping for wild furs is supplemented by mink farming. Whitefish and other fishes are caught by commercial fishermen in the northern lake area.

Power and Transportation. Hydroelectric power developments are inhibited by extreme seasonal variations in river flows. Because of the rich resources of coal, electric power generation is mainly thermal.

Cattle ranches were established in Alberta where moisture was inadequate for grain farming.

SSC/PHOTOCENTRE

The rail transportation network traces to the 1880's, when the Canadian Pacific Railway was completed. It facilitated immigration and opened southern areas to agricultural development. Major railway building continued for another 30 years, during which lines were constructed throughout the remaining areas suitable for agriculture. Later railroad construction served resource-rich northern and north-central Alberta, providing links with Dawson Creek in British Columbia and Great Slave Lake to the north.

Road systems passed through a similar process of evolution. In the period after World War II, the provincial government developed an extensive network of hard-surfaced, all-weather highways. The Trans-Canada Highway, begun in 1950, provided a continuous highway link to the Canadian Pacific and Atlantic coasts.

Aviation has been of special importance to economic development. Since the early 1920's, locally based aircraft have been used to transport people, machinery, and supplies to the relatively inaccessible areas of the Canadian north.

The city of Edmonton, known as the "Gateway to the North," is the most northerly major air center of Canada. All the larger cities have main airports, and there are several hundred minor landing strips and airfields.

Since provincial prosperity stems from the volume of exports of raw or semifinished materials, transportation is of vital importance in the area of economic growth. Like other sections of western Canada, Alberta depends on railroads for interregional and international transport of major export commodities, and on the local highway system for collection and dispersion. Pipelines are used for transporting oil and gas as well as other liquid hydrocarbons.

Tourism. Alberta's major scenic attractions have drawn large numbers of visitors since the late 19th century. Income from tourist spending has contributed consistently to the economy.

3. The People

The opening to settlement of rich farmlands provided the main impetus for immigration to Alberta during the early 1900's. Some of the immigrants moved north from the United States, drawn by the attraction of cheap and available land in

NINA RAGINSKY/CANADIAN MUSEUM OF CONTEMPORARY PHOTOGRAPHY

Hutterites are among the many religious minorities that have settled in Alberta. They retain traditional dress.

the last agricultural frontier of North America. The most suitable agricultural areas were settled during the 20 years before World War I. In 1901 the population was only 73,022. It more than quadrupled during the next decade. A second wave of immigrants, in the 1920's, was composed largely of persons escaping from the hardships of postwar Europe. Immigration all but ceased during the Great Depression and drought years from 1929 to 1939. A third wave of immigrants, following World War II, settled primarily in the cities and included a significant proportion from Asia as well as Europe.

Population Characteristics. Most Albertans are of European descent. Almost half trace their roots to the British Isles. Those of German, Ukrainian, Scandinavian, French, and Dutch background are represented in substantial numbers. There are fewer descendants of Mediterranean Europeans.

The native Indian population in Alberta is small. Among the tribes are the Blackfoot—including the Blood and the Peigan—the Cree, the Assiniboine or Stoney, the Sarcee, the Beaver, Slavey, and the Chipewyan. A considerable number live on reserves, engaging in ranching or farming. Some have entered trade or the professions. Still others, such as the Slavey in the north, maintain their traditional lifestyle, relying on hunting, fishing, and trapping.

Religion. Of the various Christian denominations, the United Church of Canada and the Roman Catholic Church have the most adherents. (The former came into being in 1925 as a union of Methodist, Presbyterian, Congregation-

POPULATION GROWTH

Year	Population	Change (%)
1901	73,022	
1911	374,295	412.6
1921	588,454	57.2
1931	731,605	24.3
1941	796,169	8.8
1951	939,501	18.0
1961	1,331,944	41.8
1971	1,627,874	22.2
1981	2,237,724	37.5
1991	2,545,553	7.6
2001	2,974,807	16.9

LARGEST CENTERS OF POPULATION

City	2001	1991	1981
Calgary	878,866	710,677	592,743
Calgary metropolitan area	951,395	754,033	592,743
Edmonton	666,104	616,741	532,246
Edmonton metropolitan area	937,845	839,924	657,057
Strathcona County	71,986		
Red Deer	67,707	58,134	46,393
Lethbridge	67,374	60,974	54,072
St. Albert	53,081	42,146	31,996
Medicine Hat	51,249	43,625	40,380
Wood Buffalo	41,466	34,706[1]	31,000[1]

[1] Fort McMurray.

The Alberta Legislative Building is in Edmonton, the most northerly of Canada's provincial capitals.

al, and various local churches.) Fewer in number are the Anglicans, Lutherans, Greek Orthodox, Baptists, Ukrainian Catholics, Mormons, Mennonites, and Hutterites. The Jewish, Islamic, Hindu, Sikh, and Buddhist faiths are represented, though in relatively small numbers.

Certain areas of the province have pronounced concentrations of a single denomination. North and east of Edmonton there are Greek Orthodox and Ukrainian Catholic populations. Mormons are numerous in the extreme southwest. Hutterites—members of a sect that originated in Moravia and Slovakia in the 16th century—are scattered in communal agricultural settlements throughout the province.

Urbanization. Before World War II the provincial economy and outlook were predominantly agricultural and rural. Farmers composed by far the largest proportion of the labor force. By 1961, however, the balance had shifted, and more than three quarters of the population lived in urban centers. Over half of the total population are in the Edmonton and Calgary metropolitan areas. Outside the cities, the central and southern plains are relatively thickly settled regions.

4. Education and Cultural Life

Among the first acts of the Alberta legislature were the creation of a university and public school system.

In the early years the population was sparse and largely rural. Education was made compulsory, but young pupils could not be expected to travel long distances. A network of one-room schools was established, with each school serving a complete range of grades and ages. A high school education and a short training period were the main qualifications for teachers. Particularly important in areas first settled by heavy concentrations of non-English-speaking people was the insistence that lessons be taught in En-

glish. As a result, English is the first language of the vast majority of Albertans.

The curricula of the public schools emphasized academic subjects. In the period following World War II major programs were inaugurated for the building of technical and vocational schools to meet the need for training in trades and service occupations. Consolidation of rural school districts proceeded during the 1940's, with the result that new large centralized schools were able to offer educational advantages formerly available only in cities.

Higher Education. The University of Alberta in Edmonton was created in 1906. The University of Calgary began as a secondary campus of the University of Alberta, but became autonomous by 1966. Lethbridge University serves the higher educational needs of southern Alberta, and Athabasca University specializes in "distance education," offering by mail a wide array of courses to the more sparsely settled areas of the province. Supplementing these, a system of junior colleges, agricultural colleges, and institutes of technology fills other educational needs in Alberta.

Museums. Alberta's natural and human history form the core of the exhibits and reference materials available at the Provincial Museum and Archives in Edmonton. A comprehensive collection of works of art, western Canadian books and manuscripts, and Indian and other ethnic artifacts are gathered in the Glenbow Museum in Calgary. Historical buildings have been brought to Heritage Parks in Calgary and Edmonton. Extensive collections of fossil remains are on exhibit at the Tyrrell Museum of Paleontology and the Dinosaur Fossil Museum and Prehistoric Park in Drumheller. The visual arts are featured prominently at the Alberta College of Art in Calgary, the Edmonton Art Gallery, and in numerous other public and commercial art galleries.

Other Cultural Organizations. The structurally identical Northern and Southern Alberta Jubilee Auditoriums, located in Edmonton and Calgary respectively, were built to mark Alberta's 50th anniversary. They were conceived as centers in which visiting opera companies, orchestras, and theater companies could perform. Of later vintage were Calgary's Centre for Performing Arts, with its three theaters and hall to serve as the home of the Calgary Philharmonic, and the similar Citadel Theatre in Edmonton.

"Little theater" groups, organized in the larger cities, have won considerable success over the years in national drama festivals. The major symphony orchestras in the province are the Edmonton Symphony and the Calgary Philharmonic. Opera and ballet are presented by associations in both major cities.

5. Recreation

Alberta offers a wide range of recreational opportunities. The nonagricultural areas support the larger types of wild animals that attract hunters. In season the lakes and streams abound in fish and offer opportunities for all types of water sports. Skiing facilities in Banff and Jasper national parks are world famous, and ski areas have been opened elsewhere. For the camper, few areas in North America can compete in scenery with the foothills and slopes of the Rockies.

National Areas. The national parks—Banff, Jasper, Waterton Lakes, Elk Island, and Wood Buffalo—were reserved "for the benefit, advantage, and enjoyment of the people of Canada." Development of the parks began after the Canadian Pacific Railway crossed the Rocky Mountains. The natural beauty of the region was recognized, and Banff was established as the first Canadian national park in 1885. Jasper National Park was established in 1907.

The Waterton Lakes area was set aside as a national park in 1895. In 1932 it was linked with Glacier National Park in Montana to form Waterton-Glacier International Peace Park.

Elk Island National Park, to the east of Edmonton, was established in 1913, chiefly to protect elk, buffalo, and other wildlife. It is relatively small and is a favorite picnic spot.

Wood Buffalo National Park, covering a large area in northern Alberta and beyond, was established in 1922 as the home of the largest remaining herds of plains and woods bison. It is also a breeding and nesting ground for the whooping crane.

Provincial Areas. The provincial government established dozens of recreational parks and a number of sites to mark and preserve places of historical interest. In general, they are provided with picnic, camping, and playground facilities. Among the better known are the Cypress Hills Provincial Park, in the Cypress Hills; the Little Bow Provincial Park, near one of the large irrigation reservoirs; and Dinosaur Provincial Park in the badlands of the Red Deer River valley. Certain wilderness areas also have been set aside to preserve the natural habitat. These areas are protected from development of any kind.

Annual Events. The Calgary Stampede, held in July, is undoubtedly the best known and most popular annual event. It features a colorful parade that includes Alberta Indians on horseback, as well as square dancing in the downtown streets. The most spectacular features of the ro-

The West Edmonton Mall opened in 1981 as the world's largest shopping facility of its type.

Banff, Canada's oldest national park, attracts visitors in all seasons. The park was established in 1885.

© O. BIERWAGEN/MILLER SERVICES

A popular feature of the annual Calgary Stampede is the chuckwagon race.

deo itself are bronco busting, Brahma bull riding, calf and steer roping, and a frenzied chuckwagon race that has been dubbed "the Rangeland Derby." Edmonton celebrates a summer festival called "Klondike Days," also in July, that harks back to the 1898 gold rush in the Yukon and Alaska. The Banff Winter Carnival, held each January, features an exhilarating blend of Nordic and Alpine skiing and other winter sports competitions.

DANIEL I. ISTVANFFY, Author of
"Alberta's Industry and Resources"

6. History

The Indians the European fur traders found when they began to arrive in the region had lived there for at least 12,000 years. The wandering hunters on the Plains relied primarily on bison for food, clothing, and utensils. The Indians of the woodlands in northern Alberta lived by fishing and hunting, supplementing their diets with wild berries and plants.

Fur Trade and Exploration. Because of the tremendous profits to be made in the fur trade, both the French and the English pushed westward, challenging each other as they established overlapping trading empires. The Hudson's Bay Company (HBC) began operations in 1670, after receiving its charter from the British crown to conduct trade in "Rupert's Land," an area comprising the lands bounded by waters draining into Hudson Bay. Rupert's Land included much of the present-day area of the Prairie Provinces and Nunavut and part of the Northwest Territories. However, the company did not send a trader to what is now Alberta until 1754, when Anthony Henday arrived and began to promote trade with the Blackfoot Indians.

After the British victory in the Seven Years' War (1756–1763), French traders abandoned their posts in the Northwest. But by 1784 the HBC was confronted with a new rival in the form of the North West Company (NWC), formed by free traders from Montreal. One of the "Nor'Westers" (as the traders of the NWC were called), Peter Pond, built a fur-trading post on the Athabasca River in 1778, thus establishing the first post in present-day Alberta. Soon after, other Nor'Westers built Fort Chipewyan on nearby Lake Athabasca, which served as the departure point for Nor'Wester Alexander Mackenzie's explorations.

The two companies, from the 1770's to their merger in 1821, established competing posts throughout central and northern Alberta. After the merger Forts Edmonton and Rocky Mountain House became centers of the reorganized fur trade.

Opening the Canadian West (1867–1896). The advance of the central Canadian frontier challenged the HBC's control over the west. In 1869 the Canadian government purchased Rupert's Land from the company, and in 1870 the area that would be Alberta became a colony of Canada, administered as part of the North-West Territories by a federally appointed lieutenant governor and council.

As part of its policy of settling the west, the federal government in 1874 sent the North-West Mounted Police (NWMP) to Alberta to establish law and order, help arrange for treaties with the Indians, and prepare the way for settlement. During the late 1860's, whiskey traders from Montana had moved into southern Alberta to trade for buffalo robes. The effect they had on the Blackfoot Indians was devastating. In response, the NWMP established Fort Macleod, chased out the whiskey traders, and helped protect the Indians from further destruction. The government signed treaties with the Indians, then placed them on reserves, and worked to assimilate them. The Indians agreed to the treaties during the late 1870's because of the rapid decline in the game population.

The ranching industry in the foothills of southwest Alberta began in the late 1870's. Well-connected friends of Canada's Conservative government received generous leases and successfully established a few large ranches. Many of the ranchers were from Britain and eastern Canada. They attempted to create for themselves a replica of aristocratic life in Victorian Britain, with sports like polo and tennis, hunting and horse racing, and with formal balls, imported governesses, private schools, and the Anglican Church. Their efforts never totally succeeded and largely ended with the decline of the ranching industry before World War I.

The transcontinental Canadian Pacific Railway (CPR), which was completed in 1885, facilitated settlement and economic activity. In 1891 a rail line from Calgary to Edmonton was completed and was extended in 1893 from Calgary to Macleod. The arrival of the railways led to the emergence of dozens of rural supply centers and created a market for coal. Lethbridge developed as a coal-mining center in southern Alberta, and eventually several other coal-mining towns grew up along railroads in the Rocky Mountains and in many other parts of the province.

Immigration and Alberta's Ethnic Diversity (1896– 1914).
Although the largest number of settlers to the west during the 1880's came from Ontario and Britain, Alberta also began to attract immigrants from the United States and from continental Europe, particularly people of German and Scandinavian origin. Most of the Germans originally came from religiously based German-speaking settlements in central and eastern Europe. But the number of immigrants remained small until the late 1890's.

After 1896 better economic conditions, new farm technology, the development of an early maturing wheat, the closing of the American frontier, and the initiation of new immigration policies under a new Liberal government in Ottawa led to a large influx of people. Cities and towns mushroomed. Because of their strategic location on rivers and railroads, Calgary and Edmonton grew most quickly.

The largest numbers of immigrants came from Britain, the United States, and continental Europe. The British immigrants included all social classes. Their influence merged with that of people of British background who moved west from central Canada. By 1911 nearly 20% of the population was British-born and had strong cultural ties with Britain.

The Americans, mostly farmers from the Midwest, constituted the largest immigrant group (22% of the population in 1911). Included among the Americans were Mormon farmers from Utah and surrounding states, who had first come in 1887 because of antipolygamy laws in the United States. They arrived in much larger numbers at the turn of the century. German-Americans and Scandinavian-Americans also arrived, and a small group of blacks immigrated from Oklahoma to escape racial persecution there.

Americans played a prominent role in rural Alberta politics and society from the 1910's into the 1930's. They supported populist farm movements like the Society of Equity and the Non-Partisan League and their successor, the United Farmers of Alberta.

Central and eastern Europeans (half of whom were Ukrainians) also came in large numbers, accounting for 20% of the population by 1911. Slavic immigrants developed farmland in the parkbelt of north-central Alberta, and they did much of the manual labor on the railroads, in the coal mines, and in the cities.

The Wheat Economy and Changing Political Status.
Wheat provided the economic base for settlement, and it continued until World War II to be Alberta's most important commodity. However, the wheat farmers faced many problems: the hazards of the physical environment, the instability of wheat prices, high railway freight rates, monopolistic practices by grain companies, high tariffs, and a banking system that seemed remote and exploitive. Farmers consequently developed a number of cooperative organizations and later joined political movements to bring about change.

Demands that the North-West Territories (NWT) be given more political autonomy dated from the early 1890's. In 1905 the territorial district of Alberta, with considerable additional territory, became, with Saskatchewan, one of the two new Canadian provinces carved out of the old NWT. (The district of Alberta had been named after Princess Louise Caroline Alberta, the fourth daughter of Queen Victoria.)

In establishing the province, Ottawa required Alberta to fund and protect Roman Catholic schools. At the same time the federal government retained control of Alberta's natural resources. Both provisions were contentious; the latter remained a source of resentment in Alberta into the 1920's and fueled a political alienation with deep roots.

The political influence of Edmonton's Member of Parliament Frank Oliver (who became minister of the interior in 1905) made Edmonton, not Calgary, the provincial capital. The first premier was A. C. Rutherford, a Liberal. The Liberals remained in power until 1921.

Indian girls at the Old Sun Anglican mission school in Calgary pose for a group portrait in 1901.

GLENBOW ARCHIVES, CALGARY, ALBERTA

Oil was discovered at Turner Valley southwest of Calgary in 1914. Above are the first two wells.

Because of a minor scandal over an overly generous railway contract, Rutherford resigned in 1910. Another lawyer, A. L. Sifton, replaced him. The Liberals faced no serious challenge until the politicization of the farmers' movement at the end of World War I. While in power, the Liberals established the civil service and the educational system, introduced state control of telephones, and encouraged the development of an extensive railway network.

World War I and Social Reform. The first two decades of the 20th century witnessed the rise of several interrelated social reform movements. The wartime sense of idealism and sacrifice provided the rationale and the stimulus for prohibition and women's suffrage. In 1915, following a plebiscite, prohibition was enacted. In 1916 the Equal Suffrage Act gave women the vote, and in 1917, Louise McKinney, a prohibition leader, became the first woman in the British Empire to become a member of a legislature.

Most Albertans supported the war and (at least initially) the wartime Union Government in Ottawa, a coalition of Liberals and Conservatives formed in 1917. A. L. Sifton resigned the premiership in 1917 to join the Union Government and was replaced by Charles Stewart.

Postwar Unrest. Labor dissatisfaction led to a series of strikes across the province in the spring of 1919. The One Big Union (OBU) was launched in Calgary in March 1919 and gained considerable support among coal miners. Opposing the workers was a powerful coalition of businessmen, political leaders, and craft unions, which led to the OBU's decline by the mid-1920's.

Agrarian protest was a more potent force than labor unrest because of the greater number of farmers. Farmers opposed the conscription of Canadian youth and gradually came to oppose the national Union Government. Postwar inflation, a recession, and the instability of the wheat economy added to their discontent.

Though Henry Wise Wood, the American-born president of the United Farmers of Alberta (UFA), opposed political action, the leaders of the small Non-Partisan League helped convince the UFA to enter politics. The UFA won a decisive victory in the 1921 provincial election. Herbert Greenfield became premier, then was replaced in 1925 by J. E. Brownlee. Brownlee led the UFA to victory in the elections of 1925 and 1930. He remained in power until 1934, when he was forced to resign because of a personal scandal. He was replaced briefly by R. G. Reid.

Once in power, the UFA government was largely dominated by a conservative group that resisted the farmers' demands that it should legislate primarily for them. Across the province the farmers turned successfully to voluntary wheat pools for marketing crops. The UFA's support for the wheat pool movement and their successful negotiations with the federal government for the transfer of jurisdiction over natural resources (completed in 1930) contributed to their reelection in 1930.

Depression Years and the Rise of Social Credit. The Great Depression of the 1930's proved catastrophic for Alberta's economy. Wheat prices plummeted. The downswing quickly affected secondary and service industries. Unemployment reached an all-time high. Natural disasters of drought, wind and dust storms, and grasshopper plagues added to the problems. Alberta farmers on highly variable incomes were faced with fixed interest charges on their debts.

The UFA government responded to the depression with a policy of fiscal frugality. At the same time it came increasingly into conflict with the federally oriented UFA political organization, which became one of the founding groups behind a new socialist party, the Co-operative Commonwealth Federation (CCF), organized in Calgary in 1932. In 1935 the farmers of Alberta expressed their feelings about the scandal-ridden UFA government with its tight money policies, bland conservatism, and internal divisions by turning en masse to the new Social Credit movement.

Social Credit had a dramatic and lasting impact. Its ideology came from the writings of Major C. H. Douglas, a Scottish engineer-economist, who believed that depressions were the result of a chronic shortage of purchasing power and could be ended by distributing dividends. The charismatic William Aberhart, a Calgary high school principal and fundamentalist religious leader, popularized Douglas' theories. When in 1935, after much debate and public controversy, the UFA government refused to embrace Social Credit, Aberhart decided to take his movement into politics. Following an emotion-charged campaign, the Social Credit movement swept the province, winning 56 of 63 seats.

Once in power, Aberhart was unable to carry out the Social Credit program. By 1937 conflict had broken out within the movement over his failure to implement Social Credit policies. After a revolt of almost half of his legislative supporters, he brought from England two Douglasite "experts" who helped draw up legislative measures. Once enacted, however, these measures were disallowed as unconstitutional by the federal government.

Despite these frustrations, some financial problems were solved by Alberta's temporary repudiation of its debt payments. The Social Credit government protected farmers' property from foreclosure. Aberhart also introduced some important changes in other areas including the creation of larger school divisions and counties, the establishment of improved public health care, and the passage of mildly progressive labor legislation.

The War Years. World War II ended the economic depression. New wartime industries emerged. Coal mining, lumbering, and agriculture boomed.

Upon Aberhart's death in 1943 the Social Credit party chose his former student and protégé Ernest Manning as his successor. Manning remained in power for 25 years. He presided over Alberta's transformation from a largely rural agricultural province to an urban industrial one. A social conservative, Manning helped transform Social Credit from a party espousing monetary reform into one favoring the economic status quo.

Oil Discoveries and the Transformation of Modern Alberta. After World War II the economic, social, and political life of Alberta changed dramatically because of major discoveries of oil beginning at Leduc in 1947. The Turner Valley field, discovered in 1914 and further expanded in the 1920's and 1930's, had been the only significant oil field in the province until this time. The development of oil and gas after the Leduc discovery resulted in a population growth of 40% between 1951 and 1961. The oil industry created wealth and promoted urbanization. Calgary grew rapidly as the head office center of the oil industry, while Edmonton developed as a refining and service center.

The cities easily absorbed those leaving the farms because of farm mechanization and consolidation. Oil replaced agriculture as the most important industry in the province, though agriculture (which became increasingly diversified) remained important. The urban labor force became increasingly well educated, skilled, and professional. The economic boom of the 1950's also attracted a new wave of immigrants.

Manning's leadership during the 1950's and 1960's was marked by financial conservatism and cautious social reform. Increased oil revenues made possible the expansion of educational facilities, social services, and highways. During the 1950's, Manning attracted the support of urban businessmen through his opposition to "socialism" and his emphasis on "free enterprise." Manning retired in 1968 and was succeeded by his minister of agriculture, Harry Strom.

In 1971 a rejuvenated provincial Conservative party led by Peter Lougheed, a Calgary lawyer, defeated the Social Credit party. Lougheed made his party the voice of the new urban Alberta. A predominantly rural, small-town, and lower-middle-class movement like Social Credit had little chance of surviving in an increasingly urban and middle-class society.

The Lougheed Years and a New Alberta. The Conservatives came to power shortly before the economic boom of the 1970's, which was based on OPEC-induced increases in oil prices. The Gross Domestic Product (in constant dollars) almost doubled between 1971 and 1981, and Alberta became Canada's wealthiest and fastest-growing province. The economic boom attracted hundreds of thousands of migrants from across Canada. With the nation's newly liberalized immigration laws, the boom also brought, for the first time, significant numbers of immigrants from Asia and the Caribbean. Alberta's cities grew rapidly.

The 1970's and early 1980's also brought increased alienation from the federal government. Many Albertans saw the national Liberal party, which was in power throughout most of this period, as representative of the interests of Quebec and Ontario and insensitive to the west. Consequently, they voted overwhelmingly for the Conservatives. Alberta's economic fortunes were not matched by a similar rise in influence on national politics, and many Albertans resented their political impotence.

Feeling powerless at the national level, many Albertans turned to the provincial government to protect them against perceived federal encroachment and to increase industrial development and diversify the economy. As the defender of "Alberta rights" against the federal government, Lougheed's Conservative party won a series of one-sided electoral victories in 1975, 1979, and 1982. The Conservatives fought numerous battles with the federal government over the control and pricing of oil, particularly in 1974 and 1980–1981. A skilled organizer and negotiator, Lougheed gained national attention as a spokesman for Alberta's interests.

Though espousing a strong "free enterprise" ideology, the Conservatives adopted a "province building" strategy of state assistance for private entrepreneurs. They provided financial support for an expanded petrochemical industry, and for the development of Alberta's heavy oil and oil sands. In order to diversify the economy and maximize provincial revenues, the Conservatives in 1976 also established the Alberta Heritage Savings and Trust Fund, which put aside a portion of oil and gas revenues for investment chiefly in provincial crown enterprises.

Conflict between the Alberta and federal governments reached its peak in 1980–1982 following the unilateral introduction of new energy and constitutional policies by the Liberal federal government under Pierre Trudeau. Following the rapid rise in oil prices in 1979, the federal government left Canadian prices far below international prices. Then, in 1980, the federal government introduced the National Energy Program (NEP), which increased federal control

E. OTTO/MILLER SERVICES

Contemporary Calgary's fortunes march in step with the oil and natural-gas industry.

over, and federal revenues from, the oil and gas industry. A protracted legal and public-opinion battle followed between the two governments, during which a right-wing separatist party, the Western Canada Concept, emerged briefly, demanding either drastic changes in the Canadian political system or the separation of western Canada.

After protracted negotiation, the two governments reached an agreement (1981) that left major elements of the NEP intact but increased the price of oil, transferred some control of the industry back to the province, and gave the Alberta government greater revenues.

One year later high interest rates, softening world oil prices, and a broader economic recession led to economic distress. Unemployment increased dramatically. In 1983 and 1984, for the first time in decades, the province's population declined slightly as people left for other parts of Canada.

In 1980 the Conservatives strongly opposed the federal government's unilateral constitutional changes, and Lougheed led the eight premiers who resisted Ottawa. After much acrimony, court battles, and negotiation, Canada's new Constitution Act (1982) included the amending formula (protecting provincial rights) that the Alberta government had proposed.

The Conservative victory at the national level in September 1984 placed Alberta on the winning side nationally, reducing its strong sense of political alienation. The federal and provincial Conservatives cooperated on a number of new policies, including dismantling the NEP.

The Need for Diversification. The subsiding of the economy and constitutional wars contributed to Lougheed's decision to retire from politics in 1985. He was replaced by his former energy minister, Don Getty. The decline of federal-provincial conflict, the change of political leadership, and further economic distress created an opportunity for the provincial opposition parties. In the 1986 provincial election, three opposition parties elected 22 members out of 83, thereby breaking a succession of lopsided Conservative majorities.

Alberta's experience in the late 19th and 20th centuries has been characterized by rapid social and economic change. This rapid change, coupled with a dependence on primary natural resources and external markets, has continually spawned political and economic insecurity. All political parties agree that Alberta's economy should become more diversified in order to avoid its recurring boom-bust cycles.

HOWARD PALMER
University of Calgary

Bibliography

Breen, David H., *The Canadian Prairie West and the Ranching Frontier* (Univ. of Toronto Press 1983).
Burnet, Jean, *Next-Year Country: A Study of Rural Social Organization in Alberta* (Univ. of Toronto Press 1978).
MacGregor, James C., *A History of Alberta* (Univ. of Wash. Press 1981).
MacPherson, Ian, ed., *Western Canada* (Sunflower Univ. Press 1985).
Mann, William E., *Sect, Cult and Church in Alberta*, rev. ed. (Univ. of Toronto Press 1972).
Thomas, Lewis G., *The Ranchers' Legacy: Alberta Essays by Lewis G. Thomas*, ed. by Patrick A. Dunae (Univ. of Neb. Press 1986).

ALBERTA, University of, al-bûrt′ə, a coeducational and nondenominational institution of higher learning in Edmonton, in the province of Alberta, Canada. The university was created by an act of the first legislature of Alberta in 1906. Classes began in Edmonton in 1908, and the first degrees were awarded in 1912. The legislature also gave the university the responsibility of setting the standards for all professional education in Alberta. In 1944 the legislature empowered the university to provide all teacher training in the province.

The Calgary division of the university was granted almost complete autonomy in 1964 and became a separate university in 1966. The Lethbridge division became the University of Lethbridge in 1967. A number of junior colleges in the province are affiliated with the university.

ALBERTI, in his design for the basilica of Sant'Andrea in Mantua, was influenced by classical architecture.

ALBERTI, äl-bâr′tē, **Leon Battista** (1404–1472), Italian architect and scholar, who was a notable example of the "universal man" of the Renaissance. In the wide range of his interests and in the high degree of his talent in both art and science, he was an intellectual forerunner of Leonardo da Vinci. Alberti's writings on architecture, painting, and sculpture contributed greatly to Renaissance theory of the arts and had a strong, continuing influence, especially on architecture, for several centuries.

Alberti was born in Genoa on Feb. 14, 1404. He received his first formal training in the humanities at Padua and studied law at Bologna. In 1428 he became an aide of the papal legates to Burgundy and Germany. In 1431 he was named a papal secretary in Rome, where he began a careful study of the city's ancient monuments. Moving to Florence in 1434, he became a member of the inner circle of humanists in Tuscany and was recognized as an authority on classical literature and art. While in Florence, he also developed an interest in contemporary architecture, especially that of Brunelleschi. He returned to Rome in 1452 and became a recorder of pagan monuments and a consultant for the papacy in the remodeling of medieval churches, including the early Christian basilica St. Peter's.

Alberti's career as an architect began when he was in his 40's. In 1450, Sigismondo Malatesta, lord of Rimini, called on him to redesign the medieval church of San Francesco in Rimini as a shrine to the Malatesta family and its court —the Tempio Malatestiano. He reworked the medieval exterior in classical terms. The main block of the building is in the form of a temple, with a tripartite triumphal arch on the façade— both ideas derived from Roman imperial architecture. For each side of the building he constructed a row of deep niches to serve as tombs for intellectuals of the court.

Alberti undertook a similar redesigning project for the Gothic church of Santa Maria Novella in Florence in 1456. Because only the façade of the church was to be rebuilt, he maintained a unity between the older and the newer parts of the building by taking his inspiration from Tuscan Romanesque, the most "classical" phase of the indigenous medieval style. He designed a light-colored marble revetment, serenely divided into simple geometric shapes by darker marble bands.

Two churches in Mantua, San Sebastiano (1460) and Sant'Andrea (1472), best exemplify the classicism of Alberti's architecture. For San Sebastiano, Alberti planned a church in the form of a square within a Greek cross, a classical central plan that was a major departure from the "T" shape usually found in medieval basilicas. The façade is a free interpretation of a Roman temple, with an austere front and a pediment lifted on a high base and articulated by tall pilasters and a broken entablature. For Sant'-Andrea he again combined the elevation of a pagan temple with that of a triumphal arch. The effect of the superimposition is especially harmonious because he chose the less complex single arch (like the Arch of Titus in Rome) to articulate the severe wall of the temple. Although Sant'Andrea is designed on the more traditional "T" plan, Alberti's treatment of the interior space, with its vast open nave, deep wall chapels, and large dome, was a forerunner of the architecture of the baroque period.

Alberti also was a major innovator in the field of secular architecture. His design for the Rucellai Palace in Florence (about 1447–1451) is one of the earliest examples of the revival of the ancient practice from Roman times of applying classical pilaster strips to the three stories of a building.

Alberti's famous treatise on architecture, *De re aedificatoria*, written about 1452 and first published in 1485, is based in part on such Roman authorities as Pliny and Vitruvius. He drew his theories of architectural aesthetics from his study of the basic mathematics of proportion in classical art. Beauty, he said, would result from harmonious proportions, simplicity of form, and judicious use of classical ornament. He also stressed the importance of freeing the architect from directing the actual construction of the building, which he believed should be carried out by skilled craftsmen. For this reason, he has been called the first architect in the modern sense of the word.

Alberti's other writings include a treatise on painting, *Della pittura* (1436), and *Della famiglia* (1441; *On the Family*) and *Della tranquillità dell'animo* (1442; *On Peace of Mind*). Alberti died in Rome on April 25, 1472.

JAMES SNYDER, *Bryn Mawr College*

Further Reading: Borsi, Franco, *Leon Battista Alberti: The Complete Works* (Harper 1977); Gadol, Joan, *Leon Battista Alberti* (Univ. of Chicago Press 1973); Wittkower, Rudolf, *Architectural Principles in the Age of Humanism* (Norton 1971).

ALBERTINELLI, äl-bär-tē-nel'lē, **Mariotto** (1474–1515), Italian painter. He was born at Florence, Italy, on Oct. 13, 1474. He was a pupil of Cosimo Rosselli and he collaborated with Fra Bartolommeo, completing the latter's *Last Judgment,* now in the Uffizi Palace in Florence. Of Albertinelli's own works, *The Visitation of the Virgin* (1503) in the Uffizi, and the *Annunciation* (1510), in the Florence Academy, are the most highly regarded. He died at Florence on Nov. 5, 1515.

ALBERTUS MAGNUS, al-bûr'təs mag'nəs, **Saint** (c. 1206–1280), German Scholastic philosopher and theologian, known in English as *Albert the Great.* Born in Lauingen, Swabia, Germany, he entered the Dominican Order in 1223 while studying at the University of Padua. After teaching theology at Cologne and other German cities, he went to the University of Paris, where he received his doctorate. Between 1245 and 1248, Albert had Thomas Aquinas among his pupils. In 1248 he returned to Cologne and was made regent of the newly established Dominican house of studies, with Thomas as his assistant. After serving as provincial of the German Dominicans, he was consecrated bishop of Regensburg (Ratisbon) in 1260 but two years later resigned the bishopric and by order of Urban IV took charge of the campaign in Germany to promote the Crusade to the Holy Land. He carried out other official missions for the church until 1267, when at his request he was allowed to resume his teaching at Cologne. In 1277 he went to Paris to defend Thomas Aquinas from attacks on his doctrine. He died in Cologne on Nov. 15, 1280. November 15 is celebrated as his feast.

Albert wrote extensively on a great variety of subjects ranging from philosophy and theology to the natural sciences. He did not develop an original and homogeneous system of philosophy; rather he attempted to synthesize the best of Aristotle's teaching with Neoplatonic elements. He clearly distinguished between philosophy and theology and inaugurated a new trend of thought by cultivating philosophy and the sciences as fields of study independent of theology. While maintaining some basic Aristotelian doctrines, he stressed the spirituality and immortality of the human soul and argued against the Averroists in favor of a separate active and passive intellect for each man. (See AVERROËS.) He accepted Aristotle's theory of abstraction and emphasized the role of sensation in knowledge. He held—in opposition to some of his contemporaries—that reason alone cannot demonstrate with certainty the world's creation in time.

Albert was a pioneer in the development of the experimental sciences and brought to the attention of the Christian world the treasures of natural truths contained in Aristotle and his Arab commentators. A chief merit of Albert consists in his having trained and encouraged Thomas Aquinas and detected his great abilities.

BERNARDINO M. BONANSEA, *O.F.M.*
The Catholic University of America

Bibliography

Albertus Magnus, *The Book of Secrets of Albertus Magnus of the Virtues of Herbs, Stones and Certain Beasts; Also, a Book of the Marvels of the World,* ed. by R. Michael Best (Oxford 1974).

Kovach, Francis, and Shahan, Robert W., eds., *Albert the Great: Commemorative Essays* (Univ. of Okla. Press 1980).

Madden, D. H., *Chapter of Medieval History* (1924; reprint, Associated Faculty Press 1969).

ALBERTVILLE, àl-ber-vēl', a small city in southeastern France that was selected as the headquarters of the Olympic Winter Games of 1992. The city is situated in the department of Savoie, on the Arly River just above its junction with the Isère. A commercial and industrial center, the city includes the medieval village of Conflans located on a ridge east of the Arly. Albertville was named for King Charles Albert of Sardinia (reigned 1831–1849), a former ruler. Population: 18,190 (1999 census).

ALBI, àl-bē', in France, the capital of the department of Tarn. It is built on a height rising nearly 600 feet (183 meters) above the Tarn River, 42 miles (68 km) northeast of Toulouse. The fortress cathedral church of St. Cecilia, built between 1282 and 1400, is one of the most notable architectural monuments of southern France. Also of great interest is the archbishop's palace (13th–15th century). It now houses a great collection of works by the painter Henri de Toulouse-Lautrec (1864–1901), who was born in Albi, as well as works by other modern painters and sculptors. The religious movement of the Albigeneses, in the 12th to 13th centuries, derived its name from the town. Modern Albi is an agricultural trading center, with variegated industries. Population: 49,106 (1999 census).

ALBIGENSES, al-bi-jen'sēz, members of a Christian sect centered in Albi, southern France, during the 12th and 13th centuries. They followed the teaching of the Catharist heresy and were known also as *Cathari.* They professed religious beliefs similar to those practiced by the Bogomils of Bulgaria and other Eastern heretical sects. It is possible that these beliefs were transmitted from the East by way of trade routes to northern, and thence to southern, France. Catharism reached Albi in 1145, or shortly thereafter, and spread throughout Languedoc. Its success posed a threat to the church, the state, the family, and society.

Catharism, or Albigensianism, was a Christian heresy of Manichaean tendencies, although no direct dependence on ancient Manicheanism has ever been proved. It taught the irreconcilability of matter and spirit and claimed that human souls were imprisoned in the bodies they inhabited.

Like Satan, the first human souls had been created pure spirits but were cast out of heaven for rebelling against God. Satan encompassed them in matter, which he created (according to the strict form of the doctrine) or found already in existence. From that time on, human souls were born imprisoned in matter. Procreation was the greatest of evils, since it prolonged this condition, and marriage was to be shunned.

Out of pity for man, Christ, a good angel, assumed the semblance of a body and came to earth to teach souls that heaven, their true home, could be attained only by efforts to rid themselves of matter. Souls already purified might hasten their liberation by starvation (*endura*). Those not yet purified at the time of bodily death would pass by transmigration into some lower bodily form. Out of reverence for inhabitant souls, therefore, the killing of men or animals was forbidden. Vegetarianism was encouraged, since meat, eggs, and dairy products were deemed contaminated and contaminating.

Only the perfect (Greek, *katharoi;* Latin, *perfecti:* both meaning "pure") were held to all obligations of the sect. Ordinary believers were bound to venerate the perfect and to strive to become members of that class, at least at the point of death. Incorporation among the perfect was effected by spiritual baptism, consisting of the imposition of hands, accompanied by prayer. This rite was believed to absolve the suppliant from sin and to impart the Holy Spirit, an assisting angel. Other practices included the study of the New Testament and the prophetic books of the Old Testament, group confession, and the sharing of a common meal (*agape*). Preaching was reserved to the perfect, from whose number were chosen the bishops and deacons.

The ascetic lives of Catharist preachers, in sharp contrast to the worldliness of many clerics and monks of Languedoc, gained them an attentive hearing and numerous converts. The determining factor in many conversions, however, was the fact that the moral commitment required of the ordinary Catharist was less strict than the requirements for members of the Catholic faith.

Since Catharism denied the reality of Christ's death and its redemptive significance, the value of Catholic Mass and the sacraments, and the existence of hell and purgatory, the heresy was condemned by church councils and the popes. Disapproval, however, had little effect, because local rulers, and some bishops, protected the Catharists. Among their supporters were Count Raymond VI of Toulouse and his son.

Pope Innocent III (reigned 1198–1216) strove by correspondence and the commissioning of legates and preachers to stem the tide of heresy. Obstruction of his efforts reached its climax in the slaying of his legate Peter of Castelnau in 1208. Innocent then called for a crusade against Toulouse. The French king, Philip II, excused himself from involvement but permitted his vassals to answer the summons.

Led successively by Simon IV de Montfort, his son Amaury, and Louis VIII of France, the northern armies were successful, despite stubborn opposition. It was not until 1229, however, when Raymond VII ceded Languedoc to France by the treaty of Meaux, that hostilities ended. Subsequent rebellions, the last and most bloody of which was that at Montségur in 1245, were quelled by the summary execution of their leaders.

The Albigensian Crusade exceeded its initial purpose and eventually became an instrument of political and private gain. Better justice was accorded the heretics by the papal Inquisition, which was set up by 1230. The Inquisition gradually eliminated Catharism by the end of the 14th century. The outcome might have been very different, however, if the political power of Catharism had not first been broken by the crusade.

See also BOGOMILS; INQUISITION; MANICHAEANS.

JOHN E. BRESNAHAN
Augustinian College

ALBINISM, al'bə-niz-əm, is a hereditary absence of pigment from the skin, hair, and eyes. It occurs occasionally in many mammals. In man, the estimated incidence of the condition is 1 in 20,000 in the general population.

Description. In generalized or total albinism, there is no pigmentation in the skin (the skin may be of a slightly pinkish color because of the blood vessels beneath). The hair is snow white, and the eyes have a pink iris and red pupil. Other conditions, especially eye abnormalities such as astigmatism and photophobia (extreme sensitivity to light), frequently occur along with albinism. Mental and physical retardation also can accompany the condition.

Causes. Albinism has several causes: a complete absence of pigment cells (melanocytes); interference in the migration of these cells during the development of the embryo; or an inability of the melanocytes to produce pigment (melanin). This inability is believed to result from a lack of the enzyme tyrosinase, an enzyme necessary for the production of melanin.

Albinism is a hereditary condition. The absence of certain genes (hereditary units) is thought to account for the lack of tyrosinase. When the gene for normal pigmentation (that is, for the production of tyrosinase) is absent and the gene for no pigmentation (that is, for no tyrosinase) is present in a double state, albinism manifests itself.

Treatment. Until a way is discovered to produce tyrosinase in the pigment cells of the albino, there will be no cure for albinism. Meanwhile, the avoidance of sunlight, for which all albinos have a poor tolerance, and early and careful treatment by an ophthalmologist for any eye abnormalities are helpful in alleviating the handicaps of the condition.

Related Conditions. There are two other pigmentation disorders of the skin that are related to albinism: *partial albinism* and *vitiligo*. Partial, or piebald, albinism causes skin changes such as white spotting and white forelock. It has about the same rate of incidence as total albinism, but it is not so disabling. Vitiligo is the absence of pigment in various areas of the body. It occurs in from 1 to 3 percent of the population. The affected areas can be of various shapes and sizes and frequently have hyperpigmented borders. Some areas can repigment, but generally the course of the disease is progressive.

REAUMUR S. DONNALLY, M.D.
Washington Hospital Center

ALBINONI, äl-bē-nō'nē, **Tommaso** (1671–1750), Italian composer and violinist, who wrote instrumental music and operas. The son of a wealthy paper merchant, he was born in Venice on June 8, 1671. Albinoni composed 50 operas between 1694 and 1740. Among these works were *Zenobia, regina de' Palmireni* (1694), *Griselda* (1703), and *I veri amici* (1722). Some of his operas, such as *Vespetta e Pimpionone* (1722), were early examples or forerunners of *opera buffa* (comic opera).

Albinoni is remembered principally, however, for his instrumental music. Johann Sebastian Bach, a contemporary of Albinoni, admired his work and arranged two fugues from Albinoni's trio sonatas, which are listed as Nos. 437 and 438 in Bach's works. Albinoni also composed chamber music and concertos for solo instruments and orchestra. He died in Venice on Jan. 17, 1750.

ALBION, al'bē-ən, was the earliest name by which the island of Great Britain was known. It was used by Aristotle in the 300's B.C. and still appears in poetry. The Greeks and Romans probably received the name from the Gauls, in whose language it would mean "mountain land" or "white land," from the Celtic *alp*, *alb*, meaning "high" or "white" (whence also Alps): This probably referred to the chalky Dover cliffs.

ALBION, al'bē-ən, a village in western New York, on the Erie Canal, 30 miles (50 km) by road west of Rochester and 10 miles (16 km) south of Lake Ontario. A residential center, it is the seat of Orleans county and a summer resort. The village stores, processes, and ships the farm produce of the surrounding district, which grows vegetables and fruit and raises dairy cattle. The Albion and Orleans correctional facilities are in the area. Albion was settled in 1811 and was incorporated in 1828. Population: 7,438.

ALBO, Joseph, äl'bō (c. 1380—1440), Spanish religious philosopher, whose major work, *Sepher ha-Ikkarim (Book of Principles*, 1485), is a carefully reasoned synthesis of Hebraic theology.

Born in Monreal del Campo, Spain, Albo became known as a preacher and theologian. His treatise, believed to incorporate the teaching of Simon ben Zemach Duran, a contemporary scholar, derives its conclusions in part from the philosophy of Maimonides (1134—1204) and in part from that of Hasdai Crescas (1340—1410). It is divided into four sections, the first presenting an exposition of the fundamentals of all religions. Albo reduces the essence of Judaism to three basic principles: the existence of God, divine revelation, and divine justice embodied in a system of rewards and punishments.

ALBOIN, al'boin (died 572), a king of the Lombards. When he succeeded his father in 565, the Lombards were in possession of the Drava River region. In alliance with the Avars, a Mongolian tribe moving west, Alboin defeated the Gepidae, a Teutonic tribe in the Danube basin. He married the Gepidae king's daughter, Rosamund.

Forced from the Drava by his former allies, the Avars, Alboin led the Lombards in an invasion of northern Italy in 568. He conquered lands as far as the western Alps and as far south as the Po River and in 572 made Pavia the Lombard capital.

After his death, the Lombards, the first barbarian invaders to treat the Romans as subjects rather than as partners in the empire, established control over much of Italy. Alboin was assassinated on Rosamund's orders at Verona in 572, after he had forced her to drink out of a goblet made from her father's skull.

ALBONI, Marietta, äl-bō'nē (1823—1894), Italian opera singer who was regarded as one of the great contraltos of her era. She was born in Città di Castello, Italy, on March 6, 1823. She studied with Gioacchino Rossini, who taught her the contralto roles in his operas.

She made her debut as Maffio Orsini in Donizetti's *Lucrezia Borgia* at La Scala, Milan, in 1843. When she sang in the United States she rivaled Jenny Lind in popularity. Retiring in 1866, she made occasional concert appearances and sang at Rossini's funeral in 1868. She died in Ville d'Avray, France, on June 23, 1894.

ALBORNOZ, Gil Álvarez Carillo de, äl-bôr-nôth' (1300—1367), Spanish prelate and cardinal. Appointed archbishop of Toledo in 1337, he served under Alfonso XI of Castile in his successful campaigns against the Moors. He fled from Alfonso's successor, Pedro the Cruel, to the court of Pope Clement VI at Avignon. Clement created Albornoz cardinal in 1350.

In 1353, Clement appointed him legate to Rome, and Albornoz spent the next years securing the restoration of papal authority over the Papal States. He first waged war against Giovanni di Vico, prefect of Rome, and defeated him in 1354. An able commander of men and a suave diplomat, he conducted successful wars against the powerful lords who held lands formerly under papal control.

In 1357, Albornoz issued the constitutions of the Papal States, a codification and revision of existing laws. Known as the Egidian Constitutions, they remained in force until 1816.

Albornoz returned to Avignon in 1357, but Roman intrigues forced him back to Rome the following year. By 1359, after a year of constant warfare, he had won back all the territory of the Papal States except Bologna, which was held by the powerful Visconti family. Bologna finally surrendered in 1364, and the Papal States were again united, allowing the pope to resume his seat at Rome.

Albornoz was appointed legate to Bologna in 1367, and he died near Viterbo on August 14. He left his money to found the Spanish College of St. Clement at Bologna.

ALBRECHTSBERGER, Johann Georg, äl'breкHts-ber-gər (1736—1809), Austrian organist, composer, and theorist who was a leading master of counterpoint. He was born in Klosterneuburg, Austria, on Feb. 3, 1736. His famous pupils included Josef Weigl, Johann N. Hummel, and, most notably, Ludwig van Beethoven. Albrechtsberger was appointed organist to the court of Vienna in 1772 and choirmaster of St. Stephen's Cathedral in 1792. He died in Vienna on March 7, 1809.

Albrechtsberger's fame rests less on his compositions than on his theoretical works, which include *Gründliche Anweisung zur Komposition* (1790) and *Kurzgefasste Methode, den Generalbass zu erlernen* (1792).

ALBRET, äl-bre', the name of a historically important family of France, taken from the seigniory of Albret, situated in the Landes.

CHARLES D'ALBRET (died 1415) became a constable of France and was in command of the French forces, numbering over 50,000 men, at the Battle of Agincourt (1415). He led his armored horsemen against the English archers and was killed in the ensuing rout.

JEAN D'ALBRET (died 1516) married Catherine of Foix and assumed the title of king of Navarre. His sister, Charlotte d' Albert, married Cesare Borgia in 1499.

HENRI D'ALBRET (1503—1555) was the eldest son of Jean. On the death of his mother in 1517, he claimed the crown of Navarre as Henry II. His title was disputed by Charles I of Spain (Emperor Charles V), but from 1517 until his death he remained titular king of French Navarre. He married Margaret of Angoulême, sister of King Francis I of France, in 1527. In 1550 he was made duke of Albret and peer of France.

JEANNE D'ALBRET (1528—1572), queen of Navarre, was the daughter of Henri d'Albret. She married Anthony of Bourbon, duke of Vendôme, in 1548. On the death of her father (1555), she succeeded to the throne of Navarre and Béarn, reigning in conjunction with her husband until his death in 1562, and afterward alone. She was the mother of Henry III of Navarre, later Henry IV of France.

She was a supporter of the reformed religion and established it in her kingdom.

ALBRIGHT, Ivan Le Lorraine, ôl'brīt (1897—1983), American "magic realist" painter whose subjects were the decaying debris of life and humanity. He was born in North Harvey, Ill., on Feb. 20, 1897. He turned from studying architecture to art after serving as a medical draftsman in World War I. From 1918 to 1924 he studied painting at, among other schools, the École des Beaux-Arts in Nantes, the Art Institute of Chicago, and the National Academy of Design in New York City. Independently wealthy, he devoted his life to art, first sharing a studio in Warrenville, Ill., with his father and twin brother, Malvin Marr, both painters, and later living in Chicago and New England. He died on Nov. 18, 1983, in Woodstock, Vt.

A painstaking craftsman, Albright worked for over a decade on *That Which I Should Have Done I Did Not Do* (1931—1941; Art Institute of Chicago), which shows a decrepit door adorned with a funeral wreath; and *Poor Room—There Is No Time, No End, No Today, No Yesterday, No Tomorrow, Only the Forever and Forever and Forever without End* (1941—1962; Art Institute of Chicago), which depicts a detritus-strewn room. Other works include *And Man Created God in His Own Image* (1930—1931; Art Institute of Chicago), *The Farmer's Kitchen* (c. 1933—1934; National Museum of American Art), and a series of portraits for the 1945 film *The Picture of Dorian Gray*, the latter executed with his twin brother.

ALBRIGHT, Madeleine Korbel, ôl'brīt (1937—), American foreign policy expert, Democratic party activist, and government official. Named permanent representative to the United Nations during the first Clinton administration, she became the first female secretary of state and the highest-ranking woman yet to serve in the federal government.

The daughter of a Czech diplomat, Albright was born Maria Jana Korbelova in Prague on May 15, 1937. Her childhood was tumultuous—the Korbels fleeing Hitler's armies to a wartime exile in London, returning to Czechoslovakia in 1945, and fleeing again after the 1948 Communist coup. Though she was reared as a Roman Catholic, it became public in 1997 that she was of Jewish heritage and had lost three grandparents in the Nazi Holocaust.

Arriving in the United States at age 11, Albright attended private school in Denver, graduated from Wellesley College in 1959 with a B.A. in political science, and married media heir Joseph Medill Patterson Albright. While rearing three daughters, she earned her master's and doctoral degrees from Columbia University, under thesis adviser Zbigniew Brzezinski. She served as chief legislative assistant to Sen. Edmund Muskie, Democratic senator from Maine, from 1976 to 1978 and later was hired by Brzezinski (then national security adviser to Pres. Jimmy Carter) as his congressional liaison.

Shortly after President Carter left office in 1981, Albright's husband abandoned their 23-year marriage, and she retreated to Georgetown University's School of Foreign Service, where she turned her town house into a salon on the European model. Key Democratic party officials, including Arkansas governor Bill Clinton, joined in wide-ranging foreign policy discussions there. During this same period, Albright conducted research at the Woodrow Wilson Center for Scholars and the Center for Strategic and International Studies in Washington, D.C., and served as chief foreign policy adviser to the vice presidential and presidential campaigns, respectively, of Geraldine Ferraro (1984) and Michael Dukakis (1988). From 1989 to 1992 she was president of the Center for National Policy.

Albright's extensive experience and contacts bore fruit when the Democrats recaptured the White House in 1992: on Feb. 1, 1993, she was named U.S. ambassador to the United Nations. An activist policymaker, she displayed an unusual combination of toughness and idealism in that post. During the first years of her ambassadorship, she enunciated a doctrine of "assertive multilateralism" for American foreign policy and successfully championed using U.S. military force for nation building in Somalia, against Serb aggression in Bosnia, and to restore democracy in Haiti.

During Albright's later years at the United Nations, however, her idealism was tempered by disaster in Somalia and by the election of a Republican Congress. Assertive multilateralism gave way to "doability," and her toughness became more public. She now opposed humanitarian intervention in Burundi, castigated Cuba for shooting down private American aircraft, and led the U.S. effort to deny Boutros Boutros-Ghali a second term as UN secretary-general. By 1996, UN colleagues complained that she was more often trumpeting the U.S. position than working for multinational agreements.

President Clinton, however, was delighted with her energetic defense of U.S. interests, her political savvy, and her media skills. On Dec. 6, 1996, he appointed Albright the 64th secretary of state, and she was confirmed 99—0 by the Republican-controlled Senate.

TERRY L. DEIBEL, *National War College*

ALBUMAZAR, al-bū-maz'ər (805?—886), Arab astrologer. Albumazar, or Abū Ma'shar Dja'far ibn Muhammad, was born in Balkh, in western Turkestan, and lived in Baghdad. He was most widely known in Christian Europe for *The Great Introduction to the Science of Astrology,* an influential work translated by Hermanus Secundus into Latin and printed in Augsburg in 1489. In this work he correctly explained the movement of tides. One of his less plausible ideas was the theory that the world was created when the seven planets were in conjunction in the first degree of Aries, and that the world would end when the same conjunction occurred in the last degree of Pisces. His reputation, even in his own time, for being a plagiarist is confirmed by modern research.

ALBUMIN, al-bū'mən, a simple protein found in plant and animal tissues. It is coagulated by heat and is soluble in water and in strong salt solutions. In animals the liver manufactures albumin. Because of its high molecular weight, albumin generally is not excreted by the kidney in animals.

The most important of the albumins are ovalbumin, which is found in the white part of eggs, and serum albumin, which constitutes 50% of the plasma protein in human blood and regulates the osmotic pressure of the plasma.

ALBUMINURIA, al-bū-mə-nūr'ē-ə, a condition characterized by the presence of increased amounts of proteins, such as serum albumin and globulin, in the urine. It is frequently called proteinuria. Although it is usually a symptom of disturbed kidney function, it may also indicate other abnormal conditions such as progressive systemic sclerosis (a disease involving the connective tissue) or multiple myeloma (a malignant proliferation of plasma cells that are too large or small).

Albuminuria generally is a result of increased permeability of the secretory and excretory tubes of the kidney, reduction of the kidney blood flow, or an increase in the plasma volume. There are, however, several other types of albuminuria. These include febrile proteinuria, which occurs during active infection; transient proteinuria, a result of severe muscular exercise; and psychosomatic proteinuria, produced by emotional stress.

ALBUQUERQUE, Afonso de, äl-boo-ker′kə (1453–1515), founder of the Portuguese empire in South Asia. He was known as the "Portuguese Mars" and also as "Afonso the Great." Albuquerque was born in Alhandra, near Lisbon, and spent his early years at the court of King Alfonso V of Portugal. In 1481 he took part in the expedition against the Turks and in the Battle of Otranto.

After further service with the king's forces, Albuquerque was sent with the Portuguese fleet to the Indian Ocean in 1503. He established a fort in southern India at Cochin and returned to Portugal in 1504. Two years later King Emanuel appointed him viceroy of Portuguese possessions in Asia. In 1507, during the voyage to India, Albuquerque left the main fleet and captured Hormuz Island, at the entrance to the Persian Gulf, but Muslims soon retook it. Albuquerque proceeded to India in 1508. At Cannanore, in India, the Portuguese viceroy, Francisco de Almeida, refused to recognize Albuquerque's commission and jailed him. When the Portuguese fleet arrived in 1509, Albuquerque was released and took office.

In 1510 Albuquerque began the conquest that firmly established the Portuguese empire in South Asia. He captured the city of Goa and made it the center of Portuguese government and commerce in the area. Within the next five years forces under his command gained control of the Malabar coast, Ceylon (Sri Lanka), the Sunda Islands, Malacca, and Hormuz Island. In 1513 he unsuccessfully attacked Aden, the fortified Muslim city at the entrance to the Red Sea.

The purpose of Albuquerque's campaigns was to secure fortified bases for the Portuguese so that they could take over Muslim trade. His capture of Malacca was important because the city controlled the spice trade from China and other regions in Asia. Although successful in India, Albuquerque had enemies at the Portuguese court, and King Emanuel appointed one of Albuquerque's opponents as viceroy in 1515. This news reached the ailing Albuquerque as he was sailing to Goa, and he died embittered on Dec. 16, 1515, before reaching the city.

ALBUQUERQUE, al′bə-kûr-kē, the largest city in New Mexico and the seat of Bernalillo county. It is situated on the Rio Grande River, 62 miles (100 km) southwest of Santa Fe. Because of its equable climate, it is famous as a health center. At an altitude of 5,314 feet (1,619 meters), Albuquerque has an annual average rainfall of only 8.13 inches (206.5 mm). Temperatures range from a January average maximum of 46° F (8° C) to a July average maximum of 91° F (33° C).

Economy. The trading center of a farm region where sheep and livestock are raised, Albuquerque is also the headquarters for banking interests and government agencies. Also important to the city's economy are nuclear research, health and medical services, and tourism. Several military installations are situated here. Kirtland Air Force Base is a weapons research center. It includes the National Atomic Museum and the Sandia Laboratories, which conducts research in solar energy and laser technology and is the state's largest private employer. Albuquerque has an international airport.

Education and Culture. The University of New Mexico, one of the largest universities in the Southwest, has a campus in Albuquerque. It contains a fine arts center, a museum of anthropology, and a museum of geology. Other educational institutions include the National College, Nazarene Indian Bible College, Southwestern Indian Polytechnic Institute, and Albuquerque Technical-Vocational Institute.

The Old Town Plaza, dating to 1706, reflects the character of 18th-century Albuquerque. Adjacent to it is the Church of San Felipe de Neri (1706), once used as a fortress against the Native Americans. The "new town" section, planned in 1880, is quite different. In the 1970s an extensive urban-renewal program included a multimillion-dollar civic plaza, convention center, and library. The city's cultural institutions comprise the Albuquerque Little Theatre, the Albuquerque Civic Light Opera, and the Albuquerque Ballet Company. The city is also the home of the New Mexico Symphony. The New Mexico State Fair is held in September on a 220-acre (90-ha) fairground in the heart of the city. The New Mexico Museum of Natural History was opened in Albuquerque in 1986. To the east of the city, the Sandia Peak Aerial Tramway lifts passengers 10,378 feet (3,163 meters) for a scenic view and excellent skiing.

History and Government. Albuquerque was founded in 1706 by the Spanish provincial governor, Don Francisco Cuervo y Valdez, who named it in honor of the duke of Alburquerque, the viceroy of New Spain. The first *r* in the duke's title was eventually omitted from the name of the city. In 1846, during the Mexican War, the area that is now New Mexico was occupied by United States troops, and it became a United States territory in 1848. Albuquerque remained an American military outpost until 1870. During the Civil War it was occupied briefly by Confederate forces. In 1883 it became the county seat, and in 1891 it was incorporated as a city. With the advent of the nuclear age after World War II, the city attained its accelerated rate of growth. Population: 448,607.

ELSA SMITH THOMPSON*
Albuquerque Public Library

ALCAEUS, al-se′əs, a Greek lyric poet of the 7th century B.C. who is said to have originated the Alcaic meter. He was born in Mytilene, Lesbos, of a noble family. He was early involved in the war between the Athenians and Mytilenians at Sigeum and with the political factions of his native city. Exiled because of his political activity, he went to Egypt but later returned home.

An elder contemporary of Sappho, Alcaeus wrote lyrical songs, many of which dealt with contemporary politics. He also wrote love songs, hymns to Apollo and Hermes, and drinking songs.

His works, originally edited in 10 volumes by Aristophanes of Byzantium, survive in fragments. He usually wrote in two- or four-line stanzas in a variety of meters, one of which, called the Alcaic, Horace was to imitate. His style was simple and direct; he was at his best in describing sights and emotions.

ALCALÁ ZAMORA, Niceto, ä-kä-lä thä-mō'rä (1877–1949), Spanish political leader who was president of the Spanish republic from 1931 to 1936. He was born in Priego de Córdoba, Córdoba province, on July 6, 1877, and was educated at Granada and Madrid universities. He practiced law and in 1905 was elected to the Cortes, the Spanish parliament. Under the monarchy he served in several liberal governments, becoming minister of works in 1917 and minister of war in 1922.

In 1930 Alcalá Zamora became a republican and began to work for King Alfonso XIII's abdication. When the king was forced to leave Spain in April 1931, Alcalá Zamora became prime minister of the provisional government. But when left-wing members of the Cortes, seeking to reduce the power of the Roman Catholic Church, passed a constitution containing anticlerical provisions, Alcalá Zamora, a devout Catholic, resigned in October 1931. Several months later, however, he accepted the presidency of the republic.

Despite his efforts to moderate the influence of the left-wing parties, Alcalá Zamora was accused by the rightists of siding with the anticlericalism of the left. At the same time the leftists criticized his amnesty of many rightists who had been convicted of political offenses under the leftist government. After the left-wing Popular Front victory early in 1936, dissatisfaction with him increased, and he was deposed as president in May 1936. Alcalá Zamora went into exile, living in France and Argentina. He died in Buenos Aires on Feb. 18, 1949.

ALCAMENES, al-kam'ə-nēz, a Greek sculptor of the 5th century B.C. Unlike his teacher, Phidias, Alcamenes chose religious subjects and worked in a variety of materials—ivory, gold, bronze, and marble. His masterpiece is said to have been a statue of Aphrodite. He worked with Phidias on the decoration of the temple of Zeus at Olympia, where he carved a relief on the west pediment representing the battle of the Centaurs and Zapithae. As a tribute to him, his portrait was carved in relief on the temple at Eleusis. None of Alcamenes' work survives. Information about him is derived from the writings of Pliny, Cicero, Lucian, and Valerius Maximus.

ALCATRAZ, al'kə-traz, an island in San Francisco Bay, California, north of San Francisco. Its area is 12 acres (5 ha). From 1859 it was the site of a U.S. Army disciplinary barracks, replaced in 1909 by a military prison. This was converted in 1934 into a federal prison, considered virtually escape proof. It was closed in March 1963. In October 1972 it became part of the National Park Service's Golden Gate National Recreation Area.

ALCESTIS, al-ses'təs, in Greek legend, the daughter of King Pelias of Iolcos. She married Admetus, the Thessalian king of Pherae. Alcestis offered herself as a willing substitute when Thanatos (death) came to claim her husband, after his aged parents had refused to die in his stead. When Alcestis died, Admetus gave himself up wholly to his sorrow and remained inconsolable until Heracles (Hercules) brought her back to him from the tomb.

The story is the theme of *Alcestis* (438 B.C.), the earliest extant play of Euripides. The portrayal of emotions is the major strength of the drama. Alcestis is presented as a woman of tenderness and nobility of soul. Admetus, a well-intentioned but mediocre man, comes to recognize his failings only after he has selfishly allowed the sacrifice of his wife.

The comic element is more pronounced in *Alcestis* than in any other Greek tragedy. It is seen in the garrulous and jovial manner of Heracles and in the happy ending, when Heracles restores Alcestis to life. Euripides employs the chorus with a high degree of success to unify the action. It is not until his later drama, the *Bacchae,* that he gives the chorus as important a part and such lines of extraordinary beauty as in *Alcestis.*

The tragedy by Euripides was the basis of *Alceste,* an opera in three acts composed by Christoph Willibald Gluck in 1767. This opera generally is conceded to be a historic musical landmark, in that it anticipates Wagner by converting opera into music-drama. Gluck freely acknowledged his indebtedness for this innovation to his librettist, Raniero da Calzabigi, crediting him with conceiving a new type of lyric drama in which flowery descriptions are replaced by strong passions. For the first time in opera, the dramatic action is well knit, and the music attempts a faithful interpretation of the story's emotional content.

Calzabigi's Italian libretto was translated into French for a Paris premiere, given on April 23, 1776. This version is presented most often today.

ALCHEMIST, The, al'kə-məst, a comedy by Ben Jonson, considered by many critics his best play. According to Samuel Taylor Coleridge, *The Alchemist* has one of the perfect plots of all literature, revolving around characters whose very extravagances broaden our knowledge of human nature.

First acted in 1610 and printed in 1612, the play was included in the folio edition of Jonson's works published in 1616. The plot concerns Love-Wit, a London gentleman, who departs for the country, leaving his town house in charge of his servant, Face, during a plague epidemic. Face invites the alchemist Subtle and the latter's accomplice, Dol Common, to his master's house, where the three embark on a series of swindles. Among the gullible victims are the greedy voluptuary Sir Epicure Mammon, the hypocritical Puritans Tribulation Wholesome and Ananias, the tobacconist Abel Drugger, and the clerk Dapper. Jonson also introduces the quarrelsome young Kastril, a country bumpkin who apes court manners, and his sister Dame Pliant, a pretty young widow. Surly, a gamester friend of Sir Epicure, sees through the swindlers' game and attempts to expose them. The unexpected return of Love-Wit forces Subtle and Dol to take hasty flight. Love-Wit, however, falls in love with Dame Pliant, marries her, and forgives Face, the unwitting matchmaker.

Bibliography: Beaurline, L. A., *Jonson and Elizabethan Comedy* (Huntington Library 1978); **Haynes, Jonathan,** *The Social Relations of Jonson's Theatre* (Cambridge 1992); **Holdsworth, R. V.,** ed., *Jonson: "Every Man in His Humor" and "The Alchemist": A Casebook* (Macmillan 1978).

ALCHEMY, al′kə-mē, is usually defined as the art of transmuting base metals into gold. However, alchemy passed through many phases during its history, and consequently the meaning of the term varied considerably.

Hellenistic Science and Alchemy. Western alchemy arose about 100 A.D. in the great meeting place of Greek and Oriental cultures, Alexandria in Egypt. It was in the fusion of these cultures that alchemy was born.

The early Greek philosophers, speculating without much actual handling of materials, had evolved a number of theories on the basic composition of matter. The system devised by Aristotle in the 4th century B.C. became the most widely accepted of these theories. In later centuries Aristotle came to be considered the final authority in science, and his views formed the basis for later scientific systems.

According to his concept, the basis of all material objects was to be found in four qualities: heat, cold, moisture, and dryness. These qualities could combine to form the four elements: earth (cold and dryness), water (cold and moisture), air (heat and moisture), and fire (heat and dryness). By altering the proportions of their qualities, these elements could be changed into each other. This theory was as close to a chemical theory of matter as the classical Greeks came, and an essential feature of it was the interconvertibility of the elements.

In the centuries following the death of Aristotle a more practical and more scientific culture arose in the Hellenistic world. The Egyptians, in particular, had long been expert artisans, working in metals and in the dyeing of cloth in rich colors. In the Mesopotamian countries a number of rather mystical ideas had dominated the minds of thinkers. These ideas found expression in astrology. One of the main ideas on which astrology was based was that the life of man on earth (the microcosm) was only a reflection of events in the great world of the stars (the macrocosm).

These three strains—Greek philosophy, Egyptian craftsmanship, and Mesopotamian astrology—met and fused in the workshops of the Egyptian artisans in Alexandria. These men were familiar with metallurgical procedures, and they knew the stability and value of gold. They therefore regarded gold as the most perfect metal. Greek philosophy taught them that the metals, like all other substances, could be converted into each other. Astrology showed that events in the outer world paralleled the life of man, and thus the metals, like plants and animals, could be born, nourished, and caused to grow through imperfect stages into a final perfect form.

The central idea of alchemy was in strict accord with the best philosophical and scientific thinking of the day, and alchemy actually was a true science in its origin. The earliest alchemists were laboratory workers who tried to carry out the processes predicted by their theory and to speed the action of nature by which, over a long interval of time, gold was perfected deep in the earth. By the application of various types of heat and by the use of various reagents, they hoped to produce gold as good as that furnished by nature, and in much less time.

These men, who came chiefly from the artisan class, had a long tradition of keeping trade secrets in their own workshops. Therefore, they often resorted to cryptic language in describing the steps they were performing. They associated gold with the sun, silver with the moon, and the other metals with the five planets known to them. Many of their reagents were given fantastic names, such as "bile of the tortoise."

The tendency to use obscure terms was intensified when a new group of thinkers began to invade the science of alchemy. Within a century of its beginnings, alchemy attracted the attention of the mystical philosophers, including some who were active in Alexandria. These men saw the search for the perfect metal as an allegory of the search of the human soul for perfection. They were little interested in practical metallurgy, but they quickly began to utilize alchemical terminology by taking the technical terms of the artisans and converting them to mystical meanings. By the 4th century, alchemy had split into two branches: the esoteric and the exoteric. Adherents of the esoteric branch drew further away from practical laboratory operations. The practitioners of the exoteric branch remained close to their furnaces and retorts. Both branches continued to survive throughout the history of alchemy, but it was the esoteric alchemist who was likely to produce a written work. Therefore, the literature of alchemy became less and less understandable to the uninitiated.

As Hellenistic interest in science weakened and the mystics gained the upper hand, the work of the practical alchemists gradually sank into obscurity. The commentaries and allegorical writings of the later Byzantine empire ceased to make any original contributions to the subject.

Interest in Greek science was not lost, however. The Nestorian church carried Greek science into the Near East in Syriac translations and eventually transmitted it to the Arabs.

Chinese Alchemy. Alchemical ideas had arisen, apparently independently, in China at about the same time as in the West. The Chinese adepts were followers of the Taoist philosophy and were seeking the "tao," or "way," of nature. They, too, felt that gold was the supreme achievement of nature, and they, too, sought to make it artificially.

In two important respects Chinese alchemy differed from that of the West. The Chinese alchemists originated the idea of adding a material substance to a base metal to bring about the desired change into gold. The later concept of the Philosopher's Stone, a sort of catalyst for transmutation, arose from this idea. The Philosopher's Stone became the goal in the searches of later alchemists. The Chinese alchemists also believed that gold was a "medicine" that could prolong life and cure disease. Not only could gold aid sick humans, it also could cure "sick" metals—that is, imperfect ones. They believed that the addition of small quantities of gold would "multiply" the amount of gold. This idea of "multiplication" became a standard feature of alchemical thinking.

Arabic Alchemy. After Mohammed had established his religion, the Arabs spread rapidly over the Near East, North Africa, and Spain. They became interested in Greek science, which they learned from the Nestorians, and they translated the Syriac manuscripts, including those on alchemy, into Arabic. Baghdad and Córdoba became centers of intellectual life, and the scientific tradition was carried on by the Arabs between 800 and 1200, when western Europe seemed uninterested in learning.

ALCHEMISTS are shown at work in these drawings from J.J. Manget's *Biblioteca Chemica Curiosa* (1702).

The Arabian alchemists were in contact with the Greek culture of the Hellenistic world and with the Chinese culture. They took ideas from both cultures and combined them into a unified alchemical theory. The Arabian alchemists were practical men, and many of them returned to the laboratory. Once again exoteric alchemy flourished, and important discoveries were made. For example, they discovered the caustic alkalis. The esoteric alchemists also flourished, and they produced a large literature that was strongly tinged with mystical and astrological ideas. Religious sects began to compile encyclopedic works on alchemical subjects. One such sect, the Ismailites, ascribed many of its writings to a reputed alchemist of the 8th century, Jabir ibn-Hayyan. It is doubtful that he actually wrote the works attributed to him, but his name became famous as the greatest Muslim alchemist.

Alchemy in Medieval Europe. After 1100, Arabic interest in science began to decline, but a new culture was ready to take over the traditions. In Sicily and in Spain, translators became active in translating the Arabic scientific works into Latin, and thus European scholars became aware of alchemical ideas. The theories of Greek and Chinese alchemy, systematized by the Arabs, fell upon fertile new soil.

Alchemy was taken up avidly in Europe, both in its exoteric and esoteric forms. The chief work of the exoteric alchemists probably was written by a practicing Spanish alchemist and metallurgist of the 14th century. Writing under the name of Geber, a Latinized form of the name Jabir, he produced four books (about 1310) in which alchemical theory and metallurgy were described. According to Geber, metals were composed of sulfur (the principle of combustibility or rusting) and mercury (the principle of fluidity, or ability to melt). Under the proper conditions the proportions of these constituents could be changed in the direction of the perfect metal, gold. The works of Geber served as a handbook of metallurgy for 300 years, and their alchemical theorizing encouraged the esoteric alchemists to continue their speculations.

During this time, alchemical terminology became more and more confused. New and fantastic terms were introduced for reagents and processes. An elaborate system of symbols was developed to hide meanings from the ordinary reader. Eventually even the alchemists found the manuscripts difficult to understand.

Alchemy in the Renaissance. Because the alchemists claimed to transmute base metals into gold, they were in great demand among princes and nobles who wished to augment their treasures. Naturally, a large number of charlatans were attracted to the profession. Certain credulous monarchs, such as Emperor Rudolf II (1552–1612), surrounded themselves with court alchemists and subsidized them heavily. The profession was not a secure one; many of those who failed to carry out their promises were exiled or executed. However, the rewards of a successful swindler were great, and there was no lack of those willing to tempt fortune in this way.

Probably the majority of educated men in the period from 1400 to 1600 believed in the reality of transmutation, although some notable exceptions are found in literature. Chaucer in the "Canon's Yeoman's Tale" and Ben Jonson in *The Alchemist* held the adepts up to merciless derision.

During this period many true believers continued to impoverish themselves in seeking the Elixir—the Philosopher's Stone. The esoteric alchemists grew more and more obscure in their writings, but the exoteric school was discovering new chemical facts, improving laboratory equipment, and gradually beginning to turn from the search for transmutation to the study of the substances themselves. They were becoming true chemists, although they continued to call themselves alchemists. In particular, this use of the name was adopted by Paracelsus (1493–1541), a German physician who introduced the use of many mineral substances as medicines. He defined alchemy as the study of any change in a natural substance that made it fit for a new use.

Alchemy After the Renaissance. As the sciences became more and more systematized, the Aristotelian and alchemical theories gave way before the attack of the physicists. The last vestige of alchemy disappeared with the establishment of modern chemistry by Antoine Lavoisier at the end of the 18th century. Alchemy was classified once and for all as a pseudoscience. However, at its inception, alchemy was a truly scientific discipline, the chemistry of its day. During the periods of greatest activity, alchemists made many discoveries that were of great value to later practical chemistry.

The modern transmutation of elements carried out by nuclear physicists cannot properly be classified as alchemy, although the nuclear physicists have achieved the goal long sought by the old alchemists. See also CHEMISTRY.

HENRY M. LEICESTER, *College of Physicians and Surgeons, University of the Pacific*

Bibliography
Cockren, A., *Theoretical Alchemy* (Alchemical Press 1987).
Pritchard, Alan, *Alchemy: A Bibliography of English Language Writings* (Methuen 1980).
Redgrove, H. Stanley, *Alchemy: Ancient and Modern* (Ares 1980).
Taylor, Frank S., *The Alchemists* (Beekman House 1977).

ALCIATI, äl-chä′tē, **Andrea** (1492–1550), Italian legal scholar, who helped introduce the scientific method into jurisprudence. He was born at Alzate, near Lake Como, on May 8, 1492, and taught law at universities in France and Italy. He was one of the first to apply the historical method to the study of Roman law through reinterpretations based on his studies of the language and literature of the ancients.

Alciati, whose name was also spelled *Alciato*, achieved notice outside the field of law for a collection of moral verses entitled *Emblemata* (1522). His collected works were published as *Opera omnia* (4 vols., 1546–49). He died at Pavia on Jan. 12, 1550.

ALCIBIADES (c. 450–404 B.C.), al-sə-bī′ə-dēz, was an Athenian aristocrat, general, and politician. He was reared in the home of Pericles, his cousin and guardian. In his youth Alcibiades was a frequent companion of Socrates. He shared Socrates' individualistic outlook but was not influenced by his moral and ethical teachings.

Alcibiades served with distinction in the army at Potidaea (432). In the early years of the Peloponnesian War against Sparta, he fought at Delium (424), where he saved Socrates' life. Alcibiades began his political career in 420 as one of the 10 generals elected annually at Athens. Radically pro-war in policy, he successfully brought about an alliance between Athens and several of Sparta's chief enemies—Argos, Elis, and Mantinea. Although he was reelected in the following year, his radical designs were held in check by the more conservative and cautious Nicias.

In 415, over the strong objection of Nicias, Alcibiades ill-advisedly encouraged Athens to send a naval force to Sicily. He accompanied this force as one of its commanders. On the eve of the departure of the fleet, a number of religious statues in Athens were desecrated. Capitalizing on the incident, his political enemies had little trouble convincing the Athenians that Alcibiades, whose impiety was well known, was involved in a plot to overthrow the government. Formally indicted in absentia, Alcibiades eluded the escort sent to take him back to Athens for trial and took refuge in Sparta.

For the next several years he resided at Sparta, serving as military adviser to the Spartans in their renewed conflict with Athens. In 412, Alcibiades headed a Spartan mission to Ionia, where he successfully convinced a number of Athenian colonies and allies to revolt. He was generally distrusted by the Spartans, however, and personally disliked by their king, Agis, whose wife he had seduced. Having lost the confidence of the Spartans, he moved to the court of the Persian satrap Tissaphernes, whom he sought to use to further his own designs.

Alcibiades now hoped to return to Athens. Realizing that the democratic government there would not recall him, he did what he could to have it overthrown. In 411 an oligarchy replaced the democratic government at Athens. But when Alcibiades failed to separate Tissaphernes from his Spartan ally, the oligarchy did not recall him. However, a group of Athenian generals on the island of Samos opposed the oligarchic government in Athens and gave Alcibiades the command of the Athenian fleet stationed at Samos.

Between 410 and 408, Alcibiades achieved several important victories, notably in 410 at Cyzicus, where 60 Spartan ships were either destroyed or captured. Subsequently he brought much of the northern Aegean back under Athenian control. Because of his success in these ventures, he was welcomed back to Athens as a hero in 407 and given command of the Athenian navy. As naval commander he achieved no immediate victories, and when an Athenian fleet was defeated at Notium in 406, his enemies used this defeat to turn popular sentiment against him. His command was not renewed, and he went into voluntary exile in Thrace. After the Peloponnesian War came to an end, the Spartan commander Lysander demanded his life. Alcibiades fled to Phrygia, where he was assassinated in 404.

Alcibiades was an egoist and an opportunist who stopped at nothing to further his own interests. Extremely handsome and endowed with a sharp, quick mind, he was a good general but a thoroughly unprincipled demagogue without respect for the law, man, or the gods.

THOMAS KELLY
University of Alberta

ALCINOUS, al-sin′ō-əs, in Greek legend, was king of Phaeacia (modern Corfu) and the father of Nausicaa. He entertained Odysseus (Ulysses) who came to Phaeacia after being shipwrecked on his homeward voyage to Ithaca from the Trojan War.

ALCIPHRON, al′si-fron, Greek writer of the 2d century A.D., was the author of a collection of 122 imaginary letters that attempt to depict Greek daily life of the 4th century B.C. Written in imitation of Lucian, Alciphron's contemporary, the letters use many of the plots of the New Attic comedy, particularly those of Menander.

ALCMAEON, alk-mē′ən, in Greek legend, was a son of Amphiaraus and Eriphyle of Argos. Suspecting Eriphyle of treachery, Amphiaraus commanded his sons to kill her if he was slain. Alcmaeon led the Epigoni against Thebes. On his return to Argos, he found that his father was dead, and so he killed his mother. He then went mad and was pursued from place to place by the Furies.

At Psophis, in Arcadia, he was absolved by King Phegeus of the murder, and he married Phegeus' daughter, Arsinoë. When the land became barren because of his presence, he took refuge near the mouth of the Achelous River and married Callirhoë, daughter of the river god. Alcmaeon was killed by Arsinoë's brothers, on the orders of Phegeus.

ALCMAEONIDAE, alk-mē-on′i-dī, an Athenian family of great political influence in the 6th and 5th centuries B.C. Alcibiades and Pericles were members of the family.

ALCMAN, alk′mən, was a Greek poet of the 7th century B.C., who was founder of the Dorian school of choral poetry. He is believed to have been a native of Sardis, in Lydia, and to have been taken as a slave to Sparta, where he was freed because of his talent. Later he was made teacher of the state choruses.

His works were originally collected in six books, but only fragments now exist. He used the broad, direct Doric dialect and wrote in varied and simple meters. His lyrical poems—love songs, hymns, and paeans—were simple, clear, and musical and were often sung at Spartan feasts and festivals. He was especially celebrated for his parthenia (choir songs for girls). His verse was unaffectedly charming and usually dealt with simple matters, such as birds, horses, and food.

Alcman is regarded as the founder of erotic poetry. The bucolic poets also considered him their predecessor. He was read widely as late as the 2d century A.D., although his dialect was then considered harsh.

ALCMENE, alk-mē'nē, in Greek mythology, was the daughter of Anaxo and Electryon, king of Mycenae. She was the mother of Heracles (Hercules) by the god Zeus, who had deceived her by disguising himself in the form of her husband, Amphitryon.

ALCOA, al-kō'ə, an industrial city located in eastern Tennessee, in Blount county, 15 miles (24 km) by road south of Knoxville. It is adjacent to the county seat and commercial center, Maryville. Alcoa was founded in 1913 by the Aluminum Company of America ("Alcoa"), which constructed large aluminum reduction plants there because hydroelectric power was available nearby. The community, which was incorporated in 1919, adopted city-manager government that year. Population: 7,734.

ALCOBAÇA, äl-kōō-vä'sə, is a village in the Leiria district of east-central Portugal, 18 miles (29 km) southwest of the city of Leiria. It is celebrated for its magnificent Cistercian monastery, established about 1150 by Alfonso I. The monastery was a center for teaching improved agricultural methods. Some of the kings of Portugal are buried there.

ALCOCK, ôl'kok, **John** (1430–1500), English prelate and statesman, who was successively bishop of three sees and lord chancellor of England. He was born at Beverley, educated in the church school there, and graduated with distinction from Cambridge University. Although educated for the church, he sought and found authority in secular as well as ecclesiastical affairs. In addition to church offices in London, he filled in 1470 and 1471 the offices of privy councillor, master of the roles, and royal emissary to Scotland. Thereafter, as a favored courtier of Kings Richard III and Henry VII, he became, in turn, bishop of Rochester, Worcester, and Ely. In 1475 he was briefly lord chancellor and, in the following year, lord president of Wales.

Toward the end of his life, he used his considerable wealth to endow Peterhouse College and found Jesus College, Cambridge. He died at Wisbeach Castle on Oct. 1, 1500.

ALCOCK, ôl'kok, **Sir John William** (1892–1919), British aviator who piloted the first nonstop airplane flight across the Atlantic Ocean. He was born in Manchester, England, on Nov. 6, 1892. In World War I he was in the Royal Air Force.

On June 14–15, 1919, he made the historic transatlantic flight with Arthur Whitten Brown as navigator. Their flight time from St. John's, Newfoundland, to Clifden, Ireland, was 16 hours 12 minutes, of which 15 hours 57 minutes was over water. After the flight, both airmen were knighted. Alcock was killed in a plane crash at Côte d'Évrard, France, on Dec. 18, 1919.

ALCOHOL, al'kə-hôl, is any of a family of organic compounds containing the atomic group —OH. This group, which largely determines the physical and chemical properties of alcohols, is attached to a chain of carbon atoms that also hold hydrogen atoms. The formulas CH_3OH (methanol), C_2H_5OH (ethanol), and $CH_3CH_2CHOHCH_3$ (2-butanol) are typical.

Ethanol, also called ethyl alcohol or grain alcohol, is familiar as the beverage alcohol. It is a member of a large family of compounds, and it is the only simple one that can be consumed safely (within limits). Some of the other members, methanol for example, are highly poisonous. The mistaken belief that the term "alcohol" applies to a single substance rather than to a group of related substances that may have widely different physiological effects has cost many lives.

The alcohols have great industrial importance as commercial solvents, antifreeze mixtures, solvents for pharmaceuticals, and intermediates in the manufacture of many other products.

Historical Background. Alcoholic beverages, such as beer and wine, that contain ethyl alcohol (ethanol), were probably made before history was recorded. The process is the fermentation of sugars or starches from plant products under the catalytic action of enzymes from yeast or malt. Fermentation stops when the alcohol concentration in the mixture reaches about 12 percent by volume. Although the primary product is ethanol, small amounts of propanol, butanols, pentanols, and higher alcohols are also formed.

Hundreds of years ago it was learned that these fermentation products could be distilled to obtain alcohol concentrations much higher than 12 percent. Distillation of fermentation products is the basis for making such beverages as whisky, gin, and rum.

In the early days of the distilled liquor industry in England, the alcohol content was measured by "proof." A mixture of alcohol and water was applied to gunpowder. The amount that would just permit the ignition of the powder was considered to be 100 proof. In England this was established as 11 parts by volume of ethanol to 10 parts of water. In the United States the proof figure is just twice the percentage by volume. For instance, a liquor that is 90 proof contains 45 percent ethanol.

Types and Nomenclature. According to one classification, an alcohol is a primary alcohol if the —OH group is attached to the end of a carbon chain. It is a secondary alcohol if the —OH group is attached to a carbon atom that has two carbon atoms attached directly to it. It is a tertiary alcohol if the carbon atom bearing the —OH group has three carbon atoms attached to it directly.

$$
\begin{array}{ccc}
& & \text{H} \\
& & \text{HCH} \\
\text{H H} & \text{H H H} & \text{H H} \;|\; \text{H} \\
\text{(a) HC–C–OH} & \text{(b) HC–C–CH} & \text{(c) HC–C–C–CH} \\
\text{H H} & \text{H O H} & \text{H H O H} \\
& \text{H} & \text{H}
\end{array}
$$

primary   secondary   tertiary

According to a common and older nomenclature, substance (a) is ethyl alcohol, (b) is isopropyl alcohol, and (c) is tertiary amyl alcohol. Many of the names of the higher alcohols (those containing more carbon atoms) are individual rather than systematic. Lauryl alcohol for example, has the formula $CH_3(CH_2)_{10}CH_2OH$.

The modern and more systematic method of naming alcohols is based on the number of carbon atoms in the longest continuous chain, the substituents being named and their positions numbered. The naming of the fundamental carbon chain follows the naming of the hydrocarbons: 1 C (1 carbon atom), methane; 2 C, ethane; 3 C, propane; 4 C, butane; 5 C, pentane; 6 C, hexane, and so on. Adding the ending "-ol" gives the alcohol name, and a number before the name gives the position of the —OH group. Numbers before the names of substituents indicate their positions. According to this system, alcohol (a) is ethanol, (b) is 2-propanol, and (c) is 2-methyl-2-butanol.

Some alcohols have two or more —OH groups in their structure. Several of these alcohols have great importance in industry. Two —OH groups cannot be held in a stable combination on a single carbon atom. Alcohols with two —OH groups are called diols. For example, ethylene glycol has the structural formula

$$\begin{array}{cc} H & H \\ | & | \\ HC & -CH. \\ | & | \\ O & O \\ H & H \end{array}$$

Its systematic name is 1,2-ethanediol.

The triols are alcohols with three —OH groups. For example, glycerin has the structural formula

$$\begin{array}{ccc} H & H & H \\ | & | & | \\ HC & -C & -CH. \\ | & | & | \\ O & O & O \\ H & H & H \end{array}$$

Its systematic name is 1,2,3-propanetriol.

Some alcohols are multiple-function compounds; that is, they contain other characteristic atomic groups besides —OH. These alcohols may exhibit modified characteristics of the chemical behavior of the attached groups. Lactic acid, present in sour milk and other food products, is a hydroxy acid with the formula

$$\begin{array}{ccc} H & H & O \\ | & | & \parallel \\ HC & -C & -C & -OH. \\ | & | & \\ H & O & \\ & H & \end{array}$$

The carboxyl group, $-\overset{\displaystyle O}{\overset{\parallel}{C}}-OH$, is a typical organic acid group.

The carbohydrates are common substances that contain multiple —OH groups. They also hold either the aldehyde group, $-\overset{\displaystyle O}{\overset{\parallel}{C}}-H$, or the ketone group, $\rangle C=O$, or structures that can be broken down to these groups by hydrolysis. The sugar glucose, $CH_2OH(CHOH)_4CHO$, is an example.

If the —OH group is attached directly to the benzene ring, $C_6H_5—$, the substance has acid properties rather than alcohol properties. Phenol, C_6H_5OH, is a weak acid but a highly corrosive and toxic substance.

Physical Properties. Methanol, the first member of the alcohol family, has a boiling point of 149° F (65° C). As the number of carbon atoms in an alcohol increases, the boiling point rises. Ethanol boils at 173.1° F (78.4° C), and 1-propanol boils at 207° F (97.2° C). Chain branching tends to lower the boiling point. Alcohols boil at much higher temperatures than hydrocarbons with an equal number of carbon atoms.

The lower alcohols—methanol, ethanol, 1-propanol, 2-propanol, and 2-methyl-2-propanol—mix with water in all proportions. The butanols are partly soluble and the higher alcohols are progressively less soluble with increasing molecular weight. The excellent solvent action that the lower alcohols have on many other organic materials is one of their most important commercial properties. An increase in the number of —OH groups present per molecule tends to increase solubility in water. It also tends to produce an increasingly sweet taste.

Chemical Properties. Of the alcohols, only ethanol is effectively intoxicating. Methanol is highly toxic when taken internally. Its vapor can also be toxic, and harmful quantities can be absorbed through the skin. Some other alcohols are poisonous to a lesser degree if ingested.

In general, primary and secondary alcohols are readily oxidized to compounds that contain an unchanged number of carbon atoms. The primary alcohols form aldehydes, and the secondary alcohols form ketones. The aldehydes are easily oxidized further to carboxylic acids. The ketones are less easily oxidized to acids that have fewer carbon atoms. Tertiary alcohols strongly resist oxidation, but under powerful oxidizing agents, they can be converted to carboxylic acids that contain fewer carbon atoms.

Primary and secondary alcohols can be dehydrogenated catalytically to produce aldehydes and ketones, respectively. The reaction is frequently carried out at temperatures of about 572° F (300° C) under the action of a copper, nickel, or silver catalyst:

$$CH_3CH_2OH \xrightarrow{\text{catalyst}} CH_3-\overset{\displaystyle H}{\underset{}{C}}{=}O + H_2.$$

Sulfuric acid is an effective dehydrating agent for alcohols. This treatment results in the formation of hydrogen sulfate esters, unsaturated hydrocarbons, or ethers, depending on reaction conditions. The commercial manufacture of diethyl ether from ethanol is an important example:

$$2\ CH_3CH_2OH \xrightarrow[150° C]{H_2SO_4} \underset{\text{diethyl ether}}{(C_2H_5)_2O + H_2O.}$$

Alcohols react directly with carboxylic acids to form compounds called esters, many of which have industrial importance as solvents. The reaction between ethanol and acetic acid is typical:

$$\underset{\text{ethanol}}{C_2H_5OH} + \underset{\text{acetic acid}}{CH_3\overset{\displaystyle O}{\overset{\parallel}{C}}-OH} \longrightarrow \underset{\text{ethyl acetate ester}}{CH_3\overset{\displaystyle O}{\overset{\parallel}{C}}-OC_2H_5} + H_2O.$$

When an active metal such as sodium combines with ethanol, there is rapid evolution of hydrogen gas, and a substance called sodium ethoxide ($NaOC_2H_5$) is formed. This reaction indicates a very slight degree of hydrogen ion formation in ethanol. Higher alcohols react with sodium less readily than the alcohols with fewer carbon atoms, and secondary and tertiary alcohols react less readily than primary ones.

Commercially Useful Alcohols.—*Methanol*. The principal industrial uses of methanol are as a component of an antifreeze mixture, as a solvent, as a denaturant for ethanol, and as a source material for the manufacture of formaldehyde and a wide range of other organic chemicals. The greatest single use is in making formaldehyde. Methanol is a nonpermanent antifreeze because of its rather low boiling point. In a one-to-one mixture with water by volume, the freezing point is $-52.6°$ F ($-47°$ C). A typical formula for its use in denaturing ethanol calls for 5 gallons of methanol to 100 gallons of ethanol.

Methanol (methyl alcohol) is produced by the direct combination of carbon monoxide and hydrogen at high temperature (350 to 400° C) and pressure (3,000 to 4,500 psi). A catalyst of the oxide of chromium and zinc is used:

$$CO + 2 H_2 \xrightarrow{\text{catalyst}} CH_3OH.$$

Methanol formerly was prepared entirely by the destructive distillation of hard woods. The wood, heated in the absence of air, produced a distillate (pyroligneous acid) that contained a mixture of organic substances. Fractional distillation of this mixture yielded methanol, acetic acid, acetone, and other materials. The process, now little used, accounts for the term "wood alcohol" for methanol.

Ethanol. Most of the ethanol produced is used in alcoholic beverages in various dilutions. In denatured form, it is used as an industrial solvent and as a raw material for the manufacture of acetaldehyde, acetic acid, and other organic chemicals. Some denatured alcohol is used for rubbing compounds, lotions, and colognes. Small amounts of pure ethanol are used in flavor extracts and medicinal tonics.

In modern distillation methods, a series of fractionating columns normally produces an efficient separation of a mixture of liquids with different boiling points. It is not possible, however, to get pure ethanol by distilling an ethanol-water mixture. Ethanol boils at 173.1° F (78.4° C) at a pressure of one atmosphere and water boils at 212° F (100° C), but a mixture of 95.6 percent ethanol and 4.4 percent water boils at an even lower temperature, 172.6° F (78.1° C). Such a mixture is said to be azeotropic. This mixed distillate constitutes the ordinary 190-proof ethanol of commerce.

About 25 percent of the commercial ethanol produced in the United States is prepared through fermentation. The source is blackstrap molasses, a byproduct of the cane or beet sugar industry. It is a syrupy mixture of sucrose and impurities that remains after several successive crystallizations of sugar from the extracted juice. The following equations describe the reactions of manufacture:

$$C_{12}H_{22}O_{11} + H_2O \xrightarrow[\text{(from yeast)}]{\text{sucrase}} C_6H_{12}O_6 + C_6H_{12}O_6$$

$$C_6H_{12}O_6 \xrightarrow[\text{(from yeast)}]{\text{zymase}} 2\ CO_2 + 2\ C_2H_5OH.$$

glucose-fructose   carbon   ethanol
mixture   dioxide

Careful government control of alcohol manufacture is necessary to avoid evasion of the tax on beverage alcohol. For most industrial purposes, ethanol can be treated with small amounts of toxic or nauseous substances to render it unfit for drinking without impairing its industrial utility. Such alcohol is said to be "denatured" and is tax exempt. Methanol, which is toxic, is the most common denaturant.

About 60 percent of the commercial ethanol produced in the United States is obtained from petroleum. Large quantities of ethylene (ethene, $CH_2{=}CH_2$) are produced as a byproduct in the cracking of petroleum fractions for the manufac-

ture of motor fuel. The ethene is treated with sulfuric acid, and the resulting acid ester is hydrolyzed in a two-stage reaction:

$$\underset{\text{ethene}}{HC{=}CH} + \underset{\substack{\text{sulfuric}\\\text{acid}}}{H_2SO_4} \longrightarrow \underset{\substack{\text{sulfuric acid ester}}}{HC{-}CH}$$

$$\underset{}{HC{-}CH} + H_2O \longrightarrow \underset{\text{ethanol}}{HC{-}CH} + H_2SO_4.$$

Propanols. 1-Propanol has some commercial use as a solvent for resins and for cellulose esters. Its isomer, 2-propanol (isopropyl alcohol), is by far the more important of the two. The chief use for 2-propanol is in making acetone. 2-Propanol is also utilized in preparing antifreeze solutions, as a solvent for gums and shellacs, for quick-drying lacquers and inks, and for hand lotions, after shave lotions, and rubbing alcohol compounds.

Commercial preparation of 2-propanol is by methods similar to the preparation of ethanol from ethene. The starting material for 2-propanol is propene, a petroleum byproduct.

Butanols. The major part of the 1-butanol production is used to make butyl acetate. This material is an important solvent in the manufacture of lacquers, photographic films, plastics, safety glass, and artificial leather. 2-Butanol is utilized in the synthesis of flotation agents for the metals industry, and for wetting agents, dyes, flavoring materials, and perfumes, and 2-methyl-1-propanol (isobutyl alcohol) is used in manufacturing flavoring essences and as a solvent for paint and varnish removers.

Fermentation is the principal commercial method of production of 1-butanol, or n-butyl alcohol. The raw materials are starch or sugar. The fermentation is promoted by enzymes from certain soil bacteria. The method was originally developed during World War I to produce acetone, a second product of the fermentation. 2-Butanol (sec-butyl alcohol) is prepared from the petroleum byproducts 1-butene and 2-butene by methods similar to those used in preparing ethanol from ethene and 2-propanol from propene.

Higher Monohydroxy Alcohols. Alcohols that have 6, 8, or 10 carbon atoms are widely used in the production of plasticizers. These materials are added to many synthetic plastics to impart properties such as moldability, toughness, and shock resistance. One such substance is dioctylphthalate, which is made from 2-ethylhexanol.

Alcohols that contain 11 or more carbon atoms are suitable for the manufacture of detergents that leave no detergent accumulation (pollution) in streams. These alcohols formerly were only available from tallow or palm oil, but they can now be prepared from ethene by the Ziegler process. This process, also called the Alfol process, uses aluminum, ethene, hydrogen, and air to produce mixtures of alcohols that can be separated by fractional distillation.

Some of the alcohols, including 1-butanol, 2-methyl-1-propanol (isobutyl alcohol) and 2-ethyl-1-hexanol, are made commercially by the oxo process. The method involves direct combination of carbon monoxide, hydrogen, and unsaturated hydrocarbon byproducts of the petroleum industry. Aldehydes are produced in the first stage of the reaction. These aldehydes are catalytically reduced to primary alcohols. In some cases, a mixture of alcohols results.

O. W. NITZ
Stout State University, Wisconsin

ALCOHOLIC BEVERAGES. See BEER; DISTILLED SPIRITS; GIN; RUM; VODKA; WHISKEY.

ALCOHOLICS ANONYMOUS, a fellowship whose members strive to recover from alcoholism through self-help and the help of recovered alcoholics. With more than 30,000 autonomous local groups in some 90 countries, AA has an estimated total membership of more than 1 million. The only requirement for membership is a desire to stop drinking. Traditionally, members are identified publicly only by first name and last initial.

AA stresses a belief in spiritual values as the way toward recovery. Members share their experience, strength, and hope with anyone who seeks help. The program is based on "Twelve Steps" for guiding individual recovery and "Twelve Traditions" for group activities.

The AA movement, begun in 1935, grew out of the efforts of a former New York stockbroker, Bill Wilson, and an Akron, Ohio, surgeon, Dr. Bob Smith, to conquer their own drinking problems and to use their experiences for the benefit of others similarly distressed. The first members published *Alcoholics Anonymous*, a textbook of their experience, in 1939.

AA is self-supporting through voluntary contributions of its members. It is not allied with any organization. The international service center and publications office, located in New York City, is administered by a nonsalaried board of trustees, some of whose members, including the chairman, are not alcoholics.

JOHN L. NORRIS, M. D., *Chairman General Service Board of Alcoholics Anonymous*

ALCOHOLISM, the most widespread form of drug abuse. It is a worldwide problem, with distinct national differences in prevalence that, in general, mirror rates of per capita alcohol consumption.

There is no single, simple definition of alcoholism. In North America a large group of people, though not addicted to alcohol, persist in drinking even though they become aggressive, cause accidents, or have other alcohol-related problems. Such people are generally known as *problem drinkers.* The term alcoholism or chronic alcoholism is applied to a behavioral disorder characterized by an excessive use of alcohol to the extent that it interferes with physical and mental health. According to the National Council on Alcoholism, alcoholism is an addiction to alcohol that entails several harmful consequences, including damage to the brain, liver, or other organs, as well as destructive effects on the alcoholic's own life and that of the alcoholic's family.

In the United States about 4 million are alcoholics, and perhaps another 6 million are problem drinkers. Together they are responsible for more than 20,000 traffic deaths each year. They make up nearly half of all people arrested, and are often involved in crimes of violence. As many as 25,000 murders and suicides yearly are associated with misuse of alcohol. In addition to the deaths and suffering associated with alcohol misuse, the economic costs of alcoholism are enormous—on the order of $60 billion a year, chiefly in lost work time, medical and hospitalization costs, property damage, and welfare services.

ALCOHOL IN THE BODY

Alcoholic beverages are so classified because they contain ethyl alcohol, or ethanol (C_2H_5OH). Once it is ingested, ethyl alcohol is absorbed from the stomach and small intestine into the bloodstream. The rate of absorption depends on various factors. Food in the stomach, especially fatty food, slows down the rate of absorption, whereas water mixed with the alcohol speeds it up. Similarly, the alcohol in carbonated beverages, such as bubbly wines and cocktails made with soda, are absorbed more rapidly. The stomach, however, has protective mechanisms for preventing too much alcohol from being absorbed too quickly. If too much alcohol is in the stomach, the stomach lining secretes a mucous coating that slows absorption, and the valve between the stomach and small intestine closes, preventing the alcohol from entering the small intestine, where it would be absorbed quickly. The closing of the valve may also cause nausea.

The elimination of alcohol from the body begins almost as soon as it is absorbed into the bloodstream. About one tenth of it is eliminated unchanged as part of sweat, urine, and exhaled air. The rest of the alcohol is broken down or metabolized, chiefly by the liver. An average-sized adult metabolizes from one-third to one-half ounce (10–15 ml) of alcohol an hour. A person drinking 4 ounces (120 ml) of whiskey will have about 1.5 ounces (45 ml) of alcohol in the blood at the end of an hour as a result of both elimination and metabolic action. The blood-alcohol concentration will be about 0.07%.

As alcohol circulates in the bloodstream, it is distributed to every part of the body. The effects of alcohol on various organs and tissues are of three types: the short-term effects of a single episode of drinking; the long-term effects of chronic alcoholism; and withdrawal symptoms. Also important is the interaction of alcohol with other drugs in the body that may result in fetal malformations in pregnant women. The amount of alcohol required to produce such malformations is not known.

Short-Term Effects. Contrary to popular belief, alcohol is not a stimulant but a depressant. The organ most affected is the brain, and as the blood level rises, the concentration of ethanol in the brain increases.

At a blood-alcohol level of about 0.05%, resulting from drinking 2 or 3 ounces (60–90 ml) of whiskey, the drinker's judgment and thinking become dulled. Feelings of tension and anxiety are relieved so that the drinker feels relaxed and inhibitions may be released.

Higher blood levels, about 0.10%, produce clear signs of intoxication—clumsy movements, slurred speech, and difficulty in maintaining balance. In many states, a blood level of 0.10% is accepted as legal evidence of intoxication.

At 0.30% the drinker is confused and close to unconsciousness. At 0.45% the drinker may sink into a coma. Usually at about 0.70% the brain areas controlling breathing and heart rate are affected, causing death. Most people rarely drink enough to raise their blood alcohol level above 0.40%; at that level they are usually in a deep sleep and cannot drink anymore.

Some alcoholics experience blackouts during periods of heavy drinking. The affected person appears to be behaving normally, but later cannot remember anything that happened during this period.

Other organs and tissues affected by alcohol include the liver, gastrointestinal tract, and kidneys. Because sugar stored in the liver is not accessible when alcohol is present, hypoglycemia (low blood sugar) may occur. Large amounts of alcohol irritate the stomach and may cause gastritis or diarrhea. Because alcohol acts as a diuretic, the kidneys are stimulated to produce more urine.

Alcohol also affects sleep. Small amounts may be an aid to sleep; however, red wines with a high tyramine content may cause insomnia. Heavy drinking just before bedtime decreases the normal extent of REM (rapid eye movement) sleep, an important phase of sleep in which dreaming occurs.

Although the underlying mechanism is not understood, large amounts of alcohol can precipitate an attack of gout. Alcohol may increase sexual desire in males but results in decreased sexual potency. The effects of alcohol on sexual desire in women appears to be changing as sexual mores evolve. In an earlier time, alcohol was more likely to decrease sexual desire in women; today, however, the data appear to be more complex.

Long-Term Effects. Chronic alcoholics suffer a number of serious physical and mental disorders, and their life span is usually 10 to 12 years shorter than that of nonalcoholics. It is not known whether many of their disorders are caused directly by the alcohol or by the effects of poor nutrition, which almost always accompanies chronic alcoholism. Because alcohol supplies the body with calories (about 150 calories per ounce), alcoholics tend to neglect other foods and develop serious nutritional deficiencies. Also, the B vitamins thiamine and niacin play a role in the metabolism of alcohol and thus are more quickly used up. Alcohol may interfere with the absorption and storage of other vitamins, and, because it increases the formation of urine, many water-soluble minerals are lost through increased urination.

Probably the best-known disease associated with prolonged drinking is cirrhosis of the liver. Cancer of the liver is also associated with alcoholism, as is a disorder called *fatty liver*, which results from the accumulation of fatty acids in the liver. Fatty liver is considered by medical authorities to be the first phase in the development of cirrhosis of the liver.

Cancers of the mouth, throat, and larynx (voice box) more commonly affect alcoholics than nonalcoholics, especially if the drinker is also a heavy smoker. Gastritis, an inflammation of the stomach, is common among alcoholics, as are ulcers, disorders of the small intestine, and inflammation of the pancreas.

The nervous system may suffer serious damage from chronic alcoholism, causing physical as well as behavioral problems. Some brain cells die, producing memory loss, confusion, and learning difficulties. Neuritis and impaired vision are also common, probably due to vitamin B deficiencies. A neurological disorder, Wernicke's syndrome, is caused by a lack of thiamine. It is characterized by neuritis, visual problems, lack of coordination, and other symptoms. Korsakoff's psychosis, which

may accompany Wernicke's syndrome, includes amnesia, confusion, and confabulation—the telling of fanciful stories. While Wernicke's syndrome can be treated with thiamine, Korsakoff's psychosis is generally not treatable.

The heart is the only organ that actually may benefit from the prolonged use of alcohol, but only if consumed in moderate amounts. Researchers have found that people who drink about 1.5 ounces (45 ml) of whiskey, or 12 ounces (360 ml) of beer, or 5 ounces (150 ml) of wine a day have higher levels of special blood proteins called high-density lipoproteins (HDL's) than either nondrinkers or heavy drinkers. These proteins seem to protect the heart against coronary artery disease, a major cause of heart attack.

Chronic heavy drinking, however, is harmful to the heart. The muscle cells may be damaged, and the heart's ability to pump may be impaired. Chronic alcoholics may develop high blood pressure, abnormal heart rhythms, and a disorder called cardiomyopathy. Prolonged use of alcohol may raise the blood level of triglycerides, fatty substances that can clog arteries.

Hormone levels also are affected by chronic alcoholism. Testosterone levels in men decrease, while liver disease interferes with the metabolism of estrogens in males and results in feminization, including breast development and shrinkage of the testicles. In both sexes the body's immune mechanisms may be impaired, making the alcoholic more susceptible to infection.

Withdrawal Symptoms. At the end of a prolonged bout of heavy drinking, as the level of alcohol in the blood drops, various withdrawal symptoms may occur. Probably the mildest form is the *hangover*, characterized by headache, nausea, thirst, heartburn, dizziness, shakiness, fatigue, and depression.

More severe withdrawal symptoms experienced by chronic alcoholics after an episode of heavy drinking include tremors, vomiting, profuse sweating, sleep disturbances, and hallucinations. Epileptic-like seizures, commonly called *rum fits,* may also occur.

The most severe form of withdrawal is a condition known as *delirium tremens,* or DT's. It usually follows a long bout of very heavy drinking and may last three to ten days. Along with tremors, restlessness, loss of appetite, and nightmares, the alcoholic experiences terrifying hallucinations. Delirium tremens is treated with bed rest, a nutritious high-calorie diet, and tranquilizers or other drugs to relieve the symptoms. If untreated, it may be fatal, especially if other physical disorders are present.

Alcohol and Other Drugs. One of the greatest dangers of alcohol is its ability to interact with other drugs in the body. The U. S. Food and Drug Administration estimates that about 2,000 deaths a year are caused by this type of interaction, most of them occurring accidentally.

Many of the most widely prescribed drugs as well as over-the-counter preparations can be harmful if combined with alcohol. Depressants, such as barbiturates and chloral hydrate, combine with alcohol synergistically—that is, their combined effects are greater than the sum of their individual effects. When these drugs interact with alcohol in the body, they may cause coma and even death.

Antihistamines, common ingredients in cold and allergy pills, motion-sickness medicine, and sleeping aids, heighten the effects of alcohol.

Drugs for high blood pressure, when combined with alcohol, may cause a sudden drop in blood pressure, 'resulting in a loss of consciousness.

Alcohol and Pregnancy. For years it was known that alcohol in the bloodstream of a pregnant woman quickly passes into the blood of the fetus. Although it was suspected that alcohol could damage the fetus, not until the late 1960's did researchers find supporting evidence.

It is now known that women who drink heavily when they are pregnant run a risk of bearing babies with a pattern of birth defects known as the *fetal alcohol syndrome*. This syndrome includes retarded physical and mental development, facial deformities, and other abnormalties. Many doctors advise pregnant women to abstain from alcohol, at least during the first three months of pregnancy.

CAUSES OF ALCOHOLISM

Nine out of ten people who drink do not become alcoholics. Why the tenth drinker falls victim to this disorde is a question that has long plagued researchers. There is no single answer. Alcoholism probably is caused by a combination of interacting factors—biological, genetic, psychological, and social.

One of the most active areas of research is heredity. Some studies have suggested that a predisposition toward alcoholism may be inherited in some people. Children of an alcoholic parent are much more likely to become alcoholics than the children of nonalcoholics. Also, alcohol is metabolized differently among some racial groups. Oriental groups appear to produce higher blood levels of acetaldehyde after alcohol consumption, resulting in facial flushing and bodily discomfort.

Although psychologists have long tried to find an "alcoholic personality," no set of personality traits predicts alcoholism. Some clinicians feel that in many alcoholics their addiction is related to deep feelings of inferiority and insecurity coupled with an inability to cope with frustration. In others, alcoholism may be rooted in a desire to escape reality or in an underlying desire for self-destruction.

Sociologists have found that family and cultural attitudes toward alcohol have an important effect on people, especially during childhood, and strongly influence their drinking habits as adults. Among some peoples, moderate or heavy drinking is an important part of social life, while among others the use of alcohol is discouraged or forbidden. Paradoxically, the rate of alcoholism among those who drink in abstinent cultures is much higher than the rate of alcoholism among drinkers in the general population.

TREATMENT OF ALCOHOLISM

Because alcoholism affects every aspect of its victim's life, treatment often consists of a combination of therapies. Before any long-term treatment can be undertaken, however, the alcoholic must be free of alcohol and treated for withdrawal symptoms.

There are two main goals of long-term treatment. One is to break dependence on alcohol so that the alcoholic can function without drinking. The other is to relieve the psychological problems that may contribute to the likelihood of relapse.

Most experts agree that the ultimate aim is to produce complete abstinence—that is, to keep alcoholics from ever drinking again—although some researchers believe that certain alcoholics can learn to drink in moderation. The latter belief is controversial and probably does not apply to alcoholics who truly have been addicted to alcohol.

Physical Forms of Treatment. For many years, a popular form of treatment was aversion therapy, to keep alcoholics from drinking by making alcohol repulsive to them. In this method, an emetic (a drug that causes vomiting) is given to the patient just before he is given a taste of his favorite alcoholic beverage. He then vomits, even before the alcohol is absorbed. Repeating this procedure every other day for several days usually produces an association between alcohol and vomiting that discourages drinking. Other forms of aversion therapy use electric shocks or drugs that cause difficulty in breathing. These treatments are controversial, and many researchers believe that they are not helpful.

The drug disulfiram (Antabuse) has been successful in treating alcoholism since the late 1940's. This drug interacts with alcohol in the body to produce very unpleasant reactions, ranging from a flushing of the face, neck, and arms to coughing spasms, difficult breathing, and a terrifying feeling of impending death. Disulfiram cannot be used in patients with cardiac or liver disease, which limits its usefulness for many alcoholics. In general, disulfiram makes alcohol symbolically unavailable to the alcoholic and thereby reduces the desire to drink. Its slow rate of metabolism in the body gives the individual pause before impulsive relapse. Studies suggest that implanted preparations of disulfiram may offer some individuals the option to avoid alcohol for long periods of time. Unfortunately, however, the disulfiram/alcohol reaction can be set off by alcohol used in food preparations or by inhaled fumes (as from after-shave lotion). Because of the danger of death from heart failure or respiratory failure during an alcohol-disulfiram reaction, the drug should be administered only under carefully controlled conditions.

Psychological Therapies. Psychological therapies are used widely for treating alcoholism. The type of therapy depends on the needs and financial resources of the individual. Group therapy has become popular, partly because it is relatively inexpensive and partly because it tends to help the alcoholic relate to others with similar problems and thus to see his own problems more clearly.

Probably the best-known type of treatment is that of Alcoholics Anonymous (AA), an organization of alcoholics who help each other overcome this disorder. Founded in 1935, AA has helped hundreds of thousands of alcoholics throughout the world. Related organizations—Al-Anon and Alateen—provide similar help to the families of alcoholics.

For additional information on alcoholism, write to the National Clearing House for Alcoholic Information, P. O. Box 2345, Rockville, Md. 20852.

Roger E. Meyer, M. D.
University of Connecticut School of Medicine

Further Reading: *Alcohol and Health*, 3d Special Report to the U. S. Congress, ed. by Ernest P. Noble (USGPO 1978); Armor, David J., and others, *Alcoholism and Treatment* (Wiley 1978); FitzGerald, Kathleen, *Alcoholism: The Genetic Legacy* (Doubleday 1988); West, Louis J., ed., *Alcoholism and Related Problems: Issues for the American People* (Prentice-Hall 1984).

ALCOTT, ôl'kət, **Amos Bronson** (1799–1888), American transcendentalist philosopher, educator, and author. He was born in Wolcott, Conn., on Nov. 29, 1799. In 1825 he began teaching in the rural schools of his native Connecticut and almost immediately attracted widespread attention. Newspapers reported his Pestalozzian educational innovations, which centered on the physical, emotional, and intellectual well-being of the pupil rather than on the conventional teaching of facts (see PESTALOZZI, JOHANN).

Famous Experiments. In 1828, Alcott moved to Boston, where he opened a school and in 1830 married Abigail May. In 1830–1834 he conducted an experimental school in Philadelphia but then returned to Boston to establish what was to become his most famous experiment, the Temple School. Elizabeth Peabody's *Record of a School* (1835), detailing his methods of instruction, aroused wide interest in his work, but his own *Conversations with Children on the Gospels* (2 vols., 1836–37), transcribing classroom dialogues, was denounced as both blasphemous and obscene, and he was eventually forced to close the school.

In 1840, Alcott moved to Concord, Mass., because of his interest in Ralph Waldo Emerson and the transcendentalists. In 1842 he visited Alcott House, an experimental school named in his honor in Surrey, England. With the aid of Charles Lane, one of his English disciples, he established an experimental community, Fruitlands, in Harvard, Mass., in 1843. Far more interested in philosophizing than in practical matters, he failed to attract sufficient members, and the community collapsed after only six months.

Activities in Concord. In 1844 he returned to Concord and devoted himself to a study of the classics and to philosophical discussions with his fellow transcendentalists. What little income he earned came from the occasional public "conversations" he was asked to conduct. In 1848, Alcott moved to Boston and, in 1855, to Walpole, N.H. He returned to Concord in 1857 and settled on a farm he named Orchard House. From 1859 to 1865 he was superintendent of schools in Concord and issued a series of annual reports on his advanced methods that received wide circulation. He basked in the reflected glory of his daughter Louisa May's fame after the success of her novel *Little Women* (1868).

From 1879 until his death, Alcott directed the Concord School of Philosophy, an informal summer school conducted on the grounds of Orchard House and devoted to the exposition of transcendentalism, Hegelianism, and educational theory. He died at Boston on March 4, 1888.

Influence and Writings. Alcott's achievements in education were not sufficiently recognized in his lifetime. His contemporaries tended to dismiss him as a dreamer, and he died without having enjoyed the fame he deserved as a pioneer in the development of the child-centered school and as a precursor of John Dewey.

Alcott's major writings on education have been collected in *Essays on Education* (1960). Among his other books are *Concord Days* (1872), *Table Talk* (1877), and *New Connecticut* (1881), an account of his childhood. His abridged *Journals* were published in 1938.

WALTER HARDING
State University College, Geneseo, N.Y.

Further Reading: Dahlstrand, F. C., *Amos Bronson Alcott* (Fairleigh Dickinson Press 1982); Shepard, O., *Pedlar's Progress* (1937; reprint, Telegraph Bks. 1986).

(ABOVE) BROWN BROTHERS;
(RIGHT) CULVER PICTURES, INC.

Louisa May Alcott (*inset*), author of *Little Women*, lived in this house in Concord, Mass.

ALCOTT, ôl'kət, **Louisa May** (1832–1888), American author, who wrote *Little Women*, a classic of children's literature. She was born in Germantown (now part of Philadelphia), Pa., on Nov. 29, 1832. During her childhood her family moved to Boston, Mass., and she lived thereafter in the Boston-Concord area. She received almost all her early education from her father, Bronson Alcott, although later she was given instruction and guidance by Ralph Waldo Emerson and Henry David Thoreau, family friends.

Her first book was *Flower Fables* (1854), a collection of tales originally written for Emerson's daughter Ellen. By 1860 both her poems and short stories began appearing in the *Atlantic Monthly*. During the Civil War she served as a nurse in 1862–1863 at the Union Hospital in Georgetown, D.C., and her letters to her family during that period were published as *Hospital Sketches* (1863). In 1864 her first novel, *Moods*, appeared, and in 1867 she became editor of a children's magazine, *Merry's Museum*.

In 1868, with the publication of the first volume of *Little Women*, Miss Alcott became a celebrated writer. A second volume was published in 1869. This novel of childhood and family life has remained one of the best-loved girls' books. In 1871 she published *Little Men*, a sequel to *Little Women*. Although *Little Men* was successful in its day, it did not attain the universal popularity of *Little Women*.

Miss Alcott spent the rest of her life traveling in Europe and writing at home. Her later works include *Eight Cousins* (1875), *A Modern Mephistopheles* (1877), *Under the Lilacs* (1879), and *A Garland for Girls* (1888). She died in Boston on March 6, 1888. See also LITTLE WOMEN.

MAY ALCOTT (1840–1879), a sister of Louisa May, was born in Concord, Mass., on July 26, 1840. She studied art at the Boston School of Design and under Edward Krug, William Morris Hunt, and Carl Müller. She lived at various times in Boston, London, and Paris. In 1878 she married Ernest Nieriker, a Swiss businessman. She died in Paris on Dec. 29, 1879.

May Alcott painted still-lifes in both oil and water colors and became known as an able copier of paintings by Joseph M.W. Turner. She published *Concord Sketches* (1869) and *Art Studying Abroad* (1879).

Further Reading: Alcott, Louisa May, *The Selected Letters of Louisa May Alcott*, ed. by J. Myerson and others (Little 1987).

ALCUIN (c. 735–804), al'kwin, English educator, scholar, and theologian, who gained renown as preceptor of the palace school of Charlemagne, king of the Franks, at Aachen (Aix-la-Chapelle) between 782 and 796. From this center of knowledge and culture came much of the light that flickered on the European continent during the Dark Ages. Intellectual progress in this period stemmed in large part from the activities of Alcuin, who was one of many Irish, Welsh, and English clergy that helped reinstitute learning in western Europe between 650 and 900.

Alcuin was born at York, England, and was educated at its excellent cathedral school. He was the school's most distinguished pupil and later taught there and became headmaster. An exemplar of the best of English scholarship, he impressed Charlemagne when they met in Italy. In the ruins of the Roman empire Charlemagne saw evidence of wisdom and attainments far beyond the accomplishments of his era. He was determined to regain the lost knowledge and glory of Rome.

The Palace School. Toward this end, Charlemagne invited Alcuin to take charge of educating his children and other youngsters in his royal court at Aachen. Assisted by several teachers he brought with him in 782, Alcuin also sought to educate the king and men and women of the nobility. The Frankish king spent many hours in the school and learned to read Latin but is said never to have mastered writing.

Alcuin's methods were largely catechetical. He prepared questions and answers to be memorized. They dealt with typical subjects of the day, including lessons from the seven liberal arts and from Scripture. Some of the lessons he developed for Pepin, Charlemagne's son, are preserved and make interesting reading. They contain many errors that reveal the limited extent of even the most advanced learning in those days.

Alcuin also wrote several executive orders to Charlemagne's bishops and priests. One of these was the famous proclamation of 787, urging them to promote learning among themselves and to establish schools. Another, that of 802, urged freemen to educate their sons.

Scholarly Work at Tours. Charlemagne, in gratitude, appointed the aging Alcuin abbot of the monastery of St. Martin at Tours in 796. Here Alcuin remained active—writing, extending the library collection, and supervising the copying of manuscripts. Impatient at the snail-like pace of individual copying, Alcuin instituted multiple reproduction. He had one monk dictate while eight or ten others printed copies simultaneously. Alcuin has been incorrectly credited with introducing script writing, but at Tours his copyists did develop the Carolingian minuscule, the antecedent of modern roman type.

Alcuin completed biographies of several saints and also wrote poems, biblical commentaries, and theological and educational treatises. His edition of the Gregorian Sacramentary was a basis for the Roman Missal and thus helped attain uniformity in the liturgy of Western Christendom.

Alcuin died at Tours on May 19, 804. From schools he had headed and helped promote came many of the scholars who were to lead in the revival of learning known as the Carolingian Renaissance.

RICHARD E. GROSS
Stanford University

ALDA, äl'dä, **Frances** (1883–1952), American soprano, who sang with the Metropolitan Opera Company in New York City from 1908 to 1929. She was born *Frances Davis* in Christchurch, New Zealand, on May 31, 1883. After studying at the École Marchesi in Paris, she made her debut at the Opéra-Comique in 1904, in the title role of Puccini's *Manon Lescaut.* In 1908 she made her American debut at the Metropolitan Opera as Gilda in *Rigoletto,* opposite Enrico Caruso. Other major roles in her repertoire included Mimi in *La Bohème,* Desdemona in *Otello,* Marguerite in *Faust,* Violetta in *La Traviata,* Aïda, and Margherita in *Mefistofele.*

Alda was married in 1910 to Giulio Gatti-Casazza, general director of the Metropolitan Opera. They were divorced in 1928. In 1939 she became a citizen of the United States. Her memoirs, *Men, Women, and Tenors,* were published in 1937. She died in Venice, Italy, on Sept. 28, 1952.

ALDAN RIVER, ul-dàn', in eastern Siberia, in the Russian Federation. A tributary of the Lena River, the Aldan is about 1,300 miles (2,100 km) long and is navigable for about 1,000 miles (1,600 km).

ALDANOV, ul-dä'nôf, **M.A.** (1886–1957), Russian novelist. His real name was *Mark Aleksandrovich Landau.* He was also known as *Landau-Aldanov.* He was born in Kiev, in the Ukraine, and studied at Kiev University, where he received degrees in chemistry and law. Aldanov played a minor role in the Russian revolution of 1917 as a moderate socialist, left Russia in 1919, and lived in Paris until January 1941, when he emigrated to America.

Opposed to the new Soviet regime, Aldanov devoted his time in France to writing historical novels that emphasized the social and philosophical conflicts of the modern world. English translations of these works include *The Ninth Thermidor* (1926), *The Conspiracy* (1927), and *The Devil's Bridge* (1928). In this period he also wrote *The Tenth Symphony,* a philosophical story laid in Vienna in the time of Beethoven.

After his arrival in America, Aldanov published *The Fifth Seal* (1943; first published in Russian in 1939), in which he depicts the general disillusionment in Europe before World War II, and *For Thee the Best* (1945), a story of Byron's participation in the Greek war for independence and of political intrigue. The latter, like most of his writings, is imbued with a skepticism that leaves little hope that human values will prevail over narrow self and group interests. Later works are *Before the Deluge* (1947), *A Night in the Airport* (1949), and *The Escape* (1950). Aldanov died in Nice, France, on Feb. 25, 1957.

ALDEBARAN, al-deb'ə-ren, is a bright, reddish star in the constellation Taurus. With a magnitude of 1.06, it is one of the 20 brightest stars in the sky. Aldebaran is 60 light years away from the earth. Its diameter has been measured with an interferometer and found to be about 33,-000,000 miles (53,000,000 km), so that Aldebaran is a larger star than the sun, although it is cooler. Aldebaran is actually a double star, or binary; its companion can be observed through a telescope. Aldebaran appears in the sky among the star cluster known as the Hyades, but the members of this cluster are much farther away from the earth than Aldebaran.

ALDEHYDE, al′də-hīd, any of a family of organic compounds characterized by the atomic group — CHO, which largely determines their chemical behavior. Aldehydes occur as intermediate stages between alcohols and the acids produced by oxidation of alcohols. Thus ethyl alcohol (CH_3-CH_2OH) is oxidized to acetaldehyde (CH_3CHO), which in turn is oxidized to acetic acid (CH_3-COOH).

Aldehydes originally were named for the acids to which they can be oxidized. Formaldehyde, HCHO, is easily oxidized to formic acid, HCOOH, and acetaldehyde, CH_3CHO, is oxidized to acetic acid, CH_3COOH. According to newer systematic nomenclature, the aldehyde name is based on the name of the hydrocarbon with the same number of carbon atoms. The ending -al is affixed to indicate an aldehyde. Thus HCHO is methanal, CH_3CHO is ethanal, and $CH_3CH_2CH_2$-CHO is butanal.

Aldehydes are made commercially by various reactions, including the oxidation of alcohols, the catalytic removal of hydrogen from primary alcohols, and the addition of water to alkynes (triple-bond hydrocarbons).

Commercially the most important aldehyde is formaldehyde, used in the manufacture of plastics, paints, varnishes, explosives, and medicinals. It is used as a germicide, disinfectant, and embalming agent. Acetaldehyde is employed in making a variety of organic chemicals.

ALDEN, ôl′dən, **Henry Mills** (1836–1919), American author and editor. Born at Mount Tabor, Vt., on Nov. 11, 1836, he graduated from Williams College (1857) and Andover Theological Seminary (1860). He settled in New York City in 1861 and became managing editor of *Harper's Weekly* in 1863 and editor of *Harper's Magazine* in 1869. One of his interests was ancient thought, religion, and literature, and in 1863–1864 he delivered 12 lectures entitled "The Structure of Paganism," at the Lowell Institute, Boston.

In his editorial work he endeavored to present in a "family" magazine the latest results of scholarship. He collaborated with Alfred Hudson Guernsey in *Harper's Pictorial History of the Great Rebellion* (1866–68), and published *A Study of Death* (1895) and *Magazine Writing and the New Literature* (1908). He died at New York City on Oct. 7, 1919.

ALDEN, ôl′dən, **Isabella Macdonald** (1841–1930), American juvenile writer. She was born at Rochester N.Y., on Nov. 3, 1841, and attended schools at Ovid and Auburn, N.Y. She wrote some fiction for adults and *The Prince of Peace,* a life of Christ. However, she was noted chiefly as the author of about 60 Sunday-school juvenile novels called the "Pansy Books." She also edited the juvenile periodical *Pansy* (1875–1896) and was on the staffs of the *Christian Endeavor World* and *Trained Motherhood.* She died at Palo Alto, Calif., on Aug. 5, 1930.

ALDEN, ôl′dən, **John** (1599–1687), Pilgrim Father who for nearly a half century held numerous public offices in the Plymouth Colony and was the last surviving signer of the Mayflower Compact. He appears as a principal character in Henry Wadsworth Longfellow's *The Courtship of Miles Standish,* but the account of him given there is based on tradition, not fact.

According to records of the Plymouth Colony, Alden was born in England in 1599. He was employed as a wine casker at Southampton when he enlisted for the *Mayflower* voyage in 1620. Accounts of a later date say he was the first Pilgrim to set foot on Plymouth Rock. Within three years of his arrival in Massachusetts, he married Priscilla Mullens, after supposedly failing to win her hand for his friend Miles Standish.

About 1627, Alden and Standish founded the town of Duxbury, where Alden worked a farm of about 170 acres (69 hectares). The two men served as joint arbitrators in boundary disputes between the colonists and the Indians. Alden also assisted Standish in raising forces to defend the colony against Indian attacks.

Alden served as assistant governor of the colony for 44 years (1633–1641, 1650–1686). He was acting governor on numerous occasions and treasurer for two years beginning in 1656. He died at Duxbury on Sept. 12, 1687, and was buried in South Duxbury, near the grave of Standish.

ALDER, äl′dər, **Kurt** (1902–1958), German chemist, who was the coinventor of a versatile and prolific chemical reaction known as the Diels-Alder synthesis. For this achievement, Alder and Otto Diels were awarded the Nobel Prize in chemistry in 1950.

Alder was born at Königshütte, Germany, on July 10, 1902. He received his education in chemistry at the University of Berlin and at the University of Kiel, which awarded him the Ph.D. degree in 1926. His sponsoring professor for the degree was Otto Diels, son of the great classical scholar Hermann Diels. Otto Diels had been a pupil of Emil Fischer, an outstanding organic chemist.

In 1928, Diels and Alder found the reaction now known by their name. They started with quinone and an organic material called a diene, which is an aliphatic compound with an alternate pair of double bonds. Although others previously had made a comparable synthesis, Diels and Alder showed its general nature and wide applicability. Their method of joining two compounds to form a ring-structured molecule now is used in the preparation of cantharidin, morphine, reserpine, cortisone, the insecticides aldrin and dieldrin, and other alkaloids and polymers. Many plant products are believed to be formed naturally by this type of synthesis.

In the Diels-Alder reaction a diene (an organic compound containing two carbon-to-carbon double bonds) is linked to a dienophile (a compound, usually containing a pair of doubly or triply bonded carbon atoms, that readily reacts with a diene) to form a six-membered ring compound called an adduct. The reaction takes place without the use of powerful chemical reagents. Alder described the reaction fully in *Newer Methods of Preparative Organic Chemistry* (1948).

Alder became a professor of chemistry at the University of Kiel in 1934. Two years later he began to work in the research laboratory of I.G. Farbenindustrie at Leverkusen. In 1940 he became professor of chemistry and director of the chemical institute at the University of Cologne. In 1955 he was one of 18 Nobel Prize winners who issued a declaration urging the renunciation of war in order to prevent a nuclear holocaust. He died in Cologne on June 20, 1958.

MORRIS GORAN, *Roosevelt University*

ALDER, ôl′dər, the common name for a group of trees and shrubs widely distributed throughout the Northern Hemisphere and in the Andes of South America. Generally found in cool climates, alders are moisture-loving plants. Most alders flower in the spring before the leaves appear, although some flower in the fall. The thick woody scales of the alder fruit persist on the branches long after the seeds and leaves have fallen off each year. The alder's soft brown wood is very durable in water and is used for piles.

The alder belongs to the genus *Alnus* in the birch family, Betulaceae. There are about 30 species, 10 of which are found in the United States. Common shrubs of the eastern United States are the green mountain alder (*A. crispa*), which does not retain the naked pistillate (female) catkins (spikelike flower clusters) all winter, but encloses them in scaly buds; the speckled alder (*A. rugosa*); and the common or smooth alder (*A. serrulata*). Two species grown in the eastern United States, *A. glutinosa* and *A. incana*, were introduced from the Old World.

Various fossil species of alder that date from as early as 40 million to 50 million years ago (the Eocene Epoch) have been found in various locations in the Northern Hemisphere.

ALDERMAN, ôl′dər-man, a title designating an officeholder in some municipal corporations of the United States and Britain. In the United States, the alderman is generally an elected member of a town's legislative body, although his or her powers and duties differ in the various states and cities. Municipal reorganizations in the 20th century have reduced the number of assemblies of aldermen in favor of smaller councils or commissions, and the title itself is increasingly being replaced by councilman.

In Britain the title generally applies to offices next in dignity to the mayor or chairman of the town or county councils. Aldermen are often elected by the council members. The title was formerly widely used to designate magistrates.

The term was first used in Anglo-Saxon England, where aldermen, or *aeldormen*, were officials of high rank. In many cases they were hereditary representatives of the crown and exercised judicial as well as administrative functions.

ALDERNEY, ôl′dər-nē, an island in Great Britain. Called Aurigny in French, it is the third in size of the Channel Islands in the English Channel. Alderney is separated from Cap de la Hague on the Normandy coast of France by an 8-mile (13-km) tidal channel, the Race of Alderney. The island is about 3.5 miles (5.6 km) long and 1.5 miles (2.4 km) wide. Its coast is rocky and barren but the interior plateau permits intensive agriculture. The island's historically significant dairy industry remains an important part of the economy. Other significant industries include quarrying and tourism.

Alderney is part of the bailiwick of Guernsey but it has a local elective legislature called the States. Justice is administered under the auspices of the royal court of Guernsey. The town of St. Anne is the capital.

Megalithic remains indicate that Alderney was inhabited in prehistoric times. In the Roman period it was known as Riduna. Old forts recall its former strategic importance. During World War II the Germans occupied the island.

ALDERSHOT, ôl′dər-shot, a municipal borough in England, 32 miles (52 km) southwest of London. The town owes its growth to the presence nearby of a major military training center. The camp was established in 1854, as a result of experience in the Crimean War, with the purchase by the government of an extensive tract of moorland on the borders of Surrey, Hampshire, and Berkshire. The object was to create a site large enough for the training of troops in units of brigade and division size, as well as to accustom the men to actual field conditions. Since its founding, the camp has been enlarged, and permanent facilities have been constructed and extended.

The town of Aldershot lies in Hampshire, south of the camp. Brewing and flour milling are local industries. Population: 53,665 (1981 census).

ALDHELM, ald′helm (640?–709), English prelate, scholar, poet, and Christian saint. His name is also spelled *Ealdhelm*. Educated at Malmesbury, he was introduced to classical studies by Hadrian, the Roman abbot of St. Augustine's, Canterbury. As abbot of Malmesbury (from 675) and bishop of Sherborne (from 705), Aldhelm was known widely for his scholarship. He founded monastic communities and built several churches, notably St. Laurence's in Bradford-on-Avon, Wiltshire.

Aldhelm was one of the first English authors to write in Latin and was noted for a treatise on prosody, for which he composed some 100 riddles to illustrate metrical rules. His poems and ballads in Old English were popular but none survive. His feast day is May 25.

ALDINE PRESS, ôl′dīn, a printing establishment founded by Aldus Manutius in Venice in 1490 and operated by his family until 1597. The press published the first printed editions of Greek and Roman classics, as well as the works of contemporary writers, including Petrarch, Dante, and Boccaccio. All its books are distinguished for the remarkable correctness of their typography, although the Latin and Italian volumes are somewhat superior to those that are in Greek.

The first editions published by Aldus Manutius (1450–1515) form an epoch in the annals of printing because they contributed immeasurably to the perfecting of type. No one before had ever used such beautiful Greek types, of which he made 9 different fonts. He also made at least 14 fonts of Roman letters. His engraver, Francesco of Bologna, invented italic type, which Manutius used for the first time in the octavo edition of ancient and modern classics, commencing in 1501 with a volume devoted to Virgil. Earlier, in 1500, Manutius had founded the New Academy, or Aldine Academy of Hellenists, an organization designed to promote the study of Greek literature and the publication of Greek authors. Its members, comprising the most distinguished Greek scholars in Italy, were required to speak Greek and, as might be expected, the rules of the organization were written in Greek.

Following Aldus's death in 1515, the Aldine Press was carried on by the "Three Asolani"— Aldus's father-in-law, Andrea Torresani of Asolo, and Andrea's two sons. In 1533, Paulus Manutius (1512–1574), Aldus's son, took over management of the press. Paulus in turn was succeeded in 1574 by his son Aldus (1547–1597).

During its more than 100 years of operation, the press printed 908 different works. The mark of the press was an anchor, entwined by a dolphin, with the motto *Festina lente* (Make haste slowly) or *Sudavit et alsit* (He sweated and was cold). Because of the demand for editions from the Aldine Press, and especially for its earlier editions, printers in Lyon and Florence, about 1502, began to issue counterfeit Aldines.

The Pierpont Morgan Library in New York City has one of the largest collections of editions from the Aldine Press, including the *Hypnerotomachia Poliphili* (1499) of Francesco Colonna, which is considered perhaps the finest work of the press.

ALDINGTON, ôl'ding-tən, **Richard** (1892–1962), English author. Baptized *Edward Godfree Aldington*, he was born at Portsmouth, Hampshire, England, on July 8, 1892. He studied four years at Dover College and a year at the University of London. Through his friend Ezra Pound, he met the poet H.D. (Hilda Doolittle), whom he married in 1913. He joined the imagist movement and for a while edited the avant-garde *Egoist*. His first book of poems, *Images, Old and New*, appeared in 1915. During World War I he fought with the British army in France. Afterward he was on the staff of the London *Times Literary Supplement*, but soon retired to the country to begin his long career as a freelance novelist, translator, editor, critic, and biographer. He died at Sury-en-Vaux, Cher, France, on July 27, 1962.

Aldington's best-known novel, *Death of a Hero* (1929), is a fictional document of World War I disillusionment. His previous publications had been mostly poems, critical studies, and translations, and he had gained distinction with *Dangerous Acquaintances* (1924), his English version of Choderlos de Laclos' *Les liaisons dangereuses* (1782). His editing of *Last Poems* (1932) and *Selected Poems* (1934) by D.H. Lawrence showed his critical discernment. During the 1930's he wrote other novels, including *All Men Are Enemies* (1933), and several volumes of short stories.

Aldington then turned mainly to biographical works, receiving the James Tait Black memorial award for *Wellington* (1946; New York ed., *The Duke*, 1943). *Portrait of a Genius, But . . .* (1950) is a sympathetic study of D.H. Lawrence. His prose writings display energetic candor and a hatred of hypocrisy and fraud, best exemplified in his autobiography *Life for Life's Sake* (1941) and in *Lawrence of Arabia* (1955).

HORACE V. GREGORY
Author of "Amy Lowell" and Other Books

ALDOSTERONE. See ADRENAL GLANDS.

ALDRED, al'dred (1000?–1069), was an English prelate. His name also is spelled *Ealdred*. As bishop of Worcester and archbishop of York, he improved church discipline and built and repaired a number of church and monastic buildings. He was the first English bishop to make a pilgrimage to Jerusalem. He submitted to William the Conqueror and crowned him king on Christmas Day, 1066. In 1068 he also crowned William's wife, Matilda. Aldred died in York on Sept. 11, 1069.

ALDRICH, ôl'drich, **Nelson Wilmarth** (1841–1915), American legislator. Born in Foster, R.I., on Nov. 6, 1841, into a farm family of modest means, Aldrich went to work at the age of 17 in Providence where his business success was rapid. At 24 he was a partner in the largest wholesale grocers' firm in Rhode Island and in later years acquired extensive interests in banking and other fields.

Aldrich chose, however, to devote his chief energies to politics rather than to business. A Republican, he was a member of the Providence common council in 1869–1875, the Rhode Island state legislature in 1875–1876, and the national House of Representatives in 1879–1881. In the latter year he won the Senate seat made vacant by the death of Gen. A.E. Burnside, and established control of Republican politics in Rhode Island.

Aldrich soon entered the inner circle of Republican leadership in the Senate. His strong yet attractive personality, the security of his political position in his home state, his skill as a parliamentary tactician, his expert knowledge of economic and financial matters, and his considerable wealth and numerous business connections combined to make him a dominating figure during his 30 years' service in the Senate.

A staunch conservative, indifferent to public opinion, Aldrich represented in the Senate the interests of Eastern industrial, commercial, and financial groups in resisting the demands for tariff and monetary reform from the insurgent West. He consistently supported high protective tariffs and the gold standard. He led the Senate in its struggle with Theodore Roosevelt for dominance in the government, yet the relations between the two men were, for the greater part of Roosevelt's presidency, amicable and mutually respectful.

The great interest of Aldrich's last years in public life was a plan of banking reform. As a result of the panic of 1907, Congress passed the Aldrich-Vreeland Act, providing for the creation of a National Monetary Commission, of which Aldrich became chairman, to investigate the banking problem. Studies of European banking and currency systems in 1908 and consultations with American bankers preceded the publication in 1911 of the "Aldrich Plan," which contained many features embodied in the Federal Reserve Act of 1913.

Aldrich retired from the Senate in 1911. He died in New York City on April 16, 1915.

ALDRICH, ôl'drich, **Thomas Bailey** (1836–1907), American writer and editor, who was noted for his refined prose and delicately wrought poetry. He was born in Portsmouth, N.H., on Nov. 11, 1836. In 1852 he accepted a job as a clerk in New York City, where he began to write poetry; his first collection, *The Bells*, was published in 1855. During the next 10 years he held various editorial positions on a number of New York publications.

Aldrich settled in Boston in 1865 and was editor of *Every Saturday* until 1872. He soon became a member of an illustrious literary group that included Longfellow, Whittier, Lowell, and Holmes. In 1870, Aldrich published his most successful work, *The Story of a Bad Boy*, an autobiographical novel about his boyhood in Portsmouth.

In 1881, Aldrich succeeded William Dean Howells as editor of the *Atlantic Monthly*. He held this post until his retirement in 1890 and spent the rest of his life traveling and writing. He died in Boston, Mass., on March 19, 1907.

Aldrich's other works included the novels *Prudence Palfrey* (1874), *The Queen of Sheba* (1877), and *The Stillwater Tragedy* (1880). His fiction, particularly his short stories in such collections as *Marjorie Daw and Other People* (1873) and *Two Bites at a Cherry, with Other Tales* (1894), was marked by technical skill and charm, although it often lacked depth. His verse, collected in *Cloth of Gold* (1874), *Flower and Thorn* (1877), *Mercedes and Later Lyrics* (1884), and *Judith and Holofernes* (1896), was noted for its craftsmanship, delicacy, and felicitous phrasing. See also STORY OF A BAD BOY.

ALDRICH, ôl′drich, **Winthrop Williams** (1885–1974), American banker and diplomat who was U. S. ambassador to Britain under President Eisenhower. The son of Nelson W. Aldrich, U. S. senator from Rhode Island, he was born in Providence, R. I., on Nov. 2, 1885. He graduated from Harvard Law School in 1910 and was admitted to the New York bar in 1912.

In 1922, at the urging of his sister's husband, John D. Rockefeller, Jr., he entered the banking field as chief counsel of the Equitable Trust Company. In 1930 he became president of the Chase National Bank and in 1933 chairman of the board. He left Chase in 1953 to become ambassador to Britain and served until 1957. He died in New York City on Feb. 25, 1974.

ALDRIDGE, ôl′drij, **Ira Frederick** (1805–1867), American actor, who was one of the great Shakespearean tragedians of his time. A protégé of the English actor Edmund Kean, Aldridge played roles that included Othello, Shylock, Macbeth, and King Lear. He also revived *Titus Andronicus*, after a century of neglect, playing the part of Aaron.

Aldridge was born in New York City, the son of a freed slave who had become a preacher in a Calvinist chapel. Although little is known of Aldridge's early life, he seems to have been preparing for missionary work when he met Edmund Kean, who was then making a tour of America. He became Kean's personal attendant and accompanied him back to England. Encouraged by Kean to prepare for the stage, Aldridge studied for 18 months at the University of Glasgow.

In January 1827, Aldridge made his debut at the Royalty Theatre in London, playing Othello. His immediate success led to appearances in Dublin, the English and Irish provinces, and later on the European continent—in Germany, Switzerland, and Sweden.

In 1830 or 1831, Aldridge made a brief, unsuccessful tour in the United States. He returned to Europe and became a British subject in 1863. He was married to an Englishwoman and, after her death, to a Swedish baroness.

Later in his career Aldridge frequently toured the Continent, where he was an immense popular success. He was on tour in Lodz, then in Russian Poland, when he died on Aug. 7, 1867.

ALDRIN, ôl′drin, **Edwin Eugene, Jr.** (1930–   ), American astronaut, who was the second man (after Neil Armstrong) to walk on the moon. Aldrin was born in Montclair, N.J., on Jan. 20, 1930. After graduating from the U.S. Military Academy in 1951, he joined the Air Force and flew combat missions in the Korean War. He later attended the Massachusetts Institute of Technology and gained a doctor of science degree in astronautics in 1963.

Selected as an astronaut by the National Aeronautics and Space Administration in 1963, Aldrin first entered space in the two-man Gemini craft in November 1966. On the historic flight of Apollo 11, Colonel Aldrin was the copilot and Neil Armstrong the pilot of the lunar module that separated from the main spacecraft (orbiting the moon with Michael Collins aboard) and landed on the lunar surface on July 20, 1969. See also ASTRONAUTS; SPACE EXPLORATION.

ALE, āl, is a fermented alcoholic beverage prepared from grain. The terms *ale* and *beer* often are used interchangeably. Both beverages contain malt and hops, but a distinction may be made according to the fermentation process used in their manufacture. If fermentation occurs on top of the brew, the product—particularly in the United States—is classified as ale; if on the bottom, it is beer. Different species of yeast are used to make the brew ferment on the top or on the bottom. Ale usually has the higher alcoholic content (about 6 percent by volume), is heavier in body, and is more bitter in taste.

The history of malt liquor—ale and beer—dates back to its manufacture in Babylonia and Egypt. The Greeks considered it a barbarian drink; they preferred wine, as did the Romans. The ancient Celts and early Teutonic tribes, however, were devotees of malt liquor. The words *ale* and *beer* are both of Teutonic origin and may originally have meant the same beverage.

In England in the 15th century, brewers drew a distinction based on the use of hops for flavoring. The liquor made of malt, yeast, and water, without hops, was called ale and became an English favorite. About a century later hops were used in all brewed liquor, but the term "ale" persisted. In Britain, ales were brewed for special times or occasions—Easter ales, October ales, and bride ales for weddings. *Pale ale*, with a strong hop flavor, is drunk in Britain and the United States, as is *brown ale*, more lightly flavored and sweeter in taste.

ALEANDRO, ä-lä-än′drō, **Girolamo** (1480–1542), Italian humanist and diplomat. Aleandro was born on Feb. 13, 1480, in Motta di Treviso, near Venice, and was educated at Padua and Venice. At the suggestion of Erasmus, he went to France to teach at the University of Paris. He became rector of the university and, while in that post, published a Greek-Latin lexicon (1512).

In 1516, Aleandro went to Rome and warned Pope Leo X of an impending schism in the German church. In 1519, Leo named him Vatican librarian and, a year later, nuncio to Germany. Aleandro played a major role in the condemnation of Luther at the Diet of Worms (1521) and thereafter concentrated on repressing Lutheranism and fostering church reform. In 1524, after his ordination, he was named archbishop of Brindisi and then nuncio to France. Later he was imprisoned with the French king, Francis I, until ransomed by Rome. After 1531, he twice returned to Germany as nuncio and, in 1538, was made a cardinal by Pope Paul II. He died at Rome on Feb. 1, 1542. His writings are a mine of information on the early Reformation.

MSGR. FLORENCE D. COHALAN, *Cathedral College*

ALEARDI, ä-lā-är′dē, **Aleardo** (1812–1878), Italian poet and patriot. He was born at Verona, Italy, on Nov. 14, 1812. His original surname was *Gaetano*. He early adopted Republican principles, and in 1848 took part in the insurrection against the Austrians in Lombardy. Imprisoned in 1852 and again in 1859, he returned to Verona after the Austrians had been expelled. From 1864 he was a professor of aesthetics and the history of art at Florence. After 1873 he served as a senator in the Italian parliament. He died at Verona on July 17, 1878.

Aleardi's verse has been criticized for its excess of description, but it helped to promote the regeneration and unification of Italy. Perhaps the most successful of his poems is *Le città italiane marinare e commercianti* (1856), an ode to the Italian commercial and maritime cities. Among his other works are *Le lettere a Maria* (1846), *Prime storie* (1846), *Raffaello e la Fornarina* (1855), *Il monte Circello* (1856), *Un'ora della mia giovinezza* (1858), *I sette soldati* (1861), and *Il canto politico* (1862). His writings were collected in one volume, *Canti* (6th ed., 1882). G. Trezza edited his correspondence, *Epistolario* (1879).

ALECSANDRI, ä-lek-sän′drē, **Vasile** (1821–1890), Rumanian poet and statesman. He was born in Bacău, Moldavia in July 1821. His name is also spelled *Alexandri*. He studied in Paris from 1834 to 1839, and then returned to Moldavia. Because he took part in the revolutionary movement against the Russian protectorate of Moldavia and Wallachia in 1848, he was compelled to seek refuge in France. Subsequently, after having once again returned to his homeland, he helped to bring about the union of the Rumanian principalities under Alexandru Ioan Cuza in 1859. In 1859–1860 he served as minister of foreign affairs, and in 1885 he was appointed minister to France.

A leader of the national cultural renaissance, Alecsandri published a collection of Rumanian folk songs, altered by him, in 1852–1853 (rev. ed. with title *Poezii populare ale Românilor*, 1865). His own verse included *Doine și Lăcrămioare-Suvenire* (1852); *Pasteluri* (1867), notable for its description of the Rumanian landscape; and *Legende-Varii* (1871). His creation of the dithyramb *Cântecul gintei latine* led to his being crowned poet of the Latin peoples at Montpellier, France in 1878. He wrote in a variety of genres, and is given credit for helping to create the Rumanian national theater, with plays such as *Despot Vodă* (1880), *Fântâna Blanduziei* (1884), and *Ovidiu* (1890). He died in Mirçesti, Rumania, on Aug. 22, 1890.

ALEICHEM, ä-lā′ᴋнәm, **Sholom** (1859–1916), Yiddish short story writer and dramatist who, with Mendele Moikher Sforim and Isaac Leibush Peretz, formed the Yiddish Classical Triumvirate. Sholom Aleichem's unheroic heroes are rooted in Biblical lore and morality. They prize learning more than wealth. They feel the sting of oppression and the pain of existence, but they retain faith in the ultimate victory of justice. Known as the "Yiddish Mark Twain," Sholom Aleichem laughed at the absurdities of his ragged, quaint characters, but never with malice or bitterness. His work exemplifies Jewish humor at its best.

Life. Sholom Aleichem was born *Solomon Rabinovitch* at Pereyaslavl (now Pereyaslav-Khmelnitski), Poltava, Ukraine, on March 3, 1859. After early unsuccessful literary efforts in Russian and Hebrew, he turned to Yiddish in 1883, choosing as his pseudonym the words of the traditional Yiddish greeting "*Sholom Aleichem*" (Peace be upon you). Immediately acclaimed, he edited (1888–1889) the literary annual *Die Yidische Folksbibliotek*, which attracted the best Yiddish writers. After losing his money as a result of an unsuccessful business speculation, he was forced to depend entirely on writing for a living. In 1906 he went to New York City where he died on May 13, 1916, while in the midst of writing an autobiography, *A Great Fair*.

Works. In his best sketches, *Tevye the Dairyman* (1895–99), Sholom Aleichem immortalized the typical East European Jewish village under the name of Kasrilevke, peopling it with an assortment of peculiar, poor, impractical, good-hearted characters. These sketches were successfully dramatized in New York's Yiddish Art Theater beginning in 1919, and in the Broadway musical *Fiddler on the Roof* in 1964.

The sketches *Mottel, the Cantor's Son* (1907–16) present an orphan boy who is unwilling to accept adult concepts of proper behavior. Cheerful, wise beyond his years, Mottel is a Yiddish Huckleberry Finn who turns situations topsyturvy. In the final sketches, Mottel emigrates to America, thus affording his creator an opportunity to interpret the American Jewish scene through the eyes of a perceptive and uninhibited lad.

The tragicomedy *Hard to Be a Jew* (1914) is a variant on Mark Twain's *Prince and the Pauper* theme. The play tells of a Gentile student who changes his name and identity with a Jew and experiences the harsh reality of being Jewish in Christian-dominated czarist Russia.

Many of Sholom Aleichem's stories have been filmed in the Soviet Union. *The World of Sholom Aleichem*, a dramatization of a number of his stories, was a Broadway success in 1953, and was adapted for television in 1957.

SOL LIPTZIN
Author of "The Flowering of Yiddish Literature"

Further Reading: Aarons, Victoria, *Author As Character in the Works of Sholom Aleichem* (Mellen Press 1985); Miron, Dan, *Sholem Aleykhem: Person, Persona, Presence* (Yivo Inst. 1972); Samuel, Maurice, *The World of Sholom Aleichem* (1943; reprint, Atheneum 1986).

ALEKHINE, u-lyā′ᴋнyin, **Alexander** (1892–1946), Russo-French chess player. The Russian form of his name is *Aleksandr Aleksandrovich Alekhin*. Born in Moscow, Russia, on Nov. 1, 1892, he was classed as a master of chess at the age of 16, when he won the Russian amateur tournament. During World War I he served with the Russian Red Cross. After the October Revolution in 1917, he was condemned to death by the Bolsheviks, but secured his freedom. He settled in Paris and, in 1927, became a French citizen.

Alekhine won the world chess championship from José Raúl Capablanca y Graupera in 1927 at Buenos Aires. Thereafter, until his death, he retained the world chess title, except for the interval 1935–1937, when the title was held by Max Euwe. In 1924, 1925, and again in 1933, he broke the world blindfold chess record. Alekhine was noted for novel treatments of situations apparently drained of possibilities. His several books on chess include *My Best Games of Chess, 1924–1937* (1939). He died in Estoril, Portugal, on March 24, 1946.

ALEKSEI, u-lyi-kysā′ (1877–1970), patriarch of Russia, leader of the Russian Orthodox Church. Born Sergei Vladimirovich Simansky in Moscow on Oct. 27, 1877, he was ordained a monk and a deacon in 1902. Aleksei rose through the hierarchy, becoming vicar of Novgorod and Petrograd (now Leningrad), archbishop of Novgorod, and metropolitan of Leningrad and Novgorod. When Hitler attacked Russia in 1941, Aleksei rallied the church to Russia's defense. He was crowned patriarch of Moscow and All Russia on Feb. 4, 1945. He worked to preserve Russian Orthodoxy in the USSR and to reunify it with divisions of the Orthodox Church in other countries. In 1964 he visited the archbishop of Canterbury and pledged his concern for Christian unity. He died in Moscow on April 17, 1970.

ALEKSEYEV, u-lyi-ksyā′yef, **Mikhail Vasilievich** (1857–1918), Russian army officer. He was born in Tver (now Kalinin), Russia, on Nov. 3, 1857. As chief of staff to Gen. N.Y. Ivanov, Alekseyev was mainly responsible for the crushing defeat of the combined Austrian-German forces in Galicia in 1914. He subsequently became chief of staff to Grand Duke Nicholas and was made commander of the general staff in 1915.

After the Bolshevik Revolution of November 1917, Alekseyev joined Gen. L.G. Kornilov and the counterrevolutionary armies. Alekseyev headed the counterrevolutionary government from March 1918 until his death in Yekaterinodar (now Krasnodar) on Oct. 10, 1918.

ALEMÁN, äl-ā-män′, **Mateo** (1547–c. 1614), Spanish novelist. He was born at Seville and graduated from the university there in 1564. In 1571 he entered government service. After a somewhat troubled life, he migrated in 1608 to Mexico, where he died about 1614.

Alemán's fame rests on his long and popular novel *Vida del picaro Guzmán de Alfarache* (1599; part 2, 1604), which ran through several editions and was translated into French, English, and Latin. This work, interspersing a picaresque narrative with moral digressions, records the author's dissatisfaction with the Renaissance faith in the senses, presenting a view of pleasure as universally transitory and depicting man as both universally corruptible and—through divine grace—individually eligible for salvation. It also is important for its picture of contemporary life.

ALEMÁN VALDÉS, ä-lä-män′ väl-dās′, **Miguel** (1902–1983), president of Mexico, whose administration stimulated industrial development of the country. He was born in Sayula, Veracruz, on Sept. 29, 1902. He graduated from the University of Mexico in 1928 and practiced law before entering the senate in 1935. He was governor of Veracruz from 1936 to 1940 and interior secretary in the government of Manuel Ávila Camacho from 1940 to 1945. His youth, attractiveness, and experience won him a large majority in the presidential election of 1946.

In foreign policy he established friendly ties with the United States, which aided Mexico in substantial industrial and agricultural projects. On the domestic scene he faced a serious financial crisis in 1948, but it was followed by an apparent improvement in Mexico's credit. However, grave financial problems appeared after Alemán's administration ended in 1952, and the succeeding regime of President Adolfo Ruiz Cortines inaugurated a vigorous campaign against government corruption. Alemán died in Mexico City on May 14, 1983.

ALEMBERT, à-län-bâr′, **Jean le Rond d'** (1717–1783), French scientist and mathematician. He was born in Paris on Nov. 17, 1717, the illegitimate son of the writer Mme. de Tencin and the Chevalier Destouches, who abandoned him on the steps of the Church of St. Jean de Rond. He was brought up in the home of a glazier named Rousseau. At first he was known as Jean le Rond; later he added the name d'Alembert.

D'Alembert earned a degree in law, studied medicine, and then achieved eminence in mathematics. He was admitted to the Académie des Sciences in 1741. In 1743 he published his classic *Traité de dynamique* (*Treatise on Dynamics*), in which he stated the law, known as *d'Alembert's principle*, that the sum of the external forces acting on a body is equal to the body's kinetic reaction. The differential equation $y = x\,f(y') + g(y')$ also bears his name, and the fundamental theorem of algebra (every polynomial equation has at least one root) is still known in France as *d'Alembert's theorem*. His publications cover a wide variety of topics, including planetary perturbations, the precession of the equinoxes, music, and philosophy.

D'Alembert collaborated with Diderot in the publication of the *Encyclopédie* and wrote the introduction and most of the encyclopedia's scientific and mathematical articles. In defending the encyclopedia against attacks he played a part in the expulsion of the Jesuit Order from France, and he was among those who paved the way for the French Revolution through the secularization of culture. He died in Paris on Oct. 29, 1783.

CARL B. BOYER
Brooklyn College

ALENCAR, ä-länng-kàr′, **José Martiniano de** (1829–1877), Brazilian novelist, who was the first great prose stylist of Brazilian literature. He was born in Fortaleza, Ceará, Brazil, on May 1, 1829. A lawyer and journalist, Alencar entered politics and rose to become minister of justice in 1868. But his fame rests on his literary work, especially his novels based on the life of the Brazilian Indians.

Though these three novels—*O Guarani* (4 vols., 1857), *Iracema* (1865), and *O sertanejo* (1876)—are psychologically weak, and are peopled with aborigines who are no more than idealized stereotypes of Chateaubriand's noble savage, they contain strong and colorful descriptions of the tropical jungles in which they are set. *O Guarani* was made into a successful opera in 1870 by the Brazilian composer Antônio Carlos Gomes. Other novels include *Diva* (1864) and *O gaucho* (2 vols., 1870). He died in Rio de Janeiro on Dec. 12, 1877.

ALENÇON, à-län-sôn′, a town in France, the capital of the department of Orne. It is on the Sarthe River, 110 miles (177 km) west-southwest of Paris. The town has long been famous for the manufacture of a type of lace called *point d'Alençon*. Alençon was captured by William the Conqueror in 1048. It later became the seat of the counts and dukes of Alençon. Population: 30,379 (1999 census).

ALEPPO, ə-lep'ō, the second-largest city of Syria and the capital of the district of Aleppo. It is situated about 30 miles (48 km) south of the Turkish frontier and about 70 miles (113 km) east of the Mediterranean Sea.

The old city of Aleppo preserves its Oriental character. In the center the imposing medieval citadel crowns a great mound. Below it the colorful bazaars wind for miles, their narrow streets cooled by an arched stone roof and lit by periodic shafts of sunlight.

Aleppo district, though semiarid, has excellent production of barley, wheat, cotton, vegetables, and fruit. Aleppo is famous for its pistachios. Although the district is cold in winter, with occasional snowfalls, and hot and dry in summer, its climate is healthy and bracing.

Economy. For centuries Aleppo was an important center for trade between the Persian Gulf and the Mediterranean. It was the chief market for northern Syria and a large part of eastern Asia Minor. Its trade suffered when it was cut off from Turkey in 1918 and from the port of Alexandretta (now İskenderun) in 1938 by the French cession of Hatay to Turkey. Aleppo later recovered its commercial importance with the large-scale development of agriculture in northeastern Syria and with the modernization of the port of Latakia, which replaced Alexandretta as an outlet for Aleppo's goods. As a transportation hub, Aleppo has rail connections with Istanbul, Baghdad, Damascus, and Beirut. Textile and other factories have put Aleppo in the forefront of Syrian industry.

History. Halab, the Arabic name of Aleppo, is of pre-Arab origin, as indicated by the forms Khalap and Halpa occurring in documents of the early 2d millennium B.C. The city was then the capital of the Amorite kingdom of Yamkhad. After conquests by the Hittites and the Hurrians, Aleppo appears to have been briefly occupied by the Egyptians in the 15th century B.C. As a Syro-Hittite principality, Aleppo enjoyed independence until the Assyrian advance in the 8th century B.C. In the time of Cyrus (6th century B.C.), Aleppo came under Persian rule. The Seleucid successors in Syria of Alexander the Great (d. 323 B.C.) gave the city the Macedonian name of Berea, which it kept under the Romans and Byzantines. The Arabs took Aleppo in 637 A.D. Since then it has remained a stronghold of Islam.

The city achieved its greatest splendor under the Arab dynasty of the Hamdanids in the 10th century. In the 12th century Saladin appointed his son Ghazi governor of Aleppo, and the citadel in its present form is mainly Ghazi's work. The Crusaders never succeeded in capturing Aleppo, though they lent a hand in its sack by the Mongols in 1260. Aleppo flourished commercially in Elizabethan times, and Shakespeare mentions the city in *Macbeth* and *Othello*.

In the 19th century, earthquakes and cholera epidemics contributed to the decline of Aleppo, which was abetted by the completion of the Suez Canal. But in the 20th century the energy of the Aleppines has brought about a vigorous revival. Established as an autonomous entity under the French mandate in 1920, Aleppo was merged with the rest of Syria in 1924. Population: 1,582,930 (1994 census).

GEORGE RENTZ
Curator, Middle East Collection
Hoover Institution, Stanford, California

ALÈS, à-les', a town in southern France, in the department of Gard. It is on the Gardon d'Alès River, at the base of the Cévennes Mountains, 30 miles (48 km) northwest of Nîmes. It was called *Alais* until 1926. The surrounding area is rich in coal, iron, and other minerals. Steel, chemicals, and ceramics are important manufactures. A statue of Louis Pasteur commemorates his work on the silkworm disease that threatened to destroy the large silk industry located around the town.

During the religious wars of the 17th century, the town sided with the Protestants. After its capture in 1629 by royalist forces representing the Catholics, the Peace of Alais was negotiated there. This agreement terminated the Huguenot wars in France. In accordance with the peace terms, the fortifications of all Protestant towns were demolished; however, the Protestants were granted religious freedom. Population: 41,054 (1999 census).

ALESIA, ə-lē-zha, is the ancient name for Mont Auxois, a hill of the Côte d'Or in France. The hill rises above Alise-Sainte-Reine, a village northwest of Dijon. Alesia was the strongly fortified encampment where Vercingetorix, the Gallic chief of the Arverni, made his last stand against Julius Caesar. This battle in 52 B.C. concluded the Roman conquest of Gaul. The place became a considerable city under the Romans, but was destroyed by the Normans in 864. A colossal statue of Vercingetorix, erected in the mid-19th century by Napoleon III, stands on Mont Auxois.

ALESSANDRIA, ä-läs-sän'drē-ä, in Italy, is the capital of Alessandria province, Piedmont. It lies along the Tanaro River, 50 miles (80 km) southeast of Turin. Notable buildings include an old castle, a cathedral (rebuilt early in the 19th century), an episcopal palace, and Palazzo Ghilini, the former royal palace. There is also a municipal museum. The city is an important rail and road junction and an industrial center with foundries, railroad shops, and manufactures of felt hats, bicycles, motorcycles, and textiles.

The city was founded in 1168 by the Lombard League—under the auspices of Pope Alexander III, whose name it adopted—as a defense against Emperor Frederick I Barbarossa. Because of Alessandria's military importance, the fortifications were gradually enlarged and strengthened. It was a free commune from 1198 to 1348, when it was included in the duchy of Milan. In 1707 it was ceded to the dukes of Savoy, rulers of Piedmont, who in 1728 erected a powerful citadel across the river to defend the Austrian frontier. Except for the French occupation (1800–1814), the city remained part of Piedmont until the kingdom of Italy was formed in 1861. Population: 85,438 (2001 census).

ÅLESUND, ô'lə-sōōn, a seaport on the west coast of Norway about 160 miles (260 km) northeast of Bergen. The port is situated on three adjacent islands at the mouth of Stor Fjord. Ålesund is Norway's largest fishing port and is the center of the nation's cod, herring, and Arctic fisheries. The processing of fish is its chief industry. It also has a well-equipped shipyard. Ålesund was rebuilt in stone after a severe fire in 1904. The name also is spelled *Aalesund*. Population: 35,862 (1990 census).

ALEURITES, al-ū-rī′tēz, a genus of trees cultivated in tropical countries, especially in eastern Asia and the islands of the Pacific, for the oils obtained from its seeds. The oils (kekuna, bankul, tung, or wood oil) are similar to linseed oil, and are used largely in the manufacture of paints and soaps. *Aleurites* is also grown as a shade tree. The genus *Aleurites,* consisting of four species, belongs to the family Euphorbiaceae.

ALEUTIAN ISLANDS, ə-loo′shən, a chain of islands extending westward from the southern tip of the Alaska Peninsula. They stretch in a 1,700-mile (2,700-km) saucer-shaped arc to within 500 miles (800 km) of the Kamchatka Peninsula in the Russian Federation, separating the Bering Sea on the north from the Pacific Ocean on the south. The Aleutians include 14 large islands, 55 small islands, and innumerable islets.

Once owned by Russia and called the Catherine Archipelago, the Aleutians became part of the United States with the purchase of Alaska from Russia in 1867. The islands form a unit of the Alaska Maritime National Wildlife Refuge, which regulates the numbers of wildlife, including the seals and sea otters that are a basic source of food for the Aleuts.

From east to west the islands are divided into five groups. The Fox Islands, named for the great number of foxes found there by Russian fur traders, includes Unimak (the largest and easternmost of the Aleutians), Unalaska, and Umnak. The Islands of the Four Mountains consist of five islands: Chuginadak, Herbert, Carlisle, Kagamil, and Uliaga. The Andreanof Islands, named for Andrean Tolstykh, a Russian explorer who traveled these islands in the early 1760s and wrote an account of his findings, includes Amlia, Atka, Great Sitkin, Adak, Kanaga, and Tanaga. The Rat Islands, where hordes of rodents were found, include Semisopochnoi, Amchitka, Kiska, Ray, and Buldir. The Near Islands, named for their proximity to Russia, are made up of the Semichi Islands, Agattu, and Attu, the terminus of the Aleutian chain. Attu is 200 miles (320 km) southeast of the Komandor Islands and 750 miles (1200 km) northeast of the Kuril Islands.

Topography.   The Aleutian Islands are the partially submerged continuation of Alaska's Aleutian Range. Largely mountainous, the islands have irregular shore lines and rocky cliffs jutting from the ocean. Small lakes are very common. Much of the ground is spongy and marshy in warm weather and completely frozen in winter. Beneath it layers of volcanic ash are usually found. Although the islands are treeless, they support several hundred species of plants, many of which have showy flowers.

There are 30 or 40 volcanoes in the islands, many of them active. The largest, located on Unimak, is Mount Shishaldin (9,387 feet, or 2,861 meters), known also as Smoking Moses. Near it are Isanotski Peak (8,088 feet, or 2,465 meters) and Mount Round Top (6,155 feet, or 1,876 meters). On Umnak is Mount Vsevidof (7,236 feet, or 2,206 meters), and on Unalaska, Mount Makushin (6,678 feet, or 2,035 meters). Mount Cleveland on Chuginadak has an elevation of 8,150 feet (2,484 meters). There are active glaciers on all these mountains.

It has often been said that the Aleutian Islands were once continuous land, connecting Kamchatka with Alaska. There is no evidence, however, that such a land bridge across the Aleutians existed in the Pleistocene or Recent periods. There are ocean depths as great as 3,000 fathoms (5,500 meters) between Attu and the Komandor Islands and Kamchatka.

Climate.   Temperatures are fairly uniform, averaging about 33° F (1° C) in winter and 50° F (10° C) in summer. Cold winds from Siberia and ocean currents from the Bering Sea meet the warm air and currents flowing eastward across the Pacific. The interaction results in high velocity winds and dense fog, mist, rain, and snow. At Attu five or six days a week are rainy, with scarcely a dozen clear days a year. Annual rainfall of the islands averages 40 to 50 inches (1,000–1,300 mm).

The sharp, sudden changes of weather make aviation dangerous. Good visibility often gives way to fog concentrations, and sudden squalls known as williwaws sweep down from the mountains and reach gale proportions within 30 minutes.

Population.   When Russian traders first went to the Aleutian Islands, nearly every island was inhabited and the native population was estimated at 25,000. After a period of mass murder and enslavement that followed, Father Ivan Venyaminov wrote in 1834 that there remained fewer than 2,500 Aleuts. Smallpox and flu epidemics in 1848 and 1918 further reduced their ranks, and in 1945 the anthropologist Aleš Hrdlička estimated their number at 1,400.

The 2000 census enumerated 8,162 residents in the Aleutian Islands, including the lower Alaska Peninsula. That represented a decrease of about 32% since 1990, owing largely to the closing of military facilities. The total included 2,834 whites; 2,059 Asians; 1,930 Alaska Natives (Eskimo or Aleut); and 210 African Americans. Hispanics, of any race, numbered 912. The principal settlements are on Unalaska and Adak.

History.   A Russian exploration party led by Vitus Bering came upon the Aleutian Islands in 1741. Drawn by reports of abundant furbearing animals, 18th-century Russian traders almost exterminated animal life on the islands.

In 1778 the English explorer Capt. James Cook surveyed the eastern Aleutian Islands. Later, Russian expeditions made scientific investigations and improved navigation charts. The maps of this region that the United States used at the beginning of World War II were based largely on Russian findings.

Aleksandr Baranov was later responsible for a migration of traders from the Aleutians to Kodiak Island and Alaska. The Russians took hundreds of Aleuts with them as slaves because of their knowledge of hunting and fishing.

In 1867 Russia sold Alaska, including the Aleutians, to the United States. The Aleutians were left open to all fur hunters, and, with no legal restraints, the combination of American, Canadian, Japanese, and Russian ships threatened the extinction of fur seals. Not until 1911 did the four countries sign a treaty that prohibited oceanic sealing. In the meantime a gold rush in Nome triggered the development of Dutch Harbor, on Unalaska, as a transshipping point.

During World War II the United States established naval and air bases on the islands and Japanese forces occupied Attu and Kiska (1942–1943). Many island residents were relocated owing to the war.

A change of military strategy led to the relocation of most military installations to the mainland in 1947 and 1949. Amchitka was the site of underground nuclear tests in 1965 and 1971, for which residents were once again relocated. Radiation leaks from the test sites were detected in the 1990s. The remaining military facilities were closed in the 1990s.

See also ALEUTS; ALASKA; BERING SEA CONTROVERSY; SEAL AND SEAL FISHERIES; also separate articles on the chief Aleutian islands and island groups; and biographies of important explorers.

Bibliography: Collins, H. B., et al., *The Aleutian Islands: Their People and Natural History*, War Background Studies No. 21 (Smithsonian Inst. Press 1945); **Garfield, Brian**, *The Thousand-Mile War: World War II in Alaska and the Aleutians* (1969; reprint, Univ. of Alaska Press 1995); **Jochelson, Waldemar**, *Archaeological Investigations in the Aleutian Islands* (1925; reprint, Univ. of Utah Press 2002); **Rennick, Penny**, ed., *Alaska Geographic: The Aleutian Islands* (Alaska Geographic Soc. 1995).

ALEUTS, a-lē-üts′, the name given to persons who are native to the Aleutian Islands (including the Shumagin Islands) and the southwestern tip of the Alaska Peninsula. *Aleut* is the Russian name for a person belonging to this group; in the Aleut language the people refer to themselves collectively as *Unangan*, meaning "real people." There are also smaller groups of Aleuts living on the Pribilof Islands in the Bering Sea and on the Russian-owned Commander Islands to the east. Culturally and linguistically, the Aleuts' nearest relatives are the Alutiiqs, formerly known as Pacific Eskimos, of nearby Kodiak Island, the Gulf of Alaska, and Prince William Sound.

The Aleut language is the second branch of the Eskimo-Aleut language family. The two derive from a common ancestral trunk but are thought to have been distinct by 1,000 B.C. Aleut is a single language having two main—eastern and western—dialects. The course of Aleut prehistory is widely debated. The earliest Aleut artifacts are from a site in the eastern Aleutians dating to about 6,000 B.C. They show marked similarities to those from northeastern Asia of similar dates. At about 2,000 B.C., an in-migration from the mainland had moved onto the Alaska Peninsula and the easternmost islands.

The Aleuts at the Time of European Contact. The Aleuts' earliest historical contacts were in 1741, when the Russian expedition led by Vitus Bering stopped at several Aleut villages. The Bering expedition's tales of vast numbers of sea otters resulted in an enormous influx of Russian fur hunters in the Aleutians. With no laws to restrain them, they savaged the Aleuts and depleted the islands' rich fur stocks. In the 1790s the Russian American Company was formed to regulate the fur trade and administer the Russian interests in Alaska. Christian influence began with the 1824 arrival of Father Ioann (Ivan) Veniaminov. A successful missionary, Veniaminov was also a scholar of Aleut language and culture.

Because the Aleuts were contacted relatively early and were subject to disruptive changes, information about their social and political organization is fragmentary. Unlike that of the nearby Eskimos, Aleut society was stratified, with separate classes of slaves, commoners, and rich men. It also had chieftains, or headmen, whose status was inherited. Although the Aleut kinship system is often portrayed as formerly matrilineal, it is more likely that it was bilateral with patrilineal tendencies.

The Aleuts traditionally lived in extended family groups, occupying semisubterranean sod houses called *barabaras*, which were grouped in small shoreline communities. The *barabara* was entered by a notched ladder descending from a large hole in the roof. The people lived mainly on sea mammals such as seals, walrus, and, occasionally, whales as well as fish. Hunting was carried out from skin *baidarkas*, which resemble kayaks. The Aleuts were unusual in hunting whales with poison-tipped harpoons, later recovering their prey when it washed ashore.

Apparently, indigenous Aleut religion was similar to that of the Eskimos. Humans exerted power over the universe by manipulating, through the use of charms, amulets, and recitations, the interaction among several forces, such as human souls and the "souls" of animals, places, and things. The Aleuts were also sophisticated in the medicinal uses of plants. Aleut art and material culture were equally accomplished, particularly the spectacular bentwood and painted chiefs' hats embellished with sea lion whiskers. Women worked in skin, sea-mammal intestine, and grass, producing elaborately decorated clothing and basketry of extreme fineness.

Of all the Alaska Natives, the Aleuts were most directly affected by World War II. Because of the Japanese attacks on the Aleutians, the U.S. government evacuated hundreds of Aleuts, leading to social disruption and, in some cases, permanent relocation.

Contemporary Situation. According to the 2000 U.S. Census, there are 10,695 Aleuts living in Alaska. The number of Aleuts residing in Russia is about 700; approximately 300 of them live in Nikolskoye on Bering Island, while the others are scattered over Kamchatka and other parts of Russia. Some Alaskan Aleuts still inhabit the coastal villages, but many have moved to Alaska's major cities. The native-language retention rate is low in both areas: fewer than 200 Aleut speakers are left in Russia and about 500 in the United States. To counter such tendencies, Alaska has instituted language programs, but with limited success.

The passage of the Alaska Native Claims Settlement Act (ANCSA) in 1971 changed the political, economic, and cultural landscape for the Alaskan Aleuts forever. Today the Aleut Corporation, along with a form of village corporation, manages the land and money transferred under ANCSA. Problems, however, such as minimal business opportunities in remote villages and attempts to mainstream U.S. Aleut culture into that of America at large, have resulted in uneasy relations between traditional Aleuts and their corporate leadership. At the same time Aleuts have been successful in reviving certain parts of their cultural heritage.

Russian Orthodoxy remains strong among the Aleuts of Alaska and Russia. The Russian Aleuts on Bering Island have recently been able to increase their efforts in the preservation of Native heritage. There are song and dance ensembles as well as an Aleut Folklore Museum.

MOLLY LEE, *Curator of Ethnology*
University of Alaska Museum
PETER P. SCHWEITZER
University of Alaska at Fairbanks

Bibliography: **Black, Lydia T.**, *Atka: An Ethnohistory of the Western Aleutians* (Limestone Press 1984); **Jochelson, Waldemar**, *History, Ethnology, and Anthropology of the Aleut* (1933; reprint, Univ. of Utah 2002); **Liapunova, Roza G.**, *Essays on the Ethnography of the Aleuts*, tr. by J. Shelest (Univ. of Alaska Press 1996).

ALEWIFE, ăl'wīf, a small fish, closely related to both the herring and the shad and found abundantly along the east coast of North America. It resembles the shad in shape and color, but it is smaller—only eight to ten inches long. It is of great importance as a food fish, and millions are caught yearly. Several varieties, which are not of good food quality, are used as fertilizers.

In the spring, the alewife swims up the coastal rivers from North Carolina to Nova Scotia to spawn. The eggs are released by the female in great quantities; they sink to the bottom and stick to rocks and debris. The young grow quickly and return to the sea at the age of six months.

The genus and species of alewife is *Pomolobus pseudoharengus.* The landlocked species is a variation, *lacustris.* The alewife is called the *gaspereau* in St. Lawrence Bay and *branch herring, ellwife,* and *sawbelly* in other places.

ALEXANDER, al-ig-zan'dər, **Saint** (died about 250), bishop of Comana, in Pontus, Asia Minor. He was known as the "charcoal burner," a trade he adopted out of humility. His merits as an administrator and his holiness were discovered by St. Gregory of Neocaesarea, who named him bishop of Comana. Alexander suffered martyrdom in the persecutions by Emperor Decius. His feast day is August 11.

ALEXANDER, al-ig-zan'dər, **Saint** (died 251), bishop of Cappadocia and first bishop coadjutor of Jerusalem. He sponsored Origen as a lay teacher and ordained him to the priesthood. (See ORIGEN.) Alexander also is noted for the theological library he built at Jerusalem. He died in prison at Caesarea during persecutions by Emperor Decius and is considered a martyr. His feast day in the Roman Catholic Church is March 18; in the Greek Orthodox Church, December 22.

ALEXANDER, al-ig-zan'dər, **Saint** (died 326), patriarch of Alexandria, whose appointment to that see excluded Arius from the honor and brought the latter's heresy into the open. Alexander is said to have made every effort to redeem Arius, but when the latter proved unrepentant, Alexander drew up the acts of the General Council of Nicaea, which condemned Arius. Alexander died at Alexandria on April 17, 326, and was succeeded by Athanasius. His feast day is April 17. See also ARIUS; ATHANASIUS.

ALEXANDER I, al-ig-zan'dər, **Saint,** pope from 105 to 115. Little is known about him, but tradition asserts that he added the words commemorating the institution of the Eucharist to the Canon of the Mass (where his name is mentioned); that he introduced the use of holy water for blessing homes; and that he suffered martyrdom. His feast day is May 3.

ALEXANDER II, al-ig-zan'dər, was pope from 1061 to 1073. Born *Anselmo da Baggio,* of a noble Italian family, he studied at Bec in Normandy under Lanfranc, whom he later made archbishop of Canterbury. An outspoken foe of simony and clerical concubinage, he was elected pope through the influence of Hildebrand and St. Peter Damian, who vainly hoped thereby to avert a possible schism. Alexander was the first pope elected under the electoral law of 1059.

His objections to Emperor Henry IV's attempt to divorce his wife were the opening phase of a conflict that reached its climax under Alexander's successor, Pope Gregory VII. Alexander was a firm supporter of the monastic clergy, whose position he strengthened everywhere. By the methodical use of papal legates he promoted widespread reform, especially in Italy, Germany, and France, and thereby made papal control of the church more effective than ever. He blessed the invasion of England by William the Conqueror in 1066. In Italy, he supported the Norman nobles who drove the Eastern Empire and the Saracens from their remaining possessions in Italy. Alexander died at Rome on April 21, 1073.
MSGR. FLORENCE D. COHALAN, *Cathedral College*

ALEXANDER III, al-ig-zan'dər, was pope from 1159 to 1181. Born *Roland Bandinelli,* of a distinguished Sienese family, he was a renowned canonist, cardinal priest, and papal chancellor. His anti-imperial attitude incurred the enmity of Emperor Frederick I Barbarossa, who fought against his election and supported an antipope, Victor IV. Both contenders were summoned by the emperor to a council at Pavia, which declared for Victor and excommunicated the absent Alexander. The latter responded by excommunicating the emperor and releasing his subjects from their oaths of allegiance. For 18 years, pope and emperor each labored to reduce the other to subservience. They were reconciled at Venice in 1177, and both church and empire survived intact.

After the murder of Thomas à Becket, archbishop of Canterbury, Alexander persuaded King Henry II of England to recognize the right of benefit of clergy for the English church and the right of appeal to papal courts. As a legislator he was second in importance only to Innocent III. During his reign, the Third Lateran Council (1179) confirmed the exclusive right of the College of Cardinals to elect the popes. He died at Civ ità Castellana on Aug. 30, 1181.

ALEXANDER IV, al-ig-zan'dər, was pope from 1254 to 1261. Born *Rinaldo Conti,* of the illustrious house of Segni, he became a worthy and experienced prelate. He came to the papal throne unwillingly and at an advanced age. He ruled the spiritual affairs of the church with dignity and prudence, but he was ineffectual in coping with the serious political problems in which the church was involved as a result of the struggle between his predecessor Innocent IV and Emperor Frederick II. He failed to unite Christendom against the threatened invasion of the Tatars, and Rome was lost to papal control during his reign. Although he defeated the tyrant Ezzelino IV in northern Italy, he did not keep the Two Sicilies out of the control of Manfred, Frederick's son. He befriended the Franciscans and canonized St. Clare. He died at Viterbo on May 25, 1261.

ALEXANDER V, al-ig-zan'dər, was antipope in 1409–1410. Born *Pietro Philargi* (or *di Candia*) in Crete, he became a Franciscan and later was archbishop of Milan. He was made a cardinal in 1405. The Council of Pisa, attempting to put an end to the schism in the church, in 1409 pronounced as heretics and schismatics both rival popes, Gregory XII (reigned 1406–1415) of Rome and Benedict XIII (reigned 1394–1417) of Avignon, and then elected Alexander pope.

He was, however, recognized by only a part of Christendom, and during his ten-month reign he never reached Rome, which was held by Ladislaus of Naples for Gregory XII. Alexander died at Bologna on May 3, 1410.

ALEXANDER VI (1431–1503), al-ig-zan'dər, was pope from 1492 to 1503. Born at Xativa near Valencia, Jan. 1, 1431, he became the ward of his maternal uncle, Cardinal Alfonso Borgia, and took the name *Rodrigo Borgia*. The cardinal educated Rodrigo and made him a canon of Valencia. Alfonso became Pope Calixtus III in 1455, and Rodrigo moved to Rome. Made a cardinal in 1456, in 1459 he became papal vice-chancellor, the highest administrative office in the Curia. He held that post during five pontificates, until 1492.

He acquired an immense fortune by accumulating as benefices dioceses in Italy, Spain, and Hungary. His liaison with Vanozza dei Catanei produced four children, the most famous of whom were Cesare and Lucrezia Borgia. Though rebuked by Pope Pius II for immorality, Rodrigo openly acknowledged his children, and providing for them became a dominant passion in his life.

In the conclave of 1492 he used bribery to win the two thirds of the votes necessary for election to the papal throne. Except in Venice, Naples, and Spain, where he was disliked for political reasons, his election was welcomed.

As pope, Alexander pledged himself to restore peace to Italy and to unite Christendom against the Turks (although at one time he was negotiating with the Turkish sultan against his enemies among the princes of Europe). Alexander fulfilled part of his pledge by restoring order to Rome.

Alexander attempted economies, but was a liberal patron of the arts. He attracted to Rome such great artists as Bramante and Pinturicchio.

In ecclesiastical affairs, Alexander was an active pontiff. He defended the rights of the Holy See in the Netherlands, tried to suppress heresy in Bohemia, and protected the religious orders, especially the Dominicans and Augustinians. He also began church censorship of books.

The Dominican friar Girolamo Savonarola denounced Alexander as a corrupt pontiff. After the friar directly attacked papal authority, Alexander excommunicated him for heresy.

Alexander's most important political act was issuing the Bull of Demarcation in 1493, which established a line separating Spanish and Portuguese lands in the New World. He also sent the first missionaries to America. Though he opposed the French king Charles VIII when Charles invaded Italy in 1494 and conquered Naples in 1495, Alexander was in too weak a position to resist him effectively. The pope sent his son Cesare as a hostage to Charles; in return, Charles spared the city of Rome and did not accede to the wishes of Alexander's enemies for a council to depose him. His efforts to crush Roman nobles like the Colonnas and Orsinis were made ineffective by his vain attempt to establish a principality for Cesare. Alexander died in Rome on Aug. 18, 1503.

Much criticism of Alexander has been calumnious. It cannot be denied, however, that he increased the secularization of the papacy and reduced its capacity to resist the Protestant Reformation. His reign was a disaster for the church.
Msgr. Florence D. Cohalan, *Cathedral College*

ALEXANDER VII (1599–1667), al-ig-zan'dər, was pope from 1655 to 1667. He was born *Fabio Chigi*, Feb. 13, 1599, of a noble family in Siena. He obtained doctorates in philosophy, law, and theology there. After Chigi had completed diplomatic missions in Ferrara, Malta, Cologne, and Münster, Innocent III made him cardinal and secretary of state. Chigi was elected pope in a conclave notable for its length and dissension.

Although he was distinguished for exalted sanctity, moral severity, and aversion to luxury, Alexander was an ineffectual pontiff. The humiliating terms of the Treaty of Pisa (1664) were the result of his trouble with Louis XIV of France and Mazarin. During his reign, papal authority began to change from monarchic absolutism to the deliberative methods of constitutional aristocracy wielded by the various congregations and the secretary of state. However, Alexander enriched Rome with masterpieces of art—notably the Bernini colonnade of St. Peter's—and he made extensive additions to the Vatican Library. He died in Rome on May 22, 1667.

ALEXANDER VIII (1610–1691), al-ig-zan'dər, was pope from 1689 to 1691. Born *Pietro Ottoboni* of a noble Venetian family, he was elected pope in 1689 after a distinguished career as an administrator. Alexander won concessions from Louis XIV of France, who relinquished Avignon and gave up the right to grant asylum long enjoyed by the French embassy in Rome. Moreover, Alexander, a resolute man, renewed the nullification of Gallican Liberties. These principles, set forth by an assembly of the French clergy in 1682, held that popes have no temporal power over princes, are subject to ecumenical councils, and are bound by customs of local churches. Alexander assisted Venice against the Turks, strengthened the finances of the church, and enlarged the Vatican Library. He died in Rome, Feb. 1, 1691.

ALEXANDER I (1857–1893), al-ig-zan'dər, was the first prince of Bulgaria. Born *Alexander Joseph*, at Verona, Italy, on April 5, 1857, he was the second son of Prince Alexander of Hesse-Darmstadt and his morganatic wife, Julia Teresa, countess von Haucke. He later received the title *Alexander Joseph of Battenberg*. After obtaining a military education in the cadet corps at Dresden, Germany, Alexander served with the Russians in the war against Turkey in 1877–1878. At the insistence of his uncle, Czar Alexander II of Russia, he was elected hereditary prince of Bulgaria in 1879. Bulgaria had just attained autonomy within the Ottoman empire.

Under Russia's influence, Alexander suspended the Bulgarian constitution in 1881 and ruled as virtual dictator for two years, until he was forced by the rising discontent within the country to restore legality. He aroused Russian and Serbian opposition in 1885, when he supported a revolution in Eastern Rumelia that brought about its union with Bulgaria. On Aug. 20, 1886, through Russian intrigue, he was kidnapped and compelled to abdicate. He was taken to the Russian town of Reni, but a counterrevolution in Bulgaria enabled him to return to Sofia almost immediately. Finding Russian and German opposition too strong to overcome, he abdicated again on Sept. 7, 1886. He spent the rest of his life in exile in Austria. He died at Graz on Nov. 17, 1893.

ALEXANDER (1893–1920), al-ig-zan'dər, was king of Greece in 1917–1920. He was born in Athens on Aug. 1, 1893, the second son of King Constantine and Sophia, a sister of German Emperor William II. In 1917, Constantine was forced by the Allied powers to abdicate in favor of Alexander. Two years later Alexander entered into a morganatic marriage with Aspasia Manos. He died of blood poisoning, caused by an animal bite, at Tatoi Palace, on Oct. 25, 1920. Aspasia gave birth to a daughter shortly after, but the child was not legitimized until 1922, and Constantine returned to the throne.

ALEXANDER I (1777–1825), al-ig-zan'dər, was an emperor of Russia. The eldest son of Paul I, he was born in St. Petersburg on Dec. 12, 1777. He was raised in the libertine atmosphere of the court of his grandmother, Empress Catherine II, who determined that he would receive a Westernized education—a startling innovation for an heir to the Russian throne. Alexander's principal tutor was César La Harpe, a Swiss revolutionary and republican, who instilled in his pupil a strong emotional attachment for the philosophy of the Enlightmenment but failed to acquaint him with Russian social and political reality. From other tutors and from his father, Alexander imbibed the traditions of Russian autocracy and acquired a passion for the military parade field. The contradictory nature of his education, the sharply conflicting demands of duty to his grandmother and loyalty to his father, and perhaps the dissonance between his political ideals and Russia's unreadiness for reform may have contributed to his instability.

Alexander ascended the throne on March 12, 1801, at the age of 23, following a palace revolution that removed Paul I from the throne and ended with Paul's murder. Alexander's compliance with the plot to remove his father from the throne is almost certain.

Domestic Policy. Alexander began his reign with a promise to right the social ills of his subjects by emancipating the serfs, reorganizing the state administration, granting a constitution, and keeping his country at peace with its neighbors. To carry out his plans he relied on the advice and help of four young aristocratic friends, N. Novosiltsev, V.P. Kochubey, P. Stroganov, and A.J. Czartoryski, and the brilliant administrator M.M. Speransky. The political idea of enlightened despotism governed Alexander's actions in these early days. Despite Alexander's professed wish to grant "liberty" to his subjects, a constitutional plan drafted by Speransky was only partially implemented. Changes made at the upper levels of the state administration only strengthened the bureaucratic framework of the state. Alexander's attempts to ameliorate the plight of the serfs and introduce enlightened education and censorship policies proved ineffectual, with the result that the social and political structure of Russia changed little during his reign. The meager results of his policies to develop manufacturing and commerce underscored the incompatibility of serfdom and nascent Russian capitalism.

Foreign Policy. In 1801, Alexander disavowed the militant foreign policy of his father and declared Russia neutral in European affairs. But faced with the threat of French hegemony on the Continent, Alexander, like his grandmother and father, could not resist the temptation to use Russian might to arbitrate European affairs. After Napoleon's declaration of a French empire in May 1804, Alexander helped to form the Third Coalition (Russia, Britain, Sweden, and Austria) against France. A succession of disastrous Russian military defeats, at Austerlitz, Eylau, and Friedland, resulted in the humiliating Treaty of Tilsit (July 7, 1807), which linked Russia to France in a military alliance and bound Russia to participate in France's economic blockade of England. Between the time of this treaty and the resumption of hostilities with France in 1812, Alexander launched costly military campaigns against Sweden and the Ottoman empire, adding Finland (1809) and Bessarabia (1812) to the Russian empire. A war with Persia begun in 1804 resulted in the recognition of Russian sovereignty over much of Georgia in 1813. Harmful economic consequences stemming from the loss of the trade with Britain, and the growing unpopularity of the Tilsit treaty forced Alexander into moves which pointed to another conflict with France. But before Alexander could complete military preparations and conclude an alliance with Britain, Napoleon invaded Russia (June 24, 1812) in a bloody campaign that culminated in the burning and sacking of Moscow. This so enraged Alexander that he refused to consider a negotiated peace, and Napoleon's weakened army began the long retreat from Russia, which set the stage for the final defeat of Napoleon.

In 1814, Alexander was the most powerful monarch in Europe, and he played a dominant role at the Congress of Vienna (1814–1815). Inspired by a growing mystical piety, he proposed to restore European peace by means of a Holy Alliance (Sept. 26, 1815) based on Christian morality. Signed eventually by nearly all the European powers, after 1822 the treaty was actively supported only by Russia, Prussia, and Austria as a means to maintain order in eastern Europe. After Napoleon's brief return to power during the Hundred Days, Alexander readily subscribed to the Quadruple Alliance of Russia, Austria, Britain, and Prussia (1815), and committed Russia to the role of "gendarme of Europe."

Personal Life. The tragedy of Alexander's public career—the failure to fulfill his promise as reformer and peacemaker—was paralleled in his personal life. He was married at the age of 16, in a political union, to the German Princess Luisa Maria Augusta of Baden (Empress Yelizaveta Alekseyevna). The marriage, an unhappy one, resulted in the birth of only one child, a girl who died in infancy. As a result, a succession crisis followed Alexander's death. Toward the end of his life an increasingly morbid religiosity produced moods of melancholy and the tendency to seek divine inspiration in matters of state. Oppressed and disillusioned, Alexander died suddenly while in Taganrog on Nov. 19, 1825. The enigma surrounding Alexander's life survived his demise. A legend grew up after his death that the unhappy emperor had not died in 1825 but had given up his crown and assumed the guise of a wandering holy man, Fyodor Kuzmich, who died in Siberia in 1864.

PETER CZAP, *Amherst College*

Further Reading: Cate, Curtis, *The War of the Two Emperors* (Random House 1985); Niven, Alexander, *Napoleon and Alexander* (Univ. Press of Am. 1978); Paleologue, Maurice, *The Enigmatic Tsar* (1938; reprint, Shoe String 1969); Troyat, Henri, *Alexander of Russia* (Fromm Intl. 1986).

ALEXANDER II (1818–1881), al-ig-zan'dər, was emperor of Russia from 1855 to 1881. Alexander was born in Moscow on April 17, 1818, the eldest son of Emperor Nicholas I. He received the traditional education for an heir apparent, which included studies in the humanities, history, statecraft, and military science. In 1841 he married a German princess, Marie of Hesse-Darmstadt (Empress Maria Alexandrovna), who bore him six sons and two daughters. Alexander was gentle, humane, and sentimental. But because he lacked deep convictions or determination, all his official acts were characterized by hesitation and vacillation.

Alexander ascended the throne on Feb. 18, 1855, during the Crimean War, on the death of his father. Conservative and instinctively sympathetic to the authoritarian, bureaucratic system perfected by his father, Alexander was nonetheless shaken by Russia's disastrous performance in the Crimean War, which revealed the need to reform the administration, stimulate the Russian economy, and end the system of bondage in which three quarters of the Russian people lived. The "Era of Great Reforms" began on Feb. 19, 1861, with the abolition of serfdom, the act that won for Alexander the epithet "Czar Liberator." This reform was rapidly followed by changes in the system of governmental finances, issuance of a charter granting a measure of academic freedom to universities, reorganization of the judicial administration, and introduction of local self-government for rural districts and cities. A relatively democratic system of universal conscription and military training was introduced.

The reforms failed to produce the rapid modernization of the Russian economy and governmental structure for which many had hoped. The peasants' and radical intellectuals' profound disappointment with the reforms led to widespread social unrest and eventually were followed by Alexander's disenchantment with the role of reformer.

The military and diplomatic defeats inflicted on Russia by the Western powers in connection with the Crimean War led Alexander to seek compensation in Asia and in the Caucasus and the Balkans. Southern Bessarabia was returned and Kars and Ardahan were added to Russia by the treaty that concluded the Russo-Turkish War of 1877–1878.

On March 1, 1881, the day on which he was to grant modest political concessions, Alexander was assassinated by a bomb thrown by members of a revolutionary terroristic organization. His heir at once canceled the concessions.

PETER CZAP, JR.
Amherst College

ALEXANDER III (1845–1894), al-ig-zan'dər, was emperor of Russia from 1881 to 1894. Alexander was born on Feb. 26, 1845, in Tsarskoye Selo, the second son of emperor Alexander II. As the second son he was destined for a military career; thus his general education was somewhat neglected. At the age of 20 he became heir apparent after the death of his older brother. He was deeply influenced at this time by his tutor, K.P. Pobedonostsev, who instilled in Alexander a religious, nationalistic, and reactionary political outlook. Alexander was a robust, gruff figure with little subtlety of personality or mind. In 1866 he married Princess Sophia Frederika Dag-

mar of Denmark (Empress Maria Fyodorovna), who had been the fiancée of his older brother. He ascended the throne on March 1, 1881, after the assassination of his father, and he rejected the modest political concessions his father had made on the morning of his death.

Alexander's strong conservative convictions led to measures reducing the autonomy of self-governing rural districts and cities and restricting the freedom of self-governing peasant communes. He introduced a Russification policy among his Baltic, Polish, and Finnish subjects. Russian Orthodoxy was promoted at the expense of minority religions, and Russian became the language of instruction in all the border provinces of the empire. Jews were persecuted, and quotas were established to reduce the number of Jews attending universities.

Alexander avoided major military conflicts while pursuing a policy of expansion in Asia and the Near East. He led Russia out of its traditional alliance with Germany and formed the Franco-Russian alliance of Dec. 31, 1893. During his reign the Russian industrial revolution was begun. Alexander died in the Crimea on Oct. 20, 1894.

PETER CZAP, JR.
Amherst College

ALEXANDER I (1078?–1124), al-ig-zan'dər, was a king of Scotland, whose rule fostered the consolidation of both church and state in Scotland, under English influence. He was one of three Scottish kings born from the marriage of Margaret, grandniece of the English king Edward the Confessor, and Malcolm Canmore, king of Scotland. All three ruled under the protection of English kings. Alexander succeeded to the throne in 1107, but he ruled only the area north of Edinburgh. His younger brother and heir, David, ruled the south. Alexander established bishoprics on the English model and furthered the assimilation of the northern Scots to the Anglicized culture of the south. At his death the kingdom was reunited under his brother David.

ALEXANDER II (1198–1249), al-ig-zan'dər, was a king of Scotland, whose prudent rule helped consolidate the kingdom and win a measure of independence from England. Alexander was born at Haddington, East Lothian, on Aug. 24, 1198, and succeeded his father, William the Lion, on Dec. 6, 1214.

Under William, Scotland had become a vassal state of the king of England and was deprived of contested lands in the border country between the two kingdoms. In 1215, during the English disorders leading up to the Magna Carta, Alexander invaded the border country and renewed Scotland's claim to Northumberland. King John of England retaliated with a punitive invasion of Scotland the next year, but the accession of Henry III opened the way to peace. In 1221, Alexander married Henry's elder sister, Joan, and in 1237 the two sovereigns agreed to an enduring demarcation of the border. A year after Joan's death in 1238, Alexander married Marie de Coucy, daughter of a French nobleman. Relations with England deteriorated until a new agreement was reached in 1244. Thereafter Alexander consolidated his rule in northern and western Scotland. While on an expedition to subjugate the Hebrides, he died on Kerrera, near Oban, on July 8, 1249.

ALEXANDER III (1241–1286), al-ig-zan′dər, king of Scotland, who conquered the Hebrides and the Isle of Man. He was born on Sept. 4, 1241, and was betrothed at the age of one to Margaret, the two-year-old daughter of Henry III of England. He succeeded his father, Alexander II, on July 13, 1249, and two years later, at the age of 10, was married to Margaret.

A regency troubled by constant intrigues governed during his minority, but in 1257 the spirited young king began to assert his independence. Between 1260 and 1264 he drove the Norwegians out of the islands west of Scotland and brought the peoples of the Hebrides and the Isle of Man under Scottish rule. Thereafter, until his death, the Scots enjoyed an unprecedented freedom from outside interference in their affairs.

Alexander lost his children—two sons and a daughter—before he died in a riding accident near Kinghorn, Fife, on March 16, 1286. His only heir was the infant daughter of his eldest child, Margaret, and King Eric of Norway. The child was declared queen of Scotland but died on the way to her coronation. A long contest for power ensued.

ALEXANDER I, al-ig-zan′dər (1888–1934), king of Yugoslavia. He was born in Cetinje, Montenegro, on Dec. 4, 1888, the second son of Peter I and grandson of Alexander I Karageorgevich. Alexander spent his early boyhood at Geneva, Switzerland, with his exiled father. In 1899 he was sent to Russia to continue his education, becoming a page at the emperor's court. In 1909 he returned to Serbia, where his father had been reigning since 1903, and took the oath as heir apparent when his elder brother, George, renounced the right of succession. Alexander distinguished himself in the wars of 1912–1913 against Turkey and Bulgaria, and in June 1914 he was appointed regent of Serbia because of his father's ill health. During World War I he was nominally commander in chief of the Serbian army, sharing with his troops the bitter retreat across Albania to the coast.

Alexander returned in triumph to Belgrade in November 1918, and on December 1 he was recognized as prince regent of the Serb-Croat-Slovene state. Following the death of King Peter in 1921, he was proclaimed king. Political conditions in the new state were chaotic, and reached a climax after Stefan Radich, the Croat leader, was assassinated on the floor of Parliament in 1928. Alexander, who had striven for harmony and tried to save democratic forms of government, proclaimed himself absolute ruler on Jan. 6, 1929, abolishing the constitution adopted in 1921. He changed the name of the country to Yugoslavia in October 1929, and governed as dictator until 1931, when he proclaimed a new constitution. Few of its provisions were carried out, however, and the king continued to control both the government and the political parties. He endeavored to establish friendly relation with neighboring countries, but he aroused bitter enmity among many elements in Yugoslavia, particularly the Croats. On Oct. 9, 1934, he arrived at Marseille on a visit of good will to France. The king entered an automobile with Jean Louis Barthou, the French foreign minister, and a few minutes later both were shot to death by an assassin.

Alexander married Princess Marie, second daughter of King Ferdinand and Queen Marie of Rumania, in June 1922. The eldest of their three sons succeeded to the throne as Peter II.

ALEXANDER, al-ig-zan′dər, **Albert Victor** (1885–1965), British public official. He was born in Weston-super-Mare, Somerset, England, on May 1, 1885. Educated in Bristol schools, he began his public life as chief clerk of higher education for the Somerset county council. About the same time he became active in the Weston Cooperative Society and espoused socialism.

Following service as an infantry captain in World War I, Alexander became nationally known in the cooperative movement. In 1922 he was elected to the House of Commons on the Cooperative party ticket and in 1924 became a junior cabinet member in the first Labour administration. In Labour's second administration, formed in 1929, he was first lord of the admiralty and was also appointed to the Privy Council.

After the government resigned in 1931, Alexander retired briefly from politics, but was reelected to Parliament as a Labour member in 1935. He returned to the Admiralty as first lord in Winston Churchill's coalition government of 1940 and served with distinction in that post throughout World War II.

When Clement Attlee formed Britain's third Labour government in 1945, Alexander was retained as first lord of the admiralty and, in 1947, was named minister of defense. His service in the last post, in which he coordinated the work of all three branches of the armed services, ended in 1950 with his elevation to the peerage. As *Viscount Alexander of Hillsborough,* he entered the House of Lords and became chancellor of the Duchy of Lancaster. He was created *Earl Alexander of Hillsborough* in 1963 and made a Knight of the Garter in 1964. He died in London on Jan. 11, 1965.

ALEXANDER, al-ig-zan′dər, **Edward Porter,** (1835–1910), American Confederate army officer who directed the artillery barrage preceding the charge of Pickett's infantry at the battle of Gettysburg. He was born at Washington, Ga., on May 26, 1835, and graduated from West Point. He helped to develop the wigwag system of flag signaling that was adopted by the U.S. Army. Alexander resigned his commission at the start of the Civil War and was named a captain of engineers in the Confederate Army. He was chief of ordnance in Gen. P.G.T. Beauregard's command and in the Army of Northern Virginia. As a colonel of artillery, he served notably at the Battle of Fredericksburg in December 1862 and at Chancellorsville in May 1863.

At Gettysburg in 1863, Alexander commanded the artillery in Gen. James Longstreet's corps. At 1 P.M. on July 3, the third day of the battle, more than 100 of his cannon aligned on Seminary Ridge began a heavy bombardment to weaken the Union lines on Cemetery Ridge in preparation for the charge of Gen. George E. Pickett's infantry. Great damage was done, but Alexander's ammunition ran low, and his fire slackened before it could be fully effective. Pickett's charge was beaten back. Alexander was made a brigadier general in February 1864.

After the war he taught engineering at the University of South Carolina and was president of the Columbia Oil Company and of the Georgia Railroad and Banking Company. In the 1890's he was a rice planter on islands off the South Carolina coast. He wrote *Railway Practice* (1887) and *Military Memoirs of a Confederate* (1907). He died at Savannah, Ga., on April 28, 1910.

ALEXANDER, al-ig-zan'dər, **Grover Cleveland** (1887–1950), American baseball player, who shared with Christy Mathewson the National League record for victories by a pitcher, with 373. He was born in St. Paul, Nebr., on Feb. 26, 1887. A 6-foot 1-inch farm boy, he was acquired by the Philadelphia Phillies for $750. The big righthander pitched four consecutive shutouts while winning 28 games in 1911, his first year in the majors.

Alexander reached his peak in 1915–1917, winning 94 games in those three years and setting major league records with four one-hit games in 1915 and 16 shutouts in 1916. In December 1917 he was traded to the Chicago Cubs, where he remained until he was sold to St. Louis shortly after the beginning of the 1926 season. He pitched for the Cardinals through 1929 and ended his baseball career in 1930 with the Phillies.

In the 1926 World Series between the Cardinals and the New York Yankees, Alexander, after winning two games for the Cards, was called in with the bases loaded in the 7th inning of the deciding game and struck out slugger Tony Lazzeri. He added two more hitless innings to win the first series for St. Louis. Alexander, or "Old Pete" as he was called, pitched in 696 games and established National League records for complete games (437) and shutouts (90). He was elected to the National Baseball Hall of Fame in 1938. He died at St. Paul, Neb., on Nov. 4, 1950.

BILL BRADDOCK
New York "Times"

ALEXANDER, al-ig-zan'dər, **Harold,** EARL ALEXANDER OF TUNIS (1891–1969), British field marshal, who was one of the most successful commanders on either side in World War II. With his military skill he possessed a charm and a diplomatic flair that made him the British general whom Britain's allies liked best.

He was born *Harold Rupert Leofric George Alexander* in County Tyrone, Ireland, on Dec. 10, 1891. In World War I he served with distinction as a battalion officer in the Irish Guards.

His service in World War II began with involvement in two withdrawals. As commander of the 1st corps in France in 1940, he conducted the final stages of the evacuation of the beaches at Dunkirk and was the last man to embark. His next field assignment was to direct the fighting retreat of the British in Burma before the first onrush of the Japanese in the spring of 1942. His discharge of these duties enhanced his reputation for coolness under fire.

In the summer of 1942, Prime Minister Winston Churchill appointed Alexander commander in chief of Britain's Middle East Command. At the same time he named Lt. Gen. Bernard L. Montgomery (later field marshal) to command the British Eighth Army. Britain's fortunes in the Middle East were low. German Field Marshal Erwin Rommel had beaten the Eighth Army earlier that summer and almost won Egypt, being stopped at El Alamein only 60 miles (95.5 km) from Alexandria.

The appointment of Alexander and Montgomery was a turning point in the desert campaign. The combination of Alexander the impresario and supreme commander and Montgomery the tactical commander in the field became legendary in the next 15 months of continuous victory. After a historic triumph at El Alamein in November 1942, they pursued the German-Italian forces across North Africa and in May 1943 met Gen. Dwight D. Eisenhower's Anglo-American army coming from the west. At Tunis the Axis forces were finally destroyed or taken.

Alexander next commanded the Fifteenth Army Group (British Eighth and U.S. Fifth armies) in the invasion of the Italian mainland. Many Americans hoped that he would be chosen also to command the British element in the invasion of northwest Europe in 1944. Churchill chose the more eccentric Montgomery instead.

Alexander continued in charge of the Allied Armies Italy (AAI), as the expanded Fifteenth Army Group (with British, American, Commonwealth, French, and Polish elements) had been renamed. Alexander's talents made him an ideal commander of such a complex army. He was made a field marshal in 1944. For the later stages of the Italian campaign he became supreme commander in the Mediterranean theater.

After the war Alexander held two civilian appointments with distinction. From 1946 to 1952 he was a popular governor general of Canada, and he was minister of defence in the Conservative government of Britain from 1952 to 1954. He was created 1st Viscount Alexander of Tunis in 1946 and 1st Earl in 1952. He died at Slough, Buckinghamshire, on June 16, 1969.

The names of Alexander and Montgomery are inevitably coupled in the story of World War II. Alexander's charm and his avoidance of public controversy, contrasted with Montgomery's often provocative egoism, have led to prejudiced judgments of their respective contributions to their joint victories. Alexander excelled as an army group or theater commander, with political duties in directing allies of various nations. Montgomery had the tactical touch, the understanding of men, and the ruthlessness to win battles.

FRED MAJDALANY
Author of "The Battle of El Alamein"

ALEXANDER, al-ig-zan'dər, **James** (1691–1756), American colonial lawyer who defended the patriot printer John Peter Zenger (q.v.). Alexander, born in Scotland, was heir to the earldom of Stirling. In 1715 he fought for the Stuart pretender to the English throne, and he fled to America when the insurrection failed. In the same year, Alexander was appointed surveyor-general of New Jersey and held other high offices in New Jersey and New York. Meanwhile he established himself as a prominent lawyer and colonial patriot. When Zenger was imprisoned for seditious libel in 1734, Alexander volunteered to defend him, but was disbarred at the trial for attacking the credentials of the judges. He returned to his profession two years later. Alexander died at Albany, N.Y., on April 2, 1756.

ALEXANDER, al-ig-zan'dər, **John White** (1856–1915), American painter, who is best known for his portraits of eminent people of his time.

Alexander was born in Allegheny (now part of Pittsburgh), Pa., on Oct. 7, 1856. He began his career as a magazine illustrator. After studying art in Germany and Italy, he lived in Paris for 11 years, returning to the United States in 1901. In addition to easel paintings, he painted murals for the Library of Congress and for the Carnegie Institute in Pittsburgh. One of his best-known portraits, of Walt Whitman, is in the Metropolitan Museum in New York City. He died at New York City on May 31, 1915.

ALEXANDER, al-ig-zan′dər, **Samuel** (1859–1938), British philosopher, who developed a neo-realistic system of metaphysics. He was born in Sydney, Australia, on Jan. 6, 1859. He studied at the University of Melbourne and at Balliol College, Oxford, where he won a prize for his essay *Moral Order and Progress* (1889). His interest in the nature of knowledge led him to go in 1890 to Germany, where he studied psychology with Hugo Münsterberg. From 1893 until his retirement in 1924 he taught in Manchester, England, at Owens College (now the University of Manchester). He died at Manchester on Sept. 13, 1938.

Alexander's most important work is *Space, Time, and Deity* (1920), delivered as lectures in 1916–1918 at the University of Glasgow. The metaphysical system he develops in this book distinguishes three levels of being—matter, life, and mind—each with an inherent urge toward the next higher level of development. The level of development toward which mind dimly gropes is "deity" in his system.

Alexander developed an aesthetic theory in *Beauty and Other Forms of Value* (1933). Among his other works were *Locke* (1908), *Spinoza and Time* (1921), and *Art and the Material* (1925).

ALEXANDER, al-ig-zan′dər, **William** (1726–1783), American general in the Revolutionary War. He was born in New York City, the son of James Alexander, who claimed descent from the Scottish earls of Stirling. The title had become extinct on the death of the 5th earl in 1739. Alexander went to England in 1756 to press his claim to the title. A jury at Edinburgh supported the claim, but its decision was reversed by the House of Lords. Nevertheless, Alexander called himself "Lord Stirling" all his life. Modern historians regard his claim as legitimate.

Alexander was commissioned a brigadier general in the Continental army in 1776. He played a leading part in the Battle of Long Island on Aug. 27, 1776, and was captured. He soon was exchanged and rejoined Washington's army. At Trenton on Dec. 26, 1776, he defeated a Hessian brigade, and later, at Scotch Plains, he blocked Cornwallis' advance. He fought in the battles of Brandywine and Germantown near Philadelphia and at the Battle of Monmouth in New Jersey. In 1781 he commanded the northern division of the American army, with headquarters at Albany, N.Y. He died there on Jan. 15, 1783. After his death Washington, in a letter to Lady Stirling, wrote in praise of his generalship.

ALEXANDER, al-ig-zan′dar, **Sir William** (1567?–1640), Scottish writer and courtier, to whom in 1621 all of then-known Canada was granted by royal decree. Born a commoner, he won recognition as a scholar, poet, and playwright, and earned royal favor. Under James I, he was knighted (1608), given charge of dispensing royal patronage (1614), and granted New Scotland, whose territory included present-day Nova Scotia and New Brunswick (1621). Charles I made him secretary of state for Scotland for life (1626) and created him *Earl of Stirling* and *Viscount Canada* (1633). Despite these and other favors, he died insolvent in London on Sept. 12, 1640. Alexander's poetry and plays had a limited audience for about a century after his death.

ALEXANDER, Romance of, al-ig-zan′dər, a medieval romance cycle based on the account of Alexander the Great's invasion of Asia. The original account was written in Greek about 200 A.D. by a historian now called the Pseudo-Calisthenes. It was translated into Latin about 300 A.D. by Julius Valerius and again about 950 by Leo, archpriest of Naples. These versions served as the basis of the cycle in most European languages. Among the best-known versions are the French *Roman d'Alexandre* (about 1100) and the Middle English *Kyng Alisaunder* (about 1275).

ALEXANDER ARCHIPELAGO, al-ig-zan′dər, an island group in Alaska, situated off the coast of the southeastern part of the territory, and extending from 54° 40′ to 58° 25′ north latitude. Of its 1,100 islands, the major ones are Admiralty, Baranof (on which Sitka is situated), Chichagof, Kuiu, Kupreanof, Prince of Wales, and Revillagigedo. The islands, which are summits of a submerged mountain range, are lofty, with steep cliffs rising from the sea.

ALEXANDER CITY, al-ig-zan′dər, a trading and industrial city located in east-central Alabama, in Tallapoosa county. It is situated 45 miles (72 km) northeast of Montgomery, the state capital. Leading manufactures are textile, cast-iron, and lumber products. Nearby are Martin Lake and Horseshoe Bend National Military Park. Alexander City, known as Youngville when first settled (approximately 1835), was incorporated and renamed in 1873. Government is by mayor-council. Population: 15,008.

ALEXANDER ISLAND, al-ig-zan′dər, in Antarctica, lies off the western side of the Antarctic Peninsula, at the peninsula's base. It is separated from the peninsula by George VI Sound. The island is roughly J-shaped, measuring about 235 miles by 150 miles. It is uninhabited.

The island was discovered in 1821 by the Russian explorer Fabian von Bellingshausen, who named it for the Russian emperor Alexander I. It was proved to be an island in 1940 by a U.S. expedition under Finn Ronne.

ALEXANDER NEVSKY (1220–1263), al-ig-zan′-dər nev′skē, a Russian national hero, was canonized a saint of the Russian Orthodox Church in 1547. Alexander was born in Vladimir, Russia, in 1220. He was the son of Prince Yaroslav II of Novgorod and was the great-grandson of Vladimir Monomachus, grand duke of Kiev. He became prince of Novgorod in 1236 and grand duke of Kiev and Novgorod after his father's death in 1246. In 1252 he was chosen by the Mongol overlords to replace his brother Andrei, who had revolted against Mongol rule, as grand duke of Vladimir.

Although he was generally a successful administrator, Alexander's fame rests mostly on his early military victories. In the 1230's Russia was threatened on the north and west by the Teutonic knights and the Swedes and on the south and east by the Mongols. Anticipating the danger from the north, Alexander was able to lead his forces to a great victory over the Swedes at the Neva River, near present-day Leningrad, on July 15, 1240. He took the name *Nevsky* ("of the Neva") after the battle. The victory strained his relations with the boyars (nobles), who were trying to limit the power of the princes, and

Alexander was forced to move temporarily to Pereyaslavl, southeast of Kiev.

In 1241 the people of Novgorod recalled Alexander to help them repel an invasion of the Teutonic knights. In the winter of 1242, Alexander won another important victory, driving back the invaders in a historic battle on the ice of Lake Peipus, in Estonia. The victory was the subject of a distinguished motion picture, *Alexander Nevsky*, directed by Sergei Eisenstein and produced in 1938. Sergei Prokofiev wrote the music for the film and in the following year expanded the score into a cantata, also entitled *Alexander Nevsky*.

Alexander led several later expeditions against the Swedes but devoted most of his time to the administration of his realm. He submitted to the demands of the Mongol overlords and so averted the continual devastating attacks that the Russians had been subjected to previously. Alexander's cooperation with the Mongols caused deep resentment among the people of Novgorod, and although he has become a national hero, his policies have been sharply criticized by some historians. He died at Gorodets, on the upper Volga River, in November 1263.

ALEXANDER OF APHRODISIAS, al-ig-zan'dər, af-rō-diz'ē-əs, was a Greek philosopher and commentator on Aristotle, who headed the Lyceum in Athens about 200 A.D. He was a native of Aphrodisias in Caria, now part of Turkey, and a student of Aristocles of Messene.

Still extant are his commentaries on Aristotle's *Prior Analytics, Topics, Meteorologica, De sensu,* and *Metaphysics.* His original works include *On Fate,* an argument against the Stoic doctrine of necessity, and *On The Soul,* in which he argues that human reason is inseparable from the body. The Alexandrist philosophers of the early Renaissance based their opposition to the Christian doctrine of personal immortality on the latter book.

ALEXANDER OF HALES, al-ig-zan'dər, hālz (died 1245), English theologian and a leading scholastic philosopher. He was born in Hales, Gloucestershire, and held several church offices before going to Paris to study theology and metaphysics. Appointed professor of theology at Paris, he taught there until 1238. He was a member of the Franciscan order from 1222. He died on Aug. 21, 1245.

Alexander was one of the first to attempt to correlate Augustinian theology with the ideas of Aristotle and the Arab commentators. In collaboration with others he produced the *Summa theologiae,* a compendium of theological knowledge, said to have influenced St. Thomas Aquinas.

ALEXANDER OF TUNIS. See ALEXANDER, HAROLD.

ALEXANDER SEVERUS, al-ig-zan'dər sə-vēr'əs, **Marcus Aurelius** (208?–235), Roman emperor. Originally named *Alexianus Bassianus,* he was born in Phoenicia, the son of Gessius Marcianus. His mother was Julia Mamaea, niece of Julia Domna, the wife of Emperor Septimius Severus. Alexander was admirably educated by his mother, and in 221 was adopted and made caesar by his cousin, Emperor Heliogabalus, at the instigation of their common grandmother, Julia Maesa. When Heliogabalus was murdered by the Prae-

torian Guard, Alexander became emperor, on March 11, 222.

For the first nine years of his reign, the government was controlled in large part first by his grandmother and then by his mother. Reforms were undertaken, and arts and letters were encouraged. The Senate's prestige was enhanced, but it received little real power, and the Praetorian Guard remained strong. In 228 the Praetorians murdered their prefect, Ulpian, chief adviser to the emperor.

In 231, Alexander went to Antioch to repel an invasion of Mesopotamia by Ardashir I, founder of the Sassanian dynasty of Persia. The campaign was indecisive, but Mesopotamia was recovered and, in 233, the emperor returned to Rome and celebrated a triumph. Meanwhile, the Alamanni were attacking along the Rhine, and Alexander left Rome to deal with the new threat. His attempt to purchase peace angered the soldiers, who murdered him near Mainz, Germany, in March 235, and elevated Maximinus as his successor.

ALEXANDER THE GREAT (356–323 B.C.), al-igzan'dər, was king of Macedon and the greatest general in ancient times. By the age of 32 he had founded an empire stretching from the Adriatic Sea to India. He was born in Pella, Macedon, in 356 B.C., the son of King Philip II of Macedon. His mother was Olympias, an Epirote princess.

Mastery of Greece. Alexander was magnetic, intensely willful, mystical in thought, while practical in action. As a pupil of Aristotle he learned the use of scientific investigation, became interested in doctoring the sick, and deeply attached to Greek tradition—having been told that Heracles and Achilles were his ancestors.

At 16, serving as regent during his father's absence in Byzantium, he subdued a rising of Illyrian tribes by attacking them. Put in command of the select Companion cavalry at 18, he spearheaded his father's victory at Chaeronea over the degenerating Greek city-states, which had been roused to resistance by the oratory of Demosthenes. A year later he was an exile, after Philip cast off his mother, Olympias.

At the age of 20 he was placed on the throne of Macedon (336 B.C.) as Alexander III by the army commanders after the assassination of Philip by unidentified enemies. In neither assassination nor election did Alexander have a hand.

Alexander faced enemies on all sides. Philip's death encouraged the tribal Thracians and Illyrians to hostility in the north, and at the same time it relieved the fears of the Greek cities in the south. When Alexander moved north, crossing the Danube to confront the savage Celts, the city of Thebes rebelled in the south. Turning south by forced marches, the Macedonians fought their way into Thebes and destroyed the city, except for its temple and the house of Pindar. Having first shown remarkable mildness to the barbarians, Alexander startled Greece by the severity of his reaction against Thebes. He was then, as Philip had been, captain-general of the Hellenes, head of the Panhellenic League. He wished to treat the Greeks as free allies, but he had no friends among them. Sparta, strengthened by Persian gold, remained antagonistic.

But the greatest danger to Alexander lay in the Persian empire, which stretched from the Dardanelles to the Indian Punjab and north into the nomadic steppes. This empire comprised loose

538

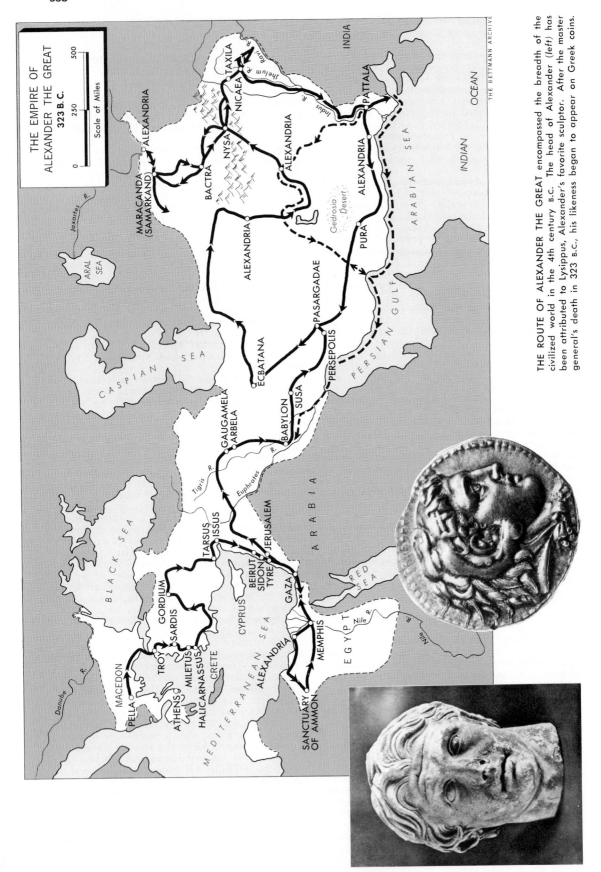

THE EMPIRE OF
ALEXANDER THE GREAT
323 B.C.

Scale of Miles
0   250   500

THE ROUTE OF ALEXANDER THE GREAT encompassed the breadth of the civilized world in the 4th century B.C. The head of Alexander (left) has been attributed to Lysippus, Alexander's favorite sculptor. After the master general's death in 323 B.C., his likeness began to appear on Greek coins.

THE BETTMANN ARCHIVE

INDIA

INDIAN
OCEAN

ARABIAN
SEA

TAXILA

NICAEA

Jhelum R.

Indus R.

PATTALA

ALEXANDRIA

NYSA

BACTRA

ALEXANDRIA

MARACANDA
(SAMARKAND)

Jaxartes R.

ARAL
SEA

ALEXANDRIA

Gedrosia
Desert

PURA

ALEXANDRIA

PASARGADAE

ECBATANA

PERSEPOLIS

PERSIAN GULF

CASPIAN
SEA

SUSA

BABYLON

GAUGAMELA
ARBELA

Tigris R.

Euphrates R.

ARABIA

JERUSALEM

TARSUS
ISSUS

GORDIUM

SARDIS

BEIRUT
SIDON
TYRE

GAZA

CYPRUS

RED
SEA

Nile R.

EGYPT

MEMPHIS

ALEXANDRIA

MEDITERRANEAN SEA

CRETE

HALICARNASSUS

MILETUS

ATHENS

TROY

PELLA

MACEDON

BLACK SEA

Danube R.

SANCTUARY
OF AMMON

Nile R.

aggregations of peoples, governed by satraps and held together only by the authority of its Great King (Darius III) and by its tight control of the sea and of the continental trade routes, which fed its well-managed finances. Alexander, though, had no semblance of a fleet. He had 70 talents in his treasury and owed 1,300. He did not make the decision to invade Persia because Philip and his commanders already had made it—ostensibly as revenge for past Persian aggressions and to free the Greek cities of the Asia Minor seaboard, but more realistically to restore the weak Macedonian economy.

Conquest of Asia Minor. In the spring of 334 B.C., Alexander crossed the Dardanelles. He did not believe himself to be, as legend has it, a god-power destined to rule the world. This inexperienced ruler was leading 35,000 veterans, who had no desire to leave their homeland, against great odds in manpower and wealth. His expedition had to supply and to pay itself as it went. Philip's genius for organization had given it able intelligence, surveyors, and engineers. Alexander added architects, scholars, naturalists, and artists. His first act in Asia was to hold a festival at the site of Troy, where he figuratively took for himself Achilles' ancient shield as a symbol of the new Greek "holy war" against Asia.

At the meeting with local Persian forces on the river Granicus, Alexander nearly lost his life through recklessness. But the defeat of the Asian horsemen and the capture of their Greek mercenaries opened the Ionian Greek ports and Sardis (334 B.C.). Only Miletus was defended by its imperial garrison. Alexander released the Ionian cities to do as they liked. They proceeded to rid themselves of the Persian-imposed tyrants and of taxation without giving any material aid to the Macedonian expedition. Alexander's novel idea was to treat such communities not as subjects but as partners in his rule. Turning inland to the Phrygian highlands, he took the submission of the mountain peoples in the same way. At Gordium he untied the Gordian knot on the enshrined chariot. He did not cut it with his sword, but pulled out the peg hiding the loose end of the knot.

Until then Alexander had followed closely the advice of his senior commanders: Antipater, who was left as viceroy in Macedon, and Parmenion. Now he overruled Parmenion and started a march around the Mediterranean's end to capture the bases of the Persian allied fleet, which cut him off from his own base in Macedon-Greece. By an unexpected night march, the expedition got through the gorge known as the Cilician Gate, leading to the fertile Syrian coast, where the expedition almost met its end. On the narrow coastal road near the village of Issus (333 B.C.) the Great King, Darius III, with a formidable field army, appeared in the rear of the Macedonians, effectively cutting them off by land as well as the sea. Caught in this manner, Alexander turned back at night, meeting the advance of the pursuing Persians at daybreak in the narrow valley of the river Pinarus.

The Macedonian army was distinguished for its mobility, the steadiness of the farmer-phalanxmen, and the impetus in attack of its heavy cavalry, composed of the Companions (Macedonian nobles) and Thessalians. It had superb officers, and now it had Alexander's alert, unquenchable determination to lead it. While Parmenion and the left flank fought, actually, in the

wash of the sea, Alexander worked his shock cavalry across the mountain slope on the right and came headlong down behind the Persian line. Darius could not stand the onslaught and fled in his chariot. His flight took the heart out of his troops, and the savage Macedonian pursuit scattered the army of the Great King so that it never assembled again. At Damascus the Persian army's treasure and supply train were captured, giving Alexander wealth for the first time. The Battle of Issus stunned the Mediterranean coast. The Phoenician port of Sidon welcomed the Macedonians.

Fall of the Levant and Egypt. Militarily, Alexander's greatest feat was the siege of Tyre (332 B.C.). Situated a quarter of a mile out in the sea, Tyre resisted him for seven months, trusting in its invulnerability. Macedonian engineers reached it by constructing the still extant mole. The capture was effected by warships, mostly from Sidon, that now served Alexander. When the Persian-commanded fleet had disintegrated because the Phoenician, Cypriote, and Egyptian crews returned to their native ports, Alexander controlled the eastern Mediterranean. After being wounded at the siege of Gaza, he could rest himself and his men in Egypt, which accepted him readily as a pharaoh—so he was proclaimed by the sacred oracle of Ammon at Siwa—since he was more akin to them than was the Great King.

In the winter of 332–331 B.C. differences arose between Alexander and Parmenion, his marshal, the spokesman for the Macedonian nationalist group of the army. All the objectives of Philip's Panhellenic plan had been gained, miraculously, and were exceeded. The historic cultural axis between Egypt and Greece had been restored. Darius, whose family had been captured at Issus, offered tempting terms of bullion payment and a frontier on the Euphrates for peace. Parmenion, reputedly, said that he would accept the peace if he were Alexander. "And so would I," Alexander—as the tale goes—answered, "if I were Parmenion." As he had been unwilling to retreat in Asia Minor with the enemy fleet a menace at sea, so he would not rest his arms on the Nile in the face of the Persian armies.

After the Battle of Issus, Alexander seems to have formed the idea that he could drive the Great King from his empire without fighting the peoples of Persia. If Greeks could be fused with Egyptians, why not Asians with Greeks? Aristotle never had believed possible such a *homonoia* (common humanity) in which civilized people would merge with barbarians. Henceforth it was to be Alexander's objective.

Final Destruction of the Persian Empire. As a first step toward this world order, Alexander founded his new capital, Alexandria, at a mouth of the Nile, where it was to become a trade terminal. There would be more than 60 Alexandrias begun by his engineers at intersections of trade routes. For he marched eastward now with a moving settlement of technicians and allied peoples, sending home all war-weary Greek and Macedonian units as fresh drafts reached him along his lengthening line of communications. With this altered army he crossed the Tigris to defeat and to dissipate the full levy of the Persian horde (331 B.C.) on the plains at Gaugamela (Arbela). Thereafter the Asian levies, loyal to the monarchy rather than to Darius, a usurper, withdrew to their distant homelands. Alexander's pursuit was pressed to the limit of endurance, down the rivers to Babylon, up to the second capital at Susa, and over the mountains to the sacred city of Persepolis, which was burned after his entrance either accidentally or to impress the Persians by destroying the Great King's sanctuary. In Susa and Persepolis his headlong pursuit won him the imperial treasure of some 180,000 talents in bullion and coin—so fabulous an amount that he demonetized the gold to equate it with the smaller Graeco-Macedonian silver coinage. Thrusting through the winter-bound mountains to the third capital, Ecbatana (Hamadan), Alexander tracked the fugitive Darius across the desert toward the Caspian Sea, where, with only 500 Macedonians keeping pace with him, he found Darius dead, assassinated by angered officials (330 B.C.).

Alexander's Cosmopolitanism. At this point Alexander had to deal with the problem of administering this new kind of empire. Originally king of Macedon and generalissimo of the Hellenes, he became the godlike pharaoh of Egypt and then Great King of Asia. His solution to the problem of governing was to leave unchanged the Persian land system and satrapy (governor) control. Over Babylon—which he intended to be his land capital, as Alexandria was to be the capital on the sea—he placed Mazai, the Persian noble, who had led the Persians at Gaugamela. He separated civil from military and financial administrations, mingling Asian with Macedonian officials, except in finances. This treatment of Asians as equals increasingly angered the Macedonian core of the army.

Alexander eagerly assimilated the religious mysticism of the Nile and of Magian Persia. Not only did he protect these religions, but also as sole ruler, he necessarily assumed the semidivine aspect of an Asian despot, wearing Persian attire at ceremonies and accepting prostration in his presence.

With much justice his own officers believed that Alexander no longer was acting as king of Macedon in conquered territory. Inevitably his concept of *homonoia* clashed with the stubborn nationalist sentiment of the Macedonians. There was a conspiracy to kill him, which resulted in his execution of Philotas, commander of the Companion cavalry, of the veteran Parmenion, father of Philotas, and of Callisthenes, a philosopher of Aristotle's school, who opposed the act of prostration.

East to India. This ideological cleavage widened as Alexander insisted on pressing into mountainous eastern Persia (329 B.C.) to end the satrap's resistance there. In so doing he ventured beyond Greek geographical knowledge. The army felt itself lost in the limbo of the world, uncertain whether it was nearing the Maeotis (Azov) or the Aral seas. The army met bitter, nationalistic resistance from the mountain peoples of what is now Afghanistan. It followed Alexander across an unknown river, the Jaxartes (Syr Darya), to meet the attack of Scythian nomads. More than two years were needed to subdue these eastern ranges, which were terrible in winter. Incredibly, while subduing them, Alexander maintained his communications, built a new chain of cities (the farthest at the modern cities of Samarqand and Khujand), and colonized his conquest. He also married Rushanak (Roxane), daughter of an enemy leader.

Hearing of the river Indus, he drove the army eastward across the Hindu Kush (327 B.C.). His army had understood the need to consolidate all the Persian dominion, but believed this new venture to be a madman's act. Actually, Alexander thought that he was entering the last peninsula of the earth: that beyond it lay the Ocean of the East. He reached the Indus with a growing following, a moving state of allied peoples and their families, while his remaining Macedonians laid down pontoon bridges, shored up roads over immense ranges, and fought battles when necessary. Passing from friendly country around Taxila (near Attock), they encountered the hostile Paurava rajah at the Jhelum River, where the Macedonian infantry had to fight against armored elephants for the first time. Alexander and his equestrian spearhead could not approach the elephants, which terrified the horses. This shook the Macedonian veterans, who mutinied en masse at the river Ravi. Deeply angered, because he believed the end of land lay not far off, at Ocean, Alexander was obliged to retreat (326 B.C.).

Returning, however, he forced his Macedonians to explore, to survey, and to build terminals along the water route down the Jhelum and the Indus to the coast. Badly exhausted by insomnia, wounds, and sickness, Alexander was critically injured in ferocious fighting against the Brahmanic peoples at the junction of the rivers. After venturing into the Indian Ocean, he made the famous journey over the Gedrosia Desert back to Babylon, while the fleet under Nearchus followed by sea. He died at Babylon, not so much from fever as from exhausted vitality. He was not yet 33 years old.

Goals and Achievements. To the end, Alexander drove himself at the task of creating a commonwealth of peoples by reorganizing his army as an allied police force, by planting colonies along the trade routes, and by commanding mass intermarriages between his Macedonians and Asians, in which he himself set the example. To Greek emissaries the young king seemed to have the attributes of a god. Eratosthenes said, "He is the reconciler of the world, pouring human beings together like wine in a loving cup."

Alexander's attempt to fuse the populations of East and West failed. Since there was no living son to succeed him, his dominion was administered, as far as the Indus, by his leading commanders: Craterus in Macedon and Greece, Ptolemy in Egypt, Seleucus along the Tigris–Mediterranean axis. These portions, which came into conflict, developed into empires: Antigonid, Seleucid, Bactrian, Ptolemaic.

But Alexander had succeeded in establishing Greek as the universal language of the East. Greek culture followed in his train and penetrated far into Asia. The trade network, the new ports, and many Alexandrias thrived. These factors gave birth to the enlightened Hellenistic age (with a unity of culture hardly equaled today), prepared the way for Roman rule, and ultimately assisted the spread of Christianity as a world religion outward from the Mediterranean's shore.

No other man has been claimed—in legends—by so many nations. Egyptian fable makes him a god. Arabo-Persian tradition represents *Iskander* as a hero-saint. Israelite lore joins him to the house of David as a precursor of the Messiah. Even Ethiopian hagiology preserves his memory as a saint. Christian tales of the medieval and Renaissance periods relate how *Alixandre le Grant* searched for paradise.

HAROLD LAMB, *Author of "Alexander of Macedon"*

Bibliography

Greek and Latin sources for Alexander's life are published in English translation in the Loeb Classical Library (Harvard Univ. Press) as follows: Arrian, *History of Alexander—Indica,* 2 vols.; Curtius, Quintus, *History of Alexander,* 2 vols.; Plutarch, *Parallel Lives,* vol. 8; Strabo, *Geography,* 8 vols.

Ashley, James R., *The Macedonian Empire: The Era of Warfare under Philip II and Alexander the Great, 359–323 B.C.* (McFarland 1998).

Bosworth, A. B., *Conquest and Empire: The Reign of Alexander the Great* (Cambridge 1988).

Hammond, N. G., *Three Historians of Alexander the Great* (Cambridge 1984).

Stoneman, Richard, *Alexander the Great* (Routledge 1997).

ALEXANDRA

ALEXANDRA (1844–1925), al-ig-zan′drə, queen consort of king Edward VII of Britain. She was born in Copenhagen, Denmark, on Dec. 1, 1844, the eldest daughter of Prince Christian of Schleswig-Holstein-Sönderborg-Glücksborg, afterward King Christian IX of Denmark, and Louise, daughter of Landgrave William of Hesse-Cassel. Her full name was *Alexandra Carolina Maria Charlotte Louise Julia.* In 1862 she was betrothed to Albert Edward, prince of Wales, heir to the British throne, and they were married in St. George's Chapel, Windsor, on March 10, 1863. That same year her father became king of Denmark, and her brother George became king of Greece.

Alexandra's first child, a son, Albert Victor (who died before his parents), was born at Frogmore on Jan. 8, 1864. Two more sons, one of whom succeeded as George V, and three daughters followed.

The early years of Alexandra's married life were taken up with domestic matters, but after 1868 she began to take a more active part in British public life. Because of Queen Victoria's seclusion, Alexandra and her husband became the real leaders of social life in Britain. She made several visits to Denmark, and a visit to Russia in 1894 at the time of the death of Emperor Alexander III, husband of her sister, Dagmar (Maria Fyodorovna).

In January 1901 her husband succeeded to the British throne as Edward VII, and as queen consort Alexandra was crowned with him in Westminster Abbey on Aug. 9, 1902. Following Edward's death in 1910 and the accession of her son, as George V, she made her London home at Marlborough House. She died at Sandringham on Nov. 20, 1925, and was buried beside her husband in St. George's Chapel, Windsor.

ALEXANDRA FYODOROVNA

ALEXANDRA FYODOROVNA (1872–1918), al-ig-zan′drə fyô′də-rôv-nə, was the wife of Emperor Nicholas II of Russia. She was the daughter of Louis IV, grand duke of Hesse-Darmstadt, and Alice Maud Mary, who was a daughter of Queen Victoria. Alexandra was born in Darmstadt, Germany, on June 6, 1872, and married Nicholas in 1894, a few weeks after he had become emperor. She was dominated by the monk Rasputin, who she hoped could cure her sickly son Alexis. She and Rasputin's protégés wielded great influence over Russian governmental affairs during World War I. (See RASPUTIN, GRIGORI.) The Bolsheviks shot the royal family at Yekaterinburg (now Sverdlovsk) on July 17, 1918.

ALEXANDRETTA. See İSKENDERUN.

CARL FRANK, FROM PHOTO RESEARCHERS

ALEXANDRIA'S EL RAMLEH STATION is in Saad Zaghlul Square in the eastern quarter of the city.

ALEXANDRIA

ALEXANDRIA, al-ig-zan′drē-ə, is the chief port and second-largest city in Egypt (United Arab Republic). First called *Racondah* by the pharaohs, then *Rhacotis* by the Greeks, the city acquired its present name in 332 B.C., when its rebuilding began under Alexander the Great. The Arab name is *al-Iskandarîyah.*

The city is situated at the western extremity of the Nile delta, on a narrow strip of land sandwiched between Lake Maryut and the Mediterranean Sea. A half-mile (0.8-km)-wide isthmus provides access to the island of Pharos, once the site of a 400-foot (122-meter) lighthouse, famed as one of the seven wonders of the ancient world. On either side of the isthmus are Alexandria's two natural harbors: the West Harbor, which handles most of Egypt's commerce, and the East Harbor, used mainly by fishing boats. The West Harbor is divided by a 1,000-yard (914-meter) mole into a large outer harbor and an inner harbor lined by 2½ miles (4 km) of quays, and can accommodate vessels of up to 28-foot (8.5-meter) draft.

Economic Life. Besides being an international seaport, Alexandria has good transportation and communications links to Egypt's major urban and agricultural centers. A main highway, 124 miles (200 km) long, connects it directly with Cairo through the Libyan desert, and a commercial road through the delta links it with Lower Egypt's main towns on the way to Cairo. A civil airport is located south of the city. Alexandria was the financial and economic center of Egypt prior to the revolution of 1952. It remains the site of the nation's stock exchange, but its economy now depends largely on trade and tourism. The inhabitants are engaged mainly in transport of merchandise, especially cotton, grains, fruits, and vegetables; in industry, especially textiles and food processing; and in harbor work, shipping, and fishing.

Points of Interest. Traditionally a delightfully cosmopolitan center, Alexandria has lost some of this quality, but it remains one of the most populous cities on the Mediterranean and a popular summer resort. Many monuments attest to its cosmopolitanism, among them the Anglican St. Mark's Cathedral, built in 1839, and the Roman Catholic St. Catherine's Basilica, named after the saint who was martyred there by order of Emperor Maximinus. Historical sites include the 88-foot (27-meter) Pompey Pillar, dedicated to Diocletian about 297 A.D.; the catacombs of Kom al-Shakafa, al-Anfushy, Mustafa Kamel, and Shatby; the 15th century fort of Qait Bay; and the 19th century fort of Caffarelli.

The city has five museums—among them the famous Graeco-Roman Museum. There are two botanical gardens, a zoological park, and a 25,000-seat stadium. Its municipal library contains a 70,000-volume multilingual collection. Alexandria University (formerly Faruk University), established in 1942, comprises ten faculties. Alexandria is the Middle Eastern headquarters of the World Health Organization.

A focal point of the city is Midan al-Tahrir (Liberation Square), named Midan Mohammed Ali in prerevolutionary days and Place des Consuls still earlier, in the 1800's. Here on July 26, 1956, President Gamal Abdel Nasser announced the nationalization of the Suez Canal. Another prominent square is Midan Saad Zaghlul, named for the nationalist hero who founded the Wafd party. The main commercial arteries are sharia Sherif, Tewfik, and Rosette. Sharia al-Geish, a breathtaking 16-mile (26-km) seacoast drive and promenade, overlooks fine sandy beaches.

History. Ancient Racondah existed as a fishing village as early as 1500 B.C., but it gained international importance only after Alexander refounded it as Alexandria in 332 B.C. As capital of Egypt under the Ptolemies, from 304 to 30 B.C., it was the hub of commerce between the classical and the Arabian and Indian worlds. By 250 B.C. the city had become the largest urban center in the West and the vortex of the Hellenistic and Hebraic civilizations. Its museum and library complex (see ALEXANDRIAN LIBRARY) was the largest of the ancient world.

The influence of Rome was gradual, but in 80 B.C. Alexandria passed officially under Roman jurisdiction. It became the largest provincial capital of the Roman empire, with a population of 300,000 free inhabitants plus slaves. Alexandria is inextricably linked with the reign of Cleopatra. It was occupied by Julius Caesar in 47 B.C. and ruled by Mark Antony and by Octavian. The obelisks now standing in parks in London and New York once adorned Cleopatra's Caesareum.

Under the Byzantine empire, Alexandria was a center of Christianity and a patriarchate. It was still relatively prosperous when, after a 14-month siege, it fell to the Arabs in 646 A.D. Thereafter the city declined to a mere relic of its glorious past.

Alexandria's comeback began when Napoleon captured it in 1798. In 1801, after the British destroyed the French fleet at Abukir (Aboukir), the city was occupied by Britain. The British remained influential in Alexandria, but its modern renaissance is credited to the Egyptian Pasha Mohammed Ali (ruled 1805–1848), who reopened a freshwater canal from the Nile. Although the center of gravity shifted to Cairo in the late 1800's, Alexandria, as Egypt's chief port, continued to be strategically and commercially important, especially during both world wars and after. Population: 3,328,196 (1997 est.).

ALFRED G. GERTEINY, *University of Bridgeport*

ALEXANDRIA, al-ig-zan′drē-ə, a city in eastern Indiana, in Madison county, on Pipe Creek, 50 miles (80 km) by road northeast of Indianapolis. It is situated in an agricultural region with extensive limestone deposits. The limestone is used in making rock wool, an insulation material, which is Alexandria's chief product. The city was settled in 1834 and is governed by a mayor and council. Population: 6,260.

ALEXANDRIA, al-ig-zan′drē-ə, in central Louisiana, a city on the Red River, 110 miles (177 km) by road northwest of Baton Rouge. It is the seat of Rapides Parish (county) and the commercial and industrial center of a farm and forest region. From the hill country and alluvial bottomlands around the city come lumber, cotton, and sugarcane for Alexandria's processing industries. The city also has oil refineries and manufactures brick, tile roofing, road machinery, turpentine, tar, valves, pipe fittings, and concrete products.

Alexandria is called the "Convention City" because many large conventions use the facilities provided in the city hall and Coliseum. Among the other important buildings are St. Francis Xavier Cathedral (Roman Catholic), St. James Episcopal Church, and the State Headquarters Building of the Baptist Church, The public park system includes a zoo. The Alexandria Campus of Louisiana State University is situated 10 miles (16 km) south of the city, and tactical jet fighters operate from England Air Force Base, 6 miles (10 km) northwest of Alexandria.

The city is situated at a point on the Red River where rapids once obstructed navigation. In the 1720s the French built a fort to guard the portage around the rapids. Alexandria was laid out in 1805 by Alexander Fulton, a wealthy landowner and merchant, who named it for his daughter. A thriving river trade promoted the community's prosperity, and Alexandria was chartered as a city in 1832. During the Civil War, Union forces captured Alexandria and tore down a number of its buildings to be used for material to dam the river, so that they could float their gunboats over the rapids. Later they set fire to the city. Alexandria was rebuilt after the war, and the rapids were eliminated. The city has a commission-council type of government. Population: 46,342.

ALEXANDRIA, al-ig-zan′drē-ə, a city located in west-central Minnesota and the seat of Douglas county. It is 130 miles (210 km) by road northwest of Minneapolis. The city has some light industry, but is primarily a trading center for a diversified farming and resort area. The countryside is dotted with small lakes whose recreational facilities draw tourists to Alexandria. Lake Carlos State Park is a few miles north of the city.

On exhibit at the Runestone Museum in Alexandria is a boulder with runic inscriptions describing a Viking exploration of this area in 1362. Found in 1898, it is called the Kensington Rune Stone because it came from a farm near Kensington, Minn., approximately 20 miles (30 km) from Alexandria. The authenticity of the inscriptions is doubtful. (See KENSINGTON RUNE STONE.)

Alexandria was settled in 1858 on land that was once part of Ojibwa and Sioux camping grounds. It was originally incorporated as a township in 1866 and was named for Alexander Kinkead, an early pioneer. Population: 8,820.

ALEXANDRIA, al-ig-zan′drē-ə, an unincorporated place in southeastern Ontario, Canada, 55 miles (88 km) east of Ottawa. It is a retail and manufacturing center and the seat of a Roman Catholic diocese. Its many ecclesiastical buildings include St. Finnan's Cathedral. Alexandria was founded in 1819 by Alexander MacDonnell, the first Roman Catholic bishop of Upper Canada. It was settled by Scottish families, but most of the inhabitants now are of French extraction. Incorporated as a town in 1903, Alexandria was merged into the new township of North Glengarry in 1998.

ALEXANDRIA, al-ig-zan′drē-ə, a residential city in Virginia, 6 miles (9.5 km) south of Washington, D.C. It is an independent city, with no county affiliation. Its 15 square miles (38 sq km) are bounded by Arlington County (north), the Potomac River (east), and Fairfax County (south and west). In the 18th century the town was a sizable port, and today oceangoing ships may dock. The "Old Port" section is now a residential area with many fine houses, old and new. But Alexandria is part of the Washington metropolitan complex, and high-rise apartment houses are being built.

The city has a growing number of industries. Principal manufactures are fertilizers, machinery, furniture, chemicals, and cinder blocks. There are also electronics and scientific research establishments.

Alexandria has a number of historic cultural and educational institutions. Alexandria Academy, now the property of the city school board, was established in 1785 and George Washington was a trustee. Two of his nephews attended the school. The Episcopal High School, begun in 1839, is a private school for boys. The Episcopal Theological Seminary was founded in 1823. Alexandria Library began as a subscription library in 1794 and became a public library in 1937. It is especially proud of its Virginiana collection. The *Alexandria Gazette*, founded in 1784, was one of the oldest continuously published daily newspapers in the United States.

The city has many places of historic interest. The Carlyle House was occupied by Gen. Edward Braddock in 1755 before his expedition against the French and Indians. In this house five royal governors met to propose the first tax on the American colonies. Gadsby's Tavern was frequented by Washington and his friends, who celebrated his last birthday here in 1799, the year he died. There are two colonial churches—the Presbyterian Meeting House, begun in 1774, and Christ Church, where Washington was a vestryman. Robert E. Lee also worshiped at Christ Church. The Stabler Leadbeater Apothecary Shop is one of the oldest in the United States.

In 1730 Scottish tobacco exporters built a warehouse on Oronoco Creek. The small settlement that developed was called Belhaven. In 1748 the Virginia House of Burgesses passed an act for the establishment of a town, and Alexandria was begun the next year. The land was owned then by the Alexander family but had been part of land grants made to others in 1654 and 1669. When the District of Columbia was created in 1791, Alexandria was included in its boundaries. It was returned to the state of Virginia as a "free city" by act of Congress in 1846. Population: 128,283.

ELLEN COOLIDGE BURKE
Alexandria Library

ALEXANDRIAN AGE, al-ig-zan′drē-ən, the period of Greek literature and learning beginning about 300 B.C. and centered at Alexandria, Egypt. The Alexandrian age began under the Ptolemy dynasty in Egypt (323–30 B.C.), continued under Roman supremacy until the 4th century A.D., and endured, in a weaker form, to 641, when Alexandria fell to the Arabs.

In the distribution of the empire of Alexander the Great in 323 B.C., Egypt came under the governorship of Ptolemy, one of Alexander's generals, who ruled as king of Egypt from 306. He made Alexandria his capital and there founded the famous Alexandrian Library (q.v.) and the Museum, a kind of academy of arts and sciences. These were greatly enlarged and scholarship was encouraged under his successors, Ptolemy II Philadelphus (reigned 285–246 B.C.) and Ptolemy III Euergetes (reigned 246–221 B.C.). Numerous scholars and people of genius thus were attracted to Alexandria, and a period of literary activity set in that made Alexandria, for centuries, the focus and center of Greek culture and intellectual effort. The subsequent rise of Syracuse, Rhodes, Antioch, and other intellectual centers in the ancient world may be traced to the influence of Alexandria, since a majority of their leaders were educated there.

Among the famous grammarians and critics in Alexandria were Zenodotus, Eratosthenes (also a noted mathematician and geographer), Aristophanes of Byzantium, and Aristarchus of Samothrace, all of the 3d or early 2d century B.C. These scholars collected, edited, and preserved the existing monuments of Greek literature. Among the poets of the late 4th and 3d centuries B.C. were Lycophron, Callimachus, Apollonius of Rhodes, Aratus of Soli, Theocritus, and Euphorion. Noted Alexandrian scientists of the same age included Euclid, the father of scientific geometry; Archimedes, great in physics and mechanics; Apollonius of Perga, known for his treatise on conic section; and, in the 2d century A.D. under the Romans, Nicomachus, the first scientific arithmetician, and the astronomer and geographer Ptolemy.

The influence of Alexandria spread through the empire under Roman supremacy, but gradually men of letters began to concentrate in Rome rather than in Alexandria. This gave rise to a new movement in Alexandria, in the direction of theology and philosophy. The principal Gnostic systems (see GNOSTICISM) had their origin there, as did the speculative Neo-Platonic school (see NEO-PLATONISM), which was established early in the 3d century A.D. by Ammonius Saccas.

ALEXANDRIAN LIBRARY, al-ig-zən′drē-ən, the most celebrated library in antiquity. It was a remarkable collection of manuscripts from all over the Hellenistic world, housed mainly in the museum and partly in the Serapeum in Alexandria, Egypt, roughly between 300 B.C. and 400 A.D. The library flourished under the Ptolemies; it survived under the Romans, but was destroyed during the Byzantine period.

Ptolemy I (reigned 323–285 B.C.) is generally credited with having founded both the museum and the library in the palace precincts, situated in the Brucheum district of Alexandria. The museum was conceived as an international academy; the library, as a collection of Greek works supplemented by works translated from other languages. The initial organization was done by

Demetrius Phalereus of Athens. Under Ptolemy II (reigned 285–247 B.C.), the museum and library were expanded, and Alexandria became the intellectual capital of the Hellenistic world. Ptolemy III (reigned 247–222 B.C.) established a subsidiary library at the Serapeum, or temple of Jupiter Serapis.

During the Ptolemaic period, the total collection of the library may have exceeded 500,000 volumes. Such distinguished scholars of the Alexandrian school as Zenodotus, Aristophanes of Byzantium, Callimachus, and Apollonius of Rhodes were associated with the institution.

The main part of the library was damaged during a fire in the Brucheum quarter when Julius Caesar besieged Alexandria in 47 B.C. It was ravaged in the civil war that occurred under Emperor Aurelian in the late 200's A.D. The Serapeum collection endured until 391 A.D., when Christians, following the edict of the Emperor Theodosius, destroyed the temple and its literary treasures. No books or buildings remain today.

ALEXANDRIAN MANUSCRIPT, al-ig-zan′drē-ən man′yə-skript, a Greek manuscript of the Bible, now in the British Museum. It is also called the *Codex Alexandrinus,* or *Codex A.* It is written in uncial (capital) letters on 773 leaves of parchment (10½ by 12¾ inches) and originally, early in the 5th century, contained the whole Bible, including the four books of Maccabees, and also the "Epistle of Athanasius to Marcellinus on the Psalter" and Eusebius' summary of the Psalms. It contains the 14 "Odes" used in the church: that is, the canticles found in both the Old and New Testament and the Gloria in Excelsis; it also has the apocryphal Psalm 151, and once contained the Psalms of Solomon. The New Testament contains most of I Clement and fragments of II Clement.

The Alexandrian Manuscript was obviously a complete Bible, meant for use in a great church. Many pages are now missing: parts of Genesis, I Samuel, Psalms 50:20 to 80:11; Matthew 1:1 to 25:6, John 6:50 to 8:52, and II Corinthians 4:13 to 12:6.

In 1624 the manuscript was offered by Cyril Lucar, patriarch of Constantinople, to King James I of England, but the gift arrived after James' death and far too late for use in the preparation of the King James Version of the Bible (1611). The codex was said to have come originally from Alexandria in Egypt, where it belonged to the patriarch of Alexandria in 1098. It was the first uncial manuscript to be used by Western scholars. Bishop Brian Walton collated it for his Polyglot (1657). J.E. Grabe published the Old Testament in 1707–1720, and F. Lee and W. Wigan completed the work after Grabe's death. H.H. Baber published the whole Old Testament in 3 volumes in 1816–1828. Other editions appeared in 1786, 1859, 1860, 1867. The entire manuscript was published in photographic facsimile in three volumes by E.M. Thompson in 1881–1883, and again in reduced facsimile in four volumes in 1909–1936, with an introduction by Sir Frederic G. Kenyon.

The term "Alexandrian manuscript" should not be confused with "Alexandrian version" (as the Septuagint is sometimes described), or the "Alexandrian type of text."

FREDERICK C. GRANT
Union Theological Seminary
Author of "Translating the Bible"

ALEXANDRINA, Lake, al′ig-zan-drē′nə, a shallow lagoon in South Australia about 40 miles southeast of Adelaide, at the mouth of the Murray River, which flows through it into Encounter Bay. Some 23 miles long and 13 broad, it has an area of 220 square miles. The Coorong, a southeasterly extension, is a narrow lagoon paralleling the coastal dunes for nearly 100 miles.

ALEXANDRINE, al-ig-zan′drən, a line of verse having 6 feet (6½ feet with feminine rhymes) equal to 12 syllables (13 with feminine rhymes), with a pause after the third foot (see VERSIFICATION). An example is the second of the following lines from Alexander Pope's *Essay on Criticism:*

"A needless Alexandrine ends the song
That, like a wounded snake, drags its slow
length along."

The name is derived from the meter used in certain 12th and 13th century French poems on Alexander the Great. As developed in France, it became known as heroic verse and also became the meter of French classical tragedy. Its use in English usually is confined to the last line of a Spenserian stanza or as a variant in a poem of heroic couplets. It was used by Michael Drayton in *Polyolbion* and by Robert Browning in *Fifine at the Fair.*

ALEXANDRITE, al-ig-zan′drīt, is a rare variety of the mineral chrysoberyl (an oxide of beryllium and aluminum), which is used as a gem. In daylight the twinned crystals of alexandrite are dark emerald to grayish green, but in artificial light they are a beautiful columbine red and have a brilliant luster. Alexandrite was first discovered in 1833 in the Ural Mountains and was named after the future czar Alexander II, who was then heir apparent to the Russian throne. It became a highly prized gem, since the red and green colors of alexandrite were those of the imperial Russian army. The finest alexandrites are found in Siberia, but good gems occasionally are found also in Ceylon.

Composition: BeO 19.8%, Al₂O₃ 80.2%; hardness, 8.5; specific gravity, 3.75; crystal system, orthorhombic.

ALEXIAN BROTHERS, ə-lek′sē-ən, a religious order devoted to the care of the sick. It was formed in 1365 by Tobias of Mechelen, Belgium, to ease the suffering caused by the Black Death and to bury its victims. Because of its origin, the order is also called *Cellites,* from Latin *cella* (cell or grave). Choosing St. Alexius (died 417) as its patron, the group expanded its work to other countries and in 1469 was organized as a religious order. Pope Pius IX confirmed its constitution in 1870.

The order's first mission in the United States was a hospital in Chicago, Ill., founded in 1866. The brothers, whose U.S. motherhouse is at Signal Mountain, Tenn., limit their work to nursing and hospital administration.

ALEXIS I (1629–1676), ə-lek′sis, was the 2d Russian czar of the Romanov line. He was born on March 9, 1629 and named *Aleksei Mikhailovich.* Alexis succeeded to the throne in 1645 on the death of his father, Michael (Mikhail Fyodorovich). The first years of his reign were marked by a series of disturbances and insurrections due in great part to his youth and inexperience. By 1655 he had restored peace at home and began to look abroad for realms to conquer. He conducted two campaigns against Poland (1654–1656 and 1660–1667), captured Smolensk, overran Lithuania, and seized several provinces. He also took part of the Ukraine, and waged a war against Sweden in 1656–1661. Alexis greatly extended Russian influence in the East, sent several raiding parties of Cossacks into Asia, and made an attack on China. At home he introduced important modifications of the legal code, had translations made of numerous scientific and military works, and also instituted some ecclesiastical reforms. His private character appears to have been above reproach. He was the father of Peter the Great.

ALEXIS PETROVICH (1690–1718), ə-lek′sis pe-trō′vich, Russian czarevitch. He was born in Moscow on Feb. 19, 1690, the oldest son of Peter the Great by his first wife, Eudoxia Lopukhina. Alexis incurred his father's wrath because of his opposition to some of the reforms Peter inaugurated. He fled to Vienna in 1717 to seek the protection of his brother-in-law, Emperor Charles VI, and thence proceeded to Naples.

Peter lured him home with promises of forgiveness, then disinherited him and extorted under torture a "confession" that he had headed a conspiracy against his father. The alleged plotters were executed and Alexis was tried by a specially constituted tribunal, which recommended further examination under torture. Severe floggings caused his death a few days later in St. Petersburg on June 26, 1718.

Alexis was married in 1711 to Charlotte Christine Sophie, daughter of the duke of Brunswick-Wolfenbüttel. She bore him a daughter and a son, the future Czar Peter II.

ALEXIUS, ə-lek′sē-əs, was the name of five rulers of the Byzantine empire.

ALEXIUS I COMNENUS (1048–1118) was the nephew of Emperor Isaac Comnenus. In his youth he proved himself an able soldier, serving with distinction in campaigns against the Seljuk Turks in Asia Minor and Greece. In 1081, when the Byzantine empire was torn by anarchy, Alexius' supporters seized Constantinople, deposed Nicephorus III, and placed Alexius on the throne. At the time of his accession, the Seljuk Turks were seizing the empire's Asian provinces, the Norman leader Robert Guiscard was attempting to take Greece, and fierce Turkish tribes from beyond the Danube River threatened the European border provinces.

During his 37-year reign Alexius managed to reorganize the army and the central government and to regain much of the territory the empire had lost in Asia. He sent support to his ally Emperor Henry IV and thus enabled Henry to attack Rome. Pope Gregory VII, a firm supporter of Guiscard and the Normans, was driven from Rome by Henry's armies. Guiscard's sudden death in 1084 ended his conquests in Greece. Alexius then was able to concentrate his forces against the Turks and the Scythians, as the Byzantines called the Turkish tribes from beyond the Danube. With the aid of Western mercenaries, Alexius finally managed, after a long and arduous struggle, to repel the Patzinak armies that were besieging Constantinople.

In 1096 the warriors of the First Crusade arrived at Constantinople. They came partly because Alexius had asked for their help against the Patzinaks, but he had some initial difficulties with them. Alexius managed to come to terms with the Crusaders, and with their help he was able to recover parts of Asia Minor that had been lost to the Turks. But when the Crusaders failed to turn over Antioch to the Byzantines, Alexius broke with them. The conflict over Antioch led eventually to war with the Latins in North Syria and the Armenians in Cilicia. In 1108, Alexius finally came to terms with the prince of Antioch, but the prince meanwhile had sown the seeds of distrust between the Greeks and Latins that underlay their relations for most of the century.

ALEXIUS II COMNENUS (1168–1183) was the son of Manuel I Comnenus. He was only 12 years old when his father died in 1180 and his mother, Mary of Antioch, became regent. Because of the traditional hostility between the Greeks and the Latins, Mary's Latin background caused some difficulty, creating an excuse for Alexius' cousin Andronicus to massacre the Latins and storm Constantinople in 1182. Andronicus overthrew Mary's government and proclaimed himself and Alexius co-emperors. A month later Andronicus had Alexius deposed and strangled.

ALEXIUS III ANGELUS (died 1210) was the brother of Isaac II Angelus, whom he blinded and succeeded as emperor in 1195. During his eight-year rule he spent money recklessly and neglected the administration. Frankish Crusaders and the Venetians replaced Alexius III in 1203, reinstating Isaac II as coemperor with his son Alexius IV, and Alexius III fled into exile.

ALEXIUS IV ANGELUS (died 1204) was the son of Isaac II Angelus. He was chiefly responsible for bringing the Crusaders to Constantinople in 1203 and reinstating his father on the throne. He became coemperor with his father, but disputes soon arose with the Crusaders, and during the struggle for power Alexius was strangled on the orders of Alexius Ducas Mourtzouphlos, leader of the Greek resistance, who secured the throne for himself as Alexius V.

ALEXIUS V DUCAS MOURTZOUPHLOS (died 1204), son-in-law of Alexius III, proclaimed himself emperor after the murder of Alexius IV in 1204. He continued the struggle against the Crusaders who were attempting to seize Constantinople, but he was unable to defend the city, and he fled to Morea, where he met the exiled Alexius III. Alexius III put out his eyes, and he then fell into the hands of the Crusaders, who put him to death for the murder of Alexius IV. Baldwin I succeeded Alexius V.

ALFALFA, al-fal′fə, is a perennial forage crop, also known as *lucerne.* Alfalfa stems usually are 2 to 3 feet (60 to 90 cm) high and may be erect or spreading. Each leaf is composed of three distinct leaflets. The flowers of the principal type of alfalfa are purple, but there is a yellow-flowered species that crosses freely with the purple. The result is variegated alfalfa and a large group of varieties which show flowers with innumerable shades of lilac, green, cream, and even white. Common alfalfa has a deep taproot which may penetrate to depths of 10 to 15 feet (3 to 4.5 meters), but a type with creeping and more shallow, fibrous roots also occurs.

Cultivation. Alfalfa should be grown on deep, well-drained, nonacid soil. It needs a good supply of phosphorus and potassium, as well as ample moisture. It adapts readily to changes in temperature and length of days. Varieties of

Alfalfa

(*Medicago sativa*)

JOHN J. SMITH

alfalfa are grown at the equator and as far north as 60°N.

Disease and injurious insects are often problems to alfalfa growers, and much of the effort at the improvement of alfalfa is directed to the development of resistance to these pests.

Pollination. Alfalfa seed production is highly specialized. The flowers must be pollinated by bees. Wild species of bees, such as leafcutter, alkali, and bumblebees, are natural pollinators, and their domestication is a phase of alfalfa research. Honey bees are ineffective except in irrigated, desert valleys where competing sources of pollen and nectar are absent.

Production. It is estimated that over 50 million acres (20 million hectares) are planted in alfalfa. Over one half of this acreage is in the United States, but the crop is important also in Canada, Argentina, France, Italy, central Europe, Russia, South Africa, New Zealand, and Australia.

Uses. Alfalfa is used mostly as feed for livestock. Hay, pasture, and silage are the principal products. A flourishing dehydration industry processes immature alfalfa into alfalfa meal and pellets—products that provide a high quality protein and vitamin supplement for all classes of livestock.

History. Alfalfa is believed to have originated in central Asia and the Middle East; probably it was cultivated also in ancient Babylon. The first definite record is its introduction into Greece about 490 B.C. From Greece it spread to Rome, through North Africa, to Spain, and then on through Europe to Russia. The Spanish conquerors brought it to Mexico and Peru; it then spread north to the United States and south to Argentina and Chile. The strain now widely adapted in the northern parts of the United States and in Canada was introduced by a German immigrant about 100 years ago.

Classification. Alfalfa belongs to the pea family, Leguminosae. Common forage alfalfa is *Medicago sativa*. Another species, *M. arborea*, is a little-known ornamental called "tree alfalfa."
J.L. Bolton, *Canada Department of Agriculture*

ALFIERI, äl-fyä'rē, **Count Vittorio** (1749–1803), Italian tragic poet, who represented the opening of a new era in the history and literature of Italy. He was a turbulent, passionate, and free spirit whose works vitally reflect his life and personality.

Early Years. In *Vita di Vittorio Alfieri scritta da se stesso* (*Life of Vittorio Alfieri Written by Himself*), published posthumously in 1804, Alfieri characterized the periods of his life. He makes four divisions: "Infancy" (Asti), "Childhood" (Turin), "Youth" (described as periods of "vegetation," "non-education," and "travel and dissipation"), and "Manhood," a vigorous period of study and creation that began in 1776 and continued uninterrupted.

Alfieri, of noble parentage, was born on Jan. 17, 1749, in Asti, in the French-dominated Piedmont. His father died when he was about a year old. In 1758, at the age of nine, he left Asti to enter the Academy of Turin, where he remained for eight years in spite of his dissatisfaction with the routine of studies. An inheritance from his father and from an uncle who died in 1763 allowed him to indulge his tastes, including a passion for horses. His studies at Turin ended in 1766.

Travels. Between 1766 and 1768, Alfieri traveled extensively in Europe. During his visit to France he conceived an ardent dislike for the French people, country, and civilization. In Holland, an affair with a married woman ended unhappily and led the romantic young man to an unsuccessful suicide attempt. Returning to Turin in 1769 he spent the winter reading Voltaire (whom he always deeply disliked), Montesquieu, Rousseau, and especially Plutarch. In the spring of 1770 he started upon a second and more extensive tour of Europe. On his visit to England he had his next serious affair with a married woman, terminating in a duel in which he was slightly wounded. In Portugal he formed a lifelong friendship with the Abbot Tommaso de Caluso, who encouraged him to read good literature and to write verses of his own.

Alfieri began to withdraw into himself, turning more and more toward introspection inspired by the romantic ennui of his life. His love for a disreputable noblewoman occasioned his first drama, *Cleopatra*, produced in Turin in 1775. A year earlier he had outlined a portion of this play to amuse his ladylove during an illness. Though the play was an immediate success, the author was displeased by its obvious faults. He determined to become a tragic poet and toward this end undertook the study of Italian and Latin. His next plays *Filippo* and *Polinice* were nevertheless written in French prose. Alfieri's own language was a mixture of Piedmontese and French.

Productive Years. Alfieri felt a strong aversion to French domination in the Piedmont, and he identified himself increasingly with the Italian patriotic movement. For these reasons he felt that he could no longer remain in the Piedmont, and in 1776 he went to live in Florence. In order to make the rupture complete, Alfieri turned over all of his property in the Piedmont to his sister in exchange for an annual pension, and settled into a life of study at Florence. There he forced himself to speak, read, write, and think in Italian exclusively.

In Florence, in 1777, Alfieri met and fell in love with the countess of Albany, wife of Charles Edward, the Stuart pretender to the English throne. The young countess, who returned his love, separated from her drunken and abusive husband and later lived with Alfieri until the end of his life. This ennobling love for the countess was the great influence of Alfieri's life. It was due largely to her inspiration that the poet wrote his greatest tragedies: *Filippo, Polinice, Antigone, Agamennone, Virginia, Oreste, La congiura dei Pazzi, Don Garzia, Maria Stuarda, Rosmunda, Ottavia, Timoleone, Merope,* and *Saul,* his masterpiece.

In 1786 the couple went to Paris to live, but they were forced to return to Italy in 1792 after the French Revolution began. In Paris, Alfieri wrote his tragedies *Agide, Sofonisba, Mirra, Abele, Bruto primo,* and *Bruto secondo,* Because of his hatred of oppression and love of liberty, he had at first looked somewhat favorably upon the revolutionary movement, but its excesses soon disgusted him. It is ironic that his tragedies became associated with the Jacobin theater, when in reality the Jacobins, with their own abuses and oppression, were more odious to Alfieri than any royal tyrant.

Back in Florence, and by now almost entirely retired from all society, he continued his studies and work with ever more intensity. In 1795 he undertook the study of Greek. The intensity of this work and his anger at the occupation of Florence by French troops in these years undoubtedly hastened his death, which occurred on Oct. 8, 1803. He is buried in the Church of Santa Croce in Florence, where the countess of Albany also was buried after her death in 1824. His monument was done by Antonio Canova.

Influence. Alfieri's tragedies are perhaps the greatest Italy possesses. Political in nature, and having human and poetic qualities, all of them have a tyrant as protagonist and the fatality of human destiny as their theme. Benedetto Croce has aptly called Alfieri a protoromantic, for whom life becomes an ideal of the heroic.

One cannot overestimate Alfieri's influence on Italian thought. His deep moral consciousness, which has its direct ancestors in Dante and Plutarch; his denunciations of all forms of tyranny and oppression; and his dream of an independent Italy—all had a vital influence in the subsequent formation of modern Italy as a unified nation.

Alfieri remains best known for his tragedies and for his biography, the *Vita.* In addition, he wrote four political comedies—*L'uno, I pochi, I troppi, L'antidoto (The One, The Few, The Too Many, The Antidote)*—and two moral comedies—*La finestrina* and *Il divorzio (The Little Window* and *Divorce);* but the comic spirit was foreign to his temperament, and these are inferior works. Other works include, in prose, *Del principe e delle lettere,* expressing the Alfierian theory that a writer is a hero in action; *La virtù sconosciuta,* on the ideal of the citizen; *Misogallo,* in verse and prose, expressing his hatred of France. He also wrote sonnets, verse epigrams and satires, odes, and verse translations from Latin and Greek classics.

ELMO GIORDANETTI
Amherst College

Bibliography

Alfieri, Vittorio, *The Prince and Letters,* tr. by B. Corrigan and J. A. Molinaro (Books on Demand 1975).
Alfieri, Vittorio, *Tragedies of Vittorio Alfiero,* 2 vols. (1876; reprint, Greenwood Press 1975).
Bondanella, Peter, *Dictionary of Italian Literature,* ed. by Julia C. Bondanella (Greenwood Press 1978).
Corrigan, Beatrice, ed., *Italian Poets and English Critics* (Univ. of Chicago Press 1969).
Dole, Nathan H., *Teacher of Dante, and Other Studies in Italian Literature* (1908; reprint, Ayer 1967).
Megaro, Gaudence, *Vittorio Alfieri, Forerunner of Italian Nationalism* (1930; reprint, Hippocrene Bks. 1971).
Whitfield, J. H., *A Short History of Italian Literature* (1960; reprint, Greenwood Press 1976).

ALFONSO, al-fon'sō, was the name of 5 kings of Aragon, 2 kings of Naples, 6 kings of Portugal, and 13 Spanish kings, several of whom ruled only parts of Spain. The Portuguese form of the name is *Afonso or Affonso.*

ARAGON

ALFONSO I (1073?–1134) was king of Aragon and Navarre from 1104 until his death. After his marriage in 1109 to Urraca, queen of Castile and León and daughter of Alfonso VI of Castile, he briefly shared in the sovereignty of Castile and León. Known as *Alfonso el Batallador (the Battler),* he was the most famous knight of his time, and he delighted in warfare. He fought against the armies of his wife when his people rejected him as king, and he was perennially at war with the Moors. In 1118 he defeated the Moors at Saragossa and in 1125–1126 drove them back from Valencia and Granada to the sea. His unhappy marriage with Urraca, his third cousin, was annulled by Pope Honorius II. He died after a battle at Fraga with Alfonso VII of Castile.

ALFONSO II (1152–1196) succeeded his father, Ramón Berenguer IV, as count of Barcelona in 1162 and became king of Aragon in 1164 when his mother renounced her rights to the throne. He inherited the French county of Provence in 1167. A writer of Provençal poetry, he was well known as a patron of the troubadours. He died in Perpignan on April 25, 1196.

ALFONSO III (1265–1291) was the eldest son of Pedro III, whom he succeeded as king of Aragon in 1285. A weak ruler, he surrendered important royal prerogatives in the "Privileges of the Union" when he agreed to summon the Cortes (a representative assembly) annually and to accept their nominees as his advisers. He first supported his brother James' claim to Sicily, but abandoned his cause in 1291. He died in Barcelona on June 18, 1291.

ALFONSO IV (1299–1336) succeeded his father, James II, in 1327. His short reign was disturbed by civil uprisings. During most of his reign he was involved in a war with the Genoese over possession of Corsica and Sardinia. He died in Barcelona on Jan. 24, 1336.

ALFONSO V (1385–1458) was king of Aragon, Naples, and Sicily. Called *Alfonso the Magnanimous,* he followed his father, Ferdinand I, to the throne in 1416. As Alfonso I, he ruled Sicily from 1416 to 1458 and Naples from 1443 to 1458. In 1420 he assisted Queen Joanna II of Naples in defeating Louis III of Anjou, her rival for the Neapolitan throne. As a reward, Joanna promised to make Alfonso her heir. In 1423, however, they quarreled, and when Joanna died in 1435, she bequeathed her domains to René of Anjou.

A few years later Alfonso attacked René, captured Naples (1442), and the next year was acknowledged its sovereign by the pope. Leaving his Spanish territory under the rule of his wife and his brother John, he went to live in Naples, where he maintained a brilliant Renaissance court and was a patron of the arts.

NAPLES

ALFONSO I was king of Sicily (1416–1458) and of Naples (1443–1458). See *Alfonso V of Aragon.*

ALFONSO II (1448–1495) was king of Naples. The son of Ferdinand I of Naples, he became duke of Calabria in 1458 when Ferdinand acceded to the throne. He commanded Neapolitan forces during the frequent wars of the day, defeating the Florentines at Poggio in 1479 and the Turks at Otranto in 1481. At his father's death in 1494 he became king. When Charles VIII of France threatened the kingdom, Alfonso abdicated in favor of his son (who ruled as Ferdinand II) on Jan. 23, 1495, and retired to Sicily. He died in Messina on Dec. 18, 1495.

PORTUGAL

ALFONSO I (1109?–1185) was the first king of Portugal. Known in Portuguese as *Afonso Henriques*, he succeeded his father, Henry of Burgundy, as count of Portugal in 1112 and was placed under the direction of his mother, Teresa, an ambitious and unscrupulous woman. In 1128 he gained control of the government, after defeating his mother in battle, and led his armies in victories over León and Castile. In 1143, to avoid vassalage to Alfonso VII of Castile he put himself under the protection of the pope. At the pope's instigation, Alfonso VII recognized Portugal as a separate state at a conference at Zamora in the same year.

One of the most famous knights of his age, Alfonso opposed the Moors and in 1139 defeated them in the battle of Ourique. After the battle he assumed the title of king of Portugal at the urging of his soldiers. In 1147 he captured the Moorish stronghold of Santarém. With the aid of English, German, and Flemish crusaders, he liberated Lisbon and the surrounding area from the Moors later in the year. At war with the Spanish in 1169, he was taken prisoner and forced to surrender several towns as a ransom. In 1171 and again in 1184 he defended Santarém against sieges by the Moors.

ALFONSO II (1185–1223) was the son of Sancho I. Called *Afonso o Gordo* (*the Fat*), he succeeded his father in 1211. He tried unsuccessfully to strengthen the crown's taxation and land policies by curtailing the powers of the church and the barons. As a result of his anti-clerical activities, he was excommunicated by Pope Honorius III. Continuing the Portuguese conflict with the Moors, he won a decisive victory over them in 1217 at Alcácer do Sal.

ALFONSO III (1210–1279) was the son of Alfonso II and younger brother of Sancho II. Alfonso received aid from the pope in deposing his brother during a civil war that ended in 1248. His strongest support came from the commoners, whom he allowed to sit in the Cortes for the first time, and from the clergy. By an agreement with Alfonso X of Castile in 1267, in which each surrendered claims to parts of the other's territory, the borders of Spain and Portugal were fixed much as they are today.

ALFONSO IV (1290–1357) was the son of Diniz, whom he succeeded in 1325. Although intermittently at war with Castile, he joined forces with it in 1340 and defeated the Moors at the important Battle of Salado. His reign was crippled by a disastrous civil war with his son Pedro, whose mistress, Inéz de Castro (claimed by Pedro as his wife after her death), was murdered at Alfonso's urging in 1355. (Inéz de Castro later became a famous figure in Portuguese literature.) Alfonso and Pedro eventually were reconciled by Alfonso's wife, Queen Beatriz. He died in Lisbon on May 28, 1357.

ALFONSO V (1432–1481) was born at Sintra. He succeeded his father, Edward I, in 1438.

During his minority his mother, Leonor of Aragon, then his uncle Dom Pedro, Duke of Coimbra, served as regents. In 1446, while Dom Pedro was regent, the Ordenações Afonsinas, Portugal's first great law code, was drawn up.

On reaching his majority, Alfonso asserted his right to the throne and in 1449 defeated and killed his uncle at the Battle of Alfarrobeira. Also known as *Afonso o Africano* (*the African*) for his invasions of Africa, which began in 1458, he won his most important victory in 1471 when he captured Tangiers. In 1476 he was defeated at Toro while trying to seize the throne of León and Castile. Compelled to abdicate, he resumed power when his son John declined the crown.

During Alfonso's reign, his famous uncle, Prince Henry the Navigator, directed the important voyages of discovery that made Portugal one of the leading sea powers of the century.

ALFONSO VI (1643–1683) was the son of John IV of the house of Braganza. He was partially paralyzed at the age of three, and on his accession to the throne in 1656 proved a dissolute and frivolous ruler. Under the influence of the unscrupulous but able Count Castelho Melhor he drove his mother, the Queen regent, from court in 1662. The count then reorganized the army and repulsed the Spanish invasion of John of Austria in 1663, thereby earning for Alfonso his ironic sobriquet of "the Victorious."

Alfonso's reign was marked by disputes with his younger brother Pedro. Alfonso married in 1666, but the new queen allied herself with Pedro. In 1667 she and Pedro overthrew Castelho Melhor and forced Alfonso to abdicate in favor of Pedro as prince regent. The queen had her marriage annulled because of Alfonso's impotence and married Pedro, who succeeded to the throne as Pedro II after his brother's death in 1683. From 1667 to 1674, Alfonso was confined in the Azores and then at Sintra, where he died.

SPAIN

ALFONSO I (693?–757), king of Asturias, succeeded his father-in-law, Pelayo (died 737), the first Christian king of Asturias. Called *Alfonso the Catholic* because of his wars with the Moors, he recovered parts of Galicia and León from them.

ALFONSO II (759?–842), king of Asturias, was the son of Fruela I and the grandson of Alfonso I. He was king of Asturias from 791 until his death. He built a new capital at Oviedo and tried to give his kingdom a national identity. While continuing the war against the Moors, he attempted to enlist the support of the Frankish king Charlemagne.

ALFONSO III (848–c. 910) king of Asturias, was the son of Ordoño I. He became known as *Alfonso the Great* because of his brilliant victories over the Moors. He greatly increased his territory at their expense. Asturias remained united until his three sons, García, Ordoño, and Fruela, forced him to divide the kingdom among them.

ALFONSO IV (died 933), king of Asturias and León, was the son of Ordoño II. He succeeded Fruela II in 925. Called *Alfonso the Monk*, he abdicated, after five years of rule, in favor of his brother Don Ramiro and retired to a monastery. Later, he invaded León in an attempt to recover his crown, but Ramiro defeated and captured him. He was imprisoned near León in the monastery of San Julián until his death.

ALFONSO V (994?–1027), king of León, ruled from 999 to 1027. During his minority the Moors under al-Mansur conducted successful campaigns against León. He died while besieging the Moorish town of Viseu.

ALFONSO VI (1030–1109), king of León and Castile, inherited León in 1065 from his father, Ferdinand I. His brother Sancho II of Castile opposed and defeated Alfonso, who took refuge with the Moorish ruler of Toledo. After Sancho's assassination in 1072, Alfonso became king of Castile. The following year he seized Galicia from his brother García. Driving south to the Tagus River, he captured Toledo in 1085 and made it his capital. Although he was defeated by the Moors in 1086 and 1108, his reign is memorable for the great impetus given to the Christian reconquest of Spain and especially for the legendary exploits of the Spanish hero the Cid (q.v.). He was succeeded by his daughter Urraca, who married Alfonso I of Aragon in 1109.

ALFONSO VII (1104–1157), king of Castile and León, was the son of Urraca, queen of Castile and León, and of her first husband, Raymond of Burgundy. Known as *Alfonso the Emperor*, he succeeded his mother in 1126 and soon recovered those parts of Castile that his stepfather, Alfonso I of Aragon, had seized. He proclaimed himself emperor in 1135, after unifying the Christian states in Spain. His conquest of Almería in 1147 was his most famous victory over the Moors. He divided his kingdom between his two sons, Sancho III of Castile and Ferdinand II of León.

ALFONSO VIII (1155–1214), king of Castile, was the son and successor of Sancho III. Called *Alfonso the Noble*, he was king from 1158 until his death. After taking control of the government, he quickly proved himself an able ruler and brought order to his chaotic realm. He married Eleanor, daughter of Henry II of England. Alfonso temporarily ended his disputes with his cousin, Alfonso IX of León, by marrying his daughter, Berengaria, to Alfonso IX. Defeated by the Moors in 1195, he subsequently led a Christian coalition against the Almohads, the ruling Moorish dynasty. When he defeated them at Navas de Tolosa in 1212, he opened Andalusia to the Christians and broke the Almohads' power in Spain.

ALFONSO IX (1171–1230), king of León, succeeded his father, Ferdinand II, in 1188. After his accession to the throne he was often at war with his cousin, Alfonso VIII of Castile. The pope annulled his marriages with Teresa of Portugal and Berengaria of Castile (daughter of Alfonso VIII) as within the forbidden degrees of consanguinity. His son by Berengaria, Ferdinand III, reunited Castile and León when he fell heir to both kingdoms.

ALFONSO X (1221–1284), king of Castile and León, followed his father, Ferdinand III, to the throne in 1252. He continued his father's campaigns against the Moors, capturing Cádiz in 1262. After twice falling to be elected emperor of the Holy Roman Empire, he renounced his claims in 1275. In the same year his heir, Ferdinand, died in battle with the Moors. In 1282 his second son, Sancho (who succeeded him as Sancho IV), rebelled against him when Alfonso recognized Ferdinand's son as heir to the throne. Sancho took control of the government at Alfonso's death in 1284.

Alfonso X was known as *Alfonso the Wise* because of his patronage of literature and learning. *Las siete partidas*, a compendium of legal knowledge, was assembled at his instruction. He also directed, in 1252, the revision of the Ptolemaic planetary tables called the Alfonsine tables.

ALFONSO XI (1311–1350), king of Castile and León, was the son and successor of Ferdinand IV. His campaign against the Moors of Granada led to their reinforcement from Morocco and their seizure of Gibraltar in 1333. Forming a Christian coalition with Portugal, Navarre, and Aragon, he helped win the important Battle of Salado in 1340 and four years later took Algeciras. He died while trying to recover Gibraltar and was succeeded by his son Pedro el Cruel (Peter the Cruel).

ALFONSO XII (1857–1885), king of Spain, was born on Nov. 28, 1857. The only son of Queen Isabella II, he left Spain with his mother in 1868 when she was driven from the throne by a revolt of liberal military officers and republican intellectuals. Two years later, Isabella abdicated in Alfonso's favor. Proclaimed king by Gen. Martínez de Campos in 1874, he entered Madrid early the next year and was acclaimed by most Spaniards. With the help of Martínez de Campos and Cánovas del Castillo, he defeated the Carlists, who supported a rival branch of the royal family, in 1876 and summoned a Cortes which drafted a new constitution.

His second wife, María Cristina, bore him two daughters and a son, Alfonso XIII, born after his father's death.

ALFONSO XIII (1886–1941), king of Spain, was the posthumous son of Alfonso XII. He was born in Madrid on May 17, 1886. He became king at birth, but his mother continued as regent until he formally acceded to the throne on May 17, 1902. He married Princess Victoria of Battenberg, granddaughter of Queen Victoria of England, on May 31, 1906. An attempt was made to assassinate the royal couple on their wedding day.

The execution in 1909 of Francisco Ferrer, accused of plotting a revolution and the establishment of an anti-Catholic state, roused considerable ill will toward the young monarch. But Alfonso's policy of keeping Spain neutral in World War I helped restore his popularity. However, his acquiescence in the Primo de Rivera dictatorship (1923–1930) was widely and vigorously criticized.

Rapidly deteriorating political and economic conditions forced him, on April 14, 1931, to "suspend the exercise of the royal power" and go into exile. After the Civil War of 1936–1939, General Francisco Franco indicated that Alfonso would not recover the throne. Alfonso delayed his abdication in favor of his third son, Don Juan, until shortly before his death in Rome on Feb. 28, 1941.

ALFORD, ôl'fərd, **Henry** (1810–1871), English clergyman and scholar. Born in London on Oct. 7, 1810, he graduated from Cambridge and was dean of Canterbury from 1857 to 1871. He is best known for his edition of the New Testament in Greek (1841–61), which incorporated the results of contemporary German Biblical scholarship and marked a turning point in New Testament study in England and the United States. He was the first editor of the *Contemporary Review*. He died at Canterbury on Jan. 12, 1871.

PICTURE COLLECTION, N.Y. PUBLIC LIBRARY

Alfred the Great, from an engraving at Oxford University.

ALFRED THE GREAT (849–899), al'frəd, was a king of the West Saxons, whose organization of his kingdom's defenses saved the English from Danish conquest. He was born at Wantage in Berkshire, the fifth (fourth surviving) son of Aethelwulf. He succeeded to the throne in 871, after the three short reigns of his brothers Aethelbald, Aethelbert, and Aethelred. Of Alfred's early years little is known. The indications are that he was a favorite son. At the age of five he was sent by his father to Rome where Pope Leo "hallowed Alfred as King and took him as his bishop's son" (Asser, *Chronicle*). The allusion to Alfred as "bishop's son" refers to his confirmation, the pope standing as his sponsor according to a not unusual practice of the times. The allusion to his hallowing as king is less clear; since his three older brothers were still alive, it probably refers to some titular dignity conferred on him. Two years later Aethelwulf himself went to Rome, and Alfred accompanied him.

The story of Alfred's learning to read falls in the period before the second pilgrimage to Rome. It is found in Asser, who states that Alfred "remained illiterate" (*illiteratus permansit*) to his 12th year or more, although he knew many Saxon poems by heart. By "illiterate" Asser undoubtedly means ignorant of Latin. Alfred certainly could read Anglo-Saxon before his 12th year, and the mother who, according to the story, promised a book of Anglo-Saxon poems to that one of her sons who first learned to read it to her was without question Alfred's own mother, Osburh. It was not until after his accession, however, that Alfred acquired a knowledge of Latin. Asser also states that at Alfred's marriage festivities in 868, he was attacked by a grievous illness that afflicted him for 20 years or longer. This story has obviously been exaggerated for hagiological purposes, although it probably has some foundation in the fact that Alfred was never in robust health.

Alfred first appears in public life in the year 866 as the assistant of his brother Aethelred in repelling the attacks of the Danes. In 871, in the midst of these Danish wars, Alfred succeeded to the throne. Nine general engagements were fought in this year.

Alfred's own wars with the Danes center in two great campaigns. As a result of the first, the Danes, in 878, promised to leave Wessex, and their king, Guthrum, received Christian baptism. But after 14 years of comparative peace the Danes returned to the attack. In the meantime, however, Alfred had strengthened his army and his defenses. At one brilliant engagement after another, the Danes were defeated, and in 897 they fled into East Anglia and Northumbria and over the sea into France. For the remaining years of Alfred's life, Wessex was at peace.

Alfred died on April 26, 899. Asser's *Chronicle* says, in recording his death, that he was king over all the English people except those living in areas under the power of the Danes. But practically all England north of the Thames was in the Danelagh, and Alfred's authority extended only over Wessex and a part of Mercia. In saving Wessex, however, Alfred had saved England for the English people; for it was from Wessex as a center that his successors began the task of reconquering England from the Danes.

In years of peace, Alfred engaged in strengthening and organizing his army, building an excellent navy, and systematizing the government of the country. The plans that he laid for advancing the intellectual interest of his people made him much more than a soldier. Unable to find teachers in England, Alfred brought scholars from abroad and with their aid planned to have translated into English all the Latin books that he considered most important for his people to know.

Alfred himself bore the greater part of this burden. His first translation was one of Pope Gregory's *Pastoral Care*, made about 894. This was followed by the *Universal History* of Orosius and Bede's *Ecclesiastical History*, although there is some question whether the latter work proceeded directly from the hand of Alfred. These were followed by his interesting version of Boethius' *Consolation of Philosophy*. His last work was a translation and adaptation of writings of Augustine and Gregory. Other undertakings undoubtedly due to Alfred's influence are a translation of Gregory's *Dialogues* (the preface of which was written by Alfred), the *Anglo-Saxon Chronicle*, and a translation of the Psalter. Popular tradition has ascribed a number of other works to Alfred that actually belong to much later periods. Asser refers to Alfred's *Handbook*, a commonplace book or anthology, but this work is no longer extant.

Historians agree in placing a high estimate on the character and achievements of Alfred. It was the greatness of his character, not the magnitude of his military achievements nor the extent of the country that he governed, that lifts him into the ranks of the world's famous men.

GEORGE P. KRAPP

Editor of "Paris Psalter and Meters of Boethius"

Bibliography

Duckett, Eleanor S., *Alfred the Great, the King and His England* (Univ. of Chicago Press 1958).
Frantzen, Allen J., *King Alfred* (G. K. Hall 1986).
Hawkins, Walter, and Smith, Edward T., *The Story of Alfred the Great* (1900; reprint, Arden Library 1980).
Helm, Peter J., *Alfred the Great* (R. West 1963).
Keynes, Simon, and Lapidge, Michael, trans., *Alfred the Great* (Penguin 1984).

ALFRED UNIVERSITY is a nonsectarian coeducational institution, located at Alfred, N.Y., controlled by a private university corporation but with divisions supported by the State of New York. It was first established as a school in 1836 and then chartered as an academy in 1843 and as a university in 1857. Units of the university are the college of liberal arts, the State University of New York College of Ceramics, the State University Agricultural and Technical Institute, the school of nursing, and a graduate school. A school of theology, begun in 1901, was discontinued in 1963. The university library includes special collections on ceramic art and glass technology.

Full-time student enrollment increased from about 600 in 1940 to 900 in 1950 and to over 1,500 in the 1960's.

ALGAE, al'jē, are a group of primitive plants, from one section of which the higher plants apparently have evolved. They are photoautotrophic (that is, they manufacture their own food by photosynthesis). The algae are not a uniform group either phylogenetically (according to their evolution) or morphologically (according to their structure), having evolved in remote geological epochs along several distinct and widely divergent lines. Some of them are microscopic and of simple, often unicellular structure; others attain very large dimensions and show a considerable degree of differentiation into parts resembling the roots, stems, and leaves of higher plants. The large majority of algae are aquatic, either freshwater or marine; however, some have become adapted to terrestrial existence, although they remain largely dependent on moisture, especially for their reproductive processes.

Classification. In currently accepted classification the algae comprise the following natural divisions: blue-green algae (Cyanophyta), golden algae (Chrysophyta), brown algae (Phaeophyta), dinoflagellate algae (Pyrrhophyta), cryptomonad algae (Cryptophyta), euglenoid algae (Euglenophyta), green algae (Chlorophyta), and red algae (Rhodophyta). As some of these names indicate, pigmentation plays an important role in their classification, and its correlation with distinctive structural and reproductive features shows that it is fundamental. In most cases, the pigmentation referred to is an accessory one that occurs in addition to the major green photosynthetic pigment, chlorophyll, which the accessory pigment often masks; thus the externally visible color in some of the groups is not green. In at least two of the divisions (brown algae and red algae) there is strong evidence that the accessory pigment is functional in photosynthetic metabolism, absorbing and transferring light energy to the chlorophyll.

Blue-Green Algae. The blue-green algae (division Cyanophyta) are considered to be the most primitive existing algal representatives. There is fossil evidence of their presence in Precambrian rocks over two billion years ago. In some respects, such as absence of an organized nucleus and of normal sexual reproduction, they show a strong resemblance to the bacteria. It seems possible that they evolved from that group, although in the living representatives of blue-green algae the divergence in size, morphology, and metabolism is considerable.

Blue-green algae owe their characteristic blue-green color to the presence of a blue pigment, phycocyanin, in addition to chlorophyll (type *a*), but their color may vary considerably. The pigments are not localized in special structures, called chromatophores, but are diffused throughout the protoplasm—another primitive character that makes them different from other algae. The products of assimilation (conversion of nutritive materials) are glycogen and glycoproteins.

The blue-green algae are small, and many of them are microscopic. They range in form from single isolated cells to simple filaments made up of single rows of cells, which often are united into colonies by colorless or pigmented gelatinous sheaths. Unicellular (one-celled) types are represented mainly by the order Chroococcales (for example *Chroococcus*), and filamentous types are represented by the order Oscillatoriales (such as *Oscillatoria, Nostoc, Stigonema*). Reproduction is asexual, either by cell division, by the formation of internal spores (endospores), or by short, detachable sections of filament (hormogonia). Movement by means of flagella (whiplike processes) is completely absent in the group, although certain of the filamentous genera, for example, *Oscillatoria*, show gliding or undulating movement.

The blue-green algae are among the most widely distributed and ecologically adaptable of all organisms, with worldwide distribution from the polar regions to the equator. Species are found in all environments—terrestrial, freshwater, and marine—and they inhabit such diverse and unfavorable situations as arid rocks, glaciers, and hot springs. Some are symbiotic (relationship in which both organisms benefit) with lichens, and others occur in the spaces between the cells of higher plants. Certain species are capable of fixing atmospheric nitrogen. Others may produce toxic "water blooms" (accumulations of algae at or near the surface of the water) in lakes and ponds.

Golden Algae. The golden algae (division Chrysophyta) range in size from microscopic, unicellular organisms, which often form colonies, to relatively small but visible, filamentous types. The three classes constituting the group—Chrysophyceae, Bacillariophyceae and Xanthophyceae—are widely divergent in form and structure but are united by certain fundamental characteristics. These are the presence (in addition to chlorophyll of the *a*-type) of specific carotinoid accessory pigments (carotins and xanthophylls) that may or may not mask the green color of the *a*-type chlorophyll, and the elaboration of oil or a peculiar carbohydrate, chrysose (leucosin), as a product of assimilation. The pigments are localized in special structures called chromatophores. Impregnation of the cell wall with silica is widespread in the group, and movement by means of flagella is common in many of the unicellular forms and in the sexual reproductive cells. The three main classes are distinguished by the following characters:

Chrysophyceae—chromatophores are golden-yellow to brown; unicellular to filamentous.

Bacillariophyceae (diatoms)—chromatophores are brown; unicellular, with an outer sheath, or frustule, of silica.

Xanthophyceae—chromatophores are green or greenish; unicellular to filamentous.

The class Chrysophyceae consists mainly of unicellular forms that move by means of two flagella of unequal length. Many of the Chrysophyceae formerly were regarded as protozoa

(Flagellata). However, some types are nonmotile, and others show creeping amoeboid movement by means of protoplasmic extrusions. Most of the forms are freshwater.

The class Bacillariophyceae, commonly known as diatoms, is peculiar in the form of the silica sheath, or frustule, that it possesses. This consists of two distinct, overlapping halves and is ornamented with symmetrically arranged pits or pores that have a complex ultramicroscopic structure. The symmetry may be radial (around a central axis), as in the order Centrales, or bilateral (right and left sides as mirror images), as in the order Pennales. Diatoms are an important constituent of marine and freshwater plankton. Some form colonies by aggregation of the individual cells.

The class Xanthophyceae shows motility by two unequal flagella in certain forms; others use creeping amoeboid movements. Some (such as *Vaucheria*) form a tubular, unpartitioned, thallus (plant body), producing multinucleate and multiflagellate zoospores. They are mainly freshwater or terrestrial.

Brown Algae. The brown algae (division Phaeophyta) include the largest seaweeds known. They commonly are called "kelps." Some genera, such as *Macrocystis*, reach a length of many yards. They are almost exclusively marine and show considerable structural complexity in the more highly evolved forms. There is differentiation into holdfast organs, stems and leaves, and air-filled flotation organs, or bladders, often are present. The motile reproductive cells have two flagella and may function sexually or asexually. Some genera, such as the well-known rockweed, or wrack (*Fucus*), have an animal-like type of life history involving the fertilization of eggs; in others the sexual process leads to the formation of distinct generations of individuals differing in cell structure and either similar or dissimilar in external appearance. The products of metabolism are peculiar carbohydrates (laminarin, mannitol). Common examples of brown algae are *Ectocarpus*, *Laminaria* (well known as devil's apron kelp), and *Ascophyllum* (the common knotweed of rocky intertidal shores).

Dinoflagellates. The dinoflagellate algae (division Pyrrhophyta) are unicellular and flagellated but rarely colonial or filamentous. Some have a cellulose wall consisting of sculptured plates; they are the so-called "armored dinoflagellates." Their chromatophores are brown (rarely reddish or bluish), and the product of assimilation is either starch or oil. Some are luminescent, such as *Gonyaulax*, and others produce a toxin lethal to fish and mollusks, often associated with a reddish discoloration of the water known as "red tides." Most are marine, but freshwater and terrestrial forms are also known.

Cryptomonad Algae. The cryptomonad algae (division Cryptophyta) form a small division of unicellular, flagellated forms that resemble the dinoflagellates in many respects.

Euglenoid Algae. The euglenoid algae (division Euglenophyta) are typically green, unicellular algae that are motile by flagella. They resemble protozoa in many respects, such as in the tendency toward loss of the green pigment chlorophyll and in the adoption of an animal-like, or heterotrophic, mode of nutrition, sometimes by ingestion of solid organic particles. They possess a small red organelle (eyespot) that is sensitive to light. Some are bounded only by a cell membrane and are capable of considerable change in form, while others are encased in a rigid, sometimes sculptured sheath. The products of assimilation are a starchlike substance (paramylum) and oil. As far as is known with certainty, only asexual reproduction by fission occurs. Euglenoids are found in both freshwater (often polluted) and marine environments.

Green Algae. The green algae (division Chlorophyta) are a large and important division showing great diversity in structure and reproduction, ranging from microscopic unicellular forms to structurally complex types of moderate size. Practically every possible type of cellular organization is found in the group—unicellular, colonial, filamentous, leafy, or tubular (siphonaceous). Occasionally, as in the class Charophyceae, there is considerable structural complexity, though not to the extent found in the Phaeophyceae. Motility by flagella (usually two, rarely four or more) is widespread, especially in the case of the reproductive cells (zoospores and zoogametes). The color is grass-green, due to the presence of unmasked chlorophylls, of the *a* and *b* types, a pigmentation characteristic of the higher green plants (mosses, ferns, and flowering plants). This fact furnishes one of the arguments in support of the hypothesis that the higher plants evolved in the past from the green algae. Starch is formed as the product of assimilation. Some forms are symbiotic with fungi to form lichens, and symbiosis with marine invertebrate animals also is known. Sexual reproduction shows a wide range of variation, from fusion of similar motile gametes (isogamy) to that of dissimilar gametes (anisogamy or oögamy) or the fusion of the entire protoplasm content of different cells, as in the filamentous freshwater genus *Spirogyra*. Six classes are recognized, of which that of the Chlorophyceae is the largest and varies the most in form.

Flagellate unicellular forms of the Chlorophyceae are placed in the order Volvocales, the representatives of which may be either single motile cells (such as *Chlamydomonas*) or colonies of cells joined together. *Volvox* is the best-known representative of the latter type. The colony is in the form of a hollow, slowly revolving sphere just visible to the naked eye. Nonflagellate unicellular or colonial forms comprise the order Chlorococcales, of which *Trebouxia*, the algal symbiont most commonly associated with lichens, is an example.

Filamentous or membranous plant body organization is shown by the orders Ulotrichales and Ulvales respectively. *Ulothrix* consists of simple unbranched filaments, each cell with a single chromatophore applied to the inner cell wall. *Ulva* (sea lettuce) forms leafy, platelike thalli, two cell layers in thickness.

The filamentous freshwater alga *Oedogonium*, placed in a separate class Oedogoniophyceae, is peculiar in its mode of intercalary cell division (addition of new cells between existing cells) and in the fertilization of eggs by zoogametes produced from small male plants that lodge on the female filaments (nannandry).

Coenocytic structure, a multinucleate mass of protoplasm, is found in the orders Cladophorales (for example, *Cladophora*), Siphonocladales (*Valonia*), Dasycladales (*Acetabularia*), Codiales (*Codium*), and Caulerpales (includes several marine genera such as *Caulerpa*, *Penicillus*, *Halimeda*, and *Udotea*).

The desmids (order Desmidiales) are microscopic unicellular forms with minutely perforated walls. The cells are constricted in the middle and show bilateral (left and right sides are mirror images) to almost radial (developed around central axis) symmetry. They occur in fresh water.

A very isolated position in the Chlorophyta is occupied by the class Charophyceae (stoneworts), a weakly calcified group of fresh or brackish water algae. They are characterized by large multicellular thalli showing division into nodes and internodes (segment between nodes), with branches in whorls at the nodes. Their reproduction is oögamous, the eggs being enclosed in a multicellular sheath. This feature is not common in the algae.

Red Algae. The red algae (Rhodophyta) owe their typically reddish color to a phycobilin pigment that is chemically similar to that found in the blue-green algae. Another characteristic that they share with the blue-green algae is the total absence of flagellated motile cells. These resemblances may indicate divergence from a common ancestral stock in the remote past, but among living forms no close relationship exists.

Nearly all the red algae are marine, although a few genera (for example, *Batrachospermum*) inhabit swiftly running fresh water. Some simple types are unicellular, but most have a basically filamentous organization, which often is elaborated into compound plant body structures that frequently show branching of great regularity. In the higher forms there are obvious pit-connections between adjacent cells of the same filament.

Sexual reproduction is highly developed and often exceedingly complex in red algae. It is based on the fertilization of egg cells by small, nonmotile, male gametes (spermatia). In many cases it involves the transfer of fertilized nuclei into specialized auxiliary cells and filaments (gonimoblasts) prior to their inclusion in spores. Alternation of cytologically different generations (usually isomorphic or identical in structure) is found in the more highly evolved genera. The reserve foodstuff is a polysaccharide known as Floridean starch.

The single class Rhodophyceae is divided into two subclasses, Bangiophycidae and Florideophycidae. The former are more primitive and lack the complicated post-fertilization processes of the latter. They also are less highly organized morphologically. A well-known representative is the genus *Porphyra*.

The Florideophycidae comprise six orders (Nemalionales, Gelidiales, Cryptonemiales, Gigartinales, Rhodymeniales, and Ceramiales), which are based on features of the life cycle and post-fertilization development. The typical life cycle of one of the higher Florideophycean red algae, such as *Polysiphonia*, may be briefly summarized as follows:

The first generation of plants (gametophytes) produces male gametes (spermatia) and female gametes (egg cells), commonly on different individuals. From the fertilized egg cell a small plant called the carposporophyte develops parasitically on the female gametophyte. It has a double number of chromosomes in the nuclei (diploid) and consists of only a few rows of cells or filaments. The carposporophyte gives rise to a cluster of spores, usually inside a protective sheath (cystocarp). These spores are released and germinate to give rise to the second (usually isomorphic) alternating generation of plants, which,

unlike the gametophytes, has diploid nuclei. The number of chromosomes is reduced by half in the developing tetrasporangia (a four-celled "case" in which the spores develop) borne on these plants, and the tetraspores, on being liberated, germinate to produce a new generation of gametophyte plants bearing sexual organs. Thus the life cycle is completed.

Certain genera of the order Cryptonemiales deposit lime in the thallus, making it rigid and stony, and either solid (as in *Lithothamnium*) or in articulated segments (as in *Corallina*).

Some of the better known representatives of the subclass Florideophycidae are *Chondrus* (Irish moss), *Rhodymenia* (dulse), and *Ceramium* (lobster claws). All are common on northern shores.

Economic Importance. The economic importance of algae always has been considerable in some countries, especially in Japan, where they are used extensively as part of the human diet. In the Western Hemisphere they are exploited mainly for the production of agar, carrageenin, and alginic acid.

From the 17th to the 19th century, algae such as dulse (*Rhodymenia*) and laver (*Porphyra*) were used quite commonly for food in western Europe. In Japan, numerous species of green, brown, and red algae are used extensively in

ALGAE (larger genera)—1, *Ulva*; 2, *Chara*; 3, *Ectocarpus*; 4, *Polysiphonia*; 5, *Laminaria*; 6, *Nemalion*; 7, *Fucus*.

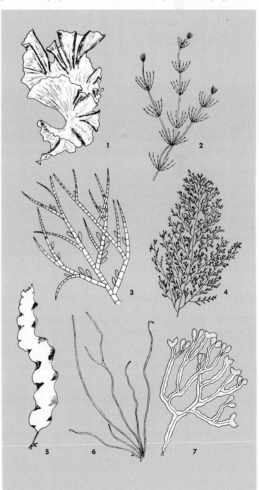

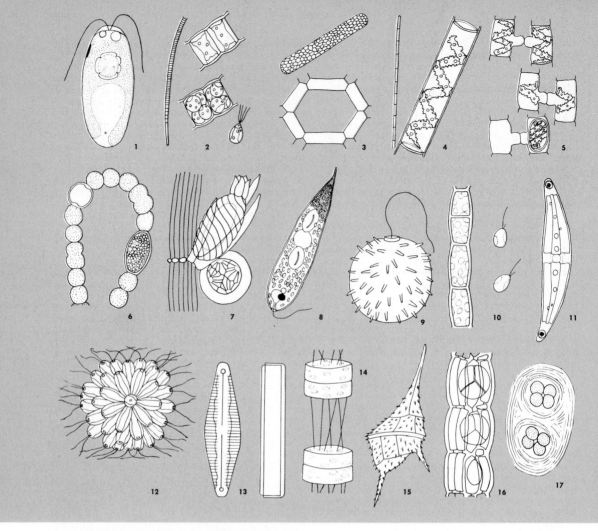

ALGAE (microscopic views)—1, *Chlamydomonas;* 2, *Ulothrix;* 3, *Hydrodictyon;* 4, *Spirogyra;* 5, *Spirogyra,* reproduction; 6, *Anabaena;* 7, *Chara,* sex organs; 8, *Euglena;* 9, *Trachelomonas;* 10, *Tribonema;* 11, *Closterium;* 12, *Synura;* 13, Diatom (Pennales), top and side views; 14, Diatom (Centrales); 15, *Ceratium;* 16, *Polysiphonia,* tetraspores (asexual spores); 17, *Gloeocapsa.*

daily diet, and *Porphyra* ("Amanori," "Asakusa-nori") is cultivated artificially on bamboo or brushwood screens sunk in estuaries. Sheep, cattle, and poultry can be fed on marine algae, and certain common brown algae (*Laminaria, Fucus, Ascophyllum*) are processed into a seaweed meal that forms a valuable supplement used in feeding livestock.

Seaweeds also have some value as organic fertilizers in agricultural districts close to seashores, where they are readily accessible. Another use of algae is the production of antibiotic substances. They have been obtained from species of *Chlorella* (Chlorophyta), *Laminaria, Ascophyllum, Halidrys, Pelvetia* and *Sargassum* (Phaeophyta) and *Polysiphonia* and *Rhodomela* (Rhodophyta).

The production of agar and carrageenin from red algae, and alginic acid derivatives from brown algae, is now a major industry in many parts of the world. Agar is used as a solidifying agent for nutrient culture media for fungi and bacteria, and it also has important applications in the food and pharmaceutical industries. It is extracted mainly from the red algal genera *Gelidium* and *Gracilaria.* Carrageenin, obtained

from Irish moss (*Chondrus crispus*), is similar in composition to agar and is put to similar uses.

Alginic acid occurs in various genera of the larger brown algae (kelps), notably *Macrocystis, Laminaria* and *Ascophyllum.* It is an extremely colloidal (hydrophilic) substance that has many applications in industry, as in the production of plastic membranes and artificial fibers and as a stabilizing agent in various dairy products, salad dressings, pie fillings, hair creams, and cosmetics.

Marine planktonic algae are of fundamental importance as one of the basic links in the food chain on which higher forms of life, and ultimately the fisheries industry, depend.

I. MACKENZIE LAMB, *Harvard University*

Bibliography

Graham, Linda E., and Lee W. Wilcox, *Algae* (Prentice Hall 2000).

Meinesz, Alexandre, *Killer Algae,* tr. by Daniel Simberloff (Univ. of Chicago Press 1999).

Round, F. E., *The Ecology of Algae* (Cambridge 1981).

Sze, Philip, *A Biology of the Algae,* 3d ed. (WCB/McGraw-Hill 1998).

Van den Hoek, C., et al., *Algae: An Introduction to Phycology* (Cambridge 1995).

ALGARDI, äl-gär′dē, **Alessandro** (1595–1654), Italian sculptor and architect, who was the principal artist for Pope Innocent X. He was born in Bologna and received training under Lodovico Carracci. Algardi settled in Rome about 1625 and was elected head of the Academy of St. Luke there in 1639. When Innocent X acceded in 1644, Algardi replaced Giovanni Bernini as the leader of baroque artists.

Algardi's first major sculpture was *San Filippo Neri and the Angel* (1640). His portrait busts of Innocent X and his family were noted for their balance between naturalism and idealism. Among his major works are the *Tomb of Leo XI* (1634–1652) and the bas-relief *Leo and Attila* (1643–1653), both in St. Peter's Basilica. His architectural works included the plans of the papal Villa Doria Pamphili and the façade of the Church of Sant' Ignazio, Rome. He died in Rome on June 10, 1654.

ALGAROTTI, äl-gä-rôt′tē, **Count Francesco** (1712–1764), Italian writer. Born at Venice on Dec. 11, 1712, Algarotti was a cultured and widely traveled person, famous for his friendships with illustrious men, including Pope Benedict XIV, Augustus III of Poland, Voltaire, and Frederick II (the Great) of Prussia, who made him a count in 1740.

At the age of 20, Algarotti went to Paris, where he came under the influence of Voltaire, and wrote *Il Neutonianismo per le dame* (1733; Eng. tr., *Sir Isaac Newton's Philosophy Explained for the Ladies*, 1739), a popularization of Newton's theory of optics.

Algarotti also wrote verse and essays, and was noted as a connoisseur of art, literature, and music, about which he wrote discerningly. He died in Pisa on May 3, 1764.

ALGARVE, äl-gär′və, is the southernmost historical province of continental Portugal, coextensive with the official administrative district of Faro. The name Algarve is derived from the Arabic *al-Gharb*, "the West (of Muslim Andalusia)." The provincial capital was the city of Faro.

Algarve is bounded on the north by the historical province of Baixo Alentejo, on the south and west by the Atlantic Ocean, and on the east by the estuary of the Guadiana River, which forms the boundary with Spain. Low mountain ranges cover the interior of the province, separating it from the rest of mainland Portugal. The chief range is the Serra de Monchique, which extends to the promontory of Cape St. Vincent, the southwesternmost point of continental Europe. The Portuguese Prince Henry the Navigator established his famous school of navigation near the cape.

The interior, which is otherwise unproductive and sparsely settled, has large stands of cork oaks. Most of the people live in the coastal plains, where almonds, figs, olives, citrus fruits, and grapes are grown. Along the coast are important sardine and tuna fisheries.

Algarve was first colonized by Greek and Phoenician traders, who settled along the coasts. The more thorough Roman occupation, beginning in the third century B.C., pacified the interior. From the 8th to the 13th centuries A.D., Algarve was a Moorish kingdom with its capital at Silves. Between 1249 and 1253, Alfonso III of Portugal conquered it from the Moors, adding "king of the Algarve" to his title.

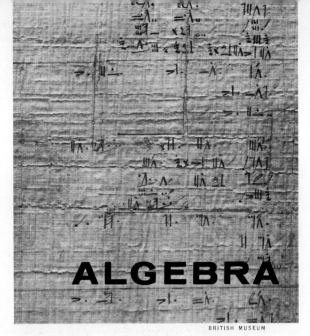

BRITISH MUSEUM

RHIND PAPYRUS (detail) is one of earliest works on algebra. It was prepared by Ahmes about 1650 B.C.

ALGEBRA, al′jə-brə, is that portion of mathematics whose primary consideration is the representation of numbers by symbols and the study of the rules of their operation inside a given set by means of the few elementary operations (addition, subtraction, multiplication, division). Such representation is of great assistance in considering the relations and properties of numbers with the aid of signs of operation (such as $+$, $-$, $\times$) and signs of relation (such as $>$, $<$, $\neq$).

1. Elementary Algebra

From a practical point of view, elementary algebra is concerned with the extension of the laws of arithmetic to include operations of symbols, usually the letters $a, b, c, \ldots, x, y, z$. It is customary to use the first letters of the alphabet (a, b, c, . . .) to represent quantities whose values are supposed to be known in any expression, and the later ones (. . . x, y, z) for quantities whose values are to be found, called unknowns. Some of the notation must be explained at the start. Suppose that a and b represent any two quantities. We shall indicate the sum of the two quantities as $a + b$ and their difference as $a - b;$ their product as $a \times b$, $a \cdot b$, or, most simply, as $ab;$ and their quotient as $\frac{a}{b}$, a/b, $a \div b$.

If we have a number associated with the letters, the number is called the *numerical coefficient* of the letters; thus, in $5ab$, 5 is the numerical coefficient of ab. It must be noted that when two or more numerals are placed together without a symbol between them, like 27 or 113, they still have their position values: 27 still means twenty-seven, not two times seven. When two or more quantities are multiplied together, each one is called a *factor*. If two or more quantities are added together, each one is called an *addend*. If we have several addends, each containing the letter b, like $3b$, $5b$, $2b$, $9b$, the expression

$$3b + 5b + 2b + 9b = 19b$$

is true for any value of b, which is often called

the *base*. In words, the sum of any number of quantities with a common base is the sum of their numerical coefficients times the base.

Signs of Aggregation. Before we can continue this discussion profitably, we must define the symbols used to indicate that a certain expression is to be treated as a single symbol in a problem. These are called signs of aggregation: parentheses ( ); braces { }; brackets [ ]; and the vinculum $\overline{}$. For example, if it is desired to think of $a + b + 2c + 3d$ as a single quantity, regardless of the values of the letters, it will be written: $(a + b + 2c + 3d)$; $\{a + b + 2c + 3d\}$; $[a + b + 2c + 3d]$; or $\overline{a + b + 2c + 3d}$. Then, $5(a + b + 2c + 3d)$ would mean five times the quantity obtained by first adding $a + b + 2c + 3d$ when, and if, their values are known. This is perfectly consistent with our previous experience with numbers. Our statement, written as a formula, is $3b + 5b + 2b + 9b = (3 + 5 + 2 + 9)b$.

Plus and Minus Quantities. In algebra, quantities are considered as having either plus or minus signs; for instance, money received is counted as plus and money spent as minus, so that a person's net worth is a combination of the two. A bit of reflection will show that for sums: the coefficient of the sum of two multiples of a given base with like signs is the sum of the coefficients preceded by the common sign; the coefficient of the sum of two numbers with different signs is the difference between the values of the coefficients preceded by the sign of the larger coefficient. Thus,

$$\begin{array}{cccc} + 3b & - 3b & + 5b & - 5b \\ + 5b & - 5b & - 3b & + 3b \\ \hline + 8b & - 8b & + 2b & - 2b \end{array}.$$

In subtraction, the above answers and one of the addends would be given; we would have to find the other addend. It is evident that if we change the sign of the number we wish to subtract and then proceed as in addition, we will obtain the other addend.

The following rules for multiplication and division can be justified: The product (or quotient) of two like-signed quantities is *plus*; of two unlike-signed quantities is *minus*.

If we wish to multiply two numbers like $+3abc$ and $-5def$, their product is made up of all the factors taken in any order and $(+3abc)(-5def) = (+3)(-5)abcdef = -15\ abcdef$. If some of the factors are repeated (see POWER), as in $(-2a^2bc^3)(+3a^3b^2c^4)$, the product is $-6a^5b^3c^7$. Multiplication is said to be *associative* because the order in which the factors are taken is not material.

$$abc = (ab)c = (ac)b = a(bc).$$

It is also *distributive*, that is,

$$a(b + c + d) = ab + ac + ad.$$

We can check the truth of these statements by substituting any numbers we wish for the letters and showing that the results are identical.

Monomials and Polynomials. A quantity made up of symbols not separated by plus or minus signs is called a *term* or a *monomial*, like $3a^2b^3c$ or $2xyz$. The combination of several terms by plus or minus signs forms a *polynomial*; in particular, if there are two terms it is a *binomial*, three terms a *trinomial*, and so on. The distributive law for multiplication makes the product of a polynomial by a monomial immediate, that is, $3a^2(ab^2 - 3ab + 4b^2) = 3a^3b^2 - 9a^3b + 12a^2b^2$. Similarly, where the parentheses make $(a + b)$

behave as a single term, we have $(a + b)(a^2 + 3ab - 2b^2) = (a + b)(a^2) + (a + b)(3ab) + (a + b)(-2b^2) = a^3 + a^2b + 3a^2b + 3ab^2 - 2ab^2 - 2b^3 = a^3 + 4a^2b + ab^2 - 2b^3$. This result can be obtained more advantageously by setting it up as:

$$\begin{array}{ll} a^2 + 3ab - 2b^2 & \text{Check: } 1 + 3 - 2 = 2 \\ a + b & \qquad\qquad 1 + 1\ \ = 2 \\ \hline a^3 + 3a^2b - 2ab^2 & \qquad\qquad \text{Product } 4 \\ \quad + a^2b + 3ab^2 - 2b^3 & \\ \hline a^3 + 4a^2b + ab^2 - 2b^3 & 1 + 4 + 1 - 2 = 4, \end{array}$$

where like terms will be in proper columns. A check on coefficients can be made by substituting $a = 1$ and $b = 1$, that is, by adding coefficients as shown to the right above. The product of these sums must equal the sum of the coefficients of the product.

The process of division of a polynomial by a polynomial may be explained by asking, "By what factor must $(a+b)$ be multiplied to obtain $a^3 + 4a^2b + ab^2 - 2b^3$?" We have shown in the previous paragraph that $a^3 + 4a^2b + ab^2 - 2b^3 = (a+b)a^2 + (a+b)(3ab) + (a+b)(-2b^2)$; so when we divide $a^3 + 4a^2b + ab^2 - 2b^3$ by $a + b$ we must obtain a quotient made of the terms a^2, $3ab$, and $-2b^2$. To accomplish this end we set up the operation as indicated below, after we have arranged the dividend and divisor in descending order of the powers of one letter, in this case of a:

$$\begin{array}{l} \qquad\qquad\qquad\qquad \text{Quotient } a^2 + 3ab - 2b^2 \\ a^3/a = a^2 \qquad\qquad a + b \ )\ \overline{a^3 + 4a^2b + ab^2 - 2b^3} \\ \text{Subtract } a^2(a + b) \qquad\quad \underline{a^3 + a^2b} \\ (3a^2b)/a = 3ab \qquad\qquad\qquad + 3a^2b + ab^2 - 2b^3 \\ \text{Subtract } 3ab(a + b) \qquad\qquad \underline{+ 3a^2b + 3ab^2} \\ (-2ab^2)/a = -2b^2 \qquad\qquad\qquad\quad - 2ab^2 - 2b^3 \\ \text{Subtract } (-2b^2)(a + b) \qquad\qquad\quad \underline{- 2ab^2 - 2b^3} \\ \qquad\qquad\qquad \text{Remainder} \qquad\qquad\qquad 0. \end{array}$$

The quotient we have obtained contains only the factors designated above.

Products by Inspection. Several kinds of products occur so frequently that we are able to type them, and write the answer by inspection. Some of the commonest are:

(P-1) $a(\pm b \pm c \pm d \pm \ldots) = \pm ab \pm ac \pm ad \pm \ldots$
(P-2) $(a + b)(a - b) = a^2 - b^2$
(P-3) $(a + b)(a + b) = a^2 + 2ab + b^2 = (a+b)^2$
(P-4) $(a - b)(a - b) = a^2 - 2ab + b^2 = (a-b)^2$
(P-5) $(x + a)(x + b) = x^2 + (a+b)x + ab$
(P-6) $(ax + b)(cx + d) = acx^2 + (bc + ad)x + bd$
(P-7) $(a + b)(a^2 - ab + b^2) = a^3 + b^3$
(P-8) $(a - b)(a^2 + ab + b^2) = a^3 - b^3.$

All of these general results can be verified by simple multiplication.

Factoring. When these forms are read from right to left, they become the rules for factoring, that is, for finding the factors whose product is a given quantity.

(F-1) Always factor out a common monomial factor, if there is one:

$$3x + 6xy - 9xy^2 = 3x(1 + 2y - 3y^2).$$

If your quantity has only two terms it must arise from (P-2), (P-7), or (P-8), so we have

(F-2) $16x^2 - 25y^2 = (4x + 5y)(4x - 5y)$
(F-7) $8a^3 + 27b^3 = (2a + 3b)(4a^2 - 6ab + 9b^2)$
(F-8) $8a^3 - 27b^3 = (2a - 3b)(4a^2 + 6ab + 9b^2).$

Special rules for factoring quantities like $a^n + b^n$ when n is an odd integer, and $a^n - b^n$ when n is either an odd or an even integer, are given in more extensive discussions.

If the quantity has three terms it must be the result of (P-3), (P-4), (P-5), or (P-6). In (F-3) and (F-4), the trinomial has two perfect square terms, and the other term is twice the product of their square roots, thus:

(F-3) $4x^2 + 12xy + 9y^2 = (2x + 3y)^2$.
(F-4) $4x^2 - 12xy + 9y^2 = (2x - 3y)^2$.

In (F-5), the trinomial has only one perfect square term like $x^2 - 3x - 18$. Here we must find two numbers a and b whose sum is -3 and whose product is -18. Inspection says that $a = -6$ and $b = 3$, hence by (P-5)

(F-5) $x^2 - 3x - 18 = (x - 6)(x + 3)$.

(F-6), a trinomial with no perfect square terms, is reserved until after we have studied the quadratic equation in a later paragraph (see section on *Equations*). It is an interesting comment that we never need to write wrong factors because the product of the factors must give the expression we are factoring.

Highest Common Factor (HCF) and Lowest Common Multiple (LCM). The HCF is the factor of highest degree that is common to all the quantities. The LCM is the expression of lowest degree into which each of the quantities may be divided without a remainder.

Example: Find the HCF and LCM of $9x^2 - 4y^2$, $9x^2 - 12xy + 4y^2$, and $6x^2 + 11xy - 10y^2$.

$9x^2 - 4y^2 \qquad\qquad = (3x + 2y)(3x - 2y)$
$9x^2 - 12xy + 4y^2 = (3x - 2y)(3x - 2y)$
$6x^2 + 11xy - 10y^2 = (3x - 2y)(2x + 5y)$.

Evidently, the HCF is $3x - 2y$, and the LCM is $(3x - 2y)^2 (3x + 2y)(2x + 5y)$ because it must contain every factor the greatest number of times it occurs in any one of the quantities.

The ability to factor algebraic expressions is necessary in performing the fundamental operations on fractions. In adding fractions it is basically necessary that all be reduced to the same denominator, the LCM of the denominators. This denominator is called the lowest common denominator (LCD).

A fraction is said to be in simplest form when there are no common factors in the numerator and the denominator. If the degree of the numerator of a fraction is lower than the degree of the denominator, the fraction is called *proper;* all others are *improper.*

Equations. When two algebraic quantities are joined by a sign of equality, the expression is called an *equation.* The term equation has two distinct meanings. Quite frequently it makes a statement like

$(3a - 4b)(3a - 5b) = 9a^2 - 27ab + 20b^2$,

which is true for all values of a and b; this is called an *identity.* On the other hand, equations like $3x + 4 = 2x - 5$ or $x^2 - 5x + 6 = 0$ ask a question: "Are there any values of x for which these statements are true?" These are the principal working tools of algebra; they are called *equations of condition.*

The following operations may be performed on an equation without changing the answer to the question above:

(1) Both sides of an equation (called its members) may be multiplied or divided by any quantity whose value is not zero.

(2) The same quantity may be added to or subtracted from both members.

(3) Both sides may be raised to the same power, integral or fractional. This will never fail to give the correct answer, but it may introduce some spurious answers.

When the value, or values, of the unknown in an equation have been obtained, we say we have *solved* the equation, and the values so obtained are called the *roots* of the equation. Once they are obtained, it is possible to verify the result, because the substitution of the value (or values) in the original equation must give rise to a numerical identity.

It is always possible to find a solution in terms of the coefficients for equations in which the variables occur only to the first or second degree. Theoretically, such solutions are also possible for third and fourth degree equations, but they have no practical value. For equations of higher degree no such solutions exist.

Any first degree equation can be written $ax + b = 0$; its solution is $x = -b/a$.

Any second degree equation, called a *quadratic equation,* can be written in the form $ax^2 + bx + c = 0$ where a, b, and c are constants, and the solution is

$$x = \frac{-b \pm \sqrt{b^2 - 4ac}}{2a}.$$

The derivation of this important formula should be clear to every student of algebra. The following method is perhaps the simplest to remember.

Solve $ax^2 + bx + c = 0$; a, b, c constants. First, multiply by $4a$: $4a^2x^2 + 4abx + 4ac = 0$. Add $-4ac$ to each member $4a^2x^2 + 4abx = -4ac$. Add b^2 to each member: $4a^2x^2 + 4abx + b^2 = b^2 - 4ac$. The first member is now $(2ax + b)^2$; hence $\qquad\qquad (2ax + b)^2 = b^2 - 4ac$.

Take the square root of both members to obtain

$$2ax + b = \pm \sqrt{b^2 - 4ac}, \text{ whence}$$

$2ax = -b \pm \sqrt{b^2 - 4ac}$ and $x = \dfrac{-b \pm \sqrt{b^2 - 4ac}}{2a}$.

If $b^2 - 4ac$ is a positive perfect square, the values of x are rational fractions, and it is possible to factor the form (F-6) omitted earlier (see section on *Factoring*).

Logarithms. A particular application of the theory of exponents makes it possible to perform multiplication by addition; division by subtraction; powers by multiplication; and roots by division (see LOGARITHMS). Tables have been devised that give the exponents of a base (10 in usual practice) that are needed to produce any number. Thus, if $10^L = N$, L is called the logarithm of N to base 10, written $L = \log_{10} N$. All the operations using the form $10^L = N$ are basically algebraic equations.

Function Notation. One of the most interesting phases of algebra is its ability to spell out more or less complicated ideas in a formula. Suppose we have a polynomial like

$$a_0x^n + a_1x^{n-1} + a_2x^{n-2} + \ldots + a_n$$

where the a's are constants, then the value of this polynomial depends entirely on the value of x. Hence we say it is a function of x, and we invent a symbol $f(x)$, called "f function of x," to stand for the polynomial. Thus

$$f(x) = a_0x^n + a_1x^{n-1} + a_2x^{n-2} + \ldots + a_n.$$

If we now wish to speak of the value of this function when $x = b$, we write simply:

$$f(b) = a_0b^n + a_1b^{n-1} + a_2b^{n-2} + \ldots + a_n.$$

In particular, suppose we define $g(x)$, called "g function of x," as follows:

$g(x) = 3x^3 - 7x^2 + 11x - 17$,
then $g(0) = 3 \cdot 0 - 7 \cdot 0 + 11 \cdot 0 - 17 = -17$
$\qquad g(1) = 3 - 7 + 11 - 17 = -10$
$\qquad g(a) = 3a^3 - 7a^2 + 11a - 17$.

Factor Theorem. Let us investigate what happens when we divide $f(x)$ by $x - a$. It is evident from our previous knowledge of division that the quotient will contain x to a degree one less than that of the dividend—we shall call it $Q(x)$—and probably a remainder R, which at worst will be a constant. In formula it will look like this:

$$\frac{f(x)}{x - a} = Q(x) + \frac{R}{x - a}$$

or, cleared of fractions, $f(x) = (x-a)Q(x) + R$. This is the method used to prove a division problem,

(dividend) = (divisor) (quotient) + remainder. This is true for any values of x. Hence,

$$f(x) = (x - a) Q(x) + R$$

must be true. If $x = a$, it becomes

$$f(a) = (a - a) Q(a) + R \text{ or } R = f(a) ;$$

that is, $f(a)$ is the remainder when we divide $f(x)$ by $x - a$. If the remainder upon such division is zero, $x - a$ is a factor of $f(x)$. This is known as the *factor theorem*; it is most convenient for determining linear factors of functions that are of higher degree than the second in x.

Abridged Division. At this stage of our thinking it will be wise to consider how certain processes can be shortened without impairing their reliability. Let us consider the division of $3x^4 - 5x^3 + 2x^2 - 4x - 11$ by $x^2 - 2x + 5$. If we lay out a skeleton division, leaving a place in the dividend and the divisor for each power of x in descending order, we can write our problem entirely in coefficients:

```
              Quotient        3 +  1 - 11
  1 - 2 + 5 ) 3 - 5 +  2 -  4 - 11
              3 - 6 + 15
              ─────────────
                  1 - 13 -  4 - 11
                  1 -  2 +  5
                  ─────────────
                     - 11 -  9 - 11
                     - 11 + 22 - 55
                     ─────────────
    Remainder           - 31 + 44
```

where the quotient is $3x^2 + x - 11$ and the remainder is $-31x + 44$. This is called division by *detached coefficients*.

Such division by a quantity like $x - a$ becomes even simpler, for example, $\dfrac{2x^3 - 7x + 15}{x - 3}$

(note that the coefficient of x^2 is zero):

```
                    2 +  6 + 11
    1 - 3) 2 + 0 -  7 + 15
           2 - 6
           ─────
               6 -  7
               6 - 18
               ──────
                   11 + 15
                   11 - 33
                   ──────
                     + 48.
```

Notice that the quantities printed in boldface type agree with those in the quotient and 48 is the remainder. This work may be shortened by omitting the second writing of the numbers 2, 6, and 11 and writing the divisor as -3 as below

```
            - 3) 2 + 0 -  7 + 15
Subtract            - 6 - 18 - 33
                 ──────────────
                 2 + 6 + 11 + 48.
```

Here is the operation: bring down the 2; multiply it by the -3, subtract from 0 to get $+6$; multiply the $+6$ by -3 and subtract from -7 to get $+11$; multiply $+11$ by -3 and subtract from 15 to get 48, which is the remainder. The other coefficients give the quotient as $2x^2 + 6x + 11$. If the divisor is changed to $+3$, the same operation can be followed but we add instead of subtract, thus

```
    +3) 2 + 0 -  7 + 15
             + 6 + 18 + 33
        ──────────────────
        2 + 6 + 11 + 48.
```

This method of dividing by a quantity like $x - a$ is known as *synthetic division*. Since the remainder is $f(a)$ when we divide $f(x)$ by $x-a$, synthetic division gives an easy method for finding $f(a)$. If $f(a)$ is zero, a is a root of the equation $f(x) = 0$.

Partial Fractions. If we have two quantities in a single variable set up on two sides of an equality such as

$$b_0x^n + b_1x^{n-1} + \ldots + b_n = a_0x^n + a_1x^{n-1} + \ldots + a_n,$$

we understand that this equation cannot hold unless the coefficients of the like powers of the variables are identical, that is, $b_0 = a_0$, $b_1 = a_1$, and so on. This leads to the principle of *undetermined coefficients*, which is particularly useful in the calculus in separating a fraction with a factorable denominator into a sum of fractions with the separate factors as denominators, called *partial fractions*. To illustrate the method, let us find the partial fractions whose sum is

$$\frac{3x^2 + 4x + 41}{(x - 3)(x + 5)(x + 2)}.$$

Suppose that

$$\frac{3x^2 + 4x + 41}{(x - 3)(x + 5)(x + 2)} = \frac{A}{x - 3} + \frac{B}{x + 5} + \frac{C}{x + 2};$$

when cleared of fractions we have

$$3x^2 + 4x + 41 = (A + B + C)x^2 + (7A - B + 2C)x + 10A - 6B - 15C.$$

This will be true only if $A + B + C = 3$; $7A - B + 2C = 4$; and $10A - 6B - 15C = 41$. The common solution of these three equations gives $A = 2, B = 4, C = -3$; hence,

$$\frac{3x^2 + 4x + 41}{(x - 3)(x + 5)(x + 2)} = \frac{2}{x - 3} + \frac{4}{x + 5} - \frac{3}{x + 2},$$

which we can easily check. See also BINOMIAL; COMBINATIONS AND PERMUTATIONS; INDUCTION, MATHEMATICAL; PROBABILITY.

WALTER F. SHENTON
American University, Washington, D.C.

Further Reading: Angel, Allen R., *Algebra: An Elementary Approach*, 2d ed. (Prentice-Hall 1988); Beckenbach, Edwin F., and others, *College Algebra*, 6th ed. (Wadsworth Pub. 1984); Matthews, P. E., and Chisko, A. M., *Elementary Algebra: An Analytical Approach* (Wiley 1986); Yamato, Yoshiko, and Cordon, Mary J., *Mastering Elementary Algebra* (Harcourt 1987).

2. Modern Algebra

Modern algebra is a branch of mathematics that has been developed, for the most part, during the 20th century, although it has its roots in earlier work. Before the modern trend toward abstraction was felt, algebra was chiefly concerned with theories for the solution of equations, finding values of the unknown quantities, or the conditions under which they can or cannot be found. During the 20th century, algebraic research has been largely concerned with studying the abstract structure of some of the algebraic systems that were introduced in the earlier work and in introducing new concepts that give a deeper understanding of these problems. Group theory, matrices, and Galois theory (all subjects that were developed extensively during the 19th century) play an important role in modern algebraic research. Some of the concepts essential to their understanding are dealt with here from a unified point of view: fields, integral domains, rings, ideals, linear algebras. (See also GROUPS, THEORY OF; MATRIX.)

The great interest in modern algebra lies in the generality and the beauty of its results and in its relations with other branches of modern mathematics such as the geometry of curves and surfaces. Through abstractions it treats many of the essential issues of ordinary algebra so that the solution of a single abstract problem gives the solution of many special formulations of it. But modern algebra seeks also to obtain general results, for example, the determination of all domains in which unique factorization is possible.

Sets and Mappings. In order to take advantage of some of the powerful abstractions of modern algebra, it is useful to begin by considering one of the most fundamental concepts in mathematics, the concept of *class* or *set*. A set is a collection of objects described by some rule that tells exactly which objects belong to the collection. Thus we can talk of the set of all even numbers, or the set consisting of John, Jerry, and Jane, or the set of all circles that are in a plane and have a radius of 3. Sets such as these may be combined by certain operations (union and intersection), similar to addition and multiplication, to form other sets, just as numbers may be combined by addition and multiplication to form other numbers. The study of these operations comprises the *algebra of sets* (or Boolean algebra), first studied by George Boole in 1854.

For the present, our concern is with the *mapping* of one set into another, an operation that enables us in suitable instances to understand the identity of the structure of two apparently distinct algebraic systems. If, by any device, every element s of a set S (symbolically $s \varepsilon S$) is made to correspond to an element r of a set R, S is said to be mapped in R. It may or may not be that every r has an element s mapped on it; and some r's may correspond to more than one s. For example, if we set up a correspondence between the natural numbers and the set $\{0, 1\}$ so that even numbers correspond to 0 and odd numbers to 1, we have a many-to-one correspondence. Such a mapping does not have an inverse. But some mappings are a one-to-one correspondence. For example, if we map the natural numbers, 1, 2, 3, . . ., on the even numbers, 2, 4, 6, . . ., by the correspondence, $n \rightarrow 2n$, this mapping can be reversed by the mapping, $2n \rightarrow n$. This example is a one-to-one correspondence. (We say that the natural numbers and the even numbers have the same *cardinal number*.) This example illustrates the fact that an infinite set may be put into a one-to-one correspondence with a part of itself.

Similarly, on a plane graph, all the points for which x and y are both integers may be put into a one-to-one correspondence with the natural numbers.

Basic Concepts. The oldest mathematical system is the set of positive integers. We shall begin our discussion, however, with the set of all integers, positive, negative, and zero, using the methods of modern algebra to describe this system; and we shall then observe the variety of other sets that are similarly described. For this purpose the term "integer" is not defined except by a set of postulates that the symbols, a, b, c, . . . are required to satisfy. Later it will be seen that these symbols may also be thought of as real or complex numbers, polynomials, matrices, ideals, or a variety of other objects. To describe the sets in which we shall be interested we need the concepts of equivalence, addition, and multiplication.

Equivalence ($\sim$) is a relation that is either true or not true for any two elements of the set, and is described by the postulates:

(1) $a \sim a$ for every a in the set.
(2) If $a \sim b$, then $b \sim a$.
(3) If $a \sim b$ and $b \sim c$, then $a \sim c$.

Clearly the integers satisfy the postulates of equivalences if $\sim$ means equality. And if $a \sim b$ means that the set a is in a one-to-one correspondence with the set b, it is clear that this relation is also an equivalence relation. But equivalence is an even more inclusive concept. For example, if a and b represent two points in a plane, and the relation $a \sim b$ means that a and b lie on the same horizontal line, we see that these three postulates are satisfied. Moreover, the set of all points p such that $a \sim p$ is the horizontal line through a. The set of all such lines gives a decomposition of the points of the plane into sets characterized by the fact that every point is in a set, and no two sets have a point in common. These lines are the *equivalence classes* defined by this particular equivalence relation. Every equivalence relation has the property that it determines such equivalence classes. Thus, if we have a set of elements S, and an equivalence relation r, a new set S of equivalence classes is determined, called the *quotient set* of S with respect to r. See also section on *Types of Algebraic Systems*.

Addition ($+$) is one of the operations characterizing an algebraic system that enables us to construct additional elements of the system from a finite number of them. The postulates assumed for addition are:

(1) For any two elements a and b of the set, there exists a sum $(a + b)$ also in the set.
(2) If $a = a_1$ and $b = b_1$ then $(a + b) = (a_1 + b_1)$.
(3) For every a and b, $a + b = b + a$, described as the commutative law for addition.
(4) For every a, b, and c, $a + (b + c) = (a + b) + c$, described as the associative law for addition.
(5) There exists an element 0 of the set such that, for every a, $a + 0 = a$. The 0 is the identity element for addition. It is the element 0 in the set of integers.
(6) For every a, there is an element $(-a)$ such that $a + (-a) = 0 = (-a) + a$. Also, $a + (-b)$ is written $a - b$.

Multiplication ($\times$ or $\cdot$) is another operation that enables us to construct additional elements of the system from a finite number of them. Among the following postulates, it satisfies (1) and (2), and some or all of the others.

(1) For any two elements a and b of the set, there exists a product $(a \cdot b)$ also in the set.

(2) If $a = a_1$ and $b = b_1$ then $a \cdot b = a_1 \cdot b_1$.

(3) For every a and b, $a \cdot b = b \cdot a$. This is the commutative law for multiplication.

(4) For every a, b, and c, $a \cdot (b \cdot c) = (a \cdot b) \cdot c$. This is the associative law for multiplication.

(5) There exists an element e of the set such that, for every a, $a \cdot e = a$. The e is the identity element for multiplication. It is the element 1 in the set of integers.

(6) If $ab = ac$, and $a \neq 0$, then $b = c$. This is the cancellation law.

(7) For every $a \neq 0$, there is an inverse a^{-1} (called reciprocal in the set of rational numbers) such that $aa^{-1} = e = a^{-1}a$.

It will be seen that the postulates for addition and multiplication are formally identical except that, in postulate seven for multiplication, there is an excluded element, zero.

A further law, the distributive law, is postulated for the two operations, addition and multiplication:

$a \cdot (b + c) = a \cdot b + a \cdot c;$
$(b + c) \cdot a = b \cdot a + c \cdot a.$

Clearly the system of integers, positive, negative, and zero, satisfy all these postulates until we reach (7) for multiplication. Such a system is called an *integral domain*. In order to secure a system satisfying *all* these postulates, we must extend the set of integers to include all the rational numbers (fractions). By this extension we obtain a *field*.

The process of extension has broad significance in modern algebra. The particular extension from integers to fractions is representative of an important class of extensions, from integral domains to fields; it can be effected by introducing as an element of the new set a *pair* of integers (a, b) with $b \neq 0$, satisfying the following definitions:

(1) $(a, b) = (c, d)$ if and only if $a = c$ and $b = d$

(2) $(a, b) \pm (c, d) = (a \pm c, b \pm d)$

(3) $(a, b) \cdot (c, d) = (ac - bd, ad + bc)$

(4) $(0, b) = 0$ (identity for addition)

(5) $(a, a) = e$ (identity for multiplication).

Under these definitions a pair (a, b) has all the properties of the familiar fraction $\frac{a}{b}$. Moreover, the system of pairs (a, b) satisfies all the above postulates of equivalence, addition, and multiplication, with $(-a, b)$ serving as the inverse of (a, b) for addition, that is $(a, b) + (-a, b) = (0, b)$; and (b, a) serving as the inverse for multiplication, that is, (a, b) $(b, a) = (ab, ab) = e$, provided $a \neq 0$.

Types of Algebraic Systems. This new system is an illustration of a *field*, an algebraic system for which all the enumerated axioms are satisfied. (If the commutative law for multiplication is not satisfied the system is sometimes called a noncommutative field.) A less familiar example of a field can be found among *modular systems*.

One of the most familiar modular systems is used in telling the time of day. If it is now 10 o'clock, and we ask what time it will be in 5 hours, we do not usually say 15 o'clock but rather 3 o'clock, because our clocks admit only

the numbers 1 through 12. Similarly, if we ask what time it will be after 18 hours, we do not say 28 o'clock but rather 4 o'clock. Thus we habitually reduce the answer by throwing away multiples of 12. In this case, 12 represents what is called in mathematics a *modulus* (M), and 15 is said to be *congruent* $(\equiv)$ to 3, while 28 is congruent to 4, modulo M. Two integers, a and b, are said to be congruent if they differ by a multiple of M. Symbolically, $a \equiv b \pmod M$ means $a = b + kM$ where k is an integer. We saw above that $15 \equiv 3 \pmod{12}$; $28 \equiv 4 \pmod{12}$. By means of a modulus, all the integers are divided into equivalence classes. In the case of modulus 12, these classes may be represented by the integers 1, 2, 3, 4, . . ., 11, 12 (or 0). This means that every integer is congruent to one, and only one, of these.

If, now, we consider this set of equivalence classes as our algebraic system, it will be seen that they satisfy all the postulates for addition (where $-a$ is the same as $12 - a$; for example, -4 is 8), and all the postulates for multiplication except (6) and (7). The cancellation law fails since, for example, $6 \cdot 9 \equiv 6 \cdot 3$ does not imply $9 \equiv 3$; and there are classes that have no inverse, for example, the class represented by 4. If, however, the modulus is a prime number, say 5, then the equivalence classes represented by 0, 1, 2, 3, 4 satisfy all the postulates for addition and multiplication and form a field.

A *ring* is a system with the two operations, addition and multiplication, satisfying all the postulates for addition and at least postulates (1), (2), and (4) for multiplication. Special types of rings satisfy additional postulates. An integral domain, mentioned above, is a ring in which all the postulates of multiplication are satisfied except postulate (7) on the existence of an inverse.

A ring without an identity is exemplified by the set of all even integers. Here postulates (5) and (7) for multiplication are not satisfied, but an easy check of the familiar properties of integers shows that all the other postulates are satisfied. A ring in which postulate (6) for multiplication (the cancellation law) is not satisfied is said to have *divisors of zero*. This is equivalent to the statement that the product of two elements may be zero, though neither element is zero. For example, the set of all second-order

matrices $\begin{pmatrix} a & b \\ c & d \end{pmatrix}$, where a, b, c, d are rational numbers, is a noncommutative ring with divisors of zero. The noncommutativity is a familiar property of matrices. The example

$\begin{pmatrix} 0 & b \\ 0 & d \end{pmatrix} \quad \begin{pmatrix} a & c \\ 0 & 0 \end{pmatrix} = \begin{pmatrix} 0 & 0 \\ 0 & 0 \end{pmatrix}$, with a, b, c, d

different from zero, illustrates the fact that the product of two elements of this system can be zero when neither element is zero.

A *group* is a system with a single operation satisfying all the postulates for addition, except possibly (3) on commutativity. If postulate 3 is satisfied, the group is called commutative or Abelian. In commutative groups the single group operation is frequently described as addition; in noncommutative groups, as multiplication. But, in the general case, the more inclusive term, composition, is often used to indicate that the operation may correspond to neither of the familiar concepts (addition and multiplication).

The group operation may, for instance, be rotation or mapping.

Homomorphisms. When we have a mapping of one group S into another group R, or one ring S into another ring R, or one field S into another field R, it may happen that the mapping always makes the sum or product of two elements of S correspond to the sum or product of the corresponding elements of R. For example, in the familiar mapping of the integers on the points of a line, beginning with an origin, and equally spaced, so that n_1 is the length of ON_1, and n_2 the length of ON_2

$$
\begin{array}{ccccccc}
O & & & & N_1 & N_2 \\
\hline
0 & 1 & 2 & 3 & n_1 & n_2
\end{array}
$$

the sum of the two integers $(n_1 + n_2)$ maps on the point obtained by the geometric addition of ON_1 and ON_2; and the product $n_1 \cdot n_2$ maps on the point corresponding to their geometric product. But this kind of correspondence after a mapping is not always preserved, as we see by considering the mapping of the natural numbers n on the even numbers $2n$. In this case it is true that the map n_1 + map n_2 = map $(n_1 + n_2)$ because $2n_1 + 2n_2 = 2 (n_1 + n_2)$, but it is not true that map $n_1 \cdot$ map n_2 = map $(n_1 n_2)$ because $2n_1 2n_2 \neq 2n_1 n_2$.

If the mapping of $S \to R$ is such that $s_1 \to r_1$, $s_2 \to r_2$, and

$$O_S (s_1 s_2) \to O_R (r_1 r_2),$$

where O_S represents all the operations in the set S, and O_R all the operations in the set R, then the mapping is called a homomorphism. If the mapping is a one-to-one correspondence, it is called an isomorphism. If the mapping carries the set into itself and is a one-to-one correspondence, it is called an automorphism. For example, the mapping of the integers on the points of a line is an isomorphism. In fact, we base our arguments on points or numbers interchangeably, using whichever is more convenient. This is a recognition of the fact that two isomorphic sets have the same structure. An example of an automorphism is the rotations of a plane through angles that are multiples of $60°$.

Now consider the mapping of the integers on the elements of the modular field 0, 1, 2, 3, 4. This mapping is described by the correspondence $5k_0 \to 0, 5k_1 + 1 \to 1, 5k_2 + 2 \to 2, 5k_3 + 3 \to 3, 5k_4 + 4 \to 4$, where k_0, k_1, k_2, k_3, k_4 are arbitrary integers. This is a many-to-one correspondence that is preserved under addition and multiplication. Therefore, the ring of integers is homomorphic to this modular field.

Extensions of Integral Domains. If we represent by D any integral domain, and if we let x be any symbol, subject to the postulates of addition and multiplication, except for postulate (7), we may form sums and products of x with itself and the elements of D. Thus we obtain a *polynomial* in the *indeterminate* x (called indeterminate because we make no assumptions on x, not even the usual assumption of elementary algebra, namely, that x is an element of D). This procedure enables us to construct all expressions of the form $a_0 + a_1 x + \ldots + a_n x^n$ with $a_0, a_1 \ldots, a_n$ in D, $a_n \neq 0$ if $n > 0$, and x^n is $x \cdot x \ldots x$ to n factors. The concepts of addition and multiplication can be extended to these new forms. For example, if D is the field consisting of all the congruence classes modulo 7, namely, 0, 1, 2, 3, 4, 5, 6, then two such polynomials might be $f(x) = 2 + 6x + 4x^2$, and $g(x) = 4x + 3x^2$. Their sum would be $(2 + 3x)$, and their product would be $(x + 2x^2 + 6x^3 + 5x^4)$.

In general, with the usual definitions of addition and multiplication, it can be proved that the set of polynomial forms in x over any integral domain D constitutes a new integral domain $D[x]$ containing D.

A number of the properties of elementary algebra hold in $D[x]$. In particular, an extension of a familiar theorem of elementary algebra is given by the theorem: A polynomial form $f(x)$ of degree n over an integral domain D has at most n zeros in D. Another theorem states that if $f \neq 0$ and h are polynomials of degree n and m, respectively, and if the coefficient of the term of highest degree in h has a reciprocal, then there are unique elements q and r in $D[x]$ such that $f = hq + r$, where q is either zero or of degree $n - m \geq 0$, and the degree of r is less than m. This is the extension of the Euclidean divisibility algorithm, familiar for integers and for polynomials in elementary algebra. For integers f and h, this algorithm is merely the statement that when f is divided by h there is a quotient q and a remainder r less than h.

The Euclidean algorithm can be used to prove that the greatest common divisor (GCD) g of two nonzero integers a and b can be expressed in the form $g = sa + tb$ where s and t are integers; or, in words, g is a *linear combination* of a and b. The Euclidean algorithm can also be used to prove the fundamental theorem of arithmetic, *the unique factorization theorem*, namely, that every positive integer N can be expressed as a product of primes in one and only one way except for the order of the factors. There are, however, quite simple domains in which this theorem fails. If, for example, we consider the set of numbers obtained by *adjoining* $\sqrt{-5}$ to the rationals, namely, all the numbers $(u + v\sqrt{-5})$ where u and v are rationals, it is easily verified that this set does not meet the unique factorization theorem although it satisfies all the postulates for a field. The concept of integer can be extended by defining the integers of such an *algebraic field* as any numbers of the field that satisfy an algebraic equation with rational integral coefficients and a leading coefficient of unity. All rational integers u (the ordinary integers) satisfy a linear equation $x - u = 0$. Also, $\sqrt{-5}$ satisfies the quadratic equation $x^2 + 5 = 0$, and it is therefore an integer of the form $R(\sqrt{-5})$. Moreover, all numbers of the form $a + b\sqrt{-5}$ are integers of the new field, if a and b are rational integers, because they satisfy the equation $x^2 - 2ax + (a^2 + 5b^2) = 0$.

The converse is also true: all integers of this field have the form $a + b\sqrt{-5}$ where a and b are integers. (The form does not generalize to all quadratic fields.) An interesting feature of $R(\sqrt{-5})$ is that an extension of the usual definition of primes does not preserve the unique factorization theorem. This is evident from the simple identity:

$$21 = 3 \cdot 7 = (1 + 2\sqrt{-5}) (1 - 2\sqrt{-5}) = (4 + \sqrt{-5}) (4 - \sqrt{-5})$$

since 3, 7, $1 + 2\sqrt{-5}$, $1 - 2\sqrt{-5}$, $4 + \sqrt{-5}$, and $4 - \sqrt{-5}$ can all be shown to be prime integers in the field.

The failure of the unique factorization theorem is related to the fact that, in this field, it is not true that every pair of integers, not both 0, have a GCD expressible linearly in terms of those integers. By the introduction of a new kind of number, *ideal* numbers, unique factorization in terms of ideals can be restored. Ideals, which have many other interesting properties, have been studied extensively by the methods of modern algebra.

Linear Sets. The concept of linear sets and, in particular, vector spaces (see VECTOR ANALYSIS) is a fundamental one in mathematics. Such sets can be defined over any ring R. However, for the purposes of this account, the discussion will be limited to the most familiar cases where the domain of definition is a field F. We need the following definition: A vector space (or linear space) V over a field F is a set of elements, called vectors, such that any two vectors α and β of V determine a unique vector $\alpha + \beta$ as a sum. Also, any vector α of V and any scalar c of F determine a scalar product $c \cdot \alpha$ in V that has the properties:

(1) V is an Abelian group under addition.
(2) $c \cdot (\alpha + \beta) = c \cdot \alpha + c \cdot \beta$.
(3) $c^{-1}(c\alpha) = (c^{-1}c) \cdot \alpha = 1 \cdot \alpha = \alpha$.

The set of all two-rowed matrices whose elements are complex numbers is a vector space over the field of rational numbers. The set of two-rowed matrices whose elements are ordinary integers is not a vector space over the rationals because a rational multiplied by such a matrix may give a matrix not in the set. For example,

$$\tfrac{1}{2}\begin{pmatrix} 1 & 0 \\ 1 & 0 \end{pmatrix} = \begin{pmatrix} \tfrac{1}{2} & 0 \\ \tfrac{1}{2} & 0 \end{pmatrix},$$

and the matrix elements are not integers. The vector space V of two-rowed matrices, with complex elements over the field F of complex numbers, has further interesting properties. It is a *linear algebra* if we define multiplication of matrices in the usual way because:

(1) It is *finite dimensional*, that is, every matrix of V can be expressed as the sum of four

matrices, $\begin{pmatrix} 1 & 0 \\ 0 & 0 \end{pmatrix}, \begin{pmatrix} 0 & 0 \\ 1 & 0 \end{pmatrix}, \begin{pmatrix} 0 & 1 \\ 0 & 0 \end{pmatrix},$ and $\begin{pmatrix} 0 & 0 \\ 0 & 1 \end{pmatrix},$

that are multiplied respectively by elements of F. These basic elements are linearly independent. (See VECTOR ANALYSIS.)

(2) The multiplication of matrices is associative.

(3) If α, β, γ are any matrices of V, and c, d are any complex numbers, then

$$\alpha(c\beta + d\gamma) = c(\alpha\beta) + d(\alpha\gamma)$$
$$(c\alpha + d\beta)\gamma = c(\alpha\gamma) + d(\beta\gamma).$$

This algebra has a unity element, $\begin{pmatrix} 1 & 0 \\ 0 & 1 \end{pmatrix} = \varepsilon,$

such that $\varepsilon\alpha = \alpha$ for all α in V. Moreover, every element has a multiplicative inverse. These properties are necessary and sufficient to show that this algebra is a *division algebra*.

A famous example of a division algebra is the algebra of quaternions introduced by Sir William Rowan Hamilton (1805–1865). These can be obtained by adjoining to the field of complex numbers another quantity j such that $j^2 = -1$. Since the equation $x^2 = -1$ can have at most the two roots $\pm i$ in any field, it is clear that the set containing i and j cannot be a field. If, however, we specify that multiplication of a

complex number by j shall be noncommutative:

$$ij = -ji;\ (a + bi)j = j(a - bi)$$

where a and b are real, and if we set $ij = k$, we obtain the following multiplication table:

·	1	i	j	k
1	1	i	j	k
i	i	-1	k	$-j$
j	j	$-k$	-1	i
k	k	j	$-i$	-1

Every number in the set of quaternions can be written in the form

$$x = x_0 + x_1 i + x_2 j + x_3 k \qquad (x_i \text{ real}),$$

and two such numbers can be multiplied, by consulting the multiplication table, to obtain a new number of the same form. Scalar multiplication (by reals), addition, and multiplication are defined in the usual way; addition and multiplication are distributive. Thus, quaternions form a linear algebra. If we make

$$1 \sim \begin{pmatrix} 1 & 0 \\ 0 & 1 \end{pmatrix}, i \sim \begin{pmatrix} -i & 0 \\ 0 & i \end{pmatrix}, j \sim \begin{pmatrix} 0 & 1 \\ -1 & 0 \end{pmatrix},$$
$$k \sim \begin{pmatrix} 0 & -i \\ -i & 0 \end{pmatrix},$$

then $i^2 = j^2 = k^2 = -1$, and these elements are linearly independent. Quaternions can thus be represented as an algebra of two-rowed matrices. In fact, it can be proved that every linear algebra of order n with a unit element is isomorphic to an algebra of $n \times n$ matrices.

The material that has been presented is introductory. Modern algebra has been undergoing substantial changes in scope and character as a result of vigorous research in a number of fields. The reader is referred particularly to the books listed in the bibliography that deal with representation theory, homological algebras, Lie algebras, nonassociative algebras, and commutative algebra.

MINA REES, *Hunter College*

Bibliography

Albert, A. Adrian, *Fundamental Concepts of Higher Algebra* (Polygonal Pub. 1981).
Angel, Allen, *Elementary Algebra* (Prentice-Hall 1985).
Beckenbach, Edwin F., and others, *Modern College Algebra and Trigonometry,* 5th ed. (Wadsworth Pub. 1985).
Bell, Evelyn, and others, *Essential Skills for Algebra* (Wiley 1987).
Birkhoff, Garrett, and MacLane, Saunders, *A Survey of Modern Algebra,* 4th ed. (Macmillan 1977).
Buchberger, B., and others, eds., *Computer Algebra* (Springer-Verlag 1983).
Diers, Y., *Categories of Boolean Sheaves of Simple Algebras* (Springer-Verlag 1986).
Dornhoff, Larry L., and Hohn, Franz E., *Applied Modern Algebra* (Macmillan 1978).
Gilbert, Linda and Jimmie, *Elements of Modern Algebra* (PWS Pub. 1983).
Hutton, Lucreda A., and others, *Success with Algebra* (Prentice-Hall 1985).
Marcus, Marvin, ed., *Introduction to Modern Algebra* (Dekker 1978).
Schafer, Richard, *An Introduction to Non-Associative Algebras* (Academic Press 1966).
Willerding, Margaret F., *Modern Intermediate Algebra,* 2d ed. (1975; reprint, Krieger 1982).
Zariski, Oscar, and Samuel, Pierre, *Commutative Algebra* (1958; reprint, Springer-Verlag 1975).

ALGEBRAIC GEOMETRY, al-jə-brā′ik jē-om′ə-trē, is the study of algebraic sets and their classification. In plane analytic geometry, the main idea is to set up a coordinate system and then to associate with an equation $f(x,y) = 0$ the set of all points (a,b) such that $f(a,b) = 0$. If $f(x,y)$ is a polynomial, the resulting set of points is called an *algebraic curve*. These points and their generalizations to higher dimensions are the concern of algebraic geometry. At first only points with real-number coordinates were allowed in algebraic geometry. Later it became necessary to allow points with complex-number coordinates. Once the transfer to complex numbers was made, the visual realization of geometric objects became little more than an aid in finding or understanding theorems.

The fundamental objects of study in modern algebraic geometry are *algebraic sets*. For any field K, we define an affine n-space $A_n(K)$ over K to be the set of n-tuples $(x_1, \ldots, x_n)$ with $x_1, \ldots, x_n$ belonging to K. Such an n-tuple is called a *point*. An *algebraic hypersurface* is the set of all such points satisfying a polynomial equation in n variables with coefficients in K. An *algebraic set* (often called an *algebraic variety*) is the intersection, or common locus, of a finite collection of algebraic hypersurfaces.

The modern period in algebraic geometry starts with the work of R.L. van der Waerden, Chow, Oscar Zariski, and André Weil. The publication of Weil's *Foundations of Algebraic Geometry* in 1947 was particularly important. The modern theory of algebraic groups starts with C.C. Chevalley and Weil; the works of Rosenlicht, A. Borel, and J.P. Serre on this subject are of basic importance. See ALGEBRA.

ALGECIRAS, äl-hā-thē′räs, is a city in Spain, in Cádiz province, on the western side of Algeciras Bay, 6 miles west of Gibraltar. Its name in Arabic is *al-Jazirah al-Khadra*. The city is a port, used primarily by vessels trading with North Africa, and a railway terminus. A mild climate, bathing beaches, and the Fuente Santa mineral springs have made it a winter resort. Tourism and fishing are the principal industries. There are also fish- and cork-processing industries and shipyards. Grain, tobacco, oranges, and livestock are raised in the surrounding area.

The city is reputedly situated on the site of the ancient Roman town of Portus Albus. The region was occupied by the Moors in 711 and ruled by them until 1344, when Alfonso XI of Castile captured the city. It subsequently was destroyed and later was colonized by Spanish refugees from Gibraltar in 1704. The modern city was built by Charles III in 1760. During the Napoleonic Wars a British fleet defeated the French and Spanish off Algeciras in 1801. In 1906 the city was the scene of the Algeciras Conference, called to settle the Moroccan crisis. Population: 101,468 (2001 census).

ALGECIRAS CONFERENCE, a 1906 international diplomatic conference in Algeciras, Spain. President Theodore Roosevelt intervened on behalf of the Germans to initiate discussion about the partition of Morocco by Spain and France, which was delayed until 1912.

ALGER, al′jər, **Horatio** (1832—1899), American author, who wrote a series of successful novels for boys on the rags-to-riches theme. He was born in Revere, Mass., on Jan. 13, 1832, the son of a Unitarian minister. His father wanted him to become a minister and, for this purpose, sent him to Harvard and to Harvard Divinity school, from which he graduated in 1860. Illness and a twice-broken arm kept Alger from joining the Union Army during the Civil War. He finally was ordained in 1864 and became minister of a Unitarian church in Brewster, Mass.

In 1866, Alger resigned from his church and moved to New York City, where he became associated with the Newsboys' Lodging House. The homeless waifs who lived there became the Ragged Dicks and Tattered Toms of his stories. He died in Natick, Mass., on July 18, 1899.

Alger was one of the New England moralizers who, though not necessarily rich or virtuous themselves, told others how to translate virtue into fortune in the rising commercial cities. He wrote about 135 books, with such titles as *Fame and Fortune*, *Struggling Upward*, and *Strive and Succeed*. The "Horatio Alger hero" became a symbol of success in an age when the legend was established that any poor boy could become president or a millionaire if he was intelligent, hard-working, and honest. Boys of the period delighted in Alger's tales of young men who won fortune's favor by leading virtuous lives and performing heroic deeds.

Cotton Mather, Benjamin Franklin, Freeman Hunt, and others had extolled the rewards of industry, frugality, and sobriety before Alger. He differed from his predecessors mainly in aiming at an audience of boys, in using the fictional form, and in setting his stories in New York City, the great mecca of success. His novels contain flimsy plots, wooden characters, and stilted conversations, which betray their hasty composition and expose the lack of imagination that made it impossible for Alger to fulfill his desire to write adult fiction.

IRVIN G. WYLLIE, *University of Wisconsin*

ALGER, al′jər, **Russell Alexander** (1836–1907), American public official. He was born in Lafayette Township, Medina County, Ohio, on Feb. 27, 1836, and was admitted to the Ohio bar in 1859. He moved in the following year to Michigan, where he eventually amassed a large fortune in the lumber industry. Serving in the Civil War, he rose from private to colonel, and in 1865 was breveted major general of volunteers for gallantry. After the war he was active in Republican politics, serving as governor of Michigan from 1885 to 1887.

In March 1897, Alger was appointed secretary of war by President William McKinley. The War Department, as he inherited it, was poorly organized and grossly inefficient, and the new secretary did nothing to improve it. This situation, which might have been tolerated in peacetime, became a matter of grave concern after the outbreak of the Spanish-American War in 1898. Poor food, inappropriate clothing, and inadequate medical services aroused widespread criticism. Finally, in July 1899, McKinley requested the secretary's resignation. A presidential commission failed to establish the extent of Alger's responsibility for the maladministration, and in 1901 he published *The Spanish-American War*, defending his conduct in office. He served as United States senator from Michigan from 1902 until his death in Washington, D.C., on Jan. 24, 1907.

Algiers, the capital of Algeria, extends up hills from a semicircular bay.

ALGERIA

CONTENTS

ALGERIA, al-jĕr′ē-ə, the second-largest country in Africa, in the Maghrib, or northwestern part of the continent. Its land mass is about as large as the combined areas of Alaska and Texas. At its farthest points, Algeria extends 1,240 miles (2,000 km) from north to south and 1,120 miles (1,800 km) from east to west. Its coastline stretches 686 miles (1,104 km) along the Mediterranean Sea, its only natural border. Algeria's name is derived from the Arabic word for "islands" (*al-jazair*) and was coined by a ruler of the Zirid dynasty on observing the islets off Algiers.

The country's topography is distinguished from north to south by approximately parallel east-west regions featuring coastal plains, mountains, plateaus, and deserts. Ethnic and cultural diversity is displayed by the Arab, Berber, and residual French and Jewish populations. Algeria presents a wide range of social contrasts, from the cosmopolitanism of the northern cities to the nomadic pastoralism of the Sahara.

Algeria's location and lack of natural barriers have made it susceptible to invasions and influences from Southwest Asia, Africa, and Europe, which have produced a multifaceted heritage. Although historically the area was not usually regarded as an independent country, local dynasties and especially the Turkish regency asserted a distinct sovereign identity. The imposition of French rule, however, subjugated Algeria politically, economically, and socially. This oppressive colonialism provoked the eight-year War of National Liberation, which led to independence in 1962.

1. The Land and Natural Resources

Algeria is a spectacular country of dramatic geographic and climatic contrasts that can be experienced in a day's drive south from Algiers. The most useful land is in the north (3% arable, 13% pasture, 2% forest), where over 90% of the population lives in a belt approximately 100 miles (160 km) deep. This area, however, has a history of disastrous earthquakes.

The rest of the country is desert. The arid zones nevertheless contain most of Algeria's economic wealth, such as impressive hydrocarbon (oil and natural gas) reserves and significant deposits of iron ore, zinc, lead, coal, and phosphates.

INFORMATION HIGHLIGHTS

Total Area: (land and inland water) 919,595 square miles (2,381,741 sq km).
Boundaries: *North,* Mediterranean Sea; *east,* Tunisia, Libya; *south,* Niger, Mali, Mauritania; *west,* Western Sahara, Morocco.
Elevations: *Highest*—Mt. Tahat (9,573 feet, or 2,918 meters); *lowest*—Shatt Melrhir (131 feet, or 40 meters, below sea level).
Population: 32,129,324 (2004 est.).
Capital and Largest City: Algiers.
Major Languages: Arabic (official), French, Berber.
Major Religion: Sunnī Islam.

For Algeria's flag, see FLAG, both illustration and text.

The Mediterranean Region. In the far north, narrow, fertile, discontinuous coastal plains, such as the Mitidja zone around Algiers, provide a rich variety of market-garden and industrial agriculture. The unnavigable Chélif River west of Algiers is valuable as a source of irrigation. The climate is temperate, with a warm summer that occasionally becomes stifling when sirocco winds blow in from the Sahara. However, these winds occur more often in the winter, which is mild and wet. Seasonal average temperatures range from 52° to 77° F (11°–25° C). The average annual rainfall for the region is 30 inches (760 mm), although less rain falls in the west than in the east. Among the most important cities are Algeria's principal ports: Algiers (the national capital), the population centers of Oran and Annaba, and the hydrocarbon harbors of Bejaïa, Skikda, and Arzew.

The Tell Atlas Region. The Tell Atlas mountain chain, with its magnificent gorges, separates the coastal zone from the plateau. This range reaches elevations of over 7,500 feet (2,300 meters). In eastern Algeria it includes the Hodna range and the very striking Djudjura massif. The Tell Atlas is much drier in the west than in the east, where the Kabylia zone receives over 40 inches (1,000 mm) a year on the seaward slopes. The average seasonal temperatures range from 47° to 83° F (8°–28° C). The mountains are forested with pine, juniper, cork oak, thuga, and cedar. Wildlife includes boars, antelope, Barbary apes, and jackals.

Among the mountains are fertile inland basins and plains. Kabylia, an important zone in this region, is the home of most of the Kabyles, the largest Berber group in the country. Its cultural capital is Tizi Ouzou. Other important cities of the Tell Atlas region are Constantine, Sétif, and Tlemcen.

The Saharan Plateau Region. The semiarid Saharan Plateau has an average elevation of 3,600 feet (1,100 meters). In the east it merges into the formidable Aurès Mountains, which include Mount Chelia, the highest peak (7,638 feet, or 2,328 meters) in northern Algeria. This region's irregular yearly rainfall of only about 8 to 16 inches (200–400 mm) inhibits extensive farming. The average seasonal temperatures range from 41° to 80° F (5°–27° C). Vegetation includes mastic trees, wild olives, and dwarf palms. Fields of alfa (esparto) produce nourishing pasture for livestock. There are also hares, jerboas, wild sheep, ibex, antelope, and gazelle. In the 1970s the Algerian government began planting a "green barrage" of drought-resistant vegetation, such as Aleppo pines, to impede the spread of the Sahara desert. Numerous shallow salt lakes and marshes—shatts, or chotts—dot this region.

The plateau has considerable mineral wealth along the Tunisian border. Iron ore is mined at Ouenza and Bou Khadra and phosphates at Djebel Kouif and especially Djebel Onk. Among the most important cities are Batna and Biskra, which flank the Aurès; Bou Saada in the central plateau; and Saïda in the west, renowned for its spring water.

The Saharan Region. The Saharan Atlas divides the plateau from the vast desert. This range averages from 4,900 feet (1,500 meters) in the east to 7,550 feet (2,300 meters) in the west and is less continuous than the Tell chain. The immense desert is characterized by a varied relief, including expanses of pebbles (reg), bare rocks (hamada), and sand (Great Western and Eastern ergs). The rocky plateau of Tassili n'Ajjer rises to 5,600 feet (1,700 meters) in the south. The far south features the surreal Ahaggar massif, the nation's highest mountain range.

Rainfall is only an annual 5 inches (130 mm), but the desert has numerous intermittent streams (wadis) and salt lakes and marshes. Subterranean rivers feed lush oases. Temperatures average seasonally from 51° to 101° F (11°–38° C) with occasional 80° F (44° C) daily temperature variations. Despite this inhospitable climate, the amount of vegetation and wildlife is surprising. Besides hardy grass such as drinn and cram-cram, there are scattered acacia and jujube trees. Algeria's oases are renowned for their groves of date palms. The varied wildlife includes antelope, jackals, hares, fennec foxes, gazelle, horned vipers, and scorpions.

The Sahara is the source of Algeria's hydrocarbon industry, with its chief fields at Hassi Messaoud (oil) and Hassi R'Mel (gas). Coal is mined near the Moroccan border at Kénadsa. A very rich iron-ore deposit lies at Gara Djebilet, southwest of Tindouf, in the far west along the border with Mali. The Ahaggar, a plateau, holds uranium. Among the most important cities of the Sahara are Touggourt; Ouargla, near the Hassi Messaoud oil field; and Ghardaïa, in the M'zab oasis.

2. The Economy

After independence Algeria attempted with mixed success to liberate itself from its "extroverted" colonial economy, so called because primary products—the output of agriculture and mining—were destined for export. Under President Boumedienne, from 1965 to 1978, state

The mountainous Ahaggar plateau in the Sahara of southern Algeria reaches the country's highest elevation.

© ROBERT EVERTS/TSW

Palms nourished by underground water in an oasis produce dates for the Algerian economy.

planning aimed at a more autarkic, or "introverted," Algeria by using hydrocarbon export receipts to build up the secondary sector (manufacturing). This strategy envisioned a multiplier effect—termed "industrializing industries"—accelerating the development of the entire economy. After 1978 President Benjedid opted for a more balanced approach to the economy, as more attention was given to the primary (agricultural) and tertiary (service) sectors. Rejecting past socialist economic projects, Benjedid promoted liberalization and privatization.

Nevertheless, Algeria's continued dependence on hydrocarbon revenues made its economy extremely vulnerable to price fluctuations. Diversification was difficult to achieve except within the hydrocarbons division. Like other developing countries, Algeria borrowed to pay for development, creating an external public debt of $23 billion by 1988. A 1989 standby credit agreement with the International Monetary Fund was expected to secure financial credibility and assistance. Massive unemployment and underemployment were compounded by the country's rapidly growing population. The economy faced enormous challenges in every sector.

Agriculture. Algeria's food deficit consumed a large portion of its revenues. In the early 1980s up to two-thirds of its cereals and three-quarters of its eggs had to be imported. Signaling its intention to increase primary production, the Benjedid government inaugurated the Agricultural and Rural Development Bank in 1982. It also replaced socialist collectives with private agricultural enterprises in 1987. Other incentives for farmers included private retail marketing of their produce. Results were encouraging, with a drop in food imports marked particularly by self-sufficiency in eggs. Nevertheless, in 1989 Algeria still imported over half of its food supply.

The agricultural north features market-garden produce such as carrots, artichokes, tomatoes, and potatoes. Industrial produce includes sugar beets, tobacco, and cotton. Rice is cultivated in the Chélif River valley. Dry legumes include broad beans, chickpeas, and lentils. Citrus, figs, and Saharan dates are important fruit products. An olive industry provides cooking oil.

Wine grapes were the mainstay of the colonial economy. After independence, cultivation of this cash crop was reduced significantly because of the need to convert fields to cereal production in order to satisfy domestic demands. Another consideration was that wine was produced in a country whose religion, Islam, forbade the consumption of alcoholic beverages. Algerian wine remains, however, an important commercial crop even though volumes have fallen by more than half.

Cereals such as wheat (soft and hard) and barley are grown especially on the inland plains and the plateau. The plateau's grass nourishes sheep, goats, and cattle.

The forests are valuable assets. Algeria ranks as one of the world's largest producers of cork.

Mining and Manufacturing. Algeria's most important industry is hydrocarbons. Though oil reserves are depleting, the country remains an important producer. Algerian oil is light and requires less refining than the heavier-density Middle Eastern crude. Algeria possesses large natural gas reserves; condensates and liquefied petroleum gas have become increasingly important exports. An ultramodern hydrocarbon infrastructure has been developed, including petrochemical and liquefaction complexes and pipelines. A trans-Mediterranean pipeline that was placed in operation in 1983 pumps natural gas to Europe through Italy.

The earnings from hydrocarbons became strategically significant because they financed Algeria's development and contributed toward paying for food imports and toward servicing debts. The initiation in 1986 of a more liberal exploration code attracted foreign companies to the Sahara to organize joint operations with the Algerian state company, Sonatrach.

The principal minerals produced are high-grade iron ore and phosphates. Modest amounts of lead, zinc, and coal are extracted.

Steelworks are located in Algiers and especially at the Hadjar complex near Annaba.

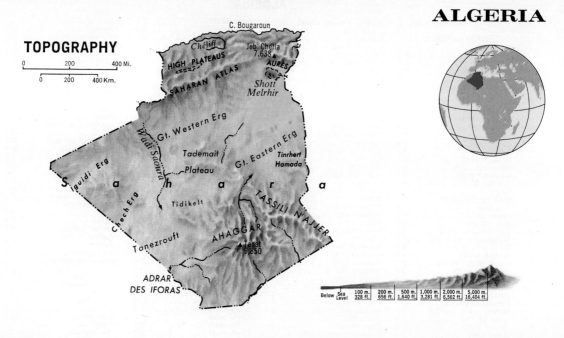

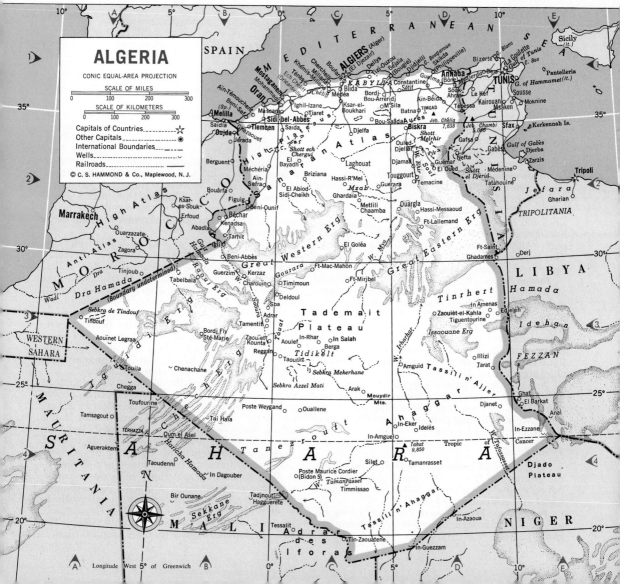

ALGERIA

Total Population, 28,539,321

CITIES and TOWNS

Abadla, 8,692 ....B 2
Adrar, 28,495 ....B 3
Aïn Beïda, 67,281 ....D 1
Aïn Sefra, 22,400 ....B 2
Aïn Témouchent, 48,935 ....B 1
Algiers (capital),
  1,687,579 ....C 1
Amguid ....D 3
Annaba, 227,795 ....D 1
Aoulef, 10,259 ....C 3
Arak ....C 3
Batna, 184,833 ....D 1
Béchar, 107,042 ....B 2
Béjaïa, 118,233 ....D 1
Beni-Abbès, 7,370 ....B 2
Beni-Ounif, 8,332 ....B 2
Beni-Saf, 30,700 ....B 1
Berga ....C 3
Bidon 5 (Poste Maurice
  Cordier) ....C 4
Biskra, 129,611 ....D 2
Blida, 131,615 ....C 1
Bône (Annaba), 168,790 ....D 1
Bordj-Bou-Arréridj, 86,997 ......C 1
Bordj Fly Sainte Marie ....B 3
Boufarik, 54,023 ....C 1
Bougie (Béjaïa), 64,876 ....D 1
Bou-Saâda, 50,000 ....C 1
Briziana, 10,000 ....C 2
Charouïn, 6,102 ....B 3
Cherchell, 32,572 ....C 1
Constantine, 449,602 ....D 1
Deldoul ....C 3
Dellys, 29,700 ....C 1
Djamaâ, 34,600 ....D 2
Djanet, 5,300 ....D 4
Djelfa, 88,929 ....C 2
Djidjelli, 35,371 ....D 1
Ech Cheliff, 103,998 ....C 1
Edjeleh ....D 3
El Abiod-Sidi-Cheïkh,
  15,300 ....C 2
El Bayadh, 44,925 ....C 2

El Djezair (Algiers) (capital),
  1,687,579 ....C 1
El Goléa, 24,400 ....C 2
El Oued, 73,093 ....D 2
Fort-Lallemand ....D 2
Fort-Mac Mahon ....C 3
Fort-Miribel ....C 3
Ghardaïa, 62,518 ....C 2
Ghazaouet, 29,795 ....B 2
Guelma, 84,826 ....D 1
Guémar ....D 2
Guerara, 22,300 ....C 2
Guerzim ....B 3
Hassi-Messaoud ....D 2
Hassi-R'Mel, 10,545 ....C 2
Idelès, 2,828 ....D 4
Ighil-Izane, 43,547 ....C 1
Igli, 4,397 ....B 2
Illizi, 4,600 ....D 3
In Amenas, 4,200 ....D 3
In-Amguel ....C 4
In-Eker ....D 4
In-Rhar ....C 3
In-Salah, 20,733 ....C 3
Kenadsa, 9,822 ....B 2
Kerzaz, 3,190 ....B 3
Khémis-Miliana,
  57,101 ....C 1
Ksar-el-Boukhari, 41,200 ....C 1
Laghouat, 71,808 ....C 2
Mascara, 70,885 ....B 1
Méchéria, 40,251 ....B 2
Médéa, 84,062 ....C 1
Metlili Chaamba, 21,300 ....C 2
Miliana, 36,400 ....C 1
Mohammadia, 58,967 ....B 1
Mostaganem, 115,302 ....B 1
M'Sila, 82,877 ....C 1
Oran, 598,525 ....B 1
Orléansville (Ech Cheliff),
  103,998 ....C 1
Ouallene ....C 4
Ouargla, 76,270 ....D 2
Ouled Djellal, 33,278 ....D 2
Poste Maurice Cortier ....C 4
Poste Weygand ....B 4
Reggan, 10,061 ....B 3

Saïda, 84,371 ....C 2
Sba, 1,441 ....B 3
Sétif, 185,786 ....D 1
Sidi-Bel-Abbès, 154,745 ....B 1
Silet ....C 4
Skikda, 128,503 ....D 1
Souk-Ahras, 85,873 ....D 1
Tabelbala, 4,028 ....B 3
Tamanrasset, 38,146 ....D 4
Tamentit, 5,300 ....B 3
Taourirt, 7,857 ....C 3
Tarat ....D 3
Tarhit ....B 2
Tébessa, 111,688 ....D 1
Temacine ....D 2
Ténès, 26,510 ....C 1
Tiaret, 105,562 ....C 1
Tiguentourine ....D 3
Timimoun, 21,556 ....C 3
Tindouf, 6,500 ....A 3
Tizi-Ouzou, 93,025 ....C 1
Tlemcen, 108,145 ....B 2
Touggourt, 75,600 ....D 2
Zaouïet-Kahla ....D 3
Zaouïet-Kounta, 10,707 ....B 3

OTHER FEATURES

Adrar des Iforas
  (plateau) ....C 4
Ahaggar (range) ....D 4
Aouïnet Legraa (well) ....A 3
Aurès (mountains) ....D 1
Azzel Mati, Sebkra
  (salt flat) ....C 3
Bougaroun (cape) ....D 1
Chech Erg (desert) ....B 3
Chélia, Jebel
  (mountain) ....D 1
Chéliff (river) ....C 1
Chenachane (well) ....B 3
Chergui, Shott ech (salt
  flat) ....C 2
Dra, Wadi (dry river) ....A 3
Gourara (oases) ....C 3
Great Eastern Erg
  (desert) ....D 2

Great Western Erg
  (desert) ....C 2
High Plateaus (ranges) ....B 2
Idehan (desert) ....E 3
Iguidi Erg (desert) ....A 3
In-Ezzane (well) ....E 4
In-Guezzam (well) ....D 5
Irharhar, Wadi (dry
  river) ....D 3
Issaouane Erg (desert) ....D 3
Kabylia (region) ....C 1
Mediterranean (sea) ....C 1
Medjerda (river) ....D 1
Mekerhane, Sebkra (salt
  flat) ....C 3
Melrhir, Shott (salt lake) ....D 2
Mouydir (mountains) ....C 3
Mya, Wadi (dry river) ....C 2
Mzab (oases) ....C 2
Raoui Erg (desert) ....B 3
Rhir, Wadi (dry river) ....D 2
Sahara (desert) ....A 4
Saharan Atlas (ranges) ....C 2
Saoura, Wadi (dry
  river) ....B 3
Souf (oases) ....D 2
Tademait (plateau) ....C 3
Tafassasset, Wadi (dry
  river) ....D 4
Tahat (mountain) ....D 4
Tamanrasset, Wadi (dry
  river) ....C 4
Tanezrouft (desert) ....C 4
Tassili n'Ahaggar
  (plateau) ....C 4
Tassili n'Ajjer
  (plateau) ....D 3
Tidikelt (oases) ....C 3
Timgad (ruins) ....D 1
Timmissao (well) ....C 4
Tindouf, Sebkra de
  (salt flat) ....A 3
Tinrhert Hamada
  (desert) ....D 3
Tni Haïa (well) ....B 4
Touat (oases) ....C 3
Touila (well) ....A 3

Trucks, refrigerators, television sets, textiles, cement, fertilizers, plastics, clothing, shoes, cigarettes, matches, and paper are manufactured nationally. Food-processing includes canning factories; mills produce pasta and semolina.

Transportation. The French left an impressive infrastructure that the Algerians have maintained and improved. National roads include the Trans-Saharan Highway. Railways transport coal, lead, zinc, and iron ore to the coast. The Algerian airline operates internationally from four major airports (Algiers, Oran, Annaba, and Constantine). The country's fleet includes ferries and LNG (liquefied natural gas) tankers.

Foreign Trade. Algerian planners have aimed at diversifying exports and trading partners. Nevertheless, hydrocarbons continue to dominate exports, contributing up to 95% of export earnings. Additional important exports are other minerals, citrus fruit, and wine. The European Community is Algeria's largest trading partner. France, in particular, has maintained its position as Algeria's chief supplier.

Among Algeria's chief imports are food, capital goods (machinery), and pharmaceutical supplies. After hydrocarbon prices dropped in the 1980s, Algeria's trading partners (especially France) offered commercial credits.

3. The People

The Algerian people are a composite of ethnic groups and traditions. This diversity has enriched the nation culturally, but it has also caused social and political problems.

Population. Though there has been a long history of intermarriage, over 80% of Algerians regard themselves as Arabs. The largest minority are Berbers, of whom the Kabyles live mainly in Kabylia, the Chaouia (Shawiya) in the Aurès Mountains, and the Mzabi (Mozabites) in the M'zab oasis. The Tuareg of the deep Sahara, also Berbers, have been traditionally nomadic, but drought during the late 1960s and early 1970s forced them to become more sedentary. Resident foreigners are mainly French. Although they make up an insignificant percentage of the population, many serve in professional positions such as technicians and teachers.

Spoken Algerian Arabic is a dialect quite different from the formal Arabic taught in the classroom. A controversial law passed in 1990 called for the complete Arabization of education and official affairs. Viewed as a means of asserting an Algerian identity, however, Arabization had been a policy since independence. Its application has provoked protests, especially by the Berber minority. The Berbers speak several dialects of their own language and have their own alphabet. Francophone Algerians feared that the elimination of French would impede technology transfers.

Islam was named the official state religion in the constitution of 1996. Over 98% of the people are Sunnī Muslims, with the vast majority adhering to the Mālikī school and some to the Ḥanīfī school; Ibadis (Khārijī) live in the M'zab. The Christian community, chiefly Roman Catholic, is small. Very few Jews remain in Algeria; after independence most immigrated to France or to Israel.

The Algerian population's high rate of natural increase remains a problem. An estimated 200,000 dwellings must be constructed yearly to meet housing needs. Infrastructure is extremely strained, especially the water supply system. The nation's population, traditionally heavily rural, is now about half urban. Most of it is also very young, with nearly half under age 17. Efforts to promote birth control and resettlement in less populous areas have been unsuccessful.

As many as 1 million Algerians live in France. While the Algerian government projects their "reinsertion," it is hard-pressed to provide housing, consumer goods, and services for the growing population at home.

Life-Styles. In Algerian cities men and women dressed in the latest European fashions are flanked by fellow citizens in traditional burnooses and *haiks* (an outergarment covering women's faces and falling to their feet). Islamic wear has become more popular with the growth of religious political parties. In the remote Aurès hardy Berbers live an existence that has not changed that much over centuries. This also applies to some Tuaregs in the southern Sahara. The Algerians in France have felt suspended between French and Algerian cultures, creating identity crises among members of the second generation (the "Beurs").

Algerian families are tightly knit. In general, Berber women enjoy more social freedom than Arab women. The growth of revivalist Islam influenced the enactment of a conservative family code (1984), which drew protests from women.

Education. After independence, Algeria allocated extraordinary sums toward education—usually about 25% of the budget. In 1962 about 800,000 Algerian children were in school; by 1990, over 5.6 million. In higher education approximately 3,000 matriculated in 1962, but over a quarter-million by the 1990s. There were eight major universities and the Emir Abdelkader Islamic University (in Constantine). Algeria's 90% illiteracy rate at independence had dropped below 50%.

Culture. The national telecommunication system broadcasts in Arabic, Berber, and French on radio and television. These media reflect the complexities of Algerian culture, for a twist of the dial can take the listener from Koranic recitations to Western-style music. Algerians also receive programs emanating from abroad. The freedom of the press allowed after 1988 produced numerous new newspapers and journals. Algerian cinema has received international acclaim, including a Grand Prize in 1975 at the Cannes Film Festival for Mohamed Lakhdar's *Chronique des années de braise.*

A great oral tradition has been complemented by *rayy* singers—folksingers who "relate" or "transmit." They earned an international reputation and also became controversial because they often expressed the social and political frustrations of the people.

Algeria has produced great literary figures. The Nobel laureate Albert Camus was born in Algeria. The writing of Kateb Yacine has been compared with that of William Faulkner. Mouloud Mammeri wrote outstanding novels and especially promoted Berber literature. Mohammed Dib was regarded as one of the greatest novelists writing in French, while Abdelhamid Benhadouga was the leading novelist and essayist writing exclusively in Arabic.

4. History and Government

Algeria was the site of active Neolithic cultures, as depicted at Tassili n'Ajjer in hunting and herding scenes of the predesiccated Sahara. These rock paintings date from approximately 6000 to 4000 B.C. The country's indigenous Berber population probably migrated to North Africa from Southwest Asia. Fiercely independent, the Berbers resisted invaders and colonizers throughout Algerian history.

History to the Arab Conquest. The arrival of Phoenician traders led to the establishment of Carthage (in Tunisia), probably in the 8th centu-

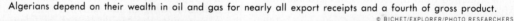
Algerians depend on their wealth in oil and gas for nearly all export receipts and a fourth of gross product.

© BICHET/EXPLORER/PHOTO RESEARCHERS

© CHRISTIAN-SAPPA/PUBLIPHOTO

Under Rome, Djemila was a military and administrative center that later flourished on agriculture and trade.

ry B.C. Carthage's expansion along the North African coast into eastern Algeria influenced the customs and language of the neighboring Berbers. In the 3d century B.C. the Massyli king Masinissa, who ruled from Cirta (Constantine), sided with victorious Rome during the Second Punic War (218–202 B.C.) and was recognized as king of Numidia. Admired today in Algeria, Masinissa was an assertive monarch whose kingdom stretched from the borders of Carthage into Morocco.

After Rome's destruction of Carthage in 146 B.C., the cooperative relationship with Numidia changed. Roman political ambitions conflicted with those of Masinissa's grandson, Jugurtha, who is regarded today as a national hero. The Jugurthine War (112–105 B.C.) ended with a Roman victory. Subsequently, North Africa was gradually integrated into the Roman Empire.

The Roman colonization of Algeria resulted in remarkable cities and agricultural development. Today ruins at Timgad and Djemila attest to the sophistication of life in Roman times. The coastal plains became one of Rome's granaries. Roman legionnaires even penetrated the Sahara. Many Berbers became romanized, though others remained restive and rebellious. The conversion of the area to Christianity created a serious problem because of the popularity of the antiauthoritarian Donatist sect. Donatism was particularly opposed by the Catholic church father St. Augustine, a native of Tagaste (Souk Ahras) and bishop of Hippo (Annaba).

The Vandal invasion of the 5th century ended Roman rule but had little effect on the Berbers in the hinterland. The Emperor Justinian restored the area to (Eastern) Roman, or Byzantine, rule in the 6th century. The Byzantines, like the Vandals, maintained merely a coastal presence.

The next invasion was that of the Muslim Arabs in the 7th and 8th centuries. Not surprisingly, the Berbers provided a stout resistance led by the chieftain Kusayla and the "prophetess" el-Kahina. The Arabs finally conquered the area and infused it with their culture, including above all Islam. The Berbers maintained their own language but became Muslims, influencing Islamic ritual with their customs.

Muslim Algeria to the Turkish Regency. Algeria was still neither a unified state nor a nation. It was highly influenced by neighboring areas and by its own local dynasties. The Ibadite Rustumid dynasty established itself in Tahert (near Tiaret) in the late 8th century. In the 9th century the Aghlabid dynasty of neighboring Ifriqiya (Tunisia) controlled much of eastern Algeria. It was displaced in the early 10th century by the Fatimids, Ismaili Shiites who controlled Ifriqiya, northern Algeria, and much of Morocco. When the Fatimids embarked for Egypt in the late 10th century, the western provinces were handed to the local Berber Zirid dynasty.

The Zirids, who are credited with the founding and naming of Algiers, were rivaled by the Berber Hammadid dynasty at Qala and afterward at Bejaïa. The onslaught of the Arab tribes known as the Banu Hilal and the Banu Sulaym pressured both the Zirids and Hammadids in the 11th century. The Almoravids swept into western and central Algeria in the late 11th century, followed in the 12th century by the Almohads, who under Abd al-Mumin united the Maghrib from the Atlantic to Ifriqiya. After the breakup of the Almohad state in the mid-13th century, the Abd al-Wadid dynasty ruled at Tlemcen. Coastal cities such as Algiers often acted as independent city-states.

The integration of Algeria into the Islamic community promoted commercial and cultural exchange. Cities such as Constantine, Tlemcen, Annaba (Bône), Bejaïa (Bougie), and Algiers were centers of religious learning and trade. The great historian and sociologist Ibn Khaldun (1332–1406), lived in Tlemcen, Bejaïa, and Biskra before settling in his native Tunis. Under the Almoravids, the Maliki branch of Islam became entrenched in Algeria. Furthermore, as a consequence of Almoravid and Almohad conquests, Algeria was influenced by the great Ibero-Islamic (Andalusian) civilization. As a result of the Christian reconquest of Spain, completed in 1492, many displaced Muslims and Jews found safe haven in Algerian cities, although the Jewish presence predated the arrival of Islam. Over the centuries Algeria received a rich and pluralistic cultural legacy occasionally revived and renewed by conquest.

The Turkish Regency. In the early 16th century, Spanish crusading and commercial incursions along the northwest African coast created enclaves such as Algiers and Oran. The militant Spaniards were matched, however, by the ambitious "Barbarossa" brothers, Aruj and Khayr al-Din. These Turko-Greek privateers took over Algiers and subsequently secured much of the Algerian littoral and hinterland as a regency for the Ottoman Empire.

The real founder of the regency was Khayr al-Din, who in 1529 reduced the Spanish fort of Peñón controlling Algiers and built up a fleet of corsairs. Though the regency was theoretically under the rule of the sultan of the Ottoman Empire, in practice it acted as an autonomous state. With its impressive navy complemented by Turkish elite troops (janissaries), the regency became a formidable Mediterranean force. In 1541 the Habsburg emperor Charles V dispatched a powerful invasion force against it but was repulsed, heightening the regency's prestige.

Headed by beylerbeys and later deys with subordinate beys ruling locally, the Turks governed northern Algeria for 300 years. The economy was based not only on piracy, which was also a common European practice, but on agricultural production and the manufactures of artisans as well. Algiers became a great cosmopolitan center. Nevertheless, European naval strength, disease, and political instability reduced the regency's power. Even the relatively weak United States imposed peace terms in 1815 in order to protect American shipping.

Relations between the regency and France deteriorated when King Charles X refused to honor an old debt owed to an Algerian exporting firm. Furthermore, the behavior of the French consul in this and other affairs offended the exasperated Dey Hussein to the point that he slapped or tapped him with a fly whisk. Charles exploited this situation because it diverted his subjects' attention from his unpopular domestic policies. In 1827 he ordered a blockade of Algiers. Then in 1830 French troops landed west of Algiers, defeated Turkish and allied Berber forces, and seized the city.

The French Colonial Establishment. After several years of indecision, France committed itself to the colonization of Algeria, but the French faced determined resistance from the indigenous population. Amir Abd al-Qadir (Emir Abdelkader) organized an Islamic state, which controlled roughly two-thirds of the inhabited part of Algeria. Applying modern statecraft, Abd al-Qadir attempted unsuccessfully to gain diplomatic recognition from Britain and Spain. Although he also encountered difficulty in obtaining modern weapons, he and his followers forced the French in 1837 to recognize his theocracy.

War resumed soon afterward, as the amir's territorial ambitions conflicted with those of France. Faced by the determined Marshal Thomas Robert Bugeaud, who commanded overwhelming forces, the amir was forced to surrender in 1847. The enduring struggle of Abd al-Qadir and his followers made him Algeria's greatest national hero. The north was divided into three departments in 1848. Nevertheless, French control of the north was not consolidated until the suppression of a Kabyle uprising in 1871.

Settler rule over Algeria was secured with the establishment of the Third Republic that year. By 1900 the French government had permitted an autonomous budget and unique institutions for Algeria. Concurrently, colonization policies transferred land and property from Algerians to settlers, because "pacification" usually led to expropriation. The period 1830–1940 was disastrous for Algerians. Almost 8.75 million acres (3.5 million hectares) were taken over by the colonialists. The severity of this economic deprivation had profound social effects.

Approximately 3 million people lived in Algeria in 1830. By 1871 warfare, disease, and famine had reduced the native population by about one-third. The gradual introduction of modern sanitation, hygiene, and medicine, however, increased the indigenous population at an extraordinary rate. In 1921 there were about 5 million Muslims. By 1956 their numbers had inflated to approximately 8.5 million. This growth created hardships such as widespread unemployment, which forced Algerians to seek work in France. The European settler population also grew—from 100,000 in 1845 to just over 1 million in 1956.

The imposition of a colonial economy impeded innovation, diversification, and consequently competition. It made Algeria's economic system externally dependent. Before the discovery of huge hydrocarbon deposits, the most significant economic event was the introduction of grape cultivation to Algeria. In order to maximize profits, cereal fields were replaced with vineyards in a land where hunger haunted millions. In 1880 some 100,000 acres (40,000 hectares) were devoted to viticulture, but this figure had increased tenfold by 1940.

Muslims fortunate enough to go to school received a French education, which impressed another culture upon their own repressed one, thus compounding an identity dilemma. Arabic was taught as a foreign language. By 1954 over 90% of the colonized were illiterate, and only one out of ten Muslim children attended school.

Algerian Nationalism. Although Algerian nationalism began before World War I, it was hardly revolutionary then. The early "Young Algerian" nationalists were educated in French schools and had "assimilated" French culture. They pointed out the paradoxes inherent in French colonialism and called for an extension of French citizenship.

Given the Algerian sacrifice of manpower during World War I, Premier Georges Clemenceau proposed legislation (the Jonnart Laws) that would have granted Muslims greater opportunities to participate in government and to acquire full French citizenship. Determined colonialist opposition, however, minimized the reform. Dissatisfied with the pace of change, Emir Khaled (Amir Khalid), a grandson of Abd al-Qadir, proposed ideas that went beyond those of the Young Algerians. Among his demands were equal political representation in colonial assemblies and French citizenship without the loss of Muslim status. Khaled's activism provoked his deportation in 1923.

The three most renowned nationalists were Ferhat Abbas, Messali Hadj (Hadj ben Ahmed Messali), and Shaykh ben Badis (Abd al-Hamid bin Badis). At first Abbas was an earnest assimilationist embracing French ideals. Nevertheless, the continuing colonial insensitivity symbolized by the rejection of the Blum-Viollette Law of 1935, which would have extended citizenship, forced Abbas and other moderates toward a more radical direction. Messali Hadj resolutely endorsed national independence and social revolution. Shaykh ben Badis organized and led the Association of Algerian Reformist Ulama, a group of religious scholars who criticized assimilation and superstitious Muslim practices.

In February 1943, during World War II, Abbas issued the Manifesto of the Algerian People. It called for an autonomous Algeria. Charles de Gaulle, who had made Algiers the capital of Free France, finally granted citizenship to tens of thousands of Algerians in March 1944. However, he had failed to satisfy nationalist aspirations. Abbas organized the Association des Amis du Manifeste, but colonialists attempted to weaken the movement by deporting its leader, Messali

Hadj. As a result, violence exploded at Sétif and Guelma in May 1945.

The violence fractured the fragile unity of the nationalists. Abbas created the Union Démocratique du Manifeste Algérien (UDMA), and Messali mobilized the Mouvement pour le Triomphe des Libertés Démocratique (MTLD). The misapplication of the Algerian Statute of 1947—which created an Algerian assembly chosen by a dual electoral college—compounded by Abbas's and Messali's policies of activism and abstention, alienated the brooding younger elite angered by the killings of May 1945. This younger group in 1947 formed the Organisation Spéciale (OS), which remained associated with the MTLD. Its fundamental tactic was armed insurrection. Colonialist police eventually suppressed it, but some of its members, who later completely broke with Messali, became the nucleus of the future revolutionary Front de Libération Nationale (FLN) in 1954.

The War of National Liberation. After the initial attacks of Oct. 31–Nov. 1, 1954, the repeated operations of the FLN's Armée de Libération (ALN) convinced French authorities that the rebellion was serious. The bloody, indiscriminate French retributions that followed the FLN massacres near Philippeville (Skikda) in August 1955 alienated the moderate Muslims such as Ferhat Abbas, who joined the FLN. The Association of Reformist Ulama also gave its support. In August 1956, undetected by the French, the FLN held the Soummam Conference in the Kabylia; there war strategy was discussed and planned, including the decision to launch a campaign in Algiers. The Battle of Algiers (1956–1957) was an ALN defeat, but their resort to torture brought the French international condemnation.

Fearing that Paris would decolonize Algeria, the French Army and insurrectionary settlers seized the offices of the governor-general in May 1958. French authority suddenly vanished, and de Gaulle was ushered to power. De Gaulle understood that France needed a new, associative relationship with Algeria. In October he proposed a massive social and economic assistance plan and called for peace. The FLN's provisional government, proclaimed on September 19 with Ferhat Abbas as its president, rejected this appeal.

Although the ALN suffered from sophisticated airmobile French tactics, it remained a threat. De Gaulle decided in September 1959 to grant Algeria "self-determination." His policies, coupled with the reassignment of the popular Gen. Jacques Massu, provoked in January 1960 a settler uprising in Algiers that de Gaulle had difficulty in ending through persuasion. A more serious threat occurred in April 1961, when four generals rebelled unsuccessfully against de Gaulle's authority.

The Transition to Independence. Formal negotiations on Algeria's future began in Évian, France, on May 20, 1961, between the French government and the FLN. On June 13 talks broke down. Terrorism in Algeria and France increased, led by the colonialist Organisation de l'Armée Secrète (OAS). Discussions resumed secretly in February 1962 at Les Rousses, where an agreement was formulated. Final negotiations at Évian resumed on March 7, and a cease-fire was proclaimed for March 19. The Évian Accords ensured Algerian political independence while preserving a French presence (for example, settler guarantees, hydrocarbons concessions, and military bases). France promised to continue social and economic aid.

Despite the signing of the Évian Accords, vindictive violence between the OAS and the FLN intensified. Even after a cease-fire was signed in June, the uncertainly facing the settlers induced hundreds of thousands of Europeans to flee to France. Furthermore, the FLN's Tripoli Program publicized the elite's choice of a "socialist option," thereby challenging the Évian Accords' neocolonial and increasingly anachronistic stipulations.

On July 1, 1962, 91% of the Algerian electorate voted in favor of independence in a national referendum. The official declaration of independence was on November 1. Liberation had come at a very high price; estimates range from 300,000 to 1 million dead as a result of the war.

The FLN's unity disintegrated as various political and military elites competed for power. The provisional government, now led by Ben Youssef Ben Khedda, clashed with the recently formed Political Bureau under Ahmed Ben Bella, who mustered the powerful support of the external ALN (soldiers mobilized in Morocco and Tunisia) commanded by Houari Boumédienne. After several pitched battles, tainting the FLN's heroic image, demonstrations organized by the Union Générale des Travailleurs Algériens (UGTA) prevented the outbreak of widespread civil war.

Ben Bella. In September 1962 an Algerian assembly with powers to draft a constitution was elected. Ferhat Abbas became its president, with Ben Bella as premier. Once in power, Ben Bella outlawed opposition political parties except for the FLN, and by the constitution of 1963 he created a presidential republic. He nationalized vacant European lands and properties, which were already being "self-managed" by Algerians. The self-management (autogestion) system was further defined by the FLN's "Charter of Algiers" in April 1964, reaffirming Algeria's socialist commitment.

In foreign affairs Algeria projected itself as a revolutionary state aiming to assist national liberation movements. Its most important relationship, though, was with France. Initially, Algeria was dependent on France in every way, especially with regard to technical and educational services. Relations became particularly strained because of French atomic testing in the Sahara and Algerian nationalization of European property. The FLN understood that decolonization was incomplete as long as France maintained an influential presence in Algeria.

Although relations with its Maghribi neighbors had been "fraternal" during the War of Liberation, they cooled after independence. President Bourguiba of Tunisia had hoped to alter Algerian borders in order to share hydrocarbon wealth. The FLN had agreed with Morocco in 1961 to address the contentious demarcation of their colonial frontiers after the war, but Ben Bella claimed that they were now unalterable. A brief border war took place in October–November 1963.

Ben Bella's authoritarianism provoked much opposition. As a symbolic protest Ferhat Abbas resigned from the presidency of the National Assembly. Ben Bella was forced to suppress a revolt in Kabylia (1963–1964) and to subdue a military coup (1964). When he moved against Boumédienne loyalists in his government, his rival retaliated by launching a bloodless coup d'état.

Boumédienne. Boumédienne headed the newly constituted Council of the Revolution. After instituting political changes, he devoted himself to state building. His main economic aim was the industrialization of Algeria, utilizing its hydrocarbon wealth for financing. Concurrently, he initiated the "Agrarian Revolution," to promote socialism through land redistribution, and a "Cultural Revolution," especially promoting Arabization.

The relationship with France was transformed. The last French base (at Bou Sfer) was handed over in December 1970. Then in February 1971, after arduous negotiations, French hydrocarbon concessions were nationalized. However, the improvement of relations was disrupted by the Madrid Accords of November 1975, which partitioned the Spanish Sahara between Morocco and Mauritania. France supported this new arrangement, whereas Algeria provided havens for Polisario, the liberation organization in the former Spanish colony.

Boumédienne faced challenges to his power in the early years of his regime, including student protests in 1965–1966, a coup attempt in December 1967, and an assassination attempt in April 1968. The mysterious murders of exiled Mohammed Khider (1967) and Belkacem Krim (1970), however, eliminated prominent political opponents. Boumédienne institutionalized his regime in 1976 with the promulgation of the National Charter, which described Algeria's socialist ideals and goals, and a new constitution.

Benjedid. Boumédienne died from a rare blood disease on Dec. 27, 1978, and he was replaced the following February by Chadli Benjedid. Although Benjedid appeared committed to Boumédienne's socialist model, he pursued a somewhat more balanced sectoral economic development over the next decade. He also initiated a gradual liberalization by reversing the Agrarian Revolution and returning land to the private sector, by "restructuring" state companies into competitive enterprises, and by loosening foreign investment laws. Benjedid also decentralized the political administration and increased the number of *wilayat* (states) from 34 to 48. The revised, or "enriched," National Charter of 1986, however, presented little substantial change from Boumédienne's original.

In foreign policy Benjedid tempered past radicalism and acted as a mediator during the American hostage crisis with Iran (1979–1981). His pursuit of Maghrib unity resulted in accords with Tunisia and Mauritania in 1983. Despite differences over Western (formerly, Spanish) Sahara, relations were restored with Morocco in May 1988. In February 1989 the Arab Maghrib Union was proclaimed, committing its member states to regional cooperation and integration.

Domestic problems, however, remained. The precipitous drop of oil prices in the mid-1980s staggered the economy. Social distress compounded by the frustrations of the emerging generation and the rising Islamist movement led to denunciations of the corruption-ridden FLN. In October 1988 rioting that resulted in heavy casualties shook the state's foundation. Benjedid quickly introduced democratic reforms. In February 1989 a constitutional amendment terminated the FLN's monopoly of power. Free local elections, the first in the country's history, resulted in the surprising success of the Front Islamique du Salut (FIS) in June 1990.

Civil Unrest. The FIS scored a stunning success in the first round of parliamentary elections in December 1991. The specter of an Islamic-controlled government alarmed the elite, especially the army, leading to the forced resignation of President Benjedid on Jan. 11, 1992. The High Council of State (HCS) then assumed power, with Mohamed Boudiaf, a former leader of the FLN, as its chairman. The HCS annulled the elections and declared the FIS illegal. This action provoked furious denunciations and assaults by the FIS, which resulted in the deaths of hundreds of members of the security forces. Thousands of FIS supporters and sympathizers were incarcerated.

Boudiaf himself was assassinated on June 29, 1992. The inconclusive investigation of his murder incriminated both the FIS and members of his own government. His successor, Ali Kafi, endeavored to address the collapsing economy and the growing Islamic rebellion but met with little success. The HCS replaced him with retired general Liamine Zéroual in January 1994.

Promising to bring peace, Zéroual was elected president in Algeria's first multiparty elections, in late 1995, in which a surprisingly high percentage of voters participated despite rebel threats and a boycott by most major parties. He then concentrated, however, on increasing his own power and lost much of his popular support. Finally abandoned by the army as well, Zéroual resigned two years before the end of his term, in September 1998. The following April Abdelaziz Bouteflika, a former foreign minister, was elected president after all the other candidates had denounced the election as fraudulent and dropped out of the race.

Addressing the insurgency, Bouteflika released several thousand detainees and proposed an amnesty for rebels who renounced violence. The amnesty law passed in a referendum in September 1999. After a decade of violence that had left at least 100,000 dead, many insurgents responded positively, and the FIS's Islamic Salvation Army dissolved itself in January 2000. Religious parties, including the FIS, remained banned, however, and fighting continued sporadically.

Violence erupted in 2001 in Kabylia, where Berbers demanded political and cultural recognition, including parity for their language, Tamazight. The legislature recognized Tamazight as a "national" language in 2002, but Arabic remained the sole "official" language. Bouteflika appointed a Berber as prime minister in 2003, but other Berbers dismissed his offers to negotiate.

By the time of presidential elections in April 2004, violence in general was easing and the economy had improved somewhat, although unemployment remained at about 25%. Unprecedentedly, the military declared itself neutral in the elections, which international observers deemed the fairest in Algeria to date. Bouteflika was reelected with 83.5% of the vote.

PHILLIP C. NAYLOR*, *Marquette University*

Bibliography

Abun-Nasr, Jamil, *A History of the Maghrib in the Islamic Period* (Cambridge 1987).

Entelis, John P., and Phillip C. Naylor, eds., *Algeria: State and Society* (Westview Press 1992).

Heggoy, Alf A., *Historical Dictionary of Algeria* (Scarecrow 1981).

Horne, Alistair, *A Savage War of Peace: Algeria, 1954–1962*, 2d ed. (Penguin 1987).

Naylor, Phillip C., *France and Algeria: A History of Decolonization and Transformation* (Univ. Press of Fla. 2000).

Ruedy, John, *Modern Algeria: The Origins and Development of a Nation* (Ind. Univ. Press 1992).

Stora, Benjamin, *Algeria, 1830–2000: A Short History* (Cornell Univ. Press 2001).

Willis, Michael, *The Islamist Challenge in Algeria: A Political History* (New York Univ. Press 1999).

ALGIERS, al-jērz′, the largest city and capital of Algeria. Situated along 10 miles (16 km) of Mediterranean coastline, Algiers extends upward from a semicircular bay onto hills facing east and north, creating the impression of a vast urban amphitheater. Named al-Jazaïr ("the islands") for its offshore islets in the 10th century, it is Algeria's economic and cultural as well as political center.

The city is distinguished by its architectural diversity. Tall modern apartment buildings contrast with colonial arcades and boulevards. The labyrinthine Casbah, with its narrow streets and terraced congestion, is one of the world's most famous urban communities.

Algiers exports vegetables, wine, and fruits from surrounding agricultural areas, especially the fertile Mitijda zone beyond the city's western Sahel Hills. Because it is one of the Mediterranean's busiest seaports, ships often wait long periods to load and unload cargoes. Algiers is the hub of the nation's rail, highway, maritime, and air networks. Local industries produce steel, trucks, cement, chemicals, and paper. In addition, the city has an oil refinery and sulfuric acid and superphosphate plants.

Places of Interest. Algiers features excellent museums surveying the country's culture from prehistoric to contemporary times. Among them are the Bardo Museum (prehistory and ethnography), the National Museum of Classical and Muslim Antiquities, and the Museum of Fine Arts. The University of Algiers was formally established in 1909. The National Library includes a collection of thousands of Arabic, Persian, Turkish, and Berber manuscripts. The city also has botanical gardens.

Among Algiers's most significant buildings are its mosques. The Great Mosque dates from the 11th century; others include the Ali Bitchine (1623), New (1660), Sidi Abd al-Rahman (1730), and Ketchaoua (1794) mosques. The Roman Catholic Basilica of Notre-Dame d'Afrique was consecrated in 1872, and the modernistic Cathedral of the Sacred Heart was completed in 1962.

The soaring Memorial of the Martyrs (302 feet, or 92 meters) contains a museum chronicling the history of Algerian nationalism and the Revolution of 1954–1962. Next to the Monument is Victory Park (Riadh el-Fath) with a modern shopping mall, gardens, and cultural center.

History. The site of the modern city was named Ikosin (Ikosim) by the Phoenicians and then Icosium by the Romans, who colonized it in the 1st century A.D. With the Christianization of North Africa, the city became the seat of a bishopric. Waves of invaders (Vandals, Byzantines, and Arabs) left the city destroyed or deserted until the middle of the 10th century. After the Zirid dynasty of Muslim Berbers reestablished the city, Algiers was governed by a variety of dynasties between the 11th and 15th centuries.

Between conquests Algiers was a city-state under the leadership of native citizenry (*baldis*, or *baladis*). The scholarly and saintly Sidi Abd al-Rahman al-Thaalibi, the author of a renowned Koranic commentary, was a distinguished citizen during the 15th century. Fugitive Andalusian Moors and Jews arrived at the end of the century, and in 1511 the Spanish commander Pedro Navarro took possession of the islet of Peñón in the harbor. Aruj Barbarossa, a Greco-Turkish corsair leader, removed the Spanish supporters from the city. His brother, Khayr al-Din, destroyed Peñón in 1529 and is credited with founding the Turkish regency.

Piracy is usually associated with the regency, though Algerines had engaged in it before the Turkish establishment. Under the Turks, captains (*raïs*) cruised the Mediterranean, even reaching the North Sea and Iceland while searching for prizes and hostages. Consequently, Algiers was often targeted by victim states and endured many bombardments. Algiers was also attacked by land. The most famous assault, by the forces of Emperor Charles V in 1541, was repulsed by the besieged and the bad weather. Finally, using a plan developed by Napoleon's staff, the French seized Algiers in 1830.

Under the Turks, Algiers underwent dramatic changes. Besides building and maintaining highly effective fortifications, the beylerbeys, pashas, aghas, and deys who ruled the regency constructed a remarkable city. The Turks, greatly influenced by Anatolian architecture, produced magnificent mosques and monuments. The construction of the Casbah began in earnest in the 16th century. Eventually the dey's palace was located there.

Algiers numbered about 60,000 inhabitants in 1580. This figure rose to 100,000 in the 17th century, including about 30,000 captives. The city was famous for its artisans and its agricultural markets. Nevertheless, epidemics, famines, and the general decline of piracy reduced the population to about 30,000 at the time of the French conquest.

French colonialism endowed Algiers with an excellent infrastructure. This included loggias and colonnades along the port and many new streets and buildings. In World War II the city was seized by the Allies from Vichy French control during "Operation Torch" in November 1942 and served as their headquarters in North Africa. It also became the provisional capital of Free France.

During the War of Algerian Independence (1954–1962), Algiers was often the site of dramatic events. The Battle of Algiers, with its intense urban guerrilla warfare and colonialist suppression, generated worldwide concern in 1956–1957. The successful colonial French military insurrection that occurred there in May 1958 ended the Fourth French Republic. In January 1960 Europeans barricaded themselves in the streets of Algiers to protest President Charles de Gaulle's war policies. In April 1961 four rebellious generals in Algiers failed to mobilize another revolt against Paris. During the last days of French Algeria, Algiers suffered from colonialist and nationalist terrorism. About 300,000 Europeans fled the city and were immediately replaced by 500,000 Muslims.

After gaining independence the city's bulging population placed its infrastructure under severe strain. The water quality deteriorated, and water was often available only intermittently. Collapsed buildings provoked outrage in the Casbah in 1985 and 1989, underscoring the immediate need for the construction of tens of thousands of new housing units throughout the metropolis. Yet even in this state of chronic crisis, Algiers remained striking, still deserving the colonial title "Alger la Blanche" ("Algiers the White"). Population: 28,566,000 (1996 est.).

PHILLIP C. NAYLOR
Merrimack College

ALGIERS, University of, al-jērz', an institution of higher education in Algiers, Algeria. The university was formed in 1909 by the union of a school of pharmacology and medicine, founded in 1859, with the schools of law, sciences, and arts, founded in 1879.

Off-campus units of the university are the two institutes of legal studies, at Constantine and Oran; an institute of political studies in another section of Algiers; and at El-Harrach, the national polytechnic school.

A library, considered the most important bibliographic center in North Africa, is on the main campus. The National Museum of Fine Arts, the archaeological Musée Stéphane-Gsell, and the Museum of Ethnography and Prehistory of Bardo are adjuncts of the university.

ALGIN, al'jən, any of a class of acidic polysaccharides obtained from various species of marine brown algae. The algins, or alginates, are used for stabilizing emulsions and suspensions in foods and cosmetics, thickening printing pastes, and coating and sizing paper.

Preparation, Structure, and Properties. The primary sources of algin are *Macrocystis pyrifera* on the American Pacific Coast, *Laminaria digitata* on the American Atlantic Coast, *L. digitata* and *Nereocystis leutkeana* in Canada, and *Ascophyllum nodosum* and *L. digitata* in Great Britain. The algin is associated with the cell walls and may have a structural function in cell walls similar to that of cellulose in land plants.

In the preparation of the polysaccharide, freshly harvested algae are washed to remove impurities. Then the polysaccharide is extracted by using a dilute alkali (sodium carbonate). The alkaline solution of sodium alginate is either acidified to precipitate alginic acid or treated with acid calcium chloride to precipitate calcium alginate.

When the purified polysaccharide is hydrolyzed, it is broken down to D-mannuronic and L-guluronic acids. The mannuronic acid makes up 35 to 65 percent of the polysaccharide, depending on the alga from which it is obtained, and the remainder is guluronic acid. As many as 1,200 of these uronic acids can be joined together by means of β 1,4-glycosidic links forming a polysaccharide with a molecular weight of 185,000. If the acid groups are in the hydrogen form (-COOH), the polysaccharide is called alginic acid, which is insoluble. When it is neutralized, the alginate (-COO⁻) or sodium alginate (-COONa) is water soluble and very surface active. If the sodium ions are replaced with calcium or beryllium, the polysaccharide chains are cross-linked by the divalent metal ions, and they become insoluble.

Uses. Because of its surface activity, dissolved sodium alginate is an excellent stabilizer of emulsions and suspensions. This property and its lack of toxicity make it useful in such diverse products as ice cream, cheese, syrups, chocolate milk, drugs, and water paints.

If paper or textiles are treated with sodium alginate and dried, the alginate forms a tough gel or sizing that gives the surface a smoother appearance. Calcium alginate can be spun into fibers that are woven into cloth along with cotton or wool. The cloth is then treated with sodium carbonate solution to remove the alginate threads, leaving behind very lightweight cloth or an unusual pattern. Dry calcium alginate is pressed into tablets with drugs. When the tablet becomes wet, the alginate swells, dispersing the drug and hastening its dissolution.

THOMAS R. PUNNETT, JR.
Temple University

ALGIRDAS (died 1377), äl'gir-däs, was a grand duke of Lithuania, who greatly extended Lithuania's frontiers. The Polish form of his name is *Olgierd*. He came to power in 1345 when he and his brother Kestutis wrested control of Vilna, the capital city, from their younger brother Jaunutis. The state that their father, Gediminas, had established was in danger of falling to the Teutonic Knights coming from Prussia in the west and Livonia to the north. Algirdas took the ducal title, but in fact he ruled jointly with Kestutis. Kestutis administered the western regions, defending them from the Knights. Algirdas held Vilna and directed Lithuania's expansion into territories inhabited by the East Slavs. Many historians maintain that the support of the Slavs was decisive in Lithuania's success in withstanding the Knights.

Although Algirdas was a pagan, his rule was well received by the Orthodox Slavs because of his willingness to leave local social, religious, and political institutions intact. By the end of his reign he had extended Lithuania's southeastern frontiers to the Black Sea.

Algirdas and his brother were hard pressed to secure Lithuania's northern and western frontiers against the Knights. In the east, Algirdas clashed with the rulers of Moscow as both sides bid for religious and political control of the East Slavs. In 1368, 1370, and 1372, Algirdas led military campaigns against Moscow, twice besieging the Kremlin.

ALFRED E. SENN, *University of Wisconsin*

ALGOL, al'gol, is a variable white star in the constellation Perseus. It has been known since ancient times. It shines at a magnitude of 2.3 for about 2½ days, then drops to a magnitude of 3.5 in 4½ hours. After 20 minutes a 4½-hour return to full brightness begins. Algol is an eclipsing binary, or double, star, rather than a true variable. The dimmer of the two stars partially eclipses the brighter one, periodically, producing the drop in magnitude. A third star circles the other two.

ALGONKIAN STOCK, al-gong'kē-ən, a North American Indian linguistic group that once comprised between 40 and 50 separate languages. The group is also known as *Algonquian*. Before the European conquest of North America, the Algonkian tribes dominated an area larger than any other Indian region, extending from Labrador to the Rocky Mountains and from Hudson Bay to Pamlico Sound and the Cumberland River. This expanse was divided only by Iroquois enclaves in the eastern Great Lakes area and by Beothuk tribes in Newfoundland. Outlying Algonkian tribes, including the Shawnee, lived to the south. The Cheyenne and Arapaho, who had crossed the Missouri into the Black Hills and later into Colorado and Wyoming, extended the stock west of this main area.

The tribes of the Algonkian stock formed a loose confederation, and many were entirely independent. They have been roughly classified into five geographical divisions. The northern division occupied the largest area, extending north of the St. Lawrence and the Great Lakes, from the extreme northwest of the Algonkian area to the extreme east. It included one of the largest groups, the Chippewa, comprising the Cree, Ottawa, Chippewa, and Missisauga; and the Algonkin group, made up of the Nipissing, Temiscaming, Abitibi, and Algonkin. The northeastern division, including the tribes in eastern Quebec, the Maritime Provinces, and eastern Maine, comprised the Nascapee, Montagnais, Mistassin, Bersiamite, and Papinachois of the Montagnais confederacy, and the Micmac, Malecite, Passamaquoddy, Penobscot, and Norridegewock of the Abnaki. In the central division—Wisconsin, Illinois, Indiana, Michigan, and Ohio—were the Menominee; the Sac, Fox, and Kickapoo of the Sac group; the Potawatomi; the Peoria, Kaskaskia, and Michigamea of the Illinois; and the Miami, Piankashaw, and Wea of the Miami. The western division, on the eastern slope of the Rocky Mountains, included the Siksika, Kainah, and Piegan of the Blackfoot confederacy, and the Arapaho and Cheyenne groups. The eastern division comprised the tribes along the Atlantic coast south of the Abnaki. The major confederacies and groups were the Pennacook, Massachuset, Wampanoag, Narraganset, Nipmuc, Montauk, Mohegan, Mahican, Wappinger, Delaware (once the most important of the stock), Shawnee, Nanticoke, Conoy, Powhatan, and Pamlico.

The Algonkians were the first Indians to come into contact with Europeans. They allied first with the French and then with the English, always against advancing settlers. As they were pushed farther west by the powerful Iroquois confederacy and by the extension of the frontier of white settlement, their great chiefs Philip, Powhatan, Pontiac, Tecumseh, and Black Hawk exacted reprisals. In the War of 1812 many Algonkians sided with the British. Later they ceded most of their land east of the Mississippi to the United States. See also INDIAN, AMERICAN and articles on individual tribes.

ALGORITHM, al'gə-rith-əm, an abbreviated, easily performed procedure for finding the result of a computational operation, such as addition or division. It is also called *algorism*. An algorithmic approach to learning arithmetic has weaknesses because the steps of the algorithm become manipulations of numbers by rote. The use of an algorithm conceals the meaningfulness of the operation as well as the logical structure of the subject.

A pure algorithmic procedure for finding sums—for example the sum of 68 and 57—is as follows: Draw a line under the column of addends. Add the numbers represented by the numerals in the ones column ($8 + 7 = 15$), place a 5 in the ones place in the sum, and carry the 1 to the top of the tens column. Add the numbers represented by the numerals in the tens column ($1 + 6 + 5 = 12$), place a 2 in the tens place in the sum, and place a 1 in the hundreds place in the sum. The result is:

$$
\begin{array}{ll}
1 & \text{(carry numeral)} \\
68 & \text{(addend)} \\
\underline{57} & \text{(addend)} \\
125 & \text{(sum)}
\end{array}
$$

An example of a modified algorithmic procedure that is more meaningful is as follows:

$$
\begin{array}{lll}
68 & = 60 + 8 & \text{(Renaming)} \\
57 & = 50 + 7 & \text{(Renaming)} \\
68 + 57 & = 110 + 15 & \text{(Adding)} \\
68 + 57 & = 100 + 10 + 10 + 5 & \text{(Renaming)} \\
68 + 57 & = 100 + 20 + 5 & \text{(Adding)} \\
68 + 57 & = 125 & \text{(Adding)}
\end{array}
$$

In computer programming, the term "algorithm" refers to any procedure, consisting of simple, unambiguous steps, that can be used to solve a computational problem. It usually refers to a procedure within a program.

LEE E. BOYER
Bureau of State Colleges, Harrisburg, Pa.

ALGREN, ôl'grən, **Nelson** (1909–1981), American novelist and short-story writer, who is noted for his naturalistic works. He was born in Detroit, Mich., on March 28, 1909, but his family soon moved to Chicago, which was to become the locale of much of Algren's fiction. He graduated from the University of Illinois with a degree in journalism and then traveled in the southern United States, working at various jobs.

Algren's first novel was *Somebody in Boots* (1935), a brutal portrayal of depression youth. This novel foreshadowed much of Algren's later work, for it contained his recurrent themes—the downtrodden, the depression, the seamier side of life. His first critical success was *Never Come Morning* (1942), a story about poverty among the Poles living on Chicago's West Side. Reviewers compared his work to that of another Chicago realist, James T. Farrell. Algren's most acclaimed novel was *The Man With the Golden Arm*, which won the National Book Award as the most distinguished American novel of 1949. This novel, which details the life of Frankie Machine, a gambling dealer, and his involvement in Chicago's underworld, is marked by Algren's characteristic unsparing realism.

Algren's other works include *Chicago: City on the Make* (1951), a prose poem; *A Walk on the Wild Side* (1956), a novel set in New Orleans; and *Notes from a Sea Diary: Hemingway All the Way* (1965), a book of travel notes and literary criticism. He died in Sag Harbor, Long Island, N.Y., on May 9, 1981.

ALHAMBRA, al-ham'brə, is a city in California, in Los Angeles County, 8 miles east of downtown Los Angeles. It stands at the gateway to the San Gabriel Valley. It is primarily a residential city, although it has diversified industries in such fields as engineering, contracting, and printing. Some of the principal manufactured products are missile and aircraft parts, air-conditioning equipment, and pressed wool felt. Transportation facilities include the Southern Pacific Railroad and the San Bernardino Freeway, which connects with the network of southern California's major highways.

Alhambra is governed by a city manager and council, and the seat of government is a new city hall, dedicated in 1961. The city supports a civic chorus and orchestra.

Alhambra is built on land purchased from the state for $2.50 an acre in 1874 by Benjamin D. Wilson. Two of his daughters chose the town's name from Washington Irving's book *The Alhambra.* Early settlers were attracted to the area because it was one of the first areas in Southern California to bring water in iron pipes to each lot. Population: 85,804.

ALHAMBRA'S Court of the Lions is named for its central fountain, which consists of an alabaster basin resting on 12 marble lions. White marble columns support the filigree walls of the arcade surrounding the courtyard.

ALHAMBRA, al-ham′brə, a Moorish fortress palace in Granada, Spain. It is the most beautiful example of Western Islamic architecture surviving in the 20th century. It was originally built as a citadel on high ground overlooking Granada in the mid-1200's, but in the next century it grew to become an entire royal city. The magnificent buildings for which it is famous were largely the work of two Moorish kings of Granada, Yusuf I (died 1354) and Mohammed V (reigned 1354–1391). Of the old citadel, called the *Alcázaba,* only the massive walls and towers remain. Next to this is the royal palace, and beyond the palace is the *Alhambra Alta,* a residence for court officials. The entire plateau of about 35 acres is surrounded by a reddish brick wall.

The royal palace is famous for the magnificent coloring of its decoration. Sunlight, freely admitted, alternates magically with shadow amid the airy grace of its Moorish pillars and arches. The palace consists chiefly of two spacious rectangular courts and the halls adjoining them. The Patio de la Alberca (or de las Arrayanes—Court of the Pool, or of the Myrtles), built by Yusuf I, is paved in marble with a large rectangular pool at the center. To one side of the court is the Sala de los Embajadores (Hall of the Ambassadors), the former throne room, with a dome that rises 75 feet.

Adjacent to the Alberca is the Patio de los Leones (Court of the Lions), which was built by Mohammed V. The court is named for its central fountain, which consists of an alabaster basin supported by 12 white marble lions. The court is surrounded by an arcade supported by 124 slender white marble columns. Several domed pavilions with filigree walls extend from this graceful colonnade. The walls of the Court of the Lions are decorated with yellow and blue tile beginning about five feet above the floor; the floor itself is covered with tiles of various colors.

On one side of the Court of the Lions is the Sala de los Abencerrajes, which derives its name from a Moorish family allegedly murdered there. It is a square room with a high dome decorated in blue, red, gold, and brown. Opposite is the Sala de las Dos Hermanas(Hall of the Two Sisters), which contains a fountain and a remarkable dome honeycombed with innumerable tiny cells.

After the surrender of Granada to the Spaniards in 1492, the palace suffered severely from neglect and from attempts to remake it in European style. Charles V destroyed one wing about 1526 to build a palace that was never completed; Philip V redecorated many of the rooms; and the French blew up some of the towers in 1812. An earthquake in 1821 increased the damage. It has subsequently been restored.

ALHAZEN (c. 965–c. 1039), al-hə-zen′, was one of the greatest scientists of medieval Islam. "Alhazen" is an abbreviated Latin form of his Arabic name, *al-Hasan Ibn al-Haytham.* Born in Basra, Iraq, he moved to Egypt during the reign (996–1021) of the Fatimid caliph al-Hakim and remained in Egypt until his death.

A medieval Latin translation of Alhazen's *Optics* strongly influenced later writers on the subject, including Kepler. In it he rejected Euclid's and Ptolemy's doctrine of visual rays and based his own system on the view that vision occurs through light coming to the eye from the object. His approach is empirical and dependent on mathematical methods. The observations and experiments relate to the camera obscura, perception, visual illusions, reflection, and refraction. He formulated a problem, now known by his name: given two points in space, find the point on a cylindrical, spherical, or conical mirror at which the light incident from one of the two points would be reflected to the other. He solved it for spherical mirrors by the intersection of a circle and hyperbola.

Following Ptolemy, Alhazen elaborated a system of physical spheres responsible for producing the apparent motions of the heavenly bodies.

ALI (c. 600–661), a-lē′, was the fourth caliph, or ruler, of the Arab empire founded by the prophet Mohammed. He was the prophet's cousin and son-in-law. Ali was born in Mecca, and because his father, Abu Talib, was poor, Ali was sent to live with Mohammed. As a boy of about ten, he accepted Mohammed's religion, becoming one of the first Muslims. When Mohammed fled from Mecca to Medina in 622, Ali was left behind to settle Mohammed's affairs in Mecca. When he rejoined Mohammed in Medina, he married Mohammed's daughter, Fatima. Ali is said to have fought bravely in battle, but this may be exaggerated.

During the reigns of the first three caliphs, Ali took little part in politics. After 650 he criticized the caliph Uthman and befriended his active opponents, but Ali himself was not implicated in Uthman's assassination in 656. The Muslims in Medina then elected Ali caliph, but his election was not universally accepted. Some Muslims of Meccan origin collected an army in Iraq but were defeated by Ali in the Battle of the Camel (December 656), fought around the camel bearing the litter of Aisha, Mohammed's widow, near Basra. The Battle of Siffin in 657 against Muawiya and the Arabs of Syria was broken off when Ali agreed to submit to two arbiters his claim to the caliphate. There are different versions of what followed. Ali had to deal with dissidents among his own supporters, whom he attacked and massacred at Nahrawan in 658. The arbiters probably decided against Ali. Further conferences did not settle matters, and Muawiya steadily increased his strength.

In January 661, Ali was assassinated by a man seeking personal revenge. Muawiya, first of the Umayyad dynasty, then became caliph and brought all the empire under his rule. Ali, though not a competent statesman, received great honor after his death from the Shiite sect of Islam, which claimed he was the rightful successor to Mohammed and should have been succeeded by his sons, Hasan and Husayn. Some later subdivisions of the Shiites paid almost divine honors to Ali.

W. MONTGOMERY WATT
University of Edinburgh

ALI (1744–1822), a-lē′, was an Ottoman governor of Yanya (Janina), who ruled a large area in Greece and Albania. He was known as *Ali Pasha, the Lion of Janina.*

The son of an Albanian chieftain, Ali was a skilled politician, and by 1787 he was appointed ruler of Janina, in Epirus (now Ioannina, Greece). In the next 15 years he expanded his domain by military conquest and treaties. After a lengthy struggle, he suppressed a rebellion of the inhabitants of Epirus against Ottoman rule in 1802 and took control of the region. In the same year he was appointed governor of Rumelia.

As a ruler Ali displayed excellent qualities. He put an end to brigandage, built roads, and encouraged trade. His court was the center of Greek culture at that time. Aiming at independent sovereignty, he intrigued against Ottoman rule with England, France, and Russia. He was actually almost independent of the government at Constantinople, which finally decided to put an end to his power. In 1820, Sultan Mahmud II announced that Ali was deposed. Ali resisted the order but finally surrendered in 1822. He was shot to death on Jan. 24, 1822.

THE RING MAGAZINE

Muhammad Ali, who as Cassius Clay first won the heavyweight boxing title from Sonny Liston in February 1964.

ALI, a-lē′, **Muhammad** (1942–   ), American professional boxer, who held the world heavyweight title three times. He was born Cassius Marcellus Clay, Jr., in Louisville, Ky., on Jan. 17, 1942. In 1960 he leaped into boxing prominence by winning the Amateur Athletic Union's light heavyweight championship, the National Golden Gloves heavyweight title, and an Olympic gold medal as a light heavyweight.

Turning professional in October 1960, Clay won 19 bouts, 15 by knockouts, before taking the championship from Charley (Sonny) Liston in the sixth round at Miami Beach, Fla., on Feb. 25, 1964. In 1965 he knocked out Liston in one minute in a rematch at Lewiston, Me. He then defeated former champion Floyd Patterson in Las Vegas. Six victories in 1966 and 1967 included one over Ernie Terrell.

In 1967, however, Clay was stripped of his title after he had refused to be inducted into the U. S. armed services. Earlier, he had embraced the Muslim religion, changed his name to Muhammad Ali, and claimed exemption from military duty as a Black Muslim minister. Granted a license to return to the ring, he began a comeback in 1970. He won twice, then lost his first fight—to champion Joe Frazier on March 8, 1971. Three months later the U. S. Supreme Court ruled that Ali had been drafted improperly.

After losing a decision to Ken Norton in 1973, Ali outpointed Joe Frazier in a rematch in January 1974. He then regained his heavyweight crown from George Foreman in Zaire on Oct. 30, 1974. He lost his title to Leon Spinks in 1978 but regained it that same year. In July 1979 he announced his retirement, but he returned to the ring and was defeated by Larry Holmes in October 1980 at Las Vegas, Nev., and again by Trevor Berbick in Nassau, the Bahamas, in December 1981, after which he again retired.

ALI BEY (1728–1773), ä'lē bā, was an Egyptian ruler. Born in Abkhazia, in the Caucasus, he was taken to Cairo and sold as a slave in boyhood. Ali joined the Mamluks, rose to the highest rank among them, and succeeded in making himself virtually governor of Egypt.

In 1769 he took advantage of a war in which the sultan was then engaged with Russia, and attempted to add Syria and Palestine to his Egyptian dominion. In this he had almost succeeded when the defection of his own son-in-law, Abu al-Dhahab, drove him from Egypt. Joining his ally Sheikh Zahir in Acre, Ali still pursued his plans of conquest with remarkable success, until in 1773 he was induced to make the attempt to recover Egypt with insufficient means. In a battle near Cairo his army was completely defeated and he himself taken prisoner. He died a few days afterward either of his wounds or by poison.

ALI PASHA (1815–1871), ä'lē pə-shä', was a Turkish diplomat and grand vizier (chief minister of the Ottoman Empire). He was born *Mehmed Emin* in Constantinople (now Istanbul). He acquired the name "Ali" when he first entered the service of the government. A more or less self-educated man from a humble background, he learned French, which qualified him for service in the government translation office in 1833. In 1836 he accompanied Turkish diplomatic missions to Vienna, Austria, and St. Petersburg, Russia. After a year as interpreter to the Divan (state council) and another as counselor to the ministry of foreign affairs, he became ambassador to Britain in 1841. In 1844 he was back in Constantinople as a member of the council of justice. He served as deputy minister of foreign affairs in 1845 and a year later became foreign minister.

Ali was elevated to the rank of vizier in 1848. He became grand vizier for the first time briefly in 1852 and for the second time in 1855. In this capacity he helped draft and promulgate, on Feb. 18, 1856, the *Hatt-i Humayun* (second imperial reform rescript). As chief Ottoman delegate to the Paris Peace Conference he signed the Treaty of Paris (March 30, 1856) that ended the Crimean War. In 1859 he was dismissed as grand vizier but was renamed in 1867. He died at Bebek, while still in office, on Sept. 7, 1871.

J. STEWART-ROBINSON, *University of Michigan*

ALIBI, al'ə-bī, in law, is the defense that, at the time of the commission of a crime, the accused was at another place. (The word *alibi* is Latin for "elsewhere.") If such a fact is established sufficiently to raise a reasonable doubt in the minds of the jury, it is a good defense, except for crimes committed through agents or others for whose acts the accused is responsible. In all cases where the presence of the accused at the scene of the crime at the time of its commission is essential to his guilt, the burden is upon the prosecution to prove such presence beyond a reasonable doubt. By interposing the defense of alibi, the accused does not assume the burden of proving that he was elsewhere as a prerequisite to establishing his innocence. The burden of proving guilt beyond a reasonable doubt on the whole case, including the issue of alibi, always rests upon the prosecution. The burden, if any, upon the accused is that of going forward with the evidence by offering some proof of the alibi. See also EVIDENCE.

ALICANTE, ä-lē-kän'tä, is a seaport and resort city in Spain, 77 miles south of Valencia. It is the capital of Alicante province and the seat of a Roman Catholic bishopric. The city manufactures textiles and cigars. Wines, fruits, and vegetables are produced nearby.

Alicante was built on the site of the Roman city of Lucentum. It was held by the Moors from the 8th to the 13th century. Population: 284,580 (2001 census).

ALICE, al'is, a city located in southern Texas, 45 miles (72 km) by road west of Corpus Christi. The seat of Jim Wells county, it is an oilfield supply center and cattle-shipping point, and the commercial center of an agricultural area. Oil refining ranks as the main industry, but other light industry is also important. The town, named Alice in honor of Alice Kleberg, owner of the million-acre King cattle ranch to the southeast, was incorporated as a city in 1910 and adopted the city-manager plan of government in 1949. Population: 19,010.

ALICE'S ADVENTURES IN WONDERLAND is a novel for children by Charles Lutwidge Dodgson, writing under the pen name Lewis Carroll. The book was published in 1865. Although intended primarily as a tale of fantasy and nonsensical humor for children, the book also achieved great popularity among adults for its parodies of serious adult situations and conventions. The story grew out of a tale that Dodgson, a mathematician and lecturer at Oxford, told to the three young daughters of his friend, the classical scholar Henry George Liddell. One of the girls was the original for the novel's main character, Alice. The success of the book led Carroll to write a sequel, *Through the Looking Glass and What Alice Found There* (1872). Both books were illustrated by Sir John Tenniel, chief cartoonist for *Punch* magazine, and the illustrations have become classics along with the books.

Alice's adventures occur during a dream. She follows a white rabbit into a rabbit hole and finds herself in a strange, irrational world peopled by characters such as the fantastic Duchess, the grinning Cheshire Cat, the Mad Hatter, the March Hare, and the King and Queen of Hearts. She plays croquet with the Queen, using live flamingos for mallets; attends a tea party with the Mad Hatter, the March Hare, and a sleepy Dormouse; and takes part in a hilarious and maddeningly unfair trial of the thief of tarts.

ALICE'S tea party with the March Hare, the Dormouse, and the Mad Hatter, as depicted by Sir John Tenniel.

ALIEN, ā'lē-ən, a foreigner; more exactly, one who was born abroad and owes allegiance to a foreign government. It is opposed to *citizen*, one who by birth, naturalization, or other legal means is a member of the nation in which he resides. United States immigration laws define an alien as any person not a citizen or national of the United States.

The status of an alien in the United States is not altered merely by length of residence or domicile. However, lawful permanent residence, usually for five years, creates eligibility for naturalization.

The Permanent Resident Alien. A lawful resident alien is one admitted permanently to the United States. He is protected by the United States Constitution and is subject to the laws enacted by Congress and the several states. The status of an alien is the same as a citizen so far as his property and liberty are concerned. He can live and work and raise a family, secure in the personal guarantees every resident has. However, an alien cannot vote, cannot run for most public offices, and is subject to the restraints of the Immigration and Nationality Act.

The Temporary Visitor. In the mid-1960's about 2 million aliens arrived in the United States yearly, most of them as visitors and students, but some as diplomats, representatives of foreign news media, exchange visitors, and temporary workers.

Aliens with temporary permits must adhere to the exact conditions of their admission and must depart when the purpose of their visit is accomplished. For example, a person admitted as a student must not only study but must also have passing grades in order to continue his stay. Aliens on temporary visas are not subject to the draft if they maintain the conditions of their admission. They are not required to pay income taxes on money earned outside the United States.

The Refugee-Parolee. Since the Hungarian uprising in October 1956 a third group of aliens has come to the United States—namely, refugees who enter neither as lawful permanent aliens nor as temporary aliens, but "on parole." The first group of about 27,500 Hungarians thus admitted by presidential invitation were later permitted by special legislation to become permanent residents. Starting in 1960, several hundred thousand Cubans arrived in the United States under this same emergency provision.

A 1965 law amending the Immigration and Nationality Act created a new concept of "conditional entry" for refugees from all but Western Hemisphere countries. The legal status of a conditional entrant is similar to that of the parolee, with the distinction that if a conditional entrant has resided in the United States for a period of two years and is admissible under all but the quota provisions of the immigration law, he may be admitted to permanent residence without the special legislation necessary for the emergency parolee.

Technically, a parolee or conditional entrant, although physically in the United States, has not been "admitted." Unless and until he has been permitted to change his status to lawful permanent resident, he is in the country on sufferance only and his parole may be revoked at the government's discretion. If he was admitted because of a specific emergency and the president or in some cases the commissioner of immigration should rule that the emergency is over, he may be ordered to leave.

The Illegal Alien. In some respects the paroled alien is less secure legally than the alien who, either because he has violated his admission status or because of some act committed after entry, is illegally in the United States. Although the latter may be deportable, deportation procedures in many respects are more formal than either exclusion procedures or revocation of parole. Parolees are subject to both of these last-mentioned hazards because technically they have not yet "entered" the country.

Alien Registration. Aliens are required to register and to be fingerprinted, although this regulation has been waived for many on temporary visits. Aliens must notify the U.S. attorney general each January of their current address. They must also inform him of any change of address and, if over 18 years old and permanent residents, must carry an alien registration card on their person. Willful failure to comply with these requirements may result in deportation proceedings or even criminal prosecution.

Immigration and Naturalization Service. Enforcement of the immigration laws and the policing of, as well as assistance to, aliens, in the United States is the responsibility of the Immigration and Naturalization Service, a bureau within the Department of Justice. It is directed by a commissioner who is responsible to the attorney general.

The alien who remains within the law will find that his life differs little from that of a U.S. citizen; but the alien in conflict with the authorities may face not only various criminal sanctions but also 18 possible grounds of deportation and 31 of excludability.

Every entry into the United States is a "new entry." As a result a long-term resident alien who after his first entry committed an act that did not then make him deportable may well find upon his return from a vacation abroad that he is an excludable alien. The law contains a number of remedies left to the discretion of the attorney general. Almost all of them require "good moral character" with very high standards.

Expulsion of Aliens. If the Immigration Service considers an alien either excludable or deportable, it cannot summarily remove him without both administrative and judicial review. However, because deportation is considered a civil and not a criminal proceeding, it is not covered by those clauses of the U.S. Constitution and the Bill of Rights that relate to criminal proceedings, including the ex post facto clause contained in Article I, section 9, of the Constitution. For example, an alien who during the 1930's briefly joined the Communist party may now be deportable under the Subversive Activities Act of 1950; or the alien convicted of a drug offense in 1945 may thus have become deportable in 1952 when such offenses were made a special ground of deportability.

Under the present interpretation of the Constitution even a "lawful permanent resident" does not have a "vested right" to remain in the country. The Supreme Court explained this in terms of national sovereignty and the fact that policies toward aliens are vitally interwoven with current foreign policy and the needs of military security.

Important Recent Legislation. In 1965, President Johnson signed an amendment to the existing law that represents a basic change in U.S. immigration policy. The new law phases out the so-called national origins quota system, in operation (with some modifications) since 1921, which was based on the ethnic composition (1920 census) of the U.S. population. It gave large quotas to British, German, and Irish immigrants but very small ones to many nationals of southeastern Europe, the Middle East, and Asia.

Under the new law, selection of immigrants on the basis of national origin was to end in 1968. But since the new system had about the same numerical ceiling on immigration (170,000 for all but the Western Hemisphere and, after 1968, 120,000 for the Western Hemisphere), a new "selection system" had to be created. This gives highest preference to close relatives of U.S. citizens and of lawful resident aliens; 20 percent of the preferences to aliens who have high skills or are otherwise needed in the nation's economy; and 6 percent to refugees. Persons without close relatives in the United States may immigrate only if they can establish (1) that they do not displace any worker from the job they expect to take and (2) that their proposed wages will not adversely affect the labor market.

EDITH LOWENSTEIN, *Attorney at Law*
American Council for Nationalities Services

Further Reading: Conover, Ted, *Coyotes: A Journey Through the Secret World of America's Illegal Aliens* (Random House 1987).

ALIEN AND SEDITION ACTS, ā'lē-ən, sə-dish'ən. In 1798, when relations between the United States and France were strained almost to the breaking point by the publication of the X Y Z correspondence, the Federalist party secured the passage, by small majorities, of four acts of Congress directed against subversive activities of foreigners in the United States and imposing far-reaching restrictions on freedom of speech and of the press. Ostensibly intended to safeguard the country during time of war, these acts also originated in the Federalists' alarm at the growing strength of the Republican party led by Thomas Jefferson and James Madison; the intemperate and slanderous attacks made upon administration leaders by Republican journalists; and the widespread fear of the "foreign menace" represented by French agents and refugee Irish and English radicals.

These acts of Congress were: the Naturalization Act (June 18, 1798); the Act Concerning Aliens (June 25, 1798); the Act Respecting Alien Enemies (July 6, 1798); and the Act for the Punishment of Certain Crimes (July 14, 1798). Of these measures, two—the Act Concerning Aliens (Alien Act) and the Act for the Punishment of Certain Crimes (Sedition Act)—were chiefly responsible for giving to this period the name of the "Reign of Terror" and for producing the opposition which culminated in the Virginia and Kentucky Resolutions.

By barring alien enemies from naturalization and requiring the registration of aliens upon arrival in the United States, the Naturalization Act gave the federal government much-needed power over aliens. But the provisions of this act raising the term of residence required before naturalization from 5 to 14 years were clearly intended to weaken the Republican party, to which most naturalized citizens gravitated. The Act Respecting Alien Enemies endowed the government with authority to arrest and deport all alien enemies in the event of war, a measure directed against French nationals resident in the United States. The Act Concerning Aliens, on the other hand, did not require a declaration of war before it went into effect; nor was it intended to apply only against French nationals. Radicals of every nationality came within its purview. By this law, the president was given power to order out of the country all aliens he deemed dangerous to the security of the United States.

Because the United States did not declare war against France, waging instead an undeclared war for over two years, the Alien Enemies Act did not go into force. Although it hung as a threat over the heads of all aliens in the United States, the Alien Act was not actually enforced. It may have played some part in the decision reached at this time by many French citizens living in the United States to return to France; it certainly prompted several foreign-born Republican journalists to take out citizenship papers. Its chief importance, however, lay in the heated constitutional debate which arose. Republicans denounced it as unconstitutional on three counts: as a deprivation of trial by jury; as an illegal enlargement of the authority of the federal government over aliens; and as an unwarranted extension of the powers of the executive. By Republican theory, resident aliens were wholly within the jurisdiction of the states; the federal government had no right to touch their persons and property. This constitutional objection was given added force by the apprehension felt in the South that the Alien Act menaced the institution of slavery; it was widely believed that the president had been given authority to deport slaves.

As exponents of the implied and inherent powers of the national government, the Federalists found sanction for the Alien Act in the right of Congress to defend the country against foreign aggression. Moreover, they insisted that the admission of foreigners to asylum is not an absolute right but a revocable privilege and that the grant as well as the revocation is at the discretion of the government.

Originally introduced into the United States Senate by Senator James Lloyd of Maryland, the Sedition Act underwent considerable revision in the House of Representatives. At the instigation of Harrison Gray Otis, Robert G. Harper, and James A. Bayard, the Federalist floor leaders in the House, provisions were inserted by which truth was admitted as a defense in cases of slander and libel, proof of malicious intent was required, the jury was permitted to determine questions of law as well as of fact, and limits were fixed upon the amount of the fine and term of imprisonment that could be imposed. In these respects, the Sedition Act was an improvement over the common law, by which, in cases of libel, truth was no defense, the judge decided upon matters of intent, the jury was confined to questions of fact, and punishment was left to the discretion of the court.

However, these safeguards to the rights of the individual proved, in the actual execution of the law, to be of little avail. Judges and juries were usually biased against defendants and, owing to the rulings of the judges, truth was ineffective as a defense. As a result, the Sedition Act bore out the Republicans' fears that it would be used to destroy freedom of speech and of the press. By its terms, the publishing or printing of any false, scandalous, or malicious writings to bring the government, Congress, or the president into contempt or disrepute, excite popular hostility to them, incite resistance to the laws of the United States, or encourage hostile designs against the United States, were declared a misdemeanor. Interpreted broadly by the courts, these powers were directed against Republican critics of administration policies. Among the victims of the Sedition Act was Matthew Lyon, a Republican congressman from Vermont, who was convicted of sedition, fined $1,000, and sentenced to serve four months in jail. Only about 25 persons were indicted under the Sedition Act, and of these hardly a dozen were ever brought to trial. But among those convicted of violating the law were some leading Republican journalists.

Republicans held the Sedition Act to be a violation of the First Amendment to the Constitution. Federalists, on the other hand, defended it as a measure necessary to the safety of the government and therefore justified by the right of self-preservation. The question of its constitutionality never was brought before the Supreme Court. Had it been, there can be little doubt that it would have been upheld by the justices who sat upon the bench during John Adams' presidency; among them were to be found its most fervent champions.

The Naturalization Act was repealed by the Jeffersonian Republicans in 1802; the Alien Act expired on June 25, 1800; and the life of the Sedition Act terminated on March 3, 1801. In January 1801, although they had lost the presidency and control of Congress in the elections of 1800, the Federalists nevertheless attempted to reenact the Sedition Law. The Republicans successfully warded off this effort, but in the final vote in the House of Representatives (where the Federalists mustered almost their entire strength, lame ducks and all) the Sedition Act received more votes than had the original act of July 14, 1798.

The unpopularity of the Alien and Sedition Acts certainly contributed to the overthrow of the Federalist party. It was not, however, until after the panic engendered by "Jacobinism" was over that the full import of these measures became clear. Much of the Federalists' social and political philosophy was outmoded in 1800; but it was the immorality of their public conduct and their disregard of the basic freedoms of Americans that completed their ruin and cost them the confidence and respect of the people.

JOHN C. MILLER, *Stanford University*

ALIGARH, u'lē-gur, is a city in western Uttar Pradesh state, India, 70 miles southeast of Delhi. Locally the city is commonly called by its old Hindu name of *Koil;* the name *Aligarh* ("high fort") refers to the fortress protecting Koil. The city is an industrial center manufacturing locks, other metal items, and cotton rugs and carpets, and it is a market center for wheat, sugar, and cotton.

In the late 1800s, Aligarh was the headquarters of the Aligarh movement, a drive launched by Sir Sayyid Ahmad Khan to introduce Western education, culture, and political ideas to Indian Muslims in order to foster loyalty to Britain and thwart the Hindu nationalist movement. The Aligarh Muslim University, founded by Sir Sayyid as the Anglo-Arabic College in 1875, remains the principal seat of Muslim education in India. Population: 667,732 (2001 census).

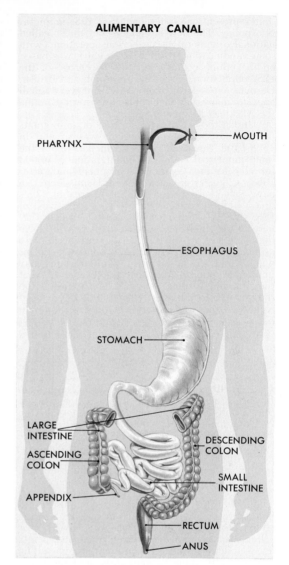

ALIMENTARY CANAL

PHARYNX — MOUTH — ESOPHAGUS — STOMACH — LARGE INTESTINE — ASCENDING COLON — APPENDIX — DESCENDING COLON — SMALL INTESTINE — RECTUM — ANUS

ALIMENTARY CANAL, al-ə-ment′ə-rē kə-nal′, a closed system beginning at the mouth and extending to the anus. It is also called the *digestive tract*. In man, the alimentary canal is approximately 29½ feet (9 meters) long. It is primarily concerned with digestion and nourishment, breaking down foods into their smallest component parts so that they can be absorbed into the blood and lymph. These circulating body fluids then carry the food elements to the cells of the body, where they provide the energy necessary for all the body's life processes.

Structure and Function. The first segment of the alimentary canal is the mouth, which breaks up food by the process of mastication, or chewing. The food mass is also lubricated, and the process of digestion is started by an enzyme secreted by the salivary glands. The act of swallowing conveys food and water from the mouth to the esophagus, or gullet, a slender tube 9 to 10 inches (23 to 25 cm) long in man. The esophagus passes the food and water downward through the chest cavity to the stomach.

The stomach is the most dilated portion of

the alimentary canal. Generally, it is a J-shaped organ, but its shape changes when it contains food or when the person is under emotional stress. In the stomach, gastric juices continue the process of digestion and convert the food mass into a thick liquid called chyme.

From the stomach, the chyme is emptied into the small intestine, a narrow coiled tube about 23 feet (7 meters) long. There, digestion is completed and the food elements are absorbed into the blood and lymph. Generally, the small intestine is divided into three sections: the duodenum, the jejunum, and the ileum.

Nearly all foods contain some indigestible matter, and this material forms the residue that is emptied from the small intestine into a blind pouch called the cecum. From the cecum it enters the colon, or large intestine, a tube about 4½ feet long (1½ meters) in man, extending to the rectum. In the colon, digestive action results mostly from mechanical churning that aids the absorption of water and inorganic salts; also, certain bacteria in the colon dissolve cellulose fibers. Anatomically, the colon is divided into four sections: ascending colon, transverse colon, descending colon, and sigmoid colon.

The rectum, the terminal portion of the canal, is a pouch that acts as a passageway to evacuate the residue. It varies in length from about 8 to 10 inches (20 to 25 cm) in man and terminates in the anus.

Diseases. Some diseases, including many infections and tumors, may occur in all segments of the alimentary canal, while others tend to occur in only one segment. The esophagus is occasionally narrowed by scar tissue formed after the ingestion of corrosives. In the stomach, irritating substances may cause an inflammatory disease or ulceration. There is also a high incidence of cancer in the stomach.

Diseases of the colon include ulceration and congenital malformation. The most common disorders of the rectum and anus include diarrheal diseases, hemorrhoids (piles), and fissures, and skin changes that cause itching. Interference with the nervous and muscular control of the rectum often causes leakage of the intestinal contents.

JOHN U. SCHWARZMAN, M.D.
Washington Hospital Center

ALIMONY, al'ə-mō-nē, is a payment ordered as part of a matrimonial proceeding in a court of law. It is the judicial measurement of a wife's (sometimes a husband's) right to financial support. Temporary alimony (*pendente lite*) is awarded until final determination of a marital action, when permanent alimony is fixed.

In the United States, the state court granting a divorce or separation decree must have jurisdiction over the marriage. It must also have jurisdiction over the husband's person in order to issue an enforceable requirement to pay alimony. While there may be collection problems if the husband leaves the state and goes elsewhere, the decree is enforceable, under the full faith and credit clause of the Constitution.

In *Williams* v. *North Carolina* (1942), the U.S. Supreme Court enunciated a doctrine of "divisible divorce"—that is, a state may effectively terminate a marriage although it is powerless to grant enforceable support. Thus a woman determined to end a marriage, but lacking grounds in one state, may establish residence in an "easy" divorce state like Nevada and secure a valid

divorce. But if her husband fails to appear personally or by counsel in the Nevada action, the alimony provisions will be unenforceable anywhere, even in Nevada, since neither Nevada nor any other state could force the husband to comply. (A wife may, however, under the Uniform Support of Dependents Act, secure child support, in whatever state the husband resides.) Similarly, a husband may migrate, secure a valid one-sided divorce, and leave the wife no legal remedy. New York State protects the wives of such errant spouses by permitting suit for support even after a valid foreign divorce.

Some states have set maximum alimony limits, but the amount usually is based on the family's pre-separation living standard and is limited by the husband's finances. Usually, the courts have discretion to fix amounts as justice and circumstances require. The primary duty of support rests on the husband, but the wife's assets, income, and earnings potential are relevant.

Pennsylvania refuses permanent alimony on the theory that support is an incident of marriage and the right to support ends with its termination. Nearly every other state recognizes the right to alimony, although standards vary.

Alimony should be differentiated from property division. Some states will divide property as recompense to the injured party in cases of marital misconduct. Except for "community property" states, most states will not divide property at all but will award alimony only, without regard to the financial or other contribution the wife has made to the husband's assets. Since divorce ends a wife's right to inherit upon the husband's death (when alimony also terminates), the practice of awarding alimony only and not dividing capital assets has been criticized as unfair. Such criticism seems especially valid when the marriage has been of long duration and when there are children, support of whom devolves upon the wife.

Conversely, husbands often are saddled by a lifetime obligation without regard to their impaired earning ability in later years. It is often urged that both parties should have easy access to relief as circumstances change. However, although most states have laws theoretically permitting such alimony adjustments, practical redress under present laws often proves impossible.

JULIA PERLES
*Chairman, Committee on Matrimonial Law
New York County Lawyers Association*

ALIPHATIC COMPOUNDS, al-ə-fat'ik kom'-poundz, are saturated or unsaturated organic compounds that have an open chain of carbon atoms, as contrasted with the ring structure of aromatic compounds. Because of the variety and numbers of aliphatic compounds, many subclasses have been recognized, including alkanes, alkenes, alkynes, alcohols, halides, carboxylic acids, esters, nitriles, amines, amides, aldehydes, and ketones. Aliphatic compounds also include more complex series such as the carbohydrates, terpenes, steroids, and polyenes. As one example, the branched alkane, 2,2,4-trimethylpentane, is the 100-octane standard of motor fuel. Its structural formula is:

$$H_3C - \underset{\underset{H}{|}}{\overset{\overset{CH_3}{|}}{C}} - CH_2 - \underset{\underset{CH_3}{|}}{\overset{\overset{CH_3}{|}}{C}} - CH_3$$

S.I. MILLER, *Illinois Institute of Technology*

ALIQUIPPA, al-ə-kwip′-ə, an industrial borough in western Pennsylvania, in Beaver county. It is situated on the Ohio River, 18 miles (29 km) northwest of Pittsburgh. Its industries include the manufacture of open-hearth and Bessemer steel, steel sheets, welded products, pig iron, electrical machinery, and stone, clay, and glass products. The site was once a trading center for Iroquois, Delaware, and Shawnee Indians, and Aliquippa was named for a notable Iroquois woman. It was incorporated as a borough in 1893. Expansion of the steel mills stimulated its growth after 1909. Heavy industry continues to influence the city's economy. Population: 11,734.

ALIZARIN, ə-liz′ə-rən, is a natural dyestuff formerly obtained from the roots of the madder plant (*Rubia tinctorum*) but now produced synthetically from coal tar. Alizarin and indigo were the two major dyestuffs known and used by man centuries ago. For example, some Egyptian mummies were wrapped in red-colored cloth dyed by alizarin. The madder plant, the source of alizarin dye in ancient Egypt, Persia, and India, still is grown and used in India.

The first synthesis of alizarin was achieved by the German chemists Karl Graebe and Karl Liebermann in 1868. This synthesis also was the first synthesis of a natural dyestuff. In 1869 Sir William Henry Perkin developed another process for producing alizarin. This synthetic product was cheaper and had a more uniform composition than natural alizarin; therefore, the madder plant rapidly was replaced as a commercial source for the dye.

Combined with various other materials called mordants (the binder between the cloth and the dyestuff), which determine color, alizarin provided red, rose, violet, dark brown, and black dyes. But dyeing with it was not easy, and alizarin now is seldom so used. It is used, however, in the manufacture of such dyes as alizarin blue (a wool dye), in other dyes for cotton and silk, and in the manufacture of artists' pigments.

In the synthetic production of alizarin ($C_{11}H_5O_4$), anthracene ($C_{14}H_{10}$), prepared from coal tar, has oxygen added to it to produce anthraquinone ($C_{14}H_8O_2$). Anthraquinone is sulfonated (sulfuric acid is added), and the product, including the sulfonic acid of anthraquinone, then is fused with caustic soda and potassium chlorate. The melt is run into hot water, and alizarin is precipitated by adding sulfuric acid.

Pure alizarin forms orange-red crystals. Alizarin melts at 554° F (290° C) and boils at 796° F (424° C). It is almost insoluble in cold water, moderately soluble in alcohol, and readily soluble in ether at 77° F (25° C).

ALKALI, al′kə-lī, is the name used for some of the compounds of the alkali metals (q.v.). The term was used in alchemy to describe the oxides of sodium and potassium that could be recovered from plant ashes. When added to water, these oxides form the hydroxides. Solutions of the hydroxides turn litmus extract blue, react with acids to give neutral salts, and have a corrosive action on the skin. All the alkali metals form similar compounds. The reaction with litmus is a property common to all alkalis, but other compounds also turn litmus blue. In the chemical industry the term "alkali" is used for sodium hydroxide (caustic soda), sodium carbonate (soda ash), and potassium carbonate (pearl ash).

Of the alkalis, only sodium carbonate occurs naturally in large quantities. The main alkalis of the chemical industry are sodium carbonate and sodium hydroxide. They are used to prepare most other sodium compounds. Where natural sodium carbonate is not available, it is prepared commercially by the Solvay process. Alkalis are used extensively in the manufacture of glass, soap, leather, paper, detergents, plastics, petrochemicals, and fertilizer.

IRVING FATT, *University of California, Berkeley*

ALKALI METALS, al′kə-lī met′əlz, are the metallic constituents of the common alkalis (see ALKALI). The alkali metal group in the periodic table consists of sodium, potassium, lithium, rubidium, and cesium. All the alkali metals are soft, and all are silvery white when freshly cut. Except for lithium, which melts at 367° F (186° C), all alkali metals melt below the temperature of boiling water. The alkali metals are less dense than other metals and water. Lithium, with a density of 0.53 gram per cubic centimeter, has the lowest density of any known solid.

The alkali metals react violently with water to form the hydroxide and hydrogen. Potassium, rubidium, and cesium react with water so violently that the evolved hydrogen ignites spontaneously.

The alkali metals do not occur in metallic form in nature. They can be prepared by the electrolysis of the molten hydroxide or chloride. Sir Humphry Davy first prepared metallic sodium and potassium in 1807 by electrolysis of their molten hydroxides. Lithium was first isolated by Robert Bunsen and Augustus Matthiessen in 1855 by electrolysis of the molten chloride. Rubidium and cesium are rare elements; they were first recognized by spectrographic analysis.

Sodium, the sixth most abundant element, constitutes 2.63 percent of the earth's crust. It is the only alkali metal of commercial importance in the metallic form, and it is the cheapest nonferrous metal on the industrial market. Industrial production is by electrolysis of a molten mixture of sodium chloride and calcium chloride. The calcium metal produced in the electrolysis separates from the sodium during cooling of the metal mixture. After filtering the molten sodium, a product of 99.9 percent pure sodium is obtained.

The largest use for metallic sodium is in the manufacture of tetraethyl lead, an additive for gasoline to improve its properties as an automobile fuel. Large amounts of sodium also are used in the manufacture of detergents and titanium. Molten sodium is used to carry heat from a nuclear reactor to steam-generating equipment.

IRVING FATT, *University of California, Berkeley*

ALKALINE EARTH METALS, al′kə-lən ərth, are a periodic-table group of elements—beryllium, magnesium, calcium, strontium, barium, and radium. Historically, this group included only calcium, strontium, and barium because these metals form hydroxides with distinctly alkaline properties.

Calcium and magnesium are the fifth and eighth most abundant elements in the earth's crust. Other alkaline earth metals are relatively rare. All the alkaline earth metals are soft, except beryllium, which is hard enough to scratch glass. All are silvery white. Their chemical properties resemble the alkali metals, but are less reactive.

Calcium, strontium, and barium were first prepared in metallic form by Sir Humphry Davy in 1807–1808 by electrolysis of their molten salts. In 1808, Davy prepared magnesium from a mercury amalgam of magnesium. Beryllium was isolated by Friedrich Wöhler in 1828. Radium, in the form of a salt, was prepared by Pierre and Marie Curie in 1898 from pitchblende. Marie Curie isolated the metal in 1911 by electrolysis of the chloride.

Magnesium, in the form of lightweight magnesium-aluminum alloys, is used for aircraft structural members. Beryllium forms strong, light alloys with copper. These alloys are used when high strength and good electrical and heat conductivity are required. Calcium metal is used in the steel industry to desulfurize and deoxidize iron alloys and in the chemical industry to dehydrate alcohol and other organic solvents.

IRVING FATT, *University of California, Berkeley*

ALKALINE EARTHS, al′kə-lən ərths, are the oxides of calcium, strontium, and barium. They were called the alkaline earths in ancient chemistry because they resemble iron oxide and aluminum oxide, common earth minerals, and because they have properties similar to those of the alkalis. From the modern point of view, the oxides of beryllium and magnesium should be included in the alkaline earth group.

Common names for these oxides are: beryllia (beryllium oxide); magnesia (magnesium oxide); lime (calcium oxide); strontia (strontium oxide); and baryta (barium oxide). All the oxides have melting points above 2000° C (3630° F), and they do not decompose up to 3000° C (5430° F). They are extremely poor conductors of heat. These properties make oxides ideal for furnace linings; large quantities of magnesia bricks are used in this way.

Calcium oxide is prepared by heating the naturally occurring calcium carbonates—limestone, chalk, or marble. When fresh oxide (quicklime) is added to water (a process called slaking), the hydroxide, also called lime, is formed. Lime has been used since prehistoric times for fertilizer, building mortar, and plaster. It continues to be used as a fertilizer and in building construction, and is used in the metallurgical and paper industries and in purifying water and treating sewage.

IRVING FATT, *University of California, Berkeley*

ALKALOIDS, al′kə-loidz, are a group of organic compounds that occur chiefly in seed-bearing plants. The word *alkaloid* means "alkalilike." The compounds were called alkaloids because, like the inorganic alkalis, they reacted with acids to form salts. The alkaline, or basic, nature of alkaloids depends on the one or more nitrogen atoms that are an invariable part of their molecular structure. Alkaloids have attracted attention for many years because some of them have profound effects on the animal body.

Classification. Alkaloids can be regarded as derivatives of ammonia (NH_3) by substitution of carbon-containing radicals for hydrogen. The nitrogen atoms in alkaloids usually are in cyclic (ring) structures. The alkaloids are subdivided into many groups according to the fundamental skeleton of carbon and nitrogen atoms in the molecule. Thus alkaloids can be described as pyrrolidines, pyridines, purines, indoles, isoquinolines, tropanes, and so on. This chemical classification is overlapped by another type of designation based on the plant source. Thus an alkaloid may be described as being of the Amaryllidaceae type. There is no great conflict between the two kinds of terminology because plants of a given group often contain alkaloids of similar chemical structures.

Properties. When isolated, most alkaloids are colorless, nonvolatile, crystalline solids. A few, such as nicotine and coniine, are liquids in their free base form but become crystalline salts when treated with acids. Many alkaloids have asymmetric structures, and therefore their solutions rotate a beam of polarized light. The direction and degree of rotation is a characteristic that is useful in identifying them. A very few alkaloids, such as berberine and sanguinarine, are colored. This coloring accounts for the yellow- to red-colored juices of such familiar plants as celandine, bleeding heart, barberry, and bloodroot. A bitter taste is a well-known characteristic of alkaloids. The reactivity of alkaloids can be related to the availability of an uncombined pair of electrons on the nitrogen atom of compounds derived from ammonia. The slight negative charge of this electron pair gives most alkaloids a capability of combining with the positively charged hydrogen ion of acids. This reaction forms salts.

Certain functional groups are found very commonly in alkaloid structures. Oxygen atoms in alcohols, ethers, or ketones are a part of most alkaloid molecules. Methyl groups also are found frequently, often as methyl ethers.

Occurrence and Function. The natural distribution of alkaloids is not highly systematic, but a few generalities can be made. Primarily, the higher plants (seed plants) produce alkaloids, although some fungi, such as ergot (*Claviceps*) of rye, are noted for their alkaloids. Lower fungi, and even animals, produce certain compounds that might be classed as alkaloids, but such compounds usually are not so classed.

One compilation lists more than 3,000 species of seed plants that contain alkaloids. Certain families are particularly rich in alkaloids. The Papaveraceae, Solanaceae, Rubiaceae, and Amaryllidaceae are prominent alkaloid-containing families. Commonly, alkaloid-bearing plants contain complex mixtures of compounds that have similar structures and properties. The opium poppy (*Papaver somniferum*) contains about 30 different alkaloids, as does the ergot fungus. A particular alkaloid may be quite restricted in its occurrence, or it may be widespread. Cocaine is found only in species of *Erythroxylon*, whereas nicotine is found in several dozen unrelated genera. Probably most often an alkaloid is found throughout the plant but most highly concentrated in a particular tissue. Quinine normally is obtained from bark, morphine from latex, cocaine from leaves, strychnine from seeds, and emetine from roots. Alkaloid formation is regularly associated with rapidly growing tissues, but alkaloids made in one part of the plant may be transported to another part. Nicotine, which is known to be made primarily in the roots of tobacco, is carried upward by the flow of sap and accumulates in the leaves.

The function and the mode of formation of alkaloids in plants are still under study. The most-favored current view is that alkaloids are merely waste products of plant metabolism. Earlier suggestions, now regarded as unfounded, were that alkaloid formation has arisen as a way for plants to protect themselves against predators.

Alkaloids do not merely accumulate in plants. They are metabolized by plants and sometimes undergo rapid fluctuations in concentration. It is difficult to reconcile this evidence and the view that alkaloids are merely waste products.

In most cases, amino acids are found to serve as precursors for the formation of alkaloids in plants. The amino acids most commonly used are arginine, tyrosine, and tryptophan; they lead to piperidine, isoquinoline, and indole-type structures, respectively. Other alkaloids evidently are derived from other plant constituents, such as acetic acid or nicotinic acid.

Preparation. Alkaloids are isolated by extraction of fresh or dried plant material, using organic solvents or water made slightly basic or acidic. At present, chromatographic methods of separation are regarded highly for isolation of pure alkaloids from mixtures. Adsorption chromatography on activated alumina or ion-exchange chromatography permits fine separations of alkaloids from each other.

Although chemical syntheses of many alkaloids are possible, the synthetic products usually are unable to compete economically with preparations of alkaloids from plant sources. However, some available synthetic materials are similar in physiological activities to natural plant alkaloids. Procaine and neostigmine, for example, are synthetic compounds that act quite like cocaine and physostigmine but only very slightly resemble their structures.

Pharmacology. The plant alkaloids continue to be of great importance in medicine. In spite of its addicting properties, morphine remains essential in alleviating severe pain. Investigations of the Indian *Rauwolfia* plant, used for centuries as a tranquilizer, led to isolation and widespread use of its active principle, the alkaloid reserpine. Still more recently, alkaloids of the periwinkle have shown promise in the treatment of certain neoplasms. Other alkaloids of fungi and some higher plants have gained notoriety because of their hallucinogenic action.

Except for very few cases, there are no biochemical explanations for the physiological action of alkaloids. Some alkaloids that act on the central nervous system are thought to increase the concentration of the hormone serotonin by causing its release from tissue stores or by inactivating enzymes that destroy serotonin. Many alkaloids have multiple physiological effects, and intimate understanding of their mechanism of action will probably remain elusive for many years.

TREVOR ROBINSON, *University of Massachusetts*

Further Reading: Cordell, Geoffrey A., *Introduction to Alkaloids: A Biogenetic Approach* (Wiley 1981); Manske, Richard H. D., and Holmes, Henry L., eds., *The Alkaloids,* vols. 1–28 (Academic Press 1950–1986); Pelletier, S. William, ed., *Alkaloids* (Wiley 1987); Robinson, Trevor, *The Biochemistry of Alkaloids* (Springer-Verlag 1981).

ALKMAAR, älk′mår, is a city in the Netherlands, in the province of North Holland. It is on the North Holland Canal, 20 miles northwest of Amsterdam and 6 miles from the North Sea.

Alkmaar is a market center for cattle, butter, and grain. It holds a famous Edam cheese market on Fridays from May to October. Its manufactures include iron, paper products, leather goods, and chocolate.

The town is intersected by tree-lined canals and has many houses that date from the 1600's. Among the notable buildings are the Gothic Church of St. Lawrence or Groote Kerk (1470–1498); the richly decorated Gothic town hall (1507); and the weighhouse, which was built as a chapel in the 1400's.

Alkmaar was founded early in the 1100's and was chartered in 1254. The city is famous in Dutch history because it resisted a siege conducted by the duke of Alba in 1573 during the Netherlands' war of independence from Spain. Population: 90,767 (1991 est.).

ALL FOURS is a card game once widely played in the United States and England, and forerunner of such American variants as *auction pitch* and *cinch.* Popular in England as early as the 17th century, it derives its name from four points—high, low, jack, and game—involved in the scoring. In the United States, all fours (also called *seven-up*) was the favorite game of professional gamblers until poker supplanted it.

ALL GOD'S CHILLUN GOT WINGS, a two-act play by Eugene O'Neill, written in 1923 and first produced and published in 1924. With O'Neill's *The Emperor Jones,* this tragedy helped attract the American theater to the rich dramatic potentialities of African American life.

Considered by one major critic as O'Neill's "most concentrated tragic work," the play is based on the problem of mixed marriage in a hostile society. It concerns Jim Harris, an ambitious and intelligent black man , who marries a white girl, Ella Downey, to whom he has been devoted since childhood days when he drank chalk and water mixtures in an effort to become more eligibly white in her eyes. After a brief but relatively calm visit to France, the young couple return to New York, where Ella crumbles before the social force of race prejudice. The resulting strain on their marriage so seriously affects her mind that she plagues Jim with insulting allusions to her supposed superiority and plots against his success in passing an examination for the bar, which he has repeatedly failed because of his extreme sensitivity to white examiners. Although Jim remains patiently loyal, Ella eventually goes insane and unsuccessfully tries to kill him. "Will God forgive me, Jim?" she asks. "Maybe He can forgive what you've done to me," Jim answers, "and maybe He can forgive what I've done to you; but I don't see how He's going to forgive—Himself." In the final scene of the play, Ella seeks tranquillity and happiness in the delusion that she is a child; and Jim, asking God's forgiveness for blasphemy, begs that their suffering make him worthy of Ella the child, sent to him in place of Ella the woman.

The tragedy is distinguished for its warm characterization, its subtle analysis of human psychology, and its poetically rich style supported with the effective use of symbolism. One of the play's most theatrically exciting scenes is that in which Jim, dressed in black, and Ella, in white, leave church between hostile lines of black and white wedding guests. This scene dramatically underlines the race distinction which later led Jim, exhausted with the eternal talk about the white and black races, to exclaim bitterly, "Where does the human race get a chance to come in?"

ALL HALLOWS. See ALL SAINTS' DAY; HALLOWEEN.

ALL QUIET ON THE WESTERN FRONT is a novel by Erich Maria Remarque (q.v.). The original German language edition was published as *Im Westen Nichts Neues* in January 1929. The English translation, by A.W. Wheen, appeared in the United States later that year.

The central purpose of the novel is stated thus by the author: "This book is to be neither an accusation nor a confession, and least of all an adventure, for death is not an adventure to those who stand face to face with it. It will try simply to tell of a generation of men who, even though they may have escaped its shells, were destroyed by the war."

A wide range of World War I experiences are seen through the eyes of a young German volunteer, Paul Bäumer, who manages to survive many kinds of terror and embitterment, both at the front and at home on leave, only to lose his life a few weeks before the armistice. His lot as a common soldier is shared with such comrades in arms as the hard-bitten Katczinsky, who has "a remarkable nose for dirty weather, good food, and soft jobs"; the huge-fisted Westhus, "who thinks of nothing but his farmyard and his wife"; the clear-headed Kropp, the first of Bäumer's companions to become lance corporal; and the ex-student Müller, who "dreams of examinations, and during a bombardment mutters propositions in physics."

All Quiet on the Western Front is one of the finest fictional re-creations of World War I and continues to attract readers by the strong appeal of its realism, humor, pathos, humanity, and a kind of bitter beauty. It was among the books publicly burned by the Nazis when they came to power in the 1930's.

A distinguished American motion picture was made from the novel in 1930. The film, which won the Academy Award for the 1929–1930 season as the best picture of the year, succeeded in capturing the harsh reality of war so well delineated in the book.

ALL SAINTS' DAY is a religious festival honoring all Christian saints. It is observed on November 1 by Roman Catholics and members of the Anglican Communion, and on the first Sunday after Pentecost (Whitsunday) by the Eastern Orthodox Church. The festival was instituted (May 13, 709) by Pope Boniface IV, who consecrated the Pantheon in Rome to the Virgin Mary and all Christian martyrs. Its date was changed to November 1 when Pope Gregory III (reigned 731–741) dedicated a chapel in the basilica of St. Peter to all saints. In 835, Pope Gregory IV ordered its universal observance. The festival originally was called *All Hallows* in English, and the night before was called *All Hallows Eve*, which became known as *Halloween*.

In many American churches a custom has developed of making the Sunday nearest November 1 the occasion of a service in memory of those who have died during the year.

ALL SOULS' DAY, in the Roman Catholic Church, is a day of special prayer for those dead who still are deprived of the sight of God because of imperfections. It is observed on November 2, or on November 3 if the 2d falls on Sunday. The custom began in the early church with a reading of the names of the dead, for remembrance by the faithful. In the 6th century the Benedictines honored their dead on Pentecost. Then in 998, St. Odilo of Cluny moved the Benedictines' rite to November 2, the day after the feast of All Saints, and the practice was adopted later by the entire church. In 1915, Pope Benedict XV decreed that priests could offer three Masses on All Souls.

The Church of England eliminated the feast at the Reformation, but it has since been restored in the Anglican Church.

ALL THE KING'S MEN is a novel by Robert Penn Warren (q.v.), published in 1946. It won the 1947 Pulitzer prize for fiction. The novel, set in the 1920's and early 1930's in the U.S. South, is a powerful and vivid portrayal of a Southern demagogue whose career shows striking parallels to that of Huey Long.

The story traces the career of Willie Stark from farm boy to unscrupulous politician. At first, Willie is honest, but his lust for power drives him to seek political success through deviousness and corruption. Originally a man of the people, he becomes wholly corrupt, and a tragic outcome is inevitable.

The narrator of the story is Jack Burden, Willie's press agent. The novel, remarkable for its rich perceptiveness, driving narrative, and effortless prose style, is as much a study of Burden's self-realization and redemption as it is of Willie's destruction.

ALLAH, al'ə, is an Arabic word meaning "God" or, more properly, "the God." When the prophet Mohammed began to preach to the pagan Arabs in the 7th century, the heart of his message lay in the declaration that Allah is the sole, unique divinity. Mohammed believed that Allah had chosen him as the messenger of Allah's Word to mankind, and that he was to transmit the revelations given him (collected in the Koran) and to summon his fellow Arabs to commitment (*islam*) to Allah.

The characteristics of Allah in His relationship to men are made clear in the Koran. Fundamental is the affirmation that Allah is the sole divinity, One without partner, unique in His deity. In addition, Allah is He who created all things by His command and who exercises absolute sovereignty over them, the One from whom nothing escapes. As the Creator of everything good, He is the great Benefactor of men but also their Just Judge. The Koran lays great emphasis on the inevitability and imminence of the Hour (the Day of Judgment) when the Sovereign Lord and King will mete out punishment to those who have been "ungrateful" for His benefactions. The Koran also asserts repeatedly the mercy and forgiveness of Allah. For those who entrust themselves to Him in gratitude for His mercy He is a Refuge, a Guide, and a Protector.

Later Muslim theologians have not been much concerned with the nature of Allah in Himself, for they consider the divine nature to be an ineffable mystery. Allah has expressed His perfection in the 99 Most Beautiful Names He has given Himself, such as the Living, the Powerful, the Real. Two problems above all have preoccupied the theologians: (1) the nature of Allah's attributes and their relation to His essence, and (2) man's moral responsibility in the light of Allah's omnipotence and absolute sovereignty.

CHARLES ADAMS
McGill University

ALLAHABAD, al'ə-hə-bad, a city in India. Allahabad is the former capital of Uttar Pradesh and administrative center for Allahabad district and division. The city is situated at the confluence of the Ganges and Jumna rivers, and is important as an educational center. Its industries include the manufacture of foot lockers and trunks, and the canning of guava products. A principal market center, Allahabad transports such regional products as grain, oilseeds, sugarcane, cotton, and ghee (butter). There is an airport at the nearby suburb of Bamrauli.

Famous landmarks in Allahabad include Alfred Park, in which is located the Thornhill and Mayne Memorial with its fine library and museum; and, west of the park, Mayo Memorial Hall. The University of Allahabad (founded 1887) enrolls about 10,000 students in 9 constituent colleges. Other educational institutions include Muir Central College and Aggarwala Agricultural College.

Allahabad is on the site of the ancient Aryan holy city of *Prayag* ("place of sacrifice"), still a sacred place of pilgrimage to the Hindus. Its prominence during the early Buddhist period is attested to by the 35-foot-high polished stone Pillar of Asoka inscribed with the famous Buddhist edicts of Emperor Asoka (about 242 B.C.). The pillar stands just inside the gateway to the Allahabad fort, which occupies a strategic position at the rivers' confluence. Both the fort (erected 1583 A.D.) and the modern city were founded by the Mughul emperor Akbar, who established the settlement *Al-Ilahbad* ("city of God"). Outside the fort is the celebrated tomb of Khusru (died 1622), the rebellious son of Emperor Jahangir. With the decline of the Mughul empire, Allahabad changed hands several times until it was ceded to the British in 1801. A disastrous massacre took place here during the Indian (Sepoy) Mutiny in 1857.

Prior to 1947, Allahabad was a center of the Indian nationalist movement. Here, on Feb. 12, 1948, the ashes of Mohandas K. Gandhi, the nationalist leader, were immersed in the waters of the two holy rivers. Following the deaths in 1964 and 1966, respectively, of India's first two prime ministers, Jawaharlal Nehru and Lal Bahadur Shastri, their ashes were also consigned to the waters at Allahabad. Population: 1,049,579 (2001 census).

ALLAIRE, a-làr', **James Peter** (1785–1858), American engineer, of French Huguenot descent. Allaire opened a brass foundry on Cherry St., New York City, in 1813. Two years later he leased the Robert Fulton engine shop in Jersey City, N.J., transferring its business to his Cherry Street shop in 1816. The Allaire works was the first plant to produce steam engines in New York City, and soon became the most important producer of steamboat engines in the United States. Allaire was also the first to build compound marine engines. He died on May 20, 1858.

ALLAMANDA, al-ə-man'də, is a genus of climbing evergreen shrubs found in Brazil and Central America, where it is cultivated as an ornamental.

About 3 feet tall, *Allamanda* has large yellow or purple flowers that are borne terminally on many-flowered stalks. The flowers are funnel-shaped, with 5-parted limbs (flattened extensions of the flower tube), and they mature to large, spiny pods that contain hairy seeds.

Allamanda belongs to the dogbane family, Apocynaceae. There are about 12 species. Among the species, *A. cathartica*, or cup of gold, is grown extensively. Native to Brazil, it has golden yellow flowers marked with white. *A. heriifolia*, also found in Brazil, has yellow flowers striped with reddish brown.

RICHARD M. STRAW
*Los Angeles State College of
Applied Arts and Sciences*

ALLAN, al'ən, **David** (1744–1796), Scottish painter. He was born at Alloa, Stirlingshire, Scotland, on Feb. 13, 1744. He studied at the Academy of Arts in Glasgow (1775–1762) and from 1764 to 1777 worked in Rome, where his painting *Origin of Painting: or the Corinthian Maid Drawing the Shadow of Her Lover* was awarded a gold medal (1773). From 1777 to 1780 he maintained a portrait studio in London. He then settled in Edinburgh, where in 1786 he became director of the Academy of Arts.

Allan became known as the "Scottish Hogarth" because of the humor of his genre pictures, such as *Scotch Wedding* and *Highland Dance*. He died at Edinburgh on Aug. 6, 1796.

ALLAMANDA, often called cup of gold, has large, showy yellow or purple flowers. Its leaves, which are from four to six inches long, are thick and leathery.

ROCHE

JOHN J. SMITH

ALLAN, al'ən, **Sir Hugh** (1810–1882), Canadian financier and shipowner. He was born at Saltcoats, Ayrshire, Scotland, on Sept. 29, 1810. Allan emigrated to Canada in 1826, and by 1835 had become a partner in a large shipbuilding and grain-shipping firm in Montreal. Subsequently, as head of the company, he founded the Allan Line. In 1852 the firm obtained a government contract for a line of iron screw steamers on the St. Lawrence River. Its first vessel, the *Canadian,* made its maiden voyage in 1855, and two others were used as transports in the Crimean War. The Allan Line, which ran from Montreal to Liverpool and Glasgow, played a large part in developing Canadian prosperity. Allan was also one of the projectors of the Canadian Pacific Railway, although the contract for its construction was ultimately taken from his company. He was knighted in 1871. He died at Edinburgh on Dec. 9, 1882.

ALLAN, al'ən, **John** (1747–1805), American soldier. He was born in Edinburgh, Scotland, on Jan. 14, 1747. His family emigrated to Halifax, Nova Scotia, in 1749. As a youth Allan was sent to Massachusetts to complete his education. He was a member of the Nova Scotia provincial Assembly from 1770 to 1776. His sympathy for the American colonies, and especially his success in organizing anti-British feeling among the Indians, caused a charge of treason to be brought against him, and he had to leave Nova Scotia.

He went first to Maine, then to Massachusetts, and in 1777 the Continental Congress made him its agent to the Eastern Indians, with the rank of colonel. He established headquarters at Machias, Me., where his skill in dealing with the Indians kept them from deserting to the British. In 1783 he resigned his commission and became a merchant on Allan's Island in Passamaquoddy Bay, retiring in 1786 to live at Lubec Mills, Me. He died there on Feb. 7, 1805.

ALLANTOIS, ə-lan'tō-is, an important organ in embryos of reptiles, birds, and mammals. It begins as a saclike outgrowth from the posterior region of the gut tube and later protrudes outside the embryonic body. Having a rich blood supply, it serves as a respiratory organ in reptiles, birds, and monotreme mammals (duckbill, echidna). In placental mammals the allantois unites with the chorion, or outer embryonic membrane, to form the fetal placenta. It brings the embryonic blood into osmotic relation with the maternal blood in the uterine lining (maternal placenta) to carry out prenatal nutrition, respiration, and excretion. The basal part of the allantois, inside the fetal body, remains after birth as the urinary bladder, except in snakes, crocodiles, and birds. See also EMBRYOLOGY—*Extra-Embryonic Membranes.*

ALLBUTT, ôl'bət, **Sir Thomas Clifford** (1836–1925), English physician. Born at Dewsbury, Yorkshire, on July 20, 1836, he attended Cambridge University, obtained a medical degree at St. George's Hospital, London, and, after graduate study in Paris, settled in Leeds as a consulting physician (1861–1889). In 1892 he became regius professor of medicine at Cambridge University. He was elected a fellow of the Royal Society in 1880, and was knighted in 1907. He died at Cambridge on Feb. 22, 1925.

Allbutt invented the short clinical thermometer (1866) and did important research on the pathology of the nervous system and the use of the ophthalmoscope. Of particular value were his discovery of the aortic origin of angina pectoris (1894) and his study of high blood pressure apart from kidney disease (1895). He wrote *System of Medicine* (8 vols., 1896–99; rev. ed., 11 vols., 1905–11). Other important works are *Diseases of the Arteries and Angina Pectoris* (1915) and the historical studies *Science and Medieval Thought* (1901) and *The Historical Relations of Medicine and Surgery* (1905).

ALLEGATION, al-i-gā'shən, a formal assertion or declaration made by a party to a legal action, setting forth what he undertakes to prove. As used in a pleading, an allegation is a statement of what can be proved, that is, what is said to be a positive declaration of fact.

When, in response to a complaint, the defendant contests the suit, the issue must be formulated by pleadings or written allegations by both sides, but particularly on the part of the defendant, as to their respective grievances and defenses. These allegations and counter allegations of what is affirmed on one side and denied on the other are the practical means used to join the issue; that is, to disclose to the court or jury the real matter of dispute between the parties. A material allegation in a pleading is one that is fundamental to the claim or to the defense. See also PLEA AND PLEADING.

ALLEGHENY COLLEGE, al-ə-gā'nē, is a private, coeducational institution in Meadville, Pa. Established in 1815 under Presbyterian auspices, it was transferred to Methodist control in 1833, but it functions on a nonsectarian basis. The curriculum stresses the liberal arts, with special emphasis on independent study under faculty supervision. The library includes special collections of early Americana. Enrollment increased from 780 in 1940 to over 1,200 students in the mid–1960's.

ALLEGHENY MOUNTAINS, al-ə-gā'nē, the high eastern margin of the Allegheny Plateau, extending from Pennsylvania to central West Virginia. The plateau is the western part of the Appalachian mountain system. It reaches from the Mohawk Valley in New York to the beginning of the Cumberland Plateau in West Virginia. The escarpment along the eastern edge of the Alleghenies, overlooking the ridge-and-valley province of the Appalachian Mountains, is known by several names. In Pennsylvania and West Virginia it is called the Allegheny Front; in Maryland, Dans Mountain; and on Virginia's border with West Virginia, Allegheny Mountain. To the west the Allegheny Plateau slopes gradually down to the interior lowland.

Although the Allegheny Mountains form a rugged mountainous terrain in many places, they are classed geologically as a dissected plateau. Their peaks are all of nearly equal height, indicating that the region was once a level tableland. Their lowlands are not typical valley lowlands, but strips of dissected plateau. Despite the sharp relief of the northern Alleghenies the mountains in central West Virginia rise only 1,000 feet (305 meters) above the 3,500-foot (1,070-meter) Allegheny Plateau.

The Allegheny Mountains form the divide between the rivers emptying into the Atlantic

ALLEGHENY MOUNTAINS in West Virginia show an unbroken ridge crest as a background for the stubby hills that swell up from the valley floor.

GRANT HEILMAN

Ocean and those draining into the Gulf of Mexico. The predominant geologic formations are limestone, sandstone, and conglomerates, ranging from the Cambrian to the Carboniferous systems. Immense coal seams occur throughout the Alleghenies, and the mountains are generally clothed with hardwood forests. Many areas are known for their scenic beauty. Historically, the Alleghenies were influential in restricting early American settlements to the eastern seaboard, and for years they delayed exploration of the West.

HAROLD C. AMICK, *University of Tennessee*

ALLEGHENY RIVER, al-ə-gā′nē, a headstream of the Ohio River. It rises in Potter County in north central Pennsylvania and flows northward through Cattaraugus County, N.Y., then generally southwest through Pennsylvania, joining the Monongahela at Pittsburgh to form the Ohio. It is 325 miles (523 km) long. Besides Pittsburgh, the chief cities on the river are Olean, N.Y., Warren, Pa., and Oil City, Pa. The Kinzua Dam, a federal flood-control project on the Allegheny in Pennsylvania, was completed in 1965. The dam required flooding of the Seneca Indian reservation in Cattaraugus County, N.Y., forcing the Indians to relocate.

ALLEGIANCE, ə-lē′jəns, is the obligation of fidelity and obedience to government in return for its protection. During the feudal period, tenants and serfs owed allegiance to the lord of the manor. Under present law, however, allegiance is owed only to the state or its symbolic head. Aliens owe a temporary allegiance to a host country and, under certain circumstances, may be subject to its law of treason.

Prior to the enactment of the 14th Amendment in 1868, the U.S. Constitution did not define the constituent elements of citizenship or of allegiance. Congress's adoption of the 14th Amendment, while intended primarily to benefit African Americans, conferred citizenship on persons of all races born or naturalized in the United States. That same year, Congress abandoned the English common law doctrine of indefeasible allegiance and issued a statute that declares that the citizen has an unqualified right to change allegiance at will.

In 1870 the British Parliament also passed a statute that formally abandoned the doctrine of indefeasible allegiance by providing that any British citizen not under mental or legal disability, on becoming validly naturalized in a

foreign country, should cease to be a British citizen. Similarly, under the terms of the British Nationality Act of 1948, a British citizen can renounce his citizenship if he either becomes a citizen of another Commonwealth country or has dual nationality in a country outside the Commonwealth. The 1948 act further provides that the terms "British subject" and "Commonwealth citizen" shall have the same meaning.

The Soviet bloc countries, as well as France, Greece, and Turkey, still fail to allow their nationals to change allegiance without consent of the head of state. Most nations, however, follow the American and British practice of free choice.

Because some states look primarily to the place of birth (jus soli) and others to nationality by descent (jus sanguinis) to determine who are their nationals, dual nationality is not uncommon. To remove conflicting claims to the allegiance of naturalized persons, the United States and other nations have entered into treaties that bar one party from imposing military service on a dual national if the dual national has closer ties with the other party.

A person who has renounced or who has been deprived of his nationality, and who has not acquired the nationality of another state, may become a so-called "stateless" person. The International Refugee Organization and the United Nations have been active in attempting to resettle stateless refugees in various states.

JOHN F. MURPHY, *Attorney at Law*

ALLEGORY, al′ə-gôr-ē, is a technique of creating or interpreting works of literature, art, and music so that they will convey more than one level of meaning simultaneously. The beast fables of Aesop and La Fontaine are simple allegories in which the reader gives human significance to the action of the animal characters. An example of a more complex allegory is John Bunyan's *Pilgrim's Progress*, which on one level tells the story of a man's journey, while on a second level it conveys the idea that a Christian life is a spiritual pilgrimage. An allegorical character (for example, Mr. Worldly Wiseman in *Pilgrim's Progress*) personifies an idea or set of ideas on the second level of meaning.

Iconography. The artistic symbolism of allegory is called *iconography*. Ornamental symbols like the scythe of Time or the dove of Peace are basic, unchanging iconographic elements. The use of such symbols occurs in literature, the visual arts, and music. Medieval church decorations, Renaissance emblem books, and painting by such artists as Titian, Bosch, Mantegna, and Dürer display an emblematic iconography that was later perpetuated in mannerist art, 18th-century landscapes, Gothic revival grotesqueries, and modern surrealism. Musical counterparts include the "imitative" melodies used in the music of Johann Sebastian Bach and other composers of the High Renaissance and baroque periods. Later, program music (such as Beethoven's *Pastoral Symphony*), Wagner's operas, with their obsessive *leitmotifs*, and Richard Strauss' tone poems all employ recurrent phrases which have double meanings.

Iconography must be interpreted by the reader, viewer, or listener in the light of his own special knowledge. Iconography can refer indirectly to either ideas or actual persons and events. Hence, it is frequently used when political censorship forces the artist to be devious.

Typology. From the 600's B.C., Greek philosophers defended Homer as a sacred author by inventing dignified allegorical meanings for the Homeric portrayals of quarrelsome, carousing gods. Early rabbinical exegeses exonerated the erotic poetry of the Song of Songs by giving it a mystical and prophetic allegorical interpretation.

For Christians, the comparable technique is "typology," a historically oriented, prophetic symbolism distinct from the unchanging iconography of moral allegory. Through typology, persons named in the Old Testament become prototypes or archetypes of actual later persons, including Jesus. See ARCHETYPE.

Allegory in Literature. All literary genres, from short lyrics to such full-scale plays as the anonymous *Everyman*, can use allegory, and most Western literature is touched, if not controlled, by allegorical intentions. Iconography was employed sporadically by the classical Greek and Roman writers, and frequently by medieval authors. Medieval literature used such popular commonplaces as the Seven Deadly Sins, the Four Daughters of God, and the Dance of Death, and produced such masterworks of allegorical romance and Christian vision as *The Romance of the Rose* by de Lorris and de Meung, and *Piers Plowman* by William Langland. A medieval Frenchman gave Ovid's *Metamorphoses* a moral purpose in *Ovide moralisé*, and Virgil was commonly granted Christian (typological) significance. Chaucer wrote allegorically in his *Book of the Duchess* and *Parliament of Fowls*. In the Renaissance, classical myths survived as moral fables, serving to dignify both the new romantic epic and its classical models. In 18th-century English literature, allegory dominated the Gothic romance and the satiric works of Dryden, Pope, and Swift.

Writers of the romantic age, following the lead of Goethe, opposed allegory on the grounds that it artificially divided reason and imagination. However, Freudian dream interpretation and Frazer's *Golden Bough* helped return allegory to a central place in modern literature. Many authors, including Henry James, James Joyce, Franz Kafka, D.H. Lawrence, George Orwell, William Faulkner, and William Golding, have used allegory, and it even has infiltrated modern realism, giving a number of novels of this type an abstract substructure of ideological message.

ANGUS FLETCHER
Author of "Allegory: Theory of a Symbolic Mode"

Bibliography
Bloomfield, Morton W., ed., *Allegory, Myth, and Symbol* (Harvard Univ. Press 1982).
Cooper, J. C., *Fairy Tales: Allegories of the Inner Life* (Borgo 1986).
Fletcher, Angus, *Allegory: Theory of a Symbolic Mode* (1964; reprint, Cornell Univ. Press 1982).
Leyburn, Ellen D., *Satiric Allegory: Mirror of Man* (1956; reprint, Greenwood Press 1978).
Quilligan, Maureen, *The Language of Allegory: Defining the Genre* (Cornell Univ. Press 1979).
Russell, Stephen, *Allegories: The Craft of Allegory in Medieval Literature* (Garland 1987).
Whitman, Jon, *Allegory: The Dynamics of an Ancient and Medieval Technique* (Harvard Univ. Press 1987).

ALLEGRI, äl-lā'grē, **Gregorio** (1582–1652), Italian composer. Born in Rome, he was a singer in the papal choir of St. Peter's Basilica from 1629 until his death. His most famous composition is the *Miserere*, based on the 50th Psalm in the Roman Catholic Bible (the 51st in the King James Version). This work, written for nine voices in two choruses in five- and four-part harmony, is still sung regularly during Passion Week in the Sistine Chapel at Rome. Allegri died at Rome on Feb. 17, 1652.

ALLEGRO, ä-lā'grō, an Italian word meaning "gay," is used in music to indicate a more or less quick rate of movement. *Allegro* without qualification denotes a rate of speed midway between *andante* and *presto*. The degrees of quickness are indicated by additional qualifying words or by derivatives of the word *allegro*. Thus *allegretto* or *poco allegro* indicates a rather lively tempo; *allegro moderato, allegro comodo, allegro giusto*, moderately quick; *allegro maestoso*, quick, but with dignity; *allegro assai* and *allegro molto*, very quick; *allegro con brio* or *con fuoco*, with fire and energy; and *allegrissimo*, with the utmost rapidity.

The rapid first movement of a composition in sonata form is often referred to as the allegro.

ALLEGRO, L', lä-lā'grō, a lyric poem by John Milton (1608–1674), companion piece to *Il Penseroso* (see *Penseroso, Il*). The Italian titles may be translated "the gay or happy or mirthful man" (L'Allegro) and "the melancholy or contemplative man" (Il Penseroso). Each character declares for his own temperament and way of life against the other, then gives an account of a typical day of recreative and aesthetic satisfaction. The contrast between the two sets of experience is carefully maintained in the poems.

L'Allegro hears the lark at dawn and goes forth to see the sunrise. He watches the plowman, the milkmaid, and the shepherd until afternoon; then he looks on at the country revels, hears the twilight stories in some upland hamlet, and finally spends a social evening, attending a play or a masque, in the towered city.

Il Penseroso begins first to enjoy himself at evening, and his pleasures are all solitary. For the lark he has the nightingale; instead of seeing comedies performed he reads tragedies; instead of listening to and perhaps taking a part in madrigals he hears the organ and the full-voiced choir at church. And being a man of studious and reflective habit, he is able, unlike L'Allegro, who lives in the present, to envisage a happy old age in a hermit's cell.

Nevertheless, the modes of pleasure that Milton is analyzing in the two poems are not essentially different. For even L'Allegro is more contemplative than he is social. He himself does not join the country dancers, and his smile, as he views the strutting cock or listens to the huntsman's horn, comes short of hearty laughter.

When and on what occasion Milton wrote these delightful poems is not really known. They do not appear in the Trinity College, Cambridge, manuscript and therefore probably antedate *Arcades* (1633). The idea, which was first advanced by E. M. W. Tillyard in 1932, that they are addressed to a student audience is supported by their kinship in theme and tone with some of the poet's college exercises. This is not to say that they are either trivial or immature. They have, in fact, always been among the most admired of Milton's minor poems.

JAMES H. HANFORD
Author of "John Milton, Englishman"

ALLEN, Ethan, al'ən (1738–1789), American Revolutionary soldier, leader of the Green Mountain Boys. Allen was born in Litchfield, Conn., on Jan. 10, 1738. He served in the French and Indian War and about 1769 settled in Bennington, Vt., where he quickly became a leader in the Vermonters' quarrel with New York.

The British Crown had given Vermont, then called the New Hampshire Grants, to both New Hampshire and New York under conflicting patents. When the dispute was settled (1764) in favor of New York, Gov. Benning Wentworth of New Hampshire had already granted over 100 townships, and he continued to grant others until the outbreak of the American Revolution. New York proceeded to regrant the same territory, but the indignant settlers, applying the "beech seal" (whipping), drove out the surveyors.

The British government ordered New York to respect the status quo and to avert further disorders by granting only ungranted land. The New York authorities nonetheless still sent surveyors. Their grantees persisted in attempting to take possession of their lands, and the New Hampshire grantees continued to eject both deputy sheriffs and claimants by armed force.

The adventurous Allen was now in his element. In 1770 the New York Supreme Court ruled that all the New Hampshire grants were invalid. Faced with the prospect of having to rebuy their lands because of New York's new attempt to enforce its rights, the settlers raised a defense regiment, called the Green Mountain Boys, of which Allen was made colonel. Governor William Tryon of New York proclaimed him an outlaw and put a price on his head. Under Allen, Seth Warner, and other able partisan chiefs, however, the settlers held New York at bay. In 1774 Allen answered publications supporting New York claims with a tract defending the Vermonters. It was reprinted in 1779.

When the American Revolution broke out, a number of patriots saw the desirability of capturing the British forts at Ticonderoga and Crown Point. At Castleton, Vt., Allen and a body of Green Mountain Boys and some Connecticut militia encountered Benedict Arnold, who was commanding revolutionary troops from Massachusetts. Both men had the same mission, and contention and confusion ensued over which of them was to lead the assault on Ticonderoga. At last, Allen and Arnold were recognized as joint commanders. The unwilling partners seized Ticonderoga and its valuable artillery stores on May 10, 1775, without a struggle. The following day, Allen took Crown Point. These actions gave the insurgents control of Lake Champlain.

Congress was now moved to grant the Green Mountain Boys the same pay as Continental soldiers and to counsel the New York Assembly to employ them in the army under their own officers. Allen and Warner went to New York and asked admittance to the session. After some grumbling over receiving proclaimed felons, a heavy majority voted to admit Allen and later to raise a regiment of Green Mountain Boys. Allen wrote a letter of thanks and proposed an invasion of Canada, which was rejected. He then joined Gen. Philip Schuyler's army as a volunteer, was sent on secret missions to Canada, and undertook an invasion of Canada with Col. John Brown. Brown left Allen in the lurch in the attack on Montreal, and Allen was taken prisoner on Sept. 25, 1775, and sent to England. He was chained and treated with great severity, but was returned on May 6, 1778, in a prisoner exchange.

Allen received the brevet rank of colonel in the Continental Army, but he played no further role in the Revolution. On returning to Vermont, he was given command of the militia with the rank of major general. Although it was not recognized as independent by the Continental Congress, Vermont had so declared itself in 1777. The old land-grant feud still raged, and Allen and his brothers Ira and Levi conducted simultaneous negotiations with the Americans and the British, exploring possible terms for joining Canada if Vermont could not achieve statehood, while steering a largely independent course for Vermont.

Allen settled in Burlington, Vt., in 1787. He died there on Feb. 12, 1789, two years before Vermont entered the union as the 14th state.

Controversial in his religious and philosophical views as well as in a number of other areas, Allen wrote *A Narrative of Colonel Ethan Allen's Captivity* (1779); *A Vindication of the Opposition of the Inhabitants of Vermont to the Government of New York* (1779); and *Reason the Only Oracle of Man.*

Bibliography: Duffy, John J., et al., eds., *Ethan Allen and His Kin: Correspondence, 1772–1819,* 2 vols. (Univ. Press of New England 1998); Holbrook, Stewart H., *Ethan Allen* (1940; reprint, Binfords & Mort 1958); Jellison, Charles A., *Ethan Allen: Frontier Rebel* (1969; reprint, Syracuse Univ. Press 1983).

ALLEN, Florence Ellinwood, al'ən (1884–1966), American judge. She was born in Salt Lake City, Utah, on March 23, 1884. After graduating from Western Reserve University in Cleveland, Ohio, in 1904, she studied music in Berlin, Germany. Returning to Cleveland in 1906, Allen became interested in civic affairs and then in law. She studied law at Chicago and New York universities and began the practice of law in Cleveland in 1914.

In 1922 she was elected judge of the Supreme Court of Ohio, the first woman judge of last resort (member of the highest court of a state) in the world. In 1934 she became the first woman to be appointed to the U.S. Circuit Court of Appeals. Judge Allen retired from active service in 1959, assuming the title of senior judge of the Court of Appeals of the Sixth Circuit. She died in Cleveland on Sept. 12, 1966.

ALLEN, Fred (1894–1956), American comedian whose nasal voice and deadpan wit were popular features of 1930s and 1940s radio. He was born

John Florence Sullivan in Cambridge, Mass., on May 31, 1894, and started out as a juggler in vaudeville, peppering his act with comic patter. He appeared in Broadway revues, including *The Passing Show of 1922* and *Three's a Crowd* (1930). Portland Hoffa, whom he wed in 1928, became his partner on the radio shows *Town Hall Tonight* (1934–1940) and *Texaco Star Theatre* (1940–1949); for the latter he created Mrs. Nussbaum, Senator Claghorn, Ajax Cassidy, and other well-known denizens of "Allen's Alley." Allen, who wrote the autobiographical volumes *Treadmill to Oblivion* (1954) and *Much Ado about Me* (1956), died in New York City on March 17, 1956.

Bibliography: Havig, Alan, *Fred Allen's Radio Comedy* (1990; reprint, Temple Univ. Press 1992); Taylor, Robert, *Fred Allen: His Life and Wit* (Little, Brown 1989).

ALLEN, Gracie. See BURNS, GEORGE, AND ALLEN, GRACIE.

ALLEN, Hervey (1889–1949), American poet, critic, and novelist. William Hervey Allen was born in Pittsburgh, Pa., on Dec. 8, 1889. In 1910 he entered the U.S. Naval Academy; he was honorably discharged in 1911 because of athletics injuries. He served in the army during the Mexican border campaign of 1916 and later saw action in France, where he was wounded.

Allen's literary career began with a volume of poems, *Wampum and Old Gold* (1921). *Anthony Adverse* (1933), a novel of Napoleonic times, filled with romance and adventure, brought him wide popularity. This was followed by *Action at Aquila* (1937), a novel dealing with the American Civil War. Allen later began work on a five-volume novel, *The Disinherited*, about pre-Revolutionary western Pennsylvania. By the time of his death, in Miami, Fla., on Dec. 28, 1949, Allen had completed the first three volumes—*The Forest and the Fort* (1943), *Bedford Village* (1944), and *Toward the Morning* (1948)—and had begun the fourth, *The City in the Dawn.* Allen's best-known critical work is *Israfel* (1926), a biographical and psychological study of Edgar Allan Poe.

ALLEN, Ira (1751–1814), American political leader who was closely allied with his brother, Ethan Allen, in achieving independence and statehood for Vermont. He was born in Cornwall, Conn., on May 1, 1751. In 1772 he and four older brothers acquired title to New Hampshire land grants totaling 77,000 acres. To protect their investment from claims made by New York State, Ira and other landholders formed the convention that declared Vermont's independence in 1777. Thereafter he negotiated successfully for recognition of the republic. In 1796, while ostensibly buying French arms for the state militia, he was arrested at sea by British agents and charged with arming Irish rebels. Acquitted after a lengthy trial in London, he returned to Vermont to find himself an outcast as a result of a change in government. He retired to Philadelphia, where he died in poverty on Jan. 15, 1814.

ALLEN, Richard (1760–1831), American religious leader. He was born to slave parents in Philadelphia, Pa., on Feb. 14, 1760, embraced the Methodist religion in 1777, and in 1782 was permitted to preach. The intense racial discrimination Allen encountered led him to found the Free African Society in 1787. Francis Asbury, the first bishop of the Methodist Church in the United States, frequently gave Allen preaching assignments, and in 1799 he ordained Allen into the ministry of the Methodist Episcopal Church.

After several ugly incidents in which whites forced blacks to leave church services, 16 black Methodist congregations from throughout the United States met in 1816 to form the African Methodist Episcopal Church, with Allen as its first bishop. In 1830 Allen led a group of blacks interested in emigration to Canada, although he opposed the African colonization movement. Allen died in Philadelphia on March 26, 1831.

ALLEN, Steve (1921–2000), versatile American television personality, comedian, musician, and writer. Stephen Valentine Patrick William Allen was born in New York City on Dec. 26, 1921, to vaudevillian parents whose stage names were Billy Allen and Belle Montrose. He briefly attended Drake University in Des Moines and Arizona State Teachers College. He served briefly in the U.S. Army before beginning to work in radio.

By 1947 Allen was a popular Los Angeles disc jockey. From 1950 to 1952 he had his own television show on the Columbia Broadcasting System (CBS), subsequently moving to the National Broadcasting Company (NBC) to be the master of ceremonies, from 1953 to 1956, of the first incarnation of the *Tonight* show, which grew to be a television fixture. Many credited Allen with the virtual invention of the late-night talk show, for which he devised bits and a format that later practitioners built upon.

Besides hosting *The Steve Allen Show* (1956–1960s) and *I've Got a Secret* (1964–1967), Allen created the cerebral Public Broadcasting Service (PBS) series *Meeting of Minds* (1977–1981), with actors portraying historical figures. Allen was a prolific songwriter and pianist; he recorded some 40 albums and allegedly wrote some 5,000 songs. He starred in the film *The Benny Goodman Story* (1955); wrote fiction and nonfiction, including murder mysteries and *Hi-Ho, Steverino! My Adventures in the Wonderful Wacky World of TV* (1992); and was a spokesman against sex and violence on the airwaves. Allen died in Los Angeles on Oct. 31, 2000.

ALLEN, William (1532–1594), English cardinal who was noted for his efforts to preserve Roman Catholicism in England. Born in Rossal, Lancashire, he graduated from Oriel College, Oxford, and was principal of St. Mary's Hall, Oxford. Allen left England in 1561 during the persecutions of the Roman Catholics and spent a year in Belgium. Returning to England, he directed missionary work there until 1565, when he again was forced to leave.

Allen was ordained a priest at Mechelen, Belgium, and undertook the task of training priests, hoping someday to return to a Roman Catholic England. To this end, he established the English College at Douai (now in France) in 1568 and was instrumental in producing the Douai (Douay) Bible. He founded similar colleges at Rome (1578) and Valladolid, Spain (1589).

Allen was created a cardinal in 1587 but lost favor with English Catholics for supporting King Philip II of Spain in his plans to invade England. He spent his last years at the English College in Rome, where he died in Oct. 16, 1594.

ALLEN, Woody (1935–   ), American film director, writer, actor, and jazz clarinetist who, as an actor-director, was best known for the mordant comedies in which he played a bumbling, anxiety-ridden but generally cultured Everyman. He was born Allen Stewart Konigsberg in Brooklyn, N.Y., on Dec. 1, 1935. At 17 he became a radio staff writer and soon began contributing jokes to newspaper columnists and sketches to television shows.

Allen's performing career began with a nightclub act in which he was the butt of his own jokes. His first screenwriting and directing project was *What's New, Pussycat?* (1965), in which he acted, as he did in the comedies *Take the Money and Run* (1969), *Bananas* (1971), *Sleeper* (1973), and *Love and Death* (1975). In the late 1970s his films began to explore more serious themes. Most were bittersweet comedies, set in New York City and starring Allen opposite Diane Keaton or Mia Farrow. *Annie Hall* (1977) won the best picture Academy Award, and Allen best director and original screenplay. He won another Oscar for the screenplay of *Hannah and Her Sisters* (1986).

Other Allen films include *Manhattan* (1979); *Stardust Memories* (1980); *Zelig* (1983), a faux-documentary about a human cipher whose variable personality puts him into many of the 20th century's major events; *Broadway Danny Rose* (1984); *The Purple Rose of Cairo* (1985); *Radio Days* (1987); *Crimes and Misdemeanors* (1989); *Mighty Aphrodite* (1995); *Everyone Says I Love You* (1996); *Sweet and Lowdown* (1999), with Sean Penn playing a 1930s jazz guitarist; and *Small Time Crooks* (2000).

Allen's first play, *Don't Drink the Water,* opened on Broadway in 1966, and he made his stage acting debut in *Play It Again, Sam* (1969), which he wrote. His books include *Getting Even* (1971) and *Side Effects* (1980). For decades he played his clarinet weekly at Michael's Pub in New York City; in 1996 the European tour of Woody Allen and His New Orleans Jazz Band was filmed by Barbara Kopple as *Wild Man Blues* (1997).

Bibliography: Baxter, John, *Woody Allen: A Biography* (1998; reprint, Carroll & Graf 2000); Brode, Douglas, *The Films of Woody Allen*, rev. ed. (Carol Pub. Group 1997); Lax, Eric, *Woody Allen: A Biography* (1992; reprint, Da Capo 2000); Meade, Marion, *The Unruly Life of Woody Allen* (Scribner 2000).

ALLEN PARK, a city in southeastern Michigan, in Wayne county, about 10 miles (16 km) southwest of Detroit. It is a residential suburb. Interstate 75 freeway passes through the city, and the Detroit Metropolitan Airport is nearby.

Allen Park was settled in 1860. One of the earliest founders was Lewis Allen, for whom the site was named. It was incorporated as a village in 1927. In 1952 the village elected a commission that prepared a charter classifying Allen Park as a city. Population: 29,376.

ALLENBY, Edmund Henry Hynman, al'ən-bē (1861–1936), British general. Allenby was born near Southwell, Nottinghamshire, on April 23, 1861, and educated at Haileybury, a then recently founded public school, and at the Royal Military College, Sandhurst. During his boyhood he acquired a keen interest in birds and plants, which he retained throughout his life. Allenby was commissioned in the Inniskilling Dragoons in 1882 and saw active service in the Bechuanaland expedition of 1884–1885 and in Zululand in 1888. He returned with his regiment to England in 1888 and was married in 1896.

During the South African War of 1899–1902, Allenby was in command of cavalry operations. He emerged from the war with a sound reputation. In 1905 he became brigadier general and in 1909 major general. From 1910 until 1914 he held the post of inspector general of cavalry.

On the outbreak of World War I, Allenby went to France in command of the British cavalry, and in 1915 he was knighted and appointed to command of the 5th Corps. He led the Third Army at the Battle of Arras in the spring of 1917, and in June he was assigned to command the British Expeditionary Force in Egypt. In the campaign to expel the Turks from Palestine, he took Beersheba, entered Jerusalem on Dec. 9, 1917, and won a sweeping victory at Megiddo in September 1918. He was promoted to field marshal in 1919 and created a peer as 1st Viscount Allenby of Megiddo and Felixstowe. From 1919 until 1925 he served as British high commissioner in Egypt. He died in London on May 14, 1936.

Allenby was the last of the great British cavalry commanders. He had a violent temper but seldom acted on it. He had a high sense of duty, and his life was marked by simplicity and sincerity. General (later, Field Marshal) Archibald P. Wavell, who served under him, wrote *Allenby* (1940) and *Allenby in Egypt* (1943).

See also LAWRENCE, THOMAS EDWARD; WAVELL, 1ST EARL WAVELL; WORLD WAR I—*Turkish Campaigns.*

ALLENDE GOSSENS, Salvador, ä-yän'dä gôs'ens (1908–1973), president of Chile and first freely elected Marxist chief of state in Latin America.

Allende early became active in radical politics, and in 1933, a year after receiving a medical degree, he helped found the Chilean Socialist party. From 1943 he was its secretary-general. He served in the Chamber of Deputies from 1937 to 1945 and in the Senate from 1945 until his election as president in 1970.

With Communist support, Allende ran unsuccessfully for the presidency in 1952, 1958, and 1964. But in 1970, backed by the Popular Unity coalition of Socialists, Radicals, Communists, and dissident Christian Democrats, he won a narrow plurality of the popular vote. Because no candidate had a majority, it was left to Congress to choose the victor. By pledging to respect Chile's democratic system, Allende won with the support of the Christian Democrats.

As president, Allende nationalized Chile's natural resources, basic industries, and banks. He raised the wages of factory workers and accelerated the redistribution of land. However, food shortages, rampant inflation, and extremist elements provoked the hostility of the middle class. U.S. economic pressure and covert Central Intelligence operations helped to destabilize the Allende regime. Strikes and political violence moved the country toward civil war. The government was overthrown by the military on Sept. 11, 1973, and Allende either committed suicide or was murdered during the coup.

ALLENTOWN, a city in eastern Pennsylvania, on the Lehigh River, 60 miles (97 km) northwest of Philadelphia. It is the seat of Lehigh county.

Economy.   Allentown is the leading industrial and commercial center of the Lehigh Valley. Limestone deposits gave rise to its important cement industry. Other manufacturing industries produce a variety of goods. These include motor trucks, electrical appliances, electronic equipment, machinery and tools, textiles, clothing and shoes, processed foods, and cigars. Mineral resources in the vicinity, besides limestone, are iron ore, anthracite coal, slate, and zinc. The fertile farmlands surrounding Allentown, which lies within the area known as "Pennsylvania Dutch Country," produce potatoes, orchard fruits, corn, wheat, and livestock. One of the state's well-known retail stores, Hess's Department Store, is situated in Allentown.

Educational Institutions. Muhlenberg College, a coeducational college in Allentown, controlled by the Lutheran Church, traces its origin to Allentown Seminary, founded in 1848. The present name, adopted in 1867, honors Heinrich Melchior Mühlenberg, who organized the first Lutheran synod in America. Cedar Crest College for women, controlled by the United Church of Christ, was chartered as Allentown College for Women in 1868. Other colleges are Eastern Pilgrim College, Allentown College of St. Francis de Sales, and a junior college campus affiliated with the Pennsylvania State University.

Points of Interest. Allentown has a large public library, a museum of fine arts, a symphony orchestra, and a civic little theater. The Lehigh County Historical Society maintains a museum of local and state history in Trout Hall, a historic house erected in 1770 by James Allen, son of the founder of Allentown.

Another point of interest is the Liberty Bell Shrine in Zion Reformed Church. This church stands on the site of a former church in which the Liberty Bell was hidden during the Revolutionary War. Trexler Memorial Park on the edge of Allentown includes a wildfowl refuge. Buffalo, elk, and deer can be seen in the Trexler-Lehigh County Game Preserve, about 10 miles (16 km) northwest of the city. Allentown Fair is held annually in August.

History. Allentown stands on a tract of land bought in 1735 by William Allen, a Philadelphia merchant and jurist. The former owner of this property, according to records of the time, had obtained it from Thomas Penn, son of the founder of Pennsylvania. Allen, who served as chief justice of Pennsylvania from 1750 to 1774, built a fishing and hunting lodge on the site in the 1750s, but a town was not laid out until the 1760s. Northampton county had been formed in this section of Pennsylvania in 1752, and the new town was given the name of Northampton. In 1811 the community was incorporated as a borough. In 1812, when Lehigh county was formed, it became the seat of that county. In 1838 the name was changed to *Allentown* in honor of the founder. Allentown was incorporated as a city in 1867. Government is by mayor and council. Population: 106,632.

ALLEPPEY, ə-lep′ē, also called Alappuzha, a seaport city in southern India, in Kerala state. It is situated on the Malabar Coast between the Arabian Sea and the Vembanad backwater.

A roadstead port protected by a mudbank, Alleppey services considerable backwater barge traffic. Its main industries are based on processing and exporting coconut products, chiefly coconut oil, coir ropes and mats, and copra. The surrounding area also produces spices and rice. Two colleges of Kerala University are within the area. Population: 177,079 (2001 census).

ALLERGY, al′ər-jē, a hypersensitive response of the body to foreign substances. Such foreign substances, known as *antigens,* stimulate the body to produce *antibodies*—molecules whose normal function is to combat antigens by destroying them or otherwise making them harmless. In allergic individuals, for poorly understood reasons, the body's antibody defense mechanism goes awry and injures the body instead of protecting it.

Antigens may include almost all substances that are foreign to the body. These substances are not necessarily toxic or irritative in the absence of an allergy. They may be inhaled (bacteria, molds, pollens), ingested (foods, drugs), injected (biologicals such as serums, vaccines, or drugs), or in some cases introduced through contact with the skin (poison oak, chemicals in cosmetics and dyes). Some chemically simple antigens have the capacity to combine spontaneously with the proteins of the subject's own tissues. The body treats the resulting combination, or complex, as foreign.

IMMUNE MECHANISMS

Allergic states are of two major categories, immediate and delayed. In immediate allergy, the subject, as a result of an initial exposure to an antigen, has developed antibodies—proteins that are highly specific in combining with the antigen that induced their synthesis. Once antibody molecules are present, reexposure to the appropriate antigen is followed by rapid combination of antibody and antigen, with consequences described below.

Delayed allergy depends on a similarly specific reactive state that is a property of certain cells of the body (lymphoid cells) rather than of molecules in solution. Upon reexposure to the antigen, the sensitized subject shows a response only after some hours, because the appropriately sensitive cells must migrate via the blood and lymph to accumulate in the organ or tissue where the antigen is present. There they produce toxic chemical mediators that cause the symptoms of the allergy.

Immediate Allergy. The categories of immediate allergic responses are referred to as atopy, anaphylaxis, and Arthus reactions. They are antibody-mediated allergies, and their immunologic mechanisms are basically the same.

Atopy. This type of reaction occurs in humans who have been sensitized spontaneously to inhaled or ingested antigens, particularly pollens and mixed dusts in the air, or milk, fish, nuts, and eggs among foods. If the reaction to inhaled substances causes inflammation of nasal passages, it is called hay fever. The symptoms of hay fever result from dilation of the capillaries in the mucous membranes of the nose, with consequent leakage of fluid into adjoining tissues. Sometimes the eyes become inflamed because of dilation of the capillaries in their mucous membranes. An attack of asthma may result, mainly from contraction of smooth (involuntary) muscle around the small bronchioles (branching tubes in the lungs). Hives, gastrointestinal distress, or infantile eczema also may develop. A single individual may show a combination of these signs and symptoms.

The class of antibody globulin concerned in atopic reaction has a marked tendency to become bound to tissues (basophilic cells) and to cause the release of pharmacologically active mediators once combination with antigen has taken place. These mediators include histamine, SRS-A (slow reactive substance-A), serotonin, bradykinin, and other substances that affect the capillaries and smooth muscles.

Atopic allergies run in family lines. Both the general capacity to become sensitized and specific reactivities to particular substances are genetically determined.

The common procedure for detecting the antigenic cause in atopic allergy involves skin tests using a variety of possible antigens. The antigens are rubbed into scratches or injected. Those to which the subject is sensitive cause a local swelling or hives within a few minutes of exposure. The tests are most successful, however, in those subjects whose seasonal difficulties are caused by pollens. Antibodies associated with atopic allergies can also be detected in the test tube.

Anaphylaxis. The term anaphylaxis is applied to allergic reactions that result in a systemic reaction affecting the whole body, especially when the reaction results from injections of antigen. Anaphylaxis may be induced in virtually anyone, provided the person has responded to a first exposure to an antigen by producing antibodies that become bound to body tissues. Following a second exposure to the same antigen, the bloodstream carries the antigen to the previously sensitized tissues. There the antigen combines with the antibodies and causes the release of histamine and other pharmacologically active substances mentioned in the preceding section. A systemic reaction, which affects the entire body, can occur within minutes, or even seconds, after injection of the antigen. Such a reaction is marked mainly by difficulty in breathing, although contractions of smooth muscle in parts of the body less vital than the lungs may also occur.

Anaphylactic reactions typically are caused by injections of drugs or by stings of bees and other insects. Physicians are particularly concerned about the severity of anaphylactic reactions to the injection of large-molecule proteins, such an antitoxins, because these substances are highly antigenic.

Local anaphylactic reactions also may occur when an antigen is injected into a tissue, such as the skin, from which diffusion does not occur readily. This may show itself as a local hive. But in a highly sensitive subject, even this route of exposure may elicit a systemic reaction. See also ANAPHYLAXIS.

Arthus Reaction. This type of reaction appears in the sensitive subject several hours after exposure to an antigen. It is manifested by local swelling and redness, which may disappear in 24 hours or progress to the local death of tissue. It differs from the more fleeting anaphylactic reaction in two main ways: the class antibody concerned in the Arthus reaction is not of the tissue-fixed kind, and a high concentration of the antibody must be present in the blood. The amount of antigen required to elicit the reaction also must be relatively large. The interaction of antibody with antigen occurs in the walls of the blood vessels as the antigen diffuses and meets the antibody from the circulation, or small complexes of antigen and antibody may invade the vessel walls.

Serum Sickness. The various categories of immediate allergic reaction are not mutually exclusive, and there may be a combination of them. Such a combination occurs in serum sickness. The term derives from the time in which serum therapy was common. Many individuals who received horse or other foreign serum developed late signs of an immediate type of allergic reaction (usually in the form of hives, pain in the joints, rash, and fever). Their appearance was delayed because the subject had not previously experienced the serum antigens and thus had to produce antibodies before a reaction could occur.

The term "serum sickness" still is applied to this syndrome even though it now appears mainly following the administration of drugs such as penicillin, streptomycin, and the sulfonamides. Although the symptoms of serum sickness usually disappear after a few days or weeks, complications in the kidneys, heart, or joints may occur following a persistent injury, especially to blood vessels, by antigen-antibody complexes.

Delayed Allergy. This is a hypersensitive state in which lymphoid cells participate as the specific reactive agents, perhaps as carriers of partial antibodies on their surfaces. Characteristically, it results from infections, especially from those in which the infecting microbe tends to reside in cells. The classical example among bacterial diseases is tuberculosis.

The same kind of allergic state results from contact of the skin with some simple chemicals, including the one responsible for poison-ivy rash. The reasons for the development of this kind of reactivity during infection or after exposure of the skin to certain antigens are not known.

A similar delayed allergy is involved in the body's rejection of tissues grafted from one to another individual and in its rejection of tumors. Donor tissues or organs are acted upon mainly by cells that have become specifically reactive against antigens contained in them. Conventional antibodies also may be produced against such tissue antigens, but these are not involved ordinarily in the rejection process, perhaps because they cannot effectively damage the cells composing a compact tissue, as infiltrating reactive cells can.

Delayed allergic reactivity also is implicated in some of the so-called "immunologic diseases," in which a subject spontaneously becomes reactive against constituents of his own tissues. This immunologic paradox is also called autoimmunization.

Hereditary Aspects. Genetic constitution influences the allergic state in two ways. In a singular sense, individuals may be unable to respond to a particular antigen because they lack the genes that direct the production of the reactive substance specific for the antigen. Heredity also influences the development of allergy in a more general sense, as exemplified by people who show an unusual capacity to respond not to particular antigens but in general to environmental antigenic agents that induce atopic hypersensitivity. Such responses may be related to genetically determined absorptions or processing of antigens by the body.

ALLERGIC DISORDERS

Allergic disorders may result from any of the immune mechanisms discussed in the preceding section. The immediate types are mediated by antibodies, and the delayed types are mediated by sensitized lymphocytes. The immediate types are more numerous and potentially more life-threatening. In severe cases they may result in a general systemic shock of the anaphylactic type. But more usually the immediate allergies manifest themselves by hives or angioedema (leakage of fluid through blood-vessel walls). The delayed reactions include contact dermatitis with localized eczema, as in reactions to poison ivy or poison oak, or a generalized rash, as in reactions following the swallowing of a drug.

Immediate. Disorders resulting from immediate hypersensitive reactivity include rhinitis, hives, asthma, serum sickness, and anaphylactic shock. All may be induced by antigens that act through respiratory and gastrointestinal membranes or by substances that are injected. These antigens may include a wide variety of pollens, dusts, foods, and drugs, including biologic products such as hormones and vaccines.

The treatment of these disorders varies with circumstances. Antihistaminic drugs may be useful for the control of hay fever but less useful for asthma. For asthma, cromolyn sodium, which hinders release of mediators by basophilic cells, may be helpful. Adrenaline or ephedrine and xanthine derivatives, such as aminophyilin, are sometimes useful. Adrenal cortical hormones (cortisone and its various analogs) may alleviate certain hypersensitive reactions by decreasing the inflammatory responses that are the hallmark of many of them or, if used in large enough quantities, by inhibiting antibody responses to some extent. Finally, in some reactive states, notably the atopic ones such as hay fever, efforts are made to desensitize the subject by means of graded injections of the antigens to which hypersensitivity has developed spontaneously.

Allergists believe that such injections, by introducing antigen through an "unnatural" route, may stimulate the formation of antibodies of a different molecular class from those induced via the natural route of sensitization through the mucous membranes. Such antibodies, which are less likely to provoke reactions when they combine with antigen, and which divert antigen from union with the spontaneously acquired kind of antibodies, are referred to as "blocking" antibodies.

Antibodies also appear to be implicated in autoimmune diseases, in which antibodies are directed against components of the subject's own tissues or against antigens attached to cells. These include hemolytic anemia (antibodies active against red cells), myasthentia gravis (antibodies against acetylcholine receptors), rheumatoid arthritis (antibodies against a blood protein), and rheumatic fever (antibodies against heart and other muscle). Treatment of these diseases varies. Corticosteroids have been used in acquired hemolytic anemia (sometimes with removal of the spleen) and rheumatoid arthritis. In rheumatic fever, penicillin is useful in preventing recurrences of streptococcal infections that make the disease process more severe.

Delayed. Diseases that may result from delayed allergic reactivity include lesions caused by allergic destruction of tissue in infections such as tuberculosis. Noninfectious afflictions may result from delayed autoimmune reactions to constituents of the body tissues.

Another category of disease of this class is dermatitis caused by contact antigens such as certain plant substances and other simple chemicals. Plant substances responsible for contact dermatitis include catechols secreted by poison oak, poison ivy, and primula. Among the offending chemicals are some antibiotics and local anesthetics.

In all these cases, the antihistaminic agents that may be of use in certain of the immediate hypersensitivities are without value. The adrenocortical steroid hormones may alleviate these conditions by decreasing inflammatory reactions. Desensitization has been disappointing in the treatment of human disease.

Common Allergies. The most familiar allergies are hay fever and asthma, which are caused by a wide variety of inhaled pollens, dusts, and other agents. Because of their importance these disorders are discussed in separate articles. See ASTHMA; HAY FEVER.

Drug Allergies. These allergies may become manifest after ingestion, injection, or contact with the skin. As in the case of foods, most allergic reactions to drugs are immediate.

Penicillin is the greatest single cause of drug hypersensitivity. The most common symptom is a diffuse rash, although anaphylactic reactions occur in about one in 10,000 persons. Serum sickness occurs occasionally, and contact dermatitis is fairly common after handling the drug or following topical applications. Many other drugs have been implicated in such allergies—including analgesics, sulfonamides, barbiturates, and even some antihistamines—but allergic reactions to drugs other than penicillin probably are rare.

Food Allergies. Food does not often cause allergic reactions. Food allergies are more common in infants than in older children and adults, probably because the infant's immature digestive tract permits more ready absorption of offending food molecules.

Manifestations of food allergies in adults are usually of the immediate kind, including hives, angioedema, eczema, gastrointestinal disorders, and general systemic reactions of the anaphylactic type. Systemic reactions occur quickly after eating. They are most frequently caused by legumes, nuts, seafoods (especially shellfish), and berries, but carbohydrates, fats, food additives, and contamination by drugs may be implicated. In infants and children, eczema is the prominent manifestation, and the most frequent causative agents include milk, wheat, eggs, fish, and soybean products.

Food allergies are diagnosed on the basis of the patient's allergic history together with trial eliminations of suspected foods from the patient's diet. Skin tests and tests for antibodies in serum are less significant, because the hypersensitive reaction may be provoked by breakdown products of the food resulting from digestion, and not by the food itself.

The management of food allergies is based mainly on avoidance of the offending foods. An antihistamine taken before a meal may be helpful if a food to which one is allergic is to be eaten. Food allergies in children tend to lessen or disappear with age, but the anaphylactic types manifested in adults do not usually improve over time.

See also IMMUNITY.

SIDNEY RAFFEL, *Stanford University*

Further Reading: Bierman, C. Warren, and Pearlman, David S., *Allergic Diseases from Infancy to Adulthood*, 2d ed. (Saunders 1987).

ALLERTON, al'ər-tən, **Isaac** (1586?–1659), *Mayflower* Pilgrim whose skill as the Plymouth Colony's negotiator in England greatly strengthened the colony. He was born in England about 1586 and worked as a tailor in London before emigrating to Leiden, Holland, in 1608. He joined the English Pilgrims, who began arriving in Holland in 1609, and helped arrange their voyage to the Americas in 1620. At Plymouth he was elected assistant governor under William Bradford and served in that office from 1621 to 1625.

For the next six years Allerton was the colonists' negotiator in England. Making frequent journeys, he settled the colony's initial debts, borrowed money, purchased supplies, stimulated emigration, and secured the patents that ensured the colonists' title to their land. In 1631 he overreached his instructions in contracting debts for trading investment; the colonists repudiated his transactions and relieved him of his responsibilities. He moved that year to Marblehead and, in 1644, to New Haven, where he died in February 1659.

ALLEYN, al'ən, **Edward** (1566–1626), renowned English actor of the late Elizabethan period. Alleyn originated the roles of the Revenger (in Thomas Kyd's *The Spanish Tragedy,* 1592) and Marlowe's formidable heroes Tamburlaine, Faustus, and Barabbas. He is not known to have acted in any of Shakespeare's plays. Alleyn earned generous praise from his contemporaries, including Thomas Nash, Thomas Heywood, and Ben Jonson.

Alleyn was born in London on Sept. 1, 1566. By 1586 he was a well-established actor with the Worcester's Men company and by 1590 was with the Lord Admiral's Men. During the plague years of 1592–1594 he acted with Lord Strange's traveling company. He married Joan Woodward, the stepdaughter of the theater manager Philip Henslowe, in 1592 and thereafter engaged in various business dealings with his father-in-law. Alleyn's profit from the bear-baiting in the Paris Garden in Southwark, rather than from his acting, established his fortunes. Astute in business, he had an interest in several London theaters and was also involved in real estate ventures.

Alleyn apparently left the stage temporarily in 1597 and permanently by about 1604. In 1599 he had begun construction of the Fortune theater, which he and Henslowe opened in 1600. (The theater burned in 1622 but was rebuilt the following year.) In 1613 Alleyn founded the College of God's Gift in Dulwich, the royal patent for which was granted in 1619. His first wife died in 1623, and within a few months he had married John Donne's eldest daughter, Constance. Alleyn died in Dulwich on Nov. 25, 1626.

ALLIANCE, ə-lī'əns, a city located in northwestern Nebraska and the seat of Box Butte county. It lies 180 miles (290 km) northeast of Cheyenne, Wyo., on a high treeless plain, making the city a center of agricultural production. It is a shipping center for grain, cattle, and seed potatoes, which are produced in large quantities. The Chicago, Burlington & Quincy Railroad developed the city as its western terminus in 1888. Alliance is a junction and repair center on this rail system. Population: 8,959.

ALLIANCE, ə-lī'əns, in international relations, any formal political commitment by two or more states to coordinate their relations in solving problems arising out of the international distribution of power. Nominally, every alliance is defensive, insofar as the participants will justify it in terms of actual or potential threats from others, but the actual purpose of alliances has often been offensive. In a narrower sense, alliances, whether defensive or offensive, may be distinguished from other political commitments—such as guarantees, confederations, nonaggression and mutual security pacts, and regional and collective security arrangements—in that they are usually concluded between a small number of states for a limited period of time and are directed, explicitly or implicitly, against a particular rival state or alliance.

Given the unpredictability of international relations and the divergent interests of nations, alliance members will tend to embody their objectives in a treaty. They intend thereby to render their collaboration legal, even if, as was the case in the alliance between Germany and the Soviet Union in 1939, it contains secret provisions.

While alliances are usually embodied in treaties, not all treaties involve true alliances. The purposes of treaties may include international cooperation, but if they are not political—that is, if they are not intended to address the acquisition, distribution, and usage of power—and have instead administrative, economic, cultural, humanitarian, or other nonpolitical purposes, such treaties do not constitute alliances. The fact that they may have political consequences is not at issue. Thus despite its name, the Alliance for Progress (1961), a program of mutual economic and social assistance concluded by the United States and all Latin American countries except Cuba, was nonpolitical and therefore not really an alliance.

Defensive and Offensive Alliances. Defensive alliances are concluded between states that are generally satisfied with existing conditions, in order to maintain the balance of power and the stability of the state system. Offensive alliances are made, usually secretly, among states that are dissatisfied with the existing situation, with the objective of upsetting the equilibrium and changing the status quo.

An offensive alliance, contemplating aggression against or partition of another state, is in principle void because international law does not recognize the validity of obligations that violate fundamental principles such as respect for the territorial integrity, sovereignty, and political independence of states. Even if an alliance is defensively intended, the targeted state will usually regard it as offensive. Thus during the Cold War, the Soviet Union regarded the North Atlantic Treaty Organization (NATO) as offensive, while the Western powers regarded the Warsaw Treaty Organization (WTO), a series of alliances between and among the Soviet Union and the surrounding member states, as offensive, although both alliances were officially arrangements for defense against attack from any quarter.

Although there is no general agreement on terminology, alliances are also classified according to whether they intend collective or mutual security. Collective alliances include all potential aggressors. Hence the United Nations, which is a collective security alliance, potentially includes all nations. NATO, on the other hand, is a mutual security alliance that excludes and is directed against immediate or potential aggressors.

Interpreting and Enforcing Alliances. Alliances usually lack precise legal definition of the *casus foe-*

deris (literally, "case of the treaty"; that is, the specific situation covered by provisions of the alliance that will activate members' obligations). They also tend to lack provision for impartial procedures of interpretation and application. Consequently, alliances have been reliable only so long as they have conformed to the interests of the parties. Members may withdraw from an alliance if they believe that their national interests are better served otherwise. Some may simply adopt a neutral position, while others may defect to a counteralliance. Allegation of failure to observe alliances, after they have been in effect for some time and the situation has changed, is common. The United States abrogated its alliance of 1778 with France when the latter was at war with most of Europe in 1793, instead declaring neutrality, alleging that the alliance was defensive and that France had engaged in aggression. Since there was no procedure for deciding whether the *casus foederis* had arisen, each ally interpreted the situation according to its interests of the moment.

While most alliances do not include means of determining the *casus foederis*, some guarantees and mutual security and collective alliances have established impartial procedures for doing so. Guarantees such as that of Belgian neutrality (1839) were to be applied by conference of the guarantors. When Germany, a guarantor, alleging military necessity, violated that neutrality in 1914 by invading Belgium, the guarantors found themselves on opposing sides, with Austria siding with Germany, and Britain, France, and Russia lining up with Belgium.

The lack of a clear definition of the term *aggression* has also posed problems for alliances. In 1974 the United Nations finally defined aggression as the first use of belligerent means to achieve political ends despite a solemn assurance not to do so. In the abstract most states agree with this definition, but they have continued to give primary consideration to their immediate interests in deciding whether aggression has occurred and whether to act accordingly. States are, however, often reluctant to stigmatize other states as aggressors precisely because such a designation may be deemed unfriendly and lead to further aggression. Thus during the Manchurian episode of 1931, none of the League of Nations' members was prepared to act on the league's decision that Japan was the aggressor. This placed the league in the worst possible position: it further alienated Japan by branding it as the aggressor and proved its own collective impotence by failing to act. These factors emboldened other revisionist powers who regarded the league as a feckless protector of the status quo. As a result, during the Ethiopian hostilities of 1935, Italy's aggression went largely unpunished because few nations were prepared to apply the league's sanctions.

Despite the existence of collective alliances intended to inhibit aggression, Hitler invaded the Rhineland in 1936 contrary to the Pact of Locarno, Mussolini intervened in Spain in the same year, Japan renewed hostilities against China in 1937, and Hitler invaded Czechoslovakia in 1939 contrary to the Munich Pact. There were discussions in the league, but no action was taken against the aggressors even though the covenant seemed to require action. The league soon ceased to exist, but the Declaration of United Nations of Jan. 1, 1942, implied that the United Nations (the Allies) would rectify Axis violations of international law

and alliances, including the Kellogg-Briand Pact (1928), a renunciation of war.

After World War II it became increasingly apparent that the destructiveness of modern war necessitated a transition from a system of power politics sustained by temporary alliances and war to a system of international law sustained by collective security and international organization. The transition has been slow and halting. From the Korean War of 1950–1953, when the United Nations faced the first test of its mandate to keep the peace and relied on voluntary member contributions to maintain a policing operation in Korea, to the Persian Gulf War of 1990–1991, when the United Nations, under U.S. leadership, pieced together an alliance that came to be known as a "coalition to address aggression," the tenuousness of alliances in response to aggression has remained a fact of international relations.

Historic European Alliances. The attitude of Europe and America toward alliances has been characteristically different. Among European governments, alliances have been major elements of policy since the secular system of sovereign states superseded the solidarity of Christendom during the Middle Ages. This change began in Italy in the 14th century and extended to all Europe at the time of the Renaissance and Reformation. Striking evidence of the change is presented by the alliance of the Christian king Francis I of France with the Muslim sultan Suleiman I (ruler of the Ottoman empire), against the Christian emperor Charles V in 1536.

The Peace of Westphalia (1648), ending the Thirty Years' War, firmly established the secular state system in Europe and laid out the principles of international law, including the sovereign equality of all states and the balance of power. After this time, most important European alliances were directed against a state that was considered so powerful as to threaten domination of the whole of Europe. Thus between 1668 and 1718 several alliances involving the major states of Europe were directed against the rising power and aggressions of Louis XIV of France.

A series of alliances checked France's power under Napoleon, culminating in the Quadruple Alliance of 1814 among Britain, Austria, Russia, and Prussia. The last three of these powers joined in the Holy Alliance of 1815 to maintain peace and Christian principles both internationally and in their domestic affairs. But this alliance, along with the conference system that arose out of the Quadruple Alliance, came to be directed against democratic and nationalistic movements to maintain the authority of legitimate monarchs.

The system of alliances that led to World War I began with the Dual Alliance made by Chancellor Otto von Bismarck with Austria in 1879. Italy became a secret party in 1882. The resulting Triple Alliance was aimed against the resurgence of France following its defeat by Prussia in 1871 and was buttressed by the League of the Three Emperors concluded by Bismarck with Austria and Russia in 1881. After Bismarck's resignation ten years later, France approached Russia, resulting in the alliance of 1894. The German emperor's intervention in the South African conflict with the Boers and his development of German naval power alarmed Britain and induced it to settle its differences with France, resulting in the Entente Cordiale of 1904. Meanwhile, Britain had made an alliance with Japan in 1902, encouraging the latter to attack Russia in Manchuria in 1904. Following this, Japan reached agreement with Russia dividing Manchuria into spheres of interest, and Britain adjusted relations with Russia, establishing the Triple Entente among Britain, France, and Russia. The bipolarization of the European world effected by the rival alliance systems soon resulted in general war.

After World War I the League of Nations became the major alliance among states. In addition, France concluded mutual assistance agreements with Belgium, Poland, Czechoslovakia, Yugoslavia, and Romania to prevent the resurgence of Germany, and encouraged the last three to form the Little Entente to prevent German-Austrian union and the resurgence of Hungary. This system, which sought to make the status quo permanent, broke down after its key mechanism, the League of Nations, was weakened by its failure to stop Japanese and Italian aggression. France made a mutual assistance pact with the Soviet Union in 1935, and both partners undertook mutual assistance obligations to Czechoslovakia. These arrangements, however, did not prevent the partition of Czechoslovakia under the Munich Pact, which was signed by Germany, Italy, Britain, and France in 1938.

Alleging French violation of the agreement of 1935, fearing that the West sought to turn Hitler against Stalin in an ideological war, and following the collapse of Anglo-Soviet negotiations, the Soviet Union made a nonaggression pact with Hitler in August 1939. In the meantime Germany and Italy had completed the Rome-Berlin Axis, and Germany and Japan had made the Anti-Comintern Pact in 1936. Alarmed by Hitler's occupation of Czechoslovakia in March 1939, Britain made alliances with Poland and Romania. Hitler and Mussolini converted the Axis into an alliance in May 1939, joined by Japan in 1940. Confident of the Soviet Union's temporary neutrality after the pact of August 1939, Hitler attacked Poland and World War II began.

U.S. Alliances. Although the United States' independent history began with an alliance with France in 1778, Pres. George Washington saw wisdom in neutrality for the United States. In his Farewell Address in 1796, Washington cautioned against permanent alliances, a theme Pres. Thomas Jefferson reiterated in his first inaugural (1801) when he warned against entangling alliances. This admonishment and a policy of political isolation remained a prevailing philosophy that guided U.S. foreign policy for over a century.

The United States entered World War I not as an ally, because it did not adhere to the September 1914 alliance treaty among Britain, France, Russia, and Japan, but as an associated power. After the war, the Senate rejected U.S. membership in the League of Nations and the United States reverted to an isolationist policy, although it initiated and, with most other nations, ratified the Kellogg-Briand Pact.

Fearing that entry into foreign disputes would both threaten its democracy and slow down its economic improvement, the United States passed neutrality legislation in 1935 and 1937 but repealed most of its provisions after the onset of the war in September 1939. Following the Japanese attack at Pearl Harbor and Germany's declaration of war against the United States, the United States took the initiative in obtaining general approval of the Declaration of United Nations

of Jan. 1, 1942, in effect a military alliance against Germany. This marked the beginning of America's recognition of the utility of alliances, a process that would continue through much of the Cold War. The United States also took the initiative of converting this wartime alliance into a permanent UN organization at San Francisco in 1945. The UN Charter combined a general system of collective security with regional and collective self-defense arrangements (Articles 51–54). The United States favored these special arrangements to prevent another great power from vetoing action within the Western Hemisphere. Thus even at this stage the fear that alliances might ensnare the United States in actions beyond its control dominated U.S. political thinking to such an extent that it compromised on a priori commitment to collective secuirty measures.

American opinion always regarded a universal system of collective security as different from a system of special alliances. Washington's farewell address had opposed only the latter. The Articles of Confederation had the character of a collective security arrangement among the states, but it forbade the states without consent of Congress from entering into any "conference, agreement, alliance or treaty" with any foreign state or into any "treaty, confederation or alliance" with another state of the Union.

Such realistic features of international relations as spheres of influence (already recognized in the Monroe Doctrine), balance of power, alliances created in advance of threats, and collaboration became part of U.S. foreign policy after World War II. This recognition was embodied in the UN Charter and in many postwar alliances.

Post–World War II Alliances. After World War II American and European attitudes toward alliances converged. Alliances became means of distributing obligations, resources, and rewards among states with shared political objectives.

Four factors distinguish traditional from postwar attitudes toward alliances. First, the alliance that defeated Germany, Italy, and Japan became responsible for the peace that followed. Therefore, it was believed that the peace could be managed as effectively as the war had been. Second, the very success of that effort generated a confidence in alliances unlike any seen since before World War I. Third, allied exertions in World War II had been unequal; some had expended lives while others, whose home territories were beyond the range of enemy weapons, had mainly contributed industrial products. Finally, technology, including nuclear weapons, which had traditionally been called on to serve political ends, now helped to shape them.

Combining these perceptions, unique to the post–World War II international system, leads to the recognition that carefully planned, preventive alliances are better instruments of foreign policy than are those that are hurriedly assembled. But this overlooks the fact that alliances may generate counteralliances. In the end the postwar superpowers collaborated, avoiding a nuclear war and maintaining their exclusive status as superpowers.

Periods of international relations are often demarcated by postwar systems generated by victors. Recently, two such alliance systems, Versailles after World War I and Yalta after World War II, reflected political realities of the moment as well as the major powers' aspirations and skills. The

Yalta alliance system legitimated Soviet and American spheres of influence. An effort to render permanent alliances created for specific wartime purposes may mean that suspicions stilled during war reemerge to become irritants in the effort to establish peace. Also inherent in this approach is the certainty that lesser states will have to sacrifice their interests to those of the larger states, which in turn creates a basis for alliance among those nations whose interests are denied. The post—World War II world became bipolar. Power revolved around the United States, which forged chains of nominally capitalistic and democratic alliances, and the Soviet Union, which established obedient regimes espousing Marxist-Leninist authoritarianism. But bipolarity ultimately surrendered to more numerous, complicated, and convoluted configurations as Soviet-American rivalries froze into well-armed, sterile blocs. Other centers of power created their own alliances. Nonaligned states, claiming independence in the Cold War and rejecting alliances with the superpowers, often created their own alliances as well.

NATO (1949) and the WTO (1955) were the primary post—World War II alliances. Responding to the image of a communist monolith, the United States embarked on containment with a continuum of alliances designed to confront the Soviet Union and its allies. The Western alliance system began in northern Europe, flanked North Africa via NATO, and extended through the northern tier of the Middle East with the Baghdad Pact (1955), which with Iraq's withdrawal in 1959 became the Central Treaty Organization. The South East Asia Treaty Organization (1955) followed France's loss in Indochina. The Japanese-American Security Treaty (1954, 1960) completed the geographical encirclement of the Soviet Union and China, in effect ignoring intracommunist realities after 1955. The Soviet Union responded to NATO by organizing the WTO. Several times between 1955 and 1989 the superpowers confronted one another, as in the Berlin Crisis (1961) and the Warsaw Pact's invasion of Czechoslovakia (1968).

The Arab League (1945) brought together 13 Islamic states for purposes of security and social, economic, cultural, and political cohesion against external threats. The Organization of African Unity (1961) included independent states organized on the basis of Pan-African interests. These regional alliances developed out of distrust of Cold War and neoimperialist intrusions but were weakened by domestic, ideological, and objective factors and by the absence of a direct and durable adversary.

The creation of alliances and counteralliances reflected and helped to produce four types of states. The superpowers possessed global reach. The major powers had receded in their ability to reach several distant areas simultaneously but remained regionally significant. A third category were the losers in World War II, who would quickly emerge from defeat to compete with the major powers. Finally, so-called take-off states were those that had not yet achieved major international status but whose assets lay in their importance to one of the superpowers.

After 1945 the superpowers wove alliances to procure human resources, to obtain essential natural resources, and to deny both of these resources to one another. These alliances often exaggerated the importance of the take-off states and encouraged them to extort their superpower mentor for continued fidelity. Such alliances also enabled some states to modernize, frequently resulting in local and regional instability followed by further superpower tensions.

Postwar alliances repeated traditional political patterns. Among other things, they limited nations' maneuverability and adaptability, suggested undue clarity and precision in the motive forces that would activate an alliance, became yardsticks for measuring nations' loyalty and morality, and encouraged outsiders to organize additional alliances.

In 1975 NATO and the WTO were augmented by the creation of the Conference on Security and Cooperation in Europe (CSCE), which legalized postwar European geographic changes and extended a European collective security arrangement across the Atlantic to include the United States and Canada. It was originally meant to overcome rigidities and uncertainties of the counterbalancing NATO alliance and Warsaw Pact by offering a forum that included nations other than alliance members.

Post—World War II alliances involved changes in states' rankings, arranged power according to the shared interests of states, and encouraged intersecting interests across and among classes of states. An apparently fixed international order resulted that rested on subtle shifts within the equilibrium and on the superpowers' muting their opposition to one another. This heterogeneous equilibrium ended with the Soviet Union's disintegration, thus illustrating the fragility of the postwar alliance system.

After the Soviet fragmentation, the CSCE's membership increased to 52, roughly the number of original UN members. After the United Nations this is the largest, most disparate and fragile alliance. Its tasks, unforeseen in 1975, include presiding over once-divided Europe's post—Cold War transition in the face of a multiplicity of long pent-up rivalries. Thus CSCE marks the maturation of alliance building. Its task is not simplified by the fact that, although NATO's *casus foederis* has been rendered unnecessary, the Western alliance remains.

See also INTERNATIONAL RELATIONS; TREATY.

QUINCY WRIGHT*, *University of Virginia*
PETER K. BREIT, *University of Hartford*

Bibliography: Degenhardt, H. W., *Treaties and Alliances of the World*, 4th ed. (Gale Res. 1987); Sabrosky, A. M., *Alliances in U.S. Foreign Policy* (Westview Press 1986); Walt, Stephen M., *The Origins of Alliances* (Cornell Univ. Press 1988).

ALLIANCE FOR PROGRESS, an economic development program established in 1961 by the United States and all Latin American nations except Cuba aimed at improving economic and social conditions in the Western Hemisphere. The Charter of Punta del Este (Uruguay) outlined the goals and dimensions of the program, calling for a massive effort in cooperative economic and social development to combat Latin America's basic problems.

The original ten-year life span of the Alliance was extended indefinitely in 1965, but operations were halted in 1974 owing to disagreements among the Latin American nations and a lack of funding. Despite encouraging improvements in economic growth, health, education, and housing, the program failed to meet its ambitious expectations.

ARTURO MORALES-CARRIÓN*, *Pan American Union*

ALLIGATOR, al'ə-gā-tər, either of two nontropical crocodilian reptiles—the American alligator and the Chinese alligator. The American alligator (*Alligator mississippiensis*) is found in the rivers and swampy lowlands of the southeastern United States and ranges west to the Rio Grande of Texas. One of the giant crocodilian species, it reaches an average length of 8 to 10 feet (2.4 to 3 meters), but it can be as long as 19 feet (6 meters). *A. mississippiensis* has webbed fingers and has no trace of bones in the skin of the ventral surface of the body. The number of teeth in its upper jaw is at least equal to that found in the lower jaw.

The Chinese species (*A. sinensis*), which is critically endangered, is confined to the lower Yangtze Valley. Its average length is only 4 to 4.5 feet (1.2 to 1.4 meters). The Chinese form has unwebbed fingers and small bones in the scutes (large scales) of its ventral skin. There is one more tooth in its upper jaw than in its lower jaw.

Reproduction. Both species of alligator have a gland on the right and the left side of the lower jaw, near the corner of the mouth. The gland secretes, through slitlike pores, an odorous, musky fluid that attracts the opposite sex during mating season. The males of the American species utter thunderous roars during the spring, when mating takes place, and engage in combat with one another. Competition ends when the loser retreats.

The female members of *A. mississippiensis* lay from 29 to 68 eggs in a large moundlike nest. The nest is built first as a cone of decaying vegetation; the top is then excavated by the female with her hind feet. She covers the eggs with dirt, which is smoothed down with water to hold in the heat produced by the decomposition of the vegetation. Since alligators are ectothermal (without internal means of regulating temperature), the decomposition-generated heat is the sole source of warmth during incubation. In the Chinese species, however, the eggs are exposed directly to the sunlight for incubation.

During the incubation period, which lasts about nine weeks for *A. mississippiensis*, the female guards the nest. The eggs are threatened by opossums, bears, and many other animals.

Once the offspring have hatched, it is doubtful that the female takes an active part in guarding them. This is probably due to the large number of alligators hatched at a single time. As a result, many of the young are killed by birds of prey, soft-shelled turtles, and even their own species, or fall victim to humans seeking curiosities. When alligators reach maturity, their only real enemies are humans, who hunt them for sport or to collect the animals' hide for commercial use. However, state and federal regulations now protect *A. mississippiensis* from being overhunted.

Habits. The Chinese and American species are similar in burrowing habits. Both dig deep holes, or dens, which may be 40 feet (12 meters) long, and use them for hibernation during the dry season. Alligators feed principally on fish, but crustaceans, insects, and small vertebrates also are included in their diet.

Alligators and Crocodiles. One difference between alligators and crocodiles is that the teeth of the alligator's lower jaw do not interlock with those of the upper jaw when the mouth is closed but instead bite inside the line of the upper dental row. Also, unlike crocodiles, there are more than 15 teeth in the alligator's lower jaw, and the fifth tooth of the lower jaw bites into a pocket, rather

© MARIAN BACON/ANIMALS ANIMALS

The American alligator (*Alligator mississippiensis*) inhabits the southeastern and southwestern United States.

than a groove, in the upper jaw. An easily recognized distinction between alligators and crocodiles, however, is that the alligator has a broad snout, whereas the crocodile has a narrow one.

Alligator belongs to the family Alligatoridae, in the order Crocodilia, class Reptilia. The name *alligator* is a corruption of the Spanish *el lagarto*, meaning "the lizard."

SAMUEL MCDOWELL*
American Museum of Natural History

Bibliography: Strawn, Martha, *Alligators: Prehistoric Presence in the American Landscape* (Johns Hopkins Univ. Press 1997); Zug, George R., *Herpetology: An Introductory Biology of Amphibians and Reptiles* (Academic Press 1993).

ALLIGATOR FISH. See POACHER.

ALLIGATOR GAR. See GAR.

ALLIGATOR PEAR. See AVOCADO.

ALLIGATOR SNAPPER, al'ə-gā-tər snap'ər, the giant snapping turtle of the southeastern United States. Also called the alligator turtle or the alligator snapping turtle, it is the largest of the freshwater turtles. Species members grow to about 5 feet (1.5 meters) in length and attain an average weight of 100 pounds (45 kg), although weights as high as 400 pounds (180 kg) have been recorded. The

Alligator snapper (*Macroclemys temminckii*).

© JOE MCDONALD/ANIMALS ANIMALS

alligator snapper uses a wormlike protuberance on its tongue to lure fish into its jaws. Popularly believed to be an aggressive animal with a powerful bite, this turtle actually is quite passive and is barely capable of breaking a pencil in two with its jaws. The alligator snapper (*Macroclemys temminckii*) belongs to the family Chelydridae, in the order Testudines, class Reptilia.

ALLINGHAM, William, al′ing-əm (1824–1889), Irish poet who figured in the flowering of Irish literature in the latter part of the 19th century. His use of Irish subjects and his interest in Irish folk songs and ballads influenced Yeats and other writers of the Irish literary revival.

Allingham was born in Ballyshannon, Ireland, on March 19, 1824. He held various posts in the Irish customs service from 1846 until 1870, when he moved to London and became an editor of *Fraser's Magazine*. In 1874–1879 he was chief editor of *Fraser's*, succeeding James Anthony Froude. He died in Hampstead, England, on Nov. 18, 1889.

Allingham published his first volume of poetry in 1850. Most of his best verse appears in his second published volume, *Day and Night Songs* (1854). His most ambitious undertaking was the long poem *Laurence Bloomfield in Ireland* (1864), depicting the social problems of rural Ireland. He also published *The Ballad Book* (1864) and *Songs, Ballads, and Stories* (1877). His poetical works were collected in 6 volumes (1888–1993).

Allingham knew many of the major literary figures of his time and was a close friend of Dante Gabriel Rossetti, whose *Letters to Allingham* were published in 1897. Allingham's *Diary* was brought out posthumously in 1907.

ALLISON, William Boyd, al′i-sən (1829–1908), American political leader who was one of the most powerful United States senators in the early 1900s. He was born in Perry Township, Ashland county, Ohio, on March 2, 1829. His parents were farmers, and he worked to put himself through Allegheny and Western Reserve colleges. He practiced law in Ashland from 1852 to 1857. In 1855 he left the Whig party to become a member of the convention that founded the Republican party. He later moved his law practice to Dubuque, Iowa, where he was elected to the U.S. House of Representatives in 1862.

As a member of the House Ways and Means Committee, Allison was regarded as a friend of railroad and other industrial interests. Partly as a result of the Crédit Mobilier scandal, which involved a number of his business and political associates, he was defeated in his first campaign for the U.S. Senate in 1870. Elected two years later, he served until his death in Dubuque, Iowa, on Aug. 4, 1908.

Allison is best remembered for the astute compromise between free silver advocates and conservative business interests contained in his key sections of the Bland-Allison Act of 1878. As chairman of the Appropriations Committee from 1881 to 1908, he dominated Senate business. He contended unsuccessfully for the Republican presidential nomination in 1888 and 1896.

ALLITERATION, ə-lit-ə-rā′shən, the succession or frequent occurrence of words beginning with the same consonant sound, as in the common phrases "kith and kin" and "safe and sound." In early Scandinavian, German, Anglo-Saxon, and English poetry, it served instead of rhyme, giving the poetry a certain regularity of accent and emphasis. For example, in Langland's *Piers Plowman* the poetic line is constructed with two hemistichs, the first with two words beginning with the alliterative letter, and the second with one, thus:

"Her *r*obe was full *r*ich/with *r*ed scarlet engreyned."

The poetry of widely separated languages and ages uses alliteration—Hindu and Finnish, ancient Greek and Latin. Early in the 17th century, English writers ran to great extravagance in the use of alliteration, both in prose and poetry, as, for example, when preachers called their congregations "chickens of the church."

Most poets use alliteration to lend musical beauty or emphasis to their verse, though it can be overused or misused. Examples of effective alliteration by 19th-century American poets are:

"And the *s*park struck out by that *s*teed in his *f*light
Kindled the land into *f*lame with its heat."
Longfellow

"It carves the *b*ow of *b*eauty there,
And the *r*ipples in *r*hymes the oar forsake."
Emerson

"Of *w*ailing *w*inds, and naked *w*oods."
Bryant

"And *h*ark! *h*ow clear bold chanticleer,
Warmed with the new *w*ine of the year."
Lowell

"Stole with *s*oft *s*teps the shining stairway through."
Holmes

"What a *t*ale of *t*error now their *t*urbulency *t*ells!"
Poe

"Across the *m*ournful *m*arbles play."
Whittier

Examples of alliteration by later poets are:

"Miniver *Ch*eevy, *ch*ild of scorn,"
Edwin Arlington Robinson

"The only singers now are *c*rows *c*rying, 'Caw caw';"
Carl Sandburg

"far from the splendor and squalor of hurrying *c*ities"
e.e. cummings

"It *s*nowed in *s*pring on earth *s*o dry and warm
The *f*lakes could *f*ind no landing place to *f*orm."
Robert Frost

"Spawned in *s*ome estaminet of Antwerp,
*Bl*istered in *Br*ussels, *p*atched and *p*eeled in London."
T. S. Eliot

ALLIUM, al′ē-əm, a genus of strong-smelling, bulbous herbs that contains such well-known food plants as onion, garlic, leek, and chives.

Allium's 300 or so species are perennial, monocotyledonous plants with narrow basal leaves and with white, yellow, or red flowers that cluster in small umbrella-shaped groups. The scape, or leafless stalk, of the flower cluster, ranges from 4 inches to 3 feet in height. The genus is widely distributed in the temperate parts of the Northern Hemisphere, with about 70 species native to the United States. Most of these species are found in the Rocky Mountains and in California.

Among the common species is *Allium canadense*, a wild garlic found in the eastern United States and Canada. One European species, *A. vineale*, or field garlic, has become a troublesome weed in the United States, especially in New England pastures. It is a rapidly spreading species that gives a garlic flavor to the milk produced by cows that ingest it.

A. *cepa* is the common onion. It is of unknown origin. It is widely grown as a crop in various forms, such as the subspecies *solanium*, the potato or multiplier onion. This form propagates quickly by natural division or separation of its bulb. Other species cultivated as food plants are garlic (*A. sativum*), which is native to Europe; chives (*A. schoenoprasum*), native to Europe and Asia, with variations found in North America; leek (*A. porrum*), a tall, stout plant found in Europe and western Asia; and Welsh or spring onion (*A. fistulosum*), whose leaves are used for seasoning.

Traditionally the genus *Allium* has been assigned to the plant family Liliaceae; however, some botanists classify *Allium* in the family Amaryllidaceae.

ALLORI, Alessandro, äl-lô′rē (1535–1607), Italian painter. He was born in Florence on May 3, 1535. Also called *Alessandro Bronzino*, he studied under his foster father, Agnolo di Cosimo, known as Il Bronzino. Like Bronzino, he was greatly influenced by Michelangelo, whose work he studied at Rome, but unlike Bronzino, he was frequently little more than a copyist whose stiffened draftsmanship marks the beginning of the rapid decline of Florentine painting. He executed many works for churches and buildings in Florence and painted portraits of contemporaries, notably that of Giuliano de' Medici. He died in Florence on Sept. 22, 1607.

ALLORI, Cristofano, äl-lô′rē (1577–1621), Italian painter. Born in Florence, on Oct. 17, 1577, he was the son of Alessandro Allori. He studied under his father and under Gregorio Pagani, from whom he adopted the rich coloring of the Venetian school combined with the draftsmanship of Michelangelo. Although he was successful as a portraitist, he is best known as a mannerist who specialized in scenes of passion and violence, such as *Sacrifice of Isaac* and *Judith with the Head of Holofernes*. His model for Judith was the lovely Mazzafirra, his mistress, and the severed head is said to be a self-portrait. He died in Florence in 1621.

ALLOSAURUS, al-ə-sôr′əs, a predatory dinosaur that inhabited much of what is now the western United States. *Allosaurus* ("different lizard") was one of the largest carnivorous dinosaurs of the Late Jurassic Period, which ended more than 140 million years ago.

A powerfully built, presumably quite agile biped with a rapid stride, *Allosaurus* may have reached lengths of up to 39 feet (12 meters), holding its back horizontally and employing its raised, stiffened tail as a counterbalance. A large horny ridge ran along both sides of *Allosaurus*'s nose, leading up to, but not connecting with, a triangular bladelike horn in front of each eye. The latter may have served both as a display feature for attracting mates and as a defensive weapon for protecting the eyes during combat.

The fingers of the dinosaur's short, muscular arms ended in large raptorial claws that were apparently used to seize prey. The jaws bore numerous sharp, curved, serrated teeth, and the surrounding skull, although quite strong, was kinetic (that is, connections between the skull bones were flexible), allowing the feeding animal to tear off and swallow enormous chunks of meat. *Allosaurus* probably hunted the many large sauropods, such as *Camarasaurus*, that shared its range. (See CAMARASAURUS.)

Serrated teeth and a powerful stride made *Allosaurus* a formidable predator during the Late Jurassic Period.

The American paleontologist Othniel Charles Marsh provided the first description of *Allosaurus*, in 1877, after examining several bone fragments discovered in Colorado, including a tooth, two dorsal vertebral centra, and a toe bone. These fossils were collected from the Morrison Formation, a 150-million-year-old geological deposit covering much of western North America. Since then *Allosaurus* specimens have accounted for about 10% of the Late Jurassic dinosaur fauna excavated from Morrison rocks, indicating the large size of the *Allosaurus* population just prior to the beginning of the Cretaceous Period, about 144 million years ago. (See MARSH, OTHNIEL CHARLES.)

The richest *Allosaurus* site in the Morrison Formation has been the Cleveland-Lloyd Quarry in east-central Utah, where the disarticulated skeletons of dozens of these carnivores have been recovered. The great number of bones at this site suggests that it had once been muddy enough to trap prey animals, attracting predators who, in turn, also became fatally mired.

Paleontologists previously subdivided *Allosaurus* into numerous species based on differing fossil skull characteristics and skeletal proportions. The majority of scientists, however, now believe that there may have been only one species, *A. fragilis*, and that the variations that were seen simply represent natural anatomical deviations among individuals or differences between males and females.

Allosaurus has been classified within the group, or clade, Allosauroidea, part of a larger clade of bipedal, meat-eating dinosaurs, Theropoda. (A clade is a designation employed in the scientific classification system known as cladistics.) The largest member of Allosauroidea appears to have been *Saurophaganax* ("lizard eater king"), a North American dinosaur from the Late Jurassic that matched *Tyrannosaurus rex* in size. (See TYRANNOSAURUS.)

Thought to have arisen during the Middle Jurassic, species of Allosauroidea were widespread across the Northern Hemisphere, with a primitive form possibly having existed in South America. Allosauroidea appears to have gone extinct by the Late Cretaceous, approximately 98 million years ago.

(See DINOSAUR; CRETACEOUS PERIOD; JURASSIC PERIOD.)

JAMES I. KIRKLAND
Utah Geological Survey

Bibliography

Chure, Daniel J., "A Reassessment of the Gigantic Theropod *Saurophagus maximus* from the Morrison Formation (Upper Jurassic) of Oklahoma, U.S.A.," in *Sixth Symposium on Mesozoic Terrestrial Ecosystems and Biota, Short Papers*, ed. by Ailing Sun and Yuanqing Wang (China Ocean Press 1995).

Currie, Philip J., and Kevin Padian, eds., *Encyclopedia of Dinosaurs* (Academic Press 1997).

Gilmore, Charles W., "Osteology of the Carnivorous Dinosauria in the United States National Museum, with Special Reference to *Antrodemus* (*Allosaurus*) and *Ceratosaurus*," *Bulletin of the United States National Museum* 100 (1920):1–154.

Madsen, James H., Jr., "*Allosaurus fragilis*: A Revised Osteology," *Utah Geological and Mineralogical Survey* 109 (1976):1–163.

ALLOTHERIA, a-lō-thir′ē-ə, one of the three subclasses of mammals, the other two being Prototheria and Theria. Now extinct, its representatives first appeared approximately 140 million years ago (Late Jurassic Period) and survived until about 50 million years ago (Eocene epoch). Their fossils have been discovered in Europe, Asia, and North America.

The Allotheria were characterized by a peculiar dentition similar to that of present-day rodents. Their upper and lower incisors were reduced to two rodentlike teeth, and the two upper and lower molars had cusps that were arranged in two or three longitudinal rows. It is believed that the structure of the Allotheria foreshadowed that of the rodents, and that perhaps competition between the two groups led to the extinction of the Allotheria.

The classification of Allotheria has been controversial. The grouping Allotheria was set up at the end of the 19th century to include mammalian fossils of 40 million to 200 million years ago (Mesozoic, Paleocene, and Eocene). However, some paleontologists believed that the allotherians were more closely related to the marsupials, and these scientists made the allotherians a suborder, Multituberculata, under Marsupialia. It was then established that the allotherians were not ancestors of marsupials, and they are now classified as a subclass with Multituberculata as the only order. There were approximately 30 recognized species of allotherians.

Although Allotheria generally is ranked as a subclass, some paleontologists include it as an infraclass under the subclass Theria.

PHILIP HERSHKOVITZ*
Chicago Natural History Museum

Bibliography: Carroll, R. L., *Vertebrate Paleontology and Evolution* (Freeman 1988); Sereno, P. C., and M. C. McKenna, "Cretaceous Multituberculate Skeleton and the Early Evolution of the Mammalian Shoulder Girdle," *Nature* 377 (1995):144–147; Simmons, N. B., "Phylogeny of Multituberculata," in *Mammal Phylogeny: Mesozoic Differentiation, Multituberculates, Monotremes, Early Therians and Marsupials*, vol. 1, ed. by F. S. Szalay, et al. (Springer-Verlag 1993).

ALLOTROPY, ə-lot′rə-pē, also called *allotropism*, the property exhibited by many chemical elements of having different forms under certain conditions. For example, a molecule of oxygen has two oxygen atoms, whereas a molecule of ozone has three oxygen atoms. These allotropic forms of oxygen have different properties, and they occur in different places. Ozone occurs at high levels in our atmosphere and helps filter out ultraviolet rays from the sun, whereas oxygen is abundant in the lowest regions of the atmosphere.

Carbon has several allotropic forms such as charcoal, diamond, and graphite. The bonds between the carbon atoms of graphite give the bulk material enough flexibility to be a lubricant. The bonds between the carbon atoms of diamond make it the hardest natural substance known. Coke, boneblack, and lampblack are other allotropic forms of carbon. As another example, allotropic forms of phosphorus have different colors—violet, black, and white.

Some elements change to allotropic forms at a definite temperature. For example, iron has several transformation points at which allotropes are formed. Alpha iron has a body-centered atomic arrangement—there is one iron atom at the center of a cube formed by eight surrounding atoms. At 912° C, alpha iron becomes another form of iron that has a face-centered atomic arrangement—a small cube with four closely packed iron atoms is the unit of structure. At 1400° C, another transition to a third form of iron takes place.

MORRIS GORAN
Roosevelt University

ALLOYS, al′oiz, substances that have metallic properties and contain at least two elements. The base element in an alloy is a metal. Metallic substances are either metallic elements or alloys. The atoms of each solid metallic element are arranged in an array that is characteristic of the element. The array is defined by the way in which the atoms are stacked and by the distance between neighboring atoms. When atoms of one or more other elements are present in the structure of the metallic element in such quantities that the properties of the metal are significantly altered, the substance is called an alloy. The presence of alloying atoms tends to change the average distance between neighboring atoms and also may alter

Alloy atoms (black or cross-hatched) can either occupy spaces between base-metal atoms (white) and form an interstitial solid solution (fig. 1A) or substitute for base-metal atoms and form a substitutional solid solution (fig. 1B).

FIGURE 1A   FIGURE 1B

the way in which the atoms are arranged. Alloying atoms may substitute for base-metal atoms, or they may occupy spaces between base-metal atoms. (See fig. 1.) When either occurs, the alloying atoms are said to be dissolved in the solid. This condition is called a solid solution. Generally, alloying atoms are intentionally added while the base metal is molten, but sometimes they may be accidentally introduced from the ore or from refining materials. Alloying elements need not be metallic substances. (See METAL; ELEMENT.)

Alloys most commonly are produced during the melting of a base metal. They can also be formed by simultaneous electro-deposition of metals from solution or by mixing elemental metal powders and then compressing and heating the mixture.

Alloys are far more common and useful than elemental metals in everyday life. The use of pure metals is restricted to applications where their superior electrical properties, electric and thermal conductivity (which alloying impairs), or corrosion resistance (which alloying sometimes impairs and sometimes improves) are required. Alloys usually are far superior to elemental metals in mechanical properties, such as strength (load-carrying), hardness, and ductility. Alloying usually lowers the melting point of the base metal. Alloys usually are superior under ordinary service conditions and very high temperatures. (See CONDUCTIVITY, ELECTRICAL; CORROSION; STRENGTH OF MATERIALS; LOAD; HARDNESS SCALE; DUCTILITY; BRITTLENESS; MALLEABILITY; EUTECTIC ALLOY.)

Ferrous Alloys. Alloys are generally classified as either ferrous (iron-containing) or nonferrous. Judged by the annual tonnage production, the ferrous alloys are by far the more important. (See IRON.)

In producing steel, the most important alloying element (carbon) comes mainly from the coke that is used to reduce iron ore. Pig iron, which is rich in carbon, is added to molten steel scrap that has been refined by removing most of the carbon. Thus, the melt is recarburized (carbon is reintroduced). Alloying elements that are not too readily oxidized, such as copper, molybdenum, and nickel, can be added to the furnace charge scrap metal before meltdown. The more easily oxidized elements, such as chromium and manganese, are added toward the end of the refining process. Very easily oxidized metals, such as aluminum, titanium, boron, and vanadium, usually are added in the ladle. Sometimes they are added to the metal as it is being poured into the ingot mold. Final minor adjustments in carbon content can also be made by ladle additions of coke, coal, or graphite. When large amounts of alloy additions must be made (as for 18%-chromium stainless steels), the master ferrochromium alloy is preheated and added in several batches to prevent undue chilling of the bath. (See STEEL; CARBON; COKE; MOLYBDENUM; CHROMIUM; MANGANESE; BORON; VANADIUM; COAL; GRAPHITE.)

Carbon Steels. Carbon steel is defined as having a carbon content that is a quite small percentage, a copper content between 0.4% and 0.6%, a silicon content of not more than 0.6%, and a manganese content of not more than 1.65%, the balance being iron. Minimum amounts of other alloying elements are neither specified nor guaranteed in carbon steels.

In order to understand the properties of carbon steel and most alloy steels, it is necessary to understand the crystal structure of iron and steel and how the structure is altered by the presence of carbon and by thermal treatment. At room temperature the atoms of pure iron are arranged in what is called a body-centered cubic (BCC) structure. (See fig. 2A.) If iron is heated to 910° C (1670° F), then the atomic arrangement shifts to a face-centered cubic (FCC) structure. (See fig. 2B.) In interstices (the spaces between the iron atoms), the BCC structure can accept only about 1.4 atoms of carbon per 1,000 atoms of iron. If the alloy contains more than this ratio of carbon and iron atoms, then the excess carbon atoms react with iron atoms to form particles of an extremely hard, brittle compound known as cementite (Fe_3C). These particles have a distinct crystal structure, and they are intimately mixed with the crystal structure of BCC iron saturated with carbon atoms. The FCC structure can accept 96 atoms of carbon for every 1,000 atoms of iron. These carbon atoms are dissolved in the spaces between the iron atoms. This is an enormous increase in the solubility of carbon as compared with the solubility limit in BCC iron. If the FCC iron contains more carbon in solution than the 1.4 carbon atoms per 1,000 iron atoms that can be dissolved in BCC iron, then the excess carbon atoms form Fe_3C during the slow cooling and transformation of FCC to BCC. The greater the amount of Fe_3C that forms, the greater is the hardness, strength, and brittleness of the alloy. Because the amount of Fe_3C that forms is directly proportional to the carbon content, the properties of the steel are directly affected by the carbon content. (See CRYSTAL.)

If the FCC iron is rapidly cooled (quenched) instead of slowly cooled, then the excess carbon atoms do not have time to react with iron atoms to form Fe_3C. In this event, the excess carbon atoms are retained interstitially in an unstable,

Pure iron atoms are arranged in a body-centered cubic structure (fig. 2A) at room temperature and in a face-centered cubic structure (fig. 2B) at a temperature above 910° C (1670° F). The former structure can accept only 1.4 carbon atoms per 1,000 iron atoms, while the latter can accept 96 carbon atoms per 1,000 iron atoms.

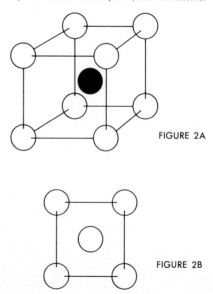

FIGURE 2A

FIGURE 2B

distorted version of the BCC structure. This structure is similar to one that would exist if a body-centered cubic structure were elongated so that the cube became a rectangular solid. This unstable, supersaturated solid solution is known as martensite. Martensite is extremely brittle and useless when freshly formed by quenching. When fresh martensite is heated after quenching (a process known as tempering), however, the excess carbon atoms it contains in solution are rejected from the interstices. The rejected carbon atoms form Fe_3C, and the remaining iron forms the stable BCC structure. The dispersion of Fe_3C in an alloy treated by quenching and tempering is extremely fine and results in a significant improvement in strength (as compared with the slowly cooled alloy) without the excessive development of brittleness (as in the freshly quenched alloy). A sufficient amount of carbon (usually more than 0.35%) must be present, however, for quenching and tempering to result in worthwhile strengthening of the alloy.

The properties of carbon steels depend on the carbon content and the thermal history of the steel. Strength and brittleness tend to increase (but not without limit) as the carbon content of slowly cooled steel increases. For any given carbon content, quenching and tempering improve the mechanical properties.

Although low-carbon steels (between 0.08% and 0.35% carbon content) are the weakest ferrous alloys, their excellent ductility (absence of brittleness) makes it possible to deform them severely without rupture or tearing. Low-carbon steels are rarely quenched and tempered, although a slightly accelerated cooling cycle (as by an air blast) results in a slight improvement in properties. Low-carbon steels are used for automobile body parts, home appliance cabinets, and tin cans. Tin cans actually are made from sheet steel coated with an extremely thin layer of tin. Low-carbon steels are also used for automobile frames, for structural shapes or beams used in building construction, and for plates used in ship construction. The low carbon content also makes it possible to weld without embrittlement.

Steels with higher carbon contents are either impossible or very difficult to weld because of the brittleness of the fresh martensite, which forms as a result of rapid cooling after welding. Medium-carbon steel (between 0.35% and 0.5% carbon content) is used where more strength is required than is provided by low-carbon steel and where some loss of ductility can be tolerated. Medium-carbon steels often are shaped by forging at high temperatures or by casting to shape rather than by cold working (deforming at room temperature). Crankshafts, steering arms, gears, and railroad axles are examples of parts made of medium-carbon steels. The carbon in the medium-carbon and high-carbon steels is much more effective as a strengthening agent if the steel is heat treated. Hence, many medium-carbon steel parts and most high-carbon steel parts are heat treated to achieve the best combination of strength and ductility. High-carbon steel (more than 0.5% carbon content) is used for railroad wheels and rails, wrenches, steel cable, piano wire, tools, and dies.

Alloy Steels. Steels that contain one or more intentionally added alloying elements, exclusive of carbon and in excess of the maximum permissible amounts found incidentally in carbon steel, are known as alloy steels. The alloy steels, if they contain sufficient carbon, are hardenable by heat treatment. Stainless steels are another major class of alloy steels. A few compositions are both stainless and hardenable.

The most important function of the alloying elements in steel is to retard the change from FCC iron to BCC iron and the accompanying precipitation of coarse Fe_3C particles. If the change can be retarded sufficiently, then the very hard, supersaturated martensitic condition can be achieved easily at room temperature. In the absence of alloying elements the change occurs so quickly that it is very difficult to obtain martensite. Alloy elements that suppress the FCC-to-BCC transformation are said to improve the hardenability of the steel. Hardenability is defined as the ease with which martensite can be formed.

Freshly formed martensite is reheated to produce a fine dispersion of Fe_3C particles throughout BCC iron. The reheated martensite provides a usefully ductile and strong steel. By retarding the formation of coarse Fe_3C particles, the slower cooling rates are able to bring the supersaturated FCC iron to temperatures at which it can change to martensite. With sufficient alloy content, quenching in oil or air can produce martensite. In the absence of alloys a more vigorous water quench would be necessary. Very large pieces of carbon steel cannot be cooled fast enough, except perhaps at the surface, to avoid the formation of coarse Fe_3C even if water is the quenching medium. Thus, alloys are essential when parts of heavy cross section are to be hardened by the formation of martensite. Furthermore, rapid cooling of intricate shapes in order to achieve martensite is likely to result in cracking during quenching. The alloy additions slow the formation of coarse Fe_3C and thereby avoid the need for very rapid cooling. A more gradual quench is effective in producing hardness, and it avoids the danger of cracking. Except for cobalt, all alloy elements, when dissolved in FCC iron at high temperatures before quenching, enhance the formation of martensite. Also, there are some alloying elements that make the martensite less susceptible to loss of hardness upon tempering. Therefore, tempered martensite in most alloy steels is more ductile and tougher than alloy-free martensite of the same hardness. In addition, some alloying elements increase the resistance to softening of the fresh martensite during tempering or exposure to high temperatures. Thus, many steels for high-temperature applications contain large quantities of alloys. Among the common alloying elements that toughen martensite and resist softening during exposure to high temperature are titanium, vanadium, molybdenum, tungsten, and chromium. (See COBALT; TUNGSTEN.)

The alloy steels are used for applications where (1) the hardenability and toughness of carbon steel is insufficient, or (2) the shape of the object is such that it would be likely to crack if hardened by the severe quench needed for carbon steel, or (3) the superior high-temperature hardness and strength of alloy steels are required. Machine parts, such as gears, axles, ball bearings, connecting rods, tools, and forging dies are examples of alloy-steel applications.

Stainless Steels. Stainless qualities are imparted to ferrous alloys that contain about one chromium atom for every six iron atoms. If there are alloying elements present in addition to chromium, the alloy is called a stainless steel. There are two major kinds of stainless-steel compositions: those that can be hardened by heat treatment and those that cannot be hardened by heat treatment. Compositions that cannot be hardened by heat treatment have either a rather stable FCC structure or a permanent BCC structure. Because the ability to harden steel depends on the change from one structure to another, these steels cannot be hardened by heat treatment. The use of sufficient chromium and a low concentration of carbon and nickel produces nonhardenable BCC structures that are called ferritic stainless steels. If the carbon content is increased or if there is a slight increase in the carbon and nickel contents, FCC-to-BCC transformations are possible and the steel is hardenable. These steels are called martensitic stainless steels. If the stainless steel contains chromium and large amounts of nickel or a combination of nickel, manganese, and nitrogen, then a rather stable FCC structure will form. This structure is incapable of hardening by heat treatment. Such steels are called austenitic stainless steels.

The ferritic stainless steels are used mainly for decorative purposes, such as automobile trim. The martensitic stainless steels are used for cutlery and surgical and dental tools. The austenitic stainless steels, which have the best corrosion resistance and resistance to high-temperature failure, are used for food-processing, textile, and chemical equipment; for combustion chambers; and for high-pressure steam equipment.

Cast Irons. Cast irons are very important ferrous materials. There are a number of different compositions, but all contain carbon and silicon as the principal alloying elements. Carbon is present in amounts between 2% and 4.5%, and silicon is present in amounts between 1.0% and 2.5%. When the percentage of carbon is high, large amounts of very coarse, unstable Fe_3C particles form in these alloys. The Fe_3C in these alloys tends to decompose into graphite and FCC iron at temperatures above 760° C (1400° F). The decomposition into graphite and FCC iron is promoted by high carbon content, high silicon content, and slow cooling of the casting after it has solidified. The advantages of cast iron over cast steel arise largely from the lowering of the melting temperature by nearly 315° C (600° F), which is achieved by using large amounts of alloying elements. Production of lower melting temperatures lowers costs and simplifies the equipment requirements for melting, handling, and casting. In addition, cast iron reproduces mold details better than do the more sparsely alloyed cast steels.

There are several varieties of cast iron: gray, white, malleable, ductile (or nodular), and alloy cast iron. Gray cast irons and white cast irons mainly contain carbon and silicon as alloy additions. Gray cast iron usually is more highly alloyed than white cast iron, and the latter is chilled during solidification. Both irons are extremely brittle. In gray cast irons, the carbon exists as flakes of graphite. These graphite flakes provide softness and good machinability, and they cause the gray color of the fractured surface. In white cast irons, most of the carbon is present as Fe_3C, an extremely hard, brittle ingredient. The Fe_3C causes the iron to be brittle, difficult to machine, and wear resistant. It also causes a white or silvery appearance of the fractured surface. Solidified white cast iron can be converted to malleable cast iron by longtime heating—for example, 50 hours at 930° C (1700° F). This heating tends

to convert the Fe_3C to iron and large spherical particles of graphite. Malleable cast iron has the properties of gray cast iron except that it is ductile rather than brittle. Ductile or nodular cast iron has properties similar to malleable cast iron, but the properties are achieved through control of composition before casting rather than by heating the solid cast shape. Alloy cast irons are compositions that contain significant amounts of alloying elements in addition to carbon and silicon. Nickel, chromium, molybdenum, and copper commonly are used. These additions are made to improve the balance among the properties of strength, wear resistance, machinability, susceptibility to heat treatment, and corrosion resistance.

Magnetic Alloys. Iron and its alloys are the basis of most, but not all, ferromagnetic substances. Although there are other kinds of magnetism, ferromagnetism is the only property considered here; it will be referred to simply as magnetism. Ferromagnetic materials have opposite poles. They strongly attract unmagnetized iron, and they concentrate lines of magnetic force. Magnetic alloys are classed broadly as either permanent magnets or temporary magnets. Some metallic substances can be made into magnets by placing them near a magnet, but these substances retain very little pole strength when the magnet is removed from the vicinity of these substances. Such substances are called temporary magnets. Other substances will retain much of the pole strength induced by the presence of the strong magnetic field of the magnet. If strong poles still are evident in the substance when the magnet is removed, the substance is called a permanent magnet. Soft iron and soft iron alloys produce temporary magnets; these materials are called soft magnets.

Permanent magnets are physically hard; they are called hard magnets. Thus, for the production of permanent magnets, alloys are added to iron to harden it or enable it to be hardened by heat treatment. All iron-base permanent magnets contain carbon. If they have a large cross-sectional area or a complicated shape, they probably will contain other alloying elements to improve hardenability. Iron-base temporary magnets, which are required for alternating-current (a-c) applications, usually contain silicon. For efficient operation, it is desirable that temporary magnet materials have a high electrical resistance. This can be accomplished in iron, as in other metals, by simple alloy additions. Such additions also harden the alloy, and this tends to produce permanent magnetism, which cannot be tolerated in a-c circuits. Silicon is selected as the alloy addition because it is known to create the greatest increase in resistance with the least increase in hardness. In addition, the silicon does not unduly impair the fabricating properties of the alloy. (See FERROMAGNETISM.)

Nonferrous Alloys. The timing and nature of alloy additions in nonferrous alloys are governed by such factors as the relative melting temperatures of the base metal and the alloy addition, the volatility of the alloy addition, the relative density of the alloy addition, and the ease of forming a solution. Thus, in making brass, zinc is added just before the brass is poured because the zinc boils away rather rapidly. When magnesium is added to aluminum, the magnesium must be submerged in the molten aluminum. When high-melting-point metals, such as nickel, are to be alloyed with aluminum, which has a lower melt-

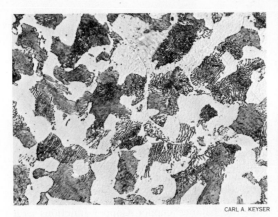

CARL A. KEYSER

Microstructure of slowly cooled medium-carbon steel shows white background of ferrite and striped and dark layers of cementite (Fe_3C) and ferrite (500X).

CARL A. KEYSER

Microstructure of quenched and tempered medium-carbon steel shows fine dispersion of Fe_3C in ferrite. Structure is much stronger than that at left (500X).

ing point, it is advantageous to use a master alloy that contains from 2% to 10% nickel and the balance aluminum in order to speed solution and prevent chilling of the melt.

Copper Alloys. Copper is widely used in unalloyed form because it has outstanding electrical and thermal conductivity. Although aluminum competes with copper as a conductor material, copper has superior conductivity and the added advantage of being easily joined by soldering. Many applications, such as electrical equipment and automobile radiators, require extensive soldering. The electrical conductivity and thermal conductivity of copper and other metals decrease as a result of alloying. Therefore, in the absence of secondary considerations, copper alloys are not used where conductivity is of prime importance. Less than half the annual copper production is used in the form of copper-base alloys. (See COPPER.)

Copper-base alloys do, however, have superior corrosion resistance, appearance, and ductility. Copper-base alloys generally are weaker than ferrous alloys, but they are stronger than aluminum- and magnesium-base alloys. Copper commonly is alloyed with zinc to make brass, with tin to make true bronze, with aluminum or silicon to make aluminum-bronze and silicon-bronze alloys, and with nickel to make cupronickel alloys. The strength and ductility of copper are improved by adding initial amounts of alloying elements. When alloys are added to copper, the color of the material gradually changes from deep red to orange, gold, lemon, and finally to a silver-white color as the percentage of the alloying element is increased. For instance, the silvery five-cent U.S. coin contains 25% nickel and 75% copper. (See BRASS; BRONZE; SILICON; NICKEL SILVER.)

The corrosion resistance of the copper-base alloys and the ease with which they can be cast, shaped, machined, and finished have led to their common use in hardware, particularly marine hardware. Copper-base alloys and other ductile alloys can be hardened by mechanical treatments, such as cold rolling of sheet and strip or reducing the diameter of a rod or wire by pulling it through a die (drawing). A few copper-base alloys, notably those containing tin, can be hardened by heat treatments that are called age hardening and precipitation hardening. In these treatments the alloy is first heated to form a saturated solid solution. If this solution is quenched, the result is an un-

stable, supersaturated solid solution. If this supersaturated solid solution is aged at room temperature for a long period of time or is heated to a slightly higher temperature for a short time, then the excess dissolved atoms precipitate as a second crystal structure throughout the base-metal crystal structure. The precipitation is accompanied by an increase in hardness and strength. This reaction is similar to the hardening of steel as a result of the formation of a fine dispersion of Fe_3C particles.

Aluminum Alloys. Aluminum and its alloys generally rank below copper and its alloys with respect to strength. If comparisons are made on the basis of strength-to-weight ratio, however, the aluminum alloys are far superior to copper alloys and to all but the strongest ferrous alloys. Pure aluminum is used only where its excellent atmospheric corrosion resistance, its electrical conductivity, or its thermal conductivity is required. Aluminum commonly is alloyed with copper, silicon, magnesium, zinc, and other alloying elements. Most of these alloys are age-hardenable or precipitation-hardenable alloys. High-strength, precipitation-hardened alloys are used as structural members when the deadweight is to be minimized and payload is to be maximized. If high-strength aluminum sheet material is to be exposed to the atmosphere, a composite material is used. This composite material has a very thin layer of high-purity, corrosion-resistant aluminum rolled onto its surface. The base metal can be hardened by a combination of mechanical work and precipitation. Most aluminum alloys are rather ductile. They are not considered to have good wear resistance because of their softness and their tendency to seize or gall. (See ALUMINUM.)

Magnesium Alloys. Magnesium and its alloys have the lowest density of the common metallic materials. There are rather limited alloying possibilities for magnesium, but aluminum and zinc are most frequently used. Aluminum forms an age-hardenable alloy system. Zinc hardens magnesium by its presence in solid solution. The strengths of magnesium alloys are generally lower than those of aluminum, and the ductility, corrosion resistance (to water), and wear resistance of magnesium alloys are not good. The chief uses for these alloys are found where light weight is important, as in aircraft and portable tools. (See MAGNESIUM.)

Titanium Alloys. Titanium alloys have strengths comparable to steel, and they have a corrosion resistance that is about equal to that of stainless steel. Titanium is a very reactive element. Alloying elements that dissolve interstitially in titanium—such as carbon, hydrogen, oxygen, nitrogen, and boron—raise the strength of titanium, but they impair ductility and toughness so severely that they are considered to be contaminants. Although alloying elements that dissolve substitutionally also impair the toughness and ductility of titanium while raising its strength, the impairment is not disastrous. Useful alloying elements include aluminum, chromium, iron, manganese, molybdenum, and vanadium. Titanium and its alloys are used principally when corrosion resistance and high-temperature strength are of primary importance. In aircraft and spacecraft applications the low density of titanium alloys (slightly more than half that of steel) and other important properties justify using them despite high cost. Titanium alloys have been used for airframes, rocket engines, and jet engine parts. (See TITANIUM.)

Nickel Alloys. Although nickel usually is used as an alloy addition to such base metals as iron (in many hardenable steels and austenitic stainless steels) and copper (cupronickel, nickel bronzes, and nickel coinage), a few nickel-base alloys are important. Monel alloys consist of almost two-thirds nickel, small amounts of silicon, aluminum, manganese, or sulfur, and the balance copper. Although hardening results chiefly from the presence of copper, these alloys can also be hardened by mechanical deformation. The monel alloys have good corrosion resistance and toughness. The machining of monel alloys, which is generally difficult, is eased by the presence of manganese and sulfur. Additions of silicon and aluminum produce age-hardenable alloys. Addition of silicon also improves the castability of monel alloys. Other nickel-rich alloys contain chromium, iron, and molybdenum in various combinations to produce alloys that resist high temperatures or severely corrosive environments. (See NICKEL; MONEL METAL; PERMALLOY.)

Zinc Alloys. Although most zinc is consumed for galvanizing sheet steel and steel wire, large quantities are used in the manufacture of die castings. Because zinc is rather soft and weak, it is alloyed with aluminum and copper to make it as strong as the magnesium alloys. In the absence of copper, zinc-aluminum alloys undergo troublesome dimensional changes after casting. Additions of copper strengthen zinc alloys and stabilize them against dimensional changes. Zinc-base die castings are widely used for decorative and functional automotive parts. Door handles, trim, and carburetors are examples. (See ZINC.)

Tin Alloys. Tin mainly is used in pure form as a protective coating on steel (tin cans). Tin alloys of importance include tin-lead solder; the most popular composition is half tin and half lead. Solders with higher tin contents are available, but the high cost of tin relative to that of lead restricts their use. Tin alloys usually are hardened by the addition of antimony, antimony and copper, or antimony, lead, and copper. The lead serves as a low-cost substitute for part of the tin content. These alloys, which are called babbitts, commonly are used for bearings, white metal (for jewelry), and pewter (for decorative articles). (See TIN; SOLDER; BABBITT METAL; PEWTER.)

Lead Alloys. Lead-tin alloys already have been mentioned as solders. Lead is hardened by adding antimony. In this form the alloy is used for such applications as sheet material, pipe, and battery grids. Type metal is a lead-base alloy that is hardened by the addition of antimony and bismuth. The composition of these materials is adjusted so that the lowest possible melting point is achieved. The lead-antimony alloys and the type-metal alloys are age hardenable. (See LEAD; ANTIMONY; BISMUTH.)

Precious-Metal Alloys. Probably the most widely used precious-metal alloys are those in which the base metal is silver, gold, or platinum. Silver alloys of importance include coinage silver, which formerly (before 1965) consisted of 90% silver with the balance copper. Sterling silver is 92.5% silver, with the balance copper. Copper functions as a hardener for both silver, which is very soft when it is pure, and gold. When added in increasing amounts, copper changes the color of gold from a yellow to a reddish color (more than 30% copper). Silver, when alloyed with gold, produces a greenish tinge. Nickel and zinc lighten the color of gold. In combination with other elements, nickel and zinc can produce green, yellow, red, and pink colors. Gold alloys are used mainly for jewelry. Platinum hardened by iridium or ruthenium additions is used for jewelry and electrical contacts. Platinum alloyed with rhodium improves the high-temperature oxidation resistance of the material and is used for thermocouples, electrical resistance windings, and crucibles. (See SILVER; GOLD; GOLDWORK AND SILVERWORK; PLATINUM; IRIDIUM; RUTHENIUM; RHODIUM.)

History. Gold and copper were known before recorded history. Tin was smelted from its ores before 3500 B.C., and alloys of copper and tin were made. The tribes with bronze tools, arms, and armor soon dominated their neighbors and made major progress in humanity's long struggle to dominate the environment. The original alloys probably were made by smelting a mixture of copper- and tin-bearing minerals. It was easier to make bronze than to make copper because of the significantly lower melting temperature of bronze. Alloys of iron and carbon also were smelted from ore at approximately the same time, and again the advantage of lower melting temperatures favored making alloys. It is likely that the first iron-carbon alloy was produced as a spongy solid rather than being cast as a liquid that was allowed to solidify. (See SMELTING.)

Adulteration of gold by alloying with copper and silver was widely practiced from ancient times through the Middle Ages. Attempts to uncover such chicanery led Archimedes (287?–212 B.C.) to the discovery of his buoyancy principle. Theophrastus (c. 370–c. 287 B.C.) described the use of the touchstone to discover adulteration. (See ARCHIMEDES; THEOPHRASTUS; TOUCHSTONE.)

Probably the greatest advances in alloying, particularly in ferrous metallurgy, came with the adoption of the Bessemer process in 1856. By this process, steel could be made from pig iron in tonnage batches in less than half an hour. Pig iron, an alloy consisting mainly of iron, carbon, and silicon, is so brittle that it is useless for modern engineering uses. Before 1856, small amounts of pig iron were converted to wrought iron by eliminating the carbon. Then small, controlled amounts of carbon were reintroduced by the cementation process (inclusion of Fe_3C) to make steel. The conversion of batches of pig iron weighing less than 45 kilograms (100 lb) required several days. The large-scale, rapid production of steel made possible great industrial progress. The German English metallurgist Karl Wilhem (Charles William) Siemens invented the open-hearth furnace in 1868, and thereafter there was a rapid proliferation in the available steel-alloy compositions. The electric furnace, invented by the French metallurgist Paul Héroult in 1899, further broadened the type and quality of available steel alloys. (See BESSEMER, HENRY; SIEMENS; HÉROULT, PAUL LOUIS TOUSSAINT.)

The scientific foundation for alloy development was laid by Henry C. Sorby in England in 1861. The German metallurgist Alfred Wilm developed age-hardenable and precipitation-hardenable alloys in 1906. The German physicist Max von Laue and the British physicists William H. Bragg and William L. Bragg used X rays to determine crystal structure in 1912. (See LAUE, MAX VON; BRAGG, WILLIAM HENRY; BRAGG, WILLIAM LAWRENCE; WILM, ALFRED.)

Modern alloys include tens of thousands of ferrous and nonferrous compositions. Near the middle of the 20th century, new alloys began receiving attention, including ones for the production of nuclear weapons and energy. Later efforts were aimed at producing ultrapure metals that contained only 1 impurity atom per 10^{10} atoms of the pure metal. Very minute controlled quantities of impurity elements are added to these ultrapure metals to produce special electronic properties. These alloys, which by ordinary standards would be considered to be very pure elements, are used in some solid-state electronic devices.

Great efforts have been made to develop superior alloys, particularly for high-temperature applications, by introducing microscopic and submicroscopic nonmetallic particles or fibers that are dispersed throughout the metallic substances. Such alloys are useful as materials for high-speed aircraft, where the weight and temperature requirements for materials are severe. These alloys are also important in developing more efficient power sources by the control of very high-temperature energy sources.

CARL A. KEYSER
University of Massachusetts

Bibliography
Cottrell, Alan, *Concepts in the Electron Theory of Alloys* (Ashgate Pub. Co. 1998).
De Gennes, P. G., *Superconductivity of Metals and Alloys* (Perseus Bks. 1999).
Durand-Charre, Madeleine, *The Microstructure of Superalloys* (Gordon & Breach 1997).
Frick, John P., ed., *Woldman's Engineering Alloys*, 9th ed. (Am. Soc. for Metals 2001).
Smith, W. F., *Structure and Properties of Engineering Alloys*, 2d ed. (McGraw-Hill 1993).

ALLPORT, Gordon Willard (1897–1967), American psychologist who was noted for his studies of personality. He was born in Montezuma, Ind., on Nov. 11, 1897, and graduated from Harvard in 1919. He began teaching psychology there in 1919 and was a professor from 1942 until his death, in Cambridge, on Oct. 9, 1967.

Setting a trend away from Freudian and developmental psychology, Allport advanced a theory of "functional autonomy" of motives. According to this theory, adult motives are independent of childhood desires, although they may have originated from such desires. His personality theory stresses present values over past orientation and emphasizes the uniqueness of each individual.

Allport was president of the American Psychological Association in 1939. He edited the *Journal of Abnormal and Social Psychology* from 1937 to 1949. His books include *Personality* (1937), *Nature of Personality* (1950), *Nature of Prejudice* (1954), and *Pattern and Growth of Personality* (1961).

Bibliography
Clark, Kenneth H., Robert Hogan, and Raymond N. Wolfe, eds., *Fifty Years of Personality Psychology* (Plenum Press 1993).
Evans, Richard I., *Gordon Allport: The Man and His Ideas* (Dutton 1971).
Maddi, Salvatore R., and Paul T. Costa, *Humanism in Personality: Allport, Maslow, and Murray* (Aldine 1972).

ALL'S WELL THAT ENDS WELL, a comedy by William Shakespeare. The play has survived only in the unsatisfactory text in the First Folio. Misprinting, inconsistencies in nomenclature, and misassignment of speeches confuse further a version that clearly is not all of one piece. Variations of style, improper joining, and contradictions have led to the view that the play was a fairly early one in Shakespeare's career, revised by him between 1602 and 1605, and perhaps disfigured by another hand. The author Francis Meres in 1598 lists a Shakespearean *Love's Labours Wonne*, a title that would accurately describe the present play and is perhaps referred to in its epilogue.

Plot.   Shakespeare's source is the story of "Giglietta di Nerbona" in Boccaccio's *Decameron*, as translated into English in William Painter's *Palace of Pleasure* (1566). (See DECAMERON; PAINTER, WILLIAM.) In Shakespeare's adaptation Helena, who lives with the Countess of Rousillon, is secretly in love with the Countess's son, Bertram, who as a ward of the king is summoned to the court of France. Helena follows him, in the hope of curing the king of a fistula and thereby winning Bertram, who is unaware of her affection. Successful in restoring the king to health, she gains the reward of selecting a husband from among his courtiers. Helena chooses the unwilling Bertram, who is ordered by the king to marry her. Bertram, who feels the marriage dishonors his rank, goes through with the ceremony but promptly sends his wife back to Rousillon and himself departs, with his companion Parolles, a boastful sycophant, to the Florentine war. Bertram informs Helena by letter that he never will be her husband, except in name, until she can "get the ring upon my finger, and show me a child begotten of my body that I am father to. . . . " Helena, although beloved by the Countess, leaves for Florence, disguised as a pilgrim, rather than keep Bertram in permanent exile. There she discovers that Bertram is attempting to seduce the virtuous Diana. By arrangement with Diana, Helena substitutes herself at an assignation in the dark, obtains Bertram's ring, and conceives a child. Back in France, where all characters now assemble, Bertram, confronted by the fulfillment of his stipulations, finally realizes the true beauty and character of Helena and accepts her as his wife.

Characters.   In his adaptation Shakespeare added to the story the warm-hearted Countess; a *miles gloriosus* (braggart soldier) figure with deep roots in Roman comedy, Parolles; a clear-sighted old lord, Lafeu; and a clown, Lavache, a role perhaps created in the revised version for the comedian Robert Armin. His principal additions to the story concern the exposure of Parolles and a highly elaborated denouement. The characters are clearly drawn, though not always consistent or filled in. Helena is beautifully realized in the first part of the play, gentle but determined, chaste but loving; later her involvement in the intrigue seems less a part of her personality than a device to complete the plot. Bertram is an average sensual young man, spirited but selfish; evidently Shakespeare imagined him as an "unbaked and doughy youth" who, after his follies, which are partially the result of Parolles' companionship, would come out all right in the end; he is truly enough imagined, but he is unconvincing in his conversion. Parolles is sharply observed in terms of the Elizabethan swaggerer; his unmasking is good comic business, and it is significant that Charles I retitled his copy of the play *Parolles*. Lavache is neither as witty nor as relevant as Shakespeare's best clowns, and some of his lines may even be Armin's. The king, Lafeu, and the Countess are well characterized and are good acting parts.

Critique. On the whole, *All's Well* must be considered among the least successful of Shakespeare's plays. Some of the difficulties must be ascribed to the state of the text and the probable revisions. The style of the writing is not homogeneous: excellent blank verse in Shakespeare's matured manner is set next to rhyme and doggerel; much of the poetry lacks the imaginative glow that transforms utterance into truth. The plot is well conducted for the most part, but the end of the play is superimposed on the characters, and even if theatrically effective, it is drawn out beyond its value.

The nature of the story also has interfered with the play's subsequent success. Many of the conventions are Elizabethan or earlier—the insistence on rank, the overt pursuit of a husband, and especially the "bed trick," as it has come to be called. However, the play was undoubtedly more romantic to the Elizabethans than to later generations. Much of the plot is based on folk material, fabliau, or romance, familiar and accepted for centuries, and the intrigue and resolution were once stock situations. Helena married Bertram and reclaimed him, and in her cleverness, patience, and true devotion she was sympathetic.

All's Well is now generally bracketed with *Troilus and Cressida* and *Measure for Measure* among the realistic or "bitter" comedies, and part of it plainly belongs to that period. Realistic it is, to a degree, in characterization; but its setting has no real atmosphere, and it is highly questionable whether Shakespeare's contemporaries thought of the play as bitter. More probably a practical playwright found a tale replete with popular themes that he thought could be dramatized for the pleasure of his audiences, but he was only partly successful.

ROBERT HAMILTON BALL
Queens College, City University of New York.

Bibliography

Text of *All's Well That Ends Well* was edited by J. L. Styan (Longwood 1984) and appears in *Three Problem Plays: All's Well That Ends Well, Measure for Measure, Troilus and Cressida* (Bantam 1988).

Cole, Howard C., *The All's Well Story from Boccaccio to Shakespeare* (Univ. of Ill. Press 1981).

Lawrence, William W., *Shakespeare's Problem Comedies*, 2d ed. (Ungar 1959).

Muir, Kenneth, *Shakespeare, the Comedies: A Collection of Critical Essays* (Prentice-Hall 1965).

Tillyard, Eustace M., *Shakespeare's Problem Plays* (AMS Press 1950).

ALLSPICE, ôl'spīs, is the dried, unripe fruit of the tree *Pimenta dioica*. The same name is applied to the spice prepared from it. It is called allspice because its pungent, aromatic flavor suggests cinnamon, nutmeg, and cloves. It is used, frequently with other spices, in pickling, seasoning, flavored wines, and in making mincemeat. It also is used medicinally. *Pimenta* and *pimento* are other names for allspice.

The tree from which allspice is derived is a member of the myrtle family, Myrtaceae. It is native to the West Indies, Mexico, and Central America. Most of the commercial allspice comes from wild plants growing in Jamaica. About 40 feet tall, *P. dioica* has oblong leathery leaves and abundant small, white, clustered flowers. The fruits are picked when they are green and nearly ripe, sun-dried to a reddish brown color, and then sifted to produce the spice.

The name allspice also is applied to *Calycanthus* (Carolina allspice), *Chimonanthus praecox* (Japanese allspice), and the spicebush, *Bensoin aestivale*. The fruit pulp of the Spanish sweet pepper *Capsicum* also is known as pimento.

ALLSTON, ôl'stən, **Washington** (1779–1843), American painter and author, who was largely responsible for introducing the romantic style of painting in the United States. He was called the "American Titian" for the rich color of his landscapes and Biblical and classical scenes.

Allston was born on Nov. 5, 1779, near Georgetown, S.C., where his father was a wealthy planter. After graduating from Harvard in 1800, he went to study painting, in spite of family opposition, at the Royal Academy in London under Benjamin West. From 1803 to 1808 he traveled on the Continent, spending most of his time in Rome, where he became a friend of the writers Samuel Taylor Coleridge and Washington Irving. When he returned to the United States in 1808, he married Ann Channing, sister of William Ellery Channing, the founder of American Unitarianism.

In 1811, Allston and his wife, accompanied by his pupil Samuel F.B. Morse, went to England, where they stayed until 1818. During this second stay in London, he painted most of his major works. *Dead Man Revived by Touching the Bones of the Prophet Elisha* (1811–1813) was awarded a prize by the British Institute. Other works of this period include *The Angel Liberating St. Peter from Prison* (1812) and *Uriel in the Sun* (1817).

In his day, Allston was also known for his poetry, prose, and theory of art.

Because of the sudden death of his wife, his own failing health, and financial difficulties, Allston returned to the United States in 1818. He lived in Boston until 1828, then in Cambridgeport, Mass., where he led a relatively secluded life. His second wife was Martha Dana, sister of the novelist Richard Henry Dana. Allston died in Cambridgeport on July 9, 1843.

Allston failed to achieve great success in the United States, but his romantic style was admired by young American artists. His most ambitious work, *Belshazzar's Feast*, begun in 1817 but unfinished, is in the Boston Museum of Fine Arts. Other paintings of his later period are *Moonlight Landscape* (1819), also in the Boston Museum of Fine Arts, and *Spanish Girl in Reverie* (1831), in the Metropolitan Museum in New York. Allston wrote *Sylphs of the Seasons and other Poems* (1813) and *Monaldi* (1841), a tragic romance.

ALLUVIUM, ə-lōō'vē-əm, the silt, mud, sand, or rock debris that a river or stream deposits in its channel, along its banks, and at its mouth. Thus the deltas of large rivers are alluvial deposits; the most famous examples are the deltas of the Nile, Ganges, and Mississippi rivers. When such deposits are composed of sufficiently fine material and contain organic matter, the alluvium eventually breaks down to form soil. The floodplain of a river such as the Nile has been enriched over the centuries in this manner, through the annual overflowing of its banks by the river.

Some rivers have alluviums of different ages deposited on the slopes of their valleys. The term *alluvium* is usually restricted to geologically recent deposits.

Marine alluvium is alluvium that has been produced by inundations of the sea, such as those that have from time to time overflowed the eastern coast of India. (See also RIVER; SOIL.)

ALLWARD, Walter Seymour, äl'wərd (1876–1955), Canadian sculptor who created the massive Canadian National War Memorial on Vimy Ridge in France. Born in Toronto on Nov. 18, 1876, he left school at the age of 14, learned to be a carpenter, and then became an apprentice to a firm of architects, where he remained for five years.

Turning to sculpture in 1895, Allward was commissioned to do the figure of Peace that surmounts the Northwest Rebellion Monument in Queen's Park, Toronto. He was then appointed to execute the busts of a number of famous Canadians for the art gallery of the Royal Ontario Museum in Toronto. After completing these, he did a series of works on a grand scale, including the heroic statue of Sir Oliver Mowat in Queen's Park; the massive National South African Memorial in Toronto; the allegorical Bell Memorial in Brantford, Ontario; and World War I memorials in Stratford and Peterboro, Ontario, and in Montreal.

Going to London in 1922, Allward began work on the Canadian National War Memorial for Vimy Ridge, which, overlooking the scene of the Canadian Corps's great victory in 1917, honors the Canadians killed in World War I. The stone monument, with its massive pylons and the figure of a woman brooding over her two dead sons, took 14 years to complete. Dedicated in 1936 by King Edward VIII, it is considered one of the grandest World War I memorials in Europe. Allward died in Toronto on April 24, 1955.

ALMA, al'mə, a commercial and industrial city in central Michigan, in Gratiot county, on the Pine River, 50 miles (80 km) by road north of Lansing. Industrial activities include oil refining, food processing, and light manufacturing. Alma College and the Michigan Masonic Home are located in the city.

Alma was settled in 1853 and was incorporated as a city in 1905. Population: 9,275.

ALMA, al'mə, a city in Quebec, Canada. It is located at the source of the Saguenay River, at the eastern extremity of Lake St. John (Lac St-Jean), 140 miles (225 km) north of the city of Quebec.

Alma is an industrial city and a regional service center in a mixed-farming and lumbering region. Its industries produce aluminum, lumber, paper, and hydroelectric power. There are granite quarries nearby. Alma is also the departure point for lake cruises.

Alma was first settled in 1863 and was called St-Joseph d'Alma until 1954. It absorbed four neighboring municipalities in 1962 and another in 2001. Population: 31,224.

ALMA-ATA, äl-mä'ä-tä', the largest city and former capital of the Republic of Kazakstan. Known as Alma-Ata from 1921, the city, after the 1991 independence of Kazakstan, adopted the Kazak form for its name, Almaty. Located in the eastern part of Central Asia near the border with China, Almaty is approximately 2,000 miles (3,200 km) east-southeast of Moscow on the Turkestan-Siberian (Turksib) Railroad.

At the southern edge of Almaty are dense orchards, which help to make it one of Central Asia's most beautiful cities. Fruit and vegetable canning are the chief industries. The city has railroad repair shops, heavy machinery plants, sawmills, and metalworks.

Almaty is the cultural center of Kazakstan. Al-Fārābī Kazak State University, formerly the S. M. Kirov State University, was founded in the city in 1934. The Kazak Academy of Sciences, founded in 1945, also is in Almaty. The city has a conservatory and opera houses and is the center of the film industry.

The present city, on the site of an old Kazak settlement called Almatay, was established as a Russian fortress in 1854 and named Verny. Although the city was destroyed by earthquakes in 1887 and 1910, it remained the administrative center of the Semirechye military district until 1917. It was renamed Alma-Ata in 1921 and replaced Qyzylorda (Kzyl-Orda) as the capital of Kazakstan in 1929. In 1997 the capital moved to Astana.

In 1930 the city entered a period of phenomenal growth when it became a terminus of the Turksib railroad, linking Siberia and Central Asia. On July 6, 1994, the Supreme Kenges, Kazakstan's parliament, approved a proposal to move the nation's capital to the city of Aqmola, later called Astana. The official transfer took place on Nov. 8, 1997. Population: 1,129,400 (1999 census).

ALMA COLLEGE, al'mə, a small, Presbyterian, coeducational liberal arts institution in Alma, Mich., founded in 1886. Beyond the liberal arts offerings, the curriculum includes courses in business, management, and education. Dual-degree programs with other institutions allow students to pursue studies in natural resources, engineering, and occupational therapy. The college also offers work experience, accelerated degree programs, and interdisciplinary opportunities in Asian studies, public affairs, and environmental studies.

ALMA RIVER, al'mə, in the Crimean peninsula of Ukraine. It rises in the central section of the Crimean Mountains, just west of Alushta, and flows west for 53 miles (85 km) into the Bay of Kalamita about 16 miles (26 km) north of Sevastopol'. The river is noted for the scenic beauty of its banks.

The Alma River was the site of a historic battle during the Crimean War. The allied armies of Britain, France, and Turkey, led by the British commander Lord Raglan and the French commander Armand de Saint-Arnaud, met the Russian army, headed by Prince Aleksandr Sergeyevich Menshikov, on Sept. 20, 1854. The Russians were outnumbered almost two to one. After a bitter struggle lasting nearly five hours, the Russians scattered in defeat.

ALMA-TADEMA, Lawrence, al′mə-tad′ə-mə (1836–1912), Anglo-Dutch painter whose sentimental historical paintings were immensely admired by his contemporaries. His subjects were drawn from bygone civilizations, beginning with a Frankish series, then a series on Egyptian life, and finally, studies of classical Greece and Rome. He was noted for accurate attention to historical detail, but his style was sometimes criticized as being coldly academic. He added "Alma" (his godfather's name) to his surname when he became a British citizen in 1873.

Alma-Tadema was born in Dronrijp, Holland, on Jan. 8, 1836. He studied at the Antwerp Academy of Fine Arts under Gustave Wappers and Baron Hendrik Leys. A visit to Italy in 1863 stimulated his lifelong interest in ancient cultures, especially those of classical Greece and Rome. He settled in England in 1870 and earned wide recognition for two paintings exhibited that year at the Royal Academy—*An Amateur Roman* and *A Juggler.* Alma-Tadema's portrayals of Greek and Roman subjects were his most admired works. Among the best known of his more than 500 paintings are *Clotilde at the Tomb of Her Grandchildren* (1858); *Egyptians, Three Thousand Years Ago* (1864), which won a gold medal at the Paris Salon; *Audience at Agrippa's* (1876); and *Roses of Heliogabalus* (1888).

Alma-Tadema became an associate of the Royal Academy in 1876 and a full academician in 1879. He was knighted in 1899 and awarded the Order of Merit in 1907. He died in Wiesbaden, Germany, on June 25, 1912.

ALMADÉN, äl-mä-thān′, a town in Spain, in Ciudad Real province, 50 miles (80 km) southwest of the town of Ciudad Real. It was called Sisapon in ancient times. Almadén is widely known for its rich mercury mines, which have been worked since the Roman period. The mines, which are government-owned, produce about one-fifth of the world's supply of mercury. The town contains a ruined Moorish castle and a school of mining. Population: 6,830 (2001 census).

ALMAGEST.   See Ptolemy of Alexandria.

ALMAGRO, Diego de, äl-mä′grō (c. 1475–1538), Spanish soldier who was a leader in the conquest of Peru. He was born near Ciudad Real in about 1475. He went to Panama in 1514 and was a partner in Francisco Pizarro's first (1524–1525) and second (1526–1528) expeditions south. Subsequently he joined Pizarro in the subjugation of Peru and in the murder of the Inca ruler Atahualpa in 1533. After frequent disputes with Pizarro about their respective shares in the conquests, Almagro was granted the region south of Cuzco (Cusco).

When Almagro's expedition (1535–1537) to his new domain proved profitless, he returned and wrested Cuzco from Hernando Pizarro. In the ensuing struggle, the Pizarro forces defeated Almagro and executed him in Cuzco in July 1538. He was avenged by his son Diego (1520–1542), who headed an insurrection in which Francisco Pizarro was assassinated in 1541. Diego was defeated at Chupas and executed.

Like most of the conquistadors, Almagro showed himself capable of enduring great privations with heroic constancy, but he was cruel and rapacious in success.

ALMANAC, ôl′mə-nak, a book or table containing a calendar of days, weeks, and months. It usually includes such data as the times of the rising and setting of sun and moon, moon phases, positions and phenomena of heavenly bodies, eclipses, times of high and low tides, a list of holy days and holidays, and other miscellaneous information.

Almanacs were among the earliest known publications in many parts of the world. An Egyptian example in the British Museum dating from the era of Ramses II (reigned 1290–1223 B.C.) shows lucky and unlucky days in black and red, notes religious festivals, and predicts the fate of children born on stated days. The Greeks of Alexandria are known to have had almanacs. The Roman *dies fasti,* listing the days for legal and public business, were precursors of the almanac.

Early Almanacs in Europe.   The horae, psalters, and missals of the Middle Ages usually included calendars of the holy days. In England Roger Bacon in his *Opus majus* (1267) first used the word *almanac* in tables recording the apparent movements of the heavenly bodies. A manuscript in the British Museum, written in English, contains a calendar and rules for its computation and predicts eclipses for a period of years beginning in 1431. There are extant manuscript almanacs written on long strips of vellum with pictorial calendars of the saints' days. On the Continent the first printed almanac appeared in 1457.

Regiomontanus (Johann Müller), a German mathematician and astronomer, produced the first almanac of real importance, *Ephemerides ab anno 1475–1506* (1473), which was used by Columbus and other navigators. Superstition, belief in the influence of the stars, and the desire to foresee the future created popular interest in almanacs, and for two or three centuries after the invention of printing, printers, astrologers, and quacks of all kinds fed on the public demand. In France prophetic almanacs were widely circulated. One of the most prominent was the *Almanach Liègeois,* which began publication in 1636.

In England almanacs were issued both as sheets to be hung on the wall and in book form. Prognostications were forbidden for a time; for these, English readers depended on translations. The *Kalendrier des Bergers* was first translated and printed in London in 1497 as *The Shepheards Calendar;* later editions followed. Although prognostications slipped in around 1540, prophecies usually were confined to the weather. There were exceptions, including *A Newe Almanacke and Prognostication for the Yere of our Lord. 1567 Wherein is Declared the Right Dysposition and State of the whole Yeare, Concerning the Weather, and Sicknesse Comming Therof: with a Prediction of such Thinges as Shall follow the Terrible Eclypse of the Sunne this Yere Appearing, by the Example and Effecte of the like Eclypse seene in the Yeare. 1540 . . .* "By Elis Bomelius Doctor in Physicke." Such almanacs were written by students or practitioners of astronomy or astrology or by physicians. Advice on the treatment of all sorts of ailments was a common feature. Each month had its herb; special days for its use were indicated. *Old Moore's Almanack,* first published in England in about 1680, was the popular home remedy book of its day. Revived in 1966, it continues the 15th-century tradition of predicting catastrophes.

After 1571, by patent of Queen Elizabeth I, all almanacs were published in London by Watkins and Roberts. A new patent was granted by

James I to the Stationers' Company and the universities of Oxford and Cambridge, the king himself profiting from the royalties. The sole right of publication later was acquired by the Stationers' Company, which always made its prophecies favorable to the ruling sovereign. In 1775 the courts declared the monopoly illegal.

Early Almanacs in America. In America *An Almanack for New England for the Year 1639*, compiled by "William Pierce, Mariner," and published in Cambridge, Mass., was the first printed almanac. Almanacs swiftly multiplied. John Tulley of Saybrook, Conn., published in 1687 the first farmer's almanac, which included a weather forecast. Benjamin Franklin's brother James began his *Rhode Island Almanac* in 1728. Outstanding were the almanacs of Nathaniel Ames, physician and innkeeper of Dedham, Mass., and his son of the same name. These almanacs, published continuously from 1725 to 1775, sold 50,000 to 60,000 copies annually. Added to the features that had become traditional in Europe were scraps of wisdom, bits of history, occasional verse, jests, and moral precepts. Ames's original almanac is important in itself and as a forerunner of *Poor Richard's Almanack*. In Philadelphia in 1687 William Bradford published a single-leaf almanac compiled by Daniel Leeds; his son Titan Leeds continued the publication (with some interruptions).

In 1732, when Benjamin Franklin launched *Poor Richard's Almanack*, Leeds's almanac was one of at least six published in Philadelphia. Having selected Leeds as his most formidable competitor, Franklin published a forecast of his approaching death on a day soon to come and then announced the sad event. The prediction and Leeds's denial were widely publicized, and *Poor Richard* was a prompt success. Under the pseudonym *Richard Saunders*, Franklin gave his wit free play. He borrowed proverbs and maxims from English and other literature and converted them to plain, rigorous prose. He attacked laziness, thriftlessness, avarice, and the deadly sins. For 25 years *Poor Richard* was a best-seller, and it proved the foundation of Franklin's fortune and career.

Contemporary Almanacs. The *Old Farmer's Almanac*, founded by Robert Bailey Thomas in 1793 and still popular, is the oldest continuously published periodical in the United States. Published by Yankee Publishing, it retains its old form and much of its old content, prophesying wind and weather and including droll anecdotes, old jokes, moral tales, and homespun verse.

The *American Almanac and Repository of Useful Knowledge*, published in Boston from 1830 to 1861, seems to have set the pattern for 19th- and 20th-century almanacs, most of which have been published by newspapers in various parts of the country. The *New York Tribune's Tribune Almanac and Political Register*, begun as the *Whig Almanac* in 1838, was an attempt to disseminate "the more important and interesting facts touching the great political struggle of the times." It supplied election statistics, political platforms, and information on national, state, and local governments until it folded in 1914. (*The Almanac of American Politics*, launched in 1972, is a modern successor.) *The World Almanac and Book of Facts*, founded in 1868, evolved into a highly successful book covering a wide range of statistical, historical, and other information. Other general almanacs followed, including the *Information Please Almanac*, begun in 1947 and later (from 1997) also

Facsimile of the title page of *Poor Richard's Almanack*.

issued as *Time Almanac*; the *Universal Almanac* (1989–1997), which became the basis for the *New York Times Almanac* (from 1997); and the *Wall Street Journal Almanac* (from 1997). Corresponding online editions also appeared.

The *British, Whitaker's, Canadian,* and *Australian* almanacs and the *Almanach national* in France have flourished for many years. Astronomical almanacs for use in sea and air navigation are published by official bodies in Britain, France, the United States, and elsewhere.

The word *almanac* has been used often in titles of books that do not include the usual almanac features. Among these are the *Almanach de Gotha*, a genealogical record of royalty and nobility in Europe; the *Almanach des lettres*, a yearbook of French literary output; the *Biography Almanac*; and the *Places Rated Almanac*. The day-by-day almanac format was loosely adapted for Minnesota Public Radio's *A Writer's Almanac*, a program hosted by Garrison Keillor featuring poetry and snippets of history keyed to the day.

HERBERT S. HIRSHBERG*, *Author of "Subject Guide to Reference Books"*

Bibliography: Capp, Bernard, *English Almanacs: 1500–1800; Astrology and the Popular Press* (Cornell Univ. Press 1979); Drake, Milton, *Almanacs of the United States*, 2 vols. (McGraw 1962); Perkins, Maureen, *Visions of the Future: Almanacs, Time, and Cultural Change, 1775–1870* (Clarendon Press 1996); Stowell, Marion Barber, *Early American Almanacs: The Colonial Weekday Bible* (B. Franklin 1977).

ALMANSA, äl-män′sä, a town in Albacete province, Spain. Formerly called Almanza, it is located 43 miles (69 km) southeast of the city of Albacete. A decisive battle was fought near Almansa during the War of the Spanish Succession. On April 25, 1707, the French, under the duke of Berwick, defeated the English, Portuguese, and Spanish forces of the Habsburg archduke Charles. Population: 23,531 (2001 census).

ALMANZOR. See MANSUR, AL-.

ALMATY. See ALMA-ATA.

ALMEIDA, äl-mā′ē-thà, a town in Guarda district, Portugal. On the river Coa, it is situated 25 miles (40 km) northeast of Guarda on the Spanish frontier. Olive oil and cheeses are processed in the vicinity. The town is noted for its sulfur waters.

Almeida was at one time one of the chief strongholds of Portugal. In 1762 it was taken by the Spaniards, who later surrendered it. A large portion of its fortifications was destroyed by the French in their retreat from Portugal in 1811. The fortifications were soon restored by the English. Population: 8,423 (2001 census).

ALMERÍA, äl-mä-rē′ä, a seaport city in Spain and the capital of Almería province. It lies 104 miles (167 km) east of Málaga, at the head of the Gulf of Almería, an inlet of the Mediterranean Sea.

Almería has one of the best harbors in Spain and is the terminus of a railroad from Sierra Alhamilla. A large export trade is carried on in white grapes and other fruits, esparto grass, iron, and lead; coal and lumber are the chief imports. Shoes, furniture, felts, flour products, and tiles are manufactured.

Places of interest include the Alcazaba, an old Moorish fort with towers rising above the city; a fortresslike cathedral dating from 1524; and a seismological station.

Almería was founded by the Phoenicians, who named it Bártulos. When the city came under Roman control, it was called Portus Magnus or Virgitanus. Under Moorish domination, beginning in the 8th century A.D., the city received its present name and became a prosperous seaport. In 1937, during the Spanish Civil War, Almería was shelled by German warships and seriously damaged. Population: 166,328 (2001 census).

ALMOHAD, äl′mō-had, a Berber dynasty that ruled over Morocco, Algeria, Tunisia, and much of Spain in the 1100s and 1200s. Its name in Arabic is *al-Muwaḥḥidūn.* It began as a religious movement founded by Muḥammad ibn Tūmart (1078?–1130) in reaction both against the puritanism of the Almoravid dynasty and against the numerous pagan survivals in Islam as it was practiced in North Africa. The call for religious reform was soon transformed into an anti-Almoravid political movement, and Ibn Tūmart became the head of a tiny state in the Atlas Mountains.

His successor, Caliph ʿAbd al-Muʾmin ibn-ʿAlī (reigned 1129–1162), carried on his cause with such skill and energy that by 1159 he had taken over all the Almoravids' African territory and added to it the territories of the Hammadids in eastern Algeria and of the Zirids in Tunisia. He also established a protectorate over most of the petty states that had succeeded the Almoravids in Muslim Spain. His conquests brought Barbary

under the rule of a single authority of native origin—for the first and last time.

Accounts of the organization of the Almohad empire indicate that ʿAbd al-Muʾmin and his successors were administrators of exceptional talent. Yūsuf (reigned 1162–1184) and Yaʿqūb al-Manṣūr (reigned 1184–1198) ruled the empire vigorously and consolidated their hold on Andalusia. Al-Manṣūr won a great victory over Alfonso VIII of Castile at Alarcos, near Ciudad Real, in 1195. This was the climax of Almohad glory. Their empire stretched from Castile to Tripoli, and intellectual and cultural activities flourished. Many of the great buildings of this period still stand, particularly those planned by al-Manṣūr, such as the Giralda at Seville.

The Almohads soon began to yield to external pressure. Alfonso VIII had his revenge at Las Navas de Tolosa, near Linares, in 1212, and the drama of the slow crumbling of Spanish Islam entered its last phase. The Berber Marinids in Morocco and the Ziyanids in Algeria gradually usurped the Almohad authority. In Tunisia the Almohad governors seized their independence in 1228, although they maintained the Almohad traditions for another three centuries. Internal strife under a succession of incompetent caliphs brought about the Almohads' final collapse in 1269.

J. F. P. HOPKINS, *University of Cambridge*

ALMOND, ä′mənd, the name of a popular edible nut of the tree that bears it. The tree (*Prunus amygdalus*) is a member of the rose family, Rosaceae. It has been in cultivation in eastern Mediterranean countries and the Middle East from very early times. Today it is widely grown in Spain, Italy, northern Africa, California (introduced about the middle of the 19th century), Australia, and southern Africa. Almonds are sold in greater quantities than any other nut.

Tree and Nut. Similar to the peach tree in appearance, the almond tree grows to about 25 feet (7.5 meters), and its white or rose flowers, 1.5 to 2 inches across (3.8 to 5 cm), appear early in spring. Unlike the peach, with its soft and juicy flesh, the flesh of the almond is dry and leathery. As this dry fruit (drupe) splits open, the seed, which has a thin brown coat (endocarp), is exposed. Commercial almonds consist of this thin, pitted, light-colored endocarp enclosing the seed, or kernel.

Several principal horticultural varieties of the tree, with innumerable forms, are generally recognized. In temperate climates the trees are usually selected for their flowers, which are often bright pink and double, rather than as bearers, whereas in warmer climates the trees are chosen for the quality of their nuts.

For commercial purposes, almonds typically are graded according to the thickness of the shell as paper-shelled, soft-shelled, or thick-shelled. Normally, two main varieties of almonds are recognized: the sweet, used in confectioneries and desserts, and the bitter, used for making oil and flavoring.

Cultivation. Successful cultivation of good bearers requires deep soil, a suitable warm climate with adequate rainfall (16 to 40 inches, or 410 to 1,020 mm, per year), and cross-pollination, as most varieties are self-sterile. Since honeybees are the most important pollinators, hives of bees are sometimes placed in the orchards at flowering time to increase the crop.

Almond trees in California (*above, left*) bloom early in the year. The green fruit (*above, right*) then forms, and its outer hull dries and splits open to expose the almond seed and kernel (*below*), which is eaten.

Over a hundred varieties, imported and new, are grown in California. Non-pareil is the best all-round variety. The bitter almond tree is often used as a stock on which sweet almond and other fruits are grafted or budded.

Almond Oil. Almond oil is volatile. It usually is derived from dried ripe kernels of bitter almond, apricot, and peach. It contains amygdalin ($C_{20}H_{27}NO_{11}$), a sugar derivative, which yields a sugar plus benzaldehyde and hydrocyanic acid with the addition of the enzyme emulsin. The hydrocyanic acid accounts for the bitter taste of bitter almond, and the benzaldehyde is responsible for the typical almond flavor. Sugar derivatives such as amygdalin, which yield cyanides, are not used widely in pharmacy and medicine because of the dangerous properties of hydrocyanic acid. They are used, however, as sedatives in cough syrups. Sweet almonds usually contain 44 to 55 percent oil; bitter almonds contain 38 to 45 percent. The oil is generally prepared from bitter almonds since they are cheaper than sweet almonds, which are preferred for eating.

In addition to these differences in taste and contents, bitter almonds are shorter and wider than sweet almonds.

THEODOR JUST, *Chicago Natural History Museum*

ALMONTE, al'mont, an unincorporated place in Ontario, Canada, 35 miles (56 km) southwest of Ottawa. It is situated on the Mississippi River, a branch of the Ottawa River. It is an agricultural-supply, electronics, and food-processing center.

The area was settled in 1821 and was first known as Waterford, for a crossing of the river. It was subsequently named Shepherd's Falls and then Shipman's Mills after early settlers. In 1856 it was renamed in honor of Gen. Juan Almonte, a Mexican military and political figure who opposed U.S. expansion. Incorporated as a town in 1871, Almonte was merged into the new town of Mississippi Mills in 1998.

ALMORAVID, al-mō'rə-vid, a Muslim Berber dynasty that ruled Morocco and part of Spain during the 11th and 12th centuries. The Arabic form of the name is *al-Murabit*.

The dynasty had its origins in a puritanical religious movement inspired by Abd Allah Ibn Yasin among the Lamtuna and Gadala Berbers of Mauritania. With missionary zeal, followers of Ibn Yasin moved southward to spread Islam among the pagan Negroes and northward to reform the decadent and heretical Berber principalities of Morocco. The firm establishment of Almoravid power in Morocco was signalized by the founding of the city of Marrakech in 1070. By 1083 all of Morocco and part of Algeria acknowledged the rule of the Almoravid leader Yusuf Ibn Tashfin (reigned 1071–1106).

Meanwhile, Islamic rule in Spain was being challenged by Christian armies that were reconquering the lands they had held before the advent of the Muslims. In 1086, Yusuf answered the call of the Abbadid rulers and crossed into Spain, where at Sagrajas he resoundingly defeated Alfonso VI of Castile. He returned to Morocco, but the corrupt and quarrelsome Spanish Muslims, whom Yusuf despised, soon had to call for his help again. Before long, Yusuf decided to take the affairs of Muslim Spain into his own hands. At his death in 1106 the Almoravids controlled more than half the Iberian Peninsula and western Africa as far as the Niger and Senegal rivers, including Morocco and part of modern Algeria. This was the culmination of Almoravid power.

Under Yusuf's son Ali (reigned 1106–1142) the empire began to decline. Christian pressure from the north was unrelenting, and the Almohad dynasty, rising in Morocco, threatened Almoravid power from the south. Added to these destructive forces were the inveterate Berber tendency to political fragmentation and the racial and cultural animosity between the Berbers and the Andalusian (Spanish) Muslims. Preoccupied by the Almohad threat, the Almoravids gradually withdrew to Morocco, yielding their Spanish possessions to a confused collection of petty rulers. With the fall of Marrakech to the Almohads in 1147, Almoravid rule finally came to an end.

By the time their power collapsed, the Almoravids had made three lasting bequests: they gave to the cities of northern Morocco and western Algeria the Andalusian stamp that they still bear; they gave to northwest African Islam a uniform Malikite orthodoxy that has never been broken; and they founded a unified Moroccan state within the boundaries that it still maintains.

See also ABBADID; ALMOHAD.

J. F. P. HOPKINS, *Cambridge University*

ALMQVIST, Karl Jonas Love, älm'kvist (1793–1866), Swedish writer. His name is also spelled *Almquist.*

Born in Stockholm on Nov. 28, 1793, he graduated from the University of Uppsala in 1815. Thereafter he had a varied career as a civil servant, farmer, teacher, cleric, and author. In 1851, accused of forgery and implicated in the attempted murder of a creditor, he fled to the United States. From 1865 he used the name Westermann and lived in Bremen, Germany, where he died on Sept. 26, 1866.

Almqvist's fame rests on his *Törnrosens bok* (*The Book of the Thorn Rose*, 14 vols., 1832–51), a remarkable series of novels, stories, plays, and poems ranging in tone from the extravagantly romantic to the realistic. He gained notoriety in 1839 with his novel *Det går an*, which defended cohabitation without marriage; it was published in English as *Sara Videbecke* (1919). Almqvist was an amateur musician and set some of his lyrics to music.

ALOE, al'ō, is a group of succulent plants native to dry areas, especially southern Africa. It is also found in northern Africa, southern Europe, Syria, and Arabia, and is cultivated in warm regions of both hemispheres. The stem of aloes generally is short, with a basal rosette of leaves. Some species, however, are treelike with forked branches and may reach a height of 65 feet (20 meters) and a width of 15 feet (4.5 meters) at the base. The leaves of aloes are usually elongated, frequently pointed, blunt- or spiny-toothed, and sometimes blotched or mottled. The red or yellow tubular flowers are formed on a stalk in simple or branched clusters.

The genus *Aloe* belongs to the lily family, Liliaceae. There are about 200 species. A common short-stemmed type is *A. aristata*, and a common treelike type is *A. bainesii*. The "American aloe" is not a true aloe, but *Agave americana*, the century plant.

ALOES, al'ōz, the dried, bitter, resinous juice prepared from the crushed leaves of various plants of the genus *Aloe.* Known to the ancient Greeks, the juice continues to be used medicinally as a purgative, especially in the East, and in the treatment of burns. It also has served as an ingredient in cosmetics.

Several species of *Aloe* are grown for aloe juice. *A. perryi*, which yields Socotra aloes, has been gathered on Socotra, an island in the Indian Ocean, for over 2,000 years. The commercial Zanzibar and Bombay aloes also are derived from this species. *A. vera*, long grown in Africa, Arabia, and India, and since the middle of the 17th century in Barbados, yields the Barbados aloes. Another commercial variety, *A. vera* var. *chinensis*, is cultivated in Curaçao. Cape aloes, from the Cape region of southern Africa, include several species—*A. africana*, *A. ferox*, *A. cuccotrina*, *A. plicatilis*, and probably some hybrids.

ALOESWOOD, al'ōz-wood, the wood of a number of species of the genus *Aquilaria*, especially *A. agallocha*, but also *A. malaccensis* and *A. sinensis.* These trees are native to tropical southeastern Asia. Their aromatic resinous heartwood (also called agalloch, eaglewood, and lignaloes) is burned as incense and used for cabinetwork. Aloeswood may have been the aloes of the Old Testament.

ALOMPRA (1714–1760), ə-lom'prə, king who reunified Burma (Myanmar) and founded its last dynasty, the Konbaung. In Burma he is known as Alaungpaya.

Alompra was a minor chief from Shwebo, in northern Burma. In 1752 the Mon king of Pegu in southern Burma captured Ava, the seat of the Toungoo dynasty, which until then had ruled the north. Refusing to take an oath to the Mons, Alompra led a resistance and declared himself king. The next year he retook Ava. In 1757 he destroyed Pegu, thus reuniting Burma.

In 1758–1759, Alompra conquered Manipur in northeastern India. Finally, in 1760 he marched through Tenasserim and invaded Siam (Thailand), hoping to repopulate devastated southern Burma with Mon refugees and Thais captured during the campaign. But after failing to take the Siamese capital, Ayutthaya (Ayuthia), he withdrew, dying on his return home.

Alompra gave the southern village of Dagon the name Yangon (Rangoon) and promoted its development as a capital and Burma's center of foreign trade.

ALONSO, Dámaso, ä-lôn'sō (1898–1990), Spanish poet and literary critic. Alonso was born in Madrid on Oct. 22, 1898. Professor of Romance philology at the University of Madrid from 1939 to 1968, he also taught at universities in Britain, Germany, and the Americas and was president of the Spanish Academy. He died in Madrid on Jan. 24, 1990.

Alonso's *Oscura noticia* ("Dark Message") and especially *Hijos de la ira* ("Children of Wrath"), both published in 1944, established him as one of the leading Spanish poets of his generation. The poem *Insomnio* (*Insomnia*), in the second of these collections, expresses his anguish, portraying Madrid as a city of the dead. In *Hombre y Dios* (1955; "Man and God"), he finally reaches an accommodation with the Deity. Alonso's criticism focused on Spanish poets of the Golden Age, particularly Góngora and St. John of the Cross; his work restored Góngora's baroque preeminence.

ALOR, a'lôr, one of the Lesser Sunda Islands of Indonesia, 20 miles (32 km) northwest of Timor. The island is 60 miles (96 km) long and 15 miles (24 km) broad, and has an area of 906 square miles (2,347 sq km). Kalabahi, the principal town, is situated on a sheltered harbor at the western end. Alor is mountainous, the highest point, at the eastern end, rising to 5,791 feet (1,765 meters). The coastal population lives on fishing and commerce, while corn (maize), cotton, and coconuts are cultivated in the interior.

ALOR SETAR, a'lôr sə-tär', a city in northwestern Malaysia. The capital of the state of Kedah, on the Malay Peninsula, it lies on the west bank of the Kedah River, 10 miles (16 km) from the Strait of Malacca and near the border of Thailand. Alor Setar has an important rice trade and a noted mosque. Population: 124,412 (1991 census).

ALP ARSLAN (c. 1030–1073), älp ärs-län', the second sultan of the Seljuk Turks. In 1060 or 1061 he succeeded his father, Chagri, as ruler of Khurasan, and in 1063 he inherited the lands of his uncle Togrul, the first sultan, in western Iran and Iraq. Thus he united the two Seljuk realms into one kingdom. He was recognized as sultan by the caliph in Baghdad.

In 1064, Alp Arslan conquered Armenia, and in 1064 and 1068 he subjugated Georgia. In 1071 he defeated and captured the Byzantine Emperor Romanus IV Diogenes in a battle near Manzikert (now Malazgirt, Turkey), north of Lake Van. Alp Arslan soon released Romanus in return for a ransom, a promised tribute, and an alliance. In 1072 the sultan advanced across the Oxus River (Amu Darya) against the Karakhanids. Wounded by a prisoner, he died in January 1073.

Alp Arslan was primarily a conqueror. Although he failed to follow up his victory at Manzikert, the Byzantines never fully recovered from the battle, which ensured the eventual Turkish conquest of Anatolia. Alp Arslan left the administration of his empire to his innovative Persian vizier, Nizam al-Mulk, who also served under the sultan's son and successor, Malik Shah.

ALPACA, al-pak′ə, a camel-like mammal (*Lama pacos*) of the family Camelidae that inhabits the central Andean highlands of South America. Closely related to the domesticated llama (*Lama glama*) and the wild guanaco (*Lama guanicoe*), it is one of the few domesticated animals native to the Western Hemisphere. Living in association with man perhaps as early as 5000 B.C., the alpaca is not a beast of burden but has been an important source of meat and wool since pre-Columbian times. Today the alpaca is found from the Pampa de Junín of central Peru south through the Lake Titicaca basin of southern Peru and western Bolivia and into northern Chile.

Description. Measuring about 2.5 to 3.5 feet (0.8 to 1.1 meters) at the shoulder and weighing from 150 to 225 pounds (68 to 102 kg), the alpaca is smaller and more compact than the llama and has shorter ears, finer wool, and a flattened, rather than erect, tail. Alpacas may be subdivided into *suri* (having long, silky, shiny fleeces) and *wakayo* (having inferior fleeces). Commercial interests generally prefer white wool, but Quechua and Aymara breeders maintain flocks in varied colors, in part for ease of identification. There are elaborate native taxonomies of colors and markings.

Adaptation and Behavior. Domesticated camelids inhabit the high-altitude grasslands known as the *puna*. More delicate and timid than the llama, the alpaca grazes primarily in well-watered environments above 13,000 feet (4,000 meters), characterized by peaty, alkaline swamps known as *bofedales,* which are sometimes expanded by irrigation. Such environments are more common in the humid Andes of southern Peru and northwestern Bolivia than in arid southwestern Bolivia and northern Chile. Because they tolerate various environmental conditions less well than do llamas, alpacas range less widely and consume a more limited variety of fodder.

Reproduction. Like the llama, the alpaca has a gestation period of 11 months, culminating with the birth of one kid in the austral summer (December–March). All camelids, including the wild guanaco and vicuña (*Lama vicugna* or *Vicugna vicugna*), can interbreed, but llama-alpaca hybrids are the most common. These are known as *wari* (Quechua) or *huarizo* (Spanish).

Value and Uses. Among experts there is a strong diversity of opinion as to the chronology of domestication, which probably resulted from human control over camelid territories leading indi-

© WAYNE BERNHARDSON

ALPACA KIDS do not produce the lustrous, silky fleece for which alpacas are prized until their second year.

rectly to control over breeding in semidomesticated animals, and eventually to herding of fully domesticated animals. In the immediate pre-Columbian era, Andean herders exchanged alpaca wool and jerked meat (*cha′rki*) for agricultural products, such as maize and coca, from lower elevations. For native Quechua and Aymara herders, the alpaca has been an important source of cash since the late 19th century, when the Peruvian southern railway facilitated wool exports to Europe via the Pacific port of Mollendo. Both freshly butchered and processed alpaca meat are locally important in urban areas of food-deficient regions such as the coastal Atacama Desert.

In addition to their economic uses, alpacas, along with other livestock, and their textiles serve important ritual functions in Andean life.

Classification. Many archaeologists believe the guanaco to be the forerunner of both llamas and alpacas, but the difficulty of identifying osteological remains of overlapping sizes and similar morphology belonging to interfertile species has confused the issue. Others believe the ancestral species to be extinct.

ALPENA, al-pē′nə, a city in northeastern Michigan, is a Great Lakes port and the seat of Alpena county. It is situated on Thunder Bay, an arm of Lake Huron, 230 miles (370 km) by road north of Detroit. The city's major industry is the manufacture of cement, the limestone for which comes from large quarries nearby. Alpena also makes machinery, automobile parts, hardboard, paper, and hydraulic cylinders. The community is a summer and winter resort, with an annual winter carnival, and good hunting and fishing areas within easy reach. Alpena Community College is situated in the city.

The first settlement at Alpena was a trading post established in 1835. It was laid out as a village in 1853 and was incorporated as a city in 1871. During the last half of the 19th century, Alpena was a major sawmilling center. Limestone quarrying began in the vicinity in 1903. Population: 11,304.

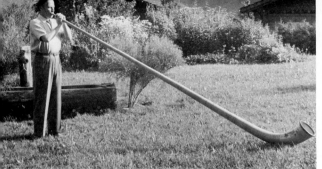

ALPENHORN, used in Alps to signal and call cattle.

ALPENHORN, al'pən-hôrn, a musical instrument used by the mountaineers in Switzerland and, with variations, by other mountain peoples. Also called the *alpine horn* or *alphorn,* it is used for signaling and for calling cattle.

The Swiss alpenhorn is 3 to 12 feet long (1 to 3½ meters), occasionally slightly curved, and made from wood covered with fiber or bark. The form varies from locality to locality. Its notes are restricted to the open harmonics of the tube ("bugle" scale). The traditional melody played on it is the *Ranz des vaches.*

ALPES-DE-HAUTE-PROVENCE, älp'də-ōt-prō-väns', a department in southeastern France, on the Italian border. The name of the department was Basses-Alpes until April 1970. Most of its area of 2,698 square miles (7,000 sq km) is mountainous. The highest point is the Aiguille de Chambeyron (11,155 feet, or 3,400 meters).

Except in the valleys the soil is not fertile, but lavender, which is widely cultivated in Provence, is processed in the department. Sheep raising is important. Digne is the capital. Population: 139,561 (1999 census).

ALPHA PARTICLES, al'fə pär'ti-kəlz, are positively charged particles emitted spontaneously from the nucleus of a radioactive element, such as radium. An alpha particle consists of two protons, which have positive charges, and two neutrons, which have no charge. When a radioactive element emits an alpha particle from its nucleus, the atomic number decreases by two because the element loses two protons. Thus, when a radioactive element emits an alpha particle, it changes to another element.

The first major step toward the discovery of alpha particles was made in 1896 by Antoine Becquerel, who observed that a photographic plate became fogged when near a uranium compound. He found that the fogging was caused by radiation given off by the uranium compound. In 1899, Ernest Rutherford discovered two types of emissions from radioactive substances. He designated these types as alpha and beta radiation. (In 1903 he discovered a third type and called it gamma radiation.) Rutherford also established that an alpha particle has two protons and two neutrons.

As early as 1910, Rutherford used alpha particles emitted by radioactive elements to bombard matter in order to determine the structure of atoms. After the development of particle accelerators in the 1930's, these machines were used to accelerate alpha particles to bombard target materials in order to find out more about the nature of matter. See also PARTICLE ACCELERATORS; RADIATION; RADIOACTIVITY.

ALPHABET, al'fə-bət, a collection of symbols (generally between 20 and 30), known as letters, that are intended to represent in writing the various elementary sounds used by the human voice in speech. Alphabetic writing now is found in most advanced cultures, with the important exceptions of Chinese and Japanese.

The term "alphabet," from the Latin *alphabetum,* was first used by the early Christian scholars Tertullian and St. Jerome. The word is derived from the names of the first two letters of the Greek alphabet—*alpha* and *beta.* These names, and most of the other names of the Greek letters, are of Semitic origin, although the Semitic names are not quite identical with the Greek. (The Hebrew word for "A" is *aleph;* for "B," *beth.*)

1. Development of Writing

Pre-Alphabetic Writing. The modern alphabet is the most recent development in a long train of events. Early man used primitive means of communication, such as memory-aid devices, notched sticks, and knotted cords. These were followed by iconography, which consists of designs, geometric symbols, and drawings of animals and natural objects. Iconographic writing found on cave walls dates back as far as 10,000 or 20,000 B.C.

Ideographic, or synthetic, writing was the first stage of true writing. This form of writing, used by many peoples in all parts of the world, consisted of a series of pictures telling connected stories. The most famous scripts of the ancient world, including cuneiform, Egyptian hieroglyphics, and Mayan and Aztec scripts, were ideographic in origin, although they became partly phonetic as they developed. Also known as "transitional" and "analytic," these scripts were more or less complete systems of writing.

Phonetic writing—such as that found in the Minoan Linear B script, which dates from about 1500 B.C., and in modern Japanese and Korean—is the graphic counterpart of speech, with each element corresponding to a specific sound in the language represented. In syllabic systems the symbols ceased to be self-interpreting pictures (as they had been in earlier stages of writing), and no connection exists between the shape of the symbol and the sound. The individual signs represent syllables or vowels, the smallest elements of words that can be isolated and spoken.

Alphabetic Writing. Alphabetic writing, the last and the most highly developed stage, is the most efficient and convenient form of writing and is the most readily adaptable to almost any language. The individual symbols, representing phonemes (consonants or vowels), are like bricks with which any word can be built.

Historians of language generally agree that all existing alphabets, as well as those no longer used, derive from one original alphabet. No other system of writing has had so extensive, so intricate, and so interesting a history. In its broad lines, this story can be traced back to the late 2d millennium B.C., but many details, particularly concerning the origin of the alphabet itself and the origin of some individual alphabets, are still uncertain.

2. Origin of the Alphabet

Over the centuries, various theories have been advanced to explain the origin of the alphabet. The Egyptian, the cuneiform, the Cretan,

FROM "WRITING" BY DAVID DIRINGER,
THAMES & HUDSON LTD.

EARLY ALPHABETIC WRITING is preserved on artifacts and stone. Bowl fragments (*center* and *right*) from the 13th century B.C. have Early Canaanite inscriptions that are among the oldest extant alphabetic scripts. Moabite stela, or stele (*left*), is from the middle of the 9th century B.C.

the Phoenican, and many other scripts, at one period or another, by one scholar or another, have been considered the prototype of alphabetic writing. The fact is, however, that scarce as the earliest extant inscriptions in alphabet writing are, they come mainly from the Holy Land and neighboring regions and date from 1700 to 1300 B.C. These inscriptions have given rise to several theories about the origin of the alphabet. One theory—based on readings of inscriptions from the Sinai peninsula, mostly of the 15th century B.C.—holds that the Paleo-Sinaitic script represented a stage of writing intermediate between Egyptian hieroglyphics and the North Semitic alphabet. This theory was advanced in 1916 by Sir Alan Gardiner, an Englishman, and Prof. Kurt Sethe, a German.

The French scholar Maurice Dunand considered the pseudohieroglyphic script of Byblos the prototype of the alphabet. He based his theory on the bronze and stone inscriptions, also of the 15th century B.C. or before, that he discovered in 1929 and later at the site of the ancient port of Byblos (now Jebel, Lebanon).

A third theory is based on an epoch-making discovery at Ras Shamra (ancient Ugarit), Syria, much farther north, on the Mediterranean coast. Thousands of clay tablets unearthed there by Claude Schaeffer in 1929 and succeeding years contain writing in a cuneiform alphabet of 30 letters. This alphabet, which was quickly deciphered, probably was in use between the 15th and 13th centuries B.C.

Opposing the theory that this was the original alphabet is the theory that the alphabet was invented by someone who knew the North Semitic alphabet already in use in the region. Because this person was accustomed to writing with a stylus on clay tablets, he borrowed the idea of an alphabet and expressed it in wedge-shaped elements. The discovery in 1948, at the same site, of a small tablet of the 14th century B.C. containing the earliest known alphabet, tends to confirm the theory, because the 30 Ugarit letters are so placed that the 22 phonemes corresponding to the phonemes in the North Semitic alphabet appear in the same order as in the North Semitic alphabet.

A theory based on enigmatic inscriptions of unknown date found in northern Egypt, at Ur (in Mesopotamia), at Baluah (east of the Jordan River), and elsewhere suggests these locations as possible sources of the alphabet.

The solution of the problem of the origin of the alphabet may come from Palestine, where, since 1929, several middle and late Bronze Age inscriptions, known as Early Canaanite, have been discovered. They can be divided into three groups (covering the 17th–13th centuries B.C.), corresponding, probably by coincidence, to the Biblical periods of the late Patriarchs, Joshua, and the Judges.

The most logical theory of the alphabet's origin is that the North Semitic alphabet, or its prototype, which may be called Proto-Semitic, was the creation of the northwest Semitic population of Syria-Palestine, and that it was based partly on a knowledge of various older scripts (Egyptian hieroglyphics, cuneiform writing, and others) employed in these and surrounding countries. Unfortunately, this theory leaves unsolved the problem of the North Semitic alphabet's connection with the Paleo-Sinaitic, the Byblos pseudohieroglyphic, the Early Canaanite, and other "alphabetic" scripts, as well as with the South Semitic alphabetic branch.

3. Main Alphabetic Branches

Around 1000 B.C. there arose four main branches of the original Semitic alphabet—South Semitic, Canaanite, Aramaic, and Greek.

South Semitic Branch. Generally speaking, this branch remained confined within the Arabian peninsula. In the south there were five pre-Islamic scripts—Minaean, Sabaean, Himyaritic, Qatabanic, and Hadhramatic—and in the north there were four—Thamudene, Dedanite, Lihyanite, and Safaitic. The Sabaean script eventually spread to the African continent. It became the progenitor of the ancient Ethiopic script, which in turn was adapted to the modern Amharic, Tigré, and other scripts of Ethiopia—the only South Semitic scripts still in use.

Canaanite Branch. This branch and the Aramaic constituted the North Semitic main branch. With some exceptions, it is almost as if an agreement had been reached between the Canaanite and the Aramaic branches. All the alphabetic scripts west of Syria-Palestine seem to have derived, directly or indirectly, from the Canaanite, whereas the hundreds of writings of the East apparently sprang from the Aramaic branch.

The Canaanite branch was subdivided into the Early Hebrew (as differentiated from the "Square Hebrew") and the Phoenician alphabets. The Early Hebrew alphabet was used by the ancient Israelites, probably until about 500 B.C., and was the original script of the Old Testament. The three eastern subdivisions of the Canaanite branch—the scripts of the Moabites, the Ammonites, and the Edomites—undoubtedly were related to the Early Hebrew alphabet.

The Phoenician alphabet was used by the ancient Phoenicians in their mother country and in their colonies, including Carthage. The scripts of the Carthaginian subbranch, which subsequently became the main branch of the Phoenician alphabet, are known as Punic (pre-Roman times) and neo-Punic (Roman and post-Roman times). The scripts of the ancient Libyans and Iberians were connected with the Carthaginian subbranch, and the script of the modern Berbers descended from the Libyan alphabet.

Aramaic Branch. This branch is comparable to the Latin alphabet in respect to its importance in the history of alphabetic writing. The Aramaic alphabet probably originated in the 10th century B.C. and subsequently became by far the most important and widespread script and language of the whole of western Asia. Between the late 3d century B.C. and about 100 B.C. various local offshoots of the Aramaic alphabet became distinctive entities. The direct and indirect descendants of the Aramaic branch include, as subbranches, the scripts used for Semitic and non-Semitic languages.

The Semitic subbranch consists of Square Hebrew (the prototype of modern Hebrew in all its styles); Nabataean and neo-Sinaitic Arabic (the latter is, after the Latin script, the alphabet most generally used in Asia and Africa); the Palmyrene alphabet (of the famous oasis of Palmyra); the Syriac-Nestorian branch (the Nestorian missionaries carried their religious teachings, language, and script into the Kurdistan highlands, southern India, Turkestan, central Asia, and even China); the peculiar Mandaean alphabet (the script of the gnostic pagan-Jewish-Christian sect known as Mandaeans, Nazareans, Galileans, or Christians of St. John); and the beautiful Manichaean alphabet (the script of Manes, or Manichaeus, who in 247 A.D. founded a religion, known as Manichaeanism, that for about 1,000 years was disseminated throughout the world from Persia to North Africa).

The non-Semitic subbranch consists of numerous scripts of direct or indirect derivation from the Aramaic alphabet that have been adopted for, and adapted to, non-Semitic languages of central, southern, southeastern, and far eastern Asia. They include, in India, Brāhmī, the great mother alphabet of the numerous Indian and Further-Indian linguistic branches (see section 4), and Kharoshthī, which came into being during the 5th century B.C. in northwestern India, at that time under Persian rule. (While the origin of the Kharoshthī from the Aramaic alphabet is not controverted, the script was influenced also by the early Brāhmī.) Persian (Iranian) scripts began to use an Aramaic non-Semitic alphabet sometime after the end of the 3d century B.C. It was known as the Pahlavi alphabet, and included Avesta, the script employed in the sacred (pre-Islamic) Persian literature. Sogdian was a non-Semitic script and language widely used in central Asia from 500 to 1000 A.D. Kök Turki was a script used from about 500 to 700 A.D. by Turkish tribes living in south central Siberia, northwestern Mongolia, and northeastern Turkestan. It was the prototype of the Early Hungarian. In about 1300 A.D. the script of the Uighurs, a Turkic-speaking people who lived in Mongolia and eastern Turkestan, and the script of the Tibetans were combined to form the Kalika (or Galica) script and adopted as the writing of the Mongolian empire. The scripts of the Mongolian peoples, including Kalmuck, Buriat, Mongolian proper, and the allied Manchu alphabet, were late adaptations from other non-Semitic languages. According to local tradition, the Armenian and Georgian (and the allied Alban) alphabets were devised in the early 400's A.D. by St. Mešrop.

Greek Branch. This branch emerged from the troubled darkness that shrouded the transition from the Bronze Age and the Mycenaean civilization to the Iron Age and the early Greek geometric art of the 800's B.C. Through its direct and indirect descendants, the Etruscan and the Latin alphabets on the one hand and the Cyrillic on the other, it became the progenitor of all the European alphabets and in the course of its history had offshoots in Asia Minor and Africa.

4. Indian and Further-Indian Branches and Korean

The Aramaic alphabet was probably the prototype of the original Brāhmī script, which seems to have arisen in the 600's B.C. It also is probable that it was disseminated by scholars and merchants for whom Aramaic was a fluent language and script. The adaptation of the Aramaic alphabet to the Indo-Aryan language, however, was neither simple nor straightforward. Although the shapes of many Brāhmī letters show clear Semitic influence and the Brāhmī originally was written from right to left, it was the idea of alphabetic writing rather than an alphabet itself that was transmitted, and the fully-developed Brāhmī alphabetic system was the outcome more of brilliant philological and phonological elaborations than of direct borrowing.

Indian Branch. In the history of Indian writing, four subbranches of Indian scripts can be distinguished. The first, the early Brāhmī styles, with approximately eight main types, were used in various parts of India from about the 6th century B.C. to the 4th century A.D. Three of these types—the Early and the late Maurya and the Śuṅga—became in the 1st centuries B.C. and A.D. the prototypes of the second subbranch, the North Indian. The early North Indian subdivision developed from the 4th to the 14th century A.D. It had seven main types, of which the most important was the Gupta style of writing (300's to 600's). Gupta, in turn, had its central Asian subvarieties Agnean and Kuchean (also known, though wrongly, as Tokharian A and B). Offshoots of Gupta included the Tibetan scripts, which arose about 639, the Siddhamātṛkā character, and the Śarada script. The most important Indian script, Dēva-nāgarī, the character employed for Sanskrit, developed from the Siddhamātṛkā.

The third subbranch of Brāhmī, the modern North Indian scripts (1300 A.D. to the present), are divided into northeastern varieties, such as Bengali, Oriya, Maithilī, Assamese, Kaithī, Gujarāti, Bihari; the eastern Hindi varieties, such as Takri and its many subvarieties; Landa, including the Sindhi varieties; and Gurmukhi, a polished form of Landa, which is the writing of the Sikh sacred scriptures. The fourth subbranch consists of the South Indian scripts (used from about 350 A.D. to the present). Some of these scripts are used for the modern Dravidian languages—Kanarese, or Kannada; Telugu; Tamil; Malayalam; and Tulu. Other scripts, such as the Kaliṅga, the early Grantha, and the Vaṭṭeḷuttu, have fallen into disuse.

Other descendants of the early Brāhmī include Sinhalese, an extremely important character of very ancient origin; the scripts of the Maldive Islands; the strange Syro-Malabaric alphabet; and the Saurashtran script.

Further-Indian Branch. In the last centuries B.C. and the first 1,000 years A.D., Indian colonization introduced Indian culture into the Indochinese and Indonesian worlds. Various new kingdoms arose, many ruled by Hindu dynasties, and Indian merchants, warriors, and magicians were accompanied by Hindu priests teaching a new ritual in Sanskrit. For daily speech the newcomers adopted the languages of the conquered peoples, but they enriched these languages with the vernacular and literary languages they brought with them. Through the Brahmans of southern India, for example, Indian civilization was carried to Champa, Cambodia, and Java. The Brahmans brought their own Early Grantha alphabet and used Sanskrit for their inscriptions.

However, the vast cultural expansion of India into Ceylon, Burma, Cambodia, Thailand, Vietnam, Malaya, and Indonesia was due mainly to Buddhism. The scripts of the Buddhist monks became the vehicle of Buddhist culture. Thus a unique empire was built up, based on the common cultural and spiritual life of peoples who were relatively independent politically. Buddhism, in fact, played a role in southeast Asia similar to that of Roman Christianity in western and central Europe in the Middle Ages.

An intermingling of peoples, languages, and scripts went on for centuries in the vast region of Indochina, as the many native tribes fought and overran each other. They spoke a number and variety of languages, classified under three great linguistic families—the Tibeto-Chinese, the Austro-Asiatic, and the Malayo-Polynesian.

The preponderance of Indian ideas in the culture of the upper classes was the result of the importation of the Buddhist religion and Indian culture—including southern Indian scripts. Buddhism was so deeply rooted in the region that it flourished into the 20th century in Burma, Thailand, Cambodia, Laos, and Vietnam, whereas in India—its place of origin—Buddhism ultimately expired through absorption by Hinduism and through Muslim destruction.

Several local scripts arose, each one having a more or less autonomous development. Several of them have long since disappeared. In Cambodia there was the Cham writing (of the shadowy kingdom of Champa, founded in 192 A.D.) and the Khmer script (the Khmers subdued the Chams in the 12th–15th centuries). In Burma there was the mysterious Pyu character from about 500 A.D. Also in Burma, but unrelated to Pyu, was the Mon script from about the same time. It had as its direct descendants the Burmese and Karen scripts. Laos has had its own character since about 500 A.D. In Thailand and in other parts of southeast Asia where Thai

dialects called Shan are spoken, there are several different Shan or Thai scripts. Of particular importance are the Pāli varieties of the Buddhist sacred scriptures.

In Indonesia there is only one script, although it has several varieties. The Javanese character has a long history and was known in its oldest phase as Kawi or Kavi. The Javanese script is used for the Javanese, Sundanese, Madurese, and Balinese languages and to some extent in Borneo. Kavi had several offshoots, such as the Batak, Redjang, and Lampong scripts of Sumatra, the Macassarese and Buginese characters of Celebes, and possibly also such Philippine scripts as Tagalog, Tagbanua, and Mangyan.

Korean. The Korean alphabet, known as Ön-mun or Un-mun, is the only native alphabet of the Far East. Some scholars consider it the most perfect phonetic system ever put to practical use. Its origin is rather controversial. It is doubtless not an independent creation but is somehow connected with the main Indian alphabetic branch and the activities of Buddhist missionaries.

5. Hebrew Alphabets

The Early Hebrew alphabet, a subbranch of the Canaanite branch, flourished in the pre-exilic period (1000 to 500 B.C.) and continued in use into the 3d century B.C. or later. The writing on Jewish coins from the Maccabaean Age to Bar Kochba's war (135 B.C. to 132–135 A.D.) is a direct derivative of the Early Hebrew alphabet. So, too, is the Samaritan alphabet, which is still in use for liturgical purposes by the small Samaritan sect.

The Square Hebrew alphabet, which was derived from the Aramaic branch of the North Semitic, was the parent alphabet of the modern Hebrew script. A distinctive Square Hebrew script can be traced from the 3d century B.C. It became standardized just before the Christian era and took the form that, with insignificant changes, is used in the ritual law-scrolls and in the printed Bible.

Generally speaking, in the evolution of classical into modern Hebrew, three fundamental types of writing were used. The square script, during its more than 2,000-year history, developed into the neat, well-proportioned printing type of modern Hebrew. The cursive book hand (handwriting used for books before the invention of printing), known as Rashi writing, was the rabbinic style of writing employed by medieval Jewish savants. Modern Hebrew handwriting is even more cursive and has many local varieties. It is or was used in the Levant, Morocco, Spain, Italy, France, Germany, Poland, and other countries. The Polish-German form has become the Hebrew hand of today.

6. Arabic Alphabetic Varieties

Because of the expansion of Islam, whose holy book, the Koran, is written in the Arabic language and script, the Arabic alphabet spread from Arabia into Syria, Egypt, Persia, the Ottoman empire, the Balkan peninsula, southern Russia, central and southeastern Asia, and a great part of Africa. It is used by such Semitic languages as Arabic and Hebrew and by such Indo-European languages as Spanish (aljamiah was the script used by the Arabs when writing Spanish), Slavonic, Iranian, and Urdu (the Hindustani-Hindu written in Persian Arabic

EVOLUTION OF THE

NORTH - SEMITIC				GREEK			ETRUSCAN		LATIN		
NORTH-SEMITIC	PHOENICIAN	NAME	PHONETIC VALUE	EARLY	CLASSICAL	NAME	EARLY	CLASSICAL	EARLY	MONUMENTAL (CLASSICAL)	RUSTIC
		'ALEPH	'			ALPHA			A	A	A
		BETH	B			BETA				B	B
		GIMEL	G			GAMMA				C	C
		DALETH	D			DELTA				D	D
		HE	H			ĔPSILON				E	E
		WAW	W			DIGAMMA				F	F
										G	G
		ZAYIN	Z								
		HETH	Ḥ			ĒTA			H	H	H
		TETH	Ṭ			THETA					
		YOD	Y			IOTA			I	I (J)	I
		KAPH	K			KAPPA				K	K
		LAMED	L			LAMBDA				L	L
		MEM	M			MU				M	M
		NUN	N			NU				N	N
		SAMEKH	S								
		'AYIN	'			ŎMICRON			O	O	O
		PE	P			PI				P	P
		SADE	S								
		QOPH	Q							Q	Q
		REŠ	R			RHO				R	R
		ŠIN	SH—S			SIGMA				S	S
		TAW	T			TAU				T	T
						UPSILON				V	V
										X	X
						CHI				Y	Y
						ŌMEGA				Z	

LATIN ALPHABET

ROMAN		ROMAN	ANGLO-IRISH	CAROLINE	BLACK LETTER	MODERN CAPITALS			MODERN LOWER CASE		
CURSIVE MAJUSCULE	CURSIVE MINUSCULE	UNCIALS	MAJUSCULE	MINUSCULE	MINUSCULE	"GOTHIC"	ITALIC	ROMAN	"GOTHIC"	ITALIC	ROMAN

A.C. SYLVESTER, CAMBRIDGE, ENGLAND

character, which is now the official script of Pakistan). The Arabic alphabet is employed for Tatar-Turkish and Malayo-Polynesian languages, and for various African tongues, including Berber, Swahili, Sudanese, and Nigerian dialects.

The Arabic alphabet developed rapidly. It probably originated in the 300's A.D., and before 650 all the Arabic letters had changed their shapes completely. In the 600's there were two main styles: Kufic, a heavy, bold, and stylized but beautiful and elegant lapidary or monumental character, and Naskhī, a round, extremely cursive hand. In the course of time the Kufic, which had several varieties, was discontinued except for formal purposes. Naskhī became the parent of a great number of styles, used in various countries and at the courts of various sultans. Naskhī eventually developed into the modern Arabic script used in both printing and handwriting.

7. Greek Alphabet and Its Descendants

The Greek alphabet occupies a unique place in the history of writing. Although the Greeks did not invent the alphabet, they transformed the consonantal Semitic script into a modern alphabet and gave it symmetry and art.

Like the Semitic scripts, the earliest Greek was written from right to left, a style that later was superseded by the *boustrophedon* (alternate lines from right to left and left to right). There are, however, some early inscriptions written from left to right. After about 500 B.C., Greek writing regularly proceeded from left to right, and top to bottom.

From the classical Greek alphabet, which is used for the capitals in the modern printed Greek alphabet and always was used in the monumental or lapidary script, there sprang the Greek uncial script, the cursive script, and the minuscule (see PALEOGRAPHY). These developments were always for the purpose of making writing easier and faster. The minuscule replaced the uncial as a book hand about 800 A.D. The cursive scripts developed into the modern Greek minuscule, although some of the capital letters of modern Greek handwriting are borrowed from Latin.

Descendants of the Greek Alphabet. Some alphabets of ancient Asia Minor, including the Lycian, the Phrygian, the Pamphylian, the Lydian, and the Carian, in one way or another were derived from the Greek. There is evidence that the first three were directly dependent on the Greek, while the last two were only partly so.

The Coptic alphabet is the only non-European descendant in Africa. (The word "Copt" is from the Arabic *qopt, qubt, qibt,* a corruption of the Greek *Aigyptios-gyptios*.) The Copts are the indigenous people of Egypt who, after the Arabic conquest of that country in 641 A.D., maintained their Christian Monophysitic faith, the Coptic religion. The Coptic language, one of the last stages of Egyptian, was spoken and written until the 1600's. Coptic (with its script) is still the liturgical language of the Coptic church, whereas Arabic is the speech of everyday life. The Coptic alphabet, which has been in use since at least the 2d century A.D., consists of 32 letters (25 were borrowed from the Greek uncial script and 7 were borrowed from a cursive variety of the ancient Egyptian demotic script to express sounds that do not exist in Greek). See also COPTIC LANGUAGE AND LITERATURE.

After the Etruscan, the Messapian was the earliest European offshoot from the Greek alphabet. It was employed for Messapian (an extinct dialect of ancient Illyrian), which was spoken on the Adriatic coast of Italy.

In the 300's A.D., in an area roughly corresponding to modern Bulgaria, the Gothic bishop Wulfila, or Ulfilas, devised an interesting alphabet for Gothic, a Teutonic language. This alphabet (which is very different from what is incorrectly called "Gothic script," the black-letter variety of the Latin alphabet) consisted of 27 letters, about 20 borrowed from the Greek uncial and the rest mainly from the Latin alphabet.

In Albania in the 1800's, three local alphabets (Büthakukye, Argyrokastron, and Elbasan), all formed on the basis of Greek cursive writing, were in use. In 1908, however, at the Monastir Congress, the Latin alphabet (with some modifications, including the addition of diacritical marks) was adopted officially.

8. Slavonic Alphabets

Between 500 and 1000 A.D. the Slavonic peoples used two alphabets, the Cyrillic and the Glagolitic. The two alphabets differed widely in the shapes of their letters and in the history of their development, but they were alike in representing adequately the many sounds of Slavonic and were richer than any other European alphabet.

Cyrillic. The Greek uncials of the 800's A.D. were the prototype of the Cyrillic alphabet. The richness of Slavonic sounds, however, involved the addition of many signs to represent sounds not present in the Greek speech; consequently, the Cyrillic alphabet at one time had as many as 43 letters. The Cyrillic alphabet developed in the course of time, with slight modifications, into the national scripts of the Slavonic peoples (Russians, White Russians, Ukrainians, Bulgarians, and Serbs) who accepted the Greek orthodox religion. For a time it also was employed for Romanian. Through the Russian script the Cyrillic was adapted to as many as 87 non-Slavonic languages, including the Finno-Ugrian group, some Turkic languages, and an Iranian language spoken in the central Caucasus. See also CYRILLIC ALPHABET.

Glagolitic. The Glagolitic alphabet, which seems to have had a common origin with the Cyrillic, consisted of 40 letters, in appearance unlike any known Greek or other variety. After general use the Glagolitic script was discontinued (although it lingered on for a long period, and it still is used as a liturgical script by some Croatian Catholics), and Cyrillic became the only writing employed for the Slavonic orthodox liturgy.

9. Etruscan Alphabet

Examples of the Etruscan language have survived in over 10,000 inscriptions belonging to the 1st millennium B.C. and in a fragmentary "book," containing about 1,500 words, written on the linen wrappings of an Egyptian mummy (in the Zagreb Museum, Yugoslavia) belonging to the Graeco-Roman period (about the 3d century B.C.). The inscriptions are on artifacts that came mainly from Tuscany (central Italy), although some were found in other Italian regions and even in other countries. Not many long inscriptions are extant, and the great majority have only a few words. They are written on various artifacts, such as mirrors, vases, and other domestic utensils, and on the walls of tombs and on tombstones and stelae.

While the Etruscan language as a whole has not been deciphered and its linguistic affiliation is not known, the reading of the inscriptions does not present difficulties. Like its prototype, early Greek, Etruscan writing nearly always goes from right to left, although there are also *boustrophedon* inscriptions. Most interesting is the ivory Marsiliana Tablet from the 8th or 7th century B.C., found at Marisiliana d'Albea. It is the earliest extant Western ABC and contains the 22 North-Semitic letters plus four Greek ones.

Etruscan Letters. In the 400's B.C. the Etruscan alphabet consisted of 23 letters. It included the *digamma* (*F*), three signs for *s*, and the letters *k* and *g*, which soon fell into disuse. When Etruria lost its political independence, it progressively gave up its script and language, although the last datable inscriptions belong to the early years of the Christian era. Nevertheless, Etruscan pronunciation influenced the Latin Tuscan dialect, which became the standard for spoken Italian.

Varieties and Offshoots. There were several varieties of Etruscan alphabets, including the South Etruscan and the North Etruscan. The North Etruscan, also known as the Alpine alphabets, were used in the inscriptions discovered in river valleys of the Italian Alps, which in pre-Roman times were inhabited by Ligurian, Lepontic, Celtic, Rhaetic, and Venetic tribes.

The most famous of all the scripts, the Latin, or Roman, alphabet, was the most important offshoot of the Etruscan. The alphabets of the Veneti and the Piceni of the 1st millennium B.C., who seem to have belonged to the same linguistic stock as the Illyrians, were direct offshoots of the Etruscan. Other descendants were the alphabets of several Italic tribes—the Osci, Umbri, Siculi, and Falisci.

10. Runes and Oghams

Runes. The runes, in all their varieties, were the scripts of the ancient northern Germanic tribes. A few runic inscriptions, however, have been found in western and southern Germany, in Austria, and even in Romania, Volhynia, Greece, and eastern France.

Of the approximately 4,000 runic inscriptions extant, the greatest number, over 2,500, come from Sweden. These belong mainly to the 11th and 12th centuries A.D.; only about 25 are of an earlier period. Denmark and Schleswig seem to have been an earlier center of runic writing: over 50 inscriptions from these regions date from the 3d to 6th centuries, and about 200 larger stone inscriptions date from about 900 to about 1050. Some 60 inscriptions from Norway belong to the period from 400 to 700. Relatively few monuments discovered in Norway are attributed to a later period. Iceland, though rich in Germanic literature, is poor in runic inscriptions. The earliest Icelandic runes date from about 1200.

About 50 inscriptions come from the British Isles. They include the artistic Northumbrian crosses, dating from about 670–680, the inscription on one of them commemorating the death of King Oswiu in 650; the *scramasax*, or sword knife (about 800) found in the Thames in 1857; and the "Franks Casket" (about 700), named for the man who presented it to the British Museum. Runic inscriptions of Norse origin were discovered at Maeshowe (Orkney), and others come from Ireland and the Isle of Man.

The runes probably originated during the 1st century B.C. and were mainly a monumental script. The theory that they derived from the North Etruscan (Alpine) alphabets is borne out by the extremely monumental aspect of the runic letters. It is substantiated by the discovery in southern Austria of small inscriptions that may be regarded as the link between the North Etruscan and the runic alphabets. See also Runes.

Oghams. The peculiar Oghamic (or Ogamic) alphabet was used by the Celtic population of the British Isles. The origin of this alphabet, in either southern Wales or southern Ireland, is uncertain but may be connected with the runic script.

11. Latin Alphabet

The Etruscan alphabet was the link between the Greek and the Latin alphabets. Most of the Latin letter names, which have descended into English and most other modern alphabets, also were taken over from the Etruscans.

Letters. The Romans adopted only 21 of the Etruscan letters. They rejected the three aspirates, *theta*, *phi* and *khi*, although they retained them, in a different form, to represent, respectively, the numbers 100, 1,000 (and 500), and 50. Of the three Etruscan sibilants, the Romans retained the *s*(*igma*), which became S. The X was added for the sound *ks* and placed at the end of the alphabet. About 312 B.C. the *z* (*eta*) was dropped, Latin having no *z* sound, and replaced by a new letter, the G, formed by adding a little stroke or bar to the letter *C*), for the sound *g* (*hard*). In the 1st century B.C., after the conquest of Greece, the symbols Y and Z, adopted for the transliteration of Greek words like *zenit* and *zephyros*, were added and placed at the end of the alphabet. The subsequent history of the Latin alphabet consisted essentially in the external transformations of the single letters, especially in the cursive styles of writing.

Transformations in the shapes of the Latin letters resulted chiefly from the desire for greater speed and changes in the nature of the writing materials. Originally there was only one style, the monumental. The main writing material was stone, and the main tool was the chisel. The principal considerations were permanence and legibility; beauty, proportion, and evenness were added later. Monumental writing gave way to cursive writing because the cursive was faster and more useful, and because it employed more convenient tools—the brush, the quill, and the pen—and writing materials—papyrus, parchment, and (later) paper.

Spread of the Latin Alphabet. Even after the various European countries had shaken off the political authority of Rome, Latin—the language of the Church of Rome—became the common language of the European intellectual world. As a result, the Latin alphabet was adapted to such Germanic languages as English, German, Swedish, Danish, Norwegian, and Dutch; such Romance languages as Italian, French, Spanish, Portuguese, and Romanian; such Slavonic languages as Polish, Czech, Croatian, and Slovene; such Finno-Ugrian languages as Finnish and Hungarian; and such Baltic languages as Lithuanian and Lettish.

Styles. With the adoption of the Latin alphabet by a large number of people speaking diverse tongues, a marked change took place in the development of the Latin literary or book hand. Several national hands or styles of the Latin cursive minuscule assumed distinctive features. Thus, on the European continent and in the British Isles five basic national hands developed, each giving rise to several varieties: Italian or Roman cursive, Merovingian (in France), Visigothic (in Spain), Germanic, and—the most beautiful and most important—the Insular, or Anglo-Irish.

At the end of the 8th century the Caroline, or Carolingian, hand developed (to some extent influenced by the Anglo-Irish style). It became the official script and literary hand of the Frankish empire and the main literary style of western Europe. During the following centuries, various styles of script developed from the Caroline, of which the most important and the most universally used was the "black letter" script (also known, though wrongly, as "Gothic" or "German" script). The black letter script was used in northwestern Europe, including England, until the 16th century and was the "national" hand of Germany until the end of World War II.

At the time of the invention of printing, about 1450, two main styles of letters were being used in Europe—the black letter and, in Italy, the more rounded *littera antiqua*, the neat humanistic or Renaissance hand that became what now is called roman type. The roman style gained ascendancy over black letter and spread throughout the world as the most widely used kind of type. In Florence there was also a more cursive form of the humanistic or Renaissance hand, with sloping letters and some joints between them. This style perfected in Venice by the printer Aldus Manutius, became the source of present-day *italics*. See also CALLIGRAPHY; HIEROGLYPHICS; PHONETICS; WRITING.

DAVID DIRINGER, *Author of "The Alphabet"*

Bibliography

Chappel, Warren, *The Living Alphabet* (Univ. Press of Va. 1980).

Clodd, Edward, *The Story of the Alphabet* (1904; reprint, R. West 1979).

Diringer, David, *History of the Alphabet* (Newbury Books 1983).

Diringer, D., *The Story of the Aleph-Beth* (Yoseloff 1960).

Diringer, David, *Writing* (Praeger 1962).

Diringer, David, and Freeman, H., *A History of the Alphabet Throughout the Ages and in All Lands* (State Mutual Bk. 1978).

Ege, Otto F., *Pre-Alphabet Days: The History of the Letters of the Alphabet* (Gordon Press 1977).

Johnston, Edward, *Writing and Illuminating and Lettering* (Taplinger 1977).

Logan, Robert K., *The Alphabet Effect: The Impact of the Phonetic Alphabet on the Development of Western Civilization* (St. Martin's 1987).

Ogg, Oscar, *The 26 Letters*, 3d ed. (Crowell 1971).

Patience, J., *Amazing Alphabet* (Outlet Bk. Co. 1985).

For Specialized Study

Awde, N., and Samano, P., *The Arabic Alphabet* (Lyle Stuart 1987).

Baker, Arthur, *The Roman Alphabet* (Art Direction Books 1977).

Briem, S. Gunnlaugur, *Sixty Alphabets* (Thames & Hudson 1986).

Driver, Godfrey, *Semitic Writing From Pictograph to Alphabet*, 3d ed. (Oxford 1976).

Friedrich, Johannes, *Extinct Languages*, tr. by Frank Gaynor (1957; reprint, Greenwood Press 1971).

Goines, D., *A Constructed Roman Alphabet* (Godine 1982).

Humez, Alexander and Nicholas, *Alpha to Omega: The Life and Times of the Greek Alphabet* (Godine 1981).

Nakanishi, Akira, *Writing Systems of the World: Alphabets, Syllabaries, Pictograms* (Tuttle 1980).

Solo, Dan X., *Classic Roman Alphabets: 100 Complete Fonts* (Dover 1983).

ALPHEUS RIVER, al-fē′əs, the chief stream of the Peloponnesus in Greece. It rises in the Taygetos mountains and flows generally northeast about 70 miles (113 km), emptying into the Ionian Sea near Pyrgos.

In Greek mythology the river was said to pass beneath the sea and rise again in Sicily. It was named for Alpheus, a river god who fell in love with the nymph Arethusa as she bathed in its waters. Artemis changed her into a fountain and removed her to Syracuse. But Alpheus pursued an underground course and emerged in Sicily to be united with the fountain Arethusa.

ALPHONSO. See ALFONSO.

ALPHONSUS LIGUORI, al-fon′səs lē-gwô′rē, **Saint** (1696–1787), Italian Roman Catholic theologian, who founded the Redemptorist order. Born near Naples on Sept. 27, 1696, Alphonsus became a doctor of law at the age of 16 but soon abandoned law for the priesthood. In 1732 he founded the Congregation of the Most Holy Redeemer (Redemptorists), an order established to preach the Gospel especially to the poor and abandoned. As bishop of Sant'Agata dei Goti (from 1762 to 1765) he was known as the father of the poor. He died in Naples on Aug. 1, 1787. He was canonized in 1839, was declared a doctor of the church in 1871, and was named patron of confessors and theologians in 1950. His feast day is August 1.

As a theologian, St. Alphonsus made significant contributions to the study of the dogma of papal infallibility, salvation, and Mariology. In moral theology he took a path between laxism and rigorism, striving to form confessors "full of charity, the essence of kindness, and maturely prudent." His spiritual treatises combated Jansenism and rigorism with the theology of the mercy of God as revealed in Christ. Croce considered St. Alphonsus a true representative of the Gospel spirit of moderation and kindness.

ALFRED C. RUSH, C.SS.R.
The Catholic University of America

ALPHORN. See ALPENHORN.

ALPINE, al′pīn, a town in western Texas, in the mountains north of the Big Bend of the Rio Grande, 220 miles (350 km) by road southeast of El Paso. It is the seat of Brewster county and a business center for ranching, with many dude ranches nearby. In the town are Sul Ross State University and the Museum of the Big Bend.

Alpine is the gateway to Big Bend National Park, 75 miles (121 km) to the south. From Fort Davis, northwest of Alpine, a 75-mile scenic loop drive winds through the mountains. It leads to McDonald Observatory and to Davis Mountains State Park, which contains a pueblo type of structure known as Indian Lodge. Alpine was incorporated in 1918. The city has a commission form of government. Population: 5,786.

ALPINI, äl-pē′nē, **Prospero** (1553–1617), Italian botanist and physician. He was born at Marostica, near Vicenza, Italy. While managing date plantations in Egypt, he discovered the sexual difference of plants and the fertilization of female flowers from the male. Linnaeus used this knowledge in his work and named the genus *Alpinia* of the order Zingiberaceae in the discoverer's honor. Alpini died at Padua, Italy.

ALPS

SNOW-COVERED MONT BLANC, the highest mountain in the Alps, towers over the gigantic neighboring peaks.

ALPS, alps, a famous mountain system in southern Europe. It occupies an extensive area including Switzerland, the northern border of Italy, several departments of France, and most of Austria, with indefinite ramifications into Germany. The mountains lie mainly between 44° and 48° north latitude and 5° and 18° east longitude, and are almost equally distant from the North Pole and the equator.

The Alps are also the focal point of lesser-known ranges—the Apennines, which traverse the length of Italy; the Dinaric Alps, which outline the rugged eastern coast of the Adriatic; the mountainous spine of the Balkans; and the Carpathians. Through the peaks of Greece and the Greek islands they may be said to continue, with slight interruptions through Asia Minor, to the loftier ranges of Iran and central Asia. This geographic panorama, though confused and ill defined, is a glimpse into the remote past, when the Alps arose in the same crustal convulsions that reared other ranges all the way from the Atlas Mountains on the Atlantic to the hinterland of China.

Origin of Name. The name *Alps* comes from *Alpes*, the Latin name for the mountains, but its origin in Latin is obscure. It apparently is derived from the Celtic *Alb*, which is thought by some authorities to signify "white," by others "height." Either would be appropriate to these snow-capped summits. In the region of the Alps themselves, the word *alp* denotes a high pasture, above the tree line and below the snow line. These pastures are sustained by mists and mountain showers and provide forage when lower lands have been seared by the sun. The early dwellers in the region were herdsmen, more concerned with their flocks and herds than with the inhospitable peaks that towered above them. Meanwhile, the word has become almost synonymous with mountains and appears in such expressions as "alpine heights" and "alpine flora."

Divisions. In conventional usage the name Alps is restricted to the sweeping arc of ridge and valley that stretches from the Gulf of Genoa on the Mediterranean Sea to Vienna, Austria. This area, though considerable, is less extensive than the more ancient Urals or the mountainous regions of Scandinavia. It is further subdivided into three main sections, the Western, Central, and Eastern Alps, all three embracing a number of prominent ridges. Some of these were differentiated by the Romans, whose knowledge of the region was fairly comprehensive; others have been given a more modern nomenclature.

Among the ranges of the Western Alps, the Maritime, Cottian, Dauphiné, Graian, and Pennine Alps are outstanding. The Maritime Alps, as their name implies, rise abruptly from the shoreline of the Riviera and the plains of Italy to form the western bastions of those mountain ramparts that Roman orators called the "Walls of Rome." They contain peaks rising over 10,000 feet, which in turn are overtopped by loftier ridges beyond.

Particularly imposing is the Pennine range, some 60 miles long, which includes the most massive, the loftiest, and the most spectacular of all Alpine summits. On its western extremity, where France and Italy meet, looms the ponderous mass of Mont Blanc, which Lord Byron termed the "Monarch of Mountains." Crowned with enormous snowdrifts, gullied by glaciers, and fringed by dizzy crags, it rises 15,781 feet above sea level, or more than 1,000 feet higher than Mount Whitney, the highest peak in the Rocky Mountains. Mont Blanc is the highest mountain in Europe, outside the Caucasus. On the other extremity of the Pennines, Monte Rosa towers 15,203 feet, while on the Swiss and Italian borders the Matterhorn, most photographed of mountains, lifts its knifelike ridges and overhanging precipices 14,691 feet, resembling, as John Ruskin observed, a colossal "rearing horse."

MAP BY DONALD T. PITCHER

Across the valley of the Rhône River are the Bernese Alps, the main ridge of the Central Alps. It has such towering peaks as the Finsteraarhorn (14,022 feet), the Aletschhorn (13,763), and the incomparable Jungfrau (13,642), admired above all other European mountains and justly acclaimed one of the most beautiful summits in the world. The Pennines and the Bernese Alps, roughly parallel and some 20 miles apart, present what is probably the grandest scenery in Switzerland. The Central Alps also have several other ranges with noteworthy features, such as the Lepontine, Tödi, Glarus, Bernina, Albula, Silvretta, and Rhaetian ranges.

The Eastern Alps, though presenting less lofty peaks, are noted for their beauty. The valleys are heavily forested, but the limestone rocks support only poor agriculture. Among their more prominent ridges are the Bavarian Alps, the Julian and Carnic Alps, and the Dolomites, famed for their precipices of crumbling limestone.

Alpine valleys vary greatly. Some are canyonlike gorges, down which foaming streams are broken into innumerable cascades and waterfalls. Others are broad valleys, which usually run parallel to the main ridges. There are also transverse valleys, usually much shorter, through which glacier-fed rivers have chiseled out passes leading into the interior. Some of these transverse valleys, however, are extensive, 150 miles long or more. From the Lepontine Alps they open into northern Italy to form the basins of beautiful Italian lakes.

Glaciers. The Alpine heights, which rise above the snow line, sustain no fewer than 1,200 glaciers and névé fields of firm granules formed from snowflakes that solidify into ice. The largest glacier is the Aletsch, 16 miles long, which covers an area of approximately 66 square miles. These curious ice rivers, characteristic of lofty mountains as well as the polar regions, were first studied in the Alps, and their slow and complex movements were carefully investigated. Like other glaciers the world over, they seem to be slowly retreating, suggesting a gradual warming of the global climate. But there is some evidence that they increased during the centuries immediately preceding the Christian era, as though the prolonged ebbing of the Ice Age had been interrupted by a period of declining temperatures. In some places they descend to an elevation of

3,200 feet, where they continue to wear down mountain flanks, widen gorgelike valleys, and build up accumulations of detritus (debris resulting from rock disintegration).

The far greater glacial action that occurred during the Ice Age is also everywhere in evidence in the Alps. Many circular basins or cirques have been scoured out by the abrasion of rock fragments gripped by moving ice. Many V-shaped valleys broadened out to the more commodious U formation as mountain flanks were worn away; many sharp crags were sculptured from the larger mountain mass. The landscape has been littered with terminal moraines (accumulations of earth and stone deposited by a glacier when the ice was at its maximum extent).

Lakes. Other relics of the Ice Age are the Alpine lakes, which are noted for their scenic beauty. Those that fan out into Italian territory from the southern border, such as Maggiore and Como, are popular tourist resorts, but others in the heart of the mountainous area, such as Geneva, Lucerne, and Constance, are equally lovely.

Since these lakes usually fill gorges that have been deepened or dammed up by glacial action, they are often very deep. Thus Geneva has a maximum depth of 1,017 feet; Maggiore, 1,220; and Como, 1,345. Geneva is also of scientific interest, for it was there that the pulsations called "seiches" were first observed. Resembling ocean tides, but quite different in origin, they have been known to cause an abrupt rise of more than five feet at one end of the lake. The north-south movements are more pronounced, but the east-west pulsations also follow a periodic rhythm. They are caused by the effect of variations in atmospheric pressure on confined bodies of water. The deeper the water, and the greater the east-west extension of the body of water, the more pronounced the oscillations are.

Rivers. Some of Europe's most important rivers bear the melted snows of the Alps to the four points of the compass. Lake Geneva is only a broadening and deepening of the Rhône River, which flows westward to turn south through the vineyards of France and empty into the Mediterranean. The Po, the major Italian river, also fed by Alpine drainage, flows easterly across the plains of Lombardy into the Adriatic. The Rhine, formed by the junction of Alpine streams, descends through winding valleys in a northerly direction to provide a busy avenue of commerce for western Germany, France, and the Low Countries until it empties through a maze of channels into the North Sea. The Danube also levies the Alps for some of its "blue" waters, which eventually reach the distant Black Sea.

Structure. Geologists have studied the Alps more intensively than any other mountains, and the picture they sketch of rock warpings and foldings tells a story of crustal disturbances extending over periods of many millions of years. The origin of these features has been traced to Mesozoic times, although some rock outcroppings date to the earlier Cambrian period. Continental outlines were far different then, and what is now the Mediterranean Sea extended far into central Asia as the Tethys Sea, while marginal areas alternately rose and sank beneath the waves. In the western sector of the Mediterranean, Europe was the northern shore and Africa the southern shore of this sea. Great troughs or geosynclines developed and were filled gradually with sediment washed down from adjacent uplands.

BRADFORD WASHBURN FROM RAPHO GUILLUMETTE

KNIFELIKE RIDGES OF THE MATTERHORN, near Zermatt, Switzerland, challenge the experienced mountaineer.

As the weakened crust sagged beneath this added weight, the slopes of the troughs were drawn together in a series of lateral thrustings that caused widespread dislocation. The African shore seems to have edged northward against the relatively stable European foreground, with much crumpling and splintering of rock strata. In some places enormous masses were thrust bodily over submerged layers, in others great folds or wrinkles in the earth crust, called "nappes," were formed. Sometimes these folds, subjected to constant and increasing pressure, virtually collapsed, their strata upheaved at every conceivable angle or even turned bodily upside down.

Certain Alpine areas have been identified as the battlegrounds where these conflicting forces strove. Thus the Jura range seems definitely a part of the European shore, the Dinaric Alps are thought to mark the African shore, and the loftier Pennine range rose from the floor of the oceanic trough, now filled with broken and distorted fragments.

This process of mountain building was no single episode. It was interrupted by prolonged periods of relative calm and by other periods when great areas alternately sank beneath or rose above the sea. Jagged crests were smoothed by long ages of weathering and then were submerged, covered with sedimentary rock, and subjected anew to the forces of erosion. Several such cataclysms marked the course of the conflicting earth movements that built up and tore down the structure of the Alps, so that the present peaks enclose cores of ancient heights long since worn away and buried by later accumulations of sediment.

The rearing of the Alps, which began in the Mesozoic era, was greatly accelerated during the more recent Cenozoic times, which also witnessed the rise of the Himalayas, the Andes, and the giant peaks of the Alaskan coast. And ,there is reason to believe that the process is still progressing. Certainly erosion is apparent enough in crumbling Alpine precipices and frequent rock slides. There is also some evidence that some of these peaks, which are comparatively youthful mountains, are still slowly rising.

In the formative period, when surface strata were subjected to prolonged strains and stresses, the weight upon the global interior was occasionally relieved so that molten magma welled up to solidify in vast sheets and provide a thickened granitic sublayer or foundation. The remains of older rock formations are sometimes embedded in this foundation; for example, Mont Blanc is an enormous batholith (mass of igneous rock originally stopped below the surface) thrust upward by a surge of viscous matter coated later with schists and gneisses and layers of sedimentary rock.

In the vast squeezing process that produced the Alps, the original area was reduced in width by as much as 150 miles, according to some estimates. It has also been estimated that the mass of the Alps has been reduced by erosion, over tens of millions of years, into little more than a fourth of its original volume.

Plant Life. Alpine plant life is rich and varied. The region is a meeting place of the northern European or Baltic zone, including many Arctic forms, and that of the warmer, sunnier, Mediterranean. To this intermingling of plant life the Alps have added a flora of their own, so that no fewer than 2,100 species of flowering plants have been identified in the region.

Along the southern slopes palms and other semitropical forms are found in what is known as

BOSSONS GLACIER on Mont Blanc is one of many ice fields that constantly change the profile of the Alps.

MASSIVE MOUNTAINS OF THE CENTRAL ALPS enclose the village of Soglio in southern Switzerland.

the olive zone. There and in the mountain valleys, vineyards climb the steep slopes in terraced gardens. The valleys and lower slopes are also the habitat of deciduous trees, particularly oak, beech, and maple. At loftier altitudes conifers are prevalent, mainly pine, larch, and spruce, although these forests have been denuded by unwise exploitation. Above them lie the high pasture lands interspersed with numerous shrubs: dwarf willows, bilberries, junipers, and rhododendrons. Alpine flowers have been admired by countless tourists. At loftier heights, usually ranging from 8,000 to 9,500 feet, vegetation is smothered by the encroaching snows, although specimens have been observed at higher altitudes. Edelweiss, the popularly adopted national flower of Switzerland, is famous for its ability to grow in inaccessible and barren rock clefts.

Animal Life. Three animals are associated with the alpine meadows above the tree line: the ibex, a wild goat once in danger of becoming extinct; the graceful chamois, a species of European antelope; and the Alpine marmot, which grows up to two feet long. Among other wildlife are the varying hare, the fox, and an occasional brown bear. The urus (a long-haired wild ox), European bison, and wolf, former inhabitants, have vanished before advancing civilization.

Bird life is fairly abundant, including grouse, woodcock, and partridge, and numerous waterfowl frequent the lakes. Golden eagles still circle the highest crags, as does an occasional lammergeier, the largest European bird of prey. Alpine choughs and ravens are not uncommon. The snowy ptarmigan finds the edge of the snowfields a congenial environment. Trout and other fish abound in many lakes and streams.

History. The Alps were the home of an early civilization, the so-called Lake Dwellers, who lived along the marshy shores or in the shallow waters of lakes in houses supported by piles driven into the mud. The earliest of these settlements dates back to the Neolithic period. Since the only implements were of stone or staghorn, the labor involved in building the houses must

have been prodigious. The best-known sites of these villages in Switzerland are along the shores of Lake Constance (where one village had over 50,000 piles) and at Robenhausen on Lake Pfäffikon. Here, when Babylon was still a village, mankind, learning by trial and error the first lessons in civilization, built dwellings of wattle work, used fishnets and spears, wore cloth, gathered edible fruits, nuts, and seeds, fashioned dugout canoes, and kept domestic animals.

Throughout history the Alpine population, though poor and ill-equipped, has been sturdy, courageous, and fired by an indomitable love of freedom. Hannibal, in his passage through the Alps in 218 B.C., was harried by the mountain tribes, who fought bravely and rolled large stones down on the invaders. This independent spirit was continued by men like the legendary Swiss hero, William Tell, and the Tirolese patriot, Andreas Hofer.

Although most of the Alpine area was incorporated in the Roman empire, it remained rather a "route than a residence," a passageway both for the Roman legions and for the armies of barbarian invaders. Yet some settlement always persisted, and as time went on, towns and cities increased in number and population. The highest permanently inhabited village is Juf in Grisons canton, Switzerland, at 6,998 feet. Several other villages are nearly as far above the sea.

For centuries the Alps were a battleground of conflicting nationalities and religious faiths. The western area was the scene of prolonged struggles between the rival powers of Savoy, Provence, and Dauphiné. From this melee France gradually emerged the victor and, as a final act in 1860, took possession of all the territory on the western slopes including Savoy and Nice.

The rise of the Habsburgs from their petty Alpine principality to the throne of the Holy Roman Empire and later of the Austrian empire gradually gave them control of the eastern Alpine region. Their power was broken during World War I, and in 1919, by the Treaty of St. Germain, Trentino was ceded to Italy. German is

THE JUNGFRAU (foreground), the Virgin, a famous height in the Bernese Alps, was first scaled in 1811.

MOUNTAIN CLIMBERS file by a cross on Säntis, the highest peak in the Alpstein range in Switzerland.

spoken in most of the Alpine area previously under Habsburg control, but Ladin, a curious variant of Latin, still survives in some isolated sections, and Slavonic in others.

Most of the Alpine region, however, is now included in Switzerland. Originally a part of the loosely organized Holy Roman Empire, it was long disturbed by the political and military adventures of the Habsburgs. A date of historic significance was Aug. 1, 1291, when the three forest cantons of Uri, Schwyz, and Nidwalden (now part of the canton of Unterwalden) united in a defensive league (the Eternal Alliance) against their Habsburg rulers. From this obscure beginning developed the Swiss Confederation of separate but united districts (cantons), the last considerable addition to which occurred in 1815.

Some 70 percent of the Swiss speak German as their native tongue, while 20 percent who live in the western part of the country write and speak French as their native language. The remainder of the population, most of whom live in Ticino and Grisons cantons, speak either Italian or Romansh, a language derived from spoken Latin. All three major languages are taught in the schools and are recognized by the state.

Some 57 percent of the people are Protestants; most of the remainder are Roman Catholics. Freedom of religious belief is part of the larger concept of freedom that has continued to unite the Swiss peoples.

Transportation. There are numerous passes in the mountains. On the French-Italian border are Montgenèvre Pass (altitude 6,083 feet), Mont Cenis Pass (6,831), and Little St. Bernard Pass (7,178), which may have been used by Hannibal. The Great St. Bernard Pass (8,110) is on the Italian-Swiss border. In central Switzerland there are the Simplon (6,589) and St. Gotthard (6,929) passes. Much farther to the east is the Brenner Pass (4,495), connecting Austria and Italy. This was the gateway to Italy for the German emperors of the Middle Ages, and it was here that Hitler conferred with Mussolini on their plans for conquest. These are the most noteworthy in a long list of 50 or more negotiable gaps in the mountain walls. Napoleon chose the Great St. Bernard for his invasion of Italy, but it is better known as the site of the Hospice of St. Bernard, which trains the St. Bernard dogs, famous for rescuing travelers lost in the snow.

Much former isolation has been overcome by roads, bridges, tunnels, and railroads. Napoleon's triumphs were not all upon the battlefield; the system of highways with which he linked France and Italy were masterpieces of engineering skill. These have been greatly extended for automobile travel. The 7.25-mile Mont Blanc tunnel, the longest automobile tunnel in the world, was completed in 1965. Connecting France and Italy, it greatly reduced travel time between the two countries. Railroads penetrate the region through some of the longest tunnels in the world, and trains on specially constructed tracks climb the slopes of Mont Blanc and ascend nearly to the summit of the Jungfrau. The larger lakes support steamer service, and airplanes find even the loftiest summits no barrier.

Industries. Alpine industries are limited by the terrain. Mining is relatively unimportant, considering the magnitude of the crustal upheaval. A mercury mine has long been operated at Idrija in northwest Yugoslavia, and lead is mined in a few locations. Rock salt is abundant in some areas. Iron, copper, zinc, gold, and silver are found in limited quantity, together with some coal. Far more abundant, however, is the "white coal" of rushing mountain streams that supplies an expanding program of hydroelectric power.

Originally a pastoral people, Alpine dwellers still have herds of cattle and flocks of sheep and goats. Grain and potatoes are grown in the plateau region, while dairying and stock raising are concentrated in the mountains. The dairy industry is noted for its fine cheeses, particularly Swiss cheese. Wine production is important in some areas. Fine craftsmanship is emphasized in wood carving and embroidery, and in the making of accurate timepieces and excellent maps.

The main industry of the Alpine region, however, is the entertainment of visitors. Besides the grandeur of the scenery, a bracing and healthful climate attracts travelers. The lower valleys, cooled by breezes from the snowfields, have a mean temperature of 50° to 60° F.

Sports. Switzerland, in particular, has become an international playground. It has long been popular with summer tourists and now is also a major center for winter sports such as skiing, skating, and tobogganing.

During the past century a growing army of enthusiasts have enlisted in the thrilling but hazardous adventure of mountain climbing. Mont Blanc was ascended in 1786, but a greater impetus was given to the movement in 1865 when the Englishman Edward Whymper, after repeated failures, scaled the Matterhorn, long thought to be unclimbable. Four of his companions plunged to their deaths in the descent. This mountain obelisk presents a perpetual challenge to ambitious climbers. The notorious Eiger also is famed for its terrifying precipices, but it has been climbed frequently during the 1960's.

In spite of the dangers, the attempt to conquer the heights has become a big business. Swiss, Italian, and French Alpine clubs have greatly increased their enrollments. Several other European countries have also had organized climbing clubs for many years. To direct these enthusiasts, mostly amateurs, Swiss guides maintain a well-equipped, highly skilled organization.

FERDINAND C. LANE
Author of "The Story of Mountains"

Bibliography

Collet, L. W., *The Structure of the Alps* (Krieger 1974).
Edwards, Amelia, *Untrodden Peaks and Unfrequented Valleys* (Beacon Press 1987).
Farrer, Reginald, *Among the Hills* (Hippocrene Bks. 1986).
Lane, Ferdinand C., *The Story of Mountains* (New York 1950).
Reifsnyder, William E., *Footloose in the Swiss Alps: A Hiker's Guide to the Mountain Inns and Trails of Switzerland,* 2d rev. ed. (Sierra Club Bks. 1974).
Reifsnyder, William E., *Hut Hopping in the Austrian Alps* (P. Smith 1983).
Spencer, Brian, *Walking in the Alps* (Hunter Pub. 1986).
Spring, Ira, and Edwards, Harvey, *One Hundred Hikes in the Alps* (P. Smith 1983).
Spring, Ira, and Manning, Harvey, *Mountain Flowers* (Mountaineering 1979).
Tranquillini, W., *Physiological Ecology of the Alpine Timberline* (Springer-Verlag 1979).
Whymper, Edward, *Scrambles Amongst the Alps, 1860–1869,* rev. ed. (David & Charles 1986).

ALS, äls, an island about 125 square miles (323 sq km) in area off the east coast of South Jutland in Denmark. The Als Sund, a narrow, swift-flowing strait, separates the island from the mainland. Als island constitutes a district of Sønderjylland amt (county). Sønderborg, on Als Sund, is the chief city and district capital.

The fertile fruit-growing island was included in the Danish duchy of Schleswig when it was created in the 1200s. Following a war with Prussia and Austria in 1864, Denmark was forced to cede Schleswig to Prussia. Together with Holstein, a neighboring region to the south, it was constituted the Prussian province of Schleswig-Holstein. As the result of a plebiscite in 1920, the northern part of Schleswig, which included Als, was returned to Denmark. The island is also known by its German name, Alsen. Population: 50,804 (1991 est.).

ALSACE, àl-zàs', is a former province of France that now is divided into the departments of Bas-Rhin, Haut-Rhin, and the Territory of Belfort. It

SWISS NATIONAL TOURIST OFFICE

MT. EIGER, renowned for its extremely dangerous precipices, is reflected in a lake in the Bernese Alps.

is situated between the Vosges Mountains on the west and the Rhine River on the east. The long border with Germany along the Rhine and on the north was often the scene of conflict between France and Germany.

History. During the 1st century B.C., Roman legions under Julius Caesar conquered Alsace (ancient name *Alsatia*). It remained Roman territory until the 5th century A.D. when it was overrun by a Germanic tribe, the Alamanni. In 496 the Franks under Clovis defeated the Alamanni and took control of Alsace. Under the Merovingians the area was colonized and Christianized. Subsequently it passed to the Carolingians. It was attached to the German holdings of the Carolingians when Charlemagne's descendants divided his empire for the second time in 870.

Political and religious conflicts disrupted Alsace during its 800-year rule by Germans. The rulers of the Holy Roman Empire, anxious to decrease the power of the local lords, encouraged the Alsatian cities to free themselves from feudal obligations. When the cities later became centers of the Reformation in Alsace, more conflict resulted. The fragmentation of Alsace, particularly after the Thirty Years' War, allowed Louis XIV of France to annex small sections, and he gained control of the area by 1681.

Although the Alsatians spoke a German dialect, they gradually became closely associated with France during the period 1648–1871. Exemption from French customs duties until the Napoleonic era greatly increased Alsace's prosperity and made the introduction of French institutions easier. The close ties with France were broken in 1871 when the peace treaty after the Franco-Prussian War required the defeated French to surrender all of Alsace except the Territory of Belfort. For Alsace's history after 1871, see ALSACE-LORRAINE.

ALSACE-LORRAINE, àl-zàs' lô-ren', a region in eastern France, composed of the departments of Bas-Rhin, Haut-Rhin, Territory of Belfort, and Moselle. It is bounded on the north by Luxembourg and Germany, on the east by Germany, and on the south by Switzerland. The Rhine River separates Alsace from Germany. Other major rivers are the Moselle, Saar, and Ill.

Although agriculture is the chief occupation, industry is also important. The principal crops are grain, tobacco, and hops. The iron and coal mines are highly productive. Manufactures include iron and steel, textiles, glass, and paper.

The great majority of the people are Roman Catholics, although some villages are almost entirely Protestant. The Alsatians speak a German dialect. French is spoken in Lorraine and in the large towns of Alsace.

History. The treaty that concluded the Franco-Prussian War in 1871 required France to cede all of Alsace, except the Territory of Belfort, and all of Lorraine to Germany. The area remained an obstacle to peaceful Franco-German relations until the end of World War II. It was retroceded to France at the end of World War I, annexed by Germany in 1940, and again returned to France in 1945.

For Germany, the acquisition of Alsace-Lorraine in 1871 was a lasting reminder of victory in the Franco-Prussian War. For France, its loss came to symbolize the eclipse of French power. From 1871 to 1914 the problem of Alsace-Lorraine played a large part in French military plans and foreign policy. Besides the region's strategic importance, the loss meant that Germany acquired valuable iron deposits, iron and steel plants, and large textile mills. French industry in these fields took many years to recover.

The people of Alsace-Lorraine protested the annexation and demanded a plebiscite, but it was denied. In 1879 some degree of local government was permitted, but the representative of the German imperial government retained supreme authority and blocked all attempts at effective self-government.

After 1895 the French government's anticlerical policy alienated the Roman Catholic majority in Alsace-Lorraine, and they sought to have the area made an autonomous state within Germany. A new constitution in 1911 pointed toward autonomy, but its political effect was counterbalanced by the number of German troops stationed in the area. As a result, there were military-civilian clashes, notably one at Saverne in 1913.

The restoration of Alsace-Lorraine to France at the end of World War I was taken as a sign of France's rebirth as a great power, and there was great rejoicing both in France and in Alsace-Lorraine. Assimilation of the area into France brought problems, however, particularly opposition to a French plan to substitute lay schools for the traditional church schools. In Alsace, efforts to replace the Alsatian dialect with French as the official language were a factor in provoking a movement for Alsatian autonomy. The French finally realized that they were proceeding too quickly and adopted more gradual methods, which proved more successful.

In World War II, Germany annexed Alsace-Lorraine after the fall of France. Attempts to germanize the area were a failure, and the people welcomed the return to France after the war. Population: 3,945,500 (1993 est.).

ALSOP, àl'səp, **Richard** (1761—1815), American poet. He was born in Middletown, Conn., on Jan. 23, 1761, and studied at Yale (M.A., 1798). Later he formed the literary group known as the Hartford Wits, which included Lemuel Hopkins and Theodore Dwight. Alsop was largely responsible for *The Echo* (1791—1805), which comprised a series of travesties and burlesques on current fads and literature; it was published in book form in 1807. His writings included *A Poem: Sacred to the Memory of George Washington* (1800) and *The Enchanted Lake of the Fairy Morgana* (1808). Alsop died in Flatbush (now in Brooklyn), N.Y., on Aug. 20, 1815.

ALSTON, àl'stən, **Joseph** (1779—1816), American public official. Born in South Carolina, he attended Princeton without graduating and then studied law. He was admitted to the bar but soon abandoned the profession for politics, serving in the South Carolina legislature from 1802.

Alston married Theodosia Burr, Aaron Burr's daughter, in 1801 and later (1806) was drawn into the "Burr Conspiracy" (see BURR, AARON). Despite this, he was elected governor of South Carolina in 1812 for a two-year term. His only child died in June 1812, and his wife perished at sea early the following year. He died in South Carolina on Sept. 10, 1816.

ALTADENA, al-tə-dē'nə, an unincorporated place in southern California, in Los Angeles county, on the lower slopes of the San Gabriel Mountains, just north of Pasadena. It covers an area of approximately 7 square miles (18 sq km), at elevations varying from 800 to 2,000 feet (245 to 610 meters) above sea level. The surrounding area grows citrus fruits and avocados.

Altadena is primarily a residential community. A majority of its people are employed in the industries of nearby Pasadena and Los Angeles. The city is known for Christmas Tree Lane, where giant deodars (cedars, native to India) are decorated with lights during the holiday season. Population: 42,658.

ALTAI, ul'tī, a territory (krai) of the Russian Federation, in south-central Siberia. It borders on Novosibirsk oblast, Kemerovo oblast, and Altai republic, all in the Russian Federation, and the Republic of Kazakstan. The capital is Barnaul. The krai's area of 65,275 square miles (169,062 sq km) includes rolling plains of fertile black earth and the foothills of the Altai Mountains. Altai is one of the most important agricultural areas of Siberia, producing wheat, corn, oats, sugar beets, and dairy products. Mineral resources include lead, zinc, tungsten, and gold. Its industries produce processed foods, machinery and equipment, chemicals, and paper. In addition to Barnaul, the krai's major cities are Rubtsovsk, Biisk, Novoaltaisk (Chesnokovka), Kamen-na-Obi, and Slavgorod. After Russians, Germans are the largest ethnic group. Population: 2,607,426 (2002 census).

ALTAI MOUNTAINS, ul'tī, a complex mountain system of central Asia, at the convergence of the former USSR, Mongolia, and China. It extends for 1,300 miles (2,090 km) from the plains of the Gobi Desert in the southeast to the margins of the West Siberian lowland in the northwest. The highest peak is Tabun-Bogdo (15,159 feet, or 4,620 meters) in Mongolia. The highest summit in the

Altai Mountains, at borders of Kazakstan, the Russian Federation, China, and Mongolia, are interspersed with glacial plateaus and lakes.

Russian Federation is Belukha (14,780 feet, or 4,500 meters), in an area of boldly cut ridges and snow-clad peaks known as the Katun Belki. The typical Altai scenery, however, is forested mountains of middle elevation (5,000–8,000 feet, or 1,500–2,400 meters) with flattened summits and steep slopes deeply dissected by erosion. Mountain ranges are separated by broad, flat-bottomed valleys.

The climate of the Altai consists of cold winters and warm summers. Precipitation varies, from 40 to 80 inches (1,000–2,000 mm) in the northwest to less than 5 inches (127 mm) in the southeast, where dry steppe and desert predominate.

The Altai is the watershed between the Ob and Irtysh rivers, which rise on the northwest slopes, and the interior drainage basins of Central Asia. Vegetation in the mountains follows a pattern of vertical zones, with grasslands on the lower slopes up to elevations of 2,000–5,000 feet (610–1,500 meters) and then forests up to about 8,000 feet. Above the forest zone, alpine pastures cover the area up to the snow zone.

Originally inhabited by Altaic tribes of Turkic language stock, the Altai Mountains attracted Russian settlement in the 1700s because of their mineral wealth, especially on the western slopes, in what is now Republic of Kazakstan.

THEODORE SHABAD
Author of "Geography of the USSR"

ALTAIC LANGUAGES, al-tā′ik, a linguistic group consisting of three subgroups—Turkic, Mongol, and Manchu-Tungus. These languages originated in the Altai Mountains region of Central Asia.

Turkic Languages. Turkic languages are divided into three types according to historical period—Old Turkic, comprising Old and Middle Uigur; Middle Turkic, including Cuman, Kipchak, Oguz, and Pecheneg; and modern Turkic languages. The latter are spoken in a vast geographical belt extending eastward from Turkey, where Osmanli Turkish is spoken, across the former Soviet Union and various eastern European countries, the border areas of Iran and Afghanistan, and into China. The use of Arabic script for Turkic languages was largely abandoned after World War I, when Turkey adopted the Latin alphabet and Cyrillic transliterations were developed for the Turkic-speaking peoples in the USSR.

The republics of the former Soviet Union have the greatest variety of Turkic languages and dialects. These are spoken in four areas: (1) the Black Sea and Caspian Sea region, where the languages include Azeri (spoken in Azerbaijan and in part of Iran), Balkar-Karachai, Kumyk, Nogai, Karaim, and Gagauz; (2) the Volga River and the Ural Mountains regions, home of Chuvash, Bashkir, and numerous Tatar dialects; (3) Siberia and the Altai Mountain range, where Oirot, Shor, Khakas, Koibal, Karaghas, and Yakut are spoken; and (4) Western Turkestan, where the languages include Uzbek, Kyrgyz, Kazak, and Karakalpak.

China has a large Turkic-speaking population in Sinkiang province, including the Uigurs, who speak modern Uigur. Most of the remainder of Turkic-language speakers in China speak Uzbek, Kyrgyz, or Kazak. (See also TURKIC LANGUAGES.)

Mongol Languages. The Mongol languages and written records date from the time of Genghis Khan (c. 1162–1227), who united the Mongols into an empire. They adopted a script that runs in vertical columns from left to right. About half of Mongol speakers live in China; most of the rest live in Mongolia and in Buryatia. There is a splinter group in Afghanistan speaking Mogholi, but the language is moribund.

Manchu-Tungus Languages. Manchu, a Tungusic language, originated in the 12th century A.D. among the Jurchen people of northern China. Manchu is nearly extinct, now spoken only by elderly villagers in northern Manchuria. Other Tungusic languages are spoken by peoples living in the subarctic taiga region of eastern Siberia.

The "Northern theory" of the origin of the Korean language, now widely although not universally accepted, places it in the Tungusic branch of the Altaic family. (See KOREA—*The People.*)

RUDOLF LOEWENTHAL*, *Author of "Turkic Languages and Literatures of Central Asia"*

ALTAIR, al-tī′ər, a yellowish first-magnitude star in the constellation Aquila. As seen from the earth it is one of the 20 brightest stars. Altair lies fairly close to the earth—about 16.5 light-years away.

ALTAMIRA Y CREVEA, Rafael, äl-tä-mē′rä ē krā-vā′ä (1866–1951), Spanish historian and legal expert. He was born in Alicante on Feb. 10, 1866. After taking a law degree at the University of Madrid, he embarked on a literary and journalistic career. His writings ranged from politics, in which he was a republican and anticlerical, to literary criticism, law, and history. He was professor of the history of Spanish law at the University of Oviedo from 1897 to 1910 and at the University of Madrid from 1914 to 1936.

The mood of pessimism that pervaded Spain after its 1898 defeat in the Spanish-American War moved Altamira to seek, in a study of Spanish civilization, the basis of a national renaissance. His four-volume *Historia de España y de la civilización española,* published between 1900 and 1911, was intended to restore national pride by reminding Spaniards of their past achievements. An English translation appeared in 1930.

He was one of a group of jurists named in 1920 by the Council of the League of Nations to draw up plans for the Permanent Court of International Justice, and he served as a judge on the court from 1922 to 1945. He died in Mexico City on June 1, 1951.

ALTAR, ôl'tər, an elevation or elevated object used for sacrifice, consecration, or prayer. An altar may be a simple stone outdoors or an elaborately carved structure in a church.

Altars are used in many of the world's religions. They mark a stage of religion well advanced above the primitive. When spirits of the dead or underworld deities were being worshiped, it was enough to place offerings on the ground. Evidence of such presentation of offerings may be found in cup markings on rocky surfaces.

Early Altars in the Middle East. When certain rocks, trees, or springs were regarded as being inhabited by a spirit, or as points where a deity might be approached with success, altars on which gifts could be placed to please or placate the spirit or god came into existence. Pillars hewn out of stone often were placed on or near the altar but were distinct from it. Although the pillar may at first have been regarded as being inhabited by a spirit, it became a symbol of the deity as religion advanced. The Old Testament story of Jacob's erection of a pillar and later of an altar gives insight into the way a cult was thought to have begun (Genesis 28:18–22; 35:6–7). At Petra, a Nabataean center in Hellenistic-Roman times (now in Jordan), there are altars with a superimposed pillar hewn out of the wall of rock. The seatlike altars shown on Babylonian boundary stones have symbols of deities placed on them. Pillars on the altars thus had become symbols.

While the pillar required an altar to supplement it, this was not the case with the rock on which gifts could readily be laid. Of surviving rock altars, one of the most interesting is that of Sarah in Palestine (now in Israel). Here the natural rock has been hewn into a blocklike shape and provided with steps leading up to it. On the surface are cup marks. As this was the locality of ancient Zorah, it may well be the altar referred to in Judges 13:19.

An early Hebrew set of laws, recorded in Exodus 20:24–26, gives several regulations for altars. First, they were to be of earth for sacrifice of burnt offerings. Second, if altars of stone were to be made, they were not to be of hewn stone. Third, altars were not to have steps leading up to them. These rules evidently were directed against imitating the altars of the Canaanites.

Altars found in Middle Eastern excavations range from the primitive marked-off spot of slaughter in an archaic temple at Ashur to the round heap of stones and rubble at Megiddo (in use 2500–1800 B.C.) and the 5-ton rectangular block with a basin hollowed out on it (13th century Hazor). In the first millennium, altars with projections at the four corners came into

ROMAN ALTAR in the Temple of Augustus at Pompeii. The sculpture shows a bull being brought for sacrifice.

vogue. In the Old Testament the projections are called "horns of the altar." They are regarded as rudimentary survivals of the stone pillar once superimposed on the altar. Blood of sacrifice was applied to these horns (Exodus 30:10), and persons seeking asylum grasped the horns (II Kings 2:28). Destruction of the horns was tantamount to destroying an altar (Amos 3:14). The horns had a special sanctity, such as had pertained to the pillars.

Special-Purpose Altars. Elaboration of worship led to the creation of altars for special purposes, such as a table for bread or cereal offerings. A separate incense altar might be a low block with horns or a high metal stand surmounted by a metal bowl. The bronze altar of the preexilic temple in Jerusalem is not described, but we hear that Ahaz moved it from its place to make way for an altar like the one he had seen at Damascus, doubtless at the camp of Tiglath-pileser (II Kings 16:10–16). The altar described in Ezekiel's vision was to be made in recessed stages (Ezekiel 43:13–17), like a Babylonian temple tower. The altar in the temple of Herod is described by the historian Josephus. It was 15 cubits (about 22 feet, or 6.7 meters) high and 50 by 50 cubits (about 75 feet, or 22.9 meters) square, and had a ramp leading to it.

Egypt. Altars in Egypt were generally simple elevations on the ground on which food was deposited. They stood in the midst of an open court. There was, however, a series of temples of the fifth Dynasty (about 2480–2350 B.C.) in which the altar stood at the farther end of an open court before a low obelisk with a pyramidlike base. The altar at Heliopolis is believed to have been of this type. Temples with altars of this style were called "the favorite seat of Re" and thus showed the sun-god particular

HIGH ALTARS of different styles and periods are shown above in the ancient Church of St. John Lateran in Rome (*left*) and the modern cathedral at Coventry, England, with its tapestry by Graham Sutherland (*right*).

honor. The altar-before-the-obelisk arrangement is like that of the altar before the pillar in Palestine.

Assyria and Babylonia. In the alluvial plain of Babylonia, clay brick rather than stone was the standard material, and altars were made of brick. In Assyria, however, they usually were made of stone. Small clay incense altars were used as far back as Sumerian times. These were two-stepped, the rear being higher than the front with windowlike openings. An archaic temple at the old Assyrian capital, Ashur, had such objects. In the center of the room was a rectangular place set off by curbing, where animal sacrifice was brought. A bowl on a stand nearby no doubt served as a receptacle for the blood. Burnt sacrifice was impossible here, and indeed there is no indication that this kind of offering played much of a role in Babylonia or Assyria, although the language has a word for it.

An instructive portrayal of a sacrificial scene is found on the white stela of Ashurnasirpal (883–859 B.C.). On a tablelike altar before a temple entrance, offerings of loaves and other foods are piled up. In front of the altar is an incense stand. The king has just thrown incense into the bowl with a cup. Behind him is an attendant with a vessel. A bull is being led to the sacrifice (presumably carried out on the ground), and on a low stand is a pot ready to receive the blood.

There was a great proliferation of altars in Babylonia in the Chaldean period. Street altars were numerous in Babylon itself. The Greek historian Herodotus speaks of a golden altar in the temple on which only a certain kind of sacrifice could be placed. Nearby, however, was another altar for general purposes.

Greek and Roman Altars. In the Greek world, altars were already well developed by the time of the Cretan-Mycenaean civilization. In historical times there were altars not only at temples but also at public buildings, in marketplaces and streets, in the courtyards of private houses, and at Athens even at the entrance to the house. There were numerous ones, too, in the countryside—often in sacred groves. The altars range from the primitive elevation of earth, accumulated ashes, or stones to the most elaborate and ornate structures. Altars were not set up within temples but in front of them. In front of the altar was a platform for the priest to stand on when officiating. From the 6th century B.C. on, altars often were made of marble and provided with sculptured ornamentation. The altar of Zeus at Olympia and one at Syracuse were large and famous. The altar of Zeus at Pergamon is well known from modern excavations.

At Rome, as at Athens, there were altars at house entrances (dedicated to the household gods, the penates), at public places of all kinds, and in front of temples. The Romans imitated the Greek custom of creating ornamented altars. A good example is the altar set up by Domitius Ahenobarbus at the temple of Neptune, which he dedicated in the Flaminian Circus shortly before his death (31 B.C.). On the front side of the altar was portrayed the marriage procession of Poseidon and Amphitrite, while on the rear was shown the sacrifice brought by the donor. To the left in this scene stands the victorious commander with his retinue, and on the right the officiating priest, while helpers are bringing forward a bull, a ram, and a pig for the offering. Greatest of Roman altars was the *ara pacis Augustae* (altar of the Peace of Augustus), which the Roman Senate had erected in 13–9 B.C. on the field of Mars in honor of Augustus, after his return from Spain and Gaul.

Christian Altars. Early Christianity knew no altar. The Eucharist was a real meal, and only the tables used at meals were needed. The early churches were house churches. About 200 A.D., Tertullian could still declare, "We have no altar." But Origen (about 225) and Cyprian (about 250) viewed the communion table as an altar, and Eusebius (about 325) saw the table as endowed with sanctity.

When the first churches were built, the table-altar stood in the apse. Behind it was the seat of the bishop. The wooden table gradually was replaced by a stone altar. Consecration of the altar by anointing is first attested to in the 5th century.

Eastern Christians have continued the idea of viewing the altar as a table and have only one altar in a church. On it are the book of the Gospels, a silver cross, and a receptacle for the elements of the sacrament. The silk altar cover is decorated with a representation of the burial of Christ, and a relic is sewn into one corner.

A change in the table form came about when relics were placed in a compartment under the table. Even the sarcophagus of a saint could be put there. The hanging in the front of the altar is reminiscent of the covers of the compartment.

In Roman Catholic churches there can be a number of altars, but traditionally the main one is the high altar at the end of the chancel. It was either placed against the wall or had a reredos behind it, blocking access from the rear. Since the liturgical renewal stimulated by the Second Vatican Council, however, there has been a trend to make the altars freestanding to allow the liturgy to be celebrated facing the congregation. Candles are now frequently placed at the side of the altar, rather than on the altar itself, so as not to impede the vision of the congregation. Similarly, the tabernacle is either placed on another altar or so constructed that it does not block vision. The altar is covered with several cloths, and either a crucifix is placed on the altar, or the cross carried in the procession of the clergy to the altar is placed on a stand in front of the altar.

The Reformation brought about a sharp devaluation of the altar among Protestants. It was no longer a place where sacrifice was brought as in the Catholic Mass. Luther was tolerant of the continued use of the altar, although he held that the clergyman should face the congregation at all times. Zwingli felt that the altar should be only a table, lest the trend toward Catholicism reassert itself. The use of a table rather than an altar became the custom in many Protestant churches.

In England altars were destroyed and replaced with wooden tables, which were moved into the body of the church at the celebration of the Lord's Supper. At the time of Archbishop Laud, in the 17th century, the altar regained sacred character and was placed against the east wall, or against a reredos near the wall, and fenced in by rails to guard against profanation. This arrangement is typical of modern Anglican church architecture.

EMIL G. KRAELING
Author of "Rand McNally Bible Atlas"

Bibliography: Humfrey, Peter, and Martin Kemp, eds., *The Altarpiece in the Renaissance* (Cambridge 1990). Limentani Virdis, Caterina, *Great Altarpieces: Gothic and Renaissance* (Vendome Press 2002). Norman, E. R., *The House of God* (Thames & Hudson 1990). Thompson, R. F., *Face of the Gods: Art and Altars of Africa and the African Americas* (Prestel 1993).

ALTAZIMUTH, alt-az'ə-məth, an instrument used in astronomy to determine the exact apparent position of a star in the heavens at any instant. The star is observed through a telescope, which is in contact with a graduated vertical circle, the telescope being free to turn about a horizontal axis through the center of the circle and perpendicular to its plane. The whole apparatus is so mounted that it can be rotated about a vertical axis, and the angle of rotation is shown by means of a graduated horizontal circle. Thus, when the telescope is pointed at a star, the reading on the graduated vertical circle

STONE ALTAR in a chapel at Villefranche, France. Murals behind the altar were painted by Jean Cocteau.

gives the altitude of the star, and the reading on the horizontal circle gives the angle through which the vertical circle must be rotated from its standard north-and-south position in order that its plane may pass through the star. This angle is called the azimuth; altitude and azimuth together determine the apparent position of the star, or except at the meridian, the sun.

ALTDORF, ält'dôrf, a town in Switzerland and the capital of Uri canton. The name is also spelled *Altorf.* The town is situated 2 miles (3 km) southeast of Lake Lucerne. William Tell is reputed to have shot an apple from his son's head in the town's marketplace. A large statue erected in 1895 and an annual performance of Schiller's *William Tell* honor the legendary patriot. Population: 8,200 (1991 est.).

ALTDORFER, ält'dôr-fər, **Albrecht** (died 1538), German artist who is sometimes called the "Father of Landscape Painting." He was renowned in his lifetime as an engraver, painter, and architect. Altdorfer was born, probably in Regensburg, Bavaria, sometime before 1480. He was an important member of the city council there, and in 1526 became city architect. He built the city's wine cellars, slaughterhouse, and the tower of the city hall, none of which survive. He died at Regensburg on Feb. 12, 1538.

In 1528, Altdorfer refused the post of mayor to work on his major painting, *The Battle of Alexander.* This huge canvas, considered his most important work, is a good example of Altdorfer's style. The battling armies of Alexander and Darius include thousands of horsemen and soldiers, painted in minute detail and set in an imaginary landscape. The painting, confiscated by Napoleon but later returned to Germany, now hangs in the Alte Pinakothek in Munich. Altdorfer's other works hang in public and private collections in Berlin, Munich, Nürnberg, and other German cities.

Altdorfer was a leading member of the "school of the Danube," a group of artists, including Lucas Cranach, who are considered the pioneers of modern landscape painting. Before their time, outdoor scenes had been used chiefly as background for the presentation of narrative themes. Their innovation was to evolve a style of pure landscape painting, telling no story, and often including no human figure. Many of Altdorfer's works, especially his water colors and etchings, show the emergence of this new style. He painted landscapes realistically and with great detail.

Altdorfer was also a master engraver in copper and wood. His movement toward pure landscape can be clearly seen in his engravings. He owed much to the influence of Albrecht Dürer, and may have been his pupil at one time.

A gradual change took place in Altdorfer's paintings after about 1510, reflecting his interest in architecture. He began to paint interiors, often influenced by Italian engravings or architectural drawings. An important example of this transition is his large *Altarpiece of St. Florian*. About 1518 he made a series of purely architectural drawings, including church interiors. These were often sketches for later paintings, such as *The Birth of the Virgin*. In these later works, the architecture became more elaborate. One of the most beautiful of his architectural fantasies is the palace that dominates the painting *Susanna at the Bath*.

ALTERNATING CURRENT, a flow of electric charge that reverses its direction periodically. For a discussion of alternating-current circuits, see under ELECTRICITY.

ALTERNATOR. See GENERATOR, ELECTRIC.

ALTGELD, ôlt'geld, **John Peter** (1847–1902), American political leader. He was born in Niederselters, Hesse, Germany, on Dec. 30, 1847. His family moved to the United States in 1848, settling in Richland County, Ohio. Altgeld received little formal education, but after serving as a private in the Union Army (1864–1865) he became a schoolteacher in Missouri, began to practice law there, and in 1874 was elected state's attorney for Andrew County. Moving to Chicago in 1875, he became an active Democrat. He was judge of the superior court of Cook County from 1886 to 1891 and was its chief justice when he retired.

Altgeld was elected governor of Illinois in 1892 by farm and labor votes. He embarked on a program of reform which included the improvement of prison conditions, education, and working conditions in factories. He appointed the well-known social worker Florence Kelley as state factory inspector.

Believing that the anarchists convicted of conspiracy in the Haymarket Square Riot of 1886 had not had a fair trial, he pardoned the three survivors in 1893. This action and his protest to President Grover Cleveland on the use of federal troops in the Pullman strike (1894) aroused considerable opposition among conservative elements, and Altgeld was not reelected in 1896.

Altgeld was a champion of free silver and an active supporter of William Jennings Bryan for the presidency in 1896 and 1900. He died at Joliet Ill., on March 12, 1902.

ALTITUDE, al'tə-tōōd, is the elevation of an object above a given level. Thus, in astronomy, navigation, and surveying, altitude is the angular height of a celestial body above the plane of the horizon (see Fig. 1). Altitude is measured in a vertical plane, from 0° at the horizon to 90° at the zenith. True altitude is calculated from observed or apparent altitude by correcting for such factors as atmospheric refraction and the dip of the horizon. Optical refraction by the earth's atmosphere has the effect of lifting the apparent position of an object above the horizon by a small amount, depending upon the local density of the atmosphere where the observation is made. The dip of the horizon is the angle between the refracted horizon and a theoretical reference horizon. Corrections must also be made for errors introduced by the observing instrument when a reading is taken.

In the case of observations of the sun and moon, additional corrections must be made. Thus, since the edge or limb of the visible disk of the sun or moon is observed, a correction is necessary to determine the position of the object's center. Another necessary correction is made for

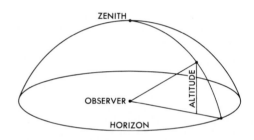

parallax. The latter error results from the observer's position at the surface rather than at the center of the earth. A nearby celestial object therefore appears nearer to the horizon than it actually is.

In geography and aviation, altitude is elevation measured above mean sea level (or above a local land-fixed reference point based upon mean sea level). Geographical altitude may be expressed numerically in feet or meters above mean sea level, or by use of contours on a map. In aviation, altitude is also measured above sea level by radar or a pressure-type altimeter. In the latter case, the reading must be corrected for local barometric pressure.

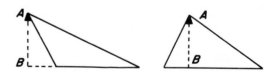

In geometry, altitude is the height of a plane or solid figure. It is measured by a perpendicular line dropped from the highest point, or vertex, of the figure, to the base (or extended horizontal base line) of the figure. The lines labelled AB in Figure 2 are representative altitudes.

See also GEODESY; HORIZON; PARALLAX; LIGHT—*Refraction;* SURVEYING

FERGUS J. WOOD
U.S. Coast and Geodetic Survey

ALTO, al′tō, is the female or boy's singing voice of the lowest range, below soprano and mezzo-soprano. It is also known as *contralto*. The normal range of the alto voice is from A (or in deep voices F) below middle C, to the F above middle C.

Alto musical instruments are those that have a range of a fifth or sometimes a fourth below their higher prototypes. They include the viola (the alto of the violin family), the English horn (an alto oboe), the alto saxophone, and the alto trombone.

ALTO ADIGE. See TRENTINO-ALTO ADIGE.

ALTON, ôl′tən, a city in Illinois, is in Madison County, 25 miles by road north of St. Louis, Mo. It is a manufacturing center and shipping point on the Mississippi River, 4 miles above the mouth of the Missouri. Alton has an oil refinery, foundries, and plants that make glass, paper, cartridges, explosives, steel products, boats, awnings, tents, clothing, plastics, automobile dies, brooms, clay and lead products, and foodstuffs. Lime and building stone are quarried in the vicinity. The city is the home of Southern Illinois University Residence Center (formerly called Shurtleff College).

The site of Alton was first settled in 1783, and by the beginning of the 19th century a fur-trading post had been established there. By 1818 there were three towns in the area. One of them, developed by Col. Rufus Easton and named Alton for his son, absorbed the other two. It was incorporated as a city in 1837. On November 7 of that year, opponents of the abolitionist (radical anti-slavery) movement rioted in Alton, and the abolitionist editor Elijah P. Lovejoy was killed while trying to defend his presses. A monument to Lovejoy's memory stands in the city cemetery. The last of the historic debates regarding the slavery question between Abraham Lincoln and Stephen Douglas during the 1858 campaign for United States senator from Illinois took place in Alton on October 15. The first Illinois state prison was located in the city, but it was abandoned after the Civil War.

Alton has a mayor-council type of government. Population: 30,496.

ALTOONA, al-tōō′nə, is a city in Pennsylvania, in Blair County, 99 miles (159.3 km) east of Pittsburgh. It is situated at an altitude of 1,160 feet (353.4 meters) at the eastern base of the Allegheny Mountains. It is the business center for a productive agricultural region and is adjacent to the rich bituminous coalfields of Pennsylvania.

The city was developed by the Pennsylvania Railroad in 1849 as a switching point for locomotives, where the more powerful engines needed to cross the Alleghenies could be kept and serviced. The Samuel Rea Railroad Shops in Altoona are now said to be the largest of their kind in the world. The city also has diversified manufacturing industries, including the production of silk, clothing, shoes, radio tubes, bearings, and candy. Commercial air service is provided at Blair County Airport, 15 miles (24 km) to the south.

On the main line of the Pennsylvania Railroad, 5½ miles (8.8 km) west of Altoona, the tracks form the famous Horseshoe Curve. This great engineering achievement is 2,375 feet (720 meters) long. It describes a curve of slightly more than 9° and rises at the rate of 91 feet per mile (17.5

meters per km). Another notable scenic attraction is Wopsononock Tableland, 6 miles (9.6 km) northwest of Altoona, at an altitude of 2,580 feet (782.3 meters), where the view extends 50 miles (80 km) over 6 counties.

Pennsylvania State University maintains a two-year undergraduate center in Altoona. The Blair County Historical Society occupies the Baker Mansion, built in 1840.

Altoona's name is believed to derive either from the former German town of *Altona*, now a part of Hamburg, or from the Cherokee word *Allatoona*, meaning "high lands of great worth." Nearby is the site of Fort Roberdeau, built in 1778 to protect a mine supplying lead for the bullets of Washington's army in the Revolutionary War.

During the Civil War the Altoona Conference of Union Governors demonstrated strong sentiment in favor of Abraham Lincoln's Emancipation Proclamation. In 1864 the first steel rails for a United States railroad were laid between Altoona and Pittsburgh. The first steel passenger car was built here in 1902.

Altoona was incorporated as a borough in 1854 and received its city charter in 1868. The city is governed by a mayor and four commissioners. Population: 49,523.

RUSSELL E. WALKER, *Altoona Public Library*

ALTRUISM, al′trōō-izəm, is a concept in psychology and philosophy developed by the French philosopher Auguste Comte. Using the term *égoïsme* as a model, Comte coined the French word *altruisme*, basing it on *autrui* (meaning "other person").

In psychology, altruism is a theory about human motivation. It holds that some things people do are done for the sake of another person or persons. It opposes the psychological theory of egoism, which holds that "everything I (the ego) do is for my own sake," that is, for the sake of what will happen to me.

Comte acknowledged his indebtedness for the concept of altruism to the British moral philosophers Joseph Butler, Francis Hutcheson, and David Hume. They had challenged egoism, which since ancient Greek times had been the dominant theory of human motivation, by arguing that altruistic habits may be formed in personalities that originally were egoistic.

In philosophy, altruism as an ethical concept appeared as soon as it was granted that it is psychologically possible to acquire habits of altruistic action, with questions arising as to whether and to what extent it is obligatory, foolish, or a matter of indifference to develop altruistic habits. Comte proposed the formation of completely altruistic personalities, each of whom would devote himself to playing his role in society for the good of humanity. John Stuart Mill claimed that a person gets more happiness from a life of altruism—from aiming at the happiness of the greater number—than from an egoistic pattern of life. Nevertheless, like his acquaintance Herbert Spencer, Mill rejected Comte's proposals, counting instead on the slow development of more and more altruism through the proper education of successive generations.

There still exist articulate defenders of the claim that ethical altruism is bad (the novelist Ayn Rand, for example). They assert that altruism tends to develop dependent, unenterprising, and sentimentalistic personalities.

WILLIAM H. HAY, *University of Wisconsin*

ALTUS, al'təs, a city located in southwestern Okla-homa, 155 miles (249 km) by road southwest of Oklahoma City. The city is the seat of Jackson county. It is the trade center of an agricultural area and has many farm-based industries. The community is the home of Western Oklahoma State College. Altus Air Force Base is situated on the northeastern outskirts. At Lake Altus, situated 20 miles (30 km) north of the city, Quartz Mountain State Park has been developed as a recreational area. The lake was created by the building of Altus Dam.

Altus was founded in the early 1890s and was incorporated in 1901. It has a mayor-council form of government. Population: 21,447.

ALUM, al'əm, is an inorganic compound that gen-erally contains two metals, two sulfate groups (SO_4), and water (H_2O). A compound of this type is called a hydrated double salt. Alums are hydrated double salts that have similar composi-tions and similar crystalline structures. The term "alum" is derived from the Latin *alumen,* which denoted the astringent properties of substances that contained aluminum sulfate. The term "alum" now is used in several different senses.

"Common alum," or "ordinary alum," means either potash alum (potassium alum), a double salt of potassium sulfate and aluminum sulfate, or ammonium alum, a double salt of ammonium sulfate and aluminum sulfate. The formulas of these double salts usually are written as KAl (SO_4)$_2$·12H$_2$O and NH$_4$Al(SO_4)$_2$·12H$_2$O.

The term "alum" also denotes a series of crys-tallized double sulfates that have the general formula M(I)M(III)(SO$_4$)$_2$·12H$_2$O, in which M(I) and M(III) represent positive ions with valences of 1 and 3, respectively. The M(I) ion must be a large, univalent ion, and the M(III) ion must be a small, trivalent ion. The univalent ions found in alums include sodium, potassium, rubidium, cesium, ammonium, and thallium. The trivalent ions include aluminum, iron, chromium, manganese, indium, gallium, iridium, titanium, vanadium, cobalt, and rhodium. A sulfate ion, SO_4^{-2}, can be replaced by a selenate ion, SeO_4^{-2}. Thus, a very large number of compounds may be classified as alums. Some examples are: cesium alum, CsAl(SO$_4$)$_2$·12H$_2$O; iron alum, KFe-(SO$_4$)$_2$·12H$_2$O; chrome alum, KCr(SO$_4$)$_2$·12-H$_2$O; and chromoselenic alum, KCr(SeO$_4$)$_2$·12H$_2$O. Although aluminum sulfate, Al$_2$(SO$_4$)$_3$, does not fit into this classification of alums, it is known as "papermaker's alum" or "filter alum."

Properties. Alums are soluble in hot water but less so in cold water. Thus, they can be crys-tallized readily from saturated solutions to form beautiful crystals. The evaporation of a solution containing potassium, aluminum, and sulfate ions in almost any proportions has been a favorite method for growing octahedral crystals of alum. In crystallized alums the 12 water molecules are an integral part of the crystal structure. Six of the water molecules associate themselves around the M(III) ion. The other six, which occupy cavities in the crystal lattice, probably are bonded to the sulfate ions by hydrogen bonds.

Manufacture. Commercially, the two most im-portant alums are ammonium alum and potassium alum. Ammonium alum is manufactured by crys-tallization from an aqueous solution of ammonium sulfate and aluminum sulfate. Ammonium alum crystals also are produced by treating a mixture of aluminum sulfate and sulfuric acid with am-monia. The crystals are colorless and have a strong astringent taste.

Potassium alum, which occurs naturally in the minerals alunite and kalinite, is manufactured by treating aluminum oxide with sulfuric acid and potassium sulfate. In another method of production, alunite is heated and treated with sulfuric acid to obtain crystals of the alum. Potassium alum is a white crystalline substance with a sweetish astringent taste.

Sodium alum, which occurs naturally as the mineral mendozite, is manufactured from a heated solution of aluminum sulfate and sodium sulfate. A slurry of potassium sulfate, sodium silicate, and sodium carbonate is added to the heated solution to improve the properties of the product. This mixture is pumped to a digest-or, where it is mixed for several hours, and then is pumped to evaporators. On discharge from the evaporators, the material forms a hard cake. After the cake is heated, it is ground to produce fine sodium alum crystals. Sodium alum forms colorless crystals that have an astringent taste.

Uses. The principal uses of alums depend pri-marily on the hydrolysis of the aluminum ion:

$$Al(H_2O)_6^{+++} \longrightarrow Al(OH)_3\downarrow + 3H_2O + 3H^+$$
aluminum ion   aluminum   hydrogen
               hydroxide   ion

The major uses of alums are based on properties related to the precipitation of aluminum hydrox-ide and on properties related to the acidity created by the production of hydrogen ions.

Uses of alums that depend on the precipita-tion of gelatinous aluminum hydroxide are:

Dyeing. Aluminum hydroxide is used as a mordant in dyeing cotton goods and other fabrics. A mordant is a substance that fixes a dye to the cloth, rendering the dye insoluble. The gelati-nous precipitate of aluminum hydroxide aids in holding the dye on the cloth.

Water Purification. The gelatinous aluminum hydroxide adsorbs dissolved and suspended im-purities from the water. These impurities are re-moved as the precipitate settles.

Sizing Paper. The weighting and sizing of paper is accomplished by the precipitation of aluminum hydroxide in the meshes of the cellu-lose fibers of the paper.

Fireproofing Fabrics. The precipitation of nonflammable aluminum hydroxide in the fibers imparts fire-resistant qualities to the fabrics.

Uses of alums that depend on the formation of hydrogen ions by hydrolysis are:

Baking Powders. The acid solution produced by the hydrogen ions releases carbon dioxide from sodium bicarbonate present in the baking powder. The release of this gas causes the dough to rise in a leavening process.

Fire Extinguishers. In some fire extinguishers the hydrogen ions react with a sodium bicarbon-ate that contains organic substances. This re-action is capable of forming very stable foams.

Uses of Alums in Medicine. Because of its astringent properties, potassium alum is used in medicine to treat certain skin conditions, to re-duce excessive perspiration, and to stop bleeding from small cuts.

Uses of Alums in Chemistry. In chemistry, alums are used as a source of M(III) ions. The advantage of alums in the preparation of these ions is that alums can be readily purified by crystallization, whereas the simple M(III) sul-fates are difficult to crystallize.

HERBERT LIEBESKIND, *The Cooper Union*

ALUM ROCK, al'əm rok, a residential area in west-central California, in Santa Clara county, on the eastern side of San Jose, 50 miles (80 km) southeast of San Francisco. Within the area, the boundaries of which are not strictly defined, is Alum Rock Park, called "Little Yosemite" because of the beauty of its canyon. The area was named for the park when, in 1956, it was first designated to be developed for homes.

Portions of Alum Rock have been incorporated into the city of San Jose, though substantial portions remain unincorporated. Part of the area is within the San Jose urban service area, and the whole of it is within the city's sphere of influence.

ALUMINA, ə-loō'mə-nə, is a compound containing aluminum and oxygen. Technically, it is aluminum oxide, Al_2O_3. It is called *corundum* when found in nature. One type of corundum includes emerald, ruby, and sapphire, which are gem stones of alumina colored by trace impurities of other metal oxides. Alumina usually is found in the earth's crust in combination with silica (SiO_2), one of the constituents of clay.

The principal use of alumina is in the production of aluminum. Bauxite ($Al_2O_3 \cdot 2H_2O$), the most important ore of aluminum, is refined chemically, and the product is heated to obtain alumina. The alumina then is dissolved, and an electric current is passed through it. The result is: $2Al_2O_3 \rightarrow 4Al + 3O_2$.

Alumina also has important uses in electronics. In its ruby form it is a basic part of one type of laser. In a thin-film form it is used as a protective surface for transistors.

Because its hardness ranks just below that of diamonds, alumina has important commerical applications as an abrasive. Bauxite is smelted with carbon in an electric furnace to remove impurities, and the molten alumina is allowed to solidify in large blocks. The crystalline product is crushed and sized as grains of alumina for grinding wheels, for abrasive papers, and for many applications in cutting, grinding, and polishing of metals and other materials.

Alumina is used in glassmaking to increase the resistance of the glass to chemical reactions. Because of its high melting point (about 3600° F or 1982° C) and chemical inertness, alumina also is used in electrical insulators, in spark plugs for aircraft engines, and in refractory brick for high-temperature furnaces.

Activated alumina, a porous, granular form of alumina, is made by heating lumps of the trihydrate of alumina ($Al_2O_3 \cdot 3H_2O$) at a temperature of about 700° F (371° C) until most of the chemically combined water is removed. Activated alumina has exceptional ability to adsorb moisture from gases, vapors, and liquids, and it is used commercially to dry liquids and gases, in air conditioners, and as a catalyst. After the alumina has adsorbed moisture, it can be reactivated by heating.

Special forms of the trihydrate of alumina of very small particle size are used as a coating pigment for paper and as a reinforcing pigment for rubber and other compositions.

As a paste, hydrous aluminum oxide is used in the drug and cosmetic industries for creams, salves, and lotions.

See also ALUMINUM; CLAY; CORUNDUM; GEMS.

JUNIUS D. EDWARDS
Aluminum Company of America

ALUMINUM, ə-loō'mə-nəm, is the most abundant metallic element, estimated to form about 8 percent of the solid portion of the earth's crust. (*Aluminum* is the accepted spelling in the United States; in other countries the name is spelled *aluminium.*) It is an important constituent of practically all common rocks except sandstone and limestone; even in these it is usually present as an impurity. Aluminum has a strong affinity for oxygen and never is found in the purely metallic condition. It occurs chiefly in chemical combination with oxygen or silicon, although there are large deposits of aluminum chemically combined with phosphorus and sulfur.

The commercially important ore of aluminum is bauxite, a claylike earth varying in consistency from mud to relatively soft rock. Bauxite may be brown, yellow, pink, red, or a mixture of colors. It consists of chemical combinations of aluminum, oxygen, and water, called hydrated oxides of aluminum, along with oxides of iron, silicon, and titanium, which are considered impurities. There are two hydrated oxides of aluminum: the monohydrate ($Al_2O_3 \cdot H_2O$), and the trihydrate ($Al_2O_3 \cdot 3H_2O$).

Bauxite contains about 50 to 60 percent alumina (aluminum oxide, Al_2O_3). It takes about two pounds of bauxite to make a pound of alumina, and two pounds of alumina to make a pound of aluminum.

The principal sources of bauxite in the United States are in Arkansas and other Southern states. Large deposits also are found in Jamaica, the USSR, Greece, Guinea, France, Surinam, Guyana, Brazil, Hungary, Yugoslavia, Indonesia, and other parts of the world.

Production. The first step in the production of aluminum is to obtain pure alumina. Alumina generally is prepared by the Bayer process, in which finely ground bauxite is mixed under pressure with hot caustic soda (N_aOH) in large tanks called digesters. The impurities, principally oxides of iron, titanium, and silicon, form a sludge known as red mud, which is filtered out. The remaining liquid, a sodium aluminate solution, is piped into precipitating tanks in which it is agitated and seeded with crystals of aluminum hydrate. As the sodium aluminate solution cools, the seeds of aluminum hydrate grow into alumina in its trihydrate form and drop to the bottom of the tank. The alumina is removed and washed, then heated to 2,000° F (1093° C) in rotary kilns to remove the water, and it emerges as a white powder.

In the second half of the process the oxygen in the alumina is removed by the use of electricity, and pure aluminum remains. In this electrolytic reduction, called the Hall-Héroult process, the alumina is dissolved in a molten bath of cryolite maintained at a temperature of about 1800° F (982° C). Cryolite is a chemical combination of sodium, fluorine, and aluminum ($3N_aF \cdot AlF_3$) that is mined commercially only at Ivigtut, Greenland, but also is produced synthetically in the United States. The molten bath or electrolyte is contained in a carbon-lined cast-iron shell that serves as the cathode. Carbon rods suspended in the electrolyte serve as the anode. The current passing through the electrolyte separates the dissolved aluminum oxide into metallic aluminum, which is deposited on the bottom of the cell, and oxygen, which is deposited on the carbon anodes and gradually consumes them. The cryolite remains substantially

1. Bauxite, the ore from which aluminum is made, is shown being taken from an open-pit mine in Arkansas. Most bauxite used by American aluminum producers comes from South America and the Caribbean area.

unaltered while alumina is periodically stirred into the bath and dissolved to maintain the continuous operation of the process. It takes about 10 kilowatt-hours of electricity to produce a pound of aluminum; therefore, a source of cheap electric power is very important for the aluminum industry.

In the 16-year period from 1948 to 1964, world production of aluminum rose from 1,235,-000 to 6,718,000 short tons. The world's largest producer, the United States, increased its aluminum production from 622,160 short tons in 1948 to 2,553,747 short tons in 1964.

Properties. Aluminum is a light metal with a bright, silvery luster. The affinity of aluminum for oxygen, which makes it so difficult to obtain the metal, is also responsible for its great stability and resistance to corrosion. Aluminum exposed to the air always is covered with a thin film of impervious aluminum oxide. This protective film is so thin that it is practically invisible.

An outstanding characteristic of aluminum is its lightness; its specific gravity is 2.70, and its density is only about one third that of the common heavy metals, such as iron, copper, nickel, and zinc. The atomic weight of the element is 26.98.

The electrical conductivity of pure aluminum is about 65 percent of that of the international annealed copper standard; the conductivity of aluminum commercial electrical conductors is 61 percent of that of copper. Being a good conductor of electricity, aluminum also has high heat conductivity, which is 0.52 in the centimeter-gram-second system, or roughly half that of silver. The pure metal melts at 1220° F (660°C).

Aluminum is an excellent reflector of radiation in the ultraviolet, visible, and infrared regions of the spectrum. Its reflectivity for light can be as high as 90 percent; and its reflectivity in the infrared regions can be as high as 97 percent.

The pure metal has a tensile strength of about 9,000 pounds per square inch (632 kg/cm²) and an elongation of 60 percent in two inches (5.1 cm) when in the annealed condition. It will regain its original shape after subjection to pressures up to 10 million pounds per square inch (703,070 kg/cm²). Although pure aluminum is soft and ductile (that is, it can be easily drawn out or hammered thin), it can be hardened by cold working and alloying. Some aluminum alloys also can be hardened by heat treatment. The most commonly used alloying elements are copper, magnesium, manganese, chromium, silicon, iron, nickel, and zinc. Both pure aluminum and its alloys are available in wrought form as plate, sheet, rod, wire, tubing, and rolled and extruded (forced through a die) sections. The workability of the metal is excellent, and it also can be formed by forging, stamping, spinning, and other metalworking methods. The alloys can be cast by the sand, permanent mold, or die-casting processes.

Aluminum is useful because of its durability in outdoor service as well as its resistance to attack by a variety of chemicals. Aluminum is not particularly resistant to alkalies (except ammonia) because of the solubility of the protective aluminum oxide film in alkaline media. In neutral solutions and in the presence of certain acids, aluminum is quite stable. Acetic acid and concentrated nitric acid, for example, are commonly shipped and stored in aluminum drums and tanks. Aluminum is attacked by hydrochloric acid, particularly when hot and strong.

High Purity. Aluminum up to 99.95 percent in purity can be produced by the Hall-Héroult process. Aluminum sheet of commerce (called 1100 alloy) has an aluminum content of 99.0 to 99.3 percent. A somewhat higher-purity aluminum is used for foil and electrical conductors, and some aluminum of 99.99 percent purity is used for electrolytic capacitors and for alloys for costume jewelry. This very high purity of aluminum is made by a double electrolytic refining process.

2. As a first step in producing aluminum, bauxite in solution is stirred in five-story precipitator tanks.

3. From the precipitator tanks comes alumina, a white powder that closely resembles coarse granulated sugar.

The impurities in commercial aluminum are principally iron and silicon with smaller amounts of copper. These act as alloying elements and increase the strength of the aluminum. The addition of 1.25 percent manganese produces an alloy (designated 3003) that is widely used for sheet, rod, and tube because of its combination of high strength, good workability, and excellent resistance to corrosion. Alloys of aluminum with various amounts of magnesium and manganese or magnesium and chromium provide a series of wrought products with tensile strengths as high as 65,000 pounds per square inch (4,570 kg/cm²) in the cold-worked condition, and many of them have excellent welding characteristics.

A substantially higher range of mechanical properties comparable with those of structural steel is obtained with certain aluminum alloys that can be heat treated. The best known of these alloys (2024) is of the duralumin type and has a composition of 4.5 percent copper, 0.6 percent manganese, and 1.5 percent magnesium. Heat treatment consists in heating to a temperature of 920–930° F (493–499° C) for sufficient time to dissolve and disperse the hardening constituents. The part is then quenched rapidly in cold water to retain the hardening elements in solid solution. After aging for four days at room temperature, this alloy has a tensile strength of approximately 68,000 pounds per

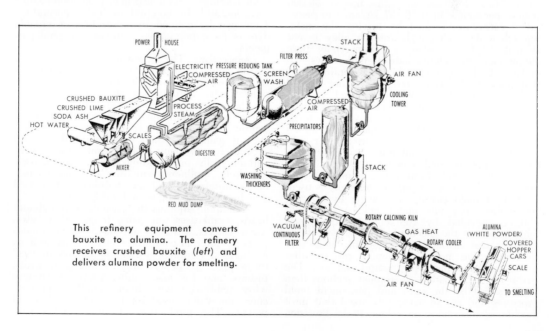

This refinery equipment converts bauxite to alumina. The refinery receives crushed bauxite (left) and delivers alumina powder for smelting.

4. A "pot puncher" breaks the top crust of alumina in an electric smelter to help it dissolve in the cryolite.

square inch (4,781 kg/cm²) and an elongation of 20 percent in two inches (5.1 cm). Another high-strength alloy (7075) contains magnesium, zinc, copper, and chromium. This alloy has a tensile strength of 76,000 pounds per square inch (5,484 kg/cm²) when it is the form of heat-treated and aged alclad-type sheets (a sheet that consists of a strong alloy core, with surface coatings of aluminum or aluminum alloys). Alclad-type sheet, having high resistance to corrosion, has excellent serviceability, particularly for aircraft. Alloy 7075 develops strengths up to 88,000 pounds per square inch (6,187 kg/cm²) in pieces called extrusions, formed by forcing the metal through a die. This high-strength alloy is not as resistant to corrosion as commercially pure aluminum or the intermediate-strength alloys. To make parts that operate at high temperatures and that must retain their strength and not expand unduly, aluminum is alloyed with nickel.

Castings. Aluminum casting alloys generally contain larger percentages of alloying elements than wrought alloys. The principal metals added to aluminum for casting alloys are copper, silicon, magnesium, zinc, and iron. For most large castings—such as crankcases for internal-combustion engines, architectural forms, or machine elements—the sand-casting process generally is used. Permanent mold castings are made by pouring the molten alloy into metal molds. The rapid chilling provided by contact with the metal mold improves the mechanical properties of the casting. Die castings are made in metal dies by forcing the molten aluminum into the dies by means of a piston or compressed air. Die castings can be made with thinner sections than are practical by the sand and permanent mold processes and are so accurately sized that most machining operations are eliminated. Precision castings with excellent surfaces and high dimensional accuracy can be made in plaster molds. Aluminum castings have been produced with a weight as great as 7,000 pounds (3,175 kg) and as little as 1 ounce (28 g).

Joining and Finishing. Aluminum alloys with strength comparable to that of structural steel and only one third as heavy have found widespread application for lightweight structures. Some of the most striking applications have been in the transportation field—in the construction of stream-lined trains, railway cars, trucks, buses, and aircraft of all types. The joining of aluminum can be accomplished by either riveting, welding, or brazing. With the use of a suitable flux, usually a mixture of fluorides and chlorides of the alkali metals, aluminum can be satisfactorily torch- or fusion-welded. Development of the inert-gas, shielded-arc method has made it possible to weld aluminum without the use of a flux. Electric resistance welding methods, such as spot welding, also are used for joining many parts. Welding, however, tends to remove the effects of cold working or thermal treatment in areas adjacent to the weld zone. This annealing effect can be controlled and minimized by some of the newer electrical welding methods. Joining by dip and furnace brazing is being used for the production of both small and large heat-exchanger units. Although aluminum is considered difficult to solder because of its surface oxide film, satisfactory soldering fluxes and techniques have been developed and are used commercially. Soldered joints are susceptible to corrosive attack, and this limits their use for some applications.

Aluminum articles can be finished in a wide variety of ways, such as by painting, lacquering, electroplating, chemical and electrochemical polishing, and porcelain enameling, as well as by sandblasting, scratchbrushing, and buffing. Anodized aluminum (aluminum that has been immersed in an acid bath, or electrolyte, and has a coating applied to it by passage of electricity) is important in the construction industry. The electrolyte most used is dilute sulfuric acid. The oxide coatings provide excellent protection against corrosion and abrasion and are highly decorative. They can be colored by adsorption of organic dyes or by impregnation with some mineral pigments.

Applications. The largest uses of aluminum are in the fields of transportation and architecture. It is used extensively in the construction of railway cars, automobiles, streetcars, truck and bus bodies, airplane wings and fuselages, and small boats. Aluminum's stability to atmospheric exposure and particularly the excellent appearance it maintains when it is anodically treated account for its many architectural uses, such as curtain walls on buildings, siding for houses, spandrels, mullions, window sash and frames, doors, storefronts, and screen frames. It is used also for highway signs and bridge railings.

Aluminum alloy castings are used for cylinder heads, crankcases, oil pans, transmission cases, water jackets, pistons, and many miscellaneous parts of internal-combusion engines, as well as jet engines. Forgings of aluminum alloys are used for airplane propellers and landing gear struts, pistons, and for many other parts. Aluminum wires reinforced with high-strength steel wire cores are widely used for transmitting electrical power. The production of aluminum cooking

5. Overhead crane (upper left) moves crucible of molten aluminum tapped from a series of reduction pots. An electrolytic process converts the alumina to molten aluminum, which is collected at the bottom of a pot.

utensils was one of the first applications of aluminum and still provides a large market for the metal. In the food-processing industries, steam-jacketed aluminum kettles and tanks are standard equipment, aluminum foil is finding widely increased uses for wrapping and packaging many foods, aluminum caps and seals are used on bottled products, and aluminum cans are for beer, soft drinks, and heat-processed foods.

Aluminum is being used in the construction of machinery and for many household appliances; in the home, the vacuum cleaner, washing machine, and flatiron are a few examples. Aluminum's resistance to attack by certain chemicals makes it a most acceptable material for the production of tanks, stills, pipes, and fittings for the production and handling of many chemicals. Aluminum also is processed into a fine flake powder that makes an excellent pigment for paint to cover wood, metal, brick, and concrete surfaces. Because of its high affinity for oxygen, aluminum is one of the best deoxidizers for iron and steel, and a substantial amount is used annually for this purpose. Aluminum also is widely used in constructing satellites and spacecraft.

History. Although Sir Humphry Davy, in 1807, was convinced that alumina had a metallic base, he was unsuccessful in his attempts to prepare

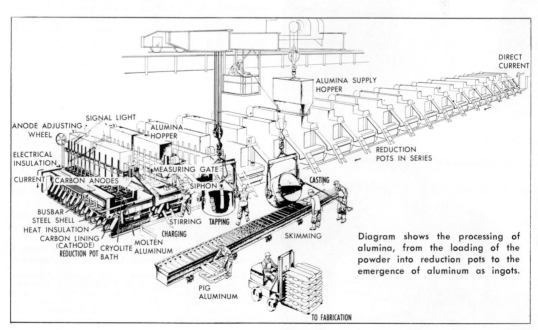

Diagram shows the processing of alumina, from the loading of the powder into reduction pots to the emergence of aluminum as ingots.

6. An ingot of aluminum weighing over 5 tons is lowered by a crane to await its turn in the hot rolling mill.

7. The console operator sends the aluminum ingot back and forth through the hot mill to squeeze it thinner.

8. A worker examines an aluminum extrusion that is being stretched with a force of three million pounds.

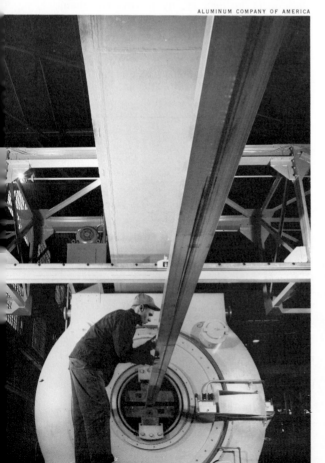

the metal by electrolysis. The element was first isolated by Hans Christian Oersted in 1825, when he reduced aluminum chloride with potassium amalgam. Friedrich Wöhler, in 1827, simplified the process by using potassium instead of potassium amalgam. The next great step in the development of a commercial process for producing aluminum was made in 1854 by a French scientist, Henri Sainte-Claire Deville, who substituted sodium for potassium. He also found that the use of sodium chloride and aluminum chloride improved the operation of the process because the salt acted as a flux and allowed the aluminum globules to coalesce to form a solid ingot. Sainte-Claire Deville's work led to the production of aluminum commercially, and a metal that once was more valuable than gold soon was being produced at $17 a pound. At this price, however, there were not many applications for the metal except for jewelry and novelties.

In 1886, Charles Martin Hall, who had been searching for a cheap method of producing aluminum, discovered that aluminum oxide could be dissolved in molten cryolite and that the dissolved oxide could be reduced electrolytically to produce aluminum. The same process was discovered almost simultaneously in France by Paul Louis Toussaint Héroult. Except for substantial improvements in equipment and for the size of the units used, the Hall-Héroult process in use today is basically the same as when it was discovered. See also BAUXITE; CRYOLITE.

FRED KELLER, *Alcoa Aluminum Research Laboratories, Aluminum Company of America.*

Further Reading: Ammen, C. W., *Casting Aluminum* (TAB Bks. 1985); Burkin, A. R., *Production of Aluminum and Alumina* (Wiley 1987); Dorre, E., and others, *Alumina* (Springer-Verlag 1984); Ferdinand, E., *Bauxite and Aluminum* (Lexington Bks. 1979); King, Frank, *Aluminum and Its Alloys* (Halsted Press 1987).

ALUMROOT, al′əm-rōōt, the common name for about 50 species of perennial plants native to western North America, constituting the genus *Heuchera* of the saxifrage family (Saxifragaceae). They usually grow as low, spreading tufts, from which rise slender panicles or spikes of small red, white, greenish, or purplish flowers. In the wild they are found mostly in hilly or mountainous terrain. The species *H. sanguinea*, with red or white bell-shaped flowers, is cultivated as an ornamental garden plant and is called coralbells. *H. americana*, with greenish flowers, is called rock geranium.

ALUNITE, al′ū-nīt, also called alumstone and alumite, a sulfate mineral that has been mined, especially in wartime, as a source of potash and alum. A brittle white or pinkish mineral with a glassy luster, alunite is found primarily in the Ukraine, Czechoslovakia, Italy, France, Spain, Mexico, and the western United States. Large deposits occur in old volcanic regions where rocks have been acted on by sulfuric acid. Its formula is $K_2Al_3(OH)_6(SO_4)_3$; its hardness, 3.5 to 4; and its specific gravity, 2.6 to 2.8.

ALVA, äl′vä, **3d Duke of** (1507–1582), Spanish general and statesman, who was chiefly famous for his governorship of the Netherlands from 1567 to 1573. The Spanish form of his title is Alba. Fernando Álvarez de Toledo was born on Oct. 29, 1507, in Piedrahita, Ávila province. His father, Don García, was killed in battle in 1510, and the boy was reared by his grandfather, Don Fadrique, the 2d duke of Alva.

Military Career. At 17, Alva fought against the French at the siege of Fuenterrabía. He continued to serve with Emperor Charles V in the latter's campaigns in Italy and against the Turks in Hungary. He led the emperor's forces at the fall of Tunis in 1535 and was placed in charge of the abortive Algerian campaign (1541) with orders to reorganize the army, which he did with the utmost severity. Alva then became commander of the imperial armies sent against the German Lutherans, and in 1547, at Mühlberg, he defeated John Frederick, elector of Saxony.

In 1555, Alva was given command of the Spanish forces in Italy. The next year, when Philip II assumed the crown of Spain, Alva moved against the forces of Pope Paul IV and the duke de Guise. Spain made peace with the pope after Alva had advanced to the gates of Rome. His campaign in Italy served Philip in forcing a break between Henry II of France and the pope.

Governor of the Netherlands. Just as Duchess Margaret of Parma, regent of the Netherlands, appeared to have settled the Protestant-Catholic conflicts in that region, Philip sent Alva there (1567) as captain general and then governor and regent. The duke began a policy of energetic repression. Although his ability as a general ultimately gave him military success, his policy ended all hope of reconciliation between the people of the Netherlands and Spain. Alva founded the infamous Council of Troubles (known popularly as the "Council of Blood") and condemned thousands to death without appeal. Among his victims were the counts of Egmont and Horn.

In 1568 open revolt against Spanish rule began in the Netherlands. Alva defeated Louis of Nassau at Jemmingen and then forced William

The 3d Duke of Alva, Spanish military commander and governor of the Netherlands, as portrayed by Titian.

the Silent of Orange to withdraw from Brabant to Germany. Oppressive tax laws enacted in 1569 caused further opposition, and the taxes were suspended. On April 1, 1572, the so-called Sea Beggars, a group of Dutch patriots, took the fortress of Briel (The Brill). William of Orange retook Brabant, and his brother Louis captured Mons and Valenciennes. Alva then enforced the new taxes and led a successful campaign with victories at Mons, Zutphen, Naarden, and Haarlem, driving William northward. But Philip wanted peace and in 1573 replaced Alva with the more moderate Luis de Requesens, although with scant success.

Last Years. The duke was received home coldly, supposedly because of an earlier slight to the king, but more probably because of the presence of his enemy Antonio Pérez as the king's secretary. Nevertheless, he was recalled from virtual imprisonment some years later to lead Philip's campaign against Dom Antonio for the throne of Portugal. His victory over Diego de Meneses on Aug. 25, 1580, at the Bridge of Alcántara, made Philip king of Portugal. Alva died in Lisbon on Dec. 11, 1582.

GREGORY RABASSA, *Columbia University*

ALVARADO, äl-vä-rä′t̲h̲ō, **Pedro de** (1485?–1541), Spanish soldier. He was born in Badajoz, Spain, and went to Hispaniola in 1510. In 1518 he commanded a vessel in the expedition of Juan de Grijalva to Yucatán, and in 1519–1521 he aided Hernán Cortés in the conquest of Mexico. Alvarado assumed command in Tenochtitlán (Mexico City) when Cortés marched to the coast to capture Pánfilo de Narváez. When the Spaniards were driven from Tenochtitlán in 1520, Alvarado saved his own life by a famous long leap with the use of his spear.

In 1523–1527, Alvarado commanded the expedition that conquered Guatemala. He founded the city later known as Guatemala la Vieja and established Puerto de la Posesión on the Pacific coast. He was received in Spain with great honor by Emperor Charles V and returned to Guatemala as governor. In 1534 he embarked on an expedition against Quito, but Francisco Pizarro paid him to withdraw. Alvarado died in Mexico on June 29, 1541, in an accident.

ÁLVAREZ, äl'vä-räs, **Juan** (1780–1867), Mexican general. He was born in Concepción de Atoyac (later, Ciudad Álvarez), Mexico, on Jan. 27, 1780, of Indian parentage. In 1810 he took part in the insurrectionary movement led by José Maria Morelos y Pavón, and in 1821 he distinguished himself during the struggle for Mexican independence. He supported Antonio López de Santa Anna in the revolt that overthrew the government of Agustín de Iturbide in 1823, fought in the war against the United States in 1846–1847, and in 1849 became the first governor of his native state of Guerrero.

In 1854–1855, Álvarez led the "revolution of Ayutla" that ended the despotic rule of Santa Anna, and in October 1855 he became acting president of the republic. Unable to establish harmony among his supporters, he resigned on December 8 in favor of Ignacio Comonfort. In the 1860's he opposed the French attempt to establish Maximilian in Mexico. He died on Aug. 21, 1867.

ALVAREZ, Luis Walter, al'və-rez (1911–1988), American physicist who won the 1968 Nobel Prize in physics for his work in elementary particle research. Born in San Francisco, Calif., on June 13, 1911, he studied physics at the University of Chicago, where he obtained his Ph.D. in 1936. During World War II he worked on the development of radar at the Massachusetts Institute of Technology, creating a ground-controlled approach system for landing aircraft. In 1944–1945 he worked on the development of the atomic bomb at the Los Alamos Laboratory in New Mexico. He spent most of his professional career at the University of California at Berkeley, where he was associate director and senior physicist at the Lawrence Radiation Laboratory. Alvarez's other scientific achievements include a color television system and the development of sophisticated particle accelerators. In the 1970s he and his son Walter proposed a controversial theory that one or more asteroids or comets struck the earth 65 million years ago, causing the extinction of the dinosaurs. Alvarez died in Berkeley on Sept. 1, 1988.

Alvarez was awarded the Nobel Prize for his discovery of a large number of resonances or higher energy levels of subatomic particles, made possible through his development of the hydrogen bubble chamber, with photographic processes and systems of data analysis. In his bubble chamber, subatomic particles passing through liquid hydrogen left trails of tiny bubbles, enabling the particles to be studied.

ÁLVAREZ DE PEREIRA Y CUBERO, äl'vä-räth thä pä-re'ē-rä ē kōō-bä'rō, **José** (1768–1827), Spanish sculptor, who did classical portrait sculptures in marble of noble personages and mythological figures. He was born in Priego, Spain, on April 24, 1768. From 1799 to 1826 he studied and worked in Paris and in Rome, where he was commissioned by Napoleon to decorate the Quirinal Palace. While in Rome, he became a friend and student of the Italian sculptor Antonio Canova.

When he returned to Spain, he executed a group representing Antilochus and Memnon, which won him appointment as court sculptor. In this capacity he made statues of King Charles IV and his consort, Queen Maria Luisa, and of Isabella de Braganza. His other work included busts of King Ferdinand VII and the duchess of Alba. He died in Madrid on Nov. 26, 1827.

ALVEAR, äl-vä-är', **Marcelo Torcuato de** (1868–1942), Argentine diplomat and statesman. He was born in Buenos Aires on Oct. 4, 1868, the grandson of Carlos María de Alvear (1789–1853), who in 1823 became the first Argentine minister to the United States. Alvear participated in revolutionary outbreaks in 1890, 1893, and 1905, and in 1912 was elected to the lower house of the Argentine Congress on the ticket of the Radical party, of which he had been one of the founders in 1893. In 1916 he was appointed Argentine minister to France.

Alvear was elected president of Argentina in 1922. During his administration he effected some social reform, notably in aiding the farmers, though he failed to implement much of the rest of his program. After his term as president expired in 1928, he took up residence in France. Returning to Argentina in 1931, he was in the following year arrested for suspected complicity in a revolt, and for a brief period he was exiled. In 1937, Alvear was again a candidate for the presidency but was defeated. He died in Buenos Aires on March 23, 1942.

ALWAR, ul'wər, a city in India, in northeastern Rajasthan state. The name is also spelled Alwur. Once the capital of the princely state of Alwar, the city is now the capital of Alwar district. It is located about 80 miles (129 km) southwest of Delhi. It markets and processes such regional products as grains, oilseeds, and cotton.

The city is set picturesquely at the base of a rocky range of quartz and slate. A large fort, reached by a moat, crowns the mountains. Near the fort stands a monument honoring the Maharaja Pratap Singh, the founder of the city. The palace of Alwar, a complex of architectural styles, contains a museum with a collection of Rajasthani and Mughul paintings, and a library of Hindi, Sanskrit, and Persian manuscripts.

Alwar was founded in 1771 as the capital of the Rajput state of Alwar. Overrun by the Marathas, the state sought British protection and concluded a treaty with Britain in 1803. After India achieved independence, Alwar state joined the Matsya union in 1948, which merged with Rajasthan in 1949. Population: 260,245 (2001 census).

ALYATTES, al-ē-at'ēz (died 560 B.C.), a king of Lydia whose victories in Asia Minor established the foundation of the Lydian empire. A ruler of the Mermnadae dynasty, he succeeded his father, Sadyattes, about 610 B.C. About 590 he came into conflict with the Median empire. On May 28, 585, a battle between Alyattes and Cyaxares, the Median king, was ended by a total eclipse of the sun. The treaty that followed established the Halys River (now the Kızılırmak) as the boundary between the two empires.

Alyattes died in 560 and was succeeded by his son Croesus. He was buried in a magnificent tomb north of Sardis, his capital city.

ALYPIUS, ə-lip'ē-əs, a Greek writer on music in the mid-300's A.D. His *Introduction to Music,* a list of symbols of scales and modes, is the chief guide to the system of musical notation employed by the ancient Greeks. In 1652, Mark Meiboom published a collection of Alypius' writings, among others, under the title *Antiquae musicae auctores septem Graece et Latine.*

ALYSSUM. See SWEET ALYSSUM.

ALZHEIMER'S DISEASE, älts'hī-mərz, the most common cause of dementia, that is, the progressive loss of intellectual abilities. First described in 1906 by Alois Alzheimer, a German neuropathologist, this devastating and incurable condition is most prevalent among the elderly, affecting an estimated 10% of Americans over age 65 and 30% to 50% of those beyond age 85. An estimated 4 million Americans have Alzheimer's disease, and the condition will present an increasing societal problem as the number and proportion of elderly people in the population grow. Data from developed nations indicate that worldwide roughly 10% of the population over age 65 suffers from the disease.

Development. Since the earliest symptoms of Alzheimer's disease develop gradually, the exact onset of the condition may be difficult to identify. Often the earliest sign is forgetfulness, which may be accompanied by subtle changes in personality. As the disease progresses, other impairments develop, including difficulties with language, perception, and complex motor skills. The patient gradually declines over a period of five to ten years and may reach a point of losing control of body functions and becoming unresponsive to those around him or her. Death often results from complications, such as pneumonia, related to the patient's lack of mobility.

Effects on the Family. Alzheimer's disease causes tremendous psychological strain on both patient and family. Legal and financial issues often become complicated when an individual is no longer competent to manage his or her own affairs. Often the most difficult decision the family faces in the later stages of the disease is whether or when to place the patient in an extended-care facility.

Effects on the Brain. Alzheimer's disease is defined by specific changes in the brain. The disease involves shrinkage of the brain together with loss of nerve cells in several areas of the brain thought to be important for intellectual activity. Under the microscope two abnormalities are usually seen. Clusters of neuritic plaques, composed of degenerating nerve-cell elements surrounding a core of the brain protein β-amyloid, are widespread. In addition, fibrous structures called neurofibrillary tangles are found in diseased neurons and may interfere with normal cell function.

Associated with these nerve-cell changes is a reduction in the brain's neurotransmitters, chemical messengers used for communication between nerve cells. Understanding the changes in these neurotransmitter levels is particularly important, since many of the drug treatments for neurological and psychiatric diseases work by way of neurotransmitter systems. A major neurotransmitter affected in Alzheimer's disease is acetylcholine (which plays an important role in memory), because the condition destroys a portion of the brain's acetylcholine-producing nerve cells. While other neurotransmitters are also affected in Alzheimer's disease, the alterations in acetylcholine are the most severe and the most consistently found.

Possible Causes. Although the precise cause of Alzheimer's disease remains a mystery, research has increasingly focused on a genetic basis for the condition. Scientists now suggest that genes on at least three different chromosomes may be responsible for Alzheimer's disease. Chromosome 19 may control the common form, which appears after age 65, while two other, relatively rare forms of the condition, occurring at an earlier age, may

be linked to genetic material on chromosomes 14 and 21. If these three chromosomes do play a developmental role, however, they may do so in combination with other factors. Some researchers have suggested that an infectious agent similar to a virus, or perhaps concentrations of aluminum in the brain, may be involved.

Scientists are also looking into the possible role of β-amyloid in Alzheimer's disease. Some researchers suggest that the protein itself may cause nerve degeneration, while others believe that, on the contrary, it is the breakdown of the cells that causes the protein to collect. However, scientists have found that, in the lab, synthetic β-amyloid can destroy neurons. If the protein does contribute to the development of Alzheimer's disease, scientists may one day discover a method to treat, or even prevent, the condition by interfering with the production of β-amyloid.

Research also indicates that a direct link exists between acetylcholine levels and the production of β-amyloid. Scientists have found evidence that levels of the protein can rise if concentrations of the neurotransmitter decline.

Diagnosis. Specific tests for Alzheimer's disease are virtually nonexistent. To make a diagnosis, a physician must generally rule out all other possible causes of dementia-like symptoms and assess whether the patient's symptoms are consistent with Alzheimer's. Although Alzheimer's disease is the most common cause of dementia, many other diseases can result in similar changes in behavior and intellect. In about 10% of patients, dementia has a potentially reversible cause such as stroke, brain tumor, head injury, liver or kidney disease, thyroid or other endocrine problems, or brain infection. In addition, some psychiatric disorders, such as depression, can be mistaken for dementia. A thorough evaluation of the patient with dementia is therefore essential before the diagnosis of Alzheimer's is accepted. Definitive diagnosis, however, is possible only through a brain biopsy of a living patient (which is rare) or through an autopsy of the brain after death.

Therapy. No specific treatment has been found that consistently ameliorates the symptoms of Alzheimer's disease or reverses the disease process. Nevertheless, a variety of therapies can be helpful for the individual affected by this disease. Research indicates that the medication known as tacrine can bring about some mental improvement, including the ability to remember and reason, in a portion of Alzheimer's patients. The drug inhibits the enzyme acetylcholinesterase, which breaks down acetylcholine.

Specific medications can also be used to treat the depression and other psychological problems that may accompany the disease and increase the symptoms of dementia. Also, psychotherapy can help both patient and family deal with the illness, and support groups such as those organized in the United States by the Alzheimer's Association offer substantial help.

Research. Considerable research is being directed toward the development of therapies for Alzheimer's disease. One potential treatment involves the implantation of fetal tissue into the brain in order to improve neurological function.

Other promising therapies may result from the contributions of a number of medical disciplines. By examining the demographic characteristics of Alzheimer's patients, for example, epidemiologists may be able to identify factors that place certain people at high risk for the disease. In addition, neurologists, psychiatrists, and psychologists are studying individual patients in the hope of better defining the nature of the intellectual impairments associated with Alzheimer's; neuropathologists are working to understand why only some nerve cells are affected by the disease; and neurochemists are analyzing the neurotransmitter changes linked to the condition. With this combined effort, it is hoped that understanding of Alzheimer's disease will substantially increase.

PETER J. WHITEHOUSE, M.D.*
Johns Hopkins University

Bibliography

Aschwanden, C., and L. Cederborg, "Could a Vaccine Prevent Alzheimer's Disease?," *Health* 13 (1999):24.

Gillick, Muriel R., *Tangled Minds: Understanding Alzheimer's Disease and Other Dementias* (Dutton 1998).

Gray-Davidson, Frena, *Alzheimer's Disease: Frequently Asked Questions: Making Sense of the Journey* (Contemporary Bks. 1998).

Hamdy, Ronald C., et al., eds., *Alzheimer's Disease: A Handbook for Caregivers*, 3d ed. (Mosby 1998).

Huffman, G. B., "Are Cholinergic Deficits Present in Early Alzheimer's Disease?," *American Family Physician* 60 (1999):1232.

Whitehouse, Peter J., et al., eds., *Concepts of Alzheimer Disease: Biological, Clinical, and Cultural Perspectives* (Johns Hopkins Univ. Press 2000).

AMADEUS, am-ə-dē′əs (1845–1890), duke d'Aosta and king of Spain. He was born in the Piedmontese city of Turin, in the Kingdom of Sardinia, on May 30, 1845, the second son of the future king Victor Emmanuel II of Italy. The Italian form of this name is *Amedeo;* the Spanish is *Amadeo.*

Amadeus was one of the European princes whom the Spanish liberal monarchists, led by Gen. Juan Prim, sought as a constitutional monarch after they overthrew Isabella II in 1868. When Leopold of Hohenzollern–Sigmaringen (whose candidacy for the Spanish throne was the immediate cause of the Franco-Prussian War) finally withdrew, Amadeus unwillingly accepted the crown, to please his father and the Italian government.

Amadeus was proclaimed king by the Spanish Cortes on Nov. 16, 1870, and reached Madrid on Jan. 2, 1871. The liberal monarchists were divided into several quarreling factions. Both the radical Republicans and the reactionary Carlists opposed Amadeus, as did the Spanish nobility and the mass of the people, who regarded him as a foreign intruder knowing neither their language nor their problems. His brief reign was a succession of ministerial crises, climaxed by a Carlist revolt that broke out in 1872. Amadeus abdicated on Feb. 11, 1873, and returned to his tranquil life in Turin. He died there on Jan. 18, 1890.

AMADIS OF GAUL, am′ə-dis, gôl, the most famous romance of chivalry in prose. The oldest extant edition of the *Amadís de Gaula* (completed about 1492; *Amadis of Gaule,* 1590–1618) was printed in Saragossa, Spain, in 1508. Its author was Garcí Rodríguez (or Ordóñez) de Montalvo, governor of Medina del Campo in Castile. Montalvo adapted the first three books from a medieval model, Spanish or perhaps Portuguese, known by the late 13th or early 14th century and clearly influenced by French Arthurian romances. Adding a fourth book, Montalvo thus started on its career a romance destined to unfold in more continuations than any other known to literary history. In Miguel de Cervantes's *Don Quixote,* the work is characterized as the "best of all books of its kind"—

splendid praise that has been echoed by later critics. (See ARTHURIAN ROMANCES; DON QUIXOTE.)

The scenes of the *Amadis* are laid in a mythical Britain and an imaginary Firm Island. (*Gaula* signifies Wales.) Amadis of Gaul is a prince of Wales, born of a secret amour, reared as a knight, and serving devotedly the fair English princess Oriana. For her sake he contends against monsters and enchantments, defends her father's kingdom from an oppressor, and opposes and finally vanquishes the Roman emperor as rival. He at last is formally united to Oriana in marriage.

High ideals mark the work—pride, honor, valor, love, loyalty to the king, and religion. *Amadis* contains none of the extravagances of later chivalric romances, which were effectively parodied by Cervantes in *Don Quixote,* and exhibits comparatively little of the absurdity characteristic of its fantastic continuations. Of these the first was Montalvo's own sequel, *Las sergas de Esplandián* (1510; *The Labors of the Very Brave Knight Esplandián,* 1992). Its hero is the son of Amadis and Oriana. Most other continuations followed the fortunes of Esplandian's descendants, professing to be additional books of the original *Amadis.*

FRANK W. CHANDLER*, *University of Cincinnati*

Bibliography: Keen, Maurice H., *Chivalry* (Yale Univ. Press 1984); O'Connor, John J., *Amadis de Gaule and Its Influence on Elizabethan Literature* (Rutgers Univ. Press 1970); Pierce, Frank, *Amadís de Gaula* (Twayne 1976); Thomas, Henry, *Spanish and Portuguese Romances of Chivalry* (Cambridge 1920).

AMADO, Jorge, ä-mä′tho̅ (1912–2001), widely translated Brazilian novelist whose works depict life in his native state of Bahia. Amado was born on Aug. 10, 1912, on his family's cacao plantation in northeastern Brazil. While studying law in Rio de Janiero, Amado began to formulate left-wing political views and to write. His first novel, *O país do carnaval* (1931; "Carnival Land"), reflects his political concerns and his sympathy for the common people. These preoccupations persisted in his next novels, *Cacau* (1933; "Cacao") and *Suor* (1934; "Sweat"), and culminated in *Terras do sem fin* (1943; *The Violent Land,* 1965), a saga of the Bahia cacao plantations in east-central Brazil that established his reputation as a master of the regional novel.

Amado's ensuing works relied less on Marxist ideology and more on magic realism, along with shrewd characterization and sympathetic portrayals of Brazilian daily life. Outstanding among the later novels are *Gabriela, cravo e canela* (1958; *Gabriela, Clove and Cinnamon,* 1962) and *Dona Flor e seus dois maridos* (1966; *Dona Flor and Her Two Husbands,* 1986), both of which were filmed; *Tenda dos milagres* (1969; *Tent of Miracles,* 1971); *Tieto do agreste* (1977; *Tieta, the Goat Girl,* 1979); *Tocaia grande* (1984; *Showdown,* 1986); and *Sumiço da santa* (1993; *The War of the Saints,* 1993). Amado, who at various times was imprisoned and exiled for his political activities, served as a Communist party representative to the Brazilian parliament from 1946 until 1948. He was awarded the Stalin Peace Prize in 1951 and France's Legion of Honor in 1985. Amado died on Aug. 6, 2001, in Salvador, Brazil.

Bibliography: Brower, Keith H., et al., eds., *Jorge Amado: New Critical Essays* (Garland 2000); Chamberlain, Bobby J., *Jorge Amado* (Twayne 1990); Mellen, Joan, *Magic Realism* (Gale 2000).

AMAGASAKI, ä-mä-gä-sä-kē, a city in Japan, in the Hyogo prefecture, on southwestern Honshu Island. It is on Osaka Bay near the mouth of the Yodo River. Part of the Osaka-Kobe industrial area, Amagasaki is known chiefly for the manufacture of iron and steel. It serves Osaka as a suburb, and has excellent railway service. Air transportation is available at Osaka International Airport. The city was heavily bombed toward the end of World War II but was rapidly rebuilt. Population: 466,187 (2000 census).

AMAHL AND THE NIGHT VISITORS, ä-mäl', a one-act opera by Gian Carlo Menotti, who wrote both the libretto and the music. Commissioned by the National Broadcasting Company for live U.S. television, the opera premiered on Dec. 24, 1951. It was so successful that it became an annual television presentation during the Christmas season; it is also popular with theater audiences worldwide. It tells the story of Amahl, a crippled shepherd boy who, upon meeting the three Magi bearing gifts for the Christ Child, offers his crutch as a gift and is then miraculously cured.

AMAKUSA ISLANDS, ä-mä-kōō-sä, an island group situated in the East China Sea off the west coast of Kyushu, Japan. They are administered by Kumamoto prefecture. Shimo and Kami are the largest of the more than 70 islands in the archipelago. The principal industries are coal mining, lumbering, and fishing. Hondo on Shimo Island is the chief city.

AMALARIC (502?–531), ə-mal'ə-rik, king of the Visigoths of Spain and Septimania (the coastal region between the Rhône River and the Pyrenees). Following the death of his father, Alaric II, in battle with Clovis in 507, the kingdom was protected until 526 by Amalaric's Ostrogoth grandfather, Theodoric, king of Italy. After Amalaric became king, he attempted to make peace with the Franks by marrying Clovis's daughter Clotilda. When he mistreated his wife, her brother Childebert came to her rescue with a Frankish army and killed Amalaric near Narbonne, France.

AMALASUNTHA (498?–535), am-ə-lə-sun'thə, queen of the Ostrogoths. The daughter of Theodoric the Great, she was born probably at Ravenna, Italy, and in 515 was married to an Ostrogoth noble, Eutharic. On the latter's death she was left with two children, one of whom, Athalaric, was heir to the throne. When Theodoric died in 526, Amalasuntha became regent during her son's minority, until his death (Oct. 2, 534), when she became queen.

At Amalasuntha's invitation, her cousin Theodahad shared the throne. Accusing her of conspiring to deliver the kingdom to Justinian, emperor of the East, Theodahad imprisoned her in a castle on Lake Bolsena, near Viterbo, Italy, on April 30, 535, and had her strangled. Her love of Byzantine and Roman learning made her unpopular among her Gothic subjects. Her name is also spelled Amalsuentha or Amalaswintha.

AMALEKITES, am'ə-lek-īts, an ancient nomadic tribe described in the Bible as a serious enemy of Israel. The Amalekites inhabited the desert south of Palestine and east of Shur on the Sinai Peninsula and penetrated northern Arabia and the region, called the Arabah, south of the Dead Sea. They frequently troubled the Hebrews during the Exodus, the Hebrews' migration from Egypt to Canaan. Deuteronomy 25:17–19 records the memory of this experience.

The Amalekites continued to be a serious problem for Israel during the period of the judges, when Gideon conquered them (Judges 6 to 7). Later, King Saul defeated them in battle but refused to destroy their livestock and their king Agag in spite of a divine command to do so (I Samuel 15). During the reign of David, the king had to rescue two of his wives from them (I Samuel 30:1–20).

The Hebrews' attitude toward the Amalekites is reflected in Balaam's prophecy (Numbers 24:20) and in Psalm 83:7, as well as in the Deuteronomy passage noted above. In the Book of Esther, Haman, the archenemy of Israel, is termed "the Agagite," emphasizing his descent from Agag, king of the hated tribe, and is opposed to Mordecai the Benjamite. Statements in the Bible about the Amalekites are obscure, however, and archaeological discoveries have contributed little toward an understanding of this people.

AMALFI, ä-mäl'fē, a town in Italy. Amalfi is in the Salerno province, in the region of Campania. It is situated about 24 miles (39 km) southeast of Naples on the Gulf of Salerno. It is a tourist center noted for its fine scenery. The breathtaking Amalfi Drive, cut from rugged cliffs along the gulf, extends west almost as far as Sorrento and east to a point just before Salerno. Amalfi's chief industry, besides tourism, is fishing.

Originally a Byzantine settlement, Amalfi rivaled Venice and Genoa as a center for trade with the East in the 800s. By 839 it had become independent of Naples and Benevento and was developing as a naval power. It became a duchy in 953 and an independent republic early in the 11th century. The *Tabula Amalphitana* (*Amalfitan Table*), its notable maritime code, was used from the 1100s to the 1500s throughout the Mediterranean area. The tablets are still kept in the town hall. The harbor has, for the most part, been filled in by periodic landslides. Population: 5,428 (2001 census).

AMALGAM, ə-mal'gəm, an alloy that contains mercury as the base metal. Most common metals react with mercury to form amalgams. Amalgams, whose exact nature is complicated, are interesting because in them a liquid metal (mercury) can be made to react with a solid metal at room temperature to form an alloy. Amalgams are used mainly for dental fillings and for extracting silver and gold from ore. In cadmium standard cells a cadmium-mercury amalgam is used to produce a standard voltage. (See also ALLOYS.)

Natural and Synthetic Amalgams. A natural amalgam of silver occurs as massive isometric crystals. A natural amalgam of gold also exists.

Amalgams can be made by exposing clean, bright, metal surfaces to mercury. The use of dilute acid often is helpful because the acid cleans the metal surface of oxide soils, which retard the reaction between the mercury and the metal. Heat, which also speeds the process of making an amalgam, makes the mercury atoms and the alloy atoms diffuse (or migrate) throughout the substance at a faster rate.

In electrochemical methods for producing amalgams, either the solid metal is dipped into a mercury salt solution or the mercury (or mercury amalgam) is placed in a solution of a metal salt. The process can be aided by the passage of an appropriate electric current, as in electroplating. (See also ELECTROPLATING.)

Uses. The amalgam used for dental fillings is an alloy that nominally contains the following weight percentages of elements: 52% mercury; 33% silver; 12.5% tin; 2% copper; and 0.5% zinc. As first formed, the amalgam is plastic. While in this condition, it is packed into the excavated tooth. If it is proportioned properly, protected from moisture prior to packing, and not excessively rubbed or packed, the amalgam will expand slightly upon hardening. Careful control of expansion is essential in order to lock the filling in place. (See also DENTISTRY.)

When used for the extraction of gold or silver from ore, an amalgam is made by placing a layer of mercury on a suitable metal plate, which frequently is made of copper. A gold-bearing water suspension, which is sometimes obtained from crushed ore, is allowed to flow over the mercury-coated plate. The heavier gold particles form an amalgam layer that is scraped off periodically. The excess liquid mercury is squeezed through canvas or chamois, which retains the pastelike amalgam layer. Mercury, gold, and other noble metals are separated from the amalgam by distillation. (The use of corduroy cloth largely has replaced the amalgam process. The ribs and valleys of the cloth mechanically trap the gold particles.) Extremely fine particles of gold do not amalgamate readily. These particles are recovered chemically from the suspension after it has passed over the mercury-coated plate. (See also GOLD; SILVER.)

CARL A. KEYSER
University of Massachusetts

AMALGAMATED CLOTHING AND TEXTILE WORKERS UNION

(ACTWU), a former AFL-CIO (American Federated Labor-Congress of Industrial Organization) union in the clothing and textile industry that pioneered in providing union assistance for employers and social services for members. In 1995 the ACTWU merged with the International Ladies' Garment Workers' Union (ILGWU) to form the Union of Needletrades, Industrial and Textile Employees (UNITE). (See also INTERNATIONAL LADIES' GARMENT WORKERS' UNION.)

The oldest segment of the ACTWU, the Amalgamated Clothing Workers of America (commonly referred to as the Amalgamated), traces its beginning to a national organization of tailors established in 1873 by the Knights of Labor. In 1895 the organization merged with the United Garment Workers, an AFL union founded in 1891. The national leaders of the United Garment Workers were native born and somewhat conservative, and most of the members were immigrants, largely eastern European. The more militant immigrant majority broke away in 1914 to form the Amalgamated Clothing Workers under Sidney Hillman. Its stock in trade was men's clothing (in contrast to the women's garments manufactured by members of the ILGWU). (See also HILLMAN, SIDNEY.)

The Amalgamated was socialist oriented in its early years but abandoned this point of view after the advent of the New Deal. In the 1920s and 1930s, attempts were made by Communists and racketeers to gain control of the union, but these failed. The Amalgamated did not affiliate with the AFL until 1933, and soon left to play an important role in founding the CIO. Hillman became a political adviser to Pres. Franklin D. Roosevelt and held high government posts during World War II. The Amalgamated helped launch the American Labor party as a third party in New York in 1936 but withdrew its support in 1948. On Hillman's death in 1946, Jacob Potofsky became president; he in turn was followed by others.

The Textile Workers Union of America (TWUA) was founded in 1939 as a means of organizing textile mill workers. One of its early successes was the elimination, in 1945, of wage disparities between mills in the South and those in the North. Within a few years the union had a substantial membership from Canada as well as from the United States. The American Federation of Hosiery Workers was incorporated into the TWUA in 1965, and in 1976 the TWUA itself merged with the Amalgamated to form the Amalgamated Clothing and Textile Workers Union.

Further changes in the industry, particularly the mass movement of apparel work overseas beginning in the 1980s, required further adaptations by labor organizations. In 1983 the United Hatters, Cap and Millinery Workers' International Union affiliated with the ACTWU. In subsequent years the ACTWU and the ILGWU collaborated in a variety of antisweatshop campaigns, and in 1995 they officially merged under the UNITE banner. Some 9,000 laundry and dry-cleaning workers joined the ranks of UNITE in 2001.

See also AMERICAN FEDERATION OF LABOR AND CONGRESS OF INDUSTRIAL ORGANIZATIONS.

AMALRIC OF BENA

(died c. 1206), ə-mal'rik, bē'nə, French theologian and philosopher. He was born at Bène (Bena), near Chartres, and is also known as Amalric (French, Amauri) of Chartres. Amalric taught philosophy at the University of Paris and was the founder of the heretical sect, the Amalricians.

The Amalricians held a pantheistic philosophy derived from Aristotle and Johannes Scotus Erigena. These doctrines were condemned by the university, by Pope Innocent III, and later by the Fourth Lateran Council (1215). As a result, ten of Amalric's followers were burned to death, and Amalric's body was exhumed and burned.

AMANA SOCIETY,

ə-man'ə, a producing and marketing cooperative in Iowa that administers the secular affairs of a community of seven villages situated on the Iowa River, 20 miles (30 km) southwest of Cedar Rapids. The villages, known as the Amana Colonies, were collectively designated a national historic landmark in 1965.

The name Amana Society is often used to refer to the Community of True Inspiration, the last extant branch of a pietistic sect founded in Germany in 1714. Led by Christian Metz, 800 sect members left Germany in 1842 and settled in Ebenezer, N.Y. In 1855 the community moved to Iowa and took the corporate name Amana Church Society. It adopted a system of communalism administered by church elders. In June 1932 its secular affairs were reorganized under the new Amana Society. Many communalistic practices were dropped; all members were issued stock in the profit-sharing society, which is supported by agriculture, handicrafts, and tourism.

AMANITA, am-ə-nīt′ə, is a genus of fungi in the gill fungi family, Agaricaceae. It has characteristic white spores, and the structure is typical of the family—a stalk (stipe) topped by an umbrella-shaped cap (pileus). It also has some additional structures: a membranous or fleshy ring (annulus) that generally surrounds the stipe just below the pileus, and a sac or cup (volva) around the base of the stipe.

The various species of *Amanita* are widely distributed; most are poisonous. The commonest species is the fly mushroom (*Amanita muscaria*), which has a variously colored (often bright red) cap and yellow or white gills. Another species, the death cup (*A. phalloides*), usually is green, brown, or gray. Both of these species are found in woods. See also MUSHROOM.

AMAPÁ, ä-mə-pá′, is a territory in northern Brazil. It is bounded on the east by the Atlantic Ocean, on the south by the Amazon River and its delta, on the west by the Jarí River, which separates it from the state of Pará, and on the north by French Guiana and Surinam. Its area is 53,694 square miles (139,168 sq km). Most of the land is less than 1,000 feet (304.8 meters) above sea level, although the Tumuc-Humac Mountains in the west rise above 2,000 feet (609 meters). The country is heavily forested, but there are some cattle-grazing lands in the east. Amapá's principal product is manganese, which is mined in the central region and shipped by railroad 100 miles (161 km) to Macapá, the territory's capital, on the Amazon. There are also iron mines. Other natural resources are rubber, gold, hardwood timber, medicinal plants, and Brazil nuts.

Possession of the territory's northern section, long in dispute between France and Brazil, was awarded to Brazil by arbitration in 1900. Amapá was part of Pará until it became a separate territory in 1943; it achieved statehood in 1990. Population: 248,100 (1989 est.).

AMARANTHUS, am-ər-an′thəs, is a genus of flowering plants found chiefly in tropical countries. The common name for the plants of the genus is *amaranth*. The genus takes its name from the Greek word meaning "unfading," because the flowers preserve their appearance after they are plucked and dried. As a result, the amaranth has been used by poets as a symbol of immortality. The plant is characterized by dense flowers that lack petals and are composed of white or reddish scales. *Amaranthus* is the typical genus of the family Amaranthaceae and has about 60 species. The plant is grown largely as an ornamental. Common garden varieties include *love-lies-bleeding, prince's feather, Joseph's coat,* and *cockscomb.* Some of the species are troublesome weeds, such as *pigweed* and *tumbleweed.* Two species are cultivated as cereals in Asia.

AMARAPURA, u-mə-rä-pōō-rä′, a town in Myanmar (Burma) and formerly the capital of the country. It is situated on the east bank of the Irrawaddy River 5 miles (8 km) south of Mandalay, of which it is a suburb. Tile, pottery, and baskets are manufactured. Founded in 1783 as a new capital of the Burmese kingdom, the town was destroyed by fire in 1810. It was abandoned as the capital in 1860. The ruins of former royal palaces and a colossal statue of the Buddha are tourist attractions. Population: 10,519 (1983 census).

AMARILLO, am-ə-ril′ō, a city in Texas, is the seat of Potter County but extends into Randall County. It is situated nearly in the center of the Texas Panhandle, at an altitude of 3,676 feet (1,120 meters). It is sometimes called "the crossroads of the Panhandle."

Amarillo is a major banking, business, and industrial center for northwest Texas and adjacent areas of New Mexico and Oklahoma, and an important market for cattle, wheat, and sorghum. Its industries include petrochemicals, grain and feed storage and processing, meat packing, and the manufacture of clothing, leather goods, and cement. The U.S. Bureau of Mines' Helium Activity, the only large-scale producer of helium in the world, has its operational headquarters and principal storage facilities in Amarillo. The city is a major railroad junction, and Amarillo Air Terminal supplies commercial air service. Route 66, the main highway from Oklahoma City to southern California, traverses the city.

Educational and cultural institutions include Amarillo College, a fully accredited two-year college; the Amarillo Symphony Orchestra; Amarillo Little Theatre; and the Amarillo Civic Ballet. Among its recreational facilities are Ellwood Park, Thompson Park, and the Tri-State Fairgrounds. Annual events include the Amarillo Fat Stock Show, a tri-state music festival, and a tri-state fair. Palo Duro Canyon State Park, 16 miles (25.7 km) southeast of Amarillo, is located in a colorful canyon, 1,120 feet (404 meters) deep, whose walls record four geologic ages.

In 1541 the Spanish explorer Francisco Vásquez de Coronado reached the vicinity of Amarillo in his search for the legendary Seven Cities of Cibola, which a previous Spanish explorer had reported to be rich in gold. A monument to Juan de Padilla, a member of Coronado's expedition who was killed by the Indians in 1544, stands in Ellwood Park.

It was not until after the Civil War that settlers were attracted to the Texas Panhandle. In the 1870's buffalo hunters swarmed into the region, killing bison for their hides, and by 1885 the animal was nearly extinct. In 1887 a construction crew of the Fort Worth and Denver City Railroad camped on the future site of Amarillo—which was then called *Ragtown.* Henry B. Sanborn, a land developer, laid out the new city and promoted it as county seat. Amarillo was incorporated in 1892. The name, which in Spanish means "yellow," was first given by Mexican herders to Amarillo Lake, for its yellow banks.

By 1890, Amarillo was one of the largest cattle-shipping points in the United States. A typical cowboy town, with hotels, cafés, saloons, and gambling houses, it was policed by the Texas Rangers until 1899. With the coming of the railroad, farmers moved in, and when cotton was introduced into the Panhandle shortly after the turn of the century, Amarillo became a ginning and cottonseed-oil mill center.

Following the discovery of the first natural gas well in the vast Panhandle field in 1918, the discovery of oil in 1921, and the subsequent development of oil production in the region, Amarillo's industrial growth began. By 1930, with increasing acreage in wheat and small grains, it also became a center for grain storage, milling, and feed production.

Amarillo has a council-manager form of government. Population: 173,627.

DORMAN H. WINFREY, *Texas State Library*

AMARYLLIDACEAE, am-ə-ril-ə-dā′sē-ē, the am-aryllis family, are a large group of perennial herbs. The plants are identified by rootstocks of bulbs, corms, or rhizomes; basal leaves; and lilylike flowers with an ovary located below the level of the outer floral envelope. The Amaryllidaceae are closely related to the lily family but are more advanced in development.

The amaryllis family has 86 genera and 1,310 species. They are found in tropical and subtropical regions. Only 8 genera with 66 species occur in the United States. *Agave,* the largest of the genera, is an important source of fiber, especially sisal hemp. Most of the other genera are cultivated as ornamentals, including *Amaryllis* (belladonna lily), *Galanthus* (snowdrop), *Hypoxis* (star grass), *Hymenocallis* (spider lily), *Leucojum* (snowflake), *Narcissus* (daffodils, jonquils), and *Zephyranthes* (zephyr lily).

AMARYLLIS, am-ə-ril′əs, is a group of bulbous, lilylike plants found in tropical America. They are often grown under glass as spring and summer ornamentals. The amaryllis has long slender leaves and large fleshy roots. Its funnel-shaped flowers, which appear in clusters, are red, white, or white-striped.

The genus *Amaryllis* belongs to the amaryllis family, Amaryllidaceae; there are about 70 species. Most of the species now classified in this genus formerly were considered members of the genus *Hippeastrum.* The belladonna lily, A. *belladonna,* is a common species that has red or salmon-red flowers four to five inches long; it is native to South Africa. A. *reticulata* has rose-pink flowers with darker rose-colored crossbars; it is found in Brazil. A. *reginiae,* which is found in Mexico, the West Indies, and South America, is identified by its bright red flower with a white star at the throat. A. *vittata* is a red-and-white-striped form that is found in the Peruvian Andes. Most of the cultivated types of *Amaryllis* are hybrid forms.

Amaryllis is also the common name for the whole plant family Amaryllidaceae (q.v.).

AMASA, am′ə-sə, in the Old Testament, was a nephew of King David. When Absalom rebelled against David, his father, he made Amasa commander of his army. The rebellion was crushed by David's forces, led by Joab, who killed Absalom. Amasa then was appointed commander of David's army, replacing Joab. His first mission was to put down a revolt led by Sheba, a Benjaminite, and he was given three days to assemble an army in Judah. When Amasa was late in returning, Abishai was put in charge of the royal army and later was joined by Joab. Amasa met them at Gibeon, where he was murdered by Joab as they were greeting each other (II Samuel 17:25, 20:4–12).

AMASIS, ə-mā′səs, was an Egyptian king of the 26th (Saite) dynasty who reigned from 570 to 526 B.C. He succeeded Apries (the Biblical Pharaoh Hophra) when his native force defeated his predecessor's mercenaries.

Amasis appears to have been a capable and judicious sovereign. He saved Egypt from conquest by Nebuchadnezzar of Babylon, who ravaged Egypt but was forced to retreat. He also preserved the land from invasion by Cyrus the Great of Persia. Maintaining friendly relations with the Greeks, Amasis promoted commerce with them and encouraged their colonization in

ROCHE

AMARYLLIS, with colorful flowers ranging from red to white, often is popularly cultivated as an ornamental.

Egypt. The excellent port of Naucratis, which he assigned to them, grew into a flourishing city. After the temple at Delphi was burned, he contributed liberally to its reconstruction. He built a Temple of Isis at Memphis and erected a colossus before the Temple of Vulcan. According to Herodotus, he was visited by Pythagoras, Polycrates, Solon, and other outstanding citizens of Greece. He was also known as *Ahmose II.*

AMASYA, ä-mä-syä′, a city in north-central Turkey. Located in Amasya province, about 90 miles (145 km) northwest of Sivas, it has been known for centuries for its manufacture of beautiful tiles. The ancient city, known as Amasia, was the capital of the kingdom of Pontus and later became one of the chief cities of the Seljuk Turks. It was the birthplace of the geographer Strabo. Population: 57,288 (1990 census).

AMATEUR ATHLETIC UNION OF THE UNITED STATES, a nonprofit organization whose aim is to promote and improve sports and games among amateurs throughout the United States. A union of 55 district associations with more than 3,500 member units, the AAU provides competitive athletic programs in 16 sports and physical fitness activities for at least eight million Americans. About 10,000 volunteers plan and conduct the sports programs at all levels of competition and in every section of the country.

Founded in 1888 to combat abuses in amateur athletics, the AAU initiated a plan to protect the eligibility of athletes through a system of registration. The organization now governs basketball, bobsledding, boxing, gymnastics, judo, luge, swimming and diving, synchronized swimming, track and field events, water polo, weight lifting, and wrestling (catch-as-catch-can and Greco-Roman)—all of which are sports represented in the Olympic calendar. It is also the single United States member in the world federations governing these sports. In addition, the AAU has jurisdiction over baton twirling, handball, horseshoe pitching, and volleyball. The group has one of the largest representations on the U.S. Olympic Committee.

The AAU pioneered the development of municipal recreation departments, including public swimming pools. It now conducts a nationwide "Junior Olympics" in seven sports for boys and girls between the ages of 9 and 17.

Membership in the AAU is open to every American without regard to race, color, creed, or education, and every amateur athletic organization in the United States is invited to become an allied member. Among the approximately 50 allied groups are the National Association of Intercollegiate Athletics, Young Men's Christian Association, National Jewish Welfare Board, Catholic Youth Organization, and the armed forces. As an "umbrella"-type association, the AAU is the "rallying group" for all amateurs participating or interested in those sports under its jurisdiction.

Prior to 1960, the National Collegiate Athletic Association (NCAA) was an allied member of the AAU. Since then the NCAA, following the abrogation of the articles of alliance, has pursued an independent course. In the 1960's the two groups became involved in much-publicized jurisdictional disputes, and a series of efforts were made by nationally prominent figures to reconcile the points at issue.

The AAU publishes *Amateur Athlete*, a monthly magazine, as well as handbooks for each of its sports. The national headquarters is in Indianapolis, Ind.

STEPHEN M. ARCHER
Captain, U.S. Navy (Retired); Secretary, AAU

AMATEUR RADIO. See RADIO—*Amateur Radio* and *CB Radio.*

AMATEURISM, in sports, is the practice of contestants' pursuing a game as an avocation, merely for the love of it, and not for any recompense. Amateurism is followed by many local, national, and international groups, such as the Amateur Athletic Union, National Collegiate Athletic Association, and National Federation of State High School Associations, all in the United States; the Amateur Athletic Association, in England; the national Olympic committee of each member country; the international sports federations governing each Olympic sport; and the International Olympic Committee.

It is almost impossible to devise rules for participation that would apply in every case of amateurism, since conditions are variable in each sport. A contestant may be rewarded or paid in many different ways, but his intent in relation to the sport is known only to himself. What constitutes amateurism is further confused by the fact that in most competitive sports both amateur and professional teams exist. In some sports amateurs may compete under certain conditions against professionals (those who receive remuneration for participating in a sport and, therefore, whose vocations are in these sports). In other sports this is not allowed without jeopardizing the status of the amateur participant.

Originally, amateur competitors paid all their own expenses (the cost of clothing, equipment, travel, food, and housing). At present, because of the widespread development of sport and the youth of most of the participants, expenses are generally assumed by the amateur organization to which the athlete belongs.

Athletes who are subsidized by commercial establishments or government agencies solely because of their athletic ability are not considered amateurs. Business and industrial firms sometimes employ athletes chiefly for the value received from the publicity given to their athletic fame. These athletes presumably are paid to devote most of their time and energies to perfecting their athletic skills. For national aggrandizement, governments occasionally adopt similar methods; they give athletes special positions in the armed services, in the police force, or in a government office. They also operate training camps for extended periods. It is thus easy for a government agency to command leaves of absence for their athletes to train for scheduled events. Recipients of these special favors, which are granted only because of athletic ability, are not amateurs.

Contestants in the Olympic Games must be amateurs. As defined in the Olympic rules, an amateur "is one who participates and always has participated in sport as an avocation without material gain of any kind." He does not qualify: "(a) if he has not a basic occupation designed to insure his present and future livelihood" (if sport is an avocation, there must be a vocation); "(b) if he receives or has received remuneration for participation in sport." In addition to the above requirements, the athlete must comply with the rules of the international sports federation that governs his sport.

The Olympic code bars from Olympic competition any athlete who has:

(1) Received prizes exceeding $50 in value or presents that can be converted into money or into other material advantages.

(2) Received payment of excessive expenses or demanded payment or expense money for a manager, coach, relative, or friend.

(3) Capitalized in any way on his athletic fame or success or accepted special inducements of any kind to participate.

(4) Secured employment or promotion by reason of his sports performances rather than his ability in the job, whether in commercial or industrial enterprises, the armed services, or branches of the press, theater, television, cinema, radio, or any other paid activity.

(5) Indicated his intention of becoming a professional athlete.

(6) Received payment for teaching or coaching others for competition in a sport.

(7) Been awarded a scholarship based mainly on his athletic ability.

(8) Interrupted his occupation (studies or employment) for special sports training in a camp for more than four weeks.

When any sport has become commercially successful as a means of entertainment (baseball, football, and basketball, for example), it is practically impossible to conduct a strictly amateur program at an international, or even at a national, level because of the large sums of money involved. Such a sport eventually may have to be dropped from the Olympic program, or it may never become a part of the program.

As long as the regulations governing amateurism in sports remain primarily the responsibility of the many separate international sports federations and their national affiliates, it will continue to be difficult to obtain a uniform code of interpretation and enforcement for the conduct of amateur sports throughout the world.

AVERY BRUNDAGE, *Former President*
International Olympic Committee

AMATI, ä-mä′tē, an Italian family of Cremona, who were celebrated as musical instrument makers, particularly of violins, in the 16th and 17th centuries.

ANDREA AMATI (c. 1530–c. 1578) was the first known member of the family to devote himself to violin making. His earliest violins are dated 1564. He is credited with introducing the modern shape of the violin (later modified by Antonio Stradivari) and the characteristic amber-colored varnish of the Amati instruments. He produced two sizes of violins, the larger of which became known as the "grand Amati." He also made a few violas and cellos.

ANTONIO AMATI (1550–1638) and GIROLAMO or GERONIMO AMATI (1556–1630), Andrea's two sons, carried on the tradition of high craftsmanship established by their father. They became known as "the brothers Amati." In addition to violins, they made a number of other types of stringed instruments, including violas and violoncellos.

NICCOLO or NICCOLA AMATI (1596–1684), Girolamo's son, inherited the business from his father and uncle and extended the fame of the family. His violins were of the highest quality, distinguished for their practical shape and for the beauty and power of their tone. He also produced violas and cellos. Niccolò was the master in whose shop Andrea Guarnieri and Stradivari, two later great violin makers, received their early training.

GIROLAMO AMATI (1649–1740), the son of Niccolò, maintained the high degree of craftsmanship of the Amati instruments for another generation. Although he produced a large number of instruments of the highest class, he was overshadowed by his contemporary Stradivari, who modified the Amati violin to produce what is now widely regarded as the classical shape of the violin.

AMATO, ä-mä′tō, **Pasquale** (1878–1942), Italian baritone. Born in Naples, Italy, on March 21, 1878, he studied at the Naples Conservatory and made his debut at the age of 22 in *La Traviata* at the Teatro Bellini in the same city. He sang at La Scala in Milan, at other leading opera houses in Italy, and elsewhere on the Continent. In 1904 he appeared in London.

In 1908, Amato went to the United States, where he first appeared at the Metropolitan Opera in New York City as the elder Germont in *La Traviata* with Marcella Sembrich and Enrico Caruso. It was at the Metropolitan that he achieved his first great successes, sharing many triumphs with Caruso. His roles included Rigoletto, Valentin, Kurwenal, Iago, Scarpia, Sharpless, and Figaro (in *The Barber of Seville*). He created the role of Jack Rance, the sheriff, in Puccini's *Girl of the Golden West*, and appeared in the American premieres of *Mme. Sans-Gêne, Cyrano de Bergerac, L'amore dei tre re*, and less well-known operas. His voice was brilliant, sonorous, and of great range, and he acted well. He left the Metropolitan in 1921, and thereafter taught voice, continued to sing on occasion, and directed operatic productions for a time at Louisiana State University. He died in New York City on Aug. 12, 1942.

AMAUROSIS, am-ô-rō′səs, is a partial or total loss of sight caused by disease of the optic nerve, retina, or brain. Amaurosis is sometimes confused with amblyopia. See also AMBLYOPIA.

AMAUROTIC FAMILY IDIOCY, am-ô-rot′ik, is a rare, lethal, hereditary disease of the brain, caused by a recessive gene. It is characterized by progressive mental deterioration and blindness (amaurosis) and by muscular weakness, spasms, and paralysis. The disease generally occurs in infancy but may begin in later childhood. It is caused by an excess of a lipid substance that accumulates in the brain because of the absence of an enzyme that normally removes the substance. In the infantile form of the disease, the appearance of a cherry red spot on the retina of the eye is an important diagnostic aid.

AMAZIAH, am-ə-zī′ə, in the Old Testament, was a king of Judah. After taking the throne he put to death all those in the court who had conspired to murder his father, Joash. He reconquered Edom, which had won its independence from Judah. He turned to the worship of idols and challenged Jehoash, king of Israel to war, but his army was routed at Beth Shamesh. He was captured and taken to Jerusalem, where the victors sacked the city. Amaziah outlived Jehoash and was restored to the throne, but after several years he was murdered by conspirators. The story of Amaziah is in II Kings 14:1–14, 17–20 and II Chronicles 24:25.

AMAZON, am′ə-zon, in Greek legend, a member of a tribe of women warriors who lived on the southern shore of the Black Sea. The Amazons were said to kill or send away their male offspring, keeping only their female children.

One story about them involved the Greek hero Heracles (Hercules). For his ninth labor, he was ordered to obtain the girdle of Hippolyta, queen of the Amazons. Although she gave it to him, the goddess Hera (Juno) caused a misunderstanding and as a result Hippolyta was slain. In another legend, Theseus, king of Athens, attacked the Amazons and carried off their queen, Antiope. When Amazon forces invaded Attica, Theseus defeated them. In the Trojan War a band of Amazons supported Troy and fought bravely until Achilles slew their queen, Penthesilea.

Herodotus, the 5th century Greek historian, reported that following one war between Greeks and Amazons, the Greek party set sail with a number of Amazon captives. The women murdered their captors and were blown ashore in the territory of the Scythians. There they seized a herd of horses and rode away, pursued by the Scythians. Eventually, they took Scythian husbands who adopted the hunting, horseback-riding life to which the Amazons were accustomed. Their descendants were the Sauromatae.

While the early legends are largely fictitious, they may have had some kernel of fact. Among early Germanic tribes, women followed their men into battle, bringing food and encouragement to the fighting men. The Mongol armies of Genghis Khan were accompanied by their families. In the 19th century, Hazara women in Afghanistan supported their men in battle, bringing up ammunition and food, and the wife of one khan wore men's clothing and led troops in war. It is thus possible that, in wars with the Greeks, tribal women joined the fighting when their fathers and husbands were hard pressed, thus giving rise to the legends. It is improbable, however, that there was ever a tribe of women warriors.

ELIZABETH E. BACON
Author, "Central Asians Under Russian Rule"

THE UPPER AMAZON, seen here at Iquitos, Peru, is dotted with houseboats and canoes, showing how the life of the people of this region centers on the mighty stream.

AMAZON RIVER, am'ə-zon. The Amazon River extends approximately 3,900 miles (6,275 km) across the northern part of the South American continent. It is the world's second longest river, surpassed only by the Nile (about 4,145 miles or 6,670 km). The Amazon's drainage basin, or water catchment area, covers 2,053,318 square miles (5,318,100 sq km) and is the largest in the world. The main body of the Amazon flows across Brazil. With its tributaries it drains half the land of that country. Other tributaries flow into the Amazon from Bolivia, Peru, Colombia, and Venezuela. Brazilians call the main part of the river *Rio Amazonas*. Upstream from its junction with the Rio Negro at Manaus, Brazil, it is called the *Rio Solimões*.

The Amazon River closely follows the line of the equator from west to east. It drains the most extensive area of high rainfall in the world. This explains why six of its tributaries, and the Amazon itself, are among the largest rivers of the world. The discharge of water near the mouth of the Amazon is greater than that of any other river. It was measured at Obidos, Brazil, in 1960 and found to be 7,638,683 cubic feet (216,332 cubic meters) of water per second—about 12 times the volume of flow of the Mississippi River.

As one flies in an airplane over the Amazon River, it is difficult at first to grasp its immensity and diversity. For example, it takes 1 hour and 15 minutes to fly in a two-engine airplane across the delta and mouth of the Amazon from Belém

to Macapá, the capital of the federal territory of Amapá. Furthermore, one island in the delta of the river—Marajó Island—is one fourth larger than the state of Rhode Island.

The flight upstream, westward from Belém, in a low-flying plane is an unforgettable experience on a clear day. The Amazon does not look like an ordinary river. It looks more like a great river-sea, or huge arm of the sea, on which ocean-going vessels are moving. Because of the breadth of the floodplain one can rarely see both margins at the same time. The river itself appears in varying shades of light tan, although a few of its tributaries have a black color. The vegetation along the banks is green and yellow.

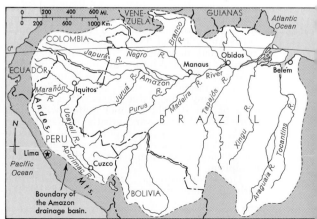

GEORGE HOLTON, FROM PHOTO RESEARCHERS

INDIANS of the upper Amazon basin. The Yahma hunter (*left*) has a blowgun for poison darts. The Shipibo mother and her child (below) reside in the valley of the Ucayali River in Peru, a headstream of the Amazon.

GEORGE HOLTON, FROM PHOTO RESEARCHERS

One way of defining the Amazon region is to call it the area covered by the Amazon tropical rain forest. This dense forest flourishes in the equatorial climate and influences almost every primary economic activity of the region. The Amazon tropical rain forest is, therefore, the element that best distinguishes the Amazon region geographically.

The area drained and served by the Amazon River has not yet been very productive or valuable to man. There have been sporadic periods of economic speculation in the area, based on forest products and rubber. But only the floodplain—comprising the two percent of the Amazon area—is reasonably well suited to agriculture. Hydroelectric potential is naturally small in rivers like the Amazon, where there are great volumes of water but little drop, or head, along their courses to turn hydroelectric turbines.

In the 1960's, Brazil began to pump resources into its vast tropical hinterland by allocating not less than three percent of its federal tax revenue to the Plan for the Economic Valorization of the Amazon. It had become apparent that the Amazon region would never progress economically with so few people spread over such a vast area, employing out-of-date technology, without economic aid. Government and private investments in the Amazon region have at last begun to integrate it economically and culturally with the rest of Brazil.

The Amazon and Its Tributaries. The sources of the Amazon River are many and scattered. The generally acknowledged source, 3,900 miles from the river's mouth, is high in the snowcapped Andes Mountains of Peru. There, icy mountain streams find their way into the Apurimac and Marañón rivers and eventually into the Solimões, or Amazon, River. The Amazon in its main course is not a meandering river like the Mississippi and so many other large rivers. It is a broad, more or less straight channel dotted with lens-shaped islands that vary greatly in length and width. However, a ship may be forced to follow a meandering course, simply because it is navigating around the many islands that lie in the floodplain.

Going downstream, as virtually all of the early explorers did, one is impressed by the monotony of the thick green wall of tropical vegetation that lines each bank. Since the Amazon provides the only surface transportation route available to the traveler, the river and its banks are the best-known portion of its basin. Most people do not venture away from the river, and therefore the vast and varied Amazon region has usually been described in terms of its antechamber—the floodplain. From this fact has come the widespread misconception that the Amazon region is a vast flooded swamp.

The principal tributaries are full-fledged rivers. The largest right-bank, or northward-flowing, tributaries and their lengths are the Xingu, 1,800 miles (2,900 km); Tapajós, 1,100 miles (1,800 km); Madeira, 2,100 miles (3,380 km); Purús, 2,000 miles (3,220 km); and Juruá, 1,500 miles (2,400 km). The main left-bank tributaries are the Japurá, 1,500 miles, and the Negro, 1,400 miles (2,250 km). Some of the tributaries, like the Rio Negro, resemble the Amazon in that they do not meander. Others, such as the Purús and Juruá, have pronounced meander patterns. The reasons for this difference are not yet well understood.

Another characteristic that differentiates the tributaries is the color of their waters. The so-called "white rivers" get their color from the yellowish clay particles, carried in suspension, which reflect the light. Both the Amazon and its tributary, the Madeira, are white-water rivers. The Rio Negro is a "black-water" river that owes its black aspect to the humic acid from decomposed organic matters on the forest floor. There are also rivers—like the Tapajós and Xingu—that run over white sands and, when seen from the air or in shallow places, have a clear, emerald-green color.

Navigation. The Amazon River and its tribu-

MANAUS, Brazil, is a commercial and shipping center of the rich region of the middle Amazon. Its river harbor accommodates seagoing vessels.

taries are navigable for long distances. The existence of this vast network of navigable water greatly influenced the original settlement of the region. People tended to establish themselves along the rivers' margins. The rivers were and still are the lifelines of the area. With the exception of the few people and goods now transported by air, everything still moves on the water. Before 1962 there was no road connecting the Brazilian Amazon with the outside world. Then the 1,250-mile (2,010-km) Belém-to-Brasília road was completed.

River navigation is heaviest along the Amazon itself and the larger tributaries like the Purús, Juruá, and Madeira, as well as on the lower courses of the smaller tributaries. The months of the high-water stage of the Amazon, from April to August, are the busiest for river navigation. Local boats are of three general types: sailing craft, which tend to be used in the outer area at the river's mouth and along the coasts of Maranhão, Pará, and the territory of Amapá; canoes, which are used everywhere; and motorboats, used on the Amazon and the larger rivers. Motorboats will often tow dugout canoes upstream for a small fee, or for nothing.

In the lower courses of the Amazon and its tributaries the ocean tides determine when boats can best move upstream (with the rising tide) or downstream (with the ebbing tide). During spring tides, when the lunar pull is strongest and other conditions of the river and sea are optimal, great tidal bores (waves) as high as 13 feet (4 meters) rush upstream with a deafening roar and are a menace to all shipping. The onomatopoeic Indian name for this fearsome tidal wave is *pororoca*.

In addition to the smaller craft there are much larger river streamers, stern-wheelers, and oceangoing freighters, tankers, and passenger ships. But small multipurpose motorboats serve the needs of most people. For example, there are several 35-foot (10-meter) motorboats based in Manaus that make an 8-hour "milk run" to Careiro Island early every morning. They pick up milk from dairy farms along the riverbank and let off and take on passengers. Gasoline, diesel oil, and kerosene are included in the cargo of practically all the boats.

The Amazon Basin. The Amazon basin is a young sedimentary plain situated between two old, but not very high, crystalline plateaus. It is flanked on the north by the Guiana Highlands, on the west by the Andean Cordillera, and on the south by the Brazilian Highlands. This vast sedimentary area, the largest in the world, is really a very low Tertiary-period plateau, most of which presents a subdued relief of hills, ridges, and tablelands. Most areas are less than 200 feet (60 meters) above sea level, but some ridges rise as high as 400–800 feet (120–240 meters).

The element in the landscape that most impresses visitors to the Amazon is its gigantic equatorial forest, the Amazon *hylea*. Like a dense mantle or carpet, the forest covers almost the entire region. It is the equatorial variant of the tropical rain forest and is typical of continental areas that have high rainfall and a uniformly warm, excessively humid climate. The forest of the floodplain has greater botanical diversity than that of higher ground, or terra firma. The quantity and variety of the seeds carried by the annual floodwaters and deposited on the rich soils of the floodplain are very great. The dryland forest on the unflooded *terra firme*, however, has a great variety of useful hardwoods. On the floodplain the so-called "white," or soft, woods predominate—among them, the rubber tree (*Hevea*) and the kapok tree (*Ceiba pentandra*).

The high-density woods of the *terra firme* include mahogany (Portuguese, *mogno*) and other fine cabinet woods, and the Brazil nut tree (Portuguese, *castanheiro*), which provides good building timber. There are many oil-yielding palms in the forest and the familiar profusion of ropelike lianas and epiphytes. The competition for sunlight forces the trees and their parasite plants to strive upward, with trees sometimes reaching 160 feet (50 meters) above the ground. There are also some fairly large areas of savanna grassland.

The basin has varied insect, reptile, and bird populations, but there are few large mammals. There are no equivalents in the Amazon region —or in South America generally—of the large animals of Africa. Much of the wild game in the more populated areas has been killed by

EWING GALLOWAY

AMAZON STEAMBOAT stops at the riverbank about 2,000 miles upstream to take on wood for its boiler fires.

hunters or driven away when forest land has been cleared for crops or pasture.

Climate. The climate over most of the Amazon basin seems monotonous to people raised in mid-latitudes, but it does have two distinct seasons: a dry season, lasting three to five months, and a rainy season. Most areas receive 80 to 120 inches (200–300 cm) of rainfall per year and experience daytime temperatures above 80° or 90° F (27° or 32° C) and nighttime temperatures above 70° (21° C) or 80° F. The warmest months are September to November, at the end of the dry season and just before the rainy season.

From May through September, during the dry season, cold waves (*friagems*), resulting from a northward movement of an Antarctic polar air mass, sometimes penetrate into the western Amazon basin. They can lower temperatures for three or four days by as much as 18° to 27° F (9°–14° C). These cold waves, further aggravated by the region's consistently high relative humidity (85 percent), damage crops, kill fish in shallow pools, and bring misery to people who are unaccustomed to low temperatures and are unprepared with warm clothing or heated houses.

Along the eastern parts of the Amazon basin, winds from the east and southeast predominate. Farther inland, variable light winds are more common. The rainy season, from December through April, actually coincides with the latitudinal migration of moist air, known as the Intertropical Convergence Zone, toward the equator and the areas where the sun's rays strike the earth's surface vertically. In general the most uncomfortable aspects of the climate can be minimized if there are shade and air movements. Modern, scientifically designed houses in Amapá have broad roofs that are insulated against the noonday heat and that shade most of the exterior walls from the sun's rays. The sides of the rooms are open and screened, allowing breezes to blow through the house. Until early in the afternoon, the atmosphere frequently absorbs the moisture that evaporates from land and water surfaces. Then a torrential thunderstorm will rage for 10 or 20 minutes, and the rest of the afternoon will be freshened and cooled by the shower. Around 4 P.M. the temperature begins to drop perceptibly—in contrast to the situation in mid-latitudes where the heat of summer days lasts longer.

Population. The population of the Amazon basin is situated almost exclusively along the rivers. Among the four million people living in the basin, probably not more than 75,000 are Indians. In Brazil alone there are probably no more than 50,000 Indians. Although the number of pure-blooded Indians is small, and most of them live far back in the remote areas of the region, a large proportion of the Amazon population has some traces of Indian blood. The largest population cluster is at the mouth of the Amazon, centered on Belém and along the coast from Bragança across Marajó Island to Amapá. The second cluster lies along the Amazon River at the junction of the Rio Negro, in and around the city of Manaus. There are, in fact, no cities of any importance that are not situated on a river. Many, like Manaus and Santarém, are found at the point where a major tributary joins the Amazon. These sites are obviously the natural locations for transshipment operations, commercial establishments, and processing activities.

Early Exploration. The Amazon River was first descended in 1541, from Peru, by the Spaniard Francisco de Orellana and his bedraggled group of soldiers. In the early decades of the 16th century the Spaniards especially, and the Portuguese to a lesser extent, were tramping all over the South American continent searching for gold and silver and for Indians who could be enslaved. Few permanent settlements resulted from these expeditions, but a vast area was explored. Sometimes observations were recorded, as, for example, an account of the "tall women warriors" of the interior of the continent. The explorers named them Amazons, after the female warriors in Greek mythology, and their name was given to that area of the continent. These "warriors" were probably Indian men who were mistaken for women because of their peculiar dress.

While the Spaniards were busy consolidating their gains in the Aztec and Inca regions of Central America and northwest South America, the Portuguese occupied the Amazon. They began in a small way in the early 16th century. Throughout that century and the 17th, there were short periods of economic activity by a handful of people, separated by long intervals of no activity. The Portuguese and their *caboclo* (copper-colored) descendants of mixed European and Indian blood carried on rudimentary subsistence agriculture, using Indian methods. They gathered *drogas do sertão* (back-country drugs), such as cinnamon, cloves, indigo, cacao, aromatic roots, sarsaparilla, and oleaginous seeds, as well as valuable woods, such as the *pau Brasil*, or brazilwood, for which Brazil was named. The first major turning point came in 1752 when the Portuguese embarked upon a kind of regional development program. They wanted to encourage colonization and establish a strong spice trade to replace the one they were losing to the Dutch and other European powers in the East Indies. The Portuguese Overseas Councils pro-

FISHERMEN paddle their boats along an inlet to the Amazon not far from Manaus.
Many tributaries, flowing out of the tropical rain forest, feed the great river.

moted agriculture and the raising of cattle. Several groups of missionaries were sent to the area to Christianize the Indians and assure their survival by encouraging farming. Military forts were built as early as 1616 at Belém, and small trading outposts were scattered over the back country.

In the 19th century some scientific expeditions were carried out in the Amazon. In the 1850's two United States naval lieutenants, William Lewis Herndon and Lardner Gibbon, traveled to Peru and the Amazon region and made a survey of its condition and future potential. Many Europeans studied and mapped parts of the area before and after the mid-19th century. One of the most recent projects was a 1960 expedition to measure accurately the Amazon River's volume. This joint Brazilian-United States venture revealed that the Amazon's outflow was much greater than had been thought.

Development of the Amazon River. The discovery of the rubber vulcanization process in 1839 had a great impact on the Amazon region. It made possible the industrial utilization on a large scale of one of the area's greatest natural resources—rubber. The zenith of the rubber boom in the Amazon, which attracted people from many parts of the world, came around 1910. This was the high point of Brazil's rubber economy. After growing steadily from the 1840's to 1913, it finally collapsed because of competition from the rubber plantations in Malaya.

The years from 1870 to 1910 also witnessed the migration of almost 200,000 refugees from northeast Brazil into the Amazon area. They fled a land of searing droughts to seek the riches of "black gold" (rubber)—or at least to achieve physical survival in the dark, dripping Amazon forests. The years following 1874 also saw a major colonization of the Belém-Bragança zone, which became the principal agricultural area of the Amazon region. The rural population densities there are still considerably higher than they are in any other part of the Amazon basin.

Since the 1930's Japanese immigrants have introduced the cultivation of black (Java) pepper and have achieved great success with it on the right-bank *terra firme*, near Belém. They also launched what is now the most successful commercial crop of the Amazon area—Indian jute. It is grown in the floodplain over much of the lower Amazon region. The gathering and collecting activities continue, but chiefly as a background for more recent and very different kinds of activities.

The 1950's and especially the 1960's witnessed striking changes in the Amazon region. The small territory of Amapá probably experienced the most impressive transformation. A large manganese deposit at Serra do Navio has been mined since the 1950's and has provided tax revenues for other activities. The mining company, Indústria e Comércio de Minério S.A. (ICOMI), was formed by 51 percent Brazilian capital and 49 percent United States (Bethlehem Steel) capital. It has invested money in subsidiary companies and projects to diversify the economy of its immediate territory and the larger region. In the mid-1960's sugarcane and *dendé* oil (from palm-nut trees) were in production, and subsistence food crops were being planned.

A plywood factory began production at Santana at an ideal location near the mouth of the river and at the terminus of the railroad running from Serra do Navio. The Regional Development Institute of Amapá (IRDA), an independent foundation receiving money from ICOMI and other sources, had urbanization plans under way for the Macapá-Santana region. Its plans included working in the areas of public health and education to achieve a balanced cultural development of the territory.

In the 1960's outside capital was attracted to north Brazil by exemption from 50 percent of the federal taxes on income derived from the Amazon. A large cement factory capable of supplying most of the whole Amazon basin was built outside of Belém in 1962. A petroleum re-

BELÉM, the port at the Amazon's eastern mouth, handles the commerce of the immense river basin. The bustle of its colorful waterfront market typifies its activity.

DAVIS PRATT, FROM RAPHO GUILLUMETTE

finery was built at Manaus, and a small industrial park was developed on the outskirts of Belém.

These developments in the private economic sector were the reflection of policies and objectives stated by the superintendent of the Plan for the Economic Valorization of the Amazon when the plan was established in 1953. Those objectives were (1) to secure the occupancy of the Amazon territory by Brazil; (2) to build an economically stable and progressive society in the Amazon region capable of fulfilling its social duties with its own resources; and (3) to develop the Amazon in a way that parallels and complements the Brazilian economy.

The government followed with other development projects for the area, such as the "poles of development" policy (1974) to promote settlement and the Carajás project (1985), centered in the state of Maranhão, to develop mining, railroads, and cities. Of special importance for the transformation of the Amazon basin was the construction of roads, starting with the Belém-Brasília highway in the 1960's and culminating with the 3,100-mile (5,000-km) Trans-Amazonian Highway from Recife to the Peruvian border in the 1970's. Road construction encouraged the migration of settlers, who burned down large swaths of the rain forest to create pasture and croplands. The result was mixed, however, inasmuch as agricultural development was limited by adverse climatic conditions, the unsuitability of the soil for crops, and the great distances to markets. Moreover, protests were raised in many countries against the burning of rare tropical plant species and the resulting emission of carbon dioxide, which exacerbated global warming.

KEMPTON E. WEBB*
Columbia University

Bibliography

Bates, Henry, *The Naturalist on the Amazons* (White Rose Press 1987).
Bunker, Stephen G., *Underdeveloping the Amazon* (Univ. of Ill. Press 1985).

Carvajal, Gaspar de, *Discovery of the Amazon According to the Accounts of Priar Gaspar de Carvajal and Other Documents*, ed. by H. C. Heaton and Bertram T. Lee (1934; reprint, AMS Press 1977).
Cousteau, Jacques-Yves, and Richards, Mose, *Jacques Cousteau's Amazon Journey* (Abrams 1984).
MacCreagh, Gordon, *White Waters and Black* (Univ. of Chicago Press 1985).
Shoumatoff, Alex, *The Rivers Amazon* (Sierra Club Bks. 1986).
Weinstein, Barbara, *The Amazon Rubber Boom, 1850–1920* (Stanford Univ. Press 1983).
Zalis, Paul, *Who Is the River?* (Atheneum Pub. 1986).

AMAZONAS, ä-mə-zō′nəs, a state in Brazil, the largest of all the Brazilian states in area. Its area is 604,032 square miles (1,564,445 sq km). It is bounded on the north by the state of Roraima and Venezuela; on the east by the state of Pará; on the south by the states of Acre, Rondônia, and Mato Grosso; and on the west by Colombia and Peru. Except for mountains on the Venezuelan border, it is a low alluvial plain crossed west to east by the middle Amazon. Most of the state, particularly south of the river, is covered by dense forests. The capital, chief city, and industrial center is Manaus.

The climate is tropical, and the soil rich and fertile. Commercial products include cacao, Brazil nuts, rubber, medicinal plants, hardwood, tobacco, hides, and skins. Rice, corn, manioc, and fruit are raised for domestic consumption. River transportation and air transport are the chief means of communication, although highways, such as the Trans-Amazonian and the Manaus-Humaita, have been built. Population: 2,320,200 (1995 est.).

AMAZONITE, am′ə-zən-īt, a green or blue feldspar, chemical formula $(K, Pb)AlSi_3O_8$. Also called amazonstone, it is a variety of the mineral microcline and occurs in crystals in granite near Pikes Peak, Colo. Inferior crystals have been found in New Jersey, the Ural Mountains, and elsewhere. Large quantities of green cleavable amazonite have been obtained in Amelia, Va., and have been worked up as semiprecious and decorative stones.

Bibliography: Deer, William A., et al., *An Introduction to the Rock-Forming Minerals,* 2d ed. (Longman 1992); Hamilton, W. R., *Henry Holt Guide to Minerals, Rocks, and Fossils* (H. Holt 1995); Klein, Cornelius, and Cornelius S. Hurlbut, *Manual of Mineralogy,* 21st ed. (Wiley 1995).

AMBARVALIA, am-bər-vā′lē-ə, a Roman festival held at the end of May. Its purpose was lustration, or ritual purification, of the fields and propitiation of the goddess Ceres. The public ritual involved a procession around the boundaries of the fields being purified, prayers, and the sacrifice of a pig, sheep, and bull and of grain. A similar private rite involved a procession around the family's property, prayers, and a sacrifice.

AMBASSADOR, am-bas′əd-ər, a diplomatic officer of the highest rank, representing one nation in the capital of another. The title also may be given to the chief of a temporary mission, or of a permanent mission to an international organization such as the United Nations.

The status of ambassador was defined by the Vienna agreement of 1815, which established three classes of diplomatic officers: ambassador, minister plenipotentiary, and chargé d'affaires. These ranks were confirmed by the Vienna treaty of 1961, which also codified the customary law of diplomatic privileges and immunities. The treaty states that there is no difference among chiefs of mission except in matters of precedence and etiquette. On formal occasions, chiefs of mission rank according to title and length of residence in a particular capital.

Like any other diplomatic officer, an ambassador must be *persona grata*, or acceptable, to the receiving state; consequently his government must obtain the consent of the government to which he is to be accredited, by a process known as *agrément* (or *agréation*). If an ambassador should become *persona non grata* to the receiving government, he may be dismissed without a statement of reasons.

In the past, an ambassador often exercised considerable discretionary authority, although in principle he was bound by instructions from his government. With modern communications media, however, he receives frequent detailed instructions. Nevertheless, an ambassador may influence his government's policies because of his greater insight into the prevailing opinion in the receiving state and the intentions of its government. Continuous reporting on these matters and skillful representation of his government's position are, therefore, his major functions.

The term "ambassador" originally was associated with monarchy, and ambassadors were exchanged only between the principal monarchies. Since other states would consider it beneath their dignity to send diplomats of higher rank than they received, the great monarchies were able to reserve the rank of ambassador to themselves by sending only ministers or chargé d'affaires to lesser monarchies and republics. The United States began sending ambassadors in 1893. By that time the term had lost its association with monarchy. The United States originally sent ambassadors to the major European states and to three Latin American republics. The principle of equality of states has since induced the United States and most nations to exchange ambassadors with nearly all nations.

QUINCY WRIGHT, *University of Virginia*

AMBASSADORS, The, a novel by Henry James, which he regarded as "quite the best 'all round' of all my productions." It was published in 1903.

The "germ" and theme, as recounted in James's preface to *The Ambassadors*, came from the advice the elderly William Dean Howells gave to a young man: "Live all you can; it's a mistake not to. It doesn't so much matter what you do . . . so long as you have your life." As he composed the work, this theme "glowed" brightly in James's mind from beginning to end. It allowed him the "luxury" of creating the character Lambert Strether, an American of sensitivity, sympathy, intelligence, imagination, and honor. Technically the novel is the epitome of James's later dramatic manner. Strether is the center of revelation; he is in every chapter and conversation, and the story unfolds through his consciousness, the author never intruding with his own ideas. The novel's 12 books are as 12 lamps illuminating the development of the novel's theme.

Strether is sent to Paris as an "ambassador" by his fiancée, Mrs. Newsome, a widow of means in Woollett, Mass. His mission is to persuade her son Chad to return from Paris, where he has lingered for several years enjoying Old World culture. Strether discovers that European ways are enchanting and that Chad has matured remarkably. After some weeks, Mrs. Newsome sends other am-

bassadors to retrieve Chad. When Strether discovers that Chad and a countess, Mme de Vionnet, a woman of mature charm and grace and understanding, are in love with one another, he can only reject his commission, assuring Chad, "you'll be guilty of the last infamy if you ever forsake her." Chad remains in Europe, but all of the ambassadors return.

LYON N. RICHARDSON*, *Western Reserve University*

Bibliography: Johnson, Courtney, Jr., *Henry James and the Evolution of Consciousness: A Study of The Ambassadors* (Mich. State Univ. Press 1987); Rosenbaum, Stanford P., ed., *The Ambassadors: The Authoritative Text, the Author on the Novel, Criticism,* 2d ed. (Norton 1994).

AMBATO, äm-bä′tō, a city in Ecuador, the capital of the province of Tungurahua. It is situated at the foot of Mount Chimborazo, on the Pan American Highway, 70 miles (115 km) south of Quito, at an altitude of about 8,400 feet (2,560 meters). The surrounding region grows a great variety of fruit, as well as vegetables, sugarcane, barley, wheat, and cinchona. Ambato is the commercial center of the area, and also manufactures boots, shoes, and textiles.

The city has been damaged by frequent volcanic eruptions and was nearly destroyed by an earthquake that occurred in 1949. Population: 124,166 (1990 census).

AMBER, um′bər, a ruined city in India, the ancient capital of Jaipur. It is picturesquely situated at the mouth of a rocky mountain gorge, in which nestles a lovely lake. The site is remarkable for its architectural remains. The chief building is the Diwan-i' Am, built by the Rajput ruler Mirza Raja (Jai Singh I) in the early 17th century. Its columns were covered with stucco to hide their magnificence from the commissioners of Mughul Emperor Jahangir, who had ordered it destroyed because it surpassed the marvels of his imperial city of Agra.

AMBER, am′bər, a fossilized resin from prehistoric trees, particularly the pine tree *Pinus succinifera.* Specimens of amber may be as much as 40 million years old. Evidence of the vegetable origin of the substance is provided by its occurrence in coal and fossil wood deposits. The soft and sticky nature of the original material is indicated by specimens that occasionally are found containing perfectly preserved insects that were trapped by the resin. Such specimens were long prized for their intriguing appearance and are valued by scientists for the record they provide of ancient insect life.

Amber is easily carved and polished and is characterized by a resinous luster. It is transparent to translucent and ranges from white or yellowish to red or brown. Specimens often are clouded or streaked. Amber softens at the relatively low temperature of 300° F (150° C).

The substance occurs abundantly and is mined on the Baltic coast of Germany and Poland as well as on the coasts of Denmark, Sweden, and the former Soviet Union. It also is found on those shores when it is washed up by the waves after a storm. Fossil resins are found in Myanmar and Sicily and on the Atlantic coast of the United States as well.

Amber has been used as a gem since the days when it was worn in strings of beads by prehistoric man. It also was employed by ancient man as a means of exchange in commerce. Medical properties were ascribed to it, and it was used as a talisman. The Greeks were familiar with amber and called it *elektron*, from which the word *electricity* is derived. (A negative electric charge is built up on a piece of amber when it is rubbed by cloth.) For the ancient Greek poets, amber was a symbol of the tears shed by the Heliades after their grief over the death of their brother Phaeton had changed them into poplars. Amber still is valued as an ornamental material and is used in certain lacquers and varnishes.

Many hardened resinous tree gums, such as the Kauri gum from New Zealand and the copal gum from Africa, sometimes are misrepresented as amber. These gums, however, will float in a brine—a solution of salt and water—whereas real amber will sink because of its higher density. Because Baltic amber has a relatively low melting point, scraps of the material are fused into cakes. These cakes, called *amberoid*, are very difficult to distinguish from natural specimens of solid amber. Other, more readily distinguished amber substitutes are easily manufactured from celluloid, bakelite, Canada balsam, or a number of modern plastics.

Composition: $C_{10}H_{16}O$; hardness, 2.0 to 2.5; specific gravity, about 1.1.

D. VINCENT MANSON
American Museum of Natural History

Bibliography: Grimaldi, David A., *Amber: Window to the Past* (Abrams 1996).

AMBERFISH, am'bər fish, a group of subtropical and tropical fishes related to the pilotfishes. The great amberfish, or amberjack, is a food fish of some importance in the Gulf of Mexico and the West Indies, reaching a weight of 100 pounds (45 kg). Other species in that region are more commonly known as medregals. A species of the Pacific Coast is the highly prized yellowtail. The amberfish is the genus *Seriola*, which belongs to the family Carangidae.

AMBERG, äm'berĸʜ, a town in Germany, in Bavaria, 35 miles (56 km) east of Nürnberg. The town stands on both sides of the Vils River. It is noted for its iron works and also produces glass, precision instruments, and textiles.

Amberg was the capital of the Upper Palatinate until 1810. The main buildings are the 15th-century Gothic church of St. Martin's, the 15th-century town house, and the palace of the counts Palatine. Archduke Charles Louis of Austria defeated the French general Jean Baptiste Jourdan there on Aug. 24, 1796, during the Napoleonic Wars. Population: 44,700 (2004 est.).

AMBERGRIS, am'bər-gris, a rare and valuable substance used in the manufacture of perfumes. It is formed in the intestine of the sperm whale, *Physeter catodon*. Sperm whales eat squid and cuttlefish, whose horny, indigestible beaks are often found in ambergris. From this it may be inferred that ambergris protects the whale's intestines against the sharp beaks. Ambergris is found floating at sea or on tropical shores, usually in small pieces; it is also taken from dead whales. When fresh from the whale, it looks like a thick black grease and has an unpleasant odor; after exposure to air and sun, however, it becomes light gray and hard, with a sweet musky fragrance.

Perfumers add ambergris to flower essences as a fixative, so that the delicate flower scent will last. Ambergris has been used since ancient times as a perfume, a spice for food and wine in the Orient, and a drug.

Ambergris consists of cholesterol (about 80%), fatty oil, benzoic acid, and an alcohol called ambrein. With heat it vaporizes or burns. Insoluble in water, it dissolves in hot alcohol, ether, chloroform, fats, or volatile oils.

AMBLER, Eric, am'blər (1909–1998), English author of realistic suspense novels and screenplays. Born in London on June 28, 1909, Ambler studied engineering at the University of London but did not take a degree. After a brief apprenticeship in engineering in 1927–1928 and an unsuccessful foray into show business, he worked as an advertising copywriter in a London agency (1929–1937), writing fiction in his leisure time. Disdain for the popular thrillers of the time led him to write *The Dark Frontier* (1936), first intended as a parody but sufficiently successful to keep him engaged in the genre. By the late 1930s Ambler was able to become a full-time writer. He served in the British Army during World War II, chiefly in making educational and training films. After the war, in addition to numerous works of fiction, he wrote screenplays, alone and in collaboration, although others wrote the screenplays based on his novels. Ambler was named an Officer of the Order of the British Empire in 1981. He died in London on Oct. 22, 1998.

Ambler's fiction of the late 1930s virtually reinvented the thriller, discarding its fantastical conventions in favor of credible heroes, believable if colorful villains, and complex social and political dimensions. Among his works of this period were the novels *Cause for Alarm* (1938), *A Coffin for Dimitrios* (1939; filmed as *The Mask of Dimitrios* by Jean Negulesco in 1944), and *Journey into Fear* (1940; filmed by Norman Foster in 1942 and Daniel Mann in 1975). Following World War II he began turning out original or adapted screenplays, including *The Magic Box* (1951), *The Cruel Sea* (1953), *A Night to Remember* (1958), and *The Wreck of the Mary Deare* (1959). Postwar novels of suspense and international intrigue that added to his fame included *The Schirmer Inheritance* (1953), *State of Siege* (1956), *A Passage of Arms* (1959), *The Light of Day* (1962; filmed by Jules Dassin in 1964 as *Topkapi*), *To Catch a Spy* (1964), *The Intercom Conspiracy* (1969), *The Levanter* (1972), *Doctor Frigo* (1974), *The Siege of the Villa Lipp* (1977; published in England as *Send No More Roses*), and *The Care of Time* (1981). Ambler's autobiography, *Here Lies*, appeared in 1985.

Bibliography

Ambler's short fiction has been gathered in *Waiting for Orders: The Complete Short Stories of Eric Ambler* (Mysterious Press 1991). His novels have been republished in various omnibus volumes, including *Intrigue*, with an introduction by Alfred Hitchcock (Knopf 1943), and *The Intriguers: A Second Omnibus* (Knopf 1965).

Ambrosetti, Ronald J., *Eric Ambler* (Twayne 1994).
Benstock, Bernard, and Thomas F. Staley, eds., *British Mystery Writers, 1920–1939*, vol. 77 of *Dictionary of Literary Biography* (Gale Res. 1989).
Lewis, Peter, *Eric Ambler* (Continuum 1990).
Symons, Julian, *Bloody Murder: From the Detective Story to the Crime Novel*, 3d ed. (Mysterious Press 1992) [first edition published under the title *Mortal Consequences: A History—From the Detective Story to the Crime Novel* (Harper 1972)].
Wolfe, Peter, *Alarms and Epitaphs: The Art of Eric Ambler* (Bowling Green State Univ. Popular Press 1993).

AMBLER, am′blər, **James Markham Marshall** (1848–1881), American surgeon, naval officer, and Arctic explorer. He was born in Markham, Va., on Dec. 30, 1848, and was educated at Washington and Lee University and the medical college of the University of Maryland.

He entered the navy as assistant surgeon in 1874 and volunteered to serve as assistant surgeon on the Arctic expedition under Lt. George Washington Delong, aboard the *Jeannette*, in 1879. After their vessel sank in June 1881, he accompanied his chief along the Lena River, in Siberia. He died in the Lena delta on Oct. 30, 1881. His body, discovered on March 23, 1882, was returned to his birthplace for burial.

AMBLER, am′blər, is a borough in Pennsylvania, in Montgomery County, 15 miles (24 km) by road northwest of Philadelphia. It has large nurseries and manufactures asbestos, chemicals, brake linings, and sheet-metal products. The Ambler Campus of Temple University was formerly the Pennsylvania School of Horticulture.

Ambler was settled in 1728 and was a major supply center for the army of George Washington when it quartered at Valley Forge in the winter of 1777–1778 during the Revolutionary War. The borough, incorporated in 1888, is governed by a mayor and council. Population: 6,609.

AMBLYGONITE, am-blig′ə-nīt, is a group of variously colored, translucent minerals that are valuable sources of lithium. In Europe, amblygonite is found in Norway, France, Spain, and Germany. In the United States, sources of amblygonite have been discovered in Maine, California, South Dakota, and Connecticut.

Composition: chemical formula, $(Li,Na)AlPO_4(F,OH)$; hardness, 6; specific gravity, 3.05.

AMBLYOPIA, am-blē-ō′pē-ə, is a partial or sometimes total loss of vision in the absence of any disease in the eye itself. Amblyopia is sometimes confused with amaurosis—a partial or total blindness resulting from disease of the optic nerve, retina, or brain.

The simplest form of amblyopia occurs as a result of disuse. This sometimes happens in a person with a strabismus, or cross-eye, that was not corrected at an early age. As a result, the person has used only his dominant eye, leaving the unused eye untrained and incapable.

Other causes of amblyopia are not clearly understood, but certain known poisons have been associated with amblyopia of either one eye or both. These poisons include wood alcohol, lead, tobacco, and the systemic poisons present in the blood as a result of uremia. Certain brain diseases may also cause amblyopia.

REAUMUR S. DONNALLY, M.D.
Washington Hospital Center

AMBLYPODA, am-blip′ə-də, an extinct order of hoofed mammals that lived 40 million to 70 million years ago (the Paleocene and Eocene epochs) in Europe, North America, and Asia. Also known as Pantodonta, they were clumsy animals identified by a primitive pattern of teeth, five-toed feet, and short heavy limbs. Later members of the order (*Barylambda* and *Coryphodon*) were about 8 feet (2.4 meters) long. Similar in appearance to the hippopotamus, Amblypoda became extinct and has no modern descendants.

AMBO, am′bō, a reading desk or pulpit placed in the choir of early Christian churches. The Epistle and Gospel were read from the ambo, and sermons sometimes were preached from it. The ambo had two ascents—one from the east side and one from the west. In many churches there were two ambos, one on each side of the choir; the Gospel was read from one, and the Epistle from the other. Two early ambos, of beautifully carved marble, are at Ravenna, Italy, in the cathedral and in the church of Sant'Apollinare Nuovo.

AMBOISE, äN-bwȧz′, **Georges d'** (1460–1510), French prelate. He was born at Chaumont-sur-Loire, France. D'Amboise became successively bishop of Montauban and archbishop of Narbonne and (in 1493) of Rouen. When Louis XII ascended the throne in 1498, d'Amboise became a cardinal and the king's chief minister.

Between 1499 and 1503, d'Amboise took part in the French campaigns in northern Italy. He failed in his ambition to secure the papacy but was appointed papal legate in France for life. He died at Lyon on May 25, 1510. His fine tomb is in the cathedral at Rouen.

AMBOISE, äN-bwȧz′, is a town in France in the department of Indre-et-Loire. It is situated on the Loire River, 15 miles (24 km) east of Tours, in a rich vineyard district. A Renaissance château, which consists of a three-story building flanked by two towers, dominates the town. The château was long a favorite residence of French kings. During its later use as a state prison, the Algerian rebel Abd el-Kader was imprisoned here in 1848–1852.

In 1560 the town was the scene of an unsuccessful Huguenot conspiracy against the Guise family. Three years later the Edict of Amboise guaranteed religious liberty to Huguenot nobility and gentry. Population: 11,968 (1999 census).

AMBON, äm′bôn, is a small island in eastern Indonesia, in the Molucca (Maluku) group. It was formerly famous for its nutmeg and cloves. The island's chief city, also called Ambon, is the capital of Maluku province, Indonesia, comprising all the Moluccas. Both island and city are sometimes called *Amboina*, or *Amboyna*.

Land. Ambon island, with an area of 314 square miles (1,813 sq km), fronts on the Banda Sea and lies about 5 miles (8 km) southwest of the larger island of Ceram. Two long, narrow bays almost divide Ambon in two. The interior is rugged, with maximum elevations exceeding 3,400 feet (1,000 meters) in the north and reaching 1,850 feet (560 meters) in the south. Upland areas consist mainly of volcanic materials and are clothed in dense tropical forests. Ambon's temperatures remain in the low 80's F (26°–30° C), and rainfall is heavy, averaging 136 inches (345 cm) annually.

Economy. Most of Ambon island's population is engaged in subsistence farming. Maize is the chief crop, and coconuts are the principal export. Nutmeg and cloves are still produced in limited quantities. Population densities are high.

History. Ambon played little part in Indonesian affairs until the 12th century, when it became a vassal of Kediri (East Java) through allegiance to Kediri's vassal, the king of Ternate. Islam spread into Ambon in the late 1400's.

A Portuguese captain was the first European

to visit the island, about 1511. Drawn by the lucrative spice trade, the Portuguese set up a fort in Ambon and converted many Ambonese to Roman Catholicism. In 1574 the Dutch drove the Portuguese from all their Moluccan empire except Ambon, where the Portuguese held their fort until 1605.

Dutch rule ended in 1949, when the island became part of independent Indonesia. In 1950, Ambon led in creating the South Moluccan republic, but resistance to the government of Indonesia was crushed by 1956. Population: city, 205,193 (1990 census).

FREDERICK L. WERNSTEDT
Pennsylvania State University

AMBROSE, am'brōz, **Saint** (c. 399–397), the first of the four great Fathers of the Roman Catholic Church. He was born in Trier, Germany. His father, Aurelius Ambrosius, who was praetorian prefect of Gaul, died when Ambrose was a young boy. His mother took him, his sister, Marcellina, and his brother, Satyrus, to Rome. Marcellina became a nun and Satyrus a provincial prefect.

As a student, Ambrose mastered Greek, and this language proved invaluable in the later years of his life. Seeking a public career, he studied law, and in about 365 was appointed an advocate to the court of Probus, praetorian prefect of Italy. About 370 he became governor of Liguria and Aemilia with headquarters in Milan.

When Auxentius, the Arian bishop of Milan, died (373 or 374), serious frictions developed between the Arians and orthodox Christians over the election of a successor. As the official responsible for maintaining order, Ambrose entered the cathedral to address the people and to calm the factions. Although still a catechumen, and contrary to his wishes, he was elected bishop by popular acclamation. He then received Baptism and, passing through the successive orders, was consecrated bishop on Dec. 7, 374—the traditional date, though recent studies point to Dec. 1, 373, as the more likely date. Under the direction of Simplicianus, who later became his successor, Ambrose pursued theological studies and read the Greek fathers. After making provisions for his sister, the new bishop gave his possessions to the church and the poor and led an ascetic life.

Ambrose was not only a capable administrator but also an effective preacher, as Augustine testifies in his *Confessions*. In his preaching he showed great preference for the allegorical interpretation of Scripture and wide familiarity with the works of Philo, Origen, and St. Basil of Caesarea. Ambrose coped resolutely with the religious and political problems of his day and wielded considerable influence in public affairs, notably under the Emperors Gratian (375–383), Valentinian II (375–392), and Theodosius I (379–395). He stemmed the tide of Arianism in Milan and opposed the efforts of the Empress Justina in behalf of its adherents. He thwarted the pagan party in Rome, led by Symmachus, in its attempts to restore the Altar of Victory in 382. The bishop's firm stand against the imperial reprisal for revolt in Thessalonica brought Theodosius I to do public penance for the massacre of 7,000 persons. Ambrose's insistence on autonomy of the church in relations with civil authority was succinctly stated: "The Emperor is within the Church, not above the Church." He thus anticipated aspects of medieval theory on relations between spiritual and temporal authority.

Among Ambrose's literary works the following are notable: *Hexaemeron,* containing vivid descriptions of nature and heavily indebted to St. Basil; *Commentary on the Gospel According to Luke,* his largest work; *On the Duties of Ecclesiastics,* the first comprehensive presentation of Christian ethics; *Concerning Virgins,* an ascetic treatise for his sister; and *On the Faith,* a defense of the divinity of the Son.

Ambrose was a pioneer in adapting the pagan funeral oration to Christian Latin use. As a composer of hymns, Ambrose is truly the father of hymnology in the Western Church, but few of the many hymns attributed to him are today recognized as his work (see also AMBROSIAN MUSIC). Ambrose's *Letters,* 91 in all, are important sources for the history of his time.

St. Ambrose died at Milan, Italy, on April 4, 397. His feast is celebrated on December 7.

HERMIGILD DRESSLER
The Catholic University of America

Further Reading: Ambrose, St., *Complete Letters* (Catholic Univ. of Am. Press 1954); id., *Hexaemeron Paradise, Cain and Abel* (Catholic Univ. of Am. Press 1961); id., *Theological and Dogmatic Works* (Catholic Univ. of Am. Press 1963); Morino, Claudio, *Church and State in the Teaching of St. Ambrose* (Catholic Univ. of Am. Press 1969); Paredi, Angelo, *A History of the Ambrosiana* (Univ. of Notre Dame Press 1983).

AMBROSIA, am-brō'zhə, in classical mythology, was the food of the gods (as nectar was their drink) and was supposed to preserve their immortality. Ambrosia also was used by the gods as a salve to anoint the body and hair; Homer wrote of the ambrosial locks of Zeus. Ambrosia was supposed to be brought by pigeons to Zeus, who distributed it to the other gods. Mortals who were permitted to eat it gained in beauty, strength, and swiftness—qualities of divinity— and were guaranteed immortality.

AMBROSIAN MUSIC, am-brō'zhən, is a type of liturgical music of the Roman Catholic Church. It resembles the Gregorian chant but is less rigid in form. Some Ambrosian music is highly florid, with several hundred notes for one syllable; some is even simpler than the Gregorian chant. See GREGORIAN CHANT.

Ambrosian music was named for Saint Ambrose, the bishop of Milan under whom it was thought to have had its beginnings. It differed from the music of the church in Rome, just as the Ambrosian rite, used in Milan, differed from the rite used in Rome. Many attempts were made to suppress Ambrosian music, but for centuries the Milanese clung tenaciously to their unique musical practice.

Scholars once assumed that the Ambrosian and Gregorian chants came from a common stem, since lost, or that Ambrosian music represented a primitive stage of the Gregorian chant. These theories were later modified by evidence pointing to the independent beginnings of each type of chant.

The earliest extant examples of Ambrosian music date from the 12th century, but fragments of music and literary evidence show that it was already distinct from Roman music by the 9th century. Scholars attribute the texts of about 14 hymns to Saint Ambrose himself, but it cannot be conclusively proved that any extant examples of Ambrosian music go back to his time.

REMBERT G. WEAKLAND
Archbishop of Milwaukee

COMMON AMEBA

The common ameba moves by forming an extension of its body, called a pseudopod, and flowing into it. Here, it is putting forth one pseudopod (right) and withdrawing another (lower left).

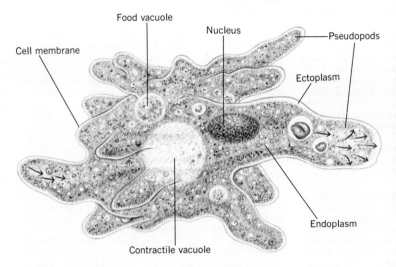

Food vacuole
Nucleus
Pseudopods
Cell membrane
Ectoplasm
Endoplasm
Contractile vacuole

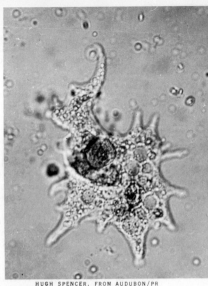

A common ameba as viewed under a 50-power microscope, showing pseudopods, nucleus, and vacuoles.

AMBUSH BUG, any of a small family of bugs that typically hide among leaves of flowers and grasp insects that happen by. Their grotesque, somewhat leaflike, appearance may serve as camouflage. The bug's forelegs are modified into powerful lobsterlike claws with sawtooth edges for grasping and holding prey.

Ambush bugs are usually about ⅜ inch (10 mm) long. They often attack much larger wasps, bees, moths, and other insects. Of about 25 species in North America, the most common is the yellowish green *Phymata erosa,* often found in the fall on goldenrod.

Ambush bugs make up the family Phymatidae of the order Hemiptera.

AMEBA, ə-mē′bə, any of a large group of tiny one-celled animals that have changeable body outlines and usually move about by forming temporary projections called pseudopods. The name is also spelled *amoeba.* Amebas are widely distributed throughout the world, occurring in salt water, fresh water, and moist soil. Although many species are free-living, others are parasitic, attacking all animal groups and sometimes causing serious diseases. In man, for example, an intestinal disorder called amebic dysentery is caused by the ameba *Entamoeba histolytica.*

Characteristics. Amebas vary greatly in size and shape, but basically they contain the same structures found in most animal cells. The cell membrane is usually highly elastic, although in one group, the verrucose amebas, the membrane is thickened and somewhat stiff. The ameba's body is divided into a relatively rigid outer zone, called ectoplasm, and a more fluid inner mass, called endoplasm. The endoplasm contains one or more nuclei, a number of mitochondria and other typical cell organelles, and several vacuoles containing food particles. Usually, a contractile vacuole that expels fluids is also present.

The most distinctive anatomical feature of amebas is their capacity to form pseudopods of strikingly different forms, and this trait is used as the basis for classifying amebas into different groups. Some amebas, including the common

ameba (*Amoeba proteus*), have bluntly rounded pseudopods, called lobopods, which are composed of both endoplasm and ectoplasm. Others have slender, tapering pseudopods, called filopods, composed only of ectoplasm. More rarely, a pseudopod may consist of a branching network, called a reticulopod, which serves to trap prey outside the body. In one special group of amebas, individual pseudopods are replaced by a broad, rippling, sheetlike expansion of the advancing end of the body.

Locomotion. Although amebas with lobopods may extend only a single pseudopod during locomotion, most others extend numerous pseudopods. As these pseudopods are being extended, the ameba's rear portion remains attached to the substrate. After they have been fully extended, the body wall at the posterior end of the body contracts, forcing this portion of the cell toward the advancing end. When this is completed, new pseudopods are extended, and the process begins again.

Feeding. The feeding behavior of amebas is strikingly similar to that observed in white blood cells. Very often, fingerlike pseudopods simply surround the food particle, a process known as phagocytosis. Occasionally the food particle first adheres to the cell membrane and is then drawn inward. Similarly, an ameba may engulf fluids and enclose them in vacuoles. This process is known as cell drinking, or pinocytosis.

Life Cycle. Amebas apparently have a simple life cycle. After a period of feeding and growth an ameba reproduces asexually by binary fission. In this process, the ameba becomes pinched in half, forming two equal-sized offspring. Sometimes, when environmental conditions become unfavorable, certain amebas form resistant stages, called cysts, in which a thick outer wall develops around the cell body. This outer wall persists until a changed environment stimulates the ameba to emerge.

WILLIAM BALAMUTH
University of California, Berkeley

AMEBIC DYSENTERY. See DYSENTERY—*Amebic Dysentery.*

AMEN, ā-men′, is a term of affirmation used by the Christian, Jewish, and Muslim faiths. Derived from the Hebrew *aman*, "to confirm," it signifies "so be it," "so it is," or "verily."

"Amen" is found in the Old Testament as ratification of a prophecy (Jeremiah 28:6) or a curse (Deuteronomy 27:15–26). The Hebrews pronounced it in their synagogues to show their acceptance of the ritual. Christ prefaced many statements with "Amen" to emphasize the truth of his words, and in Revelation, Christ himself is called "The Amen" (3:14). The Christian church uses "Amen" throughout its liturgy. Catholics pronounce it at the consecration of the Mass, their most solemn rite. Protestants use "Amen" at the end of prayers to mean "verily," signifying the affirmation of the Old Testament and Christ's guarantee of truth in the New. Muslims say it after the first chapter of the Koran.

AMENDMENT, in government usage, is a modification of a law or bill. It is also an addition to the text of a constitution or an organic act.

Article V of the U.S. Constitution provides for the adoption of amendments to that document. Amendment proceedings may be initiated either by a two-thirds vote of both houses of Congress or on the application of two thirds of the state legislatures to the Congress. To become law, amendments must be ratified by three fourths of the states by legislative action or convention. See also CONSTITUTION OF THE UNITED STATES; CONSTITUTIONAL LAW.

In law, an amendment is the correction of error in any process, pleading, or proceeding. In the absence of any statutory provision on amendments, permission to amend is left to the discretion of the court. Amendments are very liberally allowed in all formal and most substantial matters under statutes in modern practice. They are allowed either without costs to the party amending or upon such terms or conditions as the court may deem proper to impose.

AMENHOTEP, ä-mən-hō′tep, is the name of four pharaohs of Egypt's 18th dynasty (1554–1304 B.C.). The name means "Amen (Amon) is pleased," a reference to the Egyptian god Amon.

AMENHOTEP I (reigned 1529–1509 B.C.) was the son of Ahmose I, the founding king of the dynasty. He extended the empire by conducting successful campaigns in Libya and Nubia. After his death he was recognized as god and patron of the necropolis of Thebes by the workmen there. His mummy, discovered in the cache at Deir el-Bahri, is in the Cairo museum.

AMENHOTEP II (reigned 1438–1412 B.C.),

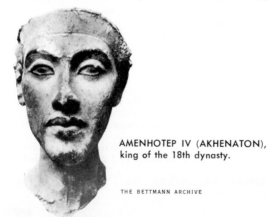

AMENHOTEP IV (AKHENATON), king of the 18th dynasty.

the son of Thutmose III and Queen Meryetre Hatshepsut, carried on several wars in Asia. His monuments extolled his strength, prowess, and bravery.

AMENHOTEP III (reigned 1403–1366 B.C.), the son of Thutmose IV, consolidated and controlled the vast empire acquired by his predecessors. During his reign Egypt was at the height of its prestige, and Amenhotep III used his wealth and power for the erection of public monuments and temples. Especially renowned was his huge funerary temple at Thebes, of which two colossi remain.

AMENHOTEP IV (reigned 1366–1349 B.C.) was the most important of the four Amenhoteps because of the revolution in art and religion that he helped create in Egypt, including the introduction of a monotheistic form of worship. However, his preoccupation with matters of mind and spirit led to neglect of the empire, and his reign marked the beginning of Egypt's decline.

Amenhotep IV was the son of Amenhotep III and Queen Tiy. His wife was the beautiful Nefertiti. His successor was his son-in-law Tutankhamen, famed for his lavish tomb, which yielded the richest royal treasure discovered in Egypt. Early in his reign Amenhotep IV abandoned his royal Amen-name and took the name of *Akhenaton* in honor of his god Aton (Aten). Variations of the name include *Akhenaten*, *Akhnaton*, and *Ikhnaton*.

Studying the traditional theology of the priests, Akhenaton conceived of a single controlling intelligence, behind and above all beings including the gods. He identified this supreme being as the sun-god Aton and elevated Aton's worship above that of all the other Egyptian deities, including Amon, the most popular god. Despite the opposition of the priesthood of Amon, Akhenaton set about systematically to abolish the worship of all cults but that of Aton and had the name of Amon obliterated wherever it occurred.

About 1365 B.C., Akhenaton left the royal city of Thebes and founded a new capital, Akhetaton ("Horizon of Aton"), at the site of modern Tell el-Amarna. Both here and at Thebes, Akhenaton and Nefertiti fostered a naturalistic school of art and literature, emphasizing sun-derived nature in accordance with Aton worship. The art of the so-called Amarna period was a striking departure from the conventional, symbolic ancient Egyptian art; its most noted example is the painted limestone bust of Nefertiti in the Dahlem museum in Berlin. The Amarna period also has yielded some 400 clay tablets from Akhenaton's foreign office archives. Excavated at Tell el-Amarna between 1887 and 1934, the Amarna tablets provide detailed knowledge of Egypt and neighboring countries in the 14th century B.C. The incursions of the Hittites and the shrinking of the Egyptian empire also are revealed in the Amarna tablets.

Akhenaton's loss of Egypt's possessions in Asia and his religious reforms alienated most of the people, and in his last years he came to be called the "criminal of Akhetaton." He prepared a tomb for himself and his family in a lonely valley east of Tell el-Amarna, but his actual burial place is uncertain.

Akhenaton's religious and artistic innovations were all nullified at his death. Tutankhamen (originally Tutankhaton) took an Amen-name on his succession. Abandoning Akhetaton, he returned to Thebes and permitted the priesthood of Amon to obliterate the remnants of Atonism.

AMERICA, Exploration of.

The first outside contact with the American continental hemisphere, a region then inhabited only by native peoples, is popularly ascribed to Christopher Columbus. Contemporary scholarship, however, grants some credit to earlier explorers.

The possibility of contact between Europe and America in ancient times cannot be discounted. Evidence suggests that Carthaginians visited the Azores, 1,200 miles west of Portugal. Greeks and Romans wrote of "Ultima Thule," which perhaps meant Iceland. However, it is doubtful that Europeans reached America until a few Scandinavians did so about the year 1000.

The ancestors of the American Indians migrated from Asia in prehistoric times. But this fact should not be confused with far-fetched claims, advanced by a few writers, of historical visits to America by civilized Orientals.

Any discovery by Europeans or Asians before the effective development of firearms could hardly have led to a rapid conquest. Moreover, Europe was thinly populated during most of the Middle Ages, and the Black Death in the 14th century reduced a population that had only started to increase. Even in 1492 most of Europe was unready for American adventure. For generations only Spain and Portugal paid much attention to the New World. Other nations destined to play roles in America waited until the 17th century, when exploration was well under way.

DERIVATION AND MEANING OF THE WORD "AMERICA"

"America" is derived from the given name of Amerigo Vespucci (1454–1512), a Florentine businessman and pilot, who sailed with both Spanish and Portuguese expeditions to the New World. When Columbus made his first voyages, Vespucci was living in Seville, where he originally represented the Medici banking interests and later engaged in private business.

Columbus' expeditions aroused Vespucci's curiosity about the new lands and persuaded him to embark on discovery expeditions of his own. He made either two or four voyages. Current knowledge of his navigations comes from maps of the period and from letters Vespucci wrote to friends in Florence. The letters have not all been accepted as genuine by all authorities. Two are considered spurious by some modern scholars.

In one of his letters, Amerigo appears to claim the discovery of a New World continent in 1497 (a year before Columbus' first continental landfall), an assertion that conflicts with other evidence. However, his report of a voyage made in 1501–1502 under Portuguese colors is undeniably authentic. On that voyage he coasted South America from above the shoulder of Brazil to southern Patagonia and discovered the Río de la Plata. Amerigo's description of the journey established a "New World" concept to replace Columbus' assertion that the new lands were part of Asia.

In 1507 a group of scholars at St. Dié in the Vosges Mountains of Lorraine produced a geography entitled *Cosmographiae introductio*, in which they took account of recent discoveries. Martin Waldseemüller, who drew the map for this work, wrote "America" across the part corresponding to Brazil, because he considered Amerigo the discoverer of that area. There was some immediate reaction against this, and Spaniards resisted the name for many years. But others soon applied it to the whole hemisphere.

PRE-COLUMBIAN VOYAGES

According to Norse sagas that survive in transcriptions made long after the events, Norsemen colonized Iceland in 860 and Greenland in 986. From the latter outpost, whose existence has been confirmed by archaeological remains, voyages to America probably were launched. The sagas suggest that the first ship to sight America was commanded by Bjarne Herjulfson. He sailed from Iceland to Greenland in 986, missed his mark, and came to a land he deemed worthless. It was probably northern Labrador or southern Baffin Island. When he finally reached Greenland, Bjarne was criticized for failing to explore the unknown country.

About 1002, Leif Ericson, a Norse colonist in Greenland, followed Bjarne's route west and south from Greenland to a place he called "Vinland" because grapes grew wild there. Vinland appears to have been northern Newfoundland.

Other Norsemen went to the new land. About 1004 a wealthy Icelander named Thorfinn Karlsefni attempted to settle there but abandoned the effort after encountering hostile natives—"Skraelings," as the Norsemen called them. Within 20 years of Leif's discovery regular voyages from Greenland to Vinland ceased, although an Icelandic record of 1121 states that a Greenland bishop went to look for Vinland in that year. Another document, of 1347, mentions a ship reaching Greenland from Markland, which neighbored Vinland, but the verified record of Norse visits to America stops at this point.

Publication by Yale University in 1965 of a recently discovered "Vinland map" aroused wide interest and stimulated debate. On an otherwise typical European world map, apparently made about 1440 (and hence well before Columbus), there appears in the western Atlantic an island labeled "Island of Vinland, discovered by Leif and Bjarni in company." Scholars differed on the date of the Vinland representation. Most considered it authentically pre-Columbian, but some did not. In any event, Yale announced in January 1974 that, as a result of tests of the ink, the map had been proved a forgery.

Evidence of other pre-Columbian explorations is less substantial. In 1898 a flat stone bearing a carved inscription was unearthed on a Swedish-American farm near Kensington, Minn. The carving was dated 1362 and proved to be runic (see RUNES). The inscription told of the plight of Norsemen who had come to that area.

Scholarly disputes began at once. Hjalmar Rued Holand, a Norwegian-American writer, championed the stone's authenticity. Others declared it a clumsy forgery. This runestone and others unearthed in the United States are now generally regarded as forgeries.

Henry Sinclair, the Scottish earl of Orkney, and Antonio Zeno, a Venetian navigator, are reported to have made a westward voyage in 1398 that perhaps took them to Nova Scotia. Zeno wrote an account of the voyage that was not published in Venice until 1558, and then in garbled form. The report nonetheless has the ring of truth. Its geographical description of the unknown land fits Nova Scotia. Most significantly, Zeno described pitch flowing out of the ground, a phenomenon that once existed in Nova Scotia. (Deposits of viscous pitch are known elsewhere in the New World only in Trinidad and Venezuela.) Traditions among the Micmac Indians of

Nova Scotia, recalling the arrival of a "prince" with some resemblance to Sinclair, lend further support to the account.

THE EPOCH OF DISCOVERY

European Preparation. The rediscovery and exploration of America was a Renaissance achievement stemming from European political and economic development, improvement of communications, and advancement of science. By 1492 several European countries were evolving from loose collections of feudal jurisdictions into consolidated monarchies ruled by absolute kings. Commerce increased rapidly as travel became safer and cities grew. Bankers with ready money to invest flourished, especially in northern Italy, the Low Countries, and the Baltic regions.

Sea voyages of a length and difficulty impossible a century earlier now became possible. In the Atlantic the lateen-rigged caravel replaced the oar-propelled galley that had been dominant in the Mediterranean since pre-Grecian times. Maps had progressed from medieval ones emphasizing religious theory to charts stressing coastlines and practical navigational problems.

The compass, an Asian invention known in crude form to Europeans as early as 1187, had been much improved. Navigators in the 15th century understood that the needle did not point true north, although no one knew why. The astrolabe, for taking the altitude of heavenly bodies, had come into wide use by 1400.

Portugal laid most of the groundwork for the discovery of America. To her salient geographical position were added the advantages of political unity and secure rulers. Portuguese expansion was encouraged by Prince Henry the Navigator (1394–1460) and King John II (1455–1495). By 1492, Portuguese navigators had rounded the southern tip of Africa and discovered or rediscovered the Madeiras, Azores, and Cape Verde Islands.

During most of the 15th century Spain was disunited and beset by domestic problems. Its principal overseas accomplishment was the partial conquest of the Canary Islands. However, the marriage of Ferdinand of Aragon and Isabella of Castile in 1469 substantially united Spain and placed her monarchs in a more favorable position to compete with Portuguese sponsors of overseas exploration.

Known World in 1492. The Martin Behaim globe, constructed at Nuremberg in 1492, gives a fair indication of what European geographers knew of the outside world at that time. It displays all the continents of the Old World and depicts the Mediterranean in easily recognizable form. Scandinavia and Russia are badly drawn, and Asia is almost imaginary, but the island of "Cipangu" (Japan), described by Marco Polo, appears to the east of Asia. Asiatic place names, furnished by Marco Polo and other travelers, are often misplaced. Islands in the Indian Ocean are also misplaced, and the peninsulas of India and Malaya are totally inaccurate.

Behaim's Africa is recognizable, thanks largely to the explorations of Africa's west coast that the Portuguese had recently made. Interior Africa was unknown to Behaim and to all Europeans until the 19th century. The archipelagos of the Azores, Canaries, and Cape Verde are included, but the latter is out of place. Several imaginary Atlantic islands are depicted. Iceland is shown, but Greenland is mentioned only in an accompanying text. In terms of the Greenwich meridian, Japan lay about 60° west of the Azores.

Although Behaim and such contemporary cartographers as Henricus Martellus confidently described Asia and Africa, much of their information was imaginary or conjectural. European knowledge of Asia practically ceased east of Persia, and acquaintance with inner Africa stopped at the northern rim of the Sahara. A few Westerners, mostly Italians, had penetrated to Abyssinia, but its location was not a matter of general knowledge.

Educated people agreed that the world was round. And old fables regarding the impassability of the tropics and the uninhabitability of the Southern Hemisphere had been disproved.

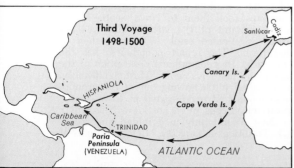

THE FOUR VOYAGES OF CHRISTOPHER COLUMBUS

First Voyage 1492-1493

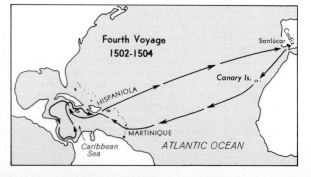

Second Voyage 1493-1496

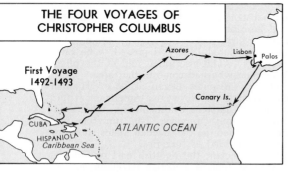

Third Voyage 1498-1500

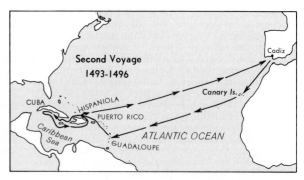

Fourth Voyage 1502-1504

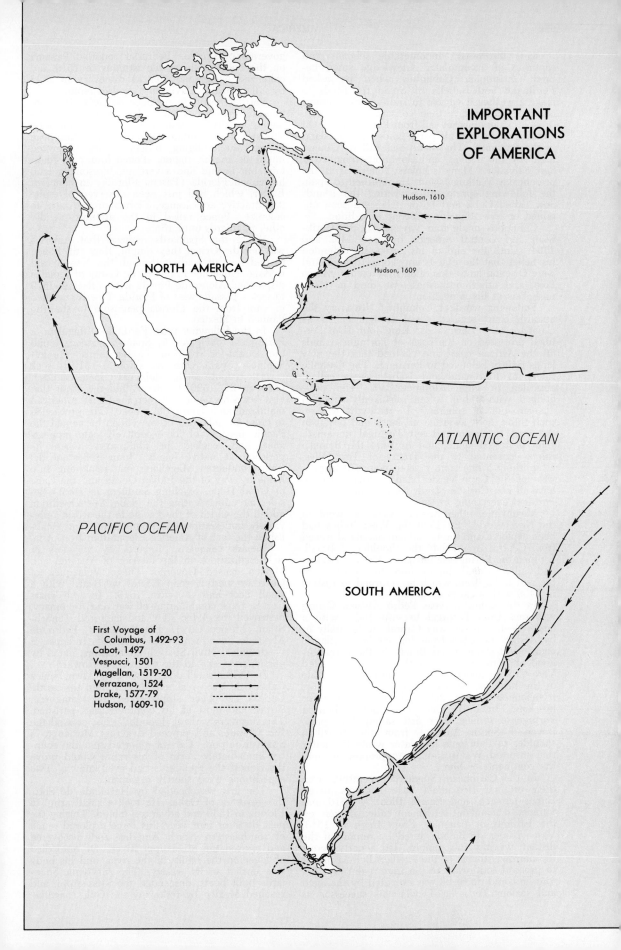

IMPORTANT EXPLORATIONS OF AMERICA

NORTH AMERICA

Hudson, 1610

Hudson, 1609

PACIFIC OCEAN

ATLANTIC OCEAN

SOUTH AMERICA

First Voyage of
  Columbus, 1492–93
Cabot, 1497
Vespucci, 1501
Magellan, 1519–20
Verrazano, 1524
Drake, 1577–79
Hudson, 1609–10

Early Discoveries. Innumerable scholars and centuries of accumulated knowledge stood behind Christopher Columbus when he asked Ferdinand and Isabella of Spain for funds to make a westward voyage to India. After numerous delays they gave their consent, and on Aug. 3, 1492, Columbus set sail from Palos, Spain. On October 12 he and his party landed on an island in the Bahamas. The island was called "Guanahani" by the natives, and Columbus renamed it San Salvador. Many scholars believe it is the present-day Watling Island. He returned to Spain the following spring, after visiting the islands now called Cuba and Hispaniola, and soon obtained underwriting for a second expedition.

Columbus made four voyages to the Caribbean and Central America between 1492 and 1504. Until the end of his career he defended his belief that the islands and adjacent mainland were Oriental lands described by Ptolemy, Marco Polo, and other authorities. He died in 1506, unshaken in his conviction.

Following word of Columbus' discovery the Spanish court secured papal recognition of its claim to the western lands. King John II of Portugal protested on the basis of Portuguese finds off the African coast and claimed that the new lands rightly belonged to Portugal. The Catholic rulers, as Ferdinand and Isabella were called, appealed to Pope Alexander VI. The pope obliged with a bull, often mistakenly called a "demarcation of spheres." In reality it was no such thing, as it awarded all lands and ocean in the west to Spain and left Portugal unnamed. John protested again, and in 1494 the Spanish rulers consented to the Treaty of Tordesillas, establishing a line from pole to pole 370 leagues west of the Cape Verde Islands. Spain was to have all non-Christian lands west of the line, and Portugal everything to the east.

Meanwhile, other Spanish voyagers went to the New World. By 1500 the West Indies had been explored and the Caribbean mainland traced from Central America to the shoulder of Brazil. By then the Portuguese navigator Vasco da Gama had sailed around the southern tip of Africa to the real India, from which he returned to Lisbon in 1499 with a cargo of spice.

In the following year Pedro Álvares Cabral was sent from Portugal to visit India with a larger fleet. On the way Cabral, accidentally or by design, deviated from his southern Atlantic course and encountered Brazil, in the neighborhood of Porto Seguro. As this land, first called Vera Cruz in honor of the Southern Cross visible in the heavens, lay east of the Tordesillas line, it belonged to Portugal. Cabral claimed it for his king. In 1501, Amerigo Vespucci, then in Portuguese service after first sailing for Spain, traversed South America from the Brazilian shoulder to Patagonia and later wrote the letter that inspired Waldseemüller to propose naming the continent for him.

In the Caribbean, Spaniards operating from their original Hispaniola base had conquered Cuba, Jamaica, and Puerto Rico by 1510 and founded a mainland settlement called Darién, on the Isthmus of Panama. From there in 1513, Vasco Núñez de Balboa, lured by rumors of the distant, wealthy Inca empire, led a party across the narrow isthmus to the Pacific. Balboa meant to proceed southward to the Inca realm, but before he could do so he was executed by the aged and jealous Pedrarias Dávila, his successor as governor of Darién. Pedrarias founded Panama on the Pacific side of the isthmus in 1519 and colonized Nicaragua after its discovery in 1522 by Gil González Dávila and Andrés Niño.

Farther north, Juan Ponce de León, the conqueror of Puerto Rico, sailed through the Bahamas in 1513 in search of a new colonization site and the "fountain of youth" that European legend and obliging Indian stories suggested might lie in this region. Ponce found no fountain, but he did find a verdant, blossoming land he named Florida (Pascua Florida) in honor of Easter, which had just been observed. Despite its attractive appearance, Florida proved hard to colonize. Ponce failed in the attempt, as did other Spaniards until 1565.

When the Spaniards realized that America was not the Orient they sought, they still hoped to find a strait leading through the New World to Asia. Governor Francisco de Garay of Jamaica dispatched Alonso de Pineda with a fleet in 1519 to seek a passage west of Florida. Pineda searched in vain from the Florida peninsula to the Río Pánuco in Mexico.

In the following year, Ferdinand Magellan, a Portuguese navigator in Spanish service, found the sought-for strait in the far south. He left Sanlúcar, Spain, with five ships in 1519 to seek a western route to the Moluccas (Spice Islands). On Oct. 21, 1520, he discovered the strait that now bears his name, between the South American mainland and Tierra del Fuego. He proceeded to cross an unknown ocean, which he named the Pacific because of its deceptively calm appearance, and reached the Philippines, where he perished at native hands. Juan Sebastián del Cano conducted Magellan's one remaining ship home by way of the Indian Ocean and the Cape of Good Hope, reaching Sanlúcar in 1522. Besides circumnavigating the globe, this expedition added the width of the Pacific to the world's previously underestimated circumference and established the fact of America's separation from Asia.

Spanish Conquests. Reports by voyagers of rich civilizations in the interior of Yucatán and Mexico caused Governor Diego Velázquez of Cuba to send Hernán Cortés westward with a small fleet and army in 1519. In two years Cortés, by a combination of war and diplomacy, destroyed the Aztec state and captured Tenochtitlán (Mexico City). His lieutenant, Pedro de Alvarado, conquered the civilized Indians of Guatemala. Other Spanish adventurers, aided by missionaries, spread the conquest northward.

In 1536 a small party headed by Álvar Núñez Cabeza de Vaca reached Mexico from the north. Cabeza had been shipwrecked off Matagorda, Texas, and most of his comrades had perished. The survivors walked through Texas, crossed the Rio Grande, and proceeded across Mexico to a Spanish outpost. Cabeza reported that the country immediately north of his route would prove the richest the Spaniards had ever known. Two expeditions were shortly organized.

The first was headed by Hernando de Soto, the governor of Cuba. He took a small army to Florida in 1539 and advanced inland. During the next three or four years his force explored much of southeastern North America and discovered and crossed the Mississippi River. De Soto died of fever on the banks of the river, and his body was buried in its waters. The surviving Spaniards built boats, descended the Mississippi, and reached Mexico by following the Gulf coastline.

The second expedition was headed by Francisco Vázquez de Coronado, governor of the province of Nueva Galicia in Mexico. In 1540 he marched north from Mexico to search for the riches that Cabeza had promised. Coronado's route took him through southwestern and central North America to the vicinity of Kansas. His journey ended in disappointment.

In 1542 a sea expedition commanded by Juan Rodríguez Cabrillo attempted a rendezvous with Coronado and sought a strait through the continent. It explored to the Rogue River in Oregon but returned to Mexico after Cabrillo's death without accomplishing either of its specific aims. Disillusionment postponed further Spanish exploration of the north for many years.

Penetration of South America was more successful. The Pizarro brothers and Diego de Almagro left Panama in 1530, and the following year they invaded the Inca empire of Peru, the largest and richest political structure in the New World. By repeating Cortés' tactics on a cruder scale, Francisco Pizarro, the leader, seized the supreme Inca, Atahualpa, and used him to govern the empire before putting him to death. Hard fighting ensued before Peru capitulated, but by 1536 it was practically subdued.

In 1540, a year before his death, Francisco Pizarro sent Pedro de Valdivia to conquer Chile. The conquest was by no means complete when the Araucanian Indians slew Valdivia in 1553. The Araucanians, in fact, fought their last fight against the Chilean republic in 1884.

In eastern South America the Spaniards entered the Río de la Plata region. They founded Buen Aire (Buenos Aires) in 1536 (the city was refounded in 1580) and ascended the Paraná to establish Asunción.

From Quito, the northern capital of the Incas, the youngest Pizarro brother, Gonzalo, and his cousin, Francisco de Orellana, led a large force across the Andes in search of cinnamon forests. When starvation threatened, Gonzalo dispatched Orellana with a boat and party down an Amazon tributary in search of food. Orellana located food but elected to reach the sea. While Gonzalo struggled back to Quito unaided, Orellana's party sailed down the great river to its mouth. On the way they skirmished with Indians whose women lent a hand in the fighting—a fact that caused Orellana to call the region "Land of the Amazons."

To enter the country of the semicivilized Chibchas in upland Colombia, Gonzalo Jiménez de Quesada in 1536 ascended the great Magdalena River. After taking the Chibcha capital of Bacatá (Bogotá) rather easily, the Spaniards went in search of El Dorado (The Gilded Man). El Dorado's prototype was one of a bygone line of Indian rulers of central Colombia who were daubed from head to foot with gold dust on ceremonial occasions. German employees of the Welser banking house, to which Emperor Charles V had temporarily leased Venezuela in discharge of a debt, assisted and competed in the search. Explorers named Alfinger, Speyer, and Federmann, who for some years roamed Venezuela and Colombia in quest of whatever wealth they could find, matched their Spanish contemporaries in cruelty to the Indians.

Portuguese Settlement. The Portuguese neglected Brazil from 1500, when Cabral discovered it, until the 1530's, when threats of French competition persuaded them to plant a thin line of colonies along the coast. However, both French and Dutch harassment prevented the Portuguese-Brazilians from doing much exploration of the hinterland until the 17th century. Then they scoured the interior in *bandeiras* (armed companies). Private individuals led the search for precious metals and Indian slaves, both of which they found. As a result, knowledge of the back country was increased and the Treaty of Tordesillas, which had originally limited Portugal to a narrow coastal strip, was abrogated in 1750.

French and English Expeditions. England entered the exploration scene early, although briefly. At an unknown date before 1497, and possibly before 1492, Bristol merchants sent an expedition to Newfoundland, then known as Brasil. In 1497, Giovanni Caboto (known as John Cabot), an Italian employed by the merchants and commissioned by Henry VII, made a voyage to Newfoundland and perhaps to the nearby mainland. He sailed from Bristol again the following year, evidently expecting to reach China by a more southerly route and open trade with the "Cathay" that Marco Polo described. The result of the second voyage is unknown. Cabot died during or immediately after it.

Cabot's son, Sebastian, also in English service, discovered what evidently was the inlet of Hudson Strait and Hudson Bay in 1509. He mistakenly claimed that he had found the Northwest Passage around America to Asia. He may have taken the combination of strait and bay for the desired route. When Sebastian returned to England, Henry VII was dead, and Henry VIII was not interested in sponsoring further voyages. Sebastian transferred to Spanish service, and England turned her attention elsewhere.

The next important move in North America came from France. In 1524, Francis I, apparently at the request of a group of interested French merchants, commissioned Giovanni da Verrazano, a Florentine, to search for the desired strait through North America. The Cabots had explored Newfoundland and perhaps south of it. Spanish explorers—Francisco Gordillo in 1521 and Lucas Vázquez de Ayllón in 1523—had explored the coast from Florida to the Pedee River of South Carolina. Verrazano logically explored the region in between. He went from the Carolinas to Nova Scotia and was the first European navigator to sail into the harbor of New York.

The next French venture, by Jacques Cartier, was made farther north. Cartier explored the Gaspé Basin in 1534. The next year he ascended the St. Lawrence to the Lachine Rapids near Hochelaga (Montreal). A subsequent voyage and an attempt to found a settlement in partnership with the sieur de Roberval failed. The French temporarily abandoned Canada.

In the second half of the 16th century France was preoccupied with internal conflicts between Catholics and Huguenots that led to civil war in 1562 and lasted until 1593. The conflicts served to thwart French efforts overseas. However, persecuted Huguenots made two attempts at colonization by themselves—one at Guanabara (Rio de Janeiro) in the 1550's and the other in Florida in the 1560's. The Portuguese ended the first effort and the Spaniards the second in a bloody massacre that seemingly enjoyed the blessing of the Catholic French monarchy.

During the reign (1558–1603) of Elizabeth I, England renewed its interest in America and became a formidable sea rival of Spain. A

EARLY 16th CENTURY EXPLORATIONS IN SOUTH AND CENTRAL AMERICA

Mexico City

Balboa Crosses the Isthmus of Panama, 1513

Lima   Cuzco

Pineda, 1519
Cortes, 1519-21
Dávila and Niño, 1522
Pizarro, 1530-31
Valdivia, 1540-41
Orellana, 1541-43

Santiago

they discovered, and Baffin Island, which they did not, commemorate their voyage.

The French in the Interior. France resumed American activity early in the 17th century. The greatest of all French explorers was Samuel de Champlain, who founded Quebec in 1608, defeated the warlike Iroquois in battle, and labored for the development of Canada. By the time of his death in 1635 he had explored westward to Lake Huron. The entire Great Lakes system was soon known to the French. (Curiously, no one knows when, or by whom, the Niagara Falls were discovered. They are first recorded as an already familiar landmark in 1648.)

French missionaries, mostly Jesuits, did much of the exploring. Their travels were widespread and numerous. By 1665 they had founded a mission station at La Pointe, near the western end of Lake Superior. Jacques Marquette, a good explorer if an indifferent missionary, accompanied the trader Louis Jolliet down the Mississippi to the Arkansas country in 1673. (They thought they were descending the Colorado and expected to reach the Gulf of California. When they realized their mistake, they turned back.)

In 1682 a French fur trader, the sieur de La Salle, sailed all the way down the Mississippi from the Illinois country to the Gulf and took ceremonial possession of the whole river valley. He meant to colonize the valley but died by a mutineer's hand before he could attempt it.

In the early 18th century French traders visited the Spanish New Mexico settlements. The La Vérendrye brothers in 1743 explored the area to the edge of the Bighorn Mountains west of the Black Hills. A few years later another French party, moving along the Saskatchewan, reached the Rocky Mountains. Their object was to reach the Pacific, but the Rockies stopped their advance. Finally, in the Seven Years' War (1756–1763) the French were expelled from almost all of North America.

Mapping South America. Magellan's discovery of the southern strait to the Pacific was followed up by many voyagers. In 1578 the English navigator Francis Drake sailed south of Cape Horn, then through the Strait of Magellan to the Pacific. Sailing northward, he reached a point on the California coast in or near San Francisco Bay, where he anchored in 1579. He named the country Nova Albion. Soon after Drake's expedition, Pedro Sarmiento de Gamboa gave the strait a more thorough exploration for Spain than it had received previously.

Surprisingly, under the circumstances, Cape Horn was not discovered until the 17th century, when the Dutch were given a strong incentive. A Dutch trading concern, formed to combat the powerful Dutch East India Company's monopoly of Orient trade, was barred by government concessions to the company from using either the Cape of Good Hope (in southern Africa) or the Strait of Magellan. Accordingly, in 1616 an expedition commanded by Willem Schouten and Jakob Le Maire ran past the strait and discovered Cape Horn. The cape was named for the Dutch town, Hoorn, where the enterprise originated.

Land exploration of South America in the 17th century consisted of filling in the details of a pattern already established by the earlier explorers. In the 18th century scientific expeditions from Europe, if they did not discover new territory, at least added to the understanding of what was already known. In 1736 the French

great deal of the English overseas effort was expended in the north, out of Spanish reach, with good results for discovery and barren ones for colonization. Martin Frobisher explored the region of Greenland, Labrador, and Baffin Island, where in 1577 he took aboard a cargo of worthless dirt, which he took to London for gold assay. John Davis, in search of the Northwest Passage, sailed up the west coast of Greenland to 72° N in 1587. Nearly three centuries earlier a small party of Norsemen had been to Upernavik, in the same vicinity. The strait between Greenland and Baffin Island received Davis' name.

Henry Hudson, who explored the Hudson River up to Albany for the Dutch East India Company in 1609, sought the Strait of Anian for England in 1610. His theory was that Asia swung far to the east above North America and was divided from it by this hypothetical strait connecting the Atlantic with the Pacific. Hudson entered Hudson Bay and reached James Bay, where the ship froze in and all hands nearly starved. In the spring of 1611 the crew mutinied. They set Hudson and a few faithful seamen adrift, to freeze or starve, and sailed for home.

The last important exploration of the far north in this era was undertaken by William Baffin in company with Robert Bylot, one of the Hudson mutineers. In 1616 they sailed up Davis Strait to 78° N. The names of Baffin Bay, which

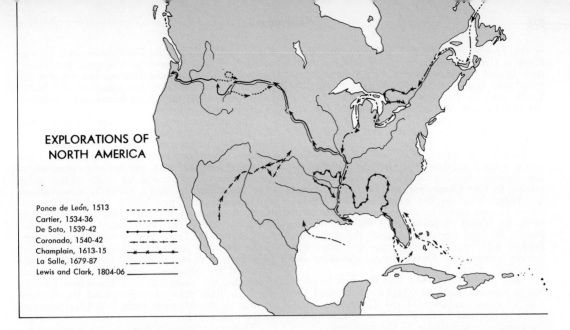

**EXPLORATIONS OF
NORTH AMERICA**

Ponce de León, 1513
Cartier, 1534-36
De Soto, 1539-42
Coronado, 1540-42
Champlain, 1613-15
La Salle, 1679-87
Lewis and Clark, 1804-06

geographer Charles Marie de La Condamine began an investigation of Peru and the Amazon
basin. Alessandro Malaspina, an Italian who entered Spanish service in 1789, surveyed the
Pacific coast from South America to Alaska,
where he discovered the great Malaspina Glacier.
Alexander von Humboldt, the famous Prussian
geographer, went to Spanish America in 1799,
remained five years, and described parts of it in
an interesting critical account, *Personal Narrative of Travels to the Equinoctial Regions of the
New Continent* (7 vols., 1818–29).

Russian Expansion in America. During the 17th
century the Russians pushed across Siberia to
the Pacific coast, where they founded a station at
Okhotsk in 1638. Just before his death in 1725,
Peter the Great issued orders for an expedition
to explore the Pacific east of Siberia and to determine where America and Asia met. Vitus
Bering, a Danish captain in the Russian navy,
was placed in command. Martin Spanberg and
Aleksei Chirikov were his lieutenants.

Using Okhotsk as their base, the explorers
investigated the Kamchatka Peninsula in 1728.
They reconnoitered the coast north of Kamchatka
to its westward bend at 67° 18′ N, where they
determined that the two continents were separated by water. Bering returned to St. Petersburg
and reported to Peter's successor, Empress Anna.

With the encouragement of the Russian Academy of Sciences another expedition was planned.
Several scientists volunteered to accompany it for
research purposes. One of the objectives of the
expedition was to investigate the remaining unknown area between Russia and America. After
many delays, Bering and Chirikov left Okhotsk in
1741. Each commanded his own ship, and they
explored separately. Bering reached the Alaskan
mainland, where he sighted Mount St. Elias and
mistook it for a volcano. He contracted scurvy
on the return voyage and died at the island near
Kamchatka that bears his name. Chirikov reached
the American coast at about 56° N, sailed for
Kamchatka, and discovered a number of Aleutian
islands on the way.

The voyages by Bering and Chirikov revealed
the shape of the great northwest shoulder of
America and showed that the Strait of Anian
could not exist in its supposed form.

Continuing Russian exploration in the north-
west Pacific stimulated a final effort by Spain.
Worried by the threat of Russian competition,
Viceroy Antonio Bucareli of Mexico dispatched
Juan Pérez northward in 1774 and Bruno Heceta
and Juan Bodega the following year. The second
expedition reached approximately the latitude of
Chirikov's landfall.

Canadian Expeditions. Employees of the Hudson's Bay Company were among the most active
agents in the exploration of northern and western Canada. Founded in 1670, the company
during most of its first century limited itself to
holding posts near the mouths of rivers flowing
into the great bay and letting the Indians bring
furs there for trade. In the 18th century, however, the company eagerly sought a navigable
route through western Canada.

In 1754, Anthony Henday left York Factory,
a trading post on Hudson Bay, and penetrated as
far southwest as the Saskatchewan River, visiting
the country of the Assiniboin and the Blackfoot
Indians. More important expeditions were undertaken by Hudson's Bay agent Samuel Hearne,
who was commissioned in 1769 to find an exit
from the bay to the west (and also to investigate
reports of rich copper deposits in the interior).
His first two attempts, in 1769 and 1770, accomplished little; but on the third try, in company with a band of Chipewyan Indians on their
way to attack Eskimo, he encountered the Cop-
permine River and followed it to the Arctic
Ocean. His charting appears to have been clumsy
and inaccurate, for he placed the mouth of the
river approximately 4° too far north. On his return to Fort Prince of Wales, Hearne swung south
and west and discovered what must have been
Great Slave Lake, although he called it the
Great Athapuscow.

The most important of all the Anglo-Canadian
explorers was the Scotsman Alexander Mackenzie.
He belonged to a small free-lance trading group
that had no affiliation with Hudson's Bay or its
formidable rival, the North West Company of
Montreal.

In search of fur and markets, Mackenzie left
his Churchill River base and proceeded to Lake
Athabasca, where his cousin, Roderick Mackenzie,
had founded Fort Chipewyan. He left Chipewyan

in the spring of 1789 and followed the Slave River to Great Slave Lake, out of which a large river flowed to the northwest. He followed this river, now known as the Mackenzie, more than 1,000 miles to its outlet in the Arctic Ocean. While returning to Fort Chipewyan in the autumn of 1789, he learned from Indians that there was an ocean to the west and also a great river, probably the Yukon.

Before attempting other expeditions, Mackenzie visited England to purchase instruments and increase his knowledge of surveying. Returning to Fort Chipewyan in 1792, he ascended the Peace River to the mouth of the Smoky, where he was joined by several other white men. With the object of pushing all the way to the Pacific, he and his party scaled the Canadian Rockies early the following year and, after trying the tempestuous Fraser River, descended the easier Bella Coola to the Pacific.

Mackenzie's expedition was the first to cross North America north of Mexico. It opened the way for other explorers—David Thompson, Alexander Henry, and Simon Fraser—who soon added abundantly to knowledge of the continent.

United States Surveys. Following the Louisiana Purchase in 1803, President Jefferson undertook to learn more about the vast territory he had added to the Union. Its northern and western boundaries were vague until treaties with England in 1818 and Spain in 1819 established them, and the sources of the western rivers flowing into the Mississippi were all but unknown.

Jefferson commissioned Lt. Zebulon Pike to locate the source of the Mississippi. In 1806 Pike erroneously reported that he had found it at Leech Lake in Minnesota. (The real source is the Itasca Basin in Minnesota.) The next year Pike went west to seek the headwaters of the Red River. His principal discoveries were Pike's Peak and the Royal Gorge. Missing the Red River, he descended the Rio Grande until he was arrested as an interloper by a Spanish force near Santa Fe. He was soon released, but some of his papers were confiscated and remained in a Mexican archive until they were found and published nearly a century later.

The most famous western expedition that the scientific-minded Jefferson sponsored was that of Meriwether Lewis and William Clark, two Army officers. Their orders were to explore the Missouri and find the most direct water communication across the continent for trade. They were also instructed to make scientific observations and examine the possibilities of the Columbia River mouth as a site for a fur post to rival a Canadian post at Nootka Sound.

Leaving St. Louis with a considerable party in the spring of 1804, Lewis and Clark completed their mission in two years and four months. They ascended the Missouri, crossed the Rockies, and descended the Columbia. On the return journey the expedition split. Lewis crossed the Rockies by way of the Missouri Falls, and Clark by way of the Yellowstone.

Their expeditionary force kept a weather record and collected valuable information about the Indians. Many details remained to be filled in, and for two generations after their expedition others, such as James Bridger, Jedediah Smith, Kit Carson, Benjamin Bonneville, John C. Frémont, and John Wesley Powell (see individual entries), contributed in numerous ways to making the map of the West more accurate.

Final Expeditions. Exploration of America ended almost where it began—in the Arctic zone. In the 19th century there was a renewed search for the Northwest Passage, although the incentives were no longer commercial but scientific. A succession of British expeditions, commanded in turn by David Buchan, John Ross, and William E. Parry between 1818 and 1829, filled in many

DISCOVERIES AND EXPLORATIONS IN AMERICA—A CHRONOLOGY

c. **1002**—Discovery of Vinland by Leif Ericson, following lead of Bjarne Herjulfson.

c. **1004**—Attempted settlement of Vinland by Thorfinn Karlsefni.

1398—Year of possible visit to Nova Scotia by Earl Sinclair of Orkney and Antonio Zeno.

c. **1440**—Postulated date of European world map displaying island labeled "Vinland."

1492–1504—Dates of Columbus' four expeditions to New World, leading to discovery of many West Indian islands and mainland coasts of Venezuela and Central America.

1497—Date ascribed to first, and doubtful, expedition of Amerigo Vespucci, reported to have discovered a New World continent.

1497—Exploration of Newfoundland and perhaps of adjacent mainland by John Cabot for Bristol merchants and Henry VII of England.

1500—Landfall of Portuguese Pedro Álvares Cabral at about 17° S in Brazil.

1501—Voyage of Vespucci, in Portuguese service, tracing South America to Patagonia; beginning of New World concept.

1507—"America" suggested as name for New World by Martin Waldseemüller.

1509—Discovery of Hudson Bay entrance by Sebastian Cabot for England.

1513—Crossing of Isthmus of Panama to Pacific by Vasco Núñez de Balboa.

1519—Exploration of Gulf of Mexico from Florida to Mexico by Alonso de Pineda.

1519–1521—Defeat of Aztec confederation of central Mexico by Hernán Cortés.

1519–1522—Circumnavigation of earth by Ferdinand Magellan's expedition.

1522—Exploration of Pacific coast of Central America by Gil González Dávila and Andrés Niño.

1524—Exploration of Atlantic coast of North America by Giovanni da Verrazano, for France.

1531—Invasion of Inca empire of Peru by Pizarro brothers and Diego de Almagro.

1534–1543—Explorations of St. Lawrence River by Jacques Cartier and sieur de Roberval, for France.

1539–1542—Explorations of southeastern and southwestern United States by Hernando de Soto and Francisco Vázquez de Coronado.

1540—Pedro de Valdivia begins campaign to conquer Chile.

1541—Descent of Amazon River by Francisco de Orellana.

1542–1543—Exploration of California and Oregon coasts by Juan Rodríguez Cabrillo and Bartolomé Ferrelo.

1579—Visit to coast of Nova Albion (California) by Francis Drake.

1608—Resumption of French exploration of St. Lawrence by Samuel de Champlain. Founding of Quebec.

1609—Exploration of Hudson River to approximate site of Albany by Henry Hudson in Dutch service.

1610–1611—Exploration of Hudson Bay for England by Henry Hudson.

1616—Discovery of Baffin Bay by William Baffin.

1616—Discovery of Cape Horn by Dutch captain Willem Schouten.

1669–1687—Exploration of central North America by Robert Cavelier de la Salle.

1728–1741—Exploration of Bering Sea, Aleutian Islands, and Alaskan mainland coast by Vitus Bering and Aleksei Chirikov.

1789–1793—Exploration of Mackenzie River to Arctic and crossing of Rockies to Pacific coast by Alexander Mackenzie.

1804–1806—Exploration of Missouri River and descent of Columbia to Pacific by Meriwether Lewis and William Clark.

1903–1905—Sailing of Northwest Passage and fixing of Magnetic Pole by Norwegian Roald Amundsen.

1909—Discovery of North Pole by Comdr. Robert Peary from Cape Columbia base in Grant Land.

blanks on the map of the great Arctic archipelago above Canada. They explored as far north as Bathurst and Melville islands, progressing as far west as Peel Sound. The shape of the entire mainland coast of Arctic Canada was established, with the benefit of knowledge gained from local land expeditions.

By 1845 the time was ripe for a voyage to traverse the entire passage. This voyage was undertaken by Sir John Franklin, an Englishman. Although he and his followers perished in the attempt, evidence later collected from Eskimos suggests that they found the correct route, east and south of King William Island, but were unable to use it. Last reported moving south by land in search of food, Franklin and his men presumably died between Adelaide Peninsula and Great Fish River.

The centuries-old puzzle of the Northwest Passage was finally solved in 1903–1905 by the Norwegian Roald Amundsen, future discoverer of the South Pole. Amundsen, using the 47-ton fishing smack *Gjoa*, took only six companions. On their way he and his crew made repeated magnetic observations and fixed the location of the Magnetic Pole at 70° 30′ N, 95° 30′ W, on the west side of the Boothia Peninsula. The explorers knew they had succeeded when, on Aug. 26, 1905, they met a whaler from San Francisco that had entered the Arctic Ocean from Bering Strait. Amundsen next planned to discover the North Pole, but in this he was anticipated by Robert Peary of the U.S. Navy. Peary made several attempts. On April 6, 1909, he finally reached the pole from Cape Columbia in Grant Land.

CHARLES E. NOWELL, *University of Illinois*
Author of "Great Discoveries and the First
Colonial Empires"

Bibliography

Babcock, William H., *Early Norse Visits to North America* (Gordon Press 1976).
Brebner, John B., *The Explorers of North America, 1492–1806* (Harper 1955).
Brotherston, Gordon, *Image of the New World: The American Continent Portrayed in Native Texts* (Thames & Hudson 1979).
Conaway, James, *The Kingdom in the Country* (Houghton 1987).
Greenlee, William Brooks, *Cabral's Voyage to Brazil and India* (Oxford 1938).
Greer, Thomas H., *A Brief History of the Western World,* 5th ed. (Harcourt 1987).
Hermansson, H., *The Northmen in America* (Gordon Press 1984).
Holand, H. R., *Norse Discoveries and Explorations in America* (P. Smith 1984).
Kamphoefner, Walter D., *The Westfalians* (Princeton Univ. Press 1987).
Kirkpatrick, F. A., *The Spanish Conquistadores,* 2d ed. (Oxford 1963).
Maynard, Theodore, *De Soto and the Conquistadores* (1930; reprint, AMS Press 1979).
Morison, Samuel Eliot, *Admiral of the Ocean Sea: A Life of Christopher Columbus* (1942; reprint, Northeastern Univ. Press 1983).
Morison, Samuel Eliot, *The Great Explorers: The European Discovery of America* (Oxford 1974; reprint, 1986).
Nowell, Charles E., *The Great Discoveries and the First Colonial Empire* (1954; reprint, Greenwood Press 1982).
Parkman, Francis, *Pioneers of France in the New World* (1865; reprint, Corner House 1970).
Parry, J. H., *The Discovery of South America* (Taplinger 1979).
Penrose, Boies, *Tudor and Early Stuart Voyaging* (Folger Bks. 1979).
Platt, Rutherford, *Wilderness, the Discovery of a Continent of Wonder* (1961; reprint, Greenwood Press 1973).
Sauer, Carl O., *The Early Spanish Main* (Univ. of Calif. Press 1966).
Skelton, R. A., and others, *The Vinland Map and the Tartar Relation* (Yale Univ. Press 1965).
Wahlgren, Erik, *The Vikings and America* (Thames & Hudson 1986).

AMERICA, ə-mer′ə-kə, is a patriotic hymn of the United States, with text by Samuel Francis Smith (q.v.). It is sung to the music of the British national anthem, *God Save the King (Queen)*. The music, generally credited to Henry Carey (q.v.), was first published with the words of *God Save the King* in a song collection called *Thesaurus Musicus* (1744). The verses of *America* are:

My country! 'tis of thee,
Sweet land of liberty,
  Of thee I sing.
Land where my fathers died!
Land of the Pilgrims' pride!
From every mountain side,
  Let freedom ring!

My native country, thee—
Land of the noble free—
  Thy name I love;
I love thy rocks and rills,
Thy woods and templed hills,
My heart with rapture thrills
  Like that above.

Let music swell the breeze,
And ring from all the trees,
  Sweet freedom's song;
Let mortal tongues awake;
Let all that breathe partake;
Let rocks their silence break—
  The sound prolong.

Our fathers' God! to Thee,
Author of liberty,
  To Thee we sing;
Long may our land be bright
With freedom's holy light;
Protect us by Thy might,
  Great God, our King!

According to the music historian John Tasker Howard, *America* was first sung in 1831 at an Independence Day celebration. An account of the affair was printed in the *Christian Watchman* of July 8, 1831. More than half a century later the author mistakenly thought he had written the verses a year later, in 1832, as is shown in the following letter:

NEWTON CENTRE, MASS., JUNE 5, 1887.
Mr. J.H. Johnston:
  Dear Sir: The hymn "America" was not written with reference to any special occasion. A friend (Mr. Lowell Mason) put into my hands a quantity of music books in the German language early in the year 1832—because, as he said, I could read them and he couldn't—with the request that I would translate any of the hymns and songs which struck my fancy, or, neglecting the German words, write hymns or songs of my own, adapted to the tunes, so that he could use the music. On a dismal day in February, turning over the leaves of one of these music books, I fell in with the tune, which pleased me—and, observing at a glance that the words were patriotic, without attempting to imitate them, or even to read them throughout, I was moved at once to write a song adapted to the music—and "America" is the result.

Respectfully yours,
S.F. SMITH.

The song attained popularity in the North during the Civil War. Since then it has been the most frequently sung "semiofficial" national anthem in the United States, second only as a patriotic song to the official national anthem, *The Star-Spangled Banner*. The former Swiss national anthem, *Rufst du, Mein Vaterland? (Callest Thou, Fatherland?)*, is set to the same music, as is a German patriotic song used in World War I, *Heil dir im Siegerkranz (Hail to the Victorious Crown)*.

See also GOD SAVE THE KING (QUEEN).

AMERICAN, The, ə-mer′ə-kən, a novel by Henry James, published in 1877 and dramatized by James himself in 1891.

The central situation of the novel, like others by the same author, is the conflict between the cultures of the Old World and the New, Europe and America. The latter is represented by Christopher Newman, a wealthy American on a visit to Paris; the former, by Claire de Cintré, a widow of aristocratic birth, half French and half English. Newman is tolerated by Mme. de Cintré's family, up to a point, because of his money, but her mother, the marquise, and her elder brother, Marquis Urbain de Bellegarde, although permitting the engagement of the pair, ultimately forbid the marriage. They persist in their refusal even when Newman confronts them with concrete evidence that the marquise murdered her husband. Though intending to expose the guilty secret in retaliation for his rebuff, Newman experiences a reversal of feeling and destroys the incriminating evidence.

Apart from those mentioned above, the important characters of the novel include Mme. de Cintré's younger brother, Count Valentin, who encourages the American's suit, and Mrs. Bread, maid to the elderly marquise, who reveals her mistress' crime to Newman.

James placed *The American* first in a recommended reading sequence of his major works. He believed that by following this sequence, the reader would acquire a fuller understanding of his progressively more subtle, involved, and leisurely creations, with their ever greater emphasis on the brilliantly precise rendering of complex and fugitive states of consciousness and conscience.

AMERICAN ACADEMY AND INSTITUTE OF ARTS AND LETTERS,

an honorary institution whose purpose is to further art, literature, and music in the United States. The institute (founded in 1898 by the American Social Science Association and incorporated by act of Congress in 1913) and the academy (created in 1904 as a section of the institute and incorporated in 1916) were amalgamated in 1976. The combined membership is limited to 250 native or naturalized citizens qualified by notable achievements in art, literature, or music. From this list, 50 members are elected to the academy for special distinction. Election to the academy-institute is an honor conferred on their peers by working artists of distinction. In order to establish cultural ties with other countries, the academy-institute has an honorary membership of 75 foreign artists, writers, and composers.

The academy-institute is governed by an 11-member board of directors. It occupies two buildings on West 155th Street in New York City, containing a library, two art galleries, and an auditorium.

The academy-institute confers awards and honors for work of excellence. Its highest honor, The Gold Medal, is given annually in two categories of the arts (there are 12 categories in all). There are 21 annual awards of $3,000 each given to artists, writers, and composers for work of outstanding merit, and the $1,000 Award for Distinguished Service to the Arts. Other awards, made possible through bequests and the generosity of donors, are: the $2,500 Marc Blitzstein Award for the Musical Theatre; the $1,000 Arnold W. Brunner Memorial Prize in architecture; the

$5,000 E. M. Forster Award; Charles Ives grants for the publication and performance of music and other works by Charles E. Ives; six annual $4,000 Charles Ives scholarships; the $2,500 biennial Loines Award for Poetry; the Richard and Hinda Rosenthal Foundation Awards ($2,000 each) for fiction and painting; the $1,500 Marjorie Peabody Waite Award to an older artist, composer, or writer (in rotation); and the $2,500 Morton Dauwen Zabel Award to a critic, poet, or novelist (in rotation).

The academy's awards consist of the Howells Medal, given every fifth year for the most distinguished work of American fiction published during that period, and the Award of Merit Medal and its accompanying $1,000 prize given in five categories of the arts (in rotation) to an outstanding practitioner of the arts who is not a member of the academy.

Exhibitions of art and manuscripts by newly elected members and recipients of honors are held following the annual May ceremonial at which members are inducted and honors and awards are bestowed. Award winners are selected by rotating juries made up of members of the academy-institute. Applications for awards are not accepted.

AMERICAN ACADEMY IN ROME,

an institution in Italy for American scholars and artists in architecture, painting, sculpture, music, landscape architecture, classics, postclassical humanistic studies, art history, and Italian studies. The academy awards annual fellowships to U. S. citizens for study at the institution. Awarded on a competitive basis, these provide a yearly stipend and travel and housing allowances.

The academy was founded in 1894 as the American School of Architecture in Rome by the American architect Charles F. McKim. In 1897, painting and sculpture were added, and it was given its present name. It was incorporated by act of Congress in 1905, and in 1913 it merged with the American School of Classical Studies in Rome. Fellowships in musical composition were added in 1921 and in creative writing in 1952.

AMERICAN ACADEMY OF ARTS AND SCIENCES,

an honorary society and interdisciplinary studies center founded in Boston, Mass., in 1780 by John Adams and others. Members include scholars and national leaders in four classes: mathematics and physical sciences, biological sciences, social arts and sciences, and the humanities. The academy meets eight times a year in Brookline, Mass. It conducts seminars that bring together scholars whose research, experience, or knowledge can help clarify contemporary problems and place them in perspective. The academy publishes a bulletin eight times yearly and *Daedalus*, a quarterly. Membership, which is by election, exceeds 2,000.

AMERICAN ANTI-SLAVERY SOCIETY,

an organization founded in 1833 by reformer William Lloyd Garrison and others who denounced the institution of slavery in the United States and demanded that it be ended. See also ABOLITIONISTS.

AMERICAN ART AND ARCHITECTURE.

See UNITED STATES—*Art and Architecture;* such articles as ARCHITECTURE, MODERN ART AND ARCHITECTURE, PAINTING, SCULPTURE; the Index entries *American Architecture* and *American Art*.

AMERICAN ASSOCIATION FOR THE ADVANCE-MENT OF SCIENCE, the largest scientific society in the United States. It was founded in 1848 "to further the work of scientists, to facilitate cooperation among them, to improve the effectiveness of science in the promotion of human welfare, and to increase public understanding and appreciation of the importance and promise of the methods of science in human progress." Membership is worldwide, but most individual members are from the United States and Canada. The membership also includes scientific societies, professional organizations, and state and local scientific academies. Many of these groups sponsor junior academies of science to promote interest in science among young people.

The association is divided into sections representing most of the branches of science. It holds an annual meeting, as well as an annual symposium and lecture. It publishes *Science*, a weekly; a series of symposium volumes; *Science Books and Films*, which appears five times a year; and a quarterly magazine, *Science Education News*. The association's headquarters are in Washington, D.C.

DAEL WOLFLE*
Executive Officer, American Association for the Advancement of Science

AMERICAN ASSOCIATION OF RETIRED PERSONS (AARP), a nonprofit, nonpartisan membership organization dedicated to addressing the needs and interests of older Americans and committed to bringing lifetimes of experience and leadership to serve all generations. Membership is open to anyone, working or retired, age 50 and older. Headquartered in Washington, D.C., AARP seeks, through service, advocacy, and education, to help older Americans achieve lives of independence, dignity, and purpose.

AARP offers its members a wide range of services and benefits, and provides legislative advocacy at the federal and state levels. Volunteers implement most of AARP's educational and community service programs through its local chapters. Educational resources offered by the AARP include publications and audiovisual materials on aging-related issues and books on topics of interest to mature readers. AARP also publishes a bimonthly magazine, *Modern Maturity*. In 1968 the AARP Andrus Foundation began to award grants for research in gerontology to U.S. universities and colleges.

AARP's national officers and its board of directors all serve in a volunteer capacity. They are elected by delegates at AARP's biennial convention.

AARP was founded in 1958 by Dr. Ethel Percy Andrus, a retired educator, who believed that older Americans could attain a sense of satisfaction and fulfillment by remaining physically and intellectually active and by serving others. Eleven years earlier, Andrus had founded the National Retired Teachers Association (NRTA) to help retired teachers whose quality of life had been greatly reduced because of inadequate pensions and inability to obtain health insurance. The successes the NRTA achieved through collective action prompted Andrus to found a similar national organization to speak on behalf of all older Americans. In 1982 the NRTA merged with the AARP.

Reviewed by the American Association of Retired Persons

AMERICAN ASSOCIATION OF UNIVERSITY PROFESSORS (AAUP), a professional organization of college and university teachers, research scholars, and academic librarians. The AAUP is the largest organization representing the general interests of the academic profession in the United States. Since its founding in 1915, the AAUP has chiefly been concerned with the defense of academic freedom and the tenure concept. Other important areas of concern include college and university government, professional ethics, standards of accreditation, and teaching standards and procedures. Its headquarters are in Washington, D.C.

AMERICAN ASSOCIATION OF UNIVERSITY WOMEN (AAUW), an association of women graduates of regionally accredited colleges. It conducts a study action program and other programs of interest in the areas of international relations, education, and culture. The AAUW awards graduate fellowships annually to women, and it finances women from other countries to go to the United States to study each year. In 1958 the association established the AAUW educational foundation to expand educational work through research and various projects. The foundation is especially concerned about evaluating AAUW programs in community leadership training as well as in women's participation in higher education.

Founded in 1882, the AAUW is headquartered in Washington, D.C.

AMERICAN AUTOMOBILE ASSOCIATION (AAA), a federation of automobile clubs that provide trip routing, travel guidebooks, insurance, bonding, and emergency repairs and other services to American motorists. The organization's chief functions are to improve motoring conditions and to aid members when they have motoring difficulties. Adequate marking of highways, elimination of abuses in the financing of automobiles and automobile accessories, and provision of adequate facilities for parking are other major goals of the AAA.

The American Automobile Association sponsors legislation and works for uniformity of motor vehicle laws. The AAA and its clubs have worked for fair taxation of motor vehicles and have opposed efforts to raid highway funds for nonhighway expenditures. The AAA's traffic safety program promotes the school safety patrol system and increased driver education in high schools.

Personal assistance to members includes emergency road service when a car breaks down on the road for any reason. Members also may request national or international routing and mapping services embracing regional road maps, tour books, tourist accommodation lists, and bridge and ferry directories.

The AAA was founded in 1902 and is headquartered in Heathrow, Fla.

R. W. TUPPER*
American Automobile Association

AMERICAN BALLET THEATRE, a ballet company based in New York City. Founded as Ballet Theatre by Lucia Chase and Richard Pleasant in 1939, it had its origins in the Mordkin Ballet, of which Chase had been prima ballerina and Pleasant had been manager. Ballet Theatre gave its first performance on Jan. 11, 1940, in New

York City. In 1957 it became the American Ballet Theatre (ABT).

The company's early style was influenced chiefly by staff choreographers Antony Tudor and Agnes de Mille. Tudor contributed masterpieces such as *Pillar of Fire* (1942), *Romeo and Juliet* and *Dim Lustre* (both 1943), and *Undertow* (1945). De Mille was responsible for such classics as *Fall River Legend* (1948) and *The Four Marys* (1965). Jerome Robbins' *Fancy Free* was introduced by Ballet Theatre in 1944 and his *Les Noces* by ABT in 1965.

Many of the world's great dancers appeared with ABT, as guests or members of the company, including Alicia Alonso, Mikhail Baryshnikov (who served as ABT's artistic director from 1980 until 1989), Natalia Makarova, and Rudolf Nureyev.

AMERICAN BANKERS ASSOCIATION, an organization that serves the banking industry by means of committees on banking as a profession, education, government relations, communications, and special activities. See also BANKS AND BANKING—*Bankers' Associations.*

AMERICAN BAR ASSOCIATION, a voluntary association of American lawyers and judges. The association's chief objectives are to uphold and defend the Constitution of the United States; to advance the science of law; and to promote the administration of justice. The association also seeks to ensure uniformity of legislation and of judicial decisions throughout the United States; to uphold the honor of the legal profession; to encourage cordial relations among the association's members; and to correlate the activities of local and state bar associations.

Organizations affiliated with the American Bar Association include the American Bar Foundation, the American Law Student Association, the National Conference of Bar Presidents, the National Conference of Bar Executives, and the National Conference of Commissioners on Uniform State Laws.

The American Bar Association was founded in 1878 on the initiative of the Connecticut State Bar Association. The organization's constitution, revised in 1936, set up a house of delegates as the policy-making body. The house is a large body, and its membership represents broad regional and philosophical differences. It meets twice a year, in winter and in summer. Between its sessions the board of governors is authorized to act for it. Members of the house of delegates are elected by individual members in each state, by state and local bar associations, and by a number of affiliated legal organizations.

The American Bar Association holds an annual meeting, usually in August, at which members may offer resolutions. The meeting also provides a forum for prominent invited speakers.

Most of the association's preliminary work is carried out by its numerous committees and subcommittees. These groups discuss subjects ranging from professional problems, such as ethics and grievances, to world peace through law. They prepare resolutions based on their discussions. They then submit these resolutions to the house of delegates or the board of governors for final action.

The association publishes the monthly *American Bar Association Journal*, the quarterly *Barrister*, and many publications in particular areas of the law, such as *Antitrust Law Journal, Criminal Justice, Family Law,* and *International Lawyer.* The association is headquartered in Washington, D.C.

JOSEPH R. TAYLOR*, *Former Managing Editor "American Bar Association Journal"*

AMERICAN BIBLE SOCIETY, a nonprofit organization founded in 1816 to encourage the circulation and reading of the Bible throughout the world. The society is interdenominational and is supported by contributions from churches and individuals. Its headquarters are in New York City.

The society assists in the preparation of new translations of the Bible, which are published in inexpensive editions. Bible reading is also promoted by such means as advertising, dissemination of literature, and daily Bible-reading services by telephone.

AMERICAN CANCER SOCIETY, a national voluntary agency composed of physicians and laypersons. Its programs include research in the prevention, diagnosis, detection, and treatment of cancer, and professional and public education. Among its special committees are groups that study new or unproved methods of treatment and the connection between smoking and cancer.

The society publishes *Cancer News* (triannually), *Cancer* (semimonthly), and *CA—A Cancer Journal for Clinicians* (bimonthly). The society was founded in 1913 and is headquartered in New York City.

AMERICAN CHEMICAL SOCIETY. See CHEMICAL SOCIETY, AMERICAN.

AMERICAN CIVIL LIBERTIES UNION (ACLU), a nationwide, nonprofit, nonpartisan organization dedicated to preserving and defending the principles set forth in the Bill of Rights. The ACLU functions in three primary ways: through litigation, through legislation advocacy, and through public education.

The ACLU's network of affiliates and chapters in every state make it the largest private law firm in the United States. The ACLU has been involved (either as direct counsel or by filing "friend-of-the-court" briefs) in more Supreme Court cases than any other organization except the U.S. government.

The ACLU's legislative office in Washington, D.C., lobbies Congress to prevent the passage of federal laws that violate constitutional rights or are hostile to civil liberties.

The ACLU's national headquarters in New York houses the public education department, which alerts the public to violations and potential violations of civil liberties, and to the importance of preserving the Bill of Rights. It publishes an annual report, a quarterly membership newsletter, and several briefing papers a year on vital civil liberties issues. It also produces publicity materials, including radio and print advertising, books on civil liberties, and pamphlets.

The ACLU was founded in 1917, under the name National Civil Liberties Bureau, with the goal of protecting the free speech rights of citizens who spoke out against U.S. participation in World War I. It adopted its present name in 1920. The ACLU immediately began to play a role in major court cases involving civil liberties.

In the 1925 Scopes "monkey trial," it sponsored a challenge to a Tennessee law prohibiting the teaching of the theory of evolution. It participated in the 1921 defense of Sacco and Vanzetti, two anarchists tried for murder; protested the internment of Japanese Americans during World War II; defended the right of Jehovah's Witnesses not to salute the flag; challenged Bible reading and prayer in public schools as violations of the constitutional principle of separation of church and state; and defended women's reproductive and privacy rights, including the right to have an abortion.

In 1978 the ACLU defended the First Amendment rights of the American Nazi Party to march in Skokie, Ill., engendering controversy both within and outside the organization. Many ACLU members resigned in protest, causing fiscal problems for the organization. But the ACLU rebounded, and membership rolls eventually surpassed pre-Skokie levels.

ACLU policy is determined by a national board and a national committee, which advises the board. Policy is carried out by national and affiliate staff. Each state affiliate also has its own board of directors, which determines affiliate policies independent of the national board.

Reviewed by
The American Civil Liberties Union

AMERICAN COLONIZATION SOCIETY, an organization established in the United States in 1816 for the purpose of aiding emigration of freed black slaves from the United States to Africa. The Republic of Liberia owes its existence to the work of the society.

Robert Finley of New Jersey, a Presbyterian minister, was the founder, but the desire for such a project had existed for many years. Going to Washington, D.C., in December 1816, Finley was encouraged to organize the society by President James Madison, Henry Clay, and other influential leaders. On Dec. 28, 1816, formal organization of the society was completed, and on Jan. 1, 1817, a meeting for the election of officers was held.

The society was supported by antislavery groups and by some slave owners, the two factions sharing a desire to provide a homeland for free blacks outside the United States. The society purchased a tract of land (now part of Liberia) on the west coast of Africa. The first groups of settlers, totaling 114, sent out in 1820–1821, were almost wiped out by disease. In 1822 another party of 37 went over, led by a white missionary, Jehudi Ashmun, whose courage and initiative enabled the colonists to establish a permanent settlement at Cape Mesurado (Montserrado) near the present site of Monrovia. Another man whose work was vital in the early years of the colony was Ralph Randolph Gurley, who was appointed by the U.S. government and the society to draw up the colony's constitution.

Branches of the American Colonization Society functioned in various states, Maryland having a particularly active group. In 1833 this branch established an African state of Maryland at what is now Harper, Liberia, on Cape Palmas. This colony became part of Liberia in 1857. Union of other settlements under the governorship of a society appointee had been achieved in 1837. Altogether, the society moved about 6,000 blacks to Liberia between 1821 and 1867, but after 1840 the work was hampered by lack of money, disputes over policy, and strong opposition in the United States. From 1865 until its dissolution in 1912, the society acted chiefly as caretaker for the colony. See also LIBERIA—*History.*

AMERICAN COUNCIL ON EDUCATION, an organization of national and regional educational associations and institutions. The council provides a center for cooperation in the improvement of education in the United States at all levels, with particular emphasis on higher education.

Founded in January 1918 to strengthen educational services to the federal government in World War I, the council became a national clearinghouse for the exchange of information. Through its staff, commissions, and committees, it conducts inquiries into educational problems, studies pending legislation affecting education, and serves as a liaison between educational institutions and government. Its publications include the *Educational Record,* a quarterly. The council's headquarters are in Washington, D.C.

AMERICAN DENTAL ASSOCIATION, a national organization of dentists. It was founded in 1859 to improve the health of the public and to promote the art and science of dentistry. The association carries on programs of dental research, inspects and accredits dental schools and hospital dental departments, reviews legislative and executive proposals affecting dentistry, maintains ethical standards, and cooperates with allied organizations throughout the world. It produces most of the material on dental-health education used in the United States. It compiles statistics on personnel practice, dental-care needs, and patients' attitudes about dental health.

Publications of the American Dental Association include the monthly *Dental Abstracts* and a biweekly *News.* The association's headquarters are in Chicago.

AMERICAN EAGLE, the national emblem of the United States since June 20, 1782, when the Continental Congress established the first great seal of the United States. Charles Thomson, secretary of the congress, proposed that the American bald eagle should appear on the seal. It was retained on the seal and appeared on various American coins. See also EAGLE; GREAT SEAL OF THE UNITED STATES.

AMERICAN ECONOMIC ASSOCIATION, an association of economists, business executives, government administrators, journalists, lawyers, and others interested in economics and its application to current problems. The purposes of the association are to encourage economic research, especially historical and statistical study; to issue publications on economic subjects; and to encourage freedom of discussion about economics.

The association conducts a visiting scholars program to prepare foreign students for graduate studies in economics in the United States. It also sponsors the National Registry for Economics, a placement service. Its publications include the *American Economic Review* and the *Journal of Economic Literature,* both quarterlies.

The association was founded in 1885 at Saratoga, N.Y. Its headquarters are in Nashville, Tenn.

AMERICAN ENGLISH. Americanisms are words or phrases peculiar to the English speech of the United States. John Pickering, who published the first vocabulary of them in 1816, divided them into three classes. First, he said, "we have formed some new words"; second, "to some old ones that are still in use in England we have affixed new significations"; and third, "others which have been long obsolete in England are still retained in common use among us." He should have added a fourth class, composed of borrowings from the Indian languages and from those of non-British immigrants. Examples of all four classes come readily to mind: of the first, *peanut, hired man, crazy quilt, schooner, movie, bootlegger, spellbinder, rubberneck, cafeteria, reliable, upstate, flatfooted, O.K., to stump, to advocate, to belittle,* and *to service;* of the second, *corn, shoe, rock, lumber, shop, cracker, dry goods, homely,* and *to haul,* all of which still have different significances in England and the United States; of the third, *andiron, offal, adze, bay window, burly, catty-cornered, to wilt, to loan,* and *to whittle;* and of the fourth, *persimmon, hominy, tomahawk, terrapin, skunk, cruller, portage, prairie, ranch, canyon, chop suey, bum, sauerkraut, spaghetti, kosher,* and *frankfurter.*

Origins. The first settlers must have begun to make Americanisms as soon as they landed, for they were confronted by a flora and a fauna that were largely unfamiliar to them, and they had to find words to designate the various species. Some of those words they borrowed from the Indians, such as *hickory, squash,* and *oppossum,* but in most cases they fashioned their novelties out of English material, as, for example, *June bug, live oak, bullfrog,* and *catfish.* Similarly, they needed names for the features of the new landscape that confronted them, and for the articles of their new domestic economy. A great many words that are still in use appear to have been those invented before the end of the 17th century. *Backlog* occurs in a writing of Increase Mather dated 1684, and *log house* in the Maryland Archives for 1669. *Clapboarded* houses, quite unknown in England, were being built in Ipswich, Mass., in 1637, and *cockroaches* (from the Spanish *cucaracha*) were mentioned in Capt. John Smith's *General Historie of Virginia, New-England, and the Summer Isles* (1624). Indeed, a number of words borrowed from the Indian languages, usually through the Spanish, were carried back to England by voyagers before there was any permanent English settlement in America, and some of them, like *alligator, sassafras,* and *sarsaparilla,* not to mention *potato* and *tobacco,* were familiar by 1600. But these were hardly Americanisms in the sense here meant, and it was not until after the founding of Jamestown that Englishmen in the New World began to concoct in earnest, and on a large scale, a really new vocabulary.

They had come from an England in which even the standard speech was still untrammeled by rule, and eagerly hospitable to picturesque neologisms. Shakespeare himself had been an ardent introducer of novelties and was the first writer, so far as the record shows, to use such now-classical words as *capable, courtship, lonely,* and *to dwindle.* In the same way Ben Jonson introduced *parody, brain-child, keystone, nonsense, exotic, narrow-minded,* and *graphic.* The American colonists, less sensitive to the sough and burble of words than these masters, con-

In 1919, H.L. Mencken (1880–1956) published the first edition of his *American Language,* one of the landmarks in the study of the English language as used in the United States. Some years before his death, Mr. Mencken wrote an article on *Americanisms* for the *Encyclopedia Americana.* Because of the historical interest of this article, it is reprinted as the first part of the coverage of *American English.* The second part, *American Usage,* which discusses the differences between "American English" and "English English" since World War II, was written by Margaret Nicholson, author of *A Dictionary of American-English Usage.*

fined themselves to homelier situations and produced mainly novelties that remained lodged in the folk-speech. But all the same, those novelties revealed a boldness that was genuinely Elizabethan, and if *hog-wallow, razorback,* (hog), *corn-dodger,* and *mossback* remain more or less inelegant to this day, they also remain pungent and highly expressive. Many of the first colonists were ignorant men, and so they made some blunders that have endured. Mistaking the native grouse for a partridge, they called it a *partridge,* and a *partridge* it continues to be. And when they mistook the American hare for a rabbit, they obliterated the whole race of hares from the new country and made them all *rabbits.*

Reaction in England. There was relatively little communication back and forth between colony and homeland in the earliest days, and in consequence the majority of Americanisms were seldom if ever heard in England. By an unhappy chance the beginnings of more frequent intercourse coincided precisely with that rise of purism in speech which marked the age of Queen Anne. The first Englishman to sound the alarm against Americanisms was one Francis Moore, who visited Georgia with Oglethorpe in 1735. In Savannah, then a village but two years old, he heard the word *bluff* applied to a steep bank, and was so unpleasantly affected by it that he denounced it as "barbarous." He was followed by a gradually increasing stream of other linguistic policemen, and by 1781 the Rev. John Witherspoon, who had come out in 1769 to be president of Princeton, was printing a headlong attack upon American speech habits, not only on the level of the folk but also higher up—indeed, clear to the top. "I have heard in this country," he wrote, "in the senate, at the bar, and from the pulpit, and see daily in dissertations from the press, errors in grammar, improprieties, and vulgarisms which hardly any person of the same class in point of rank and literature would have fallen into in Great Britain."

Witherspoon's attack made some impression, but only in academic circles. The generality of Americans, insofar as they heard of it at all, dismissed its author as a mere Englishman (he was actually a Scotsman), and hence somehow inferior and ridiculous. The former colonies were now sovereign states, and their somewhat cocky citizens thought that they were under no obligation to heed admonitions from a defeated and effete empire 3,000 miles across the sea. Even before the Declaration of Independence an anonymous author, supposed to have been John Adams, proposed formally that an American Society of Language be set up to "polish" the American language on strictly American principles, and on Sept. 30, 1780, Adams wrote and signed a letter to the president of Congress renewing this proposal. "Let it be carried out," he said, and "England will never more have any honor, excepting now and then that of imitating the Americans." He was joined in 1789 by the redoubtable Noah Webster, who predicted the rise in the new Republic of a "language as different from the future language of England as the modern Dutch, Danish, and Swedish are from the German, or from one another."

The English reply to such contumacy was a series of blasts that continued in dreadful fury for a whole generation, and then abated to a somewhat milder bombardment that goes on to this day. From 1785 to 1815 the English quarterly reviewers, then at the height of their power, denounced all Americanisms in a really frantic manner, the good along with the bad. When Thomas Jefferson, in 1787, ventured to use the verb *to belittle* in his *Notes on Virginia,* he was dealt with as if he had committed some nefarious and ignoble act. "Freely, good Sir," roared the *European Magazine and London Review,* "will we forgive all your attacks, impotent as they are illiberal, upon our national character; but for the future—oh spare, we beseech you, our mother-tongue!" All the other American writers of the ensuing quarter century were similarly belabored—among them, John Marshall, Noah Webster, Joel Barlow, and John Quincy Adams. Even Washington got a few licks—for using *to derange.* But the Yankee, between the two wars with England, was vastly less susceptible to English precept and example than he is today, and the thundering of the reviewers did not stay the hatching of Americanisms. On the contrary, it seems to - have stimulated the process.

Frontier Influences. With the opening of the West, the invention of Americanisms got a fresh start, and by the time of the Mexican War, American English was already so far differentiated from the English of England that almost every Englishman who crossed the ocean to write a book complained that understanding it as spoken had become difficult. Not only was its vocabulary enormously enriched by the movement of population beyond the Alleghanies; there was also a distinct change in American pronunciation. The influence of English example in the latter field began to be restricted sharply to the Boston area and the Tidewater region of the South. Everywhere else the English broad *a* disappeared, the *r* that the English had begun to elide reasserted itself harshly, and there gradually emerged the brisk, clear, somewhat metallic Western American that has since conquered four fifths of the whole country and seems very likely to conquer the rest. This Western American is still obnoxious to Englishmen, but its superiority to Standard English, and especially to Oxford English, is obvious. It gives nearly all sounds their full value and is quite devoid of affectation and artificiality. There is no mistaking the meaning of a person speaking it. It tends to a certain monotony, for its range of pitch is much smaller than that of Standard English, but what it thus lacks in variety it more than makes up in clarity.

It differentiates American from English much more definitely than the difference in vocabulary, but the latter is what English observers chiefly discuss, for it includes hundreds of terms that puzzle, astonish, and shock them. Their own language was so harshly regimented in the 18th century, largely under the influence of the pedantic Samuel Johnson, that it has never recovered the lively enterprise that it showed in Shakespeare's day. It takes in foreign words very reluctantly, and in making neologisms out of its own materials exhibits very little sense of the pungent and picturesque. Whenever a new situation confronts the people of the two countries, the Americans respond with much more boldness and ingenuity. Certainly it will hardly be denied that *movie* is a better word than *cinema,* and *commuter* than *season-ticket holder,* and *weather bureau* than *meteorological office,* and *steam shovel* than *crane-navvy,* and *cow-catcher* than *plough,* and *thirty-second note* than *demisemiquaver.* The English have invented nothing as magnificently expressive as *rubber-neck* in a century. Nor have they taken in the half, or even the tenth, of our rich harvest of loanwords, beginning with the French *chowder, bogus,.* and *picayune* and the Dutch *cooky, cole slaw, scow,* and *waffle* of colonial days, and running through the Spanish *stampede, tamale, lasso, corral,* and *calaboose* of the Western migration and the German *rathskeller, kindergarten, stein, delicatessen,* and *katzenjammer* of the great immigration, to the Yiddish *mazuma, matzoth,* and *oi-yoi* of our own time.

Modern Trends. There was a day when it seemed likely that the different direction and far greater impetus of American would carry it so far from English that the two would bear out Noah Webster's prophecy by becoming mutually unintelligble. But that possibility has now vanished, for since the turn of the century the influence of American upon English has been felt increasingly, and large numbers of American neologisms come into use in England almost as quickly as they circulate at home. The influence of American movies and the American radio is obvious in this process, and the American comic strip has had some influence too. But the main reason for the eagerness with which American novelties are accepted and adopted is simply the fact that they are, taking one with another, greatly superior to the home product. There is usually more humor in them, and they show better resourcefulness and ingenuity. The English, indeed, have come to look upon such novelties in speech as essentially imported goods, and no longer resist them as fiercely as aforetime. A few purists, to be sure, still denounce them violently, and now and then a storm of such denunciation runs through the letter-columns of the English newspapers. But much more frequently the papers give over their space to vocabularies of the latest comers with definitions. It is a commonplace in England that the younger generation already speaks American—if not always correctly, then at least fluently. When, during 1938 and 1939, *Punch* ran a series of amusing articles, explaining the meaning of a long series of American slang terms, it was announced frankly that they were printed for the enlightenment and edification of adults only: the assumption was that the youth of the country were already familiar with them, and skilled in their use.

A contrary movement of Anglicisms to the United States also goes on, but it is much feebler than the movement of Americanisms to England. It shows itself chiefly on the level where speech habits are rather self-conscious and there is some pretension to elegance. The use of the English *shop* in place of the American *store* began about 1910, and *shop* has now acquired the special American meaning of a relatively small establishment dealing in but one line of goods. An effort was made about the same time to displace the American *shoe* with the English *boot,* but it never made much progress, though *bootshops* still survive. Of late it has become fashionable to teach children to call their mothers *Mummy,* which is English, instead of *Mamma,* which is American, but *Mummy* is so hideous a word that it is not likely to prevail. Perhaps the most striking English contribution to the American language in recent years has been *charwoman,* which has pretty well supplanted *scrubwoman.*

H.L. MENCKEN
Author of "The American Language"

AMERICAN USAGE

In the years after the United States entered World War II, the differences between British English and American English have rapidly decreased. U.S. forces stationed in England, Telstar, the exchange of television and radio programs, the Universal Copyright Convention (making it unnecessary for American publishers to reset English books in order to secure full-term U.S. copyright)—all have been among the contributing factors. In literary and scholarly material, the distinguishing features of American English are now often only spelling and pronunciation. In popular writing and speech, however, many differences, especially in the vocabulary of everyday life, colloquialisms, and slang, are still easily recognizable. An Englishman with no personal knowledge of America might have difficulty in understanding some American words and phrases, even with the help of an English dictionary that includes definitions "chiefly" or "originally" U.S.

Although in all languages usage ultimately triumphs over etymology, spelling, and grammar, English is slower than the United States in accepting innovations. The verb *contact,* for example, after first being unrecorded in English dictionaries, has gone through successive later editions as "U.S. slang," "U.S. colloquial," "chiefly U.S.," and finally with no indications of being either "U.S." or substandard. *Recognise* and *judgement,* formerly so spelled by most British writers, now are often *recognize* and *judgment,* as they have long been in the United States. According to Sir Ernest Gowers in the 1965 revision of Fowler's *Modern English Usage,* the English have proved "ready pupils" of America's preference for phrasal verbs—*meet up with, lose out, miss out on, step off, face up to,* and similar combinations of verb and adverbial particle. But combinations such as these in both countries are used for the most part in speech and informal writing. There remain some characteristics of American speech and writing that, Gowers says, "the English continue to resist."

Pronunciation. As every American knows, one spoken sentence will identify the speaker as English, not only by the difference in pronunciation of individual vowels, sounds, and words, but also by inflection, cadence, and stress. The English can similarly identify their visitors from the United States by accent and their "nasal twang." American speech is usually slower and, as Mencken pointed out in the first part of this article, more forthright, if also more monotonous.

Although speech in the United States, as in Britain, differs geographically and among classes, most Americans pronounce *bath, fast, calf,* and usually *aunt* with the same vowel as in *cat;* British English pronounces the *a* as in *father.* In the speech of most Americans, the r in words like *father* retains its strong (retroflex) quality, which in England is almost lost. Most Americans give a more even stress to unaccented syllables than do the British or, on the other hand, drop unaccented syllables entirely. The American usually says "lit′ə-rer-ē," "lab′rə-tōr-ē"; the Englishman, "lit′rə-ri," "lə-bor′ə-tri." The *-ile* in such words as *fertile, facile,* and *hostile* is regularly pronounced "il" in the United States, in Britain usually "īl." But the English say "ēl" in *profile* and "il" in *Anglophile,* while the Americans say "īl" in both. Many words beginning with *wh* (whistle, wharf) retain the "h" in American speech but not in English. In the United States *schedule* is pronounced with an initial "sk" sound, not "sh," as in England; *clerk* rhymes with *jerk,* not, as in England, with *dark;* and *leisure* with *seizure,* not *treasure.* *Margarine* was originally pronounced with a hard "g" in England (as in *Margaret*), but now the American pronunciation with g sounded as "j" has triumphed.

Many Americans pronounce noun and verb with the accent on the first syllable in such words as *address, progress, contract,* whereas the British stress the first syllable of the noun but the second syllable of the verb. Most Americans pronounce *against* with an "e," *either* with an "ē," and *been* with an "i"; most British use "ā," "ī," and "ē," respectively, in these words. But these and other differences in pronunciation cause no misunderstanding in either country, and unless the British pronunciation comes naturally to an American, it is usually regarded in the United States as an affectation.

Spelling. The first indication that any piece of writing is by an American rather than by an Englishman is the spelling. The *-or* ending of words such as *favor, harbor, neighbor* is standard in the United States, although the British *-our* is still sometimes retained in *glamour* and *Saviour. Meager, meter, specter,* and similar words derived from French are regularly spelled with *-er,* but *theatre* is widely retained, as in Britain. The doubling of the final consonant before a suffix beginning with a vowel has now been dropped in American usage in such words as *traveling, jeweler, marvelous,* though the usual British *panelling* and *kidnapped* are still preferred by some writers. *Catalog, quartet, program* are typical of the American preference for shorter forms, while England continues the French spelling *catalogue, quartette, programme.*

Many words regularly spelled with an *-ize* ending in the United States are often spelled with *-ise* in England (*realise, recognise, scrutinise*), but English dictionaries usually include both forms. Although, as we have seen, England still prefers the long forms of some words (*programme, abridgement*), in others she uses short forms not yet generally accepted in the United States: *skilful, fulfil. Practice,* noun and verb, is so spelled in America, and *licence* is allowed for both, while in England the verbs retain the older spelling with *s*—to *practise,* to *license.* The older *t* spelling and pronunciation in the past tenses and past participles of such words as *leapt, leant, learnt, spoilt* are much more common in England. *Gipsy* and *pyjamas* are the first spellings in most English dictionaries; in America, *gypsy* and *pajamas* are given first, with former spellings as variants.

In spite of these and many other differences, neither the British nor the American reading public is as disturbed as formerly by the other's preferences. Whereas the spelling in British books used to be carefully changed to American usage before publication in the United States, and American spelling changed to British before publication in England, this is seldom now felt to be necessary in either country, except in children's books and textbooks.

Vocabulary. Although it might be hard to decide whether an essay on classical music, for example, was written by an American or an Englishman from the evidence of the vocabulary, a contemporary novel would almost inevitably contain words peculiar in their meaning to one country or the other. Most Americans know the meaning of *pram, lorry, lift,* and *petrol,* but would surely say *baby carriage* (or *baby buggy*), *truck* (or *van*), *elevator,* and *gas.* An English reader would understand *drugstore, faucet, eraser, cookie,* but would use *chemist, tap, rubber, biscuit.* Other typical examples of differences are:

U.S.	British
candy	sweets
corn	maize
checkers	draughts
apartment	flat
hood, trunk (of an automobile)	bonnet, boot (of a motor car)
pit (of a fruit)	stone
suspenders	braces
garters	suspenders
monkey wrench	spanner
(house) trailer	bus-caravan
sled	sledge
flashlight	electric torch

None of the individual words in either list is unused in the other country, but at least one sense of each is different. In addition, Americans use words in combinations not generally found in British usage—to *stop off* on a journey, for example, or *stop over* for the night; during hard times they talk of *breadlines.* In slang and colloquialisms the differences are legion: "*in*" between the pages," "*down* below the bridge" are often heard in American speech; a (U.S.) *bum* is a (British) *loafer,* and a *bouncer* is a (British) *chucker-out.*

Grammar and Idiom. Although in scholarly speech and writing Americans employ few deviations from accepted English grammar, Americans tend to discard some traditional constructions much more readily than the English. The distinction between *shall* and *will,* the use of the subjunctive, and the rules of the gerund are often not observed even by well-educated Americans. Nouns become verbs in speech and writing almost without the user's conscious thought: "He *gestured* his approval"; "he was *paged* at the hotel." Prepositions are dropped, shortened, or modified in such constructions as "I'll see you [on] Friday," "he flopped on [to] the ground," "[with] in the past four months," "the first time in [for] years"; and the American *aim to* rather than *aim at* is now becoming prevalent even in England. Americans often say *all of, in back of,* when the English would say *all* and *behind.*

Got in the United States has fallen into disgrace in many constructions in which it is standard in England. No American would think of

writing "where the book *got* published" (rather than "*was* published"). *Gotten* is the accepted past participle in most senses in the United States ("after he had *gotten* up"), and even *get* is avoided in some constructions (to some Americans "she was *becoming* fond of me" seems much more elegant than "she was *getting* fond of me"). *Fix* is almost a jack-of-all-trades in the United States: "she *fixed* up the papers before she left"; "he was in quite a *fix.*" "*I loaned* her" is more natural to Americans than the British "I *lent* her." *Around* in American usage is in most senses almost invariably *round* in British, and *until* is usually preferred to the shorter (and equally correct) *till.* However, the longer *whilst, amongst,* and to a lesser extent *amidst* and *towards* are almost obsolescent in the United States. *Woken, quieten* are accepted forms in England, but sound colloquial to the American ear.

There can be no question that America has contributed much to the English language: new words introduced by immigrants from many countries, and from pioneering into Indian country, as pointed out by Mencken; words from science, invention, and industry; shortened and more colorful forms (*colorful* in this sense was long considered an undesirable Americanism in England, but now is accepted). Few people, English or American, now contend that the forms of standard English usage are "right" and those of standard American usage are "wrong." The danger in America is in too readily accepting slang, colloquialisms, and (in eagerness to be "democratic") substandard usage in formal speech and writing. One may argue that insistence on "It is *I*" is obsolete, but even if 50 million Americans should say "between you and I," at this period in the growth of language it would still be wrong.

MARGARET NICHOLSON, *Author of "A Dictionary of American-English Usage"*

Bibliography

The American Language, by H. L. Mencken, was first published in 1919. It was enlarged in each of three subsequent editions (1921, 1923, 1936), and two supplements appeared, in 1945 and 1948. The 4th edition and the supplements were abridged by Raven J. McDavid, Jr. (Knopf 1963).
Dillard, J. L., ed., *Perspectives on American English* (Mouton 1980).
Dillard, J. L., *Toward a Social History of American English* (Mouton 1985).
Doty, Gladys G., and Ross, Janet, *Language and Life in the U. S. A.* 4th ed. (Harper 1981).
Ellins-Elmakiss, *Catching on to American Idioms* (Univ. of Mich. Press 1984).
Follet, Wilson, *Modern American Usage: A Guide,* ed. by Jacques Barzun (Hill & Wang 1966).
Key, Mary R., *Polynesian and American Linguistic Connections* (Jupiter Press 1984).
Kurath, Hans, and McDavid, Raven I., Jr., *Pronunciation of English in the Atlantic States* (1961; Univ. of Ala. Press 1983).
Marckwardt, Albert H., *American English,* ed. by J. L. Dillard, 2d ed. (Oxford 1980).
McDavid, Raven I., Jr., *Varieties of American English,* ed. by Anwar S. Dil (Stanford Univ. Press 1978).
Nicholson, Margaret, *A Dictionary of American-English Usage* (New Am. Lib. 1957).
Orr, Eleanor W., *Twice As Less: Black English and the Performance of Black Students in Mathematics and Science* (Norton 1987).
Pederson, Lee, ed., *Linguistic Atlas of the Gulf States,* Vol. 1 (Univ. of Ga. Press 1986).
Simpson, David, *The Politics of American English* (Continuum 1987).
Stevens, P., *British and American English* (Macmillan 1971).
Watts, Walter N. and Etheldra M., *Learning to Read the Language of Americans* (Irvington 1972).
Wentworth, Harold, and Flexner, Stuart B., *Dictionary of American Slang,* 2d ed. (Crowell 1975).
Wilder, Roy, *You All Spoken Here* (Viking 1984).
Williams, Roger, *Key into the Language of America* (1643; reprint, Gale Res. 1970).

AMERICAN FARM BUREAU FEDERATION, a voluntary organization of farm and ranch families forming the largest general farm group in the United States. Founded late in 1919, the AFBF has grown to a total membership of more than 3.2 million families in 48 states and Puerto Rico. The organization is nongovernmental, nonpartisan, and nonsectarian. It serves the needs of its members through a variety of informational, legislative, and cooperative activities.

The AFBF is an outgrowth of an early movement for public sponsorship of institutions to help agricultural development through research and education. A first step was taken with the passage of the federal Morrill (Land-Grant College) Act of 1862, which provided for the establishment of state agricultural colleges. The accumulation of scientific knowledge in agriculture led to the organization of private local groups for the purpose of dispersing this knowledge to farmers. The Broome County (N.Y.) Farm Bureau, founded in 1910, was the first of these groups to use the term "farm bureau."

The Smith-Lever Agricultural Extension Act of 1914, which set up a federal agricultural extension service through the land-grant colleges and provided for the employment of county agricultural agents, gave great impetus to the establishment of sponsoring county farm bureaus to help support the program. Although by 1954 the direct financial and organizational ties between county farm bureaus and county extension services had been abolished, some farm bureaus still make financial contributions to the extension program, notably in Illinois.

The first state federation of county farm bureaus was organized in Missouri in 1915. Massachusetts and Vermont followed quickly in order. With the rapid growth of the agricultural extension service and farm bureau organization, the need for action in other areas—particularly in the business, economic, and legislative fields—was foreseen. This led to the federation of 28 state farm bureaus into the AFBF in 1919 and the opening of an office in Washington, D.C., in 1920.

Soon after its foundation the AFBF set up an effective lobby in Washington, D.C., to seek the passage of legislation favored by farmers. The parity goal was developed largely by the federation. In addition, it has strongly supported soil and water conservation, the rural electrification and telephone program, rural road building, and farmer cooperatives, as well as agricultural and rural education, agricultural research, marketing research, and various other allied projects.

Most state farm bureaus have affiliates that offer insurance and various marketing and purchasing services to members on a cooperative basis. The American Agricultural Mutual Insurance Company provides reinsurance for state farm bureau insurance companies; the American Agricultural Marketing Association advises on changes in marketing practices; the Farm Bureau Trade Development Corporation promotes export sales of farm commodities; and the Farm Bureau Mutual Fund offers an investment service and a retirement plan.

AFBF publications include a monthly, *Nation's Agriculture*, and the weekly *Official News Letter*. General offices are in Park Ridge, Ill., and there is an office in Washington, D.C.

W. E. Hamilton*
American Farm Bureau Federation

AMERICAN FEDERATION OF LABOR AND CONGRESS OF INDUSTRIAL ORGANIZATIONS, the most powerful labor organization in the United States. It was formed by a merger of the American Federation of Labor (AFL) and the Congress of Industrial Organizations (CIO) in 1955. With more than 17 million members in the 1980's, the AFL-CIO included 78% of the nation's organized workers and 18% of its labor force.

History. The AFL was established in 1886 to organize skilled workers into national unions composed of members of the same craft with "pure and simple" objectives: shorter hours, higher wages, and better working conditions. Samuel Gompers was its president until 1925, when he was succeeded by William Green. The AFL had more than 4 million members by 1920, but its membership declined to 2,127,000 in 1933. Most of its members were building trades workers, coal miners, and railroad-shop craftsmen.

The CIO was formed in 1935 to organize the semiskilled and unskilled in the mass production industries, neglected by the AFL. Led by John L. Lewis, who was succeeded in 1940 by Philip Murray, the CIO conducted campaigns in the steel, automobile, textile, rubber, clothing, and electrical industries. By 1937 it claimed 3,700,000 members. It also developed a political movement with a program of social reform.

Merger. For 20 years after the CIO was formed, the two organizations struggled to control the nation's labor force. Membership in both organizations increased steadily. Negotiations for a merger occurred sporadically all through this period of warfare, but they did not become significant until the old leaders died and were succeeded by George Meany at the AFL and Walter Reuther at the CIO in 1952. When studies by "unity committees" revealed that the two organizations had become similar in structure and composition, that their jurisdictional warfare was producing little result, and that their disunity was weakening the political-economic strength of both, the merger movement proceeded rapidly, and unity was achieved at conventions held in New York City in late 1955.

The AFL-CIO named Meany president. Its constitution declared that the convention, meeting every two years, would be the supreme governing body. All existing national unions would be represented at the convention on a pro rata basis. Trade departments, state and local councils, and directly affiliated locals also were to be represented. The constitution provided for an executive council made up of the president, the secretary, and 27 vice presidents, which was given extensive powers as a governing body between conventions. The constitution also provided for a general board of all members of the executive council and a "principal officer" of each national union, which would meet each year to decide policy questions.

The constitution recognized the old structure of the AFL by providing for departments of construction trades, metal trades, union-label trades, railway workers, and maritime employees. It also recognized the CIO pattern by providing for a department of industrial organizations (headed by Reuther) to be made up of national unions of noncraft workers. Departments were expected to adopt common policies of action.

Joseph G. Rayback
Author of "A History of American Labor"

THE AFL-CIO SINCE 1955

The AFL-CIO is primarily a lobbying and not a collective-bargaining organization. Bargaining is carried on by the national unions, such as the Autoworkers and Steelworkers. (These national unions are actually referred to as Internationals because they have locals in Canada.) The AFL-CIO is deeply involved in political action as well. Here, too, however, the international unions have great independence and may take positions at odds with the federation.

The AFL-CIO also acts as a conciliator among the various member unions, trying to prevent quarrels over jurisdiction. Before the merger of the AFL and CIO, the two federations had played a fairly active role in organizing new members and fostering new unions, but by the time of the merger, such organizing as was done was left largely to the internationals.

Meany and Reuther. George Meany, the president of the merged federation, proved to be more influential than many had expected. A former plumber, he reflected the relatively conservative views of the skilled craftsmen of the building trades who had been the backbone of the old AFL. A devout Roman Catholic already past his middle years—he was 61 at the time of the merger—Meany was strongly anti-Communist. He was skeptical of both political parties, preferring the traditional positions of AFL founder Samuel Gompers: reward your friends, punish your enemies, and maintain political aloofness.

The United States was the only great industrial power to emerge from World War II undamaged, and the country generally enjoyed prosperity. Employers did well and were often willing to share their profits with the unions. Labor relations generally were placid compared with those in the turbulent 1930's, and Meany's style of leadership seemed to suit the times.

Corruption in some member unions was a problem that the merged organization faced. Dishonesty was difficult for the federation to deal with because of the autonomy of the international unions. But a congressional investigation focused so much attention on the Teamsters (truck drivers) union that they were expelled from the AFL-CIO in 1957. Congress enacted the Landrum-Griffin Act in 1959, aimed at ensuring democratic procedures and financial integrity in unions. The new law, added to the earlier Taft-Hartley Act, also served to make union organizing more expensive and cumbersome. The expelled Teamsters continued to exist as an independent union and continued to show evidence of corruption.

Walter Reuther, the former leader of the CIO, remained the president of the United Auto Workers (UAW). Reuther had hoped that the merger would bring a new wave of organizing. Meany, on the other hand, assumed that the AFL-CIO was just a continuation of the old AFL of mostly craft-oriented, skilled workers. Meany felt Reuther wanted to succeed him, and he resented the younger man's brilliance and flair for public relations.

Meany and Reuther also differed over foreign policy. Meany was a "hawk" who strongly supported the Cold War; Reuther was more interested in combating world poverty and in reducing international tensions. Other critics of Meany—such as Jerry Wurf of the State, County and Municipal Employees and Emil Mazey of the

BETTMANN NEWSPHOTOS

AFL's George Meany (*left*) and CIO's Walter Reuther officially opened the AFL-CIO merger convention in 1955.

Autoworkers—criticized Meany's support of the Vietnam War and his cooperation with the Central Intelligence Agency (CIA) against leftist unions or regimes overseas. After years of rivalry, Reuther and the UAW left the AFL-CIO in 1968.

The AFL-CIO under Meany succeeded in achieving one of the goals of the merger. The union became completely integrated racially, although this hindered organization in the South, where many new industries were locating. In the civil-rights field and other domestic social programs, the AFL-CIO was supportive of the presidencies of John F. Kennedy and Lyndon Johnson.

By the 1970's, however, other industrialized countries, such as West Germany, Japan, France, and Italy, had recovered from the devastation of World War II and vigorously reentered the world market. Further, multinational corporations moved many of their operations to newly industrialized, low-wage countries such as Taiwan, South Korea, and Brazil—causing unemployment in high-wage American manufacturing industries. The large amounts of capital, skilled labor, raw materials, and scientific resources devoted to the U.S. defense establishment also weakened the competitive position of U.S. industry.

The resulting decline in employment and union membership in manufacturing industries was partially offset by dramatic growth among college-educated, white-collar, and retail employees. The United Federation of Teachers, the American Federation of State, County, and Municipal Employees, the United Food and Commercial Workers, and the Communication Workers of America—all small unions at the time of the AFL-CIO merger—became major unions.

Kirkland as President. It was therefore a very different labor federation in 1979 when Meany, in ill health, declined to run for reelection and died a few months later. He was succeeded by Lane Kirkland, for many years the AFL-CIO secretary-treasurer and before that a member of a small union of merchant-marine officers. Aware that AFL-CIO membership had declined as a percentage of the labor force, and stung by the election of the conservative Ronald Reagan to the presidency, Kirkland launched a new course for the federation. A call for a "Solidarity Day" protest against Reagan's social policies brought hundreds of thousands to Washington, D.C., in 1981 in an impressive demonstration. His new course led the UAW to rejoin the federation in 1981. Kirkland also moved to align the AFL-CIO more closely with the Democratic party and to increase labor's voice in choosing Democratic presidential nominees.

Nevertheless the federation lost some of its former political clout, and in October 1988 its executive council voted to allow the more politically and socially conservative Teamsters to rejoin its ranks.

HUGH G. CLELAND
State University of New York at Stony Brook

Bibliography

Bok, Derek C., and Dunlop, John T., *Labor and the American Community* (Simon & Schuster 1970).
Goulden, Joseph C., *Meany* (Atheneum 1972).
Lichtenstein, N., *Labor's War at Home* (Cambridge 1987).
Rayback, Joseph G., *A History of American Labor* (Macmillan, N.Y. 1966)
Robinson, Archie, *George Meany and His Times* (Simon & Schuster 1982).

AMERICAN FEDERATION OF MUSICIANS, a union of instrumentalists affiliated with the AFL-CIO. Its full name is American Federation of Musicians of the United States and Canada. Its membership is nearly 300,000 in about 600 locals.

The organization was founded in 1896 by branches of the National League of Musicians, a professional society now defunct, and soon dominated the industry. Despite its strength, however, it has been unable to overcome the technological unemployment that has resulted from the use of recorded music in various media. James C. Petrillo, president from 1940 to 1958, failed in his efforts to force the hiring of musicians, even when recordings were used, but in the 1940's the union won the right to collect royalties on each recording made by its members. This money is used to pay unemployed members to give free public concerts. AFM publishes *International Musician*. Its headquarters are in New York City.

HUGH G. CLELAND
State University of New York at Stony Brook

AMERICAN FEDERATION OF STATE, COUNTY, AND MUNICIPAL EMPLOYEES, one of the largest and fastest-growing unions in the American Federation of Labor-Congress of Industrial Organizations (AFL-CIO). It organizes state and local government employees, but not federal workers, who belong to the American Federation of Government Employees. AFSCME was born in 1932, when a group of Wisconsin state employees formed a local of the AFL, under the leadership of Arnold Zander. The movement spread to other states and was chartered as a national union by the AFL in 1936.

Growth was slow at first, inasmuch as the National Labor Relations Act (Wagner Act) did not extend statutory bargaining rights to government employees. In 1964, Zander was defeated for the presidency by Jerry Wurf, the head of a district council of the union in New York City. Wurf soon transformed the union into a dynamic and rapidly expanding organization. He was often abrasive and confrontational, but public workers, who often had felt powerless, welcomed his style. Wurf was a frequent critic of AFL-CIO President George Meany.

The Rev. Martin Luther King, Jr., was assassinated while supporting the strike of an AFSCME local in Memphis, Tenn., in 1968.

Wurf died in 1981 and was succeeded as president by Gerald W. McEntee, who had successfully organized Pennsylvania state employees.

HUGH G. CLELAND
State University of New York at Stony Brook

AMERICAN FEDERATION OF TEACHERS, a union of educational employees, mostly classroom teachers. A constituent of the American Federation of Labor-Congress of Industrial Organizations (AFL-CIO), the AFT has a membership of about 580,000 in 2,100 locals. The union strives to improve teachers' salaries and working conditions and to foster better education.

The first local union of teachers was formed in Chicago in 1902. The national federation was chartered in that city in 1916, with John Dewey, the philosopher and leader in progressive education, as its most prominent founder. Because unionization of teachers was discouraged and often forbidden in the early years, growth of the AFT was slow. In 1929 membership totaled only 5,000; by 1960 it was still only 60,000. Growth was rapid after the United Federation of Teachers (UFT), an affiliate of the AFT, won an election in 1961 to become the bargaining agent for New York City teachers. The union's campaign was marked by one-day strikes in New York in 1960 and 1962.

The AFT represents teachers in New York, Philadelphia, Detroit, Cleveland, Chicago, Boston, Hartford, Conn., and many smaller urban areas. In 1956 its locals in Southern states were integrated. The AFT's headquarters are in Washington, D.C. It publishes *American Teacher*, a monthly magazine.

HUGH G. CLELAND
State University of New York at Stony Brook

AMERICAN FEDERATION OF TELEVISION AND RADIO ARTISTS, an organization of performers and announcers in the fields of television, radio, and recording in the United States. A constituent of the American Federation of Labor-Congress of Industrial Organizations (AFL-CIO), AFTRA has a membership of about 40,000 entertainers in its 38 locals. National headquarters are in New York City.

The organization was founded in 1937 and called the American Federation of Radio Artists until 1952. Eddie Cantor was its first president. In the 1950's the blacklisting of performers accused of having Communist ties posed a major problem for AFTRA. Because of pressure exerted on the radio and television industry not to employ such performers, many of them were denied work. AFTRA itself was divided in its attitude toward blacklisting and never was able to deal with the issue effectively.

HUGH G. CLELAND
State University of New York at Stony Brook

AMERICAN FIELD SERVICE (AFS), an organization of former American Field Service ambulance drivers and American and foreign students who have held AFS scholarships. Its purpose is to promote international understanding, primarily through the exchange of secondary school students who are 16 to 18 years old. Students from about 80 foreign countries have attended a year of high school in 3,000 U. S. communities, and American teenagers have participated in summer programs in about 60 foreign countries.

The AFS was founded in 1914. Its headquarters are in New York City.

AMERICAN FOXHOUND, a dog that hunts by scent and is primarily used for hunting foxes. It strongly resembles the English foxhound, its progenitor. Standing 21 to 25 inches (53–64 cm) at the shoulder and weighing 60 to 70 pounds (27–32 kg), it has a short, hard, glossy coat that may be of any color or colors but is commonly black, tan, and white, or tan and white.

EVELYN SHAFER

The American foxhound, like its progenitor the English foxhound, is used chiefly for hunting foxes.

Though healthy and thoroughly amiable, the American foxhound usually makes a difficult house pet. It may be hard to housebreak and will probably bay and become destructive if left alone in the house. Outdoors it is likely to wander off on its own at any opportunity. It is accustomed to being part of a pack, and is better off in a kennel than in the home.

JOHN HOWE
Author of "Choosing the Right Dog"

AMERICAN FRIENDS SERVICE COMMITTEE (AFSC), an organization that promotes peace and reconciliation through programs of social service and public information. It was founded in 1917 by the Religious Society of Friends (Quakers). Its goals are to relieve human suffering and to find new approaches to world peace and nonviolent social change.

Work in foreign countries includes refugee relief and rehabilitation, peace education, and community development. Within U. S. communities, it conducts programs concerning the problems of minority groups, such as housing, employment, and denial of legal rights. In 1947 the AFSC was awarded the Nobel Peace Prize jointly with the Friends Service Council, its British counterpart.

AMERICAN HEART ASSOCIATION, a national organization of physicians, scientists, and laymen. Founded in 1924, it gathers information on heart disease, aids in the development of new centers for cardiac work, and coordinates work in the prevention and care of heart disease. It supports research, education, and community-service programs, with the objective of reducing death and disability from heart and blood-vessel diseases. It conducts an annual fund drive.

Association publications include *Circulation,* a monthly, and *American Heart,* a quarterly. The association, with more than 100,000 members, has its headquarters in Dallas, Texas.

AMERICAN HISTORICAL ASSOCIATION, a national organization of historians, educators, and others interested in promoting historical studies and collecting and preserving historical documents. The association has a broad influence in directing and stimulating historical research, and its service center aids teachers of history by means of conferences and publications. The *American Historical Review* is published five times a year and is sent to all members. The association also publishes a variety of pamphlets on historical subjects and the biographical series *Writings on American History.*

The association, which was founded in 1884 at Saratoga Springs, N. Y., has about 15,000 members. Its headquarters are in Washington, D. C.

AMERICAN HISTORY. See UNITED STATES and Index entry *United States–History.*

AMERICAN INDIAN MOVEMENT, a militant civil rights organization in the United States and Canada. Founded in Minneapolis, Minn., in 1968, by Dennis Banks and Clyde Bellancourt, the American Indian Movement (AIM) has sought to seize control of the existing Indian reform movement and to discredit conventional Indian leadership groups. AIM's program calls for the reorganization of the U. S. Bureau of Indian Affairs (BIA), and demands strict observance of past treaties between American Indian groups and the U. S. government. To dramatize such demands, 500 AIM activists occupied the BIA building in Washington, D. C., in November 1972. In February 1973 about 200 members of AIM occupied the historic village of Wounded Knee, S. Dak., site of an 1890 massacre.

AMERICAN INDIANS. See INDIANS, American.

AMERICAN JEWISH CONGRESS, a national community relations and human rights organization in the United States. It was founded in 1918 by Rabbi Stephen S. Wise, Justice Louis D. Brandeis, and other noted Jewish leaders. The AJC works to eliminate racial and religious bias, to defend religious freedom, to promote the religious and cultural survival of Judaism, and to strengthen ties between American Jewry and Israel. It pioneered in the use of legislation to attack discrimination in education, housing, and employment. National headquarters are in New York City.

NATHAN L. ROBERTS*, *American Jewish Congress*

AMERICAN KENNEL CLUB, an association of all-breed, specialty-breed, and obedience dog clubs. It maintains a studbook registry with the pedigree records of about 13 million dogs. See also DOG.

AMERICAN LEGION, a United States veterans association–the largest organization of its kind in the world, with a membership of approximately 2,700,000. It was founded at a caucus of members of the American Expeditionary Force in Paris, France, after World War I and was incorporated by act of Congress on Sept. 16, 1919. Since its creation the Legion has dedicated itself to veterans, community, and national interests through four major programs: (1) rehabilitation, (2) child welfare, (3) national security, and (4) Americanism.

In its rehabilitation program the Legion, against powerful opposition, successfully promoted legislative measures to alleviate the plight of those disabled by war service, as well as legislation concerning compensation, insurance, and other benefits for veterans and their widows and orphans. Largely responsible for what became the Veterans Administration in 1930, the Legion counts among other legislative victories the restoration of veterans' benefits heavily cut by Congress in 1933 and the passage of the GI Bill of Rights (Servicemen's Readjustment Act of 1944). The latter, written and named by legionnaires, provided educational and economic assistance to nondisabled veterans of World War II. Over 11,000,000 veterans took advantage of the 1944 act's provisions, and other millions benefited from the Korean GI Bill (1952) and later extensions of the program.

In child welfare the Legion's work is directed at children's problems ranging from physical to social ills. The American Legion Auxiliary, which has a membership of approximately 1,000,000 women, and the Legion pioneered in this field. Together they have contributed to legislative and judicial actions affecting child welfare, while expending over $200,000,000 of their own funds.

The Legion has persevered in advocating adequate armed forces to support the foreign policy of the United States. An Air Force, a "two-ocean Navy," mechanization of the Army, a modern Merchant Marine, a strong Reserve and National Guard, unified military command, development of civil and naval aviation, and civil defense measures–all found early support in the American Legion.

The Legion's Americanism program covers a wide field of endeavor. In education, activities range from participation in community projects and cooperation with the National Education Association to assistance in the naturalization of aliens and support of federal aid to schools. In its work with youth the Legion sponsors Legion Baseball tournaments, Boys' State and Nation groups, and Boy Scout troops. Other Americanism activities include promotion of patriotic observances, support of the Federal Bureau of Investigation and various committees on un-American activities, and sponsorship of instructional efforts on communism and other subversive movements.

Although the Legion often has been embroiled in controversy, it skillfully applies power and effective public relations to advance its programs. Resolutions originate at the post level and may become mandates at the annual national conventions. Its National Executive Committee functions as a governing body. Its chief publication is the *American Legion Magazine*, a monthly. Programs are administered from headquarters in Indianapolis and in Washington, D. C.

RAYMOND MOLEY, JR.
Author of "The American Legion Story"

AMERICAN LIBRARY ASSOCIATION, the oldest and largest national library organization in the world. It is the chief spokesman for the modern library movement in North America and, to a considerable extent, throughout the world. Founded in Philadelphia in 1876, it pioneered to improve library services and to bring libraries within the reach of all. Its membership is open to any person or institution interested in libraries.

Major Objectives. Since its inauguration the ALA has worked for open access to library shelves, lending books for home reading, tax support for public libraries, development and coordination of research resources, special services for children and young people, extension of service to outlying regions, and cooperation among international libraries.

The ALA also has concerned itself with the formulation and adoption of library standards, the accreditation of library schools, and the recruitment of personnel. The program in library education expanded considerably with the establishment of the ALA Office of Library Education in 1966.

On the international level, the ALA has been active through representation at foreign library meetings, promotion of the exchange of librarians and publications, and support of the overseas library activities of the United States government. An International Relations Office coordinates and extends these activities.

Organization. The ALA is organized into divisions according to type of library, such as American Association of School Librarians, Association of Specialized and Cooperative Library Agencies, Health and Rehabilitative Library Services, Association of College and Research Libraries, and the Public Library Association; and type of activity, such as Reference and Adult Services, Association of Library Service to Children, Resources and Technical Services, and Young Adult Services.

Headquarters of the ALA are at 50 East Huron Street, Chicago, Ill. 60611. An office in Washington, D. C., maintains liaison with federal agencies and represents librarians in promoting legislative programs.

Awards and Publications. Awards given by the ALA each year include the Joseph W. Lippincott Award for professional achievement in librarianship, the Melvil Dewey Medal for creative professional achievement, the Clarence Day Award for promoting the love of books and reading, the Grolier Society Award for stimulation of reading in children and young people, the John Newbery Medal and Randolph Caldecott Medal for the most outstanding children's books, the Ralph R. Shaw Award for library literature, the John Cotton Dana publicity awards, and the Margaret Mann citation for achievement in the areas of cataloging and classification.

The association publishes books on subjects such as the administration of libraries, American library laws, library education and personnel, buildings and equipment, cataloging and classification, reference and research, vocational guidance aids, and rare book collections. Other publications include the monthly *American Libraries*, a general library periodical; *The Booklist*, a semimonthly book review journal; library journals in special fields, such as the *Journal of Library Automation;* the annual *ALA Membership Directory;* and the annual *Conference Proceedings.*

AMERICAN LITERATURE

WASHINGTON IRVING AND HIS FRIENDS AT SUNNYSIDE (1864), an imagined scene with Irving (*seated, legs crossed*) and (*left to right*) Henry Tuckerman, Oliver Wendell Holmes, William Gilmore Simms, Fitz-Greene Halleck, Nathaniel Hawthorne, Henry Wadsworth Longfellow, Nathaniel Parker Willis, William H. Prescott, James Paulding, Ralph Waldo Emerson, William Cullen Bryant, John Kennedy, James Fenimore Cooper, and George Bancroft.

AMERICAN LITERATURE, ə-mer′ə-kən lit′ər-ə-chŏŏr. Long before America got its name, there was a dream of a good land that man might find for himself, a land of material riches and spiritual hope, a recoverable Atlantis and a discoverable Indies. The prospect stirred men's imaginations as well as their explorations. The vision did not cease with the first European landings on the North American continent. The expanding frontier encouraged fresh surgings inland. The 18th century American political revolution gave promise of a freer life, and the material prosperity of the 19th century added the sustaining atmosphere of plenty to the developing democratic ideal. Both offered new definitions of a persisting promise to the restless peoples of the Old World. The 20th century did not divert the focus of attention from a nation that had emerged as the most prosperous on earth. In two world wars the Americans had swung the balance of power; in peace as in war their technologies had permeated the globe; their books were being read everywhere, not only for their vitality but out of a general curiosity about America and Americans. From the beginning, Americans have examined and attempted to explain themselves in their literature, and the perplexing question "What is an American?" has never lost its interest either inside or outside the American boundaries.

This curiosity about America and Americans has been accompanied by an increasing familiarity with American English on a global scale. Through American motion pictures the international ear has been tuned to the cadences of the American way of speaking. Through American literature the world has become familiar with the distinctive American way of writing. English, which has been adopted as a major international language, is all the more pliant because of its enrichment by American speech and writing.

There has been an increasing recognition of the excellence of American literature. Among 19th century American writers, Hawthorne, Melville, James, Whitman, and Emily Dickinson have become established as literary classics rather than as historical figures. In the 20th century, Eliot and Pound and Hemingway and Faulkner are major influences wherever English is read or its literary forms imitated. One result of the international recognition of American literature has been its introduction as an integral part of school and university courses of study throughout the world.

Since World War II, Americans themselves have become increasingly international-minded, reading more of the world's fiction, poetry, and drama. In the same way that writers abroad read Americans and assimilate them artistically, Americans have made world literature as much a part of their consciousness as the intellectual and artistic contributions of their own writers.

1. Beginnings

The earliest American writings were concerned directly with the dream of a new world and the first attempts at its realization. From both North and South came published accounts of pioneering motives and settlements. They form the picture of foundations. Today Americans remember their first colony at Jamestown, Va., on much the same terms as contemporary England knew of it through the writings of chroniclers, especially Capt. John Smith (1580–1631). After an adventurer's life, he sailed for Virginia late in 1606 with about 143 colonists on an expedition financed by the Virginia Company of London. When the vessel that had brought them returned to England in 1608, Smith sent with it a narrative for publication at home, *A True Relation of such occurrences and accidents of noate as hath hapned in Virginia since the first planting of that Collony, which is now resident in the South part thereof, till the last returne from thence* (1608). Smith's account, straightforward and precise like its title, was properly a combination of an economic report for the information of stockholders in the venture, a newsletter for the curious, and an encouragement for future settlers. Blunt and functional in its prose style, it might from a merely decorative point of view have been, as Smith was to say of his *Generall Historie of Virginia, New-England and the Summer Isles* (1624), "clad in better robes than my rude military hand can cut out in paper ornaments." But the first Virginia settlers used neither paper nor lace ornamentation in their daily living, as Smith's scornful remark indicates; theirs was a businesslike venture. Smith wrote other accounts of his sometimes quarrelsome American experiences, none of which is better known than *The True Travels, Adventures, and Observations of Captaine John Smith in Europe, Asia, Affrica, and America, from Anno Domini 1593 to 1629* (1630), the autobiography that established the legend of Pocahontas and made of Captain Smith himself a swashbuckling hero.

Other writings from the Southern settlements, like Richard Rich's poetical *Newes from Virginia* (1610) and Alexander Whitaker's sermon, *Good Newes from Virginia* (1613), gave variety to the newsletter. The uniqueness of George Sandys' *Ovid's Metamorphosis Englished* (1626), translated while he was the resident treasurer of the London Company, only served to show how much more interest there was in commercial bookkeeping than in literary bookmaking.

The chief image of the beginnings of New England comes from the pen of William Bradford (1590–1657), who in 1620 sailed with the Pilgrims to settle at Plymouth and, after the death of the first governor, succeeded him for the next 31 elections. His history, *Of Plymouth Plantation* (*Of plimoth plantation*), published in 1856, covers the years 1606–1646 in the life of the religious venture. The style expresses the grave dignity of a man completely imbued with the high seriousness of the mission in which he had joined; and by the use of Biblical analogies and overtones, he confirmed a people's exodus into a promised land. Narrative after narrative flowed from the pens of 17th century New Englanders for publications at first in England and later in the colonies. These were written with an equal sense of dedication and of the historical importance of the migration. At the close of the first century in America, Cotton Mather could still remark, "I am verily persuaded there are some already born who shall see the most glorious revolutions that ever happened in any former ages; even the glorious things that are spoken of Thee, O thou City of God! It is a privilege to be born so low, so far down in the line of time." "Yea," he said, "you and I have the lines fallen to us in such a pleasant place."

Early New England Prose. The first century, and more, of American literature is overwhelmingly dominated by the works of New Englanders. The reason for this is not to be found in an imbalance of population. By 1640 there were only 18,000 people in New England, and by the end

of the century only 160,000. Maryland and Virginia together had about the same number of inhabitants. But the southern groups wrote little in this period and nothing of importance. Integrated into the British mercantile system, they remained essentially colonial in culture as well as in trade. New England, on the other hand, felt that it represented something specific and unique in the history of commonwealths, and its insistence on its spiritual identity was as firm as its insistence on its political charters. New England was, to its inhabitants, a great experiment and example of the ideal state of educated Christians. They had the responsibility not only of preserving their experiment but of furthering the revolution that might reproduce it universally. In this effort, writing played an important role. Their concept demanded a high degree of maturity and a sense of responsibility on the part of an informed people.

Certain characteristics of such writing inevitably followed. A piece of literature must concern, they felt, first themselves and then mankind; it must be ultimately didactic and useful. In their judgment of writing, the final question was whether it tended toward good. Style must be functionally adapted to that audience with whom communication was being established. If a learned audience was being addressed, then the presentation could be elaborate and studded with similarly learned authority; if it was written for the man in the street, then it could be straightforward or even racy. In any case, the reader was seldom far from the pulpit. There was an emphasis on the pithy startling phrase that strikes the imagination and keeps the audience from sleeping. "Write," New Englanders said, "so that you send arrows into the hearts of your audience, and not over their heads." Such a principle lay in the phrase of the Puritan preacher who exampled his audience's manner of expression at the same time that he summed up their way of life when he wrote, "You can't get to heaven on a feather bed."

It is against such a background that one can read, both with understanding and a recognition of powerful feelings, the variety of personal journals, histories, and sermons that make up the body of the first century of New England prose. Not all of this writing is valued today, but included in what is remembered with profit is *The History of New England* (1790, 1825–26) by John Winthrop (1588–1649), the first governor of Massachusetts Bay Colony, a writer of simple strength. *New Englands Prospect* (1634) by William Wood is interesting as description both of flora and fauna and of the Indians; and *The Wonder-working Providence of Sions Saviour in New-England* (1654) by Edward Johnson (1598–1672) is an ornate rhapsody, interspersed with verse, yet vivid in its outlines of frontier settlements. *New English Canaan* (Amsterdam 1637), by Thomas Morton (1590?–1646/1647), presents a less pious tribute to the founding fathers, as it acidly narrates the attack of the Plymouth colonists in 1628 on Morton's own settlement at Merry Mount. He asserts that the attack was based on their dislike of his unpuritanical way of life, but they themselves attributed it to his trading of gunpowder and liquor to the Indians. Nathaniel Ward (about 1578–1652) was a stylistic maverick. In *The Simple Cobler of Aggawam in America* (1647) he describes himself as "one willing to help mend his native country, lamentably tattered, both in the upper-leather and sole, with all the honest stitches he can take." The stitches were as flamboyant as honest. Mary Rowlandson (about 1635–about 1678) wrote a grim and compelling account of frontier warfare with the Indians, *The Soveraignty & Goodness of God, Together with the Faithfulness of His Promises Displayed; Being a Narrative of the Captivity and Restauration of Mrs. Mary Rowlandson* (1682). Against this terrifying story of capture and redemption is to be placed the delightful early Bostonian urbanity of the lengthy diary of Judge Samuel Sewall (1652–1730), in which among soberer thoughts he recounts his unsuccessful wooing of Madam Winthrop with gingerbread, and the perplexing problems of whether to wear a wig or keep a coach.

However, sermons and religious tracts, many concerned with ecclesiastical controversy, provided the greatest part of New England writing in this period. John Cotton (1584–1652), the leader of local orthodoxy, probably set less store in his so-called *Milk for Babes, Drawn out of the Breasts of Both Testaments* (1646) than he did in his acid attacks on Roger Williams (about 1603–1683), which occasioned the latter's *Bloudy Tenent of Persecution . . .* (1644). Williams' text on the principle of freedom of conscience has been described as having "the moral and literary harmonies of a classic."

Cotton Mather (1663–1728). The most versatile as well as the most prolific writer of prose was Cotton Mather, who stands as a pivot between 17th and 18th century New England. "It has always been a maxim with me," he wrote, "that a power to do good not only gives a right unto it, but also makes the doing of it a duty." The descendant of founding fathers, he took his inherited responsibility seriously; 459 books appeared with his name as author. His range was wide. Essays, political fables, meditations, sermons, elegies and eulogies, narrations of warfare both with Indians and witches, tales of piracy, biographies, accounts of natural science, and general history indicated the breadth of his concern.

But it was his immense *Magnalia Christi Americana* (1702) that was his monument. An encyclopedic classic, it recounted the annals of New England. In it he reassembled many of the separate publications that he had written earlier, taking into the seven broad divisions of its structure his accounts of laymen and clergy in their struggle to preserve what had so nobly been begun. As in subject matter, so in its presentation it was a gathering of variety. Mather could range from the "plain style" to what he called a "cloth of gold . . . stuck with as many jewels as the gown of a Russian Ambassador." The over-elaborateness of much of his writing, and his often inescapable egotism, make the *Magnalia* unpalatable to many. "Proud thoughts," he wrote in his diary, a pontifical companion piece to Sewall's, "fly-blow my best performances." But the *Magnalia* has remained a treasure store both for the verities and the oddities of his time.

Early New England Poetry. Though New Englanders thought of writing as a necessary activity within their holy commonwealth, there was much that militated against the composition of poetry. The Puritans wrote it nevertheless. No funeral of a dignitary was complete unless his hearse, as it passed toward the burial ground, was covered with funeral elegies. But this use of occasional verse did not extend itself into the establishment of a role for poetry comparable to that for prose. There was no colonial writer who considered himself primarily as a poet. This is not to say that poetry was held to have no public values, for there were values of many kinds, limited though some of these might be. The public uses of poetry were indicated in the lines prefixed to later editions of the famous *Day of Doom* (1662) by Michael Wigglesworth (1631–1705):

A Verse may find him who a Sermon flies,
Saith Herbert well. Great-Truths to dress in Meeter;
Becomes a Preacher; who mens Souls doth prize.
That Truth in Sugar roll'd may taste the sweeter,
  No cost too great, no Care too Curious is
    To set forth Truth, and win mens Souls to bliss.

Despite such sugar, Wigglesworth's poem is always cited as wormwood. Written in an approximation of the ballad style, and as a kind of New England *Paradise Lost*, it was intended not so much to justify the ways of God to man as to explain them. It remains one of the clearest definitions of Calvinistic theology, composed, as Mather commented, "for such readers as are for plain truths dressed up in plain meter." Within a year of its publication 1,800 copies of the poem had appeared, and it has been said that one copy was eventually published for every 36 persons in New England. A second volume of poems by Wigglesworth, who was a minister, went into four editions, but *Meat Out of the Eater or Meditations Concerning the Necessity, End, and Usefulness of Afflictions Unto Gods Children* (1669) adds little to his fame.

In general, much that would today be composed as poetry was caught up in the exalted prose of sermons and the "divine rapture" of extemporaneous prayers. What became the most moving Puritan poetry was in reality a private poetry. Mrs. Anne Bradstreet (about 1612–1672), the daughter of a governor of Massachusetts and the wife of a holder of high office there, was brought up in the household of the earl of Lincoln before emigrating as a bride to American shores. Her first book of poems was published unbeknown to her in London, where it had been taken by an admiring brother-in-law, as *The Tenth Muse Lately Sprung Up in America* (1650). It is because of the posthumous second edition of her *Poems* (Boston 1678), with her own additions and corrections, that she gained the affection she holds today. Especially in her series of *Contemplations*, evidently composed in the intervals between household chores, one feels the personal solace and diversion that poetry brought her.

I heard the merry grashopper then sing,
The black clad Cricket, bear a second part,
They kept one tune, and plaid on the same string,
Seeming to glory in their little Art.
Shall Creatures abject, thus their voices raise?
And in their kind resound their makers praise;
Whilst I as mute, can warble forth no higher layes.

The second poet of significance, and the finest American poet until Bryant and Poe, was Edward Taylor (about 1642–1729). After leaving England in 1668 for religious reasons, he graduated from Harvard in 1671 and spent his entire adult life as a minister in the frontier town of Westfield, Mass. He published only a few public elegies and was not known in his own time as a poet. Privately, however, he wrote by far the largest body of American Puritan poetry. He left the manuscripts to his heirs, and the poems remained unknown until 1937 when the first selections appeared. A small collection was published in 1939 and a nearly complete edition in 1960. Two volumes of his religious prose, especially *Christographia* (1962), broadened his reputation.

His poetry, metaphysical and baroque in its conceits and much influenced by the English poet George Herbert, has a rugged spiritual firmness and a colloquial bounce of its own. Such short poems as *Huswifery, Upon a Wasp Child with Cold*, and *Upon Wedlock and Death of Children* show a gentle compassion not usually coupled with the Puritan temperament. They have become favorites. But it is in the 217 poems of his *Preparatory Meditations* and in *Gods Determinations touching His Elect*, a doctrinal allegory, that he achieves his significance as a poet of the affections. The meditations were disciplined spiritual exercises written after the completion of a sermon to prepare him both for its delivery and to administer and receive the sacraments. "My tazzled Thoughts twirld into Snick-Snarls run," he wrote. But the tangled search for divine truth and love led him home.

> I kening through Astronomy Divine
> The Worlds bright Battlement, wherein I spy
> A Golden Path my Pensill cannot line,
> From that bright Throne unto my Threshold ly.
> And while my puzzled thoughts about it pore
> I find the Bread of Life in't at my doore.

Taylor's poems are excellent examples of the Puritan's feeling for the privacy of the emotions and the spiritual life; hence the privacy of the poetry that dealt with them.

2. The 18th Century

The South. The general disinterest of the Southern colonies in the creation of their own literature continued during the 18th century. The center of their attention, like the source of their books, remained in England. There were a few exceptions. Robert Beverley (about 1673–1722) described in his *History and Present State of Virginia . . . by a Native of the Place* (1705), often with humor and always with balance, the historical development, natural resources, and contemporary life of his region. A little farther to the north, Ebenezer Cook, in amusing rhymed couplets, gave in *The Sot-Weed Factor* (1708) a burlesque account of an immigrating Englishman's travels in Maryland, picturing, as its subtitle states, ". . . the Feasts, Frolics, Entertainments and drunken humours of the Inhabitants of that Part of America."

William Byrd (1674–1744). A more cultivated colonial life is to be found in the writings of Col. William Byrd of Westover in Virginia, Esq., as he called himself. He was educated in England, in the best planter tradition, and from 1698 to 1704 he was the London agent for the colony. Returning to Virginia, he built Westover, a superb Georgian mansion on the James River. There, his library of 4,000 books is said to have been the largest in any of the colonies. In the *History of the Dividing Line: Run in the Year 1728*, an account of the boundary survey between Virginia and North Carolina, in *A Progress to the Mines, in the Year 1732*, and in *A Journey to the Land of Eden: Anno 1733*, about the inspection of his own landholdings, as well as in the extended notations of his personal life and of Virginian society in his "secret diaries," he gave a highly detailed picture of a Southern way of life that was cavalier at heart and a "Lubberland" at its borders.

New England and the Middle Atlantic Region— Jonathan Edwards (1703–1758). New England man-aged to hold on to the religious emphasis of its writing, even after the church had begun to lose its fullest authority. One of her greatest writers appeared in the twilight of the old Puritanism. In earlier approaches to American literary history, Jonathan Edwards has been cited chiefly as the author of a terrifying sermon, *Sinners in the Hands of an Angry God* (1741), which he delivered in the midst of the Great Awakening, an emotional revivalism that temporarily swept New England religious life. Some modification of this too-restricted view came from calling attention to such a tender and youthful composition as his apostrophe to Sarah Pierpont (Pierrepont), written in 1723, in which he addressed his fiancée in strains reminiscent of the Canticles. Her semimystical closeness to God finds its companion expression in Edwards' early song *Nature*, in which, while "the beauty of face and sweet airs in men are not always the effect of the corresponding excellencies of mind; yet the beauties of nature are really emanations or shadows of the excellency of the Son of God." But it was Edwards' increasing emphasis on metaphysics that brought him recognition as the first great philosophic intelligence in American history. In the 20th century, with a revival of interest in theology and philosophy, Edwards' chief fame lies in such works as *The Freedom of the Will* (in full, *A Careful and Strict Enquiry into the Modern Prevailing Notions of that Freedom of the Will which is Supposed to be Essential to Moral Agency, Vertue and Vice, Reward and Punishment, Praise and Blame*, 1754), where his defense of the doctrine of necessity led him to such brilliance of philosophical speculation that a modern critic like Perry Miller can say that "he was one of America's five or six major artists."

Benjamin Franklin (1706–1790). Benjamin Franklin was a contemporary of Edwards in time, but when in 1723 Franklin ran away from his birthplace in Boston to Philadelphia, he indicated by the course of his life and his way of thought the changes that were overtaking the older habits of New England. Franklin did not relinquish the precepts he had learned as a child; he simply converted them to the practicalities of business and politics. A remarkable combination of statesman, inventor, printer, and publisher, as well as writer, he exemplified what the 18th century called a "complete man," able to turn his hand to any form of activity. The direction of all activities was clear to him. "The most acceptable service to God," he said, "is doing good to man"; and to Cotton Mather's son he wrote, apropos of the father's *Essays to Do Good* (original title *Bonifacius . . .*, 1710), "If I have been, as you seem to think, a useful citizen, the public owes the advantage of it to that book." In publishing the many annual editions of *Poor Richard's Almanack* (1733–1758) he said, "I considered it as a proper vehicle for conveying instruction among the common people who bought scarcely any other books; I therefore filled all the little spaces that occurred between the remarkable days in the calendar with proverbial sentences—chiefly such as inculcated industry and frugality as the means of procuring wealth and thereby securing virtue." Critical as a later age might become of the implications of "thereby," there can be no question but that the general didactic tendency of Puritan writing was continued by Franklin, though redirected, in the pithy maxims he borrowed and then polished before establishing them in the

American memory. *The Way to Wealth* (1758), a compendium of relevant maxims, has been republished over 400 times and in many languages, helping, in its way, to define further the American dream of success. ·

Franklin's gay series of bagatelles, printed on his private press at Passy, when he was his country's coonskinned and highly successful representative at the court of France, gave a Gallic touch to his native wit, and have continued to delight his readers. But it was his *Autobiography*, begun in 1771, although never finished, which has become a classic of American literature. Started in the manner of a despiritualized Puritan's self-examination, for the benefit of his son, but continued to provide instruction by example for all sons, his self-history was published in England, France, and Germany before its first American publication in 1818, and was the first extended account to define an American by his own words, a self-portrait of confidence in material possibilities.

Other Writers. The American 18th century is not rich in literary masterpieces, but a number of books have retained a permanent interest. John Woolman (1720–1772), a Quaker born in New Jersey and trained as a tailor, is the author of a *Journal* (1774) in which the inward stillness of the Friends is effectively rendered. "Get the writings of John Woolman by heart," Charles Lamb said. Lamb was also the admirer of another book from the middle colonies, *Travels through North and South Carolina, Georgia, East and West Florida . . .* (1791), by William Bartram (1739–1823). Bartram wrote of his expeditions with the eye of a naturalist and the rich sensibility of a poet. It gave a new picture of the American landscape, lush and inviting to the romantic mind. Samuel Taylor Coleridge seems to have borrowed from its descriptions for *The Rime of the Ancient Mariner*, and William Wordsworth for passages in *The Prelude*. Robert Southey, Percy Bysshe Shelley, and Lord Tennyson were also influenced by Bartram's version of the wilds.

Once the American Revolution had been accomplished, interest in the New World and its inhabitants was quickened. A series of epistolary essays to satisfy this curiosity came from a Frenchman, Michel Guillaume Jean de Crèvecoeur (pen name J. Hector St. John, 1735–1813), who in 1765 had become an American citizen and married an American wife. His *Letters from an American Farmer* (1782) covered such homelike scenes as *A Snowstorm as it Affects the American Farmer*, a forerunner of Whittier's *Snow-Bound* (1866), and such central issues as his most famous essay, *What is an American?* America is opportunity, he said; for those who will work there can be ease and independence. "I will give thee fields to feed and clothe thee," he wrote, speaking with the voice of the new nation; "a comfortable fireside to sit by, and tell thy children by what means thou has prospered; and a decent bed to repose on. I shall endow thee beside with the immunities of a freeman. If thou wilt carefully educate thy children, teach them gratitude to God, and reverence to that government, that philanthropic government, which has collected here so many men and made them happy. I will also provide for thy progeny; and to every good man this ought to be the most holy, the most powerful, the most earnest wish he can possibly form, as well as the most consolatory prospect when he

dies. Go thou and work and till; thou shalt prosper, provided thou be just, grateful, and industrious." Many contemporary writers were to echo him, optimistic at the future of the new American nation.

Poetry can scarcely be said to have flourished during this period, although more and more verse was written. Writers like Thomas Godfrey (1736–1763) and Francis Hopkinson (1737–1791) helped to make Philadelphia a literary center, though hardly an American Helicon. Using classical pastoral figures in their lyrics, they adopted the manners of neoclassicism without its inspiration. In New England what little poetry of interest there was came from a group known as the "Connecticut Wits" (sometimes called "Hartford Wits"). John Trumbull (1750–1831) was the author of *M'Fingal* (1782), a mock epic of some stature, derivative from the English *Hudibras*, dealing with the figures of the American Revolution. Joel Barlow (1754–1812) was the author of *The Hasty Pudding* (written 1793; published 1796), a mock pastoral with flashes of homespun humor and detail, and *The Vision of Columbus*, 1787 (rewritten as *The Columbiad*, 1807), a long serious poem whose object was, in Barlow's words, "moral and political," meant to "encourage and strengthen in the rising generation a sense of the importance of republican institutions." Timothy Dwight (1752–1817), a president of Yale, turned his hand to such verse as *The Conquest of Canaan* (1785) and *Greenfield Hill* (1794) but is more palatable today in the prose of his *Travels in New-England and New-York* (1821–1822), with its detailed descriptions of the daily life he observed.

If these three members of the "Wits," and others in their group did not succeed artistically, they at least exhibited a healthy concern that their nation should have a literature worthy of it. The desire for a "national literature" was to become a preoccupation of American writers from their time on, and if sometimes chauvinistic, was nevertheless to provide an important stimulus. More successful than the "Wits" poetically was Philip Freneau (1752–1832) of New York, whose career began while he was still a student at Princeton, where he wrote *The Power of Fancy*, closely modeled· after English poetry. Yet Freneau did not apologize for this affinity, "a political and a literary independence," he said, "being two very different things. The first was accomplished in about seven years, the latter will not be completely effected, perhaps, in as many centuries." He was talking basically. The author of numerous poems on the struggle for political independence, he is best remembered for such early romantic pieces as *The Wild Honeysuckle* (1788) and *The Indian Burial Ground* (1788).

Political Writing. If one is to glance back over the course of the 18th century in America, the influence of scientific rationalism is seen to grow in importance. The shift in attitude toward nature, from the mysticism of Edwards' apprehension of it as a palpable reflection of divinity to the direct scientific observation of its phenomena, is the adoption of a new focus as well as a new immediacy of worldliness. More and more, also, the intellectual life of the colonists became concerned with the rational philosophy of politics, which affected them most directly; and in one sense there can be no question but that the significant literary success of the 18th century lies in the verbal formulation of the Declaration of Independence (1776) and the Constitution of the United States (1787). Their widespread influence not only on America but on the world at large came chiefly from the fact that they were written down on paper as a synthesis of man's belief in his own dignity and his own rights as a human being. Serving in explanation and defense of the Constitution, *The Federalist* (1787–88), written by James Madison, Alexander Hamilton, and John Jay, also remains one of the monumental political writings of the century.

Thomas Paine (1737–1809). "These are times that try men's souls," wrote Thomas Paine. " 'Tis not the concern of a day, a year, or an age; posterity are virtually involved in the contest, and will be more or less affected even to the end of time by the proceedings now." The Ciceronics of his *Common Sense; Addressed to the Inhabitants of America* (1776) helped to spread the revolutionary flame not only in the colonies, where 120,000 copies of the pamphlet were sold within the first three months, but also abroad, where it was frequently reprinted and established the importance of the American political adventure. *Common Sense* is still in print. An Englishman who was drawn to the colonies in 1774 by the rising revolt, Paine continued to follow in the path of revolution. In *The Rights of Man* (1791–92) he defended the French counterpart of the American revolt, and in *The Age of Reason* (part 1, 1794; part 2, 1795–96), a deistic exposition, he expressed through extremes the long intellectual distance that lay between the rationalistic close of the 18th century and its more theological beginnings.

3. The 19th Century

Early Period. As a new century began, American authors commenced to free themselves from the inevitable preoccupation with the establishment of a new nation. "All things have their season," Franklin had written, "and with young countries as with young men, you must curb their fancy to strengthen their judgment. . . . To America, one schoolmaster is worth a dozen poets, and the invention of a machine or the improvement of an implement of more importance than a masterpiece of Raphael." The country, he felt, like Poor Richard should first find its way to wealth. General Washington agreed with him. "Only the arts of a practical nature would be for a time esteemed," he said, adding that it was easy to perceive the causes that have combined to render the genius of this country scientific rather than imaginative. For the independence of literature, then, it was necessary for writing in America to secure its own franchise.

Washington Irving (1783–1859): First Man of Letters. The career of Washington Irving represents the restlessness of the imaginative mind in such a milieu. Ultimately the greatest of the Knickerbockers, a New York group of writers that included such men as James Kirke Paulding (1778–1860), Joseph Rodman Drake (1795–1820), and Fitz-Greene Halleck (1790–1867), he passed a lengthy period of youthful groping for a profession that would satisfy his somewhat dilettante tastes. But it was in the satiric essays, *Salmagundi* (1807–08), on which he collaborated with his brother and Paulding, and in *A History of New York . . . by Diedrich Knickerbocker* (1809), a burlesque history, that Irving began to find himself. From 1815 he passed 17 years of uninterrupted residence abroad, where, with the publication of *The Sketch Book* (1819–20), he became internationally famous as a romantic exploiter of the European past. Except for periods of employment in the American diplomatic service, he was entirely dependent on writing for his livelihood, a new status for American authors. Lord Byron, Sir Walter Scott, Samuel Taylor Coleridge, and William Godwin were among those to hail this first American in the field of belles lettres. They had no reason to think of him as one estranged from themselves since his subject matter was more characteristically drawn from their side of the Atlantic than from his own. In his introduction to *The Sketch Book*, Irving wrote: "I visited various parts of my own country; and had I been merely a lover of fine scenery, I should have felt little desire to seek elsewhere its gratification. . . . But Europe held forth the charms of storied and poetical association. There were to be seen the masterpieces of art, the refinements of highly-cultivated society, the quaint peculiarities of ancient and local custom. My native country was full of youthful promise: Europe was rich in the accumulated treasures of age."

This sense of the barrenness of America in the absence of castles, moss-covered ruins, and similar stimuli to the romantic emotions was to be a continuing factor in the frustration of American writers, impelled as they might otherwise be to form a new literature. *Bracebridge Hall* (1822), based on Irving's sentimental English experiences, and *The Alhambra* (1832), drawn from his visit to Granada, in Spain, furthered his literary fame; and his *History of the Life and Voyages of Christopher Columbus* (1828) earned him an honorary degree from Oxford. But it is for a few American tales like *Rip Van Winkle* (1819) and *The Legend of Sleepy Hollow* (1820) that he is most respected as a writer today. In the former he transplanted a figure from a German tale into the Catskill Mountains, and by identifying Rip with American nature made him an American natural.

James Fenimore Cooper (1789–1851). The impact and the continuing reputation of James Fenimore Cooper was to be greater than Irving's, both at home and abroad. Cooper was not the first American novelist. The first American novel was *The Power of Sympathy* (1789) by William Hill Brown (1765–1793), and from its publication until the appearance of Cooper's *Spy* (1821), many authors tried their hand at this increasingly appealing form of literary expression. The Gothic novels of Charles Brockden Brown (1771–1810) gained some recognition in England as well as in America. His *Wieland* (1798), *Arthur Mervyn* (1799–1800), and *Edgar Huntly* (1799) were brave attempts at psychological sensationalism and the use of American materials; but, written in haste, they show the awkwardness of an unskilled hand and the lack of an immediate tradition. *Modern Chivalry* (1792–1815), by Hugh Henry Brackenridge (1748–1816), is a novel of greater quality than any by Brown. A picaresque account of American backwoods life, the book is held together not so much by plot as by the author's inherent plea for the elevation of the practice of democracy.

Cooper himself was also to become a loyal critic of the ways of democracy, helping to establish the freedom of self-criticism that has become so characteristic of American writers and so continuing a source of surprise to readers abroad who do not understand a parent's proud desire to improve a child or, contrariwise, the child's desire to improve its parents. The views that Cooper advanced in *The American Democrat* (1838), a series of expositions written from a conservative viewpoint protesting the rule of the mob, were fictionally echoed in such books as *The Monikins* (1835), *Homeward Bound* (1838), and *Home as Found* (1838). Yet it was with such materials as he employed in *The Spy*, a novel of the American Revolution, and in *The Pilot* (1823), which made him an early master of the sea story, that he began the lasting reputation that his Leather-Stocking Tales ensured for him. In *The Pioneers* (1823), *The Last of the Mohicans* (1826), *The Prairie* (1827), *The Pathfinder* (1840), and *The Deerslayer* (1841), he established in the figure of Natty Bumppo a literary hero who possessed the virtues of a man both at ease with and in command of nature. Leather-Stocking and his exploits became known in every European country, and he came to represent the Natural Man who opposes anything that is "agin nature" or "agin reason." The figure of Leather-Stocking, in the rich landscape of the forests where he hunted, provided for generations of Europeans what the French called the "matter of America." Not until Sinclair Lewis' considerably different Babbitt was another fictional American to become so familiar to Europeans. Cooper helped to discover the romantic spirit of the frontier and frontiersmen for Americans as well, and with his help American literature began to take on a dress unmistakably its own, though not always of buckskin.

William Cullen Bryant (1794–1878). Slowly the verse of English poets like Wordsworth made its way into the American literary consciousness, replacing a nostalgia for the vanished past by a philosophical regard for nature and man's relation to it in the present, which the poet through the powers of his cultivated senses was peculiarly fitted to comprehend and express, and which gave the American poet in particular a way of approaching what was close at hand. The lyric gloss of poets like Joseph Rodman Drake and Fitz-Greene Halleck had often been attractive, but it was in the poetry of William Cullen Bryant that an innate freshening of American verse began. His reading of Wordsworth's *Lyrical Ballads* had, as he said, "caused a thousand springs . . . to gush up at once into my heart, and the face of Nature of a sudden to change into a strange freshness and life." Out of this new impulse came such still highly regarded poems as *To a Waterfowl* (written in 1815) and *To the Fringed Gentian* (written in 1829):

> Then doth thy sweet and quiet eye
> Look through its fringes to the sky,
> Blue—blue—as if that sky let fall
> A flower from its cerulean wall.

In other poems—the total poetical output of his long life was considerable—he not only gave to American literature its first published verse of stature, Edward Taylor being still unknown, but came to exercise a dominant, even a patriarchal influence. Poetry, Bryant declared, must appeal to the imagination, but "it has a still higher value when regarded as in some sort the support of our innocence." "It is the dominion of poetry over the feelings and passions of men," he said, "that gives it its most important bearing on the virtues and welfare of society. Everything that affects our sensibilities is a part of our moral education." It was this latter concern with moral education that caused Bryant to include so many "moral tags" to his poems, in which he pointed out the lesson rather than let the poetry speak for itself. He gave a dignity to American poetry, but he dressed it like a schoolmaster.

Edgar Allan Poe (1809–1849). Bryant felt at home in his society, but the same was not true of Edgar Allan Poe. One aspect of the romantic hero, when he was not to be the great leader, acknowledged his separation from his fellow men. Poe expressed this agony of alienation in his writing. While Bryant more and more drew the material of his poetry from the American landscape about him, Poe spun from the Gothic trappings of late 18th century English writing a more personally congenial world, supernatural rather than natural, one of decaying corpses, clanking chains, and howling storms, in which man wandered alone in the darkness of night. Poems like *The City in the Sea* (1831), *The Valley of Unrest* (1831), and *The Haunted Palace* (1839) are typical of his settings; his poems are peopled by *The Sleeper* (1831), *Ulalume* (1847), *Lenore* (1831), and *Israfel* (1831). His strange fantasies, rather than his sometimes pedestrian metrics, attracted the attention of such great French poets as Charles Baudelaire and Stéphane Mallarmé, and through them Poe exercised a profound influence on the use of symbolism in modern poetry. He was the first American poet to have a significant reputation outside his own country.

Poe also has his importance as the first American literary critic of stature; instead of fearing the imagination, as Bryant had done, Poe seized upon it and loved it. Toward fiction he felt as toward poetry. In a series of distinguished short stories like *The Fall of the House of Usher* (1840), *The Cask of Amontillado* (1846), and *The Tell-Tale Heart* (1843) he made the most of the psychological sensationalism that writers like Brown had introduced. Yet his most widespread influence on American fiction came through his single-handed invention of the detective story with all of its persisting tactics. *The Purloined Letter* (1845) and *The Murders in the Rue Morgue* (1841) are examples of his "tales of ratiocination." Sherlock Holmes is the literary son of Poe's brilliantly amateur detective, Dupin.

The New England Renaissance. New England literature had seemed to lie fallow since the time of Jonathan Edwards, except for the imitative writing of the "Connecticut Wits." In the second quarter of the 19th century, New England regained its literary eminence. Many elements were factors in the rejuvenation. The liberalism that movements like Unitarianism fostered, the growth of Harvard University, and an awakening receptivity to European intellectual and philosophical currents, plus a vigor that came from economic expansionism, all served to stir the blood and the self-confidence of New England's writers.

Ralph Waldo Emerson (1803–1882). Ralph Waldo Emerson was a true New Englander. He was seventh in a line of ministers. Like his brothers, Emerson went to Harvard, graduating in 1821, taught school for a while, and then attended Harvard Divinity School. In 1829 he became pastor of a Boston church, but he soon left the church "as an irrelevant refuge for Man. Could he not know God directly through Nature and his own soul?" At the age of 29, he made the first of three trips abroad, but he called Venice only "a city for beavers." He saw Walter Savage

Landor in Italy, Coleridge and Wordsworth in England, and, best of all for him, he met Thomas Carlyle with whom he became fast friends for life. Men, not places, were his goal. But despite finding the men, he returned, "glad to be back to myself again." "The soul is no traveler," he wrote; "the wise man stays at home." "The sun shines today also." It shone for him in Concord, where he spent the greater part of his life. "Trust thyself," he wrote in his aphoristic style that was a spiritual ennoblement of Poor Richard's maxims; "every heart vibrates to that iron string." Essays like *Nature* (1836), *The American Scholar* (1837), *An Address Delivered Before the Senior Class in Divinity College* (1838), and such collections as *Essays, First Series* (1841) and *Essays, Second Series* (1844) carried his self-reliant message.

What he sought for was an original relationship of man to the universe. Cotton Mather, walking the streets of Boston more than a century before, had asked of each object he passed, "What can I see of the Lord in this?" Emerson showed his inheritance, though he transcendentalized it, when he defined particular natural facts as symbols of particular spiritual facts and reemphasized Nature as the symbol of the Spirit. This transcendentalism he carried over into literature when he asserted that words are symbols of natural facts. By such a transit, the homely could become the divine, and all writing that embraced natural facts was an extended metaphor of the spiritual world. Emerson's teaching helped to break down the old antithesis between words and things. "Give me health and a day, and I will make the pomp of emperors ridiculous." He would help to make the pomp of uninspired rhetoric ridiculous by the same means.

As a writer of verse he tried to carry out the views expressed in his own essay *The Poet* (1844), that "it is not metres, but a metre-making argument, that makes a poem,—a thought so passionate and alive, that, like the spirit of a plant or animal it has an architecture of its own, and adorns nature with a new thing." He was ardent in his demand for the American poet who should know "the value of our incomparable materials. . . . Our logrolling, our stumps and their politics, our fisheries, our Negroes and Indians, our boats, and our repudiations, the wrath of rogues, and the pusillanimity of honest men, the northern trade, the southern planting, the western clearing, Oregon and Texas, are yet unsung. Yet America is a poem in our eyes, its ample geography dazzles the imagination, and it will not wait long for metres." He was not crying out for an increased patriotism: he was pleading for the capabilities of imagination. Listening, Walt Whitman gave the fullest reply.

Henry David Thoreau (1817–1862). There was a listener, however, whom Emerson had only to reach out to touch. He was Henry David Thoreau, the only member of the famous Concord group who was actually born there. A graduate of Harvard, where he would not pay his dollar for a diploma ("Let every sheep keep his own skin"), he became a natural protégé of Emerson. In *A Week on the Concord and Merrimack Rivers* (1849) and *Walden: or, Life in the Woods* (1854), Thoreau established his own Emersonian original relationship to Nature. The first book, filled with miscellaneous observations on life and literature, followed day by day a canoe trip taken with his brother. The second was his famous experiment in fundamental living that he conducted at the edge of Walden Pond to show how cluttered and hamstrung America had become through too great an emphasis on material possessions. "I went to the woods," Thoreau said, "because I wished to live deliberately, to front only the essential facts of life, and see if I could not learn what it had to teach, and not, when I came to die, discover that I had not lived. I did not wish to live what was not life, living is so dear." What resulted was a great American classic, an account of a residence that was a microcosm of man's existence, proffered with a love for nature and for man that is as beautiful as the book is distinguished. Thoreau carried his stubborn sense of the dignity of the individual over into politics in his essay, *Civil Disobedience* (1849). It became sweeping in its influence when, in the 20th century, Mahatma Gandhi adopted it as a model for his campaign of nonviolent resistance in India.

Thoreau's striking originality as a poet within his time is only now being recognized from verses tucked away among his papers. His reputation will grow from such Yankee lines as

> For though the caves were rabbited,
> And the well sweeps were slanted,
> Each house seemed not inhabited
> But haunted.

The Cambridge Poets. The lives of Henry Wadsworth Longfellow (1807–1882), Oliver Wendell Holmes (1809–1894), and James Russell Lowell (1819–1891) spread out easily and comfortably across the century. Their light made a warm glow, and far better than Poe or Thoreau they represented the popular tone and taste of the times. Viewed by any criteria, not the least of Longfellow's contributions to literature were the heroes he gave to America through his inventions of *Paul Revere's Ride* (1863), *The Courtship of Miles Standish* (1858), *Evangeline: A Tale of Acadie* (1847), and *The Song of Hiawatha* (1855). Longfellow wove them from the thinnest historical threads, but his name and theirs became household words abroad as well as in America. Longfellow established a two-way traffic with the Old World. More than any other poet in his age he helped to enrich American literature through his knowledge of European writing. A notable linguist and Smith Professor of Modern Languages at Harvard, he not only translated poetry from many tongues but carried over their metrics into American verse. Longfellow needs to be reread by critics; they will find many poems that escape the burden of sentimentality, and on technical terms rank high.

In Holmes the country had its first professional writer of "society verse." There was hardly a banquet or a convention held that was not graced by the poetry of the witty doctor on whose shingle punningly appeared, "Small Fevers Gratefully Received." To the American public Holmes was familiar also for his sprightly essays contributed to the *Atlantic Monthly* magazine and later collected in a succession of volumes of which *The Autocrat of the Breakfast Table* (1858) is the best known.

James Russell Lowell, the third of the minor planets of the Cambridge constellation, followed many orbits. He was lawyer, editor, ambassador, essayist, and poet, beginning as a mild radical and ending with the bewhiskered gentility that became an unjust catchword for the description of his group. Yet it is true that Lowell's writing seems less impressive to the present age than it did to his own. *The Biglow Papers* (first series, 1848; second series, 1867) were two sets of satirical verses self-consciously written in Yankee dialect; and he published as well several volumes of essays, of which *My Study Windows* (1871) and *Democracy and Other Addresses* (1887) serve as examples of his cultivated mind, his breadth of interest, and his moderated convictions.

John Greenleaf Whittier (1807-1892). The Cambridge group were urbanely waistcoated, but at a measurable distance from them, in the neighborhood of Haverhill, Mass., lived the homespun John Greenleaf Whittier. "I am not a builder," he said, "in the sense of Milton's phrase of one who could 'build the lofty rhyme.' My vehicles have been the humbler sort—merely the farmwagon and the buckboards of verse." Sentimentality is too often present in his renderings of rural New England, but in a poem like *Snow-Bound* (1866), his nostalgic recovery of a distant boyhood is the successful poetic equivalent of a Currier and Ives print. It has its lasting charm. Whittier was both a Quaker and an ardent abolitionist, and he wrote many poems in the abolitionist cause. Yet his innate gentleness was transcendent. Whittier's achievements include the writing of verses that have become well-known hymns.

Nathaniel Hawthorne (1804-1864). If there was an Achilles heel to the philosophy of Emerson and his followers, it lay in their too facile dismissal of a positive power of evil and the shadows of night that play a part in men's lives. The New England Renaissance was a rebirth of the former vigor of the Puritans, but it became complete in the writing of Nathaniel Hawthorne, with his equivalent emphasis on men's sense of sin and guilt What may personally have tormented this son of Salem and a long line of Puritan forebears is not known; but as a youth, and after his graduation from Bowdoin and during a long period of self-isolation, he pored over the printed records of New England history. From them he constructed the historical tales that deal with the moral preoccupations of characters involved with aspects or impacts of evil. His *Twice-Told Tales* (1837) was engrossed with such problems. *Mosses from an Old Manse* (1846), written in Concord and including some happier essays following his marriage, was, nevertheless, a continuation of the same emphasis.

Hawthorne's first successful novel, *The Scarlet Letter* (1850), is a study of the moral effects of sin on those who commit it; another novel, *The House of the Seven Gables* (1851), discusses the inherited effects of evil in a contemporary setting; *The Marble Faun* (1860), Hawthorne's last novel, is drawn from his life in Rome; it carries the theme of sin further in the sober maturing of characters whose connection with evil and a decaying culture is only as observers. A distinguished stylist, soon critically recognized as the leading American novelist of his time, Hawthorne made use of symbolist effects to portray the psychology of his characters. This, and his interweaving of their emotions with the impact of their surroundings, was to give a texture to his writing that would influence such later writers as Henry James.

Melville, Dickinson, and Whitman—Herman Melville (1819-1891). When Herman Melville came to publish his masterpiece *Moby-Dick* (1851), that whaling epic of man's tragic defiance of the mysteries of the universe, he dedicated it to Hawthorne. It was no casual tribute to their brief personal acquaintance. Both shared a knowledge of the dark heart of man, and each expressed the profundity of his themes through cunningly interwoven symbols. Melville had learned from Hawthorne's *Mosses*. Melville's early reputation had been gained by such narratives of his own adventures in the Marquesas, where he had lived briefly among the savages, as *Typee* (1846) and *Omoo* (1847); and from his life at sea, as in *Redburn* (1849) and *White-Jacket* (1850). Melville's accounts of life on a packet ship and a man-of-war were influenced by the success of Richard Henry Dana's pioneering *Two Years Before the Mast* (1840), but Melville's works have the intimate knowledge of the true sailor, though an educated one, rather than Dana's emotional distance from the crew that he had joined for recuperation.

In *Moby-Dick*, Melville was to write the greatest novel America has yet known. "Yes, the world's a ship on its passage out," the book says, and it was as a microcosm of the world he knew that Melville used the *Pequod* with its strange crew, mingled in types and nationalities, and captained by an Ahab who took his name from the wicked king of the Old Testament. The novel is stored with whaling lore and driven forward with the excitement of the chase of the great white whale on whom Ahab sought vengeance for the loss of his leg, even at the tragic expense of dragging his miniature world down with him. In his final book, *Billy Budd* (published 1924), written in his old age, Melville told the story of obedience to responsibility, in the case of a young and Christlike sailor, executed by his captain in conformity to the law. Yet Billy's acceptance of death, like Christ's, teaches the captain himself how to die when his apparently unjust turn comes. It is a second and companion masterpiece to *Moby-Dick*.

Others of Melville's novels, like the extravagant *Mardi* (1849) and *Pierre: or the Ambiguities* (1852) and his sardonic *The Confidence-Man* (1857), failed to please the public as *Moby-Dick* also, and more oddly, had failed to do. His reputation as a novelist of world stature began to emerge only in the 1920's. To that recognition is slowly being added Melville's reputation as a poet, a later aspect of his writing but with some memorable results.

Emily Dickinson (1830-1886). Melville's writing was most effective when he broke from literary conventions to establish his own giant identity as an author. In much the same way, though on a more delicate scale, Emily Dickinson unmistakably fixed her own highly individual and revolutionary personality in her elliptical and provocative poems. Like Melville she had to wait for lasting fame as a result of her unconventionality, though she was private like Edward Taylor in publishing but five poems during her life and in caring most for the act of literary creation itself. Her father's home in Amherst, Mass., was her cloistered haven where she tiptoed out her life and wrote the more than 1,000 poems that she called her "letter to the world." The first volume of her poems appeared only in 1890, after her death. "I am small like the wren," she wrote a friend, "and my hair is bold, like the chestnut burr; and my eyes, like the sherry in the glass that the guest leaves." She inherited something of the whimsical perversity of Thoreau, but she hardened it in the sure fire of her poetic instinct. In her verse she centered her attention not on the unusual thing but on the customary seen unusually. So too she syncopated syntax to joggle her readers and give tension to her poems. Slant rhymes, or no rhymes at all, and strange juxtapositions individualized her work. Yet her images were sharp and clean. Most of all she had a sensibility on which nothing impinged that could not become a poem.

Walt Whitman (1819–1892). In 1855 were published Longfellow's *Hiawatha* and the first issue of *Leaves of Grass* by Walt Whitman. Longfellow's epic, culled from books and metrically modeled after the Finnish *Kalevala*, has as its hero an American Indian chief. But the hero of the revolutionary free verses of *Leaves of Grass* is Whitman himself. America took *Hiawatha* to its heart and into its schools; *Leaves of Grass* it either ignored or, as Whittier is said to have done, threw the copy into the fire. That is, except for Emerson, who wrote to its author, "I greet you at the beginning of a great career, which must have had a long foreground somewhere, for such a start." Its beginnings, distantly but pervasively antecedent to Whitman himself, were in America's long-held belief in its divine mission; the direct link to Whitman was Emerson's own precept, "Trust thyself," and Emerson's assurance that the divine could be found everywhere.

Taking grass as the commonest vegetation (ubiquitous, utilitarian, and refreshingly beautiful), Whitman wrote his poems as though they were multiplying herbage, for he kept adding to his chief book during his lifetime until *Leaves of Grass* included the sum of his poetry. In one direction or another, Whitman celebrated a comprehensive ego that, because it encompasses all, is paradoxically therefore of the greatest humility. One cannot despise anything on such terms without despising one's self in it. "I would sing, and leave out or put in," Whitman said, "quite solely with reference to America and to-day." He meant with reference to himself too. The free-swinging, highly cadenced lines of his great collection are held together by the power of his sensibility and the comprehensive synthesis that his concept of America provided. One cannot think of single poems in the book without thinking of their relation to the whole.

Yet Whitman's later poems, especially those written after the impact of the Civil War, when he tirelessly nursed the wounded even at a permanent cost to his own health, show a mature sweetening of his barbaric yawp and even of his sprawling energetic lines. *When Lilacs Last in the Dooryard Bloom'd* (1866), his tribute at the death of Lincoln, is an important and mellowed aftermath to the sheer exuberance of his *Song of Myself* (1855) and to those poems in which the glorification of sexual energy was more startling to his day than to our own. In *Passage to India* (1871), he celebrated the joining of the corners of the earth through canal, railroad, and cable, and extended the implications of his symbol of America to involve a universal and spiritual commonwealth under the government of the unseen soul. With Whitman's poetry, a new chapter came in the history of American literature since political independence. Whitman helped it to stand on its own feet and yet to recognize its consanguinity with the brotherhood of man.

Southern Writing. On the whole, the century lay in a kind of literary doldrums for the South. Or perhaps it would be better to say that the Southern states had not learned to utilize their own materials in literature. William Gilmore Simms (1806–1870) had come the closest to it in a series of historical novels based on the Southern Indians and on the border warfare between colonials and British during the American Revolution. *The Yemassee* (1835) is one of his best. Augustus Baldwin Longstreet (1790–1870) in his *Georgia Scenes* (1835) gave glimpses into the "manners, customs, amusements, wit, and dialect" of the state that still retain their vitality. But there was little of strength that followed after Longstreet. The impact of the Civil War on the South was as shattering to its authors as to its economy. "Perhaps as you know," Sidney Lanier (1842–1881) wrote to a friend, "that, with us of the younger generation in the South since the War, pretty much the whole of life has been merely not dying." Such a feeling is reflected in the poetry of Henry Timrod (1828–1867), Paul Hamilton Hayne (1830–1886), and Lanier himself. The poetry of the first two looked backward to now debilitated models. It was Sidney Lanier who achieved the most before his death from tuberculosis. A professional musician as well as a poet, he looked on verse as a "phenomenon of sound" and in *The Science of English Verse* (1880) made an extended analysis of metrics in terms of musical notation, which anticipated many of the accentual innovations of 20th century poets. *The Symphony* (1877) and his *Hymns of the Marshes* (1884) were popular, but *The Revenge of Hamish* (1884) and certain experimental and fragmentary verse, published only after his death, were his most interesting work.

Generally the South was content to sit in the shadow of lost plantations. George Washington Cable (1844–1925) wrote pleasant local color stories, collected in such volumes as *Old Creole Days* (1879), and such novels as *The Grandissimes* (1880), also dealing with the Louisiana scene. *Uncle Remus: His Songs and His Sayings* (1881) by Joel Chandler Harris (1848–1908) was also in a sense of reconstruction of the past, in this instance of folklore. This was a firmer basis than the sentimentality of Thomas Nelson Page (1853–1922), who in countless popular novels covered the history of the South with magnolias.

Mark Twain and the West. The opening of the West and the swarming of settlers to the frontiers left little time for the creation of a written Western literature, except for the narratives of travel, especially by foreigners. The imagination of the frontiersmen themselves found its outlet in the oral "tall tales" they told each other, exaggerations of prowess and rough humor expressed with a racy inventiveness of diction. *Sketches and Eccentricities of Col. David Crockett* (1833), though obscure in its authorship, started Davy Crockett off on a notable career of wonderful exploits. *Sut Lovingood Yarns* (1867), by George Washington Harris (1814–1869), was more skilled on literary terms in its rendering of the extravagant monologues of a shambling mountaineer from the Great Smokies who was as lusty in his language as in his thirst for "corn licker." Mark Twain reviewed the book in a San Francisco newspaper, and the line between Harris' achievement and what was to make Mark Twain famous was a direct and congenial one.

ILLUSTRATIONS for two great American novels are Rockwell Kent's 1930 woodcut of Captain Ahab for an edition of Melville's *Moby-Dick* (left), and Edward W. Kemble's drawing of Huck Finn for the original edition of Mark Twain's The *Adventures of Huckleberry Finn.*

Samuel Langhorne Clemens (1835–1910), who is said to have taken his pen name, Mark Twain, from the cry of Mississippi rivermen when sounding, was born in Florida, Mo., and moved when he was four to the Mississippi River town of Hannibal. In the years before *The Celebrated Jumping Frog of Calaveras County* (1865) made him famous overnight, he had been a printer, pilot, miner, and newspaper man, wandering from the Mississippi to California. After settling in the East, in *The Innocents Abroad* (1869) he gave a scornful howl at the relics of Europe that had entranced Irving at the beginning of the century. The public took him completely to their hearts. *Roughing It* (1872) was an account of the mining days in Nevada, the best of the accounts that have been left us; and *Life on the Mississippi* (1883) was a more nostalgic but compelling reconstruction of the carefree life he had known as a pilot.

In *The Adventures of Huckleberry Finn* (1884), a delayed sequel to *The Adventures of Tom Sawyer* (1876) that employed many of the same characters, Clemens wrote what has sometimes been called America's greatest novel. Huck's journey down the Mississippi on a raft, companioned by an escaping Negro, gave Clemens the chance for a series of genre studies of river life that have become classic in their various modes. Underlying Huck's flight, however, is a serious theme of protest against the cruelty and hardly suppressed violence of so-called "civilization." No wonder that, at the end, with the Negro free at last, Huck should say: "I got to light out for the territory ahead of the rest, because Aunt Sally she's going to adopt me and civilize me, and I can't stand it. I been there before." This distrust of the progress of the century was to be further signified in Clemens' increasing bitterness, which he hid beneath the humor that made him the most popular literary man of his age. His growing pessimism resulted in such stories as *The Man That Corrupted Hadleyburg* (1900) and *The Mysterious Stranger* (1916). *Huckleberry Finn*, unlike these later works, wraps its implicit criticisms in the lively dialogue of characters who for almost the first time in American writing speak like human beings rather than bookish mouthpieces. Clemens was to do as much for the liberation of modern American prose as Whitman had done for modern poetry.

The use of frontier material in literature was not for frontiersmen. Instead, the stories were written for Eastern consumption and are mea-surably heightened for effect. This was true for Clemens and also for the method of another exploiter of the West, Bret Harte (1836–1902). Poems like his *Plain Language from Truthful James* (also called *The Heathen Chinee*, 1870) and sentimental tales like *The Outcasts of Poker Flat* (1869 and 1870) made him well known at home and abroad. Harte too had his influence. Rudyard Kipling remarked to himself, while an editor in India, "Why buy Bret Harte, when I was prepared to supply home-grown fiction on the hoof? And I did." The result was Kipling's *Plain Tales from the Hills* (1888).

Other Humorists. Mark Twain belonged to a tradition of Midwestern and Western humorists, though he transcended the tradition and outdistanced his rivals. Like him, most of them were journalists whose comic columns enlivened newspapers. They, too, used pen names and later turned to the harvests of the lecture platform. Their drawls, their frequent use of phonetic misspellings, and their wry commentaries on politics and contemporary foibles made a lowbrow appeal to highbrows and middlebrows alike. Their art was no less studied than the patrician humor of Oliver Wendell Holmes in *The Autocrat of the Breakfast Table* or the assumed crackerbox manner of James Russell Lowell in *The Biglow Papers*, which dignified the comic element in American literature as a reflection of American character.

Some of the humorists were originally Easterners: Charles Farrar Browne (1834–1867), known to his immense public as "Artemus Ward"; David Ross Locke (1833–1888), who wrote under the name of "Petroleum V. Nasby"; and Henry Wheeler Shaw (1818–1885), who became "Josh Billings." Artemus Ward was born in Maine but began his career as a contributor to the Cleveland *Plain Dealer*. *Artemus Ward: His Book* (1862) established his reputation; Abraham Lincoln admired him; Mark Twain imitated him. The comic role of Nasby was as a country preacher, and *The Nasby Papers* (1864) were widely read. He came from Vestal, N.Y., and became editor of the Toledo *Blade*. Josh Billings, who was born in Massachusetts, had many occupations before he began to write for small newspapers, and it was Ward who encouraged him to publish *Josh Billings, His Sayings* (1865), as Ward had also encouraged Nasby and Twain. Another representative figure in this gallery of colloquial humorists was Edgar Wilson Nye (1850–1896), known as "Bill" Nye after he moved from Maine westward to Wisconsin and then to Wyoming, where he edited the Laramie *Boomerang* and wrote the columns gathered in *Bill Nye and the Boomerang* (1881).

The tradition did not die with them but was carried into the 20th century by writers like Finley Peter Dunne (1867–1936), who began as an editor of the Chicago *Post* and became famous for the social and political opinions of "Mr. Dooley," an Irish saloonkeeper, in *Mr. Dooley in Peace and War* (1898) and other volumes. Will Rogers (1879–1935) was another. His humor became famous not only on the stage but in syndicated news columns. But it was not until "Ring" Lardner (1885–1933), a sportswriter for the Chicago *Tribune*, that another Twain transformed the method and manner of the vernacular humorist into serious literature. His *You Know Me, Al* (1916) was a racy and cutting commentary on baseball; *How to Write Short Stories* (1924), *The Love Nest* (1926) and *Round Up* (1929) presented common life that was comic only on the surface.

Local Color. Hawthorne's increasing attention in his later books to the "nice particularities" with which he sketched both characters and background was an indication of general drift toward realism. The first steps were gentle. Harriet Beecher Stowe (1811–1896), whose *Uncle Tom's Cabin* (1852) had played an instrumental role in preparing for the Civil War and became America's most popular novel in the century, turned to local color in such stories of Maine as *The Pearl of Orr's Island* (1862) and *Oldtown Folks* (1869). The classic in this popular genre of local color writing is also set in Maine, *The Country of the Pointed Firs* (1896), by Sarah Orne Jewett (1849–1909), which Willa Cather selected along with *The Scarlet Letter* and *Huckleberry Finn* as the three American books most likely to last. It is a pastoral, in which innocence is rediscovered by a summer visitor to the country folk and fishermen who live close to nature. Nature's transcendental reflection of God had dropped out of the picture Miss Jewett drew; her attention was on the innate sweetness of both nature and man. She represents the genteel tradition at its best.

Realism and Moral Realism—William Dean Howells (1837–1920). More and more, however, American fiction, following European models as well as its own inclination, came toughly to grips with what authors called "real life," discovering in less exotic scenes than those of local color the familiar conflicts that Americans faced. "It is the business of the novel," said William Dean Howells, "to picture the daily life in the most exact terms possible, with an absolutely clear sense of proportion." Howells himself laid great emphasis upon "proportion" and "the more smiling aspects of life, which are the more American," although later writers were to think him too moderate and label his manner "reticent realism." But his work was an important step in the concept of the novelist as a contemporary historian, almost a sociologist, in his concentration on man's place in society.

In *A Modern Instance* (1882) and *The Rise of Silas Lapham* (1885), Howells gave his best illustrations of his themes. The first is the study of a man without parents, without tradition, and without reliances other than on himself, who, in fighting the American way up, learns only what he could learn from looking around him and experiencing the social and cultural structure of his country, comparing what is said with what is actually done. The result, for Howell's hero, is catastrophic. The second novel concerns the ethical problems that confront a businessman in the new industrial age, in which his spiritual "rise" is at the cost of his economic "fall." Howell's meant both books as commentaries on his age. He was a prolific writer as novelist, essayist, and critic. He had left the Middle West for Boston, where he was the influential editor of the *Atlantic Monthly,* and finally for New York, where he was on the staff of *Harper's Magazine,* and his own career thus illustrated the literary path of empire in the closing years of the 19th century.

Henry James (1843–1916). Long regarded as a mere aesthete whose involved prose still further obscured rather than untangled the complexities of life, Henry James has become a leading figure in American literature, a bridge between the 19th and 20th centuries, whose novels and criticism are monuments of achievement. Like the fiction of Howells, whom he admired, James' works deal with the moral definition of characters as they face alternative choices in life. These choices James found best highlighted in the instances of Americans situated in an English or European milieu. Like Hawthorne, by whom James was much influenced, and encouraged by his brother William James, the distinguished psychologist and pragmatist, Henry James found the most significant field of realistic action in the psychological responses that man inevitably makes to situations.

The complex sensuousness of James' prose style, and his Hawthornesque emphasis upon symbolism as a mode of expression, were to help establish, as he put it, "the perfect dependence of the 'moral' sense of a work of art on the amount of felt life concerned in producing it." An artistic morality thus confirms "spiritual decency"; and on terms quite different from those that Bryant had established for an earlier generation of writers, literature becomes not a handmaiden nor schoolmaster of morals but morality itself. Among James' many novels, *The Portrait of a Lady* (1881), *The Wings of the Dove* (1902), *The Ambassadors* (1903), and *The Golden Bowl* (1904) are the best exemplifications of the moral education in which, though James himself had quit America for residence and finally citizenship in England, his American protagonists embody the ultimately triumphant image.

Drama. By the end of the century Henry James, Howells, and even Mark Twain had all tried their hand at playwriting. Behind them was a long struggle of American dramatists. In the 18th century there had been principally Thomas Godfrey (1736–1763), a Philadelphia poet who in 1759 had written the blank verse tragedy *The Prince of Parthia* (1767), and Royall Tyler (1757–1826), a Boston lawyer, remembered for *The Contrast,* the first comedy by a native American, produced professionally in New York in 1787.

William Dunlap (1766–1839) helped to turn the century on a native note with his historical melodrama *André* (1798). Robert Montgomery Bird (1806–1854) tailored his historical tragedy *The Gladiator* (1831) and his domestic tragedy *The Broker of Bogota* (1834) to fit the style of the actor Edwin Forrest, marking the rise of American actors who could demand such accommodation from playwrights. But the receipts went to the actors, not to the playwrights. Bird, discouraged, turned to writing novels like *Nick of the Woods* (1837).

The situation for the serious dramatist was not much better in England, where the actor also reigned, and while numerous closet dramas in verse were written by able poets, the plays were not produced. In America, Poe unsuccessfully tried his hand with *Politian* (1835). George Henry Boker (1823–1890), a lyric poet, wrote several verse dramas, but not even his masterpiece *Francesca da Rimini* (1855) brought him sufficient returns or even recognition to warrant his continuing as a playwright.

Dion Boucicault (1820–1890), an Irish-born, English-trained actor-playwright who knew the theater and what the audience liked, was more successful commercially with his melodramas. Boucicault's *The Octoroon* (1885), a play about miscegenation, was one of many among his 132 plays to enjoy long runs. Like Boucicault, David Belasco (1854–1931) was actor, dramatist, and producer, but his many adaptations for the stage had more theatrical vitality than art. The theater and the actor were still dominant as the century again turned. The play itself had not yet gained its true dignity; the successful playwright was still chiefly a handyman.

Section 4. The 20th Century

The new century in American letters brought with it a direct reflection of the disturbing impact of industrialization and urbanization on old ways of life. It also brought new definitions of reality, both scientific and philosophical, that the 19th century had been formulating at the expense of orthodox beliefs. The scope of literary reference was broadened as well as disturbed. Experimental psychology had opened a new approach to the operations of the consciousness and then, through the influence of Sigmund Freud and Carl Jung, revealed the inherent drama of the subconscious. In stylistics, as well as in subject matter, the new science had its effects on authors, leading them toward meaningful experiments in the communication of realities. The romantic efforts of earlier writers, like Whitman and Emily Dickinson, to originate styles to fit their individual personalities were extended by Gertrude Stein, Ezra Pound, and others to devise a syntax appropriate to non-Aristotelian logic and new concepts of time. They were not simply trying to be different; on their own 20th century terms they were impelled by an Emersonian intention to make patterns of words correspond to the newly defined nature of things. With such efforts went an increased sense of literary responsibility. Although the modern ways of thinking meant a temporary and confusing dislocation of the man of feeling from his traditional values and modes of expression, the birth of the century was intellectually exciting. It not only provided the writer with the material of countless and deeply felt conflicts, it also gave him a new sense of pioneering.

The Impact of Philosophy and Criticism. The late 19th century had seen the emergence of an indigenous philosophy, particularly related to the dissatisfaction of Americans with the status quo. Especially in the pragmatism of Charles Peirce (1839–1914) and William James (1842–1910), to which John Dewey (1859–1952) added a program, writers found instrumentation for their pathfinding. "A pragmatist," James had said, "turns away . . . from fixed principles, closed systems, and pretended absolutes and origins. He turns towards concreteness and adequacy, towards facts, towards action and towards power." To the writer this gave a justifying significance. "The sole advantage in possessing great works of literature," wrote George Santayana (1863–1952), himself both a philosopher and a poet, "lies in what they can help us to become." "A poet," he said, meaning also the serious author, "who turns his practised and passionate imagination on the order of all things, or on anything in the light of the whole, is for that moment a philosopher."

It is in this sense of the writer as philosopher that authors were responsive to the influence of 20th century historical events and the attempts to explain them or absorb their significance within a philosophical or theological framework. Authors were not satisfied simply to understand them on grounds of pure realism as national or international politics. The two world wars and the undeclared wars between and after them became an inescapable part of the writer's condition as man. The disorder of events became a stimulus to what the poet Wallace Stevens called "the maker's rage to order," his effort to attain "a new text of the world." A seemingly hostile universe, especially after the 1930's and World War II, at the same time developed an existentialist stress on the active role of the will rather than the reason as man confronts his problems. In the 1960's ironic pessimism became almost an orthodox literary stance, and a school of "black humor" evidenced itself in the novel and in drama as well as in poetry.

The 20th century attempt to understand the nature of things and develop a new vocabulary and syntax for expressing it led, significantly for the writer, into the development of formalized aesthetic considerations and the emergence of a mature American literary criticism. The distinguished discussions by Henry James of his own intentions and tactics were succeeded by the work of a long line of writers who in their analyses of craft paralleled the influence of their own artistic successes. Ezra Pound, T.S. Eliot, and Wallace Stevens were notable examples. Editions of the letters of Pound, Hart Crane, and Stevens deepened the influence of their formal writing. So did the critical comments of Ernest Hemingway, and Gertrude Stein's writings about writing may well prove to be her most important contribution to letters. John Crowe Ransom, Allen Tate, and Yvor Winters modified distinguished careers as poets in favor of writing criticism.

Criticism developed into a serious literary genre. Literary history gave way to literary criticism, and the contemporary importance of works like *Main Currents in American Thought* (1927–30) by Vernon L. Parrington (1871–1929) and *Makers and Finders* (1936–52) by Van Wyck Brooks (1886–1963) lessened. Academic humanists like Irving Babbitt (1865–1933) and Paul Elmer More (1864–1937) were succeeded by more broadly humane writers, such as Edmund

Wilson and Lionel Trilling, and by more purely literary critics, such as Kenneth Burke, Richard P. Blackmur (1904–1965), and Cleanth Brooks. The results of such measured examinations as they and many others gave to 20th century American writing were to provide authors not only with an elite jury but also with definitions that could clarify their own struggles for creative expression.

Indeed, the patronage of American writing by universities, expressed in the employment of serious poets and writers of fiction on faculties, tended, by the very duties of teaching, to make most writers into practicing critics in the classroom. A result was their increasing self-consciousness as artists and a consequently increased desire to write something that could be talked about as well as experienced.

Novels and Short Stories. In the career of Theodore Dreiser (1871–1945), and with the appearance of *Sister Carrie* (1900), American fiction entered a new phase of franker realism in its approach to contemporary life. Dreiser drew from the experiences of his own family for his story of the unpunished rise of a woman of easy virtue; he knew that the "way up" carried unresolved ambiguities with it. Stephen Crane (1871–1900) in *Maggie: A Girl of the Streets* (written 1892; privately published 1893) and *The Red Badge of Courage* (1895), which treated cowardice rather than cavalier glory in war, had helped to open the way for unconventional attitudes and subject matter. Many writers turned toward the dark shadows on the American dream. Frank Norris (1870–1902) in *The Octopus* (1901) dealt with the strangulation by the railroads of independent wheat growers in California. *The Jungle* (1906), by Upton Sinclair, was based on the evils of the Chicago meat-packing industry.

A new moral didacticism in fiction developed. But most novels in this literary manner of social engineering lacked the ungainly vitality and sympathetic understanding of Dreiser's amoral portraits of *Jennie Gerhardt* (1911) and of the Darwinian rise of the American business magnate in *The Financier* (1912) and *The Titan* (1914). Dreiser shifted from the purely personal ethic of these works to a social ethic in *An American Tragedy* (1925), his greatest novel. Here he indicted society in the guilt of a weak-willed youth tried for murder, for society had held up the goal of success without providing an accompanying morality. The story was an American tragedy, because in a country where the people are themselves their only king, whenever a part of society falls, all society drags itself down in a democratic version of Aristotelian tragedy.

Other writers examining themselves and their new society were as perplexed as Henry Adams (1838–1918) had been in his brilliant and ironic *Education of Henry Adams* (privately published 1907). Adams' rendering of his frustrated life seems as much of a novel as it is an autobiography, and is an early example of the many pragmatic 20th century fictions in which the author becomes his own protagonist. Jack London (1876–1916) wrote much the same kind of fictional self-analysis in *Martin Eden* (1909), although he is best known for his brutally vigorous tales of Alaska (*The Call of the Wild,* 1903) and of the Pacific (*The Sea-Wolf,* 1904).

Women writers began to look at the complexity of life more as men did. Edith Wharton (1862–1937) approached the problem through the novel of manners. *The House of Mirth* (1905) and *The Custom of the Country* (1913) are successful examples of her dissections of the upper classes. Her *Ethan Frome* (1911), a grim tragedy of the Berkshires, is less typical. Ellen Glasgow (1874–1945), whose first novel appeared in 1897, contrasted the agrarian way of life with the emergent Southern industrialism. She was no sentimentalist. "What the South needs is blood and irony," she said, disbudding the magnolias of Thomas Nelson Page.

Willa Cather (1873–1947), the finest stylist among the women writers, and a master of tonal effect, developed the same troubled response to her age. In such early novels as *O Pioneers!* (1913) and *My Antonia* (1918) she had dealt with the robust creativity of women who lived close to the Nebraskan farmlands and to life. But *A Lost Lady* (1923), a portrait of unbolstered moral dependency, began her criticism of a country she felt had lost its pioneering strength. *Death Comes for the Archbishop* (1927) was her finest novel. Set in early New Mexico, it contrasts in a succession of pastel frescoes the ordered spirituality of two French priests against the intimations of disorder on the part of those settlers for whom the chief joy became avarice and whose only altar was to Mammon. A power similar to Willa Cather's is felt in *Giants in the Earth* (1927), a novel of the Norwegian settlers in the Dakotas, by Ole Rölvaag (1876–1931).

Sinclair Lewis (1885–1951). In *Main Street* (1920), *Babbitt* (1922), *Arrowsmith* (1925), and *Dodsworth* (1929), Sinclair Lewis gave the most popularly received picture of the American tortured, as he put it, like "a god self-slain on his modern improved altar." Lewis was a graphic writer. He prepared his image-breaking novels with the precision of a sociologist, gathering characteristic details to integrate into his studies of the crippling small-town and average-city life of businessmen, scientists, preachers, and reformers. They were done with such heightened photographic verisimilitude that they replaced Cooper's version of America in the eyes of foreigners, and Deerslayer gave way to the cracked figure of Babbitt. In 1930, Lewis became the first American to win the Nobel Prize for literature.

A New Vitality in Fiction. What was more exciting in the development of a significant 20th century American fiction found its beginnings in the novels of Henry James and the strange and difficult work of Gertrude Stein (1874–1946). "Entering into her work," wrote Sherwood Anderson, thinking of Keats looking into Chapman's *Homer,* "was a sort of Lewis and Clark expedition into a new country where everything was strange." "Writing," Ernest Hemingway told her upon giving up journalism, "used to be easy before I met you." Through the effects she achieved in such revolutionary works as *Three Lives* (1909), *Tender Buttons* (1914), and *The Making of Americans* (1925), in all of which she threw orthodox prose to the winds, she had an influence even on authors who were only indirectly acquainted with her writing.

Sherwood Anderson (1876–1941), in the plotless tales of *Winesburg, Ohio* (1919) and *The Triumph of the Egg* (1921), showed the tentative gestures of man desperately groping for beauty and fulfillment in the face of personal inhibitions and social frustrations. What seemed crude and broken in his characters and narration was

PICTORIAL PARADE

Sinclair Lewis (1930)

CULVER PICTURES

Eugene O'Neill (1936)

REGINALD DAVIS

Pearl Buck (1938)

PICTORIAL PARADE

T.S. Eliot (1948)

RALPH MORRISSEY

William Faulkner (1949)

PICTORIAL PARADE

Ernest Hemingway (1954)

PICTORIAL PARADE

John Steinbeck (1962)

UPI

Saul Bellow (1976)

only a reluctant betrayal of the organically symmetrical form that both characters and author sought to fashion. *The Enormous Room* (1922) by E.E. Cummings (1894–1962), an account of his imprisonment in World War I, told the story of man's ability to refreshen his senses despite symbolic regimentation. Cummings' prose style was like fireworks. "There can be no more playing safe," John Dos Passos wrote after reading the book. Dos Passos was equally experimental in taking, as he said, "cross-bearings on every one of the abstractions that were so well ranged in ornate marble niches in the minds of our fathers." "Three words that still have meaning," he said, "that I think we can apply to all professional writing are discovery, originality, invention." Through symbolic devices, rapid juxtapositions of violently contrasting scenes, and intermittent flashes of headlines and popular songs, he portrayed in *Manhattan Transfer* (1925) and his long trilogy, *U.S.A.* (1938), the disorder he found in contemporary life. "It's hiding things makes them putrefy," a character states. Dos Passos did not hide very much. Neither did Thomas Wolfe (1900–1938) in his autobiographical novels *Look Homeward, Angel* (1929) and *Of Time and the River* (1935), where, influenced by Joyce's *Ulysses*, he became an American Werther in his lyrical but agonized search for himself. More naturalistic in its Dreiserian approach to life, yet expressed with the experimental devices that were transforming the novel, was the trilogy *Studs Lonigan* (1935) by James Farrell, in which, against the background of Chicago, his protagonist's life parallels the story of America from the birth of the century to what, to Farrell, was the death of an age in the economic disasters of 1933.

The apparently traumatic connection between the course of the American spirit and the role of wealth was thematically used even by so highly polished and sophisticated a writer as F.

Scott Fitzgerald (1896–1940), in *The Great Gatsby* (1925) and *Tender Is the Night* (1934), as well as in such superb short stories as *The Rich Boy* (in *All the Sad Young Men*, 1926), which have become classics of their period. Increasingly Fitzgerald has gained stature as a writer, and the cavils of proletarian-minded critics of the depression-torn 1930's who dismissed him for his "rather irritating type of chic," have been replaced by the recognition that his fiction dug deep into both character and culture.

Another writer of the 1930's to win posthumous stature as a writer of distinction is Nathanael West (1903-1940), whose *Miss Lonelyhearts* (1933), a satirical attack on the social and personal panaceas of his time, and more ambitious novel *The Day of the Locust* (1939), a penetrating study of Hollywood as a cultural mecca, stand firm for the future. John Steinbeck's *The Pastures of Heaven* (1932), *In Dubious Battle* (1936), and *The Grapes of Wrath* (1939) gave variant accounts of the need for love in economic, social, and personal relationships. In 1962 he won the Nobel Prize for literature.

Hemingway and Faulkner. The two most outstanding and influential American writers of fiction to emerge in the 20th century have been Ernest Hemingway (1899–1961) and William Faulkner (1897–1962). Each won the Nobel Prize. The crisply intense prose style of Hemingway was as influential in French and Italian writing as in American as he sought the direct communication of intense feeling in the fewest possible words. Decorum and personal courage become the concrete redemptions for his characters. "Morals," he said, "are what you feel good after," and in the manner of modern romantics he attempted to restore the power of the senses in man's original and pragmatically repeated facings-up to nature and his fellow man. In *The Sun Also Rises* (1926), a study of sophisticated expatriates, he wrote of the dislocated "lost generation" after World War I. *A Farewell to Arms* (1929), set in the midst of that war, is a love story that thematically is a search for meaning in the disorder that war represents; while *For Whom the Bell Tolls* (1940), set in the Spanish Civil War, is another struggle for values in a pressured time. *The Old Man and the Sea* (1952) retells a favorite Hemingway theme: undefeated courage as a spiritual goal in itself—the hallmark of Hemingway's democratic aristocracy. Hemingway was an equally distinguished writer of short stories, although in these as in his novels, his craftsmanship was more original than his message.

The scenes of Hemingway's stories were characteristically remote: France, Spain, Africa, Cuba. Faulkner, on the other hand, used his native state of Mississippi for the geography of Yoknapatawpha County, his fictional microcosm of the world. An agrarian by disposition, he, like other Southerners, saw in the incursion of commercialism a violent disruption of old virtues and of unselfish and immediate relationship to the land. Recounting man's false steps in history, he saw the Civil War as a guidepost in the culmination of a self-destructive exploitation. Faulkner's prose could be crystal clear, but at his most ambitious he constructed a highly involved syntax to represent the complexities that man must disentangle. Read as metaphors, his fictions came to stand for the perplexed condition of mankind, not simply in America but in all the modern world. *The Sound and the Fury* (1929), *As I Lay Dying* (1930), *Light in August* (1932), and *Absalom, Absalom!* (1936) represent his most difficult prose but also his best. Faulkner's troubled picture of what has happened to America is often disturbing to his countrymen and bewildering to non-Americans; but in principle his frankness not only demonstrates a freedom for independent thought but also gives evidence that the same belief in the potentialities of the American dream that characterized the prose of authors like Thoreau still maintains itself in the felt agony that man is less than he can be.

Later Novelists. For a time, American fiction was dominated by a group of writers who found in their native South a region of dramatic change and representative tensions. Of these, with the exception of Faulkner, Robert Penn Warren stood out as the most durable. A masterful rhetorician, a poet, and an influential critic and pedagogue, Warren wrote a series of deliberately melodramatic novels in which both past and present conflicts of the South were made to serve universally. *All the King's Men* (1946), a study of political morality based on the career of Huey Long, is one of the memorable novels of the century.

Among other significant representatives of the group as writers of fiction were Katherine Anne Porter, best known for her short stories and the novel *Ship of Fools* (1962), Eudora Welty, Carson McCullers, and Truman Capote. Capote's *Other Voices, Other Rooms* (1948) is a sensitively rendered account of a boy's growth. *The Grass Harp* (1951) has been called "a parable of freedom." Turned reporter, Capote became skilled in what, as in *In Cold Blood* (1966), he describes as a "nonfiction novel." Spiritedly naturalistic, it is a variation of the reportorial novel that John Hersey had earlier mastered in such works as *A Bell for Adano* (1944).

American Jews, as an ethnic group, were treated by several writers. The Jewish urban scene was forcefully, sometimes comically, rendered by Bernard Malamud in *The Natural* (1952), *The Assistant* (1957), and *A New Life* (1961), as well as by extension in *The Fixer* (1966), the story of an accused Jew in Russia. Jerome David Salinger's first book, *The Catcher in the Rye* (1951), became as widely read a classic as its prototype, *Huckleberry Finn.* Later, in a series of linked tales, Salinger made a loosely structured novel about the Glass family. Saul Bellow became an even more compelling literary figure. *The Adventures of Augie March* (1953), *Henderson the Rain King* (1959), and *Herzog* (1964) are stylistically vigorous and formally inventive; in them he explores man's difficulty in being himself or even knowing who he is.

Similar problems of identity were explored by black writers. Building on the work of Harlem Renaissance writers such as Langston Hughes, Ralph Ellison's *Invisible Man* (1952) examined alienation in the context of a racist society. His symbolic approach contrasted with the realism of Richard Wright, whose *Native Son* (1940) and *Black Boy* (1945) were powerful social statements. James Baldwin became eminent as a novelist and essayist. His *Go Tell It on the Mountain* (1953) was forceful and naturalistic, in the vein of Richard Wright; *Giovanni's Room* (1956) and *Another Country* (1962) treated controversial material: homosexual love in a racially mixed society.

World War II gave rise to a rebirth of naturalistic novels such as *The Naked and the Dead* (1948) by Norman Mailer and *From Here to Eternity* (1951) by James Jones. On the whole, however, the war resulted in fresh material rather than in enlarged understanding. Novelists like J.P. Marquand (1893–1960), James Gould Cozzens, and Louis Auchincloss wrote novels of manners and values with an artist's craft. "Black humorists" like Joseph Heller in *Catch 22* (1961), John Barth in *The Sot-Weed Factor* (1960) and *Giles Goat-Boy* (1966), and Thomas Pynchon in *V* (1963) and *The Crying of Lot 49* (1966) continued the provocative probing that the novel has always provided.

Short Story. The short story as a literary form has always been popular with Americans. In the early 19th century the brevity was a necessity. Publishers were not much interested in American novels; it was cheaper to pirate English ones. But American periodicals found a place for shorter fiction. In his prose Poe kept to short stories and developed a defensive aesthetic for them. Hawthorne published several volumes of tales before his first novel. Melville turned from the novel to poetry and the short story.

The 20th century short-story writer could look back on a distinguished tradition: Irving's *Rip Van Winkle* (1819) and *The Legend of Sleepy Hollow* (1820), Poe's body of horror tales and detective stories, and the stories of Hawthorne, Melville, and Henry James. Closer to his own time was the slicker professionalism of Bret Harte and O. Henry (William Sidney Porter; (1862–1910), although the latter's surprise endings no longer surprised. More literary and more lasting were the symbolic rendering in *A White Heron* (1886) by Sarah Orne Jewett and the varied skills of Stephen Crane in *The Open Boat* (1898) and *The Blue Hotel* (1899).

Most writers of fiction have tried their hands, at one time or another, at short-story writing. Edith Wharton began that way and was never defter with the comedy of manners than in *The*

Other Two (1904). So did Gertrude Stein in *Melanctha* and the other stories of *Three Lives* (1909), which helped to revolutionize style and structure so that, as in James, presentation took the place of plot. Sherwood Anderson followed her in *Winesburg, Ohio* (1919) and *The Egg* (1921), and his *Death in the Woods* (1933) contains perfect examples of the intensity that the form permits. Hemingway was another artist of the short story. His *Hills like White Elephants* (1927, *In Another Country* (1927), and *The Snows of Kilimanjaro* (1936) are masterpieces of their kind. Faulkner's comic *Spotted Horses* (1931) and his great story *The Bear* (1942) show that he would have been called a master even had he never written a novel. F. Scott Fitzgerald's *May Day* (1920) and *The Rich Boy* (1926 would have been enough, too, for a reputation. Steinbeck never wrote better than in the short stories of *The Pastures of Heaven* (1932) and *The Red Pony* (1937). William Carlos Williams alternated between poetry and short story; for him they were mutually congenial, a way of bringing the symbolic and the concrete sharply together. The nature and economy of the short story have often been close to those of the poem.

James Thurber (1894–1961) found a brilliant parallel to the penetrating humor of his drawings in the many stories, fables, and parables he contributed to the *New Yorker*. *The Secret Life of Walter Mitty* (1939) was one of his best. Indeed he helped to mold the manner of the *New Yorker*, which in turn molded the manner of many writers, including John Cheever and John Updike. Salinger's *A Perfect Day for Banana Fish* (1948) is a model *New Yorker* story.

The South has had its distinguished short-story writers, including Robert Penn Warren; Eudora Welty, who in *The Golden Apple* (1949) and *The Bride of Innisfallen* (1955) brought Sherwood Anderson's grotesques south; and Flannery O'Connor (1925–1964), whose last book, *Everything That Rises Must Converge* (1965), confirmed the growing appreciation of her art. But the most distinguished Southern writer of short fiction, other than Faulkner, and one of the leading literary figures of the 20th century, was Katherine Anne Porter, whose stories, beginning with those in *Flowering Judas* (1930), were brought together in the National Book Award-winning *Collected Stories* (1965). Miss Porter confirmed the short story as something more than a literary miniature.

Drama. Despite the development of a native drama, the important impacts on modern American drama came from abroad: from Ibsen and Strindberg, Chekhov and Shaw. After World War I, expressionism, especially through Kaiser and Toller, made itself felt, to be followed after World War II by the influence of Sartre, Brecht, and Samuel Beckett.

The vitalization of both the American theater and American drama came not from the Broadway stage but from the little theaters, conducted without pomp in obscure parts of Chicago and New York, later spreading to smaller cities and college campuses. Groups like the Washington Square Players in New York City and the Provincetown Players on Cape Cod (later in New York) were celebrated trailblazers.

In Eugene O'Neill (1888–1953), American literature had its first great dramatist. O'Neill's beginnings were off-Broadway efforts, but they came as a consequence of his familiarity with the working theater (his father had been a famous actor) and his study in the "47 Workshop" at Harvard under George Pierce Baker, where other playwrights of an emerging American drama, such as Philip Barry (1896–1949) and Sidney Howard (1891–1939), were also students. O'Neill's early one-act plays of the sea, such as those in *Bound East for Cardiff* (1916) and *The Moon of the Caribbees* (1919), were followed by full-length plays like *The Emperor Jones* (1921) and *Anna Christie* (1922), which established his American preeminence. *Strange Interlude* (1928) is a nine-act Freudian tragedy of frustrated desire; *Mourning Becomes Electra* (1931), a trilogy, is an American version of a Greek tragedy of fate. O'Neill was always an experimenter. In *The Iceman Cometh* (1946) he abandons physical action on the stage for a life in words, as he portrays the loss even of verbal illusion; in *Long Day's Journey into Night* (produced posthumously in 1956), one of his finest as well as most personal plays, his characters simply, but harrowingly, talk in a family living room. In 1936, O'Neill was given the Nobel Prize for literature.

The period between the two world wars saw an activity in American drama that made O'Neill part of a movement. *The Adding Machine* (1923) by Elmer Rice did much to bring the expressionist movement to the American stage. His *Street Scene* (1929) and *Judgment Day* (1934) were more topical but not less socially conscious. *What Price Glory?* (1924), by Maxwell Anderson (1888–1959) and Laurence Stallings, was a successful war play whose lusty language startled audiences. Sidney Howard, who, like O'Neill, was a student at Harvard's "47 Workshop," began a series of popular plays with *They Knew What They Wanted* (1924), which broadened the limits of dramatic subject matter by the realism of its story of unorthodox love. Philip Barry, still another "47 Workshop" student, began as a writer of urbane comedies (*Paris Bound,* 1927) but gained greater dramatic strength through more serious plays—*Hotel Universe* (1930), *The Animal Kingdom* (1932), and *Here Comes the Clowns* (1938). The finest proletarian plays of the socially conscious 1930's were by Clifford Odets (1906–1963), whose *Waiting for Lefty* (1935) and *Awake and Sing!* (1935) had a vigor that his later plays could not recapture.

Next to O'Neill's, the most distinguished American plays of the 1930's and 1940's were by Thornton Wilder, also a novelist of excellence. His *Our Town* (1938), which has become a classic, is an idyll of the meaning of existence. *The Skin of Our Teeth* (1942) is an optimistic version of the theory of cyclical history.

During the post-World War II period, four dramatists in particular left their mark: William Inge, Tennessee Williams, Arthur Miller, and Edward Albee. Of these, Williams and Miller stand out. The former showed his mastery of dialogue and movement on the stage in a series of plays of which *The Glass Menagerie* (1945), *A Streetcar Named Desire* (1947), *The Rose Tattoo* (1950), and *Cat on a Hot Tin Roof* (1955), are typical. They treat the emotional involvements and frustrations with which Williams chiefly concerned himself. His characters are fugitives from a world of reality, whose fantasies are sometimes pitiful, sometimes obscene, violations of normal living.

Arthur Miller created more directly social

plays based on an ambiguity of images, whether defined in a family or broader cultural sense. "It is not enough any more," Miller wrote, "to know that one is at the mercy of social pressures, it is necessary to understand that such a sealed fate cannot be accepted." *Death of a Salesman* (1949), the account of Willy Loman's tragic struggle with "the law of success," became another classic. *The Crucible* (1953), in which the Salem witch-hunts are used as a parable, and *A View from the Bridge* (1955) enhanced his reputation.

Inge's *Picnic* (1953), *Bus Stop* (1955), and *The Dark at the Top of the Stairs* (1957) show greater technical strength than originality of theme. At his best Inge is a master of dialogue, as he presents modern man's fear and trembling and self-deceits. So too is Edward Albee, whose savage dialogues of academic intellectuals in *Who's Afraid of Virginia Woolf?* (1962) frighteningly balance the serenity of Wilder's *Our Town* as a rendering of life in America. Albee's *The Zoo Story* (1959) and *The American Dream* (1961) were earlier studies of mankind frustrated by the imposition of an ideal. The ambitious *Tiny Alice* (1964) was a frustration for both characters and audience.

Poetry. Assessed on terms of the highest average of purely literary achievement, American poetry in the 20th century has flourished best. The wealth of talent has been astonishing and continued. The effect of mature criticism on poetry has been marked. Breaking away from the thin verse and sentimentality that had come to prevail at the end of the 19th century, Edwin Arlington Robinson (1869–1935) led the way in giving both substance and firmness to his poems, especially in his sketches of small-town New Englanders in *The Children of the Night* (1897), *Captain Craig* (1902), *The Town Down the River* (1910), and *The Man Against the Sky* (1916). Robert Frost (1874–1963) added further strength through the warmth of *A Boy's Will* (1913) and succeeding volumes, creating a modern American version of the pastoral. With dry humor and a fine dramatic ear, he wrote the most popular and most critically esteemed American poetry in the 20th century. By the end of the century's first decade many significant poets had begun to write, and by the end of the 1920's a true renaissance had come. "Anything," wrote William Carlos Williams (1883–1963), who was a doctor as well as a poet, "that a poet can effectively lift from its dull bed by force of the imagination becomes his material. Anything." Such knowledge was liberation. Poets like Edgar Lee Masters (1869–1950), in *Spoon River Anthology* (1915), Vachel Lindsay (1879–1931), with what he called the "higher vaudeville imagination" of *General William Booth Enters into Heaven* (1913) and *The Congo* (1914), and Carl Sandburg, in *Chicago Poems* (1916) and *Cornhuskers* (1918), gave a Midwestern liveliness to the poetic scene.

Poetry: A Magazine of Verse, founded in Chicago in 1912, became a mouthpiece for modern poets throughout the English-speaking world. Among those to appear in its pages was John Gould Fletcher (1886–1950), who helped to introduce the techniques of modern French poetry in *Irradiations: Sand and Spray* (1915) and *Goblins and Pagodas* (1916), but who in later writing joined the developing school of Southern poetry that followed more traditional lines. Hilda Doolittle (1886–1961), who wrote as "H.D.," joined Pound, Fletcher, Amy Lowell, and others in what was known as the Imagist school, whose influential emphasis in *Des Imagistes: An Anthology* (1914) was on the clean-cut image, immaculate diction, and a rhetoric stripped to the bone. She represented a growing emphasis on the craft itself, and the delicate purity of her work shows an exemplary control of poetic art.

Others to amplify the new resurgence of verse making were William Carlos Williams, whose many experimental volumes made poetry of what seemed unpoetic and asserted the importance of a contemporary idiom and prosody; and Marianne Moore, who showed a precision of ear and a sharpness of eye for significant detail that rank her among the finest American poets.

E.E. Cummings (1894–1962) brought gaiety and freshness in poems whose unorthodox typography is no less vital to their success than the continuing youthfulness of his responses. Hart Crane (1899–1932) may not have succeeded with *The Bridge* (1930) in his attempted epic of the American spirit, but in *White Buildings* (1926) he showed an intense verbal power. In poetry as in fiction, Southern authors became eminent. John Crowe Ransom and Allen Tate wrote with immaculate sophistication and controlled irony, while the narrative poetry of Robert Penn Warren is matched in dramatic vigor only in the work of Robinson Jeffers (1887–1962), with his California settings for violent action, and by Stephen Vincent Benét (1898–1943) in his popular Civil War poem, *John Brown's Body* (1928). Elinor Wylie (1885–1928) and Edna St. Vincent Millay (1892–1950) wrote lyrics of real beauty in the traditional manner, which has had its own continued growth. The strongest influence on younger American poets was the poetry of W.H. Auden, an Englishman who settled in America in 1939 and became a citizen in 1946.

Pound and Eliot. The most influential American poets of the 20th century have been Ezra Pound and T.S. Eliot (1888–1965). Eliot's *The Waste Land* (1922) is dedicated to Pound as the "better maker," and both men represent a revolutionary impact on modern poetic form. In rapidly shifting images in non-Aristotelian justaposition, they employed what they called a "logic of the imagination." Borrowing widely from many languages and integrating scraps and quotations from other authors and literatures, they gave new plasticity as well as new mannerisms and attitudes to poetry. Their critical writing added precept to example.

In his translations from the Provençal and the Chinese, and in such poems as *Homage to Sextus Propertius* (1919) and *Hugh Selwyn Mauberley* (1920), Pound proved himself a master of formal verse making. In *The Cantos*, begun in 1916 and added to in the years thereafter, he wrote the most ambitious poem of the century, as well as one of the most influential. Retracing history through man's willed memory of the past, the protagonist of his poem travels through the underworld of earlier cultures like an Odysseus or a Dante. He emerges toward a vision of a new City of Man that will embrace the spirit of order equally in art, music, literature, economics, and statecraft. Order is the reflection of beauty, and Pound is concerned most with man as himself the responsible agent.

Eliot, who in 1927 became a British citizen, assumed the role of leading poet at the beginning of the second half of the century, and whatever he wrote became an event. Earlier poems, such as *Prufrock and Other Observations* (1917) and *The Waste Land* (1922), were dramatic studies of man's spiritual and emotional poverty in a barren world. But in *Ash Wednesday* (1930) and *Four Quartets* (1943) and such poetic dramas as *Murder in the Cathedral* (1935), *The Cocktail Party* (1950), and *The Confidential Clerk* (1954), he affirmed a positive religious conviction that, if not jubilant, is at least sustaining.

Wallace Stevens (1879–1955). Wallace Stevens is increasingly recognized as one of the three or four major poets writing in English in the 20th century. Insurance executive as well as poet, he remained aloof from literary circles, and his first book of poems, *Harmonium* (1923), was published when he was over 40. For another 10 years he was again quiet, but from then on he composed and published steadily. *Collected Poems* (1954), *Opus Posthumous* (1957), and his book of essays, *The Necessary Angel* (1951), established the basis of his reputation. His poems are abstract and impersonal in one sense but warm and vibrant in their philosophical search for a mode of humanism in a dual world of realism and imagination. He was a metaphysical imagist of the spirit, who gave philosophical vibrancy to his thematic variation on the life of the imagination in the world of reality.

Later Poets. The renaissance of poetry continued beyond the days of the masters who established it. Good poetry became popular, and the poet on the campus or at public readings was a familiar sight. Nor did any mode or clique dominate; instead a series of traditions and innovations brought diversity of accomplishment.

Richard Wilbur, in a formalistic reaction to the metrical looseness of his elders, established an almost neo-Augustan but sensitive order in lyrics that an older generation admired and a younger generation copied. William Meredith belongs in the same impressive line. So in a slightly different sense does the very accomplished Elizabeth Bishop, who followed after Marianne Moore but in her own less-mannered style. Theodore Roethke (1908–1963) was another lyric poet of exceptional sensitivity, though more linked to Yeats than to the French symbolists who influenced Wilbur. Roethke's poems of his Pennsylvania childhood were carried on into meditations on his later life, given power by his strength of feeling both for the exhilaration of living and the foreboding of death.

Equally mystical but expressing himself with a liberating yawp inherited from Whitman was Allen Ginsberg, whose *Howl and Other Poems* (1956) led the movement of Beat Poetry that shook the orthodox rafters and permitted nonacademic poets, such as Gregory Corso and Lawrence Ferlinghetti, to have their day. Equally nontraditional but concentrating on what is called "projective verse" were Charles Olson, especially in *The Maximus Poems* (1960); Robert Duncan, in *Roots and Branches* (1964); Denise Levertov, in *The Jacob's Ladder* (1961); and Robert Creeley, in *For Love* (1962). Influenced by Whitman, Williams, and H.D., they tried to reflect the rhythms of American speech with intensity of feeling.

John Berryman, in *Homage to Mistress Bradstreet* (1956) and again in *77 Dream Songs* (1964), proved himself an impressive poet, confident of his poetic line and sensitive in his agon-

ized reflection of life. Of this generation only Robert Lowell, named for his ancestor the elder brother of James Russell Lowell, stood above Berryman. Lowell's *Lord Weary's Castle* (1946), *The Mills of the Kavanaughs* (1951), *Life Studies* (1959), and *For the Union Dead* (1964) are in a Hawthornesque fashion concerned with the burden of history, both public and private, and man's responsibility in the face of it. The two merge as part of the self. The poem *The Quaker Graveyard at Nantucket,* in *Lord Weary's Castle,* links the death of a cousin at sea to the death of a family, whether it is the fictional Kavanaughs or Lowell's own, which is portrayed in *Life Studies*. History—the Civil War—is the theme of *For the Union Dead.* Lowell knew, as all poets must know, that history, like the literature that renders it, is known and felt only in the present.

NORMAN HOLMES PEARSON, *Yale University*

Bibliography

Aldridge, A. Owen, *Early American Literature: A Comparatist Perspective* (Princeton Univ. Press 1982).

Baym, Max I., *A History of Literary Aesthetics in America* (Ungar 1973).

Bigsby, C. W., *A Critical Introduction to Twentieth Century American Drama: 1900–1940* (Cambridge 1982).

Blanck, Jacob, ed., *Bibliography of American Literature,* 7 vols. (Yale Univ. Press 1955–1973).

Brooks, Cleanth, and others, *American Literature: The Makers and the Making,* 4 vols. (St. Martin's 1974).

Chase, Richard, *The American Novel and Its Tradition* (1957; reprint, Gordian Press 1978).

Cowley, Malcolm, *Exile's Return,* rev. ed. (P. Smith 1983).

Cowley, Malcolm, *The Flower and the Leaf: A Contemporary Record of American Writing Since 1941,* ed. by Donald W. Faulkner (Viking 1985).

Cowley, Malcolm, *A Many-Windowed House* (Southern Ill. Univ. Press 1973).

Cunliffe, Marcus, ed., *American Literature to 1900* (Bedrick Bks. 1987).

Elliot, Emory, ed., *The Columbia Literary History of the United States* (Columbia Univ. Press 1988).

Feidelson, Charles, *Symbolism and American Literature* (Univ. of Chicago Press 1953).

Habegger, Alfred, *Gender, Fantasy and Realism in American Literature* (Columbia Univ. Press 1984).

Hart, James D., *Oxford Companion to American Literature* (Oxford 1986).

Howard, Leon, *Literature and the American Tradition* (1960; reprint, Gordian Press 1972).

Kaplan, Harold, *Democratic Humanism and American Literature* (Univ. of Chicago Press 1972).

Karl, Frederick R., *American Fictions 1940–1980* (Harper 1983).

Kartiganer, Donald M., and Griffith, Malcolm A., *Theories of American Literature* (Macmillan 1972).

Kazin, Alfred, *On Native Grounds: An Interpretation of Modern Prose Literature from 1890 to the Present,* rev. ed. (Harcourt 1983).

Lewis, Richard W. B., *The American Adam: Innocence, Tragedy and Tradition in the 19th Century* (Univ. of Chicago Press 1955).

Marx, Leo, *The Machine in the Garden: Technology and the Pastoral Idea in America* (Oxford 1967).

Matthiessen, Francis O., *American Renaissance* (Oxford 1941).

Miller, Perry G. E., *American Puritans: Their Prose and Poetry* (P. Smith 1959).

Miller, Perry G. E., *The New England Mind: From Colony to Province* (Beacon Press 1961).

Murdock, Kenneth B., *Literature and Theology in Colonial New England* (1949; reprint, Greenwood Press 1978).

Parrington, Vernon L., *Main Currents in American Thought,* 3 vols. (Harcourt 1955, 1963).

Pearce, Roy Harvey, *The Continuity of American Poetry* (Princeton Univ. Press 1961).

Perkins, David, *A History of Modern Poetry* (Harvard Univ. Press 1976).

Rexroth, Kenneth, *American Poetry in the Twentieth Century* (Seabury Press 1973).

Smith, Henry N., *Democracy and the Novel* (Oxford 1978).

Spiller, Robert E., *Milestones in American Literary History* (Greenwood Press 1977).

Spiller, Robert E., and others, eds., *Literary History of the United States,* rev. ed. (Macmillan 1974).

Wilson, Edmund, *The Shores of Light: A Literary Chronicle of the Twenties and Thirties* (Northeastern Univ. Press 1985).

AMERICAN MEDICAL ASSOCIATION, a federation of regional medical associations in the 50 states, the Commonwealth of Puerto Rico, and several territories under the jurisdiction of the United States. Founded in Philadelphia in 1847 by a group of 250 physicians "to promote the science and art of medicine and the betterment of public health," it is the largest and most active medical group in the world. In the mid-1970's the AMA had a membership of over 150,000—somewhat more than 40% of the nation's doctors of medicine. This enrollment represented a substantial decline, however, from the mid-1960's, when the organization had more than 200,000 members—about 70% of the doctors then practicing.

Scientific Programs. The AMA has a long and distinguished record of scientific achievement. Its scientific efforts have been numerous in the past and have continued to increase. The opening of the AMA's Institute for Biomedical Research in Chicago in 1965 marked a new departure—the association's initial effort to sponsor pure research to spur medical advances. The institute is devoted entirely to fundamental inquiry into life processes.

AMA activities cover all areas related to medicine and health care. The association early began to fight quackery, supporting in 1849 the establishment of a board "to analyze quack remedies and nostrums" and "to enlighten the public in regard to the nature and dangerous tendencies of such remedies." Since 1906 its Department of Investigation, which maintains the largest existent files on medical charlatans, has checked into fraudulent practices and provided regulatory bodies with evidence leading to conviction. Its Council on Drugs, formed in 1905, polices drug advertising and has helped establish testing procedures for new drugs and cosmetics.

Concerned over medical education, the AMA helped stimulate a housecleaning between 1905 and 1920 of "diploma mills," which awarded medical degrees for cash with little or no study. Since then, in conjunction with the Association of American Medical Colleges, it periodically inspects all medical schools. It also regularly checks on hospital internship programs and inspects and certifies schools in allied health professions, including institutions that train medical and X-ray technologists, physical and occupational therapists, and medical record librarians.

Many of the AMA's major contributions to the advancement of medicine have been made through its many scientific councils and committees, which gather and evaluate data on new findings and methods. Physicians from all over the United States serve on these bodies without pay. The AMA has councils on drugs, foods and nutrition, medical education, postgraduate education, mental health, national security, and occupational and rural health. There are committees on cutaneous health and cosmetics, medical aspects of automotive safety, rehabilitation, nursing, aging, nuclear medicine, alcoholism and addiction, and exercise and fitness.

More than 1,000 meetings are sponsored by the AMA each year. The two largest—the annual and clinical conventions in June and November—present some 400 scientific lectures and hundreds of exhibits, and serve as important postgraduate study sessions.

Washington Activities. The AMA maintains a Washington office where full-time lobbyists follow legislative action of interest to the medical profession. Over the years the AMA has recommended hundreds of constructive federal and state legislative proposals, including food, drug, and cosmetics laws, establishment of state boards of health, creation of the U. S. Public Health Service, and water pollution control.

For years, the AMA lobbied intensively (in the opinion of many, not always fairly) against health care for the aged under Social Security (Medicare). It asserted it was fighting the "invasion of the voluntary relationship between the patient and the physician." The AMA's losing battle over the Medicare issue was expensive both in money—about $7 million—and in a serious loss of prestige among much of the general public.

In the early 1970's the AMA lobbied intensively, again unsuccessfully, against a federal system of Professional Standards Review Organizations (PSROs). This system, popularly known as "peer review," involves the creation of boards of physicians to review, criticize, and if necessary penalize the medical care of beneficiaries of Medicare, Medicaid, and maternal and child-health programs. Once the system was enacted, however, the association officially cooperated in putting the peer-review program into effect, although this was done over the objections of many of its members.

The weekly *Journal of the AMA* (founded 1883) is the most widely distributed medical journal in the world. Other publications include monthly specialty journals in such areas as general psychiatry, dermatology, internal medicine, surgery, and diseases of children; *Today's Health,* a consumer magazine; numerous books, including a directory of all physicians in the United States; and *New Drugs,* an annual evaluative volume on new medications.

AMERICAN MISSIONARY ASSOCIATION, a nondenominational society that fosters improved human relations primarily by providing educational opportunities for minority peoples. It has founded 10 predominantly Negro colleges, six of which continue in close affiliation: Dillard University, New Orleans, La.; Fisk University, Nashville, Tenn.; Huston-Tillotson College, Austin, Texas; LeMoyne College, Memphis, Tenn.; Talladega College, Talladega, Ala.; and Tougaloo College, Tougaloo, Miss.

Born out of the Amistad Case, which sought and secured freedom for a group of Africans intended for slavery (see AMISTAD CASE), the American Missionary Association was incorporated in 1846. Initially interested in establishing missions throughout the world, it later turned to organizing primary and secondary schools in the southern United States. Most of the 500 schools that it founded were absorbed into the developing community public school systems.

The Association also has conducted programs for American Indians, Chinese, and migrant workers. In Puerto Rico it founded Ryder Memorial Hospital in 1914. Since 1962 the association has presented the Amistad Award in recognition of contributions to the betterment of human relations. National headquarters are in New York City.

WARREN MARR, II
American Missionary Association

The skeletons of extinct and modern mammals are among the permanent exhibitions on view at the American Museum of Natural History in New York City. Sometimes only partial skeletons survive, as in that of the huge *Indricotherium,* the largest known land mammal, whose skull is attached to an outline in steel that recreates the probable shape of the beast.

AMERICAN MUSEUM OF NATURAL HISTORY, in New York City, one of the world's preeminent science, research, and educational institutions, dedicated to the fields of natural science and anthropology. The museum occupies a four-block area of city-owned land on Central Park West, south of 81st Street. Founded in 1869, it is the world's largest natural-history museum. Its 23 buildings contain over 40 exhibition halls, more than 30 million scientific specimens and artifacts, numerous research laboratories and teaching facilities, the Western Hemisphere's largest natural-history library, and the Hayden Planetarium. The museumsponsors nearly 100 field studies and expeditions each year and is the research center for some of the country's most innovative scientists.

Exhibitions. Widely acknowledged to possess the world's most comprehensive and scientifically important collection of dinosaurs and other fossil vertebrates, the museum is creating six new halls in the 1990s to illustrate the history of vertebrate evolution. The halls are organized in the pattern of a giant family tree, based on the museum's scientific exploration of the evolutionary history and interrelationships of living things. The two halls of the Lila Acheson Wallace Wing of Mammals and Their Extinct Relatives, which opened in 1994, display the largest collection of fossil mammals in the world. Two dinosaur halls opened in 1995, and a hall of primitive vertebrates and an orientation center were scheduled for 1996.

The Hall of Human Biology and Evolution, which opened in 1993, traces human biology and anatomy, the complex pattern of human evolution, and the origins of creativity through fossil exhibits, life-size dioramas of early hominids, holographic models, and interactive multimedia technology. It is the only museum exhibition in the United States to examine in depth the mysteries of human evolution.

Since the early 1900s the museum has been famous for its mounted specimens of animals from around the world. The Hall of North American Mammals, the Akeley Memorial Hall of African Mammals, and the Frank M. Chapman Memorial Hall of North American Birds are especially well known for their spectacular dioramas portraying animals in their natural habitats. Other permanent halls include the Arthur Ross Hall of Meteorites, the Harry Frank Guggenheim Hall of Minerals, the Morgan Memorial Hall of Gems, the Hall of Ocean Life, the Hall of Reptiles and Amphibians, the Hall of African Peoples, the Margaret Mead Hall of Pacific Peoples, the Gardner D. Stout Hall of Asian Peoples, and the Hall of South American Peoples.

The Hayden Planetarium, opened in 1935, explores astronomy and discoveries in space. The 650-seat Sky Theater presents daily programs on space exploration and new technologies, using the Zeiss VI star projector and over 150 computer-controlled special-effects projectors. Visitors travel through the universe and learn about phenomena such as black holes and exploding stars.

Research. More than 200 scientists carry out research programs and produce scientific publications in the museum's nine scientific departments: anthropology, astronomy, mineral sciences, entomology, herpetology and ichthyology, invertebrates, mammalogy, ornithology, and vertebrate paleontology. Since 1887 the museum has sponsored more than 1,000 expeditions, sending scientists and explorers to every continent. Currently, some 100 field projects are conducted each year, including ongoing research programs in Chile, China, Cuba, French Guiana, Madagascar, Mongolia, and New Guinea. The museum also maintains three permanent field stations: Great Gull Island, N.Y.; St. Catherines Island, Ga.; and the Southwestern Research Station, in Arizona.

Since the museum's founding, its scientists have sought to identify and describe earth's life forms, an initiative of profound importance in light of current major losses of plant and animal species worldwide. The museum is working with the international research community to create a scientific framework for conserving and managing global biological resources.

In the state-of-the-art Molecular Systematics Laboratory, set up in 1990, museum scientists analyze the DNA of living and extinct creatures, gaining new insights into the evolution of life on earth. Discoveries have included DNA extracted and sequenced from a 25- to 40-million-year-old termite fossilized in amber.

Education. The museum's ongoing research provides the foundation for one of its other central missions, education. Its extensive educational programs seek to increase the public's understanding of current scientific theory and research, address issues affecting our daily lives and the future of the planet, and provide a forum for exploring the world's cultural diversity. In addition, the museum supports a number of publications, including *Natural History* magazine and the professional journals *Curator, Novitates, Anthropological Papers of the American Museum of Natural History,* and *Micropaleontology.*

AMERICAN MUSIC. See CANADA—*Music*; JAZZ; LATIN AMERICA—*Music and Dance;* MUSIC; MUSICAL THEATER; UNITED STATES—*Music;* and biographies of musicians and composers.

AMERICAN NATIONAL THEATRE AND ACADEMY,

an organization established to assist in the advancement of all phases of theater in the United States. Chartered on July 5, 1935, by an act of Congress, ANTA is an independent agency of the federal government, although no federal bureaus or government officials are involved in its operation. The only restrictions Congress placed on ANTA were that it should be nonprofit and nonsectarian and should have no honorary members.

Through its services department ANTA provides various types of assistance to community and educational theaters. It distributes materials on theater buildings and equipment, advises on the selection of theater sites and on staffing and fund raising, sends professional actors and directors to assist in local productions, provides job counseling, sends theatrical photographs of all types to schools and little theaters for exhibits or publications, and makes available its lists of play publishers, sources of special materials, and information on royalties. It publishes the quarterly *ANTA Newsletter* and pamphlets on subjects related to theater architecture.

ANTA is administered by an executive secretary in New York City and regional administrators in Arizona, Florida, and Minnesota. It owns and operates the ANTA Theatre, which formerly was the 52nd Street Theatre, in New York City.

WALTER ABEL, *ANTA*

AMERICAN NEWSPAPER GUILD, former name (1933–1972) of the Newspaper Guild, a labor organization of certain employees of some newspapers, wire news services, weekly magazines, and radio stations in the United States and Canada. Its purposes, as stated in its constitution, include advancing its members' economic interests, promoting unionism among employees of news media, working for honesty in news presentation, and raising standards of journalistic ethics. Headquartered in Washington, D.C., it was organized in 1933 by Heywood Broun, columnist and its first president, as a "guild" of newspaper editorial workers. Membership later was broadened to include business, advertising, and other employees and now stands at approximately 36,000.

EDWARD A. WALSH, *Fordham University*

AMERICAN NURSES ASSOCIATION, an organization of registered nurses, founded in 1896. It is concerned with economic security, pertinent legislation, professional standards, counseling, and placement for nurses. *The American Journal of Nursing* is published monthly. Membership exceeds 180,000.

AMERICAN PAINTING. See ABSTRACT ART; ABSTRACT EXPRESSIONISM; ART; CANADA—*Art and Architecture*; LATIN AMERICA—*Art and Architecture*; MODERN ART; PAINTING; UNITED STATES—*Art and Architecture*; and various biographies of American painters.

AMERICAN PARTY, the name of several political parties in United States history. The first established American party, which was also called the Know-Nothing party, was founded in New York City in 1849 as a secret patriotic organization under the name of the Order of the Star Spangled Banner. Its platform was inspired by the fear and resentment felt by native Protestants at the flood of Roman Catholic immigrants from Europe, and chiefly Ireland. Such immigrants, becoming naturalized citizens, were playing an increasingly important political role, especially in the large cities. (See KNOW-NOTHING MOVEMENT.)

Among other parties named American party was one organized in Philadelphia in 1887. At a convention in Washington, D.C., in 1888 it nominated James Curtis of New York for president. The party advocated 14-year residence for naturalization; exclusion of Socialists, anarchists, and other supposedly dangerous persons from entering the country; and a strong national defense. The party disappeared after polling only 1,591 votes in the November election.

In 1924 another American party, seeking Ku Klux Klan support, nominated Judge Gilbert Nations for president and polled 23,967 votes.

A party known as the American party—or as the American Independent party in some states—ran ex-Gov. George Wallace of Alabama for president in 1968. The party polled 10 million votes, or 13.5% of the total national vote, the highest percentage for a third party since 1924. Wallace, nominally a Democrat, ran a "law and order" campaign and criticized both major parties as too liberal. In 1972, with Rep. John Schmitz (R-Calif.) heading the ticket, the party received 1,080,670 votes. The remnants of the Wallace movement split in 1976; Lester Maddox (American Independent) and Thomas Anderson (American) polled 170,000 and 160,000 votes.

AMERICAN PHILOSOPHICAL ASSOCIATION (APA), a professional organization that exists to promote scholarly and creative work in philosophy, to support the teaching of philosophy, and to represent philosophy as a discipline. Since 1975 the association has been headquartered at the University of Delaware in Newark, Del.

The APA traces its origins to the founding, in the Midwest in 1900, of the Western Philosophical Association, followed by the founding, in the East, of the American Philosophical Association in 1901. These two organizations joined with the newly formed Pacific Philosophical Association in 1927 to form the national association now known as the American Philosophical Association. The original associations remain in existence as the APA's Central, Eastern, and Pacific divisions. Each sponsors an annual meeting at which philosophers exchange ideas and conduct business.

The APA maintains a site on the Internet and publishes three periodicals, *Proceedings and Addresses of the American Philosophical Association, APA Newsletters,* and *Jobs for Philosophers.* It also publishes *Guide to Graduate Programs in Philosophy, Guidebook for Publishing Philosophy,* and other pamphlets relating to aspects of research and teaching in philosophy.

AMERICAN PHILOSOPHICAL SOCIETY, the oldest existing learned society in the United States. The original society was founded in Philadelphia in 1743 by Benjamin Franklin "for the promotion of useful knowledge among the British plantations in America." In 1769 it was combined with the American Society, a successor of Franklin's Junto of 1727. The American Philosophical Society was modeled on the Royal Society of London (1660), of which Franklin became a fellow in 1756 and from which he received the Copley Medal for his discoveries in electricity. (See FRANKLIN, BENJAMIN; JUNTO CLUB; ROYAL SOCIETY.)

The society's members are elected on the basis of distinguished contributions to learning and public affairs. The membership is classified into five groups: mathematical and physical sciences, biological sciences, social sciences, humanities, and arts, professions, and leaders in public and private affairs. In 2000, there were 712 resident and 141 foreign members. Two general meetings of the society are held each year, in April and November; special meetings are held at other times.

The society occupies two buildings in Independence National Historical Park, Philadelphia: Philosophical Hall, erected 1787–1789, and the Library, a modern replica of the original home of the Library Company of Philadelphia (1798). The society's archives are especially rich in letters and manuscripts dealing with early colonial history and the beginnings of the American government. The library specializes in the history of American science, technology, and culture; Native American linguistics; and the publications of learned societies. Its rich manuscript collections include the papers of Franklin, Meriwether Lewis and William Clark, Charles W. Peale, and Benjamin Vaughan. Holdings include some 300,000 books and bound periodicals as well as archival materials, papers, and audio files.

The regular publications of the society began in 1769 with the *Transactions*. The first six volumes, in small quarto, constituting the first series (1771–1808), include many articles by Franklin, David Rittenhouse, Thomas Jefferson, Francis Hopkinson, Benjamin Rush, William Barton, John Morgan, and Joseph Priestley. The *Transactions* is now a monograph series, of which six volumes appear annually. The *Proceedings* began publication in 1838 and is now a quarterly journal drawing chiefly on papers presented at the society's biannual meetings. The *Memoirs*, first issued in 1935, presents scholarly studies in various disciplines. The society's activities are summarized annually in its *Year Book*.

The society administers a grant program, primarily in the form of grants in aid of research. By far the largest of the funds supporting this aspect of the society's work came as a bequest from R. A. F. Penrose, Jr., in 1931.

GEORGE W. CORNER*
American Philosophical Society

AMERICAN POLITICAL SCIENCE ASSOCIATION, an

organization that encourages the impartial study and development of government. Founded in 1903, the association has a membership of some 12,000, consisting mostly of teachers of political science in colleges and universities, public officials, and researchers. The association develops educational programs for political scientists as well as others and also works to improve the average citizen's knowledge of public affairs and participation in government.

The association serves as a clearinghouse for teaching and research positions. Its Congressional Fellowship Program enables qualified persons to study with members of Congress. The *American Political Science Review* is published quarterly. The association's headquarters are at 1527 New Hampshire Avenue, NW, Washington, D.C. 20036.

AMERICAN PROTECTIVE ASSOCIATION, an anti-

Catholic political lobby whose chief aim was to restrict immigration of Roman Catholics into the United States. It was founded as a secret society at Clinton, Iowa, in 1887, and rapidly revived the campaign of the Know-Nothing party against the growing influence of Roman Catholics in schools and other public institutions. The association's expressed program was to combat the following alleged conditions: widespread violation of the spirit of the Constitution by public officials; political corruption that resulted from voting by recent immigrants; Roman Catholic attacks on the public school system; and an increase in untaxed church property.

The APA grew slowly in the Middle West until the panic of 1893 bred a spirit of xenophobia among native Americans caught in economic rivalry with immigrants and their American-born children. Coincidentally there was a revival of Roman Catholic demands for a share of public school funds to apply to their parochial schools.

These factors contributed to a large increase of membership. Many local Republican organizations controlled by the APA carried elections throughout the Middle West. By 1896, according to APA claims, the membership numbered 2,500,000 and the association controlled 4,000,000 votes. However, that year saw the beginning of its rapid decline, as members deserted to take sides in the Bryan-McKinley campaign. Moribund after the turn of the century, it ceased activities in 1911.

AMERICAN PSYCHOLOGICAL ASSOCIATION, a soci-

ety of psychologists organized to advance psychology as a science, a profession, and a means of promoting human welfare. The world's largest psychological organization, it has more than 159,000 members and affiliates.

The American Psychological Association (APA) aids in the preparation of various publications to inform the general public about the work of psychologists, while an annual *Biographical Directory* provides information about the location, training, and professional specialties of the association's members. Headquartered in Washington, D.C., the APA was founded in 1892 and incorporated in 1925.

AMERICAN REPUBLICAN PARTY, a splinter politi-

cal party that was founded in New York state in 1843. The party's principal aim was to deny the franchise and political offices to Roman Catholics and foreigners. The organization of the party was part of a widespread reaction to the tide of immigrants arriving from Ireland and other Catholic countries of Europe in the 1830s and 1840s.

In the election of 1844 the party formed a local coalition with the Whigs and elected the mayor of New York City and four members of Congress. Strengthened by this success, the party joined with the Native American party of Louisiana and native Protestant Americans elsewhere in calling a national convention at Philadelphia in 1845. Delegates to the convention adopted the name *Native American party* and called for sweeping changes in U.S. immigration laws. However, the fact that the Native American party took no position on the war with Mexico and other issues contributed to its rapid demise. Native Americanism soon reappeared in the American party of the 1850s. (See AMERICAN PARTY.)

After news of the adoption of the Declaration of Independence reached New York, joyous patriots pulled down the statue of George III, which stood on Bowling Green.

The AMERICAN REVOLUTION

AMERICAN REVOLUTION, a conflict between Britain and 13 of its colonies on the Atlantic coast of North America. It is also called the *American War of Independence* and the *Revolutionary War.*

During the course of the American Revolution the Thirteen Colonies declared their independence from the mother country and concluded an alliance with France. As a result of their victory in the fighting that followed, the United States of America came into being. With the Declaration of Independence, the Thirteen Colonies became the states of New Hampshire, Massachusetts, Rhode Island, Connecticut, New York, New Jersey, Pennsylvania, Delaware, Maryland, Virginia, North Carolina, South Carolina, and Georgia.

The war began near Boston, Mass., in 1775 and ended formally in 1783 with a peace treaty signed in Paris. Most of the fighting had ended two years earlier, at Yorktown, Va.

This article is divided into four principal sections: (1) Origins of the American Revolution; (2) Military Campaigns; (3) Political, Social, and Economic Developments; and (4) Diplomatic Developments.

1. Origins of the American Revolution

Had Britain followed the lenient pattern of colonial administration developed in the late 17th and early 18th centuries, the American Revolution might well have been avoided. Under different historical circumstances the Thirteen Colonies might have achieved independent status through an evolutionary process, as did other members of the British Empire.

Rapidly expanding in wealth and numbers, developing a cultural identity differentiating them from Englishmen, and possessing a complex and sophisticated political life of their own, the Americans were certain to resist growing control from London. That they did resist, and finally rebel, indicates a profound change in British colonial policy after 1763. It is, however, impossible properly to understand the American Revolution apart from the 150 years of colonial history preceding it.

Old Colonial System. The British colonial effort in the 16th and 17th centuries shared certain basic concepts with the policies of France, Spain, and other European powers. Colonial interests were subordinate to those of the mother country, which regarded the colonies as sources of raw materials and as markets for manufactured goods. The British made little attempt to systematize those mercantilistic principles, designed to strengthen the mother country and render it economically independent of other nations, until after the restoration of the Stuart dynasty in 1660. In that year and in 1673 and 1696, Parliament passed the Navigation Acts. These acts reserved the whole trade of the colonies to ships of English or colonial construction, provided that trade in certain colonial "enumerated articles" be confined to the empire, and required that all European products destined for the colonies be brought to England before being shipped across the Atlantic.

A series of Acts of Trade passed in the 17th and 18th centuries were designed to prevent colonial competition with home industries and to reward with bounties the production of needed articles. The Acts of Trade and Navigation were the heart of the Old Colonial System (1660–1763), which envisioned the colonies as part of a great economic, not a political, unit.

The Revolution has been seen by some historians as a movement by the colonists to throw off the shackles of an unfair and oppressive system, stultifying to the economic development of the colonies. It has been held that the Revolution was the inevitable result of one capitalistic economy attempting to impose its interests on another. But modern scholarship indicates rather that the colonists prospered under the Old Colonial System. Although there are instances of enmity toward the [...] of Trade and Navigation, the system [...]ked to the benefit of both Englan[...]

A major r[...] [...]ial opposition to merc[...] [...]onomic benefits it a[...] [...]which the acts w[...] [...] competent bo[...] [...]ority to make an[...] [...]ed prior to the [...] [...]54–1763). Royal [...] [...]lly custom collec[...] [...]ercion, and they[...] [...]orrupt. Evasio[...] [...]and smuggling be[...] [...]n the colonies. [...] [...]l administration [...] [...] neglect," in the [...] [...]e was little serious [...] [...]er 1763, attempted [...] [...] machinery for ad[...] [...]ment, the colonists

[...]nd. The British government [...] of the American possessions a[...] [...]unit. Prior to 1763 the colonies wer[...] [...] the king's possessions, with Parliament exer[...]ng little control over them other than to regulate their trade. Basically, the Thirteen Colonies were of three types: (1) royal colonies, under the direct control of the crown; (2) proprietary colonies, under the control of a proprietor or proprietors, to whom the king granted land and political authority; and (3) "corporate" colonies, founded by various groups in conjunction with trading companies to which the king granted a charter.

The degree of political autonomy exercised through local representative bodies varied with the circumstances under which the colonies were founded. From 1660 and after the accession of William and Mary in 1689, the crown pursued a sporadic policy of royalization and centralization. By 1763, only Connecticut and Rhode Island retained their original corporate status. All of the other thirteen colonies except Pennsylvania and Maryland, which remained proprietary, had become royal colonies. This increase in direct crown control would appear to indicate a growth in royal power; but it was paralleled by the development and rise to power of the lower house of assembly in the royal and proprietary colonies.

The political history of the American colonies in the 18th century centers largely on the struggle for power between royal authority, represented by the royal governors, and the elected representatives of the colonists in their lower houses of assembly. The three branches of colonial government roughly resembled those of England: the royal governors represented the king, the councils occupied the place of the House of Lords, and the elected assemblies that of the House of Commons.

The royal governors possessed extensive powers, at least in theory. They were the chief executives and military commanders of the colonies; they possessed vetoes over all legislation passed by the assemblies, and with the councils, or upper houses, they were the supreme courts of appeal within the colonies. They could summon, prorogue, and dismiss the assemblies. The colonial assemblies viewed their struggle for power with the governors as similar to the long battle for supremacy between king and Parliament in England.

Gradually the assemblies claimed and won extensive power and privileges—or "rights," as the colonists called them. Most important, they came to possess the right to levy taxes and to grant supplies. In several royal colonies, the governors had to rely for their income on temporary grants from the assemblies. The assemblies further used their control over the purse to assume certain executive functions, stipulating how appropriations were to be spent and appointing committees to supervise expenditures.

The colonists accepted parliamentary taxation that had the purpose of regulating trade. But Parliament had never taxed the colonies for revenue; Americans certainly would have regarded such a practice as a dangerous and even unconstitutional innovation threatening their self-government. The power of taxation was indispensable to the assemblies' domination of the governors, and the colonists jealously regarded that power as the constitutional right of their elected representatives. Although acts of assembly were subject to review and veto by the Privy Council in London, the Americans believed that their representatives should decide domestic questions.

In fact, two conceptions of the constitution of the empire were developing in the 18th century. From the British point of view, king and Parliament wielded the same powers in America that they did in London. The colonial elective bodies were regarded as derivative, functioning only because they were permitted to do so. To the great majority of Englishmen, Parliament's authority was supreme, and its sovereign power extended over the colonies as well as England. The Americans, on the other hand, considered their elective assemblies to be, in essence, little parliaments—the supreme legislative power in

PATRICK HENRY MEMORIAL FOUNDATION

MUSEUM OF FINE ARTS, BOSTON

Two early leaders in the American struggle for independence. (*Left*) Patrick Henry denounces the Stamp Act before the Virginia House of Burgesses in 1765. "If this be treason, make the most of it," he declares. (*Above*) Samuel Adams, the fiery publicist of the Revolution, points to the Massachusetts charter in this painting by Copley.

domestic matters for the colonies. The tendency of their political thought was toward a conception of the empire as a federation, with one king and many parliaments.

Maintenance of the Army. Antagonism arose between the colonists and Britain during and after the French and Indian War. More properly called the Great War for Empire, this conflict was the culmination of a long struggle between England and France for hegemony in the New World. England emerged victorious, but with a heavy national debt and the immensely difficult prospect of administering vast territorial additions to the empire.

During the war the Americans had continued to trade with the French West Indies despite British efforts to prevent it. Colonial jealousy and disunity had hampered the war effort. After the war, England could reform and enforce her neglected colonial system; but the colonies, fearing the French no longer, felt less dependent on the mother country. From the English point of view, the imperial policy after 1763 was by no means designed to destroy colonial "rights and liberties," but to protect and govern an augmented empire, and to tighten a dangerously lax colonial system. The colonies, however, had passed the point where they would submit to an increase in subordination to king and Parliament.

In the early months of 1763 the ministry headed by John Stuart, 3d earl of Bute, decided that a standing army of 6,000 men should be maintained in North America to police the newly acquired lands between the Appalachians and the Mississippi; to defend them against the French, Spanish, and Indians; and to prevent clashes between the British colonists and the former enemies. The colonists, who were not asked

whether they desired the army, were naturally suspicious. Sharing the traditional Whig fear of a standing army and desiring expansion into the new territories, they could not but regard the English army as a threat to American interests.

The Bute ministry also decided that the colonists must help support the new army at an estimated cost of £350,000 a year. Since the British national debt and taxes were high, and the army was stationed in America ostensibly to protect the colonials, the Bute ministry saw no reason why the colonials should not contribute a fair share to the administration of imperial interests. But to the Americans, "imperial" interests did not coincide with their own.

Parliamentary Acts. In April 1763 a new ministry headed by George Grenville came into power and pushed through Parliament a series of measures that brought on a crisis in relations with the American colonies. That year a serious Indian uprising, known as Pontiac's Conspiracy, ravaged the English outposts in the west. To pacify the Indians, the British government issued on Oct. 7, 1763, a proclamation forbidding colonial settlement beyond the Allegheny Mountains. American pioneers and land speculators, temporarily checked by this and later measures restricting westward expansion, chafed under what they regarded as an unfair and oppressive policy.

The Currency Act of 1764 forbade the issuance of legal-tender paper money by the colonial assemblies. Lacking hard money, the colonists concluded that the measure would seriously harm their economy while benefiting English merchants who desired payment of debts in sterling. The controversy over paper currency was of long standing, going back to the 1730's in Massachusetts and the 1740's in Virginia.

In April 1764, Parliament passed the Sugar Act, imposing new restrictions on colonial trade and levying a three-penny-per-gallon duty upon molasses imported from the West Indies. Although formally a revision in the regulations of trade, the act was designed to raise revenue. Grenville also secured passage of a resolution stating that it might be necessary to levy certain stamp duties in the colonies. To ensure enforcement of this legislation, admiralty courts in the colonies, functioning without juries, were given jurisdiction over the Acts of Trade. This extended the courts' authority and further limited the cherished right of trial by jury.

In 1765 came the Quartering Act, a measure requiring the colonists to supply quarter and supplies to British troops stationed in settled parts of the colonies.

The Stamp Act Crisis. In the spring of 1765, Parliament passed the famous Stamp Act, which required the colonists to purchase stamps for newspapers, playing cards, dice, marriage licenses, and many other legal documents. Virtually every segment of the American population would be affected by this direct tax. The revenue obtained from the molasses and stamp duties was to be used to pay part of the expenses of maintaining British troops in America.

News of the passage of the Stamp Act provoked protest and open resistance throughout the American colonies. The colonists saw in the Stamp Act and the other measures of the Bute and Grenville ministries a pattern of tyranny. Following the lead of Patrick Henry and the Virginia House of Burgesses, they denounced the tax as unconstitutional, and asserted they could be taxed only by their own elected representatives. Mobs, calling themselves Sons of Liberty, threatened the stamp distributors, destroyed their property, and forced them to resign. No stamps were sold in the Thirteen Colonies except for Georgia, where they were soon removed from circulation.

Through their colonial assemblies and the Stamp Act Congress, which met in New York in October 1765, the Americans demanded repeal of the Stamp Act. Associations were formed to enforce a general boycott of British goods, and economic retaliation proved more effective than petitions and remonstrances. As British merchants and manufacturers began to suffer, they joined the Americans in opposition to the tax. In March 1766, a new ministry headed by the 2d marquis of Rockingham repealed the Stamp Act, but simultaneously Parliament rejected the American principle of "no taxation without representation." The Declaratory Act asserted that Parliamentary authority extended over the colonies "in all cases whatsoever."

Growing Resistance. The repeal of the Stamp Act was greeted with joy in America, and the colonists resumed their purchase of British goods. But in 1767 the Americans were again confronted with a Parliamentary tax for revenue. Since neither the colonial assemblies nor the Stamp Act Congress had clearly denounced the Sugar Act as unconstitutional, Charles Townshend, chancellor of the exchequer, mistakenly assumed that the colonists rejected only "internal" taxation, and would not object to an "external" import duty for revenue.

In the spring of 1767, Townshend steered through Parliament a series of duties on lead, tea, painter's colors, and various kinds of paper imported into the colonies. The Townshend Act provided that a large part of the funds received was to be used to pay salaries of royal governors and other royal officials in America, thus rendering them independent of the colonial assemblies.

Further reforms in the apparatus for enforcing the Acts of Trade and Navigation achieved the following: (1) the granting of specific legal authority to writs of assistance, or general search warrants; (2) the creation of a Board of Customs Commissioners to sit in Boston and supervise the American service; and (3) the suspension of the legislative "privileges" of the New York Assembly until it complied with the provisions of the Quartering Act of 1765.

The Townshend duties and the other parliamentary measures of 1767–1768 pushed the colo-

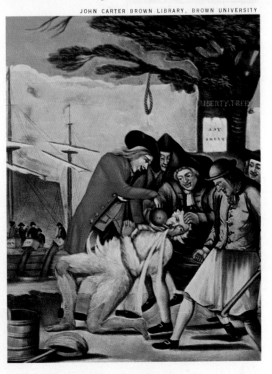

"Paying the Exciseman" depicts patriots forcing a tarred-and-feathered tax agent to toast royal family in tea.

JOHN CARTER BROWN LIBRARY, BROWN UNIVERSITY

Cartoon of the separated serpent, exhorting the colonies to unite, appeared in several versions. This one is by Benjamin Franklin.

LIBRARY OF CONGRESS

THE BETTMANN ARCHIVE

NATIONAL PARK SERVICE

(Above) Patriots in Indian dress dump 342 chests of tea into Boston Harbor during the famous Boston Tea Party on Dec. 16, 1773, to protest new British law. (Left) Years earlier, passage of the Stamp Act prompted this newspaper cartoon.

nists to a further repudiation of parliamentary authority. In his *Letters from a Farmer in Pennsylvania* (1768), John Dickinson contended that all revenue taxes on the colonists were unconstitutional, whether "external" or "internal," and the colonists generally followed his lead. The Board of Customs Commissioners, often involved in "customs racketeering," infuriated New Englanders. The act suspending the New York Assembly and the scheme to pay royal officials from the Townshend duties further convinced Americans that the right to govern themselves through representatives of their own choosing was in grave danger.

Although American resistance was not so uniform as in 1765, nonimportation and nonconsumption associations again were formed. The economic boycott led British merchants and manufacturers to request repeal of the duties.

In the spring of 1768, Governor Francis Bernard of Massachusetts and the Board of Customs Commissioners informed the British ministry that it was impossible to enforce trade regulations without the presence of British troops. Accordingly, Maj. Gen. Thomas Gage, commander in chief of the British forces in America, was ordered to dispatch at least one regiment of troops to Boston. On June 10, John Hancock's sloop *Liberty* was seized for alleged violation of the

trade acts. Three days later, the customs commissioners fled before enraged Bostonians and took refuge on board the British warship *Romney*. The British cabinet then ordered to Boston two regiments from Ireland. By the spring of 1769, four regiments were in the city. In May, Gage was authorized to withdraw the troops from Boston, but at the request of royal officials he retained two regiments.

The Bostonians had expected that all troops would be withdrawn, and trouble between civilians and soldiers increased. On March 5, 1770, a mob converged on the hated Customs House, cursing and threatening the lone sentry. Pleas for help brought Capt. Thomas Preston and a file of troops to the rescue. When the mob became violent, the troops opened fire, killing five persons and wounding several others in what became known as the Boston Massacre. Threatened by a general uprising in the wake of the incident, the Massachusetts Council arranged for the withdrawal of the troops from the city.

Under pressure from the colonial boycott and British merchants, Lord North, head of a new ministry, moved on March 5 for repeal of the Townshend duties except for the tax on tea. Parliament acquiesced. Between 1770 and 1773, the duty on tea caused little ill feeling, for the colonists bought smuggled Dutch tea that was much cheaper than English tea. The boycott on English tea was continued, but the partial repeal of duties was followed by a gradual relaxation of the nonimportation associations. The period of calm was deceptive, however. The Americans were now extremely sensitive to any exertion of British authority, and they had grown accustomed to violent resistance.

Boston Tea Party. In 1773, Lord North revived the unsettled issue of parliamentary taxation for revenue. The British East India Company, in serious financial trouble, had 17 million pounds

British troops debark on Boston's Long Wharf in 1768, as shown in this engraving by Paul Revere. Presence of the redcoats in the cities aroused colonists' ire.

The Boston Massacre, of March 5, 1770, shown in this Paul Revere engraving, climaxed a series of clashes between townsfolk and British troops. Five Americans were killed and several were wounded by gunfire during the incident in front of the Customs House.

719

of tea in its warehouses. Under North's leadership Parliament passed the Tea Act, which relieved the company of heavy duties on the tea it brought to England and enabled it to establish direct sale of the tea in America, thus undercutting American importers. The East India Company could now undersell even smuggled tea.

In the fall of 1773 the company sent several consignments of tea to America. There was little doubt that if the tea should be offered for purchase at the low price, it would be bought. But purchase of the tea would mean paying the Townshend revenue duty, and the colonial case against such taxation would be lost. The resistance leaders of 1765 and 1767, supported by the American merchants, were determined to prevent the sale of the tea. In most instances the colonists simply turned back ships carrying consignments of the tea, but in Boston it appeared that customs officials would attempt to sell some of the cargo. On the night of Dec. 16, 1773, townsmen disguised as Indians rowed out to three ships in Boston harbor and dumped the tea into the bay.

The Boston Tea Party provoked a strong reaction in London. Faced by united colonial resistance, George III and the British Parliament had twice retreated. Now they chose to stand firm, to force the colonists to obedience. The result was the passage of the Coercive (Intolerable) Acts of 1774, which closed the port of Boston and increased royal control of the government of Massachusetts. Also included in the Coercive Acts were a new Quartering Act and the Quebec Act, which extended the boundaries of that province into areas claimed by Virginia and Pennsylvania.

First Continental Congress. General Gage was sent to Massachusetts as military governor to enforce the new laws. Massachusetts refused to yield, and the other American colonies rallied to support the Bostonians. While Gage was gathering his troops in Boston and requesting instructions from London, colonial committees of correspondence decided to convene a Continental Congress in Philadelphia in September 1774. Meanwhile, extralegal conventions began to replace royal government and to assume political control in the colonies.

Delegates from all of the colonies except Georgia attended the First Continental Congress, which sat from September 5 to October 26. A redress of grievances, not independence, was the acknowledged objective. But militant leaders such as Samuel Adams and John Adams of Massachusetts and Richard Henry Lee of Virginia led the congress to reject a plan for conciliation offered by Joseph Galloway of Pennsylvania. Instead, the congress demanded repeal of all objectionable laws passed since 1763. It also provided for a Continental Association, which was to enforce a new boycott of British goods. Provision was made for another meeting by May 1775 if England did not meet the demands.

Lexington and Concord. In the early months of 1775, George III, supported by a majority in Parliament, decided to use military force to assert British sovereignty. At the same time that Lord North offered his Conciliatory Resolution, Gage was ordered to move decisively against the rebels. Accordingly he sent out troops to destroy military stores gathered by the Massachusetts patriots at Concord.

At Lexington, on April 19, 1775, British redcoats clashed with Massachusetts militia. Eight

The Battle of Lexington, from an engraving by Amos Doolittle. Minutemen fall back as British troops fire a volley that kills eight patriots and launches the war.

In the Battle of Bunker Hill, June 17, 1775, British redcoats move up heights on Charlestown peninsula (*right*) as Charlestown burns from naval bombardment.

Americans were killed and ten wounded. After marching to Concord and destroying such stores as they could find, the British returned to Boston under the harassing musket fire of thousands of enraged farmers. More than 15,000 aroused New Englanders besieged Boston. The War of Independence had begun.

Bibliography

Bailyn, Bernard, *The Ideological Origins of the American Revolution* (Harvard Univ. Press 1967).

Bridenbaugh, Carl, *The Spirit of Seventy-Six: The Growth of American Patriotism Before Independence* (Oxford 1975).

Ernst, Joseph A., *Money and Politics in America, 1755–1775: A Study in the Currency Act of 1764 and the Political Economy of Revolution* (Univ. of N. C. Press 1973).

Gipson, Lawrence H., *The British Empire Before the American Revolution,* 15 vols. (Knopf 1936–1970).

Greene, Jack P., and others, *Society, Freedom, and Conscience: The Coming of the Revolution in Virginia, Massachusetts, and New York* (Norton 1977).

Hoffer, Peter C., ed., *A Nation in the Womb of Time: Selected Articles on the Long-Term Causes of the American Revolution* (Garland 1987).

Jones, Alice H., *Wealth of a Nation to Be: The American Colonies on the Eve of the Revolution* (Columbia Univ. Press 1980).

Maier, Pauline, *From Resistance to Revolution: Colonial Radicals and the Development of American Opposition to Britain, 1765–1776* (Knopf 1972).

Martin, James K., *Rebellion: Higher Governmental Leaders and the Coming of the American Revolution* (Free Press 1976).

Morris, Richard B., *Seven Who Shaped Our Destiny: The Founding Fathers as Revolutionaries* (Harper 1973).

Nash, Gary B., *The Urban Crucible: The Northern Seaports and the Origins of the American Revolution* (Harvard Univ. Press 1986).

Schlesinger, Arthur M., *The Birth of the Nation: A Portrait of the American People on the Eve of Independence* (Houghton 1981).

Tyler, John W., *Smugglers and Patriots: Boston Merchants and the Advent of the American Revolution* (New England Univ. Press 1986).

2. Military Campaigns

The defeat of Great Britain in the American Revolution has puzzled many students of the conflict who have perhaps made too much of British strength and American weakness. Britain certainly had greater material resources than the Thirteen Colonies: a much larger population, a professional army, and an overwhelmingly superior navy. British weaknesses, however, largely offset these advantages. The prosecution of war against a people 3,000 miles (about 4,800 km) across the Atlantic Ocean posed baffling problems in transportation, communication, and strategy. The British army in America was never large enough to overwhelm and occupy the colonies, nor were there strategic centers in America which, if captured, would ensure victory. The rough, hilly, and remote spaces of North America made the traditional style of European warfare impractical.

The Americans were used to arms, and were tough-fibered mentally and physically. Although they were obliged to build a military force during the war, their incentive to win was greater than that of their opponents. Many Americans were either neutral or loyal to Britain during the conflict. Probably half the population was Patriot, however, and that half was more militant and better organized than the Loyalist (Tory) element. Even without foreign aid, the Patriots would not have been easily conquered.

THE FORCES

The American Army. The core of the American military force was the Continental, or regular, Army. Created by the Continental Congress, the regular Army, through experience and much hard work by Washington and his fellow officers,

Brandishing his sword, Ethan Allen (*at head of stairway*) surprises British commander of Fort Ticonderoga as patriots capture the post in May 1775. (*Right*) A private of the 3d Yorkers ("Ulster Regiment"), part of attacking force.

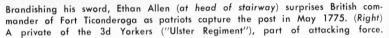

The American "Kentucky," or "Pennsylvania," rifle was accurate at long range.

gradually acquired the character of a trained professional military force.

The original army, composed of the "embattled farmers" who surrounded Boston after the Battle of Lexington (1775), enlisted for a one-year term. Thereafter the ranks were filled by voluntary enlistment according to quotas apportioned among the states by Congress. Although provision was made in November 1776 for three-year enlistments, most Patriots continued to prefer short-term enlistments, often for only three months.

The number of regulars who served during the war is uncertain. Estimates of total enlistments in the Continental Army and state militias vary from 184,000 to 396,000. Many enlisted two, three, or more times. Probably about 100,-000 actually bore arms under repeated enlistments; perhaps half this number served in the regular army. In August 1776, Washington had about 20,000 men, the largest and rawest American force of the war. At Valley Forge, his forces had dwindled to a pitiful 4,000. After 1778, the Americans were fortunate to have 10,000 long-term regulars on all fronts.

Colonial Militia and Other Forces. Supplementing the regular army were the state militia, composed of all able-bodied men between the ages of 16 and 60. Mustered, organized, and directed by the states, the militia were called out on special occasions, served for short terms, and were usually employed for action within a specific state. Washington and other officers, however, could and did call upon state militia for service in conjunction with the Continental Army. Lacking training and discipline, the militia were often untrustworthy soldiers, but on occasion they fought well, and were an indispensable part of the American military force.

Other Americans served in the small Continental Navy and Marine Corps, or as irregulars and guerrillas with such leaders as Ethan Allen of Vermont and Francis Marion of South Carolina. Scores of foreigners, especially Frenchmen, offered their services to the Patriots. Some were particularly helpful in training the raw American recruits.

The Officer Corps. The appointment of officers in the Continental Army was divided between Congress and the colony-states. Colonels and officers of lesser rank were chosen by the colonies, higher officers by Congress. In quality and experience, the officers of the Continental Army were a mixed lot. A few, such as Washington, Charles Lee, and Richard Montgomery had served in the British Army; the majority had only militia experience. Among the latter were, however, men of ability, such as John Thomas of Massachusetts and Nathanael Greene of Rhode Island, both of whom were appointed brigadier generals.

Provincial jealousy and ideas of prestige overshadowed merit in the choice of some officers, but the appointment of Washington as commander in chief was a wise one. Experienced, respected, and absolutely dedicated, he was by far the best man for a terribly difficult job. He brought to his command qualities of leadership that set him apart from the other commanders of the American Revolution. Other American officers rivaled Washington in some respects: Benedict Arnold and Montgomery in boldness

Sentinels stand guard around British army camp during the Revolution. Soldiers' laundry is draped over tents for drying. (*Left*) A private of Britain's 26th Regiment, wearing drill-order summer dress. Regiment was also known as "The Scots."

The famed British "Brown Bess" musket, named for its brown oxidized barrel.

and courage in the field; Nathanael Greene in execution of strategy; the eccentric Charles Lee in experience. It is difficult to imagine any one of them shouldering the immense and varied burdens of Washington with as much success.

The Private Soldier. Victory ultimately depended upon the fighting ability of the rank and file. The American soldier was not a professional. He was a farmer, frontiersman, or town dweller, but he proved to be a match for his adversary. Many were used to rough living. They were familiar with firearms and were, on the whole, better shots than the British.

Patriot morale rose and fell with the fortunes of war. Not all Americans shared Washington's indomitable spirit, but their tenacious will to win, spurred by the probable consequences of defeat, was generally greater than that of the British.

Discipline in the American Army was a constant and difficult problem. The lack of a military tradition, and a spirit of equality and independence, especially among the New Englanders, militated against regimentation.

Supplies, Pay, and Weapons. The American soldier was generally ill fed, badly clothed, lacking in arms and sufficient ammunition, and poorly paid. His uniform was usually whatever could be obtained, and ranged from the red garb of the Maryland line to the linen shirts and leather breeches of the frontier riflemen. Privates received $6.67 per month, of which $1.67 was withdrawn to pay for clothing. Wages for officers ranged from $18 per month for lieutenants to $166 for major generals. Pay was usually in Continental paper money and was undependable.

Both officers and men suffered from depreciating currency and high prices.

The scarcity of war materiel was often acute. The Americans built factories to manufacture gunpowder, small arms, and cannon, and imported large quantities of supplies from Europe. Most of their arms and munitions were captured from the invaders. The principal weapon was the small-bore musket, but frontiersmen from Virginia, Pennsylvania, and Maryland were equipped with a far more accurate weapon—the Pennsylvania rifle.

Tactics. American tactics, influenced by the tradition of Indian fighting, were less conventional than European linear tactics, in which troops were marched into the field in columns and deployed in three lines that delivered successive volleys. Emphasizing the loose skirmish line and individual marksmanship, the American army lacked the stability and cohesiveness of the British but was more flexible and adaptable.

The British Army. Before the Battle of Lexington, there were about 8,500 British regulars in America, most of them at Quebec and Montreal and in posts along the Atlantic coast. The 32,000 troops under Gen. William Howe in the summer of 1776 were the largest single British force during the war. The British probably had no more than 42,000 effectives available in North America at any time during the war.

The Private Soldier. The British regulars served largely in infantry, cavalry, and artillery regiments of the line, generally for the duration of the war. Voluntary enlistment prevailed before May 1778; after that date impressment laws were passed to fill the ranks. Common soldiers were

Unlikely prospects straggle after a recruiting sergeant in this British caricature
that appeared about 1780. *(Right)* Pennsylvania Loyalist battalion advertises
for "heroes" to fight the Americans, offering 50 acres of land as a reward.

drawn from vagabonds, convicts, and unemployables. *Esprit de corps* was rare except in picked regiments. But the redcoats were far more professional than their American counterparts. They were held under harsh discipline and were trained to obey orders and fight as a unit. Many were able fighting men, dedicated to the army.

The Officer Corps. Officers, especially among the higher echelons, often were mediocre or poor in quality. Social position and political influence, rather than merit, were the primary requisites for high command. Officers' commissions were usually purchased; consequently many capable officers of moderate means were confined to regimental command.

British commanders in America were not the blundering incompetents described by some historians, but with few exceptions they were too cautious and unimaginative. William Howe was slow and indolent; Henry Clinton, his successor as commander in chief in America, was insecure and afraid to take risks. John Burgoyne and Lord Cornwallis were bold but impetuous.

Mercenaries. To augment the army in America, the British government purchased the services of 30,000 soldiers from minor German princelings at great cost. Seventeen thousand were obtained from the principality of Hesse, and the term *Hessians* was applied to all the German soldiers. They were less dependable in battle than the redcoats and were inclined to desert. Of their number, 7,500 died in America and 5,000 deserted.

Loyalists and Indians. Loyalist military support in America was considerable. Approximately 50,000 Americans fought for the king. Although few joined the British Army and Navy, thousands served in provincial regiments under Loyalist officers. Loyalists fought well in most important actions after 1778, but never provided the powerful indigenous force expected by Britain.

Indians, chiefly in Canada, on the frontier, and in the South, also fought for Britain. They were generally unreliable, though ferocious, allies. They were effective in raids, and were a nuisance in extended campaigns. The use of Indians, as

well as Hessians and Loyalists, greatly increased American hatred of Britain.

Weapons. The British Army enjoyed a considerable advantage in cannon, mortars, howitzers, and other artillery. Weighted down with 60 pounds (27 kg) of equipment, the common soldier fought the Americans with the "brown Bess," a smoothbore, flintlock musket fitted with a bayonet, and probably named for its brown walnut stock. Little marksmanship was required. The object was to smash the enemy with successive volleys, then charge with the bayonet. Against undisciplined troops this method of warfare could be devastating.

Army Administration. Although the British soldier gave a good account of himself in pitched battle, winning about half of the major engagements of the war, he was hampered by factors beyond his control. Inefficiency, dissension, and diffusion of responsibility characterized the administrative machinery in London. The lines of authority among departments and officials were unclear and often overlapped. Administrative jealousy and bickering resulted in confusion and delay. Especially acrimonious were the relations between Lord George Germain, secretary of state for the colonies, and the earl of Sandwich, first lord of the Admiralty. The apparatus for transporting and supplying an army across 3,000 miles (about 4,800 km) of ocean was inadequate. The responsible departments were inefficient and often riddled with graft. In America the commissary and quartermaster services were baffled by the lack of interior communication and transport facilities. Away from the Atlantic coast and the royal navy, supply was uncertain, and the British Army courted disaster.

WAR AIMS AND STRATEGIES

The war aims of both Britain and the Thirteen Colonies were political as well as military. The British had not only to destroy American military resistance, but to restore royal rule and to bring the colonies back into the empire. While using force, the British government also sought to negotiate a reconciliation on increasingly liberal terms. The policy of political conciliation was ineffective and interfered with the military effort. Before 1776, the Americans ostensibly were fighting to defend their rights and liberties within the empire; after July 4, 1776, they fought for political independence.

British Strategic Plans. Britain had two master plans for winning the war. British grand strategy during 1776–1777 envisaged the isolation and subjection of New England, followed by piecemeal reduction of the Middle and Southern colonies. According to the "Southern strategy" of 1778–1781, the South would be conquered, restored to royal control, and used as a base to thrust northward. Neither plan worked. The distance from London to America, the vast stretches of land in America, division of command between the British forces in Canada and the Thirteen Colonies, and friction among those responsible for making and executing strategy all combined to reduce grand strategy to a series of ill-coordinated, often confused operations.

American Strategy. American strategy developed in response to British efforts and in relation to specific situations. Washington, fighting an essentially defensive war, sought to keep his army intact, offer battle on terms as equal as possible, and wear down the British will to win. The Patriot commander carried the war to the enemy when he could.

Character of the War. The War of Independence differed in several important aspects from 17th and 18th century European wars. England faced a people in arms rather than another professional army. The rebellious colonies had to be subdued and occupied, and the British Army, operating in a geographic expanse roughly 1,000 by 600 miles (1,600 by 1,000 km), was too small for the task. In its total involvement. of a people, the war resembled modern conflicts. In terms of combatants and casualties the war was small in comparison with modern contests. Casu-

alty statistics are incomplete and unreliable. By conservative count, there were slightly more than 4,000 American battle deaths in the Revolution. In the American Civil War, over 600,000 men on both sides died in action or of disease. United States dead from all causes in World War II totaled more than 400,000, and in the Korean War more than 54,000.

Scope of the War. Campaigns on the North American mainland generally progressed from north to south. The British considered New England to be the center of American resistance, and hoped to crush Washington's army at the outset. When this attempt failed they applied pressure elsewhere.

THE WAR IN THE NORTH

Operations Around Boston. Many of the New Englanders who besieged Boston after the Battle of Lexington drifted away, but by June 1775 about 7,500 men had enlisted under the authorization of the Massachusetts Provincial Congress, and the number steadily increased. On May 25, the frigate *Cerberus* had arrived from England, bringing Major Generals William Howe, John Burgoyne, and Henry Clinton to assist Gage. With them came instructions to pursue military operations vigorously.

By June 12, 1775, Gage's forces numbered about 6,000, far short of the 20,000 men he had asked for in late 1774. After conferring with his three colleagues, Gage determined to move decisively against the Patriots. He decided to take steps to occupy and fortify the heights on Dorchester Peninsula south of Boston, and prepared to move a detachment to cover Bunker Hill and Breed's Hill on Charlestown Peninsula across the Charles River to the north.

Possibly because Burgoyne had talked too much, the Patriots were aware of Gage's plans by the 14th. On June 16, American militia occupied Charlestown Peninsula and fortified

(Below) American regimental drums served the function of the bugle in later armies. *(Right)* Congress turned out vast quantities of paper money, such as this 36-shilling note engraved by Paul Revere in 1775.

GUILFORD COURTHOUSE NATIONAL MILITARY PARK

AMERICAN ANTIQUARIAN SOCIETY

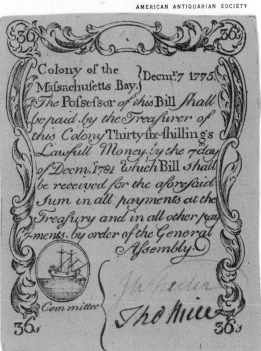

Breed's Hill. The next day, two frontal attacks on the American position were repulsed, and the British had heavy losses. Reinforced by about 700 troops from Boston, Howe led a third advance, driving the Patriots to Bunker Hill and then to the mainland.

By this engagement, known as the Battle of Bunker Hill, Gage had gained Charlestown Peninsula, but at prohibitive cost. British casualties had amounted to 271 dead and 783 wounded, compared to only 140 Americans killed and 271 wounded. Gage declined to fortify Dorchester Heights and refused to make further offensive motions. He was soon recalled to London, and Howe succeeded to the command on October 10.

Washington in Command. Meanwhile, in June and July, the Continental Congress had adopted the army besieging Boston, had promulgated a military code, and had appointed officers to the new Continental Army. Washington, named commander-in-chief, had assumed command on July 3 at Cambridge, accompanied by other officers.

Washington had found the Patriots recovering from the fierce fighting at Bunker Hill and suffering from sectional dissension and personal jealousies. During the summer and autumn, while Gage and then Howe remained on the defensive, Washington and his staff labored to create a well-regulated army. The American commander contemplated an assault on the British lines, but wisely delayed action until Congress authorized him to bombard Boston. On the night of March 4, 1776, working parties laboriously hauled cannon, brought from Fort Ticonderoga by Col. Henry Knox, to the heights of Dorchester Peninsula. Howe, realizing that the Americans could not be dislodged and that they could level Boston, reluctantly decided to evacuate the city and move to Halifax, Nova Scotia. On March 17, the British abandoned Boston to the Patriots, thus ending the preliminary stage of the war in America.

Invasion of Canada. While the British were failing to subdue New England, the Americans moved to force Canada into the family of 13 colonies. On May 10 and 11, 1775, a small expeditionary force under the joint command of Ethan Allen and Benedict Arnold captured Fort Ticonderoga and Crown Point (N.Y.), British posts at the southern end of Lake Champlain. They took Fort St. John's (Quebec) on the Richelieu River north of the lake, but were unable to hold it. But, the Americans controlled Lake Champlain, opening Canada to invasion from the south.

In late June, Congress ordered Gen. Philip Schuyler of New York to advance against Montreal, but he spent almost two months preparing for the expedition. Fortunately his second in command, Brig. Gen. Richard Montgomery, was more energetic. While Guy Carleton, governor of Canada, frantically prepared to meet the threatened invasion, Montgomery led an American force up Lake Champlain. On November 2, Fort St. John's fell to the Americans, but the resistance of Maj. Charles Preston, commander of the post, had delayed Montgomery almost three months. On November 10, the Americans entered Montreal.

They planned next to attack the city of Quebec, where Carleton had fled. Montgomery stopped for two weeks before passing on to join a larger American force under Benedict Arnold, which was already camped before Quebec. On December 5, the combined American force of about 1,000 men laid siege to Quebec. The fortress had been reinforced by Carleton and 80 troops under Allan McLean. After an exchange of artillery fire, it became clear that Quebec must be carried by storm, if at all. On December 30, under cover of a snowstorm, Montgomery attacked the west wall, Arnold the eastern defenses. The Americans were repulsed, their army cut in half. Both Arnold and Montgomery were wounded, the latter mortally. Arnold refused to admit defeat. He continued to blockade the city until relieved by Gen. David Wooster, who was superseded by Gen. John Thomas. On May 6, a British fleet brought reinforcements, and Thomas retreated toward Montreal. The Canadian invasion strategy had failed, but Montgomery and Arnold had prevented a southward thrust by the British until the fall of 1776.

British Strike at the South. In firm agreement with the King's decision to crush the American rebellion, Germain hurried reinforcements to America. Two offensive thrusts were planned. The first was by Gen. Henry Clinton with 3,000 men. He was instructed to strike at the Carolinas, supported by a naval squadron under Sir Peter Parker. The British hoped that Loyalists in the Carolinas would rise in great numbers and join the royal forces. Sailing slowly down the coast, Clinton reached North Carolina in May, 1776; Parker had arrived in April. They discovered that the Loyalists of that colony had been thoroughly cowed by a disastrous encounter with Patriots at Moore's Creek Bridge.

Frustrated and disappointed, Clinton and Parker, after several weeks' delay, decided to capture Sullivan's Island at the mouth of Charleston harbor. Clinton hoped to use the island as a base from which to attack Charleston, which was then the capital of South Carolina. While Gen. Charles Lee and Governor John Rutledge frantically prepared to defend the city, Col. William Moultrie toiled to build a fort on Sullivan's Island. On June 28, Parker sent three frigates to assail the fort from the west and seven heavier vessels to bombard it from the south. The plan was well conceived, but two of the frigates ran against a shoal, ruining the flanking maneuver. Meanwhile, Parker had begun a frontal assault, but the walls of the fort, built of palmetto logs, absorbed the cannon shot. Moultrie returned fire and after an 11-hour bombardment Parker withdrew, having suffered heavy casualties. Shortly thereafter the British sailed for New York.

British Attack on New York. The second offensive planned by the British was launched by General Howe whose army had been increased to 32,000 men. He was ordered to seize New York City and reduce New England. Washington grimly prepared to defend the city. The British did not move until late August 1776, because of the efforts of General Howe and his brother, Richard, Adm. Viscount Howe, to act as peace commissioners as well as military commanders. When their efforts to parley with influential officials in Congress and the states were unsuccessful, they resorted to force. On August 27, General Howe launched a massive attack against the American position at Brooklyn Heights on the western end of Long Island, commanded by the gallant but incompetent Israel Putnam. Howe employed a three-pronged attack, Gen. James Grant moving against the

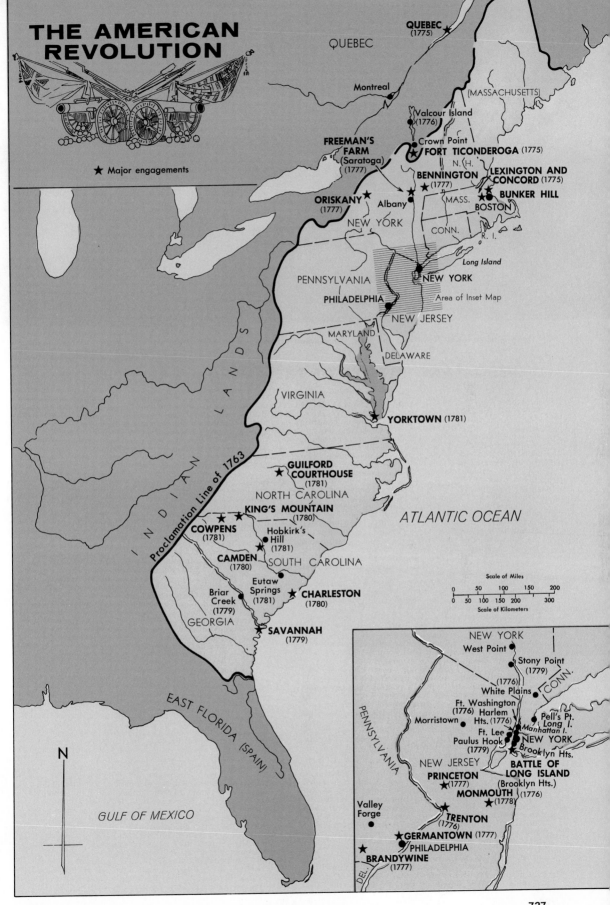

THE AMERICAN REVOLUTION

★ Major engagements

QUEBEC
Montreal

QUEBEC (1775)

(MASSACHUSETTS)

Valcour Island (1776)

Crown Point

★ FORT TICONDEROGA (1775)

FREEMAN'S FARM (Saratoga) (1777)

N. H.

BENNINGTON (1777)

LEXINGTON AND CONCORD (1775)

ORISKANY (1777)

Albany

MASS.

BUNKER HILL

BOSTON

NEW YORK

CONN.

R. I.

PENNSYLVANIA

Long Island

NEW YORK

PHILADELPHIA

Area of Inset Map

NEW JERSEY

MARYLAND

DELAWARE

VIRGINIA

YORKTOWN (1781)

GUILFORD COURTHOUSE (1781)

NORTH CAROLINA

KING'S MOUNTAIN (1780)

ATLANTIC OCEAN

COWPENS (1781)

Hobkirk's Hill (1781)

CAMDEN (1780)

SOUTH CAROLINA

Briar Creek (1779)

Eutaw Springs (1781)

CHARLESTON (1780)

GEORGIA

SAVANNAH (1779)

INDIAN LANDS

Proclamation Line of 1763

EAST FLORIDA (SPAIN)

N

GULF OF MEXICO

Scale of Miles
0   50   100   150   200
0 50 100 150 200   300
Scale of Kilometers

NEW YORK

West Point

Stony Point (1779)

(1776)

White Plains

CONN.

Ft. Washington (1776) Harlem Hts. (1776)

Pell's Pt. Long I.

PENNSYLVANIA

Morristown

Ft. Lee

Manhattan I.

Paulus Hook (1779)

NEW YORK

Brooklyn Hts.

NEW JERSEY

PRINCETON (1777)

BATTLE OF LONG ISLAND (Brooklyn Hts.)

MONMOUTH (1778)

(1776)

Valley Forge

TRENTON (1776)

GERMANTOWN (1777)

PHILADELPHIA

DEL.

BRANDYWINE (1777)

Charging with upraised sword into the fray, Washington rallies his retreating troops at the Battle of Monmouth.

IMPORTANT BATTLES OF THE AMERICAN REVOLUTION

Bennington, Aug. 16, 1777, fought in New York, 4 miles (6 km) northwest of Bennington, Vt. Gen. John Stark led 2,600 untrained Continental militia in the rout of 1,400 British and Hessians sent by General Burgoyne to capture supplies at Bennington. The Patriots suffered about 80 casualties; the British, 700 captured and 200 dead and wounded. The victory exposed the left flank of Burgoyne's army, which was moving from Canada down the Hudson River Valley.

Brandywine, Sept. 11, 1777, fought in Pennsylvania, 25 miles (40 km) southwest of Philadelphia. Gen. William Howe, moving from New York against Philadelphia, sent 15,000 men against Washington with 8,000 Continentals and 3,000 militia. While Howe assaulted the American center, Lord Cornwallis executed a flanking maneuver for which Washington was unprepared. The Patriots were forced to retreat, suffering more than 1,000 casualties to about 600 for Howe. The victory assured British occupation of Philadelphia.

Bunker Hill, June 17, 1775, fought on Charlestown Peninsula, across the Charles River from Boston, Mass. The major action occurred at Breed's Hill, just southeast of Bunker Hill. Gen. William Howe, attempting to break the siege of Boston, successfully led 2,250 British troops against about 2,200 Americans under Col. William Prescott. In gaining an outpost of little value, Howe suffered prohibitive casualties, 271 dead and 783 wounded to only 140 Americans killed and 271 wounded.

Camden, Aug. 16, 1780, fought near Camden, S.C. Gen. Horatio Gates, moving with 3,000 Continentals and militia against the British post at Camden under Lord Rawdon, was not aware that Lord Cornwallis had preceded him there, bringing the British strength up to 2,200. In the ensuing battle the American militia on the left flank fled and Gates' army was routed, suffering at least 750 killed or captured to the enemy's 68 killed and 245 wounded. The disastrous defeat exposed North Carolina to easy invasion by the British.

Charleston (siege), April 1 to May 12, 1780. After Vice Adm. Jean d'Estaing failed to take Savannah, Ga., in Oct. 1779, Gen. Henry Clinton besieged Charleston, S.C., defended by more than 5,000 troops under Gen. Benjamin Lincoln. Unable to escape, Lincoln held out for six weeks before he and his entire force surrendered. American casualties during the siege numbered 238; 76 British were killed and 189 wounded. The American army in the South was lost, and Clinton proceeded to occupy South Carolina.

Concord, April 19, 1775, fought 3 miles (5 km) west of Lexington, Mass. Following the brief skirmish at Lexington, Lt. Col. Francis Smith and 700 British regulars marched rapidly to Concord, where they dis-

covered and destroyed Patriot supplies. At the North Bridge, spanning the Concord River, a body of about 350 Patriots attacked a British covering party, killing three and wounding eight. This brief action, together with that at Lexington, aroused thousands of Massachusetts Patriots who gathered on both sides of the British route of withdrawal, pursued the British to Boston, and surrounded the city.

Cowpens, Jan. 17, 1781, fought in South Carolina, at "Hannah's Cowpens" near the Broad River. In early January, Gen. Nathanael Greene divided his army, sending Daniel Morgan with about 1,000 men to the southwest. Lord Cornwallis dispatched Banastre Tarleton with 1,100 troops after Morgan. Morgan, by using his militia to lure Tarleton's troops into devastating fire from the Continentals, routed the British. Tarleton lost 110 killed, 229 wounded, and 600 captured; Morgan suffered only 12 killed and 60 wounded. The defeat greatly weakened Cornwallis' prospects of overrunning North Carolina but he rashly pursued the fleeing Morgan.

Freeman's Farm (Saratoga), second battle, Oct. 7, 1777, fought in New York, near Bemis Heights, about 9 miles (14 km) southeast of Saratoga Springs. Moving down the Hudson valley toward Albany, Gen. John Burgoyne was confronted by more than 7,000 troops under Gen. Horatio Gates at Bemis Heights. Having failed to turn the Patriot left wing in action at Freeman's Farm, on September 19, Burgoyne attempted the same maneuver again on October 7 with 1,500 regulars and 600 Tories. Gates met him at Freeman's Farm with three columns under Daniel Morgan, Enoch Poor, and Ebenezer Learned. When the fighting ended at dusk, Burgoyne counted 700 casualties, Gates no more than 150. His lines no longer tenable, Burgoyne retreated to Saratoga (now Schuylerville) where he and his army of 5,000 surrendered to Gates on October 17. The American victory ended British plans to reduce New England, and brought France into the war as an ally of the United States.

Germantown, Oct. 4, 1777, fought in Pennsylvania, 7 miles (11 km) northwest of Philadelphia. Determined to contest British occupation of Philadelphia, Washington sent 11,000 troops in four columns against Howe's force of 9,000 deployed at Germantown. The Americans gained the initial advantage, but in the fog one Patriot column fired on another, and in the ensuing confusion the British drove them back. Howe retained Philadelphia, but occupation of the city proved to be of no strategic value, and Washington's army was left intact.

Guilford Courthouse, March 15, 1781, fought in North Carolina, 45 miles (72 km) west of Hillsborough. Having fled before the advancing Lord Cornwallis, Greene regrouped his forces, and with 1,700 Continentals and more than 2,800 militia moved across the Dan River into North Carolina. At Guilford, Cornwallis attacked with about 2,400 troops, forcing Greene to withdraw. British casualties totaled 93 killed and 413 wounded; American losses were 78 killed and 183 wounded. Cornwallis, unable to sustain such losses, began the long march to Yorktown while the Patriots began to recover the South.

Kings Mountain, Oct. 7, 1780, fought in South Carolina, about 30 miles (48 km) west of Charlotte, N. C. Inflamed by British oppression, a body of 900 militia from the North Carolina and Virginia backwoods pursued and cornered Maj. Patrick Ferguson and a party of about 1,100 Loyalists. Fighting from tree to tree, the Patriots cut Ferguson's forces to pieces, killing 225, wounding 163, and taking more than 700 prisoners. The Americans lost only 28 killed and 63 wounded. His auxiliary force destroyed, Lord Cornwallis was forced to retreat to Camden, S. C., and to assume a defensive strategy.

Lexington, April 19, 1775, fought in Massachusetts, 16 miles (26 km) northwest of Boston. Following instructions to act vigorously against the rebels, Gen. Thomas Gage sent 700 British regulars under Lt. Col. Francis Smith and Maj. John Pitcairn to destroy supplies at Concord, Mass. Warned by Paul Revere, 70 militiamen under Capt. Jonas Parker confronted an advance guard led by Pitcairn. A skirmish followed in which 8 Americans were slain, 10 wounded. One redcoat was wounded.

Long Island, Aug. 27–28, 1776, fought in Brooklyn, N. Y. Aiming at a decisive victory, Gen. William Howe landed 32,000 British regulars and Hessians at the entrance of New York Harbor. Opposing them, Washington had 19,000 poorly trained men. Howe launched a three-pronged attack against the American troops in Brooklyn, the extreme western end of Long Island. Unprepared for a flanking attack, the Americans were routed, losing 2,000 men killed or captured. British losses were under 400. The crushing defeat opened Manhattan to easy invasion and forced Washington to abandon New York City, though with most of his army intact.

Monmouth, June 28, 1778, fought in New Jersey about 50 miles (80 km) northeast of Philadelphia. Washington, with almost 10,000 troops, intercepted Gen. Henry Clinton and an army of 10,000 marching across New Jersey to New York after the British evacuation of Philadelphia. The battle ended indecisively when Gen. Charles Lee and 5,000 Patriots retreated after engaging Clinton. Casualties totaled somewhat more than 300 for both sides. Washington held the field, but Clinton was able to move his army safely to New York.

Oriskany, Aug. 6, 1777, fought in New York near Ft. Stanwix (Schuyler), between Rome and Utica. Gen. Nicholas Herkimer marched with 800 Patriot militia to relieve Ft. Stanwix, besieged by Lt. Col. Barry St. Leger. Herkimer was ambushed by 400 Indians and British rangers under Joseph Brant. Each side suffered about 200 casualties. Herkimer's stand made it possible for the garrison at Ft. Stanwix to hold out until Benedict Arnold arrived with 1,000 men from Ft. Dayton. St. Leger subsequently abandoned the siege and turned back from his march toward Albany, where he would have joined forces with Burgoyne.

Quebec, Dec. 30, 1775, fought in Canada near the city of Quebec. Attempting to carry out their mission to conquer Canada, a force of about 1,000 Americans under Brig. Gen. Richard Montgomery was repulsed by 1,200 British under Guy Carleton. Benedict Arnold and Montgomery were wounded, the latter mortally. Over half of the American force were killed, wounded, or captured. The project to conquer Canada was abandoned, and the invasion route into New York was again open to the British.

Saratoga. See *Freeman's Farm.*

Savannah, Oct. 9, 1779. In response to the Patriots' pleas for aid in recovering Savannah, Ga., Adm. Jean d'Estaing sailed his fleet to the seaport city and landed 3,500 troops, who with 1,500 Continentals and militia under Gen. Benjamin Lincoln besieged the city held by Gen. Augustine Prevost and about 2,400 troops. The allies attempted to take the city by storm and were repulsed, sustaining over 800 casualties to 155 for the British. The British victory enabled Clinton to attack South Carolina in force.

Ticonderoga (capture), May 10, 1775. Ethan Allen and Benedict Arnold led 83 Americans in the capture of the 45-man British garrison of Fort Ticonderoga, N.Y., at the southern tip of Lake Champlain. Not a shot was fired. The subsequent capture of Crown Point, N.Y., on May 11, gave the Patriots control of Lake Champlain and opened Canada to invasion from the south.

Trenton, Dec. 26, 1776, fought at Trenton, N.J. Washington, aware that the British had gone into winter quarters, led 2,400 Patriots across the Delaware River, surprised and routed the Hessian garrison of 1,500 men under Col. Johann Rall, and captured over 900. The Americans suffered 4 wounded. This brilliant victory coupled with that at Princeton on Jan. 3, 1777, led to the recovery of western New Jersey and greatly raised Patriot morale.

Vincennes, Feb. 23–24, 1779. Authorized by the Virginia Assembly to conquer the Illinois country, George Rogers Clark, with about 200 men, seized Kaskaskia (Ill.), Cahokia (Ill.), and Vincennes (Ind.) in the summer of 1778. Later that year the British retook Vincennes. Clark and 130 men, after an arduous march, reoccupied the village on Feb. 23, 1779, and attacked Fort Sackville close by. The fort surrendered the next day with its commander, Henry Hamilton, and garrison of less than 100. Clark was unable to strike at Detroit, but he had secured control of most of the old Northwest.

Yorktown (siege), Sept. 28–Oct. 19, 1781. At Yorktown, Va., occurred the decisive confrontation of British and allied (Franco-American) forces. Lord Cornwallis had entrenched there with 7,000 troops. Attempting to save him, a British fleet of 19 ships sailed to Chesapeake Bay, where Admiral de Grasse and a French fleet of 28 ships engaged them on Sept. 5, and turned them back. By September 28, Washington had covered Yorktown on the land side with 17,000 French and American troops. All hope of escape gone, Cornwallis and over 7,000 British troops surrendered on October 19, thus virtually ending the Revolutionary War. Allied casualties during the siege of Yorktown amounted to 72 killed and 180 wounded; British casualties amounted to 156 killed and 326 wounded.

The British surrender at Saratoga, Oct. 17, 1777. In this painting by Trumbull, Burgoyne presents his sword to Gates.

Henry Knox's "noble train of artillery" hauled 59 cannon from Ticonderoga and forced British out of Boston.

American right wing, Gen. Philipp von Heister pushing against the center, and Howe himself assaulting the left wing. Unprepared for a flanking maneuver, the Americans were crushed, suffering 2,000 dead or wounded and 1,000 captured.

The American Army might have been destroyed had Howe been more aggressive, but he allowed Washington to evacuate the remainder of his troops across the East River to the lower end of Manhattan Island under cover of night. General Howe again moved against Washington,

landing troops on Manhattan at Kip's Bay on September 15. The British pushed rapidly to the north and west, but were halted by the Patriots in a series of encounters at Harlem Heights in northern Manhattan on the 16th. Howe occupied and fortified New York City while Washington strengthened his position at Harlem Heights.

In early October the British resumed the offensive, planning to cut off Washington's line of retreat to the northeast. On October 18, a picked force of Hessians and redcoats landed at Pell's Point near New Rochelle. There Col. John Glover with only 850 men managed to delay the British advance while Washington retreated to White Plains, where an indecisive action was fought. Believing Washington did not intend to stand and fight, Howe swiftly attacked Fort Washington in northern Manhattan and Fort Lee, N.J., across the Hudson River. He captured both, and the loss in men, equipment, and cannon was nearly a catastrophe for the Patriot cause.

Washington retreated across New Jersey, hotly pursued by Lord Cornwallis. Again the British had great opportunities but Cornwallis, having pushed the Americans across the Delaware River, into Pennsylvania, followed Howe's orders and prepared to go into winter quarters.

American Successes. Washington's spirits had sunk low during the disorderly retreat from New York, but he was resolved to strike back. On Christmas night of 1776 he recrossed the Delaware with 2,400 men and routed the Hessian garrison at Trenton the next day. His surprise attack on Princeton, on Jan. 3, 1777, resulted in another minor but important American victory. Washington moved into winter quarters at Morristown, N.J. but his courageous action had infused new hope and vigor into the Patriot cause.

Far to the north, on Lake Champlain, Benedict Arnold had won valuable time for the embattled Americans. With a hastily built "mosquito fleet," he engaged a fleet of 20 gunboats

American Gen. Richard Montgomery (*standing, center*) sustains fatal wounds while leading attack on Quebec in 1775.

Suffering from hunger, disease, and the bitter cold, the ragged Continental Army passes in review before General Washington and his aides at Valley Forge.

under Guy Carleton at Valcour Island on Oct. 11 and 13, 1776. Arnold's fleet was almost destroyed, but his bold maneuver prevented a junction between Carleton and Howe that might have been fatal to Washington.

British Capture of Philadelphia. In the spring of 1777, the Continental Army, refitted in part with equipment secretly supplied by France, was again ready to fight. The British blundered strategically by abandoning, or at least confusing, their plans to concentrate on New England. Howe, after submitting two plans to Germain, decided to move by sea against Philadelphia, leaving a holding garrison in New York. John Burgoyne's plan, to march southward from Canada to Albany where he expected to receive support from Howe, was likewise approved. Germain ordered Howe to cooperate with Burgoyne, but his letter did not reach Howe until Howe was at sea en route to Philadelphia. So, Howe did not order troops to aid Burgoyne.

When Howe, far off schedule, landed his troops at the head of Chesapeake Bay on August 25, Washington took position in southern Pennsylvania, on the northern banks of Brandywine Creek. In an encounter on September 11, Cornwallis turned the American right flank, and the Patriots were driven back, suffering heavy losses. Placing 9,000 troops at Germantown to hold off Washington, Howe entered Philadelphia on September 25.

Washington, however, was not disposed to give up Philadelphia without a further test of arms. On the night of October 3, 11,000 Patriot troops moved in four columns against the British lines at Germantown. Next day the Americans had the advantage of surprise, but in the fog one column of Continentals fired on another, and the advance turned to disorderly retreat. Nevertheless, Washington, who moved into winter quarters, had given a good account of himself. Philadelphia was of no strategic value to Howe, and contrary to his expectations the Pennsylvania Loyalists did not rally to his banner by the thousands.

American Triumph in the Hudson Valley. While Howe posed as the conqueror, Burgoyne encountered disaster. With a force of over 7,500, Burgoyne easily took Fort Ticonderoga on July 5, but his moment of glory was fleeting. To the west, determined Patriots in the Mohawk Valley, aided by 1,000 volunteers under Benedict Arnold, turned back Barry St. Leger's expeditionary force, which was to supply a diversion for Burgoyne. Menaced by the gathering number of Patriots, who impeded his march down the Hudson valley by littering the route with fallen trees, Burgoyne was in serious trouble by mid-August. To obtain supplies Burgoyne sent Col. Friedrich Baum to Bennington (Vt.) on a foraging expedition. On August 16, Baum's troops were crushed by a force of New Hampshire militia and Continentals. The defeat cost Burgoyne about a tenth of his army.

As he pushed down the west bank of the Hudson in mid-September, Burgoyne was confronted by Gen. Horatio Gates with more than 7,000 militia and Continentals in strong fortifications at Bemis Heights, about 25 miles (40 km) north of Albany. Burgoyne tried twice to turn the American left flank. On September 19, 2,400 regulars and Hessians clashed with picked troops under Arnold and Daniel Morgan at Freeman's Farm, about a mile (1.6 km) north of Bemis Heights. The Americans were forced back at dusk, but Burgoyne's thrust had been blocked. On October 7, Burgoyne tried a reconnaissance in force against the American left, but was repulsed in the second Battle of Freeman's Farm. He was surrounded at Saratoga (now Schuylerville) and was forced to lay down his arms on October 17. Because Burgoyne surrendered at Saratoga, the fights at Freeman's Farm are often—but inaccurately—called the first and second battles of Saratoga.

In early October, Sir Henry Clinton had begun an advance from New York up the Hudson River to aid Burgoyne. He faltered and retreated, but the threat of his forces impelled

Gates to grant Burgoyne surrender terms that permitted his troops to return to England with the pledge that they would not serve in America again during the war. The agreement, known as the Saratoga Convention, was nullified by Congress, and Burgoyne's men were held as prisoners.

Burgoyne's defeat was a crushing blow for the British. Not only had they lost an army, but when the news reached Paris in early December, King Louis XVI and his ministers took France into the war as the open ally of the United States. News of the French alliance came to Congress May 2, in time to nullify the efforts of a British peace commission led by the earl of Carlisle.

Later Events in the North. In winter quarters at Valley Forge near Philadelphia in 1777–1778 Washington's army suffered terribly from cold, hunger, exposure, and disease. Possibly 2,500 perished during the six months at camp. But plans were made to reorganize the supply services. Drill and training were directed by Baron von Steuben, formerly of the Prussian Army. By spring the American Army was reinvigorated.

Clinton, who had replaced Howe as British commander in chief, evacuated Philadelphia in June 1778 immediately before the arrival of a powerful French fleet under Vice Adm. d'Estaing. As Clinton marched the bulk of the British Army across New Jersey, Washington promptly left Valley Forge in pursuit. The two armies clashed at Monmouth on June 28, but an advance American force under Gen. Charles Lee retreated in confusion until halted by an enraged Washington.

After the Battle of Monmouth, d'Estaing and Washington laid plans to move on New York City, but the admiral declined to attack the British fleet in New York harbor after discovering his heavier ships could not cross the bar. At Washington's request d'Estaing conferred with Gen. John Sullivan and agreed to a joint assault on the British garrison at Newport, R.I. On August 10, d'Estaing sailed out to engage a smaller British fleet under Admiral Howe. While the two fleets maneuvered, a violent storm arose on the night of the 11th, scattering both squadrons. D'Estaing refused to resume action against Newport, and the projected assault collapsed. In the fall of 1778 the French fleet sailed off to the West Indies, leaving the Patriots disappointed and embittered.

After 1778 there was little campaigning in the North. Clinton carried on a wasting war while Washington sought an opportunity to strike at New York. Gen. Anthony Wayne did win a small, but brilliant victory at Stony Point (N.Y.) on the Hudson River north of Haverstraw, in July 1779, and a month later Henry "Light-Horse Harry" Lee took another British post at Paulus Hook (N.J.). In the summer of 1780, after the British had evacuated Newport, a French squadron and army under Count de Rochambeau took post there.

Action in the West. Military activity on the western frontier of the American states increased after 1778. During 1777 and 1778 Tory contingents and their Indian allies under the command of Henry Hamilton, lieutenant governor of Detroit, raided settlements on the frontiers of Virginia, Pennsylvania, and New York. The excessive cruelty of these raiders provoked swift retaliation. In the fall of 1777, the Virginia

Assembly authorized a young Kentuckian, George Rogers Clark, to lead an expedition against the British in the West. After a long, hard march, Clark, with about 200 men, surprised and took the town of Kaskaskia (Ill.), on July 4, 1778. With his second capture of Vincennes (Ind.) and its fort in February 1779, he took Hamilton himself prisoner.

Though unable to attack Detroit, Clark did gain control of the old Northwest (the lands between the Great Lakes and the Ohio River), and gave the United States a technical claim to that territory at the peace table. Strong raids by Gen. John Sullivan in western New York and by Col. Daniel Brodhead in northwestern Pennsylvania ensured that American control would be firm in those areas.

THE WAR IN THE SOUTH

As the war in the North became one of attrition and endurance, Clinton mounted a major offensive against Georgia and South Carolina, where he counted on strong Loyalist support. On Dec. 29, 1778, a detachment of 3,500 men under Lt. Col. Archibald Campbell overwhelmed a small American force under Gen. Robert Howe and captured Savannah. Shortly afterwards Gen. Augustine Prevost arrived from St. Augustine (Fla.) with 2,000 British troops, and on Jan. 29, 1779, Augusta was taken by the British. Within a short time, Georgia passed under British control. Maj. Gen. Benjamin Lincoln, whom Washington had sent to command the new Southern Department in the fall of 1778, was defeated at Brier Creek (Ga.), but forced Prevost to withdraw to Savannah. In response to Patriot pleas, Admiral d'Estaing appeared off Savannah in September 1779 with his fleet and about 4,000 troops, and joined Lincoln in besieging the city. On October 9, an allied attack failed. On October 20 the siege was abandoned and the French fleet set sail for France.

Operation in the Carolinas. D'Estaing's departure enabled Clinton to attack South Carolina in great force. Leaving Baron Knyphausen to defend New York, the British commander sailed southward in December with 8,000 troops. Supported by a fleet under Adm. Marriot Arbuthnot, Clinton besieged Charleston in April 1780. After holding out for over a month, Lincoln and more than 5,000 Patriots, their escape route cut off, surrendered on May 12. After the fall of Charleston, the British occupied forts throughout South Carolina, while Tories flocked to the king's colors. Clinton returned to New York at the end of May, leaving Lord Cornwallis in command with instructions to maintain control of South Carolina and to avoid risky operations.

Cornwallis, however, was not content with holding operations. Hearing that Horatio Gates, who had succeeded Lincoln in August, was moving against the British post at Camden (S.C.), Cornwallis hurried north to reinforce Lord Francis Rawdon's garrison. The two forces collided on the morning of August 16, and Gates' army was routed. One fourth of his men were killed or wounded. Gates himself, riding hard to Charlotte (N.C.), left behind him the reputation gained at Saratoga. The disastrous defeat exposed North Carolina to invasion, and Cornwallis, intending to overrun that state and Virginia, marched on. He had hardly entered North Carolina when news came that militia from the

Rebel bayonet attack carries a British redoubt at Yorktown. On Oct. 19, 1781, Cornwallis and 7,000 men surrender in last major battle of the war.

backwoods of Virginia and North Carolina had defeated a body of Loyalists under Maj. Patrick Ferguson at Kings Mountain (S.C.). His auxiliary force destroyed, Cornwallis withdrew south of Camden where he remained for almost three months.

Greene in American Command. In January 1781, after receiving reinforcements and learning that Clinton had sent a force under Arnold to Virginia, Cornwallis resolved to return to North Carolina. Meanwhile the American army in the South had acquired a new leader, Nathanael Greene, who brought to the command courage tempered with caution, and considerable skill in strategy. At Charlotte, Greene found "only the shadow of an army," but was joined by Gen. Daniel Morgan and "Light-Horse Harry" Lee with his famous legion.

Deciding to concentrate on guerrilla tactics, Greene sent Morgan with one force toward the British post at Ninety-Six in South Carolina, while he led the main body of the army to the southeast. Cornwallis hurriedly dispatched Col. Banastre Tarleton after Morgan, and the two forces clashed at Cowpens, (S.C.) near the Broad River, on Jan. 17, 1781. Morgan performed brilliantly, placing his militia in an advance line and luring the British into heavy fire from his Continentals. Tarleton's force was routed, and the defeat greatly weakened Cornwallis' prospects of overrunning North Carolina. A more prudent man would have returned to South Carolina, but Cornwallis impetuously hurried after Morgan, who withdrew northward. Greene managed to draw back both of his contingents across the Dan River in Virginia, and Cornwallis, realizing how far he was from his base of supplies, withdrew to Hillsborough (N.C.). His army now numbered hardly more than 2,000.

With an army of over 4,500 militia and Continentals, Greene moved back into North Carolina, confronting Cornwallis at Guilford Courthouse on March 15. Greene's deployments were similar to Morgan's at Cowpens, but the militia broke and ran, and the Americans withdrew.

Cornwallis' victory was costly; almost a quarter of his army was dead or wounded. He could not ignore the fact that his triumphs in the Carolinas were empty, and that he could no longer safely remain in the interior of North Carolina. He marched off to Wilmington, and thence to Virginia, leaving the defense of the Carolinas to Lord Rawdon.

American Offensive. After the departure of Cornwallis, Greene again assumed the offensive in South Carolina and Georgia. Powerfully assisted by partisan fighters such as Francis Marion, Thomas Sumter, Andrew Pickens, and Col. Elijah Clark of Georgia, the Patriots gradually pushed the British back into Savannah and Charleston. On April 23, 1781, Fort Watson, (S.C.), one of seven British forts that protected Charleston and Savannah, was captured by Marion and Light-Horse Harry Lee. Two days later at Hobkirk's Hill near Camden, Rawdon with 1,500 men repulsed Greene with an equal number in a bloody slugging match. Unable to maintain a long supply and communication line, the British commander fell back toward Charleston. The isolated British garrisons at Forts Motte, Granby, Orangeburg, and Georgetown (S.C.) and Augusta (Ga.) were all forced to yield by June 20. Greene was repulsed in an attack on the British post at Ninety-six.

Spanish Aid to the Americans. Meanwhile the British were expelled from the colony of West Florida (parts of Florida, Louisiana, Alabama, and Mississippi) by Bernardo de Gálvez, the Spanish governor of Louisiana. In September 1779 he seized the British posts of Manchac and Baton Rouge (La.) and Natchez (Miss.). Mobile (Ala.) fell to Gálvez in March, 1780, followed by Pensacola (Fla.) in May 1781.

End of Fighting in Far South. In September 1781, Greene attempted a last major effort against Charleston. At Eutaw Springs (S.C.), about 50 miles (80 km) north of the city, he was intercepted on September 8 by Col. Alexander Stuart, who had succeeded Rawdon. After initially forcing the British to fall back, the Patriots stopped to loot the British camp. Stuart re-formed, counterattacked, and finally forced Greene to retire. Again Greene had failed to win a major engagement, but Stuart had lost more than two fifths of his force. He limited his efforts to defending Charleston. Greene remained near the city until the close of the war. Greene had committed serious tactical errors, but his strategy of maintaining his own army while wearing down the enemy had won. The British effort in the far south had failed.

Cornwallis at Yorktown. Meanwhile, Cornwallis had collected a force of 7,000 men in Virginia. After checking the Marquis de Lafayette at Greene Spring, but failing decisively to defeat him, Cornwallis abandoned all hope of conquering Virginia, moved to Yorktown, and near the end of July 1781 began to build fortifications. Clinton, appalled by Cornwallis' situation but insecure in his command, reluctantly agreed to Cornwallis' decision to make Yorktown his base.

Clinton's fear that another powerful French fleet would appear in American waters was well founded. In the spring of 1781, the French government had sent Admiral de Grasse with 20 warships across the Atlantic with orders to cooperate with Washington. Washington at first urged a land and sea attack upon New York, but then agreed with Rochambeau's suggestion to alter his objective and attempt to trap Cornwallis. Admiral de Grasse, heeding the advice of Rochambeau, appeared off the Chesapeake Bay on August 30 with a fleet of 28 ships and more than 3,000 French regulars. British admirals in the West Indies did not send enough ships to give the fleet at New York under Adm. Sir Thomas Graves equal strength.

Late in August, Rear Adm. Samuel Hood reached New York harbor with only 14 ships of the line. Graves and Hood joined their squadrons, and with 19 ships sailed on August 31 to find the French. They had no trouble finding de Grasse. On September 5 he sailed out of Chesapeake Bay to meet them. The action was indecisive, but Graves returned to New York eight days later to refit and secure reinforcements. Before his departure the French Newport squadron of seven ships under Count de Barras slipped into the bay to reinforce de Grasse. An escape by sea was impossible for Cornwallis.

Learning of de Grasse's plans on August 14, Washington boldly decided to transfer the bulk of the Franco-American army in New York to Virginia, leaving ten regiments of Continentals and militia to cover the Hudson. Moving swiftly and silently, most of Washington's force was beyond Philadelphia before Clinton could tell where it was going. On September 7, troops carried by de Grasse joined Lafayette· and took positions covering Yorktown on the land side. Adding his own allied command to these forces,

Washington had 17,000 men when he began the siege of Yorktown on September 28. On October 15 the allies seized two redoubts, forcing Cornwallis within his inner fortifications. On October 17, the British commander agreed to the surrender of all his forces, and on October 19 his army of more than 7,000 men laid down their arms. Except for minor skirmishes in the West, the war had virtually come to an end.

THE WAR AT SEA

Before the end of 1775, the majority of colonies had commissioned several craft, and Congress had established a navy and marine corps. The Continental Navy eventually put into service 50 or 60 ships; the Colonies' navies added another 40 or so. In contrast, the British Navy in 1775 had 270 ships and by 1783 had increased the number to 468. Although the combined American navies were unable to cope with the British fleets, they sank or captured nearly 200 royal ships.

The greatest damage to British shipping was inflicted by privateers, privately owned ships carrying letters of marque issued by Congress and the states. Early in 1778 approximately 10,000 Americans were engaged in privateering. After 1778, when the British had to deal with the fleets of France and Spain, American privateers multiplied. Late in the war more than 400 American vessels operated as privateers in the waters off the Atlantic coast, the West Indies, and even those surrounding the British Isles. They inflicted severe damage on British ships and trade, costing Britain about 2,000 ships, £18 million, and 12,000 men captured.

American Naval Raids. Credit for the first American naval victory belongs to Commodore Esek Hopkins. In the spring of 1776 he descended on Nassau in the Bahamas with eight ships and 200 marines, capturing the fort and carrying off powder, cannon, and other stores. By the end of 1777, United States ships had taken 464 enemy merchantmen. Britain, however, still commanded the seas with about 100 vessels in American waters, and had struck vigorously at the American commerce destroyers. In 1778, a second American raid on Nassau resulted in the capture of five ships. That year John Paul Jones, the most brilliant American naval officer of the Revolution, struck at the English border port of Whitehaven, on the Irish Sea, spiking the guns of the fort and destroying some of the vessels at the dock.

French and Spanish Action. The Franco-American alliance in 1778 and the entry of Spain into the war as an ally of France in 1779 fundamentally changed the war at sea. Thereafter, England was unable to maintain maritime supremacy, although throughout 1779 British ships dominated the waters adjacent to the American states. The cautious earl of Sandwich, first lord of the admiralty, insisted on keeping a fleet in the English Channel to guard against invasion, leaving the French and Spanish naval forces free to take the offensive where they pleased.

American Victories and Defeats. The American Navy enjoyed its most notable victory in 1779. In June of that year John Paul Jones put to sea from France in a converted 42-gun merchantman renamed the *Bon Homme Richard*. With him were the frigate *Alliance* and three French vessels. In September, in the North Sea off Flamborough Head, England, Jones engaged

Epic moonlight battle between John Paul Jones' flagship *Bon Homme Richard* (left) and the *Serapis* in 1779 ended with the American hero's capture of the British ship.

the English *Serapis* of 50 guns and the *Countess Scarborough* of 20 guns. After a moonlight battle of two hours, he captured both.

In the fall of 1779, Congress replaced its Marine Committee with a Board of Admiralty composed of experts outside Congress, but the strength and performances of the American Navy did not improve. For sea power Washington had to depend upon France.

Bibliography

Billias, George A., ed., *George Washington's Opponents* (Morrow 1969).

Bowden, R. Arthur, *Logistics and the Failure of the British Army in America 1775–1783* (Princeton Univ. Press 1975).

Bowman, Allen, *The Morale of the American Revolutionary Army* (Kennikat 1965).

Brown, Gerald S., *The American Secretary: Colonial Policy of Lord Germain* (Univ. of Mich. Press 1963).

Clark, William Bell, *Ben Franklin's Privateers* (La. State Univ. Press 1956).

Coggins, Jack, *Ships and Seamen of the American Revolution* (Stackpole Bks. 1969).

Flexner, James T., *George Washington,* 4 vols. (Little 1965–1972).

Freeman, Douglas S., *George Washington,* completed by John A. Carroll and Mary W. Ashworth, 7 vols. (Scribner 1948–1957).

Graymont, Barbara, *The Iroquois in the American Revolution* (Syracuse Univ. Press 1972).

Haas, Irwin, *America's Historic Battlefields* (Hippocrene Bks. 1987).

Higginbotham, Don, *The War of American Independence: Military Attitudes, Policies, and Practice, 1763–1789* (Macmillan 1971).

Kerber, Linda K., *Women of the Republic: Intellect and Ideology in Revolutionary America* (Univ. of N.C. Press 1980).

Mahan, Alfred T., *Major Operations of the Navies in the War of American Independence* (1913; reprint, Greenwood 1968).

Palmer, Dave R., *The Way of the Fox: American Strategy in the War for America 1775–1783* (Greenwood Press 1974).

Peterson, Harold L., *The Book of the Continental Soldier* (Stackpole Co. 1968).

Rossie, Jonathan G., *The Politics of Command in the American Revolution* (Syracuse Univ. Press 1975).

Shaw, Peter, *American Patriots and the Ritual of Revolution* (Harvard Univ. Press 1981).

Smith, Paul H., *Loyalists and Redcoats* (Univ. of N.C. Press 1965).

Symonds, Craig L., *A Battlefield Atlas of the American Revolution* (Nautical & Aviation Pub. Co. of Am. 1986).

3. Political, Social, and Economic Developments

Military conflict was but one aspect of the American Revolution. When the Thirteen Colonies severed themselves from Great Britain, they embarked upon an experiment in government that wrought fundamental changes in the political, social, and economic life of Americans. The triumph of republicanism in the establishment of state governments and a federal union was in itself a revolutionary development in an age of monarchies.

Toward Self-Government. There was no sudden, cataclysmic overthrow of constituted government. Extralegal organizations and institutions in the colonies, beginning with the nonimportation and nonconsumption associations, developed into more sophisticated and permanent bodies that gradually assumed the functions of government. Provincial conventions, generally elected by the freeholders, appeared in most of the colonies by the summer of 1774. These conventions appointed delegates to the First Continental Congress, passed laws and ordinances, and set up a system of committees of safety to combat disaffection.

Blood had already been shed at Lexington and Concord when the Second Continental Congress convened in May 1775. England's decision to use force against the Thirteen Colonies led Congress to take an aggressive stand in defense of American "rights." John Dickinson, leader of the conservative faction, prevailed on the delegates to issue one last plea for a redress of grievances in the form of the "Olive Branch Petition" to the king, adopted July 8. The effort failed when George III refused to accept the petition.

Many, perhaps most, of the delegates still hoped for a reconciliation. But Congress, under the leadership of John Adams and Samuel Adams, set about putting the colonies in a state of defense. On July 6, the "Declaration of the Causes and Necessity of Taking Up Arms" was adopted, asserting that Americans were "resolved

The Declaration of Independence is presented to Congress by the drafting committee.
The five-man group includes John Adams (*left*) and Jefferson and Franklin (*at right*).

to dye Free-men rather than live Slaves." On the last day of July, Congress adopted a report rejecting Lord North's Conciliatory Resolution.

British policy in 1775 was largely responsible for pushing the Americans toward independence. Even as the radical faction worked to prepare Congress for independence, urging the opening of colonial ports to foreign trade, alliance with France, and creation of state governments—George III declared that the colonies were in open rebellion. The Prohibitory Act, passed by Parliament in December 1775, authorized a naval blockade of America, seizure of American goods on the seas, and impressment of American sailors into the Royal Navy. The effect of this act was to reconcile hundreds of thousands of reluctant rebels to the necessity of separation from Britain.

In January 1776, Thomas Paine's *Common Sense* was published. In this most influential of American revolutionary tracts, Paine called for independence, and vigorously attacked the venerated institutions of royalty and the English constitution. Paine's plea convinced many that separation was not only inevitable but right and just.

Declaration of Independence. In response to the Prohibitory Act, Congress on April 6, 1776, resolved to open the ports of America for foreign trade. On May 10, the delegates adopted a resolution recommending that the colonies establish permanent governments. On June 7, in accordance with instructions from the Virginia Convention, Richard Henry Lee moved resolutions for independence, a general confederation, and the formation of foreign alliances. Conservatives, fearing a premature separation, managed to delay a final decision until July 2. On that day 12 states adopted Lee's resolutions (New York abstained, but gave its approval on July 9). Two days later, on July 4, 1776, Congress sanctioned the Declaration of Independence. The Thirteen Colonies were now the independent United States of America.

The Declaration of Independence was a con-vincing apologia for independence, a concise statement of the principles of the Revolution and of the nature of true government, and a magnificent assertion of the innate freedom and equality of all men. No other document so well expresses the highest ideals of the Revolution and the hopes of Americans for a better society under a government created by and functioning for the people.

Building a Government. Independence, however, was not an end but a beginning. There followed the processes of establishing constitutional state and central governments.

Many states, emulating Virginia, called special conventions for the purpose of framing their new constitutions. The "constitutional convention," transforming political ideology into practical politics, was certainly one of the greatest contributions of the American Revolution to political thought and practice. Another important innovation was the written constitution. In the 1780's the constitutional convention and the constitutional referendum, based on the principle that government must be sanctioned by the people, became American institutions.

In establishing their new constitutions, Americans did not totally reject their colonial experience and traditions. Most of the new governments were modeled on the old colonial systems, with the legislative body dominant over the judicial and executive branches.

It has been argued that the Revolution was "conservative," that Americans already enjoyed considerable democracy, and that they fought to preserve constitutional freedoms and privileges that they considered to be their rights as British subjects. This is in part true, and helps explain the broad unity of purpose among the Patriots. After 1774, however, most Patriots fought for a changed and better society, not to preserve the status quo.

Their gains were considerable. Every state acquired a bill of rights, guaranteeing trial by jury, the right of petition, freedom of speech, and other rights familiar to English law. Qualifications for the franchise and office holding were generally liberalized, although no state conceded universal manhood suffrage. In many of the states, redistricting in the interest of political justice and democracy led to increased representation in the legislatures for interior and frontier areas.

Articles of Confederation. The Patriots found it more difficult to agree on a constitution for a central government. Although virtually every Patriot acknowledged that a union was indispensable to winning and maintaining independence, jealousy among the states and fear of tyrannical rule made it difficult to achieve a satisfactory distribution of powers between the state and central governments.

On June 11, 1776, Congress appointed a committee to prepare a plan of confederation. John Dickinson reported a draft of Articles of Confederation that would, in the opinion of many delegates, create too strong a central government. Many of the most influential Revolutionary leaders feared power, especially political power concentrated in the hands of a relative few. They therefore desired that political power be diffused as much as possible—confined in the states where government officials might be more responsible to the citizens.

On Nov. 15, 1777, after long debate and many amendments, Congress adopted the Articles of Confederation and referred them to the states for ratification. Not until March 1, 1781, were the Articles formally ratified, and the United States at last had a constitutional union. The Articles of Confederation, however, proved inadequate to the political, economic, and diplomatic needs of the new nation.

The Constitution. In September 1786, delegates from five states met at Annapolis, Md., to study interstate commercial problems. Turning to broader questions, they issued a call for a special convention to revise the Articles of Confederation. The result was the Constitutional Convention, which met in Philadelphia from May 25 to Sept. 17, 1787.

Quickly discarding the old Articles of Confederation, the members of the convention produced an entirely new constitution, providing for a much stronger central government with a bicameral legislature, a federal judiciary, and a powerful executive. On Sept. 28, Congress resolved to transmit the Constitution to the states for submission to special ratifying conventions.

Debate between the proponents of the Constitution, who called themselves Federalists, and opponents, who were labeled Antifederalists, was vigorous and often bitter. Not until June 21, 1788, when New Hampshire became the ninth state to vote in the affirmative, was adoption ensured.

The addition of 10 amendments to the Constitution, known as the Bill of Rights, on Dec. 15, 1791, reconciled many Antifederalists to the new system of government. It has been asserted that the Constitution was the work of conservative forces, fearful of the democratic tendencies of the Revolution, and determined to gain control of the political and economic life of the nation. On the whole, however, the Constitution preserved, rather than destroyed, the gains made during the Revolution, and it has proved a durable, flexible, instrument of government.

Economic Upheavals. The Revolution brought economic as well as political change, together with much hardship and suffering. All of the colonies were affected by inflation and economic dislocation. Stock, grain, and tobacco, in addition to slaves, were taken from farms, warehouses, and plantations.

The shortage of finished goods, heretofore imported largely from England, led to soaring prices and an inflationary spiral. Hard money was scarce, and to finance the war effort Congress and the states resorted to the expediency of printing paper money. As the war progressed, paper money, especially Continental currency, rapidly depreciated. Efforts to establish a more stable currency supported by state taxation were fruitless.

More strenuous and somewhat more successful efforts were made to control inflation. In 1776, Connecticut, Massachusetts, New Hampshire, and Rhode Island adopted legislation to fix prices and wages. In November 1777, Congress recommended a grand program of price and wage regulation, and New York, New Jersey, and Pennsylvania instituted controls. Powerful opposition to regulation, especially from merchants who indulged in "black market" operations, undermined the program, however, and the machinery needed to enforce the laws was lacking. In June 1778, Congress recommended that attempts to set prices be abandoned. Inflation continued to plague the American economy throughout the war.

Economic dislocation and financial instability affected all Americans, but some suffered more than others, and some even prospered. Familiar channels of trade were closed to merchants, farmers, and the New England fisherman. Tobacco and rice planters in Virginia and South Carolina, heretofore assured a market in England for their produce, were forced to seek new outlets, or obtain new means of livelihood. Hardest hit by inflation were the clergy, town laborers and artisans, and the men and officers of the Continental Army. Desperate workers fought for higher wages, in some cases even went on strike, and organized committees to force merchants to lower prices. On occasion mob violence broke out, as in Philadelphia in October 1779, when angry townspeople besieged the house of James Wilson, a Loyalist counsel and commercial speculator.

Such outbursts give the impression of an internal conflict based on economic class divisions. In Pennsylvania and New York, and in some areas of other states, the struggle between privileged and nonprivileged, between upper and lower economic and social classes, was sharp. However, these clashes were not so numerous, widespread, and enduring as to support the thesis that there was an internal American revolutionary movement on the part of the poor against the rich. Many planters in the South, who rented much of their land, were seriously hurt by being obliged to accept rent payments in depreciated paper money. In such cases, the lower-class tenants, who sold their produce for high prices, were the gainers, and the "aristocratic" planters were the losers.

Among those who profited by the war were the farmers, whose products were in great demand by the Army. Privateering, which combined "business as usual" with patriotism, proved a remarkably profitable venture for thousands of enterprising Americans. Merchants and contractors—particularly men like Robert Morris of

Philadelphia, Silas Deane of Connecticut, and Benjamin Harrison of Virginia, who participated in obtaining French commercial aid for America—often realized fortunes. Many Patriots in official positions, such as Morris, who was the financial agent for the Continental Congress, carried on public and private business simultaneously, sometimes to the detriment of the former. Army commissaries and quartermasters, whose services were eagerly sought by merchants and contractors, often did the same.

Role of the Loyalists. Among those who suffered most during the Revolution were the Loyalists, or Tories. By early 1777, every state except Georgia and South Carolina had passed laws declaring as traitors those who actively supported Britain. In many states their property was seized and sold. They were denied access to the courts, the right to vote, and freedom of speech. Not less than 60,000 and perhaps as many as 100,000 Loyalists became exiles, either through banishment or refusal to submit to the hundreds of laws passed to confine and suppress them. Their property, amounting to several millions of pounds, was confiscated and sold by the states.

It is difficult, if not impossible, to ascertain the precise effect of the departure of the Loyalists, and the confiscation and sale of their property. It has been argued that they were, in the main, of the colonial aristocracy and gentry, and that their flight and the distribution of their property profoundly altered social and economic conditions in America. The Loyalists, however, were not a distinct economic and social class. Coming from virtually every station in life, they chose to support the king (or oppose the "rebellion") for a variety of reasons. The sale of their property doubtless benefited many Americans of moderate or meager means, but there followed no general leveling of social and economic status.

Perhaps those Loyalists who chose to remain in America, either as active or passive partisans of England, had the greater effect upon the course of the Revolution. Their presence and activity served to increase hatred of England, rendered immensely difficult the position of Patriot moderates and conservatives, and stiffened the determination of the majority of their countrymen to win the war.

Social and Cultural Reforms. The Revolutionary upheaval also led to important changes in the social and cultural fabric of America. The essentially democratic thrust of the Revolution can be seen in the efforts to strike at aristocracy and hereditary concentration of wealth and privilege, to obtain a large measure of religious freedom, to assail the institution of slavery and the slave trade, and to improve and extend education in the interest of an enlightened citizenry.

The principles of primogeniture and entail, designed to perpetuate wealth, social position, and political power, were abolished in every state. To be sure, they were not widely applied prior to 1776, nor, apparently, did their abolition contribute to a broad redistribution of property. Nevertheless, these legal changes did strike a blow against one prop of aristocracy. Further evidence of American distaste for rigid class or caste distinctions can be found in several of the state constitutions, which forbade hereditary distinctions, and in the Articles of Confederation and the Constitution, which prohibited

the states and the United States from granting titles of nobility.

Far more important was the movement for religious freedom and the separation of church and state. Prior to the Revolution, the Episcopal Church was established in the five southern colonies; the Congregational Church was strongly favored in three of the New England colonies. Persons of non-Christian or unorthodox Christian belief were often discriminated against. Roman Catholics could not vote in Maryland; non-Episcopalians were taxed to support the Anglican Church in Virginia. Led by Thomas Jefferson, Virginians, through the Statute of Religious Settlement (1779), made religious belief a personal matter, and disestablished the Anglican Church. Other states followed Virginia's example, although the Congregational Church retained its privileged status in Massachusetts and Connecticut well into the 19th century.

By the 1st Amendment to the U.S. Constitution, Congress was denied power to interfere with religious freedom or create an "establishment" of religion. Full freedom of religious belief, or lack of it, was not attained; but the principles of separation of church and state and the liberty of free inquiry and thought were immeasurably strengthened by the Revolution.

Not all Patriots agreed with the proposition, stated in the Declaration of Independence, that "all men are created equal" and have "certain unalienable rights." Still, thoughtful men in both the South and North agreed that Negro bondage was not morally justifiable and that slavery and the slave trade should be ended. Abolition of slavery was much easier where slaves were few. Within 30 years after the Declaration of Independence, slavery had largely disappeared in the New England states, New York, New Jersey, and Pennsylvania; and the Northwest Ordinance of 1787 forbade the institution in the Northwest Territory, from which the states of Ohio, Indiana, Illinois, Michigan, and Wisconsin were eventually formed.

In the South, manumission was made possible in Virginia and Maryland, but economic self-interest and the immense social and political problems posed by abolition led Southern reformers reluctantly to accept the institution as a necessary evil and postpone action against it to some future time.

A Beginning. In other areas the Revolutionary generation addressed itself to the construction of a better society. Jefferson, John Adams, and other foresighted leaders, convinced that a republic could not long exist without an enlightened citizenry, urged the establishment of state and national education systems. Some beginning was made toward state-supported education, but economic troubles stymied most of these efforts. The dream of education that would be open to all remained for future generations of Americans to fulfill.

It may perhaps be an exaggeration to speak of an "internal" American Revolution. The period from 1763 to 1789 was marked by social, cultural, and political continuity as well as change. It is nevertheless true that American society was in many ways transformed, and American institutions altered and reformed, during this period. Not least, a republic was established—as yet it was still an infant among nations, but it possessed vast opportunities for greatness.

Seven long years after he had been expelled by the British, General Washington makes his triumphal entry into New York in 1783. The commander in chief contributed more than any single man to the cause of American independence, confirmed by the peace treaty that became final on September 3 of that year.

Benjamin Franklin at a French reception in 1778. The American envoy captivated Paris with his wisdom and charm.

The greatest tribute to the Revolution is the fact that its ideals not only were achieved but also remained a reality two centuries later. The Constitution was still a great force for order and justice, and Revolutionary heroes were still held up to youngsters as worthy of emulation.

Bibliography

Beard, Charles A., *An Economic Interpretation of the Constitution of the United States* (Macmillan 1935).
Becker, Carl L., *The Declaration of Independence* (Harcourt 1922).
Brown, Wallace, *The Good Americans: The Loyalists in the American Revolution* (Morrow 1969).
Calhoon, Robert M., *The Loyalists in Revolutionary America, 1760–1781* (Harcourt 1973).
Conser, Walter H., Jr., and others, eds., *Resistance, Politics, and the American Struggle for Independence 1765–1775* (Lynne Rienner 1987).
East, Robert A., *Business Enterprise in the American Revolutionary Era* (1938; reprint, P. Smith 1964).
Greene, Jack P., ed., *The American Revolution: Its Character and Limits* (N.Y. Univ. Press 1987).
Greene, Jack P., compiler, *The Reinterpretation of the American Revolution 1763–1789* (1968; reprint, Greenwood Press 1979).
MacLeod, D. J., *Slavery, Race and the American Revolution* (Cambridge 1975).
Main, Jackson T., *Political Parties Before the Constitution* (Univ. of N.C. Press 1973).
Main, Jackson T., *The Social Structure of Revolutionary America* (Princeton Univ. Press 1965).
Morris, Richard B., *The Forging of the Union 1781–1789* (Harper 1987).
Royster, Charles A., *A Revolutionary People at War: The Continental Army and American Character* (Norton 1982).
Schuckers, J. W., *Finances and Paper Money of the Revolutionary War* (1874; reprint, Dent 1978).
Smith, Barbara, *After the Revolution* (Pantheon 1987).
Suggs, George G., Jr., ed., *Perspectives on the American Revolution* (Southern Ill. Univ. Press 1977).
Wood, Gordon S., *The Confederation and the Constitution: The Critical Issues* (Univ. Press of Am. 1979).

4. Diplomatic Developments

In 1776, Britain faced only 13 belligerent colonies. Within four years, France, Spain, and the Netherlands had declared war on England; the War of Independence had become a part of a vast international struggle to reduce British power in America and elsewhere, and to restore a colonial and European balance of power violently disturbed by British victory in the Seven Years' War (1756–1763).

Alliance with France. After 1763, France and Spain sought an opportunity to retaliate for the losses they had suffered at the hands of Britain. In France, Étienne François, duke de Choiseul, head of the foreign ministry, rebuilt a new and powerful navy in preparation for a war of revenge. Assuming that commerce was the real foundation of British strength, Choiseul eagerly watched the developing Anglo-American crisis after 1764. He hoped that the Thirteen Colonies would gain their independence and that their trade could be channeled to France. In this way, he hoped to strike a telling blow against British power and increase the wealth and prestige of France.

Choiseul fell from power in 1770, but his policies were continued by the Comte de Vergennes, who became foreign minister in 1774. An experienced, cautious diplomat, Vergennes embarked on a circumspect policy of encouragement to the American colonies. In September 1775 he sent an agent to Philadelphia to intimate that French ports might be opened to American ships. In March 1776, Vergennes and the playwright Caron de Beaumarchais set up a fictitious trading company—subsidized by one million livres each from the Bourbon courts in France and Spain—secretly to supply munitions and other materials to the Americans. Aid from France and from Spain, the latter largely through the services of Don Diego de Gardoqui, began to arrive after the end of 1776 and materially contributed to the American success.

In 1776, the Continental Congress sent Silas Deane, Benjamin Franklin, and Arthur Lee as agents to France to obtain a commercial and military alliance. The American agents pressed the French court to recognize American independence and to form an alliance with the struggling states. They were unsuccessful until news arrived in Paris in early December 1777 of the American victory at Saratoga. On December 17, not waiting to discover whether Spain would join France, Vergennes promised the United States formal recognition.

On Feb. 6, 1778, two treaties, one of amity and commerce, the other of alliance, were signed by France and the United States. Spain, fearful of the possible threat of an independent republic adjacent to her American colonies, refused to join the alliance. In April 1779, Spain entered the war on the side of France, although not as an ally of the United States.

In November 1780, angered by the sale of supplies to America, France, and Spain by Dutch merchants, Britain delivered an ultimatum to The Hague that brought the Netherlands into the war. In the same year Russia, Denmark, and Sweden formed the League of Armed Neutrality. Other European nations joined the league until, by 1783, Britain found itself in a position of military and diplomatic isolation.

British Conciliation Efforts. During the War of Independence, Britain was seriously torn by domestic discord at a time when political unity was indispensable for the preservation of the empire. British politics were characterized by factionalism. Corruption and place-seeking had largely supplanted political principle.

After 1770, when Lord North became prime minister and through the "King's Friends" obtained large majorities in Parliament, a semblance of political unity emerged, at least in regard to the American War. The North ministry, however, was constantly under attack by William Pitt the Elder and his following, and by other dissident factions. The war was never popular among the middle and lower classes.

At various times during the war, the North ministry made gestures toward conciliation, but the overtures were consistently too late and too little. Lord North's first plan of conciliation, embodied in a resolution of the House of Commons on Feb. 20, 1775, was regarded by the Americans as an insidious attempt to subvert their unity, and the plan was repudiated by the Continental Congress. The drift toward separation resumed and ended with the Declaration of Independence in 1776.

The news of Gen. John Burgoyne's defeat at Saratoga (October 1777) stirred panic among British officials and raised fear of a Franco-American alliance. On Feb. 17, 1778, at the behest of Lord North, Parliament repealed the Townshend tea duty, the Massachusetts Government Act, and the Prohibitory Act, and authorized the government to send negotiators to America. The Carlisle commission—composed of the earl of Carlisle, William Eden, and George Johnstone—was authorized to deal with Congress but not to recognize American independence or withdraw British forces from the 13 states.

A month before the arrival of the British commission in Philadelphia, Pa., Silas Deane delivered the Franco-American treaties to Congress. On May 4, Congress ratified both treaties. When the Carlisle commission arrived in Philadelphia in early June, it was unable to reach an understanding with the Patriots, who now would accept nothing short of independence.

Peace Negotiations. After 1778 the war went badly for England. But the king refused to consider peace negotiations even when news of Cornwallis' surrender at Yorktown reached London in November 1781. Finally bowing to the clamor for peace, George III, after briefly considering abdication, accepted in March 1782 a new ministry drawn almost entirely from the Opposition.

Sir Guy Carleton was dispatched to New York to replace Sir Henry Clinton and was instructed to withdraw British troops from the 13 states. At the same time, Lord Shelburne, secretary of state for the colonies in the ministry, sent Richard Oswald to Paris to open negotiations with Benjamin Franklin for the purpose of trying to wean the Americans away from France. The Patriots had already discovered that their interests and war aims did not entirely coincide with those of the Bourbon powers.

Franklin acted for America in the early stages of the negotiations with the British; he was later joined by John Adams, John Jay, and Henry Laurens. In September 1781, Oswald was authorized to treat with the commissioners of the "Thirteen United States," which was tantamount to informal recognition of American independence; and Jay, who had become increasingly distrustful of France and Spain, persuaded Franklin to ignore Congress' instructions that the American envoys consult fully with France.

Thereafter, negotiations moved swiftly toward a final settlement. On Nov. 30, 1782, the preliminary Anglo-American peace treaty was signed, and on Sept. 3, 1783, the treaty (called the Peace of Paris) became final.

The peace settlement was a great diplomatic achievement. The American commissioners agreed to validate private debts to British creditors, and pledged restoration of Loyalist rights and property. In addition, minor boundary concessions were made to Britain. In return, Britain recognized American independence, agreed to American fishing rights off Newfoundland and Nova Scotia, and most important, granted America the territory between the Appalachians and the Mississippi.

See also Index entry *American Revolution.*

PAUL C. BOWERS, JR.
The Ohio State University

Bibliography

Corwin, Edward S., *French Policy and the American Alliance of 1778* (Princeton Univ. Press 1916).

Coupland, Reginald, *American Revolution and the British Empire* (1930; reprint, Russell 1965).

Dull, Jonathan R., *A Diplomatic History of the American Revolution* (Yale Univ. Press 1985).

Dull, Jonathan R., *The French Navy and American Independence* (Princeton Univ. Press 1975).

Kaplan, Lawrence S., *Colonies into Nation: American Diplomacy, 1763–1801* (Macmillan 1972).

Marks, Frederick W., III, *Independence of Trial: Foreign Affairs and the Making of the Constitution* (La. State Univ. Press 1973).

Morris, Richard B., *The Peacemakers: The Great Powers and American Independence* (Harper 1965).

Ritcheson, Charles R., *British Politics and the American Revolution* (1954; reprint, Greenwood 1981).

Sosin, J. M., *Agents and Merchants: British Colonial Policy and the Origins of the American Revolution 1763–1775* (Univ. of Neb. Press 1965).

Spurlin, Paul M., *The French Enlightenment in America* (Univ. of Ga. Press 1984).

Stinchcombe, William C., *The American Revolution and the French Alliance* (Syracuse Univ. Press 1969).

Toth, Charles W., ed., *Liberté, Egalité, Fraternité: The American Revolution and the European Response* (Whitson 1987).

Van Alstyne, Richard W., *Empire and Independence: The International History of the American Revolution* (Wiley 1965).

AMERICAN SADDLE HORSE, a breed of light horse developed in the mid-1800s by Kentucky plantation owners. The foundation sire was a Thoroughbred; the breed also contains Morgan and pacer blood.

The American saddle horse is mainly bred for show. It stands an average 15 to 16 hands at the withers (a hand equals 4 inches, or 10 cm), and weighs about 1,000 to 1,200 pounds (450-545 kg). Bays, browns, chestnuts, and blacks predominate. The horse is exhibited in three classes: in light harness (at the walk and park gait, which is a showy trot), as a three-gaited saddler (at the walk, trot, and canter), and as a five-gaited saddler. To the three basic gaits, the five-gaited horse adds the slow gait (a four-beat gait, like a prancing walk) and the rack (a high-speed version of the slow gait). Flashy movement is prized.

AMERICAN SAMOA. See SAMOA.

AMERICAN SOCIETY FOR THE PREVENTION OF CRUELTY TO ANIMALS, an organization to promote kindness and prevent cruelty toward animals by education, legislation, and the enforcement of animal-protection laws. The American Society for the Prevention of Cruelty to Animals (ASPCA), founded in New York City in 1866, was the first anticruelty, or humane, society in the United States.

The ASPCA maintains shelters and adoption services for lost, abandoned, or unwanted animals. ASPCA agents can carry firearms, sue an owner for mistreatment of an animal, and, with court permission, take an animal away from its owner.

The Society for the Prevention of Cruelty to Animals (SPCA) is the name for many separate, similar organizations. In the United States they are modeled on the ASPCA, though reflecting differences in state animal-protection laws.

AMERICAN SOCIETY OF COMPOSERS, AUTHORS AND PUBLISHERS, an organization that serves as a clearinghouse in the field of performance rights. The American Society of Composers, Authors and Publishers (ASCAP) was founded in 1914 by three publishers' representatives, a librettist, and five composers, including Victor Herbert and Irving Berlin. With headquarters in New York City, ASCAP has over 63,000 members and revenues of $386 million. It grants licenses and collects fees for the public performance of the copyrighted musical works of ASCAP members on radio or television or in motion pictures, restaurants, offices, elevators, or any other place in which music is played publicly. (See HERBERT, VICTOR; BERLIN, IRVING.)

ASCAP is affiliated with similar organizations in other countries, and it protects the rights of members of those societies from copyright infringement in the United States.

AMERICAN STAFFORDSHIRE TERRIER, a tough, strong dog breed recognized in 1935 by the American Kennel Club as the Staffordshire Terrier, then given its current name in 1972 to distinguish it from England's Staffordshire bull terrier. Standard height for the males is 18 to 19 inches (45—47 cm); for the females it is 17 to 18 inches (42—45 cm). The breed's average weight is 55 to 60 pounds (25—27 kg). Its short, smooth, easy-to-groom coat may be of nearly any color or colors; its ears are usually cropped.

EVELYN M. SHAFER

The American Staffordshire terrier is a good guard dog.

Depending on its bloodlines and training, the American Staff is capable of behaving like its notorious look-alike, the pit bull terrier, both breeds having been bred originally for dogfighting and guard work. Fortunately, most American Staff breeders today are concerned with producing fine family dogs that are both protective and trustworthy. The American Staff is less exuberant than most other terriers. Many adult Staffs, however, quarrel with strange dogs and so should be kept on a leash outdoors. The American Staff is subject to hip dysplasia but has an extremely high pain threshold.

Apartment dwellers who are considering buying an American Staff should first look into the more compact Staffordshire bull terrier.

JOHN HOWE
Author of "Choosing the Right Dog"

AMERICAN STATES, Organization of. See ORGANIZATION OF AMERICAN STATES.

AMERICAN STOCK EXCHANGE (AMEX), a market in New York City for trading nearly 1,000 issues of stocks and bonds of foreign and domestic companies. In the United States, AMEX is second in size only to the New York Stock Exchange and handles somewhat lower-priced stocks of young, growing companies. It was the first exchange to introduce an automated stock quotation system (1964); to elect female members (1965); and to devise its own price index covering the entire breadth of the market (1966). This index was replaced in 1973 with a capitalization-weighted index that reflects changes in the aggregate market value of the AMEX list. With an annual trading volume of over 5 billion shares, AMEX has a daily average of over 22 million shares.

The exchange's regular membership includes nearly 500 publicly traded companies plus associates and allied members who operate in more than 4,000 offices around the world. The administration of AMEX is organized into several divisions, with emphasis on regulation and market surveillance; services to the public, investors, listed companies, and the securities industry; and planning and development. The exchange has been a leader in introducing state-of-the-art trading floor technology. As a trading facility, AMEX is an auction market in which securities' prices are determined by public bids to buy and offers to sell.

To qualify for listing on the exchange, a company must have a minimum net worth of $4 million; pretax earnings of at least $750,000; not fewer than 500,000 publicly held shares with a market value of at least $3 million; and a minimum of 800 shareholders.

The American Stock Exchange is the successor to the New York Curb Exchange, which began in the late 18th century. The Curb Exchange originally conducted its business on the street (hence the name) but eventually moved into a 14-story building. The present name was adopted on Jan. 5, 1953.

GENE SMITH, *"New York Times"*

AMERICAN TELEPHONE AND TELEGRAPH COMPANY

(AT&T), a U.S. corporation foremost in the field of telecommunications. Aside from creating, with the Bell Company, the world's largest and most advanced telecommunications network, its more distinguished achievements include development of the Gemini spaceflights network and the Telstar communications satellite, construction of early warning systems for the U.S. Defense Department, and engineering of worldwide radiotelephone and transoceanic cable systems.

Under Theodore N. Vail, the company was incorporated in 1885 as a long-line operating firm, subsidiary to the old American Bell Telephone Company. In a reorganization in 1900, AT&T took over the Bell Company by an exchange of stock. It became one of the largest corporations in the United States in terms of annual income.

In 1974 the Justice Department sued AT&T for attempting to monopolize the telephone industry. During 1982–1983 an agreement was worked out whereby AT&T would divest itself of its 22 local companies, grouped into 7 regional holding companies, effective Jan. 1, 1984. It retained the Western Electric Company (its manufacturing subsidiary), the Bell Telephone Laboratories (its research subsidiary), and its long-distance activities; it relinquished the name *Bell* to the local companies, which were permitted to sell telephones. Since 1984 AT&T has digitalized its entire network, moved into the international market and nearly 200 countries, and pursued mergers and acquisitions to provide globally networked multimedia communications and online services.

AMERICAN TRAGEDY, An,

a novel by the American writer Theodore Dreiser, published in 1925. The novel follows the life of Clyde Griffiths, son of Fundamentalist street preachers in a Midwestern town. Clyde's bleak childhood instills in him a fervent desire for wealth and elegance. After moving to Lycurgus, N.Y., to work in his wealthy uncle's mill, he becomes involved with a fellow worker, Roberta Alden, and then falls in love with the beautiful, rich Sondra Finchly. In a desperate effort to escape the mediocrity of a life with Roberta, who has become pregnant by him, Clyde murders her in a faked boat accident. A section of the book is devoted to Clyde's trial and his inner struggle to determine his own guilt or innocence. Based on an actual murder case, the novel depicts Clyde as driven to his fate by social and economic forces beyond his control.

An American Tragedy marks a high point in Dreiser's long career as the leading proponent of naturalistic determinism in American literature. A popular success, it was well received by critics who had attacked his earlier books as immoral.

AMERICAN UNIVERSITY,

a coeducational institution in Washington, D.C., founded under Methodist Church sponsorship in 1891 and chartered by Congress in 1893. Instruction began in 1914, when graduate-level courses were organized.

An undergraduate division was opened in 1925. In 1949 Washington College of Law affiliated with the university, and schools of business administration, communication, and public affairs were added. The division of general studies was established in 1957, and the school of international service and Wesley Theological Seminary were opened in 1958. Housed at the university are several academic centers and institutes, including the Center for Congressional and Presidential Studies, the English Language Institute, and the International Institute for Health Promotion. The important collections at the university's Bender Library include the Artemus Martin Collection (mathematics), the Ester Ballou Memorial Collection (music), and the Spinks Collection (Japanese culture).

AMERICAN UNIVERSITY OF BEIRUT,

bā-root', a private, nondenominational institution in Beirut, Lebanon, founded by American missionaries in 1866 as the Syrian Protestant College under a charter from the New York state board of regents. It has faculties of arts and science, engineering, agricultural sciences, and medical sciences (including pharmacy, nursing, and public health). Lectures are conducted in English and Arabic. The medical school trains physicians for the Middle East. The university's main library, the Jafet Library, was renovated and expanded in 1996 after a November 1991 bomb explosion destroyed its main hall.

AMERICAN VETERANS OF WORLD WAR II, KOREA & VIETNAM.

See AMVETS.

AMERICAN WATER SPANIEL,

span'yəl, a medium-sized liver- or dark-chocolate-colored breed of spaniel. The dog was developed about 1880 in the Middle West for hunting waterfowl and was recognized as a breed by the American Kennel Club in 1940.

The dog stands 15 to 18 inches (38–48 cm) tall at the shoulder and weighs 25 to 45 pounds

American water spaniels are popular gun dogs.

WALTER CHANDOHA

(11–20 kg). It has a closely curled coat, a moderate-sized head with short smooth hair on the forehead, generally dark eyes, strong jaws, well-developed nostrils, long and wide ears, powerful forelegs, a sturdy, well-developed body, and a tail of moderate length.

The dog has a friendly disposition and learns quickly. It is an excellent swimmer and retriever of waterfowl and has a fine nose for locating game in rough terrain. It is also a good watchdog.

AMERICAN YOUTH HOSTELS (HI-AYH), a non-profit membership organization that provides educational and recreational travel opportunities for people of all ages. The organization maintains more than 150 hostels throughout the United States in both urban and rural locations. Founded in 1934, HI-AYH is the U.S. affiliate of the International Youth Hostel Federation (Hostelling International). *Hostelling USA* is the organization's chief publication. The national headquarters is in Washington, D.C.

See also YOUTH HOSTELS.

AMERICAN'S CREED. In 1917, William Tyler Page, then clerk of the United States House of Representatives, won a national contest for the "best summary of American political faith." The city of Baltimore awarded him $1,000 for his 100-word statement, which the House of Representatives accepted on April 3, 1918. The text follows:

"I believe in the United States of America as a Government of the people, by the people, for the people; whose just powers are derived from the consent of the governed; a democracy in a republic; a sovereign Nation of many sovereign States; a perfect union, one and inseparable; established upon those principles of freedom, equality, justice and humanity for which American patriots sacrificed their lives and fortunes.

"I therefore believe it is my duty to my country to love it; to support its Constitution; to obey its laws; to respect its flag, and to defend it against all enemies."

AMERICANS FOR DEMOCRATIC ACTION (ADA), a nonpartisan political organization that supports progressive candidates for public office in the United States. It also seeks to influence legislation through public education and through testimony before congressional committees.

The ADA was organized in 1947 by a group of political leaders, trade union officials, university people, and others as a bulwark for liberalism. Its express purpose is to formulate liberal domestic and foreign policies based on the realities and changing needs of American democracy, enlist public understanding and support of these policies, and seek to put them into effect by political action through major political parties.

AMERICA'S CUP. See YACHTS AND YACHTING.

AMERICIUM, am-ə-ris′ē-əm, a silvery radioactive element and a member of the actinide series, symbol Am. Americium's atomic number is 95, its atomic weight is 243, and it is a member of Group IIIB of the periodic table. Americium was named in honor of the Americas. (See also ACTINIDE SERIES; METAL; TRANSURANIUM ELEMENTS.)

Americium does not occur naturally. It was first produced in 1944 by Glenn T. Seaborg, Ralph A. James, Leon O. Morgan, and Albert Ghiorso in Chicago while they were working on the Manhattan Project. It was produced, in the form of the isotope ^{241}Am, by the following sequence of neutron irradiations and radioactive decays:

$$^{239}Pu + n \rightarrow \, ^{240}Pu + \gamma$$
$$^{240}Pu + n \rightarrow \, ^{241}Pu + \gamma$$
$$^{241}Pu \quad\quad \rightarrow \, ^{241}Am + \beta^-$$

Other known isotopes of americium now include ^{237}Am, ^{238}Am, ^{239}Am, ^{240}Am, ^{242}Am, ^{242m}Am, and ^{243}Am. Their half-lives range from 25 minutes for ^{246}Am to 7,600 years for ^{243}Am.

The various isotopes are synthesized from elements with lower atomic numbers by means of nuclear reactions. The primary source for the production of americium isotopes is plutonium, which is made from uranium. Plutonium, produced in nuclear reactors, contains a certain percentage of the isotope ^{241}Pu. This isotope undergoes radioactive decay, forming ^{241}Am. The ^{241}Am, which has a half-life of 458 years, can then be partially converted to the long-life ^{243}Am by irradiation with neutrons in a nuclear reactor.

In the case of artificially produced elements, it is customary to give the mass number of the longest-lived isotope as the atomic weight. On this basis, the atomic weight of americium is 243.

Properties. Americium exhibits +3, +5, and +6 oxidation states in aqueous solutions. The ions and their colors are: Am^{+3}, pink; AmO_2^+, yellow; and AmO_2^{++}, red brown. Solid compounds that exhibit the +4 oxidation state, such as AmO_2 and AmF_1, have also been prepared. In its metallic form after reduction of an americium compound, americium is a typical malleable and ductile metal with a silvery luster. Its melting point is 1176 °C (2149 °F).

Isolation. In the isolation of gram amounts of ^{241}Am, plutonium containing some ^{241}Pu is purified. Then the solution is allowed to stand for several months, and some of the ^{241}Pu decays to ^{241}Am. The americium can then be separated from the plutonium by any one of several processes. An americium compound in pure form was first isolated by B. B. Cunningham in 1945.

Uses. ^{241}Am is used as the starting material for the production of curium^{242}, which is used in isotope power sources.

RALPH A. JAMES
Lawrence Livermore Laboratory

Bibliography: Emsley, John, *The Elements*, 2d ed. (Oxford 1991); **Greenwood, N. N.,** and A. Earnshaw, *Chemistry of the Elements* (Pergamon 1984); **Lide, David R.,** ed., *CRC Handbook of Chemistry and Physics*, 75th ed. (CRC Press 1994).

AMERICUS, ə-mər′i-kus, a city in Georgia, 50 miles (80 km) southeast of Columbus, and the seat of Sumter county. It is a center of agricultural production and trading. It is also a center for light industry. There is mining of bauxite and kaolin. Georgia Southwestern College is located there, and the Jimmy Carter National Historic Site is nearby. Americus was settled in 1832. In the past, the area was well known among Native Americans for the cultivation of maize. Population: 17,013.

AMERIGO VESPUCCI. See VESPUCCI, AMERIGO.

AMERIND, am′ə-rind, a word suggested by John Wesley Powell (1834–1902) as a convenient term to use for the American Indians. The term covers all Native American tribes.

AMES, āmz, **Fisher** (1758–1808), American Federalist leader, who eloquently championed strong central government based on an aristocracy of "the wise and good and opulent."

He was born in Dedham, Mass., on April 9, 1758, the son of Nathaniel Ames, an almanac maker. Fisher Ames graduated from Harvard College in 1774 and thereafter studied law with a Boston firm, being admitted to the bar in 1781. As a result of the political reputation he established with his pieces by "Lucius Junius Brutus" in the Boston *Independent Chronicle* in 1786, and his "Camillus" essays in the following year, he was elected in 1787 to the Massachusetts convention that ratified the federal Constitution and in 1788 to the Massachusetts General Court. Elected Federalist representative in the first United States Congress in 1789, he was returned to the succeeding three congresses, serving until the end of Washington's administration (1797).

A brilliant, energetic intellectual, Ames brought to the Congress a distrust of the growing Jeffersonian democracy (as represented by the new Antifederalist–or Republican–Party) and became a forceful spokesman for the rights of property, protection of the new republic's commercial interests (particularly those of New England), strengthening of ties between the legislative and executive branches of the federal government, and promotion of peace and prosperity as a means of supplanting "Jacobinism" with Federalist principles in the South. His speeches in Congress were masterpieces of eloquence. After his address to the House on April 28, 1796, in support of appropriations that would carry the controversial Jay's Treaty of 1794–1795 into effect, his opponents found it necessary to ask for an adjournment to break the spell of his oratory; and the next day the House supported his views by a majority of three votes.

Suffering from a chronic illness, he retired to Dedham in 1797, his only subsequent public service coming as a member of the governor's council in 1799–1801. In 1802 he advised the Federalists to strengthen their power in state governments, "to make state justice and state power a shelter for the wise, and good, and rich, from the wild destroying rage of the Southern Jacobins." Three years later he declined the presidency of Harvard College and in the same year wrote *The Dangers of American Liberty*, in which he expressed the fear that anarchy would be the result of Jefferson's administration. Ames died on July 4, 1808, in Dedham.

Ames' collected speeches were edited by P.W. Ames in the volume *Speeches in Congress, 1789–1796* (Boston 1871). Seth Ames assembled two volumes of his writings in *Works of Fisher Ames* (Boston 1854).

AMES, āmz, **James Barr** (1846–1910), American legal scholar, who established the case study method of teaching law. He was born in Boston on June 22, 1846, and graduated from Harvard College and Harvard Law School.

In 1873, a year after his graduation from the law school, he joined its faculty. From the outset he subscribed to the revolutionary case study method conceived by Christopher C. Langdell, the law school dean. Essentially Socratic, the method consisted of presenting students with reports of historic cases and requiring them to discover the principles contained therein. Ames' collections of cases and his successful use of them

in class proved the effectiveness of the method. When he succeeded Langdell as dean in 1895, all other methods of legal study were abolished at Harvard; many other schools adopted the case study method. His researches in Norman-French reports of early judicial decisions threw new light on the origins of the law of contracts. Ames died at Wilton, N.H., on Jan. 8, 1910.

AMES, āmz, **Nathaniel** (1708–1764), American almanac maker and physician. He was born at Bridgewater, Mass., on July 22, 1708. He founded (1725) and edited the *Astronomical Diary and Almanack*, which was similar in many respects to Franklin's *Poor Richard's Almanack*, founded in 1732. Little is known of his medical career. He was the father of Federalist leader Fisher Ames. He died at Dedham, Mass., on July 11, 1764.

AMES, āmz, **Oakes** (1804–1873), American capitalist and industrialist, who built the Union Pacific Railroad, the first transcontinental railroad in the United States. As a risk-taking organizer and manager, Ames is representative of how pioneering ventures were conducted in the 1860's.

He was born in Easton, Mass., on Jan. 10, 1804. At 16 he entered his father's shovel works as a laborer. In 1844, with his brother, *Oliver Ames, Jr.* (1807–1877), he assumed joint command of the $220,000 firm of Oliver Ames & Sons. Gold discoveries in the West and Australia, increasing rail construction, the Civil War, opening of the Northwest, and an influx of immigrant labor to the United States—all helped to boost the firm's prosperity.

In 1855, with Oliver, Jr., Ames constructed the Easton Branch Railroad to facilitate shipment of the firm's products. After two years on the Executive Council of Massachusetts, Ames was elected to the U.S. House of Representatives in 1862. He became active on House committees concerned with transportation and manufacturing and was a confidant of President Lincoln. Urged by Lincoln to attempt to build the long-sought rail link from Omaha, Nebr., to the West Coast, he inspected possible routes with John Inslee Blair in 1862. From then until the Union Pacific's tracks joined with the Central Pacific Railroad's tracks in Utah in 1869, Ames was the driving force behind the Union Pacific project.

Ames invested $1 million of his own capital in the Union Pacific, pledged the remainder of his family's funds, and raised $2.5 million from others. In 1865 the Ames brothers joined with T.C. Durant as principals—along with other large Union Pacific stockholders—in the Crédit Mobilier of America, a firm set up to construct the railroad. In his own name Oakes contracted to lay 667 miles of track. Risks ran high. Mistakes included mislocated bridges, ill-graded trackage, and failure of lines to meet. From government bonds, land-grant bonds, railroad stock, and other items paid by Union Pacific, Crédit Mobilier realized a profit of $23 million (48 percent of its total cost). But the Union Pacific itself went deeply into debt.

Ames was in a position fraught with conflicting interests. He was simultaneously promoting Crédit Mobilier, directing the Union Pacific (of which Oliver, Jr., was president), selling shovels and tools, and serving on a House committee deliberating the regulation of rail rates. In

1868, Ames sold Crédit Mobilier stock to some 22 fellow legislators at prices far below the market value. Public disclosure of the sale four years later led to three congressional inquiries and resulted in a House resolution of censure in February 1873 that said: "The House absolutely condemns the conduct of Oakes Ames . . . in seeking to secure congressional attention to . . . a corporation in which he was interested."

The House failed to expel Ames, agreeing with a later account that summed up his actions as "improper, indiscreet, but not dishonest." Nonetheless, the censure crushed Ames. He died in North Easton, Mass., on May 8, 1873. See also CRÉDIT MOBILIER OF AMERICA.

Oliver Ames (1831–1895), his son, assumed many of his father's former leadership responsibilities, paid off the estate's debts, and in 1883 won vindication for the name Oakes Ames through a resolution of the Massachusetts legislature. He later won the Massachusetts governorship three times.

FRANKLIN P. HOWARD,
University of Connecticut

AMES, āmz, **William** (1576–1633), English Puritan theologian. He was born at Ipswich, England, and studied at Christ's College, Cambridge, where he received the B.A. and M.A. degrees and was influenced by the Calvinist theologian William Perkins. Ames remained at Cambridge for a time as a fellow, but though his Puritanism was of a moderate, nonseparatist type, he had little chance for advancement in England. He therefore moved to Holland, serving English congregations and entering the lists against the Arminians. Ames was present at the Synod of Dort (1618–1619), where he took his stand with the victorious orthodox Calvinist side. He became professor of theology at the University of Franeker in 1622.

Ames was a prolific author. His Latin works were collected in five volumes (1658); not all have been translated into English. Especially important were *Medulla theologiae* (1623; *The Marrow of Sacred Divinity*) and *De conscientia* (1632; *Cases of Conscience*).

Ames was about to leave for America when he died at Rotterdam on Nov. 14, 1633. His family carried his valuable library to New England, where his theological influence was very strong. His *Medulla* was the standard textbook in theology at Harvard and Yale until the mid-18th century.

ROBERT T. HANDY, *Union Theological Seminary*

AMES, āmz, **Winthrop** (1871–1937), American theatrical producer, who was noted for his production of noncommercial plays. A grandson of the financier and politician Oakes Ames, he was born in North Easton, Mass., on Nov. 25, 1871. He graduated from Harvard in 1895, and in 1905 he became manager of the Castle Square Theater in Boston. Later he moved to New York City, where he built the Little Theatre (1912) and the Booth Theatre (1913) and attempted to establish repertory theaters in both houses.

Ames produced *Snow White*, the first play put on in New York City specifically for children. He also produced revivals of Gilbert and Sullivan's operettas. He retired from the theater in 1932. Ames died in Boston on Nov. 13, 1937.

AMES, āmz, a city in Iowa, in Story county, 30 miles (48 km) by highway north of Des Moines. It is the home of Iowa State University. The city has a number of small industries, but the university is the largest single employer. Among the points of interest on the campus of Iowa State University are the campanile, the formal gardens, and the Grant Wood murals in the library. Ames also is the headquarters of the Iowa State Highway Commission.

Settled in 1864, the city was incorporated in 1870 and adopted a council-manager form of government in 1920. Population: 50,731.

AMESBURY, āmz'bər-ē, a town located in northeastern Massachusetts, situated in Essex county, on the Merrimack River, 25 miles (40 km) by road northeast of Boston. Amesbury was settled in the mid-1600s and was once a shipbuilding center where a considerable number of the clipper ships of the late 18th and early 19th centuries were launched. Josiah Bartlett, a signer of the Declaration of Independence, was born in the town. The well-known poet John Greenleaf Whittier lived in Amesbury most of his life and is buried there. Whittier's house, containing manuscripts and many of his possessions, is open to the public.

Amesbury is administered by a town meeting. Population: 16,450.

AMETHYST, am'ə-thəst, is a transparent variety of the mineral quartz. It is characterized by a purple or bluish violet color. The name *amethyst* is derived from a Greek word meaning "not intoxicated." The ancients believed that the possessor of an amethyst would not suffer from the excess consumption of alcohol.

Amethyst has long been used as a semiprecious gem and ornamental material and has considerable folklore associated with it. It is the birthstone for the month of February and is associated with St. Matthias, the planet Jupiter, and the constellation Pisces. It was one of the stones set in the high priest's breastplate, as described in the Book of Exodus, and it has been widely used as an ecclesiastical ringstone.

The color of amethyst was long thought to be due to small quantities of manganese present as impurities in the stone. Analyses have failed to confirm this. Another view is that the color is due to imperfections in the arrangement of the atoms in the crystal structure. The color of an amethyst can be changed, through heating, to brown, yellow, or sometimes even green, although these changes are not predictable.

Amethyst is found in crystallized crusts lining the cavities in many different rock types, and localities for its occurrence are widespread. The color of the stone in most deposits, however, is neither a very deep shade of purple nor is it uniform throughout the crystal. The finest material is restricted to a few deposits. Russian (sometimes called Siberian) gem amethysts are found at several localities in the Ural Mountains. Brazilian amethysts also are of good quality, as are some from the islands of Ceylon and Madagascar and from the United States. A purple variety of corundum (see CORUNDUM) is known as *Oriental amethyst.*

Composition: SiO_2; hardness, 7; specific gravity, 2.6 to 2.7; crystal system, hexagonal.

D. VINCENT MANSON
American Museum of Natural History

AMHARA, am-har′ə, a people inhabiting central Ethiopia. They are the largest ethnic group in the country. Numbering about 17.5 million, they are closely related to the Tigrinya people, with whom they constitute over a third of the population of Ethiopia. The Amhara are almost entirely devoted to farming, with a primarily subsistence economy based on the growing of cereal grains and oil plants. Coffee is their principal export crop. The people live in compact villages, and their land is usually communally managed.

The Amhara are thought to be descendants of a Caucasian people who reached Ethiopia from southern Arabia in the first millennium B.C. The Amhara themselves believe they are descended from King Solomon and the Queen of Sheba. As they moved deeper into Ethiopia, they absorbed peoples of the kingdoms of Cush and Meroë. The Amhara were converted to Christianity in the 4th century. The Ethiopian Orthodox Church was long associated with the see of Alexandria, becoming autocephalous, with its own patriarch, in 1959.

The Amharic language, the official language of Ethiopia, is a Semitic tongue derived from ancient Ethiopic (Geez). The ancient language, no longer spoken, continues to be used as the liturgical language of the Ethiopian church.

For centuries the Amhara social and political system rested on an absolute ruler, the emperor of Ethiopia. The revolution of 1974 initiated a prolonged period of instability, but traditional cultural patterns and means of survival persisted.

L. GRAY COWAN*, *Columbia University*

AMHERST, Jeffrey, am′ərst (1717–1797), British military commander who conquered French Canada during the French and Indian War. Amherst was born in Riverhead, Kent, England, on Jan. 29, 1717. Three patrons who recognized his abilities forwarded his early career. The duke of Dorset made him his page and in 1731 obtained an ensign's commission for him in the Guards. Lord Ligonier had him as an aide-de-camp from 1742 to 1745, during the War of the Austrian Succession. The duke of Cumberland retained him as his senior aide and staff officer from 1747 to 1758.

In January 1758 Secretary of State William Pitt chose Amherst to lead an expedition against French Canada. With the rank of major general, Amherst led the successful amphibious siege of the fortress and naval base of Louisbourg in Nova Scotia. The following year, as commander in chief in North America, he took Fort Carillon (Ticonderoga) by siege. Delayed by the need to build a navy to cross Lake Champlain and by the slow pace of James Wolfe's attack on Quebec, Amherst failed to capture Montreal in 1759. But in 1760, by thorough planning, he converged three armies on the city. Montreal fell, and with it Canada.

Though lacking the impetuosity of his more famous subordinate Wolfe, Amherst achieved success by deliberate method. He adapted his regular troops to wilderness warfare and made imaginative use of the new light infantry and rangers.

Amherst was made governor-general of British North America in 1760 and was knighted the next year; however, he received the blame for Pontiac's Indian Rebellion in 1763 and was recalled to England. From then until 1768 he was governor of Virginia but resided in England. He became commander in chief of the armed forces and a privy councillor in 1772, yet he declined to command in North America during the Amer-

ican Revolution. In 1776 he was made a baron and in 1796 a field marshal, after resigning as commander in chief.

Several towns in North America are named for Amherst. He is also remembered by the Amherst College song. He died at "Montreal," his seat in Kent, on Aug. 3, 1797.

HARRISON K. BIRD
Author of "Battle for a Continent"

AMHERST, am′ərst, a town in Nova Scotia, Canada, and the land gateway to the province. It is situated on the narrow Isthmus of Chignecto, the only land connection between Nova Scotia and the rest of Canada. The town, 85 miles (137 km) northwest of Halifax (150 miles, or 240 km, by road), is the seat of Cumberland County.

Abundant coal supplies in the county have made Amherst an industrial center. The town produces structural steel, rolled-steel products, iron castings, furnaces, and various light manufactures. It also has food-processing industries and is a trading center for a fertile agricultural area.

The site was first settled by the French, who called it by the name *Les Planches.* It was renamed by the English in 1759 for Lord Jeffrey Amherst, a hero of the French and Indian War, which was then in progress. Population: 9,470.

AMHERST, am′ərst, a town in Massachusetts, situated in Hampshire county, 20 miles (30 km) north of Springfield. It is the home of Amherst College and the University of Massachusetts. Amherst has been a center of learning and literary activity since the early 1800s, when Noah Webster, a founder of Amherst College, lived in the town while working on his dictionary. Literary residents have included Helen Hunt Jackson, Emily Dickinson, Eugene Field, and Robert Frost.

Incorporated in 1759, the town was named for Lord Jeffrey Amherst, a hero of the French and Indian War. Amherst College was opened in 1821. The University of Massachusetts, an agricultural college when it opened in 1867, became the state university in 1947. Population: 34,874.

AMHERST, am′ərst, a city in Ohio, located in Lorain county, near Lake Erie, 25 miles (40 km) west of Cleveland. Amherst has a history of sandstone quarrying. One quarry that has been worked for over 100 years is 1½ miles (2.4 km) in circumference, and another is 250 feet (76 meters) deep.

Amherst was first settled in 1811 near a spring of good drinking water. A settler from Amherst, N.H., suggested the name *Amherstville,* and the town was so recorded in 1836. The name was shortened to *Amherst* in 1909. Population: 11,797.

VALERIE JENKINS, *Amherst Public Schools*

AMHERST COLLEGE, am′ərst, a private liberal arts institution situated in Amherst, Mass. It was opened in 1821 as a free college and received its state charter in 1825. The founders included Noah Webster and Samuel F. Dickinson, grandfather of Emily Dickinson. Financial support came from the townspeople of Amherst. Throughout the growth of Amherst College, the intent of the original course of study (to provide general education "in all branches of literature and science") has been maintained. Originally a men's college, Amherst became coeducational with the freshman class of 1976.

Amherst's curriculum is directed primarily toward the bachelor's degree in liberal arts. Amherst is part of Five Colleges, Inc., which allows cross-registration and other extensive programs with Hampshire College, Mount Holyoke College, Smith College, and the University of Massachusetts at Amherst. A cooperative doctoral degree is offered with the University of Massachusetts. Amherst offers study abroad in Japan through the Associated Kyoto Program. It is also a member of the Twelve College Exchange Program, which allows students to spend a semester or academic year at one of the other participating colleges.

The curriculum is designed to provide a basic foundation for subsequent specialization. Each student completes two-year sequences in humanities, social studies, and the natural sciences and masters at least one language before proceeding to his or her major. Seminars are held in the junior year, and the senior honors course requires independent research and a thesis. Classes are limited in size to permit greater attention to individual progress. Student enrollment, accordingly, has remained small.

The campus includes art, natural history, geology, and natural science museums; language laboratories; and an observatory. The main library is supplemented by numerous small libraries and by the Robert Frost Library, added in the mid-1960s. Important library collections include the Emily Dickinson Collection, the Robert Frost Collection, and the Van Nostrand Theater Collection. Museum collections at the college range from historical geology to art and include part of the Audubon bird collection. The trustees of Amherst also administer the Folger Shakespeare Library in Washington, D.C., and the Merrill Center for Economics in Southampton, N.Y.

AMHERSTBURG, am′ərst-bûrg, a historic town in southern Ontario, Canada, in Essex County. It is on the Detroit River near its outlet to Lake Erie. Amherstburg processes foods, manufactures soda ash, and is a center for marine salvaging and dredging operations. It is a resort popular with residents of the Detroit-Windsor urban area, 15 miles (24 km) north.

The town was first settled in 1784. The British established Fort Malden there in 1796 and used it as the base for their invasion of Michigan during the first year of the War of 1812. In 1813 it was captured by the Americans. The site of Fort Malden is now a national historic park. Population: 20,339.

AMIANTHIUM, am-ē-anth′ē-əm, a genus of plants commonly called *fly poison* because of their deadly effect on flies and similar insects. The plant is a perennial herb that grows from a thick bulb with a cluster of elongated leaves at the base. It has an erect stem that bears a few much-reduced leaves and ends in a dense cluster of white flowers. The genus is common in woods from southern New York to Florida, Mississippi, and Arkansas. *Amianthium* belongs to the lily family, Liliaceae. The only species in the genus is *A. muscaetoxicum.*

AMICABLE NUMBERS, am′i-kə-bəl num′bərz, any pair of numbers, *A* and *B*, such that the sum of the factors of *A* is equal to *B* and the sum of the factors of *B* is equal to *A*. (In summing the factors, the number *1* is counted but the numbers *A* and *B* are not.) For example, 220 and 284 are amicable numbers—the factors of 220 are 1, 2, 4, 5, 10, 11, 20, 22, 44, 55, and 110, and their sum is 284; the factors of 284 are 1, 2, 4, 71, and 142, and their sum is 220. Knowledge of this pair has been attributed to the Pythagoreans, who considered the pair to be supernatural. Two objects inscribed with these numbers were believed to assure perfect friendship between the wearers. The next seven known pairs of amicable numbers are as follows: (1,184 and 1,210); (2,620 and 2,924); (5,020 and 5,564); (6,232 and 6,368); (10,744 and 10,856); (12,285 and 14,595); and (17,296 and 18,416). Mathematicians have identified 236 amicable pairs below 100 million, 1,427 below 10 billion, and 3,340 below 100 billion. In 1997 American mathematician Mariano Garcia discovered an amicable pair, the largest known at the time, in which each member has 4,829 digits. Although formulas have been derived that yield some amicable pairs, no formula has yielded all known pairs.

DONALD G. OHL*, *Bucknell University*

Bibliography: Lee, E. J., and Joseph S. Madachy, "The History and Discovery of Amicable Numbers," *Journal of Recreational Mathematics* 5 (1972) : 77–93, 153–173, 231–249; Yan, Song Y., *Perfect, Amicable, and Sociable Numbers: A Computational Approach* (World Scientific 1996).

AMICIS, Edmondo De, ä-mē′chēs (1846–1908), Italian travel writer and novelist. Born in Oneglia, Italy, on Oct. 31, 1846, he attended Modena military school and served with distinction in the Austro-Italian War of 1866. After the war he wrote a series of newspaper sketches of military life. These were published in his first book, *La vita militare* (1868). In 1872 he retired from the army and devoted himself to writing. He died in Bordighera, Italy, on March 11, 1908.

During the 1870s, De Amicis traveled widely and recorded his impressions in a series of books, including *Spain* (1872), *Holland* (1874), *Morocco* (1876), and *Constantinople* (2 vols., 1878–79). De Amicis's travel writing is noted for its enthusiasm, brilliant description of scenery, and keen analytical power. His travel books have been translated into English.

He also wrote a number of novels, many of which stressed the importance of education for achieving a better life. His first such book *Cuore* (Heart), published in 1886 and translated into English in 1887 as *An Italian Schoolboy's Journal,* was intended primarily for a juvenile audience. His other novels include *Sull' oceano* (1889; Eng. tr., *On Blue Water,* 1897).

AMICUS CURIAE, ə-mē′kəs kūr′ē-ī, a legal term applied to a person who is not a participant in a dispute but who volunteers information on a point of law or of fact. The term is Latin for "friend of the court." Because the outcome of litigation can affect persons or groups who have no formal right to be heard, courts may permit them to provide information although they are not bound as parties. This occurs only when the court thinks that certain relevant issues are inadequately represented or that the proffered help would serve either some public need or a clear interest of the volunteer.

At trials the amicus is usually limited to questions of law or jurisdiction and to issues framed by the parties. On appeals there is some conflict as to the scope of his permissible contribution. On the one hand, it is asserted that he may not bring up any issue not raised by the parties; on the other, that he may advise on any issue the court itself could have raised.

PETER D. WEINSTEIN, *Member of the New York Bar*

AMIDE, am′īd, any of a group of compounds with the general formula

$$R-\overset{\displaystyle O}{\overset{\|}{C}}-NH_2$$

where R is a hydrogen atom or an aryl or alkyl radical. Except for formamide, a clear oily liquid at room temperature, the simple amides are solids with relatively low melting points. They are chemically stable, weakly acidic, and typically soluble in water, alcohol, or other solvents containing the hydroxyl group, OH. The most widely used simple amide is acetamide, which is used to denature alcohol, to improve the solvent qualities of water, as a stabilizer and plasticizer, and (in molten form) as a medium for numerous inorganic reactions. The polyamides, such as the nylons, are long-chain molecules in which amide groups—CONH—recur as integral parts of the polymer chain. Nylons and other polyamides are thermoplastic materials.

AMIEL, Henri Frédéric, à-myel′ (1821–1881), Swiss essayist, philosophical critic, and poet whose *Fragments d'un journal intime* is considered a masterpiece of confessional literature. Amiel was born in Geneva on Sept. 27, 1821. After studying in Italy, France, Belgium, and, chiefly, Germany, he returned to Switzerland, becoming professor of aesthetics at the academy in Geneva in 1849 and professor of philosophy there in 1854. He was the author of a history of literature, *Du mouvement littéraire dans la Suisse romande et de son avenir* (1849; "Of the Literary Movement in French-Speaking Switzerland and Its Future"), and of the poems "Grains de mil" (1854; "Millet Grains") and "Il penseroso" (1858; "The Contemplative"). Amiel died in Geneva on May 11, 1881.

Amiel's fame came posthumously with the publication of *Fragments d'un journal intime* (2 vols., 1883–1884; first Eng. tr., *Amiel's Journal*, by Mrs. Humphry [Mary Augusta] Ward, 1885; tr. by Van Wyck Brooks and Charles Van Wyck Brooks as *The Private Journal of Henri Frédéric Amiel*, 1935). The journal was culled from nearly 17,000 pages of a diary that Amiel kept from 1847 until his death and bequeathed to his friends. Although he led a retired and rather prosaic life, the journal reveals Amiel as an ardent intellectual, a man of delicate perceptions and acute critical ability. Yet he suffered from creative impotence, for he did not have the force to carry out his ideas. His journal depicts his long and painful struggle to arrive at positive values in an age of increasing pessimism.

AMIENS, à-myaN′, a city in France and the capital of the department of Somme. It is situated on the Somme River, 72 miles (116 km) north of Paris, and is an important marketing center for surrounding farmlands. Since the 16th century, it has been one of the textile centers of France.

The Cathedral of Notre Dame, one of the finest examples of Gothic architecture in France, is Amiens's most famous edifice. It was begun in 1220; the 360-foot (110–meters) spire was added in the 16th century. The cathedral is 470 feet (145 meters) long. The interior, where the nave rises over 140 feet (45 meters), is particularly impressive. Near the cathedral is a statue of Peter the Hermit, one of the spiritual leaders of the First Crusade, who was born in Amiens. Other interesting buildings are the 15th-century Church of St. Germain, damaged in World War II, and the Hôtel de Ville, in which the Treaty of Amiens was signed.

Amiens, also known in ancient times as *Samarobriva*, was the chief city of the pre-Roman Ambiani tribe. In the early medieval period, it was the capital of the county of Amiénois, which passed to the French crown in 1185. The county was awarded to the dukes of Burgundy by the Peace of Arras in 1435 but was returned to France in 1477. The city was captured by the Spanish early in 1597 but was retaken by King Henry IV of France later in the year.

The Treaty of Amiens, signed there in 1802 between France, England, Spain, and Holland, defined territories and marked a brief lull in the Napoleonic Wars. During the Franco-Prussian War of 1870, the Germans captured the city.

In World War I it first fell to the Germans, but it then became an important supply depot for the Allies when the Germans established their front some 20 miles (30 km) to the northeast. In World War II it was held by the Germans for over four years before being retaken by the Allies in 1944. The city was heavily damaged in both wars. Population: 139,210 (1999 census).

AMIN, Idi, ä-mēn′ (1925?–2003), Ugandan political and military leader whose bloody reign of terror lasted from 1971 to 1979. Idi Amin Dada Oumee was born in Koboko, in northwestern Uganda, probably in 1925 but possibly in 1923. He was a member of the Kakwa tribe. In 1946 he joined the King's African Rifles, a British colonial force. In the 1950s he helped suppress the Mau Mau insurrection in Kenya.

After Uganda attained independence, in 1962, Amin rose rapidly through the ranks, becoming chief of the army and air force in 1966. On Jan. 25, 1971, he led the military coup in which Pres. Milton Obote was ousted.

Amin, as president, was variously described as a shrewd politician, an arrogant buffoon, and a ruthless tyrant. He refused to delegate authority and, being illiterate, generally transmitted his orders orally. Officially sanctioned murder and torture were widespread, targeting both prominent individuals and random members of disfavored tribes. The bureaucracy became paralyzed as officials avoided decisions that could bring unpredictable retribution. An estimated 100,000–300,000 people died during his rule.

Amin's abrupt changes in mood and reckless actions also contributed to international tensions. In 1972 Amin ordered most Asians expelled from Uganda. In June 1975 he threatened to execute British author Denis Hills for describing him as a "village tyrant." At the UN General Assembly in October 1975, he called for the "extinction" of Israel. In July 1976 Amin offered the Palestinian hijackers of an Air France jetliner the use of Entebbe Airport as a base from which to press their demands. After Israeli commandos freed most of the hostages in a surprise raid, he ordered the execution of airport personnel and a hospitalized hostage. Although often at odds with neighboring countries, Amin was chairman of the Organization of African Unity (OAU) in 1975–1976.

In June 1975 the Ugandan Defense Council proclaimed Amin president for life. Insurrection followed, however, and in 1978 he ordered a diversionary invasion of northwestern Tanzania. In

April 1979 Tanzanian forces and Ugandan exiles forced him to flee to Libya. Amin died in exile, in Jidda, Saudi Arabia, on Aug. 16, 2003.

AMINE, ə-mēn', a class of chemical compounds derived from ammonia, NH_3. There are three types of amines: primary, secondary, and tertiary. When one hydrogen atom of the ammonia molecule is replaced by a hydrocarbon group, the result is a primary amine. The general formula for a primary amine is RNH_2, where R is a hydrocarbon group. Secondary amines have the general formula R_2NH (two hydrogen atoms have been replaced), and tertiary amines have the general formula R_3N (three hydrogen atoms have been replaced).

Amines are also classified by the type of hydrocarbon group that replaces the hydrogen. If the replacing hydrocarbon group has an open chain of linked carbon atoms, the molecule is called an *aliphatic amine*. If the carbon atoms of the replacing group are joined in the form of a closed ring, the molecule is called an *aromatic amine*. For example, methylamine (CH_3NH_2) is a simple primary aliphatic amine. The simplest primary aromatic amine is aniline ($C_6H_5NH_2$). Aromatic amines, such as aniline, the toluidines ($C_6H_4CH_3NH_2$), and the xylidines ($C_6H_3(CH_3)_2NH_2$), are made from coal-tar hydrocarbons.

Aliphatic Amines. Chemically, the aliphatic amines are very similar to ammonia. They are fairly strong bases and form salts with such mineral acids as hydrochloric acid. The aliphatic amines that have only a small number of carbon atoms are gases and are soluble in water at room temperature. The aliphatic amines with a medium number of carbon atoms are liquids that are soluble in water. The aliphatic amines with a large number of carbon atoms are odorless solids that are not soluble in water at room temperature. The aliphatic diamines putrescine, $NH_2(CH_2)_4NH_2$, and cadaverine, $NH_2(CH_2)_5NH_2$, are compounds responsible for the odor of decaying bodies. These two compounds are produced by the putrefying action of bacteria on animal tissue.

Aromatic Amines. The aromatic amines are much weaker bases than the aliphatic amines. The primary aromatic amines are colorless liquids and crystalline solids that are not easily soluble in water. Some secondary and tertiary aromatic amines are purely aromatic, but others also contain an aliphatic amine structure. Certain aromatic amines are among the approximately 500 known compounds that can produce tumors in animals or humans.

Tests for Amines. Tertiary amines are distinguished from primary and secondary amines by using the Schotten-Baumann reaction. The suspected amines are treated with benzoyl chloride in a basic solution. The primary and secondary amines form benzamide compounds, but the tertiary amines do not react. The benzamide compounds can be purified. Their melting points indicate which primary or secondary amines were present. The Hinsberg reaction is used to distinguish between primary and secondary amines. The suspected amine is treated with benzenesulfonyl chloride in alkaline solution. Primary amines yield sulfonamides that are soluble in basic solutions. Secondary amines yield insoluble derivatives. Tertiary amines do not react. The melting points of the sulfonamides can be used to identify the original amine. A simple test for any primary amine is the formation of isocyanides after treatment with chloroform in a basic solution. The isocyanides have an unmistakable, unpleasant odor.

It is also possible to distinguish between aliphatic and aromatic amines. Primary aliphatic amines that are treated with nitrous oxide yield nitrogen gas, whereas primary aromatic amines form diazonium compounds. These compounds form easily recognizable dye colors by coupling with a suitable chemical.

Uses. The amines are widely used. Some uses for the ethanolamines are given as an example. The ethanolamines include monoethanolamine, $(CH_2CH_2OH)NH_2$, diethanolamine, $(CH_2CH_2OH)_2NH$, and triethanolamine, $(CH_2CH_2OH)_3N$.

Monethanolamine forms soaps that can emulsify mineral oil, waxes, and resins in water. The emulsions are useful in processing textiles, cutting metals, and producing household floor waxes. Monoethanolamine is used as an acid gas absorbent, and it is used in making textile finishing agents and in manufacturing detergents and insecticides. Diethanolamine in water solution is used to remove or recover carbon dioxide from other gases. Finishing agents, dye agents, and scouring agents are made from diethanolamine. A synthetic stain remover is another product made from diethanolamine. Triethanolamine is a corrosion inhibitor in antifreeze solutions for automobile radiators. It is used in floor waxes and in the textile industry as a soap for lubricating fibers. It also is used to counteract acid conditions in the manufacture of cosmetics, insecticides, and petroleum chemicals.

MORRIS GORAN, *Roosevelt University*

AMINO ACIDS, ə-mē'nō as'əds, organic molecules that constitute a most important part of biological structure and body chemistry. They are identified by the presence of an amino group, NH_2, and an acid (carboxyl) group, COOH, the remainder of the molecule being variable. The amino group is the basic portion of the molecule, and it is capable of reacting with both inorganic and organic acids to form salts, amides, and so on, while the acid portion is capable of reacting with bases.

Amino acids are the building blocks that combine to form a protein. All of the enzymes, hemoglobins, antibodies, and many of the hormones are proteins. All structures of the body, from chromosomes found deep in the interior of cells of most organisms to hair covering the surface of the mammalian forms, are composed of protein.

Size and Shape of Amino Acids. In molecular size, a simple amino acid, such as glycine, is approximately the size of four water molecules, which have a total molecular weight of 72; a large simple amino acid molecule, such as tryptophane, has a molecular weight of 204. The average amino acid has a molecular weight of 125.

There are about 30 different amino acid building blocks, which can be linked together in different lengths (chains) and in different combinations. They may form either parallel chains or globular structures ranging from a combination of two amino acids to a large protein molecule such as nucleohistone, which has a molecular weight of 2,100,000.

From the evidence of research scientists today, it is clear that the linear sequence of the amino acids is the most important factor in determining the behavior of the molecule. For example, hemoglobin, which constitutes a major portion of red blood cells, establishes the flat, biconcave (concave on both sides) disclike structure of normal red blood cells. This hemoglobin molecule consists of two chains of acids. If one of the chains, the B chain, which has 146 amino acid units, has valine at position 6 in place of glutamic acid (which normally is there), then the hemoglobin is abnormal, and the red blood cell takes on the shape of a sickle rather than a disc. People who inherit this type of hemoglobin suffer from sickle-cell anemia.

Polymers. If two or more amino acids react with each other, long chains can be built up from the simple amino acid units. These chains are called polymers. One such polymer-producing reaction is called dehydration synthesis. In this reaction a peptide bond, COHN, is formed, and the OH group from the COOH part of one molecule combines with an H from the NH_2 part of the other amino acid to produce water. Thus, two amino acids combine to form a dipeptide; three, a tripeptide; many, a polypeptide.

Configuration. All naturally occurring amino acids, with a few exceptions, have a spatial structural arrangement, or configuration, known as the L-configuration. A solution of these amino acids is identified by its rotation of a plane of light to the left, due to the presence of an optically active carbon atom (an asymmetrically located carbon atom bearing four different substituents on its four valences).

Most other amino acids have optically active carbon atoms, except for the simplest amino acid, glycine. Certain bacteria and molds contain amino acids of the D-configuration. A solution of these amino acids rotates a plane of light to the right.

If the amino group (NH_2) and the carboxyl group (COOH) are attached to the same carbon atom, the amino acid is known as an alpha (α)-amino acid. All amino acids of dietary importance are α-amino acids.

Types of Amino Acids. Digestion or hydrolysis (chemical decomposition that splits a bond and adds elements of water) of proteins in any plant or animal will yield about 16 different amino acids. But the bulk (20 to 50 percent) of the amino acids are aspartic acid and glutamic acid.

Four additional amino acids (beyond the 16) make up the protein of some organisms. These include a rare type of amino acid (α-amino adi-pic acid), found in corn, and hydroxyproline, found in animals that have connective tissue. Monoiodotyrosine diiodotyrosine, and triiodothyronine are amino acids associated with those organisms that have a thyroid gland.

Modern Research. The synthesis of amino acids from more elementary organic molecules and the construction of peptides and the larger polymers (protein) constitute the essence of three very exciting fields of biological research today. These fields are (1) the origin of life, (2) the exact structure of protein, and (3) the synthesis of protein in cellular metabolism.

The origin-of-life investigators—Melvin Calvin, Sidney W. Fox, Stanley L. Miller, Juan Oro, and Harold C. Urey—produced amino acids from ammonia (NH_3), methane (CH_4), hydrogen (H_2), and water (H_2O) under conditions of high temperature with electrical or ultraviolet discharge as the source of energy for synthesis. Miller was able to produce three different amino acids in his system; Fox produced 11 different amino acids. Fox's "crucible of life" contained about 20 amino acids at a temperature of 200° C. These yielded simple proteinoids exhibiting many of the properties of simple, natural proteins.

Research on the analysis of the exact structure of protein received great impetus following the work of Frederick Sanger of Cambridge University in 1950 on the amino acid sequence of insulin (a protein of about 5,700 molecular weight). Sanger found a technique of identifying the end amino acid in the insulin chain by staining the amino end-group yellow with 1-fluoro-2, 4-dinitro benzene. By staining and subsequent digestion of the protein and repeated staining of protein fragments, the complete jigsaw puzzle analysis was made and the sequence of amino acids in the chain established. He found that the insulin molecule was constructed of two chains: chain A contains 21 amino acids and starts with glycine; chain B contains 30 amino acid units and starts with phenylalanine. The two chains are interconnected by sulfur (a disulfide linkage) in two of the amino acids in each chain. Other proteins have been analyzed.

A third area of investigation involves active protein synthesis occurring on tiny particles called ribosomes, which are found in the cell cytoplasm. The ultimate source of information for protein manufacture comes from genetic material within the nucleus of the cell; this material is deoxyribo-

---

AMINO ACIDS GROUPED ON BASIS OF ACIDITY

(1) **Neutral Amino Acids:**

Glycine	CH_2NH_2COOH
Alanine	CH_3CHNH_2COOH
Valine	$(CH_3)_2CHCHNH_2COOH$
Leucine	$(CH_3)_2CHCH_2CHNH_2COOH$
Isoleucine	$(CH_3)(C_2H_5)CHCHNH_2COOH$
Serine	$CH_2OHCHNH_2COOH$
Threonine	$CH_3CHOHCHNH_2COOH$
Phenylalanine	$C_6H_5CH_2CHNH_2COOH$
Tyrosine	$HOC_6H_4CH_2CHNH_2COOH$
Tryptophane	$C_6H_4NHCH:CCH_2CHNH_2COOH$
Cysteine	$CH_2SHCHNH_2COOH$
Cystine	$\begin{array}{c} SCH_2CHNH_2COOH \\ | \\ SCH_2CHNH_2COOH \end{array}$
Methionine	$CH_3SCH_2CH_2CHNH_2COOH$
Proline	$CH_2CH_2CH_2CHNHCOOH$
Hydroxyproline	$CH_2CHOHCH_2CHNHCOOH$
Asparagine (amide of aspartic acid)	
Glutamine (amide of glutamic acid)	

B-alanine	$NH_2CH_2CH_2COOH$
α-Amino-butyric	$CH_3CH_2CHNH_2COOH$
Homoserine	$HOCH_2CH_2CHNH_2COOH$
Triiodothyronine	$HOC_6H_2I_2OC_6H_2I_2CH_2CHNH_2COOH$
Tetraiodothyronine	$HOC_6H_2I_2OC_6H_2I_2CH_2CHNH_2COOH$
Dihydroxyphenylalanine	$(OH)_2C_6H_3CH_2CHNH_2COOH$

(2) **Acidic Amino Acids** (two carboxyl groups):

Aspartic acid	$HOOCCH_2CHNH_2COOH$
Glutamic acid	$HOOCCH_2CH_2CHNH_2COOH$
α-Amino-adipic	$HOOCCH_2CH_2CH_2CHNH_2COOH$

(3) **Basic Amino Acids** (two amino groups):

Histidine	$CHNCHNHCCH_2CHNH_2COOH$
Arginine	$NH_2C(NH)NHCH_2(CH_2)_2CHNH_2COOH$
Lysine	$NH_2CH_2(CH_2)_3CHNH_2COOH$
Hydroxylysine	$NH_2CH_2(CHOHCH_2CH_2CHNH_2COOH$
Ornithine	$NH_2CH_2CH_2CH_2CHNH_2COOH$
Citrulline	$NH_2COCH_2CH_2CH_2CHNH_2COOH$

nucleic acid (DNA). The DNA molecule is coded with sequences of four different nitrogenous bases. These sequences indicate a particular genetic message, and they vary according to the message. A complementary copy of the sequence of these bases in the DNA molecule is made. This is called messenger ribonucleic acid (mRNA). The mRNA then moves out of the nucleus of the cell into the cytoplasm and attaches itself to one or more ribosome particles. It provides information about the proper amino acid sequence for the protein being manufactured at the ribosome site.

Other RNA strands are dissolved in the cytoplasm. Known as transfer RNA (tRNA, also called soluble RNA), these strands are relatively large molecules. Each is specific for one of the 20 known amino acids. During protein synthesis, tRNA seeks out the particular amino acids needed in the synthesis. Thus, if there are 30 amino acids indicated on the mRNA strand sequence, there must be 30 tRNA molecules, each attaching a particular amino acid. At another site on the tRNA molecule there are three exposed nitrogenous bases (an anti-codon) that seek out and find the three appropriate complementary bases on the mRNA (a codon). This matching mechanism assures the proper sequence of amino acids in the polypeptide chain being manufactured. When the tRNA's align themselves along the ribosomes, they bring their attached amino acid molecules into juxtaposition with each other. These amino acids are linked together in proper sequence into a protein molecule under the catalytic action of the proper enzymes and the energy source adenosine triphosphate (ATP). The newly manufactured protein chain then frees itself from the ribosome sites and circulates in the cytoplasm.

The correlation between triplets of nitrogenous bases in messenger RNA and specific amino acids in the protein assembled on the RNA is known as the genetic code. By 1968 the entire code was broken, and scientists were at last able to say which amino acid is specified by which codon. Laboratory experiments with synthetic mRNA confirmed these findings. For example, synthetic mRNA with the codon UUU (three uracil bases) attracts tRNA bearing the amino acid phenylalanine, and synthetic mRNA with codon GUU (guanine, uracil, uracil) attracts tRNA bearing the amino acid valine.

Amino Acids and Nutrition. Protein is an indispensable ingredient in the living organism, and the amino acid building blocks must be available in the cytoplasm. Many amino acids are synthesized in the body; others are not. Those not synthesized are called essential amino acids. In humans these are isoleucine, leucine, lysine, methionine, phenylalanine, threonine, tryptophane, and valine. These essential amino acids must be provided in the organism's diet. For example, if in Mexico people ate only corn, their diet would lack tryptophane and lysine and their growth and tissue replacement would be impaired. Mexicans augment their basic corn diet with beans, which are richer in lysine but still tryptophane deficient. Eggs, milk, or meat would balance the diet.

A vegetarian diet is low in lysine, methionine, and cystine. Animal products provide a more complete array of amino acids. Thus inland African natives have dietary deficiencies not found in African coast natives who add fish to their vegetable diet. Children of central and southern Africa and India often suffer from protein insuffi-

ciency that leads to a disease called kwashiorkor.

See also DNA; GENE; METABOLISM; NUCLEIC ACID; NUTRITION; PROTEIN.

ALFRED NOVAK, Stephens College

Bibliography: Aida, K., and others, eds., Biotechnology of Amino Acid Production (Elsevier Pub. Co. 1986); Pfeiffer, C. The Healing Nutrients Within (Keats 1987).

AMIOT, Jean-Joseph-Marie, à-myō′ (1718–1793), French Jesuit missionary who added greatly to European knowledge and understanding of China. He was born in Toulon, France, on Feb. 8, 1718, and in 1737 joined the Society of Jesus. Sent to China as a missionary in 1740, he earned the confidence of Emperor Ch'ien Lung.

Amiot wrote extensively on many aspects of Chinese life. He compiled a Tatar-Manchu dictionary in French, making Tatar-Manchu known in Europe for the first time. Most of his important works are in the 15-volume collection *Mémoires concernant l'histoire, les sciences, les arts, les moeurs et les usages des Chinois, par les missionnaires de Pékin* (1776–1789). Amiot died in Beijing (Peking) on Oct. 8 or 9, 1793.

AMIS, Kingsley, ā′mis (1922–1995), English novelist, poet, and critic. Amis was born on April 16, 1922, in Clapham, London, and was educated on scholarships at the City of London School and at Oxford. From 1949 to 1963 he taught English literature at University College, Swansea, Wales, and at the University of Cambridge. Amis was knighted in 1990. He died in London on Oct. 22, 1995.

Amis's highly praised first novel, *Lucky Jim* (1954), satirizes the hypocrisy of academic life as perceived by a cynical young university instructor. This book and three following works—*That Uncertain Feeling* (1955), *I Like It Here* (1958), and *Take a Girl Like You* (1960)—have as protagonists members of an emerging British social group, educated beyond their working-class origins but hostile toward privileged society. This theme linked Amis with the British writers known as "angry young men." His subsequent novels covered a wide range of genres, including science fiction (*The Anti-Death League,* 1966), ghost story (*The Green Man,* 1969), mystery (*The Riverside Villas Murder,* 1973), and spy novel (*Russian Hide-and-Seek,* 1980). Later novels include *Stanley and the Women* (1984), the Booker Prize–winning *The Old Devils* (1986), *Difficulties with Girls* (1988), and *The Russian Girl* (1992). Amis also wrote short stories, verse (including *Collected Poems 1944–1979*), essays and other nonfiction (including *The Amis Collection: Selected Non-Fiction 1954–1990*), and the controversial *Memoirs* (1991). Several of his works were adapted for television, and three for film: *Lucky Jim* in 1957, *That Uncertain Feeling* (under the title *Only Two Can Play*) in 1962, and *Take a Girl Like You* in 1971. *The Old Devils* was produced as a play in 1989.

Bibliography: Fussell, Paul, The Anti-Egotist: Kingsley Amis, Man of Letters (Oxford 1994); McDermott, John, Kingsley Amis: An English Moralist (St. Martin's 1989); Salwak, Dale, Kingsley Amis, Modern Novelist (Barnes & Noble 1992).

AMISH, ä′mish, members of a religious sect, founded under the leadership of Jakob Amman, a Swiss Mennonite bishop, that broke away from the less conservative Mennonite parent body between 1693 and 1697. The schism occurred chiefly over the practice of "shunning," or complete avoidance of excommunicated persons.

As a result of the general persecution of the Mennonites, most Amish fled from Europe to North America. There are now virtually no Amish in Europe bearing the original name and upholding the early principles. In the United States there are records of Amish in Pennsylvania as early as 1727, and the largest concentrations today are in Lancaster county, Pa. There are also substantial numbers in Ohio and Indiana, and settlements in 19 other states. The Amish in Canada live chiefly in Ontario, where the first Amish community was established in 1824. From the 1850s there were internal schisms leading to the foundation of separate Amish churches. The Beachy Amish, named for their leader, Moses Beachy, divided from the Old Order Amish in 1927.

The Amish people are noted for their uniformity of dress and for the self-sufficiency of their communities. The women wear simple dresses, bonnets, and shawls, and the men wear traditionally cut pants and hats and do not shave their beards. The Amish live chiefly by farming. The most conservative, called the Old Order Amish, avoid any use of electricity or automobiles. Amish church districts, or *gemeide* ("congregations") are self-contained and self-governing. Worship services are held in members' homes or barns. Preachers, bishops, and deacons are chosen from among the male members of the district. The Amish practice adult baptism. They refuse to bear arms or swear oaths, including judicial oaths. Although they pay taxes, they do not participate in federal social security programs. Amish children attend public elementary schools but not high schools.

See also MENNONITES; PENNSYLVANIA DUTCH.

AMISTAD CASE, ä-mēs-täth′, a case tried by the U.S. Supreme Court in 1841, establishing that the United States should treat as free men any slaves escaping from illegal bondage.

In February 1839, Portuguese slave hunters abducted a large group of tribesmen from Sierra Leone and, against all the treaties then in existence, shipped them to Havana, a center of the illegal slave trade. There 53 of the Africans were purchased by two Spanish planters and put aboard the Cuban schooner *Amistad* for shipment to a Caribbean plantation. Passports for the group were obtained on perjured testimony.

On July 1, 1839, the Africans seized the ship at sea, killed two crew members, put the rest ashore in the Caribbean, and ordered the owners to sail to Africa. On August 24 the schooner was seized off Long Island by a United States brig. The planters were freed, and the Africans were imprisoned in New Haven, Conn., on charges of murder. Most of the nation's press advocated extraditing the Africans to Cuba, a course with which President Martin Van Buren sympathized. Abolitionists in the North opposed extradition and raised money for defense counsel. Despite claims to the slaves made by the planters, by the government of Spain, and by the captain of the brig, the murder case went to trial in September in the federal district court in Hartford. The court ruled that the case fell within federal jurisdiction and that the Africans, because they were illegally held, were not liable for their acts.

John Quincy Adams argued the defendants' case on review before the U.S. Supreme Court in November. Accusing the administration of President Van Buren of "utter injustice" in seeking to satisfy the Spanish claimants, he defended the right of the accused to fight to regain their freedom. The court decided for the Africans, 32 of whom were returned to their homeland. The others had died at sea or while awaiting trial.

For an interesting parallel to this incident, see CREOLE CASE.

AMMAN, Jost, äm′än (1539–1591), Swiss painter and engraver. He was born in Zürich, Switzerland, on June 13, 1539. Little is known of his personal history.

Amman did etching and wood engraving with great skill and left a considerable number of pen drawings. Of major importance are his drawings for wood engravings, through which he exercised a wide influence. Amman drew directly on the wood and sometimes cut the engravings himself. He made numerous wood engravings for illustrated editions of the Bible, and 115 wood engravings for a book on the arts and trades (1568). He also made a series of copperplate engravings of the kings of France. In Basel there is a collection of his designs for stained glass. He died in Nuremberg, Germany, on May 17, 1591.

AMMAN, äm-män′ (Arabic, ʿAmmān), the capital and largest city of Jordan. It is situated in the north-central part of the country, about 50 miles (80 km) east-northeast of Jerusalem and 25 miles (40 km) east of the Jordan River. Amman is the country's chief industrial center, manufacturing textiles, tobacco products, leather and leather goods, flour, and cement. It is connected by road and rail with most important cities of Jordan and by air with most Middle Eastern capitals and several European and African cities. The University of Jordan, founded in 1962, is near Amman.

Places of interest in Amman include the Roman amphitheater, which dates from the 2d or 3d century A.D. and has been restored. On a hilltop overlooking the city is the Citadel, which has a ruined Roman temple to Hercules; the remains of Roman walls; and a square building called El Qasr, with

Amman's amphitheater seats about 6,000 and dates from Roman times, when the city was called Philadelphia.

745

intricate stone carvings that may date from the Umayyad period (6th—7th centuries A.D.). A Byzantine gate still stands before the Citadel. The Jordan Archaeological Museum, on Citadel Hill, has a large collection of antiquities of Jordan. The Basman Palace (the palace of the king) and a guest palace face the Citadel.

In biblical times the settlement was known as Rabbah Ammon and was the chief city of the Ammonites. It was besieged and captured by Joab and David in the 11th century B.C. (II Samuel 12:26—31). Little remains from this very early period, except for a few tombs and a section of wall that was probably built in the 9th or 8th century B.C.

The city was rebuilt by Ptolemy II Philadelphus in the 200s B.C. and was named *Philadelphia* for him. In the 1st century B.C. it belonged to the commercial league of ten free cities known as the Decapolis, and it was subsequently held for a short time by the Nabataeans. They were driven out by Herod the Great, king of Judea, about 30 B.C. The Romans took the city again a few years later, and erected a number of new public buildings. A fine amphitheater built during that period still stands.

The town adopted the name *Amman*, a modification of its original name, in the 600s A.D. It declined after the Arab conquest in 635 A.D. and was little more than a village when, in 1921, it was chosen as the capital of the newly created Transjordan emirate.

In 1946 Amman became the capital of the Hashemite Kingdom of Jordan. Its population increased rapidly, partly because of the influx of Arab refugees from the Israeli sector of Palestine. Population: 1,300,042 (1994 est.).

AMMANN, Othmar Hermann, äm′än (1879—1965), American bridge builder, who designed two of the world's greatest suspension bridges. These are the 3,500-foot (1,067-meter) George Washington Bridge (1931) and the 4,260-foot (1,298-meter) Verrazano-Narrows Bridge (1964), both in New York City. He also served as a design consultant on the 4,200-foot (1,280-meter) Golden Gate Bridge (1937) in San Francisco.

Ammann was born in Schaffhausen, Switzerland, on March 26, 1879, and emigrated to the United States in 1904. He became chief engineer for the Port of New York Authority (PNYA) in 1927, in time to design the George Washington Bridge. He always was proudest of this bridge, despite his more spectacular accomplishments later. In 1957 his firm, Ammann and Whitney, was retained to add a second deck to the bridge; Ammann had designed the original structure to carry two decks. While with PNYA, Ammann directed the design and construction of Bayonne Bridge, Goethals Bridge, and Outerbridge Crossing, all between Staten Island, N.Y., and New Jersey. He also played a key role in the design of New York's Triborough, Bronx-Whitestone, and Throgs Neck bridges. He died in New York on Sept. 22, 1965.

WILLIAM W. JACOBUS, JR.
Engineering News-Record

AMMANNATI, BARTOLOMMEO, äm-mä-nä′tē (1511—1592), Italian architect and sculptor. Born in Settignano on June 18, 1511, he studied under Baccio Bandinelli and Jacopo Sansovini. He imitated the style of Michelangelo, but his work was more mannered, representing a transition from the classic style of the 16th century to the Baroque. He died in Florence on April 22, 1592.

Outstanding among Ammannati's many buildings are the Palazzo Giugni and the courtyard of the Palazzo Pitti, both in Florence, and the Palazzo Ruspoli and the Collegio Romano, both in Rome. His masterpiece was the Santa Trinita Bridge over the Arno River in Florence. Completed in 1569, it rested on three elliptic arches. It was destroyed in World War II. His greatest sculpture was the Fountain of Neptune, in the Piazza della Signoria, Florence.

AMMETER, am′mē-tər, an instrument that measures the current in an electric circuit. The principle that governs the operation of the ammeter was discovered in 1820 by the Danish physicist Hans Christian Oersted, who found that a compass needle is deflected when it is placed near a current-carrying conductor. In 1882, Jacques Arsène d'Arsonval of France devised a moving-coil, permanent-magnet galvanometer similar to the ammeter now most commonly in use.

The moving-coil ammeter consists of a horseshoe-shaped permanent magnet, a moving coil, hairsprings, a pointer, and a scale. The movable coil of fine wire is suspended in a cylindrical air gap between the permanent-magnet poles. This lightweight coil is pivoted on bearings so that only a small force is required to rotate it. The hairsprings, which are attached to the coil structure, establish the static, no-current position of the coil. The pointer, which is attached to the coil, moves over a calibrated scale to display the meter reading in units of amperes.

Direct current (d-c) passing through the coil produces a magnetic field that interacts with the permanent-magnet field. This interaction produces a torque that drives the coil against the hairsprings. The pointer stabilizes when the magnetic force is balanced by the spring force. In most ammeters the pointer deflection is directly proportional to the coil current.

For measuring alternating current (a-c), moving-coil ammeters have a rectifier that converts a-c to d-c. Many commercial ammeters are designed for both a-c and d-c measurements.

An ammeter can measure a wide range of currents because it has a device that allows only

In a moving-coil ammeter, electric current is measured by the deflection of a pointer attached to the coil.

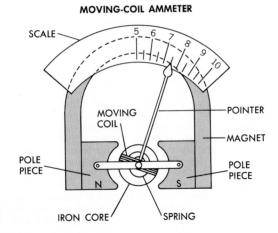

MOVING-COIL AMMETER

a portion of the current to pass through the coil. In d-c ammeters a shunt is used for this function; a-c ammeters use a current transformer.

Besides the moving-coil ammeter, there are moving-vane, electrodynamometer, and hot-wire types of ammeters. These types are used mainly for a-c measurements. Where a-c measurements must be made and it is not practical to open the circuit, clamp-on ammeters are used.

Technicians use ammeters to measure the current drain of household appliances to determine that the capacity of house lines is adequate and to troubleshoot household appliances.

MARVIN BIERMAN
RCA Institutes Inc.

AMMIANUS MARCELLINUS, am-ē-ā′nəs mär-sə-lī′nəs (c. 330—c. 398 A.D.), the last notable historian of Rome. He was born of a noble Greek family in Antioch about 330 A.D. He served in campaigns in Italy, Gaul, and Persia and also visited Egypt and Greece. These experiences lent vividness to many of his descriptions of campaigns. In his later life he settled in Rome, where, about 390, he wrote a continuation of Tacitus's history in 31 books. The work covered the period 96 A.D.—378 A.D.

Of his history, only the last 18 books have survived, covering the years 353—378, a period during the author's own lifetime. They provide a comprehensive narrative of the corruption and degeneration of the Roman empire before its fall, as reported by a well-informed contemporary with a high conception of historical accuracy. There are interesting digressions on a variety of subjects. Although his native language was Greek, Ammianus wrote in Latin, and his style is often marred by an overloading of metaphor.

AMMONIA, ə-mō′nyə, a colorless, water-soluble gas with a characteristic strong odor. Its formula is NH_3. Ammonia and some of its compounds are important in agriculture, in industry, and in the laboratory.

The name "ammonia" is said to have been derived from the name of the ancient Egyptian god Ammon, whose priests prepared the gas by heating the horns and hoofs of animals. During the Middle Ages a gas containing ammonia was obtained by distilling deer antlers. Pure ammonia was prepared and described by Joseph Priestley in 1774, and its composition was established by Claude Berthollet in 1785.

Properties and Structure. Ammonia has a boiling point of −28.3° F (−33.4° C) at one atmosphere of pressure and a freezing point of −107.5° F (−77.7° C). Its critical temperature is 271° F (133° C) at a pressure of 112 atmospheres. The heat of vaporization is 327 calories per gram. Ammonia is easily liquefied under pressure and only slight cooling, and it absorbs a relatively large amount of heat on evaporating. These properties and its low cost make it the most important industrial refrigerant for large installations. Ammonia has a density of 0.771 gram per liter at 32° F (0° C) and a pressure of one atmosphere, and a solubility of 89.9 grams per 100 grams of water. The common commercial solution contains about 28 percent ammonia.

In water solution, ammonia reacts to produce the equilibrium

$$NH_3 + H_2O \rightleftarrows NH_4^+ + OH^-.$$

The degree of ion formation is only about 0.4 percent in 1 molar solution, so water solutions of ammonia are weak bases.

The ammonia molecule can be symbolized as

$$H:\ddot{N}:H \text{ or, more} \qquad H \overset{\cdot\cdot\dot{N}\cdot\cdot}{\underset{H}{}} H$$
$$H \quad \text{exactly,}$$

Its structure resembles a pyramid with the nitrogen atom at the apex and the three hydrogen atoms at the base. The unshared electrons belong to the nitrogen atom. The electrons bonding hydrogen to nitrogen are not shared equally but are more closely associated with the nitrogen atom. This configuration results in a strongly polar molecule; there is a negative charge on the apex of the pyramid and a positive charge on the base. The water molecule is also polar, and water and ammonia have some very similar properties. Liquid ammonia as a solvent, for example, tends to produce ionization in some solutes just as water does. Like water, it ionizes to a slight extent itself, producing the equilibrium

$$2NH_3 \rightleftarrows NH_4^+ + NH_2^-.$$

Ammonia decomposes at high temperatures to produce a mixture of 25 percent nitrogen and 75 percent hydrogen. This mixture is able to be used as a commercial source of hydrogen, because it provides an inexpensive and convenient way to transport hydrogen in the form of liquid ammonia.

Ammonia burns in oxygen to form nitrogen and water vapor, and it can be oxidized by using air to form nitrogen monoxide. In general, ammonium compounds are highly soluble in water and somewhat resemble compounds of sodium, potassium, and rubidium. Stable complex ions are formed by ammonia and some metal ions, such as $Ag(NH_3)_2^+$, $Cu(NH_3)_4^{++}$, $Ni(NH_3)_6^{++}$, and $Co(NH_3)_6^{+++}$. Some of these complex ions are useful in analytical chemistry.

Production. A commercial process for fixing atmospheric nitrogen by means of calcium carbide is still in limited use for manufacturing fertilizers. Nitrogen is separated from air by liquefaction and fractionation and then is heated with calcium carbide to a temperature of about 2010° F (1100° C). The resulting compound, calcium cyanamide (CaNCN), can be used directly as a fertilizer or it can be treated with steam under pressure to produce ammonia. The ammonia is usually converted to ammonium sulfate or ammonium nitrate for use as a fertilizer.

Haber Process. The most economical method of nitrogen fixation is the direct combination of nitrogen and hydrogen. Nearly 90 percent of all ammonia is made by this method:

$$N_2 + 3H_2 \rightleftarrows 2NH_3.$$

This process, which was made commercially feasible by Fritz Haber in 1913, makes use of nitrogen from the atmosphere, and hydrogen. The more important sources for the hydrogen are the steam reforming of natural gas, the partial oxidation of natural gas or petroleum gases, the treatment of coal or coke with air and steam, and the recovery of hydrogen from petroleum refining processes. Carbon monoxide or carbon dioxide produced with the hydrogen is removed before the synthesis reaction.

The synthesis of ammonia is an equilibrium reaction that requires a high pressure for a high proportion of ammonia in the mixture. Pressures ranging between 200 and 900 atmospheres have been used commercially. At extreme pressures the ammonia yield is higher, but the cost of equipment and power is greater. The temperatures used commercially range from 750° to 1200° F (400° to 650° C). At 932° F (500° C) and a pressure of 300 atmospheres, the equilibrium mixture contains about 26.5 percent ammonia. A catalyst, consisting primarily of magnetic iron oxide (Fe_3O_4) or iron oxide mixed with the oxides of other metals, is used. The ammonia is separated from the mixture by liquefaction, and the remaining gases are recycled.

Uses. The demand for ammonia has been increasing rapidly, and the production capacity in the United States has been rising at a rate of about 25 percent annually. About 70 percent of the ammonia produced is used directly as fertilizer or is converted into nitrates or urea for fertilizers. When used directly, it is injected into the ground in anhydrous liquid form. In agricultural regions that utilize irrigation, it is added to irrigation water.

Urea. The use of urea, $(H_2N)_2CO$, as a nitrogen-bearing fertilizer is increasing rapidly as a result of decreasing production costs. Ammonia is treated with carbon dioxide to produce ammonium carbamate, $H_2NCOONH_4$:

$$2NH_3 + CO_2 \rightarrow H_2NCOONH_4.$$

The product is dehydrated to urea and water:

$$H_2NCOONH_4 \rightarrow (H_2N)_2CO + H_2O.$$

Urea is a raw material for a series of thermosetting resins that are used in molding plastic articles. In preparing them, urea is combined with formaldehyde, furfural, or resorcinol. Urea is also used in the preparation of barbiturates and other medicinals, as well as in the manufacture of cosmetics and deodorants.

Ammonium Nitrate. Ammonium nitrate is second only to anhydrous ammonia as a fertilizer material. It is prepared by direct combination of ammonia and nitric acid, followed by evaporation of the water. It may be applied to the soil in dry form or in solutions of various concentrations. The nitric acid is manufactured in a three-step process. Ammonia is oxidized with air to form nitrogen monoxide, the nitrogen monoxide is oxidized to form nitrogen dioxide, and the nitrogen dioxide is treated with water to form nitric acid. The reactions are essentially as follows:

$$4NH_3 + 5O_2 \rightarrow 4NO + 6H_2O$$

$$2NO + O_2 \rightarrow 2NO_2$$

$$3NO_2 + H_2O \rightarrow 2HNO_3 + NO$$

The process was introduced by the German chemist Wilhelm Ostwald in 1902. Several variations are used. The pressures range from 14.7 to 120 pounds per square inch, and the temperatures range from 1470° to 1740° F (800° to 950° C). An alloy of platinum and rubidium is employed as a catalyst.

Most ammonium nitrate produced in the United States is used in fertilizers but about 15 percent is used in the manufacture of explosives. It is mixed with trinitrotoluene (TNT) to make an explosive that is nearly as powerful as TNT alone but much less expensive. Dynamite and blasting gelatins frequently contain ammonium nitrate, and several other explosives contain ammonium nitrate and nonexplosive materials such as fuel oil. All common explosives contain nitrogen and oxygen. Such explosives decompose suddenly when detonated into nitrogen, nitrogen oxides, carbon dioxide, water vapor, or other gases.

Ammonium Chloride. Ammonium chloride is prepared from ammonia and hydrochloric acid, or it is obtained as a by-product of sodium carbonate production. It is widely used as a flux for cleaning metals before soldering or galvanizing. Ammonium chloride is also a major ingredient in zinc-carbon dry cells.

Liquid Ammonia. Liquid ammonia has the interesting property of plasticizing wood. When the ammonia penetrates the wood, it apparently reduces hydrogen bonding between adjacent cellulose and lignin molecules and allows them to slip in relationship to each other. The wood can then be twisted into intricate shapes. When the ammonia evaporates, new hydrogen bonds are established, and the distorted shape of the wood becomes permanently fixed. See also NITROGEN COMPOUNDS.

O. W. NITZ
Stout State University

AMMONITES, am′ə-nīts, an ancient people who lived east of the Jordan River and are described in the Bible as enemies of Israel. They are best known in Old Testament history for hiring Balaam to curse Israel when Israel came from Egypt (Numbers 22 to 24) and for their defeats by Jephthah (Judges 11), Saul (I Samuel 11:1–11), and David and his general Joab (II Samuel 10:1 to 11:1, 12:26–31). The Ammonites are accused of corrupting the Hebrew religion and nation (Amos 1:13; Nehemiah 13:23–31).

There were, however, Ammonites who befriended David when he fled from Absalom (II Samuel 17:27), and one of them was among David's 30 mighty men (II Samuel 23:37). Ammonites and Israelites intermarried, and King Solomon loved Ammonite women and constructed places of worship to the Ammonite god Molech (I Kings 11:1–8). Still flourishing at the time of Justin Martyr (about 100–165 A.D.), the Ammonites were thereafter absorbed by the Nabataean Arabs.

AMMONITES, am′ə-nīts, general name for the Ammonoidea, an extinct order of mollusks common 70 million to 200 million years ago (Mesozoic era). About 8,000 species are known. They evolved rapidly, producing a succession of types that changed rapidly in time. This, together with their abundance, has made them excellent markers of fossil zones.

The shells of ammonites vary widely in form and size, ranging from ½ inch in diameter (*Cymbites*) to over 6 feet in diameter (*Pacydiscus*). Typically, the ammonite shell is coiled in a single plane. There is a great variety in the cross section of the shells, in the degree of ingrowth, and in the surface, which may be smooth or highly ornamented with ribs, nodes, or spines. Also, the shells of younger organisms differ from those of older ones in cross section, ornament, and suture pattern. The air chambers in the shell permitted swimming to some degree. The ammonites could also retreat into the shell and close the aperture by either a pair of plates or a single plate. Because the soft parts of the ammonites did not fossilize, their nature is not known.

AMMUNITION, am-yə-nish′ən, is destructive material used against an enemy. It includes rockets, bombs, grenades, torpedoes, mines, guided missiles, pyrotechnics (for flares or smoke), and complete rounds for all types of firearms. A complete round of ammunition consists of all the necessary components to fire a weapon once. For an artillery round this includes the projectile, fuze, shell case, propellant, and primer.

Ammunition is generally classified according to use and size. Other destructive explosive devices, such as demolitions, are classified under the more comprehensive term *munitions*.

Small-Arms Ammunition. Cartridges used in rifles, pistols, revolvers, machine guns, submachine guns, and shotguns are called small-arms ammunition and are classified by the bore size (inside diameter of the barrel) of the weapon or the diameter of the projectile. The diameter is expressed in *calibers;* thus a caliber .30 rifle bullet is 30/100 inch in diameter. In countries using the metric system the caliber is given in millimeters—for example, a 9 mm projectile. *Gauge* designates the bore size of a smoothbore weapon, such as a shotgun, in terms of the heaviest lead ball the weapon will accept, and the balls are classified according to the number that weigh one pound. Thus, a 12-gauge shotgun can shoot a 12-to-the-pound ball. Types of military small-arms ammunition include armor piercing, incendiary, tracer, fragmentation, and ball. Ball ammunition is the standard jacketed bullet used against troops.

Nonmilitary Ammunition. Ammunition for handguns (pistols and revolvers), rifles, and shotguns is available in a wide variety of sizes and weights. The ammunition selected will depend on whether the round is to be used for personal defense, small-game or varmint hunting, big-game hunting, or target shooting.

While military small-arms bullets normally have a conical shape and are covered with a brass or soft-metal jacket, hunting rounds for both rifles and handguns range in shape from sharply pointed to blunt. Hunting ammunition is classified as *hollow point, soft point,* or *metal case,* depending on the design of the nose of the bullet and whether or not the jacket completely covers the nose. The advantage of the soft-point bullet, in which the tip of the lead bullet extends beyond the jacket, is that it expands on contact, thus increasing its destructive power. Commercial hunting ammunition is manufactured in all sizes from caliber .22 (5.588 mm) bullets, weighing 15 grains (7,000 grains = 1 pound; 15.43 grains = 1 gram), to the elephant-killing caliber .458 bullet, weighing 510 grains.

Many shooters cast their own lead bullets for target practice in order to reduce the cost. For accurate match shooting, the weight and shape of the bullet, as well as the amount of propellant powder used, must be controlled within close tolerances.

Shotgun ammunition consists of a cylindrical shell of plastic or heavy paper, loaded with a propelling charge and a number of steel balls called *shot.* Shot vary in size from "dust" (diameter 0.04 inches, or 1.016 mm) to BB (diameter 0.18 inches, or 4.572 mm). For every gauge of shotgun there are several types of shells, differing in the size and number of shot in the shell. The choice depends on the game being hunted. For large game (bear or deer) the shell usually contains a single rifled slug or from 10

TYPES OF AMMUNITION

SMALL ARMS AMMUNITION

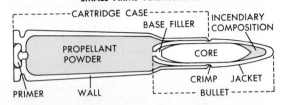

ARTILLERY AMMUNITION EXPLOSIVE TRAINS

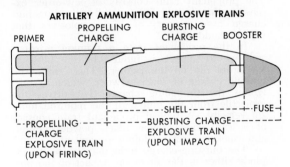

AMMUNITION consists of a projectile and a propellant, as in the rifle cartridge *(top).* In artillery ammunition *(above)* the primer, comprising a percussion element and an igniter, ignites the propelling charge. At the target, or before, a striker in the fuse ignites in turn the priming mixture, detonator, booster, and bursting charge. The artillery round *(below)* may be *fixed,* like a rifle cartridge; *semifixed,* with shell and cartridge case separate so the amount of the propelling charge can be varied; or *separate loading,* with no cartridge case, for large cannon.

THE ARTILLERY ROUND

A. FUSE
B. SHELL
C. BURSTING CHARGE
D. ROTATING BAND
E. OGIVE
F. CARTRIDGE CASE
G. PROPELLING CHARGE
H. PRIMER
I. IGNITER
J. IGNITER CHARGE ASSEMBLY

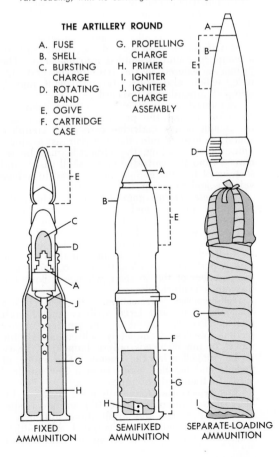

FIXED AMMUNITION   SEMIFIXED AMMUNITION   SEPARATE-LOADING AMMUNITION

to 20 pellets called *buckshot,* which may be as large as 0.36 inches (9.144 mm) in diameter.

When fired, shot pellets form a dense circular pattern. Shotgun ammunition has great destructive power at short range, but as the size of the shot pattern increases at increasing distances from the gun, effectiveness drops.

Artillery Ammunition. A complete round of artillery ammunition contains at least six different explosives divided into two explosive trains: the *propellant train,* and the *bursting-charge train.* The propellant train consists of low-order explosives that merely burn rapidly; the bursting-charge train consists of high explosives that explode suddenly.

In the propellant train a priming mixture, sensitive to impact, is ignited by the blow of the firing pin on the primer. This ignites the igniting charge of black powder, which in turn ignites the propelling charge that drives the projectile from the gun with the required muzzle velocity. A typical propellant train consists of a lead azide primer, black powder igniter, and smokeless nitrocellulose propellant.

The bursting-charge train may be set to explode either in the air or on impact of the projectile. After functioning of a fuzing device, or on impact, a striker in the fuze sets off the priming mixture. The detonator and booster, each made up of a slightly less sensitive explosive, are set off in turn. A typical bursting-charge train consists of a fulminate of mercury detonator, tetryl booster, and a TNT bursting charge.

Types of Artillery Ammunition. Ammunition for guns, howitzers, and mortars may be high explosive, armor piercing, incendiary, or chemical. Artillery ammunition is divided into three general categories: fixed, semifixed, and separate loading.

Fixed ammunition has all the components of a complete round assembled into one unit. The primer is secured in the base of the cartridge case, which also holds the propellant and is crimped around the projectile.

Semifixed ammunition differs from fixed ammunition in that the projectile fits loosely into the mouth of the cartridge case. The complete round is loaded into the weapon as a single unit. Before loading, the projectile may be removed from the cartridge case (shell case), and sections of the charge may be removed to reduce velocity and range of the projectile.

Separate-loading ammunition, in which the projectile, primer, and propellant are loaded separately, is used in weapons of large caliber where the weight would make handling difficult.

Complete rounds for recoilless rifles are similar to fixed ammunition except that the cartridge case is perforated to allow the gas to escape into the chamber of the weapon, whence it flows out through a venturi tube.

Self-Propelled Ammunition. Rockets of a "bazooka" type and large artillery and aircraft rockets also are classed as ammunition, as are guided missiles. Completely self-contained, the rocket or missile needs only a launching device to be propelled at the enemy. The range of rockets and missiles varies from a few hundred yards to thousands of miles.

CBR Ammunition. Ammunition for chemical, biological, and radiological (CBR) warfare is specialized in design and application, although it may be delivered by conventional ammunition. Nuclear warheads, chemical agents, and biologi-

cal agents may be loaded into artillery projectiles, bombs, rockets, or guided missiles. Nuclear ammunition is classified according to the equivalent yield in tons of TNT. Thus, a 20-kiloton nuclear warhead would have an explosive yield equivalent to that of 20,000 tons of TNT.

Other Military Ammunition. Bombs, torpedoes, grenades, mines, and many types of pyrotechnics are not like complete rounds of artillery ammunition, since the propelling charges of the latter are replaced by other means of delivery. Grenades are hurled by hand or by special projectors; mines are laid in water from ships, dropped from the air, or buried by hand; torpedoes are expelled by compressed air or black powder and propelled by steam or electricity. Bombs are carried to their release point by aircraft and may or may not be propelled from release to target. Mines are essentially thin-walled containers of high explosive with fuzes that function on contact, by remote control, or under an "influence" such as magnetism or pressure.

Ammunition Service. Ammunition is the cutting edge of war. The total military effort exists only so that at the right time and place a round of ammunition will defeat an enemy target.

The supply of ammunition to an army at war is a problem of great magnitude and complexity. It is not the tonnage of the ammunition that causes the chief difficulty but the unpredictability of the requirements. During periods of maneuver and dispersal of forces, small amounts of ammunition are expended. But when the proper moment comes, the army must strike with every weapon firing at its maximum rate, to reduce resistance and produce casualties. In modern warfare this rate of fire may be as high as 6,000 rounds per minute for an aircraft machine gun or one round per minute for a 16-inch (40.64 cm) gun, for which each complete round weighs about 1½ tons. With every soldier shooting an automatic or semiautomatic weapon, and with the multiplicity of automatic and quick-firing weapons for tank, aircraft, antitank, and antiaircraft use, the peak load of ammunition that must be replaced quickly runs into millions of tons. The wide extent of the theater of operations and the rapid movement of troops and weapons in the atomic age have further increased the difficulty of ammunition supply. The difficulty has been offset only partially by transportation improvements.

Ammunition service in the field operates on a continuous refill system. Ammunition supply points are set up within the combat zone, and ammunition is issued from these points directly to using units. The use of nuclear warheads has presented special problems in assembly facilities, control, and security of ammunition supply.

See also ARTILLERY; BALLISTICS; BAZOOKA; BOMB; BULLET; CHEMICAL AND BIOLOGICAL WARFARE; EXPLOSIVES; GRENADE; GUIDED MISSILES; GUNS; HYDROGEN BOMB; NUCLEAR WEAPONS; PROJECTILES; ROCKETS; SMALL ARMS; SMOKELESS POWDER; TORPEDOES.

JOHN D. BILLINGSLEY, *Colonel, USA*
United States Military Academy

Further Reading: Goad, K. J., and Halsey, D. H., *Ammunition, Grenades, and Mines* (Pergamon 1982); Hogg, Ian V., *Jane's Directory of Military Small Arms Ammunition* (Jane's Pub. 1985); Hoyem, George A., *The History and Development of Small Arms Ammunition* (Armory Pubs. 1982); Thomas, Gough, *Shotguns and Cartridges for Game and Clays,* 3d ed. (Transatlantic Arts 1976).

AMNESIA, am-nē′zhə, a partial or complete memory loss. It may be permanent or temporary.

In anterograde, or post-traumatic, amnesia, events following the incident that caused the amnesia are not retained. For example, someone who has suffered an injury to the head may be unable to recall the accident or the events that followed but may be able to perform coordinated motions and be aware of his or her surroundings. Memory usually returns within a few days. If the amnesia persists for more than a week, serious brain damage may have occurred.

In retrograde, or retroactive, amnesia, events that occurred prior to the injury or incident that caused the amnesia are forgotten. Amnesia can also be classified as anteroretrograde and retroanterograde, both of which involve memory loss for events occurring before and after the incident.

There are, in addition to head injuries, several other causes of amnesia. Hysterical amnesia, for example, is based on a person's psychoneurotic motivation to become dissociated from what he or she perceives as an intolerable situation. It often arises when the person feels the need to suppress many of his or her natural impulses and feelings. The individual may act in a normal manner, perhaps "blotting out" the events of a certain period of time; he or she may be dazed or confused; or the person may assume a new identity within which he or she can act out the repressed feelings. This type of amnesia can be treated through psychotherapy.

Amnesia can also result from complications arising from certain diseases. Cerebral malaria sometimes results in amnesia, but medical treatment of the malaria usually restores the memory. Other causative diseases are collagen diseases (diseases of a protein substance in bones and cartilage), diabetes, amyloidosis (deposit of the protein amyloid in the tissues), and sarcoidosis (which causes lesions on the skin, lymph nodes, or bones).

Toxic agents also may cause amnesia. Carbon monoxide poisoning, for example, may cause temporary (less than 72 hours) loss of memory. Alcoholism and an overdose of tranquilizers or barbiturates may also result in amnesia.

REAMUR S. DONNALLY, M.D.*
Washington Hospital Center

AMNESTY, am′nə-stē, an act by government that relieves a group of persons of punishment for a public offense, usually treason, sedition, rebellion, resistance to a wartime draft, or desertion. In a strict legal sense, amnesty (from the Greek word meaning "forgetfulness") should be distinguished from a pardon. Amnesty bars prosecution for the specified crimes, whereas a pardon is granted after a conviction.

The first recorded amnesty seems to have been granted by the Athenian general Thrasybulus in 403 B.C. Other historic amnesties were granted in England in 1652 after the civil war and in 1660 at the time of the Restoration. In the United States, President Lincoln's amnesty proclamation of 1863 was followed by amnesty acts of Pres. Andrew Johnson in 1865, 1867, and 1868. Soon after World War I the U.S. government gave amnesty or pardon to certain conscientious objectors and other violators of wartime statutes, including deserters. President Truman did likewise in the years 1945, 1947, and 1952. Between the end of World War II and the beginning of the Korean War in 1950, deserters were also granted clemency.

Amnesty became a problem during and after the Vietnam War. Never before in U.S. history had there been a war with such a high rate of desertion. As many as 50,000 draft resisters and deserters were reported living in Canada, Sweden, and elsewhere, and an estimated 9,000 served terms in U.S. jails.

In September 1974, Pres. Gerald Ford announced an earned-clemency program for Vietnam-era draft evaders and military deserters who agreed to do public service work for up to two years, but only a small portion of those eligible applied by the closing date of March 31, 1975. President Jimmy Carter pardoned draft evaders and ordered a review of 432,000 less-than-honorable discharges of Vietnam veterans for possible upgrading.

AMNESTY INTERNATIONAL, am′nə-stē, the world's largest human rights organization. Amnesty International (AI) counted more than 1 million members, subscribers, and donors in the early 1990s, along with over 6,000 volunteer groups in 74 countries, including nationally organized AI sections in 48 nations.

The organization was launched in May 1961 by British lawyer Peter Benenson. He called for an international campaign to protect human rights for persons detained or physically restricted for their beliefs, ethnic origin, sex, color, or language, so long as these persons had not advocated or used violence. The AI was established on a permanent footing following an immediate international response; the organization has continued to expand its mandate and membership. It was awarded the Nobel Peace Prize in 1977.

Amnesty International pressures governments to honor commitments made in human rights agreements. Specifically, it works to release prisoners of conscience; to ensure fair, prompt trials for political prisoners and persons detained without charge; to abolish the death penalty, torture, and other cruel, inhuman treatments or punishment; and to oppose any extrajudicial execution or "disappearance." It has also sought release for persons imprisoned solely on the basis of homosexuality.

Impartiality is safeguarded by extensive research through the AI Secretariat and by prohibiting AI members from becoming involved in cases in their own countries. The Secretariat conducts research on human rights issues, publishing detailed reports respected for their impartiality. Between 1991 and mid-1992 AI had adopted or investigated more than 43,500 cases.

CLAUDE E. WELCH, JR.
State University of New York at Buffalo

AMNIOCENTESIS, am-nē-ō-sen-tē′sis, a procedure for extracting amniotic fluid from the sac that envelops a fetus in the womb. It is performed with a long, hollow needle and with or without a local anesthetic. The procedure, though normally safe, can slightly increase the risk of miscarriage.

Amniocentesis was first done late in the 19th century to reduce abnormal accumulation of amniotic fluid. The procedure began to be used in the late 1950s to monitor the pregnancy of Rh-negative women for signs of Rh blood-group incompatibility between mother and baby. Since 1966 the procedure has been used to obtain samples of the baby's cells in order to identify an increasing number of serious genetic disorders. Amniocentesis also reveals the baby's sex—information that is important in the management of some 400 sex-linked genetic disorders, such as muscular dystrophy.

Amniocentesis is most commonly recommended for expectant mothers of age 35 or older because women in this group have a higher risk of bearing children with chromosomal disorders. The best time for amniocentesis or a prenatal genetic examination is during the 14th to 16th weeks of pregnancy. For Rh blood-group studies or for determining fetal maturity, the procedure is performed during the last three months of pregnancy.

Prenatal genetic studies are based on an examination of the chromosomes, enzyme activity, and protein content of cells originally shed by the baby itself or by its surrounding membranes. The cells are extracted from the amniotic fluid and multiplied by growing them in tissue culture. Examination of the cell's chromosomes can detect disorders, such as Down's syndrome (mongolism), that are caused by the presence of an extra chromosome.

Fatal biochemical genetic disorders, such as Tay-Sachs disease and certain diseases characterized by severe mental retardation, are revealed by deficient enzyme activity in the cell cultures. Serious defects of the brain or spinal column, such as spina bifida, can be detected before birth by measuring the concentration of alpha-fetoprotein—a protein found mainly in the developing fetus—in the amniotic fluid.

AUBREY MILUNSKY, M. D.
Author of "Know Your Genes"

AMOEBA. See AMEBA.

AMON, ä'mən, was an ancient Egyptian deity, preeminent among the gods from the 12th dynasty. His chief cult-place was Thebes, where the great temples of Luxor and Karnak testified to his glory. As Amon-Re, King of Gods, he was praised for victory in war; and his holdings, enriched by spoils and tribute, eventually rivaled the wealth of the crown. Amon was commonly shown as a ram or as a man with ram's horns or head, but he also took the form of the reigning king to beget a royal heir. An august god, charged with the welfare of the state, he was nevertheless beseeched by the lowly for justice in courts of law and for comfort and healing.

To retain supremacy over Amon's chief priests (who virtually ruled Upper Egypt), the kings of the 21st dynasty married them to their daughters; and rulers of the 25th and 26th dynasties made the high priests subservient to a high priestess, who was always a princess. As kingly power declined, royal decisions were increasingly fortified through delivery by oracle of Amon.

CAROLINE N. PECK, *Brown University*

AMORE DEI TRE RE, ä-mô'rä dä trä rä, a three-act opera by the 20th century Italian composer Italo Montemezzi. *L'amore dei tre re (The Love of Three Kings)* was first performed at La Scala, Milan, in 1913. The opera, with a libretto by Sem Benelli, based on his play of the same name, is regarded as Montemezzi's masterpiece and one of the foremost 20th century Italian operas. *L'amore dei tre re* is highly melodic, with the score depicting the events of the plot.

The opera is set in Italy in the 10th century, following a barbarian invasion of Altura, led by King Archibaldo, who is now blind. Manfredo, Archibaldo's son, is married to Fiora, an Alturan princess, who had given up her lover, Prince Avito, in order to bring peace to the land. However, Fiora and Avito meet secretly. Archibaldo, aware of her infidelity, strangles Fiora, but because of his blindness he does not know who her lover is. To entrap him, Archibaldo puts poison on the dead Fiora's lips. On her bier, Fiora is kissed by both Avito and Manfredo, and both men die. When King Archibaldo learns that his trick has killed his son as well as Avito, he dies in despair.

AMORITES, am'ə-rīts, an ancient Semitic people of Canaan, identified in the Old Testament as enemies of the Israelites. The prophet Amos described the Amorites as having the "height of cedars" and being as "strong as the oaks" (Amos 2:9). Numbers 13:29 locates the warlike Amorites in the mountains north of Palestine, and their name means "mountaineers" in Hebrew. Their strength was gradually reduced during the conquest of Canaan by the Hebrews (Judges 1:35), and Solomon forced the remnant to pay tribute. However, their prowess is demonstrated by the fact that they were among those peoples whom the Hebrews "were not able utterly to destroy" (I Kings 9:20).

AMORTIZATION, am-ər-tə-zā'shən, in finance and accounting, is the process of gradually reducing an amount over a period of time. The amount of the periodic or cumulative reduction also is called amortization. The term is applied to reducing a debt by periodic payments and reducing an amount by periodic accounting entries.

Reducing a Debt by Periodic Payments. On bonds owned by a corporation, the interest payments ordinarily diminish as the debt grows smaller. Thus for the first year, amortization may be $1,000,000 and interest $600,000, while for the second year amortization may be $1,000,000 and interest $540,000. On a mortgage loan to an individual, the periodic payments usually remain equal; as the interest diminishes, the payment on the principal increases correspondingly. The individual may pay $50 interest and $20 principal in the first month, while less than $1 of the final month's $70 payment will be interest. For obligations of both types, interest usually is figured only on the balance owed.

By contrast, on "small loans" and installment obligations, interest usually is figured on the original amount for the entire repayment period. This results in an effective interest rate about twice the stated rate. The periodic payments remain equal, but the interest and principal are not identified separately. Whatever the form of loan, shortening the amortization period reduces the total interest paid.

Reducing an Amount by Periodic Accounting Entries. The amount may be a balance sheet item such as the cost of a capital asset (for example, a building or a machine tool) or the difference between the face value and the purchase price of a bond purchased at a discount. The periodic reduction usually is a factor in determining net income (profit). For capital assets, the write-off period usually is the expected useful life, and the term usually applied is *depreciation*. Thus a $100,000 building may be depreciated at $10,000 a year for 10 years.

ERNEST L. HICKS, *CPA*

AMOS, ā′məs, the earliest of the literary prophets of the Old Testament, lived in the middle of the 8th century B.C. The book that bears his name is placed among those of the so-called "minor prophets" merely on account of its brevity (only 9 chapters), but the influence of his personality and message was greater than that of any of his successors.

According to the notice that now introduces the collection of his poems and sermons (Amos 1:1), Amos originated "from among the herdsmen of Tekoa," a mountaintop village in Judah, situated a few miles southeast of Bethlehem, just "between the desert and the sown." He migrated seasonally to the more fertile territory of Ephraim, in the northern Kingdom of Israel, where he earned his living as a tender of sycamore trees. He was therefore a southern, destitute, seminomadic "layman," not a member of the prophetic guilds (I Kings 22:6 ff.). He even refused to be called a prophet, but he admitted that he had received a compelling call to "prophesy" to his economically prosperous contemporaries of the northern state (Amos 7:14–15).

In a series of visions that probably took place from the late spring to the late summer of the year 751 or 750 B.C. (Amos 7:1–9; 8:1–3; 9:1–4), Amos slowly and reluctantly came to accept the conviction that the covenanted people was soon to be annihilated, despite its claim to deserve perpetual protection from God, who had brought it into historical existence through the exodus from Egypt. He attributed the impending destruction to the verdict of Yahweh of Hosts, the creator and sovereign ruler of nature, the righteous judge of history (Amos 3:1–2; 5:2 ff.). Such a message reveals an astoundingly bold conception of the godhead and a new conception of the relationship between religion and ethics.

Concept of God. Amos did not deny the popular belief that Israel stood in a relation of peculiar intimacy with the God of the covenant (Amos 3:2). But he asserted that the Hebrew awareness of national election created a nobility of mission and an urgency of obligation that could not be divorced from the privilege involved. Furthermore, he extended to its extreme conclusion the universalism that was inherent in the ancient faith (Genesis 12:1–3; Exodus 19:4–6), maintaining that not only Israel but all the nations of the earth were the object of divine solicitude and judgment (Amos 9:7; 1:3 to 2:3). This would include Israel's close neighbors and bitter enemies such as the Philistines in the southwest and the Syrians in the northeast, as well as racially different and almost unknown peoples like the Ethiopians in the distant south. These views constitute in effect the first concrete—although not fully explicit—formulation of ethical monotheism in the history of civilization.

Ethical Teaching. The high concern for social justice that characterized the religion of Moses and of the Hebrew ancestors in the wilderness period (14th century B.C.) underwent a slow process of disintegration when the Israelites entered the land of Canaan and gradually abandoned nomadic and tribal patterns in favor of a sedentary, agricultural, and commercial form of society. This sociological evolution produced economic inequalities and consequently gave rise to a sharp class distinction between wealthy landowners, traders, and even specula-tors in commodities, on the one hand, and, on the other, landless laborers and dispossessed farmers who were sometimes even sold into slavery for debt failure. Amos stood in the line of Hebrew reformers, like the legislators of the Code of the Covenant (Exodus 20:22 to 23:19) or the prophets Nathan (II Samuel 12:1 ff.) and Elijah (I Kings 21:1 ff.); but he went further than any of his predecessors in denouncing social injustice (Amos 2:6–8; 4:1 ff.; 6:1 ff.) More specifically, he proclaimed for the first time in the history of religions that the observance of a ritual is in itself of no significance whatever, unless it be the expression of the worshipers' dedication to moral integrity and respect for the social needs of the community as a whole (Amos 5:4 ff.). This attitude is nowhere more graphically revealed than in the oracle—spoken in the name of deity in the first person singular—which sums up the prophet's teaching:

> Take thou away from me the noise of songs; for I will not hear the melody of the viols.
> But let judgment roll down as waters, and righteousness as a mighty stream. (Amos 5:23–24)

SAMUEL TERRIEN
Union Theological Seminary

AMOY, ä-moi′, a city in southeastern China, was formerly one of China's most important seaports. It is situated on two small islands—Amoy and Kulangsu—in Fukien province, on the Taiwan Strait. Amoy has the best natural harbor on the Fukien coast and is able to accommodate oceangoing ships. There are dockyards, excellent anchorages, and with the completion of a causeway in 1956, a direct rail connection with the mainland of China. The Mandarin name for the city is *Hsiamen.*

Amoy became famous as a trading port in the late 18th century. It was captured by the British in 1841 during the Opium War and the following year was one of the five ports opened to foreign trade by the Treaty of Nanking. Thereafter, foreigners were given the right to establish a settlement on Kulangsu. Amoy's flourishing tea trade declined in the late 19th century, and with it the commercial importance of the city. For many years thereafter, however, Amoy, which has sometimes been referred to as the "Garden of the Sea," remained one of the chief ports of Chinese emigration to Southeast Asia. During World War II the city was occupied by the Japanese from 1938 to 1945. Situated only 130 miles (209 km) from Taiwan, the Chinese Nationalist stronghold, Amoy took on special strategic importance after the Communists gained control of the Chinese mainland in 1949. The port is effectively blockaded by the Nationalists on nearby Quemoy Island. Population: 697,300 (2001 est.).

AMPELOPSIS, am-pə-lop′səs, is a genus of North American and Asian woody vines, commonly cultivated to cover walls and trellises. The plants have simple or divided leaves, small greenish flowers in clusters, and small grapelike berries. The chief species cultivated is *A. brevipedunculata* var. *elegans,* a plant with variegated leaves that are white, greenish, yellowish, or sometimes pink. Ampelopsis belongs to the grape family, Vitaceae, and has about 25 species. They are easy to cultivate, as they still thrive in a variety of soils, but they must be tied to supports as they do not have sucking disks.

AMPÈRE, än-pâr′, **André Marie** (1775–1836), French physicist and applied mathematician, who helped to establish the science of electrodynamics. He made experiments and formulated laws on the electromagnetic forces between conductors carrying electric currents.

Ampère was born in Lyon on Jan. 20, 1775. Most of his education was private study under the guidance of his father, a wealthy silk merchant. At 14, Ampère had unusual competence in mathematics and a broad knowledge of science. In 1793, during the Reign of Terror, Ampère's father was executed.

After a happy marriage in 1799 and the birth of a son in 1800, he became a professor of physics in Bourg (1801–1803). A mathematical paper on game theory then gained him a post at the lycée in Lyon. On his wife's death he left in 1804 for the École Polytechnique in Paris, and he taught in Paris for the rest of his life. He was elected to the Academy of Science in 1814.

At a meeting on Sept. 11, 1820, the Academy was told about H. C. Oersted's discovery that a compass needle deflects when it is near a wire carrying an electric current. At subsequent meetings in September and October, Ampère showed that two nearby conductors carrying electric currents exert forces on each other, and he developed the mathematical laws for calculating such forces. He demonstrated that a long helical coil carrying current was magnetically similar to a bar magnet, and he showed that a piece of iron inserted in such a coil became strongly magnetized. He interpreted the magnetic forces between permanent magnets as forces between molecular electric currents in the iron. Initial criticism that part of his theory contradicted Newton's law of equality of action and reaction soon subsided, and Ampère's laws of electrodynamics gained universal acceptance and admiration. These laws became a basic element of J. C. Maxwell's electromagnetic theory in 1865.

Ampère, who was an ingenious experimenter, proposed a current-measuring galvanometer and a 26-wire electromagnetic telegraph, both based on Oersted's observation. He also suggested the rotating switch (commutator) first used on H. Pixii's electric generator in 1832. Ampère made other contributions in the fields of mechanics, optics, statistics, chemistry, and crystallography. He died in Marseille on June 10, 1836.

The ampere, the unit of electric current, is named after him. A law, now called Ampère's law, gives a quantitative expression for the force between two arbitrarily oriented current elements in a uniform medium.

Ampère's publications include *Recueil d'observations électrodynamiques* (1822) and *Théorie des phénomènes électrodynamiques* (1826).

Robert A. Chipman, *University of Toledo*

AMPERE, am′pēr, the standard unit of electric current. The current flowing in each of two parallel wires one meter apart is defined as one ampere when the force between the wires is 2×10^{-7} newton per meter of length. Before 1948 the ampere was defined in terms of the coulomb and was equal to the flow of one coulomb of charge per second. The coulomb then was redefined in terms of the ampere in such a way that this relationship still holds.

Named after the French physicist André Marie Ampère, the ampere is one of the seven basic units in the International System (SI).

AMPHETAMINE, am-fet′ə-mēn, a synthetic dependency-producing stimulant related to the hormone noradrenalin, or norepinephrine. It was first synthesized in 1887 and first used medically in 1927. Amphetamine pills are commonly called "bennies" because they are often sold under the trade name Benzedrine. Dextroamphetamine (Dexedrine, "dexies") is a more potent form of amphetamine. Drugs of the amphetamine type are known as "uppers" and "pep pills."

Amphetamines stimulate the central nervous system, dilate the pupils of the eyes, dilate the bronchial tubes, increase blood pressure, raise body temperature, and speed up heartbeat and breathing. Overdoses may cause death from heat stroke, heart irregularities, or the rupture of a blood vessel in the brain because of increased blood pressure.

Amphetamines most often are taken because of the ways they affect feelings and moods. They reduce or eliminate feelings of fatigue and depression and make users feel elated, energetic, and alert. They intensify most sensory experiences but diminish sensations of pain and reduce or eliminate hunger. For these reasons they are often abused, although they have approved medical uses for treating narcolepsy and minimal brain dysfunction and for controlling hunger in short-term weight reduction programs.

The effect of amphetamines on performance is not clear-cut. Generally they increase the alertness and motor ability of fatigued people, so that they can carry out simple repetitive tasks more effectively. But people who are not fatigued show no measurable improvement in mental or physical skills. And performance may actually deteriorate in tasks that require judgment, problem solving, or complicated thinking.

Tolerance to the effects of amphetamines usually develops after prolonged use, with the result that increasingly larger amounts are needed to produce the same effect as that of the initial dose. If a heavy user of amphetamines suddenly gives up the drugs, typical withdrawal symptoms include prolonged sleep followed by a ravenous appetite, depression, and apathy on awakening. Because these symptoms are relieved by amphetamines, heavy users tend to become dependent on the drugs. Amphetamines are sometimes taken with sedatives or narcotics. Such polydrug combinations tend to eliminate or reduce unpleasant effects caused by the drugs taken separately.

People who take large amounts of amphetamines may become paranoid and develop stereotyped behavior patterns, such as endlessly polishing an object. High doses taken over long periods of time may result in a psychotic state resembling paranoid schizophrenia.

Sidney Cohen, M. D.
University of California, Los Angeles

AMPHIARAUS, am-fē-ə-rā′əs, in Greek legend, a hero and seer of Argos. He became one of the Seven against Thebes at the urging of his wife, Eriphyle. Polynices, leader of the expedition, had bribed Eriphyle to persuade her husband to join it. Foreseeing disaster, Amphiaraus told his sons to kill their mother if he did not return. Zeus spared him from death in combat, but the god caused the ground to open up and swallow him. Carrying out Amphiaraus' orders, his son Alcmaeon killed Eriphyle. Amphiaraus became an immortal, and a temple to him was erected at Oropos, in Attica. See also ALCMAEON.

AMPHIBIA
DISTINGUISHING CHARACTERISTICS:

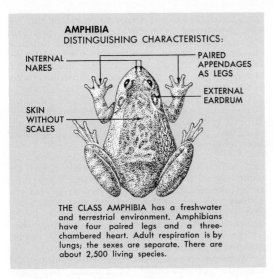

INTERNAL NARES

PAIRED APPENDAGES AS LEGS

EXTERNAL EARDRUM

SKIN WITHOUT SCALES

THE CLASS AMPHIBIA has a freshwater and terrestrial environment. Amphibians have four paired legs and a three-chambered heart. Adult respiration is by lungs; the sexes are separate. There are about 2,500 living species.

1. Caecilian

NEW YORK ZOOLOGICAL SOCIETY

2. Newt

GEORGE PORTER, FROM NATIONAL AUDUBON SOCIETY

3. Toad

W.J. SCHOONMAKER, FROM NATIONAL AUDUBON SOCIETY

MAIN CLASSES OF AMPHIBIA: 1. Apoda (caecilians), which are wormlike and have no limbs or eyes; 2. Caudata (newts and salamanders), with aquatic larvae that resemble the adult; 3. Anura (toads and frogs), with no tail or neck, long hind limbs, and webbed feet.

AMPHIBIA, am-fib′ē-ə, are a class of vertebrate animals intermediate in development between the fishes and the reptiles. The name "amphibian" literally means dual, or amphibious, life. Most amphibians live the first, or larval, portion of their lives entirely in the water, while the adults live partially or completely on land. Some species bypass the aquatic stage and spend their entire lives on land.

Along with a large number of fossil groups, the class Amphibia includes three distinct living orders: Anura, which contains the frogs and toads; Caudata, which contains the salamanders and newts; and Apoda, which contains only the caecilians.

Each of these orders may be distinguished by certain characteristics. Anurans lack tails as adults and possess hind legs that are much larger than their front legs. They are found throughout the world, except for extremely cold areas and some of the oceanic islands. Newts and salamanders, the Caudata, have long tails and usually have four nearly equal-sized legs. They are, in general, restricted to the Northern Hemisphere, with major centers of concentration in the United States, Europe, and the Far East. Caecilians are not well known. Limbless and usually blind, they look more like earthworms than like the other amphibians. They are burrowing forms and are found in southern Asia, Africa, and South America.

Physiology and Anatomy. Amphibians are ectotherms, which means that they derive their body heat from the surroundings in which they live. As a result, their temperature fluctuates directly with that of the environment and usually closely matches that of the air or water in which they live.

The skin of amphibians is thin and moist, although some caecilians have small scales embedded in the skin. The slimy, smooth feeling of their skin is due to numerous mucous glands that discharge their secretion onto the surface of the skin. Most species also possess numerous skin poison glands, which in some cases produce extremely toxic substances.

For most amphibians the moist skin serves as an important respiratory surface. In some (such as salamanders in the family Plethodontidae), lungs are absent, and the skin is the major organ of respiration. The lining of the mouth has an extensive blood supply and also serves as a respiratory surface. The lungs of amphibians are rather simple, baglike structures, which are much less efficient respiratory organs than the complex lungs of mammals and birds. In a few aquatic amphibians, the lungs serve as hydrostatic organs, aiding the animal in maintaining its position in the water.

Many amphibians have special anatomical structures associated with their habitat or habits. The blind, burrowing caecilians have tentaclelike structures on their heads. These structures are tactile and enable the animals to feel their way along their burrows. Spadefoot toads have sharp-edged cornified tubercles (lumps) on each hind foot, enabling them to burrow into the ground and to avoid hot, dry weather. Tree frogs have expanded, adhesive toe tips that aid them in climbing.

For color illustrations showing the anatomy of the frog, see the article FROG.

Life History of Amphibians—Frogs and Toads. Most frogs and toads breed and lay eggs in the water during the spring or summer months. However, frogs and toads that live in harsh, dry regions may not breed at any particular time of the year. Instead, they breed only when torrential rains occur. Thus, adequate water for the development of the young is assured. Such forms are called explosive breeders.

The males of most species have good vocal cords and vocal pouches that act as resonating chambers. The calls of each species are quite distinctive, and some can be heard as far as a mile (1.6 km) away. The females are attracted to the breeding sites by the calls of the males.

In mating, the male climbs on the back of the female and grasps her under the arms. As the female releases eggs, the male deposits sperm on them; therefore, fertilization is external. However, in two species of frogs, sperm are transferred to the body of the female, and fertilization is internal.

The clutches of eggs, which vary greatly in number according to the species, hatch into larval forms called tadpoles. Tadpoles have a long tail with a high fin (a tail that extends well up onto the body). They lack legs, eyelids, lungs, and true jaws. Tadpoles have gills for respiration and an extremely long intestinal tract that is coiled like a watch spring. They are vegetarian and eat algae with their beaks, which serve for jaws.

After a period of growth that varies from a few weeks to three years, tadpoles undergo metamorphosis into the adult form. Externally, the hind legs show first, followed by the front pair. Eyelids and jaws develop, and the tail gradually is absorbed. Internally, lungs develop, and the intestine shortens until it gains the characteristic adult form.

Some frogs, particularly in tropical areas, have life cycles quite different from the typical pattern. A few lay their eggs on the ground or in trees, and some of these species build special nests to contain the clutches. In other species the eggs may be carried in pits or pouches of the skin of one of the parents until they hatch; in one case, the father carries the eggs in his vocal pouches. In forms that lay their eggs away from water, it is common for the tadpole stage to be bypassed and for the eggs to hatch directly into miniature replicas of the parents.

The leopard frog (*Rana pipiens*) is typical of the seasonal breeding frogs. It is encountered in marshy meadows near ponds and swamps across North America, and its spots make it difficult to see unless it jumps. The leopard frog breeds in springtime, and the tadpoles metamorphose during the summer months. The adults subsist primarily on insects.

The bullfrog (*Rana catesbeiana*) also is a seasonal breeder. It is the largest frog in North America and reaches a body length of 9 or 10 inches (22.8 to 25.4 cm). Bullfrogs are insect eaters, but they have been known to eat mice, birds, and crayfish as well.

The spadefoot toads (*Scaphiopus*) of the western United States are examples of explosive breeders. Spadefoots are active at night to avoid the drying desert air. During the day and extended dry periods they burrow into the ground to avoid desiccation. Spadefoots breed immediately after heavy rains. Their eggs hatch rapidly, and the tadpoles develop quickly in order to complete their development before the water pools dry up.

The ribbed frog (*Ascaphus truei*) of the Pacific Northwest is restricted to cold mountain streams. It is a unique anuran, in that fertilization is internal and sperm are transferred to the female by an extension of the male cloaca, which serves as a copulatory organ. Breeding takes place in early fall. The eggs are laid under a rock the following summer, and two to three years are required for tadpole development. Ribbed frogs seldom leave the vicinity of streams and live primarily on insects and other small invertebrates.

Adult frogs and toads are strict carnivores and will not feed on dead material. Some are quite selective in their feeding and show definite preferences for certain types of insects. Others will eat almost anything they can catch and swallow. The tongue, which is sticky, is attached in the front of the mouth rather than at the back; it can shoot out to capture insects and other small invertebrates.

Salamanders and Newts. Unlike the anurans, the Caudata are voiceless. As a result, the males and females must find each other by smell during the breeding season. Similar to the anurans, most of the salamanders and newts breed in the water in the spring. Some, however, breed on land and some breed in the fall. In the more primitive salamanders, the male deposits sperm on the eggs as the female releases them into the water. In the advanced forms, the male deposits a packet of sperm called a spermatophore on the stream or pond bottom after a courtship consisting of rubbing and nosing. The female then picks up the spermatophore with her cloaca, and the sperm are stored in an internal structure called the spermatheca. Fertilization is internal. Eggs laid in the water hatch into larval forms, but, unlike tadpoles, the larvae of salamanders show a resemblance to their parents. Legs and jaws are present, and the intestine is similar to the adult form. Salamander larvae are carnivorous on small animals, as are their parents. The larvae have bushy, external gills and a high tail fin. In the forms that switch to terrestrial habitats in the adult stage, these structures are lost at metamorphosis.

Some salamanders, notably the plethodontids, lay their eggs on land. In these species the larval stage is passed in the egg, and small replicas of the adult are hatched. In a few species, the eggs are retained within the mother until they hatch, and the young are born either as larvae or as transformed juveniles.

The hellbender (*Cryptobranchus alleganiensis*), which lives in rapidly flowing rivers of the eastern United States, is one of the primitive salamanders with external fertilization. It is a large salamander, reaching lengths of 30 inches (76.2 cm). The hellbender has a wrinkled skin that provides more surface area for respiration than would a smooth skin. It is aquatic throughout its life, and it eats snails, crayfish, and other water animals. Fishermen occasionally catch hellbenders on their baited lines.

Salamanders of the genus *Ambystoma* are typical of the caudatans that are terrestrial as adults but migrate to the water to lay their eggs. The larval forms usually transform to the terrestrial stage within a few months. However, in some western areas where iodine, which is necessary for metamorphosis, is absent, the larvae may remain in the water and fail to transform. See AXOLOTL.

The slimy salamander (*Plethodon glutinosis*) lives under logs and rocks in forests of the eastern United States and never goes into the water. Its eggs are laid under rotten logs or in other hidden spots, and they hatch in the adult form.

Caecilians. The life history of many of the caecilians is not well known. Some of them lay eggs, while in other species the eggs are retained in the mother and are born either as larvae or in the adult form.

Development of the Class Amphibia. The modern members of the class Amphibia bear little resemblance to the first amphibians that evolved from Crossopterygian (see CROSSOPTERYGII) fishes in the Devonian period (330 million to 290 million years ago). Some of the early amphibians were as long as 15 feet (4.6 meters), and many of them had bony armor covering parts of their bodies.

It appears that limbs, lungs, and other advances the amphibians show over the fishes evolved as adaptations to allow vertebrates to remain in the water rather than to leave it. The Devonian was a period of alternating wet and dry periods. As pools dried up, most true fishes perished. Crossopterygians, with their muscular lobed-fins and lungs, were able to flop their way down the stream beds to places where water remained. Once this process was started, it is easy to envision how it expanded. Some might linger to eat insects or dying fishes. This easy life was selectively favored, and the vertebrates able to remain out of water flourished. Thus the amphibians evolved.

The Devonian was followed by the Carboniferous period (290 million to 230 million years ago) with its widespread coal swamps. The swampy conditions were favorable to the amphibians, and they rapidly evolved into many diverse forms. Some remained in the water at all times. Others with better legs and better ability to resist desiccation spent much of their time on land but returned to the water to breed and lay their eggs. Although the fossil evidence is somewhat inconclusive at this time, it appears that the ancestors to the three modern orders of amphibians had diverged into separate groups as early as the Carboniferous period. At that time, they did not resemble closely the modern forms of amphibians. Fossils that definitely can be recognized as modern-type amphibians did not appear until millions of years later, in the Mesozoic era (200 million to 75 million years ago). Fossil caecilians are not known.

Toward the end of the Carboniferous period the character of the land and the climate started to change. The coal swamps were replaced by dry, upland areas. As a result, many of the water-dependent amphibians died out. Evolution of the reptiles took place at this time from some of the amphibians that were better adapted to terrestrial life.

DEAN METTER, *University of Missouri*

Bibliography

Ashton, R. E., Jr., and P. S., *The Amphibians*, ed. by Sandra Romashko (Windward 1987).
Conant, Roger, *Field Guide to Reptiles and Amphibians*, 2d ed. (Houghton 1975).
Duellman, W. E., *Biology of Amphibians* (McGraw 1985).
Halliday, Tim, and Adler, Kraig, eds., *The Encyclopedia of Reptiles and Amphibians* (Facts on File 1986).
Norris, David O., and Jones, Richard E., eds., *Hormones and Reproduction in Fishes, Amphibians and Reptiles* (Plenum Pub. 1987).
Roth, G., *Visual Behavior in Salamanders* (Springer-Verlag 1987).

DEPARTMENT OF DEFENSE (MARINE CORPS)

AMPHIBIOUS LANDING shows Marines storming beach in landing craft and helicopters at Camp Lejeune, N.C.

AMPHIBIOUS WARFARE, am-fib′ē-əs wôr′fâr, is the doctrines, tactics, and techniques required by naval and landing forces to launch an attack from the sea on a hostile shore. Normally it requires extensive air participation, and the helicopter has become an important airborne landing craft that adds a new dimension. Special doctrine, equipment, and training are required for amphibious warfare because of the unique requirement to build combat power ashore from zero to fully coordinated striking power as the enemy defenses are assaulted. In the United States the responsibility for developing amphibious doctrine, equipment, and training has been assigned by law to the U.S. Marine Corps.

Capabilities for amphibious operations are strategically important because of the ability of an amphibious force to enter a hostile area when other means of entry may be closed. Landings often can exploit the important military element of surprise. In addition, the mere existence of an amphibious capability may cause the enemy to waste force and effort through overdispersion in an attempt to avoid surprise.

Purposes and Types. An amphibious operation is often a preliminary step to conventional land warfare, as was the case with all the major Allied landings in Africa, Sicily, Italy, and France during World War II. It also may be used to seize a site for an advanced naval and air base. This was the purpose of the first American amphibious operation of World War II—the U.S. Marine Corps landing on Guadalcanal island in the South Pacific. Another purpose might be to deny the use of an area or facilities to the enemy. An example was the landing (unopposed) of U.S. Marines in the Da Nang area of South Vietnam in March 1965. Identified by operational purpose, landings of this type are called *amphibious assaults*. They are characterized by the fact that the landing forces enter the hostile area fully deployed for fighting and seek a more-than-brief establishment of military force on the hostile shore.

Other operational types include the *amphibious withdrawal*, such as that made by U.S. forces from Hungnam, Korea, in 1950; the *amphibious demonstration*, a feint made by elements of the naval task force and landing forces to deceive the enemy as to the true objective; and the *amphibious raid*. The raid involves swift incursion into, or temporary occupancy of, an objective, followed by a planned withdrawal. Raids may be conducted to inflict loss or damage on the enemy, to obtain information, to create a diversion, or to capture or evacuate individuals and matériel. In 1965 and 1966, in South Vietnam, U.S. Marine elements afloat as the Special Landing Force of the Seventh Fleet made a number of such raids. Comparable raids made at Dieppe, on the French coast, by Canadian and British forces and on Makin Island by U.S. Marine forces in the Pacific area are among historic incidents in World War II.

Phases. The amphibious assault follows a well-defined sequence of events that usually is also recognizable in the other types of operations. These phases include (1) planning, (2) embarkation, (3) rehearsal, (4) movement to the objective, and (5) assault and capture of the objective. Planning occurs throughout the entire operation but is dominant in the period prior to embarkation.

The planning phase begins with the decision that a landing is to be made. Factors that complicate planning involve coordination of all forces —naval, air, and landing—to provide for the precise timing necessary to place deployed troops ashore to follow a scheme of maneuver that can be supported by air, naval gunfire, artillery, missiles, and logistics employed to the fullest extent, in an area where no military capability or action previously existed. The decision as to the objective of the landing normally produces the broad concept of the operation. Next an effective scheme of maneuver ashore must be designed to gain the objective. Coordinated planning among all forces then serves to assure that men, weapons, and matériel combine properly and in timely fashion. Planning, as a phase, terminates when embarkation begins.

In the embarkation phase, men and matériel are loaded aboard ships in such a way as to ensure that they will be unloaded rapidly and in the order in which they will be needed ashore. A ship is loaded first with what is calculated to be required last. This is known as combat loading. Men are designated for the successive assault waves of the landing force and are billeted aboard ship as boat teams and helicopter teams for entry into battle in the proper sequence.

Because of the overriding importance of precise timing in the amphibious operation, a rehearsal of the landing normally will be made, on friendly territory. This rehearsal phase tests the adequacy of plans, checks the efficiency of combat loading, and serves as practice for timing and a shakedown for machinery and communications.

During the movement to the objective, components of the amphibious task force move from points of embarkation to the target area. This move may be via rehearsal, staging, and rendezvous areas. This phase ends when task force elements take position in the objective area.

The assault phase is the coordination and employment of all components of the amphibious force so that they act in concert against the enemy for the maximum effect. During this phase the landing force moves from the ships to the shore in deployed assault formations, supported by air cover, naval gunfire, and missiles. This phase continues until the mission is accomplished or until conditions of combat and support ashore can be considered to be conventional land warfare. Development of the area for its ultimate use may be initiated during this period.

History. Amphibious operations as a part of warfare probably began in the Mediterranean region. In the battle of Marathon (490 B.C.) the Greeks faced an amphibious beachhead established by the invading Persians.

The Romans gave special training to some of their legions for use as marines, and Julius Caesar used amphibious operations repeatedly in the Mediterranean and in his two invasions of Britain. Much later, amphibious operations played an important role in expanding the British empire. One of the more important successes was the capture of Quebec in 1759. Probably the most notable failure of amphibious operations was at Gallipoli, Turkey, during World War I. British and French forces landed at the Dardanelles in an attempt to knock Turkey from the war and thus turn the flank of the Central Powers. Although the operation endured for nearly a year, it failed and ended in a costly withdrawal.

The operation at Gallipoli became a point of departure for studies concerning the techniques of amphibious warfare. The most notable and long-lasting of these studies began in the early 1930's at the Marine Corps Schools, Quantico, Va. By early 1934 the Marine Corps had developed fundamental doctrine for amphibious warfare. Testing and evaluation of the principles began in earnest. Tactics and techniques were devised, revised, and tested before World War II.

With the onset of World War II the United States proved itself well qualified to conduct modern amphibious operations, supported by swift and powerful Allied fleets, and covered by aircraft of increasing range and usefulness. In the Pacific the operations increased in size and complexity. The final assault of that war, against the island of Okinawa in 1945, involved 318 combat ships, 1,139 auxiliary vessels, 1,000 amphibious vehicles, and over 500,000 men.

A classic amphibious assault after World War II was made by U.S. Navy and Marine Forces at Inchon, Korea, on Sept. 15, 1950. In this case, a factor that complicated the planning, the timing, the coordination, and the execution was the tidal pattern in the area. There were only a few high tides that year that provided sufficient water for landing craft to cross extensive mud flats, and this suitable condition prevailed for only a few

PONTOON CAUSEWAY (shown here during a landing in South Vietnam) enables vehicles to be moved ashore from landing ships in shallow water.

hours on certain days. Despite this challenge, the Inchon landings were successfully executed and achieved significant tactical results.

Many landings in the Vietnam war during the 1960's were classified as amphibious raids. A number of such landings were made by U.S. Fleet Marine landing forces operating with the Seventh Fleet as the Special Landing Force.

Helicopter operations, whether executed as part of an amphibious operation or in a land-warfare mode, resemble amphibious operations in certain respects; both face the same problem of quickly building up full combat momentum from an initial zero. Marine forces and Army units, notably an airmobile division, began extensive use of these vertical envelopment tactics during the war in Vietnam.

WILLIAM R. COLLINS, *Major General, USMC*
Assistant Chief of Staff for Operations
and Training, Headquarters Marine Corps
(Specially prepared for Encyclopedia Americana.)

Further Reading: Bartlett, Merrill L., *Assault from the Sea* (Naval Inst. Press 1983); Creswell, John, *Generals and Admirals: The Story of Amphibious Command* (1952; reprint, Greenwood Press 1976); Godson, Susan H., *Viking of Assault* (Univ. Press of Am. 1982); Ladd, J. D., *Amphibious Warfare* (Pergamon 1987).

AMPHIBOLES, am′fə-bōlz, are a group of common rock-forming minerals containing varying ratios of different silicates. Chemically, the basic building block of silicate minerals is the SiO_4 unit. The amphiboles consist of continuous double chains of these units; such minerals are called *inosilicates*. The binding forces between the double chains are not so strong as the bonds between the units along the chain. Amphibole rocks tend to be fibrous or to exhibit prismatic cleavage.

Amphiboles resemble pyroxenes, another group of silicate minerals. However, all amphiboles contain hydroxyl (OH) groups in their structure. Also, their lines of cleavage intersect at angles of about 55° or 125°, while pyroxenes tend to cleave at nearly right angles.

The amphibole group as a whole has a worldwide distribution. The most common amphiboles are *hornblendes*. In addition, *amphibolites* are metamorphic rocks with hornblende as a major constituent. Fibrous amphiboles are mined as asbestos and may be used in cement or as insulating material. They include *amosite*, which forms the longest fibers of all asbestiform materials, and *crocidolite*, which is the blue asbestos of commerce. Most of the world's asbestos, however, comes from serpentine, another kind of silicate mineral with higher tensile strength. The amphiboles *tremolite* and *glauconite* are sometimes used in making ornaments.

Compositions of amphiboles can be very complex, but five distinct series are recognized (listed here according to crystal system):

ORTHORHOMBIC
(1) Anthophyllites: magnesium-iron amphiboles.
MONOCLINIC
(2) Cummingtonites: iron-magnesium amphiboles.
(3) Tremolites: calcium-magnesium-iron amphiboles.
(4) Hornblendes: similar to tremolites but with aluminum and minor amounts of sodium.
(5) Alkali amphiboles such as glaucophane, riebeckite, and arfvedsonite.

Composition: general formula $(WXY)_{7-8}(Z_4O_{11})_2(O,OH,F)_2$, in which X may be Ca, Na, and K; X may be Mg, Fe^{+2}, and Mn; Y may be Ti, Al, and Fe^{+3}; and Z is Si, sometimes partly replaced by Al. Hardness, 5 to 6; specific gravity, 2 to 3.4.

See also GLAUCOPHANE; HORNBLENDE; PYROXENE; TREMOLITE.

ARIE POLDERVAART, *Columbia University*

AMPHICTYONY, am-fik′tē-ə-nē, an association of neighboring states in ancient Greece established to protect and maintain a religious center common to all. The word is derived from the Greek *amphiktyones*, meaning "dwellers around." There were regional amphictyonies centered at Argos and Delos, but the most important was at Delphi. The Delphic Amphictyony maintained sanctuaries at the temple of Apollo at Delphi and of Demeter at Thermopylae. It was composed of 12 northern Greek states, each of which had two votes in the Council of the Amphictyony, which governed the league. Its main concerns were the safety of the shrines, the protection of pilgrims, and the maintenance of the roads leading to Delphi.

Occasionally the Delphic Amphictyony took political action. Thus, about 600 B.C., the Amphictyony, dominated by Thessaly, waged a "sacred war" on the city of Crisa, which may have levied dues on the pilgrims. Crisa was defeated, and its territory thereafter was dedicated to Apollo. Generally, however, the stronger states ignored the policies of the Amphictyony, and the association did not exercise lasting influence.

AMPHION, am-fi′ən, in Greek legend, was a son of Zeus and Antiope, princess of Thebes. He and his twin brother, Zethus, were abandoned at birth and were raised by shepherds. After Lycus became king of Thebes, the brothers learned of their royal birth, deposed or killed Lycus, and became joint rulers of Thebes.

As a boy, Amphion had been taught by Hermes (Mercury) to play the lyre and sing. The charm of his music could cause stones to form themselves into walls, and the wall around Thebes was supposed to have been built in this way.

Amphion married Niobe, who bore him seven sons and seven daughters. Proud of her fertility, Niobe challenged the supremacy of the goddess Leta (Latona), who could bear but two children. At Leta's command, Apollo and Diana slew Niobe and her children. Amphion then killed himself.

AMPHIOXUS, am-fē-ok′sas, is the common name for a small, primitive chordate that resembles a fish lacking lateral fins. It is important from an evolutionary standpoint because it has many characteristics expected of an ancestor of the vertebrates. Amphioxus inhabits shallow coastal seawaters in temperate and tropical regions. It is found in moderately fine sand or shell-gravel ocean bottoms with low silt content, and usually lies head up with its body half buried in the ocean floor.

Anatomy and Physiology. Amphioxus is about 1½ to 3 inches (4 to 7 cm) long. It has a low dorsal fin that extends the length of its body excluding the head. There is also a ventral fin on the rear third of the body. Simple V-shaped muscle segments make up most of its bulk.

At the front end of the body is a small hood edged with numerous long, slender cirri (tendril-like appendages). The mouth opening lies at the rear of the hood and leads into a large elongate pharynx extending about ⅖ the length of the body. The pharynx is pierced by as many as 180 pairs of closely placed, obliquely slanted slits separated from each other by slender bars formed from the pharynx wall. Cilia line the slits and occur in several elongate patches on the walls of the hood. The beat of the cilia causes water to flow into the pharynx and through the slits into the atrium, an ectoderm-lined cavity that completely surrounds the pharynx except at its upper attachment to the body wall. The atrium has one exit, the atriopore.

Amphioxus feeds on microorganisms that are carried into the pharynx by the water current and are caught on a food belt consisting of a sticky substance secreted by the endostyle, a gland on the floor of the pharynx. Except for a large blind pouch, or cecum, extending from the esophagus, the digestive tract extends straight to the anus, which is situated forward from the tip of the tail. The food belt passes through the stomach-intestine to a heavily ciliated section called the ileocolic ring. Fragments from the surface of the food belt are swept into the cecum, where they are slowly digested. The indigestible residue is ejected and eliminated via the intestine and anus.

A relatively thin layer of transverse muscle forms the ventral body wall forward from the atriopore. Elsewhere the body wall is formed of skeletal muscle.

The largely closed circulatory system of amphioxus has a striking similarity to that of vertebrates. It includes a ventral aorta connected by aortic arches with a pair of dorsal aortae, which unite near the rear of the pharynx, forming a single artery that extends to the tail. Other vessels return blood to the ventral aorta.

Respiration is accomplished largely through the single-layered skin covering. A mesoderm-lined, true coelom is present. Blind nephridial tubes gather excretory wastes from the dorsal coelomic spaces and release them into the atrium.

The skeletal system consists of a tough tissue, similar to a soft cartilage. This is found in the cirri, the pharyngeal bars, and the dorsal and ventral fins. A large notochord extends to the tips of the body immediately underneath a tubular dorsal nerve cord. The brain is represented by a small enlargement of the central nervous system in the rear part of the head. No paired eyes or optic or olfactory organs exist.

Reproduction. The sexes are separate. Numerous gonads lie on either side of the body cavity and against the outer wall of the atrium. Germ cells are released into the atrium where fertilization takes place; they then are swept out of the atriopore. Breeding occurs once a year in the shortlived species and twice in others. In gross anatomy the larva closely resembles the adult.

Classification. Amphioxus belongs to the genus *Branchiostoma*, which contains 27 species. There is only one other close relative, *Asymmetron*. These two genera, known as lancelets, compose the subphylum Cephalochordata, which, with the subphyla Urochordata (sea squirts) and Vertebrata, make up the phylum Chordata.

Vertebrate Relationships. The living kinds of lancelets are survivors of an extremely ancient group of animals rather closely related to the common ancestor of the phylum Chordata. They possess some features otherwise unique to the Vertebrata or to the Urochordata, but they also possess numerous specializations found in no other animals. Thus they are not a "link" between vertebrates and invertebrates.

HOBART SMITH, *University of Illinois*

AMPHIOXUS model, showing ventral and dorsal fins and characteristic V-shaped muscle segments.

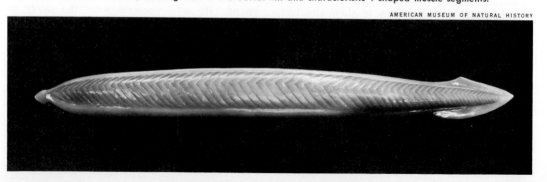

AMPHIPODS, am'fi-podz, are a group of crustaceans that includes beach flies, sandhoppers, skeleton shrimps, and whale lice. Amphipods are characterized by a flattened or compressed body with no caraprace (a bony shield covering the body) or cephalothorax (fused head and thorax). The thorax contains seven pairs of legs, and the abdomen has six pairs plus the telson, a tail-like segment. The legs are so elongated, however, that walking is difficult. Respiration is by gills. The sexes are separate. One of the most abundant forms of life found on the floors of coastal shelves, amphipods feed on aquatic plants and debris or swallow mud containing food particles. They form an important food for many commercial fishes.

The order Amphipoda belongs to the subclass Malacostraca and contains about 3,200 species in the oceans and 600 in fresh water and in moist terrestrial environments. There are four suborders of Amphipoda—Gammaridea, the largest of the four, which is principally marine but contains the only nonmarine forms; Hyperiidea, containing 300 marine species; Caprellidea, with 230 species in shallow water; and Ingolfiellidea, with only 4 species. Common examples are *Gammarus*, found in both salt and fresh water, and *Chelura terebrans*, which burrows into wood and frequently destroys pilings.

AMPHISBAENIDS, am-fəs-bē'nədz, are a group of highly specialized worm lizards found mostly in Africa and South America. Amphisbaenids have flourished without much change for over 50 million years, and many fossil forms exist.

Similar in appearance to a huge earthworm, the worm lizard has a blunt head and tail, with eyes and ears concealed beneath head shields. Because the head and tail are similar in appearance, worm lizards often are called two-headed snakes or blind snakes. Amphisbaenids have no limbs, and their shoulder and hip bones are rudimentary. Three Mexican species, however, have much-reduced forelimbs. Amphisbaenids without limbs move by means of their loose-fitting skin, which has square or rectangular vestigial scales fused in transverse and longitudinal rows. They are burrowing animals that feed on termites, ants, grubs, and earthworms.

Worm lizards belong to the family Amphisbaenidae. The family is divided into about 20 genera, with more than half of the 125 species assigned to the genus *Amphisbaena*.

Among species of amphisbaenids are the egg-laying *Rhineura floridana*, 12 inches long and found in Florida; *Monopeltis jugularis*, a West African species that is 26 inches long—the longest of the species; and *Amphisbaena alba*, the white-bellied worm lizard of South America.

AMPHITHEATER, am'fə-thē-ət-ər, an elliptical building, with seats surrounding a central arena, used for open-air spectacles. In ancient Rome, gladiatorial games, wild beast hunts, and sometimes mock naval battles and brutal plays were regularly held in amphitheaters. Such spectacles, sponsored by emperors and local magistrates, served a populace that increasingly demanded bread and entertainment. The shows at first were modest in scale, but they became increasingly extravagant and brutal. When the Colosseum was opened in 80 A.D., the games lasted 100 days, from dawn to dusk; 9,000 animals were killed, 5,000 gladiators fought, and the arena

RAPHO GUILLUMETTE

THE AMPHITHEATER AT ARLES in southern France, accommodating 26,000 spectators, is used for bullfights.

was flooded for a naval battle. No emperor dared rouse popular resentment by economizing on the spectacles. There were thousands of animals from remote lands, elaborate stage settings, and well-trained, richly rewarded gladiators.

Structure. The building form, with no known Greek precedent, apparently developed in Campania, where gladiatorial games had early popularity. The oldest extant amphitheater, dated 80 B.C., is at Campanian Pompeii. In Rome the first games were held in the Forum on temporary seats. Then, in 55 B.C., two wooden theaters, back to back, were mounted on a swivel and pivoted 180° to form an amphitheater for gladiatorial games. Whether the amphitheater was derived from the rectangular Forum or from joining two theaters, it was regularly elliptical.

The great Flavian Amphitheater, the Colosseum, represents the sophisticated culmination of the amphitheater form, grouping masses of spectators around a central arena. It is 584 feet (188 meters) long, 468 feet (143 meters) wide, and 161 feet (49 meters) high. The basic structural material is gray travertine, supplemented with masonry and concrete and faced with brick and marble. Based on piers sunk 20 feet (7 meters) underground, the façade has four stories. In the first three stories, 80 arches spring from pillars with Doric, Ionic, and Corinthian capitals. The fourth story is not arched but has 40 windows alternating with 40 bronze shields. Within the arches, arcades with barrel vaults circle the building. They open into the seating area, which is cut at regular intervals by stairways that divide the seats into wedge-shaped blocks. Above the arena, protected by a bronze balustrade, were the boxes for the emperor, magistrates, vestal virgins, and other dignitaries. Senators and equestrians sat in the first gallery, while the plebeians filled the upper marble seats. Unaccompanied women had wooden seats at the top, and above them stood slaves and others who were not citizens. An awning, drawn by sailors, could cover the crowd of 50,000. The arena was floored in timber made watertight for mock naval battles. The floor covered a subterranean complex for storage of scenery, for animal dens, and for other purposes. Now half-destroyed, the Colosseum still glorifies Roman architecture.

Later History. Lesser amphitheaters spread across the Western empire. They ranged from simple earthen banks, enlarged by timber or masonry, to handsome structures whose remains are still used for spectacles. In northern Gaul and Britain a stage for plays sometimes was built at one side of the oval arena. In the East, where the less brutal Hellenistic tradition prevailed, amphitheaters were few, but many theaters and odeums were converted into amphitheater form for Roman spectacles. By the 6th century, Christianity ended these brutalities.

ELEANOR HUZAR, *Michigan State University*

AMPHITRITE, am-fə-trī′tē, in Greek mythology, was the wife of Poseidon (Neptune), god of the sea. She was a daughter either of Oceanus and Tethys or of Nereus and Doris. When Poseidon wanted her for his wife, she hid from him. Poseidon sent a dolphin to find her. The dolphin brought her to Poseidon and, as a reward, received a place among the stars. As sea goddess, Amphitrite is represented in a chariot of shells drawn by tritons, or riding on a dolphin.

AMPHITRYON, am-fit′rē-ən, in Greek legend, was the son of Alcaeus, king of Tiryns. Engaged to marry Alcmene, he accidentally killed her father, King Electryon of Mycenae. Amphitryon fled with Alcmene to Thebes, where he was absolved of the killing by King Creon.

Before Alcmene would marry Amphitryon, she required him to avenge the deaths of her brothers, slain in battle by the Teleboans (Taphians). During his absence, Zeus impersonated Amphitryon as Alcmene's lover. Amphitryon returned and, with much difficulty, proved his identity. He married Alcmene, who gave birth to twin sons: Heracles (Hercules) by Zeus, and Iphicles by her husband.

This version of the theme of mistaken identity was the basis of comedies by the Roman playwright Plautus and by Molière and Dryden in the 17th century. Jean Giraudoux's *Amphitryon 38* (1929) is a modern rendering.

AMPHOTERIC COMPOUNDS, am-fə-ter′ik, are compounds that can act either as acids or as bases. (*Ampho* is Greek for "both.") In combination with an acid, an amphoteric compound acts as a base; in combination with a base, it acts as an acid. Aluminum hydroxide, for example, is an amphoteric compound. Two of its typical reactions are:

$$Al(OH)_3 + 3HCl \rightarrow AlCl_3 + 3H_2O$$
$$Al(OH)_3 + 3NaOH \rightarrow Na_3AlO_3 + 3H_2O$$

In the first reaction the aluminum hydroxide acts as a base in reaction with hydrochloric acid. In the second reaction the aluminum acts as an acid in reaction with sodium hydroxide, a base. In general, an amphoteric compound acts as an acid when it provides H^+ ions, and it acts as a base when it provides $(OH)^-$ ions.

AMPLIFIER, am′plə-fī-ər, a device that increases the magnitude of a varying quantity, such as an electrical voltage. The amount that the quantity is increased can be controlled. The vacuum tube, the transistor, and the magnetic amplifier are three devices that are widely used as amplifiers.

Applications. Vacuum tubes, transistors, and magnetic amplifiers enlarge or amplify tiny electrical voltages to a level at which they can operate loudspeakers, control industrial equipment, operate distant remote-control defense centers, and perform thousands of other essential tasks. Amplifiers make it possible to keep in radio contact with space probes millions of miles from earth. Amplifiers in electronic equipment on ships permit navigators to obtain precise bearings from distant ground-based loran stations. Airline pilots depend on thousands of amplifier circuits to operate their radar, navigation, communications, and identification equipment. Electronic amplifiers are used to control theater lighting, elevator speed, and traffic systems. They are used to perform hundreds of daily duties. Radios, phonographs, and television receivers have many amplifier circuits that amplify and reamplify small signals.

Amplifiers can be classified by the frequency band, or range of frequencies, that they are designed to amplify. Audio-frequency amplifiers operate in the audio-frequency range, which extends from 20 cycles per second (cps) to 20,000 cps. For example, hi-fi and stereo amplifiers accept low-level audio signals from phonograph cartridges and enlarge them to high-level signals that drive loudspeakers. Radio-frequency (r-f) amplifiers are designed to operate within the range of frequencies from about 100 kilocycles per second (Kc) to 1,000 megacycles per second (Mc). Commercial radio transmitters and receivers, for example, use r-f amplifiers. Video amplifiers, which are used in television receivers and studio camera chains, operate in the frequency band from 30 cps to 4 Mc. Microwave amplifiers, which amplify at frequencies greater than 1,000 Mc, are used in radar sets and other applications. Microwave circuits contain special-purpose tubes and circuit elements (See RADAR).

At the frequencies of operation that are used for radio and television, the circuits contain vacuum-tube amplifiers or transistor amplifiers. The type of device that is used is another way to classify amplifiers.

Diode Vacuum Tube. Although the diode vacuum tube is not an amplifier, it will be discussed first because it is the simplest type of vacuum tube. The diode vacuum tube contains two electrodes. One electrode, called the cathode, emits electrons. The second electrode, called the anode, or plate, receives the electrons. The electron flow (current flow) through the vacuum tube is influenced by two factors: (1) the temperature at which the cathode is operated and (2) the potential difference or voltage between the anode and the cathode.

When the cathode is heated, it emits electrons, which are negatively charged particles. If a negative voltage is applied between the anode and the cathode, the negatively charged electrons are repelled, and electron flow cannot take place. If no voltage is applied between the anode and the cathode, the emitted electrons will form an electron cloud, or negative charge, around the cathode. This negative charge around the cathode tends to repel the electrons emitted later, and no conduction to the anode takes place. If a positive voltage is applied between the anode and the cathode, a positive charge is produced at the anode. This positive charge counteracts the negative charge at the cathode, and electron flow from cathode to anode can take place. The negatively charged electrons are attracted by a positively charged electrode. If a positive anode voltage is increased, the electron flow increases. This increase in electron flow is limited only by the emission ability of the cathode material and the operating temperature of the cathode.

Triode Vacuum Tube. Amplification—the ability to develop or control a large output by means of a low-level input—is made possible by adding a third electrode, called the control grid, to form a triode vacuum tube. This electrode, which is a spiral of fine wire surrounding the cathode, can exercise considerable control over the electron flow because it is placed extremely close to the cathode.

When the anode is set at a high positive voltage relative to the cathode and the cathode emission is steady, the electron flow is determined by the control-grid voltage. If the control grid is placed at a highly negative voltage, the negative charge at the grid reinforces the negative charge at the cathode, and no electrons reach the anode. If the control-grid voltage is made less and less negative, there will be a point at which the positive charge on the anode overcomes the combined negative charges of the grid and cathode, and electron flow can then take place. If the control-grid voltage is made even less negative, electron flow increases further.

A small change in the control-grid voltage will cause a large change in the anode current. If a resistor R is connected between the anode and its battery (see Fig. 1), the anode current will flow through the resistor and cause a voltage drop across it. A large current produces large voltage drop, but a small current produces only a slight voltage drop. A large voltage drop across the resistor subtracts a large voltage from the fixed battery voltage applied to the anode circuit. This subtraction leaves only a small voltage between the anode and cathode electrodes. Thus the anode voltage decreases by a large amount. In summary, a small change in control-grid voltage produces a large change in anode current flow, and a large change in anode current flow produces a large change in the anode voltage.

The ability of a small voltage change at one electrode (control grid) to cause a much greater voltage change at another electrode (anode) provides amplification. The amount by which a tube amplifies is termed the "amplification factor." This factor is the ratio of the anode voltage change to the control-grid voltage change. Thus, an amplification factor, or gain, of 20 is provided by a triode when its anode voltage can be varied by 60 volts with only a 3-volt variation in the control-grid voltage. A typical triode has an amplification factor from 30 to 100. Triodes are often used as audio-frequency amplifiers.

One disadvantage of the triode is that there is a cathode-to-grid capacitance and a grid-to-anode capacitance because the tube electrodes are metallic and are separated in a vacuum. At high operating frequencies, the grid-to-anode capacitance allows some of the amplified voltage to return to the control grid, and this action upsets the performance of the amplifier.

Figure 1. TRIODE VOLTAGE AMPLIFIER

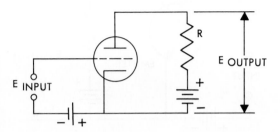

Voltage amplifier circuit includes a triode vacuum tube, a resistor, and two batteries. A small change in control-grid voltage results in a large change in output voltage.

Tetrode Vacuum Tube. To reduce this capacitance effect, a second grid, called the screen grid, is placed between the control grid and the anode. This four-electrode tube is called a tetrode. Tetrodes are seldom used because some electrons released from the anode are attracted to the positively charged screen grid. This phenomenon, called secondary emission, reduces the anode electron flow and thus reduces amplification.

Pentode Vacuum Tube. To improve the tetrode, a third grid, called the suppressor grid, is placed between the anode and the screen grid. The suppressor grid is kept at a relatively low negative voltage to repel any secondary electrons that leave the anode. This five-electrode tube, which is called a pentode, is considerably more efficient than the triode. An amplification factor greater than 1,000 is not unusual for pentodes. A pentode tube that has a heater element to cause electron emission from the cathode is shown in

Figure 2. PENTODE VACUUM TUBE

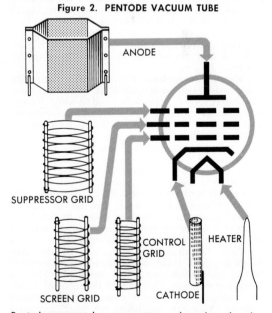

Pentode vacuum tube components are shown in conjunction with their schematic representation. Cathode is the source of electrons. The grids help to control the flow of electrons from the cathode to the anode. Heater heats cathode.

Figure 3. TRANSISTOR VOLTAGE AMPLIFIER

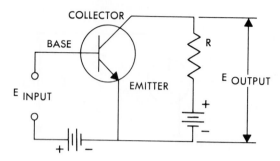

Voltage amplifier circuit includes a transistor, a resistor, and two batteries. A small change in the base voltage results in a large change in the output voltage.

Fig. 2. Pentode tubes are often used as r-f amplifiers and as video amplifiers.

Transistor Amplifier. The triode vacuum tube was invented by Lee De Forest (q.v.) in 1906. In 1948, scientists at the Bell Telephone Laboratories demonstrated a solid-state device—the transistor—that could amplify currents in solid semiconductor materials, such as germanium and silicon. Since its invention the tiny, rugged transistor has displaced the bulky, fragile vacuum tube in many applications. Although there are many differences between the two devices, some basic characteristics can be compared. In the vacuum tube the source of current carriers is the cathode; in the transistor the source of current carriers is called the emitter. In the vacuum tube the electrode that attracts the current carriers is the anode; in the transistor this electrode is called the collector. The control electrode in the tube is the control grid; the electrode that performs this function in a transistor is called the base electrode. In a transistor amplifier, small variations in the base-to-emitter voltage produce greater changes in the emitter current and the collector current, and high amplification is possible. A diagram of a simple transistor amplifier is shown in Fig. 3.

Magnetic Amplifier. The magnetic amplifier can provide such advantages as high efficiency, low input power demands, and ability to operate under adverse environmental conditions. The basis of a magnetic amplifier is the saturable reactor, which consists of two separate coils of wire wrapped around an iron core. One coil is connected to an a-c power source, and the other coil, called the control winding, is connected to a d-c power source. When the iron core is not saturated (not fully magnetized), the reactor allows only a small amount of current to flow from the a-c power source to the load, or device under control. When a small amount of direct current is sent through the control winding, the degree of saturation of the core increases, and there is a considerable increase in the alternating current to the load. Thus, a small current-flow variation in the control winding can produce a large change in the output current. Magnetic amplifiers are used to control motor speed and torque. They also are used in welding equipment and high-power lighting systems.

HOWARD BIERMAN, *RCA Institutes, Inc.*

AMQUI, äN-kē', a town in Quebec, Canada, at the base of the Gaspé Peninsula, 250 miles (400 km) northeast of Quebec City. It is situated on the Matapédia River and is the seat of Matapédia County. Amqui has food processing, textile, and woodworking plants. Dairying is the economic mainstay of the area. Population: 6,473.

AMR IBN AL–AS (594?–664), am-rōōb-nil-äs', was an Arab general and statesman who was responsible for the Muslim conquest of Egypt. He was an opponent of Mohammed until his conversion to Islam in 629. In 633, Mohammed's father-in-law and successor, Abu Bakr, entrusted Amr with a high command in the Muslim army that was about to depart for the conquest of Syria. Amr was chiefly responsible for conquering the territory west of the Jordan River. He led an army into Egypt in 639, occupied Babylon in 641, and completed his conquest of Egypt, with the surrender of Alexandria, in 642. When the Byzantines took Alexandria in 645, Amr, who had been recalled from Egypt, returned and recaptured the city in 646. He then destroyed the city's walls.

Amr supported Muawiya against Ali in the struggle over the caliphate and was thus instrumental in establishing the Umayyad dynasty, with Muawiya as its first caliph. Muawiya appointed Amr governor of Egypt, and he held the post until his death in 664. His administration of Egypt was a good one, and its moderation facilitated the spread of Islam. He cleared a canal built by the ancient pharaohs connecting the Nile River and the Red Sea, and he established a new capital city (643) called al-Fustat, later renamed Misr. In the 900's, the city was destroyed and then rebuilt and renamed Cairo.

AMRAM BEN SHESHNA (died c. 875), äm'räm ben shesh'nä, head of the Jewish Talmudic academy at Sura, Babylonia, compiled the first complete Jewish prayer book. He prepared the book, known as the *Siddur Rab Amram*, for the Jewish community of Barcelona, Spain. Arranged for daily, Sabbath, and holiday rites, the book became the authority for Jewish liturgical practice. It was first published in Warsaw in 1869, about 1,000 years after Amram compiled it.

AMRITSAR, um-rit'sər, a city in India, is the capital of a district of the same name in Punjab state, 31 miles east of Lahore, Pakistan. Favorably situated between Kabul and Delhi and Kashmir and the Deccan, Amritsar is of considerable importance as a commercial and manufacturing center. Textiles are the most important of the diversified industries located there. The manufacture of shawls and silks was formerly an important industry, and the city still is noted for its carpets. There is a large trade in agricultural products as well.

Amritsar is the principal religious center of the Sikhs. It is the site of the sacred "pool of immortality," constructed in the 16th century by Ram Das, one of the earlier pontiffs of the Sikh faith. The Sikhs immerse themselves in the pool to be purified of sin. Built of brick, the basin is 510 square feet (47 sq meters). In its center is the Golden Temple, the chief Sikh shrine, in which is kept the sacred book of Sikh religion and law, the Granth Sahib. Voluntary contributions of pilgrims and devotees support the shrine. Population: 975,695 (2001 census).

AMSTERDAM, largest city in the Netherlands, is sometimes called the "Venice of the North" because of its hundreds of miles of canals.

AMSDORF, äms'dôrf, **Nikolaus von** (1483–1565), German theologian, who was a leader of the Protestant Reformation in Germany. Born at Torgau, Germany, on Dec. 3, 1483, he was educated at the universities of Leipzig and Wittenberg and became a professor of theology at Wittenberg in 1511. Amsdorf was a devoted friend of Martin Luther and was with Luther at the Disputation of Leipzig (1519) and at the Diet of Worms (1521). He was also among the few persons who knew that Luther had gone into seclusion in Wartburg Castle in 1521. Amsdorf supervised the publication of Luther's works.

Amsdorf was appointed Lutheran bishop of Naumburg in 1542 but was expelled by the Catholics in 1547. After Luther's death in 1546, he opposed Melanchthon's compromises with the Catholics on nonessential doctrines. He died at Eisenach on May 14, 1565.

AMSTERDAM, am'stər-dam, is the largest city in the Netherlands. It is the commercial, banking, and industrial center of the country and the official capital, although the actual seat of government is The Hague.

Amsterdam's many canals add great beauty to the city, besides providing it with transportation routes. There are more than 50 canals and 500 bridges in the city. A boat trip through the canals gives a visitor a good first view of Amsterdam's attractive old houses and busy modern harbor.

Economic Life. Amsterdam depends on waterways for its commerce. Situated in the province of North Holland, the city is built on the IJ, a long bay of the IJsselmeer (a lake formed by the damming of the Zuider Zee). The Amstel River divides the city into two main parts. Amsterdam's lifeline is the North Sea Canal, which links the landlocked harbor with the North Sea, 16 miles to the west. The canal is deep enough (40 feet) and wide enough (400 feet) for large ocean vessels. Other major canals connect Amsterdam with the North Sea by a longer route to the north and with the Rhine River to the south.

The port of Amsterdam is the second busiest in the Netherlands, outranked only by Rotterdam. More than 8,000 seagoing vessels enter the port each year, loading or discharging about 15 million metric tons of cargo. Most of the imports are bulk cargoes of oil, ores, coal, and grain. Manufactured products, bulbs and seeds are exported. Much of Amsterdam's water trade is bound to or from Germany. The city is also a major fishing port.

Schiphol Airport, 6 miles southwest of Amsterdam, is the main port of entry for people arriving in the Netherlands by plane. More than 20 international airlines serve Schiphol.

The major manufacturers, banks, and insurance companies of the Netherlands have home offices or branches in Amsterdam, and more than 300 foreign companies are represented. The stock exchange is one of the most active in Europe.

One of Amsterdam's oldest industries is diamond cutting and polishing. These skills, introduced by Jewish refugees from Portugal and Spain in the 1580's, have made Amsterdam the leading diamond market of the world. The city's heavy industries produce iron and steel, machinery, locomotives and railroad cars, bridge materials, ships, motor vehicles, and aircraft. Other important industries are clothing manufacture, printing and publishing, sugar and oil refining, food processing, brewing and distilling, and the manufacture of chemical, glass, leather, paper, rubber, and plastic products.

Points of Interest. The city is laid out in the shape of a fan, with three main canals forming concentric half-circles around the business center. Amsterdam lies below sea level but is protected by dikes and floodgates. The ground is so soft that the city is built on wooden or concrete piles sunk into the earth. Because of this insecure foundation, some buildings seem to hang over the canals, out of vertical alignment.

The most attractive parts of Amsterdam are the tree-lined canals along which rich merchants of the 1600's and 1700's built their houses. These gabled brick houses are often tall and narrow because they were once taxed according to their frontage. Many buildings in the city have pulleys at the top to hoist furniture through the windows if the stairs are too narrow.

The central square of Amsterdam is the Dam, where the royal palace is situated. The palace was originally the town hall, built between 1648 and 1662. On the same square is New Church, begun in 1417. Every Dutch monarch since 1814 has been crowned there. One of the city's oldest shopping streets, Kalverstraat (Calves' Street), leads from the Dam to the old Mint Tower, a prominent landmark.

The most beautiful church in Amsterdam is Old Church. Consecrated in 1306, it is the city's most ancient building. Another historic place is the Weeper's Tower, the last remnant of the city wall of 1482. From this point, on April 4, 1609, Henry Hudson sailed in the vessel *Half Moon* on a voyage that brought him to New York harbor and the Hudson River.

A fascinating old section of the city is the Jewish quarter, where Spinoza was born and where Rembrandt lived. In another section is the warehouse in which the young diarist Anne Frank and her family took refuge from the Nazi persecution of the Jews during World War II. Here can be seen the rooms where they hid for two years before they were betrayed and captured.

Although Amsterdam is rich in historic buildings, the city also takes pride in its 20th century architecture and town plannings. Outstanding among the many modern buildings is the Stock Exchange, completed in 1903. The impressive Olympic Stadium, seating 60,000 persons, was constructed for the 1928 Olympic Games.

Amsterdam began expanding into carefully planned suburbs after World War I. These areas have houses, apartment buildings, and schools of advanced design. They are among the finest parts of the metropolitan area. Amsterdam's expansion has been planned up to the year 2000.

Amsterdam has outstanding museums and theaters. The Rijksmuseum houses the world's greatest collection of Dutch art. Its most famous painting is Rembrandt's *Night Watch*. The Municipal (Stedelijk) Museum is devoted to modern art. It contains many of the best paintings of Van Gogh. The museum of the Royal Institute of the Tropics exhibits the arts and products of the Netherlands Antilles, Surinam, and the former Netherlands East Indies (now Indonesia). Amsterdam's Concert Hall is the home of the world-renowned Concertgebouw Orchestra. Opera, ballet, and drama are presented in the Municipal Theater.

There are two universities. The University of Amsterdam, founded in 1632, has about 10,000 students and a library of over 1,500,000 books and manuscripts. The Free University, founded in 1880, has more than 3,000 students.

History. Amsterdam's origins go back to the 1200's. The city was then a fishing port. It was called *Amstelredamme* because it had grown up around a dam on the Amstel River. The place came into the possession of the counts of Holland in 1296, and by 1482 it was important enough to have a protective wall.

After the decline of Antwerp and the cities of Flanders in the late 1500's, Amsterdam became the key city of the Low Countries. Many people from Flanders fled to it to escape economic depression. Huguenots from France and Jews from Spain and Portugal went there to escape religious persecution. Many of these immigrants brought to Amsterdam valuable business experience, industrial skills, and scholarly knowledge.

The city reached a peak of economic prosperity and power in the 1600's. The Dutch East India Company, founded at Amsterdam in 1602, brought the city a rich trade in the spices, cloths, and dyes of the East. By 1622, Amsterdam had a population of 100,000. Its commerce and banking made it the richest city in Europe, and it sent out navigators to explore the world for new markets. It was also a center of philosophy and theology.

The city repulsed the armies of William II of Orange in 1650 and Louis XIV of France in 1672 by opening dikes that flooded the countryside. But in 1795 it was captured by the French. The port had already begun to decline because of the gradual silting of the Zuider Zee, which was then Amsterdam's outlet to the high seas. The British blockade during the Napoleonic wars completed the destruction of Amsterdam's commerce.

The opening of the North Holland Canal in 1825 and the more important North Sea Canal in 1876 helped to make Amsterdam once again a great port, although Rotterdam captured a larger share of Dutch and German commerce. The city's trade declined again in World War I, but after the war it grew rapidly.

Amsterdam was not bombed during World War II, but the occupying Germans destroyed much of the port before surrendering. In the final winter of the war, the inhabitants suffered great hardships from cold and hunger. Many starved. Only 10,000 of the prewar Jewish community of 86,000 survived the Nazi terror. After the war, the port was rapidly rebuilt, and the city regained its position as a world trading center. Population: 715,148 (1997 census).

Bibliography: Dunford, Martin, and Jack Holland, *Rough Guide to Amsterdam* (Methuen 1987); Heyden, A. van der, *The Glory of Amsterdam* (Elsevier Pub. Co. 1975); Kistemaker, Renée, and Roelf Van Gelder, *Amsterdam* (Abbeville Press 1983).

AMSTERDAM, am'stər-dam, an industrial city in New York, about 35 miles (56 km) by road northwest of Albany. It is situated in Montgomery county on the Mohawk River and Erie Canal.

The city, formerly known for its manufacture of gloves and carpeting, now has an economy based primarily on the production of electronic games. Fiberglass also is produced. Among the historic buildings is Guy Park Manor (1766), now a museum of Indian and colonial relics.

Amsterdam's first permanent settler was Albert Vedder, who founded the hamlet of Veddersburg in 1783 on the city's present site. In 1804 the name Amsterdam was adopted because the ancestors of most of the early residents had come from the Netherlands. The village began to grow in importance after the Erie Canal was opened in 1825. Amsterdam was incorporated as a town in 1831 and as a city in 1885. It is governed by a mayor and a city council. Population: 18,355.

AMSTERDAM, University of, am'stər-dam, a publicly financed coeducational institution in Amsterdam, Netherlands. It was founded in 1632 as the Athenaeum Illustre, a municipal academy. It achieved university status in 1877 and was then given its present name. Municipal control ended in 1961, and it is now independent, although its financial support comes from the state and the city. The university has faculties of theology, law, medicine, mathematics and natural science, arts, economics, and political and social sciences.

AMTRAK, a semipublic corporation that provides intercity passenger service by rail in the United States. Amtrak is the official nickname for the National Railroad Passenger Corporation, which was created by the Rail Passenger Service Act of 1970. Before 1970 many railroads had sought permission from the Interstate Commerce Commission to discontinue service. To ensure continuation of a viable intercity system, Congress established Amtrak and provided initial funding. The service began operations in 1971 but consistently lost money. Amtrak is governed by a nine-member board that includes the secretary of transportation.

Amtrak operates about 240 trains each day to some 500 stations on 23,000 miles (37,000 km) of track. Its busiest routes are in the Northeast Corridor, principally between Boston and Washington. Amtrak maintains its own repair and service facilities and contracts with about 20 railroads for the right to operate on their tracks. Fare hikes, cost-control measures, and aggressive marketing have led to reduced reliance on federal subsidies.

AMU DARYA, ä-mōō där′yə, one of the chief rivers of central Asia. Its classical name, still in use, is Oxus. It rises in northeastern Afghanistan and flows nearly 1,500 miles (2,400 km) west and northwest to the south shore of the Aral Sea in Uzbekistan. The Amu Darya is navigable for about 930 miles (1,500 km), as far as Chärjew, where it is crossed by a railroad.

The source streams are the Pamir and the Ab-i-Wakhan, outlets of snow-fed lakes in the Pamir Mountains. These headwaters join at the western end of the Wakhan Range, and for nearly 700 miles (1,130 km) the united stream wanders through mountains and foothills until it flows out onto a desert plain about 70 miles (110 km) below Termiz in Uzbekistan. There the Amu Darya forms part of the northern boundary of Afghanistan. The chief tributaries are the Vakhsh, Kofarnihon (Kafirnigan), and Surkhandarya from the north, and the Kunduz from the south, all entering above Termiz.

In its middle and lower reaches the river crosses a sand desert, for which it supplies irrigation water. As it nears the Aral Sea, the stream loses itself in a swampy delta.

Alexander crossed the stream in 328 B.C. In ancient geologic times the river flowed into the Caspian Sea, and in the 1950s some water was diverted into the old course to form a canal.

JOEL M. ANDRESS
Central Washington State College

AMULET, am′yə-lət, an object worn or carried on the person in the belief that it will bring good luck or ward off evil. It represents a kind of personal magic—often sympathetic or imitative magic. Used frequently to protect persons or livestock specifically against magical attack (for example, the evil eye), amulets may be thought of as countermagic.

Magic and Amulets. Some anthropologists differentiate between magic and religion. Whereas magic operates automatically and impersonally, religious practices such as prayer and sacrifice are effective only contingently, as appeals to higher powers. In anthropologist Bronislaw Malinowski's view, religion is directed toward collective goals while magic is designed to serve individual ends. This last characteristic is illustrated by belief in amulets.

Amulets are used to protect persons who are particularly vulnerable: children, the sick, and women in childbirth; persons in dangerous or frightening occupations; or persons with occupations in which luck plays a major role (the gambler, the hunter). Like many elements of magic, amulets seem to be associated with situations and activities over which man's control is slight or nonexistent. Hence the use of magic to deal with specific problems has decreased as man's rational control over his environment has increased.

Amulets must be distinguished from talismans. A talisman is believed to have the power to work wonders. Thus the legendary lamp of Aladdin is a talisman, because it could do far more than ward off evil or bring luck.

Varieties of Amulets. Although magical practices have long been decried by the Christian churches as superstitious, amulets are still very widely used in the Western world—for example, the rabbit's foot, the lucky coin, birthstones, St. Christopher medals, the horseshoe, and the four-leaf clover. Personal, nontraditional amulets may be in any form from a string of beads to a Phi Beta Kappa key.

Amulets have been made of such diverse materials as stone, metal, feathers, cloth, wood, bone, and shell. Natural objects of striking form or manufactured objects have been used. Interesting examples are the amulets found among the simple tribes of the Chaco region in South America. The men of the Mocovi tribe tied deer hooves to their ankles and wrists to acquire, by sympathetic magic, the swiftness of the deer. Among the Mocovi and their neighbors, hunting charms and love charms were widely used.

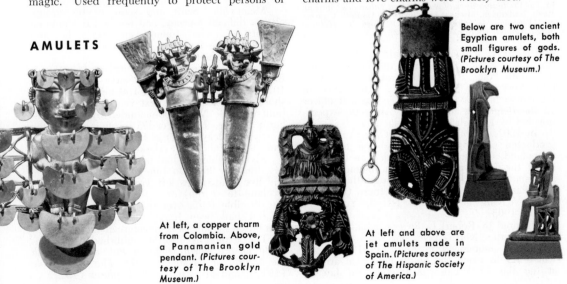

AMULETS

Below are two ancient Egyptian amulets, both small figures of gods. *(Pictures courtesy of The Brooklyn Museum.)*

At left, a copper charm from Colombia. Above, a Panamanian gold pendant. *(Pictures courtesy of The Brooklyn Museum.)*

At left and above are jet amulets made in Spain. *(Pictures courtesy of The Hispanic Society of America.)*

One notable group of amulets originated in the Middle East and were spread throughout that region, and later to the Iberian peninsula, by Arab conquests. From there many of the same amulets spread to Latin America. Among these, the most famous is the Hand of Fatima, which may be found in Peru as well as in Syria. Also, throughout the Islamic region from Africa to India the color blue is thought to defend against the evil eye, and blue beads are found on children, camels, donkeys, and water buffalo throughout the area.

Written passages from the Koran may be similarly used, since for semiliterate and nonliterate peoples the written word carries magical significance and great prestige, quite apart from its meaning. A similar use of the written word is found among Haitian peasants, who sometimes wear printed Christian prayers on a string as amulets. These magical uses of religious texts illustrate clearly the transformation of elements of religion into instruments of magic.

Amulets have been reported from all parts of the world, and there are references to them in the most ancient written sources. It is likely that many of the objects found in prehistoric burials that appear to be concerned with fertility or in some cases to have no practical utility may have been amulets.

Among ancient peoples the Egyptians were particularly famous for their great variety of amulets, many of which are found on mummies in tombs. Among these the scarab, the symbol of immortality, is very frequent. Scarabs were made of a wide variety of materials, with various methods of manufacture, often combining cameo and intaglio work. On the underside they frequently carried inscriptions, including charms. The scarab was a physical symbol of a complex religious idea, but in popular thought it was transformed into a magic amulet. The use of scarabs spread from Egypt throughout major portions of the Mediterranean world; they have, for example, been found in Etruscan and Roman representations of later periods.

ERIKA BOURGUINON
The Ohio State University

Further Reading: Budge, E. Wallis, *Amulets and Superstitions* (Dover 1978); Lippman, Deborah, and Colin, Paul, *Amulets, Charms and Talismans* (Evans & Co. 1985); Logan, Jo, *The Prediction Book of Amulets and Talismans* (Sterling 1986); Rodkinson, Michael L., *History of Amulets, Charms and Talismans* (Gordon Press 1977); Shire, T., *Hebrew Magic Amulets* (Behrman House 1982).

AMUNDSEN, ä'mōōn-sən, **Roald** (1872–1928), Norwegian explorer, who was the first to reach the South Pole. He was born at Vedsten, Østfold, Norway, on July 16, 1872. He served in the Norwegian navy and in 1897 was first officer on the *Belgica* in the Belgian Antarctic expedition led by Lt. Adrien De Gerlache.

In 1901, in the small sloop *Gjøa*, Amundsen conducted oceanographic research off northeast Greenland. In June 1903 he sailed on the *Gjøa* to fix the location of the north magnetic pole and made the first voyage through the Northwest Passage and around the northern Canadian coast, arriving at Herschel Island, Yukon, in August 1905.

Inspired by Robert E. Peary's achievement in reaching the North Pole on April 6, 1909, Amundsen announced in August 1910 that he would try to reach the South Pole. He arrived at the Bay of Whales, Antarctica, on Jan. 3,

Roald Amundsen

(1872–1928)

UPI

1911, in the *Fram,* a famous vessel that had been used by the Arctic explorer Fridtjof Nansen. His projected expedition had become a race for the pole. Capt. Robert Falcon Scott of Britain also had established an Antarctic base and was planning to move toward the pole. Scott used Siberian ponies as transport, while Amundsen relied on sledges drawn by dogs.

Amundsen's base was 60 miles (96 km) farther south than Scott's. He laid his plans with care and foresight. On a preliminary trip he deposited stores of food part way along the route he intended to take out and back.

Amundsen started for the pole on Oct. 20, 1911, with four companions, 52 dogs, and four sledges, taking enough food for four months. The weather was favorable, and all went well. In a mountain range that Amundsen named the Queen Maud Range the party climbed to 10,750 feet (3,276 meters).

On Dec. 14, 1911, celestial observations confirmed that they had reached the South Pole, in a level region that Amundsen named King Haakon VII Plateau. The Norwegian flag was raised. The party remained until December 17, making studies and taking observations, and were back at their base at the Bay of Whales on Jan. 25, 1912. He had had good fortune, but his success was due to the courage and endurance of his party and to Amundsen's care for details.

Meanwhile, Scott and some of his group, after a difficult journey, had reached the pole on January 17. They found Amundsen's flag and letters that he had left. Scott and all his men perished on their return trip.

Amundsen tried to fly an airplane from Kings Bay, Spitsbergen, over the North Pole in May 1925 but was forced down 136 miles (218 km) short of his goal. The next year, in the Italian-built dirigible *Norge,* commanded by Capt. Umberto Nobile, he succeeded in flying over the North Pole, leaving Kings Bay on May 11, 1926, and landing at Teller, Alaska, on May 13.

Flying, which he had taken up in middle age, cost him his life. On June 18, 1928, Amundsen and five companions left Tromsø, Norway, in an airplane to search for Nobile, who had flown the dirigible *Italia* over the North Pole on May 24 but had been forced down the next day. Amundsen's plane was never seen again.

The explorer's several published books include *To the North Magnetic Pole and Through the Northwest Passage* (1907), *The South Pole* (1913), and *My Life as an Explorer* (1927).

AMUR RIVER, ä-moor', a major waterway in northeastern Asia, which for more than half of its 1,770-mile (2,850-km) length forms the border between China (Manchuria) and the Russian Federation. Its Chinese name is Heilung Kiang (Black Dragon River).

The Amur is formed by the junction of the Shilka River, which rises in the Russian Federation, and the Argun, rising in Manchuria. It flows first southeast and then northeast and empties into the Tatar Straits, which separate the island of Sakhalin from the mainland of Siberia. Its chief tributaries are the Sungari, Manchuria's largest river, and the Ussuri, which also forms part of the Manchurian-Siberian border. In all, the Amur and its 200 tributaries drain an area of 712,000 square miles (1,844,000 sq km)—the tenth-largest river basin in the world and one of the largest in the Russian Federation.

The Amur is the greatest shipping artery in the Russian Far East. It has little spring flooding because of the scant snowfall in its basin; the high-water mark is attained in summer as a result of monsoon rains. When ice free (May to November), the entire Amur is open to navigation. Grain, salt, and manufactured goods are the most important cargoes moving downstream; oil, fish, and timber are the chief products moving upstream.

The shores of the Amur are partly wooded mountains and hills and partly meadows and swamps. The river has 99 known types of fish, and fishing is an important occupation for the people who live along its shores.

Russians first reached the Amur in 1644. They annexed the north bank of the river from China by the Treaty of Aigun in 1858. Amur oblast, a subdivision of the Russian Federation, lies along the north bank of the central section of the Amur River. Its area of 140,000 square miles (360,000 sq km) includes the Stanovoi Mountains in the north and the low-lying Amur swamps and a section of wooded steppe in the south. The lowlands are one of the best farming areas in the Russian Far East, and agriculture is the region's primary occupation. Grain, soybeans, sunflowers, and potatoes are the most important crops, and large herds of cattle, sheep, hogs, and reindeer are raised. Hunting, fishing, lumbering, and mining of gold, coal, and nonferrous metals are other major occupations of the population. There are also food-processing and woodworking plants. The oblast's capital is Blagoveshchensk. The people are chiefly Russians and Ukrainians.

AMVETS, am'vets, the official title of a national organization also known as American Veterans of World War II, Korea, & Vietnam. Its aims are to promote peace, preserve American ideals, and aid veterans to help themselves. Founded in December 1944 in Kansas City, Mo., it was chartered by Congress on July 23, 1947. Congress amended the charter first in 1950 to include veterans of the Korean conflict and again to include the "cold war" and Vietnam veterans. Membership, which is open to all citizens who served honorably in the armed services since Sept. 16, 1940, is about 200,000. Sad Sacks, an honor group, is part of the organization, and AMVETS National Auxiliary (women) and Junior AMVETS are affiliates. The official publication is the *National AMVET.* National headquarters are located in Lanham, Md.

RICHARD C. SULLIVAN, *AMVETS*

AMYL, am'əl, the organic radical C_5H_{11}. This group of atoms forms a part of a number of organic substances, but it is not a complete molecule and it has no independent existence. An amyl alcohol, for example, has the general formula $C_5H_{11}OH$. The —OH group is characteristic of all alcohols and is largely responsible for their chemical behavior. There are a dozen or more other characteristic organic family groups that connect with the amyl group. The amino group, —NH$_2$, the aldehyde group,—CHO, and the nitrite group, —NO$_2$, are examples.

Eight different arrangements (isomeric forms) are possible for the atoms of the amyl group. Four examples are: normal amyl, $CH_3(CH_2)_4$—; isoamyl, $(CH_3)_2CH(CH_2)_2$—; tertiary amyl, $(CH_3)_2(C_2H_5)C$—; and active amyl, $CH_3CH(C_2H_5)CH_2$—. The active amyl group is particularly interesting because it contains an asymmetric carbon atom (indicated by an asterisk). This carbon atom is surrounded by four groups of different makeup. This structure makes the molecule optically active, enabling it to rotate the plane of polarized light.

All eight of the amyl alcohols are known, but only three have industrial importance. Isoamyl alcohol and active amyl alcohol, which are formed along with ethyl alcohol in the fermentation of grain, are the chief constituents of fusel oil, at one time the chief commercial source of higher alcohols. The other commercially important amyl alcohol is normal amyl alcohol, which is used in organic syntheses and as a solvent.

Mixed amyl alcohols can be made by treating the pentane fraction from petroleum distillation with chlorine and hydrolyzing the resulting monochloropentanes in an alkaline solution. They are used commercially as solvents, as plasticizers in the plastics industries, and in the manufacture of synthetic flavors and perfumes. Isoamyl alcohol is used in the manufacture of smokeless powder and mercury fulminate, a detonator for small arms ammunition.

Some of the organic esters containing the amyl radical are important solvents. They have limited use in flavoring confectionery and in perfumes because of their pleasant fruity odors. Isoamyl acetate, $CH_3COOCH_2CH_2CH(CH_3)_2$, also called banana oil, is commercially the most important member of this ester group. It is used as a solvent for lacquers, bronzing mixtures, metallic paints, nitrocellulose, and celluloid cements. Mixed amyl acetates are frequently made by distilling sodium acetate, sulfuric acid, amyl alcohols, and water.

Normal amyl butyrate has been used to simulate the flavors of pineapple, pear, apricot, and plum. Isoamyl butyrate is used to flavor rum and confectionery. Isoamyl isovalerate simulates the flavor of apple in extracts, candies, and liqueurs. Isoamyl phthalate, a plasticizer for nitrocellulose plastics and lacquers, makes the film tough and shock resistant.

Isoamyl nitrite, $(CH_3)_2CHCH_2$ CH_2ONO, is useful in medicine as a vasodilator. When its vapors are inhaled, the walls of the blood vessels are relaxed and the blood pressure is lowered. Its primary use is to relieve pain in angina pectoris. It is also used in treating bronchial asthma and convulsions. Isoamyl nitrite, which is given by inhalation, is an effective antidote for cyanide poisoning, especially when administered together with thiosulfate.

OTTO W. NITZ, *Stout State University*

AMYLASE, am′ə-lās, any of a group of enzymes that aid in the digestion of starch and glycogen ("animal starch"). Amylases are found both in plants and in animals. Plant amylases are especially plentiful in potatoes, grains, and germinating seeds. Ptyalin, in saliva, and amylopsin, in pancreatic juice, are examples of animal amylases.

Amylases help digest large starch molecules by splitting them into smaller molecules. The smallest product is maltose, a disaccharide consisting of two simple sugars. Amylases that yield alpha-maltose, such as amylopsin, are called alpha-amylases; those that yield beta-maltose, such as most malt amylase, are called beta-amylases. The alpha-amylases include ptyalin, amylopsin, takadiastase (present in molds), and a small fraction of malt amylase. They first split starch molecules into smaller units called dextrins and then slowly split the dextrins into maltoses. Nearly all plant amylases are beta-amylases. These amylases split starch molecules completely into their component maltoses. See also DIGESTION.

AMYNODONTS, ə-min′ə-donts, a group of rhinoceroslike animals that lived 25 million to 55 million years ago (the Oligocene and Eocene epochs). The group first appeared in North America and later spread to Asia and Europe. They differ from rhinoceroses by their large canine tusks. Important genera are *Amynodon, Metamynodon,* and *Cadurcotherium.* The last of the amynodonts were the size of the present hippopotamus and had similar aquatic habits.

AMYOT, à-myō′, **Jacques** (1513–1593), French humanist and scholar. He was born in Melun, France, on Oct. 29, 1513. After teaching Greek and Latin at the University of Bourges, he became abbot of Bellozane and tutor to the sons of King Henry II, the future Charles IX and Henry III. He was appointed bishop of Auxerre by Charles IX in 1570.

Amyot is famous for translations from the Greek, which, owing to their elegant style, are considered classics: *Aethiopica* (1547) by Heliodorus; *The Seven Books of Diodorus Siculus* (1554); the *Daphnis and Chloë* (1559) of Longus; and *Plutarch's Lives* (1559). The *Lives* had an immense influence on French literature. It was used by Corneille as a source for his tragedies, and by Montaigne, who quotes from it in his *Essais.* It was also the main source for Sir Thomas North's English version of the *Lives,* used by Shakespeare. Amyot died in Auxerre on Feb. 6, 1593.

AMYOTROPHIC LATERAL SCLEROSIS (ALS), ā-mī-ō-trō′fik lat′ə-rəl sklə-rō′sis, one of a group of serious progressive neurologic disorders that affect the spinal cord and lower brainstem. They result in progressive degeneration of motor neurons together with progressive wasting and weakness of muscles. In ALS the large motor neurons of the cerebral cortex are also affected.

ALS—popularly known as the Lou Gehrig disease—usually strikes late in life, typically during the 50's, 60's, and 70's but sometimes earlier. After symptoms first appear the disease generally worsens steadily, taking as little as 18 months or as long as seven years to run its course. In most patients the disease progresses slowly. Weakness tends to develop first in the muscles of parts distant from the brain, especially the hands. Subsequently it spreads to muscles of the forearms, shoulders, and other regions nearer to the brain. The lower extremities usually are affected later than the upper extremities. Typically, patients keep control of their bladder and anal sphincter muscles, and intelligence is not affected even in terminal stages of the disease.

The cause of ALS is unknown. It usually seems to strike at random, although in some instances it runs in families—suggesting either exposure of family members to the same agent or a genetically based tendency.

There is no treatment for the disease.

ANABAPTISTS, an-ə-bap′tists, Christian sects that rejected the rite of infant baptism. Basing their convictions on a literal interpretation of the Scriptures, the members of the sects insisted that baptism be withheld until a person had made a profession of faith. Various sects that held this belief sprang up in Europe during the Protestant Reformation in the 16th century. Their unorthodox concept appeared monstrous to both Roman Catholics and Protestants, who viewed rebaptism as sacrilegious and heretical. The very name "Anabaptist," derived by Ulrich Zwingli from a Greek verb meaning "to rebaptise," had a disdainful connotation. Yet the Anabaptists, with few exceptions, were peace-loving, law-abiding people imbued with an idealistic vision of uncompromising Christian love. Neither their pacifism, however, nor their theology was the chief cause of their widespread persecution.

The Reformation was a period of religious and political unrest—an unrest personified by the Anabaptists. Dissatisfied with the slow pace of the Protestant Reformers, they established their own church of voluntary, professed members. They pleaded for religious freedom and considered themselves martyrs for the cause of a church independent of state control. These principles, though accepted in many modern countries, seemed radical in the 16th century.

The Roman Catholics were struggling to reclaim the Protestant Reformers for the church, and the adamant Reformers could ill afford division among themselves. The Anabaptists posed a threat to both sides. Furthermore, their peculiar civil ideas challenged the state's authority. They refused to bear arms, swear oaths, or assume political office. Some of the sects practiced a communistic system, and all held strict moralistic views regarding usury and taxes. For these reasons—magnified by several unfortunate acts of fanaticism on the part of Anabaptists—the sects were persecuted throughout Europe.

Swiss Brethren. Despite the objections of Zwingli and the Swiss authorities, a group of radicals founded a community of believers in Zürich, Switzerland, in 1525. Konrad Grebel, who Zwingli himself acknowledged was "a noble and learned young man," led the movement after a public disputation with Zwingli proved futile. Grebel signalized the dissolution of ties with the Protestant Reformers by baptizing Georg Blaurock, an ex-priest, at a small gathering. Blaurock, in turn, baptized the others present. The group became the core of a body of zealous missionaries, who rapidly converted large numbers in Switzerland. The disturbed authorities resorted to reprisals. Prison terms were threatened, and finally the death penalty was employed to curtail rebaptism. But this action only spread the movement; missionaries passed into North Italy.

Hutterites. The development of the Hutterite movement began with Balthasar Hubmaier. A dedicated and learned man whose philosophical tracts are still admired, he led a congregation of persecuted Swiss Brethern to Moravia in 1526. The counts of Liechtenstein gave them refuge on their estates at Nickolsburg. After a quiet year in which members of the congregation worked the land and developed small industries, they were joined by Hans Hut, a disciple of Thomas Münzer. Münzer, founder of German Anabaptism, who at one time disputed with Luther, had precipitated the Peasants' War in Germany. Like Münzer, Hut preached the imminence of the millennium (Christ's 1,000-year reign on earth), the efficacy of communal property, and the evil of paying taxes to support wars. Hubmaier stood firm against Hut's fanaticism, but many of his followers were won over. The authorities indiscriminately imprisoned both leaders.

The moderate sect members then moved on to Austerlitz where they were joined by Jakob Hutter and a group of Anabaptists from the Tyrol. Hutter, a man of great administrative abilities, organized them into communes and helped them to build a thriving economy. An unfortunate incident at Münster, however, escalated the persecution of the Anabaptists, and the Hutterites too were forced to find a new haven. See also HUTTERIAN BRETHREN; MÜNZER, THOMAS.

The Tragedy of Münster. Melchior Hoffmann, a furrier from Waldshut, Germany, had joined the Reformers in 1521. At first he espoused Lutheranism, but soon he developed a peculiar Christology of his own and preached millenarianism. Driven from place to place, he eventually met a group of Anabaptists and combined their theology with his own. Through his fiery preaching he converted thousands in the Netherlands, and as persecution persisted, his confidence in the coming of Christ increased. He prophesied that the "kingdom" would be founded by Christ at Strasbourg in 1533. When he arrived there he was arrested, and he died in prison 10 years later. The fanaticism he inspired culminated tragically at Münster.

The city of Münster was under Anabaptist control. When the city council decided to close its gates to all nonbelievers, Catholics and Protestants united in a siege of the stronghold. In April 1533 a tailor named Jan Bockelson (John of Leyden) became the Anabaptists' leader. He dismissed the council and declared himself king of "the New Zion." While the city was under siege, the male population diminished until there were four women to every man. To alleviate the situation, Bockelson declared polygamy legal. When news of this reached the combined armies of the besiegers, they redoubled their assaults, and in the summer of 1535 they overwhelmed the city and slaughtered hundreds, including Bockelson. Accounts of licentiousness in Münster were grossly exaggerated, but they heightened the general hatred of the Anabaptists.

Mennonites. As Jakob Hutter had repaired the damage done by the extremists in Moravia, Menno Simons rebuilt the movement, diminished by Münster, in the Netherlands. An ex-priest, he accepted the best of the moderate Anabaptist teachings, disavowed any connection with the Münster disaster, and advocated orthodox Christology. By his wisdom he preserved the movement from extinction. See also MENNONITES.

ANABAS, an'ə-bas, is a genus of freshwater fish with spiny fins, found in southeastern Asia and Africa. Because of its modified branchial apparatus, it can breathe free air. One species, *Anabas scandens* of India, is known as the *climbing perch* because it leaves the water and can travel some distance on land.

ANABASIS, ə-nab'ə-səs, translated usually as *The March Inland*, is a work in seven books by the Greek historian Xenophon (c. 430–c. 354 B.C.). It relates the adventures of a Greek expeditionary force in the campaign of Cyrus the Younger to seize the throne of Persia from his brother Artaxerxes II.

In the spring of 401 B.C., Cyrus assembled at Sardis in Lydia an army of mercenaries that included more than 10,000 Greeks. The Athenian-born Xenophon had joined the expedition as a junior officer. After marching inland more than 1,000 miles, Cyrus was killed and his forces defeated by Artaxerxes at the Battle of Cunaxa, near Babylon.

The Greeks, whose generals were treacherously murdered by the victors, found themselves in a rugged, hostile country. At this point Xenophon, elected senior officer, induced the remaining officers to prepare for a safe retreat. After a difficult march up the Tigris Valley, the force reached Trapezus (now Turkish Trabzon) on the Euxine (the Black Sea), where there was a Greek colony, and from there followed the coast to Chrysopolis (now Turkish Üsküdar), across the Bosporus from Byzantium (modern Istanbul).

The *Anabasis* makes fascinating reading, offering a wealth of geographical, ethnological, zoological, and general information. The narrative, historically accurate, is written in a clear, concise, and elegant style. In his record of the famous retreat, Xenophon lauds the Greeks' discipline and morale, to which he attributes their survival. The most famous passage records the joy of the Greeks, after a year of hardships in strange territory, at the sudden appearance of the friendly, familiar sea:

> They came to a mountain named Theches. Wher the vanguard reached the summit a great shout went up. Xenophon and those in the rear heard it and thought new enemies were attacking in front . . . . But the cry grew louder and louder and the men coming up from behind ran forward to join those that were shouting, and as the numbers swelled so the noise increased. Xenophon, thinking something serious had occurred, mounted his horse . . . and went to the rescue. Soon he heard the soldiers shouting: "The sea, the sea!" and passing the cry along. Then all ran, even the rear guards, and the pack animals and horses were urged on. When all reached the summit they wept for joy and embraced one another and the generals and captains. Suddenly someone gave the word and they brought stones and made a huge heap, on which they placed a great number of raw hides and staves and captured shields. . . .

The Greeks' humorous contempt for their Asian allies is illustrated by the following account of a display given for the queen of Cilicia:

> When the trumpet sounded they advanced arms and charged. And then, as they went on faster and faster, at length with a shout, the troops broke into a run of their own accord in the direction of the camp. As for the barbarians, they were terribly frightened; the Cilician Queen took flight in her chariot and the people in the market left their wares behind and took to their heels, while the Greeks with a roar of laughter came up to their camp.

The author draws a lifelike picture of Cyrus, pleasure-loving, ambitious, and generous to his friends. He gives an equally vivid account of the scheming Tissaphernes, Artaxerxes' lieutenant who, after the defeat and death of Cyrus, lured the Greek commanders to a parley and assassinated them. With the practical, undramatic simplicity of an officer interested in the supplies available for his troops, Xenophon observes the natural characteristics of the country through which he advances:

> They descended to a beautiful plain, well-watered and full of trees of all sorts, and vines; it produces an abundance of sesame, millet and panic, wheat and barley, and it is surrounded on every side, from sea to sea, by a lofty and formidable range of mountains.

Legendary and historical curiosities encountered along the retreat are reported with keen interest. For example, when the expedition arrives at Celaenae, Xenophon observes that its acropolis rises above the sources of the Marsyas River, where Apollo flayed Marsyas. He remarks that at Thymbrium he saw the spring of Midas where the Phrygian king caught the satyr by mixing wine in the spring water. By treating the satyr kindly, Midas was granted his famous disastrous wish—that whatever he touched might turn to gold. Xenophon is also interested by the ruins of the ghost towns of Larissa on the Tigris, the Assyrian Calah (Genesis 10:11), and Mespilah (Nineveh).

Like Julius Caesar, Xenophon has handed down a narrative that is alive. He possesses the concise, practical clarity of Caesar's account and far greater charm.

ANDRÉ MICHALOPOULOS
Fairleigh Dickinson University

ANABLEPS, an'ə-bleps, is a group of fishes characterized by an eye structure unique among vertebrates. The eye is divided into two parts by a horizontal septum, or membrane, each part having a separate cornea and iris. Because of this structure, *Anableps* is commonly called the *four-eyed fish.* The fish habitually swims at the surface of the water, with the dividing septum at water level, so that the upper part of the eye looks into air while the lower is directed into the water. The eye protrudes slightly above the head line, and as the fish swims at the surface, the eye is the only part visible above water, looking like a bubble.

Anableps reaches about eight inches in length. The young are born alive and well developed,

ANABLEPS has each eye divided into two sections. It swims with half of each eye above water and half below.

NEW YORK ZOOLOGICAL SOCIETY

about 1¾ inches long. A peculiar enlargement of a scale on one or the other side of the external sex organs of both sexes prevents operation of these organs from both sides, so that each individual is sexually right-sided or left-sided, and two individuals of similar polarity are unable to mate. This character also appears to be unique among vertebrates.

The genus *Anableps* belongs to the order Cyprinodontes, family Anablepidae. There are three species. The fish is native to coastal waters, both fresh and salt, from Yucatán to equatorial Brazil.

C.W. COATES
The Aquarium, New York Zoological Society

ANACARDIACEAE, an-ə-kär-dē-ā'sē-ē, are a family of trees and shrubs that are identified by their milky sap and resinous bark. Commonly known as the sumac family, it contains about 73 genera and 600 species. The family is native to the tropics but also extends to the Mediterranean, eastern Asia, and North America. It is important for edible nuts and fruits (cashews, pistachios, and mangoes), resins, oils, lacquers, and tannic acid. The family also includes poison ivy.

ANACLETUS, an-ə-klē'təs, **Saint,** pope from 76 to 88. He is also called *Cletus.* He was the second successor to St. Peter as bishop of Rome. Little is recorded of his pontificate except that he died a martyr.

ANACLETUS II (died 1138), an-ə-klē'təs, was an antipope who reigned concurrently with Pope Innocent II (1130–1143). He was born *Pietro Pierleoni,* in Rome, of a senatorial family of Jewish origin. After study in Paris he entered the monastery at Cluny but was called to Rome by Pope Paschal II, who made him a cardinal, about 1116. Anacletus was elected pope illegally in 1130, on the same day as Innocent II, but was acknowledged only in Rome and Sicily. He was opposed by saints Bernard and Norbert and by his abbot, Peter the Venerable, because of his worldly habits. Innocent excommunicated Anacletus in 1131, but Anacletus held Rome until his death on Jan. 25, 1138.

MSGR. FLORENCE D. COHALAN, *Cathedral College*

ANACONDA, an-ə-kon'də, a city in southwestern Montana, 25 miles (40 km) by road northwest of Butte. It is the seat of Deer Lodge county. Although Anaconda has historically been an industrial center, it services an important tourist industry based on Georgetown Lake and nearby national forests.

In 1883 Marcus Daly of the Anaconda Company obtained land and water rights on Warm Springs Creek for a new smelter. The city of Anaconda was established at this location the next year and was named for the company. The city was incorporated in 1887. Four years later it lost a famous political conflict with Helena to determine which should be the state capital. In 1891 the Butte, Anaconda, and Pacific Railway was constructed to carry copper ore and concentrates from Butte to a large smelter in Anaconda. The Anaconda Company was purchased in 1977 by the Atlantic Richfield Company, which, for economic reasons, found it necessary to close the smelter in 1980. Population: 9,417.

PAUL B. ALEXANDER*
University of Montana

ANACONDA, an-ə-kon′də, a semiaquatic, constricting serpent found in tropical South America east of the Andes. The anaconda, also known as the *great water boa,* is the largest of the snakes in the Western Hemisphere, sometimes reaching a length of 30 to 40 feet. Its life span is believed to be the longest among the snakes—about 28 years. It is identified by its leopardlike markings —large, blackish spots over a grayish, olive-colored background.

Although it is not poisonous, the anaconda has extremely strong muscles and can kill animals by wrapping itself around them and crushing them. Always found near or in the water, it spends most of its time partly submerged in order to prey on small aquatic animals, such as fish, swimming birds, or young tapirs. After a large meal, the snake will go several months before eating another, even in captivity. Although it is greatly feared by the Indians of South America, the anaconda is not aggressive toward man and seeks to avoid him rather than to attack.

The anaconda is similar in some respects to poisonous snakes. It has nocturnal habits and seeks its prey only at night. The female produces 20 to 40 young serpents every year, which she abandons immediately. In captivity, the births are very irregular.

The anaconda belongs to the Boidae (boa family), subfamily Boinae, and genus *Eunectes.* There are only two species—*E. notaeus,* found in the Paraguay river regions, and *E. murinus,* found in all the aquatic regions of Brazil, especially in the Amazon and the rivers of central Brazil. *E. murinus* is the largest nonpoisonous constricting serpent in the world. Although it may exceed 40 feet in length, with a circumference of 2 to 2½ feet, its usual length is between 10 and 20 feet. This species is rare and sometimes is confused with the semiaquatic snakes of the genera *Boa, Constrictor,* and *Epicrates,* which may measure 6 to 15 feet in length. These constricting serpents have the same living habits as the anaconda and are encountered more frequently than the latter.

EDUARDO VAZ
Instituto Butantan, São Paulo, Brazil.

ANACORTES, an-ə-kôr′təs, is a seaport city in Washington, on Fidalgo Island in Puget Sound, 80 miles northwest of Seattle. The island, part of Skagit County, is connected with the mainland by a bridge. Anacortes is a deepwater shipping center with oil-refining, chemical, wood pulp, plywood, hardboard, and fish-canning industries.

Mount Erie, on Fidalgo Island, affords a panoramic view of the Cascade and Olympic mountains and of the scenic San Juan archipelago. The ferry from Anacortes to Sidney, on Vancouver Island, British Columbia, stops at several of the San Juan islands. A high-level bridge between Fidalgo and Whidbey Island, to the south, spans the tidal rapids of Deception Pass. Anacortes adopted city-manager government in 1958. Population: 14,557.

ANACREON, ə-nak′rē-ən, was a celebrated Greek poet of the 6th century B.C. He was born in Teos, an Ionian city in Asia Minor. Driven out during the Persian invasion about 540 B.C., Anacreon moved to Abdera in Thrace. From Abdera he went to the court of Polycrates of Samos and then to that of Hipparchus, tyrant of Athens.

THE ANACONDA (above, the yellow anaconda, *Eunectes notaeus*) is usually between ten and twenty feet long.

Anacreon sang and wrote graceful, elegant poems about love, wine, and revelry, in a variety of lyric measures. He became the personification of the Dionysian old man, the white-haired bard of wine, love, and song. He also wrote a number of hymns to the gods and some serious epigrams.

Greek scholars in Alexandria had a collection of his poems in five books, of which approximately 15 pages of fragments are extant. Later, from the end of the Hellenistic period to the Byzantine period, it became fashionable for writers to compose poems in the style of Anacreon about the themes he had celebrated. Thus, without any conscious intention of forgery, there arose the collection of *Anacreontea,* which usurped the name and fame of Anacreon. These later poems can be distinguished from those of Anacreon because they are not in the Ionic dialect, they do not refer to the details of Anacreon's life, and they rarely, if ever, are quoted by ancient writers as being the work of Anacreon. Furthermore, the poems are not composed in a variety of Greek lyric measures, but in a monotony of tripping iambics. The later poems substitute Alexandrian or Pompeian gods of love for the god Eros.

The publication of the Greek text of the *Anacreontea* by Henri Estienne in 1554 influenced French Renaissance poetry, and in 1555 the French poet Pierre de Ronsard made a French translation. Subsequently, the popularity of the style of the *Anacreontea* spread into Italy and Germany.

The word *Anacreontics* was first used in English in 1656 by Abraham Cowley, who called a section of his poems "anacreontiques" because they were paraphrased from the so-called writing of Anacreon into a measure that was supposed to represent the meter of the Greek. Half a century later, John Phillips laid down the arbitrary rule that an anacreontic line "consists of seven syllables, without being tied to any certain law of quantity."

There are several English translations of the *Anacreontea,* but perhaps the best is by the Irish poet Thomas Moore, who called his translation *Odes of Anacreon* (1800). English writers who composed original Anacreontics included Robert Herrick, William Shenstone, and William Oldys.

ANADARKO, an-ə-där′kō, a city in west-central Oklahoma, on the Washita River, 65 miles (100 km) by road southwest of Oklahoma City. It is the seat of Caddo county and a trading center. There are oilfields nearby, but the Anadarko trading area is largely agricultural, producing cotton, peanuts, wheat, poultry, and livestock. Industrial plants include cottonseed-oil mills and a rug factory.

Anadarko is home to the Riverside Indian School, and there are various museums in the area. The Bureau of Indian Affairs area office is located within the city. Indian City U.S.A., a tourist attraction on the outskirts of Anadarko, displays many different types of Native American homes. The American Indian Exposition is held annually.

Anadarko was chartered in 1901, the year the area was opened to white settlement. The city adopted the manager-council plan of government in 1947. Population: 6,645.

ANADYR GULF, u-nə-dir′, off northeastern Siberia, in the Russian Federation. It is a northwestern arm of the Bering Sea, opposite the state of Alaska. The gulf, about 250 miles (400 km) wide at its mouth, receives the Anadyr River, which originates in the Anadyr Mountains in Siberia. The river is navigable for about 250 miles from its mouth. Its total course is 700 miles (1,125 km).

Anadyr, a village at the mouth of the Anadyr River on Anadyr Gulf, is the administrative center of the Chukchi (Chukot) national okrug. The village is connected by boat with Vladivostok and southern Sakhalin.

ANAGNI, ä-nä′nyē, is a town in Italy in Frosinone province, in Latium, about 45 miles southeast of Rome. In Roman times it was known as *Anagnia* and was the chief city of the Hernici. It was the birthplace of Popes Innocent III, Gregory IX, Alexander IV, and Boniface VIII.

In 1303 an incident called the "outrage of Anagni" occurred in the town. The incident was a milestone in the history of church-state relations. King Philip IV of France, involved in a feud with Pope Boniface VIII, sent Guillaume de Nogaret to Anagni to arrest the pope. He held Boniface under guard in his castle for several days, did not succeed in arresting him, and was finally forced to retreat. Population: 19,134 (2001 census).

ANAGRAM, an′ə-gram, a word, phrase, or sentence that is formed by transposing the letters of another word, phrase, or sentence. Examples are *dais* from *said* and *Flit on, cheering angel* from *Florence Nightingale*. Originally, a true anagram was formed only by reading the letters backward, as *evil* from *live*.

Anagrams date from ancient times. Composing them was a favorite pastime during the Middle Ages, when a mystic connection was believed to exist between the nature or fate of a person and an anagram derived from his name. A celebrated example of an anagram is *Voltaire*, the pseudonym of Francois Marie Arouet, which he probably formed from his family name by adding *l* and *j* (the initial letters of *le jeune*, the younger) and returning the *u* and *j* to their 16th century forms of *v* and *i*.

A *palindrome* is a type of anagram that forms the same word or phrase when read either forward or backward, such as *madam, Hannah, radar*, or the sentence, *Was it a cat I saw?*

ANAHEIM, an′ə-hīm, a city in southern California, is the home of Disneyland and the California Angels baseball team. It is situated in the Santa Ana Valley, 25 miles by freeway southeast of Los Angeles. The city has numerous industries, the most important of which are aerospace and electronics enterprises. Since 1950, when the population of Anaheim was less than 15,000, the city and surrounding Orange County have grown phenomenally. In 1963, Anaheim, Santa Ana, and Garden Grove were designated the urban centers of a new standard metropolitan statistical area with more than 700,000 residents.

Millions of people visit Anaheim each year. A large percentage of them are drawn by Disneyland, the world-famous amusement park, which opened there in 1955. Major league baseball was introduced to the city in 1966, when the California Angels, an American League team, moved from Los Angeles to the new Anaheim Stadium. The stadium seats 44,000 for baseball and 56,000 for football. Anaheim Convention Center is a third attraction.

Anaheim was founded in 1857 by German immigrants and was incorporated in 1878. It adopted city-manager government in 1950. Population: 328,014.

ANAIMALAI HILLS, ə-nī′mə-lī, a mountain range in southern India, in the Western Ghats, in the Coimbatore district of Madras. The range is situated south of the Palghat Gap and north of the Cardamom Hills. The highest peak is the Anai Mudi, which rises to 8,841 feet, the highest elevation in southern India. Other summits in the Anaimalai Hills rise to 8,000 feet, towering above a tableland that is partly grassy and partly forested. Teak and other valuable timbers are found on the lower slopes. The name is also spelled *Anamalai*.

ANALCIME, ə-nal′sēm, is a common mineral, a member of the zeolite family of hydrous (water-bearing) silicates. The name is derived from the Greek *analkēs*, meaning "weak," because analcime exhibits weak electric properties when rubbed. Its crystals are usually colorless or white, although they may be greenish or reddish, and they have a glassy luster. Structurally they are very similar to leucite.

Analcime occurs as crystals in the cavities of igneous rocks and is often present as a primary mineral in igneous rocks that are rich in alkalis. It is also abundant and widespread in some sedimentary formations. Beautiful crystals of analcime have been found in Nova Scotia, in Iceland, and near Mount Etna in Sicily. In the United States, fine crystals have been found in New Jersey, Colorado, and near Lake Superior.

Composition: $NaAlSi_2O_6 \cdot H_2O$; hardness, 5 to 5.5; specific gravity, 2.27; crystal system, isometric.

ANALGESIC, an-əl-jē′zik, a drug that relieves pain by raising the pain threshold (the point at which a stimulus causes a feeling of pain) without disturbing consciousness. The mechanisms by which various analgesics raise the pain threshold are not clearly understood. Some seem to act by blocking pain impulses as they are carried over sensory nerve tracts. Many analgesics also act to reduce fevers. Analgesics are usually divided into two classes: *narcotic analgesics* and *nonnarcotic analgesics*.

Narcotic Analgesics. Among the narcotic analgesics are opium and its derivatives, including morphine and codeine, obtained from the opium poppy (*Papaver somniferum*). Synthetic derivatives and related drugs including diacetylmorphine (heroin), dihydromorphinone (Dilaudid), meperidine (Demerol), and many others. Narcotic drugs are very useful to relieve pain, but generally they are not used when lesser measures will suffice because they may cause drug addiction, produce drug tolerance when used for a long time, or mask symptoms and obscure diagnosis.

Nonnarcotic Analgesics. Nonnarcotic analgesics are used in enormous quantities for a variety of aches and pains. The salicylates are among the oldest remedies, and they still occupy an important place in modern medicine. Some, such as salicin and methyl salicylate (oil of wintergreen), occur naturally in many trees and plants, notably the willow (genus *Salix*). The first synthetic salicylates were too irritating for internal use, but further modifications have resulted in the synthesis of acetyl salicylic acid (aspirin), salicylamide, and some salicylic acid salts that are effective and nonirritating.

Other types of nonnarcotic analgesic drugs include pyrazolone derivatives, aniline (coal tar) derivatives, and cinchophens. The first pyrazolone derivative was antipyrine, now abandoned in medicine because of toxicity. The newest of the pyrazolone derivatives are phenylbutazone and chemically related oxyphenbutazone and sulfinpyrazone, which are notably effective in the treatment of rheumatoid arthritis and gout. Cinchophen and colchicine are also commonly employed in the treatment of gout.

Aniline derivatives include acetanilid and acetophenetidin (phenacetin)—two analgesics that are widely used in commercial pain-relieving remedies. Acetaminophen, a related drug, is now considered less toxic than acetanilid and acetophenetidin and is used as a substitute.

Newer nonaddictive analgesics related to the opiates include ethoheptazine (Zactane) and propoxyphene (Darvon). Both are devoid of antipyretic effects but are reportedly effective analgesics with low toxicity.

GEORGE GRIFFENHAGEN
American Pharmaceutical Association

ANALOG COMPUTER. See COMPUTERS.

ANALOGY, ə-nal′ə-jē, in linguistics, is one of the fundamental processes in the evolution of languages. By analogy, new forms are created and old forms are modified under the influence of other existing morphological patterns. Analogy has had far-reaching effects in the development of the English language. For example, in Old English (Anglo-Saxon), of the five major noun declensions, only one (the masculine strong declension) had a plural ending in s. By the mid-14th century, however, at the height of the Middle English period, virtually all nouns had acquired plurals ending in s, by analogy with the nouns of the old masculine strong declension.

Analogical change is likewise responsible for the universality of the possessive inflection s, which is found in only two of the major Old English declensions. The curious double possessive forms *hers, ours, yours, theirs* were created by analogy with the possessive inflection of nouns, as was *its* (first known example, 1598),

his having been used previously for the neuter as well as the masculine pronoun.

Analogy has caused the conversion of many formerly strong verbs into weak verbs, as *help* (whose other principal parts were formerly *holp, holpen*), *glide, bow, yield;* and, on the other hand, the conversion of some weak verbs into strong ones, as *strive* (by analogy with *drive*), *wear* (by analogy with *bear* and *tear*), and *ring* (by analogy with *sing*).

Finally, the analogical process manifests itself in the formation of hybrids like the French-English combination *dukedom* for *duchy*, by analogy with the all-English word *kingdom;* back formations like *grovel* from *groveling* (mistaken for a present participle) and *beg* from *beggar;* false plurals like *riches* from *richesse;* and new singulars from older singulars mistaken for plurals, like *pea* from *pease* or *cherry* from Old North French *cherise.*

ANALOGY, in zoology. See ZOOLOGY—4. *Evolutionary Zoology* (Comparative Embryology).

ANALYSIS, ə-nal′ə-səs, is a major branch of mathematics concerned especially with the concepts of continuity, function, and limit. The most important subdivision of analysis is the calculus, which in turn has two major parts, the differential calculus and the integral calculus. Other important subdivisions are analytic geometry, differential equations, and the calculus of finite differences.

For a discussion of the major areas and topics of analysis, see CALCULUS; EQUATION—5. *Differential Equations;* GEOMETRY—*Analytic Geometry;* SERIES.

ANALYSIS SITUS. See TOPOLOGY.

ANALYTIC GEOMETRY. See GEOMETRY—4. *Analytic Geometry.*

ANALYTICAL CHEMISTRY. See CHEMICAL ANALYSIS.

ANALYTICAL PSYCHOLOGY, an-ə-lit′i-kəl sī-kol′ə-jē, is a point of view developed by Carl Gustav Jung, who in 1912 broke away from Sigmund Freud and established his own system. Jung broadened the concept of the libido (psychic energy) to include all drives that lead to the creative aims of the individual, not merely the sexual instinct. Whereas Freud's theory is said to be retrospective (that is, the roots of maladjustments lie in the early childhood of the patient's life), the Jungian analyst is concerned with the directions in which the individual is trying to move. Sex, of course, is an important drive in behavior, but other drives are of equal or greater strength

The personality consists of discrete, interacting parts. The *ego* is defined as the awareness of a continuing self. Many experiences have been forgotten or excluded from consciousness, and these make up the *personal unconscious.* One of the most interesting contributions of Jung is the concept of the *collective unconscious,* made up of racial memories called *archetypes.* Evidence from studies of dreams and of folklore is cited to justify this concept. The individual needs to conform to the demands and the expectations of society; hence, a *persona* (the "public personality") is acquired. Man has inherited concepts (archetypes) of his masculine role (the *animus*) and woman of her feminine role (the *anima*), but masculinity and femininity have become intermingled in the unconscious mind. The *shadow* consists of drives inherited from subhuman ancestors, and it may direct the individual into immoral activities. The *self* is achieved when the individual is able to bring all these parts into an integrated, purposeful coherence.

Complexes (constellations of emotionally toned ideas) indicate a lack of unity in the mental life of the individual. Psychic energies may then be expended uselessly in forms of activity that impede growth toward the self. The causes for nonpurposeful distributions of mental energy must be looked for in the past life of the patient. It is not enough, however, to discover the reasons for the present difficulties. There must be a direction toward purposeful goals in the future life of the patient. Thus, Jung's system is both reprospective and teleological (behavior directed toward ends), whereas Freud's is retrospective (the search for causes of present difficulties lying in the early childhood of the patient). All the psychic energies of the patient undergoing a Jungian analysis are directed toward the development and the completion of an integrated, harmonious self. See also INTROVERSION-EXTRAVERSION; JUNG, CARL GUSTAV.

PHILIP L. HARRIMAN, *Susquehanna University*

Bibliography

Fordham, Michael S., *Jungian Psychotherapy: A Study in Analytical Psychology* (Books on Demand 1977).
Hogenson, George B., *Jung's Struggle with Freud* (Univ. of Notre Dame Press 1983).
Mattoon, Mary-Ann, *Jungian Psychology in Perspective* (Free Press 1985).
Wilmer, Harry A., *Practical Jung: Nuts and Bolts of Jungian Psychotherapy* (Chiron Pub. 1987).

ANAN BEN DAVID, ä-nän' ben dä'vid (died 790/800), Jewish religious leader in Babylonia, who founded the Karaite sect (see KARAISM). In 760 his younger brother Josiah was elected exilarch (official lay leader of the autonomous Jewish community in Babylonia) over Anan, who had shown disdain toward traditional Judaism. Anan permitted his followers to proclaim him anti-exilarch, which led to his imprisonment and trial in Baghdad. In jail, Anan was befriended by Abu Hanifa, founder of the Hanafite school of Muslim jurisprudence. On the advice of Abu Hanifa, Anan pleaded that he was the founder of a new religion close to Islam. The caliph al-Mansur freed Anan, and he devoted himself to propagating his new religion, whose adherents later became known as Karaites.

In 770, Anan published his Hebrew *Sepher ha-Mitzvot* (*Book of Precepts*), in which he used Talmudic style to reject Talmudic lore and to give new interpretations to the laws of the Bible —the only holy book he recognized. After his death, his son Saul and his descendants became heads of the Karaite sect.

RAPHAEL PATAI, *Theodor Herzl Institute*

ANANDA, ä'nən-də, the favorite disciple of Gautama Buddha, lived and taught in the Ganges Valley of India in the 5th century B.C. Ananda's father, Amitodana, is reputed to have been Gautama's uncle. According to existing accounts, Ananda joined the order of Buddhist monks in the second year of the Buddha's ministry and became his permanent attendant in the 25th year. Because he is credited with hav-

ing persuaded the Buddha to permit women to become nuns, Ananda has always been the object of special devotion on the part of Buddhist nuns. He is supposed to have written many of the discourses in which he appears as interlocutor.

ANANDA MAHIDOL (1925–1946), ä-nän-tä mä-hē-dôn, king of Thailand. His name is also spelled *Anan Mahidon*. Born in Germany on Sept. 20, 1925, he was taken to Thailand at the age of two, and in 1933 was sent to Switzerland to attend school at Lausanne. Following the abdication of King Prajadhipok, his uncle, on March 2, 1935, Ananda was proclaimed king; during his minority a regency administered the kingdom. He paid a state visit to Thailand in 1938 but continued to reside in Switzerland thereafter through World War II. On Dec. 5, 1945, after the occupying Japanese forces had left Thailand, he returned there, and he opened the first wholly elected Thai parliament on June 1, 1946. He died at Bangkok on June 9, 1946, after being shot by an unknown assassin.

ANANIAS, an-ə-nī'əs, in the Bible, was a Christian at Jerusalem, the husband of Sapphira. A newly introduced practice among the early Christians was to sell personal property and contribute the entire proceeds to a common fund administered by the apostles. Ananias and his wife sold a property but withheld a portion of the money for themselves. When Peter confronted them with their deceit, they fell dead before him (Acts 5:1–11).

Ananias was the name of two other persons in the Bible. One was a Christian disciple whom Paul met in Damascus after his conversion; he helped Paul regain his sight (Acts 9:10–17; 22:12). The other was a Jewish high priest of the Sanhedrin before whom Paul was tried at Jerusalem (Acts 23:2).

ANAPEST, an'ə-pest, a metric foot in poetry. It consists of two short or unstressed syllables followed by one long or stressed syllable. First used in Greek drama, the anapest was particularly effective for the entrances and exits of the chorus and so came to be known as the marching rhythm. Although the English language contains few anapestic words—"domineer" is an example—anapestic verse, especially anapestic tetrameter, has established itself firmly in English literature. William Walsh (1663–1708) was one of the first to use the form. Effective use has been made of it by many other poets, notably Algernon Charles Swinburne, See also VERSIFICATION.

ANAPHYLAXIS, an-ə-fə-lak'səs, is an acute allergic reaction that occurs after a person has been injected with, or has eaten or inhaled, a substance to which he has previously been sensitized. This reaction, known also as anaphylactic shock, is brought about when the substance— called the antigen—reacts with antibodies that have previously been formed against it. Thus an injection containing a foreign protein may produce no ill effects the first time it is given; but the second time it is administered, anaphylaxis may occur. This happens because the person's body produced antibodies against the foreign protein after the first injection.

Causes. Among the most common antigens that produce anaphylaxis are certain drugs, particularly antibiotics. Penicillin is a major offender, especially when it is given as an intramuscular injection.

Other common antigens include certain foods, such as shellfish; insect venoms, particularly those produced by bees, wasps, and ants; and certain serums, including horse serum. Whole blood plasma and gamma globulin also are frequent causes of anaphylaxis, as are egg powder and vaccines such as the flu vaccine, which are grown in chick embryos. Animal danders and walnuts are also thought to be possible causes of anaphylaxis.

Symptoms. A person suffering anaphylaxis first becomes very pale and feels dizzy or faint. Soon, heart palpitations occur, accompanied by hives, a reddening of the face, and a drop in blood pressure. This condition is followed by a generalized edema, or swelling, which produces obstructions in the throat and lungs, causing a marked difficulty in breathing. Unless the victim is treated immediately, he may then enter a state of irreversible shock in which blood pressure falls drastically and death follows.

Treatment. The treatment of anaphylactic shock begins with the administration of epinephrine (adrenalin) and cortisone derivatives. In many cases antihistamines also have been helpful, but any blood plasma or serum albumin should be given cautiously, since these substances may themselves be antigens.

The patient should always be placed in the position used in treating shock, with his head lower than his feet. Often it is necessary to administer oxygen and to create a pathway to the lungs by making an incision in the trachea.

Prevention. A doctor can prevent anaphylaxis by finding out a patient's medical history and performing a skin test before injecting him with a particular drug. The doctor must be especially careful with patients who are known to have an allergy, such as hay fever, hives, or asthma. When administering penicillin, the doctor usually prescribes it in a form that can be taken by mouth. If it is necessary to inject the drug he carefully performs skin tests to observe the degree of wheal and flare reactions. In hospitals anaphylaxis caused by blood or plasma is prevented by cross-matching the blood before a transfusion is given.

For people who are known to have an allergic reaction to insect bites or stings, it is advisable to have a supply of the proper agents, such as cortisone sprays or tablets, in the medicine cabinet. It is sometimes possible to prevent anaphylaxis by desensitizing a person against a particular antigen.

REAUMUR S. DONNALLY, M.D.
Washington Hospital Center

ANÁPOLIS, ə-na'poo-lĕs, a city in central Brazil, situated in the southern part of the state of Goiás, 500 miles (804.6 km) north of São Paulo. It is an industrial center that deals in livestock and processes coffee, rice, lumber, and rock crystal produced in the region. As the northwest terminal of a railroad from São Paulo, with a branch to Rio de Janeiro, it distributes nickel, diamonds, gold, quartz, maize, and rubber from Goiás. Travelers entering the forested areas of interior Brazil stock up on supplies in Anápolis. The city has an airport, and a highway runs 82 miles (130 km) to Brasília, capital of Brazil. Population: 222,400 (1991 census).

ANARCHISM, an'ər-kiz-əm, is a theory of social organization that represents the extreme of individualism. It looks upon all law and government as invasive, the twin sources of nearly all social evils. It therefore advocates the abolition of all government as the term is understood today, except that originating in voluntary cooperation. Anarchists do not conceive of a society without order, but the order they visualize arises out of voluntary association, preferably through self-governing groups.

Anarchists do not ignore the benefits resulting from association but insist that the purposes of association will be better served in a state of freedom and in the absence of all compulsion. They believe that everything now done by the state can be done better by voluntary or associative effort and that no restraint upon conduct is necessary because of the natural tendency of men in a state of freedom to respect the rights of the individual. The repression of crime, where crime might arise, could safely be left to spontaneously created organizations, such as the vigilance committees in early California, where no state government existed. In the view of Prince Pyotr Kropotkin (1842–1921), a leading Russian anarchist, no cause for litigation would arise after the abolition of "the present system of class privilege and unjust distribution of the wealth produced by labor, which creates and fosters crime."

While agreeing that the doctrine of laissez-faire should be extended to all departments of human activity, anarchists are by no means in agreement on all points. There are evolutionary and revolutionary anarchists and communist and individualist anarchists. The points on which all are agreed are their opposition to compulsory forms of government and the view that the despotism of majorities in a democracy is only a little less hateful than the despotism of a monarchy.

Proudhon and His Followers. "Governments are the scourge of God," said Pierre Joseph Proudhon (1809–1865), the Frenchman with whom the philosophy of modern anarchism may be said to have begun. Germs of the doctrine of which Proudhon was the founder may be traced to much earlier, even ancient periods. Among his modern precursors was the English philosopher William Godwin (1756–1836), who in his *Enquiry Concerning Political Justice* (1793) advocated the abolition of every form of government and formulated the theory of anarchistic communism.

Modern anarchism as a force in sociologic thought began with the publication of Proudhon's famous essay, *What is Property?* (1840). In it he rejects all law and authority, but in a work that appeared in 1863 entitled *The Federative Principle* he modifies in a measure his former theory of government and favors the formation of self-governing communities. In *What is Property?* occurs Proudhon's famous answer to the question posed by the title: "Property is robbery." Actually, this phrase as used by the father of anarchism applied rather to modern methods of acquisition than to property itself. Proudhon was an individualist, not a communist anarchist, and he strove, however unsuccessful he was in making himself understood, rather to refine than to destroy the idea of property.

Proudhon's chief follower in the United States was Benjamin R. Tucker (1854–1939), who started the journal *Liberty* in 1881. In Germany,

Proudhon found an adherent in Moses Hess (1812–1875), who showed a strong Hegelian influence. The doctrines of anarchism in the hands of the Russian Mikhail Bakunin (1814–1876) underwent a change from the advocacy of a purely peaceful revolution to the advocacy of force. He was prominent in the Paris Revolution of 1848, was surrendered to Russia and sent to Siberia, but succeeded in making his escape. His principal work, in addition to innumerable pamphlets and addresses, is *God and the State* (1882).

As Proudhon was the father of anarchistic individualism, Kropotkin was as indisputably the father of anarchistic communism. Theoretic anarchism for some time after Proudhon was rigidly individualistic. Max Stirner (1806–1856), a follower of Proudhon in Germany, whose philosophy was more of a blank negation than that of his master, pushed individualism to a point where it resembled a caricature more than a dogma, and Bakunin hated the idea of communism. But in Kropotkin's thought the idea of property reached the disappearing point, and the ideal of anarchism became at the last purely communistic.

Anarchist Violence. "Propaganda by action" became the rallying cry of anarchists influenced by Bakunin's advocacy of force. Its aim was to inspire such dread and horror as to compel the adoption of measures of social amelioration, or perhaps the overthrow of the state itself. Incidents attributed to anarchists include the attempted assassination of German Emperor William I in 1878; the attempt on the life of the German princes in 1883; and the assassinations of President Sadi Carnot of France in 1894, of the Empress Elizabeth of Austria in 1898, of King Humbert I of Italy in 1900, and of U.S. President McKinley in 1901.

In the Haymarket tragedy of 1886, in Chicago, a number of persons lost their lives in a bomb explosion, which resulted in the trial and conviction of eight professed teachers of anarchism in that city. Seven were sentenced to die on the gallows (two sentences were later commuted to life imprisonment) and one to a prison term of 15 years. The trial aroused the attention of the whole civilized world. It is now seen, after the lapse of years, that these men, even if dangerous to the community, were convicted more by the existing state of public terror than by any actual evidence connecting them with the throwing of the bomb. The fact that the pardon of the two who escaped the gallows was petitioned for (after the terror of the time had died away) by some of the most prominent citizens of Chicago, is evidence of the change the public mind underwent regarding the accused. See also HAYMARKET RIOT.

The purely economic doctrines of anarchism have no relation to acts of murder and vengeance. "Propaganda of action" is repudiated by those who are sometimes termed "philosophical anarchists," to distinguish them from the revolutionary wing. Members of this latter school regard force as fundamentally at war with their ideals. They do not believe that social revolution can be accomplished by the methods of Bakunin and his school. Proudhon never preached force.

Further Reading: Joll, James, *The Anarchists* (Harvard Univ. Press 1980); Kline, W. Gary, *The Individual Anarchists: A Critique of Liberalism* (Univ. Press of Am. 1987); Miller, David, *Anarchism* (Biblio Dist. 1984); Wells, Robert, *Anarchist Handbook*, ed. by E. Flores (Gordon Press 1987).

ANASTASIA (1901–   ), an-əs-tā′shē-ə, was the youngest daughter of Nicholas II, last czar of Russia, and Alexandra Fyodorovna. She was probably killed by Bolshevik revolutionaries with the rest of her family in Yekaterinburg (now Sverdlovsk), Russia, on July 16 or 17, 1918. Several women have claimed to be Anastasia and, therefore, the legal heir to a Romanov fortune held in Swiss banks. They have maintained that Anastasia survived the firing squad and managed to escape from Russia. An elaboration of the story provided the plot for a play, *Anastasia*, written by Marcelle Maurette and adapted by Guy Bolton, which was produced in 1954. A movie based on the play was released in 1956.

ANASTASIUS, an-əs-tā′shəs, was antipope in 855. A Roman cardinal priest, he was excommunicated by Leo IV. On Leo's death in 855 he set himself up as pope in opposition to Benedict III, who had already been elected pope. Anastasius was deposed. Rehabilitated by Benedict III, he was later made an abbot by Nicholas I and church archivist by Hadrian II. He has been identified with Anastasius Bibliothecarius.

ANASTASIUS I, an-əs-tā′shəs, **Saint,** pope from 399 to 401. A native of Rome, he succeeded St. Siricius. During his short reign, Anastasius became renowned for the holiness of his life. Admired by Saints Augustine, Jerome, and Paulinus, he condemned some of Origen's doctrines as well as the Donatist heresy. His feast is celebrated on December 19.

See also DONATISM; ORIGEN.

ANASTASIUS II, an-əs-tā′shəs, was pope from 496 to 498. He condemned traducianism, the theory that the human soul is generated by the souls of one's parents. Although he dealt severely with schismatics, he nevertheless recognized the validity of their sacramental acts. A letter to Clovis, king of the Franks, congratulating him on his conversion to Christianity, was attributed to Anastasius, but it has been discovered to be a 17th-century forgery.

ANASTASIUS III, an-əs-tā′shəs, was pope from 911 to 913, succeeding Pope Sergius III. There are no records of the pontificate of Anastasius III except for evidence that he was active in determining the ecclesiastical divisions of Germany.

ANASTASIUS IV, an-əs-tā′shəs, was pope in 1153–1154, succeeding Pope Eugenius IV. Before becoming pope, Anastasius was cardinal bishop of Sabina. During his pontificate, he settled a long-standing controversy by recognizing the candidate of Emperor Frederick I (Frederick Barbarossa) as bishop of Magdeburg. Under the leadership of Anastasius IV the Pantheon at Rome was restored. Of his writings, a treatise on the Trinity and a number of letters are extant.

ANASTASIUS I (430?–518), an-əs-tā′shəs, was a Byzantine emperor whose reign was disturbed by religious controversy within the empire. A native of Dyrrachium (modern Durazzo, Albania), Anastasius served in Constantinople as one of the silentiaries, whose function was to act as marshals at imperial audiences. When the emperor Zeno died in 491 and the choice of the new emperor was left to the empress Ariadne, she chose

Anastasius, then about 60 years old, whom she also married. Anastasius was a deeply religious man, but his Monophysitic beliefs aroused the opposition of Euphemius, the patriarch of Constantinople, who obliged him to give written assurance that he would not tamper with the doctrine formulated at the Council of Chalcedon.

The doctrine of Chalcedon—which defined the incarnate Jesus as one person in two natures, human and divine, each independent of the other —had been rejected in the eastern provinces, notably Egypt and Syria, where Monophysitism prevailed. According to the Monophysites, the divine nature of the incarnate Jesus had absorbed the human, and so Jesus was really of one nature, the divine. At first Anastasius followed a policy of compromise, but later he tended to favor the Monophysites. The violent reactions in Constantinople and the Balkan peninsula several times endangered his throne. But Anastasius persisted in his policy to the end.

Anastasius was an able administrator, noted for his financial reforms. He was perhaps a sounder statesman than Justinian, but his reign is overshadowed by the brilliance of Justinian's.

PETER CHARANIS
Rutgers University

ANATHEMA, ə-nath'ə-mə, is a word used in the formula of excommunication from the Roman Catholic and Greek Orthodox churches. It is a Greek word and was applied originally to an object set apart and devoted to a deity, such as a gift hung in a temple. Gradually the term came to mean separation from God and man, something accursed. Finally, to pronounce an anathema or to anathematize became equivalent to pronouncing a curse upon some person or thing.

The word occurs in the New Testament, for example, in I Corinthians 16:22. The older version of this verse, "Let him be Anathema Maranatha," is now rendered (as in the Revised Standard Version), "Let him be accursed. Our Lord, come!" The imprecation was uttered in condemnation of disloyal church members who were undermining the work of the apostles by their internal division and strife, and was a term of excommunication. The Aramaic term that follows it, *Marana thá*, when properly divided and translated, was simply the early Christian prayer for the coming of Christ on the Day of Judgment (Revelation 22:20). The ultimate judgment is left to Christ.

See also EXCOMMUNICATION.

FREDERICK C. GRANT
Union Theological Seminary

ANATOL, an'ə-tōl, is a comedy in seven episodes written in 1893 by the Austrian playwright Arthur Schnitzler. Each episode shows the restless Anatol in an amusing but somewhat agonizing situation with one of the seven charming ladies with whom he is or has been amorously involved. The play was first produced in 1910, in Vienna.

ANATOLIA, an-ə-tō'lē-ə, is the modern name for Asia Minor. It is derived from the Greek *anatole*, "rising" (of the sun). The name was first used in ancient geography to designate the land mass east of the Aegean Sea. Later, under the Byzantine empire, the name was applied to one of Phrygia's three provinces. The Turkish name is *Anadolu*, and in modern times it denotes the area occupied by Asiatic Turkey. See ASIA MINOR.

ANATOMY, ə-nat'ə-mē, is the science of the structure of biological organisms. The term comes from Greek *anatomē*, meaning "dissection." In many senses, it can be used as a synonym for *morphology*, the study of form. If one classifies the domains of anatomy with respect to the nature of the living forms under study, one can speak of plant anatomy, viral anatomy, bacterial anatomy, ostracoderm anatomy, and the like. These terms denote the study of the structure of plants, viruses, bacteria, and ostracoderms, respectively.

Another way to subdivide the science of anatomy is according to the size of the structural units under consideration. For example, one may speak of *gross anatomy*, the study of structural components large enough to be examined without the aid of magnifying devices. *Microscopic anatomy* is concerned with biological structural units of a size permitting study with the light microscope. Still smaller units can be examined with the electron microscope and fall within the province of *submicroscopic anatomy*, or *ultrastructure*. The study of the structure of the molecular units of living organisms and of their arrangement is called *molecular anatomy*.

Sometimes the term "anatomy" is used in a very restricted sense, to refer only to human gross anatomy. In the present discussion the term is used more broadly and will encompass not only morpholological anatomy (gross, microscopic, submicroscopic, and molecular) but also the functional and comparative aspects of the science. Developmental anatomy (embryology), which provides valuable concepts on the origin and relationships of parts in the growth of the individual and its evolution, is discussed in the article EMBRYOLOGY.

Anatomy is one of the oldest sciences and has a noble tradition. It is a catholic science, embracing or touching on many different fields of knowledge. The study of anatomy is tremendously important to the welfare of mankind and it poses some of the most profound questions ever conceived by theorists who have sought an understanding of nature. What, then are the various branches of this field of knowledge, and how have they developed?

Gross Anatomy. We can suppose that from earliest times men have come across anatomical findings and have put them to practical use. Drawings in caves made by primitive Stone Age hunters assure us that those men knew of the heart and entrails of animals and understood that if one aimed to slaughter, a wound or a blow inflicted at certain anatomical sites had a better chance of success than at others. Animals slain in the hunt were cut up—that is, anatomized— for convenience in transport, in preparation, and in eating. In the course of this process much was learned about their internal structure. Writings of the early Egyptians tell us that surgery was practiced in the Nile Valley in the second millennium B.C. and that anatomical knowledge was beginning to find practical application in the healing arts.

The founder of anatomy as a systematic learned discipline was Herophilus of Chalcedon, a contemporary of Euclid, who carried out systematic dissections of the human body in the first half of the 3d century B.C. He made many important discoveries, describing accurately structural features of the brain, meninges, eye, genital organs, and lymphatic vessels of the abdomen.

He recognized the function of the nerves, the retina of the eye, and the differences between arteries and veins and between nerves and tendons. He was followed and his observations extended by his brilliant pupil, Erasistratus, who was the founder of physiology. The greatest of his successors was Galen of Pergamum, physician to the Roman emperor Marcus Aurelius in the 2d century A.D., and the greatest physician of antiquity save for Hippocrates of Cos, who did not, however, make any important contributions to anatomy. Galen was the founder of the science of experimental medicine. By experiment and accurate observation, he demonstrated that urine was formed in the kidneys and not in the bladder. He observed that hemisection of the spinal cord produced a paralysis on the same side below the injury. He dissected apes extensively and described a number of anatomical details for the first time. He is famed for his physiological concepts, which, although largely erroneous in the light of later experiments, dominated the thinking of European and Arabic physicians for nearly 15 centuries.

Galen represented the pinnacle of classic Greek learning in the field of anatomy. But Greek and Roman scholarship was already declining by Galen's time. The barbarian invasions and the ascendancy of Christian dogmatism led it to catastrophe. But Arab scholars preserved something of its glory, and with the revival of classic learning in medieval Europe, the surviving writings of Galen became the unchallenged authority for anatomy and medicine. However, the inquiring spirit of Galen and Herophilus was entirely wanting. Galen's errors went uncorrected, his valid observations unconfirmed, and his learning unextended. Anatomy remained stagnant for 13 centuries.

This static condition was brought to an end by a Belgian physician, Andreas Vesalius, who published in 1543 a monumental monograph reporting and depicting accurately the structure of the human body as revealed to the eye by systematic dissection. This magnificent work, entitled *De humani corporis fabrica (Concerning the Structure of the Human Body)* appeared in the same year as the great astronomical treatise of Nicolaus Copernicus' *De revolutionibus orbium coelestium (Concerning the Revolutions of the Heavenly Bodies)*. These two scientific achievements took place at a time characterized by great voyages of discovery which made known vast regions of the globe. These events marked the transition of medieval to modern times and were decisive contributions to the transition. Vesalius carried out his studies from the chair of anatomy and surgery at the University of Padua in Italy. Prior to that time, university professors, though often very learned, had not as a rule seen it as their duty to study nature directly or to advance knowledge. Vesalius set a fine example for many great scientists who have since used university posts as places for research as well as for teaching.

Vesalius can also be regarded as the founder of modern biological research. Although efforts had previously been made to catalog and recognize medicinal plants, the studies of Vesalius on the human set a pattern which was followed successfully in succeeding centuries by other biologists investigating many species of living creatures. Thus the human is the first biological species to be subjected to systematic scientific study in modern times. And Vesalius, one of the founders of modern scientific thought, wears the triple crown of the father of modern anatomy, the father of university science, and the father of modern biology.

Vesalius lived before the advent of microscopes or other instruments useful for revealing fine structural detail. He depended for dissection upon knives, probes, and similar mechanical instruments held in the hand, upon the unaided eye for observation, and upon an artist's trained hand for recording his data. These features characterize the traditional approaches of gross anatomy, which remains to this day a cornerstone of the learned and practical disciplines of medicine and of surgery and an active scholarly field in its own right.

The methods of gross anatomy suffice for studying structural details of any size above about 0.3 millimeter. Smaller details than these require optical aids for visualization.

Microscopic Anatomy. Magnifying lenses and simple but effective compound microscopes came into use about a century after Vesalius. The persons who first applied these to biological studies became the founders of microscopic anatomy. These developments occurred during the second half of the 17th century. Robert Hooke, one of the founders of the Royal Society, reported in 1667 his observations on plant anatomy as observed with a crude compound microscope. He observed that cork was composed of small compartments bounded by woody walls. He spoke of these compartments as "cells," and thereby introduced a durable term which, after 1839, came to be applied generally to a very important anatomical structural unit.

Two contemporaries of Hooke are also worthy of mention as founders of microscopic anatomy. One was an amateur scientist, the other was a professional scholar. The amateur was Anton van Leeuwenhoek, a Dutch linen draper of Delft, who ground his own lenses and constructed simple microscopes of surprising effectiveness. With these he examined a great variety of biological objects. He was the first to recognize and describe small single-celled living beings such as bacteria, protozoa, and small algae. He made some observations on the structure of higher animals, describing the red corpuscles of blood, the spermatozoa of semen, and the cross striations in heart muscle fibers.

The contributions of the Italian professional scholar Marcello Malpighi were very significant, as they comprise the first systematic studies of the microscopic anatomy of plants and animals. Malpighi also initiated the field of embryology or developmental anatomy. This division of anatomy involves the study of structural changes occurring as plants and animals grow from early stages. Using his compound microscope, Malpighi studied the structure of plant seeds at various stages of germination and recorded structural features of the developing chick embryo in the egg. He was the first to observe the blood capillaries and thus to complete knowledge of the structural basis for the circulation of the blood, discovered a few decades before by William Harvey in England. Malpighi was a professor at the University of Bologna in Italy. He was also an active man of affairs and a celebrated physician, serving for a few years as the private physician of Pope Innocent XII.

Although the field of microscopic anatomy

developed only slowly during the 18th century, the 19th century brought notable achievements in microscope optics. These were the gradual development of achromatic lenses during the first third of the 19th century, and later, the achievement of the magnificent apochromatic microscope optics by Ernst Abbe in the 1870's. Apochromatic lenses are so made as to permit all colors of visible light to be brought very nearly to focus at one setting of the lens. These accomplishments raised the resolving power of the light microscope close to its theoretical limit.

Hand in hand, improved methods of dissection were developed during the 19th century, permitting the preparation of specimens suitable for profitable study with the new lenses. These improvements involved the development of dissecting machines or microtomes (small cutters) which were capable of grasping a small bit of tissue and slicing it into a series of thin sections a few microns thick (a micron, μ, is 1/1000 of a millimeter, or about 1/25,000 of an inch). Such a slice or section can then be examined in a light microscope and is capable of revealing details down to about $\frac{1}{4}$ μ. Chemical dissection methods were also developed. These invoke the principle of loosening by chemical means the bonding forces holding together structural units in the organism such as cells, groups of cells, or portions of cells. After such treatment, the cells or other units may gently be separated and studied as individual components unencumbered by overlying or underlying extraneous material. In this procedure, the chemical agents, which may be acids or enzymes, serve the function of the knife in manual or microtome dissection. They separate and make available the parts of interest for isolation and study.

During the second half of the 19th century there appeared methods for staining sections or other bits of material prepared for examination in a light microscope. These advances were made possible by the development of the synthetic organic (aniline) dye industry. Many of the dyes manufactured for the textile industry proved to be of value to microscopic anatomists. By combining several dyes of different colors, preparations of great beauty could be obtained and many small details of structure could be recognized in contrasting colors under the microscope. Thus it became possible to stain a section of tissue in such a way that all nuclei were of one color— for example, blue, and other components would be revealed in a contrasting color such as red. By 1880 most preparations studied with the light microscope were comprised of sections cut with a microtome and stained with synthetic dyes. Such sections were usually mounted on a glass slide under a glass cover slip. They have proved to be very durable and useful preparations which lend themselves to routine use. Many specially trained persons earn their livelihood by preparing such slides in hospitals or in medical schools or research laboratories. Persons specializing in this line of work are called *tissue technicians* or *histological technicians*.

Accompanying these developments in optics, dissection, and staining, were profound advances in physics and chemistry, including the recognition of polarized light, proteins, and enzymes. These technical and conceptual accretions set the stage for a magnificent flowering of microscopic anatomy.

For certain purposes, it was useful for microscopists to focus attention primarily on the structural organization of various organs and tissues (see section *Histology*). Other problems were better served by studying the features of individual structural units called cells. This field of learning has come to be called *cytology*. Histology and *cytology* are important branches of microscopic anatomy.

Histology. This development was ushered in during the 1700's by a brilliant young French physician, Marie François Xavier Bichat, who advanced the notion of bodily tissues. He pointed out that muscles had a certain similarity wherever found and in whatever animal, and that likewise fatty portions had certain features in common, as did parts of an organism comprised largely of nerves or of tendon. These observations led him to classify a portion of an organ or of a body as belonging to a more general class of so-called tissues, such as nervous tissue, muscular tissue, connective tissue, fatty tissue, glandular tissue, or the like. The study of the detailed organization of such tissues is called histology. Histology is an important branch of anatomy and a mainstay of the clinical discipline of pathology.

The field of histology includes the study of organs, which may be made up of several kinds of tissues. Thus the liver, for example, contains connective tissue, glandular tissue, blood vessels (vascular tissue), and ducts, all arranged in an orderly manner which is closely related to the functionings of the organ. Similarly, the heart is an organ with muscular and connective tissue, along with nerve fibers, blood vessels, and other components.

The first textbook of histology was published in 1852 by Rudolf Albert von Kölliker, professor of anatomy at the University of Würzburg in Germany. For about a century the field of histology was based almost entirely on structures which could be studied with the light microscope. Since 1950, however, findings based on electron microscopy have found places of increasing importance in the field of histology.

Cytology. The development of achromatic lenses after the time of Bichat permitted a much more detailed study of anatomy than had been possible previously. By 1840 minute features within the size range of a micron or less were accessible to study and general concepts of structural organization began to emerge. Among the most important was the formulation of the "cell theory" by Matthias Jakob Schleiden (1838) and Theodor Schwann (1839). The cell theory holds that all plants and animals can be regarded as being comprised of units called cells, together with the products of cells and such material as each cell may accumulate from its environment. Thus cells are properly thought of as important anatomical units of structure. The study of the detailed structure of cells is embraced in the field of cytology. Since 1840 cytology has been an important subspeciality of anatomy. Cytology is often regarded as a special field of histology. In cytology, attention may also be focused on the functional and chemical significance of the structures observed and their roles in the overall functioning of the cell.

An important subdivision of cytology is the field of *cytogenetics*. Cytogenetics is concerned with the anatomy of the chromosomes in cells, and with the ways in which details of chromosome anatomy can be correlated with inherited characteristics of the cell or organism. Chromosomes are threadlike bodies located in the nuclei of cells. The chromosomes contain the molecules of nucleic acid (chiefly DNA), which determine many of the characteristics of the cell and of its descendants. Abnormalities in these molecular genetic determiners often produce abnormalities in the structure or configuration of the chromosomes in which they reside. The study of such chromosomal features falls within the province of cytogenetics.

Ultrastructure or Submicroscopic Anatomy. As concepts of molecular units of matter emerged in the mid-1800's, anatomists came to realize that the most minute details of biological structure discernible with the light microscope were in turn comprised of still smaller units of molecular dimensions. This concept was recognized in 1852 by Rudolf Albert von Kölliker, and in 1841 by Friedrich Gustav Jacob Henle, professor of anatomy at Zürich, Switzerland. Although the ordinary light microscope is not able to image accurately any structures whose dimensions are less than about $\frac{1}{4}$ μ, anatomical details smaller than this can be studied with the polarizing microscope, the X-ray diffraction camera, and the electron microscope. The study of biological structural units smaller than those which can be imaged accurately by the light microscope is called submicroscopic anatomy or ultrastructure (*ultra*, meaning "beyond," implying beyond the limits of the light microscope). Sometimes the term *fine structure* is used to refer to this field of anatomy.

Polarization Microscopy. The earliest successes in determining features of structure below the limits of resolution of the light microscope were achieved by examining specimens in a light microscope so fitted as to illuminate the specimen with polarized light. Such a microscope is called a polarizing microscope. By studying the interaction between the matter in the specimen and the illuminating beam of polarized light, one can deduce some of the structural properties of the specimen. The structural features so evidenced are small in relation to the wavelength of light and thus cannot be seen or imaged directly in a microscope. Yet by examining a specimen in a polarizing microscope, one can detect whether or not the specimen has submicroscopic structural units arranged in an ordered asymmetry: that is, units which are not randomly arranged, but are dispersed with a degree of order showing preferential alignment in some direction. For example, an anatomist examining a nerve, a tendon, or a muscle in a polarizing microscope can observe that the specimen affects the illuminating beam of polarized light in a certain way. By suitably analyzing the changes in the beam induced by the specimen, the anatomist can conclude that the specimen has an ordered submicroscopic structure, the units of which are too small to be distinguished individually with the microscope.

During the mid-1800's Gabriel Gustav Valentin, professor of physiology at the University of Bern in Switzerland, pioneered the application of polarization microscopy to the study of biological fine structure. The basic optical principles were understood sufficiently well by 1858 to permit Ernst Wilhelm von Brücke, an Austrian cytologist, to conclude from polarization microscopic studies that certain crossbands in striated muscle contained submicroscopic rodlike units oriented parallel to each other and to the long axis of the muscle. Von Brücke recognized that these rodlike units were of molecular dimensions far too small to be resolved with the light microscope. Nearly 90 years later, in 1946, they were visualized directly with the electron microscope by Cecil Hall, Marie A. Jakus, and Francis O. Schmitt at Massachusetts Institute of Technology. Using similar methods and arguments during the 1930's, Wilhelm J. Schmidt of the University of Giessen in Germany was able to show on the basis of polarization optical studies that the so-called "myelin sheath" of nerve fibers was composed of a framework of sheets of protein arranged circumferentially, upon which lipid (fatty) molecules were arranged radially. Once more this was confirmed in the 1940's by X-ray diffraction and in the 1950's by electron microscopy.

In order to use a polarizing microscope with full advantage, a considerable knowledge of optical theory is necessary.

Electron Microscopy. Great progress in the elucidation of the submicroscopic anatomy of animals and plants followed the introduction of the electron microscope. The development of this instrument depended on the discovery by Louis Victor de Broglie in 1924 that electrons moving at high speed have wavelike properties. This means that a beam of moving electrons can be diffracted, and the diffracted electrons can be collected and bent by magnetic or electrostatic lenses and caused to form images. Thus an electron microscope has many similarities to a light microscope, but uses a beam of electrons instead of light and focuses the beam by electrostatic plates or magnets instead of by glass lenses or curved mirrors. The first practical electron microscopes were made in Germany in the 1930's by Bodo von Borries and Ernst Ruska. By the 1960's hundreds of electron microscopes of high quality were in use in laboratories throughout the world for the study of biological fine structure.

Anatomical specimens suitable for examination in an electron microscope must be very thin. Samples more than about 5,000 A thick (1 angstrom unit = 0.00000001 cm. or 1/250,000,000 inch)—a thickness equal to the wavelength of visible light—are too thick for fruitful study with an electron microscope. The most useful range of specimen thickness is from 200 to 1,000 A. Special methods of dissection have been developed to prepare material in this fine a form. One method depends on the use of a special type of microtome called an ultramicrotome. Small specimens of plant, animal, or microbial tissue can be embedded in a suitable synthetic plastic. A block of the plastic containing the embedded material can then be placed in an ultramicrotome and sliced with a glass, diamond, or steel knife of special sharpness. By such means, sections as thin as 100 A have been obtained, though usually the thicknesses of these sections range about 500 A. A section of 500 A has a thickness equal to about $\frac{1}{10}$ the wavelength of visible light. The sections can be mounted on a specimen holder and studied in an electron microscope. Alternatively, other methods of dissection can be used. Chemical dissection, mechanical shearing or tearing forces, or ultrasonic energy can be applied to biological specimens so as to yield fragments of a size and thickness appropriate for electron microscopy.

Whereas the light microscope can image faithfully details ranging in smallest dimensions down to about $\frac{1}{4}$ μ or 2,500 A (about half the wavelength of visible light), an electron microscope in good operating condition can resolve details down to 2.5 A, thus revealing structures a thousand times smaller than can be imaged faithfully by a light microscope.

With these capabilities, electron microscopes served to mediate spectacular advances in anatomical knowledge during the decade from 1950 to 1960. Among these was the recognition that delicate membranes comprise important structural elements in all plant and animal cells. The chief such membranes are those that surround the cell and the cell nucleus and those that form the "skeletons" of cell organelles such as the endoplasmic reticulum, ribosomes, mitochondria, and lysosomes. These membranes are about 70 A thick. They are composed of protein and lipid (fat), and often assume very elaborate configurations inside cells and around their perimeters. These membranes may move about briskly during cellular activity and can carry materials with them in the course of their movements, thus facilitating exchanges of substances in cells. Upon these membranes may be arranged enzyme molecules—protein catalysts which fulfill important roles in the synthetic and energy-producing functions of cells.

Hugh E. Huxley, working in London, England, demonstrated with the electron microscope in 1957 that striated muscle fibers contain two sets of overlapping myofilaments about 100 A in diameter and 150 A apart, with frequent cross connections between members of the two sets of filaments. A myofilament is a thin protein thread-like structure, perhaps 1 or 2 μ long, with the diameters mentioned above. They comprise an essential part of the contraction mechanism of muscle. In the myofilaments lie the molecular structures that are responsible for the expanding and contracting movements of the entire muscle cell.

Anatomists working with the electron microscope are also able to image and photograph the shape and structure of certain molecules and parts of molecules, to discern much of the external and internal anatomy of viruses, bacteria, and fungi; and to achieve an understanding of anatomy far greater than is possible on the basis of light microscope studies. After 1950, the electron microscope became the most important single instrument for the advancement of the anatomical sciences.

Molecular Anatomy. X-ray diffraction became available for studying submicroscopic and molecular anatomy during the second and third decades of the 20th century. The method depends on the following circumstances: if a small object, perhaps 0.5 mm. in diameter, is placed in the path of a narrow, well-collimated beam of parallel X-rays, some of the rays are diffracted (scattered) as they encounter the electrons in the atoms in the object. Of course, most of the beam traverses the specimen straight through without deviation. It is the deviated or refracted or scattered rays which are used for analysis of the submicroscopic structure of the specimen.

Max von Laue, W. Friedrich, and P. Knipping in 1912 first demonstrated that X-rays are diffracted by crystals. William Henry Bragg and William Lawrence Bragg (father and son) by 1913 had developed basic mathematical approaches which permit one to calculate from the angles and the intensities of the diffracted rays the positions of the atoms, molecules, and chemical bonds in the crystal which give rise to the diffractions.

These methods can be applied to molecular anatomy by first performing a chemical dissection, whereby a considerable number of molecules of the same kind are separated from others in the organism (that is, purified). These molecules can then be collected and permitted to arrange themselves in an orderly, regular pattern in a crystal. The crystal, or a portion of it, can serve as the specimen and be placed in the path of an X-ray beam. The diffracted rays can be studied and an image of the molecule synthesized by mathematical means.

The commonest molecular constituent of the body is the water molecule. This can be separated from other bodily constituents by distillation and arranged in a crystalline form by freezing. The anatomy of the water molecule has become known accurately from X-ray diffraction studies of ice crystals. In a similar manner, various sugars (such as glucose), amino acids, fatty compounds, and other molecular components of living creatures have been isolated and crystallized and their molecular anatomy determined rigorously by X-ray diffraction methods. X-ray diffraction photographs played a key role in the establishment of the basic helical structure of the DNA molecule in 1953 by James D. Watson and Francis H.C. Crick. The molecular anatomy of the complex protein molecules, myoglobin and hemoglobin, was ascertained in considerable detail in 1960 by John C. Kendrew and Max Ferdinand Perutz in Cambridge, England, using X-ray diffraction. These two molecular species have an important physiological role as carriers of oxygen. Myoglobin is the oxygen carrier molecule of red muscle, and hemoglobin serves the same function in the red cells of the circulating blood.

X-ray diffraction methods can also be used to advantage in studying the submicroscopic structure of organized tissue components which have a sufficient degree of structural order. For example, a sample of ordinary mammalian tendon, such as is found in the tail of a kangaroo, when held straight and placed in the path of an X-ray beam, produces diffractions which can be attributed to a structural unit in the tendon which repeats itself regularly every 640 A along the length of the tendon. Other reflections from the tendon reveal longitudinal repeating units of 2.86 A and transverse units of 11 A and 4.6 A. These appear to be features of molecular components of the tendon. The constituent protein molecules of tendon are called *collagen*. The number and sharpness of the rays diffracted from collagen are not sufficient to permit one to conclude very much more than this about the submicroscopic structure of the collagen molecules from X-ray diffraction alone. Similar limited information can be gathered by X-ray diffraction studies of the finer anatomy of nerve, muscle, bone, cartilage, etc. These tissues all contain many species of molecules arranged with a certain degree of structural regularity, but not with sufficient order to permit detailed or complete understanding on the basis of X-ray diffraction methods.

Chemical and Functional Anatomy. An understanding of anatomy requires a recognition of the chemical composition of the various anatomical structures and a comprehension of the ways in which the several chemical and structural components participate in the reactions and functionings of the organism. The study of the disposition and localization of chemical compounds in tissues is called *histochemistry,* and a corresponding study of the localization and amounts of chemicals within cells is called *cytochemistry.* It is necessary further for anatomists to understand the functioning or workings of the various constituent parts of an organism as it goes about its activities. The study of the ways in which structural components work is called *functional anatomy.* These are all important branches of anatomy.

Functional gross anatomy is concerned with the ways in which various muscles, nerves, bones, blood vessels, or other large bodily components participate in movements and physiological workings. Thus a study of the functional anatomy of the biceps muscle of the upper arm reveals that this muscle acts to flex the elbow. Functional anatomical investigations of the alimentary canal clarify ways in which various structural components of the digestive system participate in the process of digestion and the absorption of the nutritional elements.

Functional anatomy, cytochemistry, and histochemistry are often closely related. This can be illustrated in the case of mitochondria, which are small threadlike or ovoid bodies found abundantly in most cells. The mitochondria can be seen with the light or electron microscopes and are composed of elaborately folded membranes and an intervening matrix. Cytochemical studies have shown that on the membranes of mitochondria are arranged catalytically active protein molecules called enzymes. The enzymes in mitochondria are particularly concerned with oxidation (burning) of fat or sugar, with the capture of the heat or energy of combustion, and the conversion of that heat into energy-rich phosphate bonds which can be transported to another part of the cell to power some important activity such as contractility or pumping of ions or water. Thus the functional anatomist thinks of mitochondria as serving as powerhouses or furnaces in the cell. In mitochondria fuel is burned and energy converted to a form which is readily available to the cell for useful work.

Similarly, as explained earlier, many of the delicate submicroscopic membranes in cells can serve functionally as transportation devices, as barriers between two fluid compartments, or as frameworks on which enzyme molecules may be arranged in an orderly way, serving as minute molecular assembly lines on which complex chemicals can be synthesized, or as disassembly lines upon which molecules can be taken apart piece by piece. By cytochemical methods nucleic acids have been found in the chromosomes of the nuclei of cells. The functional anatomy of these nucleic acids relates their molecular structure to the activities of genes. A functional anatomical study of the red cells of mammalian blood shows that the structure and chemical composition of these cells are well suited to the function of transporting oxygen to the peripheral tissues and carbon dioxide away from the tissues. Thus functional and chemical anatomy have important applications at the gross, microscopic, submicroscopic, and molecular levels of anatomical organization of living creatures.

Comparative Anatomy. Understanding of the significance of anatomical structures can often be enhanced by examining corresponding structures in several related or unrelated species or forms and noting the similarities and dissimilarities.

Such studies fall within the province of *comparative anatomy.* Vertebrate comparative anatomy is an important representative in this division. It is concerned with a detailed study of the anatomy of the vertebrates such as fish, amphibians, reptiles, birds, and mammals, with particular emphasis on the structural variations of corresponding parts from form to form. Thus the pectoral and pelvic fins of fish correspond to the four limbs of terrestrial animals. The fore limbs of amphibia correspond to the wings of birds and the hands and arms of primates. The homologies and similarities of structure in these corresponding parts are of great interest. Similar important homologies can be discerned in the cardiovascular, respiratory, digestive, and osseous systems of the various classes of vertebrates. See also ANATOMY, COMPARATIVE.

Comparative cytology is a branch of comparative anatomy wherein the structures of cells of various forms are studied and compared. The development of the electron microscope led to a rapid expansion of this field. With this instrument it was ascertained during the 1950's and early 1960's that cells of plants, including fungi, contain mitochondria, nuclei, and membranes similar to those in animal cells. On the other hand, bacteria have nuclei somewhat different from those of animals and lack bodies with the characteristic structure of mitochondria, yet carry out the function of mitochondria with organelles of another configuration. By extension of such studies as these, comparative anatomy becomes a coordinating and unifying discipline for all branches and subdivisions of anatomy. See also CELL; CYTOLOGY.

H. STANLEY BENNETT, M. D.
University of North Carolina

Bibliography

GENERAL

Burke, Shirley R., *Human Anatomy and Physiology for the Health Sciences,* 2d ed. (Wiley 1985).
Carola, Robert, et al., *Human Anatomy and Physiology,* 2d ed. (McGraw-Hill 1992).
Felts, William J. L., *Gross Anatomy,* 2d ed. (Springer-Verlag 1992).
Kahle, Werner, et al., *Color Atlas and Textbook of Human Anatomy,* 3 vols., 4th ed. (Thieme Med. Pubs. 1992, 1993).
Marieb, Elaine N., *Human Anatomy and Physiology,* 5th ed. (Benjamin/Cummings 2001).
Netter, Frank H., *Atlas of Human Anatomy,* 2d ed. (Novartis Pharmaceuticals Corp. 1997).
Pansky, Ben, *Review of Gross Anatomy,* 6th ed. (McGraw-Hill 1996).
Shier, David, et al., *Hole's Human Anatomy and Physiology,* 9th ed. (McGraw-Hill 2002).
Tortora, Gerald, and Sandra Reynolds Grabowski, *Principles of Anatomy and Physiology,* 9th ed. (Benjamin/Cummings 2000).
Woodburne, Russell T., and William E. Burkel, *Essentials of Human Anatomy,* 9th ed. (Oxford 1994).

HISTORY

Galen, *On My Own Opinions,* tr. by Vivian Nutton (Akademie Verlag 1999).
Persaud, T. V. N., *Early History of Human Anatomy: From Antiquity to the Beginning of the Modern Era* (Thomas, C. C. 1984).
Persaud, T. V. N., *A History of Anatomy: The Post-Vesalian Era* (Thomas, C. C. 1997).

FUNCTIONAL ANATOMY

Jenkins, D. B., *Hollingshead's Functional Anatomy of the Limbs and Back* (Harcourt 1991).
Zuidema, George D., ed., *The Johns Hopkins Atlas of Human Functional Anatomy,* 4th ed. (Johns Hopkins Univ. Press 1997).

MICROSCOPIC ANATOMY

Bergman, Ronald A., et al., *Atlas of Microscopic Anatomy: A Functional Approach Companion to Histology and Neuroanatomy,* 2d ed. (Saunders 1989).
Kelly, Douglas E., et al., *Bailey's Textbook of Microscopic Anatomy,* 18th ed. (Williams & Wilkins 1984).
Wheater, Paul, *Wheater's Functional Histology: A Text and Colour Atlas,* 3d ed. (Churchill Livingstone 1993).

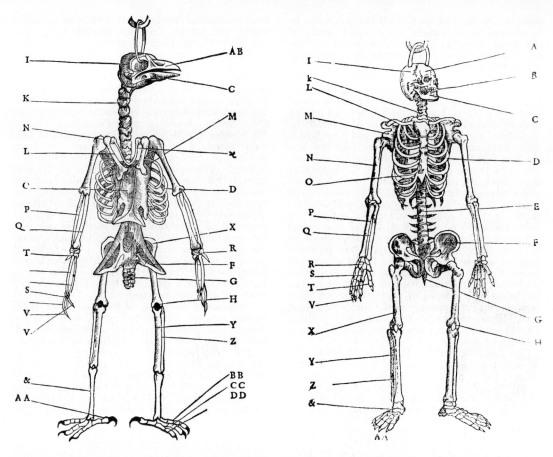

A 16th century drawing by Pierre Belon, pointing out corresponding bones in bird and human skeletons.

ANATOMY, Comparative, ə-nat′ə-mē, the study that compares the organs or organ systems in groups of related animals in order to understand the adaptive modifications that these structures have undergone in their descent from a common ancestral type. The key to the major theme of the subject is the term *homology*—the identity of a given structure throughout a series of related animals under every variety of form and function. The best proofs of homology are similarity in embryological origin, similarity in embryological form or structure even when these differ in the adult, and similar relations to adjacent structural features. In preevolutionary days, comparative studies of organs were made with reference to their similarity to or divergence from those of an idealized "archetype." Still earlier, the term "comparative anatomy" was applied to any anatomical description of organisms other than man. Although properly applicable to studies of other animal groups (or of plants), the term is now commonly restricted to studies on vertebrate animals.

HISTORICAL DEVELOPMENT

Aristotle (384–322 B.C.) dissected and described a variety of animals, and Galen (130/129–200/199 B.C.) dissected a number of mammals to reinforce his knowledge of human anatomy, but true comparative studies had to await the revival of learning and the growth of modern science. Even so, progress was slow. During the 16th, 17th, and early 18th centuries a considerable quantity of anatomical studies were made on a variety of animals as well as on man. Among workers in this field in the 16th century may be cited Guillaume Rondelet, who studied the anatomy of fishes, and Pierre Belon, who worked on birds and whales as well as fishes. In the 18th century, Pieter Camper, who produced admirable monographs on several mammals, and John Hunter, founder of the famous anatomical museum bearing his name at the Royal College of Surgeons in London, are worthy of mention. Their work, however, was mostly descriptive.

Establishment of True Comparative Methods. The first major attempts at a true comparative method were those of Count Georges Louis Leclerc de Buffon, an 18th century French naturalist with an unusually broad view of animal life, and his colleague Louis Jean Marie Daubenton. Prominent in the thinking of many comparative anatomists, as of other biologists of the late 18th and early 19th centuries, was the *Naturphilosophie* derived from the ideas of such philosophers as Immanuel Kant and, especially, Friedrich Wilhelm Joseph von Schelling, who sought to array the facts of nature in accordance with assumed basic principles of transcendental nature. Lorenz Oken and Johann Wolfgang von Goethe, although doing little actual anatomical work, were especially influential in instilling such ideas into the minds of zoologists. An early concept in this realm was that of a "scale of beings," as advocated, for example, by Charles Bonnet—a ladder on which each animal would occupy a specific rung. This proving eventually none too practical with increasing knowledge of the animal world, it was replaced by the concept that all animals could be considered as variations on a small series of structural patterns, "types" conceived in the mind of the Creator. Adherence to the concept of idealized types influenced the thinking of many comparative anatomists of the early 19th century; the attempt of Étienne Geoffroy Saint-Hilaire to reduce all animal forms to a single plan drew upon him a devastating attack by Georges Cuvier, when in 1830 he supported the idea that cephalopod mollusks and vertebrates were built on a common pattern. Cuvier was the true founder of modern comparative anatomy and perhaps the greatest figure in the history of the subject. In contrast with the nature philosophers who sought to fit facts into preconceived theories, Cuvier based generalizations on solid facts. In his *Leçons d'anatomie comparée* (5 vols., 1800–05) he unified all known anatomical data into an organized system of knowledge. To be sure, there must be some standard of reference for comparison, and in *Le règne animal distribué d'après son organisation* (1816–29), after protesting against the idea of the scale of beings, he established a series of types, based on practical study of the anatomy of the forms concerned —vertebrata, mollusca, articulata, and radiata. Except for the last, these have well withstood the test of time.

In the 19th century, Henri de Blainville was an able pupil and successor of Cuvier in France. During the same period such workers as Johann Friedrich Blumenbach, Carl Gustav Carus, Johannes Müller, Karl Theodor Ernst von Siebold, and Hermann Friedrich Stannius, advanced comparative anatomical study in the German-speaking world, and Johann Friedrich Meckel, Karl Ernst von Baer, Martin Heinrich Rathke, and Christian Heinrich Pander, combined embryological and anatomical studies.

The greatest anatomist of the preevolutionary period, apart from Cuvier, was Richard Owen. Perhaps no one individual has ever had so wide a firsthand knowledge of vertebrate structure; his *Comparative Anatomy and Physiology of the Vertebrates* (1866–68) contains a wealth of material based on personal observation. To Owen is due the development of the concept of homology. Although a disciple of Cuvier, he was strongly influenced by *Naturphilosophie*, and the concept of types is prominent in his work. For example, he put forward a theoretical archetype of the vertebrate skeleton, in which each segment consisted of variations of an idealized vertebra. He maintained (as had Oken and Carus) that the mammalian skull consisted of a series of modified vertebrae, and although this thesis was demolished by Thomas Henry Huxley, so strong has been Owen's influence that this theory still exists in some modern texts.

Influence of the Theory of Evolution. The evolutionary concept was, in general, absent from the thoughts of workers so far mentioned; indeed, both Cuvier and Owen, although major figures in the development of paleontology as well as comparative anatomy, were violent opponents. With the general acceptance of evolution in the 1860's, the study of comparative anatomy was revolutionized and for the next few decades occupied an outstanding position in zoology. The

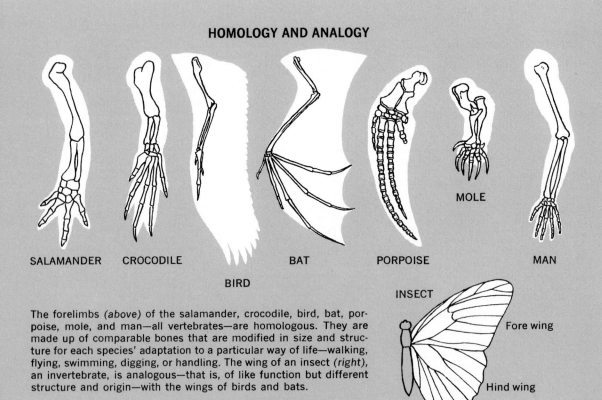

HOMOLOGY AND ANALOGY

SALAMANDER   CROCODILE   BAT   PORPOISE   MOLE   MAN

BIRD

INSECT

Fore wing

Hind wing

The forelimbs (*above*) of the salamander, crocodile, bird, bat, porpoise, mole, and man—all vertebrates—are homologous. They are made up of comparable bones that are modified in size and structure for each species' adaptation to a particular way of life—walking, flying, swimming, digging, or handling. The wing of an insect (*right*), an invertebrate, is analogous—that is, of like function but different structure and origin—with the wings of birds and bats.

consideration of differences in structure as due to variations from a mysterious, hypothetical "archetype" was replaced by the much more attractive concept that the variations had come about through descent along a variety of evolutionary lines from an actual flesh and blood ancestor. Homology had a concrete meaning, rather than a vague transcendental one. Further stimulus was added by the development of related fields. Such anatomical structures as the stomach and other organs of the digestive system are of relatively little interest from the point of view of gross anatomy; the development of microscopical techniques brought into being the realm of histology to reinforce gross study.

Post-Darwinian Developments. Embryology blossomed greatly in the post-Darwinian period and played a major part in comparative anatomical studies. Among the notable embryologists of the latter half of the 19th century, whose work contributed to the advance of comparative anatomical studies may be cited Edwin Ray Lankester and Francis Maitland Balfour in England, Wilhelm His and the brothers Oskar Hertwig and Richard von Hertwig in Germany. To Lankester and the Hertwigs are due modern concepts of the nature and development of the body cavities (the coelom). Balfour, before the close of his short but brilliant career, produced an influential treatise on vertebrate embryology. Also highly influential in stimulating work in embryology and comparative anatomy was Ernst Haeckel. Famous is his recapitulation theory, the claim that in ontogeny is to be found a recapitulation of phylogeny—in popular phraseology, that the animal during its development climbs its own family tree. Although now largely discredited, this thesis stimulated many anatomists to study embryology in the expectation that ancestral conditions of organs would be discovered.

A more enduring contribution of embryology to comparative studies was that of the concept of primary germ layers in the embryo—a concept already in the minds of earlier workers and more firmly established in post-Darwinian days by such workers as the Hertwigs. At an early stage are seen three primary tissues. An external epithelium, the ectoderm, forms the superficial part of the skin of the adult and the entire nervous system. An inner layer, the entoderm, surrounding the embryonic gut, forms the inner lining of the adult digestive tube and its outgrowths, such as the tissues of liver and pancreas. Almost all the remainder of the body—connective tissues, most of the skeleton, muscles, and so forth—arises from an intermediate embryonic layer, the mesoderm. Tracing adult structures back to their origins in these embryonic layers has been highly important in the study of homologies. In recent decades experimental work has shown that the origin of adult structures from given embryonic layers is not subject to inflexible "laws"; in general, however, the prospective fate in normal development of the germ layers and subsidiary areas of these layers is in accord with the experimentally deduced story of their potencies.

In the post-Darwinian period of the 19th century, Germany became definitely the major center of comparative anatomical studies, and Karl Gegenbaur was the outstanding figure. This forceful, positive worker was very influential throughout his life, not only through his original works but also through his texts, of which the culmination was his *Vergleichende Anatomie der Wirbeltiere*, published in 1898–1901. In gross adult structure lay his main interests; function was little regarded, histology neglected, and even embryological considerations had little attention from him. Among numerous other Germans of this general period may be noted Max Fürbringer, Gegenbaur's successor at Heidelberg, Ambrosius Arnold W. Hubrecht, and Robert Wiedersheim. Despite the predominance of German workers, able men were not lacking in other countries; representative of the period were Thomas Henry Huxley and William Kitchen Parker in England and Aleksandr Onufrievich Kovalevski in Russia.

The 20th Century. The golden age of comparative anatomy drew to a close as the 19th century ended. Since that time the subject has continued to flourish, but to flourish in more modest fashion. The reasons for this relative decline are readily discerned. New areas of biological work in cytology, genetics, physiology, and eventually biochemistry, were developing and calling for attention; further, the workers of the preceding decades had dealt with the more readily solved problems in the comparative field, forcing their successors to attack more difficult areas of work or to content themselves with relatively minor problems. In this later period active work has continued in Germany but that country has tended to lose its outstanding position, and prominent schools of comparative work have arisen in other regions, notably Great Britain and Scandinavia. Of workers of the 20th century, Edwin Stephen Goodrich of Oxford and Aleksei N. Severtsov of Russia were notable for the breadth of their interests and of their contributions.

Much of the work in comparative anatomy in its more modern period has been subject to two influences absent for the most part in the classical period: a close tie-in with paleontology, and a renewed awareness of functional implications.

A result has been a close welding of studies in comparative anatomy with those in paleontology, so that such workers of the 20th century as David Meredith Seares Watson in Great Britain, Erik A. Stensiö of Sweden, and William King Gregory of the United States could be classed as outstanding figures in either field. Of specific areas, osteological studies have, of course, profited most greatly from paleontological discoveries. However, fossil materials afford many clues as to the evolution of other organ systems such as the musculature and—particularly in the cranial region—vascular and nervous systems.

More important in many ways than the specific items of information gained from advances in paleontology is the fresh point of view on the concept of ancestral types. In the absence of a coherent paleontological record, such ancestral forms were often regarded as rather amorphous creatures, supposedly with a "generalized" structure, lacking specializations of any sort. Today many major evolutionary sequences among fossil vertebrates are becoming well known and never do we discover among ancestral types an "ideal" unspecialized ancestral form. As one, on reflection, should have concluded even in the absence of fossil data, an animal cannot, so to speak, spend its time being an ideal ancestor; it must at all stages be specifically adapted to its environment and conditions of life, and have structural as well as functional specializations to this end.

Although such early comparative anatomists as Cuvier were constantly concerned with func-

VERTEBRATE BODY PLANS

The typical vertebrate skeleton has two main divisions: the axial skeleton and the appendicular skeleton. The axial skeleton consists of the backbone, skull, and rib cage. It serves to support the rest of the body and protect vital organs. The appendicular skeleton consists of the shoulder and pelvic girdles and the paired limbs or fins attached to them. It provides a system of jointed levers that makes vertebrate locomotion highly effective. The drawings on these pages show typical skeletons of animals representing the major groups of vertebrates.

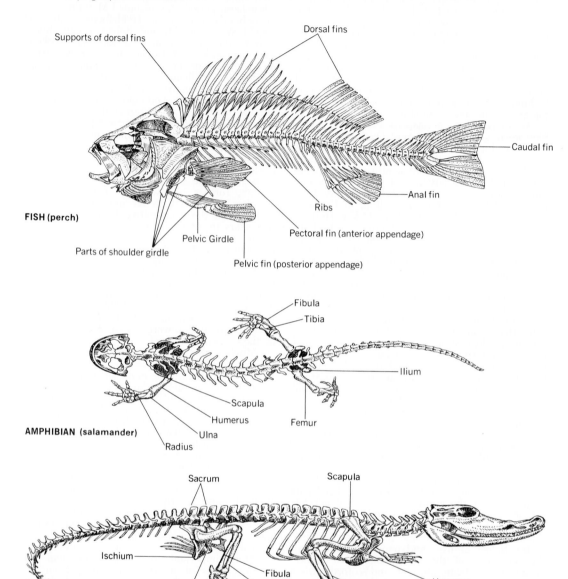

FISH (perch)

Supports of dorsal fins
Dorsal fins
Caudal fin
Anal fin
Ribs
Pectoral fin (anterior appendage)
Pelvic Girdle
Parts of shoulder girdle
Pelvic fin (posterior appendage)

AMPHIBIAN (salamander)

Fibula
Tibia
Ilium
Scapula
Humerus
Femur
Ulna
Radius

REPTILE (crocodile)

Sacrum
Scapula
Ischium
Femur
Fibula
Tibia
Humerus
Radius
Ulna

tion, this was not true of the workers of the Gegenbaur school of thought who tended to deal with "pure" morphology, with little consideration of the utility of the structures described. During the 20th century this trend has been in great measure reversed, and in many—although not all—major areas of investigation, workers have been concerned with the "why" of structural modifications in terms of their utility in the life of the organism.

BODY SYSTEMS OF VERTEBRATES

Skin. A variety of structures are found in the skin of vertebrates, both in the superficial part (epidermis) derived from the ectoderm, and the thicker dermis beneath, derived from the mesoderm. Epidermal structures include, for example, glands of various sorts, the horny scales of reptiles, feathers, and hair. In a majority of

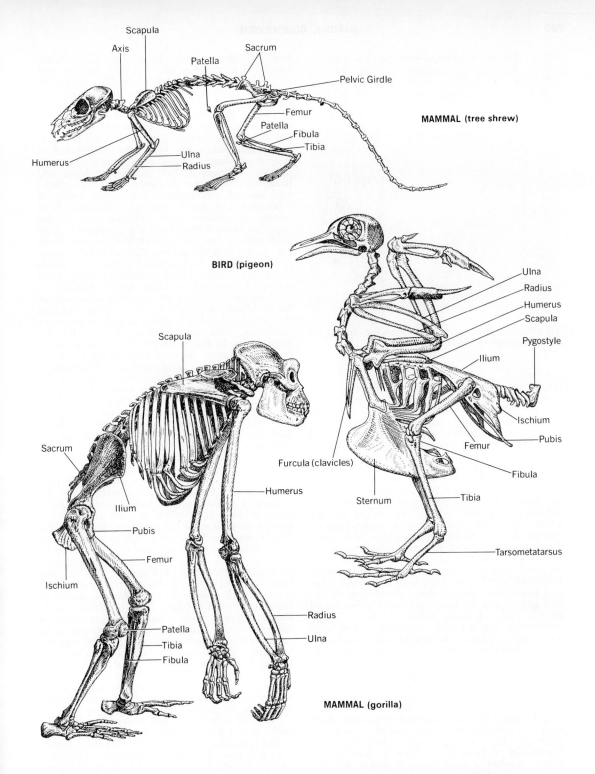

MAMMAL (tree shrew)

Axis
Scapula
Sacrum
Patella
Pelvic Girdle
Femur
Patella
Fibula
Tibia
Humerus
Ulna
Radius

BIRD (pigeon)

Ulna
Radius
Humerus
Scapula
Pygostyle
Ilium
Ischium
Pubis
Femur
Fibula
Furcula (clavicles)
Sternum
Tibia
Tarsometatarsus

Scapula
Sacrum
Ilium
Pubis
Femur
Ischium
Humerus
Radius
Ulna
Patella
Tibia
Fibula

MAMMAL (gorilla)

vertebrates the underlying dermis, constituting the greater part of the thickness of the skin, is simply formed of thick masses of connective tissue fibers. But in sharks, the skin includes a shagreen of small denticles of dermal origin; bony dermal scales are present in nearly all higher fishes; bony ossicles, scales, or plates are formed in the dermis of many reptiles (and a very few mammals). It was in the past generally assumed that in the main line of vertebrate evolution the unossified condition of the dermis was the primitive one. But paleontological discoveries in recent decades strongly suggest that, on the contrary, vertebrates acquired an armor of plates and scales at a very early stage, and that an unossified dermis is a secondary condition.

Skeleton. In the modern era, as in earlier ones, the skeleton has been a major center of interest. Because of the discrete and distinctly formed nature of skeletal elements, clear-cut descriptions

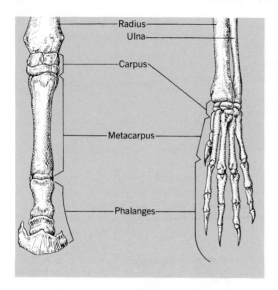

The cat's foot *(right)* is specialized for killing and climbing, the horse's foot *(left)* for running at high speed.

can be given both in adult and embryo; significant diagnostic features useful in classification and phylogeny are obtainable; skeletal materials are generally readily preserved for future reference; most especially, paleontology can, and often does, give us the actual ancestral pattern of skeletal structures.

An archaic supporting structure is the notochord, a long flexible rodlike structure running the length of the back in some lower chordates and prominent in the embryo of every vertebrate although generally reduced or absent in the adult. Apart from this, vertebrate skeletal tissues consist of two substances, cartilage and bone. Cartilage, also present in some invertebrates, is a relatively weak but pliable material generally confined to elements deep within the body. Bone, known in vertebrates alone, is of two types. Dermal bones form directly from the dermis of the skin and, except for bony scales and plates found on the body of many fishes and some higher vertebrates, are generally confined to the head and shoulder region. All internal ossifications are replacement bones, first laid down as cartilages in the embryo; during development the cartilage is resorbed and replaced by bone. No bone is to be found in cyclostomes and sharks, and cartilage persists to a considerable degree in the adult even in some more advanced fishes. It was hence long believed that the ancestral vertebrates were boneless, cartilaginous forms, and that bone was relatively late in appearance. But increased knowledge of fossil fishes, due to Stensiö and others, renders it much more probable that the reverse was the case; that bone was well developed at an early stage in vertebrate history, and that the cartilaginous condition in sharks and cyclostomes is a degenerate one.

Most complicated, most diagnostic, and most intensively studied of vertebrate skeletal structures is the skull. Typically, this is a complex of dermal bones and more deeply lying cartilages or cartilage replacement bones. Dermal bones primitively formed a solid shield over the outer surface of the skull and were also present over the sur-

faces of the palate. Internally, a braincase formed of cartilage in the embryo is present, and on either side of this a bar of cartilage forms the basis for the formation of the upper jaws. No formed skull is, of course, present in cyclostomes or sharks. Bony fishes exhibit well-developed but varied skull patterns; no common ancestral type has as yet been found. The skull of extinct crossopterygian fishes has long been recognized to bear resemblances to that of ancient amphibians. Certain contrasts in both dermal patterns and brain-case structures between the two groups long seemed irreconcilable, but recent studies of crossopterygian skulls and new discoveries of ancient amphibians have bridged most of the gap. No living tetrapod has a generalized type of skull pattern, but the work of Watson and others has shown that the ancient Paleozoic labyrinthodont amphibians had skulls of a type from which those of all other land vertebrates have been derived by gradual but often drastic changes.

The axial skeleton of vertebrates consists of the backbone, or vertebral column, formed around the notochord of the embryo, as well as accessory structures, such as the ribs, supports for the median fins in fishes, and in tetrapods a breast bone or sternum. In most regards the comparative study of these structures is well advanced but the homologies of the central region of the vertebrae in various fish and tetrapod groups is still puzzling. Hans Friedrich Gadow in 1896 put forth the theory that the primitive centrum consisted of four pairs of elements—"arcualia"— and that the centra of all existing forms are structures evolved by modification, fusion, or reduction of these primordial arches. But it is increasingly apparent that the Gadow theory must be abandoned. Much attention has been devoted to the study of the paired appendages and the associated limb girdles. Paired fins or limbs, typically two in number, are present in most vertebrate groups except where secondarily lost. Fin origins have been much debated. Gegenbaur early claimed that the original type of paired fin was one which he termed the "archipterygium," its skeleton consisting of a central axis and side branches. But although this pattern, or modifications of it, is present in a number of groups of living and extinct fishes, it is far from certain that this type is truly primitive. Many recent as well as extinct forms have, in contrast, a fin skeleton with an arrangement of parallel supporting bars. The placoderms, oldest of fishes with paired fins, show a variety of structures, with spiny supports rather than internal skeletons prominent in their patterns, and there is evidence suggesting that paired appendages evolved more than once, in parallel fashion.

In land vertebrates—the tetrapods—where the limbs have taken over the task of propulsion, the paired appendages have of course become greatly enlarged and of complex structure. The basic pattern in both front and hind limbs includes one element in the proximal limb segment (humerus or femur), two in the second major segment (radius and ulna, or tibia and fibula) and, beyond this, a series of small bones (carpus or tarsus), leading to the digits. Through the work of Goodrich and Gregory, particularly, it seems clear that the tetrapod limb pattern can be derived from that seen in crossopterygian fishes. Most of the evolutionary story of vertebrate limb structures has been clarified through increasing knowledge of fossil forms.

Of seemingly basic importance in vertebrate evolution is the fact that in contrast to the mesodermal origin of most skeletal elements—which may be termed the somatic skeleton—certain portions of the structures of the head and pharynx, designated as the visceral skeleton, do not come from the mesoderm. Instead they are derived from the neural crest—cellular materials of ectodermal origin which migrate into the interior of the head from the ridges which close to form the neural tube. Arising in this fashion are the bars which aid in stiffening the gill openings of fishes, an enlarged anterior pair of such bars which evolved to become jaw cartilages, and the forward part of the brain case. As noted below, a comparable contrast between somatic and visceral elements is seen in the muscular and nervous systems, the visceral components in each case being associated with the gut and, especially, with the anterior pharyngeal region. A suggestion arising out of this situation is that the ultimate vertebrate ancestor may have been an essentially sessile "visceral" animal, somewhat comparable to certain of the tunicates of the present seas. This would have consisted of little else than a relatively enormous pharynx as a food straining apparatus. The "somatic" animal was a phylogenetic supplement to this structure, which added to the visceral component a locomotor apparatus, with sensory and nervous systems to direct it (much as in the larva of some tunicates). Under such a speculative hypothesis the vertebrate represents essentially a dual organism.

Musculature. Histologically, vertebrate muscle tissues are of two types—smooth muscle fibers such as are found in much of the digestive tract, and striated muscles which make up the flesh of the body. In recent decades, however, it has become apparent that the major categories of musculature should not be based on microscopic structure but upon embryological origin, and that the division should be into (1) somatic muscles arising from paired segmental muscle blocks—myotomes—which form along nearly the whole length of the body at an early embryonic stage, and (2) visceral muscles, which arise in the tissues surrounding the primitive gut. All somatic muscles are of the striated sort; of the visceral muscles, those in the head and throat region are striated, those surrounding the more posterior parts of the digestive tract are smooth muscle.

Major derivatives of the somatic muscle blocks of the embryo are the axial muscles of the trunk and tail, which sheath the body beneath the skin, run between successive vertebrae and ribs, and in fishes form the main propulsive organ. Massive in fishes, they are much reduced in bulk in land vertebrates, where the limbs take over locomotion. In the throat region, ventral extensions of the axial muscle group run forward and form the musculature of the tongue. Three small muscle blocks in the eye region give rise to the muscles of the eyeball. The muscles of the paired fins of sharks appear to be directly derived in the embryo from the myotomes, and it is believed that the muscle tissues of the paired appendages of other fishes and tetrapods are ultimately derived from this same somatic source. In fishes, the paired fin musculature consists essentially of small opposed muscle masses above and below the fin. Much more complicated, of course, is the musculature of the limbs of land vertebrates. The general picture of the evolution of tetrapod limb muscles can now be made out, and

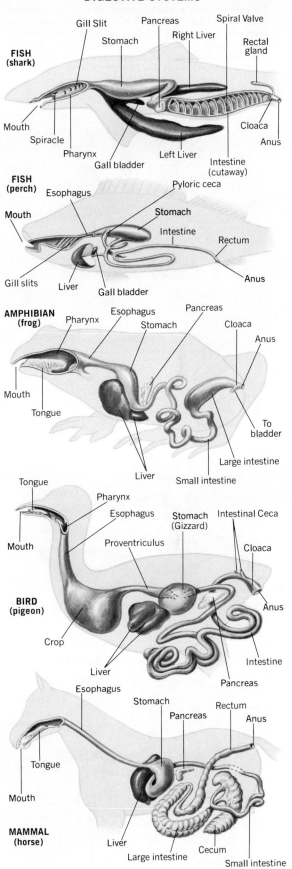

BREATHING ORGANS

The principal types of breathing organs are gills, for respiration in water, and lungs, for respiration in air. In both types, blood gives off carbon dioxide and picks up oxygen from the surrounding water or air. Birds have relatively small lungs, but their efficiency is greatly increased by associated air sacs that in effect provide one-way flow through the lungs.

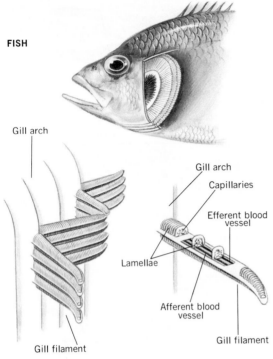

FISH

Gill arch

Gill arch

Capillaries

Efferent blood vessel

Lamellae

Afferent blood vessel

Gill filament

Gill filament

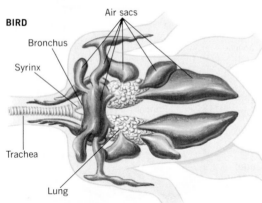

Air sacs

BIRD

Bronchus

Syrinx

Trachea

Lung

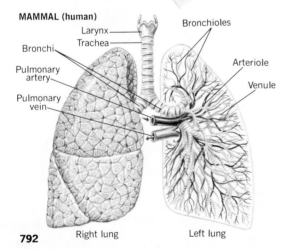

MAMMAL (human)

Bronchioles

Larynx

Trachea

Bronchi

Pulmonary artery

Arteriole

Venule

Pulmonary vein

Right lung

Left lung

it seems clear that the complex muscular system of land limbs is derivable from the simple dorsal and ventral muscle masses of the fish paired fins.

The striated visceral muscles which surround the anterior part of the digestive tract appear to have been originally functional in controlling the gill openings, as is the case today in cyclostomes. With the development of jaws, anterior members of this series became prominent as the jaw muscles. Despite the reduction of the gill region in land vertebrates, remnants of this series persist in the throat and neck regions, and in mammals fractions of the original gill musculature have had a spectacular development, spreading forward over the surface of the head as the facial muscles, or muscles of expression.

Digestive System. As seen in typical higher vertebrates, the digestive tract is divided into a familiar series of structures—mouth, pharynx, esophagus, stomach, small intestine, and large intestine. Every one of these regions, however, is subject to variation in one group or another, and some may be absent or difficult of recognition in many cases. The mouth is of variable nature. In all except the most primitive forms, it is bounded by jaws, bearing a series of teeth which in themselves constitute an interesting area for study. In tetrapods the nostrils have an internal opening, but this is absent, except for the lungfishes, in the existing fish population. A tongue, for food manipulation, is present in all land forms but little developed among fishes. The pharynx, next in order beyond the mouth, is unimportant in tetrapods but in fishes is highly developed as the area in which are located the breathing organs, the gills. The esophagus is, on the contrary, almost nonexistent in fishes, but in land vertebrates, with reduction of the pharynx and development of the neck, may be of considerable length. The stomach is highly variable both as to gross morphology and the histological nature of its glandular inner lining, and in some fishes there is no stomach—possibly a truly primitive condition in some instances. Structures similar to the mammalian small intestine—a long coiled tube of small diameter—are found in all land vertebrates and most of the higher bony fishes as well. But it appears probable that the primitive intestine was the spiral intestine found in modern sharks—a short but broad cigar-shaped structure traversed by a complex spiral passage. In mammals and some fishes the intestinal tract opens separately to the exterior; but in birds, reptiles, amphibians, and many fishes we find a surely more primitive situation in which the terminal part of the gut tract is a pocket termed the cloaca, into which are passed genital and urinary as well as digestive products. The massive liver is an outgrowth of the gut, as is the pancreas.

Breathing Organs. Primitive vertebrates were water dwellers, breathing by a unique internal gill system, not elsewhere present except in their lower chordate ancestors. Pouches grow out from the pharynx of the embryo, break through to the surface, and typically develop into slits, in the margins of which gill structures, richly supplied with blood capillaries, take up oxygen from the stream of water passing through the gills and give off carbon dioxide in exchange. Typically, six pouches are developed, but the first gill slit is generally reduced or absent. It is probable that food-filtering rather than breathing may have been the original function of the gills, as it is today in lower chordates and the lamprey larva. In land vertebrates the gill apparatus is reduced or absent in the adult, but gill pouches remain prominent in the embryo of every tetrapod.

In land dwellers paired lungs which grow out from the floor of the pharynx replace the gills as breathing organs. Simply built lungs are present in a few modern fishes. Most living bony fishes (teleosts) have instead of lungs a single dorsally placed air bladder which functions as a hydrostatic organ. It was formerly believed that the lung had evolved from this air bladder. In recent years, however, a consideration of paleontological and anatomical data leads to the opposite conclusion: that lungs probably evolved at an early stage in fish history, in relation to fish life, in inland waters subject to drought, and that if lungs and air bladder are real homologues, the bladder has evolved from the lung.

Body Cavities. In various advanced invertebrates there develop body cavities—coelomic cavities—surrounding the internal organs of the digestive and other systems. In most groups these cavities arise by cleavage of the mesodermal tissues. However, in echinoderms and lower chordates they are formed from pouches growing out from the gut cavity. It is believed that this was the condition present in ancestral vertebrates, although typical pouch formation is obscured in the development of modern forms. In the vertebrate embryo there develops a single longitudinal cavity running the length of the trunk on either side of the gut tube. Anteriorly, however, a distinct compartment develops to contain the heart, and in mammals separate pleural cavities contain the lungs.

Excretory System. Vertebrates are unique in that the microscopic functional excretory unit, in contrast to the various types of nephridia found in invertebrates, is the nephron, or kidney tubule, generally with a prominent spherical "head," the glomerulus. The glomerulus is a filtering device; along the course of the convoluted tubule salts and other useful materials are resorbed into the blood stream and the end product is generally a very dilute watery urine. It has been pointed out by Homer W. Smith that this type of structure strongly suggests that the early vertebrates inhabited fresh water. In nearly all vertebrates it is necessary for survival that the internal fluids of the body contain a certain concentration of specific salts. A freshwater fish is constantly subject to dilution of salt content through osmosis; the typical kidney tubule counteracts this by constantly "pumping out" large amounts of water (as well as waste materials). Saltwater fishes and land vertebrates, on the other hand, are in danger of overconcentration of salts; various methods of counteracting this are found, some involving modifications of the nephron.

Primitively, it is believed, the kidney gross structure consisted of a segmental series of tubules arranged the length of the trunk on either side. Such a kidney, termed a holonephros, is found today in the larval hagfish. But even in that lowly creature the most anterior, first-formed, set of tubules, termed the pronephros, disappears in the adult. In vertebrates generally there is a strong trend for multiplication of tubules and a concentration of them toward the posterior part of the trunk, although the pronephros may persist in many fishes as a specialized "head kidney." The nomenclature of vertebrate kidney types has been in general based on the embryonic picture seen in reptiles, birds, and mammals. Here, there first appears a short series of pronephric tubules, from which a primitive kidney duct—the archinephric duct—passes back to open, eventually, to the exterior. Soon there forms back of the pronephros a second series of tubules, termed the mesonephros, which functions for a time in the embryo as the pronephros disappears. Somewhat later, there develops near the back of the trunk region a massive structure containing countless kidney tubules, and in connection with it a new duct, the ureter; this structure, termed the metanephros, remains as the adult kidney. Since the adult kidney in fishes and amphibians is seldom as concentrated posteriorly as in the amniotes, it is frequently termed a mesonephros. But it includes, in its development, the regions from which both mesonephros and metanephros of amniotes are derived; and there is often a trend for development of ducts seemingly comparable to ureters. The term mesonephros is hence inappropriate and the adult kidney of lower vertebrates is perhaps best termed an opisthonephros. Bladder structures occur in variable fashion in many fishes; in land vertebrates the bladder develops as a ventral outpocketing of the cloaca.

Reproductive Organs. Almost universally the sexes are distinct in the vertebrates; in a few cases among fishes and amphibians there may be a shift from one sex to the other during the life of an individual, but never are there functional hermaphrodites. The gonads develop as a pair of longitudinal ridges projecting into the coelomic cavity dorsally on either side of the midline; for some time the embryonic gonads remain in a sexually indifferent state before developing into a definitive testis or ovary. In cyclostomes both eggs and sperm are shed into the body cavity, to make their way to the exterior through posteriorly placed pores. In all higher groups ducts are developed for transport. In the male, the archinephric duct is generally utilized as a sperm duct, the ductus deferens, a series of anterior kidney tubules being modified to pass the sperm from testis to duct. In the female, the eggs are persistently shed into the coelomic cavity; but they are at once taken up into a ciliated funnel, whence they are transported toward the exterior by a tube, the oviduct, which runs parallel to the primitive kidney duct. In sharks, the oviduct develops by splitting off from the primitive kidney duct, and hence the oviduct may have evolved by specialization from the urinary system.

In forms which have a shelled egg, a gland for shell formation may be present near the proximal end of the oviduct. Distally, an expansion of this duct allows for retention of eggs until the time of laying; in viviparous forms, development of the embryo takes place here and in typical mammals this expanded area becomes the uterus, within which a placenta may form from the membranes of the embryo and the adjacent uterine walls. The most distal portion of the two oviducts in typical mammals fuses to form a vagina. In forms with shelled eggs or in viviparous types, intromittent organs for internal fertilization may form about the distal ends of the sperm ducts, as in the claspers of the male sharks, paired penislike organs found in most reptiles, and the penis of mammals.

Circulatory System. In vertebrates, unlike some invertebrate groups, the blood flows in an entirely closed circuit, from the heart through arteries to capillaries and thence through veins

URINARY AND REPRODUCTIVE ORGANS

In typical bony fishes the urinary, genital, and digestive tracts all have separate openings at the body surface. In female mammals the three kinds of tracts also have separate openings, but in males the urinary and genital tracts combine in the urethra. In most other vertebrates the three kinds of tracts empty into a pocket — the cloaca — with a single opening to the exterior. Specialized copulatory organs occur in reptiles (hemipenes) and mammals (penis).

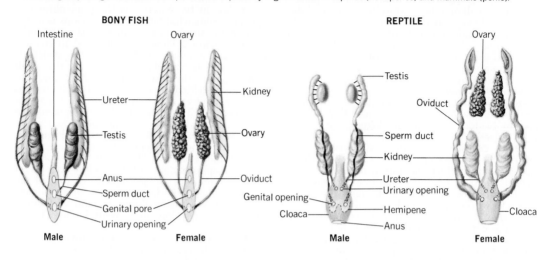

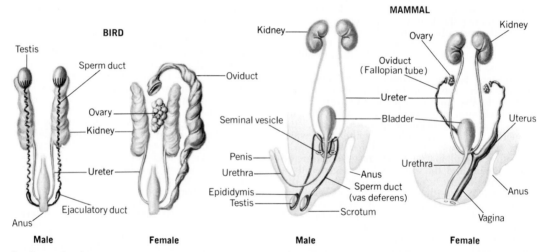

back to the heart again. In such highly developed invertebrate groups as the annelids and arthropods the major blood circuit runs forward dorsally and returns posteriorly beneath the gut; among vertebrates the reverse is the case. The primary embryonic blood circuit runs forward below the gut, ascends dorsally in the gill region and then flows backward in a major vessel lying beneath the backbone.

The heart develops in the ventral vessel just back of the gill region of the embryo, and hence the main ventral vessel back of this point is a portion of the venous system. As the liver grows in the embryo, it grows down to meet this ventral venous trunk, and interrupts it. As a consequence, blood from the digestive tract, bearing food materials, flows to the liver as a hepatic portal system and passes through the liver in a maze of small vessels, where the liver tissues may extract from or add to the blood content. Beyond, the blood continues toward the heart in one or more hepatic veins. One or a pair of small abdominal veins are found draining the belly region in lower vertebrates, and in lung-breathing tetrapods

large pulmonary veins return aerated blood from the lungs.

The venous drainage of the dorsal portions of the body and the head is effected in the lower vertebrate groups by paired cardinal veins lying dorsal to the body cavity on either side of the midline. Anterior cardinal veins run backward from the head region; posterior cardinals carry blood forward along the trunk. At a point dorsal to the heart, anterior and posterior members join and descend to the heart in paired common cardinals. Both anterior and posterior cardinals became subjected to major change as higher vertebrate groups evolved. Numerous modifications occurred in the cranial drainage, and in typical mammals both anterior vessels unite to form a single anterior vena cava. The evolution of the posterior vessels is a still more complex story. There is a strong tendency for the two vessels to unite in a single channel for much of their length. The connections with the common cardinals are reduced and finally lost, and the heart is reached through a single vessel, the posterior vena cava, which plunges down more

CIRCULATORY SYSTEMS

In the circulatory system of a fish, blood flows in essentially a single circuit from the two-chambered heart to gills to body tissues and back to heart. In amphibians, with three-chambered hearts, the circuit to respiratory organs (lungs and skin) is partially separated from the circuit to body tissues. In mammals and birds, with a four-chambered heart acting as a double pump, the circuit to the lungs is kept completely separate from the circuit to body tissues.

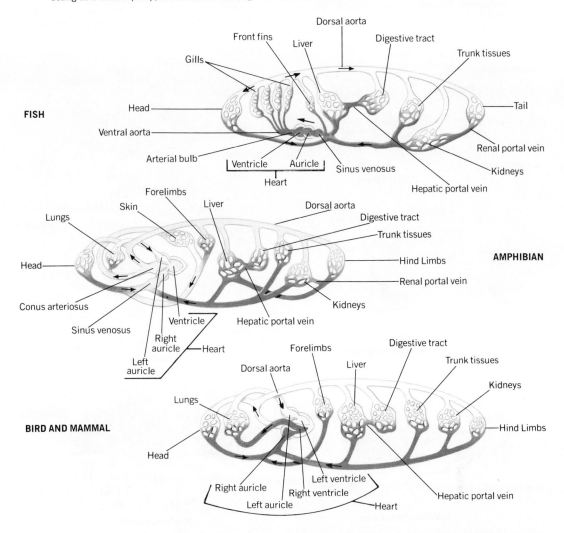

FISH

Front fins · Gills · Head · Ventral aorta · Arterial bulb · Ventricle · Auricle · Heart · Liver · Dorsal aorta · Digestive tract · Trunk tissues · Tail · Renal portal vein · Kidneys · Sinus venosus · Hepatic portal vein

AMPHIBIAN

Forelimbs · Skin · Lungs · Head · Conus arteriosus · Sinus venosus · Right auricle · Left auricle · Ventricle · Heart · Liver · Hepatic portal vein · Dorsal aorta · Digestive tract · Trunk tissues · Hind Limbs · Renal portal vein · Kidneys

BIRD AND MAMMAL

Forelimbs · Lungs · Dorsal aorta · Head · Right auricle · Left auricle · Left ventricle · Right ventricle · Heart · Liver · Digestive tract · Trunk tissues · Kidneys · Hind Limbs · Hepatic portal vein

posteriorly in conjunction with the hepatic veins. In cyclostomes, blood from the tail region flows forward without interruption into the cardinals; in sharks and other fishes, however, blood from the more posterior regions passes through the kidneys in capillaries, thus establishing a renal portal system. The renal portal persists in amphibians, but is reduced in reptiles and in birds; in mammals it has disappeared.

In fishes and in the embryos of tetrapods the heart lies close below and behind the gill region. Blood passes forward from it beneath the pharynx in a ventral aorta; this gives off paired branches, typically six in number, which pass upward between successive gill pouches. These aortic arches are, of course, continuous tubular structures in the embryo and (as far as they persist) in land animals; in fishes, however, the arches in the adult break up along their course into capillaries for gill breathing. But even in fishes the first two arches may be reduced or much modified, and further modification and reduction takes place in tetrapods, with the loss of gill breathing. The third, or carotid pair of arches, supplies

blood to the head; the fourth become the main systemic arches taking blood back to the body through a dorsal aorta; arch five disappears; the sixth pair, with the development of lungs, become pulmonary arteries. In amphibians and reptiles both systemic arches are present but in birds and mammals only a single systemic arch persists. Curiously, it is the left aortic arch which is found in mammals, the right in birds.

The lymphatic system offers a means of returning excess fluids from the tissues to the heart under lower conditions of pressure than the veins which they parallel in function and to some degree in course. Lymphatic vessels begin in tissue capillaries which, unlike those of the major circulatory system, have no arterial connections. Like the cardinal veins, these trunks appear to have had a complicated evolutionary history; this history, however, is far from understood.

The typical fish heart consists of four chambers arranged in a single series: a thin-walled sinus venous into which the veins empty, an atrium (auricle), a thick-walled, muscular ventricle, the main pumping organ, and a terminal

VERTEBRATE BRAINS

The vertebrate brain has three main divisions: the forebrain, consisting mainly of the cerebrum, thalamus, and hypothalamus; the midbrain, which includes the optic lobes; and the hindbrain, consisting of the cerebellum and medulla oblongata. The most striking change on the evolutionary scale from fish to mammal is the great increase in the size and importance of the forebrain, and especially of the cerebrum.

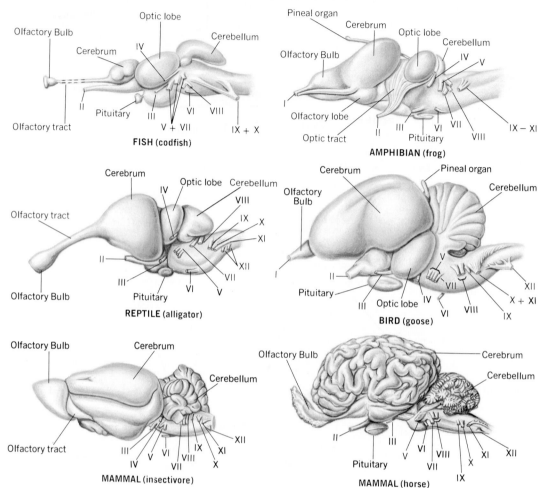

FISH (codfish)

AMPHIBIAN (frog)

REPTILE (alligator)

BIRD (goose)

MAMMAL (insectivore)

MAMMAL (horse)

conus arteriosus leading to the ventral aorta. But when gill breathing is abandoned and lungs develop as breathing organs, there is created a functional "problem" with which this simple straightforward structure cannot adequately cope, and which has been completely "solved" only when the bird or mammal stage is reached. With lung breathing there enters the back chambers of the heart not only "spent" blood from the tissues but also fresh, aerated blood from the lungs. These two blood streams should be separated and the "spent" blood delivered to the pulmonary arteries, the aerated blood to the main arterial trunk to head and body. A beginning of a separation of the heart into two sets of chambers is made in amphibians, and continued in reptiles; only in birds and mammals is the cleavage of the system into two discrete halves complete. Left atrium and ventricle receive blood from the lungs and distribute it to head and body via systemic arch; the right atrium (with which the sinus venosus is incorporated) receives the venous flow from the body and passes it, via the right ventricle, to the pulmonary trunk and lungs.

Endocrine Organs. During the last half century much work has been done on the nature and function of organs of internal secretion, which produce minute amounts of chemical materials, hormones. These act through the blood stream on structures far removed from the hormone source. The primary interest has lain in the physiological action of these chemical messengers but there has been a correlated interest in the anatomy of the glands in which they are produced. These glands do not form a coherent system of organs, but are, so to speak, specialized fragments derived from a variety of organ systems. Most important of endocrine organs is the pituitary gland, or hypophysis, lying beneath the forebrain and producing a considerable array of hormones which may influence various tissues directly or through their effect on other members of the hormone system. The pituitary has a double origin; the greater part is derived embryologically from a pouch which grows upward from the roof of the mouth; a posterior neural lobe is a ventral outgrowth of the brain.

Important endocrine structures develop in the throat region, most notably the median ventral thyroid gland, whose product is important in the regulation of growth and metabolism. Other glandular structures in the throat region develop from the gill pouches, notably the small but vital parathyroid glands of tetrapods which condition calcium and phosphate metabolism. Part of the pancreas is an endocrine structure, releasing insulin and regulating carbohydrate metabolism. The walls of the small intestine produce hormones influencing digestive activity. The tissues of the gonads produce hormones which affect other sexual organs. The adrenal glands, which in mammals cap the kidneys, consist of two types of tissue with quite different functions. One type secretes adrenaline, a general body stimulant, the other, steroid hormones which influence carbohydrate metabolism, kidney function, and so forth. If we turn to the lower vertebrate groups, we find no formed adrenals, but instead two discrete paired series of small cell aggregates, strung along above the body cavity not far from the midline, serving these two discrete functions; embryologically the adrenaline-forming cells are seen to be modified elements of the autonomic nervous system.

Sense Organs. Apart from simple sensory structures in the skin, gut, and mesenteries, vertebrates have a distinctive series of complex structures which are paralleled by analogous developments in many of the invertebrates. Taste is effected by a series of small "buds" generally located in the mouth and concentrated on the tongue in tetrapods; in some fishes (notably catfishes) numerous taste buds may be found in the skin external to the mouth. A second chemical sense is smell. In most fishes the nasal apparatus consists of paired pockets opening to the outer surface of the snout near the mouth margins. In cyclostomes, however, there is but a single median nostril which in the lamprey is situated far back on the upper surface of the head. It is uncertain whether this peculiarity is primitive or a specialization; certain of the oldest fossil vertebrates are now known to have the lamprey condition of the nostril. In all tetrapods and, we believe, in the extinct crossopterygians ancestral to them, there is an internal opening from nasal pockets to mouth cavity, facilitating breathing as well as smell. The primitive internal opening lay far forward. In mammals and some reptiles there is present a secondary palate in the roof of the mouth; as a result the internal nares lay far back, not far from the opening (the glottis) leading to the lungs. This condition facilitates continuous breathing during feeding or (in crocodilians, for example) when the mouth is water-filled in partial submergence.

An important sensory organ of fishes and larval amphibians is the lateral line system. Located in a groove or a canal, with openings to the surface, along each flank of a fish, and in similar canals, grooves, or pits arranged in patterns on the head are numerous small sensory structures termed neuromasts. These appear to respond to water currents and pressures and are important in fish navigation.

Very probably specialized developments from the lateral line system are the internal ear structures common to all vertebrates. The ear was, to begin with, primarily an organ of equilibrium rather than hearing and was thus, like the lateral line system, functionally associated with movement; further, its receptors, sensitive to movements and pressures of the liquids in which they are bathed, are closely comparable to the neuromasts of the lateral line system. The typical fish ear consists of a series of liquid-filled sacs and canals buried within the braincase. Three semicircular canals, at right angles to one another, register turning movements; two sacs, termed the utriculus and sacculus, contain major sensory areas, both of which appear to register static balance, and one of the two may be associated with hearing as well. The cyclostomes have a less highly developed apparatus. In lampreys and at least some of the oldest fossil vertebrates there are but two ear canals, and hagfishes have but one. Whether these more simplified conditions are primitive or due to degeneration is uncertain.

In tetrapods accessory structures are developed as aids in hearing air vibrations. Even in typical fishes there exists a fingerlike ventral projection from the sacculus, termed the lagena. In most land forms hearing is associated with a sensory papilla in this region of the internal ear, and this develops in mammals as the cochlea, a highly evolved hearing organ. More spectacular is the development of external structures. In nearly all tetrapods the first gill pouch of the ancestral fishes develops as a middle ear chamber, separated from the outer surface of the head by a membrane, the ear drum (tympanum). Air waves vibrating the drum are carried across the middle ear by a rodlike ossicle, the stapes, formed from a gill bar propping the jaws in fishes. At the inner end of the stapes is an opening through which the vibrations can reach the liquids of the internal ear and, eventually, the sensory areas. In mammals three auditory ossicles—malleus and incus as well as stapes—are present. More than a century ago it was suggested, on embryological grounds, that the additional ossicles represented the two bones which in other vertebrates form the joint between upper and lower jaws. In recent decades this hypothesis has received ample confirmation from the study of fossil reptiles leading toward mammals. The history of the auditory ossicles gives a striking example of the way in which changes of function may occur in organs definitely homologous, for these structures were first associated with breathing, then with eating, and, finally, with hearing.

Nature appears to have had no difficulty in the creation of light sensitive organs, and eyes are found in a variety of animal phyla. Those of vertebrates have a pattern distinct from those of other groups (although paralleled to some extent in cephalopod mollusks). External to a spherical eyeball are accessory structures, such as a set of eye muscles, and lids in many groups. The "front" surface of the eyeball is a transparent cornea; some distance back of this in the liquid-filled interior is the lens, for focusing; at the back the retina, with the actual light-perceiving cells. Focusing may be accomplished in a variety of ways, including either movements of the lens or changes in lens shape; no two major groups of vertebrates employ the same system, suggesting that the ancestral vertebrate had little focusing ability, and that the development of focusing devices has taken place a number of times in parallel fashion. The sensory retinal cells are of two types, rod cells, which respond to minute amounts of light, and cones, which require more light before being stimulated but, in contrast to the rods, perceive color and are capable of registering detail. There are numerous variations in the degree to which rods and cones are present and in their arrangement in the retina. Primitive vertebrates, as we know from the fossil record, had a smaller third eye, atop the head; this is reduced or absent in most living forms, but may be represented by internal glandlike structures.

Nervous System. The nervous system of vertebrates and certain of their chordate relatives is unique, consisting of a hollow dorsal tube, the spinal cord, which expands anteriorly into a brain of complex structure, and, emerging from cord and brain on either side, a series of nerves, more or less segmental in nature. The spinal cord as seen in sections consists of masses of "gray matter" surrounding a small central liquid-filled cavity and, superficially, white areas. The gray matter consists mainly of nerve cell bodies, the white matter of innumerable nerve fibers connecting areas of the cord with one another or with the brain.

Early comparative studies of the brain were generally confined to external, superficial features of its gross anatomy; much more important is the nature of its internal structures—the varied nerve centers and the fiber tracts connecting them—the "wiring" of the brain. Before the close of the 19th century, however, special nerve stains were developed by Ramón y Cajal and others, and there came into being a school of comparative neurologists. Ludwig Edinger of Frankfurt was a pioneer, C.U. Ariëns Kappers of Holland a further major European figure. In the United States, Charles Judson Herrick was the leader of a school of American workers, many of whose studies have appeared in the *Journal of Comparative Neurology.*

Embryology indicates that the brain primarily consists of three basic regions—fore-, mid-, and hindbrains, formally termed prosencephalon, mesencephalon, and rhombencephalon. Each appears to have been primitively associated with one of the three major sense organs—nose, eye, and ear—, although these relationships may be much altered in advanced types. In the brain, as in the cord, the primitive structure was one in which the gray cellular matter lay internally, adjacent to the liquid-filled central canal—here much expanded. In certain areas in each major brain segment, however, complex superficial areas of gray matter have developed to form important centers of nervous activity. Much of the hindbrain is formed by the medulla oblongata, basically similar to the spinal cord in nature. Above the anterior end of the medulla is found an expanded outgrowth of gray matter—the cerebellum, a major center for coordination and regulation of motor activities and posture. The midbrain is in mammals a short and relatively insignificant brain region. In lower vertebrates, however, its roof—or tectum—was an important area of gray matter which was primarily associated with sight but, more than this, wielded a major influence on body activities. In reptiles and birds the tectum is still of importance, but is rivaled by the cerebral hemispheres, to which almost all of its original functions have been transferred in mammals.

The primitive forebrain appears to have been merely an anterior unpaired terminal segment of the neural tube, which persists in all vertebrates at the diencephalon, mainly utilized in advanced forms as a relay station to and from the cerebral hemispheres. These last structures began early in vertebrate history as paired outpocketings of the primitive forebrain concerned merely with reception of olfactory sensations. The rise of the hemispheres, or cerebrum, to a dominating position in the brain of higher vertebrates is one of the most spectacular stories in comparative anatomy. Internal masses of gray matter—the striate bodies (or basal nuclei) early began to function as centers for correlation. Still more important, however, has been the trend for the development of superficial sheets of gray matter on the surface of the hemispheres, as a pallium or cortex. Most highly developed of these surface areas is the neopallium (or neocortex), present to some extent in reptiles, and in mammals constituting the greater part of the surface of the hemispheres. Of complex structure and often (as in man) deeply infolded, with a consequent increase in area, the neopallium is the seat of all the mammal's higher brain activities.

Typical spinal nerves in higher vertebrates have two roots, a ventral motor root whose fibers arise from cells within the cord, and a sensory dorsal root, the nerve cells of which are contained in a ganglion on the root. In 1895, O.S. Strong pointed out that a clear distinction could be made among the elements of both sensory and motor nerves, between somatic components, associated with the "outer tube" of the body, and visceral ones, associated with the gut and its outgrowths. This distinction has been of aid in tracing the evolution of both spinal nerves and the complex cranial nerve system. Although in mammals all, or nearly all, motor elements of spinal nerves leave the cord through the ventral root, emergence of visceral motor fibers through the dorsal root becomes common as we descend the scale, and it is not improbable that in the ancestral vertebrate segments of the spinal cord produced, on either side, two discrete nerves, a dorsal one including both sensory types plus visceral motor fibers, and a ventral one which contained only somatic motor elements. This concept is of aid in unraveling the complexities of the cranial nerves. Apart from special sensory nerves serving nose, eye, and ear, cranial nerves appear to be of two types: nerves corresponding to primitive dorsal root nerves in the cord, and potentially including motor elements to the striated visceral muscles of head and throat as well as sensory fibers, and ventral nerves supplying muscles of a somatic nature. The visceral motor elements supplying smooth musculature and glands in the gut and other areas are termed the autonomic system. They are of considerable functional interest, and are morphologically distinctive in that the fibers of two successive nerve cells are required to carry the impulse from cord to end organ. Their phylogenetic history is still incompletely known; the evidence suggests that in the vertebrate ancestor the gut was more or less autonomous and that increasing control of the gut by the central nervous system has come about through gradual development of the autonomic system.

ALFRED S. ROMER, *Harvard University*
Author of "The Vertebrate Body"
and "Vertebrate Paleontology"

Bibliography: Anderson, D. T., ed., *Invertebrate Zoology* (Oxford 1998); Butler, Ann B., and William Hodos, *Comparative Vertebrate Neuroanatomy: Evolution and Adaptation* (Wiley-Liss 1996); Kent, George C., and Robert K. Carr, *Comparative Anatomy of the Vertebrates,* 9th ed. (McGraw-Hill 2001); Moore, Janet, *An Introduction to the Invertebrates* (Cambridge 2001).

ANATOMY, Human. See HUMAN BODY.

ANATOMY OF MELANCHOLY, ə-nat′ə-mē, mel′-ən-kol-ē, Robert Burton's enormous and delightfully digressive treatise on melancholy. It was first published in 1621, under the pen name "Democritus Junior." It is the most comprehensive handling of a subject that permeated a large portion of English Renaissance literature. Burton believed the disease to be especially symptomatic of his own 17th century England. He thought he was afflicted with it personally, and he undertook this exhaustive analysis of its causes, symptoms, and cures as a purgative measure.

An Oxford divine all his life, Burton displayed his erudition in the book with a huge number of references to and quotations from classical, medieval, and contemporary works. He is probably the greatest borrower in all literature, mining every possible source for corroboration and illustration. Consequently, his work presents an extraordinary parade of melancholic humanity from all stations, lands, and ages, and it shows concretely the dispersal of the malady through all time and place.

As his title suggests, Burton divided his subject into innumerable categories: a long introduction is followed by three main partitions, each with sections, members, and subsections. The first main division is concerned with causes, and the second with treatments. The third is a vast collection of sacred and profane love stories illustrative of religious and amatory melancholy. Such careful categorization is paradoxical in light of Burton's wandering, discursive, and highly allusive style, part Latin, part English. But instruction, not beauty, was his goal, and he called his manner "a rhapsody of rags gathered together from several dung-hills . . . confusedly tumbled out without art." Despite the disorder, his prose is uniquely alive because of the curious juxtaposition of racy and scholarly vocabulary, and the pell-mell rush through time and space, from allusion to allusion and from tale to tale.

The work attained immediate popularity and continued to be popular throughout the 17th century. It fell into a decline during the next hundred years, but by the 19th century the vogue of antiquarianism resurrected it. A product of the first modern age of doubt and introspection, *The Anatomy of Melancholy* has attracted renewed interest since Freud because of its discussion of the pervasiveness of psychological disorders.

MYRNA KANNER JACKSON
University of Pennsylvania

Bibliography
Babb, Lawrence, *A Sanity in Bedlam* (1959; reprint, Greenwood Press 1977).
Burton, Robert, *Burton the Anatomist* (1925; reprint, Folcroft 1976).
Craig, Hardin, *The Enchanted Glass* (1952; reprint, Greenwood Press 1975).
Evans, Bergen, and Mohr, George, *The Psychiatry of Robert Burton* (1944; reprint, Hippocrene Bks. 1972).
Mueller, William, *Anatomy of Robert Burton's England* (Folcroft 1952).
O'Connell, Michael, *Robert Burton* (G. K. Hall 1986).

ANAWRATHA, an-ə-rath′ə, (r. 1044–1077), ruler who united Burma politically for the first time. After becoming king of Pagan in 1044, he annexed most of what is now Burma, including northern Arakan and Lower Burma, which was the home of the Mon people. The Mon religion of Theravada Buddhism became central to Anawratha's court and an important unifying force in Burmese life.

ANAXAGORAS (c. 500 B.C.–c. 428 B.C.), an-ak-sag′ə-rəs, Greek philosopher. Born at Clazomenae, Ionia, in Asia Minor, he was the first philosopher to teach at Athens, where he settled about 480 or 465 B.C. Among his pupils were Pericles, Euripides, and possibly Socrates. Pericles' political enemies indicted Anaxagoras for impiety, and, though acquitted, Anaxagoras felt compelled to go to Lampsacus, in the Troas, where he continued to teach and where he died.

Anaxagoras explained his philosophy in a treatise *Peri physeos* (*On Nature*), of which some 20 fragments from possibly 3 books remain. He was dissatisfied with the systems of his predecessors among the Ionian philosophers, who had endeavored to explain the various phenomena of nature by regarding matter in its several forms and modifications as the cause of all things. Anaxagoras conceived the need of seeking a higher cause, independent of matter, and found it in *nous*, that is, mind or intelligence. It was *nous*, he held, not blind forces, that acted upon matter, caused motion and change, and produced the rationally ordered cosmos that is evident from the universe's design, order, and harmony. To Anaxagoras *nous* was nonmaterial and incorporeal. Essentially the ground of motion, it was a world-forming, but not a world-creating, intelligence, since *nous* and matter coexist.

To the theory of the *nous* Anaxagoras owes his importance in the history of philosophy. For the first time in Western thought a definite distinction between the corporeal and the incorporeal, mind and matter, was drawn. It is also to his credit that he introduced into philosophy the idea of teleology, which explains the ends of things, to oppose his predecessors' theory of mechanism, which explains things by their causes. But it is in the development of these two antitheses—matter and mind, mechanism and teleology—that the defects of Anaxagoras' speculation appear. His separation of mind and matter ends in irreconcilable dualism, since he believed that both matter and mind coexist from creation as equally underived principles: he failed either to derive mind from matter (monistic materialism) or matter from mind (monistic idealism). His teleology becomes only a new theory of mechanism, since *nous* is only another piece of mechanism to account for the initial impulse to motion: thereafter the process of motion proceeds by itself. But Anaxagoras paved the path for Plato and Aristotle, who developed his principle of teleology and made it the central idea of their own philosophical systems.

P.R. COLEMAN-NORTON
Princeton University

Further Reading: Afnan, Ruhi, *Zoroaster's Influence on Anaxagoras, the Greek Tragedians and Socrates* (Philosophical Lib. 1969); Schofield, M., *An Essay on Anaxagoras* (Cambridge 1980); Stokes, Michael C., *One and Many in Presocratic Philosophy* (1971; reprint, Univ. Press of Am. 1986); Teodorsson, Swen-Tage, *Anaxagoras' Theory of Matter* (Humanities Press 1982).

ANAXIMANDER, ə-nak′sə-man-dər (610?–?546 B.C.), Greek philosopher and astronomer, who wrote the first prose philosophical treatise in Greek. He was born at Miletus, Ionia, in Asia Minor. He set forth his philosophical principles in a work whose title has been lost and of which only a few fragments are extant. He believed that the origin of all things was formless, illimitable, immortal matter, which he called "the boundless" (*to apeiron* in Greek). The bound-

ANCESTRAL SPIRITS are represented by a masked dancer in a village of the Ivory Coast, in West Africa.

MARC & EVELYNE BERNHEIM FROM RAPHO GUILLUMETTE

less contained the four contrary elements—earth, air, fire, and water. From these elements, by a vague process of union and disunion, innumerable worlds were created, developed, and destroyed in an endless periodic revolution. This theory was a forerunner of rational mechanistic philosophy.

Anaximander is credited with making the first geographical map, discovering the obliquity of the ecliptic (see ECLIPTIC), and introducing the gnomon or style, a rod placed upright on a horizontal plane and used as a sundial or to determine solstices and equinoxes.

As a result of Anaximander's astronomical observations he concluded that the universe is spherical with the earth as its center.

ANAXIMENES OF MILETUS, an-ak-sim′-ə-nēs, mī-lē′təs, was a Greek philosopher of the 6th century B.C. He was born at Miletus, Ionia, in Asia Minor.

Anaximenes believed that air was the first principle of the universe. Air, according to him, stretched through infinite space and by its eternal motion eventually produced the cosmos by two opposite processes: rarefaction and condensation. By rarefaction, air grew hot and became fire, which was borne upward to form the sun, moon, stars, comets, and planets. By condensation, air grew cold and became successively wind, clouds, water, earth, and stone. Thus all finite things, Anaximenes reasoned, owed their origin to a material cause and their development to physical law.

P.R. COLEMAN-NORTON, *Princeton University*

ANCESTOR WORSHIP, an′ses-tər wûr′shəp, is a form of religion emphasizing the influence of deceased kindred on the living. It is not a complete religious system in itself but one phrasing of relations beyond human control, and thus but a facet of religious expression. Among some peoples it has formed an appreciable core of their beliefs and practices, as in China, tropical Africa, Malaysia, and Polynesia. Some aspects of religion among ancient Egyptians, Romans, and ancient Hebrews—involving a more or less reverential regard for the dead—have been mistakenly described as ancestor worship. As a cult it is by no means universal nor even widespread among primitive peoples.

Ancestor worship is based on a variety of mingled motives: continuity with the past; respect for the wisdom of elders; a desire for the blessing that may be given by the dead, who are endowed with knowledge and power beyond human experience; a desire to assuage grief and to tend the dead by offerings and prayers for their wellbeing; and fear of ghostly visitors and their possible vengeful acts. The two principal ideas are (1) that "those who have gone before" have a continuing and beneficent interest in the affairs of the living; and (2) more widespread, uneasiness or fear of the dead, with practices to placate them. But the latter motive gave rise more frequently to simple routine acts to drain off emotion—or to magic—than to rites of worship.

The 19th century anthropological theorists (Edward Burnett Tylor, Herbert Spencer, Frank Byron Jevons) saw ancestor worship as a first inchoate religion (not as one phase). They assumed the inability of savages to comprehend the unseen: the dead as something unnatural and uncanny were feared and conciliated. It is now known that primitives commonly make a distinction between the dead in general—who as the unknown might be feared—and their own departed kinsmen, who are commonly thought of as reciprocating their affection. Further, ghosts are ordinarily not ancestral dead, but impersonal and unidentified, and hence unpredictable, inimical, or malignant. Such practices as ridding houses of the spirits of the dead or foiling ghosts are common, but they are magical acts rather than rites of worship and reverence.

The religious attitudes of primitives toward their ancestors vary widely. In Polynesia, where social rank depends on nearness of descent from the gods and their successors the ancestors, the attitude is one of reverence and expectation of help and guidance, but does not involve much worship. In Malaysia, family rites were addressed to dead kindred who were thought to be ever present nearby and ever concerned that traditional life should be preserved unchanged. Among Pueblo Indians, the dead were thought to become one with their mythical forebears, the kachinas; ceremonials, involving masked impersonation of the kachinas, were prayers to "the departed" to bless with rain, fertility, and happiness.

Ancestral cults are common to most of tropical Africa. Here family includes not only the living but ancestors as well; living elders have control of their juniors as the forebears had of them. The major theme of these cults is concern with the continuity of family ties. In Dahomey (West Africa) ancestral spirits are of three ranks: the spirit founders of clans, those who died before genealogical records began, and the known dead. At intervals the recent dead are established among the ancestors by a rite. Annually there is worship with dancing, when distinguished ancestral spirits "alight" on the heads of men to possess them spiritually. Each clan has a mythical pair of founders, whose son, as oldest of ancestors, stands as absolute ruler of all family ancestral spirits. The actual clan head (the oldest man) derives his absolutism from his association with the ancestral spirits, whose power he can invoke to enforce his decrees.

In China, emphasis is also on continuity of family and reverence for the wisdom of elders. The worship is very ancient (dating from before 1000 B.C.). It is essentially a family affair, involving prayer and offerings before tablets in the home and in ancestral temples. It is accompanied by an elaborate system of burial and mourning, the visiting of graves as a mark of deep respect, and a horror of trespassing on or despoiling a grave. Ethically, among the Chinese, the primary virtue is filial piety—an obligation to serve and honor the parents without any sense of fear or gain, which results in strong social solidarity of the family. The state worship of Confucius, with which this is involved, is an extension of this reverence for the wisdom of the elders, a mark of respect and honor for a great teacher rather than attributing to him power over human affairs. Today, however, there is evidence that these attitudes are no longer so prevalent among the Chinese, especially on the Communist mainland.

In the Japanese form of family worship the concept of duty to elders and ancestors—fostered by the government—is modified by reciprocal obligations of parents to children.

India's many religions are marked by respect and veneration of the past, but not of the forebears, with practice rarely warranting characterization as ancestor worship.

Ancient Egypt had an impressive cult of the dead but little trace of ancestor worship. The Egyptians believed that at death the soul could live on if the body was preserved, joining the king of the dead, Osiris, in everlasting happiness. The ordinary man did not venerate his ancestors, but he often commemorated their names.

In ancient Rome, what ancestor worship existed was a private family, not public, affair. The dead joined the *manes,* the good household gods, "visiting" the family and thus gaining immortality by "reliving" on earth. As visitors they were greeted and propitiated but with no great sense that their influence on mortals was important.

LESLIE SPIER, *University of New Mexico*

Bibliography

Antonaccio, Carla Maria, *An Archaeology of Ancestors: Tomb Cult and Hero Cult in Early Greece* (Rowman 1995).

Janelli, Roger L., *Ancestor Worship and Korean Society* (Stanford Univ. Press 1982).

Martin, Emily, *The Cult of the Dead in a Chinese Village* (Stanford Univ. Press 1973).

McAnany, Patricia Ann, *Living with the Ancestors: Kinship and Kingship in Ancient Maya Society* (Univ. of Texas Press 1995).

Smith, Robert J., *Ancestor Worship in Contemporary Japan* (Stanford Univ. Press 1974).

ANCHISES, an-kī′sēz, in Greek legend, was a hero of Troy. A handsome youth, he was loved by the goddess Aphrodite (Venus) who, disguised as a shepherdess, bore him a son, Aeneas. When Troy was burned by the Greeks, Aeneas carried the aged Anchises on his shoulders to safety and brought him to Sicily. Their voyage is described in Virgil's *Aeneid.*

ANCHOR, ang′kər, is a heavy implement that is dropped to the sea bottom to keep a ship or boat from drifting. It is attached to a line or chain cable and is carried on deck or stowed in a suitable receptacle so that it can be used quickly. When dropped, the anchor provides holding power either by digging into the sea bottom or by sheer weight.

History. The earliest anchors were probably heavy stones tied to ropes. In Egyptian tombs, ship models have been found with grooved or perforated anchor stones, some of which are shaped like a T. Crooked stocks or wooden frames weighted with stones (killicks) have been used for centuries.

It is believed that iron anchors were first forged about 575 A.D. in England. By 1600, iron anchors had a long shank (vertical bar), two sharply pointed straight arms at right angles to the shank, a large wooden stock (crosspiece) for turning the arms in a soft ocean floor, and an iron ring for attaching the mooring cable. This design was a forerunner of the all-iron Admiralty

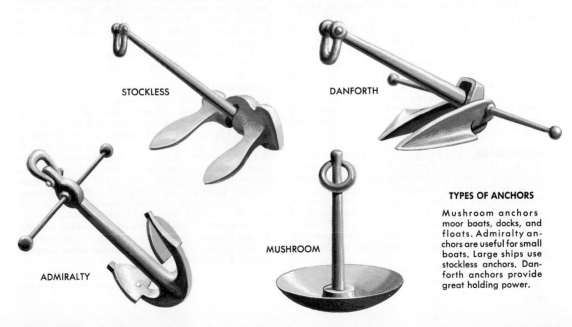

STOCKLESS

DANFORTH

ADMIRALTY

MUSHROOM

TYPES OF ANCHORS

Mushroom anchors moor boats, docks, and floats. Admiralty anchors are useful for small boats. Large ships use stockless anchors. Danforth anchors provide great holding power.

The business district of Anchorage, Alaska, with the snow-capped Chugach Mountains in the background.

anchor, which had curved arms with pointed flukes (flattened ends of the arms), a shank, a stock, and a ring. By 1852 the Admiralty anchor had gained wide acceptance by the British navy. The folding-fluke anchor was introduced in England in 1818, and the folding-fluke, stockless anchor was patented before 1840. The mushroom anchor appeared in use in 1859.

Modern Anchors. The Admiralty anchor, although no longer used on large ships, is still in use for small boats. It has great holding power in a soft bottom, but it is awkward to handle, and one fluke always projects above the sea bottom where it may foul the anchor cable. The folding-fluke, stockless anchor is used by large ships and naval vessels. It can be stowed compactly, and both flukes dig into the sea bottom, minimizing the risk of fouling the cable. This type of anchor is often carried in an opening in the bow called a hawsehole. The mushroom anchor continues to be useful for small craft. It is particularly effective in soft, muddy bottoms. Modern anchors usually are made of cast or forged steel rather than iron.

Newer anchor designs include the Danforth and Northill anchors. Tests have shown that these types have a much greater ratio of holding power to anchor weight than the older types. These newer anchors are used for sailboats, small powerboats, and large cabin cruisers. However, the selection of an anchor depends on many factors, including the type of boat, the size and weight of the boat, the type of bottom, and wind and weather conditions.

ANCHORAGE, ang'kər-ij, is the largest city in Alaska. It is situated at the head of Cook Inlet, 275 miles (442 km) by air south of Fairbanks. It is an important transportation center and a trading center for the farming, oil, and mining areas of the Matanuska Valley to the northeast and the Kenai Peninsula to the southwest. Oil is increasingly important to the city's economy. Drilling from platforms is carried on in Cook Inlet.

Anchorage is a year-round seaport, equipped to handle oil shipments. Its airport—one of the busiest in the United States—is a regular stop on transpolar flights from Scandinavia to Japan and on the route from Seattle to Tokyo. Anchorage is headquarters for the Alaska Railroad, and modern highways connect it with the Kenai Peninsula and the Richardson and Alaska highways.

Tourism is becoming increasingly important to Anchorage. Winter sports attract visitors to the Alyeska ski area, 38 miles (61.1 km) from the city, where the 1963 National Alpine ski championships were held. A highlight of the annual Fur Rendezvous, a fur buyers' market held every February in Anchorage, is the championship dog-sled race. The average temperature at Anchorage ranges from $-36°$ F ($-37.7°$ C) in winter to $86°$ F ($30°$ C) in summer. The annual rainfall averages a little over 14 inches (35.5 cm), and the snowfall averages 60 inches (152.4 cm).

Cook Inlet is named for the English navigator Capt. James Cook, who discovered it in 1778. The city was founded in 1915 as the headquarters of the Alaska Railroad, then under construction. Anchorage was incorporated in 1920. It grew rapidly during World War II when it served as headquarters for the U.S. Army's Alaska Defense Command. Elmendorf Field, the present Air Force base, and Fort Richardson were then built.

On March 27, 1964 Anchorage was struck by one of the most devastating earthquakes ever experienced in North America. Within five minutes, the city suffered municipal damage of $19 million and private property damage of $67 million. Nine persons were killed and hundreds injured. Thirty blocks of houses and commercial buildings were destroyed or severely damaged. But within two years new construction and repairs gave Anchorage even more dwellings than before the earthquake, and a $17 million urban renewal program was begun for the downtown area. The airport was modernized and enlarged, and the seaport developed for year-round use.

Educational institutions in Anchorage include Alaska Pacific University and the University of Alaska at Anchorage. Government is by council-mayor. Population: 260,283.

PHYLLIS D. CARLSON
Z. J. Loussac Public Library

ANCHORITE, ang'kə-rīt, is a holy person who retires from the world to live a solitary life of prayer and contemplation. The term is derived from the Greek *anachoreo*, "I withdraw," and is analogous to the Latin *eremita*, "hermit." Anchorites (women, anchoresses) were numerous in the early Christian Church. They lived apart from human habitation, taking shelter in caves or huts, and subsisting on such food as they could forage. Most followed a definite rule of religious life and attracted numerous disciples.

The most notable of the early anchorites was St. Anthony of Egypt (c.250–356), who drew so many followers that his cell became the nucleus of monastic life. Although anchorites, as such, disappeared from the life of the church, their way of life is incorporated in the hermitic orders of St. Augustine (Carthusians, Camaldolese). Perhaps the oddest anchorite was St. Simeon Stylites, who lived on top of a pillar. See also HERMIT.

ANCHOVY, an'chō-vē, a family of small, herringlike fish. They are common along the western coast of Europe, in the Mediterranean, in the waters near China, along the western coast of North America, and in some South American streams.

Anchovies range from 4 to 6 inches (10 to 15 cm) in length. Their bodies are slender and small and usually are silvery with a light stripe along the sides. The fish has a long mouth cleft, an underslung jaw, and small teeth. In some rare species, the body is wide in front, tapering to a small rounded tail.

Anchovies run in large schools both inshore and offshore. They usually inhabit temperate or warm salt waters, but some larger ones may go into deeper, cooler, offshore waters, and a few are found in fresh waters. They are flesh-eating fish and are themselves the prey of seabirds. They are used commercially as food and as bait.

The anchovy family, Engraulidae, includes several genera and many species.

ANCHUSA, ang-kū'sə, a genus of hardy annual or perennial herbs, comprising about 30 species native to Europe, the Middle East, and Africa. It commonly grows in clumps of coarse, hairy foliage, with tubular or funnel-shaped blue, purple, white, or yellow flowers in panicles or clusters. Anchusa is a member of the Buglossum family. It is also called bugloss or alkanet, and is an excellent plant for garden cultivation.

ANCONA, äng-kō'nä, in Italy, is an important port on the Adriatic Sea. It is the capital of Ancona province and the chief city of The Marches. Its site, 132 miles (212 km) northeast of Rome, is an amphitheater between two headlands. At the entrance to its ancient harbor is a triumphal arch designed by the Greek architect Apollodorus about 115 A.D. Nearby is a modern arch designed by Luigi Vanvitelli in the 1700's.

Ancona's chief industries, besides shipping, are shipbuilding, sugar refining, and the manufacture of silk, paper, and sailcloth. Important buildings include the Romanesque and Byzantine Cathedral of St. Cyriacus, dating from the 11th and 12th centuries, a 13th century town hall, and a museum. Ancona is believed to have been founded about 392 B.C. by Greeks fleeing from the persecutions of the Elder Dionysius in Syracuse. Population: 100,507 (2001 census).

ANCRE, äN'krə, **Marquis d'** (died 1617), Italian adventurer. He was born *Concino Concini* in Florence. Little is known of his life before 1600, when he went to France as part of the entourage of Marie de Médicis, who had just married King Henry IV of France. Concini married Leonora Galigai, the queen's companion since childhood. The Concinis sided with Marie in her frequent quarrels with Henry and became a powerful influence on the queen. After Henry's assassination in 1610, Marie assumed the regency for their young son, Louis XIII, but the Concinis became the dominant power in France.

Unfortunately for France, the Concinis were more interested in advancing themselves than in pursuing Henry's vigorous policies. A few months after the death of the king, Concini purchased the marquisate of Ancre (now Albert) in Picardy, which gave him his title, and began to dissipate the treasury left by Henry IV. Concini took over as governor of Amiens and Normandy, became marshal of France in 1614, and was, in effect, prime minister. He bought off a league of nobles, which Henri de Condé had formed against him, by loading the malcontents with money and honors (Treaty of Loudun, May 3, 1616). Condé's hatred soon revived, however, and Concini, on the advice of his protégé, the bishop of Luçon (later Cardinal Richelieu), had Condé imprisoned in 1616. A Paris mob sacked the Concini residence, and Louis XIII ordered Concini arrested. Concini resisted and was killed in Paris on April 24, 1617. His wife, accused of sorcery, was beheaded and burned in the same year.

ANCUS MARCIUS, ang'kəs mär'shəs, the legendary fourth king of early Rome (supposedly reigned 642–617 B.C.), is said to have been the grandson of Numa Pompilius, the second king. According to tradition, he established the plebeian class by bringing to Rome the conquered populations of many towns in Latium. He also reputedly founded Ostia, built a bridge across the Tiber, and fortified the Janiculum. Most likely, he was a historical figure during whose lifetime Rome expanded.

ANCYRANUM, Monumentum, an-sī'rə-nəm, an inscription written by Emperor Augustus (63 B.C.–14 A.D.) and engraved on columns before his mausoleum. It is known also as the *Res gestae divi Augusti.* The original no longer survives, but a copy in Latin and Greek was discovered at Ancyra (modern Ankara) in Asia Minor. The inscription contains Augustus' account of his accomplishments and of the history of his reign. He depicts himself, somewhat falsely, as a constitutional ruler in the tradition of the Roman republic.

ARTHER FERRILL, *University of Washington*

ANDALUSIA, an-də-lōō'zhə, a city in southern Alabama, situated 85 miles (137 km) by road south of Montgomery. The seat of Covington county, it is a trading and processing center for a farming and lumbering region. Its industries make cotton, peanut, meat, and wood products. Although Andalusia was the site of an early Spanish settlement, the present community dates from 1836. It was incorporated in 1888. Before the development of rail and highway networks, the nearby Conecuh River was used as a commercial artery by flatboats. Andalusia is governed by a mayor and council. Population: 8,794.

ANDALUSIA, an-də-loo′zhə, is the southernmost region of Spain. The Spanish form of the name is *Andalucía.* The region, which has an area of 33,675 square miles, is bounded on the south by the Mediterranean Sea, the Strait of Gibraltar, and the Atlantic Ocean. On the west is Portugal; on the north and east are the old provinces of Estremadura, New Castile, and Murcia. Andalusia was a province of Spain until 1833, when it was divided into eight modern provinces, named for their capital cities: Almería, Cádiz, Córdoba, Granada, Huelva, Jaén, Málaga, and Seville. The region is celebrated for its fertility, picturesque beauty, and the architectural remains of Moorish civilization.

Physical Features. In northern Andalusia, running through the northern sections of Jaén, Córdoba, Seville, and Huelva, are the mountains of the Sierra Morena, which have rich deposits of mineral wealth, particularly copper, iron, manganese, nickel, and coal. Another mountainous section, in the southeast, follows the Mediterranean coast through Almería, Granada, Málaga, and Cádiz. Many summits of these southern ranges, which include the Sierra Nevada, are covered with perpetual snow—such as Mulhacén, the highest point in Spain, rising 11,420 feet, and Veleta, 11,168 feet.

Between these mountains in the southeast and the Sierra Morena lies the heart of Andalusia, a fertile plain watered by the Guadalquivir River and its tributaries. This river rises in eastern Jaén in the Sierra de Cazorla and flows southwestward through Upper Andalusia, a region consisting mainly of arid tracts, lying at elevations of from 650 to 1,500 feet. After receiving the waters of the Guadalimar, the Guadalquivir flows into Lower Andalusia, which is known as the "granary of Spain." In this lower course the river receives the flows of the Guadiato, Genil, and Huelva, and the land is generally well watered and fertile, particularly in the vicinities of Córdoba and Seville. South of Seville, the river passes through the extensive marshy area of Las Marismas and empties into the Atlantic Ocean at Sanlúcar de Barrameda. Large vessels can ascend the Guadalquivir as far as Seville.

Economy. Traditionally an agricultural area, Andalusia's main farm products are wheat, barley, olives, tomatoes, grapes, and many other fruits, honey, and silk. A large portion of the soil is in pasture. Andalusia is famous for its horses, and its bulls are sought for bull-fighting throughout Spain. Sheep are raised in great numbers and bear an abundance of good but not fine wool. The chief manufactures are woolens, silk, leather, cork, and the celebrated sherry, the production of which centers around Jerez de la Frontera in Cádiz province. Along the Atlantic and Mediterranean coasts, sardine and tunny fishing are widespread.

Moorish Influences and Language. The settlement of the Moors in Andalusia from the 8th to 13th centuries (at Granada until 1492) left a permanent imprint on the region. The mosque-cathedral at Córdoba, the Alcazar and Giralda at Seville, and the Alhambra at Granada all bear witness to the splendor of the Moorish civilization at its height in the 10th to 12th centuries. The popular language spoken in Andalusia contains a greater admixture of Arabic words than is common elsewhere in Spain. Many Andalusian geographic names begin with *al* (Arabic, "the") or *guad* (from Arabic *wadi,* meaning "river").

Another peculiarity of Andalusian popular speech is the pronunciation of *z,* and of *c* before *e* or *i,* as *s,* whereas in Castilian Spanish these consonants approximate the English *th.* Since Seville and Cádiz were the centers through which trade and emigration were funneled to the Spanish colonies in America, the Spanish spoken in Latin America generally follows the Andalusian *s* rather than the Castilian *th.*

History. Andalusia was known as *Tartessus* in ancient times and probably was the place called *Tarshish* in the Bible. It was colonized by Phoenicians (who founded Cádiz in the 9th century B.C.) and by Greeks and was made subject to Carthage in the 3d century B.C. Under the Romans, who conquered Andalusia between 210 and 206 B.C., it developed a flourishing civilization. It was the birthplace of the emperors Trajan and Theodosius I and of the writers Lucan and Seneca.

In the 5th century A.D. the region came into the possession first of the Vandals and then of the Visigoths. The name "Andalusia" is thought to have arisen either from *Vandalusia,* land of the Vandals, or from *al-Andalus,* the term used by Arab geographers for Andalusia and for the Iberian peninsula.

The Arabs invaded the region in 711, and Andalusia was included in the independent Umayyad caliphate of Spain from the time of its establishment by Abd ar-Rahman III in 929 until its disintegration a century later. Separate petty emirates were set up at Córdoba, Málaga, Algeciras, and Granada, but the region was again made subject to centralized control through a second invasion from Africa, by the Berber Almoravid dynasty (1086–1147), and again by a third invasion, that of the Berber Almohads (1147–1212).

This Moorish period was the golden age of Andalusia, not even equaled during the prosperous 16th and 17th centuries when Seville and Cádiz held monopolies of the trade with the Americas. Under the Arabs, Córdoba, Granada, and Seville became centers of Muslim culture, commerce, and industry. Córdoba, in particular, under Abd ar-Rahman III and his successors, became "the Athens of the West," the seat of the arts and sciences. When the Dark Ages spread over Europe, Andalusia was perhaps the brightest spot on the Continent. But the annihilation of Almohad power by the Christian kings at the Battle of Las Navas de Tolosa (1212) left only local dynasties incapable of unified resistance, although the last Moorish stronghold, at Granada, held out until 1492.

The period of conquest and colonization in the New World channeled great wealth into Andalusia, but this prosperity did not long survive the loss by Cádiz and Seville of their trade monopolies in the 17th century. Increased mining activity in the late 19th century and the redevelopment of Seville as a modern port benefited some but not all Andalusians.

During the Spanish Civil War of 1936–1939, Cádiz and Seville were Nationalist strongholds from the beginning, while the east remained for the most part Republican. Málaga fell to the Nationalists in February 1937, and Almería was severely damaged by shells from German warships in May of that year.

In the 1960s the Andalusian seacoast, the Costa del Sol, with its pleasant resorts and its cultural and architectural variety, developed into one of the leading tourist attractions of Spain. Population: 7,357,558 (2001 census).

ANDALUSITE, an-də-lōō'sĭt, is an aluminum silicate mineral, so named because it was first discovered in Andalusia, a region of Spain. Andalusite usually occurs in coarse, nearly square crystals that have a glassy luster and vary greatly in color and degree of transparency. They may be white, pinkish, brown, or gray. Transparent crystals, sometimes used as gems, are reddish or greenish; some specimens change from one color to the other according to the angle at which they are viewed. A variety of andalusite known as *chiastolite* contains carbon particles within the crystals, distributed so as to give the appearance of a cross when the crystal is viewed in cross section. Andalusite is used in porcelains that require high heat resistance. It is most commonly found in metamorphic rocks, and occurs in many parts of Europe. Specimens also occur in the Brazilian state of Minas Gerais and, in the United States, in California, South Dakota, Pennsylvania, and New England.

Composition: Al_2SiO_5; hardness, 7.5; specific gravity, 3.16–3.20; crystal system, orthorhombic.

ANDAMAN AND NICOBAR ISLANDS, an'də-mən, nik'ə-bär, two neighboring groups of islands in the eastern Bay of Bengal, forming one of the union territories of India. The Andaman group has a population of 241,453 and the Nicobars, about 39,208. The islands are administered by the chief commissioner of the Andaman and Nicobar Islands. Port Blair (1991 population, 74,955) in the Andamans, the only town of any size in the territory, is the administrative center. The islands are connected with mainland India by air and shipping services.

There are over 200 islands and islets, some uninhabited, in the Andaman and Nicobar groups, and they form a sweeping arc 600 miles (966 km) long. The total land area is 3,215 square miles (8,327 sq km). The Andaman group to the north is separated from the Nicobars by the Ten Degree Channel, a 90-mile (145-km) stretch of water. The islands have forest-covered interior hills and highly indented shores fringed with palms or mangroves. The highest elevation is Saddle Peak (2,402 feet; 732 meters) on North Andaman Island.

Temperatures are always warm and sometimes hot, and rainfall is heavy, totaling 120 inches (305 cm) annually. Although substantial rainfall occurs every month, the rainiest months are between May and October, during the monsoon.

People. The population of the islands consists of people of foreign origin and aborigines. The majority of the nonaborigines are in the Andamans. Until about 1952 these consisted almost entirely of convicts, their descendants, and administrative personnel of the British penal settlement established here in 1858. Between 1952 and 1962, however, immigration of mainland Indians more than doubled the population.

The Andaman aborigines are a truly primitive people, essentially of the Stone Age. They are believed to be survivals of the Negrito race, perhaps the earliest inhabitants of Southeast Asia. They consist of four groups—the Andamanese proper, the Onges, the Jarawas, and the Sentinelese. The total aboriginal population, now estimated to be about 1,000, has apparently declined.

The Andamanese proper, once the most numerous group, are now almost extinct, having been decimated by measles, syphilis, and other diseases introduced from abroad. The other groups,

by remaining remote and hostile, have saved themselves from this fate. The people are of small stature, and their skin is smooth, satiny, and very black. Their traditional mode of living is hunting, fishing, and food gathering. The diet consists of fruits, seeds, roots, fish, shellfish, wild pig, turtle, and honey. The Onges and Jarawas live in villages from which they make periodic fishing and hunting excursions, but the Andamanese are nomadic, moving between customary camps where they make temporary shelters.

Most of the people living in the Nicobars are aborigines. Unlike the Andaman peoples, the Nicobarese have flourished, their population increasing from some 6,500 in 1901 to about 14,500 in 1961. They are physically and culturally a different people from the Andaman islanders. Their language belongs to the Mon-Khmer family and is not related to the Andaman tongues. They have a lighter, reddish brown skin, and they are slightly taller and heavier. Unlike the Andaman peoples, the Nicobarese are cultivators, specializing in coconut. Pigs, fowl, and fish are also eaten. Villages consist of up to 50 or more thatched houses in a circle around an open communal area. The Nicobarese are good sailors and travel by canoe over open water, using the stars and winds for navigation.

Economy. The Andaman aborigines have been largely self-sufficient, without additional benefits from trade. The Nicobarese, however, have long exchanged their coconuts and such minor products as turtle shell and edible birds' nests for cloth, tobacco, and iron.

Since the early 1950s the economy has expanded as a result of a plan to settle farm families from mainland India in the Andamans and by the development of the islands under India's five-year plans. Many refugees from Bangladesh added to the workforce. Agriculture, especially rice growing in the Andamans, is being expanded, and there have been improvements in the areas of communications and manufacturing. Employment opportunities expanded with the development of banks, bureaucracies, schools, and hotels. Port Blair has a government dockyard. Coconut palms have been introduced into the Andamans, despite the fact that they are not native, and there is a coconut-oil factory on South Andaman Island. Native timber has long been exploited in the Andamans.

History. Documented contact by Europeans dates from the 17th century in the Nicobars and from the late 18th century in the Andamans. A series of evangelizing and colonizing efforts were made in the Nicobars by the French, Austrians, and especially the Danes between 1648 and 1848, but they all failed. A British penal colony was set up in the Andamans in 1789 but was discontinued after seven years. The British again occupied the Andamans in 1858 in an effort to stop piracies and to establish a penal settlement for rebels taken in the Indian (Sepoy) Mutiny of 1857. The British took formal possession of the Nicobars in 1869, and in 1872 the Andamans and Nicobars became a single administration.

The islands remained in British hands until 1942, when they were occupied for three years by Japanese forces. At the close of World War II the penal settlement was abolished. In 1947 the islands passed to India when the country became independent. Population: 280,661 (1991 census).

JOEL M. ANDRESS
Central Washington State College

ANDANTE, än-dän-tā, is a musical direction that usually indicates a moderate but still flowing pace. It is quicker than *larghetto* and slower than *allegretto*. The word is the participle of the Italian verb *andare* (to go). The meaning of *andante* is modified when it is coupled with other terms. *Andante un poco allegretto* adds "a little bit lively" to *andante; andante con moto* adds "with movement." Both are faster than *andante* alone. *Andante sostenuto* implies a more sustained, slower tempo.

Andantino, the diminutive form of the word, has given rise to considerable confusion. Because it means "rather slow," it originally was taken to indicate a slower pace than *andante.* Many composers, however, use the term to indicate a rate somewhat faster. A famous example of the subjective and inexact nature of the *andante* tempo indications occurs in Mendelssohn's oratorio *Elijah.* Three movements of the oratorio bear identical metronome tempos, but are marked, respectively, *andante con moto, andante,* and *andantino.* In such cases, only instinct and good taste can guide the interpreter.

SHIRLEY FLEMING, *"Musical America"*

ANDERS, än'dərs, **Władysław** (1892–1970), Polish general, who commanded Polish troops with the Allied armies in North Africa and Italy in World War II. He was born in Blonie, Poland. In World War I he was a cavalry officer in the Russian army. He served against the Soviets in the Polish-Russian War of 1919–1920 and was made a general in the Polish army in 1936.

With the outbreak of World War II, he fought against the Germans and then against the Soviets, who had invaded eastern Poland. Captured by the Soviets, he was released in 1941 to lead the Polish contingent formed to fight against Germany. He saw action at Tobruk in North Africa in 1942 and commanded the 2d Polish corps in Italy in 1944–1945. His troops took the stronghold of Monte Cassino in May 1944. Toward the end of the war he became acting commander in chief of the Polish forces in the West. Refusing to recognize the Polish Communist government, he was deprived of Polish citizenship and lived in exile in England. He died in London on May 12, 1970.

ANDERSEN, än'ər-sən, **Hans Christian** (1805–1875), Danish writer of fairy tales. His many stories have been translated into most major languages and are popular with children and adults throughout the world.

Early Life and Education. Andersen was born in the slums of Odense, Denmark, on April 2, 1805. His father, a poor shoemaker, was literate; his mother, however, was uneducated and superstitious. Andersen, a highly emotional, imaginative child, with a forceful ambition to become famous, received little formal education, and was hopelessly poor at spelling. His father died in 1816. At the age of 14, young Andersen went to Copenhagen with the vague hope of becoming a singer, a dancer, or an actor. After many disappointments and much hardship, he succeeded in becoming associated with the Royal Theater in Copenhagen, but he had to leave the theater when his voice began to change.

Andersen then began to write plays, all of which were rejected by the Royal Theater. However, in 1822, with the help of Jonas Collin, one of the theater's directors and an influential

HANS CHRISTIAN ANDERSEN statue in Central Park is beloved by the small children of New York City.

government official, Andersen received a grant that allowed him to enter the grammar school at Slagelse. He lived in the home of the school headmaster, a malicious bully, and suffered unspeakably. In 1827, Collin took him out of the school and arranged private tuition for him. Soon after, Andersen gained admission to Copenhagen University, where he completed his education.

Literary Career. In 1827, Andersen's first poem, *The Dying Child,* was published in a Copenhagen journal. In succeeding years he also wrote impressionistic prose arabesques, plays, poems, and novels. A visit to Germany in 1831 inspired the first of his many travel sketches. He later wrote sketches about Sweden, Spain, Italy, Portugal, and the Middle East.

Andersen used Italy as the setting for his first novel, *The Improvisatore,* published in 1835. The book became a success throughout Europe, and during his life it remained the most widely read of all his novels, which included *O.T.* (1836), *Only a Fiddler* (1837), *The Two Baronesses* (1848), *To Be or Not to Be* (1857), and *Lucky Peer* (1870). His travel books include *A Poet's Bazaar* (1842), *In Spain* (1863), and *A Visit to Portugal* (1866).

Andersen's fame, however, rests on his *Fairy Tales and Stories,* written between 1835 and 1872. The first four of these tales, which numbered 168 in all, were *The Tinderbox, The Princess and the Pea, Little Claus and Big Claus,* and *Little Ida's Flowers.* Later well-known tales include *The Emperor's New Clothes, The Ugly Duckling, The Little Mermaid, The Nightingale, The Snow Queen, The Story of a Mother,* and *The Swineherd.*

Profoundly self-centered, Andersen wrote and rewrote his memoirs, the standard edition of which is generally considered to be *The Fairy Tale of My Life* (1855). Additional information about his life is available in his many published letters; some have been translated into English. Andersen died in Copenhagen on Aug. 4, 1875.

ELIAS L. BREDSDORFF
Author of "Hans Christian Andersen"

Further Reading: Bredsdorff, Elias L., *Hans Christian Andersen* (Scribner 1975); Lederer, Wolfgang, *The Kiss of the Snow Queen: Hans Christian Andersen and Man's Redemption by Woman,* ed. by Alan Dundes (Univ. of Calif. Press 1986); Marker, Frederick J., *Hans Christian Andersen and the Romantic Theatre* (Books on Demand 1974); Spink, R., *Hans Christian Andersen: The Man and His Work* (A. Vanous 1981).

ANDERSON, Alexander (1775–1870), American engraver. The son of a printer, he was born in New York City on April 21, 1775. He was interested in engraving from boyhood, and, entirely self-taught, he made the first wood engravings in the United States in 1794. His work included illustrations for Noah Webster's *Elementary Spelling Book*, Thomas Bewick's *Birds*, and Sir Charles Bell's *Anatomy*. He died in Jersey City, N.J., on Jan. 17, 1870.

ANDERSON, Carl David (1905–1991), American physicist who received the 1936 Nobel Prize in physics for his discovery of the positron. Anderson's most famous work began in 1930 when he was studying cosmic rays under the direction of R.A. Millikan, who had received a Nobel Prize in 1923 for his precise determination of the charge of the electron (normally a negatively charged particle).

In 1928, P.A.M. Dirac developed a mathematical theory of elementary particles that implied the existence of positively charged electrons. On Aug. 2, 1932, Anderson observed, almost by chance, the track of a curious particle in a cloud chamber. The particle behaved like a normal electron in every respect but one—the direction of its motion was opposite to that of usual electrons, indicating positive charge. Unaware of Dirac's theory of the positron, Anderson at first did further experiments to see if the particle might be a proton, the only positively charged nuclear particle then widely known. He found that the density of the particle was too small for it to be a proton. Anderson, who had subsequently learned of Dirac's theory, then concluded that the particle was a positron. His brilliant experimental analysis provided persuasive confirmation of Dirac's theory.

The discovery of the positron, along with Sir James Chadwick's confirmation of the existence of the neutron in 1932, opened the way to the more sophisticated analysis of atomic structure and to the discovery of further subatomic particles, two developments that have characterized the subsequent history of nuclear physics. The discovery of positively charged electrons also laid the groundwork for the formulation of one of the basic principles of modern physics, the law of charge conjugation symmetry. (For every charged particle, there is a corresponding particle with an opposite electric charge.)

Positrons collide with electrons shortly after creation and disappear in a burst of radiation. Shortly after detecting positrons and their mode of destruction, Anderson studied their mode of creation. He found that just as positrons and electrons conjoin to produce energy, so does energy, in the form of *gamma* radiation, occasionally change into matter, producing an electron and a positron. See also ANTIMATTER.

During 1936–1938, Anderson discovered the existence of mesons in cosmic rays. Mesons are subatomic particles intermediate in mass between the electron and the proton. During World War II he devoted himself to research questions related to national defense.

Anderson was born in New York City on Sept. 3, 1905. After receiving B.S. and Ph.D. degrees at the California Institute of Technology, he joined the faculty of the institute in 1930 and was made full professor of physics in 1939. He died on Jan. 11, 1991, in San Marino, Calif.

L. L. LAUDAN, *University College London*

ANDERSON, Clinton Presba (1895–1975), American political leader. He was born at Centerville, S.Dak., on Oct. 23, 1895, the son of a Swedish immigrant farmer. In 1918, following an attack of tuberculosis, he abandoned studies at the University of Michigan and moved to Albuquerque, N.M. There, after four years of newspaper work and recurrent illness, he became an insurance agent.

Anderson held appointive offices in New Mexico in the 1930's and entered the U.S. Congress as a Democrat from that state in 1941. Despite an independent voting record, he earned the trust of congressional leaders. As chairman of the Campaign Expenditures Committee in 1944, he uncovered evidence incriminating patrons of both major parties. His investigation of food shortages and black markets at the end of World War II impressed President Truman, who named him secretary of agriculture in 1945. He resigned that post in 1948 to seek election to the U.S. Senate from New Mexico.

From 1949 to 1973, Anderson was an influential member of the Senate and a leader in shaping the nation's aeronautical and space programs. In 1959, while chairman of the Joint Committee on Atomic Energy, he led a successful fight to defeat the nomination of Lewis Strauss, former chairman of the Atomic Energy Commission, for secretary of commerce. Anderson regarded him as too conservative. He also prevented the Navy from retiring Adm. Hyman Rickover, the controversial developer of the atomic submarine. Anderson died in Albuquerque on Nov. 11, 1975.

ANDERSON, Edwin Hatfield (1861–1947), American librarian, who for many years directed the New York Public Library. Born at Zionsville, Ind., on Sept. 27, 1861, he graduated from Wabash College in 1883 and studied at the New York State Library School in Albany in 1890–1891. In 1892 he became librarian of the Carnegie Free Library, Braddock, Pa. In 1895 he organized the Carnegie Free Library of Pittsburgh, Pa., and this institution, which he directed for nine years, became a model library.

In 1906 he became director of the New York State Library and Library School. He was appointed assistant director of the New York Public Library in New York City in 1908 and served as director from 1913 until his retirement in 1934. In 1926 he played a major role in organizing the Columbia University School of Library Service. He died at Evanston, Ill., on April 29, 1947.

ANDERSON, Eugenie Moore, (1909–1997), American diplomat, the first woman to achieve the rank of U.S. ambassador. Helen Eugenie Moore was born in Adair, Iowa, on May 26, 1909. While studying at Carleton College she married John Pierce Anderson, an art student from Red Wing, Minn.

Before World War II, Eugenie Anderson studied international relations and worked in the League of Women Voters and Minnesota state Democratic politics. Immediately after the war she helped effect a fusion of the state Democratic and Farmer-Labor parties. In 1948 she campaigned for President Truman and Hubert Humphrey, Minnesota's Democratic candidate for the Senate.

Anderson served as ambassador to Denmark in 1949–1953, as minister to Bulgaria in 1962–1964, and as a U.S. representative on the UN Trusteeship Council after 1965. She died in Red Wing, Minn., on March 31, 1997.

ANDERSON, an′dər-sən, **John Bayard** (1922–), U.S. congressman and candidate for president in the election of 1980. The son of a Swedish immigrant, he was born in Rockford, Ill., on Feb. 15, 1922. He received his B.A. and J.D. degrees from the University of Illinois and his LL.M. from Harvard. After admission to the Illinois bar in 1946 he practiced law in Rockford until 1952, when he entered the U.S. foreign service and served in West Berlin as adviser to the U.S. high commissioner for Germany from 1952 to 1955. He began his political career in 1956 with election as state's attorney. In 1960 he was elected a Republican congressman.

Anderson's early years in Congress found him espousing traditional Republican principles, but within a decade he had become more liberal in his support of social-welfare programs. In 1968 he succeeded Melvin Laird as chairman of the House Republican Conference.

Conservative in economic matters and liberal in social-welfare legislation, he became an outspoken supporter of civil-rights measures, elimination of waste in national defense, nuclear-arms limitation, and gun-control legislation.

On June 8, 1979, Anderson announced his candidacy for the Republican presidential nomination in 1980, but following six primary losses he withdrew from the race on April 24, 1980. Instead he announced his candidacy as an independent and selected Patrick J. Lucey, a Democrat, as his running mate. Although Anderson's National Unity campaign won no electoral votes in the election of Nov. 4, 1980, he emerged with about 7% of the popular vote.

ANDERSON, an′dər-sən, **Judith** (1898–1992), Australian actress whose depictions of both modern and classical roles, most calling for sustained and disciplined dramatic intensity, were milestones in 20th-century theater. Her portrayals of Lady Macbeth, in London in 1937 and in New York in 1941, and of the title role in Robinson Jeffers's *Medea* in 1947 were particularly memorable.

She was born in Adelaide, Australia, on Feb. 10, 1898. Going to the United States in 1918, she scored her first major New York success in *Cobra* in 1924. She had leading roles in *Strange Interlude* (1928), *Mourning Becomes Electra* (1932), *Come of Age* (1934), *The Old Maid* (1935), *Hamlet* (1936), *The Tower beyond Tragedy* (1939), *The Three Sisters* (1942), and *In the Summer House* (1953).

On-screen she is best remembered as Mrs. Danvers, the icily sinister housekeeper in *Rebecca* (1940). Her film career also included appearances in *Blood Money* (1933), *King's Row* (1942), *Laura* (1944), *The Ten Commandments* (1956), *Cat on a Hot Tin Roof* (1958), and *A Man Called Horse* (1970). She starred on television in *Macbeth* (1960) and *The Chinese Prime Minister* (1974), and she appeared in *Santa Barbara* (1984–1987), the daytime soap opera. She was named a Dame Commander of the British Empire in 1960. Anderson died in Santa Barbara, Calif., on Jan. 3, 1992.

ANDERSON, an′dər-sən, **Leroy** (1908–1975), American composer and conductor who became a highly successful composer of popular music. He was born in Cambridge, Mass., on June 29, 1908, and received his first music lessons from his mother, a church organist. He graduated from Harvard University in 1929 and received an M.A. degree in music there in 1930. He studied Scandinavian languages at Harvard from 1930 to 1934, during which period he was director of the Harvard University band and active as a church organist and choir director in Milton, Mass.

In 1935 Anderson decided to devote his time exclusively to music, starting out as a freelance arranger, composer, and conductor. In 1936 he began making orchestral arrangements for the Boston Pops Orchestra, and from then until 1950 he continued arranging for the orchestra.

Anderson's orchestrations have been praised for their perceptiveness, balance, humor, and fancy. Among his most popular works are *Sleigh Ride*, *Blue Tango* (the first purely instrumental composition to top the hit parade), *The Syncopated Clock*, *Fiddle-Faddle*, *Bugler's Holiday*, *The Typewriter*, and *Serenata*. Other compositions include *Jazz Pizzicato*, *Irish Suite*, and *A Suite of Carols*. He died in Woodbury, Conn., on May 18, 1975.

ANDERSON, Marian, an′dər-sən (1897–1993), American singer who was the first African American soloist to appear with the Metropolitan Opera in New York City. Anderson's deep, rich-textured contralto had a versatility that ranged from the direct simplicity of African American spirituals to the dramatic grandeur of opera. It prompted Toscanini to remark that "a voice like hers comes only once in a century."

Anderson was born on Feb. 27, 1897, in Philadelphia, Pa., where she sang in church choirs and studied voice under Giuseppe Boghetti. In 1925, after winning a competition against 300 other singers, she appeared with the New York Philharmonic. Subsequent engagements at home were few, so in 1930 she went to Europe to study and perform. From 1933 to 1935 she gave a series of acclaimed concerts abroad. Her reputation firmly established, she returned to the United States, where she gave a New York recital in December 1935, followed by a national tour.

In 1939 Anderson became the subject of a nationwide controversy. Because of her race the Daughters of the American Revolution (DAR) refused her the use of its Constitution Hall for a concert in Washington, D.C. Eleanor Roosevelt resigned from the DAR and helped sponsor a concert for Anderson at the Lincoln Memorial, where she sang for 75,000 (millions more listened over the radio).

In 1955 Anderson made her debut with the Metropolitan Opera as Ulrica in Verdi's *Un Ballo in maschera*. She resumed her concert career in 1957, singing around the world, and gave her last recital in 1965 at Carnegie Hall. She was an alternate U.S. delegate to the 13th General Assembly of the United Nations and was much honored with degrees and awards, including the Presidential Medal of Freedom (1963) and the National Medal of Art (1986). Her autobiography, *My Lord, What a Morning*, was published in 1956. She died in Portland, Oreg., on April 8, 1993.

ANDERSON, an′dər-sən, **Mary Antoinette** (1859–1940), American actress who was noted for her flexible voice and extraordinary beauty. Anderson was born in Sacramento, Calif., on July 28, 1859, and was educated in Louisville, Ky. She made her theatrical debut in Louisville at the age of 16 as Juliet in Shakespeare's *Romeo and Juliet*. Her first New York appearance was in 1877, after which she made several successful tours of the United States as the star of her own company.

During the mid-1880's, she played in London and at Stratford-on-Avon, where she portrayed the Shakespearean heroines Rosalind in *As You Like It,* Hermione and Perdita in *A Winter's Tale,* and Lady Macbeth. Sir William S. Gilbert wrote the play *Comedy and Tragedy* for her.

In 1889, when she was not yet 30, she suffered a nervous collapse during a performance in Washington, D. C., and retired from the stage. She later married Antonio F. de Navarro, an American lawyer, and the couple settled in England. She wrote two books of reminiscences, *A Few Memories* (1896) and *A Few More Memories* (1936), and with Robert Hichens dramatized his novel *The Garden of Allah.* She died at Worcestershire, England, on May 29, 1940.

ANDERSON, an′dər-sən, **Maxwell** (1888–1959), American playwright. His dramas, written in both verse and prose, touched on universal social questions, including the disillusionment of men in war, injustice, and political corruption.

He was born at Atlantic, Pa., on Dec. 15, 1888, the son of a Baptist minister. During his childhood his family moved to the Midwest, where he attended 11 different schools before entering the University of North Dakota in 1907. In college he became interested in drama and poetry. After graduating in 1911, he moved to San Francisco, where he taught high school and earned an M. A. degree at Stanford University in 1914. He then became a journalist and in 1918 moved to New York City, where he wrote for the *New Republic,* the *New York Globe,* and the *New York World.*

In 1923, with the help of Laurence Stallings, drama critic on the *World,* Anderson's *White Desert* was produced on Broadway. This effort, in verse, was a failure. Anderson and Stallings then collaborated on *What Price Glory?* (1924), a verse drama debunking war. The play was an immediate success, and Anderson thereafter devoted his full time to playwriting.

Anderson's prose comedy about marriage, *Saturday's Children* (1927), enjoyed moderate success. This was followed by the successful historical verse drama, *Elizabeth the Queen,* produced in 1930. In 1933, Anderson won the Pulitzer Prize for his prose play *Both Your Houses,* a satire on political corruption in Congress.

Winterset (1935) is generally regarded as Anderson's most successful tragedy in verse form. Based on the Sacco-Vanzetti case, it won the first New York Drama Critics Circle Award. Anderson won the same award for his comedy *High Tor* (1937), written in a combination of blank verse and colloquial prose. In 1938 he collaborated with composer Kurt Weill in the highly successful musical comedy *Knickerbocker Holiday.*

Several of Anderson's later plays deal with war themes. *Key Largo* (1939) is a verse play about an American fighting in the Spanish Civil War. *The Eve of St. Mark* (1942) and *Storm Operation* (1944) have World War II settings. His later plays on historical themes included *Joan of Lorraine* (1947), about Joan of Arc, and *Anne of the Thousand Days* (1948), about Anne Boleyn. He also wrote a number of television plays. He died in Stamford, Conn., on Feb. 28, 1959. See also WHAT PRICE GLORY?; WINTERSET.

A collection of the playwright's letters, edited by Laurence Avery, was published in 1977 as *Dramatist in America: Letters of Maxwell Anderson, 1912–1958.*

ANDERSON, an′dər-sən, **Robert** (1805–1871), American army officer, who defended Fort Sumter in the first engagement of the Civil War. He was born near Louisville, Ky., on June 14, 1805, graduated from West Point, and was wounded in the Mexican War. In 1860, when South Carolina was threatening to secede from the Union, Anderson was named commander of the U. S. troops in Charleston harbor, based at Fort Moultrie. He received no reinforcements, and on Christmas Day, five days after South Carolina seceded, he moved his garrison to Fort Sumter, a stronger post. When the U. S. government at last dispatched help, the Confederates considered it an act of war, and on April 12–13, 1861, they bombarded the fort for 33 hours. Anderson's men were weak from lack of food, and he surrendered the fort but was not taken prisoner. On April 14, 1865, after the war ended, he raised over Fort Sumter's ruins the same flag he had lowered in 1861. He died at Nice, France, on Oct. 26, 1871.

ANDERSON, an′dər-sən, **Robert Bernerd** (1910–1989), American public official. He was born at Burleson, Texas, on June 4, 1910. In 1932 he received his law degree at the University of Texas and was elected to the Texas state legislature. He was appointed assistant attorney general for Texas in 1933 and state tax commissioner in 1934. He was in business privately during the 1940's. In 1953 he was appointed secretary of the navy by President Dwight D. Eisenhower, and in 1954 secretary of defense. He resigned in 1955 to return to business.

On July 29, 1957, Anderson succeeded George M. Humphrey as secretary of the treasury. He retained this post until Jan. 15, 1961. He came to be considered one of the most influential members of the cabinet and the man chiefly responsible for the fiscal conservatism of the second Eisenhower administration.

Anderson was convicted of tax fraud in 1987 and served a brief prison term. He was disbarred in January 1988. He died in New York City on Aug. 14, 1989.

ANDERSON, an′dər-sən, **Sherwood** (1876–1941), American writer, whose naturalistic novels and short stories portray life in the small towns of Midwestern America. He is best known for *Winesburg, Ohio* (1919), a series of interrelated short stories depicting the "lives of quiet desperation" led by the inhabitants of such a town.

He was born at Camden, Ohio, on Sept. 13, 1876, the son of an itinerant saddle and harness maker. Most of his childhood was spent in Clyde, Ohio. His schooling was scattered and irregular, and he worked at various jobs to help support his family. When he was 17, he enlisted in the Army and served in Cuba in the Spanish-American War. After the war he became manager of a paint factory in Elyria, Ohio. Dissatisfied with this life, he walked out of the factory one day, determined to pursue a more meaningful life.

Anderson moved to Chicago, where he found work as an advertising copywriter. He lived with his brother Karl, who later became a well-known painter. Through his brother he met some of the members of the rising "Chicago group" of authors including Floyd Dell, Carl Sandburg, and Theodore Dreiser, who encouraged him to write. His first book, *Windy McPherson's Son,* was published in 1916. This novel, like many of his works, is heavily autobiographical, giving an account of one man's escape from the stifling effect of small-town life and commercial success. It was followed by *Marching Men* (1917), set in the coal-mining region of Pennsylvania, and then by *Mid-American Chants* (1918), a series of prose poems.

In 1919, *Winesburg, Ohio* was published, winning Anderson wide critical acclaim. In it he established his dominant theme—the conflict between the instinctive forces of human nature and the inhibiting effects of a narrowly conventional industrial society. See the article WINESBURG, OHIO.

Anderson moved to New York in 1921 and began contributing to periodicals. He visited Europe the same year and came under the influence of Gertrude Stein. In 1922 he returned to the United States, settling briefly in New Orleans, where he established the *Double Dealer,* one of the early "little" magazines. It was in the *Double Dealer* that William Faulkner was first published, and a close friendship grew up between the two writers. In 1925, Anderson bought a farm in Grayson County, Va., and began editing two weekly papers in the nearby town of Marion, Va. He died on March 8, 1941, while on a South American cruise.

Anderson's other works include *Poor White* (1920), *The Triumph of the Egg* (1921), *A Story Teller's Story* (1924), *Dark Laughter* (1925), *Tar* (1927), *Hello Towns* (1929), *Perhaps Women* (1931), *Puzzled America* (1935), and *Memoirs* (1942).

ANDERSON, an'dər-sən, in Indiana, is the seat of Madison County and a commercial and industrial city on the west fork of the White River, 35 miles (56 km) northeast of Indianapolis. Its manufacturing plants produce automotive ignition and lighting equipment, automotive regulators and pumps, fire trucks, recreation equipment, wall and floor tile, files and rasps, packaging machinery, corrugated paper boxes, mattresses, and meat products. Anderson is a trading and shipping point for a rich farming area.

The city is the home of Anderson College, founded by the Church of God, which has its national headquarters in Anderson. Mounds State Park, just east of the city, contains the largest human-made prehistoric earthwork discovered in Indiana, as well as several other mounds dating to prehistory.

Platted in 1823 by John Berry, on the site of a Delaware Indian village, the community was named *Andersontown* after a Delaware chief, Kikthawenund, whose English name was Chief Anderson. The town was incorporated in 1838, and in 1844 the name was changed to Anderson. Incorporation as a city followed in 1865.

Anderson's importance as a manufacturing center dates from 1887. It was at this time that natural gas was discovered in the region. The automobile parts industry started up and aided the city's later growth.

During the 1960s the city annexed the greater part of Anderson Township. Anderson has a mayor-council form of government. Population: 59,734.

ETHEL W. ALBRIGHT
Anderson Carnegie Public Library

ANDERSON, an'dər-sən, a city in South Carolina, is a textile-manufacturing center. The seat of Anderson County, it is situated on the Piedmont plateau in the northwestern part of the state, about midway between Atlanta, Ga., and Charlotte, N.C. Anderson manufactures clothing, cotton cloth, rayon fabrics, textile machinery, fiber glass, and fishing tackle. The surrounding agricultural area produces dairy and beef cattle.

Anderson College (a junior college) and Forest College (business) are located in the city. At Clemson University, 15 miles northwest of Anderson, stands Fort Hill, the home of John C. Calhoun. Between Anderson and Clemson, at La France, is one of the earliest cotton mills in the South, built in 1838 and still operating.

Anderson was founded in 1826 and was incorporated in 1828. It was named for Gen. Robert Anderson, a hero of the Revolutionary War. The community sometimes is called the "Electric City" because it was among the first in the South to be supplied with as much hydroelectric power as it could use. The first hydroelectric plant in the area was built in 1894 at High Shoals, on the Rocky River. In 1963, Hartwell Dam, more than 15,000 feet (4,500 meters) wide, was completed on the Savannah River about 20 miles (30 km) southwest of Anderson. The dam supplies power, and its reservoir, Lake Hartwell, has become a recreational area, with facilities for boating, fishing, and other water sports. Population: 25,514.

SARAH C. SMITH
Anderson County Librarian

ANDERSONVILLE PRISON, an'dər-sən-vil, was a Confederate stockade for Union prisoners in the American Civil War. It was situated at Andersonville, Ga., about 10 miles northeast of Americus, and was in use from February 1864 until April 1865. The prison was an open enclosure of 27 acres surrounded by a wall of 20-foot pine logs. There was a hospital but no barracks. The prisoners lived in tents without floors, or in crude huts. Designed to hold 10,000 men, it confined 33,000 at one time. The total number imprisoned there was 49,485, all of them privates.

Overcrowding, exposure, impure water, absence of sanitation, and shortage of food and medicines caused the deaths of more than 13,700 men in 13 months. At one time the death rate was 150 a day. An investigating medical commission appointed by the Confederate War Department in the spring of 1864 recommended the removal of the majority of the prisoners, and by October all but 4,000 had been transferred to camps at Florence, S.C., and Millen, Ga., where conditions were less harsh. The prison superintendent, Capt. Henry Wirz, was convicted by a United States military court of murder and was hanged in November 1865.

The graves of the prison dead now constitute a national cemetery. The prison site, with adjoining land that enlarges it to 84 acres, is a park maintained by the government of the United States.

ANDERSSON, än'dərs-sôn, **Karl Johan** (1827–1867), Swedish explorer. He was born in Värmland, Sweden. Andersson explored southwestern Africa with Francis Galton and in 1854 went alone to Lake Ngami. In 1859 he penetrated to the Okavango River. He died on July 5, 1867, in Ovamboland, South West Africa, on an expedition to the Cunene River. He wrote *Lake Ngami, or Discoveries in South Africa* (1856), *The Okavango River* (1861), and *Notes of Travel in South Africa.*

THE MASSIVE ANDES, one of the world's longest mountain systems, is topped by Aconcagua in Argentina.

ANDES

ANDES, an'dĕz, one of the world's longest and highest mountain systems, extending more than 4,000 miles (6,437 km) along the Caribbean and Pacific coasts of South America. These mountains cover parts of Venezuela, Colombia, Ecuador, Peru, Bolivia, Chile, and Argentina. Including the valleys and plateaus which they enclose, they constitute the most densely populated and economically valuable parts of several of those countries.

North of Venezuela the Andes are connected under the Caribbean Sea with the mountain arc of the West Indies (Antilles). Through spurs reaching from Colombia into Panama they are joined to the mountain systems of Central America and Mexico, which continue as the Rocky Mountains of North America. In the extreme south the Andes disappear beneath Drake Passage south of Tierra del Fuego and reemerge under other names in the Antarctic Peninsula. East of the Andes are the Orinoco Llanos (tropical grasslands), the Amazon and tributary lowlands, the Paraná plains, and the Patagonian plateau. In places the mountains are separated from the Pacific Ocean, on the west, by coastal ranges. In Chile, where these low coastal mountains are fairly continuous, a structural valley sets them apart from the true Andes; in Peru and Ecuador, the coastal ranges give way to Andean spurs of an east-west trend, which in turn are replaced by coastal ranges in Colombia.

Aconcagua, 22,834 feet (6,960 meters) high, in Argentina near the border of Chile, is the highest peak in the Andes, but nine others reach 22,000 feet (6,706 meters), and more than a dozen touch altitudes of 20,000 feet (6,096 meters). Only Asian mountains reach greater heights. On other continents, only Mt. McKinley in Alaska is as high as 20,000 feet.

HIGHEST PEAKS OF THE ANDES

Peak	Country	Height feet	meters
Aconcagua	Argentina	22,834	6,960
Bonete	Argentina	22,546	6,872
Ojos del Salado	Argentina-Chile	22,539	6,870
Tupungato	Argentina-Chile	22,310	6,800
Pissis	Argentina	22,241	6,779
Mercedario	Argentina	22,211	6,770
Huascarán	Peru	22,205	6,768
Tocorpuri	Bolivia-Chile	22,162	6,755
Llullaillaco (volcano)	Argentina-Chile	22,057	6,723
El Libertador (Cachi)	Argentina	22,047	6,720

Passes as well as peaks are lofty. From the southern border of Ecuador to Uspallata Pass, east of Valparaíso, Chile, the lowest of the east-west crossings exceeds 10,000 feet (3,048 meters). Not only do mountains and mountain passes rise high above sea level, but the ocean is very deep within a short distance of the Andes' western border. In some places, mountain heights of 15,000 feet (4,572 meters) and ocean depths of 20,000 feet (6,096 meters) are separated from one another by no more than 100 airline miles (161 km). This contrast suggests faulting of immense proportions. (A fault is a fracture of the rock strata along which there has been a significant displacement, either vertical or horizontal.) Moreover, because of the Andes, the continental divide is located very near the Pacific Ocean, with the result that the drainage of the bulk of the continent is to the Atlantic. No other continent shows such a large proportion of its area drained to one side of the land mass. Although Andean peaks are higher than the highest in North America, the widest Andean section—400 miles (644 km), in Bolivia—is not nearly so wide as the broad mountain and plateau region of the western United States.

The Andes present formidable transportation barriers, which have isolated the people. Among the obstacles to transportation by road, rail, and even airplane are great heights, steep slopes, low temperatures and low pressures in the high altitudes, treacherous air currents that result from the rugged terrain, and permanent snowfields, with lower limits at about 17,000 feet (5,182 meters) in Peru and approximately 2,300 feet (701 meters) in Tierra del Fuego. In Peru, to reach the Cerro de Pasco copper region at 15,000 feet (4,572 meters), the highest standard-gauge railroad in the world passes through 65 tunnels, runs over 67 bridges, and swings around 16 switchbacks. The rail lines from Pacific ports to Quito (Ecuador) and La Paz (Bolivia) reach elevations of over 11,000 feet (3,353 meters).

More than 400 years after the Spanish conquest of the Incas, who inhabited the central Andes, only a small part of the Andean population has become an active part of the modern world. There is little doubt that the Andes barrier can be blamed for much of this lack of progress.

On the other hand, the location of a large

Caribbean Sea · ATLANTIC OCEAN
Caracas
VENEZUELA
GUYANA · SURI-NAM · FR.GUIANA
PANAMA
Tolima · Bogotá
COLOMBIA
Amazon River
Quito
ECUADOR · Iquitos
B R A Z I L
Huascarán
Cerro de Pasco
Lima · PERU · Lake Titicaca
El Misti · BOLIVIA
La Paz
Arequipa · Sucre
PACIFIC OCEAN · PARAGUAY
Chuquicamata
Antofagasta · Asunción
Llullaillaco
Bonete · URU-GUAY
Aconcagua
Valparaíso · Buenos Aires
Santiago
ARGENTINA
CHILE
Miles
0   200   800
0   400   1200
Kilometers
Tierra del Fuego

MAP BY DONALD T. PITCHER

part of the Andean highlands in tropical latitudes makes living conditions at moderate altitudes more comfortable than in the hot insect-infested lowlands of the Amazon basin lying to the east. Largely as a result of this situation, population in the Andes is far greater than in the wet lowland plains. In rural sections of the central Andes, Indians cultivate crops and graze livestock at high as well as at medium altitudes. They grow potatoes at altitudes up to 12,000 feet (3,658 meters), raise barley in places as high as 14,000 feet (4,267 meters), and graze livestock up to the snow line. In the northern Andes, mestizos (people of mixed race) and Indians grow coffee, a commercial crop, at lower elevations, and they also practice subsistence agriculture there and at higher altitudes. Few people, however, live at either moderate or high altitudes of the southern Andes.

Although subsistence agriculture is the major activity of most Andean people, mineral products account for the bulk of the foreign trade. These metallic deposits became a part of the Andes during the long periods of geologic time involved in mountain formation.

Geology. The geology of the Andes is extremely complex. The mountains are not one continuous chain but are made up of several structural units joined more or less closely together. In general, folded and faulted structures dominate, but active volcanoes occur in four distinct areas—in southern and central Peru; in southern

Chile; along the border of Bolivia and Chile; and in Ecuador and southern Colombia. Extinct volcanoes are widespread.

While there is no complete agreement concerning the evolution of the Andes, many geologists agree upon most of the following stages. In the Paleozoic Era, which began about 600 million years ago, the Andes region comprised a subsiding trough in which thick deposits of Silurian shale and Carboniferous limestone were deposited. During the Mesozoic Era, starting about 225 million years ago, thick layers of limestone and sandstone were laid down. In the late Cretaceous period of Mesozoic time, the mountains experienced uplift, folding, and thrusting over nearly the entire length of the South American continent. With the coming of the Cenozoic (present) Era, about 70 million years ago, erosion resulted in extensive peneplanation or leveling, at least in the central Andes. In later Cenozoic time, uplift occurred again, causing a general elevation of the erosional surface to heights of between 3,000 and 7,000 feet (914–2,134 meters). This highland was in turn eroded and then reelevated during the Pliocene and early Pleistocene epochs, not more than about 10 million years ago.

Today, dissected erosion surfaces of the old peneplain reach an average elevation of approximately 12,000 feet (3,658 meters), although local elevations may range from 6,000 to 15,000 feet (1,829–4,572 meters). This ancient surface is well preserved in the high plains of Bolivia, where great lava flows and lofty volcanic cones have been superimposed upon it. Mountain growth seems in process now, if the frequent earthquakes that occur are good evidence of such movement.

While mountain growth still may be proceeding, both water and ice are actively engaged in tearing down. Erosive agencies have not, however, shaped the Andes into the gentle, rounded, and mature forms characteristic of the highlands of eastern Brazil and the Appalachians of the eastern United States, both of which are geologically older. Glaciation, now present in the southern Andes and in the high altitudes of the central and northern Andes, was more widespread and more significant as an agent of erosion during Pleistocene time.

Economic Potential and Development. The extraction of minerals is the major commercial activity of the Andean countries, with the exception of Colombia, Ecuador, and Argentina. Folding, faulting, and volcanic action—all mountain-building processes—have encouraged heavy metal-bearing molten materials to rise from the earth's interior toward the upper part of the crust, thus making them more easily available to man. Moreover, erosive activities of streams and glaciers have aided the miner by removing some or all of the rock layers that covered the metals after their upward movement toward the earth's surface.

Andean mines provided the Inca civilization with metals for tools of bronze and copper and with gold and silver for ornaments for social and religious purposes. Today, however, the extraction of Andean gold and silver is of slight commercial importance compared with the production of such metals as copper and tin. Present operations are centered largely in three main areas: central Peru; the Cordillera Oriental (Eastern Cordillera) of Bolivia; and the Cordillera Occidental (Western Cordillera), east of the nitrate zone of northern Chile.

Most Andean mining is carried on by large

ROCK FAULTING, like this vertical fracture in a Bolivian range, is typical of Andes mountain structure.

state-owned or private corporations, which are able to cope with serious problems of transport, equipment, labor, food supplies, and power. In a few cases, coal for use as fuel is found near the metallic workings—at Cerro de Pasco in Peru, for example; but in most Andean mining regions, coal is either limited or lacking, just as it is throughout all of South America. Moreover, most copper and tin mines, as well as those of other metals, lie either above the tree line or at lower elevations in deserts, where little wood is available. On many mining projects, laborers have to be brought in from more populous districts.

The Andes contribute many essential materials to the world's economy. Bolivian tin accounts for about 70 percent of that country's exports, and other minerals in the past have brought the total to 90 percent. Tin dominates Bolivian production, but significant amounts of silver, copper, tungsten, antimony, lead, and zinc also are produced, as well as some bismuth. Mines at Corocoro supply copper; those near Oruro, Potosí, and Uncía contribute tin, silver, and other metals.

The open-pit copper mines of Chuquicamata, Chile, are known throughout the world. Together with the workings at El Teniente and Potrerillos, they account for the leadership of Chile in the production of copper among all the South American countries. Nitrates are not mined in the Andes, but workings lie close to the mountains. Little mining development takes place in the Andean region of Argentina, although a variety of minerals may be present.

Peru ranks high in world production of silver, bismuth, and vanadium and also ships significant quantities of copper from Cerro de Pasco. In this area the mines, at elevations over 15,000 feet (4,572 meters), are the highest in the world where large-scale operations take place. Significant amounts of vanadium are taken from the Mina Ragra region near Cerro de Pasco.

Although metallic minerals are found in the Andes of Colombia, Ecuador, and Venezuela, petroleum is of greatest importance to these countries. In Venezuela, oil flows from the Maracaibo depression between the two great branches of the Cordillera Oriental, which divides near the boundary between Colombia and Venezuela. In Colombia, oil occurs in the Magdalena Valley, lying between the Cordillera Central and the Cordillera

Oriental. This petroleum contributes more to the nation's economy than the unique emerald deposits at Muzo, not far from Bogotá. In Ecuador, oil occurs in the Santa Elena peninsula. Explorations have convinced some geologists that rich petroleum deposits lie in the foothill country of the eastern Andes along the entire length of South America.

Andean mineral resources have contributed much to the region's commerce in the past, are of great significance to the present economy, and promise well for the commercial future. The development of other commercial resources ranks far below them. For example, tropical forest products on the eastern mountain slopes of Ecuador, Peru, and Bolivia may receive greater attention in the future, but isolation from both home and world markets is a serious handicap. Middle-latitude forest products of the Chilean Andes' western slopes already contribute to the nation's economy but do not compare with the value of Andean minerals. Finally, commercial farming operations are of minor importance except for coffee, in the northern Andes, and pyrethrum, which is becoming important in Ecuador.

Climate. The Andes form one of the greatest meteorological barriers in the world. Because they stand in the path of prevailing winds, the cordillera is watered in some sections on the east, in other sections on the west. In most sections the ranges exhibit opposite extremes on eastern and western slopes; however, to the north of Guayaquil, Ecuador, rain on both sides is usually adequate, and precipitation shows no marked contrast. From Guayaquil to 30° south latitude (northern Chile and Argentina) the eastern slopes are well watered, but western exposures suffer extreme drought. Some authorities attribute the desert condition on the coasts of Peru and northern Chile to the fact that the moisture-laden trade winds striking against the Atlantic-facing slopes fail to pass over the great heights encountered in the central Andes; others ascribe the lack of rainfall there to the stability of the atmosphere, caused by cooling of the prevailing south and southwesterly winds by the Humboldt current. Between 30° and 40° S, both sides are about equally dry. Beyond 40°, the prevailing westerlies encourage heavy rainfall on windward slopes.

The Andes exert other climatic influences.

Low atmospheric pressure accounts for the mountain sickness, or soroche, among the highland dwellers. The great lung capacity, massive chests, and abnormally large torsos of the Quechua and Aymara Indians of the high Andean plateaus may be an evolutionary response to rarefied air.

Colder temperatures generally occur with increases in elevation. The Colombian Andes provide a good example of vertical climatic zones, resulting from altitude variations. The area from sea level to 3,000 feet (914 meters) is known as the *tierra caliente* (hot country). Here mean annual temperatures ranging from 83° to 75° F (28°–24° C) favor luxuriant tropical vegetation, with such commercial crops as bananas, sugarcane, cacao, and coconuts. Between 3,000 and 6,000 feet (914–1,833 meters) the *tierra templada* (temperate country) ranges from 75° to 65° F (24°–18° C) and creates suitable growing conditions for corn (maize) and coffee. The *tierra fría* (cold country) between 6,000 and 10,000 feet (1,833–3,048 meters), with a range of 65° to 54° F (18°–12° C), is the zone of wheat, potatoes, temperate fruits, and pasture. High paramos (meadows) at 10,000 to 13,000 feet (3,048–3,962 meters) are generally too cold for trees or for cultivated crops and are suitable only for poor grazing. Above the paramos the snow line is found at about 14,000 feet (4,267 meters).

High Andean elevations also bring great contrasts in temperatures between night and day and between sun and shade exposure. Great heights increase wind velocity, account for mountain and valley winds, intensify ultraviolet radiation, lower absolute humidity, and increase relative humidity. The many differences in Andean heights and exposures produce a legion of microclimates throughout the entire cordillera.

Vegetation. The Andes provide an almost complete laboratory of the world's vegetation. The influence of elevation can be seen in the eastern ranges of Peru. Here the Amazon selva (rain forest) covers the Atlantic-facing slopes up to approximately 4,000 feet (1,219 meters); above, a subtropical forest occurs; still higher is the zone of hardier and smaller tree vegetation; beyond, bush and grasses are encountered, encroaching on alpine plants, which persist despite trying conditions until the snow line is reached.

Peru can be used again as an example to show influences of rainfall on Andean vegetation. On the lower eastern slopes, heavy rainfall and high temperatures encourage a tropical hardwood rain forest; on the lower western slopes is one of the most desolate deserts in the world, with only xerophytic (drought-resistant) plants, such as cacti, when any plants are to be found at all.

Finally, latitudinal contrasts result in temperate rain forest, even grassland, in southern Chile and an equatorial rain forest on the lower Pacific- and Atlantic-facing slopes of Colombia and northern Ecuador.

People. Population in the Andes varies in density and race. Mestizos dominate the racial pattern of the highlands of Argentina, Chile, Colombia, and Venezuela. In Andean Peru, Ecuador, and Bolivia, however, pure Indians account for over half the people. Population is sparse in the Argentine and Chilean Andes, but the central and northern Andes support a larger population than the adjoining plains.

In the central Andes the Indians are descendants of peoples once ruled by the Incas, whose great empire spread over most of what are now Peru, Ecuador, Bolivia, and northern Chile. Like their ancestors, the present-day inhabitants face a difficult environment. Stony soil, uncertain and limited rainfall, low temperatures, and poor agricultural practices provide low yields of such staple crops as potatoes, quinoa, and barley. Without coal, and living in homes well above the tree line, the Indians often use dried manure and bush growths to cook food. Good fuel is too expensive to heat their adobe huts or water for frequent baths. The Indian suffers from disease and lack of medical attention. He frequently resorts to alcoholic beverages and especially to coca to make him forget rigorous physical conditions. (See also COCA.)

Conditions are somewhat better for agriculture on the lower eastern slopes of the central Andes, but few Indians have left their isolated highland homes for still more isolated regions to the east. Nevertheless, although change is likely to come slowly in the high Andes, it will come. Already many Indians are listening to the radio

OPEN-PIT MINE at Chuquicamata, Chile, two miles long and 1,000 feet deep, is a rich source of copper ore.

CARL FRANK FROM PHOTO RESEARCHERS

(Above) INDIANS OF THE PERUVIAN ANDES are descendants of the Incas, who ruled a vast empire.

(Right) URUBAMBA RIVER CANYON, Peru, shows persistent action of water that wears down mountains.

and learning that there is another world where people possess better food, shelter, clothing, and medical care, and other comforts. The same kind of information also is spreading through more frequent contacts with visitors from the outside world. The Andean Indian is very conservative, but he is becoming dissatisfied with his miserable lot; there may be hope for improvement.

Regional Geography. The Andes may be divided into several physical regions. Probably the most practical approach is a separation into the southern, central, and northern Andes.

Southern Andes. This zone, in Argentina and Chile, begins at approximately 30° south latitude and extends to the tip of the continent. Made up essentially of one main range, the southern Andes form the most compact region of the entire cordillera. Here the highest and lowest mountains of the Andes can be seen—the high mountains, such as Aconcagua, and the low hills of Tierra del Fuego. Great piles of rocky fragments occur along the walls of many structural basins. In the far south, glaciation is active, and valley glaciers approach the coast, where they break off into icebergs. Glaciers, lakes, and mountains attract tourists, but the region is too far from densely populated lands to draw large numbers of people. Farther north, relatively good and frequent transportation service now is available by road, rail, and airplane, but the mountains cannot compete for settlement with Chile's central valley lying along their western base or with the eastern lowlands of Argentina.

Central Andes. The Altiplano, a high plateau lying mostly in Bolivia, is enclosed by two major sierras, which lose their identity north of Lake Titicaca, one of the highest navigable lakes in the world—over 12,500 feet (3,812 meters) above sea level. Three mountain groups branch from the convergence near Lake Titicaca, come together in central Peru, then separate once more and join in southern Ecuador. In Peru, such rivers as the Marañón, Urubamba, and Huallaga occupy deep canyons; some sections compare in depth and grandeur to the Grand Canyon of the Colorado in the United States. Beyond the mountain con-

vergence in southern Ecuador two great sierras extend relatively parallel to one another until they meet farther north in southern Colombia. These Ecuadorian mountains and their intervening basinlike plateau contain many imposing volcanic cones, such as Chimborazo (inactive) and Cotopaxi (active).

Besides holding records for high railroads, the central Andes have some of man's highest habitations. In Peru, shepherds' huts are found at 17,000 feet (5,181 meters), just below the snow line; in La Paz, Bolivia, one of the world's highest capitals, more than 300,000 people live in a narrow valley of the Altiplano nearly 12,000 feet (3,658 meters) high. Now the airplane is making contact between western and eastern slopes of the central Andes far easier than it used to be. Even as recently as the 1920's, journeys between Lima, on the Peruvian coast, and Iquitos, over the mountains some 650 miles (1,046 km) to the northeast in the Amazon basin, were made by ocean steamer through the Panama Canal and around the north coast of South America to the mouth of the Amazon, and thence by river steamer up the Amazon to Iquitos. Trips at present can be made by air in a few hours.

Northern Andes. This zone, in Colombia and Venezuela, includes three major, well-defined subdivisions: the Cordillera Occidental (Western Cordillera), the Cordillera Central, and the Cordillera Oriental (Eastern Cordillera). The Cordillera Occidental is the lowest, although its massive crystalline structure is quite similar to that of the Cordillera Central. The latter is the highest and is separated from the Cordillera Occidental by the Cauca Valley, in Colombia. The Cordillera Oriental, the most populous, is composed of stratified rocks folded over a crystalline core. This eastern range is set apart from the central one by Colombia's Magdalena Valley, which occupies, in part, a downfaulted section.

Near the boundary between Colombia and Venezuela at about 7° N, the Cordillera Oriental divides into the Sierra de Perijá, which extends to the north, and the Cordillera de Mérida, which trends to the east. To the west of the Sierra de

HECTOR ACEBES FROM PHOTO RESEARCHERS

FEW HIGHWAYS climb the lofty passes over the barrier that has isolated the mountain people for ages.

Perijá lies the high Sierra Nevada de Santa Marta, which extends down to the Caribbean coast. The Cordillera de Mérida is replaced near the Caribbean by the low Segovia Highlands and gives way toward the east to the Northeastern Highlands of Venezuela.

The Andes of Colombia were the home of the highly developed Chibcha civilization at the time of the Spanish conquest. Today, Indian and mestizo descendants of the Chibchas, together with some Europeans, occupy the land. The Chibcha economy was based largely on corn (maize) culture, but highland dwellers now produce much more diversified crops, with emphasis on coffee.

The northern Andes offer less hindrance to transportation than the other Andean highlands. A general north-south trend coincides with the main routes of commerce in Colombia. In Venezuela the mountains, for the most part, are comparatively low and lie close to the coast. The Andes in both countries offer greater habitability than either the central or southern Andes and as a result of this and other advantages have become the chief population centers of northern South America. The lower slopes and high basins contain the bulk of the people, with the high crests showing little attraction for man.

EARL B. SHAW, *Assumption College*

Bibliography

Baker, P. T., and Michael A. Little, eds., *Man in the Andes* (Academic Press 1976).

Bowman, Isaiah, *The Andes of Southern Peru* (1916; reprint, Greenwood Press 1968).

Engel, Frederic A., ed., *Paloma* (Humanities Press 1980).

Engel, Frederic A., ed., *Stone Typology* (Humanities Press 1983).

Frazier, Charles, and Donald Secreasi, *Adventuring in the Andes* (Sierra Club Bks. 1985).

Harmon, R. S., et al., eds., *Andean Magmatism: Chemical and Isotopic Constraints* (Birkhauser 1984).

Isbell, Billie J., *To Defend Ourselves: Ecology and Ritual in an Andean Village* (Waveland Press 1985).

Lynch, Thomas F., ed., *Guitarrero Cave: Early Man in the Andes* (Academic Press 1980).

Means, Philip A., *Ancient Civilizations of the Andes* (1931; reprint, Gordian Press 1964).

Monge, Carlos, *Acclimatization in the Andes*, tr. by Donald F. Brown (1948; reprint, Blaine Ethridge 1973).

Murphy, D., *Eight Feet in the Andes* (Overlook 1987).

Pitcher, W. S., et al., *Magmatism at a Plate Edge: The Peruvian Andes* (Halsted Press 1985).

Silvester, Hans, *The Land of the Incas*, tr. by Jane Brenton (Thames & Hudson 1986).

ANDHRA PRADESH, än'drə prə-däsh', one of the states of India. Andhra Pradesh lies on the west shore of the Bay of Bengal, in the central part of the Indian peninsula, and is bounded by the Indian states of Orissa and Madhya Pradesh on the north, Maharashtra on the northwest, Karnataka on the west, and Tamil Nadu on the south. The state has an area of 106,286 square miles (275,281 sq km) and a population (1991 census) of 66,508,008, excluding several isolated tribes. The chief cities and their 1991 populations are Hyderabad (3,145,939), the state capital; Vijayavada (Vijayawada, 701,827); Guntur (471,051); and Visakhapatnam (752,037).

Andhra Pradesh was formed in 1953 as a linguistic state, designed to encompass within its boundaries most of the Telugu-speaking people of India. Telugu, a Dravidian tongue, became the official language; it is now the language spoken by most of the people. Hindus are the largest religious group, but there are Muslim, Christian, and tribal minorities. Most of the Muslims speak Urdu, and English is widely understood.

The Land. Andhra consists of three main regions: the interior plateau, the coastal plain, and the deltas. The interior plateau is largely a gently rolling upland. In the southeast are chains of hills: the Velikonda, Nallamalai, Erramalai, Seshachalam, and Palkonda. The northern coastal plain is interrupted by branches of the rugged Eastern Ghats, which straddle the Andhra-Orissa border; the southern coastal plain is wider and more continuous. The deltas begin where the Krishna and Godavari rivers emerge from the plateau about 45 miles (72 km) from the sea. From there the fertile alluvial land slopes gently toward a coastal fringe of sand dunes and mangrove swamp.

The Penner River rises in the arid southern Deccan plateau, and its southerly location gives it a maximum flow after the autumn rains. The Krishna and Godavari, rising in the monsoon-drenched Western Ghats, flood in late summer.

Climate. The climate of most of Andhra is controlled by the southwest monsoon. October to March is warm and dry; April and May, hot and dry. In June the rains begin, bringing cooler weather until September. Along the south coast the rains continue until December. Annual rainfall ranges from 20 inches (51 cm) in the arid southwest to over 55 inches (140 cm) in the Eastern Ghats and from 40 inches (102 cm) along the south coast to over 50 inches (127 cm) along the north coast.

Soils and Vegetation. Most of Andhra has poor red soils, except in the deltas, where alluvial soils predominate, and in the Krishna and Godavari valleys, where black soils are found. The natural vegetation is mostly open, dry, deciduous thorn forest, except for the moist deciduous forest of the northeast and the coastal mangrove. Forests cover 19 percent of the land area.

Mineral Resources. The most important minerals in Andhra are coal, mined at Singareni; iron ore in Krishna district; mica in Nellore district; and manganese north of Visakhapatnam. There are small deposits of asbestos, copper, chromite, limestone, kaolin, and refractory minerals.

The Economy—Agriculture. Most of the people of Andhra are farmers. The majority of them have farms of under 10 acres (4 hectares) and use simple implements, bullock power, and much hand labor. Rice is the leading crop, grown wherever irrigation is possible, but especially in the deltas and coastal plain. Millet, grain sorghums, pulses, peanuts, and other oilseeds are raised on unirrigated land, especially on the plateau. Tobacco in the Krishna delta, cotton on the plateau, and irrigated sugarcane north of Hyderabad are important cash crops.

Irrigation. Before independence (1947), Andhra's irrigation came mainly from small, seasonally filled "tanks" or ponds. Canals irrigated 2.3 million acres (0.9 million hectares) in the deltas and small areas elsewhere. Since then major river development projects have been undertaken to assure a regular supply of water in climatically hazardous areas, expand the irrigated area for more food and cash crop production, control floods, and provide power for industry. These projects have added over 5 million (2 million hectares) irrigated acres and 2,785,000 kilowatts of hydroelectric capacity to the area's former resources. The important ones include the Tungabhadra (jointly with Mysore), Nagarjunasagar and Srisailam (on the Krishna River), Machkund (with Orissa), Prakasan, and Vamsadhara projects.

Industry. Andhra is only moderately urbanized by Indian standards and has little heavy industry. Cottage and small-scale industries, such as weaving and rice milling, predominate. In Hyderabad there are textile mills and numerous small factories making glass, sugar, paper, cigarettes, bicycles, machinery, chemicals, and metal products. Secunderabad, a military and railroad center near Hyderabad, makes machine tools. Visakhapatnam, the fifth-largest port in India and a naval base, has a shipyard and an oil refinery. Industry can be expected to increase in the state as the hydroelectric potential is further developed.

Government. The state government is parliamentary, with a governor appointed by the president of India, an elected legislative assembly, and a partly appointed legislative council. Executive functions are performed by ministers selected from the assembly by the chief minister, who is the leader of the majority political party or coalition of parties. The state has 20 districts, each administered by an appointed "collector and district magistrate," assisted by police, medical, excise, and other officers. The basic administrative unit is the village, composed of a rural settlement and its lands, with an elected village *panchayat* or council. Urban areas are governed by elected municipal boards.

EWING GALLOWAY

CHAR MINAR AT HYDERABAD, a famous landmark of Andhra Pradesh, is a double-arch gate built in 1591.

History. The Andhra people have a long history, marked by the rise and fall of successive kingdoms. The Andhra dynasty, known also as the Satavahana or Satakarni, ruled the entire Deccan region for most of the period from the 1st century B.C. to the 3d century A.D. Successor rulers, the Ikshvakus, Pallavas, Vakatakas, Vishnukundins, and others, divided the area of modern Andhra until the 9th century, when the Cholas and Chalukyas gained dominance. These in turn yielded to the Kakatiyas in the late 12th century. The Muslims began making inroads in the south in the 14th century, while the Vijayanagar dynasty conquered the north. By the 17th century the Mughul empire had absorbed most of the territory, and British colonization had begun. The coasts and southern interior came under British rule in the early 19th century, but the hereditary ruler, the nizam of Hyderabad, retained the northern interior.

Under British rule, the Telugu-speaking population was divided between Madras province and Hyderabad state. Following independence, the Indian government came under political pressure to create a Telugu linguistic state, and on Oct. 1, 1953, the Telugu areas were detached from Madras to form Andhra Pradesh, with its capital at Kurnool. On Nov. 1, 1956, the Telugu-speaking area of former Hyderabad state was added to Andhra, and the capital was moved to Hyderabad city. Population: 75,727,541 (2001 census).

HOWARD F. HIRT, *Boston University*

Bibliography

Bhandarkar, R. G., *Early History of the Dekkan* (1983; reprint, South Asia Bks. 1986).
Chanda, Asok K., *Federalism in India* (Allen & Unwin 1965).
Fadia, Babu L., *State Politics in India*, 2 vols. (Humanities Press 1984).
Government of India, *India: A Reference Annual* (annually).
Lisker, Leigh, *Spoken Telugu* (Spoken Lang. Serv. 1976).
Persad, Dharmendra, *Social and Cultural Geography of Hyderabad City* (Apt. Bks. 1986).
Prasad, Rajendra, *The Asif Jahs of Hyderabad* (Advent Bks. 1984).
Rao, V. Lakshmana, *Economic Development of Andhra Pradesh* (Apt. Bks. 1986).

ANDHRA UNIVERSITY, än'drə, a coeducational institution in Waltair, Andhra Pradesh, south India. It was founded in 1926 to serve the Telugu district of the Madras presidency. When India became independent, the charter was revised to include Srikakulam, Visākhāpatnam, East and West Godāvari, Kistna, and Guntūr districts.

Andhra University has five constituent colleges: Erskine College of Natural Sciences; a college of science and technology; and the university colleges of arts and commerce, engineering, and law. There are also more than 100 affiliated colleges, offering general and professional studies. The university library houses over 340,000 volumes. Enrollment in the mid-1990s exceeded 53,000 students.

ANDIJON, un-di-zhàn',[*] a city in Uzbekistan. Formerly Andizhan, the city, after the 1991 independence of Uzbekistan, abandoned the Russian form for the Uzbek, Andijon. It is the capital of Andijon oblast and the center of a cotton-growing area in the Farghona Valley of Central Asia. Its most important industries are cotton ginning and oil pressing. The city also has fruit canneries and machine shops as well as tile and brick factories. Andijon became part of Russia in 1875.

Andijon region, in the easternmost corner of Uzbekistan, has an area of 1,470 square miles (3,800 sq km), used mostly for irrigated cotton cultivation. Fruit, silk, and rice also are grown, and cattle are raised. After World War II, Andijon became the chief petroleum- and natural-gas-producing area of Uzbekistan. The people are Uzbek, Russian, and Kirghiz. Population: city, 323,900 (1999 est.); region, 1,899,000 (1993 est.).

THEODORE SHABAD*
Author of "Geography of the USSR"

ANDOCIDES (c. 440–c. 390 B.C.), an-dos'i-dēz, an orator of ancient Athens. He was not a trained rhetorician; his speeches are valuable mainly for their bearing on Athenian history and customs. In 415 B.C., Andocides was implicated with others in the mutilation of the Hermae, sacred pillars surmounted by busts of deities that were set up throughout Athens. The sacrilege, which occurred on the eve of a naval expedition to Syracuse, was regarded as ominous. A sentence of *atimia* (disgrace) was passed on him, and he went into exile. (See PELOPONNESIAN WAR.)

The first of Andocides' three extant speeches, "On His Return," was a plea for pardon addressed to the assembly in 410 B.C. Permitted to return in 403 B.C., he was accused of impiety in 399 B.C. for attending the Mysteries of Eleusis (religious rites) while still under sentence. "On the Mysteries" was his successful defense. His final speech, "On Peace," in which he urged peace with Sparta, was delivered in 390 B.C. after an unsuccessful mission there as peace envoy. He then again went into exile.

ANDORRA, an-dôr'ə, an independent principality in western Europe, between France and Spain. From 1278 to 1993, Andorra was under the joint sovereignty of the president of France and the Spanish bishop of Urgel. Located on the south slope of the eastern Pyrenees, it is bounded on the north and east by the French departments of Ariège and Pyrénées-Orientales; on the south lies the Spanish province of Lérida. Andorra is accessible by road or trail through several high moun-

tain passes, but the highway running from northeast to south is the only one transversing the country. Andorra has an area of 175 square miles (453 sq km). The capital, Andorra la Vella, has a population of over 20,000.

The Land and the People. Andorra has an extremely rugged terrain, with seven mountain peaks nearly 10,010 feet (3,050 meters) high. Of seven major mountain passes, six are at elevations above 6,990 feet (2,130 meters). Eight lakes lie at elevations of between 6,500 and 8,500 feet (1,980 and 2,590 meters). Several hydroelectric plants harness Andorra's considerable water power. The country is drained by the Valira River and its tributaries. The Valira has its origin in two branches, one in the north and the other in the northeast, and flows southwesterly into Spain.

The landscape is characterized by a treeless zone in the mountain peaks, wooded regions at lower altitudes, and grassy meadows along the rivers and lakes. The climate is dry and sunny, with severe winters and markedly little rainfall except in April and October. There is considerable snowfall during the winter months, however.

The origins of the people who inhabit Andorra can be traced back to Roman times, when the tribe that had settled there was referred to as the Andosians. A hardy, self-sufficient people, Andorrans constitute only about one-quarter of the state's population; the remainder are mostly Spaniards, with a small French minority. The native language is Catalan, but Spanish and French are widely spoken. The official religion is Roman Catholicism, yet religious liberty is protected by law.

Economy. Andorra's traditional economic activities, agriculture and livestock raising, have been replaced as the chief source of income by the tourist industry. Some 12 million tourists visit Andorra annually, accounting for 80% of the national income. Summer visitors are attracted by the grandeur of Andorra's mountain scenery, the area's delightful climate, and the country's relative seclusion from the outside world. Prices are reasonable, partly because there are no sales taxes or customs duties. Visitors come principally from Spain and France, but the number of tourists from other European countries and from the United States has increased considerably. Winter tourism has been stimulated by the availability of magnificent skiing sites.

Tourism, in turn, has led to the development of trade and the establishment of new business ventures. Imports have also increased, and Andor-

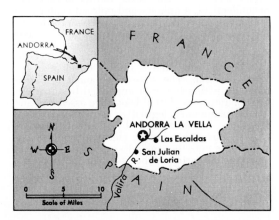

ra's dependence on food imports from France and Spain has grown as a result of increasing tourism. Only 2% of Andorra's land is arable; some 56% of the land is suitable for grazing, and cattle, sheep, and goats are raised. Apart from handicrafts, manufacturing is confined mostly to tobacco processing. Small amounts of iron ore and lead are mined.

Government and Politics. A new constitution, ratified by referendum on March 14, 1993, established Andorra as a democratic parliamentary principality. It called for the creation of an independent judiciary, the election of the legislature by universal suffrage, and the formation of political parties and trade unions.

The coprinces—the bishop of Urgel and the president of the French Republic—were retained as the constitutional heads of state with greatly reduced constitutionally defined powers. The General Council (Consell General), a 28-member unicameral legislature, elects the Head of Government (Cap de Govern). The Cap de Govern in turn selects the members of the Govern (the executive branch of the government).

Many of Andorra's newly formed political parties took part in the first multiparty election for the general council, held in December 1993. The center-right National Democratic Grouping (AND, founded in 1979) and the Liberal Union (UL) together garnered almost 50% of the vote. Other newly formed parties also won representation in the legislature, including the New Democracy party (ND), the National Andorran Coalition (CNA), and the social democratic National Democratic Initiative (IDN).

In June 1993 a treaty was signed with Spain and France that recognized the sovereignty of Andorra and subsequently established embassies in the country. Andorra became a member of the United Nations in July 1993.

History. According to tradition, Charlemagne drove the Moors out of Andorra in the early 9th century A.D. His grandson, Charles II, named the count of Urgel as overlord of Andorra, and a descendant of the latter donated these lands to the bishop of Urgel in the year 954. After the French count of Foix became heir to the count of Urgel through marriage, serious clashes occurred between the count and the bishop. In 1278 they reached an agreement called a *paréage,* whereby each was granted equal rights in Andorra.

In 1589 the count of Foix ascended the French throne as Henry IV. Thereafter, the ruler of France acted as coprince of Andorra. French and Spanish cosovereignty has continued, as the Andorrans have chosen to enjoy French protection in order to avoid exclusive domination by Spain.

Andorra's relative isolation from the outside world and its dual relationship with France and Spain have helped it to escape the great European conflagrations of the 20th century. Its ties to Spain enabled Andorra to remain neutral in both world wars, and its association with France prevented involvement in the Spanish Civil War. As a result of the growth of the tourist industry after World War II, however, Andorrans have become less isolated and more involved in the affairs of Europe, particularly in regard to those economic aspects affecting their own prosperity. Population: 65,306 (1997 census).

Bibliography: Reynolds, Kev, *The Mountains of the Pyrenees* (Hippocrene Bks. 1984).

YAN, FROM RAPHO GUILLUMETTE

A hill in Andorra is topped by Muslim ruins (*right*) and a 12th-century Roman Catholic chapel (*left*).

ANDOVER, an'dō-vər, a historic town in northeastern Massachusetts, in Essex county, 25 miles (40 km) north of Boston. It is part of the Lawrence-Haverhill metropolitan area. Settled in 1643 and incorporated in 1646, it still has many of its early buildings and is the home of a distinguished secondary school, Phillips Academy. Andover is also an industrial center.

Phillips Academy, founded as a boarding school for boys in 1778, is considered one of the leading private secondary schools in the United States. On its campus, which overlooks the town, are the Addison Gallery of American Art and the Robert S. Peabody Museum of Archaeology. In 1973 Abbot Academy, founded in Andover in 1829 and the first school for girls incorporated in New England, merged with Phillips. The Andover Theological Seminary (now Andover Newton Theological School) was situated in Andover from 1807 until 1908.

The oldest house in Andover, the Benjamin Abbot homestead, was built in 1685. The Andover Historical Society is located in the Deacon Amos Blanchard House, built in 1819. Its Barn Museum features early farm implements and an early pump fire wagon. Harriet Beecher Stowe, the author of *Uncle Tom's Cabin,* is buried in Andover.

Andover's industrial importance began in the Revolutionary War period, when Samuel Phillips, who was the founder of Phillips Academy, built powder mills there. In the 19th century, Andover became a textile-manufacturing center, but an attempt to found a silk industry failed. Andover continues to maintain light industry. Population: 31,247.

MIRIAM PUTNAM*
Memorial Library, Andover

ANDOVER NEWTON THEOLOGICAL SCHOOL,

an'dō-vər nū'tən, in Newton Centre, Mass., was formed in 1931 by the union of Andover Theological Seminary and Newton Theological Institution. Andover, founded in 1807, was the oldest Congregational seminary in the United States. Newton, founded in 1825, was one of the country's oldest Baptist theological institutions.

Andover Newton has continued the pioneering work of its affiliates in the field of theological education. This included the first acceptance, in the 1890's, of women seminarians. In 1931, Andover Newton made the first appointment of a professor of clinical psychology at a seminary. In 1953 the school initiated a fourth-year intern program that has since served as a model for schools of theology.

The historic disciplines—Biblical, theological, and historical—are the core of Andover Newton's course for the degree of bachelor of divinity. Master's degrees are offered in sacred theology and religious education. Enrollment has been held to an average of 325 students.

Andover Newton has a working library of more than 82,000 volumes on campus. In addition, there is the Andover research collection of 70,000 volumes in the Andover-Harvard Library at Harvard Divinity School. The school has an agreement with Harvard Divinity School, Boston University School of Theology, and the Episcopal Theological School whereby students registered at one institution may obtain credit for work done at any of the others.

PAUL R. DUNN,
Andover Newton Theological School

ANDRADA E SILVA,

aɴɴ-drá'thə ē sil'-və, **José Bonifácio de** (1763–1838), Brazilian patriot-statesman, scientist, and poet, who is regarded as the father of Brazilian independence. Born at Santos, Brazil on June 13, 1763, he received his early education at home from his uncle, a priest, and from the bishop of São Paulo. He was then sent to the University of Coimbra in Portugal, later to Paris, and then to Freiburg, Germany. He rendered distinguished services to Portugal as a university professor at Coimbra, administrator, and military man, and returned to Brazil in 1819 after an absence of 36 years.

The return to Portugal of King John VI in 1821 accelerated the movement for the independence of Brazil, a movement in which Andrada played an important role, using his influence to support the young prince regent, the future Emperor Dom Pedro I. After the prince proclaimed Brazilian independence on Sept. 7, 1822, Andrada was made minister of the interior and minister for foreign affairs. He worked successfully to strengthen the unity of the new empire and to obtain its recognition by foreign powers. However, his fervent advocacy of a representative constitution during the first year of independence resulted in his arrest and exile to France in November 1823. After five years, he was allowed to return, and when Dom Pedro I abdicated in favor of his son Dom Pedro II, Andrada was appointed tutor to the five-year-old emperor and his sisters. Dismissed from office two years later, Andrada retired. He was the author of many scientific and poetical works. He died at Niterói on April 6, 1838.

LUIS GARCIA DE SOUSA,
Colegio Loyola, Belo Horizonte, Brazil

ANDRAL,

äɴ-drál', **Gabriel** (1797–1876), French physician. He was born in Paris on Nov. 6, 1797. After graduating from Lycée Louis-le-Grand, he attended the University of Paris medical school and graduated as doctor of medicine in 1821. In 1828 he became professor of hygiene and in 1830 professor of internal pathology at the University of Paris. In 1839 he succeeded to the chair of general pathology and therapy and became head of the department of pathology, a post he held the rest of his career. He was a member of the French Academy of Medicine at its inception in 1820 and was elected to the Academy of Science in 1848. His first major work, *Clinique médicale*, published in five volumes beginning in 1823 and revised in many editions during his lifetime, was probably the first internal medicine textbook in the modern sense. His *Précis d'anatomie pathologique* (1829) was the first general comprehensive textbook of pathological anatomy.

Andral's main contribution, however, was in the field of blood pathology, and his *Essais d'hématologie pathologique* (1842) was a basic pioneer work on that subject. In order to find instructive comparisons with human blood he made numerous investigations of animal blood and is remembered, as well, as a pioneer comparative hematologist. He introduced the terms "anemia" and "hyperemia" into medicine, was one of the first to attempt to determine normal limits in the proportions of blood serum constituents, and one of the first to draw diagnostic relationships between disease states and alterations in serum properties. He proposed that no single part of the body undergoes modification without causing modifications elsewhere in the body, an early insight into pathophysiological interdependence of body functions and composition.

Andral's wide activities included intensive medical history researches, the editing of René Laënnec's works, and vigorous campaigns against bloodletting. He died at Châteauvieux, in Loiret-Cher department, France, on Feb. 13, 1876.

HERBERT S. BENJAMIN, M.D.

ANDRÁSSY,

on'drä-shē, **Count Gyula** (1823–1890), Hungarian statesman who was premier of Hungary and foreign minister of Austria-Hungary. One of Europe's leading political and diplomatic figures during the second half of the 19th century, Andrássy helped win domestic autonomy for Hungary within the Habsburg empire. He also was largely responsible for restoring temporarily the empire's declining prestige.

Andrássy was born in Kassa, Hungary (now Košice, Czechoslovakia), on March 3, 1823. At first he was a moderate in politics but soon switched into the camp of anti-Austrian extremists who hoped to separate Hungary from the Austrian Habsburg empire. He fought with the Hungarian independence forces in the insurrection that broke out in 1848–1849. When the revolt failed, he fled the country and was condemned to death *in absentia* for high treason.

Andrássy lived in voluntary exile in western Europe for eight years. He returned to Hungary in 1857 and was elected in 1861 to the Hungarian national assembly, where he sponsored a law to protect the national minorities in Hungary. With the Hungarian nationalist leader, Ferencz Deák, Andrássy arranged the 1867 agreement with Austria, called the *Ausgleich* (Compromise), that gave Hungary autonomy in domestic affairs. Andrássy then became Hungary's first prime minister.

Foreign Minister. Andrássy's most notable achievements were in foreign affairs, and in 1871 he resigned the premiership to take over the post of foreign minister of the Austro-Hungarian empire. Extremely distrustful of Russia, Hungary's eastern neighbor, Andrássy based his foreign policy on the establishment of close relations with Germany and Britain. He reluctantly agreed to an alliance in 1872–1873 among Russia, Germany, and Austria-Hungary, known as the *Dreikaiserbund* (League of Three Emperors). The alliance soon fell apart because Russia's expansionist goals in the Balkans conflicted with those of the Austro-Hungarian empire.

Russian ambitions in the Balkans led to a war with Turkey, which ended in a Russian victory. The victory was signalized by the Treaty of San Stefano (1878), which to all intents and purposes made the Balkans a Russian province. Attacking this settlement as an "Orthodox Slav sermon," Andrássy united with Germany and Britain to force Russia to confer in Berlin on Balkan issues. The resultant Treaty of Berlin (1878) substantially reduced Russian gains and gave Austria-Hungary a mandate to occupy Bosnia-Hercegovina, one of the Balkan provinces of Turkey.

On Oct. 7, 1879, Andrássy negotiated a secret defensive alliance with Germany, directed against Russia. He regarded the agreement as the crowning achievement of his career. But he was bitterly attacked at home for his Balkan and German policies, and he retired from office the next day. He died in Volosca, Istria (now Opatija, Yugoslavia), on Feb. 18, 1890.

ARTHUR J. MAY, *Author of*
"The Hapsburg Monarchy, 1867–1914"

ANDRÁSSY, on'drä-shē, **Count Gyula** (1860–1929), Hungarian statesman and diplomat. He was born at Töketerebes, Hungary (now Trebišov, Czechoslovakia), the second son of Count Gyula Andrássy (1823–1890, q.v.). Educated at the University of Vienna, Andrássy entered the Hungarian parliament in 1885. In time he clashed violently with Prime Minister István Tisza, chiefly over relations with Austria. He assumed leadership of an anti-Tisza coalition, and when that bloc triumphed (1905) in national elections, Andrássy became minister of the interior, retaining that post until 1910. His proposals on child welfare and emigration were passed into law, though plans for military and suffrage reform were defeated.

After 1910, as a spokesman for the opposition, Andrássy resumed his bitter feud with Tisza. Yet, when the European war started in 1914, he vigorously supported the war effort, wrote extensively on public issues, and pleaded passionately for the inclusion of Poland in the Habsburg realm. On Oct. 24, 1918, his long-standing ambition to become foreign secretary was fulfilled, but about all that he did was to apply to the U.S. government for an armistice and a separate peace.

On the passing of the monarchy, Andrássy warmly espoused the restoration of the Habsburg claimant to the throne of Hungary. At his death, in Budapest, on June 11, 1929, he was hailed by legitimists as "the most loyal of the loyalists." His book *Diplomacy and the War* appeared in English translation in 1921.

ARTHUR J. MAY, *Author of*
"The Hapsburg Monarchy, 1867–1914"

THE GRANGER COLLECTION

JOHN ANDRÉ, as he appeared in a pen drawing done by himself the day before his execution at Tappan, N.Y.

ANDRÉ, än'drā, **John** (1750–1780), British military officer, who was executed as a spy during the American Revolution. He was born in London on May 2, 1750. His father, Anthony André, belonged to a prosperous Huguenot family, with headquarters in Geneva, Switzerland, engaged in international trade. Born in Genoa, Italy, the father was a naturalized Englishman. John's mother, Marie Louise Giradot, came from Paris. John spent his childhood in and near London, studied at Geneva, and at 16 or 17 entered the family's London countinghouse, although he disliked business, being torn between artistic and military pursuits. When 19, he fell under the spell of the 26-year-old poetess, Anna Seward, who arranged a romantic engagement between him and her young ward, Honora Sneyd. The engagement was broken in December 1770.

Military Career. On Jan. 21, 1771, André bought a second lieutenant's commission in the Royal Welsh Fusiliers, but he soon secured leave to study at Göttingen in Hannover. He became intimate with a group of poets, the *Göttingen Hain.* Late in 1774 he joined his regiment at Quebec, Canada, where he pursued his interest in literature and art. After the outbreak of the American Revolution, he suffered through the siege of St. Johns, Quebec (September–October 1775), which ended with the capture of that fortress by Gen. Richard Montgomery. Interned as a prisoner at Lancaster, Pa., he considered resigning from the army to become a painter; but during his subsequent internment in the frontier hamlet of Carlisle, Pa., he received such rough treatment from the backwoodsmen that he grew to hate the "rebels." He determined to become a ruthless and efficient soldier.

Exchanged in November 1776, André joined the British army in New York City. An able report of what he had seen behind the American lines attracted the attention of the British commander in chief, Sir William Howe, who approved his purchase of a captaincy and his appointment, in June 1777, as aide to Maj. Gen. Charles Grey. During the British advance on Philadelphia that summer, André took enthusiastic part in the bloody Paoli, Pa., massacre, when an American force was exterminated. Grey's corps was held in reserve at Brandywine, but André led a charge at Germantown. In occupied Philadelphia he was a leader of the worldly group around Howe; he acted in and designed scenery for amateur theatricals, and flirted with the local belles, including Margaret Shippen. But all the while, he urged on his superiors a more aggressive military policy.

André served as Grey's aide during the retreat to New York and on a naval foray against New England. In the fall of 1778 he joined the staff of Howe's successor, Sir Henry Clinton, who fell increasingly under the influence of the brilliant young officer. In April 1779, André was put in charge of intelligence. His memoranda of prominent rebels who might be won to the British cause did not mention Benedict Arnold; but Margaret Shippen was now Arnold's wife, and in May an emissary to André offered Arnold's treason at a price. Since Clinton believed that the wounded and half-disgraced Arnold would never again secure a command, André was not allowed to meet the price, and the secret negotiations through the lines collapsed in October.

Clinton, however, promoted André to deputy, and then full, adjutant general. This unprecedentedly rapid rise was so much resented that, although the adjutant generalship usually carried with it the rank of colonel, Clinton had great difficulty getting André accepted as a major by the War Office. André took a leading part in the capture of Charleston, S.C., and continued to urge a more brutal prosecution of the war.

Arnold's Treason. In June 1780, Benedict Arnold reopened the treason negotiations; his offer was taken seriously when, in August, his appointment as commandant of West Point gave him something of value to betray. Arnold demanded a personal interview with André; Clinton warned his favorite not to assume the role of a spy by taking off his uniform or entering an enemy post. During the night of September 21, André was picked up in mid-Hudson from the British sloop *Vulture* by Arnold's emissary, Joshua Hett Smith. André wore his uniform. He was ferried to Arnold, who waited in a pinewoods on the west shore near Haverstraw, N.Y. At dawn, André rode with the traitor to Smith's house, within the American lines. Arnold gave him papers to carry to Clinton and then departed.

In the meanwhile, the *Vulture* had been fired on and forced to drop downriver. The resulting decision to carry André back to the British lines by land forced him to discard his uniform for civilian clothes. André and Smith set out on horseback at nightfall, crossed the river, and early in the morning of September 23 reached Pines Bridge. Now theoretically in British-held territory, André proceeded alone. He was stopped near Tarrytown by three American militiamen, John Paulding, Isaac Van Wart, and David Williams. Finding the papers in his shoes, they delivered André to an American outpost commanded by Lt. Col. John Jameson, who suspected Arnold's treason but did not dare violate orders by failing to notify Arnold that "John Anderson," as André called himself, had been captured. Arnold escaped.

André's Trial. André was held and tried by court-martial. Two different lines of argument were used to prove him not a spy. In letters from New York City, Clinton and Arnold insisted that all of André's equivocal acts were justified because he had obeyed orders given by Arnold, who was still legally commandant of the area. André claimed that Arnold had forced him against his will behind the American lines, making him a prisoner of war justified in attempting to escape dressed as a civilian. The two arguments were contradictory, and neither held water. A British officer is under no obligation to obey an enemy general; an escaping prisoner may not carry treasonous papers. In any case, recently discovered British documents reveal that, before he met Arnold, André had expressed willingness, if expedient, secretly to enter an American post.

André was found guilty. He petitioned George Washington to be shot like a gentleman, not hanged as a spy, a request that could not be granted lest the British propaganda machine seize on it as an admission that he was not really guilty. He was hanged at Tappan, N.Y., on Oct. 2, 1780, mourned even by his enemies, who had been moved by his gallant behavior under his misfortunes.

JAMES THOMAS FLEXNER
Author of "The Traitor and the Spy"

Bibliography

Decker, Malcolm, *Ten Days of Infamy* (Ayer 1968).
Flexner, James Thomas, *The Traitor and the Spy* (Little 1975).
Sargent, Winthrop, *The Life and Career of Major André* (1902; reprint, Somerset Pubs. 1972).
Smith, Joshua H., *Authentic Narrative of the Causes Which Led to the Death of Major André*, ed. by Malcolm Decker (1808; reprint, Ayer 1969).

ANDREA CHÉNIER, än-drä′ä shā-nyā′, is an opera in four acts by Umberto Giordano with a libretto by Luigi Illica. The work was first performed at La Scala in Milan, Italy, on March 28, 1896; its first American performance was given in New York City on November 13 of the same year. *Andrea Chénier* is Giordano's masterpiece and the most frequently performed of his operas.

The plot has as its background the turbulent years of the French Revolution. Three principals are involved: Andrea Chénier, a poet sympathetic to the ideals of the revolution; Maddalena, a young noblewoman in love with Chénier; and Gérard, a former servant in the household of Maddalena's family, who has become a popular hero of the revolution. The dramatic climax of the piece is reached in the fourth act when Chénier is unjustly sentenced to death by the revolutionary tribunal. Gérard, jealous of the lovers, has been the author of this situation, but has a change of heart and tries unsuccessfully to have the verdict reversed. Maddalena, true to her vow, joins Chénier in his cell so that they may go together to the guillotine.

The music of *Andrea Chénier* is undistinguished to the point of tedium. Its melodies are banal, and its harmony is awkward and unimaginative. Nevertheless, the spirit of Giordano's score suits the melodramatic character of the libretto. The emphasis of the music is on theatrical effect, and the success of the opera is due largely to the score's dramatic tone. See also CHÉNIER, ANDRÉ MARIE DE.

EDMOND STRAINCHAMPS, *New York University*

ANDREA DEL SARTO (1486–1530), än-drä′ä del sär′tō, Italian painter. His real name was *Andrea Domenico d'Agnolo di Francesco*. He was born at Florence, Italy, on July 16, 1486, the son of a tailor (*sarto*); hence the name used during his lifetime and ever since. He spent his life in Florence except for possible student trips to Rome and Venice and a sojourn of less than one year (1518–1519) at the court of Francis I of France. According to his contemporary Vasari, Andrea was apprenticed to a goldsmith at the age of seven, then to the painter Gian Barile. His last master was Piero di Cosimo. On Dec. 12, 1508, he entered the Florentine guild for artists, and soon after he opened a workshop with the slightly older painter Franciabigio.

His first commission was for five wall paintings in the Servite Order Church of the Annunziata in Florence. These lively frescoes were completed in 1510. Depicting scenes from the life of St. Filippo Benizzi, they reveal the novice indebted to Leonardo da Vinci and the early Raphael, among others. They nevertheless manifest a developing individual style. Andrea added a *Journey of the Magi* in 1511 and a *Birth of the Virgin* in 1514, whose figures have the breadth and ease of the High Renaissance. With Franciabigio's assistance, he did a fresco series in grisaille (1512–1526) on the story of St. John the Baptist, in a cloister belonging to the Brotherhood of the Scalzi in Florence. Compositionally these paintings follow traditional types, yet they are modernized by means of heroic, classical forms of the kind used by Raphael and Michelangelo. If occasionally somewhat overpowered by their draperies, the figures are magnificently sculptural, perhaps evidence of Andrea's friendship with Jacopo Sansovino. These paintings also borrow elements from the graphic works of Dürer. Other of Andrea's important frescoes include the *Madonna del Sacco* (1525), in a lunette in the monastery of the Annunziata, and a superb *Last Supper* (about 1526) in the refectory of San Michele a Salvi, Florence. The former, in its beauty of color, finesse of treatment, and exquisitely balanced composition, may be his greatest painting.

His work frequently has an almost Venetian charm and sensibility as well as a feeling for color and atmosphere rare among Florentine painters and revealed particularly in his panel paintings. The most famous of these is the serenely monumental *Madonna of the Harpies* (1517, Uffizi, Florence). Also notable are a pyramidal *Charity* (1518, Louvre, Paris), painted in France, and the *Dispute About the Trinity* (1517–1518, Pitti, Florence). He is famous too for his penetrating yet appealing and simple portraits, as his *Portrait of a Sculptor* (about 1524, National Gallery, London). His numerous drawings, of which the Uffizi possesses the largest collection, display great ease and delicacy.

Andrea did not have the profundity and originality of a Leonardo or a Michelangelo. Yet his technical skill, humanity, and extraordinary ability as a wall decorator place him among the outstanding representatives of the Florentine High Renaissance. His influence was felt by a number of Florentine mannerists. Andrea died at Florence on Sept. 29, 1530.

ANNE BETTY WEINSHENKER, *Art Historian*

ANDREA DEL SARTO, än-drä′ä del sär′tō, is one of Robert Browning's most famous dramatic monologues. It was first published in *Men and Women* in 1855. Based on the biography of the Italian painter Andrea del Sarto, as given in Giorgio Vasari's *Lives of the Painters*, it is an attempt to explain the meaning of the portrait that the painter did of himself and his wife, Lucrezia, now in the Pitti Gallery, Florence.

Andrea, though called the "faultless painter" by his contemporaries, lacked some essential

ANDREA DEL SARTO'S *Portrait of a Sculptor* (c. 1524), from the collection of the National Gallery, London.

quality (according to Browning, elevation of mind, aspiration) that enabled such painters as Michelangelo, Raphael, and Leonardo da Vinci, though inferior in technique, to surpass him. Browning finds in Andrea's infatuation with Lucrezia the key to this defect. This is brought out as the painter discusses himself and his art in a monologue addressed to his wife.

The poem is a three-sided study of character: of an artist who has failed to attain his ideal and who knows why he has failed; of a man who has lost his self-respect; and of a lover who has given his all without return. Yet this artist, man, and lover, though disillusioned and hopeless, is content. As a picture of Renaissance life and character, the poem should be read in contrast with Browning's *Fra Lippo Lippi*.

MARION TUCKER
The Polytechnic Institute of Brooklyn

ANDREA DEL VERROCCHIO. See VERROCCHIO, ANDREA DEL.

ANDREA PISANO. See PISANO, ANDREA.

ANDRÉE, àn-drä, **Salomon August** (1854–1897), Swedish aeronautical engineer and polar explorer. Born at Grenna, Sweden, on Oct. 18, 1854, he was educated as an engineer at the Stockholm technical college, where he taught from 1886 to 1889. In 1892 he was awarded a grant by the Swedish Academy of Sciences to experiment with scientific aerial navigation. Thereafter he devoted himself to aeronautics.

In 1895 he launched a project for exploring the north polar region by balloon and made an unsuccessful attempt at such an expedition in 1896. Then, on July 11, 1897, under the patronage of the academy and financed by a national subscription that included contributions from the king of Sweden and Alfred B. Nobel, he started from Danes Island, Spitsbergen (Svalbard), with two companions, Nils Strindberg and Knut Frænkel, in a well-equipped balloon. Two days later a message from Andrée was brought by carrier pigeon to a sealer in the vicinity of Spitsbergen, reading: "July 13, 12:30 P.M. 82° 2′ N. lat., 15° 5′ E. long. Good journey E. 10° S. All well on board."

This was the last word received from him. Several search expeditions proved fruitless, but on Aug. 6, 1930, members of the crew of a Norwegian sealer, carrying the Arctic expedition of Gunnar Horn, accidentally found the bodies of Andrée and Strindberg on White Island. Frænkel's body was found later. Andrée's diary and the log of the expedition were beside him, carefully wrapped in a shirt. Evidence indicated that they died sometime after Oct. 2, 1897.

ANDREINI, än-drä-ē′nē, **Francesco** (c. 1548–1624), Italian actor and playwright. He was born at Pistoia, Italy. In 1578, at Florence, he joined the Gelosi, one of the most renowned of the *commedia dell'arte* troupes, which he later directed and took on tour throughout Italy and France. His early stock role of the lover was succeeded by that of the ambitious, boastful soldier, Capitan Spavento, in which he won lasting distinction. On the death of his wife in 1604, he retired to Mantua and gave all his time to writing scenarios, among them *Bravure del Capitan Spavento* (1607) and *Ragionamenti fantastici* . . . (1612). He died at Mantua.

ISABELLA ANDREINI (1562–1604), the wife of Francesco, was a famous actress and also a writer. Born at Padua, Italy, she married Francesco at 16 and with him joined the Gelosi. Well educated, beautiful, and dignified, she achieved stardom in the character of the prima donna in love. So forcibly did she impress her personality on the role that the name Isabella was later given to the heroines she portrayed. Though she was not a major poet, her graceful verse won the praise of the poets Torquato Tasso and Giambattista Marini. Her published works include the pastoral fable *Mirtilla* (1588), a volume of lyric verse (1601), and a collection of letters published posthumously (1607). She died at Lyon, France.

GIOVANNI BATTISTA ANDRIEINI (1578–1654), son of Francesco and Isabella, was a poet, playwright, and actor. He was born in Florence and began his career with the Gelosi, where he originated the role of the lover under the name of Lelio. When the Gelosi were disbanded in 1604, he joined the Fedeli troupe, and as manager took it to Paris in 1620, where he won added fame as Lelio. Among his writings was the sacred drama *L'Adamo* (1613), which is believed to have influenced John Milton's *Paradise Lost*. He died at Reggio nell'Emilia in June 1654.

ANDREW, an′droo, **Saint** (died 60 or 70), one of the Twelve Apostles. According to John, he was the first of the disciples of Jesus. His name, meaning "manly" in Greek, was common among Jews and testifies to the strong Hellenic influence that permeated Jewish life.

Like his brother Simon Peter, Andrew was a fisherman on the Sea of Galilee, living in Bethsaida. All the Gospels as well as the Acts have references to him. Four of these references suggest that Andrew shared with Peter, James, and John the inner circle of intimacy with Jesus. Andrew tells Simon, "We have found the Messias . . . the Christ," and brings him to Jesus (John 1:40–42). In the miraculous feeding of the five thousand, it is Andrew who tells Jesus of the boy with five barley loaves and two fishes (John 6:8–9). On the request of some Greeks to see Jesus, Philip seeks Andrew's advice before consulting the master (John 12:20–22). Three days before the Crucifixion, Andrew is in the company of Peter, James, and John when they take Jesus aside to ask him to explain his pronouncement on the destruction of the temple; to these four Jesus reveals the awesome signs attendant upon the end of the world and his Second Coming (Mark 13:3–37).

Andrew's apostolate was served among the Gentiles, and tradition assigns him a wide field of missionary activity, ranging over Cappadocia, Galatia, Bithynia, Scythia (now part of Russia), Thrace, Macedonia, Thessaly, and Achaea. The place, date, and manner of his death also are traditional. He is supposed to have been crucified in Patras, Greece, by the Romans on a decussate (X-shaped) cross, the so-called cross of St. Andrew (see CROSSES AND CRUCIFIXES). Because he was bound rather than nailed, his torment is said to have lasted two days.

Andrew is the patron saint of Scotland and Russia. The Eastern Orthodox, Roman Catholic, and Anglican churches observe his feast day on November 30.

ANDREW, an′droo, was the name of three kings of Hungary, of the Arpad dynasty. The name in Hungarian is *Endre*.

ANDREW I (died 1060), a cousin of Hungary's first king, Stephen I, reigned from 1046 to 1060. After his father's death in the 1030's, Andrew lived in exile at the court of Yaroslav the Great of Kiev. In 1046, however, he was recalled and crowned king of Hungary. He zealously protected the newly established Christian church against paganism and engaged in a series of struggles with Emperor Henry III for Hungary's independence. He was killed in a war that he brought on himself by revoking a promise that his brother Béla would succeed him.

ANDREW II (1175–1235), a son of Béla III, succeeded his older brother Imre and reigned from 1205 to 1235. To finance his reckless military campaigns and extravagant court, he virtually gave crown lands to the nobles and initiated a policy of currency depreciation. In 1217 he undertook an ill-starred crusade to the Holy Land. When he returned, his rebellious subjects forced him to issue the Golden Bull (1222), sometimes called the Hungarian Magna Charta. It guaranteed the privileges of the nobles against encroachment by the king, but also protected the lesser gentry against the great feudal lords. One of Andrew's daughters was St. Elizabeth of Hungary.

ANDREW III (died 1301), the last king of the Arpád dynasty, was called *Andrew the Venetian*. The grandson of Andrew II, he succeeded Ladislas IV and reigned from 1290 to 1301. In the early years of his reign he was involved in struggles with two contenders for the throne: Charles Martel of Anjou and Albert of Habsburg. Andrew defeated Charles in 1291 and made peace with Albert by marrying his daughter in 1296. Andrew died childless and was succeeded by Wenceslas III, first of the elected kings of Hungary.

ANDREW, James Osgood, an'drōō (1794—1871), American Methodist Episcopal bishop. Born in Wilkes County, Ga., on May 3, 1794, he was admitted at the age of 18 to the South Carolina Annual Conference of the Methodist Episcopal Church. For the next 20 years he served as a minister in Georgia and the Carolinas. His ability as a preacher and pastoral leader earned him election as a bishop at the General Conference in Philadelphia in 1832.

In 1844 his second marriage, to a woman who was a slaveowner, brought on a heated controversy in the Methodist Church. At the General Conference in New York City in May 1844 a resolution was passed suspending Andrew until his wife divested herself of her slaves. The Southern delegates to the conference protested the action, asserting that the best way for the church to combat slavery was to continue its mission to both slaves and slaveholders, working to arouse the national conscience in favor of emancipation. Unable to resolve their differences, delegates from all the Southern annual conferences met in Louisville, Ky., in May 1845 and created the Methodist Episcopal Church, South. At the first General Conference of the newly organized church, held in Petersburg, Va., in May 1846, Bishop Andrew became one of the first two bishops of the Southern jurisdiction. He died in Mobile, Ala., on March 2, 1871.

ANDREW, John Albion, an'drōō (1818—1867), American political leader who was governor of Massachusetts during the Civil War. Born in Windham, Maine, on May 31, 1818, he graduated from Bowdoin College in 1837 and practiced law in Boston from 1840 to 1861. An ardent opponent of slavery, he was one of the organizers of the Free-Soil party in 1848, and in 1854 joined the new Republican party. Andrew's eloquent defense of John Brown's part in the raid at Harpers Ferry thrust him into prominence on the eve of the Civil War. In 1860 he was chairman of the Massachusetts delegation to the Republican National Convention, and later in the year he was elected governor.

Andrew properly evaluated the danger of civil war and in his inaugural message announced his intention to ready the state militia for possible action. He carried out the mobilization so promptly that when Lincoln issued his historic call for troops on April 15, 1861, the 6th Massachusetts Regiment reached Washington only four days later. After the Emancipation Proclamation, Andrew obtained permission from the secretary of war to activate black units, and in May 1863 he sent out the 54th Massachusetts, the first black regiment. Later he fought the ruling that black troops should be paid as laborers and won for them pay equal to that for white troops.

Andrew was reelected governor in 1864 but retired from active politics in 1866 to resume private law practice. In the Reconstruction period he spoke out against the use of vindictive or humiliating measures against the prostrate Southern states and opposed the immediate and unconditional enfranchisement of the blacks. He died in Boston on Oct. 30, 1867.

ANDREW OF CRETE, Saint, an'drōō, krēt (c. 660—720/740), Byzantine prelate and hymnologist. Born at Damascus, Syria, he entered a monastery in Jerusalem at the age of 15. He is alternately known as Andrew of Jerusalem. He became a deacon about 685 and was appointed metropolitan of Gortyna in Crete about 711.

It is believed that he originated the musical or Greek canon; 14 canons definitely known to be his are still used in the Eastern Church, and many others are ascribed to him. He was also one of the great Byzantine preachers. He died on the island of Lesbos. His feast day is July 4.

ANDREW OF WYNTOUN. See WYNTOUN, ANDREW OF.

ANDREWES, Lancelot, an'drōōz (1555—1626), English bishop, preacher, and translator of the Bible. The son of a merchant, he was born at Barking, Sussex, England, and was educated at Merchant Taylors' School and Pembroke Hall, Cambridge, where he was elected a fellow in 1576. In 1589 he became vicar of St. Giles, Cripplegate, and prebend of St. Paul's Cathedral, and later in the year was appointed master of Pembroke Hall. Queen Elizabeth I named him dean of Westminster Abbey in 1601, and under James I he was successively bishop of Chichester (1605), Ely (1609), and Winchester (1619). In the controversy over the oath of allegiance imposed after the discovery of the Gunpowder Plot (1605), Andrewes wrote two spirited polemics, *Tortura Torti* (1609) and *Responsio ad Apologiam Cardinalis Bellarmini* (1610), replying to attacks made on King James by Robert Cardinal Bellarmine, who used the pen name Matthaeus Tortus.

Andrewes took part in the Hampton Court Conference (1604), which selected him as one of the translators of the Authorized Version of the Bible. The Pentateuch and the historical books were largely his work. He was particularly renowned for his sermons, and on the great feast days he was called to preach at court. Though highly mannered and abstruse, his homilies continue to rank among the great Anglican classics.

Andrewes was exceptionally learned; he is said to have mastered 15 languages. As a theologian he opposed both Roman Catholicism and Calvinism, and he strongly influenced the formation of a distinctive Anglican theology, of a generally Arminian cast. A collection entitled *Ninety-six Sermons* (1629) was published after his death. *Preces Privatae* (rev. ed., 1648; *Manual of Private Devotions*, 1903) contains prayers he composed in Greek and Latin for his own use.

Bibliography: Davies, Horton, *Like Angels from a Cloud: The English Metaphysical Preachers, 1588—1645* (Huntington Lib. Publs. 1986); Lossky, Nicholas, *Lancelot Andrewes, the Preacher (1555—1626),* tr. by Andrew Louth (Oxford 1991); Reidy, M. F., *Bishop Lancelot Andrewes* (Loyola Univ. Press 1955).

ANDREWS, Charles McLean, an'drōōz (1863—1943), American educator and historian. He was born of Puritan ancestry in Wethersfield, Conn., on Feb. 22, 1863. His B.A. (1884) came from Trinity College, Hartford, Conn., and his Ph.D. (1889) from Johns Hopkins. In the latter year he began teaching at Bryn Mawr College; in 1907 he went to Johns Hopkins. Three years later he became Farnam professor of American history at Yale, where he remained for the rest of his life. He died in Vermont on Sept. 9, 1943.

By 1893, Andrews had decided to devote himself to American colonial history. To ground himself thoroughly he felt it necessary to study the source materials in England. Out of his deep knowledge of sources there came works invaluable to other students as research tools. To these were added his illuminating surveys of life in the colonial period.

Andrews' first major work was *Colonial Self-Government, 1652–1689* (1904). *The Colonial Period* appeared in 1912. In it he clearly presented the "imperial viewpoint," which he did much to implant in the minds of other American historians. Formerly, he said, the colonies had been discussed apart from the mother country. The point to stress, he insisted, was the dependence and interdependence of the colonies and the mother country.

Andrews' great work was *The Colonial Period of American History* (4 vols., 1934–38), awarded the Pulitzer Prize. Conservative in tone, it was largely a history of institutions, of governmental agencies, charters, and land titles. Economic and social history was treated lightly, and the narrative left much of the 18th century untouched. Had Andrews lived, he planned to portray in future volumes of this series the rise of a more distinctively American civilization. But his completed work and that of his many students gave a new direction to American scholarship.

MICHAEL KRAUS
Author of "The Writing of American History"
City College of the City University of New York

ANDREWS, an'drōōz, **Elisha Benjamin** (1844–1917), American educator. Born at Hinsdale, N.H., on Jan. 10, 1844, he served in the Union Army in the Civil War. He graduated from Brown University in 1870 and from Newton Theological Institute in 1874, and held a Baptist pastorate for a year. He then turned to education and was professor of history and economics at Brown University from 1883 to 1888. In 1888 he went to Cornell University as professor of political economy and finance, but returned to Brown in 1889 as president of the university. Brown experienced a remarkable period of growth under his direction. He was chiefly responsible for the establishment of the university's women's branch, now known as Pembroke College.

Andrews served as a United States commissioner to the International Monetary Conference in Brussels in 1892. He then advocated international bimetallism—the use of both silver and gold as mediums of exchange. When university authorities tried to curb expression of these views in 1897, he resigned as president, but withdrew his resignation at the trustees' urging.

In 1889, however, he left Brown to become superintendent of the Chicago public schools. From 1900 to 1908 he was chancellor of the University of Nebraska. He died at Interlachen, Fla., on Oct. 30, 1917.

His books include *Institutes of General History* (1885; 1895), *Institutes of Economics* (1889; 1900), and *The Call of the Land* (1913).

ANDREWS, an'drōōz, **Frank Maxwell** (1884–1943), American army officer and airman, who foresaw the importance of air striking power before World War II. In 1938 he pleaded unsuccessfully for the United States to build fleets of heavy bombers, contending that they were the only practicable defense in the air, since they could strike at an enemy's bases and destroy its planes on the ground.

Frank Andrews was born in Nashville, Tenn., on Feb. 3, 1884. A graduate of West Point in 1906, he learned to fly during World War I. Af-

ter training at the Air Corps Tactical School and the Command and General Staff School, he was attached to the General Staff in 1934–1935. During the next four years he organized and commanded the General Headquarters Air Force, molding the Army's underequipped air combat squadrons into a small but efficient unit. In 1939 he was promoted to brigadier general and given a General Staff command.

After World War II broke out, Andrews was sent to take charge of the Panama Canal defenses and later, as lieutenant general, of all Army units in the Caribbean. In 1942 he was made commander of U.S. forces in the Middle East. Early the following year, as a U.S. commander in the European theater, he helped launch the effective daylight bombing campaign against Germany. Andrews was killed in a plane crash in Iceland on May 3, 1943.

ANDREWS, an'drōōz, **Julie** (1935–   ), English actress and musical comedy star who achieved fame in the role of Eliza Doolittle in the stage production of *My Fair Lady*. She was born *Julia Elizabeth Wells* at Walton-on-Thames on Oct. 1, 1935. When she was a child, her mother divorced her father and married Edward Andrews, a music hall singer. At the age of twelve, Julie Andrews made her stage debut as a singer at the London Hippodrome. In 1953, while acting the title role in *Cinderella* at the London Palladium, she was discovered by Vida Hope, director of *The Boy Friend*, who signed her for the female lead role in the New York production of the show. Early in 1956, Miss Andrews made her television debut opposite Bing Crosby in a musical adaptation of Maxwell Anderson's *High Tor*.

On March 15, 1956, Julie Andrews opened in the Broadway production of *My Fair Lady*, the Alan Jay Lerner and Frederick Loewe musical adaptation of George Bernard Shaw's *Pygmalion*. As the ragged cockney flower girl who is transformed into a lady by the ill-tempered Professor Higgins, she became an immediate star and received wide critical acclaim. She recreated the role in London in 1958.

In 1960 she returned to Broadway in the production of Lerner and Loewe's *Camelot*. She also appeared in motion pictures, and in 1964 she won the Academy Award as best actress for her performance in *Mary Poppins*. Her other films include *The Americanization of Emily* (1963) and *The Sound of Music* (1965).

JULIE ANDREWS in the Lerner-Loewe musical *Camelot*.

FRIEDMAN-ABELES

ANDREWS, an'drōōz, **Lorrin** (1795–1868), American missionary. He was born at East Windsor, Conn., on April 29, 1795, and was educated at Jefferson (now Washington and Jefferson) College and at Princeton Theological Seminary. Ordained a Congregational minister in 1827, he served as a missionary in Hawaii from 1828 to 1841. In 1831 he founded a school at Lahainaluna and was its principal for 10 years. From 1845 to 1859 he was a judge in various Hawaiian courts, and from 1846 to 1859 he was a member of the privy council. He died at Honolulu on Sept. 29, 1868.

Andrews published the first newspaper in Hawaii (1834) and translated the Bible into Hawaiian. His other works include a Hawaiian grammar and the *Dictionary of the Hawaiian Language* (1865; rev. by H.H. Parker, 1922).

ANDREWS, an'drōōz, **Roy Chapman** (1884–1960), American explorer, zoologist, and author, who led several important zoological expeditions and also served as the director of the American Museum of Natural History from 1935 to 1941. In addition to being a world authority on whales, Andrews led expeditions that discovered the first dinosaur eggs known to science; the first evidence of dinosaurs in Asia north of the Himalayas; remains of the first titanotheres discovered outside North America (the titanotheres were hoofed mammals that lived 30 million years ago); skulls and parts of the skeleton of the *Baluchitherium*, the largest land mammal known to have existed on earth; and evidence that men of the Old Stone Age lived in central Asia.

Andrews was born in Beloit, Wis., on Jan. 26, 1884. He graduated from Beloit College in 1906 and went to work for the Museum of Natural History in New York the same year. His study of whales began as a result of an assignment to secure the skeleton of a whale beached at Amagansett, Long Island. He carried out an expedition to the whaling stations of Vancouver Island and Alaska in 1908, served as special naturalist on the U.S.S. *Albatross* on an exploring voyage to the Netherlands East Indies in 1909–1910, and hunted the gray whale in the waters around Korea in 1911. He subsequently built the museum's collection of cetaceans (whales, dolphins, and porpoises) into one of the best in the world.

His first important land exploration, in 1911–1912, led him into then unknown country around Paektu-san, Korea, near the Manchurian border. He was with the Borden Alaska Expedition in 1913.

Andrews led expeditions into the mountains of southwestern China and Burma in 1916, to northern China and Outer Mongolia in 1919, and to central Asia between 1921 and 1930. The scientific reports of the Asian expeditions were published in 12 quarto volumes, under the title *The Natural History of Central Asia.*

Andrews resigned his museum post in 1941 to devote himself to writing. He died in Carmel, Calif., on March 11, 1960. His books include *Whale Hunting with Gun and Camera* (1916), *Camps and Trails in China* (1918), *Across Mongolian Plains* (1921), *On the Trail of Ancient Man* (1926), *Ends of the Earth* (1929), *The New Conquest of Central Asia* (1932), *This Amazing Planet* (1940), *Under a Lucky Star,* autobiography (1943), *Meet Your Ancestors* (1945), *An Explorer Comes Home* (1947), *Quest in the Desert* (1950), *Heart of Asia* (1951), and *Beyond Adventure* (1954).

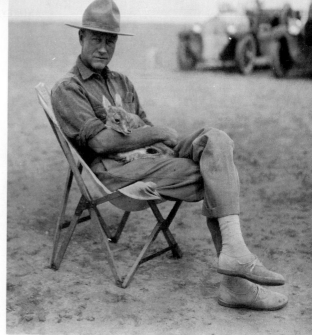

ROY ANDREWS, explorer and zoologist, holds a baby antelope caught during a Mongolian expedition in 1919.

ANDREWS, an'drōōz, **Stephen Pearl** (1812–1886), American reformer who invented the theory of "universology," a deductive science of the universe. Born at Templeton, Mass., on March 22, 1812, he practiced law in New Orleans, La., and Houston, Tex. In 1843 he was driven out of Houston because of his antislavery views. He went to England where he attempted to borrow money to buy and free the slaves of Texas.

While in England, Andrews learned the Isaac Pitman system of shorthand and later successfully introduced a system of his own in the United States. He mastered more than 30 languages and dialects, advocated greater attention to foreign languages in American schools, and originated an international language known as *Alwato.*

Andrews considered that his greatest achievement was the formulation of the theory of universology, which he introduced in *The Basic Outline of Universology* (1877). It included proposals for a utopian, semianarchistic society that he called the "pantarchy." Andrews died in New York City on May 21, 1886.

ANDREWS, an'drōōz, a city in western Texas, is the seat of Andrews County. It is situated approximately 35 miles north of Odessa by road. The city serves as a service, supply, and retail center for one of the richest oil- and gas-producing regions in the United States. Other products of its trading area are cotton, corn, and grain sorghums.

Among major annual events in Andrews are a trade fair, a junior rodeo, and a track and field competition called the Mustang Relays.

The community was settled in 1876 and was named for Richard Andrews, the first soldier killed (1835) in the Texas revolution. The city's major growth dates from 1930, when oil was discovered in the county. Andrews was incorporated in 1937. The city adopted a city-manager plan of government in 1959. Population: 9,652.

ANDREYEV, än-drä′yəf, **Leonid Nikolayevich** (1871–1919), Russian short-story writer, novelist, and playwright. His work mirrored the disillusionment of contemporary intellectuals during the last years of the czarist regime.

Born in Orel on June 18, 1871, Andreyev studied at St. Petersburg University and graduated from Moscow University with a law degree. After practicing law briefly, he began his writing career as a police court reporter for the Moscow *Courier*, which published his first short story, *Bergamot and Garaska*, in 1898. The story caught the attention of Maxim Gorky, who introduced Andreyev to Russian literary society and encouraged him to continue writing.

In 1901, Andreyev's first collection of short stories was brought out by Gorky's publisher. The book met with immediate success, selling 250,000 copies within a short time of its publication. When Andreyev's drama *King Hunger* was published in 1907, it enjoyed an even more spectacular success, with its entire first printing sold on the day of publication. From this time on, Andreyev's plays were produced regularly in Russia until the Bolshevik Revolution.

Andreyev declared himself an enemy of Bolshevism at the outbreak of the Revolution in March 1917, and this statement contributed to a break between him and Gorky, who was a supporter of Lenin. Andreyev became a member of the Kerensky government and was forced to flee Russia when the Bolshevik regime came into power in November 1917. He went to Finland, where he died in poverty at Kokkola on Sept. 12, 1919.

Andreyev's voice is anarchic, and the recurrent themes in his work are the inadequacy of man's intellect and the omnipotence of death. His early style was realistic, but allegory and symbolism became increasingly dominant as his writing evolved. *King Hunger*, a symbolic play, is a merciless dissection of contemporary Russian society. His last play, *He Who Gets Slapped* (1914), an allegorical work with a circus setting, portrays man's attempts to escape from the responsibilities of life. See also the article HE WHO GETS SLAPPED.

Andreyev's other works include the plays *The Days of Our Life, Black Masks, Anfissa, Gaudeamus, Catherine Ivanovna, Professor Storytzyn,* and *The Sabine Women* and the novel *The Red Laugh*. A collection of Andreyev's short stories was published in English in 1958 as *The Seven That Were Hanged and Other Stories*.

ANDRIA, än′drē-ä, is a commercial and manufacturing city in the Apulia region of southeast Italy. It is situated in Bari province, about 31 miles northwest of the city of Bari. The city manufactures food products and textiles, and is a trade center for the surounding district's olives, grain, and almonds.

The seat of a bishop, Andria has a number of old religious buildings. These include a Gothic cathedral; the Church of Sant' Agostino, which has a fine Gothic portal; and the churches of Santa Croce and Santa Maria dei Miracoli, which contain Byzantine frescoes.

Andria was founded about 1046 by Peter, first Norman count of Andria. The city was a stronghold and favorite residence of Emperor Frederick II (reigned 1215–1250) during his struggle with the papacy. Frederick built the imposing Castel del Monte nearby.

Andria was sacked by the French in 1527 and again in 1799. During World War II it was captured by the Allies in September 1943. Population: 95,653 (2001 census).

ANDRIĆ, än′drich, **Ivo,** Yugoslav novelist and short-story writer. He won the Nobel Prize for literature in 1961—the first Yugoslav to receive this honor. In making the award, the Swedish Academy cited him for "the epic force with which he has depicted themes and human destinies drawn from the history of his own country."

Writings. Andrić first became known for his collections of poetry, *Ex Ponto,* published in 1918, and *Unrest,* published in 1919. He later turned to prose, in which he revealed an original talent and great narrative power. He wrote many short stories of life in Bosnia during the period when that province was under oppressive Turkish rule. These stories were published in three collections—*Tales I* in 1924, *Tales II* in 1931, and *Tales III* in 1936.

During World War II, Andrić wrote three novels that placed him in the front rank of European writers. They were *The Bridge on the Drina, Bosnian Chronicle,* and *The Woman from Sarajevo.* Often called a "Bosnian trilogy," all three books were published in Belgrade in 1945. They were later translated into many languages.

The best-known of the three novels, *The Bridge on the Drina,* tells of the loves, hopes, and sufferings of generations of Bosnians living in the shadow of an ancient bridge. This book was specifically praised in the Nobel citation, although the prize was awarded for the whole body of Andrić's work. *Bosnian Chronicle* is a tapestried and many-faceted story of foreigners and Bosnians in the city of Travnik during the Napoleonic era. *The Woman from Sarajevo* is a study of the warped and misused life of a woman during the upheaval of World War I.

Andrić's later works include a number of short stories and novellas, notably *New Tales* (1948), *The Vizier's Elephant* (1948), *Under the Hornbeam* (1952), *Devil's Yard* (1954), and *Faces* (1960).

Life. Andrić, the son of poor Serbian parents, was born near Travnik, Bosnia, on Oct. 10, 1892, when Bosnia was under Austro-Hungarian rule. He attended school at Sarajevo and then studied philosophy and history at major universities in eastern Europe. In 1923 he received a Ph.D. from the University of Graz in Austria.

An ardent nationalist, he was jailed by Austro-Hungarian authorities during World War I for his activities on behalf of Slav independence. After the war, when the new state of Yugoslavia was created, he entered its diplomatic service. He became minister to Germany just before that country invaded Yugoslavia in 1941. During World War II he was kept under virtual house arrest in his Belgrade apartment and devoted himself entirely to writing. He continued writing after the liberation of Yugoslavia, while serving also as a member of parliament until 1952. He died in Belgrade, March 13, 1975. In 1959, Andrić had married Milica Babić, a scene designer at the Belgrade National Theater. She died several years before him.

Andrić was honored also by the Writers Federation and Union of Publishers of Yugoslavia.

JOSEPH HITREC
Novelist and Translator of Andrić's "Bosnian Chronicle" and "The Woman from Sarajevo"

ANDROCLES, an'drə-klēz, also spelled *Androclus,* is the hero of a story by Aulus Gellius (c. 123–165 A.D.) Androcles is an escaped Roman slave who hides in a cave where he befriends a lion by removing a thorn from its paw. Years later in an arena, the lion recognizes Androcles and refuses to harm him. The story was interpreted satirically in *Androcles and the Lion* by George Bernard Shaw.

ANDROGEN, an'drə-jən, is the name for several sex hormones secreted principally by the testes in males but also by the adrenal cortex. Androgens maintain proper functioning of the male reproductive organs; stimulate the development of secondary sex characteristics, such as hair growth pattern and voice quality in humans; induce the formation and maturation of sperm; and influence metabolic activity, such as the manufacture of protein and general growth factors. Their secretion is controlled by the front part of the pituitary.

The principal androgen produced by the testes is *testosterone.* Other androgens are *androstenedione, androsterone,* and *adrenosterone.*

In the female, androgens are produced by the ovary, and during pregnancy, by the placenta. They help prepare the uterus for pregnancy. If present in abnormal quantities, they interfere with the proper functioning of the ovaries and induce the development of male secondary sex characteristics.

ANDROMACHE, an-drom'ə-kē, in Greek legend, was the wife of Hector, the Trojan hero who was slain by Achilles in the Trojan War. After Troy was captured, Andromache's young son, Astyanax, was killed by the Greeks, and she was carried off by Achilles' son Neoptolemus (Pyrrhus). Eventually, she was married to Helenus, brother of Hector, with whom she reigned over a kingdom in Epirus.

A memorable tragic figure in Homer's *Iliad,* Andromache is noted for her affection for her husband and son and for her nobility in suffering after their deaths. The farewell scene between Andromache and Hector (*Iliad,* book 6) was a popular subject of painting. She is also the subject of tragedies by Euripides and Racine.

ANDROMEDA, an-drom'ə-də, in Greek legend, was the daughter of Cepheus, king of Ethiopia, and Cassiopeia. When Cassiopeia boasted that Andromeda was more beautiful than the Nereids (sea nymphs), the sea god Poseidon (Neptune), to avenge the insult, sent a monster to ravage the coast. Advised by oracles that only the sacrifice of their daughter would save the country, the king and queen had her bound to a rock on the coast for the monster to devour. Andromeda was rescued by Perseus, who killed the monster and married Andromeda. After her death Andromeda was made a constellation in the heavens.

The legend, one of many on the theme of the rescue of a princess from a dragon, was the precursor of that of St. George and the dragon.

ANDROMEDA, an-drom'ə-də, is an autumn constellation of the Northern Hemisphere. No star in the constellation is brighter than the second magnitude, but such stars as Alpheratz, Almach, and Mirach were well-known to the ancients. In Greek mythology Andromeda was the princess rescued from a sea monster by the hero Perseus.

LICK OBSERVATORY, UNIVERSITY OF CALIFORNIA

ANDROMEDA, an inconspicuous constellation (*inset*), is interesting because it contains the Great Nebula, the most distant object visible to the naked eye. The nebula's position in Andromeda is marked by a cross.

The region of sky occupied by the constellation is of great interest, because in it is found the most distant object visible to the naked eye —the Great Nebula of Andromeda. On a clear, moonless night this object appears as a faint, hazy patch of light. It is actually a vast star island, or galaxy, that lies about 1,500,000 light years beyond our own Milky Way galaxy and contains as many as 200 billion stars. The Great Nebula of Andromeda, the Milky Way, and a number of smaller galaxies together constitute what is known as the *local group* of galaxies.

The Andromeda galaxy was involved in the redetermination of the size of the universe by the German-American astronomer Walter Baade in the 1950's. Baade's studies led to the discovery that this galaxy was twice as large and twice as far away as had been thought. All other distances beyond our own galaxy had to be doubled as well. See also NEBULA.

ANDRONICUS I COMNENUS (1110?–1185), an-drə-nī'kəs kom-nē'nəs, was a Byzantine emperor. He was one of the most adventurous figures in the history of Byzantium. Intelligent, elegant, and attractive, but utterly unscrupulous and completely lacking in moral sense, he scandalized Constantinople by his love affairs. His cousin, Emperor Manuel I, pardoned his escapades, though he knew Andronicus desired the throne. When Manuel died in 1180, Andronicus was governor of the district of Pontus.

The news of the general discontent aroused by the incompetence of the regency appointed to guide Alexius II, the 12-year-old son and successor of Manuel, brought Andronicus to Constantinople. Acclaimed by the populace, Andronicus first disposed of the young emperor's mother, Marie, who headed the regency. Shortly afterward he disposed of Alexius himself and became emperor in his place in 1183. But his reign was a short one. The violence with which he tried to reform the administration, together with unfavorable developments abroad (particularly the sack of Thessalonica by the Normans), brought about a reaction that led to his overthrow and death.

PETER CHARANIS
Rutgers, the State University

ANDRONICUS OF CYRRHUS, an-drə-nī′kəs, sir′əs, a Greek architect who lived about 100 B.C. He built an octagonal marble tower at Athens, called the Tower of the Winds, which still stands. A sundial and carved figures representing the eight principal winds surmount each side of the monument. The roof originally was crested by a weather vane in the form of a triton, and a water clock was within the tower.

ANDROPOV, än-drô′pôf, **Yuri Vladimirovich** (1914– 1984), Soviet public official, who succeeded to the leadership of the USSR on the death of Leonid I. Brezhnev in November 1982.

The son of a railway laborer, Andropov was born on June 15, 1914, in Nagutskoye in the Stavropol krai in the northern Caucasus. He attended Petrozavodsk University in the Karelian ASSR and then began his rise to power through the Komsomol (Communist Youth League). After the Soviet-Finnish War of 1939–1940, Andropov became head of the Komsomol in the newly organized Karelo-Finnish republic. In 1951 he advanced to a staff position with the party's Central Committee in Moscow. He served as ambassador to Hungary from 1954 to 1957 and was active in the suppression of the Hungarian revolt in 1956. From 1957 to 1962 he handled party relations with the Communist parties in other Communist countries.

Andropov entered the hierarchy of Soviet politics in 1961 when he was elected to full membership in the Communist party's Central Committee. In 1962 he was promoted to membership in the Secretariat of the Central Committee. He left the Secretariat in 1967 to become chairman of the KGB (Committee on State Security), which placed him in charge of state security, espionage, and the suppression of political dissidence. In the same year he joined the Politburo as a candidate member, and in 1973 he became a full member.

On May 24, 1982, Andropov was named a national party secretary, and on May 26 he resigned his KGB post. On Nov. 12, 1982, two days after the death of Leonid Brezhnev, Andropov was chosen to succeed him as secretary-general of the Communist party. He completed his sweep of the top positions that Brezhnev had held by becoming chairman of the Defense Council and, on June 16, 1983, president of the USSR as chairman of the presidium of the Supreme Soviet. But by then a chronic kidney ailment had become life threatening. By August 1983 he was permanently confined to his home, and on Feb. 9, 1984, he died in Moscow.

In his short tenure he had emphasized tightening discipline in the workplace, eliminating corruption in the bureaucracy, intensifying the drive against dissidents, and reducing central planning constraints on the economy.

ANDROPOV, än-drô′pôf, a city in the Russian Federation. Known as Andropov from 1984 to 1987, Rybinsk had been renamed to honor the recently deceased Soviet leader Yuri Vladimirovich Andropov, whose political career had begun there.

The city is on the Volga River, about 150 miles (240 km) northeast of Moscow. It is a river port and manufacturing center and the site of a hydroelectric dam built on the Volga near the mouth of the Sheksna River. The dam, completed in 1941, created a reservoir with an area of 1,800 square miles (4,660 sq km). This, together with improvements in the nation's canal system, enhanced the city's commercial importance. The city produces river craft, printing and power machinery, cables, matches, and lumber.

First mentioned in the ancient Russian chronicles, the town was originally within the jurisdiction of the princes of Novgorod. From the 15th to the 18th century, the principal economic activity of the town, then known as Rybnaya Sloboda, was fishing. Both that name and Rybinsk, which it received in 1777, derive from the Russian word *ryba*, meaning "fish." Its commercial importance began with the opening of the Mariinsk Canal in 1810, linking the Volga with St. Petersburg. By 1910 it was the busiest port on the upper Volga. From 1946 to 1957 it was known as Shcherbakov, after a Bolshevik leader born there. Population: 222,653 (2002 census).

W. A. DOUGLAS JACKSON*
University of Washington

ANDROS, an′dros, **Sir Edmund** (1637–1714), British colonial governor in America, who is remembered chiefly for his governorship of the Dominion of New England. He had previously been governor of New York and later was governor of Virginia. In these offices he demonstrated military efficiency, technical skill, and personal strength, but he never fully comprehended American views. The restrictive policies of the crown during most of his stay in America also contributed to the problems that he faced.

Andros was born on Guernsey on Dec. 6, 1637, the son of a gentleman who served as bailiff of the island and in the household of Charles I. Becoming a soldier early in life, Andros first served in a foot regiment in the West Indies in 1666. Six years later he was a dragoon major, and in 1674 he replaced his father as bailiff of Guernsey. During these years Andros became the friend of the duke of York (later James II), who in 1674 appointed him governor of New York, his feudal domain in America.

Within the colony, Andros was virtually all-powerful, and he used his power energetically, for he knew that the duke expected his lands to return a profit. At the same time, Andros resisted popular demands that he call a representative assembly; the duke supported his governor's policy on this matter. The decision against representative government probably reduced the opportunities for making the colony pay. The towns at the eastern end of Long Island opposed Andros' authority, and he declared them in rebellion. Conflict with Connecticut and East Jersey over boundaries also increased his difficulties. Andros seized Governor Philip Carteret of East Jersey for his alleged exercise of authority over an area within the duke's colony. This act proved too extreme for the duke of York, who recalled Andros in 1681.

Governor of New England. In December 1686, Andros returned to America in the service of his old master, now James II. The crown had determined to implement a policy of political consolidation and royal control of the colonies. The first great step was the creation of the Dominion of New England, a single province composed of the colonies and regions of New England, to which New York and the Jerseys were added in 1688. In the Dominion, Governor Andros and his council had complete control.

Andros enjoyed considerable success in the first year of the Dominion. He reformed the judicial system of New England; he enforced the Navigation Acts, which previously had been ignored in New England; he provided protection to the Anglican Church; and he increased government revenues through a land tax and import duties.

These were significant achievements but cost Andros the support of important groups. Many merchants opposed enforcement of the Navigation Acts; the Puritans despised the Anglican Church; and landowners believed that Andros' land and tax policies put land titles in jeopardy. In addition, the governor's defense measures, which concentrated on Boston, left the frontier still vulnerable to attack by the French and Indians.

In April 1689, when news of the deposition of James II reached Boston, the colonists were ready for rebellion. They rose on April 18, and the Dominion speedily collapsed. Andros was imprisoned and then sent to England for trial. There charges were dropped, and Andros went into brief retirement.

Later Years. Andros' last period of service in America began in July 1692 when he arrived as governor in Virginia, where he proved popular. The large planters admired his aristocratic style, and many shared his dislike of Commissary James Blair, the bishop of London's representative in the colony. During his administration Andros presided over a gradual economic expansion. He also gave his support to the founding of the College of William and Mary (1693), now the second-oldest college-level institution (after Harvard) in the United States. But despite his success and popularity, he was recalled in 1697 at the instigation of Blair.

From 1704 to 1706, Andros was governor of the island of Jersey, one of the Channel Islands. After his retirement he lived in London, where he died on Feb. 27, 1714.

ROBERT MIDDLEKAUFF
University of California

ANDROSCOGGIN RIVER, an-drəs-kog'in, in New Hampshire and Maine, formed in Coos County, northeastern New Hampshire, by the junction of the Magalloway River and the outlet of Umbagog Lake. It flows south and southeast, entering Maine near Gilead, and joins the Kennebec River near Bath, forming Merrymeeting Bay, which empties into the Atlantic Ocean through a narrow inlet. The river's length is about 175 miles (280 km). It drops about 1,200 feet (365 meters) from its source to its mouth, and its falls supply power to mills in the Maine cities of Rumford, Auburn, Lewiston, and Brunswick. Logs for pulpwood are floated down the river.

ANDROUET DU CERCEAU. See DU CERCEAU.

ANEMIA, ə-nē'mē-ə, a deficiency of red blood cells, hemoglobin, or both. Normally, each drop of blood contains about 250 million red blood cells. These tiny disk-shaped cells are filled with hemoglobin, a reddish pigment that carries oxygen from the lungs to the body cells and also carries some carbon dioxide from the cells back to the lungs. When the number of red cells or the amount of hemoglobin within them falls below certain levels, a person is said to be anemic.

Kinds. Anemias are generally divided into three basic groups depending on their cause.

One kind of anemia is due to the loss of large amounts of blood from the body, usually from a profusely bleeding wound or an ulcer. Another kind of anemia occurs when too few red blood cells are produced. The third kind of anemia is due to the formation of red blood cells that are defective in some way and have a short life span.

Insufficient Production of Red Blood Cells. Normally, about 250 billion red cells are manufactured each day to replace those that are worn out and destroyed. Sometimes, the production is insufficient because of a lack of the substances needed for red-cell formation, such as iron, vitamin B_{12}, or folic acid. The most common anemia of this type is *iron-deficiency anemia.* Except in infants and children, iron-deficiency anemia is not due primarily to a lack of iron in the diet. Rather, it is usually the result of iron loss due to bleeding or pregnancy. Thus, changing the diet to include liver or vitamins has little or no effect on this anemia, which is cured by treating the source of bleeding. Iron, in the form of tablets or rarely, by injections, should also be administered.

Pernicious anemia is due to the body's inability to absorb vitamin B_{12} from ingested foods. The absorption of this vitamin is normally aided by a special substance secreted in the stomach. In people with pernicious anemia, this substance is lacking, and the disorder can be cured only by injections of vitamin B_{12}. Closely related to pernicious anemia is *folic-acid-deficiency anemia,* which often occurs in people whose diet does not include vegetables. This form of anemia is readily cured by the administration of very small amounts of folic acid.

People afflicted with cancer, tuberculosis, or chronic kidney disease sometimes suffer from a type of anemia, called *simple chronic anemia,* which is not due to the lack of iron, vitamin B_{12}, or folic acid. This anemia can be cured only by correcting the underlying disease.

Sometimes, insufficient production of red blood cells occurs when the bone marrow is damaged or diseased. One anemia of this type is *aplastic anemia,* which may result from the use of certain drugs, such as chloromycetin, or from exposure to irradiation. Aplastic anemia is difficult to treat and almost always requires the administration of blood transfusions. Cortisone-like drugs and male sex hormones have also been found to be helpful.

Defective Red Blood Cells. The most common of this third group of anemias is *sickle-cell anemia,* in which the red blood cells are misshapen and resemble tiny sickles. Sickle-cell anemia occurs most frequently in blacks and is inherited as a recessive trait. It is estimated that about 10 percent of all American blacks carry this trait. A similar disorder is *congenital spherocytosis,* in which the red blood cells are shaped like tiny spheres.

In some hemolytic anemias, known as *congenital nonspherocytic hemolytic anemias,* the red blood cells are short-lived even though they are normal in shape. Sometimes, the red blood cells have a short life span, not because they are defective, but because the person's body develops antibodies against his own red cells. This type of anemia is known as *autoimmune hemolytic anemia* and it can sometimes be treated with cortisone or cortisone-like drugs.

ERNEST BEUTLER, M.D.
City of Hope Medical Center

ANEMOMETER, an-ə-mom'ə-tər, an instrument for measuring the rate of flow of air or other gases. It is used primarily to measure wind speed in order to provide data for aircraft flights, weather forecasts, and weather records. A wind direction vane generally is used with the anemometer so that the wind velocity (both speed and direction) is measured.

Several types are in use, including *rotating-cup* and *propeller anemometers*. Each type has specific advantages in cost or performance that make it suitable for particular applications.

The rotating-cup anemometer in general use has three conical-shaped cups mounted on radial arms supported by a common hub. Energy from the rotation of the cups can be used to drive a mechanical counter to show wind speed.

The propeller anemometer usually has three blades mounted on a common hub; the blades move in a vertical plane. A vane is required to keep the blades facing directly into the wind. Small propeller anemometers often are used as flow-measuring instruments in ventilation ducts.

Less commonly used types include pressure-tube anemometers (or Dines) and hot-wire, bridled-cup, pressure-plate, drag-sphere, and sonic anemometers.

HERMAN H. CROUSER, *U.S. Weather Bureau*

ROCHE

Anemone (*A. coronaria*)

TAYLOR INSTRUMENT COMPANY

ROTATING-CUP ANEMOMETER and wind vane combine to provide wind velocity readings on meter at the left.

ANEMONE, ə-nem'ə-nē, is a group of spring, summer, and autumn flowering perennials found in the north temperate zone and in mountain areas. Also known as *windflowers*, they are hardy garden plants. Anemones are about 2 to 3 feet high and have erect stems. The compound leaves usually appear in whorls at the base of the stem or near the flowers. The flowers lack petals, but the sepals form the showy, colored part of the flower. There are many short stamens.

The genus *Anemone* belongs to the crowfoot family, Ranunculaceae. There are between 85 and 100 species. Common among the anemones is the poppy anemone, *A. coronaria*. Native to the Mediterranean region, it has red, blue, or white flowers and is the species usually sold by florists. The snowdrop anemone, *A. sylvestris*, has white flowers and is found in Europe and southwest Asia. The candle anemone, *A. cylindrica*, has greenish white flowers and is found in woods from New Brunswick, Canada, to New Jersey, and westward to Kansas, New Mexico, and British Columbia. Several forms also are cultivated in greenhouses as winter flowers. These are *A. hortensis*, *A. coronaria*, and *A. fulgens*.

For the marine animal of the same name, see SEA ANEMONE.

ANERIO, ä-nâ'rē-ō, **Giovanni Francesco** (1567?–1630), Italian composer who wrote church music in the tradition of Palestrina. In his secular works he introduced innovations, such as the addition of continuo parts to his madrigals. His compositions include nine books of motets, written between 1609 and 1619.

Born in Rome, he was a choir boy under Palestrina at St. Peter's, but virtually nothing else is known of his life until 1600, when he became choirmaster at St. John Lateran in Rome. He was appointed musician at the court of King Sigismund III of Poland, probably in 1606, but by 1608 he had returned to Rome.

In July 1609, Anerio was appointed choirmaster at Verona Cathedral and remained there until 1611, when he assumed the same post at the Seminario Romano. In 1613 he received an appointment as choirmaster of the Church of Santa Maria dei Monti in Rome. Anerio was ordained into the priesthood in 1616. He died while on a journey from Poland to Italy.

FELICE ANERIO (1560–1614), his older brother, succeeded Palestrina as composer to the papal chapel at St. Peter's in 1594. He composed numerous hymns, masses, and madrigals, as well as an *Adoramus te, Christe* and a *Stabat Mater* that once were attributed to Palestrina.

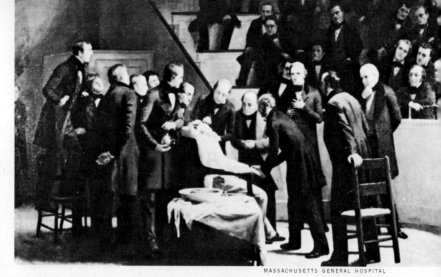

ANESTHESIA was first demonstrated to the medical profession on Oct. 16, 1846, when Dr. William T.G. Morton (left center, with a flask in his hand) administered ether to a patient and removed a tumor of the jaw at Massachusetts General Hospital, in Boston, Mass.

MASSACHUSETTS GENERAL HOSPITAL

ANESTHESIA, an-əs-thē′zhə, literally means insensibility. The word was coined by Oliver Wendell Holmes to describe the state of reversible consciousness induced by drugs to make surgery painless. Today anesthesia may refer to insensibility of any area of the body, however caused. Anesthesia in this sense may be induced by drugs, by physical agents such as cold or electricity, or by disease. Anesthesia must be distinguished from *analgesia,* which is the loss only of the sense of pain.

Anesthesia is given by an *anesthetist.* An *anesthesiologist* is a specialist physician, whose training in the United States includes at least two years of full-time residency in the specialty of anesthesiology. The American Board of Anesthesiology, which examines and issues diplomas to trained anesthesiologists, defines the specialty as follows:

"Anesthesiology is a practice of medicine dealing with (1) the management of procedures for rendering a patient insensible to pain during surgical operations; (2) the support of life functions under the stress of anesthetic and surgical manipulations; (3) the clinical management of the patient unconscious from whatever cause; (4) the management of problems in pain relief; (5) the management of problems in cardiac and respiratory resuscitation; (6) the application of specific methods of inhalational therapy; (7) the clinical management of various fluid, electrolyte, and metabolic disturbances."

Surgical anesthesia may be *general anesthesia,* in which the patient is asleep, or *local anesthesia,* in which a part of the body is rendered insensible but the patient is not unconcious. Local and general anesthesia may be combined in *balanced anesthesia.*

General Anesthesia. The exact manner in which general anesthetics act is unknown. Two theories are favored at present. According to the lipoid theory, anesthetic agents dissolve in the fatty tissues of the brain and interfere with nervous activity. The hydrate microcrystal theory, advanced by Nobel prizewinner Linus Pauling in 1959, suggests that anesthetics interlink with water in the brain to form tiny crystals. Such crystals would reduce the energy available in the brain.

History. The search for a pain-free sleep that can be turned on and off at will is as old as the story of Adam's rib. For centuries mankind had only opium, alcohol, and the legendary mandrake to provide pain relief or induce unconsciousness during surgical operations. These drugs had to be taken by mouth and, once administered, could not be controlled. Often the patient felt pain and sometimes he died.

The famous English scientist Sir Humphry Davy (q.v.) was the first to point out the only route by which drugs can be withdrawn as easily as they can be administered; this route was the lung. In 1799 he noted the pain relief obtained during the inhalation of nitrous oxide (which he named laughing gas), and suggested its use during surgery.

Davy's work was extended to ether by his pupil Michael Faraday (q.v.). Nitrous oxide, and especially ether, became popular intoxicants but remained unused by surgeons. In 1842 a doctor in Georgia, Crawford Long (q.v.), painlessly removed a tumor from a student's neck while the student was sniffing ether from a towel. Long did not publish his results until 1849.

In 1844, Horace Wells (q.v.), a Connecticut dentist, while watching a demonstration of nitrous oxide inhalation, once again noted the freedom from pain conferred by this gas. The next day Wells had one of his own teeth pulled while inhaling nitrous oxide. The experiment was a success, and Wells began using the gas in his practice. But it was William Thomas Green Morton (q.v.), a pupil of Wells, who finally demonstrated ether anesthesia successfully before an audience of surgeons in 1846. Morton generally is considered to be the father of general anesthesia.

Agents. The following general anesthetic agents are in common use today.

(1) *Gases* (compressed in tanks).

Nitrous oxide (gas, laughing gas) is an excellent analgesic but a very weak anesthetic agent. It causes little stress to the body. The gas is nonexplosive, but it is too costly and cumbersome for use in many areas of the world. Where available, nitrous oxide is a major constituent of most anesthetic mixtures.

Cyclopropane is a powerful anesthetic agent that can be administered with a high proportion of oxygen. Induction is rapid and there is no irritation. Because this gas is highly explosive and can have unfavorable effects on the heart and lungs, it is used only by experts, in whose hands it is an excellent, flexible agent.

(2) *Volatile agents* are supplied as liquids that, at room temperature, give off enough vapor to induce and maintain inhalation anesthesia. They often are carried to the patient on a stream of nitrous oxide or oxygen.

Ether, because of its safety record, remains the nearest to the ideal anesthetic. Of all agents now

833

used, ether is the only one that by itself can provide the anesthetic state necessary for any operation. It can be used without cumbersome apparatus and is not explosive in air. It is explosive, however, when mixed with oxygen. Because it is slow, irritant, and more liable than most agents to cause nausea, ether is no longer used widely where more sophisticated anesthesia can circumvent these hazards.

Divinyl ether and ethyl chloride are less irritant and more powerful than ether, and they are often used to put patients, especially children, to sleep before ether is introduced. Neither can be used for prolonged anesthesia, and both are explosive.

Chloroform is very potent, but most anesthesiologists feel that its disadvantages far outweigh its advantages. It rarely is used now.

Trichlorethylene (Trilene) is a cheap, nonexplosive agent that is a potent analgesic though a weak anesthetic. It is a valuable agent in childbirth, and, with proper precautions, can be administered by the patient to herself.

(3) *Fluorinated volatile agents* are a new group of anesthetics that were first introduced in the late 1950's. They are unique in that they contain fluorine in their chemical structure. They are mainly nonirritant, potent, and nonexplosive. Some of them, especially halothane (Fluothane), have been taken up enthusiastically by anesthetists the world over because they feel that the advantages of these agents far outweigh the disadvantages (for example, expense). The safety record of halothane, after ten years of use, was found to be as good as that of ether.

(4) *Intravenous agents.* A simple way to maintain anesthesia is to feed the anesthetic directly into a vein of the patient. Such intravenous anesthesia is used widely. The drug, once injected, cannot be withdrawn and must leave the blood stream through the kidneys or the lungs, or must be rendered harmless in the liver. Unless a fine balance can be maintained between the injection of the drug and its elimination, overdosage can easily occur. Such techniques are therefore only for those trained in their use, especially since dosage varies from person to person.

The most important intravenous anesthetics are members of the barbiturate group of drugs. The most popular, Sodium Pentothal (sodium in a barbiturate usually shortens its action), was introduced in the United States by John Lundy in 1933. Pentothal and drugs like it are cleared from the blood stream so rapidly that moment-to-moment control of the depth of anesthesia is possible. For this reason, these agents are called ultrashort-acting. However, after leaving the bloodstream, Pentothal is stored in the fat and leaves the body over a period of hours. Hence a patient who has received large amounts of Pentothal may wake up, then go back to sleep as more drug is released from the body fat.

Barbiturates do not eliminate pain reflexes. For this reason, anesthetists use them only for very brief or painless procedures; to maintain sleep during local anesthesia; or to induce anesthesia. Barbiturate induction is rapid and pleasant, and it eliminates the struggle against the effects of the anesthesia often seen with ether or nitrous oxide inductions.

(5) *Muscle relaxants.* One problem with almost all anesthetic agents is that very deep anesthesia is needed to relax the muscles for operations on the abdomen or for manipulations. In 1942 a Canadian anesthesiologist, Harold Griffith, revolutionized anesthesia by using curare, the South American arrow poison, to relax muscles during light anesthesia. The action of curare can be reversed by drugs.

Another group of muscle relaxants cannot be reversed but usually is destroyed so rapidly by the body that reversal by drugs is unnecessary. The most popular of this group, succinyl choline, acts so briefly that it allows moment-to-moment control of relaxation. Since relaxants paralyze all muscles, including those of respiration, the patient under relaxants usually needs artificial respiration.

Combination Anesthetics. The ideal general anesthetic agent should accomplish three things: sleep, pain relief, and muscle relaxation. It should be cheap, nonirritant, nonexplosive, easy to administer, and pleasant to take. It should cause no untoward effect during or after anesthesia.

Since such an agent does not exist, anesthesiologists often use a combination of drugs that will effect, separately, sleep, pain relief, and muscular relaxation, while changing the patient's condition as little as possible.

An innovation popular in Europe is the use of an anesthetic that combines a powerful analgesic and a neurolept agent. The latter acts on the brain stem to protect the patient from harmful reflexes and to erase memory of the surgical experience. Usually very light nitrous oxide anesthesia is added to sustain sleep.

Techniques. Morton dripped ether on a sponge; Long used a towel. Such open methods of administering anesthesia are still practiced, but a gauze-covered wire-mesh mask is now used.

Gases must be administered by gas-tight masks made of rubber or plastic. The mask is connected by large-bore tubes to a rubber bag, the reservoir bag, which is continuously filled with an anesthetic mixture, and from which the patient breathes. Nowadays the bag usually is attached to a machine that delivers gases and contains a means of measuring gas flows and devices by which volatile agents can be added to the gases. The exhaled gases from the patient may be recirculated to him, if oxygen is added first and harmful carbon dioxide is removed by an absorption canister.

A major advance in anesthetic technique was the introduction of a tube into the windpipe (trachea). This endotracheal tube may be inserted into the windpipe while the patient is asleep or under topical anesthesia (see below). The tube enables the anesthetist to retain control over the patient's airway during operations on the head and neck. An air-inflated cuff, which establishes an airtight fit between the tube and the trachea, has been added to this apparatus. This cuff prevents the aspiration of stomach contents and blood, and makes artificial respiration easy. Insertion of the tube and control of the lungs through it is one of the special lifesaving skills of the trained anesthesiologist.

Local Anesthesia. Anesthesia with drugs like cocaine, which block sensation in limited regions of the body, is called local anesthesia. For centuries the South American Indians knew the numbing effect of the leaves of the coca plant. About the middle of the 19th century, naturalists brought some coca leaves back to Europe, and in 1860, Albert Niemann, in Germany, extracted crystals of the numbing agent and called it cocaine. In 1884, Sigmund Freud (q.v.), then working on its use in treating narcotic addiction, suggested its use for surgery to the Viennese eye surgeon Carl Koller. One year later, in Baltimore, the eminent surgeon William Stewart Halsted began to inject cocaine around nerve trunks to block sensation in limited areas of the body.

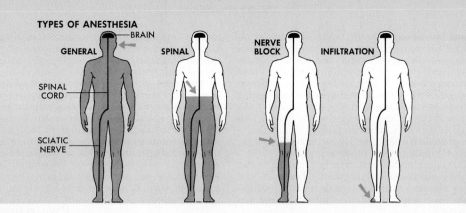

TYPES OF ANESTHESIA

GENERAL — BRAIN — SPINAL — SPINAL CORD — SCIATIC NERVE — NERVE BLOCK — INFILTRATION

Cocaine, however, is very toxic. The drug remains the best surface anesthetic, but it has been replaced for most uses by synthetic agents. Important agents include Novocaine (procaine), Xylocaine, Carbocaine, Metycaine, Nupercaine, and Pontocaine. By combining a local anesthetic drug with a drug that constricts blood vessels, a pain-relieving effect may be prolonged for hours.

A nerve block, such as Halsted used, spinal anesthesia, and epidural anesthesia are varieties of regional anesthesia. Anesthesia by application of a drug to a surface rather than by injection is topical anesthesia. Anesthesia given by injecting local anesthetic drugs in the area that is about to be cut is infiltration anesthesia.

Surgeons of the late 19th century took up all these types of local anesthesia with enthusiasm, believing that the patient was safer when awake. This is no doubt true when unskilled members of the surgical team administer general anesthesia. In countries where skilled anesthesiologists are still a rarity, surgeons use infiltration anesthesia for most major operations.

Infiltration and Topical Anesthesia. At present infiltration anesthesia is widely used for minor surgery, dentistry, and the relief of persistent pain. Topical anesthesia is particularly useful in examinations and in operations of the nose, throat, eye, and bladder.

Nerve Blocks. Nerve blocks also remain important. The nerves to the outlet from the womb can be obstructed by pudendal block, outstandingly useful in childbirth. The nerves to the hand and arm are blocked by a brachial block. Dentists use a mandibular block for surgery on the lower jaw. By a paravertebral block, any nerve can be blocked as it leaves the vertebral canal, for instance to relieve the pain of broken ribs. In addition, blocks of the sympathetic nerve chain in the neck and in the lumbar (lower back) area are used widely to diagnose and treat disorders of the blood vessels supplying the limbs.

Spinal and Epidural Anesthesia. One year after the introduction of local anesthesia, James Leonard Corning in New York City suggested a bold new approach to the blocking of the nerve supply to a larger, but still limited, area of the body.

The spinal cord, together with the nerve roots arising from it, is enveloped in a fibrous sac, the dura mater (dura). The dura also contains a clear fluid, the cerebrospinal fluid (CSF). Several nerve roots can be blocked at once if local anesthetic solution is injected either into the CSF or around the dura. Injection into the dural sac, usually performed below the level where the spinal cord ends, is spinal anesthesia. Spinal anesthesia renders insensible and flaccid the whole area below the level at which the anesthetic is placed. Injection outside the dura is epidural, or peridural, anesthesia. Epidural anesthesia covers only the area at the level at which it is placed.

The German surgeon August K.G. Bier was the first to use spinal anesthesia in man, in 1898. Early spinals were crude and gained the technique an undeservedly bad reputation. Many patients had severe headaches for long periods following their surgery, and in a few rare but well-publicized cases, paralysis of the legs developed. Techniques for dealing with complications arising during surgery were not then available.

By contrast, modern techniques make spinals safe and comfortable. With the use of very fine needles and other refinements, headaches have become uncommon and usually are mild and easily relieved. There have been no recent recorded cases of paralysis. During the operation the patient, unaware of the anesthetized area, may remain awake, or he may be put to sleep with an intravenous agent. Nausea and vomiting are rare, and patients may be out of bed a few hours after the anesthesia wears off.

Spinals are used mainly in operations on the lower half of the body. They are valuable in emergency situations, when the patient's stomach may be full and vomiting is a risk during general anesthesia. Saddle block is a spinal affecting only the areas around the anus and genital area; it is valuable in operations on these areas and especially in childbirth.

The Spanish surgeon Fidel Pagés reintroduced the use of epidural anesthesia in 1921. This is an excellent anesthetic technique, with even fewer complications than spinal anesthesia.

For caudal block, the epidural needle is introduced from the lower end of the vertebral canal. The block covers about the same area as a saddle block and is used widely in childbirth.

Any block may be made continuous by threading a very fine plastic tube through the needle and leaving it in place after the needle is removed. Repeated injections then can be made, if necessary, over a period of days.

A local anesthetic agent, in addition to its previously described use, can be given intravenously. This may eliminate pain, or, for instance, itching over the whole body. Intravenous injection into a limb may produce anesthesia in that limb only, if the outflow of blood is first obstructed by a tourniquet.

Refrigeration anesthesia is induced by packing a limb in ice. It is very effective for amputations when the patient is very ill.

Other Techniques. Anesthetic agents may be introduced through the rectum, but full anesthesia by this route is unpredictable and therefore dangerous. Small doses of Sodium Pentothal or other agents may be used rectally for young children to make the trip to the operating room uneventful.

Electrical anesthesia may be achieved by a mixture of direct and alternating currents. This method is still very unpredictable.

Hypnosis has been used for major surgery alone or in combination with other agents.

Computers have been attached to electrodes recording electrical activity of the brain. As the activity changes with varying levels of anesthesia, more or less anesthetic solution is injected automatically.

Patient Care. During an operation, the anesthesiologist, in addition to managing the anesthetic procedure, monitors the patient's vital signs and counteracts dangerous changes. He is in complete control of the flow of air to the patient's lungs, using artificial respiration as necessary, either by squeezing the reservoir bag or by using one of a number of respirators now available (most of which have been developed by anesthesiologists). He may use sophisticated devices to check temperature, the function of the heart and lungs, and muscular relaxation. He replaces water, salt, and blood as needed. If the patient suffers from diseases such as diabetes, asthma, or conditions of the heart, kidney, or liver, the anesthesiologist adjusts his anesthesia, gives medication, and treats any complications.

OLIVER H. FRENCH, M.D.
South Nassau Communities Hospital

Bibliography: Dripps, Robert D., and Vandam, Leroy D., *Introduction to Anesthesia* (Saunders 1988); Tolme, J. D., and Birch, A. A., *Anesthesia for the Uninterested,* 2d ed. (Aspen Systems Corp. 1986).

ANEURYSM, an′yə-riz-əm, a saclike enlargement of an artery, usually the aorta. An aneurysm occurs when the artery is weakened by disease or injury, allowing the artery walls to balloon out and form a sac. Most aortic aneurysms occur in men between the ages of 40 and 70, and they are usually located in the portion of the aorta that passes through the chest and abdomen.

The most common cause of aneurysms is atherosclerosis, a condition in which fatty deposits line the artery walls. Birth defects, trauma, and infections, such as syphilis, are also causes of aneurysms.

Symptoms. The symptoms of an aortic aneurysm depend on its size and location. Sometimes an aneurysm ruptures, causing a hemorrhage. It may also compress the surrounding tissues, producing pain and various other symptoms. A syphilitic aneurysm may cause a painful erosion of the chest vertebrae or breastbone, an obstruction of the windpipe and bronchi, causing shortness of breath and coughing, and an obstruction of the flow of blood in the veins, producing a swelling of the face. An atherosclerotic aneurysm occurring in the abdominal aorta may stretch suddenly and cause severe pain in the abdomen and back. There may also be massive bleeding.

A dissecting aneurysm occurs when the middle layer of the aortic wall splits. This condition is usually associated with severe chest pain, and it may also obstruct the arteries arising from the aorta, causing a stroke, a heart attack, kidney failure, or gangrene of the intestine. Sometimes, an aneurysm produces no symptoms at all and can be diagnosed only through a physical examination and X rays.

Treatment. It is often possible for a surgeon to remove an aortic aneurysm and replace the tissue with a graft made of a synthetic material. Generally, an abdominal aneurysm is more easily corrected than one located in the chest. The surgical treatment of an aneurysm that has ruptured is difficult and risky, but under the circumstances there is no alternate treatment. In cases where there is no real emergency, the decision regarding surgical treatment is largely influenced by the patient's general health.

J. WILLIS HURST, M.D.
Emory University School of Medicine

ANGARA RIVER, än-gə-rä′, in the Russian Federation, in south-central Siberia. The outlet of Lake Baikal, the Angara flows 1,151 miles (1,852 km) north and west, emptying into the middle section of the Yenisei River. The river flows mostly through Siberian coniferous forest that was virtually uninhabited until the 1950s. Because of the sparse settlement along its banks and because it is icebound from November to May, the river is not important for navigation.

The river's steep downhill gradient and the vast natural reservoir of Lake Baikal make the Angara highly suitable for generating water power. Large hydroelectric stations have been built at Irkutsk, the largest city along the Angara, and at Bratsk, an industrial city that developed in the 1960s. The dams have transformed the Angara from a torrential stream into a slow-flowing series of reservoirs.

THEODORE SHABAD
Author of "Geography of the USSR"

ANGARSK, un-gärsk′, a city in the Russian Federation, in Irkutsk oblast, in eastern Siberia. It is situated 30 miles (48 km) northwest of Irkutsk, at the junction of the Angara and Kitoi rivers. The city was founded after World War II.

Angarsk is one of the Russian Federation's largest chemical centers. The industry is based on a refinery that processes crude oil transported by a trans-Siberian pipeline from the Tatar and Bashkir oil fields on the western slopes of the Ural Mountains. The city's petrochemical products include synthetic alcohol, artificial fibers, plastics, mineral fertilizers, and detergents. There is also a cement mill.

In contrast to the older cities of Siberia, Angarsk is laid out in rectilinear fashion, according to the principles of modern city planning. Construction of the city began in 1947, when a German hydrogenation plant was shipped to Siberia and located on the site. The plant converted coal from the nearby Cheremkhovo mines into gasoline and oil. When the oil refinery was completed in 1960, Angarsk's chemical industry shifted from coal to oil. Population: 267,000 (1994 est.).

THEODORE SHABAD
Author of "Geography of the USSR"

ANGAUR, äng-our′, an island in the Palau group of the Caroline Islands, in the western Pacific Ocean. It contains deposits of phosphate. Saipan, on the west coast, is the chief village. Angaur is a part of the Republic of Palau, which gained independence from the United States in 1994.

ANGEL, ān′jəl, a spiritual being created by God to serve the heavenly throne and to act as a messenger between the Creator and mankind. The name "angel" comes from the Greek word for "messenger."

Angels are pure spirits, that is, entirely unrelated to matter although, like man, they possess the attributes of intelligence and free will. This freedom of will was shown in the angelic rebellion led by Lucifer (Satan) that resulted in the banishment of many angels from the sight of God. Christian exegesis, based on the Bible and tradition, gives the number of angels as legion and their creation as coming either at the time of the creation of the earth or shortly before this event.

According to *De coelesti hierarchia*—attributed to St. Denis (Dionysius) the Areopagite—and to the writings of the church doctors and Old and New Testament references, there are nine orders of angels. These orders are divided into three hierarchies, each containing three orders. In descending rank of importance they are: Seraphim, Cherubim, Thrones, Dominations, Principalities, Powers, Virtues, Archangels, and Angels. The lowest order, which gives the generic names to all, is the one from which the guardians of men and nations are selected.

Angels are mentioned in the Bible from the Book of Genesis through the Apocalypse. The first mention is of the cherubim whom God set before the Garden of Eden after the fall from grace of Adam and Eve (Genesis 3:24). The last is in the "Final Attestation" of the Apocalypse (Revelation 21). Between are countless references: in the Old Testament angels fill Jacob's vision; one serves as a guide to Lot; and one, as counselor to Daniel. In the New Testament they are present from John the Baptist's birth through all of Christ's earthly presence. Only three, all archangels, are named: Gabriel, whose name means "Hero of God"; Raphael, "God has healed"; and Michael, "Who is like God." See also ARCH-ANGEL; GABRIEL; MICHAEL; TOBIT, BOOK OF.

Angelology, or a belief in angels, has been a tenet of faith from early recorded history. Zoroastrianism, founded in the 5th century B.C., held that six archangels guarded the presence of Ahura Mazda (Ormuzd, the Wise Lord). Known as the Amesha Spentas, they personified Good Wind, Excellent Truth, Wished-for Kingdom, Devotion, Wholesomeness, and Nondeath.

Islam adapted many practices from Christianity, including a belief in angels. In Islamic theology the angelic hierarchy is headed by Gabriel. Islamic angels are said to have been created before man and to be of a finer nature.

Wherever they appear in religion, angels—that is, those who remained faithful to the power of good—are honored for themselves and for their power before the Creator. In the Christian church, veneration of angels was practiced from the church's founding. The Roman Church honors angels in its liturgy, particularly on the feast of St. Michael and All Angels (September 29). See also MICHAELMAS.

In art, angels are depicted in human form. Usually they are portrayed with wings, signifying their role as heavenly messengers. See also ANNUNCIATION.

ANGEL FALLS, the world's highest waterfall, located in southeastern Venezuela. Its greatest uninterrupted drop is 800 m (2,640 ft).

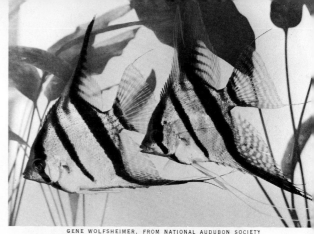

Angelfish

ANGELFISH, ān′jəl-fish, a term applied to fishes of the family Chaetodontidae, but usually limited to two genera, *Pomacanthus* and *Angelichthys*. These brightly colored fishes are widely distributed in tropical waters from low tide mark to a depth of 165 feet (50 meters), usually around coral reefs. Their distinguishing characteristics are the laterally compressed body form, the head spines, and the prolongation of dorsal fin rays backward in long, thin streamers. Angelfishes eat coral polyps and algae. Some are "cleaners" that nibble parasites off other fish.

Two typical angelfishes, both from the West Indies, are the queen angel, a blue and yellow fish with a dark blue ocellus (eyespot) in front of the dorsal fin, and the French angel, whose black scales are edged with yellow.

The name "angelfish" is also used for a raylike shark, *Squatina,* and by aquarium fanciers for the small fresh-water fishes of the genus *Pterophyllum,* of which there has been intensive and selective breeding.

ANGELICA, an-jel′ik-ə, is a group of perennial herbs that are native to the Northern Hemisphere and New Zealand. The leaves are in groups of three, and the flower clusters are white or greenish. The candied stems may be used in decorating pastries or in flavoring certain liqueurs.

The genus *Angelica* belongs to the parsley family, Umbelliferae. There are about 50 species. Of these, *A. archangelica* is found in Europe and Asia. It is about 6 feet (2 meters) tall and has long leaves. *A. curtisii* is native to the area from Pennsylvania to North Carolina.

Angelica

FRA ANGELICO'S *Madonna of the Linen Drapers' Guild*, in the Museo di San Marco, Florence, is a representative work of the artist's mature style.

ALINARI-ART REFERENCE BUREAU

ANGELICO, än-jä'lē-kō, **Fra** (1400?–1455), Italian painter, who was one of the great artists of the early Italian Renaissance. He was born *Guido di Pietro* at Vicchio, near Florence. The name "Angelico" (sometimes "Beato Angelico") was not applied to him until late in life or after his death. In contemporary documents he is called *Giovanni da Fiesole* or *da Firenze.*

He was a Dominican friar whose style preserved the religious piety and many of the artistic conventions of the Middle Ages. His modeling of forms and his use of spatial perspective show, however, that he was responsive to the innovations of such contemporaries as Masaccio.

Unlike other painters of his time, Fra Angelico painted only religious subjects. Most of his works are traditional altarpieces for private devotions, many of them painted for monasteries at Fiesole and Florence and for the Vatican. Giorgio Vasari, a painter and biographer of the 16th century, said of Fra Angelico that "he would often say that whoever practiced art needed a quiet life and freedom from care, and that he who occupied himself with things of Christ [in art] ought always to be with Christ."

Vasari, by erroneously reporting Fra Angelico's death at 68 or 69, raised problems about the artist's early life and the attribution of his works. Also, Fra Angelico's conservative style was formerly attributed by some critics to a period of training in a monastic workshop. However, recently discovered evidence indicates that he was already well known as a painter in 1417, before he entered the Dominican order, in which he was ordained sometime between 1423 and 1425. It is clear, in any case, that his art developed out of the international Gothic style of Lorenzo Monaco and Gentile da Fabriano.

The earliest surviving painting that can be attributed to Fra Angelico with certainty is the *Madonna of the Linen Drapers' Guild,* or Linaiuoli altarpiece, now in the Museo di San Marco, Florence. Commissioned by the guild in 1433, the painting is in the artist's mature style. Although it is typical of the international Gothic style in many ways, the painting substitutes a monumental simplicity for the Gothic profusion of detail. And although he used the pure or unmixed colors characteristic of the Gothic painters, Fra Angelico's colors assume symbolic values in representing the pure light of heaven and the glow of untainted celestial beings.

Fra Angelico's paintings of the later 1430's and the early 1440's include the *Coronation of the Virgin* (Louvre, Paris), and the *Deposition* and the *Madonna Annalena,* an altarpiece of the Virgin and Child with saints (both in the Museo di San Marco). During this period, Fra Angelico placed his large and simply modeled figures in an earthly environment enriched with delicate Tuscan loggias and porticos or in idyllic landscapes.

Around 1438, under the patronage of Cosimo de' Medici, Fra Angelico decorated the newly rebuilt Dominican monastery of San Marco in Florence. He painted a large *Crucifixion* for the refectory, an *Annunciation* at the head of the stairs in the dormitory, and, with his assistants, 45 frescoes in individual cells. These works have an iconic monumentality that eliminates all distracting details of narrative.

Pope Eugene IV summoned Fra Angelico to Rome around 1445 to decorate the Chapel of the Sacrament in the Vatican. Pope Nicholas V, succeeding Eugene in 1447, commissioned the artist to paint the great frescoes representing the lives of St. Lawrence and St. Stephen for his private chapel. In 1447, Fra Angelico and his assistants worked briefly in Orvieto decorating the vaults of the chapel of San Brizio in the cathedral. He died in Rome.

JAMES SNYDER, *Bryn Mawr College*

Bibliography: Guillaud, Jacqueline, and Maurice Guillaud, *Fra Angelico* (Potter 1986); Morachiello, Paolo, *Fra Angelico: The San Marco Frescoes,* tr. by Eleanor Daunt (Thames & Hudson 1996); Pope-Hennessey, John, *Fra Angelico,* rev. ed. (1974; reprint, Scala Bks. 1982); Spike, J. T., *Fra Angelico* (Abbeville Press 1997).

ANGELL, ān'jəl, **James Burrill** (1829–1916), American educator and diplomat. He was born in Scituate, R.I., on Jan. 7, 1829. He graduated from Brown University in 1849 and was appointed professor of modern languages there in 1853. During the Civil War he edited the *Providence Journal.* He was president of the University of Vermont from 1866 to 1871 and of the University of Michigan from 1871 to 1909. He twice left the latter university temporarily for diplomatic missions. He served as U.S. minister to China in 1880–1881 and to Turkey in 1897–1898. He died in Ann Arbor, Mich., on April 1, 1916.

At Michigan, Angell pioneered in teacher training and is credited with establishing (in 1879) the first separate chair in America for the study of the "Art and Science of Teaching." He also set up programs to evaluate the curriculum and teaching in high schools in the state for the purpose of admitting graduates of qualified schools to the university without examinations. He favored coeducation and promoted higher education for women.

RICHARD E. GROSS, *Stanford University*

ANGELL, ăn'jəl, **James Rowland** (1869–1949), American educator and psychologist. The son of James Burrill Angell, he was born in Burlington, Vt., on May 8, 1869. He gained his B.A. from the University of Michigan in 1890, earned an M.A. there and another at Harvard, and then studied in Germany, Austria, and France. He was appointed instructor in philosophy at the University of Minnesota in 1893. In 1894 he began 25 years of service with the psychology department of the University of Chicago. During that period the department won international renown, and Angell became known as one of the founders of the functionalist school of psychology. His *Psychology* (1904) ran into four editions. He served as president of the American Psychological Association in 1906. In 1918–1919 he served as acting president of the University of Chicago but resigned to become president of the Carnegie Corporation.

In 1921, Angell was appointed 14th president of Yale University, serving until his retirement in 1937. He was the first president of Yale who was not an alumnus. Yale's endowment increased by over $20 million during his first decade of service. The residential college plan was introduced in 1933. Angell sponsored intensive development of the undergraduate program, especially in the social and natural sciences. His chief aim was to cultivate character and public responsibility, but within this effort, development of intellect was the keystone.

After leaving Yale, he served as an educational consultant and as a public service counselor for the National Broadcasting Company. He died at Hamden, Conn., on March 4, 1949.

RICHARD E. GROSS, *Stanford University*

ANGELOU, an'jə-lō, **Maya** (1928–), American author, educator, performer, and feminist, whose writing is remarkable for its fidelity to black vocal rhythms. Marguerite Johnson was born in St. Louis, Mo., on April 4, 1928. She was nicknamed "Maya" by her brother, and her surname is adapted from that of her first husband. She presents an unsparing yet affectionate portrait of her formative years in *I Know Why the Caged Bird Sings* (1970), which was nominated for a National Book Award. After moving to San Francisco at age 16, she studied music, dance (with Martha Graham and others), and drama. She appeared in an international tour of *Porgy and Bess* sponsored by the U.S. Department of State (1954–55) and then performed in Off-Broadway productions, including *Cabaret for Freedom* (1960), which she also wrote (with Godfrey Cambridge) and produced. She was active in the civil rights movement and served as northern coordinator of the Southern Christian Leadership Conference in 1959–1960, a post for which she was chosen by Martin Luther King, Jr. Associate editor of an English-language weekly in Cairo in 1960–1961, she then was an editor and administrator at the University of Ghana (1963–1966). A series of autobiographical volumes—*Gather Together in My Name* (1974), *Singin' and Swingin' and Gettin' Merry Like Christmas* (1976), *The Heart of a Woman* (1981), and *All God's Children Need Traveling Shoes* (1986)—recounts her journey from obscurity to an established reputation as a performer and activist.

Angelou made her Broadway debut in *Look Away* (1973), earning her a Tony nomination. She directed films and plays, worked in television, composed music, and was a writer-in-residence and lecturer at several universities. She also published poems, articles, and stories. Her first book of poems, *Just Give Me a Cool Drink of Water 'fore I Diiie* (1971) drew a Pulitzer Prize nomination. Her other books of poetry include *Shaker, Why Don't You Sing* (1983) and *I Shall Not Be Moved* (1990).

ANGELUS, an'jə-ləs, a Catholic prayer that is recited at early morning, noon, and evening in commemoration of the Incarnation. Each devotion consists of an Ave Maria (Hail Mary) recited three times with verses and responses. The time for the prayer is announced by the tolling of a bell, usually in three units of three strokes each, followed by nine strokes. The Angelus takes its name from its opening: "The Angel [in Latin, *angelus*] of the Lord declared unto Mary."

ANGERS, äN-zhā', is a city in France and the capital of the department of Maine-et-Loire. It is situated on the Maine River, 165 miles (265 km) southwest of Paris. The most important of the city's numerous medieval buildings is the Cathedral of St. Maurice, dating from the 12th century. Others include the Abbey of St. Aubin, two early churches, and a castle built in the 13th century. Angers' educational institutions include faculties of theology, law, science, letters, and agriculture, and a national school of arts and trades. There are slate quarries in the area. Industries include liqueur distillation and the manufacture of cables, ropes, and leather goods.

In Roman times, Angers was known as Juliomagus. It suffered severely from Norse invasions in the 9th century and from English attacks in the 12th and 15th centuries. The Huguenots took the city in 1585, and the Vendean royalists were repulsed near there in 1793. Population: 156,327 (2001 census).

ANGEVIN. See ANJOU.

ANGINA PECTORIS, an-jī'(an'jə)nə pek'tə-ris, is a disease characterized by a distinctive tightness, compression, or pain in the chest, front or back. It is more common in men than in women. The pressure or pain often extends to the left arm or both arms, or occasionally only to the right arm; it also occurs, rarely, in other parts of the body. Often the pain is associated with a choking in the throat and less frequently with pain or discomfort in the jaws or face. Even when the pain is mild, it has a distinctive quality that gives the patient anxiety and sometimes fear of death (*angor animi*). Patients with angina pectoris may complain of difficulty in breathing, breathlessness, or inability to take a breath because of the pressure on their chest, and they may not mention pressure or pain. But this complaint must not be confused with true breathlessness (dyspnea) such as the rapid or heavy breathing experienced when running rapidly. This has a different significance from angina pectoris.

Occurrence. Regardless of the nature of the chest pain or discomfort or of its particular location in the chest, a distinctive feature of the pain of angina pectoris is that it occurs when the patient is walking outdoors and subsides rapidly when the patient stops walking. Rarely, a pain in the abdomen occurs under these circumstances and has the same significance as angina pectoris even though there is no chest discomfort.

Anger, fear, or any other emotional excitement, exposure to the cold or wind, hurrying, rapid heart action (tachycardia), and even swallowing may also precipitate the pain. It may also occur for no apparent reason.

Cause. Angina pectoris is caused by a narrowing (stenosis) or closure (occlusion) of the coronary arteries by atherosclerosis (q.v.). It may also be caused by a narrowing or leak (regurgitation) of the aortic valve, or it may develop sometimes as a result of syphilis or other diseases. The actual pain is thought to be caused by a temporary inadequacy of blood and therefore of oxygen in a portion of the heart muscle and the consequent local accumulation of waste products that cause pain by irritating nerve endings. The electrocardiogram is often normal, since there is no damage to the heart muscle in uncomplicated angina pectoris. But the electrocardiogram may be abnormal if the heart muscle has been damaged by a previous heart attack or associated disease.

Pains Confused with Angina. The pain of angina pectoris should not be confused with pain in the chest due to other causes. The pain or distress caused by heartburn or indigestion does not extend to the arm or jaw. It is not clearly related to walking or emotion and is not relieved by nitroglycerine. The pain caused by a complete and sudden closure of a large coronary artery by a clot (thrombus), as in coronary thrombosis (acute myocardial infarction, or heart attack), is similar in location and quality to that of angina but is more severe and prolonged (lasting for hours). It is unrelieved by rest or nitroglycerine and occurs without any apparent provocation. There are distinctive electrocardiographic changes in acute myocardial infarction.

Treatment. When angina pectoris occurs, exertion should be discontinued and excitement avoided. A tablet of nitroglycerine melted under the tongue usually affords relief within two or three minutes. Many such tablets may be taken daily if necessary; the value of "long-acting" nitrate drugs is not proved.

Associated conditions, such as anemia, should be treated. If aortic narrowing or leak is present, the diseased valve may have to be replaced surgically by a plastic valve or a valve homograft. If the angina occurs frequently and without any apparent unusual cause, hospitalization, sedation, and complete isolation from environmental stresses are often effective. If intractable angina persists for more than six months despite appropriate medical treatment, it may be helpful to reduce metabolism with antithyroid drugs or radioactive iodine. Operations to improve the blood supply to the heart are still experimental, and their value is not proved.

CHARLES K. FRIEDBERG, M.D.
The Mount Sinai Hospital, New York City

ANGIOSPERMS. See PLANTS AND PLANT SCIENCE —1. *Classification, Morphology, and Evolution* (Seed Plants): Angiospermae.

ANGKOR, ang′kôr, is an ancient city, now in ruins, situated just north of the western end of the Tonle Sap (Great Lake) in Cambodia. For six centuries it was the center of the Khmer empire. Its principal monuments are the temple complex of Angkor Wat, the Bayon temple in Angkor Thom, and the city walls and gates.

The site first became a settlement in 819 A.D.

THE GATEWAY TO ANGKOR THOM, with its imposing four-faced tower, is a relic of the Khmer period.

under the founder of the empire, King Jayavarman II (reigned 802–850). The first city at the exact location of Angkor was *Yasoharapura,* built almost a century later by King Yasovarman I (reigned 889–900). It became the center of an extensive system of agricultural facilities, including reservoirs, dikes, and irrigation channels, all traversed by elevated roadways, As rebuilt by King Rajendravarman II (reigned 944–968), Angkor included the terraced Phnom Bakeng (one of the lesser monuments) and smaller temples.

The Vishnu temple of Angkor Wat, one of the architectural masterpieces of all time, was constructed by the great Cambodian ruler Suryavarman II (reigned 1113–1150). The limestone temple covered an enclosed rectangular area approximately 2,800 by 3,300 feet (850 by 1,000 meters), featuring several concentric square gallery corridors surrounding a central mass that was crowned by five huge lotus-shaped towers, elaborately designed and gilded with gold leaf. The entire Vishnu legend was depicted in relief carvings on the interior wall of the innermost corridor along with pictorial representations of Cambodian life. King Suryavarman employed Thai mercenaries to stave off the threat of Cham enemies, but after his death the city was virtually destroyed by the Cham invasion of 1177.

The last of the great Khmer rulers, Jayavarman VII (reigned 1181–1219), after conquering the Chams, built Angkor Thom as a new capital adjacent to the Phnom Bakeng and Angkor Wat monuments. At the city's center was the Bayon, a Buddhist temple with some 50 towers decorated with the monarch's half-smiling face.

Beginning in the mid-1200's, the Cambodians suffered incursions by the Thai, and about 1431 they were forced to abandon Angkor and relocate their capital farther south near Phnom Penh. Irrigation and roadway systems fell into disuse, and all of Angkor was eventually swallowed by the jungle. The ruins were discovered by the French in 1861, and restoration began during the 1920's.

JOHN F. CADY, *Ohio University*

ANGLE, ang'gəl, is the figure formed by drawing two straight lines from a point. The lines are the sides of the angle, and the point is the vertex of the angle. The two sides can be designated B and C, and the vertex can be designated A. Then the angle is written as ∠ BAC or ∠ CAB.

The magnitude of an angle is measured by placing the vertex of the angle at the center of any circle. The sides of the angle cut off an arc of the circle. To divide the length of this arc by the radius of the circle is the proper theoretical way to measure the magnitude of the angle.

One unit of measurement for the magnitude of an angle is the degree. An angle of 1° cuts off a length of arc of the circle that is equal to 1/360 of its circumference. Another unit of measurement for the magnitude of an angle is the radian. When the length of the arc, S, cut off between the sides of the angle is equal to the radius, R, of the circle, the measure of the angle is one radian. The radian is a dimensionless quantity because it is the ratio, S/R, of two lengths. The radian has a maximum value of 2π and a minimum value of zero. For conversions between radians and degrees, one radian equals $(180/\pi°)$ (about 57.3°), and 1° equals $\pi/180$ radians.

An angle that has a magnitude greater than zero radian and less than $\pi/2$ radians is called an *acute angle*. An angle of $\pi/2$ radians is called a *right angle*. An angle that has a magnitude greater than $\pi/2$ radians but less than π radians is called an *obtuse angle*. An angle of π radians is a *straight* line. An angle greater than π radians is called a *reflex angle*.

Consider ∠ CAB where the vertex A is at the center of the circle, side B remains fixed as the horizontal right-side radius of the circle, and side C, originally overlapping side B, rotates counterclockwise about the center of the circle. When side C has rotated $\pi/2$ radians, ∠ CAB measures $\pi/2$ radians. As side C continues to rotate in a counterclockwise direction, angles of π radians, $3\pi/2$ radians, and 2π radians occur. The rotation of 2π radians brings side C back to its starting position. Thus, an angle measures the amount of rotation of one straight line (C) about a fixed point (A) on an initial fixed line (B).

In addition to the property of magnitude, the measure of an angle depends on the direction of rotation of side C. By convention, the measure of an angle is a positive number if the rotation is in a counterclockwise direction and is a negative number if the rotation is clockwise. Two angles are equal if they have the same sign and equal magnitudes.

The study of relationships involving angles and the sides of angles was greatly advanced by the Greek astronomer Hipparchus (about 160–125 B.C.), who invented or developed trigonometry. (The word "trigonometry" is derived from the Greek words *trigōnon*, triangle, and *metria*, measurement.)

In modern mathematics there are six trigonometric functions of an angle. These are called the *sine, cosine, tangent, cotangent, secant,* and *cosecant.* The trigonometric functions are very important because they are used to represent periodic phenomena that occur in nature or that are man-made, such as an alternating current.

See also TRIGONOMETRY.

ANGLER. See GOOSEFISH.

ANGLES, ang'gəlz, a Germanic tribe that probably lived originally on the east side of the Elbe River, between the Saale and Ohre rivers. From there they moved to what became the district of Angeln, in Schleswig-Holstein, between the territories of the Jutes and the Saxons. In the 5th century the Angles joined the Saxons and Jutes in effecting the conquest of Britain. See also ANGLO-SAXONS.

From their name, the name *England* was derived. A part of the tribe remained in their continental home and gave their name also to the district of Angeln.

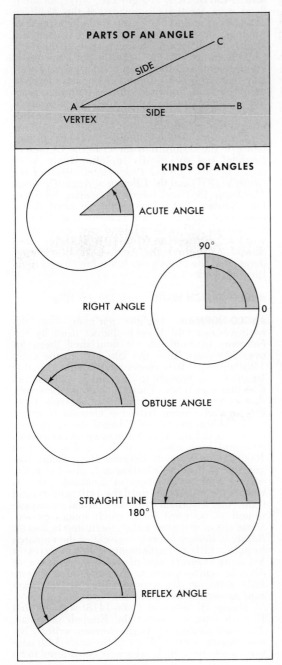

PARTS OF AN ANGLE

C

SIDE

A — VERTEX — SIDE — B

KINDS OF ANGLES

ACUTE ANGLE

90°

RIGHT ANGLE — 0

OBTUSE ANGLE

STRAIGHT LINE 180°

REFLEX ANGLE

ANGLESEY, ang'gəl-sē, is an island off the northwest coast of Wales, in the Irish Sea. Called Ynys Môn in Welsh, it is part of Gwynedd county. The island is separated from the mainland of Wales by Menai Strait, a narrow channel spanned by vehicular and railroad bridges. Anglesey, known also as Anglesea, is about 25 miles (40 km) long and 20 miles (32 km) wide. The islets along its shores include Holy Island, just off the west coast. This islet rises to only 720 feet (219 meters), but it seems to tower over Anglesey proper, which is quite low. Anglesey is flat or rolling, with moorland and marsh extending northeast to southwest. The highest point is Parys Mountain, which rises to 418 feet (127 meters) in the north.

Farming and stock raising long have been the chief economic activities on Anglesey. Other traditional occupations are fishing and seafaring. Copper mining once flourished at Parys Mountain, and anglesite was discovered on the island, but mineral working now is insignificant except for stone quarrying. The administrative center is Llangefni, a market town. Holyhead, on Holy Island, is the chief port.

The Celts colonized the island in pre-Roman times, and it became a stronghold of the Druid priesthood. The Romans (who called the island Mona) destroyed this stronghold in the 1st century A.D. Edward I established English power in the area in 1282 and founded a castle at Beaumaris, now a seaside resort, in 1295.

ANGLICAN COMMUNION, ang'gli-kən, the fellowship of churches that share the beliefs and traditions of the Church of England. These churches aim to preserve the creeds, sacraments, and ministry of the ancient and medieval church, while welcoming the Biblical insights of the Reformation and the spirit of Christian humanism. Thus, Anglicanism combines Catholic, Evangelical, and Liberal strands.

Besides the Church of England, the Anglican Communion includes other British churches not founded by it but strongly influenced by Anglican history: the Church of Ireland, the Church of Wales, and the Episcopal Church in Scotland. Overseas Anglican churches were established partly as a result of immigration from the British Isles and partly through missionary activity. These include the Protestant Episcopal Church in the United States, organized in 1789, and the Brazilian Episcopal Church, which became autonomous in 1965.

Since 1867 the Anglican Communion has had an informal organ of unity in the Lambeth Conference. This meeting of bishops from all churches in the communion is convoked by the archbishop of Canterbury, normally every 10 years. The Anglican churches also have taken an interest in the unity of all Christians. Principles for Christian unity were laid down in the Lambeth Quadrilateral of 1888. In 1931 sacramental communion was established with the Old Catholic churches of Europe, and Anglicans have taken part in discussions of plans for reunion.

EDWARD R. HARDY
Berkeley Divinity School

ANGLIN, ang'glin, **Margaret** (1876–1958), Canadian-American actress. She was born in Ottawa, Ontario, on April 3, 1876, and was educated in Toronto and Montreal. In 1892 she enrolled at the Empire School of Dramatic Acting in New York. She caught the attention of producer Charles Frohman and made her Broadway debut in his staging of *Shenandoah* in 1894.

In 1898 she played opposite Richard Mansfield in *Cyrano de Bergerac* at the Garden Theatre in New York and achieved stardom. Thereafter she appeared in plays produced by James O'Neill, Frohman, and Henry Miller. Her long list of notable portrayals included roles in *Mrs. Dane's Defence, The Great Divide, Antigone, Medea,* and *Electra.* She made her last stage appearance with a touring company production of *Watch on the Rhine* in 1943. In 1911 she married Howard Hull, American author and playwright. She died in Toronto on Jan. 7, 1958.

ANGLO-CATHOLICS, ang'glō kath'ə-liks, an unofficial term for those members of the Anglican churches who emphasize the Catholic aspects of Anglicanism. They commonly are called the High Church group, in contrast with the Low Church group. Anglo-Catholics put more stress on vestments and the ceremonial aspects of worship than do Low Churchmen, who tend more to the Protestant tradition. Anglo-Catholics practice frequent private confession. They promote religious orders comparable to those in the Roman Catholic Church.

The term Anglo-Catholic owes its prominence to the Oxford movement in the Church of England and specifically to John Henry Newman's *Lectures on the Prophetical Office of the Church* (1837) and the *Library of Anglo-Catholic Theology* (1841 and later). Newman, John Keble, Edward Pusey, and other leaders of the movement stressed the ancient traditions of the church. Their work produced controversy within the Anglican churches, but this died down. As a group the Anglo-Catholics neither dominated the church nor left it but shared in its life and work.

ANGLO—DUTCH WARS. See DUTCH WARS.

ANGLO-NORMAN, ang'glō nôr'mən, was the northwestern Old French dialect used by the Normans in England. It flourished there for over 200 years, from the late 11th to the early 14th century. It is commonly thought that this language was brought to England by William the Conqueror in 1066. There is no doubt, however, that well before then, from about the year 1000, the time of Queen Emma—"Gemma Normannorum"—the mother of Edward the Confessor, there was in England a Norman-speaking aristocracy and high clergy. With the Conquest in 1066, Anglo-Norman became the official language of state administration and, after Latin, the second literary language of England. It was used at the royal court until the 14th century, and some Anglo-Norman or French formal terms continued to be used for a much longer period. Some are in use even today, including *le Roy (la Raine, la Reyne) le veult*—assent of the monarch to public bills of Parliament; *le Roy remerciant Ses bons Subjects, accepte leur Benevolence, et ainsi le veult*—assent to financial bills; *a ceste bille avecque des amendments les Seigneurs sont assentus*—assent of the Lords.

Henry IV (reigned 1399–1413) was the first English king to master the English language. The most prolific of Anglo-Norman writers, Nicole Bozon, a Friar Minor of the early 14th century, wrote in French, which he considered to be

England's common language. It was not until 1363 that the English parliamentary session was opened in English. In the civil service, Anglo-Norman or French was used until the reign of Henry V (1413–1422), and its use in the law courts continued into the 18th century. Anglo-Norman or Anglo-French is still in use in the British Channel Islands.

By about the year 1000 the Normans or Northmen in France had become Frenchmen in every way, and until the reign of King Philip II Augustus of France (1180–1223), Anglo-Norman was hardly different from contemporary French. Later, however, it assumed several features that distinguished it from the French spoken in France. Differences occurred in the pronunciation of several vowels and some consonants, and in spelling. Also, Anglo-Norman used the imperfect as the perfect tense, and retained the accusative case.

An interesting macaronic language developed out of Anglo-Norman mixed with early English, an example of which is *il ject un brickbat a le dit justice que narrowly missed* (he threw a brickbat at the said justice that narrowly missed him). A rich Anglo-Norman literature—*chansons de geste*, religious legends, tales or fables, and historical works—was produced from the 12th to the early 14th century. See also ENGLISH LITERATURE—*Anglo-Norman Period.*

DAVID DIRINGER
Author of "The Story of the Alphabet"

ANGLO-SAXON CHRONICLE, ang′glō sak′sən, the main source of English history of the Anglo-Saxon period. Written in English, it was compiled in the late 9th century from earlier sources and traces the history of Britain from the Roman conquest to the time of Alfred the Great. The original manuscript and copies of it are lost. Altered versions survive in seven manuscripts that were continued in chronicle form and amplified from other sources for as long as 250 years after the date of the original.

The surviving manuscripts are generally designated by letters of the alphabet. The oldest and best manuscript, Ā, is at Corpus Christi College, Cambridge. It was written by one hand, possibly at Winchester, up to 891, and later was taken to Canterbury, where it was altered in the 11th century. A, a copy of it, transcribed before the alterations were made, survived until 1731, when it was almost totally destroyed by fire. A 16th century transcript survives.

Two Anglo-Saxon manuscripts based on a lost copy kept at Abingdon are preserved: *B* was continued up to the late 10th century at Abingdon and then sent to Canterbury; *C* was transcribed about 1050 and sent to Canterbury, where it was continued to 1066. Both are in the British Museum.

A northern copy, now lost, was made at Ripon or possibly York. It was expanded with local materials from the *Mercian Register*, Bede's *Historia Ecclesiastica,* and the *Northumbrian Gesta.* The *D* manuscript, at the British Museum, is a copy of this made about 1050 and continued to 1079. Another lost northern copy, less full than the one *D* is based on, was sent to Canterbury. *E*, at the Bodleian Library, Oxford, was copied from it about 1122 in the north and continued at Peterborough until 1154. *F*, also at the British Museum, is an English and Latin summary made in Canterbury about 1100.

ANGLO-SAXONS, ang′glō sak′sənz, a term first used on the continent of Europe to differentiate the Saxons of Britain from the "Old" Saxons of Germany. It is first recorded toward the end of the 8th century A.D., a datable instance being 786, and it was used occasionally in England from the latter part of the 10th century. Modern historians have adopted it as being clearer and more comprehensive than the terms "English" or "Saxons," which were the expressions normally used in England before the Norman conquest.

Origins. The people designated as Anglo-Saxons were, according to Bede (673–735), descended from three Germanic peoples—the Angles (from whose name the word "English" is derived), the Saxons, and the Jutes. He traces the descent of the East and Middle Anglians, the Mercians, and the Northumbrians from the Angles; the East, West, Middle, and South Saxons, from the Saxons; and the people of Kent, the Isle of Wight, and the district opposite Wight on the mainland, from the Jutes. In reference to this last area, southern Hampshire, the term "of the Jutes" is used by a 12th century writer, but otherwise Jutes are mentioned only by Bede and writers using Bede.

While there is some basis of truth for Bede's account of the threefold origin of the Anglo-Saxons, Bede himself does not keep to this differentiation, and his contemporaries do not observe it. They speak of Angles or Saxons with reference to all the Germanic settlers in Britain. "English" is the commonest name for the language they spoke. Bede appears to say that the three tribes came from the Cimbric Peninsula (Jutland, comprising mainland Denmark and German Schleswig) and the North Sea coastlands of Germany, but some modern scholars believe that the Jutes had had at least a temporary sojourn in the Rhineland. The civilization of Kent had marked differences from that of the rest of England and close affinities with the lands of the Middle Rhine.

Settlement in Britain. The Anglo-Saxons normally calculated their stay in Britain from the year 449 A.D., but in fact the precise date is not recoverable, as the evidence is conflicting. The settlement began some time about the middle of the 5th century with, according to Welsh and English tradition, the cession by a British king of a part of his territory to a band of raiders, on condition that they should defend him from the Picts and Scots. Tradition calls the Anglo-Saxon leaders Hengist and Horsa.

Archaeology has shown that there were early settlements in the coastal plains from Southampton Water to the Wash, in the Plain of York and the East Riding, in the middle reaches of the Nene, the Welland, and the Great Ouse (with its tributaries the Cam and the Lark), and in the valley of the Upper Thames. The first reliable historical accounts show that several kingdoms were established: Kent, Sussex, Essex, Wessex, Mercia, East Anglia, and Northumbria. Essex included Middlesex and perhaps Surrey. Wessex was formed by a coalition of settlers along the Upper Thames, with others spreading north from the south coast. Mercia, originally the most westerly outpost, along the Upper Trent and its tributaries, later conquered other Midland tribes and absorbed the Middle Anglians, the Hwicce of the Severn Valley, and the Magnonsæte of Hereford. Northumbria was a union of the ancient kingdoms of Deira and Bernicia.

Lindsey (formerly a district between the Humber and the Witham in Lincolnshire) had had a royal line of its own, but in historic times the territory was possessed alternately by Northumbria and Mercia. The lands on both sides of the Upper Thames were fought over by Mercia and Wessex. The Thames finally became the boundary between these two kingdoms in the middle of the 9th century.

All the lands south of the Humber generally owed allegiance to a common overlord, to whom a 9th century authority gives the title of *Bretwalda* (ruler of Britain). Northumbrian kings held this dignity during much of the 7th century; in the 8th century Mercia was the chief power. It was no empty title, for the overlord had very effective powers over the subkingdoms. The Mercian king Offa (reigned 757–796) dealt with Charlemagne as if empowered to act for the whole country. Egbert of Wessex obtained overriding power for a single year (829–830). As the royal houses of the other kingdoms came to an end during the Viking invasions, it was left to his descendants in the 10th century to reconquer the Danelaw, the area ruled by Danish Vikings, and thus to become rulers of all England.

The Anglo-Saxon invaders were heathen. Place-name evidence provides proof that they worshiped the Teutonic gods Woden, Thunor, and Tiu (Tiw) in Britain. Bede provides the names of two goddesses, Hretha and Eostre (from whom the name Easter is derived). But the Anglo-Saxons were not savages. They brought over with them a settled order of society and a far from primitive legal system.

Legal Customs. Lawsuits were dealt with at the popular courts, called *folkmoots*. While the settlements were small, one folkmoot probably was adequate, but division into separate districts became necessary later. A 10th century reorganization appears to have been responsible for a division of the country into areas of uniform size known as *hundreds*. (In the northern Danelaw the term used was *wapentake*). However, some similar system of small jurisdictional areas must have been in existence some time before the 10th century.

Above these small courts were the *shire moots* and the *borough moots*. All these assemblies met for various purposes besides the exercise of justice. Transactions requiring witnesses could be carried out conveniently there, and there, too, the king could make known his will to his people.

In the exercise of law the Anglo-Saxons depended on the oath and the ordeal. The defendant, unless the circumstances were particularly suspicious, usually produced an oath of his innocence with the help of a fixed number of compurgators, or oath helpers. Otherwise his case was tried by the ordeal, the judgment of God. The church then took control of these proceedings, and the plaintiff decided whether the ordeal should be of water or of iron. Accused clerics were tried by the ordeal of the consecrated morsel. See also ORDEAL.

Whether the accused should be allowed to produce an oath was decided by the assembled court, not by the official in charge of the court. Judgments likewise were rendered by the assembled court. This practice checked abuses of power, for the king often granted to favored individuals jurisdiction within their own lands. In that event, fines collected by the court went to the holder of the king's grant of jurisdiction.

How soon a gift of the profits of jurisdiction included a right to hold a court is a disputed question, but some evidence suggests it did so by the early 9th century. Certain serious pleas were almost always reserved for the crown.

The penalty for such crimes as treason, secret slaying, and serious theft was death. Most offenses were compoundable, by payment of compensation to the persons injured (including persons whose "mund," or right of protection over their own, had been infringed) and by payment of fines to the state (or to the holder of the jurisdictional grant). Failure to pay resulted in penal slavery. Failure to appear to answer a charge made one an outlaw.

Government. From earliest times the Anglo-Saxons were governed by kings, men of families who regarded themselves as descendants of the old gods. Theoretically the people chose their king from the adult members of the royal family, but in practice the eldest son of the last king was most often selected. An ecclesiastical ceremony of coronation was not introduced until the late 8th century, though even earlier documents speak of kings reigning "by the grace of God."

As kingdoms grew in size, deputies were appointed to deal with routine business in the various districts. The deputies were called *ealdormen* until the term was superseded in the early 11th century by *earl*—under the influence of the Scandinavianized parts of England where the same official bore this title. There were more ealdormen in earlier times than later, when several shires were combined under a single ealdorman. In consequence, charge of a single shire increasingly was given to an official called a *sheriff*, an office that first appears in the 10th century.

By this time the country had been divided into shires, somewhat as at present. Those in the lands south of the Thames were of ancient origin. Those in the districts north of the Thames were formed after the Viking Age, and conditions before this time are little known.

The sheriff, like the ealdorman, was appointed by the king, and he looked after the royal interests in his shire. Sheriffs and ealdormen usually were chosen from among the king's *thegns*, that is, from a body of nobles who (like the retainers of the Germanic chiefs described by Tacitus) were the king's companions, serving in rotation in his household in peace and attending him in war. They usually possessed, by his gift and by inheritance, large estates and exercised great influence in their districts. Together with the archbishops, bishops, and great abbots, they formed the king's council, which the king customarily consulted on important matters of policy, the enactment of laws, and the alienation of land.

The king had ancient and well-defined rights. He possessed extensive estates and received a "farm," or food-rent, from land held by others. He also could claim rights of hospitality for his officials, messengers, huntsmen, and others and various other minor services. He sometimes forgave these obligations when he made grants to individuals by title deed. Estates so granted were called *bookland*. The term *folkland*, contrasted with this, probably meant land not freed from these royal dues. The king only rarely granted immunity from the rights he had over all men: his claim to military service and to the building or repair of bridges and fortresses. The ealdorman also had official lands and in late times, at any rate, received a third of the profits of jurisdiction in his area and of the income from the boroughs.

Social Structure. Two main ties of society were recognized. That between lord and man was a voluntary association in which the man gave unquestioned loyalty (even to the extent of refusing to return alive from a field where his lord lay dead) in return for maintenance and gifts of weapons, horses, treasures, and endowment with land. The other bond was one of kinship, on which the individual depended for security and help in all the normal affairs of life.

The kindred were duty bound to exact compensation or take vengeance for injuries done to their members. They also were jointly responsible for bringing a member to answer a charge and for payment of damages and fines.

Society was made up of nobles, churls, and slaves. Members of the first two classes were distinguished by their *wergilds*—the prices to be paid to their relatives if they were killed (see also Wergild). Nobles everywhere were valued at about the same worth—1,200 West Saxon or Mercian shillings being close to 300 gold shillings in early Kent. Churls were valued at 200 shillings except in Kent, where their lives commanded twice that price.

Until the late 9th century there was an intermediate class, everywhere but in Kent, with a wergild half that of the highest class. Compensations and liabilities of many kinds were equated with the individual's wergild, and higher rank carried with it greater responsibilities. The slave had no wergild, only a price, to be paid to his lord. By custom he had rights to an established amount of provisions and to his earnings in his leisure. Slaves sometimes were able to buy their freedom. Freeing slaves was considered a meritorious act, and it often was done. Although slaves could be sold as chattels, frequent attempts were made to stop any sale outside the country.

The slave class was made up of captives, men enslaved for crime or debt, and people born in slavery. It included subject Britons. In Wessex, however, there were Welshmen above the rank of slaves, though with lower wergilds than Englishmen of the same rank. Kentish men with lower wergilds than the churl, who were called *læts,* also may have been part of a subject population.

The churl class probably included men of many different grades of prosperity, from the freeholder who worked his own land, paying only the king's farm and other public dues, to the landless man who rented a small holding from a lord and paid him rent and services. The various men of special crafts, huntsmen and fishermen, smiths, carpenters, leatherworkers, and the like, were men of the churl class or, less often, slaves.

Evidence suggests that the ordinary freeman became more and more dependent as the period advanced. Many men had to buy assistance and protection in times of dearth and unrest, at the expense of independence.

Commerce and Industry. The majority of the population engaged in agriculture. Land was cultivated in many parts of the country on an open field system. Each member of the community had his strips in the arable and cultivated meadow and his rights, proportionate to his holdings, in the pastures, woods, fisheries, or other appurtenances of the village. Some specialized industries existed from very early times. Salt was produced at Droitwich and in Cheshire. Iron was mined in Gloucestershire, and lead in Derbyshire. Trading communities grew up on good harbors and navigable rivers and at the junctions of important routes.

The growth of towns was given an impetus by the policy of Alfred the Great and his son Edward. Their resistance to the Danes compelled them to build fortified centers at strategic points and provide for their permanent manning and repair. The Danish settlers were great tradesmen and increased the amount of foreign trade.

London was a great mart of nations as early as Bede's time. By the late 10th century it was visited habitually by traders from all parts of France, the Low Countries, and Germany. York and Lincoln were sought especially by merchants from Scandinavia. Chester and Bristol conducted a flourishing trade with Ireland.

Imports included wine, copper, tin, spices, sulfur, glass, and such luxury goods as silk, precious garments, and furs. England exported wool, hides, cheese, and cloth. English cloaks were exported as early as the 8th century, and English embroideries and goldsmiths' work later were greatly prized abroad.

The boroughs, in the charge of a town reeve (*portgerefa*), had their own courts and specialized law. Each had a mint. They were connected closely with the king, and the Domesday Book records the considerable variety of terms that they had made with him. In many places the earl shared with the king, in a proportion of one to two.

Religion. Christianity first reached England in 596, when Augustine arrived from Rome. During the 7th century all Englishmen accepted the new religion, either its Roman form or the Celtic Christianity that Iona introduced into Northumbria in 633. Differences in usage caused friction. Late in 663 or in 664 a Northumbrian synod accepted the Roman usages, and within the next few years the whole English church was organized on the Roman model by Archbishop Theodore of Tarsus.

When Augustine landed, the Kentish king was overlord south of the Humber, so that Canterbury became the metropolitan see. From 735 there was a second metropolitan see at York. Early in the 8th century the episcopate had taken approximately the form it was to retain until after the Norman Conquest, although three southwestern sees were added to Wessex early in the 10th century, and other modifications were caused by the Viking invasions.

The general plan was a suffragan for each tribe. Monasteries were more frequently built than parish churches in the period soon after the conversion, but numbers of local churches eventually were built. Several large churches, known as *minsters,* that supplied the needs of areas far larger than villages, were served by priests.

Permanent endowment for the church was supplied gradually. A due called *churchscot* dates from early times, and there were various minor dues as well. *Tithe,* the church tax, was compulsory by the late 10th century.

The first century after the conversion to Christianity was one of great monastic fervor. It also witnessed a remarkably rapid flowering of scholarship, literature, and the arts. Northumbria produced, in Bede, one of the greatest of medieval scholars. Its masterpieces include the Lindisfarne

Gospels and the great Anglican crosses. During the 8th century, after Christianity was well established in England, missionaries took the faith to Frisia and Germany. The English missionary St. Boniface initiated reform of the Frankish church and forged a link between the papacy and the Frankish rulers which profoundly influenced the history of western Europe.

After the Viking invasions, English missionary zeal converted the Scandinavians who densely settled the north and east of England. Later, missionaries from England played an important part in the conversion of the Scandinavian lands.

Meanwhile, in the 10th century, the English church underwent a monastic revival emanating from the Continent. Monks replaced secular canons in many monasteries. The great abbeys of the Fenlands were restored. New establishments were founded, and a revival of learning and art resulted. The Danish conquest of England by Canute (Cnut) caused no setback. The king came under the influence of such ecclesiastics as Wulfstan, archbishop of York, and was inspired to reign as a Christian king. The next foreign influences on the English church came as the period closed, with the Norman Conquest.

DOROTHY WHITELOCK, *Cambridge University*

Bibliography

Blair, P. H., *An Introduction to Anglo-Saxon England*, 2d ed. (Cambridge 1975).
Hooke, D., *The Anglo-Saxon Landscape* (Longwood 1985).
Houghton, Leighton, *In the Steps of the Anglo-Saxons* (Darby Bks. 1984).
Scott, A. F., *The Saxon Age: Commentaries of an Era* (Longwood 1979).
Stenton, Frank M., *Anglo-Saxon England*, 3d ed. (Oxford 1971).
Whitelock, Dorothy, and others, eds., *The Anglo-Saxon Chronicle* (1961; reprint, Greenwood Press 1986).
Woods, J. D., and Pelteret, D., eds., *The Anglo-Saxons: Synthesis and Achievement* (Humanities Press 1986).

LITERATURE

Anglo-Saxon, or Old English, literature begins theoretically with the arrival of Germanic tribes in Britain (mid-5th century) and extends to the Norman Conquest (1066). The earlier limit precedes by at least 200 years the oldest extant literary remains, but the later date is more than an arbitrary historical boundary, since one consequence of Norman rule was the decline of English as a written literary language during the next 250 years.

The extant corpus of Old English literature—one can only speculate how much has been lost through the ravages of time and the arbitrary choices of clerical copyists—is best divided into prose, which can be categorized chronologically and often by author, and verse, which responds only to criticism by genre. The difference in approach is necessitated by the Germanic heritage of oral heroic poetry, highly conventional in form and style, which underlies Old English poetry. Because the Anglo-Saxons took with them to Britain no tradition of written prose, the growth of prose literature among them is traceable from its beginnings. The major factor in this development was the written Latin culture to which the English were exposed on their conversion to Christianity. The preservation in Old English verse of the Germanic legacy and its traditions of expression, on the other hand, obscured individual and chronological distinctions among poets. These traditions include: an often archaic vocabulary; heavy dependence upon stock phrases or formulae, originally developed to help the oral poet fill out his lines extem-

poraneously; the incorporation of linguistic features from various dialects; and usually, though not always, the poet's anonymity.

Prose. The earliest prose in Anglo-Saxon England was written in Latin. Aldhelm (about 639–709) and Bede (673–735) are the outstanding representatives of this phase, and the greatest achievement among the extant works is the latter's famous *Historia ecclesiastica gentis Anglorum* (731), a national history written from a Christian perspective.

Old English literary prose came into its own through the efforts of King Alfred (849–899) of Wessex, who, after saving the English from domination by Scandinavian invaders, set out to restore the ruined cultural life of his war-ravaged nation by undertaking the translation and dissemination of standard religious, historical, and philosophical texts. Alfred made some of the translations himself and commissioned others from learned clerics whom he had invited to his court. His aims and methods are described in the preface he added to the translation of Pope Gregory the Great's *Cura pastoralis*. Among the other products of the Alfredian revival are translations of the histories of Bede and Orosius, Boethius' *Consolation of Philosophy*, and St. Augustine's *Soliloquies*. Original material of great interest is sometimes added to the translation, as in the description of lands and customs of the far north, recounted to Alfred by two sailors, Ohthere and Wulfstan, and included by him in the first book of Orosius' universal history. The *Anglo-Saxon Chronicle* also took shape during this period (see ANGLO-SAXON CHRONICLE).

In the late 10th and early 11th centuries Old English prose reached the height of its artistic achievement in the writings of ecclesiastical teachers, preachers, and reformers. The most accomplished artist was Aelfric, abbot of Eynsham (about 955–about 1012), whose homilies and saints' lives combine patristic traditions of teaching and exegesis with a complete mastery of expression in the vernacular and a taste for highly sophisticated rhetorical and rhythmic effects. Aelfric's contemporary Wulfstan (died 1023), bishop of London and Worcester and archbishop of York at various times, wrote an equally accomplished though very different prose. The author of several legal works, he is best known for his fiery, eschatological sermons, especially the *Sermo Lupi ad Anglos*.

During the last century of Old English prose a secular literature of the marvelous also grew up, including a translation of *Apollonius of Tyre*, a widely circulated Greek romance.

Poetry. Most of the surviving Old English poetry is contained in four manuscripts, all dating from about 1000. The basic verse unit is the alliterative long line, divided in half by a caesura (break), and having the half-lines linked across the caesura by alliterating stress syllables. This line developed while Germanic poetry was still orally composed and recited to a harp accompaniment (as was Old English verse in recitation), and since it remained standard throughout the Old English period, it is impossible to discover the point at which Anglo-Saxon clerks began to compose written poems using the formulaic diction of Germanic tradition.

The early interaction between Christianity and traditional heroic poetry in England is attested to by Bede's famous story of Caedmon in the *Historia ecclesiastica*. Caedmon was an il-

Noe frume. ppa hine nengehv hehr· hynbe þam hal
gun·heðpon cyninge· ongan· ofoft·lice·þhof·pyrcan·
roicle mihe eaftee· magum fugoe·þyaf þnfalue þmig·
þeþbum toptmb· neðe·pitt· hie· nepoheon þær·ge
rah þa ymb pinena pofin· pam fafe mæoð· gbþon
hifa mafe· gtuo hlipigtun· innan jutan· ðonðan
time· gefafmoð þit floðe· þeji·nofð· þy peljfan·
þit fynðfig cynn· Symle·bið þy heanðona· peðic hmdoh
þaiði· ffalnce· fæ fenðamar· fþ oðn bðarcð·

THE BETTMANN ARCHIVE

ANGLO-SAXON POEM, from the Junius manuscript at Oxford, is based on the Book of Genesis. The illustration gives an Old English conception of Noah's ark.

literate herdsman who miraculously received the gift of composing and singing poetry when a mysterious young man appeared to him one night and commanded him to sing of God's glory. Caedmon's *Hymn* is preserved in the Old English translation of Bede's account and shows how the formulaic element of Germanic verse was adopted by Christian poetry. It contains in its nine lines several epithets for God that are standard formulas throughout Old English poetry.

Bede credits Caedmon with composing many poems based on the Bible after his miraculous "conversion"; the existence of three poems of this type—*Genesis, Exodus, Daniel*—long led scholars to attribute them to Caedmon. The attribution is now universally denied, and indeed one of the poems, *Genesis*, contains a long interpolation on the fall of man translated from the Old Saxon (Continental) language into Old English. These poems, and other Biblically inspired epics like *Andreas* (on St. Andrew and St. Matthew) and *Judith*, are notable for their adaptation of heroic language and values to the Biblical or pseudo-Biblical narrative.

More complex is the relationship between Christianity and the heroic ideal in *Beowulf*, the longest and greatest Anglo-Saxon poem. *Beowulf* admirably fulfills the potentialities of the epic mode in its portrayal of the steadfast hero, whose adherence to his ideals ultimately dooms him, and in its evocation of triumphant and tragic heroic civilizations and their leaders. The interweaving of Christian elements in the fabric of pagan-heroic rhetoric and values has often been condemned as Beowulf's great weakness, but the coexistence of these ultimately opposed world views—the tension between prov-

idence's protection and fate's destruction of the hero and his society—is actually most effective. Through the juxtaposition the reader is brought face to face with the question of the significance of human endeavor and is implicated in Beowulf's struggle to impose order upon a mysterious and apparently arbitrary universe.

In contrast to the heroic and Biblical epic narratives are the religious narratives of Cynewulf, which apparently belong to a later generation. Cynewulf alone among Anglo-Saxon poets has left his signature worked into the text of four of his poems. These include two hagiographic narratives, *Elene* (on the discovery of the Cross) and *Juliana*, a devotional poem on the Ascension and a brief account of the fate of the apostles. Cynewulf's poetic style is less heroic than that of the "Caedmonian" poems.

Among a wide variety of shorter poems on religious subjects the *Dream of the Rood* stands out. This piece recounts a vision of an alternately bloody and bejeweled cross, which describes its unwilling role in Christ's Crucifixion and offers a message of final triumph to the sin-stained, despairing narrator.

Aside from *Beowulf* the most striking achievement of Old English poetry is a group of "elegiac" poems that manifest a (perhaps Germanic) preoccupation with the transitory nature of all earthly phenomena. A special, related genre are the philosophical *persona* narratives *Wanderer* and *Seafarer*, in which the comments of a stock figure, such as the exiled retainer, on the hardships of his life serve as the starting point for a consideration of human existence from a double perspective of secular resignation and Christian expectation of salvation. Lyric complaints, charms, riddles, and gnomic maxims are also represented in Old English verse.

There seems to have been a revival of interest in heroic poetry and traditions in the 10th century. Two remarkable products of this revival are the *Battle of Brunanburh*—a brief, vigorous, heavily formulaic poem inserted in the *Anglo-Saxon Chronicle*—and *Maldon*, which, in describing an English defeat by Scandinavian forces in 991, brilliantly recreates the heroic ethic of bravery and loyalty. The contemporaneous compilation of the four main manuscripts of Old English poetry in this era seems to be owing to the same antiquarian enthusiasm.

The literary accomplishment of the Anglo-Saxons is all the more remarkable in that theirs was the only written vernacular language in constant literary, legal, and ecclesiastical use in early medieval Europe. The chief later influence of Old English poetry was on the works of the "alliterative revival" of the 14th century in England—works whose vitality and artistry indicate the worth of their inheritance.

ROBERT W. HANNING, *Columbia University*

Bibliography

Alexander, Michael, tr., *Earliest English Poems* (Penguin 1966).

Chance, Jane, *Woman as Hero in Old English Literature* (Syracuse Univ. Press 1986).

Cook, Albert S., and Ticker, Chauncey B., eds., *Select Translations from Old English Prose* (1908; reprint, Gordian Press 1968).

Greenfield, Stanley B., *A Critical History of Old English Literature* (N.Y. Univ. Press 1965).

Hollister, C. Warren, *Monarchy, Magnates and Institutions in the Anglo-Norman World* (Hambledon Press 1986).

Kennedy, Charles W., tr., *Early English Christian Poetry* (Oxford 1963).

Wormald, P., and others, eds., *Ideal and Reality in Frankish and Anglo-Saxon Society* (Basil Blackwell 1984).

© DIANE RAWSON/PHOTO RESEARCHERS

Luanda, the capital of Angola. The country's colonial masters hoped to develop Angola as an overseas Portugal.

ANGOLA, ang-gō′lə, a country on the west coast of southern Africa. It won its independence from Portugal in 1975 after nearly 15 years of armed struggle.

1. The Land and the Economy

Angola has a South Atlantic coastline of 1,000 miles (1,600 km) between the Congo and Cunene rivers and extends inland a rail distance of 838 miles (1,348 km) from the port of Lobito to the Democratic Republic of the Congo border. The small Angolan exclave of Cabinda, which lies north of the Congo River, is separated from the rest of the country by a narrow strip of land belonging to the Democratic Republic of the Congo.

Physical Features and Resources. Angola's dominant landform is a plateau occupying most of the country. Called the *planalto* in Portuguese, it rises from a coastal lowland no wider than 100 miles (160 km) and reaches maximum elevations of over 8,000 feet (2,440 meters). The average elevation ranges between 3,300 and 5,900 feet (1,000–1,800 meters).

Climatically the plateau is the more favored region, with cooler temperatures and four times more rainfall than the coastal lowland. Angola's vegetation varies from tropical rain forest in the north to desert types in the south, but primarily the country is woodland with shrub or grass.

The Economy. Most of Angola's economically active population is engaged in subsistence farming, with maize (corn), cassava, and beans the chief crops. The cultivation of crops for export was the main source of income during the late colonial period but has declined in relation to mineral exports. Coffee, the traditional cash crop, exceeds in value all other farm exports combined. Sisal and bananas are of secondary importance. Poor pasture and the prevalence of tsetse flies have inhibited the development of commercial livestock raising.

Forests in Cabinda and eastern Angola are a source of timber, while softwood plantations along the main rail line support wood pulp and paper industries. The chief marine product is fish meal, an animal and poultry feed.

Angola's vast mineral wealth includes petroleum, diamonds, iron, manganese, copper, bauxite, lead, zinc, gold, and phosphate rock, but few minerals have provided significant income. Crude petroleum, chiefly from the offshore deposits of Cabinda, is the mainstay of the export economy. Diamonds, mostly gemstones and mined principally in northeastern Angola, have alternated with coffee in value of exports. The production and export of iron ore has come largely from high-grade deposits near the Namibian border.

The manufacturing sector of the economy began to expand rapidly in the 1960s but from a very small base. In comparison with agriculture and mining, it continues to account for only a small percentage of gross domestic product and national employment. It contributes petroleum products to the inventory of Angolan exports but otherwise serves mainly the domestic market, where buying power is low. Production is best developed in the category of foods, beverages, and tobacco products, followed by textiles. Several dams, such as the Camambe on the Cuanza River, are the country's main source of electricity.

Transportation difficulties have impeded economic development. After independence the government gave high priority to improving the road network, partly for economic reasons but also to contain guerrilla opponents. The railroads run from the interior to the coast without lateral connecting lines. The longest route, the Benguela Railway, crosses the middle of Angola from the Democratic Republic of the Congo (the Congo) to the Atlantic Ocean at Lobito and is a strategic outlet

ANGOLA

0   300 Mi.
0   300 Km.

AFRICA

ANGOLA

for minerals from the Congo and Zambia. Angola's leading ports are Cabinda, Luanda, Lobito, and Namibe. Air transportation, which is better developed than surface systems, greatly increased in importance after independence, with the comparative security of air travel a major factor in passenger increase.

2. The People

Although Angola is 13 times the size of Portugal, the two countries are roughly comparable in population. About 60% of the people occupy only 12% of the national territory, chiefly the higher western parts of the plateau and the coastal zones that include major seaports. The only large city is Luanda, the seaport capital, in the north. Midcoast Lobito and Benguela make up the second-biggest urban concentration. The largest highland city is Huambo, on the Benguela Railway.

Bantu-speaking peoples constitute the vast majority of the population. The largest groups are the Ovimbundu (37%) of the central-western highlands, the Mbundu (22%) farther north, the Kongo (13%) of the far northwest, the Lunda-Chokwe (5%) of the east, and the Luimbe-Nganguela (5%), who are split by the Lunda-Chokwe. Only the Ovimbundu and Mbundu live entirely within Angola. Mestiços (of mixed African and European ancestry) form 0.5% of the population and tend to be urban. Before 1975 Angola had some 350,000 Portuguese settlers, many of whom had never seen Portugal and who represented one of the largest white minorities in sub-Saharan Africa.

The Portuguese language, however, remained the official and most convenient means of communication. In addition, according to 1997 estimates, some 43% or more of all Angolans have adopted the religion of Portugal, Roman Catholic Christianity, and perhaps 13% of the people are Protestants. The remainder adhere to traditional African religious beliefs and practices, which also are accepted by many of the Christians.

Until the 1950s the Portuguese did little to educate their Angolan subjects and left schooling largely to Roman Catholic missionaries. Afterward the colonial government attempted to provide at least primary education to Angolans but

reached no more than a third of the primary school-age population. Few Africans went on to secondary school, let alone higher education, although the University of Angola was founded in 1963. After independence the new government emphasized free primary education for all children, technical and ideological training, and adult literacy programs.

3. History, Government, and Politics

Bantu-speaking Africans originating in what is now the Nigeria-Cameroon border region migrated southward via the Congo Basin and began settling in Angola in about 500 A.D. By 1500 they had overwhelmed and replaced the area's first inhabitants, thinly spread hunter-gatherer peoples related to the present Khoisan peoples of southwestern Africa. Over time the crop-growing, iron- and copper-toolmaking Bantu speakers established increasingly sophisticated social structures, most notably the Kongo kingdom that straddled what later became the northwestern Angola—Democratic Republic of the Congo border.

Colonial Rule. Seafaring Portuguese made their first contact with the region in 1483, when Diogo Cão sailed into the mouth of the Congo River. They established ties with the royal court at Mbanza Kongo, where, by 1530, their missionar-

Offshore oil sustains the Angolan economy. The country also has rich resources of diamonds and iron ore.

© CHIASSON/LIAISON

ies had converted the Kongolese king to Roman Catholicism. The main role of the Portuguese, however, rapidly assumed the destructive form of an expansive and prolonged slave trade, which depopulated the interior and fueled interethnic conflict. Quests for slaves for a growing market in Brazil led Portuguese forces southward to conquer Mbundu country (the Ngola kingdom, for which modern Angola is named) and establish a slave port at Luanda (1576). From there they extended the trade down the coast, creating another port at Benguela (1617), through which they trafficked in people of the deep interior captured and sold by agents of the Ovimbundu kingdoms of Angola's central highlands. By the 1850s, when international (largely British) pressure forced an end to the trade, at least two million Angolan slaves had reached the Americas and another two million had died in transit.

Following the Berlin Conference of 1884–1885, which set the territorial limits of Portuguese colonial jurisdiction, Portugal mounted sporadic but costly military campaigns to extend the range of its effective political control beyond a few coastal enclaves to all the territory that it claimed. At the same time it replaced slave trading and local slavery with a new system of conscript labor under which thousands of Angolans built roads for the state or cultivated crops for colonists—all without pay. Diamonds were discovered in the northeastern region, Lunda, in 1912; but the Angolan economy remained essentially inert. The colony, which was not fully subdued until the 1920s, was a drain on the Portuguese treasury into the 1950s.

Under the authoritarian right-wing government of António Salazar (1932–1968), Portugal's overseas possessions were declared to be provinces, not colonies, and the state subsidized efforts to ensconce large numbers of Portuguese settlers in what were depicted as integral parts of a multicontinental Portuguese-speaking realm. However, it was not until a post–World War II boom in robusta coffee production and trade that the Angolan economy began to develop and Portuguese settlement rose significantly, from 80,000 in 1950 to some 350,000 by 1974. A few thousand of the Portuguese-educated Africans and mestiços were accorded full citizenship, but 90% of the population were left illiterate and essentially without political rights.

African Nationalism. Before World War II, Angolan nationalists were harshly repressed and could make only ineffective political and cultural protests. During the 1950s, however, influenced by the rise of anticolonial sentiment throughout Africa, they created and sustained clandestine political movements. Early in 1961 a series of violent upheavals aimed at liberating political prisoners and retaliating against exploitative farm labor triggered an ongoing, low-intensity insurgency and related exile political activity centered on three competing, regionally based nationalist movements.

The National Front for the Liberation of Angola (FNLA) was led by a Kongo émigré and avowed anti-Communist, Holden Roberto. With support from a succession of Zairian governments, it fought from bases within the forested coffee country of the former Kongo kingdom in the northwest. The Popular Movement for the Liberation of Angola (MPLA), an Mbundu-based movement centered on Luanda but with support among urban, educated elites elsewhere in the country, was led by a socialist-oriented physician and intel-

lectual, Dr. António Agostinho Neto. The MPLA organized armed resistance in the Dembos area northeast of Luanda and in the Moxico and Lunda regions of the east. Finally, the National Union for the Total Independence of Angola (UNITA), with support among the Ovimbundu and other communities less influenced than the Mbundu by Portuguese culture, was led by a political pragmatist, Jonas Savimbi. It organized a small guerrilla force in eastern Angola but relied ultimately on political mobilization tactics.

At first the Portuguese army was able to contain and even reduce the level of Angolan insurgency. The discovery and exploitation of oil in the Cabinda exclave covered the costs of counterinsurgency and sparked economic growth in coffee, diamonds, iron, and fish meal. Meanwhile, Portuguese military forces confronted more effective challenges from African rebellions that broke out and persisted in Guinea-Bissau (1963) and Mozambique (1964). Junior officers commanding overstretched and demoralized Portuguese troops in these territories, impressed by African commitment to the cause of national independence, organized a military coup in 1974 that overthrew the conservative government of Salazar's successor, Marcelo Caetano. This "captains' coup" signaled the end of the world's last colonial empire.

Civil War and Independence. Portugal's new military rulers reached cease-fire agreements with Angola's three nationalist movements by mid-1974. Then on Jan. 15, 1975, they signed the Alvor Agreement with them, under which a tripartite transitional government was established in Luanda and free elections were promised, to be followed by independence on November 11. Distrust among the competing Angolan movements soon led to violent encounters that, in a context of crumbling Portuguese political resolve, escalated to the level of civil war, with outside powers supporting their clients. In July 1975 the transitional government collapsed.

As Soviet and Cuban assistance to the MPLA poured into Luanda and other ports, a motorized column of South African troops sped northward in support of UNITA and Zairian soldiers joined FNLA units occupying the Kongo-speaking areas of the northwest. The United States provided covert assistance to the FNLA and UNITA. The arrival of a major Cuban expeditionary force in aid of the MPLA was legitimated in the eyes of previously neutral Africans and others by the dramatic invasion of troops from South Africa. The Cubans enabled the MPLA to rout its foes and secure military control over most of the country by February 1976.

The People's Republic of Angola. Portugal's last high commissioner for Angola had fled Luanda on Nov. 10, 1975, the day before scheduled independence. The next day the locally dominant MPLA proclaimed the independent People's Republic of Angola (PRA). In October 1976 Pres. Agostinho Neto signed a Treaty of Friendship and Cooperation with the Soviet Union. Cuban military units supplemented by health, education, and transportation personnel, totaling in all between 25,000 and 35,000, provided crucial support.

After prevailing militarily over their Western-backed rivals and politically over internal dissidents, the MPLA leadership converted their movement into a "party guided by Marxism-Leninism." At its First Congress, in December 1977, it became the MPLA–Party of Workers (MPLA-PT). The po-

The vast, thinly populated savanna of southern Angola provided bases for antigovernment guerrillas after 1975.

litical bureau at the top of its pyramidal hierarchy exercised full control over the press, curtailed religious freedom, and set out to create a centralized socialist society. No free elections were held.

After a brief pause during the civil war, oil production in Cabinda resumed. Although the rest of the economy had collapsed with the panic exodus of some 300,000 resident Portuguese, the destruction of transport and manufacturing facilities, and the abandonment of coffee plantations, iron mines, and other enterprises, expanding oil production and exports were realized in collaboration with a widening range of European and American companies. Oil kept the country afloat.

But by the late 1970s resentment had arisen over heavy-handed collectivization, antireligious policies, the continued presence of Cuban forces, and a scarcity of food. Popular discontent, combined with the political tenacity of Jonas Savimbi and his followers, who received military supplies and training from South Africa, enabled UNITA to rekindle its military activity. UNITA's leaders appealed for Western assistance, and in 1986 the U.S. government resumed military aid.

President Neto, who died in September 1979, was succeeded by José Eduardo dos Santos in a smooth transfer of power. Confronted with economic disaster, the government began liberalizing its policies in the mid-1980s. It decentralized some governmental authority, allowed for a greater measure of private enterprise in trading and agriculture, and sought association with Western and international financial institutions. Yet the MPLA's dependency on Cuban troops and its unwillingness to negotiate with UNITA locked it into continued civil war. In December 1988 U.S.-sponsored negotiations produced an agreement on the withdrawal of Cuban and South African forces from Angola and the independence of Namibia. Fighting resumed, however, between the government and UNITA. Renewed negotiations resulted in a peace treaty between them on May 31, 1991. Under the accord the two sides agreed to establish a multiparty democracy and a market economy and

to integrate UNITA forces into a national army.

In August 1992 Angola's parliament changed the country's name to the Republic of Angola. In elections in September the MPLA won a legislative majority, but UNITA disputed the results of the presidential election, and civil war resumed. UN-brokered peace talks produced a new peace treaty on Nov. 20, 1994. Key issues, however, remained unresolved, including the extension of government administration to UNITA-held territory, UNITA's role in a coalition government, demobilization, and the integration of UNITA fighters into the national army. Mutual recrimination over these issues and over UNITA's control of the diamond-producing regions of the northeast continued for years. A Government of Unity and National Reconciliation was finally formed in April 1997, but then MPLA and UNITA armed forces actively supported opposing sides in the civil war in Congo (Zaire). In 1998 fighting resumed once again in Angola, and once again neither side was capable of defeating the other.

New prospects for peace came only on Feb. 22, 2002, when UNITA leader Savimbi died in a government ambush. Weary of war, his successors signed a cease-fire with the government on April 4. Poverty, in the meantime, had grown ever more severe, despite repeated announcements that oil revenues would be spent increasingly on popular needs rather than armaments.

Section 3 by JOHN A. MARCUM*
Author of "The Angolan Revolution"

Bibliography

Black, Richard, comp., *Angola* (Clio Press 1992).
Broadhead, Susan H., *Historical Dictionary of Angola* (Scarecrow 1992).
Collelo, Thomas, ed., *Angola: A Country Study* (USGPO 1991).
Guimarães, Fernando Andresen, *Origins of the Angolan Civil War* (St. Martin's 1998).
Heywood, Linda, *Contested Power in Angola, 1840s to the Present* (Univ. of Rochester Press 2000).
Hodges, Tony, *Angola: From Afro-Stalinism to Petro-Diamond Capitalism* (Ind. Univ. Press 2001).
Marcum, John A., *The Angolan Revolution*, 2 vols. (MIT Press 1969, 1978).

ANGOULÊME, äN-gōō-lâm′, a town in France and the capital of the department of Charente. It is situated on a bend of the Charente River, 65 miles (105 km) northeast of Bordeaux. A commercial center, it also manufactures various products, principally paper.

The Cathedral of St. Pierre is a Romanesque edifice particularly distinguished for its heavily sculptured west facade. The mid-19th century town hall preserves two towers of the former château of the counts of Angoulême.

Founded in the 4th century, the town came under Frankish control early in the 6th century. A fief of Aquitaine in the early Middle Ages, it was acquired by France's Philip the Fair in 1308, then passed to England (1360–1373) during the Hundred Years' War by the Treaty of Brétigny. It was permanently joined to France in 1515. Population: 46,324 (1999 census).

ÅNGSTRÖM, ông′strûm, **Anders Jonas** (1814–1874), Swedish physicist, who was one of the founders of the science of spectroscopy. Ångström was born in Lögdö, Sweden, on Aug. 13, 1814. He studied at Uppsala University and remained there the rest of his life as a professor of physics, a research scientist, and a member of the staff of Uppsala Observatory. He died in Uppsala on June 21, 1874.

Ångström was a pioneer in using the spectroscope to study light and chemical elements. In 1861 he began to analyze the solar spectrum by using a spectroscope and photographic plates. The spectroscope separates the sunlight into its component wavelengths, and the photographic plate records the various wavelengths as a series of spectral lines. From an analysis of the spectral lines, Ångström showed that the sun contains hydrogen. In 1869 he made a map of the entire solar spectrum by carefully locating the positions of lines on the photographic plate. Unlike others, he measured the wavelengths of light in units that now are named in his honor. (One angstrom unit is 10^{-8} centimeter, or 10^{-10} meter.) Ångström also studied the spectrum of the aurora borealis and detected and measured lines in the yellow-green region of its visible light spectrum. His works include *Optiska undersökningar* (1853).

MORRIS GORAN, *Roosevelt University*

ANGSTROM UNIT, ang′strəm, abbreviated A or AU, a unit of length that is equal to 1×10^{-10} meter (1 meter = 39.37 inches). It was named for Anders Jonas Ångström (1814–1874), a Swedish physicist and spectroscopist who made important studies of light. The Angstrom unit is used in designating the wavelengths of light. For example, red light has a wavelength of 6500 A (about 1/40,000 inch). The micron, another unit of length, is equal to 10,000 A.

ANGUILLA, ang-gwil′ə, a British dependent territory in the Caribbean Sea, formerly part of St. Kitts–Nevis–Anguilla in the Leeward Islands. The flat, rocky island has an area of 35 square miles (91 sq km). Its chief products are salt, boats, livestock, and fish.

Discovered by Columbus in 1493, Anguilla became a British colony in 1650. With St. Kitts and Nevis, it became part of Britain's Leeward Islands colony in 1871. In 1967 it declared its independence, as the Republic of Anguilla, from the Associated State of St. Kitts–Nevis–Anguilla.

British troops occupied the island briefly in 1969, and by 1971 colonial status had been restored. On Feb. 10, 1976, with Britain's approval, a new constitution recognized Anguilla's separate status as a self-governing territory within the Associated State of St. Kitts–Nevis–Anguilla. Anguilla obtained formal separation from the state as a dependent territory of Britain in December 1980. Under its constitution (1982) it has a House of Assembly of 11 members. Population: 6,680 (1984 census).

ANGUS, ang′gəs, formerly a county (earlier known as Forfarshire) in east central Scotland, bounded on the east by the North Sea and on the south by the Firth of Tay. The county town was Forfar, and the largest city was the port of Dundee. With the reorganization of 1975, Angus was made part of the Tayside region.

The county was the center of Scotland's textile industry, which dated back to the 12th century, when Flemish immigrants introduced wool and linen manufactures into the region.

ANGUS, Earls of. See DOUGLAS—*Earls of Angus.*

ANHALT, än′hält, a historical region of Germany lying athwart the Elbe River and its tributaries, the Saale and Mulde rivers. Its rulers were descended from Albert the Bear, who conquered Brandenburg in the 12th century. Albert passed the county of Anhalt on to his son Bernhard, later duke of Saxony. Bernhard's son Henry, as prince of Anhalt, separated his lands from Saxony. There followed a long sequence of dynastic partitions illustrative of the less fortunate aspects of German political history.

Temporarily reunited in 1570 under Prince Joachim Ernst, Anhalt was divided among his five sons into the lines of Anhalt-Dessau, -Bernburg, -Plötzkau, -Zerbst, and -Cöthen. In 1863 the five areas were united under Leopold of Anhalt-Dessau, but some of the duchy's sections were separated from one another by parts of Prussia and Saxony. In 1871, Anhalt became a state in the German Empire and in 1919 a state in the Weimar Republic. After World War II, Anhalt was merged with Saxony as a state in the German Democratic Republic (East Germany).

GERALD STRAUSS
Indiana University

ANHINGA, an-hing′gə, any of a family of slender web-footed birds closely related to cormorants. They are sometimes known as snakebirds or darters. Anhingas are found in the warmer parts of all continents except Europe. They usually inhabit the wooded shores of freshwater lakes, rivers, and swamps, and they frequently skim underwater.

Anhingas are from 32 to 36 inches (80–90 cm) long. They have very small heads with slender, sharply pointed beaks, elongated bodies, long pointed wings, and short legs. Their long necks are peculiarly joined to allow them to make rapid, darting stabs at fish, their favorite prey. Their coarse plumage is mostly black or dark brown with white streaks on the upper parts. Colonial breeders, anhingas build bulky stick nests in trees near water. The three to six eggs are bluish.

Anhingas make up the family Anhingidae of the order Pelecaniformes.

CARL WELTY, *Beloit College*

ANHUI, än'hwā', an island province in east central China. The province is a region of transition between the North China plain and the hills of the Yangtze River (Chang Jiang) valley.

The name Anhui, also spelled Anhwei, is compounded from the first syllables of Anqing and Huizhou (now Shexian), two ancient cities of the region. The province's area of 54,000 square miles (139,900 sq km) falls into two distinct geographical regions separated by the Wan Mountains. From 1949 until 1952 the two regions were separately administered as North and South Anhui.

The northern region, drained by the Huai (Hwai) River, is an extensive plain deposited by the Huai and its many tributaries and by the Yellow River (Huang He), which usurped the channel of the Huai from 1194 to 1855. Agriculture in this fertile alluvial plain is, however, limited by cold winters and moderate precipitation. The principal crops of the plain are wheat, millet, and beans.

The southern region is hilly, rising to an elevation of 6,040 feet (1,841 meters) in the Huang Mountains. Drained by the Yangtze River system, the south is studded with small alluvial basins and lakes. The climate is subtropical, with hot, wet summers. Rice, cotton, ramie (cultivated for its fiber), and silk are the major agricultural products. The southern region also leads the nation in tea production; Tunxi is famous for its green tea, and Qimen is known for its black tea.

Anhui province is rich in coal and iron deposits. Huainan and Liehshan are among China's leading coal-mining centers. Fanchang and Dangtu are major sources of iron ore. The industrial city of Ma'anshan is one of China's most important producers of both pig iron and ingot steel.

The Yangtze and Huai systems, augmented by connecting railroads, provide the province with its chief transportation arteries. Hefei, situated at the geographical center of the province, is the provincial capital. Other important cities include Anqing, the historical capital; Wuhu, an industrial and rice-trading center; and Bengbu, the leading commercial city in the Huai Valley. Xuancheng is well known for the manufacturing of *xuan* paper, and Shexian for China's best India ink—the two items essential to Chinese watercolor painting and calligraphy.

In the northern region of the province a dialect similar to Mandarin is spoken. Several dialects are spoken in the south of Anhui, including the isolated Huizhou dialect of the Tunxi area. Anhui was part of the province of Jiangnan until 1667, when the Manchus divided Jiangnan into Anhui and Jiangsu. Population: 58,999,948 (2000 census).

KUEI-SHENG CHANG
University of Washington

ANHYDRIDE, an-hī'drīd, an oxide that combines with water to form either an acid or a base. An acid anhydride is one that combines with water to form an acid, and may in turn be formed by withdrawing water or the elements of water from the acid. A basic anhydride is one that combines with water to form a base, and may in turn be formed by withdrawing water or the elements of water from the base. The anhydride of an organic body is the substance obtained from it by the elimination of water.

ANHYDRITE, an-hī'drīt, a calcium sulfate mineral similar to but rarer than gypsum. It differs from gypsum in being anhydrous (containing no water), and is used commercially as a drying agent. Anhydrite most commonly occurs in massive form, as layers in gypsum beds and salt deposits. Its crystals have a glassy or pearly luster and are usually colorless to white. The best deposits of anhydrite are found in Europe.

Composition: $CaSO_4$; hardness, 3 to 3.5; specific gravity, 2.89 to 2.98; crystal system, orthorhombic.

ANICETUS, an-ə-sē'təs, **Saint,** pope from about 155 to 166. Probably born in Syria, he succeeded Pope Pius I. Polycarp, bishop of Smyrna, tried but failed to persuade him to adopt the practice of the churches of Asia Minor in celebrating Easter on the 14th day of the Jewish month of Nisan, the day of the Passover. His feast day is April 17.

ANILINE, an'ə-lən, an organic chemical extensively used in the rubber, dye, pharmaceutical, explosives, and many other industries. A colorless oily liquid that turns brown in air, it is a poison, of acrid taste and aromatic odor. It boils at 364° F (184.4° C) and freezes at 21° F (−6° C). Aniline was discovered among the decomposition products of indigo by Otto Unverdorben in 1826, and its name comes from the Sanskrit word for "indigo." Its first commercial use was in 1856, when Sir William Henry Perkin used a crude aniline with chromic acid in an attempt to synthesize quinine and succeeded instead in making mauve, the first synthetic dye.

About 65 percent of the aniline produced is used in rubber—to speed its processing, prolong its life, and give it desired qualities. The second-largest use is in preparing dyes of many colors, along with related uses in paint, varnish, ink, and photographic materials. It is the basis of all the sulfas and of other drugs. An aniline explosive was important in World War I. Aniline is a component of several rocket fuels.

Because aniline occurs in the products of the destructive distillation of coal, dyes containing it are called coal-tar dyes. Commercial production of aniline, however, has been almost entirely from benzene (C_6H_6) by substitution of NH_2 for an atom of hydrogen to obtain aniline ($C_6H_5NH_2$). In the original process, which is still in use, nitric and sulfuric acids are added to benzene to produce nitrobenzene ($C_6H_5NO_2$); iron filings and hot water then are added to this in the presence of a catalyst, such as hydrochloric acid. The resulting liquid is distilled to produce aniline. The sludge, magnetic iron oxide (Fe_3O_4), is used as a paint pigment or to filter hydrogen sulfide from coal gas. Another important process involves adding chlorine to benzene to produce chlorobenzene (C_6H_5Cl), which is heated with a mixture of copper chloride (Cu_2Cl_2) and copper oxide (Cu_2O) at very high pressure. In the 1960's processes were introduced in which nitrobenzene is vaporized. Hydrogen then is added in the presence of a copper or nickel-aluminum-sulfide catalyst. Another method starts with cyclohexane (C_6H_{12}) instead of benzene.

Aniline poisoning, called "the blues" by chemical workers because it turns the skin blue, is caused by swallowing aniline, breathing its vapors, or absorbing it through unbroken skin.

ANIMAL

Reptiles like these were the dominant animals in the Mesozoic Era, 50 million to 200 million years ago.

ANIMAL, an'ə-məl. Most people consider a living organism to be either a plant or an animal. Indeed, many organisms are quite obviously plants and many others are quite obviously animals. But sometimes it is difficult to distinguish between the two groups, and a specific set of criteria must be used to identify each. If we disregard protozoa for the time being, a living organism can be identified as an *animal* if it exhibits the following traits:

> *Multicellular body organization.*
> *Capacity for active locomotion at least at*
> *some stage of the life cycle.*
> *A form of nutrition requiring preexisting*
> *foods (heterotrophism).*
> *Production of sex cells (gametes) of two*
> *different types (sperms and eggs).*
> *Formation of an embryo and often also a*
> *larva during development.*

1. Animal Characteristics

General Organization. All life, including animal life, depends on the functions of metabolism and self-perpetuation. Metabolism comprises three main kinds of activities: procurement of raw materials, or nutrition; liberation of internal energy from some of the nutrients, or respiration; and manufacture of new structural components from the remaining nutrients, or synthesis. These metabolic processes keep the living machinery running and in working condition. Self-perpetuation also includes three principal kinds of activities: maintenance of optimum conditions in living units for the longest possible periods, or control of steady states; propagation of living units in space and time, or reproduction; and long-term change of living units in line with changes in the environment, or adaptation. This last activity includes the subordinate processes of sex, heredity, and evolution. Self-perpetuation as a whole provides control over metabolism; it

permits the living machinery to continue to run, despite the potentially destructive effects of the environment.

The life-maintaining functions of metabolism and self-perpetuation are made possible by the structural organization of animals. There are several levels of increasing complexity that may be distinguished here: *chemical constituents* are organized into *cells;* cells form *tissues;* tissues are joined into *organs;* and organs are combined into *organ systems.* Some animals contain tissues only, and others possess tissues and organs; however, in the majority, the highest level of complexity is the organ system.

Chemicals and Cells. Some 60 to 80 percent of an animal consists of inorganic chemicals, such as water and mineral solids; the rest of the animal is composed of organic chemicals. About half the organic portion is protein, and a similar amount is lipid (fatty) material; all other compounds, including carbohydrates, nucleic acids, and others, generally do not exceed 1 percent of the total weight of the animal.

The most important organic compounds are the nucleic acids, deoxyribose nucleic acid (DNA) and ribose nucleic acid (RNA). DNA forms the genes, which directly or indirectly govern all the characteristics of an animal. The most basic role of DNA is that it controls what kinds of proteins an animal can manufacture. Different types of DNA molecules represent chemical codes, and by means of certain reactions these code "messages" can become transferred into the structure of RNA molecules. The RNA molecules then serve as chemical "blueprints" for the construction of particular protein molecules.

Formed in this way under nucleic acid control, proteins are the main architectural components in animal structure. As proteins of animals differ, so do the animals differ structurally. Moreover, proteins are also reaction-accelerating catalysts, or enzymes. These, in effect, determine what kinds of chemical processes are possible in an animal and therefore what functions the animal can perform.

Thus the entire nature of an animal is protein-dependent, hence also DNA-dependent. Genes ultimately control all structural characteristics as well as all metabolic and self-perpetuative capacities.

The chemical constituents of an animal are grouped into microscopic complexes called cells. A cell is the minimum structural unit capable of metabolism and self-perpetuation and thus of exhibiting life. Animal cells have an average diameter of 7 to 10 microns ($1\mu = 1/1000$ mm), and they typically consist of three principal parts: a globular central nucleus, a surrounding cytoplasm, and an outer cell membrane.

In the nucleus are the genes, which are organized into threadlike bodies called chromosomes. The number of chromosomes is fixed for each animal species; for example, there are 46 in a human cell. The chromosomes are suspended in a semifluid nucleoplasm, and a nuclear membrane separates the whole nucleus from the cytoplasm.

The bulk of the cytoplasm is a semifluid substance in which various microscopic and submicroscopic bodies are suspended (see CELL). Each of these consists of particular chemical components and, under the control of the nuclear genes, serves in particular metabolic or self-perpetuative functions. At the surface of the cytoplasm, the cell membrane is the gateway for all molecular traffic into and out of a cell. Many cells that are exposed directly to the physical environment possess an additional covering cuticle or other protective layer. The cell surface also functions importantly in cell movement. Thus, many cell types (for example, certain blood cells) move in amoeboid fashion, a process in which the cell puts out temporary fingerlike extensions called pseudopodia. Other cell types move or create currents by means of fine permanent outgrowths, either long, whiplike flagella, as in sperm cells, or shorter cilia, as in the lining of the windpipe.

Animal cells are specialized in various ways; any given cell usually does not perform all the functions necessary for life. For example, nerve cells, liver cells, and skin cells perform different functions, and only the collective totality of the different cell types composing an animal can maintain life. Cells differing in specific function also differ in detailed structure. The chemical components, microscopic inclusions, and overall shapes of cells vary considerably, even though all cells contain nucleus, cytoplasm, and cell membrane.

Tissues and Organs. Just as groups of co-operating chemicals form a cell, so groups of cooperating cells form a tissue. Most animal tissues are either *connective tissues* or *epithelia.*

In a connective tissue the cells are separated by comparatively large amounts of intercellular deposits. Such deposits can be gelatinous, as in jelly-tissues (for example, within the eyes); fibrous, as in tendons and ligaments; or hard, as in cartilage and bone. The most abundant type is loose fibroelastic tissue, in which tough as well as elastic fibers form an irregular meshwork. Imbedded in it are the fiber-secreting cells and also fat-storing cells, pigment cells, embryonic reserve cells (mesenchyme), and various others.

THE CELL

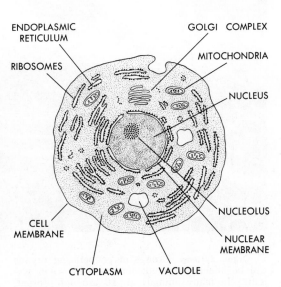

ENDOPLASMIC RETICULUM

GOLGI COMPLEX

RIBOSOMES

MITOCHONDRIA

NUCLEUS

CELL MEMBRANE

NUCLEOLUS

NUCLEAR MEMBRANE

CYTOPLASM

VACUOLE

THE CELL is the basic unit of animal life. It is the smallest structural unit capable of metabolism and reproduction. Microscopic in size, its main parts are a nucleus, the cytoplasm, and a cell membrane.

Connective tissues typically interconnect body parts and provide a structural scaffolding. Secondarily, they store nutrients as in fat-storing adipose tissues; serve protective functions, for example, skull bones; and provide mobility, for example, in permitting the skin to slide over underlying muscle.

Those body parts for which connective tissues form a structural framework usually are composed of epithelia. An epithelium typically consists of closely packed cells, and the tissue may be organized as a single-layered sheet, as in the lining of ducts; as a multilayered sheet, as in skin; or as a bulky, irregularly shaped cell mass, as in liver.

Three of the most abundant tissues—muscle, blood, and nerve—usually are not classified as either epithelia or connective tissues. Nevertheless, muscle in most respects is like an epithelium, being composed of closely packed contractile cells. Blood exhibits characteristics of a connective tissue, inasmuch as it consists of separated cells suspended in fluid. And nerve tissue has attributes of both epithelia and connective tissues; it is formed by closely packed cells that often possess long cytoplasmic extensions (nerve fibers) that pass to other parts of the animal body.

A combination of one or more epithelia and one or more connective tissues represents an organ. The epithelia perform the characteristic functions of the organ, and the connective tissues provide the structural framework, carry nerves and blood vessels, and form the general link with other body parts. In a compact organ, such as the liver or a gland, numerous connective tissue partitions usually traverse and subdivide the organ, and the epithelia occupy the regions between the partitions. In sheetlike organs, such as skin or the intestinal wall, epithelia and connective tissues are arranged in adjacent, often alternating layers.

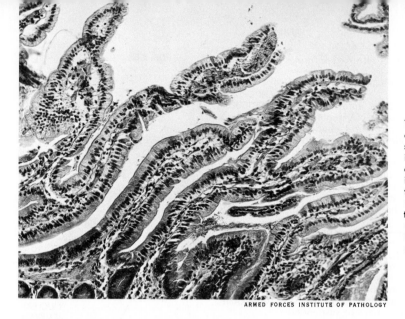

TISSUES are made up of groups of cells that have a similar structure and perform a specialized function. An example of a tissue is epithelium, a covering and lining tissue. One of the body parts it lines is the ridged inner surface of the intestine. Columnar epithelial cells with large nuclei are shown in this microphotograph of tissue that lines the small intestine.

ARMED FORCES INSTITUTE OF PATHOLOGY

Organ Systems. Groups of cooperating organs can be joined into a maximum of 10 organ systems. In many animals all 10 are not present, however, and the functions of the missing systems then are carried out by separate organs or tissues. The 10 systems are:

Integumentary System. It includes the skin and all associated structures, for example, skin glands, cutaneous sense organs, and such appendages as hair, feathers, scales, and hooves. In different animals the system contributes to nutrition, breathing, excretion, temperature regulation, locomotion, skeleton formation, protection, mate selection and mating, species recognition, expression of behavior, and other functions.

Skeletal System. It forms either an external skin-secreted cover (exoskeleton) or an internal supporting framework (endoskeleton). The hard components are in some cases organic and horny, in others inorganic calcium or silicon compounds. The system serves primarily in protection and mechanical support, but it also contributes to motion and locomotion.

Muscular System. It provides the means of motion and maintains posture and shape. It also lends mechanical support, particularly in animals lacking a skeleton (for example, worms).

Nervous System. It coordinates the activities of all body parts and, on the basis of sensory information received, also governs overt behavior. The structural components are nerves, bundles of nerves forming nerve cords, collections of nerve cells called ganglia, groups of ganglia forming brains, and sensory structures of various kinds.

Endocrine System. It consists of glands that produce hormones functioning as chemical coordinators. Like the nervous system and often in conjunction with it, the endocrine system regulates numerous metabolic and self-perpetuating activities, including the overt behavior of an animal.

Circulatory System. It transports and distributes chemicals throughout the body (for example, nutrient molecules, gases, wastes, and hormones) and also provides internal defense against invasive, potentially injurious agents, such as viruses and bacteria. In a closed circulation, blood flows entirely within a circuit of vessels, chemical exchanges taking place through the vessel walls. In an open circulation (as in mollusks and insects), blood flows out from open-ended vessels, circulates freely through the body, and then passes back into the vessels.

Alimentary System. It procures foods from the external environment (ingestion), decomposes them into usable molecules (digestion), and eliminates unusable components (egestion).

Excretory System. It maintains a chemical steady state within the body. As part of this function it retains chemicals in short supply and eliminates those present in excess. Skin, gills, lungs, alimentary organs, and kidneys of various types contribute to this chemical regulation.

Breathing System. It maintains a steady state of gaseous chemicals. As part of this function it procures environmental oxygen for internal use in cellular respiration and eliminates water and carbon dioxide resulting from cellular respiration. The same body parts that contribute to excretion also serve variously in breathing.

Reproductive System. It produces gametes and in many cases also provides a site for fertilization and offspring development. An animal is a hermaphrodite if it possesses both a male and a female reproductive system.

Development. An adult animal arises from a reproductive unit that subsequently develops either *vegetatively* or *sexually*. In vegetative development, the reproductive unit is a greater or lesser portion of the parent body. It may be a group of cells representing a bud, as in sponges, or a fragment separated from the parent by injury, as in a cut worm. Vegetative development of such a unit consists of formation of body parts originally missing. Not all animals can develop vegetatively, but all are capable of developing sexually. In this case the reproductive units are gametes—sperms and eggs. During the production of animal gametes meiosis occurs. (Meiosis is a process in which the chromosome number of each sex cell becomes reduced by half, or to the haploid number). A mature sperm must fuse then with a mature egg, and this fertilization reestablishes the species-specific (diploid) chromosome number.

Most animals spawn, that is, they release gametes into environmental water. Fertilization and development then take place in this external medium (as in most fishes, for example). In other animals, notably terrestrial ones, copulation occurs, and the male deposits sperms directly into the reproductive system of the female.

Here fertilization is internal, and the fertilized eggs then are either released to the outside (as in birds) or retained within the female reproductive system, in a uterus. In some animals the uterus provides protection only (as in certain fishes and reptiles), but in others (most mammals) it also supplies nourishment to the developing offspring. Animals in the latter category are said to become pregnant, and their offspring are born.

Regardless of whether an egg develops externally or internally, the first phase of development always consists of a succession of embryonic stages. Initially an egg undergoes repeated cell divisions. This cleavage process produces a blastula, a ball of cells arranged somewhat differently in different animal groups. Then, again by various specific means in different cases, the blastula transforms into a gastrula, an embryo composed of an outer cell layer (ectoderm) and an inner cell mass or layer (endoderm). Later a third layer (mesoderm) develops between the first two. These three tissues, the primary germ layers, are the source from which all organs and systems will be constructed subsequently.

Thus, the bulk of the ectoderm becomes the integumentary system, and a tubular infolding from the ectoderm produces the nervous system. The endoderm gives rise to the alimentary system, with oral and anal openings to the outside breaking through later. The mesoderm forms the muscular, circulatory, and reproductive systems. All other systems develop from different germ layers in different animal groups, largely by outfoldings or infoldings of portions of the primary layers. For example, localized outfoldings from ectoderm and mesoderm develop into limbs or the gills of many animals, and outfoldings from various levels of the endoderm become lungs and alimentary organs, such as liver, pancreas, or salivary glands.

If an offspring develops within a uterus, the embryonic period continues essentially until birth. But if development occurs outside the female, the embryonic period terminates at hatching, a process that usually liberates a free-living larva. The larva ultimately becomes a young adult form through a transformation process called metamorphosis. In some animals metamorphosis is a slow, gradual event (as in fishes), but in others it involves more or less rapid and drastic changes (for example, from caterpillar to butterfly).

2. Animal Ways of Life

Animals must interact with their physical surroundings, which provide living space and raw materials, and with their biological surroundings, which provide food and mates. Survival evidently requires group association among animals and interaction with the total environment. Such groupings and interactions form the subject matter of the science of ecology (q.v.).

Nutritional Interrelations. One of the most fundamental ecological interrelations is the dependence of animals on plants, the ultimate food suppliers. It happens that the chemical creativity of animals is far more limited than that of plants. For example, animal cells are unable to create basic organic food substances, such as carbohydrates, out of the inorganic raw materials available in the physical world. But green plants can do so through photosynthesis, a light-requiring chemical process in which water and

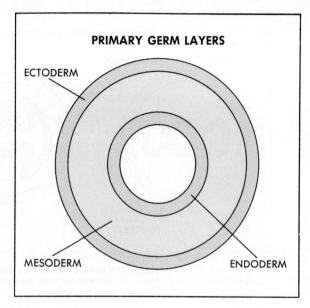

PRIMARY GERM LAYERS

ECTODERM

MESODERM

ENDODERM

aerial carbon dioxide are transformed into carbohydrates and other foods. Animal chemistry also cannot incorporate inorganic nitrogen into organic nutrients. By contrast, plants can make use of inorganic nitrogen available in soil (and soil fertilizers). Further, animal cells are incapable of manufacturing various vitamins and other essential compounds, whereas plant cells synthesize such materials quite readily. Consequently, green plants are food creators, and animals are primarily consumers.

Animals usually are specialized with respect to the kinds of foods they consume. Some animals are plant-eating herbivores. Others, the carnivores, obtain required plant-derived nutrients indirectly, by eating herbivores. A third group, the omnivores, can eat plants, animals, or both. Plant tissues generally contain a high proportion of water and correspondingly less organic material, hence most herbivores must eat more or less continuously to obtain sufficient quantities of nutrients. Also, plants are stationary and hardly can avoid being eaten. Correspondingly, the general behavior of herbivores tends to be noncombative, often furtive, and oriented toward defense. By contrast, carnivores necessarily must be aggressive predators, mentally geared toward offense. And since animal matter usually contains more organic chemicals than equivalent amounts of plant matter, carnivores consume comparatively smaller quantities of food, in fewer meals.

Many animals solve the problem of food supply by giving up a free-living existence and becoming symbiotic instead: one animal, the symbiont, lives directly on or within another animal, the host. The host obtains food both for itself and for the symbiont. Some forms of symbiosis offer mutual benefits to host and symbiont, but in the most widespread form, parasitism, only the symbiont (parasite) benefits; the host is harmed to a greater or lesser extent. All parasites have evolved from free-living ancestors, and the parasitic way of life has become so advantageous that parasites usually harbor smaller parasites of their own. For example, man may be infected with parasitic

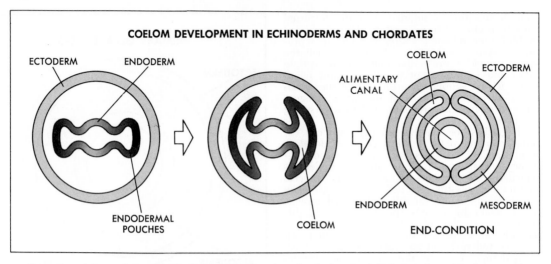

COELOM DEVELOPMENT IN ECHINODERMS AND CHORDATES

ECTODERM ENDODERM

ENDODERMAL POUCHES

COELOM

ALIMENTARY CANAL

COELOM ECTODERM

ENDODERM MESODERM

END-CONDITION

Formation of the coelom, or the body cavity, in the subgrade Coelomata (which includes echinoderms and chordates) is shown here. In the embryo, the mesoderm grows out from the endoderm, forming lateral pouches which then separate from the endoderm. The coelom is the cavity within the mesodermal pouches.

worms, these may contain parasitic protozoa, the latter may become invaded by parasitic bacteria, and the bacteria in turn may support parasitic viruses.

Population and Species. Many ecological interactions of animals are associated closely with geography. A geographically localized group of animals of the same kind forms a population, and all populations of a given type of animal constitute a species. For example, all men now in existence are members of the same species, and the men within a city district, village, or rural locality represent a population. The main identifying characteristics of a population is that its members interact (for example, interbreed) more extensively with one another than with members of neighboring sister populations. In some instances such interactions are so highly organized that the population becomes a society. Social populations are most characteristic of certain insects (bees, ants, wasps, termites), and a good many vertebrates (some fishes, birds, and many mammals, man included).

A species as a whole represents an evolutionary unit; its members are related more closely to one another than to members of other species. Secondly, a species is also a reproductive unit; interbreeding normally can occur only among animals within a species but not (or at best only rarely) among animals belonging to different species. Thirdly, each species is an ecological unit, and it is defined by a unique ecological niche, or place in nature. It inhabits a particular territory, requires a particular set of foods and other raw materials in this territory, produces a particular set of byproducts, and in general interacts with its total environment in a very particular, species-specific manner.

No two species have completely identical ecological niches, although various degrees of partial overlapping may occur. For example, the food organisms of man include plants that also are eaten by numerous insect species. The ecological niches of man and many insects thus overlap partially. Such common food requirements and also the partial sharing of the same geographic living space lead to competition among species. If two niches overlap greatly, competition tends to be correspondingly severe and actually becomes quite unequal sooner or later. The "losing" species then may become extinct or, by evolving into a new species, may find means of subsisting on other food. Changes in the physical environment likewise promote species extinction or evolution.

Community and Ecosystem. A given locality normally is occupied by populations of many different plant, animal, and microorganismic species. Such an association of different coexisting populations represents a community, and a community together with the physical environment in which it lives constitutes an ecosystem.

The nonliving, or abiotic, part of any ecosystem provides the basic inorganic raw materials that support the producers, which are largely food-creating green plants. The consumers, or animals, depend on the producers. The excretion products and dead bodies of both producers and consumers sustain the decomposers of an ecosystem, the bacteria and fungi. These bring about decay, and thereby they return to the abiotic portion the raw materials removed from it originally.

In such nutritional cycles the successive transfers of material are not 100 percent efficient; it takes more than 500 pounds (227 kg) of grass, for example, to maintain a 500-pound cow. The result is the existence of food pyramids in ecosystems. A given number of tons of abiotic material in soil or ocean can sustain only fewer tons of producers such as grasses or algae. A given quantity of grass in turn can support only a much smaller quantity of grass-eating consumers. And a given number of herbivores can support only a still smaller number of carnivores. A terrestrial ecosystem therefore might contain billions of grasses but only dozens of cows and perhaps no more than two or three men.

During these nutritional cycles the materials within an ecosystem become redistributed extensively, and the very nature of the environment undergoes gradual change. Later populations may find the changed environment no longer suitable and must either emigrate, evolve into new types, or die out. Vacancies arise in this manner that may be filled by immigrating populations of other species. This continuing process of gradual replacement of populations, called ecological succession, may lead ultimately to establishment of a climax community—a set of populations that alters the environment in such a way that the original conditions are re-created repeatedly. Steady states of this sort are maintained by, for example, the communities in the ocean, in large lakes, and in extensive prairies and forests. Climax communities normally persist until profound geologic or climatic changes, or interference by man, make communal life no longer possible.

Habitats and Zoogeography. In any ecosystem the kind of community present is determined primarily by the physical nature of the environmental home, or habitat.

Several distinct habitats exist in the ocean. The intertidal zone is the densely populated region between the tide lines. The benthonic zone is represented by the ocean floor. The pelagic zone constitutes the open water of an ocean. Within the latter the photic zone is the surface water as far down as sunlight can penetrate—250 to 600 feet (76 to 183 meters) in different regions—and the aphotic zone is the eternally dark water underneath.

Animals in these habitats fall into three general categories—plankton, nekton, and benthos. Plankton comprises the microscopic types that float and drift. They depend on photosynthesizing algae for food and thus occur only in the photic zone. Nekton consists of active swimmers, mainly fishes, whales, squids, and other strongly muscled types. Herbivorous forms among them stay in or near the photic zone, close to the planktonic food supply, but the carnivorous nekton ranges throughout the pelagic region. Indeed, the deep aphotic zone is inhabited exclusively by nektonic carnivores (that include bioluminescent, large-mouthed, long-toothed fishes). The benthos comprises the sessile and creeping animals along the sea bottom. Sponges, reef-forming and other corals, starfishes and sea urchins, and a large variety of clams, snails, and worms are characteristic inhabitants of these regions.

Like the ocean, fresh water also contains distinct kinds of habitats, each suitable for specific kinds of communities. Planktonic, nektonic, and benthonic groups again are encountered in very large lakes, but smaller lakes, ponds, bogs, and rivers contain rather different ecosystems. The communities in them vary in line with physical variables, such as strength of currents, bottom deposits, oxygen content, water chemistry and temperature, and geographic location at particular latitudes and altitudes.

The nature of terrestrial habitats is determined principally by latitude and altitude, amount of precipitation, and the annual temperature range. As these vary, some six or seven major kinds of habitats are formed. Two of them, the desert and the rain forest, are particularly characteristic of tropical and subtropical regions. Deserts appear when precipitation amounts to less than 10 inches (25.4 cm) per year, and rain forests arise where the winter is a rainy season with daily torrential cloudbursts. In deserts the growing season is limited to a few days or weeks. Plants generally tend to be small and spiny, and the animals too are small, many of them being burrowing types. In rain forests, by contrast, plant growth tends to occur the year round, "jungles" being the typical result.

Also present in some parts of the tropics but extending well into the temperate zone are the grasslands. The annual precipitation in such habitats totals some 10 to 40 inches (25.4 to 101.6 cm), and plant growth tends to slow down or cease entirely during the winter. Animal life is probably more abundant and more diverse here than in any other terrestrial habitat. Similarly characteristic of the temperate zone is the habitat of the deciduous forest, where most of the trees hibernate by shedding their foliage in winter. Many of the animals present hibernate also.

At higher latitudes are the taiga and the tundra, habitats characterized by long, severe winters and correspondingly brief growing seasons. The taiga is predominantly a zone of coniferous forests, with single tree species (such as spruce) covering large areas. Trees do not occur in the tundra, the plants there being mainly low shrubs, herbs, mosses, and lichens. In the polar habitat, terrestrial plant life is absent completely and animal life, such as seals, walruses, and penguins, is sustained by the sea.

The horizontal sequence of habitats between equator and pole is repeated in a vertical direction along the slopes of mountains. Thus, a high mountain in the tropics generally supports a rain forest at the base, deciduous forest and grassland at progressively higher altitudes, then coniferous forest, then a tundralike treeless region up to the snow line, and finally a permanently ice-bound "polar" zone.

3. Animal Diversity

Classification. On the basis of their similarities and differences, organisms can be assigned to variously inclusive classification groups, or taxonomic categories. In one of the earliest scientific systems of taxonomy, formulated in the 18th century by the Swedish naturalist Linnaeus, living creatures were classified into two main groups, the plant kingdom and the animal kingdom. It has since become clear, however, that these two groups cannot be defined adequately, for the identifying traits supposedly characteristic of one kingdom are encountered also in the other. Today, therefore, it is technically no longer adequate to regard any living organism simply as either a plant or an animal. For example, many fungi, bacteria, blue-green algae, and viruses have traits that are not completely plant-like or animallike. Consequently, the number of kingdoms recognized by biologists and other scientists has been increased from two to as many as six in modern classification systems: the Monera (bacteria, blue-green algae); the Protista (protozoa, some single-celled algae); the Fungi; the Plantae or Metaphyta (plants proper); the Animalia or Metazoa (animals proper); and the Viruses. In these systems algae are not strictly considered "plants," and protozoa are not considered "animals" but do exhibit animallike traits.

Apart from such redefinitions of the very large taxonomic groups, the basic features of the Linnaean system are still in universal use today. Thus, each large group is classified into a hierarchy of subgroups on the basis of progressively greater similarities among organisms. A group such as the Metazoa, for example, is subclassified into *phyla;* each phylum contains *classes;* a class is composed of *orders;* an order consists

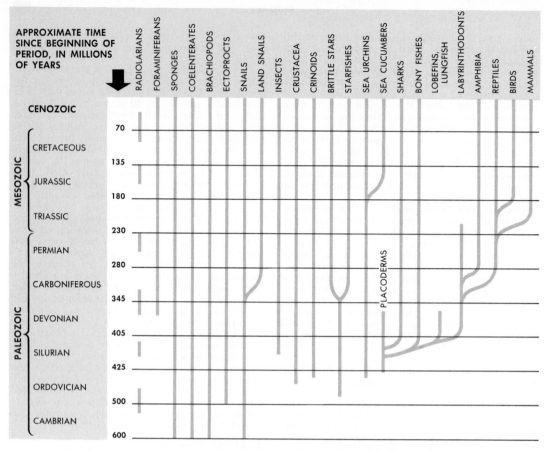

APPROXIMATE TIME SINCE BEGINNING OF PERIOD, IN MILLIONS OF YEARS

FOSSIL RECORDS of many of the animal groups are summarized here. The vertical lines indicate the periods during which each animal group is present in the fossil record. For example, insects began to appear in the fossil record in the middle of the Silurian period.

of *families;* each family is made up of *genera;* and a genus encompasses one or more *species.* Each organism is identified by two names, the first designating the genus and the second the species to which it belongs. For example, the techncial name for man is *Homo sapiens. Homo* represents the genus that includes all past and present human species, and *H. sapiens* identifies the sole human species now in existence. Where necessary, intermediate ranks (subphyla, super-orders, subfamilies) can be established as well. As will become apparent presently, several additional ranks above the phylum level actually are required in Metazoan classification.

Metazoan Categories. The subclassification of the Metazoa is based in part on the important observation that the earlier a given trait appears in development, the more animals share this trait in common. Accordingly, the highest, most inclusive subdivisions of the Metazoa are defined by the earliest, most common trait, namely, the level of organization attained by an animal. Some animals develop only up to the tissue level, whereas others become elaborated further into organs and organ systems. On this basis, two *branches* are recognized within the Metazoa. In the branch Parazoa, the highest organizational level attained is the tissue. The only animals belonging to this group are the sponges, representing a single phylum. All other animals form the branch Eumetazoa, characterized by an organizational complexity beyond that of the tissue level.

After level of organization, one of the earliest traits to appear during development is that of body symmetry. The early embryos of all animals tend to exhibit an initial radial symmetry (that is, they are equal around a central axis). In some Eumetazoa this radiality persists right into the adult stage, but in all others the symmetry changes; later embryos, larvae, and typically also the adults are bilaterally symmetrical (that is, the left and right halves are mirror-images). Accordingly, the eumetazoan branch is subclassified into two *grades,* the grade Radiata and the grade Bilateria. The Radiata comprise two phyla, the coelenterates (jellyfishes, corals) and the comb jellies. In all these the highest level of complexity is the organ. All remaining animals belong to the Bilateria, in which the highest organizational level is the organ system.

After symmetry, the next embryonic trait important in classification is the development of the third germ layer, the mesoderm. According to the different later fates of the mesoderm, the grade of Bilateria is subdivided into three *subgrades.* In some Bilateria, mesoderm comes to fill all spaces that appear between the outer, ectoderm layer and the inner, endoderm layer of the embryo. Such animals are therefore without internal body cavities (apart from the cavity of the gut), and they represent the subgrade Acoelomata. Two phyla are so classified—flatworms (planarians, tapeworms) and ribbon worms.

In another group of Bilateria, mesoderm accumulates only in limited regions, leaving a free

RELATIONSHIPS BETWEEN ANIMAL PHYLA

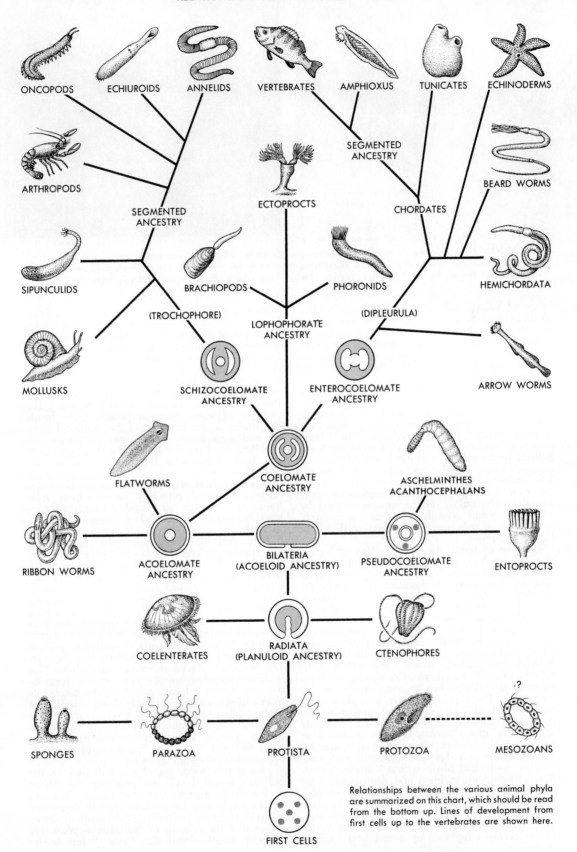

Relationships between the various animal phyla are summarized on this chart, which should be read from the bottom up. Lines of development from first cells up to the vertebrates are shown here.

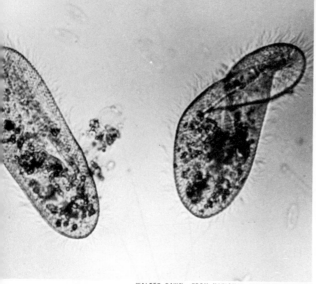

PROTOZOA. Two representatives of *Paramecium* are shown at left. Their microscopic bodies are covered with tiny locomotor structures called cilia, identifying them as members of the ciliate subphylum. Foraminifers, members of the subphylum Sarcodina, secrete chalky shells (*right*). Pseudopodia protrude from the holes.

space between ectoderm and endoderm. Such a space represents a body cavity, in this case a so-called "false" body cavity. Animals possessing it form a subgrade Pseudocoelomata. This category includes three phyla, the most familiar animals among them being the rotifers and the roundworms.

In all remaining Bilateria, mesoderm comes to form two sublayers, one lying along the ectoderm, the other along the endoderm. The space left between these sublayers again represents a body cavity. This space is a "true" body cavity, or coelom. A coelom is a space enclosed entirely by mesoderm, and particularly by a mesodermal lining membrane called a peritoneum. The animals possessing a coelom represent the subgrade Coelomata, a group containing some 14 phyla. Depending on the specific method by which a coelom actually arises in the embryo, coelomate animals are subclassified further into three *superphyla*.

In one of these, the superphylum of lophophorates, coeloms form by several quite unique processes. The group includes three small phyla, none of them generally familiar. In another superphylum, the schizocoelomates, the coelom arises by a splitting of an originally solid mesoderm layer into outer and inner sublayers. Of the six phyla in this group, several include well-known animals: snails, clams, and other mollusks; earthworms, leeches, and other annelid worms; and spiders, insects, and other arthropods. In all remaining Coelomata, coeloms form as paired pouches growing out from the endoderm. These pouches later lose their connection with the endoderm and persist as independent mesoderm sacs enclosing coelomic spaces. The group encompasses five phyla. One of these is the phylum Chordata, which includes all vertebrates and therefore mammals and man.

The individual phyla within a higher classification group are defined and distinguished by a wide variety of traits that appear during later developmental stages. For example, the Chordata are identified by a notochord, a skeletal supporting rod, which in the later embryos of vertebrates becomes replaced by a vertebral column.

Within a given phylum, analogously, successive lower ranks are defined by progressively later developmental traits. For example, some vertebrate embryos develop skin with a potential of growing hair, one of the traits identifying the class Mammalia. Some of the mammalian embryos in turn later develop fingers with flat nails, one of the traits identifying the order Primates. Among the animals in this order, the embryos of some come to possess large heads and brains, a characteristic of the family of man. In analogous manner, other animal groups are classified (and usually also named) according to the most conspicuous traits developed at successive stages.

Evolutionary History. Because taxonomic classification is based primarily on structural relations, and because structural relations in turn tend to suggest historical relations, taxonomy generally is considered to provide a rough outline of evolutionary histories. In many cases, evolutionary inferences can be made more certain by independent direct evidence obtained from fossils. Unfortunately, however, a reasonably extensive fossil record does not go back more than about 500 million years, to the beginning of the Paleozoic era. At that time all animal phyla now known were already in existence. Fossil evidence thus is unavailable for the entire previous history of animals, that is, the periods during which the Metazoa evolved into the various branches, grades, subgrades, and phyla. This early history consequently must remain speculative and can be inferred only from the taxonomic interrelations among currently living phyla. For groups down to the phylum level, therefore, the taxonomic pattern also must serve as an evolutionary pattern; and the taxonomic diagram on page 861 may be regarded as a presumptive evolutionary diagram as well.

From the beginning of the Paleozoic to the present, animal fossils are available in greater or lesser abundance, and evolutionary histories within phyla can be studied through taxonomy as well as through fossils. Such fossil evidence shows that the animals of 500 million years ago differed greatly from the kinds living today;

within each phylum, extinction of ancient types and evolution of new groups occurred repeatedly. None of the animals of the early Paleozoic was terrestrial as yet. The fauna was predominantly marine and it included various archaic sponges, jellyfishes, worms, lamp shells, ectoprocts, mollusks, starfishes, sea lilies, and others. Among the mollusks the nautiloids, distant relatives of the present squids, attained lengths of several yards. Particularly abundant were the trilobites, from which the insects and all other arthropods later evolved. The only chordates of the time were tunicates; vertebrates did not appear until the Ordovician period, about 400 million years ago, when the jawless fishes came into prominence. They were ancestors of the class of placoderms, armor- and jaw-possessing fishes that became extinct some 300 million years ago (Devonian period). Before the placoderms died out, they gave rise to sharks and bony fishes.

During the Silurian period (370 million to 340 million years ago), plants managed to colonize the land and animals soon followed. Scorpions, spiders, and early insects were the first terrestrial animals. Amphibia, descended from ancestral bony fishes, appeared on land during the Devonian. From them, in turn, evolved the reptiles, which became well established by Permian times. At the end of the Paleozoic era, about 200 million years ago, large-scale extinctions occurred within most phyla, and new groups came to replace the earlier types. During the ensuing Mesozoic era (200 million to 70 million years ago) the bony fishes became the dominant animals in the sea, a status they still have today, and insects and reptiles attained dominance on land. Insects continued to diversify steadily and they are now the most numerous of all living organisms. Reptiles flourished at first and produced, for example, many gigantic dinosaurian types. But most of the reptiles died out at the end of the Mesozoic, and only a few relatively small groups now survive. However, from reptilian ancestors evolved the mammals and birds, and these two vertebrate classes became dominant during the last 75 million years, the Cenozoic era. Some 30 million years ago, tree-living mammalian types gave rise to a ground-living stock, which eventually produced man. True men are known to have existed at least 2 million years ago, and our own species appears to be at least 500,000 years old.

The fossil record as a whole shows, and taxonomic studies likewise indicate, that the pattern of past evolution has the form of a branching bush. All currently living groups are at the tips of the branches and a given group is neither "higher" nor "lower" than any other. All are simply contemporaries, existing at the same uppermost time level of the evolutionary bush, the present; and their independent histories go back to more or less remote common ancestors at the fork points of this bush.

THE ANIMAL PHYLA

Phylum **Protozoa**: *heterotrophic Protista, largely unicellular and motile; with evolutionary affinities to algae; not strictly "animals," but the most animal-like Protista; a subkingdom in traditional Linnaean classification*
Subphylum Mastigophora: flagellate protozoa
Subphylum Sarcodina: amoeboid protozoa
Subphylum Sporozoa: spore-forming protozoa
Subphylum Ciliophora: ciliate protozoa

PORIFERA. Sponges, such as this basket sponge, constitute the branch Parazoa. They are sessile (permanently attached), colonial, and generally marine.

Abundant in all environments containing moisture, protozoa possibly may number 100,000 or more species. The usually microscopic body of a protozoon is either naked or covered with a secreted cuticle. On the surface also are the locomotor structures—flagella, cilia, or pseudopodia. Feeding is accomplished by permanent gullets in flagellates and ciliates, by pseudopodia in the sarcodines, and directly through the cell surface in sporozoans. Many protozoa possess internal contractile fibrils and neurofibrils, and freshwater types also contain contractile vacuoles that expel excess water entering by osmosis. All subphyla include multinucleate types. Ciliates always possess two different kinds of nuclei—micronuclei, which control sexual processes, and macronuclei, which control all other processes of life. Protozoa reproduce by cell division. In most cases the sexual process involves fusion of two entire cells (syngamy), but in ciliates conjugation occurs—a mutual exchange of gamete nuclei takes place between two temporarily fused cells.

The most familiar flagellate protozoa are parasitic, for example, the trypanosomes, causative agents of sleeping sickness. Sarcodina include the planktonic Foraminifera and Radiolaria, the shells of which form the bottom ooze of many seas. The most familiar sarcodine type is *Amoeba*, a specialized sexless form. Related to it is the parasitic, dysentery-causing *Entamoeba*. Sporozoa are all parasitic. These organisms undergo complex life cycles, including stages at which the cell subdivides all at once into numerous offspring cells (spores). The best-known sporozoon is *Plasmodium*, various species of which produce malaria. Parasitic types are rare among ciliate protozoa. A well-known member of this subphylum is *Paramecium*, one of the most studied of all organisms.

Metazoa: *animals proper; multicellular, heterotrophic, motile at some stage of life cycle; originated from unknown protistan ancestors; a subkingdom in traditional Linnaean classification*

Branch **Parazoa**: *animals at tissue level of complexity; Porifera*

CHARLES WALCOTT   R.C. HERMES, FROM NATIONAL AUDUBON SOCIETY

CNIDARIA. Also called coelenterates, representatives of this phylum are the hydra (*left*) and the jelly-fish (*right*). The hydra is a freshwater member of the class Hydrozoa. It has tentacles at its top and the buds of offspring along its sides. The jellyfish, a marine scyphozoan, has tentacles on the underside of its body.

*Phylum **Porifera** (sponges; 5,000 species)*
   Class Calcarea: calcareous sponges
   Class Hexactinellida: silica sponges
   Class Demispongiae: horny sponges

A few horny sponges live in fresh water; all others are marine. Adults are sessile and grow in colonies. The body is radial to asymmetrical and in the simplest types forms a sac with a three-layered wall. The outer layer is an epithelium of flat cells (pinacocytes). The middle layer (mesogloea) consists of jelly-secreting and amoeboid cells of various types. Some of these manufacture needlelike skeletal supports (spicules), composed of calcareous, silicaceous, or horny materials according to the class. The innermost layer is an alimentary epithelium containing food-trapping flagellate cells (choanocytes). The beat of the choanocyte flagella maintains a food-bearing water current that passes through pores in the body wall into the cavity (spongocoel) of the saclike body, and out from there through the upper main opening of the sac (osculum). In more complex sponges the spongocoel is a branched system of canals and spaces, lined by choanocytes. Sponges are without nerve cells or specialized muscle cells and their capacity of responding to external stimuli therefore is limited greatly.

*Branch **Eumetazoa**: adults above tissue level of*
   complexity
*Grade **Radiata**: animals at organ level of complexity, all stages typically radially symmetrical; Cnidaria, Ctenophora*
*Phylum **Cnidaria** (coelenterates; 10,000 species)*
   Class Hydrozoa: both medusae and polyps; hydras, millepore corals, Portuguese man-of-war
   Class Scyphozoa: medusae dominant; jelly-fishes
   Class Anthozoa: polyps only; corals, sea anemones, sea fans

Cnidaria are named after their cnidoblasts, stinging cells containing capsules (nematocysts) with coiled, hollow threads. The latter turn inside out when discharged and release paralyzing or toxic poisons. The body of a coelenterate is basically a sac, a single opening serving both as mouth and as anus. If the main axis is long relative to the diameter of the body, the animal is a cylindrical, usually sessile polyp. But if the main axis is short relative to the diameter, the animal has an umbrella-shaped medusa form and is typically free-swimming. Both forms are equipped with cnidoblast-bearing tentacles around the alimentary opening. The body wall consists of three main layers: an outer epidermis, which contains sensory cells and also secretes a calcareous or horny exoskeleton; a middle mesogloea, which contains jelly-secreting and other types of connective tissue cells; and an inner gastrodermis, which is digestive and contains food-absorbing amoeboid and flagellate cells. Under the epidermis lies a nerve net. True muscle cells occur in all but the Hydrozoa.

Coelenterates develop by way of planula larvae, each composed of an ectoderm layer and an inner mass of endoderm-mesoderm cells. The larva settles and grows into a polyp. In Hydrozoa this individual often gives rise to a branching colony of polyps. Medusae then bud off from some of these. The medusae are sexual and complete the life cycle. In Scyphozoa, the original polyp produces medusae directly, but in Anthozoa medusae never form, the polyp phase eventually becoming sexual. Some anthozoan polyps, such as sea anemones, remain solitary; and others become colonial, for example, the reef-forming corals. Only a few coelenterates live in fresh water (for example, *Hydra*).

*Phylum **Ctenophora** (comb jellies; 80 species): marine; body often globular, with eight rows of ciliary comb plates and a pair of long tentacles containing food-trapping adhesive cells; hermaphroditic; evolutionary affinities to medusalike coelenterates*

•   •   •

*Grade **Bilateria**: animals at organ-system level of complexity, adults typically bilateral; tubular alimentary tract with separate mouth and anus in all but the flatworms*

Subgrade Acoelomata: mesoderm fills space between ectoderm and endoderm, hence internal body cavity not present; Platyhelminthes, Nemertina

Phylum Platyhelminthes (flatworms; 10,000 species) Class Turbellaria (planarians and related types): free-living
Class Trematoda (flukes): bulk-feeding parasites
Class Cestoidea (tapeworms): fluid-feeding parasites

In these flattened, elongated animals the alimentary system is a sac, with a single mouth-anus opening on the underside. The nervous system consists of anterior ganglia and of two or more interconnected nerve cords passing posteriorly. The regions between the body surface and the alimentary system are occupied by connective tissues, muscles, and excretory and reproductive organs. The worms are hermaphrodites.

The free-living types are believed to have evolved from planulalike coelenterate ancestors. Marine Turbellaria develop from free-swimming larvae, but larvae are not formed by freshwater groups and the few representatives in moist terrestrial environments. Ancestral turbellarians probably have given rise to the flukes and tapeworms, all of them parasitic. Flukes exhibit complex life cycles requiring two or three hosts, man often being the final host. For example, the Chinese liver fluke (*Clonorchis sinensis*) passes through successive larval stages in two intermediate hosts, a snail and a fish. The final host is man, who becomes infected by eating raw fish. Complex life histories are characteristic also of tapeworms. The head of such a worm is attached to the intestinal wall of a host, and the main parts of the body consist of a series of segments (proglottids) in which the reproductive systems mature. The oldest, most posterior proglottids contain fertilized eggs, and such segments detach from the worm and escape with the host's feces. If such eggs are deposited on grass, they may be eaten by cattle. Tapeworm embryos then develop in beef muscle and man may become infected by eating undercooked beef.

ROBERT C. HERMES, FROM ANNAN PHOTOS

CTENOPHORA. The bright bands along the body surface of these comb jellies are the locomotor comb rows. Parts of the gastrovascular system also can be seen.

Phylum Nemertina (ribbon worms; 600 species): mostly marine, some freshwater and terrestrial; most primitive phylum with tubular alimentary system; most primitive phylum with circulatory system, composed here of 2 or 3 interconnected longitudinal vessels; eversible proboscis (a tubelike organ that can be turned inside out) in chamber above mouth, used in food-trapping

• • •

Subgrade Pseudocoelomata: mesoderm in limited regions, leaving pseudocoelic body cavity between ectoderm and endoderm; distant evolutionary affinities to flatworms; Aschelminthes, Acanthocephala, Entoprocta
Phylum Aschelminthes (sac worms; 15,000 species) Classes Rotifera, Gastrotricha, Kinorhyncha, Priapulida, Nematoda, and Nematomorpha

The two most important classes are the rotifers and the nematodes. Rotifers are microscopic,

PLATYHELMINTHES. Two flatworm representatives are the planaria (*left*) and the tapeworm (*right*). The planaria is a free-living form that has two eyes located at the anterior end. The tapeworm portion (shown here) has a knoblike head, a short neck, and a series of identical segments forming most of the body.

HUGH SPENCER   ARMED FORCES INSTITUTE OF PATHOLOGY

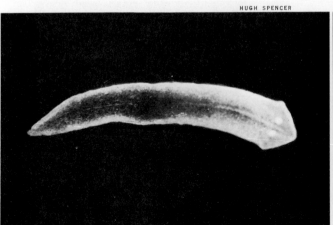

NEMERTINA. The ribbon worms are the most primitive phylum having a tubular alimentary system and a circulatory system. A characteristic proboscis is retracted here.

largely freshwater types bearing an identifying anterior crown of cilia. The latter are locomotor and also create food-bearing water currents. Propulsion may be achieved additionally by inch-wormlike creeping. A rotifer is covered with a thin, transversely creased cuticle that permits telescopelike extension and contraction of the body. Like sac worms generally, rotifers exhibit cell constancy: individuals of any species are composed of a fixed number of identically positioned cells or cell nuclei. Under dry conditions, freshwater rotifers may shrivel into cystlike bodies and persist in this state for very long periods, until water is again available. The animals exhibit natural parthenogenesis (eggs develop into females without being fertilized). In some species males are unknown altogether. In most cases the spring and summer animals are females, and males are produced only during the fall. Fertilized eggs then winter over and give rise to new female generations the next spring.

Nematodes, or roundworms, are slender, tapered at both ends, and covered with a tough,

resistant cuticle. The worms are probably among the most abundant of all animals. Although only 12,000 species have been described to date, the actual species number may be about 500,000. Free-living roundworms abound in all aquatic environments as well as in soil, and even more types are parasitic in plants and animals. Nematodes usually are implicated when an animal suffers from "worms." Man is infected by some 50 species, a few of them producing serious diseases (trichina worms, filaria worms, guinea worms, hookworms). Many of the parasitic types have complex life histories with several hosts.

Phylum **Acanthocephala** *(spiny-headed worms; 600 species): parasites with arthropod intermediate and vertebrate final hosts; without alimentary system, food absorbed through body surface; spiny retractible proboscis at front end*

Phylum **Entoprocta** *(entoprocts; 60 species): marine, one genus freshwater; adults sessile, stalked, solitary or colonial; filter-feeding by means of crown of ciliated tentacles; alimentary tract U-shaped, mouth and anus inside tentacle crown*

• • •

Subgrade **Coelomata:** *mesoderm forms outer and inner layers, leaving a coelom lined by mesoderm, particularly a mesoderm-derived peritoneal membrane*

Lophophorates: *coelom formed in various ways; adults with lophophore, a feeding organ composed of tentacle-studded arms; sessile, with U-shaped alimentary tract; development via various free-swimming larvae; Phoronida, Ectoprocta, Brachiopoda*

Phylum **Phoronida** *(phoronids; 16 species): marine, wormlike, in secreted upright tubes; lophophore horseshoe-shaped, projecting from tube*

Phylum **Ectoprocta** *(ectoprocts; 5,000 species): microscopic, sessile, always in budding colonies; anus outside lophophore crown; marine types with boxlike calcareous exoskeletons, forming encrustations on seaweed and other objects; freshwater types with extensive gelatinous housings*

ASCHELMINTHES. The most important sac worm classes are the rotifers (*left*) and the nematodes, or round worms (*right*). Rotifers have a crown of cilia called the wheel organ at the front end and a narrow foot at the rear. The trunk has a creased cuticle. The nematode body has a cuticle and is tapered at both ends.

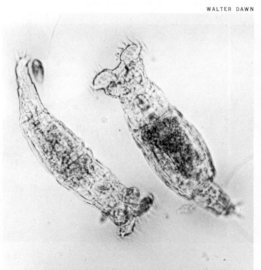

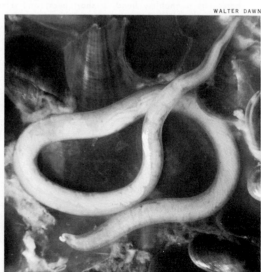

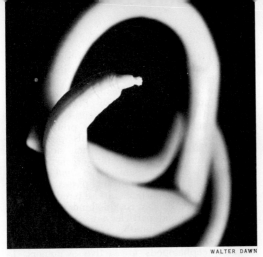

ACANTHOCEPHALA. Known as the spiny-headed worms, this phylum has a proboscis (extended here) at the forward tip. The proboscis is armed with curved hooks.

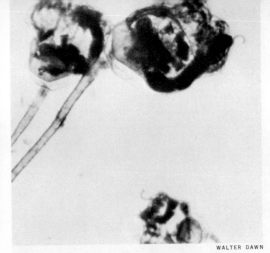

ENTOPROCTA. One characteristic species, *Barentsia*, is shown here. It is a stalked, marine animal with a tentacle crown surrounding the alimentary tract openings.

Phylum **Brachiopoda** (lamp shells; 300 species): marine, clamlike; adult with upper and lower shell; lophophore can be protruded between shells; usually attached by stalk

Schizocoelomates: coelom forms by splitting of mesoderm into outer and inner layers; development primitively through ciliated trochophore larvae, secondarily through variously modified larvae or without larvae; Mollusca, Sipunculida, Echiuroida, Annelida, Oncopoda, Arthropoda

Phylum **Mollusca** (mollusks; 100,000 species)
    Class Amphineura: chitons
    Class Gastropoda: snails
    Class Scaphopoda: tusk shells
    Class Pelecypoda: clams
    Class Cephalopoda: squids, octopuses

All members of this huge phylum share a common anatomical makeup. The body consists of a muscular locomotor foot, a visceral hump that contains most of the internal organs, and a mantle that covers the visceral hump and secretes an exoskeleton. A head is typically

present as well but is reduced or absent in chitons and clams. The nervous system consists basically of a series of interconnected nerve cords, thickened in various regions into ganglia. Breathing is accomplished by gills, and the circulatory system is open in all but the cephalopods. Trochophore larvae generally are characteristic of the phylum. Additional larval forms (veligers) occur in snails and clams, but larvae are absent altogether in cephalopods.

In chitons, the foot is a broad, flat platform, and the visceral hump above it is dome-shaped. The covering mantle secretes eight overlapping calcareous shell plates. Chitons, like snails, feed by means of a radula, a rasping organ that can be protruded from the mouth and scrapes off pieces of aquatic vegetation. In snails the visceral hump develops at different rates at the left and right sides. Various degrees of coiling result, seen most clearly in the shell. Some snails have reduced shells or lack an exoskeleton altogether. In scaphopods, the visceral hump remains uncoiled but becomes greatly elongated and tapered in a dorsal direction. The animal thus acquires

PHORONIDA. These are marine, wormlike animals that are in secreted upright tubes. Pictured here are the tentacular lophophore and a portion of the trunk region.

ECTOPROCTA. Members of the marine genus *Bugula* are illustrated. Microscopic in size, the individuals of such a colony live in secreted exoskeletal housings.

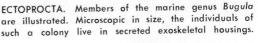

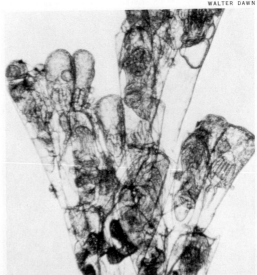

BRACHIOPODA. Two members of the genus *Terebrat-ulina* are shown. The side view at left shows the larger ventral and smaller dorsal shell valves.

a conical tusklike shape, with a tubular shell open at both ends. Tusk shells are marine sand burrowers.

Clams are flattened from side to side, and the two hinged shells (valves) cover the visceral hump and the foot. In many cases the foot is a burrowing organ that may be protruded between the valves. These animals possess enlarged, ciliated gill plates on each side of the visceral hump, and the cilia create a water current that enters a clam at the hind end (incurrent siphon). This current passes over the gills, where food particles are filtered out, and eventually leaves again at the hind end (excurrent siphon). Food particles are carried forward on the gills to the mouth.

Whereas other mollusks are sedentary and sluggish, cephalopods are active swimmers. In these animals the foot is represented by a crown of sucker-studded tentacles emanating from the head. The chambered *Nautilus*, sole survivor of the ancient nautiloids, still possesses an external shell, formed into a flat coil in this case. But in squids and octopuses the shell either is reduced to an internal plate (for example, a cuttlebone) or is absent completely. Cephalopods possess highly developed nervous systems, with large brain ganglia and eyes as complex as those of vertebrates.

As a group mollusks are largely marine, but clams and snails are conspicuous also in fresh water and some snails are terrestrial. In the latter the gill apparatus has become modified into lung chambers. Mollusks include the largest invertebrates, namely giant clams, which may weigh up to 500 pounds (227 kg), and giant squids, which can be more than 50 feet (15.3 meters) long.

Phylum **Sipunculida** *(peanut worms; 250 species): marine sand burrowers with plump trunk and slender, mouth-bearing extension that can be retracted into the trunk; with trochophore larvae*

MOLLUSCA. The snail (*left*), a member of class Gastropoda, has a coiled shell and a tentacle-bearing head. Scallops (*bottom left*) are members of class Pelecypoda. In the top scallop, the mantle tissue can be seen between the rims of the opened shell valves. Squid (*below*), in class Cephalopoda, has tentacles and large eyes.

*Phylum **Annelida** (segmented worms; 15,000 species)*
  Class Polychaeta: tube-formers and burrowers
  Class Oligochaeta: earthworms
  Class Hirudinea: leeches

In these animals all systems except the alimentary tract are subdivided into a series of segments from front to hind end. Apart from the segments at the head and hind ends, all others are very much alike; each contains its own nervous ganglia, blood vessels, muscles, excretory organs, and reproductive structures. Adjacent segments are marked off internally by a peritoneal partition, but nervous and circulatory connections (as well as the alimentary tract) pass through it. In polychaetes each trunk segment also bears an external pair of parapodia, flaplike appendages equipped with chitonous bristles. Parapodia serve partly in locomotion and partly in providing a large surface for breathing through the skin. Earthworms are without parapodia, but bristles (reduced in number) are present. In leeches even bristles are absent. The head contains brain ganglia, sense organs (for example, eyes in polychaetes), and mouth and associated structures. At the hind end is the anus.

Polychaetes develop by way of trochophore larvae, and for this reason the worms are believed to have evolved from ancestors that also gave rise to the mollusks. Early polychaetes, in turn, appear to have been ancestral to the earthworms and leeches. Some polychaetes live in temporary sand burrows, others in secreted tubes or in permanent mud or sand burrows. Earthworms are mostly freshwater and terrestrial forms. They and the leeches differ from polychaetes in being hermaphroditic and in forming cocoons in which the eggs develop without larval stages. Leeches are predominantly freshwater animals, some living as carnivores, most as bloodsucking parasites.

*Phylum **Echiuroida** (spoon worms; 60 species): marine sand burrowers with plump trunk and nonretractile, proboscislike extension; larvae segmented, adults unsegmented*

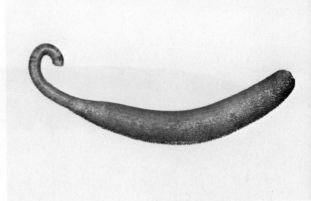

SIPUNCULIDA. Although unsegmented, sipunculids are related to the annelids. Sipunculids, also called peanut worms, live in shallow burrows along seashores.

*Phylum **Oncopoda** (500 species): segmented, claw-footed; evolutionary status transitional between annelids and arthropods*
  Subphylum Onychophora (Peripatus): terrestrial, wormlike, with segmental pairs of claw-bearing legs
  Subphylum Tardigrada (water bears): terrestrial, microscopic, barrel-shaped; six segments, four with claw-bearing legs
  Subphylum Pentastomida: bloodsucking parasites of vertebrates; adults wormlike, with claws at side of mouth
*Phylum **Arthropoda** (jointed-legged animals; 1 million species)*
  Subphylum Chelicerata: without antennae or jaws
  Class Xiphosurida: horseshoe crabs
  Class Pantopoda: sea spiders
  Class Arachnida: scorpions, spiders, ticks, mites

ANNELIDA. The clam worm *Nereis* (*left*), has segmental parapodia—flaplike appendages along the sides of the animal. The tube-dwelling peacock worm (*right*) has a crown of food-catching tentacles protruding from its shell.

ONCOPODA. The peripatus is a slender wormlike animal that lives under logs and debris in tropical rain forests. At night it comes out to feed, using its two short antennae to feel its way about.

ARTHROPODA. The wolfspider has four pairs of walking legs and a cephalothorax and abdominal divisions.

ARTHROPODA. The sand crab, a member of the class Crustacea, has stalked eyes and specialized appendages.

ARTHROPODA. A millipede, belonging to the class Diplopoda, has two pairs of legs per body segment.

ARTHROPODA. The luna moth is in the class Insecta. Its feathery antennae are characteristic of moths.

Subphylum Mandibulata: with antennae and
jaws
Class Crustacea: crustaceans
Class Chilopoda: centipedes
Class Diplopoda: millipedes
Class Insecta: insects

CHAETOGNATHA. In this arrow worm, the head (near the center of the photo) bears curved spines on each side. The trunk has lateral and tail fins for stabilizing.

This largest of all phyla appears to have evolved from ancient polychaete ancestors. Arthropods possess segmented bodies and paired, jointed appendages on the segments. But in contrast to the segments of an annelid those of an arthropod are mutually different in structure and function, and distinct body divisions, such as head, thorax, and abdomen, are clearly in evidence. Arthropods are further distinguished by unique compound eyes, each composed of numerous separate visual units. Simple eyes are present in addition. Particularly characteristic of the phylum is an all-enveloping chitinous exoskeleton. This cover is molted periodically, either throughout life (as in crustacea) or during preadult stages only (as in insects). Size increase can occur only after a molt, before a new exoskeleton has hardened.

The nervous system is basically annelidlike, but the brain ganglia are large, and some or all of the segmental ganglia often are fused together. Breathing is accomplished in aquatic forms by feathery gills or sets of gill plates (gill books), and in terrestrial forms by lung books and especially by tracheal systems. Lung books are structured like gill books but are adapted for air breathing. A tracheal system consists of a series of branching, chitinous channels leading from the body surface to all interior tissues. The circulation is open and consists of a dorsal open-ended vessel that also serves partly or wholly as a contractile heart. Endocrine systems are highly developed in crustacea and insects. The hormones produced by these systems regulate, for example, reproductive activities and especially the molting processes during development.

In chelicerates, the head and thorax form a fused cephalothorax developed from eight embryonic segments. Six of these bear paired appendages, of which four pairs are walking legs. The animals are without jaws, and they feed by crushing food with their appendages and then sucking out the juices. On the abdomen are gill books in horseshoe crabs, lung books in scorpions, and lung books or tracheal openings in spiders. At the tip of the abdomen of spiders are spinnerets, organs that release the silk secreted by interior silk glands. Spiders are the most numerous chelicerates, some 30,000 species being known.

In mandibulates, the head consists of six fused segments and bears a pair of mandibles (jaws) as well as antennae. There are two pairs of antennae in crustacea and one pair in insects. The structure of thorax and abdomen differs in different groups. In a lobster, for example, the thorax consists of eight segments, the abdomen of six. One pair of thoracic appendages forms the large claws, and four pairs are walking legs. In an insect the thorax is composed of three segments, each with a pair of legs. Two of these segments typically also carry paired, chitinous wings. The insect abdomen, composed of 11 segments, is without appendages.

Crustacea include waterfleas, copepods, barnacles, shrimps, prawns, lobsters, crayfishes, crabs, and related types in ocean and fresh water. Some crustacea, such as woodlice, sowbugs, and slaters, are terrestrial. Many members of the class are minute and planktonic and constitute important food organisms (particularly copepods and krill). But the class also contains the largest arthropods, namely, the giant crabs, with leg spans over 10 feet (3.1 meters), and lobsters, which can weigh well over 40 pounds (18 kg). Some 50,000 crustacean species have been described.

Centipedes live predominantly in dry, tropical environments. They are carnivores, with poison fangs on the first trunk segment. All other segments of the trunk bear legs, and the animals are efficient runners. About 3,000 species are known. Millipedes, encompassing 8,000 known species and possibly 25,000 species altogether, are herbivorous. The trunk consists largely of fused double segments, each carrying two pairs of legs. Yet despite their more numerous appendages, they are poor runners.

Among insects, the most primitive group (Subclass Apterygota) comprises wingless types (for example, silverfish). The hatched young here are essentially adults, and larval stages and metamorphosis do not occur. All remaining insects (Subclass Pterygota) typically are capable of flight, although some are secondarily wingless (for example, fleas). In one superorder (Exopterygota) the hatched young are larvae that transform gradually into adults through a series of molts. Wings grow progressively larger on the outside of these larvae. To this group belong, for example, grasshoppers, earwigs, stone flies, termites, various types of lice, dragonflies, mayflies, scale insects, and true bugs (such as plant bugs, bedbugs). In a second superorder (Endopterygota) the hatched young are larvae (often caterpillars) that molt several times and eventually transform into pupae. The latter then molt in their turn and produce adults. In these insects the wings grow within the larval and pupal body, and they become external within a few minutes after the pupa metamorphoses into the adult. Included in this group are scorpion flies, dobson flies, caddis flies, moths and butterflies, houseflies and mosquitos, fleas, beetles and weevils, and bees, ants, and wasps.

HEMICHORDATA. The acorn worm represents a small subphylum of marine animals belonging to the phylum Chordata. The worm's body is divided into a proboscis, short collar, and trunk.

Some 80 percent of all arthropods, and thus more than all other organisms combined (plants included), are insects.

Enterocoelomates; coeloms form as cavities within mesoderm pouches growing out from endoderm; Chaetognatha, Pogonophora, Hemichordata, Echinodermata, Chordata

Phylum Chaetognatha (arrowworms; 50 species): marine, planktonic; torpedo-shaped, head with grasping spines, trunk with lateral and tail fins formed by extensions of cuticle

Phylum Pogonophora (beard worms; 50 species): tube-dwellers in deep-sea bottoms; with crown of anterior tentacles; alimentary system absent, feeding process not observed

Phylum Echinodermata (spiny-skinned animals; 6,000 species)
Class Crinoidea: sea lilies, feather stars
Class Holothuroidea: sea cucumbers
Class Asteroidea: starfishes, sea stars
Class Ophiuroidea: brittle stars
Class Echinoidea: sea urchins, sand dollars

Echinoderms develop via larvae that, in many cases, are very similar to the tornaria larvae of hemichordates. This and other developmental correspondences suggest that hemichordates and echinoderms are fairly closely related. Echinoderm larvae are bilateral and free-swimming, but the adults are radially symmetrical and sessile or sluggish. In these radial adults the body parts occur in sets of five or multiples of five (for example, the five arms of a starfish). Echinoderms possess an endoskeleton, composed of flat, calcareous plates underneath the epidermis. The most characteristic feature of the phylum is the water-vascular system, a hydraulic apparatus used in feeding, locomotion, or both. The system consists of a series of branched, water-filled ducts open to the external seawater at a sievelike pore. Called a madreporite, the pore in a starfish is a small red-brown spot on the upper side. Internally the ducts terminate at numerous blind-ended tube feet projecting from the body surface. In a starfish, for example, rows of tube feet are located on the underside of each arm. Sets of tube feet are used as little legs or as food-trapping and food-holding organs.

Echinoderms are exclusively marine. Sea lilies are stalked, sessile, deepwater forms. Their feathery arms are studded with tube feet, which trap food and convey it to the mouth in the center of the upper side. Feather stars are unstalked and unattached, and they use their arms for swimming as well as for feeding. In sea cucumbers the main body axis is horizontal, the animals lying on the side. The skin is leathery, and the skeleton in reduced. In all other echinoderm classes, the mouth is on the underside of the body. Brittle stars resemble starfishes superficially, but these animals lack tube feet. Instead, locomotion is brought about by the serpentine movements of the highly mobile arms and food is trapped directly by the mouth. In sea urchins and sand dollars the skeletal plates are fused into a rigid shell. Pores in this shell permit protrusion of the tube feet, which in these animals serve primarily in breathing. The tooth-equipped mouth functions in feeding directly, and movable spines hinged to the skeletal shell serve in locomotion.

Phylum Chordata (chordates; 50,000 species): with notochord, hollow dorsal nerve cord, and pharyngeal gill slits at least at some stage of life cycle

Subphylum Cephalochordata (amphioxus): marine sand burrowers; body segmented, tadpolelike, without head, but with permanent tail, notochord, nerve cord, and gill system

Subphylum Urochordata (tunicates): marine; larvae are tailed tadpoles with notochord, nerve cord, and developing gill slits; adults mostly sessile, with elaborate system of gill slits used in filter-feeding and breathing, but without tail, notochord, or nerve cord

Subphylum Hemichordata (acorn worms and related types; 100 species): marine, wormlike, solitary in sand or colonial in secreted housings; with ciliated gill slits serving in filter-feeding and breathing; development often by way of tornaria larvae

Subphylum Vertebrata (vertebrates): primitively in fresh water, secondarily in all environments; body segmented, with head and permanent tail; notochord in embryo and larva, supplemented or replaced in adult by vertebral column of cartilage or bone; nerve cord becomes brain and spinal cord; breathing by gill system in aquatic forms, by lungs in terrestrial forms; blood circulation closed, with heart, arteries, veins, and capillaries; usually with paired appendages, forming fins or legs

Class Agnatha (jawless fishes): freshwater and marine; notochord throughout life, supplemented in adult by cartilage skeleton; heart 2-chambered; with single nostril; skin glandular; lampreys, hagfishes (50 species)

Class Chondrichthyes (cartilages fishes): marine; notochord largely replaced in adult by cartilage skeleton; heart 2-chambered; with jaws, teeth, and paired nostrils; skin with toothlike denticles; sharks, rays (600 species)

Class Osteichthyes (bony fishes): freshwater and marine; skeleton of bone; heart 2-chambered; skin with bony scales; swim bladder usually present; gills covered by bony plate; fins supported by internal bones or by hard or soft rays; all other fishes (25,000 species)

ECHINODERMATA. The starfish (*left*), seen from the upper side, shows the typical radial symmetry of adults of this phylum. The body parts occur in sets of five, as shown here, or in multiples of five. The sea urchin (*below*) has thick spines growing from its shell. Its long slender tube feet protrude through the pores of the shell.

Class Amphibia (amphibians): freshwater and terrestrial; heart 3-chambered; skin glandular; aquatic adults with gills or lungs, terrestrial adults with lungs only; eggs laid in water; salamanders, newts, toads, frogs (3,000 species)

Class Reptilia (reptiles): largely terrestrial; heart 4-chambered; lung breathing; skin with horny plates or scales; fertilization internal; shelled eggs laid on land; turtles, lizards, snakes, crocodiles (6,000 species)

Class Aves (birds): terrestrial, aerial, and aquatic; heart 4-chambered; internal temperature constant ("warm-blooded"); skin with feathers; forelegs and wings, some groups secondarily flightless; teeth absent, mouth with horny beak; fertilization internal, shelled eggs laid on land (9,000 species)

Class Mammalia (mammals): terrestrial, aerial, and aquatic; heart 4-chambered; red blood corpuscles without nuclei; internal temperature constant; skin with hair; coelom subdivided by diaphragm; fertilization internal; young nursed with milk (5,000 species)

Subclass Prototheria (egg-laying mammals): shelled eggs laid on land; duck-billed platypus, spiny anteaters

Subclass Metatheria (marsupial mammals): young born in immature condition, development completed within skin pouch (marsupium) of female; opossums, kangaroos, wombats, koalas, and related types

Subclass Eutheria (placental mammals): young develop entirely within uterus of female, nourished through umbilical cord and uterine attachment region (placenta); all other mammals

Chordates exhibit evolutionary affinities to ancestral echinoderm stocks. The phylum originated in the sea, and the primitive representatives (tunicates, amphioxus) still are marine. The tailed amphioxus appears to have been the evolutionary source that gave rise to the chordates—that is to say, the tunicates, hemichordates, and vertebrates.

The first vertebrates probably were freshwater forms that were capable of maintaining station against river currents by means of their muscular tails. These animals presumably were filter-feeders, as is the case even now in tunicates, amphioxus, and to some extent also in lampreys. In this feeding method, water and microscopic food enter the mouth, food particles are strained out in the pharynx by the gill slits and are conveyed into the esophagus, and water leaves the body through the gill slits. In the process, blood in the gills is oxygenated as well.

Later descendants of these original vertebrates evolved jaws and teeth and filter-feeding then ceased; the mouth trapped large food organisms directly and the gill apparatus came to serve only in breathing. This is still the pattern in the cartilage and bony fishes. As freshwater animals, primitive bony fishes must have been subjected to periodic droughts. Presumably in adaptation to this hazard, the animals evolved a pouch attached to the pharynx that could serve as a temporary air sac and oxygen supplier when water was in short supply. Some present-day descendants of such fishes still use this sac as a lung, and from the same ancestral stock the terrestrial vertebrates appear to have evolved. In all other descendant bony fishes, however, the

873

MARINELAND OF FLORIDA

CLINTON L. HOFFMAN, FROM BLACK STAR

CHORDATA. Representatives of three classes of vertebrates are shown here. The mullet (*upper left*), a bony
fish in the class Osteichthyes, is an aquatic vertebrate
that breathes through gills. The chuckwalla lizard
(*above*), which is a member of the class Reptilia, has
a typical vertebrate head and tail and paired appendages. The leopard (*left*), like man, is a mammal.

SATOUR

original air sac now functions as a swim bladder.

In the amphibia the ancestral fins with their
internal bony supports have become elongated
into legs. But apart from being able to walk and
breathe air, the animals still are aquatic in most
respects; they require a moist environment generally, their eggs must be laid in water even if
the adults live on land, and the tadpoles must
develop in water. By contrast, the reptiles
evolved a complex water-containing and shell-en-
closed egg capable of being laid and hatched
out on land. Thus, even sea turtles and all other
aquatic reptiles come to land for egg-laying. The
birds arose from one group of ancestral reptiles.
The feathers of these animals not only make
flight possible but also aid in regulating body
heat to a constant level. Such warm-bloodedness,
in turn, permits a bird to remain highly active
even if the environmental temperature is low.

Another group of ancestral reptiles gave rise
to the mammals. Like birds, mammals adopted
exceedingly active ways of life, largely on land,
but also in the air and in water. High levels of
body activity here again are correlated with a
heat-regulating skin cover (hair) and also with
a highly efficient breathing system (aided by a
diaphragm) and oxygen-supply system (aided by
specialized red corpuscles). In further correlation with the fast tempo of mammalian living,

the ancestral method of laying and leaving eggs
came to be replaced in most cases by pregnancy;
the developing eggs are carried about within the
female and are nourished by means of a placenta.
Moreover, since fewer embryos can be carried
about than could be left to develop independently, the fewer offspring produced receive correspondingly more parental care. Nursing is one
expression of this increased postnatal attention,
and training of young within family, herd, or
society is another.

PAUL B. WEISZ, *Brown University*

Bibliography

Alcock, John, *Animal Behavior: An Evolutionary Approach,* 7th
  ed. (Sinauer Assocs. 2001).
Alexander, R. McNeill, *Principles of Animal Locomotion* (Prince-
  ton Univ. Press 2002).
Arthur, Wallace, *The Origin of Animal Body Plans: A Study in
  Evolutionary Developmental Biology* (Cambridge 1997).
Baker, Steve, *Picturing the Beast: Animals, Identity, and Repre-
  sentation* (Univ. of Ill. Press 2001).
Burnie, David, and Don E. Wilson, eds., *Animals: The Defini-
  tive Visual Guide to the World's Wildlife* (Smithsonian Inst.
  2001).
Burton, Robert, ed., *Animal Life* (Oxford 1991).
Calder, William A., III, *Size, Function, and Life History* (1984;
  reprint, Dover 1996).
Caro, Tim, ed., *Behavioral Ecology and Conservation Biology* (Ox-
  ford 1998).
Carroll, Sean B., et al., *From DNA to Diversity: Molecular Genet-
  ics and the Evolution of Animal Design* (Blackwell 2001).
Foster, Susan A., and John A. Endler, *Geographic Variation in
  Behavior: Perspectives on Evolutionary Mechanisms* (Oxford
  1999).
Fryxell, John M., and Per Lundberg, *Individual Behavior and
  Community Dynamics* (Chapman 1998).
Maier, Richard, *Comparative Animal Behavior: An Evolutionary
  and Ecological Approach* (Allyn & Bacon 1998).
McGowan, Christopher, *A Practical Guide to Vertebrate Mechan-
  ics* (Cambridge 1999).
Romer, Alfred S., and Thomas S. Parsons, *The Vertebrate Body,*
  6th ed. (Saunders 1986).

ANIMAL BEHAVIOR, the focus of a scientific discipline aimed primarily at discovering why different organisms exhibit various behaviors. In their search for the origins of behavior, scientists have traditionally subscribed to one of two major theories. The so-called hereditarians state that behavior results mainly from an individual's genetic endowment, while the environmentalists propose that past experiences are the most important determinant of behavior.

Opinion regarding behavioral origins has shifted over time, with scientists favoring first one position and then the other. Yet the question of whether a given behavior pattern is innate or learned is both restrictive and misleading. The idea that such a pattern's development is solely genetic or nongenetic prohibits the discovery of any interactions between heredity and environment and also fails to allow for the effects of certain variables that might be neither innate nor learned.

Basic Principles of Animal Behavior. While the study of animal behavior extends at least as far back as ancient Greece, 19th-century British naturalist Charles Darwin was responsible for turning it into a true scientific discipline. The field grew from two concepts that Darwin set forth, the first being that behavior patterns have biological adaptiveness (that is, they contribute to the survival of the individual and its species) and thus are subject to selection pressures similar to those affecting morphological characters. Second, according to Darwin a continuity exists in the mental processes of various species of animals, including humans.

These two insights led to the development of the independent scientific disciplines known as ethology and comparative psychology, which together form the two major branches of the science of animal behavior. Comparative psychologists are concerned for the most part with gaining an understanding of learning and behavior, obtaining their knowledge primarily through laboratory research that requires strictly controlled variables and complex statistical analyses. Mammals are often used in these experiments, particularly common laboratory species, such as rats, mice, and monkeys.

Ethologists usually are trained in zoology and conduct research through observation and experimentation in an animal's natural habitat. Ethological experiments typically involve birds, fish, and insects and emphasize both instinctive behavior patterns, rather than learned ones, and the evolution and biological adaptiveness of these patterns.

Ethology and comparative psychology are obviously complementary approaches. After an early period of distrust and disagreement, the two approaches have reached the present state where each recognizes the significance of the other.

The bringing together of comparative psychology and ethology has gone hand in hand with recognition by both schools that few, if any, behavioral traits are either completely innate or completely learned. Animal behaviorists now recognize that the normal development of behavior depends on the interaction of the behaving organism with its environment, both past and present. Interest is centered on the determinants of an animal's behavior, including those that are historical (maturational and experiential), environmental, and organismic (physiological).

Modern Research in Animal Behavior. The following review describes six areas of current research in animal behavior. These six areas by no means exhaust the possibilities for research in the field, nor are they intended to be mutually exclusive. Rather, the intent is to provide a sampling of the questions currently being asked and the kinds of research currently being conducted to answer the questions. The discussion begins by reviewing basic organismic determinants of relatively simple behavior patterns and ends with a consideration of the behavior of animals in groups.

Behavior Genetics. Investigators in the field of behavior genetics are concerned with the effects of an organism's genetic makeup (genotype) on its behavior, conducting their research on the role that genotypic differences play in the determination of behavioral differences. Suppose, for example, that all males of a given fish species establish similar territories and build identical nests, in identical fashion, at a particular time of the year. This species-specific behavior pattern might suggest a long series of experiments for animal behaviorists concerned with the development of those aspects of behavior that appear to be relatively unchangeable. In contrast, because there are no apparent behavioral differences involved, the raw material for a behavior genetics study is not present. But should individual males of the fish species construct nests either made up of different materials or made at different times of the year, an experiment in behavior genetics would be possible. By making appropriate genetic crosses between subgroups exhibiting differing behavior patterns, researchers could determine whether or not genotype affects behavioral patterns such as nest building, nest-material selection, and breeding season.

What behavior geneticists require, then, is variation in the traits that they study. Any traits, whether morphological or behavioral, may vary within a population in two primary ways. The first type of variation may be referred to as qualitative, which means that the members of the population may be placed in mutually exclusive categories on the basis of the trait. For example, the flowers of certain species of plants may be classified as red or pink or white. It was such qualitatively varying traits that Gregor Mendel used in establishing the basic principles of genetics. (See MENDEL, JOHANN GREGOR.)

Second, traits may vary in a quantitative fashion. Height and weight in the human population offer good examples. Traits that vary quantitatively usually can be shown to result from the interaction of many different genes with each other and with the environment. A branch of genetics called quantitative genetics specializes in the study of such traits. Since most behavioral traits may be said to vary quantitatively rather than qualitatively, the methods of quantitative genetics have a wide application to experiments of behavior genetics.

Obviously, if the effects of genotype are to be studied in an experiment, the experimenter must be able to manipulate and vary genotype while holding other variables constant. Two major methods of manipulating genotype are available to the behavior geneticist. One is selective breeding. In the usual selection experiment, animals with high values of the trait under study are mated, while simultaneously, animals with low values are mated. If such selective breeding for several generations results in discrete (distinct) populations, one has demonstrated that genotype affects the behavioral trait in question. Selection experiments with a number of different species have shown that genotype affects traits such as maze-learning ability, temperament, motivation, sexual behavior, and social behavior.

The second major method of varying genotype in an experiment is the use of inbred strains. Inbreeding has been defined as the mating of close relatives. In a selection experiment the object is to increase or decrease the value of a certain trait in the population. The objective of inbreeding is quite different. The mating of close relatives (for example, brother crossed with sister) over several generations results in the highest possible degree of homozygosity in the population. Since chromosomes usually occur in pairs, each gene can be said to have a "partner" located at the corresponding locus, or point, of the homologous, or matching, chromosome. *Homozygosity* refers to that condition in which the members of each pair of genes are identical. For example, if a gene for brown coat color occurs on one chromosome, an identical gene for brown coat color must occur on the other chromosome in order for the pair to be described as homozygous. (See also GENETICS.)

Inbreeding has the further effect of producing genetically similar animals. All males of a given inbred strain will have the same, or nearly the same, genotype as all other males of that strain. The males of such a strain then may be considered as a large group of identical twins, and all the females of that strain may be considered as a second large group of identical twins, which differs from the males only in regard to the sex chromosomes. House mice have been used often in the development of inbred strains, with these strains offering a degree of genetic control that has proved invaluable in many different areas of research.

Neural, Hormonal, and Chemical Control of Behavior. As noted in the preceding section, genotype can be shown to affect many different types of behavior. The logical question that evolves from behavior genetic research is, How does genotype affect behavior? While the answers to this question represent one of the great challenges to modern science, it is possible to set forth some general statements concerning the physiological mechanisms by which genes affect behavior. Most scientists agree that the primary function of genes lies in the control of enzymes and enzyme systems. The function of enzymes is to mediate the metabolic activities necessary for the development and differentiation of cells, tissues, and organs. Behavior ultimately depends on the resulting morphology and physiology. One should bear in mind, however, that these morphological and physiological bases of behavior are not necessarily unchangeable. Scientific literature contains many examples of behavioral and environmental effects on physiology and anatomy.

In terms of behavioral research the most key parts of the organism are the nervous system and the endocrine system. Consequently, much emphasis in animal behavior experimentation has been placed on neural function and the effects of hormones on behavior. (See ENDOCRINE GLANDS; NERVOUS SYSTEM; HORMONE.)

Recent experiments in brain function have used the techniques of implanted electrodes and implanted chemicals in the brain. These experiments have led to the discovery of hitherto unsuspected pleasure and pain centers and to the more accurate mapping of the functions of the various parts of the brain. Specific areas responsible for specific patterns of behavior have been discovered. For example, certain areas of the cat's brain, when stimulated, yield attack behavior; other areas of the brain yield escape behavior.

It has been known for many years that one of the primary functions of hormones is that of activating certain neural centers. This activation results in predictable types of behavior. For example, if mating behavior is abolished in a male animal by castration, it can be reinstated by appropriate hormone replacement. A recent discovery has shown that hormones have a different effect prenatally, that is, before the birth of the organism. Before birth, hormones act as "organizers" rather than as "activators." This effect is demonstrated by injecting male hormones into pregnant females. Female embryos carried by the injected mothers are born with genitalia resembling that of males. Furthermore, behavioral tests indicate that their nervous system has been altered by the presence of the prenatal androgen (a male hormone) so that they behave more like males than females in both sexual activity and play patterns. This extremely important area of research is greatly increasing our understanding of the hormonal determinants of behavior.

Behavior can be controlled by stimulating parts of the brain. This cat was raised in friendship with the rat.

ARTHUR LEIPZIG

Stimulation of the hypothalamus initiates attack behavior in the cat until the electric current is stopped.

ARTHUR LEIPZIG

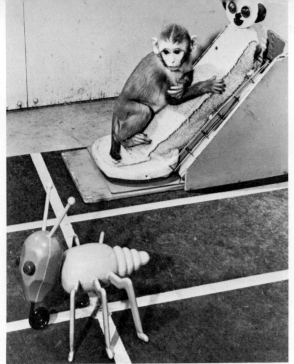

Depriving this monkey of its natural mother during a critical period of development caused abnormal behavior toward intruders until a mother-substitute was provided.

As noted before, the fact that hormones affect behavior has been known for some time. A more recent discovery is that feedback occurs from behavior to the hormone-producing glands. Furthermore, it has been shown that external stimuli (including those emanating from another animal) affect the secretion of certain hormones. For example, in certain species of birds the visual presence of the mate and of nesting material results in enlargement of the ovaries and in the onset of incubation behavior after a certain period of time.

Studies of the chemistry of the brain represent another important area of research on the physiological determinants of behavior. Experiments have shown that both genotype and past experience can affect the balance of certain chemicals in the brain and that these chemicals are somehow correlated with learning ability. This research some day may lead to an understanding of individual differences in mental ability.

The Development of Behavior: Critical Periods and Imprinting. This area of investigation is concerned primarily with environmental determinants of behavior. The emphasis is on early experiential factors that influence later behavior. Progress in this key area has been so encouraging that one might speculate that the results of these investigations, combined with those of behavior genetics and behavioral physiology, may in fact represent the area where the next major breakthrough in science will occur.

One important insight that has developed as a result of these studies is that certain periods occur in the development of an animal when the animal is particularly sensitive to certain experiences. These periods are called "critical periods." For example, it has been shown that if dogs between three and seven weeks of age do not have contact with humans, their later behavior in response to humans is abnormal. On the other hand, if puppies between three and seven weeks of age do not have contact with other dogs, their later behavior toward other dogs is abnormal. Critical periods in development have been discovered for many different species and for many different types of behavior. Critical periods in human development have also been hypothesized.

Other research in this area has been concerned with the effects that long periods of social isolation early in life have on later behavior. Experiments with Rhesus monkeys have shown that if these animals do not have contact with members of their own species during the first year of life, later social responses are greatly impaired. The animals do not play normally, and they can be bred only with great difficulty. Experience with other monkeys during the first year seems essential for learning adequate patterns of monkey behavior.

Another discovery concerning the effects of early experience on later behavior is that of imprinting. Imprinting has been defined as very rapid learning during an early critical period in the development of certain animals. For example, freshly hatched ducks and geese have a tendency to follow the first moving object that they see. Normally, this object is the mother duck or goose. However, ethological research has shown that if the first moving object that the ducklings or goslings see is a human being, they tend to follow the person. Later, when the human being is placed in direct competition with the natural mother, the ducklings and goslings prefer to follow the human being. Furthermore, in adult life, animals imprinted to a person will direct social responses to people in preference to members of their own species. The universality of this phenomenon and factors affecting the critical period for its occurrence are under investigation. (See also IMPRINTING.)

Sensory Processes, Communication, and Orientation. Human beings have long speculated about the mental life of the animals that share the earth with them, and many questions concerning the existence of processes such as consciousness in animals have been posed. Although most of these questions may be forever unanswerable, experiments have shown conclusively that many animal species possess senses and means of communication and orientation that humans do not have. Research in this area is difficult and demanding, but it can be most rewarding, since many of the most interesting problems in animal behavior are found in the areas of sensory processes, communication, and orientation. A few examples will illustrate some of the rather startling findings in this field.

Perhaps the earliest, and certainly the most famous, modern research in this area concerns the ability of bees to communicate a food source to other members of the hive. They do this by means of various "dances," which they execute on the combs of the hive. The dances indicate the distance and the direction in which other bees must fly in order to locate the food source. Furthermore, it has been discovered that different species of bees have different "dialects"—that is, the pattern of the dance and the information conveyed by the dance differ from species to species. It has also been shown that bees can orientate by means of polarized light in the sky and that they are sensitive to ultraviolet light. The human eye is incapable of detecting either of these stimuli.

An active field of research has been concerned with abilities of various animals to use reflected sound waves in finding their way in their environment and in securing food. It has been demonstrated that bats can locate small flying insects by means of echolocation (a sonarlike process). It has also been discovered that certain moth species have evolved a behavior pattern that affords some protection from predatory bats. On hearing a bat's cry, these moths power-dive into the grass. Porpoises also have an excellent sonar system, and these marvelously intelligent animals are proving of great value in behavioral research. Echolocation systems have been analyzed in detail and have been shown to depend on frequencies higher than the upper limit of hearing in humans.

Yet another fascinating discovery is that certain fish possess an electric sense. Specialized organs located in the tails of these fish send out electric pulses at a constant frequency. This emitted current then is sensed by other specialized organs located in the head region and along the sides of the body. Objects in the environment distort the flow of current, and the fish respond to this change with appropriate behavior. They are astonishingly sensitive to changes in the electric field. If a comb that has been passed through someone's hair is moved near the side of the aquarium, they respond violently. Certain species of these fish can be taught to select objects that they cannot see on the basis of the electrical properties of the objects. All fish that possess this electric sense swim by means of undulating fins or rays. It is necessary for these fish to swim with the spine held very straight so that movements of the tail will not distort the electric field.

The abilities of animals to migrate from place to place and to "home" have interested many scientists. Certain species of fish, for example, find their way over long distances to a particular segment of a particular stream when in reproductive phase. They seem to have been imprinted to the chemical conditions of that section of the stream during their early development. The homing ability of pigeons has also been investigated, with the discovery that pigeons flying near the home loft are able to find their way to the loft by means of landmarks, which they have learned during previous flights. Pigeons released in unfamiliar territory, at some distance from the loft, however, orient themselves in the direction of the loft by means of a little understood "navigational grid."

Learning and Motivation. Learning and motivation are the experimental psychologist's favorite topics. They have been investigated intensively, and several theories about them have been formulated.

An accepted generalization in this area is that the intelligence of animals is correlated with their position on the evolutionary scale. A chimpanzee is capable of solving more difficult problems than a rat, and a rat, on most problems, can learn better than can a frog. However, behaviorists have had great difficulty in devising experiments that would separate the learning abilities of animals in other than a very crude fashion. Modern experimentation in this area has reformulated the questions, and the results to date appear very promising. (For information on learning and motivation, see ANIMAL INTELLIGENCE; PSYCHOLOGY.)

Social Behavior, Ethology, and Evolution. Social behavior has been defined as the behavior of an animal or group of animals in response to others of the same or different species. The social behavior of an animal obviously is of great importance in determining biological adaptiveness. For this reason ethologists have conducted many experiments on the social behavior of animals. These experiments generally have involved a combination of careful observation of the animal in its natural setting with field experiments, in which models are often used. Emphasis continually is placed on the biological adaptiveness and the evolutionary antecedents of the behavior.

The following example illustrates a typical ethological experiment. Most species of birds dispose of the empty eggshell shortly after the young birds have hatched. Through experimentation with certain species of gulls, ethologists have demonstrated that eggshell removal contributes to the survival of the species. Although the eggshell has an outer camouflage, the inside of the shell is white. Empty shells have been shown to attract predators. Thus birds that remove shells from their nest would reduce the chances of their young being eaten by a predator. Ethologists were also interested in the stimuli that provoked the behavior of eggshell removal in these gulls. What is there about an empty shell that results in the parent bird's removing it from the nest? By ingenious use of models, ethologists have learned that gulls tend to remove objects that are khaki or white much more frequently than they discard objects of other colors. Furthermore, they have discovered that the critical stimulus for shell removal is not the weight of the shell, or its shape, but rather its thin edge. If a blown (hollowed-out) egg to which has been glued a small piece of shell is put in the nest, the parent birds in two out of three cases will remove it. If an eggshell is placed on the rim of the nest of an inexperienced bird, it is removed; if an intact egg is placed on the rim of the nest, it is rolled into the nest by the birds. However, learning also enters into the behavior pattern. If plaster eggs are introduced into the nest before the normal eggs are laid, the birds will incubate the plaster eggs. Gulls that incubated black plaster eggs tended to remove black shells when tested later. Similarly, gulls that incubated green plaster eggs tended to remove green shells when tested. Ethological experiments, such as this one, have shed much light on problems of the evolutionary development of behavior. (See also ETHOLOGY.)

An area of research that has developed rapidly is the social behavior of primate groups studied under natural conditions. Field-workers have published accounts of the social organization of chimpanzees, gorillas, orangutans, and many species of monkeys, including baboons. The observations have revealed a great variety of patterns of social organization and have even led to hypotheses concerning the development of social organization in human beings. Fuller understanding of these and other factors of animal behavior will provide a better understanding of human behavior.

THOMAS E. MCGILL
Williams College

Bibliography: Barnard, C. J., *Animal Behaviour* (Wiley 1983); Dugatkin, Lee A., *Cooperation among Animals* (Oxford 1997); Gould, James L., and Carol Grant Gould, *The Animal Mind* (Freeman 1994); McFarland, D., ed., *The Oxford Companion to Animal Behavior* (Oxford 1982); Zahavi, Amotz, and Avishag Zahavi, *The Handicap Principle: A Missing Piece of Darwin's Puzzle* (Oxford 1997).

ANIMAL EXPERIMENTATION, research or tests using live vertebrates, especially mammals. Sometimes the term is used more broadly to refer to experiments with all animals, including invertebrates.

It is estimated that 25 million mammals are used annually in research in the United States alone. Rodents, mainly rats and mice, make up about 90% of the test animals; cats and dogs, about 2%; and nonhuman primates, about 1%. The rodents are raised specifically for this purpose, and a variety of pure genetic strains are available for specific types of experiments. Of the approximately 10 million dogs and cats taken in by pounds and shelters every year, about 2% are used in research.

Types of Experiments. Most Nobel Prize—winning work in medicine and physiology has depended on animal experiments whose major objective has been to provide fundamental physiological knowledge on which the prevention and treatment of human and animal disease can be based. The Belgian scientist Corneille Heymans, for example, received the 1938 prize for experiments that showed that stimulating or cutting nerve pathways in the neck and aorta of dogs had important effects on respiration and circulation. The Argentinian physiologist Bernardo Houssay was similarly honored with the 1947 prize for demonstrating in dogs the role of the pituitary gland in regulating sugar metabolism.

Animals also provide models for the study of human disease. Strains of rodents with hereditary diabetes, hypertension, and atherosclerosis have yielded information of great value. Disease-causing agents often have been isolated from animals that were intentionally infected, and this has led to the development of vaccines. Animals are also used for developing and testing new surgical procedures and medical devices. New drugs are tested on animals to help determine their potential for causing cancer or other diseases or for harming embryos and fetuses in the womb.

Behavioral studies of animals in psychology laboratories have revealed much information about reactions to stress, pain, and other types of stimuli. Experiments of this kind may cause pain to the subjects if the nature of the experiment precludes the use of analgesics or anesthetics. Most experiments, however, involve no pain to the test animals.

Many experiments are brief procedures in which the animals are killed while under anesthesia. Others are long-term tests, sometimes lasting several years. In long-term tests the animals are normally kept in optimal surroundings to prevent illness, which could harm the subjects and thereby destroy the validity of the observations.

Benefits of Animal Experimentation. Nearly every advance in health care and combating human disease has been based on animal research. Vitamins and hormones, polio vaccines and other vaccines, new cancer treatments, modern advances in immunology, and scores of surgical operations were discovered or developed with the help of animal experimentation. Two very common diseases, heart disease and diabetes, provide typical examples of the value of experiments on animals.

Heart Disease. In 1628 the English scientist William Harvey published his description of the circulation of the blood, based on observations made on a variety of invertebrates and vertebrates, including dogs. In 1733 Stephen Hales, an English clergyman, made the first measurement of blood pressure, using a mare as the experimental animal for his cumbersome apparatus. A century later

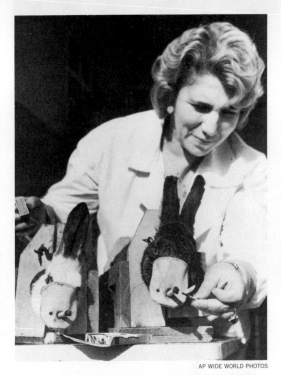

AP WIDE WORLD PHOTOS

Rabbits are forced to inhale in a Soviet project to determine the physiological effects of cigarette smoke.

the French physiologist Jean Poiseuille invented a mercury manometer that eventually made blood pressure measurements feasible in clinical practice, using dogs as his experimental subjects. In the early 20th century the British physiologist Ernest Starling devised a heart-lung preparation in dogs to study the mechanics of heart contractions. Numerous animal experiments such as these demonstrated the mechanisms underlying the symptoms of heart disease.

In the 1950s animal studies made it possible to develop the pump oxygenator, used to support circulation while the heart is stopped for major heart surgery. All organ transplantation techniques have been developed with animal subjects. Similarly, the development of artificial hearts has required years of experiments.

Rodents, cats, dogs, primates, and other mammals are widely used to perfect techniques for heart surgery; to study atherosclerosis, which causes most coronary artery disease and most strokes; and to develop effective drugs for hypertension, heart failure, angina pectoris (heart pain due to inadequate coronary blood supply), and arrhythmias (abnormal heart rhythms that can cause sudden death).

Diabetes. In 1923 two Canadian physiologists, F. G. Banting and J. J. R. Macleod, received a Nobel Prize for the discovery that diabetes produced in dogs by removing the pancreas could be treated with insulin. Millions of diabetics owe their relatively normal lives to this discovery.

To provide models for research, investigators produce diabetes in animals by one of several chemical or surgical methods. For example, rabbits with artificially induced diabetes were used to develop laser treatment for retinal disease caused by diabetes. Similarly, dogs are used to develop methods for treating diabetes by transplanting pancreatic cells from healthy donors.

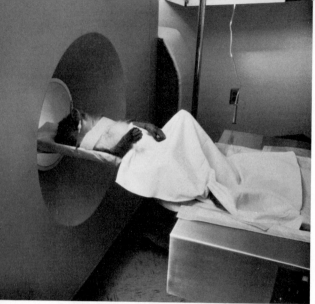

A monkey is positioned for a PET (positron-emission tomography) brain scan in a brain-research project. PET scanners picture brain activity as well as structure.

© NUBAR ALEXANIAN/STOCK, BOSTON

Controversy over Animal Experimentation. The antivivisection movement began in Britain in the 19th century, when groups opposed to the use of animals in research persuaded Parliament to legislate severe restrictions on animal experimentation.

By the turn of the 20th century in the United States, attempts to pass similar laws were under way in several states and the District of Columbia. These attempts were opposed vigorously by the scientific community. Since then animal experimentation has become an emotional political issue throughout the developed countries.

Animal Welfare and Animal Rights. Modern opposition to animal experimentation falls under two headings: animal welfare and animal rights. Animal welfare groups, such as the Animal Welfare Institute and most humane societies, do not categorically oppose the use of animals in biomedical research. Instead, they seek to prevent abuse of animals by requiring researchers to substitute research models for live animals whenever possible, to use no more animals than necessary, to provide anesthetic and analgesic drugs when appropriate, and to keep the animals as clean and comfortable as possible.

In contrast to animal welfare advocates, many animal rights advocates believe that the lives of humans and animals are equally valuable and that their interests should count equally. For some, the belief in the rights of animals justifies illegal entry into research laboratories to destroy records and equipment. A group known as the Animal Liberation Front, for example, staged more than a dozen raids on laboratories to liberate research animals in 1984. Records representing years of work were destroyed, as well as expensive equipment and facilities. (See also ANIMAL RIGHTS.)

Regulation of Experimentation. Lobbying by animal welfare groups has resulted in federal, state, and local legislation severely restricting animal experimentation. Some of this legislation has been very beneficial. Under the provisions of the U.S. Animal Welfare Act, for example, all animals used in biomedical research must be bought from vendors licensed by the U.S. Department of Agriculture (USDA). The USDA inspects laboratories where animals are used and enforces federal laws governing care and treatment.

Biomedical scientists, too, have acted to prevent abuses, in part because abused animals may not provide reliable data. The American Physiological Society, the National Institutes of Health (NIH), and other scientific organizations have joined to lay down clear guidelines for the use and humane treatment of experimental animals. The American Association for the Accreditation of Laboratory Animal Care is a voluntary organization formed by universities, pharmaceutical companies, and other sponsors of animal research laboratories to establish and enforce criteria for the care of experimental animals. Many universities have animal welfare committees that review animal research protocols and animal care facilities and oversee experiments. To receive NIH funding, an animal research project must be approved by its local committee.

Substitutes for Mammals. Partly because of rising costs of research animals, scientists have sought to develop reliable substitutes as research models. These include lower vertebrates, invertebrates, microorganisms, cultures of cells and tissues, and computer simulations. As a result, the use of primates, dogs, and cats is declining. Despite increasing use of nonmammalian research models, however, studies using live mammals provide information that can only be obtained in this way.

JOHN C. ROSE*, M.D., *Georgetown University*

Bibliography: Groves, Julian McAllister, *Hearts and Minds: The Controversy over Laboratory Animals* (Temple Univ. Press 1977); Orlans, F. Barbara, *In the Name of Science: Issues in Responsible Animal Experimentation* (Oxford 1993); Salem, Harry, ed., *Animal Test Alternatives: Refinement, Reduction, Replacement* (Dekker 1995); Tuffery, A. A., ed., *Laboratory Animals: An Introduction for Experimenters*, 2d ed. (Wiley 1995); Walker, S. R., and A. D. Dayan, eds., *Long-Term Animal Studies: Their Predictive Value for Man* (Kluwer 1986).

ANIMAL FARM. A satire (1945) on the Russian Revolution and its aftermath. (See ORWELL, GEORGE.)

ANIMAL HEAT, the heat produced by the body cells of an animal. In each cell heat is given off by the process of catabolism, which breaks down food materials and provides the cell with the energy needed to carry out its life processes. If an animal's body temperature falls below a certain level, the animal's cells cannot function and the organism dies.

Animals are usually divided into two groups with respect to how their temperature is regulated. Most animals are poikilotherms, which means that their body temperature varies greatly but is always about the same as the temperature of their surroundings. These creatures are also referred to as being cold-blooded, but this term is misleading because some poikilotherms, especially those in warm regions, may have a high body temperature. The second group, the homeotherms, have a body temperature that is maintained at a fairly constant level, even though the temperature of their environment may vary. Members of this group are called warm-blooded animals.

Poikilotherms. Poikilothermic animals include all insects, worms, fishes, amphibians, and reptiles. Although these animals have no inner mechanism for regulating their body heat, they can control their temperature to some extent by moving to different environments. For example, a lizard may raise its body temperature by basking in the sun.

It is estimated that an animal's rate of metabolism doubles with every increase of 18° F (10° C) in its body heat. Thus poikilothermic animals are virtually dependent on the external temperature for regulating their degree of activity.

Homeotherms. Birds and mammals are the only homeothermic animals, maintaining a body temperature that usually varies no more than a few degrees. In mammals the body temperature is controlled chiefly by the hypothalamus of the brain. If the body temperature is too low, the hypothalamus stimulates the body muscles to produce shivering. If the body is too warm, the hypothalamus stimulates the sweat glands to become more active and also dilates the blood vessels of the skin, allowing more heat to be lost to the air from the blood. In addition to this temperature-regulating mechanism, mammals are well insulated by fur or by a layer of fatty tissue under the skin.

Birds are insulated by a layer of feathers, and their body temperature is partially regulated by special air sacs that extend from the lungs. If the bird's body becomes too warm, the rate of breathing increases, and as more air is pumped in and out of the body, more heat is lost to the air.

ANIMAL INTELLIGENCE, a characteristic expressed through traits such as the ability to learn, reason, and form concepts. All animals, except the least complex, exhibit some degree of intelligent behavior, ranging from learned responses to complex reasoning.

Although many methods exist for studying this complex behavior in animals, serious problems arise in applying the concept of intelligence to nonhuman animals. For example, in an early research technique, the anecdotal method, animals' intelligence level was measured in terms of human capacities required to perform parallel acts. Such a method, used uncritically and without suitable observational or experimental controls, led to gross overestimation of the intelligence of the animal being studied. As a result, British psychologist C. Lloyd Morgan (1852–1936) proposed his now famous canon, "In no case may we interpret an action as the outcome of the exercise of a higher psychical faculty, if it can be interpreted as the outcome of the exercise of one which stands lower in the psychological scale." This dictum prompted scientists to reexamine evidence of intelligence and to divide complex animal behaviors into simpler components. Researchers found that many anecdotal descriptions could be reinterpreted in terms of instinctive or learned responses.

Later testing methods have sought to measure intelligence factors such as the ability to learn, solve new problems, or create novel solutions to familiar problems. In addition, problems such as differences of intelligence among kinds of animals, loss of intelligence in brain-injured or drugged animals, and correlation of intelligence with nervous system complexity are studied. Results of such experiments not only provide information about animal intelligence but can also aid in the study of human intelligence.

Factors in Intelligence. One factor in intelligence is the ability to learn. Learning refers to a relatively enduring change in an animal's behavior, owing primarily to experience. Sometimes, as in classical conditioning experiments, the animal is merely subjected to repeated paired presentations of two stimuli, with the result that the response characteristic of one of the stimuli (the unconditioned stimulus) can be elicited by the other stimulus (the conditioned stimulus). If, for example, a brilliant flash of light (which characteristically elicits an eye blink) is repeatedly accompanied by a musical tone, conditioning will take place and the musical tone alone will elicit the eye-blink (a conditioned response to the tone). Usually, however, learning involves responses by which an animal avoids punishment or obtains a reward.

Learning is probably beyond the capacity of, for example, protozoa and starfish. Such lower animals instead exhibit instinctive behavior. (See ANIMAL BEHAVIOR.) However, learning has been demonstrated in sea anemones. In one experiment, pieces of filter paper were placed on some of the tentacles of sea anemones. At first the tentacles grasped the paper and brought it to the mouth, where it was swallowed and later rejected. After several trials the paper was not swallowed. Finally, the particular tentacle being trained failed to grasp the paper at all. The untrained tentacles still accepted the paper, but they learned to reject the paper, and they did so in many fewer trials than had been required by the first tentacle. These results indicated that the learning in the sea anemone involved central as well as local nervous modification.

A simple apparatus for measuring learning is the T-maze, which consists of a straight runway leading to a perpendicular cross arm. Animals are trained to run down the runway and to make an appropriate left or right turn in order to obtain a reward or to escape or avoid an unpleasant stimulus. Because of its simplicity the T-maze has proved useful for the study of learning in animals ranging from earthworms to primates. Snails have been found to learn faster than do earthworms and insects. Ants can learn complex mazes that involve many alternative paths to the goal.

American psychologist Edward Lee Thorndike (1874–1949) used the discrimination-learning method, in this case by requiring an animal to learn which of two or more stimuli signified food reward. Performance was measured by the number of trials the animal needed to learn. Thorndike stressed the gradual improvement in proficiency and the role of trial and error as opposed to insight.

Problem solving is demonstrated by sea otters, who open clams by smashing them on a rock on their chest.

STUART B. HERTZ

Various studies have shown that learning and memory are closely linked with protein synthesis. Some of these experiments have demonstrated that if protein synthesis in the brain is blocked during learning, the learning is not transferred from short-term to long-term memory and thus is not retained. Other experiments have shown an increase in the concentration of ribonucleic acid (or RNA, a molecule essential to protein synthesis) in the brain cells of animals shortly after a learning session.

Learning to Learn. The procedures used in the study of learning can, with appropriate elaboration, be made suitable for the study of complex behavior. The researcher H. F. Harlow extended Thorndike's studies by presenting several hundred discrimination-learning problems to monkeys in rapid succession. Whereas Thorndike measured the learning that took place within a single problem, Harlow measured the improvement over the series of problems. Harlow referred to this improvement as learning to learn, or the formation of learning sets. The proficiency of higher primates at this task was superior to that of either lower primates or carnivores.

Concept-Forming Ability. The ability to form concepts is another characteristic of intelligence. Concept formation is the process whereby an animal develops a consistent response to all the members of one class of stimuli but not to others. For example, an animal that selects all of the red stimuli regardless of their shades or the variety of contexts in which they appear has a concept of "redness."

One of the highest forms of concept formation, called conditional matching, has been demonstrated in monkeys and apes. In this problem, the subject chooses which of two objects matches a third, or sample, object in color or form in accordance with an independent background cue.

Reasoning. Through reasoning, another characteristic of intelligence, an animal combines two disparate experiences into a single pattern to achieve an end. Psychologist Norman Maier arranged three different tables—X, Y, and Z—interconnected by runways that rats were allowed to explore. This exploration he called Experience 1. The rats were then placed on table X and given food there. This was Experience 2. After eating some of the food, the rats were placed on one of the other tables, perhaps Z. Maier's rats could combine Experience 1 with Experience 2 and go directly from table Z to table X.

Although German-American psychologist Wolfgang Köhler (1887–1967) observed many species, he is famous for his work with chimpanzees. In one typical "detour" problem he suspended a banana from a wire, with a long pole being the only other object in the room. Instead of using the pole to knock down the food as Köhler expected, the chimpanzees stood the pole on end, quickly climbed it, and grabbed the banana before the pole fell over. This was a novel solution. The chimpanzees also stacked boxes and climbed on them to reach the food. Once an insight was achieved, the animals could solve similar problems. Various studies have reported a correlation between the problem-solving proficiency of rats and the brain concentration of an enzyme, cholinesterase, that catalyzes one of the chemical transmitters in the central nervous system.

Benefiting from Vicarious Experience. The ability to benefit from the experiences of others also has been cited as a characteristic of intelligent behavior. White rats can be trained to follow another rat down a maze to obtain food reward, and cats have demonstrated a limited ability to learn by observing other cats work a puzzle box. Monkeys can learn a simple discrimination problem merely by watching another monkey perform a single trial on that problem. During the 1950s, at the Yerkes Laboratory of Primate Biology, in Atlanta, researchers Catherine and Keith Hayes observed many instances in which a chimpanzee named Vicki, which was raised in a human home, imitated ordinary household activities like sweeping and opening doors. Vicki even learned to imitate on the command "Do this."

Evolutionary and Developmental Effects. Behavior evolves with increasing complexity of structure. Thus simple animals have only limited sensory and response capability, while larger, more complex animals respond in increasingly diverse ways to a wide range of environmental influences. Complexity increases the organism's ability to integrate and to organize its experiences and responses. One-celled animals have not shown learning distinct from sensitization, adaptation, or fatigue. Simple organisms show only limited capacity to vary their response to intermittent or continuous stimulation.

The profound growth in behavioral capacity from simple, one-celled animals to primates resulted from the progressive differentiation of the nervous system into specialized tissues and the change in the organization of these tissues from a diffuse system to one in which clusters of nerve-cell bodies develop into centralized integrating structures. In the simpler invertebrates the nervous system is merely a diffuse, undifferentiated network of nerve cells running through the organism. In spiny-skinned animals, such as the starfish, the nervous system is simply a complication of a nerve ring. But in higher invertebrates, such as the worms, a ladderlike organization of separate structures exists for sensing, moving, and

Concept formation is demonstrated by a chimpanzee who can match the peg shape with the correct hole.

LILO HESS, FROM THREE LIONS

conducting. The vertebrate nervous system, although retaining some of the features of the worm, collects the neural elements to form a brain and spinal cord that serve to integrate the activities in widely separated parts of the body.

In proceeding toward the primate end of the phyletic scale, the degree of development of the organism increases, especially at the head end. This is known as the principle of encephalization. Thus the head of an insect is more highly developed than that of a tapeworm, and that of a monkey more highly developed than an insect's. This increased development of the brain and the sensory receptors provides better reception of environmental stimuli.

Encephalization reaches its peak in mammals, in which the outer layer of the brain becomes very large relative to the brain's total volume. The cortex, as this layer is called, forms about 30% of the total brain in rodents, 40% to 46% in carnivores, and 46% to 58% in primates. These percentages reflect the increasing functional importance of the cortex in higher animals, as shown by the effect its removal has on behavior. In the absence of the cortex, the fish and the bird show no detectable disturbance, while the rat, cat, and dog show impaired posture but can stand and walk. The monkey can sit but is unable to walk, but the human without this part of the brain can neither walk nor maintain a normal posture.

When part of the brain is removed, a rat's behavior deteriorates in proportion to the amount of tissue lost. The behavior of primates is determined much more specifically by discrete parts of the brain. For example, discrimination learning is greatly impaired following removal of the temporal lobes but not of the frontal lobes.

Intelligence and Heredity. It is well known that particularly intelligent people tend to have particularly intelligent offspring; this is also true for nonhuman animals. Successive generations of highly intelligent rats, that is, those who made few errors on a maze, and of less-intelligent rats, who made many maze errors, were produced by successively interbreeding the smarter rats with one another and the less-intelligent rats with one another, forming two separate groups. In seven generations the progeny of the smarter rats were vastly superior to the offspring of the other group. Experiments of this kind have not been performed on more complex mammals, such as primates, because their life span is so long that experimentation becomes far more difficult to conduct and interpret.

ARTHUR J. RIOPELLE*
Delta Regional Primate Research Center

Bibliography

Dugatkin, Lee A., *Cooperation among Animals: An Evolutionary Perspective* (Oxford 1997).
Hoage, R. J., and Larry Goldman, eds., *Animal Intelligence: Insights into the Animal Mind* (Smithsonian Inst. Press 1986).
McFarland, David J., and Thomas Bosser, *Intelligent Behavior in Animals and Robots* (MIT Press 1993).
Mortenson, Joseph, *Whale Songs and Wasp Maps: the Mystery of Animal Thinking* (Dutton 1987).
Patterson, Francine, and Eugene Linden, *The Education of Koko* (Holt, Rinehart & Winston 1981).
Vauclair, Jacques, *Animal Cognition: An Introduction to Modern Comparative Psychology* (Harvard Univ. Press 1995).

ANIMAL PSYCHOLOGY. See ANIMAL BEHAVIOR.

ANIMAL RIGHTS, a term denoting an international movement aimed at raising the theoretical and practical moral status of animals in society and manifested in social thought and action. More specifically, the notion of animal rights is expressed in differing, sometimes mutually exclusive ideas stemming from varying philosophical approaches to morality. For example, whereas American philosophers Tom Regan and Bernard Rollin each maintain that animals should have, and are demonstrably worthy of, moral and legal rights, Regan, unlike Rollin, believes such rights to be incompatible with agricultural animal use. Australian philosopher Peter Singer centers his moral theory not on a concept of rights for either humans or nonhumans but instead on the supposition that humans are obligated to minimize pain and maximize pleasure for members of their own and other species.

Animal rights concerns additionally extend to a social activist movement analogous politically to those advocating civil rights and women's rights. Influenced by philosophers but primarily action oriented, hundreds of activist groups have emerged. Among the most prominent have been People for the Ethical Treatment of Animals (PETA), Mobilization for Animals, Animal Rights International, and the Animal Liberation Front (ALF). More-specialized rights groups, including the Farm Animal Reform Movement and Britain's National Anti-Vivisection Society, are constituted according to issue-specific goals or, in the case of the Animal Legal Defense Fund (formerly, Attorneys for Animal Rights), Psychologists for the Ethical Treatment of Animals, and the Association of Veterinarians for Animal Rights, according to professional expertise.

In most cases specialized associations seek "animal liberation," desiring, for example, an end to the use of animals as livestock or in scientific research. De facto, however, these organizations tend, like the more conservative animal welfare groups, such as the Humane Society of the United States or the American Humane Association, to address relatively moderate goals by working to reform these practices rather than to effect a complete, immediate elimination of such activities.

The animal rights movement evolved not only from pertinent concerns among activists but from societal attitudes as well. The 18th-century Scottish philosopher David Hume asserted that most people are willing to assume that animals are conscious, sentient beings, a presupposition that would permit extending to nonhumans the notions of rights and protection. Starting in 1988 a series of coordinated surveys conducted in 15 nations questioned whether or not respondents opposed research into human disorders if the associated test animals suffered pain and injury. According to the studies 42% of both the American and the Japanese, 49% of the Canadian, and 68% of the French respondents were against such practices. Other research has indicated that, more broadly, over 80% of the U.S. population believes that animals have some rights (although roughly the same percentage considers it permissible for animals to serve humankind's purposes if the animals are maintained under humane conditions).

The Rise of Activism. American animal rights activist Henry Spira is generally credited with orchestrating the first animal rights demonstration, a protest organized in 1975 against invasive experiments being conducted by the Museum of Natural History in New York City on feline sexual behavior. After 18 months of picketing, the research was stopped, and the publicity generated by Spira's campaign in turn stimulated general social unease regarding animal experimentation, a concern that grew significantly over the next decade.

In the late 1970s Rollin attempted to outline in ethical terms the elements behind the general public's emerging interest in animal welfare. He ultimately distinguished six reasons that he believes account for the ascension of animal welfare concerns during the 1970s:

• The increasing urbanization of society led to companion animals, that is, household pets, becoming the paradigm for animals in the social mind.

• The mass media discovered that animal rights issues capture public attention, leading to greater coverage of these topics.

• Rising social and economic complexities that made people feel increasingly powerless in the face of uncontrollable social forces fueled empathy toward animals. This supposition originated with British scientists, who attributed growing concern for animal rights on the part of the country's blue-collar population to economic troubles among the working class.

• The ethical spotlight that illuminated social inequities in the treatment of women and minorities was inevitably shone on animals. Indeed, many animal advocates have earlier histories in other social movements, such as those for civil and women's rights.

• Philosophers as well as scientists, including British ethologist Jane Goodall, eloquently articulated their perceptions of human obligations to animals and so helped to shape public opinion.

• Finally, and most important, beginning in the mid-20th century, after thousands of years of what had been perceived as relatively fair and stable animal use by humankind, animals came to be exploited in ways and placed in environments that together sparked an interest in a more carefully structured animal rights ethic.

Animal Rights throughout History. For most of human history, social ethics regarding animal use existed only to the point of condemning individuals who harmed animals under their care through outrageous neglect or the deliberate, sadistic, and purposeless infliction of pain and suffering. This minimalist ethic was deemed socially adequate because the vast majority of animal use was agricultural and thus dependent on animal husbandry. In essence, livestock best served the purpose of humankind when maintained in an environment for which the animals were well suited by virtue of both natural and artificial selection. Because animals' natural ability to survive was augmented with additional food and water along with medical attention and protection from predators, agriculture was regarded as a fair contract between humans and animals through which both parties benefited. (See also AGRICULTURE, HISTORY OF.)

Changes in Animal Use. Following World War II both the advent of large-scale, industrialized agriculture and the growing availability of antibiotics and vaccines for livestock prompted the replacement of traditional animal husbandry with strategies for animal-based mass production. It had by this time become possible to raise thousands of animals in a single building, a practice that would previously have caused the animals to perish from disease. Livestock now existed under crowded living conditions that prevented many natural behaviors that had once been accommo-

dated, severing the connection between productivity and animal well-being. The postwar period also witnessed a significant rise in funding for biomedical animal research, including funding for an increasing number of studies that exposed test subjects to disease and deprivation and for which the animals sustained wounds, burns, and other trauma, again violating the ancient contract between humans and nonhumans. A new set of ethical concepts arose as a consequence of social concern for pain and suffering that was not the result of deliberate cruelty. (In the United States, animal rights concerns were first focused primarily on animal research. In Britain, owing to British journalist Ruth Harrison's groundbreaking book *Animal Machines* (1964), the concern was directed toward the torturous conditions of livestock kept in confinement for purposes of maximum agricultural production.) (See also ANIMAL EXPERIMENTATION; MEDICAL ETHICS.)

Animal Rights Philosophies. The quest for a contemporary animal rights philosophy has spawned debate not only with regard to humankind's obligations toward other species but also over the validity of applying to creatures other than *Homo sapiens* the moral tenets that normally influence human behavior.

Peter Singer. As demonstrated in his pioneering work *Animal Liberation: A New Ethic for the Treatment of Animals* (1975), Singer bases his ideas on classical utilitarian moral theory, agreeing with British philosopher Jeremy Bentham (1748–1832) that the capacity to feel pain and suffer is sufficient for inclusion within a society's moral notions. Given that nonhuman animals can experience pleasure and pain, Singer believes that ignoring an animal's interests simply because the creature is not human constitutes an indefensible, morally arbitrary form of behavior that he terms speciesism. Animal and human interests, Singer insists, must carry equal weight when decisions affecting animal welfare are made.

Singer does not, however, maintain that animals have inalienable rights, and as a utilitarian, he cannot categorically dismiss the use of agricultural livestock if the animals can live comfortably and be killed painlessly. The same utilitarian approach prevents Singer from unconditionally attacking animal research, provided that sacrificing a few test subjects will prevent great harm to a vast animal population, either human or nonhuman. He also asserts, however, that if physically damaging, invasive animal experiments are deemed to be acceptable because the test subject, apparently lacking the mental capacity to "grasp that it is a 'self,' a mental entity existing over time," cannot conceive of and desire a continued existence, then in utilitarian terms such research should also be permissible on humans suffering from severe mental retardation or profound brain damage.

Bernard Rollin. Because new ethical beliefs evolve from preexisting ones, Rollin maintains, society inevitably derives its ethics for the treatment of animals from its guidelines for human interactions. Specifically, according to Rollin, society constructs this new set of ethics by examining the concept of rights, which, as the Bill of Rights of the U.S. Constitution demonstrates, is a moral and legal notion that helps to protect the interests of a human individual from being submerged by society's pursuit of the general welfare. In the absence of financial incentives to safeguard animal interests, says Rollin, such protection must be morally (or legally) guaranteed. His goal is the exposure of society's underlying thoughts regarding the moral status of animals, bringing into sharp focus the ideas that have existed within the population but that have not been clearly and formally articulated by its members.

Tom Regan. *The Case for Animal Rights* (1983), by Regan, presents an absolutist condemnation of most animal use. Regan theorizes that rights are applicable to humans in general and to other mammals over one year of age, at which time, according to him, the nonhumans are "subjects of a life," possessing beliefs, desires and inherent value, regardless of their value to humankind. On the basis of his arguments, Regan indicts most types of animal use and calls unequivocally for their abolition. He is also noteworthy for pressing for the involvement of religious leaders in the campaign for animal rights.

Steve Sapontzis. Believing the "routine and avoidable" sacrifice of animal interests to be inherent in most of humanity's social practices, the American Steve Sapontzis is another philosopher who argues for the elevation of the moral status of nonhumans. In his 1987 book, *Morals, Reason, and Animals,* he grounds his case in what he considers to be commonsense moral intuition. He also makes the assertion, denied by most other philosophers, that animals can be viewed as moral agents, that is, beings who display behaviors to which humans give moral approval, such as bravery and self-sacrifice.

Other Philosophers. Along with the philosophers cited above, a number of their contemporaries have written extensively, and from various perspectives, on the moral status of animals. It is fair to say that the overwhelming majority of these philosophers have been animal advocates. Exceptions include American philosopher Carl Cohen, whose 1986 paper in the *New England Journal of Medicine,* "The Case for the Use of Animals in Biomedical Research," supported increased use of experimental animals. Cohen argued that moral concepts represent an ideological agreement between rational beings, leading him to further maintain that, since nonhumans cannot enter into such an agreement, such concepts are not applicable to them.

Canadian philosopher Michael Allen Fox initially defended invasive animal experiments in his 1986 book, *The Case for Animal Experimentation: An Evolutionary and Ethical Perspective,* basing his view on the opinion that animals are not self-aware. Within months of the book's publication, however, Fox repudiated this philosophy, asserting instead that animal experimentation is parallel to social injustice toward women in male-dominated societies and to careless exploitation of the environment. In his 1992 book, *The Animals Issue,* British philosopher Peter Carruthers, presenting an idea first championed by the 17th-century French philosopher René Descartes, denied the existence of consciousness in nonhuman animals. This lack of cognition, says Carruthers, excludes nonhumans from moral considerations. (See also DESCARTES, RENÉ.)

Social and Commercial Influence of Animal Rights. While ascribing to different philosophies, animal rights activists, by tapping into strong social concerns, have together effected major international changes in the treatment and use of animals, including the severe curtailment of invasive ani-

mal use as a teaching tool on the high school, university, and graduate level; reductions in the commercial use of animal fur and the employment of animals in cosmetics testing; the closing of many substandard zoos; and the banning of steel-jawed traps in numerous parts of the United States and in a significant number of other countries. By spawning greater public sensitivity to animal issues in general, activism also gave rise to major legislation during the 1980s in the United States, Great Britain, and elsewhere, protecting animals used in research. Additionally, various European nations and the European Union have put major constraints on industrialized agriculture, including a 1988 law, passed by the Swedish parliament, that gradually phases out such agriculture in Sweden altogether.

The extent and power of animal rights sentiments in the United States are best illustrated by enactment of the Health Research Extension Act of 1985 and the amendments, also in 1985, to the Animal Welfare Act, both designed to protect the interests of animals used in research. The laws not only require the proper administration of anesthetics, analgesics, and tranquilizers to control pain, suffering, and distress but also empower local Animal Care and Use committees, comprising researchers, veterinarians, and also lay citizens, to review various research projects, teaching protocols, and scientific facilities in an attempt to insure the appropriate use and treatment of the animals.

Fearing that their work would fall victim to extensive government control, many individuals in the biomedical research community initially fought the passage of such legislation, perceiving it as a threat to the advancement of medical knowledge and care. Animal activists responded by publicizing severe cases of research-related trauma, including two discovered in the United States during the early 1980s: the brutal restraint of baboons during one neurological study and the poor treatment of baboons in a head-injury research project. The resulting public outcry made the passage of legislation virtually inevitable.

Animal rights issues are likely to keep fueling major ethical concerns within society. New scientific and technological advances, such as the cloning and genetic engineering of animals, will undoubtedly continue to raise major questions regarding humankind's obligations toward other species.

BERNARD E. ROLLIN, *Colorado State University*

Bibliography

Carruthers, Peter, *The Animals Issue* (Cambridge 1992).

Coetzee, J. M., et al., *The Lives of Animals* (Princeton Univ. Press 1999).

Finsen, Lawrence, and Susan Finsen, *The Animal Rights Movement in America: From Compassion to Respect* (Twayne 1994).

Francione, Gary L., *Introduction to Animal Rights: Your Child or the Dog?* (Temple Univ. Press 2000).

Petrinovich, Lewis F., *Darwinian Dominion: Animal Welfare and Human Interests* (MIT Press 1999).

Pluhar, Evelyn, *Beyond Prejudice: The Moral Significance of Human and Nonhuman Animals* (Duke Univ. Press 1995).

Regan, Tom, *Defending Animal Rights* (Univ. of Ill. Press 2001).

Regan, Tom, and Peter Singer, eds., *Animal Rights and Human Obligations,* 2d ed. (Prentice-Hall 1989).

Sapontzis, Steve, *Morals, Reason, and Animals* (Temple Univ. Press 1987).

Varner, Gary E., *In Nature's Interests? Interests, Animal Rights, and Environmental Ethics* (Oxford 1998).

Wise, Steven M., *Rattling the Cage: Toward Legal Rights for Animals,* foreword by Jane Goodall (Perseus Bks. 2000).

ANIMAL WORSHIP. See ANIMALS, SACRED.

ANIMALS, Domestication of. Animals are said to be domesticated when they are kept under human control and also regularly breed in captivity. Animals born wild and later tamed, such as elephants or sea lions, are not domesticated. Some species of animals regularly breed only in the wild state and cannot be domesticated. Long-domesticated species are likely to differ biologically from their wild relatives because of selective breeding and mutation.

Animals have been domesticated for a number of reasons: as hunters or as pets (dogs and cats), for ornament (swans and peacocks), for sport (horses, bulls, and gamecocks), and for religious reasons (cats, in Egypt). The primary motive in domesticating animals, however, has been to have them available as a source of food, skins, or other products, or to do work. Animal domestication has thus been a major factor in the development of farming. Both animal and plant domestication began relatively late in man's existence. Man was associated with animals—as hunter (or hunted)—for many thousands of years before he began to keep and breed animals.

Dogs. The dog, probably the first domesticated animal, is found nearly worldwide in cultures of the most diverse character. Dogs seem to have attached themselves voluntarily to man; perhaps they were attracted to the hunting camps of early man by refuse and were tolerated as scavengers and sentinels. They also came to be used in hunting.

It is possible that dogs were domesticated in several regions independently, 10,000 to 12,000 years ago, if not earlier. However, the oldest skeletal remains of unquestionably domesticated dogs date from around 6500 B.C. in Jordan (at Jericho) and also in Britain and Denmark. Some of the Jericho dogs resembled modern terriers. By 4500 B.C. greyhound-type dogs were present in predynastic Egypt.

Sheep and Goats. Archaeological evidence indicates that the next animal to be domesticated was the sheep. At Zawi Chemi in Iraq, archaeologists have found bones of sheep dating from around 9200 B.C., at about the time that the first grain cultivation was beginning in southwestern Asia. Sheep or goats (their bones are hard to differentiate) appear early in that region, and could have been domesticated from wild relatives still found in the uplands.

The initial motive in domesticating sheep and goats was to have a source of meat when game was scarce. Wool had not yet developed in sheep, and goats were presumably not yet regularly milked.

Cattle. Next to be domesticated were bovines. Cattle were derived from very widespread Eurasian and North African wild bovines, with which they were later frequently recrossed to yield new breeds. The advent of cattle herding added a new dimension to animal husbandry. Kept in large numbers, cattle could provide the entire subsistence for a human community.

There is no definite proof of cattle domestication before about 4000 B.C., and the actual date may be later. Numerous finds of bones in ancient Middle Eastern sites may be those of domestic livestock or wild bovines that were still being hunted. Clear traces of dairying, in the form of pictures of milking scenes, go back only to about 3000 B.C. in Iraq and Egypt. Regular milking of cattle and goats probably came before, however. Zebu or humped cattle were domesti-

cated about 3000 B.C. in Baluchistan and the Indus Valley.

A momentous innovation around 3000 B.C. in Iraq and Egypt was the plow. The invention of this tool probably coincided with the discovery that the castration of bulls produces a more docile work animal, the ox. Ox-drawn carts appeared about the same time in Iraq. The spread of plowing and of the idea of using animals to save human labor, combined with the invention of the wheel, initiated a chain of inventions.

Pigs. After cattle, the next major animal to be domesticated on a large scale was the pig. Archaeologists have found some evidence of domestic pigs by 5500 B.C.—even before there is evidence for cattle—in southern Turkey. There is stronger evidence from Anau, in southern Soviet Turkmenistan, from around 4000 B.C. Pigs do not congregate in large herds and are far less mobile than sheep, goats, or cattle; thus they fit well into sedentary village economies. Like dogs, pigs could have been self-domesticated, attracted by opportunities for scavenging.

Donkeys and Horses. Around 3000 B.C. asses or donkeys were domesticated in the Nile Valley from the wild Nubian ass. This useful animal later spread to most of the Mediterranean Basin, across southwestern Asia, and into North China, chiefly as a pack animal.

At some time around 3000 B.C. tribes north of the Caucasus or in the Ukraine were domesticating horses. A light two-wheeled vehicle, the chariot, was developed about 1,000 years later, and this military vehicle was taken by raiders westward into Europe and southward into the old centers of Bronze Age civilization. Chariot-using armies of the Hyksos invaded Egypt around 1700 B.C. and northwestern India about 1500 B.C. War chariots also appear about this time in North China. The regular use of cavalry dates from 900–800 B.C. in southern Russia.

As work animals, horses were limited by the fact that their necks could not carry the heavy yokes used for oxen. The Chinese invented the horse collar around the start of the Christian era, and this device made it possible to use horses for plowing and for hauling carts. The use of the horse collar spread slowly to the West.

Poultry. Ducks and geese were domesticated fairly early, probably in several places independently. Chickens are of more restricted origin, coming from southeast Asia. They reached Europe and Africa only in Roman times. Southeast Asians kept chickens for their eggs or meat, and for cockfighting, religious offerings, and as handy alarm clocks.

Camels and Reindeer. Camels were late in being domesticated. They were used as mounts by the Assyrians and by others in southwest and central Asia, but were not brought to North Africa until Roman times. The two-humped Bactrian breed was used in central Asia, notably as a pack animal on the great trans-Asian silk caravan route. The one-humped dromedary is a general-purpose animal in southwestern Asia and North Africa, especially among nomadic groups, who ride, pack, milk, and eat their camels.

Reindeer occur wild in a wide zone of northern forest and tundra from Scandinavia to northern Canada (where they are known as caribou). They were domesticated relatively late—not much more than 2000 years ago—and possibly in several different regions independently. The peoples of northern Eurasia, from the Lapps to the Chukchi, use reindeer in varied ways—from dairying and sled pulling to riding, or just for meat and skins. Neither the Eskimo nor the northern Indians domesticated the American caribou.

New World Animals. Most of the important domestic animals first appeared in Europe, Asia, and Africa. No comparably important domestic animals (except the dog) were available to the inhabitants of the New World until the Europeans brought them in the 16th century. In the Old World, agriculture developed alongside animal husbandry, but American Indian farming was practically limited to crop production. Eventually the Indians of Mexico domesticated a local duck, stingless bees, and turkeys. Turkeys spread to the Indians of what is now the southwestern United States. The Indians of the Andean region in South America had a few more promising animals, notably the llama and alpaca. Llamas were used as pack animals and for meat, hair, and hides; alpacas were kept for their wool.

Although wild horses existed in the Americas in prehistoric times, they became extinct before 6000 B.C. and had never been domesticated. American Indian use of horses in modern times resulted from Spanish and other European contacts, notably in the North American Great Plains and in the grass and steppe lands of Argentina.

Domesticated Animals and Civilization. The availability of livestock has had profound influences on the growth of civilization. For example, the way of life called pastoral nomadism is built around flocks and herds. In this economic system, livestock are the basis of subsistence, and agriculture is absent or marginal. Anthropologists once believed that pastoralism was a widespread stage in economic evolution in the Old World. However, this stage is now seen as a comparatively late development in regions poorly suited to crop raising. For example, central Asia did not become a major pastoral region until the 1st millennium B.C.

At times in history, such nomadic peoples as the Scythians, Huns, Sarmatians, and later Turkic and Mongolic tribes were able to dominate the inhabitants of agricultural oases. But in the world generally, pastoral nomadism declined as more diversified farming developed. The dominant food-producing pattern of the modern world combines animal husbandry with crop raising. Much land that once was used for range has been taken over for planting.

At the same time, there have been great advances in livestock raising and the use of animal products. No important new species have been added to the roster of domestic animals. Improvements have come from more systematic animal breeding, increasing control over animal disease, advances in the study of animal nutrition, and improvements in food processing, storage, and transport. Animal husbandry in the more advanced countries has been transformed from a local and rather primitive system of production for subsistence to an increasingly complex commercial economy. In the world as a whole, however, the need for food has grown faster than the supply of domesticated animals.

See also AGRICULTURE, HISTORY OF.

GORDON W. HEWES, *University of Colorado*

Bibliography: Blakely, James, and David H. Bade, *The Science of Animal Husbandry*, 6th ed. (Prentice Hall 1994); Taylor, Robert E., and Thomas G. Field, *Scientific Farm Animal Production: An Introduction to Animal Science*, 7th ed. (Prentice Hall 2001).

ANIMALS, Sacred. Animals have been connected with religious beliefs and practices from prehistoric times. Particularly among peoples who live by hunting or by raising flocks and herds, animals have had major roles in religious as well as economic and social life.

The religious significance of animals can take various forms. Hunting peoples may show reverence to animals as a way of trying to ensure a supply of game. Cave paintings of bison by Old Stone Age artists may have been created for such magical purposes. Among North American Indians each species of animal was believed to have a spirit "boss." This "boss" rewarded the hunter if certain conditions were observed. For example, animals were not to be killed wantonly and were to be treated with respect whether alive or dead. Indians often believed that animals, or their spiritual counterparts, appeared in visions and dreams to grant special blessings. The bear was the most important cult animal in many parts of North America and is still sacred among the Ainu of northern Japan.

Another form of sacred relationship between men and animals is found in totemism, which reached its most complex development among Australia's aborigines. There, kinship is believed to link certain clans and certain animal species. The human group and the animal species are believed to share a common ancestor. Human members of the totemic group may be reincarnated in the form of the totem animal. Various taboos are observed. Most important are a ban on marriage or sexual relations with members of the same totem group and a prohibition against eating animals of the totem species.

In some religions animals are closely associated with gods. The ancient Egyptians, for example, believed that certain animals were divine incarnations. Thus a bull, called Apis, was considered the representative of the god Osiris, was venerated during its life, and was ritually entombed after its death. Other animals, including lions, jackals, wolves, and antelopes, had sacred significance in Egypt. Cats received extraordinary attention, as shown by the number of cat mummies that have been found. The ibis was sacred to the god Thoth.

In India, too, gods were at times believed to take on animal form. In Hindu myths the god Vishnu appeared at one time as a wild boar and in another story as a giant turtle. Many animals are closely associated with gods in Hindu belief. As is widely known, the cow is revered by Hindus. However, the so-called "sacred cows" are not worshiped. Nor, contrary to popular belief, are these cows economically useless or a burden on the people. In fact, cows are an important economic asset for India. Cattle provide power for farming and also a source of leather and of milk. They provide meat for certain non-Hindu portions of the population.

In many cases animals have sacred characteristics or significance but are not worshiped. Among peoples who have sacred animals, the more sophisticated individuals regard animals as symbolically rather than literally sacred.

ERIKA BOURGUIGNON, *The Ohio State University*

Further Reading: Kroeber, L., *Anthropology* (Harcourt 1963); Levi-Strauss, *Totemism* (Beacon Press 1963;) Wood, J. G., *Animals in the Bible* (Foundation for Classical Reprints 1986).

ANIMATED CARTOON. See CARTOON, ANIMATED.

ANIMISM, an′ə-miz-əm, is a term used in several senses to describe primitive religion. The term was first used by the English anthropologist Sir Edward B. Tylor. In *Primitive Culture* (1871) he described animism as "the general belief in spiritual beings," and called this a minimum definition of religion. Tylor held that animism, so defined, was the core of all religion, and that no primitive or crude society had been found which did not exhibit such a belief in spirits. The term "spirits," according to Tylor, applied not only to gods and divinities, but also to souls of the living and the dead. Tylor held that belief in spirits arose because primitive man wondered about the phenomena of death, dreams, cataleptic and trance states, and other seeming mysteries for which they attempted to find an explanation. Wherever this belief in spirits existed, there was evidence of worship and ritual.

Tylor's book constitutes an elaborate review, based on the descriptive materials then available, of the religious beliefs and practices of mankind. Of particular significance is his approach. Tylor viewed his topic as a natural scientist rather than as a religionist. He clearly demonstrated that, hypothetically, it was possible that there were primitive peoples who had no religion. When a definition of religion unbiased by the models of universal religions was applied, however, no such peoples were found. Tylor has been criticized for an unduly rationalistic approach to the origin of religion. His very concern for origins has been criticized, since it is only possible to speculate about the nonmaterial elements of prehistoric cultures.

Other theories for the origins of religion were developed by other anthropologists. Bishop R.H. Codrington in his study, *The Melanesians* (1891), reported on the Melanesian belief in *mana*—a concept of immaterial, impersonal power which "works to effect everything which is beyond the ordinary power of men, outside the common process of nature." The English anthropologist Robert R. Marrett in his work, *The Threshold of Religion* (1909), defined this belief in mana as *animatism*. Discussions soon arose as to whether animatism should be thought of as an older or earlier stage in religion than Tylor's animism. Such priority is no longer important since, as previously mentioned, evidence for origins cannot be found. Tylor's book continues to be of great value for its clarification of concepts and its presentation of illustrative materials.

Since Tylor's day, the term animism has frequently been used to imply the attribution of spiritual qualities to inanimate matter. It is doubtful that any human group does in fact do so indiscriminately. The Ojibwa Indians of North America, for example, believed that certain rocks had animate qualities, but they did not stretch this belief to include *all* rocks. The Swiss psychologist Jean Piaget held that animism, in this sense, is a characteristic stage in the development of a child's concept of the world.

The term animism has also been used as a census category. Those people, particularly of Africa, Asia, and the Pacific, who do not adhere to one of the universal religions, are classified as animists. About 135 million animists are thought to live in various remote areas. It would be inaccurate, however, to infer that they do in fact believe in animism in either of the senses of the term indicated above.

ERIKA BOURGUIGNON, *Ohio State University*

ANIMUCCIA, ä-nē-mōō′chä, **Giovanni** (1500?–1571), Italian composer of sacred music. He was born in Florence. From 1555 he was choirmaster of St. Peter's Basilica in Rome. His *Laudi spirituali* (songs of praise), which were performed with the oratories of St. Philip Neri, contain dramatic elements that prefigure the formal religious oratorio. Animuccia also composed masses, motets, psalms, and madrigals. Volumes of his *laudi* were issued in 1563 and 1570, though the bulk of his work has remained in manuscript. He died in Rome on March 25, 1571.

ANISE, an′əs, is an aromatic annual plant native to Egypt. It grows two feet high and has several slender branches. It is cultivated for its seeds, called *aniseeds*, which are used to flavor food and liqueurs. Anise oil is used in medicine, and in perfumes and dentifrices. The anise belongs to the Umbelliferae family.

ANJOU, äN-zhōō′, was a former province of western France. It centered around the capital city of Angers, on the Maine River. Primarily an agricultural area, the region is watered by the Loire, Mayenne, Maine, and Sarthe rivers. It is noted for Vouvray and Saumur wines.

Anjou was organized as a province by the Carolingians and became a countship in the 9th century. Important counts were Fulk I the Red, founder of the countship; Fulk III Nerra, who enlarged the family holdings; and Fulk V the Young. Fulk V's son Geoffrey married Matilda, daughter of Henry I of England, in 1129. Their son Henry started the Angevin, or Plantagenet, line of English kings when he ascended the throne in 1154 as Henry II. The house of Plantagenet retained the English crown until 1399 when Henry IV of Lancaster seized it.

The Plantagenets continued to rule Anjou until Philip II of France conquered the province and added it to the royal domain in 1205. In 1246, Louis IX gave Anjou to his brother Charles, who extended Angevin influence to Italy in 1266 when he assumed the crown of Naples and Sicily as Charles I. His son, Charles II, succeeded him as king of Naples in 1285, but a revolt had ended Angevin rule in Sicily earlier.

Five lines of European rulers descended from Charles II's five children. From Charles Martel, the eldest, came the Angevin kings of Hungary. Between 1309 and 1443, Robert, John, and Margaret, and their descendants held the throne of Naples at different times. Their rivalries did much to prevent Italian unification. Blanche, youngest child of Charles II, married James II of Aragon, and started the Spanish family that held the throne of Naples from 1443 to 1496.

Margaret's son Philip, count of Anjou, became king of France as Philip VI in 1328 and reunited Anjou with the crown. Philip's son, King John II, gave Anjou to his son Louis as a duchy. When Louis' grandson René died in 1480, Anjou was permanently incorporated into France.

ANJOU, äN-zhōō′, an industrial and residential town in southern Quebec, Canada. It is situated on Montreal Island, about 6 miles (10 km) east of Montreal, of which it is a suburb. Anjou, formerly the parish of St.-Leonard-de-Port-Maurice, was incorporated as a town in 1956, with a population of 2,140. Since then, numerous industries have established branches there. Population: 38,015.

Neymeyr U., Die christlichen Lehrer im zweiten Jahrhundert: Ihr Lehrtätigkeit, ihr Selbsverständnis, und ihre Geschichte, in *Supplements to VCh* 4, (Leiden: E.J. Brill 1989).

Nock A., Orphism or popular philosophy? in *HThR*, 33 (1940), p. 301-315.

Nogara B., *Guida ai Musei del Laterano*, (Vatican: Rome 1948).

Nohlac P. de, Notes sur Pirro Ligorio, in *Mélanges Léon Renier*, in *Bibliotèque de l'Éclole des Hautes Études* 73 (Paris: Vieweg 1887).

———, *La Bibliothèque de Fulvio Orsini*, (Paris: Honoré Champion 1976).

Nolan L., *The Basilica of San Clemente in Rome*, (Rome: Vatican 1934).

Nolte, Ein Excerpt aus dem zum grössten Theil noch ungedruckten Chronicon des Georgius Hamartolus, in *ThQ* (1862), p.467.

Norman A.F., Libanius: Orations, in *Loeb Classical Library*, (Cambridge Mass.: Harvard U.P. 1969).

Notopoulos J.A., Studies in the Chronology of Athens, in *Hesp.* 18 (1949), p. 26-27.

Ogg G., Hippolytus and the Introduction to the Christian Era, in *VCh* 16 (1962), p. 1-18.

Oggioni G., La questione di Ippolito, in *ScuCat* 78 (1950), p. 126-143; p. 315-322.

———, in *ScuCat* 43 (1951), p. 75-85.

———, Ancora sulla questione di Ippolito, in *ScuCat* 80 (1952), p. 513-525.

Oliveira C.-J.P., Signification sacerdotale du Ministère de l' Evêque dans la Tradition Apostolique d' Hippolyte de Rome, in *FZPhTh* 25 (1978), p. 398-427.

Oliver J.H., The Diadoché at Athens under the Humanistic Emperors, in *AmJPhil* 98 (1977), p.160-169.

Oltramre A., *Les origines de la diatribe romaine*, (Université de Genève, Faculté des Lettres Thesè no 47), (Geneva: 1926).

Omont H., Minide Mynas et ses missions en Orient (1840-1856), in *Memoires de l'Académie des Inscriptions et Belles-Lettres XL*, (Paris: 1916).

Osborne C., *Rethinking Early Greek Philosophy: Hippolytus of Rome and the Presocratics.* (London: Duckworth 1987).

Palachkovsky V., La Tradition hagiographique sur S. Hippolyte, in *StudPatr 3TU* 78 (Berlin: 1961), p. 97-107.

Parsons E.A., *The Alexandrian Library: Glory of the Hellenic World*, (London: Elsevier 1952).

Paulys-Wissowa A., *Real-encyclopädia der classischen Altertumswissenschaft*, 3 Band, (Metzler: Stuttgart 1899).

Pearson B.A., Gnosticism as Platonism with special reference to Marsanes (NHC 10,1), in *HThR* 77,1 (1984), p. 55-72.

Pekáry T., Statuen in der Historia Augusta, in *Antiquitas* 4,7 (1970), p. 151-172.

Périer J., Les 127 Canons des apôtres. Texte arabe en partie inédit publié et traduit d' après les manuscrits de Paris, de Rome et de Londres, in *PO* VIII,4, (1912).

Perkins A., *The Art of Dura-Europos*, (Oxford:Clarendon 1973).

Perler O., Melito de Sardis sur la Pâque et fragments, in *SC* 123, (1966).

Peterson E., La traitement de la rage par les Elkésaites d'après Hippolyte, in *RecSciRel* 34 (1947), p. 232-238.

Peterson E., Meris, Hostien Partikel und Opfer-Anteil, in *EphL* 61 (1947), p. 3-12.

Pietri C., *Roma Christiana: Recherches sur l'Eglise de Rome, son organisation, sa politique, son idéologie de Miltiade à Sixte III (311-440)*, (Rome: École Francais de Rome, Palais Farnèse 1976).

Pistolesi E., *Il Vaticano descritto e illustrato, III. Con disegni a contorni diretti dal pittore Camillo Guerra*, (Roma: Vaticano 1829).

Platner S.B. and Ashby T., *A Topographical dictionary of Ancient Rome*, (Oxford: U.P. 1929).

Platthy J., *Sources of Earliest Greek Libraries*, (Amsterdam: Hakkert 1968).

Plecket H.W,. and Stroud R.S. et al. (Ed.), *Supplementum Epigraphicum Graecum* (Amsterdam: Gieben 1976-).

Plümacher E., Apostel/ Apostolat/ Apostolizität, in *Theologische Realenzyklopädia*, Band III (Berlin: Walter de Gryter 1978).

Poschmann B., Zur Bussfrage in der cyprianischen Zeit, *ZKTh* (1913), p. 25-54.

——, Paenitentia Secunda: Die kirchliche Busse im ältesten Christentum bis Cyprian und Origenes: Eine dogmengeschichtliche Untersuchung, in *Theoph* 1 (1940).

Powell D.L., Ordo presbyteri, in *JThS* 26 (1975), p. 290-328.

——, The Schism of Hippolytus, in *StudPatr* (*TU* 115) 12,1 1975, p. 449-456.

Prestige L., Callistus, in *Fathers and Heretics,* (London: S.P.C.K. 1954).

Preysing von K., Der Leserkreis der Philosophoumena Hippolyts, in *ZKTh* 38 (1914), p. 421-445.

——, Hippolyts Ausscheidung aus der Kirche, in *ZKTh* 42 (1918), p. 177-186.

——, Existenz und Inhalt des Bussediktes, in *ZKTh* 4 43 (1919), p. 358-362.

——, Des heiligen Hippolytus von Rom Widerlegung aller Häresien, in *Bibliothek der Kirchenväter* 40, (München: Kösel und Pustet 1922).

——, „δίθεοι ἐστε" (Hippolyt. Philos. IX. 12,16), in *ZKTh* 50 (1926), p. 604-608.

Prigent P., and Stehly R., Citations d'Hippolyte trouvées dans le ms. Bodl. Syr. 140, in *ThZ* 30,2 (1974), p. 82-85.

Prigent P., Hippolyte, commentateur de l'Apocalypse, in *ThZ* 28,6 (1972), p. 391-412.

——, Les fragments du De Apocalypsi d'Hippolyte, in *ThZ* 29,5 (1973), p. 313-333.

Prinzivalli E., Due passi escatologici del Peri pantos di Ippolito, in *Vetera Christianorum* 16 (1979), p. 63.

——, Note sull'escatologia di Ippolito, in *Orpheus* 1 (1980), p. 305.

——, Gaio e gli Alogi, in *Studi storico-religiosi*, 5 (Japadre Editore L'Aquila: Rome 1981), p. 53-68.

——, Ippolito (statua di), in *Dizionario Patristico e di Antichità Cristiane* 2, (Casale Monteferrato 1984), coll. 1798-1800.

Puchulu R., *Sur le Contre Noet d'Hippolyte- les attaches littéraires et doctrinales de la doxologie finale.* (Thèse de Doctorat presentée à la Faculté de Théologie de Lyon, Année académique 1959-1960).

Quacquarelli A., L'antimonarchisanesimo di Tertulliano, in *Rassegna di scienze filosophische*, 3 (1950), p. 31-63.

Rabe H., *Ioannes Philoponus: De Aeternitate Mundi Contra Proclum*, (Leipzig: Teubner 1899).

Rackham H., Cicero: De Finibus Bonorum et Malorum, in *Loeb Classical Library,* (Cambridge Massachusetts: Harvard University Press 1914).

——, Pliny: Natural History, in *Loeb Classical Library,* (Cambridge Massachusetts: Harvard University Press 1952).

Rahmani I.E., *Testamentum Domini nostri Iesu Christi nunc primum edidit, Latine reddidit et illustravit*, (Mayence:Kirchheim 1899).

Rankin D., *Doctrines of Church and Ministry in Tertullian*, unpublished PhD thesis, Melbourne College of Divinity 1991.

——, *Tertullian and the Church,* (Cambridge: U.P. 1995).

Ratcliff E.C., Justin Martyr and Confirmation, in *Liturgical Studies*. Edited by CouratinA.H., and Tripp D.H. (London: S.P.C.K. 1976), p. 110-117.

——, The Eucharistic Institution Narrative of Justin Martyr's "First Apology,". in *Liturgical Studies*. Edited by CouratinA.H., and Tripp D.H. (London: S.P.C.K. 1976), p. 41-48.

——, "Apostolic Tradition": Questions Concerning the Appointment of the Bishop. in *Liturgical Studies*. Edited by Couratin A.H. and Tripp D.H. (London: S.P.C.K. 1976), p. 156-60.

Raubitsche A.E., Greek inscriptions, in *Hesp.* 35 (1966), p. 241-251.

Rauer M., Origene Werke: Bd. 9: Die Homilien zu Lukas in der Übersetzung des Hieronymus und die griechischen Reste der Homilien und des Lukas-Kommentars, in *GCS* (1959).

Reekmanns L., L'implantation monumentale chrétienne dans la zone suburbaine de Rome du IVe siècle, in *RivAC* 44 (1968), p. 196-199.

Rehm B., Zur Entstehung der pseudoclementinischen Schriften, in *ZNW* 37 (1938), p. 77-184.

Reichardt G. (Ed.), Filopono Giovanni, De opificio mundi, (Leipzig: Teubner 1897) text also in *PG*. X,296.

Reicke Bo., *Diakonie, Festfreude und Zelos in Verbingdung mit der altchristlichen Agapenfeier*. (Uppsala Univ. Arsskr.), (Uppsala: 1951).

Reutterer R., Legendenstudien um den heiligen Hippolytos, in *ZThK* 95 (1973), p. 286-310.

Réville J., *La religion à Rome sous les Sévères*, (Paris: Leroux 1886).

Richard M., Sainte Hippolyte, «Hippolyte e Josipe»: Bulletin de Patrologie, in *MSR* 5 (1948), p. 294-308.

——, Comput et chronographie chez Saint Hippolyte, in *MSR* 7 (1950), p. 237-268.

——, Comput et chronographie chez Saint Hippolyte, in *MSR* 8 (1951), p. 19-51.

——, Encore le problème d'Hippolyte, in *MSR* 10 (1953), p. 13-52, 145-180.

——, Dernières remarques sur S. Hippolyte et le soi-disant Josipe, in *RecSciRel* 43 (1955), p. 379-394.

——, Le Florilège Eucharistique du Codex Ochrid, Musée National 86, in Quelques nouveaux fragments des Pères Anténicéens et Nicéens, in *Symbolae Osloenses*, 38 (1963), p. 76-83, reprinted in ——, *Opera Minora*, (Turnhout/Leuven: Brepols/U.P.) 1,6.

——, Notes sur le comput de cent-couce ans, in *RevEtByz* 24 (1966), p. 257-277.

——, Hippolyte de Rome, in *Dictionnaire de spiritualité* VII (1969), p. 533.

——, Les difficultés d'une édition des oeuvres de S. Hippolyte, in *StudPatr* 12,1 (*TU* 115), (1975), p. 51-70.

Richardson C.C., A note on the epiclesis in Hippolytus and the Testamentum Domini, in *Rechthéolancmédiév* 15 (1948), p. 357-359.

Richter G.M.A., *The Portraits of the Greeks*, (London: Phaidon 1965).

Richter K., Zum Ritus der Bischofsordination in der „Apostolischen Überlieferung" Hippolyts von Rom, in *ALw* 17 (1975), p. 7-51.

Roberts C.H., Early Christianity in Egypt, in *JEgArch* 40 (1954), p. 92-96.

Rolfe J.C., Ammianus Marcellinus, Vol. 2 in *Loeb Classical Library*, (Cambridge Mass.: Harvard U.P. 1972).

Rolffs E., Das Indulgenzedikt des römischen Bischofs Kallist, kritisch untersucht und reconstruiert, in *TU* 11, 3 (1893).

——, Urkunden aus dem antimontanistischen Kämpfe des Abendlandes, in *TU* 12,4) (1895).

Rondeau M-J., Les polémiques d'Hippolyte de Rome et de Filastre de Brescia concernant le psautier, in *RevHisRel* 171 (1967), p. 1-51.

Rordorf W., L' Ordination de l' évêque selon la Tradition apostolique d' Hippolyte de Rome, in *QLP* 55 (1974), p. 137-150.

Rose A., La prère de consécration pour l' ordination épiscopale, in *Au service de la parole de Dieu. Mélanges offerts à Msgr. A.-M. Charue*, (Gembloux 1969), p. 129-145.

Rostovtzeff M.I., *Dura-Europos and Its Art*, (Oxford: Clarendon 1938).

——, *Social and Economic History of the Roman Empire*, (Oxford: Clarendon 1957)

Routh M.J., *Scriptorum Ecclesiasticorum Opuscula praecipua quaedam*, I (Oxford: U.P. 1832).

Rubach G., Das Eindringen des Christentums in die gebildete Welt, in *Kirchengeschichte als Missionsgeschichte*, Vol.1 Die alte Kirche, (München: 1974), p. 293-310.

Rucker I., Florilegium Edessenum anonymum (syriace ante 562), in *SbMn* 5 (1933).

Ruggieri, *De Portuensi S. Hippoyti sede. Dissertatio*, (Rome: 1771).

Ruhbach G., Klerusbildung in der alten Kirche, in *WuD* 15 (1979), p. 107-114.

Salmon G., The Chronology of Hippolytus, in *Hermath* 1 (1873), p. 82-128.

Saltet L., Les sources de l'Eranistes de Théodoret, in *RevHE* 6 (1905), p. 513-536; 741-754.

Salvatore P., Osservazioni sulla Struttura Letteraria del «De Christo e Antichristo» di Ippolito, in *Orpheus* 12 (1965), p. 133-155.

Sanders J.N., *The Fourth Gospel in the Early Church: Its Origin and Influence on Christian Theology up to Irenaeus*, (Cambidge: U.P. 1943).

Savile H., *Rerum Anglicarum Scriptores Post Bedam, praecipui, ex vetustissimis codicibus, manuscriptis nunc primum in lucem editi*, (Frankfurt: Wechelianis apud Claudium 1601).

Saxer V., Figura corporis et sanguinis Domini. Une formule eucharistique des premiers siècles chez Tertullien, Hippolyte, et Ambroise, in *RivAC* 47 (1971), p. 65-89.

——, Note di agiografia critica: Porto, l'Isola Sacra e Ippolito a proposito di studi recenti, in *Miscellanea A.P. Frutaz*, (Roma 1978), p. 110-121.

——, La questione de Ippolito Romano: a proposito de un libro recente, *StEphAug* 30 (1989), p. 43-59.

Schaeffer E., *Die Bedeutung der Epigramme des Papstes Damasus für die Geschichte der Heiligenverehrung*, (Rome: 1932).

Schermann Th., Eine neue Handschrift zur Apostolischen Kirchenordnung, in *OrChr* 2 (1902) p. 398-408.

——, Eine Elfapostelmoral oder die X-Recension der „beiden Wege," in *Veröffentlichungen aus dem Kirchenhistorischen Seminar München*, 2,2 (Lentner: München 1903).

——, *Die allgemeine Kirchenordnung, frühchristliche Liturgien und kirchliche Überlieferung*. 1. Die allgemeine Kirchenordnung des zweiten Jahrhunderts, (Studien zur Geschichte und Kultur des Altertums), (Paderborn: Schöningh 1914).

Schmid J., Studien zur Geschichte des griechischen Apocalypse-Textes, 1. Der Apocalypse-Kommentar des Andreas von Kaisareia, in *Münchener Theologische Studien*, (München: Karl Zink 1955).

Schmidt C., Studien zu den Pseudo-Clementinen, in *TU* 46,1, (1929).

Schoedel W.R., Theological Method in Irenaeus. (Adversus Haereses 2. 25-28, in *JThS* n.s. 35,1 (1984), p. 30-49.

——, Athenagoras, *Legatio* and De Resurrectione, in *OECT* (1972).

Scholl R., Das Bildungsproblem in der alten Kirche, in *Zeitschrift für wissenschaftliche Pädagogik* 10 (1964), p. 24-43.

Schöllgen G., Hausgemeinden Oikos-Ekklesiologie und monarchischer Episkopat. Überlegungen zu einer neuen Forschungsrichtung, in *JbAC* 31 (1988), p. 74-90.

——, Monepiskopat und monarchischer Episkopat: Eine Bemerkung zur Terminologie, in *ZNW* 77 (1986), p. 146-157.

Schubart W., Ägyptische Abteilung (Papyrussammlung): Ptolemaeus Philopator und Dionysos, in *Amtliche Berichte aus den preussischen königlichen Kunstsammlungen* (= *Beiblatt zum Jahrbuch der preussischen königlichen Kunstsammlungen*) 38 (1916/1917), p. 189-198.

——, *Das Buch bei den Griechen und Römern*, (Berlin: De Gruyter 1921), p. 36-75.

Schuhmacher W.N., Prudentius an der Via Tibertina, in *Spanische Forschungen der Görresgesellschaft*, 1 Reihe, (Gesammelte Aufsätze zur Kulturgeschichte Spaniens 16 Band), (Münster: 1960), p. 1-15.

Schürer W., *The History of the Jewish People in the Age of Jesus*, (Ed.) G. Vermes, F. Millar, and M. Black, (Edinburgh: T. and T. Clark 1979).

Schwartz E., Über den Tod der Söhne Zebedaei. Ein Beitrag zur Geschichte des Johannesevangeliums, in *AKWG* Phil.-Hist. Kl. N.F. 7,5, p. 29-30.

——, Über die pseudapostolischen Kirchenordnungen, in *Schriften wissensch. Gesellschaft im Strassburg*, 6, (Strasbourg: 1910).

——, Codex Vaticanus Graecus 1431: Eine antichalkedonische Sammlung aus der Zeit Kaiser Zenos., in *ABAW* Philos. und hist. Klasse 32, 6 (1927).

——, Publizistische Sammlungen zum accacianischen Schisma, in *ABAW* Phil. Hist. Abt. N.F., Heft 10, (1934).

——, Christliche und jüdische Ostertafeln, in *AKWG* Phil.-Hist. Kl., N.F. 8,6 (1905), p. 1-194.

Schweizer E., Der Johanneische Kirchenbegriff, in *TU* 73 (1959), p. 263-268.

Segal J.B., *Edessa "the Blessed City,"* (Oxford: Clarendon 1970).

Segelberg E., The Benedictio Olei in the Apostolic Tradition of Hippolytus, *OrChr* 48 (1964), p. 268-281.

——, The Ordination Prayers in Hippolytus, in *StudPatr* 13 (1975), p. 397-408.

Seni F.S., La Villa d' Este in Tivoli, in *Memorie Storiche tratte da documenti inediti*, (Roma: Tata Giovanni 1902).

Seston W., L'Église et le baptistère de Doura-Europos, in *Annales de l'école des hautes études de Grand*, (Paris: 1937), p. 161-177.

Settis S., Severo Alessandro e i suoi Lari. (SHA, 29, 2-3), in *Ath* 60 (1972), p. 237-251.

Simonetti M., *La letteratura cristiana antica greca e latina*, (Milano: 1969).

——, Note di cristologia pneumatica, in *Aug* 12 (1972), p. 201-231.

——, Due Note su Ippolito, in *StEphAug* 13 (1977), p. 121-136.

——, A modo di conclusione: una ipotesi di lavoro, in *StEphAug* 13 (1977), p. 151-156.

——, Prospettive Escatologiche della Cristologia di Ippolito, in *La Cristologia nei Padri della Chiesa*, (Accademia Cardinale Bessaronis: Rome 1979), p. 85-101.

——, Un falso Ippolito nella polemica monotelita, in *Vetera Christianorum* 24, (1987), p. 113-146.

——, Aggiornamento su Ippolito, in *StEphAug* 30 (1989), p. 75-130.

——, Il problema dell'unità di Dio da Giustino a Ireneo, in *Rivista di storia e letteratura religiosa*, 22 (1986), p. 201-239 reprinted in Simonetti (1993), p. 71-107.

——, Studi sulla cristologia del II e III secolo, in *StEphAug* 44 (1993).

Simpson A.D., Epicureans, Christians and Atheists in the Second Century, in *Transactions of the American Philological Association* 72 (1941), p. 372-381.

Smith M.A., The Anaphora of the Apostolic Tradition Reconsidered, in *StudPatr* 10,1 (TU 107), (1970), p. 426-430.

Smolak K., *Christentum und Römische Welt* (Orbis Latinus), (Hilder Pichler Tempsky: Wienna 1988).

Spanneut M., Hippolyte ou Euststathe? Autour de la Chaîne de Nicetas sur l'Evangile selon Saint Luc, in *MSR* 9 (1952), p. 215-220.

Stam J.E., *Episcopacy in the Apostolic Tradition of Hippolytus*, Basel 1969 (ThDuss 3).

———, Charismatic Theology in the "Apostolic Tradition" of Hippolytus, in *Current Issues in Biblical and Patristic Interpretation. Studies in honour of Merill C. Tenney presented by his former students*, Ed. G.F. Hawthorn, (Grand Rapids 1975), p. 267-276.

Stanton G.N., Aspects of Early Jewish Polemic and Apologetic, in *NTS* 31 (1985), p. 377-392.

Stauffer E., Zum Kaliphat des Jacobus, in *ZRGG* 4 (1952), p. 193-214.

Stead C., Review of Ricerche su Ippolito, in *JThS* n.s. 30,2 (1979), p. 549-551.

Stevenson J., *The Catacombs: Rediscovered monuments of early Christianity*. (London: Thames and Hudson 1978).

Straub J., Heidenische Geschichtsapologetik in der Spätantike. Untersuchungen über Zeit und Tendenz in der *Historia Augusta*, in *Antiquitas* 4,1 (1963).

Strecker G., Das Judenchristentum in den Pseudoclementinen, in*TU* 70 (1958 and 1981).

Strocka V.M., Römische Bibliotheken, *Gym* 88 (1981), p. 289-329.

Stroux J., Die Constitutio Antoniana, in *Phil* 88 (1933), p. 272-295.

Styger P., *Die Römischen Katakomben*, (Berlin: Verlag für Kunstswissenschaft 1933).

———, *Die Römischen Martyrgrüfte*, Vols I and II, (Berlin: Verlag für Kunstswissenschaft 1935).

Sundberg A., Canon Muratori: A Fourth Century List, in *HThR* 66 (1973), p. 1-41.

Swete H.B., *Essays on the Early History of the Church and Ministry*, (London: MacMillan 1918).

Syme R., *Historia Augusta* Papers, (Oxford: Clarendon 1983)

Taft R., The Dialogue before the Anaphora in the Byzantine Eucharistic Liturgy II: The Sursum Corda, in *OrChrP* 57 (1988), p. 47-77.

Tateo R. (Ed.), *Ippolito de Roma. Tradizione apostolica*, (Roma 1972).

Tattam H., *The Apostolical Constitutions or Canons of the Apostles in Coptic with an English translation*, (London: Oriental Translation Fund 1848).

Telfer W., Episcopal Succession in Egypt, in *JEH* 34 (1952), p. 1-13.

———, *The Office of a Bishop*, (London: Darton, Longman and Todd 1962).

———, Was Hegesippus a Jew? in *HThR* 53,2 (1960), p. 143-153.

Testini P., *Le catecombe e gli antichi cimiteri cristiani in Roma*, (Roma Cristiana 2), (Bologna: Capelli 1966).

———, Di alcune testimonianze relative ad Ippolito, in *StEphAug* 13 (1977), p. 45-65.

———, Sondaggi a s. Ippolito all'Isola Sacra. I depositi, reliquiari scoperti sotto l'altare, in *RendPontAcc* 46 (1973-1974), p. 165-179.

———, Indagini nell'area di S. Ippolito all'Isola Sacra. L'iscrizione del vescovo Heraclida, in *RendPontAcc* 51-52 (1978/79-1979-1980).

———, Vetera et nova su Ippolito, in *StEphAug* 30, (1989), p. 7-22.

———, Damaso e s. Ippolito di Porto, in *Studi di Antichità Cristiana* XXXIX, Saecularia Damasiana, p. 293-303.

Theissen, G., Die soziologische Auswertung religiöser Überlieferungen, *Kairos* 17 (1975), p. 284-299.

Till W., and Leipoldt J., Der koptische Text der Kirchenordnung Hippolyts herausgegeben und übersetzt, in *TU* 58,5 (1954).

Torrès F. and Possevino A., *Apparatus Sacer*, (Cologne 1608).

Toynbee J., and Ward Perkins, J. *The Shrine of St. Peter and the Vatican Excavations*, (London: Longmans Green 1956).

Treadgold W.T., The nature of the Bibliotheca of Photius, in *Dumbarton Oaks Studies*, XVIII (Washington: Harvard U.P. 1980).

Trevissoi M., Diogene Laerzio, L'età in cui visse, in *Rivista di Storia Antica* xii (1908), 482-505.

Troiano M.S., Alcuni aspetti della dottrina dello Spirito Santo in Ippolito, in *Aug* 20 (1980), p. 615-632.

Turner C.H., The Early Episcopal Lists, in *JThS* 1 (1899- 1900), p. 181-200, 529-553.

——, Tertullianea, in *JThS* 14 (1913), p. 556-564.

——, The Ordination Prayer for a Presbyter in the Church Order of Hippolytus, in *JThS* 16 (1915), p. 542-547.

——, The Early Episcopal Lists, in *JThS* 18 (1916-17), p. 103-34.

——, The "Blessed Presbyters" who condemned Noetus, in *JThS* 23 (1921), p. 28-35.

——, Cheirotonia, cheirothesia, epithesis cheiron, in *JThS* 24 (1923), p. 496-504.

Urlichs C.L., *Codex Urbis Romae Toptographicus*, (Wirceburgi: Ex Aedibus Steahelianis 1871).

Ursinus Fulvius, *Imagines et Elogia Virorum Illustrium,et Eruditorum ex Antiquis Lapidibus et Numismatibus expressae cum annotationibus*, (Lafrery-Formeis: Rome 1570).

Usener H., *Epicurea*, (Leipzig: B.J. Teubneri 1887).

Valentini R. and Zucchetti G., *Codice topografico della città di Roma*, Vol. 2, (Rome: Istituto Storico Italiano 1942).

Vallée G., A Study in Anti-Gnostic Polemics: Irenaeus, Hippolytus, and Epiphanius, in *Studies in Early Christianity and Judaism* 1, (Canada: William Laurier University Press 1981), (Canadian Corporation for Studies in Religion).

Vellico A.M., „Episcopus Episcoporum" in Tertulliani libro De Pudicitia, in *Antonianum* V (1930), p. 25-56.

Veloccia Rinaldi M.L., and Testini P., *Ricerche archeologiche nell'Isola Sacra*, (Rome 1975).

Verhoeven T., *Studiën over Tertullianus' Adversus Praxean*: Voornamelijk Betrekking hebbend op Monarchia, Oikonomia, Probola in verband met de Triniteit, (Amsterdam: N.V. Noord-Hollandsche Uitgevers Maatschappij 1948).

Viellefond J.-R., *Les "Cestes" de Julius Africanus: Étude sur l'ensemble des fragments avec édition, traduction, et commentaires*, (Firenze: Sansoni/ Paris: Didier 1970)

Villette J., Que représente la grande fresque de la maison chrétienne de Dura? in *Rbib* 60 (1953), p. 398-413.

Voicu S.J., Pseudoippolito in Sancta Theophania e Leonzio di Constantinopoli, in *StEphAug* 30 (1989), p. 137-146.

Volkmar G., *Die Quellen der Ketzergeschichte bis zum Nicäum. I, Hippolytus und die römischen Zeitgenossen*, (Zürich: 1855).

——, *Die Zeit der ältesten Haeresis und die Quellen ihrer Geschichte, mit besonderer Beziehung auf Lipsius' neue Untersuchung*, (Jena: Dufft 1875).

Vööbus A., The Synodicon in the West Syrian Tradition, in *CSCO* 367, Scriptores Syri Tom. 161.

Wagner G., Zur Herkunft der Apostolischen Konstitutionen, in *ZKG* 68 (1957), p. 1-47.

Waitz H., Pseudoclementines, in *TU* 25,4 (1904).

Walls A.F., A Note on the Apostolic Claim in the Church Order Literature, in *StudPatr* 2,2 (1957), p. 83-92.
———, The Latin Version of Hippolytus' Apostolic Tradition, in *StudPatr* 3 (1961), p. 155-162.
Watzinger C., Die Christen Duras, in *Theologische Blätter* 18 (1938), p. 117-119.
Wegman H., Généalogie hypothétique de la prière eucharistique, in *QL* 61 (1980), p. 263-278.

———, Une anaphore incomplète? Les Fragments sur Papyrus Strasbourg Gr 254, in *Studies in Gnosticism and Hellenistic Religions presented to Gilles Quispel on the Occassion of his 65th Birthday*, Ed. R. van den Broek and M.J. Vermaseren, (Leiden 1981), p. 432-450.
Wegner M., *Die antiken sarcophagsreliefs*, Vol. 5,3.
Wendel C., Versuch einer Deutung der Hippolyt-Statue, in *TheolStKrit*, 26 (1937-1938), p. 362-369.
Wendland P., Philo und die kynisch-storische Diatribe, in *Beiträge zur Geschichte der griechischen Philosophie und Religion*, (Ed.) P. Wendland und O. Kern, (Berlin: 1895).
———, Die hellenisch-römische Kultur in ihren Beziehungen zu Judentum und Christentum, in *Handbuch zum neuen Testament* 1,2, (Tübingen: 1912).
———, Hippolylus Werke: 3.: Refutatio Omnium Haeresium, in *GCS* (1916).
Whittaker M., Tatian: *Oratio ad Graecos* and Fragments, in *OECT* (1982).
Wiefel W., Die jüdische Gemeinschaft im antiken Rom und die Anfänge des römischen Christentums, in *Judaica* 26 (1970), p. 65-68.
Wilamowitz-Möllendorff U. von, Antigonos von Karystos, in *Philologische Untersuchungen*, (Ed.) A. Kiesing und U von Wilamowitz-Möllendorff, Heft 4 (Berlin: 1881).
Wilken R.L., Collegia, Philosophical Schools, and Theology, in *The Catacombs and the Colosseum*, (Valley Forge: 1971), p. 268-91.
———, Early Christian Chiliasm, Jewish Messianism, and the Idea of the Holy Land, in *HThR* 79 (1986), p. 298-307.
Williams M. Gilmore, Empress Julia Domna, in *Am. J. Arch.* 6 (1902), p. 259-305.
Wilpert G., *I sarcofagi cristiani antichi*, Vol. 1 (Rome 1929).
Wolf J.C., *Compendium historiae philosophae antiquae, h.e. Pseudorigenis Philosophumena, ex ipso M.S. Mediceo denuo collato et alio Taurinensi repetita vice emendata*, (Hamburgi: Christ. Liebzeit 1713).
Wolfson H.A., *The Philosophy of the Church Fathers: Faith, Trinity, and Incarnation*, (Cambridge Massachusetts: Harvard U.P. 1976).
Wordsworth C., *St. Hippolytus and the Roman Church in the Earlier Part of the Third Century, from the Newly Discovered Philosophumena*, (London: Rivington 1853).
Wright W.C., Vita Philosophorum, in *Loeb Classical Library*, (Cambridge Mass.: Harvard U.P. 1921).
———, Julian: Letters, in *Loeb Classical Library*, (Cambridge Mass.: Harvard U.P. 1969).
Wycherley R.E., Peripatos: The Ancient Philosophical Scene I, in *Greece and Rome* 8 (1961), p. 152-163.
———, Peripatos: The Ancient Philosophical Scene II, in *Greece and Rome* 9 (1962), p. 1-21.

Zani A., La Cristologia di Ippolito, in *Ricerche di Scienze teologiche* 22, (Brescia: Morcelliana 1984), (Publicazioni del Pontifico seminaro lombardo in Roma).

Zollitsche R., Amt und Funktion des Priesters: Eine Untersuchung zum Ursprung
und zur Gestalt des Presbyterats in den ersten zwei Jahrhunderten, in *F.ThSt* 96,
(Freiburg-Basel- Wein: 1974).
Zuchschwert E., Das Naziräat des Herrenbruders Jakobus nach Hegesippus, in
ZNW 68 (1977), p. 176-87.

INDEX

1. Biblical Citations

2. Ancient Authors

3. Modern authors

4. Manuscripts and Inscriptions Cited

5. Greek Words and Phrases

6. Latin Words and Phrases

SUPPLEMENTS TO VIGILIAE CHRISTIANAE

21. HENNINGS, R. *Der Briefwechsel zwischen Augustinus und Hieronymus und ihr Streit um den Kanon des Alten Testaments und die Auslegung von Gal. 2,11-14.* 1994. ISBN 90 04 09840 2
22. BOEFT, J. DEN & HILHORST, A. (eds.). *Early Christian Poetry.* A Collection of Essays. 1993. ISBN 90 04 09939 5
23. McGUCKIN, J.A. *St. Cyril of Alexandria: The Christological Controversy.* Its History, Theology, and Texts. 1994. ISBN 90 04 09990 5
24. REYNOLDS, Ph.L. *Marriage in the Western Church.* The Christianization of Marriage during the Patristic and Early Medieval Periods. 1994. ISBN 90 04 10022 9
25. PETERSEN, W.L. *Tatian's Diatessaron.* Its Creation, Dissemination, Significance, and History in Scholarship. 1994. ISBN 90 04 09469 5
26. GRÜNBECK, E. *Christologische Schriftargumentation und Bildersprache.* Zum Konflikt zwischen Metapherninterpretation und dogmatischen Schriftbeweistraditionen in der patristischen Auslegung des 44. (45.) Psalms. 1994. ISBN 90 04 10021 0
27. HAYKIN, M.A.G. *The Spirit of God.* The Exegesis of 1 and 2 Corinthians in the Pneumatomachian Controversy of the Fourth Century. 1994. ISBN 90 04 09947 6
28. BENJAMINS, H.S. *Eingeordnete Freiheit.* Freiheit und Vorsehung bei Origenes. 1994. ISBN 90 04 10117 9
29. SMULDERS s.J., P. (tr. & comm.). *Hilary of Poitiers' Preface to his* Opus historicum. 1995. ISBN 90 04 10191 8
30. KEES, R.J. *Die Lehre von der* Oikonomia Gottes in der Oratio catechetica *Gregors von Nyssa.* 1995. ISBN 90 04 10200 0
31. BRENT, A. *Hippolytus and the Roman Church in the Third Century.* Communities in Tension before the Emergence of a Monarch-Bishop. 1995. ISBN 90 04 10245 0
32. RUNIA, D.T. *Philo and the Church Fathers.* A Collection of Papers. 1995. ISBN 90 04 10355 4